AGE, WEIGHT &

For use with Tim

Distance	Age	Mar.	Apr.	May	June	July	Aug.	Sept.	Oct.	Nov.
5f	4	10-0	10-0	10-0	10-0	10-0	10-0	10-0	10-0	10-0
	3	9—0	9—2	9—4	9—6	9—8	9-10	9-11	9-12	9-13
	2	6—8	6-13	7—3	7—7	7-11	8—1	8—5	8—8	8-11
6f	4	9-13	10-0	10-0	10-0	10-0	10-0	10-0	10-0	10-0
	3	8-11	9—0	9—2	9—4	9—6	9—8	9-10	9-11	9-12
	2			6-13	7—3	7—7	7-11	8—1	8—5	8—8
7f	4	9-12	9-13	10-0	10-0	10-0	10-0	10-0	10-0	10-0
	3	8—8	8-11	9—0	9—2	9—4	9—6	9—8	9-10	9-11
	2					7—4	7—8	7-12	8—2	8—5
1m	4	9-11	9-12	9-13	10-0	10-0	10-0	10-0	10-0	10-0
	3	8—6	8—9	8-12	9—1	9—3	9—5	9—7	9—9	9-10
	2							7—9	7-13	8—2
9f	4	9-11	9-12	9-13	9-13	10-0	10-0	10-0	10-0	10-0
	3	8—4	8—7	8-10	8-13	9—2	9—4	9—6	9—8	9—9
1¼m	4	9-10	9-11	9-12	9-13	10-0	10-0	10-0	10-0	10-0
	3	8—2	8—5	8—8	8-11	9—0	9—3	9—5	9—7	9—8
11f	4	9—9	9-11	9-12	9-13	9-13	10-0	10-0	10-0	10-0
	3	8—0	8—4	8—7	8-10	8-13	9—2	9—4	9—6	9—7
1½m	4	9—9	9-10	9-11	9-12	9-13	10-0	10-0	10-0	10-0
	3	7-12	8—2	8—5	8—8	8-11	9—0	9—3	9—5	9—7
13f	4	9—8	9-10	9-11	9-12	9-13	9-13	10-0	10-0	10-0
	3	7-11	8—1	8—4	8—7	8-10	8-13	9—2	9—4	9—6
1¾m	4	9—7	9—9	9-10	9-12	9-13	9-13	10-0	10-0	10-0
	3	7—9	7-13	8—3	8—6	8—9	8-12	9—1	9—3	9—5
15f	4	9—6	9—8	9-10	9-11	9-12	9-13	10-0	10-0	10-0
	3	7—8	7-12	8—2	8—5	8—8	8-11	9—0	9—2	9—4
2m	4	9—6	9—8	9-10	9-11	9-12	9-13	10-0	10-0	10-0
	3	7—7	7-11	8—1	8—5	8—8	8-11	9—0	9—2	9—4
2¼m	4	9—6	9—8	9—9	9-11	9-12	9-13	10-0	10-0	10-0
	3	7—6	7-10	8—0	8—4	8—7	8-10	8-13	9—1	9—3
2½m	4	9—5	9—7	9—9	9-10	9-11	9-12	9-13	10-0	10-0
	3	7—5	7—9	7-13	8—3	8—6	8—9	8-12	9—1	9—3

For 5-y-o's and older, use 10-0 in all cases.

4

**14 Primed athletes aimed for the 1986 Classics . . . .
representing WATERFORD FARM's strongest-ever yearling consignments & including another potential Nijinsky champion to be sold at Saratoga, following in the footsteps of the 1981 champion turf filly, De La Rose, sold for a then record price of $500,000.**

Keeneland

c. **FORLI/CANDY ECLAIR** – 1st foal of Champion 2-y-o filly

f. **IN REALITY/EGYPTIAN ROSE** – out of a ½ sister to **De La Rose** and **Upper Nile**

c. **HALO/HEAVENLY ADE** – out of a Gr. I. winner

c. **KEY TO CONTENT/TAKE WARNING** – ½ brother to 3 stakes winners

c. **SIR IVOR/TATALLAH** – ½ brother to Stakes winner and Stakes producer **Joi'ski**

c. **CURE THE BLUES/CANANEA**– out of a ½ sister to dual classic winner **Blue Wind**

Write, telephone or telex
Dr. and Mrs. R. Smiser West or Bob West
Post Office Box 638
Midway, Kentucky 40347
Telephone 606/846-4149 or 846-4417
Telex 467165

Saratoga

c. **NIJINSKY/ZERELDA** – dam a Stakes placed ½ sister to **Tanagra**

c. **FORLI/PASHAMIN** – ½ brother to **Properantes**

c. **HALO/FILLE DU NORD** – family of Champion **Victorian Prince**

f. **HONEST PLEASURE/ERIN'S WORD** – dam 4th High-weighted filly behind **Genuine Risk** and **Bold 'n Determined**

f. **TOPSIDER/SEARCHING MAGIC** – ½ sister to New York Stakes placed **Stashed**

c. **BORZOI/LEMON PEEL**– ½ brother to **Front Limited**, Horse of the Year in Puerto Rico

f. **PRIVATE ACCOUNT/MILLINERY LADY** – ½ sister to Stakes placed **Fancy Hatter**

c. **HAWAII/MARVELOUS MONA** – dam a New York Allowance winner, family of **Gay Style**

UUATERFORÖ FARCO

Breeders of :
**DE LA ROSE, TECORNO,
AIR DISTINGUE, EASTERN DAWN,
PROPERANTES,
WANDA.**

9

Established 1890

HEATHORNS

BOOKMAKERS

OVERSBY HOUSE
ONSLOW STREET
GUILDFORD
SURREY GU1 4SR
Telephone: (0483) 31233

11

RACEHORSES
OF
1983

A Timeform Publication   Price £45.00

A Timeform Publication

Compiled and Produced under the direction of
Phil Bull, B.Sc., and Reg Griffin

by members of the Timeform Organisation
G. Greetham, B.A. (Deputy Managing Director),
J. G. Clarke (Director), G. F. Walton, Dip.A.D.
(Director), J. D. Newton, B.A. (Editor), J. P.
Early, B.A. (Deputy Editor), D. P. Adams, A. M.
Caulfield and G. C. J. Dench, B.A.; also D. P.
Cleary, B.A., P. Morrell, G. J. North, B.Sc., and
G. A. Willstrop.

© **Portway Press Limited 1984**

ISBN 0 900599 38 3

CONTENTS

Foreword

"Racehorses of 1983" deals individually, in alphabetical sequence, with every horse that ran under Jockey Club Rules in 1983, plus a number of foreign-trained horses that did not race here. For each of these horses is given (1) its age, colour and sex, (2) its breeding, (3) a form summary giving details of all its performances during the past two seasons, (4) a rating of its merit, (5) a commentary upon its racing or general characteristics as a racehorse, with some suggestions, perhaps, regarding its potentialities in 1984 and (6) the name of the trainer in whose charge it was on the last occasion it ran.

The book is published with a twofold purpose. Firstly, it is designed to provide the betting man with data for practical use in analysing the racing programmes from day to day, and instructions as to its use in this capacity will be found in the Explanatory Notes which follow this Foreword; and secondly, the book is intended to have some permanent value as a review of the exploits and achievements of the more notable of our thoroughbreds in 1983. Thus, while the commentaries upon the vast majority of the horses are, of necessity, in note form, the best horses are more critically examined, and the short essays upon them are illustrated by half-tone portraits and photographs of the finishes of some of the races in which they were successful.

The attention of foreign buyers of British bloodstock, and others who are concerned with Timeform Ratings as a measure of absolute racing class in terms of a standard scale, is drawn to the section headed "The Level of the Ratings" in the Explanatory Notes on page 29.

February, 1984.

17

INDEX TO PHOTOGRAPHS
PORTRAITS & SNAPSHOTS

19

21

RACE PHOTOGRAPHS

Daniel Prenn Royal Yorkshire Stakes (York)	*A. Russell*	737
David Dixon Sprint Trophy Handicap (York)	*A. Russell*	139
Derby Stakes (Epsom)	*Sport and General*	832
Derby Stakes (Epsom)	*A. Russell*	833
Diadem Stakes (Ascot)	*George Selwyn*	712
Doonside Cup (Ayr)	*A. Russell*	92
Dubai Champion Stakes (Newmarket)	*John Crofts*	198
Duchess of Kent Maiden Stakes (York)	*A. Russell*	498
Duke of York Stakes (York)	*A. Russell*	892
Earl of Sefton Stakes (Newmarket)	*A. Russell*	402
Erroll Stakes (Ascot)	*George Selwyn*	879
Esal Bookmakers Handicap (Doncaster)	*A. Russell*	146
Esher Cup (Sandown)	*George Selwyn*	785
Extel Stakes (Goodwood)	*John Crofts*	538
Firth of Clyde Stakes (Ayr)	*A. Russell*	687
Fitzroy House Stakes (Newmarket)	*A. Russell*	458
Flying Childers Stakes (Doncaster)	*George Selwyn*	816
Gallinule Stakes (the Curragh)	*E. G. Byrne*	163
Galtres Stakes (York)	*A. Russell*	389
Geoffrey Freer Stakes (Newbury)	*George Selwyn*	434
Gerry Feilden Memorial Stakes (Newmarket)	*John Crofts*	922
Gilltown Stud Stakes (the Curragh)	*E. G. Byrne*	534
Gimcrack Stakes (York)	*Press Association Photos*	641
Goffs Irish One Thousand Guineas (the Curragh) ..	*E. G. Byrne*	454
Gold Cup (Ascot)	*John Crofts*	475
Goodwood Cup	*John Crofts*	477
Gordon Stakes (Goodwood)	*John Crofts*	413
Grand Criterium (Longchamp)	*P. Bertrand*	865
Grand Prix de Saint-Cloud	*P. Bertrand*	235
Granville Stakes (Ascot)	*E. G. Byrne*	430
Great Voltigeur Stakes (York)	*John Crofts*	738
Happy Valley Stakes (York)	*A. Russell*	322
Hardwicke Stakes (Ascot)	*A. Russell*	794
Harry Rosebery Challenge Trophy (Ayr)	*A. Russell*	629
Haynes, Hanson and Clark Stakes (Newbury)	*John Crofts*	664
Henry II Stakes (Sandown)	*John Crofts*	608
Highland Spring Derby Trial Stakes (Lingfield)	*W. Everitt*	831
High Steward Stakes (Yarmouth)	*John Crofts*	537
Holsten Diat Pils Final (Doncaster)	*A. Russell*	189
Hoover Fillies Mile (Ascot)	*John Crofts*	580
Horris Hill Stakes (Newbury)	*John Crofts*	257
Houghton Stakes (Newmarket)	*A. Russell*	193
Hyperion Stakes (Ascot)	*John Crofts*	540
Intercraft Fillies Stakes (Kempton)	*W. Everitt*	734
Irish Guinness Oaks (the Curragh)	*E. G. Byrne*	329
Irish Sweeps Derby (the Curragh)	*E. G. Byrne*	745
Japan Cup (Tokyo)	*Japan Racing Association*	796
Jefferson Smurfit Memorial Irish St Leger (the Curragh) ...	*M. Ansell*	563
Jersey Stakes (Ascot)	*A. Russell*	829
Jockey Club Cup (Newmarket)	*A. Russell*	424
Jockey Club Stakes (Newmarket)	*John Crofts*	255
Joe McGrath Memorial Stakes (Leopardstown)	*E. G. Byrne*	795
John Porter Stakes (Newbury)	*John Crofts*	234
John Smith's Magnet Cup (York)	*A. Russell*	106
July Scurry Handicap (the Curragh)	*E. G. Byrne*	191
King Edward VII Stakes (Ascot)	*A. Russell*	744
King George Stakes (Goodwood)	*John Crofts*	775
King George VI and Queen Elizabeth Diamond Stakes (Ascot) ...	*W. Everitt*	848
King's Stand Stakes (Ascot)	*A. Russell*	724
Kiveton Park Stakes (Doncaster)	*A. Russell*	69

Prix Perth (Saint-Cloud)	*P. Bertrand*	668
Prix Robert Papin (Maisons-Laffitte)	*P. Bertrand*	578
Prix Royal-Oak (Longchamp)	*P. Bertrand*	601
Prix Saint-Alary (Longchamp)	*P. Bertrand*	772
Prix Thomas Bryon (Saint-Cloud)	*P. Bertrand*	636
Queen Anne Stakes (Ascot)	*A. Russell*	882
Queen Elizabeth II Stakes (Ascot)	*John Crofts*	703
Reg Day Memorial Trophy (Newmarket)	*E. G. Byrne*	70
Ribblesdale Stakes (Ascot)	*John Crofts*	373
Rockfel Stakes (Newmarket)	*A. Russell*	506
Royal Hunt Cup (Ascot)	*A. Russell*	532
Royal Lodge Stakes (Ascot)	*W. Everitt*	336
Sancton Stakes (York)	*A. Russell*	346
Scarbrough Stakes (Doncaster)	*A. Russell*	776
Sceptre Stakes (Doncaster)	*A. Russell*	694
Shaw Maiden Stakes (Newbury)	*George Selwyn*	168
Sir Charles Clore Memorial Stakes (Newbury)	*Press Association Photos*	768
Somerville Tattersall Stakes (Newmarket)	*John Crofts*	690
St Hugh's Stakes (Newbury)	*John Crofts*	113
St James's Palace Stakes (Ascot)	*Press Association Photos*	383
St Leger Stakes (Doncaster)	*Sport and General*	812
St Simon Stakes (Newbury)	*George Selwyn*	419
Sun Chariot Stakes (Newmarket)	*A. Russell*	197
Sussex Stakes (Goodwood)	*E. G. Byrne*	588
Temple Stakes (Sandown)	*John Crofts*	286
Tia Maria Autumn Handicap (Newmarket)	*John Crofts*	90
Timeform Race Card Stakes (Thirsk)	*A. Russell*	750
Tote Cesarewitch Handicap (Newmarket)	*A. Russell*	91
Tote-Ebor Handicap (York)	*John Crofts*	418
Troy Stakes (Doncaster)	*George Selwyn*	863
Trusthouse Forte Prix de l'Arc de Triomphe (Longchamp)	*P. Bertrand*	50
Trusthouse Forte Prix de l'Arc de Triomphe (Longchamp)	*P. Bertrand*	51
Trusthouse Forte Prix Vermeille (Longchamp)	*P. Bertrand*	741
Turf Classic (Aqueduct)	*Rich Eng*	53
Two Thousand Guineas Stakes (Newmarket)	*John Crofts*	480
Vernons Sprint Cup (Haydock)	*A. Russell*	355
Washington D.C. International (Laurel)	*Frutkoff–Laurel Photo*	54
Waterford Candelabra Stakes (Goodwood)	*John Crofts*	754
Waterford Crystal Mile (Goodwood)	*Sport and General*	554
William Hill Cambridgeshire (Newmarket)	*A. Russell*	709
William Hill Cheveley Park Stakes (Newmarket)	*John Crofts*	230
William Hill Dewhurst Stakes Newmarket)	*A. Russell*	260
William Hill Futurity Stakes (Doncaster)	*E. G. Byrne*	61
William Hill July Cup (Newmarket)	*John Crofts*	353
William Hill Middle Park Stakes Newmarket)	*John Crofts*	205
William Hill November Handicap (Doncaster)	*A. Russell*	80
William Hill Sprint Championship (York)	*A. Russell*	354
William Hill Stewards' Cup (Goodwood)	*John Crofts*	85
William Hill Trophy (York)	*A. Russell*	85
Windsor Castle Stakes (Ascot)	*John Crofts*	227
Wokingham Stakes (Ascot)	*A. Russell*	527
Yorkshire Cup (York)	*A. Russell*	471
Yorkshire Oaks (York)	*John Crofts*	811

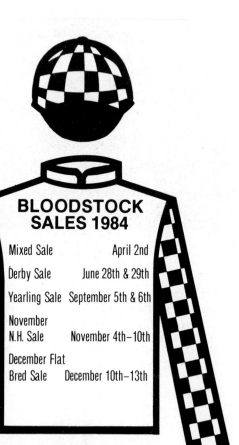

**BLOODSTOCK
SALES 1984**

Mixed Sale	April 2nd
Derby Sale	June 28th & 29th
Yearling Sale	September 5th & 6th
November N.H. Sale	November 4th–10th
December Flat Bred Sale	December 10th–13th

Ballsbridge Tattersalls Ltd.,
Anglesea House, RDS., Anglesea Rd., Ballsbridge,
Dublin, 4, Ireland. Telephone Dublin 605544
Telex 30854 BIBS EI

Brindley

EXPLANATORY NOTES

TO assess the prospects of any horse in a race it is necessary to know two things about him: first, how good he is; and second, what sort of horse he is. In this book the merit of each horse is expressed in the form of a *rating* (printed on the right); and the *racing character* of the horse is given in the commentary.

TIMEFORM RATINGS

The Timeform Rating of a horse is simply the merit of the horse expressed in pounds. More precisely, it is *the number of pounds which, in our opinion, the horse would be entitled to receive in an average Free Handicap.* Thus, a horse which we regard as worth 9 st 7 lb in an average Free Handicap, i.e., 133 lb, would receive a rating of 133: and one regarded as worth 8 st (112 lb) would receive a rating of 112; and so on.

This explains what the ratings are; but of course individual ratings are not actually allocated in this way, merely by "inspection". The rating of any horse is a result of careful examination of its running against other horses. We maintain a "running" handicap of all horses in training throughout the season, or, to be strictly accurate, two handicaps, one for horses aged three years and over, and one for two-year-olds.

THE LEVEL OF THE RATINGS

At the close of each season all the horses that have raced are re-handicapped from scratch, and each horse's rating is revised. It is also necessary to adjust the general level of the handicap, so that the mean of all the ratings is kept at the same standard level from year to year. Left to itself, the general level of the ratings, in each succeeding issue of Timeform, tends to rise steadily. For technical reasons it is desirable to allow it to do so during the season: but, in the winter, when the complete re-handicap is done, the ratings must, of course, be put back on their proper level again.

This explains why, in this book, the ratings are, in general, different from those in the final issue of the 1983 Timeform series.

RATINGS AND WEIGHT-FOR-AGE

These matters, however, are by the way. What concerns the reader is that he has, in the ratings in this book, a universal handicap embracing all the horses in training it is possible to weigh up, ranging from tip-top classic performers, with ratings from 130 to 145, down to the meanest selling platers, rated around the 40 or 50 mark. And what we now have to explain is the practical use of these ratings in the business of weighing up a race.

Before doing so, it is important to mention that all ratings are at weight-for-age, so that equal ratings mean horses of equal merit: perhaps it would be clearer if we said that the universal rating handicap is really not a single handicap, but four handicaps side by side: one for 2-y-o's, one for 3-y-o's, one for 4-y-o's and one for older horses. Thus, a 3-y-o rated, for argument's sake, at 117 is deemed to be identical in point of "merit" with a 4-y-o also rated at 117: but for them to have equal chances in, say, a mile race in June, the 3-y-o would need to be receiving 13 lb from the 4-y-o, which is the weight difference specified by the Age, Weight and Distance Table on the page facing the front cover. However, let us to cases!

USING THE RATINGS

In using Timeform Ratings with a view to discovering which horses in any race have the best chances at the weights, we have two distinct cases, according to whether the horses taking part are of the same age or of different ages. Here is the procedure in each case:—

A.   Horses of the Same Age

If the horses all carry the same weight there are no adjustments to be made, and the horses with the highest ratings have the best chances. If the horses carry different weights, jot down their ratings, and to the rating of each horse add one point for every pound the horse is set to carry less than 10 st, or subtract one point for every pound he has to carry more than 10 st. When the ratings have been adjusted in this way the highest resultant figure indicates the horse with the best chance at the weights.

Example (any distance: any month of the season)

2 Good Girl (9-6)	.. Rating 119. . . .	add 8. . . .	127
2 Paulinus (9-4)	.. Rating 113. . . .	add 10. . . .	123
2 Abilene (8-11)	.. Rating 107. . . .	add 17. . . .	124
2 Bob's Joy (8-7)	.. Rating 108. . . .	add 21. . . .	129
2 Time Warp (8-2)	.. Rating 100. . . .	add 26. . . .	126
2 Eagle Eye (7-7)	.. Rating 92. . . .	add 35. . . .	127

Bob's Joy (129) has the best chance; Good Girl (127) and Eagle Eye (127) are next best.

B.   Horses of Different Ages

Take no notice of the weight any horse receives from any other. Instead, consult the Age, Weight and Distance Table on the page facing the front cover. Treat each horse separately, and compare the weight it has to carry with the weight prescribed for it in the table, according to the age of the horse, the distance of the race and the month of the year. Then, add one point to the rating for each pound the horse has to carry less than the weight given in the table: or, subtract one point from the rating for every pound he has to carry more than the weight prescribed by the table. The highest resultant figure indicates the horse most favoured by the weights.

Example (1½ miles in July)

(Table Weights: 5-y-o 10-0; 4-y-o 9-13; 3-y-o 8-11)

6	Nimitz (9-12)	. .	Rating 115. . . .	add	2. . . .	117
4	Red Devil (9-9)	. .	Rating 114. . . .	add	4. . . .	118
6	Sweet Cindy (9-5)	. .	Rating 115. . . .	add	9. . . .	124
3	Jailhouse (8-12)	. .	Rating 120	subtract	1. . . .	119
4	Haakon (8-11)	. .	Rating 101. . . .	add	16. . . .	117
3	Fine Strike (8-7)	. .	Rating 112. . . .	add	4. . . .	116

Sweet Cindy (124) has the best chance at the weights, with 5 lb in hand of Jailhouse.

JOCKEYSHIP AND APPRENTICE ALLOWANCES

There is just one further point that arises in evaluating the chances of the horses on the basis of their ratings: the question of jockeyship in general, and apprentice allowances in particular. The allowance which may be claimed by an apprentice is given to enable apprentices to obtain race-riding experience against experienced jockeys. For the purposes of rating calculations it should, in general, be assumed that the allowance the apprentice is able to claim (3 lb, 5 lb, or 7 lb) is nullified by the boy's inexperience. Therefore, the *weight adjustments to the ratings should be calculated on the weight allotted by the handicapper, or determined by the conditions of the race,* and no extra addition should be made to a rating because the horse's rider claims an apprentice allowance.

The above is the general routine procedure. But of course there is no reason why the quality of jockeyship should not be taken into account in assessing the chances of horses in a race. Quite the contrary. Nobody would question that the jockeyship of a first-class rider is worth a pound or two, and occasionally an apprentice comes along who is riding quite as well as the average jockey long before he loses the right to claim. There is no reason whatever why, after the age and weight adjustments have been made to the ratings, small additional allowances should not be made for these matters of jockeyship. This, however, is a matter which must be left to the discretion of the reader.

WEIGHING UP A RACE

It having been discovered, by means of the ratings, which horses in a particular race are most favoured by the weights, complete analysis demands that the racing character of each horse, as set out in the commentary upon it, shall be checked to see if there is any reason why the horse might be expected not to run up to his rating. It counts for little that a horse is thrown in at the weights if he has no pretensions whatever to staying the distance, or is unable to act on the prevailing going.

These two matters, suitability of distance and going, are, no doubt, the most important points to be considered. But there are others. For example, the ability of a horse to accommodate himself to the conformation of the track. Then there is the matter of pace versus stamina: as between two stayers of equal merit, racing over a distance suitable to both, firm going, or a small field with the prospect of a slowly run race, would favour the one with the better pace and acceleration, whereas dead or soft going, or a big field with the prospect of a strong gallop throughout the race, would favour the sounder stayer. There is also the matter of temperament and behaviour at the start: nobody would be in a hurry to take a short price about a horse with whom it is always an even chance whether he will consent to race or not.

A few minutes spent checking up on these matters in the commentaries upon the horses concerned will sometimes put a very different complexion on a race from that which is put upon it by the ratings alone. We repeat, therefore, that the correct way to use Timeform, or this annual volume, in the analysis of individual races is, first to use the ratings to discover which horses are most favoured by the weights, and second, to check through the comments on the horse to discover what factors other than weight might also affect the outcome of the race.

Incidentally, in setting out the various characteristics, requirements and peculiarities of each horse in the commentary upon him, we have always expressed ourselves in as critical a manner as possible, endeavouring to say just as much, and no whit more than the facts seem to warrant. Where there are clear indications, and definite conclusions can be drawn with fair certainty, we have drawn them: if it is a matter of probability or possibility we have put it that way, being careful not to say the one when we mean the other; and where real conclusions are not to be drawn, we have been content to state the facts. Furthermore, when we say that a horse *may not* be suited by hard going, we do not expect the reader to treat it as though we had said that the horse is *not* suited by hard going. In short, both in our thinking and in the setting out of our views we have aimed at precision.

THE FORM SUMMARIES

The form summary enclosed in the round brackets shows for each individual horse the distance, the state of the going and where the horse finished in each of its races on the flat during the previous two seasons. Performances are in chronological sequence, the earliest being given first.

The distance of each race is given in furlongs, fractional distances being expressed in the decimal notation to the nearest tenth of a furlong.

The going is symbolised as follows: h=hard or very firm; f=firm; fg=fairly good, or on the firm side of good; g=good; d=dead, or on the soft side of good; s=soft, sticky or holding; v=heavy, very heavy or very holding.

Placings are indicated, up to fourth place, by the use of superior figures, an asterisk being used to denote a win.

Thus, 1983 10s* 12f^3 11.7g signifies that the horse ran three times in 1983, winning over 10 furlongs on soft going first time out, finishing third over twelve furlongs on firm going next time out, and then unplaced, not in the first four, over 11.7 furlongs on good going. NR means that the horse did not race.

Included in the pedigree details are the highest Timeform Annual ratings during their racing careers of the sires, dams and sires of dams of all horses, where the information is available.

Where sale prices are given F denotes the price in guineas sold as a foal, Y the price in guineas sold as a yearling. The prefix IR denotes Irish guineas.

THE RATING SYMBOLS

The following symbols, attached to the ratings, are to be interpreted as stated:-

p   the horse is likely to make more than normal progress and to improve on his rating.

P·   there is convincing evidence, or, to say the least, a very strong presumption that the horse is capable of form much better than he has so far displayed.

+   the horse may be rather better than we have rated him.

d   the horse appears to have deteriorated, and might no longer be capable of running to the rating given.

§   a horse who is somewhat ungenerous, faint-hearted, or a bit of a coward: one who may give his running on occasions, but cannot be relied upon to do so.

§§   an arrant rogue or thorough jade; so temperamentally unsatisfactory as to be not worth a rating.

?   if used in conjunction with a rating this symbol implies that the rating is based upon inadequate or unsatisfactory data, upon form which it is impossible to assess with confidence. The use of a query without a rating implies that although the horse has form, his merit cannot be assessed on the data at present available.

SALES
DATES
for 1984

RACEHORSES OF 1983

ABA NABEEM (USA) 2 ch.c. Fire Dancer–Penny Hughes (Penny Trumpet 99) (1983 7fg 7d⁴ 7g) rangy, deep-girthed colt; half-brother to 3 winners in USA, including very useful 1979 2-y-o sprinter Solo Legacy (by Solo Landing); dam won 5 small races in USA; sire unraced son of Northern Dancer; consistent but quite modest form in autumn maiden events; on second outing well-backed favourite at Warwick. *G. Harwood.*   **70**

ABC SUPERSTAR 3 b.c. Undulate–Paddy's Rose 81 (St Chad 120) (1982 NR 1983 10.4fg) half-brother to middle-distance winner Earl's Court (by Lord Gayle); dam 2-y-o 5f winner; 100/1, tailed off a long way out in 13-runner maiden race won by Home Secretary at Chester in July. *C. Crossley.*   **–**

ABDALI 2 b.c. Top Ville 129–Abalvina 119 (Abdos 134) (1983 8fg*) Mar 16; first foal; dam won Prix Cleopatre and stayed 1½f well; second favourite, put up a very pleasing first effort when beating more-experienced Commerce by 1½ lengths in maiden race at Longchamp in October, keeping on well after holding a good place throughout; promises to make a very smart middle-distance performer. *A. de Royer Dupre, France.*   **103 p**

ABDOUN 4 b.c. Luthier 126–Afrique (Exbury 138) (1982 12f* 14fg⁴ 14g* 13.3f* 14fg 13.3g⁴ 14g 1983 14s* 12f 12g⁴ 14g² 14.6fg 18fg) small, sparely-made colt; good walker and very good mover; useful handicapper; beat Popsi's Joy by ¾ length at Newmarket in May; ran creditably next 3 starts, including when fourth to Regal Steel in Old Newton Cup at Haydock and 1½ lengths second to Jupiter Island in Tote-Ebor at York; suited by 1¾m and should stay further; acts on any going; sweated up at York; runs the odd moderate race, and did so on fifth start; appears to go particularly well when fresh. *M. Stoute.*   **99**

ABE MY BOY 2 ch.g. Absalom 128–Balidium 69 (Psidium 130) (1983 5v 5v 7fg 5g) May 8; 5,000Y; sturdy, good-bodied gelding; fourth reported foal; dam stayed long distances and is half-sister to Pugnacity; no worthwhile form, including in Catterick seller; trained by R. Boss until after third outing. *A. Balding.*   **–**

ABERFIELD 6 ch.g. Northfields–Abergara (Abernant 142) (1982 12fg² 10fg* 10f 11.1g* 12f 10.2g² 10.5f³ 10g* 12f* 13.3g⁴ 10g² 9d 10v 8s³ 12s 1983 10fg³ 12f² 12fg 10f 12f² 11s 12fg⁴ 12fg 10.2fg³ 12fg) leggy, narrow gelding; middle-distance handicapper; acts on any going but is ideally suited by top-of-the-ground; blinkered once in 1980; good mount for an inexperienced rider. *P. Kelleway.*   **93**

ABERRATION 3 b.c. Abwah 118–Pilamenon 90 (Parthia 132) (1982 7s 1983 8.2s 10fg 10fg 12f 10.2fg 10g 10g* 10fg) quite a well-made colt; plater; blinkered, showed improved form when making most to win at Leicester in October (bought in 1,600 gns); had stiff task only subsequent outing; stays 1¼m. *M. McCormack.*   **70**

ABERSEA 2 b.f. Silly Season 127–Aberklair 72 (Klairon 131) (1983 5v 5v⁴ 6s 5.8g 5fg 7f) May 7; 1,900Y; lengthy filly; plating-class maiden; dead. *J. Benstead.*   **61**

ABJAD 2 b.c. Mummy's Pet 125–Maxim's 88 (Major Portion 129) (1983 6g 5f 6h 7d) Mar 19; 32,000Y; big, rangy colt; has a round action; brother to useful sprinter Amorous, and half-brother to numerous winners, including useful miler Deadly Nightshade (by Floribunda); dam 2-y-o 5f winner; plating-class maiden; stays 7f. *G. Huffer.*   **69**

ABLE ALBERT 3 gr.c. Abwah 118–Polly Peachum 123 (Singing Strand) (1982 5s* 5f* 5f* 5f* 1983 7s³ 7d³ 6d 6f 7g* 7fg⁴ 6s) big, strong, rangy, good sort; unbeaten in 4 early-season races as a 2-y-o; met with a setback afterwards and was off course 10 months; ran very well when third in spring in £3,100 event at Leicester (to Proclaim) and Ladbroke European Free Handicap at Newmarket (to Boom Town Charlie after swerving badly leaving stalls); didn't run up to his best next 2 starts but really took the eye and returned to form after a 2-month absence in 6-runner City of York Stakes in August, beating Spanish Place gamely by ½ length; ran a bit freely when 4 lengths fourth of 8 behind Annie Edge in Kiveton Park Stakes at Doncaster in September; seems suited by 7f nowadays; acts on any going; genuine. *M. H. Easterby.*   **111**

ABLE DAN 2 ch.g. Full of Hope 125–Set Piece 69 (Firestreak 125) (1983 5v 6fg 5f 5.1f² 5.1f² 5f) half-brother to a winner in Norway; dam prolific winner in   **54**

City of York Stakes, York—Able Albert runs on gamely from Spanish Place and Coquito's Friend

Norway; plater; should stay at least 6f; changed hands 1,800 gns Newmarket September Sales. *P. Brookshaw.*

ABORIGINE (FR) 3 b.f. Riverman 131–Prima 75 (Alcide 136) (1982 9s* 1983 **117**
9s⁴ 10fg² 12fg⁴ 13.5d³ 12s 12g³ 12s*) half-sister to several winners, including useful 1¼m winner Laska Floko (by Thatch) and good Italian performers King Jay (by King Emperor) and My Royal Prima (by Captain's Gig); dam half-sister to very useful stayer Saraceno; didn't get off mark in 1983 until October, when beating Brezzo by 4 lengths in 90,000 francs event at Saint-Cloud; in frame earlier at Saint-Cloud (twice, shaping very well when close fourth to Escaline in Prix Vanteaux on reappearance after which she was off course 2½ months), Evry (also twice) and Deauville; stays 13.5f; probably acts on any going, but is well suited by plenty of give underfoot. *E. Bartholomew, France.*

ABOUDI 2 br.c. Frimley Park 109–Young Mementa (Young Christopher 119) **79**
(1983 5d 5f⁴ 5f 5fg* 5g 5g) Apr 5; neat colt; half-brother to several winners, including useful 1980 2-y-o 5f and 6f winner Mementa Mia and 3-y-o 5f winner Django (both by Music Boy); dam never ran; won 15-runner maiden race at Bath in September; trained by K. Brassey first start. *B. Hills.*

ABOUSHABUN (USA) 3 b.g. Halo–Dear Editor (Prince John) (1982 NR 1983 —
8s 12g 13fg⁴ 13f 14f 14f) $25,000Y; close-coupled, good-topped gelding; not a good walker; fourth foal; half-brother to stakes winners Lt. John (by Lt. Stevens) and Writin' Mama (by Gleaming); dam won over 6f at 4 yrs; fourth in maiden race at Nottingham in July; should stay 1¾m; blinkered fifth start; sold to J. Jenkins 1,600 gns Newmarket Autumn Sales. *G. Huffer*

A BOY NAMED SIOUX 3 b.g. Idiot's Delight 115–Susanella 83 (Eborneezer —
105) (1982 NR 1983 12v 11.7s 11.7v) fourth foal; half-brother to a disqualified winner by Native Bazaar; dam needed long distances; beaten a long way in maiden races at Wolverhampton and Bath (2) in spring. *W. R. Williams.*

ABSAROKE (USA) 3 ch.c. Crow 134–Scarlet My Dear (Grey Dawn II 132) **87**
(1982 NR 1983 8d³ 11v 10s³ 13d* 12f³ 13fg* 14f³ 14d 14g³) tall, quite attractive colt; half-brother to 4 winners in USA, including stakes-placed Mouse Corps (by Within Hail); dam third once from 11 starts; successful in maiden race at Ayr in June and slowly-run minor event on same course in July, in latter event quickening into

lead 3f out and beating Misty Halo by 2 lengths; third to Gildoran in £4,900 handicap at Goodwood later in July and to Same Again in Norwegian St Leger at Ovrevoll in October; stays 1¾m; acts on any going; tends to get stirred up in preliminaries. *G. Pritchard-Gordon.*

ABSOLVE 2 gr.f. Absalom 128–Lemon Blossom 83 (Acropolis 132) (1983 7f 7h 7f³ 8.2s) Mar 9; 11,000Y; good-topped filly; half-sister to very useful 1981 2-y-o 6f winner Foam Bath (by Wollow), useful 1½m performer Cima (by High Top) and a winner in Austria; dam won over 11f; just over 3 lengths third of 19 to Circus Plume in maiden race at Salisbury in September, only indication of merit; favourite, last of 11 in Hamilton nursery the following month; sold 8,400 gns Newmarket Autumn Sales. *Sir Mark Prescott.* **80 ?**

ACADIE (FR) 3 ch.f. Caracolero 131–Djallybrook (Djakao 124) (1982 6f 7fg* 8fg 7g³ 1983 8.5g 8.5fg 9f 10fg 8f 8f 8fg 7.6fg 12d) sparely-made filly; won minor event at Doncaster as a 2-y-o; raced in USA early in 1983 and was unplaced at Gulfstream (twice) and Hialeah; didn't show much on her return; should stay 1½m; acts on a firm surface; blinkered last 5 starts; retained 1,700 gns Newmarket Autumn Sales. *M. Ryan.* **—**

ACAMONT 2 b.c. Acamas 130–Battlemaid (Captain's Gig) (1983 6fg³ 7fg³ 8s* 6.5g⁴) Feb 2; IR 36,000Y; fourth foal; half-brother to a winner in Malaysia by Tyrant; dam third over 6f and 7.5f at 2 yrs in Ireland; made virtually all when winning 11-runner minor event at Evry in September most impressively by 10 lengths; faded in final furlong when 4¾ lengths fourth of 14 to Diamada in Prix Eclipse at Saint-Cloud the following month; probably found 6f too sharp at 2 yrs and will stay 1¼m; acts well on soft going. *F. Boutin, France.* **106**

ACCLAIM 3 b.g. Record Token 128–Acolyte 86 (Roan Rocket 128) (1982 NR 1983 8f 10.1f 10h 12fg) sturdy, workmanlike gelding; first foal; dam, 1m winner, is half-sister to smart sprinter Acquit; showed a little ability on second and final outings. *N. Henderson.* **—**

ACCLIMATISE 3 b.f. Shirley Heights 130–Habituee (Habitat 134) (1982 7d* 7g² 8g⁴ 8g* 1983 10.5s 12g² 12g³ 10f* 12d⁴) **115**
Acclimatise, who'd been one of the leading winter fancies for the Oaks on the strength of winning the Hoover Fillies Mile only to drift to 20/1 as a result of a poor showing in the Musidora Stakes on her seasonal reappearance, came out best of the fourteen fillies outclassed by Sun Princess at Epsom. Fourth into the straight in pursuit of the eventual winner, she ran on strongly past Ghaiya and Cormorant Wood and ultimately kept New Coins out of second place decisively by two and a half lengths. Sun Princess was a vintage Oaks winner, but the field she beat was ordinary. New Coins and the next two home, Shore Line and Ski Sailing, failed to win in twelve further starts between them; the admirable Cormorant Wood and Royal Heroine, who came next, were nowhere near their best on the day. Acclimatise made three subsequent starts: she finished third of thirteen to Give Thanks and Ski Sailing in the Lancashire Oaks at Haydock, beaten two lengths and the same apparently on merit though she didn't have much room on the last turn; next she won a six-runner Nassau Stakes at Goodwood; finally, she turned in a lacklustre performance in the Yorkshire Oaks, admittedly just twelve lengths down on Sun Princess as at Epsom but also soundly beaten by Green Lucia and Give Thanks, done with two furlongs out, in fact. There is a certain inconsistency in

Nassau Stakes, Goodwood—Acclimatise quickens clear from Air Distingue (later disqualified), La Grigia (No.7), Gaygo Lady (No. 5) and Elysian

Acclimatise's form which might have been the result of temperament—she seemed keener some days than others (her trainer said of her 'you have almost got to be a psychiatrist to deal with this one'). Her performance in the Nassau Stakes contrasted sharply with that in the Yorkshire Oaks. She was impressive in the Nassau, quickening really well when sent after the strong-looking Air Distingue inside the last two furlongs and eventually beating her subsequently-disqualified opponent by three lengths. Acclimatise was unquestionably the deserving winner of a controversial contest: Gaygo Lady posed no threat to Acclimatise when hampered by Air Distingue inside the final furlong, and the others had every conceivable chance.

Acclimatise (b.f. 1980)	Shirley Heights (b 1975)	Mill Reef (b 1968)	Never Bend
			Milan Mill
		Hardiemma (b 1969)	Hardicanute
			Grand Cross
	Habituee (b 1971)	Habitat (b 1966)	Sir Gaylord
			Little Hut
		Participator (ch 1960)	Petition
			Participation

Had she shown up better in the Yorkshire Oaks Acclimatise would have been a serious candidate for the Park Hill Stakes over the St Leger course at Doncaster. Although she gained her only win as a three-year-old at a mile and a quarter on fast ground she usually gave the impression that she would have no difficulty in staying a mile and three quarters. Furthermore her half-sister Ma Femme (by Bustino), who won the Galtres Stakes at York incidentally, finished a creditable third in the Park Hill in 1981. The dam never raced beyond nine furlongs; she won over a mile at Saint-Cloud as a three-year-old. Her dam, Participator, won over a mile at Lanark and a mile and a half at Pontefract and Leicester as a four-year-old; she disappointed the only time she was tried over two miles but she also gave the impression that a mile and a half wasn't her limit. Participator, a half-sister to numerous winners including the Doncaster Cup runner-up Alexis and another smart staying horse Partner, was out of a winning daughter of the very speedy Arabella, winner of the Queen Mary Stakes, Champagne Stakes and Imperial Produce Stakes. This family has been a very successful one, and Habituee was sold for 1,850,000 dollars at Keeneland in November. The number of Habituee's winning produce isn't confined to Acclimatise and Ma Femme. She is also the dam of Bruckner (by Wollow), who had definite stamina limitations; a seven-furlong winner early in his three-year-old career, he was put to sprinting after finishing down the field in Assert's Irish Sweeps Derby, and ultimately won the Seven Springs Sprint over six furlongs at the Curragh.

Both Ma Femme and Acclimatise are substantially-made fillies; Acclimatise is also a particularly attractive one. Though Acclimatise won on softish going first time out as a two-year-old she showed easily her best form on a sound surface and was probably suited by one. Further evidence on the point isn't likely to be forthcoming, since she's almost certainly been retired. *B. Hobbs.*

ACCURACY 2 ch.f. Gunner B 126–Veracious 86 (Astec 128) (1983 5g 6g 6f 7f) May 9; well-made filly; third foal; half-sister to 3-y-o So True (by So Blessed), a very useful middle-distance filly; dam effective from 1¼m to 2m; behind in sizeable fields of maidens in the South; should stay quite well. *G. Balding.*   –

ACCUSED (USA) 3 br.c. Alleged 138–Pas de Nom (Admiral's Voyage) (1982 7fg² 7fg³ 8g³ 1983 10.6v⁴ 8g⁴ 10g) tall, quite attractive colt; good mover; not seen out here after July and was rather disappointing; fourth in maiden races at Haydock and Newmarket, looking short of speed on latter course; should be suited by middle distances; probably unsuited by heavy ground; has a tendency to break blood vessels; sent to USA. *I. Balding.*   **89 d**

ACE OF ACES 2 ch.c. Continuation 120–Stevie 79 (The Phoenix) (1983 6fg) Mar 22; brother to 2 poor animals and half-brother to several winners; dam sprinting half-sister to Deep Diver; 33/1, tenth of 14 in minor event at Nottingham in July. *J. Hardy.*   –

ACE OF SPIES 2 b.g. He Loves Me 120–Belle Bergere 104 (Faberge II 121) (1983 6fg⁴) Mar 28; 1,850Y; second reported foal; dam won at up to 1½m; 20/1, shaped well (finishing very strongly indeed) when 7 lengths fourth of 17 behind Taqdir in maiden race at Lingfield in October; sure to improve. *P. Cole.*   **70 p**

ACERCATE 2 b.c. Town and Country 124–Cotillion 73 (Gala Performance) (1983 7fg 7g⁴ 7fg⁴ 8d) Mar 30; 3,900Y; sturdy colt; third foal; dam 2-y-o 5f winner; 4½ lengths fourth of 11 to Ministerial in Hyperion Stakes at Ascot in October, third outing and best effort; should stay 1m; acts on a firm surface. *M. Francis.*   **88**

ACER LAD 2 b.g. Abwah 118–Avon Royale 66 (Remainder 106) (1983 5s 5v 5v **47** 5s² 6fg) Mar 31; plain, good-topped gelding; second foal; dam won over 7f and 1m; plater; should stay 6f; best run on soft going; not seen out after June. *D. Wintle.*

ACHERON 3 ch.c. Bay Express 132–River Aire 82 (Klairon 131) (1982 5d* 5fg 6f⁴ 7fg⁴ 8.2d 8s 6s 1983 7v 8s 7d 7v⁴ 7fg 8.3f) small, well-made colt; plater; stays 7f; probably acts on any going; blinkered final outing (finished last). *C. Wildman.*

ACID ANT 2 b.f. Owen Anthony 102–Acid Drop (Acer 123) (1983 5f 5g 5fg 6g) – third reported foal; dam placed over hurdles; of no account. *H. Beasley.*

ACK ACK REGIMENT (USA) 2 b.c. Ack Ack–En Tiempo (Bold Hour) (1982 **71** 8g 1983 11s 11.7s 10f⁴ 11.7h³ 12f 16f² 16fg 16d⁴ 18fg⁴) big, lengthy, fair sort; ran on strongly when ½-length second to Night Eye in handicap at Newcastle in August, best effort; clearly suited by a test of stamina. *P. Cole.*

ACKA'S GEM 2 b.f. Tower Walk 130–Ackabarrow 97 (Laser Light 118) (1983 5fg **71** 5g*) Apr 14; second foal; dam won 6 times over 5f; made all to win 11-runner minor event at Edinburgh in October by a neck from Sister Hannah. *Mrs. A. Cousins.*

ACORA'S PREDICTION 3 gr or ro.f. Scallywag 127–Royal Ribston (Ribston – 104) (1982 7fg 7g 1983 10v 8g 12g 8f 7fg⁴ 8f 8d 16fg) big filly; little worthwhile form in varied races, including 1000 Guineas and Oaks. *M. Haynes.*

ACQUISITOR (USA) 2 b. or br.f. Tom Rolfe–Ecstacism (What A Pleasure) **79 p** (1983 6fg 7fg) Feb 5; $80,000Y; smallish, lengthy filly; first foal; dam, unplaced in 4 starts, is out of sister to French Oaks winner Belle Sicambre; noted running on strongly when unplaced in big fields of maidens at Newmarket in the autumn, particularly on second occasion when 5¾ lengths fifth of 22 behind Travel Away; will be much better suited by longer distances, and should stay 1½m. *B. Hills.*

ACRUX 2 b.c. Keren 100–Windblown (Ribston 104) (1983 5d⁴ 6f 7f) Apr 1; small – colt; poor mover; bad plater; not raced after July; blinkered final outing. *N. Chamberlain.*

ACTION BELLE 3 b.f. Auction Ring 123–Tavella 98 (Petingo 135) (1982 6g 8f – 1983 8s 8s 8d 7v² 7d 8g 12f 12fg 10fg) quite well-made filly; second in maiden race at Newcastle in April, easily best effort; behind in a seller final start; gives impression she should stay 1m; sometimes blinkered; sold to M. Tate 2,100 gns Ascot October Sales. *C. Booth.*

ACTION TIME 2 ch.c. Sagaro 133–Royal Declaration 78 (Breeders Dream 116) **81** (1983 7f³ 7f⁴ 7fg³ 8fg⁴ 8.2fg 10fg) rather leggy, lengthy colt; first known foal; dam won over 11f; often faced difficult tasks, and usually ran well; should stay 1½m; acts on firm going; capable of winning maiden event; to be trained by P. Makin. *D. Morrill.*

ACTON TURVILLE 2 ch.f. Porto Bello 118–Canteen Katie (King's Troop 118) – (1983 5v 5s 5g 5.8g 6fg) Mar 30; 2,500F, 1,250Y; workmanlike filly; half-sister to 1981 2-y-o 5f winner Broadway Lodge (by The Go-Between) and 3 winners in Italy; of no account. *C. Wildman.*

ACUSHLA MACREE 6 ch.m. Mansingh 120–Cannie Cassie 70 (Canisbay 120) **47** (1982 10.2g 8d 10f 10.1fg 10fg 10.6f 10fg³ 8g³ 10d 8fg 10f 10f² 10g² 8fg* 8fg⁴ 10.6s 1983 10.2d 8v 8g 8fg 10f 10f* 8f 8f 10f 10f) neat mare; poor handicapper; sometimes runs in sellers; readily won amateur riders event at Folkestone in July; stays 1¼m well; acts on any going, except possibly very soft; wears blinkers or a hood; good mount for an inexperienced rider; sometimes bandaged behind. *F. J. Houghton.*

ADAM CRAIG 5 b.g. Connaught 130–Karenina 95 (Silver Shark 129) (1982 12f* – 12f⁴ 13g 20fg 20g 1983 13g 15.8d 15g) lengthy gelding; poor handicapper; stays at least 1½m; acts on any going; has sweated up; blinkered second start. *M. Naughton.*

ADAM'S PEAK (USA) 2 b.c. Riva Ridge–Baussibay (Sanctus II 132) (1983 5s⁴ **89 ?** 6s⁴ 6s 6f² 7f³ 7f² 6fg² 7s 7fg 6fg²) Feb 20; $55,000Y; strong, compact colt; good walker and mover; first foal; dam, lightly-raced 1m winner in France, is granddaughter of very smart Bubunia; good second in Gimcrack Stakes at York in August, on seventh appearance, but nowhere near that form in his other races; bred to stay 1m; suited by fast ground; ridden in paddock first 3 outings, after having to be withdrawn on intended debut; not to be trusted. *D. Elsworth.*

ADAY EARLY (CAN) 3 b.f. Cojak–Susie's Valentine (Winning Hit) (1982 NR – 1983 8s 8f 10f 11f 12fg) $36,000Y; lengthy filly; first foal; dam won 7 races at up to 7f, including claiming events; well behind in maiden races; blinkered last 2 outings. *S. Norton.*

ADDAANA 2 gr.f. Mill Reef 141–Pasty 122 (Raffingora 130) (1983 6f 6f 5f⁴ 5fg²   **78**
5s*) Apr 14; smallish, close-coupled, fair sort, lacking in scope; third foal;
half-sister to 1m winner Cornish Granite (by Ragstone); dam best English 2-y-o filly
of 1975; blinkered, made all in 8-runner maiden race at Hamilton in October; clearly
thought best at 5f; probably acts on any going. *H. T. Jones.*

ADEEB 2 b.c. Artaius 129–Calamarie (Deep Diver 134) (1983 6f 6f 7f² 6f³ 6f* 6f   **80**
7g 6fg) Mar 23; good-quartered, attractive colt; second foal to Northern
Hemisphere time; half-brother to 3-y-o Forever Mary (by Red Alert); dam, Irish 6f
winner, is half-sister to very smart Greenland Park; made all in 3-runner minor
event at Yarmouth in August, winning by a short head from odds-on Paramaribo;
stays 7f; has raced only on a sound surface. *W. O'Gorman.*

ADEEBAH (USA) 3 br.f. Damascus–Transylvania (Bold Ruler) (1982 6fg³ 5fg*   **89**
5g³ 6g³ 6g 5s² 5g 1983 5fg 5f⁴ 5fg 5f). close-coupled filly; fourth of 15 to Django
in handicap at Doncaster in June, best effort; stays 6f; seems to act on any going;
blinkered second and final outings. *H. T. Jones.*

ADELONG 2 b.f. Free State 125–Eastern Romance 73 (Sahib 114) (1983 5v 6s)   **—**
Apr 11; 5,200Y; lengthy, good sort; third foal; sister to 7f and 1m winner State
Romance and half-sister to 3-y-o Tez Shahzada (by Mummy's Pet); dam won 6f
seller at 2 yrs; backward, showed little in modest company at Newbury and
Leicester in May. *R. Laing.*

ADIRONDACK 8 br.g. Wolver Hollow 126–Palgal (Le Prince 98) (1982 10f³ 11g   **—**
12g 14s 18s 1983 12s) lengthy ex-Irish gelding; poor mover; poor performer
nowadays; stays 1¼m; suited by firm going; has worn blinkers. *G. Lockerbie.*

ADIYAMANN 2 ch.c. Nishapour 125–Adayra (Le Haar 126) (1983 6f 6f 7fg² 7g⁴   **87**
8g*) Feb 10; attractive, quite well-made colt; good walker and excellent mover
with a smooth light action; half-brother to 3 winners, including 11f winner Ardar (by
Relko) and stayer Ayyabaan (by Sun Prince); dam, placed over 10.5f in France, is
half-sister to high-class 7f to 1¼m winner Sharapour; won 10-runner minor event at
Bath in October by ¾ length from Worth While; will be suited by 1¼m+; yet to race
on soft surface; type to train on and make quite a useful 3-y-o. *F. J. Houghton.*

ADJUSTED 4 ch.g. Busted 134–Angel Row 96 (Prince Regent 129) (1982 7d   **62**
8.2v 6f⁴ 5g 6fg³ 6g⁴ 5g 6s 1983 6f* 7h⁴ 7f 7fg) big, strong, plain gelding; plater;
bought in 1,000 gns after winning at Yarmouth in July; stay 7f; acts well on fast
ground; trained by R. Hobson first start. *R. Hollinshead.*

ADMINISTRATOR 6 b.g. Gay Fandango 132–Maureen's Slipper (Gratitude   **46**
130) (1982 NR 1983 8f 10f²) lengthy gelding; former plater; stays 1¼m; seems to
act on any going; has run respectably for an amateur; used to be none too reliable;
has been taken down early. *H. O'Neill.*

ADMIRAL GRENVILLE 7 b.g. Sweet Revenge 129–Soverena 98 (Sovereign   **48**
Lord 120) (1982 NR 1983 12f 12f² 11.7f 11.7fg) big, rangy gelding; suited by 1½m;
acts on any going; has been tried in blinkers; suitable mount for an apprentice.
J. Jenkins.

ADMIRAL'S RULER 3 ch.g. Anax 120–Lancashire Lass 73 (King's Troop 118)   **—**
(1982 NR 1983 7.6v⁴ 7g 6f 8.2g) 13,500Y; useful-looking gelding; good walker;
half-brother to 2 winners, including 1981 2-y-o 5f winner Petworth Park (by
Mummy's Pet); dam sprinter; ran a creditable first race when fourth in maiden
event at Lingfield in May but was very disappointing afterwards; possibly needs
plenty of give in the ground. *P. Cole.*

ADMIRAL STEVE 3 ch.g. Home Guard 129–Sardinia (Romulus 129) (1982 5d   **73**
5fg 6s 5g³ 5s⁴ 6s 1983 6d 6g 7f² 6fg 7fg 7f³ 8g 7₅; 7.6d 6d* 7f) rather leggy, quite
attractive gelding; none too consistent, but beat Master Cawston by a short head in
19-runner handicap at Newbury in October; stays 7f; acts on any going; blinkered
nowadays; exported to Malaysia. *R. Hannon.*

ADOCENTYN (USA) 2 b.f. Upper Nile–Liz. Piet (Piet) (1983 6d) Apr 29;   **– p**
$230,000Y; closely related to 3-y-o Northern Adventure (by Far North), and
half-sister to numerous winners, including Father Hogan (by Dewan), a smart
winner at up to 1¼m, and to Salieri's dam; dam won at up to 9f; 12/1 and apprentice
ridden, about 10 lengths fifth of 12 behind Visible Form in maiden event at Yarmouth
in September; will be much better suited by longer distances; sure to improve. *H.
Cecil.*

ADONIJAH 3 ch.c. High Line 125–Shadow Queen (Darius 129) (1982 6d³ 6g³   **126**
1983 8d* 10v* 12f⁴ 10f* 10.5d* 8fg² 8fg² 10fg)
    Prices realized at the record-breaking Newmarket December Sales of 1982
ranged from the minimum bid of 500 guineas to 1,020,000 guineas laid out for

Mr K. Abdulla's "Adonijah" (L. Piggott)

Tenea, a once-raced three-year-old half-sister to Tachypous, Taxiarchos, Tromos, Tyrnavos and Tolmi from Bruce Hobbs's stable; the average was over 18,000 guineas. Since trading mainly concerned broodmares, prospective broodmares, foals and yearlings, time must pass before we can see how wisely most of the money was spent, but few better bargains are likely to emerge than one already come to light. Tenea's stable-companion Adonijah, a two-year-old in training with quite useful maiden form, sold for 38,000 guineas. Six months later Adonijah started favourite for the prestigious King Edward VII Stakes at Royal Ascot. He failed to show his best form in finishing fourth of six to Shareef Dancer on that occasion but later in the season he ran well in top company over shorter distances, picking up second-place money in the Waterford Crystal Mile and the Queen Elizabeth II Stakes. In all he won four out of eight races, was out of the frame only in the Dubai Champion Stakes, and earned almost as much as he fetched at Tattersalls.

That sale wasn't the last for Adonijah: following easy victories in a maiden race at Newbury in April (from Seymour Hicks) and a relatively minor event at Lingfield in May (from Soldier Ant), and just before he stepped up in class at Royal Ascot, he was bought privately by another patron of his stable. Adonijah's performance in the King Edward VII Stakes can't have been too encouraging for the new owner. However, it could be explained at the time on grounds of distance or going. Adonijah ran like a horse who didn't get a mile and a half, leading into the straight, soon being pressed then quickly headed. Without being punished he finished four

41

and a half lengths down on Shareef Dancer. Events soon showed that firm going wasn't against Adonijah; so, whether or not he gets a mile and a half, the likelihood is that he's better over shorter distances. His trainer never raced him over further than ten and a half furlongs again. For a while the horse was returned to less exacting contests. At Newbury in July he resumed winning ways in the Steventon Stakes, a seven-runner race for under £5,000 in which one of his opponents was the eight-year-old steeplechaser Fishleigh Gamble. Predictably Fishleigh Gamble finished virtually tailed off while the odds-on Adonijah came home two lengths ahead of Sailor's Dance. At York in August the High Line Stakes disappointingly attracted a field of three—Adonijah, St Boniface making his first appearance of the season, and Shackle Pin who'd shown no form for a long time. Allowing for the limitations of the opposition Adonijah was still a very impressive winner: he was always moving strongly, and ran right away in the last two furlongs, showing the commendable attitude to the job in hand that we'd noticed more than once previously. The High Line Stakes was Adonijah's last easy race; it was also the last race he won, but it should not have been. He was desperately unlucky to be beaten by Montekin in the Waterford Crystal Mile at Goodwood later in August. The post came just too soon after he'd had the greatest difficulty in finding room to make his run; he was only half a length down at the end, closing fast. Adonijah had Montekin four lengths behind in third place when second to Sackford in the Queen Elizabeth II Stakes at Ascot in September. Sackford was too good for him and beat him in clear-cut fashion by a length and a half, taking over inside the last furlong from Adonijah who'd gone on early in the straight. This was Adonijah's best performance, and although he gave the impression in achieving it that a return to a mile and a quarter would suit him he again finished behind Sackford in the Champion Stakes at Newmarket in October: they were fifth and sixth respectively to Cormorant Wood, separated by three parts of a length; Montekin was seventh.

Adonijah (ch.c. 1980)	High Line (ch 1966)	High Hat (ch 1957)	Hyperion
			Madonna
		Time Call (b 1955)	Chanteur II
			Aleria
	Shadow Queen (ch 1965)	Darius (b 1951)	Dante
			Yasna
		Shadow (ch 1960)	Alycidon
			Sunshade

Adonijah's dam has proved a far better broodmare than racemare; decidedly short of ability on the track she had already produced three winners from five runners when Adonijah came along. The pick of these was another horse named after one of King David's disloyal sons, the high-class sprinter Absalom (by Abwah), winner of the Vernons Sprint Cup, the Diadem Stakes and the Cornwallis Stakes. Stamina used to be the family's strong suit. Shadow, the second dam, was out of a winning half-sister to the Cesarewitch and Yorkshire Cup winner Woodburn; she herself won over thirteen furlongs and was placed in the Ribblesdale Stakes and Lingfield Oaks Trial.

Adonijah will, no doubt, continue to do his racing at distances of a mile to a mile and a quarter. He looks a likely horse, all remaining well with him, for such races in the first part of the next season as the Earl of Sefton Stakes and the Westbury Stakes (both won by the stable with Ivano in 1983). A small, sturdy colt who walks well, a grand little workman, Adonijah acts on any going. He has a good turn of foot. *H. Cecil.*

ADVANCE 2 b.c. Habitat 134–Gay Trinket 72 (Grey Sovereign 128§) (1983 6f⁴)   **74 p**
May 7; strong, good sort; good walker and mover; half-brother to several winners, including fairly useful 1½m winner Goumi (by Grundy) and useful sprinter Nusantara (by Lorenzaccio); dam headstrong half-sister to French Derby second Patch; 4/1 and just in need of race, had unlucky run when 4 lengths fourth of 7 to Creag-an-Sgor in maiden event at York in July on only appearance, having to be snatched up when challenging 1f out and no time to recover; looks the sort to win races. *J. Tree.*

AESCULAPIUS 2 ch.g. Mansingh 120–Silver Love (The Axe II 115) (1983 6fg²)   **72 p**
Feb 12; 9,800F, 19,000Y; quite attractive gelding; second foal; dam ran 4 times; 10/1, staying-on 2 lengths second of 7 to Kayus in maiden race at Ayr in July; gelded subsequently; promises to stay 7f. *P. Haslam.*

AFFAIR 2 ch.f. Bold Lad (Ire) 133–Guest Night 109 (Sir Ivor 135) (1983 6f⁴ 6f 6f*   **78**
8fg 7fg) Feb 22; compact filly; fourth foal; half-sister to 3 winners, including 1979 2-y-o 7f winner Downderry (by English Prince); dam, daughter of high-class filly

Mesopotamia, won over 7f and 9f; won 23-runner maiden race at Lingfield in August; showed nothing under stiffish weights in nurseries afterwards, on final outing blinkered and last of 14; should stay beyond 6f; raced only on fast ground. *H. T. Jones.*

AFRICAN ABANDON 2 b.f. African Sky 124–Saintly Angel 87 (So Blessed **104** 130) (1983 5d* 5d* 5d4 5s4 5f 5f4 5f 5fg3 5s 5s2 6fg 5fg) Mar 12; IR 10,500 Y; fair sort; good mover; third foal; half-sister to 3-y-o Seraphim (by Oats) and fairly useful 1981 2-y-o 5f winner Shared Moment (by Bay Express); dam lightly-raced 2-y-o 5f winner; justified favouritism early in season in maiden race at Doncaster and minor event at Newmarket; usually faced stiffish tasks subsequently, running easily best race when second to Petorius in Harry Rosebery Challenge Trophy at Ayr in September; best form at 5f; acts on any going but is evidently in her element on soft; below form in blinkers fifth outing; often sweats up. *C. Brittain.*

AFRICAN CONNECTION 2 b.g. African Sky 124–Turkish Song (Aglojo 119) **74 §** (1983 6fg3 6g 5g 5fg 5fg) Apr 7; 9,400GY; quite attractive gelding; second produce; dam, half-sister to Irish Oaks second Indian Melody, won over 5f in Ireland; disappointed badly after finishing promising third in minor event at York in June; off course (coughing) for 2 months after second start; gelded after fourth; one to leave alone. *R. Hollinshead.*

AFRICAN DREAM 3 b.f. African Sky 124–Jabula 99 (Sheshoon 132) (1982 5f3 6g **70** 5.8g 8.2d3 1983 10fg 8.2h 8f4 8f2 8d3 8.2g) rather lightly-made filly; evidently suited by 1m and is worth another chance at 1¼m; ran moderately final start. *P. Cole.*

AFRICAN HERON 2 b. or br.f. African Sky 124–Clear Belle (Klairon 131) (1983 — 7f 7fg 7h) May 11; 12,500Y; half-sister to 3 winners including Italian 1000 Guineas third Laser Belle (by Laser Light); dam showed only poor form; well beaten in maiden races and a minor event; blinkered final start; sold 600 gns Newmarket September Sales. *B. Swift.*

AFRICAN IMAGE 2 b.c. African Sky 124–Imagem (Dancer's Image) (1983 5d 5f **76** 5f* 5f 5fg4 6g 5g) Apr 21; IR 3,000Y; lightly-made colt; first foal; dam winning Irish sprinter; won 10-runner maiden race at Catterick in July; fourth of 5 in Beverley nursery in September, best other form; should stay 6f. *R. Hollinshead.*

AFRICAN JOY 4 b.c. African Sky 124–Baby Elli (Diplomat Way) (1982 8d 7fg **116** 7f2 7s 8s 7g 1983 8v4 8s* 8v 8v4 9.7v 8s2 8.5v* 8s4 8fg* 7d* 9g 6.5fg3 6f3 8fg4 8g 5f 7f3 7fg 8g) tall colt; second foal; closely related to a useful winner in Spain by Averof; did well at 4 yrs and showed himself a smart performer, winning gentlemen riders race at Saint-Cloud, handicaps at Longchamp and Chantilly and Prix de la Porte Maillot at Longchamp again; beat Geral by ½ length in last-named in June; in frame several starts afterwards, including in Prix Maurice de Gheest (behind Beaudelaire), Prix de Meautry (behind Maximova) and Prix Quincey (behind Great Substence), all at Deauville; best at up to 8.5f; acts on any going; tough. *D. Smaga, France.*

AFRICAN PEARL 5 b.h. African Sky 124–Stickpin 74 (Gulf Pearl 117) (1982 **70** 10g* 10fg* 8f2 9fg3 9g2 10fg* 10fg* 1983 12f3 8fg 10.5f 10g 10g) quite attractive horse; won handicaps at Folkestone, Epsom (City and Suburban), the Curragh and Leopardstown at 4 yrs; below form in 1983; stays 1¼m; yet to race on very soft going, but acts on any other; sometimes sweats up; has been bandaged; sold to J. S. Wilson 3,500 gns Doncaster November Sales. *R. Simpson.*

AFRICAN TUDOR 3 b.c. African Sky 124– Spare Filly 95 (Beau Sabreur 125) (1982 **96** 5d 6f3 5g* 5fg* 5g2 5.3g2 6d3 1983 5fg 6fg 5f2 6f4 6d 5. 6fg4 6s 5fg 5d4 6fg) rather leggy colt; ran well sixth and seventh starts to be fourth of 15 behind Out of Hand in Portland Handicap at Doncaster and close fifth of 28 behind Polly's Brother in Ladbrokes (Ayr) Gold Cup, both in September; creditable equal fourth of 13 to Massorah in Premio Omenoni at Milan in October; stays 6f; blinkered second and eighth outings, but seems better without; has raced with his tongue tied down. *M. Stoute.*

AFZAL 3 b.c. Sassafras 135–Afrique (Exbury 138) (1982 NR 1983 12g4 10.1fg4 **79** 12f* 14.6f3 12.3g 10f) lengthy, quite useful-looking colt; good walker; fifth foal; half-brother to fairly useful 1½m to 1¾m winner Abdoun (by Luthier); dam, half-sister to Val de Loir and Valoris, won over 1½m in France; stayed on strongly to beat Jobroke by 2 lengths after pulling quite hard in maiden race at Beverley in July; finds 1¼m too sharp and should be suited by 1¾m; acts on firm going; sold to R. Hollinshead 15,000 gns Doncaster November Sales. *M. Stoute.*

AGAINST THE GRAIN 2 b.c. Oats 126–Bench Game (King's Bench 132) (1983 **78** 8g 7g2) May 29; 6,800Y; half-brother to numerous winners, including very smart 1m to 1¼m performer Record Run (by Track Spare); dam half-sister to smart

1961 2-y-o Gustav; 25/1, failed by head to catch all-the-way winner Talk of Glory in 13-runner maiden event at Lingfield in October; will stay at least 1¼m; should win races. *G. Pritchard-Gordon.*

AGINCOURT 4 b. g. St Columbus 98–Barslipper 76 (His Slipper) (1982 NR 1983   –
14.7d) half-brother to 2 winning jumpers; dam won over 7f and 1m and dead-heated in novice hurdle; apprentice ridden when well tailed-off last of 15 in maiden race at Redcar in May. *Ronald Thompson.*

AHMAD (USA) 2 b. c. Lyphard 132–Envidiada (Con Brio 121) (1983 6g 6fg⁴ 7f 7f   **74**
7f 7f 8d) Mar 14; smallish, quite well-made colt; good mover; half-brother to 3-y-o 1m and 9f winner Fluid Mechanics (by Sir Ivor); dam good winner in Argentina; quite a moderate maiden; best form at 7f, but probably stays 1m; blinkered sixth outing. *M. Albina.*

AHOHONEY 2 b. f. Ahonoora 122–Honey Buzzard (Sea Hawk II 131) (1983 6f²   **97**
6fg* 8f² 8fg*) Apr 3; IR 6,200F; lengthy, quite attractive filly; third foal; dam, second 3 times at up to 2m at 4 yrs in Ireland, is daughter of Italian 1000 Guineas and Oaks winner Dolina; won maiden race at Pontefract in August and Rowley Mile Nursery (stayed on strongly to beat Maruthayoor ¾ length) at Newmarket in September; narrowly beaten on her other starts, on second occasion appearing somewhat unlucky; suited by 1m, and may well stay further; yet to race on a soft surface; likely to make up into useful 3-y-o. *S. Norton.*

AIR CADET 3 br. g. Air Trooper 115–Modom 81 (Compensation 127) (1982 5s 5g   –
1983 8v 10s 7fg) fair sort; in rear in maiden races and handicaps. *W. Wightman.*

AIR COMMAND 3 ch. c. Air Trooper 115–Snotch (Current Coin 118) (1982 5f   **92**
5fg 5f 5g² 6g⁴ 5d3 5g² 5s 5g* 1983 6d* 7d* 6f 7.2g 6fg³ 7g 6s 6fg) strong, good-bodied colt; poor mover; successful in handicaps at Pontefract and Doncaster, making all on latter course in May; ran moderately next 2 starts; stays 7f well; acts on a firm surface but seems ideally suited by some give in the ground; trained by D. Smith until after fifth outing (off course 3 months before his next race). *Mrs G. Reveley.*

AIR DISTINGUE (USA) 3 b. f. Sir Ivor 135–Euryanthe (Nijinsky 138) (1982   **120**
6g* 8d* 8s 1983 10.5f³ 10f² (dis) 10f²) tall, lengthy ex-French filly; half-sister to American winner Steambath (by Honest Pleasure) and smart French 2-y-o Eastern Dawn (by Damascus); dam unraced sister to high-class middle-distance stayer Caucasus and half-sister to several very good performers; won newcomers race at Deauville and Prix d'Aumale at Chantilly as a 2-y-o when trained by F. Boutin; ran very well indeed when 1¼ lengths third of 17 behind Escaline in Prix de Diane Hermes at Chantilly in June on reappearance, battling with second-placed Smuggly up straight until pair were passed by fast-finishing winner close home; odds on when second of 6 in Nassau Stakes at Goodwood the following month (beaten 3 lengths by Acclimatise and was subsequently disqualified for hampering another runner when ducking right under whip) and Virginia Stakes at Newcastle in August (never landed a blow and was beaten similar distance by Cormorant Wood) on only subsequent outings; may prove suited by 1½m; acts on any going with possible exception of really soft; said to have returned lame at Goodwood. *R. Hern.*

AIREDALE TRAVEL 2 br. g. Air Trooper 115–Miss U.K. (Primera 131) (1983   **64**
5v 5d 6f 6f* 6f 7h 6f) Apr 24; well-grown gelding; attracted no bid after winning 7-runner seller at Pontefract in June by 4 lengths from Highford Lad; showed little in his other races, in final one tried in blinkers; should stay at least 1m; inconsistent. *M. W. Easterby.*

AIRFIELD 3 ch. c. Northfields–Easy Landing 110 (Swing Easy 126) (1982 6f³ 7s   **103**
1983 8v* 9s* 8.2v² 10.5f² 10f 10g² 10fg) tall, lengthy, quite attractive colt; won 23-runner maiden event at Warwick in April (made virtually all) and handicap at York in May, latter easing up by ¾ length from Rangefinder; second subsequently in Cecil Frail Handicap at Haydock later in May (beaten 4 lengths by Schuss), £5,000 event at York in June (outsprinted by Seymour Hicks in a slowly-run race and beaten 2 lengths) and Peter Hastings Handicap at Newbury in September (no match for Mauritzfontein and beaten 3 lengths); stays 1¼m; has run respectably on firm going but is much better on soft; had stiffish task and made little show on final start; sold privately to race in USA. *J. Tree.*

AIR GIRL 3 ch. f. Air Trooper 115–Bosworth Moll (Henry the Seventh 125) (1982   –
5fg 5fg 5.8f 6f 6g 1983 10d 7g) lengthy filly; of little account. *W. Wightman.*

AIRLING 2 b. g. Import 127–Cooling 89 (Tycoon II) (1983 5v⁴ 5g 6f 6f 5h* 6fg)   **75**
Mar 27; compact, useful sort; first foal, dam won over 1¼m and 13f; showed

improved form when winning 7-runner maiden race at Beverley in July by 1½ lengths from Pershing; disappointing favourite in Redcar nursery early the following month, and subsequently gelded; free-running sort, best at 5f; acts on hard going. *M. H. Easterby.*

AIRSHIP 5 br. h. Manado 130–High Sphere (St Paddy 133) (1982 7s 7.6g 8f* 8f* 9fg² 8f 9g 1983 8d 9fg⁴ 8f 8f 10.6gh⁴ 9f 8fg 8f² 8.2fg³ 9g 8fg 8f 8d) rather lightly-made horse; poor mover; quite a moderate handicapper on his day; promises to stay 1¼m; acts on any going, but seems suited by firm; blinkered final start; has run respectably for an apprentice; started slowly fourth outing; sold to M. Bradley 560 gns Newmarket Autumn Sales. *R. Hollinshead.*   **70**

AIR STRIKE 2 b. g. Air Trooper 115–Penstemon (Pendragon) (1983 5fg 6fg 6fg 6g) half-brother to 2 winning jumpers; dam unraced half-sister to Champion Hurdle winner Bandalore; fair sixth of 20 under big weight in selling nursery at Lingfield in October, final outing and best effort; bred to be much better suited by longer distances, and should stay at least 1¼m. *B. Stevens.*   **60**

AIYANA (USA) 3 b. f. Giacometti 130–In Full Bloom (Fleet Nasrullah) (1982 NR 1983 8d 12f* 12g⁴ 11f*) $50,000Y; rather sparely-made filly; first foal; dam unraced half-sister to smart 1979 2-y-o Thousandfold and high-class Faliraki; successful in maiden race at Redcar in June and handicap at Wolverhampton in August, on latter course holding on by a head from Lady Moon (pair clear); had still looked green in between; suited by 11f+; acts on firm going. *M. Stoute.*   **94**

AKEED (USA) 2 br. c. Honest Pleasure–Turban (Bagdad) (1983 6fg) Apr 10; $100,000Y; neat, quite attractive colt; half-brother to several winners, notably very useful 1977 2-y-o 6f and 7f winner Turkish Treasure (by Sir Ivor); dam, minor 6f winner, is half-sister to smart Sir Wimborne and Irish 1000 Guineas winner Lady Capulet; 20/1, close up 4f when 9½ lengths sixth of 13 to disqualified Bluff House in minor event at Goodwood in August; should stay 1m; sure to do better. *P. Walwyn.*   **71 p**

Beckhampton Ltd's "Airfield"

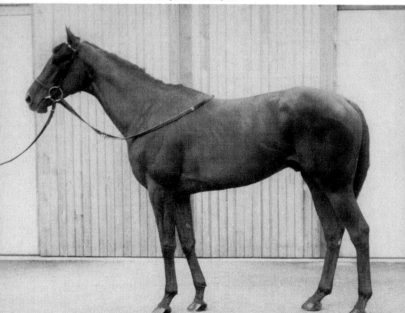

AL-ABJAR 3 b.c. Blakeney 126–Glamour Girl (Riverman 131) (1982 8d 8s 10s[2]   **61**
1983 12s[2] 17v 14g) neat colt, lacking in scope; second in handicap at Leicester in
April; off course 4 months before last outing; lacks pace and should be suited by a
thorough test of stamina; acts on soft going; wears blinkers; sold 2,600 gns
Newmarket Autumn Sales. *P. Walwyn.*

AL AHMAR 3 b.c. Mill Reef 141–Hatter's Dream 103 (Buckpasser) (1982 NR   **59**
1983 8d 11.7v 12f 12f[4] 13f[4] 12.3f[2] 15.5s[3]) good-topped, lengthy, attractive colt;
half-brother to winners here and abroad, including fairly useful French middle-
distance winner Dream Top (by High Top); dam, daughter of 1000 Guineas winner
Glad Rags, won over 5f at 2 yrs and is half-sister to Gorytus; in frame in maiden
races; suited by a test of stamina; blinkered final outing. *F. J. Houghton.*

ALAKH 3 ch.c. Sharpen Up 127–Gold Rupee 86 (Native Prince) (1982 NR 1983   **91**
6v* 6s* 6f 6fg[2] 7f 6d 6fg[3] 6fg) 28,000Y; tall, lengthy, fair sort; dam,
winner twice over 5f, is half-sister to dam of smart Captain Nick (by Sharpen Up);
favourite when beating Manimstar in maiden race at Nottingham in April and
handicap at Lingfield in May; placed in 2 handicaps at Newmarket afterwards, but
ran below form final outing; seems best at 6f; acts on any going. *J. Tree.*

AL AMEAD 3 br.c. Brigadier Gerard 144–Hatta 114 (Realm 129) (1982 NR 1983   **60**
8d 6v 6v[4] 7d[2] 7f[3] 6f 6fg 6fg 5g[3] 5.8fg) big, strong, deep-girthed colt; first foal;
dam won Molecomb Stakes; placed in maiden and minor events; should be suited by
longer distances but takes a good hold and may be best at up to 7f. *J. Benstead.*

ALAN STUART 3 b.c. Town Crier 119–My Sweet Afton 73 (Javelot 124) (1982   **–**
6f 5fg 5d 6f 6fg[3] 7f 8fg 8fg 1983 12d 8fg 6v 10f) compact colt; poor plater; stays 6f;
blinkered 3 times in 1982. *W. Barrett.*

AL-ASTAKAA 2 ch.f. Tumble Wind–Frensham 67 (Floribunda 136) (1983 5f 5f[4])   **64**
May 26; half-sister to 1980 2-y-o 5f winner Tough an Rough (by Saulingo) and a
bumpers winner who later won over hurdles; 20/1, 3½ lengths fourth of 19 to
Costalotta in maiden race at Folkestone in September; should stay 6f. *M.
McCormack.*

ALASTOR O MAVROS (USA) 4 gr.c. Tentam–Carte Noire (Native Charger)   **–**
(1982 12fg 12fg 16fg 16d* 16.5f* 16.5fg* 16fg[2] 1983 16fg 18fg) rangy sort; not a
good mover; staying handicapper; in rear both starts at 4 yrs in the autumn; seems
to act on any going; best in blinkers; refused to enter stalls once. *J. Gifford.*

A LA VAI 5 ch.g. Gay Fandango 132–Solo Stream 106 (Jolly Jet 111) (1982 10d   **–**
1983 7s 6d 6h 6f 6f[4] 7f 6f) lengthy, rather plain gelding; poor maiden; stays 6f; will
be more at home in sellers. *J. Spearing.*

ALAWIR (FR) 3 br.c. Riverman 131–Reine du Chant 112 (Premier Violon) (1982   **97**
6s 1983 6v* 7g[2] 8f 8g[2] 8fg) stocky colt; 50/1 and ridden by an apprentice unable to
claim his allowance when beating Conrad Hilton gamely by ½ length in 25-runner
minor event at Newbury in May; second in minor events at Epsom and Newbury
afterwards, showing improved form on latter course in September when going
down by a head to Hungarian Prince; stays 1m; best form with some give in the
ground, and acts on heavy going. *H. T. Jones.*

ALAYYAM 2 b.f. Pollerton 115–Kiss (Mark Ye Well) (1983 8g 7.2g* 8.2fg[4]) Apr   **70**
18; IR 6,000Y; useful-looking filly; half-sister to several winners in France; dam,
half-sister to high-class Miletus, placed 5.5f to 7.5f in France; bought in 5,200 gns
after beating Tapouscha by 3 lengths in 13-runner seller at Haydock in September;
creditable fourth of 17 in nursery at Nottingham the following month; will stay at
least 1¼m. *P. Cole.*

ALBADEEAH (USA) 3 b.f. Nashua–Precious Girl (Intentionally) (1982 6g*   **79**
1983 7fg 7f[4] 7s) strong, rangy filly with scope; creditable fourth behind Ampersand
in handicap at Epsom in August, best effort of 1983; stays 7f. *H. T. Jones.*

AL BAYAN (USA) 2 b.f. Northern Dancer–Bold Melody (Bold Reason) (1983   **82**
7f[3] 6fg) Mar 23; $1,000,000Y; rangy, attractive filly; good walker; second foal;
sister to 1982 2-y-o 6f winner Northair; dam, winner 5 times at up to 1m at 3 yrs, is
half-sister to Prix Morny winner Broadway Dancer (by Northern Dancer);
favourite, clear 2f out and looked likely winner until weakening badly in final
furlong, when 3 lengths third of 18 behind Our Island Story in maiden event at
Salisbury in September; again favourite, never-dangerous 4 lengths sixth of 12 to
Rappa Tap Tap in Blue Seal Stakes at Ascot later in the month; bred to stay at least
1m. *H. T. Jones.*

ALBERTAT 3 gr.g. Habat 127–Albertina 102 (Great Nephew 126) (1982 5f 5f 5f   **74**
7g 7fg 7f 8f 8.2s 1983 8d[3] 9s[2] 8fg[2] 11d* 11d[2] 10f[3] 11fg 9fg 10f) lengthy gelding;

gamely won maiden race at Redcar in May (ridden by 5-lb claimer); stays 11f; acts on any going, but is probably ideally suited by some give. *D. Smith.*

ALCANON 2 ch.c. Nonoalco 131–Countess Palotta 98 (Brigadier Gerard 144) — (1983 7f 6f 8fg 8d) Feb 10; quite attractive colt; first foal; dam, daughter of German 1000 Guineas and Oaks winner Oraza, won from 1m to 2m; no form, including in Warwick nursery when apprentice ridden at 7-7; sold 2,600 gns Newmarket Autumn Sales. *H. Candy.*

ALCINOUS 2 b.c. Averof 123–Floral Palm 69 (Floribunda 136) (1983 5g⁴ 6fg² **77** 7fg² 7d 7g 6fg) May 8; 13,000Y; leggy, rather plain colt; half-brother to several winners, including useful 3-y-o 5f winner Debaj (by Blue Cashmere) and very useful Italian sprinter Dublin Taxi (by Sharpen Up); dam won 5f seller at 2 yrs; quite a modest maiden; stays 7f; acts on a firm surface; ran moderately in blinkers on final appearance. *R. Boss.*

ALCMENE (USA) 2 b.c. Marshua's Dancer–Faye Mar (What A Pleasure) (1983 **65** 7f 7fg) Mar 28; $20,000Y; resold 112,000 gns Y; strong colt; sixth foal; half-brother to 2 minor winners; dam, half-sister to Hello Gorgeous, ran 5 times unplaced; 9½ lengths fifth of 12 to Mafoo's Image in maiden race at Salisbury in September, second outing. *C. Brittain.*

ALDENHAM (USA) 5 ch.g. His Majesty–Mama's Silver (Silver King 119) (1982 — 10f 10g 11.7fg³ 10fg* 12fg 10d 10f³ 10f 12fg² 11.7fg⁴ 10g³ 10fg⁴ 10.2f* 10v* 10v² 10.2d 1983 10v 10g) smallish, fair sort; quite a modest handicapper; stayed 1½m; acted on any going; blinkered once; sometimes made the running; dead. *G. Balding.*

ALDERN STREAM 3 gr.f. Godswalk 130–Betsy Ross 100 (Petingo 135) (1982 **102** 5fg* 6s⁴ 6s³ 1983 7d 7g 6d 8f 7fg 8f 7f* 7f⁴ 9fg) lengthy, useful-looking filly; good walker with a smooth, light action; by no means the most consistent of animals but won handicap at Salisbury in August by a neck from One Degree, making relentless progress; stayed on when good fourth of 10 behind Silverdip, beaten about 2 lengths, in Strensall Stakes at York later in month; should stay 1m; acts on firm going and action suggests she's possibly not at her best on soft ground; usually blinkered in her later races; sold 48,000 gns Newmarket December Sales. *G. Wragg.*

ALDERSHAWE HALL 4 b.c. Wollow 132–Hatha 78 (Bold Reason) (1982 8g **49** 8fg 8f² 8f² 8g 9.4fg³ 8g 8.2fg² 8g 8g³ 8f 10fg 8g³ 8d 8g 1983 9f 10f 10f 8.2fg 10f⁴ 10h²) smallish, fair sort; poor walker; plater nowadays; promises to stay beyond 1¼m; acts well on firm going; sold 800 gns Doncaster November Sales. *R. Hollinshead.*

ALDHABYIH 2 b.f. General Assembly–Pampered Dancer (Pampered King 121) **86** (1983 6f⁴ 5g* 6g² 5fg) Feb 20; 220,000Y; lengthy filly; good walker and mover; half-sister to 4 winners, including very smart 1982 2-y-o sprinter Kafu (by African Sky) and smart 7f to 1¼m winner Moomba Masquerade (by Gay Fandango); dam once-raced half-sister to Irish 1000 Guineas winner Royal Danseuse; made heavy weather of landing odds of 6/4 on in minor event at Wolverhampton in July; second to Fawzi in Schwarzwald-Rennen at Baden-Baden in August, best subsequent effort; disappointing co-favourite (last of 10) in nursery at Newmarket in September; needs at least 6f, and will be better suited by 7f+. *H. T. Jones.*

ALDINGTON MILL 3 b.g. Legal Eagle 126–Dear Catalpa (Dear Gazelle 113) — (1982 7d 7f 7fg 7f 6g³ 7f 8.2d 1983 8.3fg 6g 6fg 7fg) leggy, rather lightly-made gelding; plater nowadays; stays 1m; acts on firm going; blinkered final outing at 2 yrs. *C. Trietline.*

ALDO KING (FR) 2 b.c. King of Macedon 126–Aldonza (Exbury 138) (1983 7g) — Apr 8; 250,000 francs Y (approx £20,800); lengthy colt; half-brother to winners in France and Italy, notably very useful middle-distance performer Dom Aldo (by Hard to Beat); dam, winner over 1½m, is daughter of top-class La Bamba; 25/1 and distinctly backward, tenth of 12 to stable-companion Lucky Scott in £5,000 event at Kempton in September. *P. Cole.*

ALEOS (FR) 6 b.g. Faunus–Aphytis (Crepello 136) (1982 10.2f 12d⁴ 1983 10g — 13.1h) workmanlike gelding; fairly useful in 1980; lightly raced and soundly beaten on flat since; stays 1¼m; acts on firm going; looked ungenuine when blinkered once. *J. Old.*

ALERTED 3 ch.f. Red Alert 127–Ladies Night 65 (Midsummer Night II 117) (1982 — 6fg 6d 6s 1983 9f 6fg) strong filly; lightly raced and disappointing; should be suited by 7f+; behind in a seller final start. *Miss S. Hall.*

47

ALETIS 2 ch.g. Hot Grove 128–Lady Chrystal 53 (Sparkler 130) (1983 5s 5d³ 6fg   **69**
7.2fg⁴ 6f 6fg⁴) Mar 25; 4,500Y; sturdy, deep-girthed gelding; seems to carry
plenty of condition; first foal; dam is out of sister to High Line; plating-class
maiden; better suited by 7f than 6f, and will stay further; probably acts on any
going; consistent. *K. Brassey.*

ALEV 4 ch.g. Hot Spark 126–St Citrus 108 (Relic) (1982 6fg 6fg 5f² 5g* 5g 6g 5fg   **94**
5g 6v 5s 1983 5g 6.5d 7.5s 5g* 5v* 5v* 5d⁴ 5.6fg 6s 6s 5g* 5fg) lengthy,
useful-looking gelding; won race at Cagnes-sur-Mer in March and handicaps at
Lingfield and Goodwood (apprentice event) in May and Sandown in October; beat
Ferryman 1½ lengths on last-named; speedy and is best at 5f; acts on any going;
best in blinkers. *P. Mitchell.*

ALEXANDRA PALACE 2 b.c. Warpath 113–Alexandra 81 (Song 132) (1983   **–**
7fg 8g) Jan 20; big, lengthy colt; second foal; dam third over 6f and 7f at 2 yrs;
made late headway when remote sixth of 18 in 1m maiden event at Ayr in
September; sold 7,500 gns Doncaster November Sales. *C. Thornton.*

ALEXANDRIE (USA) 3 b. or br.f. Val de l'Orne 130–Apache (Sir Gaylord)   **114**
(1982 8v* 1983 10.5v³ 10.5v* 12g 10g² 9g² 9.2f 10.5g 8g) strong, deep-girthed,
good-looking filly; shows a pronounced knee action; first foal; dam, half-sister to
high-class French filly Aryenne, was a very useful winner at around 1¼m in France;
ran out a comfortable winner of 7-runner Prix Cleopatre at Maisons-Laffitte in May,
beating Aunty by 3 lengths after leading 2f out; also placed in Prix Penelope at
Saint-Cloud (under 2 lengths third of 9 to Smuggly), Prix de Malleret at Longchamp
(2 lengths second of 6 to comfortable winner Chamisene) and Prix Chloe at Evry (4
lengths second of 5 behind Verria), but finished only eleventh of 15 behind
runaway-winner Sun Princess when favourite for Oaks at Epsom on third start
(looked extremely well but was never better than mid-division and seemed ill at
ease running down hill); should stay 1½m; acts on heavy going; sent to USA. *A.
Head, France.*

ALFIE DICKINS 5 ro.h. Spanish Gold 101–Vila Real 76 (Town Crier 119) (1982   **47**
8f⁴ 11fg⁴ 12f 12f² 12fg² 12g³ 12d³ 12f 12f 12fg² 12g⁴ 12g⁴ 12fg⁴ 12fg³ 13s⁴ 12g⁴
1983 12s² 12fg 12s 12d 12fg³ 12f⁴ 12fg⁴ 12f* 12f 12f³ 12f 12d²) robust horse; not a
good mover; middle-distance handicapper; won at Carlisle in July; acts on any
going; has run respectably in blinkers; suitable mount for an apprentice; none too
genuine. *R. Hollinshead.*

ALFRED DOUGLAS 3 b.g. Grundy 137–Gay Surrender 70 (Sir Gaylord) (1982   **– §**
NR 1983 11.7s 11.7v 16f 16g 17g 12f 12fg) 12,000Y; tall, fair sort; second foal;
dam, half-sister to very smart Double-U-Jay, won over 1¼m; no worthwhile form,
including in claiming company, and is ungenuine; blinkered final outing; sold 1,000
gns Newmarket September Sales. *M. McCormack.*

ALFRED'S CHOICE 4 br.c. So Blessed 130–Scamperdale 81 (French Beige   **110**
127) (1982 8s* 10.5d 10.5fg² 12fg⁴ 12.5d⁴ 12f² 10s 10v² 1983 10s 10v 10.5v²
12s⁴ 11s⁴ 11f⁴ 12.5fg³ 12fg² 12s 11g² 10g⁴) 15,000F, 9,600Y; rangy, attractive colt;
good walker; fourth foal; half-brother to 2 winners, including Lady Peg (by Young
Emperor), fairly useful winner at up to 1m here and also successful in Norway; dam
stayed well; ran respectably most starts, notably when fifth to Imyar in Prix
Exbury at Saint-Cloud, fifth to Welsh Term in Prix d'Harcourt at Longchamp, head
second to Mariacho in 80,000 francs race at Saint-Cloud, about 2 lengths fourth to
Diamond Shoal in 1½m Grand Prix d'Evry, fourth to Prima Voce in Grand Prix
Prince Rose at Ostend on sixth start and nose second to Zalfa in 1½m Grand Prix de
Clairefontaine; stays 1½m; acts on any going. *E. Bartholomew, France.*

ALGHUZAYLAH 2 ch.f. Habitat 134–Asian Princess (Native Prince) (1983 5s³   **84**
5g* 6d) Apr 3; IR 330,000Y; robust, deep-girthed filly; half-sister to 3 winners,
notably very smart French 5.5f to 10.5f winner Pitasia (by Pitskelly); dam of no
account; won Hilary Needler Trophy at Beverley in June; not seen out again until
October when remote fifth of 6 to Sally Chase in nursery at Lingfield; may stay 1m.
H. T. Jones.

ALHARGAH 2 gr.f. Be My Guest 126–Fair Melys 81 (Welsh Pageant 132) (1983   **–**
6f 6f 5g) Mar 25; 20,000Y; first foal; dam, 7f and 1m winner, is half-sister to
high-class middle-distance colt Pelerin; behind in maiden and minor events; bred to
need 7f+. *J. Benstead.*

AL HEBAAB (USA) 2 b.c. Native Royalty–First Sky (Sky Clipper) (1983 6f 6fg   **72**
7f 7g) Apr 10; $12,500F, $27,000Y, resold 23,000 gns Y; workmanlike colt; good
walker; half-brother to numerous winners in USA; dam, from family of Nashua,
won twice at up to 6f at 3 yrs; beaten little more than 2 lengths when seventh of 9 to

Lord Lux in maiden race at Yarmouth in August, third outing and only sign of ability; sold 8,200 gns Newmarket Autumn Sales. *H. T. Jones.*

ALIANNA 2 ch.f. Nebbiolo 125–Flying Anna (Roan Rocket 128) (1983 5v⁴ 5s 6fg⁴   **92** 6f 7f² 7.9f* 8.5g*) Mar 11; IR 14,500 Y; first foal; dam won over 5f and 1m in Ireland; showed improved form when given a test of stamina, winning maiden race at Dundalk in August by 2½ lengths from Tolstoya and 14-runner Waterford Crystal Nursery at Gowran Park in September by 5 lengths from Action Girl; promises to stay 1¼m; acts on firm going. *A. Redmond, Ireland.*

ALIAS (USA) 2 ch.c. Nodouble-Profiterole (Candy Spots) (1983 8g 7fg) Mar 28;   — $90,000Y; tall, rather lightly-made colt; half-brother to several winners, notably Ile Flottante (by Go Marching), a good winner from 7f to 11f in France and Italy; dam placed at 3 yrs; no show in big fields at Newbury and Newmarket in September. *F. J. Houghton.*

ALIMONY 3 ch.f. Sallust 134–Constanza 94 (Sun Prince 128) (1982 6f 6g² 1983   **71** 7h³ 8f 8fg⁴ 10fg² 9d) rangy, quite attractive filly; in frame in maiden races; looked uncooperative in blinkers on fourth outing; stays 1¼m; seems rather short of pace; sold to Mrs G. Forbes 10,500 gns Newmarket December Sales. *R. Hern.*

A LITTLE MORE 2 b.f. Mr Bigmore 123–Manicou's Dream (Manicou) (1983 6g   — 6fg 7f 6fg 7fg) Mar 29; fourth reported foal; dam fair hurdler; no worthwhile form in varied company, including selling; likely to need a thorough test of stamina. *R. Smyth.*

ALJADEL 3 b.f. Habitat 134–Petocracy 102 (Petingo 135) (1982 NR 1983 7fg   — 6fg) 44,000Y; well-made filly; good walker; third foal; sister to useful 1981 2-y-o 5f winner Hampton Bay; dam, daughter of Italian Oaks winner Anticlea, stayed 1¼m; not seen out after finishing seventh of 23 behind Rare Honour in maiden race at Lingfield in July. *L. Cumani.*

ALJAZAAR 3 ch.c. Jaazeiro 127–Celina 115 (Crepello 136) (1982 NR 1983 11.5fg   **59** 14f 14f 12g 11.7g² 16d³ 12.2g) 92,000Y; big, well-made colt; half-brother to 3 winners, including fairly useful middle-distance filly Calf of Man (by Derring-Do); dam won 1968 Irish Guinness Oaks; placed in handicaps at Bath and Warwick in October, best efforts; stays 2m. *J. Benstead.*

AL KHASHAB 6 ch.g. Habat 127–Parlais 101 (Pardao 120) (1982 10d 12g* 12f*   **43** 12f 12f 12f 10.6s 12s 10d 1983 12d 12.3f 12.2fg 13.8f 12f⁴ 12f²) workmanlike gelding; poor mover; disappointing handicapper; stays 1½m; acts on any going. *R. Hollinshead.*

ALLADO 7 b.g. Crooner 119–Head On (Never Say Die 137) (1982 10f 1983 10s   — 15.5f 16fg) soundly beaten in varied company. *A. Neaves.*

ALL AGREED 2 b.g. Jaazeiro 127–Tynwald Hill (Rarity 129) (1983 5g⁴ 5v* 5f²   **103** 5fg³ 5g² 5f 5fg* 6fg 6d⁴) Mar 22; 12,000F, 44,000Y; neat, good-quartered gelding; first foal; dam won over 5f and 7.5f in Ireland; won maiden race at Kempton in May and £3,200 event at Thirsk in September; placed, including good second in Windsor Castle Stakes at Royal Ascot, in 4 of his other runs, and on last 2 outings ran well under big weights in nurseries at Newmarket and Newbury; better suited by 6f than by 5f; acts on any going. *J. Winter.*

ALL ALONG (FR) 4 b.f. Targowice 130–Agujita (Vieux Manoir 132) (1982 10d*   **134** 10.5d* 10v² 12f 10.5v 12.5d* 12f* 12s 12f² 1983 12f³ 12.5fg 12s² 12f* 13d* 12g* 12d*)

Any racing enthusiast subscribing to Martin Luther's extreme opinion that 'Never any good came out of female domination' would probably have viewed the 1983 season with even more suspicion than its immediate predecessors. Fillies have indeed done remarkably well against colts in top races of late, and while it is worth recalling that considerable success for the so-called weaker sex is nothing new—in 1882, for instance, all five British classics went to fillies—the present trend is noteworthy in its persistence. Since 1978 twenty-eight fillies aged three or above have won European Group 1 races open to both sexes, and in 1983 there were no fewer than eleven of them, namely All Along, Awaasif, Cormorant Wood, Habibti, High Hawk, Luth Enchantee, Ma Biche, Mountain Lodge, Stanerra, Sun Princess and Time Charter, as well as the two-year-olds Masarika and Treizieme.

For much of the season it looked unlikely that All Along would become a member of this select group, let alone one who would set up a tremendous sequence of victories in top races on both sides of the Atlantic. Early on little went right for the 1982 Prix Vermeille winner and Japan Cup second who took a long time to come to herself and consequently was not seen out until La Coupe at

Chantilly on French Oaks day in June, having been withdrawn from the Coronation Cup on the morning of the race. All Along, a short-priced favourite, lay close up from the start, went past the front-running Darine a couple of furlongs out and made the best of her way home until lack of peak fitness told in the final furlong; at the line she was under three lengths third to Zalataia.

It seemed fair to expect improvement on this display in the Grand Prix de Saint-Cloud the following month but unfortunately All Along dropped out in the straight and came home a moderate seventh of nine to Diamond Shoal, reportedly suffering from back trouble and internal bleeding. The King George VI and Queen Elizabeth Diamond Stakes unsurprisingly went by without All Along and though she was mentioned as a possible starter for the Benson and Hedges Gold Cup it was not until September, two months after her abortive Saint-Cloud venture, that she again saw a racecourse. Like much of fashionable French society she had spent part of the time between at Deauville to obtain a change of air, and if her performance in the Prix Foy is anything to go by a few more trainers may follow Biancone's example.

The race for the Prix Foy exploded one belief about All Along, one that we and apparently her connections had long held, namely that she needed to be ridden up with the pace. It was in this way that she had won the Vermeille, lying up behind the leaders before going to the front over two furlongs out and staying on strongly, and these tactics were the ones used on her in La Coupe. Biancone had clearly changed his thinking, no doubt partly because All Along was not a strong puller and could probably be settled anywhere in a race without fear of her becoming frustrated in the way some horses suited by enterprising tactics are when their jockeys try holding them up. Our doubt about the advisability of using waiting tactics on All Along rested principally on the fact that she seemed to lack the powerful acceleration usually required in horses that come from behind, but the Foy left this view if not in tatters at least rather frayed. Settled in the middle of the field by Head, All Along could be seen lobbing along happily in about seventh place as they came towards the straight headed by Indian Prince, but once round the turn the runners quickly bunched up with the result that when Head tried to make progress he found the route blocked. Forced to switch to the wide outside, as also was the King George winner Time Charter, All Along followed the latter through and made excellent headway without her jockey resorting to the whip to pass six horses, among them Welsh Term, Khairpour and Great Substence, in the final furlong. At the post she went down by a length to the English filly who was conceding her 7 lb.

Considering that she was sympathetically handled and that the decidedly soft conditions did not suit her ideally All Along had evidently put up a most encouraging performance, one that indicated her earlier ailments no longer presented a problem. Even so, her chances of winning the Trusthouse Forte Prix de l'Arc de Triomphe the following month looked only average, and to judge by the

Trusthouse Forte Prix de l'Arc de Triomphe, Longchamp—Sun Princess leads them early in the straight; All Along is fifth-left, on the rails

Trusthouse Forte Prix de l'Arc de Triomphe, Longchamp—All Along comes with a strong run to beat Sun Princess (rails), fast-finishing Luth Enchantée, and Time Charter (partially hidden). Salmon Leap (No. 19), Stanerra (No. 13) and Lovely Dancer (No. 17) finish close up

difficulties All Along's connections had in finding a jockey for their filly one might have thought her a no-hoper. For one reason or another Head, Starkey, Piggott, Moore, Asmussen and Mercer did not take the mount, Piggott's decision to ride Awaasif resulting in public recriminations which saw M Wildenstein stating his determination not to have Piggott put up on any of his horses again, including those with Cecil. Eventually Swinburn, without a mount after the withdrawal of Shareef Dancer, came in for the ride, proving that for him at least seven is a lucky number.

The Arc is one of the year's great racing events and as a sheer spectacle it has the edge on the King George since it tends to have more runners. The twenty-six-strong field in 1983 matched that of 1977 as the fourth-largest to have contested the Arc since it was increased considerably in value in 1949—the record is held by the 1967 race with thirty runners, followed by 1949 (twenty-eight) and 1973 (twenty-seven). There were several in the race with no prospects of success, notably the 1978 French Derby winner Acamas making a come-back after fertility problems at stud, but as usual the overall quality was high notwithstanding a lack of top-class three-year-old colts—between them the contestants had won fifty-eight races, thirty-eight of them pattern races, during the current season. From England came Time Charter, the dual classic winner Sun Princess with her pacemaker Sailor's Dance, the much-travelled and highly successful Diamond Shoal, the Great Voltigeur winner Seymour Hicks, Awaasif, third in the race in 1982, Guns of Navarone and Prima Voce; from Ireland the recent Joe McGrath Memorial winner Stanerra and Derby fourth Salmon Leap; from Germany the good-class Orofino; while the home defence included All Along herself, the Prix de Diane winner Escaline, Prix Vermeille winner Sharaya, Prix Ganay winner Lancastrian and Prix Jacques le Marois and Prix du Moulin winner Luth Enchantée having her first attempt at a mile and a half. The ground had dried

51

up markedly since the Foy and was officially firm, a point in All Along's favour and against some of her rivals, but in a market headed by Time Charter, the coupled Sun Princess and Lancastrian, and Diamond Shoal, All Along started at a shade over 17/1, coupled with her stable-companion Sagace.

Once Sailor's Dance took up his allotted position at the head of affairs after half a furlong the pattern of the race did not alter appreciably until past halfway, the pacemaker being pursued to that point by a group including Diamond Shoal, Time Charter, Sun Princess, Stanerra and Sharaya: All Along, steadily taken across the course to the stand rail from her outside draw, was settled towards the back with Lancastrian, very slowly away, bringing up the rear. With Sailor's Dance palpably tiring half a mile out—the eventual time was only a tenth of a second outside Detroit's record—Carson pushed Sun Princess into the lead followed by Diamond Shoal, and the two British challengers swung into the straight ahead of Stanerra, Time Charter, the strongly-ridden Seymour Hicks and Guns of Navarone. Diamond Shoal, already under pressure, proved incapable of keeping up with Sun Princess as the latter went for home for all she was worth, and though Stanerra and Time Charter each came with a promising run on the outside they, too, could not maintain their momentum after reaching the leader's quarters. A furlong and a half out Sun Princess led by a length and showed no signs of stopping but any thoughts of there being a British-trained Arc winner for the first time since Rheingold in 1973 soon received a nasty jolt. Travelling smoothly in about twelfth place, still on the rails, rounding the final turn, All Along had not been asked a serious question by Swinburn until a couple of furlongs out whereupon she had begun to make significant progress, obtaining a clear run by virtue of Seymour Hicks's hanging away from the rails under pressure. All Along had some five lengths to make up on Sun Princess halfway up the straight but proved more than equal to the task. Accelerating in devastating style she was switched away from the rails and made ground relentlessly, passing the weakening Diamond Shoal, then Time Charter and Stanerra and finally, fifty yards from home, Sun Princess who had no reserves left with which to withstand this assault. The final margin of success was a length; Luth Enchantee, who had started her run on the outside at about the same time as All Along, finished strongly to be third, a short neck away and a nose ahead of Time Charter, while Salmon Leap, in a seemingly hopeless position at the rear two and a half furlongs out, ran on as well as anything to be a further half length back in fifth, just ahead of Stanerra and the equally fast-finishing Prix du Prince d'Orange winner Lovely Dancer. There has been no shortage of exciting results to the Arc over the years but in only one, that of 1959, have so many horses finished so close to the winner. In 1959 when Saint Crespin III dead-heated with the subsequently-demoted Midnight Sun II the tenth home was beaten about two and a half lengths: in 1983 the twelfth horse, Diamond Shoal, finished within five lengths of All Along. Would that there were more finishes of this type in a season.

After the race, several commentators expressed something approaching astonishment that fillies had occupied five of the first six places, but there is really no justification for such a reaction. On top of the fact that there were more fillies in the race than ever before, ten, it was clear prior to the contest that these fillies included the best of their respective generations while the colts, Diamond Shoal excepted, did not. None of the first three in the Derby, Irish Sweeps Derby or Prix du Jockey-Club took part and none of the seven three-year-old colts that did had won a Group 1 race, so it is obvious the classic crop of colts was rather poorly represented. The fillies, on the other hand, had rattling good representatives, numbering eight Group 1 winners among them. From the fact that Salmon Leap finished a close fifth it is safe to assume that at their best Caerleon and Shareef Dancer to name but two would have been involved in the finish and in their absence the fillies' success came as no surprise at all.

While history appeared to counsel caution regarding the plan to continue racing All Along after the Arc—of the eight previous Arc winners since 1949 to have run again during the same season only Ribot and Molvedo had managed to win—there were good reasons for the decision. All Along had enjoyed a relatively easy season, and now that she had hit top form the temptation to try and pick up more big prizes with her was understandable. With the improvement in international travel over the past twenty years making it a relatively simple matter to transport horses anywhere in the world, there is much less reason nowadays for a top-class horse to end its season with the Arc, especially as the enterprise of racecourse executives in North America and Japan has resulted in four very valuable international contests being run between mid-October and the end of November. The four races involved are the Rothmans International at Woodbine, the Turf Classic at Aqueduct, the Washington International at Laurel and the Japan Cup at Tokyo, and to add to the attraction of the first three the executives concerned obtained an insurance policy in 1983 to guarantee any horse winning these races a million-dollar bonus.

Soon after the Arc All Along was announced as a possible runner in all four events and a fortnight after the Arc she lined up against a tip-top field for the Rothmans International. Three of her ten opponents, Majesty's Prince, Nijinsky's Secret and the ex-French Palikaraki, had already won Grade 1 races in the States in 1983 and another, Thunder Puddles, had run second to Majesty's Prince in the previous year's Rothmans International, while Escaline, Welsh Term and Load the Cannons were additional challengers from France. All Along started a warm favourite despite the ground being on the soft side of good and she justified the support in style, moving through to challenge Nijinsky's Secret and Thunder Puddles early in the straight and going away to beat the latter convincingly by two lengths with Majesty's Prince three quarters of a length away third.

On the evidence of this display All Along didn't have a great deal to fear from any of her rivals in the Turf Classic two weeks later and she went to post at odds on to beat a field of nine, best of whom looked to be Thunder Puddles, Erins Isle, successful in three top-class races early in 1983 though not in such good form of late, Welsh Term again and the Foy third Great Substence. Her performance was simply breathtaking: her opponents could do nothing as she breezed to the front rounding the home turn and drew away with incredible ease to administer an eight-and-three-quarter-length beating to Thunder Puddles with Erins Isle third. This was M Wildenstein's second success in the race—Waya won the second running in 1978—and the fourth in succession for a French-trained filly following Anifa in 1980 and April Run in 1981 and 1982.

The co-operation between the Woodbine, Aqueduct and Laurel executives which led to the creation of the International Classic Series in 1983 resulted in there being a gap of two weeks between each of the races when in most previous years the Turf Classic and Washington International had been separated by only six days. This naturally has made it easier to run a horse in all three events though the

Turf Classic, Aqueduct—All Along wins with incredible ease

Washington D.C. International, Laurel—All Along wins easily from Welsh Term

schedule is still an extremely punishing one, especially for a European horse with the vast amount of travelling involved. The Turf Classic suggested that far from being weakened by her exertions All Along, like Youth in 1976, had in fact improved after arriving in North America, and despite the rain-softened going she started at long odds on to follow eleven previous French-trained horses by winning the Washington International. The race clashed with the Oak Tree Invitational on the west coast in which Zalataia, John Henry, Awaasif and Thunder Puddles ran. Thunder Puddles' connections had clearly decided it was a waste of time opposing All Along again; those of Majesty's Prince, Palikaraki, Welsh Term and Lovely Dancer thought otherwise since all four horses ran at Laurel where new members of the cast were Cormorant Wood, Give Thanks and the good American mare Hush Dear. All Along treated them all with disdain, taking up the running half a mile out and cruising home by three and a quarter lengths from Welsh Term with Majesty's Prince third and Give Thanks and Cormorant Wood back in fifth and sixth.

In every sense of the term All Along had come a long way from Amiens where she had begun her career almost exactly two years before by dead-heating in a maiden race. The million-dollar bonus she earned at Laurel took her into fourth place in the list of all-time money earners behind John Henry, Spectacular Bid and the Venezuelan filly Trinycarol. On its own money won is not necessarily proof of exceptional merit—Trinycarol finished soundly beaten in the States after being sent there to be trained in the second half of 1983—but we don't think anyone would be foolish enough to play the doubting Thomas regarding All Along's ability. It would be all but impossible to surpass and very difficult to equal her brilliant autumn campaign, and it is good news indeed that she stays in training.

The first four home in the Arc were all European-bred but ironically only one of the sires involved is at present standing in Europe. Saritamer, sire of Time Charter, is in Saudi Arabia; Be My Guest, sire of Luth Enchantee, is in Ireland; English Prince, sire of Sun Princess, is dead and had been at stud in Japan anyway; and Targowice, sire of All Along, is still standing in Japan. It often seems to happen that the exploits of a sire's progeny after he has been exported make the loss look

54

substantial, and in some respects Targowice exemplifies this tendency. The highest-weighted two-year-old in the French Free Handicap but a disappointment at three, he stood in Ireland then France prior to being sent to Japan in 1980 at which time his runners had done little of note. No sooner had he gone than Ukraine Girl won the French Guineas, Prince Mab showed himself a good sprinter/miler, Tipperary Fixer won the Prix Kergorlay and All Along proved to be out of the top drawer, though to maintain a sense of proportion it is worth mentioning that Targowice's 1980 and 1981 crops appear not to contain anything out of the ordinary. All Along is the fifth foal of the smart if slightly inconsistent middle-distance

All Along (Fr) (b.f. 1979)	Targowice (b 1970)	Round Table (b 1954)	Princequillo
			Knight's Daughter
		Matriarch (b 1964)	Bold Ruler
			Lyceum
	Agujita (b 1966)	Vieux Manoir (b 1947)	Brantome
			Vieille Maison
		Argosy (b 1950)	Coastal Traffic
			Prosodie

performer Agujita, successful in the Prix de Royaumont; best of the other four was Abala (by Baldric II and thus closely related to All Along), a very useful miler who numbered the Prix de la Calonne among her three wins. Agujita's 1980 foal, the Carvin filly Addenda, was placed over a mile and a half in 1983 and the 1982 foal, a filly by New Chapter, failed to reach her reserve at the Deauville Sales in August. The latter was being carried by Agujita when M Wildenstein sold the mare for what turned out to be a song, 2,400 guineas, at the 1981 Newmarket December Sales; Addenda fetched a great deal more at the same venue two years later, going for 230,000 guineas. The once-raced grandam Argosy produced two other winners one of whom, Autre Prince, ran second in the Prix Royal-Oak and third in the Gold Cup, while the third dam, a granddaughter of the Oaks winner Brulette, ran twice unplaced and foaled seven winners on the flat in Brazil and the United States.

All Along, a strong, attractive individual who in appearance was undoubtedly the pick of the fillies contesting the Arc, stays thirteen furlongs and while unlikely

M. D. Wildenstein's "All Along" (F. Head)

ALL

to be given the opportunity will get further. Though she has won on soft ground it bears repeating she is ideally suited by a sound surface, and should the going be on top for the 1984 Arc de Triomphe All Along could again take all the beating. Either way, we look forward to seeing her using her formidable turn of foot to add further lustre to an already magnificent record as a five-year-old. *P.-L. Biancone, France.*

ALLAN WELLS 4 ch. g. Queen's Hussar 124–Baggage 86 (Zeus Boy 121) (1982 8g4 10s 8f3 7f 8g 7f 8.2g 1983 6f 8.2fg) compact gelding; plater; stays 1m; acts on firm going; usually wears blinkers. *A. Watson.* —

ALL BRONZE 3 ch. c. Cavo Doro 124–Bronze Princess 72 (Hul a Hul 124) (1982 6g 5.1fg 8d 7.2s 10d 1983 12v) poor plater; ran best race over 1m at 2 yrs. *T. Bill.* —

ALLECTA 2 b. f. Bustino 136–Mineown 85 (Roan Rocket 128) (1983 7f2) Feb 6; quite attractive filly, but a bit unfurnished; sister to 3-y-o middle-distance winner Mytinia and very smart 1½m winner Bustomi; dam, placed over 5f and 6f, is half-sister to top Italian horse Weimar; 11/1, finished to some purpose after having plenty to do at halfway when 2 lengths second of 18 to Our Island Story in maiden race at Salisbury in September; should have no difficulty in winning, and is probably useful stayer in the making. *R. Hern.* **83 p**

ALLEGING (USA) 2 b. c. Alleged 138–Sweet Habit (Habitat 134) (1983 7fg* 8.2fg*) May 2; smallish, sturdy colt; first foal; dam unraced daughter of Prix de Diane winner Sweet Mimosa; looked a useful colt in the making when running on strongly to beat Razyana decisively by 2½ lengths in 26-runner maiden race at Newmarket (sweated up) in September; confirmed that impression when 7/2 on for £3,400 event at Nottingham the following month, winning by 3 lengths from Nelsons Dockyard with 14 others well beaten off; will stay 1¼m; sure to win more races. *H. Cecil.* **96 p**

ALLEGORY (USA) 3 b. f. Alleged 138–Justaguest (Groton) (1982 NR 1983 11v 10g) $105,000Y; big, rangy, quite attractive filly; fourth foal; half-sister to American winner Just Good (by Shecky Greene); dam won 3 races at up to 6f, including a minor stakes at 2 yrs; behind in maiden and minor events at Newbury; sold 100,000 dollars Keeneland November Sales. *J. Dunlop.* —

ALL EXPENSE 5 ch. g. Crash Course 128–Yellow Mel (Yellow God 129) (1982 NR 1983 12d4) ex-Irish gelding; first foal; dam never ran; placed in bumpers race and successful over hurdles; over 10 lengths fourth of 8 to Seabattle in amateur riders race at Redcar in May, first outing on flat; will stay well. *H. Bell.* —

ALL FAIR 2 b. c. Free State 125–Be Honest 95 (Klairon 131) (1983 7fg 7g3 8.2s* 7fg) Apr 22; 6,800Y; big, useful sort; half-brother to 2 winners, including 1m and 9f winner Honest Record (by Record Token); dam won over 1m; won 9-runner maiden event at Haydock in October easing up by length from Jerry Can; modest sixth of 20 under 8-9 in nursery at Doncaster the following month; will stay 1¼m; acts well on soft ground. *R. Whitaker.* **88**

ALLGATE 2 gr. f. Habat 127–Lenana (Never Say Die 137) (1983 7.2g 7d 7fg 6fg) Apr 14; 6,000Y; big filly; sixth foal; half-sister to a winning plater; dam unraced daughter of Coronation Stakes winner Aiming High; in rear in the autumn in varied company, including selling. *D. H. Jones.* —

ALL HELL LET LOOSE 2 b. c. Star Appeal 133 Justine (Luciano) (1983 6f 7fg 7g 7fg* 7fg4 7fg*) Feb 14; 9,800F; quite attractive, short-coupled colt, has a round action; third foal; half-brother to a winner in Germany by Lombard; dam won at 2 yrs and 4 yrs in Germany; much improved in blinkers, making all in 17-runner maiden race at Leicester in September and in 13-runner mixed-aged event (beating Ziggurat short head in very tight finish) at Newmarket in October; good fourth in competitive nursery in between; suited by 7f; yet to race on a soft surface. *G. Pritchard-Gordon.* **94**

ALLICANCE (USA) 3 b. f. Alleged 138–Runaway Bride (Wild Risk) (1982 8s4 7.5s2 1983 12v2 10.5s3 12fg3 10fg3 12g2 10.5fg* 12.5f4 10.5g2 10f4 12.5g) $1,000,000Y; half-sister to numerous winners, notably French 2000 Guineas winner and Derby third Blushing Groom and very smart 6f to 1m performer Bayraan (both by Red God); dam placed over 1½m in Ireland as a 4-y-o; showed plenty of promise as a 2-y-o, but didn't get off mark until beating Sulemeif by 3 lengths in 65,000 francs race at Maisons-Laffitte in September; ran well on other occasions, including when close third to Marie de Litz in Prix de Royaumont at Chantilly on second outing, 2 lengths fourth of 10 behind High Hawk in Prix de Royallieu at Longchamp and 2½ lengths second of 10 behind Fly Me in Prix de Flore at Saint-Cloud, last 2 races in October; stays 1½m; acts on any going; sent to USA. *F. Boutin, France.* **113**

56

ALLIED KINGSWOOD 3 ro.g. Mandrake Major 122–Fair Jacqueline 79 —
(Fortino II 120) (1982 6d 1983 7s 7.6v 8fg 8h 7f) compact, good-bodied gelding;
poor walker; plating-class maiden; ran best race in apprentice event third start.
S. Harris.

ALLIED LONDON 4 ch.g. Jimmy Reppin 131–Yofi (Articulate 121) (1982 7f³ 6f —
6fg 8g 1983 8fg) strong gelding; plating-class maiden; best run at 7f on firm going;
sold 700 gns Ascot August Sales. *S. Harris.*

ALLIGATRIX (USA) 3 br.f. Alleged 138–Shore (Round Table) (1982 6g⁴ 7fg* —
8g³ 1983 7d 12fg 12g 10g) close-coupled, quite attractive filly; very useful as a
2-y-o, when winning maiden race at Newmarket and finishing third in Hoover Fillies
Mile at Ascot; ran well for a long way when seventh of 14 behind High Hawk in
Ribblesdale Stakes at Royal Ascot in June but finished last on her only subsequent
outing, Lancashire Oaks at Haydock; disappointing. *R. Armstrong.*

ALL IS FORGIVEN 3 b.g. Mummy's Pet 125–Condonna 92 (Constable 119) **108**
(1982 6fg 6fg 6g³ 6g 6f³ 6s 1983 5g 5fg² 5fg² 5f² 6fg* 5.1fg* 6f³ 6f* 6f 6fg² 5fg*
5fg) quite attractive gelding; has a round action; often disappointed early in his
career but made up for it by winning handicaps at Newmarket (2), Yarmouth and
York; beat Sharpish by 2 lengths in £7,100 Innovative Marketing Sprint Handicap
on last-named course in September, travelling well most of way and running on
strongly once given a couple of smacks; stays 6f; acts on firm going; blinkered
nowadays; suited by strong handling and goes particularly well for L. Piggott;
sweated up and unseated his rider in parade ring at York. *D. Thom.*

ALLODIUM 3 gr.g. Dragonara Palace 115–Pepperita 79 (Nelcius 133) (1982 6g —
6g 7fg 8s 1983 7f 10f 8f) compact, good-bodied gelding; soundly beaten, including
in a £5,000 seller as a 2-y-o; bandaged off-hind second outing; sold 3,500 gns Ascot
October Sales. *M. W. Easterby.*

ALLORETTE 4 b.f. Ballymore 123–Alcidette 110 (Alcide 136) (1982 7v 8s⁴ **100**
12fg³ 12g² 12g 10g 10g² 11.5s 12d 9v² 12s* 10d 1983 8s 9v 13g 14v* 14fg³ 12f 9fg
14f² 14f⁴ 14f* 12g² 11g) first foal; dam very useful at up to 1½m in Ireland; trotted
up in handicap at Leopardstown in May and won 3-runner handicap at Tramore in
August; improved on that form on eleventh start, coming home 1½ lengths second
of 9 to Bay Empress in Brownstown Stakes at the Curragh; suited by 1½m+; acts
on any going; tough. *P. Mullins, Ireland.*

ALL SAINTS DAY 2 ch.f. Artaius 129–Red Letter Day 100 (Crepello 136) (1983 – p
7f) Apr 15; fair sort; second foal; half-sister to 1982 2-y-o 5f winner Holy Day (by
Sallust); dam won over 6f and 1m; 20/1, prominent 5f in £4,600 event won by
Mahogany at Newbury in September; will be suited by 1m+; should do better. *P.
Walwyn.*

ALL SEASONS 4 b.f. Silly Season 127–Little Rapide 90 (Rapace 130) (1982 10f —
12.2f² 12fg 12.2f⁴ 1983 12f 14.6f) plating-class maiden; suited by 1½m; sometimes
bandaged; sold 800 gns Doncaster November Sales. *Ronald Thompson.*

ALL SECRET 2 br.f. Continuation 120–Hillset (Hill Clown) (1983 5f⁴ 5f 6f² 6f⁴ **60**
5g⁴) Apr 2; rather lightly-built filly; sister to a winning 2-y-o plater and half-sister
to two 2-y-o winners; dam of no account; plater; will be suited by 7f and 1m; acts on
firm ground; consistent. *J. Hardy.*

ALL SYSTEMS GO 3 ch.c. Bay Express 132–Omnia 80 (Hill Clown) (1982 6fg² **113**
6d* 7f* 7f* 7g* 7fg 1983 7d³ 8g 6f 7fg⁴ 7.6g⁴ 7f³ 10f 8fg⁴ 7g³) well-made, quite
attractive colt; good walker; smart performer as a 2-y-o, and a tough one too;
didn't recapture his sparkle in 1983 but was in frame in goodish company at
Newbury, Newmarket, Lingfield, Newcastle, Baden-Baden and Goodwood; finds 6f
on sharp side and should stay 1m; acts well on a sound surface and has also won on
dead going; blinkered fourth and sixth outings; sent to race in USA. *G.
Pritchard-Gordon.*

ALLTEN LIMITED 2 ch.c. Majority Blue 126–Nora's Choice 110 (King's Leap **78**
111) (1983 5g⁴ 6fg 6f³ 6fg 6fg⁴ 7.2g³ 6d²) Mar 29; IR 3,000F, 3,000Y; lengthy
colt; poor mover; dam sprinter; in frame in varied company, having remainder well
beaten off and putting up a game effort when head second of 18 to Fill The Jug in
valuable seller at York in October; best at 6f; acts well on a soft surface. *M.
Naughton.*

ALL THE QUEENS MEN 3 br.g. Undulate–Crusheen (Typhoon 125) (1982 —
NR 1983 10d 12fg) half-brother to several winners, including sprinters H. R.
Micro (by High Award) and Out Of Hand (by Some Hand); dam ran twice at 2 yrs in
Ireland; running-on seventh of 16 behind Fighter Pilot in maiden race at Redcar in
May; poor last of 7 in similar event on same course in August, only subsequent
start. *M. Lambert.*

ALLURED 4 b.f. Decoy Boy 129–Charter Belle 60 (Runnymede 123) (1982 7f 8s **54**
7g 9.4f⁴ 9g 8g⁴ 8fg 8.2g* 10.6s 1983 8s³ 8s⁴ 8.3s³ 7s 8g 10.1fg* 8.3f² 10f*) rangy
filly; plater; bought in 1,500 gns after winning at Windsor in June and 1,050 gns
after scoring at Salisbury in July; suited by 1¼m; acts on any going; wears blinkers
and sometimes a hood as well. *J. Jenkins.*

ALLUVIA (FR) 3 br.c. Riverman 131–Alea II (Galivanter 131) (1982 6s³ 7fg* 6.5d **115**
7.5v³ 7s 1983 8v³ 11s³ 12s 9fg³ 9.2d 6.5fg 7f 8g) half-brother to several winners,
notably high-class 7f to 1¼m winner Noalcoholic (by Nonoalco); dam won Italian 1000
Guineas; won maiden race at Chantilly as a 2-y-o; third in Prix de Fontainebleau (6½
lengths behind Castle Guard) and Prix Noailles (beaten 3 lengths by Jeu de Paille after
losing ground at start) at Longchamp in the spring, and in Prix Jean Prat at Chantilly in
June, beaten under a length by Ginger Brink in last-named; needs further than 6.5f and
evidently stays 11f (soundly beaten in Prix Hocquart at Longchamp over further); acts
on any going, except possibly very firm. *R. Collet, France.*

ALLVERTON (USA) 3 b.c. Alleged 138–Royal Honoree (Round Table) (1982 **112**
8f* 10v² 1983 9.7s³ 8g 9fg) good-bodied colt; half-brother to Irish St Leger
runner-up Father Rooney (by Val de l'Orne); showed smart form in 2 races at
Longchamp at 2 yrs, winning newcomers event and finishing second in Prix de
Conde; ran respectably when 2¼ lengths third to Pluralisme in Prix de Guiche on
same course in April and about 2 lengths fifth of 10 to Ginger Brink in Prix Jean Prat
at Chantilly in June; never-dangerous twelfth of 16 behind Lomond in 2000 Guineas
at Newmarket in between; would have stayed 1½m; acted on any going; died of
twisted intestine in summer. *F. Boutin, France.*

ALLYANZA 3 ro.f. Swing Easy 126–Sunny Sovereign 85 (Lucky Sovereign) (1982 **58**
5fg 5fg 6g 5fg* 6f 5g⁴ 5g* 1983 6d 5g 5fg⁴ 6fg 5s⁴ 6fg⁴ 5fg) rather sparely-made
filly; stays 6f; seems to act on any going; sold 2,300 gns Ascot November Sales,
reportedly for export to Italy. *P. Rohan.*

ALMA-CANDY 3 b.c. Tudor Music 131–Autumn Glory (Silly Season 127) (1982 **–**
6v 8s 1983 8v⁴ 10fg 12fg 10s 10.5d) useful-looking colt; fourth of 24 behind
Spanish Bold in maiden race at Kempton in April, easily best effort; blinkered when
behind in a £4,000 seller final start; stays 1m. *J. Bethell.*

AL MAMOON (USA) 2 ch.c. Believe It–Lady Winborne 98 (Secretariat) (1983 6f* **105 ?**
6f* 6fg 6fg) Mar 9; \$310,000Y; tall, leggy colt; first foal; dam, half-sister to Allez
France, won over 9f in Ireland from 2 starts; won his first 2 races, at York and Thirsk in
July, in style of high-class 2-y-o, but failed to go the right way; beat only one home in
Gimcrack Stakes at York and William Hill Middle Park Stakes at Newmarket, and in
Gimcrack was badly behaved (sweating profusely and very much on his toes) into the
bargain; bred to stay beyond 6f; one to be wary of. *H. T. Jones.*

ALMA REAL 2 ch.f. Red Alert 127–Lipizza (Acropolis 132) (1983 6g) May 24; **–**
6,600Y; sturdy filly; half-sister to a minor 2-y-o winner; dam lightly-raced daughter
of very smart 1952 2-y-o Pirouette; 50/1, behind in 27-runner maiden race at
Newmarket in July. *P. Haslam.*

ALMEIRA (FR) 2 b.f. Gay Merene 128–Armida (Caro 133) (1983 6.5fg* 7fg* **118 p**
8f*)
  In the early 'seventies, soon after winning the Prix de l'Arc de Triomphe with
San San, the Poule d'Essai des Poulains and the Prix Ganay with Caro and the Prix
Royal-Oak with Samos, Countess Margit Batthyany appeared to be severing her

Prix Marcel Boussac, Longchamp—Almeira gains her second pattern win of the season, beating Masarika and Feerie Boreale

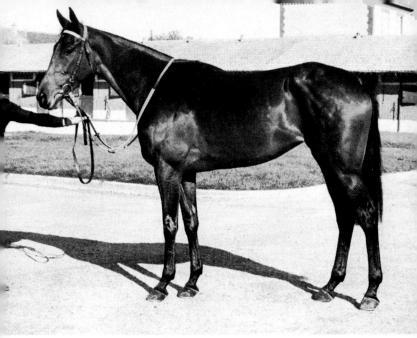

Countess M. Batthyany's "Almeira"

links with French racing: in 1973 she sold a batch of twenty-seven in-foal mares and the following year disposed of twenty-eight horses in training and forty-eight home-bred yearlings. However, the Countess still owns the Haras de Bois Roussel, the home of the promising stallion Pharly, and in 1983 her colours were carried by another potential champion in the unbeaten Almeira. Oddly enough Almeira is a daughter of one of the yearlings sold in 1974 then re-purchased cheaply after an undistinguished racing career.

Almeira began her racing career by accounting for ten other maiden fillies in the Prix Tanit early in the Deauville August meeting. Her only other starts were in pattern events, the Prix du Calvados on the same course and the Prix Marcel Boussac at Longchamp on Arc day, and she ran out a clear-cut winner on each occasion. The eight-strong field for the Calvados included six other previous winners, with the two top weights, the Robert Papin third Harifa and the Criterium de Bernay winner Perdomi, both starting at a shorter price than Almeira. Harifa ran below her best but Perdomi was fighting for the lead at the distance where Almeira was looking for an opening. Once a gap appeared the race was as good as over; Almeira produced easily the best acceleration, quickening away to win by two lengths from Premium Win, who got the better of Perdomi by a length.

Almeira succeeded in the Prix Marcel Boussac where the previous Calvados winner, Maximova, had failed. Whereas Maximova was made a very short-priced favourite at Longchamp Almeira was only second choice in the betting behind the Aga Khan's very fast filly Masarika, the conqueror of Superlative in the Prix Robert Papin. None of the five remaining runners, which included the wide-margin Chester winner Lallax from England and the Silken Glider Stakes winner Shindella from Ireland, started at shorter than 8/1. As the betting suggested it might, the race developed into a battle between Almeira and Masarika, with Almeira settling in second place behind the free-running favourite who had pulled her way to the front after only a furlong. Despite showing surprising signs of greenness when asked to challenge Masarika in the straight, Almeira had taken her measure before the final furlong and eventually beat her weakening opponent pretty comfortably by two lengths. The firm ground didn't inconvenience Almeira in the slightest; indeed she has the unusual record for a French filly of never having raced on an easy surface.

Almeira (Fr) (b.f. Feb 24, 1981)	Gay Mecene (b 1975)	Vaguely Noble (b 1965)	Vienna
			Noble Lassie
		Gay Missile (b 1967)	Sir Gaylord
			Missy Baba
	Armida (ch 1973)	Caro (gr 1967)	Fortino II
			Chambord
		Andrea II (br 1955)	Ticino
			Adriana II

Normally victory in the Marcel Boussac gives a filly very strong claims to be regarded the best young staying filly in France but Treizieme's defeat of the colts in the Grand Criterium a week later entitles her to be regarded as Almeira's superior. However, there may well be little to choose between the pair at three; Almeira, a big, rangy filly, has bags of scope for further improvement and she's a daughter of Gay Mecene, something of a late-developer who didn't reach his best until raced over middle distances. We mentioned earlier that Almeira's dam Armida had an undistinguished career on the racecourse—she was third once over a mile from five starts—but she was a well-bred filly, so much so that at 210,000 francs she was the highest priced of Caro's first-crop yearlings sold in France. Two of her half-sisters had already shown smart form, with Anna Karenina winning the Prix d'Arenberg and Arosa the Prix Messidor. Their dam Andrea II was also an excellent performer; she was rated the best two-year-old in Germany in 1957 after winning all her three starts and she stayed well enough to finish a close second in the Preis der Diana, as well as taking fourth place in both the Deutsches Derby and St Leger. Other notable members of the family were Andrea's brother Ataturk, who represented Germany in the 1955 Washington International after winning over a wide range of distances, and her half-brother Anatol, the champion German two-year-old of 1962. It's not too surprising that Countess Batthyany should be tempted to buy back Armida in 1977 when carrying her first foal, a colt by Satingo subsequently named Albertas; the price was only 110,000 francs (around £10,000). Albertas has met with much more success than Armida's only other previous produce, the Pharly gelding Augis, winning a small race over a distance just short of a mile and a half on the flat in addition to doing well over jumps. There is no shortage of stamina in Almeira's make-up and she'll be very well suited by middle distances. She's certain to remain very hard to beat. *J-C. Cunnington, France.*

ALMIGHTY ZEUS 6 ch.g. High Line 125–Zeus Girl 75 (Zeus Boy 121) (1982 NR 1983 17.1g) staying maiden on flat though has won over jumps. *D. Elsworth.*   —

AL MUNDHIR (USA) 2 b.c. Seattle Slew–Huggle Duggle (Never Bend) (1983 7fg 7fg⁴) Apr 8; $570,000Y; big, rangy colt; good walker; has a powerful, round action; first foal; dam at her best at 4 yrs when smart stakes winner over 8.5f; 3 lengths last of 4, after none too clear a run, to Bonne Ile in Newmarket Challenge Cup in October; will stay 1½m. *H. T. Jones.*   **61 p**

AL MURTAJAZ (USA) 2 b.c. Damascus–Pantomime (The Axe 115) (1983 6fg) May 8; $850,000Y; good-bodied, attractive colt; third foal; half-brother to a winner by Olden Times; dam, very useful 8.5f stakes winner, is half-sister to very smart filly Grafitti; 16/1, tenth of 23 to Optimistic Lass in maiden race at Newmarket in October; sure to do better over further, and will stay at least 1¼m. *H. T. Jones.*   **— p**

AL NASR 5 b.h. Green Dancer 132–Padrona 103 (St Paddy 133) (1982 12.2d² 13f 14fg³ 12f³ 12g 12.2s 12s 1983 12s⁴ 12d³ 14s⁴ 15.5v² 12d³ 14fg 16g³ 12.2fg² 16.5f² 16.5f² 13h*) rangy, good-looking horse; won handicap at Nottingham in September; stays very well; acts on any going; has been tried in blinkers; not the greatest of battlers but is consistent. *J. Benstead.*   **59**

ALNOOD 2 b.c. Habitat 134–Lucky For Me 116 (Appiani II 128) (1983 6f 7fg⁴ 7g² 6g* 7fg*) Mar 3; IR 330,000Y; rather lightly-made, quite attractive colt; half-brother to 3 winners, including Grand Prix de Paris winner Yawa (by Luthier) and very useful 1980 Irish 2-y-o 6f and 1m winner Euclid (by Lyphard); dam middle-distance filly; a progressive colt who won his last 2 races, Buggins Farm Nursery at Haydock in October by 3 lengths from Mr Meeka and Tankerville Nursery at Ascot later in the month on disqualification of neck winner Leipzig for hampering him in final furlong; will stay 1m; acts on a firm surface; sort to make a very useful 3-y-o, and seems sure to win more races. *J. Dunlop.*   **105**

ALOICIOUS 2 gr.c. Malicious–Venturesome Lass (Right Boy 137) (1983 5s 6fg   **51**
5f⁴ 6f⁴ 7f³ 8f 8g 8d 6g) Mar 16; narrow colt; plater; stays 7f; ran very wide on
turn at Beverley sixth outing; blinkered penultimate appearance. *D. Leslie.*

ALPHABATIM (USA) 2 b.c. Verbatim–Morning Games (Grey Dawn II 132) **122**
(1983 8d³ 8fg* 8fg*)

Buying as many yearlings as he does nowadays James Delahooke is bound to
have the occasional failure. Three of them showed up at the 1983 Newmarket
Autumn Sales—the two-year-old colts Apodemus, Poetic Justice and Santella Pal
who were sold, without having reached the racecourse, for a total of only 2,650
guineas just a year after being bought for 35,000 guineas, 56,000 guineas and
55,000 dollars respectively. On the other side of the coin there have been some
spectacular examples of good judgement over the years, the most recent being
Lear Fan and Rousillon, both bought for sums well below their sire's average;
Raft, whose price of 140,000 dollars fell over 30,000 dollars short of the average
price at Saratoga; Rainbow Quest who may one day be labelled 'cheap' at 950,000
dollars; and Alphabatim.

Alphabatim, a 23,000-dollar purchase at the Keeneland September Yearling
Sale, was perhaps the shrewdest buy of all. At the time his sire Verbatim had
sired only three winners in Britain in a fairly lengthy stud career, and his dam
Morning Games, unplaced on her only appearance, came from a none-too-
successful family in recent generations. Alphabatim has now put his sire on the
map over here and boosted his family's reputation with a well-deserved victory in
Britain's richest race for two-year-olds, the William Hill Futurity Stakes at
Doncaster in October. Despite its value the Futurity rarely attracts as strong a
field as it once regularly did, and the subsequent failure of recent winners Take
Your Place, Sporting Yankee, Dactylographer, Count Pahlen and Dunbeath have
led to the race's acquiring the unfortunate nickname of William Hill Obscurity. As
the founders and first sponsors of the race—the race was first run in 1961 as the
Timeform Gold Cup and won by Miralgo—we find it sad to have to say that the
1983 field looked distinctly substandard. Of the nine runners four were maidens
and the only one to have gained a place in a pattern race was the French colt
Mendez, an easy winner of the Prix des Chenes before finishing an unlucky third
in the Grand Criterium. Alphabatim, on the strength of a very encouraging third
to his stable-companion Gambler's Cup at Goodwood in September and an
impressive four-length victory over twenty opponents in the Soltikoff Maiden
Stakes at Newmarket early in October, was made second favourite ahead of the
Grand Criterium International d'Ostende winner Beldale Lear. Making up the
field were the Newbury maiden race winner Lake Valentina, the promising
maidens Falstaff and Ilium, the dual York winner Great Western and the
long-shots Bounty Hawk and Petrizzo. In the race the runners were closely
grouped early on, Alphabatim turning into the straight in fourth place behind Lake

*William Hill Futurity Stakes, Doncaster—Alphabatim (No. 2) gets the best of a driving
finish with French challenger Mendez (stripes) and Ilium (rails)*

Valentina, Ilium and Petrizzo, with the hard-pulling Mendez being restrained not far behind. When Alphabatim moved up to tackle the new leader Ilium inside the last two furlongs he had already been niggled at for some time and his prospects of winning looked none too bright as Mendez loomed up on his outside. However, Mendez didn't get things all his own way, and he looked less than fully genuine under pressure, whereas Alphabatim responded in fine style to strong driving, forcing his head in front well inside the last furlong to beat the favourite by half a length. Ilium held on well to be third, just a head further behind. Time may prove the principals well up to classic standard but Petrizzo's proximity in seventh place, less than eight lengths behind Alphabatim, suggests they have a long way to go—Petrizzo had recently been beaten a similar margin in a maiden race at Warwick and received a five-length beating in maiden company at Beverley. While the Futurity result was unenthusiastically received by the leading bookmakers—even the sponsors of the race made Alphabatim no better than a 33/1-chance for the Derby—it was a triumph for the winner's connections, not least Khaled Abdulla who had purchased the colt privately after his Newmarket success.

			Prince John
		Speak John	Nuit de Folies
	Verbatim	(b 1958)	
	(b or br 1965)	Well Kept	Never Say Die
Alphabatim (USA)		(b 1958)	Bed o' Roses
(b.c. Jan 27, 1981)		Grey Dawn II	Herbager
	Morning Games	(gr 1962)	Polamia
	(gr 1976)	Major Play	B. Major
		(b 1971)	Rich Royalty

Alphabatim's big-race win gives us a chance to say something about Verbatim, hitherto little known outside the USA. He was a tough performer, racing fifty-one times over four seasons for a total of eleven wins and 415,802 dollars, a sizeable amount of money for a horse rated over 7 lb inferior to the best of his age in each season he raced. His stakes successes were gained at seven furlongs to a mile and a quarter, his most valuable wins coming in the Governor Nicolls Stakes and the Amory L. Haskell Handicap. He has done well at stud in the States, siring the winners of over 10,000,000 dollars including the Belmont Stakes winner Summing and the top filly Princess Rooney who won all her six starts as a two-year-old in 1982. Much of Verbatim's stock stays reasonably well by American standards and Alphabatim races as though he'll be suited by a mile and a quarter or more. He's the first winner bred by Morning Games whose third produce, a yearling colt by High Tribute, was sold for only 4,500 dollars in 1983. His grandam Major Play, the winner of six small races at up to eleven furlongs as a three-year-old, has bred three minor winners and is a half-sister to the very useful sprinter Royal Villa. The only high-class winner from the family in recent generations is the tough filly Oil Royalty, a half-sister to Rich Royalty who won over 330,000 dollars in one hundred and seven appearances.

Like so many of his stable's horses, Alphabatim is a sizeable, attractive individual and a good walker, all in all the type to make a better three-year-old. Consequently it would be foolish to write him off as a potential Derby winner, but it must be stressed that he needs to make more than normal improvement if he's to reach such heights. *G. Harwood.*

ALPHA OMEGA 4 b.g. Auction Ring 123–Hey Dolly (Saint Crespin III 132) (1982 10s² 12s² 12f* 12.3fg* 12f² 12f³ 16fg 12.3d³ 11.7g² 11.5g² 13s² 12v⁴ 12g 1983 16v* 16d² 20fg 16f 18.4fg² 15fg 15.8fg 18.8f³) workmanlike gelding; good mover; modest handicapper; always prominent and kept on strongly to beat Popsi's Joy 7 lengths in Queen's Prize at Kempton in April; ran creditably on occasions afterwards; stays well; acts on any going; suited by front-running tactics; blinkered once at 2 yrs; has had tongue tied down; genuine. *R. Williams.* **88**

ALPHA PLUS 3 ch.f. Anax 120–Argo 64 (Decoy Boy 129) (1982 NR 1983 5fg 6fg 6fg) second foal; dam sprint plater; no worthwhile form, but didn't run in a seller. *A. W. Jones.* **–**

ALPINE AIR 3 br.g. Sparkler 130–Argitone (Aureole 132) (1982 7fg 7fg 8s 1983 10s) big, workmanlike gelding; behind in maiden races. *J. Cann.* **–**

ALPINE SILK 3 b.f. Malinowski 123–Shortia (Shantung 132) (1982 7d 7g 1983 8s 8g) small filly; well beaten in varied races, including sellers; started slowly when blinkered final start. *G. Pritchard-Gordon.* **–**

ALPINE STRINGS 2 b.c. Stradavinsky 121–Kanvita (Home Guard 129) (1983 5v 7fg 6fg* 6g* 5fg* 6fg²) Apr 6; lengthy, quite attractive, dipped-backed colt; third foal; dam never ran; in fine form in August and September, winning minor **103**

events at Windsor and Lingfield and 5-runner Kensington Palace Stakes (finding impressive turn of foot to beat El Gazebo going away by 3 lengths) at Ascot; no match for top-weighted Forzando when short-priced favourite for 13-runner Martini Trophy Nursery at Newmarket in October and went down by 3 lengths (had a shoe removed at start); stays 6f well; acts on a firm surface; the type to win more races. *R. Armstrong.*

ALPINE WAY 4 gr.g. Dragonara Palace 115–Country Ramble 93 (Kribi 110) (1982   **64**
7g² 12fg³ 9s* 12.2d⁴ 8g 12d⁴ 1983 8d 9g 8f² 8h 9fg⁴ 10f* 10s³ 10.6g 8.2s) short-coupled gelding; apprentice ridden when winning handicap at Beverley in September; suited by 1¼m but possibly doesn't stay 1½m; acts on any going. *Miss S. Hall.*

ALRIGGA (USA) 2 b.f. Bold Bidder–Mauna Loa (Hawaii) (1983 5fg) May 6;   **–**
$325,000Y; third foal; half-sister to 3-y-o middle-distance stayer Exceller, won 7f claiming race at 2 yrs; never dangerous in maiden race at Lingfield in October; bred to need much further than 5f, and should stay at least 1¼m. *H. T. Jones.*

ALSHAHEER 3 b.c. Great Nephew 126–Word from Lundy 93 (Worden II 129)   **–**
(1982 NR 1983 8d 10fg 10fg) 200,000Y; big, strong, rangy colt; brother to Derby winner Grundy and smart middle-distance colt Centurius; dam stayed 2m; in rear in big fields of maidens at Newmarket (2) and Sandown; sold 7,200 gns Newmarket Autumn Sales. *J. Benstead.*

ALSHANDEGHA (USA) 2 b.f. Alydar–Eyeshadow (My Babu 136) (1983 5fg 5f   **70**
5f⁴ 8d) Apr 29; $320,000Y; lightly-built, unimpressive filly; half-sister to numerous winners, including Irish Sweeps Derby winner Malacate (by Lucky Debonair); dam ran only twice; sire, son of Raise A Native, was top-class winner of 14 races from 5.5f to 1¼m; always outpaced when 4 lengths fourth of 8 to Sarab in minor event at Beverley in August, best effort; should stay 1¼m. *H. T. Jones.*

ALSUFUUH 2 b.c. Welsh Saint 126–Good Opportunity (Hail to Reason) (1983 5f)   **–**
May 19; IR 37,000Y; big, strong-quartered colt; half-brother to 1m winner Northern Chance (by Northfields) and winners in Italy and France; dam twice-raced half-sister to Bold and Brave, a very smart winner at up to 1m; weak in market and in need of race, last of 7 in maiden event at Sandown in July. *J. Benstead.*

ALTDORFER (USA) 2 gr.c. Caro 133–Abala (Baldric II 131) (1983 5s* 6d³ 5fg³   **90**
7f) May 13; useful-looking colt; second foal; half-brother to 3-y-o Absalon (by Crow); dam, very useful French miler, is closely related to top-class filly All Along; won 8-runner newcomers race at Goodwood in May; took on useful opposition subsequently, best effort when 9 lengths third of 5 behind Masarika in Prix du Bois at Longchamp (blinkered first time) on third appearance; should stay 1m; sent to France. *P. Kelleway.*

AL TRUI 3 gr.c. Scottish Rifle 127–Sweety Grey (Young Emperor 133) (1982   **87**
5.1g⁴ 5f* 5g* 5g³ 5d⁴ 5f* 5v² 1983 5f³ 5f³ 5fg² 6f* 6f 6f³ 6s 6fg 5g) small, compact colt; won handicap at Ripon in August; close fourth behind Saxham Breck in similar race at Newmarket in September, best subsequent effort; stays 6f; acts on any going; suitable mount for an apprentice. *W. Musson.*

ALUWHITE HABIT 4 b.g. Hittite Glory 125–Tritonia 69 (Tyrant) (1982 7d   **48**
8.2fg 7f 8fg 8.2s 6s 7s 7s 1983 8g 11.5s⁴ 10fg² 9d 10g 11s²) workmanlike gelding; has a round action; plater; stays 11.5f; acts on soft going; sometimes sweats up. *G. Fletcher.*

ALVA GLEN 2 b.g. Absalom 128–Badwell Ash (Morston 125) (1983 6s) Mar 14;   **–**
7,000Y; good-bodied gelding; first foal; dam, who never ran, is closely related to Cheshire Oaks winner Hunston; 10/1 and in need of race, never-dangerous seventh of 10 in minor event at Ayr in September. *W. Musson.*

AL WASHL (USA) 3 b.f. The Minstrel 135–Velvet Flight (Stewvard) (1982 5fg²   **–**
6h² 6fg² 6d² 1983 6g 7h 5.3f) leggy, quite attractive filly; has a round action; didn't recover her form in 1983 (blinkered last 2 starts); should stay beyond 6f; possibly not at her best on a soft surface. *H. T. Jones.*

ALWAYS NATIVE (USA) 2 b. or br.c. Our Native–Mountain Memory (Groton)   **88**
(1983 5f* 6g) Apr 13; $38,000Y; well-grown colt; brother to a stakes-placed winner and to stakes winner Mountain Native; dam, half-sister to 4 stakes winners, won over 4f on only start at 2 yrs; very fit, led over 2f out to win 13-runner maiden race at Newcastle in August by 2½ lengths from Be There Baby; over 7 lengths fifth of 15 to Round Hill, after pulling very hard, in minor event at Doncaster the following month; headstrong and may prove best at 5f. *M. Albina.*

ALY

ALYCHANT 3 b.f. Chantro 104–Alice Springs 83 (Coronation Year 124) (1982 NR 1983 6f* 6fg 6f⁴) half-sister to 2 winners, including sprinter Gentle Springs (by Gentle Art), a smart winner at 2 yrs; dam middle-distance performer; ran moderately after making a successful first appearance in seller at Carlisle in June (apprentice ridden); will stay 7f. *D. Smith.*   **56**

ALZAO (USA) 3 b.c. Lyphard 132–Lady Rebecca (Sir Ivor 135) (1982 9s* 8v* 1983 10v³ 9s* 10v⁴ 10fg² 10fg 8g) strong, compact colt; third foal; dam, half-sister to top-class American colts Tom Rolfe and Chieftain, was very useful French middle-distance winner; very useful at 2 yrs, when winning both his races; put up a good performance when holding off Ginger Brink by a neck in Prix Matchem at Evry in May; in frame subsequently in Prix la Force at Longchamp later in month and in La Coupe de Maisons-Laffitte in September, going down by ½ length to Bylly The Kid in latter; creditable eighth of 19 to Cormorant Wood in Dubai Champion Stakes at Newmarket in October; stays 1¼m; yet to race on really firm ground, but seems to act on any other. *F. Boutin, France.*   **117**

AMAL LEES HOPE (FR) 2 b.c. Irish River 131–Oak Hill 119 (Sheshoon 132) (1983 6f 7f² 8s 8g) Apr 19; 140,000Y; medium-sized, attractive colt; third reported foal; half-brother to 3-y-o Oak Ridge (by Shirley Heights) and very useful French 1½m winner Oak Dancer (by Green Dancer); dam won Criterium des Pouliches; 4 lengths second of 11 to odds-on El Hakim in maiden race at Yarmouth in August, best effort; unimpressive on way to start final appearance; should stay 1¼m; acts on firm going. *H. T. Jones.*   **74**

AMANDA MARY 5 b.m. Wishing Star 117–Marchpane (Parthia 132) (1982 6fg 5f 7f 6f² 6f² 6fg 6g 7f4 8.2s 8.2v⁴ 1983 6v⁴ 6s⁴ 6fg⁴ 7f 8f4 6fg 7f4 10f* 10fg 10.4fg 10f 10s 12fg³ 10.6g 7g 10g²) lengthy mare; plater; attracted no bid after winning at Nottingham in July (apprentice ridden); suited by middle distances; acts on any going but goes well on firm; effective with or without blinkers; usually bandaged nowadays; hasn't always looked genuine; sold 2,500 gns Ascot December Sales. *W. Stubbs.*   **45**

AMANZIMTOTI (USA) 3 b.f. Accipiter–La Fantastique (Le Fabuleux 133) (1982 NR 1983 10s 12g 10g 8f 8f 7s 8.2g⁴ 8g) $75,000Y; third foal; half-sister to a minor winner; dam unraced half-sister to champion American sprinter Chou Croute; only quite moderate form in maiden races; blinkered last 2 outings; sold 3,100 gns Newmarket December Sales. *G. Hunter.*

AMARACH 5 ch.g. Deep Run 119–Irish Halo (Macherio) (1982 13.8f 1983 9s² 9g⁴) smart hurdler; second in amateur riders race at Ripon in April, only form on flat; will stay 1½m. *R. Fisher.*   **51**

AMARONE 3 b.c. Realm 129–Misacre 66 (St Alphage 119) (1982 5d* 5fg³ 5f4 5f 7f² 6fg 7v 8.2s 1983 7v 8d³ 8v 8s* 7s³ 8.5g 6f 10g 8d³ 7f*) well-made, quite attractive colt; has a round action; fair handicapper on his day, as he showed when winning decisively at Brighton in May and Leicester in November (ridden by 7-lb claimer both times); stays 1m; acts on any going; blinkered once in 1982; tends to sweat up. *R. Simpson.*   **89**

AMAZON PRINCE (USA) 3 b. or br.c. Native Royalty–Bright n' Gay (Citation) (1982 6g 6fg 7fg² 7s³ 1000 12v 7d² 8f² 7f* 7.2g 7g³ 7g⁴ 8fg²) useful sort; made all and easily landed the odds in minor event at Folkestone in June; also placed in varied races, including when second in Britannia Stakes at Royal Ascot earlier in month (to Teleprompter) and minor event at Doncaster in November (below form when narrowly beaten by Scoutsmistake); likely to prove best at up to 1m; acts on soft going but best form on firm; suited by forcing tactics. *G. Hunter.*   **83**

AMBER BAY 3 b.g. Orange Bay 131–Amber Flyer 91 (Amber Rama 133) (1982 5fg² 5fg² 5fg 7fg 1983 6s) tall, lengthy, leggy gelding; plating class at 2 yrs; behind only outing of 1983; dead. *R. Hoad.*   **—**

AMBER FIZZ (USA) 2 ch.f. Effervescing–Amber High (Ambiopoise) (1983 7f) Feb 24; $90,000Y; half-sister to numerous winners, including very smart 1978 2-y-o Groton High (by Groton); dam comes from same family as Bold Ruler; 14/1 and apprentice ridden, well behind in 15-runner maiden race at Lingfield in October. *J. Dunlop.*   **—**

AMBER HEIGHTS 3 ch.g. Relkino 131–Jackie's Joy (Skymaster 126) (1982 NR 1983 12v 12s* 13fg³ 14d 15s⁴ 11g⁴ 15.8d) lengthy, rather sparely-made gelding; half-brother to several winners, including Amber Vale (by Warpath) and Amber Valley (by Forlorn River), both fairly useful middle-distance performers at their best; dam well beaten all outings; 20/1 when making all to beat Clearly Bust by 2½ lengths in 10-runner maiden race at Doncaster in May; in frame at Ayr (twice)   **83 d**

64

and Hamilton subsequently; promises to stay 1¾m+; ideally suited by soft going. *J. Hanson.*

AMBER VALE 6 gr.m. Warpath 113–Jackie's Joy (Skymaster 126) (1982 10d 12f 10f 8.2g 12f⁴ 12f² 12f² 10g³ 9g 10fg 10d 11f 8fg 8s 1983 11g³ 10v⁴ 8d 10f 16f⁴ 15.8f 16f* 12f⁴ 16f³ 16f 15.8f 16f 15.8g³ 12s 14.7fg) poor handicapper nowadays; won at Beverley in July; stays 2m; acts on any going; blinkered several times in 1982; inconsistent and not entirely genuine. *D. Chapman.* **51**

AMBER WIND 3 ch.g. Tumble Wind–Super Amber (Yellow God 129) (1982 5f 5f³ 5f* 5d 5g 1983 5v 7v) leggy, narrow gelding; soundly beaten since winning maiden race at Folkestone as a 2-y-o; bred to stay further than 5f; blinkered final start in 1982. *M. Blanshard.* **–**

AMBER WINDSOR 3 ch.f. Windjammer (USA)–Rose Amber (Amber Rama 133) (1982 7d 7g 1983 7s 8.5d² 7d² 7fg⁴ 8fg³ 6fg 7g* 8d 8.2s² 7fg) fair sort; poor walker and mover; plater; bought in 1,750 gns after winning at Edinburgh in September; gives impression she'll stay beyond 1m; sometimes bandaged; looks a difficult ride; trained by N. Tinkler. *N. Tinkler.* **52**

AMBIANCE 4 gr.g. Three Legs 128–Ambient 68 (Amber Rama 133) (1982 8s² 9g⁴ 10f* 12fg* 12g* 12f 12fg* 12f 14fg⁴ 12.5g⁴ 1983 12f 14f³ 16f² 14g 14.8fg) compact, useful-looking gelding; fairly useful performer; placed in handicaps at Sandown in July and Lingfield in August, going down by a neck to Prince of Princes on latter; stays 2m; acts on any going; blinkered once at 3 yrs. *R. Hannon.* **92**

AMEGHINO 3 gr.g. So Blessed 130–Maruka 70 (Abernant 142) (1982 5.8f³ 5.8f* 6f³ 6d³ 6g⁴ 1983 8v 6d 6fg 7f 5g* 5fg 6d) workmanlike gelding; returned to form and landed a tremendous gamble in handicap at Goodwood in September, beating Cheri Berry readily by 2½ lengths; didn't reproduce the form; stays 6f (last both outings over further); yet to show he can handle really soft going, but acts on any other. *M. McCourt.* **98**

AMEL 2 b.g. Raga Navarro 119–Windy Breeze 77 (Pindari 124) (1983 7f 7f⁴ 7fg³) Apr 8; IR 1,700Y, 16,000 2-y-o; workmanlike gelding; seventh reported foal; dam won at up to 2m; favourite, looked unsuited by course and was ridden along throughout when 3¾ lengths third of 11 to Marzia's Hollow in maiden race at Chester in August; had shown promise in quite useful maiden company at Goodwood on previous appearance; will probably be better suited by 1m+; acts on firm going; gelded at end of season; capable of winning maiden event. *B. Hanbury.* **86**

AMENDOLA 3 br.f. Ercolano 118–Crab Apple (Nelcius 133) (1982 7d 7g 1983 11.7v 16s⁴ 12g) big, rangy, useful sort; only poor form; promises to stay middle distances at least. *H. Candy.* **–**

AMERICAN MINSTREL (USA) 3 b.c. The Minstrel 135–American Legacy (Hail to Reason) (1982 7f 7d³ 7s 1983 8g 10v 7fg) tall, leggy, rather narrow colt; not disgraced when tenth of 29 to Socratic in 1m maiden at Newmarket in April (sweated up); possibly unsuited by really soft ground; dwelt final start (June). *R. Sheather.* **–**

AMERICAN WINTER (USA) 2 b.f. Lyphard 132–American Legacy (Hail to Reason) (1983 5d 7f⁴ 7g² 7fg³ 8f³) Mar 26; $325,000Y; close-coupled, quite attractive filly; has a round action; closely related to 3-y-o American Minstrel (by The Minstrel) and modest middle-distance maiden Czar's Bride (by Northern Dancer); dam, unplaced 5 times, is half-sister to top-class filly and broodmare Fanfreluche; placed 3 times in modest company, twice favourite; will probably stay beyond 1m; acts on firm going. *G. Harwood.* **78**

AMERICK 3 ch.c. High Line 125–Paripan (Pardao 120) (1982 7fg 1983 12d 13.3g 11.7f² 14f⁴ 15.5f* 17f² 16.1g) rangy, angular colt; landed the odds by 15 lengths in 3-runner maiden race at Folkestone in August; 5/2 on when going down by 6 lengths to Fortune's Guest in minor event at Wolverhampton later in month; suited by a test of stamina; acts on firm going; soundly beaten in apprentice race final start. *G. Harwood.* **91**

AMIGO ALEGRE 3 ch.c. Great Nephew 126–Pardina 98 (Pardao 120) (1982 6fg 1983 10v 10fg 10f 7f 12g 7fg 7.6d) rangy, workmanlike colt; behind in varied races; blinkered final outing. *P. K. Mitchell.* **–**

AMIGO LOCO 2 ch.g. Whistling Deer 117–Chive (St Chad 120) (1983 6fg 5f 5f³ 5g* 6g⁴ 5fg³ 6g 5d⁴) Apr 17; IR 800F, IR 5,800Y; workmanlike gelding; first foal; dam never ran; won maiden race at Haydock in September, having been disqualified from first place and placed third in maiden event at Wolverhampton 3 **82**

weeks previously; not disgraced in nurseries and a £5,200 event afterwards; appears equally effective at 5f and 6f; yet to race on very soft going but acts on any other; wears blinkers. *K. Brassey.*

AMILA 3 gr.f. Great Nephew 126–Allara (Zeddaan 130) (1982 7.2s* 1983 10.6v⁴ **80** 8f 9f⁴ 12.2g² 12g) wiry filly; went down by short head to Hasty Goddess in handicap at Catterick in September, and would probably have won had she settled better early on; needs further than 9f; acts well on soft going; ran very wide on home turn when blinkered at Edinburgh on final start. *M. Stoute.*

AMORATA (USA) 3 b.f. Nordic Prince–Our Taska (Our Native) (1982 5f⁴ 6g — 8.2s 7s 1983 12.2d 11d) rather leggy, narrow filly; plating-class maiden; seemed to stay 1m; blinkered final start (April); covered by Castle Keep. *S. Norton.*

AMORE BELLO 2 b.c. Mummy's Pet 125–Avahra 108 (Sahib 114) (1983 6fg 5g — 6d) Apr 22; 10,000Y; useful-looking colt; fourth foal; brother to fairly useful sprinter Pavahra, and half-brother to 11f and 13f winner Savahra (by Free State); dam stayed 6f; well beaten in maiden and minor events; sold 2,600 gns Ascot December Sales. *P. K. Mitchell.*

AMOREUSE 2 ch.f. Artaius 129–Roselyn 80 (Mill Reef 141) (1983 5v) May 6; — 6,400Y; second foal; dam won over 6f at 2 yrs in England and later won 4 times in Italy; poor fifth of 8 in maiden race at Newcastle in May. *N. Tinkler.*

AMOROUS 5 b.g. Mummy's Pet 125–Maxim's 88 (Major Portion 129) (1982 7s **96** 8d 6g² 6fg² 6f⁴ 6g* 6fg 6f² 6f* 6f 6f³ 6g 7fg 5s 5s 1983 6s 7s 6g* 6f 6f² 6s² 5fg 6fg* 5g) lightly-made, leggy gelding; sprint handicapper; won at Lingfield in June and October; ran well in between to be beaten a head by Autumn Sunset in William Hill Stewards' Cup at Goodwood and by Polly's Brother in Ladbrokes (Ayr) Gold Cup; suited by 6f; acts on any going; blinkered once in 1981; game, though ran badly final start, behaved rather mulishly once in 1982 and bolted before start second outing. *M. McCourt.*

AMPERSAND (USA) 3 b.f. Stop the Music–Quicksand (Mill Reef 141) (1982 **86** 5f² 5g⁴ 5g 7g³ 7d³ 1983 8s⁴ 8d* 7v 8g* 8.5g 8f 7f* 8fg 8g³) short-backed, quite attractive filly; ridden by apprentice J. H. Brown when successful in maiden race at Thirsk and handicaps at Brighton and Epsom; made excellent headway from back of field to lead close home and beat Vatican Way by a length on last-named course in August; stays 1m; seems to act on any going, with possible exception of heavy. *I. Balding.*

AMPHITHEATRE 3 ch.f. Relkino 131–Drury Lane 83 (Gala Performance) (1982 **70** 7g² 1983 10.5s³ 8g 12f 10f) big, lengthy, useful-looking filly; has a long stride; gained only placing of year when moderate third in minor event at York in May (looked fit but hadn't got her coat); suited by 10.5f and promises to stay 1½m; sold 37,000 gns Newmarket December Sales. *M. Jarvis.*

AMRULLAH 3 br.g. High Top 131–Ravenshead (Charlottown 127) (1982 7g 8g 8s **73** d 1983 9v 11d² 12f 16f⁴ 14.7f⁴ 12.2fg 14g) big, strong, good sort; walks and moves well; disappointing maiden; stays 11f; often blinkered; sold out of M. H. Easterby's stable 4,700 gns Newmarket September Sales after sixth start. *J. Bridger.*

AMYNDAS 5 b.h. Sparkler 130–Gem of Gems 106 (Grey Sovereign 128§) (1982 **114** 12fg² 12fg³ 10f³ 12f 12f² 12g* 10.5fg³ 12d 10d 1983 12d³ 12d³ 12fg⁴ 11g 12f⁴) strong, compact, attractive horse; smart performer on his day; always prominent and kept on well when 4 lengths third to Diamond Shoal in John Porter Stakes at Newbury in April and just over a length third to Electric in Jockey Club Stakes at Newmarket later in month, best efforts at 5 yrs; stayed 1½m; acted on any going; game; stud in Czechoslovakia. *B. Hobbs.*

ANCAT 3 b.c. Lochnager 132–Bovick 75 (Compensation 127) (1982 5fg 6d 1983 **54** 10f 7g⁴ 5f 8.2g 7g 7fg) plating-class maiden; stays 7f; has worn a bandage on his near-fore. *M. W. Easterby.*

ANCESTRAL 3 b.c. Habitat 134–Ampulla 110 (Crowned Prince 128) (1982 6d* **106** 6.3g* 6g 1983 7s* 5d) 350,000Y; well-made, handsome colt; has a round action; second foal; brother to winning Italian filly Steel Habit; dam, winner of Cherry Hinton Stakes, is half-sister to high-class sprinter Steel Heart (by Habitat); won his first 2 races as a 2-y-o, including Railway Stakes at the Curragh; held on to dead-heat with Cremation (rec 5 lb) when odds-on for 5-runner McCairns Trial Stakes at Phoenix Park in April; only seventh of 11 behind Bri-Eden when favourite for Ballyogan Stakes at Leopardstown 2 months later; suited by 6f and stays 7f; yet to race on a firm surface; sent to race in USA. *V. O'Brien, Ireland.*

ANCIENT MARINER 2 b. or br.c. Wollow 132–Idle Waters 116 (Mill Reef 141) **63+** (1983 7f 7f 7f 8fg 7g) Mar 20; lengthy, quite attractive colt; second foal;

half-brother to 3-y-o Silent Pool (by Relkino); dam won Park Hill Stakes; only plating-class form, mainly in useful company; will be suited by 1¼m+; blinkered final outing. *F. J. Houghton.*

ANDALAS 3 ch.c. Vitiges 132–Ixia (Le Fabuleux 133) (1982 NR 1983 12.3v 13.8g 10f) 2,000Y; workmanlike colt; half-brother to middle-distance winner Tajonski (by Bolkonski) and 2 winners in France; dam French 1¼m winner and also won over jumps; towards rear in maiden and minor events; blinkered last 2 outings; sold 700 gns Doncaster August Sales. *M. Camacho.*

ANDRESS 2 b. or br.c. Persian Bold 123–Claremont Girl (Will Hays) (1983 5s 5s* 5f 7f³ 6g*) May 1; IR 9,200F, IR 15,500Y; tall, quite attractive colt; poor walker; third produce; half-brother to a winner in Switzerland; dam Irish 1½m winner; won maiden race at Down Royal in May by 8 lengths from Erins Star and collected a valuable prize when beating Nosey 3 lengths in 9-runner Fasig-Tipton Nursery at Phoenix Park in October; co-favourite when 6½ lengths third of 11 to Executive Pride in Hennessy V.S.O.P. Stakes at Leopardstown in July; should stay 7f+; possibly needs some give in the ground; became very upset in stalls and missed break badly third outing (Windsor Castle Stakes). *M. Kauntze, Ireland.* **106**

ANDSON 3 ch.g. Sagaro 133–Forty Love 79 (Fortino II 120) (1982 5d 5fg* 1983 8s 5s 6d²) small, lengthy gelding; plater; should stay at least 1m; acts on a firm and a soft surface; has run creditably in blinkers; sold 825 gns Ascot 2nd June Sales. *P. Cundell.* **–**

ANGELA EDELSON 4 b.f. Owen Dudley 121–Mauritania 74 (The Brianstan 128) (1982 8g 7s³ 7g 8d 1983 8d 7fg 7d 7.6fg 8g 10.1f 8f⁴ 8.2g) lightly-made filly; poor handicapper; has been beaten in a seller; stays 1m; acts on any going; blinkered fourth and fifth starts. *N. Guest.* **–**

ANGELA'S GIRL 2 b.f. Bigivor–O'Penport (Porto Bello 118) (1983 5d 5g) June 10; fifth foal; dam never ran; last in Midland maiden races in October. *R. Griffiths.* **–**

ANGELUS CHIMES 4 b.f. Northfields–Twelve O'Clock (Hardicanute 130) (1982 8.5fg 10fg⁴ 12fg² 12f² 12f⁴ 10fg 11.7s 10s² 1983 16s⁴ 9fg 14f² 12g* 10d² 11.5s² 10fg) lightly-made, lengthy ex-English filly; quite modest in this country at 3 yrs; won handicap at Roscommon in September; runner-up afterwards in similar events at Listowel and Down Royal; blinkered when towards rear in valuable handicap won by Bahoor at Newmarket on final outing; stays well; acts on any going. *J. Oxx, Ireland.* **67**

ANGLEMAN (USA) 2 b.c. Angle Light–Mary Biz (T. V. Lark) (1983 6f 7g³ 7fg² 6g* 6g*) Apr 23; $75,000Y; useful-looking colt; brother to 1m and 9f winner Angle Fire and half-brother to 3 other winners, including Gimcrack winner Full Extent (by Full Out); dam, unplaced 4 times, is half-sister to smart Terrible Tiger; won twice in September, maiden race at Yarmouth and minor event at Lingfield, both times leading throughout; clearly suited by 6f and forcing tactics; yet to race on a soft surface; sent to USA. *M. Jarvis.* **98**

ANGMERING 3 b.f. Raga Navarro 119–Tamarisk Way 92 (Tamerlane 128) (1982 5f 5g 5s 1983 5v 5g 5f 6fg 6f 5h 8g 6fg) well-made filly; good walker; poor maiden; should be suited by 7f; sold 9,600 gns Newmarket December Sales. *J. Winter.* **–**

ANIECE 5 br.g. Ballymoss 136–Gay Maria (Tacitus 124) (1982 16.1s 12fg 12f³ 14fg 14fg 16.1s 15d² 1983 18d 14fg 14.7f* 16f 16.1fg) well-made gelding; poor mover; inconsistent handicapper; won at Redcar in June (apprentice ridden); very well suited by a test of stamina; probably acts on any going; ran badly first and final starts (gelded after latter). *F. Durr.* **61**

ANITA'S PRINCE 2 b.c. Stradavinsky 121–Get Ready 91 (On Your Mark 125) (1983 5fg 7g 5g 6d² 5d* 6d² 7d) Apr 1; IR 4,200Y; third foal; half-brother to 6f winner In Slips (by Mount Hagen); dam best at 5f; 12/1, always close up when winning 8-runner Goffs Stakes at the Curragh in September by ½ length from odds-on Grey Dream; also creditable second in 2 races, going down by 1½ lengths to newcomer Argosy in maiden race on same course and by 3 lengths to top-weighted Western Symphony in 10-runner Birdcatcher Nursery at Naas; likely to prove best at sprint distances; acts on a soft surface. *R. Lister, Ireland.* **101**

ANKARA (USA) 3 ch.c. Northern Dancer–Rule Formi (Forli) (1982 7g* 1983 7g* 10fg* 12f² 10f 8d) brother to top 1981 Irish 2-y-o filly Woodstream and half-brother to 2 winners, notably high-class miler Jaazeiro (by Sham); dam never ran; successful twice at Phoenix Park, beating Source of Success by a length in 12-runner race in May and Bold Connection by ¾ length in £10,700 Woodland Stud **106**

Mr R. E. Sangster's "Ankara"

Stakes in June; met first defeat when short-head second of 8 finishers behind Condell in Royal Whip Stakes at the Curragh in July and was subsequently down field behind Mourjane in Prix de la Cote Normande at Deauville in August and behind Persian Royale when favourite for Irish Cambridgeshire at the Curragh in September; stays 1½m; acts on firm going; sent to Australia. *V. O'Brien, Ireland.*

ANNAMOE BRAY 3 ch.g. Whistling Deer 114–Evening Sky 74 (Skymaster 126)   **83**
(1982 5s 5f 5f 6g³ 6g 6g* 7f³ 6fg² 7g³ 6g* 6g 6s* 6s 6v 1983 7d 7v* 6v⁴ 8.2v 8f 8f³ 7.6fg*) lengthy, workmanlike gelding; ridden by 7-lb claimer when winning Northern Free Handicap at Newcastle in April (by ½ length from High Cannon) and handicap at Chester in July; ideally suited by a strongly run 7f or 1m; acts on any going; ran poorly in blinkers once as a 2-y-o; tough and genuine; sent to Hong Kong. *J. Wilson.*

ANNAN MAJIC 3 b.f. Majestic Streak–Masandra 100 (Whistling Wind 123) (1982   **34**
NR 1983 9v 6d 9.4d 5f 6g³ 6f) third foal; dam useful 2-y-o sprinter; third in selling handicap at Ayr in August, only form; fell third start; dead. *T. Barnes.*

ANNESLEY 4 b.c. Relkino 131–My Candy 81 (Lorenzaccio 130) (1982 10.1fg   **—**
10.8fg 11.7g 1983 10g) well-made, attractive colt; good walker and mover; fair performer at his best but has shown no form for a long time; sweating and backward only start at 4 yrs in September; should be suited by middle distances; blinkered once. *N. Gaselee.*

ANNE TUDOR 2 b.f. Whitstead 125–Tudor Link 77 (Manacle 123) (1983 5v 5f 5f   **—**
7f) of no account; has worn blinkers; sold 320 gns Ascot November Sales. *A. Ingham.*

ANNIE EDGE 3 ch.f. Nebbiolo 125–Friendly Court (Be Friendly 130) (1982 5f*   **118**
5f² 5fg³ 6g³ 7fg² 1983 7d² 8g 8v³ 8f 8g 7fg* 7fg) workmanlike filly; third foal; half-sister to fairly useful Irish 6f and 7f winner Maiacourt (by Malacate) and a winner in USA; dam fairly useful 2-y-o 5f winner in Ireland; a useful performer as a 2-y-o and was even better in 1983; gained only success however when beating Salieri (gave 13 lb) by a short head in 8-runner £13,600 Kiveton Park Stakes at Doncaster in September, getting up near finish under very strong pressure; had run well in spring when 1½ lengths second of 9 to comfortable winner Favoridge in Nell Gwyn Stakes at Newmarket, sixth of 18 behind Ma Biche in 1,000 Guineas on same course (later moved up a place) and excellent 2½ lengths third of 18

behind L'Attrayante in Goffs Irish 1000 Guineas at the Curragh; stays 1m well; acts on any going; genuine; ran well in blinkers once at 2 yrs; had stiffish task final outing; sold 330,000 gns Newmarket December Sales, reportedly to race in USA. *D. H. Jones.*

ANNIE GET YOUR GUN 3 br.f. Blakeney 126–Cheyenne 83 (Sovereign Path 125) (1982 NR 1983 10f 12f³ 15.8g³ 12s⁴ 15fg²) small, strong, sturdy filly; second foal; dam, 2-y-o 6f winner, is sister to very useful Warpath and half-sister to very smart Dakota; placed in maiden races and handicap; needs a test of stamina. *C. Thornton.* **69**

ANNIE GO QUICKLY 3 b.f. Anax 120–Miss Swift 79 (Canisbay 120) (1982 6f 5fg 6f 1983 7s 7v 7fg 7fg) strong filly; little worthwhile form in varied company, including selling; should stay 1m; blinkered final start; sold 420 gns Newmarket July Sales and resold same price Ascot September Sales. *N. Callaghan.* **–**

ANNIE OKE 2 b.f. Anax 120–Reppeve 45 (Jimmy Reppin 131) (1983 7.6fg 8d 7.6d 6fg 7g) May 10; fifth produce; dam plater; of no account. *Peter Taylor.* **–**

ANNIESLAND 2 b.f. Wolver Hollow 126–Roseanne 68 (St Paddy 133) (1983 6f 6fg 7d) Apr 3; 3,700F, 14,000Y; attractive, well-made filly; good walker and mover; third foal; half-sister to a winner in Trinidad; dam won over 1½m and is half-sister to Derby third Mount Athos and smart sprinter John Splendid; in rear in valuable newcomers event at Ascot and 2 maiden races at Brighton, twice starting none too well; sold to BBA 6,200 gns Newmarket December Sales. *J. Dunlop.* **–**

ANNIVERSARY TOKEN 3 ch.f. Record Token 128–Josceline (Knightly Manner) (1982 7g 8s 6d 1983 9v 10f 8fg 10.8g³ 12f 13.8f² 10h* 12fg 13.8g 15fg) lengthy filly; plater; bought in 5,300 gns after winning decisively at Chepstow in August; disappointing afterwards, and was pulled up penultimate start; stays 1¾m; acts well on top-of-the-ground; trained by R. Hollinshead until after eighth start. *J. Wilson.* **54**

ANOTHER DEB 2 b.f. African Sky 124–Suffice 84 (Faberge II 121) (1983 6g 6f 5f*) Apr 30; 1,000F, 12,500Y; good-quartered filly; half-sister to 1¼m sellers winner Never Enough (by Sandford Lad); dam won over 8.5f and 1½m; made virtually all to win 16-runner maiden race at Beverley in August by a neck from Conrara; probably stays 6f. *P. Haslam.* **78**

ANOTHER GENERATION 6 ch.g. Fine Blade 121–Brig O'Doon (Shantung 132) (1982 NR 1983 16f 14h) useful stayer in 1980 when he won 5 times; tailed-off last both starts at 6 yrs (bandaged); acts on any going; has won for an apprentice; winning hurdler. *R. Howe.* **–**

Kiveton Park Stakes, Doncaster—Annie Edge (right) returns to form, and gets up under strong pressure to beat Salieri

ANOTHER GUNNER 2 ch.c. Gunner B 126–Wheel Grace 69 (Gulf Pearl 117)   –
(1983 7f) Apr 9; 1,150 2-y-o; resold 440 2-y-o, good-bodied colt; first foal; dam,
plater, won at 1¼m and 13.8f; last of 8 in minor event at Salisbury in July; dead. *A.
Barrow.*

ANOTHER HIT 3 b.f. Hittite Glory 125–Partridge 65 (Mossborough 126) (1982   **53**
5.1g 6fg 5.1fg⁴ 6fg 1983 8s 7d³ 6v² 6v* 6d 7f 7fg) lightly-made filly; plater; bought
in 2,000 gns after winning at Ripon in June; stays 7f; acts on heavy going; exported
to Algeria. *G. Blum.*

ANOTHER REALM 5 gr.h. Realm 129–Tiara III (Persian Gulf) (1982 ran 10   –
times in USA, placed once 1983 6fg 6fg) a smart miler (rated 118) in 1981, when he
won Clerical, Medical Greenham Stakes at Newbury and ran creditably in several
top races; raced in USA at 4 yrs, being placed third once; beaten in 2 handicaps in
the autumn on return to this country, running respectably at Newmarket on first
occasion; suited by 1m; acts on any going, with possible exception of very soft. *F.
Durr.*

ANOTHER RISK 3 b.c. The Brianstan 128–Sally Ann III (Port Corsair 98) (1982   **109**
5d² 5f* 6f² 6fg² 6d² 6fg* 5f³ 6f 5g³ 5g 1983 5g⁴ 6v* 6s 5f 6f 5f 6s 5fg) robust,
deep-girthed non-thoroughbred colt; ran very well indeed when 4 lengths fourth of
17 behind On Stage in Palace House Stakes at Newmarket in April and beat Justus
by 4 lengths when odds-on for 8-runner Benazet-Rennen at Baden-Baden the
following month; usually had stiffish tasks afterwards; effective at 5f and 6f; seems
to act on any going; has run well for an apprentice; blinkered final start; sold 19,000
gns Newmarket Autumn Sales, reportedly for export to Malaysia. *P. Mitchell.*

ANOTHER RUMBO 5 ch.g. Royben 125–Fiord (Mountain Call 125) (1982 5g   –
8g 8g 8.3g 8.3g 8fg 6g 1983 8v 5v 7s) workmanlike gelding; disappointing
handicapper; behind in sellers on occasions; often blinkered; dead. *K.
Cunningham-Brown.*

ANOTHER SAM 6 b. or br.h. Comedy Star 121–Balandra Star 92 (Blast 125)   **113**
(1982 16s 14f 18.4fg³ 14fg* 16g⁴ 16.1f² 16fg 16fg² 16g 16fg* 19f 14g* 14.6g 18d
1983 13.3v 13.3g 16f 16f 16.1fg* 15fg⁴ 16.1fg² 14g 18fg 16fg* 16fg² 15.5f³) leggy,
narrow horse; smart handicapper on his day but is unreliable; stayed on well to beat
Voyant by 1½ lengths at Newmarket in July and Valuable Witness by 2 lengths in
Gordon Carter Stakes at Ascot in September; excelled himself on final 2 starts,
going down by ¾ length to Karadar in Jockey Club Cup at Newmarket and coming
home 1¼ lengths third of 14 to Old Country in Prix Royal-Oak at Longchamp;
suited by a test of stamina; acts on any going; often drops himself out in early
stages and is not an easy ride; ran abysmally eighth start. *R. Hannon.*

ANOTHER SPECIAL 5 b.m. Space King 115–Pip's Princess (Border Chief 101)   –
(1982 12fg 10d⁴ 10s 12d 1983 10f 10f 12d) small mare; poor maiden. *D. Francis.*

ANOTHER THRILL 4 b.c. Morston 125–Another Treat 92 (Derring-Do 131)   –
(1982 12f* 17.1s 1983 12.2g 12d) attractive colt; readily won maiden race at
Brighton early in 1982; lightly raced and well beaten all subsequent starts; should
stay beyond 1½m; has been bandaged; presumably difficult to train. *J. Parkes.*

*Reg Day Memorial Trophy, Newmarket—Another Sam (No. 4) stays on well to win from
Voyant (chevrons) and Manor Farm Toots (noseband)*

ANSTRUTHER 4 b. or br.c. Oats 126–St Tropez 99 (Princely Gift 137) (1982 8g **93** 6fg² 6f 6fg 7g 5g 5v⁴ 6d⁴ 1983 6s 7s² 6v³ 6f 6f 6d³ 6fg 6s 7.2g² 7g² 7fg³ 6d) big, strong, good-bodied colt; excellent mover; won handicap at Haydock in September by a length from Swingin' Cowboy; stays 7f well; acts on firm going but is ideally suited by some give; blinkered eighth start; sent to USA. *C. Brittain.*

ANTONIAZZO 2 ch.c. Kashmir II 125–Afasheen (Sheshoon 132) (1983 7f) Mar 22; **78 p** IR 30,000F; useful-looking colt; has a very nice, smooth action; half-brother to 2 minor French middle-distance winners; dam, placed in France, is half-sister to dam of Blushing Groom; 20/1, 5¾ lengths sixth of 14 to Rule Of The Sea in maiden race at Sandown in July; will stay at least 1m; should improve; sent to France. *P. Kelleway.*

ANTONITA 2 ch.f. Anton Lad 103–Orbenita (Orbit 106) (1983 5fg 5f 5f 7g 6d) of — no account. *J. Mulhall.*

ANTON PILLAR (USA) 2 b.c. No Robbery–Fast Time (Time Tested) (1983 **103** 6f² 5fg* 5fg⁴ 5.3fg* 5fg) Mar 18; $130,000Y; smallish, rather lightly-built colt; first foal; dam, winner of 2 small sprint races, is half-sister to dams of good fillies Mitey Lively and Dainty Dotsie; won minor events at Windsor in August and Brighton (beating Derry River a neck) in September; disappointing favourite at Thirsk in between; will be suited by a return to 6f; yet to race on a soft surface; not particularly consistent; sent to USA. *H. Cecil.*

ANVIL INN 5 b.g. Roi Soleil 125–Floor Show 78 (Galivanter 131) (1982 12g⁴ 12.3fg 8f² 11g 9g 10fg* 9g³ 10f 13.8d 12g² 1983 12d 8g² 8fg 10f 8f) compact gelding; plater; stays 1¼m; well suited by a sound surface; has been bandaged; inconsistent. *T. Craig.*

ANY BUSINESS 2 br.c. Music Maestro 119–Princess Nefertiti (Tutankhamen) **99** (1983 5v³ 5v³ 6s* 6fg 6fg 6g²) Apr 5; 5,400F; quite attractive colt; half-brother to several winners here and abroad; dam ran twice; won maiden race at Kempton in April by 3 lengths from Time Machine and 10-runner Woodcote Stakes at Epsom in June by 6 lengths from Captain Crumpet; 2¼ lengths second of 5 to Water Moccasin in Moet and Chandon Zukunfts-Rennen at Baden-Baden in September, easily best subsequent effort; a free-running colt but suited by 6f; acts well on very soft ground and seems unsuited by a firm surface. *G. Lewis.*

ANYTHING ELSE 2 gr.g. Absalom 128–Silette 84 (Siliconn 121) (1983 5v⁴ 6s **94** 7f* 7f² 7fg⁴ 7g) Apr 20; stocky gelding; second foal; half-brother to 3-y-o 1m winner Elisetta (by Monsanto); dam top-of-the-ground 1¼m performer; showed much improved form when making all to win maiden race at Brighton in July by 3 lengths from Bonnement; put up best subsequent effort when 1½ lengths second of 8 to Northern Tempest in £3,300 event at Sandown later in month (again made running but hung badly left from over 2f out and was caught inside last); well suited by 7f and forcing tactics; form only on firm ground. *R. Hannon.*

APERITIVO 5 ro.g. Sharp Edge 123–Feasting (Sayajirao 132) (1982 10s 10f* **71** 10f⁴ 10fg² 12fg³ 10f 10fg 10d³ 8f* 8g 9d 8s 1983 12v 10s² 10v⁴ 10f) lengthy gelding; fair handicapper at his best; stays 1¼m; acts on any going; can produce a useful turn of foot when in the mood but is unpredictable and inconsistent. *R. Atkins.*

APHRODISIAC 2 b.f. He Loves Me 120–Comfrey 60 (High Top 131) (1983 5fg **69** 5g 6f 5f 7.2g*) May 10; 3,500Y; lengthy filly; first foal; dam slow maiden; apprentice ridden, won 12-runner seller at Haydock (no bid) in September by 1½ lengths from Domanus; had shown up in non-sellers previously; suited by 7f, and will probably stay further; appears to act on firm going; sold to R. Morris 1,450 gns Ascot December Sales. *H. Candy.*

APPEAL COURT 3 b.g. Star Appeal 133–Misnomer 85 (Milesian 125) (1982 **61** NR 1983 10v³ 10.5f 12f 12.3fg) lengthy, quite useful sort; has a round action; half-brother to 3 winners, including fairly useful 1½m winner York Cottage (by Royal Palace); dam, winner at up to 1½m, is daughter of St Leger third Cold Storage; soundly beaten after dead-heating for third in minor event at Ripon in June (had stiffish tasks on first 2 occasions); should be suited by 1½m; gives impression he'll always be seen to best advantage with some give in the ground. *W. Elsey.*

APPEAL TO ME 3 b.g. Star Appeal 133–Monagram 77 (Mon Fetiche 120) (1982 **87** NR 1983 12v² 12v 12v 14s 20f 14f* 12fg² 19f 14d) 7,800Y, 35,000Y; lengthy, rather wiry gelding; half-brother to 3 winners, including useful 1976 2-y-o 5f winner Japora (by Raffingora); dam won at 1m; led on post to beat Whiskey Time a head in 12-runner maiden race at Sandown in July; second to easy 5-length winner Horton Line in 5-runner minor event at Lingfield later in month; had stiff tasks most other starts; suited by a test of stamina; blinkered third and fourth outings. *P. Kelleway.*

APPLANTE 8 br. g. Alto Volante 109–Pomme (Polic 126) (1982 NR 1983 8fg   –
10f⁴) winning jumper; little worthwhile form on flat. *R. Armytage.*

APPLE BLOSSOM 4 ch. f. Orange Bay 131–Appleshaw (St Alphage 119) (1982   §§
10d⁴ 8.5f 7.6f² 7f⁴ 7fg² 7d* 8g 7f 7fg 7g 1983 12g 10.2fg) tall, leggy filly; has a
round action; has ability but is thoroughly temperamental and best left severely
alone; sometimes blinkered; cost 1,500 gns Ascot March Sales. *B. Stevens.*

APPLEJADE 2 br. c. Fair Season 120–Jedburgh Justice (Mossborough 126) (1983   44
5v 5v 5v 5s 6d 6f 6fg 6f⁴ 6d 6g) Mar 4; 2,700Y; compact colt; bad plater; has worn
blinkers; virtually refused to race on debut; sold 540 gns Ascot December Sales.
M. Bolton.

APPLE ORCHARD 3 b. g. Shirley Heights 130–Apple Peel 109 (Pall Mall 132)   –
(1982 8s 8g 1983 11d 11f 15.8g) lengthy, rather angular gelding; no worthwhile
form; often slowly away. *P. Rohan.*

APPLE WINE 6 ch. g. Ribston 104–Ruffino 99 (Como 120) (1982 10d 12fg 10.6s   63
10.2d 1983 10.2d 10v² 12d* 12v 12s 12v 10f 10f 12fg* 12f² 12f 12h 12f³ 12f 14fg⁴
15.8f 12f 14fg 11f) good-topped, workmanlike gelding; won handicaps at
Edinburgh in April, Hamilton in June and Beverley in July; suited by 1½m+; acts
on any going; blinkered twice at 2 yrs; suitable mount for an inexperienced rider;
none too consistent. *D. Chapman.*

APRIL FOR EVER 2 ch. f. Whistlefield 118–Royal Elegance 63 (Coronation Year   50
124) (1983 5v² 5s⁴ 5s 6fg 5f² 5f 6f) May 22; small, sturdy filly; half-sister to 1m
winner Not Amused (by Blast); dam won twice at 1m; plater; should stay at least
6f; acts on any going; sold 300 gns Doncaster October Sales. *L. Leslie.*

APRIL LUCKY 10 b. g. St Alphage 119–Susceptible 86 (Supreme Court 135)   58
(1982 6f 6fg² 6f⁴ 6fg* 6g 6g 6g⁴ 6g 6f 7.2s 1983 6s 6d 6g³ 6f³ 6fg* 6fg² 6f 6h⁴ 7g)
leggy gelding; won handicap at Pontefract in July; stays 7f; acts on any going;
tried in blinkers at 3 yrs; sometimes sweats up; good mount for an inexperienced
rider; needs to be held up; has won 7 times at Hamilton; has occasionally broken a
blood vessel and did so when pulled up on final outing. *C. Crossley.*

APRIL MEMORIES 4 b. f. Rolfe 77–Sweet Memories 58 (Runnymede 123)   58
(1982 6g 6f² 6fg² 5g² 6fg³ 5d 5fg² 6d 1983 6v 5d⁴ 6d³ 6fg² 8g⁴ 7g² 6g³ 6s 6fg)
rather sparely-made filly; plater; stays 7f; seems to act on any going but goes well
on fast ground; sometimes sweats up; suitable mount for an apprentice; pulled up
lame final start. *M. Blanshard.*

APRIL WIND 2 gr. f. Windjammer (USA)–Georgie Girl 96 (Crocket 130) (1983   91
5s 5fg² 5f² 5f* 5f⁴) Apr 14; sister to successful Italian horse Win The Wind and
half-sister to 2 winners, including useful 1980 Irish 2-y-o 5f winner Crimson
Heather (by Red Alert); dam beat at 5f; made all to land the odds by 2 lengths
from Desert Walk in maiden race at Naas in July; beaten only a length when
second previously in 2 much more valuable events, namely Goffs Silver Flash
Stakes won by Welsh Dancer at Phoenix Park and Nishapour Curragh Stakes won
by Safe Home; ran poorly when odds on for quite valuable race at Limerick
Junction in August and wasn't seen out again; acts well on firm going; blinkered
third and fourth outings and possibly needs them nowadays; sold 92,000 gns
Newmarket December Sales. *L. Browne, Ireland.*

APRON BLUE 2 ch. f. Crooner 119–Mahnaz (Deep Diver 134) (1983 8g /fg) Apr   –
3; big, plain, lengthy filly; second foal; dam never ran; behind in maiden races at
Leicester in September and Newmarket (last of 22 after moving badly to start) in
October. *H. Collingridge.*

AQABA PRINCE 3 br. g. Sweet Revenge 129–Lady Anita 72 (Como 120) (1983   78 d
6g 5fg 6f 6f² 6g⁴ 6fg³ 6g 5d⁴ 6v² 5g⁴ 1983 6v³ 5s⁴ 6d 7f 7f 7f 7.6fg) workmanlike
gelding; ran best races in spring; suited by 6f; acts on any going but is best served
by some give in the ground; blinkered once at 2 yrs; trained by R. Hannon until
after fourth start. *R. Howe.*

AQUARIUS SPIRIT 2 ch. c. Gay Fandango 132–That's Better (Mourne 126)   –
(1983 6fg) May 18; IR 11,000Y; half-brother to 2 winners, including useful 1977
Irish 2-y-o 6f and 1m winner Dolly Dewdrop (by On Your Mark); dam won over 5f at
2 yrs; 50/1, behind in 22-runner maiden race at Newmarket in July. *W. Musson.*

ARAFY 2 b. f. Sharpen Up 127–Rotisserie 106 (Tesco Boy 121) (1983 6f⁴ 7f⁴ 7f   80
7h² 7g 7fg) Apr 20; 35,000Y, 42,000Y; close-coupled filly; half-sister to 3 winners,
including useful 1½m and 1¾m winner Rowlandson (by Blakeney); dam won Fred
Darling Stakes; in frame in maiden races, including staying-on neck second of 8 to
Silver Ikon at Chepstow in August; never going well when well-backed favourite for
nursery at Leicester in September on penultimate appearance; will stay 1m; acts on
hard going. *H. T. Jones.*

ARAGON 3 b.c. Mummy's Pet 125–Ica (Great Nephew 126) (1982 5fg* 6fg* 6g2 **118**
6f3 7f 7v2 7s3 1983 7d4 7s2 8v* 8.5s2 7f3 7fg3 8g)

The decision to bring back Aragon for an autumn campaign after a break of more
than four months, during which he reportedly suffered from a serious blood disorder,
was justified by his third to Ma Biche and Pampabird in the Prix de la Foret at
Longchamp, his first outing in Group 1 company. Looking very well and on particularly
good terms with himself there, he never really threatened to win but kept on well up
the straight to finish within three and a half lengths of Ma Biche. It was an effort which
will have done his appeal as a stallion no harm at all. Aragon would have gone close to
winning the Prix Perth at Saint-Cloud had he reproduced the form, but he was a
disappointing favourite and finished only fifth of fifteen behind Rare Roberta.

Aragon only just scraped into the Free Handicap as a two-year-old but after
finishing fourth in a handicap at Doncaster on the first Saturday of the new season
he quickly left his previous form well behind. A fortnight later he ran the smart
Proclaim to half a length in the Salisbury Two Thousand Guineas Trial and followed
that with a half-length defeat of Ginger Brink in the Prix de la Jonchere at
Longchamp in May, in which race he produced a tremendous burst on the outside,
under typical Piggott assistance, which took him to the front in the last few strides.
Aragon subsequently had only two more races before his lay-off began and
acquitted himself really well in both of them, finishing a short-head second to Lofty
in a thrilling finish to the Pacemaker Diomed Stakes at Epsom on Derby Day and a
four-length third to Tecorno in the Jersey Stakes at Royal Ascot. The penalty that
he was obliged to carry in both races for his Longchamp win meant that at weights
carried he worked out the best horse in each: the conditions of the Jersey Stakes
required him to concede as much as a stone to the winner. A stiff task indeed!

Aragon is fashionably-enough bred for a stallion. Mummy's Pet had another
highly successful year in 1983 with the leading sprinting two-year-olds Precocious
and Petorius also representing him. Aragon is the second foal of Ica, an unraced
half-sister by Great Nephew to the top-class sprinter Song. Ica's first foal Sun And
Shine (by African Sky) was a useful winner over five furlongs in France as a
two-year-old and has since won stakes races in the United States, including the
Riggs Handicap and the Red Bank Handicap in 1983; Sun And Shine's sire and
Aragon's are both sons of Sing Sing, incidentally. Ica's third foal Aseel (by Homing)

Lady Macdonald–Buchanan's "Aragon"

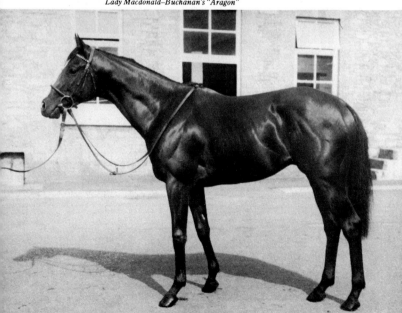

is also a winner; he was awarded a maiden race at Salisbury in June after finishing second to House Hunter.

Aragon (b.c. 1980)	Mummy's Pet (b 1968)	Sing Sing (b 1957)	Tudor Minstrel
			Agin the Law
		Money for Nothing (br 1962)	Grey Sovereign
			Sweet Nothings
	Ica (gr 1974)	Great Nephew (b 1963)	Honeyway
			Sybil's Niece
		Intent (gr 1952)	Vilmorin
			Under Canvas

Aragon will be standing at the Egerton Stud, Newmarket, in 1984 where he'll be joined by his year-older stable-companion Jalmood. Shares in Aragon were offered at £7,500 each, with nominations priced at £2,000 with the October 1st concession. A quite attractive, full-quartered, close-coupled colt and a good mover, he stayed a mile and evidently acted on any going. *J. Dunlop.*

ARAHAB 2 b.f. Hittite Glory 125–Araby 82 (Sweet Revenge 129) (1983 5d³ 5v* 5s 6f 6s 6fg 6d³ 6s³) Apr 12; 1,500Y; fair sort; second foal; dam won twice over 5f; won 23-runner maiden auction event at Doncaster in May; kept her form well afterwards, and on last 2 outings was placed in good-class sellers at York and Haydock in October; will stay 7f; appears to act on any going; consistent. *J. Etherington.* **68**

ARALA 2 gr.f. Fordham 117–Allara (Zeddaan 130) (1983 6g 6fg³) Apr 3; compact filly; half-sister to 2 winners, including 1982 2-y-o 7f winner Amila (by Great Nephew); dam, closely related to Nishapour, won small 7f race in France; not seen out until October, and ran fairly well in minor event at Pontefract and maiden race (apprentice ridden) at Leicester; will be suited by 7f. *M. Stoute.* **67**

ARAMINTA MAVIS 2 br.f. Owen Dudley 121–Fair Marina 93 (Hethersett 134) (1983 6f 7f 7f 5fg 6fg²) Mar 18; sturdy, good-bodied filly; half-sister to 2 winning platers and a winning jumper; dam 2-y-o 6f winner; dropped in class, finished strongly after being outpaced when 1½ lengths second of 22 to Parveno in seller at Newmarket in October; capable of winning similar event at 7f+; acts on firm going. *R. Smyth.* **68**

ARAS AN UACHTARAIN 3 b.c. Habitat 134–Galletto 111 (Nijinsky 138) (1982 6s³ 5s* 1983 6s* 8v 8s³ 7f² 6fg³ 7g 5s³) short-backed, rather sparely-made colt; second foal; dam, daughter of Irish Guinness Oaks winner Gaia, was very useful at up to 1½m; favourite when winning 7-runner Coolmore 'Godswalk' Stakes at Phoenix Park in April by a length from Glorious Jane; placed on same course (3 times) and at the Curragh; stays 1m; acts on any going; blinkered last 3 starts. *D. O'Brien, Ireland.* **101**

ARATI 2 ch.f. Record Run 127–Ranjitara (Right Boy 137) (1983 5d 5d 5f 5f 7h 7f 7g) Apr 13; 800Y; leggy filly; bad plater; sold 380 gns Doncaster September Sales. *A. Smith.* **–**

ARBITRAGE 2 b.c. Monsanto 121–Sideshow 103 (Welsh Pageant 132) (1983 6g 7f³ 7fg 7fg²) Apr 24; sturdy colt; second foal; dam, half-sister to Oaks second Vielle, won 4 times over 1¼m; placed in maiden race at Yarmouth in July and 4-runner Newmarket Challenge Cup in October; will be suited by 1¼m; sold 5,000 gns Newmarket Autumn Sales. *B. Hobbs.* **67**

ARBOR LANE 2 b.f. Wolverlife 115–Suburb's Queen (Levanter 121) (1983 7fg 7f 8fg) Mar 4; IR 2,100Y; fourth produce; dam never ran; showed no form; backed from 10/1 to 5/2 in Redcar seller in October on final outing; sold to M. Haynes 1,650 gns Ascot November Sales. *I. Walker.* **–**

ARCHIMBOLDO 5 b.g. Midsummer Night II 117–Quenilda 101 (Fair Copy) (1982 5d 6f 8f 8f 7f 6f 6fg 6g 6f 6s 5d 5g 1983 6g* 6s 6f 6fg) lightly-built gelding; showed first form for a long time when narrowly winning handicap at Hamilton in September; should stay 7f; acts on any going except perhaps very soft; has been tried in blinkers; sometimes sweats up badly. *W. A. Stephenson.* **52**

ARCHWAY SPARKLE 2 ch.f. Sparkler 130–Shahbanou 89 (Darius 129) (1983 5f⁴ 5f⁴ 5f) Mar 12; half-sister to Emerald Palace (by King Emperor), successful in France and Belgium; dam 5f performer; bad plater; sold 1,500 gns Newmarket Autumn Sales. *W. Musson.* **–**

ARCKARINGA 2 b.f. Persian Bold 123–Aspasie (Milesian 125) (1983 6g³ 6fg⁴ 6h² 6fg 8g) May 9; IR 50,000Y; tall, short-coupled filly; sister to 3-y-o Sir Siegfried, and half-sister to several winners, including useful 1m to 1¼m winner Nonchalant (by Wolver Hollow); dam won over 1m in Ireland; placed in maiden **79**

events on first and third outings, but did nothing in 2 nurseries; will be suited by 7f. *D. Morley.*

ARCTIC LORD 3 br.c. Lord Gayle 124–Arctic Chimes (Arctic Slave 116) (1982 **106**
7d 9v* 1983 12v 10g³ 12g² 11g* 14s⁴ 12g²) half-brother to several winners, including 1m to 1½m winner Polar Star (by Rarity); dam sister to excellent broodmare Arctic Melody, the dam of Arctique Royale and grandam of Ardross; placed in handicaps at Phoenix Park and Naas before beating Ounavarra comfortably by 2½ lengths in one at Phoenix Park again in October; always prominent when 6½ lengths fourth of 10 behind Mountain Lodge in Jefferson Smurfit Memorial Irish St Leger at the Curragh later in month; suited by a test of stamina; acts on heavy going (hasn't raced on a firm surface). *D. O'Brien, Ireland.*

ARDENT ROSE 2 ro.f. Roan Rocket 128–Pomegranite 59 (Ragstone 128) (1983 **–**
5g) Apr 26; 150F; plain filly; second produce; dam in frame in maiden events and a seller; tailed-off last of 13 in maiden race at Wolverhampton in September. *D. Wintle.*

ARDENT WARRIOR 4 b.g. Roman Warrior 132–Ardent Belle (Buisson Ardent **42**
129) (1982 6g 6g 1983 8.2v 8s⁴ 8g⁴ 7d 10f 6g* 6f 6h 5s) big gelding; plater; attracted no bid after winning at Ayr in August; effective from 6f to 1m; acts on soft going; usually wears blinkers. *A. W. Jones.*

ARDOONY 5 b.h. Ardoon 124–Linbel (Linacre 133) (1982 8fg⁴ (dis) 8f 8fg 7fg³ 8g **70**
7.6d² 9d² 8. 2f 8d⁴ 10.5s² 10d 10.2d 1983 6.5d 12s* 12g 12. 2v³ 12g 11v 12d² 12f² 12fg⁴ 12.3fg* 13g² 13f³ 12.3g³ 12g 12.2g 12fg 12g⁴ 14d 12d) neat horse; unreliable handicapper; won race at Cagnes-sur-Mer in February and handicap at Chester in July; stays 13f; acts on any going; suitable mount for an apprentice; sometimes sweats up; none too genuine and is suited by waiting tactics; trained by C. Milbank first 3 starts. *R. Hollinshead.*

ARDROX LAD 3 ch.c. Roi Soleil 125–Petalina 93 (Mummy's Pet 125) (1982 5f **96**
6fg² 5g* 5fg* 5g² 6fg² 6g 6g* 6fg² 6g² 6s² 6g² 5s⁴ 1983 6d 6v² 6s 6v⁴ 6s² 5.8g 6fg 6f² 7f 6f 6fg 6fg² 6g 6fg³) smallish, lengthy colt; relegated to second after dead-heating with Dual Investment (whom he accidentally interfered with) in apprentice race at Nottingham in October; creditable second 3 times earlier and ran well when third to Battle Hymn in apprentice event at Doncaster on last day of season, but also ran some moderate races; should stay 7f; acts on any going, but is ideally suited by some give in the ground; blinkered 4 times in latter part of season but ran better without on final start. *M. Blanshard.*

ARDVERIKIE 3 b.f. Red Alert 127–Black Gnat (Typhoon 125) (1982 6d 6g 7f **–**
1983 11v 7fg 8.3f) smallish, lengthy filly; behind in varied races, including in sellers; sometimes blinkered. *D. Morley.*

ARENA 3 b.f. Sallust 134–Melodramatic 112 (Tudor Melody 129) (1982 6d 1983 **69**
7fg 8f⁴ 7f) quite attractive, well-made filly; good walker; modest fourth in 1m maiden event at Pontefract in June; ran too freely when blinkered only subsequent start. *M. Stoute.*

ARGOSY (USA) 2 b.c. Affirmed–My Charmer (Poker) (1983 6d*) **105 P**
One of the features of American racing in the 'seventies was the sustained duel between Affirmed and Alydar. They met six times at two years, Affirmed winning four times, and in all the triple crown races at three when Affirmed beat Alydar each time—by a length and a half in the Kentucky Derby, by a neck in the Preakness Stakes and by a head in the Belmont Stakes. Affirmed won twenty-two of his twenty-nine races in three seasons, only once finishing out of the first three, when his saddle slipped. Though Affirmed was marginally superior to Alydar as a racehorse, the latter has made the much more spectacular start at stud with two Grade 1 stakes winners in his first crop. Although Affirmed has made a comparatively quiet start none of his three runners in Britain and Ireland has been beaten: these are Claude Monet, out of the dual French classic winner Madelia;

		Exclusive Native	Raise A Native
	Affirmed	(ch 1966)	Exclusive
	(ch 1975)	Won't You Tell	Crafty Admiral
Argosy (USA)		(b 1962)	Scarlet Ribbon
(b.c. Feb 16, 1981)		Poker	Round Table
	My Charmer	(b 1963)	Glamour
	(b 1969)	Fair Charmer	Jet Action
		(ch 1959)	Myrtle Charm

Easy To Copy, a daughter of Talking Picture, the champion American two-year-old filly of 1973; and Argosy, at 1,500,000 dollars Affirmed's most expensive first-crop yearling, who is a half-brother to Seattle Slew and Lomond. Argosy made his only appearance so far in the eleven-runner Kildare Maiden over six furlongs at the Curragh in September. Starting at 3/1 on, he tracked the leaders, moved up two furlongs out and led just inside the distance to win easily by a length and a half from Anita's Prince, who won a listed race on his next start, with Arranan, subsequently third to Without Reserve in the Ashford Castle Stakes, another three lengths away third. Argosy's time was only a fifth of a second slower than the filly Gala Event's for the Moyglare Stud Stakes later in the afternoon.

Argosy is said to be one of his stable's principal Two Thousand Guineas candidates, and though it is impossible to say how good he is Argosy is clearly a highly-regarded colt with the potential to be top class at distances of a mile or more. *V. O'Brien, Ireland.*

ARGUING 2 ch.f. Pharly 130–Arantelle (Tapioca 123) (1983 7d 7fg 7g) Feb 9; $200,000Y; half-sister to numerous winners, notably Washington International winner Argument (by Kautokeino); dam, French middle-distance winner, is out of smart Neptune's Doll; quite a moderate filly; ran best race on second outing; will stay at least 1m. *M. Stoute.*   **71**

ARIBIAN 2 ch.f. Anax 120–Falahill (Romulus 129) (1983 7s 6fg 10.2fg) Mar 19; workmanlike filly; half-sister to fair 1977 2-y-o 5f winner Toco Tommy (by Great Nephew); dam once-raced half-sister to So Blessed and Lucasland; plating-class maiden; stays 1¼m. *R. Hollinshead.*   **66**

ARIES DO 3 br.f. Swing Easy 126–Floradora Do 85 (Derring-Do 131) (1982 NR 1983 7v⁴ 8f⁴ 8f* 10f 8f² 7fg 8d) 8,600Y; quite an attractive, good-quartered filly; half-sister to very useful middle-distance stayer Capricorn Line (by High Line) and quite useful middle-distance filly Rosaceae (by Sagaro); dam won at up to 7f; quickened nicely to beat Most Honourable by 2 lengths in 18-runner maiden race at Yarmouth in June; ran well when second to Vitigeson in handicap at Redcar in July and wasn't disgraced after a lay-off on penultimate start; will probably stay beyond   **95**

Mr R. E. Sangster's "Argosy"

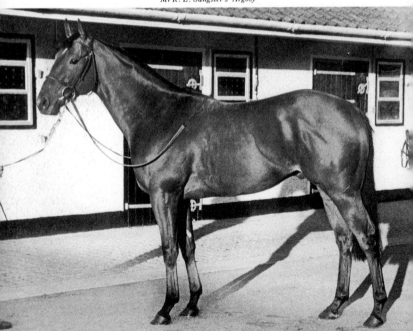

1m (given a lot to do when tried at 1¼m); best form on a sound surface and acts on firm going; sold 10,500 gns Newmarket December Sales. *L. Cumani.*

ARIKARA 2 ch.g. Mandrake Major 122–Hoppity 72 (Negotiation) (1983 5s 7fg **66** 6f⁴ 7f² 7fg) Apr 3; 3,800F; 11,500Y; close-coupled, workmanlike gelding; half-brother to 11f winner Space Dancer (by Roan Rocket); dam half-sister to smart sprinter Hopiana; plating-class maiden; stays 7f; exported to Singapore. *P. Haslam.*

ARISTA (FR) 2 b.f. Thatching 131–La Bellissima (Rose Laurel 125) (1983 5fg **79** 7.6d 6fg²) Mar 28; 120,000 francs Y (approx £10,000); first foal; dam, half-sister to very smart French middle-distance filly Floressa, won small 10.5f race in France; backed from 33/1 to 12/1, caught close home and beaten head by Swift Return in 13-runner maiden event at Leicester in October; stays 6f; acts on a firm surface. *A. Jarvis.*

ARISTO TREAT 4 ch.g. Be My Guest 126–Betsy Ross 100 (Petingo 135) (1982 **–** 8fg 11f 13g² 13f 15.5fg 14fg 12v 1983 12.2g) tall, useful-looking gelding; plating-class maiden on flat but has won over hurdles; appears not to stay 1¾m; apparently needs some give in the ground; usually wears blinkers. *M. Lambert.*

ARITIMA 3 br.c. Manado 130–Westgate Sovereign 89 (Sovereign Path 125) (1982 **–** 5s² 5s² 5f² 5f³ 6fg 5d 6d 1983 8s 6v³ 5v 6d 6s 5g 5.1g 6f⁴ 6fg) small colt; keen walker; sprint maiden; acts on any going; blinkered eighth outing; sold 390 gns Ascot August Sales and exported to Singapore. *K. Ivory.*

ARKENGARTHDALE 9 b.m. Sweet Story 122–Fortzeno 78 (Fortino II 120) **–** (1982 16g 1983 15.8d) sturdy mare; lightly raced and no sign of ability on flat though has won over hurdles; has been bandaged. *N. Bycroft.*

ARMALOU 4 gr.f. Ardoon 124–Sweet Rocket (Roan Rocket 128) (1982 6g 7d 7g **–** 8fg 8fg 10v* 12d 1983 8v 10v 8s 8s 10s 8d 10g) robust filly; plater; stays 1¼m; acts on heavy going; has been tried in blinkers but didn't wear them when successful. *D. Sasse.*

ARMATEX 6 b. or br.g. Kambalda 108–Marina (Supreme Court 135) (1982 NR **–** 1983 12fg) strong gelding; poor form, including in a seller; stays 1½m; acts well on soft going; has worn blinkers. *M. Bolton.*

ARMENISTIS 4 b.c. Relkino 131–Persian Market 105 (Taj Dewan 128) (1982 **–** 16f³ 16f* 15.5f 16h 17fg 16fg 14g 1983 15fg 18f 15f 13f) compact, quite useful sort; poor mover; poor staying handicapper nowadays; yet to race on a soft surface; sometimes blinkered. *S. Leadbetter.*

ARMONIT 3 ch.f. Town Crier 119–Wasdale 97 (Psidium 130) (1982 5fg 5g⁴ 5f 5fg **81** 7fg 7fg 6d 7f⁴ 1983 10.2v 10v⁴ 8.3f⁴ 8f 8g 10g 10.2g³ 10.6s* 11d 8fg) tall filly; always prominent when beating Record Dancer by 2½ lengths in minor event at Haydock in October; good third to Bahoor in apprentice event at Bath earlier in month; suited by 1¼m+; seems to act on any going, but is probably ideally suited by give in the ground. *R. Hannon.*

ARNAB 3 b.g. Pitskelly 122–Reelin Bridge (New Day) (1982 5s 5fg³ 5fg 5fg 6g **–** 7fg* 7g³ 7fg 7.6fg² 1983 6s 7fg 10g 12f) little worthwhile form in 1983; yet to show he stays middle distances; blinkered once at 2 yrs. *R. Smyth.*

ARNALDO 5 b.g. Upper Case–Flower Petals (Busted 134) (1982 10.1d 1983 **–** 12fg 12.3g) neat gelding; middle-distance plater; acted on firm going; often bandaged; usually a front runner; dead. *Mrs C. Lloyd-Jones.*

ARNEDA (FR) 2 b.f. Green Dancer 132–Hagerstown (Ruysdael II 122) (1983 **104** 6f² 7g⁴ 7.5f³ 8s² 9fg* 8.5d³ 10fg*) fifth foal; half-sister to smart French 5f to 10.5f winner Daeltown (by Dictus); dam won over 5.5f and 7f in France; a useful young stayer who won a maiden race in September and 4-runner Prix Isonomy in October, both at Evry; came through in final furlong to beat Broadsound ¾ length in latter; will stay 1½m; probably acts on any going. *D. Smaga, France.*

ARNOLD'S AGENT 2 b.f. Goldhill's Pride 105–Spring Secret 71 (Hillary) (1983 **56** 5v⁴ 5s) Apr 27; 1,500Y; small, sparely-made filly; half-sister to a winner in Italy; dam 1m winner; poor form in spring maiden auction events; dead. *G. Blum.*

AROMA 2 ch.c. Be My Guest 126–Abergara (Abernant 142) (1983 8fg) Apr 8; **–** 42,000Y; closely related to fairly useful middle-distance winner Aberfield (by Northfields) and half-brother to 3 winners, including useful middle-distance performer Paternoster Row (by Godswalk); dam last only start; unquoted, last of 21 in maiden race at Newmarket in October. *G. Huffer.*

AROUND TOWN 2 br.g. Town and Country 124–Scottish Circuit 87 (King's **71** Bench 132) (1983 7f 8f 8.2g⁴) Feb 20; 3,500Y; strong gelding; half-brother to several minor winners; dam 6f to 1m handicapper; 7 lengths fourth of 10 to For Sure For Sure in maiden race at Hamilton in September; stays 1m. *R. D. Peacock.*

ARRABIDA 4 b.f. Bold Lad (Ire) 133–Chippings (Busted 134) (1982 9.5fg 10.5d 12s 1983 7s 9s 10s 8f⁴ 7f) good-bodied, useful-looking ex-French filly; poor mover; second foal; half-sister to useful Irish 7.5f to 1½m winner Red Chip (by Red God); dam unraced half-sister to smart 5f performer Silver God; useful at her best in France; sold out of F. Boutin's stable 24,000 gns Newmarket December (82) Sales and didn't show much form in this country, best effort when 2½ lengths fourth to Hodaka in handicap at Doncaster in July; seems to stay 1½m; probably acts on any going. *J. Etherington.* —

ARRANAN (USA) 2 b.c. The Minstrel 135–Society Column (Sir Gaylord) (1983 6d³ 8d³) Mar 15; $350,000Y, resold $1,150,000Y; half-brother to 1½m Princess Royal Stakes winner Sylph (by Alleged) and 2 winners by Hoist the Flag, namely very useful stakes winner Present The Colors, successful at up to 11f, and very useful Crown Thy Good, a winner at up to 9f; dam, stakes-winning half-sister to top-class Typecast, won at up to 1¼m; put in best work in closing stages when 4½ lengths third of 11 to Argosy in 11-runner maiden race at the Curragh in September and when 2½ lengths third of 7 to Without Reserve in Ashford Castle Stakes on same course the following month; will be well suited by 1¼m+; yet to be subjected to a punishing race and is sure to do a good deal better. *D. O'Brien, Ireland.* 95 p

ARRAS GIRL 4 br.f. Rapid River 127–Arras Gem 82 (Three Wishes 114) (1982 7g* 6fg 7fg 1983 7d 5f 6f 5f 5g) neat filly; has a round action; poor plater; suited by 7f and may stay 1m; possibly needs some give in the ground. *A. Smith.* —

ARRAS LASS 3 b.f. Tycoon II–Arras Gem 82 (Three Wishes 114) (1982 NR 1983 10.5s 7g 10d 7d 8f 7f 6f 8f 8g 7g 7g) good-bodied filly; second foal; half-sister to 7f seller winner Arras Girl (by Rapid River); dam won twice over 1m and also won over hurdles; towards rear in varied races. *A. Smith.* —

ARROGANCE 3 ch.g. Lepanto–Rustic Tweed (Fighting Charlie 127) (1982 NR 1983 12g 12g 12d) first foal; dam novice hurdler; behind in minor events at Lingfield (2) and Newbury (last of 12) in autumn. *D. Elsworth.* —

ARROW BEAK 2 gr.c. Sagaro 133–Lovely Beak (Counsel 118) (1983 5v 5d) Mar 9; 4,000Y; well-grown, strong, close-coupled colt; half-brother to 2 winners, including useful 1m and 1¼m winner Starfen (by Comedy Star), also smart winner over jumps; dam ran once; very weak in market, didn't break on terms in 14-runner seller at Thirsk in May on second outing but without being knocked about unnecessarily ran on to some purpose from halfway to finish 3½ lengths sixth to Pamela Jane; claimed afterwards for 5,000 gns. *W. Musson.* —

ARROWOOD JUNCTION (USA) 3 b.g. Junction–Promised Princess (Promised Land) (1982 8g 8g 1983 10s⁴ 11d 11.5fg 10g 10fg) strong, compact, attractive gelding; only poorish form and looks rather one paced; never going when blinkered final outing; sold to C. Trietline 2,500 gns Newmarket September Sales. *G. Pritchard-Gordon.* —

ARTHUR'S DAUGHTER 3 b.f. Artaius 129–State Pension 112 (Only for Life 126) (1982 NR 1983 10.5s 10fg³ 10fg 8f³ 10fg²) big, rangy filly; half-sister to several winners, including smart 1975 2-y-o State Occasion (by Roan Rocket) and very smart 6f to 1m winner Kampala (by Kalamoun); dam second in Oaks; placed in maiden and minor races at Newmarket (2) and Nottingham; stays 1¼m. *P. Walwyn.* 77

ARTISTE 3 b.f. Artaius 129–Val's Girl 113 (Sir Ivor 135) (1982 6g 8f* 1983 8s* 8f 8.2h* 10h⁴ 8g³) quite a well-made, attractive filly; successful in handicaps at Bath in April (leniently treated) and Nottingham in August; beat Worlingfoot decisively by ½ length in 17-runner event on latter course; stays 1½m; acts on any going; ran moderately second start and wore blinkers subsequently; doesn't look a particularly easy ride, and may need a strongly-run race. *J. Tree.* 89

ARTIST'S REEL 3 ch.c. Artaius 129–Come Dancing 91 (Northern Dancer) (1982 5f² 6fg 7fg² 7g* 7g⁴ 8g² 8g 1983 8s⁴ 8d 10.2s³ 11.7fg 10.1fg 10g 10g⁴) small, fair sort; in frame in handicaps at Newbury, Doncaster and Chepstow, best efforts; stays 1¼m; sold to G. Huffer 6,200 gns Newmarket Autumn Sales. *P. Walwyn.* 81 d

ART SYMPHONY (USA) 3 b.c. Arts and Letters–Am Desirable (Red Monk) (1982 NR 1983 12g 12d⁴) $50,000Y; neat, quite attractive colt; first foal; dam very useful sprint winner; second favourite when about 20 lengths fourth of 13 behind Sikorsky in maiden race at Lingfield in September; sold to P. Mitchell 1,750 gns Ascot December Sales. *G. Harwood.* —

ARUN'S DELIGHT 3 b.g. Furry Glen 121–Aran Jacket (Le Levanstell 122) – (1982 5fg 7f 1983 12fg 10f 12f) smallish gelding; little worthwhile form in varied races, including sellers; sold 1,250 gns Doncaster August Sales. *Miss S. Hall.*

ASCENDROSS 2 ch.g. Ascendant 96–Impossible Dream 56 (Will Somers 114§) – (1983 7h 6g 8fg) Apr 23; tall, plain gelding; third known foal; brother to a poor plater; dam sister to very useful sprinter Willipeg; no worthwhile form in sellers, on debut very slowly away. *R. Hobson.*

ASCOT BELLE (USA) 2 b.f. L'Enjoleur–Native Berry 76 (Ribero 126) (1983 – 5f 5fg 6d) first foal; dam won 4 times at up to 6f here and in France; poor form in maiden and minor events. *D. Hanley.*

ASCOT BLUE 10 b.g. Majority Blue 126–Pebble Ridge 107 (Big Game) (1982 5d **46** 5fg 5fg 5g 5fg 5fg 5fg⁴ 5d 5s 6s 1983 5.8s 5fg³ 5f) sprint handicapper; has been beaten in a seller; ideally suited by some give in the ground nowadays; suitable mount for an inexperienced rider; has occasionally worn blinkers. *M. Bradley.*

ASCOT STRIKE (USA) 2 b. or br.f. Mr Prospector–Queen's Turf (Round **85** Table) (1983 5f³ 5.8h² 7g² 8fg³) Apr 24; $150,000Y; close-coupled, lightly-made, quite attractive filly; half-sister to 2 winners by Spanish Riddle; dam, placed twice in 9 starts, is half-sister to very smart staying 2-y-o Hang Ten; placed in varied company, putting up easily best effort when 2½ lengths second of 10 to Troyanna in minor event at York in October on penultimate appearance; will stay 1¼m; appears to need some give in the ground to be seen to best advantage. *R. Hern.*

ASEEL 2 gr. or ro.c. Homing 130–Ica (Great Nephew 126) (1983 6g³ 7f* 7f⁴ 6f 7g) **89** May 10; 20,000Y; useful-looking colt; has a round action; third foal; half-brother to smart 3-y-o Aragon (by Mummy's Pet), successful at up to 1m, and useful 1981 French 2-y-o 5f winner Sun And Shine (by African Sky), subsequently a stakes winner in USA; dam unraced half-sister to Song; awarded race after being beaten ¾ length on merit by House Hunter in 13-runner maiden race at Salisbury in June; sweated up when good fourth of 6 to Falstaff in £3,800 event at Newmarket in July, best subsequent effort; will probably stay 1m. *M. Blanshard.*

ASH FAIR 2 b.c. Ashmore 125–Travelling Fair 95 (Vienna 127) (1983 7fg) Apr – 21; IR 6,800F, 9,500Y; half-brother to several winners, including fairly useful 1m and 1¼m winner Dibbinsdale Lad (by Sandford Lad); dam best at around 1m; 50/1 and apprentice ridden at overweight, behind in 23-runner maiden race at Newmarket in June. *A. Jarvis.*

ASHGAR (USA) 2 gr.c. Caro 133–Anafa (Faristan 123) (1983 7f* 8g*) Feb 1; **99 p** leggy, quite attractive, rather finely-made colt; good walker; first foal; dam, half-sister to very smart sprinter Adraan, won over 1m and 9f in France; won 16-runner maiden race at Yarmouth in August and 5-runner minor event (upsetting by 2½ lengths odds laid on Van Dyke Brown) at Leicester in October; suited by 1m and will stay further; promises to make very useful 3-y-o. *M. Stoute.*

ASH KING 4 b.c. Ashmore 125–Four Queens (Quorum 126) (1982 8g 12f 12f³ **49** 13.8f 10d* 10fg²(dis) 12g² 10g³ 10v 11v* 12g 1983 12v² 12s 12fg) rather lightly-made colt; poor mover; former plater; worth another try at 1¾m; acts on any going but is ideally suited by soft ground; used to wear blinkers; fairly useful hurdler. *W. Musson.*

ASHLEY ROCKET 2 b.c. Roan Rocket 128–City Sound 63 (On Your Mark 125) **69** (1983 5v 5v* 5d*) Mar 19; 4,500Y; lengthy, sparely-made colt; first foal; dam won over 6f; landed gambles in sellers at Goodwood (bought in 3,200 gns) and Doncaster (retained 9,600 gns) in May; will stay 6f. *W. Musson.*

ASH WARRIOR 3 ch.g. Roman Warrior 132–Hepash 81 (Henry the Seventh – 125) (1982 NR 1983 11d) half-brother to 1m winner Zaccio (by Lorenzaccio); dam best at 1m; dwelt when behind in maiden race at Redcar in May; sold 1,400 gns Doncaster June Sales, for export to Norway. *M. Camacho.*

ASIA A LA CARTE 3 b.c. Wolver Hollow 126–Grass Emerald (Alcide 136) – (1982 NR 1983 11.5fg 12f) 28,000Y; attractive, good-topped colt; fourth foal; half-brother to fairly useful stayer The Bedford (by English Prince); dam, from very good family, ran only at 2 yrs; tailed-off last in maiden races at Sandown (backward) and Brighton (blinkered). *A. Pitt.*

ASIA MINOR 3.b.g. Hittite Glory 125–Paresseuse 114 (Relko 136) (1982 6fg – 7.2g³ 7d⁴ 8f 1983 7d 10.2v) strong, full-quartered, good-bodied gelding; good walker; rather a disappointing maiden on flat; should be suited by 1m; possibly needs some give in the ground. *G. Pritchard-Gordon.*

*William Hill November Handicap, Doncaster—Asir comes late to beat Free Press
(noseband), Sikorsky (right) and Keelby Kavalier*

ASIAN KING 2 ch.c. Roman Warrior 132–Night Cap (Hornbeam 130) (1983 6g — 7g 7fg) Mar 18; 4,000Y; strong colt; no worthwhile form; blinkered when tailed-off last of 28 in valuable seller at Newmarket in September on final outing; apparently of no account. *I. Walker.*

ASIR 3 b.c. High Top 131–Twelve O'Clock (Hardicanute 130) (1982 NR 1983 12f* **109** 12f3 12fg*) 54,000Y; rangy, attractive colt; third foal; half-brother to Irish 1½m winner Angelus Chimes (by Northfields); dam, very useful French 2-y-o 6f winner, is half-sister to Irish Sweeps Derby runner-up Lombardo; won 2 of his 3 races and developed into a very useful performer; accounted for 3 previous winners when beating Aylesfield by 3 lengths in 5-runner minor event at Salisbury in August and for a big field of seasoned campaigners when getting home by 1½ lengths from Free Press in William Hill November Handicap at Doncaster (did particularly well in latter as he was last of 25 turning for home); never really got into race when 4½ lengths third of 6 behind Dancing Affair in minor event at York in between (moved short to post); will stay beyond 1½m; may well have further improvement in him and is the type to win more races. *G. Harwood.*

ASK JOHN 2 b.g. Legal Eagle 126–Rhodia (Parthia 132) (1983 7f 8g 10fg) Feb — 20; 1,200F, 4,000Y; fair sort; half-brother to 3 winners by Blast, including very useful 7f to 1m performer Rhodomantade, and to another winner; dam once-raced half-sister to Champion Hurdle winner Saucy Kit; no form in varied company. *C. Horgan.*

ASK THE WIND 3 ch.f. Run The Gantlet–Arburie (Exbury 138) (1982 7v* 10v* **106** 10v 9v 1983 10s* 12fg4 12g) narrow, rather lightly-built filly; half-sister to a winner in USA by Kalamoun; dam won over 13f in Ireland; won at Saint-Cloud and Evry as a 2-y-o when trained by F. Boutin; made a successful reappearance in 10-runner Hard Fought 3-Y-O Fillies Stakes at Phoenix Park in May, beating Erins Glen by 2½ lengths; ran most respectably when 4½ lengths fourth of 14 behind High Hawk in Ribblesdale Stakes at Royal Ascot in June, better subsequent effort; well suited by 1½m; acts on a firm surface, but is the type who'll probably always be ideally served by soft ground. *D. K. Weld, Ireland.*

ASMALWI 3 gr.f. Averof 123–Sylvanecte 70 (Silver Shark 129) (1982 5g 5f 8fg **61** 7s 1983 8d2 8f 8.2fg 8g 10f) tall, lengthy filly; showed easily best form when ¾-length second to Teleprompter in handicap at Carlisle in May; off course 3 months after next outing; stays 1m; suited by some give in the ground; blinkered last 2 starts. *W. Musson.*

ASSADAA 3 b.c. Habitat 134–Gallissa (El Gallo 122) (1982 6g 5d 6d 6g4 1983 **84** 6d4 7v* 7s2 7v 7g 7.3g 7g 8d4) tall, good-topped colt; poor mover in his slower paces; 3-length winner of handicap at Wolverhampton in April; stays 1m; acts on heavy going (has yet to race on a firm surface); wears blinkers. *H. T. Jones.*

AS SAKAB (USA) 2 br. c. Nodouble–Fancifool (Vaguely Noble 140) (1983 7f) — Apr 12; $160,000Y; short-coupled colt; second foal; dam, second twice from 10 starts, is sister to Touching Wood's dam Mandera; 10/1 and in need of race, eighth of 19 in maiden event at Redcar in October; should stay quite well. *H. T. Jones.*

ASSERTER (USA) 4 b. c. Go Go Roger–Laura Dora (Pleiades 115) (1982 10.6s **69** 12f³ 12f 12f² 12f* 12f* 12d² 13g 12.2f 13s 18s 1983 12g² 12d 12g 14.7f 12f 18.4fg* 19h⁴ 16.5fg³ 15.8fg⁴ 16fg 16fg 18fg 15fg) leggy, fair sort; sweated up badly when winning handicap at Chester in July; stays well; acts well on fast ground; sometimes blinkered. *S. Norton.*

ASSUMED (USA) 3 ch. g. Annihilate 'Em–Gypsy Clara (Tinajero) (1982 NR — 1983 10s) first foal; dam won over 1m at 4 yrs; 25/1 and backward when behind in maiden race at Leicester in March; sold 1,700 gns Doncaster May Sales. *M. Jarvis.*

ASSWAN 3 ch. c. Sharpen Up 127–Wild Romance 96 (Pirate King 129) (1982 6g* **101** 1983 8f 6fg² 7fg 7f³ 6h* 8g* 8s⁴) rangy, attractive colt; got up close home to land the odds by a neck from Northair in apprentice event at Nottingham in August and readily beat Ajoute by 3¾ lengths in Blanquet-Rennen at Baden-Baden later in month; had run well in handicaps earlier and had been placed at Newmarket and Newcastle; finds 6f on sharp side and stays 1m; acts on hard going (didn't run up to his best but wasn't disgraced on soft in a ladies race). *J. Hindley.*

ASTARA 3 gr. f. Nishapour 125–Astana (Arbar 135) (1982 5g 5fg 5g² 6fg 7f* 6s³ **83** 7d 1983 10fg⁴ 10f² 11.5f* 10f² 10f⁴ 10f² 10g) close-coupled, sharp sort; beat Flying Palace by 6 lengths in handicap at Yarmouth in July; wandered right and left when caught on line by Honeybeta in similar event on same course next time; played up a bit in preliminaries second start and sometimes pulls hard; suited by 11.5f; probably acts on any going; didn't have smoothest of runs final start. *M. Stoute.*

ASTERION (USA) 2 gr. c. Star de Naskra–Roman Blue (Charlottown 127) (1983 **65** 6f 6fg 7g 7fg 7g 7fg) small, fair sort; second foal; dam won 1977 Italian 1000 Guineas and was second in Italian Oaks; plating-class maiden; form only at 6f, but should stay further; blinkered final outing; sold 4,200 gns Newmarket Autumn Sales. *G. Pritchard-Gordon.*

ASTONISHING 3 ch. f. Jolly Good 122–Intrusion 101 (Aggressor 130) (1982 NR — 1983 15.5f² 16f 14g 15.8g 12g) small filly; half-sister to 3 winners, including very smart stayer Mr Bigmore (by Mandamus); dam soft-ground stayer; beaten 15 lengths by Americk in a 3-runner maiden race at Folkestone in August. *F. Durr.*

ASTONISH ME 3 ch. f. Levanter 121–Criffel 99 (Malhoa) (1982 NR 1983 12f — 13.1fg) workmanlike filly; ninth foal; half-sister to a fair hurdler; dam won at 1½m and 1¾m; tailed off in maiden race at Newbury and minor event at Bath. *K. Brassey.*

ASTRAL DANCER 2 b. f. Wolverlife 115–Petite Gazelle (Star Gazer 123) (1983 **74** 5s³ 5v* 5d 5s² 5s³ 5f 6fg 6fg 5g) Apr 2; 1,200Y; lengthy, useful sort; sister to a winner in Trinidad and half-sister to 2 winners, including useful sprinter Deer Leap (by Deep Diver); dam Irish 2-y-o 6f winner; won 20-runner maiden auction event at Kempton in April; second to Pageantic in minor event at Goodwood the following month, best subsequent effort; showed nothing in nurseries on last 4 appearances; should stay 6f; probably requires soft ground; has run well for an apprentice. *C. Wildman.*

ASTRAL KING 2 ch. c. Balidar 133–King's Gem 88 (King's Troop 118) (1983 5s³ **91** 5v* 6f 6fg³ 6f) Apr 5; smallish, rather lightly-built colt; good walker; half-brother to 3 winners, including fairly useful 1972 2-y-o African God (by Runnymede); dam sprinter; won 9-runner maiden race at Lingfield in May; 5½ lengths third of 6 to Petorius in minor event at Windsor in July, easily best subsequent effort; stays 6f; sent to Trinidad. *J. Winter.*

ASTRAVEST 2 b. c. Artaius 129–Kissing 98 (Sing Sing 134) (1983 6fg 7g) Apr — 26; 20,000Y; quite attractive colt; half-brother to several winners, including fairly useful 1981 Irish 2-y-o 7f winner Karissima (by Kalamoun); dam won twice over 5f at 2 yrs; behind in 19-runner events at Newmarket in August and York in October; sold 7,800 gns Ballsbridge December Sales. *J. Bethell.*

ATAMAN 3 ch. c. Ashmore 125–Selenis 95 (Huntercombe 133) (1982 8s 1983 10s **65** 16v² 17v³ 16s² 14f 15.5f² 16g³ 16f⁴ 16.5f 16d) fair sort; placed in maiden and minor races and a handicap; evidently suited by a test of stamina; acts on any going, but is probably ideally suited by some give in the ground; had stiffish task when blinkered final outing; sold to M. Pipe 10,500 gns Newmarket Autumn Sales. *F. J. Houghton.*

ATAVA 3 b.g. Artaius 129–Lady Beck 104 (Sir Gaylord) (1982 NR 1983 6fg³)   **60**
second foal; half-brother to 1980 2-y-o 5f winner Malia (by Malacate); dam won over 1m at 2 yrs in France; 33/1, finished strongly and ran a creditable first race when going down by a neck to dead-heaters Dual Investment and Ardrox Lad (who was subsequently demoted) in apprentice race at Nottingham in October; should do better over further. *D. Arbuthnot.*

ATHENIA (USA) 2 ch.f. Mr Prospector–Bonavista (Dead Ahead) (1983 6fg*)   **89 p**
May 11; tall filly; closely related to 4 winners, including very smart French 6f and 7f winner Exclusive Order and smart American 5f to 9f winner Teddy's Courage (both by Exclusive Native), and half-sister to 3 other winners; dam stakes-placed winner over 4f at 2 yrs and 3 yrs; heavily-backed favourite, won 15-runner maiden race at Doncaster in October by ¾ length from Native Charmer; sure to improve, and is probably useful filly in the making. *H. Cecil.*

ATHENS STAR 8 b.g. Athens Wood 126–Maushe Joan 78§ (Major Portion 129)   **–**
(1982 10fg 1983 12g) of little account on flat. *M. Bradley.*

ATHERSTONE 2 ch.c. Monseigneur 127–Dreamy Idea 68 (Double Jump 131)   **– p**
(1983 7fg) May 15; 15,000Y; big colt; good walker; half-brother to several winners, including 1981 Irish 2-y-o 6f winner Oileann Carrig (by Pitcairn); dam ran twice at 2 yrs; 100/1 and distinctly burly, wasn't given hard time after chasing leaders 5f when remote tenth of 18 to Seismic Wave in £5,000 event at Doncaster in September; sure to improve. *C. Booth.*

ATITHASSOS 2 br.c. Sparkler 130–Tegleaze 81 (Galivanter 131) (1983 5fg³ 6f   **72**
7g 7fg 7fg⁴ 6d 7fg) Feb 13; 6,000Y; useful-looking colt; has a round action; half-brother to 1980 2-y-o 1m winner Jade And Diamond (by Bold Lad, Ire); dam 2-y-o 5f winner; quite a moderate maiden; apparently best at 6f. *M. Francis.*

ATKINS 2 b.g. Captain James 123–Sea Dog (Sea Hawk II 131) (1983 8fg 8d 7g⁴)   **73**
Apr 16; IR 12,500F, IR 15,000Y; fair sort; not a good walker or mover; half-brother to Irish 3-y-o Mighty Sea (by Godswalk) and 1m and 1¼m winner Seaway (by Kalamoun); dam useful middle-distance performer; not seen out until October, running best race when 2¼ lengths fourth of 13 to Talk of Glory in maiden event (blinkered) at Lingfield; should be suited by 1m+. *B. Swift.*

ATLANTIC AIR 3 ch.f. Air Trooper 125–Atlantica (Tulyar 134) (1982 5f 7fg   **–**
1983 9d 10fg 14f 10.1fg 10.1f 9d 11.7g) close-coupled filly; plating-class maiden; sometimes blinkered. *Mrs R. Lomax.*

ATLANTIC SALMON (USA) 2 b.c. Lyphard 132–Cloonlara 130 (Sir Ivor 135)   **94 p**
(1983 5g*) Mar 11; third foal; closely related to 3-y-o Glenstal (by Northern Dancer), a smart winner at up to 9f, and to 1981 2-y-o 6f winner Chivalry (by Nijinsky); dam, 6-length winner of Phoenix Stakes, is half-sister to top-class Kings Lake; accounted for experienced colts and fillies in excellent style in 13-runner maiden race at Phoenix Park in October on first appearance, quickening away in final furlong to beat Formalist 3 lengths; has the makings of a very good colt over longer distances. *V. O'Brien, Ireland.*

ATLANTIC TRAVELLER (USA) 6 b.g. Noholme II–Mlle Quille (On-and-On)   **–**
(1982 16s 18.4fg 18f² 20fg 20.4g³ 19f* 20g² 18d 20g 1983 14s 15g 20fg 16f 19f 16.5fg⁴) rather sparely-made gelding; out-and-out staying handicapper; below form in 1983; well suited by top-of-the-ground; blinkered fourth and sixth starts; ideally suited by strong handling. *M. Naughton.*

ATOMIC FORCE (USA) 2 b.c. Matsadoon–Synoble (Vaguely Noble 140)   **87**
(1983 7fg 7f² 8d) Mar 3; $160,000Y; deep-girthed colt; first foal; dam unraced daughter of very useful 6f stakes winner English Toffee; comfortably accounted for 13 others when ½-length second to Jamais Derierre in maiden race at Redcar in September, best effort; should stay 1m. *M. Albina.*

A T S PRINCE 4 b.g. He Loves Me 120–Miss Holborn (Pall Mall 132) (1982 10g   **–**
8fg² 8fg³ 12f 9g 12fg 1983 12.2g 16fg 12f 12fg 10f) lengthy, angular gelding; plater; stays 1m; acts on any going except perhaps soft; blinkered last 2 starts; has run moderately when sweating up; none too consistent. *K. Stone.*

AT TALAQ (USA) 2 b.c. Roberto 132–My Nord (Vent du Nord) (1983 6g* 8g²)   **102 p**
Mar 6; $800,000Y; quite attractive, well-made colt; fourth foal; half-brother to fairly useful 3-y-o 1m winner Northern Script (by Arts and Letters); dam, winner of 2 sprint claiming races, is half-sister to very useful 6f to 9f stakes winner Biller; looked a useful colt in the making when winning 20-runner maiden race at Newmarket in August, quickening in very good style entering last furlong and

striding clear to beat Defloreur by 2 lengths; no match for odds-on Rousillon in 3-runner minor event at Goodwood the following month, going down by 3 lengths after coming under pressure 3f out; will stay 1¼m. *H. T. Jones.*

AT TARF 2 ch.c. Tap On Wood 130–Innocent Air 75 (Court Martial) (1983 7g⁴) —p Feb 17; 400,000Y; half-brother to 4 winners, notably top-class French and American middle-distance performer Perrault (by Djakao); dam won 3 small races at up to 10.5f in France; 7/1, shaped quite well when over 10 lengths fourth of 15 to Bold Patriach in minor event at Chepstow in October, doing all his best work in last 2f; will be suited by 1m; sure to leave this form behind. *H. T. Jones.*

ATTEMPT 2 b.c. Try My Best 130–Wild Asset (Welsh Pageant 132) (1983 6fg 7f² **116** 7f² 7.2fg* 7f* 7f² 8g* 7fg³) Mar 22; 56,000Y; well-made, good sort; first foal; dam poor maiden; had an excellent season, winning minor event at Haydock, £3,500 race at Sandown and 11-runner Kinrara Stakes at Goodwood; particularly impressive at Goodwood, being clear long way out and winning by 5 lengths and 6; very good third under 9-7 to Free Guest in well-contested nursery at Newmarket in October on final appearance; stays 1m; acts on firm going; suited by forcing tactics; genuine. *G. Harwood.*

ATTICUS 2 ch.c. Sagaro 133–My Candy 81 (Lorenzaccio 130) (1983 7f⁴ 7.2fg² **78** 8fg 8.2fg) Apr 25; close-coupled, fair sort; fourth foal; half-brother to 2 winners, including fair 1981 2-y-o 6f winner Annesley (by Relkino); dam placed over 7f at 2 yrs; moderate maiden; lacks pace, and will be suited by 1¼m+; acts on firm going. *R. Hern.*

ATTRATZKY 3 br.g. Radetzky 123–Attractive II (Faberge II 121) (1982 NR 1983 — 7s 8s 8s 7fg 10f 10f 10.8g) 320 2-y-o; small, sparely-made, plain gelding; half-brother to 1978 2-y-o 7f winner Roxy Lad (by Sahib), subsequently successful in Malaya, and to another winner abroad; dam won 4 times in Norway; well beaten in maiden races, sellers and an amateur riders event; often ridden by 7-lb claimer. *M. Hinchliffe.*

ATTWOOD KEN 2 b.c. Wollow 132–Feminist 65 (Reform 132) (1983 5g) May — 26; 1,800Y; second foal; dam plating-class maiden; blinkered, tailed-off last of 13 in seller at Lingfield in July; sold 410 gns Ascot July Sales. *R. Akehurst.*

Mr S. S. Niarchos' "Atlantic Salmon"

AUBRETIA (USA) 2 ch.f. Hatchet Man–Rock Garden 86 (Roan Rocket 128) **84**
(1983 7f 7f* 7g 8fg 8fg) lengthy filly; closely related to 3-y-o Quiet Field (by Stop
the Music) and half-sister to useful 1981 staying 2-y-o Rockfest (by Stage Door
Johnny) and a winner in Scandinavia; dam, half-sister to very smart Glen Strae,
won over 1m; won 13-runner maiden race at Sandown in July; favourite, seemed
unsuited by track when beaten 4 lengths in nursery at Chester on next appearance;
should stay 1m; sold 17,000 gns Newmarket December Sales. *J. Tree.*

AUDACIEUX SOURIRE (USA) 2 b.f. Bold Forbes–Share A Smile (Hagley)   –
(1983 7g) Feb 14; $20,000Y; second foal; dam won 6f claiming race at 4 yrs in
USA; 50/1, in rear in 13-runner maiden event at Lingfield in October. *D. Sasse.*

AUDIT 5 ch.g. Henry the Seventh 125–Red Again (Red God 128§) (1982 13.8f   –
1983 12f 12.2g) small, stocky gelding; plater; stayed 1¾m; seemed to act on any
going; effective with blinkers and without; dead. *D. Yeoman.*

AUGUST (USA) 2 b.c. Sensitive Prince–Polynesian Charm (What A Pleasure) **85**
(1983 6fg² 7d³ 7fg) Mar 8; $250,000Y; robust, good-bodied colt; has a powerful
action; half-brother to 3 winners, including 6f winner Tiger Trap (by Al Hattab);
dam half-sister to numerous winners, including smart 1969 American 2-y-o Clover
Lane; sire high-class winner of 14 of his 20 starts, scoring at up to 1¼m; raced in
useful company, and though usually well backed (clearly quite highly regarded)
showed form no better than fair; co-favourite when 5½ lengths sixth of 8 behind
Round Hill in Somerville Tattersall Stakes at Newmarket in September on final
appearance; will probably be better suited by 1m+. *B. Hills.*

AULAIT 3 ch.c. Gay Fandango 132–Rings 104 (Realm 129) (1982 7g 7d 1983 6v **89**
8fg² 8f³ 7f* 8h²) sturdy, hollow-backed colt; good walker; made all to beat
Perfect Host by 2 lengths in maiden race at Epsom in August; put head in air but
ran well at weights when 2½ lengths second to Marshalla in handicap at
Pontefract the following month; stays 1m; acts on firm going; doesn't look
entirely genuine. *B. Hills.*

AULD LANG SYNE 4 b.g. Warpath 113–Eternally 85 (Ballymoss 136) (1982 **62**
10fg 12d* 16g³ 12g 13d 1983 13v⁴ 12d 13d³ 16fg 14.7f 16f 20.4f³ 13g* 17.4g*
16.1g) lengthy, workmanlike gelding; good walker; won handicaps at Ayr in
August and September, beating Tentwort a head in Eglinton and Winton Memorial
on latter occasion; stays very well; acts well on soft ground; blinkered last 4
starts; tailed-off last final outing (reportedly injured after colliding with tree in
paddock). *Mrs M. Nesbitt.*

AUNT JUDY 2 ch.f. Great Nephew 126–Juliette Marny 123 (Blakeney 126) (1983   – p
7f 7.6fg) Apr 15; 100,000Y; medium-sized, quite attractive filly; half-sister to 2
winners, including useful 3-y-o 1¼m winner Jolly Bay (by Mill Reef), and to fairly
useful maiden Sans Dot (by Busted); dam won Oaks and Irish Guinness Oaks and is
sister to St Leger winner Julio Mariner; given 2 races in autumn maiden events,
looking decidedly green and burly in first, and showing up for long way in second;
almost certain to do better in time. *I. Balding.*

AUNTY (FR) 3 ch.f. Riverman 131–Aunt Zara (Great Nephew 126) (1982 NR 1983 **113**
10v* 9s² 10.5v² 10.5f 8s⁴ 9.2f⁴ 10.5g³) 1,750,000 francs Y (approx £159,000);
strong, compact filly; second living foal; dam, very useful French middle-distance
performer, is half-sister to 2 very useful winners; won newcomers race at
Saint-Cloud in April by 2 lengths from Califlora; in frame 5 times afterwards,
including in Prix Cleopatre at Saint-Cloud (3 lengths second to Alexandrie), Prix de
l'Opera at Longchamp (less than 2 lengths fourth to Royal Heroine) and Prix de
Flore at Saint-Cloud again (about 2½ lengths third to Fly Me); suited by 1¼m+;
acts on any going. *J. C. Cunnington, France.*

AUSPICIUM 3 b.f. Record Token 128–Sultan's Slipper (Saint Crespin III 132)   **43**
(1982 5f⁴ 5f 5g 5f 1983 5d 6d⁴ 5v⁴ 6v⁴ 5g 5h 5f 5g 5g) small filly; sprint plater;
probably acts on any going. *E. Weymes.*

AUSSIE RULES 2 b.f. Homeboy 114–Lucky Run 101 (Runnymede 123) (1983 5v **54**
5v⁴ 5fg 5f 6fg 6d⁴ 7fg 6fg) Mar 23; compact filly; half-sister to minor winners by
Master Sing and Crooner; dam won over 5.9f at 2 yrs; moderate plater; stays 7f;
sold 4,000 gns Newmarket Autumn Sales. *R. Smyth.*

AUST FERRY 3 b.c. Welsh Pageant 132–Severn Bridge 81 (Hornbeam 130) (1982 **74**
8s 8s² 1983 8fg* 7f) useful-looking colt; won maiden race at Warwick in July by a
length from Flying Gayle; found pace far too hot and got going much too late on only
subsequent start; will be suited by 1¼m; acts on a firm surface but may possibly
prove best with some give in the ground. *B. Hills.*

William Hill Trophy, York—the most valuable event on Timeform Charity Day which raised in the region of £100,000 for cancer charities. Autumn Sunset gets up from the almost-hidden Jonacris and Bold Secret

AUTOLYCUS 2 ch.c. Bold Lad (Ire) 133–Claretta 82 (Roberto 131) (1983 6fg) **71** p
Feb 5; IR 4,200Y; first foal; dam, 2-y-o 7f winner, is half-sister to Italian 1000 Guineas winner Rosananti and good English and German performer Claddagh (by Bold Lad, Ire); 7/1, not knocked about when promising 4½ lengths fifth of 20 to Godstone in £4,400 maiden race Lingfield in July; will stay 7f; sure to improve. *J. Dunlop.*

AUTUMN SUNSET 3 b. or br.c. African Sky 124–Merrie Moira (Bold Lad, Ire **106** 133) (1982 6fg⁴ 5fg² 5d³ 1983 5v* 5g* 6f* 5f³ 6f* 6f⁴ 6fg) attractive ex-Irish colt; excellent mover; was given a very lenient mark after making hard work of winning maiden race at Thirsk in heavy ground on reappearance, and was subsequently well placed to win handicaps at Sandown, York and Goodwood, picking up major prizes on last 2 courses; got home by a neck from Jonacris in £13,400 William Hill Trophy at York in June (tended to idle in front and wasn't all that impressive) and by similar distance from Amorous in £25,000 William Hill Stewards' Cup at Goodwood in July (got up gamely close home under hard driving), starting favourite both times; didn't run particularly well last 2 starts, although had stiff task on final one; suited by 6f; not at his best on really soft ground and is well suited by firm; blinkered fourth outing; tends to sweat up. *M. Stoute.*

William Hill Stewards' Cup, Goodwood—Autumn Sunset is a game winner from Amorous (No. 17)

AUTUMN WALK 3 br.f. Tower Walk 130–Autumn Double 72 (Double Jump 131)   –
(1982 5fg 6g 6g 5d 6g 6s 1983 12v 8fg 10fg 8.2s) leggy filly; bad plater; best effort
on soft going at 2 yrs; sometimes blinkered. *Hbt Jones.*

AVABAY 3 b.c. Averof 123–Targos Delight (Targowice 130) (1982 NR 1983 8d   –
5v 8v 10f 8.2g 8g) 4,000Y; rangy colt; poor mover; first foal; dam unraced
half-sister to top 1974 Irish 2-y-o Sea Break; well behind in varied races; sold 360
gns Doncaster October Sales. *H. Collingridge.*

AVENITA LADY 3 b.f. Free State 125–Square Note 85 (High Top 131) (1982 7fg   **57**
7g 8s 8g 1983 8s³ 7fg 10f 12f⁴ 13.8f* 12fg³ 17.1h) hollow-backed filly; plater; held
up when winning at Catterick in August (bought in 1,700 gns); had made running on
her 2 previous starts; suited by 1¾m (had stiffish task over further); probably acts
on any going. *R. Sheather.*

AVERAGE 2 ch.f. Julio Mariner 127–Sahibs Daughter 88 (Sahib 114) (1983 7fg   –
7s 7fg) Mar 25; 4,800F; compact, quite attractive filly; third foal; dam won 5
times at up to 7f; showed only a little ability in big fields of maidens. *G.
Pritchard-Gordon.*

AVERAYR 3 b.c. Averof 123–Mingalles 65 (Prince de Galles 125) (1982 6g 6g   –
1983 6s 6g 6d 5f 5s) neat colt; little worthwhile form, including in sellers;
blinkered last 2 starts; sold 360 gns Doncaster October Sales. *P. Cole.*

AVERON 3 b.c. Averof 123–Reluctant Maid 94 (Relko 136) (1982 5g³ 5g 6f 7.3g   **66**
1983 10s 7v* 7v² 7.3v 7v³ 10g) tall, workmanlike colt; ran best race for a long time
when making virtually all to win handicap at Warwick in April by 7 lengths; placed
twice more in spring, spoiling his chance by hanging on first occasion; should stay
beyond 7f; acts well on heavy going; off course almost 5 months before final start.
C. Wildman.

AVISFORD 3 br.c. Averof 123–Galoprise 88 (Tudor Music 131) (1982 7f 7f 8fg   –
1983 12v 8f) strong, well-made, good sort; has shown no ability and would seem
to be nowhere near so good as he looks. *J. Dunlop.*

AVON BELLE 3 ch.f. Balidar 133–Destiny Girl 112 (Karabas 132) (1982 5f 6g   –
5.8g³ 5g² 6f 5d 5fg⁴ 7g³ 8s 6s 1983 6fg 6fg 7fg) well-made filly; plater; best at 5f or 6f;
suited by a sound surface; sweated up when blinkered once in 1982. *P. Cundell.*

AVON EXPRESS 3 ch.g. Bay Express 132–Mehudenna 77 (Ribero 126) (1982   –
6f 5f 1983 6v⁴ 5f 5fg) lengthy, workmanlike gelding; showed signs of ability as a
2-y-o but was well beaten in a seller on first outing of 1983; sold 500 gns Ascot
July Sales. *P. Cundell*

AVONMORE WIND 4 b.c. Tumble Wind–Gay Friend (Be Friendly 130) (1982   **86**
6d 6g 5f⁴ 5f* 5g* 6f 6f 5g 5s* 5v 5s³ 5s 1983 6d³ 6s 6g 6f) quite attractive,
useful-looking colt; usually impresses in appearance; sprint handicapper; fair
seventh of 27 to Melindra in Wokingham Stakes at Royal Ascot on final start; stays
6f; acts on any going; sometimes sweats up; sent to USA. *S. Mellor.*

AVON VALE 2 ch.g. Vitiges 132–Vendemmia (Silly Season 127) (1983 7f 7f 8fg   **65**
8.2fg 8d) Feb 20; 16,000Y; smallish, workmanlike gelding; half-brother to quite
useful 1979 2-y-o 5f winner Stout (by Bold Lad, Ire) and a good winner in Belgium;
dam poor maiden; best effort on fourth start when staying-on seventh of 19 to
Bonnement in nursery at Nottingham in September; suited by 1m; blinkered final
outing. *P. Cundell.*

AVRAEAS (USA) 4 b.c. Key To The Mint–Rosewater (Sir Ivor 135) (1982 8.2f   –
8d 11.5f 7s 6s 1983 7d 9v 8.2fg) small, strong colt; soundly beaten in varied
company, including selling; blinkered last 3 starts in 1982, looking ungenuine on
first occasion. *R. Morris.*

AWAASIF (CAN) 4 b.f. Snow Knight 125–Royal Statute (Northern Dancer) **127**
(1982 8d 10fg* 12f⁴ 12fg* 12f 12s³ 12d 1983 12fg⁴ 12fg⁴ 12f 12d* 12g)
Awaasif's four-year-old campaign in Europe was rather like Belshazzar's
feast in reverse, ending in better style than it started. In fact mid-October
arrived before she showed form strictly comparable to that which had seen her
finishing a fine third to Akiyda in the 1982 Arc de Triomphe besides winning the
Yorkshire Oaks, so she could hardly have left it much later.

When we interviewed John Dunlop for *Timeform* in April he told us that
although Awaasif had done well physically over the winter the weather had been
appalling for fillies, especially those who, like Awaasif, had been turned out. Dunlop
planned to run Awaasif in the Hardwicke but that race went by without her and she
put in her seasonal reappearance in the Princess of Wales's Stakes at Newmarket
in July. Looking as if the run would benefit her she tracked the leaders, lost her place

two furlongs out and then stayed on again to be a well-beaten fourth of eleven to Quilted. Awaasif looked fitter a couple of weeks later for the King George VI and Queen Elizabeth Diamond Stakes and put up a better effort. Soon close up, she was pushed along at halfway, took second place early in the straight as Diamond Shoal went for home but could find no extra acceleration in the closing stages and finished under four lengths fourth to Time Charter.

Awaasif came out of the King George slightly stiff, and her trainer could not get her right in time for a crack at either the Geoffrey Freer Stakes or the September Stakes, races in which he had hoped to run her as preliminaries to another attempt at winning the Trusthouse Forte Prix de l'Arc de Triomphe. The Arc was thus only Awaasif's third race of the year; Piggott rode her and no doubt to his chagrin the very firm going at Longchamp did no favours to his mount while benefiting immensely All Along on whom he had apparently been offered the ride. In the middle of the field on the outside after half a mile, Awaasif made a little ground three furlongs out, reached eighth place early in the straight but could do no more and ran on at one pace to be thirteenth of twenty-six to All Along, albeit beaten only about five and a half lengths.

Time seemed to be running out for Awaasif in Europe but Dunlop, never afraid to run his horses abroad, identified a fine opportunity for the filly in the Group 1 Gran Premio del Jockey Club at Milan midway through October. No British-trained horse had won this event since Chicago in 1968; in the intervening period the French had won it five times, the Germans three and the Italians six. There were representatives from all four countries in the eleven-runner field in 1983, among them My Top and Celio Rufo, successful respectively in the Italian Derby and St Leger, the smart German colt Tombos, the ex-Italian filly Right Bank, now trained in France and with good form to her name in both countries, and Awaasif herself. Overnight rain made the ground on the soft side, which suited Awaasif, and starting at odds on she put up a majestic performance, leading two furlongs out and drawing right away to beat Right Bank by six lengths, presumably to the great satisfaction of her jockey Piggott after the Arc debacle. Piggott's post-race comment—'I went to the front early in the straight because there was nothing to beat'—was a bit of an exaggeration since it decidedly undervalued Awaasif's opponents. Admittedly the

Sheikh Mohammed's "Awaasif"

Italian three-year-old colts were not a bright bunch but Right Bank's and Tombos' form bears the closest inspection and the Gran Premio del Jockey Club clearly showed that Awaasif had returned to something very near her best. Unfortunately on her only remaining start she finished last in the Oak Tree Invitational at Santa Anita, apparently suffering from a high temperature.

Awaasif (Can) (b.f. 1979)	Snow Knight (ch 1971)	Firestreak (br 1956)	Pardal / Hot Spell
		Snow Blossom (br 1957)	Flush Royal / Ariana
	Royal Statute (b 1969)	Northern Dancer (b 1961)	Nearctic / Natalma
		Queen's Statute (b 1954)	Le Lavandou / Statute

The 1974 Derby winner Snow Knight stands in the States but significantly his two best runners so far, Awaasif and Ivano, have raced in Europe. Awaasif cost 325,000 dollars as a yearling and on the dam's side her pedigree matches her form since she is the fifth winning foal out of the two-year-old five-furlong winner Royal Statute, the others including One Thousand Guineas runner-up Konafa (by Damascus) and the top-class American colt Akureyri (by Buckpasser). Royal Statute's 1981 foal, the filly Royal Lorna (by Val de l'Orne), fetched 240,000 dollars as a yearling and is in training with Konafa's trainer Cumani. The second dam did not race but proved a grand broodmare, foaling thirteen winners, notably the Canadian Oaks winner Menedict and Dance Act, a brother to Royal Statute twice named champion handicap horse in Canada.

Awaasif visits Seattle Slew in 1984. At a mile and a half she needed an end-to-end gallop to be seen to best advantage since this helped to blunt the finishing speed of her opponents, and with stamina her strong suit we should have liked to have seen her given a chance over a mile and three quarters. A good-looking filly and a game one, she went particularly well on soft ground and was ideally suited by a galloping track. *J. Dunlop.*

AWESOME FOURSOME 2 b.c. Saritamer 130–Seven Gates 77 (Henry the Seventh 125) (1983 5v 6f) Mar 30; 500F; seventh produce; dam 2-y-o 5f winner; last on both outings; dead. *J. Berry.* —

AXIANE 2 b. or br.f. Mill Reef 141–Acoma 121 (Rheffic 129) (1983 6g) Jan 30; lengthy, quite attractive filly; excellent mover; third reported foal; half-sister to 1¾m winner Acclaimed (by Luthier); dam, very smart winner of 2 of her 3 starts, over 1¼m and 1½m, is half-sister to high-class Ashmore; heavily-backed favourite, had every chance until unable to quicken in last 2f when 4 lengths fifth of 23 behind Miss Beaulieu in newcomers event at Goodwood in September; bound to do a lot better over longer distances; sent to France. *P. Kelleway.* — 74 p

AXIOS 2 b.c. Shirley Heights 130–Lady Gaylass (Sir Gaylord) (1983 7fg 7d² 8d) Feb 21; 84,000Y; compact, good-bodied, attractive colt; first foal; dam, out of half-sister to Blakeney and Morston, won at up to 1m in France; 2 lengths second of 13 to Elusive in Acomb Stakes at York in August, easily best effort; disappointing favourite in £4,400 event at Goodwood the following month; should stay 1½m; acts on a soft surface. *B. Hobbs.* — 92

AXKERNISH (USA) 3 br.f. Drone–Cynthiana (Nashua) (1982 5f 7f³ 7f 8f* 8g³ 1983 8d 10fg 8f 8.3f 8fg 8d² 8g) long-backed filly; rather disappointing, although finished second to Under the Hammer in handicap at York in October; should stay 1¼m; yet to race on really soft ground, but acts on any other; blinkered last 2 outings. *J. Tree.* — 84

AYAABI 2 b.c. Habitat 134–Demare (Pardao 120) (1983 6f 6g) Apr 23; 370,000Y; half-brother to 3-y-o Still More and Irish 1000 Guineas winner More So (both by Ballymore), latter also a smart winner at up to 1m in USA, and to 2 other winners; dam placed over 5f at 2 yrs; quite modest form in maiden events at Yarmouth in August and September; poorly drawn on second occasion; may improve. *M Stoute.* — 70 p

AYAD 3 b.g. Prince Tenderfoot 126–Bench Game (King's Bench 132) (1982 NR 1983 8v 7d 10.1d 10.1s³ 12v⁴ 8.5d) 29,000Y; smallish, good-topped, quite attractive gelding; half-brother to numerous winners, including very smart 1m to 1¼m performer Record Run (by Track Spare); dam half-sister to smart 1961 2-y-o Gustav; in frame in minor and maiden events at Windsor and Folkestone in May; suited by middle distances; dropped out quickly after making running when blinkered in a seller final start (June). *G. Huffer.* — 66

AYLESFIELD 3 b.c. Busted 134–Woodwind 103 (Whistling Wind 123) (1982 NR 1983 10.2v 10fg 11f* 12f² 12fg) strong, good-bodied colt; third foal; brother to — 84

88

fairly useful stayer Bulldozer and half-brother to a winner; dam won twice over 6f at 2 yrs; showed first worthwhile form when 33/1-winner of 15-runner maiden race at Newbury in July, beating Insular by a length; made running but had no answer to winner's late burst when 3 lengths second of 5 to Asir in minor event at Salisbury the following month, better subsequent effort; will stay at least 1¾m; acts on firm going, but gives impression he'll be seen to much better advantage when racing on an easy surface again. *G. Wragg.*

AYMAN (USA) 3 b.c. Raja Baba–I Understand (Dr Fager) (1982 5f* 5f³ 7f² 7fg³ 1983 8s⁴ 8d² 7d⁴ 8f 8f 8fg 8fg* 9g 10fg) medium-sized, good-bodied, attractive colt; stayed on well to beat Bold Mover by 1½ lengths in handicap at Pontefract in August; never going well next time, but had a stiffish task; suited by 1m; acts on any going; blinkered last 4 starts and also wore them when winning void race at Carlisle on fifth outing. *H. T. Jones.* — **88**

AYNHO HILL 2 gr.f. Godswalk 130–Rough Love 105 (Abwah 118) (1983 5f 6h 5f 7d 6fg) May 7; neat, sharp sort; good walker; first reported foal; dam sprinter; failed to show any form; blinkered when well beaten under low weight in Nottingham nursery on final appearance. *H. Candy.* — **–**

AZAAM 5 b.h. Mummy's Pet 125–Emperor Star (King Emperor) (1982 7f⁴ 7g 6g² 7fg 6fg 8f 6s* 6s 6s² 7d 1983 6s² 5s 6f 6f 6fg* 6f² 6s 6fg 6g²) useful-looking horse; fairly useful handicapper; beat Return To Me by 1½ lengths going away at Newmarket in August; neck second to Never So Bold in Great St Wilfrid Handicap at Ripon on next start; best at up to 7f; acts on any going; below form when tried in blinkers on occasions; inconsistent. *W. O'Gorman.* — **96**

AZARA 3 b.f. Quiet Fling 124–Alangia 101 (Shantung 132) (1982 7f⁴ 7fg 1983 11.7s² 17v⁴ 16g* 14f⁴) lengthy, good sort; beat Hal's Joy by 1½ lengths (pair well clear) in 20-runner maiden race at Lingfield in June; had stiffer task and ran well when fourth of 7 to British in minor event at Sandown the following month on only subsequent outing; suited by a test of stamina; acts on any going with possible exception of heavy. *H. Candy.* — **80**

B

BABA ANN (USA) 2 b.f. Raja Baba–Tenderly (Native Charger) (1983 6d 6fg 7s) Mar 29; $240,000Y; strong, good-topped filly; second foal; closely related to Meru (by Dewan), a stakes-placed winner at up to 6f; dam stakes-placed winner of 7 sprint races; ninth of 29 to Capricorn Belle in maiden race at Newmarket in September, good outing; not sure to stay 7f. *A. Stewart.* — **71**

BABY BOY 2 b.c. Mummy's Pet 125–Lucent 117 (Irish Ball 127) (1983 7f 7d²) Apr 20; 31,000Y; strong, good-topped colt; second foal; dam, daughter of very good sprinter Lucasland, was smart winner from 1m to 1½m from 2 yrs to 4 yrs; off course since June, made much of running when 2 lengths second of 19 to Dorset Venture in maiden race at Warwick in October; stays 7f; sure to win maiden event. *Sir Mark Prescott.* — **75**

BABY'S SMILE 3 b.f. Shirley Heights 130–Two's Company (Sheshoon 132) (1982 7f 1983 12s 12s 10s 16g 11.7fg 12f³ 17.1g 18fg 16fg³) attractive, good-bodied filly; poor maiden; suited by a test of stamina; sold 7,400 gns Newmarket December Sales. *J. Benstead.* — **51**

BACHAGHA (USA) 2 b.g. Marshua's Dancer–Green Carnation (Exbury 138) (1983 7fg 8fg³) Apr 13; $17,000F, $37,000Y; $110,000 2-y-o; leggy gelding; third foal; dam second once from 8 starts in USA; 5½ lengths third of 11 to Caro's Gift in maiden race at Newcastle in October; a free-running sort, not certain to stay beyond 1m; gelded at end of year. *M. Jarvis.* — **77**

BACK'HUS BOY 3 b.c. Workboy 123–Knocknashee 70 (Astec 128) (1982 5g 7d 7fg* 7g* 7fg 7.6fg* 7v 1983 7d 7s 7g 6f 8f 8fg 8f) compact, good sort; useful performer as a 2-y-o but rather disappointing in 1983; suited by 7f+ and a sound surface; sent to Hong Kong. *G. Harwood.* — **–**

BACK STAGE 4 b.c. Busted 134–Bold Words (Bold Ruler) (1982 12fg 14g 13f 1983 12s) big, rangy, quite attractive colt; poor mover; soundly beaten in varied company. *M. Albina.* — **–**

BADACHRO BOR 4 br.g. Import 127–Right Beauty 66 (Right Boy 137) (1982 7f 7g 6fg 6g 6g 7s 1983 6v 6d³ 5g 5g 5fg 8f 6f 5f 6f 5f) poor plater; stays 6f; acts on a soft surface. *D. Chapman.* — **–**

BAD HABITS 3 b.g. Habat 127–Ribofleur 74 (Ribero 126) (1982 7g 7fg 8s 1983 12v 11.7fg 16g) robust gelding; no worthwhile form in maiden and minor events and a handicap, although finished sixth of 20 on final start. *B. Swift.* — **–**

Tia Maria Autumn Handicap, Newmarket—Bahoor is in tremendous form

BAFFLE BAY 2 b.c. Bay Express 132–Baffle 87 (Petingo 135) (1983 5g 5d² 6g **80**
5f⁴ 5fg³ 6f² 6fg* 6g³ 6fg) Apr 27; 6,000Y; fair sort; second foal; dam won over
13.3f and comes from good staying family; won nursery at Windsor in August by 1½
lengths from Double Room; will stay 7f; best form on a sound surface; wears
blinkers. *M. Tompkins.*

BAHHR 3 b.g. Bay Express 132–Sixandahalf (Thirteen of Diamonds 126) (1982 **58**
7fg 7g 8s 8g 1983 7d 10d² 8s² 8.3s 8f) lengthy gelding; good walker; plater;
second twice in spring; stays 1¼m; acts on soft going. *N. Callaghan.*

BAHIA BLANCA 3 gr.c. Galivanter 131–Spanish Gal (El Gallo 122) (1982 NR **–**
1983 12v 8s 8g 10.2g 10.1f) 330 2-y-o; half-brother to a winning plater; dam ran
only once; behind in a maiden race and 4 sellers. *M. Bradley.*

BAHOOR (USA) 3 br.c. L'Enjoleur–Jalapa 117 (Luthier 126) (1982 7g 8g³ 1983 **109**
12d* 10v² 12v 10g* 10fg² 10.2g* 12g* 10.2fg* 10fg* 10g*) big, strong, good-looking
colt; not the best of movers; developed into a very useful performer and was
skilfully placed to win 7 times from 10 starts, despite missing more than 4 months in
mid-season; gained most important win when quickening up well to beat Miramar
Reef in good style by 3 lengths in valuable Tia Maria Handicap at Newmarket in
October on penultimate start; also won a maiden race at Doncaster, apprentice
events at Leicester, Bath, Pontefract and Doncaster again and amateur riders race
at Lingfield, most of them very easily; stays 1½m; yet to race on really firm going,
but acts on any other; reportedly choked when running poorly third start; the type
to make a very smart 4-y-o. *G. Harwood.*

BAHRAIN PEARLS (USA) 3 ch.c. Annihilate 'Em–My Blue Jay (Royal Note) **–**
(1982 5fg³ 6f³ 6d 6f 7g 10s 7s 1983 8s) well-made colt; disappointing maiden;
should stay 1m; ran very freely when blinkered once at 2 yrs; bandaged off-hind on
only outing of 1983 (March); sold 1,900 gns Doncaster November Sales. *N. Guest.*

BAJAN BOY 3 ch.c. Mandao–Cardio-Vanter (Galivanter 131) (1982 5fg 5fg 6fg 6g **48**
6f 1983 10f 10.1f 8.3f³ 8h) lengthy, lightly-made colt; poor plater. *J. Jenkins.*

BAJAN SUNSHINE 4 b.g. Reliance II 137–Nyanga (Never Say Die 137) (1982 **87**
10g² 12f⁴ 12f³ 14g* 14f⁴ 15.5fg* 16fg* 19s² 18d 18d* 18s⁴ 1983 14fg⁴ 16f 16h³
18.1d² 19g³ 17.1g* 18fg*) good-topped gelding; fairly useful handicapper; took
time to reach best at 4 yrs but did so when winning at Bath and Newmarket in
October; got the better of Popsi's Joy by ¾ length after a fine tussle in Tote
Cesarewitch on latter; stays well; acts on any going but is ideally suited by some
give in ground; has won for an amateur rider; tough and genuine; sold privately
before final start and to be trained by M. Tate. *R. Simpson.*

BAKERS DOUBLE 2 br.f. Rapid River 127–Mrs Dumbfounded (Adropejo 114) **75**
(1983 5s³ 5f 6fg⁴ 5fg³ 5h² 5f² 5fg 5fg²) Apr 16; quite a well-made filly; first foal;
dam bad plater; runner-up in a maiden race and 2 nurseries; seems best at 5f;
consistent. *R. Hollinshead.*

BAKUNIN (FR) 3 b.c. Riverman 131–Hairbrush (Sir Gaylord) (1982 5f³ 7g 7d⁴ **–**
6s 6s 7v 1983 10d 8d 8s⁴ 8fg³ 9.4d) small, quite attractive colt; fit from racing at
Cagnes-sur-Mer when in frame in maiden races at Doncaster and Edinburgh in
spring; should be suited by 1¼m; blinkered last two starts in 1982. *M. Ryan.*

BALAASH (USA) 2 ch.c. Cox's Ridge–Lots of Flair (Bold Native) (1983 7f⁴ 7fg **62**
7g) Mar 23; $85,000Y; big, rangy colt; first foal; dam, winner of 4 sprint claiming

races, is half-sister to smart 1975 American 2-y-o Root Cause; sire top-class winner of 16 races at up to 9.5f; showed a little ability in maiden races; may improve. *J. Hindley.*

BALABIL 2 ch.c. Mount Hagen 127–Lady Exbury 111 (Exbury 138) (1983 9s) May 10; IR 16,500Y; fourth foal; half-brother to 1m and 1¼m winner Maybury (by Manado); dam, half-sister to very smart Boreen, stayed 1½m well; 16/1, eighth of 10 in maiden race at Wolverhampton in October. *Sir Mark Prescott.* —

BALACLAVA HUSSAR 2 ch.c. Queen's Hussar 124–Balaclava Maid (Crimea 107) (1983 6fg) May 5; half-brother to 5f winner Miss Cameron (by Decoy Boy); dam never ran; 33/1, slow-starting last of 12 in maiden race at Folkestone in October. *M. Haynes.* —

BALANCHINE 4 b.g. Ballymore 123–Ambuscade 77 (Relko 136) (1982 10d⁴ 10.6fg³ 11f² 12d³ 12fg* 12f* 12g* 12g3 1983 13.3f 14.6fg) well-made, attractive gelding; poor walker; good mover; developed into a useful handicapper at 3 yrs but well beaten in 1983; wasn't seen out until August and still needed race on second start; should stay 1¾m; acts on any going; coltish in paddock on reappearance. *D. Nicholson.* —

BALATINA 5 ch.m. Balidar 133–Toccatina 79 (Bleep-Bleep 134) (1982 5d* 6fg³ 5fg* 5fg³ 5.1f³ 5.1g* 5.3fg* 5f 5.6f* 6g* 6g 5fg⁴ 1983 6g⁴ 5v² 5s* 6v 6f 5fg 5g 5fg) fair sort; sprint handicapper; always going well and strode clear in fine style to beat Morse Pip 4 lengths at Newmarket in May; below form most subsequent starts; stays 6f; acts on any going; suitable mount for an apprentice; often used to wear blinkers and wore them again final outing; withdrawn after giving a lot of trouble in stalls once in 1982; game. *H. Westbrook.* 85

BAL-A-VERSAILLES 3 ch.g. Bustino 136–Bedouin Dancer 79 (Lorenzaccio 130) (1982 6g 7g 1983 10.6v 16fg²) tall, rangy gelding; not seen out after finishing 2½ lengths second of 5 behind Thoughtless in maiden race at York in June; had proved difficult to settle when last in better company previously; stays 2m. *J. Hanson.* 80

BALDINGSTONE BOY 5 b.h. Seaepic 100–Vivyiki (Kirtonian 88) (1982 12f 12f 10fg⁴ 1983 10f 10fg 10fg 12d 12g 18g) compact horse; poor middle-distance plater; acts on firm going; often apprentice ridden; has been blinkered; sold 580 gns Doncaster October Sales. *A. Balding.* —

BALEARICA 2 b.f. Bustino 136–Cala-Vadella 110 (Mummy's Pet 125) (1983 6fg²) Feb 3; first foal; dam, sister to Runnett, won 4 times over 5f at 2 yrs; 33/1 and backward, clear running into the Dip until caught close home when beaten a length by stable-companion Optimistic Lass in 23-runner maiden event at Newmarket in October; speedy, and seems sure to win races. *M. Stoute.* 90 p

BALGOWNIE 3 br.f. Prince Tenderfoot 126–Grandee Ann (Cyane) (1982 5f 5f 6f 6s 1983 12.2g⁴ 12.2d 12f) fair sort; fourth in seller at Catterick in May; fell next time; blinkered third start in 1982; trained by R. Woodhouse first 2 starts. *W. Stubbs.* —

Tote Cesarewitch Handicap, Newmarket—Bajan Sunshine (noseband) gets the better of a fine tussle with Popsi's Joy

BALIBURN 3 b.g. Balidar 133–Golden Apple 68 (Athens Wood 126) (1982 7g⁴ 8d 8s 1983 11v⁴ 9.4d 8f 12fg² 12.3fg) sturdy gelding; good walker; second in seller at Pontefract in August (sweated and pulled hard); stays 1½m; blinkered last 3 starts; bandaged in front third outing; looks to have more than his share of temperament; sold 400 gns Doncaster September Sales. *P. Asquith.* **42**

BALIDAMSEL 3 br.f. Balidar 133–Mam'selle Marron 72 (Quayside 124) (1982 5fg 5fg³ 6fg³ 6g⁴ 6g² 7g² 7.2s 1983 6g 6fg 6fg) plater; stayed 7f; blinkered final start; dead. *P. Cundell.* **–**

BALI DANCER 4 ch.c. Habitat 134–Miss Bali 95 (Crepello 136) (1982 8f* 8.2f⁴ 8fg* 8f² 10f² 9g* 10.5g 10g 1983 9d² 10.2v 8fg 10f 10f 8g) lengthy colt; good walker; ran well to be 6 lengths second to Ivano in Earl of Sefton Stakes at Newmarket in April; didn't reproduce that form, best effort when fifth of 10 to Valiyar in Queen Anne Stakes at Royal Ascot on third start, and ran atrociously final outing; stayed 1¼m; possibly unsuited by heavy ground; best in blinkers; suited by waiting tactics and wasn't an easy ride; sold 16,000 gns Newmarket December Sales and to stand at Blakeley Stud, Shropshire. *M. Stoute.* **105 §**

BALINESE 3 b.f. Balidar 133–Gleaming Horn 97 (Hornbeam 130) (1982 5fg³ 5fg 5fg 7g² 7fg² 7f* 7fg 7.3g 7d 1983 7v 7g 7.6g* 8fg 7f* 7f⁴ 8f 7f 7d 7fg) good-quartered, useful-looking filly; successful in handicaps at Lingfield in June and Sandown in July, beating Admiral Steve a head when ridden by 7-lb claimer on latter course (made much of running); suited by 7f+; acts well on a sound surface; didn't run particularly well last 2 starts. *R. Smyth.* **86**

BALITOU (FR) 4 ch.c. Margouillat 133–Dynamite (Marino) (1982 10s* 11fg⁴ 12s 10.5f 13.5g 15f* 15.5v 12s*(dis) 1983 15.5v 20f 20g* 15.5f⁴ 14g²) lengthy colt; brother to a modest French maiden and half-brother to 3 minor winners in France and Spain; dam won 5 times over middle distances in France; got the better of Kelbomec by a length in Prix Gladiateur at Longchamp in September; in frame afterwards in Prix Royal-Oak on same course (4¼ lengths fourth to Old Country) and Premio Roma (went down by short head to High Hawk after showing a tendency to hang); finished very sore when tailed-off last behind Little Wolf in Gold Cup at Royal Ascot second start; suited by a test of stamina; acts on any going. *P.-L. Biancone, France.* **108**

BALKAN 3 b.c. Balidar 133–Self Satisfied 100 (Great Nephew 126) (1982 5fg 6f 5fg 6f 5f² 6fg 5d 1983 6s 5.8v 5f² 5fg 5f 5.3f 6f³ 5g 6d 6g 6g²) strong-quartered, useful-looking colt; sprint maiden; acts on firm going; sometimes blinkered (ran well in them final start); has raced with tongue tied down; sold 3,900 gns Newmarket Autumn Sales. *W. Wightman.* **62**

BALLACOREY 7 b.g. Sallust 134–Broad River 75 (Chieftain) (1982 NR 1983 12s³ 15.5f⁴ 17f⁴) poor handicapper; stays well; acts on any going. *M. Usher.* **34**

Doonside Cup, Ayr—Balladier (right) runs on strongly to hold Say Primula (noseband)

BALLADIER 3 b.c. Busted 134–Ring Rose 86 (Relko 136) (1982 7g 7fg 1983 **111**
11s* 12g³ 14s³ 11g⁴ 12g 11g* 12d) tall, useful-looking colt; successful in
17-runner maiden race at Newbury in April (beat Hot Touch by 1½ lengths) and
6-runner Doonside Cup at Ayr in September (made all and ran on strongly to hold
Say Primula by 1½ lengths); in frame in between in minor events at Newmarket
and York and Mecca Bookmakers' Scottish Derby at Ayr, easily best effort in
last-named event when just over a length fourth of 11 behind Dazari (made
running and stayed on well); bred to stay 1¾m but best form at shorter distances;
acts on soft going; suited by front-running tactics (couldn't get to front final
start); sent to Sweden. *H. Candy.*

BALLAD ISLAND 3 b.f. Ballad Rock 122–Taggs Island 76 (Silly Season 127) **77**
(1982 6f 8s* 1983 8.2v² 8d* 8v 7.3v² 7g* 7f² 7f³ 7g³ 7fg) leggy filly; won
handicaps at Thirsk in April (by 8 lengths) and Brighton in May; ran well on her
other starts too, including when third of 17 to Gradille in handicap at
Wolverhampton in October (having first race for nearly 3 months and ridden by an
inexperienced boy); stays 1m; acts on any going, but has done all her winning with
some give in the ground; often ridden by apprentice W. Ryan. *M. Jarvis.*

BALLAGARROW GIRL 3 ch.f. North Stoke 130–Capule (Middlegroun) (1982 **66**
5f 8s 7.2s 1983 8d 8d 12f 8fg 8.2f 8.2h 8h 10d³ 10.6g 9fg² 10f 10fg 10fg) quite
well-made filly; placed in maiden race at Beverley in September and handicap at
Redcar in October; suited by 1¼m. *R. Hollinshead.*

BALLARD ROCKET 2 gr.f. Roan Rocket 128–Razor Blade 65 (Sharp Edge 123) **–**
(1983 6g 7f 7f 8fg 8fg) Jan 27; small filly; first foal; dam won over 5f and 7f at 2 yrs
but didn't train on; little worthwhile form, including in nurseries. *R. Baker.*

BALLASAYLE LAD 2 b.c. He Loves Me 120–Mil Pesetas (Hotfoot 126) (1983 **–**
7g) Apr 30; IR 9,400F, 1,000Y; leggy, close-coupled colt; second foal; dam Irish
6f winner; 66/1, backward and green, tailed off after missing break in 17-runner
maiden race at Leicester in September. *R. Hollinshead.*

BALLET DE FRANCE (USA) 2 b.f. Northern Dancer–Fabulous Native (Le **101**
Fabuleux 133) (1983 6fg* 6d 7g*)
A career analysis of the past winners of the C.L. Weld Park Stakes, run at
Phoenix Park in October, doesn't augur well for the latest winner Ballet de France.
Only the 1975 winner Capricious, successful in the Galtres Stakes at York the
following year, won a race of any prestige as a three-year-old. Once again the Park
Stakes took little winning for an event carrying Group 3 status. Ballet de France
started at 10/1; Rustic Lace and Reo Racine, first and second in the one-mile Silken
Glider Stakes at Leopardstown the previous month, occupied first and second
positions in the market here at 5/2 and 4/1 respectively. Rustic Lace and Reo Racine
made the running, until the former came wide into the straight. Having tracked the
leaders Ballet de France went second at halfway, challenged well over two furlongs
out and was driven clear to win by two and a half lengths and a neck from Lady Aura
and Miss Turnberry, each a winner on her previous outing. Reo Racine finished
fourth. Successful in a maiden event at Phoenix Park on her debut in July, Ballet de
France had been defeated in her race immediately prior to the Park Stakes. She'd
reportedly hit a couple of false patches of ground when a disappointing fifteenth of
twenty behind Gala Event in that race, the more strongly-contested Moyglare Stud
Stakes at the Curragh in September.

		Northern Dancer	{ Nearctic	{ Nearco
		(b 1961)	(br 1954)	Lady Angela
	{		Natalma	{ Native Dancer
Ballet de France (USA)			(b 1957)	Almahmoud
(b.f. Apr 29, 1981)			{ Le Fabuleux	{ Wild Risk
		Fabulous Native	(ch 1961)	Anguar
	{	(ch 1974)	{ Alyne Que	{ Raise A Native
			(ch 1970)	Mellow Marsh

Ballet de France, an attractive filly, is the second foal of her dam Fabulous
Native, a lightly-raced half-sister to several winners including the useful Irish
six-furlong to nine-furlong winner Muscovite and Exclusive Air, a winner over a mile
and a quarter in Ireland at three years. Fabulous Native's dam, Alyne Que, a winner
over six furlongs as a two-year-old, is a sister to the very useful sprinter L'Natural
and closely related to Yale Coed (who has since produced the smart French and
American colt Interco). She is also closely related to the champion American sire
Exclusive Native, so Ballet de France, by Northern Dancer, might be said to be bred
well enough to win almost anything. So far Ballet de France may be regarded as
having shown promise rather than having shown enough to suggest she is capable of
winning in the best company. Only time will tell how good she is. The chances are

that if she is to improve on previous Park Stakes winners and run well in a classic it will be in one over a distance of a mile, probably the Irish One Thousand Guineas. She should get a mile and a quarter, but perhaps not much further: her pedigree on the whole contains more speed than stamina. *D. O'Brien, Ireland.*

BALLIMA (NZ) 5 b.g. Bally Royal 109–Lazer Ray (Globe of Light 111) (1982 NR   –
1983 15.5f) New Zealand-bred gelding; last of 5 in maiden race at Folkestone in
August. *D. Grissell.*

BALLINLEG PRINCE 3 b.c. Crooner 119–Greasby Girl (John Splendid 116)   –
(1982 NR 1983 8s 7fg) first foal; dam bad plater; last in 2 sellers. *P. Butler.*

BALLNACARN 4 ch.c. Firestreak 125–Deer Forest (Huntercombe 133) (1982   **64**
8.2d 9f³ 8f² 8fg³ 8.3fg* 8.3g 8fg² 8s² 7d* 7g 1983 7.2v⁴ 7g 8s³ 7s² 7f* 7f 8.3f² 7f
7f² 7s³ 7g 7fg) very lightly-made colt; won handicap at Beverley in June; stays 1m
well; acts on any going. *J. Toller.*

BALLY 3 ch.f. Balidar 133–Lipizza (Acropolis 132) (1982 NR 1983 8f⁴ 8f)   **74**
5,600Y; strong, workmanlike filly; has an enlarged near-hock; half-sister to 1978
2-y-o 5f winner Fraserfield Boy (by Frankincense); dam lightly-raced daughter of
very smart 1952 2-y-o Pirouette; kept on quite well when just over 6 lengths fourth
of 11 behind easy winner Remembering in minor event at Newmarket in July, better
effort; sympathetically handled next time; possibly capable of better. *J. Toller.*

BALLYCRACKERS 2 ch.g. Vitiges 132–Love and Care 96 (Ballymoss 136)   –
(1983 5s 7f) Mar 15; 10,500Y; compact gelding; fourth living foal; half-brother to
a winner in Italy; dam, daughter of Gimcrack winner Be Careful, won over 5f at 2
yrs; not fully wound up, soundly beaten in maiden race at York in May and £3,100
event at Redcar in July; subsequently gelded. *M. H. Easterby.*

BALLYDURROW 6 ch.g. Doon 124–Even Tint (Even Money 121) (1982 13d   **51**
1983 13.8g³ 9.4f) big gelding; winning hurdler; only poor form on flat; will stay
2m. *R. Fisher.*

Mr R. E. Sangster's "Ballet de France"

BALLYFEE 6 br.m. Sovereign Bill 105–Ballyarctic (Arcticeelagh 119) (1982 12s   –
1983 13v 12s) plain mare; of little account; cost 750 gns Ascot January Sales; has
been very troublesome at start and was banned from racing by Stewards of the
Jockey Club in July. *K. Bridgwater.*

BALLYLUMMIN 2 ch.g. Tumble Wind–Native Charm (Red God 128§) (1983 5s   **68**
5fg 5fg 6fg 5fg) May 16; IR 16,000Y, resold 26,000Y; compact gelding; closely
related to winning Irish stayer Wingate (by Windjammer) and half-brother to
another winner in Ireland; dam, who never ran, is closely related to winning
Greenland Park and Red Sunset; plating-class maiden; usually shows early pace;
blinkered final outing; gelded subsequently. *I. Balding.*

BALLYMENOCH 4 ch.g. Relkino 131–Latin Verses (Appiani II 128) (1982 10s   –
9g4 14f2 12g2 12g* 16f2 12f* 12f3 1983 12d 8fg 10g) ex-Irish gelding;
good-topped individual; won handicaps at Naas (apprentice event) and Tramore
(odds on) in 1982; didn't show much in this country at 4 yrs; stays well; acts on
firm going and is probably not at his best on soft; has won over hurdles. *J. Old.*

BALLYREEF 3 br.f. Ballymore 123–Belle Reef 98 (Mill Reef 141) (1982 6g 7d   –
1983 10s 8v4 10.6g) small filly; only poor form in maiden races; sold to Mrs G.
Forbes 5,600 gns Newmarket Autumn Sales. *P. Walwyn.*

BALLYSEEDY HERO 5 gr.g. Supreme Sovereign 119–Knocknagrena   **55**
(Worden II 129) (1982 7f 8f3 10.1g3 8fg3 10.2f3 10v 1983 10.2g3 10fg* 10.6fg3)
tall, lengthy gelding; plater; won claiming race at Brighton in August; stays 1¼m;
suited by a sound surface; blinkered once. *D. Elsworth.*

BALMACARA 2 b.g. Free State 125–Deer Forest (Huntercombe 133) (1983 5fg   **62**
6f 5f4 5f 5fg) Mar 26; 3,000 2-y-o; fair sort; has a slightly round action; third foal;
half-brother to 7f and 1m winner Ballnacarn (by Firestreak); dam showed no form in
3 outings; 3 lengths fourth of 11 to Singerman in maiden race at Newcastle in
August, best effort; should be suited by 6f; brought down on debut; blinkered final
start. *P. Feilden.*

BALMENOCH 2 b.f. Queen's Hussar 124–Immatation 67 (Polyfoto 124) (1983   –
5g 6g 7s) Mar 29; 4,000Y; second living foal; dam won 4 races at 4f and 5f; behind
in minor and maiden events; off course 4 months after second start and backward
on return. *D. Hanley.*

BALMORAL BONNET (NZ) 2 ch.f. Balmerino 133–Header 78 (High Hat 131)   –
(1983 8g 8.2fg) Jan 25; stocky filly; keen walker; half-sister to 2 winners, including
useful 1976 2-y-o 6f winner Rockery (by Roan Rocket); dam half-sister to good
stayer Charlton; behind in sizeable fields at Leicester and Nottingham (led to
halfway) in the autumn. *R. Hern.*

BALTIC AIR 3 b.g. Stradavinsky 121–Grunhilde 54 (Mountain Call 125) (1982 6d   –
7d 6f 6f 6fg4 7f 7f 8fg 1983 12d 8s) neat gelding; poor plater; stays 1m; sometimes
blinkered. *R. Asquith.*

BALUCHI 2 b.c. Gunner B 126–Atlantica (Tulyar 134) (1983 7fg) June 12;   –
narrow, fair sort; has rather a round action; half-brother to a winning plater and a
winner in Austria; dam never ran; soon tailed off in 11-runner Hyperion Stakes at
Ascot in October. *Mrs R. Lomax.*

BAMBA 2 b.f. Dance In Time–Brescianina (Hugh Lupus 132) (1983 6f3 6f4 7s*   **82**
7d3) May 1; rather lightly-built filly; half-sister to very useful 6f and 1m winner
Bancario (by Owen Dudley) and several winners in Italy; dam useful at up to 11.5f in
Italy; held on gamely to beat Nadia Nerina a short head in 16-runner maiden race at
Ayr in September; fair third of 6 to Derrygold in minor event at Catterick the
following month; should stay 1¼m; best run on soft going. *E. Weymes.*

BAMDORO 4 br.f. Cavo Doro 124–Pat 98 (Ennis 128) (1982 12s 1983 12g 10fg   **54**
8d 8.2s3 8fg* 7fg) plater; bought in 900 gns after winning at Edinburgh in
November; stays 1m; seems to act on any going; sometimes blinkered (wore them
at Edinburgh). *W. Stubbs.*

BANCHORY BRIDGE 4 ch.g. Bay Express 132–Renoir Picture 90 (Relko 136)   –
(1982 8g 8f 10fg 8fg 8.2s 7d 8s 1983 11.7h) strong gelding; poor maiden; probably
stays 1m; sometimes blinkered. *M. Pipe.*

BAND 3 b.c. Blakeney 126–Zither 72 (Vienna 127) (1982 6d2 7g4 1983 10v2 12f*   **123**
11.5f* 12f* 14g4 14fg* 12f* 14s2 15.5f2)
Long-distance racing is presently at a fairly low ebb. Competition in the top
grade is particularly weak and seems likely to remain so, since very few owners
with the right sort of horse are willing to run in the Cup races. However, there
will be fresh names in the long-distance events in 1984, among them Carlingford

Mr K. Abdulla's "Band"

Castle and Band who were placed in classics in the latest season. Carlingford Castle faced tougher assignments as a three-year-old than Band, and showed better form; he looks the better prospect for the Gold Cup, too. But Band made pleasing progress through the season, and should have a part to play in some of the good staying races.

Band reached his peak in the autumn, when he won the Cumberland Lodge Stakes at Ascot and ran second in the Jefferson Smurfit Memorial Irish St Leger at the Curragh and the Prix Royal-Oak (the French St Leger) at Longchamp. He'd arrived at that level via maiden races, handicaps and the March Stakes at Goodwood. He first won a race at York in July, on the fourth outing of his career and his first over a distance as long as a mile and a half: he won in good style. Before the month was out he'd followed up by winning handicaps at Sandown and Goodwood, so outclassing the opposition for a £6,500 prize on the latter occasion that he started 7/1-second favourite for the Tote-Ebor Handicap with a weight of 9-3. At the time, his failure to get to grips with the leaders in the Ebor was a trifle disappointing; in retrospect, his finishing fourth of sixteen to Jupiter Island was a highly creditable performance, that of a developing young stayer. Band's very easy win in the March Stakes at Goodwood ten days later revealed little new about him—he was up against only Bold Connection, Ring Of Greatness, Current Raiser, and The Liquidator who hadn't been out for four months—but then came the Cumberland Lodge. Although returning to a mile and a half from a mile and three quarters Band needed to win or be thereabouts to be worth his place in the Irish St Leger field. Band won by a length from Looking For, the pair of them clear of Lyphard's Special, Zilos and four others, including the four-year-old Khairpour who ran well below his best. Band found a turn of foot at the end of a truly-run race. Settled with only two behind him for much of the way, he was in trouble early in the straight and had to be switched outside for a run; faced with at least eight lengths to make up on the leaders he quickened sufficiently to reach the front inside the last hundred yards, and at the post he was going away from his field.

Underfoot conditions for the Irish St Leger and the Prix Royal-Oak could scarcely have contrasted more sharply—mud at the Curragh, firm at Longchamp. In our opinion Band was the more impressive at Longchamp, but he ran very well on each occasion, whereas Mountain Lodge who beat him two lengths in Ireland was put completely out of court in France. The 6/4 favourite in Ireland, Band was gradually worn down by Mountain Lodge after taking the lead over a furlong and a half from home; though very tired he stayed on too well for the pursuing Khairpour, who did show his form here. In France Band started at 6/1. He went down by a neck to Old Country in an all-British finish (Another Sam was third, a length down on the second). Band had a desperately unlucky run. He was badly checked when attempting to make progress early in the straight and had to be switched outside, forfeiting much more ground than that by which he was ultimately beaten. He finished very strongly indeed but had just too much to do; he must have made up all of five lengths on the winner in the last two furlongs. As in several of his other races Band gave the impression over the first two thirds of the journey that he was running lazily or was slow to warm up.

Band (b.c. 1980)	Blakeney (b 1966)	Hethersett (b 1959)	Hugh Lupus
			Bride Elect
		Windmill Girl (b 1961)	Hornbeam
			Chorus Beauty
	Zither (ch 1965)	Vienna (ch 1957)	Aureole
			Turkish Blood
		Electronic (b 1956)	Borealis
			Metallic

Band's half-brother Pop Song (by Silly Season) was placed in the Cumberland Lodge Stakes in 1974; he won a maiden race at a mile on the same course and later won over hurdles before breaking a leg in a novice chase at Chepstow. Two other foals of the dam Zither won over hurdles—Fighting Fiddler (by Derring-Do) and Queen's Music (by Queen's Hussar), the latter also a winner on the flat—and three more won on the flat. They were Cithern (by Canisbay), a two-year-old winner; Cymbal (by Ribero), a middle-distance performer; and Zimbalon (by Ragusa), the best of all her foals until the arrival of Band. Zimbalon won six races, including the Ormonde Stakes at Chester, the King George V Stakes at Royal Ascot and the Rosebery Handicap at Kempton; he improved significantly from three years to four years, and perhaps Band will do likewise. Zither herself was a minor ten-furlong winner, so was her grandam Metallic; Zither's dam Electronic never ran.

Band is an attractive, close-coupled colt. He stays two miles so well there's little doubt he'll get further especially since he's by Blakeney, a close second in the Gold Cup of 1970 and a strong influence for stamina at stud. Band acts on any going; nevertheless a firm surface suits him particularly well. Band was sold privately to Khaled Abdulla after the Cumberland Lodge Stakes; previously he'd been owned by Mr R. D. Hollingsworth, his breeder. *R. Hern.*

BANDELERO 3 br.c. Relkino 131–Siouan 78 (So Blessed 130) (1982 6fg 7fg 8d **74** 8.2s⁴ 1983 11v* 12d⁴ 14.7d 12g 13s³ 15.8d³ 12fg) compact colt; had opposition well strung out when successful in maiden event at Ayr in March; ran best race and put up a good performance when 3¾ lengths third of 11 behind Prince of Peace in minor event on same course in September on fifth start; stays at least 13f; acts on heavy going; sold to R. Holder 8,800 gns Doncaster November Sales. *C. Thornton.*

BANDIT KING 2 b.c. Cavo Doro 124–Candid Queen 80 (Good Bond 122) (1983 — 7f 8d) Mar 30; second foal; dam won over 1¼m; well beaten in £3,500 race at Sandown in August and maiden event (blinkered) at Brighton in September; sold 500 gns Ascot October Sales. *P. Mitchell.*

BANNA'S RETREAT 2 b.f. Vitiges 132–Buff Beauty 92 (Mossborough 126) — (1983 7f 8d) Feb 17; 3,200F; half-sister to winning stayer Cavalier's Blush (by King's Troop) and a winner in Italy; dam well suited by a distance of ground; little worthwhile form in maiden races at Yarmouth in August and Beverley in September. *A. Stewart.*

BANNONWARD 7 b.m. Forlorn River 124–Double Bank 80 (Double Jump 131) — (1982 NR 1983 6g) neat mare; of little account and a short runner; has worn blinkers. *K. Bridgwater.*

BANOCO 5 b.h. Nonoalco 131–Denaneer 78 (Green God 128) (1982 7.5g 6.5fg² **66 §** 8s 7.5d* 8g 7d 8g 7f 7.2fg 8f 7fg 9fg 8f³ 8fg 8fg 8.2g⁴ 10g⁴ 8.2g³ 8d² 8d* 8s 7g⁴ 8s

1983 8d 9d* 8g³ 9g³ 9fg* 8d 8f 9f 10fg⁴ 10fg) quite moderate; won handicaps at Hamilton in May and York in June; stays 9f; acts on firm going but is suited by some give underfoot; tends to sweat up; has won for an apprentice; sometimes bandaged on off-hind; inconsistent, probably ungenuine and is suited by waiting tactics. *T. Craig.*

BANTEL BANDIT 2 br. g. Rhodomantade 110–Right On Time 78 (Right Boy 137) (1983 6d⁴ 7f⁴ 5f 7f 6f* 6f² 7f 6g* 7d 7f) Mar 31; 1,150Y; big, strong gelding; fourth foal; dam 5f performer; bought in 4,000 gns after staying on gamely under pressure to beat Trengale a length in £3,500 seller at York in July; ran creditably in better company before and afterwards, on eighth outing dead-heating with Fawzi in nursery at Ayr in August; finds 5f a bit sharp and stays 7f; suited by a sound surface. *H. Bell.*   **78**

B. A. POUNDSTRETCHER 4 b.f. Laser Light 118–Grecian Flame (Sound Track 132) (1982 5d 6fg 5.8f 6fg 6g 1983 7s 7d² 7f⁴ 7f 6f⁴ 6f 7g⁴ 6g⁴ 6fg) lengthy, workmanlike filly; in frame in handicaps and a seller; doesn't quite stay 7f; seems to act on any going; has twice been blinkered; has worn bandages behind; has run respectably for an apprentice. *E. Eldin.*   **64**

BARA GILL 3 gr. g. Baragoi 115–Gill Breeze (Farm Walk 111) (1982 5fg⁴ 6f³ 6g 8fg 8f 7.2s* 1983 8s 8d³ 8g³) lengthy gelding; stays 1m; appears to act on any going; exported to Singapore. *W. Haigh.*   **63**

BARAN (ITY) 4 br. c. Windjammer (USA)–Bridge Four (Roi Soleil 125) (1982 7.5g⁴ 7g* 6g² 5g³ 6g² 6v 6g² 12g 6g³ 7g³ 7g 6g* 7.5g² 7.5g 6g⁴ 1983 6g² 6g³ 5g⁴ 6g 5g 8g* 8g 9d² 7s³) attractive ex-Italian colt; first foal; dam half-sister to very smart Irish sprinter Cinerama Two; won 3 times at Milan at 2 yrs (given 8-8 in Free Handicap) and twice at Turin in 1982 (given 7-1 in Free Handicap); placed twice at Pisa before winning at Milan in June; made running and kept on quite well to be 2 lengths second of 3 to long odds-on Spanish Place in slowly-run minor event at York in October, and finished creditable third to Nandino in Premio Chiusura at Milan later in month; has raced mainly over sprint distances but evidently stays at least 1m. *L. Cumani.*   **?**

BARASTAR 4 bl. or br. g. Baragoi 115–Lyrical Star 62 (High Table 105) (1982 NR 1983 12.3v 9d 9g) first foal; dam plating class at 2 yrs; well beaten in minor events. *T. Cuthbert.*   **–**

BARATERRE (USA) 2 b.f. J. O. Tobin 130–Shamme (Sham) (1983 7fg) Apr 25; $150,000Y; big filly; third foal; half-sister to a winner; dam unraced half-sister to smart milers Out of the East and Painted Wagon; unquoted, 9½ lengths tenth of 22 to Travel Away in maiden race at Newmarket in October; will stay 1m; sure to improve. *M. Jarvis.*   **70 p**

BARBARA ANN 3 ch.f. Nebbiolo 125–Miss Anna (King's Company 124) (1982 NR 1983 7.6v 7f 8f 10g 10fg⁴) workmanlike filly; second reported foal; half-sister to quite useful 1980 Irish 2-y-o 7f winner Lady Nightingale (by Martinmas); dam, half-sister to Providential, showed no form; showed signs of ability on several occasions, including when staying on to be about 8 lengths fourth of 11 behind Polestar in maiden event at Newmarket in October; stays 1¼m. *A. Turnell.*   **–**

BARBARESCO 4 ch.c. Nebbiolo 125–Firstville (Turn-to) (1982 NR 1983 8fg 9d³ 10v 7fg 8f 7f 9f) IR 4,400Y; 820 3-y-o; sturdy colt; fourth foal; dam, closely related to Sir Gaylord, ran 7 times unplaced in USA; poor maiden. *J. Gilbert.*   **–**

BARBICAN AIRE 2 b.c. Crooner 119–Laura Lou (Lauso) (1983 5d² 5s⁴ 5s⁴ 7f 7f 5f 7fg 6fg 6g) workmanlike colt; not a good walker; third reported foal; dam tailed off only outing; seems to stay 7f; acts on any going. *R. Hoad.*   **66**

BARBRANCER 3 b.g. Carnival Dancer 113–Denita (Saintly Song 128) (1982 5f⁴ 6f 6f 6g 6d 1983 8fg 8d 12f² 10fg) compact, plain gelding; plater; stays 1½m; acts on firm going; blinkered last 2 starts in 1982. *G. Richards.*   **–**

BARDAN 3 b.c. Dom Racine 121–That Girl (Breeders Dream 116) (1982 7g 7s 1983 8v 9f 10g² 10fg 10.5d) lengthy, rather leggy colt; ¾-length second to Thessaloniki in handicap at Yarmouth in September; made little show next time and found very little on final start; will possibly benefit from a return to shorter distances than 1¼m. *R. Armstrong.*   **74**

BARDSEY POET 3 ch.f. Monsanto 121–Barlow Fold 99 (Monet 126) (1982 5f 7fg 7d 7d 1983 9f 8f) workmanlike filly; quite a moderate maiden; not seen out after July; tends to sweat up. *G. Huffer.*   **–**

BARE ESSENCE 2 gr. c. Mount Hagen 127–Robinie (Fortino II 120) (1983 6g 7g³ 7f 7.3d) Mar 18; 45,000F; big, well-made colt; particularly good mover; half-brother to useful French 7.5f and 1¼m winner Running Back (by Great   **82 +**

Nephew); dam unraced half-sister to Blushing Groom; 20/1, shaped most promisingly when ½-length third of 10 behind Elegant Air in £4,100 event at Newmarket in July, travelling smoothly on bridle 2f out and finishing very strongly indeed; ran badly in Sandwich Stakes at Ascot later in the month (found to be suffering from a liver complaint) and was off the course afterwards until October, when always behind in Horris Hill Stakes at Newbury; will stay 1m; grand type, who must be kept on right side. *J. Dunlop.*

BARE MINIMUM (USA) 2 b.c. The Minstrel 135–Barely Even (Creme dela **99 p** Creme) (1983 8g² 7d*) Apr 28; closely related to French 3-y-o Sulemeif (by Northern Dancer) and half-brother to 2 winners, including stakes-placed Golden Highlights (by Secretariat); dam, high-class winner at up to 1m, was successful in 17 of her 30 starts; drew well clear of 13 others when failing by ¾ length to catch Yashgan in newcomers event at Saint-Cloud in October; bandaged when landing the odds by a short neck from Welsley in maiden race on same course following month; will stay 1¼m; a very well-bred colt who should make a decent 3-y-o. *O. Douieb, France.*

BARGOUZINE 2 ch.f. Hotfoot 126–Right as Rain 96 (King's Bench 132) (1983 **63 +** 6d 6fg) Feb 26; 17,000Y; sparely-made, workmanlike filly; half-sister to several winners, including very useful sprinter As Friendly (by Be Friendly); dam 2-y-o 5f winner; showed up in big fields of maidens at Newbury in October and Doncaster (third favourite) in November; may do better. *M. Jarvis.*

BARLEY BIRCH 5 b.g. Crooner 119–Bella Sandra 88 (Botticelli 129) (1982 10f² **–** 12f³ 10s⁴ 10fg 9g 10fg⁴ 12f² 12fg 1983 12s 12s³ 10.8v) compact, short-legged gelding; poor maiden; stays 1½m; acts on any going; sold 490 gns Ascot October Sales. *M. Pipe.*

BARNABY GRANDE 2 ch.c. Record Run 127–Daughter of Song 73 (Song 132) **–** (1983 5s 5v 6fg 7h 5.3fg 6fg 6g) Apr 30; 2,700Y; workmanlike colt; bad plater; has worn blinkers. *P. K. Mitchell.*

BARNABY SAM 4 br.g. Comedy Star 121–Balandra Star 92 (Blast 125) (1982 **–** 12fg 8f 14d 10.1g 10.1g 10.1g 13.1f³ 12v 1983 12d 12s) useful sort; good walker; quite a modest maiden at his best; seems to stay 13f; blinkered second start; sold 1,400 gns Ascot 2nd June Sales. *P. Mitchell.*

BARNALYRA 2 b.c. He Loves Me 120–Wild Orchid (Sassafras 135) (1983 7fg **–** 8d) Apr 14; IR 9,200F; lengthy colt; second produce; half-brother to 3-y-o Ming Village (by Persian Bold); dam never ran; last but one in good-class autumn races at Ascot and Newbury. *M. McCormack.*

BARNBROOK AGAIN 2 b.c. Nebbiolo 125–Single Line (Rash Prince) (1983 **69** 7fg 8g) Apr 19; IR 12,500Y; workmanlike colt; half-brother to Ski Lift (by Mount Hagen), successful at around 1¼m; dam, closely related to CCA Oaks winner Magazine, won at up to 6f in USA; 3¾ lengths fifth of 8 to Bonnement in minor event at Wolverhampton in August; no show in much better company at Newbury the following month. *D. H. Jones.*

BARNET HEIR 5 ch.g. Great Nephew 126–Right as Rain 96 (King's Bench 132) **68** (1982 6d 6d³ 6fg⁴ 6g* 7f 6g 6fg 5g² 5.3fg² 5f 5g 5g² 5fg² 5d 1983 5d 6v 5s³ 5d 5.3f⁴ 6g) small, sturdy, very attractive gelding; good mover; sprint handicapper; stays 6f; acts on any going; suitable mount for an apprentice. *B. Swift.*

BARNEY MILLER 3 b.g. Monseigneur 127–Etta (Umberto 118) (1982 5fg 7f **75** 1983 8g 10.1d 11.5fg⁴ 11.7fg⁴ 11g 12.3fg 11.5g² 12f² 13fg 12fg³ 12s³ 12.2g) big, rangy gelding; quite a modest maiden; gives impression he'll be suited by a test of stamina; often blinkered; sold to M. Pipe 6,200 gns Doncaster November Sales. *M. Ryan.*

BARNLOUGH 5 br.m. Blue Cashmere 129–Stick 'Em Up (Burglar 128) (1982 7f **–** 6f 5.3g 5fg 1983 6v 8g) compact mare; poor maiden; stays 7f. *J. Jenkins.*

BARN PIECE 2 b.f. High Line 125–Buckham Barn (Lorenzaccio 130) (1983 6f) **–** Mar 28; lengthy, plain filly; second foal; half-sister to a minor winner in France; dam never ran; unquoted and sweating, no show in maiden race at Salisbury in July. *N. Gaselee.*

BARN ROD 2 b.f. Gold Rod 129–Barneo (Dumbarnie 125) (1983 6d 5f) Apr 27; **–** sixth foal; dam won over hurdles; in rear in minor event and a seller in the Midlands. *R. Whiston.*

BARNUM 2 b.c. Auction Ring 123–Blanche Hardy (Ribot 142) (1983 5s⁴ 6g 6f 6fg **83** 7h*) Mar 5; neat, attractive colt; third foal; half-brother to a winning plater and a winning hurdler; dam won over 1½m in Italy; won 13-runner nursery at Bath in August by a neck from Mr Chromacopy; will be suited by 1m; best run on hard going but ran respectably on soft; sold 19,000 gns Newmarket Autumn Sales, for export to Hong Kong. *P. Walwyn.*

BARODA BAY 2 b.g. Prince Tenderfoot 126–Victorian Pageant 95 (Welsh —
Pageant 132) (1983 6s 6f) Mar 3; 7,000F; well-made gelding; second produce;
half-brother to 3-y-o Blushing Girl (by Blushing Groom); dam lightly-raced 1¼m
winner; behind in June in Woodcote Stakes at Epsom and £5,700 maiden race at
York. *P. Kelleway.*

BARON BLAKENEY 6 gr.h. Blakeney 126–Teleflora 89 (Princely Gift 137) —
(1982 17f² 18.8fg⁴ 20fg² 16.1g² 16.1f⁴ 19f² 18.8fg 18g⁴ 19s 18d 20g 1983 18d 17.1v
18.8v 20fg 22.2f 20.4g) neat horse; poor staying handicapper nowadays; acts on
any going; suited by strong handling; blinkered once at 3 yrs. *M. Pipe.*

BARON HOPKINS 9 ch.g. Frankincense 120–Jolie 64 (Jolly Jet 111) (1982 8.2s —
8f 8.2fg 10g 8fg 8.2g 8fg 1983 8.2d 10f) poor plater. *A. W. Jones.*

BARONY 2 ch.f. Ribston 104–Sherry (King's Coup 108) (1983 7f 8.2f 7g 8.2g) of —
no account. *N. Chamberlain.*

BAROOQ (USA) 4 br.c. Turn and Count–Ballet Pleasure (What A Pleasure) 102
(1982 8.2s 8fg 10f 8g² 9d 1983 10.2v 8v 7g 8.3f* 8h* 8.3fg² 8.3fg* 8.3fg* 8fg)
well-made colt; good mover; hasn't always been reliable but did well at 4 yrs and
made most to win handicaps at Windsor (3) and Beverley; stays 1m well; acts well
on fast ground; tends to pull hard and has been taken down early; bandaged in
front first outing (rather fractious in preliminaries). *F. Durr.*

BARRA HEAD 3 b.g. Nonoalco 131–Bruntlaw 94 (Bounteous 125) (1982 7g 1983 85
8f 10g 8f⁴ 8h* 10s³ 8.2g² 8d³ 8.2fg⁴ 10.2fg*) good-bodied gelding; chipped a bone
in a knee on only outing as a 2-y-o; ran creditably most outings in 1983 and won
weakly-contested maiden race at Chepstow in August and very slowly-run
apprentice event at Doncaster in November, latter by a head from Country Charm;
stays 1¼m; acts on any going. *J. Dunlop.*

BARRANCA 2 b.g. Pitskelly 122–Val d'Or 57 (Gulf Pearl 117) (1983 5.3f 6g 7f 7h) —
May 10; 7,200Y; lightly-made gelding; first foal; dam won twice over 2m at 4 yrs;
little form, including in Sandown seller; retained by trainer 750 gns Ascot August
Sales after fourth appearance and was then gelded. *R. Smyth.*

BARREL ORGAN 2 ch.g. Homing 130–Hurdy-Gurdy 90 (Espresso 122) (1983 —
6fg 8s) Feb 28; lengthy, fair sort; half-brother to 3 winners, notably very smart
middle-distance filly Vielle (by Ribero); dam won at up to 1¼m; behind in minor
event at Newmarket in August and maiden race at Yarmouth in September; sold
2,200 gns Newmarket Autumn Sales. *B. Hobbs.*

BARRERA LAD (USA) 3 ch.c. Barrera–Misty Joy (Misty Day) (1982 5f³ 5f 5f — §
5f⁴ 5s² 1983 5v 6s 7d 7g) temperamental sprint maiden; has been tried in
blinkers; one to treat with caution. *D. Elsworth.*

BARRIE BABY 3 b.f. Import 127–Even Song (Falcon 131) (1982 NR 1983 7d* 85
8f² 8fg 8g 8s* 8fg³) 750Y; lengthy, workmanlike filly; fourth living foal; half-sister
to 6f to 1½m winner Winter Sunshine (by Crisp and Even); dam showed little sign
of ability; ran creditably all starts and won minor event at Leicester in June (in good
style by 8 lengths) and £4,000 ladies race at Doncaster in September (beat Darting
Groom by 2½ lengths, going away); creditable third to Dinner Toast in £10,800
handicap at Ascot later in September; gives impression she'll stay beyond 1m; acts
on any going, but is very much at home on soft; game. *C. Booth.*

BARROW STRAND 3 br.g. Mansingh 120–Vaunt (Hill Rise 127) (1982 6g 1983 —
6s) well-made gelding; well beaten in maiden and minor events. *D. Whelan.*

BARRYPHILIPS DISCO 6 br.g. Firestreak 125–Appollo Fourteen 78 (Space —
King 115) (1982 18d 12d 1983 13s 16.1v³ 15.8d 16fg 16f 16f) strong gelding;
winning hurdler; plating class on flat; stays well. *R. Whitaker.*

BARRY SHEENE 2 b.c. Camden Town 125–La Gamberge 87 (Vieux Manoir 90 p
132) (1983 7fg² 7g*) Mar 14; 11,500F, 46,000Y; quite attractive, rather
unfurnished colt; good mover; half-brother to 3 winners, including fairly useful
middle-distance performer French Lane (by Boreen); dam Irish stayer; odds on,
got up close home to beat Wunderkind a neck after coming under pressure fully 2f
out in 16-runner maiden race at Leicester in September; had shaped promisingly
previous month when 4 lengths second of 17 to odds-on Carocrest in minor event
at Lingfield, keeping on well; will be well suited by longer distances; the type to
make a useful 3-y-o. *J. Dunlop.*

BARYSHNIKOVSKY 3 b.c. Manado 130–Neriad (Princequillo) (1982 8s 8.2s² —
1983 9d 10g 10.1f) tall, leggy, rather narrow colt; should have been suited by
middle distances; dead. *R. Boss.*

BASH-UM-BABY 2 gr.f. Dragonara Palace 115–Bashi 73 (Zarathustra 131) (1983 63
5d 5s² 5f⁴ 6g) May 8; 2,000F; rather lightly-made filly; half-sister to several

100

winners, including quite useful sprinter Attymon Place (by Mummy's Pet); dam ran only at 2 yrs; plating-class maiden; not raced after July; not certain to be suited by 6f; sweated up third start. *E. Weymes.*

BASICALLY BRIGHT 3 b.f. Sparkler 130–Rosetown 84 (Charlottown 127)   **59**
(1982 5.8f3 5.8g3 7f4 1983 7s4 7s4 9v2 7s4 7f 7f 10g 9fg 10fg) rather sparely-made filly; disappointing maiden; stays 9f; acts on any going; brought down on her last outing; sold to BBA 2,600 gns Newmarket December Sales. *B. Hills.*

BASIE 2 b.c. Jaazeiro 127–Orchestration 116 (Welsh Pageant 132) (1983 7fg) Mar   **–**
27; 28,000F; close-coupled, sparely-made, fair sort; first foal; dam won Coronation Stakes; 25/1, no show in 26-runner maiden race at Newmarket in September. *H. Candy.*

BASIL BOY 4 b.c. Jimsun 121–Slick Chick 89 (Shiny Tenth 120) (1982 8d 7g4 8f   **88**
7f3 7f3 6fg 7.2g 7.6g 7f2 7g3 7fg* 8g3 8f3 10s 7s 8v4 8s 1983 8d3 10v 8d 8d 7.6v 8.5g4 8f 8fg* 10f4 8f3 8f3 8f4 9g 8g3 8fg* 9fg3 9d4 8g4) strong, sturdy colt; fair handicapper; won at Salisbury in June and Ascot (apprentices) in September; creditable 1¾ lengths third to Sagamore in William Hill Cambridgeshire at Newmarket in October; stays 1¼m; seems to act on any going but goes well on firm; blinkered sixth and seventh starts; tends to get behind in early stages and is suited by strong handling; has his share of temperament. *R. Hannon.*

BASSETT BOY 2 ch.c. Crimson Beau 124–Saintly Chorus 65 (Saintly Song 128)   **87**
(1983 7f 7f2 7f2 8fg4 8fg 8g2 7g) Mar 5; useful-looking colt; first foal; dam stayed 9f; second in maiden races at Brighton, Newbury and Sandown, going down by ½ length to Forest of Dean on last-named in October; better suited by 1m than by 7f, and will stay further; yet to race on a soft surface; blinkered fifth outing. *R. Hannon.*

BASSETT GIRL 2 b.f. Brigadier Gerard 144–Greek Opal (Furry Glen 121) (1983   **–**
8f) Mar 30; first foal; dam Irish 1m winner; 33/1 and backward, behind in 18-runner maiden race at Leicester in November. *J. Bethell.*

BASTA 4 b.f. Busted 134–The Woodbird (Tudor Melody 129) (1982 11g3 12f 12fg   **66**
14.7f4 14d2 14g 10s* 12d* 1983 10s 10g 12d 12d4 10fg 10.2f 12h3 12fg4 12f* 12f3 16fg 16.1g3 12s2 18fg2 14.7fg 18fg*) rangy, attractive filly; good walker; awarded handicap at Ripon in August on a technicality and held on gamely to win similar event at Doncaster in November; stays well; acts on any going; has won for an apprentice; tended to hang third start; doesn't always find much off bridle. *R. Hollinshead.*

BASTILLE 2 ch.c. Vitiges 132–Criminelle (Crepello 136) (1983 7f 7fg 7d* 7fg*)   **97**
Mar 2; rather leggy colt; half-brother to Pagan Deity (by Brigadier Gerard), a fair winner at around 1¼m; dam lightly-raced sister to 2 winners; successful in maiden race at Brighton and nursery at Doncaster (strongly ridden to get up close home) in the autumn; will be suited by 1m+; acts on a firm and a soft surface; ran too freely when apprentice ridden on second outing and is clearly suited by waiting tactics. *J. Dunlop.*

BASTIONS LADY 2 b.f. Frimley Park 109–Alexzena (Upper Case) (1983 5v 6f3   **63**
6fg 7fg 8.2fg 7d) May 19; small filly; first foal; dam plating class; 3¾ lengths third to Seattle Rose in 12-runner maiden event at Brighton in June, only indication of merit. *D. Arbuthnot.*

BATHING BELLE 2 ch.f. Wollow 132–Regal Splendour 76 (Sovereign Path   **–**
125) (1983 6d 6g) Apr 21; smallish filly; half-sister to 3 winners, including useful sprinter Think Ahead (by Sharpen Up); dam 6f winner; little worthwhile form in maiden race at Yarmouth (speed 4f) in September and minor event at Pontefract in October; sold 2,100 gns Ascot December Sales. *H. T. Jones.*

BATON BOY 2 ch.c. Music Boy 124–Lobela 77 (Lorenzaccio 130) (1983 6g4 7g)   **79**
Mar 24; first foal; dam won at 1m and 1¼m; had quite a hard race when 3½ lengths fourth of 23 to Miss Beaulieu in newcomers event at Goodwood in September, better effort; pushed along throughout when fifth of 16 in maiden race at Leicester later in month. *R. Williams.*

BATONI 4 b.c. Realm 129–Marthe Meynet (Welsh Pageant 132) (1982 7f 6f 5s   **77**
6s2 6s 5s 1983 6s* 5v2 6v 6d) lengthy colt; good mover; sprint handicapper; well-backed favourite when winning at Thirsk in April and when second to Singing Sailor in £6,400 race at Doncaster in May; better suited by 6f than 5f; acts on heavy going. *M. H. Easterby.*

BATSHEEBA 3 br.f. Olden Times–Forward Princess (Forward Pass) (1982 NR   **–**
1983 12fg 13f) IR 21,000Y; lengthy, workmanlike filly; first foal; dam, out of sister to Ribocco and Ribero, was placed in USA; soundly beaten in maiden races at Newmarket (apprentices) and Nottingham in summer; sold 8,800 gns Newmarket December Sales. *M. Jarvis.*

BATTALION 5 br. g. Bustino 136–True Love 89 (Princely Gift 137) (1982 10.2g²   **63**
13d³ 8f² 8f 8fg 12f 8f⁴ 8fg 8fg 12f 1983 7d 7fg³ 7d³ 8fg 8f 7f 7g 7.2g 6s 7g* 7g)
useful-looking, though rather hollow-backed gelding; made all to win handicap at
Edinburgh in October; best at up to 1¼m; acts on any going, but is ideally suited by
some give in the ground nowadays; has run respectably for an amateur rider. *D.
Chapman.*

BATTLE CHANT 3 gr. g. Runnymede 123–Boating Song 59 (Crewman) (1982   –
NR 1983 5d 5fg 9d 6f) 1,100 2-y-o; second foal; dam placed over 6f; towards rear
in maiden and minor races and a seller. *F. Watson.*

BATTLE DRUM 2 b. or br. c. Bustino 136–Ring Rose 86 (Relko 136) (1983 7g   –p
8fg) Apr 27; strong, well-made colt; third foal; closely related to very useful
middle-distance 3-y-o Balladier (by Busted); dam, winner of 3 middle-distance
races, is daughter of very smart Heath Rose; out of first 10 in big fields of maidens
at Goodwood in September and Newmarket in October; likeable sort, almost
certainly capable of improvement. *H. Candy.*

BATTLE EVE 3 b. f. Le Johnstan 123–Wellington Girl 62 (Tribal Chief 125) (1982   –
NR 1983 5f 5s) smallish, strong filly; second foal; dam plating class at 2 yrs;
showed some early speed before finishing towards rear in minor events at Redcar
in September and Haydock in October. *W. C. Watts.*

BATTLE HYMN 4 b. c. Music Boy 124–Wild Words 76 (Galivanter 131) (1982   **103**
6g 6fg* 6fg² 8.2f 6fg* 7f 6g 7f⁴ 1983 6d⁴ 6s 7fg³ 6fg² 6fg² 6fg² 6fg*) big,
handsome colt; useful handicapper; not seen out until August after suffering from
hepatitis but ran creditably to be second at Lingfield, Newmarket and Doncaster
before getting the better of Saxham Breck by ½ length in apprentice event at
Doncaster again in November; stays 7f; ideally suited by fast ground; sometimes
hangs and is ideally suited by strong handling. *G. Harwood.*

BATTLE MASTER 2 br. g. Thatching 131–Maiberry 92 (Supreme Court 135)   **80**?
(1983 5fg 5f 6fg 7d⁴ 7g 6fg) May 6; small gelding; has a smooth action;
half-brother to 3 winners, all at least fairly useful, including sprinter Cock of the
Walk (by Takawalk II); dam sprinter; 4¾ lengths fourth of 16 to Bastille in maiden
race at Brighton in September, best effort; stays 7f; suited by a soft surface;
blinkered last 2 starts; gelded after final outing. *N. Vigors.*

BATTLING AGAIN 3 ch. f. Crooner 119–Battling 75 (Pinza 137) (1982 5fg 5g   –
5.3fg 6g 1983 7g 8.5d 7f) behind in maiden and minor races and an apprentice
event, 3 times last. *M. Haynes.*

BAVAL (FR) 6 b. g. Baroque 128–Valse des Coeurs (Homere) (1982 NR 1983   **44**
15.8d* 13.8g) tall gelding; not a particularly good walker or mover; made all to win
handicap at Catterick in March (well backed); off course subsequently until
October; stays 2m; yet to race on a firm surface. *D. Yeoman.*

BAY CITY ROLLER (USA) 3 b. c. Groshawk–Lady Kaps (Lurullah) (1982 NR   –
1983 8f) $21,000F, $25,000Y; good-bodied colt; half-brother to several winners,
including useful 1981 French 2-y-o 1m winner Abraje (by Accipiter); dam won 2
claiming races at up to 1m; unquoted and burly when last of 12 behind Trakady in
maiden race at Newbury in July; sold 1,000 gns Doncaster October Sales to Miss
S. Morris. *R. Simpson.*

BAY EMANUELLE 3 b. f. Anax 120–Khotso (Alcide 136) (1982 5f³ 5f 5f⁴   –
1983 6d 5d 8s 8d 8v 9f 9f) rather lightly-made filly; poor maiden; well beaten in a
seller final start. *Mrs M. Nesbitt.*

BAY EMPRESS 3 b. f. Empery 128–Not Mistaken (Mill Reef 141) (1982 7d 6s³   **105**
6s 1983 6s 8v 8fg* 10f³ 12fg 12g* 8d³ 10g) IR 10,500Y; compact filly; first foal;
dam never ran; first past post at Punchestown as a 2-y-o but was relegated to third
after running left; successful in 1983 in minor event at Navan in June and
Brownstown Stakes at the Curragh in August, keeping on to beat Allorette by 1½
lengths on latter course; also creditable third twice at the Curragh, beaten length
by Flame of Tara in Pretty Polly Stakes in between and a neck and a short head by
Mighty Fly and El Kantaoui (after looking to be going best early in straight) in
Gilltown Stud Stakes in September; below form on her other starts, including when
eleventh of 12 in Irish Guinness Oaks; effective at 1m and stays 1½m; acts on any
going. *T. Burns, Ireland.*

BAY FELLA 3 b. g. Bay Express 132–Felipa (Philip of Spain 126) (1982 6s 7.6v   –
6g 1983 6v 6s 6s 6v 7.6g 6fg 6f 6fg 7fg 10g 10g) lightly-made, fair sort; no
worthwhile form, including in a seller; blinkered sixth outing. *J. O'Donoghue.*

BAYFORD 4 ch.c. Brittany–Sweet Silhouette 70 (Setay 105) (1982 5f 8f 1983 7s 8s 8.3s 5f 5f 6fg) workmanlike colt; poor plater; blinkered nowadays; has sweated up. *Mrs B. Waring.* —

BAYNOUN 2 br.c. Sassafras 135–Busarella (Busted 134) (1983 7fg³) June 6; third foal; half-brother to 3-y-o 1½m winner Bayrak (by Rheingold); dam, from excellent family, ran only once; weak in market and apprentice ridden, showed promise when 1½ lengths third of 13 to Jabaraba in maiden race at Redcar in October; will be much better suited by 1¼m+; sure to improve. *F. J. Houghton.* **84 p**

BAYRAK 3 br.c. Rheingold 137–Busarella (Busted 134) (1982 NR 1983 10.1fg³ 14.7f² 12f* 12g³ 13.3d) big, rangy colt; second foal; dam, from excellent family, ran only once; kept on dourly to beat Barney Miller a length in 17-runner maiden event at Redcar in September; hampered in early stages next time; will stay 2m+; acts on firm going and ran very disappointingly on dead last time out; sold to M. Pipe 21,000 gns Newmarket Autumn Sales. *F. J. Houghton.* **77**

BAY SHADOW (USA) 2 b. or br.c. Caucasus 127–Shady Hill 82 (Hillary) (1983 7g 8d) Mar 16; $100,000Y; small, compact colt; fourth foal; half-brother to 2 winners by Decidedly; dam, placed over 1¼m, is sister to high-class 1m and 1¼m filly Hill Shade (dam of J. O. Tobin and Mysterious); backward, behind in good-class races at Kempton in September and York (seventh of 12 to Corinth) in October; should do better over further. *M. Jarvis.* **– p**

BEACH LIGHT 3 ch.f.Bustino 136–Street Light 120 (St Chad 120) (1982 7g⁴ 7g 1983 10g* 12g 10f) IR 50,000Y; lengthy, rather shallow-girthed filly; third living foal; half-sister to 2 winners, including useful 5f and 6f winner Highland Light (by Home Guard); dam smart sprinter; ran on really well under pressure to beat Sibley by ½ length in 9-runner minor event at Newbury in June; had stiff tasks when in rear in Lancashire Oaks at Haydock and small handicap at Newmarket afterwards; suited by 1¼m. *M. Jarvis.* **89**

BEACH PALACE (USA) 3 b.c. Barrera–Ocean Palace (Hail to Reason) (1982 NR 1983 8v 10.1f) $275,000Y; first foal; dam twice-raced half-sister to Sporting Yankee and Amazer; last in maiden race at Kempton in April and minor event at Windsor in July; sold 825 gns Ascot August Sales. *J. Dunlop.* —

BEACON HEIGHTS 6 b.g. Guillaume Tell 121–Moana (Zucchero 133§) (1982 NR 1983 14f) well beaten in minor and maiden events though is a winner over hurdles; has worn blinkers. *J. Cann.* —

BEAKER (USA) 3 ch.c. Crow 134–Tucked In (Jim J) (1982 7s⁴ 1983 10.1s² 10d³ 10.1fg 12g 12d⁴) close-coupled, quite attractive colt; placed in maiden and minor events at Windsor and Epsom (didn't come down hill well); off course almost 3 months afterwards and didn't run particularly well on his return; should stay 1½m. *P. Walwyn.* **71 d**

BEAMING ANNE 3 ch.f. The Go-Between 129–Ann's Beam (Bold and Free 118) (1982 5fg² 5fg 6g 6f 5v 5v 1983 5fg 5f 6fg) plater; no form in 1983 (blinkered final start). *J. Scallan.* —

BEAN BOY 5 ch.g. Some Hand 119–Battling 75 (Pinza 137) (1982 12f⁴ 12.3fg³ 15.8f* 12fg 15.8f* 1983 12d 12fg² 12v 12d 15fg* 14.6f² 15f* 19f 15.8f³ 15.8fg³ 18f² 16fg²) workmanlike gelding; won handicaps at Edinburgh in June and July; stays very well; acts well on firm going; blinkered last 3 outings in 1981; suitable mount for an apprentice. *D. Smith.* **69**

BEAT THE DRUM 3 b.f. Brigadier Gerard 144–Tantara (Pakistan II 84) (1982 6fg 8.5g* 7g² 1983 8s 7s³ 8v 6fg² 10f 8fg³ 7g* 8d) strong, short-legged filly; half-sister to winning hurdler Roll of Drums (by Royal Prerogative); dam won 5 times in New Zealand; cost only 720 gns at 1982 Newmarket May Sales and proved quite a bargain; beat Erin's Hope by a short head in 10-runner Red Mills Stakes at Phoenix Park in September; had run respectably most previous starts, including when 1½ lengths third of 10 behind Flame of Tara in Athasi Stakes at the Curragh, about 6 lengths sixth of 18 behind L'Attrayante in Goffs Irish 1000 Guineas on same course and 4 lengths fifth of 14 to Flame of Tara in Pretty Polly Stakes at the Curragh again; finds 6f on sharp side and stays 1¼m; acts on any going. *M. Connolly, Ireland.* **94**

BEAT THE RETREAT 2 b.g. Town and Country 124–Mrs Bacon 82 (Balliol 125) (1983 7g 7g 8g) Mar 20; 7,600Y; strong, good sort; first reported foal; dam, 2-y-o 5f winner, didn't train on; in rear in maiden and minor events, on final outing last of 5; has worn a tongue strap. *C. Horgan.* —

BEAUDELAIRE (USA) 3 ch.c. Nijinsky 138–Bitty Girl 123 (Habitat 134) **125**
(1982 5fg* 7fg* 1983 8s² 8f² 7f* 6.5fg* 6g)

Owner Robert Sangster has had several attempts at winning the Vernons Sprint Cup at Haydock, sponsored by his own company, and in 1983 he appeared to have a really strong contender in Beaudelaire who started second favourite and seemed sure to give a better account of himself than Sangster's other recent runners Jester, Miami Springs and Mofida, none of whom finished better than sixth. Beaudelaire ran badly though, struggling from halfway and trailing in last of six behind Habibti, beaten almost twenty lengths. Even at his very best he wouldn't have been up to troubling Habibti in the form she was in that day, but he most certainly should have finished closer. It is probably significant that he missed several attractive opportunities afterwards and wasn't seen out again.

Prior to the Vernons Beaudelaire had seemed to improve with virtually every race. Unbeaten in two races at Leopardstown as a two-year-old, he had been beaten narrowly by Iron Leader and Burslem respectively over a mile at Phoenix Park and the Curragh in June before reverting successfully to shorter distances in the Beeswing Stakes at Newcastle in July and the Prix Maurice de Gheest at Deauville in August. At Newcastle he readily quickened past the front-running five-year-old I'll See You when shaken up inside the last furlong and swept clear to win in good style by two and a half lengths, knocking more than a second and a half off the course record in the process. At Deauville, facing stronger opposition and starting at odds against for the first time in his career (though still favourite) he took the eye and was always going strongly once more. He took up the running a furlong and a half out and needed only to be kept up to his work to make sure, passing the post half a length ahead of the filly Maximova, with the tough four-year-olds African Joy and Pampabird a length and a half or so back in third and fourth. Beaudelaire's win maintained his trainer's fine run in France, following the successes of Caerleon, Glenstal and Solford.

Beaudelaire (USA) (ch.c. 1980)	Nijinsky (b 1967)	Northern Dancer (b 1961)	Nearctic Natalma
		Flaming Page (b 1959)	Bull Page Flaring Top
	Bitty Girl (b 1971)	Habitat (b 1966)	Sir Gaylord Little Hut
		Garvey Girl (ch 1960)	Princely Gift Tekka

As one best at distances short of a mile Beaudelaire is something of a rarity among Nijinsky's progeny, and his speed is clearly inherited from the dam's side. Bitty Girl, a sister to the high-class sprinter Hot Spark, was a very speedy two-year-old indeed, the winner of her first five races including the Queen Mary, the Molecomb and the Lowther Stakes. As a three-year-old she finished a half-length second to Bay Express in the King's Stand Stakes, and as a four-year-old she won three times at up to a mile in the United States. Beaudelaire

Prix Maurice de Gheest, Deauville—Beaudelaire accounts for strong opposition, holding on from Maximova

Mr R. E. Sangster's "Beaudelaire"

is her fourth foal and third winner; Nijit, also by Nijinsky, was a stakes-placed winner in the States and Memento, by Roberto, was a useful winner over seven furlongs in Ireland who is now at stud in Australia. Since producing Beaudelaire Bitty Girl has foaled two fillies by Northern Dancer and another by Northjet.

Beaudelaire has been sold privately and is to stand at stud in Florida. A rather short-coupled, attractive colt with a sharp action, he was a very smart performer at' his best and one capable of an excellent turn of finishing speed. Although he ran respectably over a mile on soft ground Beaudelaire showed much his best form over shorter distances and did all of his winning on firm ground. *V. O'Brien, Ireland.*

BEAU FILS 2 b.g. Crimson Beau 124–Kantado 93 (Saulingo 122) (1983 5f² 6fg² 6h³ 6g⁴) Mar 30; 8,200F, 8,000Y; quite attractive, lightly-built gelding; first produce; dam raced mainly over 5f; in frame in a variety of races, including 2¾ lengths fourth of 16 to Melaura Belle in valuable nursery at York in October; will be suited by 7f; possibly not at his best on hard ground; sweated up last 2 starts and subsequently gelded. *G. Lewis.* **82**

BEAUFORTWOOD (CAN) 2 gr.c. Caucasus 127–Dancing Angela (Dancer's Image) (1983 6s 6g 7f⁴) Apr 16; $95,000Y; compact colt; half-brother to 3 winners, notably high-class Canadian colt Le Danseur (by Lord Durham) and good Canadian stakes winner Bejilla (by Quadrangle); dam, half-sister to champion Canadian filly Square Angel, won over 5f at 2 yrs; 8 lengths fourth of 8 to Northern Tempest in £3,300 race at Sandown in July; will be better suited by 1m+; blinkered last 2 outings. *B. Hills.* **74**

BEAULAH 7 ch.g. Track Spare 125–Rippling Water 80 (Star Moss 122) (1982 NR 1983 12s 10f 12f 11.5f) poor form, including in sellers; cost 650 gns Ascot January Sales; sold 880 gns Doncaster November Sales. *M. Chapman.* **–**

BEAU NAVET 2 ch.g. Meldrum 112–Lady Loveliness (Flush Royal 127) (1983 7.6fg 10d 8f) Mar 19; 2,600 2-y-o; workmanlike gelding; half-brother to a minor winner; dam hurdler; poor form, including in a seller; stays 1¼m. *T. Bulgin.* **54**

BEAU'S GIRL 2 ch.f. Crimson Beau 124–Eilan Aigas 93 (Counsel 118) (1983 5d 6fg 6fg⁴ 7fg 7f 7d) Apr 20; 1,300Y; tall, leggy, rather narrow filly; half-sister to several winners, including useful miler Geoffrey's Sister (by Sparkler); dam won at **53**

1m and 11f; poor form in varied company, including selling; will stay 1¼m. *B. Gubby.*

BEBE HATTIE 3 ch.f. Gracious Melody 117–Tennis Girl 79 (Ennis 128) (1982   –
7f 8.2d 8s 1983 8f) sturdy filly; seems of little account. *J. Doyle.*

BECHAMEL (USA) 2 ch.f. Sauce Boat–Bold But Baffled (Bold and Brave) (1983   **87** p
6f⁴ 6fg³ 5g*) Feb 24; $100,000Y; strong, lengthy filly; half-sister to several
winners, including Amazing Love (by Advocator), a very useful stakes winner at up
to 1m; dam, half-sister to high-class 5.5f to 9f winner Baffle, ran 3 times unplaced;
beat a seemingly modest field in good style when odds on for 13-runner maiden race
at Wolverhampton in September, winning by 4 lengths from Some Would;
previously had faded in final furlong, possibly through lack of peak fitness, when in
frame in maiden race at Yarmouth (favourite) and £4,000 event at York
(co-favourite); highly regarded, and almost certainly capable of further
improvement. *L. Cumani.*

BECTIVE BABY 3 ch.f. Nebbiolo 125–Rose Princess (Princely Gift 137) (1982   **57**
5s⁴ 5f³ 5f² 5f² 6g³ 5f 5g² 6s 1983 5fg 6fg 6f³ 8f 8f 8f 6fg⁴ 6g 6fg) IR 9,000Y;
lengthy ex-Irish filly; half-sister to several winners, including fair Irish 1m to 11f
winner Welsh Steel (by Welsh Saint); dam never ran; quite useful as a 2-y-o when
trained by L. Collins in Ireland; fairly prominent in maiden races on 4 occasions in
1983; stays 6f, and doesn't settle well enough to get much further; started slowly
fifth outing; usually bandaged nowadays; didn't impress in appearance fourth and
fifth outings. *G. Huffer.*

BEDTIME 3 ch.g. Bustino 136–Sweet Hour 91 (Primera 131) (1982 NR 1983   **119**
10.1d* 10.1s* 10.5f* 14d⁴ 10.5fg*)
    Given the chance, and he probably will be one day since he is a gelding,
Bedtime could go a long way as a hurdler: he is a grand stamp of animal, big and
rangy, possessing the speed to win in more-than-useful company at a mile and a
quarter. No doubt he figures on the shopping list of most jumping trainers who
might afford him. Bedtime's immediate future would seem to be as a flat racer,
though. In just five races as a three-year-old (he wasn't seen out at two) he
developed into a tip-top handicapper, and it would be a surprise if he failed to win
more decent prizes for his present stable.
    Bedtime's racing experience has been acquired on just two courses, Windsor
and York; he began his education in relatively small events on the former, both of
which he won, before taking on much stiffer opposition in the John Smith's Magnet
Cup on the latter. The Magnet Cup, a £20,000 handicap run over ten and a half
furlongs in July, attracted a small but competitive field which included four older
horses, Farioffa, Miramar Reef, African Pearl and Lion City. Of the three-year-
olds, the public knew as little about Bedtime as any in the race, except perhaps for
Vaisseau who hadn't run since the previous season. A good deal about Bedtime had

John Smith's Magnet Cup, York—Bedtime wears down Gay Lemur (right)

to be taken on trust, not least his ability to handle the firm ground: the ground had been dead or soft at Windsor, soft certainly when he'd won easily from Beaker the second time. However, his physical appearance suggested he was well worth his place in the field. On a mark of 7-9 he started co-favourite at 7/2 with Majestic Endeavour, who was giving him 6 lb as a result of winning the fairly valuable Esal Handicap at Sandown the previous month. Three-year-olds took the first three places, but it was Gay Lemur not Majestic Endeavour who quickened away with Bedtime from the rest at the three-furlong pole; from that point the first two had the race between them, and Majestic Endeavour just stayed on for third. For such a big, inexperienced horse running on firm ground Bedtime kept amazingly straight and well balanced; he gradually wore Gay Lemur down, led inside the final furlong and won by half a length.

Bedtime, by Bustino, promised to be well suited by a longer distance, but he is out of a sprinting mare and judging by his performance in the Melrose Handicap at York five weeks later he'll never again be seen over so great a distance as a mile and three quarters, on the flat at any rate. Favourite, he finished fourth of thirteen behind Incredible Idea, beaten twenty lengths by the third horse Fighter Pilot: he ran like a non-stayer, floundering three furlongs out and finishing very tired after momentarily looking as though he'd come right through from the back of the field where he'd been settled with a lot to do, moving easily, until making the home turn. Significantly, when returned to the Magnet Cup course to contest the Fernedge Garrowby Handicap, he won decisively by three parts of a length from Elect: he managed to improve all the way to number-one spot this time after again being waited with, and he stuck on well under pressure to hold his advantage through the last furlong, edging slightly left as he did so.

		Busted		Crepello
	Bustino	(b 1963)		Sans le Sou
	(b 1971)	Ship Yard		Doutelle
Bedtime		(ch 1963)		Paving Stone
(ch. g. 1980)		Primera		My Babu
	Sweet Hour	(b 1954)		Pirette
	(br 1968)	Daylight		Princely Gift
		(br 1958)		Light of Day

Bedtime's dam Sweet Hour has had four other runners. They are Honeypot Lane (by Silly Season), a quite useful winner at up to a mile and a half; Lake Naivasha (by Blakeney), who won at a mile and a quarter annual and finished a good second in the Cheshire Oaks; Shadows Lengthen (by Star Appeal), placed over five furlongs and six furlongs as a two-year-old in her only season; and Shuteye (by Shirley Heights), the winner of a controversial one-mile maiden at Beverley as a two-year old in 1983. Sweet Hour herself won over five furlongs at York as a two-year-old; the following season she was raced only in six-furlong and seven-furlong handicaps, and was unplaced under stiff weights. The next dam was a miler out of that prolific winner producer Light of Day, the 1942 One Thousand Guineas third. There have been notable stayers in the family in fairly recent times, among them the Queen Alexandra Stakes and Prix Gladiateur winner Hickleton (out of Daylight's half-sister Fan Light) and the Northumberland Plate winner Grey God. The latter is bred on very similar lines to Bedtime, since he's by Bustino's sire Busted out of Daylight.

All things considered, Bedtime will probably stay a mile and a half; we should back him to do so. He acts on any going. He has had comparatively little taken out of him so far, and should do well as a four-year-old. *R. Hern.*

BEDWELL BOY 2 b.g. Will Somers 114§–Sweet Alyssum (Gala Performance) — (1983 5fg 6fg 7f 7fg 7g 7.6fg 7fg) Apr 6; IR 2,100F; lengthy gelding; fourth foal; dam of little account; seventh of 16 to Barry Sheene in maiden race at Leicester in September, fifth outing and only sign of ability; unseated rider after swerving badly and attempting to jump rails soon after halfway on second outing; blinkered final appearance. *N. Guest.*

BEECHWOOD SAILOR 2 b.g. Owen Dudley 121–Ma Mitte (Faristan 123) 39 (1983 7f 7f 8f 8.2g) Mar 14; 800Y; bad plater. *K. Stone.*

BEE'S DANCE 2 b.c. Dance In Time–Honey Portion 107 (Major Portion 129) 85 (1983 7fg 6g 6fg 6g*) May 29; fair sort; half-brother to numerous winners, including Irish Guinness Oaks third I've a Bee (by Sir Ivor) and smart French stayer Honeyville (by Charlottesville); dam miler; 20/1 and apprentice ridden, showed much improved form when winning 19-runner nursery at Leicester in October by 3 lengths from Simon; should be suited by 7f+. *F. Durr.*

BEE SQUARED 3 b.f. Star Appeal 133–Silesca (Silent Screen) (1982 NR 1983   –
7h⁴ 6fg 10.6g) 6,000Y, 1,800 2-y-o; third foal; half-sister to a minor winner by
Song; dam won over 7.5f at 2 yrs in France; plating-class maiden; should be suited
by 1m+. *D. Marks.*

BEFORE THE DAWN (USA) 3 b.c. Roberto 131–Lover's Quarrel (Battle   71
Joined) (1982 NR 1983 8d⁴ 11.7v² 9.4d 10fg 12g 10d² 10.2g 10g) $100,000Y;
medium-sized, compact colt; half-brother to several winners, including very smart
Girl In Love (by Lucky Debonair), a stakes winner at up to 9f; dam won California
Oaks; in frame in Wood Ditton Stakes at Newmarket and maiden races at Bath and
Beverley; ran some moderate races too; stays 1½m; sold 7,400 gns Newmarket
Autumn Sales. *B. Hills.*

BEGET 3 ro.c. Be Friendly 130–Easy to Love 90 (Infatuation 129) (1982 NR 1983   –
10.1fg 10.1fg) brother to Molecomb Stakes winner Be Easy, closely related to 5f
and 7f winner Nelski (by Skymaster) and half-brother to a winner abroad; dam 1m
to 1¼m handicapper; soundly beaten in 2 minor events won by Millfontaine at
Windsor in June; sold 675 gns Ascot July Sales. *J. Dunlop.*

BELA KUN 2 b.f. Monseigneur 127–Magyar Melody (Prince Tenderfoot 126)   –
(1983 6f 5f 5f) May 10; small, workmanlike filly; second live foal; sister to fairly
useful 3-y-o miler Hungarian Prince; dam won over 5f and 1m at 2 yrs in Ireland;
soundly beaten in maiden and minor events; got very stirred up and sweated badly
on second outing; sold 520 gns Ballsbridge December Sales. *P. Makin.*

BELDALE CONCORDE (USA) 3 b.c. Super Concorde 128–My Gal Lucky   114
(Gallant Man) (1982 5f³ 7fg* 7g⁴ 8.2fg² 8s² 8d 1983 7s⁴ 8g² 8f* 8fg) $70,000
2-y-o; rangy, attractive colt; has a free but round action; first foal; dam third once
from 10 outings; about 4½ lengths fourth of 6 behind Proclaim in £3,100 event at
Leicester in March; ran in Italy next 3 starts, finishing length second to Drumalis in
Premio Parioli (Italian 2000 Guineas) at Rome in April, winning 8-runner Premio
Nearco on same course in May (odds on, beat Okay For Sound by 2 lengths) and
finishing only seventh of 9 to Bold Run in Premio Emilio Turati at Milan in June;
probably finds 7f too sharp and will stay 1¼m; acts on any going; sent to race in
USA. *M. Jarvis.*

BELDALE CURRENT (USA) 2 b.c. Little Current–Hello Theo (Pronto) (1983   79
5s² 6f 7fg⁴) May 8; $21,000Y, $80,000 2-y-o; rather finely-made, close-coupled
colt; good mover; brother to Red Current, a stakes-placed winner at up to 1m, and
half-brother to 3 winners, including stakes winner My First Fling (by Olden
Times); dam, a sprinter, won a small stakes race; 2½ lengths second of 8 to
Altdorfer in newcomers race at Goodwood in May, best effort; beaten favourite in
Chesham Stakes at Royal Ascot (last of 13) and small race at Chester; should be
well suited by 6f+; possibly needs some give in the ground; disappointing. *M.
Jarvis.*

BELDALE LEAR (USA) 2 b.c. Majestic Light–Solabar's Finale (Funny   109
Fellow) (1983 7g² 7f² 7f* 8fg) Feb 11; $110,000 2-y-o; strong, deep-girthed colt;
good mover; first foal; dam, stakes-placed winning sprinter, is half-sister to 2
stakes winners; won 4-runner Grand Criterium International d'Ostende in August
by a length from unlucky-in-running Blushing Scribe; showed deal of promise
previously in 2 races at Newmarket, failing by only a head to catch Elegant Air in
£4,100 event and going down by a length to newcomer Raft in maiden race;
disappointed when third favourite for 9-runner William Hill Futurity at Doncaster in
October, fading to finish eighth to Alphabatim after being niggled at soon after
halfway; should be suited by 1m; yet to race on a soft surface. *M. Jarvis.*

BELDALE PROSPECT (USA) 2 b.c. New Prospect–Bouncing In (No   77
Robbery) (1983 7f 8.2f 8fg⁴) Apr 20; $23,500Y, $45,000 2-y-o; lengthy,
lightly-made colt; second foal; half-brother to stakes-winning American 3-y-o
Hotsy Totsy (by Noholme II); dam won twice at up to 1m; sire, son of Never
Bend, was smart winner from 6f to 1m; 5½ lengths fourth of 13 to Feasibility
Study in maiden race at Newcastle in October; stays 1m. *M. Jarvis.*

BEL ESPRIT 4 b.f. Sagaro 133–Esprit d'Or 86 (Jolly Jet 111) (1982 11.7f 7fg   –
11.5fg 16fg 1983 12f) dipped-backed, sparely-made filly; behind in varied company,
including selling. *T. Bulgin.*

BELFE 4 ch.f. Tachypous 128–Appian Way 89 (Romulus 129) (1982 10.6s⁴ 12g 12f   68
12g 14g² 14fg 16.5fg* 16s 16.5s 1983 16s 17.1v 20fg 18f 16.1fg² 14f 14.7f* 16.5fg²
14fg⁴ 15.8fg 16h) rather unfurnished filly; staying handicapper; made virtually all
to win 4-runner event at Redcar in July; ran creditably next time but was below
form afterwards; acts well on fast ground; suited by forcing tactics; sold 10,500
gns Newmarket December Sales. *R. Hollinshead.*

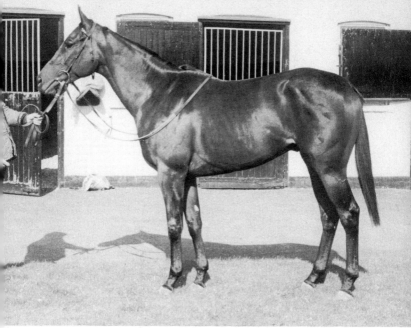

Beldale Bloodstock Investments Ltd's "Beldale Lear"

BELINDA BROWN 3 br.f. Legal Eagle 126–Port Meadow 83 (Runnymede 123)   **81 d**
(1982 5g* 5g⁴ 5f³ 6d⁴ 5fg 5s 5g 1983 5g² 6v 5f 6f⁴ 6f 5g 5f⁴ 5g 5d) smallish,
workmanlike filly; sprint handicapper; stays 6f; well beaten when blinkered eighth
outing. *T. Barron.*

BELLAMAY 2 ch.f. Porto Bello 118–Salvo of Conkers 79 (Salvo 129) (1983 5d   **46**
5d 5.1f 5f 5f 6fg) May 13; 800Y; plain filly; poor plater; blinkered third to fifth
outings; dead. *A. Cawley.*

BELLAMONTI 3 gr.c. Godswalk 130–Marta 87 (Aureole 132) (1982 5g 5fg 5g⁴   **60**
6fg 1983 6v 10.1fg² 10f² 10f⁴ 11fg⁴ 10f³ 10.6f³) close-coupled, quite attractive
colt; runner-up in handicap at Windsor and maiden race at Folkestone in June;
gives impression he'll be suited by 1½m; acts on firm going; blinkered final start;
sold 6,400 gns Newmarket September Sales. *B. Hills.*

BELLAMUSE (USA) 3 ch.g. Apalachee 137–Colinear (Cohoes) (1982 NR 1983   **72**
10s 12d 14g 14g 16.5f* 16fg* 16g) $65,000Y, 5,000 2-y-o; workmanlike gelding;
half-brother to 2 good winners by Irish Castle, including Richmond Stakes winner
Castle Green and very smart 6f to 1¼m winner Hardgreen; dam won 6f claiming
race; showed himself well suited by a thorough test of stamina when winning
handicaps at Redcar in September and Lingfield in October, latter by ¾ length from
The Pawn; never on terms final outing however; acts on firm going. *E. Eldin.*

BELLARIBO 3 ch.f. Porto Bello 118–Dorriba (Ribero 126) (1982 6fg 6f 7.6v 1983   **–**
12g 8f) small, lengthy filly; in rear in varied races, including a claimer when
blinkered on final start. *R. Simpson.*

BELLARY 2 gr.f. Bellypha 130–Manoline (Vieux Manoir 132) (1983 6f) May 19;   **–**
31,000F, 15,000Y; half-sister to fairly useful miler Ramannolie (by Caro); dam
unraced half-sister to Prix Morny winner Princeline; out of first 10 of 20 in maiden
race at Windsor in July; sold NBA 4,600 gns Newmarket Autumn Sales. *P. Cole.*

BELLA TRAVAILLE 5 b.m. Workboy 123–Thorganby Bella (Porto Bello 118)   57
(1982 5fg 5fg 5f 5f² 5fg² 5fg² 5.1g⁴ 7f 5f² 5fg* 6fg 5g² 6d 5d 5g 5.8f 5fg 5d 5g 1983
5g 5d* 5fg³ 5f³ 5.1fg² 5f* 5f² 5f² 5.6f* 5fg² 5f 5g 5g) lengthy mare; sprint
handicapper; won at Hamilton in May and Catterick (apprentices) and Doncaster
in July; best at distances short of 6f; probably acts on any going; occasionally
blinkered and has also worn hood; good mount for an apprentice; has won when
sweating up; consistent. *R. Hobson.*

BELLAURA 2 b.f. Monsanto 121–Sylvan Path 69 (Sovereign Path 125)   (1983 5d   53
5fg 5f 5f 5f 5g) May 12; 2,000Y; narrow filly; half-sister to 2 winning platers; dam
won over 2m; modest plater; bred to need 7f+. *E. Eldin*

BELLEKINO 2 b.f. Relkino 131–Miss Wrekin 97 (Pardao 120)   (1983 6fg 7fg 8g 9g   –
7s) Apr 28; 3,600Y; rather lightly-made, fair sort; half-sister to several winners,
including useful stayer Peter Wrekin and useful 1½m winner Lakin (both by Lauso)
and 7f to 13f winner Jamestino (by Bustino); dam 2-y-o 5f winner; poor maiden. *R.
Hollinshead.*

BELLE VUE 10 b.g. Track Spare 125–Royal Camp 91 (Sovereign Path 125)   (1982   43
8f 7f 10d 7.6fg 8fg 8f³ 8f² 8.2g 8fg 12fg³ 8fg 10d 10.2d⁴ 1983 10.6s 10d 10g⁴ 10f³ 8f
10fg² 10h 10.6fg 10f 10f 10f 10s 10.2g 11fg 10g³) neat gelding; plater; stays at least
1¼m; acts on any going; used to wear blinkers; suitable mount for an
inexperienced rider. *R. Hollinshead.*

BELLS OF ST MARTIN 3 b.f. Martinmas 128–Trackalady 96 (Track Spare   74 d
125)   (1982 5g* 5g⁴ 5fg³ 5d³ 6s 6s 1983 7f 6d⁴ 5.8fg 6fg 6fg 7fg) leggy filly;
seemed to run well when fourth of 9 behind Overtrick in minor event at Brighton in
September but didn't reproduce the form, including when dropped to selling
company; stays 6f (last both outings over 7f); often apprentice ridden. *R. Laing.*

BELOW THE LINE 2 ch.c. Music Boy 124–Visitation 84 (Tarqogan 125)   (1983   87
6g⁴ 6g) Apr 17; 6,800Y; strong, compact colt; brother to 3 winners, including
3-y-o 6f and 7f winner King of Rock, and half-brother to a winner; dam stayed 1½m;
showed up well in useful maiden company, finishing 5¾ lengths fourth of 13 to
Double Schwartz in £5,300 event at York in August and 7¾ lengths fifth of 19 to
New Dimension at Goodwood in September; promises to stay 7f; should win at one
of the smaller meetings. *K. Brassey.*

BELROSE 4 ch.f. Music Boy 124–Red Form (Reform 132)   (1982 6s³ 5g³ 5fg⁴ 6g   –
1983 5g 6s 7f) fair sort; plater; stays 6f. *S. Norton.*

BELTURBET BRIDGE 3 b.c. Stradavinsky 121–Sandolett (Nimbus 130)   (1982   –
7d 7fg 1983 8d 8s 8.3s 10.2g 10.1fg 8fg) useful-looking colt, but is only a poor
plater; blinkered final start. *D. H. Jones*

BELVOIR PATROL 2 b.c. Raga Navarro 119–Suir (Palestine 133)   (1983 6g 6fg   64
8f 8d) June 1; IR 780F (privately), 1,400Y; big, rangy colt; second produce; dam
won 2m bumpers race on a disqualification; 4¾ lengths seventh of 23 finishers
behind Tophams Taverns in maiden auction event at Redcar in September, third
outing and only indication of merit; acts on firm going. *J. Toller.*

BELVOIR ROSE 5 b.m. Dubassoff–Rothwell Rose (Henry the Seventh 125)   –
(1982 NR 1983 8g 5f 6fg) poor maiden. *H. O'Neill.*

BE MY DARLING 3 b.f. Windjammer (USA)–Kilcurley Lass (Huntercombe   82
133)   (1982 5d 6fg 6fg³ 5s⁴ 1983 6d* 6d³ 8.5g² 8f 7f 10g² 8fg 10g³ 10fg) quite an
attractive filly; 4-length winner of handicap at Brighton in April; ran best
subsequent races when second to Sedra in Ebbisham Handicap at Epsom in June
and Intercraft Fillies Stakes at Kempton in September, and when unlucky third to
Folly Hill in handicap at Sandown in October; suited by 1¼m; probably acts on any
going; not particularly consistent. *G. Lewis.*

BE MY LADY 3 ch.f. Be My Guest 126–Image Intensifier (Dancer's Image) (1982   –
7g 1983 9v 9f4 10fg 7f 8g 7.6d) tall filly; good mover; little worthwhile form,
although showed a bit of promise over 9f on second outing; started slowly fourth
outing; sometimes bandaged in front; trained until after third start by P. Haslam.
G. Lewis.

BE MY NATIVE (USA) 4 br.c. Our Native–Witchy Woman (Strate Stuff)   (1982 122
10f² 10.5f³ 10v* 9fg³ 10fg 10.5fg 10f² 10s³ 12f 1983 9d 10v 12d* 12f³ 12fg 10g 10fg)
   Be My Native chose the right day on which to run up to his best as a
four-year-old. Successful in the Prix La Force and a fine second in the Budweiser
Million in 1982, he lined up for the Coronation Cup at Epsom in June having run
decidedly modestly in the Earl of Sefton Stakes at Newmarket and the Westbury
Stakes at Sandown on his first two starts, finishing a long way behind Ivano each
time despite looking reasonably fit. According to his trainer, Be My Native's

110

problems resulted from a thin skin which meant he had suffered badly from the poor weather in the spring, and the fact he was backed from 14/1 to 8/1 at Epsom indicated that his stable at least did not lack confidence in his ability to return to top form.

In terms of prestige the Coronation Cup is second to only the King George VI and Queen Elizabeth Diamond Stakes in the list of British mile-and-a-half races open to horses above the age of three, but as often as not it has a small field, averaging just six per year since its institution in 1902. The 1983 edition of the event suffered a double blow on the day with the defection of All Along and Time Charter, the latter of whom had bruised a foot, and the six runners left consisted of Be My Native and his ex-Australian stable-companion My Sir Avon, good winners in Electric, Diamond Shoal and Old Country, and Lafontaine, usually a front runner. With the last-named held up for once Diamond Shoal became an uncomfortable pacemaker, setting a modest gallop while Piggott, probably scarcely able to believe his luck, settled Be My Native in last place. Diamond Shoal quickened the pace from halfway but by this time the damage had been done as far as he was concerned; coming down Tattenham Hill there was not much more than six lengths between first and last with Be My Native seemingly travelling extremely smoothly in fifth. Diamond Shoal and his closest pursuers Old Country and My Sir Avon soon came under pressure in the straight, and immediately Piggott asked Be My Native to improve the colt did so in great fashion, going through a gap towards the rails then accelerating into a lead of over a length about a furlong out. Thereafter he always looked the winner despite Electric's strenuous efforts to reduce the deficit and at the line he had three parts of a length to spare over the latter with Old Country and Diamond Shoal next to finish. We gained the impression that on a more orthodox track Electric, who had never looked happy on the course and had been niggled at a long way out, would probably have won, but be that as it may Be My Native was a worthy winner by virtue of the fact that he alone produced a turn of foot when necessary.

For all the good he did during the remainder of the season Be My Native might as well have concluded his campaign with the Coronation Cup, or with Royal Ascot

Coronation Cup, Epsom—Be My Native keeps on strongly to beat Electric (left)

Mr K. Hsu's "Be My Native"

at the latest. His next start at least saw his gaining a place in the Hardwicke Stakes, albeit a long way behind Stanerra and Electric after being easily outpaced over the last two furlongs, but in his three subsequent races he managed to finish ahead of only five out of forty-one opponents. Ninth of eleven in the Princess of Wales's Stakes at Newmarket and eleventh of fourteen in the Budweiser Million at Arlington Park, he ran miserably when a 50/1-shot for the Dubai Champion Stakes at Newmarket again on his final start, ending up tailed-off last of nineteen after dropping out quickly in the last quarter mile. Try as we might we cannot think of a satisfactory explanation for Be My Native's in-and-out form and are forced to conclude that game as he was he simply lacked the consistency one likes to see in a horse of his ability. He will be standing at the Ballylinch Stud in Ireland in 1984 at IR £3,500.

Be My Native (USA) (br.c. 1979)	Our Native (b or br 1970)	Exclusive Native (ch 1965)	Raise A Native
			Exclusive
		Our Jackie (gr 1964)	Crafty Admiral
			Rakahanga
	Witchy Woman (ch 1972)	Strate Stuff (ch 1965)	Noholme II
			Lady Vale
		Witchy Norma (ch 1967)	Crimson Satan
			Tomratta

Be My Native, the second foal of the sprinter Witchy Woman, cost 45,000 dollars at the 1980 Keeneland September Sale and has repaid the investment handsomely. Since foaling him his dam has produced colts by Full Out and Master Derby and fillies by Plum Bold and Be My Native's sire Our Native; the Master Derby colt, named Master Wit, won over seven furlongs at Leicester for Cecil during 1983. The next two dams, neither of whom raced, foaled a total of seven fairly ordinary winners between them, and the only other good-class performer from the family in recent years was Tomratta's brother Chompion, successful fourteen times in the States with earnings of over 600,000 dollars.

A neat, attractive colt with a look of quality, Be My Native is a good walker with a fluent though slightly round action. Blinkered once at two, he stayed a mile and a half and acted on any going while always giving the impression some give in the ground suited him ideally. *R. Armstrong.*

BE MY PRINCESS 3 b.f. Try My Best 130–Mare D'Erba (Habitat 134) (1982 7g 6g 1983 7v 7fg 6fg⁴ 7f 6f²) fair sort; in frame in maiden event at Lingfield and handicap at Hamilton in summer; should stay 1m. *P. Haslam.*   **64**

BE MY QUEEN 2 ch.f. Be My Guest 126–Tulalanee (Habitat 134) (1983 6fg⁴) Apr 15; 56,000Y; fair sort; second foal; sister to disqualified 3-y-o middle-distance winner Guess Who; dam, half-sister to Derby runner-up Cavo Doro, showed only a little ability; 20/1, always prominent and wasn't knocked about when 1¾ lengths fourth of 12 to Rappa Tap Tap in Blue Seal Stakes at Ascot in September; will do better over longer distances. *M. Jarvis.*   **84 p**

BE MY VALENTINE 2 ch.f. Be My Guest 126–Red Laser 95 (Red God 128§) (1983 5g* 5f*) Feb 14; 64,000Y; neat, sharp, active sort; has sharp action; half-sister to fairly useful sprinters Regal Ray and Gamblers Dream (both by Prince Regent) and to a winner in France; dam 5f sprinter and closely related to very speedy Ruby Laser; quickly asserted her superiority entering final furlong when landing the odds by 4 lengths from Rizla Blue in maiden race at Newmarket in April; looking very fit despite a long absence, ran on most gamely to pip Brave Advance (originally deemed to have dead-heated but was declared outright winner a week later) in 9-runner St Hugh's Stakes at Newbury 4 months later; will probably stay 6f; acts on firm going; sent to USA. *H. Cecil.*   **98**

BE MY WINGS 2 ch.c. Be My Guest 126–Wingau 70 (Hard to Beat 132) (1983 6fg 7g) Mar 18; 28,000F; big, workmanlike colt; first foal; dam middle-distance handicapper; in rear in October maiden races at Folkestone and Leicester. *G. Lewis.*   **–**

BENGAL LANCER 3 b.g. Mandrake Major 122–Rose Petite 66 (Negotiation) (1982 7fg 6s 8s 8d 1983 7f 12fg 8f 9f 8.2s) neat gelding; poor plater; by no means sure to stay 1½m; sold 300 gns Doncaster November Sales. *Miss L. Siddall.*   **–**

BEN JARROW 4 ch.c. Roman Warrior 132–Shady Desire 88 (Meldrum 112) (1982 6s³ 7g 6f 6f* 5f⁴ 6fg³ 6f² 6g 5fg² 6f 6fg* 7fg² 6fg 7f* 6d⁴ 7g 7f* 6g 7s 6s⁴ 7d 1983 6s 6s 7g 6fg² 6f 6f* 6f 8fg 7f 8fg) big, workmanlike colt; good walker; won handicap at Pontefract in June; suited by 7f but has yet to show he stays 1m; acts on any going but is ideally suited by top-of-the-ground; usually wears blinkers; sometimes bandaged; has been ridden by lad in paddock; successful 3 times at Redcar. *T. Fairhurst.*   **78 d**

BENJEYA 3 br.g. Golden Mallard 103–Dearon II (Ron 103) (1982 6fg 1983 7f 5g 6d 7.6d) fair sort; little worthwhile form, but hasn't run in a seller. *J. O'Donoghue.*   **–**

St Hugh's Stakes, Newbury—Be My Valentine runs on gamely to pip Brave Advance (rails)

BEN'S BIRDIE 3 ch.g. Track Spare 125–Gold Topaz 76 (Goldhill 125) (1982 6g **67** 8.2s⁴ 1983 8s 12s³ 10v² 9g² 11d* 10.2f 10f⁴ 10f 12d* 10g⁴ 11g³ 12.2g⁴ 10g) plain gelding; successful in handicaps at Ayr in June (showed a good turn of foot in a slowly-run race) and Wolverhampton in September (apprentice event); suited by 1½m; acts on any going, but is well suited by some give underfoot. *M. Tompkins.*

BENTELER 3 b.g. Bay Express 132–Green Chartreuse 91 (French Beige 127) **–** (1982 NR 1983 7fg 6f) 650Y; half-brother to three winners, notably Middle Park winner and 2000 Guineas second Mattaboy (by Music Boy); dam won over 5f and 7f at 2 yrs; bandaged when tailed-off last at Newmarket and Yarmouth (blinkered). *G. Blum.*

BENTY HEATH 2 br.g. Home Guard 129–Vestina 85 (Run The Gantlet) (1983 **–** 7f) May 3; 5,400Y; rangy gelding; first living foal; dam, winner over 7f and 1¼m, is daughter of Irish 1000 Guineas winner Cloonagh; unquoted and backward, never in hunt in £3,800 event won by Raft at Salisbury in August. *J. Bethell.*

BENZ 2 b.c. Free State 125–Irish Isle 67 (Realm 129) (1983 6g* 6fg* 6s³ 6fg² 7fg) **99** Mar 29; 8,800Y; lengthy colt; poor mover; first foal; dam 1m winner; successful in maiden race at Haydock in July and nursery (beating Throne of Glory a neck after being hampered early on) on same course in August; should stay 1m; seems to act on any going. *M. H. Easterby.*

BE ON TIME 3 b.g. Be My Guest 126–Deep Brook (Wolver Hollow 126) (1982 7f **59** 7fg 8s 1983 7.6v³ 8f⁴ 8h³ 8.2f² 8f 8h⁴) quite attractive gelding; probably ran best races when placed in apprentice event at Bath and handicap at Nottingham in July; will be suited by 1¼m; seems well suited by top-of-the-ground conditions; tends to sweat up; rather disappointing fifth start and ran in snatches on his last. *P. Walwyn.*

BERGERAC 3 ch.g. Sweet Revenge 129–Lady Whistler (Whistling Wind 123) **57** (1982 6fg 6g 6g⁴ 6f 7fg 6g³ 1983 8d² 11v 10s) big gelding; second in seller at Doncaster in March; ran in non-sellers afterwards; probably stays 1¼m; needs some give in the ground. *J. Holt.*

BERKELEY COURT 2 b.f. Mummy's Pet 125–Karmala (Tanerko 134) (1983 **102** 4.5g 6fg 5.5fg⁴ 6.5fg⁴ 8g³ 8fg* 8fg* 8s 8g³ 6.5g 8d³) Apr 19; 6,000F, IR 10,500Y; fifth foal; half-sister to 3-y-o 7f winner Princess Zita (by Manado); dam placed at up to 12.5f in French Provinces; won minor event at Clairefontaine and Prix Herod at Evry within 4 days in mid-season (by 6 lengths on former occasion); later ran respectably in pattern company when 4½ lengths third to Mendez in Prix des Chenes at Longchamp and 1½ lengths third to Sly Moon in Premio Dormello at San Siro; improved with distance and is well suited by 1m; acts on any going. *R. Collet, France.*

BERNARD SUNLEY (USA) 4 ch.c. Rainy Lake–Charling (Charabanc) (1982 **78** 6g* 6fg⁴ 6g 5d³ 6fg 6v² 6d⁴ 6s 1983 6v 6v 5.8s 5g 6fg⁴ 5fg* 5f* 5fg 5f 5d 5fg³) strong, good-bodied colt; poor mover; won handicaps at Warwick and Hamilton in July; stays 6f; acts on any going; has run respectably for an apprentice; blinkered nowadays; below form on eighth outing and ran badly on ninth. *G. Hunter.*

BERRY VILLE 2 ch.c. Silly Season 127–Fair Louise 72 (Blakeney 126) (1983 6f³ **62** 6f 5f 7f) strong, workmanlike colt; second foal; dam 1½m winner; ran well in seller on debut, but showed little in non-sellers subsequently; should stay 1¼m; worth noting in plating company. *M. W. Easterby.*

BERTHA 3 ch.f. Filiberto 123–Petchora 64 (Le Haar 126) (1982 6fg 7g 1983 10g **75** 9f³ 10.1fg³ 10d 10g³ 10.6s³ 10f* 12fg) fair sort; third 4 times before holding on by a head from Chic Boutique in handicap at Redcar in October; stays 1¼m well; acts on any going. *R. Baker.*

BERTHON GOLD 3 b.g. Averof 123–Buff Beauty 92 (Mossborough 126) (1982 **–** 5g 5f 1983 8g) of little account; sold 625 gns Ascot July Sales. *M. Bradley.*

BERTIDA 5 b.m. Porto Bello 118–Miss Bubbly 78 (Track Spare 125) (1982 8.2g² **76** 8fg 10f* 10d* 10.2g³ 8g* 1983 8fg 10f 11.5g⁴ 9d* 11fg³ 10.2fg) useful sort; quite a modest handicapper; won at Wolverhampton in October; stays 11f; acts on any going; suitable mount for an apprentice; sold 5,000 gns Newmarket December Sales. *E. Eldin.*

BERTORELLA 2 ch.f. Import 127–Falcrello 51 (Falcon 131) (1983 6fg 6g 6fg) **65** Mar 28; sturdy filly; second foal; sister to useful 3-y-o Wiki Wiki Wheels, a winner at up to 7f; dam won 11f seller; 7 lengths fifth of 18 to Real Silver in minor event at Pontefract in October, second outing. *S. Pritchard-Gordon.*

BERYLS DREAM 2 ch.f. Garda's Revenge 119–Trigonella (Balliol 125) (1983 5v **77** 5s 5d³ 6d² 5fg 5fg 5g³ 6fg⁴ 7g³ 6g⁴ 6g² 6g) Apr 9; IR 1,600F, 900Y; fair sort;

second foal; dam never ran; quite a moderate filly; stays 7f; acts on a firm and a soft surface. *N. Guest.*

BESPOKE 2 ch.g. Relkino 131–Hors Serie 103 (Vaguely Noble 140) (1983 7f 7g³ **83** 8g⁴ 8.2fg) Apr 7; useful-looking gelding; fourth foal; half-brother to useful 1978 2-y-o 5f winner St Hubert (by Derring-Do); dam stayed 1½m; in frame in maiden race at Leicester and minor event at Bath in the autumn; should stay 1½m. *R. Hern.*

BESSACARR BOY 2 b.g. Ahonoora 122–Falcade (Falcon 131) (1983 7f) Apr — 22; IR 4,800Y; rangy gelding with scope; half-brother to 2 winners, including fairly useful 1977 2-y-o 6f and 7f winner Badsworth Boy (by Will Hays), subsequently a top-class chaser; dam ran only at 2 yrs; 15 lengths sixth of 9 behind Meig in maiden event at Wolverhampton in June; subsequently gelded. *J. Berry.*

BEST BIDDER 3 b.f. Auction Ring 123–Storming Finish (Arctic Storm 134) **61** (1982 5fg 5fg⁴ 5fg³ 5fg 5g 5g* 5d 5s⁴ 1983 5s 6v* 6d 6s 6fg 6g² 6f⁴ 6f³ 6fg⁴ 5g⁴ 6f 6s 5g 6s) neat, sturdy filly; won handicap at Haydock in April and ran creditably on occasions afterwards; suited by 6f; acts on any going; dwelt tenth outing. *R. Hollinshead.*

BEST LADY 2 b.f. Try My Best 130–Sandra II (Le Haar 126) (1983 5d) Jan 20; — 24,000Y; small, quite attractive, chunky filly; half-sister to 3 winners, including fair miler Fandangle (by Gay Fandango); dam placed over 1m at 2 yrs in France; second favourite, disputed lead until weakening after 3f in maiden race at Sandown in May. *M. Jarvis.*

BEST VENTURE 2 b. or br.c. Derrylin 115–Skipton (Breton 130) (1983 5f) Mar — 20; 4,700F, 640Y; third living produce; dam never ran; last of 8 in seller at Beverley in June. *D. Garraton.*

BE THERE BABY 2 b.f. The Brianstan 128–Jackyda 71 (Royal Palm 131) (1983 **84** 5g³ 5f² 6fg² 5s*) Jan 20; 5,400F; smallish, well-made filly; half-sister to several winners, including useful sprinter Overtrick (by Great Nephew); won 12-runner nursery at Haydock in October by a head from Lak Lustre; best form at 5f; acts on firm going but is evidently better on soft; sold Mrs G. Forbes 13,000 gns Newmarket Autumn Sales. *J. W. Watts.*

BETH OF HOUNDHILL 3 b.f. Filiberto 123–Teenager 71 (Never Say Die 137) — (1982 5g 7fg 6s 1983 12fg 12.2f 12f) leggy, lightly-made filly; in rear in varied company, 4 times last; looks temperamental. *T. Taylor.*

BETHSITA 3 b.f. Balidar 133–Takarabune 72 (Martinmas 128) (1982 NR 1983 **68** 7.6v 7d³ 7fg² 6f 7.6d) 3,700Y; quite a well-made filly; first foal; dam 1¼m winner; placed in maiden race at Sandown in May and fairly weakly-contested minor event at Salisbury in June; off course 2½ months afterwards; will stay 1m. *K. Cunningham-Brown.*

BETSEY SHANNON 3 b.f. Hittite Glory 125–Skewy Bay 86 (Tamerlane 128) — (1982 7f 6g 6d 8s 1983 10v 8s 6g⁴ 6v 6f) plain filly; well beaten in sellers on occasions; sold 700 gns Ascot 2nd June Sales. *D. Morley.*

BETSY BAY (FR) 2 b.f. Bellypha 130–La Menandiere (Roi Dagobert 128) (1983 **107** 6s³ 6fg³ 5g² 6fg* 6g* 7.3d*) Jan 30; strong, lengthy, attractive filly; third re-ported foal; dam plating-class French maiden; improved with her races, winning her last 3, maiden at Nottingham, minor event at York and 14-runner Rochford Thompson Newbury Stakes (beating Calaloo Sioux by 1½ lengths), in space of 3 weeks during the late autumn; will stay 1m; game and genuine. *M. Jarvis.*

BETTABET GERAGHTY 5 b.g. Blue Cashmere 129–Piccadilly Etta 76 **74 §** (Floribunda 136) (1982 6f 6fg³ 6f 6f* 6fg 6f⁴ 6g 6f* 6g⁴ 6d 6d 6fg 7f² 6f 1983 6v* 6v 7d 6fg* 5f³ 6f 6d 6g 7g) neat, strong gelding; has a fair amount of ability when in the mood to produce it but is most unreliable; won handicaps at Nottingham (made all) in April, and Hamilton (apprentices) in July; stays 7f; acts on any going; usually blinkered; trained by G. Huffer first 7 starts. *Miss S. Hall.*

BETTER BID 3 b. or br.c. Auction Ring 123–Wigeon 80 (Divine Gift 127) (1982 — 5fg 6g 7fg 7f 6g 6fg 6s 8s 1983 10g 12fg) leggy, good-topped colt; little worthwhile form, including in sellers; changed hands 650 gns Ascot 2nd June Sales. *T. Kersey.*

BETTER PORTION 4 ch.g. Music Boy 124–Shirwani 77 (Major Portion 129) **71** (1982 7d 8g 7fg 7fg 7s 6s 6v 1983 8s 8s² 6g 7s² 8g 9g 8f 6.3f 6d 9g 7g² 9g² 8s) quite a well-made ex-English gelding; runner-up in 4 handicaps at Phoenix Park; behind in Royal Hunt Cup at Royal Ascot on seventh start; has run creditably for an apprentice; sometimes taken early to post; trained most of season by P. Mullins. *T. Casey, Ireland.*

BETTYKNOWES 5 b.g. Satingo 129–Djimbaran Bay (Le Levanstell 122) (1982   **71**
10fg 10d² 10f* 12g 10g 10s 1983 12.2v 10v² 10v⁴ 10g) lengthy, workmanlike
gelding; 3 lengths second to easy winner Cannon King in City and Suburban
Handicap at Epsom in April; possibly doesn't stay 1½m; acts on any going; has
twice been blinkered; sold to S. Pattemore 7,000 gns Ascot May Sales. *A.
Ingham.*

BEV'S GIRL 3 gr.f. Beatic–Enniris Wood (Precipice Wood 123) (1982 NR 1983   –
7d 7.2fg 10.4fg 8.2fg 9fg 8fg) plain filly; third foal; dam never ran; no worthwhile
form, including in a seller on final start (blinkered). *M. James.*

BEZARA (USA) 2 b.c. Barrera–Alan's Princess (Distinctive) (1983 6g 5fg⁴ 6fg*   **80**
5fg) Mar 22; $37,000Y; big, strong colt; second foal; dam, winner of 7 sprint
claiming races, is half-sister to very useful British performers Bass Rock and St
Puckle; won 12-runner maiden race at Folkestone in October; probably found 5f too
sharp when behind in nursery at Newmarket later in month; a grand type who will
prove his Newmarket form all wrong when returned to 6f or more. *J. Sutcliffe.*

BHAIBUNDI CHEWUNJA 4 b.g. Spanish Gold 101–Pensong 84 (Pendragon)   –
(1982 8f 9.4f 12f 10d 12g 13.8f⁴ 10f 13.8f⁴ 12s⁴ 13.8d* 12s³ 1983 15.8d 12.3fg 10fg
12f) lightly-made, narrow gelding; plater; stays 1¾m; best with some give in the
ground; blinkered once; has run respectably for an apprentice; sold 1,300 gns
Doncaster August Sales. *J. Wilson.*

BHARAT 3 br.g. Ballymore 123–Alcidette 110 (Alcide 136) (1982 NR 1983 12v   –
14f) IR 15,500Y; well-made gelding; second foal; brother to Irish middle-distance
stayer Allorette; dam very useful at up to 1½m in Ireland; slowly away when
soundly beaten in maiden races at Folkestone in May and Sandown in July; sold
1,450 gns Ascot Sales later in July. *J. Sutcliffe.*

BIBI BELLE 3 ch.f. Morston 125–Parmesh 105 (Home Guard 129) (1982 7s 1983   –
7.2fg 6f) lightly-made filly; little worthwhile form in maiden events. *G. Huffer.*

BIC CRYSTAL 2 b.f. Hittite Glory 125–Jebs Junior (Huntercombe 133) (1983   –
5fg 5g 6fg) Apr 23; second foal; dam unraced granddaughter of Gimcrack winner
Be Careful; little worthwhile form in late-season maiden events. *G. Balding.*

BICKERSTAFFE 2 br.g. Workboy 123–Siciliana 77 (Sicilian Prince 126) (1983   **60 §**
5d 5d 6f⁴ 6f² 7f³ 6f 7f 7.2fg 5f 8fg) May 27; 450Y; fair sort; good walker;
half-brother to a winning plater and a winning hurdler; dam stayer; ran second
in maiden auction event at Nottingham in June, but was basically
disappointing; best form at 6f; acts on firm going; blinkered 3 of his last 4 starts;
one to be wary of. *M. W. Easterby.*

BID AGAIN 3 b.c. Auction Ring 123–Another Flutter 75 (Credo 123) (1982 5fg³   **108**
5fg* 6f* 5fg² 6f* 6d³ 6d² 1983 7g* 6d 7f⁴ 7.6fg) neat, good-looking colt;
extremely good mover; put up an excellent performance under top-weight when
beating Travelguard by ¾ length in £8,300 Ward Hill Handicap at Newmarket in
April, getting up in last 50 yards after having to wait for an opening; ran another
good race when less than 5 lengths fourth of 13 behind Tecorno in Jersey Stakes at
Royal Ascot in June (looked in tremendous shape) but finished last of 6 to Lyphard's
Special in valuable race at Lingfield in July; suited by 7f; well suited by
top-of-the-ground conditions and has yet to race on really soft going; sent to race in
USA. *M. Stoute.*

BIDDABLE 4 b.g. Auction Ring 123–Imperial Levee (Levmoss 133) (1982 7g 6f   **43**
5fg³ 5f 6d 5fg 6f⁴ 5fg 6f 6g 6g 6s³ 6s⁴ 1983 6s 6v 7v 8g 6s 6f 7f³ 8f 7g) fair sort;
poor walker; plater; stays 7f; acts on any going; sold 1,050 gns Ascot November
Sales. *W. Elsey.*

BIDDOUR 2 b.f. Bold Lad (Ire) 133–Witch of Endor 80 (Matador 131) (1983 6g 6f   **79 ?**
5g* 5g) Apr 4; 22,000Y; strong, good sort; half-sister to 4 winners here and
abroad, including 1m to 1¾m winner High Old Time (by Mount Hagen); dam won
over 9f; didn't impress on way down but ran out a decisive winner of 20-runner
minor race at Catterick in September, quickening clear 2f out to beat Rare Gal 2½
lengths; never going well after starting slowly when odds on for minor event at
Edinburgh the following month; should stay 6f. *A. Stewart.*

BID HIGH 2 b.f. Auction Ring 123–Doushiska 78 (Hornbeam 130) (1983 7g) Apr   – p
20; lengthy, light-framed filly; half-sister to several winners, including very useful
7f and 10.5f winner Bozovici (by Queen's Hussar) and very useful 1m to 13f winner
Serge Lifar (by Lyphard); dam won at 1½m; unquoted, chased leaders to past
halfway and wasn't disgraced behind stable-companion Mahogany in 21-runner
£4,600 event at Newbury in September; likely to improve. *C. Nelson.*

BIDIVERA 2 b.f. Auction Ring 123–Veronica Heron 79 (Crooner 119) (1983 6fg)   – p
Feb 14; 16,500Y; third foal; sister to 3-y-o Delta Lad; dam middle-distance winner;

weak in the market, staying-on seventh of 22 behind Tender Moon in maiden race at Leicester in October; should do better. *Sir Mark Prescott.*

BIEN NOBLE (ITY)   3 ch.f. Mannsfeld 125–Brigitte D'Assche (Clouet 113) (1982 NR 1983 8.2fg 9f 10s) workmanlike filly; half-sister to Italian winner Berta Filava (by Toulouse Lautrec); dam unraced half-sister to smart French 1m and 1¼m winner Brustolon; behind in maiden and minor races. *E. Incisa.*   —

BIG-ED   4 ch.c. Sparkler 130–Ours 76 (Yours 125) (1982 7g 7f 8fg 12d* 12f² 10fg³ 12fg⁴ 14fg 14g 16g 14g 1983 13v* 14s⁴ 16g 12v 12d³ 12g 12g) tall colt; good walker; decisively won amateur riders race at Nottingham in April; stays 13f; acts on any going; suitable mount for an inexperienced rider. *R. Hollinshead.*   59

BIGEE   2 ch.c. Windjammer (USA)–White Shoes (Tiepolo II 121) (1983 6g 7fg 10fg) May 21; good-topped colt; fifth foal; dam never ran; behind in autumn maiden races. *D. Oughton.*   —

BIG JAY TEE (USA)   2 ch.c. Big John Taylor–Miss San-Jo (Amarullah) (1983 6f 7g) May 28; $14,000Y; well-made colt; half-brother to several winners, including smart 1975 staying 2-y-o Native Goal (by Exclusive Native); dam won at up to 1m, including claiming events; sire smart stakes winner from 6f to 9f; in rear in maiden races at Epsom in August and Leicester in September; sold 1,600 gns Ascot October Sales. *J. Sutcliffe.*   —

BIG LAND   4 ch.c. Habitat 134–Bay Triumph (Canisbay 120) (1982 8g 7f³ 7f³ 9f³ 8g⁴ 10f 8f 8fg 7fg² 7f² 6d³ 6g 6f³ 6g 6s 1983 7fg 6f² 7f 6fg 7f 10h 8fg) neat colt; poor walker and mover; best at up to 7f; seems to act on any going; usually blinkered nowadays; has run respectably for an apprentice. *Mrs N. Macauley.*   57 d

BIG OAR (USA)   3 b. or br.c. Big Spruce–Bend an Oar (Never Bend) (1982 NR 1983 9v³ 8.2s* 8s 10fg 10f³ 12f² 14fg³ 14f²) big colt; half-brother to several winners, including fairly useful 6f and 7f winner Miss Taymore (by Sham); dam won 3 times at up to 6f; apprentice ridden when winning maiden race at Hamilton in April; placed 4 times afterwards, including in amateur riders race and a ladies event; suited by 1¾m; acts on any going; has worn bandages; blinkered last 2 outings; sent to race in USA. *S. Norton.*   80

BIG PAL   8 gr.g. Pals Passage 115–Queen's Honey (Tudor Treasure 119) (1982 10fg 10fg* 8g* 8f* 10fg* 10fg* 10g* 10fg 10d 1983 10s 8f 10f² 10fg 10f* 10d* 10.2fg 10fg* 10.2fg) big, rangy gelding; won handicaps at Folkestone and Brighton (2); stays 1½m, but is best at up to 1¼m; acts on any going; a thoroughly genuine front runner who is an excellent mount for an apprentice and a credit to his trainer. *G. Harwood.*   90

BIG SMILE (FR)   2 b.f. Northern Treat–Do Up (Breakspear II) (1983 5f 6f) May 11; 120,000 francs Y (approx £10,000); small, good-bodied, sturdy filly; half-sister to 3-y-o My Best Friend (by Rex Magna) and French middle-distance winner Miranda's Inn (by Versailles); dam won over jumps at 3 yrs; sire, closely related to Golden Fleece, won 7f maiden race in USA; behind in July maiden races at Sandown and Nottingham; sold 420 gns Doncaster November Sales. *P. Kelleway.*   —

BIG SPIEL (USA)   3 b.g. To The Quick–Gorgeous Gay (Blue Gay) (1982 6f 7fg 1983 8f 8h) well-made, quite attractive gelding; little worthwhile form, including in a seller. *M. Pipe.*   —

BIG STEVE   3 b.g. Malinowski 123–Itinerant 69 (Sky Gipsy 117) (1982 6f 7f 7fg 7g 8s 1983 12f) lengthy gelding; good walker; plating-class maiden; blinkered final outing as a 2-y-o. *A. Ingham.*   —

BILDARA   4 br.f. Balidar 133–Dido's Grandaughter (By Thunder! 122) (1982 8f 10h 10g 10fg 1983 8s 10d 8s) big, strong filly; poor plater; didn't look a suitable mount for inexperienced apprentice first start. *W. Clay.*   —

BILL BAUGH   2 br.c. Mister Tudor–Masami (King Log 115) (1983 7g 8g 7.2g 6fg) first foal; dam of no account; well beaten in sellers and a claiming race; sold 1,350 gns Doncaster November Sales. *R. Hollinshead.*   —

BILLILOV   2 b.g. Anax 120–Miss Quay (Quayside 124) (1983 7f 6g 8g) unimpressive individual; first foal; dam, half-sister to unbeaten hurdler The Grey Bomber, was fairly useful staying hurdler; poor form in modest company. *D. Smith.*   —

BILL SPEAKER   3 ch.c. Double Jump 131–Star Speaker (Philemon 119) (1982 NR 1983 10g) 470Y; first foal; dam won over hurdles; unquoted when last of 14 behind Sunoak in amateur riders race at Lingfield in October. *J. Long.*   —

BINCLEAVES   5 ch.h. Tumble Wind–Pink Doll (Palestine 133) (1982 6s 5g² 1983 6v² 6v 5fg* 5g 6g) close-coupled, quite attractive horse; not a good mover in   53

his slower paces; plater; won non-selling handicap at Beverley in June; stays 6f; seems to act on any going. *M. McCormack.*

BIONDONI 3 ch.g. Carnival Dancer 113–Duresme 76 (Starry Halo 122) (1982 NR 53 1983 8f 8f 8f² 12.2f 8f 8f 7g) 310F; 1,600Y; workmanlike gelding; fifth foal; brother to 1981 2-y-o 5f seller winner Anniversary Waltz and half-brother to middle-distance winner Palmero (by Palm Track); dam third twice over 7f at 2 yrs; held up when second in maiden race at Beverley in July, best effort; stays 1m (pulled hard over 1½m). *J. McNaughton.*

BIONIC BILL 8 b.g. Sovereign Bill 105–Soldier Girl (Queen's Hussar 124) (1982 — NR 1983 10d 8h 7fg 8f) poor plater nowadays; best form at 1m on firm going; good mount for a boy. *J. Old.*

BIRDSEDGE (USA) 3 b.c. Giacometti 130–Featheredge 110 (Nashua) (1982 7d 57 8d 1983 110v³ 12v* 12s 14s 12f 12f 12f 16fg 12.2g⁴) tall colt; mainly disappointing after winning maiden race at Haydock in April; needs at least 1½m; acts on any going; blinkered last 5 starts (ran respectably first time); sold to M. Bradley 2,800 gns Newmarket Autumn Sales. *S. Norton.*

BIRDS OF A FEATHER 3 gr.f. Warpath 113–Yours and Mine 83 (Tin Whistle 41 128) (1982 NR 1983 8v 9f⁴ 12fg* 13.8f 10h⁴) lengthy filly; sister to Sioux and Sioux, a winner several times over 7f and 1m at 2 yrs in 1977; dam stayed 9f; ran easily best race when winning seller at Pontefract in August (no bid); looks slow and is suited by 1½m; sold 1,350 gns Newmarket September Sales. *C. Thornton.*

BIRDWOOD 2 b.f. Pitskelly 122–Sarsgrove 70 (Hornbeam 130) (1983 6fg 6f⁴ 84 6fg² 7f* 7.3g) Feb 6; strong, good-topped filly; half-sister to several winners, including fairly useful 6f and 7f winner Pay Roll (by Burglar) and fairly useful 1981 2-y-o 7f winner Northleigh (by Reform); dam won at up to 1½m; second twice in August, failing by a head to catch Petsy in maiden race at Haydock and being caught close home and beaten ¾ length by Gilt Star in minor event at Brighton; subsequently awarded latter race because winner's rider drew wrong allowance; will stay 1m; has raced only on a sound surface. *J. Dunlop.*

BIRTHRIGHT 3 b.c. Free State 125–Oudalia 107 (Gala Performance) (1982 6s — 6g 1983 6v 7v⁴ 6v) good-bodied colt; only poor form in varied company. *J. Benstead.*

BISHOP BRAY 2 ch.g. Monseigneur 127–Miss Holborn (Pall Mall 132) (1983 — 8s 7f) Apr 14; 3,000F, 2,000Y; heavy-bodied gelding; half-brother to several winners, including fair 7f and 1m winner Ring Bidder (by Auction Ring) and useful 1m to 1¼m winner Saffron Hill (by Gulf Pearl); dam sister to very smart sprinter Holborn; in rear in autumn maiden races at Beverley and Redcar. *M. Lambert.*

BISHOPS PANTO 2 ch.f. Lepanto–Bishops Down (Crozier 117) (1983 7f 8g) — Mar 6; angular filly; second foal; dam poor novice hurdler; backward, behind in maiden races at Salisbury and Leicester in September. *R. Baker.*

BISHOPSPORT (USA) 3 b.g. Amasport–Lil Teresa (Traffic Mark) (1982 6g 5d — 1983 8d 8g) leggy, sparely-made gelding; no form, including in sellers; has been tried in blinkers. *G. Huffer.*

BISHOPS RIDE 4 ch.g. Hot Spark 126–Montcall (Mountain Call 125) (1982 7f 7f — 11f 10d 8f⁴ 8.3fg 1983 12s 12fg 12g) stocky gelding; poor maiden; stayed 1m; sold 3,100 gns Doncaster November Sales; dead. *R. Baker.*

BISHOPS ROYAL (USA) 3 ch.g. King's Bishop–Vircan (Bold Reason) (1982 — NR 1983 13f 16g 16h 12g 15.8g) $60,000Y; third foal; half-brother to 2 winners in USA, including a minor stakes winner; dam unraced half-sister to very smart John William; little worthwhile form; has worn a tongue strap; sold out of P. Cole's stable 2,000 gns Newmarket September Sales after third start. *A. Potts.*

BISKERYL 6 b. or br.m. Biskrah 121–Keryl 106 (Infatuation 129) (1982 NR 1983 — 17d) staying handicapper; acts on a firm and a soft surface; has worn blinkers; has been bandaged. *K. Stone.*

BIT OF A STATE 3 b.f. Free State 125–On A Bit 66 (Mummy's Pet 125) (1982 60 6fg 7d 6f⁴ 7fg 6g 6g² 7fg 7g 7.2s³ 6s 6s 1983 7d³ 8d² 8f³ 8fg 8.2f⁴ 8f⁴ 10f 8h 9f² 9g* 8.2g 9fg 10g) compact filly; attracted no bid after winning seller at Hamilton in September by 7 lengths; didn't run well afterwards; stays 9f; seems to act on any going; blinkered nowadays; finds little off bridle. *S. Wiles.*

BLACK COUNTRY 2 ch.f. Dominion 123–Black Crow 72 (Sea Hawk II 131) 91 (1983 5d* 5s² 5s* 5v* 5g³ 5f) Mar 25; 7,000F, 9,000Y; compact filly; second produce; half-sister to 1982 2-y-o 7f seller winner Viceroy Princess (by Godswalk); dam won over 9f and 1½m; a very speedy filly who justified favouritism in maiden race at Leopardstown in March, 17-runner minor event at Naas in April and 7-runner M. C. Collins Marble Hill Stakes at the Curragh in May; soon cruising in lead at the Curragh but weakened well inside final furlong and got home by only a length from Welsh Dancer, after looking likely to win in style at distance; odds on when 2¾ lengths third of 5 to Gimme Pleasure in Marwell Stakes at Phoenix Park at end of May; probably needs some give in the ground (only ninth of 15 to Night of Wind in Queen Mary Stakes at Royal Ascot on firm); sent to USA. *J. Bolger, Ireland.*

BLACK FALCON (USA) 3 b.c. Irish Ruler–Sebago (Day Court) (1982 6f³ 6fg **88 d** 5d 7g* 1983 7.6v* 8d 10.1fg⁴ 10g 8h² 8.3fg² 7f 8fg) rather lightly-made, fair sort; won handicap at Lingfield in April by length from Zaheer; ran best subsequent races when in frame at Windsor (twice) and Bath (apprentice event); stays 1¼m; acts on any going; sold 4,400 gns Newmarket Autumn Sales. *P. Cole.*

BLACKFEET 4 b. or br.g. Import 127–Sky Hostess 72 (Skymaster 126) (1982 **52** 7fg 6g 8.2fg 1983 6v* 7v 5g² 6g 6d⁴ 6g) made all to win seller at Ayr in March (no bid); possibly stays 7f; acts well on heavy going; has run respectably for an amateur rider. *J. S. Wilson.*

BLACK GLAZEPTA 3 br.c. Mansingh 120–Kareela (Deep Diver 134) (1982 – 5s* 5f* 5fg³ 5f³ 5f³ 5.1f* 5fg³ 5fg³ 5s⁴ 5d⁴ 6d³ 1983 6g 6d 5s 6g 5fg 7f 7f) quite attractive, robust, well-made colt; quite useful as a 2-y-o but disappointing in 1983; sometimes blinkered nowadays. *A. Jarvis.*

BLACKGUARD 2 b.c. Bustino 136–Noirima 110 (Right Tack 131) (1983 7g – 8.2fg) Mar 25; 18,500F, 21,000Y; neat colt; third foal; half-brother to 1m and 1¼m winner Noirio (by Blakeney); dam very useful at up to 1m; showed ability in first of 2 runs in useful company in the autumn; should stay 1¼m. *P. Walwyn.*

BLACK LABEL 2 b. or br.g. Town and Country 124–Black Mink 83 (Gratitude – 130) (1983 6f 6fg 6fg) Apr 24; 6,400F; half-brother to several winners here and abroad, including fair sprinter Brentex (by Birdbrook); dam won twice over 5f at 2 yrs; no worthwhile form; sold privately 620 gns out of Doncaster seller on final appearance. *B. Hills.*

BLACK MIKE 8 b.h. Hardicanute 130–Sariette (Barbare II 128) (1982 10fg 8fg⁴ – 10d² 11.7fg⁴ 12f* 14g 12fg 1983 12d 12d 11d 12f) smallish, strong sort; well beaten in 1983; suited by 1½m; seems to act on any going. *D. Garraton.*

BLACKPOOL BELLE 2 br.f. The Brianstan 128–Sovereign Swop 53 (Goldhill **70** 125) (1983 5v² 5s* 5v* 6d² 5f³ 6f⁴ 6g 6f 6d) Feb 28; 640F; small filly; first produce; dam third in 5f seller at 2 yrs; successful in sellers at Hamilton and Wolverhampton (retained 1,500 gns) in April; not disgraced most subsequent starts (very much above herself on sixth); stays 6f well; acts on any going; consistent. *J. Berry.*

BLACK SPOUT 2 b.c. Nonoalco 131–One In A Million 125 (Rarity 129) (1983 7g – 7fg) Feb 26; 80,000Y; compact colt; first foal; dam won 1000 Guineas; well beaten in October in maiden race (moved poorly to start) at York and William Hill Dewhurst Stakes at Newmarket. *C. Brittain.*

BLACK VEIL 3 b.f. Blakeney 126–Kaftan 68 (Kashmir II 125) (1982 7d 1983 **53** 11s 10s 8v 12g 12.2f 10.2h 12f² 10f 12fg 12f 11.5s² 12g* 12fg) small, rather sparely-made filly; has a round action; attracted no bid after winning seller at Goodwood in September; suited by 1½m; acts on any going; none too consistent. *M. Blanshard.*

BLAKESWARE DANCER 3 br.f. Dance In Time–Carlton's Girl 87 (Hotfoot – 126) (1982 5.1f⁴ 5d⁴ 8f 7.6v 8s 1983 11v 12f 10.1fg) lengthy filly; no form in 1983, including in a seller on final start (blinkered); should stay middle distances; appears to act on any going; sold 950 gns Ascot July Sales. *M. Tompkins.*

BLAKESWARE GIFT 2 b.f. Dominion 123–Presentable 60 (Sharpen Up 127) **74** (1983 6f 7g 7.2s³ 8fg⁴) Feb 21; smallish, rather lightly-built filly; dam, half-sister to Gimcrack winner Wishing Star, was placed over 1½m; in frame in October in minor event at Haydock and maiden race at Redcar; suited by 1m. *M. Tompkins.*

BLAKEY BANK 4 b.g. Blakeney 126–Be Tuneful 130 (Be Friendly 130) (1982 – 10d³ 10f⁴ 17f² 13.8f* 13.8f* 12f⁴ 17fg² 16fg 16d 15f³ 14g 10.2s 1983 12g 12v 14.7f⁴ 14.6f⁴ 16f 13.8f 15.8f 15.8g 12fg² 12fg 14.7fg) small, sturdy gelding; poor walker; plater in latter stages of career; stayed well; acted on firm going; blinkered last 4 starts; collapsed and died at Redcar in October. *Hbt Jones.*

BLAME (USA) 2 b.f. Far North 120–Patty's Fault (Bronze Babu) (1983 7fg 7fg) **68** Apr 1; $52,000Y; useful sort; half-sister to several winners, including very useful sprinter Pretty Angela (by Son Ange), successful in 11 minor stakes races; dam won claiming races at up to 1m; beaten about 10 lengths in 2 late-season races in quite useful company at Doncaster and Newmarket. *B. Hills.*

BLANCHE NEIGE 2 gr.f. Forlorn River 124–La Magna 104 (Runnymede 123)   **75**
(1983 5d* 6g 5fg 6fg) May 10; 24,000Y; small, sharp sort; good walker and mover; half-sister to high-class French sprinter Kind Music and very useful 3-y-o 5f performer Boy Trumpeter (both by Music Boy); dam won twice over 5f at 2 yrs; won 18-runner minor event at Windsor in May by ¾ length from Lily Bank; soundly beaten afterwards in Kingsclere Stakes at Newbury and 2 nurseries, and evidently failed to progress; blinkered final outing. *M. Jarvis.*

BLAZE OF TARA 2 b.c. Nonoalco 131–Welsh Flame 106 (Welsh Pageant 132)   **101**
(1983 6g4 7fg4 7fg* 6.3g2 7g* 8d)
    How blinkers can transform certain horses is made clear by the career of the good Irish two-year-old Blaze of Tara. After being nearest at the finish on his first two appearances—and having started none too well on the second of them–Blaze of Tara sported blinkers for the first time when favourite for a maiden race at Leopardstown in August. What a difference they made! This time Blaze of Tara was able to race with the leaders from the start before forging away in the straight to win by six lengths from Cerussite. Not surprisingly Blaze of Tara wore blinkers in all his subsequent starts, putting up splendid efforts in the P. J. Prendergast Railway Stakes at the Curragh and in the valuable Bright Highway Stakes at Phoenix Park on the first two of them. Although there didn't seem to be much confidence behind him at the Curragh, where he drifted from 3/1 to 8/1, he gave supporters of the odds-on El Gran Senor a fright. As Blaze of Tara took a definite advantage on the stand side two furlongs out, El Gran Senor quickened very smoothly into the lead on the other side, so smoothly that Blaze of Tara looked sure to be beaten decisively. However he kept on so strongly that, with the favourite edging off a straight course, he went down by only a neck. Blaze of Tara then made all to win easily by five lengths when odds on at Phoenix Park, a performance which

Bright Highway Stakes, Phoenix Park—Blaze of Tara wins impressively

suggested he would take all the beating despite top weight in the Ashford Castle Stakes at the Curragh in September. Not only was he beaten, he finished all of ten lengths behind Without Reserve after dropping out very quickly with two furlongs to run. When the stewards inquired into his running neither his rider nor trainer could offer much in the way of an explanation. Possibly the soft surface was against Blaze of Tara but his subsequent absence from the course suggests that, temporarily at least, all might not have been well with him.

Blaze of Tara (b.c. May 12, 1981)	Nonoalco (b 1971)	Nearctic (br 1954)	Nearco / Lady Angela
		Seximee (ch 1966)	Hasty Road / Jambo
	Welsh Flame (br 1973)	Welsh Pageant (b 1966)	Tudor Melody / Picture Light
		Electric Flash (b 1962)	Crepello / Lightning

Blaze of Tara and his year-older half-sister Flame of Tara (by Artaius), winner of the Coronation Stakes, combined to make 1983 a year to remember for their owner-breeder, Miss O'Kelly of the Kilcarn Stud. Miss O'Kelly must consider herself very fortunate to own them still, as Flame of Tara missed being sold only because of a high temperature on the day of the sales and Blaze of Tara was reportedly retained because of a slight bone enlargement. Their dam Welsh Flame, who is due to Artaius in 1984, was a useful filly and won four times over a mile as a three-year-old. She comes from a good family, being out of a half-sister to the Derby winner Parthia, and she's made an excellent start at stud with three winners from her first four foals. Her other winner is Nacibi, a brother to Blaze of Tara, who scored over seven furlongs as a two-year-old in France. Flame of Tara stays a mile and a quarter well but Blaze of Tara gives the impression that a mile will prove his best trip. He should again make his presence felt in the top Irish races. *J. Bolger, Ireland.*

BLESSED SILENCE 5 b.g. So Blessed 130–Cease Fire 112 (Martial 131) (1982 6f 6f³ 7fg 6s 6fg 6g² 6fg* 6f 5d 6s* 6s 6s⁴ 1983 6s 6d 6f 6f² 6fg 6f* 6h⁴ 6d 6fg⁴ 6g 6g 6f 6fg) fair sort; narrowly won handicap at Redcar in July; ran creditably final start; best at 6f; acts on any going; has sweated up; successful with and without blinkers; suited by forcing tactics; sold 3,300 gns Doncaster November Sales. *P. Asquith.*   **61**

BLESSIT 3 br.f. So Blessed 130–Habanera (Habitat 134) (1982 NR 1983 5v² 6v 5fg 6fg) lengthy filly; second foal; dam ran only twice; on backward side and showed signs of greenness when excellent ½-length second of 10 finishers behind Conrad Hilton in maiden race at Sandown in April; didn't fulfil that promise however; should stay 6f; sold only 2,600 gns Ascot August Sales. *M. Jarvis.*   **79**

BLITHE BARD (USA) 3 b.c. The Minstrel 135–Silk Hat (Shantung 132) (1982 7s 1983 7s 10v 10d) \$170,000Y; small, quite attractive colt; half-brother to 3 winners, including Bold Chapeau (by Bold Bidder), a smart winner at up to 9f; dam very useful winner at up to 1m in USA; soundly beaten in maiden and minor events in spring; blinkered final outing. *F. J. Houghton.*   **–**

BLOCHAIRN SKOLAR 5 ch.m. Most Secret 119–Olibanum 61 (Frankincense 120) (1982 6f 5f⁴ 5f 5fg* 6g* 5fg³ 6f 6g 5d 6g 8fg 6s 5g² 1983 6v² 5d 6s⁴ 5fg 6f 5f 5f³ 6fg³ 5fg 5. 6f 5f 5f² 5f 5fg* 5g 5g³ 6g 6fg 5s) compact mare; sprint handicapper; won at Hamilton in September; stays 6f; acts on any going; effective with and without blinkers; suitable mount for an apprentice. *N. Bycroft.*   **48**

BLOCK OF GRANITE 2 b.c. Fordham 117–Laurel Wreath (Sassafras 135) (1983 6f³ 6fg³ 6g² 7f 6fg) Apr 1; IR 25,000Y; second foal; closely related to 3-y-o Loca Mia (by Home Guard), winner of a 7f seller in France in 1982 and subsequently successful in Italy; dam never ran; quite a modest maiden; ran badly at 7f but should stay a good deal further than 6f; had stiff task in nursery final start. *R. Armstrong.*   **77**

BLOEMFONTEIN 4 ch.g. Free State 125–Belligerent 74 (Roan Rocket 128) (1982 7g⁴ 5fg² 6f* 6g⁴ 6f⁴ 6g⁴ 7.2g 7f 8g 7g 6g 7s 1983 6v 6fg 7g 7f 11.7fg 10.4fg) neat, strong gelding; poor handicapper; sometimes beaten in sellers; stayed 7f; acted on firm going; virtually refused to race final start; dead. *M. Chapman.*   **–**

BLONDE BOMBSHELL 5 ch.m. Warpath 113–Poncho 80 (Ragusa 137) (1982 NR 1983 10f 11.7h) strong mare; poor maiden; has had tongue tied down. *I. Wardle.*   **–**

BLONDELLO 4 ch.c. High Line 125–Mink Mini 103 (Martial 131) (1982 14f 1983 12fg) in rear in maiden race and minor event. *R. Sturdy.*   **–**

BLONDIN (USA) 3 ch.c. The Minstrel 135–Fair Renown (Stage Door Johnny)   –
(1982 7f³ 8g 8s 1983 10v 10f 13f 17f) fair sort; has a round action; disappointing
maiden; has worn a bandage on his off-fore. *J. Dunlop.*

BLOOD ORANGE 8 ch.g. Warpath 113–Sunflower 96 (Paveh 126) (1982 NR   –
1983 14.6f 12f 16f 19h) workmanlike gelding; poor maiden on flat though has won
over hurdles; stays 1¾m; sometimes has tongue tied down; sold 1,400 gns
Doncaster September Sales. *J. Leigh.*

BLOOMSDAY 2 ch.f. Sparkler 130–Bas Bleu 117 (Abernant 142) (1983 6fg) Feb   –
25; useful-looking filly; fourth foal; half-sister to useful miler Baccalaureate (by
Crowned Prince); dam, best at sprint distances, stayed 1m; unquoted, backward
and green, missed break and was always struggling in 29-runner maiden race at
Newmarket in September. *G. Wragg.*

BLOWING BUBBLES 3 b.f. Native Admiral–Out of Depth 65 (Deep Diver 134)   **57**
(1982 NR 1983 6f 8f 7fg 6f⁴ 7.6fg⁴ 6fg³ 8g) well-made filly; second foal; dam 5f
winner; in frame in varied races, last of them an apprentice handicap; stays 7f well.
R. Howe.

BLOW MY TOP 4 gr.f. Some Hand 119–Tempered Wind (Fleece 114) (1982 8g   **52**
8.2d 9f 10f 10.1d 8g² 9f² 8g⁴ 8g* 1983 8v* 8v) plain filly; plater; won non-seller at
Warwick in April; stays 9f; acts on any going; suitable mount for an apprentice; not
seen out after April. *R. Holder.*

BLOW YOUR MIND 3 b.g. Take a Reef 127–Living For Kicks (Murrayfield 119)   –
(1982 5f 1983 8d 12s 12v 10s⁴ 13fg 12f) lengthy, fair sort; little worthwhile form,
including in sellers, although finished fourth under bottom weight in apprentice
handicap at Goodwood in May. *W. Musson.*

BLUE AZURE 2 br.f. Blue Cashmere 129–Azure (African Sky 124) (1983 6f 6g 7f   **43**
7g 7.2g 6fg) May 3; lengthy, sparely-made filly; first foal; dam never ran; bad
plater; showed form only on fourth outing; sold 600 gns Ascot November Sales. *I.
Walker.*

BLUE BABY 5 br.m. The Brianstan 128–Le Brillante (Eudaemon 129) (1982 8fg   –
8g 6fg² 6fg 5fg 5fg 5g 7s 1983 6f 8.2fg) small, sturdy mare; sprint plater; has
sweated up. *D. Francis.*

BLUEBIRDINO 4 ch.g. Bustino 136–Blue Bird 84 (Majority Blue 126) (1982 8s   –
8g 1983 12fg 12g) big, attractive gelding; has rather a round action; little
worthwhile form in maiden races and a valuable selling handicap; sold to D.
Chapman 900 gns Doncaster November Sales. *Miss S. Hall.*

BLUE BREEZE (USA) 3 b.f. Blue Times–Nuturf (Noble Union) (1982 6s 1983   **70**
8v² 9s 10.5s 12.2d 12fg⁴ 12f³ 12.2f 12f 14.7f* 17f⁴ 12.2g 13.8g² 12s⁴ 14.7fg)
compact filly; 6-length winner of poor maiden race at Redcar in August (made all);
also ran some moderate races; seems suited by a test of stamina; acts on firm
going; sometimes blinkered (wore them at Redcar); bandaged off-hind final start.
S. Norton.

BLUE BROCADE 2 b.f. Reform 132–Bridestones 92 (Jan Ekels 122) (1983 5d   **91** d
6f² 7f 6fg² 6fg⁴ 7d³ 7g³) May 12; quite attractive, lightly-made filly; first foal;
dam, half-sister to high-class stayer Crash Course, won 4 middle-distance events;
placed 4 times in varied company, running best race (somewhat disappointing
afterwards) when beaten short head in nursery at Windsor in August on fourth
appearance; bred to stay at least 1m. *J. Hindley.*

BLUEBUTTON 3 b.f. Blue Cashmere 129–My Candy 81 (Lorenzaccio 130) (1982   –
5g 5fg² 5f⁴ 1983 9v 7d 16f) neat filly; little form in 1983, but isn't certain to stay 9f,
let alone 2m; sold 580 gns Newmarket Autumn Sales. *N. Gaselee.*

BLUE CLOUD 4 ch.f. Blue Cashmere 129–Hill Cloud 60 (El Gallo 122) (1982 5f   –
5g 5fg 5fg⁴ 6f² 6g 6fg 5fg 6s 6s 7s² 1983 7s 10d) strong, good-bodied filly; poor
performer; stayed 7f; acted on any going; dead. *Mrs R. Lomax.*

BLUE DO 4 b.g. Swing Easy 126–Nylon Pirate 80 (Derring-Do 131) (1982 11s   –
11g² 9g 9fg⁴ 10f 8.2fg 12f 12g 11fg 12fg 10d 8g 8d 1983 11fg 12g 12d 8g 8g 12.3fg)
workmanlike gelding; poor plater; stays 11f; sometimes blinkered; sold 420 gns
Doncaster October Sales. *T. Craig.*

BLUE DONNA 2 b.f. Blue Cashmere 129–Happy Donna 106 (Huntercombe 133)   **70**
(1983 5g 6fg) May 31; second foal; dam won 3 times over 5f at 2 yrs; 100/1, 4
lengths eighth of 20 to Tug Top in maiden race at Doncaster in November, second
outing. *C. Spares.*

BLUE EMMANUELLE 4 b.c. Lochnager 132–Julie Be Quick (Selari) (1982 5g   **93**
6.5g² 6.5v 6s³ 6s* 6d² 6f 6fg 6g 7f* 6fg³ 7.2g* 7fg* 6g 1983 6d 8v 7s 7s 8f 7f* 7f³

7fg 7f) big, rangy colt; returned to form when running on strongly to beat Grey Desire by ¾ length in £5,000 handicap at Newcastle in June; ran creditably next time; stays 1m; acts on any going; blinkered once at 3 yrs; slowly away when apprentice ridden eighth outing; racing in USA. *N. Callaghan.*

BLUEGANBY 2 b. or br.f. Blue Cashmere 129–Thorganby 75 (Decoy Boy 129)   **61**
(1983 5f 5.1fg 5g 5f 5f 5g) Mar 19; 3,600Y; lengthy, strong-quartered filly; not a good mover; first foal; dam won eight 5f races; plating-class maiden; showed form only on fourth outing; blinkered fifth start. *R. Hobson.*

BLUE GRASS 3 br.c. Warpath 113–Delphinium 93 (Tin King 126) (1982 7s 1983   **77**
8d* 10s) strong, good sort; good walker; made a successful reappearance in maiden event at Pontefract in April despite looking on backward side, producing a strong run to beat Regal Express by 1½ lengths; looked well but ran as if something was wrong with him at Ayr in September on only other outing; should be suited by middle distances; has raced only on soft ground. *C. Thornton.*

BLUE HEN BLEND 2 b. or br.f. Artaius 129–Secala (Secretariat) (1983 5s 7d*)   **79 p**
Apr 1; 30,000Y; second foal; half-sister to useful Irish 3-y-o middle-distance winner Sir Simon (by Sir Ivor); dam won at up to 1m in USA and is daughter of very smart Aladancer; having first race for over 4 months when winning 12-runner minor event at Naas in October by a length from Action Girl; likely to improve a good deal over longer distances. *K. Prendergast, Ireland.*

BLUE HILL (FR) 3 b.c. Artaius 129–Summer Bloom 68 (Silly Season 127) (1982   **—**
NR 1983 10f 10f⁴ 14f⁴ 16fg) deep-girthed colt; keen walker; second foal; half-brother to minor French middle-distance winner Pinka (by Tachypous); dam won over 1¼m and is half-sister to very smart 6f to 1¼m winner Cistus; remote fourth in maiden races; runs like a stayer; sold out of F. J. Houghton's stable 3,000 gns Newmarket September Sales after third start and finished last of 21 on only subsequent outing. *M. Haynes.*

BLUE LAMA 2 ch.f. Laxton 105–Mablon 76 (Majority Blue 126) (1983 5fg 6fg)   **68**
Mar 30; smallish, strong filly; half-sister to useful 5f performer Mayab (by Maystreak) and a winner in Malaya; dam placed over 5f at 2 yrs; fair sixth of 12 in maiden event at Haydock in August, second outing. *H. Wharton.*

BLUE REALM 4 b.f. Realm 129–Honey Tower 70 (Tower Walk 130) (1982 6s 8fg   **—**
8f 6g* 8f³ 6g 7fg* 10d 8.2s 6s 8s 1983 8d 7.6fg 8fg 6h 8.2g 5s 7fg) leggy, close-coupled filly; plater; ran poorly in 1983; best at up to 7f; suited by a sound surface; blinkered penultimate start; retained 1,500 gns Doncaster June Sales. *R. Ward.*

BLUE RHAPSODY 5 ch.h. Sandford Lad 133–Sovereign Court 87 (Sovereign   **—**
Path 125) (1982 10f 1983 6v) strong, useful sort; poor plater; has worn blinkers; one to be wary of. *A. Neaves.*

BLUESHOES 3 ch.f. Blue Cashmere 129–Lady Helen 63 (Majority Blue 126)   **—**
(1982 5d 5f* 5fg* 5f 1983 5s 5s 5fg 5g 5.3f 6fg 5fg 8.3fg⁴ 6fg 8fg 10g) leggy, sparely-made filly; plater; promises to stay 1m; suited by firm going. *C. Wildman.*

BLUE STONE 2 ch.c. Mansingh 120–Irma Flintstone 110 (Compensation 127)   **—**
(1983 5d) May 16; 2,600Y; fifth foal; dam 5f performer; behind in 17-runner maiden auction event at Redcar in May; dead. *T. Fairhurst.*

BLUE WATERS 2 b.f. Blue Cashmere 129–Evvoia 53 (Khalkis 127) (1983 6fg   **—**
7g) Apr 4; stocky filly; half-sister to fairly useful 1976 2-y-o 6f winner Firemaiden (by Firestreak) and 2 winners in Sweden; behind in minor event at Newmarket in August (moved badly to start) and £5,000 race at Lingfield in September. *M. Jarvis.*

BLUE WONDER 2 gr.f. Idiot's Delight 115–Rainbow Wonder (Runnymede 123)   **81**
(1983 6f 7fg 8g 9g³ 8fg*) Apr 11; rangy, rather sparely-made filly; good mover; half-sister to 1½m winner Sunset Wonder (by Tickled Pink); dam apparently of little account; 7/1 and dropped in class, routed her 15 opponents in valuable seller at Newmarket in October, leading over 2f out and drawing clear to beat Kansas Bob by 7 lengths; sold 12,500 gns afterwards; had shown ability in maiden races previously; stays 9f; clearly a cut above a plater and can win in better company. *D. Elsworth.*

BLUFF 2 ch.f. Nebbiolo 125–Hidden Hand (Ribocco 129) (1983 7g) Apr 30; IR   **—**
10,500F, 10,000Y; big, lengthy filly; half-sister to 3 winners, including 3-y-o stayer Rare Friendship (by Rarity) and fair 6f and 1m winner Hugo di Tours (by African Sky); dam, daughter of high-class Hidden Meaning, won 7f claiming race in USA; 25/1, never going well in 19-runner maiden race at York in October. *J. W. Watts.*

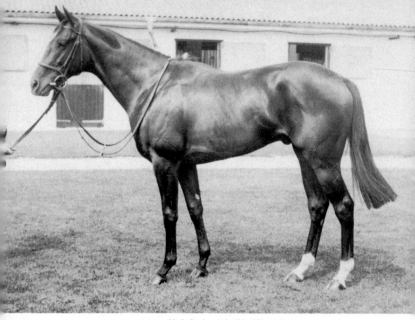

Mr J. B. Austin's "Bluff House"

BLUFF HOUSE (USA) 2 b.c. Irish Castle–Trenthor Star (Reneged) (1983 6f* **107**
7d 6fg*(dis)) Mar 27; $35,000Y; fine, big, rangy colt; third foal; half-brother to a
stakes-placed winner; dam won 12 times at up to 1m, including claiming events;
successful twice at Goodwood in the summer, wearing down Anton Pillar to win
newcomers event by 2½ lengths, and then beating Round Hill on merit by ½ length
in minor event only to be disqualified for hampering fourth when switched to
challenge; ran moderately (possibly unsuited by ground) in between; acts well on
firm going. *G. Harwood.*

BLUNT (FR) 3 b.g. Sharpen Up 127–Cesarine (Royal Palace 131) (1982 6g 1983 **62**
8f 8fg 7f² 7f 7h) 380,000 francs Y (approx £35,000); lightly-built, quite attractive
gelding; first foal; dam lightly-raced half-sister to Brigadier Gerard; in rear in
newcomers race at Chantilly as a 2-y-o; didn't have best of runs twice over here,
including when second in modest maiden event at Thirsk in July; ran moderately
subsequently though (blinkered fourth start); sold 1,300 gns Newmarket Autumn
Sales. *P. Makin.*

BLUSHING NURSE 3 gr.f. Saritamer 130–Red Cape 84 (Matador 131) (1982 8g **–**
1983 12g³ 12g) of little account. *N. Bycroft.*

BLUSHING RIVER 3 ch.c. Blushing Groom 131–Lys River 119 (Lyphard 132) **96**
(1982 6f³ 7fg⁴ 7g* 7g² 8g⁴ 8g² 1983 8s³ 10.1s 7fg³ 7f³ 7f 7f³ 7g 7fg) small,
close-coupled colt; third in handicaps at Newbury, Warwick (dead-heated),
Yarmouth and Brighton; best at up to 1m; acts on any going; well beaten last 2
starts. *H. T. Jones.*

BLUSHING SCRIBE (USA) 2 ch.c. Blushing Groom 131–Takealetter **107**
(Monitor) (1983 5s 7fg 7g* 7fg* 7d* 7f² 7s³) Mar 14; useful-looking colt; third
foal; half-brother to stakes winner Addressee (by George Navonod); dam very
useful winner of 14 races at up to 1m, including 3 minor stakes races; showed an
excellent turn of foot when successful in maiden race at Ayr and nurseries at
Newmarket and York in the summer; put up a useful effort at York, catching Mr

Meeka on line with 14 others well beaten off; also ran very well in 4-runner Grand Criterium International d'Ostende, failing by only a length to catch Beldale Lear after stumbling 2f out, and was far from disgraced when 6½ lengths third of 5 to Seattle Song in Prix de la Salamandre at Longchamp in September; will be suited by 1m; seems to act on any going; game and genuine. *B. Hanbury.*

BLYTHE-BOY 2 br.c. Heres 81–Gayella (Communication 119) (1983 6fg 6f) Apr 16; 300Y; first foal; dam never ran; behind in sellers at Nottingham and Pontefract in June. *W. Clay.* —

BLYTHE KNIGHT 2 br.g. Martinmas 128–Relza 91 (Relko 136) (1983 7fg 8g 8.2s) Apr 7; 3,000F; tall, leggy gelding; half-brother to fairly useful middle-distance winner Toussaint (by So Blessed) and a winner in France; dam stayer; soundly beaten in minor and maiden events. *E. Carter.* —

BLYTHE WARRIOR 2 gr.c. Roman Warrior 132–Palestra 92 (Palestine 133) (1983 6f 7f) Apr 19; 9,000Y; rangy colt; brother to Irish 5f winner Roman Consul and half-brother to several other winners here and abroad, including fairly useful 7f to 1½m winner Cyprus Sky (by Redundant); dam stayed 7f; 50/1, behind in maiden races at Thirsk in July and Redcar in September; sold 3,000 gns Doncaster October Sales. *E. Carter.* —

B.M.C. SPECIAL 8 gr.h. Supreme Sovereign 119–Agapimou (Great White Way) (1982 8fg4 8fg 8f4 8f 15f 1983 10g 8fg 8fg) plater; poor walker; suited by 1m; seems to act on any going; blinkered once; bandaged nowadays. *J. Gilbert.* —

BOARDMANS DELIGHT 2 gr.f. Sexton Blake 126–Naval Artiste (Captain's Gig) (1983 5g2 5f* 6fg) Apr 14; 750Y; fair sort; fifth foal; dam Irish 2-y-o 5f winner; led near finish when beating Trim Taxi a head in maiden auction event at Redcar in June; second favourite, sixth of 7 in nursery on same course in August; should be suited by 6f. *J. Berry.* **65**

Mr S. T. Wong's "Blushing Scribe"

BOARDMANS STAR 4 ch.f. Cawston's Clown 113–Weewanda 94 (Cagire II — 122) (1982 6d 5f 6f 1983 8f) small, lightly-made filly; good mover; poor performer; form only at 5f; collapsed and died at Brighton in June. *R. Hannon.*

BOAS FESTAS 3 b.g. Golden Dipper 119–Rebecca (Quorum 126) (1982 NR — 1983 10v 10v 10.1fg 12g 10.1f 8fg) 4,400Y, 2,100 2-y-o; strong, sturdy gelding; half-brother to winners here and abroad, including 7f and 1m winner Swinging Rebel (by Swing Easy); dam poor half-sister to Steel Pulse; behind in varied races, including a seller. *P. K. Mitchell.*

BOATROCKER 4 b.g. African Sky 124–Cheap and Sweet (Rising Market) (1982 — 6s³ 6g* 6f² 6f² 1983 6g 7s) quite useful-looking gelding; quite modest; not seen out after April; stays 6f; acts on any going. *S. Norton.*

BOB BACK (USA) 2 br.c. Roberto 131–Toter Back (Carry Back) (1983 7fg 8fg* 110 ? 8g*) May 26; $150,000f; big, good sort; half-brother to a winner by Sensitivo; dam stakes winner at up to 9f; third favourite, always prominent and stayed on strongly to lead near finish when winning 28-runner maiden race at Newmarket in October by a length from Commanche Run; won 9-runner Premio Tevere at Rome the following month, beating a useful Italian 2-y-o 2½ lengths into second place; will be suited by 1¼m+; likely to make smart 3-y-o. *M. Jarvis.*

BOBBIE JAMES 2 ch.c. Balidar 133–Layer Cake (Levmoss 133) (1983 6f² 6g 85 6fg²) Feb 20; 7,800F; strong, workmanlike colt; second foal; dam won over 1½m in Ireland; second in maiden races at Yarmouth in July and Brighton in October; will be suited by 7f+. *L. Cumani.*

BOBBINETTE 3 b.f. Whitstead 125–Rosehill 59 (Stupendous) (1982 NR 1983 — 12v 12.2g 8d 12f) 3,000Y, 420 2-y-o; third live foal; dam ran only 3 times; tailed off in sellers. *D. Chapman.*

BOBBY BUSHTAIL 3 ch.c. Porto Bello 118–Rich Harvest (Bounteous 125) 65 (1982 6f 6f* 6d⁴ 8.2d 8s 1983 8s 8s 7fg 7h 7g 8g 10f*) smallish, good-topped colt; good walker; apprentice ridden when winning seller at Leicester in November by 3 lengths, despite wandering badly left; bought in 1,400 gns afterwards; suited by 1¼m; seems best on a firm surface; sometimes blinkered (wore them at Leicester); sold out of J. Dunlop's stable 1,300 gns Ascot July Sales after third start. *R. Thompson.*

BOBBY DAZZLER 2 ch.c. Sparkler 130–Philigree 84 (Moulton 128) (1983 99 5.8g³ 7f² 7fg 6g² 7.6fg² 7g 7fg*) Mar 19; 4,000Y; compact, quite attractive colt; first foal; dam stayed well; blinkered first time, made all under top weight of 9-7 in 20-runner nursery at Leicester in October; will stay 1m; yet to race on a soft surface; missed break sixth outing. *R. Laing.*

BOB-DOUBLE 2 ch.g. Import 127–Two's Up (Double Jump 131) (1983 6fg) May — 22; sturdy gelding; first foal; dam never ran; 100/1 and backward, behind in 20-runner maiden race at Doncaster in November. *R. Whitaker.*

BOCA RATON 2 gr.f. Sweet Revenge 129–Regency Girl 89 (Right Boy 137) 88 (1983 5d² 5v* 5s* 5g* 5g 6f 5fg⁴ 6f³ 6s 5s) Feb 12; IR 5,800F, 3,400Y; rather leggy filly; half-sister to 2 winners, including sprinter Blakesware Saint (by Welsh Saint); dam stayed 6f; successful in maiden race at Haydock in April and minor events at Ripon and Catterick in May; also ran very well when length third of 11 to Forzando after showing up throughout in nursery at Haydock in September; stays 6f; acts on any going; has won for an apprentice but is better with strong handling. *J. Berry.*

BOCCACCIO (USA) 3 b.c. Full Out–Mindy's Hurricane (Noble Commander) 80 (1982 6f³ 6f³ 6d 1983 7v⁴ 6d 9.4d 8.2g³ 10f⁴ 8f³ 8.2fg* 8.2f* 9f* 9f² 9fg* 10.5d 11fg) strong, attractive, good-quartered colt; good walker; in good form in summer and made nearly all to win maiden and minor events at Hamilton and handicaps at Ripon and Wolverhampton; below form last 2 starts; stays 1¼m; very well suited by top-of-the-ground conditions; blinkered second and third outings; genuine; sent to USA. *S. Norton.*

BOCODA LAD 2 ro.c. Oats 126–Takawin 109 (Takawalk II 125) (1983 5s 5fg 6f 69 7f⁴ 7fg⁴ 7f) Mar 27; tall, good-bodied colt; half-brother to several winners, including fairly useful sprinter Welwyn and very useful sprinter Welshwyn (both by Welsh Saint); dam sprinter; plating-class maiden; best efforts when fourth in maiden race and a £3,900 nursery at Brighton in the summer; stays 7f; acts on firm going. *J. Benstead.*

BOEZINGE 2 b.f. Derrylin 115–Gay City 99 (Forlorn River 124) (1983 6f 5.8h* 102 6fg* 5g*) Mar 15; 4,500F; short-legged, useful-looking filly; half-sister to 1978 2-y-o 5f winner Blessingtonia (by So Blessed) and a winner in Malaya; dam sprinter; had 4 races, winning last 3, maiden at Bath in August, and Dick Poole Stakes (beating Malaak) at Salisbury and 15-runner Champagne Louis Roederer Trophy Nursery (by neck from Rio Riva) at Newbury in September; equally effective at 5f and 6f; yet to race on a soft surface. *M. Smyly.*

BOHEME 3 b.g. Lypheor 118–Sweet Jewel (Will Somers 114§) (1982 7fg 8s 7s 1983 9d 7f 7f 9f 8d) short-coupled gelding; soundly beaten, including in sellers; sold 300 gns Doncaster November Sales. *D. Garraton.*   –

BOHEMOND 2 b.c. Auction Ring 123–Kaftan 68 (Kashmir II 125) (1983 7f 7g 8g) Apr 12; 9,400Y; strong, good sort; second foal; half-brother to 3-y-o 1½m seller winner Black Veil (by Blakeney); dam, sister to high-class 5f to 6f performer Blue Cashmere, won over 1¼m; no worthwhile form in modest company; looks capable of better. *D. Smith.*   –

BOLD AND WOOLLY 3 br.g. Kashmir II 125–Tarakanova (Bold Lad, USA) (1982 6g² 7d* 7v⁴ 6v* 7d 1983 8.2v 7s 6s* 6s⁴ 7d²) leggy gelding; won handicap at Brighton in May; apprentice ridden when in frame in similar races afterwards; suited by 7f and should stay 1m; has raced only on an easy surface; exported to Hong Kong. *B. Hanbury.*   **85**

BOLD APPAREL (FR) 3 br.f. Bold Forbes–Gay Apparel (Up Spirits) (1982 6g² 5v 5s* 6.5v* 6v* 1983 7v³ 7.5v 6f 5d*) first foal; dam very useful Canadian 2-y-o, winning 2 sprint stakes races, and is sister to 2 other stakes winners; won 3 of her 5 races as a 2-y-o, including Premio Umbria at Rome; only lightly raced as a 3-y-o, but showed herself a smart sprinter in 8-runner Prix du Petit Couvert at Longchamp in October when having first race for 5 months, leading inside last furlong to beat Sky Lawyer by ½ length; had put up best earlier effort when 4½ lengths third of 7 to Ma Biche in Prix Imprudence at Maisons-Laffitte; stays 7f but is better at sprint distances; acts well on heavy going. *R. Collet, France.*   **116**

BOLD BEE 2 ch.f. Bold Lad (Ire) 133–In The Clover (Meadow Mint 120) (1983 6f 6fg 5fg 5f* 5.3fg) Mar 30; third foal; half-sister to 3-y-o 5f winner Lady Clementine (by He Loves Me) and 6f to 1¼m winner Music Lover (by Gay Fandango); dam won over 7f at 2 yrs in Ireland; dropped in class, beat Miami Prince comfortably by a neck in 12-runner seller at Windsor in August (bought in 1,200 gns); stays 6f; has raced only on fast ground; blinkered third outing. *D. Morley.*   **61**

BOLD BLAIZE 2 ch.c. Diamonds Are Trump 108–Philistia (Palestine 133) (1983 5fg 5.8h² 5fg⁴ 5d 5g) May 18; 3,000Y (privately); half-brother to 5f to 1m seller winner Isobel's Choice (by Green God) and 2 winners abroad; dam never ran; quite a modest maiden; stays 5.8f; acts on hard going. *S. Matthews.*   **71**

BOLD BOB 3 ch.c. Sharpen Up 127–Finest View 66 (Bold Lad, Ire 133) (1982 5fg² 5fg* 5f⁴ 5f² 5f⁴ 5g⁴ 5f² 1983 5f 5fg 6fg² 5fg⁴ 5g² 5fg 5d) strong, attractive, rangy colt; second in minor events at Salisbury and Newbury in September, making winner pull out all the stops when going down by a head to Fine Edge on latter course; about 3 lengths fourth of 8 behind Soba in Scarbrough Stakes at Doncaster in between; stays 6f; acts on firm going; below form last 2 outings, wearing blinkers and sweating on first occasion. *C. Brittain.*   **99**

BOLD BUCCANEER 2 b.c. Decoy Boy 129–Sea Tycoon 80 (Tycoon II) (1982 NR 1983 8v 12v³ 12g) 3,600Y; 880 2-y-o; fourth foal; half-brother to 3 winners, including quite useful sprinter Davenport Boy (by Workboy); dam stayed 1½m; 33/1 when 8¾ lengths third of 12 behind Colonel Godfrey in maiden race at Folkestone in May; well beaten only subsequent outing (September); evidently suited by 1½m. *A. Pitt.*   **66**

BOLD CONNECTION 3 ch.c. Persian Bold 123–Lady Tyrrel (Pall Mall 132) (1982 5g⁴ 7g² 7.5f² 7fg³ 7fg³ 8d³ 1983 9s² 10s⁴ 8g 12g* 9g³ 10g² 10fg² 9fg 9.5f* 14f* 8f³ 11.5f³ 12f⁴ 14fg²) IR 7,000Y; big, rangy colt; third foal; half-brother to useful 1981 2-y-o Irish 7f winner More Heather (by Ballymore); dam Irish 11f winner; won maiden race at Limerick, minor event at Dundalk and handicap at Gowran Park in summer; ran well on several other occasions during a busy season, including when ¾-length second to Ankara in Woodland Stakes at Phoenix Park on seventh outing and 3 lengths second to odds-on Band in 5-runner March Stakes at Goodwood in August on final start, in latter event running on pretty well under pressure; stays 1¾m, but is clearly effective at much shorter distances; acts on any going; often blinkered (has won in them). *L. Browne, Ireland.*   **100**

BOLD DECEPTION 7 br.g. Bold Lad (Ire) 133–Classical Music 85 (Santa Claus 133) (1982 NR 1983 14f) probably of little account. *S. Pattemore.*   –

BOLDERA 2 b.f. Persian Bold 123–Wolverina 71 (Wolver Hollow 126) (1983 5h 7fg 8g) Feb 19; 6,200F; first produce; dam 2-y-o 5f winner; beaten less than 5   **69**

lengths when ninth of 17 to Signorina Odone in maiden race at Beverley in September, second outing; sold to D. Chapman 1,050 gns Doncaster November Sales. *M. Camacho.*

BOLD FISHER (USA) 2 b.c. Bold Forbes–Pond (Hawaii) (1983 7g) Apr 24; $120,000Y; good-looking colt; second foal; dam, placed once in 7 outings, is sister to very useful Frond, successful at up to 1m; 20/1, no show in 18-runner maiden race at Goodwood in September; looks capable of much better. *G. Harwood.* — p

BOLD FORT 4 b.c. Auction Ring 123–Via Mala 81 (Pall Mall 132) (1982 8fg 6fg 6f 6g 5s 6d 6s 1983 6.5d³ 6.5d⁴ 7.5s³ 5g 6d 7g 7d 7.2s 8f 5f⁴ 7.6g⁴ 7g 8g² 8.2g 8.2s 8.2fg) small colt; good mover; found 5f too sharp and stayed 1m; acted on any going; blinkered final outing in 1982; trained by R. Hollinshead first 10 starts; stud. *D. Smith.* — 69

BOLD INDIAN 2 b.c. Bold Lad (Ire) 133–Sassalya (Sassafras 135) (1983 6fg³ 7fg³) May 3; close-coupled, rather finely-made, quite attractive colt; good walker and excellent mover; third foal; dam useful Irish 7f and 1¼m winner; promising third, sympathetically handled, in newcomers race won by Keen at Ascot in July and in 26-runner maiden event won by Alleging at Newmarket in September; was clearly trained and raced with his 3-y-o career in mind, and has makings of useful performer. *G. Wragg.* — 88 p

BOLD MAID 3 b.f. Persian Bold 123–Gold Pollen 110 (Klondyke Bill 125) (1982 5f² 5.8f⁴ 7f 6f 5fg 5fg⁴ 5fg 5s 1983 7g 5s² 5g⁴ 6fg 6fg) lightly-made filly; second in all-aged seller at Beverley in September; best form at 5f; has been tried in blinkers. *R. Williams.* — 46

BOLD MAJOR 3 ch.c. Orange Bay 131–Armelle 87 (Tribal Chief 125) (1982 6f 7g³ 6f² 6g* 6s* 8f⁴ 7s 1983 8f) useful-looking colt; good walker; useful as a 2-y-o; exported to Hong Kong after finishing respectable sixth of 15 to Full Rainbow in quite valuable handicap at Sandown in July; stays 1m; acts on any going. *E. Eldin.* — 93

BOLD MANEUVER (USA) 3 gr.f. Par Excellent–Bold Fascinator 122 (Bold Lad, USA) (1982 6fg 6s 1983 10g 10f³ 11f 8f⁴ 9fg⁴ 10fg* 10g 10fg 10fg) strong, workmanlike filly; beat Alimony by 2 lengths in maiden race at Salisbury in September; stays 1¼m; acts on firm going. *M. Francis.* — 75

BOLD MEADOWS 2 b.f. Persian Bold 123–Spare Filly 95 (Beau Sabreur 125) (1983 6.9g* 6d) Mar 22; neat filly; half-sister to numerous winners, including quite useful 3-y-o sprinter African Tudor (by African Sky) and fairly useful 1m to 1¼m performer Manfilia (by Mandamus), herself dam of African Hope and Kilijaro; dam soft-ground stayer; favourite when winning 16-runner maiden race at Limerick in September by a length from Can't Argue; 12/1 when fourteenth of 20 to Gala Event in Moyglare Stud Stakes at the Curragh 2 days later; will be suited by 1m+; likely to improve. *J. Bolger, Ireland.* — 80 p

BOLD MOVER 3 b.c. Bold Lad (Ire) 133–Short Rations (Lorenzaccio 130) (1982 6fg* 6s² 7v 1983 6d 8v 7fg³ 7.2g 8f² 8fg² 9f³ 8s) quite well-made, attractive colt; good mover; placed under 9-7 in handicaps at Sandown, Yarmouth, Pontefract and Ripon; 1¾ lengths third to Monongelia on last-named in August; stays 9f; acts on any going; not the easiest of rides. *M. Stoute.* — 95

BOLDNINE 2 ch.c. Bold Lad (Ire) 133–Donine (Soleil II 133) (1983 6d 6f 7f) May 10; 11,500F, 14,000Y; small, well-made colt; half-brother to 2 winners, including middle-distance winner Rapide (by Gulf Pearl); dam unraced half-sister to smart middle-distance filly Nanticious; quite a modest colt; showed ability only when ninth in maiden race at Chester in August on final outing; evidently stays 7f; may be capable of improvement. *C. Brittain.* — 67

BOLD PATRIACH (CAN) 2 b.c. Bold Forbes–Spit and Polish (Herbager 136) (1983 6f 6f² 7g³ 6fg³ 7g* 7g* 7fg) Mar 18; $105,000Y; robust, well-made, good sort; half-brother to several winners, including Rich and Ready (by Stage Door Johnny), a very useful winner at up to 11f; dam, out of sister to champion filly Silver Spoon, won at up to 1m; won maiden race at Leicester in October by ¾ length from Raami, and minor event at Chepstow later in the month by 3 lengths from Jabaraba; favourite, disappointing fifth behind Jabaraba in nursery at Doncaster in November; will stay 1m; possibly requires some give in the ground to be seen to best advantage. *J. Dunlop.* — 98

BOLD PRINT 4 ch.g. High Line 125–Star Story 117 (Red God 128§) (1982 10.1fg³ 10.1d* 12fg⁴ 8s 1983 10s 12d² 12v² 11.7d 12fg 12g 12fg⁴ 12g) rather lightly-made gelding; suited by 1½m; acts well on soft ground; has run creditably for an apprentice; rather inconsistent. *F. J. Houghton.* — 68

BOLD QUEEN 3 b.f. Persian Bold 123–Queen of Time (Charlottown 127) (1982 —
6s 1983 8.5v 12g 12g) fair sort; little worthwhile form in maiden and minor events;
last of 20 when blinkered final start. *M. Haynes.*

BOLD REALM 2 b.g. Bold Lad (Ire) 133–Elm 88 (Realm 129) (1983 5s 5v 5.1g² **79**
6f 5fg² 5fg 6s) Apr 16; IR 20,000Y; strong, heavy-bodied, lengthy gelding; good
walker; third foal; brother to a disappointing gelding; dam won over 5f on her first 2
starts; runner-up in maiden races at Yarmouth in June and Windsor in July;
apparently best at 5f; best form on a sound surface; ran much too freely when tried
in blinkers on final outing. *A. Jarvis.*

BOLD ROWLEY 3 br.c. Persian Bold 123–Lady Rowley 114 (Royal Levee) (1982 **73**
6f 6s² 1983 7s 6v 7f⁴ 7f² 7f⁴ 7f 7f⁴ 7g) tall, good-topped colt; in frame in 3
handicaps and a maiden race; stays 7f; acts on any going. *G. Lewis.*

BOLD RUN (FR) 4 b.c. Tyrant–Bold Cherry (Bold Reason) (1982 8.5s* 8d* **117**
10g* 9g 1983 including 8g* 8g² 8g* 8fg* 9d⁴ 8f 10g 11f² 10f³ 12g) 205,000 francs
Y (approx £20,500); first foal; dam unraced daughter of smart stakes winner
Cherry Sundae; successful 7 times in Italy when trained by A. Botti, including at 4
yrs in Gran Premio Citta di Torino and Premio Emilio Turati at Milan; beat Drumalis
a nose in latter in June; subsequently raced in France and USA, putting up
creditable performances in Prix d'Ispahan at Longchamp (3¾ lengths fourth to
Crystal Glitters) and Louisiana Downs Handicap (second to Late Act); stays 11f;
acts on any going; best in blinkers; trained in Italy by A. Botti and in France by O.
Douieb. *C. Whittingham, USA.*

BOLD SCUFFLE 5 b.g. Bold Lad (Ire) 133–Cloe (Shantung 132) (1982 5g 5fg §§
6fg 6g³ 6d 5g² 5f 5.6f 5fg 5fg 5fg 1983 5s⁴) useful-looking gelding; not a good
mover; sprint handicapper; ran respectably on only start at 5 yrs in October;
suited by 6f; gives impression he needs some give in the ground nowadays;
blinkered once in 1982; moody and thoroughly inconsistent. *R. Hollinshead.*

BOLD SECRET 3 b.g. Auction Ring 123–Whispering Star 78 (Sound Track 132) **103**
(1982 6g 1983 6s* 6d* 6f³ 5f 6fg 6fg) compact, quite attractive gelding; won in
taking style at Newmarket on first 2 starts, beating Conrad Hilton by 6 lengths in
9-runner maiden race in April and Misguided by 3 lengths (value 5) in 10-runner
£8,200 Holsten Diat Pils Handicap in May; lightly raced afterwards, best effort
when close third of 17 to Autumn Sunset in William Hill Trophy at York in June; ran
quite well after a lay-off on penultimate start, but was well beaten final outing;
suited by 6f (outpaced throughout over 5f); acts on any going but is ideally suited
by some give underfoot. *G. Pritchard-Gordon.*

BOLD SPINNEY 3 ch.f. Bold Lad (Ire) 133–Stunog Wood 98 (Falcon 131) (1982 **72**
7fg 7g⁴ 7d² 1983 10v² 12s 13d² 13.4fg 14f² 14f* 17.1h² 16.5f 16fg⁴) workmanlike
filly; won maiden race at Yarmouth in August and was second on 4 other
occasions; suited by a test of stamina; acts on any going; ran moderately in
blinkers fourth start; sold to BBA 12,500 gns Newmarket December Sales. *J.
Hindley.*

BOLD THOUGHTS 3 b.f. Diamonds Are Trump 108–No Fooling 83 (Narrator —
127) (1982 6g 7f 8f 1983 9f 6f 9fg 10fg) rangy filly; no worthwhile form in 1983,
including in a seller; stays 1m. *A. Jarvis.*

BOLD TUDOR 2 b.c. Thatching 131–Annacloy (Majority Blue 126) (1983 6d) —
Feb 17; IR 150,000Y; lengthy, useful sort; third foal; half-brother to 1981 2-y-o 7f
winner Pamparino (by Pampapaul), later a winner in Italy; dam speedy early-season
2-y-o in Ireland; 7/1 but green, showed little after missing break when 10 lengths
eighth of 16 to Turn The Key in maiden race at Newbury in October; sold 5,400 gns
Newmarket Autumn Sales. *B. Hills.*

BOLTRANS 3 br.f. Monsanto 121–Brush's Choice (Robson's Choice 105) (1982 —
5d 5fg 6d 1983 7.2fg) rather leggy filly; poor form in maiden and minor events.
J. Berry.

BOLT THE GATE 4 ch.g. Bustino 136–Madame Quickly 80 (Saint Crespin III —
132) (1982 14s⁴ 16.4s⁴ 1983 12d⁴ 12v 14.7d 14.6f) big, rather dipped-backed
gelding; has shown a little ability in varied company in the North; promises to stay
1¾m; blinkered third start; sold 2,300 gns Ascot August Sales. *W. Elsey.*

BOMBARD 2 b.g. Gunner B 126–Asturia 104 (The Phoenix) (1983 6d 7f) Apr —
26; 2,000Y; strong, good-bodied gelding; half-brother to numerous winners,
including Musidora Stakes winner Escorial (by Royal Palace); dam 2-y-o 5f winner;
last in maiden auction events at Epsom in June and Doncaster in July. *D. Thom.*

BOMBILI 4 ch.g. Native Bazaar 122–Curry Favour 72 (Negotiation) (1982 7g² —
7fg 10.1fg 8fg² 8.2s³ 8g 10s 1983 10s 14fg) workmanlike gelding; stays 1m;
trained first start by G. Balding. *M. Tompkins.*

BOMBPROOF 2 ch.f. Roan Rocket 128–Surety 56 (Sheshoon 132) (1983 6f) Mar 8; 800Y; half-sister to 3 winners abroad, including French 3-y-o 9f winner Surety Bank (by Oats); dam second over 1½m; destroyed after breaking leg in maiden race at Redcar in August. *W. Elsey.* —

BOND DEALER 6 gr.g. Habat 127–Sounion 69 (Vimy 132) (1982 8g 7f⁴ 8g 7f* 7g* 8fg² 7f² 8fg* 8f² 8f* 8fg 8fg 1983 7.6v* 8v³ 7s² 7.6v³ 7fg* 8f² 7g² 8f² 7fg* 8f 8h⁴ 8fg 7g 7fg) good-looking gelding; a grand individual who won handicaps at Lingfield in April, Yarmouth (apprentices) in June and Lingfield (apprentices) again in July; best at up to 1m; acts on any going; best in blinkers; excellent mount for an apprentice; usually makes running; genuine and consistent; changed hands 6,400 gns Ascot March Sales. *B. Swift.* 71

BOND HOUSE 4 ch.g. Tumble Wind–Rold Gold (Bold Combatant) (1982 10.1fg 7g 8fg 1983 7s 6fg) big gelding; poor form in varied company, including selling; blinkered once. *N. Vigors.* —

BOND MARKET 2 ch.c. Native Bazaar 122–French Bond (Prince de Galles 125) (1983 5fg 6fg) Feb 12; third foal; brother to 2 poor animals; dam never ran; behind in maiden race at Bath in September and claiming event at Nottingham in October. *S. Matthews.* —

BONDOE (AUS) 3 ch.f. Ksar 126–Bete a Bon Dieu (Herbager 136) (1982 NR 1983 10g) Australian-bred filly; half-sister to outstanding stayer Buckskin (by Yelapa) and very useful French middle-distance winner Belawan (by Beau Garcon); dam won over 1¾m in France and was placed over jumps; backward and 50/1, finished creditable eighth of 20 to Staravia in maiden race at Sandown in October; the type to do better over longer distances. *R. Williams.* —

BONDOR 7 b.g. Good Bond 122–Floradora Do 85 (Derring-Do 131) (1982 NR 1983 10f) poor plater; has been bandaged. *L. Barratt.* —

BONFIRE 2 ch.g. Thatch 136–Dancing Fire (Crepello 136) (1983 5f 5.8h 6f) Feb 28; 6,800Y; rangy, useful-looking gelding; third foal (first to Northern Hemisphere time); half-brother to Australian 6f winner Be My Fire (by Be My Guest); dam once-raced sister to smart stayer Pink Gem; no worthwhile form; blinkered when last of 11 in good-class maiden race at Goodwood in July on final start. *D. Sasse.* —

BON HOMMAGE (USA) 2 ch.c. L'Heureux–Fine Tribute (Diplomat Way) (1983 6fg 7f 6f² 7g³ 7fg²) Apr 23; $20,000Y; compact, fair sort; first foal; dam, daughter of good Canadian filly Royal Spirit, was placed twice from 9 starts; runner-up in maiden race at Epsom in August and valuable 28-runner seller at Newmarket in September; will stay 1m+; yet to race on a soft surface. *M. Stoute.* 73

BONJOUR TRISTESSE (USA) 2 b.c. Grey Dawn II 132–Ciao (Silent Screen) (1983 7f² 7fg²) Mar 28; $360,000Y; strong, rangy, deep-girthed colt, with plenty of scope; third foal; half-brother to smart 2 yrs when winning 4 times at up to 7f from 7 starts; failed by ½ length to hold off Ashgar when favourite for maiden race at Yarmouth in August but nonetheless shaped well, easily accounting for 14 others; came up against an above-average newcomer in Rainbow Quest when short-priced favourite for 30-runner maiden event at Newmarket later in month and was beaten 2 lengths into second place; will stay 1m; sure to win races. *H. Cecil.* 91

BONNE BAISER 4 ch.f. Most Secret 119–Condonna 92 (Constable 119) (1982 5v² 6f 5f² 5f 1983 5d* 5d² 5.1g* 5fg 6f 5f³ 6s 5d) leggy filly; sprint handicapper; won at Thirsk in May and Yarmouth in June; ran creditably in between; stays 6f; acts on any going but seems best with some give in the ground (moved badly to start on very firm sixth start); suitable mount for an apprentice. *A. Jarvis.* 81

BONNE ILE 2 b.f. Ile de Bourbon 133–Good Lass (Reform 132) (1983 7fg*) Mar 8; compact, deep-bodied filly; second foal; dam, out of half-sister to Blakeney and Morston, was 2-y-o 1m winner in France; despite running green, justified favouritism by ½ length from Arbitrage in 4-runner Newmarket Challenge Cup in October; will be suited by 1¼m+; sure to improve. *B. Hobbs.* 65 p

BONNEMENT 2 br.c. Blakeney 126–Maruka 70 (Abernant 142) (1983 7fg 7f² 7fg* 7fg³ 8fg 8.2fg* 8fg 8.2s) Mar 14; neat colt; half-brother to three winners, including 3-y-o sprinter Ameghino (by So Blessed); dam 2-y-o 5f winner; won 8-runner minor event at Wolverhampton in August and 19-runner nursery under joint-top weight of 9-7 at Nottingham (blinkered first time) in September; suited by 1m; acts well on fast going; sold 11,000 gns Newmarket Autumn Sales, probably for export to Italy. *J. Dunlop.* 89

BONNIE DE LYON 10 ch.m. Jukebox 120–Gorgeous Gael (Atan) (1982 NR 1983 8fg 12f) of little account. *J. Edmunds.* –

BONNY GOLD 5 br.g. Goldhill 125–Politely 55 (Polic 126) (1982 12s⁴ 1983 12v 12s 12s⁴) strong gelding who carries plenty of condition; good walker; poor performer; stays 1½m; acts on any going. *P. Rohan.* –

BONNY SHIELDS 3 gr.f. Owen Dudley 121–Saragail (Warpath 113) (1982 5g* 5g* 5fg³ 5f² 6f⁴ 6d³ 5d³ 7f³ 6fg 6fg 6s 8d 8.2s 1983 7v 8d 8v 9s 9s* 10.6v 9f 8fg 8g 10f) workmanlike, slightly hollow-backed filly; showed only form of year when 33/1 for minor event at Ripon in May, leading 3f out and holding on by ¾ length from Say Primula; suited by 9f, but seems to find an extended 1¼m beyond her; possibly best with some give in the ground. *K. Stone.* 94

BOO 3 b.f. Bustino 136–Shoshoni 72 (Ballymoss 136) (1982 NR 1983 10s 10.6g 12s² 12g 18fg²) fifth foal; half-sister to fairly useful 1977 2-y-o 1m winner Apache Dancer (by Sovereign Path); dam, 1¼m winner, is half-sister to Warpath and Dakota; second in maiden race at Hamilton in October and handicap at Doncaster in November, going down by ½ length to Basta in latter event; suited by a test of stamina. *C. Thornton.* 77

BOOM SHANTY 2 ch.f. Dragonara Palace 115–Pegs Promise (Tumble Wind) (1983 5s 5f 5fg 5g 6f 6f 5f* 5fg 5g) Apr 21; 5,000Y; fair sort; third foal; half-sister to a winning 2-y-o plater; dam well beaten in 2 starts at 2 yrs; put up best effort when running in selling company for first time, making all to win £3,300 event by 1½ lengths from Lady of Leisure at York (bought in 3,100 gns) in August; a free-running sort not sure to stay 6f; acts on firm going; sweated up third and fourth outings; sold 4,000 gns Doncaster October Sales. *P. Brookshaw.* 66

BOOM TOWN CHARLIE (USA) 3 ch.c. Silent Screen–Serica (Silky Sullivan) (1982 6f 7g* 6f* 7f 6f³ 6d* 1983 7d⁷ 8v) $55,000Y; tall, quite attractive colt; half-brother to 3 minor winners in USA; dam stakes-placed winner of 6 races at up to 7f; won Ladbroke European Free Handicap at Newmarket in April by 1½ lengths from Salieri (gave 10lb), racing prominently throughout and keeping on strongly; didn't look at his best and weakened a furlong out when 7 lengths sixth of 10 behind Wassl in Airlie/Coolmore Irish 2000 Guineas at the Curragh the following month; didn't run again, but was entered up at back-end of season; should stay 1m; acts on firm going, but has shown best form on a soft surface; genuine. *W. O'Gorman.* 113

Ladbroke European Free Handicap, Newmarket—Boom Town Charlie keeps on strongly to account for Salieri

BOOTH'S TOWN BOY 3 b.g. Decoy Boy 129–Aldbury Girl 79 (Galivanter 131)   **64**
(1982 5g⁴ 6fg 5d⁴ 6s 6s 6v⁴ 5g² 5d²   1983 6v² 6v* 6v 6s) leggy, workmanlike
gelding; made virtually all to win small seller at Haydock in April by 15 lengths (no
bid); soundly beaten in non-sellers subsequently; stays 6f well; acts on heavy
going; usually blinkered nowadays; ridden by 7-lb claimer; seldom impresses in
paddock. *J. Berry.*

BORDER SIGNAL 4 b.g. Pitcairn 126–Strong Light 103 (Fortino II 120) (1982   –
NR 1983 14f) 25,000F, 400 3-y-o; rangy gelding; has been hobdayed; brother to
1,000 Guineas third Yanuka and half-brother to 2 winners; dam genuine miler; won
NH Flat race at Folkestone in May; unquoted when last of 12 to British in maiden
race at Sandown in July. *A. Pitt.*

BOREALE (FR) 2 b.f. Bellypha 130–Princesse Tora (Prince Taj 123) (1983 5v³   **114**
5.5fg² 6.5fg³ 6.5fg* 7g* 8fg*) closely related to very useful French 1m and 9f
winner Cabbaliste (by Lyphard) and half-sister to 2 winners, notably high-class
1974 French 2-y-o Princesse Lee (by Habitat), herself the dam of Prix Morny and
Prix de la Salamandre winner Princesse Lida; dam, very useful at around 1m, is
half-sister to top-class miler Carlemont; developed into a very useful filly, winning
maiden race at Deauville in August, 90,000 francs race at Longchamp in September
(by ½ length from Toll Teller) and Prix des Reservoirs, also at Longchamp, in
October (gave weight to all but one of her 5 opponents and led close home to win by
a head from subsequently-disqualified Misbehaving); suited by 1m; acts on a firm
surface. *Mme C. Head, France.*

BOREHAM DOWN 4 b.g. High Top 131–Woodwind 103 (Whistling Wind 123)   –
(1982 12fg 12fg 10s* 1983 10v 12g) big, rangy gelding; stays 1¼m; acts on soft
going; trained by M. Lambert first start; sold 1,700 gns Ascot October Sales. *J.
Jenkins.*

BORJANA (USA) 2 ch.f. To The Quick–Scotch Hop (Ben Lomond) (1983 6s⁴)   –
Feb 24; $210,000Y; half-sister to several winners, including 11f winner At The
Dance (by Speak John); dam, winner of 6f claiming race, is half-sister to Verbatim,
a good winner at up to 1¼m; 10/1, shaped reasonably well after being bit slowly
away in maiden race at Leicester in May to finish 8 lengths fourth of 17 to Bryony
Rose; sent to France. *M. Albina.*

BORODINO 2 ch.c. Bustino 136–Alma 87 (Shiny Tenth 120) (1983 7f 7f 7fg) Apr   –
17; robust colt; second foal; dam, daughter of high-class stayer Almeria, won over
5f and 1m; soundly beaten in maiden races and a minor event; blinkered final outing;
sold to T. Fairhurst 3,200 gns Newmarket September Sales. *R. Hern.*

BORUSHKA 2 b.f. Bustino 136–Valdavia (Ribot 142) (1983 7.6d³) May 7; fourth   **66 p**
foal; half-sister to very useful 3-y-o Vahila (by Relko); dam, half-sister to Prix de
Diane winner Crepellana, won over 1½m in France; weak joint third-favourite, had
every chance 2f out when 8 lengths third of 18 to Channel Affair in maiden race at
Lingfield in October; will be suited by further, and should stay at least 1½m; sure
to improve. *F. J. Houghton.*

BOSSANOVA BOY 4 b.c. Rhodomantade 110–Samba 69 (Sammy Davis 129)   **67**
(1982 8d 7f* 8f 8g4 10g 10.2d 10d² 1983 10s³ 11s² 10v* 11.1v* 10d³ 10fg 12f* 12fg)
smallish, fair sort; won handicaps at Kempton (2) and Salisbury (apprentices);
stays 1½m; acts on any going but goes well on soft; effective with and without
blinkers; suitable mount for an apprentice; sweated up final start. *P. Makin.*

BOSSEY 3 br.g. Oats 126–Sinful 72 (Grey Sovereign 128§) (1982 8g 6d 1983 6s   –
5v 5v) tall, narrow gelding; only poor form in maiden and minor races; blinkered
final start (June). *J. Berry.*

BOSSY BOOTS (USA) 2 b.c. Cornish Prince–Maui Maid (Kauai King) (1983   **72**
6fg 6g 6f 5s) Mar 10; $50,000Y; rangy, good sort; half-brother to 3 minor winners;
dam, minor 6f winner, is half-sister to high-class filly Singing Rain; 25/1, chased
leaders for long way when 6¼ lengths sixth of 7 to Keen in valuable newcomers
race at Ascot in July; brought down by a faller when co-favourite for maiden race at
Newmarket on next start and subsequently finished in rear in maiden race at Epsom
(co-favourite) and Flying Childers Stakes at Doncaster. *M. Jarvis.*

BOTH ENDS BURNING (USA) 3 b.g. Nalees Man–Star Game (Pia Star) (Pia Star)   **93**
(1982 6f 5d² 6f* 1983 7.3v 7f 7f 8fg4 10f³ 10f 10fg 10g 12fg* 12fg* 12fg) strong,
lengthy, useful-looking gelding; good walker; well ridden by T. Williams when
successful in handicaps at Ascot in September (apprentice event) and Newmarket
in October; beat Cristalga by 1½ lengths in a driving finish on latter course; suited
by 1½m (none too consistent over shorter distances); seems to act on any going,
but goes well on firm; ran badly in blinkers eighth start; hampered on first outing.
H. Candy.

BOTTERSLOW 2 b.f. Sowerby Sovereign 76–Politely 55 (Polic 126) (1983 5v 5s) leggy, lightly-made filly; half-sister to 1980 2-y-o 7f and 1m winner Bonny Gold (by Goldhill); dam won over 1m; backward, behind in May in big fields of maidens at Thirsk and Wolverhampton (tailed-off last of 18). *W. Clay.*   –

BOTTESFORD BOY 3 b.g. Record Token 128–Facetious 88 (Malicious) (1982 5f³ 5fg* 5fg² 7f 5d* 5g³ 6g   1983 7v 6v 6s 6fg 5fg 8h 7fg) small, sturdy gelding; little form in 1983, but had some stiffish tasks; best form at 5f; dwelt when blinkered fifth start; sold 1,900 gns Doncaster November Sales. *M. Lambert.*   –

BOTTLE AND GLASS 2 b.g. Hot Spark 126–Queen's Penny (Queen's Hussar 124) (1983 5g 6d) Mar 24; 7,000Y; half-brother to several winners, notably smart 5f to 7f winner Hillandale (by Crossing The T); dam never ran; soundly beaten in the autumn in maiden race at Haydock (slowly away) and valuable seller at York. *M. W. Easterby.*   –

BOUNTEOUS SPIRIT 3 ch.c. Mossberry 97–Bounteous Sport 70 (Bounteous 125) (1982 NR   1983 8fg) neat colt; fifth live foal; dam won 5f seller at 2 yrs; needed race when last of 25 in minor event at Doncaster in November. *J. Townson.*   –

BOUNTY HAWK 2 b.c. High Top 131–Northern Tavern (Charlottesville 135) (1983 6f² 6f³ 7fg³ 8fg) Mar 12; strong colt; half-brother to 3 winners, including fairly useful middle-distance filly Taverne de France (by Caracolero); dam, smart winner at up to 10.5f, is half-sister to smart animals Dominion Day, Sir Penfro and Padroug; turned in a very good first effort when head second of 7 to Creag-An-Sgor in maiden race at York in July; ran well but was generally out of his depth subsequently, particularly when last of 9 in William Hill Futurity at Doncaster (blinkers) in October; will stay 1¼m; sure to win maiden event. *W. Elsey.*   85

BOURBONIEN 2 b.c. Ile de Bourbon 133–Tour des Dames (Nonoalco 131) (1983 6f* 7fg*) Mar 11; 70,000Y; medium-sized, useful-looking colt; has a smooth action; first foal; dam unraced half-sister to Criterium des Pouliches winner Oak Hill; justified favouritism in pleasing style in 9-runner maiden race at Newcastle in June, moving strongly into lead 2f out and keeping on to win by a neck from El Capistrano; toyed with the opposition in small race at Leicester the following month, cruising home 1½ lengths clear of Maricourt; will stay at least 1¼m; almost certainly much better than we are able to rate him, and seems sure to win more races. *H. Cecil.*   93 +

BOUTADE 3 b.f. Bold Lad (Ire) 133–Turiana (Citation) (1982 6g 6g⁴ 6f 7.6v 7d 1983 8s 12s) neat, quite attractive filly; quite a moderate maiden; should stay beyond 6f; not seen out after April. *B. Hobbs.*   –

BOWIE BOY 3 b.g. Tachypous 128–Miss Poker Face (Raise You Ten 125) (1982 6g   1983 7d* 8f 8g) workmanlike gelding; 33/1 when beating Al Amead by 1½ lengths in minor event at Leicester in May; in rear both subsequent outings, but had stiff task and needed race after a longish lay-off on final start; should be suited by 1m and more. *O. Brennan.*   61

BOXBERGER BEAUTY (HOL) 4 ch.f. Filandre–Cook (Hail to All) (1982 10d² 9g² 12fg 12.5g* 14.5d² 12.5g³ 10.8s*   1983 8d 9s 12v* 15.8f 10.8f⁴ 10.5g²) fair sort; won race at Duindigt in May; well beaten over here; stays 1¾m; suited by some give in the ground; sometimes blinkered (has won in them). *M. Ryan.*   ?

BOXBERGER MEKKA (HOL) 2 b.f. Mount Hagen 127–Boxberger Queen (Hotfoot 126) (1983 7fg 6.5g⁴ 9v³) Feb 4; strong, deep-girthed filly; first foal; dam won Dutch 1000 Guineas and Oaks and scored from 5f to 12.5f; took the eye on way to start and showed some promise when remote seventh of 20 to Lear Fan in maiden race at Newmarket in August; in frame subsequently in Holland, notably just over a length third of 9 to Sparkos in Criterium at Duindigt; suited by a test of stamina. *M. Ryan.*   ?

BOXBERGER NANCY (HOL) 2 b.f. Filandre–Nancy (Compromise 109) (1983 7f 5f³ 6fg 6.5g² 9v) Mar 7; sister to useful 1982 2-y-o 5f and 6.5f winner Boxberger Oscar; dam won 1972 Dutch Oaks and St Leger; placed behind stable-companion Boxberger Ster in 2 races at Duindigt, Holland, in the summer; soundly beaten both outings in this country; should be suited by 7f+. *M. Ryan.*   ?

BOXBERGER OSCAR (HOL) 3 ch.c. Filandre–Nancy (Compromise 109) (1982 5fg 6f⁴ 7g 7f² 5d* 6.5g* 9g²   1983 9v 12f 14.5f³ 10fg 10.7d³) strong, well-developed Dutch-bred colt; useful as a 2-y-o; ran mainly in Holland in 1983, and was third there twice, including in St Leger; ran well for a long way before finishing in rear under very stiff weight in handicap at Ascot on fourth outing; possibly stays 1¾m. *M. Ryan.*   ?

BOXBERGER ROMEO (HOL) 2 b.c. Filandre–Nevada Squaw (Bon Mot III 132) (1983 7fg 5f 9v⁴) Apr 2; big, useful-looking colt; brother to Boxberger Squaw, placed twice in Holland at 2 yrs; dam unraced half-sister to very smart French miler Nurabad; 50/1, prominent 5f when out of first 11 of 25 in maiden race won by Roussillon at Newmarket in July, first outing; beaten in Holland subsequently, running respectably when 3¾ lengths fourth of 9 to Sparkos in 9f race in September. *M. Ryan.*   ?

BOXBERGER STER (HOL) 2 b.f. Tumble Wind–Dolphinetta 88 (Gulf Pearl 117) (1983 7f 5f* 6.5g* 6fg 6g) Feb 14; big filly; half-sister to Dutch 1000 Guineas winner Boxberger Dream (by My Swanee) and useful jumper Sea Image (by Our Mirage); dam 1m winner; successful twice at Duindigt, Holland, in the summer, beating stable-companions Civano and Boxberger Nancy respectively by a neck in Van Brienens Memoriaal and by 3¾ lengths in Clingendaalren; subsequently in rear in £3,500 race at Salisbury and minor event (tailed off by halfway) at York; should stay 7f+. *M. Ryan.*   ?

BOXBERGER TAMARA (HOL) 3 ch.f. Shiny Tenth 120–Alison's My Girl 77 (Appiani II 128) (1982 7d 6.5g 9g 1983 9v 16f 12f) close-coupled, plain filly; little worthwhile form here or in Holland. *M. Ryan.*   –

BOXBERGER TRIX (HOL) 3 ch.f. Mount Hagen 127– Lady Alpha (St Alphage 119) (1982 5.1f 1983 9v 8f 6fg 6.5fg³ 5f² 5fg 5fg 6g³ 5.1s 6g³) Dutch-bred filly; placed in varied races, including an amateur riders event; seems best at sprint distances; has worn bandages; well beaten in blinkers ninth start. *M. Ryan.*   51

BOYD'S PRIDE 3 b.g. Tudor Rhythm 112–River Belle 72 (Divine Gift 127) (1982 5f 5fg 6f 7f 6fg 6g 8d 8.2s 8d 1983 7d 9f² 10f 10.8fg² 13.8f) plain gelding; plater; stayed 1¼m; acted on firm going; blinkered last 2 starts; dead. *W. Ryan.*   43

BOYNE 3 b.c. Grundy 137–Orange Triumph (Molvedo 137) (1982 NR 1983 8d 14f* 12f³ 14f⁴ 16f) medium-sized, lengthy colt; half-brother to several winners here and in Italy, notably top-class middle-distance performer Orange Bay (by Canisbay); dam ran once at 2 yrs; stayed on well to win 11-runner maiden race at Salisbury in July by 1½ lengths from Fortune's Guest; suited by 1¾m (ran very badly over 2m however); acts on firm going. *P. Walwyn.*   83

BOY PIPER 4 br.g. Bold Lad (Ire) 133–Pipeline 85 (Gulf Pearl 117) (1982 8fg 8fg 8g³ 8f⁴ 7fg 7.3g 8s 1983 8v 8d 8s 6v 7s) good-bodied gelding; not the best of movers; plating-class maiden; will stay 1¼m; has worn bandages in front; has worn blinkers; sold 1,050 gns Ascot July Sales. *M. Haynes.*   –

BOY SANDFORD 4 br.g. Sandford Lad 133–Perldia (Diatome 132) (1982 6g 6fg 8g 8fg 1983 13s 8.2d* 8g* 12f⁴ 7f 8f 8.2f³ 9f* 8g² 8.2f) plater; won at Hamilton (no bid) and Ayr (no bid) in May and Hamilton again (bought in 920 gns) in July; not sure to stay 1½m; probably acts on any going. *H. Bell.*   61

BOYS IN BLUE 2 ch.c. Tap On Wood 130–Light Opera 101 (Vienna 127) (1983 5s 7fg 6f 8.2f³ 8.2fg) Mar 29; IR 13,000Y; sturdy, good-bodied, compact colt; half-brother to numerous winners including useful 1980 2-y-o 5f winner Vienna Miss (by Thatch); dam, closely related to smart sprinter Laser Light, stayed 7f; moderate plater; stays 1m; acts on firm going; normally blinkered; sold 4,400 gns Newmarket Autumn Sales. *M. Jarvis.*   57

BOY TRUMPETER 3 ro.c. Music Boy 124–La Magna 104 (Runnymede 123) (1982 5fg³ 5fg* 5g³ 5.3g* 6s² 5d* 1983 5s 6d 5d² 5fg) smallish, strong, good-quartered, sprint type; very good walker; third foal; brother to good French sprinter Kind Music; dam won twice over 5f at 2 yrs; showed useful form as a 2-y-o; ran easily best race of 1983 and put up an excellent performance when neck second of 11 behind Fearless Lad in Temple Stakes at Sandown in May, showing good speed and keeping on well; showed early speed but was beaten 2f out when eighth of 10 to Rutland in £4,700 race on same course in June (finished distressed, reportedly having pulled a muscle in back and suffered a splinter fracture of a knee bone); likely to prove best at 5f; probably acts on any going. *B. Hobbs.*   114

BRACAGH LADY 5 b.m. Wishing Star 117– Josephine Blatt (Super Sam 124) (1982 NR 1983 14.7d) workmanlike ex-Irish mare; first foal; dam well beaten both starts; little worthwhile form in maiden races though has won over hurdles; sold 1,100 gns Doncaster September Sales. *E. Carter.*   –

BRACKEN GILL 5 gr.h. Ribston 104–Gill Breeze (Farm Walk 111) (1982 6s 6s 6fg 7f 5fg 5f³ 6fg 6g 5fg* 5g⁴ 5g 1983 5d 5g 5fg 5f) sprint plater; best form on a sound surface; sometimes blinkered; has won for an amateur rider; inconsistent. *Mrs A. Bell.*   –

BRACKEN REED 4 b.g. Welsh Saint 126–Argentessa 80 (Sing Sing 134) (1982   –
NR 1983 8g) 1,000Y; big, rangy, workmanlike gelding; turns his front feet out
badly; half-brother to 3 winners, including 7f and 1m winner Silver Ruler (by
Sovereign Path), and fairly useful 6f to 7.6f winner Nantucket (by Pall Mall); dam
placed at 2 yrs; tailed off in 10-runner £4,100 event at Newbury in June. *I. Walker.*

BRAE DOWNE 2 b.g. Riboboy 124–Strathoykel 94 (Aberdeen 109) (1983 7g)   –
Feb 15; second foal; half-brother to fairly useful 1981 2-y-o 7f winner Cassley River
(by Relkino); dam best at sprint distances; unquoted, distant eighth of 15 in maiden
race at Lingfield in October. *Sir Mark Prescott.*

BRAEMAR ROAD 2 ch.c. John de Coombe 122–Tantra 72 (Song 132) (1983 5fg   **66**
5.8h³ 6fg 5fg 5fg) Mar 12; 10,000Y; robust colt; first foal; dam won 3 sprint races
at 2 yrs; plating-class maiden; stays 5.8f. *D. Sasse.*

BRAGADO 2 b.c. Daring March 116–Cithern 91 (Canisbay 120) (1983 7fg 7d 5d)   **74**
Apr 8; 3,000F, 2,800Y; fair sort; not a good walker; half-brother to fair 1981 2-y-o
5f and 6f winner Ten-Traco (by Forlorn River); dam, 2-y-o 7f winner, is half-sister
to smart performers Zimbalon and Band; finished creditable sixth of 21 behind
stable-companion Chelkov in maiden race at Newmarket in September on debut,
but didn't reproduce that form, including in an auction event; probably needs
further than 5f; possibly not at his best on soft surface. *R. Armstrong.*

BRAKA (USA) 2 b.c. Lyphard 132–Forest Friend (Linacre 133) (1983 7fg⁴) May   **87 p**
14; $160,000Y; small colt; half-brother to numerous winners, including 3-y-o
Onaizah (by Bold Bidder), successful at up to 1¼m, and smart Irish stayer Moss
Trooper (by Levmoss); dam half-sister to Vaguely Noble's dam; 33/1 and very
green, showed up well, pushed along throughout, when 3¾ lengths fourth of 26 to
stable-companion Alleging in maiden race at Newmarket in September; sure to
improve. *H. Cecil.*

BRANCH LINE 3 ch.c. Dom Racine 121–Sapling 78 (Hornbeam 130) (1982 7fg*   ?
1983 10g³ 12f) half-brother to 2 winners, including useful 1974 2-y-o 7f and 1m
winner Estructura (by Gulf Pearl); dam won over 13f and is half-sister to smart
miler Prince Midge; won maiden race at Leopardstown on only start as a 2-y-o;
ran extremely well when length third of 10 behind Solford and Caerleon in £4,400
event at Phoenix Park in May (clear of remainder) but was never going well when
sixth of 7 behind Shareef Dancer in King Edward VII Stakes at Royal Ascot the
following month on only other start; sent to USA. *E. O'Grady, Ireland.*

BRANDO 6 ch.h. Busted 134–Cafe au Lait 97 (Espresso 122) (1982 16fg 1983   –
17.1v 16.5f) leggy, lightly-made horse; fairly useful stayer at 3 yrs; lightly raced
since; probably acts on any going. *G. Thorner.*

BRANKSOME TOWERS 3 b.f. Hotfoot 126–Let Slip 77 (Busted 134) (1982   –
5fg* 5f 5fg 5g⁴ 5d³ 5d 1983 7f 6g 6g 6fg) leggy, quite useful sort; moderate form
as a 2-y-o; soundly beaten in 1983, best effort third start; bred to stay much
further; acts on a firm and a soft surface; tailed off in blinkers on final outing; sold
800 gns Newmarket December Sales. *E. Eldin.*

BRAVE ADVANCE (USA) 2 b.f. Bold Laddie–Osculate (Forli) (1983 5s² 5v³   **98**
5f 5fg* 5g² 5f* 5f² 5fg) Apr 20; $25,000Y; good-bodied, useful sort; half-sister to 2
winners, one stakes-placed; dam unraced half-sister to Robellino's dam; sire,
winner at up to 6.5f, was very smart at 2 yrs; proved herself a game and useful
performer when failing by a short head to hold off Be My Valentine in 9-runner St
Hugh's Stakes at Newbury in August (originally deemed to have dead-heated but
was placed second a week later); had previously won 15-runner maiden race at
Chester and £5,000 nursery at Goodwood; last of 9 to Sicyos in Prix d'Arenberg at
Longchamp in September; very speedy and is suited by a sharp 5f; best form on a
sound surface; sweated up at Goodwood. *G. Hunter.*

BRAVE BRIDGE 4 b.g. Jolly Me 114–Spaniard's Darling (Darling Boy 124)   –
(1982 10f 12fg 14fg 15.8f⁴ 12fg 16s 12g 1983 10.6s 10g 10f) quite attractive
gelding; poor plater; has twice worn blinkers; bought 480 gns Doncaster March
Sales. *S. Wiles.*

BRAVE MAIDEN 4 gr.f. Three Legs 128–Julie's Gi-Gi (Brave Invader) (1982   **62 §**
10g* 12.2g³ 12f² 12f³ 12fg³ 16.5g² 15.8d 16fg 16d² 16s 16s 1983 16v 17.1v 12s²
12s* 13d⁴ 16f 12f 15.8fg 12d 12g³ 12d) lightly-made filly; former plater; won
apprentice handicap at Leicester in May; stays well; acts on any going; effective
with or without blinkers; has her share of temperament (often starts slowly and
was reluctant to race final start); sold to M. Pipe 5,000 gns Newmarket Autumn
Sales. *J. Bethell.*

BRAVE MEMORY (USA) 3 b.c. Crow 134–Out Of The Past (Olden Times) **89**
(1982 7f² 8d³ 1983 8d² 11.5fg* 10f* 12f² 10f4 11g 10g² 10.2s) lengthy, long-striding
colt; won maiden race at Yarmouth (readily) and minor event at Brighton in June,
getting home by a neck from Feather Flower when 9/4 on in latter; in frame most
other outings, including when 4 lengths second of 10 behind Shaftesbury in Oslo
Cup at Ovrevoll in July and 1½ lengths second to Sharp End in Preis der Stadt
Baden-Baden in September; suited by 1½m; probably unsuited by really soft going,
but acts on any other; brought down in Germany sixth start. *J. Hindley.*

BRAVE WORDS 2 b.g. Bold Lad (Ire) 133–Quite Sweet 100 (Super Sam 124) **75**
(1983 7fg 7fg 7g) May 18; 5,200Y; good-topped, rather plain gelding; half-
brother to 3 winners, including 3-y-o 1m winner Sugar Loch (by Lochnager) and
fairly useful 5f to 7f winner Lucky Man (by Manacle); dam best at up to 1¼m; 6
lengths fifth of 11 to Marzia's Hollow in maiden race at Chester in August, second
outing and best effort; gelded after third start. *P. Rohan.*

BREEZE HILL 4 b.c. Swing Easy 126–Jester's Girl 71 (Will Somers 114§) (1982
8d* 7g³ 7g4 10.2f² 12d 8fg 8f 1983 10g) rangy colt; very good mover; stays 1¼m;
seems to act on any going; has run respectably for an apprentice. *A. Moore.*

BREEZE LINE 2 b.c. On Your Mark 125–What A Breeze (Whistling Wind 123) **60**
(1983 5g4 5f4 6f* 6fg4 7h) May 20; 5,400Y; workmanlike colt; half-brother to fairly
useful Irish 6f and 7f winner Mistral Man (by Sweet Revenge); attracted no bid
when beating Discreetly Yours by ½ length in 12-runner seller at Ripon in June,
best effort; best form at 6f; acts on firm going; twice ran moderately at Beverley;
inconsistent. *D. Garraton.*

BREEZY GLEN 3 b.g. Furry Glen 121–What A Breeze (Whistling Wind 123) **–**
(1982 6f 7fg 1983 8v 16g 14f 17f 18f) lengthy gelding; good walker; poor staying
maiden; often blinkered; slipped up fourth outing. *A. Jarvis.*

BREEZY MORNING 2 ch.f. Persian Breeze 121–Quartette Royale 65 (Jukebox **–**
120) (1983 5f 5.3fg) Feb 24; IR 2,100F; second produce; dam placed over 5f at 2
yrs; in rear in September in maiden race at Folkestone and minor event at
Brighton; sold 280 gns Ascot December Sales. *M. Haynes.*

BREGA BOY 2 b.c. Kala Shikari 125–Vivaz (Reform 132) (1983 5fg* 5d³ 5s² 5fg³ **101**
5d* 6f³ 6fg* 5s 5s) Apr 9; 3,600Y; strong, robust colt; not a good mover in his
slower paces; first foal; dam never ran; developed into a useful colt and had a fine
season, winning maiden auction event at Edinburgh in April, £3,000 race at Ayr in
June and 6-runner Strathclyde Stakes, again at Ayr, in July; 20/1, ran well over 3f
when seventh of 10 to Superlative in Flying Childers Stakes at Doncaster in
September on eighth outing; suited by 6f; acts on any going; blinkered last 5 starts;
consistent. *T. Fairhurst.*

BREIDDEN ROCK 3 ch.g. Pretty Form 97–True Verdict (Hopeful Venture **–**
125) (1982 NR 1983 6f 8fg 7f 8fg 7f) workmanlike gelding; first foal; dam of little
account; poor plater; wears blinkers; sold 500 gns Ascot September Sales. *B.
McMahon.*

BRENDAN'S CHOICE 3 ch.c. Flashback 102–Dumette 89 (Dumbarnie 125) **–**
(1982 6g 6s 1983 7v 10.1fg) workmanlike colt; has been tubed; of no account. *A.
Davison.*

BRENTEX 5 gr.h. Birdbrook 110–Black Mink 83 (Gratitude 130) (1982 6fg 5d* **63**
5fg² 5g4 5f³ 5fg 5g 5g 5fg4 5fg4 5.8f³ 5s² 5d 5s² 6s³ 5s 1983 5v 6v 5v 6g 5.8g 5fg³
5f³ 5fg4 5f³ 5f 7fg 7g 5g 6fg) neat horse; sprint handicapper; acts on any going;
occasionally blinkered; suited by waiting tactics. *N. Vigors.*

BRENTHURST 2 ch.g. Shack 118–Bacchante (Immortality) (1983 7fg 7f 6f 5fg³ **68**
5fg4 5g 7g) May 3; IR 800F, 7,000Y; workmanlike gelding; fifth produce; dam
unraced daughter of smart sprinter Devon Vintage; in frame in minor event at
Windsor and maiden race at Wolverhampton in August; evidently suited by 5f;
blinkered fourth to sixth starts. *R. Laing.*

BRETTON PARK 5 b.g. Mummy's Pet 125–Trickster 92 (Major Portion 129) **§§**
(1982 6s 7f 8f 8f 8f 8f 8fg 8fg² 8f 1983 6fg 7f) strong, fair sort; has a round action;
ungenuine and unreliable handicapper; stays 1m; acts on any going; often
blinkered (has worn them with some success). *M. McCourt.*

BREVET 4 b.c. Busted 134–Major Barbara 90 (Tambourine II 133) (1982 9fg 10f² **102**
13.3f* 13.3f² 1983 12v4 12v 12v 13.3g³ 12f 13g* 12g4) most attractive colt; good
walker but not a good mover; useful performer; stayed on well to beat Ardoony
1½ lengths in handicap at Ayr in July; will stay 1¾m; acts on firm going but gives
impression he'll always be best with some give in the ground; sold 18,000 gns
Newmarket December Sales. *P. Walwyn.*

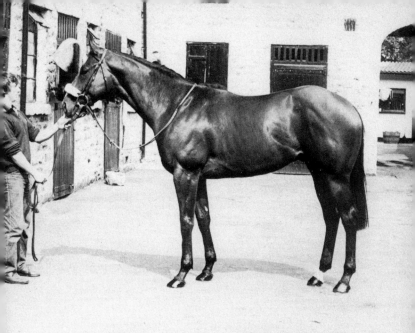

Mr R. Burke's "Brega Boy"

BREWIS 2 gr.g. Bruni 132–Saufina 106 (Hard Sauce 131) (1983 6f 6f 6fg 8s 8.2fg 8fg 8fg² 8fg) Apr 29; lengthy gelding; good walker; half-brother to 2 winners, including quite useful 6f winner Sienna (by Richboy); dam 5f sprinter; 33/1 and dropped in class, caught on line and beaten a head by Russborough in 20-runner selling nursery at Doncaster in October, easily best effort; stays 1m; unseated rider after 1f fourth start; blinkered sixth and seventh outings. *M. W. Easterby.* — 73

BREWMASTER 10 br.g. John Splendid 116–Ronelda (Tyrone 130) (1982 8.2g 1983 10fg) poor plater. *J. Mulhall.* — –

BREZZO (FR) 4 b.c. Gift Card 124–Brezette (Mossborough 126) (1982 10.5d² 12s 10v² 12s* 12d³ 12d* 12.5g² 13.5g 12v 12v* 12v* 10v* 1983 10v 12s³ 12s² 12v² 12.5fg 12.5g 10fg 12s² 12g 12g 12s*) half-brother to 2 winners in France; dam placed at around 9f in France; smart performer at his best; won minor event at Maisons-Laffitte in December; ran particularly well third and fourth starts when going down by 1½ lengths to Diamond Shoal in Grand Prix d'Evry and by 2½ lengths to Welsh Term in Prix Jean de Chaudenay at Saint-Cloud, both in May; stays 1½m well; revels in the mud. *N. Pelat, France.* — 113

BRIAN MARK 2 ch.c. On Your Mark 125–Bright Diadem (Pall Mall 132) (1983 5d 7f 6fg 7f 5f) Apr 15; workmanlike colt; soundly beaten in maiden auction events and sellers; dead. *M. W. Easterby.* — –

BRIANS BOY 2 gr.c. Scallywag 127–Florica 80 (Floriana 106) (1983 7fg 7g⁴ 8fg) Mar 12; big, workmanlike colt; fourth foal; half-brother to a winning plater; dam won sellers over 1m and 1¼m; 66/1, 5½ lengths fourth of 17 to All Hell Let Loose in maiden race at Leicester in September, only indication of merit; always struggling in better company the following month; will stay 1¼m. *N. Guest.* — 77

BRIAREAN 2 b.c. Ile de Bourbon 133–Latin Verses (Appiani II 128) (1983 8fg 8s² 8fg² 8.2s² 8g) Apr 26; IR 115,000Y; deep-girthed, quite attractive colt; — 84 half-brother to useful 6f winner Blessed Soandso (by So Blessed) and Irish 1m and 1½m winner Ballymenoch (by Relkino); dam, Irish 1½m winner, is half-sister to Mesopotamia; second in autumn maiden races, going down by 2 lengths to Flame Bearer at Beverley, by 2½ lengths to Caro's Gift at Newcastle and by a head to Laurie's Panther at Haydock; will stay 1¼m; yet to race on very firm going but acts on any other; blinkered last 2 outings; sold Mrs G. Forbes 13,500 gns Newmarket Autumn Sales and exported to Trinidad. *G. Harwood.*

BRIAVAN 3 br.f. Saulingo 122–Miss Season (Silly Season 127) (1982 5s³ 5fg² 6f⁴ **69**
5.8g³ 5fg 5d 5s 6g 1983 6s 5s 5s 6fg 5f* 5fg⁴ 5f⁴ 5f² 6fg² 6f² 6fg 6fg 6f 5.8fg 6fg) small filly; made all and kept on gamely to beat Balkan by ¾ length in minor event at Chepstow in June; stays 6f; seems to act on any going, but is best served by a sound surface; sometimes blinkered at 2 yrs; genuine. *M. McCourt.*

BRIDGE OF JOY 2 gr.f. Town Crier 119–Rose Bridges 63 (Calpurnius 122) **68**
(1983 6f 7f 6f⁴ 8f⁴ 8.2fg 8.2s) Mar 14; 4,000Y; lengthy filly; first foal; dam, plater, stayed 1¼m; plating-class maiden; suited by 1m; probably acts on any going. *J. W. Watts.*

BRIDGE STREET LADY 2 b.f. Decoy Boy 129–Diamond Talk (Counsel 118) **62 p**
(1983 5f 5fg, big, lengthy, fair sort; sister to fairly useful miler Corn Street, and half-sister to 2 winners, including fair sprinter Pusey Street (by Native Bazaar); dam never ran; prominent some way in 2 maiden races and a well-contested minor event; has scope and is the type to improve with racing. *J. Bosley.*

BRIDGE THE GAP 2 ch.c. Run The Gantlet–Pas de Probleme 99 (Sir Gaylord) **62**
(1983 7.6fg 9s) May 2; second live foal; half-brother to French 9f winner Rock Dancer (by Dance In Time); dam, 7f winner, comes from family of Rock Roi; modest sixth of 8 to Sassagrass in 9f maiden race at Wolverhampton in October, dropping out in last 3f; sold 1,800 gns Ascot November Sales, probably for export to Italy. *J. Dunlop.*

BRIDGTOWN-CASTLE 2 b.c. Porto Bello 118–Princess Elise (Prince Regent **–**
129) (1983 5d 7f) Feb 25; 1,100Y; lightly-built colt; first foal; dam never ran; in rear in maiden races at Leicester (started slowly) and Wolverhampton in June. *W. Clay.*

BRIDOON 8 ch.m. Brigadier Gerard 144–Keadby Bridge (Petition 130) (1982 NR **–**
1983 10.2g 6h) has been pin-fired; of little account; has been tried in blinkers. *B. Forsey.*

BRI-EDEN 9 b.g. The Brianstan 128–Dainty Eden 53 (Orbit 106) (1982 5g⁴ 5fg **105 d**
5fg 5f* 5fg³ 5f 5g* 5fg* 5f* 5g² 5fg² 5g* 5g⁴ 5f* 5fg³ 5v* 1983 5v 5s* 5g⁴ 5d* 5f 5f 5f³ 5fg 5fg 5fg)
The miserably wet spring resulted in regular laments from trainers concerning the problems they faced getting their charges ready to run when the horses were more backward than usual and a number of gallops remained waterlogged for weeks at a stretch. There was one notable exception to the prevailing air of pessimism though, for by the first of June Jack Berry had sent out no fewer than thirty-three winners (one was later disqualified on a technicality) from his fifty-six-box yard at Lancaster, a yard filled mainly with cheaply-bought horses who tend to run in ordinary races rather than fashionable ones. Interestingly, Berry's total at this stage of the season exceeded the combined tally of Harwood and Cecil, who eventually headed the trainers' list in number of races won, and while the phenomenal strike rate of the first months of the season was not maintained later on this in no way detracts from Berry's splendid achievement.

The brightest star of the string was its oldest member, the nine-year-old Bri-Eden, whose win in the Group 3 Ballyogan Stakes at Leopardstown in June made him one of the oldest horses ever to win a pattern race. Successful nine times for Berry from 1978 to 1981, Bri-Eden improved tremendously as an eight-year-old, picking up seven races including the Bovis Stakes at Ascot, and his form early in 1983 showed he had not gone back in the slightest. Quite the reverse, for after a pipe-opener at Doncaster early in May he went to York just over a week later to compete in the valuable David Dixon Sprint Trophy, giving weight to all but one of his eight opponents. He looked magnificent beforehand and put up a game display, making the running and responding enthusiastically to strong pressure in the final furlong to hold off Cree Song by a neck.

On the strength of this display Bri-Eden started favourite to win a handicap at Redcar on the last day of the month but finished only fourth. This form suggested he had no better than average chance of making the frame in the Ballyogan Stakes seven days later and he started at 10/1 in a field containing the CBA Greenlands Stakes winner Curravilla, the McCairns Trial winner Ancestral and useful sprinters

David Dixon Sprint Trophy Handicap. York—Bri-Eden responds enthusiastically to the challenge of Cree Song (No. 7)

of the order of Royal Hobbit and Tilden. Swiftly away, Bri-Eden had a commanding advantage over Tilden after a quarter of a mile, and though pressed by Royal Hobbit with a couple of furlongs to go he quickened away again to defeat the fast-finishing Hot Princess by three quarters of a length with Tilden third and Curravilla fourth. We are of the opinion that several of those behind Bri-Eden did not run up to their best—on his next start, for instance, Curravilla ran a close second in the Cork and Orrery, while Tilden proved good enough to finish fourth in the Prix de l'Abbaye four months later—but notwithstanding this Bri-Eden's performance was an excellent one, far in advance of anything he had achieved hitherto.

Unfortunately the old campaigner did not reproduce his Leopardstown form in six races afterwards, making the frame in only the Rous Memorial Stakes at Ascot and putting up probably his best effort when sixth of eight to Soba in the Scarbrough Stakes at Doncaster on his penultimate outing. Bri-Eden has already earned a special place in the affection of racegoers, but how long he can go on is anyone's guess. Certainly we hope that his substandard form towards the end of the year was nothing more than a temporary aberration for flat racing needs all the characters it can get, needs the Baronets, Be Hopefuls, Boldboys, Le Garcon d'Ors, Morris Dancers, Sea Pigeons and Bri-Edens since these do as much for the sport and its popularity as any number of Group 1 winners.

Bri-Eden (b. g. 1974)	The Brianstan (b 1967)	King's Leap (b 1959)	Princely Gift Impala
		Sissi (br 1953)	Walvis Bay September Lady
	Dainty Eden (br 1968)	Orbit (b 1958)	Ribot Eyewash
		Finger-Print (b 1957)	High Treason Fingertip Control

As pedigrees go Bri-Eden's is uninspiring but that has never hindered him in the slightest. His sire, a nailing good sprinter at his best, has had only one other pattern-race winner to represent him, the 1976 Richmond Stakes winner Stand to Reason, while his dam, a plater who won over a mile at Carlisle and stayed two miles, has foaled no other winners whatsoever. The second dam hardly set the world alight either, winning a six-furlong seller at Carlisle and producing one winner

besides Dainty Eden. Bri-Eden has been fired and operated on for a soft palate; he has worn bandages but didn't do so in 1983. A thoroughly genuine individual who has won for an amateur, he is evidently best at the minimum trip and acts on any going. *J. Berry.*

BRI-ETTE 2 gr.f. Brittany–Sweet Minuet (Setay 105) (1983 5g 5f 6f 7f 6fg) May 6; lengthy filly; sister to useful sprinter Tinjar and half-sister to winners here and abroad; dam ran once on flat and once over hurdles; little worthwhile form in maiden events and a nursery; worth bearing in mind if dropped to selling company. *J. Holt.*   **53**

BRIGADIER GREEN 6 b.g. Brigadier Gerard 144–Queen's Parole (Worden II 129) (1982 12f³ 10.6f 12d 10f 15.8f³ 1983 14fg 14.6f 10f⁴ 8g) neat gelding; poor handicapper; stays well; probably acts on any going; ran badly in blinkers once. *B. Richmond.*   **–**

BRIGADIER HAWK 5 b.h. Brigadier Gerard 144–Flibbertigibbet 97 (Klairon 131) (1982 12d 14² 16fg 16fg 12f 12fg 12g⁴ 10g 12fg* 14f⁴ 12g 11.7g 14.6g 12d 12s 1983 18d 14s 12s 10g 12f 12f² 14f 13.1h* 16f⁴ 13.1h³ 18.8f 12fg 16fg 12s) compact, good-bodied horse; won handicap at Bath in July; beaten in seller sixth start; stays 2m; probably acts on any going but is ideally suited by fast ground; sometimes blinkered; races with tongue tied down; inconsistent and unreliable. *C. Austin.*   **62 §**

BRIGADIER VICTOR 5 br.g. Brigadier Gerard 144–Humming Top 92 (Tudor Melody 129) (1982 NR 1983 15.8f 12.2f⁴) workmanlike gelding; has a very round action; poor performer; has been beaten in a valuable seller; suited by 13f; has worn bandages. *W. A. Stephenson.*   **–**

BRIGG MELODY 2 ch.f. Oedipus Complex–In For A Penny (Soletra 94) (1983   **65**
5g 6g 5d⁴ 6fg 6fg) fair sort; second live foal; dam never ran; 3½ lengths fourth of
14 to easy winner El Gazebo in maiden race at Catterick in October, best effort;
should stay 6f; blinkered final appearance. *A. Smith.*

BRIG GROVE 3 b.f. Brigadier Gerard 144–Sarsgrove 70 (Hornbeam 130) (1982   –
NR 1983 10fg) 760 2-y-o; half-sister to 4 winners, including fairly useful 1981
2-y-o 7f winner Northleigh (by Reform); dam won at up to 1½m; unquoted when
behind in 22-runner minor event at Nottingham in June. *G. Blum.*

BRIGHT CAMELLIA (USA) 2 b.f. Cannonade–Bold Amelia (Bold Reason)   **75**
(1983 6g 7f 7fg 7f 7.6d 7.3d) Apr 1; $35,000Y; rangy, quite useful-looking filly; first
foal; dam never ran; showed worthwhile form only when fifth of 13 in Sandown
maiden event in July on second outing; well-backed second favourite fifth start, and
blinkered on sixth; acts on firm going. *R. Armstrong.*

BRIGHT CECILIA 2 b. or br.f. Welsh Saint 126–Music Mistress 83 (Guide 118)   **–p**
(1983 6fg) May 30; lengthy, quite attractive filly; half-sister to several winners,
including useful 1977 2-y-o 6f winner Discreet (by Jukebox); dam ran only at 2 yrs;
20/1, moved nicely and shaped promisingly in 29-runner maiden race at Newmarket
in September, keeping on steadily without being knocked about; sure to improve.
M. Stoute.

BRIGHT CONE (USA) 3 gr.f. Giacometti 130–Lovelight 112 (Bleep-Bleep 134)   –
(1982 5fg² 6g* 6f 7fg 8g 6s³ 7d* 1983 7s³ 7s) big, well-made, quite attractive
filly; good walker; half-sister to very smart 5f to 1m winner Motavato (by
Apalachee); quite useful as a 2-y-o; ran only twice in 1983, keeping on steadily
when creditable third of 8 behind Silverdip in Salisbury 1000 Guineas Trial in April
but dropping out after 5f when disappointing sixth of 7 to Glasson Lady in Mulcahy
Stakes at Phoenix Park later in month; stays 1m; appears to act on any going. *B.
Hills.*

BRIGHTER BITE 2 br.f. Fordham 117–Sciure (Sea-Bird II 145) (1983 6g 6f 5f²   **66**
6f 5d) Apr 27; neat filly; fourth reported foal; dam French 1m winner; 2½ lengths
second of 19 to Costalotta in maiden race at Folkestone in September; should stay
beyond 5f. *D. Morley.*

BRIGHT FOLLY 2 b.c. Dublin Taxi–Irish Holiday 73 (Simbir 130) (1983 7f 5f   –
8.2f) Mar 15; workmanlike colt; not a good mover; first foal; dam won over 1¾m;
in rear in sellers, on final start last of 11; blinkered second outing; apparently of
no account. *N. Tinkler.*

BRIGHT HOLLOW 2 br.c. Wolver Hollow 126–Miss Legend (Bold Legend)   –
(1983 5s 7f 5f 6f) Apr 22; 12,000Y; small, attractive colt; brother to 3-y-o
Legendary Queen, and half-brother to useful 1978 Irish 2-y-o 5f performer Devilish
(by Red God); dam won twice over 6f in USA; in rear in varied company, twice
tailed off; blinkered third start; sold 1,650 gns Newmarket September Sales. *B.
Swift.*

BRIGHT SCOT 3 b.g. Shiny Tenth 120–Scots Bloom (Jock Scot 121) (1982 NR   –
1983 12s 14d 7fg) big, plain gelding; fourth foal; dam won over fences; well behind
in minor events at Beverley, York and Newmarket (blinkered). *H. Collingridge.*

BRIGHT SPIRIT 3 br.c. Quiet Fling 124–Liberation 63 (Native Prince) (1982   –
6fg³ 6s 1983 7s 7fg 8fg 10f 10f) tall, leggy colt; no form in 1983; should be suited
by 7f+; sweating badly fourth start. *R. Baker.*

BRIGHT WIRE 4 ch.g. Condorcet–Fairy Tree (Varano) (1982 10s* 10g³ 10f 16f   –
16d 16d 16.1s 1983 18f) lengthy gelding; stays 2m; acts on any going;
unimpressive in paddock and bandaged when tailed off only start (August). *J.
McNaughton.*

BRIGOMEIDE 2 ch.f. Brigadier Gerard 144–Sea Lichen 106 (Ballymoss 136)   **64**
(1983 6g 6f 5d⁴ 5g 5fg) Mar 27; tall, narrow filly; good walker; half-sister to
several winners here and abroad, including quite useful 1¼m and 11f winner
Rockeater (by Roan Rocket); dam fourth in 1000 Guineas; only plating class on
form in 5 races, one a nursery; not bred to sprint, and may do better at 1m or
more; sold 6,200 gns Ascot November Sales, probably for export to Italy. *G.
Wragg.*

BRILLANTE (FR) 3 gr.f. Green Dancer 132–Belga (Le Fabuleux 133) (1982 7g   **118**
8v* 1983 11v* 10v 10.5fg² 10.5fg³ 8fg 8s) sister to a disappointing animal and
half-sister to 3 winners, notably top-class miler Bellypha (by Lyphard) and very
smart middle-distance colt Bellman (by Riverman); dam, a winner over 9f at 3 yrs,
is half-sister to smart 1969 French 2-y-o Belmont; held up when beating Miss
Mulaz cheekily by ½ length in 100,000 francs event at Longchamp in April; placed
subsequently in Prix de Royaumont at Chantilly (short-neck second of 11 to Marie

de Litz) and Prix Fille de l'Air at Saint-Cloud (about 2 lengths third of 5 to Darine), both in June; off course 2 months after latter and was below best on her return; suited by middle distances; probably acts on any going. *Mme C. Head, France.*

BRILLIANT CUT 2 br.c. Diamonds Are Trump 108–Lucky Kim (Whistling Wind 123) (1983 5d 5v³ 6g 6d 6fg) Apr 11; 4,000Y; lightly-made colt; first foal; dam of little account; just over 5 lengths third of 12 to All Agreed in maiden race at Kempton in May, best effort; in rear under top weight in claiming nursery final start. *A. Jarvis.* **79**

BRILLIANT ROSA 3 b.f. Luthier 126–Raduga (Counsel 118) (1982 7d* 1983 12d 10f⁴ 12g² 12f² 12fg² 12d* 13.3d) tall, leggy, rather sparely-made filly; runner-up in 3 handicaps before beating Corduroy very easily by 2 lengths in one at Wolverhampton in October; suited by 1½m (had stiff task when tried over further); yet to race on really soft going, but acts on any other; didn't handle track well at Epsom on first outing. *M. Stoute.* **91**

BRINY 2 ch.f. Grundy 136–Bedeni 100 (Parthia 132) (1983 8d⁴) Mar 19; strong, sturdy, slightly hollow-backed filly; half-sister to several winners, including very useful 1976 2-y-o 5f to 7f winner Sky Ship (by Roan Rocket) and smart 1¼m filly Upper Deck (by Sun Prince); dam disappointing half-sister to smart animals Torpid and Admirals Launch; 33/1 and very green, ran well for long way and wasn't punished once chance had gone when promising 10 lengths fourth of 14 to Corinth in £4,000 event at Newbury in October; will be suited by 1¼m+; sure to improve. *R. Hern* **77 p**

BRISBANE ROAD 3 b.g. Pitskelly 122–Gamma (Zank) (1982 6d 7d 6f⁴ 6g 8d 1983 8v⁴ 7v 8s 8f) short-backed gelding; poor plater; possibly stays 1m; has twice worn blinkers. *C. Williams.* **—**

BRITISH 3 br.c. Blakeney 126–Saucy Flirt 102 (King's Troop 118) (1982 NR 1983 8d 12g 14f* 14f* 14f² 16g 18fg 16fg²) big, well-made, attractive colt; particularly good walker; half-brother to 3 winners, notably Prix de Diane winner Madam Gay (by Star Appeal); dam stayed 6f; won maiden race and minor event at Sandown in July, in latter event wearing down Dancing Admiral after rare duel and winning by a head; subsequently good second in quite valuable handicaps won by Gildoran at Goodwood and Hi Love at Newmarket, on latter course beaten only a short head under 9-7; by no means disgraced in better company in between; stays well; acts on firm ground; genuine; blinkered last 2 starts; sold 47,000 gns Newmarket Autumn Sales, reportedly for export to Australia. *R. Hern.* **98**

BRITISH PRINCE 4 b.g. Duc d'Orleans 76–What a Performance (Gala Performance) (1982 NR 1983 12v 12f 10.2f) dipped-backed gelding; poor walker; brother to a poor animal; dam probably of little account; poor maiden. *T. Kersey.* **—**

BROAD BEAM 3 b.g. Averof 123–Angel Beam 115 (Hornbeam 130) (1982 8s* 1983 8s² 10s 8s 8.3fg) rangy, quite attractive gelding; ran pleasingly when neck second to Rock's Gate in 10-runner minor event at Wolverhampton in April, but disappointed afterwards and wasn't seen out after July; should be suited by 1¼m; started slowly final outing; winning hurdler. *P. Walwyn.* **85**

BROADLEAF 2 b.c. Welsh Pageant 132–Pulchra 107 (Celtic Ash) (1983 6f) Apr 16; 7,000Y; big colt; brother to 14.7f winner The Professor and half-brother to 2 winners; dam won Nassau Stakes; unquoted, burly and in need of experience, behind in £3,100 event at Salisbury in August. *D. Hanley.* **—**

BROADWATER MUSIC 2 b.c. Music Boy 124–La Presidente 69 (Primera 131) (1983 5.1g 5g 5fg⁴ 5f² 5fg 5g* 5fg* 5g* 5fg) Mar 21; 7,600F; strong, workmanlike colt; half-brother to useful 1979 2-y-o 7f winner Black Earl (by So Blessed); dam won over 1½m; showed much improved form in the autumn, winning maiden race at Catterick by 5 lengths, making all under a 7-lb penalty to win Bloodstock and General Insurance Stakes (Nursery) at Newmarket by ¾ length from Reesh and then carrying a big weight to a ½-length success over Yallah in 12-runner apprentice nursery at Sandown; speedy but may well stay 6f; yet to race on a soft surface; ran well when sweating up. *M. Tompkins.* **100**

BROBURY 4 gr.g. Bladon 85–Ramona (Quorum 126) (1982 NR 1983 10.1f) third foal; half-brother to a winning hurdler; dam poor maiden; successful over hurdles; tailed off in minor event at Windsor in August. *D. H. Jones.* **—**

BROCKLEY BELLE 4 ch.f. Track Spare 125–Just Jolly 80 (Jolly Jet 111) (1982 7f⁴ 7g³ 8fg 7g 8s⁴ 8d 8s³ 1983 7d² 8d 8d⁴ 7d 7d² 7fg 7f 7.6fg² 7f 9f⁴ 8g³ 8d 10.2g) tall, light-framed filly; not a good walker or mover; placed in handicaps and a valuable seller; stays 1m; acts on any going; good mount for an apprentice; blinkered ninth start. *C. Spares.* **54**

Mr J. B. Moseley's "Brogan"

BROCKTON 2 gr. or ro. g. Broxted 120–Khotso (Alcide 136) (1983 6fg 6f 6h 7g) — Feb 16; fifth foal; half-brother to a winning jumper; dam never ran; poor form in maiden races and a nursery. *J. Smith.*

BROGAN (USA) 3 b. c. Nijinsky 138–Drumtop (Round Table) (1982 7fg⁴ 8fg² 110 8s* 1983 12v 12f² 15d³ 15fg* 15g 12h³) strong, good-bodied, attractive colt; from a very successful family and is brother to useful 11f to 13f winner Bedford and stakes-placed winner Kyra's Slipper; dam top-class American middle-distance filly; improved in 1983 and was placed in Derby Italiano at Rome (1½ lengths second to My Top) and Prix de l'Esperance at Longchamp before beating Ponty Pool impressively by 6 lengths when favourite for 9-runner Prix Berteux at Chantilly in June; last subsequently in Grand Prix de Paris won by Yawa at Longchamp (dropped out quickly before home turn) and 3-runner Welsh Derby at Chepstow (beaten 9 lengths by Russian Roubles); met with a setback afterwards and was sent to USA; suited by a test of stamina; seems to act on any going, but is well suited by a sound surface; blinkered nowadays and has also raced in a tongue strap. *I. Balding.*

BROKEN CHORD (USA) 2 gr. f. Stop the Music–Break a Heart (T. V. Lark) — (1983 7f 7f) Mar 20; $32,000Y; good-bodied filly; second foal; dam unplaced in 3 starts; unquoted, outpaced throughout in 2 races at Salisbury, £3,800 event in August and 18-runner maiden in September. *D. Elsworth.*

BROKENCROSS 3 b. c. The Brianstan 128–Aurelia 68 (Aureole 132) (1982 6d — 7g² 7d 8g 8s 1983 11.7s 8f 8f 8f) sturdy colt; no form in 1983; yet to show he stays beyond 7f; blinkered last 3 outings. *J. Douglas-Home.*

BROKEN HABIT (USA) 3 b. f. Habitony–Split Personality 68 (Home Guard 96 129) (1982 5g² 6d⁴ 5.8g* 5g* 5g² 5g 5s* 5g² 1983 6v 7g 5g 5g⁴ 5.8f² 6fg⁴ 5.3f* 5fg) smallish, lengthy, quite attractive filly; steadily recovered her form, and beat Guntrips Centenary in good style by 2½ lengths after being held up in handicap at Brighton in August; moved short to post and was never going only subsequent start; bred to stay beyond sprint distances; acts on any going; good mount for an apprentice; genuine; sold 40,000 gns Newmarket December Sales. *I. Balding.*

BROKEN RAIL 4 b.c. Busted 134–First Huntress 64 (Primera 131) (1982 **113** 10.4g* 14fg* 14.6f 1983 12d 14v³ 16g²) big colt; poor walker and has a round action; smart stayer; placed in Yorkshire Cup at York in May (still not fully wound up when 4½ lengths third to Line Slinger) and Henry II Stakes at Sandown later in month (1½ lengths second to Ore); not seen out again; stays well; evidently acts on a firm surface but gives impression he'll always be suited by some give in the ground. *R. Hern.*

BROKEN SEAL 4 br.f. Privy Seal 108–Histoun (Behistoun 131) (1982 12.2g² **73** 16f² 16fg* 16d⁴ 15.8f² 19f* 16f⁴ 17.4d 1983 18d 12v⁴ 18d* 15.8d³ 18f 16s) leggy, narrow filly; doesn't impress in appearance; has a round action; battled on gamely to win handicap at Doncaster in May; suited by a test of stamina; acts on any going; bandaged when well beaten last 2 starts. *C. Gray.*

BROMWICH BOY 3 b.g. Headin' Up–Will's Girl 76 (Will Somers 114§) (1982 **–** NR 1983 6s 5v 5f 5g 7.6g 8h³ 8f 8d 8.2g 6fg) strong, plain gelding; half-brother to successful sprinter Will's Star (by Dunoon Star); dam won 2-y-o 5f seller; showed only form when third in 1m maiden race at Chepstow in August (went left in last furlong). *L. Barratt.*

BRONDESBURY 3 br.c. Welsh Saint 126–Whistling Tudor (Whistling Wind 123) **110** (1982 5g* 5fg* 5fg² 5g* 5f* 5f* 5f* 1983 5d 5f) strong, attractive colt; good walker and exceptionally good mover; brilliantly speedy as a 2-y-o and won 6 of his 7 races, including Norfolk Stakes at Royal Ascot, invariably starting extremely fast and usually having his races sewn up by halfway; had a couple of minor setbacks afterwards and didn't recover his sparkle in 1983; appeared to have conditions ideal for him in King George Stakes at Goodwood in July on second start but was headed over a furlong out and finished only seventh of 14 to Soba; most unlikely to have stayed beyond 5f (even that distance stretched his stamina on a stiff track, especially when the ground was on the soft side); acted well on firm going; reportedly sold for stud duties in Southern Hemisphere. *W. O'Gorman.*

BRONISLAVA 2 ch.f. Nonoalco 131–Neriad (Princequillo) (1983 5f 5g 6fg) Feb **68** 27; lengthy, rather narrow filly; sister to very useful French 6f and 7f winner Firyal and to useful Irish 1m winner Delaneige, and half-sister to several winners, notably top-class 1½m filly Comtesse de Loir (by Val de Loir); dam never ran; 7 lengths fifth of 20 to Mrs Bennet in maiden race at Newbury in September, second outing and best effort; bred to be better suited by 7f+; very slowly away on debut. *J. Dunlop.*

BRONSKI 2 ch.c. Tower Walk 130–Princess Tavi (Sea Hawk II 131) (1983 6f 7g **–** 8d) Apr 15; useful-looking colt; second foal; half-brother to fairly useful 1981 2-y-o 6f and 7f winner Straeker (by Sharpen Up); dam well beaten all starts; behind in maiden races. *P. Felgate.*

BROOKLANDS BELLE 2 ch.f. Dublin Taxi–Pat's Fancy 82 (Falcon 131) (1983 **57** 5s 5s³ 5d² 5f³ 6fg 5fg 6g² 6f² 7g 6s) Apr 6; tall, leggy, rather narrow filly; half-sister to a minor 2-y-o winner; dam stayed 7f; placed in a maiden race and several sellers, one a nursery; should stay 7f; acts on any going; sold 1,000 gns Doncaster October Sales. *J. Berry.*

BROON'S LADY 2 b.f. Rapid River 127–Devil's Moon (Sheshoon 132) (1983 5v⁴ **55** 5d⁴ 6d 6f* 6fg³ 7h⁴ 7f² 6g) June 23; 100F; small filly; third foal; dam showed no ability; favourite and dropped in class, won 5-runner seller at Carlisle (no bid) in June by a length from Cross Farm Boy; stays 7f; acts on any going; consistent. *G. Lockerbie.*

BROON'S SECRET 9 b.g. Most Secret 119–Vaudaville 77 (Vigo 130) (1982 **–** 6fg* 6f* 6f* 6fg 6f³ 6fg* 5g 6fg 6fg* 1983 6g 6f 6f 6f 6fg 6fg) strong gelding; sprint handicapper; below form most starts in 1983; acts on any going, but clearly goes well on top-of-the-ground; has twice worn blinkers; usually apprentice ridden. *A. Jarvis.*

BROTHER GEOFFREY 4 b.g. Sheshoon 132–Eilan Aigas 93 (Counsel 118) **–** (1982 10.2g 12g³ 14.6g 1983 15.8d 13h 17.4g 16.1g) big, lengthy gelding; staying maiden. *C. Thornton.*

BROTHERLY (USA) 2 ch.c. The Minstrel 135–Politely (Amerigo 116§) (1983 **80** p 8fg) Apr 25; brother to 3-y-o Minstrely, closely related to very useful stakes winner Northerly (by Northern Dancer), successful at up to 1¼m, and half-brother to useful Irish 1m winner Salutely (by Hoist the Flag); dam high-class winner of 21 races at up to 11f; second favourite, never-dangerous ninth of 21 to

Alphabatim in maiden race at Newmarket in October; should do a good bit better in time. *R. Hern.*

BROTHER PARTISAN 2 b.g. Hillandale 125–Resist 55 (Reliance II 137) (1983 7fg 8g) Apr 17; first foal; dam won selling hurdles; in rear in autumn minor events at Brighton and Bath. *J. Old.* —

BROUGHTON STAR 3 ch.g. Mossberry 97–Monet Royal 79 (Monet 127) (1982 8g 8s 1983 13fg) lightly-raced maiden; seventh of 15 behind Westview at Nottingham in July. *J. Etherington.* —

BROWN RIFLE 3 bl.g. Scottish Rifle 127–Mother Brown 103 (Candy Cane 125) (1982 6d 6g 7.2s 8d 1983 8.2s) leggy gelding; modest plater; should stay 1¼m; sold 675 gns Ascot July Sales. *M. Naughton.* —

BROWN SANDS 3 b.f. Radetzky 123–Double Sands (Double Jump 131) (1982 5g 6g 7g 8fg 5s 1983 6f) workmanlike filly; behind in maiden and minor races; blinkered last 3 starts. *D. Sasse.* —

BROWN'S CAY 2 ch.f. Formidable 125–Queen of Twilight 107 (Off Key 121 or Twilight Alley 133) (1983 7s 8.2fg³) May 5; 26,000Y; good mover; half-sister to several winners, including smart stayer Antler (by Northfields); dam won at up to 1¾m, including Jockey Club Stakes; 8 lengths third of 16 to Alleging in £3,400 event at Nottingham in October; will stay middle distances. *F J. Houghton.* **71**

BROWN SHADOW 3 b.g. Hittite Glory 125–Pop Gun ᴏ5 (King's Troop 118) (1982 5fg² 6fg* 6g³ 8.2s 1983 10s 8.3s* 8v 7f) lengthy, rather dipped-backed gelding; good walker; plater; bought in 1,350 gns after winning at Windsor in May; stays 1m well; probably acts on any going. *M. Pipe.* **72**

BROWN TAW 2 b.f. Whistlefield 118–Taw Court 58 (Lear Jet 123) (1983 5s 5v 5g³ 5f 5.8h 5.8h²) Mar 28; second foal; dam sprint plater; plating-class maiden; not seen out after July; best form at 5f on a sound surface; blinkered last 2 outings. *J. Hill.* **66**

BROWN VELVET 3 b.f. Mansingh 120–Luckhurst (Busted 134) (1982 5fg 5fg 5.3g⁴ 5g 1983 6s 5g 6f 5.3f 5g 6fg) compact, workmanlike filly; plating-class maiden; gives strong impression she's a short runner; trained by B. Swift first 3 outings. *M. Haynes.* —

BROXADELLA 3 br.f. Broxted 120–Addie (Klairon 131) (1982 5d 1983 5v 5s² 5fg 6fg 6fg³ 5fg) lengthy filly; placed in small race in Isle of Man and handicap at Pontefract; stays 6f; swerved at start first and last outings, taking no part on first occasion and unseating rider on second. *A. W. Jones.* – §

BRUALILAD 2 ch.g. Whitstead 125–Minna 59 (Pirate King 129) (1983 5v³) Apr 9; 2,100Y; useful-looking gelding; half-brother to Brown Gold, placed over 7f here as a 2-y-o and subsequently successful in USA, and to a winner in Austria (both by Cavo Doro); dam half-sister to 2000 Guineas winner Only for Life; 5/4 favourite, kept on at one pace when 5 lengths third of 6 to Oyston's Special in minor event at Newcastle in April; gelded subsequently; likely to need a test of stamina. *M. H. Easterby.* —

BRUMMENDELLE 4 gr.f. Bruni 132–Make Amends 74 (Tutankhamen) (1982 8d 9g⁴ 11.7f 12f 12f 17.1s 1983 10.8v³ 12fg 17f 12g) lengthy, plain filly; plating-class maiden; stays 11f; acts on heavy going; blinkered second start. *D. Wintle.* —

BRYMA 3 b. or br.g. Rymer 121–Saucy Walk (Saucy Kit 76) (1982 5d 7fg 6f 1983 11.7v 10.1fg 10.1f 10f 16h) tall, rangy, slightly dipped-backed gelding; poor form in maiden and minor events. *B. Palling.* —

BRYONY ROSE 2 gr.f. Bruni 132–Pritillor 93 (Privy Councillor 125) (1983 6s* 6fg* 7f³ 6g 6f³) Mar 10; lengthy filly; good walker and a good, easy mover; half-sister to 1m and 1½m winner Robert Adam (by Mansingh); dam best at up to 1¼m; won 17-runner maiden race at Leicester in May and 15-runner minor event at Windsor in July; ran well subsequently in useful company, on fourth outing finishing close-up sixth in Lowther Stakes at York; should stay at least 1¼m; acts on any going; game and genuine. *A. Jarvis.* **96**

BUCKALEX (USA) 2 b.f. Buckaroo–Ricara (Thorn) (1983 5f 5f 7d) May 3; $14,000Y; leggy filly; first foal; dam unraced half-sister to high-class Australian 5f to 1m winner Citius; sire, son of Buckpasser, was very smart at up to 9f; in rear in maiden races. *D. Morley.* —

BUCKLOW HILL 6 b.g. Rheingold 137–Parmassia (Pampered King 121) (1982 12fg 12f 12fg² 14.7f* 14g 12fg* 14.6g² 13d 12s 1983 14.7f² 12g 14g 12f*(dis) 14.6fg* 14d 12fg⁴) tall gelding; won handicap at Beverley in August on merit but **91**

Esal Bookmakers Handicap, Doncaster—Bucklow Hill wins in good style from Jupiter Island

was disqualified for hampering fourth horse; gained handsome compensation in £20,000 Esal Bookmakers Handicap at Doncaster the following month, travelling well throughout and beating Jupiter Island in good style by 3 lengths; stays 1¾m well; ideally suited by fast ground; sometimes sweats up. *J. Fitzgerald.*

BUCKMINSTER BOY 2 ch.g. Sweet Revenge 129–Tintale (Tin Whistle 128) (1983 5d* 5d² 5d⁴ 5s³ 6f⁴ 6g 7fg) May 21; IR 2,000Y; workmanlike gelding; half-brother to several minor winners here and abroad; dam ran 4 times; won maiden race at Doncaster in March; off course 4 months after fifth outing, and ran poorly in nurseries on return; stays 6f; acts on any going. *W. Wharton.* **68**

BUCKS FIZZ MUSIC 3 ch.f. Be Friendly 130–Hastily 99 (Hornbeam 130) (1982 5.8g 5d² 5fg 1983 6fg 7f² 6fg 7f 8f 6fg² 6g 5g) workmanlike filly; second in maiden race at Leicester and apprentice handicap at Folkestone; ran moderately last 2 starts; stays 7f; yet to race on really soft going but acts on any other; blinkered last 3 outings. *B. Gubby.* **65**

BUD'S GIFT 4 ch.g. Tudor Music 131–Recapped (Sallust 134) (1982 7d 7f 6f³ 7fg 8g 6fg 7f 1983 10d³ 10.1d² 10.8v 10.1fg) neat gelding; plater; stays 1¼m; acts on any going; suitable mount for an apprentice; has worn blinkers. *G. Balding.* **37**

BUGSY MALONE 2 ch.c. Music Boy 124–Lady Of York 75 (Double-U-Jay 120) (1983 6f 6f 7fg) Feb 19; IR 13,500Y; small, strong colt; second foal; dam won 3 times over 1½m; poor maiden; blinkered final outing; sold 2,500 gns Newmarket Autumn Sales; sent to Singapore. *Sir Mark Prescott.* **–**

BULANDSHAR 4 ch.g. Royal Palace 131–Castle Mona 78 (Sound Track 132) (1982 11.5fg 10.1g 1983 8d) fair sort; poor maiden. *D. Jermy.* **–**

BULLOM 3 b.g. Bustino 136–Romella (Romulus 129) (1982 7g⁴ 7g⁴ 7fg 8.2d 1983 8fg² 9d* 8f⁴ 12.3f² 9.4f² 12.2f⁴ 12.2f4 12.3f⁴ 8fg 11fg) big, useful-looking gelding; good walker, but by no means the best of movers; beat Fai La Bella in good style by 4 lengths in minor event at Redcar in May; second in 2 handicaps afterwards; probably stays 1½m; yet to race on really soft going, but seems to act on any other; pulled hard and raced with head high on sixth start. *D. Smith.* **83 d**

BUMPKIN 3 b.f. Free State 125–The Country Lane 90 (Red God 128§) (1982 5f³ 5fg* 5f³ 5fg 6fg* 6g 5fg² 6d* 1983 7g 6v⁴ 6f 6fg 6f*) well-made, attractive filly; good walker; returned to form and put up a very useful effort in apprentice handicap at Newbury in August, beating Briavan in great style by 4 lengths after being held up; headstrong and unlikely to get 7f, or even 6f in testing conditions; acts on firm going and a soft surface; sweated up fourth start. *I. Balding.* **108**

BUNCE BOY 7 b.g. King Emperor–All Hail 112 (Alcide 136) (1982 12f² 12f* 12f 12g 12f³ 12g² 12fg 12g⁴ 12g 1983 12d⁴ 12s⁴ 10f² 12fg² 12f 12f* 12d³ 12fg⁴) useful sort; middle-distance handicapper; goes well at Brighton and won there in August; ideally suited by top-of-the-ground conditions and forcing tactics; occasionally blinkered; suitable mount for an apprentice. *Miss A. Sinclair.* **72**

BUNCH OF THYME 3 b.f. Owen Dudley 121–Annabel Lee (Crooner 119) (1982 NR 1983 8v) 700Y; first foal; dam never ran; 50/1 when remote fifth of 7 behind Galetzky in maiden race at Newcastle in April; sold 300 gns Doncaster November Sales. *P. Calver.* **–**

BUNDABURG 3 ch.c. Creetown 123–Maple Syrup 89 (Charlottown 127) (1982   85
5fg 5fg⁴ 1983 6s³ 5v 8f⁴ 7f* 8f* 8f³ 8f 8.3fg) workmanlike colt; ran on well to win
handicaps at Salisbury in June and Brighton in July; suited by 7f and 1m; probably
acts on any going, but is well suited by firm; retained 4,000 gns Doncaster October
Sales. *S. Matthews.*

BUNTER 5 b.h. Prince de Galles 125–New Flag (Royal Serenade 131) (1982 8g   –
8fg 7fg 8g 1983 8d 7.6v 10fg 8f) quite attractive, good sort; useful at his best but
has deteriorated; best at 1m; seems to act on any going. *A. Moore.*

BURAAG 2 b.c. Shirley Heights 130–Star Court 102 (Aureole 132) (1983 7g) Mar   – p
4; 120,000Y; fair sort; third foal; half-brother to 2 winners, including useful 1978
2-y-o 7f winner Etoile des Indes (by Kashmir II); dam won over 7f at 3 yrs and is
half-sister to Owen Dudley and Abwah; second favourite but backward, always
behind in 18-runner maiden race at Leicester in October; should do better. *P.
Walwyn.*

BURBRIDGE DANCER 2 br.c. Stradavinsky 121–Bristol Milk 88 (Raise You   85
Ten 125) (1983 5v 5d 6g 6fg* 7f⁴ 5g 6fg³ 6f* 6f⁴) May 26; quite a useful-looking
colt; half-brother to 3 winners, including useful middle-distance winner Corked (by
Tumble Wind) and 1m to 1¼m winner Majestic Nurse (by On Your Mark); dam
stayed 1½m; won 2 races, seller at Warwick (bought in 2,600 gns) by 15 lengths and
nursery at Catterick; other form a bit mixed; suited by 6f; best form on fast ground;
acts well on sharp tracks; blinkered at Warwick and twice afterwards. *N. Tinkler.*

BURBRIDGE KING ST 2 b.g. Dublin Taxi–Granny Smith 76 (Tiger 125) (1983   40
5s³ 5d 6g 5d 6f 6f) Feb 27; 2,300Y; sturdy gelding; half-brother to out-and-out
stayer Golden Apple (by Athens Wood) and a winner in Hong Kong; dam needed
long distances; soundly beaten, including in sellers; blinkered final start. *N.
Tinkler.*

BURGLARS WALK 3 b.g. Godswalk 130–Pay Roll 94 (Burglar 128) (1982 5fg²   –
6fg 6f⁴ 1983 8d 6d 12.3f 11fg⁴ 15f 12fg 16f) big, rangy individual; rather a
disappointing maiden; possibly stays 11f; last when blinkered sixth outing; trained
by R. Williams first outing. *W. Stubbs.*

BURGOS 3 ch.g. Grundy 137–La Speroana 68 (Roan Rocket 128) (1982 NR 1983   85
10v 13.3g* 14h⁴ 16fg 14g) strong, well-made gelding; half-brother to 3 winners
by Mill Reef, including 1000 Guineas third Dione and smart middle-distance
stayer Beau Reef; dam 1m winner; 20/1 and sweating quite badly, ran easily best
race when winning 12-runner maiden event at Newbury in June by ¾ length from
Horton Line; should be suited by 1¾m+; unruly in paddock and ran
disappointingly last time out. *J. Dunlop.*

BURGUNDY STAR 2 b.g. Averof 123–Pellarosa (Crepello 136) (1983 6f² 6g   77
5f) May 28; 6,000Y; close-coupled gelding; first reported live foal; dam unraced
half-sister to very useful fillies Denosa and Rimosa's Pet; ran well for a newcomer
when short-head second of 12 to Emergency Plumber in maiden race at Nottingham
in July, being caught close home after running green in final furlong; faded after
showing good early pace on subsequent starts, wearing blinkers third outing
(apprentice ridden); bred to stay 7f+ but needs to learn to settle to do so. *P.
Kelleway.*

BURLEY GRIFFIN 3 b.c. Octavo 115–Whispering Breeze (Caliban 123) (1982   93
7g⁴ 8d 7d² 1983 9v* 10.5f 10g² 13g) big, strong colt; carried plenty of condition;
won maiden event at Newcastle in May impressively by 10 lengths from Let Me
Play; head second to Dick 'E' Bear in handicap at Ayr, best subsequent effort;
would have stayed 1½m; possibly needed some give in the ground; broke a leg and
was destroyed at Ayr in July. *D. Smith.*

BURLEY HILL LAD 3 b.c. Anax 120–Home Sweet Home (Royal Palace 131)   –
(1982 5f 1983 5g 8d 12fg 12f 18f) compact colt; seems of little account; blinkered
final start. *A. Cawley.*

BURLINGTON LAD 4 ch.c. Sweet Revenge 129–Allegretto (Preciptic 122)   46
(1982 6d 5d 6g 5f 5g 5d 6g 7s* 1983 8d 8v 9s 8s 7s² 6fg 6g 6s 8.2s³) small colt;
plater; sometimes runs respectably in better company; suited by 7f+; acts well on
soft going; has worn blinkers once. *J. Perrett.*

BURNS LAD 2 b.g. Balidar 133–Petitt 60 (Mummy's Pet 125) (1983 7f 6g 6g)   –
May 8; robust, good sort; second foal; dam sprint plater; soundly beaten in autumn
maiden and minor events. *P. Asquith.*

BURNT ASH 2 b.g. Firestreak 125–Glebe 83 (Tacitus 124) (1983 5d 6f 6f³ 8.2g   –
7fg) May 14; half-brother to several winners, including 7f winner Cannon Hall (by
Singing Bede); dam, winner over 2m, is half-sister to high-class filly Bringley; poor
maiden. *W. Holden.*

Lord Iveagh's "Burslem"

BURN UP 4 b.f. Blue Cashmere 129–Stick 'Em Up (Burglar 128) (1982 7f 7f 6g 7s **65**
7d 6s 7s 1983 6s 6s 6fg² 6f* 6f 7f⁴ 6g* 6f 6h) neat filly; sprint handicapper; won at
Ripon in June and Ayr in August; sometimes runs in sellers; acts well on fast
ground; suitable mount for an apprentice; sold 800 gns Doncaster November Sales.
P. Asquith.

BURSLEM 3 ch.c. Nebbiolo 125–Spice Road (Gallant Man) (1982 5g* 5f 7fg* **123** d
6.3fg³ 7d² 8s² 1983 8f* 8fg* 12f³ 10.5d 8d³) medium-sized, workmanlike colt;
half-brother to numerous winners here and abroad, notably smart 1979 Irish 2-y-o
6f winner Noble Shamus (by Royal and Regal); dam won at up to 1m in USA; not
seen out until June, but put up good displays to win 13-runner Coolmore Hello
Gorgeous Stakes at the Curragh and 5-runner Guinness Golden Fleece Stakes at
Phoenix Park; beat odds-on Beaudelaire by ¾ length in former and held on by a
short head from Montekin in latter; third behind Condell in Royal Whip Stakes at
the Curragh and behind Erin's Hope in Desmond Stakes on same course
afterwards, but was one of first beaten when only eighth of 9 behind Caerleon in
Benson and Hedges Gold Cup at York in between; effective at 1m and seemed to
stay 1½m; acted on any going; standing at Ashleigh Stud, Meath, fee IR £4,000
(Oct 1st). *K. Prendergast, Ireland.*

BUSACO 4 b.g. Bustino 136–Deed 86 (Derring-Do 131) (1982 10.4fg 8.2f 10g* **—**
10f* 10v⁴ 10s* 10g 1983 10.2v 12g³ 22.2f 12g⁴) strong, compact gelding;
showed a bit of knee action; a smart handicapper at his best; showed only form at
4 yrs when fourth of 10 to Jupiter Island in valuable event at Newmarket in
August; stayed 1½m; acted on any going; suited by waiting tactics; dead. *S.
Mellor.*

148

BUSHTI MUSIC 3 b.f. Bustino 136–Light Link 99 (Tudor Music 131) (1982   **63**
6.3fg 7f² 6fg³ 7g² 6f 1983 8g⁴ 9f³ 10fg 7f 9f⁴) leggy, rather lightly-built ex-Irish
filly; has a round action; third foal; half-sister to very useful sprinters Hanu (by
Hot Spark) and Sanu (by Steel Heart); dam won over 5f and 6f at 2 yrs; placed in
Ireland as a 2-y-o when trained by D. K. Weld; in frame over here at Bath and
Wolverhampton in June but didn't run well afterwards; stays 9f; bandaged behind
first outing. *F. Durr.*

BUSHY TOP 2 ch.f. Thatching 131–Right Now 100 (Right Royal V 135) (1983 7f²   **83**
7f² 7f³ 8d) Feb 19; IR 10,000Y (privately); good-bodied filly; half-sister to several
winners, including useful hurdler Exalted (by King Emperor); dam 1½m winner and
half-sister to Mon Fils and Son of Silver; modest maiden; consistent until running
poorly at Beverley in September on final appearance; should stay 1m; possibly
unsuited by softish ground. *D. Morley.*

BUSORM 3 ch.g. Bustino 136–Wrekinianne 96 (Reform 132) (1982 5f* 6f² 1983   **–**
7v⁴ 8v 10v 8v) medium-sized, quite attractive gelding; quite useful at 2 yrs; having
first race for 10 months when nearly 10 lengths fourth of 11 behind Annamoe Bray in
Northern Free Handicap at Newcastle in April (didn't seem to last the trip out in
testing ground and probably needed run); didn't run particularly well afterwards
and wasn't seen out after May; bred to stay quite well. *M. H. Easterby.*

BUSTED FLAVOUR 2 b.c. Busted 134–Minarika (Djakao 124) (1983 8fg) Apr   **74 p**
7; fifth foal; dam dead-heated in small 9f race in France; 50/1, burly and green,
showed up in 28-runner maiden race won by Bob Back at Newmarket in October.
M. Albina.

BUSTLING NELLY 2 gr.f. Bustino 136–Flying Nelly 107 (Nelcius 133) (1983   **92 p**
6f²) May 16; smallish, well-made filly; fourth foal; sister to fairly useful 1½m
winner Neltino, closely related to quite useful stayer Morning After (by Busted)
and half-sister to a winner; dam stayed 13f but was best at 1m to 1¼m; well-backed
co-favourite, led 2f out until close home when beaten ¾ length by Rusticello in
8-runner Virginia Water Stakes for newcomers at Ascot in July; sure to win races
over longer distances. *B. Hills.*

BUSTOFF 3 b.g. Bustino 136–Magical 95 (Aggressor 130) (1982 8g 1983 10fg   **–**
12f 12g) strong, good-topped, attractive individual; good mover; ninth of 27 behind
Zaheer in maiden race at Sandown in June; still looked as if he needed more time
when last of 6 to Society Boy in Churchill Stakes at Ascot later in month and was off
course afterwards until November, when in rear in maiden event at Redcar (needed
race); sold privately out of M. Jarvis's stable after second outing. *Miss S. Hall.*

BUTTON BRIGHT (USA) 3 br.c. Honest Pleasure–Admiring (Hail to Reason)   **–**
(1982 8g 1983 8d 8v 10d) rangy colt; little worthwhile form in maiden and minor
events. *I. Balding.*

BUY INTERSPORT 3 br.c. Track Spare 125–Last Stop (Charlottown 127)   **39**
(1982 5fg 7fg 8s 1983 7v 8fg 7f 8g 8f³ 9fg³ 10h 9f 10g⁴ 12.2d 10g) plater; stays 9f;
acts on firm going; blinkered eighth outing; sold out of J. Etherington's stable 1,250
gns Doncaster September Sales after ninth start. *A. Potts.*

BUZZLER 2 b.c. Comedy Star 121–Malina 94 (Astec 128) (1983 5d 5v 6d² 7fg*   **97**
7fg⁴ 6fg* 7g² 7.2g* 8fg 7fg) May 19; 6,400Y; fair sort; third foal; half-brother to
2m winner Palikari (by Petingo) and a winner in Italy; dam won over 6f at 2 yrs from
only 3 starts; successful in maiden auction event at Warwick in June (made all under
top weight) and in nurseries at Pontefract in August and Haydock (under 9-7) in
September; stays 1m; acts on a firm and a soft surface; genuine. *J. Bethell.*

BYDAR 2 b.g. Balidar 133–Real Party 68 (Realm 129) (1983 5fg² 5fg³ 6fg 5g⁴ 5g)   **78**
Mar 25; 17,000Y; second foal; dam, half-sister to dam of Madam Gay, won over 5f
at 2 yrs; quite a modest maiden; apparently best at 5f; blinkered final outing;
disappointing. *W. O'Gorman.*

BY DECREE (USA) 3 gr.c. Caro 133–Lindaria (Sea-Bird II 145) (1982 7fg 7s*   **95**
1983 10fg 12f 8g 10.5fg 10g³ 8fg 10.8d⁴) big, rangy, good sort; good walker; very
useful as a 2-y-o; didn't run particularly well in 1983, best efforts when in frame in
handicap at Goodwood in September and minor event at Warwick in October;
stays 1¼m; possibly needs some give in the ground; blinkered last 3 outings; best
with strong handling. *G. Harwood.*

BYE APPEAL 7 ch.g. Busted 134–One Extra 85 (Abernant 142) (1982 15.5fg*   **59**
16f⁴ 15.5f* 20fg 1983 14fg 15.5f³ 16.5f) rangy gelding; staying handicapper;
suited by top-of-the-ground; often makes the running; has worn bandages; ran
badly final start. *J. Winter.*

BYE BYE BIRDIE (FR) 2 ch.c. Anne's Pretender 124–Love For Love (Abdos   **88 p**
134) (1983 10fg³) Mar 23; 115,000 francs Y (approx £9,600); close-coupled colt;

half-brother to minor winners in France and USA; dam, placed from 6.5f to 11.5f in France, is half-sister to very useful Danestic; 12/1 and bit backward, always prominent when promising 2 lengths third of 9 to High Debate in Jennings The Bookmakers Zetland Stakes at Newmarket in October; will stay 1½m. *P. Kelleway.*

BYKER 3 ch.g. Vitiges 132–Upper Deck 115 (Sun Prince 128) (1982 NR 1983 — 10fg 10fg 10g4) 1,100 3-y-o; first foal; dam very useful 1¼m filly; never-dangerous fourth to wide-margin winner Bahoor in amateur riders race at Lingfield in October; in mid-division in seller on same course earlier in month. *R. Hoad.*

BYLLY THE KID (FR) 7 ch.g. Yours 125–Bycorne (Prominer 125) (1982 10d 116 9.7fg4 10.5d3 9g 9d* 12g 10fg4 10fg 9.7f* 10s2 10g 1983 10s 10.5s 10.5fg 9g2 9fg3 10fg 10f* 10fg* 10fg4) French gelding; a tough campaigner who won valuable handicap at Deauville in August by a nose from Abdonski and La Coupe de Maisons-Laffitte in September by ½ length from Alzao; best at around 1¼m; acts on any going; smart. *R. Touflan, France.*

BYROC BOY 6 b.g. Runnymede 123–Royal Pat 80 (King's Troop 118) (1982 5d 52 6g 5f 5g* 5.8f2(dis) 6f 5.8f 5g2 1983 5v 5d3 5fg4 5g 5.3f3 5f 6fg 5f2 6fg 6g) strong, sprint type; former plater; stays 6f; probably acts on any going; sometimes blinkered; suitable mount for an apprentice. *D. Jermy.*

BYRON LANE 3 ro.f. North Stoke 130–Casino Queen (Silver Shark 129) (1982 NR 1983 9f 12f 14f 9d 8d) 1,500Y; big, strong, good-topped filly; half-sister to successful Irish sprinter King Song (by Song); dam never ran; behind in maiden and minor events. *B. McMahon.*

BY SURPRISE 2 ch.f. Young Generation 129–Ambuscade 77 (Relko 136) (1983 71 p 7fg) Apr 1; sturdy, lengthy filly; half-sister to 3 winners, including useful 6f to 1½m winner Balanchine (by Ballymore); dam, winner over 1½m, is half-sister to Smuggler and Little Wolf; 25/1 and backward, 9 lengths ninth of 22 to Travel Away in maiden race at Newmarket in October; will be suited by 1m; sure to improve. *Sir Mark Prescott.*

C

CABALLO 4 ch.g. Track Spare 125–Colinetta (Alba Rock 107) (1982 8fg 9g 8fg2 86 12fg4 10fg2 12v 10s 1983 8d 10s 8fg 8f* 8fg* 10g3 8f 8h 9fg2 10g4 10d3 8fg2 10.2fg3) rangy gelding; good mover; won apprentice race and handicap at Brighton in June; best at up to 1¼m; acts well on fast ground; suitable mount for an inexperienced rider. *K. Brassey.*

CABALLEROS 3 ch.c. Sallust 134–Hidden Key 110 (Sing Sing 134) (1982 NR 1983 7d 7f) IR 27,000Y; good-bodied colt; half-brother to 3 winners here and abroad, including Irish 1m winner Celera (by Sun Prince); dam very speedy 2-y-o; behind in newcomers race at Doncaster in March (dwelt) and maiden race at Folkestone in August. *R. Simpson.*

CADDAGAT 3 b.g. Be My Guest 126–Merry Mate 109 (Ballymoss 136) (1982 8d 10s 8s4 1983 10s 10s 9.5g3 10g 10s4 10v4 12v2 17v 13.1v 11f 14fg 13.3d 16g) big, tall gelding; in frame in 2 races at Pisa, handicap at Kempton and maiden race at Doncaster in spring; ran moderately afterwards; suited by 1½m, but has yet to show he stays further; occasionally blinkered. *D. Sasse.*

CADOUDAL (FR) 4 br.c. Green Dancer 132–Come To Sea (Sea Hawk II 131) 124 (1982 10d* 10.5d3 12s* 12fg 12f 12s 12v4 1983 10v2 10.5d2) 180,000 francs Y (approx £18,000); third foal; half-brother to French 1¾m winner Come To Reef (by Mill Reef); dam very useful middle-distance performer in France; very smart performer; ran well in 2 races at Longchamp early in year, going down by 4 lengths to Welsh Term in Prix d'Harcourt and just failing to get up when short-head second to Lancastrian in Prix Ganay; sustained an injury in latter and did not race again; stayed 1½m; revelled in the mud; bandaged once at 3 yrs; retired to Haras du Hoguenet at 30,000 francs + 20,000 francs Oct 1st. *B. Secly, France.*

CAEDMON 2 gr.c. Bruni 132–L'Aventura 65 (Elopement 125) (1983 5g 7f 9f 71 10fg4) May 3; 12,500Y; good-topped colt; half-brother to several winners here and abroad, including quite useful sprinter Chin-Chin (by Sing Sing); dam won at 1m and 1¼m; 2 lengths fourth of 19 to subsequently-demoted My Aisling in maiden race at Nottingham in October; suited by a stiff test of stamina; retained 7,800 gns Newmarket Autumn Sales. *C. Brittain.*

CAERHAGEN 2 ch.f. Mount Hagen 127–Caerinion 76 (Royal Palace 131) (1983 **81** 5g³ 5fg 5f⁴ 6fg 6g²) May 14; 6,600Y; small filly; quite attractive; third foal; sister to a plating-class animal; dam, daughter of 1000 Guineas winner Caergwrle, placed over 1m; put up easily best effort when short-head second of 10 to Speak Nobly in minor event at Chester in August, leading over 5f and fighting back well; will be suited by 7f and 1m; best form with some give in the ground; clearly suited by a sharp track. *D. Arbuthnot.*

CAERLEON (USA) 3 b.c. Nijinsky 138–Foreseer (Round Table) (1982 6g* **132** 6.3fg* 1983 10s 10g² 12fg* 12f² 12fg 10.5d*)
The names change—The Minstrel giving way to Alleged, Alleged to such as Golden Fleece and Assert, Golden Fleece and Assert to such as Caerleon, Lomond and Solford—but the Sangster bandwagon rolls on. The sun, it seems, hardly ever sets on Robert Sangster's racing empire nowadays; a week seldom passes without his being represented somewhere round the world by a big-race contender. In Britain alone, Mr Sangster's familiar green and blue silks were carried to success in forty races on the flat in 1983 and he ended the season as leading owner with record earnings of £461,488. It was the fourth time in seven years that he had topped the list, a degree of domination not seen since the days of the present Aga Khan's grandfather.
Sangster heads one of the richest bloodstock buying groups in the world which concentrates on purchasing fashionably-bred, good-looking yearling colts, the types Sangster and his associates have been convinced from the outset would appreciate in value provided they met with some sort of racecourse success. The Sangster syndicates, which made their first substantial yearling purchases in 1975, have had some multi-million-dollar payoffs—they have sold stallions consistently successfully for big money to the Americans—and have also built up an impressive array of sires at the Coolmore Stud complex in Ireland. Among those joining the likes of Be My Guest, Golden Fleece, Hello Gorgeous, Kings Lake, Pas de Seul and Thatching at Coolmore in 1984 will be the classic winners Lomond and Caerleon, the former a son of Northern Dancer, the stallion who has been at the hub of the Sangster success story, and the latter sired by Northern Dancer's son Nijinsky. Lomond won the latest Two Thousand Guineas while Caerleon, who gave Sangster his second successive winner of the Prix du Jockey-Club (French Derby) in June, contributed £93,980 to his owner's 1983 first-prize money earnings in Britain when winning the Benson and Hedges Gold Cup at York in August. Solford, who won the Coral-Eclipse Stakes, and El Gran Senor, winner of the William Hill Dewhurst, also carried the Sangster colours to success in Group 1 pattern races in Britain during the season.
Caerleon, Lomond, Solford and most of their well-bred contemporaries in

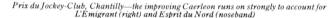

Prix du Jockey-Club, Chantilly—the improving Caerleon runs on strongly to account for L'Emigrant (right) and Esprit du Nord (noseband)

Benson and Hedges Gold Cup, York—Caerleon puts up another fine effort, resisting Hot Touch's strong challenge

the O'Brien stable were only lightly raced in their first season. Caerleon won both his races, including the Ballsbridge-Tattersalls Anglesey Stakes, a pattern race at the Curragh, and officially rated the second best of his age to race in Ireland. Caerleon's form at two didn't match up to that of another highly-regarded inmate of Ballydoyle stables Danzatore—we had 10 lb between the pair compared to the Irish Classification's 5lb—but Caerleon seemed sure to improve a good deal over middle distances and, with Danzatore not certain to stay the Derby distance, looked likely to develop into the stable's chief Derby hope. His training programme was geared to Epsom and he made his reappearance in the mile-and-a-quarter Rogers Gold Cup Ballymoss Stakes at the Curragh towards the end of April. Rarely can a classic winner have made such an inauspicious start to his three-year-old career! Starting at 7/4 on in a field of ten Caerleon was towards the rear throughout, dropped to next-to-last rounding the home turn and managed to beat only two home. Allowing for his having looked backward in his coat beforehand, Caerleon would—in the words of our representative at the Curragh—'have to improve a hell of a lot to make up into a classic contender.' Caerleon performed much better on his next outing, running Solford—who received 8 lb—to three quarters of a length over a mile and a quarter at Phoenix Park in May; but with Branch Line, winner of a maiden race on his only previous start, a close third to the O'Brien pair Caerleon still had a fair way to go to rekindle serious hopes of a classic victory. Eddery incidentally, who had ridden Caerleon in his previous races, deserted him for Solford at Phoenix Park.

Caerleon was one of six Sangster-owned horses to appear among the thirty-two four-day acceptors for the Derby—Lomond, Salmon Leap, Shearwalk, Solford and The Noble Player were the others—but both Caerleon and Solford were kept in reserve for races at Chantilly, Caerleon for the Prix du Jockey-Club four days after the Derby and Solford for the Prix du Lys, a Group 3 pattern race run a week later than the Prix du Jockey-Club over the same distance. Caerleon's task looked a tough one and he would have started at much longer odds had not the pari-mutuel coupled him for betting purposes with L'Emigrant, whose owner was a shareholder in Caerleon, and with Pietru owned by the son of L'Emigrant's owner. Why three horses in different ownership should be coupled for betting purposes is hard to understand. It has no basis in logic. Why shouldn't the punter have a free choice of which horse, or horses, he backs in a race? Why should he be obliged to bet on a horse, or horses, which he does not wish to? Caerleon, L'Emigrant and Pietru were coupled at 14/10. L'Emigrant had good form in France and seemed to hold a chance second to none at Chantilly, having won both the Poule d'Essai des Poulains (French Two Thousand Guineas) and the Prix Lupin, the two most important events for a horse of his type in France at up to that time. Margouzed, third in the Poule d'Essai, and Lovely Dancer, runner-up in the Lupin, were also in the field for the Prix du Jockey-Club, along with Jeu de Paille and Esprit du Nord, first and second in the Prix Hocquart, and Dom Pasquini who had won the Prix Greffulhe early in the season from Lovely Dancer and Esprit du Nord; Cock Robin, an eleventh-hour withdrawal from the Derby, and Jasper were the British-trained challengers in a field of twelve. Caerleon's victory was achieved in similar manner to that of Assert twelve months earlier: he was kept in a handy position from the start, began his challenge in earnest as soon as the field straightened up for home and stretched out with a will to beat L'Emigrant by three lengths, the same as Assert's winning margin over Real Shadai. Esprit du Nord came third to Caerleon, half a length behind L'Emigrant and three quarters of a length in front of fourth-placed Jeu de Paille; Jasper finished sixth and Cock Robin ninth.

After the Prix du Jockey-Club, Caerleon ran in the Irish Sweeps Derby, the King George VI and Queen Elizabeth Diamond Stakes and the Benson and Hedges Gold Cup, races contested by Assert the previous year. If Caerleon's performance at Chantilly was probably the equal of Assert's, the same cannot be said of their respective performances at the Curragh and at Ascot. Assert's performance in the 1982 Irish Sweeps Derby in particular was one of the most impressive seen in a classic in recent times—he won with great ease by eight lengths (we made it ten) from the Derby third Silver Hawk. Caerleon finished second to Shareef Dancer at the Curragh, beaten a long-looking three lengths in a field that admittedly looked a good deal stronger at the time than that faced by Assert, seeing that it included the Derby first and second Teenoso and Carlingford Castle and the Airlie/Coolmore Irish Two Thousand Guineas winner Wassl. Caerleon it must also be said didn't have the best of luck on Sweeps Derby day, having to be switched to the wide outside of the field after being trapped on the rails early in the straight. Caerleon, who was in close touch from the start, momentarily had no room to challenge as Shareef Dancer, Teenoso and Wassl moved up on his outside at the same time as the weakening Carlingford Castle and Sir Simon dropped back into his path. Once Eddery had extricated him, Caerleon again showed admirable resolution, running on strongly to finish a most creditable second, two lengths ahead of third-placed Teenoso. Caerleon ran poorly in the King George VI and Queen Elizabeth Diamond Stakes four weeks later (Assert had been narrowly beaten by Kalaglow in 1982) but his connections offered the excuse that Caerleon lost both his front shoes during the race; he lost his place rapidly approaching the straight and was virtually pulled up in the closing stages.

Caerleon followed in Assert's footsteps by winning the Benson and Hedges Gold Cup at York's August meeting. The Benson and Hedges comes at an awkward stage of the season for a top three-year-old who has been campaigned at middle distances; like Assert, Caerleon was facing his fourth major racecourse

Mr R. E. Sangster's "Caerleon"

test in the space of ten weeks. A good deal of the interest in the Benson and Hedges disappeared when Shareef Dancer defected at the last minute. But Caerleon's victory will remain in our memory for some time to come: if there was a gamer performance all season we didn't see it. Taken into the lead soon after the start, Caerleon made a good pace but he could never set up a clear advantage and early in the straight the challengers began to close in, Hot Touch, Gorytus and John French looking the most dangerous. These three and Caerleon were almost in line abreast at the two-furlong marker, Caerleon looking for all the world as if he was all out and nearing the end of his tether. Some horses would have capitulated but, with Eddery throwing everything at him, Caerleon stuck his neck out in grand style, almost as though striving for the line, determined to get there first, and held off Hot Touch by a neck; the next four home, John French, Gorytus, Electric and Guns of Navarone, all finished within three lengths of Caerleon. Caerleon's Benson and Hedges victory was the sixth in a row by a three-year-old after four of the first six runnings had gone to older horses; Caerleon was also the fourth winning favourite in the past six years, a period which has gone a long way to redressing the balance after the unhappy record of favourites during the early history of the event.

Caerleon didn't race again. There was talk of his running in the St Leger, and later of his running in the Prix de l'Arc de Triomphe. After first announcing Caerleon a likely runner for the St Leger his connections had a change of heart after rain fell at Doncaster on the Thursday of the meeting, a decision which looked premature when the course dried out the next day. In the event further heavy rain produced soft going for the St Leger, conditions which Caerleon's connections regarded as being against him; he wasn't risked on very soft ground after his poor performance in the mud on his first outing as a three-year-old. Caerleon acted well on firm going and won the Benson and Hedges Gold Cup on ground which was on the soft side. He stayed a mile and a half well. Caerleon's two poor performances as a three-year-old were out of character: gameness was one of the hallmarks of his best performances and he seemed a genuine type. It's of interest that Caerleon had his tongue tied down at York though whether his reported tendency to choke had any bearing on his performances at the Curragh in April and in the King George we have no way of knowing.

		Northern Dancer	Nearctic
Caerleon (USA) (b.c. 1980)	Nijinsky (b 1967)	(b 1961)	Natalma
		Flaming Page (b 1959)	Bull Page
			Flaring Top
	Foreseer (b or br 1969)	Round Table (b 1954)	Princequillo
			Knight's Daughter
		Regal Gleam (b or br 1964)	Hail to Reason
			Miz Carol

The very attractive, medium-sized, compact Caerleon was purchased at the Keeneland Summer Select Yearling Sale which has become the most important talent-spotting arena for the world's richest racehorse owners; the Sangster syndicates bought The Minstrel and Golden Fleece at this particular sale and are nowadays always among the sale's leading buyers. At 800,000 dollars, Caerleon cost considerably less than the two highest-priced lots at the 1981 sale, the Sangster-purchased Ballydoyle, who didn't live up to his 3,500,000-dollar price tag, and Shareef Dancer who cost 3,300,000 dollars. Caerleon comes from a highly successful family. His dam Foreseer, a daughter of the champion two-year-old filly of 1966 Regal Gleam and a sister to the top-class middle-distance horse Royal Glint who won twenty-one races and more than a million dollars in prize money, was a very useful racemare at up to a mile; she is the dam of five other winners, notably the very useful Forli filly Palmistry and Caerleon's brother the 1983 two-year-old Vision, both stakes winners at around nine furlongs in North America, and the 1980 Irish St Leger runner-up Good Thyne (by Herbager). Caerleon will stand at a fee of IR 80,000 guineas in 1984. *V. O'Brien, Ireland.*

CAESAR'S COMMAND 2 b.g. Roman Warrior 132–Julie Be Quick (Selari)   — (1983 6fg) May 14; big, workmanlike gelding; half-brother to fairly useful 6f and 7f winner Blue Emmanuelle (by Lochnager) and quite useful 1980 2-y-o 5f performer Queen of Prussia (by Bay Express); dam won at up to 1m in USA; 25/1 and backward, behind in 24-runner maiden race at Doncaster in October; sent to Singapore. *R. Armstrong.*

CAESAR'S GHOST 4 gr.g. Young Emperor 133–Xanthoria (Levmoss 133)   — (1982 6fg 6g 6f⁴ 7g 8.3g 1983 8s 8s) plater; stays 6f; has worn blinkers. *D. H. Jones.*

154

CAJOLERY 7 br.h. Pall Mall 132–Do Please (I Say 125) (1982 7.2s 7f 7f² 7g⁴ 7g³   –
7f 7d 1983 7s 7.6v 8f 7fg 7f 7g 7fg) lightly-made horse; fair handicapper at his best
but has deteriorated; best at around 7f; seems to act on any going; sold 3,600 gns
Newmarket Autumn Sales. *I. Walker.*

CALALOO SIOUX (USA) 2 ch.f. Our Native–Roshanndra (Mill Reef 141)   **100**
(1983 6f 6fg³ 7.6fg² 7.3d²) Apr 2; $97,000Y; quite an attractive filly; good walker;
first foal; dam twice-raced half-sister to very speedy fillies Mange Tout, Rose
Dubarry and Hecla; staying-on 1½-length second of 14 to Betsy Bay in Rochford
Thompson Newbury Stakes in October, final outing and easily best effort; will be
well suited by 1m+; acts on a firm surface but is evidently much better with some
give in the ground; sure to win a race. *R. Laing.*

CALEDONIAN 7 b.h. Philip of Spain 126–Blasllyn 88 (Blast 125) (1982 5d 5f 5f³   –
5f 5f* 5fg 6f² 6d 6g² 6g 5f² 6g 5fg 5d 6f³ 5g 6s 6s 5s 1983 5v 5g 5fg 5f 5d 6g 6f) tall
horse; sprint handicapper; acts on any going, but is well suited by top-of-the-
ground; wears blinkers; sometimes bandaged; suitable mount for a boy; sold 620
gns Newmarket Autumn Sales. *W. Stubbs.*

CALFUCCI 2 b.c. Great Nephew 126–Calahorra 116 (The Marshal 118) (1983   **82 p**
7g³) half-brother to 3 winners, including useful 6f and 7f winner Cartridge (by Jim
French) dam smart at up to 1m; 4/1, 7½ lengths third of 13 to Royal Halo in maiden
race at Lingfield in October; will be suited by 1m; sure to improve. *H. Cecil.*

CALICO GIRL 2 b.f. Saritamer 130–Twice Shy (Lord of Verona 120) (1983 6f)   –
Apr 17; 1,600 2-y-o; workmanlike filly; half-sister to 2 winning platers; dam of little
account; last of 13 in maiden race at Doncaster in June: sold 410 gns Ascot
September Sales. *L. Lightbrown.*

C A LIGHTING 2 b.c. Monsanto 121–Miss Brecqhou 58 (Linacre 133) (1983 7fg   –
7g 8d) Mar 7; fair sort; fourth reported foal; brother to poor 3-y-o Patination; dam
second over 9f and 1¼m; in rear in maiden races. *Mrs B. Waring.*

CALIPH 2 b.c. Saritamer 130–Daphne's Dilemma (Mummy's Pet 125) (1983 5.3f⁴   **65**
6fg⁴) Mar 3; first foal; dam poor maiden; fourth in maiden events at Brighton in
June; may prove better suited by 5f than 6f. *R. Simpson.*

CALISOLON 9 b.g. Caliban 123–Solensister 100 (Ennis 128) (1982 12d 10g 12fg   **68 ?**
8g 12fg 7g 10g⁴ 10v 10v⁴ 1983 12s 8d 7.6v* 8g* 10s⁴) former plater; won
handicaps at Lingfield and Sandown (apprentices) within space of 3 days in May;
stays middle distances; acts on any going; has worn blinkers and bandages; not
seen out after June. *P. K. Mitchell.*

CALLING BIRD 3 b.f. Warpath 113–Hirondelle 86 (Falcon 131) (1982 6fg 1983   –
12.3fg 12fg) sturdy filly; well beaten, including in a seller; sold 700 gns Doncaster
November Sales. *C. Thornton.*

CALL OF THE SEA 2 b.f. Decoy Boy 129–Sea Tune (Klairon 131) (1983 5fg 5g   **70**
6d) Apr 26; lengthy, sparely-made, plain filly; half-sister to fairly useful Melanesta
(by Estaminet), successful at up to 7.3f, and to a winner in Italy; dam won over 6f at
2 yrs in Ireland; 5¼ lengths fifth of 16 to Turn The Key in maiden race at Newbury
in October, final outing and best effort; stays 6f; sold 4,300 gns Newmarket
Autumn Sales. *H. Candy.*

CALL UP 3 b.g. Headin' Up–Skye 62 (Mountain Call 125) (1982 NR 1983 9g 7f   –
10f) plain gelding; second foal; dam placed in 7f seller at 2 yrs; behind in maiden
races and a seller. *A. Bailey.*

CALORIFIC 2 b.f. Hotfoot 126–Pavillon 88 (French Beige 127) (1983 6fg) Feb   – p
14; workmanlike filly; half-sister to several winners, including useful stayer Elusive
(by Blakeney) and fairly useful 1m and 13f winner Uppety (by Rouser); dam 1¼m
winner; 50/1 and backward, 11 lengths eleventh of 23 to New Generation in minor
event at Redcar in September; not bred to sprint, and should do better at 1¼m or
more. *E. Incisa.*

CALPOPPY 2 ch.f. Be My Guest 126–Panetona (Pan II 130) (1983 6fg 6g 6fg³   **90**
7g² 6g 6d⁴) May 29; 50,000Y; rather lightly-built filly; half-sister to several
winners, including smart French middle-distance performer Mazus (by Major
Portion) and very useful French and American winner Planing (by Daring Display),
successful at up to 1½m; dam won over 10.5f in France; beaten neck by Mystery
Ship in Sweet Solera Stakes at Newmarket in August, easily best effort; clearly
needs further than 6f, and should stay at least 1¼m; blinkered last 4 outings. *W.
O'Gorman.*

CALSONG 4 b.c. Song 132–Calspea 81 (Calpurnius 122) (1982 7f² 7f⁴ 7f* 6f² 7f   –
1983 7g 7f 8f) fair sort; poor mover; plater; stays 7f; acts on firm going; cost 680
gns Doncaster January Sales. *A. Watson.*

CALYPSA (USA) 2 ch.f. The Minstrel 135–Fast Approach (First Landing) (1983   **83**
6f⁴ 7g* 7.2s²) Apr 5; tall, lengthy filly; closely related to several winners,
including very useful Summer Fling (by Nijinsky), successful at up to 1m, and smart
First Approach (by Northern Fling), a winner at up to 11f, and half-sister to 2
winners; dam once-raced half-sister to 2 stakes winners; won 16-runner £5,000
event at Lingfield in September by 1½ lengths from American Winter; beaten 6
lengths by My Tootsie when odds on for minor event at Haydock the following
month; should stay at least 1¼m; appears to act on any going. *I. Balding.*

CALYPSO QUEEN (FR) 2 b.f. Prince Regent 129–Rostadalen (Val de Loir 133)   **83**
(1983 5fg 7f² 7f⁴ 7h 6fg⁴ 6d) Feb 8; 105,000 francs Y (approx £8,750); rangy filly;
first foal; dam placed at 3 yrs in Italy; modest maiden; should stay at least 1m; acts
on hard going; blinkered final outing. *A. Jarvis.*

CAMACHO (USA) 8 b.g. Mickey McGuire–To My Lady (Amber Morn) (1982 8f   **73**
12h³ 16fg 12fg² 13.1f* 14f* 13.1g* 13.3g 12g 1983 12s 16f 16f² 12f² 13.1h² 16h³
17d³ 16fg³ 16fg*) genuine and consistent handicapper; beat Dark Proposal at
Ascot in October; stays 2m; acts on any going but goes well on top-of-the-ground;
good mount for an inexperienced rider; does best when ridden up with pace; game.
G. Cottrell.

CAMBERLOT 3 b.g. Solution–Miss Worden 40 (Worden II 129) (1982 6f 6fg 6s   –
6v 1983 8f) plating-class maiden; should stay 1m; best form in blinkers final outing
in 1982. *B. Wise.*

CAMBRIDGE CIRCUS (USA) 2 b.c. Graustark–Dos A Dos (Advocator)   **72**
(1983 8d 7g⁴) Apr 20; $75,000Y; rangy, useful-looking colt; third foal;
half-brother to a winner; dam very useful winner at up to 1m; quite modest form
in fair company at the back-end; should stay 1¼m; may improve. *R. Laing.*

CAMBRIDGE GOLD 9 b.g. Sassafras 135–Greyia (Grey Sovereign 128§)   –
(1982 NR 1983 17d 18.8v 17f 17fg) strong gelding; lightly raced and of little
account on flat; dead. *M. Tate.*

CAMBRIDGE LODGE 2 ch.f. Tower Walk 130–La Conistrano 86 (Capistrano   – p
120) (1983 7fg) May 7; 11,500Y; fair sort; half-sister to a winning plater; dam
showed ability at 2 yrs and is half-sister to Italian Oaks winner Val D'Erica; 20/1 in
need of race, ran on steadily when in mid-division in 30-runner maiden won by
Rainbow Quest at Newmarket in August; clearly has ability and is worth keeping an
eye on in Northern maiden company. *K. Stone.*

CAMDEN LAD 2 br.c. Camden Town 125–Backwoodsgirl (Young Emperor 133)   **72**
(1983 5s⁴ 5d² 5g 5d⁴ 6f 5f 6fg 6f 5g 7fg) Feb 26; IR 14,500F, 21,000Y; leggy,
close-coupled, fair sort; first produce; dam never ran; beaten length by African
Abandon in 9-runner minor event at Newmarket in April on second outing, but on
balance is not much better than a plater; should stay 1m; probably acts on any
going. *R. Hollinshead.*

CAMDEN LOCK 2 b.c. Camden Town 125–Reliable Rosie (Relko 136) (1983   **82** p
6fg⁴) Apr 26; IR 17,000F, 24,000Y; half-brother to 3 winners abroad; dam won
from 8.5f to 11.5f in Ireland; weak in market, 4¼ lengths fourth of 5 to Stinging
Nettle in Duke of Edinburgh Stakes at Ascot in October; will be much better suited
by further; sure to improve. *G. Lewis.*

CAMDEN MILLY 2 b.f. Camden Town 125–Milly Whiteway 112 (Great White   **77**
Way) (1983 7fg 6fg) Apr 6; 20,000Y; lengthy filly; third foal; half-sister to 2
winners, including fairly useful 1978 Irish 2-y-o 6f and 1m winner Saylers Creek (by
Wolver Hollow); dam very useful over 5f and 6f at 2 yrs in Ireland; 50/1 and ridden
by apprentice unable to claim her 5-lb allowance, showed up throughout when 8½
lengths fifth of 18 to Seismic Wave in £5,000 event at Doncaster in September;
eighth of 12 in Blue Seal Stakes at Ascot later in month; will stay 1m. *P. Kelleway.*

CAMDEN PASSAGE 2 gr.g. Camden Town 125–Duotone (Sweet Revenge 129)   **57**
(1983 6f 6f 7fg 7fg) Mar 21; 6,000F, IR 9,000Y; close-coupled, useful sort; second
foal; dam twice-raced half-sister to Cambridgeshire winner King Midas; unquoted
and blinkered, ninth of 28 in valuable seller at Newmarket in September, final outing
and best effort; stays 7f. *G. Balding.*

CAMDORE BOY 3 b.c. Anax 120–Paddy's Daughter (St Paddy 133) (1982 NR   –
1983 9d 8d) fair sort; third reported foal; dam of little account; behind in sellers at
Wolverhampton. *D. H. Jones.*

CAMERONIAN LAD 4 b.g. Bay Express 132–French Maid 89 (Shantung 132)   55
(1982 12fg 1983 13s 9d* 12g 11g 13g) 33/1 when winning 13-runner minor event at
Hamilton in May; has no other form of comparable merit; stays 9f. *J. S. Wilson.*

CAMIONNAGE 2 b.c. Take a Reef 127–Nasty Niece (Great Nephew 126) (1983   70
6g 6d 6f 7g 8fg 10d*) May 13; big, workmanlike colt; third foal; half-brother to 1m
winner Tender Niece (by Prince Tenderfoot); dam won over 7f at 2 yrs in Canada;
won seller at Leicester (bought in 1,500 gns) in October by neck from Sergiades,
having shown nothing at all in his previous races; evidently suited by 1¼m;
blinkered last 2 outings. *E. Carter.*

CAMISADO 3 ch.c. Mill Reef 141–Goosie 112 (Sea-Bird II 145) (1982 7s⁴ 1983   101
8f* 10fg² 9g³ 10g* 10d⁴) Irish colt; landed the odds by a length from Nonno in
5-runner £3,450 race at Phoenix Park in July and beat long odds-on Colonial Flag by
¾ length in similar race on same course in October (slowly-run affair); placed in
minor event and Pacemaker International Whitehall Stakes on same course in
between, finishing 5 lengths third of 8 behind Salmon Leap in latter; will stay 1½m;
acts on firm going. *D. O'Brien, Ireland.*

CAMISITE 5 ch.h. Hittite Glory 125–Camisole 94 (Psidium 130) (1982 6fg* 7fg³   107
6fg* 6fg² 6d* 6g* 6f 6fg* 6g³ 6g 6d³ 6s* 1983 6d³ 6v 6d 6v² 5g³ 6f 6f 6fg* 6fg
6fg⁴) leggy horse; doesn't impress in his slower paces; smart performer at his
best; led near finish to beat Battle Hymn a neck in £5,200 handicap at Newmarket in
October (first outing for 3½ months); looked unlucky final outing; best at 6f; acts on
any going; blinkered fifth start. *W. O'Gorman.*

CAMPS HEATH 2 ch.c. Ahonoora 122–Our Bernie (Continuation 120) (1983   79
5fg² 6f 6g 6f³ 5s⁴) May 10; IR 8,000F, IR 4,400Y; fair sort; first live produce;
dam second 3 times at up to 1m in Ireland; well-backed favourite, moved
appallingly to start and gave impression ground was against him when 2¾ lengths
third of 8 to easy winner Throne of Glory in nursery at Salisbury in September;
had previously shown form in maiden company; stays 6f; not disgraced when
blinkered final outing; sold F. Durr 7,400 gns Ascot November Sales. *I. Walker.*

CAMPUS BOY 2 ch.g. Stanford 121§–Naughty Lass 82 (Run The Gantlet) (1983   68
6f 7fg 8fg 6fg) May 28; IR 8,200Y; useful-looking gelding; third foal; half-brother
to Irish 3-y-o 1½m winner Northern Game (by North Stoke) and quite useful stayer
Protos (by Tumble Wind); dam won over 1¼m and 1½m in Ireland; plating-class
maiden; stays 7f. *D. Morley.*

CANARIM 2 b.g. Fordham 117–Super Fly (Above Suspicion 127) (1983 8s) May   –
26; 10,500 2-y-o (privately); second foal; dam maiden hurdler; unquoted and
backward, in rear in 15-runner maiden race at Beverley in September. *T. Bulgin.*

CANDAULES 5 b.g. Supreme Sovereign 119–Sweet and Naughty 76 (Connaught   –
130) (1982 8f 1983 10.6s) strong, quite attractive gelding; poor performer
nowadays; has been beaten in a seller; stays 7f; acts on hard going; sometimes
blinkered. *C. James.*

CANDY BURN 3 br.f. Lucky Wednesday 124–Threshoon 81 (Sheshoon 132)   –
(1982 5g 1983 8.2fg 9g) of little account. *Mrs A. Bell.*

CANDY CREEK 2 ch.f. Sandy Creek 123–Picnic Time (Silly Season 127) (1983   –
5g) May 5; neat filly; second foal; half-sister to 3-y-o 1m and 1¼m winner Time
For A Laugh (by Cawston's Clown); dam poor maiden; last of 10 in maiden race at
Warwick in July; dead. *M. Lambert.*

CANIF 2 gr.g. Saritamer 130–Couteau 92 (Nelcius 133) (1983 7fg 7d³ 6fg³) May   77
16; deep-girthed gelding; third reported foal; dam, daughter of very smart Panga,
won over 1m and later over hurdles after birth of first foal; third in autumn maiden
races at Yarmouth and Folkestone; stays 7f. *M. Ryan.*

CANIO 6 b.g. Welsh Pageant 132–Nedda 113 (Alcide 136) (1982 12d³ 12fg 12fg   65
1983 12s³ 10g 12s² 12s³ 12v 12s²) lightly-made gelding; middle-distance
handicapper; seems to act on any going; blinkered once at 3 yrs. *R. Hodges.*

CANLAS 3 ch.f. Master Sing 109–Blue Oak (Blue and Grey 93) (1982 5fg 6s 1983   –
5v 5fg 5f 5f) small filly; poor sprint maiden; trained until after third start by K.
Bridgwater. *R. Thompson.*

CANNON KING 7 b.h. Owen Anthony 102–Primmy 56 (Primera 131) (1982 10f⁴   113
10g³ 10fg⁴ 10f* 12fg² 10.5f² 12g² 11d⁴ 9d 10g* 1983 10v 10v* 10v 10fg⁴) smallish
horse; very useful handicapper; won City and Suburban at Epsom in April,

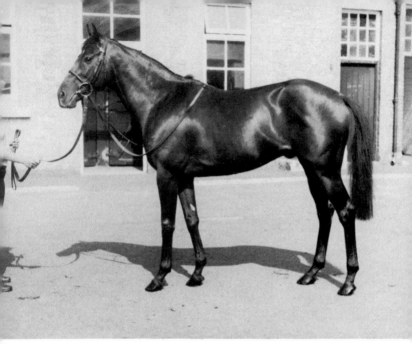

Mr E. Penser's "Cannon King"

accounting for Bettyknowes very easily by 3 lengths; creditable fourth of 11 to Stanerra, beaten about 5½ lengths, in Prince of Wales's Stakes at Royal Ascot; not seen out again; stays 1½m; acts on any going and any track; suitable mount for an apprentice; genuine. *J. Dunlop.*

CANONBURY FLYER 2 b.g. Lucky Wednesday 124–Symphonie (Tambourine II 133) (1983 7.6fg) Apr 30; half-brother to 2 winners; dam never ran; unquoted, tailed-off last of 18 in maiden race at Lingfield in October. *P. K. Mitchell.* —

CANONESS 2 b.f. St Paddy 133–Sea Fable 51 (Typhoon 125) (1983 5d 7s) Mar 25; small filly; second foal; dam poor plater; in rear in October maiden races in the Midlands. *J. Fox.* —

CAN'T SWIM 4 b.f. Bruni 132–Out of Depth 65 (Deep Diver 134) (1982 8d 12f 1983 8s 10f) compact, strong-quartered filly; plater; best run at 6f; blinkered last 3 outings in 1981; has sweated up badly. *R. Howe.* —

CANUCK CLOWN 2 br.c. Cawston's Clown 113–Cartlone (Escart III) (1983 8g 8.2fg) Apr 17; IR 3,100F, 4,000Y (privately); half-brother to 1¼m winner Cardinal Puff (by St Alphage), subsequently successful in Malaya; dam, daughter of Cesarewitch winner Prelone, won 17f amateur riders race in Ireland; 50/1, 11 lengths fifth of 16 to Alleging in £3,400 event at Nottingham in October, second outing; likely to stay quite well. *C. Horgan.* — **67**

CANVAS SHOE 2 br.f. Hotfoot 126–Cesarea 108 (Raeburn II) (1983 5v 5fg 6h* 5fg) May 21; half-sister to 2 winners, including fairly useful 7f winner Cassina (by Habitat); dam game winner of 5 races from 5f to 1½m; sold out of P. Walwyn's stable 3,100 gns after winning 8-runner seller at Nottingham in August; needs further than 5f and will be suited by 7f+; acts on hard going. *E. Weymes.* — **57**

CAPA 3 ch. g. New Member 119–Poshteen 86 (Royal Smoke 113) (1982 NR 1983   –
10g) first foal; dam 2-y-o 5f winner; unquoted when towards rear in amateur riders
race at Goodwood in September. *O. O'Neill.*

CAP D'AZURE 3 b. f. Majority Blue 126–Fravelot (Javelot 124) (1982 5g⁴ 5g 6s²   **64**
6v³ 1983 6d⁴ 6s³ 8d 7s 8f² 8fg³ 8.2f 8.2fg 10s² 8fg⁴ 8g⁴ 9s² 10fg⁴) neat filly;
placed on several occasions; possibly doesn't quite stay 1¼m; acts on any going;
blinkered last 5 outings. *S. Norton.*

CAPISTRANO PLAYA 2 b. g. Monseigneur 127–Statira 103 (Skymaster 126)   **80**
(1983 6f* 7fg⁴ 8fg) Apr 14; IR 8,000Y; big gelding; half-brother to 2 winners
including Ludova (by Right Tack), successful at up to 6f at 2 yrs in France and
subsequently a stakes-placed winner in USA; dam, half-sister to smart sprinters
Most Secret and Artaxerxes, was a useful 5f winner at 2 yrs; won 7-runner
maiden race at Carlisle in July; ran badly in nursery final outing; subsequently
gelded. *Sir Mark Prescott.*

CAP OF FREEDOM 4 b. c. Thatch 136–Parolee 88 (Sing Sing 134) (1982 7fg   –
8d⁴ 8fg² 7s* 1983 10d 10fg 8f 8.2fg 8.3fg 8.3fg) strong, attractive colt; good
mover; didn't find his form at 4 yrs; promises to stay 1¼m; acts well on soft going;
blinkered final start; has won for an apprentice. *J. Dunlop.*

CAPPADOCIA 2 ch. f. Roman Warrior 132–Miss Taurus 79 (Bullrush 106) (1983   –
7s 6fg) Apr 11; IR 620Y; big filly; seventh foal; dam sprinter; tailed-off last in
maiden races at Leicester in October; no prospects. *R. Hollinshead.*

CAPRICORN BELLE 2 b. f. Nonoalco 131–Supremely Royal (Crowned Prince **106** p
128) (1983 6fg* 7fg³) Mar 10; big, quite attractive filly with plenty of scope; has a
rather round action; second foal; half-sister to 6f and 10.2f winner Royal
Invitation (by Be My Guest); dam, poor maiden, comes from top American family;
led 3f out and kept on really well to win 29-runner maiden race at Newmarket in
September by 1½ lengths from Coda; good third to Mahogany in Rockfel Stakes
on same course the following month; will stay 1m; likely to continue to progress,
and is probably very useful filly in the making. *L. Cumani.*

CAPRICORN SAINT 3 b. f. Welsh Saint 126–January 68 (Aggressor 130) (1982   **63**
5.1f 1983 8v 7fg*) sturdy filly; dropped in class when winning 16-runner seller at
Newmarket in June; bought in 4,200 gns afterwards; suited by 7f; acts on a firm
surface. *C. Spares.*

CAPTAIN BLUE 3 b. c. Captain James 123–Edansa (Majority Blue 126) (1982   **41**
5.8g 7fg 7fg 8s 10d 1983 10s 11.7s 16s³ 16g 16g 17g) lengthy colt; moderate plater
at 2 yrs; ran best race of 1983 on third start; evidently stays 2m; soon struggling
when blinkered final start (July). *M. Usher.*

CAPTAIN BONNIE 2 b. f. Captain James 123–Bonne Esperance (Venture VII   **60**
129) (1983 5fg³ 5fg 5f 5f³ 5fg 6fg) Mar 17; smallish, fair sort; half-sister to
winners in France and USA, including very useful French 6f and 7f winner Goodmor
(by Morston); dam French 1¼m winner and half-sister to speedy Hodell;
plating-class maiden; tailed off in nursery final outing; should stay at least 1m; acts
on firm going. *B. Hanbury.*

CAPTAIN CRUMPET 2 gr. g. Home Guard 129–Farmers Daughter (Red   **83**
Slipper 126 or Javelot 124) (1983 5s⁴ 6s² 5f 5fg 5fg⁴ 5f² 6fg* 7fg) Feb 19; IR
10,000Y; strong, good-bodied gelding; half-brother to numerous winners here
and abroad, including French 3-y-o Saltoki (by Ballad Rock), a winner at up to 1m,
and speedy 1979 2-y-o Titauri (by Wishing Star); dam ran only 3 times; won
9-runner nursery at Windsor in August by a head from Tom Forrester; suited by
6f (never going well when tried over 7f); acts on any going; blinkered last 4
starts; gelded after final outing. *N. Vigors.*

CAPTAIN FREDDIE (USA) 2 b. c. Explodent–Continuance (Round Table)   **99**
(1983 6g⁴ 6fg* 6f* 6fg) Apr 1; $160,000Y; half-brother to several winners,
including very useful sprinter Brian's Babe (by Olden Times), minor stakes
winner Dr Neale (by Herbager) and very useful middle-distance winner
Continuing (by Vaguely Noble); dam, winner at 2 yrs, is half-sister to 5 stakes
winners, including very smart List and Yamanin; won twice at Phoenix Park in
July, scoring by 2½ lengths in maiden race and by a neck from Late Sally when
giving weight to his 4 opponents in valuable Barry Weisbord and Johnny Jones
Stakes; not seen out again after finishing just over 4 lengths seventh of 13 to King
Persian in Heinz '57' Phoenix Stakes on same course the following month; will be
suited by 1m. *D. O'Brien, Ireland.*

CAPTAIN HENRY 4 ch.g. Bay Express 132–Astraline 97 (Skymaster 126) – (1982 6s 6fg 6g 6g 6fg 1983 6d 7d) small gelding; good mover; has shown no form since 1981 and was well beaten in seller first start; stays 6f; probably acts on any going. *M. Lambert.*

CAPTAIN OATES 4 b.c. Oats 126–Gay Signal (Lord Gayle 124) (1982 10.1fg 10f – 14f⁴ 16fg 15.5fg⁴ 16fg⁴ 16s* 16s 1983 15.5f 16f 14.8fg 18.1d 15.5fg³) close-coupled, narrow colt; poor handicapper; has been beaten in a seller; suited by a test of stamina; acts well on soft going. *M. Hinchliffe.*

CAPTAIN'S BIDD 3 ch.g. Captain James 123–Muffet 75 (Matador 130) (1982 – 6g 6s 5d 5g 1983 6fg 5fg 6f 5d) sturdy, workmanlike gelding; no worthwhile form in varied company. *L. Lightbrown.*

CAPTAIN'S GIFT 2 ch.g. Captain James 123–Stop Thinking (Divine Gift 127) – (1983 5v⁴ 5v 7d 6g) May 11; 12,000Y; useful-looking gelding; half-brother to 2 winners, including Santellas (by Arch Sculptor), fair winner at around 1m; poor form in maiden races. *A. Ingham.*

CAPTAIN'S GOLD (USA) 2 gr.c. Riverman 131–Old Goldie (Young Emperor **100** p 133) (1983 5fg*) very attractive colt and a good walker; half-brother to 4 winners, including high-class miler Lot O'Gold (by Lothario) and very smart Golden Derby (by Master Derby), successful at up to 7f; dam won 5 times at sprint distances; held on to win 4-runner Prix Yacowlef (newcomers race) at Deauville in August by a short head (hung badly under pressure closing stages); bred to stay 1m; seemed to feel the ground at Deauville and possibly needs an easier surface. *F. Boutin, France.*

CAPTAIN SINGLETON (USA) 2 b.c. Best Turn–Candid Catherine (T.V. **106** Lark) (1983 5d 5s* 5.8s* 6g³ 7f³ 8.2f²) Feb 11; $160,000Y; strong, compact, full-quartered colt; good walker but doesn't impress in his slower paces; third foal; half-brother to a winner by Forceten; dam, smart stakes winner at 2 yrs and 3 yrs,

Mr A. P. Ward's "Captain Singleton"

won at up to 7f; was raised considerably in class after winning in modest company at Newmarket and Bath (12 lengths) in May, finishing creditable third in Anglia Television July Stakes at Newmarket and Lanson Champagne Stakes at Goodwood, and good second to Crampon (rec 8lb) in £3,100 event at Haydock; stays 1m; acts on any going. *G. Harwood.*

CAPTAIN TEMPEST 3 b.c. Manado 130–Calibina 101 (Caliban 123) (1982 5g 73
6v* 7s 7s 1983 5v³ 6d 5s² 6d² 6d⁴ 5f 6f 6g³ 6f³ 6f² 6fg² 6s 6g) lightly-made colt; close second in handicaps at Hamilton, Redcar, Ripon and Thirsk; finds 5f on sharp side and should stay 7f; acts on any going; swerved badly and unshipped his jockey leaving stalls on twelfth outing; didn't run well in blinkers next time. *T. Barron.*

CAPTAIN TOMBIE 2 gr.g. Record Token 128–Micrippina (Saritamer 130) (1983 58
5s 5d 6f 7f 5f 5f 6d) Apr 20; IR 4,100F, 5,000Y; small, strong gelding; second foal; dam twice-raced daughter of smart 1½m filly Star Ship; plater; needs at least 6f, and should stay further; acts on firm going. *Miss S. Hall.*

CAPTAIN TWINKLE 3 b.c. Royalty 130–Miss Vanadium (Helmar) (1982 NR –
1983 8v 12fg 15f³) third living foal; dam ran once in USA; showed signs of a little ability all outings, but was beaten almost 20 lengths when third to Castle Douglas in maiden race at Edinburgh in July. *J. Toller.*

CAPTAIN VIGILANTE 2 br.c. Home Guard 129–Darada (Relko 136) (1983 5s 89
5fg 6f 5f⁴ 8g*) Apr 30; strong, good sort; half-brother to 3 winners, including useful Scandinavian colt Tahoe (by Dancer's Image); dam won twice over 9f in France; backed from 16/1 to 8/1, showed much improved form to win 14-runner nursery at Pontefract in October by a length from Our Lady; suited by 1m. *J. Etherington.*

CAPTAIN WEBSTER 3 ch.c. Sandford Lad 133–Maynooth Belle (Busted 134) 69
(1982 6f 7fg 8s 8s 10s* 1983 10v 10s⁴ 10s* 10v 11g 16f⁴ 12fg 16fg 13.3d) smallish, lengthy colt; won handicap at Goodwood in May; respectable fourth of 6 to Frantonios in minor event at Chepstow following month; seems to stay 2m; acts on any going, but goes particularly well on soft; blinkered final outing. *V. Hide.*

CAPTIVA 2 b.f. Bay Express 132–Reltop 72 (High Top 131) (1983 5.1f* 7g 5d) 58
Mar 20; 6,000Y; first foal; dam won over 1½m; sold out of J. Hindley's stable 4,800 gns after winning 10-runner seller at Yarmouth in August; showed nothing in nurseries afterwards; should stay beyond 5f. *G. Blum.*

CAPTIVATE 3 b. or br.f. Mansingh 120–Mildura 98 (Vilmorin) (1982 6s 1983 79
5fg³ 5f² 5f 5g* 5f* 5d) fair sort; has been tubed; in good form in September and won maiden race at Lingfield and minor event at Redcar; form only at 5f; yet to show she can handle really soft ground, but acts on any other. *A. Hide.*

CAPTIVATOR 3 b.c. Artaius 129–Sorbus 121 (Busted 134) (1982 NR 1983 8s* 119
8s* 9fg 8d 10g 8d²) 148,000Y; neat colt; first foal; dam disqualified winner of Irish Guinness Oaks; looked very promising when winning twice at Phoenix Park in spring, quickening very nicely 2f out and winning easing up by a length from Slaney Prince in maiden event and beating Senior Citizen by a length in 6-runner Coolmore/Pas de Seul Stakes; made most and ran easily best subsequent race when short-head second of 7 behind Erin's Hope in Desmond Stakes at the Curragh in September (blinkered); should be suited by further than 1m. *V. O'Brien, Ireland.*

CAPTURE HIM (USA) 2 b.c. Mr Prospector–A Streaker (Dr Fager) (1983 103P
7d*) Feb 12; $775,000Y; first foal; dam, who never ran, is sister to smart 8.5f stakes winner Plastic Surgeon and daughter of Fashion Verdict, a leading American 2-y-o filly in 1962; looked a potentially top-class colt when slamming his 15 opponents in maiden race at the Curragh in September, bursting away inside final ¼m to win most impressively by 8 lengths from Tomriland; will be suited by 1m; held in high esteem by his trainer and looks to have a very bright future. *V. O'Brien, Ireland.*

CARABIN 3 b.c. Scottish Rifle 127–Quick Burn 94 (Carnival Dancer 113) (1982 –
5f² 5fg³ 6f⁴ 6f 5g³ 5fg 5fg* 5g 5d 1983 5s 5fg 5f 5g) workmanlike colt; no form in 1983; had to be put down at Goodwood in September; was best at 5f; sometimes wore blinkers. *S. Matthews.*

CARABINEER 2 b.c. Formidable 125–Caramel 93 (Crepello 136) (1983 5v* 5s² 91
5g² 6f² 7f² 7g) Feb 6; 32,000F, 31,000Y; neat, quite attractive colt; half-brother to numerous winners, including very useful middle-distance performer Northern Princess (by Sir Ivor); dam won at 1½m; stayed on extremely well to wear down Time Machine close home when winning maiden race at Sandown in April by a head, the pair clear; runner-up afterwards in Salisbury Stakes, National Stakes at

161

Sandown (2 lengths behind very comfortable winner Precocious), minor event at Doncaster and £4,800 race at Newbury; well beaten under 9-7 in nursery at Chester in August; stays 7f; acts on any going; genuine. *H. Candy.*

CARADO 2 b.f. Manado 130–Kaniz (Darius 129) (1983 6fg³ 7h⁴ 7d² 8g² 8.2s*)   **82**
Feb 14; 8,200Y; half-sister to several winners, including Irish 1½m and 2m winner Triple Venture (by Realm) and prolific Italian winner Kadievka (by Saulingo); dam won over 1m in Ireland; won 11-runner nursery at Hamilton in October by 1½ lengths from Quiet Country; will stay 1¼m; acts on any going. *C. Nelson.*

CARA FLORA 3 br.f. Scottish Rifle 127–Aracara (Prince Tenderfoot 126) (1982   **–**
7g 6fg 8fg 1983 10g 12f 10fg 10g 10d⁴) small, close-coupled filly; plater; sold 825 gns Ascot November Sales. *W. Wightman.*

CARALIST 7 ch.g. Traditionalist–Hy Carol (High Hat 131) (1982 12s 1983 8v   **–**
11.7s) strong, attractive gelding; poor performer nowadays; has been beaten in a seller; stays 1½m; acts on hard going and is probably unsuited by soft; races with head high. *Dr A. Jones.*

CARAN D'ACHE 4 ch.g. Huntercombe 133–Alfambra (Nashua) (1982 6s⁴ 5f 6fg   **67**
6g⁴ 6g⁴ 7fg² 6fg⁴ 6g³ 7d 6s 1983 6d* 6v 6s³ 6d³ 7d 6fg² 6f 7fg) quite well-made gelding; plater; sold out of G. Balding's stable 3,100 gns after scoring at Thirsk in April; placed in non-sellers afterwards; stays 7f; seems to act on any going; suitable mount for an apprentice; played up badly in stalls second start; sold 1,400 gns Doncaster October Sales. *M. H. Easterby.*

CARDIGAN 3 ch.g. Blue Cashmere 129–Alma 87 (Shiny Tenth 120) (1982 NR   **–**
1983 8fg 10d 8fg) 1,750 3-y-o; first foal; dam, daughter of high-class stayer Almeria, won over 5f and 1m; behind in maiden and minor races in latter half of season, twice last. *L. Lightbrown.*

CARDINAL FLOWER 6 ch.h. Sharpen Up 127–Ixia 91 (I Say 125) (1982 8g* 8f   **80**
9.4f² 8f³ 8.3fg³ 8fg 8fg² 1983 8d 8g 11s⁴ 9fg 10.2fg) good sort; good mover; fair handicapper at his best and a fairly useful hurdler; stays 11f; acts on any going; has run respectably for an amateur. *A. Scott.*

CARDINAL PRINCESS 2 ch.f. Moulton 128–Formana (Reform 132) (1983   **–**
8fg) Feb 27; first foal; dam, winner over 13f in France, is half-sister to smart French filly Ranimer; 25/1 and in need of race, 11 lengths seventh of 12 to Raami in maiden event at Redcar in October. *R. Whitaker.*

CAREEN 2 b.c. Shirley Heights 130–Strip the Willow 79 (Native Dancer) (1983   **90**
7f 7f² 7fg² 8g) Feb 4; strong, well-made, attractive colt; carries plenty of condition; good mover; half-brother to several winners, notably very smart 7f to 1m filly Joking Apart (by Jimmy Reppin); dam unplaced 5 times; creditable second in 20-runner maiden race at Newbury in July and 9-runner Sancton Stakes at York in September; should stay 1½m; acts on firm going; sure to win maiden event. *I. Balding.*

CAREGAN 4 ch.f. Galivanter 131–Esquire Maid 86 (Aureole 132) (1982 NR 1983   **–**
12.3v) half-sister to several winners here and abroad; dam won at 1¼m; 50/1 when tailed off in minor event won by Elect at Newcastle in May. *T. Barnes.*

CARIBLUE 6 b.g. My Swallow 134–Double Powered (Double Jump 131) (1982   **–**
NR 1983 12v 15.5v) lengthy gelding; no form, including in sellers; has worn bandages. *A. Davison.*

CARIELLOR (FR) 2 b.c. Fabulous Dancer 124–Bonicarielle (Bourbon 129)   **115**
(1983 7g² 7.5f* 8s* 8f) Mar 30; first foal; dam useful winner at around 1½m in France; looked very promising when making all to win maiden race at Deauville in August by 10 lengths and when getting the better of Truculent by ½ length in Prix La Rochette at Longchamp the following month; looked past his best for year when 4¼ lengths seventh of 9 to Treizieme in Grand Criterium, again at Longchamp, in October; will be suited by 1¼m+; probably better than his Grand Criterium running suggests. *A. Fabre, France.*

CARLINGFORD CASTLE 3 ch.c. Le Bavard 127–Rachel Ruysch 81 **126**
(Skymaster 126) (1982 8d³ 10v² 1983 10s* 12v* 12s² 12f 12fg 14.6s³)
     Warren Place stables, which have provided the Gold Cup winner in four of the last five seasons, have a strong candidate for the race in 1984 in the shape of the ex-Irish Carlingford Castle. Le Moss provided the stable's victories in 1979 and 1980 and Ardross succeeded him as champion stayer, winning at Royal Ascot in 1981 and 1982. Like many true stayers, Le Moss and Ardross didn't reach their best until after three years of age—Le Moss was at his peak in his final season, as a five-year-old, while Ardross, in our view, was at his very best as a six-year-old.

Gallinule Stakes, the Curragh—Carlingford Castle holds off the odds-on Give Thanks

Carlingford Castle too is a fairly lightly-raced type one would expect to continue to train on. He has the makings of a first-class Cup horse.

Like Le Moss, Carlingford Castle ended his three-year-old campaign in the St Leger, his first race for his new stable since being bought privately for an undisclosed sum out of L. Browne's yard. Carlingford Castle gave every indication at Doncaster that he will prove well suited by two miles or more. Always in the first four or five, he was sent up to dispute the lead with Esprit du Nord three furlongs out and battled on bravely to finish third to Sun Princess and Esprit du Nord, beaten only three quarters of a length and a short head after looking momentarily chopped for speed when Sun Princess delivered her challenge. In terms of merit, Carlingford Castle's St Leger performance was probably at least as good as that of Le Moss who was runner-up in Julio Mariner's year.

Le Moss never raced at a shorter distance than a mile and three quarters as a three-year-old but both Ardross, who was trained in Ireland until he was five, and Carlingford Castle began their three-year-old careers at a mile and a quarter. After winning a quite well-contested minor event over that distance in good style at the Curragh in April Carlingford Castle followed in Ardross' footsteps by taking the mile-and-a-half Gallinule Stakes, a Group 2 pattern race at the Curragh in May. The Gallinule was poorly contested for a race of its status the year Ardross won it at 50/1, but Carlingford Castle put up a good performance in very testing conditions to hold off the odds-on Give Thanks who was fresh from wide-margin victories in the Esal Bookmakers Oaks Trial at Lingfield and the Musidora Stakes at York. Carlingford Castle made all to beat Give Thanks fairly and squarely by a length and a half. The month of May continued as it began—wet—and Carlingford Castle's proven stamina and ability to handle the mud led, understandably, to his connections' saddling him for the Derby for which he started at 14/1. Further heavy rain the night before the race resulted in ground conditions the like of which are rarely seen for an Epsom Derby; Teenoso's winning time was the slowest this century and almost fifteen seconds slower than that of Golden Fleece twelve months earlier. After a slightly tardy start Carlingford Castle was pushed along to take up a good position on the heels of the leaders and was still well placed at the entrance to the straight despite having lost a little ground after becoming slightly unbalanced on the pronounced downhill gradient approaching Tattenham Corner. Carlingford Castle seemed poised to make his challenge on the outside but his rider elected instead to make his run through the middle of the field, between Guns of Navarone and his weakening stable-companion Neorion. Squeezed for room, Carlingford Castle became pocketed and by the time he had managed to extricate himself fully, approaching the two-furlong marker, Teenoso was gone beyond recall and Guns of Navarone was also some way ahead. Galloping on resolutely, Carlingford Castle moved past Guns of Navarone into second place approaching the final furlong and cut steadily into Teenoso's lead all the way to the post, his long, raking stride really catching the eye in the closing stages. Carlingford Castle went down by three lengths, the same margin by which he beat third-placed Shearwalk.

The St Leger was also run on soft ground and Carlingford Castle is clearly in his element in such conditions. He has encountered a firm surface only twice in his career, both times facing arguably stiffer tasks than he did at Epsom and Doncaster. In the Irish Sweeps Derby he finished seventh to Shareef Dancer, separated from third-placed Teenoso by about the same distance as at Epsom; and in the King George VI and Queen Elizabeth Diamond Stakes he came sixth to

Time Charter, beaten almost twelve lengths by the winner. Our representative at Ascot reported that Carlingford Castle moved to post that day 'like a cat on hot bricks', giving the impression that he was completely unsuited to firm ground.

Carlingford Castle (ch.c. 1980)	Le Bavard (ch 1971)	Devon (ch 1958)	Worden II / Sees
		Lueur Doree (ch 1964)	Le Haar / Lueur d'Espoir
	Rachel Ruysch (b 1966)	Skymaster (ch 1958)	Golden Cloud / Discipliner
		Sip (b 1956)	My Babu / Asti Spumante

The grand-looking Carlingford Castle takes much more after his sire Le Bavard than after his dam Rachel Ruysch, a small, light-framed type who showed ability at two years but was only plating class as a three-year-old. Rachel Ruysch has bred three other winners including the fairly useful sprinter-miler Exhilarate (by Wolverlife) who was placed at 50/1 in a pattern race, the Tetrarch Stakes at the Curragh, in 1982. Le Bavard was regarded principally as a potential sire of jumpers before Carlingford Castle put him on the map—Carlingford Castle, who changed hands in Ireland for 1,200 guineas as a foal and 7,400 guineas as a yearling, was apparently once nearly sold to a leading British jumping trainer as a potential steeplechaser. Le Bavard won the Prix du Cadran (French Gold Cup) as a four-year-old, proving exceptionally well suited by the trip, and was afterwards second (promoted from third) to Sagaro in the Gold Cup; Carlingford Castle's grandsire Devon came third in a Prix du Cadran. Both Le Bavard and Devon appeared to act on any going, although Devon went particularly well in the mud. Like his sire, Carlingford Castle is a genuine racehorse. All being well, he'll give the older horses plenty to do in the Gold Cup; if there's some give in the ground we'll be backing him to win it! *H. Cecil.*

CARLO OLIZ 3 b.g. Relevant–Gypsy Queen (Pelso Lad 87) (1982 NR 1983 8f 12fg 10.6fg) rather lightly-built gelding; third foal; dam won a selling hurdle; behind in sellers. *D. McCain.* —

CARLTON STAR 2 ch.f. Quayside 124–Sailor's Saint (Saint Crespin III 132) (1983 5f 7f) Apr 28; IR 800F, 1,750Y; half-sister to several minor winners; dam ran 4 times in Ireland; in rear in maiden race at Catterick in August and seller at Redcar in September. *D. Smith.* —

CARMELINA 2 b.f. Habitat 134–Heavenly Form 107 (Reform 132) (1983 7.5g*) Apr 23; sister to very useful 1979 French 2-y-o 6.5f and 1m winner Suvero, and half-sister to winners in Austria, Ireland and France; dam, useful at up to 7f at 2 yrs, is daughter of smart 5f performer Heavenly Sound; made all to win a maiden race at Saint-Cloud in November comfortably by 2½ lengths from Dancing Place; will be suited by 1m; promising and will win more races. *F. Boutin, France.* 98 p

CARNEADES 3 b.g. Homing 130–Connarca (Connaught 130) (1982 7d² 7g* 7g² 8d 1983 8.2v 8v 8s 8f 12f 12.2f 10.6f 12.2g 16.5f) workmanlike gelding; quite useful as a 2-y-o but seemed not to train on; gives impression he should be suited by 1¼m+ now; acts on a soft surface and doesn't impress in his slower paces on firm; blinkered sixth and last outings. *M. H. Easterby.* —

CARNET DE DANSE 2 b.f. Dance In Time–Yorktown (Charlottown 127) (1983 6g⁴ 7s³) Apr 5; small, lightly-made filly; second foal; dam placed from 7.5f to 10.5f in France; ran on without being knocked about when in frame in minor event at Lingfield and maiden race at Leicester in the autumn; will be suited by 1m; capable of winning a small race. *J. Dunlop.* 77

CARNIVAL PRIZE 3 b.g. Carnival Dancer 113–Bath Miss 83 (Appiani II 129) (1982 5g 5d³ 5g 5g 6d 7fg 8d 1983 12.2g 9d 9f 9f⁴ 10fg 8f* 10fg 9f) plain, compact gelding; plater; attracted no bid when winning at Carlisle in July; best form at 1m; yet to race on really soft going, but acts on any other; often blinkered and has worn bandages. *D. Yeoman.* 47

CAROCREST (USA) 2 b.c. Caro 133–Irish Course (Irish Lancer) (1983 7f⁴ 7f² 7fg* 8fg*) Mar 9; $550,000Y; strong, handsome colt; excellent mover; half-brother to several winners, notably North Course (by Northern Jove), a very smart winner at up to 1m; dam very useful winner at up to 1m; improved with his races, on last 2 outings making all in 17-runner minor event at Lingfield in August and 13-runner £3,900 race at Salisbury in September; will stay 1¼m; almost certainly has further improvement in him, and appeals strongly as a good 3-y-o in the making. *G. Harwood.* 109 p

Lady Harrison's "Carocrest"

CAROLINA 2 b.f. Martinmas 128–Dolly Grey (My Swanee 122) (1983 7f) May 5; IR 3,400Y; smallish filly; third foal; half-sister to Irish 1½m winner Ashford Doll (by Pitcairn); dam poor maiden; tailed off in 17-runner claiming race at Leicester in August; sold M. Haynes 640 gns Ascot November Sales. *I. Walker.* —

CAROLINE'S GIRL 2 b.f. Roman Warrior 132–Sovereign Game 60 (Sovereign Path 125) (1983 5v 6fg3 5.3fg 5d4 6fg) Feb 15; 960Y; workmanlike filly; half-sister to a minor winner; dam, maiden sprint handicapper, is half-sister to very smart Record Run; close-up eighth of 22 in maiden event at Leicester in October, final outing and best effort in 5 races, one a seller; suited by 6f; acts on a firm surface. *M. Hinchliffe.* **58**

CAROLSIDE 3 br.f. Music Maestro 119–Primrose Bank 91 (Charlottown 127) (1982 5fg* 5f* 5fg3 6f2 6fg 6g 1983 7d 6d 5fg4 6fg) smallish, lengthy filly; good walker and mover; useful at her best as a 2-y-o; ran well for quite a way when 7 lengths fifth of 9 behind Favoridge in Nell Gwyn Stakes at Newmarket in April on first outing; ran best subsequent race when 3½ lengths fourth of 10 behind Runnett in £4,700 event at Sandown in June; may stay beyond 6f. *P. Walwyn.* **95**

CARO NOME 4 b.f. Jolly Good 122–Gilda 65 (Connaught 130) (1982 14g 14d 12fg* 16fg3 1983 10.2d 13v 12d 12v 10fg 20.4g 16.5f4 14f3 16.5f* 14f 15.8fg 16h 15.5f4 15g) lengthy, workmanlike filly; poor handicapper; won at Folkestone in August; acts on firm going; suitable mount for an inexperienced rider; sold 3,800 gns Newmarket Autumn Sales. *A. Bailey.* **54**

CARO'S GIFT (USA) 2 gr.c. Caro 133–Christmas Belle (Santa Claus 133) (1983 6g 7fg 7fg4 8s3 8fg*) Mar 4; $60,000Y; half-brother to 2 winners, including useful 7f and 1½m winner Lyphmas (by Lyphard); dam, Irish middle-distance winner, is half-sister to smart Royal Sword; improved with distance and stayed on in fine style **89**

165

to win 11-runner maiden race at Newcastle in October by 2½ lengths from Briarean; will be suited by 1¼m; probably acts on any going. *G. Pritchard-Gordon.*

CARO'S LAD 2 gr.c. Caro 133–Favoletta 115 (Baldric II 131) (1983 6fg 6g 6g)   **72 p**
Apr 3; close-coupled, rather lightly-made colt; excellent walker and good mover; half-brother to numerous winners, notably very smart 3-y-o Favoridge (by Riva Ridge), successful at up to 1m, and smart 5f performer Amaranda (by Bold Lad, Ire); dam won Irish 1000 Guineas; 9 lengths seventh of 15 to Round Hill in minor event at Doncaster in September, final outing and best effort; will be better suited by 7f and 1m; almost certainly capable of improvement, and could pay to follow. *G. Wragg.*

CAROUSER 6 b.g. Warpath 113–Brandy (Busted 134) (1982 12g 12g 8f 11fg 8f²   **–**
11g 10d 12fg⁴ 19f 12g 1983 12f) lightly-made, lean gelding; plater; stays 1½m; acts on a firm and a soft surface; has run creditably for an amateur rider; has worn bandages; has worn blinkers. *J. Doyle.*

CARO WOOD 2 b.c. Raga Navarro 119–Tiefland (Right Tack 131) (1983 5s 6g)   **–**
Feb 25; IR 3,400F, 800Y; big, leggy colt; first foal; dam never ran; in rear in maiden race at Kempton in April and minor event at Lingfield in September. *M. Haynes.*

CARREG CENNEN 4 ch.g. Native Bazaar 122–Cennen-Olive (Wolver Hollow   **–**
126) (1982 6d 5fg² 5.8f² 5f 5h 5g 5.3f³ 5fg 5f² 6fg 6g 5d 1983 5f 6h 5f 8d) tall, leggy gelding; sprint maiden; acts on any going; usually bandaged off-fore. *Dr A. Jones.*

CARREG-WENNOL 2 ch.f. Dublin Taxi–Cennen-Olive (Wolver Hollow 126)   **–**
(1983 5g 5.8h 5fg) May 7; half-sister to a winner in Trinidad; dam of no account; well beaten in maiden races in the summer. *B. Palling.*

CARRIAGE WAY 9 br.h. Track Spare 125–Polyandrist 92 (Polic 126) (1982 8g   **71**
8.2v³ 8d* 8f4 8g 8f 8fg 8.2f 8g 8fg* 7.2s² 7s 9s* 8.2s³ 8.2s³ 8s 1983 9fg² 8fg 8d 8fg 9d 9d³ 8.2s* 10fg 8.2fg 8fg) workmanlike horse; quite a modest handicapper; won at Haydock in October; stays 9f; acts on any going, but is very much at home with give in the ground; blinkered once; good mount for a boy; covered several mares in spring. *W. Stubbs.*

CARRIEMEAR 3 b. or br.f. Averof 123–Party Royale (Busted 134) (1982 NR   **–**
1983 12s 12.2d 14.6f) compact filly; first foal; dam never ran; ran a respectable first race when 16 lengths fifth of 10 behind Shenton Way in maiden race at Haydock in May, staying on steadily after missing break; still needed race next time; probably needs some give in the ground; wears bandages in front. *K. Stone.*

CARRY ON AGAIN 5 ch.g. Swing Easy 126–Hi-Conkers 86 (Sica Boy 132)   **–**
(1982 12fg 12f 1983 8v 10s 10v 12fg 12fg⁴) lengthy gelding; of little account nowadays; has shown signs of temperament. *G. Fletcher.*

CARTERS WAY 3 b.g. Farm Walk 111–Darling Do (Derring-Do 131) (1982 7d   **83**
1983 9v 9s 9g³ 10f 9f 10f³ 12fg* 12s 9g* 9fg² 10f) neat gelding; held up when successful in 2 minor events at Hamilton in September, showing improved form in latter to win by 2½ lengths from Gentle Down; had stiffish task in between; stays 1½m; probably acts on any going (showed distinct promise on soft in spring); tends to hang and isn't an easy ride; sold 8,000 gns Doncaster November Sales. *Miss S. Hall.*

CASAL ROYALE 5 b.m. Netherkelly 112–Composite 61 (Compensation 127)   **–**
(1982 8fg 1983 8fg 9.4f) poor maiden. *D. McCain.*

CASANNA 4 b.f. Star Appeal 133–Try-Gun (Combat 123) (1982 10.2g 12.3g⁴   **–**
12fg² 12fg⁴ 12fg 15.8d 1983 12d 12.2fg 12fg 12f 13h⁴ 12d⁴ 12.2g) fair sort; poor maiden; stays 13f; sometimes blinkered. *A. Hide.*

CASBAR KID 2 b.c. Native Bazaar 122–Avengeress 73 (Aggressor 130) (1983   **–**
5v⁴ 5s 5v 6fg 5g 6fg) May 3; smallish, workmanlike colt; brother to a winning plater over 7f and a winning hurdler; dam won at up to 13.8f; poor form, including in sellers; blinkered last 2 starts. *S. Matthews.*

CASCABEL 2 b.f. Matahawk 127–Belle Margot (Counsel 118) (1983 7fg 7g 7fg)   **67**
Apr 20; workmanlike filly; has a round action; half-sister to 1982 2-y-o 6f winner La Perricholi (by Targowice); dam won over 1½m at 5 yrs in France; 11½ lengths sixth of 21 to Mahogany in £4,600 event at Newbury in September, second outing and best effort; bred to stay well. *D. Marks.*

CASHMERE QUEEN 2 b. or br.f. Blue Cashmere 129–Knavesmire 82   **45**
(Runnymede 123) (1983 5d⁴ 5d 5v) Feb 22; first foal; dam at her best at 2 yrs

when winning over 5f; poor form, including in a seller; exported to Algeria. *M. Hinchliffe.*

CASHMOOR 5 b.g. Ashmore 125–Go Friendly (Be Friendly 130) (1982 8d³ 10f — 8g² 8f4 10fg 10f 12d* 12g 12.2fg* 11.7g* 11.7fg* 1983 12f 10fg 12.2d) strong, close-coupled gelding; quite a modest handicapper at his best; well beaten at 5 yrs; stays 1½m; yet to show he acts on extremes of going; sometimes makes the running. *R. Baker.*

CASH OR CARRY (USA) 3 b.c. Naskra–Pay Cash (Whistler 129) (1982 5fg⁴ 72 6fg³ 6g 8.2s² 7.6v⁴ 7s 7s 1983 6s 7fg⁴ 8f 9f² 7.6g 9fg 8g³ 8.2g³ 9g³ 10.5d 8g²) quite an attractive colt; placed in varied races, but became a little disappointing and was beaten in a £4,000 seller tenth start; possibly doesn't stay 1¼m; acts on any going; blinkered third outing; has worn a tongue strap. *B. Hanbury.*

CASSIO LIL 4 b. or br.f. Scottish Rifle 127–Solway Bay 86 (Tamerlane 128) (1982 — 12g 10d² 13.8f* 12fg³ 12g 12.2f² 12g³ 13.8d 1983 12d 12v 12.2g⁴ 10f 10f 10h) leggy, lightly-made filly; plater; stays 1¾m; seems to act on any going but goes well on firm; effective with or without blinkers; has worn bandages; has sweated up. *D. Morley.*

CASTANET 3 ch.c. Green Dancer 132–Pampas Flower 80 (Pampered King 121) 82 (1982 6fg* 7s 1983 8s 8f* 8f4 8fg) rangy colt; won handicap at Pontefract in June all out by a short head from Darting Groom after being held up; not seen out after July; suited by 1m; a good-moving colt who is very well suited to top-of-the-ground. *P. Walwyn.*

CAST A SHADOW 3 b.c. Welsh Saint 126–Predestination 73 (Premonition 130) — (1982 5fg 5f² 5f* 6f 6g4 6fg 6s 1983 8g 10.5s 6v 6f 7.6fg 8fg 9f 10f 14d 7g) tall, lengthy colt; poor mover; showed very little in 1983, but often had stiffish tasks and is unlikely to stay beyond 1m; bit coltish on second outing at 2 yrs and often sweated up; blinkered eighth start; slowly away final outing. *J. McNaughton.*

CASTAWAY (FR) 4 ch.f. Filiberto 123–Castania (Orsini 124) (1982 5fg 6g 7fg 6fg — 7fg 7f4 8g 5fg 7g 1983 8g 5.1g 7f 11.7fg 7fg 8d 9s 6fg) workmanlike filly; poor maiden; virtually refused to race third start. *C. Austin.*

CASTELLITA 2 br.f. Homing 130–Claironcita 97 (Don Carlos) (1983 6f4 6fg 7g) 68 Apr 14; tall, rather shallow-girthed filly; second foal; dam won 6 times over middle distances; quite a modest maiden; will be better suited by 1m+. *F. J. Houghton.*

CASTLE DOUGLAS 3 b.g. Amboise 133–Linguistic 95 (Porto Bello 118) (1982 68 8.2s 1983 11.7s4 12g4 16f² 14f³ 15f* 16f² 15.5f* 16.5f³ 16fg) rangy gelding; made all and had opposition well strung out at finish when winning maiden race at Edinburgh in July and amateur riders race at Folkestone in September (odds on both times); suited by a test of stamina; acts well on firm going; ran poorly final start; sold to I. Dudgeon 16,500 gns Newmarket Autumn Sales. *Sir Mark Prescott.*

CASTLE GUARD 3 br.c. Home Guard 129–Perldia (Diatome 132) (1982 6fg³ 116 7d* 6f* 7f 8s 1983 8s* 8v* 8v 10.5v4 9fg 10f 8fg) well-made, useful-looking colt; superb mover; second foal; half-brother to a winning plater; dam won over 4.5f at 2 yrs in France; showed very useful form at 2 yrs in this country when trained by R. Price; improved in 1983 and won Prix Omnium at Saint-Cloud in March and Prix de Fontainebleau at Longchamp in April (beat Saint Cyrien 2½ lengths in latter); also finished creditable 6¼ lengths fourth of 7 to L'Emigrant in Prix Lupin at Longchamp again in May and respectable sixth of 14 to Mourjane in Prix de la Cote Normande at Deauville in August on sixth outing; stays 1¼m; acts on any going but revels in the mud. *J. Fellows, France.*

CASTLE RISING 3 b.c. Blakeney 126–Christchurch 88 (So Blessed 130) (1982 116 10.2s 1983 11v* 15g4 13.3f² 12d4) good-looking colt; good mover; third foal; half-brother to smart 6f to 10.5f winner Church Parade (by Queen's Hussar) and 1½m winner Glastonbury (by Grundy); dam, 1½m winner, is half-sister to 1000 Guineas and Oaks winner Highclere; confirmed the promise of his only race as a 2-y-o when beating Oregon Trail by 2½ lengths in 17-runner maiden race at Newbury in May; really took the eye and ran well when about 4 lengths fourth of 7 to Yawa in Grand Prix de Paris at Longchamp in June and length second of 7 to Khairpour in Geoffrey Freer Stakes at Newbury in August (made running), but was given plenty to do and didn't run up to his best when just under 3 lengths fourth of 11 behind Jupiter Island in St Simon Stakes at Newbury again in October (favourite, lost second close home); gives impression he's a thorough stayer;

Shaw Maiden Stakes, Newbury—Castle Rising wins decisively from Oregon Trail and Danseur de Corde (right)

acts on any going, but seems to go particularly well on firm; the sort to win more races where stamina is at a premium; to be trained by I. Balding in 1984. *R. Hern.*

CATALDI 2 b.c. Wolver Hollow 126–Gerona (Herero) (1983 7f 8fg⁴) Apr 14; IR 170,000Y; attractive colt; good mover; half-brother to 2 winners in Germany, including German Derby third Gare du Nord (by Levmoss); dam versatile winner of 7 races, including 1¼m Preis der Diana (German Oaks) and 6f Goldene Peitsche; improved a good deal on first effort when 2½ lengths fourth of 28 to Bob Back in maiden race at Newmarket in October, looking likely winner until unable to quicken from the Dip; has further improvement in him and seems sure to win races. *G. Harwood.* — **91 p**

CATCHER IN THE RYE 3 ch.c. Tudor Music 131–Lake Constance 85 (Star Gazer 123) (1982 NR 1983 6fg*) IR 4,400F, IR 3,000Y; half-brother to useful 1976 2-y-o sprinter Bodensee (by Wolver Hollow) and a winner in Denmark; dam best at sprint distances; 16/1 when leading in final furlong and beating It's A Pleasure by ¾ length in 10-runner minor event at Brighton in August; wasn't seen out again. *D. Arbuthnot.* — **86**

CATCHPOLE 2 b.f. Fair Season 120–Warm Slipper (King's Company 124) (1983 5d 6fg 6fg) Jan 23; small filly; a twin; of no account. *C. Spares.* — **–**

CATCHING 2 b.c. Thatching 131–Blue Parrot (Lyphard 132) (1983 5s 5d⁴ 6d² 6f³ 6fg* 7d 6fg* 6fg) Apr 20; 12,000Y; close-coupled, robust colt; first foal; dam won small 11f race at 4 yrs in France; successful in nurseries at Redcar (apprentice ridden) and Newmarket in August, at Newmarket putting in a terrific last-furlong run to snatch victory by ½ length from Throne of Glory in Philip Cornes Nickel Alloys Stakes Final; beaten some way out when tried over 7f; best form on fast ground. *J. Fitzgerald.* — **91**

CATCH THE THATCH 2 b.c. Thatch 136–Lady Morgan (Levmoss 133) (1983 7g) Apr 24; first foal; dam Irish 1½m winner; 25/1, modest sixth of 10 in minor event at Chepstow in October. *D. H. Jones.* — **–**

CATHERINE CLARE 2 b.f. Sallust 134–Awakening Rose (Le Levanstell 122) (1983 6f 6f 6d 6g) Mar 9; 15,500Y; close-coupled, fair sort; second foal; dam, — **58**

168

French 10.5f winner, is half-sister to Rose Laurel and Rambling Rose; plating-class maiden; showed form only on final start, when blinkered; should stay 1m; sold 1,550 gns Doncaster November Sales. *G. Pritchard-Gordon.*

CATHERINE'S CHASE 2 b.f. Hotfoot 126–Santa Caterina 83 (Bold Lad, Ire 133) (1983 5.8h) May 4; first foal; dam showed ability on all 3 starts at 2 yrs; 8½ lengths eighth of 14 to Boezinge in maiden race at Bath in August; sold 310 gns Ascot October Sales. *J. Tree.* —

CATMAN 2 b.c. Crawter 97–Camina 55 (Don Carlos) (1983 6fg 7f 7g 6fg) Mar 29; workmanlike colt; second foal; dam won 1¼m claiming race and poor novice hurdle; seventh of 24 in maiden race at Doncaster in November, best effort; will be suited by 1m; trained first 2 outings by R. Sturdy. *M. Francis.* —

CAT O'NINE TAILS 3 b.c. Le Johnstan 123–The Dupecat 75 (Javelot 124) (1982 5fg³ 5f* 5g* 5fg² 5g* 6f³ 6.5d³ 7s 1983 7s) quite well-made, useful-looking colt; good walker and mover; smart performer as a 2-y-o when trained by R. Price; weak in market, ran badly and was soon beaten when fifth of 6 in Salisbury 2000 Guineas Trial in April, only outing of 1983; should stay 7f; has won on firm going but is probably suited by some give in the ground. *C. Horgan.* —

CATS 2 b.f. Dance In Time–Catalpa 115 (Reform 132) (1983 6g 7g²) Apr 3; sturdy filly; third foal; half-sister to 3-y-o 1½m winner Shawnee (by Grundy) and Ribblesdale Stakes winner Strigida (by Habitat); dam and grandam won Ribblesdale Stakes; third favourite, 1½ lengths second of 10 to Soosjoy in minor event at Catterick in October; burly and didn't move well on debut; will be suited by further; should win a race. *E. Weymes.* **85**

Lady Trina Stanhope's "Catching"

CAUNSALL BEAU 2 b.c. Proud Knight–Woodland Dell (The Dell 94) (1983 —
5.8h) Apr 22; small colt; fourth foal by a thoroughbred stallion; dam of little
account on flat and over jumps; last of 13 in maiden race at Bath in July. *R.
Griffiths.*

CAUSE CELEBRE 3 gr.c. Habitat 134–Canton Silk 108 (Runnymede 123) (1982 —
5f2 5fg* 5f4 7g2 6g2 7g2 7s 1983 7.6v3 7d 6d3 7fg 6fg4 6fg) smallish, lengthy,
attractive colt; very useful as a 2-y-o; ran disappointingly in varied company in
1983, although reached frame in minor events at Lingfield and Brighton and an
apprentice race at Nottingham; suited by 7f; best form on a sound surface;
blinkered second outing. *J. Hindley.*

CAUTIOUS STYLE (USA) 2 b.c. Caucasus 127–Impressive Style (Ready Say 81 p
Go) (1983 6s 5f*) Mar 30; $60,000Y; big, well-made colt, with plenty of scope;
half-brother to Impressive (by Vaguely Noble) and 3 winners in USA,
including a minor stakes winner; dam won 19 races at up to 1m, showing smart form
from 2 yrs to 6 yrs; led 2f out and soon went clear to beat Faridpour by 2½ lengths
in 14-runner maiden race at Salisbury in June; had also shown excellent speed on
introduction; bred to stay at least 1m; acts on firm going; type to train on into useful
performer. *P. Cole.*

CAVALIER SERVENTE 5 gr.h. Barbaro–Quoro Star (Quorum 126) (1982 12s 62
12.2f2 12f2 10fg2 12f4 13.8f3 16g 16fg 12g4 12s2 12s 1983 12d* 12g 12s3 12f 14.6f*
16f* 14fg* 16f 18fg) strong horse; won handicaps at Pontefract in April, Doncaster
in July and Newcastle and Haydock in August; stays 2m; acts on any going; has
worn bandages; suited by waiting tactics (doesn't find much off bridle) *P. Wigham.*

CAWSTON'S KID 3 ch.f. Cawston's Clown 113–Giddy Goat (Hill Clown) (1982 —
NR 1983 5f) 130Y; fifth living foal; dam unraced half-sister to very smart Fool's
Mate; started slowly when last in apprentice race at Edinburgh in July. *Mrs A.
Bell.*

CAWSTON STAR 4 br.f. Comedy Star 121–Telouet 90 (Sing Sing 134) (1982 5fg 40
5f 5f 5fg 5.3f4 5f3 5fg 5g2 5g 1983 5f 6fg 5f 5f3 5f3 5fg) smallish, fair sort; sprint
plater; sometimes blinkered; occasionally starts slowly. *H. Collingridge.*

CAYLA 3 ch.f. Tumble Wind–Relicia (Relko 136) (1982 NR 1983 7f4 6fg 5g 5g —
7.6fg) close-coupled filly; half-sister to several winners; dam, from a very
successful family, showed smart form over middle distances in France; showed
signs of ability on first 2 outings. *R. Boss.*

C B M GIRL 2 br.f. Diamonds Are Trump 108–Frontier Princess 86 (Crocket 130) 62
(1983 5s 5g2 6g 5f3 5f2 6d 6s 6fg) Apr 1; 2,500Y; big filly; half-sister to a winner in
Switzerland; dam best at around 1m; modest plater; stays 6f; acts on any going;
gave a mulish display and fell after getting loose on way to start on sixth outing. *K.
Stone.*

CECILE 3 b.f. Captain James 123–Spring Again (Primera 131) (1982 5f3 5fg* 5d2 78
5fg3 5g 6g 1983 6g 5s 7f 8fg4 8f 7f* 7fg) rather leggy, narrow filly; made all and
beat Socratic in good style by 3 lengths in handicap at Redcar in August; stays 1m;
yet to race on really soft ground but acts on any other; none too consistent; sold
10,000 gns Newmarket September Sales, reportedly for export to California. *J.
Fitzgerald.*

CEDAR HALL 2 ch.g. Record Run 127–Picnic Dancer 71 (Hul a Hul 124) (1983 —
6fg 7fg) Feb 17; strong, workmanlike gelding; half-brother to 1978 2-y-o 5f winner
Sand Dancer (by Sandford Lad); dam placed over 5f at 2 yrs; soundly beaten in
August in maiden race at Pontefract (dwelt) and £3,800 event at Newcastle. *M. W.
Easterby.*

CEDARWAY 2 ch.g. Sandy Creek 123–Call Me Mrs (Charlaway) (1983 5s 5v3 63
5d) Apr 18; 10,500Y; lengthy, useful sort; reportedly third foal; half-brother to a
placed animal in Australia; dam unraced daughter of Molecomb Stakes winner
Royal Indiscretion; plating-class maiden; not raced after April. *W. O'Gorman.*

CEDEES 3 b.f. Habat 127–Water Rat 83 (Hard Tack 111§) (1982 5g 5g 5fg 1983 —
7g 8f 7g 10fg) sturdy filly; soundly beaten, including in sellers; blinkered final start.
D. Ringer.

CEDILLA (USA) 2 ch.f. Caro 133–Mashteen (Majestic Prince) (1983 8g 8fg*) 108 p
Jan 28; $135,000Y; good-bodied, attractive filly; second foal; dam, smart winner at
up to 7f, is half-sister to dam of very smart Smuggly (by Caro); still looking short of
peak fitness, led early in straight and never looked likely to be caught when winning
8-runner maiden race at Longchamp in October by ½ length from Reine d'Egypte;
will stay 1¼m; the type to make a good 3-y-o. *F. Boutin, France.*

CEEDEE REVENGE 3 b.g. Garda's Revenge 119–Fiddle Myree 69 – (Frankincense 120) (1982 8fg 8d 6g 1983 13fg 12f) strong, well-made gelding; behind in varied company; sold 410 gns Ascot August Sales. *P. Haslam.*

CEE MAC CEE 2 ch.c. Anax 120–First Gain (Psidium 130) (1983 5v*) Apr 15; 52 920F, 3,200Y; workmanlike colt; fifth produce; dam won a selling hurdle; bought in 3,000 gns after winning 12-runner seller at Warwick in April by ¾ length from April For Ever. *W. O'Gorman.*

CELERITAS 2 ch.f. Dominion 123–Contadina (Memling) (1983 6fg 7.6d) Mar – 19; good-bodied filly; excellent walker; half-sister to several winners, including very useful sprinter Manor Farm Boy (by Mansingh) and very useful 7f performer Conbrian (by The Brianstan); dam never ran; unquoted when in rear in 12-runner Blue Seal Stakes at Ascot in September and 20-runner maiden race at Lingfield in October; looks capable of better. *A. Pitt.*

CELESTIAL AIR 3 br.f. Rheingold 137–Cloudbreak 95 (Nimbus 130) (1982 NR 96 1983 12d* 11.7fg 12h* 11fg 12f) big, quite attractive filly; good walker; sister to modest middle-distance winner Palatinate, and half-sister to several winners, including useful 1976 2-y-o 5f and 7f winner Beriosova (by Lorenzaccio); dam 2-y-o 5f winner; successful in 18-runner maiden race at Thirsk in May and small handicap at Beverley in July, winning impressively by 8 lengths on former course; well below that form other starts, twice finishing last; stays 1½m well; seems to act on any going; most inconsistent. *M. Stoute.*

CELESTIAL BRIDE 3 b.f. Godswalk 130–Light Diamond (Florescence 120) – (1982 6f 6fg 1983 9v 10s) fair sort; lightly raced and little worthwhile form; has worn a tongue strap. *H. Candy.*

CELESTIAL DANCER 4 b.c. Godswalk 130–Oulanova (Nijinsky 138) (1982 114 6fg² 6fg*(dis) 6f* 6f³ 6g* 6d⁴ 6g 1983 5f⁴ 6fg 6f 6fg³) big, strong, rangy colt; carries plenty of condition; smart performer; ran very well in King's Stand Stakes at Royal Ascot, keeping on strongly to be 4½ lengths fourth of 16 to Sayf El Arab; ran respectably afterwards to be about 4½ lengths fifth of 9 to Maximova in Prix de Meautry at Deauville in August on third start and 5½ lengths third of 8 to Gabitat in Goldene Peitsche at Baden-Baden later in month; suited by 6f; acts on any going; needs to be held up, has a tendency to hang and isn't an easy ride; consistent. *A. Hide.*

CELTIC ASSEMBLY (USA) 2 b.f. Secretariat–Welsh Garden 123 (Welsh Saint 95 126) (1983 6f 6f 7f³ 7fg 7.3d) Feb 20; $175,000Y; strong, compact, sturdy, quite attractive filly; second foal; dam, half-sister to very good American performer Galaxy Libra, was top 2-y-o filly in Ireland in 1975 when successful 5 times from 5f to 7.9f; ran creditably in 2 good 7f races in October, finishing 7 lengths sixth of 13 to Mahogany in Rockfel Stakes at Newmarket and 4¾ lengths sixth of 14 to Betsy Bay in Rochford Thompson Newbury Stakes; will stay 1m; the type to make a useful 3-y-o. *J. Dunlop.*

CELTIC BIRD 3 b.f. Celtic Cone 116–Bird Cherry 61 (Falcon 131) (1982 5f 5f² 77 ? 5f* 5g* 5fg 5fg 5d⁴ 5s 1983 5s 6f² 5f³ 5f* 5fg⁴ 5f 5g⁴ 5s*) small, strong filly; had a good season and won handicap at Redcar, seller at Edinburgh (no bid) and minor event at Haydock; appeared to show vastly improved form when beating quite useful Irish sprinter Pampas decisively by 2 lengths on last-named course in October; stays 6f, but has done all her winning at 5f; acts on any going; genuine; excellent mount for an apprentice. *A. Balding.*

CELTIC PROMISE 3 b.g. Martinmas 128–Irish Bride (Track Spare 125) (1982 73 7s⁴ 1983 8v² 8v² 8f 9f) leggy gelding; second in 2 maiden races at Warwick in spring but became rather disappointing; gives impression he'll stay 1¼m; didn't look particularly keen in blinkers third start; sold to P. Mitchell 7,400 gns Newmarket Autumn Sales. *I. Balding.*

CENTIMETER 3 b.c. Thatch 136–Millimeter (Ribocco 129) (1982 7g 8g 1983 71 8v 10fg 10fg² 10f² 11.5g³) sturdy, attractive colt; placed in maiden races at Pontefract and Yarmouth (2); suited by middle distances. *L. Cumani.*

CENTRAL CARPETS 4 b.f. Garda's Revenge 119–Homecomings (Primera 63 131) (1982 6g 5s 5fg 6fg 6fg³ 5f 5f* 6fg 6f 6h 6g 5fg 6g 5fg 5d 5d² 5g 5s 1983 5v² 5v* 5s 5v⁴ 5v³ 5v 5f 5.6f 5f 5s 5g 5fg) lightly-made filly; poor mover; sprint handicapper; won at Warwick in April; acts on any going; suitable mount for a 7-lb claimer; blinkered once in 1982. *W. Stubbs.*

CENTROLINE 5 b.h. High Line 125–Centro 86 (Vienna 127) (1982 12fg⁴ 14f 111 1983 12d⁴ 16g 20f 15fg) small, lightly-made horse; good walker; very smart stayer at his best; stayed on at one pace when 5½ lengths fourth to Diamond

Shoal in John Porter Stakes at Newbury in April; outpaced in closing stages when respectable fifth of 7 to Ore in Henry II Stakes at Sandown in May; well beaten afterwards in Gold Cup at Royal Ascot and Tennent Trophy (Handicap) at Ayr; stays very well; possibly not at his best on very firm going; tends to pull hard nowadays; suited by a strong gallop; sold to C. Bell 28,000 gns Newmarket December Sales. *H. Candy.*

CENTRUST (USA) 3 b. or br.c. Mr Prospector–Rock Fever (Hawaii) (1982 5g*   **92** 5g⁴ 5f² 6fg⁴ 6fg 1983 6d 7d 7f² 7f³ 8fg² 7g) neat, attractive colt; fairly useful top-of-the-ground handicapper; suited by 7f+; sold 27,000 gns Newmarket Autumn Sales, reportedly to race in USA. *P. Walwyn.*

CERUSSITE 2 b.c. Malinowski 123–Icing 112 (Prince Tenderfoot 126) (1983 6v²   **97** 6f³ 7f⁴ 7fg² 7g* 7d 8d² 8s² 7d) Feb 12; strong, lengthy, good-looking colt; second foal; half-brother to useful Irish 1m to 1½m performer Meringue (by Ballymore); dam won from 5f to 1m at 2 yrs; won 19-runner maiden race at the Curragh in August by short head from Prince of Rondo; subsequently ran in valuable races, notably finishing creditable 1½ lengths second of 7 to Without Reserve in Ashford Castle Stakes and 6 lengths runner-up to odds-on Sadler's Wells in Panasonic Beresford Stakes, both at the Curragh; will probably stay 1¼m. *K. Prendergast, Ireland.*

CHA CHA CHA 2 ch.f. Julio Mariner 127–Kitten 102 (Pardal 130) (1983 7fg 7f   **–** 7.6fg) Apr 18; smallish, rather lightly-made filly; half-sister to very useful middle-distance stayer Grand Chat (by Grand Roi) and fairly useful middle-distance winner Mon Chat (by Great Nephew); dam beat at up to 7f; beaten in minor and maiden events. *B. Swift.*

CHACONIA 2 b.f. Record Run 127–St Pauli Girl 114 (St Paddy 133) (1983 7fg⁴   **81** 7f* 7fg) Feb 12; 5,000Y; big filly; half-sister to several winners, including useful 1¼m performer and smart jumper Major Thompson (by Brigadier Gerard); dam runner-up in 1000 Guineas and Oaks; won 12-runner maiden race at Yarmouth in July by ¾ length from Shadiliya; soundly beaten in £3,800 event won by Golden Flute at Newcastle the following month; will be suited by 1m+; acts on firm going. *F. Durr.*

CHAD'S DELIGHT 3 br.f. Idiot's Delight 115–Bonnie Bladnoch (Lord of Verona   **–** 120) (1982 NR 1983 10fg) 800Y, 2,200 3-y-o; sister to a bad animal, and half-sister to very useful staying hurdler Garliestown and leading point-to-pointer Glasserton (both by Sea Wolf); dam poor stayer; backward and sweating when last of 12 in minor event at Nottingham in September. *O. Brennan.*

CHADS GAMBLE 8 ch.g. St Chad 120–Another Flutter 75 (Credo 123) (1982   **–** 6f³ 7h² 7fg 8fg 6f 7fg⁴ 6f⁴ 7g 7f³ 1983 7f 8.2fg 8h 8fg 8f 7f⁴ 7h 8f) poor handicapper nowadays; stays 1m; appears to act on any going but is suited by a sound surface; used to wear blinkers; has run creditably for an apprentice. *J. Bethell.*

CHALET WALDEGG 3 ch.f. Monsanto 121–Glistening 84 (Aureole 132) (1982   **64** 5fg 7fg 7fg 1983 12s³ 11v* 12s 12f) small, rather unfurnished filly; 33/1-winner of handicap at Wolverhampton in April; ran moderately both subsequent starts; stays 1½m; acts well on heavy going. *D. Gandolfo.*

CHALK FARM 2 b.c. Camden Town 125–Sigtrudis (Sigebert 131) (1983 5.8g 7f   **68** 6f) Mar 13; IR 4,000Y; third living produce; dam, placed in Germany as a 2-y-o, is from a good German family; showed a little ability on debut but soundly beaten both subsequent outings, on final one blinkered; should be suited by 7f; sold 2,900 gns Newmarket September Sales for export to Italy. *K. Brassey.*

CHALKIES PET 3 b.f. Reliance II 137–Solentown 72 (Town Crier 119) (1982 6d   **–** 8f 8.2d 7g 8s³ 10d 1983 12f 10.2f) leggy filly; bad mover; plater; should stay 1¼m; sold 420 gns Ascot October Sales. *D. Marks.*

CHALLANGING 3 b.f. Mill Reef 141–Vital Match 113 (Match III 135) (1982 7f*   **–** 7f⁴ 7fg² 1983 10d 10g 12g) small, close-coupled filly; nice easy mover; quite useful as a 2-y-o but was well beaten in 1983, including in Pretty Polly Stakes at Newmarket and Galtres Stakes at York; should stay at least 1½m; acts on firm going; didn't impress in appearance first 2 starts. *B. Hobbs.*

CHAMISENE (FR) 3 b.f. Pharly 130–Tuneria (Tanerko 134) (1982 7.5d² 1983   **120** 8s³ 8v² 8v⁴ 8d⁴ 8v* 8s* 10g*) 950,000 francs Y (approx £86,000); attractive filly; half-sister to several winners, notably very smart French miler Lou Piguet (by Habitat); dam French middle-distance winner; developed into a very smart filly and on last 2 starts in June held off Luth Enchantee by a neck (pair clear) in Prix de Sandringham at Chantilly and won most decisively by 2 lengths and 1½ lengths from

Alexandrie and Sharaya in Prix de Malleret at Longchamp; flattered by her relationships to both Luth Enchantee and Sharaya however as neither had found her very best form at that stage; had got off mark in maiden race at Longchamp the previous month (beat Luth Enchantee by ¾ length) and had previously twice run well when acting as a pacemaker for stable-companion Mysterieuse Etoile, finishing fourth of 11 to her in Prix de la Grotte and just over 2 lengths fourth to L'Attrayante in Poule d'Essai des Pouliches, both at Longchamp; stays 1¼m; yet to race on a firm surface; genuine and consistent. *M. Saliba.*

CHAMPAGNE CHARLIE 6 br.h. Charlottown 127–The Guzzler 69   –
(Behistoun 131) (1982 17f³ 16fg³ 16fg 16.9fg² 1983 14s⁴ 17.1g 16g⁴ 17.1h⁴)
compact horse; staying handicapper; appears to act on any going; blinkered last 2
starts; suitable mount for an inexperienced rider; inconsistent. *N. Gaselee.*

CHAMPAGNE GLORY 4 b.c. Hittite Glory 125–Tilt Guard 75 (Crepello 136)   –
(1982 10g 1983 8f 10.1f) short-backed colt; poor plater. *M. Bradley.*

CHAMPAGNE MANDY 3 b.f. Mandrake Major 122–Champagne Party (Amber   **59**
Rama 133) (1982 5f⁴ 5f 5g 5fg⁴ 7g³ 7.2s 8d 1983 8d 6d 6d 8d⁴ 7d 7f 8f² 8g³ 7f² 7f
9f* 8.2g³ 12f* 12.2g 10f⁴) lightly-made, plain filly; plater; won at Redcar in
September (bought in 1,050 gns) and October (no bid); stays 1½m; best form on a
sound surface. *R. Hollinshead.*

CHAMPERS CLUB 6 ch.m. Run The Gantlet–Vein (Kalydon 122) (1982 NR   –
1983 16f 18f) fair sort; probably of little account nowadays. *D. Weeden.*

CHAMPIONS DAY 2 ch.g. Sagaro 133–Gerfalcon 105 (Falcon 131) (1983 7f 8fg   **75**
8s³ 8.2fg) Apr 4; slightly hollow-backed, useful sort; brother to lightly-raced
maiden and half-brother to a winning sprinter by Roan Rocket; dam best at 7f; quite
a modest maiden; will stay 1¼m; probably acts on any going. *J. Dunlop.*

CHANCES ARE 2 b.f. He Loves Me 120–Damson 66 (Dike) (1983 6f) Mar 24;
rather leggy, narrow filly; first foal; dam won over 1¼m; fourteenth of 15 in maiden
race at Yarmouth in July. *W. Holden.*

CHANCEY 2 b. or br.f. Porto Bello 118–Kings Fillet (King's Bench 132) (1983   **60**
5d² 5s⁴ 5f 6f 5f) Apr 6; 1,000F; sparely-made filly; half-sister to winning sprinter
My Raff (by Raffingora) and a winner in Belgium; dam poor plater; poor maiden;
exported to Algeria. *M. H. Easterby.*

CHANDRA 3 b.f. Artaius 129–Daidis 66 (Welsh Pageant 132) (1982 NR 1983 7fg   –
9f 10fg⁴ 10.1fg 12fg⁴ 12d 10g) IR 40,000Y; compact filly; first foal; dam, placed
over 1½m, is daughter of high-class stayer Attica Meli; fourth in maiden races at
Brighton and Wolverhampton; promises to stay 1½m. *G. Lewis.*

CHANEY 5 b.g. Sparkler 130–Anippe 102 (Aggressor 130) (1982 9fg 10f³ 10.6f   –
14.6g 1983 10f⁴ 10fg 10fg 10f⁴) strong, compact gelding; bad mover; plater;
stays 1¼m; acts on firm going; has been tried in blinkers. *G. Fletcher.*

CHANGAN 3 ch.f. Touch Paper 113–Tin Tina 72 (Tin Whistle 128) (1982 5s³ 5g   –
6fg 7.2f 7f 1983 6s) sparely-made filly; good walker; plating-class maiden; stays
7f; acts on any going. *R. Hollinshead.*

CHANGATRE 3 ch.f. Malinowski 123–Good Reliance (Good Bond 122) (1982 6f   **57**
6g 8f 7d² 10s⁴ 7g 1983 12.2d 12s 10fg 10f 10f 10f 10h 8f 10f 8.2h⁴ 10g* 9fg 10.2fg)
small, rather shallow-girthed filly; dropped in class when winning seller at
Leicester in September (bought in 1,500 gns); stays 1¼m; acts on any going; badly
hampered fourth start; changed hands 1,000 gns Doncaster September Sales. *R.
Hollinshead.*

CHANGED HIS MIND 3 b.c. Pitskelly 122–Miskish (Gallant Man) (1982 8g²   **83** d
5d² 7fg² 7g² 7d 1983 7d* 7v 7fg 8.2fg* 8g 9g 8fg 8.2h 8d) IR 5,400Y; smallish
colt; second foal; dam, plating-class Irish maiden, comes from good family;
second in maiden races as a 2-y-o when trained in Ireland by A. Maxwell;
successful in similar event at Edinburgh in April and small handicap at Hamilton in
June; stays 1m; acts on a firm and a soft surface (very coltish when running
moderately on heavy and is worth another chance); bandaged near-fore fifth
start; not disgraced in blinkers seventh outing. *C. Nelson.*

CHANNEL AFFAIR (USA) 2 br.f. Le Fabuleux 133–Simple English (Raja   **84**
Baba) (1983 7f 7f³ 7h³ 8g² 7.6d*) May 7; $48,000Y; close-coupled, useful-looking
filly; first foal; dam, stakes-placed sprint winner, is half-sister to smart 1980 2-y-o
Panjandrum; favourite, won 18-runner maiden race at Lingfield in October
comfortably by 3 lengths from Southern Dynasty; stays 1m; probably acts on any
going. *P. Cole.*

CHANNING GIRL 4 b.f. Song 132–Maternal 93 (High Top 131) (1982 6g 8.5fg   **59**
8f² 8fg 8d² 10fg 10.1g³ 12g* 12g 14.7fg³ 16g² 14g² 16s 1983 18d 16g 14s 12d 12g⁴
17.1g 12.2g 18fg) lengthy filly; well beaten most starts at 4 yrs; stays well;
probably acts on any going; blinkered twice at 2 yrs; sweated up and looked
unimpressive second start; trained by C. Brittain first 5 outings; sold 1,100 gns
Newmarket Autumn Sales. *M. McCormack.*

CHANTRY 3 b.f. Habitat 134–Chappelle Blanche 96 (Olden Times) (1982 5s 1983   **86**
8f² 9fg 8f* 8d* 8.2g 7.6d) strong, rangy filly; won maiden race at Salisbury and
minor event at Brighton in September, seeming to show improved form on latter
course when beating French Pleat by 2 lengths; ran moderately in 2 handicaps
afterwards however; stays 1m; yet to show she can handle really soft going, but
acts on any other; moved short to start at Salisbury. *G. Harwood.*

CHAPEL COTTAGE 2 br.f. Homing 130–Mayday Melody 117 (Highland Melody   **111**
112) (1983 5s 5fg* 6fg* 6g³ 5s³)
    'She's the best filly in Europe' enthused Mick Easterby after Chapel Cottage
had won the Cherry Hinton Stakes at Newmarket in July comfortably by four
lengths. Easterby, who trained the 1977 One Thousand Guineas winner Mrs
McArdy, rates Chapel Cottage, a good-actioned, rangy filly with lots of scope, in
the same class. We aren't so enthusiastic as her trainer about Chapel Cottage's
classic prospects: her display at Newmarket stamped her as a very useful
performer but we doubt whether she'll stay the Guineas trip. Chapel Cottage
started favourite for the Cherry Hinton on the evidence of a well-publicised home
reputation and a victory over Red Line Fever in a maiden event at York the
previous month. The nine runners at Newmarket included seven other previous
winners, notably the Queen Mary winner Night of Wind. Chapel Cottage looked
well beforehand and was always moving well in the race. Eased out with two
furlongs to run she quickened clear, ridden with hands and heels, to come home
four lengths ahead of Nophe, despite drifting off a true line, a tendency also
revealed on her previous outing.
    After Newmarket, Chapel Cottage was seen out in the Lowther Stakes in
August and the Flying Childers Stakes in September (she was also an intended
runner for the William Hill Cheveley Park Stakes but was withdrawn on the eve of
the race with a temperature). At York Chapel Cottage finished a creditable third
to Prickle and Desirable, both of whom received 5 lb. Put back to five furlongs at
Doncaster she met with bad luck in running after a furlong and a half, clipping the
heels of another horse, stumbling and almost unseating her rider, and was then

*Cherry Hinton Stakes, Newmarket—Chapel Cottage produces a fine turn of foot to win from
Nophe and Sajeda (blinkers)*

Mr R. E. Sangster's "Chapel Cottage"

denied a clear run in the closing stages, doing extremely well in the end to dead-heat with Reesh for third, three and a half lengths behind the winner Superlative.

Chapel Cottage (br. f. Mar 26, 1981)	Homing (b 1975)	Habitat (b 1966)	Sir Gaylord
			Little Hut
		Heavenly Thought (b 1967)	St Paddy
			Wishful Thinking
	Mayday Melody (b 1970)	Highland Melody (br 1962)	Tudor Melody
			Follow Elizabeth
		Tread Softly (br 1965)	Poaching
			Blue Valley

Chapel Cottage, who cost 16,000 guineas at the Doncaster Sales, is likely to prove best at up to six furlongs. Her sire Homing was a miler and her dam Mayday Melody, whose second living foal she is, was a sprinter, winner of five races and good enough to reach the frame in the Vernons Sprint Cup and the Prix de Meautry. Mayday Melody's earlier foal Maybe So (by So Blessed) was a sprinter, and won over five and six furlongs. Chapel Cottage seems to act on any going. Whatever her fate in the One Thousand Guineas she should win more races. *M. W. Easterby.*

CHAPLINS CLUB (USA) 3 ch.c. Parade of Stars–Nautical Rose (Henrijan) **87** (1982 5fg² 5g³ 6g³ 6g 6d² 5v* 5g* 1983 5s⁴ 5s 5s⁴ 5g³ 5fg 5f 6f 5g³ 5d⁴ 6g) small colt; sprint handicapper; didn't win in 1983 but put up several creditable efforts; best form at 5f, but stays 6f; acts on heavy going but is possibly best on good ground; genuine; sold to R. Thompson 8,000 gns Ascot November Sales. *I. Walker.*

CHARIOTS OF FIRE 2 br.f. Kala Shikari 125–Fire and Flame (Bold — Commander) (1983 5f 7.6d 8d) Mar 28; 2,000F; first produce; dam never ran; behind in maiden and minor events, twice last. *G. Kindersley.*

CHARLES STREET 6 ch.g. Huntercombe 133–Limerick Queen (Whistling 64 Wind 123) (1982 5d³ 6g³ 7.6g 6fg 5.3g* 6g 5s 5s 1983 5v 5v 6g 6g³ 6fg 6g 6fg) neat gelding; stayed 6f; acted on any going but was well suited by some give in the ground; often blinkered; dead. *P. Haynes.*

CHARLES STUART(FR) 4 b.c. Anne's Pretender 124–Kerline (Spy Well 126) 52 (1982 8fg 10fg 8g 8d 10.8fg⁴ 12f 12g 11.7fg 12fg⁴ 1983 12s 14s 12d 16g² 20.4g* 16f 16.5fg 20f⁴) big, rangy colt; won handicap at Ayr in July; evidently suited by a thorough test of stamina; ran as if something was wrong with him seventh start. *R. Baker.*

CHARLIE KILGOUR 4 b.g. Pitskelly 122–Nuageuse (Prince Regent 129) — (1982 10f³ 10.8fg 12g 12v 1983 11.7d 12s) plating-class maiden; best run at 1¼m on firm going; blinkered final start in 1982. *A. Pitt.*

CHARLIE NOVEMBER 3 br.c. Sandford Lad 133–Lavarna (Le Levanstell — 122) (1982 NR 1983 6v 7d 10fg 8f 7f 6fg) 2,500F, 4,600Y; lightly-made colt; half-brother to several winners, including useful miler Brian's Venture (by Sallust); soundly beaten in varied races, including a seller on final start (blinkered). *K. Ivory.*

CHARLIE POOLE 2 b. or br.g. Mr Bigmore 123–Polly Poole 68 (Silent Spring 40 102) (1983 5d 5s⁴ 6fg 5f 7h 6f) Mar 28; bad plater; swerved start first outing; slowly away when apprentice ridden fourth and fifth starts. *K. Ivory.*

CHARLIE'S ANGEL (USA) 2 b.f. Halo–Queen's Ballad (King Emperor) (1983 66 p 9g 8.2fg) Feb 10; \$80,000Y; fair sort; first foal; dam unraced half-sister to smart stakes winner Lou Rosenbush; showed a little ability in 2 late-season races in the Midlands; will stay 1¼m; should improve. *I. Balding.*

CHARLIE'S SUNSHINE 6 b.m. Jimsun 121–Dracaena 62 (Double Jump 131) — (1982 12.2fg 1983 17.1d 16s² 19h) small mare; poor performer; stays well. *J. Townson.*

CHARLOTTE AMALIE 4 br.f. No Mercy 126–Penhill Point 84 (King's Leap — 111) (1982 8g 12fg 10fg 1983 6f 8f 12f 8f) of little account; has worn bandages and blinkers; sold 380 gns Doncaster September Sales. *A. Smith.*

CHARLOTTE BONNIE 2 br.f. Kala Shikari 125–Derry Willow (Sunny Way — 120) (1983 5d 5.8g 6fg 7f) May 5; 1,500F, 1,550 Y; closely related to 3-y-o 1m winner Some Sunny Day (by Radetzky); bad plater; sold 560 gns Ascot October Sales. *R. Akehurst.*

CHARLOTTE'S CHOICE 8 b.g. Blakeney 126–Queendom 109 (Quorum 126) — (1982 12.2d 16fg² 13.1f 13.3f³ 16.1g 16fg⁴ 12fg³ 1983 12s 12g 12.2fg 12.2fg) neat, attractive gelding; stays well; acts on any going; has been tried in blinkers; sometimes bandaged in front. *W. Wightman.*

CHARLOTTE'S DUNCE 3 br.c. Sit In The Corner–Bollin Charlotte 79 — (Immortality) (1982 5fg 6f* 6fg⁴ 7f² 7f² 7g* 8fg* 1983 7d 8d 8f 8f) compact colt; fair performer at 2 yrs; below form in 1983 and wasn't seen out after June; will probably stay 1¼m; possibly needs a sound surface. *M. H. Easterby.*

CHARMED LADY 3 b.f. Scottish Rifle 127–Credo's Daughter (Credo 123) (1982 — NR 1983 10.1f 10.1f 10.1f 8.3f 10f.) small, quite well-made filly; of little account; dead. *A. Ingham.*

CHARMED LIFE TOO 3 ch.f. Dominion 123–Party Girl 96 (Pardao 120) (1982 58 5f 6g 7fg 7.6v 7d 1983 8g⁴ 8.5d⁴ 10.2f² 10f*) quite well-made filly; good walker; sold 4,700 gns after winning slowly-run selling handicap at Newmarket in July; suited by 1¼m and a sound surface; sent to race in Italy. *J. Bethell.*

CHARMING LIFE 4 b.f. Habitat 134–Fighting 105 (Aggressor 130) (1982 NR 88 1983 6v² 5fg³ 7f* 7f 6f 7f 8g 8d) 100,000Y, 360,000 francs 3-y-o (approx £36,000); lengthy, sparely-made filly; fourth foal; half-sister to 3 winners, including Kri Kri (by Karabas), 3 times winner at around 7f in Ireland, and fairly useful 1978 2-y-o Balilla (by Balidar); dam a miler; landed odds with minimum of fuss in minor event at Folkestone in June; ran creditably most subsequent starts, on seventh having no luck in running when staying-on fifth to Hungarian Prince in minor event at Newbury in September; suited by 7f+; probably acts on any going. *M. Stoute.*

CHARTFIELD 3 ch.g. Whitstead 125–Appian Way 89 (Romulus 129) (1982 NR — 1983 10g) half-brother to several winners here and abroad, including very useful middle-distance stayer Valentinian (by Morston); dam won over middle distances; unquoted when towards rear in 16-runner amateur riders race won by Kuwait Team at Goodwood in September. *S. Mellor.*

CHASE THE CLOUDS 2 ch.f. Nearly A Hand 115–Fair Georgina 71 (Silver Cloud 121) (1983 5s 5s) Apr 5; close-coupled filly; second reported foal; dam, winner from 1m to 1½m, ran over hurdles and fences after birth of first foal; in rear in May in maiden race at Salisbury and seller at Chepstow. *W. R. Williams.*   –

CHASE THE LADY 4 ch.f. Ginger Boy 101–Paddy's Amour 88 (St Paddy 133) (1982 NR 1983 16d) sixth foal; dam stayed 1¼m; well beaten in seller at Lingfield in October. *A. Moore.*   –

CHASTE 2 b.f. Slim Jim 112–Baran Kuh (Coronation Year 123) (1983 6f) May 23; third foal; dam of no account on flat but won a point-to-point as a 12-y-o when only finisher; 50/1, behind in 12-runner maiden event at Brighton in June. *R. Smyth.*   –

CHASTITY BELT 6 b.g. So Blessed 130–Queen's Keys 84 (Right Royal V 135) (1982 NR 1983 8v) workmanlike gelding; bad maiden on flat though has won a selling hurdle; has been blinkered; sold 1,150 gns Doncaster August Sales. *R. Allan.*   –

CHATLEY'S SEEDLING 3 b.g. Young Nelson 106–Chatley Pippin 53 (Kribi 110) (1982 NR 1983 8f) neat filly; second foal; dam a point-to-point winner; 50/1, dwelt and was tailed off when pulled up in maiden race at Beverley in August. *T. Taylor.*   –

CHATTER 2 b.f. Free State 125–Tudor Whisper 53 (Henry the Seventh 125) (1983 6f 6g 7.6d[4]) May 23; small, lightly-built filly; first foal; dam half-sister to Grundy; 8 lengths fourth of 20 to Risk All in maiden race at Lingfield in October; will stay 1¼m. *F. J. Houghton.*   66

CHAUMIERE 2 ch.c. Thatching 131–Cafe Au Lait 98 (Espresso 122) (1983 6fg[2] 7fg[2]) Apr 23; IR 14,500Y; rather narrow, light individual; good walker; half-brother to several winners, including fairly useful stayer Brando (by Busted); dam stayed 1½m; good second, running on, in Duke of Edinburgh Stakes at Ascot in October (behind Stinging Nettle) and Houghton Stakes (to Condrillac) at Newmarket a week later; will be suited by 1m; sure to win a race. *R. Williams.*   95

CHEEKY MONKEY 4 ch.f. Shiny Tenth 120–Evvoia 53 (Khalkis 127) (1982 8d 8f 8fg 8g 8fg 8g 7g 8d[4] 7g 1983 10f 8f 10f) sparely-made filly; plater; stays 1m; sometimes blinkered. *D. Morrill.*   –

CHEEKY ROSES 2 b.f. Crimson Beau 124–Friendly Neighbour 88 (Mansingh 120) (1983 5.1fg 6fg[3] 7f 7f[4] 8d) Feb 20; 6,400Y; rather leggy filly; first foal; dam sprinter; plating-class filly; in frame in maiden event at Haydock and nursery (favourite) at Newcastle in the summer; stays 7f. *G. Pritchard-Gordon.*   64

CHEEKY RUPERT 3 b.g. Runnymede 123–Peachy (Reliance II 137) (1982 NR 1983 14g 13fg 14.6f 16h) 3,100Y; big, rangy gelding; second foal; dam fair hurdler; poorish form in maiden races. *E. Eldin.*   –

CHEEKY STREAK 2 b.c. Streak 119–Treasury (Henry the Seventh 125) (1983 6g) Apr 15; sixth foal; brother to a poor animal; dam of little account; 50/1, tailed off in 19-runner maiden race at Goodwood in September. *N. Mitchell.*   –

CHEHO 4 b.g. Parade of Stars–Flower Basket (Mr Leader) (1982 8g 13.3f 13g 10fg 14fg 10s 1983 10f 12f 12fg 14fg 8fg[3] 10fg* 10d[3] 10g) leggy gelding; carries plenty of condition; plater; bought in 1,700 gns after winning at Nottingham in September; stays 1½m; seems to act on any going; effective with or without blinkers. *R. Akehurst.*   54

CHEKA (USA) 7 b.g. Russian Bank 110–Sweet Seventeen (County Delight) (1982 18g* 16s* 16fg* 18.4fg 16g 14fg 16d 16.1s 18d 1983 18d[2] 16.1v[3] 17.1g 18f[4] 16f[3] 19f[2] 16.1fg 20f[3] 17g 17d) strong gelding; good walker; out-and-out staying handicapper; acts on any going; versatile (also a winner over hurdles and fences). *I. Balding.*   67

CHEKIKA 3 gr.g. Warpath 113–Border Honour 76 (Above Suspicion 127) (1982 7g 7f 7fg 8d 1983 11v[2] 16v 14s 12s 16g 15.8g 12s 16fg 15.8g) big gelding; disappointing maiden; should stay quite well; blinkered fourth outing; sold to G. Lockerbie 2,500 gns Doncaster November Sales. *C. Gray.*   71 d

CHELKOV (FR) 2 ch.c. Fabulous Dancer 124–Dudinka (Mossborough 126) (1983 7fg 7fg* 7fg) Apr 23; strong, deep-girthed, good sort; good walker; half-brother to winners in Italy by Mill Reef and Blakeney; dam, rated second best 3-y-o filly in Italy in 1973, won 1¼m Premio Lydia Tesio; second favourite, disputed lead throughout and ran on strongly to win 21-runner maiden race at   91

Newmarket in September by 1½ lengths from Shipwright; 20/1, out of his depth and dropped right away in last 3f when eighth of 10 to El Gran Senor in William Hill Dewhurst Stakes on same course 2 weeks later; will stay 1¼m. *R. Armstrong.*

CHELLASTON PARK 4 b.f. Record Token 128–Acquire 105 (Burglar 128) **110** (1982 5s* 6f3 5s3 5f2 5fg2 5f 5g2 5g2 1983 5v2 5g 5s 5d3 5f 5f3 5fg3 6fg) small, well-made, lengthy, strong-quartered filly; good mover; smart sprinter at her best; placed in Field Marshal Stakes at Haydock in April, Temple Stakes at Sandown in May (½-length third to Fearless Lad), King George Stakes at Goodwood in July (blinkered, came from a long way back and didn't enjoy best of runs when about 2½ lengths third to Soba) and William Hill Sprint Championship at York in August; moved up a place after finishing over 8 lengths fourth to Habibti in last-named; has distinct stamina limitations; acts on any going; suited by waiting tactics; sold 165,000 gns Newmarket December Sales. *B. Hobbs.*

CHELSEA MAID 4 b.f. So Blessed 130–De Nada 79 (Ragusa 137) (1982 NR 1983 10s 12s 10f 12d 12fg 16d2 16g) second in seller at Lingfield in October; suited by a test of stamina. *R. Laing.*

CHELSEA PARK 2 ch.f. Mansingh 120–Davina (Darius 129) (1983 6f 6f 5g 6s) — Apr 26; 2,100F, 3,000Y; rather narrow filly; half-sister to winners in Hungary and Italy; no form, including in a valuable seller; trained by D. Morley first two starts. *D. Smith.*

CHENKYNOWA 3 b.f. Connaught 130–Paperwork (Brigadier Gerard 144) (1982 — 5f 5fg2 5fg 6g 1983 5f 7g) small filly; second in seller at 2 yrs, only form; tailed off both outings of 1983; trained by A. Smith first start. *N. Guest.*

CHEQUERED LIFE 3 b.f. Wolverlife 115–The Chequer (Majetta 115) (1982 — 6fg 7s 1983 8fg 10.2h 12g 15.5fg4) big, lengthy, shallow-girthed filly; poor form, including in sellers; blinkered and bandaged final start. *R. Laing.*

CHERI BERRY 4 b.f. Air Trooper 115–Diorina 91 (Manacle 123) (1982 6fg 6f3 **78** 6fg 6f2 6g 5fg 6d 6s* 5s 1983 6v 7s 5.8s 6fg 6g 6f4 5.8h 5f 6f 5g 5g2 5g* 5g 5d* 5g) small, lengthy filly; poor mover; sprint handicapper; made most to win at Wolverhampton and Newbury in October; stays 6f; acts on any going; best in blinkers; inconsistent and seems to need to have things her own way; retained 5,000 gns Newmarket December Sales. *W. Wightman.*

CHERRY HILL 2 b.c. Shirley Heights 130–Spring in Rome (Forli) (1983 7fg3) **86 p** Mar 21; 17,000F, 25,000Y; well-made, attractive colt; good walker; first foal; dam once-raced granddaughter of champion American filly Cicada; got jarred up when highly promising third, 2¼ lengths behind Rousillon, in 25-runner maiden event at Newmarket in July, and wasn't seen out again; has only to return fit and well to be certain of winning races at 1¼m or more. *J. Dunlop.*

CHERRY HILL GIRL 2 b.f. Orange Bay 131–Borbonica (Dark Star) (1983 5v **46** 5fg 6f 6fg 6fg) May 5; IR 4,000F, IR 5,000Y; half-sister to 3 winners in Italy; dam won 7 races in Italy, including good-class 1¼m event; poor plater; bred to be much better suited by 7f+. *M. McCormack.*

CHERRY SEASON 3 gr.f. Silly Season 127–Tudor Gus 64 (Gustav 121) (1982 **52** 6g 7fg 6g 7fg2 8s 8d 1983 8s 7fg2 7f4 7f* 7f 9fg 7f 8.2g 7fg) leggy, lightly-made filly; not a good walker and has a round action; plater; stayed on when winning narrowly at Beverley in July (no bid); should stay 1m; seems to require a sound surface; usually blinkered. *Hbt Jones.*

CHERRY SINGH 2 b.f. Mansingh 120–Cherry Picking 85 (Queen's Hussar 124) — (1983 6f 5f 8fg) Mar 15; 800Y; smallish filly; good walker; first foal; dam, middle-distance winner, is half-sister to very smart 1m to 1¼m handicapper Hardy Scot; in rear in maiden and minor events; retained by trainer 390 gns Ascot December Sales. *W. Elsey.*

CHERRY WALK 2 ch.f. Private Walk 108–Palmaria (Be Friendly 130) (1983 6f — 5.8h 5f) Apr 24; first foal; dam showed a little ability at 2 yrs in Ireland; behind in maiden race and sellers. *B. Swift.*

CHESHIRE HOUSE 2 b.c. Relkino 131–God Sent 75 (Red God 128§) (1983 **66** 5d3 5g 7fg) Feb 25; 8,200Y; fair sort; half-brother to 2 winners by Rheingold, including 8.5f to 11f winner Uplands Park; dam placed over 5f at 2 yrs; plating-class maiden; will stay 1m. *S. Mellor.*

CHESTNUT PALE 4 ch.f. Record Token 128–Whitestake 74 (Compensation **48** 127) (1982 6fg 6f 7fg 10f4 10d4 13.8d 12s3 12g 12s 1983 10d2 12d 8s*) stocky filly; poor mover; sold to D. Yeoman 2,500 gns after winning at Pontefract in May; stays 1½m; suited by some give in the ground; usually wears blinkers. *Hbt Jones.*

CHESTY 4 b.g. Wrens Hill 115–Scotspree (Lone Star 97) (1982 NR 1983 13s — 13.4f3 10g3) ex-Irish gelding; first foal; dam won at 2m in Ireland; third in amateur riders races at Dundalk in August and Lingfield in October; runs as though he'll stay further than 13f; acts on firm going; trained by J. Cox first two starts. *M. Ryan.*

CHEUNG SING 4 b.c. Vitiges 132–Singing Witch 71 (Sing Sing 134) (1982 5f 8g 1983 8s 10v 7g 5f 10f 10f 10g 10fg 16d) small, compact colt; poor plater. *P. K. Mitchell.*   –

CHEVANTER 3 br.g. Levanter 121–Little Charter 65 (Runnymede 123) (1982 NR 1983 12v³ 11.7v) half-brother to a winning 2-y-o plater by Royal Smoke; dam won 1m seller; showed a little ability in maiden races at Wolverhampton and Bath. *D. Gandolfo.*   –

CHEVELEY STAR 4 b.c. Roman Warrior 130–Tipsy Rider 60 (Hard Ridden 131) (1982 7f 7g² 8f² 7g 7fg 8.2s 8s 1983 8d 10v 9v⁴ 10g 10d² 12f) tall, fair sort; hung right and was relegated to second after winning handicap at Leicester in June; stays 1¼m; acts on any going; blinkered once in 1982 and is not entirely genuine. *M. Ryan.*   **61**

CHEVENING 5 b.g. Prince Tenderfoot 126–Sunny Nest 99 (Habitat 134) (1982 10g 12g 10s 10v 10s 1983 8g 10f) heavy-topped ex-French gelding; second foal; dam 1m winner and half-sister to Sun Prince; showed fairly useful form at 3 yrs; well beaten all subsequent starts, running abysmally on final outing at 5 yrs; stays 1¼m; acts on soft going; sometimes blinkered; suitable mount for an apprentice. *D. Sasse.*   –

CHEZZY GIRL 2 ch.f. Manor Farm Boy 114–Petit Secret 64 (Petingo 135) (1983 5fg) Apr 5; 3,000Y; fifth foal; half-sister to useful 1982 2-y-o Secret Miracle (by Abwah) and a winner in Trinidad; dam placed over 1m; 50/1, in rear in 15-runner maiden race at Bath in September. *S. Mellor.*   –

CHIAVARI 3 b.c. Try My Best 130–Bracey Bridge 115 (Chanteur II 135) (1982 NR 1983 9v* 9s³ 9v* 12v³ 11.5f⁴ 9g²) half-brother to two winners and smart but lightly-raced The Parson (by Aureole); dam won Ribblesdale Stakes and Park Hill Stakes; successful in 18-runner maiden race at Mallow in April and 8-runner minor event at Naas in May, beating Tetradrachm by 1½ lengths in latter race; ran very well when 4½ lengths third to Carlingford Castle and Give Thanks in Gallinule Stakes at the Curragh in May and when 2½ lengths second of 8 behind Salmon Leap in Pacemaker International Whitehall Stakes at Phoenix Park in September but ran moderately in Ulster Harp Derby at Down Royal in between; stays 1½m; best form with some give in the ground. *D. O'Brien, Ireland.*   **106**

CHICAGO BID (USA) 2 b.c. Bold Bidder–Shore (Round Table) (1983 6fg* 6g³ 6g) May 13; $150,000Y; well-made, attractive colt; half-brother to several winners, including very useful 1982 staying 2-y-o Alligatrix (by Alleged); dam, very useful at 2 yrs, won at up to 9f and is sister to very smart animals Cabildo and Canal; put up a very pleasing effort in 22-runner maiden race at Newmarket in July, scoring by 4 lengths from Alcinous after leading on bridle 2f out; fell just after post when very good third to Defecting Dancer in BonusPrint Sirenia Stakes at Kempton 2 months later, and was possibly not at his best (appeared to walk stiffly) when running moderately in Mill Reef Stakes at Newbury 2 weeks afterwards; will stay 7f+. *R. Armstrong.*   **108**

CHIC BOUTIQUE (USA) 3 ch.c Wajima–Chain Store (Nodouble) (1982 7g 1983 7d 12.3f² 14f² 13.4fg 12f* 12f 12f³ 12fg 11g 10f² 12fg) quite a useful-looking colt; not the best of movers; won 3-runner maiden race at Hamilton in July from odds-on Loyal Subject; stays 1¾m; acts on firm going; has run creditably in blinkers. *B. Hanbury.*   **84** d

CHICKEN AGAIN 6 b.g. Royalty 130–Dust Sheet (Silly Season 127) (1982 6d 6s 6s 1983 6v) tall gelding; lightly raced and seemingly of little account nowadays. *C. Crossley.*   –

CHIEF BLACKFOOT 4 ch.g Kashiwa 115–Indian Graduate (Chieftain) (1982 5f 9f 5f 7.9f 9f 8g² 9.5f 11.5f⁴ 1983 8fg 8f 10.1f) IR 6,000Y; sturdy ex-Irish gelding; half-brother to 3 winners, including useful 1980 Irish 2-y-o 5f winner Lady Blackfoot (by Prince Tenderfoot); dam won at up to 1½m; in frame in maiden races at Laytown and Down Royal in 1982; behind in varied company over here though has won over hurdles; seems to stay 11.5f. *J. Old.*   –

CHIEF SINGER 2 br.c. Ballad Rock 122–Principia (Le Fabuleux 133) (1983 6fg* 6g)   **119**

    One of the major disappointments of the season was the failure of Chief Singer to confirm the tremendous impression he created when winning the Coventry Stakes at Royal Ascot on his first appearance in public. No newcomer had won the Coventry since Messmate in 1956 and Chief Singer, at 20/1, seemed unlikely to change matters; among his thirteen opponents were the winners of twenty-one races and four of them, Executive Pride, Gimme Pleasure, Our Dynasty and Superlative, were unbeaten. Chief Singer's chance appeared more forlorn when he missed the break completely, but by halfway he had made up much of the lost ground and was clearly travelling very strongly. After briefly looking in trouble when the leaders bunched in front of him two furlongs out, Chief Singer produced an extraordinary turn of foot, bursting through most impressively to win going away by four lengths from the best of Ireland's three challengers, Hegemony. This scintillating display apparently came as no surprise to Chief Singer's trainer. The story goes that Chief Singer had worked with the useful miler Teamwork just a week before Royal Ascot and that the two-year-old had trounced the older horse despite giving him start and meeting him at two stones worse than weight-for-age!

The rangy, good-topped Chief Singer already stood 16 hands 2½ inches and he looked sure to have improvement in him. Predictably, when he reappeared in the Anglia Television July Stakes at Newmarket the following month he was made a very short-priced favourite to beat his five opponents. His supporters had cause to worry even before he reached the stalls; he tore down to the start, giving his rider a tough time. Unfortunately that wasn't the end of his headstrong behaviour, for he took a strong hold in the early stages. Not surprisingly his exertions took their toll and Chief Singer was quickly beaten when pushed along to challenge inside the final two furlongs. He crossed the line only fifth, over nine lengths behind Superlative, after being eased. Following this poor display Chief Singer's connections were probably almost relieved to discover there was a physical explanation for it, variously described as a dirty nose and a broken blood vessel. Any relief must quickly have turned to dismay when the colt showed no signs of recovering form. Two months later his trainer was quoted as saying 'We have had a string of vets examine Chief Singer, and we are no nearer the solution. When he walks or trots he is perfectly sound – but canter him and he's like a cripple. I'm convinced it is connected with the virus we've had. Two years ago, I had similar problems and the horses began to lose their hair. I cannot believe it's a muscle complaint, because if horses are jarred up they won't walk or trot'. Hopefully a speedy cure will be effected once the cause of the problem is identified. However, it would be most unwise to support Chief Singer until he has given concrete proof that his difficulties are behind him.

Chief Singer (br.c. Mar 19, 1981)	Ballad Rock (ch 1974)	Bold Lad (b 1964)	Bold Ruler / Barn Pride
		True Rocket (gr 1967)	Roan Rocket / True Course
	Principia (b 1970)	Le Fabuleux (ch 1961)	Wild Risk / Anguar
		Pia (br 1964)	Darius / Peseta II

Chief Singer's sire Ballad Rock has also had physical problems, of a very different sort. He contracted contagious equine metritis early in his stud career and as a result had only thirteen reported living produce in 1980, ten in 1981 and ten again, this time from a limited book, in 1982. He has reportedly now made a full recovery, covering full books with satisfactory results in each of the last two seasons, and he will now have every chance to fulfil the promise he's shown with his first runners, which also include the smart sprinter Prince Spy. Ballad Rock also stands well over 16 hands and his size led to difficulty in squeezing him into the stalls in his racing days. His career suffered as a consequence but he still managed to win five of his ten starts, showing that he stayed six furlongs well. Chief Singer must have reasonable prospects of staying a furlong or two further. His dam Principia, a daughter of the Oaks winner Pia, won over a mile and a mile and a

Coventry Stakes, Ascot—a remarkable debut by Chief Singer

quarter in France, showing useful form. Principia's previous living foals are the Spanish winner El Muneca (by Malacate) and the 1977 Irish two-year-old mile winner Querida (by Habitat). This is a good family and Chief Singer's size was no doubt responsible for his fetching no more than 10,000 guineas as a yearling. *R. Sheather.*

CHIKALA 3 br.f. Pitskelly 122–Ballychord (Ballymoss 136) (1982 5f² 5d* 5fg³ 6g⁴ 6f² 6fg 1983 6d 8s 8d⁴ 8f 7.2g 7g) strong filly; carries plenty of condition; ran best race of year when fourth of seven behind Tender Bender in handicap at Ayr in June; suited by 1m; seems to act on any going; has worn a tongue strap; sometimes blinkered. *Miss S. Hall.*   —

CHILDOWN (USA) 3 b.c. Sadair–Swoonson Gal (Swoon's Son) (1982 7g 1983 8v 9.4d² 12f³ 12g² 10.8g² 10f² 10f² 14g² 12f³ 14g* 14.7fg*) deep-girthed, good sort; ridden by apprentice K. Bradshaw when winning minor event at Sandown and handicap at Redcar in October, latter by 2½ lengths from Sallametti; frequently placed earlier; suited by a test of stamina; acts on firm going; sometimes blinkered (not when successful) and has worn a hood. *M. Stoute.*   **86**

CHILD'S GAME (USA) 3 ch.c. Cyane–Musical Chairs (Swaps) (1982 NR 1983 8d 8f³ 8f³ 8g* 10h* 10s 10fg) lengthy, workmanlike colt; half-brother to several winners in USA, notably very smart Woodchopper (by Hatchet Man), a winner at up to 9f; dam twice-raced sister to very smart 6f to 9f winner No Robbery; won maiden race at Ayr (comfortably) and handicap at Sandown in August; quickened up well in a slowly-run race to land a gamble on latter, beating Holmbury a head; suited by 1¼m; acts on hard going (never in race on soft, sixth start); genuine; retained by trainer 6,800 gns Newmarket Autumn Sales. *J. Hindley.*   **80**

CHI MAI 3 b. or br.g. Home Guard 129–Mythical Lady 86 (Track Spare 125) (1982 6.3fg 7.9f4 8.5g 1983 7g 6fg) IR 18,000Y; ex-Irish gelding; third foal; half-brother to 2 winners, including fairly useful 7f and 1m winner Beeleigh (by Sallust); dam won from 5f to 1¼m; soundly beaten in varied company; best run at 7.9f on firm going as a 2-y-o; has worn blinkers; sold 920 gns Doncaster October Sales. *R. Simpson.*   —

CHIMERA 2 br.f. Hittite Glory 125–Mandilinee 77 (Star Envoy) (1983 5v 5v 6fg² 5.1fg 7f 7d) May 17; 820Y; first foal; dam won from 5f to 7f; plater; stays 7f; acts on firm going; capable of winning a seller. *M. Hinchliffe.*   **57**

CHINA GOLD 4 b.g. Blue Cashmere 129–China Girl 76 (Shantung 132) (1982 5fg 5fg 8fg 6s 1983 6fg 6f* 6g 6d 5f* 5f 6g 5fg) lengthy gelding; gambled on when making most to win seller at Redcar in July decisively (bought in 4,000 gns) and was well backed again when narrowly winning handicap at Ripon in August; has shown little other worthwhile form; stays 6f; acts on firm going; blinkered last 4 starts. *Miss L. Siddall.*   **63**

CHINA PEAK (USA) 3 ch.c. Key To The Mint–Another Treat (Cornish Prince) (1982 7g 7d 1983 11v 13fg³ 12.2f 16.5fg) leggy, rather sparely-made colt; third in maiden event at Nottingham in July; in front when saddle began to slip inside last 2f in handicap at Catterick next time (possibly unlucky); will stay 1¾m; probably unsuited by heavy going and looked extremely uncomfortable on firmish going final start (August). *B. Hills.*   **74**

CHLOSTERLI 3 ch.f. Wollow 132–Anadyomene 101 (Sea Hawk II 131) (1982 6g 1983 11.5fg 12g² 12g 14g) lengthy filly; having first race for 3 months and 25/1 when 3 lengths second to Killifreth in minor event at Lingfield in September, best effort; stays 1½m; sold 2,500 gns Newmarket December Sales. *C. Horgan.*   **81**

CHOCOLATE ECLAIR 2 b.f. Daring March 116–Lilian Clare 79 (Ribero 126) (1983 5d 5f* 5f 5f³ 5f 6f) May 15; 480Y; small filly; first foal; dam won 1¼m seller; plater; bought in 1,300 gns after beating Torski by a neck at Beverley in June; should be suited by 6f; acts on firm going; sweated up third start; exported to Algeria. *W. Bentley.*   **51**

CHOIR 3 br.f. High Top 131–Land of Song 82 (Sing Sing 134) (1982 7fg 7g 8s 1983 11.5fg) lengthy filly; good mover; behind in maiden races, starting 25/1 or more each time. *B. Hobbs.*   —

CHOPINA 2 ch.f. Import 127–Rota 58 (Reliance II 137) (1983 5fg 5f) June 2; tall, robust filly; third foal; dam won 1¼m claiming race; backward, soundly beaten in June maiden races at Sandown and Salisbury. *W. Wightman.*   —

CHRISMAL 2 ch.g. Free State 125–Dorchester 50 (Connaught 130) (1983 5v 5fg³ 5g⁴ 6f 5fg 7f 6f³ 7fg 6f 5fg⁴ 8.2g 8g 8.2s³) Apr 22; 2,000F, 2,000Y; sturdy gelding; second foal; half-brother to 1982 2-y-o 6f winner Trumpery (by Diamonds   **68**

Are Trump); in frame in varied company in Scotland; only sixth of 17 in valuable seller on ninth outing; stays 1m; ran wide into straight penultimate start (apprentice ridden); sometimes wears blinkers but is probably better without; none too consistent; gelded after final outing. *D. Smith.*

CHRISTMAS COTTAGE 5 br.g. Lochnager 132–Nelski 83 (Skymaster 126)   **92** (1982 8g² 7d* 8g 8f 6d 7d 7s⁴ 1983 7v* 8d² 7s 8v 8f³ 7f 7s* 9fg) workmanlike gelding; poor mover; fairly useful handicapper; won McEwan's Lager Handicap at Newcastle in April and Holsten Diat Pils Handicap at Ayr in September; beat Cyril's Choice in fine style by 4 lengths on latter; ran creditably several other starts, including when 1½ lengths third to Mighty Fly in Royal Hunt Cup at Royal Ascot and under 5 lengths fifth of 30 to Sagamore in William Hill Cambridgeshire at Newmarket in October on final outing; gives impression 7f is an absolute minimum for him nowadays and stays 9f; acts on any going but seems ideally suited by some give in the ground; has won with and without blinkers. *J. Mason.*

CHRISTMAS HOLLY 2 b.c. Blind Harbour 96–Holly Doon (Doon 124) (1983 6f   – 6f 9f) workmanlike colt; third foal; brother to a winning plater and half-brother to another; dam poor plater; soundly beaten in maiden and minor events. *N. Tinkler.*

CHRISTMAS ORNAMENT 2 gr.f. Raga Navarro 119–Tinsel 95 (Right Boy   – 137) (1983 5g 5fg) Apr 30; sister to 3-y-o 6f winner Sylvan Navarro, closely related to successful Irish sprinter Monetary Wish (by Wishing Star) and half-sister to several winners, including very useful sprinter Sparkling Boy (by Comedy Star); dam raced 5f to 7f handicapper; apprentice ridden, showed little in 2 races in modest company at the back-end. *R. Simpson.*

CHROME MAG 5 br.m. Prince de Galles 125–Pat 98 (Ennis 128) (1982 8f 8f 8f   **49** 10fg 8fg 8fg 8f 8g 8d 10g² 8d* 1983 8d 8fg 9f 10fg* 10f² 8.2fg 10f) leggy, rather sparely-made mare; plater; bought in 1,300 gns after winning at Nottingham in July; stays 1¼m; acts on any going; has twice worn blinkers. *W. Bentley.*

CHRONICLE LADY 2 b.f. Martinmas 128–London Spin 86 (Derring-Do 131)   **68** (1983 5s⁴ 6f 6fg 5f 7g 6fg 9f 8g) May 14; 5,800 F, IR 5,000Y, 6,600 2-y-o; rather leggy, fair sort; good mover; third foal; half-sister to fair 1982 2-y-o 5f winner Mama Leone (by Young Emperor); dam stayed 1m; plating-class maiden; probably stays 9f. *M. Jefferson.*

CHRYSICABANA 3 b.f. Home Guard 129–Copocobana 67 (Petingo 135) (1982   **88** NR 1983 10.2h 9f 10.1fg* 12fg³ 12fg 10fg 10.6s⁴) big, strong, deep-girthed filly; half-sister to 1m winner Mar del Plata (by Crowned Prince); dam slow half-sister to very smart animals Averof and Falkland; 50/1 when beating Slix by 2½ lengths in 8-runner minor event at Windsor in August; seemed to run well when about 5 lengths third of 5 behind Trakady in Troy Stakes at Doncaster in September, but didn't reproduce the form; suited by 1½m; best form on a firm surface. *C. Brittain.*

CHRYSIPPOS (USA) 6 ch.g. Damascus–Better Begin (Buckpasser) (1982   – NR 1983 11.7fg 11.7f) big, rangy, attractive gelding; fairly useful at 3 yrs but no form since; stays 1m; acts on any going; often sweats up. *M. Scudamore.*

CHUMMY'S BOY 3 ch.g. Cawston's Clown 113–Barbara Bryce (Yellow God 129)   **63** (1982 5.8f 1983 6s 8g 7v 8v* 8d³ 10f 10f) workmanlike gelding; plater; attracted no bid after winning at Doncaster in May; ran creditably in non-seller next time; stays 1m; acts on heavy going and is probably unsuited by firm; blinkered third start; bandaged sixth outing. *N. Callaghan.*

CHURCHES GREEN 4 b.g. Sassafras 135–Alice Johnston (Majetta 115) (1982   **59** 12g 12fg 10.1fg 10.1fg 11.7fg⁴ 12fg² 1983 12s 13g* 12f 12s) good sort; won handicap at Ayr in May; will stay 1¾m; form only on a sound surface; has run creditably for amateur rider; has given trouble at start. *S. Mellor.*

CIDELSIA (USA) 3 b.f. Honest Pleasure–Dancing Lark (Native Dancer) (1982   – NR 1983 8s) $325,000Y; closely related to Gustoso (by What A Pleasure), a very useful winner from 5.5f to 9f, and half-sister to numerous winners, including smart Sonny Says Quick (by Stevward), successful at up to 1m; dam stakes-placed winner; 33/1 when twelfth of 13 behind Fluid Mechanics in maiden race at Leicester in March (soon behind). *R. Smyth.*

CIDER WITH KATHY 3 b. or br.f. Relko 136–Talarea 76 (Takawalk II 125)   – (1982 NR 1983 10s 11.7v 10s 10.2f 12g 16d) big, lengthy filly; second foal; dam, 5f winner, stayed 7f; in rear in varied company, including selling. *C. Wildman.*

CIEL BLEU 2 ch.f. Sassafras 135–Quelle Blague (Red God 128§) (1983 7fg) June   – 3; smallish filly; sister to Irish and American winner Galland and 7.5f to 10.8f winner Veramente, and half-sister to numerous winners; dam fair Irish miler; very weak in market, eleventh of 12 behind stable-companion Miss Saint-Cloud in minor event at Doncaster in October. *M. Stoute.*

CIMA 5 br. g. High Top 131–Lemon Blossom 83 (Acropolis 132) (1982 12.2d* 12fg² 12f 12s⁴ 12s* 12s 1983 12s) quite well-made gelding; good mover; useful handicapper at his best on flat and a very useful hurdler; didn't impress in appearance when well beaten at Doncaster only start at 5 yrs in March; suited by 1½m; acts on any going but is ideally suited by some give underfoot; doesn't seem to find much off bridle. *J. Old.*   –

CIMARRON 5 ch. m. Carnival Dancer 113–Duresme 76 (Starry Halo 122) (1982 8fg 9f 9fg³ 8f³ 10.8fg 8g 7f 8f 9g 9g 8g 1983 8v³ 9f 6fg 6f) leggy mare; plater; stays 1¼m; acts on any going; has worn blinkers and a hood. *Mrs N. Macauley.*   –

CINQUIEME ROUE (USA) 2 ch. c. Damascus–Better Begin (Buckpasser) (1983 7f 7g) Mar 4; $32,000Y; rangy colt; brother to fairly useful 1979 2-y-o 5f winner Chrysippos; dam, winner twice at up to 1m, is half-sister to Gorytus; third favourite, showed up well until lack of peak fitness told from 2f out when about 12 lengths seventh of 16 to Raft in maiden race at Newmarket in July; not seen out again until October when seventh of 19 to Secret Way in similar event at York; has scope and is sure to do better in due course. *G. Pritchard-Gordon.*   – p

CIRCASSIAN CIRCLE (FR) 3 b. g. Dance In Time–Circlet 97 (Baldric II 131) (1982 6f 6d² 5s 1983 5.8v) sturdy, full-quartered, good sort; excellent walker; second in maiden race at Brighton as a 2-y-o; showed speed before finishing last in handicap at Bath in May on only outing of 1983. *I. Balding.*   –

CIRCUIT 2 b. f. Mandamus 120–Span (Pan II 130) (1983 6g) May 1; smallish, quite attractive filly; half-sister to winning stayer Cantilever (by Crooner); dam placed over 1½m; 13½ lengths eleventh of 27 to Desirable in maiden race at Newmarket in July; likely to need 1m+. *B. Hobbs.*   – p

CIRCUMSPECT 2 b. g. Court Circus 97–Dites Donc 34 (I Say 125) (1983 6f 5fg³ 6fg 8fg) Apr 28; fourth foal; dam, half-sister to very good NH performer Easby Abbey, won over hurdles and fences; poor plater; should stay at least 1m; blinkered second outing. *D. Chapman.*   **40**

CIRCUS PLUME 2 b. f. High Top 131–Golden Fez (Aureole 132) (1983 7f³ 7f* 8fg³) Apr 17; 98,000F; well-made, quite attractive filly; has a round action; half-sister to useful French middle-distance stayer Marriageable (by Great Nephew) and fairly useful 7f to 11f winner Golden Brigadier (by Brigadier Gerard); dam, daughter of 1000 Guineas winner Zabara, won over middle distances in France; well-backed favourite, forged clear from 2f out to win 19-runner maiden race at Salisbury in September in splendid style by 3 lengths from Troyanna; 1¾ lengths third of 8 to Nepula in Hoover Fillies Mile at Ascot later in the month; will stay 1¼m; acts on firm going; looks sure to win more races. *J. Dunlop.*   **101**

CIRCUS TRICK 2 b. f. Court Circus 97–French Secret (Most Secret 119) (1983 5s 6f² 6f³ 6f) Feb 5; smallish, lengthy filly; first foal; dam never ran; modest plater; will stay 7f; acts on firm going. *D. Chapman.*   **52**

CITY LINK EXPRESS 6 ch. g. Dubassoff–Chaddy (St Chad 120) (1982 10g 1983 8d 10s³ 12f 10f 13.1h⁴ 16fg 16g) leggy gelding; former plater; stays 13f; acts on any going; sometimes wears blinkers; has run creditably for a boy. *D. Wilson.*   **33**

CITY LINK ROSE 2 b. f. Lochnager 132–City Link Lass 92 (Double Jump 131) (1983 5d) May 20; useful-looking filly; first foal; dam at her best at 2 yrs when winner over 5f and 6f; 50/1 and poorly drawn, eleventh of 17 in maiden race at Sandown in May. *D. Wilson.*   –

CITY'S SISTER 5 ch. m. Maystreak 118–Must Improve 47 (Lucky Brief 128) (1982 6f 8f 8fg 10fg² 12.2f² 12g* 12.2f 13s* 12g 12s² 12v² 12s 1983 13g 12s) lengthy, rather lightly-made mare; quite modest at her best; occasionally runs in sellers; tailed off both starts at 5 yrs; suited by 1½m+; acts on any going, but is very well suited by plenty of give in the ground; sometimes sweats up; usually apprentice ridden. *G. Richards.*   –

CITY SWINGER 3 b. f. Derrylin 115–Free and Easy (Liberator III) (1982 NR 1983 7.6v⁴ 8s 7v) 4,900Y, 3,000 2-y-o; strong filly; half-sister to numerous winners, including smart 5f sprinter Bold and Free (by Bold Lad, Ire) and good miler Watergate (by Sovereign Path); dam useful Irish miler; little worthwhile form in a minor event and 2 sellers; hampered on second start. *D. Sasse.*   –

CIVANO (HOL) 2 b. c. Gunner B 126–Cupid's Dart (Levmoss 133) (1983 7fg 5f² 6f⁴ 9v²) Apr 15; workmanlike colt; has a round action; second foal; half-brother to   ?

183

Dutch 1000 Guineas and Dutch St Leger winner Carmona (by Track Spare); dam blinkered when withdrawn, not under orders, on only appearance; second twice at Duindigt, Holland, going down by a neck to Boxberger Ster in Van Brienens Memoriaal and by a length to Sparkos in 9-runner Criterium; 3½ lengths last of 4 to Nasr in maiden race at Yarmouth in between; will stay 1½m; acts on any going. *M. Ryan.*

CIVILITY 3 b.f. Shirley Heights 130–Makeacurtsey (Herbager 136) (1982 7g **108** 1983 11s³ 12s² 11.7v* 12f 12g² 14.6fg⁴) lengthy, fair sort; first past post in minor event at Salisbury in May (beat Elect a length, but placings were reversed) and in maiden event at Bath later in month (beat Killifreth by 5 lengths); ran best subsequent races when 2½ lengths second of 12 behind Hymettus in Galtres Stakes at York in August and just under 5 lengths fourth of 7 behind High Hawk, after making running, in Park Hill Stakes at Doncaster in September; suited by 1¾m; possibly not at her best on very firm going but acts on any other. *J. Tree.*

CLACHAN 3 ch.c. Habitat 134–Padrona 103 (St Paddy 133) (1982 6fg 7g² 1983 — 7s 8g 8fg 8f 7g) compact, attractive colt; promising second to Cock Robin in Ribero Stakes at Doncaster as a 2-y-o in 1982 but was very disappointing as a 3-y-o (last three times); should stay 1m. *G. Wragg.*

CLANGERWINSTANLEY 3 ch.c. Homing 130–Lady of Chalon (Young **65** Emperor 133) (1982 6d 7d 7f 7f² 8d 1983 7s 8s 7fg⁴ 8f*) quite attractive, smallish colt; a twin; 5-length winner of claiming race at Brighton in June; claimed £2,550 afterwards and exported to Malaysia; stays 1m; acts on firm going; usually blinkered. *R. Laing.*

CLANRALLIER 3 b.g. Captain James 123–Mary Campbell (Mossborough 126) **81** (1982 7f⁴ 7fg² 8d³ 8s⁴ 1983 8d³ 9.4f* 11f* 11g* 12f⁴ 10fg³) good sort; has a long, raking stride; gained successive wins in minor event at Carlisle, small handicap at Hamilton and minor event at Ayr in summer; creditable third to Deutschmark in another handicap at Newmarket in September; suited by middle distances; acts well on a sound surface; sweated up and found little under pressure fifth start. *J. W. Watts.*

CLANTIME 2 ch.c. Music Boy 124–Penny Pincher 95 (Constable 119) (1983 5v* **99** 5d² 5s* 5s* 5s* 5f³ 5f 5fg) Mar 5; 4,600F, 11,500Y; smallish, fair sort; keen walker; half-brother to 2 winning sprinters, including fairly useful Tobermory Boy (by Mummy's Pet); dam 5f sprinter; fit early, won 4 races in first part of season, minor events at Ayr and Thirsk, Tattersalls' Yorkshire Stakes (beating Lade Lustre short head) at York, and Great Surrey Stakes at Epsom; gave every indication of having trained off when well beaten in good-class company at Goodwood and York (sweated up) on last 2 appearances; acts on any going; ridden by apprentice S. Morris first 2 starts. *J. Berry.*

CLARE BRIDGE (USA) 2 ch.f. Little Current–Gliding By (Tom Rolfe) (1983 **92 p** 7.3d) Mar 9; big, rangy filly; first foal; dam, winner of 6f maiden race at 3 yrs on only start, is closely related to top-class Key To The Mint and half-sister to American Horse of the Year Fort Marcy; co-favourite, had none too clear a run, after being chopped for speed early in straight, when strong-finishing 5 lengths seventh of 14 behind Betsy Bay in Rochford Thompson Newbury Stakes in October; will be suited by 1¼m+; certain to be better for the experience, and is clearly thought capable of winning good races. *I. Balding.*

CLARENDON 6 gr.g. Brigadier Gerard 144–France (Milesian 125) (1982 12s — 1983 13v 12s 17.1v 16f 12f 18g) modest at his best but had deteriorated markedly; blinkered once; pulled up lame final start; dead. *J. Yardley.*

CLARYON 2 ch.g. On Your Mark 125–Carnoch Walk 82 (Tower Walk 130) (1983 **49** 5s³ 5v 5d 5d 7f 7g 6fg⁴) Mar 7; 7,400Y; neat gelding; first foal; dam 2-y-o 5f winner; showed only a little ability, including in claiming races; blinkered fourth outing. *M. Ryan.*

CLASS AGENT (USA) 3 b.f. Mr Leader–Millinery Lady (In Reality) (1982 7fg **68** 6fg 5f⁴ 6d⁴ 6g 1983 7v*) rather leggy filly; led near finish when beating Meadeway in handicap at Warwick in May; not seen out again; stays 7f; acts on any going. *H. T. Jones.*

CLASSICAL VINTAGE 2 b. or br.f. Stradavinsky 122–Spoiled Wine **80** (Pampered King 121) (1983 5s² 5v² 5d 5s* 5s³ 6f⁴ 5f⁴ 6f 7.3g 6fg 5s) Apr 11; IR 2,600Y; rather leggy, good-topped filly; sister to Irish 3-y-o 7f to 9.5f winner Sunder and half-sister to numerous winners; dam won at up to 1½m in Ireland; won maiden race at Salisbury in May by a short head from Street Venture; good fourth of 10 to Brave Advance in £5,000 5f nursery at Goodwood in July; bred to stay 1m; acts on any going; disappointed third appearance (reportedly in season). *R. Hannon.*

CLASSIC JEWEL 2 gr.f. Native Admiral–Alvada (Dankaro 131) (1983 5f 6f 8g 7fg) Mar 31; first foal; dam never ran; well beaten in maiden events. *Mrs A Cousins.* **54**

CLASSIC OWEN 2 ch.c. Owen Anthony 102–Classic Lady 103 (Gratitude 130) (1983 5v 5fg 6f 8d 8fg 7.6fg) Feb 24; seventh reported foal; dam won twice over 5f at 2 yrs as Cool in the Pool; no form in maiden and minor events; blinkered fifth start. *T. M. Jones.* **–**

CLASSY DEB 5 b.m. Abwah 118–Near The Line 88 (Nearula 132) (1982 NR 1983 12d 8s⁴ 12v 13.8g 10f) sturdy mare; of little account; has worn a tongue strap. *J. Townson.* **–**

CLAUDE MONET (USA) 2 ch.c. Affirmed–Madelia 127 (Caro 133) (1983 7fg*) May 4; tall, rather narrow colt; second foal; half-brother to smart 3-y-o 7f winner Magdalena (by Northern Dancer); dam, half-sister to Mount Hagen and Monsanto, won all her 4 starts, including Poule d'Essai des Pouliches and Prix de Diane; 2/1 on, won 14-runner minor event at Doncaster in October untroubled by ½ length from Coulee Queen; looks sure to make a useful performer over longer distances. *H. Cecil.* **85 p**

CLAUDIUS CROZET (USA) 4 b.c. Halo–Ima Roan (Determine) (1982 8fg 12f⁴ 14f⁴ 12g* 11.5fg* 14s² 12g* 14g 1983 12s² 12.2v 12fg³ 12d* 12f 11g 12d 12fg) neat, strong colt; good mover; blind in near eye; a modest handicapper; narrowly won at Leicester in June; suited by 1½m or more; seems to act on any going; suited by front-running tactics; wears an eye shield; has won for a lady rider; ran moderately second start. *G. Huffer.* **80**

Clantime Ltd's "Clantime"

CLAUDIUS SECUNDUS 6 b.g. Idiot's Delight 115–Versailles 93 (Never Say **99**
Die 137) (1982 NR 1983 9f² 10g*) big gelding; fairly useful handicapper;
quickened in great style to beat Sagamore comfortably by 2½ lengths at
Newmarket in August; had run well previous start (first for nearly 2 years); stays
1¼m but not 1½m; acts on any going; bandaged in 1983; has a useful turn of foot;
game. *M. Jarvis.*

CLAY PIGEON 2 gr.f. Bold Lad (Ire) 133–Marcrest (On Your Mark 125) (1983 **72**
5f 5f⁴ 5f⁴ 5f² 5s 5g⁴) May 12; 12,000Y; lengthy, rather dipped-backed filly; second
foal; half-sister to fairly useful Nadasdy (by Queen's Hussar), a winner at up to 9f in
Ireland; dam won 5 races in Italy; in frame in maiden and minor events; speedy and
unlikely to stay 6f; ran poorly only outing on soft going; blinkered final appearance.
G. Hunter.

CLAYTON KING 2 b. or br.g. Anax 120–Crowned Princess (Taj Dewan 128) **–**
(1983 5v 5f) June 25; 360Y; small gelding; first foal; dam poor maiden on flat and
over hurdles; behind in maiden race at Newcastle in May and seller at Beverley in
June; sold 360 gns Doncaster August Sales. *E. Alston.*

CLEAN LIVING 2 b.c. Try My Best 130–Flying Spear 94 (Breakspear II) (1983 **–**
6f³) Mar 1; IR 4,000Y; robust colt; half-brother to winners here and abroad,
including useful 1976 2-y-o 5f winner Stradey Park (by Murrayfield); dam won over
5f at 2 yrs; 7/4 on, dwelt slightly and was never going particularly well when 4
lengths last of 3 behind Jack Tar in minor event at Catterick in July. *H. Cecil.*

CLEARLY BUST 3 ch.c. Busted 134–Crystal Light 114 (Never Say Die 137) **92**
(1982 NR 1983 12s² 12fg* 14fg² 12fg³ 14fg³ 12fg) 46,000Y, 14,000 2-y-o; strong,
good-topped colt; half-brother to 4 winners, including very smart sprinter Street
Light (by St Chad) and very useful performers Headlamp (by High Hat) and Flash
On (by Sea Hawk II); dam very useful winner over 1m; beat Sea Raider by 2 lengths
in minor event at Leicester in June; placed most other starts, on final occasion 4
lengths third of 12 behind Statesmanship in handicap at Newmarket in October
(first race for 3 months); stays 1¾m; yet to race on really firm going, but acts on
any other. *D. Morley.*

CLEOBURY KATE 3 gr.f. The Brianstan 128–Sovereign Comment (Sovereign **–**
Path 125) (1982 5fg 5fg 6s 1983 5v 9v 5f 7f) small filly; behind in varied races,
including sellers; sold 390 gns Doncaster October Sales. *J. Tierney.*

CLEODOE STAR 4 ch.g. Ascertain–Alvette (Alcide 136) (1982 NR 1983 16f) **–**
first foal; dam pulled up in novice hurdles; apprentice ridden when tailed-off last in
maiden race at Newcastle in June. *J. Parkes.*

CLEWISTON 7 b.g. Manacle 123–Blue Bird 94 (Majority Blue 126) (1982 6d 8fg **50**
1983 8d* 8f 8.2fg² 8f 8g) leggy gelding; made virtually all to win handicap at
Redcar in May; stays 1m; probably unsuited by very soft going but acts on any
other; sometimes sweats up; trained by A. Cawley first 4 starts. *K. Morgan.*

CLICKHAM LAD 5 ch.g. Keren 100–Native Queen (Native Prince) (1982 NR **–**
1983 12v⁴) poor maiden; has been blinkered; has worn bandages; possibly
temperamental. *N. Chamberlain.*

CLIFTON PRIDE 2 b.c. Palm Track 122–Miss Warwick (Stupendous) (1983 5v **65**
5d⁴ 6d³ 7f 6f⁴ 6f 7f³ 6fg) Mar 29; well-grown colt; brother to 3-y-o plater Marsh
Track; dam never ran; in frame in maiden races and a claiming event; stays 7f; acts
on firm going and a soft surface; blinkered last 2 outings; sent to Singapore. *W.
Haigh.*

CLINKER 3 gr.g. Saritamer 130–Burning Deck 56 (Fighting Ship 121) (1982 8g **70**
1983 12v³ 10.1d 11.7v⁴ 14f 12g 12g 12g* 16g) workmanlike gelding; held clear lead
all way up straight and appeared to show much improved form when beating Royal
Brigadier by 5 lengths in gentleman riders handicap at Ascot in October; didn't
reproduce it next time; suited by 1½m. *J. Bosley.*

CLOCK 'EM (USA) 2 br.f. Bold Hour–Points Gal (Pine Point) (1983 5g³ 5f 5fg² **81**
5f³ 6fg) Feb 27; $30,000F, $50,000 2-y-o; lengthy filly; second foal; dam won 3
times at up to 5f, including a claiming race; placed in 15-runner maiden races at
Newbury and Chester and in 7-runner Molecomb Stakes at Goodwood; should be
suited by 6f (ran no sort of race when favourite for nursery over trip); yet to race
on a soft surface; stumbled and unseated rider leaving stalls on second outing; sold
to NBA 31,000 gns Newmarket December Sales. *M. Jarvis.*

CLOISTERED 2 b.f. Godswalk 130–Parmassia (Pampered King 121) (1983 6fg **75**
7fg⁴ 7s 7fg) Mar 27; fair sort; half-sister to fair middle-distance stayer Bucklow
Hill (by Rheingold) and a winner in Austria; dam French 2-y-o 1m winner; 25/1,
made much of running when 2¼ lengths fourth of 17 to Signorina Odone in maiden

race at Beverley in September, only indication of merit; will probably stay 1m; acts on a firm surface; sold 2,000 gns Newmarket December Sales. *R. Williams.*

CLOSE TO YOU 3 b.f. Nebbiolo 125–Etoile Freda (Florescence 120) (1982 6fg 5.8g 6s 1983 7.6g 6f 7fg 8f 7fg*) won selling handicap at Brighton in October by ¾ lengths from Tender Gift, first form; sold 4,000 gns afterwards, but was later returned to same connections; stays 7f. *P. K. Mitchell.*   **44**

CLOUDS DAUGHTER 4 br.f. Rheingold 137–Clouds 70 (Relko 136) (1982 6f 10g* 10f* 10g* 10g4 10v 1983 8d 10s3 10s 9g 9fg 8.5f 11.5f* 10fg2 9fg3 11.5g 10g 10fg) IR 2,000Y; plain filly; half-sister to 2 winners in Italy; dam, half-sister to Mountain Call, stayed 1¼m; made all and held on by a neck from Littleton Rory in handicap at Galway in July; twice ran well in better company at Phoenix Park the following month, finishing 2 lengths second to Homeowner in Shanbally House Stud Stakes and 3 lengths third to Senior Citizen in Coolmore Be My Guest Stakes; well beaten behind Cormorant Wood in Sun Chariot Stakes at Newmarket in October on final start; stays 11.5f; seems to act on any going but goes well on a firm surface; good mount for an apprentice; has sweated up and doesn't always impress in appearance. *W. Durkan, Ireland.*   **96**

CLUNK CLICK 2 ch.f. Star Appeal 133–Double Lock 104 (Home Guard 129) (1983 8g 6g4) June 7; 17,000Y; lengthy filly; second foal; half-sister to 3-y-o 1m to 1¼m winner Only A Pound (by Sharpen Up); dam won over 1¼m; 10/1, 4¼ lengths fourth of 9 to Betsy Bay in minor event at York in October; should stay 1¼m. *J. Hindley.*   **72**

COARSEGOLD 2 b.c. Import 127–Two Bells 75 (Foggy Bell 108) (1983 5v 5f 6f) May 28; second foal; dam won from 1m to 11f; last in maiden and minor events. *N. Chamberlain.*   **–**

COASTAL RUN 4 b.g. Morston 125–Shipshape (Shantung 132) (1982 NR 1983 12fg4) second foal; dam never ran; remote fourth of 9 behind Khyber in gentleman riders race at Brighton in October. *P. K. Mitchell.*   **–**

COBBY CASTLE 2 gr.f. Palm Track 122–Sweet Dough 66 (Reindeer 124) (1983 7fg 8fg) Apr 27; well-grown, lengthy filly; first foal; dam, half-sister to very useful animals Slaney Idol and Slaney Maid, won over hurdles; in rear in £3,800 event and a maiden race at Newcastle. *R. Johnson.*   **–**

COCKED HAT PIPPIT 4 b.f. Farm Walk 111–One-Only (Prince Richard 103) (1982 NR 1983 12.2f 16f) small filly; third reported foal; half-sister to a winner over jumps; dam of no account; tailed off in 2 maiden races in the North. *Miss S. Hall.*   **–**

COCK ROBIN (USA) 3 gr.c. Raise A Native–Flyingtrip (Vaguely Noble 140) (1982 7fg* 7g* 8d2 1983 10v 12fg 8fg) rather finely-made, medium-sized colt; very good walker; developed into a very smart performer as a 2-y-o, winning his first 2 races and finishing second to Dunbeath in William Hill Futurity at Doncaster; below form in 1983 in slowly-run Guardian Classic Trial at Sandown in April (about 4 lengths fifth of 7 to Gordian), in Prix du Jockey-Club at Chantilly in June (ninth of 12 to Caerleon) and St James's Palace Stakes at Royal Ascot later in June (14 lengths fifth of 7 to Horage); reportedly chipped a bone in his near-fore in last-named event but made a full recovery and was back in training towards end of season; should stay middle distances; acts on a firm and a soft surface. *M. Stoute.*   **–**

CODA 2 b.f. Reform 132–Grace Note 104 (Parthia 132) (1983 6d2 6fg2) Apr 22; compact, good-quartered filly; half-sister to several winners, including fairly useful 6f and 7f winner Gregorian (by So Blessed); dam appeared to stay 7f; good second in maiden events at Yarmouth and Newmarket in September, at Newmarket running Capricorn Belle to 1½ lengths in 29-strong field; will be suited by 7f+; sure to win maiden race. *B. Hobbs.*   **91**

CODY JONES (USA) 2 br.c. Soy Numero Uno–Indian Maiden (Chieftain) (1983 5f4 5fg3 5g3 5fg2 5d2 5d) Apr 11; $50,000Y; second foal; brother to very useful 1982 American 2-y-o 5f winner Delicate Treasure; dam never ran; failed to land odds of 5/2 on in maiden race at Wolverhampton in August on first outing, and continued to disappoint afterwards, although placed 4 times; will be suited by 6f; acts on a firm and a soft surface; blinkered fourth and fifth outings; sold 7,800 gns Newmarket Autumn Sales. *M. Stoute.*   **79**

COEUR VALLIANT 5 b.g. Grundy 137–Petalca 81 (Dewan) (1982 NR 1983 10.2d 9s 12d) very big gelding; poor performer nowadays; has been bandaged. *V. Thompson.*   **–**

COFFEE HOUSE 8 br. g. Silly Season 127—Village Gossip 69 (Narrator 127)   **45**
(1982 NR 1983 10s 8v 10s 10g 8g 12f 12.2fg⁴ 12f 12d 12d² 12g 12g³) poor
handicapper; used by stable to educate apprentices; stays 1¾m; acts on any going;
blinkered once at 4 yrs. *I. Balding.*

COLD FEET (FR) 2 ch. c. Arctic Tern 126—Ballarina (King of the Castle) (1983   **114**
8g* 9f² 10d² 10g) first foal; dam third in 13.5f Prix de Pomone; runner-up in 2
pattern races at Longchamp in October, going down by a short head to Truculent in
Prix Lord Seymour and by 3 lengths to impressive winner Long Mick in Prix de
Conde; had earlier beaten Polly's Ark 2½ lengths in newcomers race at Evry in
September; ran poorly in Criterium de Saint-Cloud in November; will be suited by
1½m; seems to act on any going. *J. de Choubersky, France.*

COLDHARBOUR GIRL 2 ch. f. Town Crier 119—Pepperita 79 (Nelcius 133)   –
(1983 7fg 8d 10d 10fg) May 19; 940Y; of little account; blinkered final outing. *D.
Dale.*

COLERANO BAY 3 b. f. Ercolano 118—Thunder Bay 64 (Canisbay 120) (1982   –
NR 1983 14g 10fg) fourth foal; dam stayed 1½m; behind in minor race at Sandown
and maiden race at Nottingham in October. *N. Gaselee.*

COLEY 4 b. g. Morston 125—Consistent 90 (Connaught 130) (1982 11s 9g³ 8f³ 8f   **63**
9fg³ 8g* 8g 9g 8d 10s 8.2s 10d 1983 10v 11g⁴ 7fg* 8fg⁴ 8f³ 8f³ 7f 8f² 8fg 8fg² 7f 9g
8g 11g 12g) neat gelding; poor walker and mover; won handicap at Edinburgh in
May; best at up to 9f; seems to act on any going but goes well on a sound surface;
sometimes blinkered but is effective without. *D. Smith.*

COLLECTORS GIRL 2 br.f. Mr Bigmore 123—Peace of Mind 81 (Midsummer   –
Night II 117) (1982 7d 1983 17v 14g) smallish, lengthy filly; seventh of 16 in 1¾m
maiden race, only sign of ability. *M. Ryan.*

COLLEGE ARM'S 3 b.f. Decoy Boy 129—Her Worship 61 (Privy Councillor 125)   **54**
(1982 5f⁴ 5fg 5fg⁴ 6fg 6f³ 6g 6fg 7g 6s 1983 8.3s 7v* 7fg) lengthy, light-framed
filly; 20/1-winner of 16-runner seller at Kempton in May (no bid); possibly stays
1m; acts on any going; exported to Malaysia. *S. Matthews.*

COLLEGIAN 2 ch.f. Stanford 121§—Arodstown Tan (Atan) (1983 6g 6f* 6f* 6g   **90**
6fg) Mar 19; IR 10,000Y; lengthy, useful-looking filly; closely related to 2 winners
by St Alphage, including fairly useful 1976 Irish 2-y-o 7.5f winner Snap Happy, and
half-sister to 2 other winners; dam never ran; put up a smooth display in 13-runner
maiden race at Yarmouth in August, quickening clear to win by 4 lengths from
Vernair; dead-heated with newcomer Leipzig in 15-runner minor event at Ripon
later in month; not disgraced in nursery after being drawn in stalls and dwelling on final
start; promises to stay 7f; acts on firm going. *M. Jarvis.*

COLLINSWOOD 2 ch.f. Red Regent 123—Whitewood 74 (Worden II 129) (1983   –
5v 5d 6f 6fg) May 5; half-sister to several winners, including useful Irish
middle-distance winner Welshwood (by Welsh Saint) and quite useful out-and-out
stayer Amberwood (by Amber Light); dam ran only at 2 yrs; behind in maiden and
minor events; off course 3 months after second start; sold 500 gns Ascot
December Sales. *J. Benstead.*

COLLY CONE 3 ch.f. Celtic Cone 116—Columba (Star Gazer 123) (1982 NR 1983   –
10fg 10fg) sister to a winning hurdler; dam ran at 2 yrs; dwelt when behind in
maiden race at Nottingham and minor event at Leicester in October. *R. Laing.*

COLONEL GODFREY (USA) 3 b.c. Far North 120—Fleet Judy (Fleet   **86**
Nasrullah) (1982 NR 1983 10.1d³ 12v* 12fg 11.7g³ 10.2fg) $110,000Y; rather a
narrow colt; half-brother to several winners, including Windy's Daughter (by Windy
Sea), a very smart winner at up to 9f of 12 of her 17 starts; dam never ran; made all
when easily winning maiden race at Folkestone in May; disappointed next time, and
was off course nearly 4 months before finishing length third to Statesmanship in
handicap at Bath in October; suited by 1½m and will stay further; seems to need
some give in the ground and acts on heavy going; went to post very freely indeed
final outing; sold to J. Old 9,600 gns Newmarket Autumn Sales. *M. Stoute.*

COLONEL MONCK 5 b. g. Connaught 130—Mwanza 93 (Petition 130) (1982 NR   **66**
1983 8d 12fg 16f 14f 13.4fg² 14f³ 16.5f² 16.1g²) big, deep-girthed, rangy gelding;
poor mover; second in maiden races and an apprentice handicap; stays 2m; acts on
firm going. *E. Witts.*

COLONIAL FLAG (USA) 3 b.c. Hoist the Flag—Northern Gem 121 (Northern   **104**
Dancer) (1982 NR 1983 10s² 9f* 10d* 10g² 14s) fourth foal; half-brother to
smart 1¼m winner Dreaming Away (by Sir Ivor) and 2 useful winners by
Secretariat, including 9f and 1¼m winner Government Program; dam won Fred
Darling Stakes and was second in Champion Stakes; came from behind when

beating Nonno by 1½ lengths in 8-runner £3,450 event at Phoenix Park in August and Borraderra easily by 2 lengths in 10-runner handicap at the Curragh in September; started 11/4 on when ¾-length second of 4 to Camisado in another £3,450 event at Phoenix Park again (slowly-run affair) and second favourite when remote seventh of 10 behind Mountain Lodge in Jefferson Smurfit Memorial Irish St Leger at the Curragh (blinkered), both in October; should stay beyond 1¼m; sent to Australia. *V. O'Brien, Ireland.*

COLOSSAL 2 ch.f. Formidable 125–Malossol 62 (Gulf Pearl 117) (1983 5f² 5f⁴ 5fg³ 7fg⁴ 7g⁴ 6g 7s 6fg⁴) Apr 17; leggy, fair sort; second foal; dam sister to top-class sprinter Deep Diver; in frame in maiden races and nurseries; stays 7f; acts on any going; ran creditably in blinkers seventh outing; consistent; sold 20,000 gns Newmarket December Sales. *B. Hanbury.* **72**

COLTSFOOT 3 ch.c. Decoy Boy 129–Groundsel 72 (Reform 132) (1982 NR 1983 12v 10s) second foal; dam third over 9f at 2 yrs; well beaten in maiden races at Wolverhampton and Leicester in spring. *M. Smyly.* **–**

COLUMBOOLA 4 b.f. Rapid River 127–Heckley Royal (Lord of Verona 120) (1982 NR 1983 9.4f 7f) poor maiden; sold 1,500 gns Doncaster October Sales. *W. A. Stephenson.* **–**

COLWAY BOY 9 b.g. Faraway Son 130–Crassula (Canisbay 120) (1982 NR 1983 15.5v 15.5f) lightly raced on flat nowadays and probably of little account. *O. Jorgensen.* **–**

COMASCAN 3 b.g. Cawston's Clown 113–Duns Tew 70 (Mandamus 120) (1982 5f 5fg 5d 6s 1983 10.1f 7f 8h) of little account. *D. Wintle.* **–**

COMBLAST 8 b.g. Blast 125–Heron's Dolly (Combat 123) (1982 NR 1983 12.2fg) poor maiden on flat though has won over hurdles; has worn blinkers. *J. Peacock.* **–**

COMEDY FAIR 3 b.g. Comedy Star 121–Fair Saint 79 (Bleep-Bleep 134) (1982 6fg 6fg 6g⁴ 6g² 8f 1983 10.6v 8.2s 8f 8f 8f* 7f² 8fg⁴ 8fg 10.2s* 8s² 10.5d) big, strong gelding; not particularly consistent, but won £2,700 maiden race at Beverley in July (made all) and £11,000 Holsten Diat Pils Final (Handicap) at Doncaster in September, starting at 20/1 both times; galloped on in most determined fashion to beat Red Minstrel by 6 lengths on latter course, despite appearing to face a stiff task; evidently suited by 1¼m; acts on any going; blinkered third start; suited by forcing tactics; had a particularly stiff task final start. *M. H. Easterby.* **92**

Holsten Diat Pils Final, Doncaster—Comedy Fair gallops clear of Red Minstrel

COME ON DOLL 3 ch.f. True Song 95–Spartan Doll (Spartan General 109)   –
(1982 NR 1983 10f) first foal; dam never ran; unquoted when behind in maiden
event at Nottingham in July. *B. Morgan.*

COME ON GRACIE 2 b.f. Hardiran–Pharaoh's Bride (Pharaoh Hophra 94)   –
(1983 5s 5s 5s 5s) Apr 21; well-grown, workmanlike filly; first reported foal; dam
won a selling hurdle; poor form, including in a seller; bred to need long distances
not short. *W. R. Williams.*

COME ON THE BLUES 4 b.g. Blue Cashmere 129–Floral Gift 84 (Princely   **94**
Gift 137) (1982 6s* 7fg 8fg 7f 7g* 8.5d 7fg 7g³ 8f³ 7fg 7g 7f⁴ 7g 7s⁴ 6g 1983 7.6v
6v 6f 6h³ 7g 7fg 8g 6fg 8fg) quite attractive, lengthy gelding; good walker and
usually a good mover; useful performer at his best; generally disappointing in 1983;
stays 1m; acts on any going but seems ideally suited by some give in the ground;
sometimes blinkered; has shown a tendency to hang, is suited by strong handling
and goes well for W. Carson. *C. Brittain.*

COME PLAY WITH ME 8 b.g. Jukebox 120–Compatriot (Pindari 124) (1982   –
8fg 10g 1983 8v 16s 11.7fg 12d) poor handicapper; has been beaten in a seller; has
been tried in blinkers; has worn bandages. *R. Atkins.*

COMING AND GOING (USA) 3 b.f. Roberto 131–Honor An Offer (Hoist the   **83**
Flag) (1982 8g* 8v² 1983 12v 8f³ 8g 8fg) big, lengthy, shallow-girthed filly;
seemed useful as a 2-y-o; had stiffish task when 11 lengths third of 7 behind
impressive Linda's Fantasy in Atalanta Stakes at Sandown in August, first outing
for 3 months and best effort as a 3-y-o; should be suited by middle distances; sold
70,000 gns Newmarket December Sales. *M. Jarvis.*

COMMANCHE RUN 2 b.c. Run The Gantlet–Volley (Ratification 129) (1983 8fg   **95** p
8fg²) May 1; 9,000Y; lengthy colt; half-brother to fair 1973 2-y-o 6f winner Irish
Paul (by Double Jump) and 2 winners abroad; dam once-raced daughter of Park Hill
Stakes winner Mitrailleuse; showed plenty of promise in 2 maiden races at
Newmarket in October, particularly when length second to Bob Back, after
travelling strongly throughout, in 28-runner event; the type to make a very useful
middle-distance 3-y-o. *L. Cumani.*

COMMANDER FLYING 2 br.g. Averof 123–Mustardor (Relko 136) (1983 6d   –
7g) first foal; dam poor maiden; unquoted, behind in October maiden races
at Newbury and Lingfield; sold 775 gns Ascot December Sales. *P. M. Taylor*

COMMITTED (USA) 3 b.f. Hagley–Minstinguette (Boldnesian) (1982 6.3fg 7f*   **116**
7fg* 6d³ 1983 7s⁴ 7g 7.9g* 6fg* 6.3f* 7f* 6fg* 7g*) Irish filly; had a terrific season
and won her last 6 races, 4 of them at Phoenix Park and one each at Dundalk and
the Curragh; picked up quite valuable prizes at Phoenix Park in her last 3 races,
namely £7,200 Hardwicke Cup Stakes, £8,400 Orchardstown Stud Stakes and
£10,600 Swordlestown Stud Stakes, landing the odds by 1½ lengths from Sir Prince
John in last-named event in October; effective at sprint distances and stays 1m;
seems to act on any going, but goes well on a sound surface; genuine and
consistent. *D. K. Weld, Ireland.*

COMMODORE BATEMAN 3 br.c. Tarboosh–Hellspear (Breakspear II) (1982   **77** d
6f 7d⁴ 7f* 6fg² 8g 7g 1983 8v² 8f 7fg 7f 8.2g) fair sort; made virtually all to beat
Dodgy Future a neck in handicap at Ripon in June but hung left throughout last 3f
and was relegated to second; inconsistent afterwards, and was well beaten in a
seller final start; stays 1m; seems to act on any going; sometimes blinkered. *I.
Walker.*

COMMODORE BLAKE 6 br.h. Blakeney 126–Ribamba 82 (Ribocco 129) (1982   **119**
12g 11.1fg² 10f³ 9d 8s* 8v* 1983 8v 10d 10fg³ 10fg² 10g⁴ 8fg 8g) neat, quite
attractive horse; very smart performer at his best; ran respectably most starts at 6
yrs, including when 3½ lengths fifth to Stanerra in Brigadier Gerard Stakes at
Sandown in May, just over 4 lengths third to same mare in Prince of Wales's Stakes
at Royal Ascot and 4 lengths fourth behind Morcon in Valdoe Stakes at Goodwood in
September; effective from 1m to 11f but doesn't get 1½m; acts on any going but
clearly revels in the mud; occasionally runs a very poor race, and has done so twice
in William Hill Cambridgeshire. *M. Stoute.*

COMMONTY (USA) 5 b.h. Empery 128–Duke's Little Gal (Duke of Dublin)   **71**
(1982 10d 10.6s 10.4g 10fg² 10fg² 10s³ 10.6g³ 8.2s⁴ 10fg 10s* 8v 10s⁴ 1983 10s
12s11.7s* 11.7d² 12v² 12v⁴ 12f 11g 12g⁴ 12s³ 11d) well-made, quite attractive
horse; won handicaps at Bath in April and Windsor in May; stays 1½m; acts on any
going but has shown most of his best form with some give in the ground; not
particularly consistent; sold to C. Bell 10,000 gns Newmarket Autumn Sales. *J.
Bethell.*

July Scurry Handicap, the Curragh—Committed wins from Sir Prince John and Wolverglen (rails)

COMPACTOR 4 br.g. Silly Season 127–Rubbish (Major Portion 129) (1982 12f 12f 13g 12f 1983 16fg 16.5fg⁴) workmanlike gelding; of little account; has worn blinkers. *R. Hobson.*   –

COMPOSER 5 ch.h. Music Boy 124–Contadina (Memling) (1982 8.2v⁴ 8g 6fg 7g² 7f 8d 1983 8g 8f*) big, lengthy horse; plater nowadays; bought in 1,600 gns after winning at Edinburgh in July; stays 1m; acts on any going; blinkered once; sold 2,000 gns Ascot July Sales. *H.O'Neill*   **66**

COMPOUND 9 b.g. Siliconn 121–Compose 94 (Compensation 127) (1982 7f 8g 7f³ 8f* 7g⁴ 8fg 8f* 7fg 8.3g⁴ 7g* 8g 1983 7g 8h 8f 8.3fg² 7g 7.6fg) plater; stays 1m; acts particularly well on firm going; has won for an apprentice; sometimes starts slowly; has run respectably in blinkers. *Mrs N. Kennedy.*   –

COMTEC PRINCESS 4 ch.f. Gulf Pearl 117–Miss Hart 75 (Track Spare 125) (1982 8.2d* 8f 9.4fg 8fg 8.3g 8.2g 8.2s 10s* 10.2s 1983 12s 10d 10s 12d² 10fg² 12f 10g⁴ 10f* 10fg³ 10.2fg*) leggy, lengthy filly; successful in handicaps at Leicester in August and Doncaster in September; didn't find much off bridle in between; stayed 1½m; acted on any going; ran creditably when sweating badly; in foal to Raga Navarro. *M. Ryan.*   **68**

COMTINA 3 gr.f. Comedy Star 121–Quortina 88 (Quorum 126) (1982 6g 6fg 7d 1983 8v 10v 8s 8s³ 8fg 10.2g) quite attractive filly; bad mover; third in seller at Brighton in May, only form; sold 1,500 gns Ascot 2nd June Sales. *J.Holt.*   **50**

CONCANNAN 6 ch.g. Malicious–Six Wives 80 (Royal Record II) (1982 15d 1983 10.2d) sturdy gelding; winner over hurdles; well beaten on flat. *M. Lambert.*   –

CON CARNI 2 b.f. Blakeney 126–Chili Girl 112 (Skymaster 126) (1983 7g) Mar 9; half-sister to fairly useful 6f and 7f winner Hot Case (by Upper Case) and a winner in Italy; dam, very useful sprinter, is half-sister to Steel Heart; 15/2 and ridden by 5-lb claimer, modest seventh of 13 in maiden race at Lingfield in October; should do better. *J. Dunlop.*   – p

CONCAVE 3 b.f. Connaught 130–Aberangell 96 (Abernant 142) (1982 8s 1983 10fg 8g) strong, good-topped filly; lightly-raced maiden; last-but-one when favourite at Edinburgh on final outing. *Sir Mark Prescott.*   –

CONCERT PITCH 4 ch.g. Royal Match 117–Ballychord (Ballymoss 136) (1982 7g 7g 8f³ 12.2f3 9g* 9.3fg³ 11fg* 8g³ 9g 10s 9s 10s 1983 11g* 12d 10.2f 9fg* 11fg 10f 12g) strong, dipped-backed, lengthy gelding; won handicaps at Edinburgh in May and Hamilton in July; seems to stay 1½m; best form on top-of-the-ground; blinkered last 4 starts. *Miss S. Hall.*   **68**

CONDELL 4 ch.c. Condorcet–Liberty Nell (Weavers' Hall 122) (1982 10s³ 14f* 13f* 14g* 12g 1983 12s 16f³ 12fg 12f* 18fg 10g⁴) big colt; good walker; first foal; dam, an unraced twin, is half-sister to top-class mare Park Top; put up an improved performance in Royal Whip Stakes at the Curragh in July, battling on gamely to beat Ankara a short head; also in frame in Queen's Vase at Royal Ascot (4 lengths third to Santella Man) and Joe McGrath Memorial Stakes at Leopardstown (5¾ lengths fourth to Stanera); stays 2m (held up in a slowly-run race and never got in a blow   **115**

191

Mr P. J. Barrett's "Condell"

when 6½ lengths fifth of 8 to Karadar in 2¼m Doncaster Cup); acts on any going but is ideally suited by fast ground; well beaten in blinkers third start (Princess of Wales's Stakes at Newmarket). *J. Bolger, Ireland.*

CONDRILLAC (USA) 2 b.c. Sensitive Prince–Catty (Never Bend) (1983 7fg*)   **100 P**
Apr14; $190,000Y; well-made colt; good mover; first foal; dam, successful at up to 1m, is half-sister to 2¼m stakes winner Field Cat; justified support in fine style when heavily-backed favourite for 14-runner Houghton Stakes at Newmarket in October, going clear up hill to beat more-experienced Chaumiere by 1½ lengths; clearly has a lot of ability and seems sure to win good races at 1¼m+; one to note. *H. Cecil.*

CONGRESS PALACE (USA) 2 b.c. Key To The Kingdom–Pretty Puffin 115   **93**
(Sea-Bird II 145) (1983 7g* 7g) Mar 1; IR 255,000Y; half-brother to 3-y-o The Axe Bird (by Executioner), placed in a stakes race at 2 yrs, and minor winners in USA and France; dam smart middle-distance performer; probably didn't have a lot to beat when favourite for 15-runner maiden race at Naas in September but nonetheless showed plenty of promise in winning by 5 lengths from Stefan Batory; 4½ lengths sixth of 7 to Fiery Celt after making much of running when third favourite for valuable Tap On Wood Stakes at Phoenix Park the following month; should stay at least 1m. *D. O'Brien, Ireland.*

CONMAYJO 2 b.c. Condorcet–Pricey Maid (Home Guard 129) (1983 5v* 5s*   **83**
6fg⁴ 6fg 7d 6fg) May 27; IR 2,000Y (privately); fair sort; second foal; dam won over 6f at 4 yrs in Ireland; won 16-runner maiden race at Bath and 4-runner minor event at Chepstow in May; had stiff tasks in nurseries last 3 starts, running well final occasion; should stay at least 1m; acts on heavy going and a firm surface. *D. H. Jones.*

CONNAUGHT PRINCE 2 ch.c. Connaught 130–Severn Bridge 81 (Hornbeam   **84**
130) (1983 7.2g 7d 7f⁴ 7g 7fg 10fg² 10.2fg) Jan 22; 8,200F, 17,000Y; well-made, useful sort; good walker; half-brother to several winners, including very useful 1977 2-y-o 5f winner Swing Bridge (by Swing Easy); dam won over 9f; showed

ability in maiden and minor events, notably strong-finishing neck second of 13 to Worth While at Nottingham in October; clearly suited by 1¼m; blinkered, went to post very freely and pulled hard when running poorly fifth start; not particularly consistent. *R. Hollinshead.*

CONNECTOR 4 ch.g. Red Alert 127–Polana 68 (Silver Shark 129) (1982 8g 7d 9s 8d³ 8f 10f 8fg 9g⁴ 12f* 14s 1983 13v 12fg) small gelding; poor mover; plater; suited by 1½m; seems to act on any going. *J. S. Wilson.* —

CONNEX 2 ch.g. Connaught 130–Expo 80 (Sheshoon 132) (1983 6fg 8g 8s 8fg) Apr 9; 5,600Y; angular gelding; has a round action; half-brother to Italian St Leger second Ridex (by Ridan) and a winner in Spain; dam stayed at least 1¼m; beaten some way in maiden races and a selling nursery. *D. Plant.* —

CONOR'S ROCK 3 br.g. Rheingold 137–Captains Queen (Captain's Gig) (1982 6f 7g 7g 7fg² 8f² 8g³ 1983 10d 10s 9.5s 10d 11.7fg 12f 12g 11.7fg) small, useful-looking colt; disappointing maiden; should stay beyond 1m; acts on firm going; sold 3,100 gns Newmarket September Sales. *R. Armstrong.* —

CONRAD HILTON 3 b.c. Be My Guest 126–Bentinck Hotel 74 (Red God 128§) (1982 6g³ 1983 6s² 5v* 6v²) big, good-bodied colt; first foal; dam 2-y-o 5f winner; outstandingly pick of paddock when beating Blessit by ½ length in maiden race at Sandown in April, needing to be hard ridden after looking likely to win comfortably; second in similar race at Newmarket and 25-runner minor event at Newbury, finding very little when beaten ½ length by Alawir in latter in May; will be suited by 7f; yet to race on a firm surface. *H. Cecil.* **96**

CONRARA 2 ch.f. Balidar 133–Treasure Seeker 93 (Deep Diver 134) (1983 5f³ 5f² 5f² 5g⁴) Feb 22; 7,800Y; good-bodied filly; second foal; half-sister to leading 1982 Austrian 2-y-o Montesoro (by Mount Hagen); dam won over 5f at 2 yrs but didn't train on; second twice in August, going down by 2 lengths to Maajid in £4,500 event at Ripon and by a neck to Another Deb when drawn none too well in maiden race at Beverley; acts on firm going. *M. H. Easterby.* **77**

CON'S BOY 2 ch.g. Sexton Blake 126–Kinnerton Street (Accordant) (1983 7fg 7fg² 7f*) Apr 30; 4,200Y; leggy gelding; half-brother to several winners, including disappointing Avgerinos (by Welsh Pageant), a very smart performer at 2 yrs, and very useful American sprinter Relent (by Crimson Satan); sold 3,900 gns after winning 12-runner seller at Wolverhampton in August by 5 lengths from Mr Caractacus; exported to Singapore. *M. Jarvis.* **60**

Houghton Stakes, Newmarket—Condrillac goes clear in fine style

CONSCRIPT 2 gr. g. Warpath 113–Scrub Oak 84 (Burglar 128) (1983 6g² 6d* 7f² **94**
7f² 7d³ 8s²) May 24; leggy, rather lightly-built gelding; second foal; dam 2-y-o 6f
winner; won 14-runner maiden race at Carlisle in June; ran well subsequently,
particularly when placed in good nurseries at York in August and Ayr (blinkered)
in September on last 2 appearances; stays 1m; acts on any going; consistent; sold
12,000 gns Newmarket Autumn Sales, probably for export to Italy. *J. W. Watts.*

CONSCRIPTION 3 ch.g. Gunner B 126–Needless 81 (Petingo 135) (1982 7d –
1983 11s 13f 16f⁴ 15.8g 14d 15.8g 18fg) strong, lengthy, useful-looking gelding;
poor maiden; didn't move well in his later races; promises to stay 13f+; blinkered
fifth outing; trained until after first start by F. J. Houghton. *J.Leigh.*

CONSINGH 2 ch.g. Mansingh 120–Confleur 81 (Compensation 127) (1983 6d) –
Apr 22; 4,800F, 820Y; first produce; dam 6f winner; 20/1, last of 14 in maiden race
at Carlisle in June. *H. Bell.*

CONSORTIUM 6 b.h. Targowice 130–Annerbelle 108 (Aureole 132) (1982 –
10.1fg 10fg 10g² 10g³ 11.7g² 14f 10g 12fg 8g⁴ 10v 9g 7s 1983 8v 8g 11g⁴ 10f⁴ 10fg)
strong horse; plater; stays 1½m; acts on any going but is suited by some give in
the ground; often blinkered; suitable mount for a boy; front runner. *K. Ivory.*

CONTESTER 3 ch.c. Connaught 130–Mitigation 91 (Milesian 125) (1982 5fg **89**
5.8f³ 7f⁴ 7g 8fg 8f³ 8.2s* 7g⁴ 8.2v³ 1983 12d 14.7d² 14f 13fg³ 13g⁴ 15s 14d 18fg³)
strong, well-made colt; 40/1, ran easily his best race of season and put up an
astonishing performance when 1½ lengths third of 28 to Bajan Sunshine in Tote
Cesarewitch at Newmarket in October on final outing, making up ground hand over
fist in last half mile after being a long way behind, and finishing so well he'd have
won with another 50 yds to go; needs a thorough test of stamina; acts on any going;
has been tried in blinkers but didn't wear them at Newmarket; to be trained by P.
Cundell in 1984. *F. Watson.*

CONVEYOR BELLE 3 ch.f. Gunner B 126–Thorganby Bella (Porto Bello 118) –
(1982 5fg³ 5g² 5f³ 5d* 6f 6fg⁴ 5g 1983 6d 6d 6d 7d⁴ 6f 7f) leggy, close-coupled
filly; plater; stays 7f; didn't handle bend at Catterick fourth start; sold 640 gns
Ascot September Sales. *J. Berry.*

CONWAY GROVE 3 b.g. Pongee 106–Sherry (King's Coup 108) (1982 6fg 7g 7g –
8.2s 1983 12.3fg 14.7f) plain gelding; behind in varied company. *N. Chamberlain.*

CONYGARTH HILL 2 b.f. Thatch 136–Bowerbird 88 (Herbager 136) (1983 5s –
5s) Mar 15; useful-looking filly; first reported foal; dam, granddaughter of
champion American filly Bayou, won over 7f at 2 yrs; well beaten both outings, on
second co-favourite in June maiden at Catterick; looks capable of better. *J.
Etherington.*

COOKS CHOICE 2 ch.f. Roman Warrior 132–Rockaway 62 (Siliconn 121) (1983 –
5s 5v 6fg) Jan 31; first foal; dam 5f winner; behind in big fields of maidens and a
Warwick seller; not seen out after June; probably of little account. *P. Burgoyne.*

COOKS FLANAGAN 2 b. or br.c. Shiny Tenth 120–Prompt Delivery (Catullus) –
(1983 6g 7g 6fg 5g 6g) June 16; small colt; brother to 2 winners, including 5f to 7f
winner Webbs Jewel, and half-brother to a winner in USA; dam won over 5f and 6f
in USA; behind in varied company, including selling; of no account. *P. Burgoyne.*

COOLCHAIN 2 b.c. Pitskelly 122–Relko's Pride (Relko 136) (1983 6g) Mar 30; –
IR 3,600Y; half-brother to winners here and in USA, including 1979 2-y-o 5f winner
Welsh Pride (by Welsh Saint); dam unraced half-sister to Bold Lad (Ire); 50/1, ninth
of 10 in minor event at Lingfield in July. *S. Mellor.*

COOL DECISION 6 b.g. Furry Glen 121–Aran Jacket (Le Levanstell 122) (1982 **81**
10.2g 12fg 12f² 12fg* 13fg² 12d⁴ 12f* 12f⁴ 14g 12fg* 11d* 9s⁴ 10g 12s 1983 12g
12g⁴ 12f³ 13fg⁴ 15fg 12g² 12f 11s 12fg) lengthy gelding; fair performer at his best;
ran best races when sticking on well to be 2½ lengths second to Path of Peace in
Great Yorkshire Handicap at York in August and fifth of 25 to Asir in William Hill
November Handicap at Doncaster; suited by middle distances; acts on any going;
good mount for an inexperienced rider; blinkered at Doncaster; inconsistent. *Miss
S. Hall.*

COOLINEY PRINCESS 4 ch.f. Bruni 132–Windfield Lily (Hard Tack 111§) **98**
(1982 8g 7d⁴ 12fg 7fg² 10f⁴ 1983 8g² 9g² 9fg² 11fg² 12f* 8d 12g⁴ 12d) IR 61,000Y;
strong, good-bodied filly; half-sister to 3 winners, including Irish St Leger winner
Conor Pass (by Tiepolo II) and useful 1975 Irish 2-y-o Lace Curtain Lil (by
Whistling Wind); dam prolific winning Irish sprinter; quickened clear over 1f out to
beat Noble Gift easily by 5 lengths in Moet and Chandon Silver Magnum (gentleman

riders) at Epsom in August; also in frame in quite valuable handicaps at Phoenix Park (3) and Naas and in Princess Royal Stakes at Ascot (about 6½ lengths fourth of 11 to Sylph); suited by 1½m; acts on firm going; blinkered final start at 3 yrs. *M. Cunningham, Ireland.*

COOL JAMIE 2 b.g. Pals Passage 115–Shangara (Credo 123) (1983 10.2fg) Apr 13; IR 1,250Y; brother to useful middle-distance stayer Pal's Bambino and a winning hurdler, and half-brother to 2 other winners; dam won twice over 5f at 2 yrs in Ireland; 50/1 when last of 24 to Raami in minor event at Doncaster in November. *J. Wilson.*   —

COOL WIND 4 ch.f. Windjammer (USA)–Cool Mistress 59 (Skymaster 126) (1982 5s 5v* 5g* 5f³ 5f 5f³ 5h 5fg 5fg 5fg 5d 5d 1983 5.8s³ 10.8v* 5f 10f 5g 8g 5g) neat filly; made much of running and trotted up in handicap at Warwick in May; often raced over sprint distances but is evidently suited by middle distances; acts on any going but goes well in the mud; has run creditably for an apprentice and when sweating up. *G. Price.*   **55**

COOMBE SPIRIT 3 ro.g. Grundy 137–Dame Clara 95 (Manacle 123) (1982 7fg 8s 1983 8d 10s⁴ 10s³ 8g 12g 11.7h² 11.7fg³ 10.1fg⁴ 12f⁴ 10.2g⁴ 12d) rather leggy, close-coupled gelding; good walker; showed some ability in maiden races and handicaps (2 of them apprentice events), but ran poorly on final outing; stays 1½m; acts on any going; blinkered ninth start. *H. Candy.*   **65**

COOPERHOLME 2 b.f. Joshua 129–Miss Hubbard (New Brig 120) (1983 7d) Mar 19; smallish, rather narrow filly; second known foal; half-sister to a winning hurdler; dam unplaced over hurdles after birth of first foal; 50/1, slow-starting last of 13 in Acomb Stakes at York in August. *A. Cawley.*   —

COOPERS KING 2 ch.c. Monsanto 121–Gesticulate 83 (Some Hand 119) (1983 7g 8d 8f) Apr 10; plain colt; first foal; dam 2-y-o 5f winner; soundly beaten in autumn maiden races. *J. King.*   —

COPING 2 br.c. Thatching 131–Top Call 89 (High Top 131) (1983 6fg 6g³ 7f*) Feb 2; smallish, strong, chunky colt; first foal; dam, half-sister to Final Straw and Achieved, won over 7f and 1m at 2 yrs; improved with his races; finished about 5 lengths third to Sir Humpherson in 14-runner minor event at Lingfield in September; won 17-runner maiden event at Redcar later in month easing up by ½ length from Life Guard; suited by 7f and may well get 1m; yet to race on a soft surface. *M. Stoute.*   **86**

COPPER BEECHES 6 b.g. Owen Anthony 103–Primmry 56 (Primera 131) (1982 6f 6f 5g² 6g² 6fg⁴ 5d 1983 5s⁴ 8s 6fg 6f 6f² 6f) quite attractive, lightly-made gelding; quite a moderate handicapper; stays 6f but not 1m; acts on any going; often blinkered, but seems better without nowadays. *J. Jenkins.*   **60**

COPT AGAIN 5 ch.m. Copte–Annie 65 (Damremont 120) (1982 12f⁴ 10d 15g 10.8fg³ 10fg³ 12d 1983 11s) compact mare; plater; stays 1¾m; acts well on firm going; has run creditably in blinkers. *T. Fairhurst.*   —

COQUELIN (USA) 4 ch.c. Blushing Groom 131–Topolly (Turn-to) (1982 9fg² 10d* 10fg 12v* 10g³ 10s* 12v 1983 10.5s 9.7d 12f 8fg 9fg² 10g² 10s 9f* 8g*) 220,000Y; good walker; half-brother to Turn Back The Time (by Youth), successful at up to 1¼m, and French 1½m winner Meg's Pride (by Sparkler); dam, French 9f winner, is granddaughter of top-class filly Bella Paola; very smart at 3 yrs when he won 3 races, including Prix du Lys and La Coupe de Maisons-Laffitte; not quite so good in 1983 but won 80,000 francs race at Longchamp and Premio Vittorio di Capua at Milan in October; beat Solarstern by ½ length in latter; had run respectably earlier when 2½ lengths fifth of 9 to Welsh Term in Prix Dollar at Longchamp on second start, 3 lengths second of 4 to Great Substence in apprentice event at Evry and 2 lengths second of 8 to Prince du Bourg in 70,000 francs race at Deauville; stayed 1½m; acted on any going; retired to Baroda Stud, Newbridge, Co. Kildare at a fee of IR £7,000 no foal no fee. *F. Boutin, France.*   **115**

COQUITO'S FRIEND 3 b.c. Owen Dudley 121–Kissin' Cousins (Be Friendly 130) (1982 6fg* 6fg² 6s* 6g³ 1983 6d 6v³ 6v 6f 6f* 6f² 7g³ 6fg* 6s* 6fg⁴ 6fg²) good-bodied colt; very useful performer; had a good season and was successful in £3,300 race at Newbury in July (beat Diamond Cutter shade comfortably by 3 lengths), similar event at Salisbury in September (won by 2 lengths from Bold Bob) and £15,000 SAS Open Sprint at Taby, Sweden, later in September (beat Tresor by a length); ran well most other starts too and was placed 4 times, when 2½ lengths third behind Deputy Head in handicap at York, ½-length second of 7 to same colt in Northumberland Sprint Trophy at Newcastle, 1½ lengths third of 6 to Able Albert in City of York Stakes and neck second of 11 to Kirchner in Premio   **111**

Mr A. Alvarado's "Coquito's Friend"

Umbria at Rome; stays 7f, but probably best at 6f; acts on any going; usually waited with and has a good turn of foot. *B. Hanbury.*

COQUITO'S STAR 2 ch.c. Nebbiolo 125–Please Oblige (Le Levanstell 122)   **84**
(1983 7fg 6f* 7f³ 6f* 7f 6fg 8.2g⁴ 7g² 8.2s⁴) Feb 23; IR 21,000Y; medium-sized, angular colt; first living foal; dam unraced half-sister to very useful Irish middle-distance performer Gargano and Irish 2000 Guineas fourth Staplestown; won maiden race at Hamilton in July and nursery at Leicester in August; best form at 6f and 7f, but probably stays 1m; acts on a firm going and wasn't disgraced only outing on soft; usually blinkered. *B. Hanbury.*

CORAL HEIGHTS 2 b.f. Shirley Heights 130–Chieftain Girl (Chieftain) (1983   **– p**
7.6d) Mar 16; 70,000Y; half-sister to numerous winners, including fair stayer Shaab (by Busted); dam, daughter of sister to Sir Gaylord, won at up to 1m; 12/1, prominent long way when remote sixth of 20 behind Risk All in maiden race at Lingfield in October; will be suited by 1¼m+; sure to do better. *C. Brittain.*

CORALLIAN 2 b.c. Jaazeiro 127–Coralivia (Le Levanstell 122) (1983 6f 7f 7g)   **–**
Mar 14; 7,600Y; big, rangy colt; half-brother to 3 winners, including 3-y-o 1¼m winner Cristalga (by High Top) and 7f and 1¼m winner Countess Olivia (by Prince Tenderfoot); dam, half-sister to very smart Ballyhot, won over 1½m in Ireland; soundly beaten in varied company; blinkered when last of 16 final outing. *C. Wildman.*

CORALS SECRET 3 b.f. Most Secret 119–Flicka (Balidar 133) (1982 NR 1983   **55**
5v 5v 7s 8d⁴ 8f) workmanlike filly; fourth foal; half-sister to winning sprinter Mary Maguire (by Warpath) and a winner in Norway; dam of little account; modest fourth in maiden race at Ayr in June. *M. Jefferson.*

COR ANGLAIS (USA) 2 b.f. Nijinsky 138–Royal Dilemma (Buckpasser) (1983   **78 p**
7f⁴ 7f²) May 8; tall, rangy filly; closely related to good-class 6f and 7f performer

Silverdip (by The Minstrel) and smart 5f and 1½m winner Imperial Fling (by Northern Dancer), and half-sister to 2 winners; dam, stakes-placed winner at up to 6f, is daughter of champion 1964 American 2-y-o filly Queen Empress; in frame in maiden races at Sandown in July and Brighton in August; will stay 1¼m; looks the type to improve. *I. Balding.*

CORBALLY 3 br.f. Wolverlife 115–Grindelwald 76 (Le Levanstell 122) (1982 7.6v 55 8s 6g 1983 8v 6s³ 15s 5s 5s³) tall, lengthy filly; plater; seems best at sprint distances. *A. Ingham.*

CORDITE SPEAR (USA) 4 br.c. Explodent–Lovely Lance (Assagai) (1982 – 7g³ 8.2s* 8f² 10f³ 10.6h³ 10g 8fg³ 8g 8g² 8s* 8v² 8s 1983 8d 8fg) well-made colt; very good mover; fairly useful handicapper at 3 yrs; well beaten in handicaps at Doncaster in March and November in 1983; stays 1¼m; acts on any going but goes well on soft; suited by a strongly-run race; trained by D. Nicholson first start. *J. Bosley.*

CORDUROY 7 ch.h. Hotfoot 126–Twill 89 (Crocket 130) (1982 12s 10v 12v 12s 58 1983 12s³ 12v* 12v 12d² 12.2d⁴) rangy horse; middle-distance handicapper; well ridden when scoring at Kempton in April; acts on any going; needs strong handling. *D. Nicholson.*

CORINTH (FR) 2 b.c. Troy 137–Cendres Bleues (Charlottesville 135) (1983 8g⁴ 107 p 8d* 8d*) May 3; big, rangy colt; good mover; half-brother to several winners, including very smart 1m to 1½m filly Calderina (by Lyphard) and very useful middle-distance filly Cattarina Ginnasi (by Tierceron); dam very useful over middle distances in Italy; favourite, made all in £3,500 race at York in October, holding on by a length from San Carlos Bay after looking likely to win easily 2f out; very confidently ridden, won 16-runner £4,000 event at Newbury later in the month by 1½ lengths from Little Look, coming through strongly to lead in final furlong; has plenty of scope, and looks sure to make up into smart 3-y-o over 1¼m+. *I. Balding.*

CORMORANT WOOD 3 b.f. Home Guard 129–Quarry Wood 89 (Super Sam 125 124) (1982 6g 7d* 1983 12s² 12g 12fg 12fg 10f* 10fg* 10fg* 12d)
The Champion Stakes goes from strength to strength. The latest running, sponsored once again by the Al-Maktoum family of Dubai, attracted as large a field as there has been since the beginning in 1877. A field of nineteen went to post, short of a horse of the calibre of the Champion Stakes' many great winners but a high-class field nonetheless, whose efforts resulted in a finish to grace the occasion–one of the best, most thrilling, to a big race for many a day. The winner Cormorant Wood, a filly as were twelve of the preceding twenty-five winners of this event including Time Charter, Rose Bowl, Hula Dancer, Petite Etoile and Bella Paola, produced a performance that had to be seen to be believed. With superb assistance from the in-form Cauthen and no small measure of good fortune, too, she came from last to first in the final three furlongs, squeezing past tightly-packed contestants being buffeted by a gale-force side wind; she swept up the hill on the bridle and at the very last found enough room between Tolomeo and the only other filly in the race, Flame of Tara, to allow her to lift the prize. She ·won by a head from Tolomeo; Flame of Tara was only a short head further behind, a length and a half up on the latest of the numerous rank outsiders to have excelled themselves, Miramar

Sun Chariot Stakes, Newmarket—Cormorant Wood runs on too well for Sedra (right)

Reef. The favourite Salmon Leap seemed to find the trip too sharp, though for him, as for even better horses in years gone by (Nijinsky and Park Top to name two of the more notable), the race might have come too soon after the Prix de l'Arc de Triomphe.

The last three runnings of the Champion Stakes have ended in controversy of one sort or another. The winner in 1981, Vayrann, was ultimately allowed to keep the race after traces of a prohibited substance, self-produced apparently, had been found in his routine urine sample. 1982 brought entirely justified criticism on the official handicappers, who grossly underestimated Time Charter's merit in the International Classification. In 1983 it was the long-suffering stewards' turn once again, as the unenviable task of apportioning blame for what had been, apparently, a very rough race fell on their shoulders. As a result of their deliberations Tolomeo was relegated to fourth place for causing interference. Whatever the merits of the decision, no blame whatsoever attached to Cormorant Wood or her extremely cool partner; incredibly they were able to obtain a clear run up the rails and switch to deliver the coup de grace without recourse to any barging.

The merit of Cormorant Wood's performances in the autumn was well in advance of that of her earlier ones. It would be rash, though, to attribute such improvement wholly or largely to the change in the seasons. Significantly, we feel, she obtained her three successive victories, of which that in the Champion Stakes was the third, on being switched to a mile and a quarter from a mile and a half. At a mile and a half in the spring she'd run a highly promising second to the five-length winner Give Thanks in the Esal Bookmakers Oaks Trial at Lingfield, then fallen short of fulfilling that promise in the Oaks (she finished a tired sixth behind Sun Princess, gradually giving up a long-held prominent position after reaching the two-furlong marker) and the Princess of Wales's Stakes at Newmarket (again her run petered out in the last quarter of a mile, and she was soundly beaten behind Quilted). And on her only appearance after the Champion Stakes Cormorant Wood failed to reach her best in the Washington International: she gave the distinct impression she barely got the trip while finishing sixth of eight behind an admittedly far superior winner. Cormorant Wood emulated Time Charter by winning the Sun Chariot Stakes at the Newmarket meeting prior to that which features the Champion Stakes. She won by a slightly greater margin than Time Charter in a very similar style, running on too strongly for the others once established in front about two furlongs out; Sedra finished second, beaten a length, Elect came next. Before that Cormorant Wood had won the Virginia Stakes at Newcastle in August, a quite valuable event confined to fillies and mares put on with commendable enterprise and at considerable risk by the racecourse executive. Fortunately for the day's card, the race attracted three runners of an appropriate standard in Air Distingue, Funny Reef and Cormorant Wood. Air Distingue started at odds on but Cormorant Wood beat her by three lengths, quickening well when her jockey kicked on three furlongs from home and keeping on well towards the end; Funny Reef was a well-beaten third of six. Cormorant Wood is to remain in training by all accounts. The Prix de l'Arc de Triomphe is said to be on her agenda but we should not have thought her the right type for such a race. A mile and a quarter, preferably on

Dubai Champion Stakes, Newmarket—Cormorant Wood (centre) bursts through to touch off Tolomeo and Flame of Tara (left). Miramar Reef (right) finishes fourth

Mr R. J. McAlpine's "Cormorant Wood"

top-of-the-ground though she can act on any, should be very much more her cup of tea.

Cormorant Wood (b.f. 1980)	Home Guard (bl 1969)	Forli (ch 1963)	Aristophanes / Trevisa
		Stay at Home (br 1961)	Bold Ruler / Alanesian
	Quarry Wood (b 1968)	Super Sam (br 1962)	Above Suspicion / Samaria
		Phrygia (ch 1957)	Mossborough / Lenaea

Cormorant Wood's sire Home Guard, best at six furlongs, stayed a mile and a quarter; her dam Quarry Wood stayed considerably further. Quarry Wood won four races at a mile and a half to a mile and three quarters, and stayed further; a fair handicapper, she finished fifth of sixteen behind Eric in the Chester Cup of 1972. She has had one other runner, the filly Hot Stone (by Hotfoot) who was a poor third in a Hamilton maiden race as a three-year-old. The second dam, winner of a seven-furlong apprentice maiden race at Baldoyle at the same age, foaled four other winners of whom Quarry Wood's brother Super Trojan, the Great Metropolitan Handicap winner Cullen and Davett stayed particularly well.

Cormorant Wood is big, rangy and quite attractive, physically the type to go on at four years. She's also a thoroughly likeable sort as a racehorse, and we hope she does well enough to encourage owners to keep their good fillies longer in training; that is, if they need any encouragement after the magnificent example set by All Along and others of her sex in 1983. *B. Hills.*

CORNBOY GIRL 2 b.f. Owen Dudley 121–Ribble Girl 96 (Trouville 125) (1983 5fg 5f 7f) Apr 26; 11,000Y; lightly-built filly; good mover; half-sister to several —

winners, including very useful 1981 2-y-o 5f and 7f winner Chulia Street (by Dragonara Palace); dam won twice over 5f at 2 yrs; well beaten in maiden races, starting slowly when second favourite on first 2 outings, and wearing blinkers when last of 11 on third. *W. O'Gorman.*

CORNCHARM 2 b.c. Thatch 136–Just Larking (Sea-Bird II 145) (1983 6fg[4] 7fg[2] 8g 7fg) Apr 24; 6,200F, 11,500Y; good-bodied colt; fifth living foal; half-brother to 1½m winner Tharsus Girl (by Blakeney); dam won at up to 1m in USA; 6 lengths second of 12 to Mafoo's Image in maiden event at Salisbury in September; hopelessly out of his depth in William Hill Dewhurst Stakes at Newmarket on final appearance; should stay 1m. *M. McCormack.*   **74**

CORNEILLE 3 b.g. Dom Racine 121–La Reine Margot 76 (Pampered King 121) (1982 NR 1983 10v 16v* 14f) sparely-made gelding; half-brother to 2m winner Honey Tower (by Tower Walk); dam, placed over 7f at 2 yrs, is half-sister to top-class middle-distance filly Paulista; battled on well under pressure when beating Ataman by ½ length in maiden race at Thirsk in April; had stiffish task only subsequent start (sweating and unimpressive in paddock); clearly relishes a test of stamina. *J. W. Watts.*   **66**

CORNISH GEM 4 br.c. Cornish Prince–Jeanie Duff 83 (Majestic Prince) (1982 7d[3] 7fg[2] 8fg 10g[3] 7fg[3] 8fg[3] 8g 1983 10s[4] 10v 8s 8.5g 8fg* 8d[4] 8fg[3] 8fg* 8fg[2] 8g[2] 8.2fg*) good-bodied, attractive colt; carries plenty of condition; not the best of movers nowadays; won gentleman riders race at Goodwood in August and handicaps at Brighton in September and Nottingham in October; stays 1¼m; seems to act on any going; blinkered once in 1982 and on fourth start; suitable mount for an inexperienced rider; coltish in paddock first outing. *G. Lewis.*   **77**

CORNISH GRANITE 5 gr.g. Ragstone 128–Pasty 122 (Raffingora 130) (1982 13.1f 1983 17.1h) plain gelding; quite moderate at his best; unlikely to stay 2m; best form with some give in the ground; has worn blinkers. *M. Pipe.*   **–**

CORN STREET 5 ch.g. Decoy Boy 129–Diamond Talk (Counsel 118) (1982 7s[4] 8d[3] 8f 7fg 8g 8fg* 8g* 8g 8fg* 8v* 8s* 8s 1983 8d 8v[3] 8d[4] 8v 8s* 8d[3] 8f 8fg 8fg 8d 8fg) workmanlike gelding; fairly useful handicapper; easily beat Hello Sunshine by 5 lengths at Goodwood in May; ran creditably several other starts, notably when fifth of 10 to Noalcoholic in Lockinge Stakes at Newbury on fourth; suited by 1m; acts on any going but is particularly well suited by some give; suitable mount for an inexperienced rider; genuine. *J. Bosley.*   **94**

CORRAGARY 2 gr.c. Royben 125–My Diana 94 (Sovereign Path 125) (1983 6f 7fg) Apr 29; 940F; close-coupled colt; half-brother to numerous winners here and abroad; dam sprinter; behind in 17-runner events at Windsor in August and Salisbury in September. *K. Brassey.*   **–**

CORRIB MASTER 2 b.g. Anax 120–Doubtful Request (Cheveley Lad 105) (1983 6f 5d) Apr 11; slightly hollow-backed, useful-looking gelding; half-brother to 2 winners, including 5f winner Five Aces (by Some Hand); dam never ran; soundly beaten in newcomers race at Goodwood in July and maiden event at Wolverhampton in October. *J. King.*   **–**

CORSTON LAD 3 ch.g. Orange Bay 131–Corston Lass (Menelek 114) (1982 7g 1983 10d[3] 10fg 8d[2] 8f[4] 10s 10fg) lengthy, useful-looking gelding with plenty of scope; good walker; beat The House Builder by ½ length in maiden race at Ayr in June but edged left in closing stages and placings were reversed; bred to stay further than 1¼m. *J. Winter.*   **78**

CORSTON VELVET 2 br.f. Bruni 132–Corston Lass (Menelek 114) (1983 6d 7fg 7.6d 10.2fg) Mar 23; light-framed filly; second foal; half-sister to 3-y-o disqualified 1m winner Corston Lad (by Orange Bay); dam placed over hurdles; quite a modest maiden; ran easily best race when sixth of 24 behind easy winner Raami in minor event at Doncaster in November on final appearance; needs test of stamina. *J. Winter.*   **66**

CORVELLE 3 ch.f. Reliance II 137–Corvette (Biarritz 115) (1982 6fg 7fg 8fg 1983 12fg 10.1fg 13h 7.6g) sparely-made, plain filly; little worthwhile form, although was ninth of 25 finishers in a handicap on final start. *P. Cole.*   **–**

COSHLEA 3 ch.f. Red Alert 127–White Legs (Preciptic 122) (1982 6fg 8fg 1983 11d[2] 12g[2] 12g[2] 12.3f 15g[3] 16fg 15fg) strong, compact filly; placed in varied races at Edinburgh (3) and Beverley; appears suited by a test of stamina; wears blinkers; tends to sweat up; ran deplorably fourth start and was off course 3 months afterwards. *J. W. Watts.*   **63**

COSMIC 6 b.m. Foggy Bell 108–Lunar Bug (Master Rocky 106) (1982 NR 1983   –
8fg 13.4fg 12g 17.1g) third reported foal; dam winning hurdler; soundly beaten in
varied company. *J. Old.*

COSMOPOLITAN 3 ch.c. Great Nephew 126–Monashka 73 (Sica Boy 132)   –
(1982 NR 1983 10d 12f 14.7f) 26,000F; robust colt; half-brother to several
winners here and abroad; dam half-sister to Altesse Royale, Imperial Prince and
Yaroslav; in rear in maiden races at Redcar, finishing tailed-off last on final occasion;
sold to R. Ward 800 gns Doncaster November Sales. *C. Thornton.*

COSSACK DANCER 2 ch.c. Be My Guest 126–Bolkonskina (Balidar 133)   –
(1983 5fg 5fg 6fg) Feb 19; 9,400Y; first foal; dam, sister to Bolkonski, won twice at
2 yrs in Italy; behind in maiden and minor events; blinkered final start. *Peter
Taylor.*

COSTALOTTA 2 ch.f. Music Boy 124–Loweswater 74 (Saint Crespin III 132)   81
(1983 5d 5f 5fg 5f⁴ 5f² 5fg 5h³ 5f* 5g² 5fg³) Apr 14; 7,400Y; stocky filly; half-sister
to winning stayer Village Swan (by My Swanee) and a winning hurdler; dam won
over 1½m; made all in maiden race at Folkestone in September; clear of remainder
when 1½ lengths second of 14 to Jamra in minor event at Bath the following month;
speedy and unlikely to stay 6f; acts well on firm going; blinkered second and third
outings. *B. Swift.*

COSTOCK BUNNY 2 b.f. Young Generation 129–Abbotsinch 72 (Bold Lad, Ire   –
133) (1983 5fg 5g 5g 5g) Mar 31; 1,500Y, 1,250 2-y-o; sturdy, heavy-topped filly;
first foal; dam 2-y-o 5f winner, poor form, best effort when staying-on seventh of
20 behind Biddour in small race at Catterick in September on third outing; will stay
6f. *L. Lightbrown.*

COTHAY 2 br.f. On Your Mark 125–Corsuedei (King's Troop 118) (1983 5d 5fg   65
5.8f 6f³ 5.8h⁴ 7fg 7g 7.2g³ 8f) Mar 10; IR 3,600Y; tall, lengthy, light-framed filly;
closely related to 1978 2-y-o 5f winner First Class Mail and a winner in Italy (both
by Windjammer) and half-sister to another winner; dam unplaced 4 times at 2 yrs in
Ireland; fair plater; suited by 7f, but isn't sure to stay 1m; acts on firm going; ran
too freely in blinkers seventh outing. *R. Hannon.*

COTTAGE STYLE 4 ch.f. Thatch 136–Toast Record (El Gallo 122) (1982 7d⁴   –
7.2g 7d⁴ 1983 8d⁴ 6s 9.4f 8f 7f 8fg) good-topped filly; poor maiden; possibly stays
1m. *W. A. Stephenson.*

COTTAM ELITE 2 b.f. Lochnager 132–L'Elita 83 (Porto Bello 118) (1983 5s 6f⁴   55
6f 5f 6f 8f* 8d 7.2g⁴ 8fg) Mar 25; lengthy, light-framed filly; half-sister to 2
winners, including 1980 2-y-o 5f winner Zoilo (by Workboy); dam 2-y-o 5f winner;
plater; attracted no bid when 1½-length winner from Shamrock Princess in
nursery at Beverley in September; evidently suited by 1m; acts on firm going. *M.
W. Easterby.*

COTTON PRINT 2 b.c. He Loves Me 121–Cannon Ball 91 (By Thunder! 122)   83
(1983 6f 6g 7d 6h⁴ 7f 7fg 7fg) May 20; 14,000Y; lengthy, sparely-made colt; has a
good, long stride; half-brother to numerous winners, including good French
stayer A Chara (by Worden II); dam daughter of top-class Bebe Grande;
moderate maiden; best race when fifth of 13 in good nursery at Newmarket in
October on penultimate appearance; suited by 7f; acts on hard going. *R.
Armstrong.*

COULEE QUEEN 2 b.f. Bustino 136–Lady Oriana 91 (Tudor Melody 129) (1983   81 p
7fg²) Apr 22; lightly-made filly; third foal; half-sister to a winning plater; dam,
daughter of very smart sprinter Merry Madcap, won over 7f at 2 yrs; third
favourite, strong-finishing ½-length second of 14 to Claude Monet in minor event at
Doncaster in October; will be suited by further; sure to win a race. *B. Hills.*

COUL WOLLOW 2 b.c. Wollow 132–Coulisse 85 (Right Royal V 135) (1983 5d   –
5.8g 7f 7g) May 26; 1,100F; workmanlike colt; dam, daughter of
very speedy Couloir, won over 6f at 2 yrs and stayed 1m; no form in maiden races;
had been off course 3 months when last of 16 final start. *R. Cambidge.*

COUNTACH 4 br.g. Balidar 133–Fiji Express (Exbury 138) (1982 5d* 6s³ 5g⁴   –
5fg* 5f* 5fg* 5h⁴ 6fg⁴ 7f 6f 5d 1983 5v 6g 6f 5f) quite attractive gelding; sprint
handicapper; below form at 4 yrs; stays 6f; seems to act on any going; ran freely in
blinkers last 2 starts. *P. Cole.*

COUNT BERTRAND 2 b.c. Brigadier Gerard 144–Gingerale (Golden Horus   77
123) (1983 6fg² 6f⁴) Apr 22; lengthy colt; has a rather round action; brother to 3
winners, including 1m winner Countess Walewski; dam useful at up to 9.5f in
France; modest maiden; will stay 1m; capable of winning small race. *W. Holden.*

COUNT D'ARCY 2 b.c. Balidar 133–Princess Katzie (Crowned Prince 128)   **65**
(1983 5s 5s 6f 6f 6f* 6f) Apr 12; small, hollow-backed colt; first foal; dam poor
daughter of very smart miler Katie Cecil; sold out of B. Hills's stable 1,400 gns
after winning 18-runner seller at Windsor in August; tailed off in blinkers fourth
start; exported to Algeria. *G. Blum.*

COUNT DERRY 3 ch.c. Derrylin 115–Noble Countess (Mossborough 126) (1982   **84**
7fg 8g 8.2s² 1983 10fg 12f²) big, workmanlike colt; ran respectably both outings in
1983, including when 2½ lengths second of 5 behind Sea Raider in slowly-run
handicap at Salisbury in June; suited by 1½m; acts on any going. *R. Hannon.*

COUNTESS CONCORDE (USA) 2 b.f. Super Concorde 128–Count to Ten   **91**
(Zip Pocket) (1983 6fg 6f* 6f² 5f³) Mar 3; $60,000F, $30,000Y; useful-looking
filly; second foal; dam won twice over 6f, including a claiming event; made all after a
fast start when easy 3-length winner from Ghanayem in minor event at Windsor in
July; ran well later in the month in St Catherine's Stakes at Newbury (second to
Rocket Alert) and £4,700 nursery at Goodwood; better suited by 6f than 5f; acts on
firm going. *B. Hanbury.*

COUNTESS MARA 3 gr.f. Moulton 128–Princess Supreme (Supreme   –
Sovereign 119) (1982 NR 1983 8d) big filly; good mover; sister to a winner
abroad, and half-sister to 2 more; dam never ran; third favourite when about 9
lengths fifth of 29 behind Rodners in maiden race at Newmarket in May, racing
prominently on favoured far side for a long way and not being unduly knocked
about; wasn't seen out again. *G. Wragg.*

COUNT OF SICILY 4 b.c. Dubassoff–Sicilia (Die Hard 127) (1982 13g 15fg³   –
14.6g 16.5fg² 15.8d 18d 1983 15g 16f 16f) big colt; staying maiden; best form on
a firm surface; blinkered last 2 starts. *P. Calver.*

COUNT PAHLEN 4 gr.c. Hotfoot 126–Tanara 93 (Romulus 129) (1982 8.5fg*   **103**
10.5f⁴ 12f 10s 10d 1983 9d⁴ 10v) strong, good sort who carries plenty of
condition; put up a high-class display to win William Hill Futurity at Doncaster in
1981; didn't reproduce that form though won Blue Riband Trial at Epsom and ran
respectably in Mecca-Dante Stakes at York, Derby and Dubai Champion Stakes at
Newmarket at 3 yrs; about 9 lengths fourth of 7 to Ivano in Earl of Sefton Stakes
at Newmarket in April; ran moderately in blinkers in Westbury Stakes at Sandown
won by Ivano again later in month and was subsequently sent to be trained by S. di
Mauro in USA; promises to stay 1½m; has won on a firm surface but is ideally
suited by some give in the ground. *B. Hobbs.*

COUNTRY BREEZE 2 br.f. Vitiges 132–The Country Lane 90 (Red God 128§)   **65**
(1983 5s⁴ 5s 6s² 5f³ 7g 6fg) Mar 8; fair sort; half-sister to several winners,
including very useful 3-y-o sprinter Bumpkin (by Free State) and prolific 7f to 9f
winner On Edge (by Sharp Edge); dam won 4 times over 6f; plating-class maiden;
stays 6f; probably acts on any going; off course nearly 3 months after fourth outing;
sweated up very badly and ran poorly when blinkered final start. *M. Blanshard.*

COUNTRY CHARM 3 ch.f. Northfields–Be Gyrful 89 (Gyr 131) (1982 NR 1983   **95**
8g* 9fg* 9f 10g³ 10fg 8d³ 10.2fg²) IR 30,000Y; big, rangy filly; fourth foal; closely
related to a winner in Italy by Habitat; dam, winner over 5f and 1m, is daughter of
Gimcrack winner Be Careful; won her first 2 starts, beating Leighmor by 6 lengths
in minor event at Ayr in July and Most Honourable by 1½ lengths in much more
strongly-contested minor event at Wolverhampton in August; slipped on turn third
start but ran well afterwards, gaining places in handicaps at Yarmouth and Newbury
and an apprentice event at Doncaster, and finishing fifth of 9 behind Cormorant
Wood in Sun Chariot Stakes at Newmarket; stays 1¼m; acts on a firm and a soft
surface; sold to BBA (Ireland) 96,000 gns Newmarket December Sales. *J.
Hindley.*

COUNTRY PRINCE 2 b.c. Town and Country 124–Dake (Floribunda 136) (1983   **74**
5s 7f 7f 7d 7fg) May 9; 10,000Y; small, useful-looking colt; half-brother to a winner
in Belgium; dam won from 5.5f to 1½m in France and also over jumps; quite a
moderate maiden; should stay 1¼m; acts on firm going. *R. Smyth.*

COUNTRY SONG 4 br. or gr.f. Pongee 106–Vulruska (Vulgan 123) (1982 NR   –
1983 17d) eighth foal; dam never ran; well tailed off in seller at Catterick in March.
T. Kersey.

COUNTY BROKER 3 b.g. Kashiwa 115–Ardrionn (Wolver Hollow 126) (1982   –
5fg* 5g* 5f⁴ 6d³ 6f³ 6g 5fg³(dis) 5g 5v 1983 5s 5fg 5f 5f 5fg) strong, good sort;
useful on his day in 1982 but didn't recover his form; apparently better suited by 6f
than 5f as a 2-y-o; acts on firm going; best with strong handling; trained until after
first outing by A. Jarvis. *P. Mitchell.*

COURAGEOUS BOY 2 br.c. Mansingh 120–Il Regalo (Meadow Mint 120) (1983   **57**
5fg 5fg 6g 6fg³) June 6; second foal; dam placed over 1m and 1¼m; 7 lengths third
of 15 to Mister Merlin in claiming race at Nottingham in October; stays 6f;
blinkered last 2 starts. *N. Guest.*

COURAGEOUS BUZBY 7 b.g. Communication 119–Courageous Chic 75 (Cash   **72**
and Courage 116) (1982 6f² 6f 5fg⁴ 6fg 6fg 6g 6f 5d* 6s 6s 5s 1983 6d 6d 5fg 5f* 5f
5.6f 5fg² 6h 5g² 5fg 5g³ 5g 5d*) workmanlike gelding; sprint handicapper; won at
Wolverhampton in July and Catterick in October; best at 5f nowadays; acts on any
going; occasionally sweats up; has been taken down early; usually wears a tongue
strap. *B. McMahon.*

COURT AND SPARK 2 ch.c. Relkino 131–Amadina 96 (Great Nephew 126)   **90**
(1983 6g 7f* 7fg² 7fg) Mar 29; 25,000Y; quite attractive, well-made colt; good
walker; second foal; half-brother to 7f to 10.5f winner Boldie (by Bold Lad, Ire);
dam, half-sister to very useful 1972 2-y-o Claudius, won from 6f to 8.5f; won
12-runner maiden race at Salisbury in July; ran well subsequently in nursery at
Goodwood and Somerville Tattersall Stakes at Newmarket; will be suited by
1m+; yet to race on a soft surface. *H. Candy.*

COURT CAVALIER 6 ch.g. Simbir 130–Rosenkavalier 88 (Vienna 127) (1982   **–**
NR 1983 13.8f) quite a modest handicapper at his best; tailed-off last only start at
6 yrs in July (needed run); stays 1¾m. *D. Yeoman.*

COURTFIELD (USA) 3 ch.g. Meadow Court 129–Front Page News (Dare Do   **67**
Well) (1982 NR 1983 8f 12f 11.7h⁴ 13fg⁴ 14d⁴ 13.3d⁴ 16g) lengthy, fair sort; first
known foal; dam never ran; ran respectably in varied races, including handicaps;
should be suited by long distances. *D. Arbuthnot.*

COURT GATE 3 ch.f. Hell's Gate 99–Court Amour 76 (Irish Ball 127) (1982 5g   **–**
7fg 1983 10h 9d) plain filly; in rear in sellers. *D. Wintle.*

COURT GOSSIP 2 ch.f. Imperial Fling 116–Babble On 79 (Acropolis 132) (1983   **–**
5.1fg 7f) May 10; 28,000Y; fair sort; good walker; half-sister to numerous
winners, including useful middle-distance performer Kings General (by St Paddy)
and useful 1979 2-y-o 6f and 1m winner Home Ground (by No Mercy); dam, sister
to Espresso, won at up to 11f; beaten some way in maiden races at Yarmouth in June
and Wolverhampton in July. *G. Pritchard-Gordon.*

COURT HUSSAR 2 b.f. Queen's Hussar 124–High Drama 90 (Hill Clown) (1983   **–**
8d 9g 10fg) May 14; quite well-made filly; third foal; dam stayed well; well beaten
in the autumn in £4,400 race at Goodwood (very backward) and maiden events at
Wolverhampton and Nottingham. *Mrs J. Reavey.*

COURTING SEASON 2 gr.c. Silly Season 127–Courting Day 90 (Right Boy   **103**
137) (1983 5s 6d³ 7f* 7f³ 7d 7fg⁴ 8fg³ 8s* 8s* 8d) May 29; 4,200Y; leggy, plain
colt; first living foal; dam won twice over 1m; successful in maiden auction event
at Catterick (apprentice ridden) in July and in quite valuable nurseries at
Doncaster and Ayr (8lb penalty) in September; well suited by 1m; acts on any
going but is in his element on soft; best efforts when ridden by N. Connorton;
sold 20,000 gns Doncaster November Sales. *C. Gray.*

COURT PROCEDURE (USA) 3 b.c. Valid Appeal–New Hat (Tim Tam) (1982   **68**
5d³ 5fg² 5.8f² 6fg 6d³ 6v² 6g 1983 6g²) small colt; placed 5 times in maiden
events as a 2-y-o; pick of paddock, wandered left and right under pressure when
½-length second to Qui Son in minor event at York in October on only outing of
1983; should stay beyond 6f; acts on any going; sold to NBA 7,200 gns
Newmarket Autumn Sales. *J. Tree.*

COUTURE LEG AFFAIR 2 b.f. Brigadier Gerard 144–Sera Sera 88 (Hill   **77**
Clown) (1983 5s 5g 6f 7s³ 8d) Mar 20; 4,700 2-y-o; rather lightly-built, narrow
filly; fourth foal; half-sister to 3-y-o 1m winner Whistle Hill (by So Blessed) and
11f winner Willerby (by Great Nephew); dam 7f winner; 2 lengths third of 16 to
Bamba in maiden race at Ayr in September; should stay 1m; acts well on soft
going. *R. Woodhouse.*

COWDENBEATH (USA) 6 b.h. Buffalo Lark–Intervene (Prince John) (1982   **54**
18g⁴ 14g 18.4g 14f³ 16.1f 17f* 16.5g 18.8g 16.9fg³ 16g 18d 20g 1983 14.6f 17f³
20.4g⁴) good-bodied, attractive horse; stays well; probably acts on any going but
goes well on a sound surface; ran well once when tried in blinkers; inconsistent.
R.Hollinshead.

COXWELL EAGLE 3 ch.g. Mandrake Major 122–My Bushbaby 100 (Hul a Hul   **75**
124) (1982 5g 6g* 7g 6g 6v 1983 5.8v 6d 6f³ 6f² 5.8h² 6f² 7f 6f* 7h 6g⁴ 6d) big,
strong gelding; won handicap at Hamilton in August; not certain to stay 7f; needs a

sound surface; usually blinkered nowadays, and has also worn a hood, but is effective without; trained by C. Nelson until after third outing. *M. Pipe.*

COY FIOLA 2 b.f. Decoy Boy 129–Fair Fiola (Green God 128) (1983 7.2g 8d) – Apr 26; 300Y; first foal; dam never ran; in rear in autumn sellers at Haydock and Warwick. *W. Clay.*

COY MAID 2 ch.f. Decoy Boy 129–Babe in the Wood (Athens Wood 126) (1983 5s 55 5s* 7f 6fg4 7f 6d) Mar 21; 800Y; second foal; dam ran only 3 times; bought in 1,500 gns after winning seller at Chepstow in May; stays 7f; acts on any going; sold 560 gns Doncaster October Sales. *M. Hinchliffe.*

COYOR (USA) 3 b.or br.c. Clev Er Tell–Bee's Oro (Ben Lomond) (1982 6g 1983 – 8f4 8fg4 10fg 12f2 16h 14g) big, good-topped colt; in frame in maiden and minor races, best effort when 2½ lengths second of 12 to Mikro Poulaki in a fast-run race at Leicester in August; suited by 1½m, but well beaten over further; doesn't look an ideal ride for an inexperienced rider; sold to R. Blakeney 4,100 gns Ascot October Sales. *D. Arbuthnot.*

CRACKERJILL 6 b.m. Sparkler 130–Token Girl 116 (Bolinas Boy) (1982 8f 8f – 7d 8g3 8fg 8v3 6s 1983 8d 10v 7f 8f) poor maiden; last in seller final start; stays 1m; has worn blinkers. *R. Carter.*

CRACKHILL 4 b.g. Legal Eagle 126–Mexican Music 71 (Aztec 128) (1982 7fg* – 9g* 8fg 8f2 8d 8d 9s 1983 10.2d4) lengthy, good-bodied gelding; fair performer at his best; ran respectably in amateur riders race only start at 4 yrs in March; stays 1¼m; seems to act on any going. *Miss S. Hall.*

CRADLE OF JAZZ (USA) 3 b.g. Verbatim–Louisiana (Nadir) (1982 7fg 7g3 88 1983 9d 11.5fg* 12f 10.1fg 11.5g) good-topped, attractive gelding; quickened up well to beat Kaprielian in pretty good style when odds on for 13-runner maiden race at Yarmouth in June; should stay at least 1½m; gelded after running below his best in blinkers fourth start, and ran badly on his return. *J. Hindley.*

CRAIGOUR 5 br.h. Mill Reef 141–Sudden Glory 98 (Luthier 126) (1982 9d 10.5fg 52 12d 12f 12s 10g 10fg* 10d 12d 9g4 10.5v 10.5s 10.5v 11d 1983 8d 10v 7s 10s 10g 7s 8fg 10g4 8f 16.5f 10f3 10f 8fg 9d) small horse; unreliable handicapper; stays 1½m; seems to act on any going; often blinkered; has worn a tongue strap. *C. Austin.*

CRAIG STEWART 2 b.c. Stanford 121§–Fanlight Fanny (Sky Gipsy 117) (1983 77 5s 6fg* 6fg3 6f 7g 6fg3 6fg) Mar 12; IR 8,200F, 10,000Y; good-bodied colt; third foal; dam ran once; heavily backed, made all in 22-runner seller (bought in 6,000 gns) at Windsor in June; not sure to stay 7f; acts on a firm surface; ran well in blinkers final start; consistent. *J. Sutcliffe.*

CRAMPON 2 br.c. Shirley Heights 130–Base Camp 80 (Derring-Do 131) (1983 100 7fg4 7f 8.2f*) Mar 14; tall, lengthy, attractive colt; good walker; first foal; dam won 3 times over 1¼m; overcame difficulties in running to beat Captain Singleton (gave 8lb) by ¾ length in £3,100 event at Haydock in September; had run moderately in maiden event at Goodwood on previous outing; well suited by test of stamina; acts on firm going; possibly requires galloping track. *R. Hern.*

CRAVEN BOY 2 b.g. Casino Boy 114–Freehay-Lady (Vimadee 120) (1983 5fg 7g – 8d) Apr 9; fifth reported foal; dam unraced; unquoted, in rear in maiden races in the Midlands; subsequently gelded. *R. Griffiths.*

CRAY 3 b.g. Mummy's Pet 125–Kiara (Great Nephew 126) (1982 6fg 6g 5g 7f 7s – 1983 7fg 10f 17f 16f) compact gelding; good mover; no form in 1983 (hampered third start); not at all sure to stay long distances; suited by an easy surface; hung under pressure when tried in blinkers on final appearance at 2 yrs. *P. Felgate.*

CREAG-AN-SGOR 2 b.c. Captain James 123–Happy Thought 57 (Kauai King) 122 (1983 6f4 6f* 6f2 7g4 6fg*)
The May issue of *Pacemaker* published an interesting table listing the top-priced yearlings at the 1982 sales. It showed that forty-one yearlings were bought for the equivalent of 110,000 guineas or more in Britain and Ireland and that twenty-six European-bound yearlings fetched a minimum of 750,000 dollars in America. No doubt many of these animals, which include Rainbow Quest, Sicyos and Trojan Fen, will retire with their value increased but it's most unlikely that they will win anything approaching their cost during their racecourse careers. At the end of 1983 the position was that the European group, which cost the equivalent of 8,069,602 guineas, had produced nine winners of fifteen races worth about £66,200 while of the American group, whose total cost was 35,345,000 dollars, seven have won eight races worth approximately £21,800. Ironically three of the four William Hill sponsored Group 1 juvenile events in the autumn fell to animals bought

William Hill Middle Park Stakes, Newmarket—Creag-An-Sgor holds on strongly from Superlative and odds-on Vacarme (left)

relatively cheaply at auction, the Cheveley Park winner Desirable for only 10,000 Irish guineas, the Futurity winner Alphabatim for just 23,000 dollars and the Middle Park victor Creag-An-Sgor for 20,000 Irish guineas.

Creag-An-Sgor's success in the Middle Park in September provided one of the biggest surprises of the season. He had won only one of his four previous starts, a maiden race, and at 50/1 was the rank outsider in a nine-strong field which included the odds-on Vacarme, fresh from a decisive victory in the Mill Reef Stakes; Superlative, who numbered both the July Stakes and the Flying Childers Stakes among his successes; the Irish challenger Hegemony who hadn't been out since finishing an honourable second in the Coventry Stakes; and other pattern race winners in Water Moccasin and Executive Man, successful respectively in the Zukunfts-Rennen and the Premio Primi Passi, and Godstone, who had been awarded the Richmond Stakes amid great controversy. Creag-An-Sgor beat them all decisively, in thoroughly workmanlike style. His rider Cauthen, who had forced Desirable up on the line in the Cheveley Park the day before, used completely different tactics here, taking Creag-An-Sgor to the front from Superlative and Godstone soon after the start. Coming to the last quarter mile Creag-An-Sgor responded well when asked to quicken the pace, so much so that his rivals were in trouble from then on. Vacarme managed to reach his heels entering the final furlong but Creag-An-Sgor proved much the stronger up the hill and crossed the line a length and a half ahead of Superlative, who rallied to pip Vacarme on the post.

This very smart display marked a distinct improvement on Creag-An-Sgor's previous form. It had taken him a while to realise fully what was required of him. On his debut at York in June he was a little coltish in the paddock and when returned to the same course the following month for the Philip Cornes Nickel Alloys maiden he nearly threw away his chance of success by hanging to the left. Although in the end he managed to repel Bounty Hawk's challenge by a head, we thought him somewhat fortunate to survive an inquiry. He wasn't so lucky in the very valuable OCL Richmond Stakes at Goodwood later in July. There, while Vacarme was bursting through most impressively to beat him by three quarters of a length, Creag-An-Sgor drifted to his right in the closing stages, hampering the long-time leader Godstone whose rider promptly objected on the grounds of bumping and boring. The stewards sustained the objection, promoting Godstone ahead of Creag-An-Sgor and at the same time disqualifying Vacarme outright for a separate offence. Creag-An-Sgor next tried seven furlongs for the only time in the Laurent Perrier Champagne Stakes at Doncaster in September. In finishing last of four, over eleven lengths behind Lear Fan, he ran well below form. The way he began to struggle before he'd even reached the two-furlong marker suggested that the distance wasn't the cause, or at least not the sole cause, of his poor effort and a different explanation came to light after the Middle Park. His trainer told the Newmarket stewards that Creag-An-Sgor had jarred himself slightly at Goodwood and consequently had had an interrupted preparation.

There is no reason on breeding why Creag-An-Sgor shouldn't stay seven

Mrs W. Tulloch's "Creag-An-Sgor"

furlongs or a mile as a three-year-old; his sire Captain James won the Waterford Crystal Mile and his dam Happy Thought seemed to stay a mile and three quarters. Creag-An-Sgor is easily the best representative so far of Captain James, who was sent to stand in the USA in 1983 after finishing well down the 1982 list of first-season sires. Happy Thought's previous foal is the fairly useful Tulsa Flyer (by He Loves Me) who stays a mile and a quarter well despite being a free-running sort like his half-brother. Happy Thought didn't have the ability to match her good looks and attractive pedigree and was sold out of training in 1976 for only 5,000 guineas, changing hands again two years later for 11,000 guineas when carrying Tulsa Flyer. She has proved well worth 11,000 guineas; Tulsa Flyer and Creag-An-Sgor were sold for 29,000 and 20,000 Irish guineas respectively as yearlings and her next foal, a yearling filly by Ile de Bourbon, must now be very valuable. Happy Thought is a half-sister to the St Leger fourth Stetchworth and a daughter of the very useful Grenadiere, who was second in both the Lancashire Oaks and the Cesarewitch as a three-year-old. Several of Grenadiere's half-sisters were also good performers with Full Dress II winning the One Thousand Guineas, Reload the Park Hill Stakes and Boulette taking second place in the Park Hill.

Creag-An-Sgor (b.c. Mar 25, 1981)	Captain James (b 1974)	Captain's Gig (br 1965)	Turn-to Make Sail
		Aliceva (b 1966)	Alcide Feevagh
	Happy Thought (b 1973)	Kauai King (b 1963)	Native Dancer Sweep In
		Grenadiere (ch 1967)	Right Royal V Fusil

Creag-An-Sgor, a rangy colt, looks the type to train on and if he can maintain the improvement he showed in the Middle Park he must figure prominently in the top races at around a mile. As yet he has raced only on a sound surface. It's worth pointing out that he was ridden by Cauthen when putting up his best efforts. *C. Nelson.*

CREE BAY 4 b.g. Bay Express 132–Porsanger (Zeddaan 130) (1982 5f 5f 5f 5f* 5fg* 5g³ 5g* 5fg* 5f* 5fg* 5.8f³ 5g² 5.6g 5g 5s* 5s 1983 5v 5g⁴ 5f⁴ 6f 5f 6f 5fg 5f 5.8fg³ 5fg² 5d⁴ 5s³ 5g³ 6fg) useful-looking gelding; sprint handicapper; ran creditably in second half of season; best at 5f; acts on any going; blinkered once at 2 yrs. *J. Spearing.* **87**

CREE SONG 7 b.h. Song 132–Gentle Gael 97 (Celtic Ash) (1982 6fg 5fg³ 6f* 6fg⁴ 6d 5f² 5fg⁴ 1983 5v² 5v³ 5s² 6v 5f⁴ 6f) strong horse; poor mover in his slower paces; sprint handicapper; didn't battle it out so well as winner when neck second to Bri-Eden in David Dixon Sprint Trophy at York in May on third start; stays 6f; acts on any going; effective with and without blinkers. *P. Calver.* **81**

CREETOWER 2 b.c. Creetown 123–Sally Light Foot (Hul a Hul 124) (1983 8s 8fg 8.2s) May 7; big colt; half-brother to at least 2 poor animals in Holland; dam in frame from 5f to 1m in Ireland; in rear in maiden races. *C. Brittain.* **–**

CREG-NA-BAA 4 b.g. Imperial Crown 96–Rose of France 83 (Grand Roi 118) (1982 10d 8d 7fg 1983 10d) small, lightly-made gelding; behind in maiden races and sellers. *D. Jermy.* **–**

CREMATION 3 b.c. Ashmore 125–Sacred Ibis (Red God 128§) (1982 5g² 5f* 6g² 6fg² 7fg⁴ 6f³ 7fg² 8s² 8g⁴(dis) 1983 7d 7s* 8v 8f 7fg 9g 8g) close-coupled Irish colt; keen walker; excelled himself when 20/1 for 5-runner McCairns Trial Stakes at Phoenix Park in April, forcing a dead-heat with odds-on Ancestral; ran far better than finishing position suggests when seventh of 10 to Wassl in Airlie/Coolmore Irish 2000 Guineas at the Curragh the following month, but was soundly beaten afterwards; stays 1m; acts on any going. *M. Connolly, Ireland.* **101**

CREMETS 2 b.f. Mummy's Pet 125–Rennet 109 (King's Bench 132) (1983 5g⁴ 6d*) Apr 8; well-made, good sort; sister to 5 winners, including high-class sprinter Runnett, very useful 1979 2-y-o 5f performer Cala-Vadella and useful 3-y-o sprinter Rutland, and half-sister to 3 more; dam stayed 1¼m; well-backed favourite, won maiden race at Newbury in October by 2 lengths from Saturnian; stays 6f well; is a useful sprinter in the making. *J. Dunlop.* **94 p**

CRESTED LARK 7 ch.h. Crowned Prince 128–Bird of Dawning (Sea-Bird II 145) (1982 12d* 12d 13fg* 12f* 12g 12fg 1983 12g 12g 12f* 13g 14f*) big, rangy horse; genuine front-running handicapper who won at Salisbury in July and Sandown in August; stayed 1¾m; ideally suited by top-of-the-ground; standing at Kingshill Stud, Warwickshire. *M. Smyly.* **78**

CRI DE COEUR (USA) 2 ch.f. Lyphard 132–Weeping Well (Dike) (1983 6f 7f³ 6f 7f 8fg³ 9f*) Mar 22; $150,000Y; smallish, lightly-made filly; second foal; dam, half-sister to very smart Delmora, won over 1m at 2 yrs in France; showed improved form when given a stiff test of stamina and came out best in tight finish to 13-runner maiden event at Redcar in October; acts on firm going. *F. Durr.* **82**

CRIGGELLE 3 ch.f. Blue Cashmere 129–Balholm 61 (Le Levanstell 122) (1982 NR 1983 8f.9fg 10s) strong filly; half-sister to 2 winning platers; dam ran only 3 times; not disgraced in maiden races at Doncaster in July (running-on ninth of 18 to Valerio) and York in September (fifth of 7 to Fluke) on first 2 outings; sold 1,800 gns Doncaster November Sales. *P. Asquith.* **–**

CRIME OF PASSION 3 b.f. Dragonara Palace 115–Catriona 96 (Sing Sing134) (1982 5g* 5f* 5fg² 6f* 5.5g³ 5g² 1983 8d 5d 5f 5fg) lengthy, workmanlike filly; a smart performer at 2 yrs, who won 3 of her 6 races, including Cherry Hinton Stakes at Newmarket; raced in top company in 1983 and didn't recover her form, although showing good speed on occasions; most unlikely to stay beyond 6f; acts well on firm going; hampered at start when blinkered final outing. *R. Laing.* **–**

CRIMSON KNIGHT 4 b.g. Blushing Groom131–Sirnelta (Sir Tor) (1982 7.2h 10s³ 1983 12g² 10s⁴ 12g³ 12g 15.8fg) leggy, rather lightly-made gelding; excellent mover; won handicap at Thirsk in April; suited by 1½m but isn't sure to get 2m; suited by some give in the ground; has run respectably for an apprentice; sold 4,600 gns Newmarket September Sales. *F. J. Houghton.* **73**

CRIMSON QUEEN 2 b.f. Crimson Beau 124–Noor 76 (Mill Reef 141) (1983 7f 8g 8.2fg 8d) Mar 4; 8,500F, 6,200Y; fair sort; first foal; dam, daughter of Cheshire Oaks winner Yelda, won over 1¼m at 2 yrs; poor plater; best form in non-seller on first outing; will stay 1¼m. *P. Cole.* **49**

CRISP 2 b.c. Sallust 134–Arctic Lace 106 (Arctic Chevalier) (1983 6g 8d²) May 10; IR 30,000Y; half-brother to 4 winners, notably high-class 7f to 13.4f winner **87**

Oats (by Northfields); dam third in Irish 1000 Guineas; second favourite, had rest well beaten off when 2 lengths second of 19 to Librate in maiden event at Warwick in October; will probably stay beyond 1m; sure to win at the minor meetings. *J. Tree.*

CRISP AND KEEN   5 ch.m. Crisp and Even 116–Anxious Coin (Prince Silver 98)   **43** (1982 NR 1983 10.6s 10f 10fg 8g 9fg² 12f) plater; stays 9f; seems to act on any going; has run respectably for an apprentice; has sweated up; sometimes bandaged. *L. Barratt.*

CRISPIN   6 b.g. Welsh Pageant 132–Syrona 113 (Salvo 129) (1982 NR 1983 14s   **79** 14s³ 13.3g 16f 16f⁴ 16f⁴ 17d⁴ 16fg 16.1g 16.1s) attractive gelding; staying handicapper; acts on any going; blinkered last 2 starts; suitable mount for an inexperienced rider nowadays (used to hang under pressure on occasions). *J. Dunlop.*

CRISTALGA   3 br.f. High Top 131–Coralivia (Le Levanstell 122) (1982 6fg 7g³   **90** 7d² 1983 7s³ 10s* 12fg 12g⁴ 12g 12d⁴ 12fg² 12fg) medium-sized, quite attractive filly; good walker; won maiden event at Leicester in May; not all that consistent afterwards, but ran very well when second to Both Ends Burning in handicap at Newmarket in October (was closing fast on winner at the end); will be suited by further than 1½m; seems to act on any going. *G. Pritchard-Gordon.*

CRITERION   4 b.c. Royal Palace131–Climbing Rose 81 (Pirate King 129) (1982   **98** 10.6s* 12g* 12fg⁴ 12fg 10g³ 10fg* 11.1fg³ 10fg⁴ 12d² 10d 1983 10s 10d 12f⁴ 11f 12f) tall, quite attractive colt; a smart and game performer at 3 yrs; mainly disappointing in 1983, putting up best effort when over 14 lengths fourth of 10 to Stanerra in Hardwicke Stakes at Royal Ascot; stayed 1½m; seemed to act on any going; had run well when sweating up; dead. *G. Harwood.*

CRITICAL PATH   4 ch.g. Shiny Tenth 120–Tamaqua 69 (Tamerlane 128) (1982   **–** 8d 10f 12f* 12fg² 13d 12v² 12d 1983 17.1g 16g 12f) big, strong gelding; plater; suited by 1½m; acts on any going; suitable mount for an inexperienced rider. *G. Balding.*

CROCSOX   2 b.c. Mandamus 120–Tavaro (Gustav 121) (1983 5v⁴ 5d 5d³ 8g) Mar   **65** 31; third foal; dam won in Norway; beaten around 5 lengths in 3 maiden and minor events in the spring, and was then off course until October; should stay 1m. *H. O'Neill.*

CROGHAN HILL   8 b.h. Lord Gayle 124–Good Report (Golden Cloud) (1982   **97** 10d 16fg⁴ 12g² 16fg⁴ 11.5g* 11d 12g 12s 1983 12s* 10s* 10s⁴ 16s 12s*) tall, leggy Irish horse; useful performer; won Mooresbridge Stakes at the Curragh in March (beat Standing Ovation 2 lengths), Camas Park Stud Stakes at Phoenix Park in April (gamely beat Love Tangle by 3 lengths) and minor event at Limerick Junction in June; effective from 1¼m to 2m but didn't stay extreme distances; acted on any going; consistent; stud. *D.K. Weld, Ireland.*

CROONTIME   2 ch.g. Crooner 119–Coffee Bob (Espresso 122) (1983 6fg 8g)   **–** Apr 28; attractive, stocky gelding; first living foal; dam winning hurdler; in rear in well-contested minor events at Goodwood in August and September; sold 640 gns Ascot November Sales. *A. Moore.*

CROOZA   2 ch.c. Crooner119–Zanya 70 (Will Somers 114§) (1983 5fg 6fg) Apr   **–** 25; small, sturdy colt; first foal; dam at her best at 2 yrs when placed over 5f; behind in August in maiden race (slowly away) at Windsor and minor event (blinkered, soon tailed off) at Goodwood; sold 370 gns Ascot November Sales. *P. Butler.*

CROSBY HILL   2 b.c. Frimley Park 109–Spring Walk (Tower Walk 130) (1983 5s   **76** 5fg 5f⁴ 5.8h 5f* 5h*) Apr 2; well-made colt; first reported foal; dam never ran; successful in nurseries at Windsor in July and Nottingham in August; probably best at 5f; acts on hard going; best in blinkers. *K. Brassey.*

CROSBY LOVE   2 br.f. He Loves Me 120–Primed (Primera 131) (1983 5f 6f 8f)   **–** Apr 24; 5,800F, 1,000Y; lightly-built filly; half-sister to several winners, including 1¼m and 1¾m winner Georgina Girl (by Prince Tenderfoot); dam well bred but of little account; no sign of ability in maiden company. *J. Carr.*

CROSS FARM BOY   2 ch.g. Manor Farm Boy 114–Beyond The Rainbow (Royal   **52** Palace 131) (1983 5d 5d 5s³ 6f³ 6f 6f² 6fg 5fg 6g³ 7f 7g 6s) Apr 25; IR 1,800Y; small gelding; poor walker; quite a moderate plater; best form at 6f on a sound surface; blinkered fifth and twelfth starts; retained by trainer 500 gns Doncaster October Sales. *J. Wilson.*

CROSSWAYS 4 b.c. Habitat 134–Silky 112 (Nijinsky 138) (1982 9fg³ 10fg² 10f* 8f **100** d
11g 12g 10d 10g 1983 8d⁴ 8d 8s* 8f 9f 8f 9fg 8d) strong, good-bodied, good-looking
colt; useful performer at his best but is inconsistent; got the better of Felthorpe
Mariner by a neck in Hambleton Stakes (Handicap) at York in May; had previously
run very well from an unfavourable draw in William Hill Lincoln Handicap at
Doncaster, finishing clear of stand-side runners when fourth of 26 to Mighty Fly;
effective at 1m when conditions are testing and stays 11f; acts on any going;
blinkered last 2 outings in 1982; has twice run moderately when sweating up badly;
coltish in paddock fourth start; sold to BBA 30,000 gns Newmarket December
Sales. *G. Wragg.*

CROWDOWN 5 ch.g. Morston 125–Barlassina (Taine 131) (1982 NR 1983 –
15.5f) poor performer. *D. Mills.*

CROWFOOT'S COUTURE 2 ch.c. Sweet Revenge 129–Soft Moss **79**
(Santamoss 110) (1983 5s 5v³ 5s⁴ 5d 5d 5fg 5fg³ 5f² 5fg 5fg⁴ 5fg² 6f) Apr 28; IR
2,600F, 2,500Y (privately); small, strong, lengthy colt; third produce; half-brother
to 1981 Irish 2-y-o 6f winner Duncor (by Furry Glen); dam poor Irish maiden; in
frame in varied company, on final occasion looking unlucky to go down by short head
to Sing To Me, after being switched over 1f out, in 6-runner nursery at Goodwood
in August; not disgraced over 6f; best form on a firm surface; blinkered fifth outing.
P. Brookshaw.

CROWN 4 b.c. Realm 129–Moneycashen 72 (Hook Money 124) (1982 8g 8s³ 8d* **91**
7g* 8.2d⁴ 7fg* 8fg³ 7.2g² 7fg 8s* 8v 1983 8s⁴ 7v³ 8v 9fg 8fg 9g 8fg³) sturdy,
compact colt; fair handicapper at his best; possibly does not stay 9f; acts on a firm
surface but is ideally suited by some give in the ground; blinkered once at 2 yrs;
sometimes makes the running; racing in USA. *C. Booth.*

CROWN AND SCEPTRE 2 b.f. Sparkler 130–Circlet 97 (Baldric II 131) (1983 –
7fg) Mar 22; quite attractive filly; third foal; half-sister to fairly useful
middle-distance winner Round Tower (by High Top); dam, half-sister to 1000
Guineas and French Oaks winner Highclere, stayed 1½m; 20/1, moved badly to
start but showed up for 4f in 22-runner maiden race won by Travel Away at
Newmarket in October. *I. Balding.*

CROWN COUNSEL 4 ch.g. Simbir 130–Edie's Court (Barron's Court) (1982 12fg **66**
14fg 11g 8fg* 8fg³ 8fg 10.6s 1983 8d 8f* 8fg 7f 8f³ 8s) big gelding; poor walker;
returned to form when decisively winning lady riders handicap at Redcar in June;
suited by 1m; acts well on fast ground; sweated up quite badly third start; suitable
mount for an inexperienced rider; inconsistent. *P. Feilden.*

CROWN EAGLE (USA) 2 b.c. Crow 134–Pile (Bald Eagle 119) (1983 7f⁴ 7f² **79**
7f⁴ 7f) Mar 19; $110,000Y; small, close-coupled colt; half-brother to several
winners, including smart middle-distance performer Paico (by Silly Season) and
very useful American stakes winner Polynesienne (by Relko); dam quite a useful
miler in France; moderate maiden; not seen out again after sweating up and running
poorly (out of first 10 of 17) behind Lake Valentina at Newbury in August; should
stay 1¼m; acts on firm going. *D. Elsworth.*

CROWN GODIVA 3 b. or br.f. Godswalk 130–Princess Tiara 111 (Crowned **83**
Prince 128) (1982 NR 1983 8f* 8f 7f 7.2g³ 10.5d³) quite an attractive filly;
second foal; half-sister to smart French 7f to 1¼m winner What A Guest (by Be
My Guest); dam won over 7f at 2 yrs and appeared to stay 1¼m at 3 yrs; favourite
but looking as if race would do her good when comfortably winning maiden race at
Newbury in July; third afterwards in handicaps at Haydock (didn't handle bend
well) and York; stays 1¼m; yet to race on really soft going, but acts on any other;
had stiff task second outing and a poor run on third. *B. Hills.*

CRUMBLE 3 b.f. Thatch 136–Small Dessert (Derring-Do 131) (1982 5g² 5g² **82**
1983 6d* 7fg 6fg² 6f) neat filly; made a highly impressive reappearance in maiden
event at Pontefract in April, jumping out smartly, and winning as she liked by 10
lengths from Gale Boy; ran creditably under top weight in handicaps next 2 outings,
including ½-length second to Memoria In Eterna at Nottingham in July; bred to stay
1m; acts on a firm and a soft surface; sold to NBA 4,800 gns Newmarket December
Sales. *B. Hobbs.*

CRUNCHER 3 b.g. Tachypous 128–Marphousha (Only for Life 126) (1982 6f 6g⁴
6g³ 7f³ 8.2fg² 8.2d 10d³ 1983 12d² 16fg 16f⁴) big gelding; has a growth above
off-fore knee; in frame in sellers and a maiden race; stays well; yet to race on really
soft going but acts on any other. *W. Wharton.*

CRUSADER CASTLE (USA) 4 ch.c. The Minstrel 135–Mille Fleurs 100 **117**
(Jacinto) (1982 11g 12f² 14g² 14d* 12f² 14f² 14fg² 14.6g 14v* 14v 1983 17.1d* 14v

Lonsdale Stakes, York—Crusader Castle wins from Voyant

16.1v² 16f⁴ 15fg 21f⁴ 16g*) big, handsome colt; easily justified long odds-on favouritism in minor event at Pontefract in April and put up a fine display when giving weight all round in Lonsdale Stakes at York in August, leading 1f out and staying on well to beat Voyant by 2½ lengths; in frame in between in minor event at Haydock, Miner's Northumberland Plate at Newcastle (2½ lengths fourth of 14 to Weavers' Pin under top weight) and Goodwood Cup (remote fourth to Little Wolf); suited by a test of stamina; acted well on any going but revelled in the mud; sometimes bandaged off-hind; not particularly consistent; fractured a cannon bone in autumn and has been retired. *I. Balding.*

CRYMLYN 3 b.f. Welsh Pageant 132–Cribyn 96 (Brigadier Gerard 144) (1982 6g **68** 1983 8f 8f 8fg 7s 6fg) lengthy, useful-looking filly; fifth in maiden company at Doncaster, Goodwood, Yarmouth and Nottingham on last 4 starts; will be suited by a return to 1m or more. *C. Brittain.*

CRYSTAL DANCER 2 ro.f. Roan Rocket 128–Targuette (Targowice 130) (1983 **38** 5v 5s⁴ 5v 5v) very small filly; first foal; dam poor plater; bad plater; not raced after May. *C. Wildman.*

CRYSTAL GLITTERS (USA) 3 b.c. Blushing Groom 131–Tales To Tell **127** (Donut King) (1982 6g* 7f³ 6.5d* 7s³ 1983 8s⁴ 8v² 8v⁴ 9.2d* 8f 8g 10fg)
In terms of races won Crystal Glitters experienced a lean season for a horse of his ability; his splendid performance in the Prix d'Ispahan at Longchamp in June turned out to be his only winning one in seven starts. The main reason for this state of affairs is that he was kept regularly in the best company. He wasn't the leading miler in France and there were several better in Europe. Furthermore he didn't always show top form when he needed to—the victim of sheer bad luck on one occasion, and excused by his connections on three others. Crystal Glitters had no chance of showing his worth in the Dubai Champion Stakes at Newmarket in October in his final appearance, since his jockey Saint-Martin had to ride without irons for most of the journey. According to his connections Crystal Glitters had

210

suffered from more than his share of misfortune before that. He carried a throat infection on returning from Ireland in May, where he had been a somewhat disappointing fourth in the Airlie/Coolmore Irish Two Thousand Guineas, almost four lengths down on Wassl, unable to quicken over the last three furlongs; he ran a temperature after finishing a respectable seventh of ten to Luth Enchantee in the Prix Jacques le Marois at Deauville in August, and he was found to be lame after finishing a well-beaten seventh of eight to the same filly in the Prix du Moulin de Longchamp.

A good horse at two—he'd beaten Drumalis in the Prix Eclipse and been placed in the Prix de la Salamandre and Criterium de Maisons-Laffitte—Crystal Glitters thrust himself bang into the reckoning for the Irish Guineas with a very promising display in the French equivalent, the Poule d'Essai des Poulains, three weeks earlier. Longest priced bar two, at 33/1, he was always close up with the eventual winner L'Émigrant and kept on well for second place; he went down by only a length and beat the fourth-placed English runner Sackford by almost two. Following his defeat in Ireland, where he was pick of the paddock incidentally and started 9/2 second favourite to Lomond, Crystal Glitters couldn't be given much chance of turning the tables in the Prix d'Ispahan on L'Emigrant, who'd since finished second in the French Derby. He could be given less if there was anything at all in his trainer's improbable assertion that fast ground suited the horse best. Torrential rain which had begun before the preceding Grand Prix de Paris continued unabated, delaying the start of the Prix d'Ispahan for fifteen minutes and, more importantly, softening the ground. When the race did get under way Crystal Glitters for once enjoyed a stroke of good fortune, in as much as the odds-on favourite L'Emigrant wasn't given a good ride and several of the others met trouble in running. The first to run into trouble was a horse of no consequence, Soliloquy, who missed the break and then hit the rails when attempting to assume his role of pacemaker for L'Emigrant, badly hampering the Premio Emilio Turati winner Bold Run. The pacemaker's job fell instead to Darly: he was a very useful customer, second to Pampabird in the Prix du Chemin de Fer du Nord and third to Welsh Term in the Prix Dollar, and he set a scorching gallop the others ignored at their peril. Saint-Martin, replacing the stable-jockey Gibert on Crystal Glitters, had no intention of ignoring Darly; he tracked him down the hill. Crystal Glitters always seemed at ease in the strongly-run race and halfway up the straight was able first to take over the lead and then draw clear of Darly who wasn't exactly stopping despite all his hard work. At the point the winner went on L'Emigrant had an enormous amount of ground to make up. No challenge materialised from any of the others, who included Pampabird, Drumalis, the French Oaks fourth Right Bank, the Epsom Derby seventh Pluralisme and the horse who'd beaten Diesis at Kempton, The Noble Player. Crystal Glitters ran on strongly to win by three lengths from Darly, with L'Emigrant a good third in the circumstances, a head further behind. This impressive display from Crystal Glitters made it all the more disappointing that he should go through the rest of his season without gaining so much as a place.

Crystal Glitters is another racehorse well bought by his owner, Mr Fustok; he cost 105,000 dollars. Previous shrewd purchases we can think of are the Turf Classic winner Anifa (62,000 dollars), the Poulains winner In Fijar (36,000 dollars), the outstanding Green Forest (100,000 dollars), the Cadran winner El Badr (17,000 guineas) and the top miler Hilal (9,000 guineas). Crystal Glitters was bought at the Keeneland Yearling Sales, a quite well-bred colt by Blushing Groom (covering fee in 1979 in his second season at stud 35,000 dollars, fee in 1984 200,000 dollars) out of

Prix d'Ispahan, Longchamp—a clear win for Crystal Glitters over Darly (rails) and L'Emigrant

a stakes-winning winner-producer. Crystal Glitters' dam won several races at up to a mile in the United States, among them the California Oaks at Golden Gate. She was one of the better representatives of her whimsically-named sire Donut King, a tough stakes-winning contemporary of Jaipur, Crimson Satan and Sir Ivor's sire Sir Gaylord, all of whom he beat over a mile as a two-year-old. None of Tales To Tell's four previous winners, all in the United States, was remotely in the same league as Crystal Glitters. The second dam, a minor sprint winner, produced another stakes winner to Donut King; he was called Modern Spirit and proved to be one of his sire's biggest money-earners with just over 100,000 dollars. Probably the best runner produced by the second dam, though, was Shake A Leg, the dam of none other than Danzatore who appeared in the same Keeneland catalogue as Crystal Glitters.

Crystal Glitters (USA) (b.c. 1980)	Blushing Groom (ch 1974)	Red God (ch 1954)	Nasrullah Spring Run
		Runaway Bride (b 1962)	Wild Risk Aimee
	Tales To Tell (b 1967)	Donut King (br 1959)	Determine Strayed
		Fleeting Doll (b 1961)	Fleet Nasrullah Chinese Doll

Crystal Glitters is a well-made colt. Nine furlongs suits him so well that he's sure to stay a mile and a quarter and may be worth a chance at an even longer distance. He acts on any going. *M. Saliba, France.*

CRY TO THE MOON 3 b.f. Ballad Rock 122–Wolveriana 78 (Wolver Hollow 126) (1982 NR 1983 7d) lengthy filly; first foal; dam 1m winner; never promised to take a hand when remote tenth of 11 behind Malacca Street in newcomers race at Doncaster in March. *J. Winter.* —

CUBIC ZIRCONIA 3 b. or br.g. Averof 123–Whistling Waltz (Whistler 129) (1982 5fg² 5g³ 5fg* 5fg³ 6f³ 7g⁴ 7g 8.2g 8g 1983 12s* 12s 11d³ 14d⁴ 13.1f 12g² 12d 12.2g³) rather leggy gelding; won claiming race at Leicester in March, and was subsequently placed in handicaps; suited by 1½m and is well worth another chance over further; acts on any going but seems suited by some give underfoot nowadays; blinkered final outing in 1982. *R. Williams.* 61

CUDGEL 10 br.g. The Brianstan 128–Pelta (Border Chief 101) (1982 6f⁴ 5fg³ 6g 6f⁴ 6fg 6d³ 7g³ 8f⁴ 7s 6s 1983 6v⁴ 6s 7d 6d* 7.6fg 6f 6fg 6h 6s 6f) one-time fairly useful handicapper; won apprentice event at Ayr in June; stays 1m but has done all his winning at shorter distances; acts on any going; ideal mount for an inexperienced rider; has won 5 times at Redcar. *P. Rohan.* 78 d

CUE-T-MISS 2 b.f. Leander 119–Lady Alexandra (Czar Alexander 112) (1983 5d 5v 6f 7f) May 29; small filly; bad plater; not raced after July. *R. Ward.* —

CULLEN'S EAGLE 2 br.c. Legal Eagle 126–Megans Girl 58 (Workboy 123) (1983 5v 6fg 6fg 5f 6h 7f) Mar 12; 350Y; bad plater; blinkered first two starts. *K. Bridgwater.* —

CULMINATE 2 br.c. African Sky 124–Metrovision (Golden Vision 105) (1983 6s 5g 6d) May 7; 3,200Y; leggy, rather narrow colt; half-brother to several winners, including Ébor winner Anji (by Gulf Pearl); dam poor middle-distance maiden; behind in minor and maiden events. *D. Plant.* —

CUMREW 3 b.g. Gunner B 126–Almadena 73 (Dairialatan 111) (1982 7d 7fg 7g 1983 8g 10fg 10g* 10f 10f) useful-looking gelding; good walker; beat Élite Syncopation in great style by 6 lengths in £4,800 handicap at Newmarket in July (ridden by 5-lb claimer); stays 1¼m; possibly not at his best on really firm ground. *N. Vigors.* 77

CUMULUS 5 br.h. Relko 136–Nuageuse (Prince Regent 129) (1982 6fg⁴ 6f* 7g³ 7fg⁴ 7g 7fg³ 7d 7f³ 7.2s³ 1983 8d 10v 8s 8d³ 10fg) strong, compact, good-bodied horse; poor walker; stays 1m; acts on any going; has run creditably for an apprentice. *R. Atkins.*

CUNARD 8 gr.h. Crooner 119–Emerald Flag 77 (St Paddy 133) (1982 NR 1983 15fg) one-time very useful middle-distance handicapper; tailed off only start at 8 yrs in November; acts on any going but is ideally suited by top-of-the-ground. *J. S. Wilson.* —

CURRAVILLA 3 gr.c. Nishapour 125–Domination (Luthier 126) (1982 5f* 8d³ 8s⁴ 1983 6s⁴ 6s³ 6v* 5d⁴ 6f² 6f⁴ 6.5fg) leggy, rather lightly-made colt; has a round action; developed into a smart performer; quickened to lead below distance 115

Mrs M. Togher's "Curravilla"

after being held up when beating Doc Marten fairly comfortably by a length in 10-runner CBA Greenlands Stakes at the Curragh in May; in frame most other starts, running extremely well on fifth when short-head second of 17 to Sylvan Barbarosa in Cork and Orrery Stakes at Royal Ascot in June; ran creditably over 1m as a 2-y-o but is evidently regarded as a sprinter; acts on any going. *J. Oxx, Ireland.*

CURRENT RAISER 3 b.f. Filiberto 123–Miss Budock Vean (Never Say Die **108** 137) (1982 6g 7fg 7g 6d 7g^2 1983 8v^4 7.3s 10d 12v* 12g 12fg^2 14fg^4 14.6fg) big, lengthy filly; second foal; dam poor maiden; 33/1, settled better than before and showed much improved form when beating Mytinia in good style by 6 lengths in 8-runner Lupe Stakes at Goodwood in May; ran easily best subsequent race when 1½ lengths second of 14 behind High Hawk in Ribblesdale Stakes at Royal Ascot; suited by 1½m and promises to stay further; yet to race on really firm going, but acts on any other; bandaged in front and moved badly to start seventh outing. *C. Brittain.*

CURZO 2 ch.c. Bolkonski 134–Quibala 83 (Crepello 136) (1983 7fg) Mar 25; IR — 17,000Y; big, fair sort; third foal; half-brother to a winner in French Provinces; dam, middle-distance winner, is a half-sister to top-class sprinter Realm; unquoted and burly, moved badly to start and finished some way behind in 30-runner maiden race at Newmarket in August. *P. Calver.*

CURZON HOUSE 6 ch.m. Green God 128–Laburnum Grove 70 (Pall Mall 132) — (1982 6d 5d 5fg^3 5f^4 6f 5g 6fg 5g 5fg 5.8f 1983 5s 7s 5.8s 6d 5f 6h 5.8h 5s) short-coupled mare; sprint plater; probably acts on any going; sometimes blinkered. *J. Perrett.*

CUTACROSS (USA) 3 b.g. Cutlass–Mother Superior (Bold Ruler) (1982 5fg –
7fg 1983 7s 7v³ 10s 7s 8.2g) quite attractive, well-made gelding; good walker;
stays 7f; trained until after third start by G. Harwood. *A. Potts.*

CUTE FACE 3 ch.g. High Award 119–Consequently 101 (Con Brio 121) (1982 5fg –
5d 5d 1983 6v 5v 6v 5s⁴ 5f 7f 6f 10.6g 8d 6fg) plain gelding; best form at 5f; acts on
any going; trained by D. Leslie until after seventh outing. *J. Smith.*

CUTLERS CORNER 2 ch.f. Sharpen Up 127–Solar 120 (Hotfoot 126) (1983 **81**
5d³ 5f 5f* 5g) big, rangy filly with plenty of scope; good mover; fourth foal;
half-sister to 3-y-o 1¼m winner Harbour Bridge (by Blakeney) and useful 1980
2-y-o 5f winner Ashbrittle (by Great Nephew), subsequently successful in USA;
dam, one of leading 2-y-o fillies in 1975, is half-sister to smart sprinter Smarten Up
(by Sharpen Up); having first race for 2 months, won 12-runner maiden event at
Salisbury in August, getting the better of His Dream by a head after being held up
and looking difficult to settle; ran more freely on other starts and seemed barely to
get 5f; acts on firm ground; has sweated up. *W. Wightman.*

CUT'N DRY 3 b.c. Dubassoff–Dissipation 83 (Disciplinarian) (1982 6f 7f³ 8d 1983 –
12fg) lightly raced and no form; slipped up only outing of 1983; sold 550 gns
Doncaster August Sales. *G. Pritchard-Gordon.*

CUT THE GRASS 4 b.g. Pongee 106–Sea Echo (Sea Hawk II 131) (1982 NR –
1983 12f) workmanlike gelding; fifth live foal; dam unraced half-sister to Boldboy;
16/1 and backward when never-dangerous tenth of 16 to Treasure Hunter in minor
event at Thirsk in June; sold 850 gns Doncaster June Sales. *M. H. Easterby.*

CUTTING COMMENT 8 b.g. Sharpen Up 127–Mrs Hauksbee 102 (Pindari 124) §§
(1982 13s 11s 12d 7.6fg 12g⁴ 1983 8.2d⁴ 15fg) of little account nowadays and
unreliable into the bargain. *T. Taylor.*

CUTTING EDGE 3 b.c. High Top 131–Cutle 86 (Saint Crespin III 132) (1982 –
NR 1983 8v) attractive colt; brother to St Leger winner Cut Above and smart 1¼m
filly Cut Loose, and half-brother to 3 winners including Irish 2,000 Guineas winner
Sharp Edge (by Silver Shark); dam, daughter of Park Hill Stakes and Yorkshire Cup
winner Cutter, won at up to 13f; showed promise when about 15 lengths fifth of 15
behind Deutschmark in maiden race at Goodwood in May; sold to M. Chapman only
620 gns Newmarket Autumn Sales. *R. Hern.*

CUTTING WIND 2 ch.c. Sharpen Up 127–Tumble Judy (Tumble Wind) (1983 6f **103**
6f 6f* 7f* 8d² 6fg* 6g⁴) Apr 30; 12,000Y; quite attractive, useful-looking colt;
second foal; dam never ran; put up a splendid effort under 9-3 in 11-runner Golden
Gates Nursery at Ascot in September, winning by a head from Kings Island after
being held up; had previously won maiden race at Yarmouth after making all and
minor event (beating Attempt) at Epsom; below his best final start (on toes in
paddock); best at distances short of 1m; acts on firm going and a soft surface. *B.
Hanbury.*

CYPRUS SKY 6 ch.g. Redundant 120–Palestra 92 (Palestine 133) (1982 12f 12f⁴ **68**
10d² 12d 7.6f 16g³ 12v³ 1983 8d 10v³ 10s⁴ 7.6v 8f) tall, close-coupled gelding;
stays at least 1½m; acts on any going; blinkered fourth start; does best when
ridden up with pace; sometimes owner ridden. *R. Smyth.*

CYRANO 2 ch.c General Assembly–True Rocket 116 (Roan Rocket 128) (1983 **86**
7g² 7g² 8d²) Apr 4; IR 215,000Y; half-brother to several winners, notably very
smart Irish sprinter Ballad Rock (by Bold Lad, Ire.); dam very speedy 2-y-o;
came up against very useful newcomers on first 2 outings, being beaten 6 lengths
by Sadler's Wells in 16-runner maiden race at Leopardstown in September and 2½
lengths by The Miller in similar event at Phoenix Park the following month; odds
on when going down by 3 lengths to Star Spartan in 21-runner maiden race at
Leopardstown later in August; probably stays 1m; should win races. *D. O'Brien,
Ireland.*

CYRIL'S CHOICE 4 b.c. Malicious–Saran (Le Levanstell 122) (1982 8.2d 6f* **104**
6g⁴ 5fg² 6fg* 5.8g 6f² 6f 6g³ 6g* 6fg*(dis) 6s² 6d 1983 6v³ 7g² 6f 7fg 7s² 7fg) neat
colt; ran creditably most starts, including when going down by ½ length to
Portogon in quite valuable handicap at Ayr in May and by 4 lengths to Christmas
Cottage in similar event on same course in September; stays 7f; acts on any going;
genuine and consistent though has a tendency to hang and isn't an easy ride. *S.
Mellor.*

CZERNIN 6 b.g. Forli–Nonsensical 99 (Silly Season 127) (1982 NR 1983 14.7f) –
workmanlike gelding; not a good walker; poor form on flat, including in sellers, but
is a winner over hurdles; has been blinkered. *D. Smith.*

D

DABDOUB 3 ch.c. Habat 127–No Cards 109 (No Mercy 126) (1982 7fg³ 7fg² 8s³ 96
7g² 7s* 7s⁴ 1983 8d* 10v⁴ 8.2v 8f 10f⁴) tall, strong colt; beat Ayman
impressively by 8 lengths in 16-runner £3,100 event at Brighton in April; less
than a length fourth to General Concorde in XYZ Handicap at Newcastle the
following month, best subsequent effort; stays 1¼m; best form with some give in
the ground; genuine; exported to Hong Kong. *P. Cole.*

DADDIES INVESTMENT 4 ch.f. Imperial Crown 96–Copper Queen (Sir –
d'Orient 90) (1982 NR 1983 10f) fourth reported foal; dam never ran; 20/1 when
tailed-off last of 6 in seller at Folkestone in September. *J. Gifford.*

DADDY'S PLEASURE 2 b.c. Mummy's Pet 125–Lovelorn 56 (Forlorn River –
124) (1983 5f 5g) May 16; 4,800 2-y-o; rather leggy, fair sort; half-brother to a
minor winner; dam stayed 7f; in rear in maiden races at Hamilton (slowly away) in
August and Haydock (last of 14) in September. *P. Brookshaw.*

DAGEEGAH (USA) 4 b.c. Timeless Moment–Pia's Lady (Pia Star) (1982 10f⁴ 82
12f 10g 12g⁴ 10fg 13d 10.2s* 12g 1983 12d 10s 12v 10g 10f³ 14f* 12fg* 14fg² 14h*
14.8fg³ 14.6fg 12fg 14d 14g) strong, attractive colt who carries plenty of condition;
usually a good mover; fair performer on his day; won 2 handicaps at Sandown and an
amateur riders event at Redcar in summer; suited by 1¾m; acts on any going; often
sweats up; blinkered fifth start; suitable mount for an inexperienced rider though
looked mulish fourth outing; suited by forcing tactics; sold to NBA 12,000 gns
Newmarket Autumn Sales. *F. Durr.*

DAHAAM 2 br.c. Ile de Bourbon 133–Stogumber 96 (Habitat 134) (1983 7g) Apr –
7; tall, lengthy, light-bodied colt; third foal; half-brother to Emperador (by
Empery), successful at around 1¼m, and to a winner in Italy; dam, 2-y-o 6f winner,
comes from family of Great Nephew; 14/1 and backward, slow-starting last of 7 in
minor event at Sandown in October. *F. J. Houghton.*

DAHA (USA) 3 b.f. What A Pleasure–Mostly (Grey Dawn II 132) (1982 6fg 6g ?
6g 1983 6v⁴ 6d 9g*) moderate filly; remote fourth to easy winner Loch Pearl in
maiden race at Ayr in March; odds on when winning 13-runner race at Sterrebeek
by 25 lengths in June; stays 9f; well beaten in blinkers second outing. *J. Dunlop.*

DALBREAC 4 br.f. Bustino 136–Corriefeol 102 (Jaipur) (1982 7f 10fg 10g 1983 –
12s 8g 6fg) rather leggy, lightly-made filly; poor maiden; stays 1¼m. *J. Spearing.*

DALBURY 5 b.g. Royal Palace 131–Tikki Tavi 92 (Honeyway 125) (1982 8fg³ –
10f* 12f 10.2g* 10fg 10g 1983 10d) sparely-made gelding; stays 1¼m; acts on firm
going; possibly isn't one to trust implicitly. *P. Haynes.*

DALESIDE REDWOOD 2 b.c. Captain James 123–Tudor Bay (Canisbay 120) 95
(1983 7f³ 7f* 7g⁴ 8f* 7fg) Mar 15; IR 15,000F; rangy colt; good walker; has rather
a round action; second foal; dam won over middle distances in French Provinces;
won £3,300 race at York in July and £4,000 nursery under 9-7 on same course in
August; last of 8 in Somerville Tattersall Stakes at Newmarket in September;
suited by 1m; acts well on firm going. *T. Fairhurst.*

DALLAS SMITH (USA) 2 b.c. Sir Ivor 135–Sahsie (Forli) (1983 8d 10fg) Apr –
25; 13,500Y; second foal; half-brother to American 3-y-o Sauce of Life (by Sauce
Boat); dam, winner from 4f to 1m, was very useful at 2 yrs; in mid-division in
sizeable fields of maidens at Warwick and Nottingham in October. *R. Akehurst.*

DALMANE 3 br.c. So Blessed 130–Opium 97 (Espresso 122) (1982 6f² 7g⁴ 7g 82
1983 8d² 8f 7f 10.1f²) tall, rather leggy, attractive colt; broke a leg and was
destroyed after finishing second to Pip in minor event at Windsor in July; was suited
by 1¼m; wore blinkers third start. *P. Burgoyne.*

DALTAGH 3 b.f. Tachypous 128–Crisalgo 83 (Miralgo 130) (1982 NR 1983 8v 8f –
10f 10h) fourth foal; dam won Chester Cup; towards rear in maiden races and a
seller. *G. Thorner.*

DALTON WOOD 2 br.c. Persian Breeze 121–Kalyanda 77 (Kalydon 122) (1983 –
5v 5d 5fg) Feb 13; 850Y; lightly-made colt; last in maiden races and a seller; of no
account. *M. W. Easterby.*

DAMASCUS PRINCE (USA) 3 b.c. Damascus–Durga (Tatan) (1982 8g 1983 79
10g 10.2f³) attractive colt; showed only form when 2½ lengths third of 18 behind
Holkham in maiden race at Doncaster in June; gives impression he'll be suited by
1½m. *M. Stoute.*

DAME ASHFIELD 3 b.f. Grundy 137–African Dancer 116 (Nijinsky 138) (1982   90
7d 8fg⁴ 7g³ 1983 10d 12s 12.2fg² 12g⁴ 12f² 12f⁴ 12fg 12g⁴ 12f* 12s² 12d* 12fg)
sparely-made, fair sort; didn't look entirely reliable in first half of season but did
little wrong later on and won maiden race at Ripon in August and handicap at
Leicester in October; beat Obadiah rather cleverly by 1½ lengths in latter; will be
suited by further than 1½m; acts on any going; blinkered second and seventh
starts; sold to BBA 100,000 gns Newmarket December Sales. *G. Wragg.*

DAME CAROLINE 2 ch.f. Wollow 132–Dame Clara 95 (Manacle 123) (1983 7f   –
8g 7.6d) Mar 25; 4,000Y; tall, lengthy, rather shallow-girthed filly; third foal; dam,
who stayed 7f, is half-sister to very smart 1977 2-y-o John de Coombe; showed
little worthwhile form in big fields of maidens in the autumn. *M. Blanshard.*

DAME PEGGY 3 gr.f. Comedy Star 121–Peggy Wig 55 (Counsel 118) (1982 5g 6f   49
1983 9v 8fg 7f 9d⁴ 8fg⁴ 7g⁴ 6fg²) compact filly; plater; effective at 6f and stays 9f;
usually blinkered, but has run creditably without. *J. Old.*

DAMION 2 b.g. Dominion 123–Classy Dame 94 (Jukebox 120) (1983 5v 5g 6g 6f)   52
Mar 12; small, well-made gelding; first foal; dam won 7 times over 6f; plating-class
maiden; blinkered final start. *J. W. Watts.*

DAMKINA 2 gr.f. Hittite Glory 125–Charter Island 88 (Runnymede 123) (1983   68
5d³ 5v² 6g) Mar 4; workmanlike filly; good mover; half-sister to very useful
Watership Down (by Murrayfield), a winner at up to 1m in France, and to a winner
in Italy; dam stayed 7f well; 2 lengths second of 10 to Gentle Gypsy in maiden race
at Kempton in April; not seen out after June. *R. Sheather.*

DANCE AWAY (USA) 2 ch.c. Naskra–Dance Across (Sword Dancer) (1983   75
8fg 8f³) May 20; $100,000Y; smallish, lightly-made colt; half-brother to
disappointing 1981 2-y-o Bronowski (by Raja Baba) and several winners, including
smart French 1m to 10.7f winner Silver Bells (by Tambourine II); dam from same
family as 2000 Guineas winner Baldric II; 25/1, 5 lengths third of 14 behind Hidden
Destiny in maiden race at Leicester in November; will probably stay 1¼m. *G.
Pritchard-Gordon.*

DANCE CARD 3 ch.f. Be My Guest 126–Ivor's Honey 91 (Sir Ivor 135) (1982 7g   69
1983 8d² 10fg 10.2h 10fg 15.8g⁴ 12s) quite attractive filly; disappointing after
finishing second in 1m maiden race at Thirsk in April. *M. Jarvis.*

DANCE OF LIFE 4 b.g. Green Dancer 132–Petrovna (Reliance II 137) (1982   –
7fg 6g 8g 10f 8.2f² 8.3g 7s 8.2s 1983 6fg 8.2fg) sturdy gelding; quite a modest
handicapper on his day; will be suited by a return to 1¼m; acts on firm going and is
probably unsuited by soft; blinkered nowadays. *Mrs P. Sykes.*

DANCE QUEST (FR) 2 b.f. Green Dancer 132–Polyponder 124 (Barbizon)   117
(1983 5.5fg* 6fg* 5f²) Feb 16; $165,000Y; second foal; half-sister to French 3-y-o
1m winner Riverquest (by Riverman); dam, winner from 4f to 1m in France, was
probably best over 5f; won a newcomers event at Chantilly in June by a head from
Speedy Girl and a minor event at Maisons-Laffitte the following month; just failed
to regain advantage from Reine Caroline in Prix de la Vallee d'Auge at Deauville in
August, going down by a short head; should stay 7f; acts on firm going. *Mme C.
Head, France.*

DANCER IN PARIS (FR) 3 b.g. Green Dancer 132–Au Pair in Paris (Sir   –
Ribot) (1982 NR 1983 8f 10d) $110,000Y, 8,200 2-y-o; big gelding; third foal;
half-brother to French 1¼m winner Alone in Paris (by Bel Baraka); dam poor sister
to very smart French and American performer Riot in Paris; behind in maiden race
at Newbury in July (trained by A. Pitt) and 26-runner minor event at Leopardstown
in November. *M. O'Toole, Ireland.*

DANCER'S EMULATION 3 gr.g. Dancer's Image–Mossinella 69 (Ballymoss   69
136) (1982 5f 7fg 7.6v 6s 1983 7.6v 8g² 7fg 8f 7f³) robust, workmanlike gelding;
placed in handicaps at Newbury (apprentices) and Folkestone in summer; ran
respectably in between; stays 1m. *M. Masson.*

DANCIMMO 2 b.f. Dance In Time–Bourton Downs 74 (Philip of Spain 126) (1983   64
6f 6f 7f 7g² 7fg 8fg) Mar 16; 7,400Y; useful-looking filly; second foal; dam 2-y-o
winner who didn't train on; beaten ½ length in 19-runner claiming race at Yarmouth
in September; stays 1m; acts on firm going. *R. Williams.*

DANCING ADMIRAL 3 b.c. Julio Mariner 127–Autumn Ballad 75 (Tudor   92
Melody 129) (1982 7g 8d 1983 12d⁴ 14fg* 14f² 14fg 14d² 14.6s 14fg) tall, quite
attractive colt; having first race for 3 months when winning minor event at
Yarmouth in June; very good second in similar event at Sandown in July and
Melrose Handicap at York in August, beaten narrowly by British and Incredible
Idea respectively; didn't move well to post and ran poorly in between however;

will stay 2m; yet to show he can handle really soft going, but acts on any other; seems to benefit from strong handling; out of his depth sixth start and had a stiffish task final outing. *C. Brittain.*

DANCING AFFAIR 3 b.f. Quiet Fling 124–Misalliance 87 (Royal Palace 131)   **110** (1982 NR 1983 12f* 12f* 12fg 12fg) lengthy, quite attractive filly; has rather a round action; second foal; dam suited by a test of stamina; successful in maiden race at Newbury and 6-runner minor event at York in August, putting up a good effort on latter course to win by 2 lengths from His Honour (gradually wore down leader and was well on top at finish); fifth afterwards behind Trakady in 6-runner event at Newmarket in September (outspeeded in a slowly-run race) and behind stable-companion Sylph in 11-runner Princess Royal Stakes at Ascot in October (faded in last furlong after having every chance); essentially a stayer and will be seen to better advantage over 1¾m or more; has raced only on firm ground; sold 34,000 gns Newmarket December Sales. *J. Tree.*

DANCING BARRON 2 b.c. Tanfirion 110–Absuleno 78 (Above Suspicion 127)   **93** (1983 5v³ 5s 6fg* 7fg* 7f 7fg⁴ 7fg) May 11; IR 4,600F, 6,400Y; small, attractive colt; half-brother to several winners here and abroad; dam placed at up to 1½m; won minor event at Windsor in June and £3,900 nursery under top weight at Brighton in August; suited by 7f; best form on a firm surface. *J. Dunlop.*

DANCING DAUGHTER 3 b.f. Dance In Time–Timur's Daughter 103   **77** (Tamerlane 128) (1982 6g³ 6g³ 6g⁴ 7v 1983 9f² 13.4fg* 10.1f 12f 12.3g) small, lengthy filly; grand walker; beat Colonel Monck easing up by 5 lengths in 13-runner maiden race at Chester in July; didn't run well afterwards; suited by 13f; acts on firm going; wore small bandage on off-hind final start. *F. J. Houghton.*

DANCING FEET 2 br.f. Malinowski 123–Cancaniere 86 (Hotfoot 126) (1983 6f³   **64** 6f⁴ 6f³ 6fg³ 5d) Mar 10; IR 2,100Y; small, lightly-built filly; second foal; dam, half-sister to Gold Cup winner Shangamuzo, won over 1m at 2 yrs; in frame in a variety of races, on fourth outing starting favourite when 3 lengths third of 24 to Owen Joseph in valuable seller at Doncaster in September; finds 5f too sharp and should be suited by 7f +; acts on firm going. *R.Hannon.*

DANCING FEVER 4 br.f. Sweet Revenge 129–Great Emerald 75 (Great   **–** Nephew 126) (1982 8fg 7f 12.2f 8f 9g 1983 9f 11g 12.3fg) poor plater; sometimes blinkered; has been bandaged on near-fore. *I. Jordon.*

DANCING GUY (FR) 2 br.c. Green Dancer 132–Melancolie (Petingo 135) (1983   **–** 8fg 10.2fg) Apr 27; $50,000Y; half-brother to 1m winner Petite Joie (by Canisbay) and to winners in Italy by Reform and Prince Tenderfoot; dam, winner 4 times at 3 yrs in Italy, is daughter of Italian Oaks winner Macrina d'Alba; little show in 2 races in fair company right at the back-end. *M. Jarvis.*

DANCING HARLEQUIN 3 b.g. Cawston's Clown 113–Jig (St Paddy 133) (1982   **–** NR 1983 11v 10s) strong, useful-looking gelding; fourth foal; closely related to a winner in USA by Comedy Star; dam never ran; behind in maiden races at Newbury (last of 17) and Leicester in May. *M. Blanshard.*

DANCING KATE 8 ch.m. Jukebox 120–Epee (Cranach) (1982 12s 10.6f 10fg²   **–** 12fg 12fg 10.8s 1983 10.2d 8v 8.2d 10g 7f 8f) workmanlike mare; poor plater; stays 1¾m; probably acts on any going; sometimes wears blinkers; suitable mount for an apprentice; has been bandaged behind. *M. James.*

DANCING LIGHTS (USA) 3 b.c. Northern Dancer–My Great Aunt (Bold   **66** Ruler) (1982 6d 1983 6f² 6f³) close-coupled, good-topped colt; very well bred, but only lightly raced; placed in minor event at Brighton and maiden race (blinkered) at Folkestone in July; will possibly do better over further. *J. Tree.*

DANCING MEG (USA) 3 b.f. Marshua's Dancer–Coxswain's Meg (Sailor)   **104** (1982 5fg 6g* 6fg 7f² 8g* 8g² 1983 7s 8g 12fg 12g 12fg 8f) rangy filly; good mover with lovely, long stride; very useful staying 2-y-o in 1982; unplaced in good company in 1983, best effort on fourth start when running on strongly to be 7½ lengths fifth of 13 to Give Thanks in Lancashire Oaks at Haydock in July (needed to be settled after taking strong hold, and as result had plenty to do); suited by middle distances; acts on soft going; dwelt and was always trailing when blinkered final outing. *R. Laing.*

DANCING NYMPH 4 ch.f. Dance In Time–Constant Nymph 85 (Venture VII   **–** 129) (1982 12.2f 12g⁴ 12.2f² 12d² 10d³ 10.6s 12d² 1983 12.2g 12f 12.2g) strong, deep-girthed filly; plating-class maiden; stays 1½m; acts on firm going and a soft surface; retained 3,900 gns Newmarket Autumn Sales. *J. Fitzgerald.*

DANCING ORANGE 2 b.f. Orange Bay 131–Musical Piece 91 (Song 132) (1983   **65**
5f 6fg* 6f² 7f⁴(dis) 6fg 6s 7fg) May 16; compact filly; third foal; dam best at sprint
distances; bought out of B. Hanbury's stable 4,600 gns after slamming 9 opponents
in seller at Pontefract in July; beaten ½ length by Knights Secret in nursery at
Redcar the following month; stays 7f; acts well on firm going. *A. Balding.*

DANCING SOVEREIGN 4 b.g. Dance In Time–Golden Treasure 106   **66**
(Crepello 136) (1982 11f 12f 11.7fg⁴ 12f* 12f² 11.1fg 16.9fg 12g 12g 1983 14s²
13.3g) strong, rangy gelding; has a rather round action; suited by 1¾m and will
get further; acts on any going. *Mrs N. Smith.*

DANCING VALERINA 3 br.f. Comedy Star 121–Polyandrist 92 (Polic 126)   **61**
(1982 6f 6g 5.8g 7g 7d 1983 7v 8d 7fg 10.2f⁴ 10f* 12g) quite attractive filly;
dropped in class and held up when winning seller at Nottingham in July in good
style (apprentice ridden); sold out of C. Horgan's stable 1,900 gns afterwards;
had stiffer task and didn't look 100% wound up only subsequent start; suited by
1¼m; acts on firm going; blinkered last 4 starts. *J. Etherington.*

DANCING WIND 3 b.f. Dance In Time–Winden (Worden II 129) (1982 7g 1983   **–**
7s 6v 8g) lengthy, attractive filly; showed signs of ability in big fields of maidens
but finished in rear on last 2 outings and wasn't seen out after June. *P. Walwyn.*

DANDY AL 2 ch.c. Red Alert 127–Trusian (Milesian 125) (1983 6g 7fg 6fg 7fg⁴ 7f   **52**
7h) Apr 14; 10,500Y; lengthy, workmanlike colt; brother to 1980 2-y-o 5f winner
Robin Red Breast; moderate plater; will be suited by 1m; blinkered third and
sixth outings; looked unsuited by Catterick track fifth start; sold 1,100 gns
Newmarket September Sales. *R. Williams.*

DANGEROUS MELODY 2 b.f. Tower Walk 130–Thorganby Melody (Highland   **–**
Melody 112) (1983 5fg 5g) Mar 9; 13,500Y; well-made filly; second foal; half-sister
to speedy 1982 2-y-o In Motion (by Monsanto); dam never ran; unquoted, behind in
20-runner maiden races at Sandown in May and Newbury in September. *P.
Mitchell.*

DANIELLE DELIGHT 2 gr.f. Song 132–Sylvanecte 70 (Silver Shark 129)   **–**
(1983 6fg 6g 6f 6fg) May 7; 45,000Y; strong, useful-looking filly; sister to 2
winners, including very useful Shark Song, successful here and in USA at up to 9f,
and half-sister to useful 6f and 7f winner Silver Lord (by Abwah); dam won over
1¼m; soundly beaten in 3 races at Newmarket and one at Windsor; blinkered third
start. *B. Hanbury.*

DANISH EXPRESS 4 ch.c. Music Boy 124–Ptarmigan 75 (Hill Clown) (1982   **70**
6fg 8.2fg³ 8g 8d 8s* 8d 7d 8s 1983 7f 6f 7f³ 8fg* 7.6g 8f 7g² 8g³ 8d⁴ 7.2g)
powerful, deep-girthed colt; quite a modest handicapper; won at Ayr in July; stays
1m; acts on any going; ran respectably in blinkers third start; has won for an
apprentice; no battler, and is suited by waiting tactics; sold to M. Bradley 5,500 gns
Doncaster October Sales. *M. H. Easterby.*

DANSE DU NORD 2 ch.f. Northfields–Melbourne Miss (Chaparral 128) (1983   **97** p
8g*) Jan 23; 12,500Y; first foal; dam, unraced, is closely related to Grand Prix de
Paris winner Tennyson; finished strongly to win newcomers race at Evry in
September by a neck from Arrusa; will be suited by 1¼m+; the type to leave this
form behind. *P. Bary, France.*

DANSEUR DE CORDE (USA) 3 b.c. Foolish Pleasure–Danseuse Etoile 102   **83**
(Buckpasser) (1982 NR 1983 8g 11v³ 10f* 10f² 10h²) well-made, good-bodied,
quite attractive colt; first foal; dam, sister to top-class North American filly La
Prevoyante, won over 1¼m in France and up to 9f in USA; odds on when decisively
winning 17-runner maiden event at Nottingham in July; second in minor events at
Ripon (beaten short head by River of Kings) and Nottingham afterwards; probably
stays 11f; sent to France. *H. Cecil.*

DAN ZAKI (USA) 3 b.c. Accipiter–Patrina (Olympia) (1982 7d 6s 1983 12v 11f⁴   **–**
14f⁴ 13g 12d) angular colt; running-on fourth in maiden race at Yarmouth in August
on third outing, best effort; evidently suited by a test of stamina *P. Haslam.*

DANZATORE (CAN) 3 b.c. Northern Dancer–Shake A Leg 106 (Raise A   **120**
Native) (1982 7fg* 8d* 8s* 1983 9s* 8fg)
    Judging by Press reaction, Danzatore's defection from the Two Thousand
Guineas eight days before the race left a nasty taste in many mouths. His
withdrawal had been anticipated in betting circles for several days before the
official announcement was made. The sequence of events began when Hills and
Mecca suspended ante-post betting on the Two Thousand Guineas on Monday April
18th in the face of rumours that all was not well with Danzatore, who had been as

short as 7/4 in some books the previous week. A spokesman at Ballydoyle countered the rumours with a statement the same day that Danzatore was 'in excellent form'. 'I cannot imagine how these stories get about', he said. Next day the stable reported that Danzatore 'worked satisfactorily here this morning . . . he's in fine form'. But the rumours persisted and Danzatore went out in the market to 4/1; one punter, who had a long-standing bet on Danzatore at 20/1 with Kinghorns, reportedly had his offer to cancel the bet turned down. The sensitive nose of the bookmaking fraternity proved reliable, as it so often does, and an announcement was made through the Press Association on Friday April 22nd that Danzatore 'will not run in next week's Two Thousand Guineas'. Danzatore's trainer was at some pains afterwards to point out that it was not until the Friday, when Danzatore had worked disappointingly, that a decision was taken to miss Newmarket. O'Brien insisted that on the Tuesday Danzatore had worked satisfactorily, although he also reportedly admitted to having felt concern about some of Danzatore's other recent work, which he hoped 'signified no more than that the colt had become lazy'. O'Brien ← who won the Two Thousand Guineas with Lomond – appealed to bookmakers to offer an 'O'Brien stable' bet in future on races with ante-post betting.

Few would deny that a trainer's first duty is to his owners and his primary concern must be for their interests. But a trainer has other duties too and one of them is to avoid giving the impression—no doubt erroneous—that the betting public is being misled. The betting public contributes a good deal to racing through the levy and it is deplorable that there should ever be the slightest suspicion of its being taken for a ride. The public should not be kept in the dark a moment longer than necessary about the progress of any horse about whom there has been substantial ante-post betting. If O'Brien had indeed felt concern about some of Danzatore's work in the days or weeks before April 22nd then surely the proper course would have been for him to have made it public knowledge. That said, we are aware that such courtesies can sometimes rebound on a trainer when a horse recovers in time to run in a big race after a premature announcement that it might not do so. The world being as it is, there are always those ready to believe that the market has been rigged when such a horse wins at odds longer than those available ante-post. Indeed, O'Brien himself—after following what most thought at the time was an admirably open policy with the public—was called before the Epsom stewards after Larkspur's success in the 1962 Derby to explain why he had stated a few days before the race that the horse was a doubtful runner. The stewards on this occasion expressed themselves perfectly satisfied with his explanation but their action was hardly calculated to encourage future announcements by trainers of set-backs to their big-race hopes!

Danzatore was unbeaten in three races in Ireland as a two-year-old and ended the season officially rated the joint-third best of his age in Europe, behind only the leading British-trained two-year-old Diesis and the top French juvenile Saint Cyrien. Danzatore had seemed sure to put up a very bold show in the Guineas, and before the new season opened O'Brien stated in a television interview that Danzatore had done extremely well over the winter months. 'He looks a stronger horse now', he said of the big, rangy, well-bred Danzatore, expressing the view

The Minstrel Stakes, Phoenix Park—Danzatore makes all to win easing up

that Danzatore had been a 'rather overgrown two-year-old.' Danzatore reappeared in The Minstrel Stakes at Phoenix Park in April and most observers were impressed, Danzatore shortening from 7/2 in the ante-post market after winning easing up, by a length from Quilted. We found ourselves out on a limb after The Minstrel Stakes. Danzatore's demeanour, in particular, didn't impress us—he seemed edgy and sweated up in the paddock, and he had to be blindfolded after two unsuccessful attempts to get him into the stalls. In the race he didn't slaughter the

		Nearctic	Nearco
	Northern Dancer	(br 1954)	Lady Angela
	(b 1961)	Natalma	Native Dancer
Danzatore (Can)		(b 1957)	Almahmoud
(b.c. 1980)		Raise A Native	Native Dancer
	Shake A Leg	(ch 1961)	Raise You
	(b 1970)	Fleeting Doll	Fleet Nasrullah
		(b 1961)	Chinese Doll

opposition as he was entitled to do—he started at 7/2 on—and Eddery, who was niggling at him three furlongs from home, had to push him to get on top before easing him down in the closing stages. When Danzatore lost his unbeaten record on his next appearance—he finished last of five in the Guinness Golden Fleece Stakes at Phoenix Park in July—it was decided not to persevere with him. We need not concern ourselves with him further as he has reportedly been sent to New Zealand as a stallion. Extensive pedigree details appeared in *Racehorses of 1982*. V. O'Brien, Ireland.

DANZIG 6 b.g. Wolver Hollow 126–None So Pretty (Never Say Die 137) (1982 6g⁴ 6s 6g² 8.5f 8g 8fg 11.5f 7fg 1983 10f 12f 7f) compact gelding; plater nowadays; stays 1½m, but seems reasonably effective at sprint distances; acts on firm going. D. Morrill. —

DARE YOU 2 ch.g. Dominion 123–Tactless 91 (Romulus 129) (1983 5s 5s³ 7f⁴ 7f³ 7fg³ 8fg 8fg) medium-sized gelding; half-brother to 3 winners, including very useful Padro (by Runnymede),a winner at up to 7f; dam won over 1¼m; moderate maiden; stays 1m; best form on a firm surface; gelded after final appearance. R. Smyth. 78

DARINE 5 b.m. Nonoalco 131–Be Noble (Vaguely Noble 140) (1982 12d* 13d 12f⁴ 15g 12g³ 11.7g* 10fg* 8f 12d* 10g⁴ 12v 10.2d⁴ 1983 8v 12.5s² 10d³ 12f⁴ 10.5g* 12.5g 10f 8fg 10fg³) strong, good sort; ex-English; has improved remarkably over past 3 years and is now a smart performer; put up a very game display when getting the better of Rudolfina by a short head in Prix Fille de l'Air at Saint-Cloud in June; in frame several other starts, including when fourth of 8 to Zalataia in La Coupe at Longchamp and third of 11 to Bylly the Kid in La Coupe de Maisons-Laffitte; suited by middle distances; acts on any going; suited by forcing tactics; genuine; trained by F. Durr in 1982. R. Collet, France. 114

DARING DISPLAY 2 b.f. Daring March 116–Right Barnie (Compensation 127) (1983 7f 8g 6d) Apr 21; strong, quite well-made, attractive filly; half-sister to minor winners here and in Italy by Birdbrook; dam never ran; prominent in big fields on all outings, notably 5 lengths fifth of 24 to Preobrajenska in minor event at Lingfield in October on final start; may prove best at distances short of 1m. G. Hunter. 74

DARING ELLA 2 b.f. Daring March 116–Portalla 72 (Porto Bello 118) (1983 5s 6f 7fg 6fg 7.2s) Apr 12; workmanlike filly; no sign of ability; last under a big weight in selling nursery final appearance. M. Blanshard. —

DARING PRANK 2 b.f. Daring March 116–Princess Dido 63 (Sayajirao 132) (1983 5.8s 6d 6f 7s) Apr 17; 1,500Y; rather leggy filly; half-sister to winners here and abroad; dam, 1m winner, is half-sister to very smart colts Florescence and Prince Poppa; no worthwhile form, including in maiden auction events. G. Balding. —

DARK AMBER 2 b.f. Formidable 125–Supper Time 71 (Shantung 132) (1983 6g) Apr 11; second foal; half-sister to a winner in Italy; dam lightly-raced 1½m winner; 100/1, 9 lengths fifth of 9 to Visible Form in minor event at Goodwood in September; will stay 7f+; should improve. G. Balding. 68 p

DARK MYSTIQUE (USA) 4 b. or br.f. Fleet Allied–Zerosa (Silky Sullivan) (1982 6f 7f³ 6f 5fg³ 7fg 6f³ 6g 6f⁴ 1983 7f 7g 7fg 10fg 6fg) compact filly; poor maiden; stays 7f; acts on firm going; blinkered last 2 starts in 1982. P. Haslam. —

DARK PROPOSAL (USA) 5 b.h. Blood Royal 129–Lady Gertrude (Mr Leader) (1982 13fg 14g 16fg* 17f* 18.8fg⁴ 16f 17f² 18d 18.1g² 19s 20g 1983 16.1fg 76

16f 16f* 16.5fg* 16f³ 20f 16fg 16fg² 18fg 18fg 16g* 18fg) rather leggy, quite useful sort; inconsistent handicapper; won at Newcastle in July, Redcar in August and Lingfield in October; a thorough stayer who is suited by a strong gallop; suited by firm going; needs plenty of driving, veered badly right at Redcar and is not an ideal mount for an apprentice; has raced with tongue tied down. *B. Hanbury.*

DARLY (FR) 4 ch.c. Pharly 130–Delphinia (Marino) (1982 8.5s² 10d* 10fg 10fg   **118**
10.5d 12v 10g* 10v 1983 10s 8v 8d⁴ 9.7d³ 8f² 9.2d² 8fg 10s² 10f) 440,000 francs Y (approx £44,000); half-brother to several winners in France, including very useful 9f and 10f winner Dauphin du Roi (by King of the Castle); dam very useful French middle-distance performer; improved at 4 yrs and developed into a very smart performer; excellent second in Prix du Chemin de Fer du Nord at Chantilly (2½ lengths behind Pampabird), Prix d'Ispahan at Longchamp (went down by 3 lengths to Crystal Glitters) and Prix du Prince d'Orange at Longchamp again (beaten ¾ length by Lovely Dancer); stays 1¼m; acts on any going but seems ideally suited by soft ground; suited by forcing tactics. *D. Smaga, France.*

DARSHAAN (FR) 2 br.c. Shirley Heights 130–Delsy (Abdos 134) (1983 8s 8d*   **121**
10g*) Apr 18; fourth living foal; half-brother to 3 winners, including useful French middle-distance winner Dalal (by Labus); dam useful middle-distance filly; a very promising colt who won twice at Saint-Cloud in November, beating Alliston 6 lengths in maiden race and justifying favouritism by ¾ length from Grand Orient, after leading early in straight, in 12-runner Criterium; will be suited by 1½m; should make a leading 3-y-o. *A. de Royer-Dupre, France.*

DARTCAN 4 ch.f. Streak 119–Canamour (Canisbay 120) (1982 7fg 8fg⁴ 10.1g   –
8fg 1983 8v 8g 12.2fg) plating-class maiden; stays 1m; looked sour in blinkers second start. *D. C. Tucker.*

DARTING GROOM (USA) 3 ch.c. Blushing Groom 131–Mystery Mood (Night   **93**
Invader) (1982 7fg 7fg² 7d² 8d² 8g* 8g 1983 8.2v⁴ 8s 10v 9d⁴ 8f³ 8f² 8f² 7.6fg 8.2f⁴ 8h² 10f² 10.6fg² 10.5fg⁴ 8s² 10fg*) lengthy, good-bodied, strong-quartered colt; ungenuine and a difficult ride but managed to beat Bahoor by a short head in 12-runner minor event at Nottingham in September, just getting home under very hard riding after being held up; second earlier in 5 handicaps and a ladies race; stays 1¼m; acts on any going; usually blinkered nowadays; gave impression track didn't suit him at Chester on eighth start. *S. Norton.*

DASH 2 ch.f. Connaught 130–Wounded Knee 78 (Busted 134) (1983 7.6d) Apr   –
24; fourth foal; half-brother to 3-y-o 1½m winner Pine Ridge (by High Top); dam won over 1½m and 1¾m; unquoted, remote eighth of 20 in maiden race at Lingfield in October. *P. Feilden.*

DASHING DEANO 4 b.g. Full of Hope 125–Lillima 73 (Crooner 119) (1982   –
11.7f 1983 8f 8h) rather leggy gelding; soundly beaten in varied company; has been blinkered. *I. Wardle.*

DASHING LIGHT 2 b.f. Tachypous 128–Spanish Lantern 92 (Don Carlos) (1983   **81**
5fg 6fg 7f 7f 6f⁴ 6f 7d² 6fg³ 8d³ 8.2fg) May 21; rangy filly; third foal; dam stayed well; moderate maiden; good third in well-contested nursery at Warwick in October on penultimate appearance; will probably stay beyond 1m; has run respectably on firm surface but is probably better on a soft one; blinkered last 3 outings. *G. Lewis.*

DASSELLS 2 b.g. Thatching 131–Fallen Rose (Busted 134) (1983 6fg) May 30;   –
second foal; half-brother to 3-y-o Floating Petal (by Wollow); dam, half-sister to high-class filly First Bloom, won small 11.5f race in France; 33/1, moved moderately to post and made little show in race when tenth of 20 in maiden event at Doncaster in November. *M. Jarvis.*

DATATEXT 3 b.c. Raga Navarro 119–Ribara (Barbare II 128) (1982 5fg 6f 5.8f   –
6f 6fg 7fg 8s 8d* 1983 8.2v 11v 10fg 13fg 12f) workmanlike colt; no form in 1983; evidently suited by 1m; acts on a soft surface; usually blinkered nowadays. *M. Usher.*

DAVENPORTS LADY 5 b.m. Panco 91–Lira (Souverain 135) (1982 NR 1983   –
13.4g 11.7h) well beaten in 2 maiden races; sold 980 gns Doncaster November Sales. *C. V. Miller.*

DAVIDGALAXY AFFAIR 6 b.h. Tower Walk 130–Lady's Walk (Pall Mall 132)   –
(1982 13.1f 10d 10g 8g 5fg 1983 7.2s³ 7s 8d⁴) poor handicapper nowadays; best at up to 1m; acts on any going; sometimes blinkered; suitable mount for a boy. *J. Edmunds.*

DAVID HENRYS 3 ch.g. Proud Challenge–Meadow Nymph (Meadow Court   –
129) (1982 NR 1983 12f 13.1fg 10fg 16g) smallish, sturdy gelding; first foal; dam of no account; well behind in maiden and minor events, including a seller. *M. Usher.*

DAWNBALLET (USA) 4 ch.c. Nijinsky 138–Dauntu (Grey Dawn II 132) (1982 –
11g⁴ 12g 16fg³ 16fg³ 17.1s 1983 12s 12f 17.1h) big, rangy colt; poor walker but
good mover; disappointing staying handicapper; best form on fast ground;
sometimes blinkered; usually sweats up. *J. Thorne.*

DAWN DANCER 2 ch.f. Mandrake Major 122–My Audrey 100 (Pall Mall 132) 50
(1983 5d 5v 5d 5g 6f 5f² 6f³ 6fg³ 6g⁴ 6f) June 1; 1,000Y; small filly; half-sister to
winning plater and winners in Italy and Brazil; dam, who stayed 1m, won
Wokingham Stakes; modest plater; stays 6f; acts on firm going; blinkered sixth and
tenth outings; exported to Algeria. *N. Tinkler.*

DAWN DITTY 4 ch.f. Song 132–Chick 106 (My Swanee 122) (1982 7fg 6fg 7f –
5.3f² 6f² 5fg* 5s 1983 6s 5d 5f 5f² 5fg 5fg) big filly; doesn't impress in
appearance nowadays; sprint handicapper; seems to act on any going; wears
blinkers. *J. W. Watts.*

DAWN RIVER (USA) 3 b.c. Grey Dawn II 132–Relifordie (El Relicario 125) 104
(1982 6f³ 7f 8fg* 8d* 10g 1983 12s⁴ 12fg³ 11.7fg⁴ 12fg³) rangy, attractive colt; not
the best of walkers; in frame in Schroder Life Predominate Stakes at Goodwood (12
lengths fourth to Morcon) and handicaps at Brighton, Windsor and Newmarket;
scratched down to start and ran lifelessly when 7½ lengths third to Jupiter Island on
last-named course in September; appears to stay 1½m. *G. Harwood.*

DAWN'S DELIGHT 5 b.g. Dawn Review 105–Bird of Passage (Falcon 131) –
(1982 6s* 6d³ 6f 7f 6fg³ 7g 6g⁴ 6g 6fg 6g³ 6d 6s 6v 6g 6d* 1983 6fg 6fg⁴ 7g 6f 6g 6s
6d⁴) leggy, lightly-made gelding; former plater; ran best race at 5 yrs on final start;
best form at 6f; acts on any going, but has done all his winning when there's been
some give underfoot; blinkered once at 2 yrs; suitable mount for an apprentice;
sometimes bandaged; none too consistent; slowly away fifth start. *K. Ivory.*

DAWN'S DREAM 3 ch.f. Sandford Lad 133–Humble Portion 73 (Mossborough –
126 or Major Portion 129) (1982 5f³ 5f⁴ 6d* 7s 1983 8.2h 6fg) quite well-made
filly; soundly beaten in 1983 (not seen out until September); stays 7f;
suited by a soft surface. *C. Horgan.*

DAWN STAR 2 ch.f. High Line 125–My Therape 112 (Jimmy Reppin 131) (1983 79 p
7fg³) Jan 27; 43,000Y; medium-sized, lengthy filly; second foal; half-sister to very
useful 1982 2-y-o 5f and 6f winner Domynsky (by Dominion), subsequently a stakes
winner over 8.5f in USA; dam won 7 times at up to 1m; favourite and pretty fit, ran
on well after taking time to get going when 3½ lengths third of 21 to Chelkov in
maiden race at Newmarket in September; will be suited by 1m+; shouldn't be hard
pressed to win in ordinary maiden company. *M. Stoute.*

*Mecca Bookmakers' Scottish Derby, Ayr—Dazari (blaze) holds on by a neck from fast-
finishing Seymour Hicks (out of picture) with Hot Touch (noseband) and
Balladier (right) close up*

DAYTON LEGACY 4 b.g. Auction Ring 123–Mansi (Pardao 120) (1982 6fg 5fg
6fg3 8g 6s 1983 8v 8g 12.2fg) rangy gelding; plating-class maiden; should stay 1m;
sold 1,100 gns Ascot November Sales. *I. Walker.*

DAZARI 3 br.c. Relkino 131–Damosa (Abdos 134) (1982 8g2 1983 12v* 10.2v2 **119**
12f* 11g* 12g2 14.6s)
The state of the going is more important to Dazari than his form figures
suggest, for although he has won on heavy he is very much better on a sound
surface. It was, therefore, unfortunate for his connections that despite the
unusually dry autumn the going came up soft on St Leger day. Judged on his best
form Dazari had good prospects of making the first four at least in the Leger; in the
event he trailed in only eighth of ten behind Sun Princess, failing to quicken after
racing close up into the straight. Dazari is, of course, much better than that
performance suggests, and since he's to be kept in training as a four-year-old he
should have ample opportunity of demonstrating it.
Dazari had begun the season with a decisive win over Tom Okker in a
better-than-average Wolverhampton minor event and his subsequent record had
been one of steady improvement, interrupted only when he was beaten by Funny
Reef in a slowly-run affair on heavy ground at Doncaster. He won the highly
competitive King George V Stakes at Royal Ascot in June a shade comfortably on
his third outing, despite appearing harshly handicapped with top weight; and then
he went on to register his most important win so far in the Mecca Bookmakers'
Scottish Derby at Ayr the following month, a race whose stature has grown since
its modest start in 1980. Favourite in a field of eleven, Dazari was prominent
throughout and after taking a slight lead about two furlongs from home he held on
under pressure to win by a neck and half a length from the fast-finishing Seymour
Hicks and the stiffly-penalised Mecca-Dante winner Hot Touch. Seymour Hicks
looked unlucky, having had to be switched from the rails to the wide outside for a
run, and the result of the Great Voltigeur Stakes at York in August probably

H. H. Aga Khan's "Dazari"

provides a better indication of their respective merits. The pair occupied the first two places again in a race that had seemed likely to be dominated by Teenoso and Solford, but this time Dazari, who is essentially a staying type, was completely outpaced by Seymour Hicks in the closing stages and beaten three lengths.

		Relko	Tanerko
	Relkino	(b 1960)	Relance III
	(b 1973)	Pugnacity	Pampered King
Dazari		(b 1962)	Ballynulta
(br.c. 1980)	Damosa	Abdos	Arbar
	(b 1974)	(br 1959)	Pretty Lady
		Damo	Sicambre
		(b 1967)	Arbela

Dazari is from the second crop of Relkino, and until Trakady's emergence in the second half of the season he was easily Relkino's best representative on the racecourse. The dam Damosa, whose second foal he is, was acquired by the Aga Khan upon the dispersal of the Boussac breeding empire, and she descends from the brilliant broodmare Astronomie, dam of the top-class performers Arbar, Asmena, Caracalla, Marsyas and Arbele; the last-named, winner of the Prix Jacques le Marois and Prix d'Ispahan, is Damosa's great-grandam. Damosa herself won an eleven-furlong minor event at Longchamp on the first of four outings, but the family fortunes had tended to decline over the last twenty years or so.

There are more races to be won with Dazari in 1984, and obvious early targets could include the John Porter Stakes at Newbury and the Yorkshire Cup, in both of which Dazari will be unpenalised since he has yet to record a pattern-race victory. The one and three quarter miles of the Yorkshire Cup should suit him particularly well, and it is likely that he'll stay even further given the opportunity. A lengthy, good sort who impressed us with his demeanour on several occasions, Dazari is a good mover and really took our eye when cantering to the start on the very firm ground at Royal Ascot. *M. Stoute.*

DEALAWAY (USA) 2 b.c. Mr Leader–Away (Blue Prince 123) (1983 7fg 7fg)   – p
Mar 24; $100,000Y; brother to Lead Astray, a very useful 2-y-o in 1981, and half-brother to 3 winners, including Sweet Revenge (by Raja Baba), a leading 2-y-o filly of 1980; dam smart winner at up to 1m; showed promise both starts, on second keeping on steadily to finish 13 lengths sixth of 17 to Passing Affair in maiden race at Salisbury in September; will stay 1m. *G. Lewis.*

DEAL ON 4 b.g. Quiet Fling 124–Remould 83 (Reform 132) (1982 10f³ 11.5f 14g   81
12fg² 11.5g* 10.6s 11s² 12g 1983 11.7d 11.1v 10fg 10f* 10f²) useful sort; won handicap at Pontefract in June; stayed 1¼m; acted on any going; dead. *M. Ryan.*

DEALT 2 ch.g. Decoy Boy 129–Shoe 82 (Shoolerville 121) (1983 5.8g 5g 6fg) Mar   –
22; 1,700Y; workmanlike gelding; first foal; dam, second twice over 5f, is sister to useful 7f performer Banco; in rear in maiden company. *J. Toller.*

DEANSCROFT STAR 2 ch.c. Manor Farm Boy 114–Miss Chianti (Royben 125)   –
(1983 5fg 5f 6d) May 5; first foal; dam poor sprint plater; in rear in minor and maiden events. *A. Pitt.*

DEAR ALICIA 5 gr.m. Runnymede 123–Dibby's Cousin (Be Friendly 130) (1982   –
10f 8g 1983 15.5f) workmanlike mare; poor maiden; has worn blinkers; pulled up lame only start at 5 yrs in September. *E. Witts.*

DEAR CLAUDIA 2 ch.f. Royal Match 117–Cigarette 61 (Miralgo 130) (1983 6h   41
7f 8.2g4) Apr 10; 2,300Y; rather plain filly; half-sister to 3 winners, including useful 1974 Irish 2-y-o Say Cheese (by Polyfoto); dam plater; poor plater; will stay beyond 1m. *G. Huffer.*

DEAR EMPEROR 2 b.c. Sensitive Prince–Happy Kin (Bold Hitter) (1983 5f 7fg   73
8d 8f4 9fg) Feb 14; strong, sturdy, good sort; good mover; first foal; dam won from 6f to 8.5f in USA; quite moderate; blinkered when 6 lengths fourth of 18 behind Sam M in maiden race at Leicester in November, best effort; subsequently sent to race in Italy; will stay 1¼m. *I. Balding.*

DEASY'S DELIGHT 2 b.c. Tanfirion 110–Opening Flight (Falcon 131) (1983 5s   96
5s² 5s² 5s* 5g² 6f³ 6fg) Apr 12; IR 32,000Y; first live foal; dam Irish 9f winner; had rest well beaten off when getting better of Tomard by a head in 16-runner Heron Bloodstock Race at Phoenix Park in April; came out best horse at weights when neck second of 5 to Gimme Pleasure in Marwell Stakes on same course the following month and again ran well when narrowly-beaten third of 17 to Paymaster in Tyros Stakes at Curragh in June; wasn't seen out again after finishing only eleventh of 13 behind King Persian in Heinz '57' Phoenix Stakes in August; stays 6f well; acts on any going. *D. K. Weld, Ireland.*

DEBACH RIVER 4 b.g. Forlorn River 124–Debach Game 69 (Darius 129) (1982   –
8.5f 8g³ 10f 10g 12fg 10v 7d 1983 8s⁴ 8.2v 7d 8f 10fg⁴ 10.8fg 8f) plain gelding;
plater; possibly stays 1¼m; sometimes blinkered; sold 590 gns Doncaster
November Sales. *M. Chapman.*

DEBAJ 3 b.c. Blue Cashmere 129–Floral Palm 69 (Floribunda 136) (1982 7fg 5s*   **100**
1983 5s² 5s 5g 5fg* 5f³ 5f⁴ 5g 5fg⁴ 5fg* 5g) lengthy, quite attractive colt;
successful in handicaps at Sandown in June and Ascot in October, just getting up to
force a dead-heat with Young Inca in Bovis Stakes on latter course; in frame in
between at Newmarket, Goodwood and Ascot; has stamina limitations and is best
at 5f; acts on any going; needs to be waited with (made running final outing, and his
defeat is best ignored); sold to NBA 18,500 gns Newmarket Autumn Sales. *P.
Walwyn.*

DEBAYO 3 ch.f. Music Boy 124–Belle Berners 65 (Sharp Edge 123) (1982 NR   **57**
1983 5v³ 5v³ 6g 5f 5f 5g³ 5g² 5d 5g) 2,600F, 6,000Y; small filly; first foal; dam
poor maiden; third in maiden races and a handicap; best form at 5f; seems to need
some give underfoot; blinkered sixth to eighth starts. *S. Norton.*

DEBONA 3 b.f. McIndoe 97–Perky 47 (Three Wishes 114) (1982 NR 1983 8f 9f   –
11f 10f) 440F, 180Y; workmanlike filly; half-sister to a winner abroad; dam stayed
2m; fifth of 9 in 11f maiden race at Hamilton in August, only sign of ability; looked
thoroughly temperamental and had to be withdrawn on one occasion. *Mrs M.
Nesbitt.*

DEBUTINA PARK 3 b.f. Averof 123–Debutante 78 (Silly Season 127) (1982   –
5fg² 5f³ 6f⁴ 7d 6fg* 6g³ 6g* 6s 1983 8v) lengthy filly; fair performer as a 2-y-o;
had stiffish task on only outing of 1983 (April); should stay beyond sprint distances;
acts well on a sound surface. *E. Eldin.*

DECCAN QUEEN 2 ch.f. Decoy Boy 129–Queen's Herald (King's Leap 111)   **102**
(1983 5s² 5d* 5s² 5g² 5f 6f* 6f³ 6fg 5g 5fg²) Apr 19; 600Y; smallish, lengthy,
shallow-girthed filly; second foal; dam Irish 2m winner; made all in minor events at
Thirsk in April and Pontefract in July; placed in quite valuable events on fourth and
seventh outings and ran very well when caught on line by Meis El-Reem (had Reesh
and Anton Pillar behind) in minor race at Doncaster in October; best form at 5f on a
firm surface; apprentice ridden most starts (rider unable to claim on 3 of them);
tough and genuine. *E. Eldin.*

DECKI'S PRIDE 2 b.f. Goldhills Pride 105–Dark Echo (News Item 115) (1983
5d) Mar 25; first known foal; dam bad NH performer; remote seventh of 8 in seller
at Wolverhampton in May. *J. Harris.*

DECORATED 3 ch.f. Gunner B 126–New Ribbons 79 (Ribero 126) (1982 5f 5f³   **81**
5s 7fg⁴ 8.2d* 8.2s 1983 8s 8v 10s³ 12.2fg 12fg³ 12g 10f 10f 12g⁴ 12d 10.2fg) leggy,
rather lightly-built filly; poor walker; third in handicaps at Salisbury and Brighton in
June; had no sort of run penultimate start; suited by 1½m; acts on any going;
wandered badly, ridden by a girl apprentice, when successful as a 2-y-o; trained by
F. J. Houghton until after sixth start; sold to Mrs G. Forbes 10,000 gns Newmarket
December Sales. *J. Leigh.*

DECORATIVE 6 b.h. Martinmas 128–War Ribbon (Anwar 120) (1982 10f 10fg   **62**
10g⁴ 10.6g 10.5s 1983 12fg³ 10.2v 11.7d² 11.1v³ 10v 11.7f) compact, attractive
horse; middle-distance handicapper; ideally suited by an easy surface; usually
blinkered at 4 yrs and 5 yrs; has run well for an apprentice; sent to Italy. *C.
Mackenzie.*

DECOY DUCK 2 ch.f. Decoy Boy 129–Razia 97 (Martial 131) (1983 5s 5d² 6d*   **67**
6fg 7fg 6fg) May 4; 800Y; tall, leggy, wiry filly; sister to a winning 2-y-o plater and
half-sister to winners here and abroad; dam won over 5f at 2 yrs; ran on gamely to
justify favouritism by 1½ lengths from Beryls Dream in 15-runner maiden auction
event at Epsom in June; off course nearly 2 months afterwards and in rear in
nurseries on return; stays 6f; possibly requires a soft surface; sold 700 gns
Doncaster November Sales. *G. Blum.*

DEEP IN DEBT 4 b.f. Deep Run 119–Owenette (Master Owen) (1982 NR 1983   –
12g 11.5fg 16g³ 16fg) 3,000 3-y-o; small, useful-looking filly; second foal; dam
never ran; showed only sign of ability when remote third of 20 to Azara in maiden
race at Lingfield in June (apprentice ridden); stays well. *P. Haynes.*

DEEP ROOTS 3 b. or br.c. Dom Racine 121–La Paqueline (Sassafras 135) (1982   **117**
5d* 5g³ 5.5g² 6fg* 7f* 8s⁴ 1983 7.5v³ 6.5fg 8f) good-topped French colt; tough
and game as a 2-y-o, when winning 3 of his 6 races including Prix Morny and Prix de
la Salamandre; finished respectable 2½ lengths third of 7 to Ice Hot in Prix
Montenica at Saint-Cloud in April but was below form on only subsequent outings at

225

Deauville in August, finishing seventh of 14 behind Beaudelaire in Prix Maurice de Gheest and eighth of 10 behind Luth Enchantee in Prix Jacques le Marois; should have been well suited by 1m; probably acted on any going; standing at Haras du Petit Tellier, fee 30,000 francs. *P. Bary, France.*

DEFECTING DANCER 2 b.c. Habitat 134–Running Ballerina 87 (Nijinsky 138) **115** (1983 5. 1g* 5f* 5fg* 6g⁴ 6g* 5s² 5fg)

Sheikh Mohammed's purchase of the Dalham Hall Stud in October, 1981, together with the resident mares, foals and yearlings, paid its first sizeable dividend in 1983 when one of the foals, Defecting Dancer, developed into a leading two-year-old sprinter. Defecting Dancer has a fine record, winning four times and only once finishing out of the frame in seven starts while accumulating nearly £30,000. Admirable colt though he is, he missed the top class as a two-year-old and it's significant that he was beaten each time he ventured into pattern-race company, in the Prix Morny, the Flying Childers Stakes and the Cornwallis Stakes.

Defecting Dancer shared favouritism with the unbeaten Masarika in the Morny at Deauville in August, although he had yet to meet opposition of the calibre of that which was defeated by Masarika in the Prix du Bois and the Prix Robert Papin. Indeed Defecting Dancer had met with so little competition on the first and third of his outings that he started at 7/2 on for a maiden race at Yarmouth in June, which he won easily by two and a half lengths, and at 9/2 on in the Chesterfield Stakes at Newmarket, which he took by three lengths without coming off the bridle. The Windsor Castle Stakes at Royal Ascot, contested by six other previous winners, had provided him his only serious test. He again justified favouritism, winning going away by a length from All Agreed, needing to be chased along to get on top entering the last furlong. At Deauville Defecting Dancer always found the two-length winner Siberian Express going too fast for him and he was beaten a further neck and head into fourth place behind Ti King and Masarika; he wasn't at all disgraced.

We gained the impression at Deauville that seven furlongs would suit Defecting Dancer and soon afterwards his trainer said that he thought the colt should stay a mile. However, Defecting Dancer was kept to sprint distances, with some success. Next time out he picked up a valuable prize when landing the odds in the six-furlong BonusPrint Sirenia Stakes at Kempton in September. Whether he would have won had the runner-up Double Schwartz seen daylight in the last furlong is open to doubt but Defecting Dancer, who wasn't asked a serious question, may well have been able to pull out extra. Both of Defecting Dancer's subsequent races were over five furlongs. His display in the Flying Childers, when he battled on well to be beaten only half a length by Superlative, was one of his best but he disappointed in the Cornwallis at Ascot a month later, coming home only ninth behind Petorius when second favourite.

Defecting Dancer (b.c. Mar 22, 1981)	Habitat (b 1966)	Sir Gaylord (b 1959)	Turn-to
			Somethingroyal
		Little Hut (b 1952)	Occupy
			Savage Beauty
	Running Ballerina (b 1975)	Nijinsky (b 1967)	Northern Dancer
			Flaming Page
		Running Blue (ch 1957)	Blue Peter
			Run Honey

Defecting Dancer, a strong, rangy, quite attractive colt, is by the wonderfully successful Habitat out of Running Ballerina, a daughter of the similarly successful Nijinsky. Habitat's daughters have already produced the pattern-race winners Beaudelaire, Sicyos, Ghadeer and Princesse Lida to stallions from the Northern Dancer line. Defecting Dancer is the second foal and first winner bred by Running Ballerina, a filly who never fulfilled the promise she showed when landing something of a gamble on her only appearance as a two-year-old, in a six-furlong newcomers race at Lingfield. She promises to make amends at stud and her next foal, a yearling filly by Troy, should prove worth watching. Running Ballerina certainly has something to live up to as a broodmare: her dam, the Lingfield Oaks Trial winner Running Blue, was exceptionally successful, producing ten foals, nine of them winners while the one maiden, Santa Vittoria, finished fourth in the Irish One Thousand Guineas. Among Running Blue's winners were the smart middle-distance performers Dominion Day, winner of the Blandford Stakes, Northern Tavern, successful in the Prix Fille de l'Air, and Sir Penfro, winner of both the Gallinule and Desmond Stakes. Others to do well were the Ashford Castle Stakes winner Padroug and the Somerville Tattersall Stakes winner Burleigh, while one of her daughters, Relkarunner, produced the very smart Persian Bold, who has made a very promising start to his stud career. Lord Gayle, a half-brother to Running Blue, is another successful stallion from the family and Defecting Dancer has only

Windsor Castle Stakes, Ascot—Defecting Dancer wins going away from All Agreed and Shindella

to win a pattern race to become a valuable stallion prospect. We think he needs to improve if he's to do so but he may well improve if tried over seven furlongs and a mile. He's a consistent performer and acts on any going. *H. Cecil.*

DEFLOREUR (USA) 2 b.c. L'Enjoleur–Bed Shy (Bye and Near) (1983 6g²) Jan 21; $60,000Y; big, rangy colt; first foal; dam, smart winner at up to 9f in Canada, is half-sister to top Canadian filly Not Too Shy; weak 6/1-shot but looking to have done a fair amount of work, showed plenty of promise when 2 lengths second of 20 to At Talaq in maiden event at Newmarket in July, running on really well after a slowish start without being at all hard ridden; will stay at least 1¼m; sure to improve. *G. Harwood.* **84 p**

DELIGHTFUL TERN 3 ch.f. Towern 96–Mossy's Delight 44 (Mossy Face 98) (1982 7f 7fg 8s 1983 8s 10f 7f 12fg⁴) little worthwhile form in sellers. *P. Wigham.* **–**

DELIRAH 3 ch.f. Mansingh 120–Joie de Galles 72 (Welsh Pageant 132) (1982 5g 6g 6fg⁴ 6g 7d² 7d 7g 8s 8s 1983 8g⁴ 7f 10fg) rather lightly-made filly; plating-class maiden; stays 1m; appears to act on any going. *W. Elsey.* **–**

DELLWOOD IRIS 2 b. or br.f. Firestreak 125–Hindu Flame 83 (Shiny Tenth 120) (1983 5v³ 5g* 5f³ 6f 6g 6g 7fg) Mar 21; 450Y; second foal; dam 2-y-o 5f winner; made all in 15-runner maiden auction event at Brighton in May; apprentice ridden, finished well when good third in nursery at Folkestone nearly 2 months later, only subsequent form; should stay beyond 5f; acts on firm going. *W. Holden.* **71**

DELLWOOD JET 3 ch.g. Firestreak 125–Chebs Honour 70 (Chebs Lad 120) (1982 NR 1983 6v 7s 8s 7d 7f 8f 8f) big, lengthy, plain gelding; poor plater. *W. Holden.* **–**

DELTA LAD 3 b.c. Auction Ring 123–Veronica Heron 79 (Crooner 119) (1982 NR 1983 8f 8f) 14,500Y; lengthy colt; has been tubed; second foal; dam middle-distance winner; weak in market when towards rear in maiden races at Newbury in July and Sandown in August. *P. Walwyn.* **–**

DELTA QUEEN 4 gr.f. Warpath 113–Shenandoah 88 (Mossborough 126) (1982 10fg 12.2f 12d 14.7f² 15.8f² 15.8d 18d⁴ 20g² 1983 16.1v* 17d³ 18.8v 20fg 13h 17.4g) lengthy filly; won handicap at Haydock in April; needs further than 13f nowadays; acts on any going but goes well on heavy; has been bandaged in front; off course 3 months before fifth start. *C. Thornton.* **57**

DELUCYN 2 b.f. Moulton 128–Condora 99 (Matador 131) (1983 7fg) Apr 6; 2,000Y; half-sister to a winner in France and a winning hurdler; dam won 4 times over 6f; 50/1, dropped right away after 5f to finish last of 14 in minor event at Doncaster in October. *M. Tompkins.* **–**

DEM AN DOZE 4 b.c. Malacate 131–Cinquapace 61 (Tudor Melody 129) (1982 8d 7fg 10f 7.2f 6f⁴ 7g 7g³ 7g 8.3fg² 10.1g 8fg* 8s² 10v 1983 8v 10g 7s 8fg 7fg 8g 7.6fg 7fg) stocky colt; poor mover; plater; didn't show much at 4 yrs; suited by 1m; seems to act on any going; has run respectably for an apprentice. *P. Ashworth.* **–**

DEMON KING 4 ch.g. Hell's Gate 99–Ammeline (Never Say Die 137) (1982 NR 1983 12f 12s) small gelding; second reported foal; dam never ran; tailed-off last in 2 races at Beverley. *A. Smith.* **–**

DENEL (FR) 4 ch.c. Devon III 125–Vernel (Lionel 128) (1982 10.5s³ 11fg 12d³ **124** d
12d⁴ 12fg 12s⁴ 15.5v* 15.5v* 1983 15.5v* 15.5v³ 20v³ 12d 15.5f 14g) 30,000
francs Y (approx £3,000); leggy colt; has a round action; fourth foal; half-brother to
a minor winner in France by Phaeton; dam French middle-distance maiden; very
smart stayer; won Prix de Barbeville at Longchamp in April by ¾ length from
Kelbomec; creditable third on same course in Prix Jean Prat later in month (¾
length behind Kelbomec after being given too much to do) and Prix du Cadran in
May (about 5 lengths behind Karkour after again being given plenty to do); off
course subsequently until October and didn't run up to his best; revels in the mud;
blinkered penultimate start. *B. Secly, France.*

DENMORE 7 ch.h. Moulton 128–Dugo 90 (Dumbarnie 125) (1982 6d 6fg 6g 6f* **65**
6f 6g 6g² 6f 6f 6f 6f⁴ 5.8f 6s 7s 1983 7f 6f 6f 6f 7s⁴ 6g⁴ 6fg 6f) sturdy, good-bodied
horse; moderate mover; fair handicapper at his best but has deteriorated; best
form at 6f and 7f; acts on any going; sometimes blinkered, but not when successful;
has run respectably for an apprentice. *R. D. Peacock.*

DENO'S SONG 2 br.c. Wollow 132–Singing (Petingo 135) (1983 6f 7.2fg⁴) Mar **59**
23; 4,200Y; big, strong colt; has rather a round action; fourth foal; half-brother to
winning miler Smashing Fellow (by Dragonara Palace) and a winner in Italy; dam
never ran; soundly beaten in maiden auction event at Newcastle and minor race at
Haydock in the summer; exported to Singapore. *K. Stone.*

DENVER 3 b.c. Welsh Saint 126–Indian Runner (Sallust 134) (1982 7fg 7s 8s 1983 **65**
8s³ 10f² 10.8g) good sort; placed in handicap at Goodwood in May and amateur
riders event at Newmarket in July, best efforts; suited by 1¼m; sold to I. Vickers
10,500 gns Newmarket Autumn Sales. *B. Hills.*

DENVER ROYAL 3 b.g. Royal Match 117–Wilden (Will Somers 114§) (1982 6g **–**
8s 1983 8d 10.1d 10.1s 11.7v 8f 6f) no worthwhile form in maiden and minor
races. *M. McCourt.*

DEPORTMENT 3 b.f. So Blessed 130–Lady's Walk (Pall Mall 132) (1982 5fg* **89**
5fg* 5fg 6f 6f 1983 5g* 6d⁴ 7d 6fg) attractive filly; has a round action; returned to
form when beating Belinda Brown by a head in 10-runner handicap at Thirsk in
April; pulled hard in early stages when staying-on fourth of 10 to Bold Secret in
valuable handicap at Newmarket in May, best subsequent effort; stays 6f; possibly
not at her best on very firm going. *B. Hobbs.*

DEPOSIT 2 b.f. Thatch 136–Gay France 91 (Sir Gaylord) (1983 5fg 7f⁴ 6f² 7d⁴ **73**
5d) Apr 22; neat filly; first foal; dam 2-y-o 6f winner; quite moderate maiden;
stays 7f; acts on firm going and a soft surface. *R. Smyth.*

DEPUTY HEAD 3 b.c. Tower Walk 130–Ista Jil 97 (Gratitude 130) (1982 6f 6g⁴ **95**
5fg* 6fg 1983 6v 5s³ 6d 6v* 5g 6g³ 5f 5f 6fg³ 5f 6f* 6fg 6fg 6g) good-bodied, quite
attractive colt; poor mover; struggled to go pace when winning handicaps at York
in May and Newcastle in August; led inside last furlong and beat Coquito's Friend
by ½ length, despite edging left and right, in £9,700 Northumberland Sprint
Trophy on latter course; may well stay beyond 6f; acts on any going; genuine,
although was never going well final start. *J. Holt.*

DERBY ARMS 2 b.c. Owen Anthony 102–Tilting 74 (Galivanter 131) (1983 5v **–**
5v 5v) Feb 23; first foal; dam stayed 7f; of no account. *R. Smyth.*

DERBY DAY 2 b.c. Shirley Heights 130–L'Anguissola 102 (Soderini 123) (1983 **–**
6g 7f 7fg 8g) June 3; shapely, attractive colt; half-brother to smart sprinter
Smarten Up (by Sharpen Up) and very useful fillies Solar (by Hotfoot) and Walk
By (by Tower Walk); dam won three 6f races at 2 yrs; behind in maiden races, on
third outing moving badly to start and finishing last of 17. *W. Wightman.*

DERETA'S DUDLEY 2 br.c. Owen Dudley 121–Dereta 92 (Aggressor 130) **79**
(1983 7g 9s² 10.2fg) Apr 27; half-brother to 3 minor winners; dam stayer; shaped
like a thorough stayer when 4 lengths second of 10 to Prince Crow in maiden race at
Wolverhampton in October; suited by soft going. *C. Brittain.*

DERINGA 2 b.c. Daring March 116–Eringa 101 (Saint Crespin III 132) (1983 **–**
7.6fg 6d 7g) May 7; 4,100Y; rangy, quite attractive colt; half-brother to 2 winners,
including fairly useful 1½m winner Bewick (by Blakeney); dam disappointing
half-sister to Huntercombe; towards rear in October maiden races. *C. Horgan.*

DERIVATION (USA) 2 ch.f. Upper Nile–Fly Me First (Herbager 136) (1983 6f **–**
8g) Jan 11; $70,000Y; first foal; dam unraced half-sister to Chevron Flight, one of
best American 2-y-o's of 1971; kept on steadily to finish 12 lengths sixth of 17 to
Senane in 1m maiden race at Leicester in September; likely to stay well. *I.
Balding.*

DEROULEDE 4 b.c. Blakeney 126–Set Free 90 (Worden II 129) (1982 11f 54
13.3f² 14d 14fg⁴ 12f 14s 1983 17.1v 14fg 15.5f² 12fg³) attractive, rangy colt; good
walker; staying maiden; form only on a firm surface; blinkered fourth and fifth
starts in 1982; has run creditably for an apprentice; successful hurdler. *G.
Balding.*

DERRY DANCER 2 br.g. Derrylin 115–Deer Leap 106 (Deep Diver 134) (1983 74
6fg 7f 7f 6fg 8fg 8f) Feb 11; 5,400Y; strong, heavy-bodied gelding; has a round
action; second foal; dam Irish 5f winner; quite a moderate maiden; best effort on
second outing; blinkered final appearance; disappointing. *H. Collingridge.*

DERRY DON 3 b.c. Derrylin 115–Sugar Plum 103 (Zucchero 133§) (1982 NR –
1983 8f 10.1f 8f 9d 7g 6g) small, good-bodied, fair sort; half-brother to 3 winners,
including very smart 1m filly Greengage (by Primera); dam sprinter; little
worthwhile form in varied races; blinkered last 2 outings. *N. Vigors.*

DERRYGOLD 2 br.f. Derrylin 115–Krugerrand 74 (Goldhill 125) (1983 5s 5s 6f* 97
6f² 6fg 7f* 8.2f³ 7d⁴ 7d* 7fg) May 16; strong filly; has an enlarged near-hind
fetlock; third foal; dam won over 9f; won maiden race at Redcar in June, nursery
at Beverley in August and minor event at Catterick in October; ran well under 9-9
in Doncaster nursery final outing; stays 1m; acts on firm going and a soft surface
(did nothing on very soft going first 2 starts); genuine and consistent. *R. D.
Peacock.*

DERRY RIVER 2 br.c. Irish River 131–Duboff 120 (So Blessed 130) (1983 5s* 102
5s³ 5g³ 6fg 6f² 6g² 5.3fg² 5fg 5fg³) Apr 18; smallish, quite attractive colt; poor
walker and has a round action; third foal; half-brother to 2 winners, including fair
middle-distance winner Durun (by Run The Gantlet); dam won 11 races, including
Sun Chariot Stakes and Child Stakes; won 20-runner maiden race at
Wolverhampton in April by ¾ length from Street Level; subsequently ran creditably
in varied company, on final outing finishing excellent third of 17 under top weight of
9-7 in Potter Trophy Nursery at Newmarket in October; bred to stay at least 1m
but is clearly considered a sprinter; acts on any going; wears blinkers; tough and
consistent. *R. Laing.*

DESERT AIR 4 b.g. St Columbus 98–Lady Impeccable (Dalesa 109) (1982 6d 7f 40
8f 11.7f 8.2g 1983 12.2g 10g³ 12f 10f 8d 10fg 11s) short-backed gelding; poor
plater; has worn blinkers; trained by B. Morgan first 4 starts. *K. Bridgwater.*

DESERT BROOM (USA) 3 b.f. Hoist the Flag–Priceless Gem (Hail to Reason) 84
(1982 NR 1983 7v³) big, rangy, rather plain filly; has a good long stride; closely
related to Irish 1m winner Kimberley Mine (by Tom Rolfe) and half-sister to
several winners, notably outstanding filly Allez France (by Sea-Bird II), and to
outstanding New Zealand stallion Noble Bijou (by Vaguely Noble); dam second
best 2-y-o of her year and is half-sister to champion American filly Affectionately;
heavily-backed second favourite when 4 lengths third of 17 behind Magdalena in
maiden race at Goodwood in May; looked very promising indeed, but wasn't seen
out again. *J. Tree.*

DESIRABLE 2 gr.f. Lord Gayle 124–Balidaress (Balidar 133) (1983 6g* 6fg* 6g² 115
6d² 6fg*)
At 12/1 Desirable became the longest-priced winner of the Cheveley Park
Stakes since the 100/8-shot Berkeley Springs beat Right of the Line back in 1965.

Princess Margaret Stakes, Ascot—Desirable wins from Rocket Alert

William Hill Cheveley Park Stakes, Newmarket—a smart performance by Desirable
who challenges between Pebbles (blaze) and Prickle,
with Gala Event (left) close up

Whereas Berkeley Springs' form fully justified her starting price—she had been beaten over ten lengths in the Queen Mary Stakes at Royal Ascot on her only previous start—Desirable's odds seemed generous for a filly with her record. She had been a most impressive winner on her debut in the Princess Maiden Stakes at the Newmarket July meeting, bursting clear of her twenty-six opponents in the last furlong to beat Inspire five lengths, and then had followed in the footsteps of other recent winners of the race, Royal Heroine, Circus Ring, Tolmi and Luck of the Draw, in going on to success in the Princess Margaret Stakes at Ascot later in the month. Desirable wasn't so impressive at Ascot as some of her predecessors, needing to be given a couple of cracks before landing the odds by two lengths from the top-weighted Rocket Alert, but she was well on top by the finish, giving the strong impression that another furlong would be very much to her advantage. However she was kept to six furlongs, following the path taken by Royal Heroine and Circus Ring by reappearing in the Lowther Stakes at York in August. As Royal Heroine the previous year, Desirable found one too good for her; she was always chasing the favourite Prickle and was still two and a half lengths adrift at the line, despite running on strongly in the closing stages. Her trainer was later to excuse Desirable's defeat on the grounds that the pace had been too slow to suit her. While this excuse probably holds water we must point out that the onus was on her jockey to ensure that the race was truly run, and a little more enterprise might have seen her finish a good deal closer to the winner.

Desirable's trainer himself showed plenty of enterprise shortly after, in deciding to send her to Ireland for the Moyglare Stud Stakes at the Curragh in September. The only other English-trained runner was Ispahan, from the Dunlop stable which had sent out Habibti to win the year before's race, and it seems amazing that Britain's other leading trainers, several of whom have fifty or more two-year-olds, were unable to produce a challenger for a race which not only carries Group 1 status, but also a first prize of over IR £50,000. Although Desirable found one too good for her, going down by three quarters of a length to Gala Event, she ran well and rewarded her connections to the tune of IR £15,375. Desirable therefore came to the Cheveley Park (which incidentally was sponsored by the William Hill Organization for the eleventh and final time) having lost to only two horses in four outings. The only two horses to beat her were in the twelve-strong field and headed the betting, with Prickle at 11/8 and Gala Event at 6/1. Also at shorter odds were the French filly Island Smile, the winner of a newcomers event on her only start, and Prickle's stable-companion Jameelapi who was unbeaten after two outings in minor company. Prickle attempted to lead throughout as she had at York but she was never clear of her field and Desirable was hot on her heels passing the halfway mark. Other challengers soon appeared in the shape of Gala Event, Malaak and Pebbles and the race provided a thrilling finish, with Desirable staying on most gamely to hit the front in the last strides. Pebbles, finishing perhaps strongest of all, snatched second place from Prickle on the line, just a neck behind the winner. Less than two lengths covered the first six and the proximity of Malaak and Rocket Alert in fifth and sixth places suggests that this was far from a vintage Cheveley Park. Incidentally, although Desirable carries the colours of Mrs Corbett, a half-share in her is owned by Robert Sangster, bought from the trainer's wife after

230

the filly's impressive debut. Sangster therefore has now owned or part-owned four of the last eight Cheveley Park winners, the others being Durtal, Sookera and Woodstream. Let's hope Desirable fares better than the others as a three-year-old: Durtal's career was severely curtailed by an injury when getting loose on the way to the start of the Oaks, for which she was favourite; Sookera had to be retired to stud without racing again; and Woodstream disappointed so badly on her second outing at three that she was retired immediatelly.

Desirable (gr.f. Mar 29, 1981)	Lord Gayle (b 1965)	Sir Gaylord (b 1959)	Turn-to
			Somethingroyal
		Sticky Case (ch 1958)	Court Martial
			Run Honey
	Balidaress (gr 1973)	Balidar (br 1966)	Will Somers
			Violet Bank
		Innocence (gr 1968)	Sea Hawk II
			Novitiate

Desirable isn't a prepossessing filly, being lightly built and rather narrow, but then neither was Blue Wind, another of Lord Gayle's daughters, who won the Oaks by seven lengths. The chances are that Desirable will train on; indeed she should improve over longer distances. Her grandam Innocence, by that strong influence for stamina Sea Hawk II, won twice over nine furlongs at three years in Ireland. Her only living foal before her death as a six-year-old was Balidaress who stayed well for a filly by the sprinter Balidar, winning over seven furlongs and a mile at three and over a mile and a quarter the following year. Balidaress has produced two winning fillies by the miler Sallust both of whom stayed quite well, Salidar winning once over nine and a half furlongs and Braneakins three times over a mile and a half. Desirable, her third foal, cost only 10,000 Irish guineas as a yearling but her success boosted demand significantly for Balidaress' next produce, a filly by Ahonoora which sold for 62,000 guineas at the 1983 Newmarket Open Yearling Sales.

The Cheveley Park shows how little there is between the leading English

Mrs J. M. Corbett's "Desirable"

fillies and at this stage it's difficult to say who'll prove best at three. A lot depends on how they do during the winter. What we are able to say of Desirable is that she had few equals at two years, is thoroughly dependable and most certainly won't be found wanting for courage. She hasn't yet raced on very firm or very soft going but seems to act on any other. *B. Hills.*

DESTROYER 2 br.c. Lombard 126–Mary Green 81 (Sahib 114) (1983 7f 7g² 8d² 9s²) Mar 26; quite attractive colt; first foal; dam won from 1½m to 17f; second in autumn maiden events, going down by 1½ lengths to All Hell Let Loose at Leicester, by ½ length to Maypole Dancer at Warwick and by 4 lengths to Sassagrass at Wolverhampton; will stay well; should win at one of the minor meetings. *K. Brassey.*   **87**

DESTROY (USA) 4 b. or br.c. Annihilate 'Em–Nun Better (Bupers) (1982 7.6fg 12f 11f 10f 9g 8g² 8.2s 8g 7g 1983 17d⁴(dis) 16f) tall, rather narrow colt; has a marked knee action; possibly doesn't stay 2m; seems to need some give in the ground; trained by S. Harris first start. *M. Blanshard.*   **–**

DETAILS GALORE 2 ch.c. Octavo 115–Barefoot Contessa (Homeric 133) (1983 5fg 5fg 5fg 5g) Mar 17; IR 6,800F, IR 6,600Y; second foal; dam, an unraced twin, is a half-sister to high-class sprinter/miler Record Token; was surprisingly (considering her breeding) raced only at 5f, and showed no form at all after second appearance; appears to act on a firm surface. *K. Brassey.*   **64**

DETENTE 3 ch.f. Dominion 123–Dove 92 (Sea Hawk II 131) (1982 7d 10s 1983 8d 10s³ 12s⁴ 9f⁴ 10g 12fg* 12.2f* 12fg* 13.8f⁴ 10f 11.1g 12fg 11.7g) good-topped filly; improved, and in mid-season was ridden by claimer when winning minor events at Ripon and Catterick and handicap at Brighton; suited by 1½m and will stay 1¾m; has run creditably on soft going but is clearly very well suited by firm; suited by a strong gallop; saddle slipped tenth outing; sold 6,200 gns Newmarket December Sales. *P. Kelleway.*   **87**

DETROIT SAM (FR) 2 br.c. Green Dancer 132–Tocqueville (Sir Gaylord) (1983 6fg⁴ 7g*) May 4; 10,000Y; first living foal; dam, half-sister to very speedy Princesse Lee, was third over 4.5f and 7.5f at 2 yrs in France; upset by head, after good battle over last 2f, odds laid on Little Look in 14-runner maiden race at Lingfield in October; should stay at least 1¼m; evidently useful. *R. Akehurst.*   **98**

DEUCES WILD 2 ch.c. Malicious–Turandot (Golden Mallard 103) (1983 5d 5.1g 6fg 5.1f* 7fg 7f 5d 6fg) May 21; 1,000 2-y-o; smallish, sturdy colt; second foal; dam never ran; won seller at Yarmouth (bought in 2,000 gns) in June by 2 lengths from Mikev; seemed to find trip too far when first tried over 7f; acts well on firm ground. *C. Drew.*   **58**

DEUTSCHMARK 3 b.c. Nebbiolo 125–Santa Luciana (Luciano) (1982 6d 6s 1983 8s 8v³ 8v* 8.2v 8f 8f 10s⁴ 10fg* 10fg) strong, lengthy colt; none too consistent, but won maiden event at Goodwood in May and £4,300 handicap at Newmarket in September; ran on strongly to beat Soldier Ant by 2½ lengths on latter course; suited by 1¼m and will stay further; probably acts on any going; didn't have best of runs final start; sold 13,500 gns Newmarket Autumn Sales. *G. Wragg.*   **94**

DEVIL MAY CARE 6 b.g. Galivanter 131–Taffimai (Never Say Die 137) (1982 8fg 8fg⁴ 7fg² 8.3g 8g² 8fg³ 7s² 7g 8.2s 1983 8s 12g) strong, good sort; carries plenty of condition; stays 1m well; seems to act on any going; has run well for an apprentice. *J. Old.*   **–**

DEVIL QUEEN 3 ch.f. Queen's Hussar 124–God Sent 75 (Red God 128§) (1982 5d ⁴ 5d³ 5f 5f⁴ 6s 6g 7f 6fg 6f³ 6g 6d 7g 1983 7d 8f 8f 8f³ 11.5s 10fg) poor plater; stays at least 1m (wasn't disgraced over 11.5f); sometimes wears blinkers; sold 360 gns Ascot October Sales. *D. Dale.*   **45**

DEVIL'S ARROW 2 ch.g. Derrylin 115–Blessed Again 90 (Ballymoss 136) (1983 5fg) May 29; half-brother to several winners, notably high-class 5f to 7f performer Blue Cashmere; dam daughter of good stayer No Saint; 10/1, under pressure at halfway when distant sixth of 11 to Anton Pillar in minor event at Windsor in August; probably needs much further. *H. Candy.*   **–**

DEVISDALE 4 b.g. Swing Easy 126–Miss By Miles 91 (Milesian 125) (1982 7g 10f⁴ 8f⁴ 7.2f⁴ 6fg 9fg³ 8g⁴ 1983 7d⁴) most attractive gelding; good walker; disappointing maiden; seems to stay 1¼m; seems to act on any going; sometimes blinkered; sold 4,000 gns Ascot May Sales and subsequently gelded. *J. Fitzgerald.*   **–**

DEVON LAD 2 b.c. Tycoon II–Rye Grass 71 (Ribero 126) (1983 8g 7g) Apr 12; –
first foal; dam winning hurdler; 50/1, in rear in minor events at Bath and Chepstow
in October. *N. Kernick.*

DEVON MINSTREL 2 ch.g. Music Boy 124–Penny Bazaar 67 (Native Bazaar –
122) (1983 5s 5.8s 5h) May 1; good-quartered gelding; first foal; dam 7f winner; in
rear in maiden and minor events, at Chepstow in July on final outing bad last of 5.
M. McCourt.

DEW 2 ch.f. Sparkler 130–Vernier 94 (High Hat 131) (1983 7fg) Feb 6; fair sort, 76 p
rather unfurnished; third live foal; half-sister to useful middle-distance stayer
Voyant (by Star Appeal); dam won over 1½m and 13f; 50/1, last of 13 to Mahogany
in Rockfel Stakes at Newmarket in October; should do better in time. *B. Hobbs.*

DHANTERAS 5 b.g. Nonoalco 131–Classic Tune (Ribero 126) (1982 8s 1983 8d –
7s 6s 10g) rangy gelding; poor performer nowadays; has been beaten in a seller;
may stay 1¼m; best form on a firm surface; trained by G. Lewis part of season. *P.
Mitchell.*

DHOFAR 3 ch.g. Octavo 115–Cress (Crepello 136) (1982 5g 6fg³ 6fg³ 7fg⁴ 8g³ 89 d
8s² 1983 10v* 10d⁴ 10.2s⁴ 8f 8f⁴ 8f) workmanlike gelding; trotted up in maiden
event at Newcastle in April, but didn't run particularly well afterwards; stays
1¼m well; best form with some give in the ground. *G. Pritchard-Gordon.*

DIABOLICAL LIBERTY 2 ch.c. High Line 125–Rexana (Relko 136) (1983 73 p
7.6fg 8g) Mar 14; 8,400F, 32,000Y; second produce; dam, granddaughter of
Yorkshire Oaks winner Tenacity, won over 1m and 1½m in France; 20/1, ran well
for a newcomer when 7 lengths fifth of 16 to Judex in maiden race at Lingfield in
October; unquoted, again shaped promisingly when fifth of 15 to Leadburn in
similar event at Sandown later in month, coming through from rear to be beaten
less than 10 lengths; certain to win races over a distance of ground. *J. Sutcliffe.*

DIAMADA (FR) 2 gr.c. Dictus 126–Flota Armada 100 (Sovereign Path 125) 118
(1983 5.5d³ 6fg* 8s 6.5g*) second reported foal; half-brother to French 9f winner
Fusillade (by Run The Gantlet); dam won 7f Prix Imprudence; put up best effort
when 29/1-winner of Prix Eclipse at Saint-Cloud in October, finishing well to beat
Reine Caroline a length; had previously won a minor event at Evry in July by 3
lengths and finished 5 lengths sixth to Cariellor in Prix La Rochette (faded final
furlong); bred to stay 1m; acts on firm surface and is possibly not at his best on soft
going. *G. Bridgland, France.*

DIAMOND CUTTER 4 b.c. Song 132–Lucinda Anne (Abernant 142) (1982 5f ?
6g* 6f* 6f⁴ 6f* 6d² 6d 1983 6g 6f 5fg 6f² 6f 5.3fg² 6f 6d) strong, good-topped
colt; smart performer at his best; below form most starts at 4 yrs, best efforts
when second in £3,300 event at Newbury in July (behind Coquito's Friend) and
small race at Brighton in August (to Spark Chief); suited by 6f; seems to act on any
going; used to give trouble at start. *R. Williams.*

DIAMOND GEORGE 3 b. or br.g. Diamonds Are Trump 108–Flighty Hussy –
(Flit-To) (1982 NR 1983 12g 13f 12f) IR 2,400F, 5,800Y, 900 2-y-o; angular
gelding; bad mover; third foal; dam never ran; in rear in maiden races and an
amateur riders event, and seems of little account. *Peter Taylor.*

DIAMOND GIG 2 b.f. Pitskelly 122–Gem of Gems 106 (Grey Sovereign 128§) –
(1983 6s 7f) May 3; IR 41,000Y; robust, well-made filly; half-sister to several
winners, notably very smart middle-distance colt Amyndas (by Sparkler); dam won
at up to 1½m but was better at shorter distances; in rear in maiden races at
Lingfield in June and Sandown in July. *P. Mitchell.*

DIAMOND HILL 3 b.f. High Top 131–Montania 68 (Mourne 126) (1982 7g 1983 70
7v 8g 9f* 10.1f) good-topped filly; enterprisingly ridden when beating Trendy
Philly by 1½ lengths in 15-runner minor event at Wolverhampton in June; should
stay 1¼m; acts on firm going and has run respectably on heavy. *J. Winter.*

DIAMOND KING 4 ch.c. Music Boy 124–Long Valley 71 (Ribero 126) (1982 6s⁴ –
5f 7d 6fg 6fg 7s 6s² 6d 6s 1983 6v 7s 6d 6fg 7.6g 6h 7f⁴ 7f) strong, lengthy colt;
carries plenty of condition; has a round action; poor handicapper; stays 7f; acts on
any going; ran badly in blinkers once; sweated up second outing; sold to BBA 1,400
gns Newmarket Autumn Sales. *J. Benstead.*

DIAMONDS HIGH 2 ch.c. Diamonds Are Trump 108–Easy Path (Swing Easy 85
126) (1983 6g 6g 7.6fg² 7d²) Feb 23; 7,600F, 7,600 2-y-o; well-grown colt; third
reported produce; dam never ran; showed much improved form when 1½ lengths
second of 19 to Lexis in maiden race at Lingfield in October; co-favourite, could
stay on only at one pace when beaten 3 lengths by Derrygold in minor event at
Catterick later in month; will be suited by 1m. *P. Mitchell.*

John Porter Stakes, Newbury—Diamond Shoal runs on well from Little Wolf and Amyndas

DIAMOND SHOAL   4 b.c. Mill Reef 141–Crown Treasure (Graustark) (1982   **130**
12f* 12f 12fg² 12.5d 12s² 12g² 14.6f³ 12v³ 12d⁴ 1983 12d* 12d 12s* 12d⁴ 12fg*
12.5fg* 12fg² 12g* 12f)

When Paul Mellon decided to send his mare Crown Treasure to Mill Reef for
successive coverings in 1977 and 1978 it is doubtful whether even the rosiest pair
of spectacles could have led him to anticipate how successful the venture would
be. British racing has plenty of examples of full brothers making their mark on the
racecourse, starting with the 1790 and 1794 Derby winners Rhadamanthus and
Daedalus, and the matings of Mill Reef with Crown Treasure produced another
in Glint of Gold and Diamond Shoal. Both colts developed into top-class
performers, winning over £550,000 and picking up nine Group 1 races between
them, thus proving that repetition does not always have dullness as one of its
consequences.

Successful once and placed several times as a three-year-old, including in the
Great Voltigeur and St Leger, Diamond Shoal improved in his third season yet it
was not until the King George VI and Queen Elizabeth Diamond Stakes that he
showed British racegoers his top form. True, he had won the John Porter Stakes
at Newbury on his reappearance in fine style by three lengths from Little Wolf,
leading over a furlong out and staying on powerfully, but in both the Jockey Club
Stakes at Newmarket and the Coronation Cup at Epsom he had not run up to his
best. Ridden for speed at Newmarket, a strategy that was not repeated in his
later races, he began to struggle as soon as the pace increased half a mile out and
finished fifth to Electric, while at Epsom he set a modest gallop for much of the
race and consequently had no answer to the acceleration of Be My Native in the
last furlong and a half, ending up fourth, beaten also by Electric and Old Country.

Diamond Shoal's three other races before the King George were all abroad,
two in France and one in Italy, and he won the lot. Over the past few years we
have regularly sung the praises of British-based trainers for their enterprise in
sending horses to contest foreign races, and the level of success in 1983 was
unparalleled. Of the two-hundred-and-twenty pattern races run in France,
Germany, Ireland and Italy, thirty-five, including fourteen Group 1 events, were
won by horses trained in England while second places were obtained in
thirty-four. Add to this Tolomeo's Budweiser Million success along with a number
of wins in non-pattern races and the overall amount of money earned exceeded
two million pounds, a remarkable figure.

Ian Balding has always been quick to identify opportunities for his horses
wherever they may arise, and during 1983 members of his team won races in
Belgium, France, Germany, Ireland and Italy. Diamond Shoal, like Glint of Gold
the previous year, contributed most to the tally. His first foreign venture at four
came in the Grand Prix d'Evry, in which his behaviour immediately after the race
turned out to be more interesting than the contest itself. Favourite as he was
entitled to be, Diamond Shoal hit the front fully two furlongs out after being close
up from the start and stayed on altogether too strongly for his rivals, eventually

234

winning by a length and a half from Brezzo. Just after the post Asmussen, who had not ridden Diamond Shoal before, relaxed his hold on the colt who veered to the right in startling fashion, catching third-placed Kelbomec a blow in the process. Fortunately no damage was done to either horse, Asmussen managing to stop Diamond Shoal before they collided with the stand rail. Asmussen explained the incident by saying Diamond Shoal felt his work had been done and that it was time to leave the course, an understandable if in the event rather perilous intention. To our way of thinking this behaviour was merely an indication of the fact that Diamond Shoal, who lacked for nothing in courage or consistency, is a bit of a character—according to his trainer he did not enjoy having other horses around him and as he showed in the King George when he flashed his tail several times under pressure, resented being hit with the whip.

Diamond Shoal was returned to France in July for the Grand Prix de Saint-Cloud, a race Glint of Gold had won in 1982. In the meantime he had scored a facile victory in the Gran Premio di Milano, leading early in the straight and accounting for Easter Sun by four lengths to gain the first British success in a race instituted in 1924. At Saint-Cloud Diamond Shoal faced eight opponents and good as they were it was astonishing that he should be only eighth favourite behind the Ganay winner Lancastrian, Electric, All Along, the very smart three-year-olds Jeu de Paille and Esprit du Nord, the ex-American Lemhi Gold and the recent winner of La Coupe, Zalataia. Diamond Shoal maintained the family tradition in good style. With Lemhi Gold in the field there was likely to be no hanging around and he set off at the expected fast pace, soon having a lead of five lengths followed by Diamond Shoal and All Along. Turning into the straight the remainder had closed on Lemhi Gold whose advantage stood at not much more than a length over Diamond Shoal with All Along next, Electric, already being ridden along, in fourth and Zalataia and Lancastrian towards the rear. As the leader came under pressure, Cauthen sent Diamond Shoal on over a furlong and a half out and from that point he looked an assured winner; keeping on resolutely he saw off the challenges of Zalataia and Lancastrian to win a shade comfortably by three quarters of a length from the latter who had also been second to Glint of Gold in 1982. Zalataia finished a similar distance away third with Lemhi Gold, running by far his best race in Europe, fourth and All Along and Electric soundly beaten.

The strong pace at Saint-Cloud had suited Diamond Shoal ideally and with Lemhi Gold in the field for the King George VI and Queen Elizabeth Diamond Stakes three weeks later Diamond Shoal looked to have a good chance of improving on his brother's third place in the race twelve months before. Piggott, on Diamond Shoal for the only time, rode him to perfection. Settled beside Awaasif in second once Lemhi Gold had adopted his customary front-running position after half a furlong, Diamond Shoal travelled smoothly until easily passing the leader, who had clearly shot his bolt, with three furlongs to travel. Stealing a couple of lengths as they rounded the home turn, Piggott went for home and for much of the straight it looked as though the lead he had poached would stand his mount in good stead. Sun Princess, a length adrift a furlong and a half out, tried to get to Diamond Shoal but couldn't muster the necessary pace while Awaasif equally failed to quicken. A far more serious challenge had materialised on the outside, however, as Time Charter made ground steadily, and by the time they reached the furlong pole Diamond Shoal's lead had diminished to half a length or so. Gamely as he kept on, Diamond Shoal had no reply to Time Charter's superior turn of foot, losing the lead a hundred and fifty yards out and finally going down by three parts of a length, a length ahead of Sun Princess. This

Grand Prix de Saint-Cloud—another excellent victory for Diamond Shoal who wins a shade comfortably from Lancastrian and Zalataia

time Lancastrian finished some eight lengths behind his Saint-Cloud conqueror in fifth.

With no appropriate races left for him in Britain after the King George Diamond Shoal once more went off on his travels, first trying to follow his brother's example by winning the Grosser Preis von Baden. The race was no contest. Up against the English colt Prima Voce, the Grosser Preis von Berlin winner Abary and five others, Diamond Shoal led at least half a mile out and cantered home by three and a half lengths from Abary with Prima Voce five lengths back in third. This result meant that all nine of the Group 1 races won by Glint of Gold and Diamond Shoal had taken place abroad, a noteworthy achievement, and whereas injury had prevented Glint of Gold from contesting the Trusthouse Forte Prix de l'Arc de Triomphe Diamond Shoal lined up for that race in an attempt to increase the total. Understandably one of the most fancied of the twenty-six runners he regrettably failed to run up to his very best though by no means disgraced. Close up from the start and alongside Sun Princess entering the straight, he could only keep on at one pace thereafter, being swamped in the closing stages and coming home twelfth to All Along, beaten about five lengths. We thought Diamond Shoal did not look quite so well here as earlier in the year, and it is likely that his arduous season had taken its toll. A plan to give him a late-autumn campaign in the States and Japan had to be abandoned when he sustained an injury to his hock on the gallops, and it was finally announced that he had been syndicated to stand alongside such as Alleged and Nureyev at the Walmac-Warnerton complex in Kentucky at a fee of 25,000 dollars, live foal.

Diamond Shoal has a first-class pedigree. Another good son of Mill Reef following Acamas, Glint of Gold, Milford, Main Reef, Pas de Seul and Shirley Heights, his breeding on the dam's side is no less impressive. Crown Treasure, successful over five furlongs and placed in the Grade 3 Schuylerville Stakes over six furlongs at two, is a half-sister to two smart American winners, Diomedia and Gold Treasure, out of the very useful six-and-a-half-furlong and one-mile stakes winner Treasure Chest. Since foaling Diamond Shoal Crown Treasure has visited Mill Reef twice more, producing the most disappointing three-year-old filly Emerald Reef and a colt foal who has a lot to live up to, plus the two-year-old Glimmering (by

Mr Paul Mellon's "Diamond Shoal"

Troy), a most promising third on her only outing to date, and a yearling colt by Shirley Heights. The third dam, successful five times from fifty-three starts, foaled five other winners, the best of them the top American two-year-old filly of 1959 My Dear Girl, subsequently dam of the tip-top runner and sire In Reality.

Diamond Shoal (b.c. 1979)	Mill Reef (b 1968)	Never Bend (b 1960)	Nasrullah
			Lalun
		Milan Mill (b 1962)	Princequillo
			Virginia Water
	Crown Treasure (b 1973)	Graustark (ch 1963)	Ribot
			Flower Bowl
		Treasure Chest (b 1962)	Rough 'n Tumble
			Iltis

With this breeding and his excellent record the admirable Diamond Shoal, who was a great credit to his trainer, should develop into a highly popular stallion. An attractive individual and a good mover who acted on any going, he stayed a mile and three quarters and required a strong gallop to be seen to best advantage over a mile and a half. *I. Balding.*

DIANA'S DELIGHT 2 ch.f. Some Hand 119–Bonham Hill (Armagnac Monarch 91) (1983 5s 8g 9g) Apr 5; sturdy filly; has a round action; second foal; dam won 4 point-to-points; behind in maiden races and a seller. *D. C. Tucker.* —

DIANA'S PET 3 b.g. Mummy's Pet 125–Charonne 87 (Charlottown 127) (1982 5d 6fg² 6f4 6g* 6f4 7fg4 6s 1983 12f 8f) shallow-girthed, fair sort; good walker and mover; quite useful as a 2-y-o but was well beaten in 1983; best form at 6f and is unlikely to stay 1½m; appears to act on any going. *S. Pattemore.* —

DICK 'E' BEAR 3 gr.g. Rupert Bear 105–Silent Swindler 59 (Tacitus 124) (1982 5g² 6f² 6g* 7d 6fg³ 8d 1983 8fg 8f 8f 10g* 8fg 10f² 10f 10s 10fg) sparely-made gelding; ridden out to beat Burley Griffin a neck in 5-runner handicap at Ayr in July; ran easily best subsequent races on next 2 starts; ran in a void race third start; stays 1¼m; acts on firm going; game. *M. Jefferson.* 82

DICK KNIGHT 2 ch.c. Owen Dudley 121–Illumination 86 (St Paddy 133) (1983 8fg 7f) May 18; 20,000Y; workmanlike colt; first foal; dam, daughter of 1000 Guineas winner Honeylight, won over 1m and 9f on only starts; possibly flattered when beaten less than 4 lengths in slowly-run £3,200 event at Newmarket in October, and failed to reproduce the form when fifth of 8 behind Jabaraba in minor event at Leicester soon afterwards; will stay 1¼m. *A. Bailey.* 84 ?

DICK'S FOLLY 4 br.g. Martinmas 128–No Princess (Prince Regent 129) (1982 10.4fg 9fg 8fg² 8fg* 8d³ 8d4 8.2s 8s 1983 7s) quite attractive gelding; often pulls hard and isn't certain to stay 1¼m; acts on a firm and a soft surface. *R. Hodges.* —

DIDO 3 b.f. Full of Hope 125–Correct Approach 77 (Right Tack 131) (1982 5fg³ 5fg* 6g* 5f 6fg 6g² 6fg 6d 1983 6d 6fg³ 6f² 6fg 5fg³ 6fg 5.1s 5g) leggy, useful-looking filly; plater; stays 6f; acts on firm going; suitable mount for an apprentice; sometimes blinkered. *P. Cole.* 47

DIE IN THE SKY 2 ch.c. Welsh Pageant 132–Heaven and Earth (Midsummer Night II 117) (1983 7fg 7g 8fg) Feb 25; 4,500Y; strong, stocky colt; half-brother to fairly useful 1979 2-y-o 5f winner Our Mother (by Bold Lad, Ire) and a winning hurdler; dam ran only twice; behind in varied company in the autumn. *S. Norton.* —

DIENAU'S TROVE 2 b.c. Hot Grove 128–Dienau 68 (Connaught 130) (1983 7.6fg 8.2fg) Apr 27; first foal; dam, plating class at 2 yrs, ran without success over hurdles and fences; unquoted, in rear in October in maiden race at Lingfield and £3,400 event at Nottingham. *H. Collingridge.* —

DIESIS 3 ch.c. Sharpen Up 127–Doubly Sure 59 (Reliance II 137) (1982 6f 6g* 6g* 7g* 1983 8g 7d²) 120
'I think all the first four classics come too early . . . you only need a bad winter and spring and you've really got to start pushing it'. The words are those of Henry Cecil, trainer of the winter favourites for both the 1983 Two Thousand Guineas (Diesis) and Derby (Dunbeath). Quoted in the same article, published in *The Sporting Life* in March, Cecil also made the prophetic statement: 'You've got to force the horses along which is rather like forcing anything. You'll get a bloom all right, but it won't be natural, and unless you're clever and careful it will fall in a heap'. The problems of preparing horses for the Newmarket and Epsom classics were highlighted in the latest season because of the abnormally wet spring; gallops were waterlogged and race meetings were abandoned up and down the country with the loss of several events which traditionally serve as preparatory races for

classic contenders. With Diesis, Cecil's problems were compounded when the colt was stopped in his work for a week after pulling up lame on the gallops in early April. In the time that remained at their disposal Cecil and his team achieved a notable feat in getting Diesis to post at Newmarket, particularly after Diesis suffered a further leg injury a few days before the race. The affected leg filled when the bandage was removed the night before the Guineas and Diesis' participation was in doubt until the very last moment. In the circumstances, it was perhaps hardly surprising that Diesis—winner of three of his four races as a two-year-old including the William Hill Dewhurst—failed to do himself justice. He moved feelingly to post and finished eighth to Lomond, halfway down the field. It should be recorded here that the connections of Diesis showed a commendable openness about the colt's training problems, issuing frequent statements in April about his condition.

	Sharpen Up (ch 1969)	Atan (ch 1961)	Native Dancer
			Mixed Marriage
		Rocchetta (ch 1961)	Rockefella
Diesis			Chambiges
(ch. c. 1980)	Doubly Sure (b 1971)	Reliance II (b 1962)	Tantieme
			Relance III
		Soft Angels (ch 1963)	Crepello
			Sweet Angel

Diesis was seen out only once after the Two Thousand Guineas—he was beaten by The Noble Player at 3/1 on over seven furlongs at Kempton in May—and will take up stud duties at Mill Ridge Farm, Kentucky in 1984 at a fee of 35,000 dollars (live foal). Diesis is the second of three sons of Sharpen Up and Doubly Sure to reach the racecourse: Diesis' elder brother Kris won fourteen of his sixteen races while the two-year-old Keen created a very favourable impression when winning the Granville Stakes as Ascot on his only outing in 1983. Doubly Sure is expecting another foal by Sharpen Up in 1984. Diesis, a sparely-made, attractive colt, who didn't make the same amount of physical progress as Kris from two to three, should have stayed a mile. *H. Cecil.*

DIFFERENT CLASS 3 b.g. The Brianstan 128–Acknowledgement (Fleet Nasrullah) (1982 6fg 5d 1983 11.7s) leggy gelding; no sign of ability in maiden events. *Mrs B. Waring.* —

DIGNIFIED AIR (FR) 3 b.f. Wolver Hollow 126–Dismantle 77 (Aureole 132) (1982 6s³ 1983 8f 10f 8f 7.6d 8g) tall, leggy, quite attractive filly; little form in 1983; should stay 1m; trained by M. Jarvis until after third start. *K. Brassey.* —

DIMITRI 4 ch.c. Sharpen Up 127–Doushiska 78 (Hornbeam 130) (1982 8fg² 11f 10fg² 10.1d³ 10.1fg⁴ 10g* 1983 8v 10g 10h 11.7fg⁴ 11.7fg* 11.7f* 12h) well-made, attractive colt; made most to win 2 handicaps at Windsor in August; ran poorly final start; stays 1½m; seems to act on any going. *C. Nelson.* 73

DINADAN 2 b.g. Swing Easy 126–Grace (Gratitude 130) (1983 5v 5fg 6g 6g 5g³ 5g) Mar 7; light-framed gelding; half-brother to 3 winners; dam apparently of little account; easily best effort when 2 lengths third of 7 to Preobrajenska in minor event at York in October, making up an enormous amount of ground from halfway; lost chance at start when favourite for maiden race at Sandown later in month; should be suited by 6f; gelded after final outing. *J. Holt.* 78

DINGLE BELLE 3 ch.f. Dominion 123–Temple Wood 105 (Sweet Revenge 129) (1982 6d 1983 8s 8d³ 12g³ 13.8s* 12f³ 13.8f) small filly; kept on well when winning handicap at Catterick in June; stays 13.8f; acts on any going. *W. Wharton.* 63

DINNER TOAST (USA) 3 b.or br.f. Raise a Cup–Dinner Meeting (Bold Ruler) (1982 6g 1983 7fg 7.2fg* 8f 7f² 7.2g⁴ 7f* 8fg* 7fg) useful-looking filly; wide-margin winner of modest maiden race at Haydock in July and handicap at Redcar in September prior to making most of running and staying on well to account for Miss Bali Beach by ¾ length in valuable Taylor Woodrow Team Charity Stakes (Handicap) at Ascot later in September; stays 1m; acts on firm going; didn't run up to her best final start, but carried 6-lb penalty and 4 lb overweight. *R. Armstrong.* 101

DISCOURSE 2 ch.c. Record Token 128–River Aire 82 (Klairon 131) (1983 5v 5v 6fg 6f) Mar 20; small, compact colt; of no account. *B. Swift.* —

DISCREETLY YOURS 2 b.or br.f. Averof 123–Charlotte Helen 65 (Sweet Revenge 129) (1983 5v 5s 6fg* 6f² 7fg 7f*) Apr 1; 1,100Y; rather leggy filly; good walker; first foal; dam half-sister to smart Escapologist; successful in sellers at Yarmouth (bought in 1,000 gns) in June and Newcastle (retained 2,300 gns) in July; stays 7f well; form only on fast ground; blinkered at Newcastle; sold privately 2,250 gns Doncaster November Sales for export to Barbados. *W. Musson.* 56

DISTANT SOUND 2 b.f. Faraway Times 123–Some Say (I Say 125) (1983 5s 5d — 5v 5f) Apr 10; leggy filly; second foal; dam apparently of little account; poor form in maiden events; not raced after June. *M. Smyly.*

DISTANT THUNDER 3 b.c. Wolver Hollow 126–Trusted Maiden (Busted 134) 73 (1982 7g 8g 1983 8d 8v⁴ 10.4fg² 12f) well-made, attractive colt; in frame in maiden races at Warwick in May and Chester in July; should stay 1½m; seems suited by top-of-the-ground; sold to BBA (Ire) 4,000 gns Goffs November Sales. *B. Hills.*

DISTURBANCE MONEY 4 b.c. Busted 134–Refifi 87 (Reform 132) (1982 8s 91 12fg* 14f* 14fg³ 10g 1983 10s 12s³ 20f 12f 16fg) 2,000Y; big, lengthy colt; second foal; dam won over 9f; 1½ lengths third of 16 to Croghan Hill in minor event at Limerick Junction in June, best effort at 4 yrs; moved poorly to post when tailed off behind Little Wolf in Gold Cup at Royal Ascot third start; suited by 1¾m and should get further; acts on any going. *J. Bolger, Ireland.*

DIVINE DEACON 2 br.f. Roman Warrior 132–Samia 73 (Galivanter 131) (1983 — 8g 7f) Feb 20; leggy, lightly-made filly; behind in September in maiden race at Leicester and seller at Redcar; dead. *T. Fairhurst.*

DIZZY HEIGHTS 5 b.m. Daring Display 129–Balholm 61 (Le Levanstell 122) — (1982 10.1fg 10f 8fg 10fg 10d 10g 10f 8g 10g⁴ 1983 10f 10fg⁴ 10f⁴ 10f⁴) small, lengthy mare; plater; stays 1¼m; acts on any going; occasionally blinkered; suitable mount for an apprentice. *H. Fleming.*

DJANGO 3 br.c. Music Boy 124–Young Mementa (Young Christopher 119) (1982 98 5f* 5g² 5g 1983 6v 5f 5f* 5f² 5f² 6f³ 5g² 6fg) rangy colt; good walker; won handicap at Doncaster in June, despite wandering right; narrowly beaten subsequently in more strongly-contested handicaps at Newmarket, Goodwood, Newcastle and York; stays 6f but probably best at 5f; acts on firm going; blinkered nowadays; sweated up fifth start; not himself when well beaten final outing. *K. Brassey.*

D'LO 5 b.g. Sovereign Path 125–Blaskette 99 (Blast 125) (1982 11f³ 12fg* 12fg⁴ — 12.2fg² 12.2fg³ 12f* 13.1g 12fg 1983 12f) rangy, quite attractive gelding; stays 1½m; acts well on firm going; best in blinkers; not particularly consistent, and finished last of 20 only start at 5 yrs; sold 1,600 gns Doncaster November Sales. *J. Old.*

D NOTICE 2 ch.c. Most Secret 119–Come North 72 (Track Spare 125) (1983 5v — 5v 5s) May 12; 320Y; small colt; turns off-hock out badly; of no account. *C. Wildman.*

DOC MARTEN 5 b.h. Hotfoot 126–Rockney 84 (Roan Rocket 128) (1982 7fg 7f³ 104 7f³ 6fg 6g³ 7f⁴ 6fg³ 6f³ 6fg⁴ 6fg 6g* 1983 6g³ 6v² 6v 6f 7fg 6f² 8.3fg 6f⁴ 6s 6g* 6fg³ 6fg³ 6fg⁴) quite useful sort; useful performer; beat Azaam a length in Otis Handicap at Haydock in October; creditable second earlier in CBA Greenlands Stakes at the Curragh (outpaced near finish when length behind Curravilla) and handicap at Newmarket; stays 7f; acts on any going. *A. Hide.*

DOCTOR'S ORDERS 2 b.c. Nonoalco 131–Enchanted 116 (Song 132) (1983 79 5v³ 6h⁴ 6f* 6f) Mar 23; quite attractive, lengthy colt; fourth foal; half-brother to 2 winners, including very useful 3-y-o Lofty (by High Top), a winner at up to 8.5f; dam smart sprinting 2-y-o; won 10-runner maiden race at Epsom in August; favourite when twelfth of 16 in Redcar nursery the following month; will stay 7f; acts very well on firm going; sold P. Brookshaw 17,000 gns Newmarket Autumn Sales. *H. T. Jones.*

DODGY FUTURE 3 b.c. Nebbiolo 125–Taking Silk (Shantung 132) (1982 5fg 84 7d⁴ 6f 1983 8d² 8v* 8d* 10g* 9d) big, quite well-made colt; awarded handicap at Ripon in June after going down by a neck to Commodore Bateman, who quite badly interfered with him; off course afterwards until September when winning amateur riders race at Goodwood and 16-runner handicap at Newbury, latter by neck from Jimjams; stays 1¼m well; acts on heavy going; below his best final outing. *S. Mellor.*

DOLLAR DREAMER (USA) 2 b.f. Buckfinder–Let Me Sleep (Cyane) (1983 55 5v 6s 5fg 5g 5g 5g⁴) Jan 24; $50,000Y; rangy filly; first foal; dam, winner at up to 1m, is half-sister to Washington International winner Johnny D; plating-class maiden; may do better at 7f+; blinkered fourth outing; sold 4,000 gns Newmarket December Sales. *G. Hunter.*

DOLLYMIXTURE BOY 5 b.g. Connaught 130–Country Niece (Great Nephew — 126) (1982 12f* 12fg* 10f* 10f* 12f* 12g 10g 10g⁴ 10f 10d⁴ 10d 1983 10g 10g 10f 10f 10f 11.5g) small, stocky gelding; good walker and mover; didn't find his form in 1983; suited by middle distances and top-of-the-ground; used to wear blinkers and has worn a hood but is better without; successful 3 times for apprentice S. Dennison; suited by front-running tactics. *R. Armstrong.*

DOMANUS 2 b.c. Le Johnstan 123–Par Bloom (Pardal 130) (1983 6g 6f² 5.8f⁴ 7.2g² 6fg) May 22; 3,800Y; leggy colt; half-brother to 5 winners, including fairly useful 6f and 7f winner Mummy's Pleasure (by Mummy's Pet) and successful jumper Alick (by Abwah); dam placed at up to 11f in France; in frame in maiden auction events and a seller; stays 7f well. *C. Spares.* **69**

DOMICILE 3 b.f. Dominion 123–Siliciana 113 (Silly Season 127) (1982 5g 5.8g 8s 7d 1983 8.2s 10fg 10.6g 10fg) strong, good-bodied filly; sixth in maiden race at Salisbury in September on second start, best effort; trained first outing by E. Incisa; sold 3,000 gns Newmarket Autumn Sales. *I. Balding.* **–**

DOMINATE 2 b.c. Pitskelly 122–Elvina (Dancer's Image) (1983 5v 5d⁴ 7f 6f 7f 6h⁴ 7g 7d) Jan 14; close-coupled, fair sort; first foal; dam Irish 6f and 1¼m winner; plating-class maiden; will stay 1m; apparently suited by a sound surface; sold P. Mitchell 3,200 gns Newmarket Autumn Sales. *D. Whelan.* **67**

DOMINION BLUE 2 ch.f. Dominion 123–Blue Book 101 (Majority Blue 126) (1983 5fg 5d³) June 5; 6,200Y; half-sister to 4 winners, all successful at 2 yrs, including useful La Voleuse (by Burglar); dam, winner twice over 5f at 2 yrs, stayed 1m; ran respectably in maiden races at Bath and Catterick in the autumn; will stay 6f. *J. Spearing.* **66**

DOMINION GIRL 3 ch.f. Dominion 123–Blue Book 101 (Majority Blue 126) (1982 6fg 7s 1983 10.1s 10s 8f 8g 10.8g) small filly; little worthwhile form, including in sellers. *K. Cunningham-Brown.* **–**

DOMINION PRINCESS 2 b.f. Dominion 123–Eastwood Bounty 87 (Bounteous 125) (1983 6f) Apr 3; 4,500F, 5,000Y; rangy, workmanlike filly; half-sister to several winners, including 1982 2-y-o 6f winner Fiefdom (by Home Guard) and smart Woodsome (by Runnymede), winner at up to 8.5f in England and USA; dam effective from 5f to 1¼m; unquoted, never-dangerous eighth of 13 in maiden race at Doncaster in June. *P. Rohan.* **–**

DOMONIK SAVIO 2 ch.c. Music Boy 124–Rubella (Buisson Ardent 129) (1983 6h 5g 5d) Mar 25; half-brother to numerous sprint winners, including speedy 1975 2-y-o Alacriter (by Mountain Call); dam ran once; little worthwhile form in maiden races; blinkered final outing. *P. O'Connor.* **–**

DOM PASQUINI (FR) 3 gr.c. Rheffic 129–Boursonne (La Varende 125) (1982 10v* 1983 10.5v* 12v* 10.5v* 12fg 13.5fg² 14.6s⁴ 12f) tall colt; half-brother to 3 winners in France; dam won twice in France at up to 10.5f; sold out of F. Mathet's stable 580,000 francs (approx £53,000) in March, having won 18-runner maiden race at Saint-Cloud as a 2-y-o; showed himself a smart performer when winning first 3 starts of 1983, 2 minor events at Saint-Cloud and 6-runner Prix Greffulhe at Longchamp; having second race in 3 days when winning latter in April, leading early in straight and holding off Lovely Dancer by 1½ lengths; ran moderately in Prix du Jockey-Club at Chantilly in June (said to have been coughing afterwards) but subsequently finished in frame in Grand Prix de Deauville in August (1½ lengths **122**

Prix Greffulhe, Longchamp—Dom Pasquini holds off Lovely Dancer to win his second race in three days

second to Zalataia) and St Leger at Doncaster in September (about 7 lengths fourth to Sun Princess, staying on well after taking time to get going); handaged when tailed off in Trusthouse Forte Prix de l'Arc de Triomphe on final start; stayed well; probably acted on any going but went extremely well in the mud; standing at Haras de Victot at a fee of 25,000 francs (Oct 1st). *R. Collet, France.*

DOM PERIGNON 8 b.g. Sparkler 130–Breathalyser (Alcide 136) (1982 13f⁴ 12f⁴ 12f 15f 1983 12fg) middle-distance handicapper; acts on any going. *Mrs R. Lomax.*

DON AVANTI 3 br.c. Dom Racine 121–Injection 94 (On Your Mark 125) (1982 5fg 7g 7g 1983 10v³ 8f² 8f) robust colt; ran well when placed in minor event at Kempton in May and £5,100 maiden race at York in June, finishing 1½ lengths second to Prego in latter, but was out of first 11 of 27 in Britannia Stakes (Handicap) at Royal Ascot on only subsequent outing; stays 1¼m. *A. Jarvis.*   74

DON BASILE (FR) 2 b.c. Bellypha 130–Ladona (Don II 123) (1983 8g 8fg 8s* 8f*) fourth foal; dam, half-sister to Monteverdi, won over 1¼m in France; improved with experience and beat Dictallino by ½ length in maiden race and Grausberry by a nose in 80,000-franc event, both at Longchamp in October; suited by 1m; acts on any going. *A. Head, France.*   105

DONEGAL PRINCE 7 b.g. Prince de Galles 125–Serena Rose 76 (Hethersett 134) (1982 18g 16fg 18.4fg 16f⁴ 22.2fg 16.1f 18g 16d⁴ 16v 18s 1983 18d 16g³ 16fg⁴ 18fg) quite attractive gelding; useful out-and-out staying handicapper at his best but has deteriorated; acts on any going; effective with or without blinkers; suited by a strong gallop; smart hurdler on his day. *P. Kelleway.*   74

DONE GOOD 4 gr.g. Jolly Good 122–Donna Julia 79 (Don II 123) (1982 7g 10f 10f 8f² 8fg 8fg 10fg 8.2s³ 10.6s 10g 12d³ 10.2s 1983 8.2s* 8s 9d) lengthy gelding; plater; bought in 1,100 gns after winning at Hamilton in April; possibly doesn't stay 1½m; acts on any going; blinkered nowadays; hung and found little second start; sold 480 gns Doncaster October Sales. *J. Parkes.*   36

DON MARTINO 2 br. or gr.g. Martinmas 128–Silbadora 67 (Don II 123) (1983 5s 6f) Apr 22; IR 18,500Y; lengthy, workmanlike gelding; fourth foal; half-brother to 2 winners, including fairly useful 1982 2-y-o 6f winner Gangawayhame (by Lochnager); dam ran only at 2 yrs; in rear in maiden races at Salisbury (last of 14) in May and Goodwood (ninth of 11) in July. *G. Balding.*   –

DONNA GREY 3 gr.f. Joshua 129–Empress Donna 48 (Don II 123) (1982 5fg 7.2s 6s 1983 5s 6v 5f 5f 6f 5f) leggy, sparely-made filly; little worthwhile form, including in sellers; blinkered last 2 starts; sold 510 gns Doncaster August Sales. *W. Stubbs.*

DONNA SIRENA 2 br.f. Julio Mariner 127–Donnarose (Fighting Don) (1983 6g⁴ 6f 7g 7.6g 7.6d) Mar 31; quite attractive, rangy filly; half-sister to several winners, including fairly useful 7f and 1m winner Summer Madness (by Silly Season) and useful 7f performer Fighting Lady (by Chebs Lad); dam of little account; quite a moderate maiden; will be better suited by 1¼m+. *R. Laing.*   72

DONNYSNOOKERCENTRE 2 br.g. Mandrake Major 122–Emerald Rocket 69 (Green Ruler 128) (1983 6d 6f 6fg⁴ 7f 7f 8h 8f) Apr 17; 2,100F, 2,600Y; big, workmanlike gelding; first produce; dam 1m winner; plating-class maiden; stays 1m; acts on firm going. *E. Weymes.*   69

DON PRESTO (FR) 9 b.g. Presto–Donna Speranza (Stani) (1982 9f² 16.1f 12fg³ 12g 12f³ 10g 11.7fg 12fg 12d³ 12s 1983 12s 10v³ 8g³ 12f 8f³) strong gelding; plater nowadays; probably best at middle distances; probably acts on any going; suitable mount for an amateur rider. *D. Morley.*   52

DON'T ANNOY ME 3 b.g. Manado 130–Embarrassed 81 (Busted 134) (1982 6fg 6g 6d 8fg 7d 7s 1983 5v 5v 6d 6g* 6f 7.2g 8f 8f 8.2g 6g 7g 7fg³ 9fg 7fg) IR 2,100Y; leggy, rather narrow ex-Irish gelding; first foal; been twice at around 2m; ran brave races here when winning maiden race at Ayr in May and when third in handicap at Doncaster in October; had some stiffish tasks in between; best form at up to 7f, but promises to stay further; blinkered tenth outing. *R. Whitaker.*   70

DONZEL (USA) 2 ch.c. Lyphard 132–Lindaria (Sea-Bird II 145) (1983 7fg* 7.3d) Apr 5; $150,000Y; quite attractive, good-bodied colt; very good mover; closely related to Linda North (by Northern Dancer), a very useful stakes winner at up to 1m, and half-brother to 3 winners, including very useful 1982 2-y-o 7f winner By Decree (by Caro) and good French middle-distance performer Vagaries (by Vaguely Noble); dam placed twice from 8 starts; won 8-runner Mornington Stakes at Ascot   100

Mr K. Abdulla's "Donzel"

in September by ¾ length from Ministerial; disappointing last of 7 in Horris Hill Stakes at Newbury the following month; will stay 1¼m. *J. Tree.*

DOON SILVER 9 gr.m. Doon 124–Silver Pin (Pindari 124) (1982 NR 1983 15.5f 10g) of little account. *J. Long.* —

DO OR DIE 6 b.g. Warpath 113–Shenandoah 88 (Mossborough 126) (1982 NR 1983 12g) strong, good sort; good walker; suited by a test of stamina. *O. O'Neill.* —

DORA MAAR (USA) 3 gr.f. Native Charger–Pan Shot (Northern Dancer) (1982 6f 6g 1983 8v 6s² 6f 6fg 6f⁴ 6g² 6fg³ 6g) quite attractive, well-made filly; second in handicaps at Goodwood in May and Yarmouth in September; stays 6f. *L. Cumani.* — 62

DORAME 2 ch.f. Music Boy 124–Petit Trianon 93 (Princely Gift 137) (1983 5fg 5g) Mar 25; 4,000F; half-sister to Louise Valliere (by St Paddy), a fair winner at up to 1½m; dam, half-sister to very smart stayer Petty Officer, stayed 7f; well beaten in October maiden events at Lingfield and Sandown. *B. Swift.* —

DORA'S ROCKET 2 ch.f. Roan Rocket 128–Cantadora 107 (Matador 131) (1983 5d 5f 6g² 6fg² 7f) Apr 24; sister to very useful sprinter Rory's Rocket, and half-sister to 4 winners; dam sprinter; runner-up in maiden races at Ayr in July and Pontefract in August; appears to need at least 6f. *J. Etherington.* — 69

DOREE MOISSON (FR) 3 ch.f. Connaught 130–Bombazine 110 (Shantung 132) (1982 8f³ 8s³ 1983 11fg* 12.2f³ 12g⁴ 13fg) small, fair sort; good mover; won maiden race at Hamilton in June cleverly; in frame afterwards in minor event at Catterick (possibly unsuited by the track) and handicap at Paddock, but was most disappointing final start; stays 1½m; suited by a sound surface. *J. W. Watts.* — 84

DORIS'S CHOICE 10 gr.g. Doon 124–Dalcourt 77 (Fidalgo 129) (1982 NR 1983 10.2g) of little account nowadays. *R. Thompson.* —

DORNEY 3 b.c. Tachypous 128–School Road 88 (Great Nephew 126) (1982 NR 1983 8d 8.2s) 3,000F, 4,000Y; strong, good-bodied colt; first produce; dam, sister to smart miler Saher, ran only at 4 yrs when winner over 6f and 7f; in rear in maiden race at Newmarket (needed race and missed break) and minor event at Haydock in May; sold to A. Davison 1,050 gns Newmarket September Sales. *B. Hobbs.* —

DOROTHY BREWIS 4 ch.f. Gulf Pearl 117–Dubarry (Quisling 117) (1982 9.4f3 9f 10.4d 1983 8d 11g 10.6s 10f 12f 12d) leggy, sparely-made filly; little worthwhile form, including in a seller. *G. Richards.* —

DORSET VENTURE 2 b.c. John de Coombe 122–Kayandjay 93 (Midsummer Night II 117) (1983 7fg 8fg 7d* 7f) Apr 5; lengthy, angular colt; dam stayed 1m well; ran easily best race when staying on strongly to win 19-runner maiden event at Warwick in October by 2 lengths from Baby Boy; should stay 1m; evidently well suited by a soft surface. *B. Morgan.* 80

DOUBLE DEALER (FR) 2 b.c. Habitat 134–Fanghorn 117 (Crocket 130) (1983 6g) Apr 1; brother to top-class sprinter Double Form, and half-brother to 3 winners, including very useful 5f to 1m winner Gradiva (by Lorenzaccio); dam placed in French 1000 Guineas; weak in market, remote ninth of 14 in minor event at Lingfield in September. *F. J. Houghton.* —

DOUBLE DISCOUNT 5 b or br.g. Double-U-Jay 120–Quick Sort (Henry the Seventh 125) (1982 10f 10d 1983 12s* 12d) leggy, lightly-made gelding; won poor race in Isle of Man in May; very slowly away next start in October; stays 1½m; probably acts on any going; tends to pull hard. *C. James.* —

DOUBLE FLORIN (USA) 6 b.g. His Majesty–Stamp and Cash (Roi Rouge) (1982 14f 17.1f 16g 16f3 20fg 16fg 14f 18.8fg 16d 1983 16f4 16f 14f4) small gelding; good mover; staying handicapper; needs a sound surface; sometimes sweats up; has worn bandages; tends to pull hard and is suited by strong handling. *A. Turnell.* 60

DOUBLE MARTINI 3 ch.f. Ardoon 124–Swinging Time (High Treason 126) (1982 NR 1983 6d 8d) IR 1,200F, IR 4,400Y; sister to fairly useful 1981 2-y-o 5f performer Martini Time; dam Irish 6f and 7f winner; in rear in maiden races at Pontefract and Thirsk in April. *D. Morley.* —

DOUBLE OPTION (USA) 2 b.c. Quack–Swagger 107 (Prominer 125) (1983 7g4) Mar 10; $50,000Y; good-bodied colt; first foal; dam, half-sister to smart sprinter Petipa, won from 5f to 7f here and over 6f in USA; weak in market, not given hard time when 5 lengths fourth of 12 to Lucky Scott in £5,000 event at Kempton in September; will stay at least 1m; sure to improve and win races. *G. Harwood.* 75 p

DOUBLE QUICK TIME 2 br.g. Daring March 116–Dualvi 91 (Dual 117) (1983 5v 6g 7f 7f 7fg4 8fg3 8d2 8fg*) Apr 8; robust, well-made gelding; third foal; dam won over 7f at 2 yrs; won 12-runner nursery at Brighton in October by a length from Green Mist; much better suited by 1m than by shorter distances; best form on a firm surface. *R. Smyth.* 91

DOUBLE ROOM 2 b.f. Shack 118–Flighty Hussy (Flit-To) (1983 6f* 6fg2 5f* 5s) May 23; IR 2,000F, 3,800 2-y-o; fair sort; fourth foal; half-sister to a winning hurdler; dam never ran; won seller (retained 5,000 gns) at Yarmouth in August and nursery at Redcar in September; equally effective at 5f and 6f; acts well on firm going. *W. O'Gorman.* 63

DOUBLE SCHWARTZ 2 b.c. Double Form 130–Cassy's Pet 89 (Sing Sing 134) (1983 6g3 6g* 6g2 6.5g) 111

There wasn't an unluckier loser all season than Double Schwartz, second in the BonusPrint Sirenia Stakes at Kempton in September. He had one of the worst runs imaginable. After being waited with at the rear of the field Double Schwartz quickened up to challenge the leaders approaching the final furlong, only to find his path blocked. He was then switched to the inside rail where he met with more interference all the way home. With nowhere to go in the last hundred yards he was literally pulling up, but despite this he was beaten only a length by Defecting Dancer who was able to win a shade cleverly. After watching Double Schwartz's unfortunate experiences it was easy to sympathise with his jockey's claim that he should have won ten lengths, though whether the horse would have won so far is another matter. Double Schwartz's display at Kempton established him as one of the better sprinting two-year-olds, and represented a considerable advance on his earlier form. Double Schwartz had won one of his two previous races, the Moorestyle Convivial Stakes at York in August, in which he'd been sympathetically ridden to hold Tocave Botta's persistent challenge by a short head. Double Schwartz's performance at Kempton earned him a crack at Vacarme in the Mill Reef Stakes at Newbury but he was found to be running a temperature and had to be withdrawn. Instead, he took his chance in the Prix Eclipse at Saint-Cloud in October

243

Mr R. E. Sangster's "Double Schwartz"

but finished a disappointing ninth behind Diamada, after holding a prominent position for over half a mile. Perhaps he hadn't fully recovered from his illness.

Double Schwartz (b.c. Mar 17, 1981)	Double Form (b 1975)	Habitat (b 1966)	Sir Gaylord
			Little Hut
		Fanghorn (ch 1966)	Crocket
			Honeymoon House
	Cassy's Pet (br 1971)	Sing Sing (b 1957)	Tudor Minstrel
			Agin the Law
		Cassydora (b 1948)	Nasrullah
			Glen Line

Double Schwartz is from the first crop of the Prix de l'Abbaye and King's Stand winner Double Form, who had to be put down in April after clipping his near-hind and severing the main artery, only a matter of days after his first runner Novello had given him his initial success as a stallion. Double Schwartz's dam Cassy's Pet, who has also bred the prolific Italian winner Face of Love (by My Swallow), won over five furlongs, and is a half-sister to several winners, notably the King's Stand winner Cassarate. Double Schwartz, a 13,000-guinea yearling, was purchased by Robert Sangster shortly after Kempton, obviously with an eye to the future. A big, strong, rather close-coupled, useful sort, Double Schwartz has the scope to improve at three years, and could develop into a good sprinter. *C. Nelson.*

DOUBLE SHUFFLE 4 b.f. Tachypous 128–Ali Drake (Dicta Drake 126) (1982 **102** $10f^2$ $11f^4$ $12d^*$ $12fg^2$ $16g^2$ 14.6g $12s^*$ $12v^4$ $12s^*$ 1983 $11v^2$ 12v 10.5g) big, rangy filly; useful performer at her best; finished clear of remainder when caught near finish and beaten ½ length by Forward in 9-runner handicap at Newbury in May; ran moderately afterwards; stayed 2m; acted on any going but went well on soft; best in blinkers; game; stud. *G. Pritchard-Gordon.*

DOUBLE STITCH 3 b.f. Wolver Hollow 126–Tactless 91 (Romulus 129) (1982   **65**
6d² 1983 8.2fg* 9.4f 8.2f² 8f² 10f 9fg) strong, attractive filly; won apprentice
maiden race at Hamilton in June; second in minor event on same course and
handicap at Newcastle, best subsequent efforts; stays 1m; yet to race on really
soft going but acts on any other. *Sir Mark Prescott.*

DOUBLE SWING 2 b.g. Swing Easy 126–Kiyofuji 98 (Grey Sovereign 128§)   **52**
(1983 6d 7f 8.2fg) May 23; 1,600F, 900Y; lengthy gelding; moderate plater; stays
1m. *A. Pitt.*

DOUBLETON 2 b.c. Double Form 130–Hello Honey 105 (Crepello 136) (1983   **91** p
8fg²) Mar 19; rangy colt; half-brother to 3 winners, including fairly useful
middle-distance winner Concert Hall (by Connaught); dam won 4 times at up to
1½m; 25/1 and apparently backward, made winner pull out all the stops when neck
second of 7 to Sassagrass in £3,200 event at Newmarket in October; promises to
stay beyond 1m; should win a race. *P. Walwyn.*

DOUBLE WRAPPED 7 ch.m. Double-U-Jay 120–Christmas Gift (Princely Gift   **90**
137) (1982 14g² 16f* 13d² 14g* 14fg* 16g² 16s 12s 1983 12.8g 14fg* 12f 16f* 14f²
16g 13f* 16g* 16s) workmanlike Irish mare; very useful hurdler and a useful
handicapper on flat; won at Navan in June, Galway in July (valuable amateur riders
event for second year in succession by a head from Northern Sky), Tralee in
August (accounted for Pearlstone decisively by 5 lengths in valuable race) and
Listowel in September; soundly beaten behind Crusader Castle in Lonsdale Stakes
at York in August on sixth start; suited by a test of stamina; acts very well on fast
ground; does best when ridden up with pace. *W. Durkan, Ireland.*

DOUSSARD 2 b. or br.g. Double Form 130–Ragatina (Ragusa 137) (1983 6f) May   **79** p
4; IR 21,000F, 19,000Y; good-bodied gelding; good walker; third living foal; dam,
placed over 1m, is half-sister to very useful sprinters Rollahead and Glenturret;
third favourite but distinctly backward, showed good speed until lack of condition
told from distance when 9 lengths fifth of 8 behind Bluff House in newcomers race
at Goodwood in July; subsequently gelded. *J. Tree.*

DOWEGIAN 2 ch.c. Town Crier 119–Marie Nicole (Santa Claus 133) (1983 7fg   **68**
8g 8g⁴) Apr 6; 6,800Y; half-brother to a bumpers winner and a winner in Austria;
dam unraced half-sister to high-class 1¼m to 1¾m performer Calaba; plating-class
maiden; lacks pace, and will be suited by further. *C. Nelson.*

DOWN FLIGHT 3 ch.c. Run The Gantlet–Feather Bed 111 (Gratitude 130) (1982   **90**
7g 7fg 7g 1983 12d² 12v* 14s* 16f) medium-sized, workmanlike colt; beat
Meaume by 10 lengths in maiden race at Wolverhampton in April and Rig Steel
easing up by 2 lengths in quite well-contested minor event at York in May; third
favourite when in rear behind Santella Man in 17-runner Queen's Vase at Royal
Ascot in June, only subsequent start; suited by a test of stamina; acts on heavy
going. *G. Wragg.*

DOWN THE LINE 3 b.f. Brigadier Gerard 144–Sizzler 67 (Blakeney 126) (1982   **74**
NR 1983 10s² 9f 10.4g² 12fg 10g 10fg) 8,600Y; small, deep-girthed filly; second
foal; dam, closely related to More Light and half-sister to Shoot A Line, won over
11f; ran best race on first outing, when second in maiden event at Chepstow in May;
suited by 1¼m+; probably ideally suited by some give in the ground; sold 4,000
gns Newmarket December Sales. *J. Toller.*

DOWNTOWN CHICAGO 2 br.c. Raga Navarro 119–Lepe 65 (Exbury 138)   **67**
(1983 5s* 5d³ 6g 6f 7fg 7g 7g 8.2g 8g 8.2s) May 15; 7,600Y; leggy, workmanlike
colt; poor walker; brother to Irish 3-y-o Ragabury, closely related to 2 winners by
Wishing Star, including Irish 7f to 1½m winner No Messing Sally, and half-brother
to a winner; dam needed at least 1½m; went down by 2 lengths to Lucky
Boardman's in maiden race at Hamilton in April but was awarded race over 3
months later after winner failed dope test; placed in only the first of his other
races, and was running badly in the autumn; stays 7f; acts on soft going; blinkered
sixth and eighth last 2 outings; trained by D. Smith first 6 outings. *Mrs G. Reveley.*

DOWNTOWN FOXY 2 b.f. Master Sing 109–Stolen-Secret (Burglar 128) (1983   –
5s) Apr 1; 3,700Y; first living foal; dam, closely related to very smart 5f horse
Singing Bede, ran only once; unquoted, never-dangerous 9 lengths fifth of 24 to
Filia Matris in maiden race at Windsor in May. *D. Ringer.*

DOWNTOWN HUSTLER 2 b.c. Julio Mariner 127–Greek Money (Sovereign   **80**
Path 125) (1983 7d 7.6fg) Apr 28; 940Y; second foal; half-brother to 3-y-o 1¼m
winner Sir Humphrey (by High Line); dam Irish 1¼m and 1½m winner; unquoted, 4
lengths fifth of 19 behind Lexis in maiden race at Lingfield in October, second
outing; will be better suited by longer distances. *D. Ringer.*

DRAGEDA 2 br.f. Dragonara Palace 115–Gedoparonija 88 (Right Boy 137) (1983   –
5f 6fg) Mar 28; 2,000Y; rather leggy filly; half-sister to several minor winners;
dam ran only at 2 yrs when winner over 5f; behind in September in minor events at
Catterick (early speed) and Redcar; sold 820 gns Doncaster November Sales. *W.
Haigh.*

DRAGONADE 2 b.or br.g. Dragonara Palace 115–La Sarmate (Hard Sauce 131)   –
(1983 7f) Mar 31; 5,000Y; half-brother to 2 winners abroad and a winning jumper;
dam never ran; 50/1, behind in 17-runner maiden race at Redcar in September. *C.
Booth.*

DRAGONARA PRINCE 2 br.g. Dragonara Palace 115–Arodstown Alice (Sahib   **65**
114) (1983 5v 5d 6fg 8d 7g) Mar 11; 4,500Y; strong, compact gelding; half-brother
to 2 winning sprinters, including Looking Glass (by Lochnager); dam ran only 3
times; plating-class maiden; not sure to stay 1m; blinkered final start. *D. Ringer.*

DRAGONARA'S PET 2 b.f. Dragonara Palace 115–Regal Silk (Henry the   **55**
Seventh 125) (1983 5d 5v 5v 5v 5g⁴ 5.1f³ 5f* 6f³ 5.1f*) Mar 30; 1,300Y;
sparely-made filly; plater; successful in July at Wolverhampton (bought in 1,100
gns) and Yarmouth (no bid); best at 5f; acts on firm going; wears bandages behind;
best in blinkers. *K. Ivory.*

DRAGON FIRE 4 b.f. Dragonara Palace 115–Firella 56 (Firestreak 125) (1982   **57**
8g² 7f 7f 7f 10f³ 11.5f 11.5f⁴ 8.3g* 9g³ 8d 8.3g⁴ 8fg³ 8fg 8.2s³ 8s 1983 8d 8v³ 8v
10f⁴ 12.2fg* 12.3fg³ 11.7f³ 12f 12h 12d) lightly-made filly; former plater; won
handicap at Warwick in June; suited by 1½m; acts on any going; blinkered once at 3
yrs; doesn't always impress in appearance; trained part of season by D. Wintle. *M.
Eckley.*

DRAGONLEA 3 gr.f. Dragonara Palace 115–Murton Crags 81 (No Argument   **85**
106) (1982 5f⁴ 5f* 5d 6f² 6f* 7d⁴ 6g³ 6fg 7s³ 1983 8v 8s⁴ 8s³ 8f 8f³ 10f² 10f*)
leggy, light-framed filly; 20/1-winner of Andy Capp Handicap at Redcar in August,
leading 2f out and holding off Teleprompter by a short head; subsequently won a
claiming race in USA; stays 1¼m; acts on any going; has worn a bandage on
off-hind. *W. Haigh.*

DRAGON PRINCE 3 ch.c. Nishapour 125–Nanno (Busted 134) (1982 5f 6g³   –
7g⁴ 6g³ 7s 1983 6d⁴ 7f³ 6f) big, strong colt; below his best in 1983; bred to stay
1m but is a strong-pulling sort who is far from certain to do so. *J. Etherington.*

DRAGON ROCKET 3 gr.c. Dragonara Palace 115–Running Firework 106   –
(Runnymede 123) (1982 5d 7.2s 6s 1983 6g) no sign of ability, including in sellers.
J. Fort.

DRAGUNN 4 ch.g. Dragonara Palace 115–Maria Bicknell (Jolly Jet 111) (1982 5g⁴   **48**
5s³ 5f* 6fg 5f⁴ 5f³ 5h 5g 5fg³ 5fg 5f 6g 5d⁴ 5d⁴ 5d 5g 5s 1983 5d 5v 5f 5g 5fg 5f 5fg
7f 6f³ 5fg³ 6g 5fg⁴ 6f) rather sparely-made gelding; poor mover; sprint
handicapper; best at 5f though has run respectably over 6f; acts on any going;
wears blinkers; has worn a bandage on his near-fore; not the heartiest of battlers.
R. Hollinshead.

DRAMA SCHOOL 2 br.f. Young Generation 129–Curtains 113 (Busted 134)   **72 p**
(1983 7g 7.6g) Apr 16; fifth foal; half-sister to 2 winners, including useful
middle-distance performer Heighten (by High Top); dam, half-sister to Final Straw
and Achieved, won three 1½m races; third favourite, showed ability on second
outing when close-up seventh of 19 in maiden race at Lingfield in October; will be
suited by 1m; likely to do better in time. *R. Hern.*

DRAMATIC 2 gr.f. Dragonara Palace 115–Faridetta 107 (Good Bond 122) (1983   **54**
5v 5v 5v³ 6fg 5f* 5f³ 5f) May 16; 2,700F, 3,600Y; second foal; dam won four 5f
races at 2 yrs; won seller at Folkestone (bought in 1,550 gns) in June by 3 lengths
from Philcrop; not raced after August; not sure to stay 6f; acts well on firm going.
R. Smyth.

DR BRODIE 3 ch.g. Monseigneur 127–Power Girl 77 (Tyrant) (1982 6s 1983   –
8fg 6fg) sturdy gelding; poor form, including when blinkered and tailed-off last in
seller final outing; has given trouble at start. *A. Jarvis.*

DREAM AGAIN 3 b.f. Blue Cashmere 129–Sundream (Petingo 135) (1982 5v²   **79**
5f* 5fg* 5f⁴ 5g 5g 5fg 1983 5v 5s 5g 5f⁴ 5fg 5f⁴ 5fg 6f 8s 5g) smallish, lengthy
filly; ran well when fourth of 16 behind Sharpish in valuable handicap at Ascot in
June on fourth outing, but became rather disappointing; best form at 5f on firm
ground, although promises to stay further and has run respectably on soft. *J.
McNaughton.*

DREAMCOAT (USA) 2 gr. or ro.c. Jig Time–Restless Polly (Restless Wind)   **65**
(1983 5fg⁴ 5fg 5fg) Apr 4; $75,000 2-y-o; third foal; half-brother to 2 winners by
Buccaneer, one stakes placed; dam, 2-y-o 5f winner, is daughter of smart 1961

Irish 2-y-o sprinter Polly Toogood; sire, son of Native Dancer, was very useful stakes winner over 8.5f; favourite, 4 lengths fourth of 10 behind Refueled in maiden race at Windsor in July, best effort; favourite again next time; disappointing. *D. Sasse.*

DREAM ONCE MORE 2 ch.f. Ashmore 125–Sundream (Petingo 135) (1983 6g) Apr 14; 5,000Y; half-sister to 3-y-o Dream Again (by Blue Cashmere), a fair 5f winner at 2 yrs, and a winning plater; dam unraced half-sister to speedy Song of Songs; unquoted, behind in 22-runner maiden race at Redcar in May. *J. McNaughton.* —

DROMODAN 3 b.g. Dance In Time–Wordrone (Worden II 129) (1982 7fg² 7g³ 8d⁴ 9s⁴ 1983 12s 12.3f 10f 14.7f) lengthy, slightly dipped-backed gelding; rather disappointing in 1983; one paced and should be suited by middle distances. *M. H. Easterby.*

DR PAVLICK 3 ch.g. Gunner B 126–Startop 72 (Divine Gift 127) (1982 7d 7f 1983 10.1f 10.1fg 12f) workmanlike gelding; in rear in maiden and minor events. *J. Bosley.* —

DRUMALIS 3 b.c. Tumble Wind–Virna (Coursing) (1982 6f 6f* 6.5d² 7s² 1983 7s² 8g* 8g 8fg² 9.2d 8f 7.3f⁴ 8fg* 7fg³) 8,000F; strong, well-made, quite attractive colt; half-brother to 2 winners in Ireland, including 1¼m winner Crowned Hare (by Crowned Prince); dam won from 6f to 9f in France; won 2 good prizes abroad, beating Beldale Concorde decisively by a length in Premio Parioli (Italian 2000 Guineas) at Rome in April and Lofty, who received 5 lb, by ¾ length in Oettingen-Rennen at Baden-Baden in August; in frame in between in Premio Emilio Turati at Milan and in Hungerford Stakes at Newbury (blinkered, made up quite a lot of ground to finish 6½ lengths fourth to Salieri after being slowly away) and subsequently in Kiveton Park Stakes at Doncaster in September (about 2½ lengths third to Annie Edge, staying on); also ran creditably when 6½ lengths seventh of 16 behind Lomond in 2000 Guineas at Newmarket on third outing; suited by 1m; acts on any going; sent to race in USA. *I. Balding.* 125

Greenland Park Ltd's "Drumalis"

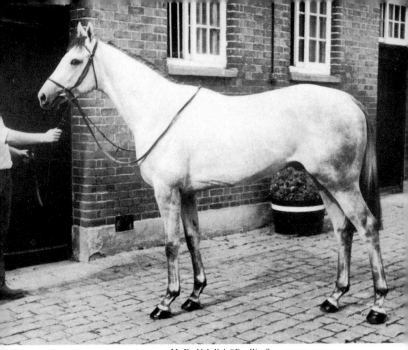

Mr K. Abdulla's "Duelling"

DRUMAPORT 2 ch.g. Import 127–Drumadoll 70 (Meldrum 112) (1983 6f 6fg) — Feb 20; lengthy gelding; first foal; dam won from 1m to 1½m; burly, last in maiden and minor events at Redcar in July and October. *P. Wigham.*

DRUM MAKER 3 br.c. Scottish Rifle 127–Ardice 91 (Hard Tack 111§) (1982 7f 66 d 7g⁴ 7s 1983 11v 11.7v⁴ 10v² 10d 8f 8.2f 7.6d) quite attractive colt; quite a modest maiden; suited by 1¼m+; acts on any going; blinkered final outing. *N. Vigors.*

DRUMMOND STREET 4 ch.g. Ragstone 128–Scottish Lullaby 92 (Aberdeen — 109) (1982 11s 12s 12f 14fg 16s 16s 1983 13v 12d) lengthy gelding; poor mover; poor maiden; beaten in seller final start; stays 1½m; has worn blinkers. *A. Jarvis.*

DRY LAND 3 b.f. Nonoalco 131–Land Ho (Primera 131) (1982 5s 5s* 1983 6v 84 5s*) good-topped filly; has a smooth action; improved greatly on her first start (last in handicap at Kempton) when battling on gamely to beat Shanleys Style a head in handicap at Newbury in April; was covered by Troy shortly afterwards; should have stayed 6f; sold 360,000 gns Newmarket December Sales. *J. Tree.*

DUAL INVESTMENT 3 b. or br.c. The Brianstan 128–Charlies Double 64 (Fighting Charlie 127) (1982 5g 6f 6g 5s 1983 6d⁴ 5v⁴ 6s 6s 7g⁴ 7fg 8f 9f 7fg 6fg* 6fg⁴) quite attractive, lengthy colt; good walker; awarded race outright after dead-heating with Ardrox Lad in apprentice event at Nottingham in October; beaten in a seller previous outing; best at up to 7f; possibly unsuited by really firm going, but acts on any other; blinkered sixth and ninth starts; sent to Singapore. *P. Mitchell.*

DUBAI RUBY (USA) 3 ch.f. The Minstrel 135–Kesar Queen 117 (Nashua) — (1982 6s 6d 1983 8.5d 6f 8g⁴) rather small filly; lightly-raced maiden; fourth of 16 behind Gentle Down at Warwick in October. *P. Walwyn.*

DUBAI SPRING (USA) 2 b.f. Broadway Forli–Fleet Empress (Young Emperor 133) (1983 6fg) Apr 25; $150,000Y; tall filly; half-sister to 3 winners, including useful 1980 Irish 2-y-o Band Practice (by Stop the Music); dam, minor 6f winner, is half-sister to very smart Fleet Victress, successful at up to 9f, and smart Flit-To, a winner at up to 13f; 14/1 and in need of race, out of first 9 in 29-runner maiden event at Newmarket in September. *H. T. Jones.*

DUBAVARNA 2 ch.f. Dubassoff–Holiday Hymn 72 (Saintly Song 128) (1983 7f 6f 8d 8fg 10.2fg) Mar 15; fair sort; first foal; dam, disappointing maiden, was placed from 1m to 1¾m; quite a modest filly; best run on fourth outing; should stay 1¼m. *C. Gray.* — 72

DUBLIN GIRL 2 ch.f. Dublin Taxi–Irresistable (Siliconn 121) (1983 5.8h) May 12; third live foal; half-sister to 3-y-o 1m seller winner Resister (by Monsanto); dam ran twice; 50/1, last of 14 in maiden race at Bath in August. *P. M. Taylor.* — —

DUBLIN ROCK 3 b.f. Dublin Taxi–Demi Rock (Double-U-Jay 120) (1982 5fg 5g 6fg 5g 1983 6fg 6fg) little worthwhile form, including in a seller. *A. Moore.* — —

DUBREE 2 br.f. Crooner 119–Royal Pat 80 (King's Troop 118) (1983 5v 5d 5v 5f³) Apr 23; fourth foal; half-sister to 5f winner Byroc Boy (by Runnymede); dam 2-y-o 5f winner; bad plater; not raced after June. *D. Jermy.* — 39

DUELLING (USA) 2 ro.c. Vigors–Irish Sword (Irish Lancer) (1983 8g² 8fg⁴) Feb 18; $330,000Y; well-made, attractive colt; quite a good mover; closely related to 2 winners by Grey Dawn II, notably smart French and American miler Carolina Moon, and half-brother to a winner; dam second in Prix Robert Papin; acquitted himself extremely well when 50/1 for £4,100 race at Newbury in September, coming with an excellent run in last 2f to finish 1½ lengths second of 21 to stable-companion Rainbow Quest; short-priced favourite, every chance when 4 lengths fourth of 21 behind Alphabatim in maiden event at Newmarket the following month; should win races. *J. Tree.* — 97

DUFFY MCGOVERN 2 ch.g. Absalom 128–Miss Candine 66 (King Emperor) (1983 7f 7g 8d 8fg) Feb 11; 12,000Y; heavy-bodied gelding; second reported foal; dam, half-sister to very useful sprinters Canteen and Staincross, was placed over 1¼m and 2m; no form, including in claiming race and a seller; sold 2,200 gns Newmarket Autumn Sales. *Sir Mark Prescott.* — —

DUKANCE (FR) 2 b.f. Iron Duke 122–Bizance (Le Haar 126) (1983 5f) Apr 26; 105,000 francs Y (approx £8,750); half-sister to numerous minor winners in France; dam won from 6f to 1¼m in French Provinces; behind in 16-runner minor event at Warwick in August; dead. *P. Kelleway.* — —

DUKAYNA 2 b.f. Northfields–Dumka 117 (Kashmir II 125) (1983 7fg³) Feb 23; good-topped filly; third foal; closely related to good miler Dalsaan (by Habitat) and half-sister to Dayzaan (by Riverman), very useful winner in France at up to 10.5f; dam won French 1,000 Guineas; short-priced favourite, finished well after running green early on when 1¼ lengths third of 22 behind Travel Away in maiden race at Newmarket in October; will be suited by 1m; sure to improve, and will probably make useful 3-y-o. *M. Stoute.* — 90 p

DUKE OF BRITTANY 5 gr.h. Saritamer 130–Belle Bretonne 90 (Celtic Ash) (1982 12s 1983 12f 12fg 12g 16g) compact horse; poor maiden. *S. Woodman.* — —

DUKE OF DOLLIS 4 b.g. Condorcet–Evening Primrose (Varano) (1982 7d 8f 10fg² 16fg 12d 12f² 12fg 12f³ 11.1fg 1983 12v 14s 12f 10.1fg 16.5f 16.5f³ 15.5f³ 12fg 16fg³ 18fg 20fg) workmanlike ex-Irish gelding; staying handicapper; favourite when beaten in seller fourth start; best form on a sound surface; has run creditably for a lady rider; has sweated up; blinkered second start; trained part of season by D. Elsworth. *R. Simpson.* — 52

DUKE OF SILVER 2 ch.c. Son of Silver 123–Irish Song (Dapper Dan) (1983 7g* 7g² 8fg* 8g* 9f4 7.5s²) half-brother to 2 winners in France, including 1¼m and 1¾m winner Beg of Allen (by Iron Duke); dam half-sister to top-class miler Irish River; in fine form in mid-summer, winning minor events at Compiegne and Clairefontaine and Prix des Foals at Deauville, last-named by ½ length from Nikos; also ran creditably when fourth, beaten 2 lengths by Truculent, in Prix Lord Seymour at Longchamp, and a fast-finishing second, beaten ½ length, to Polly's Ark in Prix Thomas Bryon at Saint-Cloud, both in October; should stay 1¼m+; acts on any going. *A. Fabre, France.* — 114

DUKE OF WELLINGTON 3 b.c. Wollow 132–Lady Dacre 86 (Queen's Hussar 124) (1982 6g 1983 10g) lightly-made colt; behind in maiden races at Newmarket. *W. Holden.* — —

DUKE'S HEIR 4 gr.g. Saritamer 130–La Pitore (Will Somers 114§) (1982 11.5fg 12f 12fg³ 10v 12s 1983 12v 16d) poor plater; stays 1½m; acts on a firm surface; sold to NBA 2,500 gns Newmarket Autumn Sales. *W. Musson.* — —

DUN

DUNANT 2 ch.c. Sallust 134–Lady Littlepace 109 (African Sky 124) (1983 5g 5v 6s 6f 5f³ 5f* 6f⁴ 5f* 5g 5fg) Mar 2; 9,000Y; well-grown, workmanlike colt; first foal; dam Irish sprinter; won maiden race (very gamely by a head) at Sandown in July and nursery (cleverly by ¾ length) on same course in August; better at 5f than 6f; acts very well on firm going. *C. Brittain.* **94**

DUNBEATH (USA) 3 b.c. Grey Dawn II 132–Priceless Fame (Irish Castle) (1982 7f² 7f* 7g* 8s* 8d* 1983 10g² 10.5s³ 8fg³) **115**

Dunbeath's overwhelming defeat in the Mecca-Dante Stakes at York in May provided one of the major upsets of the spring. He had won the last four of his five races as a two-year-old, including the Royal Lodge Stakes and the William Hill Futurity (after which he had changed hands for a reported six million pounds) and was a top-priced 4/1 favourite for the Derby on the morning of the Mecca-Dante; already he had won under his belt a highly encouraging length second to Shearwalk in the mile-and-a-quarter Heathorn Stakes at Newmarket, the best Derby trial seen at that stage and had convinced us that he had trained on. But Dunbeath, heavily backed down to 2/1 on in a field of nine for the Dante, trailed in only third behind Hot Touch and Guns of Navarone, eleven and a half lengths behind the winner. Although he had sweated slightly and hadn't pleased everyone in his appearance beforehand, all had seemed well as he'd begun moving up smoothly on the outside in the straight from his usual position towards the back of the field. At around the two-furlong marker though he began to struggle as if something was wrong with him and it was soon clear he wasn't going to peg back the principals. Piggott reportedly considered that Dunbeath hadn't lasted the distance in the heavy going—entirely possible considering Dunbeath's pedigree, by Grey Dawn out of a sprint-winning mare, and the finishing speed that had been a trademark of most of his races. Trainer Cecil didn't immediately subscribe to that view, but significantly Dunbeath was brought back to a mile in the St James's Palace Stakes at Royal Ascot, where he wasn't disgraced in finishing about four lengths behind Horage in third. This time he ran as if finding the trip on the sharp side: he never looked likely to get to grips with the all-the-way-winner and was beaten soon after the turn. This further somewhat puzzling effort turned out to be Dunbeath's last in Europe. Despite a report at one stage that he was to be retired to stud Dunbeath was sent to the United States towards the end of August, reportedly to continue his racing career.

	Grey Dawn II (gr 1962)	Herbager (b 1956)	Vandale
Dunbeath (USA) (b.c. 1980)			Flagette
		Polamia (gr 1955)	Mahmoud
			Ampola
	Priceless Fame (b 1975)	Irish Castle (b 1967)	Bold Ruler
			Castle Forbes
		Comely Nell (b 1962)	Commodore M.
			Nellie L.

Dunbeath is from a good American family that was discussed in detail in *Racehorses of 1982*. His year-younger half-sister Khwlah (by Best Turn), in training with H. T. Jones, made a successful first appearance in a big field of maidens at Newbury in August and ran respectably in much stiffer company on her only subsequent appearance. The dam's second foal, a colt by Alydar, was the second highest-priced yearling at the Saratoga Sales the week before Khwlah's debut, falling to a bid of 2,200,000 dollars from the California-based trainer D. Wayne Lukas; interestingly the underbidder was Colonel Dick Warden, acting for Dunbeath's owner. Priceless Fame herself was sold for 3.2 million dollars at Keeneland in November.

Dunbeath has joined the powerful stable of Charlie Whittingham, a man noted for his success with ex-European horses, and the ten-furlong Budweiser Million is said to be one of his principal targets in 1984. He stays the distance of that race, at least when conditions aren't too testing, and we'll be interested to see whether he can re-establish himself sufficiently to be started. An attractive, deep-girthed colt who moves with a nice, easy action and is an impressive loose-limbed walker, he'd certainly be well worth a place in the line-up on his very best form. *H. Cecil.*

DUNCES PEARL 2 br.c. Coded Scrap 90–Dunedela 60 (Dumbarnie 125) (1983 7f 6f 8g 7f) seventh foal; dam ran twice at 2 yrs; apparently of no account. *T. Fairhurst.* –

DUNFELL 3 br.f. Tower Walk 130–Queen Donna (Thatch 136) (1982 5f 6g 5g 5g 7fg 7g 6s 5d 1983 6v 6fg) leggy filly; poor plater; stayed 7f; sold, covered by Last Fandango, 2,000 gns Newmarket December Sales. *W. Haigh.* –

DUNFORD 3 b.f. Legal Eagle 126–Ol Arabel (Relic) (1982 5g 5fg 1983 5s 12f 5f) of little account; has been tried in blinkers. *M. James.* –

DUNHAM PARK 6 b.g. Manacle 123–Sweet Reproach 94 (Relic) (1982 7f* 7f³   **87**
8g³ 7f³ 8fg² 7g* 7g⁴ 7f 7g 7s⁴ 8s³ 1983 7d* 7fg² 8f 7fg 7f* 8.2fg 7f 7g 7g 8fg) tall,
useful sort; won handicaps at Catterick in June and Doncaster in July; stays 1m;
acts on any going; blinkered twice at 2 yrs; sometimes sweats up; suitable mount
for an apprentice; doesn't find a great deal in front. *J. Fitzgerald.*

DURANDAL 6 br.h. Bay Express 132–High Ransom 88 (High Treason 126) (1982   **72**
6f 6fg 5.8f² 5g 5g 5fg³ 5fg⁴ 5g 5g³ 5fg 5fg 5.8f 8d 5s 1983 6s 6g 5g 5s 5.8g 5f² 5f²
5f 5fg² 5h 5fg 5.6fg 5fg 5d 5d 6g) strong, good sort; poor walker; sprint
handicapper; second at Sandown twice and at Haydock in summer; short head
behind Reggae in Coral Bookmakers Handicap on latter; probably acts on any going
but is best served by fast ground; sometimes blinkered; inconsistent and
unreliable. *D. Wilson.*

DURANGO 2 ch.c. Octavo 115–Mainvilliers (Prudent II 133) (1983 6s 7fg) May   –
8; IR 4,000F, IR 6,000Y; good sort; half-brother to several winners here and
abroad, including Irish 1m winner Hunterville (by Huntercombe); dam third in 5f
claiming race at 2 yrs in France; ninth of 15 in minor event at Goodwood in May and
ninth of 20 in maiden race at Newmarket (sweating, showed up to halfway) in
August. *A. Jarvis.*

DUST CONQUERER (USA) 2 b.c. Dust Commander–Ivory Star (Sir Ivor   –
135) (1983 7f) Mar 8; $135,000Y; strong, compact colt; first foal; dam, who ran 3
times in France, is daughter of smart 1972 American 2-y-o Double Your Fun; 25/1
and burly, moved badly to start and made no show in 17-runner maiden race at
Newbury in August; looks capable of better in time. *G. Harwood.*

DUSTY FARLOW 4 b.g. Jukebox 120–Reelin Bridge (New Day) (1982 7fg 7f 9g   **43**
6g² 8.2g³ 8fg 8.2s 1983 12d² 12fg) former plater; stays 1½m; acts on a soft
surface; has twice worn blinkers; has worn bandages. *R. Morris.*

DUSTY LETTER (USA) 2 ch.f. Run Dusty Run–Nicoletta 81 (Busted 134)   **78**
(1983 7g 7.6d²) Mar 19; first foal; dam, successful over 9f, is half-sister to Irish
1000 Guineas winner Favoletta and Teenoso's dam Furioso; showed promise both
starts, notably when running all-the-way winner Katies to a length, well clear of
remainder, in 20-runner maiden race at Lingfield in October; should stay 1¼m; sure
to win maiden event. *G. Wragg.*

DUSTY PATH 5 gr.g. Warpath 113–The Squeeze 85 (Bing II) (1982 12f 16d   –
15.8f 13.8f 12fg 12d 1983 12d 12f 8f 10f 13s 12fg³) workmanlike gelding; poor
maiden; has been beaten in a seller; stays 13f; often used to wear blinkers. *W.
Bentley.*

DUTY PAID 2 ch.c. Import 127–Lady Tarcherio 65 (Pontifex) (1983 5fg 5d) May   –
3; 1,600F, 3,300Y; second foal; half-brother to winning staying plater Just Gunner
(by Gunner B); dam won over 7f; last in maiden company at Nottingham and
Wolverhampton in the autumn. *H. Collingridge.*

DUTY WATCH 4 ch.f. Import 127–Radar Girl 75 (Bleep-Bleep 134) (1982 5g⁴ 6f   **40**
6f 7f 5fg 5g 1983 5fg² 5f 6f) small filly; sprint plater; blinkered in 1983. *W. C. Watts.*

DUVESSA 4 b.f. Glen Quaich–Razor Bill (Fine Blade 121) (1982 NR 1983 10.2d)   –
1,500 2-y-o; first foal; dam never ran; well beaten in amateur riders race at
Doncaster in March. *P. Kelleway.*

DYNAMIC LEADER 2 ch.c. Lyphard 132–Diomedia (Sea-Bird II 145) (1983   **91**
6f⁴ 6f⁴) neat, strong-quartered colt; good walker and mover; half-brother to 3
winners, including very useful 1979 American 2-y-o Diorama (by Secretariat) and
minor 8.5f stakes winner Direct Answer (by Honest Pleasure); dam, half-sister to
dam of Glint of Gold and Diamond Shoal, was smart winner at up to 9f; favourite,
fair fourth in July maiden races at Yarmouth and Goodwood; will be much better
suited by 7f+; sent to Ireland to be trained by D. K. Weld. *H. Cecil.*

E

EAGLE COURT 3 b.g. Legal Eagle 126–Privy Court 73 (Adropejo 114) (1982   –
5.8g 5.8f 7fg 8s 6s 1983 5s 10.2g⁴ 8f) poor plater; best run at 1¼m. *M. Pipe.*

EAGLESFIELD 6 ch.h. Mountain Call 125–Rubella (Buisson Ardent 129) (1982   **64**
7f 6f 6g 6fg 7f³ 7f³ 7fg² 7g⁴ 7f 1983 6v 6fg 7f⁴ 7f⁴ 7f² 7fg 7h³ 8fg 6d) good mover;
poor handicapper; has been beaten in sellers; suited by 7f nowadays; acts on any
going; blinkered once in 1981; has run respectably for an apprentice; has been
bandaged. *C. Nelson.*

EARL'S COURT 7 ch.h. Lord Gayle 124–Paddy's Rose 81 (St Chad 120) (1982   **61**
12.3fg³ 12f* 12fg² 12fg³ 12g² 18.4g⁴ 10.6g² 12.3d 12fg 12s 12s⁴ 1983 12d* 12d²
12fg² 12.3fg 12f 12g 12s) small horse; genuine middle-distance handicapper at his
best; put up a gritty performance to win at Thirsk in May; ran well next 2 starts but
was below form afterwards; acts on any going; suitable mount for a boy; suited by
front-running tactics. *C. Crossley.*

EARLY JAZZ 2 b.f. Swing Easy 126–Persian Breakfast 50 (Deep Diver 134)   –
(1983 5d 5v 5d 5fg) Apr 23; 5,000Y, 7,000 2-y-o; tall, lengthy, rather unfurnished
filly; first foal; dam plater; soundly beaten in maiden races. *D. Chapman.*

EARLY PROMOTION 3 ch.c. High Echelon–Endeavorer (Forward Pass) (1982   –
7.6v 8g 1983 11v 11.7v) strong, useful-looking colt; well beaten in maiden and
minor events; sold 1,450 gns Ascot 2nd June Sales and resold 660 gns Doncaster
November Sales. *G. Hunter.*

EARLY SUPRISE 3 b. or br.f. Oats 126–Dawn (Moutiers 127) (1982 6g 6fg 6s³   **56**
1983 12s 8s 7d⁴ 8v 8f² 7fg 6f³ 7f* 7f 8f⁴) small filly; plater; won at Newcastle in
July (no bid); stays 1m; acts on any going; exported to Algeria. *D. Morley.*

EASTBROOK 3 b. or br.c. Lochnager 132–Lush Gold 91 (Goldhill 125) (1982 5d   –
5g³ 5d² 5f 6fg 6s 6s 1983 5v 7f 7g 5fg 8g) strong colt; good walker and mover;
disappointing maiden; best form at 5f. *M. H. Easterby.*

EAST COAST GIRL 4 ch.f. Relko 136–Starboard Belle 85 (Right Tack 131)   –
(1982 8.2g 12fg⁴ 12f 13.8f 16d 1983 12fg 15fg) lightly-made filly; poor plater; has
worn blinkers; has been bandaged. *J. Gilbert.*

EASTER CANDLE 7 b. or br.m. So Blessed 130–Palmitin 68 (Crepello 136)   –
(1982 NR 1983 17d) winning hurdler but is poor handicapper on flat; has worn
blinkers and bandages. *J. Edmunds.*

EASTER JANE 3 b.f. Palm Track 122–Jane Again (Spartan General 109) (1982   –
6f 7f 8.2fg 8s 10.2s 1983 8s 12.2g 8f 12f 9f 12fg 13.8g 12.2d) compact filly; poor
plater; has been tried in blinkers. *W. Haigh.*

EASTERLY GAEL 3 b.f. Tudor Music 131–Rathcoffey Deer (Pals Passage 115)   **49**
(1982 6g 6fg 7f 7fg 8f 1983 7fg³ 10f⁴ 10.8g* 10fg 10f³ 11.5s³) small, lightly-made
filly; bought in 750 gns after winning seller at Warwick in July by 5 lengths; stays 11f
well; trained by R. Williams first 2 outings. *J. Jenkins.*

EASTERN DAWN (USA) 2 b.f. Damascus–Euryanthe (Nijinsky 138) (1983 6f*   **115** p
8s*) third foal; half-sister to French Oaks third Air Distingue (by Sir Ivor) and a
winner in USA; dam unraced sister to high-class middle-distance stayer Caucasus
and half-sister to several very good performers; won newcomers race at Deauville
in August and accounted for six other useful previous winners in excellent style in
Prix d'Aumale at Longchamp the following month; came with a strong run to beat
Feerie Boreale decisively by ¾ length in latter, the pair 5 lengths clear; will stay
1¼m; probably acts on any going; very promising. *J. de Roualle, France.*

EASTERN LEGEND 2 b.g. High Top 131–Chinese Legend (Shantung 132)   –
(1983 5f 7f 7f 7f 7d) Feb 12; compact, useful-looking gelding; in rear in maiden and
minor events, three times last; sold P. Mitchell 2,500 gns Newmarket Autumn
Sales, and subsequently gelded. *D. Whelan.*

EASTERN TREASURE 4 b.f. Flashback 102–Eastern Lullaby (Zulu 94) (1982   –
9f 11d 8.2s 8s 8s 1983 6v 5f 6f 8f 5f 5f 5g 6fg) tall, rather leggy filly; behind in
varied company. *J. Smith.*

EASTER SUN 6 b.h. Bustino 136–Magical 95 (Aggressor 130) (1982 13.3f* 12f*   **120** d
12fg 13.3g³ 13.5g 1983 12d 12fg² 11f³ 13.3f 11g³) good-bodied, useful sort; very
smart performer at 5 yrs; didn't run up to that form in 1983, best efforts when 4
lengths second to Diamond Shoal in Gran Premio di Milano in June and 5½ lengths
third to Prima Voce in Grand Prix Prince Rose at Ostend in July; suited by 1½m+;
seemed to act on any going but went well on fast ground; blinkered last 4 starts;
sweated up and pulled hard when running moderately fourth start; standing at
Haras d'Ayguemorte at 10,000 francs Oct 1st. *M. Jarvis.*

EASTFORM 3 b.g. Reform 132–Nip in the Air 114 (Northern Dancer) (1982 5f²   **79**
5f* 5f 6fg² 6d⁴ 6g³ 6fg² 8g³ 7s 1983 9s 9d 9.4f 8fg 9f 8f² 8f 8.2fg³ 8.2g 8g* 10f
8fg) strong gelding; has a round action; inconsistent nowadays, but made all in
22-runner handicap at Pontefract in October and won decisively by 3 lengths from
Lady Donaro; should stay 1¼m; seems to act on any going with possible exception
of very soft; trained by M. H. Easterby until after second outing. *D. Chapman.*

EASTLEA COURT 2 b.f. Frimley Park 109–Frimley's One Oak 64 (Pieces of Eight   –
128) (1983 6d) June 14; big, lengthy filly; first foal; dam poor maiden; 50/1 and
backward, behind in 17-runner maiden race at Newbury in October. *S. Matthews.*

Prix d'Aumale, Longchamp—Eastern Dawn beats Feerie Boreale

EASY AIR 3 b.g. Mummy's Pet 125–Kushi 65 (Paridel 112) (1982 6fg 6g 7g 6d 1983 6v⁴ 6s³ 7g 6fg* 6g³ 6f 7f 6f⁴) rangy gelding; not particularly reliable, but won small handicap at Yarmouth in June; stays 6f; probably acts on any going; blinkered third start; exported to Singapore. *R. Armstrong.*   **73**

EASY LISTENING 4 ch.c. Jukebox 120–Misquote (Quorum 126) (1982 NR 1983 8fg 10v⁴ 12.2f 12f 10.6fg⁴ 10g) IR 44,000Y, 800 3-y-o, resold 3,000 3-y-o; workmanlike colt; brother to very useful 6f to 1m winner Star of Erin, subsequently a smart stakes winner at up to 1¼m in USA, and half-brother to 2 winners; dam prolific winner over hurdles; plating-class maiden; stays 1¼m; best run on heavy going; has run respectably for an apprentice; wears blinkers. *C. Mackenzie.*   **–**

EASY STAR 3 ch.g. Red Alert 127–Jantu 81 (Deep Diver 134) (1982 5f 6fg 6fg⁴ 5g 5.1d² 6d² 6g 6s³ 6d³ 5s 5g 1983 7fg 6f 6fg 6fg* 6fg 6g⁴ 6fg* 6fg 6g 6fg²) neat gelding; plater; bought in for 1,250 gns and 5,200 gns respectively after winning at Windsor (apprentices) and Newcastle (apprentice ridden) in summer; needs at least 6f; acts on a firm and a soft surface; sometimes blinkered (not when successful); occasionally bandaged and has worn a tongue strap; sometimes sweats up. *B. Hanbury.*   **63**

EASY TO COPY (USA) 2 br.f. Affirmed–Talking Picture (Speak John) (1983 8d*) Mar 8; half-sister to 2 winners in USA by Hoist the Flag; dam, top American 2-y-o filly of 1973, won at up to 7f; made a very impressive debut at Leopardstown in October, easily drawing clear in the final furlong to beat Quick Reference by 2 lengths (backed from 5/1 to 6/4 on); will be suited by 1¼m+; a very interesting prospect. *D. K. Weld, Ireland.*   **87 p**

ECONOMY GIRL 3 b.f. Scottish Rifle 127–Choralist 77 (Polyfoto 124) (1982 7fg 8d² 8.2d 8d 1983 12s 8s 7d 10h³ 7f 8f 9d 8d) small filly; bad plater nowadays; sometimes blinkered; left at start sixth outing; trained by Mrs J. Reavey until after third start. *K. Bridgwater.*   **–**

EGERTON 3 ch.g. Welsh Pageant 132–Visite Royale (Dapper Dan) (1982 7g 1983 8fg) no form, including in a seller; dead. *W. Haigh.*   **–**

EGIDIA 2 b.f. Welsh Saint 126–Jillette (Fine Blade 121) (1983 7d 7d*) Mar 22; second foal; dam Irish 1½m winner; got behind in 11-runner minor event at Naas in October but came through strongly, without being subjected to pressure, to win by a neck from odds-on stable-companion Miss Turnberry; will stay at least 1m; almost certainly still has improvement in her. *D. K. Weld, Ireland.*   **88 p**

EIGHTH WONDER 3 b.c. Octavo 115–Carrig Rose (Florescence 120) (1982 NR 1983 8v 10v 8s 10g 8f² 7fg* 7h 7fg 7fg) IR 2,500F, IR 8,800Y; fair sort; half-brother to useful Irish 9f to 1½m winner Carrig Willy (by Will Hays); dam won over 7f in Ireland; bought in 2,000 gns after winning seller at Brighton in June; ran respectably in non-seller next time; stays 1m; best form on a sound surface. *M. Haynes.*   **61**

253

ELAINE ANN 2 br.f. Garda's Revenge 119–Gavotte (Queen's Hussar 124) (1983   **66**
5g 5f 6f 5g³) Mar 19; 2,000Y; small, quite well-made filly; half-sister to 2 winners
by Sterling Bay, including fairly useful 1975 2-y-o winner Swedish Gavotte; dam
of little account; plating-class maiden; should stay 6f. *I. Walker.*

ELARIM 4 br.c. Meldrum 112–Souriciere 73 (Count Albany 99) (1982 8f 8f² 8fg   **62**
10g⁴ 11fg² 10fg 10d⁴ 9s 1983 8d 8d 8g 9g 9f* 9.4f⁴ 13fg 8f³ 10f³ 8.2f 10f³ 11f* 10s
8fg³ 11fg²) compact, workmanlike colt; won handicaps at Ripon (apprentice event)
in June and Redcar in September; suited by middle distances; probably acts on any
going but goes well on top-of-the-ground; good mount for an apprentice; sweated
up at Ripon. *T. Fairhurst.*

ELBURY COVE 4 ch.g. Kashiwa 115–Passing Glory 68 (Majority Blue 126)   **—**
(1982 8.2fg 1983 9s 10s 8g 7g) compact gelding; well beaten in varied company.
W. Wharton.

EL CAPISTRANO 2 b.c. Song 132–Abide 80 (Habitat 134) (1983 6fg 6f² 7fg*   **101**
7f* 7h³ 7g) Apr 3; 16,000Y; well-made, attractive colt; good walker and mover;
first foal; dam 1m winner; won maiden race at Chester and £3,100 event at Redcar
in July; 4½ lengths third of 4 to Falstaff in Solario Stakes at Sandown the following
month, better subsequent effort; suited by 7f. *G. Pritchard-Gordon.*

EL CAPISTRANO DAWN 2 ch.c. Octavo 115–Silk Gown (High Hat 131) (1983   **70**
7d 8fg⁴ 8.2s) Mar 15; IR 4,200F, 14,000Y; compact, quite useful-looking colt;
third foal; half-brother to a winner in Trinidad; dam placed up to 9f in Ireland; quite
a moderate maiden; lacks pace and will probably stay well. *G. Pritchard-Gordon.*

ELCIJ 2 ch.f. Crooner 119–Jamuna (Canisbay 120) (1983 5g 6fg) Mar 2;   **—**
half-sister to 1978 2-y-o 5f and 6f winner Royal Connection (by Royalty); dam
placed over 1m in France; unquoted, in rear in minor events at Lingfield in June and
Windsor in July. *D. Jermy.*

EL CITO 6 b.h. Ridan–Airgead Beo (Hook Money 124) (1982 8fg 12d 12s 1983   **42**
17.1g 12f 12f³ 17.1h² 13.1h) small horse; poor performer nowadays; beaten in
seller third start; suited by a test of stamina; acts on any going; suitable mount for
an apprentice; has worn blinkers, including when successful once at 2 yrs. *N.
Mitchell.*

EL DJEM 4 br.g. Mansingh 120–Mumtaz (Sheshoon 132) (1982 10f 9fg 9g 12fg⁴   **—**
12fg 12fg 13.8d 1983 12d) neat gelding; poor plater; has been bandaged in front.
P. Wigham.

ELECTO 2 b.f. Julio Mariner 127–As Blessed 101 (So Blessed 130) (1983 6f 7s)   **—**
May 5; leggy, lightly-made filly; third foal; half-sister to 3-y-o 1¼m seller winner
Have Blessed (by Averof); dam, 2-y-o 5f winner, stayed 1m; well beaten in
newcomers race at Ascot in June and maiden event (pulled hard) at Leicester in
October. *C. Brittain.*

ELECTRIC 4 b.c. Blakeney 126–Christiana (Double Jump 131) (1982 9fg² 10fg*   **123**
12f³ 12f 12f* 12g* 14.6f 1983 12d* 12d² 12f² 12.5fg 10.5d)
    The nineteenth-century political diarist Charles Greville once wrote that
'Racing is like dram-drinking; moments of excitement and wretched intervals',
and through no fault of his own Electric combined the exciting with the wretched
in his career. At his best undoubtedly a high-class colt with a good turn of foot he
was, like his contemporary Jalmood, unfortunately prone to muscle trouble in his
back which sometimes caused him to run miserably. Given this weakness,
Electric's connections must be grateful that the colt managed to collect three
top-class races, the Gordon Stakes and Great Voltigeur at three and the Jockey
Club Stakes at four.
    The Jockey Club Stakes, the highlight of the Friday card at the Newmarket
Guineas meeting, was as strongly contested as usual in 1983 with Time Charter,
Diamond Shoal, Old Country and Electric among the eleven runners. Diamond
Shoal, with the benefit of a successful run in the John Porter behind him, started
favourite ahead of the much-vaunted Simply Great and Time Charter, who
reportedly needed the run; Electric was relatively unfancied at 12/1. The first
mile takes little describing for Zilos and the ex-Irish Future Spa cut out the
running with Diamond Shoal held up in the middle of the field and Electric towards
the rear in company with Time Charter. Less than half a mile out Electric
occupied last place but he was still travelling smoothly and once switched to the
outside began to quicken well. Even so, he had at least five lengths to make up on
Zilos, Old Country and Amyndas, who were battling for the lead, with not much
more than a furlong and a half to go, while Time Charter was starting to make
significant progress on the inside. Producing storming runs, Time Charter and

Jockey Club Stakes, Newmarket—a fine performance from Electric who gets up near the finish to touch off Time Charter (centre) and Amyndas (spots)

Electric picked off the leaders well inside the final furlong and in the dying strides the colt poked his head in front to beat the sympathetically-handled Time Charter narrowly; Amyndas and Old Country came next, a length and three quarters of a length further back.

The Jockey Club Stakes was without any doubt the highlight of Electric's season, for although he ran creditably in three of his four remaining races the best he could manage was second place in two of them. The ease with which he raced at Newmarket, and the confidence of his jockey there, were much less in evidence in the Coronation Cup at Epsom where he ran in snatches, possibly owing to his back giving trouble again or because the track did not suit him. Niggled at after four furlongs and driven along vigorously to keep his place with the race only half over—an astonishing state of affairs considering the modest gallop set by Diamond Shoal—Electric once more took hold of his bit coming down Tattenham Hill and lay fourth entering the straight, not far behind Diamond Shoal, Old Country and My Sir Avon. It took Electric a good deal longer to overtake Diamond Shoal than in the Jockey Club Stakes, and by the time he had struggled past him Be My Native had swept into a lead of over a length. Hard as he tried Electric could not produce sufficient pace to peg back the leader who had three quarters of a length to spare at the line. It was much the same story in the Hardwicke Stakes at Royal Ascot. Ridden along from an early stage, Electric had no answer to Stanerra's exceptional turn of foot from the turn and though drawing twelve lengths clear of third-placed Be My Native he never looked likely to reach the Irish mare who won virtually unchallenged by a length and a half.

Electric's two subsequent races added nothing to his reputation. In the Grand Prix de Saint-Cloud he ran as if something was amiss, trailing in last of nine to Diamond Shoal after dropping out in the straight, while in the Benson and Hedges Gold Cup he ran well enough but showed a mile and a quarter to be too sharp for him, gamely staying on again to be fifth to Caerleon after being outpaced once the leaders quickened three furlongs out. A plan to run Electric in some valuable end-of-season races in the States came to nothing when he wrenched a joint on the gallops in September, and he has been retired to the Whitsbury Manor Stud in Hampshire with twenty-five shares on offer at £25,000 apiece placing a value of one million pounds on him. His fee will be £3,000 plus £3,000 (October 1st).

			Hethersett (b 1959)	Hugh Lupus
	Blakeney (b 1966)			Bride Elect
			Windmill Girl (b 1961)	Hornbeam
Electric (b.c. 1979)				Chorus Beauty
			Double Jump (ch 1962)	Rustam
	Christiana (ch 1967)			Fair Bid
			Mount Rosa (ch 1957)	Hill Gail
				Vestal Virgin

On his day Electric wasn't much inferior to his sire Blakeney's two best sons, the classic winners Julio Mariner and Tyrnavos. He is the sixth winner out of the useful Christiana who ran only at two when successful over five furlongs; of the others Chalet (by Luthier) showed smart form at seven furlongs and a mile and the three-year-old Schuss (by High Top) developed into a very useful miler in 1983, trotting up in the Cecil Frail Handicap. The second dam won twice at two and produced several winners, notably the smart miler Calpurnius. A well-made, quite attractive colt, Electric sometimes moved magnificently to post but on several

255

Mr R. Clifford-Turner's "Electric"

occasions when we saw him he did not impress anything like so much, perhaps because of his back trouble. Ideally suited by a mile and a half—when tried over further in the St Leger he had one of his off days—he appeared to act on any going. *M. Stoute.*

ELECTRICAL WIND (FR)   2 b.c. Green Dancer 132–Caretta (Caro 133) (1983 6fg⁴)   Mar 8; $475,000Y; big, fair sort; third foal; half-brother to French 3-y-o 1½m winner Jabal Tarik (by Riverman) and high-class French 1m to 11f winner Al Nasr (by Lyphard); dam, minor winner over 9.5f and 11f in France, is half-sister to 3 good winners; 10/1, reluctant to go to start but ran creditably when 4¼ lengths fourth of 20 to Saturnian in maiden race at Newmarket in October, racing smoothly with leaders to past halfway; will do quite a lot better, especially over longer distances. *M. Albina.*   **79 p**

ELECTRIC FAIRY   2 b.f. Malicious–Brava 71 (Gala Performance) (1983 5f 6fg 8g 5fg 6f)   Apr 10; compact filly; fifth foal; half-sister to 2 winners abroad; dam second over 6f at 2 yrs; in rear in varied company, including selling. *W. Elsey.*   **–**

ELECTRIFIED   2 b.f. Gunner B 126–Elected 74 (Red God 128§) (1983 6fg)   Apr 15; half-sister to several winners, notably very useful sprinter Pace Jean (by Tudor Melody); dam won at 1m; unquoted and in need of race, wasn't knocked about when never-dangerous 8¾ lengths ninth of 17 to Seattle Siren in £4,000 event at York in September; will do better over further. *W. Elsey.*   **67 p**

ELECTRIFYING   2 br.c Formidable 125–Edellette (Edellic 124) (1983 5f³ 5d* 6g)   May 12; robust colt; half-brother to several winners, including very useful 1980 French 2-y-o 5f winner Enigma (by Habitat) and very useful middle-distance performer Eddystone (by Barbare); dam won over 1¼m and 1½m in French Provinces; led throughout to win 10-runner maiden race at Wolverhampton in October by ¾ length from Quality Chorister; should stay beyond 5f. *P. Calver.*   **78**

ELECT (USA)   3 b.f. Vaguely Noble 140—Monade 129 (Klairon 131) (1982 NR 1983 12s* 12.3v* 10.6v³ 12.2fg³ 13.3f 12f³ 12g³ 10.5fg² 10s* 10fg³ 12g) big, quite attractive filly; not the best of movers; half-sister to quite useful middle-distance winner My Maravilla (by Blushing Groom) and numerous winners in USA, notably very smart Pressing Date (by Never Bend), a stakes winner at up to 1m; dam won Oaks; successful in minor events at Salisbury (awarded race after going down by a   **113**

length to Civility) and Newcastle in May and Yarmouth in September; placed on most other starts, on last 3 occasions in Galtres Stakes and valuable handicap at York and in Sun Chariot Stakes (3½ lengths third to Cormorant Wood) at Newmarket; seventh of 13 to Hush Dear in Long Island Handicap, Aqueduct on final outing; stayed 1½m well; acted on any going, but gained all her wins in the mud; stud. *L. Cumani.*

ELEGANT AIR 2 b.c. Shirley Heights 130–Elegant Tern 102 (Sea-Bird II 145) 114
(1983 7f* 7g* 7f² 7d⁴ 7.3d*)

Ian Balding told *Timeform* subscribers in the autumn that his fillies, generally, were as good-looking and well-bred a bunch as any trainer could wish for. The same could be said of his colts who include Troy's very useful son Corinth, of whom the best is most definitely yet to come, the Royal Lodge winner Gold And Ivory, the Zukunfts-Rennen winner Water Moccasin and the highly promising Elegant Air, winner of the Horris Hill Stakes.

Balding's summary of Elegant Air's four runs prior to the Horris Hill matches our reading of those races so closely that we reproduce it here. He said 'When Elegant Air first came in he looked very backward indeed, and I anticipated that he would be one of our very back-end colts. However, he seemed ready for a run in mid-June, so I ran him in a maiden race at Salisbury and to my slight surprise and great pleasure he came through and won nicely in the end. We then took him for quite a hot sort of maidens-at-closing race up at Newmarket. He was slightly inconvenienced by a slow pace there, but he took up the running with about a furlong and a half to run; in the end he tired, I thought, and just hung on to beat Beldale Lear narrowly. We then decided to go for the Champagne Stakes at Goodwood at the end of July where, unfortunately, we bumped into Trojan Fen who obviously is one of the top colts in the country. However, Elegant Air ran extremely well and was only mastered inside the last furlong. I felt that we should have one crack at a pattern race this season and rather than take on Lear Fan and Trojan Fen again in the Laurent Perrier Champagne Stakes at Doncaster, decided instead to tackle the best of the Irish in the BBA (Ireland) Goffs National Stakes at the Curragh. Elegant Air was never really going like a winner but stayed on well to finish a reasonably close fourth'.

Balding added that he thought Elegant Air had probably done enough for the season. However, he was obliged to change his mind. The colt continued to thrive physically and his work at home was reportedly so impressive that his trainer felt he must be allowed to take his chance in the Horris Hill at Newbury towards the end of the season, especially as his American owner-breeder was in the country at the time. Elegant Air thoroughly justified the decision with a smart display. Cauthen wisely decided to allow Elegant Air to stride along in front once it became clear that none of the six other runners was prepared to go on. The improving My Volga Boatman moved up to challenge him coming to the final quarter mile, looking

Horris Hill Stakes, Newbury—Elegant Air makes virtually all to beat My Volga Boatman (rails) and Round Hill

Mr Paul Mellon's "Elegant Air"

very dangerous, and quite a protracted struggle followed before Elegant Air, who wasn't subjected to so hard a race as My Volga Boatman, forged clear in the final furlong to win by two and a half lengths. The favourite Round Hill, winner of the Somerville Tattersall Stakes, was just a neck back in third place, while the other strongly-fancied runner, the Mornington Stakes winner Donzel, ran unaccountably badly in finishing last. Incidentally Elegant Air handled the softish ground admirably here and he's also shown he acts on firm going.

Elegant Air (b.c. Apr 8, 1981)	Shirley Heights (b 1975)	Mill Reef (b 1968)	Never Bend / Milan Mill
		Hardiemma (b 1969)	Hardicanute / Grand Cross
	Elegant Tern (b 1971)	Sea-Bird II (ch 1962)	Dan Cupid / Sicalade
		Prides Profile (b 1963)	Free America / Hillbrook

Before Gold And Ivory's victory in the Royal Lodge, his trainer described Elegant Air as the stable's brightest hope for 1984, a colt whom he hoped very much would make a Derby-class three-year-old. In our opinion Elegant Air needs to make a good deal more than normal improvement if he's to reach the first three in the Derby but there are grounds for thinking he may just do so; he's a splendid individual, big, strong and good-topped, and in action he's very difficult to fault, being both an excellent walker and a lovely mover. He's also likely to prove extremely well suited by middle distances: his sire Shirley Heights is, predictably, proving a strong influence for stamina and his dam Elegant Tern, a daughter of the Derby winner Sea-Bird, stayed well enough to finish third in the Ribblesdale Stakes. Elegant Tern is one of six winners produced by Prides Profile, a smart winner at up to nine furlongs who earned over 300,000 dollars in the States. Best of the others was the very useful eleven-furlong stakes winner Winds of Thought, while another of them, Pride's Palace, is the dam of the good 1983 Irish two-year-old Executive Pride. Elegant Tern has had three previous foals, all fillies, including two, Pelican Point and Fairy Tern, by Elegant Air's grandsire Mill Reef. Pelican Point was a disappointing maiden over middle distances but Fairy Tern was a more-than-useful performer who won three times at up to seven furlongs. Fairy Tern was described by her trainer as having 'considerable character' and her headstrong nature was no doubt the reason why she was kept to distances up to a mile. Elegant Air has shown none of Fairy Tern's quirks, indeed he seems extremely relaxed, and we're sure he'll stay much better that she appeared to. He promises to become the third high-class descendant of Mill Reef raced by Mr Paul Mellon in as many years, following Glint of Gold and Diamond Shoal. *I. Balding.*

ELEGANT NELL 2 ch.f. Free State 125–My Bushbaby 100 (Hula Hul 124)   –
(1983 6fg 6s) Mar 26; 3,000Y; neat filly; half-sister to 3 winners, including fairly useful 1978 2-y-o 6f winner Bushwhacker (by No Mercy); dam won over 5f at 2 yrs; 14/1, 10 lengths fifth of 10 to Lovers Bid in minor event at Ayr in September, second outing. *R. D. Peacock.*

EL GAZEBO 2 b.c. Tumble Wind–Vivungi (Exbury 138) (1983 6fg 5g³ 5fg² 5d*   **97**
5g*) May 3; IR 7,800Y, IR 26,000Y; neat colt; brother to minor 6f winner Patas Blancas; dam placed at around 7f in France and Ireland; was improving fast at the back-end, and on last 2 outings easily landed the odds in maiden race at Catterick and minor event at Redcar; will stay 6f; acts on a firm and a soft surface; sure to win more races. *J. Sutcliffe.*

EL GITANO 3 ch.c. Wollow 132–Welsh Miniature 85 (Owen Anthony 102) (1982   **98 §**
7f 8f 8s* 1983 7d* 8fg 8f* 8g 7s 8s 8fg² 8fg) lengthy, narrow, shallow-girthed colt; won £4,600 handicap at Doncaster in March and 6-runner £9,600 Food Brokers Trophy (Limited Handicap) at Newmarket in July, on latter course leading 2f or so out and keeping on to beat odds-on Muscatite by ½ length in slowly-run affair; 5 lengths second to Habitassa in handicap at Newmarket in October, only other form; suited by 1m; acts on any going; blinkered sixth start; tends to sweat up and to flash his tail under pressure; trained by R. Boss first start; thoroughly inconsistent. *A. Hide.*

EL GRAN SENOR (USA) 2 b.c. Northern Dancer–Sex Appeal (Buckpasser)   **131**
(1983 7f* 6.3g* 7d* 7fg*)
  When we saw El Gran Senor win the BBA (Ireland) Goffs National Stakes at the Curragh in September we frankly found his performance puzzling. He impressed enormously in the paddock, one of the nicest sons of Northern Dancer we'd seen, and he also impressed tremendously for the major part of the race, coming to the last two furlongs travelling so much better than his seven opponents that the only question seemed to be just how far he would win. However, by the time he'd crossed the line we weren't quite sure what to think. Instead of cutting down the front-running filly Sign-of-Life in a matter of strides as seemed likely, he managed to peg her back only a hundred yards out, eventually beating her three

BBA (Ireland) Goffs National Stakes, the Curragh—El Gran Senor (spotted cap) masters Sign-of-Life close home

quarters of a length with Red Russell taking third place a further two and a half lengths behind. Although there were grounds for thinking the result represented smart form—the next three home were the English challenger Elegant Air who had given Trojan Fen a good fight at Goodwood, the unbeaten winner of the Heinz '57' Stakes King Persian, and the promising Executive Pride, beaten only once in four starts—the prominent displays of the 33/1 shot Sign-of-Life and Red Russell suggested otherwise. These last two horses had managed only one win apiece in maiden company from a combined total of eleven previous outings. Sign-of-Life had, in fact, been beaten much more convincingly by El Gran Senor in the P. J. Prendergast Railway Stakes at the Curragh a fortnight before. El Gran Senor, a 9/4-on chance on that occasion following a smooth success in a maiden race at Phoenix Park on his debut early in August, had then had five lengths to spare over the fourth-placed Sign-of-Life. However, this performance was also difficult to assess. After looking to be going much better than the stand-side leader Blaze of Tara as he struck the front towards the far side with a quarter of a mile to run, El Gran Senor failed to draw away. Instead he tended to run green, edging to his left, and in the end scraped home by only a neck from the persistent Blaze of Tara.

After the National Stakes Vincent O'Brien intimated that El Gran Senor wouldn't race again as a two-year-old. Fortunately he had a change of heart which resulted in our obtaining a much better appreciation of the colt's capabilities. In October El Gran Senor represented the stable in the William Hill Dewhurst Stakes at Newmarket, a race it had won six times in the past, four times with sons of Northern Dancer and once with a grandson. The presence in the field of the Prix Morny winner Siberian Express, the July Stakes and Flying Childers winner Superlative and the highly promising Rainbow Quest virtually guaranteed that we'd find out much more about El Gran Senor in this one race than all his Irish races put together. El Gran Senor answered with a display which proved him beyond doubt a top-class colt and at the same time confirmed that he is indeed lazy once in front. Favourite, he was soon close up with Superlative as Siberian Express made the running ahead of the rank outsider Corncharm, and began his effort on the bridle after halfway. He hit the front two furlongs out, where Superlative and Rainbow Quest were also trying to improve, and ran down into the Dip with a two-length

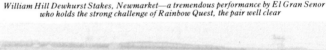

William Hill Dewhurst Stakes, Newmarket—a tremendous performance by El Gran Senor who holds the strong challenge of Rainbow Quest, the pair well clear

Mr R. E. Sangster's "El Gran Senor"

advantage over the only remaining danger, Rainbow Quest. The pair fought out a splendid battle under pressure up the hill, with El Gran Senor doing no more in the closing stages than required to hang on to an advantage narrowed to half a length at the line. The rest, headed by Siberian Express, were left toiling at least six lengths behind and if any doubts remained about El Gran Senor's merit they were dispelled by his time of 1m 24.90sec, which represents a timefigure of 1.22 fast, the best of the season by a two-year-old. Incidentally, the fast ground suited the sharp-actioned El Gran Senor extremely well, and it's worth pointing out here that his brother Try My Best didn't look nearly so good on a soft surface as he did on firm going.

So El Gran Senor ended his first season the unbeaten winner of four races, among them the most valuable race open to two-year-old colts in Ireland and the most prestigious one in Britain: such a record would have made its holder a fairly short-priced favourite for the Two Thousand Guineas in some years. However, El Gran Senor was generally offered at 10/1 immediately after the Dewhurst, with Lear Fan as short as 6/1. In our opinion there isn't much between the best performances of El Gran Senor and Lear Fan: the probable reason why El Gran Senor is available at such generous odds is the subsequent failure of recent Dewhurst winners in general and of the O'Brien-trained winners in particular. Not one of the Dewhurst winners from 1978 to 1982—Tromos, Monteverdi, Storm Bird, Wind and Wuthering and Diesis—managed to win again and the 1977 winner Try My Best wasn't seen out again after trailing home last of nineteen when an even money favourite for the Two Thousand Guineas. However, there seems to be little logic in judging El Gran Senor's prospects on the subsequent records of his predecessors, and we don't propose to do so. We believe he'll make a first-rate three-year-old. As we said earlier he is one of the nicest sons of Northern Dancer in our experience, a most attractive, good-bodied individual who is altogether bigger, stronger and more imposing than most of his sire's stock and, what's more, by far the best-looking Dewhurst winner for a number of years. Interestingly, though, his trainer, no doubt with Danzatore and Lomond very much in mind, was at pains afterwards to recommend that ante-post backers support the stable as a whole for the Guineas if they must have a bet, adding that besides El Gran Senor he had three other unbeaten colts, Argosy, Capture Him and Sadler's Wells, any of whom could develop into the stable's leading contender. This advice is well worth noting and the

Tote's offer of 6/1 the O'Brien stable at the time of writing represents very sound value when compared with the 8/1 offered against El Gran Senor alone.

El Gran Senor (USA) (b.c. Apr 21, 1981)	Northern Dancer (b 1961)	Nearctic (br 1954)	Nearco Lady Angela
		Natalma (b 1957)	Native Dancer Almahmoud
	Sex Appeal (ch 1970)	Buckpasser (br 1963)	Tom Fool Busanda
		Best in Show (ch 1965)	Traffic Judge Stolen Hour

Finding something new to write about El Gran Senor's family isn't easy. Hardly a year seems to pass without a notable winner out of either his dam, the unraced Sex Appeal, or grandam, the very useful Best in Show whose five wins included one in the seven-furlong Comely Stakes. El Gran Senor is the eighth foal produced by Sex Appeal in as many years at stud, and the fifth by Northern Dancer following Try My Best, the unraced Northern Guest who is now at stud in South Africa, the maiden Compliance who is at stud in the States after showing fairly useful form over seven furlongs in Ireland, and the unraced three-year-old filly Northern Prancer. Only one of her three other foals raced, the unbeaten Halo filly Solar, one of the best two-year-old fillies in Ireland in 1978. Solar has visited Northern Dancer in three of her five years at stud and was in foal to him when sold for 3,000,000 dollars in November 1983. Surprisingly none of Best in Show's first eleven foals was by a stallion from the Northern Dancer line. Six of them were by Sir Ivor, including Malinowski, Monroe and Gielgud, winners respectively of the Craven, Ballyogan and Laurent Perrier Champagne Stakes, while the best of her other progeny is the very smart Blushing Groom filly Blush With Pride. Blush With Pride did extremely well as a three-year-old, winning four very valuable stakes races including one over eleven furlongs, the Golden Harvest Handicap. She showed a good deal more stamina than her five half-brothers and half-sisters who raced in Europe, none of whom won beyond a mile. It's doubtful whether El Gran Senor will stay the Derby distance and he's likely to have his campaign planned very much around the Guineas. Let's hope he trains on well enough to take his chance—a rematch between El Gran Senor and Rainbow Quest, with Lear Fan there to take them on, should be worth travelling a long way to see. *V. O'Brien, Ireland.*

EL HAKIM (USA) 2 b.c. Roberto 131–Remedia (Dr Fager) (1983 7f* 7fg2) Mar 21; $475,000Y; half-brother to Too Chic (by Blushing Groom), a very smart winner at up to 1m; dam, daughter of Oaks winner Monade, won at up to 7f; did all that could be expected of him when 5/2 on for 11-runner maiden race at Yarmouth in August, winning by 4 lengths from Amal Lees Hope despite showing signs of greenness; injured a knee when excellent second, beaten neck, to Seismic Wave (rec 8lb) in 18-runner £5,000 event at Doncaster the following month; will be well suited by 1m+; acts on firm going. *H. Cecil.*   103 p

ELIASO 2 b.c. Be My Guest 126–Limuru 83 (Alcide 136) (1983 7.6fg 7g4) Mar 9; 110,000Y; closely related to poor 3-y-o Try Your Best (by Try My Best) and half-brother to numerous winners, including Derby runner-up Cavo Doro (by Sir Ivor); dam, 1m and 1¼m handicapper, is half-sister to good miler Saintly Song; reasonably close up, showing promise, in 2 maiden races at Lingfield in October; sure to improve. *G. Lewis.*   79 p

ELISETTA 3 b.f. Monsanto 121–Silette 84 (Siliconn 121) (1982 6g 5.8g 5fg 1983 9s2 8d 8s* 7d 9f 8fg4 8f 8.3f 10f 10g 7fg) compact filly; 20/1 and apprentice ridden when winning handicap at Chepstow in May; stays 9f; acts well on soft going. *M. Blanshard.*   54

ELITE SYNCOPATION (USA) 3 ch.c. Lyphard 132–Zaire (Sir Gaylord) (1982 6fg 6d* 7s3 1983 8s3 10g2 10f3 10g) small, strong, quite attractive colt; placed in minor event at Wolverhampton and 2 handicaps at Newmarket; ran moderately final outing; stays 1¼m; acts on any going; bandaged in front third start. *H. Cecil.*   90

ELITIST 2 b.f. Keren 100–Queen's Lane 107 (Tamerlane 128) (1983 6d 7fg 8.2f 7s4 7g 7fg) Jan 21; sturdy filly; half-sister to fairly useful 1975 2-y-o 6f winner Midnight Melody (by Linacre) and a winner in Malaya; dam stayed 9f; 4½ lengths fourth of 16 to Bamba in maiden race at Ayr in September, only indication of merit; should stay 1m; evidently well suited by soft going. *N. Chamberlain.*   72

ELIZA DE RICH 6 b.m. Spanish Gold 101–Dumb Kathy (Dumbarnie 125) (1982 8s 8f 8f* 7fg 7g4 8fg* 8f 8.2fg* 8d3 8fg 8fg 7g 1983 8d 8d* 8.2s4 8fg2 8f4 8f4 8.2f)   57

lightly-made mare; former plater; won handicap at Pontefract in April; stays 1m; seems to act on any going; occasionally sweats up; usually held up. *D. Smith.*

ELJAZZI 2 b.f. Artaius 129–Border Bounty 113 (Bounteous 125) (1983 7s*) Apr 12; 100,000F, 92,000Y; strong, sturdy, attractive filly; half-sister to numerous winners, including high-class miler Pitcairn and very smart middle-distance stayer Valley Forge (both by Petingo); dam runner-up in Yorkshire Oaks and Park Hill Stakes; odds on, didn't impress on way to start in 19-runner maiden race at Leicester in October but came back much better, lengthening her stride in last 2f to win impressively by 4 lengths; will stay 1½m; a very likeable filly, sure to win more races. *H. Cecil.*   85 p

EL KANTAOUI 3 ch.f. Wolverlife 115–Lula 86 (Never Say Die 137) (1982 5f 6g2 7.9g* 7f3 7g2 7g* 8d 6d3 8fg 1983 6s 6s 8f2 8.5f 8.5f 8g4 7fg 7fg 8d2 8g* 10g*(dis) 10d* 12g3 12g) Irish filly; fourth live foal; half-sister to Irish 1¼m winner Musical Boy (by Tudor Music), also successful in USA; dam won over 7f at 2 yrs; in great form in September and after finishing neck second of 15 to Mighty Fly in Gilltown Stud Stakes at the Curragh was first past post in handicaps at Navan and Listowel (2); gained her 2 wins at Listowel on successive days, but was disqualified on first occasion for carrying 1lb too little; probably stays 1½m; probably acts on any going; blinkered seventh outing. *N. Meade, Ireland.*   95

ELKIE BROOKS 2 b.f. Relkino 131–Cresset 107 (Henry the Seventh 125) (1983 7.6d 6fg2) Feb 7; 5,200F; third produce; half-sister to a winner in USA; dam 2-y-o 6f winner; led until close home in 20-runner maiden race won by Tug Top at Doncaster in November; should stay 7f+. *D. H. Jones.*   82

ELLAN VRETYN 3 b.f. Crooner 119–Rose of France 83 (Grand Roi 118) (1982 NR 1983 8s 8s 10v) third foal; dam won over 1¼m at 3 yrs and over 11f at 9 yrs, latter after birth of first foal; behind in sellers in spring. *D. Jermy.*   –

ELLENSLAD 8 ch.g. Souvran 98–Sally Bee (Sallymount 125) (1982 NR 1983 8f) lightly raced and probably of little account towards end of career; dead. *C. Drew.*   –

ELLERWOOD 3 b.f. So Blessed 130–Angello 87 (Crepello 136) (1982 NR 1983 9f 10s 8g 8f) half-sister to several winners, including 1981 2-y-o 6f winner Pamperdale (by Hotfoot) and Royal Lodge winner Adios (by Silly Season); dam won at 1m; little worthwhile form in maiden and minor events. *D. Smith.*   –

EL MANSOUR 4 b.g. Tower Walk 130–Gay Amanda 75 (Counsel 118) (1982 7fg 6fg 6g 6f2 6g 1983 7s* 7s) rangy gelding; useful at his best; won handicap at Salisbury in May; suited by 7f; acts on any going but is ideally suited by soft ground; not raced after May. *N. Gaselee.*   87

ELMAR 4 b.f. Lord Gayle 124–Regal Step 101 (Ribero 126) (1982 7g 7g3 7g* 8f2 7g* 8.5fg2 8g2 9s2 1983 8v2 8d 8v* 10v3 10s2 8f 10f 12fg 8fg3 9fg 10g) quite attractive, lightly-made filly; fair handicapper; beat Minmax smoothly by 2 lengths in Jubilee Stakes at Kempton in May; ran creditably several subsequent outings, notably when 5 lengths second to Florida Son in Daily Mirror Handicap at Epsom in June and about 5 lengths sixth of 30 to Sagamore in William Hill Cambridgeshire at Newmarket on tenth start in October; stayed 1¼m (well beaten over 1½m); acted on any going but well on soft; visits Bustino. *J. Dunlop.*   87

ELMDON 3 b.g. Hittite Glory 125–Margaret's Ruby (Tesco Boy 121) (1982 7d 6g 1983 7d 6s* 7fg 6fg 6f2 6f 6f 6d2 7g) attractive gelding; beat Quilting a short head in minor event at Brighton in May; inconsistent afterwards, but was second at Beverley and Brighton again; stays 6f; acts on any going; sometimes blinkered (wore them when successful but not when placed); sold 3,500 gns Newmarket Autumn Sales. *J. Winter.*   77

ELMSDALE 3 b.g. Derrylin 115–Vale of Honey (Mourne 126) (1982 NR 1983 10.1s 10g 10f) 7,000Y, 400 2-y-o; half-brother to a winning hurdler; dam, very useful at up to 7.5f in France, is half-sister to good sprinter Mountain Call; well beaten in maiden and minor events. *J. O'Donoghue.*   –

ELSELL 8 ch.m. Grey Mirage 128–Mary's Twiggy (Queen's Hussar 124) (1982 16d2 16f 12s 1983 16v2 16.1s) narrow, lightly-made mare; former plater; stays well; acts on heavy going. *M. Eckley.*   –

ELUSIVE 2 b.f. Little Current–Tartan Pimpernel 109 (Blakeney 126) (1983 6f3 7d*) Mar 10; well-made, attractive filly; good walker; second foal; half-sister to 3-y-o Emmuska (by Roberto); dam, half-sister to Dunfermline, won May Hill Stakes at 2 yrs and Galtres Stakes at 3 yrs; won Acomb Stakes at York in August,   94 p beating Axios by 2 lengths; outpaced at Goodwood in ordinary maiden company previously; will need test of stamina to be seen to best advantage; acts on a soft surface; sure to win more races, and seems likely to develop into pretty good filly. *R. Hern.*

ELYSIAN 3 b. or br.f. Northfields–Elizabethan 89 (Tudor Melody 129) (1982 6fg² 6g* 8fg³ 1983 8v 12v 10f² 10f² 12g 10s³ 10.2fg) neat filly; ran best race in Nassau Stakes at Goodwood in July on fourth start, being moved up a place after finishing 3 lengths third to Acclimatise; 9 lengths fifth of 12 behind Hymettus in Galtres Stakes at York in August (sweated up and unshipped her rider in preliminaries) and 3 lengths third of 6 behind Elect in minor event at Yarmouth in September on next 2 starts; seems to stay 1½m; acts well on firm going. *P. Walwyn.*   **94**

EMAD 3 ch.c. Hot Spark 126–Sky Miss (Skymaster 126) (1982 5d 6f 8s 1983 7s* 8s 7.2s⁴ 7fg⁴ 7f³ 8.3f*) fair sort; successful in handicaps at Salisbury in May and Brighton and Windsor in August, making all on last 2 courses; below form second and third starts; stays 1m well; acts on any going; exported to Hong Kong. *R. Hannon.*   **80**

EMALINE (FR) 2 ch.f. Empery 128–Chere Alise (Caro 133) (1983 7fg* 7.5s⁴) second foal; half-sister to 3-y-o Dear Boy (by Youth); dam, very useful from 1m to 1¼m in France, is sister to very useful miler Cenerentola; justified favouritism when winning a 15-runner newcomers event at Maisons-Laffitte in September by a length from Vichy Spring; ruined her chance by wandering when a close fourth to Polly's Ark in Prix Thomas Bryon at Saint-Cloud the following month; will stay 1¼m; probably acts on any going; looks a smart filly in the making. *J. Cunnington, jnr, France.*   **105**

EMERALD EAGLE 2 ch.f. Sandy Creek 123–Double Eagle 71 (Goldhill 125) (1983 6fg⁴ 5f⁴ 6fg² 5g² 5fg⁴) May 20; IR 46,000Y; lengthy, workmanlike filly; half-sister to several winners, including 3-y-o 6f winner Rumz (by Gay Fandango) and useful Irish sprinters Flaming Eagle (by Green God) and Do The Hustle (by Sun Prince); dam won 5f seller at 2 yrs; second to Preobrajenska in 2 autumn races, running her to 2 lengths in maiden at Nottingham and to a length on terms 7 lb better in minor event at York; will be suited by a return to 6f; dwelt first outing and swerved badly start on second. *C. Booth.*   **78**

Acomb Stakes, York—Elusive wins well from Axios

EMERALD REEF 3 b.f. Mill Reef 141–Crown Treasure (Graustark) (1982 7f — 8g 8g 1983 10s³ 11.7s² 12s⁴ 11v 13d 14f 12f 17.1h 10fg) lengthy, attractive filly; sister to Glint of Gold and Diamond Shoal; ran creditably when 14 lengths fourth of 12 to Give Thanks in Esal Bookmakers Oaks Trial at Lingfield in May but became most disappointing; stays 1¾m; blinkered final outing. *I. Balding.*

EMERGENCY PLUMBER 2 b.g. Sallust 134–Cratloe (African Sky 124) (1983   **81** 6f 6fg² 6f* 6f² 6fg³ 7g⁴ 6g) Apr 10; IR 6,000Y; rather sparely-made gelding; poor mover; first foal; dam never ran; won 12-runner maiden race at Nottingham in July by a short head from Burgundy Star; stays 7f; acts on firm going; consistent until showing nothing when blinkered in nursery at York in October on final appearance; subsequently gelded. *B. Hanbury.*

EMILY ETHEL 5 b.m. Impecunious–Edith 90 (French Beige 127) (1982 NR   — 1983 12g) of little account; has worn bandages. *R. Blakeney.*

EMLYN PRINCESS 3 ch.f. Julio Mariner 127–Rotondo (Royal Buck) (1982 7f   — 7fg 1983 12f 14f 17g 12d) workmanlike filly; excellent mover; well beaten in maiden events and a handicap on flat, but is a useful hurdler. *B. Swift.*

EMMA ALISON 3 ch.f. Mansingh 120–Tanzanite (Mongo) (1982 6g 5.1fg 7g   — 1983 12s) of little account. *H. Beasley.*

EMMA ROYALE 4 b.f. Royal and Regal–Moment To Remember (Assagai) (1982   **57** 10s 12g 12fg 13.8f 10f⁴ 10.6s 12.2d³ 12d* 12g 1983 12v⁴ 12fg 12f⁴ 14.6f 17d 15.8g 16s³ 16.1s⁴ 12fg* 15fg) fair sort; poor handicapper; occasionally runs in sellers and gamely won valuable event at Doncaster in October; attracted no bid afterwards; possibly stays 2m; acts on any going; has won for an apprentice; does best when ridden up with pace. *R. Hollinshead.*

EMMA'S STAR 3 b.f. Comedy Star 121–Dancin In The Wind 61 (Aureole 132)   — (1982 8s 1983 11.7s 12d 12.2d 12g 17g 8f 8fg) leggy, close-coupled filly; in rear in varied races, including a seller; blinkered third start. *M. Blanshard.*

EMMUSKA (USA) 3 br.f. Roberto 131–Tartan Pimpernel 109 (Blakeney 126)   **68** (1982 NR 1983 7d 12fg³ 12g⁴ 10d) big, rather leggy filly; first foal; dam, half-sister to Dunfermline, won May Hill Stakes at 2 yrs and Galtres Stakes at 3 yrs; having first race for nearly 4 months and very much on toes in preliminaries when 2½ lengths third of 10 behind Hymettus in maiden race at Haydock in August, best effort (pulled hard and was hampered on bend); suited by 1½m; sold 88,000 gns Newmarket December Sales. *R. Hern.*

EMOTIONAL (USA) 2 ch.f. Sensitive Prince–Aristocracy (Cornish Prince)   **71** (1983 6fg⁴ 6g⁴ 7f) May 1; $87,000F, $82,000Y; fourth produce; half-sister to a minor winner in the USA; dam, second 3 times from 7 starts, is half-sister to dam of Spectacular Bid; quite a modest filly; beaten at Ayr and Yarmouth on last 2 outings; will stay 1m; disappointing. *J. Hindley.*

EMPEROR'S PALACE 3 gr.c. Dragonara Palace 115–Emperor Star (King   **58** Emperor) (1982 7g 1983 7d 6f 7f² 7f 5f 7s) strong, good-bodied colt; well backed when second in handicap at Yarmouth in August; ran moderately afterwards (blinkered fifth start); stays 7f; sold 5,200 gns Newmarket Autumn Sales. *M. Jarvis.*

EMPRESS CATHERINE 2 b. or br.f. Welsh Pageant 132–Empress of Russia   — 79 (Royal Palace 131) (1983 7f 8g) Mar 9; good-bodied filly; third foal; dam, half-sister to Connaught, won over 1½m at 4 yrs; unquoted, in rear in maiden races at Sandown in July and October. *A. Ingham.*

EMPRESS CORINA 2 ch.f. Free State 125–Emperor Star (King Emperor)   **74** (1983 6fg 7d³ 7fg 7s 6fg) Apr 3; 3,100Y; workmanlike filly; half-sister to 2 winners by Mummy's Pet, including very useful 6f and 7f winner Not For Show; dam of little account; prominent in maiden races, running well for a 7-lb claimer when 2¾ lengths fifth of 17 to Signorina Odone at Beverley in September on third outing; will stay 1m. *R. Williams.*

ENBYAR DAN 3 ch.c. Porto Bello 118–Alleyn (Alcide 136) (1982 5fg 5.1g⁴ 7f²   — 7f* 7g² 7fg 1983 7.6v² 8v 7g 10fg 10g 11.5g 12g 13g) workmanlike colt; second to easy winner Whisky Talk in small race at Lingfield in April; didn't show much afterwards, including in claiming race; yet to show he stays beyond 7.6f; acts on any going; blinkered last 4 starts. *M. Tompkins.*

ENCHANTED CASTLE 2 ch.c. Fordham 117–Castletimon (Tudor Music 131)   **87** (1983 7f 7g³ 6g² 6fg) Feb 4; IR 54,000Y; shapely, quite attractive colt; fourth living produce; half-brother to a prolific winner in Italy; dam lightly-raced half-sister to very useful middle-distance performer Shamsan; prominent on last 3 outings in big fields of maidens at Goodwood (2) and Newmarket; stays 7f; well up to winning at the minor meetings. *P. Cole.*

ENCOURAGING (AUS) 2 br.c. Bletchingly–Dangerous Dawn (Crepello 136) 75 p
(1983 6g) half-brother to several winners in Australia, including Grade 1 Caulfield
Guineas winner Kenmark and sprint winner Sweet (both by Vain); dam well behind
in 3 races at 2 yrs in this country before being sold for 420 gns; sire, grandson of
Star Kingdom, was good winner over 5.5f and is sire of outstanding Australian
performer Kingston Town; weak 10/1-shot, in touch until finding no extra in last
furlong when promising 4¾ lengths sixth of 23 to Miss Beaulieu in newcomers
event at Goodwood in September; sure to improve. *R. Hern.*

END OF THE ROAD 3 gr.g. Warpath 113–Eternally 85 (Ballymoss 136) (1982 80
NR 1983 10f 12.3fg 16f² 14.7f* 14.7fg) big, fair sort; third living foal; brother to
winning stayer Auld Lang Syne and half-brother to a winner; dam needed long
distances; driven out to beat Bayrak by 2 lengths in 16-runner maiden race at
Redcar in September; hadn't handled bend well when second at Beverley previous
start; suited by a test of stamina; has raced only on firm ground; pulled up when bit
slipped through mouth second outing; ran moderately final start; sold to J. King
15,000 gns Doncaster November Sales. *C. Thornton.*

ENDOW 3 b.f. Mr Bigmore 123–Fulfilment (David Jack 125) (1982 6f 1983 12.2f⁴ –
14f 15.5f 15.8g 16d 12g) small filly; stumbled 1½f out when fourth of 8 in maiden
race at Catterick in August, best effort; should be suited by a test of stamina. *F.
Durr.*

ENERGY PLUS 8 b.h. Tyrant–Reformed Maid (Reform 132) (1982 6fg 6d 7g 6f –
6s 1983 8g⁴ 7d) neat, strong horse; poor mover; poor handicapper; has been
beaten in a seller; stays 1m; often bandaged. *K. Stone.*

ENGLISH MASTER (USA) 3 b.c. Master Derby–Final Quote (Minnesota 49
Mac) (1982 7g 1983 10v 8f 7fg⁴ 7f) tall, good-topped colt; fourth in seller at
Brighton in June; had stiffer task only subsequent outing; blinkered last 2 starts.
J. Sutcliffe.

ENGLISH MUFFIN 3 gr.f. Owen Dudley 121–Pure Honey 94 (Don II 123) (1982 53
5g³ 5fg³ 6g 6f² 5.8f² 6d 5d⁴ 6s 1983 7g 7fg 7fg² 8.3f⁴ 7f³ 12g) maiden plater;
races mainly at around 7f, but not entirely disgraced over 1½m; seems to act on
any going; has run creditably in blinkers; trained by R. Laing until after fifth start.
N. Tinkler.

ENGLISH STAR 3 gr.g. English Prince 129–Scargill's Girl 56 (St Alphage 119) –
(1982 5fg³ 5fg² 5fg 5g 7g 6d⁴ 5g 5fg* 5s 5g 1983 6d 5s 5g 5.3f) workmanlike
gelding; didn't recover his 2-y-o form; best form at 5f on a sound surface;
blinkered fourth outing in 1982; inconsistent. *D. Oughton.*

ENSEMBLE (USA) 2 b.c. Key To The Mint–Shuvee (Nashua) (1983 7g³) Mar 78 p
2; $1,400,000Y; brother to Shukey, a very useful stakes winner over 8.5f, and
half-brother to 4 winners, including useful 1980 Irish 2-y-o 1m winner Benefice (by
Damascus) and 13f stakes winner Tom Swift (by Tom Rolfe); dam top-class
performer at up to 2m, winning 16 races from 2 yrs to 5 yrs including CCA Oaks and
Jockey Club Gold Cup (twice); weak second favourite, ran on strongly after slow
start to finish close third of 13 behind Talk of Glory in moderate maiden at Lingfield
in October; certain to do better. *G. Harwood.*

EPETIOS 3 b.g. Wolver Hollow 126–Treechka (Reform 132) (1982 7s⁴ 1983 8f 80
12f³ 12f 10h* 12h² 12f 10d 10g) strong, good sort; favourite when 5-length winner
of maiden race at Nottingham in August and when second in handicap at Chepstow
later in month; stays 1½m; acts on any going; ran moderately third and last 3
starts, on one occasion pulling hard in an apprentice event; sold 11,500 gns
Newmarket Autumn Sales. *G. Harwood.*

EPIC MAKING (USA) 3 ch.f. Le Fabuleux 133–Bold Queen (Bold Ruler) (1982 –
NR 1983 10g 12f) half-sister to several winners in USA; dam, smart stakes winner
over 8.5f at 3 yrs, is sister to What A Pleasure and to Clear Ceiling, the dam of
Quick As Lightning and Stratospheric; well beaten in maiden races at Brighton in
May and June (last of 11). *J. Dunlop.*

EPRYANA 3 b.f. English Prince 129–Ayana (High Flown 117) (1982 7fg 8f 7d –
1983 10s 12g 17g 15.5f 10h) no form, including in a seller on final start (blinkered);
sold 660 gns Ascot September Sales. *P. Makin.*

EQUANAID 3 b.c. Dominion 123–Jungle Queen (Twilight Alley 133) (1982 7g 88
8.2s* 8.2s 1983 8.2v* 10v² 11g⁴ 10s 9fg) tall, good-bodied colt; not a good walker
and is a poor mover in his slower paces; beat Sugar Loch by 2 lengths in £7,500
Valspar Paints Handicap at Haydock in April; went down by head to General
Concorde in very close finish to XYZ Handicap at Newcastle the following month,

best subsequent effort; suited by 1¼m; well suited by plenty of give underfoot; off course more than 3 months before fourth start. *C. Nelson.*

EQUINOL (USA) 2 b.c. Nijinsky 138–Equal Honor (Round Table) (1983 7d* 8s)   **109**
second foal; half-brother to French 3-y-o Honorine (by Blushing Groom); dam, a stakes-placed winner, is half-sister to His Honor (by Nijinsky), a smart stakes winner at up to 9f; never a threat when fifth (beaten about 2½ lengths) to Cariellor in Prix La Rochette at Longchamp in September; had earlier won a maiden at Saint-Cloud by a length from Blue Whale; will be suited by 1¼m+; the type to make a better 3-y-o. *F. Boutin, France.*

ERIC'S WISH 3 b.g. Cawston's Clown 113–Sirette (Great Nephew 126) (1982   –
7fg 6fg 6s 1983 6v² 7v 8s 6f 7f 8fg) leggy, close-coupled gelding; bad plater; stays 6f; blinkered final outing. *A. W. Jones.*

ERIN'S GLEN 3 br.f. Royal and Regal–Erin Blu (Noor 123) (1982 NR 1983 7v²   **97**
8d* 10s² 10v* 10f 10fg 8d⁴ 10g⁴) half-sister to 2 winners in USA by Amazing, including Amazing Man, a stakes winner at 2 yrs; dam won over 6f at 3 yrs; successful in maiden race at Leopardstown in April and 11-runner £5,800 Browne/Doyle Stakes at the Curragh in May; also ran well to be 2½ lengths second to Ask The Wind in 10-runner Hard Fought 3-Y-O Fillies Stakes at Phoenix Park in between and less than 3 lengths fourth of 15 behind Mighty Fly in Gilltown Stud Stakes at the Curragh in September on penultimate start; stays 1¼m; acts well on soft ground and has run moderately on firm. *M. Connolly, Ireland.*

ERIN'S HOPE 4 b.c. Manado 130–Chemise 75 (Shantung 132) (1982 8d² 9s*   **117**
12g 10s² 10d³ 1983 7s³ 10v² 10d³ 10fg 10fg³ 8f 9fg² 7g² 8d* 7g) IR 6,000Y; big, lengthy colt; has a round action; half-brother to Erins Isle (by Busted), a very smart middle-distance performer here and in USA, and to a winner in Malaya; dam won over 1¼m; gained a well-deserved success in Desmond Stakes at the Curragh in September, getting the better of Captivator by a short head; placed most other starts, notably in Gladness Stakes at the Curragh, Nijinsky Stakes at Leopardstown (head second of 7 to Salmon Leap), Brigadier Gerard Stakes at Sandown (1¾ lengths third to Stanerra) and Coolmore Be My Guest Stakes at Phoenix Park (length second to Senior Citizen); pulled very hard when soundly beaten in Prince of Wales's Stakes at Royal Ascot on fourth appearance; will probably stay 1½m; ideally suited by some give in the ground; blinkered sixth outing; genuine; smart. *J. Bolger, Ireland.*

EROSTIN STAR 3 b.c. Red Regent 123–Ruche (Soleil II 133) (1982 NR 1983   –
8g 8v 7f 8fg) IR 1,500F (privately), 4,400Y (privately also); big, good-topped colt; half-brother to a winner abroad; dam unraced half-sister to very useful sprinter Stung; sixth of 15 in maiden race at Goodwood on second start; blinkered final outing; dead. *A. Jarvis.*

ERRIGAL 3 b.g. Guillaume Tell 121–Levrosa (Levmoss 133) (1982 8.2s 8s²   **68**
1983 10.2f 10.4fg 10f 12f³ 10d 12d 12s 12g⁴) quite attractive gelding; in frame in maiden races; will be suited by 1¾m; acts on any going. *R. Hollinshead.*

ESAL CONDOR (CHI) 6 b.g. Iram–Walewska (Court Martial) (1982 NR 1983   –
10s) Chilean-bred gelding; behind in apprentice event at Brighton in May, only outing on flat in this country. *P. Mitchell.*

ESCALINE (FR) 3 ch.f. Arctic Tern 126–Esdee (Hail to Reason) (1982 8f² 8s*   **123**
10v* 1983 10.5v² 9s* 10.5v³ 10.5f* 12f 13d)
We saw few more spectacular finishing bursts in 1983 than that with which Escaline took the Prix de Diane Hermes at Chantilly in June. Just when the race was apparently developing into a match between the hot favourite Smuggly and the English-trained Air Distingue, Escaline was produced from a hopeless-looking position among the backmarkers with an astonishing run on the outside which took her to the front with only thirty yards or so to go. She must have made up all of eight lengths on the leaders in the last couple of furlongs, and was travelling so fast at the finish that she won comfortably by three quarters of a length from Smuggly, with Air Distingue half a length further away in third and the Italian One Thousand Guineas and Oaks winner Right Bank a similar distance back in fourth. The ride was a most fortuitous one for Hong Kong-based jockey Moore who was holidaying in France at the time, as he had been when he came in for the ride on the 1981 Prix de l'Arc de Triomphe winner Gold River; following a disagreement with Escaline's regular rider Philipperon, trainer Fellows reportedly approached three or four other jockeys before Moore.

Escaline went to post for the Diane with sound prospects of reaching the first four but without an obvious chance of beating Smuggly who had beaten her twice already, by a short neck in the Prix Penelope at Saint-Cloud in April and by six

267

lengths into third in the far more prestigious Prix Saint-Alary at Longchamp in May. However, there were grounds for thinking that Escaline wasn't seen at her best in either: Smuggly had the advantage of a previous race at Saint-Cloud while it was reportedly Philipperon's riding at Longchamp that caused the rift between trainer and jockey. In between those two outings Escaline had landed the Prix Vanteaux at Longchamp by a neck and a nose from Soigneuse and Little Meadow, both also in the Diane line-up, where she had a little more in hand than the winning margin suggests. Interestingly all three of those races were run on really soft ground—as were most of the trials up to that time—yet the going at Chantilly was decidedly firm. Escaline was one of the few runners with any form on firm (she'd finished a creditable second in a newcomers race as a two-year-old before going on to win twice on heavy) and it clearly didn't inconvenience her in the least.

Plans were for Escaline to be brought back in the autumn for the Trusthouse Forte Prix Vermeille and the Trusthouse Forte Prix de l'Arc de Triomphe after a rest. Unfortunately she was cast in her box and couldn't run in the Vermeille, and for some time her participation even in the Arc was in the balance. Her preparation was interrupted to such an extent, apparently, that she still had a slightly swollen hock during the week preceding the Arc; on the day, she wore bandages behind. Escaline reportedly did some good work before the race but she didn't do herself justice in it. Although she raced in the first dozen or so for most of the way and was still well placed turning for home, much closer than she had been at Chantilly, she produced no acceleration; rather she faded steadily to finish among the backmarkers in nineteenth. A fortnight later Escaline was sent to Canada for the Rothmans International at Woodbine, on a wild goose-chase as things turned out since she was never able to get in a challenge and finished well beaten behind All Along again, out of the money in seventh. Possibly the distances of the last two races were too far but judging from her breeding and the fact that she won over a mile and a quarter in the mud as a two-year-old we should have expected her to get at least a mile and a half.

Escaline is an attractive filly, by Arctic Tern who has made such a good start to his career at stud that it came as no surprise to hear in late-summer that he had been sold to stand in the United States; he'll be at the Walmac-Warnerton Farm in Kentucky in 1984, alongside Diamond Shoal. Arctic Tern was a high-class colt on

Mrs J. Fellows' "Escaline"

*Prix de Diane Hermes, Chantilly—Escaline (No. 4) finishes well to catch Smuggly (rails)
and Air Distingue*

his day—one of the very best sons of Sea-Bird II—and he beat a very strong field in
the Prix Ganay when trained by Escaline's trainer. His first crop at stud included
the 1982 Prix de Diane winner Harbour and the very smart middle-distance stayer
Khairpour; his second crop includes the Prix Noailles second Pietru, the goodish
handicapper Preponderant and the smart Italian winner Angela Serra. Arctic Tern
was also represented by some promising two-year-olds in 1983, notably Polly's Ark
and Ti King, and his yearlings were in great demand; a daughter of Glena named
Actress fetched a French record price of 4,600,000 francs at the Deauville Sales in

		Sea-Bird II	Dan Cupid
	Arctic Tern	(ch 1962)	Sicalade
	(ch 1973)	Bubbling Beauty	Hasty Road
Escaline (Fr)		(ch 1961)	Almahmoud
(ch.f. 1980)		Hail to Reason	Turn-to
	Esdee	(br 1958)	Nothirdchance
	(b 1971)	Stormy Love	Promised Land
		(ch 1964)	Michaels Angel

August. Escaline herself went through the same ring as a yearling, incidentally, but
though the record books show she was sold for 90,000 francs she was in fact bought
back by her breeder who then leased her to the trainer's wife for racing. Neither
Escaline's dam Esdee nor her grandam Stormy Love managed to win although both
were placed, Esdee finishing second over a mile and a quarter at Chantilly. Escaline
is Esdee's fourth foal and her second winner, following the middle-distance winner
Escalibur (by Caracolero) who was successful several times in the Provinces in
1983. Esdee had another filly by Arctic Tern in 1981 named Encorelle, which has
yet to be seen on the racecourse. *J. Fellows, France.*

ESCAPIST 4 b.g. Run The Gantlet–Chappelle Blanche 96 (Olden Times) (1982
11s* 12.3fg 16.1h[3] 16fg[3] 1983 14s[3] 17d) attractive gelding; one paced and stays
very well; acts on any going; blinkered second start; bandaged in 1983. *J. W.
Watts.* —

ESCARENE 2 ch.f. Dominion 123–Estate 49 (Amber Rama 133) (1983 6g 7f 7f)
Apr 5; 4,200Y; useful-looking filly; first foal; dam, second in a 7f seller, is daughter
of smart 2-y-o 5f performer Summer Day; unquoted, beaten some way in maiden
races. *R. Armstrong.* —

ESKER HOUSE 2 b. or br.c. Raga Navarro 119–Bonnemahon (Polyfoto 124)   **64**
(1983 5s 5s² 5v⁴ 6fg 7fg 7.2s² 6g*) May 18; IR 1,050F (privately); small colt;
closely related to 1980 Irish 2-y-o 7f winner Nohamnob (by Wishing Star); dam
placed at up to 7.5f in Ireland; won 20-runner selling nursery (bought in 2,100 gns)
at Lingfield in October; stays 7f; suited by some give in the ground; trained by W.
Stubbs first 3 outings; off course for over 4 months afterwards. *E. Eldin.*

ESPANITA 3 b.f. Riboboy 124–L'Aventura 65 (Elopement 125) (1982 6fg 8s 7d   –
1983 12g³ 12f 12f 12d² 12.2d) modest maiden; ran easily best races when placed
at Lingfield in June and September; suited by 1½m; evidently needs some give in
the ground. *A. Pitt.*

ESPIGA 3 ch.f. English Prince 129–Estructura 102 (Gulf Pearl 117) (1982 7g 7d²   –
1983 11d 12g 10f 10.4g) robust filly; didn't run particularly well in maiden events,
twice finishing last; possibly needs further; sold to BBA 6,000 gns Newmarket
December Sales. *G. Pritchard-Gordon.*

ESPRIT DU NORD (USA) 3 b.c. Lyphard 132–Rajput Princess 118 (Prince Taj   **126**
123) (1982 8v* 1983 10.5v³ 12s² 12fg³ 12.5fg 12.5fg* 14.6s² 12fg* 14g⁴ 12f³)
    It was a wise move on the part of Esprit du Nord's connections to sidestep the
Prix de l'Arc de Triomphe in favour of the far less competitive Preis von Europa at
Cologne a week later. Good horse that he is Esprit du Nord would have been
extremely hard pressed to make the first half dozen in the Arc, particularly in the
prevailing fast conditions, whereas in the Europa he was an odds-on chance for a
prestigious race of Group 1 status with prize money of more than £60,000. Esprit
du Nord made the most of his opportunity, but his rider Piggott had to work hard
most of the way before landing him the winner by a neck from Abary, a leading
German three-year-old who had won the Grosser Preis von Berlin. After making
much of the running Esprit du Nord was headed inside the last two furlongs by
Terreno and the outsider Katapult, and it was only in the last fifty yards or so that
he regained the lead. It was a courageous performance from a colt who clearly
found the mile and a half of the race a bare minimum.
    Esprit du Nord's victory in Cologne provided well-deserved reward for some
sterling efforts which up to then had yielded only one success as a three-year-old, a
length win from Full of Stars in the comparatively modest Prix de Menneval at
Deauville in August. He had shown markedly better form than that in defeat on
other occasions, and after gaining places in the Prix Greffulhe and the Prix
Hocquart in the spring he had been third in the Prix du Jockey-Club and second in
the St Leger. At Chantilly, where Piggott took over from Philipperon for the first
time, Esprit du Nord had little chance with the three-length winner Caerleon in the
straight but plugged on so well under pressure that he finished only half a length
behind second-placed L'Emigrant and a little more than that in front of Jeu de Paille,
who had beaten him narrowly in the Hocquart. The going, much firmer than he'd
hitherto encountered, obviously didn't inconvenience him. On soft again at
Doncaster, where Moore took over from Piggott (claimed for Derby runner-up
Carlingford Castle), Esprit du Nord possibly put up an even better effort. Sixth
favourite in a field of ten, Esprit du Nord took over from the pace-setting Sailor's
Dance with Carlingford Castle at around the three-furlong marker and battled on
exceptionally well, despite edging left to the rails under pressure. He went down
by only three quarters of a length to Sun Princess and kept Carlingford Castle out of
second by a short head; the other French challenger Dom Pasquini, who went off at
a shorter price than Esprit du Nord, was six lengths further away in fourth. The
Leger distance clearly suited Esprit du Nord well, and the manner of his finishing
left little doubt that he'd get further. Esprit du Nord did have another opportunity
over a similar distance in the Premio Roma in which he was beaten little more than
half a length into fourth behind High Hawk. His third to Stanerra in the Japan Cup on
his only subsequent outing, beaten a head and the same, was a much better effort
though.

		Northern Dancer	Nearctic
Esprit du Nord (USA) (b.c. 1980)	Lyphard (b 1969)	(b 1961)	Natalma
		Goofed	Court Martial
		(ch 1960)	Barra II
	Rajput Princess (ch 1961)	Prince Taj	Prince Bio
		(b 1954)	Malindi
		Royal Arrival	Vieux Manoir
		(ch 1954)	Bellatrix II

    Esprit du Nord is a tall colt, by Lyphard out of Rajput Princess whom Piggott
got home by a whisker in the 1964 Poule d'Essai des Pouliches. Rajput Princess has
bred six other winners, the best of them being the fine staying filly Regal Exception

(by Ribot), also trained by Fellows, who in 1972 was the all-the-way winner of the Irish Guinness Oaks, second to Ginevra in the Oaks and fourth to San San in the Arc. Rajput Princess herself was a daughter of Royal Arrival, a modest racemare who stayed well.

Esprit du Nord's best chances of enhancing his reputation as a four-year-old would seem to lie in stayers' events. He's unlikely to have the pace to beat the top mile-and-a-half horses unless conditions are testing; furthermore he'll be stiffly penalised in Group 2 and Group 3 races. He could probably be placed to advantage again over middle distances in Germany or Italy but, as we said, long distances would be the best answer. Esprit du Nord is a somewhat lazy sort with a stayer's temperament and stamina is clearly one of his strong suits. Given the chance he could turn out a good Cup horse. *J. Fellows, France.*

ESSAM 5 b.g. Sallust 134–Bold Words (Bold Ruler) (1982 8f 8f* 8fg 8.2g 8g 8fg 8g 1983 8fg) strong, compact gelding; not a good mover; has shown no form for a long time; stays 1m; acts on firm going; usually blinkered; ungenuine; sold 1,500 gns Ascot November Sales. *H. Wharton.* — §

ESSEX 8 b.g. Tudor Melody 129–Fashion Model 100 (Road House II) (1982 NR 1983 12d) lightly raced and probably of little account on flat nowadays. *D. McCain.* —

ESTIVAR 2 ch.f. Import 127–Duresme 76 (Starry Halo 122) (1983 6fg) May 6; half-sister to a winning plater and 13f winner Palmero (by Palm Track); dam third twice over 7f at 2 yrs; 50/1, tailed-off last of 23 in minor event at Redcar in September. *Mrs N. Macauley.* —

ESTRAPADE (USA) 3 ch.f. Vaguely Noble 140–Klepto (No Robbery) (1982 NR 1983 10fg* 12g* 12s²) half-sister to leading Italian miler Isopach (by Reviewer); dam smart stakes winner at up to 1m; won maiden race at Deauville in August and 90,000 francs event at Longchamp in September, latter in really good style by 3 lengths from Fly Me; put up a very good effort in defeat, despite injuring her near-hind when struck into, in 12-runner Trusthouse Forte Prix Vermeille at Longchamp again later in September, finishing 2 lengths second to Sharaya; suited by 1½m; probably acts on any going, but best form on soft; looked likely to develop into a high-class filly at the time of her injury. *M. Zilber, France.* 118

ESTUARY 2 ch.f. Busted 134–Gold Coast 100 (Mourne 126) (1983 7f 7.6d) Mar 23; first foal in this country (mare has produce in Australia); dam won twice over 7f at 2 yrs and is granddaughter of 1000 Guineas and Oaks winner Sun Stream; well beaten in maiden races at Yarmouth (slowly away) in August and Lingfield in October. *J. Winter.* —

ETOILE D'ARGENT 3 ch.f. Scallywag 127–Carmarthen-By-Pass (Marine Corps) (1982 NR 1983 12s 12f 10fg 10g) useful-looking filly; second foal; dam never ran; soundly beaten in maiden and minor races; bandaged in front on first start and wore boots behind on fourth. *R. Simpson.* —

ETOILE D'OR 4 b. or br.g. Comedy Star 121–Burdigala (Tudor Music 131) (1982 5d⁴ 5v 5fg 5f 1983 7d) fair sort; poor mover; plater; best at 5f; wears blinkers. *A. Watson.* —

ETTA GIRL 2 b.f. Bay Express 132–Piccadilly Etta 76 (Floribunda 136) (1983 6fg 6fg³) Apr 27; 16,500Y; big, rangy filly; half-sister to 3-y-o 1m winner Vitigeson (by Vitiges) and 2 winning sprinters, including fairly useful Jose Collins (by Singing Bede); dam won from 1½m to 2m; shaped well in October maiden events at Newmarket and Leicester (2 lengths third of 13 behind Swift Return); will stay beyond 6f; certain to improve. *A. Hide.* 73 p

EUCRATES (USA) 2 b. or br.c. Cyane–Fast Line (Mr Busher) (1983 8g) Apr 20; $185,000Y; half-brother to numerous winners, including Kentucky Oaks winner White Star Line (by Northern Dancer) and Prix Morny winner Filiberto (by Ribot); dam won at 2 yrs; weak in market, eighth of 15 in maiden race at Sandown in October. *J. Tree.* 70 p

EUROLINK BOY 4 b.g. Sit In The Corner–Spring Romance 83 (Silly Season 127) (1982 NR 1983 10.2d 8d) 550Y, 2,200 3-y-o; half-brother to 2 winners; dam 2-y-o 5f winner; well beaten in amateur riders race at Doncaster and £3,100 event at Brighton early in year. *R. Hoad.* —

EURYCLEIA 2 ch.f. Music Boy 124–Hannah Darling 108 (Match III 135) (1983 5fg 6g 6f³ 7fg 7d 8f³ 8s 8.2fg 8d) Apr 12; small filly; good walker; sister to 3-y-o Sandy Looks and half-sister to 2 winners, including French 7f and 11f winner Zertxuna (by Averof); dam second in Irish 1000 Guineas; quite a moderate maiden; suited by 1m; best form on firm ground; game. *C. Brittain.* 78

EVANS EXPORT 2 ch.c. Import 127–True Dresden 58 (Vilmoray 126) (1983   **70**
5d³ 5s³ 5v² 5d² 5g³ 6g 6fg³ 8.2g) Mar 25; 8,200F, 8,800Y; narrow colt;
half-brother to several minor winners; dam sprint maiden; quite a moderate colt;
probably stays 6f but is unlikely to stay 1m; yet to race on very firm going but acts
on any other; blinkered seventh outing. *J. Berry.*

EVEN BANKER 4 ch.c. Lombard 126–Eventura 87 (Huntercombe 133) (1982   **67**
8d² 8.2d² 7fg² 8fg² 10.1fg³ 10d⁴ 10f* 10fg 10g⁴ 10.2g* 10g³ 1983 11.1v 10s 8f 10f
8fg 10fg 10g 12fg) workmanlike colt; below form most starts at 4 yrs; stays 1¼m
well; acts on any going; sweated up and pulled hard once in 1982; suited by waiting
tactics; sometimes bandaged in front; moved badly to post and ran atrociously
fourth start; trained part of season by R. Hannon. *D. Sasse.*

EVENING M'LORD 3 ch.g. Lord Gayle 124–Evening Slipper (Above Suspicion   **100**
127) (1982 7.5f³ 8.5s³ 10v* 1983 10s* 10s³) Irish gelding; good walker; second
foal; dam useful winner over 7f at 2 yrs in Ireland; 25/1 when showing improved
form to beat Karol and Nokuru by neck and same in Rogers Gold Cup Ballymoss
Stakes at the Curragh in April, getting up near finish; outpaced in closing stages
when about 8 lengths third of 7 to Salmon Leap in Nijinsky Stakes at
Leopardstown in May; was subsequently sent to race in USA, where he was
stakes-placed; will stay 1½m; acts on any going but is well suited by the mud. *P.
Prendergast, Ireland.*

EVENING STANDARD 3 b.f. Realm 129–Evening Blaze (Soderini 123) (1982   **61**
5fg⁴ 6f² 5fg 6fg 1983 8g 8.5s 8d³ 8d 8v⁴ 8g 7f⁴ 7f 7.2g 8fg 8.2g) sparely-made,
attractive filly; in frame at Cagnes-sur-Mer and Newcastle (twice) in first part of
season; suited by 1m; well beaten when blinkered final outing; sold 1,100 gns Ascot
October Sales. *C. Booth.*

EVER GREAT 4 b.g. Grundy 137–Forever 68 (Never Say Die 137) (1982 12s   **–**
12g³ 14fg³ 14f 13d⁴ 16g 1983 16v² 17.1v 14s 16fg) compact, strong gelding; one
paced and is suited by a test of stamina; acts on heavy going. *D. Oughton.*

EVERSEAL 3 ch.g. Patch 129–Dunstells (Saint Crespin III 132) (1982 6fg 7g 7f²   **77**
8s 1983 11.7s* 13.1v³ 11.7fg³ 11.7fg² 11f² 12.2f* 12fg⁴ 11f⁴ 12f² 12g 11.7g)
useful-looking gelding; successful in handicaps at Windsor in May and Catterick in
July; should stay beyond 1½m; acts on any going. *G. Hunter.*

EVES LAD 3 ro. or gr.c. Bustino 136–Princess Runnymede 108 (Runnymede 123)   **–**
(1982 NR 1983 9g 12f 15f) 1,100 2-y-o; fourth foal; brother to fairly useful staying
handicapper Prince of Princes; dam stayed 6f; tailed off in maiden races in summer.
A. Cawley.

EVIPPOS (GR) 2 ro.c. Stavraetos–Spinning Top 89 (Bleep-Bleep 134) (1983 5g   **81**
7fg³ 7f⁴ 8fg* 8.2fg³) Mar 20; leggy, lightly-built Greek-bred colt; half-brother to
quite moderate 1977 2-y-o Svoura (by Aetos); dam won over 5f at 2 yrs in England
and also several races in Greece; upset by ½ length odds laid on Questella in
£4,100 nursery at Thirsk in September; moved down a place after hampering
third horse when neck second to Bonnement in similar event at Nottingham later
in month; clearly suited by 1m; yet to race on a soft surface. *B. Hobbs.*

EWE LAMB 2 b.f. Free State 125–Mummy's Darling 114 (Mummy's Pet 125)   **86**
(1983 5fg* 6fg²) Mar 12; 4,000F, 3,600Y; second foal; dam won five 5f races; got
up close home to win 13-runner maiden race at Lingfield in October by a neck
from Powder Puff; strong-finishing ½-length second of 17 to Turkish Delight in
nursery at Nottingham later in month; suited by 6f. *A. Hide.*

EWELL PLACE 2 ch.c. Persian Bold 123–Much Pleasure (Morston 125) (1983   **68**
6f 7g 6g 7fg 6fg 10fg) Apr 18; 17,500Y; good-topped colt; second foal; half-brother
to very useful 3-y-o 1m and 1½m winner Trakady (by Relkino); dam unraced
half-sister to high-class Hard Fought; 8 lengths fifth of 14 to Angleman in minor
event at Lingfield in September, third outing and only sign of ability; should stay
beyond 6f. *A. Ingham.*

EWEN'S ROCK 9 b.g. Stephen George 102–Bravadora (Cash and Courage 116)   **–**
(1982 10fg 1983 8v 12g 10.2g) poor plater nowadays; has worn blinkers; often
bandaged. *M. Bradley.*

EXACTLY LIKE YOU 2 b.f. Sassafras 135–Persian Apple (No Robbery) (1983   **77 §**
7fg 7f² 7f 8fg 7g⁴ 6fg) Mar 19; IR 44,000Y; good-bodied filly; sister to 2 winners,
including smart 6f and 1¼m winner Sarania, and half-sister to 2 others, including
3-y-o stayer Faroor (by Jaazeiro); dam won over sprint distances in USA; very
disappointing maiden; went from bad to worse after finishing good second to
Satinette in valuable fillies' maiden at Goodwood in July; one to leave alone. *F.
Durr.*

EXCAVATOR EXPERT 3 gr.g. Celtic Cone 116–Dardanella Lady 66   **77** d
(Samothraki 108) (1982 6g 7.2s 8s³ 8d 1983 11d 12fg³ 12.3g 12fg 12f) plain
gelding; plater at 2 yrs; good third in maiden race at Edinburgh in June; suited by
1½m; probably acts on any going; blinkered last 2 outings. *Mrs M. Nesbitt.*

EXCAVATOR LADY 4 b.f. Most Secret 119–Forgets Image 87 (Florescence   **43**
120) (1982 6g 7f 7f² 7f² 8f 8.2g³ 11g² 11g 9.4f* 11fg⁴ 13.8f 8d 8f³ 8.2g 8.2s² 1983
12f 13.8f³ 12f⁴ 16f 8f) compact filly; former plater; stays 1¾m; acts on any going;
has run creditably in blinkers; changed hands 1,550 gns Doncaster March Sales.
Mrs M. Nesbitt.

EXECUTIVE MAN 2 ch.c. Nebbiolo 125–Glen Devon (Klairon 131) (1983   **119**
5d*6fg* 6f³ 6fg⁴ 6fg⁴ 8g)
Executive Man was the first two-year-old in fifteen years to contest the
six-furlong Diadem Stakes at Ascot in September; there are so many
opportunities for two-year-olds to compete against horses their own age that
they seldom take on older horses. In 1983 four two-year-old pattern races
besides the William Hill Middle Park Stakes were within thirteen days of the
Diadem, each worth more than the Diadem's £14,728 first prize. Perhaps
Executive Man would have been better employed in one of them since all he had
to show for a fine and improved performance at Ascot after a three-month
absence from the racecourse was fourth place behind Salieri, Silverdip and Soba;
a 50/1-shot, he finished less than four lengths down. Executive Man confirmed his
improvement in the Middle Park at Newmarket seven days later. Urged along all
the way, he kept on well to finish three lengths fourth to Creag-An-Sgor.
Executive Man's stable, which has had rather a quiet time in the last few seasons,
had earlier received fitting reward for enterprise when Executive Man picked up
the four-runner Group 3 Premio Primi Passi at San Siro in June by a length from
Sinio, three weeks after his initial success in a maiden race at Hamilton. He
possibly hadn't recovered from his travels abroad when third to Kalim in the
Champagne Stakes at Salisbury later in the month. Executive Man was returned
to Italy in October to contest the one-mile Gran Criterium but started slowly and
finished only fifth, seven lengths behind Northern Tempest.

	Nebbiolo (ch 1974)	Yellow God (ch 1967)	Red God
			Sally Deans
Executive Man		Novara (b 1965)	Birkhahn
(ch.c. Feb 20, 1981)			Norbelle
	Glen Devon (ch 1966)	Klairon (b 1952)	Clarion III
			Kalmia
		Babble On (ch 1959)	Acropolis
			Babylon

Executive Man, a rather lightly-made, fair sort who cost 8,200 guineas as a
yearling, is a son of the Two Thousand Guineas winner Nebbiolo, and a half-brother
to two minor winners at up to thirteen furlongs in France. The dam, Glen Devon, a
successful miler in the French Provinces, is out of a sister to Sagaro's sire,
Espresso. Executive Man has won on both a firm and a soft surface. He should
eventually prove well suited by a mile. Whilst he would have to make more than
normal improvement to have any chance in the Two Thousand Guineas, he is the
type likely to do well abroad. *D. Sasse.*

EXECUTIVE PRIDE 2 b.c. General Assembly–Pride's Palace 85 (Majestic   **120**
Prince) (1983 6g* 6fg⁴ 7fg* 7fg* 7d 8f⁴)
Irish breeders should be grateful that Mr and Mrs Bertram Firestone have
proved such staunch supporters of the breeding industry in Ireland since their
purchase of the Gilltown Stud from the Aga Khan in 1971. The Firestones have so
far brought over three top-class American colts to stand at Gilltown, the champion
turf performer Run The Gantlet, the versatile General Assembly and the
second-best two-year-old of 1980, Cure The Blues. Run The Gantlet sired the
outstanding performers Ardross, April Run, Providential and Swiftfoot before
being returned to the States in 1980 and General Assembly also looks likely to
make his mark at stud. As General Assembly did all his racing in the USA perhaps
some details of his breeding and achievements are appropriate here. He has a
first-class pedigree, with the triple crown winner Secretariat as his sire and the
very useful Exclusive Dancer, a close relative of the champion American sire
Exclusive Native, as his dam. He also had the performances to match his pedigree.
At two he ranked third in the Experimental Free Handicap after winning both the
Saratoga Special and the Hopeful Stakes and finishing second to the brilliant
Spectacular Bid in two very valuable races at around a mile, the Champagne

Stakes and the Laurel Futurity; and at three he did even better, winning the Gotham Stakes over eight and a half furlongs, the Travers Stakes over a mile and a quarter (by an astonishing fifteen lengths in track record time) and finally the Vosburgh Stakes over seven furlongs, as well as finishing second to his old rival Spectacular Bid in the Kentucky Derby and the Marlboro Cup. He ended his career the winner of seven of his seventeen starts and a total of 463,245 dollars. As was to be expected General Assembly was very well received at stud and despite failing to get those excellent mares A1, Altesse Royale, Hardiemma, Money for Nothing, Silky and Sweet Mimosa in foal during his first season, he has made a pleasing start with his first runners—such a start no doubt contributing to his second-crop yearling out of Sarah Siddons (Fr) making 1,400,000 guineas. Without having a great number of runners General Assembly sired winners in Britain, France, Ireland and the USA, and appropriately his best representative is the smart Irish performer Executive Pride, a colt owned and bred by the Firestones.

Until his final appearance Executive Pride seemed no more than useful. He had a good record in Ireland, winning a seventeen-runner maiden race at Phoenix Park in May before running out a length-and-a-half winner of two fairly valuable races at Leopardstown, the Hennessy VSOP Stakes in July and the Ardenode Stud Stakes in August, in which he beat Shubumi and Reo Racine respectively. However his limitations appeared to be thoroughly exposed on ventures into pattern company on his second and fifth outings, in the Coventry Stakes at Royal Ascot and the BBA (Ireland) Goffs National Stakes at the Curragh. He didn't cut much ice in either; after tearing down to the start at Ascot he was beaten over nine lengths into fourth place behind Chief Singer, and at the Curragh, where the soft surface was possibly against him, he faded to finish sixth of eight, six and a half lengths behind El Gran Senor. Consequently when Executive Pride turned out in October for France's top juvenile race, the Grand Criterium, just four weeks after the National Stakes, it was no surprise to see him start the rank outsider of nine at 41/1. He ran much better than his odds suggested to finish fourth and with better luck would have finished even closer. After being badly hampered and, it transpired, injuring a knee

Bertram R. Firestone's "Executive Pride"

in the early stages, Executive Pride was quickly in last place, a position he maintained until after the final turn. Although his rider seemed by then to have almost given up hope of cutting back the deficit, Executive Pride responded well once pressure was applied. He still appeared out of it at the distance but he finally found his stride, finishing best of all to force a dead-heat with Green Paradise, just over two lengths behind Treizieme. Evidently the waiting tactics here were unintentional but they certainly seemed to suit Executive Pride better than the more forcing ones used when meeting his previous defeats.

Executive Pride (b.c. May 16, 1981)	General Assembly (ch 1976)	Secretariat (ch 1970)	Bold Ruler
			Somethingroyal
		Exclusive Dancer (ro 1967)	Native Dancer
			Exclusive
	Pride's Palace (b 1975)	Majestic Prince (ch 1966)	Raise A Native
			Gay Hostess
		Prides Profile (b 1963)	Free America
			Hillbrook

Executive Pride, a well-made colt, is the second foal of Pride's Palace, a filly who ended her career by refusing to race when blinkered for the first time. She had won a five-furlong maiden race at two years the previous season. Pride's Palace is a sister to a minor winner and a half-sister to four others, the best of them the very useful Winds of Thought, successful in the eleven-furlong Century Handicap, and the Princess Elizabeth Stakes winner Elegant Tern, herself the dam of a good 1983 two-year-old in Elegant Air. Executive Pride's grandam, the smart Prides Profile, held her form well during a lengthy racecourse career, and numbered such good races as the Astarita Stakes and the Gazelle and Diana Handicaps among her nine wins at up to nine furlongs. The next dam Hillbrook was a half-sister to an even better performer in Hillsdale, the winner of the mile-and-a-quarter Hollywood Gold Cup and twenty-two other races. There is a fair amount of stamina in the family and Executive Pride will stay a mile and a quarter. Although he needs to improve still further if he's to hold his own at the highest level, he should be able to win a decent prize or two in Ireland. Watch out too for his year-younger sister. *D. K. Weld, Ireland.*

EXHIBITOR (USA) 3 b.g. Cannonade–Detangle (Quadrangle) (1982 NR 1983   –
7s 12fg 13fg 15.5f) $35,000F, IR 86,000 gns Y; good-bodied gelding; third living foal; half-brother to a minor winner in USA by Exceedingly; dam poor half-sister to Alleged's dam Princess Pout; in first 6 in middle-distance maiden races at Newmarket (apprentices) and Nottingham, running better race on latter course in July; not seen out after running badly later in month; sold 2,800 gns Newmarket Autumn Sales. *F. Durr.*

EXONERATE 2 ch.c. Troy 137–Expansive 111 (Exbury 138) (1983 7fg) Apr 25;   – p
first foal; dam, sister to very smart Example, won Ribblesdale Stakes on last of only 3 starts; weak in market and coltish in paddock, went to post very freely indeed and faded after showing up 5f to finish eighth of 9 behind Great Western in £3,900 event at York in September; apparently rather headstrong, but has only to settle down to be certain of doing much better at 1¼m or more. *R. Hern.*

EXPEDITIOUS 3 b.c. Tachypous 128–My Own II 96 (El Relicario 124) (1982   **91** d
6f⁴ 7g³ 7fg³ 7d 1983 7s 8.5v* 10g 8fg 10fg 8d) big, rangy colt; had his opponents well strung out at finish when beating Star of Ireland by 8 lengths, after disputing lead throughout, in 13-runner minor race at Epsom in April; off course afterwards until September, and finished towards rear all outings; stays 1¼m; has run creditably on firm ground, but possibly needs some give nowadays. *R. Hannon.*

EXPLETIVE 3 ch.f. Shiny Tenth 120–Pemba (Sodium 130) (1982 5fg* 5fg* 6f²   **61**
6g³ 6fg 1983 7v⁴ 7v 7s 8s 8f 7.6fg 7h³ 8.3f 7h 8d* 7g 7s³ 7f) lengthy, sparely-made filly; ran respectably on occasions before winning handicap at Wolverhampton in September; stays 1m; acts on any going; blinkered nowadays. *D. H. Jones.*

EXPRESS DELIVERY 3 b.c. Bay Express 132–Oakwoodhill (Habat 127) (1983   **90**
5v⁴ 5f⁴ 5f* 6f) Mar 9; 19,500Y; neat colt; second foal; half-brother to fair 1982 2-y-o 5f winner Blue Times (by Blue Cashmere), subsequently successful in Italy; dam never ran; won minor event at Sandown in July by 1½ lengths from Beau Fils; not raced after July; should stay 6f; acts on firm going; exported to Hong Kong. *E. Eldin.*

EXPRESSLY YOURS 4 ch.f. Bay Express 132–Never Part (Never Say Die   **77**
137) (1982 6fg³ 6f 7d 6f* 6g* 7fg⁴ 6g 1983 6v⁴ 6f 6f* 6f* 6f 6f 6f⁴ 6h 6s 5d) lengthy filly; poor mover; won handicaps at Pontefract and Thirsk in July;

creditable seventh to Autumn Sunset in William Hill Stewards' Cup at Goodwood later in month on fifth start; stays 6f; acts on any going but goes well on firm; sold 10,000 gns Doncaster November Sales. *P. Asquith.*

EXPRESS MISS 3 b.f. Bay Express 132–Miss Portal (St Paddy 133) (1982 5d 6g 6s 1983 7s 7f) neat, strong filly; little form in varied company, including selling; blinkered final start. *D. Garraton.* —

EYE DAZZLER (USA) 3 ch.f. Nijinsky 138–First Squaw (First Landing) (1982 6f 7g 7s² 1983 10d 8.5g 10f 8f* 7fg² 8g) strong, rangy filly; nice, easy mover; looked well and moved nicely to post when beating Garden Route gamely by ½ length in 11-runner maiden race at Sandown in August; odds on when 2½ lengths second to Miss Henry in minor event at Salisbury in September; suited by 1m and should stay further; acts on any going; blinkered second to fifth outings; didn't have best of runs final start. *R. Hern.* 79

EYELIGHT 6 gr.g. Roan Rocket 128–Pie Eye 88 (Exbury 138) (1982 8f* 8f 8f 8f⁴ 7f 8fg⁴ 7.6fg 8fg³ 8f³ 8f 7g² 8fg 10g 9g² 8.2s 8s 1983 8d³ 7d³ 8.2v⁴ 8d 8fg³ 8f 7.6fg 8g* 8fg 8f³ 8fg⁴ 8.2fg 8f* 8g⁴ 8d 9d² 8.2s² 8.2fg) robust, short-legged gelding; poor handicapper; won at Wolverhampton in July and Ripon in August; sometimes runs in sellers; stays 1¼m; acts on any going; good mount for an inexperienced rider; goes well at Beverley; doesn't always look genuine. *R. Hollinshead.* 58

F

FABULOSA (USA) 3 ch.f. Mateor–Fabulous Native (Le Fabuleux 133) (1982 5f² 6g 8g 8g⁴ 1983 10s 10f³ 13s) narrow, sparely-made filly; quite a moderate maiden; worth another chance over further than 1¼m (off course almost 3 months before last start). *N. Guest.* 68

FABULOUS HABIT 2 b.c. Tanfirion 110–Heure de Pointe (Le Fabuleux 133) (1983 7fg) Mar 20; IR 5,000F, IR 31,000Y; fifth produce; dam half-sister to Grand Prix de Paris runner-up Point de Riz; 50/1 and in need of race, 11 lengths tenth of 26 to Alleging in maiden event at Newmarket in September; will be better suited by longer distances; sure to improve. *P. Haslam.* 71 p

FACE FACTS (USA) 2 b.c. Verbatim–Deep Powder (Le Fabuleux 133) (1983 7d⁴) Mar 28; $70,000Y; second foal; dam once-raced daughter of sister to 1000 Guineas winner Waterloo; weak in market, 6 lengths fourth of 14 to Trial By Error in maiden race at Yarmouth in September; will stay 1m; bound to be better for the experience. *H. Cecil.* 75 p

FACING 4 b.f. Quiet Fling 124–Facade 99 (Double Jump 131) (1982 12d³ 8fg³ 10f 10f 8g⁴ 10.1fg 8fg 10d 10.8s⁴ 1983 8v 8d 8fg 9f 10fg² 8.3f³) leggy, lengthy, slightly hollow-backed filly; plater; stays 1¼m; acts on firm going; best in blinkers; sold 1,100 gns Newmarket July Sales. *D. Dale.* 49

FAHDI 2 ch.c. Manado 130–My Sierra Leone (Relko 136) (1983 6g⁴ 6f² 6g) Apr 22; 28,000Y; lengthy, good sort; third reported living foal; half-brother to smart 3-y-o Royal Heroine (by Lypheor), a winner at up to 9.2f, and to useful sprinter Betsy Red (by Mount Hagen); dam ran twice; second favourite, soon off bridle but ran on strongly to finish neck second of 11 to Keep Tapping in £4,500 maiden race at Goodwood in July, best effort; 7/2, never looked like taking a hand and was eased once chance had gone when 11 lengths sixth of 13 behind Double Schwartz in similar event at York the following month; will be well suited by 7f and 1m; acts on firm going; said not to have been himself at York, and is sure to win a race. *J. Dunlop.* 99

FAIDROS (FR) 2 b.c. Dance In Time–Full of Courage (Bold Ruler) (1983 7fg 7f⁴ 8.2s⁴ 10fg) Apr 1; 170,000Y; strong, good-topped colt; half-brother to 3 winners, including French 3-y-o Full of Stars (by Tennyson), a very useful winner at up to 1½m, and very smart 1975 French staying 2-y-o Four Spades (by Sassafras), subsequently successful in USA; dam lightly-raced daughter of champion American 2-y-o and 3-y-o filly Doubledogdare; 2½ lengths fourth of 17 to Coping in maiden race at Redcar in September, second outing and easily best effort; should stay 1m; possibly unsuited by soft going; blinkered final start. *H. T. Jones.* 80

FAI LA BELLA (USA) 4 b.f. Fifth Marine–No Need Askin (Reflected Glory) (1982 8fg 10d 1983 9d² 10s³ 10fg* 10f* 10f 10f* 10f³ 10f* 9fg 10fg) quite attractive filly; improved in 1983 and won handicaps at Nottingham and Yarmouth (3); stays 1¼m; acts on any going but goes well on firm ground; does best when ridden up with pace; game though was well beaten last 2 starts. *L. Cumani.* 85

FAIR AND WISE 2 ch.f. High Line 125–Flaming Peace 104 (Queen's Hussar 124) (1983 7fg) Apr 19; half-sister to winning 3-y-o stayer Paradise Straits (by Derrylin) and 1980 2-y-o 6f winner Sovereign Flame (by Supreme Sovereign); dam won twice over 7f at 2 yrs; 25/1, kept on well without threatening leaders when 14 lengths sixth of 17 behind Carocrest in minor event at Lingfield in August; will be suited by test of stamina; sure to improve. *H. Candy.* — p

FAIRBEN 3 b.f. Royben 125–Fairabunda 59 (Floribunda 136) (1982 5fg 1983 8s 10v 8.3f 10g) strong, plain filly; little worthwhile form, including in sellers. *D. Jermy.* —

FAIR DOMINION 2 br.f. Dominion 123–Dame Julian 84 (Blakeney 126) (1983 5fg* 6f³ 6g*) Apr 14; well-made, quite attractive filly; good mover; first foal; dam, half-sister to smart sprinter Daring Boy and smart Daring March, won over 1m; won 20-runner maiden race at Sandown in June and £3,400 nursery at Kempton in September, at Kempton having her 11 opponents well strung out and winning impressively by 3 lengths; will be suited by 7f and 1m; yet to race on soft going; sweated up second outing (ran creditably). *J. Bethell.* 104

FAIR DUEL 6 b.g. Status Seeker–Double Irish (Dual 117) (1982 10fg 1983 10.6s⁴ 10.2g 10fg³) sturdy gelding; plater; stays 1¼m; acts on any going; sometimes wears blinkers; sold to W. Clay 1,050 gns Ascot August Sales. *P. Makin.* 27

FAIR EMMA 2 ch.f. Song 132–Fair Sarita 95 (King's Troop 118) (1983 6s) Mar 18; third foal; half-sister to 3-y-o 7f winner Redgrave Creative (by Swing Easy); dam sprinter; unquoted, modest sixth of 12 in maiden race at Catterick in June. *P. Rohan.* —

FAIR GLORY 5 ch.m. Hittite Glory 125–Travelling Fair 95 (Vienna 127) (1982 NR 1983 10s 8h 8h 6h 6fg) no worthwhile form, including in a seller; has worn blinkers; trained part of season by J. Roberts. *D. Wintle.* —

FAIRGREEN 5 b.g. Music Boy 124–Sunny Bloom 71 (Forlorn River 124) (1982 6d 5fg⁴ 5d 5g 6s² 5s² 6s 5d* 5s 1983 5d 5v* 5d³ 6s 5v⁴ 5g 6f 6f 6f⁴ 5f³ 5fg³ 5f⁴ 5g 5d 5g⁴ 5g³ 5fg) big, strong gelding; bad walker and mover; sprint handicapper; won at Newcastle in April; better at 5f than 6f; acts on any going but is very well suited by soft ground; has been tried in blinkers; has run creditably for an apprentice. *D. Chapman.* 69

FAIR HABIT 2 b.f. Habitat 134–Fair Salinia 125 (Petingo 135) (1983 6fg 6s³ 7fg) May 26; deep-girthed, attractive filly; second foal; dam won Oaks and was awarded Irish Guinness Oaks; favourite, made running to past halfway when 3¾ lengths third of 7 to Rocket Alert in Firth of Clyde Stakes at Ayr in September; looked past her best but wasn't disgraced when over 9 lengths seventh of 13 to Mahogany in Rockfel Stakes at Newmarket the following month; will stay at least 1m; won't have any difficulty in winning in maiden company. *M. Stoute.* 90

FAIRHAM 3 ch.f. Porto Bello 118–Impromptu 88 (My Swanee 122) (1982 5d 5g⁴ 6h 5fg 6g³ 6g⁴ 7g 6fg² 6fg² 6g 5g 7g* 7.2s* 7s 1983 8.2v 8v³ 8v⁴ 8d* 9f 9f 8fg 9fg³ 9fg) lengthy filly; plater; bought in 1,600 gns after winning at Carlisle in June (apprentice ridden); stays 9f; has run creditably on a firm surface but is better with some give in the ground; effective with and without blinkers; sold 1,750 gns Doncaster August Sales. *E. Carter.* 54

FAIRLAWNE 3 b.f. Northfields–Isobelline (Pronto) (1982 6g 5.8g² 5f* 5fg³ 6g 1983 7s 7g 6fg⁴ 6d 6fg⁴ 7.3fg) quite attractive filly; carries quite a lot of condition; fourth in handicaps won by Matou at Newmarket in July and August; should stay 7f; acts on firm going. *F. J. Houghton.* 99

FAIR MADAME 3 b.f. Monseigneur 127–Fair Mark 95 (On Your Mark 125) (1982 5f 5f 5g⁴ 5f* 5g² 5g⁴ 5f³ 5f³ 6fg² 6g 6s³ 6d* 6g 1983 7g 8g 6g 6fg 6f* 6f⁴ 5fg⁴ 6g³ 6s² 6f) small, lightly-made filly; returned to form when winning handicap at Catterick in August in good style; stays 6f; acts on any going; usually blinkered (also wore a hood once in 1982) but has run well without them; had stiff task seventh outing. *C. Booth.* 79

FAIR MARINER 3 b.g. Julio Mariner 127–Fair Samela 108 (Constable 119) (1982 NR 1983 6d 8s³ 8.2fg⁴) lengthy, fair sort; half-brother to winners here and abroad, including useful sprinter Fair Sarita (by King's Troop); dam very game 6f and 7f performer; in frame in seller at Thirsk in April and apprentice maiden race at Hamilton in June; will be suited by further than 1m; wears bandages in front. *P. Rohan.* 52

FAIRMILE GAMBLER 2 ch.g. Streak 119–Judiciary 74 (Above Suspicion 127) (1983 5d² 5.1f⁴ 6f⁴ 5f 8d⁴ 5g) Apr 24; 1,250F, 2,000Y; closely related to a winner in Sweden by Runnymede and half-brother to several winners, notably very smart 57

miler Legal Eagle (by Manacle); dam stayed middle distances; moderate plater; best form at 5f; blinkered third to fifth outings; sold 600 gns Doncaster October Sales. *J. Berry.*

FAIR SARA 5 br.m. McIndoe 97–Fairstar 86 (Star Moss 122) (1982 NR 1983   –
12g 12.2fg⁴ 10f) won seller at 3 yrs; showed little in non-sellers at 5 yrs; promises to stay 1½m; seems to act on any going; has worn bandages; sold 1,400 gns Doncaster September Sales. *I. Wardle.*

FAIRSTEAD BELLE 2 b.f. Bay Express 132–Armelle 87 (Tribal Chief 125)   **79**
(1983 5s 5s² 5.1fg² 6f* 6fg) May 21; 3,500Y; sturdy, fair sort; good walker; third living foal; half-sister to useful 1982 2-y-o 6f winner Bold Major (by Orange Bay); dam 2-y-o 5f winner; won 13-runner maiden race at Doncaster in June by 5 lengths from Our Lady; not seen out again until October when faced with stiff task and well beaten in valuable nursery at Newmarket; suited by 6f; acts on any going. *E. Eldin.*

FAIR TEST 2 br.f. Fair Season 120–Persevering 95 (Blakeney 126) (1983 5s*   **95**
5g⁴ 6fg² 6fg³ 6g²) Apr 3; second living foal; dam won 4 times at up to 2m; accounted for 4 previous winners in fine style in minor event at Chepstow in May, drawing clear to beat Deccan Queen 6 lengths; good second subsequently in minor events at Windsor and Goodwood; better suited by 6f than 5f and will be even better suited by 7f and 1m; seems to act on any going. *I. Balding.*

FAIR TRADER 2 br.f. Porto Bello 118–Skilla (Mexico III) (1983 5v 5s 5g 5s³ 6fg   **65**
7f*) May 17; 1,200Y; seventh foal; half-sister to winning sprinter Silent Tears (by Weepers Boy); dam French 11f winner; having first race for 3 months, showed much improved form to win 16-runner seller (bought in 1700 gns) at Chepstow in September by ½ length from Gracious Homes; suited by 7f and firm ground; blinkered fourth and sixth starts; sold 1,500 gns Ascot December Sales. *D. Elsworth.*

FAIR TRADE (USA) 2 b. or br.f. Hawaii–Negotiating (Round Table) (1983 6f   –
8g) Feb 25; tall, close-coupled filly; sister to Native Trader, a winner of 3 sprint races in USA, and half-sister to useful stakes-placed winner Hopeful Contract (by Bold Reason); dam, from same family as Great Nephew, won over 1m; behind in maiden races at Newbury in August and Leicester (prominent long way) in September. *I. Balding.*

FAIR TUNE 2 b.f. Fair Season 120–Boating Song 59 (Crewman) (1983 6f) Mar   –
31; third foal; dam placed over 6f; unquoted, behind in 19-runner maiden race at Windsor in July. *M. Madgwick.*

FAIRY BLUEBIRD 2 b.f. Be My Guest 126–Fair Filly (Silver Shark 129) (1983   –
6fg) Apr 8; fourth foal; half-sister to Irish 3-y-o King's Chapel (by Acamas); dam, Irish 11f winner, is half-sister to top 1974 Irish 2-y-o Sea Break; 50/1, last of 20 in maiden race at Newmarket in October. *R. Armstrong.*

FAIRY DEAN 3 b.f. Balidar 133–Shardia 91 (Shantung 132) (1982 NR 1983 7f   **60**
7s³ 8g*) lengthy, sparely-made filly; first foal; dam won over 7f at 2 yrs and stayed 1½m; hung left and was all out at finish when winning maiden race at Edinburgh in October; stays 1m. *J. W. Watts.*

FAIT ACCOMPLI 4 ch.g. Sagaro 133–Fell Swoop 66 (Falcon 131) (1982 10s   –
1983 8g 10f 16g) workmanlike gelding; well beaten in varied company. *J. Dunlop.*

FAITHFUL DON (USA) 4 br.c. Dawn Flight–Always Faithful 103 (Super Sam   **51**
124) (1982 10.1fg 10f³ 10g 10g 10.1g 9fg 10v² 10.2s³ 1983 8g 10fg 10f 10f 10.1fg⁴ 10h² 10f 12fg) useful-looking colt; former plater; should be suited by 1½m; acts on any going, but goes well in the mud. *G. Balding.*

FALA KALIMA 3 b.f. Sousa 97–Ukundu 60 (Tudor Treasure 119) (1982 5f 5f 5f   **42**
1983 11f 8fg 10fg² 10g 9f 12f) fair sort; plater; best run at 1¼m; has been tried in blinkers. *T. Craig.*

FALASION DREAM 3 br.f. Dragonara Palace 115–Double Reception (Siliconn   –
121) (1982 6f 5g⁴ 6fg² 6f 6s 1983 6v 6fg 5f) small filly; plater at 2 yrs; well beaten in non-sellers in 1983 (blinkered last outing). *Mrs J. Reavey.*

FALCON FURY 2 b.c. The Verger 75–Light Tilia (Light Thrust 114) (1983 6fg   –
6h 7f) small, lightly-built colt; of no account. *J. Smith.*

FALCON'S HEIR (USA) 4 b.c. Accipiter–Famous Princess (Diplomat Way)   **75**
(1982 7g 8.2s 7f³ 8f* 7fg² 7f* 8f 7fg 8.2s* 8s³ 8s 1983 8v* 10s 8v* 7s² 8g 8fg 8fg⁴ 8g) lengthy, quite attractive colt; made most and kept on very gamely to win 2 handicaps at Kempton in April, one an apprentice event; not disgraced last 2 starts; appears not to stay 1¼m; acts on any going but revels in the mud; blinkered sixth start; sold to M. Bradley 4,800 gns Doncaster October Sales. *P. Cole.*

FALKLAND SOUND (USA) 3 b.c. Plotting–Alamosa Kitty (Cougar) (1982 –
6fg 8d 1983 7f 10h 6fg 7fg) sparely-made colt; no worthwhile form, including in
sellers, and is possibly temperamental; sold out of P. Haslam's stable 520 gns Ascot
July Sales after first start. *T. Kersey.*

FALKLANDS RULER (USA) 2 b.c. Batonnier–T.V. Shock (T.V. Lark) (1983 –
7f) Apr 19; $16,500Y; good mover with a long stride; second foal; half-brother to
3-y-o General H (by Unconscious); dam won 6f maiden race; sire, son of His
Majesty, was very smart winner at up to 9f at 3 yrs; third favourite, not knocked
about after showing up to past halfway when out of first 10 of 17 in maiden race at
Newbury in August; clearly thought capable of better. *P. Cole.*

FALL GUY 2 b.c. Tumble Wind–Jennybell (High Hat 131) (1983 5f 5fg³ 5fg*) Apr   81
25; IR 2,600F, 7,000Y; half-brother to a minor winner; dam lightly-raced half-sister
to very useful Plotina; got up close home to win 12-runner maiden race at
Wolverhampton in August by short head from Making Hay; dead. *G. Lewis.*

FALLIG SCHNELL 7 ch.g. King's Leap 111–Sea Melody 79 (Tudor Minstrel –
144) (1982 8.2s 1983 17fg) workmanlike gelding; poor plater; cost 2,000 gns
Doncaster May Sales; dead. *J. Howell.*

FALLING STAR (FR) 3 ch.f. Mount Hagen 127–Free French (Northern   120
Dancer) (1982 NR 1983 8s² 8s* 8f² 8fg³ 8g) third foal; half-sister to useful 1981
Irish 2-y-o 7f winner Fly Start (by Run The Gantlet); dam unraced daughter of
high-class American filly Forward Gal; won maiden race at Saint-Cloud in June by a
length from Florenly; placed in 100,000 francs race at Chantilly and Prix d'Astarte
at Deauville afterwards, putting up a smart effort when about 1¾ lengths third of 12
behind Luth Enchantee in latter race in August; well below form final outing
however; has raced only at 1m; acts on any going. *P.-L. Biancone, France.*

FALMOUTH HARBOUR 2 b.c. Bold Lad (Ire) 133–Handa 102 (Roan Rocket   80
128) (1983 7f 8g 8d⁴ 10fg) Mar 17; IR 13,500Y; strong, good sort; excellent
mover; second living foal; dam, 2-y-o 6f winner, is daughter of smart 2-y-o Hecla;
2½ lengths fourth of 16 to Maypole Dancer in maiden race at Warwick in October;
not sure to stay 1¼m. *P. Cole.*

FALSTAFF 2 b.c. Town and Country 124–Cappuccilli 111 (Lorenzaccio 130)   106
(1983 5s 6d 7fg* 7f* 7f² 7h* 7f*) Mar 16; neat, strong, attractive colt; had a nice,
easy action; third foal; half-brother to a winning plater; dam very useful staying
2-y-o but failed to train on; a thoroughly game colt who had a splendid summer,
running out a narrow winner of minor event at Chester, £3,800 race at
Newmarket, 4-runner Solario Stakes at Sandown and 3-runner Gilbey Champion
Racehorse Futurity at York, at York leading throughout and holding on
courageously by a neck from Head For Heights; also ran well, although no match
for winner, when 4 lengths second of 15 to Raft in £3,800 event at Salisbury;
needed at least 7f; acted well on very firm ground; wore a tongue strap; got loose
at exercise in September and was fatally injured. *R. Hern.*

FALSTAFF (USA) 2 ch.c. Lyphard 132–Ivorina 109 (Sir Ivor 135) (1983 7fg³   115
8fg³ 8fg⁴) small, strong colt; good walker; has a quick action; first foal; dam won
over 1m and 1¼m in Ireland; shaped very well on all appearances, finishing third in
2 huge fields of maidens at Newmarket and then being beaten little over 2½ lengths
when fourth of 9 to Alphabatim in William Hill Futurity (pulled a shoulder muscle) at
Doncaster; will stay 1¼m; sure to win races. *M. Stoute.*

FAMOUS STAR 4 ch.c. Sharpen Up 127–Hecla 117 (Henry the Seventh 125)   102
(1982 5f* 6d* 6fg³ 5.6g² 6g* 5v 1983 6d² 6d⁴ 6v 6f) strong, close-coupled colt;
creditable neck second to Vorvados in Cammidge Trophy at Doncaster in March;
also ran respectably to be fourth to Sweet Monday in Abernant Stakes at
Newmarket in April and seventh to Sylvan Barbarosa in Cork and Orrery Stakes
at Royal Ascot on fourth outing; suited by 6f+; acts on any going; has won for an
apprentice but is not an easy ride (sometimes pulls hard); sweated up badly once
at 3 yrs; sometimes coltish in paddock; slowly away in blinkers third start; sent to
USA and won over 7½f at Bay Meadows in September. *M. Albina.*

FAN CLUB 2 ch.c. Gay Fandango 132–Callistro 65 (Song 132) (1983 7f⁴ 7d 7fg*   91
8g) Apr 3; IR 105,000Y; good-topped, useful-looking colt; dam
plating-class maiden; always going well and quickened in good style in final furlong
to win going away by 1½ lengths from My Volga Boatman in maiden race at
Salisbury in September; 8 lengths sixth of 21 to Rainbow Quest in £4,100 event at
Newbury later in month; possibly better at 7f than 1m; acts well on a firm surface.
C. Nelson.

FANCY FLIGHT (FR) 2 gr.f. Arctic Tern 126–Foolish Fancy (Silly Season 127)   **74**
(1983 6f 6g 7.6fg) Mar 28; light-framed filly; second foal; half-sister to French
middle-distance maiden Fancy Dancer (by Green Dancer); dam, successful at up to
10.5f in France, is half-sister to very smart French 1m and 1¼m winner Bally
Game; showed ability in maiden races and a minor event, best effort when 3½
lengths sixth to Paramaribo in 20-runner maiden event at Newmarket in July on
first start; should be suited by 1¼m+. *R. Armstrong.*

FANDANGLE 5 ch.h. Gay Fandango 132–Sandra II (Le Haar 126) (1982 8d² 8f   **85**
8fg* 8f* 8fg 8f² 8.2f* 8d 8s⁴ 1983 8d 8v 8d² 8f² 8f² 8g 8fg⁴) well-made, quite
attractive horse; has been hobdayed; fair handicapper; runner-up at Sandown in
May, Royal Ascot following month (went down by 1½ lengths to Mighty Fly in
Royal Hunt Cup) and York in July; stays 1m; probably acts on any going; has won
for an apprentice though hung once in 1982; suited by waiting tactics and
sometimes meets trouble in running. *J. Tree.*

FANDANGO LIGHT 2 ch.c. Gay Fandango 132–Crystal Light 114 (Never Say   **75** p
Die 137) (1983 6f⁴) Apr 30; IR 25,000Y; quite attractive colt; half-brother to 5
winners, including very smart sprinter Street Light (by St Chad) and very useful
performers Headlamp (by High Hat) and Flash On (by Sea Hawk II); dam very
useful winner over 1m; third favourite, 3 lengths fourth of 8 to Rocket Alert in
minor event at Chepstow in June; sweated up badly and gave a lot of trouble when
withdrawn at Chester the following month; will stay 1m; the type to do better,
temperament allowing. *D. H. Jones.*

FAN THE FLAME 3 b.f. Grundy 137–Cendres Bleues (Charlottesville 135)   **68**
(1982 8s 1983 10v 12s 12d 13f³ 12f² 13fg² 11.5g³ 12g* 12s³ 11.5s) tall, leggy,
unimpressive ex-English filly; placed in maiden races, including in one at
Nottingham, before winning a similar event at Roscommon in September; will
stay 1¾m; formerly trained by I. Balding. *C. Collins, Ireland.*

FAQIR 2 b.g. Swing Easy 126–Miss Frenchy (Exbury 138) (1983 6f 7fg 7.2g) Mar   **–**
7; 6,000Y; quite a useful-looking gelding; fourth foal; dam poor maiden; well beaten
in varied company, including selling. *K. Brassey.*

FARASHA 2 ch.f. Bay Express 132–Chalumeau 109 (Relko 136) (1983 5d* 5g³)   **81**
Feb 8; 14,500Y; quite attractive, rangy filly; first foal; dam at her best at 2 yrs
when 7f winner; put up an encouraging display when second favourite for 9-runner
minor event at Thirsk in May, overcoming difficulties to win going away by 2
lengths from Lochfen; 4½ lengths third of 5 to very comfortable winner Precocious
in National Stakes at Sandown later in month; will stay beyond 5f; exported to USA.
W. O'Gorman.

FARAWAY FORTUNE 2 br.f. Faraway Times 123–Fingeroffortune 100 (Fortino   **46**
II 120) (1983 5fg 5f 5g) Feb 18; 3,100F, 1,800Y; lightly-built filly; half-sister to 3
minor winners; dam won at up to 7f; poor form in maiden auction events and a minor
race; unseated rider on way to start on second outing and wore blinkers on third;
retained 825 gns Ascot November Sales, and sold 460 gns Doncaster November
Sales. *A. Bailey.*

FARAWAY PRINCESS 2 b. or br.f. Faraway Times 123–Malpighia (Mourne   **75**
126) (1983 6f³ 6fg³) May 21; smallish filly; half-sister to several winners in
France; dam won over 11f in France; third in maiden races at Redcar in August and
Hamilton in September; should stay beyond 6f. *G. Huffer.*

FARGAZE (USA) 2 b.f. Lyphard 132–Gazala 124 (Dark Star) (1983 7s*⁴ 7g³   **108**
8fg²) Mar 17; half-sister to 6 winners, notably top-class Mississipian and 1980
Irish St Leger winner Gonzales (both by Vaguely Noble) and tip-top 1976 3-y-o
Youth (by Ack Ack); dam won French 1,000 Guineas and Oaks; ran well in 3 races at
Longchamp in autumn, winning 5-runner Prix de Toutevoie (newcomers race) by a
neck from Sara Lee and twice finishing third to Boreale, beaten 2 lengths in 90,000
francs event and ½ length in Prix des Reservoirs (moved up a place on
disqualification of second); will stay at least 1¼m; seems to act on any going. *M.
Zilber, France.*

FARHAAN 2 b.c. Shirley Heights 130–Game All 109 (Alcide 136) (1983 6fg 7fg)   **77** p
Mar 23 35,000F; quite attractive, well-made colt; good mover; half-brother to
numerous winners, including very smart French 1m and 1¼m winner Bally Game
(by Ballymoss); dam, half-sister to Birdbrook, was game performer at up to 11f;
spoilt chance by dwelling in £6,000 maiden race at Ascot in September but put in
some good late work to finish 7½ lengths sixth of 11 to Miss Silca Key; dropped out
quickly after showing up for long way in 14-runner Houghton Stakes at Newmarket
the following month; will probably need 1¼m+ to be seen to best advantage; may
improve. *H. T. Jones.*

FARHOOD 2 b.c. High Top 131–Shebeen 124 (Saint Crespin III 132) (1983 7fg³ 7f 7fg 8.2fg 8.2s) Feb 15; 30,000Y; sturdy colt; carries plenty of condition; third live foal; half-brother to 3-y-o Hossam (by Artaius), a winner at up to 13f, and disappointing Pedometer (by Great Nephew); dam very smart middle-distance performer; quite a moderate maiden; will stay beyond 1m; acts on a firm surface; twice slowly away. *H. T. Jones.*   **70**

FARIDPOUR (USA) 2 b.c. Blushing Groom 131–Felix Culpa (Kashmir II 125) (1983 5f² 7fg³) Jan 17; neat, strong, good-quartered, attractive colt; first foal; dam very useful at around 1¼m in France; placed in maiden events at Salisbury in June and September (favourite); will be suited by 1m; appeared not fully wound up on second outing, and may improve. *F. J. Houghton.*   **74**

FARIOFFA 4 gr.c. Hotfoot 126–Lapis Lazuli 84 (Zeddaan 130) (1982 7fg 10g⁴ 8f* 10fg 8g 10g* 10s* 1983 9d 10.2v* 10s² 10d 10fg 10.5f 11.1g⁴ 12fg³ 12d³) big, strong, rangy colt; put up a smart display under 10-0 in Sporting Chronicle Spring Handicap at Doncaster in May, showing a good turn of foot to beat Hill's Pageant a length; in frame several starts afterwards, best efforts when head second to Fine Sun in Clive Graham Stakes at Goodwood later in May (looked unsuited by course and didn't get going until too late) and 2 lengths third to Jupiter Island in St Simon Stakes at Newbury in October on final outing; stays 1½m; acts on any going; often sweats up; best on a galloping track; suited by strong handling; sometimes starts slowly and found little under pressure fifth start; sent to USA. *L. Cumani.*   **115**

FAROLITO (USA) 4 b.g. Foolish Pleasure–Dotty Jay Jay (Lurullah) (1982 10f 11f 12fg 1983 10.2d 12d² 12v* 12fg⁴ 12fg⁴ 13fg 12f* 13f² 17fg) big, strong, lengthy gelding; good walker; won poor maiden race at Beverley in July; promises to stay 2m; acts on firm going; blinkered at 3 yrs; sold to W. H. H. Williams 2,600 gns Newmarket Autumn Sales. *R. Hollinshead.*   **54**

FAROOR 3 ch.c. Jaazeiro 127–Persian Apple (No Robbery) (1982 NR 1983 7d 16g² 16.5fg* 13.8f² 16g⁴) IR 54,000Y; good-bodied colt; half-brother to 3 winners, including smart 6f and 1¼m winner Sarania (by Sassafras); dam won over sprint distances in USA, and is out of sister to Prix de l'Arc de Triomphe winner Migoli; shaped with promise in maiden events before winning one at Redcar in August by 4 lengths; ran well at Catterick and York later in month on only subsequent outings, putting up a particularly fine effort in stiffish company when about 5 lengths fourth of 13 behind Crusader Castle in Lonsdale Stakes on latter course (didn't look particularly well in paddock); stays well; acts on firm going. *F. Durr.*   **105**

FAR TOO YOUNG 2 b.f. Young Generation 129–Taj Princess 88 (Taj Dewan 128) (1983 6d) Mar 22; 4,100Y; first living foal; dam won over 5f and 1m; 20/1, ninth of 17 in maiden race at Newbury in October; may do better. *M. Smyly.*   **–**

FASCADALE 9 br.g. Frankincense 120–Straight Off 88 (Straight Deal) (1982 12fg 12fg 12g 12fg⁴ 12g 11d³ 11s* 10d 1983 12d³ 12.3v* 12d² 12fg 12f 11s 12s) quite a modest handicapper; won at Newcastle in May; stays 1½m; acts on any going; suitable mount for a boy; sometimes sweats up; needs to be held up and is suited by a strong gallop. *J. W. Watts.*   **83** d

FASHION LOVER 3 ch.f. Shiny Tenth 120–Glencora (Ribero 126) (1982 6g 7g 8d³ 8.2d 7g² 8s 8d² 1983 8d* 9d 8v 7f³ 7fg³ 7f 8d) workmanlike filly; sold out of M. Ryan's stable 4,600 gns after winning seller at Doncaster in March; ran creditably in non-sellers several times afterwards; stays 1m; probably acts on any going. *A. Balding.*   **59**

FAST BAY 2 b.f. Bay Express 132–Hardware 86 (Hard Sauce 131) (1983 5g 5f) Mar 27; 8,000F, 32,000Y; attractive, well-made filly; half-sister to 3 winners, including useful 1977 5f and 6f winner Sarissa (by Reform); dam won at up to 1m; no worthwhile form; impressed as an individual when third favourite for 15-runner maiden race at Newbury in June on debut; should do better. *G. Lewis.*   **– p**

FAST CURRENT 2 ch.c. Double Form 130–Oscilight 107 (Swing Easy 126) (1983 6fg) Apr 5; tall colt; first foal; dam sprinter; 33/1, backward and green, behind in 20-runner maiden race at Newmarket in October. *G. Wragg.*   **–**

FAST DANCER 3 ch.f. Hotfoot 126–Mixed Melody 82 (Alcide 136) (1982 5f 5f 5g 8f 8.2s 7g 7d 1983 8d⁴ 12g 8d 9f 8fg 8f 9d 9g 12g) neat filly; poor plater; stays 1½m. *G. Richards.*   **–**

FAST SERVICE 4 ch.g. Sharpen Up 127–Ginnies Pet 106 (Compensation 127) (1982 5d 5fg³ 5fg³ 5f 5f 5g 5fg 1983 7f 8f* 7fg 7g 8g) small, strong, close-coupled gelding; attracted no bid after winning seller at Bath in July; stays 1m; acts on firm going; blinkered twice at 2 yrs; apprentice ridden when successful. *C. Horgan.*   **55**

FAST TORPIDO (USA) 3 ch.c. Wajima–Morelle (Vitelio) (1982 6g 7fg 7fg² **68**
7d 1983 8v 8f 8f 8f³ 8f³ 10f) tall, quite attractive colt; never-dangerous third in
maiden races at Yarmouth and Doncaster in July; should be suited by 1¼m; best
form on a firm surface; blinkered first 2 starts of 1983. *M. Albina.*

FATHER BILL 3 b. or br.g. Be My Guest 126–Side Step (Double Jump 131) **72**
(1982 7f 7f 7d 8s 1983 10s² 10d⁴ 8g³ 8f 8f 8f 8g⁴ 8.2g² 8d 8f) tall, close-coupled
gelding; quite a modest maiden; probably needs further than 1m and will stay 1½m;
blinkered sixth and final outings; sold 20,000 gns Newmarket Autumn Sales. *R.
Sheather.*

FATHER MAC 2 b.g. Great Nephew 126–Lantana 74 (St Paddy 133) (1983 6s 7f **–**
8fg) Mar 17; 2,000Y; lengthy, useful-looking gelding; brother to 1½m winner
Nepotism; dam won over 1½m; little worthwhile form in maiden and minor events;
gelded after final appearance. *M. Naughton.*

FATHER REEN 2 ch.c. Bolkonski 134–Sound Number 103 (Sound Track 132) **–**
(1983 6f) May 21; half-brother to several winners, including prolific 1976 2-y-o
sprint winner Hand Canter (by Mummy's Pet); dam, a sprinter, is half-sister to
smart Some Hand; ridden in paddock and made no show at 100/1 in 17-runner
maiden race at Thirsk in July. *A. Balding.*

FATIH (USA) 3 b.c. Icecapade–Native Nurse (Graustark) (1982 6fg² 5s⁴ 1983 **69 §**
8d* 8d 6s 7f 7.6fg² 7h 7f³ 7.6g 7f) strong, close-coupled, quite attractive colt;
good mover; won 3-runner private sweepstakes at Newmarket in April; placed in
handicap at Chester and maiden race at Folkestone, best subsequent efforts; stays
1m; gives impression he's no great battler; often blinkered nowadays. *H. T. Jones.*

FATOUM 3 ch.f. Sassafras 135–Swift Protectress (Court Martial) (1982 6fg **–**
1983 7d 12d 13fg 14fg⁴ 14.6f) rather unfurnished filly; ridden by 7-lb claimer when
showing a little ability on second and third starts; ran as though she didn't get the
trip on final outing; sold to BBA (Ire) 2,300 gns Newmarket December Sales. *F.
Durr*

FATTY'S CHOICE 3 b.c. Realm 129–Bonne Esperance (Venture VII 129) (1982 **76**
NR 1983 7s³ 7.6v 6v 6g 5f 5f² 5h⁴ 5f 5g 6s 5fg) 8,200Y; quite attractive colt;
half-brother to winners in France and USA, including very useful French 6f and 7f
winner Goodmor (by Morston); dam French 1¼m winner and half-sister to
speedy Hodell; in frame in varied races; probably best at sprint distances; doesn't
find a great deal off bridle. *G. Balding.*

FAVOLOSO 4 b.c. Sun Prince 128–Lovely Clare 106 (Sing Sing 134) (1982 12fg* **104 +**
10fg 12fg 12f 12g⁴ 1983 15.5v 12d 10f 10f² 9g 8g³ 9fg 10g 10fg 8g³) rangy, quite
attractive colt; ran by far his best race at 4 yrs in Prix Perth at Saint-Cloud in
November on final start, coming home 3¼ lengths third of 15 to Rare Roberta; had
earlier run respectably to be 4 lengths second to Morcon under 9-5 in Trident
Chesterfield Cup at Goodwood; best at up to 1¼m, though stays further; seems to
act on any going; trained by R. Boss first start. *J. Winter.*

*Nell Gwyn Stakes, Newmarket—Favoridge quickens in good style to win from Annie Edge
(rails) and Royal Heroine*

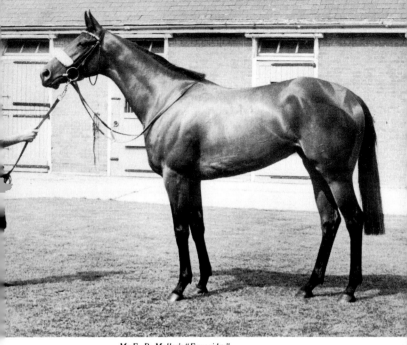

Mr E. B. Moller's "Favoridge"

FAVORIDGE (USA) 3 b.f. Riva Ridge–Favoletta 115 (Baldric II 131) (1982 **121**
5g* 5f² 5g* 6g² 1983 7d* 8g² 8d* 8f² 8g⁴ 6fg² 7fg)

Fears that Favoridge might not train on proved groundless. A high-class
sprinting two-year-old with unusual powers of acceleration, but apparently
lacking in physical scope, she came out in the spring to run the best possible
Guineas trial in the Nell Gwyn Stakes and went on to be placed in the One
Thousand Guineas and Coronation Stakes. However, she didn't hold her form
throughout a long season. In none of her three races after Royal Ascot was she
seen at her best. She finished in what was, for her, a modest fourth place behind
Royal Heroine in the Child Stakes at Newmarket; she did better when four
lengths second to Gabitat, ahead of Celestial Dancer and Prince Reymo, in the
Goldene Peitsche at Baden-Baden; then, at a time when paddock inspection
pointed firmly to her reproducing her best in the Bisquit Cognac Challenge Stakes
at Newmarket in October, she finished a disappointing seventh of ten behind
Salieri, beaten in a matter of strides two and a half furlongs from home.

Favoridge had been highest-weighted of her sex in the European Free
Handicap of 1982 apart from Ma Biche, who'd beaten her three parts of a length in
the Cheveley Park Stakes, and another French filly Maximova. In the absence of
Maximova, Favoridge appeared to hold a chance second only to Ma Biche's in the
Guineas following her run in the Nell Gwyn at Newmarket in April. On that
occasion she'd been held up until the distance, picked off her opponents with
ease, gone clear and finally won easing up by a length and a half and a head from
Annie Edge and Royal Heroine. She hadn't grown much during the winter, but she
was quite an attractive filly nonetheless and looked particularly well in herself.
The main reservation about her chance in the Guineas was not her lack of inches

283

but her ability to stay the trip. By now the balance of probabilities weighed in her favour since she had got the seven furlongs of the Nell Gwyn so well, and was clearly amenable to restraint unlike the best of her dam's previous foals, the exceptionally speedy Amaranda (by Bold Lad, Ire). The dam herself had won the Irish One Thousand Guineas after disappointing at Newmarket, and had produced four winners who stayed at least a mile—Pipina (by Sir Gaylord), Ash Ridge (by Bold Reason), Good Fellow (by Queen's Hussar) and Audley End (by Nijinsky); Favoletta's sire Riva Ridge had won ten stakes races over a mile or more and her grandam Violetta III had dead-heated in the Cambridgeshire. On the other hand, Favoridge did have this tremendous burst of acceleration at shorter distances; it might be run out of her in top-class company at a mile.

Events showed that Favoridge stayed a mile: just. At that distance she could sustain her effort for a very short time only, presenting her regular jockey Eddery with the problem of producing her at the right moment. In the Guineas Ma Biche solved Eddery's problem for him, since she was always moving at least as easily as Favoridge and went for home so strongly coming out of the Dip that Eddery was forced to make his move in order to stay in close touch. Favoridge was still almost alongside the winner with about two hundred yards to go, but slowly she lost ground under hard riding and just before the line was re-overtaken by the one-time leader Royal Heroine, Ma Biche having pulled a length and a half clear by then. Ultimately Favoridge got the second place she'd lost so narrowly in the race: Royal Heroine's failing a routine test automatically handed it to her. Favoridge had had enough after a mile in considerably less exacting company in her next race, the International Stakes at Kempton in May contested by herself (at 7/1 on), Page Blanche, Spanish Bold and Nikara. Until required to stretch to hold Page Blanche in the closing stages she was as impressive as ever, really sparkling as she quickened a length and a half ahead after hacking along in a truly-run race. On her three performances in the season thus far the most suitable race for Favoridge at Royal Ascot would have been the seven-furlong Jersey Stakes; she had a 10-lb penalty as a Group 3 winner in that, though. Receiving 4 lb from Sweet Emma and at level weights with the rest in the Group 2 Coronation Stakes (why, oh why, not Group 1?), Favoridge lost by a neck to the best Irish-trained one-mile filly, Flame of Tara. Eddery did everything he could to conserve her energy for a final sprint, and Favoridge to her credit was able to remain on the bridle until well inside the last furlong. Once let down, she went to nothing almost at once.

		First Landing	Turn-to
	Riva Ridge	(b 1956)	Hildene
	(b 1969)	Iberia	Heliopolis
Favoridge (USA)		(ch 1954)	War East
(b.f. 1980)		Baldric II	Round Table
	Favoletta	(b 1961)	Two Cities
	(b 1968)	Violetta III	Pinza
		(b 1958)	Urshalim

Favoridge has been retired, and will be covered by Be My Guest. She may be on the small side but is worth a fortune as a broodmare with a racing record and pedigree like hers. The family is, as we often seem to have cause to say, one of the best in the Stud Book. So many high-class winners have come from it since Favoridge's fourth dam Horama went to stud that on the rare occasion one of its members is auctioned a full page in the catalogue is scarcely adequate space to list them. To be brief—Urshalim, winner of the Molecomb Stakes and second in the King's Stand Stakes, produced eight winners including three fine broodmares, the Irish One Thousand Guineas winner Lacquer, Coronation Stakes winner Sovereign and Violetta. The last-named produced ten winners, among them the four mares who did most to keep the family in the limelight in the latest season, Furioso (dam of Teenoso), Parthica (dam of Give Thanks), the pint-sized Little Miss (dam of Old Country) and Favoletta.

Favoridge is a good walker and usually showed a smooth action at the canter (she moved noticeably short on the way down to the start of the Child Stakes). She seemed to act on any going, though she never raced on very soft. Really testing going might have been against her in as much as the demands on her stamina would have been all the greater. *G. Wragg.*

FAVOURITE NEPHEW 2 ch.c. Be My Guest 126–Aunty Mable (Sir Ivor 135)   **73**
(1983 7f 7fg 7f² 7f 7f 8fg 8fg⁴ 10fg²) Mar 18; sturdy, compact colt; fifth foal; dam lightly-raced half-sister to Great Nephew; quite a modest maiden; best run when blinkered on final outing; suited by 1¼m; acts on firm going. *F. Durr.*

Mr John T. Sullivan's "Fawzi"

FAWAZ 2 b.c. Decoy Boy 129–Jendean 68 (Florescence 120) (1983 6fg 8g 7.6fg) **74**
Mar 25; 1,500Y; workmanlike colt; fourth foal; dam placed over 5f at 2 yrs; eighth
of 21 to Rainbow Quest in £4,100 event at Newbury in September, second outing
and best effort. *M. Haynes.*

FAWG (USA) 3 b.c. Hagley–One Spot (Cavan) (1982 7d 1983 10v* 10d* 10d **93**
10fg² 12g 12g 12fg) strong colt; won maiden race at Folkestone in March (made all)
and quite well-contested minor event at Brighton in April (got up near finish to beat
Lochboisdale and High Hawk); caught close home when good head second to
No-U-Turn in handicap at Lingfield in August; best form at 1¼m; seems to act on
any going; does best when ridden up with pace; sold 21,000 gns Newmarket
Autumn Sales. *G. Harwood.*

FAWZI 2 b.g. Young Generation 129–Little Loch Broom 60 (Reform 132) (1983 **110**
6g² 6d* 6fg² 6g* 6g* 6h* 6g² 7fg⁴ 5fg⁴) Mar 31; 12,000Y; neat, strong gelding;
first foal; dam, placed over 1m and 1¼m, is daughter of very useful Sleat; proved
himself a very useful performer in 7-runner Mill Reef Stakes at Newbury in
September, keeping on extremely well to finish 2½ lengths second to Vacarme; had
previously won maiden race and a nursery (dead-heated with Bantel Bandit) at Ayr,
Schwartzwald-Rennen at Baden-Baden and well-contested event at Pontefract;
also ran well when less than 2 lengths fourth of 14 to Petorius in Cornwallis Stakes
at Ascot in October on final start; effective at 5f and 6f (weakened significantly up
hill when tried over 7f in Somerville Tattersall Stakes at Newmarket in September);
yet to race on very soft ground but acts on any other; most genuine and
consistent. *J. Hindley.*

FAYETTE 3 ch.f. Dom Racine 121–Cordon 89 (Morston 125) (1982 NR 1983 **80**
8s² 10s* 12.2fg⁴ 10f⁴ 10h 10h⁴ 10g) IR 8,800Y; workmanlike filly; bad mover; first
foal; dam won over 7f and 1½m; won maiden race at Chepstow in May by 3 lengths

285

but became disappointing; suited by 1¼m and promises to stay further; probably acts on any going, but goes well on soft; usually apprentice ridden; sometimes sweats up. *P. Cole.*

FAYLASOUF 3 b.c. Brigadier Gerard 144–Sassanian (Sassafras 135) (1982 NR 1983 8d 8d⁴ 11d⁴ 12f³ 11g 14f³ 16.5fg) tall, close-coupled colt; second reported foal; dam won 5 races in Spain; in frame in maiden races; stays 1¾m; blinkered last 4 starts; sold 7,000 gns Newmarket September Sales. *H. T. Jones.* **79**

FEALTY (FR) 3 b. or br.g. Blakeney 126–Noble Duty (Reliance II 137) (1982 8s 1983 13.3g³ 16f²) big gelding; placed in maiden races at Newbury and Nottingham in June, going down by 4 lengths to Sneak Preview when 9/4-on in latter event (made heavy weather of getting to front and didn't find a great deal when he got there); stays 2m; sold to P. Brookshaw 7,600 gns Newmarket Autumn Sales. *J. Sutcliffe.* **81**

FEARLESS LAD 4 ch.c. Import 127–No Fear 91 (Quayside 124) (1982 6f 6f⁴ 5fg* 5fg* 5f 5g 6f³ 5s² 1983 5v* 5g² 5d* 5f 6fg) **126**

The system of pattern-race penalties is at times beyond all understanding, in few places more so than in certain sprints. The European turf authorities offer owners little in the way of incentives to keep top-class sprinters in training at the best of times, and this particularly applies in the months before the King's Stand Stakes in mid-June. Of the nine pattern races run over five and six furlongs in Europe before Royal Ascot, only one, the Premio Melton, has no penalties and of the remainder six have penalties for Group 1 winners of 11 lb or 12 lb, a substantial burden for even a tip-top performer. On the whole milers and middle-distance horses come out of the system better though it has to be said stayers do not, since the Mono Sagaro Stakes and Henry II Stakes for instance have swingeing penalties for Group 1 winners. It follows that a sprinter of the calibre of Fearless Lad, who won the King's Stand and ran second in the Abbaye in 1982, might just as well be trained purely with a view to the valuable events run from June onwards rather than taking on a number of the same horses on disadvantageous terms in the early-season contests. This is hardly likely to benefit racing in the long term.

It was consequently fortunate for the racing public and to the credit of Fearless Lad's connections that they ran their colt in the Palace House Stakes and Temple Stakes, and to Fearless Lad's credit that he managed to win one of these races and run well in the other. Not fully wound up for his reappearance in the Field Marshal Stakes at Haydock, Fearless Lad nonetheless proved too good for his opponents, beating Chellaston Park easing up despite having had not the best of runs. This performance augured well for Fearless Lad's campaign and in the seventeen-runner Palace House Stakes at Newmarket on Two Thousand Guineas day he started second favourite to On Stage who met him on terms 12 lb better than weight-for-age. We do not think any horse in training except Habibti could have beaten On Stage on these terms, and in going down to him by two and a half lengths, finishing powerfully after being outpaced, Fearless Lad ran splendidly.

The Temple Stakes at Sandown a month later once more saw Fearless Lad conceding weight all round, this time to a field containing the very speedy Brondesbury, having his first outing of the year, the Duke of York winner Vorvados, the Abernant winner Sweet Monday and Chellaston Park. A warm favourite, Fearless Lad was again outpaced in the first couple of furlongs as Brondesbury set up a lead of four lengths or so but he began to make a forward move from halfway and under the strongest pressure from Piggott got up near the

Temple Stakes, Sandown—Fearless Lad (rails) finishes well to catch Boy Trumpeter (centre) and Chellaston Park (No. 9) with Sylvan Barbarosa, Winter Wind and Sweet Monday (left to right) in close attendance

Mr G. Soulsby's "Fearless Lad"

finish to pip the three-year-old Boy Trumpeter by a neck with Chellaston Park, Sweet Monday and Winter Wind close behind. Brondesbury finished well beaten.

The Temple suggested Fearless Lad was about as good as ever and in the King's Stand he started second choice in the market behind On Stage to win the race two years running, a feat last accomplished by Gold Bridge in the 'thirties. He did not emulate his illustrious predecessor. Physically he impressed us less than at Sandown, where he had looked particularly well, and he tended to sweat up as he had when running moderately once at three. In the race he was tapped for speed as Sayf El Arab set a hell-for-leather gallop followed by Soba, and though making some progress from halfway he was already beaten when hampered at the distance, eventually finishing fifth to Sayf El Arab. On Stage finished nearly two lengths ahead of him on terms much less favourable to the three-year-old than in their previous encounter, a sure sign that Fearless Lad had not run up to his best.

Fearless Lad (ch.c. 1979)	Import (ch 1971)	Porto Bello (ch 1965)	Floribunda
			Street Song
		Immortelle (ch 1960)	Never Say Die
			Thunder
	No Fear (ch 1973)	Quayside (ch 1967)	London Gazette
			Wong
		My Plucky Lady (gr 1963)	Cash and Courage
			Blue Robe

Hopes that Fearless Lad would become a leading contender for the sprint championship received a blow in the King's Stand; they evaporated in the William Hill July Cup at Newmarket, run over a distance that ought to have favoured him

287

on the evidence of his recent displays over the minimum trip. After again sweating up and failing to impress in the paddock he never threatened the leaders, coming under strong pressure two furlongs out, being eased when he could clearly take no hand in the finish and coming home ninth of fifteen to Habibti. The July Cup turned out to be Fearless Lad's final appearance of the season. Although spoken of as likely to contest some of the top late-season events he did not run in any of them, apparently because of minor training problems.

Fearless Lad, the best horse sired to date by the Wokingham winner and July Cup third Import, is the first foal of No Fear who stayed a mile and a half but showed her best form when hacking up in a mile-and-a-quarter maiden race in the mud at Doncaster wearing blinkers for the first time. No Fear has since foaled the unraced two-year-old Crowned Lady (by Mandrake Major) and a foal brother to Fearless Lad. No Fear's dam, successful from five furlongs to a mile, including in sellers, produced several other winners, none of them of note, and until Fearless Lad turned up this was a pretty undistinguished family. A big, strong colt and a game one, he stays six furlongs and acts on any going. *R. D. Peacock.*

FEARLESS MOVER 3 gr.g. Dragonara Palace 115–Ash Fell 83 (Bleep-Bleep 134) (1982 6s 6d 1983 10.1f 10.1f) fair sort; behind in minor events. *D. Wintle.* —

FEASIBILITY STUDY 2 br.c. Welsh Pageant 132–Yelming 76 (Thatch 136) (1983 8g³ 8fg* 7fg) Apr 6; 34,000Y; good sort; first foal; dam, placed at up to 7f, is half-sister to very useful 2-y-o sprinter Glancing; landed the odds comfortably by 1½ lengths from Marlion in maiden race at Newcastle in October; gave at least 7 lb all round when 5½ lengths sixth of 14 to Condrillac in Houghton Stakes at Newmarket later in month; will be suited by a return to 1m; acts on a firm surface. *G. Harwood.* **93**

FEATHER FLOWER 3 b.f. Relkino 131–Antonietta Corsini (Herbager 136) (1982 NR 1983 10f² 12f 12s) 22,000F; closely related to 2 winners by Relko, including very smart middle-distance stayer Relay Race, and half-sister to 2 winners; dam won 8 races in Italy and is sister to Italian Derby winner Appiani II; 50/1 and apprentice ridden when neck second of 16 to odds-on Brave Memory in minor event at Brighton in June; beaten a long way both subsequent starts, one of them in a maiden race at Hamilton (last of 14); should stay 1½m. *J. Dunlop.* **74**

FEBRUARY THE FIFTH (USA) 2 ch.c. Raise A Native–Tudor Velvet (Tudor Grey 119) (1983 6f) $157,000Y; second foal; dam minor sprint stakes winner; unquoted and backward, behind in 20-runner maiden race at Newmarket in July. *J. Sutcliffe.* —

FEELINGS (FR) 6 b.h. Green Dancer 132–Fast Iron (Iron Peg §§) (1982 14.7f³ 14g 12.2f³ 14g 12fg 13d 12g²(dis) 15.8d 1983 15.8d⁴ 20.4g 15fg 16f⁴) well-made, quite attractive horse; stays well; seems to act on any going; usually blinkered nowadays; has often made running. *T. Craig.* —

FEELS RIGHT 3 br.c. Busted 134–Sandarey 94 (Darius 129) (1982 NR 1983 12g 14d 14f 14g⁴ 16fg⁴ 14g) 18,000Y; strong colt; half-brother to numerous winners, including St Leger second Zilos (by Grundy); dam won at 1m and 11f; fourth in maiden race at Yarmouth and £5,000 handicap at Newmarket in September; suited by his best final outing; suited by a test of stamina. *L. Cumani.* **69**

FEERIE BOREALE (FR) 2 gr.f. Irish River 131–Skelda 117 (La Varende 125) (1983 7.5f* 8s² 8f³) tall, leggy, rather unfurnished filly; half-sister to several winners, notably Grand Prix de Paris winner and St Leger second Soleil Noir (by Exbury) and very useful middle-distance winner Jeune Loup (by Mill Reef); dam good stayer at 2 yrs and 3 yrs; put up 2 good performances at Longchamp in the autumn; headed in the final furlong when beaten ¾ length by Eastern Dawn (pair clear) in Prix d'Aumale, and stayed on strongly when about 2 lengths third to Almeira in Prix Marcel Boussac; had earlier won a maiden at Deauville in August; will be suited by 1¼m+; probably acts on any going; should win a good race in 1984. *A. Fabre, France.* **113**

FEI LOONG 2 ch.g. Music Boy 124–Dimione (Tompion) (1983 6f 6f 7d 7.6fg 7fg³) Apr 2; 5,600F, 5,000Y; half-brother to French 1m winner Dimiane (by Taj Dewan); dam won twice over 9f in France; 2½ lengths third of 20 to Bobby Dazzler in nursery at Leicester in October; suited by 7f. *E. Eldin.* **80**

FELIXSTOWE 5 b.g. Moulton 128–Laughing Girl 110 (Sassafras 135) (1982 NR 1983 15.5f³) first foal; dam very useful at up to 1¾m; poor last of 3 in maiden race at Folkestone in August. *R. Howe.* —

Mrs Robin Hastings' "Fenny Rough"

FELSTED ADMIRAL 4 b.g. Chantro 104–Maureen's Star 67 (Live Spirit 121) —
(1982 NR 1983 9d 12f 10f) compact gelding; poor mover; well beaten in minor
events and a maiden race in the North. *N. Bycroft.*

FELTHORPE MARINER 4 b.c. Be My Guest 126–Sea Horse 98 (Sea-Bird II 91
145) (1982 8d* 8.2s³ 8f 8d* 8f 8fg⁴ 8s 1983 8v 8d 8s² 10s³ 8f* 9g 8f⁴ 8fg 9fg 8d
8f⁴ 8fg) quite attractive, lengthy colt; not the best of movers; fairly useful
handicapper on his day; got the better of Fandangle by a short head at York in July;
creditable neck second to Crossways in Hambleton Stakes on same course earlier;
stays 1¼m; acts on any going but is ideally suited by some give in the ground. *C.
Brittain.*

FENCHURCH COLONY 2 b.g. Tachypous 128–Katebird 89 (Birdbrook 110) 78
(1983 5s² 6g³ 6f² 7f 6f⁴) Apr 8; tall gelding; fourth foal; half-brother to a winning
plater; dam, best at sprint distances on flat, won over hurdles; second in minor
event at Thirsk in April and maiden race (beaten short head) at Redcar in June; not
raced after July; best form at 6f on firm going. *M. H. Easterby.*

FENNY ROUGH 3 br.f. Home Guard 129–Geraldville (Lord Gayle 124) (1982 114
5f* 6fg⁴ 6f² 6f* 6g⁴ 1983 7f* 7f² 8d 7g) good-quartered, quite attractive filly;
good walker and mover; first foal; dam Irish middle-distance winner; weak in
market but looking well, made a successful reappearance in 6-runner £9,000 Oak
Tree Stakes at Goodwood in July, leading 2f out and running on strongly to hold
odds-on Silverdip by a length, pair clear; ran creditably when ½-length second to
same filly in 10-runner Strensall Stakes at York the following month but
subsequently ran below her best in Gilltown Stud Stakes at the Curragh (ninth of 15
to Mighty Fly) and Harroways Stakes at Goodwood (fifth of 9 to Larionov); suited
by 7f and should stay further; seems to need firm surface. *B. Hills.*

FEN TIGER 2 b.c. Morston 125–Brass Finisher 93 (Cash and Courage 116) (1983 84
6f² 7.2fg³ 7fg 6fg³ 7d 5d³ 7fg 8f) Feb 18; 2,500Y; neat, strong colt; half-brother to
3 winners, including very useful 1977 2-y-o 5f performer Emboss (by Tribal Chief)
and 1½m winner Groovy Girl (by Averof); dam, sister to smart Sol'Argent, won at
up to 1¼m and also won over hurdles; ran well in big fields of maidens at
Newmarket in the summer on first and third starts and when length fourth of 10
(promoted to third) in £4,500 nursery at Redcar in September; best form at 6f, but
stays 7f; acts on firm going; not particularly consistent. *R. Hollinshead.*

FERNDALE LAD 2 ch.c. Take a Reef 127–Geri's Jewel (Seaepic 100) (1983 6g –
7fg 7g 10fg 8f) Apr 6; fair sort; second foal; dam of little account; well beaten in
maiden races. *P. Burgoyne.*

FERRERO ROCHER 2 ch.f. Roan Rocket 128–Miss Argyle 92 (Mountain Call 76
125) (1983 8g 8g³ 8g) Apr 1; rangy, good-bodied filly; fourth foal; half-sister to 2
winners, including sprinter Marmagoa (by Saritamer); dam won over 5f at 2 yrs;
co-favourite, 3 lengths third of 13 to Springle in maiden race at Edinburgh in
September; stays 1m. *Sir Mark Prescott.*

FERRIBY FLYER 4 b.g. Vitiges 132–Lily Langtry 102 (Prince de Galles 125) –
(1982 NR 1983 12v 12d 8s) fair sort; has a round action; poor plater; has been
blinkered. *A. Smith.*

FERRIBY HALL 6 ch.g. Malicious–Gallic Law 91 (Galivanter 131) (1982 5f* 5f 76
5fg 5fg 5fg 5g 1983 6v 5s 5fg 5f 5f 5f 6h 6g* 5fg 6g 6s⁴ 7fg 5fg 8fg) strong gelding;
narrowly won handicap at Catterick in September; stays 6f; acts on any going;
effective with and without blinkers; sometimes sweats up; has run well for an
apprentice. *A. Smith.*

FERRYBOAT 3 ch.f. Silly Season 127–Aberklair 72 (Klairon 131) (1982 5f³ 5fg² 50
6s 1983 5f 5f²) lengthy filly; plater; bred to stay beyond 5f; sold 400 gns
Doncaster October Sales. *J. Hardy.*

FERRY LANE 3 ch.f. Dom Racine 121–Nana's Girl 109 (Tin Whistle 128) (1982 –
5fg 1983 7v 7f 6fg) compact filly; soundly beaten in maiden and minor events,
although probably isn't entirely lacking in ability. *P. Mitchell.*

FERRYMAN 7 b.g. Forlorn River 124–La Miranda 80 (Miralgo 130) (1982 5f⁴ 6g 90
5f³ 6fg 5g 6f 5g 5g 5fg² 5d 5d* 5v 5s* 5s 1983 6v 5s 5.8s² 6g 5.8g 5f⁴ 6f 6f 6f 6d*
5fg 5fg³ 5g² 6g*) small gelding; sprint handicapper; won at Goodwood in
September and Lingfield in October; stays 6f; acts on any going, but is ideally
suited by some give underfoot; occasionally blinkered; sometimes sweats up. *D.
Elsworth.*

FESTAL SPIRIT 4 b.f. Jimmy Reppin 131–Celebrate 85 (Rockavon 120) (1982 86
10f 10.5fg 12f⁴ 12d² 12f 12.3fg³ 12d 13d³ 14g* 15g³ 15d* 1983 12d⁴ 13fg 16fg 14d*
12fg) big, strong filly; ran on strongly to win handicap at York in October by 3
lengths from Path of Peace (raced inside on better ground); suited by a test of
stamina; well suited by some give in the ground; suited by enterprising riding
tactics; game. *W. Elsey.*

FEUTERSOEY 3 ch.f. Run The Gantlet–Time Was 76 (Crowned Prince 128) –
(1982 NR 1983 8f 8f 10f 12g 12g) lengthy, heavy-bodied filly; first foal; dam 1¼m
winner; behind in maiden and minor events. *P. M. Taylor.*

FEYDAN 2 ch.c. Double Form 130–Baby Brew 123 (Green God 128) (1983 7g 6g⁴ 71
6fg) Mar 31; lengthy, quite attractive colt; first foal; dam very smart sprinter
from family of Deep Diver and King's Company; 2 lengths fourth of 14 to
Angleman in minor event at Lingfield in September. *J. Dunlop.*

FIBOFF 2 b.f. Dubassoff–Fibeel 72 (Most Secret 119) (1983 7s 8.2s 8g) Mar 31; –
rather leggy filly; third foal; half-sister to 5f winner Mrs Love It (by Rapid River);
dam won three 5f races; in rear in Scottish maiden and minor events; blinkered final
outing. *H. Bell.*

FIDATO 7 br.g. Reliance II 137–Sealed Order (Aureole 132) (1982 NR 1983 –
10.2g 10f) temperamental and of little account. *A. Andrews.*

FIDELITY (USA) 2 b.f. Sir Ivor 135–Northern Gem 121 (Northern Dancer) –
(1983 6f 7fg 6g) May 16; neat filly; good mover; sister to very useful 1¼m winner
Dreaming Away and half-sister to 3 winners, including 3-y-o Irish 9f and 1¼m
winner Colonial Flag (by Hoist the Flag) and useful 9f and 1¼m winner Government
Program (by Secretariat); dam won Fred Darling Stakes and was second in
Champion Stakes; no show in sizeable fields of maidens at Newbury (twice) and
Pontefract. *I. Balding.*

FIDESSA 7 br.m. Fine Blade 12–Sky Hostess 72 (Skymaster 126) (1982 NR 1983 –
13s) probably of little account. *W. H. H. Williams.*

FIDURI 4 b.f. Wolver Hollow 126–Sans Blague (Above Suspicion 127) (1982 —
10.1d 8fg 10.1g 13d 1983 12f 10fg 10f 8fg) of little account; has worn blinkers. *D. Jermy.*

FIEFDOM 3 ch.c. Home Guard 129–Eastwood Bounty 87 (Bounteous 125) (1982 **94**
6g* 1983 8fg² 8g4 9fg 10g4 10fg) big, quite attractive colt; ran well when making a
belated reappearance in handicap at Newmarket in August, keeping on nicely to
finish 2 lengths second to Hollywood Party; ran best subsequent races when
seventh of 30 behind Sagamore in William Hill Cambridgeshire at Newmarket and
2¾ lengths fourth of 15 to Folly Hill in handicap at Sandown in October; probably
stays 1¼m; sold to G. Vergette 12,800 gns Ascot December Sales. *B. Hobbs.*

FIELD CONQUEROR 2 b.c. Busted 134–Divine Thought 102 (Javelot 124) **78 p**
(1983 8fg 8f4) Apr 24; 44,000Y; strong, good-bodied colt; good walker; fourth
foal; half-brother to Dee Stakes winner Great Idea (by Great Nephew); dam,
half-sister to high-class 1969 2-y-o Divine Gift, won from 1¼m to 12.5f; ridden by
inexperienced apprentice at 6-lb overweight, came from well back without
receiving deal of assistance to finish 6½ lengths fourth of 14 behind Hidden Destiny
in maiden race at Leicester in November; will be suited by 1¼m+; certain to
improve. *H. Cecil.*

FIELDS OF SPRING (USA) 3 ch.f. The Minstrel 135–Memory Lane 100 **102**
(Never Bend) (1982 NR 1983 8v 10d² 10.5s 12g 12.2fg* 12g 12fg 10.5g* 10fg
10s4) attractive, well-made filly; good walker; third foal; half-sister to 1981
American 2-y-o winner Tides of Chance (by Little Current) and 1½m winner Green
Memory (by Forli); dam, sister to Mill Reef, won Princess Elizabeth Stakes; ran
very well when ¾-length second of 17 to Jolly Bay in Pretty Polly Stakes at
Newmarket in April; probably ran best subsequent races when winning Warwick
Oaks in June (easily by 4 lengths from Dame Ashfield) and Herbst-Stutenpreis um
den Gatzweilers Alt-Pokal at Neuss in August (by neck from Bebe Arlette); stays
1½m; probably acts on any going; races with her tongue tied down. *I. Balding.*

FIERY CELT 2 b.c. Ballad Rock 122–Fiery Diplomat 120 (Diplomat Way) (1983 **102**
7g* 7d) Mar 11; IR 23,000F, 5,200Y; third foal; half-brother to a winning hurdler;

Mrs Catherine M. Shattuck's "Fiery Celt"

291

dam very smart 5f to 7f winner at 2 yrs; put up a splendid first effort in valuable Tap On Wood Stakes at Phoenix Park in October, leading inside final furlong and keeping on well to beat Western Symphony a length; never a threat when nearly 7 lengths sixth to the same horse in the Group 3 Larkspur Stakes at Leopardstown later the same month; may stay 1m. *N. McGrath, Ireland.*

FIERY CROSS 3 ch.g. North Stoke 130–Ladys View 109 (Tin Whistle 128) — (1982 NR 1983 11s 10s 10.2g 10g) IR 5,200Y; strong, deep-girthed gelding; half-brother to winning miler Al-Allam (by Sun Prince) and a winner in Denmark; dam speedy 2-y-o; in rear in maiden races and sellers; sold out of P. Cole's stable 400 gns Newmarket July Sales after third outing. *M. Chapman.*

FIFTY QUID SHORT 2 b.c. Import 127–Maryland Star 76 (I Say 125) (1983 5s | 72 5s² 6v² 6d⁴ 6g⁴ 6g 6s² 6f 6g 6s²) Apr 5; 1,000F; big, lengthy colt; good walker; sixth produce; half-brother to a winner in Norway; dam won at up to 11f; in frame in a variety of races, including a seller, putting up easily best efforts in testing conditions; not certain to stay beyond 6f; revels in the mud. *Mrs M. Nesbitt.*

FIGHTER PILOT 2 b.c. Warpath 113–Brief Flight 108 (Counsel 118) (1982 7s | 79 8.2s 1983 9d 10d* 12g⁴ 12f 13g³ 13g² 14d³ 17.4g 16.5f) lengthy, sparely-made colt; good walker; decisively won maiden race at Redcar and small handicap at Beverley in June; placed at Ayr (twice) and York afterwards; runs like a thorough stayer; probably acts on any going; tends to drop himself out and needs a deal of driving; sold to M. Pipe 14,000 gns Doncaster November Sales. *C. Thornton.*

FIGHTING JIMMY 2 ch.c. Captain James 123–Sweet Sharlie 77 (Fighting | 61 Charlie 127) (1983 5v 5s 5d 5s 5g 5fg 5g⁴ 5g) May 15; IR 3,600Y; sturdy, fair sort; half-brother to fairly useful 1981 2-y-o winner Sharlie's Wimpy (by Tumble Wind) and successful sprinter Effect (by Martinmas); poor maiden; beaten in seller fourth outing; suited by a sound surface. *D. Wilson.*

FIGHTING TRACK 2 ch.c. Palm Track 122–Freda's Hope (Fighting Don) (1983 — 8g 8.2s 6fg) Mar 14; tall, leggy colt; half-brother to a winning plater; dam of little account; well beaten in October maiden races. *S. Norton.*

FIGURE DE DANSE (FR) 3 b.f. Dancer's Image–Figure de Proue (Petingo — 135) (1982 5fg³ 5fg³ 6d³ 6f³ 7f 7g 6g 8f* 8s³ 10f 1983 12s 10v 10fg 8f⁴ 8f 8f 8d 8fg) useful sort; mainly poor form in 1983; suited by 1m; acts on any going; often blinkered; sold 660 gns Newmarket Autumn Sales. *R. Sheather.*

FILARIO (FR) 4 b.g. Filiberto 123–Escaria (Right Royal V 135) (1982 8d 8g* | 56 8fg* 9g²) 1983 12s*) strong, lengthy gelding; bandaged in front when winning handicap at Wolverhampton in April; not seen out again; stays 1½m; seems to act on any going; has run creditably for an apprentice. *M. Pipe.*

FILIA MATRIS 2 b.f. Welsh Saint 126–Maryfield (Hul a Hul 124) (1983 5d⁴ 5s* | 71 5g² 5s 5.1f³) Mar 6; 3,600F, 4,000Y; sturdy filly; sister to 1980 2-y-o 5f winner Highcroft; dam never ran; won maiden race at Windsor in May; sent to Italy after running poorly in claiming event at Yarmouth in July on fifth outing, and winner there at Livorno and Florence; acts on soft going and is probably unsuited by firm; wears blinkers. *W. O'Gorman.*

FILIPPO (USA) 2 b.c. Gallant Romeo–Queenly Gift (Princely Gift 137) (1983 — 8fg) Apr 7; $100,000Y; half-brother to numerous winners, including useful middle-distance performer Noble Gift (by Vaguely Noble) and stakes winners Princely Axe (by The Axe) and Linda Summers (by Crozier); dam unraced sister to 2000 Guineas fourth Fidelio; unquoted, behind in 21-runner maiden race won by Alphabatim at Newmarket in October. *L. Cumani.*

FILLE DE BOURBON 2 gr. or ro.f. Ile de Bourbon 133–Belligerent 74 (Roan | 71 Rocket 128) (1983 5v 5d 7f² 7h⁴ 7g 7d 8d⁴) Mar 28; 42,000F; small, sturdy, quite attractive filly; half-sister to several winners, including 3-y-o 7f winner Star of Ireland (by Star Appeal) and useful sprinter Goldhills Pride (by Goldhill); dam half-sister to very good French miler Kenmare; quite a modest maiden; should stay 1¼m; acts on firm going and a soft surface. *R. Laing.*

FILL THE JUG 2 br.f. Derrylin 115–Fleur d'Amour 85 (Murrayfield 119) (1983 | 76 5g 5fg 5f 5f² 5f 5f³ 5fg³ 8d³ 6fg 6d* 7g 6g³) Mar 28; 2,200Y; sturdy filly; third foal; dam won over 6f and 7f; attracted no bid after winning valuable 18-runner seller at York in October by a head from Allten Limited, the pair 5 lengths clear; previously placed in maiden races, best effort on eighth outing when 4 lengths third of 15 to Shuteye at Beverley; stays 1m; yet to race on very soft going but acts on any other; goes well for apprentice C. Coates. *T. Fairhurst.*

FINAL CAST 4 b.f. Saulingo 122–Speyside 84 (Live Spirit 121) (1982 7.6f 6f 6g **50**
8fg 6s 1983 5f⁴ 6fg 6f 6g 5f* 5f 6h 5g 5fg 5g 5g 5d 7fg⁴ 5g) good-topped filly;
seemed to show improved form when beating Touch Boy a short head in trainers
invitation race at Catterick in August; not disgraced on occasions afterwards; stays
7f; acts on firm going; usually blinkered nowadays (wore them first time at
Catterick); has run creditably for an apprentice; has worn bandages in front. *D.
Chapman.*

FINALE SEPT 3 b.g. Malinowski 123–Desertville 92 (Charlottesville 135) (1982 **73** d
7g 7fg 6fg* 1983 12s* 12s² 13.8s³ 12f 16f⁴ 16f 16.5f⁴ 16.1g⁴ 16.1s) medium-sized,
sparely-made gelding; good walker and mover; held up when readily winning
handicap at Ripon in April; in frame in similar races afterwards, including an
apprentice event; suited by a test of stamina; acts on any going; sometimes
blinkered; sold to H. Fleming 3,000 gns Doncaster October Sales. *M. H. Easterby.*

FINAL THATCHING 2 ch.c. Ahonoora 122–La Quinta (Thatch 136) (1983 **82** p
5s*) Apr 10; 11,500Y; first living foal; dam once-raced granddaughter of high-class
miler Lucyrowe; favourite, got the better of Deasy's Delight by a neck (pair 2½
lengths clear) in 15-runner maiden race at the Curragh in April; will stay 6f; looked
promising but wasn't seen out again. *J. Bolger, Ireland.*

FINE AND DANDY 2 ch.c. Tap On Wood 130–All Glorious 82 (Crowned Prince **–**
128) (1983 5g) Feb 25; first foal; dam won over 7f and 1m; 33/1, in rear in
14-runner maiden race at Catterick in September; likely to need further. *W.
Holden.*

FINE EDGE 3 ch.c. Sharpen Up 127–Metair 118 (Laser Light 118) (1982 5fg* 5f* **115** §
6g 1983 6d⁴ 6v 5f 5f² 5fg² 5fg³ 5g* 5fg³) good-quartered, medium-sized,
attractive colt; a good walker and a smooth, easy mover; gave an unattractive
performance when landing the odds in 5-runner minor event at Newbury in
September, failing to quicken when let down, after appearing to be travelling very
easily indeed, and only scrambling home from Bold Bob; placed earlier in stiffer
company behind Soba in King George Stakes at Goodwood and Scarbrough Stakes

Mr K. Abdulla's "Fine Edge"

at Doncaster and behind Habibti in William Hill Sprint Championship at York in between, being promoted from third in last-named after second-placed Soba was disqualified; stays 6f; acts on firm going and may well be unsuited by heavy; usually taken down early nowadays and gives impression he's no longer entirely genuine. *J. Tree.*

FINE PROSPECT 3 ch.c. Homing 130–Shanghai Lady 87 (Crocket 130) (1982 NR 1983 8d4 7.6v 10s4 11.7fg 8f) 12,000Y; sturdy, strong-quartered, plain colt; third foal; dam sprinter; fourth in maiden races at Newbury and Leicester in spring; yet to prove he stays middle distances; sold to F. Walwyn 4,500 gns Newmarket September Sales. *P. Cole.* — 75

FINE RECOVERY (USA) 2 ro.c. Northern Jove–Campaign Speech (On-and-On) (1983 5s 5g 6g 8g 8g 7d4 7fg) May 19; $32,000Y; small colt; fifth foal; dam unraced half-sister to 2 stakes winners; quite a modest maiden; best effort on sixth outing; better suited by 7f than 1m; evidently acts well on a soft surface; sold 2,100 gns Doncaster November Sales. *J. Hanson.* — 73

FINE ROMANCE 2 ch.f. Star Appeal 133–Pas de Deux 80 (Nijinsky 138) (1983 7fg) Apr 7; rather close-coupled, narrow filly; keen walker; second foal; half-sister to 3-y-o 1½m to 1¾m winner Insular (by Moulton); dam, daughter of very smart Example, won over 1¼m; 20/1, out of first 10 of 22 maiden race at Newmarket in October. *I. Balding.* — –

FINE SCHOLAR 4 b.g. Touch Paper 113–Speed Writer (Saulingo 122) (1982 12d 10d 1983 12fg 11g4 16f) ex-Irish gelding; first foal; dam never ran; seems only plating class; promises to stay 1½m. *J. Spearing.* — –

FINE SUN 6 ch.g. Fine Blade 121–All Sunshine (Miralgo 130) (1982 11d* 9d4 10v* 10g2 11.2d3 1983 10.2v 10s* 10fg 10g 10g 9fg) fair sort; reportedly acid-fired — 110

Mr Bill Hobson's "Fine Sun"

after injuring himself early in 1982; smart performer; battled on well to hold off strong-finishing Farioffa by a head in 8-runner Clive Graham Stakes at Goodwood in May; not disgraced in valuable handicaps last 2 starts; stays 11f; needs some give in the ground to show his best form; often sweats up; genuine, but seems to need holding up. *M. Lambert.*

FINIAN'S RAINBOW 2 b.c. Relkino 131–Rainbow's End 83 (My Swallow 134)   **94**
(1983 6s* 6f⁴ 7f⁴ 8g³) Mar 12; tall, quite attractive, lightly-made colt; shows quite a bit of knee action; second foal; dam 2-y-o 6f winner; had plenty to do at halfway in 15-runner minor event at Goodwood in May but kept on strongly to catch Rex Lake (gave 7 lb) close home, winning by a short head; subsequently came up against Vacarme at Ascot, Trojan Fen at Newbury and Rousillon at Goodwood, being beaten at least 6 lengths each time and finishing last on last 2 occasions; probably stays 1m; acts on any going. *I. Balding.*

FIONA'S PRIDE 4 gr. or ro.f. Runnymede 123–Crowberry (Crozier 117) (1982   **– §**
10s 10s 1983 11.5f 12f 14fg 16f 15g) compact filly; temperamental plater. *E. Carter.*

FIONA THE FAIR 3 ch.f. Balidar 133–Excitation (Brigadier Gerard 144) (1982   **–**
NR 1983 10g 10fg) 400 2-y-o; first foal; dam never ran; well-beaten ninth of 11 in 2 sellers at Lingfield in October. *A. Neaves.*

FIORENZO 3 b.g. Filiberto 123–Guiletta 63 (Runnymede 123) (1982 6d 6g 6fg   **66**
1983 8d 12d 12g³ 12.3f* 13.8f* 12fg² 13.8f* 11f 13fg 14fg) lightly-built gelding; settled better than before when winning small handicaps at Newcastle and Catterick (2) in quite good style in summer; stays 1¾m; acts on firm going. *M. Camacho.*

FIRAAZA 3 ch.f. Nishapour 125–Falassa (Relko 136) (1982 NR 1983 5v 9f 8f   **66**
8f⁴) small, quite attractive filly; fourth foal; half-sister to 2 winners, including 7f and 1m winner Falaka (by Sparkler); dam, placed at up to 1¼m in France, is half-sister to top-class Silver Shark; kept on steadily when about 2 lengths fourth of 16 behind Chantry in maiden race at Salisbury in September; stays 1m; sold to Susan Piggott Bloodstock 15,000 gns Newmarket December Sales. *F. J. Houghton.*

FIRE OFF 3 b.f. Averof 123–Fiery Kiss 82 (Floribunda 136) (1982 5fg 5f 1983 5d   **–**
5v 5f 6g 6fg) lightly-made filly; well beaten in maiden events and sellers; twice blinkered; sold 360 gns Doncaster September Sales and resold 340 gns Ascot December Sales. *W. Stubbs.*

FIRESPARK 4 ch.f. Hot Spark 126–Kari Simbi 63 (Galivanter 131) (1982 5f² 6h   **46**
7d 6fg² 6g* 6g* 7.2f 6s 1983 6v 7d³ 6fg) strong, compact filly; former plater; stays 7f; ideally suited by top-of-the-ground; best in blinkers; has run respectably for an apprentice. *M. Camacho.*

FIRE-THATCH 3 ch.c. Thatch 136–Gigiolina (King Emperor) (1982 5.1f* 5f²   **111**
5f* 1983 6fg 5f⁴) short-coupled, deep-girthed colt; won small races at Yarmouth and Newmarket and was second in Windsor Castle Stakes at Royal Ascot as a 2-y-o; never really on terms in William Hill July Cup at Newmarket or King George Stakes at Goodwood later in July but came through strongly in closing stages on latter course to finish just over 2½ lengths fourth of 14 behind Soba; likely to prove best at sprint distances; acts on firm going but moved scratchily to post at Goodwood and would possibly be seen to better advantage on an easy surface; sent to Italy. *H. Cecil.*

FIRMAMENT 3 b.g. Relkino 131–Lady Of The Moon 89 (Crepello 136) (1982 7g   **–**
7d 1983 11s 12v³ 14d) big, lengthy gelding; good mover; third to very easy winner Tom Okker in 1½m maiden race at Doncaster in May, best effort; looks slow; sold to C. Postlethwaite 5,600 gns Newmarket Autumn Sales. *P. Walwyn.*

FIRM EVALUATION (USA) 4 ch.g. Vaguely Noble 140–Valmara 104 (Fleet   **88**
Nasrullah) (1982 12fg 12f² 12f* 14f 12f 1983 14s 14s 10g² 12f 10.2f⁴ 12.3fg² 12fg* 12.2f² 12d 10d 12fg* 10fg²) big, rangy gelding; won handicaps at Brighton in August (made all) and September (dead-heated with Hysterical); below form in between; best at middle distances; needs a sound surface and acts well on firm going; one paced; sold to M. Pipe 17,000 gns Newmarket Autumn Sales. *J. Hindley.*

FIRM FOUNDATIONS 6 br.g. Pieces of Eight 128–Streetcar 87 (Crocket 130)   **–**
(1982 17.1f 12d³ 12fg³ 12g² 1983 16s 12f 12f 12f⁴ 18g) plater; stays well; acts on a firm and a soft surface; sometimes blinkered; changed hands 750 gns Ascot August Sales; pulled up lame final start. *M. Hinchliffe.*

FIRST BANQUET (USA) 2 ch.c. Banquet Table–Romance First (Ambernash) 68 p
(1983 6f 7f 7g) May 25; $37,000Y; quite well-made colt; third foal; half-brother to
moderate 1981 2-y-o Prince Gleam (by Son Ange); dam ran 4 times unplaced; in
mid-division in sizeable fields of maidens at Newmarket, Yarmouth and Goodwood;
certain to do better, and impresses as one to keep an eye on in handicap company at
1m+. *M. Jarvis.*

FIRST BOUT 2 b.g. Nishapour 125–Right Swinger (Forward Pass) (1983 7fg 72
7g) Mar 13; first foal; dam, lightly-raced sister to Irish Sweeps Derby winner
Malacate, was fourth over 10.5f in France; showed ability in quite useful company
at Doncaster and Lingfield in October; will be suited by further; may improve. *B.
Hanbury.*

FIRST CRY 2 gr.f. Town Crier 119–The Guzzler 69 (Behistoun 131) (1983 5v⁴ 7f 64
6f 7f 6fg 8fg² 8fg⁴ 8.2fg) Apr 20; fair sort; half-sister to 3 winners, including 1m to
19f winner King's College Boy (by Andrea Mantegna); dam won 6f seller; showed
improved form in 1m nurseries, finishing 4 lengths second of 17 to Maruthayoor at
Bath and 3 lengths fourth of 12 to Double Quick Time at Brighton; suited by 1m;
acts on firm going. *N. Vigors.*

FIRST GROOM (USA) 2 ch.f. Blushing Groom 131–Prima Ballerina (Royal Vale –
106) (1983 7f 6f) Apr 22; $125,000Y; half-sister to several winners, including
Cordial Prince (by Cornish Prince), a minor stakes winner over 1m; dam won at up
to 7f at 2 yrs; weak in market, soundly beaten in maiden races at Yarmouth
(prominent 2f out) and Windsor in July. *B. Hanbury.*

FIRST IMAGE (USA) 3 ro.c. Caucasus 127–Image's Sister (Native Dancer) –
(1982 7fg 1983 8v 10f 10.1fg 12g) good-bodied colt; didn't show much in 1983,
although wasn't totally disgraced last 2 starts; promises to stay at least 1½m;
retained 2,800 gns Ascot December Sales. *J. Benstead.*

FIRST MOVEMENT 5 b.h. Music Boy 124–Lunar Princess 109 (King's Bench – §
132) (1982 6fg³ 6fg 6g 6fg 6s 1983 7d 7.6v 7f 7f³ 6s 7.6fg 6g 7fg) strong, good
sort; fairly useful on his day but is inconsistent and unreliable; stays 7f; acts on any
going; blinkered final start; has run creditably when sweating up; has been taken
down early. *C. Brittain.*

FIRST NIGHT FLIGHT 5 b.g. Tumble Wind–Aracara (Prince Tenderfoot 126) –
(1982 NR 1983 15.8d) of little account and possibly temperamental. *K. Ivory.*

FIRST OF MANY 2 b.c. Chantro 104–Miss Friendly 72 (Status Seeker) (1983 –
5fg 6g 8g 7g) Apr 5; 1,350 2-y-o; of little account; blinkered final outing. *J.
Roberts.*

FIRST PHASE (USA) 4 b.c. Cannonade–Precious Elaine (Advocator) (1982 77 §
7g⁸ 8.2fg* 8.2f² 10.6h 8f* 8fg* 10f 1983 10v 8d 7g⁴ 8f 8f² 8fg 8fg) small, quite
attractive colt; poor mover; fairly useful handicapper at his best; below form most
starts at 4 yrs; yet to prove he stays beyond 1m; suited by fast ground; blinkered
final start; possibly not much of a battler nowadays and needs to be held up. *G.
Hunter.*

FIRST PLEASURE 2 b.f. Dominion 123–First Delight 80 (Primera 131) (1983 53
5v 5s 5d 6f) Feb 8; 2,800Y; small filly; good walker; half-sister to useful 9f to 1½m
winner Celtic Pleasure (by Irish Ball); dam won at 9f and 1¼m; plating-class
maiden; better suited by 6f than 5f, and should be well suited by 7f or 1m; probably
acts on any going. *W. Wharton.*

FISHLEIGH GAMBLE 8 gr.g. Tudor Bar 91–Pourquoi II (Question) (1982 NR –
1983 10f 21f) winning point-to-pointer and chaser; beaten a long way in £3,100
event at Newbury and Goodwood Cup in July. *W. R. Williams.*

FISHPOND 2 b.f. Homing 130–Lake Naivasha 101 (Blakeney 126) (1983 6f 8d³) 71
Mar 23; well-made filly; second foal; dam middle-distance performer; 2½ lengths
third of 14 behind July in maiden race at Beverley in September; will stay beyond
1m; sold 4,300 gns Ascot November Sales and is to be trained by R. Holder. *R.
Hern.*

FIT FOR A KING 4 b.f. Royalty 130–Confidante (Gulf Pearl 117) (1982 8d⁴ 10f³ –
8.5f 8g 7f 7f. 1983 10f 9d) smallish, unfurnished filly; plating-class maiden; stays
1¼m; seems to act on any going; suited by enterprising riding tactics; winning
hurdler. *J. Webber.*

FITZ ITCHING 5 b.g. Tickled Pink 114–King's Wench 61 (Kibenka 119) (1982 –
NR 1983 10.2g 8f) of little account; sold 560 gns Ascot July Sales; dead. *J.
Roberts.*

FITZPATRICK 4 b.c. Oats 126–Shannon Princess (Connaught 130) (1982 11g –
12f² 14fg³ 12f² 12f³ 12fg* 12f* 12g 12g⁴ 13.3g* 12g 1983 12d 12f 16f)

close-coupled, robust colt; good mover; fairly useful at 3 yrs; respectable eighth of 14 to Weavers' Pin in Miner's Northumberland Plate at Newcastle in June on final start, best effort in 1983; promises to stay 2m; acts well on firm going; has won for an amateur rider. *P. Walwyn.*

FITZROY 5 b.g. Furry Glen 121–Miss Wittington (Red God 128§) (1982 8f 10fg 10d² 12fg* 10fg² 10.6s* 12v 1983 12v² 12s 11.7s 12fg 12d) lengthy, hollow-backed gelding; has rather a round action; middle-distance handicapper; probably acts on any going; has won for an amateur rider; sold out of I. Dudgeon's stable 4,000 gns Ascot May Sales after third start; resold same venue 875 gns in November. *G. Thorner.* –

FITZWARREN 4 ch.c. Busted 134–Dove 92 (Sea Hawk II 131) (1982 12fg 12fg³ 12fg* 12f 12f 1983 16d 12d 14fg) strong colt; should stay 1¾m; blinkered last 2 starts. *G. Balding.* –

FITZWILLIAM (USA) 3 ch.c. Raja Baba–Muriels Dream (Blue Prince 123) (1982 NR 1983 6s) $250,000Y; tall, strong colt; brother to stakes-placed winner, and half-brother to several winners, including smart 1980 Italian 2-y-o 1m winner Panjandrum (by His Majesty); dam, half-sister to smart 6f and 9f winner Double Edge Sword, won over 5f and 6f; looked very green and struggled throughout when last of 9 behind Bold Secret in maiden race at Newmarket in April; sold only 2,400 gns Ascot May Sales. *G. Harwood.* –

FIZZER 3 ch.c. Roi Soleil 125–Caught Speeding (Psidium 130) (1982 8s 8.2s 1983 8v 10.1d 10d 10g 11.7fg 10g 10g) workmanlike colt; probably stays 1¼m; off course nearly 4 months before fourth start; has been tried in blinkers. *R. Hannon.*

FIZZMASTER 3 ch.c. Porto Bello 118–Taranari (Grand Roi 118) (1982 5fg 6v 5s 6g 1983 6s) small, useful-looking colt; sixth of 18 behind Bold and Woolly in handicap at Brighton in May. *P. Ashworth.*

FLAME 2 br.f. Firestreak 125–Chebs Lass 84 (Chebs Lad 120) (1983 5d 6f 7h² 7f 8f) Mar 17; sturdy, compact filly; sister to 3 winners, including middle-distance performer Ridgefield; dam won twice over 7f at 2 yrs; showed ability only when failing by a short head to catch Torski in 8-runner seller at Beverley in July; should be suited by 1m; acts on hard going. *W. Holden.* 49

FLAME BEARER (USA) 2 ch.c. Mr Leader–Celestial Goddess (Pronto) (1983 6f⁴ 7f³ 8s*) May 25; $65,000Y; smallish colt; second foal; dam, unplaced in 11 starts, is granddaughter of outstanding broodmare Grey Flight; improved with each outing, on final appearance winning maiden race at Beverley in September by 2 lengths from Briarean; will be suited by middle distances; probably acts on any going. *H. Cecil.* 87

FLAME LILY 2 ch.f. Dublin Taxi–Twyford Ridge (Schapiro 99) (1983 6d) Apr 28; half-sister to 5f and 1½m winner Comedy Croft (by Comedy Star); dam ran 3 times; unquoted; ran on steadily without being knocked about to finish ninth of 16 in maiden race at Newbury in October. *R. Hannon.* –

FLAMENCO (USA) 3 b.f. Dance Spell–Santiago Sweetie (Boldnesian) (1982 6f* 7g* 7fg* 7g⁴ 1983 7.3s⁴ 8g 8g² 8fg 8s² 8d⁴) strong, robust, well-made filly; second foal; half-sister to a minor winner in USA by Tentam; dam, sister to very smart 1975 2-y-o Bold Laddie, won 6f maiden race at 3 yrs; won 3 races at 2 yrs, including Waterford Candelabra Stakes at Goodwood; ran best races of 1983 when going down by 2 lengths to Royal Heroine in 8-runner Child Stakes at Newmarket in July and by a neck to same filly in 6-runner Sceptre Stakes at Doncaster in September, finishing as though she'd have been suited by a bit further than 1m both times; favourite when 4 lengths fourth of 7 behind Erin's Hope in Desmond Stakes at the Curragh later in September on final start; acted on any going; blinkered third and fourth starts; stud. *I. Balding.* 116

FLAME OF TARA 3 b.f. Artaius 129–Welsh Flame 106 (Welsh Pageant 132) (1982 6f* 6fg* 6d* 5fg⁴ 1983 8s* 7s* 8v⁴ 8f* 10f* 10g² 10fg² 10f) 124
Jim Bolger has made great strides in the last few years and he concluded the 1983 season in second place behind Dermot Weld in the trainers' list in Ireland, just in front of Kevin Prendergast and twenty or so winners ahead of Vincent O'Brien. He has sent out good winners both on the flat and over jumps, but it is his skilful handling of fillies that has attracted particular attention in recent seasons. A filly named My Hollow, who had made an inauspicious start to her career over hurdles with another trainer, was improved to such an extent that she won five races as a five-year-old in 1980, including the Royal Whip Stakes and the Desmond Stakes. The following year the stable had even better fillies in Condessa, winner of the Musidora Stakes and the Yorkshire Oaks and second to

Coronation Stakes, Ascot—Flame of Tara outstays Favoridge (rails) in a close finish.
Magdalena finishes third

Blue Wind in the Irish Guinness Oaks, and Happy Bride, who won the Pretty
Polly Stakes and was second to Tolmi in the Coronation Stakes. And in 1983
Bolger had his strongest hand yet with the formidable pair Flame of Tara and Give
Thanks backed up by the useful German-bred Glasson Lady. Between them they
lifted a high percentage of the top fillies' races run in England and Ireland up to
mid-summer. Flame of Tara won four of her first five races, including the
Coronation Stakes and the Pretty Polly Stakes; Give Thanks won six of her first
seven, notably the Esal Bookmakers Oaks Trial, the Musidora and the Irish Guinness
Oaks; and Glasson Lady won her first three, including the Mulcahy Stakes.

Flame of Tara's two-year-old form was no more than useful, although she won
three of her four races, and she ended the season just outside the top twenty in the
Irish Classification. Her improvement in the spring was quite dramatic, and she was
sufficiently impressive in the Thomastown Castle Stud Race at Phoenix Park and
the Athasi Stakes at the Curragh in April to challenge for favouritism in

Pretty Polly Stakes, the Curragh—another success for Flame of Tara who gives weight to
Ghaiya (rails) and Bay Empress

the following month's Goffs Irish One Thousand Guineas at the Curragh again. A 5/1-chance in a field of eighteen, at only a point longer than the French Guineas winner L'Attrayante, Flame of Tara justified her position as the shortest-priced home-trained runner but was beaten four lengths into fourth behind L'Attrayante, Maximova and Annie Edge; she was running on again at the finish after tending to falter in the heavy going two furlongs or so from home. Conditions could hardly have been more different when Flame of Tara made her first appearance outside Ireland in the Coronation Stakes at Royal Ascot, up against the Guineas third Favoridge, who started hot favourite, the lightly-raced Magdalena and Annie Edge again in a field of six—the smallest since 1971. Flame of Tara put up a high-class and most courageous effort. Sent all out for home at the two-furlong marker with Favoridge pulling over her, she eventually wore Favoridge down and succeeded in holding on by a neck in a fascinating finish. Whilst on the subject of the Coronation Stakes it strikes us as rather odd that the present conditions require Group I winners, which in 1983 included an outsider in Sweet Emma, to carry a 4-lb penalty whereas in the colts' equivalent, the St James's Palace Stakes (also Group 2), all the runners carry the same weight. The Coronation still often attracts one or more of the Guineas winners but the conditions can hardly be said greatly to encourage their participation.

There was talk after Royal Ascot of Flame of Tara's being returned for the King George VI and Queen Elizabeth Diamond Stakes, her trainer reportedly harbouring no doubts about her ability to last the extra half mile. Instead though the remainder of her campaign was restricted to races of a mile and a quarter, a distance that suited her extremely well as things turned out. Back at the Curragh for the Pretty Polly Stakes ten days after the Coronation Stakes she put up another resolute performance to get the better of English-trained Ghaiya, who received 4 lb, by a short head after a prolonged battle. Then, after a longish lay-off, she was brought back in October to finish second to Kalaglow's half-sister Glowing Embers in the ITB Prince's Polly Stakes at Phoenix Park, giving weight all round, and a very close third to Cormorant Wood in the Dubai Champion Stakes

Miss P. F. O'Kelly's "Flame of Tara"

at Newmarket, in which she ran the race of her life. A 25/1-chance in a field of nineteen and up against the toughest opposition she'd ever encountered Flame of Tara travelled strongly in mid-division near the rails until produced with a great challenge from the Dip. She was just getting the worse of a drawn-out battle with Tolomeo when the winner squeezed through near the line to win by a head and a short head, but after a controversial stewards inquiry she was moved up to second. Even now her season wasn't quite over. Three weeks later Flame of Tara was in the United States for the Yellow Ribbon Stakes at Santa Anita, where for the first time in her career she failed to make the frame, coming home only ninth of twelve behind Sangue, last of the four European challengers who were headed by second-placed L'Attrayante. After such an arduous season Flame of Tara needed no excuse, but it turned out that she was coughing badly afterwards.

			Round Table	Princequillo
	Artaius		(b 1954)	Knight's Daughter
	(b 1974)		Stylish Pattern	My Babu
Flame of Tara			(b 1961)	Sunset Gun
(b.f. 1980)			Welsh Pageant	Tudor Melody
	Welsh Flame		(b 1966)	Picture Light
	(br 1973)		Electric Flash	Crepello
			(b 1962)	Lightning

Flame of Tara's sire Artaius, a top-class racehorse and a commendably versatile one, has made a satisfactory, if unspectacular, start to his career at stud: Flame of Tara is his best representative so far and in 1983 his other principal winners in Britain and Ireland were Captivator and the handicapper Littleton Rory. The dam Welsh Flame, a daughter of a lightly-raced half-sister to Derby winner Parthia, was a useful performer who won four times over a mile as a three-year-old for Hobbs but disappointed when seemingly leniently treated in Intermission's Cambridgeshire. She has done extremely well at stud and in 1983 was also represented by the good two-year-old Blaze of Tara (by Nonoalco), in the same ownership as Flame of Tara and also trained by Bolger. Welsh Flame's only other foals both showed decent form, her Rheingold filly Fruition finishing second in the Lupe Stakes and another Nonoalco colt named Nacibi winning over seven furlongs as a two-year-old in France. Welsh Flame was barren in 1982 but she's reportedly carrying again to Artaius. *J. Bolger, Ireland.*

FLAMINGO GARDENS 4 b.f. Ercolano 118–Foolhardy 101 (Sicambre 135) — (1982 9fg 12f 1983 10.2d 13s 12s 12f) lengthy filly; well beaten in varied company; blinkered last 2 starts; sold, reportedly for export to South Africa, 11,500 gns Newmarket July Sales. *J. Etherington.*

FLAMING PEARL 2 b.f. Junius 124–Carol Barnett (Frigid Aire) (1983 6f 6fg) — Mar 14; 4,200F, 8,400Y; rather lightly-made filly; third foal; dam won several times at around 1m in Ireland; no form in maiden events, at Newmarket in September on second outing showing good speed in 29-runner event until beaten and eased right up after 3f; may do better. *M. Jarvis.*

FLAMTEX LAD 6 ch.g. Ribero 126–Island Lore 60 (Court Martial) (1982 NR — 1983 15.5v) no sign of ability on flat though is a winning point-to-pointer; has worn blinkers. *R. Hoad.*

FLASHRAY 5 ch.h. Flashback 102–Dumette 89 (Dumbarnie 125) (1982 10fg 7fg — 1983 10.1d 7s 8fg) poor plater; has been tried in blinkers. *J. Long.*

FLASHY GAL 3 b.f. Continuation 120–Hillset (Hill Clown) (1982 5f 6g 1983 5fg — 5f 5f) leggy, narrow filly; little sign of ability in varied races, including a valuable seller. *J. Hardy.*

FLASHY VYNZ 3 ch.c. Whitstead 125–Noaxe To Grind (The Axe 115) (1982 6f 65 7.2s⁴ 8g 1983 6v 9s³ 12v*) workmanlike colt; has a round action; beat Jay Elle Thaw in good style by 6 lengths in seller at Thirsk in May; sold 6,400 gns afterwards and subsequently raced in Italy, winning at Varese and Milan; suited by 1½m and plenty of give in the ground. *W. H. H. Williams.*

FLATTERY'S CAP 3 b.f. Tarboosh–Flattery (Atan) (1982 7g 1983 7fg 8d) — lengthy, lightly-made filly; behind in maiden and minor events. *Peter Taylor.*

FLECHA 8 ch.g. Duke of Ragusa 120–Zabbotina (Welsh Abbot 131) (1982 NR — 1983 10fg) winning hurdler; poor form on flat, including in a seller; has worn blinkers and bandages; cost 660 gns Ascot May Sales. *M. Chapman.*

FLEDGE 6 ch.g. Sharp Edge 123–Flotsam 67 (Rustam 127) (1982 NR 1983 16s — 10s 10.2g) poor performer nowadays; well beaten in seller final start; cost 1,750 gns Ascot January Sales. *P. Cundell.*

FLEET BAY 3 gr.g. Bay Express 132–Porsanger (Zeddaan 130) (1982 5g⁴ 5f³ 82 d 5f* 6f³ 6g⁴ 1983 5g 6d³ 6s³ 5f 6f* 6f 6d 6fg 6s) lightly-made gelding; won handicap at York in July; stays 6f; acts on any going; often blinkered; hung on first outing and didn't find much on third; sold 9,000 gns Newmarket Autumn Sales. *J. W. Watts.*

FLEET BUILDER 2 ch.g. Monsanto 121–Brush's Choice (Robson's Choice 105) 67 (1983 5v² 5s 5fg² 6g 5fg² 5f⁴ 5f² 5f 5fg) Mar 7; 5,000Y; leggy, quite useful-looking gelding; half-brother to 2 winners, including fairly useful miler Town Farm (by Tycoon II); dam of little account; second in maiden races at Haydock, Edinburgh, Hamilton and Newcastle; form only at 5f; acts on any going; sold out of J. Berry's stable 6,000 gns Doncaster August Sales after seventh start; gelded after final appearance; sent to Singapore. *E. Carter.*

FLEETING KNIGHT 3 b.c. Artaius 129–Fleet Wahine 121 (Fleet Nasrullah) 83 (1982 7g 1983 14f 12f 12g² 12s* 14d³ 14g²) good-bodied colt; ran on strongly to beat Dame Ashfield by 2½ lengths in minor event at Beverley in September; placed in similar races at York and Sandown afterwards, starting well-backed favourite when 1½ lengths second of 19 to Childown on latter occasion; suited by 1¾m; has shown easily best form with some give in the ground. *J. Dunlop.*

FLEETING SHADOW 2 gr.f. Absalom 128–Partridge 65 (Mossborough 126) 69 (1983 5v 5g 5.8g 6f 6fg³ 6fg* 6f³) Mar 11; 800Y; narrow, close-coupled filly; half-sister to 3 winners, including middle-distance performers by Hittite Glory and Silly Season; dam suited by a test of stamina; plater; showed improved form when beating Who Knows The Game by 5 lengths at Haydock in August (no bid); favourite; missed break completely and in circumstances wasn't disgraced when 3 lengths third of 12 to Starjay in selling nursery at Ripon later in the month; will be suited by 7f and 1m; acts well on a firm surface. *M. Hinchliffe.*

FLEETWOOD GIRL 2 b.f. Frimley Park 109–Curry Favour 62 (Negotiation) 63 (1983 5d⁴ 5s 6fg 6f* 6fg³ 6f 6fg) Apr 14; close-coupled, fair sort; half-sister to 1978 2-y-o 5f winner Foul Fella (by Native Bazaar); dam plater; bought in 1,100 gns after winning 9-runner seller at Leicester in July by 2 lengths from The Four Ays; creditable 2¾ lengths third to Benz in 7-runner nursery at Haydock the following month; last subsequently in nurseries at Salisbury (unseated rider and bolted before start) and Windsor; suited by 6f; acts on firm going. *M. Blanshard.*

FLEMING 3 ch.c. Royalty 130–Zulaika 75 (Worden II 129) (1982 6g 1983 12d — 12fg) big, plain colt; soundly beaten in maiden and minor events. *W. Holden.*

FLEUR-DE-CHRIOSE 2 b.f. Dragonara Palace 115–Bodega 87 (Espresso 122) 62 (1983 5f 5f⁴ 5fg 5g 5g 5g) Apr 27; 4,000 2-y-o; rather leggy, close-coupled filly; half-sister to a winner in Denmark and a winning hurdler; dam 6f winner; poor maiden; well beaten in Catterick seller final start; should be suited by 6f; suited by give in the ground; usually blinkered, but ran best race on fourth outing when not. *A. Balding.*

FLEUR DE LYPHARD (USA) 2 b.f. Lyphard 132–Super Flower 64 (Super 73 § Sam 124) (1983 5f 5f² 5f³ 5fg² 5g) Jan 21; $550,000Y; tall, good-topped, attractive filly; half-sister to 4 winners, notably smart 1979 Irish 2-y-o Thousandfold (by Forli) and very smart Faliraki (by Prince Tenderfoot), a sprinter here but a winner over 9f in USA; dam, half-sister to high-class Typhoon, stayed 7f; disappointed badly after second outing; should be well suited by 6f+; best left alone. *J. Dunlop.*

FLEURISTE 2 br.f. Ile de Bourbon 133–Helcia 86 (Habitat 134) (1983 7s) Apr — p 21; rather shallow-girthed filly; fourth foal; half-sister to 3 winners, including useful 1980 2-y-o 6f winner Chirk Castle (by Welsh Pageant); dam runner-up 5 times from 6f to 11.5f; 18/1 and both green and backward, soon pushed along when ninth of 19 behind Ophrys in maiden race at Leicester in October; should do better. *P. Walwyn.*

FLEXIBLE LAD 2 b.c. Ballad Rock 122–Fire Bell 93 (Firestreak 125) (1983 76 6fg³ 6g 6fg) Mar 30; IR 21,000Y; sparely-made, fair sort; half-brother to several winners, including fairly useful 1981 Irish 2-y-o sprinter Ormsary (by Jukebox); dam half-sister to very useful stayers Khalekan and Aegean Blue; favourite; 4¼ lengths third of 22 to Chicago Bid in maiden race at Newmarket in July, only indication of merit; weakened very quickly after showing excellent speed 4f in £5,300 maiden event at York the following month on next appearance. *J. Winter.*

FLIGHT OF TIME 3 b.g. Stradavinsky 121–Kelso's Niece (Herbager 136) (1982 70 6f 6g 5fg⁴ 1983 8s* 8d⁴ 7fg 8f 8fg² 8.3fg* 8fg 8g 10fg 8fg) neat gelding; good mover; apprentice ridden when winning handicaps at Ripon in May and Windsor in July, latter by 5 lengths; below form afterwards, although by no means disgraced eighth start; suited by 1m; probably acts on any going; sweating and unimpressive final outing. *B. Hills.*

FLIGHT PLAN 2 b.c. Try My Best 130–Exemplary 106 (Sovereign Lord 120)   **86 p**
(1983 6g²) Feb 18; 68,000Y; closely related to prolific Italian winner Vipera Bionda (by Northfields) and half-brother to another winner in Italy; dam best at 5f; 5/4-on, made a promising debut when head second to Omar Mukhtar in maiden race at Naas in November (caught near finish after leading 2½f out); should stay 1m; will leave this form behind at 3 yrs. *D. O'Brien, Ireland.*

FLOATING 2 b.f. Rapid River 127–Royal Bally 71 (Bally Russe 113) (1983 6f 6fg   **41**
8.2g 6fg) May 22; smallish, lengthy filly; second foal; dam won over 10.8f and was quite a useful hurdler; bad plater. *W. A. Stephenson.*

FLOATING JOKER 2 b.c. Dance In Time–Pardina 98 (Pardao 120) (1983 5fg   **84**
5.3f² 6f⁴ 7f² 7h² 6fg⁴ 7f 7d) Apr 28; 8,400Y; lengthy colt; good walker; half-brother to several winners here and abroad, including fair 1979 2-y-o 5f winner Swinford Rose (by Upper Case); dam won from 6f to 1¼m; runner-up in maiden race at Brighton, £3,300 event at York and nursery (beaten short head) at Beverley; below form, apprentice ridden, last 3 starts; suited by 7f; acts on firm going; blinkered sixth outing; sold 7,000 gns Doncaster November Sales. *P. Kelleway.*

FLOATING PETAL 3 ch.f. Wollow 132–Fallen Rose (Busted 134) (1982 6g   **79**
1983 7s² 8.5d² 10.2f 8f⁴) small, well-made filly; runner-up in maiden races at Newmarket in April and Epsom (flashed tail and put head in air under pressure) in June; promises to stay 1¼m (ran below her best over trip, but was staying on at finish); best form with some give in the ground; sold 4,000 gns Newmarket December Sales. *G. Wragg.*

FLODABAY 2 b.g. Bay Express 132–Rosaberry 94 (Rockefella) (1983 6fg) Apr   **–**
23; 16,000Y; good-topped gelding; brother to 6f winner Dewberry and half-brother to 2 winners; dam placed over 7f at 2 yrs; unquoted, ninth of 23 in maiden race at Newmarket in October; subsequently gelded. *R. Armstrong.*

FLORIDA DANCER 4 b.f. Realm 129–Cambus O'May 100 (Sing Sing 134)   **–**
(1982 6fg 1983 7s 6g) good sort; soundly beaten in varied company. *Peter Taylor.*

FLORIDA FALLS 2 ch.c. Miami Springs 121–Polly Flinders (Polly's Jet) (1983   **73**
5f 5fg* 5f⁴) Apr 12; IR 10,000F, 7,200Y; workmanlike colt; closely related to a winning hurdler by Northfields and half-brother to several winners, including Suspicious Polly (by Above Suspicion), the dam of Irish 1000 Guineas winner Prince's Polly; dam won from 7f to 9f in Ireland; justified favouritism by 3 lengths from Fleet Builder in maiden race at Hamilton in June; soon pushed along when poor last of 4 in small race at Edinburgh the following month; will be suited by 6f+; sent to Singapore. *C. Thornton.*

FLORIDA SON 4 b.c. Busted 134–Peach Stone (Mourne 126) (1982 10.5f 12f   **89**
14fg 8s 1983 8d 10v* 12g⁴ 10v 10.2v 10s* 8f 8d² 8.2s 8fg) big, strong colt; poor walker and bad mover; won handicaps at Newcastle in April and Epsom in June; one of only 3 runners to race on far side when beating Elmar 5 lengths in 15-runner Daily Mirror Handicap on latter; suited by 1¼m but appears not to stay 1½m; needs some give in the ground and revels in the mud; inconsistent. *J. Hanson.*

FLORITA 3 br.f. Lord Gayle 124–Golden Moss 91 (Sheshoon 132) (1982 7g³ 1983   **75**
8v³ 8f 9fg² 7s³ 8.2g³ 9d³ 8f) compact, workmanlike filly; quite a modest maiden; will be suited by 1¼m. *G. Pritchard-Gordon.*

FLORI WONDER 3 b.f. Floriana 106–Greek Wonder 52 (Veiled Wonder) (1982   **–**
6f 6f 6g 7g² 8g 8d 1983 8.5v 7v 10.2g 10fg 6fg 8.3f 10d) workmanlike filly; bad mover; plater; stays 1m; suited by some give in the ground. *R. Atkins.*

FLOTANGO 3 ch.f. Gay Fandango 132–Flotilla 64 (Alcide 136) (1982 NR 1983   **–**
10.1fg 6fg 8fg) IR 3,100Y; fourth foal; dam staying half-sister to good 1964 2-y-o Leonardo; behind in varied races; sold 480 gns Ascot October Sales. *D. Wilson.*

FLOUT (USA) 3 ch.c. Bold Bidder–Manta (Ben Lomond) (1982 6f 1983 7d 10s²   **92**
10g* 12f⁴ 10.1fg² 11.5f⁴ 10.1fg) strong, good sort; has a badly scarred off-fore; smoothly won maiden race at Sandown in May; in frame in King George V Stakes (Handicap) at Royal Ascot, minor event at Windsor and small handicap at Sandown afterwards; gives impression 1¼m is his trip; probably acts on any going; shade disappointing final start. *J. Tree.*

FLOWER DELL 3 b.f. Wolver Hollow 126–Floraventure 89 (Floribunda 136)   **72**
(1982 NR 1983 6g 8f 8.2fg 7f³ 6fg² 6f³ 6s 6fg) 31,000Y; wiry filly; half-sister to 3

winners, including useful Irish 5f performer Solo Venture (by Sing Sing); dam, a sprinter, is half-sister to Italian Oaks winner Claire Valentine; placed in handicaps in summer, on last occasion giving impression she'd be suited by return to 7f or more; possibly unsuited by soft going; didn't run up to her best in blinkers final start. *J. W. Watts.*

FLOWERFARM 3 b.g. The Brianstan 128–Hope Baggot (Hopeful Venture 125) (1982 6f⁴ 6f⁴ 7g 6f⁴ 7g 1983 8d 9v³ 9.4d 13d 11fg 15f⁴) leggy, lightly-made gelding; plating-class maiden; stays at least 9f; blinkered last 2 starts; sold to M. Bradley 880 gns Doncaster October Sales. *D. Smith.* —

FLOWER PRINCE 4 ch.c. Sassafras 135–Jasminia 92 (Zeddaan 130) (1982 10v² 12g* 12d² 12g* 15g 12.5g 13.5g 1983 12s* 12f² 12.5g³ 12.5fg² 13.5fg 12d4) big, rangy ex-French colt; fourth foal; dam, half-sister to 1967 Derby third Dart Board, ran well over 1¼m on only start; convincingly beat Un Etendard by 5 lengths in 90,000 francs event at Saint-Cloud in June; ran well afterwards to be placed in La Coupe at Chantilly (2 lengths second to Zalataia), Prix Maurice de Nieuil at Saint-Cloud (4 lengths third to Load the Cannons) and Prix de Reux at Deauville (short-neck second to Oak Dancer); soundly beaten in Grand Prix de Deauville in August and £3,000 event at York in October on last 2 starts; best at around 1½m though stays further; acts on any going; trained most of season by J. Cunnington, jnr. *R. Hern.* 115

FLOYD 3 ch.c. Relko 136–Honey Palm 86 (Honeyway 125) (1982 NR 1983 12v⁴ 10d 10s 10.1fg* 10f⁴ 10d⁴ 13.3d 12.2g) quite a well-made colt; keen walker; half-brother to 3 winners, including fair 1m and 1¼m winner Honegger (by King's Troop); dam a sprinter at her best at 2 yrs; showed rather mixed form, and was 25/1 when making virtually all to beat Master Carver by ½ length in 14-runner maiden race at Windsor in August (first outing for new trainer); stays 1¼m; trained early in season by P. Cole. *M. Madgwick.* 73

FLUCTUATE 2 b.f. Sharpen Up 127–Hay Reef 72 (Mill Reef 141) (1983 5g 5g*) Apr 30; tall, sparely-made filly; first foal; dam, 1¼m winner, is closely related to Irish 2000 Guineas winner Wassl; won 16-runner maiden race at Newbury in October by 2 lengths from Tahiche; likely to show improvement at 6f+. *F. J. Houghton.* 87 p

FLUELLA 3 br.f. Welsh Pageant 132–Ya Ya 84 (Primera 131) (1982 6d 7g 1983 8v³ 9f 10d⁴ 10.6g 14g 12.2g²) tall, leggy, angular filly; has a round action; beat Tivian by 3 lengths in maiden race at Beverley in September; second in handicap at Warwick the following month; seems to stay 1¾m; may well need some give in the ground; sold 20,000 gns Newmarket December Sales. *G. Wragg.* 74

FLUID MECHANICS (USA) 3 ch.f. Sir Ivor 135–Envidiada (Con Brio 121) (1982 6g⁴ 7d⁴ 7g 1983 8s* 9s* 10d) strong, lengthy filly; made virtually all when winning maiden race at Leicester in March; beaten a head by Pomade in minor event at Wolverhampton later in month but was rallying gamely when squeezed well inside last furlong and placings were reversed; well beaten in Pretty Polly Stakes at Newmarket in April on only subsequent start; will probably stay 1¼m; acts well on soft going. *M. Albina.* 85

FLUKE (USA) 3 b.f. Sham–Scoring Play (Reviewer) (1982 7g 1983 8v 8g³ 9fg* 8d 10fg4 9.2f) big, good-topped filly; having first race for 3 months when making fairly hard work of beating Florita by ¾ length in a 7-runner maiden race at York in September; ran well afterwards when 3½ lengths fifth of 15 behind Mighty Fly in Gilltown Stud Stakes at the Curragh and close-up ninth of 18 behind Royal Heroine in Prix de l'Opera at Longchamp in October, but got bit warm and looked short of pace when fourth behind Soldier Ant in £5,900 handicap at Ascot in between; promises to stay beyond 1¼m; evidently unsuited by heavy going; changed hands 900,000 francs at Arc de Triomphe Sale before final outing. *J. Dunlop.* 91

FLY DIRECT 2 b.c. Direct Flight–Cassiar 84 (Connaught 130) (1983 7fg 6g 6g) Mar 11; second foal; half-brother to 3-y-o Conaught Light (by Lightning); dam, daughter of very speedy Fortune's Darling, won over 11.5f; behind in minor and maiden events. *M. Haynes.* —

FLY FREE (FR) 2 b.c. Blakeney 126–Blue Linnet 96 (Habitat 134) (1983 5v 6d⁴ 7f 7h) Apr 15; close-coupled, quite attractive colt; second foal; dam won 4 times over 5f; showed only a little ability, including in a nursery; sold BBA 950 gns Newmarket Autumn Sales. *A. Ingham.* 58

FLYHOME 2 ch.c. Home Guard 129–Western Gem 86 (Sheshoon 132) (1983 6fg) Apr 21; 17,000Y; tall, useful-looking colt; second foal; dam, half-sister to very 76 p smart animals Western Jewel and Mr Fluorocarbon, was placed over 7f and 1½m; 20/1, never-dangerous seventh of 11 to Miss Silca Key in £6,000 maiden race at Ascot in September; will stay beyond 6f; should improve. *P. Cundell.*

FLYING EASY   3 b.f. Swing Easy 126–Flying Sovereign 74 (Sovereign Bill 105)   – (1982 5fg 6fg 7f 1983 10s 11.7v 10s 12f) plain filly; good walker; soundly beaten in maiden races and a handicap. *R. Hannon.*

FLYING FANTASY   3 b.f. Habitat 134–Formentera (Ribot 142) (1982 5fg⁴   – 1983 8g 7fg 10f 10.4g 12d) small filly; disappointing maiden; promises to stay 1m; pulled hard third start and wore blinkers on fourth (looked light). *H. Candy.*

FLYING FRIEND (USA)   3 br.f. Accipiter–Friendly Neighbour (Deck Hand)   – (1982 6fg 1983 12f 12fg) well-made filly; last or last-but-one all outings, including at Hamilton. *F. J. Houghton.*

FLYING GAYLE   3 b.c. Lord Gayle 124–Wood Grouse 56 (Celtic Ash) (1982 NR   **79** 1983 6v 8f⁴ 8fg² 10f 10.8d 12d³) IR 10,000F, 35,000Y; big, strong colt; half-brother to 3 winners, including very smart French miler Pampabird (by Pampapaul); dam, half-sister to Pitskelly, stayed 13f; in frame in maiden and minor events; stays 1½m; acts on a firm surface but is possibly better suited by some give in the ground; sold to Susan Piggott Bloodstock 16,500 gns Newmarket Autumn Sales. *G. Lewis.*

FLYING LANCER   3 gr.c. Runnymede 123–Torlonia 63§ (Royal Palace 131)   – (1982 5d 7g 8s 1983 8v² 10.1fg 8f) sturdy, workmanlike colt; plater; promises to stay 1¼m; blinkered once; exported to Malaysia. *Mrs R. Lomax.*

FLYING OATS (USA)   3 b.c. Delta Flag or Empery 128–Kelly Keim (Needles)   **61** (1982 NR 1983 11f 15.5f³ 17.1h 17.1g) $15,000Y; big, rather leggy colt; half-brother to 3 winners, including stakes-placed Needle Me On (by Executioner); dam stakes-placed winner at up to 9f; well beaten after finishing third in maiden race at Folkestone in August; sold 3,200 gns Newmarket Autumn Sales. *G. Harwood.*

FLYING OFFICER   6 b.g. Warpath 113–Rosie Wings 102 (Telegram II 120)   **78** (1982 12f* 15g 14f 20fg 16d* 20.4g² 16fg⁴ 16d* 16.9fg 16.1s 14s³ 18s 1983 17.1v* 18.8v* 20fg 16fg* 17f* 19f) neat, rather lightly-made gelding; good walker; had a good year, winning handicaps at Bath and Warwick in May, Lingfield in June and Wolverhampton in July; stays very well; acts on any going; has won for an apprentice; tailed himself off early on third start and finished well beaten final outing in July. *M. Pipe.*

FLYING PALACE   3 b.c. North Stoke 130–Splosh (Silly Season 127) (1982 6g   **71** 1983 8v 8g 10fg³ 10f 11.5f² 11g 12d 12g) medium-sized, lengthy, fair sort; keen walker; ran creditably in handicaps in summer but was rather disappointing last 3 starts; stays 11.5f. *R. Williams.*

FLYING POSTMAN   2 ch.c. Tachypous 128–Royal Message 57 (Town Crier   – p 119) (1983 6f) Apr 30; 3,700F, 6,000Y; third foal; half-brother to French 3-y-o Sans Commission (by Averof); dam, winner over 6f, is half-sister to smart middle-distance filly Reprocolor; 10/1, 11 lengths seventh of 13 to Cutting Wind in maiden race at Yarmouth in August; may do better. *L. Cumani.*

FLYING SCOTSMAN (DEN)   3 b.c. Tower Walk 130–Scotch Thistle 73   **81** (Sassafras 135) (1982 6f 5f 6g 5f 5d² 5s 1983 6v 8v 8.2g² 8f* 8.2fg² 8f 7.2fg 8f 8.2fg² 10fg 8d⁴ 8g 7f) strong, workmanlike colt; won handicap at Ripon in June and was second 3 times at Hamilton; stays 1m; acts on any going. *R. Hollinshead.*

FLYING TENDERFOOT   2 b.c. Prince Tenderfoot 126–Bracken Girl   **77** (Skymaster 126) (1983 6fg 6g⁴ 7fg 6f 8.2h 8fg 8.2fg 7d²) May 4; IR 13,500Y; workmanlike colt; half-brother to winning sprinter Spanish Point (by Malacate); dam, placed in Ireland, is half-sister to useful milers Golden Mean and Owen Anthony; quite moderate; best effort when 1½ lengths second of 17 to Paramaribo under 2 lb overweight in nursery at Wolverhampton in October; stays 7f; appears to need some give in the ground, and acts well on a soft surface; usually blinkered. *D. H. Jones.*

FLYING TONY   2 ch.c. On Your Mark 125–Prima Bella 76 (High Hat 131) (1983   **71** 7fg 6f 7f⁴ 7fg 7g 7fg³ 8fg 8fg 10fg) May 26; IR 19,000Y; strong, good-bodied colt; brother to prolific Italian winner Erlinda; dam stayed well; in frame in maiden race at Brighton in August and valuable seller at Newmarket in September; also ran well when blinkered in 1¼m maiden race at Nottingham in October; suited by 1¼m; acts on firm going; sold 525 gns Goffs November Sales. *R. Sheather.*

FLYING TROVE (USA) 2 ch.c. Super Concorde 128–Miss Treasure (Candy Spots) (1983 9s*) Apr 8; $100,000Y; brother to stakes winner Jetta J, and half-brother to 5 winners, one stakes placed; dam, 2-y-o 5f winner, is half-sister to dam of Glint of Gold and Diamond Shoal; ran on inside final furlong to land the odds by 1½ lengths from Sally's River in minor event at the Curragh in October; will stay 1¼m+; promising. *D. O'Brien, Ireland.*   **87** p

FLY ME (FR) 3 ch.f. Luthier 126–On The Wing (Tanerko 134) (1982 NR 1983 12v³ 10v* 10.5fg⁴ 12g² 9.2f² 10.5g*) 700,000 francs Y (approx. £64,000); tall filly; sister to Grand Prix de Paris winner Galiani and half-sister to winners by Green Dancer and Royal and Regal; dam won over 11f; returned from a 3-month lay-off in excellent form and, after finishing second in 90,000 francs race and 18-runner Prix de l'Opera at Longchamp (went down by 1½ lengths to Royal Heroine after being given a lot to do in latter), was successful in 10-runner Prix de Flore at Saint-Cloud in October, beating Allicance in very good style by 3 lengths; had won a maiden race at Longchamp and been in frame at Saint-Cloud and Chantilly (Prix de Royaumont) in first half of season; stays 1½m, but better form at shorter distances; acts on any going. *A. Fabre, France.*   **116**

FOCHE 2 gr.c. Godswalk 130–All at Sea 107 (Sea Hawk II 131) (1983 6d⁴ 6fg²) Mar 21; 21,000Y; big, rangy colt; first foal; dam, half-sister to very smart Miletus, won over 1½m and 2¼m; 2 lengths second of 20 to Godstone in £4,400 maiden race at Lingfield in July; will be well suited by longer distances. *P. Cole.*   **78**

FOGGY BUOY 9 b.g. Foggy Bell 108–Chancer 78 (Chamier 128) (1982 NR 1983 12f²) strong gelding; fair performer over jumps; ran creditably on debut on flat to be 1½ lengths second to Misty Halo in amateur riders race at Beverley in July (33/1); will stay further. *P. Calver.*   **65**

FOIL 'EM (USA) 3 ch.f. Blade–Spookem Joanne (Skookum) (1982 6d* 1983 6f 6f 7.2fg⁴ 6f⁴ 7.2g 5g 5g 5fg) quite a useful sort; good walker; fourth in handicaps at Haydock and Hamilton in August; seems to stay 7f; occasionally blinkered. *M. Jarvis.*   **64**

FOLGOET (FR) 3 b.f. Pharly 130–Renee Martin (Crepello 136) (1982 NR 1983 8g² 7fg 8f 8f⁴ 7fg³) 66,000Y; light-framed filly; closely related to a moderate animal by Lyphard; dam, half-sister to Italian Derby winner Ruysdael II, won in Italy at 3 yrs; rather an inconsistent maiden; stays 1m; slowly away final outing. *H. T. Jones.*   **75**

FOLKLAND 2 b.f. Auction Ring 123–Oriental Star 94 (Falcon 131) (1983 7f 6fg 7f 7f⁴ 7f) May 21; second foal; dam won 7 times from 5f to 1½m; 1½ lengths fourth of 16 to Fair Trader in seller at Chepstow in September; will stay 1m; blinkered final appearance. *B. Hills.*   **62**

FOLKLAW 5 ch.g. Song 132–Judiciary 74 (Above Suspicion 127) (1982 NR 1983 11g 8.2f) big gelding; poor maiden; has twice worn blinkers. *T. Barnes.*   **–**

FOLLOW ME FOLLOW 2 br.f. Wollow 132–Gay Shadow 99 (Northfields) (1983 5g* 6fg³ 5f 5s) Feb 18; lengthy filly; good walker and mover; third foal; half-sister to a winner in Sweden; dam, winner over 5f and 6f at 2 yrs, is half-sister to very smart sprinter Honeyblest; 4-length winner from Pictorial in 15-runner maiden race at Newbury in June; ran well in good-class fillies events on next 2 starts; out of her depth in Flying Childers Stakes at Doncaster in September; stays 6f. *J. Winter.*   **92**

FOLLOW THAT CAB 2 ch.f. Dublin Taxi–Senna (Sica Boy 132) (1983 5f 5fg 6fg 7f² 8g 8d) Apr 21; 3,500F; good-bodied filly; half-sister to several winners, including sprinter My Jem (by My Swallow); dam won over 11f in France; showed form only when going down by a head to Shamrock Princess in 9-runner seller at Catterick in August; suited by 7f. *P. Felgate.*   **57**

FOLLOW THE STARS 3 ch.f. Sparkler 130–St Citrus 108 (Relic) (1982 5g 5f³ 7.6v 6g² 1983 8d 8.5d* 8f² 8f 8fg³ 8d) good-topped filly; won maiden race at Epsom in June; good third to Habitassa in handicap at Newmarket in October, but disappointed only subsequent start; will probably stay 1¼m; yet to show she can handle really soft going, but acts on any other; sometimes sweats up. *D. Elsworth.*   **86**

FOLLY HILL 3 b.g. Moulton 128–Molly Polly (Molvedo 137) (1982 NR 1983 10s 10.1fg³ 10.1f⁴ 10fg* 11.7fg 11.7fg⁴ 11g² 10g*) half-brother to 3 winners, including useful 1974 2-y-o Fair Parrot (by Sahib); dam won 5 races in Italy; won maiden race at Pontefract in August and 15-runner handicap at Sandown in October, beating Ven Matrero by a length on latter course (25/1-shot); stays 11f; acts on firm going; apprentice ridden with overweight at Sandown. *J. Bethell.*   **89**

FONABY 3 b.g. Lord Henham 110–Millipede (Military 112) (1982 NR 1983 10.2v — 10fg 11s*(w.o.) 12g) light-framed gelding; first foal; dam of no account; showed a little ability before walking over in seller at Hamilton in October (no bid); well behind in similar race afterwards; trained part of season by J. Leigh. *J. Etherington.*

FONDU 3 ch.c. Nonoalco 131–Moon Min (First Landing) (1982 7fg 8fg 8.5s 8d[4] — 1983 11.7s 11.7v 8d) 20,000F, 26,000Y; compact ex-Irish colt; raced under wrong pedigree all outings, with dam incorrectly shown as Habanna (by Habitat); half-brother to quite useful Irish 7f and 1¼m winner Millrock (by Bustino); dam unraced half-sister to very smart 1963 American 2-y-o Traffic; showed some ability in Ireland as a 2-y-o (blinkered final start); in rear in maiden races at Bath and trainers race at Kempton in spring; not certain to stay 1½m. *C. Nelson.*

FOOLISH FLING 2 b.f. Imperial Fling 116–Grandee Ann (Cyane) (1983 5d 5s 51 5d[4] 5d 5s) May 17; strong filly; half-sister to 1m winner Maris Quest (by Windjammer); dam won 6 times at up to 7f in USA; plating-class filly; raced in Italy after fifth outing. *H. Blackshaw.*

FOOLISH WAYS 4 b.c. Comedy Star 121–Susie Hall (Gold Rod 129) (1982 10s 65 8.2fg 8f[4] 8f[4] 8f[2] 8.2fg* 7fg[4] 8.2g* 8.2g* 8.2fg[3] 9g 1983 8s 8.2fg 8f 8.2f 8f 8.2f[4] 8f[2] 8g 7g 7.2g 8.2s 7fg) strong, deep-girthed colt who carries plenty of condition; stays 1m well; acts on firm going; blinkered final start; has won 3 times at Hamilton. *A. Balding.*

FOOL'S PLEASURE 2 b.f. Idiot's Delight 115–Evada 78 (Eborneezer 105) — (1983 6f) May 11; tall, leggy filly; seventh reported foal; dam staying maiden; 25/1 and backward, no show in 20-runner maiden race at Newmarket in July. *N. Guest.*

FOOT PATROL 2 br.c. Daring March 116–Molly Polly (Molvedo 137) (1983 5d 88 5fg 6fg 7g 6fg*) Apr 6; shallow-girthed colt; excellent mover; half-brother to several winners, including useful 1974 2-y-o Fair Parrot (by Sahib); dam won 5 races in Italy; won 16-runner claiming nursery at Newmarket in October by 2 lengths from Hellcatmudwrestler, and was claimed to join W. O'Gorman's stable; apparently better at 6f than 7f; acts on a firm surface. *J. Bethell.*

FOOTWORK (USA) 3 ch.g. Dance Spell–Laraka (Impressive) (1982 7fg[3] 7g 59 7fg 7d 1983 6f 7h 7h 7f 7f[3]) sturdy, short-legged gelding; disappointing maiden; stays 7f; has given trouble at start and is doubtful temperamentally; sold 5,000 gns Newmarket September Sales. *F. J. Houghton.*

FORABELLE (USA) 2 b.f. Broadway Forli–Esprit Belle (Ack Ack) (1983 5s[3] — 5s) Mar 24; $47,000Y; lengthy, quite attractive filly; half-sister to a winner by Drone and to fair 1981 2-y-o maiden Hunt The Thimble (by Turn and Count); dam once-raced daughter of smart 1969 American 2-y-o Belle Noire; poor form in May in minor event (second favourite) at Goodwood and maiden race (favourite) at Haydock. *B. Hills.*

FORAGE 2 ch.c. Orange Bay 131–Forhat (Habat 127) (1983 6d) Feb 4; first foal; — dam out of half-sister to 2000 Guineas third Balustrade; 10/1, behind (slowly away) in 17-runner maiden race at Newbury in October. *P. Walwyn.*

FORDANESS 2 b.g. Fordham 117–Martianess 101 (Red God 128§) (1983 5v 5fg) — Jan 31; 5,000Y; well-made, quite attractive gelding; half-brother to minor winners here and abroad; dam speedy sister to high-class 5f to 7f winner Red Alert; showed up to halfway in maiden race at Kempton in May and minor event at Windsor in June. *C. Horgan.*

FORDEL 8 b.g. Tyrant–Fig Roll (Hard Tack 111§) (1982 NR 1983 12f 12f) poor — maiden on flat though has won selling hurdles; has been bandaged; cost 500 gns Doncaster March Sales. *Ronald Thompson.*

FORELIE 2 br.f. Formidable 125–Forgotten Dreams 82 (Shoemaker 121) (1983 88 6f* 6fg 8g 7fg) May 6; big, strong, rangy filly; fourth foal; half-sister to 3-y-o My Top (by High Top), winner of Italian Derby, and another winner; dam won 3 times over 2m; won 9-runner Fenwolf Stakes (newcomers event) at Ascot in June by 1½ lengths from Lightning Girl; poor form subsequently, including in a nursery. *R. Laing.*

FORESTERS BOY 6 br.g. Swinging Junior 118–Wilden (Will Somers 114§) (1982 36 7fg 7f 8f 7f 1983 8d[3] 12.2g[3] 8d) leggy, lop-eared gelding; plating-class maiden; stays 1½m; probably acts on any going; effective with and without blinkers. *N. Crump.*

FOREST OF DEAN 2 gr.c. Tap On Wood 130–Betsy Ross 100 (Petingo 135) 88 (1983 6fg 7fg[4] 8g*) Feb 11; strong, close-coupled colt; good mover; third foal;

half-brother to 5f and 7f winner Aldern Stream (by Godswalk) and a winning hurdler; dam useful at up to 1¼m; short-priced favourite, won 10-runner maiden race at Sandown in October by ½ length from Bassett Boy; promises to stay 1¼m. *H. Candy.*

FOREST TRACK 2 b.f. Track Spare 125–Forest and Vale 84 (March Past 124)   62
(1983 5v 5s 5f⁴ 6f 5.8h 5h 5g 5fg) Mar 26; rather lightly-made filly; first foal; dam 2-y-o 6f winner; plating-class maiden; stays 6f; acts on firm going. *J. Cann.*

FOREVER MARY 3 ch.f. Red Alert 127–Calamarie (Deep Diver 134) (1982 6fg   –
6g² 5v² 1983 6s⁴ 5d 5f) lengthy filly; good walker; sprint maiden; acts on heavy going; swerved start and was quickly tailed off when blinkered on final start (June); sent to USA. *W. O'Gorman.*

FOREVER PROMISE (USA) 3 b.f. Vaguely Noble 140–Summertime Promise   –
(Nijinsky 138) (1982 NR 1983 8f) first foal; dam very smart stakes winner of 10 races at up to 1m; favourite when out of first 10 of 17 behind Noble Blood in maiden race at Warwick in August, only outing. *G. Harwood.*

FOREWARN 2 b.c. Fordham 117–Mark My Word (On Your Mark 125) (1983 7g   –
8g 8d) Mar 21; 7,000Y; strong, sturdy colt; fourth foal; half-brother to 3-y-o 9f seller winner Maujendor (by Rose Laurel) and French 9f winner Jetstream (by Direct Flight); dam placed over 4.5f at 2 yrs in France; soundly beaten in maiden and minor events. *J. Dunlop.*

FORGE CLOSE 2 b.c. Swing Easy 126–Sweet Relief 90 (Sweet Revenge 129)   81
(1983 5d 6d⁴ 5.8g² 7f 7g* 7f* 7d 7fg³ 7.3g³ 7d 6g) Mar 25; 1,600F, 1,700Y; light-framed colt; second produce; dam won three 6f races; successful in seller at Wolverhampton (bought in 1,700 gns) in July and nursery at Lingfield in August; will probably stay 1m; suited by sound surface; sweated up badly at Wolverhampton. *M. Blanshard.*

FORK BALL (USA) 3 b.c. Little Current–No No Nanette (Pass The Word)   80
(1982 second in USA on only start 1983 8v⁴ 13s* 16f 14fg³ 14s) good-quartered, attractive colt; seventh foal; half-brother to 6 winners in USA, including Happy Olympian (by Fleet Kirsch), a minor stakes winner as a 2-y-o; dam, minor winner at up to 1m, is half-sister to 2 stakes winners; second in USA on only start as a 2-y-o; won maiden race at Dundalk in May; 8/1 when never-dangerous ninth of 17 behind Santella Man in Queen's Vase at Royal Ascot the following month; stays 1¾m; yet to show he can act on really firm ground, but seems to act on any other; off course 3 months before final start (last-but-one in Irish St Leger). *D. K. Weld, Ireland.*

FORLORN PRINCE 4 br.g. Forlorn River 124–Martinique II (Relko 136) (1982   –
NR 1983 12.2f) big gelding; fifth foal; brother to 1979 3-y-o 6f winner Lorna Crique; dam ran once; tailed off in maiden race at Catterick in July. *W. Clay.*

FORMIDO 2 b.f. Formidable 125–Tick Tock Baby (Dr Fager) (1983 6g 5fg 6d)   –
Apr 23; 19,000Y; half-sister to Irish 1½m winner Rough Justice (by Welsh Pageant) and 2 winners in France, including middle-distance filly Tripolitaine (by Nonoalco); dam lightly-raced daughter of 1000 Guineas winner Fleet; no worthwhile form in modest company. *J. Benstead.*

FORM MASTER 2 b.g. Music Boy 124–Klontina (Klondyke Bill 125) (1983 5v   73
5f⁴) May 25; fourth foal; brother to 1981 2-y-o 5f winner Scottish Boy; dam in rear in maiden races; creditable fourth from bad draw in maiden race at Carlisle in June. *D. Smith.*

FOR SURE FOR SURE 2 ch.c. Northfields–Catherine Linton (High Echelon)   86
(1983 7d² 8.2g* 8.2s² 10fg) Apr 3; IR 26,000F; rather leggy, fair sort; third produce; closely related to modest 1m winner Perplex (by Be My Guest) and half-brother to a winner in Italy; dam, who never ran, comes from same family as Malinowski, Gielgud, Try My Best and El Gran Senor; landed the odds in 10-runner maiden race at Hamilton in September; stays 1¼m; probably acts on any going; consistent. *C. Nelson.*

FORT LAUDERDALE (USA) 3 br.g. Holy War–Sis Gallamar (Royal   –
Dorimar) (1982 6fg 1983 5fg 5f 7g 7g) lengthy, good-topped gelding; towards rear in varied races. *M. Francis.*

FORT NAYEF 3 b.c. Sharpen Up 127–Sacred Way 88 (Milesian 125) (1982 7g   80
1983 8s² 9v* 8.5v 8f) tall, quite attractive, long-striding colt; ran with plenty of promise before landing the odds in maiden race at Newcastle in April; ran poorly at Epsom later in month (reportedly returned bleeding from the mouth) and was off

course until August, when in rear in handicap at Newbury (dropped out after pulling very hard); gives impression he'll be suited by further than 9f; shows a bit of knee action and probably needs some give in the ground. *J. Dunlop.*

FORTUNE'S GUEST 3 ch.c. Be My Guest 126–Fortune's Lady 93 (Fortino II **94**
120) (1982 8fg 1983 10f4 10f 14f2 14f3 16h3 17f* 16g 18.8f* 17d2 16fg 16fg 18fg 12d) IR 40,000Y; big, good-bodied, quite attractive ex-Irish colt; half-brother to 2 winning 2-y-o's, including fairly useful 1976 5f performer Spring Dive (by Deep Diver); dam won twice at around 1m; improved and was successful in minor event at Wolverhampton (by 6 lengths) and handicap at Warwick in August; seventh of 28 to stable-companion Bajan Sunshine in Tote Cesarewitch at Newmarket in October on penultimate outing; suited by good test of stamina; yet to race on really soft going but acts on any other; hung badly and ran in snatches fifth start, and subsequently wore a hood or blinkers; often apprentice ridden (sometimes unable to claim). *R. Simpson.*

FORTYSECOND STREET 2 ch.f. Sharpen Up 127–Dare Me 101 (Derring-Do **94**
131) (1983 5f* 5f4 5g 6fg) Mar 3; sparely-made, quite attractive filly; first foal; dam won three 5f races from 5 starts; won 9-runner maiden race at Newbury in July in good style by 3 lengths from Woodfold; generally had lot to do subsequently, and on final outing was by no means disgraced though only ninth of 12 in William Hill Cheveley Park Stakes at Newmarket; stays 6f; yet to race on soft surface. *R. Hern.*

FORWARD (USA) 4 b.c. Caro 133–Tipping Time (Commanding II) (1982 8.2fg **111**
8g 10f2 12f* 12f3 13g* 12f 12fg4 13d 12g 1983 12v2 11v* 12d 12f 15fg* 16g3 13s* 12fg4 12fg) well-made colt; good walker; has a round action; very useful handicapper; won at Newbury in May, Ayr in July (beat Weavers' Pin 3 lengths in Tennent Trophy) and Ayr again in September (showed a good turn of foot to beat Master Boatman 1½ lengths in Bogside Cup); suited by a test of stamina; acts on any going; suited by a galloping track. *J. Dunlop.*

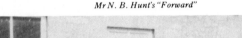

Mr N. B. Hunt's "Forward"

FOR YOUR EYES 3 b.f. Gay Fandango 132–Miller's Lass 103 (Mill Reef 141)   **75**
(1982 6fg 7fg² 7f 1983 7v² 8s 7s² 7f 6fg 6f* 7f 6g) quite attractive; good-topped
filly; well beaten after winning handicap at Folkestone in August; bred to stay at
least 1m; acts on any going; blinkered nowadays. *P. Walwyn.*

FORZANDO 2 b.c. Formidable 125–Princely Maid 71 (King's Troop 118) (1983 **122**
5d² 6s 6fg 6fg* 6f* 6f² 6f* 6fg* 6fg*)
'Like father like son' fits the two horses Formidable and Forzando well.
Although Formidable is bigger than his son each resembles the other strongly,
being good-quartered, robust and almost identically marked. The two horses'
racing careers as two-year-olds are also strikingly similar: Formidable, after losing
his first three starts, improved so dramatically that he won all his last five, proving
himself one of the best six-furlong performers with victories in both the Mill Reef
and Middle Park Stakes; Forzando, also beaten in his first three races, won five of
his last six starts, eventually showing form which would have seen him go close in
the Middle Park had he been able to run.
Unfortunately Forzando's connections hadn't entered him for the Middle Park,
nor for any other of the big autumn events. Most of these races, including the
Middle Park, closed on July 6th by which time Forzando had been beaten twice,
first at Newmarket, when a very promising second to Maajid in May, and then at
Epsom, when a most disappointing favourite for the Woodcote Stakes on soft
ground on Derby Day. His third defeat, when only eighth to Chicago Bid in a
Newmarket maiden race, came on July 7th and must have reassured his
connections that they had made the right decision in leaving him out. However,
Forzando soon showed himself to be very much on the upgrade, and before the
month was out as well as winning a maiden race at Pontefract and a small race at
Redcar he had finished a creditable second to Shoot Clear in the valuable Tolly
Cobbold Trophy nursery at Newmarket. Forzando was giving 3 lb to Shoot Clear, a
task whose magnitude became apparent a month later when Shoot Clear accounted
for the likes of Satinette and Pebbles in good style at Goodwood. Forzando wasn't
seen out again until September, returning to carry big weights to success in
nurseries at Haydock, Doncaster and Newmarket. His first two wins showed him to
be still progressing rapidly but even his greatest admirers must have been
surprised by his splendid effort in the Martini Trophy at Newmarket, two days after
the Middle Park. He had top weight of 9-7, 12 lb more than the favourite Alpine
Strings, another rapidly-improving colt who had won his last three races, the latest
at Ascot by three lengths, and 5 lb more than Kings Island, a colt who had himself
come within a head of defying top weight in a well-contested nursery on his last
appearance. Forzando beat them in sparkling style, coming through strongly to
lead in the Dip and then sprinting away up the final hill to win easing up by three
lengths from Alpine Strings. Forzando was clearly very much at home on the fast
ground here and it seems significant that he raced exclusively on a sound surface
after his poor display at Epsom.
Forzando is a splendid advertisement for his sire who met with plenty of
success with his first runners in 1983: Carabineer, Electrifying, Forelie, Visible
Form, Neeyef and Triagonal took his total to seven winners in Britain while two
others won in France and another in Italy. Naturally there was plenty of demand for
Formidable's yearlings at the 1983 sales, five of them, including a brother to
Forzando who fetched 115,000 guineas at the Highflyer Premier Sales, selling for
over 100,000 guineas. Forzando had failed to find a buyer when sent up a year

*Martini Trophy Nursery, Newmarket—the tough Forzando bursts clear to win easing up
from Alpine Strings*

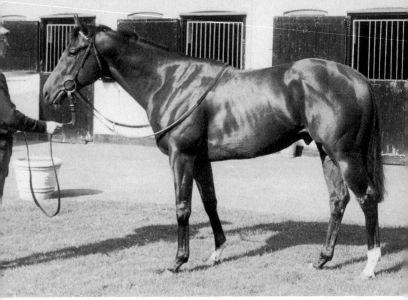

Mr T. G. Warner's "Forzando"

earlier. Forzando's dam Princely Maid, a winner over five furlongs as a two-year-old, has now had eight foals to race, all winners—a fine achievement, although it must be said that some of the eight had to be sent as far afield as Austria and Malaysia before managing to win. Best of Forzando's predecessors were the very useful fillies Pennina (by Great Nephew) and Lady Constance (by Connaught), both seven-furlong winners who showed their best form at shorter distances;

Forzando (b.c. Feb 11, 1981)	Formidable (b 1975)	Forli (ch 1963)	Aristophanes / Trevisa
		Native Partner (b 1966)	Raise A Native / Dinner Partner
	Princely Maid (b 1967)	King's Troop (b 1957)	Princely Gift / Equiria
		Moss Maid (gr 1959)	Mossborough / Jules Magic

Pennina's five sprint successes at two included one in the Chesters Stakes, while the high point of Lady Constance's career was her close third to Haveroid and Godswalk in the William Hill Sprint Championship. Forzando has already shown he's better suited by six furlongs than five and his trainer believes he'll stay seven furlongs, possibly a mile, a view we concur with. We look forward to seeing how Forzando fares against the established leaders of his generation—we're sure he'll acquit himself with credit. *M. Jarvis.*

FOSCARINI 2 gr.c. Rusticaro 124–Busted Flush 103 (Busted 134) (1983 6g 7f³ 7fg² 7g² 8d²) Apr 10; 17,000Y; half-brother to very smart middle-distance winner Guns of Navarone (by Bold Lad, Ire) and smart 1979 staying Irish 2-y-o Cobblers Cove (by Realm), subsequently a winner over 1¼m; dam, half-sister to many winners, won over 6f at 2yrs; found one too good for him on three occasions, running well under top weight when neck second to Martina's Pearl (pair clear) in apprentice nursery at the Curragh in September on final start; should do better over longer distances. *C. Collins, Ireland.* **91**

FOSTON BRIDGE 2 b.f. Relkino 131–Freia 91 (Rheingold 137) (1983 7fg³ 7f **68**
7fg 8g) Mar 23; 19,000Y; quite a well-made filly; second foal; dam, 1m winner, is
sister to Lancashire Oaks winner Rhein Bridge and half-sister to very smart
Connaught Bridge; plating-class maiden; lacks pace, and will be suited by
1¼m+. *J. Etherington.*

FOUDROYER 3 ch.f. Artaius 129–Foudre 76 (Petingo 135) (1982 NR 1983 8f –
8.2g) sparely-made filly; first foal; dam, half-sister to smart animals Lighted Glory
and Torus, won over 1¼m; showed a bit of promise when fifth of 16 behind Silk
Sash in minor event at Salisbury in June; soundly beaten only subsequent outing
(October). *F. J. Houghton.*

FOUNTAIN GIRL 2 ch.f. Monsanto 121–Arethusa 94 (Acropolis 132) (1983 6fg –
7g) Mar 24; strong, good-bodied filly; good walker; half-sister to winners here and
abroad, including 3-y-o Sparks (by Hot Spark), a winner at up to 1m; dam stayed
1½m; behind in September in good-class events at York and Newbury won
respectively by Seattle Siren and Mahogany; sold 2,000 gns Ascot November
Sales. *B. Hobbs.*

FOUR CHARACTERS 4 br.g. Reformed Character 107–Blase Rose (Blue Cliff **76**
85) (1982 NR 1983 10f* 12fg² 12f) IR 1,000Y, IR 1,000 3-y-o; quite useful-looking
gelding; fourth live foal; half-brother to a winning point-to-pointer; dam half-sister
to Hennessy Gold Cup winner Red Candle; 33/1 when narrowly winning 15-runner
maiden race at Pontefract in June; just failed to get up when head second to odds-on
Misty Halo in minor event on same course in August; ran moderately only
subsequent start; suited by 1½m and will get further; yet to race on an easy
surface. *R. Baker.*

FOUR FATHOMS 9 ch.g. Gulf Pearl 117–Capule (Middleground) (1982 NR –
1983 15.8d 12d) poor handicapper nowadays; effective at 1½m and stays well;
acts on any going; has worn bandages. *J. Parkes.*

FOUR OF EACH 3 ch.g. Roan Rocket 128–Painter's Bay 75 (Monet 127) (1982 –
NR 1983 12d 16v 12fg 17f 13.8g) seems of little account. *N. Bycroft.*

FOURTH OF APRIL 2 b.f. Mister Tudor–Bontet (Bounteous 125) (1983 5f 5f –
5f 7g) Apr 4; short-coupled filly; bad mover; half-sister to 1m seller winner Frank
Stewart (by Grey Mirage); soundly beaten in maiden races and a seller; has worn
bandages; probably of no account. *R. Ward.*

FOXLEY MEL 7 b.m. Owen Anthony 102–Westerlands Prism (Primera 131) –
(1982 NR 1983 10.2g 16g 12f 11g 10.6s) of little account; has sweated up badly;
sold out of H. Beasley's stable 620 gns Ascot August Sales after third start. *M.
James.*

FOXTROT TANGO 5 ch.g. Patch 129–Gallant Breeze (Mongo) (1982 9f 10fg² **56**
12d 9f 10d⁴ 13f 10d⁴ 14v 16s 1983 16f⁴ 12f* 12h⁴ 16h² 16g²) strong gelding;
always prominent when beating Tudor Sandy easily by 6 lengths in handicap at
Laytown in August; in frame in 3 handicaps afterwards, including 2 at Chepstow
later in August; stays 2m; acts on hard going; suited by forcing tactics. *Miss J.
Morgan, Ireland.*

FOXY QUEEN 4 b.f. Simbir 130–Riboellina (Ribero 126) (1982 10.1fg 1983 10v –
10.1f) of little account; dead. *G. Blum.*

FOZZE 2 ch.c. Malinowski 123–Exmoor Lass 86 (Exbury 138) (1983 7fg 7f⁴ 6f³ **73**
7.2fg 7fg 6s) Mar 29; IR 5,800Y; robust, useful-looking colt; brother to American
3-y-o Amazing Amanda, and half-brother to a winner in South Africa; dam 2-y-o 7f
winner; quite a modest maiden; in frame at Catterick and Nottingham in July; stays
7f; acts on firm going. *G. Huffer.*

FRANK BERRY 5 ch.h. Lorenzaccio 130–Bora Bora 91 (Hethersett 134) (1982 –
7g 8g² 7g³ 7.6f 8.2fg 7f 7fg 7g² 8s 1983 8s) lengthy horse; good walker; plater;
stays 1m; acts on any going, except possibly soft; best in blinkers; sold to O.
Carter 940 gns Ascot November Sales. *V. Thompson.*

FRANTONIOS 3 ch.g. Thatch 136–Slavissima (Sea Hawk II 131) (1982 8g 8g³ **83**
1983 10v³ 14g* 16f*) rather lightly-made, useful-looking gelding; has a round
action; won last 2 of his 3 races, both in June, namely maiden race at Yarmouth
and minor event at Chepstow; beat Westview by 2½ lengths in former and Hi
Easter readily by a length in latter; stays very well; seems to act on any going;
sent to Singapore. *J. Hindley.*

FRASASS 6 b.g. Sassafras 135–Desert Flame 96 (Baldric II 131) (1982 NR 1983   **69** §
9s 12.3v³ 12fg 13g² 15fg 18f 20.4g 13s 12g 15fg) strong, compact gelding; stays
well; seems to act on any going; has been taken down early; temperamental. *D.
Chapman.*

FRAYLAND 3 b.f. Sallust 134–Flying Escape 74 (Hook Money 124) (1982 5f 5f   –
5v 1983 6s 5.3f 5fg 5f 5g 5g) compact filly; towards rear in maiden races and
handicaps. *J. Benstead.*

FRED 2 b.c. Kala Shikari 125–Royale Final (Henry the Seventh 125) (1983 5v 5v³   **45**
6g 5.1f³ 5.8h 6f³ 6fg 6f 7fg 5g 6g) May 18; very small colt; poor plater; stays 6f;
blinkered final outing. *A. Bailey.*

FREDERIC THE GREAT 3 b.g. Ballymore 123–Bold Words (Bold Ruler)   –
(1982 7g 7d 1983 10s) smallish, good-bodied gelding; last in maiden races; sold
500 gns Newmarket Autumn Sales. *M. Ryan.*

FREE AGAIN 2 b.c. Song 132–Katira 83 (Paveh 126) (1983 5v 5v 5fg 6fg 5f 7f   **53**
7.6fg) May 16; 4,200Y; deep-girthed, close-coupled colt; closely related to a
winner in Belgium and half-brother to 3-y-o 6f and 7f winner Some Yoyo (by
Lochnager); dam, half-sister to high-class sprinter Royben, won over 2m;
plating-class maiden; stays 7f; blinkered fourth and sixth outings. *M. Haynes.*

FREE AS AIR 2 b.c. Free State 125–Whitestake 74 (Compensation 127) (1983   **75**
7fg 6f 7fg) Apr 20; 4,500Y (privately); strong, good-bodied colt; half-brother to
several winners here and abroad, including useful sprinter Palmvinnia (by Royal
Palm); dam won 5f seller at 2 yrs; quite a moderate colt; showed up in big fields of
maidens at Newmarket first and third outings; suited by 7f. *B. Hobbs.*

FREEBIE 3 ch.f. Free State 125–Mehir 71 (King's Company 124) (1982 6g 6fg 6g   **63**
7g 5v 6g 1983 6v 7d² 6v* 6f 6g 8g 8d 8fg 7fg³ 7.6d⁴ 7s) stocky, short-legged filly;
second in seller at Newmarket before winning apprentice handicap at Folkestone
in May; promises to stay 1m; acts on any going, except possibly very firm. *M.
Haynes.*

FREEDOM GLORY 3 ch.f. Hittite Glory 125–Liberty Light 82 (Henry the   –
Seventh 125) (1982 5f³ 5f² 5f 5fg⁴ 5f 5fg 6g 6g⁴ 6f⁴(dis) 6fg 6d⁴ 8.2fg⁴ 8fg⁴ 7fg*
8s 1983 8s 7d 7d³ 7fg 7f 6f 8.2fg) neat filly; plater; ran best race fourth start;
best form at 7f; seems to act on any going, with possible exception of soft;
occasionally blinkered. *T. Fairhurst.*

FREEDOM OF FLIGHT 3 b.g. Wolver Hollow 126–La Creperie 70 (Crepello   –
136) (1982 NR 1983 8.5v 7.6v 6s 8fg 10g 12fg) 16,500Y; quite an attractive
gelding; second foal; half-brother to 1½m winner Brandon Creek (by Be My
Guest); dam stayed well; little worthwhile form, although was second favourite for
a handicap on fourth start. *J. Sutcliffe.*

FREEFALL 3 ch.f. Air Trooper 116–Rota 58 (Reliance II 137) (1982 6fg 1983 8v   –
7fg 6fg) big, useful-looking filly; little worthwhile form in maiden and minor races;
sometimes blinkered; sold 1,150 gns Ascot October Sales and resold 700 gns same
venue in December. *W. Wightman.*

FREEFLOW (USA) 2 b or br.g. Giboulee–Karen Mulholland (Pago Pago) (1983   **77**
6d 6g* 6f 6f⁴ 7h³ 7fg 8f³ 8h³) Mar 29; $16,000Y; robust gelding; third foal;
half-brother to a winner; dam sister to Pago Hop, winner of stakes races over 4.5f
and 1m; won 13-runner maiden event at Hamilton in June; not disgraced
subsequently in minor events and nurseries; stays 1m; occasionally blinkered;
gelded after final appearance. *S. Norton.*

FREE GUEST 2 ch.f. Be My Guest 126–Fremanche (Jim French) (1983 7g 7d*   **94** p
7fg*) May 2; quite attractive, well-made filly; good mover; third foal; half-sister to
2 winners in Italy, notably good 3-y-o middle-distance filly Fresh (by High Top);
dam won over 9f in Italy; won maiden race at Brighton in September and £5,400
nursery (getting up close home after wandering badly) at Newmarket in October;
will be suited by 1m+; likely to make a useful 3-y-o. *L. Cumani.*

FREE LIGHT LASER 2 b.f. Free State 125–Abrill (Laser Light 118) (1983 5f   **58**
6fg 5fg³ 6f³ 6f 6fg 8d² 5g) May 2; sturdy, dipped-backed filly; third foal;
half-sister to 1982 2-y-o 5f winner Peg's Petal (by Ardoon); dam never ran;
ridden by girl apprentice at overweight, placed in sellers at Ayr, Ripon and
Warwick; stays 1m; yet to race on very soft going but acts on any other; slowly
away final outing. *J. Gilbert.*

FREEMASON 2 b.g. Free State 125–Red Velvet 114 (Red God 128§) (1983 8f)   –
May 6; tall, unfurnished gelding; brother to 1¼m winner Fox and half-brother to 4

winners, including very useful 1974 2-y-o Red Cross (by Crepello) and useful 1¼m winner Red Rufus (by Busted); dam at her best at 2 yrs; 9/1 and backward, soon pushed along when behind in 14-runner maiden race at Leicester in November; subsequently gelded. *P. Walwyn.*

FREE PRESS 4 b.g. Free State 125–Miss McWorden 75 (Worden II 129) (1982   **98** 10s* 10g* 10.6fg* 10fg 10f³ 10.1fg² 1983 10v 10v 11.1v⁴ 10d* 10f* 12g 12f⁴ 12f⁴ 10g⁴ 12fg* 12fg²) lengthy gelding; has a round action; fairly useful handicapper; won at Redcar in May (Zetland Gold Cup by 2½ lengths from Ski Run), Salisbury in June and Ascot in September (accounted for Nikiforos by ¾ length in Red Deer Stakes); also ran well to be 1½ lengths second to Asir in William Hill November Handicap at Doncaster; stays 1½m; acts on any going; often sweats up; has won for an apprentice; behaved rather mulishly sixth outing. *I. Balding.*

FREE RANGE 4 gr.f. Birdbrook 110–Micky Goleah (Quorum 126) (1982 5h 6g   **73** 5g 6fg* 5fg² 5g* 6fg² 5g 5fg 5g⁴ 6g 5fg 1983 6fg 5f 6fg⁴ 6h² 5f³ 6f⁴ 6f 5f⁴ 7h* 7g* 7fg 7fg² 6g³) leggy, lengthy filly; former plater; won handicaps at Chepstow in August and Lingfield in September; suited by 6f and 7f; form only on a sound surface; good mount for an inexperienced rider. *J. Holt.*

FRENCH ART 11 gr.g. Articulate 121–Moselle Mist (Sovereign Path 125) (1982   – NR 1983 15.8fg) winning jumper; of little account on flat. *N. Bycroft.*

FRENCH GEMMA 3 b.f. Manado 130–French Cracker (Klairon 131) (1982 7f   – 8fg 8fg 1983 12.2d 10v 12s 7d 8g 16g) small, rather leggy, narrow filly; poor form in varied company, including selling; blinkered second and fourth outings. *P. Kelleway.*

FRENCH GENT 4 b.c. Sassafras 135–Nom de Plume 70 (Aureole 132) (1982   **82** § 12.3g 12fg³ 8fg² 10g⁴ 12g 10g⁴ 1983 10.2v 9s⁴ 10s 10.6fg 12g³ 14fg 12fg 10.5d 12fg 10fg) compact colt; doesn't always impress in paddock; useful handicapper on his day but is unreliable and inconsistent; suited by middle distances and some give in the ground (appears not to stay 1¾m); ran atrociously when blinkered final start; a strong puller; sometimes taken down early. *S. Norton.*

FRENCH GREY (USA) 3 gr.g. Al Hattab–Francie T (Grey Dawn II 132) (1982   – 8s 8s 1983 12v 12v 14g) well-made, robust gelding; soundly beaten in maiden events (blinkered second start); trained by H. Candy part of season; sold 1,000 gns Ascot September Sales. *G. Thorner.*

FRENCH NEPHEW 2 ch.c. Great Nephew 126–French Fern 118   – p (Mossborough 126) (1983 7d 8g) June 8; 9,200Y; lengthy, good-bodied colt; half-brother to numerous winners, including Gold Cup winner Shangamuzo (by Klairon); dam won 1960 Ribblesdale Stakes; not fully wound up, no worthwhile form in maiden events at York in August and Ayr (weighted of 18) in September; will be better suited by 1¼m+; likely to improve. *Miss S. Hall.*

FRENCH PLEAT 3 b.f. Take a Reef 127–Boudoir 95 (Klairon 131) (1982 6g⁴ 6f³   **73** 7fg³ 7d² 1983 10fg 8f⁴ 8d²) lightly-made, racy filly; didn't recover her 2-y-o form, but wasn't disgraced when second in minor event at Brighton in September; should stay 1¼m; sold 2,600 gns Newmarket December Sales. *B. Hobbs.*

FRENCH TOUCH 6 ch.m. Dieu Soleil 111–Fabric 77 (Sheshoon 132) (1982 6g⁴   **48** 5fg 6f 5f* 7g 5g⁴ 5fg 1983 6d* 6v 5d² 6g 5f 5f³ 5fg² 5f 5f 5g 5s 5d) strong mare; plater; bought in 1,150 gns after winning at Pontefract in April; stays 6f; acts on any going. *A. Balding.*

FRIDAY STREET 4 ch.g. Town Crier 119–Honey Palm 86 (Honeyway 125)   – (1982 7fg 7.3fg 6f² 7f³ 7d⁴ 10.2g⁴ 8.3g 8.3g 1983 10s 6v 7.6fg) quite attractive gelding; showed no form at 4 yrs; promises to stay 1¼m; seems to act on any going; has run respectably when sweating up. *R. Smyth.*

FRIENDLY BOBBY 3 b.g. Coded Scrap 90–Friendly Jester 90 (Be Friendly   **69** 130) (1982 6f 6fg 5f* 5g 5g⁴ 5d² 5g 1983 5s³ 6v⁴ 5fg 5s⁴ 5g³ 5fg² 5fg 5f 6f 6f 8d 7g) big, strong, lengthy, good-quartered gelding; best form at 5f; acts on any going; ran moderately in apprentice event third start; sometimes blinkered. *T. Fairhurst.*

FRIENDLY HENRY 3 ch.g. Be Friendly 130–Henry's Lady 64 (Henry the   – Seventh 125) (1982 5d 5g 8s 1983 10h 16d) big, plain, good-bodied gelding; poor walker; in rear in maiden races and a handicap. *W. Wharton.*

FRIENDLY LASS 3 ch.f. Be Friendly 130–Friston Mist (Silver Cloud 121) (1982   – 5g 1983 6v 7fg 6g) small, workmanlike filly; behind in varied company. *P. Mitchell.*

FRIESTON FLIER 2 ch.g. Swing Easy 126–Pams Gleam 86 (Sovereign Gleam   59
117) (1983 5d 5fg 5f⁴ 5fg* 6f 6h² 6f) Apr 18; 1,300Y; workmanlike gelding; first
foal; dam, very genuine handicapper, won at up to 1¼m; plater; successful in
6-runner race at Ayr (no bid) in July; stays 6f; goes well on hard ground; none too
well away third and fourth starts; ran badly in blinkers final appearance. *A.
Balding.*

FRIMLEY PARK ROW 2 b.c. Frimley Park 109–Frimley Street (Crooner   –
119) (1983 6fg 5g) May 27; 340 2-y-o; good-topped colt; first foal; dam ran only
once; in rear in October in seller (missed break) at Newmarket and maiden race
(last of 14) at Warwick. *D. Leslie.*

FRISKY WHARF 2 ch.c. Julio Mariner 127–Noirmont Girl 95 (Skymaster 126)   93
(1983 7f 7f* 8f* 8s) May 3; 19,000F; small, lightly-made colt; half-brother to 5
winners, including very useful 1977 5f performer Noiritza (by Young Emperor);
dam ran only over 5f; won twice in August, 15-runner maiden event at Brighton by
2 lengths from Bassett Boy, and 6-runner nursery at Warwick by 3 lengths from
Seattle Rose under 9-7; stays 1m well; acts on firm going. *J. Dunlop.*

FROGMOOR 2 b.c. Tickled Pink 114–Free Girl 70 (Free Boy 96) (1983 5g 6d   61 §
5.1f² 5f 5.3f 5f⁴ 7.6fg 5fg) Apr 9; 6,400Y; robust colt; shows some knee action;
poor walker; first foal; dam won sellers from 1m to 11f and also won over hurdles;
1½ lengths second of 8 to Sams Wood in claiming race at Yarmouth in July, easily
best effort; only fourth when favourite for seller at Windsor the following month;
should stay 6f; best run on firm going; blinkered second and sixth outings;
unreliable. *N. Callaghan.*

FROGMORE SWEET 3 ch.f. Morston 125–Sweet Relief 90 (Sweet Revenge   37
129) (1982 5fg 5f 5g 7f 10d 1983 11.7s 16s 12v 10.8fg 10f 13.8f³) neat filly; poor
plater; probably stays 1¾m. *R. Thompson.*

FRONTLET 3 b.f. Moulton 128–Facade 99 (Double Jump 131) (1982 5fg 5g 5fg   –
5fg 5fg 6g 6fg 7fg² 7g⁴ 1983 12g 8.2g 8f) compact filly; should stay beyond 1m;
blinkered once in 1982; sold 540 gns Ascot 2nd June Sales. *Mrs N. Smith.*

FROSTYCARO 2 gr.c. Rusticaro 124–Frosty Stare (Targowice 130) (1983 6fg)   72 p
Apr 22; 26,000Y; first foal; dam, half-sister to very useful animals Frigid Aire and
Barclay Joy, was fairly useful winner over 5f and 7f in Ireland; 33/1, 7½ lengths fifth
of 10 to Innamorato in maiden race at Brighton in October; will be suited by 7f+;
should improve. *C. Brittain.*

FRUITBERRY 3 ch.f. Filiberto 123–Wimberry 78 (Hotfoot 126) (1982 6g 6g³   45
7f⁴ 8.2fg 1983 8v 9f² 12fg) lightly-made filly; plater; should stay 1¼m+; acts on
any going; sold 350 gns Ascot October Sales. *P. Rohan.*

FUBYMAM DU TENU (FR) 3 ch.c. Funny Hobby 126–Tamam (Blockhaus   119
125) (1982 8v* 1983 11v* 12s* 11s⁴ 12s³ 15g² 15s³ 12s 14g) lightly-built colt;
half-brother to 4 minor winners in France; dam never ran; a smart staying 3-y-o
who was in frame in 4 good races at Longchamp, Prix Noailles, Prix Hocquart,
Grand Prix de Paris and Prix de Lutece; clear second-best when going down by 2
lengths to Yawa in Grand Prix in June (off course nearly 3 months afterwards);
had earlier won his first three races, newcomers event at Maisons-Laffitte as a
2-y-o and minor events at Maisons-Laffitte again and Saint-Cloud; suited by a test
of stamina; yet to race on a firm surface; below his best last 2 starts. *J. de
Chevigny, France.*

FUEGO DIABLO 6 br.g. Sparkler 130–Black Fire 92 (Firestreak 125) (1982   –
NR 1983 17f) poor maiden. *P. Bevan.*

FULAASA PRINCE 2 b.c. Free State 125–Tribal Princess 90 (Tribal Chief 125)   –
(1983 7g 7g) Apr 5; 8,000Y; tall colt; first foal; dam best over 5f at 2 yrs; remote
sixth in October maiden races at Leicester and Lingfield. *G. Pritchard-Gordon.*

FULL BRIGADE 3 b.c. Full of Hope 125–Leaplet (Alcide 136) (1982 7d 7f 8s   53
1983 8s 8s² 10v² 10s 10.1fg 12f 10g² 10d 10fg) lengthy colt; poor walker; second in
3 sellers, best efforts; stays 1¼m; trained by R. Hannon until after second start.
R. Howe.

FULL CIRCLE 3 ch.f. Condorcet–Contourno (Continuation 120) (1982 NR 1983   –
7d 7s 7fg 12.3fg) IR 3,000Y; quite an attractive, lengthy filly; half-sister to fairly
useful 1975 2-y-o 5f to 1m winner Shukran (by Illa Laudo); dam unraced half-sister
to Queen's Vase winner Tara Brooch; has shown signs of a little ability in varied
company, including selling; trained by H. Candy first start. *N. Tinkler.*

FULL OF DREAMS 2 ch.g. Maystreak 118–Panda's Gambol 65 (Richboy 117)   –
(1983 5s 5v 6fg 6f 8fg 6fg) May 4; 400Y; short-coupled gelding; third foal; dam won

over 1½m; beaten some way in varied company, mainly selling; blinkered first and fourth outings and swerved start on second. *R. Hobson.*

FULL OF RUM 2 b.f. Swing Easy 126–Tudor Sea (Welsh Pageant 132) (1983 6g 6fg 5fg* 6fg 5g³ 6fg) Feb 28; 2,000Y; lightly-made filly; good walker; first foal; dam, from good family, never ran; plater; well-backed favourite, led inside final furlong to win 18-runner event at Ripon (no bid) in August by ½ length from Peter's Kiddie; stays 6f. *I. Walker.* **62**

FULL OF SPEED 2 ch.c. Full of Hope 125–Queen of the Realm 81 (Realm 129) (1983 6fg) May 9; 3,000Y; second foal; dam winning 5f performer; 50/1, behind in 20-runner maiden race at Lingfield in July. *D. Weeden.* **–**

FULL OF STARS 3 b.c. Tennyson 124–Full of Courage (Bold Ruler) (1982 9d⁴ 8s* 1983 12v⁴ 10.5f* 10d 12.5fg² 12.5f² 12s³ 12d³ 12g* 10g) tall, rangy colt; half-brother to 2 winners, including very smart 1975 French staying 2-y-o Four Spades (by Sassafras), subsequently successful in USA; dam lightly-raced daughter of champion American 2-y-o and 3-y-o filly Doubledogdare; won 90,000 francs event at Maisons-Laffitte in June easily by 6 lengths from Vilagro, after making all, and Grand Prix de Bordeaux in November by a length from So Good (with English-trained New Coins 3 lengths further away in third); ran well in between when second twice at Deauville (beaten length by Esprit du Nord in Prix de Menneval on first occasion) and when third to Sagace in Prix Niel and Prix du Conseil de Paris, both at Longchamp; will probably stay 1¾m; acts on any going, with possible exception of heavy; consistent (unlucky in running when behind final start). *F. Boutin, France.* **118**

FULL RAINBOW (USA) 3 b.c. Forli–Loop (Round Table) (1982 7g³ 8g² 8s* 8d² 1983 8f* 8f² 8f³ 8.5f³) good-topped, quite attractive colt; led 1½f out and stayed on strongly to beat Riverside Artist and Tetron Bay by 1½ lengths in quite valuable handicap at Sandown in July; placed at Yarmouth, Goodwood and Epsom afterwards, travelling like a winner until coming off bridle at Goodwood; stays 1m; acts on any going; sometimes sweats up; blinkered last 2 starts. *M. Stoute.* **92**

FULVIO (USA) 3 b.c. Full Out–Instant Beauty (Pronto) (1982 7f⁴ 7d⁴ 6v⁴ 1983 10s 10s 8g 9s* 8g³) strong, well-made, quite attractive colt; 5-length winner of maiden race at Hamilton in October; promises to stay 1¼m; suited by some give in the ground; blinkered last 2 outings; sold to J. Jenkins 10,500 gns Newmarket Autumn Sales. *P. Walwyn.* **77**

FUNDA 2 br.c. Persian Bold 123–Catchatartar 82 (Tamerlane 128) (1983 5g 7g) Mar 5; 5,000Y; closely related to a winner in Austria and half-brother to numerous winners, including Premier Harde (by Hardicanute), a smart winner at up to 11f in France; dam 2-y-o 5f winner; in rear in October in maiden auction race at Warwick and minor event at Chepstow; sold 500 gns Doncaster Autumn Sales. *M. McCormack.* **–**

FUN GALORE (USA) 2 b.c. Banquet Table–My Malissa (The Axe 115) (1983 5s³ 6s 5g* 6g* 6ff 6fg 6d² 6d²) Mar 21; $30,000Y; strong, useful-looking colt; not a good walker; third foal; half-brother to a winner; dam unraced half-sister to smart 8.5f stakes winner Innuendo; won minor events at Lingfield in June and July, on second occasion battling on gamely to get up close home and beat Pacific King by a length; second in 2 nurseries subsequently, going down by only a head to Redhouse Charm in £4,300 event at Newbury in October on final start; suited by 6f and some give in the ground; spoilt chance by stumbling at start sixth outing. *R. Akehurst.* **99**

FUNNY REEF (FR) 3 b.f. Mill Reef 141–Fancy's Child (Nijinsky 138) (1982 NR 1983 7d³ 10d³ 10.2v* 12fg³ 12g⁴ 12fg 10f³ 10s) rangy, attractive filly; has a nice, long stride; first living foal; dam, who never ran, is out of half-sister to very good animals Jaipur and Rare Treat; quickened clear in last 2f and beat Dazari in good style by 3 lengths in 13-runner minor event at Doncaster in May; in frame in Ribblesdale Stakes at Royal Ascot (2½ lengths third to High Hawk), Lancashire Oaks at Haydock (6 lengths fourth to Give Thanks) and Virginia Stakes at Newcastle (7 lengths third to Cormorant Wood) afterwards; stays 1½m; acts on any going. *F. J. Houghton.* **107**

FUNNY SPRING 8 b.g. Rheingold 137–Lotus 79 (Aureole 132) (1982 10s* 10f³ 10g 10d 1983 10v 10v 10s 10g 10.2f) stocky gelding; carries a lot of condition; fair handicapper at his best; below form in 1983; best form at up to 1¼m; acts on any going, but is well suited by soft; genuine but needs strong handling; trained by G. Pritchard-Gordon first start. *L. Cumani.* **–**

FUNTLEY 3 b.g. Streak 119–Belinda Pocket 84 (Pampered King 121) (1982 5g⁴ 5fg 5fg 6d* 7f 6fg 7d 1983 7v 8.2f 8.2h 6f) big, workmanlike gelding; poor performer nowadays; stays 7f; appears to act on any going; sometimes bandaged. *B. Palling.* **–**

FURRY FRIEND (USA) 3 b.f. Bold Bidder–Funny Cat (Tom Cat) (1982 6g – 1983 7s 10.6g) strong, lengthy, short-legged, attractive filly; showed promise as a 2-y-o but didn't show much worthwhile form in 1983. *R. Hern.*

FURZY LEAZE 2 b.f. Reform 132–Shineberry 93 (St Paddy 133) (1983 6fg) Apr 2; half-sister to 2 winners in Italy and another in Argentina; dam stayed 1½m; weak in the market, in rear in 13-runner maiden race at Leicester in October; will need further. *P. Walwyn.*

FUTURE LAW 2 b.c. Hittite Glory 125–Liberty Light 82 (Henry the Seventh – 125) (1983 5v 6g 6f 7g 5f) Mar 2; 6,000Y; strong, burly sort; brother to 1982 2-y-o 7f seller winner Freedom Glory; poor form in maiden and minor events; dead. *T. Fairhurst.*

FUTURE SPA 4 b.c. Ballymore 123–Breakage (Breakspear II) (1982 10s² 12g⁴ **95** 11.5fg⁴ 13d* 14s⁴ 1983 12d 13.3v² 16.1v* 16f 16g) big, workmanlike ex-Irish colt; good mover; beat Crusader Castle a length in 5-runner minor event at Haydock in May; had stuck on well though no match for winner when 6 lengths second to Ore in £3,900 event at Newbury previous start; stays 2m; revels in the mud. *C. Brittain.*

FYEDD 2 b.c. Shirley Heights 130–Aries (Acropolis 132) (1983 6d 6d) May 1; – 24,000F, 45,000Y; half-brother to several winners, including smart 1m to 1¼m performer Air Trooper (by King's Troop); dam, from excellent family, never ran; behind in October in minor event (swerved start) at Lingfield and maiden race (last of 17) at Newbury; likely to need 1¼m+. *J. Benstead.*

G

GABBLE 2 gr.f. Town Crier 119–Stuff and Nonsense 86 (Crooner 119) (1983 6f 6d **71** 5fg 5fg) Mar 29; sparely-made filly; first foal; dam best at 1¼m; showed early speed in varied company, on final start 7 lengths last of 6 to Meis El-Reem in minor event at Doncaster in October. *B. Hobbs.*

GABITAT 5 ch.h. Arch Sculptor 123–Golden Hostess (Kythnos 126) (1982 6f* **119** 6g* 6f 6f 6f 6d 6d³ 6g 5v 1983 6g 6v 5d 6f* 7f⁴ 6f² 6fg* 6fg) useful-looking horse; has been hobdayed; half-brother to 2 winners by Virginia Boy, including fairly useful 1975 2-y-o 5f winner Hotcakes; dam placed over 5f at 2 yrs in Ireland; smart performer; excelled himself on sixth and seventh starts in August, going down by a head to Maximova in Prix de Meautry at Deauville and decisively beating Favoridge by 4 lengths in Goldene Peitsche at Baden-Baden; had earlier won Home Ales Gold Tankard at Nottingham; stays 7f but is best at 6f; acts on any going but goes particularly well on firm; blinkered nowadays; has sweated up; ran moderately final outing. *B. Gubby.*

GABLES FLIGHT 3 gr.f. Tack On 114–Gables Grey 66 (Colonist II 126) (1982 – 5d 5g 1983 10fg 14g) in rear in minor events. *D. Grissell.*

GADDY 2 b.f. Buckskin 133–Galadriel 83 (Track Spare 125) (1983 5v⁴ 5s 5.8g 7fg **39** 8g 10d) Feb 22; 3,100F, 800Y; lightly-made filly; first produce; dam very tough winner of 10 races over 7f and 1m; bad plater. *Mrs J. Reavey.*

GAELIC HARP 8 ch.g. Paddy's Birthday 110–Condicote Lane (Sunny Way 120) – (1982 16f 1983 16f) workmanlike gelding; winner over jumps; poor maiden on flat; has worn bandages. *G. Lockerbie.*

GAELIC JEWEL 3 br.f. Scottish Rifle 127–Red Ruby 113 (Tudor Melody 129) **89** (1982 7g 1983 10s* 9s³ 11g² 12f⁴ 12g 10f⁴ 11f) lightly-made, quite attractive filly; ran best races when winning maiden race at Salisbury in April and finishing second in handicap at Newbury in June; suited by 1¼m+; best form with some give in the ground and acts on soft going; ran rather in snatches sixth outing. *J. Dunlop.*

GAINVILLE LAD 2 ch.g. Raga Navarro 119–Sagotox (Die Hard 127) (1983 5f **55** 8f 7.2g 10d³ 8fg 10fg 10.2fg) Mar 14; IR 2,000F, 1,200Y; workmanlike gelding; poor mover; half-brother to useful Irish sprinter Bibilah (by Continuation); dam won from 1m to 1½m in Ireland; moderate plater; suited by 1¼m; pulled up second start. *R. Whitaker.*

GAIUS 2 ch.c. Sallust 134–Sandford Lady 116 (Will Somers 114§) (1983 5d* 5g* **96** 6f*) Apr 1; IR 21,000Y; compact, good-bodied colt; good walker; second living foal; dam, half-sister to top-class sprinter Sandford Lad, won 6 times at around 6f; not troubled to land the odds in small races at Wolverhampton, Catterick and Pontefract in early part of season; suited by 6f. *H. Cecil.*

Moyglare Stud Stakes, the Curragh—left to right, Gala Event, Desirable and Welsh Woman fight it out

GALA EVENT 2 b.f. Sallust 134–Rosemarin (Mossborough 126) (1983 6fg* 6f* **112**
6fg³ 6.3f* 6d* 6fg⁴)

Irish trainer Ted Curtin met with notable success with two two-year-old fillies in the early 'seventies, sending Marble Arch to trot up in the 1972 Norfolk Stakes and Gentle Thoughts to take both the Flying Childers Stakes (the renamed Norfolk Stakes) and the William Hill Cheveley Park in 1973. Curtin hasn't had a winner in Britain since Gentle Thoughts' Cheveley Park victory. He looked to have a reasonable chance of resuming winning ways with Gala Event, second favourite behind Prickle for the latest Cheveley Park, but she proved unequal to the task: she simply couldn't quicken after having every chance at the distance, and was beaten just a length into fourth place behind Desirable, beaten also by Pebbles and Prickle.

Gala Event's record thoroughly justified her prominent position in the betting at Newmarket; she had won four of her five races, one of them the Group 1 Moyglare Stud Stakes at the Curragh, and she had a valid excuse for her defeat, having lost a shoe while finishing a close third to King Persian when favourite for the Heinz '57' Phoenix Stakes. She had created a very favourable impression when making a successful debut in a maiden race at Navan in June, an impression more than confirmed by her subsequent displays. When returned to Navan for the fairly valuable Woodford Stakes later the same month she cantered over her eight opponents, and when odds on for the Ballsbridge Tattersalls Anglesey Stakes at the Curragh just a week after her Phoenix Park defeat, she made nearly all to win comfortably by a length and a half from Late Sally. Although Gala Event had demonstrably better form than the seventeen other home-trained runners in the Moyglare Stud Stakes in September, the position of favourite went to one of the two English challengers, the Lowther Stakes runner-up Desirable. Very few of the field were still in with a chance coming to the last two furlongs where the long-time leader Welsh Woman had the edge over the two market leaders. Gala Event moved ahead before another furlong had been covered and once there never seemed likely to relinquish her advantage, crossing the line three quarters of a length to the good. Desirable narrowly got the better of Welsh Woman for second place. Gala Event's splendid effort credited her owners with the very worthwhile sum of IR £50,437 (£39,404 sterling) and provided her rider, the Australian Kevin Moses, with a major success in his first season in Ireland. Moses ended the season with the creditable total of twenty-six winners; it will be interesting to see if, in due course, he can match the achievements in Europe of his compatriots Breasley, Williamson, Moore and Hutchinson.

Gala Event has proved an extremely good buy at 25,000 guineas as a yearling, her earnings exceeding £62,000. Her dam Rosemarin stayed quite well, winning five times at up to a mile and a half in Ireland as a three- and four-year-old, her last success coming in the Naas November Handicap. Rosemarin has been mated exclusively with sprinter/milers with varying results. To Sovereign Path she produced the winning Irish stayer Regal Way and the useful seven-furlong performer Oldstock; her Tower Walk filly Set-Emal won two six-furlong nurseries; her Prince Tenderfoot filly Pendulina was a useful miler; and Salsa Rosa, by African Sky, was a two-year-old six-furlong winner. One of Rosemarin's half-sisters, Helen

317

Traubel, has also made her mark at stud, producing the top American middle-distance horse Noble Dancer; other top-class performers from the family are the Belmont Stakes winner Cavan and the St Leger winner Indiana, both half-brothers to Rose Bay Willow. Interestingly, Gala Event's trainer has said he can't compare her with Marble Arch and Gentle Thoughts because 'they tended to be speed merchants and this filly settles well'. Gala Event gave the impression in the

Gala Event (b.f. Feb 24, 1981)	Sallust (ch 1969)	Pall Mall (ch 1955)	Palestine Malapert
		Bandarilla (ch 1960)	Matador Interval
	Rosemarin (b 1966)	Mossborough (ch 1947)	Nearco All Moonshine
		Rose Petal (br 1954)	Flocon Rose Bay Willow

Cheveley Park that six furlongs was becoming a bit sharp for her and she'll be well suited by a mile at three. Although an attractive filly, she was rather on the leg at two and may improve further as she lets down. If she does she will prove a formidable opponent for the best of the English fillies. She has yet to race on very soft going but acts on any other. *T. Curtin, Ireland.*

GALA LAD 9 ch.g. Gala Performance–Land 62 (Baldric II 131) (1982 12g 13g 15.8d 1983 15.8f 16f) poor middle-distance handicapper; blind in right eye; acts on any going; suitable mount for a boy; has worn blinkers. *N. Bycroft.*   —

GALANT VERT (FR) 3 b.c. Luthier 126–Emeraldine (Tanerko 134) (1982 NR 1983 10.5v* 11s* 12fg 10d 15s* 12d²) medium-sized colt; fourth foal; half-brother to 2 winners, including Nain Bleu (by Lyphard), successful in France and subsequently a stakes winner at around 1m in USA; dam won at 1½m in France; developed into a very smart performer and won two 100,000 francs races at Longchamp in spring and 6-runner Prix de Lutece on same course in September; having first race for 2 months and looking well, galloped clear in tremendous style in last 2f to beat So Good and Fubymam du Tenu by 5 lengths and ¾ length in last-named event; clear second best when going down by 1½ lengths to Sagace in 12-runner Prix du Conseil de Paris at Longchamp again in October; finds 1¼m too sharp nowadays and stays well; acts on heavy going and finished respectable fifth to Caerleon in Prix du Jockey-Club on only outing on a firm surface; genuine. *A. Fabre, France.*   **124**

GALAXY GEMINI 7 br.g. So Blessed 130–Riddels Bay (Primera 131) (1982 NR 1983 8fg) sturdy gelding; has shown no form for a long time; has been blinkered and bandaged; sold 600 gns Ascot October Sales. *Mrs N. Smith.*   —

GALE AGENCY 4 ch.g. Hittite Glory 125–Tale of Two Cities (Charlottesville 135) (1982 NR 1983 10f 10f) poor maiden; has been beaten in a seller; wore blinkers and a hood once. *D. Oughton.*   —

GALE BOY 3 b.g. Bay Express 132–Morning Cloud 79 (Hard Tack 111§) (1982 5fg 5g 5g 6g 5s 6s⁴ 8s 1983 6d² 8fg 8s* 8v* 8d 8g 9g⁴ 8.2fg⁴ 9g⁴ 8.2g 8.2s 8fg) fair sort; attracted no bid after winning sellers at Thirsk and Newcastle (very easily) in spring; didn't run well afterwards, but seldom had the soft ground that suits him ideally; stays 1m; blinkered final start. *J. Berry.*   **71 d**

GALETZKY 3 br.f. Radetzky 123–Gallant Bid 109 (Galivanter 131) (1982 6fg 6g³ 7f 6fg⁴ 6fg 1983 8v* 8d³ 8s* 8.5g 8g² 8f 8d) big, well-made filly; made all when winning maiden race at Newcastle in April and handicap at York in May, latter by 1½ lengths from Gaygo Lady; also placed at Newmarket (sweated up badly) and Warwick; will stay beyond 1m; probably acts on any going but is evidently well suited by some give; genuine; seemed ill at ease on course and had a poor run at Epsom on fourth start; sold to CBA 5,400 gns Newmarket Autumn Sales. *C. Brittain.*   **86**

GALFORRO 2 br.c. Great Nephew 126–La Pythie 89 (Filiberto 123) (1983 7d) Feb 10; 31,000F; first produce; dam, granddaughter of top-class La Sega, won twice over 7f at 2 yrs; 50/1, 13 lengths sixth of 13 to Van Dyke Brown in maiden race at Yarmouth in September; should do better. *B. Hobbs.*   **— p**

GALIGNANI (FR) 2 br.f. Trepan 133–Contarini Fleming 68 (Abdos 134) (1983 7f³ 7f⁴ 8fg) 130,000 francs Y (approx £10,800); leggy, useful-looking filly; fourth foal; half-sister to 3-y-o Rossetti (by Bolkonski) and 2 winners in France, including 1½m winner Brandegee (by Brigadier Gerard); dam second over 1½m at 4 yrs; modest maiden; will be suited by 1¼m+; acts on firm going. *P. Kelleway.*   **82**

GALLANT BUCK 3 ch.c. Derrylin 115–Petite Gazelle (Star Gazer 123) (1982   77
NR 1983 8s 10s 10s² 12f⁴ 11f⁴ 11.7fg 12s⁴ 10.5d) 6,000Y; medium-sized,
good-topped colt; half-brother to 2 winners, including useful sprinter Deer Leap
(by Deep Diver); dam Irish 2-y-o 6f winner; middle-distance maiden; hampered
fourth start and was off course 2 months afterwards, reportedly with an injury;
behind in a £4,000 seller final outing; sold 4,500 gns Newmarket Autumn Sales.
M. Jarvis.

GALLEA 5 b.g. Prince de Galles 125–Russellia (Red God 128§) (1982 8.2g 8fg 8f   45
8f 6g 7f 8fg³ 7.2s⁴ 8v 1983 7d 7fg³ 7f 7.6g 7f 10f) leggy, narrow gelding; stays 1m;
acts on any going; suitable mount for an apprentice; blinkered fourth start. *N.
Guest.*

GALLICA ROSE 2 b.f. Guillaume Tell 121–Levrosa (Levmoss 133) (1983 6g 7f   –
7d) Apr 7; IR 5,000F; lengthy, plain filly; third produce; sister to 3-y-o Errigal and
half-sister to fair maiden Mean Francine (by African Sky); dam never ran;
unquoted, behind in maiden races. *J. Douglas-Home.*

GALLIC WIT (USA) 3 ch.c. Roberto 131–Gallina 120 (Raise A Native) (1982 7d   80
7fg² 7g 7fg* 8d³ 1983 10v³ 11v⁴ 12v 12d 12f* 13.1f³ 12g) strong, good sort;
carries plenty of condition; middle-distance handicapper; beat Vigorous Vigors by
½ length at Pontefract in June; acts on any going but is ideally suited by
top-of-the-ground; suited by forcing tactics (didn't get them final start, first race
for almost 3 months) *I. Balding.*

GAMBLER'S CUP (USA) 2 b.c. Raise A Cup–Gambrel (A Gambler) (1983 7fg   98 p
8d* 8g*) Apr 27; $75,000Y; rangy colt; second foal; half-brother to 1982 2-y-o 6f
winner Lebanese Song (by Shecky Greene); dam, out of half-sister to top-class
Olden Times, won twice at up to 7f; won minor events at Goodwood (£4,400 race)
in September and Bath in October, at Bath needing only to be pushed along to beat
Lord Butch (rec 7 lb) by 4 lengths; stays 1m well; sure to win more races. *G.
Harwood.*

GAMBLERS DREAM 6 b.or br.g. Prince Regent 129–Red Laser 95 (Red God   88
128§) (1982 6f 6g 6fg⁴ 6d 5fg 6f 6f 6g³ 5.6g⁴ 6g 5d 6g 5s⁴ 1983 6v³ 6g 6f 7f 7fg²
6f⁴ 7f 7s 7.3g* 7fg⁴ 7fg 8g² 8d) strong, attractive gelding; good mover; fair
handicapper; beat Jade Ring a short head at Newbury in September; good neck
second to Mummy's Pleasure in Ward Hill Bunbury Cup at Newmarket earlier;
suited by 7f+; acts on any going; effective with or without blinkers; suited by
waiting tactics. *D. Wilson.*

GAMBLING LORD 4 b.c. Lord Gayle 124–Gambling Queen 80 (Pretendre 126)   –
(1982 8g 10d 8fg 7.6f* 8fg 8.2f 1983 8d 10v³) quite attractive colt; should stay
1¼m; acts on firm going; sold 2,500 gns Newmarket Autumn Sales. *M. Jarvis.*

GAME FOR A LAUGH 2 b.f. Martinmas 128–Tia Polly (King's Leap 111) (1983   72 p
7f) Apr 6; 3,000F, 4,800Y; second foal; dam poor half-sister to very smart sprinter
Great Bear; unquoted, 7½ lengths fifth of 12 to Shadiliya in maiden race at
Yarmouth in August; should improve. *A. Stewart.*

GAMEGUARD 3 ch.c. Roman Warrior 132–Love Beach 75 (Lorenzaccio 130)   –
(1982 NR 1983 5s 7d 6f) 1,700F, 3,000Y; fair sort; first foal; dam showed form
only at 2 yrs; towards rear in varied races; retained by trainer 480 gns Doncaster
November Sales. *M. McCormack.*

GAME ON 3 ch.c. Continuation 120–Eve Darlin 50 (Arcticeelagh 119) (1982 7f⁴   –
8.2fg³ 1983 12f 16g) good-bodied colt; plater at 2 yrs; poor form in maiden races
in 1983; should stay beyond 1m. *J. Hardy.*

GAME ROCKET 3 ch.g. Roan Rocket 128–Debach Game 69 (Darius 129) (1982   61
7s⁴ 1983 8d 9d 8v³ 9f³ 13.8f⁴ 9f 10fg 12f³ 12g) workmanlike gelding; plater; stays
1½m; acts on any going; blinkered nowadays and has also worn bandages; didn't
look all that keen third start. *Hbt Jones.*

GAMESMANSHIP 2 b.c. Lepanto–Silly Games 62 (Siliconn 121) (1983 7fg 7f 7g   75
8fg) Apr 26; big colt; first foal; dam showed a little ability on first of 2 starts at 2
yrs; quite a moderate colt; gives impression he'll make a better 3-y-o. *W. Elsey.*

GAMON 3 b.g. Be My Guest 126–Au Revoir 79 (Ballymoss 136) (1982 5f³ 6f³   80 §
7.2g 1983 10g 10d³ 12f 12f³ 12.2f⁴) tall, close-coupled gelding; good walker;
third as a 3-y-o in slowly-run handicap won by Quite A Night at Newmarket
(proved difficult to settle) and 5-runner maiden race won by Band at York (made
running); sweated and ran moderately when blinkered at Catterick in July on final
start, and was subsequently gelded; may prove best at distances short of 1½m;
doesn't seem to have the ideal temperament for racing and is difficult to assess.
B. Hills.

GANGAWAYHAME 3 b.f. Lochnager 132–Silbadora 67 (Don II 123) (1982 5d²   **83**
5g³ 5g³ 6f* 6g² 6fg* 6s 1983 5.8v 7d⁴ 6f 8f 6f 6f) small filly; had stiffish task when
strong-finishing fourth to Krakow in handicap at Epsom in June; showed little
afterwards, but didn't have best of runs on final start (August); stays 7f; acts on any
going with possible exception of very soft. *G. Balding.*

GANGLION 2 b.f. Martinmas 128–Cambrian Angel (Welsh Saint 126) (1983 6g   **61**
6f⁴ 9g) Apr 15; IR 3,800F; leggy filly; second produce; dam Irish middle-distance
winner, also won over hurdles; 3½ lengths fourth of 18 to Inset Lady in maiden race
at Folkestone in August; should stay 9f. *M. McCormack.*

GAN ON LAD 2 ch.g. On Your Mark 125–Fado (Ribero 126) (1983 5v² 5v* 5g³   **72**
6f⁴ 6g 7f 6g) Apr 7; 3,000Y; neat, lightly-made gelding; second foal; dam Irish 2m
winner; won 10-runner maiden race at Newcastle in May; showed nothing in
nurseries last 3 outings, once blinkered; should stay 7f; acts on any going. *D.
Smith.*

GARABANDAL 3 b.g. Lypheor 118–Icy More (Ballymore 123) (1982 NR 1983   **–**
9d 8.2g 8f 8f 8g) lightly-made gelding; first foal; dam won over 1¾m in Ireland and
is half-sister to smart French miler Costly Wave; towards rear in varied races;
blinkered last 2 starts; sold 460 gns Doncaster November Sales. *A. Balding.*

GARDENERS ARMS 3 b.c. Double Jump 131–Early Morning 81 (Dual 117)   **–**
(1982 NR 1983 8g 8d 12s) workmanlike colt; first foal; dam won over 5f at 2 yrs
and ran in sellers until a 7-y-o; little worthwhile form; blinkered final outing; trained
part of season by P. Feilden. *M. Ryan.*

GARDEN ROUTE 3 b.c. Star Appeal 133–Nyeri 104 (Saint Crespin III 132)   **81**
(1982 NR 1983 8f³ 10g² 10f 8f² 8f² 8f* 9d* 10fg 9fg³) 10,000Y; close-coupled
colt; half-brother to several winners here and in Scandinavia, including useful
middle-distance stayer Greatham House (by Run The Gantlet); dam stayed 1½m;
narrowly won maiden race at Salisbury and minor event at Wolverhampton (just
got up to beat Zabeel), both in September; rather disappointing final start; bred to
be suited by 1½m but is clearly effective at 1m; acts on firm going but is possibly
ideally suited by some give in the ground; needs holding up and isn't the easiest of
rides. *F. Durr.*

GARDEZ MOI (FR) 2 b.f. King of Macedon 126–Gardegan (Weavers' Hall 122)   **55**
(1983 5d 5fg 6fg 7fg³ 6f 9fg² 7.2g) Mar 25; 100,000 francs Y (approx £8,300);
lightly-made filly; third foal; closely related to minor French 11f winner Gaffeliere
(by Margouillat); dam ran only once; placed in seller (blinkered) at Newmarket in
August and selling nursery at Redcar in September; suited by 9f. *P. Kelleway.*

GARFIELD 2 gr.c. Young Generation 129–Miss Caribbean 74 (Sea Hawk II 131)   **79**
(1983 5g 5d* 5d³ 5s⁴ 7fg² 7f) May 15; 7,000Y; big, lengthy, good sort; second foal;
dam, half-sister to very smart 1973 2-y-o Welsh Harmony, won over 1½m; won
15-runner maiden race at Windsor in May; in frame subsequently in minor events,
notably 2½ lengths second of 8 to very easy winner Trojan Fen at Yarmouth in June;
stays 7f; acts on a firm and a soft surface (hampered twice only outing on very soft
going); sometimes very much on toes in paddock (had to be led by 2 lads when
blinkered at York on final outing); exported to Hong Kong. *M. Ryan.*

GARFUNKEL 4 b.g. Music Boy 124–First Court 82 (Primera 131) (1982 8g 8f   **–**
8fg 10f 10fg 11.7d 8fg⁴ 1983 10f 8d) big, good-topped, quite attractive gelding;
good mover; has shown no form on flat for a long time but is a fairly useful hurdler;
sometimes blinkered; often sweats up. *P. Mitchell.*

GARGANTIAN 2 ch.c. Grundy 137–Harmonise 113 (Reliance II 137) (1983 7g)   **–**
Apr 27; well-grown colt; fifth foal; half-brother to a winning hurdler; dam, at her
best at 2 yrs, stayed 1½m; 7/1 but green, no show in 17-runner maiden race at
Leicester in September; sold 2,100 gns Ascot October Sales. *R. Hern.*

GARRULOUS 2 b.c. Thatch 136–Garryfine (Realm 129) (1983 6f* 6f² 6fg 6f³   **101**
5fg) Apr 23; robust, good-topped colt; good walker and mover; first foal; dam
unraced daughter of half-sister to Kentucky Derby winner Forward Pass; backed
from 50/1 to 16/1, won 8-runner minor event at Doncaster in June by ¾ length from
Carabineer; consistent in useful company subsequently until outpaced last-of-five
in £3,200 race at Thirsk in September on final appearance; probably needs further
than 5f; has raced only on fast ground. *J. Leigh.*

GARY SHAW 3 br.c. Wolver Hollow 126–Early Release (Prince Regent 129)   **–**
(1982 7g³ 1983 8g 10fg 12g 10.5d 12fg) narrow, rather leggy colt; no form as a
3-y-o, including in sellers; should stay at least 1m; blinkered fourth outing; sold
1,550 gns Ascot November Sales. *I. Walker.*

GAS LIGHTER 2 ch.f. Lighter 111–Royal Fashion (Salvo 129) (1983 6f 8g) May 4; first living foal; dam well beaten on flat and over hurdles; apparently of no account. *W. Storey.* –

GAS ONLY 3 ch.f. Northfields–Coquette (St Paddy 133) (1982 6fg 1983 8v 10g 9.4d 10.2f* 8fg³ 9f* 10h) quite attractive filly; showed improved form in July, winning handicaps at Bath (apprentices) and Redcar (apprentice ridden); suited by 9f+; suited by firm going; well below her best final start (August). *F. J. Houghton.* **63**

GASOOF (USA) 3 b. or br.c. Stop the Music–Fantastic Miss (Jacinto) (1982 NR 1983 7d 8v 10fg 10.1f 16.5f⁴ 12fg⁴ 10f 10d⁴ 12d 12g⁴) $250,000Y; quite a useful-looking colt; second foal; brother to a stakes-placed winner; dam, winner of 2 sprint races at 2 yrs, is half-sister to high-class 1980 American 2-y-o Staunch Avenger; quite moderate form in varied races; not sure to stay long distances; sold 8,400 gns Newmarket Autumn Sales. *F. Durr.* **64**

GASTRONOMIC 2 ch.g. Anax 120–Lancashire Lass 73 (King's Troop 118) (1983 6f 7fg³ 6f² 8fg) Mar 3; 4,400Y; fair sort; brother to 3-y-o Admiral's Ruler and half-brother to two 2-y-o winners; dam sprinter; quite a moderate maiden; stays 7f. *D. Morley.* **77**

GATE-CRASH 2 ch.f. Import 127–Pranky 55 (Bold Lad, Ire 133) (1983 6g) May 4; leggy filly; first foal; dam poor maiden; 20/1 but very fit, always-struggling 8 lengths fifth of 9 to Betsy Bay in minor event at York in October; sold 1,900 gns Doncaster November Sales. *J. W. Watts.* –

GATEMASTER (USA) 3 b.c. L'Enjoleur–Sun Gate (Bull Lea) (1982 7d³ 6s 1983 8s 8v 7d 6d 6f 6f 7fg) close-coupled colt; no worthwhile form in 1983, including in a seller; should be suited by 1m; sometimes blinkered; virtually refused to race fifth start; sold 560 gns Newmarket September Sales. *F. Durr.* –

GAUHAR 2 ch.c. Nebbiolo 125–Solar Jinks (Immortality or Delirium 126) (1983 5.8s³ 5g² 6g 5.8h 7fg² 8s 7g 7d³) Mar 11; IR 22,000F, 30,000Y; smallish, sparely-made colt; half-brother to several winners, including useful 1982 2-y-o sprinter Solar Rock (by Ballad Rock) and useful Irish 5f and 1¼m winner Jinkitis (by Irish Love); dam ran once; second in maiden race at Hamilton in June and nursery at Salisbury in September; well suited by 7f; acts on soft going and a firm surface. *M. Blanshard.* **71**

GAVO 4 b.g. Windjammer (USA)–Eleanor Clare 89 (Petingo 135) (1982 7g 6g² 7fg* 7.6fg* 7f* 8.2f³ 7.6f³ 8fg 7g 7f 1983 7.6v 7fg 7f² 6f 7.3f 8f 8f² 9fg) neat, strong, good-bodied gelding; has an excellent smooth action; fairly useful handicapper; ran creditably last 2 starts when ½-length second to Steeple Bell in Ripon Rowels Handicap in August and eighth of 30 behind Sagamore in William Hill Cambridgeshire at Newmarket in October; stays 9f; gives impression he will always be suited by top-of-the-ground; usually blinkered nowadays; has run creditably for an apprentice; suited by front-running tactics; sent to USA. *P. Kelleway.* **89**

GAWAINE 4 gr.g. Three Legs 128–Fei-Hoo 65 (Dionisio 126) (1982 6d 6g 8.3g 6g 7fg 8fg 10v³ 10v* 12s³ 1983 10.2d 12v 10s 10fg 12f 12g 12g⁴ 12g) lengthy gelding; plater; suited by 1¼m+; revels in the mud; suitable mount for an apprentice. *J. Holt.* –

GAWNMYSUN 5 br.g. Furry Glen 121–Fair Colleen (King Emperor) (1982 5d 6g 7g 1983 12f 8.3fg³ 8f) neat gelding; poor form, including in a seller; stays 1m. *M. Madgwick.* –

GAY BARBARELLA 2 b.f. Gay Fandango 132–Karella 88 (Jukebox 120) (1983 5s 5.1fg 6f 5d 5g) Feb 20; IR 13,000F, 7,600Y; small filly; second produce; half-sister to 1981 Irish 2-y-o 7f winner Ulpha (by Red Alert); dam 2-y-o 5f winner; poor form in maiden races; should be suited by 6f; trained by C. Brittain first 3 starts; sold 420 gns Ascot December Sales. *D. Elsworth.* –

GAYBELLS 3 b. or br.f. Gunner B 126–Haybells (Klairon 131) (1982 NR 1983 10g 11g³ 10.6g 12s 12fg) half-sister to 2 winners, including winning stayer Haywire (by Galivanter); dam lightly-raced half-sister to smart Haymaking; third in minor event at Ayr in August; should stay 1½m. *W. Elsey.* –

GAY BROAD 3 ch.f. Gay Fandango 132–Broad River 75 (Chieftain) (1982 5d 5g 6g 5.8g³ 6d 7d³ 1983 7v 7fg* 10f 7h 7.3g) small, well-made filly; good walker and mover; ridden by 7-lb claimer when winning minor event at Salisbury in June; well beaten in handicaps afterwards; stays 7f; acts on a firm and a soft surface. *R. Hannon.* **70**

GAYGARDEN LADY 3 b.f. Anax 120–Reppeve 45 (Jimmy Reppin 131) (1982 NR 1983 10.1f 10f 10f 12g 16g 10g 10f) of little account. *Peter Taylor.* –

Happy Valley Stakes, York—Gay Lemur has his opponents well strung out

GAY GEORGE 7 br.h. Prince Regent 129–Kazanlik 116 (Ommeyad) (1982 NR   **82**
1983 16f² 16.1fg³) strong, compact horse; fairly useful performer on flat and very
smart hurdler; placed in handicaps at Newbury (unlucky) and Newmarket in
summer; stayed 2m but seemed better at shorter distances; appeared to act on any
going but went well on fast ground; dead. *F. Walwyn.*

GAYGIG 3 b.g. Lord Gayle 124–Gig (Dionisio 126) (1982 6fg⁴ 6f* 6g 1983 6s 7v   **56**
6s 8f 8fg³ 9fg 9f³ 6fg⁴ 8h 8d 10fg⁴ 9fg 7fg) plater nowadays; stays 9f; sometimes
blinkered. *D. Chapman.*

GAYGO LADY 3 ch.f. Gay Fandango 132–Bally Keys 72 (Bally Russe 113) (1982   **113**
6f 6fg³ 7g² 7s 1983 8s² 8g* 8f* 10f⁴ 10f 8fg² 8s³ 8fg 8fg³) useful-looking filly; won
£4,100 race at Sandown in May (made nearly all and beat Magdalena quite
comfortably by 2 lengths) and Fern Hill Stakes (Handicap) at Ascot in June; went
down by a head to Page Blanche in latter but placings were reversed; ran best
subsequent races when about 1½ lengths fifth of 12 to Green Reef in Prix de
Psyche at Deauville in August, ¾-length second to Zaheendar in £8,000 handicap at
Newcastle later in month and just over a length third of 6 behind Royal Heroine in
Sceptre Stakes at Doncaster in September; stays 1¼m; acts on any going; quite
seriously interfered with on fourth start; gave impression she was past her best
last 2 outings. *B. Hills.*

GAY LEMUR 3 b.c. Lord Gayle 124–Coming-of-Age 93 (Majority Blue 126) (1982   **113**
6f⁴ 7g² 7s² 1983 7d⁴ 7g 10.5s* 10.2s* 10.5f² 10f² 12f³ 12fg² 12d* 12d) strong,
good-bodied colt; developed into a smart middle-distance performer and won
£4,500 Glasgow Stakes at York, slowly-run handicap at Doncaster and quite well
contested £3,000 event at York again; had his 4 opponents well strung out when
beating Nestor by 4 lengths in last-named race in October; also placed in good
handicaps won by Bedtime at York and by Millfontaine at Goodwood and Newbury,
and also in Troy Stakes at Doncaster (went down by a neck to Trakady when 2/1
on); effective at 1¼m and seems only just to stay 1½m; acts on any going; game
and genuine and races with tremendous enthusiasm. *B. Hobbs.*

GAY RHYTHM 3 b.f. Quiet Fling 124–Gay Jennie 69 (Lord Gayle 124) (1982 NR   **–**
1983 14f 10.1fg) second foal; half-sister to a winning plater; dam won over 1½m;
last in maiden race at Salisbury and minor event at Windsor in summer. *C.
Wildman.*

GAY TARA 3 ro.f. Gay Fandango 132–Portden (Worden II 129) (1982 NR 1983 6f   **–**
8f 9fg 8f 8g) IR 14,000Y; lengthy filly; half-sister to several winners including
Redden (by Red God), successful at up to 1¼m; dam Irish 9f winner; little

322

worthwhile form, including in a seller when blinkered final start; sold 2,400 gns Newmarket September Sales, for export to Norway. *B. Swift.*

GAY TWENTIES 9 b.m. Lord Gayle 124–Schull (Yorick II 127) (1982 NR 1983   –
12fg) winning hurdler; poor maiden on flat; has been tried in blinkers. *C. Drew.*

GAZAAN 5 ch.g. Margouillat 133–Goldena (Relko 136) (1982 22.2fg 15.5f 1983   –
16g 15.5f⁴) lightly-built gelding; staying maiden; blinkered second start. *B. Wise.*

GAZELLE D'OR 2 gr.f. Rusticaro 124–Gazelle (Tudor Music 131) (1983 7.6d   65
7g⁴) Apr 29; 13,000Y; fourth living foal; half-sister to a winner in Canada; dam placed over 7f and 1m in Ireland; apprentice ridden, 12 lengths fourth of 14 behind Detroit Sam in maiden race at Lingfield in October. *R. Smyth.*

GEM DIAMOND (USA) 5 b.h. Riva Ridge–Bold Place (Bold Bidder) (1982 6v²   121?
6.5s 6s⁴ 5g 6fg 5d* 8s 8.5v 6.5v⁴ 8v 1983 5g* 6.5d* 5d* 6v 7fg 5fg* 7d 6.5fg) 420,000 francs Y (approx £50,000); second foal; dam won 9 races, including minor stakes events at up to 1m; claimed out of J. C. Cunnington's stable 70,844 francs after winning claiming race at Chantilly in 1982; has proved a bargain and did well at 5 yrs, winning 3 races at Cagnes-sur-Mer early in year and Prix du Gros-Chene at Chantilly in June; accounted for Massorah by 2 lengths in last-named; clearly best at sprint distances; seems to act on any going. *C. da Meda, France.*

GEM-MAY 3 ro.f. Mansingh 120–Unclaimed Treasure 61 (Nice Guy 123) (1982   48
5f³ 5fg³ 5f 6g² 6g 5f 6g 7d 6s⁴ 5v 1983 8fg⁴ 8g 7s 8f 9f 9f² 10.4g 12fg² 9f 13.8g 10fg 12f) lengthy filly; plater; stays 1½m; probably acts on any going; sometimes blinkered; refused to race final start. *T. Fairhurst.*

GENERAL CONCORDE 3 b.c. Radetzky 123–Concorde Lady 66 (Hotfoot   96
126) (1982 5g 5fg 7fg 6f⁴ 8fg* 8f 8s² 8.2s² 7s 1983 8s 10s* 10v* 12f 10g 13.3f* 12f 14.6fg 13.3g) useful-looking colt; always prominent when winning handicaps at Salisbury and Newcastle in May and Newbury in July; picked up useful prizes on last 2 courses, beating Equanaid in very close finish to £11,000 XYZ Handicap at Newcastle and Gildoran by a length in £6,100 Morland Brewery Trophy at Newbury; finds 1¼m on a sound surface too sharp now and stays 13f well; acts on any going; occasionally blinkered; game and genuine, although below his best seventh and eighth starts (moved very badly to post in latter); sold 30,000 gns Newmarket December Sales. *R. Hannon.*

GENERAL HOLME (USA) 4 ch.c. Noholme II–Generals Sister (Count Fleet)   121
(1982 8d* 10fg* 10.5s* 9d* 10fg* 10f* 1983 10v 10v* 10g³ 12f) $200,000 2-y-o; half-brother to numerous winners, notably smart stakes winner Commissary (by To Market); dam won at 2 yrs in USA; high class at 3 yrs when unbeaten in 6 races; didn't run up to top form in 1983, best effort when accounting for Great Substance readily by 1½ lengths in Prix Gontaut-Biron at Deauville in August; stayed on when 5 lengths third of 11 to Stanerra in Joe McGrath Memorial Stakes at Leopardstown in September; gave impression at Leopardstown that 1½m would suit him but was only seventeenth of 26 to All Along in Trusthouse Forte Prix de l'Arc de Triomphe at Longchamp in October when tried at trip; possibly unsuited by heavy ground but acted on any other; syndicated for a reported 19 million francs and is to stand at Haras de Meautry at 60,000 francs. *O. Douieb, France.*

GENERAL WADE 8 b.h. Bold Lad (Ire) 133–Zerbinetta 96 (Henry the Seventh   67 d
125) (1982 6f⁴ 6f² 6fg⁴ 6f³ 6fg⁴ 6g⁴ 5fg⁴ 5fg⁴ 5fg 6fg 5.8f 6s* 1983 7s 5.8s 6d 6fg 6f* 6h⁴ 6g³ 6f 6h 6f 6fg 5g) strong, rather dipped-backed horse; sprint handicapper; won at Newcastle in June; acts on any going; wears blinkers; sometimes sweats up. *P. Makin.*

GENNARO 3 gr.c. Dance In Time–Landed Lady 89 (Realm 129) (1982 6g 6d 6g   57
1983 8v² 7.6v 10g 8.2h 8h⁴) rangy, good sort; nice, easy mover; plating-class maiden; probably stays 1¼m; sold 4,200 gns Ascot September Sales. *J. Dunlop.*

GENTLE DOWN (USA) 3 ch.f. Naskra–First Fluff (Olden Times) (1982 7g   70
7d³ 1983 10.2h 9fg³ 10f³ 10fg³ 9g² 8g* 8fg) fair sort; placed several times before beating Montrevie by 4 lengths in 16-runner maiden race at Warwick in October; gives impression 1¼m stretches her stamina. *G. Hunter.*

GENTLE GODDESS 2 b.f. Import 127–Observation 81 (Coronation Year 124)   51
(1983 5g 5g 5fg 5g³ 5f² 5f 5.3f) Apr 24; 3,000Y; well-made, quite attractive filly; half-sister to several winners, including fairly useful 1979 2-y-o 5f winner Ayoub (by The Go-Between); dam stayed 1m; placed in July sellers at Lingfield and Folkestone; blinkered last 3 starts; exported to Algeria. *P. Cundell.*

GENTLE GYPSY 2 gr.f. Junius 124–Rossaldene 79 (Mummy's Pet 125) (1983   94
5d² 5v* 5s 5g² 5f 6f 5fg⁴ 5g 5g² 5d* 5fg) May 23; IR 10,500Y; small, good-

quartered filly; second foal; dam 2-y-o 5f winner; won maiden race at Kempton in April and 12-runner nursery under top weight at Wolverhampton in October; ran creditably over 6f but is clearly thought better at 5f; acts on any going; tough and genuine. *J. Winter.*

GENTLE RHYTHM 3 ch.f. Ballad Rock 122–Super Restless (Restless Wind) (1982 6fg 1983 6s 8v 10.2f 11f 14f 14g 10fg 8f 9fg²) strong, full-quartered filly; improved in autumn and finished close second in handicap at Redcar; stays 9f; sold to CBA 7,600 gns Newmarket December Sales. *F. Durr.* **67**

GENTLE STAR 4 b. or br.f. Comedy Star 121–Super Princess 85 (Falcon 131) (1982 5g 5d 6f 6f 10.1fg 7g 6f* 6fg³ 6fg* 6f² 6fg 6g³ 6f 6f 6d³ 6s 1983 6d³ 6v² 6s 6g 6d 6fg 6g² 5.1fg 6f³ 5f 6fg) lightly-made filly; former plater; best form at 6f; acts on any going; effective with or without blinkers; has run well for an apprentice. *K. Ivory.* **50**

GENZYME GENE 2 b.f. Riboboy 124–Giglet (Frankincense 120) (1983 7fg 7f 7fg 7s) May 10; small, close-coupled filly; half-sister to 2 winners, including 3-y-o 1m winner Waljat (by Bay Express), and to disappointing Match Master (by Roman Warrior); dam showed no form; unquoted, behind in maiden races; blinkered third outing; retained 1,300 gns Doncaster October Sales. *D. Dale.* **–**

GEORGE WILLIAM 2 b.c. Import 127–Bloomsbury Girl 63 (Weepers Boy 124) (1983 5d 6fg) May 22; half-brother to 1m winner T.V. Star (by St Columbus); dam won 5f seller; 50/1, in rear in October maiden races at Catterick and Doncaster. *R. D. Peacock.* **–**

GERAL 4 b. c. Brigadier Gerard 144–Bresilia (Habitat 134) (1982 won 5 out of 11 starts in Italy 1983 10s 8v 8d 7d⁴ 8f³ 7d² 8fg² 6.5fg 8fg) 36,000,000 lire Y (approx £17,500); second foal; dam, half-sister to high-class French colts Beaugency and Bourbon, won in Italy; raced in Italy at 3 yrs and won 5 races, including Premio d'Estate at Milan; showed smart form in France in 1983 without winning, finishing fourth to Honeyland in Prix du Palais Royal at Longchamp, third to Pampabird in Prix du Chemin de Fer du Nord at Chantilly, ½-length second to African Joy in Prix de la Porte Maillot at Longchamp and ¾-length second to Pampabird again in Prix Messidor at Maisons-Laffitte; stays 1m; seems to act on any going; sent to USA. *G. Bonnaventure, France.* **115**

GERARDINA'S BOY 4 ch.c. Music Boy 124–Solace (Floribunda 136) (1982 5fg 5f 5s⁴ 6d 1983 5fg 5f) good-quartered, workmanlike colt; sprint handicapper; best at 5f; needs some give in the ground; blinkered last 2 outings in 1982. *C. Mackenzie.* **–**

GERYON 2 b.c. Exdirectory 129–Floreat Salopia 85 (Pieces of Eight 128) (1983 7fg 7f 7fg³ 8f 8s⁴) Apr 9; 3,000Y, resold 13,500Y; rangy, attractive colt; first foal; dam won over 1m and 9.4f; fair but one-paced maiden; beaten no more than 1½ lengths on last 3 outings, last 2 in good-class nurseries at York and Doncaster; better suited by 1m than by 7f, and will be suited by 1¼m+; best form on soft ground; sure to win a race. *B. Hills.* **90**

GET THE MESSAGE 2 ch.c. Grundy 137–Home Fire 99 (Firestreak 125) (1983 6f 7fg³) Mar 23; 11,500F, IR 30,000Y; rangy, useful-looking colt; half-brother to 9f winner Royal Home (by Royal Palace); dam sprinter; ran with considerable promise in Chesham Stakes (fifth of 13) at Royal Ascot in June and Somerville Tattersall Stakes (1¾ lengths third of 8 behind Round Hill) at Newmarket in September; will be suited by 1m+; sure to win a race. *P. Cole.* **94**

GETTING PLENTY 4 b.f. Oats 126–Allander Girl (Miralgo 130) (1982 12f 17fg 12f 12g 10v³ 13.8d⁴ 1983 16s*) sparely-made filly; plater; attracted no bid after winning at Lingfield in May; not seen out again; stays well; acts well on soft going and is possibly unsuited by firm; has worn a tongue strap. *M. Pipe.* **47**

GET WISE 2 ro.c. Master Sing 109–Pipemma 76 (Compensation 127) (1983 5v 5s⁴ 6d 7f 6f 6f 8f⁴ 8d 7.2fg 8fg) Apr 27; 1,250 Y; workmanlike colt; dam placed in 6 sprint races at 2 yrs; moderate plater; best run on final appearance; stays 1m; blinkered ninth start. *K. Stone.* **56**

GHAIYA (USA) 3 b.f. Alleged 138–Proud Pattie (Noble Commander) (1982 7g 8fg* 1983 12s 12g 10f² 12fg² 12g³ 11g⁴ 12fg) quite attractive, lengthy filly; ran very well when runner-up in Pretty Polly Stakes at the Curragh in June (went down by a short head to Flame of Tara, who gave 4 lb) and Prix de Minerve at Evry in July (had no answer to Rajpoura's late burst and was beaten 2½ lengths); rather disappointing afterwards, although finished in frame in Brownstown Stakes at the Curragh again in August and Doonside Cup at Ayr in September (never going particularly well); stays 1½m; suited by fast ground. *J. Dunlop.* **110**

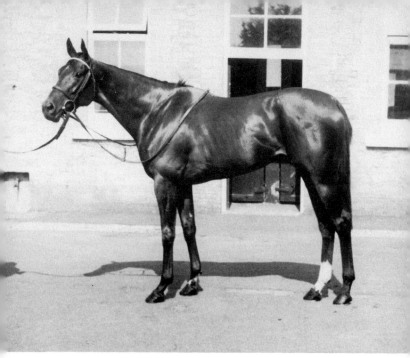

Sheikh Mohammed's "Ghaiya"

GHANAYEM 2 ch.f. Ballad Rock 122–Carcajou (High Top 131) (1983 6f² 6f⁴ 6g   76
7.6d) Mar 27; IR 10,000F, 8,000Y; second foal; dam lightly-raced daughter of very
useful stayer Wolverene; quite a moderate maiden; ran poorly after first outing;
should stay beyond 6f; acts on firm going. *R. Laing.*

GHAZGOUZ 2 gr.c. Habat 127–Planta Genista 89 (Princely Gift 137) (1983 5d   –
5fg 5f 7f 5f) Mar 10; 4,700F, 13,000Y; compact colt; half-brother to several
winners here and abroad, including 1977 2-y-o 6f winner Plant at Dusk (by
Crepello); dam 2-y-o 5f winner; soundly beaten in maiden and minor events;
blinkered fourth outing. *E. Witts.*

GHAZIBAY 2 br.c. Frimley Park 109–Kentucky Blues 83 (Royal Record II) (1983   86
5f 5fg 5f 6f* 7f⁴ 6f⁴ 5h² 5fg² 6g 5fg) Apr 18; 1,000Y, 16,000 2-y-o; compact colt;
half-brother to moderate 1¼m winner Shuwaiman (by Alcide) and a winning
jumper; dam showed ability over sprint distances at 2 yrs; won 15-runner maiden
race at Yarmouth in July at 66/1; placed afterwards in 2 nurseries; best form at 5f
and 6f, but stays 7f; has raced only on a sound surface; unseated rider at start on
debut and wore blinkers next time out; ran creditably for a 7-lb claimer sixth outing;
wears bandages. *E. Witts.*

GIADA (USA) 3 ch.f. Vaguely Noble 140–Flo's Pleasure (What A Pleasure) (1982   80
NR 1983 12.2d 8fg²) $90,000Y; tall, rangy filly; half-sister to 3 winners,
including Swirlaway (by Sir Ivor), a very useful winner at up to 7f; dam very
useful winner of 12 races at up to 1m; having first outing for 5 months, took a long
time to get going when strong-finishing length second of 9 to Jhansi Ki Rani in
maiden race at Goodwood in August; injured a leg there but is said to have made a
full recovery; will be suited by 1¼m; remains in training and should win a race.
L. Cumani.

GIBBON 7 br. g. Swing Easy 126–Fearless 77 (Derring-Do 131) (1982 NR 1983   **54**
10v 10g 5fg 7f 8f³ 8f* 8f 10fg* 8.2fg 9fg 10f 12d 8.2g 18g) strong, good-bodied
gelding; won apprentice handicap at Carlisle in July and seller (no bid) at
Pontefract in August; stays 1¼m; suited by fast ground; blinkered once; suitable
mount for an apprentice; inconsistent and hasn't always looked genuine. *N.
Bycroft.*

GIDIAN 6 ch. g. Brigadier Gerard 144–Jovian 88 (Hardicanute 130) (1982 10fg 10g   –
10d⁴ 10f² 12f² 12fg 12g 10fg² 10g⁴ 10s 1983 10g 10f) lengthy, dipped-backed
gelding; poor middle-distance handicapper; stays 1½m; acts on any going. *C.
Brittain.*

GIGONDAS 4 b. f. Brigadier Gerard 144–Gingerale (Golden Horus 123) (1982   **53**
7.6fg 10g 8.5fg⁴ 7g 1983 9v 9f 10f 8.2g*) smallish, slightly dipped-backed filly;
20/1-winner of handicap at Hamilton in September; stays 1m well; has given trouble
at start. *W. Holden.*

GILDED STRACOMER 3 b. g. Averof 123–Peta's Bay 67 (I Say 125) (1982 5fg   –
5g⁴ 5fg 7fg 6f 6fg 6g 9v 7s 1983 7d 8v 9v² 10s 10v 10fg 8f 12fg) good-topped
gelding; plating-class maiden; second at Mallow in April when trained in Ireland by
T. Gallagher, best effort; should stay 1¼m; acts on heavy going; blinkered sixth
start. *G. Lockerbie.*

GILDORAN 3 b. c. Rheingold 137–Durtal 121 (Lyphard 132) (1982 7v 7d⁴ 1983   **117**
10.2s³ 10.5s 12fg* 11.7f* 13.3f² 14f* 14g 18fg²) well-made colt; won apprentice
maiden race at Newmarket (by 6 lengths), minor event at Bath (apprentice
ridden) and £4,900 handicap at Goodwood; made a lot of running when gaining last
2 wins in July and got home by ¾ length from British at Goodwood; well beaten in
Tote-Ebor (Handicap) at York the following month, but showed much improved
form when given a stiff test of stamina in Doncaster Cup in September, keeping on
very well to finish 2½ lengths second of 8 behind Karadar; acts on any going, but
seems suited by firm; a smart performer who should win another race or 2 when
stamina is at a premium. *B. Hills.*

GILGIT POLO 2 b. c. Persian Bold 123–Monkey Tricks 85 (Saint Crespin III   **89**
132) (1983 8fg 8fg) Mar 14; half-brother to 1982 Irish 2-y-o 7.9f winner Inner
Spirit (by Pitskelly); dam won over 1¼m, and is half-sister to Oaks second Maina;
ran well in 2 maiden races at Newmarket in October, finishing seventh of 21 to
Alphabatim and 3½ lengths sixth of 28, staying on strongly, to Bob Back; will be
suited by 1¼m; well up to winning a maiden event. *J. Hindley.*

GILLIE'S PRINCE 4 b. or br. c. Furry Glen 121–Rosy O'Leary (Majetta 115)   **69**
(1982 7fg 9g³ 8f² 12f⁴ 9f* 8d 10d 1983 12fg 8d 9g 10.2f 10f² 12f* 10f³ 11fg³
10.6fg 12f² 14fg⁴ 12fg² 12d 10.5d* 12fg 10.2fg 10fg) leggy, lightly-made colt; has a
round action; former plater; won handicaps at Newmarket in July and York in
October; best at middle distances; probably acts on any going. *K. Stone.*

GILT STAR 2 ch. f. Star Appeal 133–Demeter 83 (Silly Season 127) (1983 6f³   **92**
7f*(dis) 8fg 7fg³) Apr 2; 6,400Y; quite well-made, useful-looking filly; excellent
walker and good mover; second living foal; half-sister to useful 5f to 7f performer
Mother Earth (by Jukebox); dam 2-y-o 7f winner; won 7-runner minor event at
Brighton in August by ¾ length from Birdwood but was disqualified nearly 2 weeks
later because apprentice rider drew wrong allowance; afterwards took on stronger
company at Ascot, finishing 6 lengths sixth of 9 to Nepula in Hoover Fillies Mile and
3½ lengths third of 11 to Ministerial in Hyperion Stakes; will stay 1¼m; sure to win
if not tried too highly. *P. Kelleway.*

GIMME PLEASURE (USA) 2 b. c. Honest Pleasure–Gimme Love (Dr Fager)   **94**
(1983 6v* 5g* 6fg 7g 8s⁴) Mar 15; $65,000Y; good mover; second foal;
half-brother to a winner; dam 2-y-o 6f winner; won twice in May, making much of
running to beat Cerussite a length in maiden race at the Curragh and getting the
better of Deasys Delight by a neck in 5-runner Marwell Stakes at Phoenix Park;
about 10 lengths fifth to Chief Singer in 14-runner Coventry Stakes at Royal Ascot
in June; off course until October when beaten 4½ lengths in Tap On Wood Stakes at
Phoenix Park and last of 4 Panasonic Beresford Stakes at the Curragh; stays 7f. *E.
O'Grady, Ireland.*

GINGER BRINK (FR) 3 ch. c. Brinkmanship 125–La Roussiere (Le Fabuleux   **117**
133) (1982 5g⁴ 5.5g 5.5d² 7g 7g² 7fg³ 7.5g 8g³ 7.5fg⁴ 8s² 7g* 8f 7f 8s⁴ 8s 8.5v*
7s⁴ 10v 1983 7v² 7.5v 8v 8s³ 9s² 8v² 10v³ 9fg* 7.5g* 8f³ 9f* 11g) half-brother to
2 winners, including middle-distance performer Tarsiere (by Tarbes); dam won 2
small middle-distance races; kept busy again in first part of season, as he had been
throughout 1982, but held his form really well and picked up a good prize when

beating Welsh Idol by ¾ length in 10-runner Prix Jean Prat at Chantilly in June; placed on 5 previous occasions, on last 2 going down by ½ length to Aragon in Prix de la Jonchere and finishing about a neck third to White Spade in Prix La Force, both at Longchamp in May; sent to race in USA in second half of season, where he won allowance race at Bay Meadows and Hollywood Derby (Division 2) at Hollywood Park; stays 1¼m; acts on any going; admirably tough and game. *R. Collet, France.*

GIN N' LIME 9 ch.g. Divine Gift 127–Fruit Cup 72 (Silver Shark 129) (1982 12.2fg 11.7f 1983 13.4fg) poor maiden on flat; has been tried in blinkers. *C. V. Miller.* —

GIN ROYALE 2 br.g. Royal Smoke 113–Ginger Jane 69 (Hornbeam 130) (1983 5f 6fg 7fg 8d 6g) fair sort; in rear in varied company, including selling. *M. Madgwick.* —

GIRL FRIDAY (USA) 2 ch.f. Secretariat–Patience Worth (Mr Prospector) (1983 8g* 8fg⁴) Feb 9; $335,000Y; big filly; first foal; dam very useful sprint stakes winner; moved up easily to join leaders in straight and quickened away in last furlong to win £3,400 event at Goodwood in September by 3 lengths from Superbia; looked to have lost a lot of condition when favourite for 8-runner Hoover Fillies Mile at Ascot later in month and finished in final furlong to finish 2 lengths fourth to Nepula, a useful performance nonetheless; needs to strengthen up, but should win more races. *I. Balding.* 100

GIRL FROM RIO 2 ro.f. Town Crier 119–Coy Lady (Damremont 120) (1983 5s 5d) May 12; 3,100Y; angular filly; half-sister to 3 winners, notably very smart middle-distance stayer Sir Montagu (by Connaught); dam showed no form; destroyed after breaking a leg at Thirsk in May. *N. Tinkler.* —

GIRSEACH 3 b. or br.f. Furry Glen 121–Happy Lass (Tarqogan 125) (1982 8.5d 8d 1983 10g* 12v 10s³ 16f 12g 14g⁴ 16s 12d⁴ 16d) IR 800F, IR 500Y; half-sister to Irish 2½m winner Dunabunk (by Brave Invader) and a bumpers winner, both also successful over hurdles; dam won at up to 1½m in Ireland; 25/1-winner of maiden race at Navan in April; in frame at Gowran Park, Leopardstown and Naas (blinkered) afterwards; stays 1¾m (well beaten in Queen's Vase at Royal Ascot on first attempt at 2m). *J. Kavanagh, Ireland.* 79

GITAINE 6 ch.g. Royal Smoke 113–Dancing Lane (Domaha or Drury 91) (1982 NR 1983 14f) poor performer over jumps; well behind in maiden race at Sandown in June, first outing on flat. *D. Ancil.* —

GIVE THANKS 3 b.f. Relko 136–Parthica 98 (Parthia 132) (1982 7fg 7fg 8d³ 1983 10v* 9s* 12s* 10.5s* 12v² 12g* 12f* 12d³ 14.6fg² 12d) 123
Not every high-class horse is wrapped in cotton wool; some are campaigned vigorously and fearlessly to the immense benefit of the interested public. Largely because of financial considerations most of the recent examples have been provided by the so-called weaker sex, one of the most striking that by the three-year-old Give Thanks, an Irish-trained filly who responded to a long and arduous programme in a way that would have done credit to the redoubtable Sceptre. She proved herself exceptionally tough, and among the best of her generation too. Before July was out Give Thanks had won six races, including the Irish Guinness Oaks, from seven starts, the majority of them in testing

Musidora Stakes, York—Give Thanks wins her second race in five days

Lancashire Oaks, Haydock—Give Thanks makes another successful raid; Ski Sailing beats Acclimatise for second

conditions, and had performed the nowadays-rare feat, one to be repeated by her compatriot Stanerra, of winning two pattern races inside seven days.

Give Thanks won the Esal Bookmakers Oaks Trial at Lingfield on the Friday of the first week in May and the Musidora Stakes at York on the Tuesday following. Before arriving in England she had had two races already and had won them both, a maiden at Navan and a more valuable event at Phoenix Park, the latter by three lengths. Give Thanks was never entered for the Oaks—her trainer said she would be unsuited by the Epsom track—so her victories at Lingfield and York weren't quite so significant as they might have been. Still, they were significant enough in all conscience, for she beat the Oaks probable Cormorant Wood by five lengths into second place in the Esal Bookmakers Trial and she had a field of hopefuls strung out like washing in the Musidora, winning by eight lengths, three lengths, eight, eight again and twelve from So True, New Coins, Nibabu, Acclimatise and Fields of Spring.

After these last two displays it came as a great surprise to see Give Thanks beaten a length and a half on merit by the colt Carlingford Castle in the Gallinule Stakes run in similar conditions at the Curragh later in May; she started at 5/4 on. Her prospects appeared a little less rosy now, especially with the ground likely to dry up at any time. However, it soon transpired that she'd been taking on something in Carlingford Castle; and we didn't have to wait much longer to find out she wasn't beholden to the ground, for she came out again in July and won the Lancashire Oaks on good going at Haydock and the Irish Guinness Oaks on firm at the Curragh with a degree of authority. Strange to relate now, Give Thanks was strongly opposed in the market at Haydock—by Ski Sailing and Acclimatise who'd been well beaten behind Sun Princess at Epsom though Acclimatise had finished second, and by Jolly Bay who'd been off the course since showing great promise in the early spring. Give Thanks won a slowly-run race gamely by two lengths and the same from Ski Sailing and Acclimatise. The trip seemed a minimum for her, for she was in trouble and under strong pressure early in the straight and took until inside the last furlong to get her head in front; by the line she was well on top and staying on stoutly.

The visitors have enjoyed much the better of the argument in the Irish Guinness Oaks in the last few years. On this occasion though there were no French challengers and only two from England, High Hawk and Shore Line—Sun

328

Princess having been reserved for the King George VI and Queen Elizabeth Diamond Stakes. Give Thanks started 7/4 favourite, the rapidly-improving Ribblesdale Stakes winner High Hawk at 9/4 and the Oaks fourth Shore Line 6/1 third favourite. The gallop set by the pacemaker Hocus Pocus was a good one, much stronger than that for the Lancashire Oaks, and Give Thanks ran a different type of race. She was able to improve smoothly into the lead entering the straight a good three furlongs from home and to muster the pace to move quickly clear. Once ahead she never looked in danger. High Hawk, who'd had a poor run in the early stages, chased her up the straight but was beaten by two and a half lengths. Green Lucia finished third, another two and a half lengths away; Shore Line was sixth.

Though as consistent as almost any horse in training and an above-average Irish Oaks winner Give Thanks never won again. She ran the one moderate race of her three-year-old season in the Yorkshire Oaks next time out, to the disappointment not least of those who looked forward to discovering how she compared with Sun Princess. She would never have beaten Sun Princess at level weights but at her best she wasn't so inferior as the seven-length drubbing suggests; even Green Lucia ran on much the better in the last two furlongs to deprive Give Thanks of second. Subsequently Give Thanks was found to have too high a white cell count. The information was made public after she had shown in the Park Hill Stakes at Doncaster in September that her loss of form had been only temporary. She ran well—well enough to encourage keeping her in training to represent Ireland in the Washington International—in finishing second of seven to a still-improving High Hawk. We thought the winner slightly the better suited by the distance of a mile and three quarters as we watched the pair fight out the finish with Give Thanks deprived of the lead just inside the final furlong and beaten a shade under a length. Good filly that Give Thanks was, All Along was a decidedly better one. In Washington Give Thanks was beaten around six lengths by the winner; she narrowly missed third place as she took fifth, a head in front of the English-trained three-year-old filly Cormorant Wood.

Give Thanks cost a mere 33,000 guineas as a yearling at the December Sales. She has appreciated considerably in value since then, not solely as a result of her

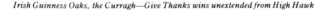

Irish Guinness Oaks, the Curragh—Give Thanks wins unextended from High Hawk

Mrs Ogden White's "Give Thanks"

own magnificent efforts either. Such were the achievements of other members of
her family in 1983 that the reader may turn to several other commentaries for some
of the details of her breeding. Teenoso, Old Country and Favoridge are also, like
Give Thanks, out of daughters of Violetta III. Give Thanks's dam Parthica, a quite
useful mile winner, was not so well established as a broodmare as many of her
relatives at the start of the season; in fact she owes it to Give Thanks for putting
her on the map. She had three runners from seven previous foals of whom the
sprinter/miler Baby Blair (by Forlorn River) and the Cyprus-trained Zoe (by Irish
Ball) won races. Parthica's two-year-old Celestial Storm, an unraced chesnut sister
to Give Thanks, is in Bolger's yard.

		Tanerko	Tantieme
	Relko	(br 1953)	La Divine
	(b 1960)	Relance III	Relic
Give Thanks		(ch 1952)	Polaire
(b.f. 1980)		Parthia	Persian Gulf
	Parthica	(b 1956)	Lightning
	(ch 1965)	Violetta III	Pinza
		(b 1958)	Urshalim

Give Thanks has been retired and visits Kings Lake. Workmanlike in
appearance, thoroughly workmanlike on the racecourse, she was an enormous
credit to her trainer. *J. Bolger, Ireland.*

GLASSON LADY (GER) 3 b.f. Priamos 123–Georgie Girl (Exbury 138) (1982 **108**
7g* 6f² 7fg⁴ 7g³ 8fg 7.5g³ 1983 7s* 7s* 7s* 10s³ 8v 8s⁴) sister to 2 winners in
Germany, including Georgie's Prince, winner of good races over 6f and 1m, and
half-sister to 3 others; dam won small 11f race in France; quite useful at 2 yrs;
improved in 1983 and did well, although not seen out after June; won minor event

at Naas, Ardoon Stud April Fillies Stakes at the Curragh and Mulcahy Stakes at Phoenix Park, beating Hole in the Wall in good style by 5 lengths in last-named race; far from disgraced in defeat subsequently in Hard Fought 3-Y-O Fillies Stakes at Phoenix Park, Goffs Irish 1000 Guineas at the Curragh (4¾ lengths fifth of 18 to L'Attrayante) and Kilfrush What A Guest Stakes at Phoenix Park; possibly best at up to 1m; acts on any going but clearly goes very well on soft. *J. Bolger, Ireland.*

GLENANNA 3 b.f. Furry Glen 121–Annatown 68 (Charlottown 127) (1982 7.6v⁴   **70**
7d 1983 9v 10v 16g* 16.5f³) big, rangy, fair sort; beat Hal's Joy a neck in 19-runner maiden race at Lingfield in July; third in handicap at Folkestone later in month; stays very well; probably acts on any going. *C. Horgan.*

GLEN COTTAGE 3 b.f. Blakeney 126–Paltrasse 84 (Palestine 133) (1982 NR   **–**
1983 12d 8d 10fg) half-sister to 3 winners, including very smart 1976 2-y-o Anax (by Right Tack); dam, 1m winner, is sister to Bay Express' dam Pal Sinna; ran best race when about 8 lengths fifth of 10 behind stable-companion Chantry in 1m minor event at Brighton in September (nearest finish); unruly in stalls previous start; sold 10,500 gns Newmarket December Sales. *G. Harwood.*

GLENFIELD CLEANER 2 b.c. Tower Walk 130–Hecuba 112 (Relic) (1983   **–**
7f) Apr 15; IR 17,500F, 9,000Y; fair sort; half-brother to a winner by Mountain Call; dam second in 1000 Guineas; last of 16, after moving badly to post, in maiden race at Newmarket in July. *P. Brookshaw.*

GLENFIELD PORTION 3 b.f. Mummy's Pet 125–Shirwani 77 (Major Portion   **–**
129) (1982 5g² 5g 5g 5d³ 5fg* 5fg 5f* 5d³ 5g³ 1983 5s 5.8g 5f) small filly; lightly raced and well beaten in 1983; unlikely to stay beyond 5f; probably acts on any going; tends to sweat up; trained by P. Brookshaw until after second outing. *G. Huffer.*

GLENHAWK 7 b.g Furry Glen 121–Genazzano (Shantung 132) (1982 18g 15.5fg³   **72**
1983 10g* 12fg* 8fg 11fg² 10f 11.7f² 12g³ 11.5g) strong, rangy gelding; good walker and mover; won amateur riders event at Lingfield in June (66/1) and handicap at Leicester in July; best at middle distances; acts on any going; tends to sweat up; pulls hard and is suited by a strongly-run race. *M. Ryan.*

GLEN ISLE 2 b.f. Auction Ring 123–Hunter's Isle 87 (Huntercombe 133) (1983 6g   **65**
5fg 6fg 7f 5fg⁴ 5fg) May 10; 10,500Y; strong, attractive, medium-sized filly; second foal; dam won twice over 5f; plating-class maiden; best form at 5f. *B. Swift.*

GLEN KELLA MANX 2 b.f. Tickled Pink 114–Joshua's Daughter 60 (Joshua   **71**
129) (1983 6g² 5fg 5d³ 5g⁴ 6d) Apr 18; lengthy, sturdy filly; second foal; half-sister to a winning plater; dam stayed 1½m; ran well in better company after finishing second in seller at Lingfield in June on first outing; stays 6f; best form with some give in the ground. *J. Fox.*

GLEN MAYE 4 b.f. Maystreak 118–Charlies Mate (Prince Regent 129) (1982 NR   **–**
1983 10f 12f⁴ 10.6fg 10h⁴ 12g) sturdy filly; first foal; dam ran once; poor form, including in sellers; stays 1½m. *D. Francis.*

GLEN NA SMOLE 2 br.f. Ballymore 123–Kix 71 (King Emperor) (1983 6g 6d)   **– p**
Mar 7; fourth foal; dam in frame in early-season maiden races at 2 yrs; showed a little ability in newcomers race at Goodwood in September and minor event at Lingfield in October; should do better over longer distances. *J. Sutcliffe.*

GLENN'S SLIPPER 2 b.f. Furry Glen 121–Grannies Slipper (Allangrange 126)   **62**
(1983 5d 6g 6f 6fg² 7f* 8h 8fg) Apr 14; IR 5,800F, IR 7,000Y; small filly; good walker; third foal; sister to a winner in Malaya; dam never ran; bought in 2,600 gns after winning 7-runner seller at Thirsk in July; will be suited by 1¼m; acts well on firm going; sweated up profusely fourth outing. *J. Mason.*

GLENSIDE LADY 4 b.f. So Blessed 130–Croomedale (Alcide 136) (1982 7d 7g   **–**
8g 6f 8g 10v² 10d 8s⁴ 7s 1983 8.2s⁴ 8.2s 10.1f 8g) short-backed filly; poor walker; plater; stays 1¼m; suited by some give in the ground; wears blinkers. *K. Ivory.*

GLENSTAL (USA) 3 b.c. Northern Dancer–Cloonlara 130 (Sir Ivor 135) (1982   **118**
6.3fg* 7d* 1983 6s² 8fg 9fg*) medium-sized, attractive colt; good walker; second foal; closely related to Irish 1981 2-y-o 6f winner Chivalry (by Nijinsky); dam brilliant 2-y-o who was disappointing at 3 yrs, though fourth in 1000 Guineas, is half-sister to Kings Lake; won both his starts as a 2-y-o, including National Stakes at the Curragh; lightly raced again in 1983, but picked up another good prize in 7-runner Prix Daphnis at Evry in July, making all, quickening 3f out and holding on by a short neck from Luderic; had previously been second to Sir Prince John in £3,500 event at Phoenix Park in April (about 6f too sharp) and tailed-off sixth of 7 behind Horage in St James's Palace Stakes at Royal Ascot in June (looked in the pink of condition but played up in stalls and was never going well); stayed 9f;

Mr R. E. Sangster's "Glenstal"

seemed to act on any going; standing at Longfield Stud, Co. Tipperary, fee IR 20,000 guineas (Oct. 1st). *V. O'Brien, Ireland.*

GLEN VINE 3 b.f. Artaius 129–Charlotteen 96 (Charlottown 127) (1982 7g 1983 8f 8f²) smallish, useful-looking filly; made running when 4 lengths second of 17 behind Noble Blood in maiden race at Warwick in August, first outing for 2½ months; will stay 1¼m; sold 27,000 gns Newmarket December Sales. *R. Hollinshead.*   **55**

GLIMMERING 2 ch.f. Troy 137–Crown Treasure (Graustark) (1983 7g³) May 1; workmanlike, rather unfurnished filly; fourth foal; half-sister to 3-y-o Emerald Reef and top-class middle-distance stayers Glint of Gold and Diamond Shoal (all by Mill Reef); dam very useful winner at 2 yrs in USA; stayed on very strongly after getting well behind through greenness when most promising 3½ lengths third of 8 behind stable-companion Troyanna in £3,800 event at York in October; will be well suited by 1¼m+; sure to improve a good deal and win races. *I. Balding.*   **83 p**

GLINT OF SILVER 2 b.f. Sallust 134–Silver Shoals 98 (Mill Reef 141) (1983 5f 5fg 6f² 6f⁴ 5d 6fg) Mar 12; 5,000Y; rather lightly-built filly; second foal; dam won over 5f and 6f at 2 yrs; in frame in large fields of maidens in August; bred to be better suited by 7f+; acts on firm going, and ran poorly only outing on a soft surface. *I. Walker.*   **69**

GLITTER BROOK 2 gr.c. Diamonds Are Trump 108–Burnside 82 (Roan Rocket 128) (1983 5v³ 5d³) Apr 3; 5,000Y; lengthy, plain colt; first foal; dam 2-y-o 7f winner; placed in maiden race at Nottingham and minor event at Newmarket. *N. Callaghan.*   **55**

GLITTERING GEM 3 b.f. Silly Season 127–Arrival 102 (Henry the Seventh 125) (1982 6g 7fg 7f² 7.6v 1983 9s 8g 10fg 12f 12f² 12fg 10f³ 12f² 12fg) strong filly; placed at Folkestone (twice) and Epsom; stays 1½m; acts on firm going. *K. Brassey.*   **62**

GLORIA MUNDI 3 b.f. Blakeney 126–Final Orders (Prince John) (1982 7fg³ 7f 7.6v² 7.2s² 8d³ 1983 12g 12d³ 12.2d³ 10.2f 12f³ 11f 11.7h² 11.1g² 12d² 10fg 12.2g) small, close-coupled filly; frequently placed but doesn't seem all that genuine; will   **73**

stay well; appears to act on any going; trained by B. Hobbs until after fourth start. *R. Baker.*

GLORY BIRD 4 ch.c. Hittite Glory 125–Partridge 65 (Mossborough 126) (1982   **59**
10s* 10d³ 10f 10d 12d 12d⁴ 1983 10v* 12v 12v²) useful-looking colt; former
plater; won apprentice handicap at Ayr in March; second in similar event at Naas in
May; stays 1½m; revels in the mud; ran respectably in blinkers once; sold 3,700
gns Ascot October Sales and sent to Switzerland. *P. Rohan.*

GLOSSY TIPS 2 ch.f. Shiny Tenth 120–Indian Tea (Taj Dewan 128) (1983 6f 5fg³   **–**
7f 6f 6g 5s) May 8; 540Y; smallish, plain filly; bad plater; has worn blinkers. *W. Stubbs.*

GLOWING EMBERS 3 ch.f. Nebbiolo 125–Rossitor 78 (Pall Mall 132) (1982   **107**
7fg 8.5d² 1983 7v* 7s² 7s⁴ 10v 10s 8fg² 12f 10f² 12g 10g* 10g* 12g) strong,
attractive, most taking filly; half-sister to top-class middle-distance colt Kalaglow
(by Kalamoun); dam, winning stayer, raced and produced in error as Aglow;
successful in maiden race at Naas in March, minor event at Navan in September and
ITB Prince's Polly Fillies Stakes at Phoenix Park in October; put up an excellent
performance in last-named event, leading 2f out and drawing clear to beat odds-on
Flame of Tara (gave 9 lb) by 5 lengths with remainder well strung out; also second 3
times, on first occasion to Glasson Lady in Ardoon Stud April Fillies Stakes at the
Curragh; only eighth of 12 behind Hymettus in Galtres Stakes at York however on
ninth outing and also ran moderately final start; stays 1¼m; probably acts on any
going; best in blinkers nowadays (didn't wear them at York). *D. K. Weld, Ireland.*

GLOWING WITH PRIDE 2 b.f. Ile de Bourbon 133–Be Easy 110 (Be Friendly   **85 p**
130) (1983 6fg³) Mar 2; rangy, deep-girthed, attractive filly; second foal;
half-sister to 3-y-o 1½m winner Majors Cast (by Morston); dam best at up to 7f;
12/1, but pick of the paddock, ran green and had to be pushed along throughout
when very promising 1¼ lengths third of 12 behind Rappa Tap Tap in Blue Seal
Stakes at Ascot in September; type to do a great deal better with time and longer
distances. *G. Wragg.*

GNOS 9 b.g. Song 132–No Recall 85 (Tutankhamen) (1982 NR 1983 5d 7fg 6d)   **–**
dipped-backed gelding; moody and inconsistent handicapper; usually wears
blinkers; sometimes sweats up; has worn a tongue strap; wears bandages; sold 440
gns Doncaster June Sales. *Ronald Thompson.*

GO BANANA'S 2 b.c. Young Generation 129–Miss Lucian (Athens Wood 126)   **60**
(1983 5v 5f³ 5.1fg² 7f⁴ 7f 6fg) Mar 16; 1,100Y; big, workmanlike colt; second foal;
dam once-raced half-sister to very smart sprinter Broxted; in frame in maiden
auction events; stays 7f; acts on firm going; slowly away when last in nursery
penultimate start. *K. Ivory.*

GO DIANA 6 gr.m. The Go-Between 129–My Diana 94 (Sovereign Path 125)   **–**
(1982 8f 8fg⁴ 5.3fg 1983 10d 10.2g 16g 16.5f) leggy mare; poor plater; often
blinkered; sold 950 gns Ascot December Sales. *H. Beasley.*

GODLORD 3 gr.c. Godswalk 130–Gay Pariso 92 (Sir Gaylord) (1982 5f² 1983 6d   **–**
5v³ 5v 6d 5fg 5fg 5g 5fg 5fg 5g) strong, good-bodied colt; plating-class sprint maiden.
T. Taylor.

GODLY 4 ro.c. Godswalk 130–Desert Pet 77 (Petingo 135) (1982 6s* 8.2fg 6d   **69**
7fg* 6fg² 6g 7g 8g 8d 8d 6s 6s 7d 1983 8f 12f³ 7f) strong colt; stays 1½m; acts on
any going; blinkered twice in 1982. *Miss A. Sinclair.*

GODOLPHIN 3 gr.c. Godswalk 130–Lilgarde 83§ (Hugh Lupus 132) (1982 5f⁴   **65 §**
5f⁴ 5f³ 5f² 5f⁴ 5f² 5g 1983 5v 5s² 5f 5f* 6f 5f 6f) short-coupled colt; apprentice
ridden when winning handicap at Beverley in July; gives impression 5f is his trip;
acts on any going; usually blinkered nowadays, and has been ridden by jockey in
spurs; very slowly away sixth start and refused to race final outing. *M. W. Easterby.*

GOD'S IMAGE 4 gr.g. Godswalk 130–Pink Larkspur (Ragusa 137) (1982 6g   **–**
7.6f4 8fg⁴ 7f 7f* 8g 1983 7f 10fg 7g 8.2g⁴) sparely-made, workmanlike gelding;
poor handicapper; fourth in seller final start; stays 1m; acts on firm going; has worn
bandages; sold to D. Wilson 1,650 gns Ascot November Sales. *I. Walker.*

GODS LAW 2 b.g. Godswalk 130–Fluently (Ragusa 137) (1983 5g 5g 6f 6fg 6f 5g   **56**
6d 6s) Feb 23; 800Y; leggy gelding; poor mover; dam won over 1¼m in France;
modest plater; will probably be better suited by 7f+. *A. Smith.*

GODSTONE 2 gr.c. Godswalk 130–Ansedonia (Captain's Gig) (1983 5f² 6fg* 6d*   **115**
6fg 5fg³)
    Few who witnessed Godstone's defeat in a maiden race at Carlisle in June
could have imagined his winning the Group 2 OCL Richmond Stakes at Goodwood

OCL Richmond Stakes, Goodwood—a fortunate success for Godstone (striped sleeves), awarded the race on the disqualification of Vacarme (rails), and demotion of Creag-An-Sgor (star on cap)

the following month. Godstone, who was successful in a valuable maiden race in excellent style at Lingfield in the interim, was an extremely fortunate Richmond winner, awarded the race on the disqualification of both first-past-the-post Vacarme and runner-up Creag-An-Sgor, each of whom arguably beat him on merit.

Esal Commodities Ltd's "Godstone"

Nevertheless, Godstone showed at Goodwood that he was one of the speediest two-year-olds of the season: prominent throughout, he kept on extremely well to pass the post third, beaten three quarters of a length and a length by Vacarme and Creag-An-Sgor. Godstone's rider objected to Creag-An-Sgor on the grounds of bumping and boring inside the last furlong. The stewards sustained his objection and as a result of the inquiry found that Vacarme had interfered with fifth-placed Pacific King; Vacarme's rider was adjudged guilty of careless riding which resulted in mandatory disqualification for Vacarme. Godstone was absent from the racecourse for two months after Goodwood, until contesting the William Hill Middle Park Stakes at Newmarket in September, where, looking a little burly, he finished seventh of nine to Creag-An-Sgor. In the five-furlong Cornwallis Stakes at Ascot nine days later Godstone put up another smart performance to finish third, beaten a head and the same by Petorius and Pacific King; he led until drifting off line well inside the final furlong.

Godstone (gr.c. May 28, 1981)				
	Godswalk (gr 1974)	Dancer's Image (gr 1965)	Native Dancer	Noor's Image
		Kate's Intent (b 1964)	Intentionally	Julie Kate
	Ansedonia (br 1973)	Captain's Gig (br 1965)	Turn-to	Make Sail
		Heron Bay (br 1954)	Honeyway	Borobella

Godstone is unlikely to stay beyond sprint distances. His sire Godswalk, who now stands in Australia, was a top-class sprinter and his dam, a winner over five furlongs in Ireland as a two-year-old, was also a sprinter. The dam has produced Solo Star (by Jukebox), a useful 1980 Irish two-year-old six-furlong winner, in addition to a winner in Malaysia. Godstone, a strong, compact colt, acts well on firm going. Whether he'll ever win another race as valuable as the Richmond—worth £34,760 to the winner in 1983—must be regarded as highly unlikely. Unless he makes more than normal progress he'll almost certainly find one or two too good for him in the important weight-for-age sprints. Ultimately he may have to take his chance in handicaps. *P. Haslam.*

GODSTRUTH 4 gr. or ro.g. Godswalk 130–Light Opera 101 (Vienna 127) (1982 6d* 6f 5g 6fg 6v⁴ 6d 6g 1983 5s 6v 5f 5.1fg 6fg 6h 5f) small, strong gelding; well beaten in 1983; suited by 6f; acts on any going; usually blinkered nowadays; looked a handful for apprentice rider sixth start. *H. T. Jones.* —

GOESWELL 3 gr.f. Roan Rocket 128–Mockbridge 106 (Bleep-Bleep 134) (1982 NR 1983 6v 7v) rangy filly; half-sister to 3 winners, including quite useful 7f to 13f performer Bines Bridge (by Lorenzaccio); dam won over 5f and 7f at 2 yrs from 4 starts; showed a bit of promise after dwelling when remote sixth of 11 behind Lyphnap in minor race at Kempton in May; started slowly again and was never placed to challenge only subsequent start; will be suited by 1m+. *G. Lewis.* —

GOING BROKE 3 b.c. Bustino 136–Spring Maiden 90 (Silly Season 127) (1982 NR 1983 12v 17v 12g* 12f 13.1f⁴ 17fg 11.7fg⁴ 12f 12g) quite attractive colt; sixth foal; dam 7f winner; won maiden race at Brighton in May; yet to show he stays beyond 1½m. *P. Cole.* 59

GOING GOING 4 b.g. Auction Ring 123–Whitethorn (Gulf Pearl 117) (1982 8fg³ 8fg 10f 10.2s² 10d 12s² 1983 10.1fg 8f³ 12f* 12g* 10.2fg 12.2d² 12fg²) compact, attractive gelding; good walker; won apprentice handicaps at Epsom in August and Goodwood in September; also first past post in handicap at Warwick in October on sixth start but was moved down a place for hampering runner-up; suited by 1½m; acts on any going; good mount for an apprentice. *H. Candy.* 88

GOLD AND IVORY (USA) 2 b.c. Key To The Mint–Ivory Wand (Sir Ivor 135) (1983 7f³ 8fg² 7g* 8fg*) 128

It's a sign of the times that 202,000 dollars now seems quite an ordinary price for a foal–750,000 dollars was paid for an Alydar filly in 1983–but when a filly foal by Sir Ivor out of Natashka was knocked down to Paul Mellon's Rokeby Stables for that amount in November 1973 the price not only constituted a new record, it nearly doubled the previous one set in 1969. The investment has proved a wise one. The filly, named Ivory Wand, developed into a smart performer, winning the seven-furlong Test Stakes and three other races from six starts at three, and retired with earnings only a little short of 100,000 dollars. Also, if Ivory Wand's pedigree was highly attractive in 1973, it makes most impressive reading now: Natashka, a very good winner at up to a mile and a quarter, had produced two

Royal Lodge Stakes, Ascot—Gold And Ivory shows improved form to beat Rousillon and Trojan Fen (rails)

winners at the time of Ivory Wand's sale, notably the Irish One Thousand Guineas and Irish Guinness Oaks runner-up Arkadina. Natashka's total now stands at seven, among them the high-class stayer Blood Royal, the Joe McGrath Memorial winner Gregorian and the filly Truly Bound, who ranked among the best of her sex in the States both at two and three years. Moreover, Arkadina's son South Atlantic won the 1983 Blandford Stakes and another of Natashka's daughters, Mild Deception, produced the 1983 National Jockey Club Handicap winner Determined Bidder. Fillies from this family remain extremely valuable and Mellon is in the happy position of owning three out of Ivory Wand—a four-year-old by Nijinsky called Leap of the Heart who has won over 100,000 dollars, a yearling by Foolish Pleasure and a foal by The Minstrel. Mellon also owns a very promising colt in Ivory Wand's only son, Gold And Ivory, a strong, good-looking individual bred along the same lines as Arkadina and Blood Royal, both of whom were by his great-grandsire Ribot, and Gregorian, who was by his grandsire Graustark.

Gold And Ivory (USA) (b.c. Apr 5, 1981)	Key To The Mint (b 1969)	Graustark (ch 1963)	Ribot
			Flower Bowl
		Key Bridge (b 1959)	Princequillo
			Blue Banner
	Ivory Wand (b 1973)	Sir Ivor (b 1965)	Sir Gaylord
			Attica
		Natashka (br 1963)	Dedicate
			Natasha

Gold And Ivory's season divides neatly in halves. The first consists of pleasing if immature performances in the Sandwich Stakes at Ascot in July, where he put in some attractive work under tender handling to finish third of nine to the four-length winner Harvard, and the Fitzroy House Stakes at Newmarket a month later, where, despite receiving 11 lb, he was completely outpointed by Lear Fan. Much better was to follow, in the shape of victories in September in an eighteen-runner maiden race at Goodwood, the Rhine and Moselle Stakes, and the Royal Lodge Stakes at Ascot. His Goodwood win showed that the penny had finally dropped: he raced with the leaders from the start and was in no danger in the final quarter mile, winning by two lengths and four lengths from Alnood and Enchanted Castle. Admirable though his effort was, it didn't seem to give Gold And Ivory much chance of beating the unbeaten colts Trojan Fen and Rousillon in the Royal Lodge, winners between them of six races by an aggregate of fifteen lengths. In a five-strong field he started at 25/1, with Trojan Fen and Rousillon sharing favouritism at 6/5. The 200/1-shot Mellow Dance usefully provided an excellent gallop from the off, leading from Gold And Ivory, Trojan Fen, Rousillon and Great Western. Cauthen on Gold And Ivory was the only one to attempt to stay within striking distance as Mellow Dance quickened the pace, and the colt turned into the straight with a clear advantage over Trojan Fen and Rousillon. The favourites were quickly sent in hot pursuit but it was obvious Trojan Fen wouldn't win fully two furlongs out, where Gold And Ivory hit the front. The same couldn't be said of Rousillon though and Gold And Ivory was quickly passed, with the race looking as good as over. However Gold And Ivory didn't weaken in the slightest and, with Rousillon suddenly coming to the end of his tether, he was not only able to regain the lead but to put two lengths between himself and Rousillon well inside the last furlong. Trojan Fen held on to third place a further two and a half lengths behind. The change in Rousillon's fortunes was so dramatic it tended to draw attention away from Gold And Ivory's thoroughly-deserved success which showed him beyond question a high-class performer, with abundant courage and stamina. Gold And Ivory must be regarded as a leading candidate for the top middle-distance races after that performance, and his trainer is most fortunate to have both Gold And Ivory and Elegant Air in his stable. Incidentally, although Gold And Ivory seemed perfectly at home on the firmish surface at Ascot and has yet to race on going softer than good, his trainer believes he's well suited by some give in the ground. *I. Balding.*

GOLDBAG 2 b. or br.g. Laxton 105–Bambag (Goldhill 125) (1983 5fg 5.8h) Mar 13; first foal; dam unraced half-sister to very smart Commodore Blake; poor form in July maiden events at Windsor and Bath (second favourite); subsequently gelded. *B. Hills.*   –

GOLD BUILDER 2 ch.g. Wolverlee 115–Lady Marigot (Lord Gayle 124) (1983 5s⁴ 5d⁴ 5g) Mar 10; 5,000F, IR 1,600Y; close-coupled gelding; first foal; dam won over 1¼m in Ireland; plating-class maiden; bred to stay beyond 5f; off course 4 months after second outing. *A. Turnell.*   **67**

GOLD CHANCE 5 b.g. Incas 88–High Gamble (Gambling Debt 98) (1982 NR 1983 10fg 8.3fg) beaten a long way in claiming race and seller; sold 525 gns Ascot November Sales. *R. Atkins.*

GOLDEN ALMIDA 2 b.f. Master Sing 109–Sincerity 91 (Soderini 123) (1983 5v 5v 5d) Apr 25; 800Y; rather plain filly; of no account; sold 430 gns Doncaster November Sales. *K. Stone.*

GOLDEN ARUM 2 b.f. Home Guard 129–Gilded Lily (Sparkler 130) (1983 5d³ 6s 6f 6f 8f) May 26; 16,500F; second produce; half-sister to American 3-y-o 6f winner Rock'n Express (by Bay Express); dam unraced half-sister to smart miler Richboy; plating-class maiden; no form after first outing; should stay at least 6f. *P. Cole.*   **67**

GOLDEN BRIGADIER 5 b.g. Brigadier Gerard 144–Golden Fez (Aureole 132) (1982 10.6s² 10fg² 10.4g 11f* 10f 12g 12fg 1983 12d⁴ 11v 12s⁴ 12s 12d) strong, good sort; modest handicapper at his best; stays 1½m; seems to act on any going; occasionally blinkered, and has won in them; has sweated up; sometimes bandaged behind; often apprentice ridden; ungenuine. *J. Old.*   §§

GOLDEN CAPISTRANO 2 b.c. Dominion 123–Blaskette 99 (Blast 125) (1983 6h* 6f) Apr 30; 18,000Y; half-brother to 3-y-o Master Silca Key (by Homing) and 2 minor winners; dam middle-distance handicapper; upset by ½ length odds laid on Ubique in 7-runner newcomers event at Chepstow in August; short-priced favourite, last of 8 in all-aged race at Folkestone the following month; should be well suited by 7f+. *Sir Mark Prescott.*   **85** ?

GOLDEN DECOY 3 b.f. Decoy Boy 129–Nina's Gold 55 (Nina's Boy) (1982 5.8g 8s 7d 6s 1983 7s* 7v³ 6s³ 7.6v⁴ 7s* 7f 8g 7.6d) good-topped, workmanlike filly; ran consistently well in first half of season and won maiden race at Leicester and handicap at Lingfield; off course for 3 months before seventh start and didn't   **73**

recapture her form; suited by 7f+; acts well on soft going; usually ridden by 7-lb claimer. *D. C. Tucker.*

GOLDEN ECSTASY 2 br.f. Derrylin 115–True Delirium 87 (Delirium 126) (1983 5g4 5s) May 1; 8,400Y; half-sister to several winners here and abroad, including useful 1972 2-y-o 5f and 6f winner Golden Treasure (by Crepello); dam showed fair form at 2 yrs but became temperamental; poor form in October in minor event at Bath and maiden race (favourite) at Hamilton; sold 4,300 gns Newmarket Autumn Sales. *P. Walwyn.*   **59**

GOLDEN FAME 3 ch.f. Goldhill 125–Famished (Arctic Chevalier) (1982 NR 1983 9s 9d 12f) fourth foal; dam won 2m bumpers race; last in maiden and minor races at Hamilton (2) and Carlisle. *J. Haldane.*   **–**

GOLDEN FLAME 2 b. or br.c. Hot Grove 128–Misacre 66 (St Alphage 119) (1983 8d 7f4) Apr 11; heavy-topped colt; third reported foal; half-brother to 3-y-o Amarone (by Realm), a winner at up to 1m; dam plating class; not seen out until right at the back-end, and seemed still to be carrying plenty of condition when 5½ lengths fourth of 8 behind Jabaraba in minor event at Leicester; likely to improve. *R. Simpson.*   **80 p**

GOLDEN FLUTE (USA) 2 ch.c. Full Pocket–Lauravella 108 (Aureole 132) (1983 5d* 5fg 7f* 7fg* 7fg) Feb 28; quite a useful sort; brother to useful 1982 2-y-o 5f to 7f performer Arrowood Bob and half-brother to numerous winners, 2 of them minor stakes winners; dam, half-sister to very smart sprinter Creetown, third in Irish 1000 Guineas; won maiden race at Carlisle in May, minor event at Beverley in July and £3,800 race (giving weight to all his 17 rivals) at Newcastle in August; never-going seventh of 8 in Somerville Tattersall Stakes at Newmarket in September; will stay 1m. *S. Norton.*   **101**

GOLDEN GRUNDY 2 ch.f. Grundy 137–Pale Gold (New Chapter 106) (1983 7fg*) Apr 7; 11,000Y; third foal; dam, minor winner over 6f and 11.5f in France, is half-sister to smart animals Pale Ale and Polynikis; 7/4 on, beat 3 more-experienced fillies in minor event at Leopardstown in August, winning easily by 4 lengths from Finuge Lady after leading 1f out; will be suited by 1¼m+; a useful filly in the making. *L. Browne, Ireland.*   **86 p**

GOLDEN HOLLY 5 ch.g. Golden Mallard 103–Holly Doon (Doon 124) (1982 NR 1983 8g 7d 6f 9f 7f) plater; best at sprint distances; occasionally blinkered. *G. Harman.*   **–**

GOLDEN LADDIE 4 ch.c. Northern Flash–Annalie (Crepello 136) (1982 10d4 8.5fg 8g 10fg* 11.7fg 10d2 10f 1983 10v) compact, short-legged colt; poor handicapper; should stay 1½m; acts on a firm and a soft surface. *M. Haynes.*   **–**

GOLDEN MATCH 5 ch.g. Royal Match 117–Hunea (Hornbeam 130) (1982 12f 12d 10.1d 1983 10fg 8h 11.7h) big gelding; poor maiden; blinkered last 2 starts in 1982. *J. Baker.*   **–**

GOLDEN OCTOBER 2 ch.f. Young Generation 129–Affection 110 (Compensation 127) (1983 6f 5g) Mar 8; 22,000Y; compact filly; half-sister to fairly useful 5f performer Cockney Rebel (by Sparkler); a winner in Italy; dam very useful sprinting 2-y-o and later won over 1m; poor form in newcomers event at Ascot in June and small race at Catterick 3 months later. *M. Jarvis.*   **–**

GOLDEN RHYME 3 ch.f. Dom Racine 121–Silly Song (Silly Season 127) (1982 7fg4 7.2s3 1983 9v 7fg* 8f 7fg2 7f* 7.3f 7f) lengthy, rather sparely-made filly; won valuable maiden race at Sandown in June narrowly from Starlit Sky and kept on strongly to beat Comedy Fair by ½ length in £4,800 handicap at Newcastle in July; also ran well twice behind Silverdip, finishing 1½ lengths second in £6,600 handicap at Newmarket in between and 7 lengths sixth of 10 in Strensall Stakes at York in August on final start (50/1-chance and facing stiff task in latter); should stay 1m; acts on any going; sent to USA. *G. Hunter.*   **87**

GOLDERAMA 2 ch.f. Golden Dipper 119–Lamara (Major Portion 129) (1983 6f) Apr 23; a twin; first produce; dam of little account; last of 18 in maiden race at Folkestone in August. *M. Madgwick.*   **–**

GOLD HARMONY 4 ch.f. Goldhill 125–Bishop's Song 67 (Bishop's Move 92) (1982 10fg 1983 7d 11d) sturdy filly; well beaten in maiden races and a seller. *J. Parkes.*   **–**

GOLD HEART 3 ch.g. Roman Warrior 132–Pickling Spice 79 (Frankincense 120) (1982 6f 6g 7g 7fg 6s 6g4 5d 1983 10s 10f 6f 7fg) short-backed, plain gelding; plater; best form at 6f as a 2-y-o and by no means certain to stay 1¼m; best in blinkers; sold out of A. Bailey's stable 540 gns Ascot March Sales. *R. Voorspuy.*   **–**

Mrs S. R. Brook's "Golden Flute"

GOLD HUNTER 3 b.c. Rheingold 137–Mothers Girl (Huntercombe 133) (1982 —
8g 1983 10s 11.5fg 8f 7h) quite an attractive colt and a good walker, but little form
over a variety of distances. *J. Sutcliffe.*

GOLD INLAY (USA) 3 ch.g. Le Fabuleux 133–Pamlisa (What A Pleasure) (1982 —
8g 10s 1983 10v 16v 14g 16f) leggy, close-coupled gelding; poor maiden on flat, but
is a hurdles winner. *R. Williams.*

GOLDLINER BONUS 2 br.g. Goldhills Pride 105–Bright and Early (Rise 'N 66
Shine II) (1983 5f³ 6fg 5s³ 6s²) Apr 9; fair sort; half-brother to winners here and
abroad, including 1980 2-y-o 7f winner Goldliner Abbey (by Abwah); dam never
ran; placed in big fields of platers late August onwards; stays 6f; acts on any going;
will win a seller. *J. Hardy.*

GOLD MASCOT 2 ch.g. Stanford 121§–Mollies First 59 (Songedor 116) (1983 61
5v 5fg) May 6; IR 8,000F; half-brother to several winners here and abroad; dam
won at up to 11f; poor form in early-season maiden events at Doncaster and
Nottingham. *E. Eldin.*

GOLDORATION 8 b.g. Gold Rod 129–Fair Jinks 65 (Tudor Jinks 121) (1982 8s² —
10fg⁴ 1983 6v) plater; needs further than 6f and stays 1¼m; probably acts on any
going. *H. O'Neill.*

GOLD SPRING 3 gr. or ro.c. Goldhill 125–Another Spring 66 (Town Crier 119) —
(1982 5g 5d 7fg 8s 1983 8s 6d) neat colt; of little account. *J. Mason.*

GOLD TOBY 2 ch.c. Porto Bello 118–Goldprize (Goldhill 125) (1983 5f 5f 5f) Apr —
22; 1,300F; second produce; dam unraced sister to useful sprinter Goldhills Pride;
in rear in August in maiden race and 2 sellers. *P. Felgate.*

GOLDWATER 3 b.c. Rheingold 137–Niltava (Habitat 134) (1982 7g 1983 8d³ —
10g) close-coupled colt; last of 3 to Fatih in private sweepstakes at Newmarket in

April; behind in amateur riders race on only subsequent outing (September); should stay middle distances; sold out of B. Hobbs's stable 2,700 gns Ascot 2nd June Sales. *P. Mitchell.*

GOLDYE'S MISS (USA) 2 b. or br.f. Nijinsky 138–Miss Suzakai (Tompion) (1983 8.5g³ 7fg 8.5s*) Mar 14; $210,000Y; rangy, unfurnished filly; half-sister to several winners, notably Coverack (by Cornish Prince), a smart winner at up to 1¼m, and Go To The Bank (by Bold Hour), a very useful winner at up to 1m; dam 9f stakes winner in Canada; favourite when 5-length winner from Mayoress in maiden race at Gowran Park in October; had previously run well for long way when seventh of 11 to Ministerial in Hyperion Stakes at Ascot; should stay 1¼m+. *M. Cunningham, Ireland.*　　**89**

GOLFERS DREAM 4 b.f. Carnoustie 132–Dream (Hornbeam 130) (1982 10fg⁴ 10.1d 8d 1983 6d 6v 6s) small, workmanlike filly; has shown little form since 1981; should stay 1¼m; blinkered last 2 starts. *W. Stubbs.*　　**–**

GOLF GIRL (USA) 3 b.f. Vigors–Caption (Riva Ridge) (1982 5g 1983 10.2h 9fg 12f 8.2g 8g) sparely-made filly; behind in maiden and minor races; blinkered last 2 starts (unseated rider in early stages on first occasion); sold to BBA 6,400 gns Newmarket December Sales. *G. Hunter.*　　**–**

GONE BANANAS 2 b. or br.f. Take a Reef 127–Maretta (Sicambre 135) (1983 5s 5s 5s 7fg³ 7f⁴ 7f 8g) Apr 19; 500F, 880Y; good-bodied, workmanlike filly; first foal; dam never ran; plating-class maiden; will stay 1¼m; apparently suited by a firm surface. *B. McMahon.*　　**56**

GOOD AS DIAMONDS 3 b.c. Persian Bold 123–Aliceva (Alcide 136) (1982 6d⁴ 7fg³ 7g² 7s⁴ 1983 7g 10fg² 10fg² 10.5f 10f⁴ 12f² 12f⁴ 10f* 10.2s⁴) smallish, well-made, attractive colt; got off mark at last in 8-runner maiden race at Epsom in August, landing the odds smoothly after being held up; had acquitted himself well most previous starts and put up a remarkable performance when 2½ lengths second of 6 to easy winner John French in 1½m Gordon Stakes at Goodwood in July (clear most of way); stays 1½m; acts well on firm going, but has also run creditably on soft; pulls hard and isn't an easy ride. *B. Hills.*　　**86**

GOODBYE SHELLEY (FR) 3 b.f. Home Guard 129–Filiform 76 (Reform 132) (1982 6h 7d* 7fg³ 7g² 8ng³ 8s* 1983 7.3s* 8d 8v 10.5f 12g 9.2f) strong, quite attractive filly; made an impressive reappearance when beating Nibabu by 3 lengths in 9-runner Gainsborough Stud Fred Darling Stakes at Newbury in April, bursting through about a furlong out after having difficulty getting a run; didn't manage to reach the frame in top company afterwards, although on next 3 starts was seventh behind L'Attrayante in Poule d'Essai des Pouliches at Longchamp (reportedly in season and tended to hang under pressure) and Goffs Irish 1000 Guineas at the Curragh in May and eighth of 17 to Escaline in Prix de Diane Hermes at Chantilly in June; should have stayed at least 1¼m but was clearly effective at around 1m, at least when conditions were testing; best with some give in the ground and acted very well on soft going; not the easiest of rides; often blinkered; ran too freely on fifth start but was never going well on only subsequent start 3 months later; sold for stud in USA. *S. Norton.*　　**113**

GOOD FRIENDSHIP 2 gr.f. Touch Paper 113–Pale Maid 93 (Rise 'N Shine II) (1983 5d 5f 7fg 7fg 7.2s) May 26; 3,000Y; rangy filly; half-sister to 3 winners, including fairly useful 1981 Irish 2-y-o 5f winner Wolver Maid (by Wolverlife) and fair 1¼m winner Carved Opal (by Arch Sculptor); dam won over 6f at 2 yrs and stayed 1½m; moderate plater; stays 7f; appears to act on any going. *P. Rohan.*　　**55**

GOOD GOING GIRL 3 b.f. Import 127–Comedy Spring (Comedy Star 121) (1982 NR 1983.7f 7.2f 6fg 6s 5s) 900Y; strong, compact filly; first foal; dam never ran; showed only glimmer of ability in a seller on third outing; not sure to stay 7f; blinkered final start; sold 1,100 gns Doncaster October Sales. *R. Whitaker.*　　**–**

GOOD MAN FRIDAY (USA) 4 b.g. Noble Commander–Tinker Jet (Hi Hasty) (1982 10s 8f⁴ 10g 10f 10.1fg 13g 9s³ 16s 10s 10.2s⁴ 1983 11d³ 12fg* 12fg 14fg⁴ 12.2fg) small, lightly-made gelding; made all to win handicap at Edinburgh in April; will stay beyond 1¾m; seems to act on any going; sold 2,800 gns Newmarket September Sales. *D. Thom.*　　**54**

GOOD N SHARP 2 b.c. Mummy's Pet 125–Sharp Lady 70 (Sharpen Up 127) (1983 5fg*) Apr 7; 22,000Y; first foal; dam won five 6f races; apprentice ridden and backed from 16/1 to 5/1, recovered from poor start to win 10-runner maiden event at Nottingham in September going away by 1½ lengths from Mantel Oak; will probably stay 6f; sure to improve. *A. Jarvis.*　　**81 p**

Mrs S. R. Brook's "Goodbye Shelley"

GOOD OFFICES 5 br.g. Murrayfield 119–Sun Queen 76 (Lucky Sovereign) (1982 NR 1983 10g 10.6g 10.6s) has shown no form on flat for a long time; sometimes blinkered. *R. Griffiths.* —

GOOD PERFORMER 4 b.g. Sun Prince 128–Haymaking 115 (Galivanter 131) (1982 8g⁴ 10s⁴ 8d 11s 8.5f⁴ 7g* 7g 7f 7fg 1983 6d 8s) leggy, workmanlike gelding; plater; stays 1m well; has worn blinkers. *D. Yeoman.* —

GOOSE GREEN 3 ch.f. Celtic Cone 116–Fanny Green 68 (Space King 115) (1982 6s 1983 12d 12.2d 13.4fg 10f⁴ 12g) smallish filly; ran best race in a slowly-run 1¼m seller; should stay further. *P. Rohan.* **49**

GOOSEY GANDER 4 gr.g. Warpath 113–Snow Goose (Santa Claus 133) (1982 NR 1983 12d 16f⁴ 15g⁴) big gelding; has a round action; brother to middle-distance winner Obergurgl, to Wild Goose Chase, a winner at up to 2m, and to 2 winners over hurdles; dam never ran; second in NH Flat races; fourth in maiden race at Beverley in June and amateur riders event at Ayr in September; saddle slipped first start; suited by a test of stamina. *C. Thornton.* —

GORDIAN 3 ch.c. Grundy 137–Mrs Tiggywinkle 109 (Silly Season 127) (1982 6f⁴ 7fg* 7g³ 7g² 1983 10v* 12s 11.1g 12g) quite a well-made colt; grand walker and superb mover; looked to have done extremely well when reappearing in 7-runner Guardian Classic Trial at Sandown in April and won shade cleverly by ½ length from Neorion in a very slowly-run race, despite tending to hang; never really going and was disappointing when tenth of 20 finishers behind Teenoso in Derby at Epsom, and was off course 3 months afterwards; about 2½ lengths fifth of 11 behind Tombos in 1½m Preis des Landes Nordrhein-Westfalen at Dusseldorf in October, **112**

341

Mr S. S. Niarchos' "Gordian"

better effort on his return; has won on heavy going and on a firm surface. *G. Harwood.*

GORDONUS 3 b.g. Crooner 119–Whitton Lane (Narrator 127) (1982 NR 1983 8v 16g) lengthy gelding; fifth foal; dam of little account; tailed off in maiden races at Goodwood in May and Lingfield in July. *P. Mitchell.*   —

GORSKY 7 b.g. Dubassoff–Artistically (Ribot 142) (1982 16g 14g 1983 11fg 16h[4] 14f) small gelding; of little account; used to wear blinkers; not resolute. *B. Richmond.*   §§

GORYTUS (USA) 3 b.c. Nijinsky 138–Glad Rags 118 (High Hat 131) (1982 7fg* 7fg* 7g[4] 1983 8g 10.5d[4] 8fg)   **123**
     The fall of Gorytus from Olympus was tragedy of an Homeric order. Praised to the skies after impressive victories in his first two races as a two-year-old, Gorytus never fulfilled the exceptional promise of those early days and became increasingly the object of denigration in some quarters as a three-year-old. Such was the impression created by Gorytus' victories in the Acomb Stakes and the Laurent Perrier Champagne Stakes that he was offered at the short odds of 4/1 favourite for the Guineas and 5/1 for the Derby with those races still over seven and eight months ahead. His abject failure, still unexplained, when odds on for the William Hill Dewhurst Stakes on his only other outing as a two-year-old seemed to dent the confidence of Gorytus' supporters only temporarily. In spite of his being denied a preparatory race by the wet weather, Gorytus started 7/2 second favourite for the Two Thousand Guineas, his trainer reporting that Gorytus hadn't turned a hair when sent to Newmarket ten days before the Guineas to be exercised and to be walked round the paddock where he had appeared before the Dewhurst. Gorytus

looked in peak form on Guineas day, well muscled up with a beautiful bloom on his coat, but after disputing the lead briefly running into the Dip he faded into fifth, beaten just over three and a half lengths by the winner Lomond. It was more than fifteen weeks before Gorytus was seen out again. He missed a succession of engagements, including the Derby (fears of soft ground), the St James's Palace (mild bout of coughing) and the Coral-Eclipse and the Sussex (training set-backs). When he returned to action in the Benson and Hedges Gold Cup at York's August meeting Gorytus again looked outstandingly well. There was plenty of money for him—he started second favourite behind the Prix du Jockey-Club winner Caerleon—and he ran creditably, finishing about two lengths behind Caerleon in fourth place, keeping on well until faltering near the finish. Some of those who had kept loyal to Gorytus after the Guineas (believing he had needed the race), were also heard to excuse him in the Benson and Hedges on the score of the softish going. The ground was on the firm side—as it was on the occasion of Gorytus' victories—for the Waterford Crystal Mile at Goodwood eleven days later; but, starting 6/4 favourite, Gorytus could manage only fifth-of-six placing, just over two lengths behind the winner Montekin, finishing rather tamely after coming with a promising run on the outside in the straight. This turned out to be Gorytus' last racecourse appearance in Britain; shortly afterwards he was sent to the United States where, we understand, he is to continue his racing career.

Gorytus (USA) (b.c. 1980)	Nijinsky (b 1967)	Northern Dancer (b 1961)	Nearctic
			Natalma
		Flaming Page (b 1959)	Bull Page
			Flaring Top
	Glad Rags (ch 1963)	High Hat (ch 1957)	Hyperion
			Madonna
		Dryad (ch 1950)	Panorama
			Woodside

Gorytus is a commanding individual, rangy and exceptionally handsome; as we said in *Racehorses of 1982* only rarely does one see an individual like him. He's a grand mover in all his paces, too. His physique and his pedigree—his sire is one of the world's most sought-after stallions and his dam won the One Thousand Guineas and has bred several other winners—will stand him in good stead when the time comes for him to be retired to stud. *R. Hern.*

GO SPECTRUM 3 br.g. Malinowski 123–Alli-Bee 57 (Violon d'Ingres) (1982 5f² 5f 5f⁴ 7d 6s 1983 5s 5g³ 6d 6g 5f 7f 5f 6g) neat, useful-looking gelding; should stay 7f; sometimes blinkered. *J. McNaughton.* —

GO TO SLEEP 3 b.c. Ercolano 118–Precious Light 90 (Psidium 130) (1982 7g 7g 7fg 8g 1983 12v 10g 14g 11.5f 12f) close-coupled colt; disappointing maiden. *A. Jarvis.* — §

GOUMI 4 b.c. Grundy 137–Gay Trinket 72 (Grey Sovereign 128§) (1982 10f² 12f* 12d* 1983 12d 11v³ 12v 12f² 11.7f 14f⁴ 13.3g 12fg*) well-made, quite attractive colt; didn't have best of runs when quickening well to win amateur riders race at Redcar in September; stays 1½m and is worth another try over 1¾m; acts on any going; sometimes hangs quite badly. *M. Stoute.* 96

GOUVERNO 4 b.c. Star Appeal 133–Gundula (Mercurius) (1982 10fg 10.4fg 8g 12f² 10fg² 12s 10g 8fg 8g³ 8fg³ 8fg* 9s* 9s⁴ 1983 8s* 8d² 8d 8fg³ 8fg 8f 8fg* 8f* 9fg⁴ 8fg* 8fg 8fg⁴ 8d² 8d) lightly-made, fair sort; good mover with a long stride; won handicaps at Salisbury in May, Brighton and Sandown (apprentice event) in August and Salisbury in September; won well by 1½ lengths from Rana Pratap for final success; stays 1½m but is better at shorter distances; evidently acts on any going. *F. Durr.* 93

GO WORKING 2 br.f. Workboy 123–Continental Divide (Sharp Edge 123) (1983 6fg) Mar 1; first foal; dam poor plater; last of 15 in claiming race at Nottingham in October. *P. Felgate.* —

GRACIOUS HOMES 2 ch.f. Porto Bello 118–Fair Fabiola 94 (Acropolis 132) (1983 5s 5s⁴ 5fg 6f³ 6fg 7g 7f² 6d) Feb 25; 1,600Y; workmanlike filly; third foal; half-sister to middle-distance winner Faridella (by Silly Season); dam won three 5f races at 2 yrs; modest plater; stays 7f; probably acts on any going; ran poorly in blinkers sixth outing. *D. H. Jones.* 64

GRADILLE 3 br.f. Home Guard 129–Gradiva 110 (Lorenzaccio 130) (1982 5.8g 6fg 6d 6s⁴ 1983 8v 6s 6d* 6f⁴ 6fg 7.6fg 7f 6f³ 6f 6h² 6g 7g* 6fg 7s⁴ 7f) leggy, rather lightly-made filly; successful in handicaps at Carlisle in June and 72

Wolverhampton (ridden by 7-lb claimer) in October; stays 7.6f; acts on any going; blinkered nowadays. *F. J. Houghton.*

GRAFTON 3 b.g. Great Nephew 126–Hazy Idea 118 (Hethersett 134) (1982 7g 1983 7s 10s) smallish, quite attractive gelding; good mover; little worthwhile form in maiden races; sold 3,000 gns Ascot May Sales. *H. Candy.* —

GRANADOS KING 3 b.g. Whitstead 125–Esquinade 84 (Silly Season 127) (1982 7d 8s 10s 8s 1983 12v 12v 17v) workmanlike gelding; poor walker; well beaten in maiden and minor races; often blinkered. *W. Turner.* —

GRAND ALLIANCE 6 b.g. Sweet Revenge 129–Lima 105 (Abernant 142) (1982 8g 6g 5f 8.2fg 6f 5f 1983 7f 10f 7f) strong gelding; has had a soft palate operation; plater; stays 7f; acts on firm going; sometimes sweats up; has raced with tongue tied down; usually blinkered. *E. Alston.* —

GRANDE MADAME 2 b.f. Monseigneur 127–Miss Pinkerton (Above Suspicion 127) (1983 5d³ 5s 5v³ 6d 6f 6f 8.2fg* 8.2fg 7fg) Apr 17; 2,800Y; small, lengthy filly; half-sister to several winners, including Tumbledownwind (by Tumble Wind), a smart performer at up to 1m; dam won over 1½m in Ireland; won 18-runner seller at Nottingham (bought in 2,200 gns) in September; suited by 1m; possibly unsuited by very firm going but acts on any other; usually blinkered and has shown a tendency to sweat up. *C. Booth.* **64**

GRANDE MODELE 3 b.f. Brigadier Gerard 144–Grande Maison (Crepello 136) (1982 6g 7g 1983 12s⁴ 9v) ex-French filly; first foal; dam, placed over 7f and 10.5f in France, is daughter of very speedy Obelisk; lightly-raced maiden; found nothing and gave impression she possibly didn't get trip when fourth in 1½m claiming race at Leicester in March. *P. Cole.*

GRAND ENTRANCE 2 ch.f. Town and Country 124–Grecian Bridge 90 (Acropolis 132) (1983 6d 5.8g 5fg 5.1f) Apr 11; 3,600Y; workmanlike filly; good mover; half-sister to 3 winners, including good-class 1m to 1¼m performer Roy Bridge (by March Past); dam from same family as Ribocco and Ribero; poor maiden; not raced after July; bred to need further than 6f, and should stay at least 1¼m; best form on a soft surface. *N. Vigors.* **61**

GRAND GRUNDY 4 ch.g. Grundy 137–Dudinka (Mossborough 126) (1982 14f 14fg 1983 12v 10d) well beaten in varied company, including selling. *P. Ashworth.*

GRAND HARBOUR 3 br.c. Dragonara Palace 115–Top Of The Tree 66 (Lorenzaccio 130) (1982 5d⁴ 5g 5fg² 6f 6g⁴ 5g³ 6fg³ 7g² 1983 7g 7fg 7f³ 8f 8fg 8g⁴ 7fg) tall, good-topped colt; in frame in a variety of races; stays 1m; acts on firm going; sold 4,700 gns Newmarket Autumn Sales. *R. Baker.* **75**

GRAND MARCH 5 b.g. Song 132–Calleva (Worden II 129) (1982 10fg 10d 1983 12v 10s 8f 8f) big, useful-looking gelding; good walker and mover; poor handicapper nowadays; not sure to stay middle distances; has sweated up badly. *K. Cunningham-Brown.*

GRAND ORIENT (USA) 2 b. or br.c. Far North 120–Martessana (Sir Ivor 135) (1983 7g³ 7.5g* 10g²) Mar 21; half-brother to French 9f to 10.5f winner Valley Mills (by Val de l'Orne); dam, winner of small 1¼m race at 4 yrs, is half-sister to top 1972 French 2-y-o Targowice; won a maiden race comfortably by 2 lengths from Oldoway at Saint-Cloud in November; bettered that effort in Criterium de Saint-Cloud later in month, going down by only ¾ length to Darshaan; will stay 1½m; looks sure to win more races. *A. Head, France.* **120**

GRAND PALACE 4 b.f. Royal Palace 131–Grand Central 79 (Grand Roi 118) (1982 11.7f³ 10f 13fg⁴ 11.7g 12v 12s⁴ 12d 1983 12v 10g 12s) big, rangy filly; well beaten at 4 yrs; stays 1½m; acts on firm going; blinkered final start in 1982. *R. Laing.*

GRANDREAMS 3 ch.f. Some Hand 119–Scottish Peace (Aberdeen 109) (1982 7d 8s 1983 8v 10s) well beaten in maiden and minor events; sold 390 gns Ascot 2nd June Sales. *J. King.*

GRAND UNIT 5 b.h. Home Guard 129–Silken Topper (High Hat 131) (1982 10d 10d* 10g² 11.1g² 12fg* 12f⁴ 12.3g 10f* 12f* 10g² 10g* 12fg 10d 1983 10g 12d 12v² 12g* 12f* 10f³ 10f³ 12fg² 10fg 12s) strong horse; successful in handicaps at Newbury, Royal Ascot (decisively beat Aberfield by 3 lengths in Bessborough Stakes) and Sandown; held off Miramar Reef by a short head in Royal Hong Kong Jockey Club Trophy on last-named at 4 yrs; stays 1½m; acts on any going but is ideally suited by top-of-the-ground; has worn bandages; ran as though something was wrong with him second start and tended to hang on third. *E. Eldin.* **95**

GRANGE GLEN 6 ch. g. Deep Run 119–Gleannagross (Prince Hansel 118) (1982   –
NR 1983 12g) ex-Irish gelding; first foal; dam showed no ability in bumpers races;
placed in bumpers events in 1982; 33/1 when well beaten in amateur riders race at
Hamilton in June; sold 6,000 gns Ascot July Sales. *J. S. Wilson.*

GRANGE OF GLORY 2 ch.c. Hittite Glory 125–Neptune's Daughter 76   **65**
(Neptunus 132) (1983 5s 6f* 6fg 7d) May 5; 1,300F, 8,000Y; rather leggy colt;
half-brother to several winners, including fair stayer Rodman (by Relko),
subsequently a good winner over jumps; dam won over 9f; bought in 10,000 gns
after winning £2,900 seller at Newcastle in June by a neck from Musical Love; out
of first 6 in nurseries at Windsor and York subsequently; should be suited by 7f;
acts on firm going. *W. Musson.*

GRAPHICS SOLAR 5 b.h. Royal Palace 131–Tina Fort (Fortina) (1982 16s*   **59**
16d 17.1f² 17f 16fg 16fg 1983 18d³ 17.1d³ 17d 16fg 12f* 12f 12fg⁴ 14fg² 15.8fg 16f*
17d 16g) leggy horse; staying handicapper; won amateur riders events at Carlisle
in June and Beverley in August; acts on any going; has won when sweating badly;
usually ridden up with pace. *B. McMahon.*

GRATCH 2 ch. c. Grundy 137–Palatch 120 (Match III 135) (1983 7fg 9s⁴) Apr 18;   **75**
small, well-made, attractive colt; tenth foal; brother to a lightly-raced maiden and
half-brother to top-class middle-distance performer Patch (by St Paddy); dam won
Musidora Stakes and Yorkshire Oaks; quite modest form in fair company at the
back-end; looks capable of better in time. *P. Walwyn.*

GRAUSBERRY (USA) 2 ch.c. Graustark–Brown Berry (Mount Marcy) (1983   **105** p
9fg* 8f²) May 4; $750,000Y; brother to top-class American colt Avatar and
high-class French middle-distance colt Monseigneur, closely related to 2 winners
by Prince Royal II, notably very good American middle-distance performer
Unconscious, and half-brother to several other winners; dam won 6f stakes race;
put up an encouraging display when winning 8-runner newcomers event at Evry in
October by 1½ lengths from Seconde; narrowly beaten by Don Basile in better race
at Longchamp later in month; will stay 1½m; sure to go on to better things. *F.
Boutin, France.*

GREASY JOAN 2 br.f. Workboy 123–Cronella 63 (Crozier 117) (1983 5v⁴ 5fg³ 5f   **40**
5f⁴) May 19; compact filly; first foal; dam won 1½m seller; bad plater; will be
suited by 6f+; blinkered final start; exported to Italy. *M. W. Easterby.*

GREAT DANCER 3 ch.f. Great Nephew 126–Bally Tudor 75 (Henry the   –
Seventh 125) (1982 NR 1983 7v 8f 7h 7s) narrow, lightly-made filly; second foal;
dam won 3 times over 1¼m; little worthwhile form; should be suited by 1m;
trained by C. Brittain first 3 starts. *M. Camacho.*

GREATEST HITS 6 b. g. Derring-Do 131–Vallota 85 (Klairon 131) (1982 10fg   **67**
8d² 10f⁴ 8f 10g⁴ 10.6g 10.6s 1983 12s⁴ 10d 12s⁴ 10.2g*) attractive, well-made
gelding; plater nowadays; readily won at Bath in June (bought in 2,000 gns); stays
1½m; has run creditably on firm going but is ideally suited by some give in the
ground; best in blinkers; suitable mount for an apprentice. *R. Holder.*

GREATHAM HOUSE 7 b. g. Run The Gantlet–Nyeri 104 (Saint Crespin III 132)   –
(1982 NR 1983 16fg) has shown no form on flat for a long time but is a fair hurdler;
stays well; has worn blinkers. *N. Gaselee.*

GREAT PRETENDER 3 ch.g. Anne's Pretender 124–Pampas Miss (Pronto)   –
(1982 5fg 6f² 6d 8g 1983 9s 12s⁴ 10s 10.2g) useful-looking gelding; rather a
disappointing maiden; should be suited by 1m+; has worn blinkers; trained until
after third start by P. Kelleway. *T. Hallett.*

GREAT SHADOW 3 ch.g. Grundy 137–Plant at Dusk 83 (Crepello 136) (1982   –
8g 8s 1983 11.7s³ 16g 17g 11.7h) big, workmanlike gelding; turns his near-fore
out; slow maiden; blinkered third start; sold 4,100 gns Newmarket September
Sales. *P. Walwyn.*

GREAT SUBSTENCE (USA) 5 b.h. Pretense–Gay Northerner (Northern   **118**
Dancer) (1982 10s³ 9g³ 8d 10fg* 11g² 10s² 8s 1983 8v⁴ 8d 9.7d 8f 9g 8fg* 10f²
8fg* 12s³ 12d 12g) neat, attractive horse; half-brother to 3 minor winners; dam
won 6f stakes race at 2 yrs in Canada; very smart performer who excelled himself
on ninth start when keeping on well to be just over a length third of 11 to Time
Charter in Prix Foy at Longchamp in September; had previously won apprentice
event at Evry and Prix Quincey at Deauville, beating Pampabird a head in latter,
and had run well to be second to General Holme in Prix Gontaut-Biron at Deauville
again; soundly beaten in Turf Classic at Aqueduct final start; effective at 1m and
stays 1½m; acts on any going; blinkered fourth start. *M. Saliba, France.*

Sancton Stakes, York—Great Western beats Careen

GREAT VINTAGE 2 ch.c. Great Nephew 126–Light Lager 91 (Crepello 136)   **69**
(1983 6fg 7g 8g) May 30; smallish, sparely-made colt; second foal; dam stayed 2m;
sixth last 2 starts in maiden races at Leicester and Sandown in the autumn; will be
suited by 1¼m+. *D. Morley.*

GREAT WESTERN 2 b.c. Hittite Glory 125–Ruddy Duck 84 (Dicta Drake 126)   **106**
(1983 7f 7fg* 8fg⁴ 7d* 8fg) Mar 20; big, lengthy colt; excellent mover;
half-brother to numerous winners, including smart middle-distance fillies Bonnie
Isle and Flighting (both by Pitcairn); dam won at up to 1½m and also over hurdles;
won Sancton Stakes at York in September and nursery gamely under 9-7 on same
course in October; also ran creditably in Royal Lodge Stakes at Ascot and William
Hill Futurity at Doncaster; stays 1m really well; acts on a firm and a soft surface;
genuine and consistent. *J. Dunlop.*

GREED 2 br.g. Great Nephew 126–Francoise 109 (French Beige 127) (1983 6d⁴   **86**
6f 7f³ 7f* 7fg² 6f³ 7f² 8s) Mar 26; 12,000F; slightly dipped-backed, fair sort; none
too good a mover in his slower paces; half-brother to 3-y-o 1¼m winner Swing To
Me (by Swing Easy) and fair 1977 2-y-o 7f winner French Swallow (by My
Swallow); dam middle-distance performer; won 7-runner minor event at Catterick
in July; placed the following month in nurseries at Brighton, Catterick (found 6f too
sharp) and Newcastle; will stay 1¼m; acts well on firm going and is possibly not at
his best on soft; very troublesome in preliminaries when blinkered sixth start;
gelded after final appearance. *D. Morley.*

GREEK BANKER 2 ch.g. Avgerinos 121–Banking Coyne 76 (Deep Diver 134)   —
(1983 5v 6fg 7g) Mar 24; workmanlike gelding; first foal; dam best at 5f; of little
account. *J. Holt.*

GREENACRES JOY 3 b.f. Tycoon II–Moon Lady 78 (Cash and Courage 116)   **49**
(1982 NR 1983 9s 12v³ 17v 12.2g³ 12.2d 10g) small, sturdy filly; second reported
foal; half-sister to fairly useful plater Moon Lad (by Virginia Boy), successful
over 7f and 1m; dam won over 1m and 1¼m; off course nearly 5 months after
finishing third in 2 sellers in spring; runs like a stayer. *B. McMahon.*

GREENFLY (USA) 3 b.f. What A Pleasure–Green Girl 124 (Petingo 135) (1982   —
NR 1983 8f⁴ 12d⁴ 10fg 9s) tall, quite attractive filly; first foal; dam very smart at 7f
and 1m; plating-class maiden; well beaten in blinkers last 2 starts. *G. Harwood.*

GREEN GYPSY 2 b.f. Creetown 123–Moorgreen 68 (Green God 128) (1983 5g⁴   **83**
5f 6f² 6h* 5g 6fg 6fg 7fg²) Apr 2; lengthy, useful-looking filly; first foal; dam placed
over 5f; won 4-runner maiden race at Nottingham in September; excellent

second to Bobby Dazzler following month in 20-runner nursery at Leicester; suited by 7f; yet to race on a soft surface. *B. Hanbury.*

GREENHAM LADY 2 ch.f. Levanter 121–Star of Cranford (Starry Halo 122) (1983 5v 6fg 6fg) May 2; second foal; dam won a selling hurdle; of no account. *P. Burgoyne.* —

GREEN HEIGHTS 2 br.c. Green Dancer 132–Guernsey (Hornbeam 130) (1983 7fg 7fg 8d3) Mar 15; 19,500F, 22,000Y; good sort; half-brother to winners in Holland and France; dam won over 7f at 2 yrs in France; blinkered, 7 lengths third of 19 to Librate in maiden race at Warwick in October; will stay 1¼m. *I. Balding.* 76

GREEN LUCIA 3 ch.f. Green Dancer 132–Cockade 104 (Derring-Do 131) (1982 6g* 6f4 8fg2 1983 10s* 12f3 12d2 12s 10fg) strong, close-coupled filly; second foal; dam, 1m winner, is sister to High Top and Camden Town; beat Rose's Best by 1½ lengths in Ballylinch and Norelands Stud 3-y-o Fillies Stakes at Gowran Park in May; improved considerably on her next 2 starts, staying on to finish 5 lengths third of 12 behind Give Thanks in Irish Guinness Oaks at the Curragh in July and 4 lengths second of 6 behind Sun Princess (3 lengths clear of Give Thanks) in Yorkshire Oaks at York in August; only seventh of 12 however behind Sharaya in Trusthouse Forte Prix Vermeille at Longchamp in September and eighth of 9 behind Cormorant Wood after looking edgy in paddock in Sun Chariot Stakes at Newmarket in October; will be suited by 1¾m; acts on any going, but seems well suited by soft. *J. Oxx, Ireland.* 116

GREEN MIST 2 ch.c. Derrylin 115–Stony Ground (Relko 136) (1983 6f 7f* 7fg 8d 8s4 8fg2 8d 8.2fg 7fg) Apr 5; IR 10,500F, IR 8,600Y; smallish, chunky colt; first produce; dam Irish 1½m winner; put up an extraordinary performance in 12-runner maiden race at Catterick in August, coming from last place 2f out to win by a length from Rihab; good second in nursery at Brighton in October; will stay 1¼m; probably acts on any going; wore blinkers fifth to eighth outings and ran creditably without them on ninth. *A. Jarvis.* 88

Mr Gerald W. Jennings' "Green Lucia"

GREEN PARADISE (USA) 2 gr.c. Vigors–Tell Meno Lies (The Axe 115) 120
(1983 6g³ 6.5fg⁴ 8g* 8f⁴ 8f⁴) Apr 2; $300,000Y; fourth foal; half-brother to
top-class miler Green Forest (by Shecky Greene) and to Honest and True (by Mr
Leader), a very smart filly at around 1m in USA; dam won over 5f and 1m in USA;
won 11-runner maiden race at Deauville in August by ¾ length from Lyphard's
Trick; fourth in much better races at Longchamp subsequently, beaten 5 lengths by
Mendez in Prix des Chenes and 2¼ lengths by Treizieme after disputing lead
throughout in 9-runner Grand Criterium; will stay 1¼m. *M. Saliba, France.*

GREEN POOL 2 ch.f. Whistlefield 118–Maiden Pool 85 (Sharpen Up 127) (1983 –
5g 6fg 7s) Mar 11; neat filly; good mover; first foal; dam won 3 times at 5f; little
worthwhile form in autumn maiden events. *G. Hunter.*

GREEN REEF 3 ch.f. Mill Reef 141–Infra Green 121 (Laser Light 118) (1982 8g² 121
1983 10v³ 10.5v⁴ 10.5v 10f* 8f 10f* 10fg² 9.2f 10.5g) second foal; dam won from 6f
to 1½m, including Prix Ganay; won valuable handicap at Chantilly in June (beat
Maganyos by 2½ lengths) and 12-runner Prix de Psyche at Deauville in August (by
a short neck from Sedra); ran a fine race when 2 lengths second of 13 behind
Sharaya in Prix de la Nonette at Deauville again later in August but disappointed
afterwards in Prix de l'Opera at Longchamp and Prix de Flore at Saint-Cloud; stays
1¼m; acts on any going, but is suited by firm; sent to USA. *J. Cunnington, jnr,
France.*

GREEN ROCK (FR) 2 ch.f. Mill Reef 141–Infra Green 121 (Laser Light 118) 86 p
(1983 7fg) Mar 19; good sort; keen walker and good mover; third foal; sister to
smart French 3-y-o middle-distance filly Green Reef and half-sister to a minor
winner in USA; dam won from 6f to 1½m, including Prix Ganay; 25/1, showed
definite ability although always towards rear when tenth of 13 in Rockfel Stakes at
Newmarket in October; sure to do a lot better over middle distances and win races.
B. Hills.

GREEN RUBY (USA) 2 br.c. Shecky Greene–Ruby Tuesday (T.V. Lark) (1983 78
7f 7g⁴) Feb 24; $55,000Y; workmanlike colt; dam, half-sister to very smart Cresta
Rider, was second once from 5 starts; 5¾ lengths fourth of 18 to Bold Patriach in
maiden race at Leicester in October; will stay 1m. *A. Jarvis.*

GREENWOOD BELLE 3 ch.f. Gay Fandango 132–Matty (Sailor) (1982 5.8g 53
6g 8f 1983 10v 7fg³ 8.2f 7f 8.3fg 10f³ 10g 8d 8d) lengthy filly; plater; probably
stays 1¼m; blinkered eighth start; sold 2,800 gns Newmarket Autumn Sales. *G.
Hunter.*

GREGORY'S LADY 2 br.f. Meldrum 112–Rosa Lewis 65 (Relic) (1983 6fg 7fg) –
Mar 9; good-topped, fair sort; half-sister to several minor winners here and
abroad; dam maiden miler; 9 lengths seventh of 23 to New Generation in minor
event at Redcar in September, first and better effort. *J. W. Watts.*

GREINTON 2 b.c. Green Dancer 132–Crystal Queen 111 (High Top 131) (1983 112
7g* 8fg⁴) Mar 5; first foal; dam very useful middle-distance stayer from family
of Crocket; won a maiden race comfortably by 2½ lengths at Saint-Cloud in July and
held on well to land 90,000-franc event at Deauville by a head from Sicyos in
August; disappointing last of 4 behind Duke of Silver when carrying top weight in
Prix des Foals later in month (beaten over 1f out); should stay at least 1m; acts on
fast ground. *F. Boutin, France.*

GREY AT LAST 5 gr.m. Copte–Marie Denise 68 (Dual 117) (1982 NR 1983 6s –
8g) compact mare; well beaten in varied company, including selling; sometimes
blinkered. *J. Parkes.*

GREY BEARD 2 gr.c. Sexton Blake 126–Saintliness 99 (St Alphage 119) (1983 –
7f) May 16; IR 5,000F, 12,000Y; second foal; half-brother to 3-y-o Andarta (by
Ballymore); dam won over 6f and 7f at 2 yrs in Ireland; 50/1, never-dangerous 14
lengths seventh of 16 to Ashgar in maiden race at Yarmouth in August. *P. Haslam.*

GREY CARD 2 gr.c. Habat 127–No Cards 109 (No Mercy 126) (1983 6f 8f 7f) Apr –
17; 3,300F, 4,000Y; workmanlike colt; second foal; brother to useful 3-y-o 7f and
1m winner Dabdoub; dam won at up to 1m; in rear in varied races, including a
valuable seller. *D. Plant.*

GREY CHARM 2 gr.f. Habat 127–Caitlin 78 (Abernant 142) (1983 5f 6fg 6f 6f 7f) –
Apr 21; 1,100Y; lengthy filly; bad mover; sister to fairly useful 1981 2-y-o 5f and 6f
winner Steel Stockholder; bad plater. *D. Plant.*

GREY CHARTER 3 gr.f. Runnymede 123–Lovely Beak (Counsel 118) (1982 5fg –
6g 5g 5g 6s 1983 6d 6v 7fg 6fg) compact, sturdy filly; plater; best form over 5f as a
2-y-o; blinkered final outing; possibly not the easiest of rides. *P. Rohan.*

GREY DESIRE 3 gr.c. Habat 127–Noddy Time 97 (Gratitude 130) (1982 5fg 5g* 103
5g³ 5fg* 8fg³ 5f* 7d² 1983 6d 5g³ 6f 7f² 6fg² 7f) workmanlike colt; useful

Mrs D. M. Solomon's "Grey Dream"

performer; ran creditably most starts and put up a particularly good effort under a
stiff weight when ¾-length second of 14 behind Blue Emmanuelle in £5,000
handicap at Newcastle in June on fourth; had very stiff task indeed final outing
(July); suited by 7f nowadays and is worth another chance at 1m; yet to race on very
soft going but acts on any other; trained by J. Fort first 3 starts. *D. Plant.*

GREY DOLPHIN 8 gr.g. Cratloe Rocket 95–Cheering Crowds 75 (Entente   —
Cordiale 119) (1982 NR 1983 11.7h) of little account on flat though is a tough and
genuine performer over jumps; has worn blinkers. *M. Bradley.*

GREY DREAM 2 gr.f. Auction Ring 123–Dream (Roan Rocket 128) (1983 5d²   **101**
5s* 6fg² 6fg* 5d²) Feb 23; IR 8,000Y; leggy, sharp sort; third foal; half-sister to
useful 1979 2-y-o 6f winner Lingdale (by Crooner); dam ran only 3 times; put up
good efforts at Phoenix Park in August on third and fourth starts, failing by only a
short head to hold off King Persian in 13-runner Heinz '57' Phoenix Stakes and then
justifying favouritism by ½ length from So Fine in Oldtown Stud Stakes; had earlier
won minor event at Phoenix Park by ¾ length from Black Country; 9/4 on for
8-runner Goffs Stakes at the Curragh in September but went down by ½ length to
Anita's Prince; gives impression 6f is her limit; seems to act on any going; sold
220,000 gns Newmarket December Sales and is to be trained by M. Stoute. *K.
Prendergast, Ireland.*

GREY LINE 4 ch.g. Run The Gantlet–Grey Shoes 104 (Grey Sovereign 128§)   —
(1982 NR 1983 14.7d) big gelding; has been hobdayed; well beaten in maiden
races. *J. Fitzgerald.*

GRISE MINE (FR) 2 gr.f. Crystal Palace 132–Katie May 103 (Busted 134) (1983   **104** p
8f*) third foal; dam, winner over 7f and 1m, is daughter of top 1970 2-y-o filly
Cawston's Pride and half-sister to top-class sprinter Solinus; put up a good display
to win 6-runner maiden race by 1½ lengths from Sara Lee at Longchamp in October
despite a poor start; will probably stay 1¼m; promises to make a very useful 3-y-o.
A. Fabre, France.

GRIZABELLA 3 b.f. Bustino 136–Hurdy-Gurdy 90 (Espresso 122) (1982 8g   **76**
1983 12g² 12s³ 12fg) lengthy, good-quartered filly; excellent walker; just failed to
get up when short-head second of 15 to Shanipour in minor event at Newmarket in
April; disappointing afterwards, better effort when 13 lengths third behind
impressive Jasper in maiden race at Goodwood in May; suited by 1½m; possibly not
at her best on soft going; sold 21,000 gns Newmarket December Sales. *B. Hobbs.*

GROAT 5 b.g. Connaught 130–Grisbi 96 (Grey Sovereign 128§) (1982 12d 12f³   –
1983 12v³ 14s) big, good-topped gelding; quite moderate but reportedly suffers
from back trouble and is very lightly raced; should be suited by 1¾m (tailed off
when tried at trip); acts on any going. *B. Hobbs.*

GROSZEWSKI 3 gr.c. Godswalk 130–Claddie (Karabas 132) (1982 5g⁴ 5f² 6g 7g   **80**
6g 6s* 6g² 6s* 7s 1983 6v 6d³ 6d 6s* 6fg⁴ 7f 6f 6fg* 6fg² 6fg 6d) fair sort; best
races when winning small handicaps at Chepstow in May and Goodwood in August,
and when second in similar race at Newmarket; best form at 6f; acts on any going;
used to wear blinkers. *J. Sutcliffe.*

GROUP VENTURE 3 gr.f. Bay Express 132–Kutelamara 81 (Quorum 126)   –
(1982 NR 1983 6d³ 7fg 7g) 920F, 1,250Y; lengthy filly; half-sister to several
winners here and abroad; dam won over 1¼m; plater; stayed 6f; dead. *M.
Tompkins.*

GRUINASTORM 2 b.c. Grundy 137–June's Storm 65 (Arctic Storm 134) (1983   –
7fg 7fg 7f) May 17; fair sort; half-brother to 1¼m winner Starry Crocket (by
Crocket); dam, 1½m winner, from family of Montverdi; behind in maiden races.
N. Callaghan.

GRUNDY GLOW 3 b.c. Grundy 137–Party Tricks (Tom Fool) (1982 6g 8fg   **57** §
8.5s² 1983 12d 12g 14d 13.8g² 16g⁴ 16.5f 12fg) tall ex-Irish colt; third foal;
half-brother to 1980 2-y-o 5f winner Steel Garrison (by Steel Heart); dam never
ran; second in maiden race at Catterick in May; looked ungenuine when blinkered in
selling company on final start; best form at up to 1¾m; sold 4,600 gns Newmarket
September Sales. *J. Hindley.*

GUARD THE FORT 3 br.g. Home Guard 129–Rustling Waters (Ballymoss 136)   –
(1982 NR 1983 16f) 1,000Y; strong gelding; half-brother to 3 winners, including
useful middle-distance performers Shallow Stream (by Reliance II) and Danish King
(by Hardicanute); dam disappointing half-sister to St Leger winner Cantelo;
withdrawn after being unruly at start of minor event at Doncaster as a 2-y-o; raced
from a flag start when tailed-off last of 17 in Queen's Vase at Royal Ascot in June. *R.
Hollinshead.*

GUESS AGAIN (GER) 2 b.f. Stradavinsky 121–Galka 98 (Deep Diver 134)   **76**
(1983 5f³ 6fg⁴ 6f³ 5fg³ 5g⁴ 5fg² 5g) Mar 8; medium-sized, useful sort; first foal;
dam, half-sister to top-class sprinter Double Form, won twice over 5f at 2 yrs; in
frame in maiden races, minor events and nurseries; promises to stay 7f; has
raced only on a sound surface; blinkered last 4 starts; consistent until running
poorly in apprentice nursery final appearance. *F. J. Houghton.*

GUESS WHO 3 b.f. Be My Guest 126–Tulalanee (Habitat 134) (1982 7g 7g 8s   **76**
1983 8d 10g 10fg 7fg 6fg 10f²(dis) 10.4g*(dis) 12g³ 10.6g² 10g 10fg³ 10fg⁴) leggy,
sparely-made filly, lacking in scope; won maiden race at Chester in August by 7
lengths from Madame Dancer, but was disqualified 2½ weeks later, her apprentice
rider having drawn wrong allowance; needs 1¼m+; blinkered fifth outing; sold
38,000 gns Newmarket December Sales. *P. Kelleway.*

GUITELL 2 ch.c. Guillaume Tell 121–Lady Talisman (Continuation 120) (1983 5v)   –
Apr 2; 3,000F; eighth produce; half-brother to a bumpers winner; dam poor Irish
maiden; backward, well behind in 15-runner maiden race at Doncaster in May. *J.
Fort.*

GUN-CARRIAGE 3 b.g. Gunner B 126–Miss Little 78 (Dunoon Star 110) (1982   **66** d
8g 8d 1983 8.2s² 8d 11d 8.2g 8g 9fg) workmanlike gelding; best runs at 1m, but
should stay further. *A. W. Jones.*

GUNGA DIN 3 br.g. Mansingh 120–Mow Meadow (Acropolis 132) (1982 6g 1983   –
8v 8d⁴ 8fg) only poor form, including in an Edinburgh seller; sold 1,500 gns
Doncaster August Sales. *R. Allan.*

GUNNARD 3 ch.f. Gunner B 126–La Conistrano 86 (Capistrano 120) (1982 6h 7d 7g 7g 8s* 1983 8.2v 12s 12.2g 10fg 8fg 10f 9fg 9f 9g³ 10fg* 10f) small filly; plater; held up when winning at Newmarket in October (no bid); promises to stay 1½m; acts on any going, except possibly very firm; well beaten in blinkers fifth start. *K. Stone.* — 51

GUNNER GIRL 2 ch.f. Gunner B 126–Swakara 92 (Porto Bello 118) (1983 5g 6fg³) May 28; second foal; sister to 3-y-o 6f winner Son Of A Gunner; dam won 10 sprint races and was well suited by give in the ground; 2 lengths third of 24 behind Native Charmer in maiden event at Doncaster in November; stays 6f well; should win small race. *R. Holder.* — 82

GUNNER ROYAL 2 b.g. Gunner B 126–Faridina 100 (Sky Gipsy 117) (1983 7.2fg 8f) Apr 15; 4,600Y; strong gelding; has a round action; third living foal; dam soft-ground 5f performer; in rear in maiden auction events at Haydock in August and Redcar in September. *J. Etherington.* — –

GUNNER'S BELLE 3 ch.f. Gunner B 126–Crimson Belle 80 (Red God 128§) (1982 NR 1983 10s 11.7v 8f 7.2fg 7f* 8.2h 7f 8.2h 8d² 10.2fg⁴ 10fg 10g) workmanlike filly; half-sister to numerous winners, notably very smart 1¼m horse Crimson Beau (by High Line); dam 7f winner; showed first form when winning maiden race at Leicester in July; ran creditably on occasions afterwards; stays 1¼m; yet to prove she can handle really soft going but acts on any other; tends to sweat up. *M. Blanshard.* — 67

GUNS OF NAVARONE 3 b.c. Bold Lad (Ire) 133–Busted Flush 103 (Busted 134) (1982 6f⁴ 6f² 1983 8v³ 8g³ 8g 10.5s² 12s 10fg* 10f 10.5d 10g² 12f 10fg) — 121

Guns of Navarone's stable doesn't shrink from tackling the best. Once again it had a runner in a good many of the big races; with some reward, too, though not on the scale of several previous seasons. As the stable's leading three-year-old Guns of Navarone was regularly called on to do duty in the top class or just below it, without ever managing to win; his only success came in a Newmarket maiden in June, where he safely took the one easy opportunity offered him. He was placed

Captain M. Lemos' "Guns of Navarone"

on occasions–second to Hot Touch in the Mecca-Dante Stakes and to Morcon in the Valdoe Stakes, third to Sackford in the BonusPrint Easter Stakes and to Muscatite in the Craven–and went near to picking up prize money in the Derby and Coral-Eclipse. At Epsom he approached the furlong pole in second place but faded into fifth, beaten eight and a half lengths by Teenoso; at Sandown he was fifth behind Solford in that memorable finish of heads and necks, after running short of room to make his challenge. Guns of Navarone suffered a poor run in two other races besides the Eclipse, to an extent as a result of his being held up as he usually is. In the Valdoe Stakes, at Goodwood in September, he was in a pocket going into the last two furlongs. His jockey Piggott managed expertly to extricate him but by that time Morcon had taken an advantage of a length and a half to two lengths, and although Guns of Navarone quickened well to pull the leader back he was still a short head down at the post. The unfortunate runner-up carried 2 lb overweight. In the Dubai Champion Stakes at Newmarket in October on his final appearance of the season Guns of Navarone was in contention running into the Dip when hampered beyond hope of recovery.

		Bold Ruler (b 1954)	Nasrullah
	Bold Lad (b 1964)		Miss Disco
		Barn Pride (ch 1957)	Democratic
Guns of Navarone			Fair Alycia
(b.c. 1980)		Busted (b 1963)	Crepello
	Busted Flush (ch 1970)		Sans le Sou
		Donna (gr 1956)	Donore
			Bashful

For a son of Bold Lad out of a mare who seemed not to get a mile and a half (she won over six furlongs as a two-year-old) Guns of Navarone stays remarkably well: a mile and a quarter suits him better than a mile. However, judging by his running in the Derby a mile and a half is a shade too far for him. His running in the Trusthouse Forte Prix de l'Arc de Triomphe supports this, though it has to be borne in mind the Arc took more winning than even the Derby. He turned for home in a good sixth or seventh place in the Arc then faded to sixteenth of twenty-six in the end; he started at 100/1. The ground was soft at Epsom, firm at Longchamp. Guns of Navarone acts on any going, but less testing conditions at Epsom would have helped his cause. He is, incidentally, not the best of movers in his slower paces.

Guns of Navarone, a big, well-made, attractive colt who cost 98,000 guineas as a yearling, is the third living foal of Busted Flush and her second runner and winner following Cobblers Cove (by Realm), placed in the National Stakes and Beresford Stakes in 1979 and successful over a mile and a quarter at three. The dam's latest runner, Foscarini (by Rusticaro), was quite a useful staying two-year-old in Ireland in 1983. Busted Flush herself is half-sister to numerous winners at up to a mile produced by Donna, notably the One Thousand Guineas second Gwen. Donna was a useful filly at up to seven furlongs. *C. Brittain.*

GUNTRIPS CENTENARY 3 br.c. Manado 130–Bantam 64 (Combat 123) (1982   **80**
5s 6g 1983 6v 5f4 5fg* 5h2 5.3f2 6f* 6f2 6fg 6g) compact colt; successful in maiden race at Nottingham (made nearly all) and handicap at Salisbury in summer; second on 3 other occasions; stays 6f; form only on fast ground. *G. Hunter.*

GURUVAYOOR 2 gr.c. Fordham 117–Miss Knightsbridge 90 (Sovereign Path   **67**
125) (1983 7fg 7f 7fg) Apr 29; IR 15,000Y; big, strong colt; second living foal; half-brother to quite useful Irish 1981 2-y-o 5f and 6f winner Miss Behaving (by Steel Heart); dam won from 5f to 7f; plating-class maiden; stays 7f. *P. Cole.*

GUSTY'S GIFT 9 ch.g. Divine Gift 127–Gusty Girl 71 (Darling Boy 124) (1982   **–**
NR 1983 7f) quite a modest handicapper at his best; suited by 7f; acts on any going but is suited by a sound surface; effective with and without blinkers; suitable mount for an inexperienced rider. *N. Henderson.*

GUY'S GOLD 2 b.c. Tap On Wood 130–Kilfenora (Tribal Chief 125) (1983 6f2   **73**
6fg3 7f3 7g2 6g) Feb 22; IR 10,500Y; strong, quite useful-looking colt; first foal; dam Irish 2-y-o 5f winner; placed in maiden events and a nursery in the North; has shown a tendency to pull, and seems unlikely to stay beyond 7f; acts on firm going; sold 11,000 gns Newmarket Autumn Sales. *Sir Mark Prescott.*

GWEN JOHN 2 ch.f. High Line 125–Romany 87 (King's Bench 132) (1983 7s)   **– p**
Apr 25; half-sister to several winners, including fairly useful stayer John O'Groats (by Welsh Pageant); dam best at sprint distances; 50/1 and green, 12½ lengths eleventh of 19 to Eljazzi in maiden race at Leicester in October; should do better. *J. Winter.*

GWYN 2 ch.f. Flashback 102–Mingwyn Wood (Pirate King 129) (1983 5v 5v 6g 6f   **42**
8g 8.2fg) Mar 25; tall, rather leggy filly; bad plater. *A. Davison.*

GWYNPRIDE 3 b.f. Val de l'Orne 130–Foresighted Lady (Vent du Nord) (1982   –
6fg 5g 7g 7g   1983 12s 9f)   plain filly; little form in maiden and minor events; sold
575 gns Ascot September Sales.   *D. Marks.*

H

HABALLOO 5 ch.g. Habat 127–Calloo 99 (Ballyciptic 122) (1982 NR 1983 12d   –
8fg) good-topped gelding; poor plater. *B. Stevens.*

HABANNE 3 gr.g. Habat 127–Sister Anne 74 (Mourne 126) (1982 7s 8d 1983   –
12.2s³ 13.4fg⁴ 14.6f⁴ 12.3fg 15.8g) sturdy gelding; in frame in maiden and minor
events; runs as if he'll stay 2m; below his best in blinkers last 2 starts; sold to D.
McCain 3,000 gns Doncaster November Sales. *J. Etherington.*

HABAT RAAPHORST (HOL) 4 ch.c. Hittite Glory 125–Reedy 81 (Klairon 131)   72
(1982 including 8.5g* 9d 10d⁴ 10d³ 1983 7s 9s 12v 5g 6.5fg* 7f* 7f* 7f* 7h 7g 7.2g) big
ex-Dutch colt; first foal; half-brother to 2 winners in Holland; dam won over 7f at 2 yrs;
won once and was placed once from 5 starts in Holland at 3 yrs; in good form in summer
and won quite valuable event at Duindigt and handicaps at Folkestone (apprentices),
Newcastle and Yarmouth; stays 1m; acts well on fast ground; blinkered final start; has
sweated up; goes well for apprentice C. Allen. *M. Ryan.*

HABAT'S MELODY 2 gr. or ro.c. Habat 127–Celtic Melody (Tudor Melody 129)   –
(1983 8s 8fg 8.2s) Apr 13; good-topped colt; second foal; dam unraced daughter of
Irish Guinness Oaks winner Celina; in rear in autumn maiden races. *K. Stone.*

HABIBTI 3 br.f. Habitat 134–Klairessa 88 (Klairon 131) (1982 6fg* 6g* 6d* 1983   136
7.3s³ 8g³ 8v 6fg* 5fg* 6g* 5f*)
A closing tribute to Marwell in *Racehorses of 1981* suggested in all sincerity
that 'Sprinting will be fortunate to see her like among the so-called weaker sex
inside another few seasons'. Even before those words had been written Soba had
embarked on a career which was to blossom unforeseen into one that would capture
public imagination in a remarkable way; and the ink had scarcely dried when a
younger filly, Habibti, took the first steps towards attainments that clearly surpass
Marwell's. Habibti dominated the sprinting stage in 1983, relegating Soba to a
supporting role. Such was Habibti's superiority over a filly behind Marwell in
ability, and over the rest of her numerous opponents, that we have no hesitation in
rating her the best sprinter of her sex in our experience; in so doing we also regard
her as good as any in the much stronger group of colts in the last thirty-seven years
with the exception of Abernant (142), Pappa Fourway (139), and Moorestyle,
Princely Gift and Right Boy (all 137). In our opinion her efforts won her the race for
Horse of the Year hands down. Habibti received all bar three of the twenty-six
votes in the official end-of-season poll of racing journalists for that honour. Some of
those who voted may find it astonishing that the International Classification of 1983
rates Habibti as low as 91 against a norm of 100. Believe it or not, Habibti doesn't
scrape into the top six sprinters of the last nine years according to the International
Classification: since the system began in its present form in 1975 Flirting Around
(International Classification 100), Lochnager (94), Bay Express (93), Gentilhombre
(93), Lianga (92), Roman Warrior (92) and Thatching (92) have been assessed her
superior. How ludicrous!
Had she stuck to sprinting Habibti might well be unbeaten. However, the

*William Hill July Cup, Newmarket—Habibti reverts to six furlongs, and races home from
Soba (right) and On Stage (blinkers)*

opportunity of running for the One Thousand Guineas is not one to be passed up lightly and on her two-year-old form she had an excellent chance if she could last out a mile. On her two-year-old form, in particular her convincing defeat of Royal Heroine in the Lowther Stakes at York, she represented England's best hope of beating the Cheveley Park winner Ma Biche. The omens for her staying a mile were conflicting. Habibti's sire, the sire also of Marwell, is no great influence for stamina, while many of her immediate relatives on the dam's side were speedy animals; and her running on her reappearance when third to Goodbye Shelley in the Gainsborough Stud Fred Darling Stakes at Newbury could be interpreted as evidence of her failing to stay a distance rather less than a mile. But her great-grandam Tessa Gillian had finished a creditable second in the Guineas; furthermore Habibti showed an excellent, relaxed temperament that ought to be in her favour, and her fading at Newbury could as easily be attributed to her needing the outing—she carried lots of condition, as a horse just short of peak racing fitness might. Habibti started at 10/1 for the Guineas and finished fourth (she was promoted to third much later, upon the technical disqualification of Royal Heroine), beaten one and a half lengths, a head and half a length behind Ma Biche. Oddly enough, Habibti couldn't be said to have failed to stay the trip; without showing the dazzling turn of foot of her two-year-old days, she ran on nicely through the last two furlongs and was going on at the finish. Largely on the strength of this performance she was allowed to take her chance in the Goffs Irish One Thousand Guineas three weeks later. She was soundly beaten in considerably more testing conditions there, with the happy result that she was returned to sprinting.

Habibti couldn't return to sprinting in time to emulate Marwell's victory in the King's Stand Stakes, but she had the opportunity to improve on that filly's record in the remaining part of the season. Marwell had gone on from Royal Ascot to win the William Hill July Cup at Newmarket and Prix de l'Abbaye de Longchamp and finish second in the other two recognised legs of the European sprint championship, the William Hill Sprint Championship at York and Vernons Sprint Cup at Haydock. No horse had managed to win all five races in one season; Lianga (another filly), Lochnager, Solinus, Double Form, Moorestyle and Sharpo besides Marwell had won three. The July Cup promised to put Habibti's ability to a stiff test, for although the latest King's Stand winner Sayf El Arab missed the race the second, third, fourth, fifth and seventh—Soba, On Stage, Celestial Dancer, Fearless Lad and Salieri—stood their ground. There were other good horses to contend with in the field of fifteen, even if two of the best of them, Noalcoholic and the Irish Guineas runner-up Maximova, weren't recognised sprinters exactly. Any significant reduction in racing distance is apt to face a horse with the problem of adjusting to a faster gallop; a reduction from a mile to six furlongs is highly significant, and the change in tempo from an Irish Guineas run in the mud to a July Cup run on top-of-the-ground would normally be held to be among the most pronounced. The possibility that Habibti might be a top sprinter gradually turned to probability as on this, her first encounter with the speed merchants since her two-year-old days, she was able to move well within herself from the start. By the end of the race, when she'd delivered her challenge to the front-running Soba at a point over a furlong out which Carson her jockey had the luxury of choosing, quickly gained the upper hand

William Hill Sprint Championship, York—Habibti confirms her superiority over Soba

Vernons Sprint Cup, Haydock—one of the best sprinting performances for years

and gone two and a half lengths clear, there was no doubt about the matter whatsoever. On Stage finished an outpaced third, another length down, ahead of Salieri and Noalcoholic.

Habibti confirmed her superiority over Soba in her three remaining races, in the course of which she also confirmed her superiority, directly or indirectly, over all the other sprinters around. In the second of them, the Vernons Sprint Cup, she put up one of the best performances ever likely to be witnessed at Haydock or anywhere else with a majestic seven-length victory. On that occasion we were treated to the sight of Carson sat still with two furlongs to go, content to have a lead from Sayf El Arab or Soba, seemingly under no threat from the three other runners On Stage, Vorvados and Beaudelaire. As soon as he moved the race was over; Habibti passed the leader Soba and drew right away, able to dominate her field to an extent rare in a top-class sprint. Things had been a lot closer two weeks earlier in the William Hill Sprint Championship at York, over probably Soba's ideal distance of five furlongs, and they were closer still afterwards in the Prix de l'Abbaye in which Soba enjoyed five furlongs again plus a slight advantage at the weights compared with the Jockey Club's weight-for-age. But there was little argument about Habibti's superiority; no argument at all unless allowance is made for the fact that Soba cut a knee in a rough flight over to Paris. At York Habibti had an unflattering length and a half to spare over Soba who was later disqualified for causing interference to another runner very early on. Habibti ran her usual race, coming from behind; she went three lengths clear of Soba before being eased, the pair of them a long way ahead of the King George Stakes runner-up Fine Edge and the previous year's William Hill Sprint Championship runner-up Chellaston Park. In

Prix de l'Abbaye de Longchamp—Habibti beats Soba for a fourth time

Paris she had a length in hand. She looked well, brighter in her coat than Soba, but took longer than previously to shake off her perennial rival. Habibti began her run two furlongs out, went into a narrow lead a furlong later and was then pressed to the line by Soba who on this occasion had never quite managed to get to the front. The French two-year-old Sicyos finished third, three lengths behind Soba, after showing tremendous speed. Sayf El Arab was seventh, Vorvados eighth and last.

All Habibti's winning timefigures in England were top class, that at Haydock a brilliant 1.69 fast, that is to say 1.69 seconds faster than standard after all the relevant factors—going, wind, weight, age—have been properly taken into account. It is one of the best timefigures we've ever encountered. Officially, Habibti came near to Deep Diver's course record at York (set in the Nunthorpe Stakes in 1972) and she beat the previous course record at Longchamp (set by the three-year-old colt Adraan in the Prix de Saint-Georges in 1980) by 1.20 seconds. We find the time at Longchamp puzzling, regard it as highly dubious though we've had it confirmed as official, and reserve judgement. What is most puzzling is not that the record should go by a margin equivalent to at least 21 lb, or over seven lengths, when conditions were at their most favourable to exceptionally fast times since the course was altered a few years ago, but that the time of 54.30 seconds for five furlongs (or to be precise for 1,000 metres which is six yards shorter) seems scarcely credible for any course in the world except Epsom, which unlike Longchamp is downhill virtually throughout and sharply downhill to halfway. Still, Habibti's time for the Prix de l'Abbaye, whatever its actuality, is not and never will be important in appreciating her ability: there is an abundance of evidence for that purpose without it. She is a magnificent sprinter who if she goes the right way as a four-year-old may conceivably have written of her, as was written of her sixth dam Mumtaz Mahal, that 'It may be doubted whether a faster filly—or colt for that matter—has been seen on our Turf.'

Mr M. A. A. Mutawa's "Habibti"

Mumtaz Mahal need hardly concern us here, though her name is still regarded important enough by the catalogue compilers to be set in black type towards the foot of the page on most of the occasions that a direct descendant of hers comes up for auction. Her presence hardly seems necessary in the numerous instances where modern generations of her family going back to the nineteen-twenties are performing with distinction. When Habibti came under the hammer as a yearling for example (she made 140,000 guineas by the way), her family had plenty of much more up-to-date form to recommend it. Klairessa her dam was a winning sister to the high-class sprinter D'Urberville and had produced two winners—the filly Great Klaire (by Great Nephew) who was successful in Australia and the fairly useful sprinting colt Khedive (by Habat). The next dam Courtessa, an unraced twin, was a full sister to the Gimcrack Stakes winner Test Case and a half-sister to several other winners including the very smart sprinting two-year-old Gentle Art. The same year that Habibti was sold the future One Thousand Guineas winner On The House had run second in the Cheveley Park Stakes. On The House is out of Lora, a daughter of Courtessa by Klairon's son Lorenzaccio and thus a close relative of Klairessa's. Since Habibti, Klairessa has produced another filly by Habitat, who unfortunately died, a colt by Northern Baby and a colt by General Assembly.

Habibti (br.f. 1980)	Habitat (b 1966)	Sir Gaylord (b 1959)	Turn-to
			Somethingroyal
		Little Hut (b 1952)	Occupy
			Savage Beauty
	Klairessa (b 1969)	Klairon (b 1952)	Clarion III
			Kalmia
		Courtessa (b 1955)	Supreme Court
			Tessa Gillian

Habibti is well made and strong quartered, quite an attractive filly. She is also a good mover who has shown by far her best form on a sound surface though she won the Moyglare Stud Stakes on a soft one at the Curragh as a two-year-old; the ground was soft for the Fred Darling and heavy for the Irish Guineas. Extremely genuine, Habibti settles unusually well for a sprinter. Unlike many great sprinters of the past she has never won her race out of the stalls, but we shouldn't care to bet heavily against her doing so if her jockey announced his intention to attempt such a feat; she wins by producing a turn of finishing pace that none of her opponents at five furlongs or six furlongs has yet been able to match. *J. Dunlop.*

HABITASSA 3 b.f. Habitat 134–Sassabunda 108 (Sassafras 135) (1982 6g 7d 1983 10.5s 10g 8g² 9d* 8fg* 10.2fg*) strong, rangy filly; has a round action; really came to herself in autumn, and won her last 3 races, maiden event at York and handicaps at Newmarket and Doncaster; beat El Gitano easing up by 5 lengths at Newmarket, but had to fight hard to beat Rio Deva a head when completing her hat-trick; stays 1¼m; seems to act on any going. *B. Hills.* **100**

HABIT FORMING 3 gr.f. Habat 127–Hi Jay (Double-U-Jay 120) (1982 6g 6g 1983 7v 7f 7fg³ 8f* 8g) workmanlike filly; plater; bought in 3,000 gns after winning by 5 lengths at Brighton in August; behind in non-seller only subsequent start; stays 1m; acts on firm going. *D. Ringer.* **52**

HABIT ROUGE 3 b.c. Habitat 134–Bombshell 76 (Le Levanstell 122) (1982 8d 1983 9v 10.6s) strong colt; very lightly raced and no form in maiden and minor events. *J. Hanson.* **–**

HABOOB (USA) 4 b.g. Graustark–Angenora (Two Relics) (1982 11fg 10f 8f 10fg 10fg⁴ 7g 9.4fg 8g 8.2s⁴ 8s 1983 10s 11.7d 10v 8f 10f 10f) smallish, strong gelding; poor middle-distance plater nowadays; acts on soft going; sometimes blinkered; has run respectably for an apprentice though tended to hang quite badly fifth start. *J. Douglas-Home.* **–**

HABUS 5 b.h. Habitat 134–Rebus 97 (Busted 134) (1982 10fg 12fg³ 11.7g 10fg 10fg 12d 12g 12s 12s 1983 12s 12f* 10f³ 12f⁴ 12f) strong horse; poor walker and mover; won handicap at Ripon in June; suited by 1½m+; acts on firm going; has won for an apprentice; blinkered last 2 outings in 1982; trained by C. Brittain first start; sold 1,850 gns Newmarket September Sales. *M. H. Easterby.* **48**

HADA RANI 3 ch.f. Jaazeiro 127–Fast Line (Klairon 131) (1982 6fg 1983 6fg) no worthwhile form in minor event at Epsom as a 2-y-o and maiden race at Nottingham in September, but showed some speed in latter; sold 2,400 gns Newmarket Autumn Sales. *G. Lewis.* **–**

HADDAK (USA) 2 b.c. Cyane–My Guest (Mister Gus) (1983 8fg) Apr 9; $90,000Y; half-brother to several winners, including stakes winners Native Guest **94 p**

and Raise Your Sights (both by Raise A Native), former a smart winner at up to 1m; dam unraced half-sister to good animals T.V. Commercial and Coraggioso; third favourite, showed up well long way when 5¾ lengths sixth of 21 to Alphabatim in maiden race at Newmarket in October; bound to improve. *H. Cecil.*

HADITOS 4 b.f. Averof 123–Peta's Bay 67 (I Say 125) (1982 7d 5f 5g³ 5fg 5g 5fg² 5fg* 5f 5g 1983 6v 5g 5f 5f 5fg) big, workmanlike filly; sprint handicapper; best at 5f; acts on a firm and a soft surface; sometimes blinkered; tends to swish her tail; bought 20,000 gns Ascot March Sales. *J. Etherington.*   –

HAD TO BE YOU 2 b.c. Mummy's Pet 125–Alauda (Shantung 132) (1983 6g) May 16; 36,000Y; half-brother to 4 winners, including very useful 1974 Irish 3-y-o 6f to 1m performer Matuno God (by Red God); dam unraced daughter of very useful stayer Rising Wings; 12/1, never-dangerous seventh of 19 to New Dimension in maiden race at Goodwood in September; will stay 7f; should do better. *H. Candy.*   – p

HAFEAF 2 ch.c. Sandy Creek 123–Angkor Vat (Vienna 127) (1983 6g⁴ 7g²) Mar 25; 17,000F, IR 115,000Y; useful-looking colt; fifth live foal; dam, winner over 1¼m in France, is sister to prolific winner Kursaal; showed fair form in maiden events at Yarmouth and York (favourite) in the autumn; will stay 1¼m; sure to win a race. *H. T. Jones.*   85

HAGEN QUEEN 4 b.f. Mount Hagen 127–Fenland Queen (King's Troop 118) (1982 8f 10.6f⁴ 11fg² 12g² 10.6f 14.7fg 12s³ 12s 1983 12v⁴ 12v 12v 16.1fg 20.4g 12f 12f⁴ 12d 10g 10.6s) fair sort; poor middle-distance handicapper; seems to act on any going; blinkered nowadays; has shown signs of temperament. *C. Crossley.*   –

HAGEN'S BARGAIN 3 ch.f. Mount Hagen 127–Titmouse (Petingo 135) (1982 5fg 5d 5g* 5f³ 5f 7fg 7g 6s² 6s³ 1983 8s 7v 6fg³ 7f 8f 10g 8d 8d) rather leggy, lightly-made filly; plater; probably stays 1m; acts on any going; dwelt when blinkered sixth and seventh starts; changed hands 620 gns Doncaster November Sales. *J. Yardley.*   52 §

HAGEN'S HOLLY 3 ch.f. Mount Hagen 127–Holiday Inn (Le Haar 126) (1982 NR 1983 10s 10.2v 12g 8.2fg) IR 5,800Y; leggy, narrow, sparely-made filly; fourth foal; dam unraced half-sister to smart French miler Gracious Knight and very useful 9f to 1¼m winner Christmas Box; behind in varied races, including Oaks; blinkered final start. *W. Stubbs.*   –

HAIFFAN 2 b.c. Mummy's Pet 125–Friendly Jester 90 (Be Friendly 130) (1983 6g³ 5d*) Mar 23; 15,000F, 6,200Y; second reported foal; closely related to 1982 2-y-o 5f winner Friendly Bobby (by Coded Scrap); dam, half-sister to the dam of Jester, won twice over 5f; won 8-runner maiden race at Wolverhampton in October; stayed 6f; dead. *G. Huffer.*   84

HALCYON AGE 3 b.f. Silly Season 127–Wax Fruit 91 (John Splendid 116) (1982 5g 5fg⁴ 5f² 6f 6fg 6g 6f 5g 5f 5fg 6d 1983 6v 6fg 5fg 5f 8f 8.2fg) leggy, light-framed filly; plater; stays 6f; probably acts on any going; often blinkered. *A. Cawley.*   –

HALCYON HOURS 2 ch.f. Shiny Tenth 120–Chinese Princess (Sunny Way 120) (1983 5s) Apr 29; half-sister to 2 winners, including middle-distance stayer Sunshine Gal (by Alto Volante); dam unraced half-sister to very smart Streetfighter; slow-starting last of 12 in maiden race at Catterick in June. *H. Blackshaw.*   –

HALF ASLEEP 2 b.f. Quiet Fling 124–Misnomer 85 (Milesian 125) (1983 7f 8fg) Feb 7; lengthy filly; half-sister to 3 winners, including fairly useful 1½m winner York Cottage (by Royal Palace); dam, winner at up to 1½m, is daughter of St Leger third Cold Storage; behind in fair company at Redcar right at the back-end; likely to need a stiff test of stamina. *W. Elsey.*   –

HALF SHAFT (USA) 2 b.g. Broadway Forli–One Quest (One-Eyed King) (1983 7g 6fg⁴ 7d 6s² 7f 6fg) Apr 18; $60,000Y; leggy gelding; half-brother to numerous winners, notably smart 9f and 1¼m winner Judgable (by Delta Judge); dam placed at 2 yrs; sold out of J. Hanson's stable 5,000 gns Doncaster September Sales shortly after finishing 3 lengths second of 10 to Lovers Bid in minor event at Ayr; should stay 1m; best form on soft going; gelded after final appearance. *W. A. Stephenson.*   76

HALLO CHEEKY 7 ch.m. Flatbush 95–Artlight (Articulate 121) (1982 NR 1983 8g 10g 15f⁴ 15fg) plater; has worn blinkers; has run respectably for an apprentice. *W. Storey.*   –

HALLO ROSIE 3 gr.f. Swing Easy 126–Mary Crooner 57 (Crooner 119) (1982 6fg⁴ 5g³ 6s 1983 6v 5v 6s 5s* 5fg 5g 5g 6fg) plater; bought in 2,200 gns after winning at Chepstow in May; seems best at 5f; acts on soft going. *J. Holt.*   67

HALL'S PRINCE 2 b.c. Stanford 121§–Desertville 92 (Charlottesville 135)   53
(1983 5.1g 5.8g 8.2fg 8d⁴ 10d) Mar 6; IR 3,000Y; dipped-backed colt; half-brother
to several winners, including very useful stayer New Jerusalem (by Reform) and
smart 1975 French staying 2-y-o Empty Jest (by Bon Mot III); plater; backed from
20/1 to 7/1, 7½ lengths fourth of 19 to Spiv's Right in apprentice event at Warwick in
October, best effort; stays 1m; acts on a soft surface; blinkered final start. *C.
Spares.*

HAL'S JOY (USA) 4 b.g. L'Heureux–Majestic Flight (Majestic Prince) (1982   69
12fg 12f 12f 14f 14.7fg 12v⁴ 14s³ 15.8d³ 18d³ 1983 20fg⁴ 16g² 16g² 16f) smallish,
good-bodied gelding; stays very well; acts on any going with possible exception of
very firm; useful hurdler. *M. Pipe.*

HALYARD 3 gr.g. Gaberdine 106–Cabotage 54 (Sea Hawk II 131) (1982 7f 7g 10d   59
10d⁴ 1983 9v⁴ 11d² 12f² 12.3f³ 11g² 12.2f³ 11f) useful-looking gelding; good
walker; will be suited by further than 1½m; occasionally blinkered; trained by A.
Young until after fourth start. *D. Smith.*

HAMBLETON LADY 2 br.f. Blue and Grey 93–Balsarroch Lady 56 (Manacle   –
123) (1983 5d 5fg 5f 5s 5g 5g) Feb 3; smallish filly; of no account. *J. Carr.*

HAMPSHIRE 9 b.g. Silly Season 127–Pirate Queen 77 (Pirate King 129) (1982   –
10g 10fg 10f³ 10fg² 12g⁴ 10fg² 10f³ 10g 10f⁴ 1983 12g 10f 10f) middle-distance
handicapper; acts on any going; wears blinkers; usually bandaged in front. *A. Pitt.*

HAMPTON WALK 2 b.g. Tower Walk 130–Wong Way Girl 99 (Kibenka 119)   –
(1983 5fg 6d) fourth foal; half-brother to 7f and 1m winner Rawlinson End (by
Song); dam won at up to 7f; in rear in minor event at Windsor in August and maiden
race at Newbury in October; subsequently gelded. *J. Holt.*

HANABI 4 b.g. Hittite Glory 125–Derry Willow (Sunny Way 120) (1982 7d 7d 11f   –
8f⁴ 8d³ 8fg 8.3g 7fg 7fg³ 8d⁴ 7s² 1983 8s 8s 7s⁴ 8f 10f 8f 8fg 8.3fg 8f) quite
attractive gelding; below form most starts at 4 yrs; stays 1m; suited by some give
in the ground; often blinkered; does best when ridden up with pace; sold 2,100 gns
Newmarket Autumn Sales. *W. Wightman.*

HANADI 3 b.f. Blakeney 126–Upanishad 85 (Amber Rama 133) (1982 8fg 7s 1983   –
14g 16f 16g 17g⁴ 16h) rather sparely-made filly with a round action; staying
maiden. *G. Huffer.*

HANDSOME BLAZE 8 b.g. Some Hand 119–Court Whisper 83 (Queen's   59
Hussar 124) (1982 8g 8fg 10fg 8.2g² 8.3g 1983 8v² 8.2v* 8d² 8g* 8f² 7f⁴ 8f⁴ 8f)
plater; bought in 1,600 gns after winning at Haydock in April; often runs well in
non-sellers and won handicap at Ayr in May; stays 1m well; acts on any going but is
suited by some give in the ground; has run well for a lady rider; sometimes sweats
up and is taken down early; invariably held up and sometimes meets trouble in
running; broke blood vessel final start. *C. Booth.*

HANDSTAND 2 ch.c. Thatching 131–Moorland Chant (Double Jump 131) (1983   107 ?
5s* 6fg² 6f³ 7g³ 6g) Apr 16; IR 14,000Y; strong, compact colt; half-brother to
several winners, including Irish 3-y-o 1½m and 13.5f winner Mexican Chant (by
Solinus) and very useful Nedsatki (by Realm), successful at up to 7f in France;
dam won over 9f in France; won 14-runner Scarborough Stakes at York in May,
beating Knoxville short head; placed in varied company subsequently, running
easily best race when 9 lengths third of 4, after 2-month absence, to Lear Fan in
Laurent Perrier Champagne Stakes at Doncaster in September; much better
suited by 7f than by shorter distances, and will stay 1m; seems to act on any
going. *J. W. Watts.*

HANDYLAD 4 b.g. Mandamus 120–Rosie Crucian (Polkemmet 91) (1982 10fg   49
1983 12d 10f³ 12fg³ 12.2fg) robust, good sort; poor maiden; stays 1½m; blinkered
last 3 starts. *W. Wharton.*

HANDYLOU 4 br.f. Downstream 105–Steak House 68 (Road House II) (1982 NR   –
1983 6fg) sister to 1m winner Helandy and half-sister to a winner abroad; dam won
6f seller at 2 yrs; last of 11 in minor event at Ayr in July. *T. Barnes.*

HANHAM ROAD 5 b.h. Shiny Tenth 120–Prompt Delivery (Catullus) (1982 7s²   44
7f 8g 7h³ 8f² 8fg 8fg 8fg 8s⁴ 8g 1983 8s* 8s²) lengthy horse; poor handicapper;
won race in Isle of Man in May; stays 1m; acts on any going; often blinkered, but
has run well without; has run respectably for an apprentice; not seen out after May.
D. Marks.

HANNAH LIGHTFOOT 4 b.f. Royalty 130–Gay Charlotte 95 (Charlottown   69
127) (1982 12f 12fg* 1983 12fg 13.3g⁴ 16fg) leggy, sparely-made filly; quite
moderate; not seen out until September but ran respectably in handicaps at
Doncaster and Newbury on first 2 starts; will stay 1¾m (well beaten over 2m);
sweated up and was very much above herself in paddock first outing. *J. Winter.*

HANNAH MOORE 2 ch.f. Grundy 137–Jeanie Duff 83 (Majestic Prince) (1983 —
8fg) Feb 22; 22,000F; small, compact filly; half-sister to 1m winner Cornish Gem
(by Cornish Prince) and a winner in USA; dam, daughter of smart stayer Turf, won
over 1¼m and 1½m; 33/1 and very wintry, out of first 10 of 28 in maiden race at
Newmarket in October. *B. Hobbs.*

HANSE 3 ch.f. Mount Hagen 127–Kissing 98 (Sing Sing 134) (1982 7d 1983 10fg)
workmanlike filly; behind in big fields of maidens at Leicester as a 2-y-o and
Newmarket in June. *G. Pritchard-Gordon.*

HAPPY ALWAYS 3 br.f. Lucky Wednesday 124–Mary of Scots 84 (Relic) (1982 —
5f 5f³ 6fg⁴ 7f 8fg 7g⁴ 8s 1983 8s 9f 7f 7f 6g 6f⁴ 6fg) poor plater; should stay 1m;
blinkered last 4 outings. *I. Jordon.*

HAPPY EATER 3 b.g. Furry Glen 121–Barby Road 62 (Tin Whistle 128) (1982 —
5fg 6d 5f 6d 7fg 1983 12fg 11fg) rather dipped-backed gelding; poor form in maiden
races and sellers. *F. Watson.*

HAPPY MOO 4 b.f. Williamston Kid–Tartarbee 72 (Charlottesville 135) (1982 —
8fg 1983 8fg 11.7h) poor maiden; blinkered in 1983. *J. Peacock.*

HAPPY RHYTHM 3 b.g. Tudor Rhythm 112–Happy Donna 106 (Huntercombe —
133) (1982 5fg 5g 8.2s 6s 8.2v³ 1983 11g 8.2g 7d 9f) lightly-built gelding; poor
walker; well beaten in varied company, including plating; sold 640 gns Doncaster
August Sales. *J. S. Wilson.*

HAPPY SEASON 3 b.c. Silly Season 127–My Shoon (Sheshoon 132) (1982 6f 6d 54
6g 7s 6d² 6s 1983 5fg 6f 5f 8f² 10d 8.2g³ 10.6s 12fg⁴) lengthy colt; in frame in
maiden and minor races; probably stays 1½m; acts on any going; blinkered third
start; trained part of season by J. Etherington. *J. Fitzgerald.*

HAPPY WONDER 3 ch.f. Levanter 121–Gretna Wonder 46 (Elopement 125) —
(1982 6fg 5f 7fg 1983 10.1f 11.7f 10.1f 10f) lengthy filly; little worthwhile form in
varied races. *D. Elsworth.*

HARBOUR BAZAAR 3 gr. or ro.g. Native Bazaar 122–Overseas 48 (Sea Hawk —
II 131) (1982 5fg 7g 8d 5g⁴ 8s 6d 6s 1983 5v 5s² 6fg 7fg 6f 8.2h 13h 10g 6fg) leggy,
shallow-girthed gelding; plater; form only at sprint distances; acts on soft going;
bandaged off-hind and blinkered final start at 2 yrs. *M. Chapman.*

HARBOUR BRIDGE 3 b.c. Blakeney 126–Solar 120 (Hotfoot 126) (1982 7f 78
7fg³ 7s 1983 12d 10s* 12v 11g 12f 12g³ 11.5f³ 12f² 12f² 11.7fg 12fg⁴ 12g 16fg)
lengthy, good sort; good walker and mover; ran on dourly when winning maiden
race at Salisbury in May; placed in handicaps several times afterwards; should be
suited by further than 1½m; acts on any going; occasionally blinkered (has run
creditably in them); sometimes bandaged near-hind. *W. Wightman.*

HARBOUR MUSIC 3 br.g. Tudor Music 131–Sark (Chamier 128) (1982 6g 6g 58
7fg 6d 1983 8f 10.6fg 10f 11f 12.3fg 8.2fg* 9g) strong, compact gelding; attracted
no bid after winning seller at Hamilton in September; little other form; stays 1m;
sometimes blinkered (wore them at Hamilton); sold to T. Craig 2,600 gns
Doncaster October Sales. *R. Whitaker.*

HARD BARGAIN 5 ch.g. Native Bazaar 122–Curry Favour 62 (Negotiation) —
(1982 NR 1983 10.2g 12fg 10f) small gelding; third foal; brother to a winning 2-y-o;
dam plater; tailed off in varied company, including selling. *P. Makin.*

HARDIHOSTESS 3 b.f. Be My Guest 126–Hardiemma 81 (Hardicanute 130) 97
(1982 5g 7fg³ 7fg* 7fg* 8f 1983 12s³ 12v³ 12g) rather dipped-backed,
good-quartered, small filly; has a sharp action; half-sister to Shirley Heights (by
Mill Reef); showed useful form as a 2-y-o; modest third behind Give Thanks in Esal
Bookmakers Oaks Trial at Lingfield and behind Current Raiser in Lupe Stakes at
Goodwood, both in May; well beaten in Lancashire Oaks at Haydock in July on final
outing; stays 1½m; probably acts on any going. *M. Stoute.*

HARD KINGDOM 3 b.c. Realm 129–Hard To Tell 68 (Buckpasser) (1982 6fg⁴ ?
6fg 1983 7v* 8d 7.3v) big colt; good walker; landed the odds a shade comfortably
in 5-runner maiden race at Newcastle in April; finished distressed in quite valuable
handicaps at Newmarket and Newbury subsequently, on latter course in May being
pulled up over 2f out, reportedly after breaking a blood vessel; should stay 1m; one
to be wary of; sold to W. Clay 1,350 gns Ascot July Sales. *G. Wragg.*

HARDWICK AMBER 2 b.f. Tanfirion 110–Super Amber (Yellow God 129) (1983 58
5s⁴ 5v 5s 6f 6g 7f 9fg³ 7.2g⁴) May 20; 3,600Y; fair sort; half-sister to 3 winners,
including two 2-y-o 5f winners; dam never ran; in frame in sellers at Redcar
(nursery) and Haydock in September; stays 9f. *M. Jefferson.*

HARDWICK EAGLE 3 b.f. Legal Eagle 126–Keenland (Weensland 121) (1982 –
5f² 6g 5fg⁴ 6g 5g 5g 1983 8.2s 12d 6f) maiden plater; form only at sprint distances
and is unlikely to stay 1½m; blinkered once at 2 yrs. *M. Jefferson.*

HARIFA (FR) 2 b.f. Green Dancer 132–Hamada 116 (Habitat 134) (1983 6f* 113
5.5g* 5.5g³ 7fg 6.5g³ 7g³) third foal; closely related to a middle-distance winner
in France by Nijinsky and half-sister to another by Busted; dam won 7f Prix de la
Porte Maillot; ran creditably in 3 pattern races, beaten under 4 lengths into third
each time, in Prix Robert Papin (won by Masarika) at Maisons-Laffitte in July,
Prix Eclipse (won by Diamada) at Saint-Cloud and Criterium de Maisons-Laffitte
(won by Procida) in October; had earlier won a 90,000-franc event at last-named
track and newcomers race at Chantilly; should stay 1m; acts on a firm surface.
Mme C. Head, France.

HARI-HARI-MOU 3 b.c. Malinowski 123–Shangara (Credo 123) (1982 6f* 6g³ 77
8.2g 8.2d 8.2s³ 1983 8s 10fg 10f 9f 10g 9d³ 13g) smallish, fair sort; didn't recover
his 2-y-o form when trained over here by R. Armstrong, but finished creditable
third in gentleman riders race at Evry in October on first outing in France
(blinkered); should stay 1¼m. *M. Blackshaw, France.*

HARLEYFORD MAID 3 gr.f. The Go-Between 129–Comprella 54 58
(Compensation 127) (1982 5f 5f² 5g 5fg⁴ 5f³ 5f 5g² 5g³ 5v⁴ 1983 5d³ 5fg² 5g 5f* 5f
5f 6fg) small, narrow, close-coupled filly; ran moderately after winning apprentice
race at Edinburgh in July; form only at 5f; acts on any going; didn't move
particularly well in her later races. *D. Smith.*

HARLOWS BOY 3 b.g. Ercolano 118–No Man's Land (Salvo 129) (1982 7fg 7fg –
7g 7d 8.2fg 8g⁴ 1983 12s) lengthy, good-bodied gelding; plating-class maiden;
should stay at least 1½m; wears blinkers; sold 2,600 gns Ascot May Sales. *P.
Brookshaw.*

HARLY (FR) 3 b.c. Pharly 130–Helvetique (Val de Loir 133) (1982 7d 7g* 8d⁴ 107
8g 1983 10v* 12v* 11g² 14f 12f⁴ 11g* 12g² 12d) small, fair sort; improved and won
handicap at Kempton, Warren Stakes at Epsom (made most to beat Shanipour
decisively by ¾ length) and Group 3 Furstenberg-Rennen at Baden-Baden;
accounted for Novelle by 1¾ lengths in last-named in August; also second twice in

Mr N. A. Shuaib's "Harly"

Germany, beaten 4 lengths by Ocos in Grosser Hertie-Preis at Munich (didn't have best of runs) and a short head by Tombos in Preis des Landes Nordrhein-Westfalen at Dusseldorf; stays 1¾m; probably acts on any going, but revels in the mud; tough and genuine. *J. Dunlop.*

HARLYN BAY 2 b.c. Wolver Hollow 126–Capsville (Cyane) (1983 7g 8d 9f³ | 84
10.2fg) Feb 22; IR 22,000Y; big, rangy colt; half-brother to several winners here and abroad, including 3-y-o sprinter Martial Fitzgerald (by Tower Walk); dam, placed in USA, is sister to smart stakes winner Pinch Pie; still bit burly, put up easily best effort when close third of 13, staying on, behind Cri de Coeur in maiden race at Redcar in October; evidently needs 9f+; should win a race. *S. Norton.*

HARRY FLASHMAN (USA) 2 b.c. Elocutionist–Right Turn (Turn-to) (1983 | – p
7fg 8fg) Mar 25; $90,000Y; quite attractive, lengthy colt; half-brother to Rich Cream (by Creme dela Creme), a very smart winner at up to 9f, and to another winner; dam never ran; backward, showed a little promise in the autumn in Mornington Stakes at Ascot and maiden race at Newmarket; should do better in time. *J. Sutcliffe.*

HARRY HASTINGS (USA) 4 b.g. Vaguely Noble 140–Country Dream (Ribot | 78
142) (1982 11f 13.3f 10f⁴ 8s 8.2s 1983 10h* 8.2g² 13.8g* 18fg) big, rangy gelding; won seller at Pontefract in September (bought in 2,100 gns) and handicap at Catterick in October (made all and trotted up); suited by 1¾m (ran too freely when well beaten over 2¼m but was only running at trip because balloted out of William Hill November Handicap for which he had been a hefty ante-post order); acts on hard going; has been bandaged. *J. S. Wilson.*

HARTBURN RELIANCE 3 b.g. Reliance II 137–Helgonet (Soueida 111) (1982 | 50
6g³ 6g 5g² 5d³ 1983 6v 10f 8.2fg³) sturdy, good-bodied gelding; plater; promises to stay 1¼m. *I. Vickers.*

HARTBURN ROYALE 3 b.g. The Brianstan 128–Aequanimitas (Infatuation | –
129) (1982 8s 1983 11v) strong gelding; tailed off in maiden races. *I. Vickers.*

HARTBURN SARAH 2 gr.f. Royal Match 117–Haunting 79 (Lord Gayle 124) | –
(1983 5g 6fg) Jan 28; 2,000Y; rather narrow, plain filly; fourth foal; half-sister to Norsk St Leger winner Our Martin (by Martinmas); dam stayed 1m; soundly beaten in minor events at Catterick and Redcar (twelfth of 23) in September. *I. Vickers.*

HARTFIELD LAD 4 br.g. Jimsun 121–Julita 87 (Rockavon 120) (1982 10g 10f | –
10.1fg 10g² 10d 1983 16f 10f 10.8g² 18g) neat gelding; plater; stays 1¼m; suited by some give in the ground; has worn blinkers. *J. Hardy.*

HARTS DESIRE 2 b.f. Frimley Park 109–La Mariposa (T.V. Lark) (1983 6g | –
7.6d) compact, rather narrow filly; half-sister to a winner in Hungary; dam placed at around 1m in France; behind in big fields in newcomers event at Goodwood in September and maiden race at Lingfield in October. *D. Arbuthnot.*

HARVARD 2 ch.c. Mansingh 120–La Melodie 77 (Silly Season 127) (1983 5v³ 6f⁴ | 96
6f³ 7f* 7f 7fg) Mar 29; 4,000F, 9,200Y; useful-looking colt; good mover with a light action; half-brother to 2 minor winners; dam stayed 1m; showed much improved form when put to 7f, winning Sandwich Maiden Stakes at Ascot in July by 4 lengths from Attempt, and finishing creditable sixth in sponsored race at Salisbury in August and William Hill Dewhurst Stakes at Newmarket in October; clearly needs at least 7f; acts well on firm going. *R. Boss.*

HARVEST 3 ch.c. Continuation 120–Polly Bellino 56 (Dadda Bert 95) (1982 7fg | –
1983 10f) well beaten in maiden races. *J. Hardy.*

HARVESTER GOLD 3 gr.c. Rheingold 137–Colloquy (Quorum 126) (1982 7fg | 75
8fg⁴ 8d 1983 10v 10.5f⁴ 10fg 10.4fg 10.6fg² 10f⁴ 10fg³) quite attractive, lightly-made colt; quite a moderate middle-distance maiden; seems unsuited by heavy ground; has run respectably when sweating badly; ran moderately fourth start. *M. Jarvis.*

HARVEST FORTUNE 3 b.c. Oats 126–Fortellina (Fortino II 120) (1982 7f 7d | 57
8s 1983 12d 12v 14g 16f 16g 12f 12fg 11.5s* 12g) rangy colt; bought in 1,200 gns after winning seller at Yarmouth in September; yet to show he stays long distances; probably acts on any going, but goes well on soft; sometimes blinkered. *H. Collingridge.*

HARVEST PRINCESS 2 b.f. Dragonara Palace 115–Harvest Reap (Majority | –
Blue 126) (1983 7s 6fg) Mar 8; 5,000Y; second foal; dam, of little account on flat, won over hurdles; behind in sizeable fields of maidens at Leicester in October. *R. Williams.*

HARWOOD BAR 4 br.f. Wollow 132–Princess Ayesha (Bold Lad, Ire 133) (1982   –
7d 6s 8g 1983 8v 11fg 14.7d 12d) poor plater; has given trouble at start and looks
highly strung. *D. Chapman.*

HASSI R'MEL 5 ch.g. Clear Run 109–Nuchiru (Chingnu 99) (1982 NR 1983 16f)   –
plater; stays 1¾m. *J. Yardley.*

HASTY FLIRT (USA) 3 b.c. Vitriolic–Lucky Flirt (Lucky Debonair) (1982 7g⁴   109
7g⁴ 7f* 7fg 8g 8g* 8g² 8d² 8g* 1983 8g⁴ 10g 8f 7f) quite attractive colt; put up
useful performance at Rome in April when 3½ lengths fourth of 9 to Drumalis in
Premio Parioli (Italian 2000 Guineas); behind subsequently in Heathorn Stakes at
Newmarket later in month and quite valuable handicaps at Sandown and Leicester
in July; stays 1m well; seems to act on any going; blinkered final outing. *B.
Hanbury.*

HASTY GODDESS 4 ch.f. Nebbiolo 125–No Delay 72 (Never Say Die 137)   65
(1982 10s³ 12fg³ 13f³ 14.7f 12d³ 14.7f⁴ 14.7fg 1983 12.3f 15f² 12f* 12f 13h³ 12.2g*
12g* 11fg 13.8g) workmanlike filly; won handicaps at Edinburgh in July, Catterick in
September and Edinburgh again in October; stays well; acts on any going; often
races with head in air. *W. A. Stephenson.*

HASTY THIEF (USA) 2 b.c. No Robbery–Step On It (Bold Lad, USA) (1983 6f   –
7d 8fg 7g 8fg) Mar 24; $55,000 2-y-o; rather sparely-made colt; half-brother to 3
minor winners; dam, 2-y-o 5f winner, is half-sister to very smart 1978 2-y-o
Fuzzbuster (by No Robbery); behind in maiden races; wore blinkers and a tongue
strap fourth start. *B. Hanbury.*

HATAL BOY 2 ch.c. Virginia Boy 106–Cloghersville (Sweet Revenge 129) (1983   –
6fg 6d) Apr 28; IR 2,100Y, 4,100 2-y-o; strong, heavy-topped colt; first foal; dam
ran only twice; in rear in October maiden races at Folkestone and Newbury. *P.
Mitchell.*

HATCHING 2 b.c. Thatch 136–Bantam 64 (Combat 123) (1983 5d 5fg) May 12;   –
quite a useful-looking colt; half-brother to several winners, notably high-class 1m to
1¼m performer Gold Rod (by Songedor); dam won 5f seller at 2 yrs; showed a little
ability in June in maiden race at Leicester and minor event at Windsor. *F. J.
Houghton.*

HATHAWAY 4 ch.f. Connaught 130–Ragirl (Ragusa 137) (1982 10fg 10fg 12fg 16f   –
1983 20.4g 11.7h) lightly-made filly; poor maiden. *A. Ingham.*

HATIM (USA) 2 ch.c. Exclusive Native–Sunday Purchase (T. V. Lark) (1983   102 P
6fg²) Apr 25; $1,100,000Y; nice, rangy colt; fifth foal; dam, 1m winner, is half-sister to high-class
notably 1979 Horris Hill Stakes winner Super Asset and 1983 Santa Anita Handicap
winner Bates Motel (both by Sir Ivor); dam, 1m winner, is half-sister to high-class
1971 USA 2-y-o Rest Your Case; second favourite, acquitted himself extremely
well in 11-runner Clarence House Maiden Stakes at Ascot in September, going
down by only a short head to Miss Silca Key despite running distinctly green and
not being given hard race; will improve considerably, especially over further; one
to follow. *J. Tree.*

HATTAN 5 b.g. Rheingold 137–Bally's Gift 83 (So Blessed 130) (1982 NR 1983   59 d
12v² 16v* 12g 19g 16fg 16g⁴) good-looking gelding; easily won handicap at
Lingfield in April; stays well; revels in the mud. *P. Mitchell.*

HATTERAS 3 ch.g. Sharpen Up 127–Shesells Seashells (Roi Soleil 125) (1982   –
NR 1983 10.2v 10f) 6,200F; tall, plain gelding; second produce; dam unraced
half-sister to dams of Pistol Packer and Saritamer; soundly beaten in minor event at
Doncaster (needed outing) and maiden race at Ripon; sold 1,550 gns Doncaster
September Sales. *M. H. Easterby.*

HATTIE JAY 2 b.f. Comedy Star 121–Babington Fats (Varano) (1983 5.8g 7fg 6fg   –
5.8h 7f 7f) Apr 8; 800Y; leggy filly; poor mover; behind in maiden auction events
and sellers; often blinkered. *M. Usher.*

HAUTE HAT (USA) 3 b.f. Exclusive Native–Lady Marguery (Tim Tam) (1982   60
7fg 8f 1983 8d 12d 11f³ 9.4f 12fg² 12.2f* 12f) rangy filly; won maiden race at
Catterick in August (didn't go to post well); acts on firm going; sent to race in USA. *S. Norton.*

HAUTES TERRES 2 b.c. Swing Easy 126–Reine d'Etat 53 (High Hat 131) (1983   –
6g 7.6fg 6d) half-brother to 3 winners here and abroad, including 1980 2-y-o 5f
winner Fleur de Galles (by Prince de Galles); dam placed over 1½m; behind in
autumn maiden and minor events. *A. Moore.*

HAVARA 4 b.f. African Sky 124–Arriva (Disciplinarian) (1982 5fg² 5g² 6g* 7fg³   —
7.3g² 7s 1983 8v 8d) big, well-made filly; modest at her best; virtually tailed off
both starts at 4 yrs in spring; should stay 1m; form only on a sound surface. *J.
Sutcliffe.*

HAVE A BALL 2 b. or br.c. Sallust 134–Haymaking 115 (Galivanter 131) (1983   — p
6g 7fg 7g) Feb 10; well-made, quite attractive colt; good mover; half-brother to
several winners, including very useful 1975 2-y-o 5f winner Hayloft (by Tudor
Melody); dam won Coronation and Nassau Stakes; eighth in big fields of maidens at
Newmarket and York in the autumn on last 2 starts; will probably improve. *F. J.
Houghton.*

HAVE BLESSED 3 b.g. Averof 123–As Blessed 101 (So Blessed 130) (1982   60
5fg⁴ 6f⁴ 7g⁴ 7fg 8d 8d 1983 10s 12fg 12fg 9f³ 10fg 10f 10g² 10g* 16g) compact
gelding; sold out of C. Brittain's stable 4,400 gns after winning seller at Lingfield
in October by 5 lengths; promises to stay beyond 1¼m (fifth of 19 over 2m);
blinkered final start in 1982. *R. Smyth.*

HAVE FORM 3 b.f. Haveroid 122–Good Form 54 (Deep Diver 134) (1982 6g 7g   —
7fg 1983 7h 8f 7f 10.1fg 10h 8fg 7fg 7s) compact filly; poor form in varied company,
including selling; stays 7f; occasionally blinkered. *R. Laing.*

HAVEN BLESSED 3 b.f. So Blessed 130–Haven Bridge 88 (Connaught 130)   60
(1982 7g 1983 9s 10f 10.2h 7f 8f 6d⁴) good-bodied, slightly hollow-backed filly;
fourth in handicap at Brighton in September, first form; somewhat headstrong, and
probably best at sprint distances; blinkered third start. *C. Nelson.*

HAVEN'S PRIDE (USA) 4 b.c. Dewan–Victoire (Crafty Admiral) (1982 7fg   —
7.6f 8f² 10.6h* 12d 10.8fg 12fg 14g 8g* 8.2g 8fg 8d 10.6s 1983 9v 8g 12f 10f 7.6fg
9fg 8.2f 8fg 10.6fg 7h 8g 8.2g 7fg) small, lightly-made colt; plater; well beaten at
4 yrs, mainly in non-sellers; stays 1¼m; acts on any going; has twice been
blinkered; trained first 2 starts by W. Charles. *M. James.*

HAVENWOOD 4 br.c. Relko 136–Pepin (Midsummer Night II 117) (1982 10f*   57
12fg 10f 12g 10d 10d 1983 10s 12d³ 11s⁴ 12d⁴ 12s 10v 11fg 12fg) leggy colt; in
frame in handicaps but found little under pressure when gambled on second outing;
stays 1½m; seems to act on any going; sometimes wears bandages. *K. Stone.*

HAVERHILL LASS 4 b.f. Music Boy 124–March Queen 88 (March Past 124)   —
(1982 6fg 6g 5f² 5g 5.1g 6f 5f³ 5d* 6g 5d 5g 1983 5.1fg 5f 5.6f) sturdy filly; sprint
handicapper; best at 5f; acts on any going; often blinkered. *G. Huffer.*

HAVERS ROAD 2 b.g. Town and Country 124–Paripan (Pardao 120) (1983 7fg³   72
7f 7f) Apr 23; 5,000Y; workmanlike gelding; half-brother to useful 1977 2-y-o 1m
winner Economy Drive and winning 3-y-o stayer Americk (both by High Line);
dam never ran; 5½ lengths third of 23 to Running Bull in maiden race at
Newmarket in June, best effort; will stay 1¼m; gelded after final appearance. *M.
Tompkins.*

HAVE YOU TIME 2 gr.g. Sweet Revenge 129–Just Frolicking (Pals Passage   —
115) (1983 6h) Feb 27; IR 1,450Y; first foal; dam ran 4 times in Ireland; eleventh of
12 in maiden race at Nottingham in August. *W. Wharton.*

HAVON AIR 5 ch.m. Celtic Cone 116–Mary's Date 60 (The Phoenix) (1982 NR   —
1983 16fg) lightly-built mare; little worthwhile form. *J. Spearing.*

HAVON COOL 7 b.h. Celtic Cone 116–Lucky Affair 83 (Stephen George 102)   —
(1982 8s 7.2s* 7.2fg³ 7.6g² 7f 6d 6g⁴ 8.3fg⁴ 7f² 7.6d 9d 7fg 6s⁴ 6s 7s 1983 8d 7.2v
7s 6fg 8.2fg⁴ 8f 8f⁴ 8.3fg³ 7.6g 7.3g 8d 7fg) neat, strong horse; poor mover; poor
handicapper nowadays; needs further than 6f, and stays 1m well; acts on any
going; usually wears blinkers; suitable mount for a boy; inconsistent; sold 500 gns
Ascot November Sales. *K. Brassey.*

HAWA BLADI 3 gr.c. Nishapour 125–Nofertiti (Exbury 138) (1982 7fg³ 7fg²   111
8fg³ 1983 10s* 10v* 12f³ 10d² 10f) medium-sized, quite well-made colt; first foal;
dam, second over 1½m in France, is half-sister to high-class 1m to 1¼m performer
Nadjar; won maiden race at Salisbury and 21-runner minor event at Kempton in
May in very good style, quickening up well when asked both times and in latter race
landing the odds by 3 lengths from Bandi; beaten for speed in closing stages but ran
very creditably when placed in King Edward VII Stakes at Royal Ascot in June (3½
lengths third of 7 behind Shareef Dancer) and Prix Eugene Adam at Saint-Cloud in
July (¾-length second of 11 to Mourjane); below best final outing (August); stays
1½m; acts on any going. *P. Walwyn.*

HAWAIIAN HEIR (USA) 4 b.c. Hawaii–Madam Fox (Rising Market) (1982   —
12g⁴ 14fg 12f 10.2g 16fg 12f 10f 1983 10.6s) quite attractive, useful-looking colt;
poor plater nowadays; has twice been blinkered. *W. Clay.*

364

Prince F. Khaled's "Hawa Bladi"

HAWK LADY (USA) 3 b. or br.f. Accipiter–Nova Miss (Great McGow) (1982   **70**
6fg 6g 6s* 1983 6s² 6d³ 8f 8f 7g 7g 7.6d 6g) strong filly; quite a modest
handicapper; probably stays 7f; acts on soft going. *Mrs R. Lomax.*

HAWKLEY 3 br.g. Monsanto 121–Varvel (Falcon 131) (1982 5f² 5fg² 5g* 6g² 6d   **91** d
7fg³ 7v 1983 7d³ 8s* 7v 7.6v 8f 8f 8f⁴ 10fg 8g³ 8fg) fair sort; good walker; ran on
well to beat Mandelstam by 2½ lengths in handicap at Newbury in April; in-and-out
form afterwards, but finished creditable third to One O'Clock Jump in handicap at
Sandown in October; promises to stay 1¼m; acts on any going; blinkered once at 2
yrs; trained much of season by K. Brassey. *P. Haslam.*

HAWTHORN ARCH 5 b.m. Wishing Star 117–River Leaves (Varano) (1982 12s   **–**
9.5g 12f² 13g⁴ 10.2s² 1983 10.2d 13v 14s⁴ 12v) small, lightly-made ex-Irish mare;
poor performer; has been beaten in sellers; stays 1¾m; acts on any going. *J. Fox.*

HAYASHI 2 gr.c. Crystal Palace 132–Absaretch (Dancer's Image) (1983 6f 7fg   **75**
8.2s³) Feb 4; 33,000Y; good sort; half-brother to 3 winners, notably French
Derby third Gap of Dunloe (by Sassafras); dam won 7f maiden race at 2yrs in USA;
not disgraced last 2 starts, particularly when just over 4 lengths third of 6 to
Laurie's Panther in maiden race at Haydock in October; will probably stay 1½m;
looks the type to win races. *C. Booth.*

HAYATILA 2 gr.f. Nishapour 125–Hadala (Le Levanstell 122) (1983 6s 6f 7h 6f)   **62**
Mar 1; first foal; dam, minor French 11.5f winner, is daughter of top 1960 2-y-o
Opaline II; plating-class maiden; should stay at least 1m; acts on hard going; sold
8,600 gns Newmarket December Sales. *M. Stoute.*

HAY FEVER 2 ch.f. Hotfoot 126–Mow Meadow (Acropolis 132) (1983 5s 5v 5s   **–**
6f) May 20; 2,000Y; quite a useful sort; half-sister to Irish 1m winner Our David
(by Great Nephew); dam sister to Craven Stakes winner Corifi; behind in maiden
and auction events; not seen out after June. *P. Brookshaw.*

HAY FIELDING 4 ch.g. Riboboy 124–Jailhouse Rock (Gulf Pearl 117) (1982 NR —
1983 14f) 1,500 3-y-o (privately); refused to race in 12-runner maiden event at
Sandown in July. *J. O'Donoghue.*

HAY GUINNESS 5 b.m. Birdbrook 110–Molvitesse 75 (Molvedo 137) (1982 11s —
12fg 11f 1983 11fg3 8g 12f) plater; stays 11f. *R. Allan.*

HAY HABIT 4 ch.c. Habitat 134–Hayrake 98 (Galivanter 131) (1982 6g* 7g4 6g* **83**
7fg2 6.3g3 7g 7fg3 7g 7g 8g3 6s4 6d 1983 7v 6g 8s 7fg4 6f3 7f) close-coupled
ex-Irish colt; in frame in handicaps at York and Pontefract in June; stays 1m; acts on
any going; blinkered last 4 starts; racing in Italy. *M. Jarvis.*

HAYMAN 3 b.g. Habitat 134–Paddy's Princess (St Paddy 133) (1982 7fg 8f2 8g —
1983 8.2v 12fg 12.3f 8f) lengthy gelding; disappointing maiden; not certain to stay
1½m; sometimes blinkered; sold 3,400 gns Newmarket September Sales. *J.
Hindley*

HAYS 4 b.c. Wolver Hollow 126–Sing a Song 115 (Sing Sing 134) (1982 7d* 8fg 8fg4 **107**
7.3g3 7s* 7g 1983 8v4 7fg 8f 7fg 8f 8fg) tall, good-looking colt; smart performer on his
day but ran some unaccountably modest races; not disgraced in Lockinge Stakes at
Newbury in May (6½ lengths fourth to Noalcoholic) and Van Geest Stakes at
Newmarket in June (3¼ lengths fifth to Thug); coltish and sweating in paddock
when running miserably in Sussex Stakes at Goodwood in July and Queen Elizabeth
II Stakes at Ascot in September; stayed 1m; ideally suited by soft ground;
unreliable; standing at Cleaboy Stud at IR £2,000 n.f.n.f. *G. Harwood.*

HAY STREET 2 gr.c. Relkino 131–Novina 72 (Connaught 130) (1983 6f 7g 6f **68**
6s3) Apr 3; close-coupled, smallish colt; first foal; dam stayed 7f; plating-class
maiden; should stay 1m; appears to act on any going. *C. Brittain.*

HAZARDOUS 3 br.g. Idiot's Delight 115–Fool 'Em 49 (Dadda Bert 95) (1982 7f **56**
6d 1983 6f2 5f) leggy, lightly-made gelding; showed plenty of speed when second
in seller at Yarmouth in July; sold 480 gns Doncaster October Sales. *J. Hardy.*

HAZEL BANK 4 gr. or ro.f. Pongee 106–Petoria 74 (Songedor 116) (1982 8f3 8g **49**
12f4 12.3g 12g 12f 1983 13v* 12.3v 13d4) won handicap at Ayr in March; tailed off
next time; suited by 13f and will get further; acts on any going but goes well in the
mud; blinkered first 2 starts; not seen out after May. *R. Allan.*

HAZEL BUSH 3 b.f. Sassafras 135–Selham 71 (Derring-Do 131) (1982 8s 1983 **71**
11d* 12s3 11g 12d3 12g2 12fg*) rangy filly; has a round action; successful in
maiden race at Edinburgh in April and handicap at Leicester in October (apprentice
ridden); suited by 1½m; yet to race on really firm ground, but acts on any other;
ideally suited by a galloping track. *Sir Mark Prescott.*

HAZEL COVE 2 b.f. Orange Bay 131–Coppice (Pardao 120) (1983 7fg 6f 7g **60**
7.6d) tall, leggy, shallow-girthed filly; fourth foal; half-sister to a winner in Italy
and to quite modest 1980 2-y-o Marston Magna (by Morston); dam second in small
9f race in France; plating-class maiden; showed form only on second outing; should
be suited by 7f+. *M. Blanshard.*

HAZUZU 2 br.c. Junius 124–Hunting Call (Averof 123) (1983 5f 6g 5d) May 17; —
22,000Y; medium-sized, lengthy colt; first foal; dam won over 1½m in Ireland;
soundly beaten in maiden and minor events; blinkered final outing; sent to
Malaysia. *G. Hunter.*

HEAD FOR HEIGHTS 2 b.c. Shirley Heights 130–Vivante 87 (Bold Lad, Ire **105**
133) (1983 6g2 6f* 7f2 7f2) Apr 2; 19,000F, 24,000Y; rangy colt; half-brother to
several winners, including useful 1982 Italian 2-y-o Very Sharp (by Sharpen Up) and
Majestic Star (by Star Appeal), a useful winner at up to 1¼m here and in Ireland;
dam stayed 1m; won 12-runner Chesham Stakes at Royal Ascot in June, beating
Adam's Peak 1½ lengths; good second afterwards in small fields to Trojan Fen in
Washington Singer Stakes at Newbury, and to Falstaff, beaten neck after being
outpaced as tempo quickened 2f out, in Gilbey Champion Racehorse Futurity at
York; will be extremely well suited by 1m+; sure to win more races; sold after York
to join R. Hern's stable. *R. Hannon.*

HEARTFELT 2 b.f. Be My Guest 126–Carved Beads (Levmoss 133) (1983 6fg **74**
7g) May 13; IR 25,000Y, resold 100,000Y; close-coupled filly; first foal; dam
once-raced half-sister to very useful 1973 staying 2-y-o Silk Buds; on backward
side, 2¾ lengths fifth of 7 to Test of Time in minor 7f event at Sandown in October;
likely to need 1m+. *B. Hills.*

HEARTLAND 2 ch.f. Northfields–Gwendolyn (Bagdad) (1983 6g 6f) May 6; IR — p
31,000Y; quite attractive, well-made, good-quartered filly; good walker; half-sister
to 3 winners, including 3-y-o middle-distance stayer Katie Koo (by Persian Bold);

dam, placed 3 times in USA, comes from good family; unquoted and still carrying a lot of condition, under 8 lengths seventh of 25, running on, behind Khwlah in maiden event at Newbury in August; a nice type of filly, certain to improve. *G. Wragg.*

HEART OF STEEL 4 ch.c. Steel Heart 128–Tetrazzini 70 (Sovereign Path 125) (1982 8.2fg 8g³ 8fg 8fg 8fg 8g³ 8s² 8s* 8.2s 1983 8d² 7.6v³ 8d 8f 8.3fg 8d) strong, useful-looking colt; stays 1m; ideally suited by some give in the ground; suited by forcing tactics; has run creditably for an apprentice; ran moderately third outing. *M. Albina.*   **70**

HEARTWOOD 3 b.f. Hittite Glory 125–Cursorial 115 (Crepello 136) (1982 6fg² 5.8g* 7.3g 1983 10h 10f) fair sort; won maiden event at Bath as a 2-y-o; not seen out until August in 1983, when last in handicap at Sandown (sweated) and Virginia Stakes at Newcastle, facing stiff tasks both times; will stay 1m. *G. Pritchard-Gordon.*   **–**

HEATHER CROFT 3 bl.f. Kala Shikari 125–Asail (Atan) (1982 5fg 5fg² 5f* 5h² 5f 5f 5d 5fg* 5g 5s 1983 6fg 6fg 6fg 5h³ 5g 5g 6fg 6g 6g*) useful sort; won handicap at Chepstow in October; stays 6f; acts on hard going; not particularly consistent. *R. Hannon.*   **69**

HEATHER PRINCE 3 b.g. Lochnager 132–Gym Slip 64 (Mummy's Pet 125) (1982 6g 5g 5f 5s 1983 7g 6d 7f 10h) light-framed gelding; behind in varied company, including selling. *A. W. Jones.*   **–**

HEAVENLY PLAIN 2 gr.c. Mount Hagen 127–Nuageuse (Prince Regent 129) (1983 6g 6g³ 6f 7f* 7f* 7fg³) Feb 26; half-brother to 5f to 7f winner Cumulus (by Relko); dam won 4 times over 5f at 3 yrs in Ireland; proved himself well suited by 7f when successful twice at Galway at end of July, beating Shubumi 3 lengths in maiden race and Action Girl 2½ lengths in minor event; having third race in space of 8 days when creditable 1½ lengths third of 7 to Executive Pride in valuable Ardenode Stud Stakes at Leopardstown in August; acts well on firm going and has yet to race on a soft surface; tough and quite useful; sent to USA. *P. Prendergast, Ireland.*   **88**

HEAVENLY PRIDE 2 b. or br.f. Goldhills Pride 105–Blou Hemel 47 (Virginia Boy 106) (1983 5fg 5f 6f 5g 5.1f 5s 5g) Mar 30; lightly-made filly; poor form, including when blinkered in sellers fifth and sixth starts. *G. Blum.*   **47**

HEAVENLY PRINCESS 3 gr.f. Godswalk 130–Inquisitive Girl 97 (Crepello 136) (1982 NR 1983 7d⁴ 8v⁴ 8d 8fg 7f 8.2fg) 5,400F; workmanlike filly; half-sister to several winners here and abroad; dam stayed 1m; little worthwhile form in varied races; has been tried in blinkers. *A. Bailey.*   **–**

HECKLEY HINNY 3 b.f. Decoy Boy 129–Heckley Surprise (Foggy Bell 108) (1982 6fg³ 7d 7g 1983 8v³ 8d² 10v³ 8.5d 8f⁴ 10.2f 8f 10fg) rangy filly; in frame in varied races, best effort when fourth of 17 behind subsequently-demoted Page Blanche in well-contested handicap at Ascot in June (50/1-chance); didn't run particularly well afterwards (looked bit light on final outing in August); stays 1¼m; acts on any going. *G. Balding.*   **67**

HEDGE CUTTER 2 br.f. Moulton 128–Hedge Warbler 89 (Sing Sing 134) (1983 7f 6d 7s) Feb 9; half-sister to 1980 2-y-o 5f winner Super Smile (by High Top) and to a winner in Italy by Blakeney; dam won at 6f and 1m; little worthwhile form in maiden races. *A. Hide.*   **–**

HEGEMONY 2 br.c. Godswalk 130–Second Bloom 64 (Double Jump 131) (1983 5s 5s³ 5s* 5v³ 6v* 6s* 6fg² 6fg) Mar 13; 16,500F, 15,500Y; compact colt; half-brother to several winners, including Mr Iconoclast (by Dike), a smart 2-y-o sprinter in Ireland who later did well in USA; dam placed over 5f at 3 yrs; showed very good speed and kept on gamely to hold second place behind 4-length winner Chief Singer in 14-runner Coventry Stakes at Royal Ascot in June; had previously won 3 of his 6 races in Ireland, maiden race and valuable Maginn TV Stakes at the Curragh (both impressively, making much of running) and valuable Steven D. Peskoff Stakes at Phoenix Park in June; looked well despite having been off course for over 3 months when respectable 5¾ lengths sixth of 9 to Creag-An-Sgor in William Hill Middle Park Stakes at Newmarket in September; stays 6f well; seems to act on any going. *M. O'Toole, Ireland.*   **106**

HEIGHLIN 7 b.g. High Line 125–Filiform 76 (Reform 132) (1982 16fg² 14f⁴ 16g* 16f³ 22.2fg 21f* 16g⁴ 18g² 16d² 18d 1983 22.2f²) good hurdler and smart stayer on flat at his best; 2½ lengths second to Sandalay in Queen Alexandra Stakes at Royal Ascot only start at 7 yrs in June; stays extremely well; acts on any going; needs to be covered up for a late run and is suited by a strong gallop. *R. Holder.*   **130**

HEIGHT OF GLORY 2 b. or br. g. Hittite Glory 125–Sarah Siddons (Reform –
132) (1983 5v 5f 5f) Apr 1; 3,600Y; third foal; half-brother to 3-y-o 1m winner
Saratino (by Bustino); dam, French 8.5f winner, is sister to top 1982 Italian 2-y-o
Anguillo; in rear all starts, breaking blood vessel when last of 18 in seller on final
appearance; subsequently gelded. *D. Plant.*

HEIGHT OF SUMMER 2 b. or br. c. Shirley Heights 130–Midsummertime **87** p
(Midsummer Night II 117) (1983 7f 7fg[3]) Jan 15; good-looking, short-legged colt;
closely related to Park Hill winner Idle Waters (by Mill Reef) and half-brother to 2
winners, including 1981 2-y-o 7f winner Melting Snows (by High Top); dam never
ran; showed considerable improvement on debut performance 2 months previously
and shaped extremely well when 4¾ lengths third of 8 behind Donzel in Mornington
Stakes at Ascot in September; will be much better suited by 1¼m+; certain to
continue to progress, and win races. *F. J. Houghton.*

HEISENBERG 3 b. c. Stradavinsky 121–Mudela (Sir Gaylord) (1982 7fg 6g[4] **89**
1983 8s 6s[2] 7s[3] 7g* 7fg[4] 6f* 5fg* 5g) 5,200Y; half-brother to 6 winners including
fairly useful middle-distance performer Oisin (by Bold Lad, USA) and useful 1977
2-y-o 7f winner King For A Day (by Crowned Prince), subsequently a winner
abroad; dam, useful Italian winner, is half-sister to Gyr; won maiden race at
Tralee in June and minor events at Naas in July and Leopardstown in August; also
in frame in varied races, including when third of 5 behind dead-heaters Ancestral
and Cremation in McCairns Trial Stakes at Phoenix Park; stays 7f; acts on any
going. *N. Meade, Ireland.*

HELAPLANE (USA) 3 b. f. Super Concorde 128–Dihela (Hitting Away) (1982 **68**
5g 7f 1983 7.2fg[2] 8f 8f 9s) narrow, close-coupled filly; plating-class maiden; should
stay 1m; hasn't much scope. *H. T. Jones.*

HELDIGVIS 3 b. f. Hot Grove 128–Twin-Set (Double Jump 131) (1982 5g 5g 5fg **54**
7fg 6g[3] 6g 8.2s* 7g* 1983 10v[3] 8.2s[3] 12s[2] 12d[4] 11d[4] 9.4f 12.3f 13.8f[4]) small filly;
ran moderately in a seller final start; suited by 1½m; needs some give in the
ground; trained first part of season by R. Allan. *E. Weymes.*

HELEN'S CHOICE 2 br. f. Coded Scrap 90–Noammo (Realm 129) (1983 5f –
6fg) well-grown filly; first foal; dam unraced daughter of very useful 6f sprinter
Cease Fire; poor form in £3,300 seller at York in August and maiden race at Redcar
2 months later. *A. Smith.*

HELEWISE 3 ch. f. Dance In Time–Wether Fell (Klairon 131) (1982 6f 6f 7g 8d* –
1983 7v 10f[4] 9.4f 7f 9fg 8.2g 9fg) lightly-made filly; mainly poor form in 1983;
possibly stays 1¼m; blinkered final outing. *R. D. Peacock.*

HELEXIAN 6 b. h. Song 132–Permutation 79 (Pinza 137) (1982 7s 7g 7.6g[4] 7g[2] **72**
7f[3] 7g 7fg 8fg 8s 8s 1983 8d 7.2v* 7v* 7s[4]) compact, good sort; good mover; won
handicaps at Haydock in April and Newcastle in May; best at around 7f; acts on any
going but goes well in the mud; has worn blinkers but does at least as well without;
has occasionally looked ungenuine, needs to be held up and is suited by strong
handling; not raced after June. *N. Tinkler.*

HELLCATMUDWRESTLER 2 b. c. Tumble Wind–Fairy Books (King's Leap **72**
111) (1983 7f 7fg 6fg 6fg 6fg[2]) Apr 23; IR 2,000F, 4,000Y; narrow, fair sort;
seventh foal; dam second twice over 5f at 2 yrs in Ireland; second favourite, 2
lengths second of 16 to Foot Patrol in claiming nursery at Newmarket in October,
first indication of merit; will be suited by a return to 7f; sure to win a seller. *N.
Callaghan.*

HELLO CAMPERS 3 ch. g. Wolverlife 115–Forever Wild (Eighty Grand) (1982 –
5d 5fg 1983 8v 8fg[4] 8f) plating-class maiden; showed only form in apprentice
event on second start; sold 420 gns Ascot November Sales. *S. Mellor.*

HELLO CUDDLES 4 b. f. He Loves Me 120–Royal Sensation 103 (Prince **90**
Regent 129) (1982 8g 8fg 5fg 5f[2] 5fg* 6f 5f[3] 5d 6s 1983 6g[2] 6v 6f 5f 6f 7g 8fg) quite
a well-made filly; good mover; useful on her day but isn't consistent; put up best
effort in 1983 when 1½ lengths second to On Stage in Thirsk Hall Stakes in April;
stays 6f; acts on any going; tended to hang once in 1982; trained by R. Hollinshead
first 5 starts. *D. Smith.*

HELLO GYPSY 2 b. c. Tumble Wind–Shirotae (Florescence 120) (1983 6fg[3] 6g **85**
7fg 6f[2] 6g 6fg[2]) May 9; IR 7,800Y; lightly-made colt; third foal; half-brother to
Irish 3-y-o 1½m winner Sheer Gold (by Yankee Gold); dam Irish 1¾m winner;
second in nursery and a maiden race at Redcar in the autumn; best form at 6f, but
should be suited by 7f+; yet to race on a soft surface; dwelt fifth start. *I. Walker.*

HELLO SUNSHINE 4 b.c. Song 132–Tropical Fruit (Tropique 128) (1982 6s
7fg 6d³ 6f 7f³ 7g 7f* 7s* 7d² 8g 1983 8v 8d 7s⁴ 8s² 7g 8f 7f* 8f² 8f 8fg 7s³ 7g³)
small, lengthy colt; poor mover; won handicap at Newbury in July; acts
on any going but revels in the mud; good mount for an apprentice. *J. Holt.*   **86**

HELMSTONE 2 b.f. Dominion 123–Brightelmstone 105 (Prince Regent 129)
(1983 5d⁴ 5fg 5g 7.2fg 5f) Mar 21; 1,600Y; neat, dipped-backed filly; second foal;
half-sister to 1981 2-y-o 5f winner Debian (by Relko); dam useful at up to 7f; poor
maiden; not seen out after August; will be more at home in sellers. *W. Wharton.*   **57**

HELP 3 b.c. Thatch 136–Escape Me Never 75 (Run The Gantlet) (1982 NR 1983
8g 8f* 8fg³ 8f* 8d²) 13,000F, 15,000Y; strong, compact, good sort; first produce;
dam, half-sister to smart miler Trusted, won over 1m; successful in maiden race at
Pontefract in July and handicap at Yarmouth in August, latter by 2½ lengths from
Worlingfoot; also placed in handicaps on the same 2 courses, one of them an
apprentice event; will stay 1¼m; yet to race on really soft going, but acts on any
other; sold 14,000 gns Newmarket Autumn Sales. *L. Cumani.*   **89**

HELPLESS HAZE (USA) 2 b.f. Vaguely Noble 140–Lodeve (Shoemaker 121)
(1983 7fg 7fg) May 12; $190,000Y; neat, quite attractive filly; third foal; half-sister
to 2 winners, notably smart French 1¼m filly Doubling Time (by Timeless
Moment); dam unraced half-sister to high-class French colts Faraway Son and
Liloy; 20/1, ran on well in last 2f when 4 lengths fifth of 14 to Condrillac in Houghton
Stakes at Newmarket in October, second outing; looks sure to win a race at 1¼m or
more. *B. Hills.*   **87**

HELTON TARN 7 b.g. Laurence O 111–Apple Tart (Shackleton 119) (1982 NR
1983 10f) robust, stocky gelding; winning hurdler; taken quietly to start when well
beaten in amateur riders event at Newmarket. *P. Butler.*   –

HELVIC (USA) 5 b. or br.g. Angle Light–Red River (Diatome 132) (1982 8g² 7f
8fg 7f 7fg 7fg² 7g 7.6f³ 8fg 7f⁴ 8.3fg 8g² 1983 8d 7s³ 8g 8f 10f³ 8fg 10f) poor
handicapper; sometimes runs in sellers; stays 1¼m; best on a sound surface;
effective with blinkers and without; has run respectably for a lady rider; has worn
a tongue strap; sold out of M. Haynes's stable 1,500 gns Ascot July Sales after
sixth outing. *S. Woodman.*   **39**

HEND 3 b.f. Dominion 123–Deodar 88 (Hopeful Venture 125) (1982 5fg 5g 6f 7f
1983 7d 7fg 10f) fair sort; soundly beaten in maiden races and sellers. *D. Thom.*   –

HENRICUS (ATA) 4 br.c. Honorius 111–Princess G (Orsini 124) (1982
including 8g* 10g³ 12g* 12s⁴ 10g* 14g² 1983 17.1d² 12d 14v 20fg³ 22.2f³ 18.4fg
16.1g* 14g 14.8fg² 12fg) strong, rangy Austrian-bred colt; poor walker; the top
colt of his generation in native country in 1982 when he won German 2,000
Guineas, Austrian Derby and Mercedes-Preis, all at Vienna; also ran second in
Austrian St Leger on same course; led 1½f out and ran on gamely to beat Another
Sam by a neck in handicap at Newmarket in August; also ran well to be 5½ lengths
third to Right Regent under top weight in Ascot Stakes at Royal Ascot on fourth
start and 2 lengths second to Hi Easter in handicap at Newmarket in August;
needs further than 1½m nowadays, and may prove best at around 2m; acts well
on top-of-the-ground; genuine; retained 23,000 gns Newmarket Autumn Sales. *J.
Hindley.*   **99**

HENRY BEAUCLERC 2 br. or ro.c. Remainder Man 126§–Che Bella (Beau
Sabreur 125) (1983 7.6fg 7g) May 28; neat colt; half-brother to several winners,
including useful 7f to 1¼m winner Pabella (by Pardao); dam won Irish
Cambridgeshire; tailed off in October maiden races at Lingfield and Leicester. *D.
Wilson.*   –

HENRY GEARY STEELS 3 br.c. Connaught 130–Halkissimo 61 (Khalkis 127)
(1982 5g 7f 1983 10.5s 8g² 8d² 8f² 8f⁴ 7f³ 8fg 7fg) rather leggy colt; second in
handicaps at Beverley, Ayr and Ripon in June; gives impression 7f is a bit on sharp
side, and should stay at least 1¼m; tends to sweat up a bit; sold to R. Champion
5,800 gns Newmarket September Sales. *D. Smith.*   **69**

HENRY'S SECRET 3 b.f. Solinus 130–Katie Cecil 120 (Princely Gift 137) (1982
5fg* 5fg* 5fg* 6fg² 6g 6g³ 1983 8g 6v² 6f) neat filly; good mover; useful
performer as a 2-y-o; 40/1, travelled strongly on bridle to halfway when eleventh
of 18 behind Ma Biche in 1000 Guineas at Newmarket in April; beaten 10 lengths
when second of 6 behind On Stage in Sandy Lane Stakes at Haydock the following
month and was in rear behind Sylvan Barbarosa in Cork and Orrery Stakes at
Royal Ascot on final outing; not sure to stay 1m. *M. Stoute.*   –

HERALDRY 2 br.c. Ile de Bourbon 133–Metair 118 (Laser Light 118) (1983 6g⁴
6f 6f⁴ 6fg²) Apr 2; small, well-made colt; good walker and mover; second foal;   **85**

369

half-brother to very useful 3-y-o sprinter Fine Edge (by Sharpen Up); dam game winner of 7 races over 5f and 6f; fair form in quite useful company; off course for 3 months after third outing; will be suited by 7f; acts on firm going; sold Mrs G. Forbes 14,000 gns Newmarket Autumn Sales; sent to Trinidad. *J. Tree.*

HERE COMES SPRING 2 b.f. Captain James 123–Spring Again (Primera 131) (1983 5f) Mar 9; IR 7,000Y; useful-looking filly; sister to 5f and 7f winner Cecile and half-sister to a winner; dam behind in maiden races; backward, always behind in 12-runner maiden race at Pontefract in June. *J. Fitzgerald.*   —

HERE I AM 2 b.c. John de Coombe 122–High Ransom 88 (High Treason 126) (1983 7f 6g 7fg 7.6fg) Apr 20; neat, strong colt; half-brother to several winners, including very useful 2-y-o sprinters Sanders Lad (by Amber Rama) and Durandal (by Bay Express); dam won over 7f; beaten some way in maiden and minor events; will do better in sellers. *D. Wilson.*   —

HERES-A-RISK 2 br.c. Heres 81–Talisker (Tutankhamen) (1983 6fg 7f 7.2g 8d) half-brother to 3 minor winners; dam never ran; bad plater; blinkered final start. *R. Hannon.*   47

HERE'S SUE 4 b.f. Three Legs 128–Gaino (Chaparral 128) (1982 5f 6f 5fg 6g3 6fg 6f 6g 6g* 7d 6g 1983 8d 7fg4 6fg 6h 5g* 5d 5g) fair sort; won handicap at Warwick in October; best at sprint distances; acts on a firm and a soft surface; best in blinkers; often apprentice ridden. *A. Jarvis.*   59

HER EXCELLENCY 6 b.m. Dragonara Palace 115–My Paddy 83 (St Paddy 133) (1982 8f 6f 8f 10g 8fg2 8f 8.2g 8fg 1983 8.2d 7f 7.6fg 6fg) poor plater; stays 1m; acts on firm going; has run respectably for a boy; blinkered once. *R. Morris.*   —

HERMES BELLE 2 b.f. Quiet Fling 124–Angelica (Hornbeam 130) (1983 7f 7h3 8.2f2) smallish filly; half-sister to 3-y-o Rathdowney May (by Derrylin); dam unraced sister to smart 1971 2-y-o Angel Beam; placed in good-class sellers at Sandown in August and Haydock (favourite) in September; will be suited by 1¼m+; acts on hard going; exported to Algeria. *R. Akehurst.*   64

HERMITAGE WALK 2 ro.f. Abwah 118–Eurolink (Current Coin 118) (1983 5f 5f 6f 5f 5g 6fg) Feb 18; neat filly; third foal; sister to a poor animal; dam poor plater; plating-class maiden; form only at 5f. *W. Bentley.*   66

HERODOTE (USA) 3 b.g. Super Concorde 128–Heiress (Habitat 134) (1982 6f3 7s3 8d2 7g* 1983 6d 8f 8g2 8fg 10s3 10fg) deep-girthed, quite attractive gelding; good mover; ran best races when placed in handicaps won by Tetron Bay at Kempton and Onslow at Ayr, both in September; never showed in between and on final start was soundly beaten after running wide into straight and being taken back sharply to far rails; stays 1¼m; possibly needs some give underfoot nowadays; blinkered last 2 outings; trained by H. Cecil until after first start. *P. Kelleway.*   98 d

HERRADURA 2 b.c. Malinowski 123–Blakeney Belle (Blakeney 126) (1983 7fg 8g 9s3) Mar 7; 17,000Y; lengthy, heavy-topped colt; good mover; third foal; half-brother to 2 winners, notably smart 7f to 1¾m performer Rocamadour (by Royal Match); dam poor half-sister to smart Daring Boy and Daring March; 6 lengths third of 8 to Sassagrass in maiden race at Wolverhampton in October; will be suited by 1¼m+. *Sir Mark Prescott.*   77

HESHAM (USA) 3 b.c. Annihilate 'Em–Rule Me Lucky (Lucky Debonair) (1982 6f 7g3 7s 1983 8s) big, rangy, quite attractive colt; third in big field of maidens at Newmarket as a 2-y-o; had stiff task when well beaten in handicap at Goodwood in May on only outing of 1983; should stay 1¼m; sold 1,450 gns Goffs November Sales. *G. Harwood.*   —

HESLA 3 b.f. Mandrake Major 122–The Bolter 81 (Road House II) (1982 NR 1983 7.6g 8fg4 8.2g 6fg 7g) strong filly; half-sister to 2 winners, including useful 1979 2-y-o sprinter Sandon Lad (by Mountain Call); dam won over 1¼m; plating-class maiden; best run at 6f. *R. Hollinshead.*   —

HETTY GREEN 2 b.f. Bay Express 132–Londonderry Air 84 (Ballymoss 136) (1983 5fg 5f 6f 6g 5fg 5fg 7fg) May 19; 5,400Y; compact filly; half-sister to useful 1m winner Persian Market (by Taj Dewan), Irish 1¼m winner Vitalise (by Vitiges) and 2 winners in Italy; dam won over 5f at 2 yrs; poor maiden; sold 2,000 gns Ascot December Sales. *J. Benstead.*   —

HI-BUCK 3 ch.g. Runnymede 123–Pibroch III (Specific 103) (1982 5s 5d 5fg4 5f 5g 1983 6s 5s 8f) non-thoroughbred gelding; bad plater; blinkered second start. *P. Burgoyne.*   —

HIDDEN DESTINY (USA) 2 b.c. Alydar–Masked Lady (Spy Song) (1983 7.6fg 8g3 8f*) Mar 28; $2,200,000Y; rangy colt; closely related to 3 winners, notably very smart 1974 French 2-y-o 5f winner Raise A Lady (by Raise A Native),   86

and half-brother to several more, including a minor stakes winner; dam stakes winner over 6.5f; improved with his races, on final outing readily landing the odds in maiden event at Leicester in November; will be well suited by 1¼m; likely to continue on the upgrade. *J. Dunlop.*

HIDDEN WARNING 2 br.f. Troy 137–Boldmani 105 (Bold Hour) (1983 6fg 7g*) May 20; half-sister to 2 winners, including Bold Green (by Green Dancer), a winner at up to 1m in France; dam won over 5f and 1m in Ireland; led inside final furlong to win by a neck from Golden Tan in 7-runner minor event at Sligo in August; wasn't seen out again; will stay at least 1m. *D. K. Weld, Ireland.*   **76**

HI EASTER 3 ch.c. High Line 125–Decked Out 77 (Doutelle 128) (1982 7fg 7g 8f² 7.6v³ 1983 12v³ 12s 12g² 16f* 16f² 16f* 19f 14.8fg* 17d 18fg) smallish, useful sort; good mover; successful in maiden race at Beverley, 5-runner minor event at Thirsk and handicap at Newmarket in summer, on last-named course beating Henricus by 3 lengths (pair well clear); also ran creditably several other starts; stays well; best form on a sound surface and acts well on firm going. *H. Candy.*   **86**

HIERONYMOUS 2 b.c. General Assembly–Suni 114 (Crepello 136) (1983 7fg) Apr 3; 40,000Y; second foal; half-brother to 3-y-o Sibley (by Northfields); dam third in Oaks; 16/1, not punished after showing up 5f when ninth of 12 to Miss Saint-Cloud in minor event at Doncaster in October; likely to need further. *C. Brittain.*   **–**

HIGHAM GREY 7 gr.g. Warpath 113–Jackies Joy (Skymaster 126) (1982 10d 10f 10.2f⁴ 12.3fg 12.3g* 12d* 11g³ 13g 14.6f* 13fg³ 12g 12fg 17.4d 12fg* 16.1s 18s 1983 12f 12f 13fg 15fg 16.5fg 16f) useful-looking gelding; inconsistent handicapper; well beaten in 1983; needs at least 1½m and stays 2m; seems to act on any going; as effective with blinkers as without; has won for an amateur rider. *D. Chapman.*   **–**

HIGH AUTHORITY 4 b.f. High Award 119–Elia (Narrator 127) (1982 5g 6.5v 6g 5fg 5fg 5d⁴ 7f 5f 5d 6s 5s 1983 5v 5s* 6d 6fg) workmanlike filly; good mover; inconsistent sprint handicapper; won narrowly at Wolverhampton in April; best form with some give in the ground; sometimes troublesome at start and was taken down early at Wolverhampton; has sweated up. *D. Leslie.*   **38**

HIGH CALORY 3 ch.f. High Line 125–Calloo 99 (Ballyciptic 122) (1982 6g 8s* 1983 10.2v* 8.5g³ 10g) fair sort; good mover; beat Miss Zhivago smoothly by 3 lengths in handicap at Bath in May; 2 lengths third to Sedra in Ebbisham Handicap at Epsom the following month, better subsequent effort (didn't impress in paddock on final appearance in July); stays 1¼m; acts well on heavy going (yet to race on a firm surface); sold to BBA 18,000 gns Newmarket December Sales. *J. Tree.*   **86**

HIGH CANNON (USA) 3 b.c. Cannonade–So High (Sea-Bird II 145) (1982 8f 8.2s 8s* 8.2v* 8d* 1983 7v² 12d* 12f³ 10d³ 15s* 14s)   **105**

High Cannon's trainer has usually done well with his North American purchases. In High Cannon, a bargain-basement 25,000-dollar buy at the Fasig-Tipton Kentucky Fall Preferred Yearling Sales, he obtained a horse who turned out to be one of the better stayers in the North: as evinced by High Cannon's fifth to Mountain Lodge in the Jefferson Smurfit Memorial Irish St Leger, his third to My Top and Brogan in the Derby Italiano earlier and, to a lesser degree, by his defeats of Moon Mariner in a small race at Thirsk in the spring and in a more strongly-contested race at Ayr in September. High Cannon was beaten only seven lengths on soft going in the Irish St Leger and only four lengths on firm in the Italian Derby; he was unlucky to find the going much faster than it usually is in Rome in the spring. High Cannon beat Moon Mariner by six lengths at Thirsk and by two, despite looking in need of the outing after a long lay-off, at Ayr. On his other appearances High Cannon ran very well over a distance too short to be second to Annamoe Bray in the Northern Free Handicap at Newcastle and third behind Free Press and Ski Run in the Zetland Gold Cup at Redcar. He's altogether a genuine, consistent animal.

High Cannon (USA) (b.c. 1980)	Cannonade (b 1971)	Bold Bidder (b 1962)	Bold Ruler
			High Bid
		Queen Sucree (b 1966)	Ribot
			Cosmah
	So High (ch 1969)	Sea-Bird II (ch 1962)	Dan Cupid
			Sicalade
		Twinkle Twinkle (ch 1957)	Tom Fool
			Moon Star

High Cannon is by the Kentucky Derby winner Cannonade out of a sprint-winning Sea-Bird II mare who had previously produced two relatively minor

Mr N. Granata's "High Cannon"

winners by Dynastic. The second dam Twinkle Twinkle was a stakes-placed winner out of a mare well known in England: Moon Star, by Hyperion, finished third in the Oaks of 1952 and won the Park Hill Stakes the same year. High Cannon is a useful-looking colt who acts on any going but is ideally suited by some give underfoot. He almost certainly has further improvement in him, the more so since he is a June foal, and should continue to pay his way over the longer distances. *S. Norton.*

HIGH COMMANDER 2 b.c. Mill Reef 141–Laxmi 108 (Palestine 133) (1983 7g³ 7g³) Mar 30; 390,000Y; seventh live foal; half-brother to 1,000 Guineas winner Enstone Spark (by Sparkler); dam best at 5f; finished third in maiden events at the Curragh in August (beaten 2 lengths by Cerussite) and Naas in September (beaten 2¼ lengths by March Song); will probably stay 1m+. *D. O'Brien, Ireland.*   **85**

HIGH DEBATE 2 ch.c. High Line 125–Debatable 84 (Counsel 118) (1983 8g³ 7fg 10fg*) Mar 21; 4,800F, 3,600Y; very tall, angular colt; half-brother to smart 7f to 1½ m winner Brandon Hill (by Wolver Hollow), to a winner in Denmark and a winning jumper; dam stayed 1¾m; won Jennings The Bookmakers Zetland Stakes at Newmarket in October by 4 lengths from Yankee Bond; likely to develop into useful stayer. *M. Jefferson.*   **92 p**

HIGHDRIVE 3 b.f. Ballymore 123–River Craft (Reliance II 137) (1982 NR 1983 11.7h 13.1fg) fourth foal; half-sister to quite moderate stayer Wet Bob (by Run The Gantlet) and 1979 Irish 2-y-o 7f winner Private Craft (by Private Walk); dam, sister to very smart 1m and 1¼m winner Rymer, was last on only start; well beaten in maiden race at Bath in July (third favourite, started slowly) and minor event on same course in September (unquoted). *R. Holder.*   **–**

HIGHEST TENDER 2 b.f. Prince Tenderfoot 126–Tender Valley (Royal Vale   **56**
106) (1983 6fg 6f 6f[4] 7f 7g 7fg 7d 8fg) Mar 9; IR 1,700F, 8,600Y; lengthy,
good-quartered filly; third foal; dam won 5 of her 56 races in USA at up to 1m;
plating-class maiden; stays 7f; acts on firm going; blinkered last 2 starts. *K.
Stone.*

HIGH FANDANGO 3 b.c. Gay Fandango 132–Miss Africa (African Sky 124)   **78**
(1982 7.6v 7s 1983 8g[3] 7.6v[3] 7g 7f[2] 8f 7g[3] 9s[3]) medium-sized, sturdy, attractive
colt; placed in maiden and minor races in goodish company in spring, but was
beaten at Catterick and Hamilton in autumn; finds 7f on sharp side and stays at least
1m; moved poorly on fifth start and was off course over 2 months afterwards; sold
to BBA 7,400 gns Newmarket Autumn Sales. *B. Hills.*

HIGHFORD LAD 2 b.g. John de Coombe 122–Sanaara (Mourne 126) (1983 5v   **55**
5d[4] 5fg[2] 6f[2] 7f*) Apr 25; 1,100Y; lightly-made gelding; half-brother to 2 winners
including 1¼m to 15f winner Beechwood Lad (by Skymaster); dam never ran;
sold privately after winning seller at Beverley in July, and exported to Malaysia;
will stay beyond 7f; acts well on firm going. *M. Camacho.*

HIGH HAWK 3 b.f. Shirley Heights 130–Sunbittern 112 (Sea Hawk II 131)   **124**
(1982 7g 8s[4] 1983 10v[2] 10v* 10d[3] 12s* 11v[2] 12fg* 12f[2] 14.6fg* 12.5f* 14g* 12g)
    The three-year-old staying filly High Hawk produced a transformation every
bit as dramatic as the sprinter Soba's the previous year. She began an extremely
busy season in a modest race at Folkestone in March and ended it running for
approximately £200,000 in the Japan Cup in Tokyo in November. She won neither,
finishing second to Fawg at Folkestone and thirteenth of sixteen to Stanerra in
Tokyo, but she well earned her invitation to the Far East through a series of
magnificent efforts that stretched right through to autumn from spring and saw her
winning the Ribblesdale Stakes at Royal Ascot, the Park Hill Stakes at Doncaster,
the Prix de Royallieu at Longchamp and the Premio Roma in Rome, and finishing
second in the Italian Oaks and Irish Guinness Oaks besides. She was one of the
toughest, most genuine, enthusiastic fillies of her generation.
    By the time she turned out for the Ribblesdale Stakes High Hawk had had a
further four races since Folkestone, of which she'd won two at Lingfield;
immediately prior to Royal Ascot she'd finished a three-quarter-length second to
what seemed likely to be a more-than-useful Italian filly, Right Bank, well ahead of
Emerald Reef, in the Oaks d'Italia in Milan. In contrast, only one of her thirteen
opponents at Ascot, the Lupe Stakes winner Current Raiser, had been subjected to
as many as four runs during the season. Plenty of competitive work is not always
desirable or appropriate for a Ribblesdale candidate but in this instance the hardest

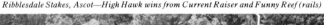

Ribblesdale Stakes, Ascot—High Hawk wins from Current Raiser and Funny Reef (rails)

raced in the field finished first and second in order. High Hawk won in really good style by a length and a half from Current Raiser who simply couldn't hold her after the winner had moved up strongly in the straight and gone quickly on a furlong out. The next three home had also won earlier in the season, Funny Reef at Doncaster, Ask The Wind the listed Hard Fought Stakes in Ireland and So True the Esher Cup at Sandown in which she'd beaten Shareef Dancer. So True had also run a remote second in the Musidora Stakes to Give Thanks, one of High Hawk's opponents in the last-named's next race, the Irish Guinness Oaks. Up to the middle of May it would have been long odds against High Hawk's being seen in the same race as a filly as good as Give Thanks, and that she could be so strongly fancied for the Irish Guinness Oaks speaks volumes for her rate of improvement. She started much shorter at the Curragh than the Epsom fourth Shore Line—second favourite at 9/4. High Hawk's improvement continued. She finished a clear second of twelve to the 7/4 favourite Give Thanks, beaten two and a half lengths, chasing the winner all the way up the straight without managing to get to grips. High Hawk might well have gone closer given a clear passage throughout: she had a poor run in the early stages.

When the pair met again in the Park Hill Stakes in September they were almost inseparable in the market, Give Thanks again favourite. Further improvement was anticipated from High Hawk, especially over the longer distance, and if that improvement materialized the normally ultra-reliable Give Thanks would have to be in better form than when a disappointing third to Sun Princess in the Yorkshire Oaks on her previous outing to hold her. High Hawk hadn't been seen out since the Irish Guinness Oaks; she'd never gone so long without a race during the season. Both fillies ran well, only three quarters of a length apart at the end with the winner slightly the better suited by the mile and three quarters in our opinion. Give Thanks came through to strike the front two furlongs out but High Hawk, who'd been ridden along from three out in a truly-run race, caught up running into the final furlong and maintained a strong gallop the rest of the way home. The well-backed, much less experienced Sylph also stayed on to be best of the five others, a further three lengths behind; Shore Line and Current Raiser both disappointed, Current Raiser actually coming in last.

Whether she outstayed Give Thanks or not, there's no doubting that stamina was a strong point of High Hawk's. She ran very much as a stayer in the Prix de Royallieu the following month, a race at just over a mile and a half for fillies of three years and upwards in which she faced nothing of the calibre of Give Thanks. She scrambled home by a neck and the same from Radiance and Quemora, partly through her jockey Carson's mistaking the winning post and partly through her losing her place when the pace quickened sharply. She needed the usual

Park Hill Stakes, Doncaster—High Hawk stays on from Give Thanks

Sheikh Mohammed's "High Hawk"

power-driven ride from her jockey to get her into contention after the last bend, but was about to win by at least a length when allowed to slacken off passing the first of Longchamp's two posts. Fortunately Carson realized his error in the nick of time and was able to keep her ahead to the right one. Italy, Ireland, and now France; and still there were long journeys to come. Although she started favourite for the Japan Cup High Hawk was basically a stand-in for her owner's other good staying filly in the stable Awaasif, and if she ran in a manner that suggested she'd also had enough by then it was no less than she was perfectly entitled to. Only three weeks previously she'd been involved in a tight finish to the Premio Roma, forcing her way between the French colts Balitou and Esprit du Nord to land the prize by a short head. At the end of this fourteen-furlong race contested by eleven runners the distances were short head, neck and neck, with Balitou second, the English-trained Looking For third and Esprit du Nord fourth.

High Hawk (b.f. 1980)	Shirley Heights (b 1975)	Mill Reef (b 1968)	Never Bend
			Milan Mill
		Hardiemma (b 1969)	Hardicanute
			Grand Cross
	Sunbittern (gr 1970)	Sea Hawk II (gr 1963)	Herbager
			Sea Nymph
		Pantoufle (b 1964)	Panaslipper
			Etoile de France

High Hawk cost only 31,000 guineas as a yearling. At that time her now highly promising sire Shirley Heights had still to have his first runner. Her dam Sunbittern was a very useful two-year-old six-furlong and seven-furlong winner who became temperamental; she received 8-3 in the Free Handicap. Again at the time of High Hawk's sale Sunbittern had produced three winners from three runners—Seriema (by Petingo), Herons Hollow (by Wolver Hollow) and Entre Nous (by Rheingold); the second-named was a useful miler, runner-up in the William Hill Lincoln Handicap, and the third-named was placed in the Irish Lincolnshire Handicap. High Hawk is the dam's fifth foal. The sixth, Tapaculo (by Tap On Wood), improved an already excellent producing record by showing quite useful winning form in 1983. Had temperament not got the upper hand Sunbittern would probably have stayed well. She is out of a staying mare and quite closely related to Irvine, the Premio Roma and Jockey Club Cup winner of 1972 who is by Sunbittern's sire Sea Hawk II out of Sunbittern's grandam Etoile de France. The Irish Derby winner Fidalgo was a full brother to Etoile de France.

High Hawk, though quite attractive, is only light framed and it was remarkable how she kept coming back for more; she really was a tough little filly. In a way it's a pity she'll be at stud in 1984—there's no reason why she shouldn't have been as good or even better over two miles or more. She acted on any going. *J. Dunlop.*

HIGH IMP 3 ch.g. Import 127–High Walk (Tower Walk 130) (1982 5f 5f 1983 7d⁴ 9.4d 6f) strong, workmanlike gelding; moderate fourth in 7f minor event at Leicester in May. *E. Carter.*

HIGHLAND BEAUTY 4 ch.f. High Line 125–Fire Queen (Prince Hansel 118) (1982 13g 14g 12v 1983 12fg 12fg 14f 15.5f) fair sort; well beaten in varied company. *D. Thom.*

HIGHLAND MAJOR 2 b.c. Mandrake Major 122–Manche 82 (Palestine 133) — (1983 5g 5g) Apr 20; smallish, lightly-made colt; fourth foal; dam second in three 5f races at 2yrs; in rear in modest company at Catterick in May and September. *F. Watson.*

HIGHLAND ROSSIE 3 b.f. Pablond 93–Highland Lassie 62 (Highland Melody 49
112) (1982 5fg 6fg 8.2fg 7fg 8d 8.2d⁴ 7g* 6s 7s 1983 8s 8s 8d 8v 10fg 10f 10h* 12fg 10fg⁴ 10fg² 11s³ 10.8g⁴ 10f³) lengthy filly; plater; won comfortably at Nottingham in August (no bid); stays 1¼m; acts on any going. *R. Hollinshead.*

HIGHLY TUNED 3 ch.f. Music Boy 124–Alchorus 78 (Alcide 136) (1982 NR — 1983 7d 6h 7.6g 8f 10.6s) strong, good sort; half-sister to 2 winners, including top-class 6f and 7f winner Be Tuneful (by Be Friendly); dam won over 9f; never-dangerous fifth of 17 behind Noble Blood in 1m maiden race at Warwick in August. *G. Huffer.*

HIGH MOON 2 b.c. Star Appeal 133–High Move (High Top 131) (1983 8d) Mar — 10; rather leggy colt; dam poor maiden; 100/1, never-dangerous ninth of 12 in £3,500 race at York in October. *J. Leigh.*

HIGH MORALE 2 b.c. High Line 125–Cecilia Gallerani (Pinturischio 116) (1983 88
7fg 7f 8g³) Apr 18; tall, good sort; fifth reported living foal; half-brother to 3 winners, including useful 5f to 1m winner Tudor Maid (by Henry the Seventh); dam poor maiden; showed ability in maiden events, running best race when 2¾ lengths third of 15 to Leadburn at Sandown in October; will be suited by 1¼m+. *J. Winter.*

HIGHNESS 2 ch.c. Mount Hagen 127–Tzaritsa 113 (Young Emperor 133) (1983 — 6f 6f 7d 8d) May 14; 6,000Y; well-grown, workmanlike colt; third live foal; half-brother to 7f and 1m winner Norroy (by Northfields); dam, at her best at 2 yrs, won at up to 1m; behind in maiden races and a nursery, twice last; sold 1,400 gns Ascot November Sales. *W. Musson.*

HIGH OLD TIME 7 ch.h. Mount Hagen 127–Witch of Endor 80 (Matador 131) — (1982 12g 10fg* 12f* 12fg* 1983 12fg 12g 12.2d) big horse; well beaten in 1983; effective at 1¼m and stays at least 1¾m; acts on any going, but seems suited by firm; suited by strongly-run race; used to wear blinkers. *J. Harris.*

HIGH PITCHED 4 ch.g. Crooner 119–Lucky Run 101 (Runnymede 123) (1982 — 8g* 8fg³ 8.2fg² 7s 7s* 8.2s* 8s² 8s 1983 8d 7.2v³ 8v 9fg 7g 8.2s 8.2fg) sparely-made gelding; stays 1m well; seems to act on any going but goes well on soft; has run creditably when sweating up; good mount for a boy. *I. Walker.*

HIGH POPPA 4 b.g. Mummy's Pet 125–Two For Joy 77 (Double-U-Jay 120) — (1982 5f 6f 8fg 6s 7g 1983 10f) lengthy, lightly-made gelding; poor mover; has shown no form for a long time; not sure to stay 1m; possibly needs some give in the ground; blinkered once. *O. Brennan.*

HIGH PORT 4 b.g. Import 127–High Walk (Tower Walk 130) (1982 8fg 8f 10f 7f 6g 7f 6f² 6g² 6g² 6f 7f 6s 6s 6s³ 6s 7d³ 1983 8fg² 7.6fg 8s 7s 10.6g) compact, quite attractive gelding; good mover; stays 1m; acts on any going; has run creditably for an amateur rider; suited by enterprising riding tactics; sometimes goes very freely to post; cost 5,000 gns Doncaster January Sales. *A. W. Jones.* –

HIGH RAINBOW 6 b.g. High Line 125–Darwin Tulip (Campaign 106 or Pirate King 129) (1982 12g 16.1s* 16.1fg² 12fg 16.1g 1983 16.1v⁴) useful-looking gelding; suited by a test of stamina; acts on any going; sometimes sweats up; bandaged only start at 6 yrs in April; not the easiest of rides. *J. Fitzgerald.* –

HIGH RATED 3 ch.g. High Line 125–Raflex 72 (Skymaster 126) (1982 NR 1983 12g) 3,000Y; rangy gelding; has rather a round action; half-brother to 3 winners, including fairly useful 6f and 1m winner Intercontinental (by Hot Spark); dam placed at 5f and 6f; needed race when tailed-off tenth of 11 behind easy winner Bahoor in apprentice race at Pontefract in October. *D. Plant.* –

HIGH REEF 2 br.c. Take a Reef 127–Hi Tess 65 (Supreme Court 135) (1983 5d³ 5d² 6f 6f⁴ 8d² 8fg*) Apr 6; narrow colt; won 16-runner seller (no bid) at Redcar in October; will be suited by 1¼m; acts on a firm and a soft surface. *Hbt Jones.* 64

HIGH RENOWN (USA) 3 br.c. Raise A Bid–Starlet O'Hara (Silent Screen) (1982 8s 8s 1983 10s⁴ 11f 12.3fg² 12g*) strong, good-bodied colt; shows a bit of knee action; ran on strongly to beat Northern Trip by 4 lengths in 16-runner gentleman riders maiden race at Kempton in September; will stay 1¾m; sold 17,500 gns Newmarket September Sales. *B. Hills.* 88

HIGH STATE 3 b.f. Free State 125–High Society 96 (So Blessed 130) (1982 5fg 7f 6g² 6fg³ 6f³ 6g² 7g 6d 8fg² 7.2s³ 7.2s⁴ 8d³ 5d 1983 6v 5f 9f 9f* 8fg 8h 8fg⁴ 8.2h³ 8f⁴ 8f) neat filly; bought in 3,900 gns after winning selling handicap at Newcastle in June; stays 9f; seems to act on any going; sometimes blinkered at 2 yrs; has worn a bandage on near-fore. *M. W. Easterby.* 63

HIGHVIEW 2 b.g. Hotfoot 126–Sunny Bloom 71 (Forlorn River 124) (1983 5f 5fg 6fg) Apr 11; half-brother to 2 winners, including fairly useful 1979 2-y-o 5f winner Marmau (by Manacle); dam stayed 6f; poor form in maiden races; sold D. Chapman 1,400 gns Doncaster November Sales. *H. Westbrook.* –

HIJAZIAH 4 ch.f. High Line 125–Keadby Bridge (Petition 130) (1982 11.5f 14g³ 14.7f* 16.5fg 14g 1983 12g* 14fg³ 14.7f 14f 12f 12f² 12.2d 12d) fair sort; won apprentice handicap at Brighton in May; stays 1¾m; acts on firm going; reluctant to go down and dwelt fifth start; sold 7,400 gns Newmarket December Sales. *A. Hide.* 66

HILL OF FARE 2 ch.f. Brigadier Gerard 144–Mountain Rescue 95 (Mountain Call 125) (1983 5h⁴ 5g 6fg 5g) Feb 17; fair sort; second foal; closely related to a modest maiden; dam 2-y-o 6f winner; poor form; last when blinkered in nursery final start; sold 420 gns Ascot October Sales. *N. Gaselee.* –

HILLSDOWN GOLD 6 b.g. Goldhill 125–Dumana 96 (Dumbarnie 125) (1982 10f 8f 10f 8fg 8.2g⁴ 8fg* 8fg⁴ 1983 10v 8g 8g 7f 8f² 7f³ 10f³ 10s* 12g 11fg) neat gelding; won handicap at Beverley in September; second in seller earlier; stays 1¼m; acts on any going; wears blinkers; has won for an apprentice; sometimes sweats up. *I. Vickers.* 65

HILLSDOWN LAD 5 b.h. Forlorn River 124–Alchorus 78 (Alcide 136) (1982 6f 7f 7f² 7f* 7d 1983 7fg 6fg 7f 10f 10g 8fg³ 9d 10.8d) rangy horse; good mover; poor handicapper; stays 1m; acts on any going; has twice worn blinkers; has won for an apprentice. *J. Harris.* 61

HILL'S GUARD 4 b.g. Home Guard 129–Ballinkillen (Levmoss 133) (1982 8.2fg 8fg² 7fg 8g 1983 12.3v⁴) quite attractive gelding; poor performer on flat but is quite a useful hurdler; has been beaten in a seller; possibly stays 1½m; best run in blinkers on firm ground. *A. Scott.* –

HILL'S PAGEANT 4 b.c. Welsh Pageant 132–Reita 87 (Gilles de Retz 132) (1982 8g 8f³ 9fg 10fg* 10.1fg* 10f* 10fg* 10f 10g³ 9d 1983 10v² 10.2v² 10s⁴ 10fg² 12g³ 10fg* 10f 10fg) good-looking colt; shows quite a bit of knee action; beat Lasolo by 1½ lengths in Group 3 Hessen-Pokal at Frankfurt in July; second previously in handicaps at Kempton (Rosebery Stakes), Doncaster (length behind Farioffa in Sporting Chronicle Spring Handicap) and Sandown; stays 1½m; acts on any going; sold 28,000 gns Newmarket December Sales. *P. Walwyn.* 92

HILLY'S DAUGHTER 2 b.f. Hillandale 125–Dorriba (Ribero 126) (1983 5fg 7g 6fg) May 18; second foal; dam never ran; no form in modest company. *R. Simpson.* –

HI LOVE 3 b.f. High Top 131–Love Story 79 (Aureole 132) (1982 6fg 7d 1983 9d² 83
10s³ 12f* 12f 12f³ 16fg* 14fg) lengthy, sparely-made, useful sort; successful in
maiden race at Brighton in June and £5,000 handicap at Newmarket in September;
led near finish to beat British and Orange Reef gamely by a short head and the same
on latter course; suited by a test of stamina; acts on any going; genuine; returned
bleeding from her off-hind after running respectably final start. *B. Hills.*

HILTON BROWN 2 br.c. Daring March 116–Holiday Season 60 (Silly Season 93
127) (1983 5s* 5v² 6s 5s*(dis) 5g 5fg4 5s³ 5g) Mar 7; quite attractive colt; has a
round action; first foal; dam placed over 1½m; successful in 20-runner maiden race
at Bath in April and 5-runner minor event at Leicester in May, only to be
disqualified at Leicester for interference; not seen out during summer, but on
return ran well in nurseries; apparently best at 5f, but is bred to stay further; acts
on heavy going and a firm surface. *P. Cundell.*

HIMORRE 4 b.c. Song 132–Monagram 77 (Mon Fetiche 120) (1982 7fg4 8g* –
7.3fg³ 10g 9g* 8f 1983 10g 10f4 10f) lengthy, good-quartered, attractive colt;
good walker; ran respectably though last of 4 to Lion City in handicap at Sandown
in July (pulled hard); will be suited by a return to 1m or 9f; gives impression he's a
top-of-the-ground performer. *C. Horgan.*

HIMSELF 2 b.c. He Loves Me 120–Makura (Pampered King 121) (1983 5fg* 5f 81
5fg 6g) May 14; big, strong-quartered colt; half-brother to 2 winners, including
very smart sprinter Abdu (by Balidar); dam well beaten all 3 outings; made all in
maiden race at Nottingham in June; ran moderately when favourite for minor event
at Sandown the following month and was then off course for nearly 3 months,
running well in nursery first time back; should stay at least 6f; seems to do best
when fresh. *W. Wharton.*

HINNENI 3 br.g. Lyphoor 118–Emarbee § (Will Somers 114§) (1982 6f 7d 6f 6f4 71
1983 10v 10s 8.3fg 10.2fg 8.2g) close-coupled, useful-looking gelding; ran best
race of 1983 when staying-on fifth of 11 to Barooq in handicap at Windsor in August
on third start; should stay 1¼m; blinkered final start. *R. Hannon.*

HIP HIP HIP (USA) 3 ch.c. To The Quick–Sugarberry (King's Bishop) (1982 76
5f³ 6s4 1983 6v4 6s 6s 5f* 6g 5.3f) attractive, full-quartered colt; held on by a
head from Fatty's Choice in minor event at Chepstow in June; stays 6f; acts on
any going; blinkered last 3 starts; not seen out after August. *G. Lewis.*

HIPPARION 11 gr.g. Sayfar 116–Grecian Palm 78 (Royal Palm 131) (1982 13d 12d –
12fg 1983 12v 12s 10g 8d 10.6g 16fg) poor performer on flat nowadays but is a
winning jumper; has been tried in blinkers; good mount for an inexperienced rider.
S. Mellor.

HIPPOLYTUS 2 b. or br.c. Faraway Times 123–Queen Hippolyta (Bend A Bow) –
(1983 7fg 6fg 7f 7d) Apr 20; first foal; dam never ran; little worthwhile form in
maiden races. *J. Toller.*

HIRE A BRAIN (USA) 2 b.f. Seattle Slew–Grenzen (Grenfall) (1983 8d³) Apr 86 p
28; second foal; half-sister to 3-y-o 9.5f winner Irish Edition (by Alleged); dam
high-class winner at up to 9f; second favourite, made a pleasing debut when under
½-length third of 19 to Lady Fawley in maiden race at Leopardstown in October;
will stay 1¼m; an interesting prospect. *K. Prendergast, Ireland.*

HIS DREAM 2 ro.c. Godswalk 130–Persian's Glory (Prince Tenderfoot 126) 84
(1983 5fg³ 5f² 5f 5fg² 6fg³ 6d) Mar 16; IR 57,000Y; useful-looking colt; good
mover; first foal; dam, sister to smart 1976 2-y-o 5f performer Athlete's Foot, won
over 5f at 2 yrs in Ireland; beaten a head in maiden races at Salisbury in August and
Bath in September; creditable 4½ lengths third of 13 to Forzando under a low
weight in valuable nursery at Newmarket in October; stays 6f but gives impression
5f suits him better; acts well on fast ground; the type to make a successful sprint
handicapper. *P. Cole.*

HIS HONOUR 3 b. or br.c. Bustino 136–Honerko 112 (Tanerko 134) (1982 7g 112
1983 12d 11v 12f* 12fg* 12f² 12f² 13.3g² 12d²) attractive colt; good walker and has a
good, long stride; awarded minor event at Newmarket in July after being hampered
by ½-length winner Prince of Peace and justified favouritism decisively by 3 lengths
from Brilliant Rosa in handicap at Goodwood following month; ran well afterwards
when second to Dancing Affair in minor event at York later in August, to Jupiter
Island in Coral Autumn Cup (Handicap) at Newbury in September and to Kesslin in
handicap at York again in October, staying on particularly well at Newbury; will be
extremely well suited by 1¾m+; probably acts on any going; a very useful
performer who should win a decent race as a 4-y-o when stamina is at a premium.
R. Hern.

HIS HOUSE 2 b.g. He Loves Me 120–Town House 91 (Pall Mall 132) (1983 6g 7f **84**
7f 7fg 8g⁴) May 8; 5,800Y; fair sort; half-brother to 2 minor winners; dam, sister
to Reform, won at up to 9f; 2½ lengths fourth of 12 behind Strathearn in small race
at Redcar in November; last 3 times previously; suited by 1m; possibly requires
some give in the ground. *Hbt Jones.*

HIS MASTER'S VOICE 5 ch.g. Brigadier Gerard 144–Heavenly Sound 115 –
(Sound Track 132) (1982 NR 1983 8fg 12f) strong, useful sort; well beaten in
1983; stays 1m well; acts on firm going; gives impression he's suited by strong
handling; winning hurdler. *P. Bailey.*

HIS REVERENCE 7 ch.g. The Parson 119–Ankole 85 (Crepello 136) (1982 NR –
1983 16fg 18f 12f 12fg) big gelding; poor maiden on flat though is a winning jumper.
G. Harman.

HIT RECORD 5 ch.g. Record Token 128–Silk Willoughby (Pirate King 129) (1982 –
7s 7f⁴ 7fg 7f 1983 8v 7fg 7fg 10g) quite attractive, well-made gelding; poor
performer nowadays; stays 1m; acts on any going, but is well suited by some give
underfoot; trained by D. Wilson first outing. *F. Durr.*

HIT THE HEIGHTS 2 b.c. Thatching 131–Hakima 77 (Hardicanute 130) (1983 **98**
5s.6d* 7f⁴ 6g 7.3g⁴ 6fg 7fg) Apr 14; 10,500F, 25,000Y; good-bodied, quite
attractive colt; second produce; dam 2-y-o 5f winner; 33/1, won 14-runner Staff
Ingham Stakes at Epsom in June, leading after halfway and holding off odds-on King
of Clubs by 1½ lengths; good fourth in 7.3f nursery at Newbury in September; stays
7f; none too well away fifth and sixth starts. *G. Lewis.*

HITTITE AL ARAB 2 ch.c. Ahonoora 122–Santa Brigida (Rarity 129) (1983 –
5fg) Apr 10; IR 8,200Y; first foal; dam Irish 2-y-o 7f winner; broke his back when
falling in maiden race at Windsor in June and had to be destroyed. *G. Huffer.*

HIVE OFF 2 b.c. Home Guard 129–I've A Bee 114 (Sir Ivor 135) (1983 7g 7.6fg –
7g) May 6; medium-sized colt; fourth foal; closely related to Irish 3-y-o Glendale
(by Thatch); dam won over 7f and 1m and was third in Irish Guinness Oaks; little
worthwhile form in varied company, on debut slowly away. *J. Dunlop.*

HIYA JUDGE 5 b.g. Ashmore 125–Grey Home 110 (Habitat 134) (1982 8g 7f 7fg² **64**
8g⁴ 8f² 8fg² 8f² 7fg* 8g⁴ 8fg³ 8g 1983 8g 7fg² 8fg³ 7f⁴ 7f 8.3fg 7f 8h³ 8f⁴ 8fg⁴ 8fg*
7.6fg 7fg³) rather plain gelding; decisively won apprentice handicap at Redcar in
September; stays 1m; acts on any going; blinkered last 4 starts; good mount for
an inexperienced rider; sold 5,000 gns Ascot October Sales. *A. Bailey.*

HOBOURNES LAD 4 ch.c. Palm Track 122–Magic Garden (Florescence 120) –
(1982 8s³ 6s 7f 6f 6fg 6fg 6fg 1983 8fg 10.8fg) neat colt; plater; stays 1m; acts on
soft going. *J. Howell.*

HOCUS POCUS 3 b.f. Wolver Hollow 126–Jungle Trial 86 (Run The Gantlet) –
(1982 7.9g 9g 7d⁴ 7v 1983 10v 12g 12f 11.5f⁴ 12g 8g) 2,400F, 6,000Y; compact,
well-made filly; first produce; dam 2-y-o 1m winner; ran best race when acting as a
pacemaker for winning stable-companion Give Thanks in Irish Guinness Oaks at the
Curragh in July on third outing, finishing around 10 lengths seventh of 12; only
eleventh of 12 behind Hymettus in Galtres Stakes at York on penultimate start;
suited by middle distances; blinkered last 4 starts. *J. Bolger, Ireland.*

HODAKA (FR) 6 b.h. Sir Gaylord–Chigusa 89 (Skymaster 126) (1982 9.1g* **68**
9.2g* 8d³ 9s⁴ 7g 10g 10f 8.2f 9g 10d 1983 10v 7f 8g 8f* 8f* 8.3fg⁴ 8g* 8d⁴ 8g)
small, strong ex-French horse; bought in 6,200 gns after winning valuable selling
handicap at Doncaster in September in fine style; had earlier won non-selling
handicaps at Doncaster and Salisbury (apprentice race); stays 9f; acts on any going;
best in blinkers; sold 2,600 gns Ascot November Sales. *I. Walker.*

HODNET 2 b.c. Mount Hagen 127–Sirnelta (Sir Tor) (1983 7fg³ 7g) Mar 4; –
medium-sized, close-coupled colt; fourth reported foal; half-brother to 7f and
1½m winner Crimson Knight (by Blushing Groom) and 3-y-o middle-distance
winner Lady Gerard (by Brigadier Gerard); dam, daughter of sister to top-class
Sanctus II, won from 1m to 1¼m in France; plating-class form in maiden events at
Chester in July and Leicester in September; will be better suited by 1m+. *F. J.
Houghton.*

HOLD TIGHT 4 b.g. Reform 132–Silk Rein 107 (Shantung 132) (1982 12fg 10f **83**
12f* 12g⁴ 12g 12fg* 12s³ 1983 12g 14v 12g² 16f 16f 12g 12f² 14g 12f* 13s 12g 14d
12fg) big, handsome gelding; has a round action; won handicap at Hamilton in
August; beaten in valuable seller final start; should be suited by 1¾m but has been
well beaten when tried at trip; acts on any going; sometimes blinkered (was at
Hamilton); has sweated up; has run respectably for an amateur rider. *R. Whitaker.*

HOLE IN THE WALL 3 b.f. Windjammer (USA)–Just A Glimmer 75   **94**
(Dumbarnie 125) (1982 7f 7fg 6g² 6d* 7.5s³ 7d* 1983 8s 7s² 7s 10.5s 7g² 8fg)
quite an attractive filly; second in Mulcahy Stakes at Phoenix Park in April (beaten
5 lengths by Glasson Lady) and handicap at Naas in June; looking well but facing a
stiff task, never really landed a blow when seventh of 8 behind Give Thanks in
Musidora Stakes at York on fourth start; suited by 7f; acts on soft going. *M.
Cunningham, Ireland.*

HOLKHAM 3 ch.c. Morston 125–Midsummertime (Midsummer Night II 117)   **84**
(1982 NR 1983 8d 11v 10.2f* 10.1f 12f⁴) quite an attractive colt; half-brother to
1981 2-y-o 7f winner Melting Snows (by High Top) and Park Hill winner Idle
Waters (by Mill Reef); dam never ran; 20/1-winner of 18-runner maiden race at
Doncaster in June, getting up on line to beat Valerio; had stiff task when fourth to
easy winner Band in quite valuable handicap at Goodwood in July, better
subsequent effort; suited by 1½m; evidently needs top-of-the-ground conditions;
sold 3,000 gns Newmarket Autumn Sales. *F. J. Houghton.*

HOLLINGREEN 3 ch.g. Malinowski 123–Laconia 58 (Great Nephew 126) (1982   **56**
6g 6d 1983 9.4d 8.2g 8d 8fg² 8f 7f² 8fg³ 8.2fg² 7g) plain gelding; plater; stays 1m;
tends to sweat up; dwelt when blinkered final start. *E. Weymes.*

HOLLOWAY WONDER 3 b. or br.f. Swing Easy 126–Laconsu (Blakeney 126)   **85**
(1982 6fg 7fg⁴ 5s* 7s* 1983 8s 7fg 7fg 7f 8fg 6fg³ 5f 5.6fg 6fg 6g²) lengthy, leggy,
light-framed filly; not disgraced in handicaps most starts, and was head second to
Ferryman at Lingfield in October; stays 7f, but probably best at 6f; seems to act on
any going. *B. McMahon.*

HOLLOWELL 3 b.g. Wolver Hollow 126–Shooting Season 91 (Silly Season 127)   **70**
(1982 6g 7f 7fg 8g 8d³ 1983 8f*) good mover; has been hobdayed; won maiden
event at Edinburgh in July; suited by 1m; yet to race on really soft going but acts
on any other; sold 7,200 gns Ascot July Sales and resold 2,500 gns same venue in
November. *Sir Mark Prescott.*

HOLLY BUOY 3 b.c. Blind Harbour 96–Holly Doon (Doon 124) (1982 5g 5d 7g*   **45**
7f 6f 8fg 7f 1983 10f³ 12f 8fg 8f 8f³ 10f 10f) lightly-made colt; third in slowly-run
handicaps at Beverley and Newcastle in summer, best efforts; stays 1¼m. *R.
Robinson.*

HOLLYWOOD PARTY 4 ch.g. Be My Guest 126–Western Goddess 95 (Red   **102**
God 128§) (1982 6g 6g 7f² 6fg 6f 5fg 6g 6g 6s 6g 1983 7fg 8f 7fg³(dis) 7f² 6f 7f*
7.6g* 8fg* 6s 8fg*) strong, quite attractive gelding; good mover; hasn't always
been reliable but did well at 4 yrs, decisively winning handicaps at Goodwood,
Chester and Newmarket and apprentice race at Ascot; finds 6f too sharp and stays
1m; acts on any going but seems ideally suited by some give in the ground;
blinkered once in 1981; has won for an apprentice; rather highly strung. *B. Hills.*

HOLMBURY LAD (USA) 5 gr.g. Al Hattab–Fairly Faithful 87 (Prove It) (1982   **46**
10g 8g 1983 8g 7g³ 7fg 10f² 10f* 10f 10f³) plater nowadays; bought in 1,150 gns
after winning at Folkestone in August; stays 1¼m; acts on firm going; has run well
for an apprentice; has been tried in blinkers; seemed reluctant to race once in 1982.
A. Pitt.

HOLMBURY (USA) 3 ch.c. Quack–Riganda (Ribot 142) (1982 5fg 7fg² 8d 1983   **80**
10v 12s 12f* 10f 10.1fg² 10h³ 11g 10g 13g³ 13.8g) rangy, useful-looking colt;
returned to form when getting home narrowly in maiden race at Folkestone in July;
placed in varied races afterwards; suited by 1½m+; best form on firm ground, but
has run respectably on a soft surface; sometimes blinkered. *G. Huffer.*

HOLME RIVER 2 b.f. Rapid River 127–Mary H (Le Tricolore 118) (1983 5f 6f   **55**
7f⁴ 7f³ 7f 8f³ 7g² 8d 8fg 8fg) May 16; smallish filly; third living foal; dam in rear in
novice hurdles; moderate plater; beaten short head in 16-runner event at Catterick
in September on seventh outing; apparently best at 7f; acts on firm going; blinkered
last 5 starts. *W. Bentley.*

HOLT ROW 2 ch.c. Vitiges 132–Lady Rowley 114 (Royal Levee) (1983 5.8s³ 6v   **86**
5fg* 5f² 5g 5f 6f⁴ 7h) Apr 16; 10,000F; short-backed, workmanlike colt;
half-brother to 3-y-o Bold Rowley (by Persian Bold) and 1m winner King's Holt (by
Royal Palace); dam very useful 2-y-o sprinter; won 15-runner maiden event at
Warwick in June; not raced after August; best form at 5f; acts well on firm going and
is possibly unsuited by very soft ground. *M. McCormack.*

HOLY DAY 3 b.f. Sallust 134–Red Letter Day 100 (Crepello 136) (1982 5f 6f 5d   —
6fg⁴ 5s* 1983 5g 5h 6f) neat, quite attractive filly; didn't quite recover her form,

although not disgraced last 2 starts; should stay beyond 6f; acts on any going. *P. Walwyn.*

HOLY SPARK 3 b.c. Sparkler 130–Saintly Miss 63 (St Paddy 133) (1982 8g* 8.2s* 10.2s² 1983 10g³ 12d 12fg) big, lengthy colt; excellent mover; reappeared in Peter Hastings Stakes (Handicap) at Newbury in September and ran very well considering his absence from the course, racing close up throughout and running on well to finish 3¾ lengths third of 9 behind Mauritzfontein; well beaten at York (didn't look right in his coat) and Doncaster afterwards; stays 1¼m well; acts on soft going. *G. Harwood.* **98**

HOLYWELL CAGRRY 2 b.f. Mandrake Major 122–Aureole's Image 78 (Saintly Song 128) (1983 5.8s 6d) Mar 25; 300Y; leggy filly; first foal; dam disappointing maiden; in rear in maiden races at Bath in May and Newbury in October. *Mrs N. Kennedy.* **–**

HOME ADDRESS 2 b.f. Habitat 134–Full Dress II 115 (Shantung 132) (1983 6f 6fg 6g²) May 2; small, good-bodied filly; closely related to useful 1m winner Fairly Hot (by Sir Ivor), the dam of Hot Touch; dam won 1969 1000 Guineas; 1½ lengths second of 15 to Angleman in maiden race at Yarmouth in September; will be better suited by 7f and 1m. *G. Wragg.* **83**

HOME AND TRADE 2 br.c. Fordham 117–Lovison (Irish Love 117) (1983 7g) Apr 2; IR 3,000Y, 4,100 2-y-o; good-bodied colt; first foal; dam fourth once over 9f in Ireland; 66/1 and very burly, moved badly to start and finished last of 17 in maiden race at Leicester in September. *B. McMahon.* **–**

HOME COMMAND 3 ch.g. Home Guard 129–Fleurie 81 (Reliance II 137) (1982 7fg 7f 8g 6d⁴ 5g 1983 7v 11v 10f) quite well-made gelding; quite a moderate maiden; promises to stay middle distances; sometimes blinkered. *C. Williams.* **–**

HOMEOWNER (USA) 3 b.c. L'Enjoleur–Zeal (Round Table) (1982 8fg* 8s³ 1983 10fg* 10g) rather a shallow-girthed colt; weak in market when making a successful reappearance in 7-runner Shanbally House Stud Stakes at Phoenix Park in August, beating Clouds Daughter by 2 lengths; 25/1, flashed his tail under pressure and ran rather wide on bend when about 8½ lengths seventh of 11 behind Stanerra in Joe McGrath Memorial Stakes at Leopardstown on only subsequent outing; may well get further than 1¼m. *D. O'Brien, Ireland.* **106**

HOMER 2 b.f. Streak 119–Lucky Pigeon (The Mongoose 108) (1983 5s) Apr 30; rather angular, workmanlike filly; half-sister to 2 winners, including fair 1973 2-y-o 7f winner Jolly Lucky (by Jolly Jet); dam Irish 1m and 1¼m winner; tailed off in maiden race at Wolverhampton in May; dead. *T. Taylor.* **–**

HOME SECRETARY 3 ch.c. Homing 130–Albany 120 (Pall Mall 132) (1982 6fg 7fg⁴ 1983 10g⁴ 10.4fg* 10.8g 10.4fg⁴ 10.6f² 10g*) good-looking colt; quite useful on his day, as he showed when winning maiden race at Chester in July (by 6 lengths after making all) and handicap at Leicester in September (by a neck from Obadiah); ran moodily twice in between though, including in an apprentice event; stays 1¼m well; acts on firm going; blinkered nowadays; sold to NBA 11,000 gns Newmarket Autumn Sales. *R. Hern.* **93**

HOME SOLUTIONS 2 ch.f. Home Guard 129–Purple Goddess 69 (Red God 128§) (1983 7fg 8g 9g⁴ 10fg) Feb 4; 10,500Y; fair sort; half-sister to several winners, including fairly useful 7f to 1¼m winner Celestial Gem (by Gulf Pearl); dam placed over 5f at 2 yrs; plating-class maiden; showed no form until blinkered on last 2 outings; stays 1¼m; acts on a firm surface. *R. Williams.* **67**

HOMME DE PAILLE (USA) 3 b.c. Vaguely Noble 140–Hay Patcher (Hoist the Flag) (1982 NR 1983 10v* 10.5v² 12d² 15d² 15g 12f² 15fg) $170,000Y; second foal; dam, from same family as Exceller, was very useful sprint stakes winner at 3 yrs; won newcomers race at Saint-Cloud in March by 6 lengths; second 4 times afterwards, including in Prix de l'Avre and Prix de l'Esperance at Longchamp in May, beaten short neck by Fabuleux Dancer and a length by Rutheford respectively; not seen out after finishing modest fifth of 8 behind Kelbomec in Prix Kergorlay at Deauville in August; stays well; has run respectably on firm ground but is well suited by soft ground. *F. Boutin, France.* **112**

HONEST PENNY (USA) 3 ch.f. Honest Pleasure–Saratoga Trunk (Raise A Native) (1982 5g² 5f² 5fg³ 5g 1983 10s 5fg 7f 9g) fourth foal; half-sister to American filly Every August (by Key To The Mint), a winner of 2 of her 4 starts at 2 yrs in 1981; dam winning half-sister to very smart animals Filiberto, Fairway Fun and White Star Line; placed in maiden races as a 2-y-o when trained by D. K. Weld; no form in 1983, including in similar event at Salisbury on reappearance (trained by **–**

K. Brassey at time); possibly unsuited by soft going; refused to race third outing. *C. Collins, Ireland.*

HONEST TOKEN 4 b. or br.g. Record Token 128–Be Honest 95 (Klairon 131) 64 (1982 7g 7g 1983 8d 8g* 8g 7g 8fg 8.2s 8fg²) compact gelding; plater; attracted no bid after winning at Ayr in July; stays 1m. *C. Thornton.*

HONEY 2 b.f. He Loves Me 120–Stickpin 74 (Gulf Pearl 117) (1983 6g 7f³ 6f 7.6d² 79 7fg) Feb 10; 11,000Y; lengthy filly; half-sister to 3-y-o Sheldan (by African Sky) and 2 winners, including fair 6f and 1¼m winner African Pearl (also by African Sky); dam placed over 5f and 7f at 2 yrs; placed in maiden races at Yarmouth in July and Lingfield in October; disappointing favourite (appeared not to have good chance at weights) in nursery at Redcar later in October; will stay 1m; acts on firm going and a soft surface. *M. Jarvis.*

HONEYBETA 3 b.f. Habitat 134–Attica Meli 125 (Primera 131) (1982 NR 1983 105 8d 9v* 10g 12g* 10f* 10f² 12f³) deep-girthed, fair sort; third foal; half-sister to smart 1979 2-y-o 6f and 7f winner Marathon Gold (by Derring-Do); dam won Yorkshire Oaks, Park Hill Stakes and Doncaster Cup; successful in minor event at Wolverhampton in May and slowly-run handicaps on same course in July and at Yarmouth in August; ran well when facing stiff tasks afterwards, particularly when about 1½ lengths third of 11 behind Sylph in Princess Royal Stakes at Ascot in October; suited by 1½m; acts on any going; genuine. *H. Cecil.*

HONEYLAND (USA) 4 ch.c. Stop the Music–Honey Pot (Drone) (1982 8d⁴ 118 10fg² 8v 8d 8d⁴ 10v 10v⁴ 1983 10s³ 7v* 8v⁴ 7d*) \$75,000F; second foal; half-brother to a minor winner in USA; dam, stakes-placed winner over 5f at 2 yrs, is out of half-sister to top-class broodmare Alanesian; lightly raced at 4 yrs but did well, winning handicap at Longchamp in April and Prix du Palais Royal on same course in June; wore blinkers when accounting for Negundo by 2 lengths in latter; subsequently sent to USA; stays 1¼m but is better at shorter distances; ideally suited by some give in the ground. *A. Head, France.*

HONORARY CONSUL 2 b.c. Bruni 132–Isadora Duncan (Primera 131) (1983 – p 8fg) Feb 23; 11,000F, 20,000Y; half-brother to a winner in USA by Lorenzaccio; dam, placed in small 7.5f race in France, is half-sister to very useful Fishermans Bridge; unquoted, backward and sweating, noted staying on steadily after being outpaced in 28-runner maiden race at Newmarket in October; should do better at 1¼m or more. *R. Laing.*

HONOURABLE ADMIRAL 2 br.g. Rolfe 77–Welsh Mistress 113 (Abernant – 142) (1983 6fg) May 17; half-brother to several winners, notably smart French 1975 2-y-o Charlie Man (by Habitat); dam 5f performer; in rear in 12-runner maiden race at Folkestone in October; subsequently gelded. *D. Arbuthnot.*

HONOUR'S IMP 2 b.f. Import 127–Border Honour 76 (Above Suspicion 127) 66 (1983 5s 5g 7s 7.2g 5d²) May 14; rather sparely-made filly; half-sister to 7f and 1¾m winner Border Squaw (by Warpath); dam, who stayed 1½m, is half-sister to dam of Pitcairn; second of 14 to easy winner El Gazebo in maiden race at Catterick in October; beaten in seller previous start; should be suited by 6f; acts on a soft surface. *C. Gray.*

HOODORY 2 ch.f. Hittite Glory 125–Godhood 86 (Green God 128) (1983 6f 6f 7f 66 6s) Mar 24; compact filly; second foal; dam 2-y-o 6f winner; plating-class maiden; stays 7f. *A. Stewart.*

HOODWINK 5 br.g. No Mercy 126–Rose Blanche 89 (French Beige 127) (1982 46 8d 10f² 7fg⁴ 8f 8g 8.3fg³ 10.1fg 10f⁴ 10fg 1983 10.1d 12v 10.2g 10f² 12f* 10f 12f³ 12f 12d 17.1g) plater; bought in 3,500 gns after winning narrowly at Brighton in July; stays 1½m; acts on firm going; often blinkered and probably isn't entirely genuine. *N. Vigors.*

HOOGE MARKET 2 ch.c. Import 127–Brighton Jet 69 (Jolly Jet 111) (1983 5.3f – 6g 5f 5f 7g) Apr 18; 1,500F (privately), 1,800Y; bad plater. *D. Wilson.*

HOOLIGAN 3 br.g. Mummy's Pet 125–Trickster 92 (Major Portion 129) (1982 5f 84 5g⁴ 6g³ 7s³ 1983 7v 8v² 8f² 8.2fg³ 7.6g* 8s 7.2g² 8g) fair sort; trotted up by 10 lengths from Pittsfield in 20-runner maiden event at Chester in August, but doesn't always co-operate; stays 1m; acts on any going, but seems particularly well suited by some give in the ground; sometimes starts slowly and is unreliable. *P. Rohan.*

HOORAH HENRY 3 br.c. Relko 136–Bold Lass (Bold Lad, Ire 133) (1982 NR 88 1983 10s² 10d² 10fg* 12f²) 6,200Y; half-brother to 1¼m winner Julesian (by High Top) and a winning plater; dam twice-raced sister to useful Lufar, dam of very

smart Relfo (by Relko); well-backed favourite when beating Tropical Mist by a neck
in 22-runner minor event at Nottingham in June; second on his 3 other starts (not
seen out after July); will stay 1½m; acts on any going. *L. Cumani.*

HOOTON LANE 2 b.f. Master Sing 109–Makinlau 88 (Lauso) (1983 6fg 7f 7f   44
7.2g 8fg) May 9; lightly-built, narrow filly; third foal; dam won from 1m to 1½m;
poor plater; stays 7f. *M. Camacho.*

HOPEFUL WATERS 3 br.f. Forlorn River 124–Hopeful Way 72 (Hopeful   59
Venture 125) (1982 5f 6g 6fg 6fg² 7g 6s 6s 5s 5d⁴ 6s* 1983 6f 6f 6s 6g 6g 7g 7s 6fg
6fg* 7fg) lightly-made filly; attracted no bid after convincingly winning
apprentice selling handicap at Leicester in October; stays 7f; possibly not at her
best on really firm going, but acts on any other. *J. Spearing.*

HOPSTONE 7 ch.g. Queen's Hussar 124–Vistella 100 (Crepello 136) (1982 NR   55
1983 6d 8.2v 8s 8v 8.2d 8g² 9f 10fg² 8f³(dis) 8g² 8f 8g* 8.2fg 8f 8f 8g 8g³) big,
rangy gelding; plater; won non-selling handicap at Ayr in August; stays 1¼m;
suited by top-of-the-ground conditions; wears bandages. *R. Hobson.*

HOPWOOD 2 b.c. Be Friendly 130–Jeldi 58 (Tribal Chief 125) (1983 5s 5v* 5d⁴   71
5f 7fg) Feb 24; 1,600F; useful-looking colt; has a long stride; half-brother to a
winning plater and a winner in Malaya; dam ran only at 2 yrs; won 10-runner maiden
race at Warwick in April; no form afterwards, including in 2 sellers; possibly
requires plenty of give in the ground; off course 3 months after fourth outing. *B.
Hills.*

HORAGE 3 b.c. Tumble Wind–Musicienne (Sicambre 135) (1982 5s* 5g* 5fg* 5f*   124
6f* 6f* 6f* 6g* 6g* 6g4 1983 8g³ 8fg* 7.3f 8g 8fg4)
Of the top seven two-year-olds in the 1982 International Classification, only
Horage won a pattern race in his second season. Indeed only Horage and
Danzatore–successful at Phoenix Park in April–won a race of any description at
three. In truth, Horage had seemed one of the least likely of the leading
two-year-olds of 1982 to make his mark at three. While admitting to immense
admiration for him as a two-year-old–he won nine races off the reel including the
Coventry Stakes, the Anglia Television July Stakes and the Gimcrack—we weren't
sure he'd be so effective another year. It was noticeable that some of his
contemporaries in his first season made much greater physical progress. However,
gameness was one of the hallmarks of Horage's performances as a two-year-old and
his exceptional courage saw him through in the St James's Palace Stakes at Royal
Ascot, where, very well ridden, he gave one of the bravest front-running
performances seen all season.
Horage started the outsider of seven in the St James's Palace, having been

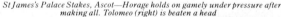

*St James's Palace Stakes, Ascot—Horage holds on gamely under pressure after
making all. Tolomeo (right) is beaten a head*

written off by many after finishing a well-beaten third when odds on for the Timeform Race Card Stakes at Thirsk in mid-April. Horage wasn't seen out between Thirsk and Royal Ascot, having reportedly returned from Thirsk with a bruised heel and missed the Two Thousand Guineas for which he had been quoted at around 12/1 in the winter ante-post betting. The Two Thousand Guineas second and third Tolomeo and Muscatite were among Horage's rivals at Royal Ascot. Cauthen, who passed the one hundred-winner mark for the second successive year in Britain, rode one of his best races in the St James's Palace, jumping Horage smartly out of the gate and, after allowing him a short breather at halfway, dashing him into a four-length lead rounding the home turn, securing an advantage which served him to the end. Only Tolomeo, coming from well back, was able to find the pace to get to grips with Horage in the straight. Horage held on very gamely under

Horage (b.c. 1980)	Tumble Wind (b 1964)	Restless Wind (ch 1956)	Windy City Lump Sugar
		Easy Stages (b 1953)	Endeavour II Saturday Off
	Musicienne (ch 1968)	Sicambre (br 1948)	Prince Bio Sif
		Musical II (ch 1961)	Prince Chevalier Musidora

strong pressure inside the final furlong, passing the post with a head to spare over the fast-finishing Tolomeo; Dunbeath came third, four lengths behind Tolomeo and a neck in front of Muscatite. A good performance by Horage and a fine example of vigorous, opportunist jockeyship by Cauthen! Horage didn't reproduce his St James's Palace form in three later races: he was soundly beaten in the Hungerford

Mr A. R. Rachid's "Horage"

Stakes and the Prix du Moulin de Longchamp and finished fourth of nine to Sackford, beaten seven lengths by the winner, in the Queen Elizabeth II Stakes at Ascot on his final outing.

Horage is a strong, compact, useful-looking colt, and a good mover. His sire Tumble Wind had another winner at Royal Ascot in 1983 when Night of Wind, a stable-mate of Horage, was successful next day at 50/1 in the Queen Mary Stakes. Horage's dam Musicienne, who ran only once, had a moderate record at stud before Horage came along but she comes from an excellent family, being a granddaughter of the One Thousand Guineas and Oaks winner Musidora and a half-sister to the Irish Sweeps Derby third Master Guy and a useful French staying filly called Musique Royale. Horage stayed a mile and acted very well on firm ground (he also won on soft on his debut, the only time he encountered such conditions on a racecourse). He has been retired and will stand at the Ballygoran Stud, County Kildare at a fee of IR 6,000 guineas (October 1st concession). *M. McCormack.*

HORSFORD HENRY 3 b.g. Duc d'Orleans 76–Kempton Princess (Defence 93) (1982 NR 1983 11.5fg 16f 11.5fg[4]) leggy gelding; has rather a round action; first known foal; dam poor maiden on flat and over hurdles; staying-on fourth in maiden race at Yarmouth in September; will stay beyond 11.5f, but was tailed off over 2m. *I. Walker.* —

HORTON LINE 3 ch.f. High Line 125–Jamaya 71 (Double-U-Jay 120) (1982 NR 1983 12s 12s 10s 13.3g[2] 12g* 12fg* 13.3f 12g 14g) 3,200 2-y-o; workmanlike filly; good mover; second foal; dam won 11f seller and also won over hurdles; below form after winning a 20-runner maiden race and a 5-runner minor event at Lingfield in summer; made all and beat Appeal To Me easily by 5 lengths in latter; suited by 1½m+; acts on a firm surface. *D. Elsworth.* — 89

HOSSAM 3 b.c. Artaius 129–Shebeen 124 (Saint Crespin III 132) (1982 6fg* 6s 1983 8s[4] 10d[2] 10d 12f 13.1f* 13.3f[3]) medium-sized, good-topped, fair sort; apprentice ridden when beating Rikki Tavi a shade comfortably by 2½ lengths in handicap at Bath in July; ran well most other starts, including when length third to General Concorde in £6,100 handicap at Newbury later in July on only subsequent start; will be suited by 1¾m; acts on any going, but is particularly well served by fast ground. *P. Walwyn.* — 92

HOT ANNA 4 ch.f. Hotfoot 126–Lantana 74 (St Paddy 133) (1982 7d 11.5f 10g[4] 11d 12d 12g 10g 1983 10.2d 10d 10d 8.3s 8f[4] 6fg 9fg 10f 8fg) tall filly; good mover; poor plater nowadays; sometimes blinkered. *P. Feilden.* —

HOT BETTY 3 b.f. Hotfoot 126–Sunstrucks Betty (Sunstruck) (1982 7g 1983 7s[4] 9v 7f 10f[2] 10fg) medium-sized, lengthy filly; finished well after wandering badly when ¾-length second to Tharaleos in 18-runner maiden race at Ripon in August; suited by 1¼m; acts on any going; very slowly away second outing. *L. Cumani.* — 65

HOT CAPTAIN 4 b. or br.g. Roi Soleil 125–Telling 91 (High Treason 126) (1982 11g 9.4fg 11fg 13.8f 9s 1983 10d) neat gelding; poor plater; sold 550 gns Doncaster May Sales. *G. Richards.* —

HOTEL DE VILLE 2 b.f. Top Ville 129–Knighton House 113 (Pall Mall 132) (1983 7g 7.6d) Apr 7; lengthy filly; keen walker; half-sister to several winners, including smart 1977 French 2-y-o 6f and 1m winner River Knight (by Riverman) and very useful middle-distance winner Open Day (by Northfields); dam, sister to Reform, was very useful at up to 1¼m; modest fifth of 18 in October maiden race at Lingfield, second outing; will be better suited by 1¼m+; sent to France. *I. Balding.* —

HOT GOLD 3 b.c. Hot Grove 128–Lumiere 56 (Siliconn 121) (1982 6fg 8.2s 1983 6v 10fg 7f 7g) lengthy, leggy, shallow-girthed colt; evidently of little account; blinkered final start. *H. Collingridge.* —

HOTKOLE 2 ch.g. Hotfoot 126–Ankole 85 (Crepello 136) (1983 5v 5d 5fg[4] 7f 8h 8.2g) Mar 3; 4,300F; compact, sturdy gelding; brother to 3-y-o Waldron Hill, and half-brother to numerous winners, including useful miler Horbury (by Sing Sing); dam won at up to 13f; plating-class maiden; should stay 1½m; acts on firm going; blinkered final outing; subsequently gelded. *J. W. Watts.* — 64

HOT MELODY 2 ch.f. Hot Spark 126–Mellila (Tudor Melody 129) (1983 5s 5d 5g 5f[2] 5fg 5g[3]) Apr 10; sturdy filly; second foal; half-sister to a winner in Italy by Connaught; dam poor French maiden; quite a modest maiden; appears only just to stay 5f; form only on a sound surface; blinkered fourth and fifth outings. *N. Guest.* — 74

HOT POTATO 3 ch.g. Class Distinction–Cateryne (Ballymoss 136) (1982 5d[2] 6d* 7s[4] 7d 1983 8d[3] 7v[2] 7d[4] 8f 7.6fg 7f[4] 8.2g) lengthy, workmanlike gelding; has a roundish action; ran creditably in non-sellers, including when second in handicap at — 77 d

Thirsk in May; will stay 1¼m; acts on heavy going; sold to M. Tate 4,800 gns Ascot October Sales. *C. Booth.*

HOT PRINCESS 3 ch.f. Hot Spark 126–Aspara 58 (Crimson Satan) (1982 5g 5fg 5f* 6d² 5fg 6f* 5s 6d 1983 6s 6s² 6v 5d² 5fg⁴ 7fg*) Irish filly; not seen out after leading inside last furlong to beat Laois Princess by ¾ length in 5-runner £5,800 Ballycorus Stakes at Leopardstown in July; runner-up earlier in BBA Sprint Stakes at Phoenix Park and Ballyogan Stakes at Leopardstown, going down by only ¾ length to Bri-Eden after losing ground at start on latter; stays 7f; acts on any going with possible exception of heavy; wears blinkers; sent to USA. *D. K. Weld, Ireland.*   **97**

HOT RODDER (USA) 2 b.c. Forli–In Hot Pursuit (Bold Ruler) (1983 8fg) Mar 24; tall colt; brother to top-class miler Posse and half-brother to American winner Kleiglight (by Majestic Light); dam, sister to 2 stakes winners, was one of best 2-y-o fillies in USA in 1973; 14/1, created a most favourable impression when eighth of 28 in maiden race won by Bob Back at Newmarket in October, travelling easily on heels of leaders for long way and being handled very sympathetically as lack of experience told; looks sure to make a good 3-y-o. *J. Dunlop.*   **82 P**

HOT ROLL 3 b.f. Hot Spark 126–Charming Roll (Droll Role) (1982 6g 7fg³ 8fg 1983 7s 6f² 6fg³ 6f 6f* 6f⁴ 6s 6d) ex-Irish filly; first foal; dam won over 1m in USA; ridden by 7-lb claimer when beating Guntrips Centenary by a short head in handicap at Yarmouth in August; stays 7f; acts on firm going; bandaged behind fourth start; dwelt seventh outing; sold 2,000 gns Newmarket September Sales and resold to BBA 4,000 gns Newmarket December Sales. *B. Hanbury.*   **73**

HOT RUBY 2 ch.f. Hot Spark 126–Rubenesque (Busted 134) (1983 5d 7s 7f) Mar 18; 3,000Y; first foal; dam unraced half-sister to very smart middle-distance stayer Relay Race; poor maiden; well beaten in Redcar seller final outing; stays 7f; acts on soft going. *D. Plant.*   **52**

HOT SPIRIT 7 b.m. Hot Brandy 119–Rocita (Roc du Diable 125) (1982 NR 1983 11.7h) tailed off in maiden race at Bath in July. *M. Bradley.*   **–**

HOT TOUCH 3 b.c. Moulton 128–Fairly Hot 109 (Sir Ivor 135) (1982 8d⁴ 1983 8d 11s² 10.5s* 12f 11g³ 10.5d² 11.1g² 10fg)   **126**

Hot Touch reserved his best for York, where he won the Mecca-Dante Stakes and came within a neck of emulating his sire, Moulton, by winning the Benson and Hedges Gold Cup. His other races in top company were largely disappointing, though he often faced stiff tasks. On his first visit to York in May Hot Touch, with seven others, opposed the Derby favourite Dunbeath. His previous best run was a second to Balladier in a Newbury maiden race and consequently he was behind The Noble Player and Welsh Idol in a market in which Dunbeath started at 2/1 on. In the race Hot Touch, given an enterprising ride by Pat Eddery, quickened a few lengths clear three furlongs out and maintained that lead till eased near the line. Hot Touch beat Guns of Navarone a length and a half with Dunbeath a poor third. This proved to be Hot Touch's only victory; indeed, the nine runners managed only three subsequent wins between them, two gained by warm favourites in maiden races.

Between the York May meeting and the York August meeting Hot Touch was well beaten behind Shareef Dancer at Royal Ascot and then finished a neck and a half length third, giving 9 lb, to Dazari and Seymour Hicks in the Mecca Bookmakers' Scottish Derby at Ayr. In the Benson and Hedges Gold Cup, Hot Touch again met Guns of Navarone, though the Prix du Jockey-Club winner Caerleon, Gorytus and John French, who had won the Gordon Stakes, looked more dangerous rivals. Always well placed behind Caerleon, Hot Touch closed to

Mecca-Dante Stakes, York—Hot Touch never looks like being caught by Guns of Navarone

Mr E. B. Moller's "Hot Touch"

challenge three furlongs out and kept on well under pressure, just giving best to Caerleon in a finish where no more than three lengths covered the first six. This was a high-class performance, Hot Touch's best so far, and made his next one, in Kempton's September Stakes, all the more disappointing—he was never going particularly well and he hung quite badly under strong pressure before finishing two lengths second to Lyphard's Special. He wore blinkers in his only subsequent race, the Dubai Champion Stakes, in which he started at 20/1 and showed up well for a long way before fading into ninth of nineteen, one place ahead of Lyphard's Special.

		Pardao	Pardal
	Moulton	(ch 1958)	Three Weeks
	(b 1969)	Close Up	Nearula
Hot Touch		(br 1958)	Horama
(b.c. 1980)		Sir Ivor	Sir Gaylord
	Fairly Hot	(b 1965)	Attica
	(b 1974)	Full Dress II	Shantung
		(b 1966)	Fusil

Hot Touch is an attractive, good-bodied colt. His sire, Moulton, who died in 1981, was generally disappointing at stud, Stone and John de Coombe being about the pick of his other runners. As a four-year-old Moulton won the Benson and Hedges and finished second to Scottish Rifle in the Eclipse. Hot Touch, a half-brother to the fair middle-distance performer Mill Plantation (by Northfields), is the second foal of Fairly Hot, a mare who won a minor event at Newcastle and was placed in very good company, notably when third to Freeze The Secret in the Nell Gwyn Stakes and to Triple First in the Musidora Stakes. She lacked resolution on occasions, though is clearly her dam's best foal. Full Dress II, the 1969 One

387

Thousand Guineas winner, has also produced Hussar, a winner in Belgium, and the temperamental maiden Susanna. Fusil, the dam of Full Dress II, had a number of very useful daughters who stayed further than Full Dress II did. Hot Touch remains in training to contest the top mile-and-a-quarter races; he will need to improve from three to four, as his sire did, to win in the best company. He appears best suited by a mile and a quarter and some give in the ground; there's a doubt about his staying a mile and a half. *G. Wragg.*

HOUDINI'S MARK 2 ch.c. Royalty 130–Carolinda 63 (Grand Roi 118) (1983 7g) June 5; good-bodied colt; second foal; dam ran only 4 times; very backward, tailed-off last of 18 after moving very badly to post and starting slowly in maiden race at Leicester in October. *D. H. Jones.*   –

HOUGHTON WEAVER 4 b.g. Warpath 113–Broughton Flyer (Huntercombe 133) (1982 7g 7g2 9fg 8.2f 8.2g4 6f 6d 8.2s 6s 7g 1983 8.2s2 8v 8s 10g) leggy, rather narrow gelding; poor walker; plater nowadays; stays 1m; probably acts on any going; blinkered once in 1982. *J. Berry.*   43

HOUSE GUEST 3 b.f. Be My Guest 126–Plum Fool (Silly Season 127) (1982 5fg4 6fg2 6fg* 7d 6s 1983 7v 8f 8.2fg) leggy, lightly-made filly; no form since winning at Pontefract as a 2-y-o; should be suited by 7f; sent to USA. *B. Hanbury.*   –

HOUSE HUNTER 2 ch.g. Dubassoff–Sambell 71 (Sammy Davis 129) (1983 5v3 5d4 6g 7f2 7f 8.2h 8g 7fg) Mar 29; 1,000F; leggy, good-topped gelding; half-brother to 1981 2-y-o 5f winner Sammy Waters (by Rapid River); dam won 1m seller; moderate colt; disqualified, for taking runner-up's ground, after passing post first in maiden event at Salisbury in June on fourth start; stays 1m; acts well on hard going; blinkered final appearance; gelded subsequently; trained by R. Simpson first 5 outings. *C. Horgan.*   78

HOUSE WARMER 2 b.f. Petitioner 83–Flying Glory (Flying Mercury) (1983 5v 5.1f) May 20; leggy, narrow filly; first foal; sire, son of Petingo, won twice in Denmark; well beaten in sellers at Warwick in April and Yarmouth in June. *G. Fletcher.*   –

HOWZAT 3 gr.f. Habat 127–Heaven Knows 113 (Yellow God 129) (1982 NR 1983 7.6v) sturdy filly; second foal; dam won Lingfield Oaks Trial but was best at up to 9f; unquoted and poorly drawn when fourteenth of 19 behind Seymour Hicks in £4,300 maiden race at Lingfield in May. *R. Smyth.*   –

HOYER 2 b.c. Rarity 129–Mombones (Lord Gayle 124) (1983 6f2 7.2g* 7f* 7f3 7f3 8g2) Mar 20; IR 54,000Y; neat, attractive colt; good walker and mover; second foal; dam unraced half-sister to Lincoln winner King's Ride (by Rarity) and high-class 6f and 7f performer Court Chad; won Cock of the North Stakes at Haydock in July and minor event the same month at Salisbury; placed in races won by Trojan Fen, Beldale Lear and Attempt subsequently; will stay 1¼m; yet to race on a soft surface. *H. T. Jones.*   98

H. R. MICRO 5 br.m. High Award 119–Crusheen (Typhoon 125) (1982 6g 6fg 5f2 5fg* 5f2 5g2 6s2 6g2 5g3 6f 5f3 5fg 7f 8fg 6s 1983 6d* 5d* 6s 6g4 5fg 5f 5f4 5f3 5.6f 6fg 6fg 5f) sturdy, good-quartered mare; sprint handicapper; won at Catterick in March and Edinburgh (dead-heated with Pergoda) in April; stays 6f; probably acts on any going; occasionally blinkered but is effective without; good mount for an apprentice. *M. Lambert.*   56

HSIAN 3 b.f. Shantung 132–Blue Shadow 97 (Crepello 136) (1982 NR 1983 9f 8f 10g) sturdy, useful-looking filly; half-sister to several winners, including smart 6f to 1m winner Bas Bleu (by Abernant) and very useful middle-distance performer Primerello (by Primera); dam won over 6f at 2 yrs; soundly beaten in maiden and minor events. *G. Wragg.*   –

HUAPANGO 2 br.f. Rhodomantade 110–Samba 69 (Sammy Davis 129) (1983 5d 5f3 6f 6s* 7fg) Feb 6; 1,300Y; fair sort; sister to 7f to 1½m winner Bossanova Boy and half-sister to successful 5f performer Sammy Bear (by Rupert Bear); dam won over 5f; well-backed second favourite, put up easily best effort when winning £4,200 nursery at Ayr in September comfortably by 2½ lengths from Fifty Quid Short; should stay 7f+; clearly suited by soft going. *J. W. Watts.*   84

HUMBERSIDE LADY 2 b.f. Jellaby 124–Joseagle (Jock Scot 121) (1983 6h 7f 7.6fg 6fg) May 9; 2,000Y; fifth foal; dam never ran; soundly beaten in maiden races; dwelt third outing. *G. Huffer.*   –

HUMBOLDT 7 b.g. Levmoss 133–Bonne Femme (Bold Lad, Ire 133) (1982 NR 1983 13v) has been fired; poor performer; wears bandages. *M. McCormack.*   –

HUNGARIAN PRINCE 3 b.g. Monseigneur 127–Magyar Melody (Prince Tenderfoot 126) (1982 7g3 8.2s* 1983 9d3 12v 10v3 8g2 8f 12d 8g* 8d 12d) strong,   97 compact, good sort; carries plenty of condition; blinkered first time when beating Alawir by a head in 14-runner minor event at Newbury in September, running on strongly to lead near finish after being last turning for home; started slowly and finished last when blinkered again both subsequent starts; had run well when placed earlier at Newmarket, Newcastle and Newbury; stays 1¼m well; acts on heavy going; none too reliable; sold 7,400 gns Newmarket Autumn Sales. *R. Sheather.*

HUNTER HAWK 4 ch.g. Huntercombe 133–White Legs (Preciptic 122) (1982 –
10d 6f³ 6g 5g 5g² 6f³ 5f 5f 1983 5d 6v 8d 9.4f 8f 8fg 8f 8g³ 7f 7f 8fg 7fg) neat, strong gelding; poor maiden; has been beaten in a seller; not sure to stay 1¼m; acts on firm going; sometimes blinkered; trained part of season by A. Balding. *D. Chapman.*

HURRY DOWN 2 ch.f. High Line 125–Bird Reserve 74 (Blakeney 126) (1983 7s) –
Apr 5; fair sort; first foal; dam disappointing daughter of smart staying 2-y-o Never a Fear; 10/1, never-dangerous eighth of 18 in maiden race at Leicester in October; likely to need a stiff test of stamina. *H. Candy.*

HUTTON GLORY 3 b.g. Hittite Glory 125–Dividend 74 (Busted 134) (1982 5g –
7g 8s 1983 6s 11v 8g 8fg) smallish, plain gelding; little worthwhile form, including in a seller; sold 440 gns Newmarket July Sales. *I. Walker.*

HUYTON'S HOPE 2 b.c. Full of Hope 125–Bella Musica (Sing Sing 134) (1983 –
5s 5fg 5g 5d) May 7; 1,700Y; leggy, short-backed colt; half-brother to winning miler Sir Pelleas (by Sahib) and 1980 2-y-o 5f winner Reidor (by Roi Soleil); dam ran 3 times; behind in maiden company. *T. Taylor.*

HYDRANGEA 4 b.f. Warpath 113–Hitesca 110 (Tesco Boy 121) (1982 8fg 12fg –
15fg² 16.5f* 16g³ 16.1s 16.1s 16s* 18s 1983 15.8d 18d 15.8d² 16fg 12fg 14fg 14fg 15.8fg 17.4g 15fg) small filly; good walker; lacks pace and is suited by a test of stamina; acts on any going; has run moderately in blinkers several times; retained 1,000 gns Doncaster October Sales. *D. Chapman.*

HYMETTUS 3 b. or br.f. Blakeney 126–Honeypot Lane 91 (Silly Season 127) 103
(1982 NR 1983 10fg 12g 12fg* 12g* 12f⁴ 12fg) rather sparely-made filly; second foal; half-sister to fair 1¼m winner Fanny's Cove (by Mill Reef); dam middle-distance winner; ran easily best race when beating Civility decisively by 2½ lengths in 12-runner Galtres Stakes at York in August, leading over a furlong out after being held up and never looking likely to be caught; never going particularly well when about 5 lengths fourth of 6 behind Dancing Affair in minor event on same course later in month, better subsequent effort; had earlier won a maiden event at

Galtres Stakes, York—Hymettus runs easily her best race

Haydock; will be suited by further than 1½m; acts on a firm surface; blinkered last 3 outings, running sourly on last occasion. *J. Dunlop.*

HYMNOS (FR) 6 ch.h. Luthier 126–Hairbrush (Sir Gaylord) (1982 12g 13.3f 12g³ 12f 12f 13.1f⁴ 10f³ 10g 10fg* 11f 12v³ 1983 12g) workmanlike horse; stays 13f; acts on any going, but seems suited by a sound surface; best in blinkers; has run respectably for an amateur rider; none too genuine; sold privately 5,000 gns Ascot May Sales. *D. Elsworth.*   —

HYPERION PALACE 2 gr.f. Dragonara Palace 115–Hyperion Girl 59 (Royal Palm 131) (1983 7s) May 23; third foal; dam placed over 6f at 2 yrs; last of 19 in maiden race at Leicester in October. *W. Wharton.*   —

HYPERION PRINCE 2 b. or br.c. Mansingh 120–Hyperion Lass (Punchinello 97) (1983 5s 5d 5d) Apr 9; fair sort; brother to winning sprinter Hyperion Chief; dam point-to-pointer; behind in maiden races; blinkered at Leicester in June on final appearance. *W. Wharton.*   —

HYSTERICAL 4 b. or br.f. High Top 131–Madame's Share 115 (Major Portion 129) (1982 NR 1983 8f⁴ 10f³ 10h³ 12fg*) lengthy, good-bodied filly; second foal; dam, daughter of 1000 Guineas winner Night Off, was smart 2-y-o 6f winner in England and very useful miler at 3 yrs in France; rallied gamely to dead-heat with Firm Evaluation in handicap at Brighton in September; suited by 1½m; has raced only on firm ground; has run respectably for an apprentice; sold 36,000 gns Newmarket December Sales. *H. Candy.*   **68**

I

I APPEAL 2 b.f. Star Appeal 133–Harriet Air 80 (Hardicanute 130) (1983 5fg 6f 7f 6s) May 21; 5,000F; small filly; half-sister to Txuri (by Warpath), a winner at up to 9.5f in France; dam 2-y-o 1m winner; no sign of ability, including in a seller. *R. Hannon.*   —

Lord Halifax's "Hymettus"

IBADIYYA 2 ch.f. Tap On Wood 130–Insolite (Charlottesville 135) (1983 8d²) Apr 24; half-sister to 2 minor winners and a winning jumper in France; dam won 10.5f Prix Cleopatre; ran on strongly to finish neck second to Normia in maiden race at Maisons-Laffitte in November; will probably stay 1¼m+; promising. *A. de Royer Dupre, France.*   99 p

I BIN ZAIDOON (USA) 2 b.c. Damascus–Charvak (Alcibiades 95) (1983 6fg 7f) May 5; $500,000Y; shapely, attractive colt; half-brother to several winners, including 11.7f winner Cairnfold (by Never Bend) and Majestic Kahala (by Majestic Prince), a smart winner at up to 1¼m; dam unraced half-sister to top American stallion Exclusive Native; 6 lengths fifth of 7 to Keen in valuable newcomers race at Ascot in July, better effort; soon behind and chased along in 17-runner maiden race at Newbury the following month; should stay 1¼m. *P. Walwyn.*   73

IBOLYAN SOUND 4 ch.g. Music Boy 124–Ibolya Princess 87 (Crowned Prince 128) (1982 NR 1983 8v 6d 9s 6v* 6g 6f 6f 6fg* 6g 5fg 6fg³ 6f 6fg) strong gelding; inconsistent handicapper; won at Thirsk (apprentices) in May and Chester (made all) in August; stays 6f; seems to act on any going; blinkered sixth start. *S. Norton.*   61

IBTISAMM (USA) 2 ch.f. Caucasus 127–Lorgnette 107 (High Hat 131) (1983 6f 7h² 6g⁴) Feb 12; $150,000F; attractive, lengthy filly; closely related to Au Printemps (by Dancing Champ), a stakes winner at up to 9f in Canada, and half-sister to a winner who has bred 2 stakes winners; dam showed useful form without winning at up to 1¼m; in frame in maiden races at Chepstow in August and Hamilton in September; will be better suited by 1m+. *G. Hunter.*   70

ICE 5 b.g. Northfields–Carmine City 104 (Charlottesville 135) (1982 10fg 10fg 10fg 10g 10fg* 10f³ 10f² 10fg³ 1983 12s 10g 10f 10g 12f 8fg 14f) well-made, attractive gelding; poor handicapper; stays 1½m; yet to show he can handle really soft going, but acts on any other; ran rather freely when tried in blinkers once. *G. Thorner.*   –

ICE GALAXIE (USA) 3 b.f. Icecapade–High Galaxie (Irish Castle) (1982 6fg 6s 7d 1983 7d 8f 7.2fg² 8d 8g) small filly; showed only worthwhile form when 5 lengths second to Dinner Toast in maiden race at Haydock in July; stays 7f; blinkered third and fourth outings; tends to sweat up. *R. Laing.*   –

ICE HOT (USA) 3 b.c. Icecapade–Beau Fabuleux (Le Fabuleux 133) (1982 7fg* 8.5v² 7s 1983 8v³ 7.5v* 8v 8v 10.5f³ 9fg⁴ 8f 8g³ 7¹g³ 8g* 7f*) $90,000Y; first foal; dam, from same family as high-class stayer Astray, won at up to 9f; successful in Prix Montenica at Saint-Cloud in April, 130,000 francs handicap at Maisons-Laffitte in September and Prix du Pin at Longchamp in October; got home by ½ length from Lichine in last-named race; ran respectably on other occasions, including in Prix de la Jonchere at Longchamp on fourth start (fifth to Aragon) and Prix Daphnis at Evry (fourth to Glenstal); stays 1¼m; acts on any going. *C. Beniada, France.*   118

ICEN 5 b.g. Tycoon II–Pepstep 88 (Polic 126) (1982 10s 10g* 8fg* 9g 8f 1983 8f 8fg 10f 10.2fg 10fg) lightly-made gelding; has been pin-fired; fair handicapper at his best, but showed little at 5 yrs and ran deplorably fourth start; stays 1¼m; suited by a sound surface. *M. Smyly.*   –

ICE PATROL (USA) 3 b.c. Far North 120–Mary Biz (T.V. Lark) (1982 7fg 8s 7s* 1983 8g² 10.5s 12s 8f⁴ 10f 10h⁴ 7fg) smallish, close-coupled, quite attractive colt; ran very well indeed when 5 lengths second of 9 to Shearwalk in Timeform Race Card Stakes at Thirsk in April; wasn't disgraced when about 20 lengths fifth of 9 behind Hot Touch in Mecca-Dante Stakes at York the following month but showed moderate form in variety of company afterwards; promises to stay middle distances; probably needs some give in the ground; a difficult ride and was withdrawn after taking charge of his apprentice rider on one occasion. *S. Norton.*   94 d

IDEAL HOME 2 br.f. Home Guard 129–Milk and Honey 102 (So Blessed 130) (1983 5s* 6f⁴ 6s 6g² 6fg³) May 7; leggy filly; second foal; half-sister to 3-y-o middle-distance winner Kondair (by Record Run); dam won over 5f and 6f at 2 yrs but didn't train on; made a promising debut in £3,400 maiden race at York in May, quickening up really well to beat Rosana Park by 1½ lengths after missing break; ½-length second of 16 to Melaura Belle under a big weight in very valuable nursery on same course in October; suited by 6f; needs some give in the ground to be seen to best advantage. *M. H. Easterby.*   104

IDLE MATINEE (USA) 2 b.c. Bold Forbes–Matuta 115 (Stage Door Johnny) (1983 8fg 8.2fg) Jan 28; tall, rangy, good sort; good mover; half-brother to a winner in USA; dam third in Oaks; seventh of 16 to Alleging in £3,400 event at Nottingham in October, second outing; sure to do good deal better over longer distances. *J. Dunlop.*   – p

Mr Norman A. Blyth's "Idolized"

IDOLIZED 2 b. or br. c. Mummy's Pet 125–Darlingka 77 (Darling Boy 124) (1983   **110**
5d 6g⁴ 6f² 6f* 7d⁴ 6f* 6g 7fg²) Mar 4; big, useful-looking colt; fifth foal;
half-brother to a winner in USA; dam won twice over 1½m; won 6-runner Chesters
Stakes at Newcastle in June and 8-runner Champion Two Yrs Old Trophy (beating
Maajid a length) at Ripon in August; came from a long way back to finish neck
second of 8 to Round Hill in Somerville Tattersall Stakes at Newmarket in
September; stays 7f well; acts well on fast ground. *E. Weymes.*

I HAD A DREAM 2 b. f. Ribston 104–Mistaya 69 (Welsh Rake 118) (1983 7.6d   –
7g) third foal; dam lightly-raced half-sister to very useful miler Caius; well beaten
in maiden events at Lingfield in October, on first occasion last of 18. *H. Beasley.*

IKAAYA 2 gr. f. Nishapour 125–Irova (Iron Liege) (1983 7d) Apr 3; half-sister to 4   – p
winners, including Irish middle-distance winner Ormus (by Faunus); dam, French
1m winner, is daughter of high-class Cordova; 8/1, never-dangerous 9 lengths sixth
of 10 to Free Guest in maiden race at Brighton in September; should do better. *M.
Stoute.*

IKE'S MISTRESS (USA) 3 b. f. Master Derby–Ike's Gamble (Correlation)   –
(1982 7f 5g* 5g 5s³ 1983 7s 7v 5.1g 6fg 9g 7g³(dis) 5g 6d 6d) workmanlike
ex-English filly; disqualified after finishing third at Galway in September, best
effort of 1983; stays 7f; blinkered fourth start; trained until after that outing by J.
Hindley. *B. Kelly, Ireland.*

392

ILE D'AMOUR 2 b.f. Sassafras 135–Castleisland (Deep Diver 134) (1983 7f 7f) —
Apr 2; IR 14,000Y; first foal; dam Irish 1½m winner; poor form in Yarmouth maiden
events in July and August; sold 10,000 gns Goffs November Sales. *G.
Pritchard-Gordon.*

ILIUM 2 b.c. Troy 137–Glamour Girl (Riverman 131) (1983 7fg² 8fg³)   121
    Expectations that we should be entertained by masterly examples of the art
of naming a racehorse, classical allusions to the fore, when names were
registered for Troy's first crop, went largely unfulfilled. Troy's son out of Fenella
is known as Trojan Fen; his colt out of Topsy and filly out of Queen's Castle are
unimaginatively named Troytops and Trojan Queen respectively; and others bear
such names as Troyanna, Troyenne and Troyanos. A few have been named more
deftly: Lord Porchester's filly Cassandra is named after the daughter of Priam,
king of Troy, Sheikh Mohammed owns a filly called Helen's Dream, and Hadi
Al-Tajir's colt out of Glamour Girl carries the Latin name for Troy, Ilium.
    Ilium ran only twice in his first season, appearing firstly in the Hyperion
Stakes at Ascot in October, the race chosen by his stable for the introduction of
Touching Wood two years earlier. A compact colt, he impressed both on the way
to post and in the race, faring better than Touching Wood; he finished a
two-and-a-half-length second to the more-experienced Ministerial, realising what
was required of him only entering the final furlong. Ilium took on even better
opposition in the William Hill Futurity at Doncaster later in the month, and started
seventh choice in a field of nine at 12/1. He ran particularly well, turning into the
straight in second place behind Lake Valentina and then taking up the running a
quarter of a mile out. As soon as he'd done so he was hard pressed by Falstaff
(USA) and the market leaders Mendez and Alphabatim, but he held on splendidly,
battling on so gamely that Alphabatim and Mendez took his measure only in the
closing stages. Although we don't rate the Futurity form highly, there was a lot to
like about Ilium's performance, especially as it came only a fortnight after his

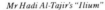

Mr Hadi Al-Tajir's "Ilium"

debut. There are clearly good prizes to be won with him when he gets a stiffer test of stamina as a three-year-old.

Ilium (b.c. Apr 22, 1981)	Troy (b 1976)	Petingo (b 1965)	Petition Alcazar
		La Milo (ch 1963)	Hornbeam Pin Prick
	Glamour Girl (b or br 1975)	Riverman (b 1969)	Never Bend River Lady
		Glamour (br 1960)	Djebe Tudor Gleam

Ilium's trainer bought Glamour Girl on behalf of Mr Tajir for 43,000 guineas at the 1978 Newmarket December Sales. She had won two races at Rouen earlier in the year, a maiden over nine and a half furlongs and a handicap over seven, without showing anything like the same ability as some of her eight winning half-brothers and half-sisters. Best of the eight were the smart fillies Gleam, runner-up in the One Thousand Guineas, and Glaneuse, who ended her career with a win in the Gran Premio del Jockey Club over a mile and a half. Glaneuse had three foals by Riverman in the mid-'seventies, all of whom won and one of whom, the filly Gold River, did outstandingly well. Among Gold River's successes were those in the Prix Royal-Oak in 1980 and both the Prix du Cadran and the Prix de l'Arc de Triomphe in 1981, which must have boosted considerably the value of her close relative Glamour Girl. However there appears to have been a slight hiccup, after a smooth start, in Glamour Girl's stud career; after visiting the Derby winner Blakeney in her first year at stud (to whom she produced the slow maiden Al-Abjar) and another Derby winner Troy in her second, she wasn't covered in 1981 despite having foaled Ilium in April. Her 1982 mate wasn't another Derby winner, either, but the sprinter Blue Cashmere, one of whose nominations was sold at auction for as little as £760 that year; her colt by him wasn't foaled until June 16th. But even if Glamour Girl never produces another animal of note, her owner is likely to more than recoup his investment with Ilium. *H. T. Jones.*

ILLICIT 4 b.g. He Loves Me 120–Princess Parthia (Parthia 132) (1982 6fg⁴ 7fg 6g 8g 7fg 6g⁴ 1983 7fg) tall, sparely-made gelding; has a round action; disappointing handicapper; has been beaten in a seller; has twice been blinkered. *J. Harris.* —

I'LL SEE YOU 5 b.h. Averof 123–Keeps (Roan Rocket 128) (1982 7d 8g 7fg 8f 8.5f 8fg* 8g* 8fg* 8f* 7.3g 8s 8fg² 1983 8d⁴ 8.5s 8f 7.6fg² 7f² 7.3f) rangy horse; good mover; returned to form when battling well on to be 1½ lengths second of 6 to Lyphard's Special in valuable event at Lingfield in July; good 2½ lengths second to Beaudelaire in Beeswing Stakes at Newcastle later in month; stays 1m; acts on firm going; hasn't run well when tried in blinkers; often sweats up; suited by forcing tactics; wears a tongue strap; goes well on switchbacked tracks; smart; winner in USA. *C. Brittain.* 117

IL PONTEVECCHIO 3 b.c. Tumble Wind–Netherside 73 (Alcide 136) (1982 6fg 7g 7g² 7g³ 7.3g 7s² 1983 12d³ 12v 10.1fg* 10.1fg⁴ 10.1fg² 10g) neat, strong, quite attractive colt; returned to form in 14-runner minor event at Windsor in July when having first race for 3 months, quickening clear in last furlong to beat Mullet by 6 lengths; ran creditably on same course next 2 starts; stays 1½m; yet to race on really firm going, but acts on any other; didn't show much sparkle final start; sold to D. Murray-Smith 16,500 gns Newmarket Autumn Sales. *B. Hobbs.* 84

IL SARACENO 2 ch.c. Roman Warrior 132–Birdcage 78 (Manacle 123) (1983 6f 6h 7g) Feb 12; 4,000Y; close-coupled colt; brother to winning sprinter Dungeon Ghyl and half-brother to another winner; dam seemed to need at least 6f at 2 yrs; soundly beaten in maiden races. *P. Burgoyne.* —

IL TIGRE 2 b.c. Bellypha 130–Tour Nobel (Habitat 134) (1983 6fg 6fg³) May 18; medium-sized colt; has a round action; half-brother to 2 winners, including minor French 1980 2-y-o 7f winner Touraine (by Luthier); dam, half-sister to very good colts Carlemont and Avaray, was very useful French sprinter; 20/1, wandered badly in the Dip after making strong progress from halfway, when 1¼ lengths third of 20 to Saturnian in maiden event at Newmarket in October; will stay 7f; sure to win a race. *L. Cumani.* 88

I'M COMINGYOURWAY 3 ch.g. Music Boy 124–Observation 81 (Coronation Year 124) (1982 5s 6d 6d 1983 7s 6s 6v 6d*) tall, lengthy gelding; short-priced favourite and dropped in class when easily winning seller at Leicester in May (no bid); stays 6f; yet to race on a sound surface; sold 780 gns Newmarket July Sales and exported to Malaysia. *N. Callaghan.* 58

IMMACULATE GIRL 3 b.f. Habat 127–Irish Elegance 60 (French Beige 127) (1982 6g⁴ 6g 1983 10d 10f) fair sort; poor walker; should stay 1¼m. *R. D. Peacock.* –

IMPECCABLE LADY 4 br.f. Silly Season 127–Gorse Bush (Hallez 131) (1982 10.1d 8g 8f³ 7f 7g* 7fg⁴ 10f² 10g 1983 8f³ 8fg⁴ 8f² 8fg* 8g* 7g⁴) leggy, narrow, lightly-made filly; poor walker and mover; plater; attracted no bid after being awarded race at Wolverhampton in August; retained 2,900 gns after trotting up at Kempton in September; stays 1¼m; acts on firm going; has been tried in blinkers; has run creditably for an apprentice. *C. Williams.* **59**

IMPEL 2 ch.f. Import 127–Elbeam (Hornbeam 130) (1983 5fg 5f 5f) May 5; 2,800Y; of little account; blinkered final appearance; sold 340 gns Ascot October Sales. *D. Dale.* –

IMPERIAL CHAMPAGNE 3 gr.c. Imperial Crown 96–Blue Champagne (Raffingora 130) (1982 NR 1983 17v) leggy, sparely-made colt; first reported foal; dam never ran; looked immature when behind in maiden race. *W. Turner.* –

IMPERIAL IMPORT 2 ch.c. Imperial Fling 116–Charites (Red God 128§) (1983 7f 7f 6fg 6d) Mar 17; deep-girthed colt; good mover; third foal; dam poor sister to top-class sprinter Green God; plating-class maiden; showed form only on second appearance; blinkered final outing. *C. Horgan.* **61**

IMPERIAL PRINCESS 2 b.f. Mansingh 120–Pladda (Reliance II 137) (1983 5fg 6fg) Apr 14; small, workmanlike filly; sister to 9f winner Naishapur and half-sister to winners here and in Italy; dam won 3 times over 1½m in Ireland; behind in maiden events at Windsor in July and Newmarket in September; possibly needs further. *P. Haslam.* –

IMPERIAL SALUTE 2 b.c. Imperial Fling 116–Saltation 111 (Sallust 134) (1983 6g 6f³ 7f³ 8d³ 8fg 8.2fg) Feb 27; compact, good-bodied colt; good mover; first foal; dam won 5 times over sprint distances; fair maiden; improved with each outing, on last 2 appearances running creditably in blinkers in nurseries at Newmarket and Nottingham; stays 1m well; acts on firm going and a soft surface; sure to win a race. *H. T. Jones.* **89**

IMPLICATION (USA) 4 b.c. Tentam–Caught in the Act (Nijinsky 138) (1982 10s² 10fg* 12.3f* 12fg³ 16s 17.1s 1983 16fg) rangy colt; stays 1½m (well beaten over further); acts on any going. *A. Moore.* –

IMPORT DUTY 2 ch.f. Import 127–Radar Girl 75 (Bleep-Bleep 134) (1983 5g 5fg 5f⁴ 5fg 5s) May 2; leggy filly; sister to a poor animal; dam won over hurdles; quite a modest plater; acts on firm going. *W. C. Watts.* **53**

IMPOUND 4 ch.g. Import 127–Douane 87 (Runnymede 123) (1982 NR 1983 12v 10fg) 2,100Y, 1,800 3-y-o, resold 2,500 3-y-o; beaten a long way in maiden race and seller; trained part of season by P. Haynes. *B. Stevens.* –

IMPRESS 4 gr.f. Warpath 113–Sica Wood 94 (Sica Boy 132) (1982 NR 1983 12v 12d⁴ 10s 12f 12fg 15.8g 12f) smallish, lengthy filly; half-sister to 2 winners, including fair middle-distance performer Elegant Star (by Star Moss); dam won over 6f and 7f at 2 yrs; little worthwhile form, including in a seller; broke a leg at Redcar in September and was destroyed. *T. Fairhurst.* –

I'M VEXED 4 b.c. High Top 131–Sassalya (Sassafras 135) (1982 8.2s 9v 1983 12v 8s² 8d 9f 8f 8g) strong, quite useful sort; poor mover; plater nowadays; second at Ripon in April (led on bridle 2½f out and would undoubtedly have won had he been sent about his business at that point); claimed out of M. W. Easterby's stable afterwards; finished distressed third start. *J. Parkes.* **47**

IMYAR 4 b.c. Labus–Iroma (Iron Liege) (1982 10v* 12s 12g² 12g² 1983 10s* 10v⁴ 10f) brother to French middle-distance maiden Imtiyaaz and half-brother to 4 winners; dam won twice at middle distances in France; very useful hurdler and a smart performer on flat; made all to beat Welsh Term by ¾ length in Prix Exbury at Saint-Cloud in March; ran respectably afterwards to be fourth of 10 to Welsh Term in Prix d'Harcourt at Longchamp in April and fifth of 8 to General Holme in Prix Gontaut-Biron at Deauville in August; stays 1½m; acts on any going but revels in the mud. *A. Fabre, France.* **111**

IN A NUTSHELL 2 ch.g. Crimson Beau 124–Concisely (Connaught 130) (1983 5v 6s 7f³ 7fg 7f 7fg 6fg³ 6g 7fg 6fg 6fg 6fg) Apr 30; 4,000Y; close-coupled gelding; third foal; dam unraced half-sister to very useful Giriama; quite a moderate maiden; beaten in sellers on 2 occasions; headstrong, and seems unlikely to stay beyond 7f; best form on a firm surface; usually blinkered. *D. Thom.* **70**

INA SEVILLE 2 b. or br.f. Orange Bay 131–Carsina 110 (Hethersett 134) (1983 **103**
7g³ 8g* 8s 8g² 10d³) Mar 28; half-sister to numerous winners, including useful
1977 2-y-o 6f winner Kehaar (by Caliban); dam at her best at 2 yrs; won a maiden
event at Deauville in August by 2 lengths from Blushet; kept on well when 2½
lengths second to Mendez in Prix des Chenes at Longchamp the following month;
disappointing 11 lengths third of 5 to Long Mick in Prix de Conde at same track in
October; should stay at least 1¼m; possibly unsuited by a soft surface. *P. Lallie,
France.*

INCARNADINE 3 ch.f. Hot Spark 126–Scarlet Thread 80 (Joshua 129) (1982 **67**
6s⁴ 7g* 1983 8d* 8f 9d 7.6d 8.2fg) short-coupled filly; beat Dodgy Future
decisively by ¾ length in handicap at Wolverhampton in May but was pulled up after
being badly hampered next time and showed little on her return in the autumn; will
probably stay 1¼m; acts on a soft surface. *P. Makin.*

INCENSE 3 b.g. Martinmas 128–Cabochard (Nelcius 133) (1982 7f⁴ 7f 7.2s³ 1983 **58**
8g 12.3f 12.2f 12fg 13.8g³ 12g*) fair sort; sold to P. Bevan 1,700 gns after winning
seller at Wolverhampton in October; had looked ungenuine previous start; suited
by 1½m+. *J. Etherington.*

INCESTUOUS 4 b.g. Mummy's Pet 125–Autumn Breeze (King's Bench 132) **51**
(1982 6s 7f² 7g 6g 8f 7g 6d 6s 7s 1983 6d² 6v 7d) fair sort; good walker; former
plater; stays 7f; seems to act on any going; usually blinkered nowadays. *B.
McMahon.*

INCHGOWER 6 b.g. Ribero 126–Lutine Belle 82 (Luthier 126) (1982 10.2g 8f **56**
10f² 10fg* 12fg 11.7g* 12g* 12fg 12g² 1983 12.2v⁴ 12d 12s² 12d* 12fg* 14f 12f 12f
12fg 16fg³ 18fg 16g) workmanlike gelding; good walker; won handicaps at
Leicester in May and Brighton in June; stays 2m; acts on any going; has run
moderately when sweating up. *W. Wightman.*

INCISIVE 2 ch.c. Sharpen Up 127–Fair Sousanne 75 (Busted 134) (1983 7f 7fg **72**
7f) May 17; tall colt; first foal; dam, in frame over 6f and 1¼m, is daughter of very
smart French filly Army Court; quite modest form in autumn maiden events at
Redcar; will stay 1m. *E. Weymes.*

INCREDIBLE IDEA (USA) 3 b.f. Youth 135–Fascinating Girl (Sir Ivor 135) **86**
(1982 NR 1983 12d 11.5fg³ 12f* 12fg² 14d* 13.3g 14fg) quite attractive, rangy
American-bred filly; first foal; dam smart winner at up to 9f; won maiden race at
Carlisle in June (by 6 lengths) and Melrose Handicap at York in August, in latter
event staying on in gutsy fashion to catch Dancing Admiral close home and win by a
neck, with most of remainder well strung out; suited by a test of stamina; seems to
act on any going; genuine; probably went too fast for her own good sixth start. *A.
Stewart.*

INDIAN 3 ch.c. Great Nephew 126–Ardneasken 84 (Right Royal V 135) (1982 7d **–**
8d 1983 11d 12f 14f 14.7f 16.5f) neat, quite attractive colt; slow maiden; well
beaten last 2 starts, wearing blinkers on first occasion. *C. Thornton.*

INDIAN CALL 4 br.f. Warpath 113–Sing High 85 (Sound Track 132) (1982 8f 10d **–**
7fg* 8g³ 7fg³ 7s 1983 7g 8g 8fg 15.8f 8.2g 12fg 10g) useful sort; good walker;
plater; stays 1m; best in blinkers; has worn a tongue strap. *Hbt Jones.*

INDIAN DAWN 2 ch.f. On Your Mark 125–Indian Beauty 93 (Indiana 129) (1983 **73**
5fg⁴ 5f 5f 6fg 6fg 6g 6s* 7fg 7fg) Apr 25; IR 6,600F, IR 6,600Y; workmanlike filly;
half-sister to 2 winners, including fairly useful 1975 2-y-o 6f winner Suncharmer (by
Roi Soleil), and 2 winning jumpers; dam won over 1¼m; blinkered first time, won
8-runner nursery at Hamilton in October by 2 lengths under 5 lb overweight; should
stay 7f; appears to need the mud. *S. Norton.*

INDIAN DREAM 2 b.g. Streak 119–Dorothy Darling 76 (Red God 128§) (1983 **–**
5f 5h 7f) Jan 24; 600F; deep-girthed gelding; apparently of little account; blinkered
final outing. *H. Wharton.*

INDIAN LADY 3 b.f. African Sky 124–Engage (Whistling Wind 123) (1982 5fg 5f **82**
5.3fg³ 5g 5f³ 5f⁴ 5d* 6fg* 5fg 1983 8g 5d 6s 5f 6f 5fg* 5f 5g³ 5g) neat, well-made
filly; returned to form when making virtually all to win handicap at Wolverhampton
in August; ran best subsequent race eighth start; stays 6f (had very stiff task in
1000 Guineas over 1m); yet to race on very soft going, but acts on any other;
blinkered twice in 1982; sold 14,500 gns Newmarket Autumn Sales. *G. Lewis.*

INDIAN MOONSHINE 3 ch.f. Warpath 113–Midsummer Madness 66 (Silly **60**
Season 127) (1982 6s 9s 1983 9.4d³ 12.2d 12f 10.5d 12f² 12fg* 12fg³) lengthy
filly; good walker; odds on, attracted no bid after winning maiden seller at Redcar in
October by 8 lengths; suited by 1½m; probably acts on any going; sold to A.
Balding 5,100 gns Doncaster November Sales. *C. Thornton.*

INDIAN PRINCE (FR) 4 ch.c. Margouillat 133–India (Hautain 128) (1982   118
including 11g* 12g* 12g 14g*) 1983 15.5v 15.5v4 20v2 20f3 12s 12s4 12g3) 56,000
francs Y (approx £5,600); rangy colt; half-brother to several winners in France;
dam won at around 1m in France; one of leading colts of generation in Spain who
won 4 of his 6 starts there in 1982, notably Gran Premio Duque de Toledo at San
Sebastian and Premio Villamejor (Spanish St Leger) at Madrid; ran well in France
at 4 yrs, best efforts when just over 3 lengths fifth to Denel in Prix de Barbeville,
about 6½ lengths fourth to Kelbomec in Prix Jean Prat and head second to Karkour
after making running in Prix du Cadran, all at Longchamp; outpaced in closing
stages when 6½ lengths third to Little Wolf in Gold Cup at Royal Ascot on fourth
start (bandaged); suited by a test of stamina; acts on any going but goes well on
heavy; trained first 4 starts by O. Douieb. *J-C. Cunnington, France.*

INDIAN RAJAH 3 b.c. Sallust 134–Light House (Primera 131) (1982 6g* 6fg*   96
7v*) 1983 7s4 7g) quite attractive colt; unbeaten in 3 races at Windsor and
Lingfield (2) as a 2-y-o; eased when beaten when less than 10 lengths fourth of 6
behind Proclaim in Salisbury 2000 Guineas Trial in April; behind in handicap at
Newmarket later in month on only subsequent start; will stay 1m; acts on a firm
surface, but clearly goes extremely well in the mud. *J. Sutcliffe.*

INDIAN SAHIB (USA) 2 ch.c. Raja Baba–Super Sally (Noholme II) (1983 5g)   – p
Apr 25; $80,000Y; third foal; dam, very useful at 3 yrs, won at up to 1m; tenth of 16
in maiden race at Sandown in October. *G. Hunter.*

INDIAN SIGN 2 b.g. Hittite Glory 125–Ouija 104 (Silly Season 127) (1983 6fg)   – p
Apr 29; excellent mover; half-brother to useful 3-y-o 1m winner Teleprompter (by
Welsh Pageant) and useful 7f and 1m winner Rosia Bay (by High Top); dam best at
1m; 50/1, ran on from halfway when in mid-division in 20-runner maiden event won
by Saturnian at Newmarket in October; will improve and should win races in the
North. *J. W. Watts.*

INDIGO JONES (USA) 2 ch.c. Northern Jove–On Second Thought (Raise A   105
Native) (1983 5v4 5v2 5d* 5f2 6g4 6f3 6g) Feb 11; $65,000Y; neat, strong,
attractive colt; has a smooth action; first foal; dam, who never ran, is closely
related to very smart French 6f and 7f winner Exclusive Order; landed a gamble in
poor maiden race at Epsom in June; ran with considerable credit against good
2-y-o's subsequently, on sixth outing beaten only 1¾ lengths when promoted
to third place on disqualification of Vacarme in OCL Richmond Stakes at Goodwood;
best form on firm going; tough and courageous; sent to USA. *J. Sutcliffe.*

INDY 3 ch.f. Indigenous 121–Dracula's Daughter (Hook Money 124) (1982 5f 5g   54
5fg 5f2 6fg2 5s 5s 6g) 1983 5v 5fg* 5g 5fg 5fg 8g 7g 7fg 6g3 6g 5g4) workmanlike
filly; won maiden race at Edinburgh in April; ran best subsequent races in autumn;
promises to stay beyond 6f; best form on top-of-the-ground; has worn bandages in
front; trained by A. Bailey until after second start. *C. Wildman.*

IN FAVOUR 3 b.f. Bustino 136–Grazia 90 (Aureole 132) (1982 7fg3 7f 1983   72
10v2 12fg 10f2 10g 10.4g 9d2 10fg) attractive, useful sort; runner-up in maiden and
minor events at Lingfield, Nottingham and York, easily best efforts; should stay
1½m (had stiff task when tried at trip); acts on any going; blinkered fifth start
(sweated and looked bit light). *P. Walwyn.*

INFELICE 3 gr.f. Nishapour 125–Quenelle 82 (Roan Rocket 128) (1982 NR 1983   –
8f 7f 7f 7s) 7,000F; smallish filly; second foal; half-sister to a prolific winner in
Italy; dam, sister to Catherine Wheel, probably stayed 1¼m; behind in maiden
races; last when blinkered final outing. *A. Hide.*

INFINITY RULES 2 b.c. Mandamus 120–Catherine Rose 59 (Floribunda 136)   68
(1983 5d 6d 7fg4 7g) Feb 28; strong, medium-sized, fair sort; brother to 1m
winner Same Date and 1½m winner Dame Sue; dam won over hurdles; 8½
lengths fourth of 12 to Mafoo's Image in maiden race at Salisbury, only indication
of merit; will stay 1m. *S. Mellor.*

INFLATION BEATER 2 b.c. General Assembly–Border Dawn 99 (Pitcairn   90 p
126) (1983 6f*) Apr 6; first foal; dam, half-sister to smart French stayer Chawn,
won 5 middle-distance races; 15/8 favourite, led around halfway and kept on well to
win maiden event at the Curragh in August by ¾ length from Prince of Rondo,
despite missing break; bred to stay 1¼m+; promising. *D K. Weld, Ireland.*

IN FOCUS (FR) 2 b.c. Sharpman 124–Model Girl (Lyphard 132) (1983 8g*) first   91 p
foal; dam useful at around 1¼m; decisively won 15-runner newcomers event at
Maisons-Laffitte in November by 2 lengths from Dauphin du Bourg; will stay 1¼m;
promising. *D. Smaga, France.*

IN FORM 2 b.f. Formidable 125–Rally 88 (Relko 136) (1983 7.6d 8fg²) Feb 25; 76
second foal; half-sister to a winner in Belgium by Mansingh; dam, sister to very
smart Relay Race, won over 1½m; 2 lengths second of 11 to Miami Star in maiden
race at Edinburgh in November; will probably stay beyond 1m. *Sir Mark Prescott.*

INGLYFACH 2 ch.f. Whistlefield 118–Carningly (King's Leap 111) (1983 9g 8.2s —
5g) Apr 28; neat filly; first foal; dam showed no ability; well beaten in autumn
maiden events, twice last. *M. Eckley.*

INLANDER 2 b.c. Ile de Bourbon 133–Blissful Evening §§ (Blakeney 126) (1983 — p
7g) Mar 24; smallish, fair sort; first foal; dam, closely related to high-class 1¼m
horse Rarity, became temperamental; 14/1, 13 lengths fifth of 18 to Bold Patriach
in maiden race at Leicester in October; will be much better suited by longer
distances; sure to improve. *H. Candy.*

INNAMORATO (USA) 2 ch.c. Blushing Groom 131–Out Draw (Speak John) 107 p
(1983 6f² 6fg* 6s*) Apr 27; $90,000Y; rather leggy, fair sort; half-brother to 4
winners, including Miss Magnetic (by Nodouble), a smart stakes winner at up to
9f; dam won at up to 1m; landed the odds in 2 races in October, beating Heraldry
easily by 3 lengths in maiden at Brighton and having his 5 opponents well strung
out in minor event at Leicester; will be suited by 7f and 1m; promises to develop
into a smart 3-y-o. *H. Cecil.*

INNOCENT MAID 2 b.f. Reform 132–Wedding Day (Tambourine II 133) (1983 78
5fg 5fg² 6g² 6fg) Apr 29; IR 6,000F; compact filly; none too good a mover;
half-sister to Irish 7f and 1¼m winner Registry (by Sharpen Up); dam, half-sister to
1000 Guineas and Oaks winner Never Too Late II, won over 10.5f in France;
second in maiden races at Chester in August and Hamilton in September; will be
much better suited by 7f+; acts on a firm surface; should win in the North. *P.
Rohan.*

IN RHYTHM 6 ch.h. Gay Fandango 132–Procession 118 (Sovereign Path 125) 80
(1982 6d⁴ 6f² 7f 7fg 6g* 6g* 6fg² 6fg³ 7fg 6g² 6fg³ 7s 6s² 1983 6s³ 6v 6g* 6fg* 6f²
6fg³ 6d 6s 6f) strong horse; won handicaps at Ayr in May and Hamilton in June;
best at 6f; acts on any going; good mount for an apprentice; blinkered last 3 starts
in 1981. *P. Makin.*

INSET LADY 2 b.f. Hittite Glory 125–Miss Jack 97 (Pampered King 121) (1983 82
7f³ 6f* 7fg 7f³ 7d 8d 6g³ 6fg) Feb 19; 1,600Y; close-coupled filly; half-sister to 2
winners, including useful stayer Nopac (by King's Leap); dam, sister to very
smart David Jack, won at up to 2¼m; won 18-runner maiden race at Folkestone in
August; third subsequently in minor event at Chepstow and 19-runner nursery
(running on strongly after being outpaced) at Leicester; gives impression 7f is her
trip. *M. Ryan.*

INSPIRED 3 ch.g. Star Appeal 133–Easy Swinger (Swing Easy 126) (1982 6f 7f³ 53
7f 7g⁴ 1983 12g 11v 12f 16g 13fg 13.8f⁴ 10f 10g³ 10g) compact gelding; plater;
probably stays 1¾m; blinkered second start; trained by P. Kelleway until after
sixth outing; sold 1,000 gns Ascot October Sales. *J. Jenkins.*

INSPIRE (USA) 2 b.f. Tell–Colnesian (Boldnesian) (1983 6g² 6f* 7fg) Feb 18; 90 +
rangy filly; half-sister to American 3-y-o Casianne (by Talk About Luck); dam won 3
sprint claiming races; sweating quite badly, put up quite an impressive display in
13-runner maiden race at Goodwood in July, being well in command 2f out and
winning easing up by 1½ lengths from Tapaculo; 7/2, weakened from distance, after
pulling hard, when seventh of 8 in Waterford Candelabra Stakes on same course the
following month; found to be lame on her return home, and might not have been at
her best; should stay 7f (sire won 1¼m Hollywood Derby); probably better than we
are able to rate her. *I. Balding.*

INSULAR 3 b.g. Moulton 128–Pas de Deux 80 (Nijinsky 138) (1982 NR 1983 10v 100
11.5fg² 11f² 12g* 13.1fg* 14fg* 13.3d*) big, well-made gelding; good walker; first
foal; dam, daughter of very smart Example, won over 1¼m; in good form in
autumn and won 4 races in a row, maiden event at Goodwood, minor event at
Bath, apprentice event at Newmarket and handicap at Newbury; gave a really
genuine performance when holding on by a length from Paris North on last-named
occasion, in October; runs like a horse who'll stay further than 1¾m; seems to act
on any going; a progressive sort who should win more races. *I. Balding.*

INTENSE (FR) 6 gr.m. Sassafras 135–Dancing Sher (Dancer's Image) (1982 NR 50
1983 8f² 10.2fg) second in seller at Warwick in August; stays 1m. *R. Thompson.*

INTERCO (USA) 2 ch.c. Intrepid Hero–Yale Coed (Majestic Prince) (1982 116
5.5s* 7g³ 5.5g 7g 8fg³ 5g² 7f⁴ 7.5v⁴ 1983 including 8s* 8v³ 9f² 9f* 9s* 9d*)
$200,000Y; attractive colt; third foal; half-brother to a winner in USA by Triple
Bend; dam, very useful winner at up to 6f at 2 yrs in USA, is granddaughter of

398

outstanding broodmare Exclusive; very useful performer as a 2-y-o; ran only twice in France in 1983, beating Bal des Fees readily by 1½ lengths when favourite for 90,000 francs race at Saint-Cloud in May and finishing most creditable ¾-length third of 7 behind Aragon in Prix de la Jonchere at Longchamp later in month; subsequently did very well in USA, finishing ¾-length second to Royal Heroine in Hollywood Derby (Div 1) and winning 4 races, including Spence Bay Stakes, Bay Meadows Handicap and Bay Meadows Derby; suited by 9f; acts on any going. *F. Boutin, France.*

IN THE BREEZE (FR) 2 ch.c. Mount Hagen 126–Starval (Val de Loir 133) (1983 6f3) Feb 9; fifth reported foal; half-brother to French 3-y-o By The River (by Riverman), successful over 5.5f and 1m; dam won poor race over 1m at 4 yrs in France; unquoted and blinkered, staying-on 3¼ lengths third of 13 to Cutting Wind in maiden race at Yarmouth in August; will be better suited by 7f+. *M. Albina.* **83 p**

IN THE PINK 2 b.f. Tickled Pink 114–American Playgirl (Knightly Manner) (1983 5g3 5f 5.1f 5f) May 3; 300Y; small filly; no worthwhile form in sellers; fell second outing; blinkered final start; sold 300 gns Doncaster August Sales. *W. Stubbs.* **–**

IN TOP FORM 4 br.f. Lochnager 132–Lady Jester 108 (Bleep-Bleep 134) (1982 5f 1983 6v4 5g 6v 6d 6fg) lengthy filly; little worthwhile form; best run at 6f on heavy going; sweated up badly third outing; trained by R. Boss first start. *A. Hide.* **–**

INTO THE FIRE 2 b.f. Dominion 123–Pollinella 108 (Charlottown 127) (1983 6f 7f 7.6d) Mar 25; good-topped filly; half-sister to a minor winner; dam stayed 1½m; quite a moderate maiden; best effort on second outing; will be suited by 1m+. *D. Elsworth.* **73**

INT' SIN BIN 4 b.g. Pauper–Kilvellane Cherry (Raise You Ten 125) (1982 NR 1983 12f4) smallish gelding; first foal; dam never ran; poor last of 4 in minor event at Pontefract in July. *Mrs C. Lloyd-Jones.* **–**

INUVIK 3 b.c. Ashmore 125–Star Relation (Star Gazer 123) (1982 7g 7fg* 8s 1983 10v2 10fg4 10f3) attractive, shapely colt; good walker; has a nice, easy action; in frame in handicaps at Ayr, Sandown and Nottingham in first half of season; stays 1¼m; seems to act on any going; sent to USA. *B. Hills.* **76**

INVERSALE 3 b.g. Touch Paper 113–Hello Amy 70 (Forlorn River 124) (1982 5s4 5f3 6f 7fg 6g 1983 8.5d 7fg 8f4) quite attractive gelding; good walker; plater; not certain to stay beyond sprint distances; sometimes blinkered. *A. Jarvis.* **–**

INVINCIBLE PINK 2 ch.g. Tickled Pink 114–Solsbury Hill (Firestreak 125) (1983 7fg 8d 8f) Apr 21; workmanlike gelding; first foal; dam poor maiden; little worthwhile form in autumn maiden events. *R. Laing.* **–**

INVINCIBLE SHADOW 3 b.f. Abwah 118–Pardilly 71 (Pardao 120) (1982 5fg 7g 8s 10s 1983 10s 12s 12s 17v 10fg) tall, strong, close-coupled filly; behind in varied company; has twice worn blinkers; trained by D. Sasse until after fourth start. *B. McMahon.* **–**

INYATI 3 ch.f. Brigadier Gerard 144–Wind Break 81 (Borealis) (1982 NR 1983 9f3 10f 12f2 12g2 12.2g 12g) half-sister to several minor winners; dam 2-y-o 7f winner; placed in varied races, including an apprentice event; rather disappointing last 2 starts (blinkered final outing); suited by 1½m. *A. Hide.* **74**

IOKASTI 2 ch.f. Imperial Fling 116–Turnbeam (Hornbeam 130) (1983 6g 6f 6fg 7g) May 5; half-sister to several winners, including very useful sprinter Oscilight (by Swing Easy); dam won at 2 yrs in Sweden; soundly beaten in maiden and minor events; likely to need further; off course 3 months after second start. *J. Dunlop.* **–**

IOWA 4 br.c. So Blessed 130–Montana (Mossborough 126) (1982 8s* 9f 8f 10f2 9g4 10d3 11s4 1983 8v2 8g 8g2 8g 10s) leggy, narrow colt; second in handicaps at Newcastle in April and Doncaster (valuable seller) in September; suited by 1¼m; acts on any going; sold to C. Wildman 3,600 gns Doncaster November Sales. *C. Thornton.* **66**

IQUACU 5 b.g. Porto Bello 118–Finest View 66 (Bold Lad, Ire 133) (1982 NR 1983 6s 8d 7s 7s) poor performer; acted on a firm and a soft surface; blinkered final start; bandaged in front in 1983; dead. *P. Cundell.* **–**

IRAN FLYER 2 br.f. Persian Bold 123–Route Royale (Roi Soleil 125) (1983 5v 5s 6f 5fg 6fg*) Mar 9; IR 7,600Y; good-topped filly; sister to Irish 3-y-o 1m and 1¼m winner Persian Royale and half-sister to 1979 2-y-o 6f winner Another Signcentre (by Pitskelly); dam never ran; second favourite, made virtually all in 15-runner seller (bought in 2,600 gns) at Lingfield in August; should stay 1m; wears blinkers. *B. Swift.* **64**

IRENE'S PRIDE 3 b.f. The Brianstan 128–Zip Flip (Bleep-Bleep 134) (1982 5g **33**
5f⁴ 5f⁴ 5.8f* 5g⁴ 6fg 6g³ 8.2g 6s 1983 7g 8s³ 7v 8.2d 7d 7fg 7f 8fg 8g⁴ 7f 8f² 7g
7fg) lightly-made filly; plater; stays 1m; acts on any going; often apprentice ridden;
sometimes blinkered; sold 1,000 gns Newmarket Autumn Sales. *A. Bailey.*

IRISH CAVALIER (USA) 3 br.c. Irish Castle–Faithful Voyage (Admiral's
Voyage) (1982 NR 1983 7d 12f 10d 7g 8g) $75,000Y; strong, useful-looking colt;
brother to a minor winner and half-brother to 3 winners, including stakes winner
Rambling Native (by Native Royalty); dam won over 2f and 4f; behind in varied
company; seems headstrong; sold out of M. Stoute's stable 1,200 gns Newmarket
July Sales after first outing. *D. Morrill.*

IRISH CLIPPER 3 b.f. Windjammer (USA)–Rachel Rose (King's Company 124) **65**
(1982 5d 1983 6v⁴ 5s² 7d² 6fg³ 8fg³ 8fg) good sort; quite a moderate maiden;
stays 1m; yet to race on really firm ground, but acts on any other; sold 2,300 gns
Ascot December Sales. *P. Cole.*

IRISH CORN 3 b.f. Oats 126–Belleek (Never Say Die 137) (1982 8fg 1983 12g
12.2f 16d) of little account; trained part of season by P. Haslam; sold 480 gns Ascot
November Sales. *P. Burgoyne.*

IRISH GUEST 2 b.g. Northern Guest–Laikipia 89 (St Paddy 133) (1983 6g 6fg –
6f) Mar 18; IR 7,000F, IR 8,000Y; robust, quite attractive gelding; seventh
produce; dam placed at up to 7f; sire unraced brother to Try My Best; well beaten
in varied company; not raced after July; blinkered final outing. *P. Mitchell.*

IRISH PIPER 2 b.f. Homing 130–Rickadoo 85 (Round Table) (1983 6g⁴ 7g*) **84**
Mar 30; third foal; dam, sister to smart middle-distance performer Corby, won 4
races from 11f to 13.1f; ran on well to lead close home when beating Flingamus ½
length in maiden race at Naas in September; had started favourite for a similar
event at the Curragh the previous month; will be suited by 1¼m. *D. O'Brien,
Ireland.*

IRISH SEA 2 b.f. Irish River 131–Sea Venture 98 (Diatome 132) (1983 6fg 7.6d³) **66**p
Mar 18; well-made filly; half-sister to 3 winners, including useful French 1980 2-y-o
6f winner Grecian Sea (by Homeric) and French 10.5f winner Venture To Say (by
Luthier); dam, from same family as Reform, won over 6f at 2 yrs and stayed 1¼m;
improved a good deal on first effort when 6 lengths third of 20 to Katies in maiden
race at Lingfield in October; will stay 1m. *I. Balding.*

IRISH WILLIAMS 3 ch.g. Shiny Tenth 120–Tweetie Pie (Falcon 131) (1982 6g **54**
1983 8d 7v² 8g 7d 8h) big, lengthy, light-framed gelding; close second in seller at
Kempton in May; should stay 1m; met difficulties in running fourth start and his
performance can be ignored. *D. Marks.*

IRON LEADER (USA) 3 b.c. Mr Leader–Iron Hinge (Iron Ruler) (1982 7fg **102**
7fg³ 6d* 7d 1983 9s³ 7s* 7s⁴ 10s² 10v 8s* 8fg 8f) $31,000Y; second foal;
half-brother to a minor winner by Executioner; dam lightly-raced half-sister to Belmont
Stakes winner Pass Catcher; won Madrid Extended Handicap at the Curragh in
April and 5-runner Kilfrush What A Guest Stakes at Phoenix Park in June, in latter
event wearing down Beaudelaire to win by a head; in frame in between in H.M.
Hartigan Tetrarch Stakes at the Curragh (about 5 lengths fourth of 6 to Salmon
Leap) and handicap at Leopardstown (beaten a short head by Gods Will); had
stiffish task and was beaten over 13 lengths when sixth of 10 behind Valiyar in
Queen Anne Stakes at Royal Ascot on penultimate start; stays 1¼m; suited by
some give in the ground. *D. K. Weld, Ireland.*

ISHKOMANN 4 b.g. Faunus–Irova (Iron Liege) (1982 10s 9g 11.7f⁴ 11.7f⁴ 11.7f*
16h 12d³ 12g³ 12f³ 10.1d 12fg 11.7s 13.8d⁴ 1983 12s) strong gelding; stays 13f;
seems to act on any going. *J. Spearing.*

ISLAND HOPPER 2 b.g. Captain James 123–Pagan Times 72 (Native Prince) –
(1983 5f 7d) May 14; fourth living produce; dam lightly raced; second favourite,
prominent to past halfway when ninth of 12 to Bold Bee in seller at Windsor in
August (trained by D. Gandolfo at time); unquoted when last of 12 in minor event at
Limerick Junction in October. *P. Doyle, Ireland.*

ISLAND MILL 2 b.f. Mill Reef 141–Siliciana 113 (Silly Season 127) (1983 6g 7f⁴ **79**
7.6fg³ 7s) Feb 11; quite attractive, well-made filly; good walker; sister to 1979
2-y-o 7f winner Cabana and half-sister to 2 winners, including useful 7f and 11f
winner Junta (by Brigadier Gerard); dam won 1973 Cambridgeshire; beaten only 2
lengths, despite being hampered, when third of 16 to Judex in maiden race at
Lingfield in October, best effort; disappointing favourite in similar event at
Leicester later in month; will stay at least 1¼m; acts on firm going. *I. Balding.*

ISLAND SMILE (FR) 2 br.f. Ile de Bourbon 133–Princesse Smile 99 (Balidar **105**
133) (1983 7fg* 6fg) rangy filly; third live foal (second to Northern Hemisphere

time); half-sister to minor French 3-y-o 1¼m winner Somerford (by Solinus); dam, sister to 2000 Guineas winner Bolkonski, won 5 times at up to 9f in Italy; justified favouritism in excellent style in 8-runner newcomers race at Chantilly in July, winning by 3 lengths from Boldtender after being in front rank throughout; 15/2, probably found 6f too sharp when eleventh of 12 to Desirable in William Hill Cheveley Park Stakes at Newmarket in September; should stay 1¼m. *F. Boutin, France.*

ISLAND WALK 5 b.m. Palm Track 122–Ladyfold 60 (Never Dwell 89) (1982 6s* 6f⁴ 6d 6fg 8f 8.2s 1983 8v³ 8.2v² 8fg⁴ 7f 6f) small mare; plater; stays 1m well; probably acts on any going; has sweated up; sold to M. McCausland 680 gns Doncaster November Sales. *W. Haigh.*   42

ISMORE (USA) 3 b.c. Libra's Rib 121–Lesse (Noblesse Oblige 99) (1982 5fg 6f 6f 7f 5fg³ 5g* 5g⁴ 5g 6s² 7v³ 1983 8d 8v 6s³ 6f 6fg 5fg* 6f 5f³ 5.3f³ 6f³ 6f 5.6fg² 6s 5fg) compact, sturdy colt; made all in handicap at Chester in July and was placed several times afterwards; ideally suited by 5f on top-of-the-ground, but stays further and acts on any going; good mount for an apprentice; has run well in blinkers; has worn a small bandage on off-hind; stumbled and unseated rider start seventh outing. *N. Guest.*   88

ISOLA VERDE 2 br.c. Ile de Bourbon 133–Green Glade (Correspondent) (1983 8fg⁴) Apr 28; 40,000Y; unfurnished, fair sort; good mover; half-brother to several winners, including useful 1980 staying 2-y-o Wicked Will (by Mill Reef), subsequently a stakes-placed winner at up to 13f in USA; dam smart stakes winner at up to 9f in USA; 25/1, ran on nicely without rider resorting to whip when 3 lengths fourth of 7 to Sassagrass in slowly-run £3,200 event at Newmarket in October; sure to leave this form behind over longer distances. *M. Jarvis.*   85 p

ISOM DART (USA) 4 b.c. Bold Forbes–Shellshock 110 (Salvo 129) (1982 12f 11.7f 14g² 1983 12g) neat, well-made, attractive colt; good walker; quite modest at his best; ran abysmally in blinkers only start at 4yrs in May; stays 1¼m. *T. Hallett.*   –

ISPAHAN 2 gr.f. Rusticaro 124–Royal Danseuse 111 (Prince Chevalier) (1982 6f 6fg* 6d 6g) May 17; IR 62,000Y; quite well-made filly; half-sister to numerous winners, including smart middle-distance performer Bog Road (by Busted) and very useful Irish sprinter Royal Hobbit (by Habitat); dam won Irish 1000 Guineas; won 19-runner minor event at Newmarket in August; well beaten in Moyglare Stud Stakes at the Curragh the following month and £9,100 nursery at York in October; should be suited by longer distances. *J. Dunlop.*   85

ITALIAN SECRET 2 ch.f. Most Secret 119–Grecian Cloud 76 (Galivanter 131) (1983 5fg⁴ 5f* 6f 5fg* 5d) Apr 18; leggy filly; fourth foal; half-sister to a winning plater; dam won 7f seller at 2 yrs and stayed 13f; won maiden race (on a disqualification) at Wolverhampton in August and 5-runner nursery at Beverley in September; speedy, and seems best at 5f; acts on firm going. *B. McMahon.*   83

ITALIAN SUNRISE 3 b.g. The Brianstan 128–Roman Dawn 87 (Neron 121) (1982 7.6v 8s 8s 1983 10fg 14f³ 14g*) well-made, good sort; having first outing for new trainer when getting up on line to beat Childown a head in maiden race at Yarmouth in September; suited by 1¾m and will probably stay further; formerly trained by C. Horgan. *D. Oughton.*   83

IT'M FOR GALA 2 ch.c. Most Secret 119–Straight Lemon (Straight Lad 110) (1983 5d 5d⁴ 6g 7f 8f 6s 6fg) May 25; 1,100Y; compact colt; third reported foal; dam winning hurdler; quite a modest maiden; stays 6f; acts on soft going and a firm surface. *N. Bycroft.*   68

IT'S A PLEASURE 3 gr.f. Runnymede 123–Ginger Puss (Worden II 129) (1982 5fg 5fg 5d² 5f² 5f 5fg² 5f³ 5s³ 5v³ 1983 5s³ 6s⁴ 5s 6g 5fg² 6fg² 6f 5g² 6fg* 6fg 6g) compact filly; good walker; placed on numerous occasions before beating Louisa Anne by 1½ lengths in 26-runner maiden race at Nottingham in September; ran well 2 days later; gave impression she didn't last 6f out in testing conditions second start; acts on any going; consistent. *W. Wightman.*   82

IT'S FOR SURE 3 br.f. Ardoon 124–Schull (Yorick II 127) (1982 5g 5f⁴ 5s 1983 5fg 5g) quite attractive filly; good walker; little worthwhile form; has been tried in blinkers. *B. Gubby.*   –

IT'S FOR YOU 3 gr.g. Town Crier 119–Flora Day 92 (Floribunda 136) (1982 5fg⁴ 6f 6g² 6g 1983 8g 10.1d 6fg 7f) close-coupled, fair sort; no form in 1983; should stay beyond 6f; has worn blinkers. *B. Gubby.*   –

IT'S HEAVEN 3 b.f. African Sky 124–Coumfea (Gulf Pearl 117) (1982 5g 5fg⁴ 6f³ 6g 1983 6f 5f⁴ 6h 6fg 6fg 6g 6g 6fg) narrow, unimpressive filly; in frame in maiden races; suited by 6f; sometimes sweats up. *R. Hollinshead.*   –

IT'S KELLY 3 b.g. Pitskelly 122–Reelin Star (Star Gazer 123) (1982 5fg⁴ 5fg 5f⁴ **78**
1983 6s² 6s⁴ 7d² 7fg 7f 8.3fg³ 8.3f² 8g 10g 8.2g* 8d 8fg) smallish, useful-looking
gelding; good walker; placed in several handicaps before winning maiden race at
Haydock in October; seems to stay 1¼m; seems to act on any going; tends to start
rather slowly. *G. Balding.*

IT'S THE BEST 2 b.f. Artaius 129–Be Best (Santa Claus 133) (1983 5v 5s 5fg⁴ **69**
7f 6f³ 7fg² 8s 6fg) Apr 26; 1,800Y; smallish filly; half-sister to minor French 1½m
winner Be A Lady (by Roi Dagobert); dam, daughter of Gimcrack and Champagne
Stakes winner Be Careful, won small 9f race in France; placed in 2 nurseries in the
Midlands in August; should stay at least 1¼m; seems best on firm ground; moved
badly to start final outing; not particularly consistent. *R. Hollinshead.*

IVANO (CAN) 4 ch.c. Snow Knight 125–Smiling Jacqueline (Hilarious) (1982 **124**
9fg* 10.4fg* 12fg³ 8fg³ 1983 9d* 10v* 10d² 8fg⁴)
Anyone bold enough to have forecast in March that just four of Henry Cecil's
fifty or so three-year-olds and upwards would win pattern races during 1983 would
probably have been laughed out of court since the stable contained such as Simply
Great, Dunbeath, Diesis, Polished Silver and The Fort, each of whom was
expected to make his presence felt in top company. In the event none of these won
any type of race and it was left to Ivano, John French, Salieri and Valiyar to carry
the flag successfully for the stable in pattern events with only Ivano and Salieri
winning more than one.
As in 1982 when he ran only four times Ivano had a relatively light season as a
four-year-old and wasn't seen out after Royal Ascot. In that time he collected the
Earl of Sefton Stakes at Newmarket and the Westbury Stakes at Sandown, in the
former gaining one of the easiest wins all year by an older horse in a pattern race.
Looking hard and well although it was his first outing for nearly ten months, Ivano
was ridden confidently, cruising to the front over a quarter of a mile out and rapidly
drawing clear to account for the useful Bali Dancer by six lengths easing up with the
backward favourite Peacetime third. In retrospect the form of the Earl of Sefton
probably did not amount to much since Bali Dancer subsequently failed to make the
frame in five starts, yet there was no getting away from the style of Ivano's win and
ten days later he started at odds on to add the Westbury to his tally. The conditions
at Sandown were among the worst for any flat racing in 1983 and Piggott gave Ivano
with a view to giving him as easy a race as possible. Never far behind, Ivano came
through smoothly in the straight, looked likely to hack up two furlongs from home
but had to be rousted in the end to hold the persistent challenge of Rocamadour
who got to within a neck of him at the distance before going down by two and a half
lengths. The remainder, headed by Jalmood, were well strung out behind.
The Brigadier Gerard Stakes, run over the same course and distance as the
Westbury, had a stronger field than the latter race but Ivano again started at odds
on. Giving weight to all the nine other runners apart from Commodore Blake he
faced a particularly stiff task and in running second to Stanerra, conceding her 9 lb,
he ran his best race to date. Though not in quite the form she was to show later the
Stanerra who ran in the Brigadier Gerard was a very different mare from the one

Earl of Sefton Stakes, Newmarket—Ivano races clear of Bali Dancer and Peacetime

Mr C. d'Alessio's "Ivano"

who had run last in the Earl of Sefton. Held up as usual, Ivano followed her through in the straight and got to within a length of her outside the distance before failing to make any further progress; at the line he was still a length behind, three quarters of a length ahead of Erin's Hope who had given Salmon Leap's supporters a fright in the Nijinsky Stakes.

Cecil left it to Sabre Dance, fourth in the Brigadier Gerard, to oppose Stanerra in the mile-and-a-quarter Prince of Wales's Stakes at Royal Ascot, preferring to run Ivano over a mile in the Queen Anne Stakes. We think it would have been wiser to have run Ivano over the longer trip. His career had already shown that a mile on fast ground was too sharp for him—he hardly saw the way Dara Monarch went in the previous year's St James's Palace Stakes—and it was no surprise to see his struggling to go the pace in the Queen Anne. The writing was on the wall with two furlongs left, for Ivano was already under pressure, and he eventually came home fourth, ten lengths behind his stable-companion Valiyar. Ivano did not race again and in September came the news that he had been sent to Italy to be trained by Botti.

Ivano (Can) (ch.c. 1979)	Snow Knight (ch 1971)	Firestreak (br 1956)	Pardal Hot Spell
		Snow Blossom (br 1957)	Flush Royal Ariana
	Smiling Jacqueline (b 1969)	Hilarious (b 1950)	Bimelech Laughter
		Fulfiliole (ch 1960)	Beau Gar Filiole

Ivano, an attractive colt who is suited by middle distances and acts well on soft ground, cost 100,000 dollars at the Fasig-Tipton Kentucky Fall Preferred Yearling Sale. He is the first foal of Smiling Jacqueline, successful nine times from

403

forty-three starts at up to a mile and a quarter in America and one of eight winners out of Fulfiliole. Fulfiliole won a small race in the States and came from the family of the top 1952 Italian three-year-old filly Filatrice and the highly successful Australian stallion Le Filou. *H. Cecil.*

IVELOSTMYWAY 3 br.f. Relko 136–Lost Path (Sovereign Path 125) (1982 NR 82 1983 12.2f 14f⁴ 14f* 14f* 14fg*) 6,400F, 14,000Y; rangy filly; half-sister to several winners abroad; dam of little account; successful in maiden event and ladies race at Yarmouth and apprentice handicap at Goodwood in August; suffered a hairline fracture of a pastern when beating Kate Kimberley narrowly in last-named, but is said to have made a full recovery and remains in training; will stay 2m; acts on firm going. *L. Cumani.*

IVER SAGA 3 ch.f. Sagaro 133–Florrie Ford 79 (Kelly 122) (1982 7d² 6s 1983 – 10.1s 11.5fg 12f 12g 11s) sparely-made filly; well beaten in 1983, including in sellers; should stay 1¼m+; retained 400 gns Ascot July Sales. *R. Williams.*

IVOR STAR (USA) 3 b.g. Sir Ivor 135–Oraza (Zank) (1982 NR 1983 14g) – $30,000F, 13,500Y; fourth foal; half-brother to 3 winners, including fairly useful 1m and 1½m winner Countess Palotta (by Brigadier Gerard); dam won German 1,000 Guineas and Oaks; 50/1, last of 19 behind Childown in minor race at Sandown in October. *D. Oughton.*

IVY THORNE 4 b.f. Relko 136–Calling The Tune 94 (Tudor Melody 129) (1982 43 10h 14fg 14g 9v³ 10g 1983 12.3v 14fg 12fg 12f⁴ 14f 18f 15g* 13.8g) strong, useful-looking filly; made all to win handicap at Edinburgh in September; stays well; acts on firm going; suitable mount for an inexperienced rider; has run respectably when sweating up badly. *A. Hide.*

J

JABAL TARIK (FR) 3 ch.c. Riverman 131–Caretta (Caro 133) (1982 8g² 9s² 109 8v² 1983 12v³ 12s* 12d⁴ 12f³ 12.5g 12.5fg⁴) 290,000Y; second reported foal; half-brother to very smart French middle-distance colt Al Nasr (by Lyphard); dam, minor winner over 9.5f and 11f in France, is half-sister to smart French animals Kebah and L'Ensorceleur and to very speedy Klaizia; looked fortunate winner of 5-runner maiden race at Longchamp in April, getting home by 2 lengths from Sagace who swerved right across course when having race at his mercy; in frame most other outings, including when 3½ lengths third of 6 behind Solford in Prix du Lys at Chantilly in June; suited by 1½m; acts on any going; wears blinkers. *J. de Chevigny, France.*

JABARABA (USA) 2 b.c. Raja Baba–Time to Step (Time Tested) (1983 6f 7fg 109 6f 7fg³ 6fg⁴ 7fg* 7g² 7f* 7fg*) Mar 15; $160,000Y; strong, useful-looking colt; third foal; half-brother to minor winners by Hempen and Navajo; dam, placed twice from 12 starts, is sister to very useful sprinter Mary Dugan; not of much account early on (beat only 2 home in 15-runner maiden at Yarmouth in July on first outing), but really came good at the back-end, winning maiden race at Redcar, minor event at Leicester and nursery at Doncaster; put up plucky and very useful display at Doncaster, pegging back Track Deal close home to win by a length with majority of a big field well beaten off; will be suited by 1m; acts on firm going; genuine. *F. Durr.*

JABBOUR 3 b.c. Quiet Fling 124–Caught In The Rye 97 (Manacle 123) (1982 – NR 1983 10f 16g) 18,000Y; big colt; not the best of movers; third foal; half-brother to fair sprinters Sanjarida (by Sandford Lad) and Curve the Wind (by Windjammer); dam won 3 times over sprint distances at 2 yrs; stayed on a bit in closing stages when ninth of 15 behind Underbid in maiden race at Pontefract in June, first outing and better effort; not sure to stay 2m. *P. Haslam.*

JACAJANDA 2 ch.f. Porto Bello 118–Pato Bravo 53 (Willipeg 112) (1983 6fg 5f) – Jan 22; first foal; dam won 5f seller; in rear in August in seller (last of 17) at Windsor and minor event at Warwick; sold 310 gns Ascot October Sales. *J. Holt.*

JACINTO TIMES (USA) 4 b.g. Olden Times–Jacinto Rose (Jacinto) (1982 – 8fg² 9.4fg² 10g* 10fg⁴ 12.3d 11.5g 1983 10v 11g 12fg 9g 10fg 12.2g 10s 11fg⁴) lengthy gelding; poor handicapper; stays 11f; ran deplorably first outing and is possibly unsuited by heavy ground; has twice been blinkered. *Mrs M. Nesbitt.*

JACKDAW (USA) 3 b.c. Crow 134–Lycabette 64 (Lyphard 132) (1982 6fg 7d² 91 1983 8s³ 10.5s 12d 11g 12f⁴ 14d 14f² 14.7f⁴ 14.7fg² 14d² 14fg 12fg²) small, quite attractive colt; in frame in maiden and minor races and a handicap, running well when second to Neorion at Haydock and Redcar in September and to Valuable

Witness at York and Sikorsky at Newmarket in October; also ran moderately in weaker company however and isn't one to rely on; suited by 1¾m; acts on any going. *R. Hollinshead.*

JACK GAGGER 2 ch.c. On Your Mark 125–Lake Constance 85 (Star Gazer 74 123) (1983 5s³ 5v 5v* 5s³) Mar 24; IR 6,000F, IR 3,400Y; strong, compact colt; has a sharp action; half-brother to 3 winners, including 3-y-o 6f winner Catcher In The Rye (by Tudor Music); dam best at sprint distances; easily justified heavy backing in valuable seller at Newbury in May, and was made favourite in 8,000 gns; seen only once afterwards (poor third in small race at Chepstow just over 2 weeks later) and was then exported to Algeria; raced only on very soft going. *J. Sutcliffe.*

JACKIE BERRY 2 ch.f. Connaught 130–Chokeberry (Crepello 136) (1983 7g⁴ 97 6d³ 8.5g* 7d³) Apr 26; 6,200Y; half-sister to 3-y-o Spindle Berry (by Dance In Time), a fairly useful 5f winner at 2 yrs; dam unraced sister to smart 1¼m filly Cranberry Sauce; favourite when winning 16-runner maiden race at Gowran Park in September by 4 lengths from Lady's Guest; promoted to third place after finishing 3¼ lengths fourth of 9 to Western Symphony in Larkspur Stakes at Leopardstown the following month; will stay 1¼m; missed break second outing. *J. Bolger, Ireland.*

JACK RAMSEY 3 b.c. Tudor Rhythm 112–Top Soprano 89 (High Top 131) (1982 53 6g 1983 7v³ 8f 11.7h 8f 10g³ 10fg²) lengthy, good-topped, short-legged colt; plater; stays 1¼m; blinkered fifth outing. *M. McCormack.*

JACKS FOLLEY 2 b. or br.f. Netherkelly 112–Mandy's Melody (Highland – Melody 122) (1983 5v 6fg 8g) Mar 27; leggy, narrow filly; sister to a poor animal and half-sister to a winning hurdler; dam never ran; poor form in sellers. *J. Harris.*

JACK TAR 2 b.c. Stanford 121§–Into Harbour (Right Tack 131) (1983 5s³ 5s³ 6s³ 92 6g* 6fg 6fg* 6f* 6f 5h⁴) Mar 28; IR 10,000Y; deep-girthed, quite attractive colt; third foal; dam ran only 3 times; won 22-runner maiden race at Redcar in May and weakly-contested minor events at Leicester and Catterick 2 months later; not raced after August; suited by 6f; seems to act on any going; tough and consistent. *K. Brassey.*

JACORAN 2 ch.c. Sweet Revenge 129–Penny Levy 69 (Levmoss 133) (1983 5v³ 83 5d² 5d* 5f² 7f² 7d 6f 6fg* 6g) Mar 12; 550Y; small colt; second foal; dam won over 1m; won 17-runner maiden auction event at Redcar in May and £4,500 nursery (on disqualification of neck winner Manerly) on same course in September; stays 7f; acts on any going. *E. Eldin.*

JACQUEMONTII 3 ch.g. Gay Fandango 132–Jemake 85 (High Treason 126) – (1982 NR 1983 8v) 5,000F; half-brother to fairly useful 5f to 1¼m winner Court Lane (by Mandamus) and a winner in France; dam stayed 7f; collapsed when tailed off in maiden race at Warwick in May; dead. *W. Holden.*

JADE RING 4 b.f. Auction Ring 123–Msida (Majority Blue 126) (1982 6f² 5g 7f² 83 7.2f³ 7d* 7g 1983 7s* 8d⁴ 8f 10f 8f⁴ 7.3g² 7fg* 7fg 7f⁴) neat, attractive filly; poor mover; won handicaps at Newmarket in May and September; stays 1m; acts on any going but seems best with some give underfoot. *J. Toller.*

JAI-ALAI 2 ch.g. Grundy 137–Blakewood 75 (Blakeney 126) (1983 8g) May 13; – 7,400Y; neat gelding; second foal; half-brother to 3-y-o Rose Glow (by Moulton), a winner at up to 1¼m; dam winning stayer; 25/1, in rear in minor event won by stable-companion Strathearn at Redcar in November; subsequently gelded. *J. Fitzgerald.*

JAIN 3 b.f. Condorcet–Surfacing (Worden II 129) (1982 5f 6fg 5f 5fg 5fg 7f 7.6v – 1983 12v 10fg 10.2f 10f 12f 10f 10d) small, lightly-made filly; plater; of little account. *P. Butler.*

JALEELA (USA) 2 b.f. Star de Naskra–Haneena 118 (Habitat 134) (1983 5s 6f 68 5fg⁴ 5g⁴ 6g) Mar 1; small, sturdy filly; half-sister to a poor animal by Chieftain; dam smart 2-y-o sprinter; plating-class maiden; off course 2 months before final start; stays 6f; wears blinkers; has little scope. *H. T. Jones.*

JALMOOD THE STONE (USA) 3 br.c. Herculean–Tish (Porterhouse) (1982 91 5fg² 6g* 7g⁴ 7g² 7d* 7.3g² 7g* 7d* 1983 8s 7g³ 7fg² 7fg³ 7.2g 7f*) fair sort; good walker; shows a bit of knee action; placed in 3 handicaps before landing the odds by a length from Gavo in apprentice event at Catterick in July on final start; suited by 7f; yet to show he can handle really soft going but acts on any other; genuine and consistent; tends to make running nowadays; good mount for an apprentice. *P. Cole.*

JALMOOD (USA) 4 b.c. Blushing Groom 131–Fast Ride (Sicambre 135) (1982 119 10f³ 12f* 12f 11g* 12f³ 14.6f 1983 10v³ 10fg* 12f 11f² 13.3f⁴ 12fg) well-made, attractive colt; did well physically over the winter; has a rather round action;

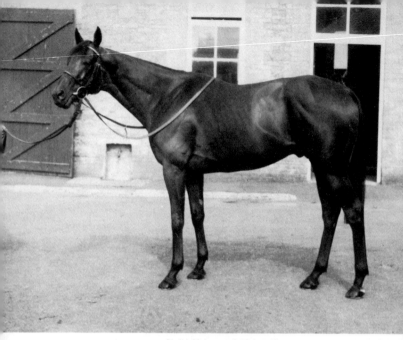

Sheikh Mohammed's "Jalmood"

very smart at 3 yrs when he won Highland Spring Derby Trial at Lingfield and
Mecca Bookmakers' Scottish Derby at Ayr; didn't strike top form in 1983 though
landed the odds by 1½ lengths from Bater in Premio Presidente della Repubblica at
Rome in May; also placed in Westbury Stakes at Sandown (third to Ivano) and
Grand Prix Prince Rose at Ostend (3 lengths second to Prima Voce); stayed 1½m;
acted on any going; genuine but ran some poor races in his career, occasionally
because of muscle trouble and once because of a broken blood vessel; slipped on a
bend when well beaten in Germany final start; standing at Egerton Stud,
Newmarket at £2,500 + £2,500 Oct 1st. *J. Dunlop.*

JAMAIS DERIERRE 2 ch.c. Monsanto 121–Boyne Saint (Saint Crespin III   **102**
132) (1983 6g⁴ 7f* 6g*) Mar 23; 4,400F, 4,600Y; half-brother to winners in
Belgium and Italy; dam won 3 times over 1½m in Ireland; won 15-runner maiden
race at Redcar in September and £2,900 event (beating Lak Lustre a length) at
York in October; bred to be suited by longer distances, and could prove a force to
be reckoned with in handicap company in the North at 1m to 1¼m. *C. Booth.*

JAMBALAYA 3 b.f. Amboise 113–Monkey Palm 111 (Royal Palm 131) (1982 NR   **–**
1983 12s 12s⁴ 16g³ 12g 17g) angular, deep-girthed filly; fourth living foal;
half-sister to very smart 6f and 7f winner Palm Track (by Track Spare) and a winner
in Austria; dam useful at up to 7f; staying maiden; ran moderately in blinkers fourth
start. *H. Candy.*

JAMEELAPI (USA) 2 ch.f. Blushing Groom 131–Itsamaza (Limit To Reason)   **94 +**
(1983 6h* 6f* 6fg) Mar 28; $675,000Y; big, workmanlike filly; second foal; dam,
successful at up to 1m, was at her best at 2yrs when smart stakes winner over 7f;
odds on when winning 10-runner maiden race at Nottingham in August in very good
style by 5 lengths from Arckaringa and 8-runner minor event at Epsom later in
month with minimum of fuss by 2 lengths from Nawal, leading over 1f out each

406

time; spread a plate before start and never got into race when 8 lengths eighth of 12 to Desirable in William Hill Cheveley Park Stakes at Newmarket in September; will be suited by further; almost certainly much better than we are able to rate her, and will probably make a very useful 3-y-o. *H. Cecil.*

JAMEENA 2 gr. f. Absalom 128–Ranikhet (Tanerko 134) (1983 5v 6s 6fg 6f² 6g 5f 65 7f 8d⁴ 8fg) Mar 22; 2,000F; half-sister to French 1½m and 1¾m winner Nanital (by Exbury); dam placed over 1¼m in France; in frame in seller and a maiden race at Brighton; suited by 1m; acts on firm going and a soft surface. *R. Simpson.*

JAMES EDWARD 2 b. g. Full of Hope 125–Sweet Rosina 61 (Sweet Revenge 56 129) (1983 5s⁴ 5v 5f* 6f 6g) Apr 22; leggy, narrow sort; second foal; dam in frame over 5f and 6f; changed hands 2,600 gns after winning 6-runner seller at Folkestone in July by ¾ length from Gentle Goddess; should be suited by 6f (had stiff tasks in nurseries over trip); acts on any going; gelded after final appearance; sent to Malaysia. *R. Howe.*

JAMESMEAD 2 ch. c. Import 127–Cathy Jane 86 (Lauso) (1983 10fg 10fg³) Apr 77 13; fair sort; half-brother to winning stayer Man On The Run (by Mandamus) and 6f to 1¼m winner Hot Trail (by Hot Spark); dam stayed extremely well; 7 lengths third of 24 behind Raami in minor event at Doncaster in November; shapes like a stayer. *A. Bailey.*

JAMESTINO 5 ch. g. Bustino 136–Miss Wrekin 97 (Pardao 120) (1982 12d² 13g⁴ 65 14.7f² 16g² 14g 14.6g 1983 12v³ 12d²) strong gelding; possibly doesn't truly stay 2m; evidently acts on any going; occasionally blinkered; has run creditably when sweating up; suitable mount for an inexperienced rider. *M. H. Easterby.*

JAMESTON 3 ch. c. Captain James 123–Copstown (Sovereign Gleam 117) (1982 78 NR 1983 5fg² 6f* 6fg⁴ 6g 7g² 7g) 7,400Y; useful-looking colt; first foal; dam poor half-sister to smart miler All Friends; won maiden race at Nottingham in July a shade comfortably; in frame at Brighton and Goodwood afterwards, making running when head second to Jhansi Ki Rani in a handicap on latter course; suited by 7f; well below best final start. *R. Armstrong.*

JAMES WINKLE 2 b. g. Wolver Hollow 126–Semantic 78 (Tudor Melody 129) 79 (1983 7fg² 7fg² 6f² 7g² 6fg) Mar 20; 1,900F; IR 51,000Y; sparely-made gelding; first produce; dam, half-sister to numerous winners, won twice over 1½m; placed in modest company at Newmarket, Ayr (twice) and Doncaster; better suited by 7f than 6f, and should stay 1¼m; acts on firm going; gelded after final outing; exported to Hong Kong. *J. Hindley.*

JAMRA (USA) 2 gr. f. Icecapade–Kankakee Miss (Better Bee) (1983 6fg 6f 5fg³ 82 5g* 6fg³) May 29; $90,000Y; quite attractive filly; sister to high-class sprinter/ miler Clever Trick and half-sister to 3-y-o Misinskie (by Nijinsky) and several winners, 2 of them of stakes; dam stakes-placed winner at up to 1m; won 14-runner minor event at Bath in October by 1½ lengths from Costalotta; creditable third of 17 in nursery at Nottingham later in month; stays 6f; yet to race on a soft surface. *C. Horgan.*

JANICOLANE 2 b. f. Tumble Wind–Holy Terror 68 (Divine Gift 127) (1983 5v 80 5g⁴ 5.8g* 5fg³ 5f 5fg) Apr 13; IR 3,600F, 1,000Y; good-bodied, useful sort; fifth foal; dam 2-y-o 5f winner; won maiden auction event at Bath in June; respectable third of 10 to Susa Steel in nursery at Lingfield the following month; stays 5.8f; acts on a firm surface; exported to Algeria. *R. Hannon.*

JANUS 5 ro. g. Ragstone 128–January (Sigebert 131) (1982 12fg⁴ 11.7fg 1983 77 12v* 12s³ 12s* 12v* 12v² 12d* 12g⁴ 10g) smallish, strong, workmanlike gelding; in fine form early in year and won handicaps at Folkestone in March (easily), Brighton and Goodwood in May and Epsom in June; beat Earl's Court unchallenged by 7 lengths in quite valuable event on last-named; effective from 1½m to 2m; revels in the mud; consistent; off course over 4 months before final start; useful hurdler. *Mrs N. Smith.*

JARALL 3 b. f. Le Johnstan 123–Compro 66 (Como 120) (1982 5fg 7g 7f 8.2fg – 8.2d 1983 12v 12.2g 8d) bad plater; has worn blinkers. *Mrs A. Cousins.*

JARB 3 gr. f. Bruni 132–Make Amends 74 (Tutankhamen) (1982 7fg 1983 9s⁴ – 11.7s 8v 16s 8f 10.1f) quite an attractive, deep-girthed filly; poor maiden; should stay at least 1½m; blinkered final start. *D. Wintle.*

JASIC 2 ch. c. No Loiterer 90–Sealady (Seaepic 100) (1983 5d* 5v 5f⁴ 6fg² 6f⁴ 6f 97 6g) Mar 13; sturdy, useful sort; keen walker; third foal; half-brother to fairly useful sprinter Singing Sailor (by Mansingh); dam never ran; won 23-runner

Mr D. D. Prenn's "Jasper"

maiden race at Thirsk in May at 33/1; showed quite useful form subsequently, on fourth appearance running Brega Boy to a neck in £3,900 race at Ayr in July; suited by 6f; possibly unsuited by heavy going; had stiff task when blinkered final outing but nonetheless ran poorly. *M. Tompkins.*

JASPER 3 ch.c. Busted 134–Riboreen 116 (Ribero 126) (1982 8s² 1983 12s* 12fg **116** 15g³ 12d³) rangy colt; second foal; dam won Oaks Trial at Lingfield; easy in market and carrying plenty of condition when beating Red Duster very comfortably indeed by 5 lengths in maiden event at Goodwood in May; ran very well in France next 2 starts in June, finishing less than 10 lengths sixth of 12 behind Caerleon in Prix du Jockey-Club at Chantilly and 4 lengths third of 7 to Yawa in Grand Prix de Paris at Longchamp; off course afterwards until October, when moderate third of 5 behind Gay Lemur in £3,000 race at York (sweated up and injured a foreleg); suited by a test of stamina; yet to race on really firm going, but probably acts on any other. *J. Dunlop.*

JASPER'S MOUNT 3 b.c. Sparkler 130–Fratini 69 (Reliance II 137) (1982 7f — 1983 12v⁴ 16v 17v) rangy colt; good walker; first foal; dam placed over 2m; stayed on when about 20 lengths fourth of 12 to Down Flight in 1½m maiden race at Wolverhampton, best of 3 efforts in spring. *N. Vigors.*

JAT 3 ch.c. English Prince 129–Sweet Rocket (Roan Rocket 128) (1982 7d 1983 — 12d 12v³ 12v 12g 16.5f 12f) strong, rangy colt; plating-class maiden; stayed 1½m; dead. *R. Hollinshead.*

JAVA JIVE 2 ch.f. Hotfoot 126–Glebehill 76 (Northfields) (1983 7g 7g) Mar 14; — first foal; dam, 2-y-o 6f winner, is daughter of smart sprinter Pendlehill; beaten some way in £5,000 race at Lingfield in September and minor event at Catterick in October. *P. Mitchell.*

JAVA LIGHTS 5 b.g. Manado 130–Sea of Light (Aureole 132) (1982 NR 1983 11f) tall, lengthy, attractive gelding; quite modest at 3 yrs; last in handicap only start of 1983 in August; stays 13f; yet to race on very soft going but acts on any other. *Miss S. Morris.*   —

JAY ELLE THAW 3 b.g. Owen Dudley 121–Pure Magic 94 (Pinza 137) (1982 5s⁴ 5fg 5f 8.2s² 7.2s 1983 12v² 12d* 14.7d³ 13.8s⁴ 13h 12g 16.5f) rather lightly-built gelding; runner-up in sellers before winning handicap at Redcar in May by eight lengths; suited by 1½m+ and some give in the ground, although not disgraced in a slowly-run race on hard when having first race for 3 months; blinkered once at 2 yrs. *T. Fairhurst.*   **55**

JAYVEE 3 b.g. Monsanto 121–Festival Night 115 (Midsummer Night II 117) (1982 7g 7fg² 1983 8f 8g 10fg) fair sort; well beaten in 1983 (not seen out until September); should stay 1m; usually taken down early; sold 390 gns Ascot November Sales. *P. Haynes.*   —

JAZZ FORTESCUE 4 gr.f. Song 132–Porto Novo (Sovereign Lord 120) (1982 10g 1983 7s 10.1fg 8f 8g) lengthy, workmanlike filly; poor plater. *A. Davison.*   —

JEANJIM 4 b.f. Homeric 133–Dance Mistress (Javelot 124) (1982 10s 8d 9f 12.2f 10g 1983 8fg) lightly-made filly; plater; has shown no form for a long time; has worn blinkers. *C. Spares.*   —

JECKEL 5 ch.g. High Award 119–Reina Isabel 69 (St Alphage 119) (1982 6g 6g 6fg² 5f 6f 6v 6g 1983 6v 6v 7s 7fg 7g 7g) smallish gelding; poor handicapper; stays 6f; apprentice ridden; usually bandaged in front; has worn blinkers. *E. Eldin.*   —

JEEMA 2 b.f. Thatch 136–Monaco Melody 103 (Tudor Melody 129) (1983 5fg 5f* 5f* 6fg² 5fg* 5s⁴) Mar 27; leggy, quite attractive filly; has a rather sharp action; third foal; half-sister to 2 winners, including 1982 2-y-o 6f winner Raashideah (by Dancer's Image); dam 6f winner; successful in maiden race (by 6 lengths) at Pontefract in June, well-contested minor event (beating Tina's Express a head) at Beverley the following month, and in nursery (putting up game effort under top weight to get home a head) at Chester in August; creditable 2¾ lengths fourth of 5 to Petorius in Harry Rosebery Challenge Trophy at Ayr in September; speedy and is probably better suited by 5f than 6f; acts on any going; goes well on left-handed courses. *H. T. Jones.*   **102**

JEMEELA 3 b.f. Windjammer (USA)–King's Darling (King of the Tudors 129) (1982 6g 6fg³ 6s⁴ 6s 1983 7.2fg 7.2g² 7d⁴ 7s⁴ 7fg⁴ 8fg 7f²) small, lengthy filly; not seen out until August but ran well on occasions, was second in handicaps at Haydock and Leicester (blinkered, hung quite badly); should stay 1m; seems to act on any going. *G. Huffer.*   **90**

JENDOR 3 b.f. Condorcet–Windy Lady (Whistling Wind 123) (1982 5s* 5fg 6f 6fg 6f 8.2d² 8d 8.2s 1983 8s 8s* 8g* 10.1fg 12fg³) fair sort; has a round action; bought in after winning sellers at Newmarket (4,100 gns) and Brighton (4,900 gns) in May, better effort on former course when scoring by 8 lengths; stays 1½m; acts on a firm surface but revels in the mud; hung badly final start (August). *R. Hannon.*   **82**

JENNY WYLLIE 2 ch.f. Nishapour 125–Godwyn (Yellow God 129) (1983 5fg 6d⁴ 6fg) Mar 24; IR 9,600Y; good-bodied, useful-looking filly; third foal; half-sister to 2 winners in Ireland, including fairly useful 1982 5f winner Kimbernic (by Lord Gayle); dam, half-sister to very useful Pianissimo, won over 6f in Ireland; plating-class maiden; will stay beyond 6f. *W. Wharton.*   **66**

JE REVIENS 3 b.f. Streak 119–Bodicea (King's Troop 118) (1982 5fg 6fg 5fg 5s 1983 7fg) lengthy filly; soundly beaten, including in a seller (blinkered); sold 800 gns Ascot December Sales. *C. James.*   —

JERRY CAN (USA) 2 br.c. Roberto 131–Bold Flourish (Bold Lad USA) (1983 7f³ 7fg² 8.2s²) Feb 15; $150,000Y; good-topped colt; fourth foal; half-brother to 2 minor winners; dam, half-sister to champion filly Gallant Bloom, won at up to 1m; placed in varied races, on final outing starting odds on when runner-up behind easy winner All Fair in maiden event at Haydock in October; will be suited by 1¼m; seems to act on any going; should win a race. *H. T. Jones.*   **86**

JESSAM 2 b.f. Hillandale 125–Wessex Lady (Communication 119) (1983 5s) May 29; third foal; dam never ran; poor fifth of 9 in seller at Lingfield in June. *R. Simpson.*   —

JESTER 4 b.c. Song 132–Trickster 92 (Major Portion 129) (1982 6fg² 6f* 5fg 6f 6f 6g 5s 7v 6s² 1983 6d 6d 7s² 8s 6f 6f* 6.5fg) rangy, attractive ex-English colt; smart performer at his best but became inconsistent; beat Sir Prince John by 2½ lengths in Baroda Stud Seven Springs Sprint at Phoenix Park in July; had run well previous start when strong-finishing fifth of 27 behind Melindra in Wokingham   **116**

Mr J. P. Kelly's "Jester"

Stakes at Royal Ascot; stayed 7f; acted on any going except possibly heavy; suited by waiting tactics; had a tendency to hang left; sold privately out of B. Hills's stable after fifth outing; retired to Ballykisteen Stud, Co. Tipperary at IR£2,000 Oct 1st. *A. Redmond, Ireland.*

JESTERS PET 2 ch.f. Cawston's Clown 113–Mummys Colleen 75 (Mummy's Pet 125) (1983 5s 5fg 5f 5f 5f* 5f 5fg³ 5f³ 5g⁴ 5g) Feb 16; 3,500Y; small, sturdy filly; first foal; dam won twice over 5f; won 8-runner maiden race at Redcar in July; not disgraced most starts subsequently; acts on firm going; stumbled and unseated rider 2f out third outing. *R. Whitaker.*   **68**

JE T'AIME 3 ch.f. Ballad Rock 122–Pipeline 85 (Gulf Pearl 117) (1982 6fg 1983 5d³ 6v² 6d² 6v³ 6f 5f 7s* 7g 8fg 7s) rangy filly; showed ability in varied company before winning maiden race at Yarmouth in September (first outing for 3 months); suited by 7f; acts on heavy going; had stiff tasks when blinkered fourth to sixth outings, but ran well in them on first occasion; sold 14,000 gns Newmarket December Sales. *R. Williams.*   **77**

JET SIOUX 3 b.f. Jolly Good 122–Hillsquaw (Hillary) (1982 NR 1983 8g 9f 12f² 12fg 10g) 1,500Y; tall, leggy filly; half-sister to 1979 2-y-o 7f winner Nahane (by Porto Bello); dam won over 7f in USA; 33/1 when ½-length second to Holmbury in maiden race at Folkestone in July, best effort; suited by 1½m; trained by P. Walwyn until after fourth outing. *J. Bolger, Ireland.*   **76**

JEU DE PAILLE (FR) 3 b.c. Lightning 129–Serbie (Breton 130) (1982 7.5d⁴ 10s² 8s* 1983 10v² 11s* 12s* 12fg⁴ 12.5fg 12s⁴ 15.5f) third foal; half-brother to minor winners in France by Rose Laurel and Crystal Palace; dam useful winner at up to 1½m; successful in Prix Noailles and Prix Hocquart at Longchamp in spring, beating Pietru by 2½ lengths in former and Esprit du Nord by ½ length in latter; put up a very sound performance when 4½ lengths fourth of 12 behind Caerleon in Prix   **126**

du Jockey-Club at Chantilly in June; not disgraced afterwards, finishing 3¾ lengths fifth to Diamond Shoal in Grand Prix de Saint-Cloud, 4 lengths fourth of 5 behind Sagace in Prix Niel at Longchamp and dead-heating for seventh behind Old Country in Prix Royal-Oak at Longchamp again; suited by 1½m+; probably acts on any going. *A. Fabre, France.*

JEWEL CHEST 2 b.f. Busted 134–Red Ruby 113 (Tudor Melody 129) (1983 7.6d) May 12; third foal; half-sister to 3-y-o 1¼m winner Gaelic Jewel (by Scottish Rifle) and 1m winner The Ripleyite (by Northfields); dam, half-sister to smart sprinter Laser Light, was very useful miler; 14/1, behind in 20-runner maiden race at Lingfield in October; sure to do better in due course. *J. Dunlop.* — p

JHANSI KI RANI (USA) 3 b.f. Far North 120–Ghost Rider (Gray Phantom) (1982 NR 1983 7f³ 7f³ 10f 8fg* 7g* 7d³ 7g*) $75,000Y; quite an attractive filly; fourth foal; half-sister to 2 winners in USA; dam won 6 small races at up to 1m and is half-sister to very smart El Pitirre; did well and was gaining her third win in little over 4 weeks when beating Jameston by a head in 17-runner handicap at Goodwood in September; had earlier made all in maiden event on same course and beaten Red Zephyr gamely in a handicap at Kempton; stayed 1m; tended to sweat up; stud. *G. Lewis.* 94

JILLYDO 2 b.f. Morston 125–Dinah Do 77 (Derring-Do 131) (1983 10d²) Apr 15; 1,600Y; sturdy, fair sort; half-sister to winners in Belgium, Malaysia and France; dam won over 1m; 14/1 and in need of run, led 2f out until outpaced final furlong when 4 lengths second of 12 to Simcoe Star in seller at Leicester in October; stays 1¼m well; should win seller. *R. Akehurst.* 60 p

JIMJAMS 3 b.g. Jimsun 121–Gamlingay (Daring Display 129) (1982 5f 7d 7g 7g⁴ 7g³ 7fg⁴ 8fg² 7.3g* 7v 1983 8s⁴ 7.3v 7fg 8f 8fg 8.3fg⁴ 8fg 10g² 10g³) big, strong, lengthy gelding; not the best of movers; ran respectably most starts but wasn't placed until blinkers were fitted in September, finishing neck second to Dodgy Future in handicap at Newbury and third to Home Secretary in similar race at Leicester; suited by 1¼m; yet to show he can handle really soft going, but acts on any other. *R. Hannon.* 88

JIMMY EDWARDS 2 gr.g. Comedy Star 121–Forty Lines (Fortino II 120) (1983 7f 6f 7fg 7g 8fg) Apr 7; 4,100Y; big, strong gelding; second foal; dam won over hurdles and fences after birth of first foal; plating-class maiden; best effort on penultimate appearance, when blinkered first time; should stay at least 1m; gelded after final outing. *D. Elsworth.* 67

JIMMY PERI 4 ch.g. Jimmy Reppin 131–Periplus 85 (Galivanter 131) (1982 NR 1983 6d 12d) leggy, sparely-made gelding; poor plater. *C. Gray.* —

JIMMY RAINE 3 b.c. Jimmy Reppin 131–La Raine 93 (Majority Blue 126) (1982 5s⁴ 5fg² 5f 5g³ 5f 5d 1983 6v 5d⁴ 5d⁴ 5fg³ 5g 5s 5fg⁴ 5f³ 5f* 6f³ 6g 8h 6g) neat, strong colt; plater; bought in 1,200 gns after winning at Catterick in July; stays 6f (had stiffish task at 1m); acts on firm going; blinkered nowadays and has tended to sweat up when wearing them; has run respectably for an apprentice; sold out of T. Barron's stable 1,400 gns Doncaster August Sales after eleventh outing. *W. Elsey.* 59

JINNY BEAUMONT 3 br.f. Blakeney 126–Grey Home 110 (Habitat 134) (1982 NR 1983 12fg² 11.5g* 12s³ 10.6g⁴) useful-looking filly; third foal; half-sister to 7f and 1m winner Hiya Judge (by Ashmore); dam very useful 5f winner from only 3 starts; stayed on well when beating Barney Miller by 1½ lengths in maiden race at Yarmouth in September; in frame in minor events at Beverley and Haydock later in month; stays 1½m. *H. Cecil.* 72

JIZAN 2 ch.c. Jaazeiro 127–Westgate Sovereign 89 (Sovereign Path 125) (1983 5d 5v² 5g* 5d 6fg) Mar 2; 11,000Y; neat colt; second foal; half-brother to 3-y-o Aritima (by Manado); dam won over 5f at 2 yrs; made all in 9-runner £3,600 event at Bath in June; taken down very quietly when disappointing in £3,000 race at Ayr later in the month and minor event at Chester (blinkered) in July; exported to USA. *W. O'Gorman.* 85

JOAN ADDISON 2 b.f. Jolly Good 122–Gilead 90 (Quorum 126) (1983 6fg) June 6; fair sort; sixth foal; half-sister to a winner in Holland; dam, a plater, placed at up to 9f; out of first 9 in 29-runner maiden event at Newmarket in September. *A. Jarvis.* —

JO-ANDREW 3 ch.g. Joshua 129–Mild Wind (Porto Bello 118) (1982 NR 1983 5v 5v* 5s 6d 5g 6s) big, rangy gelding; second living foal; half-brother to high-class and exceptionally tough sprinter Soba (by Most Secret); dam of no account; easily won maiden race at Newcastle in May; unplaced in handicaps afterwards, but far from disgraced fifth start; should stay 6f; yet to race on a firm surface; blinkered last 2 starts. *D. Chapman.* 74

JOANN'S LAD (USA) 2 b. or br. g. Irish Castle–Step Smartly (Restless Native)   –
(1983 6fg 8f) Apr 2; $9,000Y; good-bodied gelding; second foal; dam won 6f
claiming race; behind in the autumn in minor event at Nottingham and maiden race
(blinkered) at Leicester. *A. Jarvis.*

JOBROKE 3 b. c. Busted 134–Joey 110 (Salvo 129) (1982 6g 1983 7s² 8d⁴ 9d⁴   **85**
12f² 11.5f⁴ 8.2h 8f* 7g 8g* 8g) fair sort; made all when decisively winning maiden
race at Beverley in August and handicap at Goodwood in September; needs at least
1m and stays 1½m; tends to pull hard; blinkered fifth outing; moved badly to post
sixth start; inconsistent, and probably needs to dominate affairs; sold to CBA
15,500 gns Newmarket Autumn Sales. *G. Wragg.*

JOCA 2 b. f. Rarity 129–Plymouth Sound 89 (Tudor Melody 129) (1983 7f 8.2f) Mar   –
16; 1,000 2-y-o; half-sister to fairly useful stayer Spanish Armada (by Levmoss);
dam, daughter of smart stayer Seascape, won over 1¼m; well behind in minor
event at Redcar and good-class race at Haydock in the summer. *J. Parkes.*

JOE CHURCH 2 ch. c. Monseigneur 127–Whispering Star 78 (Sound Track 132)   **81**
(1983 7fg 8fg 7f³) May 16; 10,500Y; rather short-coupled colt; half-brother to
numerous winners, including very useful performers Seadiver, Pearl Star and
Portese (all by Gulf Pearl), useful 3-y-o sprinter Bold Secret (by Auction Ring) and
smart sprinter Blue Star (by Majority Blue); dam won over 5f on only start; showed
up well in 2 races at Newmarket (first a seller) and one at Redcar in the autumn;
stays 1m; acts on firm going; sold Susan Piggott Bloodstock 15,000 gns Newmarket
Autumn Sales. *J. Hindley.*

JOEYSAN (USA) 2 ch. c. Peter Vadnais–Merrybidder (Bold Bidder) (1983 5d 5g   **81**
5.1g 5f³ 5f³ 5fg* 6f 6f 5fg 6g 7fg³) Apr 11; $26,000Y; rather sparely-made, fair
sort; fourth foal; dam won 4 sprint races at 3 yrs and is sister to smart stakes
winner Bold Ballet, the dam of high-class Tap Shoes; sire, son of Crimson Satan,
won 3 times at up to 9f including a claiming race; won nursery at Leicester in July;
other form bit mixed, but on final appearance finished good third in similar event
at Redcar in October; suited by 7f; acts on firm going; sometimes starts none too
well; blinkered second outing. *W. O'Gorman.*

JOG 6 b. g. Mount Hagen 127–Strolling Sweetly (Le Levanstell 122) (1982 9f 1983   –
10s 10.2g 10f 12f² 12f 14f) ex-Irish gelding; winning hurdler; poor form on flat,
including in a seller; suited by 1½m and will probably get further; probably acts on
any going; has worn blinkers; sold 760 gns Newmarket Autumn Sales. *W. Musson.*

JOHNATHON SILVER 2 ch. g. Manado 130–Silver Seekers (Silver Shark 129)   –
(1983 7.6fg) Apr 25; 3,000F; half-brother to 2 winners, including French 1½m
winner Pirandello (by Condorcet); dam granddaughter of Yorkshire Oaks winner
Feevagh; 50/1, tailed off in 18-runner maiden race at Lingfield in October. *R.
Champion.*

JOHN DOYLE 3 b. g. Import 127–September Fire (Firestreak 125) (1982 5f³   – §
5g² 5d 5f² 6g 5.3g 5s 6s 1983 5fg) big, rangy gelding; untrustworthy sprint
maiden; has been tried in blinkers. *M. Pipe.*

JOHN FEATHER 4 b. g. Gulf Pearl 117–Galtee Princess (Varano) (1982 9s*   **55**
12.3d 13g 16g⁴ 13s³ 1983 12.3v² 17d 15g³ 16fg 13g⁴ 17.4g³ 16.1s 18f)
workmanlike gelding; suited by a test of stamina; acts on soft going; blinkered fifth
and final starts; has run creditably for an apprentice; sold 6,800 gns Doncaster
November Sales. *J. W. Watts.*

JOHN FRENCH 3 ch. c. Relko 136–Anegada 79 (Welsh Pageant 132) (1982 7g⁴   **123**
7fg* 7g* 7s* 10g* 1983 12v³ 12fg³ 12f* 10.5d³)
'Ten furlongs is probably his best trip' commented trainer Cecil after John
French had won the Gordon Stakes in July. Nevertheless, the manner in which the
horse comfortably accounted for Good as Diamonds at Goodwood by two and a half
lengths suggested he was extremely well suited by the extra two furlongs. John
French was ridden with great confidence: held up at the back of the field, he came
to challenge the front-running Good as Diamonds on the bridle two furlongs out
and, given his head, quickly sprinted clear. John French had finished third in both
his previous attempts at one and a half miles, probably needing the race when
beaten one and a half lengths by Harly, who received 5 lb, in the Warren Stakes at
Epsom in April, and running right up to his best when three lengths third to Quilted
in the Princess of Wales's Stakes at Newmarket in July. After his impressive display
at Goodwood, John French was put back to ten and a half furlongs in the Benson and
Hedges Gold Cup at York the following month. Once again he was settled at the
rear but made steady progress in the straight to reach a challenging position two

Gordon Stakes, Goodwood—John French quickens away in great style from Good as Diamonds (rails) and Majestic Endeavour

furlongs out. He kept on very well to finish third to Caerleon and Hot Touch, beaten a neck and a length and a half. John French sustained a tendon injury at York and wasn't seen out again. He seems unlikely to be kept in training.

John French (ch.c. 1980)	Relko (b 1960)	Tanerko (br 1953)	Tantieme
			La Divine
		Relance III (ch 1952)	Relic
			Polaire
	Anegada (ch 1974)	Welsh Pageant (b 1966)	Tudor Melody
			Picture Light
		Antigua (ch 1958)	Hyperion
			Nassau

John French's pedigree was fully documented in *Racehorses of 1982*. His dam, Anegada, put up easily her best effort when fourth in a large field of maidens at Newbury as a two-year-old; she was well beaten in six outings from six furlongs to a mile and a quarter at three. Anegada is well bred, however, being a half-sister to Derrylin, who won the Horris Hill and the Greenham, and the useful middle-distance filly Fiesta Fun who finished third in the Yorkshire Oaks. John French's great-grandam Nassau was a very smart two-year-old and bred six winners. John French is Anegada's second foal; her first, Antilla (by Averof), was a fair five-furlong winner at two. A subsequent foal by Wollow was sent to Italy and, in 1983, Anegada foaled a filly by Habitat. John French, a rangy colt, stayed one and a half miles. He acted on any going and was tough and genuine. *H. Cecil.*

JOHN HUNTER 3 b. or br.g. Majestic Streak–Misty Belle (Foggy Bell 108) (1982 8fg 7.6v 1983 10v 8s) good-topped gelding; behind in varied races, including a seller. *M. Bolton.* —

JOHNNIE KLAIRO 2 ch.c. Red Johnnie 100–Klaire 85 (Klairon 131) (1983 6fg 7f) May 21; neat colt; third foal; half-brother to 1m seller winner Klairove (by Averof); dam, half-sister to high-class stayer Proverb, won over 7f at 2 yrs; sixth in maiden races at Brighton and Redcar in October; sold 3,600 gns Newmarket Autumn Sales. *C. Brittain.* 67

JOHNNY CROWN (USA) 2 ch.c. Stage Door Johnny–Fujiana (Nashua) (1983 7fg 7fg) Mar 30; $50,000Y; workmanlike colt; half-brother to 2 minor winners; dam, unraced sister to middle-distance winner Vanua, is closely related to Yorkshire Oaks winner Fleet Wahine; 20/1, showed distinct promise when 4¾ lengths fifth of 26 to Alleging in maiden race at Newmarket in September, running on strongly without rider resorting to whip; third favourite, disputed lead over 5f when 6 lengths eighth of 14 behind Condrillac in Houghton Stakes on same course the following month; will be well suited by longer distances, and should stay at least 1½m; sure to improve. *L. Cumani.* 85 p

JOHNNY FRENCHMAN 2 gr.g. John de Coombe 122–Amaryllis 92 (Tudor Melody 129) (1983 5v² 5d 5.3f 5f 5f 6fg 5fg 5fg 5fg⁴ 6d 6g³) Apr 23; fair sort; half-brother to minor winners here and in Belgium; dam won over 5f at 2 yrs; in frame in a variety of races, including selling nursery; will probably stay 7f; virtually 69 refused to race fourth outing and sweated up quite badly on fifth; blinkered fourth, ninth and tenth appearances. *R. Hannon.*

JOHNNY NOBODY 3 b.c. Derrylin 115–Crystallize (Reliance II 137) (1982 5d² 6fg* 6f³ 7g 7f⁴ 6f* 6d² 6f³ 8d² 8g* 1983 8g 8.2v 8fg) deep-girthed, sturdy colt; won 3 races at 2 yrs when trained by A. Jarvis; put up a splendid effort under 10-0 when close-up fifth of 27 behind Star of a Gunner in handicap at Doncaster on last day of season; had looked on backward side when in rear twice here in the spring, but had subsequently shown some form in Italy, reportedly winning at Milan; suited by 1m; seems to act on any going. *H. Blackshaw.* — 110

JOHNNY SOME BODY 2 br.g. John de Coombe 122–Dame Fortune 84 (Kashmir II 125) (1983 5d 5g) May 27; 1,200F, 1,600Y; small gelding; half-brother to 2 winners, including fair 1978 2-y-o 7f winner Avanti Carlo (by Lorenzaccio); dam won over 9f; in rear in modest company at Catterick in the spring; blinkered second occasion; subsequently gelded. *H. Blackshaw.* — —

JOHN PATRICK 2 b.c. Home Guard 129–De Milo 89 (Busted 134) (1983 6g 7fg 7g 7g³) Mar 1; 7,400Y; deep-girthed, heavy-topped colt; third foal (first to Northern Hemisphere time); dam, half-sister to smart No Alimony, won over 7f; improved with racing, on final outing finishing just over length third of 15 behind Leysh in maiden event at Lingfield in October; will stay 1m. *P. Mitchell.* — 90

JOHNSHAVEN 2 gr.g. John de Coombe 122–Snow Chief 90 (Tribal Chief 125) (1983 6f) Apr 4; 2,000F; first foal; dam won over 1m; backward, tailed off in 17-runner maiden race at Thirsk in June. *M. W. Easterby.* — —

JOHN SILK 2 gr.c. John de Coombe 122–Tartan Silk 84 (Scottish Rifle 127) (1983 7fg 7f) Mar 8; smallish, lengthy colt; first foal; dam won over 1m and 1¼m; in rear in August in minor event at Wolverhampton and claiming race (blinkered) at Leicester. *M. Blanshard.* — —

JOLIE COURTISANE 3 b.f. Owen Dudley 121–Oh Well 61 (Sahib 114) (1982 5fg⁴ 5g* 5g* 6fg 5f 1983 5f 6fg 5fg 5fg 5g 5g³ 5s 5g) workmanlike, good-quartered filly; plater; best form at 5f; trained by P. Haslam until after fourth start. *J. S. Wilson.* — 52

JOLI WASFI (USA) 2 gr.c. L'Enjoleur–Pampa Grey (Grey Dawn II 132) (1983 8fg 9f²) Apr 6; $37,000Y; very big, workmanlike colt; first foal; half-brother to 3 minor winners; dam stakes-placed winner at up to 1m; neck second of 13 to Cri de Coeur in maiden race at Redcar in October; will be suited by 1¼m. *A. Jarvis.* — 84

JOLLY BAY 3 b.f. Mill Reef 141–Juliette Marny 123 (Blakeney 126) (1982 NR 1983 10d* 12g 10g 10fg⁴) rangy, attractive filly; fourth foal; half-sister to 1½m winner North Briton (by Northfields) and fairly useful maiden Sans Dot (by Busted); dam won Oaks and Irish Guinness Oaks and is sister to St Leger winner Julio Mariner; put up a very taking first performance in 17-runner Pretty Polly Stakes at Newmarket in April, moving through to lead inside final furlong and account for Fields of Spring cheekily by ¾ length; ante-post favourite for Oaks for a while afterwards but missed that race; ran only 3 more times, finishing ninth of 13 behind Give Thanks in Lancashire Oaks at Haydock in July (favourite, but still a bit green), about 5 lengths fifth of 6 behind Morcon in Valdoe Stakes at Goodwood in September and 6½ lengths fourth of 9 to Cormorant Wood in Sun Chariot Stakes at Newmarket in October; should stay 1½m. *J. Tree.* — 108

JOLLY BURGLAR 4 b.g. Jolly Good 122–Moaning Low 75 (Burglar 128) (1982 6f 8f 7f⁴ 7f² 7g* 7g 6fg 7fg 9f 9s² 7s 6s³ 1983 7d 10d 8g 8.2d² 7d 8f²(dis) 9f 8f⁴ 8fg) small, workmanlike gelding; plater; stays 9f; acts on any going; usually wears blinkers but has run well without; used to be a suitable mount for an apprentice but hung left several times in 1983 and needs strong handling nowadays; sent to Singapore. *E. Carter.* — 51

JOLLY SARA 3 ch.f. Jolly Good 122–Sarasingh 93 (Mansingh 120) (1982 6s 1983 8d 7v² 5s 6fg 6fg 7f⁴ 7f³) lengthy, plain filly; plater; stays 7f; acts on any going; sometimes blinkered and doesn't look entirely genuine; sold to NBA 500 gns Newmarket Autumn Sales. *M. McCormack.* — 47

JONACRIS 3 ch.c. Broxted 120–Squires Girl (Spanish Gold 101) (1982 5fg 5g* 5f* 5fg² 5f* 5fg* 5fg* 5g² 5fg² 5g* 1983 6g 5g 6f² 5f 5f* 5f 5f 5fg 5fg³ 5fg) strong, full-quartered sprint type; good mover; a really tough colt, and a useful one too; showed speed throughout and put up a typically gutsy performance when beating Mummy's Treasure by a neck under 9-7 in £10,000 Gosforth Park Cup (Handicap) at Newcastle in June; placed twice at York, running a particularly fine race when dividing Autumn Sunset and Bold Secret in a close finish to William Hill Trophy; stays 6f; form only on a sound surface; got loose before start and didn't run up to his best sixth outing and got a bit above himself final appearance; dwelt eighth start. *P. Felgate.* — 112

JONDALE 6 b.g. Le Johnstan 123–Levandale 102 (Le Levanstell 122) (1982 8g 7.2s³ 7.6g 9fg 10d 8f 9g 7g 9s 10.2d 8.2s 1983 8v² 8d³ 8g 9fg 12.3fg⁴ 9fg 11f) workmanlike gelding; good walker; fair handicapper at his best but has deteriorated markedly and is inconsistent and unreliable; stays 1¼m; seems to act on any going but is ideally suited by some give in the ground; suitable mount for an apprentice; suited by front-running tactics; blinkered once. *M. Lambert.* 57 §

JONDAO 2 ch.c. Le Johnstan 123–Viadao 87 (Pardao 120) (1983 5s 5f⁴ 5fg² 5f⁴ 6f 5f 5s 7fg) May 27; 300Y; small, sparely-made colt; dam won twice over 5f at 2 yrs; modest plater; form only at 5f; acts on firm going; often blinkered. *W. Bentley.* 55

JONESEE 2 ch.f. Dublin Taxi–Precious Light 90 (Psidium 130) (1983 5d 6s 6f 5f³ 6f 5d 5d 5d 5g³) May 16; 5,400Y; big, workmanlike filly; half-sister to 2 winners abroad; dam won over 1m; plating-class maiden; stays 6f; acts on firm going and a soft surface; blinkered last 3 starts. *A. Jarvis.* 64

JONIX 2 b.g. Crooner 119–Samoa Tan 89 (Pago Pago) (1983 7f) May 5; strong, deep-girthed gelding; third foal; half-brother to a winning plater; dam 1¼m winner; 50/1 and decidedly burly, last of 13 in £5,600 maiden race at Goodwood in July. *H. Beasley.* –

JONNY ZERO 2 b. or ro.c. Palm Track 122–Russet Lady (Wolver Hollow 126) (1983 5g 5fg 5g 8fg) of no account; blinkered third start. *E. Alston.* –

JOPHIL 3 gr.f. Town Crier 119–Sounding Star 71 (Bleep-Bleep 134) (1982 7fg 6f 7g 1983 5s 7f 10f) tall, sparely-made filly; poor walker; poor form, including in sellers; sold out of J. Tierney's stable 560 gns Doncaster June Sales after first outing. *M. Chapman.* –

JORGE MIGUEL 4 b.g. Welsh Pageant 132–Smeralda 105 (Grey Sovereign 128§) (1982 9s² 10f³ 12fg⁴ 10fg³ 10g* 10fg² 10fg 10s³ 10s³ 1983 12d) well-made, good sort; fair at his best; below form only start at 4 yrs in April; stays 1½m; acts –

Mr J. I. Morrison's "Jolly Bay"

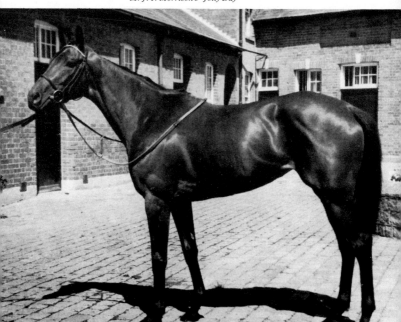

on any going but goes well on soft; has run creditably when sweating up; has run respectably for an amateur rider; quite a useful hurdler. *G. Pritchard-Gordon.*

JOSCELINE WINIFRED 2 b.f. Tachypous 128–Betony 76 (Sovereign Path 125) (1983 5d⁴ 6f 5fg 5g 6f* 6fg⁴ 6f² 6f² 7d) Apr 22; neat, good-quartered filly; half-sister to 1980 2-y-o 5f seller winner Steel Lady (by Continuation); dam 2-y-o 5f winner; won 8-runner seller (no bid) at Ripon in August; should be suited by 7f; acts on firm going. *R. Hollinshead.* **62**

JOTA 7 gr.g. Dragonara Palace 115–Aspiration 53 (Roan Rocket 128) (1982 12f 12f² 12f* 12f² 12s* 12d 12fg⁴ 12d 1983 12s) short-coupled gelding; middle-distance handicapper; acted on any going; dead. *W. Wharton.* **–**

JOUCAS 4 b.c. High Top 131–Alezan Dore 82 (Mountain Call 125) (1982 7fg 10f³ 10g 7f⁴ 8g* 8f* 7fg⁴ 8f 8s 1983 8v 7.6v⁴ 8fg 7.6g 8g 8f 8d 7.6fg 8g) strong, lengthy colt; below form in 1983; suited by 1m; acts on any going. *J. Winter.* **–**

JOURNEY HOME (USA) 3 b.f. Windy Sands–Carry Me Home (Coursing) (1982 6fg 7s 7g⁴ 1983 8s⁴ 8s 9f³ 10f⁴ 10fg⁴ 10fg) leggy, shallow-girthed filly; has a round action; stays 1¼m; possibly not at her best on really firm going; blinkered fifth start. *G. Wragg.* **73**

JOVE'S VOODOO (USA) 2 gr.f. Northern Jove–Doll Dreams (Reliance II 137) (1983 6g⁴ 7f 6d³) Jan 27; $55,000Y; smallish, well-made filly; has a smooth action; first foal; dam very useful French middle-distance filly; in frame in maiden races at Newmarket in July and Yarmouth in September; should stay 1¼m. *J. Hindley.* **74**

JOWOODY 3 b.c. Tudor Rhythm 112–Strawberry Ice (Arctic Storm 134) (1982 5d⁴ 7g³ 7.2g 7f 7fg 8f 8.2d 8s 1983 12s* 13.1v* 14d* 14f* 12g 14f 13.3g 16fg³) lengthy colt; good walker; improved enormously on his 2-y-o form and won his first 4 starts, handicaps at Leicester, Bath, Sandown and York (ridden by apprentice T. Quinn each time); ran on with great gusto when beating Shenton Way by 1½ lengths in £5,200 Elisabeth Hambro Memorial on last-named course in June; didn't run particularly well afterwards however, and gained only placing when about 13 lengths third of 5 behind Karadar in Jockey Club Cup at Newmarket in October; well suited by front-running tactics and a test of stamina (appeared to resent being restrained on sixth outing); evidently acts on any going; thoroughly game and genuine; trained by R. Sturdy first 5 starts. *B. Hills.* **101**

JOYFUL DANCER 3 ch.c. Gay Fandango 132–Sheer Joy (Major Portion 129) (1982 7s 7.6v* 1983 8v 8d 8f 10f 7h* 7fg⁴ 7g⁴ 7.6d³ 7f) big, strong, lengthy colt; won handicap at Bath in July and ran respectably afterwards; should stay 1m; acts on any going; pulls quite hard, and doesn't find much off the bridle. *P. Cole.* **73**

JOY OF MUSIC 3 b.c. Music Maestro 119–Blak-En-Bloo 72 (Blakeney 126) (1982 6f 6g 6d 8f 1983 11d 12f 10f 12g 12.2d³) quite well-made colt; tended to hang under pressure when third in seller at Catterick; stays 1½m. *P. Rohan.* **46**

JOY RIDE 3 b.g. Jolly Good 122–Hard to Follow (Roi Lear 126) (1982 NR 1983 10v¹ 11.5fg* 12fg*) good sort; first foal; dam well behind in 3 races at 2 yrs; quickened well when winning 10-runner maiden race at Sandown and 7-runner handicap at Haydock; tended to hang before getting up near finish to beat Wonderful Surprise by ½ length (pair 15 lengths clear) on latter; will stay beyond 1½m; wasn't seen out after July. *B. Hobbs.* **95**

JR DISCOUNTS 2 gr.g. Bruni 132–Tin Mary 96 (Tin King 126) (1983 8fg 9f) Mar 12; 2,800Y; half-brother to several winners, including useful 1m to 1¾m winner Gallant Welsh (by Welsh Pageant); dam stayed 1m; in rear in maiden races. *M. Lambert.* **–**

JT'S TRIUMPH (USA) 2 b.f. Big John Taylor–Triggs'z (Successor) (1983 6f 6f 7h) Mar 10; lightly-made filly; half-sister to several winners, including very useful 1980 2-y-o 6f to 7.6f winner Admiral's Heir (by Crafty Admiral); dam won over 6f; behind in maiden races. *P. Cole.* **–**

JUBILEE BILL 6 b.g. Sovereign Bill 105–Macera 85 (Acer 123) (1982 NR 1983 10f) fairly useful at his best but is only lightly raced nowadays; stays 1¼m; suited by some give in the ground; best in blinkers; has worn bandages; bought 1,050 gns Ascot March Sales. *D. Oughton.* **–**

JUDEX (USA) 2 b.c. Forli–Cecelia (Royal Levee) (1983 7.6fg* 7g³) May 3; $400,000Y; big, useful-looking colt; half-brother to several winners, including useful French miler Absentia (by Raise A Cup), subsequently a 9f stakes winner in USA; dam unraced daughter of half-sister to top American colts Chieftain and Tom Rolfe; won 16-runner maiden race at Lingfield in October by a length from Luminate; favourite, never going well when 2 lengths third of 7 behind Test of Time **87**

in minor event at Sandown later in the month; will be suited by 1¼m; acts on a firm surface. *G. Harwood.*

JUDY'S DOWRY 2 gr.f. Dragonara Palace 115–In Leiu (Tutankhamen) (1983 5g **80** 5v* 5fg 6f 6fg 6g 6fg) Apr 15; sparely-made filly; half-sister to two 2-y-o 5f winners and a winner in Barbados; dam of little account; won minor event at Ripon in June; beaten subsequently in nurseries, last one a claimer; seemingly best at 5f; acts on heavy going; sometimes starts none too well. *W. Wharton.*

JUED LAD 4 ch.g. Tower Walk 130–Super Satin (Lord of Verona 120) (1982 NR **–** 1983 10s 12fg) 4,200Y, 1,050 3-y-o; sturdy gelding; third foal; dam placed over hurdles; beaten a long way in minor events. *W. Stubbs.*

JUJU 4 b.f. Dragonara Palace 115–Go Too 78 (Goldhill 125) (1982 6f 7f 7f 5d 1983 **56** 5d 6s 5s 7f 6fg 6f 7.6fg² 6g 7fg) very leggy filly; poor handicapper; has been beaten in a seller; stays 7f well; ran moderately in blinkers once. *D. Elsworth.*

JULESIAN 5 b.g. High Top 131–Bold Lass (Bold Lad, Ire 133) (1982 NR 1983 **64** 10.2g² 11.7f) strong gelding; close second in seller at Bath in June; stays 1½m; acts on any going. *D. Elsworth.*

JULIA 3 b.f. Moulton 128–Cesarea 108 (Raeburn II) (1982 NR 1983 9s 12f² 12.2f **–** 11.7h⁴ 12f 12s) fair sort; half-sister to 2 winners, including fairly useful 7f winner Cassina (by Habitat); dam game winner of 5 races from 5f to 1½m; well clear of remainder when 4 lengths second to Hi Love in maiden race at Brighton in June, best effort; stays 1½m. *P. Walwyn.*

JULIA FLYTE 3 gr.f. Drone–Miss Upward 77 (Alcide 136) (1982 6g³ 6fg* 7g **85** 1983 10d 8f 7f 7fg 7fg) well-made filly; won maiden race at Salisbury as a 2-y-o; had stiffish tasks in 1983 (far from disgraced second outing); should stay 1¼m. *G. Harwood.*

JULIE SIMONE 8 ch.m. Some Hand 119–Esquire Maid 86 (Aureole 132) (1982 **–** NR 1983 8f 12fg) of little account. *T. Kersey.*

JULIETTE 3 ch.f. Julio Mariner 127–Oglala 61 (Sovereign Path 125) (1982 NR **–** 1983 10s 10.6g 15.8g 18fg) first living foal; dam, placed over 11f, is sister to very useful Warpath and half-sister to high-class stayer Dakota; little worthwhile form, best effort in a handicap on final start. *C. Thornton.*

JULIETTE MARINER 2 ch.f. Welsh Pageant 132–Algarve 94 (Alcide 136) **–** (1983 7f 8d) May 2; 3,000Y; fair sort; half-sister to fairly useful sprinter Swinging Trio (by Swing Easy); dam won over 1¼m and 1½m and is daughter of 1000 Guineas and Oaks runner-up Spree; showed little in maiden events at Sandown in July and Beverley in September. *C. Brittain.*

JULY 2 b.f. Warpath 113–Midsummer Madness 66 (Silly Season 127) (1983 6g 7s **77** 8d* 8.2s) Jan 26; workmanlike filly; sister to 1½m winner Dangerous Moonlite and a winning plater, and half-sister to a winner; dam won over 1½m; head winner of 14-runner maiden race at Beverley in September; eighth of 11 in nursery at Hamilton the following month; will be suited by 1¼m+. *C. Thornton.*

JUMBLIE 2 b.f. Town and Country 124–Aunt Jobiska 71 (Grey Sovereign 128§ or **65** Aureole 132) (1983 5s 5f² 6f 5fg 5d³ 5g) Mar 23; smallish, lengthy filly; poor mover; half-sister to a winner in Trinidad; dam, who stayed 1¼m, is half-sister to Queen's Hussar; placed in valuable seller at York in June and maiden race at Wolverhampton in October; should be suited by 6f; sold 6,600 gns Newmarket Autumn Sales and exported to Trinidad. *I. Balding.*

JUMPING GREY (USA) 2 gr.c. Jumping Hill 119–Soft 'n' Pretty (Minnesota **–** Mac) (1983 7fg) big colt; second foal; dam won 6f claiming race; 33/1, reluctant to go to post prior to finishing tailed-off last of 14 in Houghton Stakes at Newmarket in October; sold 600 gns Newmarket Autumn Sales. *G. Harwood.*

JUMP JAR 4 b.g. Lochnager 132–Light Jumper 100 (Red God 128§) (1982 7g³ 7f **62 d** 1983 6v² 6d² 8s* 12d* 8g⁴ 10.2f 10fg 12f) rangy, good sort; good walker and mover; plater nowadays; won readily at Brighton (bought in 2,700 gns) and Thirsk (no bid) in May; stays 1½m; needs some give in the ground; bandaged final start (finished sore). *D. Chapman.*

JUNGLE ROMEO (USA) 3 b.c. Jungle Savage–Baby Louise (Exclusive **79** Native) (1982 7s* 1983 8d⁴ 8.2v⁴ 8f 10.2fg 10g 10g) lengthy, rather sparely-made colt; respectable fourth in £4,200 handicap at Newmarket (to Sugar Loch) and Cecil Frail Handicap at Haydock (to Schuss) in spring; promises to stay 1¼m; best form on soft ground; blinkered final start; sold to J. King 9,400 gns Newmarket Autumn Sales. *M. Stoute.*

417

Tote-Ebor Handicap, York—a convincing win for Jupiter Island from Abdoun (almost obscured), Morgans Choice (light colours) and Band

JUPITER ISLAND 4 b.c. St Paddy 133–Mrs Moss 81 (Reform 132) (1982 **119**
10.5f⁴ 10g 10f 12fg* 12g⁴ 12fg³ 11.5g* 12s* 10v²·12s 1983 10.2v³ 12v 12f 12g*
14g* 14.6fg² 13.3g* 12fg* 12d*)

It is probably fortunate for the official handicappers' peace of mind that there
are not more horses of Jupiter Island's type around. No more than fairly useful at
three, he came on by leaps and bounds as a four-year-old and ended the year a
very smart performer, one whose astonishing progress can best be appreciated
by comparing the result of the Sporting Chronicle Spring Handicap at Doncaster
in May with that of the Group 3 St Simon Stakes at Newbury in October. In the
former Jupiter Island carried 8-5 and came home a respectable four lengths third
to Farioffa who gave him 23 lb; in the latter he gained a splendid victory and had
Farioffa two lengths and a short head back in third at levels.

The St Simon climaxed a marvellous year for Jupiter Island, providing him with
his fifth win and taking his first-prize earnings for the season to almost £65,000.
The first indication that he was on the upgrade came in the Tote-Ebor Handicap at
York in August, the fifth start of his campaign. He had won the valuable Air New
Zealand Handicap at Newmarket eleven days previously gamely by a neck from
Keelby Kavalier but the 7-lb penalty he had to carry at York seemed to put him out
of the reckoning, especially as the Newmarket second was in the field. Not only did
Jupiter Island win the Ebor, with Keelby Kavalier back in fifth, he won it without
undue fuss. Remarkably for a seemingly competitive event worth over £27,000 to
the winner the race developed into a two-horse affair from some way out. Ridden
for the first time by Piggott, who gets on with him particularly well, Jupiter Island
was always going nicely in the middle of the field, made rapid headway from the final
turn to challenge the leader Abdoun and after a brief tussle raced into a
three-length advantage with under two furlongs left. From this point he looked a
certain winner barring an accident and eventually won easing up by a length and a
half from Abdoun with Morgans Choice third and Band fourth.

At the time the result of the valuable Esal Bookmakers Handicap at Doncaster
the following month seemed to indicate that the handicapper had probably taken

Jupiter Island's measure for the colt never looked like getting to Bucklow Hill and went down by three lengths. This opinion had to be revised after the Coral Autumn Cup at Newbury ten days later. Ridden with exceptional confidence by Piggott, seeking his first win in the event, Jupiter Island made incredible progress from the rear in the last half mile, hitting the front at the distance and having little trouble holding off the strong-finishing His Honour by a length and a half.

By now there looked to be a case for giving Jupiter Island a chance in a pattern race and that chance came in the St Simon; in between, though, he carried on the good work by winning another handicap at Newmarket in pretty facile fashion from Thorndown, once again showing too much pace for his opponents. The St Simon Stakes, first run in 1969 after being called the Ormonde Stakes previously, has been won by some good horses, among them Knockroe, Dakota, Hot Grove and Main Reef. In all probability the latest race did not take so much winning as most of its predecessors but the field of eleven still included several smart performers, notably the Geoffrey Freer Stakes runner-up Castle Rising, the Doonside Cup winner Balladier, the much-travelled Harly and Farioffa. Jupiter Island, ridden by Robinson because Piggott had commitments at Doncaster, started a well-supported second favourite behind Castle Rising. Towards the rear early on as his stable-companion Lafontaine made the running, Jupiter Island turned into the straight in seventh and then produced his customary burst of speed to cut down his rivals in the space of a furlong or so, depriving Lafontaine of the lead fully three furlongs out. Once in front he never looked like surrendering his advantage as he saw off Castle Rising, whose promising challenge petered out at the distance, and kept on strongly to beat the Musidora Stakes second So True by two lengths.

After the St Simon Clive Brittain, who sometimes rivals Don Quixote in his tendency to tilt at windmills but deserves nothing but praise for his handling of Jupiter Island, claimed that the colt could even develop into an Arc de Triomphe candidate at five. While such a view seems distinctly hopeful it must be admitted that any prediction early in 1983 that Jupiter Island might win a pattern race would have been regarded as eccentric, so it would be dangerous to be dogmatic about his prospects. What can be said is that unless he improves further he is likely to find

St Simon Stakes, Newbury—a first pattern victory for the improving Jupiter Island

Mr S. M. Threadwell's "Jupiter Island"

things appreciably tougher in the races he will probably contest if the Arc is his ultimate objective. That, though, is in the future, and whatever happens to him in 1984 Jupiter Island, a thoroughly admirable sort, has already contributed a great deal to the good of the sport.

Jupiter Island (b.c. 1979)	St Paddy (b 1957)	Aureole (ch 1950)	Hyperion / Angelola
		Edie Kelly (br 1950)	Bois Roussel / Caerlissa
	Mrs Moss (ch 1969)	Reform (b 1964)	Pall Mall / Country House
		Golden Plate (ch 1964)	Whistler / Good as Gold

Jupiter Island's sire St Paddy, who retired from stud duties in 1981, has been represented by numerous good performers, including Connaught, Parnell, Patch, and Welsh Saint, but oddly his progeny have won more races abroad than in Britain. On the dam's side Jupiter Island is one of a host of winners out of Mrs Moss, full details of whom can be found in the essay on the Gimcrack winner Precocious, and it was surprising that he fetched only 10,000 guineas as a yearling in a season that had seen his half-sister Pushy (by Sharpen Up) winning the Queen Mary and Cornwallis Stakes. Jupiter Island is a close-coupled, quite attractive colt, and a good mover. A genuine individual, he is suited by a mile and a half or more and though effective on a firm surface is best served by some give in the ground. *C. Brittain.*

420

JUST A THOUGHT 2 b.f. Homing 130–Sugar Queen (Yelapa 130) (1983 6s 6f 68
6fg 7g) Apr 16; 8,000Y; leggy filly; half-sister to French 3-y-o 10.5f winner Sweet
Format (by Reform) and Irish 5f and 1m winner Dancing Light (by Dancer's Image);
dam, lightly raced, was in frame at up to 1¼m in France; plating-class maiden; best
effort on third outing; should stay at least 1m; trained first start by Peter Taylor.
M. H. Easterby.

JUST AUTUMN (USA) 2 b.c. Empery 128–Seasoning (Bold Reasoning) (1983 77
6f 8g) Feb 28; lengthy, quite attractive colt; first foal; dam won over 6f and 1m in
USA; ninth of 13 in Chesham Stakes at Royal Ascot in June, and fifth of 18, beaten
15 lengths, in maiden race (second favourite) at Ayr in September; will stay 1¼m.
A. Jarvis.

JUST BEAU 2 b.f. Busted Fiddle 90–Cider Drinker (Space King 115) (1983 5v 5v –
5v 5d) Apr 5; rather shallow-girthed, plain filly; first foal; dam poor maiden on flat
and over hurdles; bad plater; not raced after May. *M. Bradley.*

JUST BLAKE 2 b.c. Blakeney 126–Just A Dutchess (Knightly Manner) (1983 7f 75 p
7fg) May 15; neat, attractive colt; half-brother to 3 winners, notably very smart
sprinter Miami Springs (by Northfields); dam won 7 times at up to 1m in USA; 9½
lengths sixth of 12 to Court And Spark in maiden race at Salisbury in July and eighth
of 11 to Ministerial after showing up 5f in Hyperion Stakes at Ascot in October; will
be suited by 1m+; should do better. *B. Swift.*

JUST GUNNER 3 ch.c. Gunner B 126–Lady Tarcherio 65 (Pontifex) (1982 6fg 48
8.2fg 6g 7.2s⁴ 8s² 8d 10s 10.2s 1983 8.2v 12v 10f⁴ 12f³ 13.8f* 12fg³) small colt;
plater; attracted no bid after winning at Catterick in July; stays 1¾m; seems to act
on any going; often blinkered; trained early in 1983 by A. Balding; sold 2,000 gns
Doncaster August Sales. *S. Norton.*

JUSTICE LEA 3 b.g. Kinglet 98–Evada 78 (Eborneezer 105) (1982 NR 1983 –
9.4f 8f) 200F; sixth reported foal; dam staying maiden; in rear in minor event at
Carlisle and maiden race at Edinburgh in summer. *T. Craig.*

JUST IRENE 2 b.f. Sagaro 133–Erminia 61 (Gulf Pearl 117) (1983 5v³ 5s² 5d 5fg 50
6f 6fg 6f 5f 6d 7fg 8g 6g⁴) Mar 12; 1,250Y; workmanlike filly; half-sister to winners
in Belgium and Italy; dam won 6f seller and also a selling hurdle; quite a moderate
plater; best run on final appearance; should stay much further than 6f; trained first
3 starts by A. Young. *A. Ingham.*

JUST MAGGIE 3 b.f. So Blessed 130–Balnespick 101 (Charlottown 127) (1982 –
5f 1983 8v 9s 8v 8g) little worthwhile form; dead. *J. Bosley.*

JUST ONE MORE TIME 3 ch.f. Bonne Noel 115–Dialectic (Red God 128§) 60
(1982 6g 1983 10.2h 9.4f³ 12d) leggy, sparely-made filly; third in maiden event at
Carlisle in July; looked very light only subsequent start; stays 1½m; sold 1,300
gns Newmarket December Sales. *Sir Mark Prescott.*

JUST QUAIL 2 b.c. Welsh Pageant 132–Naughton Park 66 (Lorenzaccio 130) –
(1983 7fg 7fg 7g) June 16; 10,000 2-y-o; leggy, narrow colt; first foal; dam second
in 2 sprint races at 2 yrs; little worthwhile form in maiden and minor events. *G.
Lockerbie.*

JUST RAIN 3 b.f. Blue Cashmere 129–Aqua Nimba (Acropolis 132) (1982 6fg 56
1983 8d 9d 8fg³ 7f² 8fg 8f 8.2s) lengthy, fair sort; plater; suited by 1m; probably
needs a sound surface; blinkered sixth outing; sold to I. Vickers 950 gns Doncaster
November Sales. *P. Asquith.*

JUST TAMARA 3 b.f. Blue Cashmere 129–Countesswells (Behistoun 131) (1982 –
NR 1983 8fg⁴ 9.4f 8.2fg⁴ 9.4f 7f⁴) 1,150Y; lengthy filly; third foal; dam never
ran; plater; trained by J. Fitzgerald first outing; sold 640 gns Doncaster
September Sales. *G. Richards.*

JUST WILMUR 3 b.f. Home Guard 129–Mountain of Mourne 87 (Mountain Call –
125) (1982 NR 1983 6fg 8f 8g) 6,000Y; third foal; dam stayed 1m; unquoted when
behind in maiden and minor races. *R. Hollinshead.*

JUVITA 2 br.f. Junius 124–Tack 88 (Tacitus 124) (1983 5g 7.6d) June 9; quite – p
well-made, sturdy filly; good mover; half-sister to several winners, including
Trevita (by Tyrant), a smart winner from 6f to 1m here and a good winner in the
USA; dam stayer; showed up in 20-runner maiden races at Newbury (ninth) and
Lingfield in the autumn; will do better if looks count for anything. *H. T. Jones.*

K

KABOUR 5 b.h. Habitat 134–Kermiya (Vienna 127) (1982 6d 6fg* 7f 6s 5f 6f³ 6g –
5g 5g 1983 6f 5f) strong, quite attractive horse; has an enlarged off-fore joint and

is a poor mover; poor sprint handicapper; stayed 6f; acted on any going; sometimes bandaged; stud. *D. Chapman.*

KA BU NOR (USA) 3 b.c. Cannonade–Miss Berta (First Landing) (1982 NR 1983   **71** 7g 7f 7f* 7fg³ 7g⁴ 8g² 7.6fg 8g) $55,000Y; tall colt; has been tubed; second foal; dam won at up to 1m; showed first form when winning maiden race at Folkestone in August; in frame in handicaps afterwards; suited by 1m; acts on firm going; sold to race in Italy 3,200 gns Newmarket Autumn Sales. *G. Harwood.*

KAFU 3 b.c. African Sky 124–Pampered Dancer (Pampered King 121) (1982 5g²   **–** 5g* 6f² 6f³ 5f* 5f* 6g² 6g⁴ 1983 5g) big, well-made, quite attractive colt; excellent walker; won three 5f races from 8 starts as a 2-y-o, notably Molecomb Stakes at Goodwood and Flying Childers Stakes at Doncaster; never got into race and was disappointing when among backmarkers in 17-runner Palace House Stakes won by On Stage at Newmarket in April on only outing of 1983; stayed 6f; never raced on a soft surface; needed holding up; standing at Irish National Stud, fee £3,750 (live foal). *G. Harwood.*

KAIMLAW 9 ch.g. Native Prince–Misty Morn 70 (Worden II 129) (1982 5fg* 5fg   **–** 5g⁴ 5g 5f⁴ 5fg² 5fg 5g 5d³ 5g 5d* 5fg 1983 5g 5f 5f 5f4) sprint handicapper; has run tubed; best at 5f; acts on any going, except perhaps really soft; sometimes blinkered; suitable mount for an apprentice. *H. Bell.*

KALACHANCE 2 b.g. Kala Shikari 125–Run The Risk (Run The Gantlet) (1983   **49** 5d 5d 5fg 6f 7g 9fg 5g 6fg) May 31; 3,000F, 300Y; leggy gelding; poor plater; best run at 5f on penultimate appearance. *A. Smith.*

KALAGIRL 2 b.f. Kala Shikari 125–Valiretta (Go Marching) (1983 6f 7f 6fg   **–** 8.2fg) May 3; 1,500Y; lightly-built filly; of no account; sold 340 gns Ascot October Sales. *M. Blanshard.*

KALAMAIDAN 3 b.f. Kala Shikari 125–Buttermilk Sky (Midsummer Night II   **55** 117) (1982 5fg 5fg³ 6g 5fg 6f⁴ 6s 5v 1983 5s 5g² 5.3f 5h³ 5fg² 5fg² 5g⁴ 5g) lightly-made filly; plater at 2 yrs; placed in non-sellers in 1983; best form at 5f; appears to need a sound surface. *M. Blanshard.*

KALAMONT 4 gr.g. Kalamoun 129–Obelisk 122 (Abernant 142) (1982 8d² 10s⁴   **82** 8d² 10.5g³ 9s⁴ 1983 11.5fg 10.2f⁴ 10f* 10f* 12f² 12f⁴) big, strong ex-French gelding; half-brother to 8.2f winner The Britisher (by English Prince); dam won Nell Gwyn Stakes; won minor event at Brighton, amateur riders race at Newmarket and handicap at Epsom in summer; beat No-U-Turn ¾ length in last-named; stays 1½m; acts on any going; blinkered last 2 starts in 1982; has run creditably when sweating up; sold to J. Gifford 19,000 gns Newmarket September Sales. *J. Dunlop.*

KALAROSE 2 b.c. Kala Shikari 125–Queen's Rose 85 (Queen's Hussar 124)   **60** (1983 6f 5.1f 7f 8g 8.2fg⁴ 8fg⁴ 10d) May 9; 1,400F, 2,700Y; strong colt; poor mover; half-brother to a winning plater and to a winning hurdler; dam appeared to stay 1¾m; moderate plater; disappointing favourite at Leicester (blinkered) in October on final appearance; suited by 1m; acts on a firm surface; sold 1,500 gns Doncaster October Sales. *J. Hardy.*

KALI GANDAKI 2 br.g. Rapid River 127–Rochelle 70 (Road House II) (1983   **–** 5fg 5fg 5f) small, lightly-built gelding; of no account. *H. Bell.*

KALIM 2 br.c. Hotfoot 126–Khadaeen (Lyphard 132) (1983 6g* 6f* 6g² 7f² 7g²)   **121** Kalim had a highly satisfactory first season, never finishing out of the first two in five starts while earning over £37,000, and in one respect he might have done even better; unluckily he ended the year without a pattern-race success despite emerging the best horse at the weights in both the Anglia Television July Stakes at Newmarket and the Seaton Delaval Stakes at Newcastle. Kalim, a robust colt, came to the July Stakes unbeaten in two races in June, the twenty-seven-runner Kennett Maiden Stakes at Newbury, where he beat Head For Heights narrowly despite appearing to be carrying plenty of condition, and the Champagne Stakes at Salisbury, where he landed the odds smoothly enough from Meraval. The value of the Salisbury race meant that Kalim had to carry 3 lb more than four of his five rivals at Newmarket and he started at 7/1 in a market dominated by the top-weighted Coventry Stakes winner Chief Singer. With the stable jockey Reid suspended, Kalim was ridden by Cauthen, his third rider in as many races, and right well he ran for him. Most of the field were still in with a chance entering the last quarter mile where the well-backed Superlative, in front from the start, set sail for home with a vengeance. Kalim was the only one to come close to pegging him back, running on so determinedly under strong driving up the hill that he'd narrowed the gap to a head by the post.

Kalim's Newmarket display suggested strongly that the extra furlong of the Seaton Delaval would suit him admirably. Unfortunately he wasn't, in our view, ridden to best advantage. When the 66/1-shot Waggish ran out of steam after leading at a steady pace for half a mile, Reid found himself in front on Kalim. Instead of utilising his mount's stamina by kicking for home, the jockey waited until the distance before asking Kalim to quicken away—why we don't know, as there is no racecourse evidence to suggest that Kalim needs holding up. Kalim then found the lightly-weighted maiden Knoxville too strong in the last strides and went down by a short head. Kalim needs no excuse for his last defeat, at the hands of Lear Fan in the Laurent Perrier Champagne Stakes at Doncaster in September. He simply came up against a much better colt and he was struggling from the moment Lear Fan quickened the pace after halfway. To his credit he plugged on gamely to finish clear of the two other runners but he was flattered in finishing as close as three lengths to the winner, who was eased a couple of lengths close home.

		Hotfoot (br 1966)	Firestreak (br 1956)	Pardal
Kalim (br.c. Mar 11, 1981)				Hot Spell
			Pitter Patter (br 1953)	Kingstone
				Rain
		Khadaeen (b 1975	Lyphard (b 1969)	Northern Dancer
				Goofed
			Gioia (b 1959)	Crepello
				Bara Bibi

Kalim's dam Khadaeen wasn't one of the Aga Khan's more notable racehorses. She ran only as a three-year-old, gaining places in one-mile maiden events at Vichy and Maisons-Laffitte before finishing only fourth in modest company at Amiens on her final start. She is a half-sister to five winners in France, the best of them the very useful mile-and-a-quarter performer Kalkeen, but she was probably retained for the Aga's stud because she's a daughter of the highly successful Lyphard, a granddaughter of the Park Hill winner Bara Bibi and a great-granddaughter of the excellent Masaka, winner of the Oaks and Irish Oaks in 1948. She has been mated so far with relatively inexpensive stallions, producing the disappointing Kalyoub to Sallust, Kalim to Hotfoot, a yearling filly to Shakapour and a colt foal to Niniski, while in 1983 she visited African Sky. Now that Kalim has proved himself a smart animal Khadaeen will no doubt be sent to one of the leading sires. While we don't envisage Kalim's developing into a leading classic contender, he may well improve on his two-year-old form when tried over a mile or a mile and a quarter, and that elusive pattern-race win may yet come his way. All his races so far have been on a sound surface. *F. J. Houghton.*

KALLIBARA 2 b.f. Baragoi 115–Calloo 99 (Ballyciptic 122) (1983 5g 7fg³ 7f 8.2fg 8d) May 14; compact, good sort; half-sister to 2 winners, including 3-y-o High Calory (by High Line), a fairly useful winner at up to 1¼m; dam 2-y-o 6f and 7f winner; plating-class maiden; suited by 1m; acts on a firm surface. *H. Candy.* **67**

KALLISTA ANTARTIS 3 ch.c. Jimmy Reppin 131–Cuddly Toy (Sovereign Lord 120) (1982 5fg⁴ 5fg 5fg 6fg 1983 10s 8g 8.5d 7f 7fg 10fg) tall, narrow colt; plater; not disgraced over 1m second outing; sometimes blinkered; trained most of season by P. K. Mitchell. *H. Collingridge.* **–**

KALOOKI BERT 2 b.g. Persian Bold 123–Almanac 89 (London Gazette 117) (1983 7fg 8f 7g) Apr 27; 7,600F, 16,000Y; tall colt; third produce; dam won over 7.5f at 2 yrs and also over hurdles; last in September in maiden race at Salisbury and quite valuable races at Newbury and Goodwood (blinkered); subsequently gelded. *D. Elsworth.* **–**

KALYOUB 3 ch.c. Sallust 134–Khadaeen (Lyphard 132) (1982 6fg² 5g⁴ 1983 6s³ 7s³ 8d 10.1fg 10.2fg³ 10.8g 10h³) small, strong, chunky colt; good walker; placed in maiden and minor events; probably stays 1¼m; finds little at the end of his races; sold 6,200 gns Newmarket September Sales. *F. J. Houghton.* **70**

KAMENEV 6 b.g. Ribero 126–Welsh Mistress 113 (Abernant 142) (1982 6f 8fg 8.2fg 8g 1983 10f) short-backed gelding; good mover; poor plater nowadays; has worn blinkers; has been bandaged. *Ronald Thompson.* **–**

KANO FLOWER (USA) 4 b.c. Far North 120–Flower Vase (Round Table) (1982 7.6f 10f 10fg² 10s² 10.2f 12fg 9v² 10.2s 1983 8d 6s² 6s² 6s² 7.2s* 7fg 6fg 7g) small, useful-looking colt; won handicap at Haydock in May; effective at 6f in testing conditions and stays 1¼m; seems to act on any going but goes well in the mud; sold 5,300 gns Ascot November Sales. *I. Walker.* **65**

KANSAS BOB 2 b.c. Blakeney 126–Welsh Jewel 72 (Welsh Pageant 132) (1983 5v 5g 6d 7fg² 7f² 7f³ 8h⁴ 8.2fg 8fg²) Mar 10; 1,900Y; fair sort; has a crooked **68**

off-hock; third foal; dam in frame in 5f maiden events at 2 yrs; quite a moderate maiden; second of 16 behind runaway winner Blue Wonder in seller at Newmarket in October on final appearance; will probably stay beyond 1m; acts on firm going. *R. Akehurst.*

KANZ (USA) 2 b.f. The Minstrel 135–Treasure Chest (Rough 'n Tumble) (1983 7f³ 8g* 7fg) Apr 13; $2,100,000Y (the highest price paid for a yearling filly at auction to end of 1982); well-made, attractive filly; closely related to Gold Treasure (by Northern Dancer), a very useful winner at up to 1m, and half-sister to several other winners, notably Diomedia (by Sea-Bird II), a smart winner at up to 9f, and Crown Treasure (by Graustark), the dam of Glint of Gold and Diamond Shoal; dam very useful stakes winner over 6.5f and 1m; 7/4 on, slammed her 14 opponents in the style of a high-class filly in maiden race at Leicester in September, cruising into an 8-length lead inside last 2f and winning eased right up by 4 lengths from Rasseema; favourite, dropped out quickly after leading for long way when disappointing ninth of 15 behind Mahogany in Rockfel Stakes at Newmarket the following month; possibly not at her best on a firm surface; worth keeping on the right side. *G. Harwood.* **90 +**

KAPRIELIAN (USA) 3 b.c. The Minstrel 135–Rainbow's Edge (Creme dela Creme) (1982 7g 1983 11.5fg² 12.3f³ 13f* 12f* 13.8f* 14h² 18.1d 16fg) tall, attractive colt; won maiden race at Nottingham, amateur riders event at Newmarket and slowly-run 4-runner minor event at Catterick in summer, last-named by 1½ lengths from Faroor; stays 2m; acts on hard going; sold to race in Italy 17,000 gns Newmarket Autumn Sales. *M. Stoute.* **90**

KARABLAKE 3 b.c. Blakeney 126–Karenina 95 (Silver Shark 129) (1982 7fg³ 1983 10g² 12.3fg* 11.7fg* 13.1fg³ 16.1s³ 14g² 12fg) strong, medium-sized colt; keen walker; won maiden race at Newcastle in August and minor event at Windsor (by 4 lengths from Sikorsky) in September; staying-on second to Nassipour in handicap at Sandown in October, best subsequent effort; stays 2m; seems well suited by a sound surface. *G. Harwood.* **93**

KARADAR 5 b.h. Rheingold 137–Shahinaaz (Venture VII 129) (1982 14g² 12fg* 16.1f* 16fg³ 14g³ 14.6g* 16d 1983 16.1v⁴ 16f² 16f³ 21f² 16g 18fg* 16fg*) **118**
Karadar emulated Buckskin by winning the Doncaster Cup and Jockey Club Cup in the same season, becoming only the second horse to win both since the Jockey Club Cup reverted to two miles from a mile and a half in 1963. Karadar's overall record doesn't compare to that of Buckskin but these victories provided deserved reward for this exceptionally game stayer. The conditions of the Doncaster Cup in September favoured Karadar: he received weight from three of his seven rivals, including 7 lb from the four-year-olds Santella Man and Condell, and Eddery put up 2 lb overweight on one of the others, Mountain Lodge, one of the main dangers if she could handle the ground. Starting 2/1 favourite Karadar

Jockey Club Cup, Newmarket—Karadar accounts for Another Sam

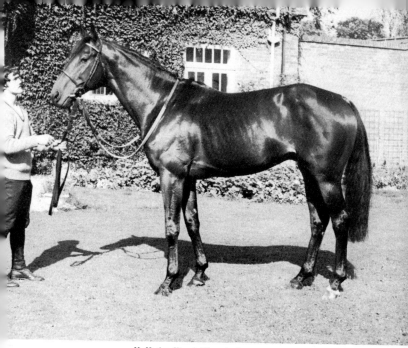

H. H. Aga Khan's "Karadar"

was enterprisingly ridden. He was sent on after half a mile, quickened entering the straight and stayed on strongly all the way home to pass the post two and a half lengths clear of Gildoran with Mountain Lodge third. Karadar was also favourite to win the five-runner Jockey Club Cup at Newmarket the following month—even money this time. His main rival Old Country was withdrawn at the start, but he had to display all his best qualities to account for Another Sam by three quarters of a length; after Karadar had led from some way out Another Sam drew almost level at the furlong marker before Karadar managed to fight him off. Karadar had served notice in June that he had improved from the previous season: he was a short-head second to Santella Man at levels in the Queen's Vase at Royal Ascot and came a close third behind Weavers' Pin and Prince Santiago in the Miner's Northumberland Plate at Newcastle. Even so he seemed to have a lot on against the Gold Cup winner Little Wolf in the Goodwood Cup in July, and he excelled himself in finishing well clear of five others as he ran Little Wolf to half a length; Karadar rallied strongly in the closing stages.

Karadar (b.h. 1978)	Rheingold (br 1969)	Faberge II (b 1961)	Princely Gift
			Spring Offensive
		Athene (b 1960)	Supreme Court
			Necelia
	Shahinaaz (b 1965)	Venture VII (br 1957)	Relic
			Rose O'Lynn
		Cherry (b 1959)	Prince Bio
			Baghicheh

It's no great surprise that Karadar stays as well as he does. His sire Rheingold, who won the Prix de l'Arc de Triomphe and finished second in the

Derby, has proved an influence for stamina. Karadar's dam Shahinaaz was very useful in France as a three-year-old, winning at a mile and at thirteen furlongs. She is a half-sister to a French middle-distance winner, out of the Irish Oaks runner-up Cherry. Karadar is Shahinaaz's sixth foal to win, best of the others being the smart middle-distance performers Kalidar (by Vienna) and Karamita (by Shantung), and the filly Khalida (by Tanerko) who showed useful form at up to thirteen furlongs. Karadar usually sweats up though he didn't when running badly on his seasonal reappearance. Incidentally, he had another untypically poor performance to his name—in the Lonsdale Stakes at York in August on his fifth outing, between Goodwood and Doncaster—which was explained by a ricked back. Karadar remains in training, and his tremendous courage makes him one to keep on the right side: he will continue to be difficult to beat in all but the best staying company. He acts on any going. *M. Stoute.*

KARAMOUN (USA) 2 ch.c. Blushing Groom 131–Korinetta (Petingo 135) (1983   **81**
7g⁴ 7f³) Mar 14; rangy, good sort; first foal; dam, useful over 1¼m, is daughter of French 1000 Guineas winner Koblenza and half-sister to Prix du Cadran winner Karkour; soon showed up and kept on nicely without being punished when 12 lengths fourth of 18 to Gold And Ivory in maiden race at Goodwood in September; odds on, unable to quicken when 3 lengths third of 15 behind Jamais Derierre in similar event at Redcar later in the month; will be better suited by 1m+; should do better in due course. *M. Stoute.*

KARENA PARK 3 b. or br.f. Hot Spark 126–Dunmore Lass II 94 (Nashua) (1982   **–**
5g 1983 9d 11.5fg 8f 7f⁴ 7s 6fg 7g 7s) workmanlike filly; fourth in 7f maiden race at Leicester in July, only form; blinkered nowadays. *M. Ryan.*

KAREN KELLY 3 b.f. Pitskelly 122–Karen Sissy 53 (Karabas 132) (1982 NR   **–**
1983 7fg 7fg) 525 2-y-o; first foal; dam poor maiden; lightly-raced plater; ran better race on first outing. *J. Bethell.*

KAREN'S STAR 6 b.g. Aglojo 119–Colate 59 (Como 120) (1982 6f 6f 5f 5fg 5fg⁴   **76**
5g 5g 6f* 5.6f² 5f⁴ 6g* 5fg 6d 5d 5fg 5s 6s 5s⁴ 1983 5g* 5d 5g 5f 6f 6fg 5f 6f⁴ 5fg* 6h² 6fg³ 6f 6fg* 5fg 6g² 6s³ 5s* 6fg) lightly-made gelding; bad mover; sprint handicapper; won at Edinburgh (apprentices) in May, Wolverhampton in August, Thirsk in September and Hamilton in October; acts on any going; has twice been tried in blinkers; good mount for an apprentice; tough. *D. Chapman.*

Prix du Cadran, Longchamp—Karkour (No. 3) gets the better of Indian Prince after a good battle

KARKISIYA (USA) 3 b.f. Caro 133–Kalkeen (Sheshoon 132) (1982 NR 1983 **112**
10s* 10.5v³ 10f* 10v*) second foal; half-sister to Kadissya (by Blushing Groom),
a useful winner over 1¼m in France at 2 and 3 yrs; dam very useful over 1¼m in
France; readily won maiden race at Saint-Cloud in April and ran well considering
her inexperience when 4 lengths third of 7 behind Alexandrie in Prix Cleopatre on
same course following month; off course 5 months afterwards, but returned in
fine form to beat Compte Rendu in very good style by 4 lengths in Prix d'Automne
at Longchamp in October and Midway Dancer comfortably by 1½ lengths in
Premio Roma Vecchia in November; stays 1¼m well; acts on any going; smart.
A. de Royer Dupre, France.

KARKOUR (FR) 5 b. or br.h. Relko 136–Koblenza 118 (Hugh Lupus 132) (1982 **115**
12fg 12s 12.5v² 12g⁴ 15g 12g* 13.5g⁴ 12f 12v³ 12v 1983 15.5v³ 15.5v² 20v* 12.5g⁴
12s 15.5f 14g)
    The fortunes of long-distance racing have declined sharply in Europe in the
post-war period: the Cup races, for example, once an automatic target for the best
of the previous year's staying three-year-olds, take much less winning most years
than they did in the period up to the end of the 'forties. The British turf authorities
have made some attempt in recent years to remedy a sad situation—the first prize
for the Gold Cup has risen from £17,837 to £43,146 since 1977—but the French
have meanwhile taken further repressive measures against the stayers. The Grand
Prix de Paris, which before 1965 always carried greater prize money than the Prix
du Jockey-Club (French Derby), has had its prize money slashed, its first prize
falling from a peak of £124,924 in 1975 to £36,463 in 1983. The Prix Royal-Oak
(French St Leger) and the Prix du Cadran, the latter until fairly recently the most
valuable race in Europe for out-and-out stayers, have also had their values cut
dramatically. The Cadran, for example, which had a first prize well-nigh double that
of the Gold Cup in 1977, was worth £25,818 to the winner in 1983, almost £10,000
less than in 1977. The status of long-distance racing in France has seldom, if ever,
been lower.
    The French have traditionally had a strong hand in Europe's top staying
events—they have won five of the last sixteen Gold Cups—but they had no

Ecurie Manhattan's "Karkour"

out-and-out stayer in 1983 approaching the calibre of such recent Prix du Cadran winners as Sagaro, Buckskin and Gold River. The best of the French stayers in 1983 were Karkour, Kelbomec, Denel and the pair that were sent over for the Gold Cup, Indian Prince (who came third to Little Wolf) and Balitou (who went lame at Royal Ascot). After a ding-dong battle, Karkour won the Cadran by a head from Indian Prince with Denel (who had earlier won the Prix de Barbeville narrowly from Kelbomec and Karkour) five lengths back in third place; the Yorkshire Cup fourth Top Creator, the only British-trained challenger, came fifth of six. On his previous outing Karkour had been beaten a head by Kelbomec (who wasn't eligible for the Cadran because of the absurd rule excluding geldings from Group 1 events) in the Prix Jean Prat, with Denel only half a length behind, Indian Prince fourth and Balitou fifth. Balitou, off the course for three months after Royal Ascot, won the Prix Gladiateur from Kelbomec on his return. Karkour failed to gain a place in his four races after the Cadran; none of them posed so stiff a test of stamina as the Cadran or its traditional preparatory events the Barbeville and the Jean Prat.

			Tanerko		Tantieme
	Relko		(br 1953)		La Divine
	(b 1960)		Relance III		Relic
Karkour			(ch 1952)		Polaire
(b. or br.h. 1978)			Hugh Lupus		Djebel
	Koblenza		(b 1952)		Sakountala
	(br 1966)		Kalimara		Norseman
			(b 1960)		Montana

Like many a true stayer, Karkour was a slow developer. Trained in his early days by Mathet, he didn't race at two but made his mark as a three-year-old, winning at a mile and a quarter and twice at a mile and a half from four starts, developing into a smart performer. After changing hands at the Arc de Triomphe Sale for approximately £44,000, Karkour again showed smart form the next season, winning the Grand Prix de Vichy and finishing in the frame in several pattern races. Both Karkour's sire and dam were trained by Mathet for the Dupres: Relko, who died in 1982, was one of the best winners of the Derby in the 'sixties and Koblenza won the Poule d'Essai des Pouliches (French One Thousand Guineas). Koblenza bred several other winners before Karkour, including Reine de Lenza (by Roi Dagobert) and Korinetta (by Petingo), both useful winners at a mile and a quarter. Karkour was suited by some give in the ground and acted well on heavy going. He has reportedly been retired to the French National Stud. *J. Audon, France.*

KARLIAN 3 br.g. Ercolano 118–Madam Jane 58 (No Mercy 126) (1982 8s 8s 10s 8s 1983 8v 8.5d 10f) compact gelding; poor maiden; ran respectably in a seller second start. *R. Hannon.*   –

KARNATAK 2 b.c. Artaius 129–Karera (Kalamoun 129) (1983 6g 6fg) Apr 21; medium-sized, close-coupled colt; second foal; dam French 9f winner; second favourite, 8 lengths sixth of 12 to Que Marido in minor event at Nottingham in September, second start; sold to J. Spearing 1,100 gns Doncaster October Sales. *M. Stoute.*   70

KAROL 5 b.h. Kalamoun 129–Le Melody 102 (Levmoss 133) (1982 10s 14f³ 14fg⁴ 14fg² 12g* 1983 12s³ 10s² 12s 11g²) attractive horse; second foal; half-brother to top-class stayer Ardross (by Run The Gantlet); dam, daughter of Musidora Stakes winner Arctic Melody, won both her starts over 7f and 1¼m; placed in Mooresbridge Stakes at the Curragh in March (2½ lengths third to Croghan Hill), Rogers Gold Cup Ballymoss Stakes on same course in April (went down by a neck to Evening M'Lord) and Grand Prix de Lyon in June (4 lengths second to Un Etendard); will stay 2m; probably acts on any going. *D. O'Brien, Ireland.*   97

KASHIDA 2 b.f. Green Dancer 132–Buz Kashi 123 (Bold Lad, Ire 133) (1983 6f 6d) Feb 16; first foal, dam, disqualified winner of Coronation Stakes, was unreliable; fifth in maiden races at Yarmouth in August and September; should do better with time and longer distances. *G. Wragg.*   68 p

KASROY 5 gr.g. Young Emperor 133–Welsh Rhythm (Abernant 142) (1982 NR 1983 8f) rangy, workmanlike gelding; poor maiden; has worn blinkers. *P. Ashworth.*   –

KASSAK 7 gr.g. Dragonara Palace 115–Dauphiness 74 (Supreme Sovereign 119) (1982 6s 6fg 6g 6f⁴ 6f³ 6f 5.3g² 6g 6g³ 5.3fg³ 5.8f⁴ 6v 6v 6s 1983 8v 7.6v 6fg 7f 6fg) leggy gelding; poor sprint handicapper; acts on any going; has worn blinkers   –

but does as well without; sometimes bandaged off-fore; has run well for an amateur rider. *P. Ashworth.*

KATADA 2 ro.f. Nishapour 125–Cardamus (Sassafras 135) (1983 6fg⁴) Mar 22; 84 p neat filly; first foal; dam, granddaughter of brilliantly speedy Texana, was placed from 1m to 10.5f in France; third favourite, ran on steadily after having to be switched when promising 3¾ lengths fourth of 10 to Boezinge in well-contested race at Salisbury in September; will stay at least 1m; likely to improve. *F. J. Houghton.*

KATE KIMBERLEY 4 b.f. Sparkler 130–Ma Griffe (Indian Ruler 89) (1982 8f 50 8fg 8s ³ 10g 1983 11.7s 11.7d 10f 8f 10f 8f 14fg² 16f 12d³ 16fg² 17.1g³ 16.1s 16g) big, lengthy filly; good walker; stays well; probably acts on any going; good mount for an apprentice. *M. Usher.*

KATE THE SHREW 3 b.f. Comedy Star 121–Fiery Romance (Fighting Don) – (1982 5fg 5g 5.8g 1983 8v 8g 6fg) of little account; has worn blinkers. *C. James.*

KATHLEEN'S MONEY 3 b.f. My Swanee 122–Philanderess (Philemon 119) 56 (1982 5f² 6g 5fg 8s 1983 5v 5.8g 6fg 5h 5g* 5fg 5fg 6f 6d) workmanlike filly; won handicap at Wolverhampton in July; form only at sprint distances; usually apprentice ridden, often at overweight; blinkered last 3 outings. *J. Fox.*

KATHRED 5 b.m. Starch Reduced 112–Kathy King (Space King 115) (1982 6s² 85 d 6d 6fg² 6f⁴ 6g 6fg 6d⁴ 6f² 6f 6fg 6g⁴ 6fg 5.6g 6s* 5v³ 6s² 6d 1983 6v⁴ 6g 6s⁴ 6v* 6fg 6f 5.6fg 6s 6g 6g 6fg 6fg) sprint handicapper; made all and kept on well to beat Camisite a length in quite valuable event at Doncaster in May; well beaten most subsequent starts; acts on any going but has done most of her winning on an easy surface; suitable mount for a boy. *R. Hollinshead.*

KATIE BOURNE 3 br.f. Jimsun 121–Wilsome (Will Somers 114§) (1982 5g 5v³ 66 5f 7g 8fg 8.2g 9s 8s 1983 12.2d² 11v 12v 12d 12.2g* 13.8s² 13fg 12.2g 16d) fair sort; attracted no bid after making virtually all in seller at Catterick in May; neck second in non-seller on same course next time; stays 1¾m; acts on soft going. *E. Carter.*

KATIE KOO 3 br.f. Persian Bold 123–Gwendolyn (Bagdad) (1982 7g 1983 7v 82 10f² 10.2h 11.7h* 12fg³ 13.1h* 12fg⁴ 11.5g³ 12d) rangy, useful-looking filly; won maiden race and small handicap at Bath in summer; in frame in handicaps afterwards, swerving left 2f out on first occasion; stays 13f; goes well on top-of-the-ground. *B. Hills.*

KATIES 2 b. or br.f. Nonoalco 131–Mortefontaine (Polic 126) (1983 6fg 7.6d* 85 7.3d) Apr 22; 11,000Y; big, rangy filly with plenty of scope; half-sister to very useful 3-y-o middle-distance winner Millfontaine (by Mill Reef) and quite useful 1978 French 2-y-o 6f and 7.5f winner Polifontaine (by Bold Lad, USA); dam, sister to very smart Polyfoto, won over 1m in France; landed odds of 11/10 on by length from Dusty Letter (pair well clear) in 20-runner maiden race at Lingfield in October; every chance 2f out when eleventh of 14 in Rochford Thompson Newbury Stakes later in the month; will stay 1m. *M. Ryan.*

KAUKAS 4 b.g. So Blessed 130–Balnespick 101 (Charlottown 127) (1982 8fg 10f⁴ 58 10.1fg 10.2g² 10f⁴ 10f* 10fg* 10d* 10s 1983 10v 10v 10d 10s 10f 10h 10f² 10fg⁴ 10d³) well-made gelding; plater nowadays; stays 1¼m; seems to act on any going; raced very freely seventh start. *G. Balding.*

KAYED (USA) 2 br.c. Mr Leader–Queenies Polly (Roman Colonel) (1983 8fg – 10fg) Apr 13; $100,000Y; half-brother to several winners, including smart 1979 American staying 2-y-o Irish Gentry (by The Irish Lord); dam ran 6 times unplaced; no show in maiden races at Newmarket and Nottingham (blinkered) in October; sold 2,600 gns Newmarket Autumn Sales. *J. Hindley.*

KAYSARIYYA 3 br.f. Shirley Heights 130–Kermiya (Vienna 127) (1982 7.6v⁴ 69 1983 10.2f 10.2h² 12f 12f² 12g) smallish, rather lightly-made filly; second in maiden races at Bath (sweated badly) and Beverley in summer; suited by middle distances; sold to CBA 66,000 gns Newmarket December Sales. *F. J. Houghton.*

KAYTU 2 b.c. High Top 131–Arawak 109 (Seminole II) (1983 7g³ 8d³) Apr 15; 97 p 50,000Y; quite attractive colt; half-brother to several winners, notably Spring In Deepsea (by Captain's Gig), a smart winner at up to 9f here and in USA; dam third in Yorkshire Oaks and Irish Guinness Oaks; third twice in October, 3 lengths behind stable-companion Secret Way in maiden race at York and 1¾ lengths behind Corinth in £4,000 event at Newbury; the type to improve further over middle distances, and seems sure to win races. *R. Hern.*

KAYUDEE 3 ch.g. Nebbiolo 125–Wet Powder (Above Suspicion 127) (1982 5f 7g 90 8s⁴ 1983 12.3v³ 12s 16g* 16.1fg* 18.4fg 16f² 17.4g 18fg) sturdy gelding; successful in maiden race at Beverley in June and handicap at Haydock in July, beating Belfe by a head in latter; excellent fifth of 28 to Bajan Sunshine, beaten about 4 lengths, in Tote Cesarewitch at Newmarket in October on final outing; well suited by a test of stamina and a sound surface; sweated up fifth start; the type to win more races when conditions are in his favour. *J. Fitzgerald.*

KAYUS 2 b.c. Junius 124–Kind Thoughts 71 (Kashmir II 125) (1983 5fg⁴ 6g³ 6fg* 6f* 6g) Apr 18; 80,000Y; attractive, well-made colt; has a very nice, easy action; first foal; dam, sister to Blue Cashmere, stayed well; made all in 7-runner events at Ayr in July and Newcastle in August, on second occasion beating Water Moccasin a neck and breaking course record; will probably stay 7f; acts on firm going; spoilt chance final start by being bit slowly into stride. *G. Hunter.*   **97**

KAZAROW 2 ch.c. Blue Cashmere 129–Sardara 106 (Alcide 136) (1983 6fg 5g*) Apr 7; 18,000Y; leggy, rather unfurnished colt; half-brother to Irish 2000 Guineas winner Dara Monarch (by Realm); dam staying half-sister to St Leger winner Intermezzo; 25/1, drew away from distance to win 16-runner maiden race at Sandown in October by 3 lengths from Mattagirl; tailed off on previous start (reportedly suffered from very sore shins afterwards); should be suited by 6f+; fairly useful. *H. Collingridge.*   **90**

K-BATTERY 2 ch.c. Gunner B 126–Kajetana (Caro 133) (1983 5v⁴ 6f⁴ 7g 7d 6fg⁴ 7d 7g 7fg*) Apr 26; strong, compact colt; first foal; dam never ran; improved late in season and won 14-runner nursery at Redcar by a neck from Silver Token; finds 6f a bit sharp and will be suited by 1m+; wears bandages behind. *W. Elsey.*   **82**

KEBIR (FR) 4 ch.c. Bolkonski 134–La Theve (Red God 128§) (1982 8d 8v 8g⁴ 8g³ 8fg 8v* 1983 8s* 8d 8f 9fg* 8fg 8g) 150,000 francs Y (approx £15,000); fourth live foal; half-brother to 2 winners in France; dam won twice over 1m in France; beat Great Substence by a length in Prix Edmond Blanc at Saint-Cloud in March and Torgos by ½ length in Grosser Preis von Dortmund in June; ran respectably several other starts; stays 9f; seems to act on any going; accompanied stable-companion All Along to North America in autumn. *P.-L. Biancone, France.*   **113**

KEDRA 2 b.f. Welsh Pageant 132–Grey Shoes 104 (Grey Sovereign 128§) (1983 6d) June 3; rather unfurnished filly; fifth foal; half-sister to Irish 1½m winner Shoemender (by Busted); dam sprinter; 14/1, not disgraced after missing break when 9 lengths seventh of 16 to Turn The Key in maiden race at Newbury in October; sure to improve. *J. Ciechanowski.*   **– p**

KEELBY KAVALIER 5 b.h. Ardoon 124–Elegant Lady 69 (Round Table) (1982 12f² 12fg⁴ 12fg* 12fg 12g 12g³ 14g 12fg² 12fg³ 12g² 12s 1983 12g³ 12v³ 12v* 12d³ 12f 12g² 14g 13s 12fg² 12fg³ 12fg⁴) compact horse; fairly useful handicapper; beat Grand Unit by ½ length at Doncaster in May; ran creditably in races won by Jupiter Island at Newmarket (beaten a neck in Air New Zealand Handicap) and York (fifth in Tote-Ebor) in August and finished good fourth to Asir in William Hill November Handicap at Doncaster; stays 1¾m; acts on any going; effective with and without blinkers; has run creditably for an amateur rider; best on a galloping track. *J. Etherington.*   **91**

KEEN 2 ch.c. Sharpen Up 127–Doubly Sure 59 (Reliance II 137) (1983 6fg*) Apr 12; big, rangy, handsome colt; brother to top-class colts Diesis and Kris; dam, placed over 1½m, is daughter of high-class staying 2-y-o Soft Angels; looking to   **90 P**

Granville Stakes, Ascot—the promising Keen is shaken up to win by two lengths from August

have done plenty of work, stood out in a good-looking field when co-favourite for 7-runner Granville Stakes (newcomers event) at Ascot in July and proved similarly superior in race, leading from start and keeping on well when shaken up to win by 2 lengths from August; will stay 1m; has the pedigree and looks of a top-class colt and must have a very bright future indeed. *H. Cecil.*

KEEP IT DARK 3 b. or br. g. Welsh Pageant 132–Rotisserie 106 (Tesco Boy 121) —
(1982 7g 1983 10v⁴ 12v 11.7v) neat gelding; ridden by 7-lb claimer when distant fourth in minor event at Nottingham, probably best effort; blinkered final start (May). *H. Candy.*

KEEP SHINING (USA) 3 ch.f. Stage Door Johnny–Carolina Moon 116 (Grey   77
Dawn II 132) (1982 8s⁴ 1983 10s*) rangy filly; showed promise on only outing as a 2-y-o and confirmed it when beating Virgin's Smile by a neck in maiden race at Chepstow in May on only outing at 3 yrs; will stay 1½m; has raced only on soft going. *J. Tree.*

KEEP SMILING 4 b.g. Tumble Wind–Retiro (Pardal 130) (1982 7g 7g⁴ 8fg 10f   —
8g³ 8fg 10fg⁴ 1983 8fg) quite attractive gelding; plater; possibly stays 1¼m. *L. Lightbrown.*

KEEP TAPPING 2 b.c. Tap On Wood 130–Windy Cheyenne (Tumble Wind)   100
(1983 5g 6f* 6f²) May 4; IR 41,000Y; strong, close-coupled, attractive colt; excellent mover; second produce; dam won 5 times at up to 6f in USA, including a stakes race at 2 yrs; won Selsey Maiden Stakes at Goodwood in July and 11-runner £3,100 race (beating Rio Riva short head) at Salisbury in August, only to be disqualified on second occasion for causing slight interference; will stay 7f; acts well on firm going; game and genuine. *B. Hills.*

KELBOMEC (FR) 7 b.g. Direct Flight–Piqueuse (Piqu'arriere) (1982 15.5v²   115
15.5fg⁴ 12s 15g³ 15fg² 20s* 1983 15.5v² 15.5v* 12s³ 15fg* 20g² 12d) strong French gelding; a tough competitor to beat in good French staying races; held on by a head from Karkour in Prix Jean Prat at Longchamp in May and easily beat Petit Montmorency in Prix Kergorlay at Deauville in August; also ran well to be ¾-length second to Denel in Prix de Barbeville at Longchamp, 1¾ lengths third to Diamond Shoal in Grand Prix d'Evry and length second to Balitou in Prix Gladiateur at Longchamp again; stays very well; acts on any going but goes well in the mud; consistent. *J-C. Cunnington, France.*

KELLATHI (USA) 3 b.c. Seattle Slew–Desert Law (Court Martial) (1982 NR   99
1983 8d 10s 8f* 8g⁴ 8f³ 7.2fg² 8g4 8fg 8g* 8fg⁴) $650,000Y; big, quite attractive colt; half-brother to several winners in USA; dam, half-sister to high-class American stayer Astray, was a very smart stakes winner at up to 9f in USA; a useful colt who ran out a 3-length winner of minor event at Doncaster in June (from Barrie Baby) and handicaps at Warwick in July (from Galetzky) and Bath in October (from Mouslat); in frame on several other occasions too; should stay beyond 1m; acts on firm going. *F. Durr.*

KELLET 3 ch.f. Palm Track 122–Goldwis 94 (Golden Cloud) (1982 NR 1983   —
9.4d) half-sister to 2 winners by Sit In The Corner, including dual 1977 2-y-o 5f winner Dollar-A-Corner; dam won from 5f to 7f; unquoted when behind in maiden race at Carlisle in May. *H. Wharton.*

KELLY BAY 2 b.f. Pitskelly 122–Columbella (Jukebox 120) (1983 5d 5f 6f 6d 6fg   49
8fg 6fg) May 24; 1,250Y; small filly; sister to Irish 7f and 1m winner Shannon View and half-sister to another winner; dam ran only twice; plater; suited by 1m; acts on firm going; off course for 3 months after third outing. *S. Norton.*

KELLYS REEF 2 b.f. Pitskelly 122–Reflex 80 (Mill Reef 141) (1983 5d* 5g 5d²   92
5fg*) Apr 7; IR 4,800Y; small, sturdy, good-quartered filly; first live foal; dam ran only at 2 yrs when winner over 6f; ran on strongly to win 15-runner maiden race at Thirsk in May by ½ length from Oystons Propweekly; returned in excellent form after a 4-month absence, and showed lot of speed when winning 17-runner nursery at Newmarket in October from Philstar; bred to stay 6f+ but gives strong impression 5f will be her trip; acts on a firm and a soft surface. *E. Eldin.*

KELLY'S SHADOW 3 b.f. Bruni 132–Palesa (Palestine 133) (1982 6s⁴ 6s 1983   —
10v 8.5d 12f 8f) leggy, short-backed filly; plater; should stay 1¼m; blinkered final start; sold 350 gns Ascot October Sales. *M. Haynes.*

KELLY'S STAR 2 b.f. Pitskelly 122–Regal Miss 90 (Sovereign Path 125) (1983   59
5fg³ 5.1fg⁴ 7f 5.3f³ 6f) Jan 2; 2,400Y; small, rather lightly-made filly; fourth foal; half-sister to winning sprinter Regal Jim (by Jimmy Reppin); dam ran only at 2 yrs when winner at up to 6f; in frame in maiden auction events and a claiming race; finds 5f a bit sharp but ran moderately over 7f; blinkered final start; exported to Algeria. *P. Haslam.*

KELLY THORPE 3 ch.f. Le Johnstan 123–Pinzica (Pinza 137) (1982 6s 5d 1983   **49**
8d 8s² 8v 9d⁴ 8g 10f³ 10f³ 10.6fg 12fg 13.8g² 12fg) narrow filly; plater; stays 1¾m;
acts on any going. *C. Gray.*

KELSEY LADY 5 gr. or ro.m. Pongee 106–Aquagold (Goldhill 125) (1982 NR   **–**
1983 14.7d² 16f 16f 12f 14.7f³ 12f) compact mare; fourth foal; dam poor plater;
winning hurdler; placed in 2 maiden races at Redcar; appears not to stay 2m;
wears blinkers. *M. Lambert.*

KENTUCKY 5 b.m. Warpath 113–Shenandoah 88 (Mossborough 126) (1982   **–**
15.8g 13v 12f 15g² 15.8f 12f³ 12.2f⁴ 15f⁴ 12fg⁴ 1983 12s 17.1g 15.5f) big, strong
mare; poor performer; suited by a test of stamina; blinkered final start; has run
respectably for an amateur rider; sold 825 gns Ascot September Sales. *G.
Thorner.*

KERFUFFLE 3 b.f. Lochnager 132–Right Barnie (Compensation 127) (1982 NR   **–**
1983 5g 8d) big, rangy filly; good walker; half-sister to 1m winner Nae Bird and a
winner in Italy (both by Birdbrook); dam never ran; last-but-one and last in maiden
race at Kempton and minor event at Brighton in September. *R. Smyth.*

KEROINE 3 b.f. Keren 100–Ribera (Ribston 104) (1982 6d 1983 11d 9.4d)   **–**
probably of little account. *N. Chamberlain.*

KEROSA 3 ch.f. Keren 100–Lindosa 104 (Aureole 132) (1982 NR 1983 12d   **–**
14.7d) small filly; half-sister to a winner in Belgium; dam useful winner at 1m;
tailed off in minor and maiden races in spring. *N. Chamberlain.*

KESSELRING 2 b.c. Brigadier Gerard 144–Cartridge 108 (Jim French) (1983   **77**
6d 7f 7g 8.2g 7g) Mar 30; lengthy colt; first foal; dam, daughter of smart French
filly Calahorra, won over 6f and 7f; quite a moderate maiden; form only at 7f;
sweated up badly on second appearance; ran freely in blinkers fourth outing; sold
German International Bloodstock 7,800 gns Newmarket Autumn Sales. *B. Hills.*

KESSLIN 3 b.g. Derrylin 115–Kessella (Le Levanstell 122) (1982 NR 1983 11.7v   **99**
11.7v³ 13.3g 12f⁸ 11.5f² 12f 12d*) compact, workmanlike gelding; half-brother to

Mr Ian M. Jewell's "Kesslin" (S. Dawson)

several winners, including Irish middle-distance winner Rathconrath (by Wolver Hollow); dam never ran; successful in handicaps at York in July (apprentices) and October, quickening clear to beat His Honour by 4 lengths, with remainder well strung out, in latter event when having first race for nearly 2 months; ran well when 2½ lengths second of 5 to Band at Sandown in between; stays 13f; probably acts on any going; has a useful turn of foot; should win another race or 2. *N. Vigors.*

KESTREL QUEEN 4 b. or br.f. Roman Warrior 132–Rana (Welsh Pageant 132) — (1982 NR 1983 9s 12f 10f 7.6fg 6g 6h) workmanlike filly; first foal; dam unraced daughter of half-sister to Raffingora; well behind in varied company, including selling; sold 1,350 gns Doncaster September Sales. *J. Wilson.*

KEYALA (USA) 2 b. or br.c. Key To The Kingdom–Alathea (Lorenzaccio 130) **108** (1983 7g³ 9fg* 8d* 10g) Feb 24; 105,000Y; first living foal; dam, half-sister to very smart 2-y-o R. B. Chesne, showed little worthwhile form; won twice in the autumn, beating Royal Tap 2 lengths in maiden race at Evry and Vercors 2½ lengths in 4-runner Prix de Martinvast at Longchamp; probably past his best for year when modest sixth to Darshaan in Criterium de Saint-Cloud in November; should stay 1¼m; will win more races. *F. Boutin, France.*

KEYBOARD 3 br.f. High Top 131–Happy Music 84 (Hethersett 134) (1982 7g³ — 7.6v* 1983 8d 8v 8f) neat, good sort; disappointing as a 3-y-o, including when blinkered final start (June); bred to be suited by 1¼m+; evidently a nervous type. *G. Pritchard-Gordon.*

KEYCORN 3 br.g. Sit In The Corner–Key Harvest (Deep Diver 134) (1982 NR — 1983 10v 12fg 12f 10d 10.5d) compact gelding; first foal; dam never ran; respectable fifth in maiden event at Beverley in September but finished towards rear in a £4,000 seller on only subsequent appearance. *M. H. Easterby.*

KEYOPS 2 b. or br.c. Shirley Heights 130–Temple Wood 105 (Sweet Revenge **71 p** 129) (1983 7fg 8d) Mar 30; 135,000Y; rangy, attractive colt; good walker; second foal; half-brother to winning 3-y-o stayer Dingle Belle (by Dominion); dam, winner from 5f to 1m, is half-sister to very smart Town and Country; faded in last 3f when nearly 14 lengths eighth of 14 to Corinth in £4,000 event at Newbury in October, second outing; a very taking individual who should leave this form well behind in due course. *G. Hunter.*

KEY ROYAL (USA) 2 br.f. Key To The Kingdom–Cool Value (Cool Moon) (1983 — 9g) Apr 3; $60,000Y; narrow, rather leggy filly; first foal; dam won over 4f and 5f in USA; 16/1, never-dangerous sixth of 13 to My Tootsie in maiden race at Wolverhampton in October. *A. Jarvis.*

KEY TOTHE MINSTREL (USA) 3 ch.f. The Minstrel 135–Seven Locks — (Jacinto) (1982 6g² 6f* 7fg 8g⁴ 1983 10v⁴ 12fg) medium-sized, lengthy, attractive filly; good walker; useful performer at 2 yrs; looked just in need of run and was by no means disgraced when remote fourth of 7 to Ski Sailing in Sir Charles Clore Memorial Stakes at Newbury in May, making a lot of the running; not seen out after finishing only twelfth of 14 behind High Hawk in Ribblesdale Stakes at Royal Ascot the following month; promises to stay 1¼m; best form on a sound surface. *M. Stoute.*

KEY WIND 3 b.f. On Your Mark 125–Key Note (Kythnos 126) (1982 5fg 5f² 5.1f* — 6g⁴ 5f³ 5fg² 5g 5d 5g 1983 5g 5fg 5h 5f 5f 5g) rangy, useful sort; didn't recover her 2-y-o form; best at 5f; acts on firm going; blinkered third outing. *A. Jarvis.*

KHACHATURIAN (USA) 2 ch.c. To The Quick–Fraga (Misti IV 132) (1983 7f) — p Feb 28; $165,000Y; useful-looking colt; half-brother to 3 winners, notably smart middle-distance stakes winner Ardiente (by Fiddle Isle); dam won over 9f in France and also won over jumps; second favourite although in need of race, faded under pressure soon after halfway when behind in 19-runner maiden race at Redcar in October; should do better. *S. Norton.*

KHAIRPOUR 4 gr.c. Arctic Tern 126–Khayra (Zeddaan 130) (1982 8g² 12f* **119** 10fg* 11f* 12f² 12f* 13.3f 12.3d* 12fg* 14.6f 12g* 1983 12d 14v² 16g³ 20f² 16fg² 13.3f* 12s 12fg 14s³)) The Yorkshire Cup in May produced one of the most remarkable incidents of the season as well as one of the most surprising results. The incident happened two furlongs out. Challenging the eventual winner Line Slinger and looking as if he might succeed, the second favourite Khairpour ducked left then violently right under the whip, veering dangerously across the track and losing several lengths; back in contention inside the final furlong he veered again when shown the whip, but was still beaten only one and a half lengths into second. Khairpour had wasted a golden opportunity, but he put the race behind him. As a three-year-old he had

Geoffrey Freer Stakes, Newbury—Khairpour gains a well-deserved success from Castle Rising (rails) and Yawa

made steady progress, winning on seven of his eleven starts and showing enough in handicaps to earn a run in the St Leger (he finished seventh to Touching Wood at Doncaster, beaten just over seven lengths). He continued to make progress as a four-year-old, and after York was placed in the Henry II Stakes at Sandown in May, the Gold Cup (second, beaten five lengths by Little Wolf) and the Princess of Wales's Stakes at Newmarket in July before gaining a well-deserved victory in the Geoffrey Freer Stakes, a Group 2 pattern race run at Newbury in August. Favoured by the conditions of the Geoffrey Freer he started 7/4 favourite but gave his supporters an anxious moment. After being ridden up with the pace, he drew into a three-length lead, looking sure to win impressively with under a furlong to run; then he appeared to try to pull himself up in the closing stages, and had to be nursed home to hold off Castle Rising by a length, his jockey—no doubt remembering York—careful not to pick up the stick. Khairpour ran three more times, his best effort a respectable third, beaten three and a half lengths, to Mountain Lodge in the Jefferson Smurfit Memorial Irish St Leger on his final outing; he didn't show a lot in finishing eighth of eleven to Time Charter in the Prix Foy, and ran without zest when a disappointing sixth to Band in the Cumberland Lodge Stakes.

			Sea-Bird II	Dan Cupid
Khairpour (gr.c. 1979)	Arctic Tern (ch 1973)		(ch 1962)	Sicalade
		Bubbling Beauty	Hasty Road
		(ch 1961)	Almahmoud
	Khayra (gr 1975)	Zeddaan	Grey Sovereign
		(gr 1965)	Vareta
		Khairunissa	Prince Bio
		(gr 1960)	Palariva

Khairpour is the first foal of his dam, an unraced sister to the top-class Kalamoun and a half-sister to several other winners at up to eleven furlongs, who is

434

a daughter of the smart 1962 two-year-old Khairunissa; the family has produced many speedy horses over the years. Khairpour's sire Arctic Tern is a Prix Ganay winner who stayed a mile and a half; he seemed more likely to sire a stayer than the dam did to produce one, though that Khairpour should turn out to stay as well as he does is something of a surprise. Despite Khairpour's quirks which make him anything but an easy ride (he ran freely when tried in blinkers in the Henry II Stakes) he is a pretty good racehorse at his best. A medium-sized, quite attractive colt, a good walker and mover, he acts on any going. *F. J. Houghton.*

KHAIZARAAN (CAN) 3 br.f. Sham–Beautiful Sister (Hail to Reason) (1982 6s* 1983 8g) well-made filly; really good mover; looked very promising when beating Sun Princess in Blue Seal Stakes at Ascot as a 2-y-o but was never travelling well and finished tailed-off seventh of 8 behind Royal Heroine in Child Stakes at Newmarket in July on only outing of 1983 (looked pretty fit but went down rather freely). *H. T. Jones.* —

KHLOUD 3 b.f. Pitskelly 122–Brig O'Doon (Shantung 132) (1982 NR 1983 7v 7fg 7.2fg³ 8f 9s) 16,000Y; fine, big, rangy filly; half-sister to numerous winners, notably high-class miler Young Generation (by Balidar); dam poor maiden; looked quite promising early on, but ended season by finishing in rear in maiden race at Hamilton in October; should stay 1m; didn't handle bends well at Sandown and Haydock on second and third outings and moved short to post on fourth. *J. Dunlop.* — 76

KHWLAH (USA) 2 b.f. Best Turn–Priceless Fame (Irish Castle) (1983 6f* 7fg) Apr 13; $550,000Y; tall, lengthy, lightly-made filly; good mover; second foal; half-sister to high-class 1982 staying 2-y-o Dunbeath (by Grey Dawn II); dam, sprint winner, is sister to Kentucky Derby and Belmont Stakes winner Bold Forbes; favourite, won 25-runner maiden race at Newbury in August by 1½ lengths from Lovers Bid after making nearly all; 10 lengths eighth of 13 behind Mahogany in Rockfel Stakes at Newmarket 2 months later; will stay 1m. *H. T. Jones.* — 91

KHYBER 3 b.c. Oats 126–Mahlene (Pontifex) (1982 7f 8s⁴ 8s⁴ 10s³ 1983 12d² 14d² 12v² 14g³ 16f 10f 12d 12fg*) well-made colt; poor walker and mover; returned to form when blinkered in gentleman riders race at Brighton in October, beating Our Caro by 10 lengths; had been runner-up at Newmarket (2) and Folkestone in spring; suited by 1½m+ (had stiff task over 2m); possibly unsuited by really firm going, but acts on any other. *G. Pritchard-Gordon.* — 86

KID 'EM (USA) 2 b.f. Sham–Necaras Miss (Ambernash) (1983 6fg 7s) Apr 10; $25,000 2-y-o; sturdy filly; half-sister to several winners, notably Drop the Pigeon (by No Robbery), a very useful winner at up to 1m; dam won 7f claiming race; put up a pleasing first effort in £4,000 event at York in September, staying on nicely to be 5½ lengths fifth of 17 to Seattle Siren; favourite, beaten over 2f out when 10 lengths seventh of 16 behind Bamba in maiden race at Ayr later in the month; should stay at least 1m; possibly unsuited by soft ground and is worth another chance on faster going. *M. Jarvis.* — 75

KIDSWOOD 2 ch.c. Lombard 126–Venetia 67 (Song 132) (1983 5fg 6fg 6g) June 9; second foal; dam won over 7f and 1m; in rear in minor events, twice last. *P. M. Taylor.* —

KIEV (BEL) 2 ch.g. Targowice 130–Biguine (Jim French) (1983 5v³ 5g 5g⁴ 6g 7fg 8.2h⁴ 7g⁴ 7g⁴ 8d⁴) Apr 3; 105,000 francs Y (approx £8,750); light-framed, unimpressive gelding; first foal; dam 2-y-o 1m winner in French Provinces; won 12-runner nursery at Goodwood in September in good style by 3 lengths from Our Lady; apparently best at 7f; blinkered fourth outing. *P. Kelleway.* — 78

KIKALONG 3 gr.f. Runnymede 123–Scoop (Bleep-Bleep 134) (1982 5fg 6d 5s 7g 1983 10v 8s⁴ 8.3s) strong, compact filly; plater; stays 1m. *P. Ashworth.* —

KILCORAN WOOD 3 b.g. Filiberto 123–White Cliffs (Hill Rise 127) (1982 NR 1983 16f) 420 2-y-o; tall, leggy gelding; third foal; dam poor daughter of very useful Victoria Quay; 100/1 and bandaged when tailed-off last of 5 behind Hi Easter in minor event at Thirsk in July. *G. Harman.* —

KILLIFRETH 3 ch.f. Jimmy Reppin 131–Spring River 66 (Silly Season 127) (1982 5g 6g 1983 10s² 12s³ 11.7v² 10s⁴ 12g* 10fg² 12fg) good-bodied, quite attractive filly; having first race since spring when making all to beat Chlosterli by 3 lengths in minor event at Lingfield in September; good second to Only A Pound in similar race at Brighton later in month; runs as though she'll stay beyond 1½m; had stiff task final outing. *H. Candy.* — 87

KILLINGHOLME CLAY 4 b.c. Targowice 130–Patricia (Sovereign Path 125) (1982 8.2s 8fg² 8fg 10f² 8fg 10d 1983 10g 10g 7f 6f) leggy colt; has a round action; fair handicapper at his best but is inconsistent; stays 1¼m; suited by a sound — 72 surface; hung very badly once in 1981; sold 920 gns Newmarket September Sales. *G. Pritchard-Gordon.*

KILLYCURRA 2 b.f. Raga Navarro 119–Uranus (Manacle 123) (1983 5fg*) Apr **80 p**
18; IR 8,200Y; half-sister to several winners, including smart 7f and 1m winner
Tellurano (by Guillaume Tell); dam won twice over 5f at 2 yrs in Ireland; 9/1, won
19-runner maiden race at Windsor in July by 2 lengths from Plaits, leading inside
final furlong; will stay 6f. *R. Williams.*

KILSYTH 4 b.f. Jolly Good 122–Harmony Thyme 73 (Sing Sing 134) (1982 7g 8g3   –
8f 9g 8fg 7d 10.6s 9s 8g 1983 7d 10d4 8.2v 8s4 8g) compact filly; plater; probably
stays 1¼m; sometimes blinkered; sold 500 gns Doncaster May Sales. *D.
Chapman.*

KILTTALEY 2 ch.f. Tower Walk 130–Starkist 81 (So Blessed 130) (1983 5fg 6fg **74?**
7.2g4 6fg 6fg 6fg) Apr 30; smallish filly; fourth reported foal; half-sister to 3-y-o
1m winner Star of a Gunner (by Gunner B); dam 2-y-o 5f winner; plater, and a
moderate one apparently, until finishing close up in maiden race at Doncaster in
November on final appearance; acts on a firm surface; blinkered fifth outing. *D.
H. Jones.*

KIMBERLEY MINE 2 b.f. Stanford 121§–Bonny Rand (Hillary) (1983 7.6d)   – p
Apr 17; IR 11,000F; third foal; dam once-raced daughter of half-sister to top-class
filly and outstanding broodmare Gazala; weak in market, never-dangerous eighth of
18 in maiden race at Lingfield in October; will probably do better. *J. Dunlop.*

KIMBLE GIRL 3 ch.f. Some Hand 119–Tacoma 89 (Hard Tack 111§) (1982 5g   –
5d2 5g2 1983 6s 5v 6f 6h 7.6d 8g 7g) big, lengthy, workmanlike filly; below form in
1983; trained until after fourth outing by R. Baker. *W. Musson.*

KINBARRA 2 b.f. Run The Gantlet–Aabora (Don II 123) (1983 7.6d) Apr 12;   –
sister to fair middle-distance stayer Aaborun and half-sister to 3 winners; dam well
beaten all outings; behind in 20-runner maiden race at Lingfield in October. *J.
Dunlop.*

KINBOSHI 3 b.g. Mummy's Pet 125–Grove Hall 66 (Hook Money 124) (1982 NR   –
1983 7f 8f 7.6g) 2,000Y; strong gelding; half-brother to numerous winners,
including smart stayer Hazard (by Sheshoon) and useful miler Hornton Grange (by
Hornbeam), herself dam of Swiss Maid; dam won over 1m; in mid-division in
maiden races; moved poorly first start; sold 740 gns Doncaster October Sales.
Miss S. Hall.

KINCS 3 b.f. Comedy Star 121–Miss Merida 64 (Midsummer Night II 117) (1982   –
7d 1983 9s4 9fg 8fg 10fg 7.6fg) big, strong filly; good mover; has shown only a
little ability; seems to stay 9f. *G. Balding.*

KIND MUSIC 4 gr.c. Music Boy 124–La Magna 104 (Runnymede 123) (1982 7s4 **120**
7.5s 5s2 6s* 5fg* 6f 5g3 5s3 5v* 1983 5s2 5fg3 5f 6fg) strong, well-made colt;
good walker and excellent mover; the top French-trained sprinter in 1982; didn't
run up to his best at 4 yrs though placed in Prix de Saint-Georges at Longchamp in
May (head second to Sky Lawyer in blanket finish) and Prix du Gros-Chene at
Chantilly in June (3½ lengths third to Gem Diamond); well beaten behind Sayf El
Arab in King's Stand Stakes at Royal Ascot and behind Habibti in William Hill Sprint
Championship at York in August on last 2 starts; hampered soon after start when
blinkered in latter; best at 5f; acted on any going; often sweated up; retired to
Haras de Victot. *R. Collet, France.*

KING ARFER 2 ch.c. Downholme 97–Grand Velvet 83 (Grand Roi 118) (1983   –
5v) May 18; 2,600Y; neat colt; half-brother to 3 winners, notably very smart 6f to
1¼m winner Go Leasing (by Star Appeal); dam stayed well; behind in 20-runner
maiden race at Thirsk in May; dead. *J. Etherington.*

KING CHARLEMAGNE 4 gr.g. Habat 127–Calibina 101 (Caliban 123) (1982 8g **62**
8.2g 9fg 8g 8.2g 8d 8.2g 12v 12s 1983 7d 6g 5f2 5f* 5f* 5f* 6g2 5f 5fg2 5g 5fg 5g
5s2 5g*) strong gelding; had a good year and won handicaps at Edinburgh
(amateurs), Beverley, Hamilton and Edinburgh again; clearly best at sprint
distances; acts on any going but goes well on firm; blinkered once in 1982; suitable
mount for an inexperienced rider; has worn bandages. *Mrs G. Reveley.*

KING HARRY 2 br.c. Relko 136–Mertola (Tribal Chief 125) (1983 7g 7fg) May   –
14; medium-sized, rather leggy, close-coupled colt; third live foal; half-brother to
1½m winner Haresceugh (by Andrea Mantegna) and a winner in Hong Kong; dam
ran once; backward, behind in maiden races at Leicester (eighth of 16) and
Newmarket in September. *N. Vigors.*

KINGKAID 4 ch.g. Scottish Rifle 127–Miss Lollypop (St Paddy 133) (1982 NR   –
1983 12g) half-brother to several winners, including fair stayer Morlolly (by

Morston); dam never ran; tailed off in modest maiden race at Brighton in May. *A. Pitt.*

KING OF CLUBS 2 ch.c. Mill Reef 141–Queen Pot (Buckpasser) (1983 5g² 5v* 6d² 6f³ 7f* 7f⁴ 6fg² 8g²) Feb 26; rather lightly-made, quite attractive colt; good walker; half-brother to winners in France and USA, including 1½m winner Gallantsky (by Nijinsky); dam, daughter of champion 1966 American 3-y-o filly Lady Pitt, won 3 times over sprint distances; successful in minor event at Newbury in May and 11-runner Limekilns Stakes at Newmarket in July; in frame all other starts, on sixth finishing very good 3 lengths fourth of 6 to Knoxville in Seaton Delaval Stakes at Newcastle in August and on eighth going down by 2½ lengths to Northern Tempest in Gran Criterium at Milan in October; finds 6f on sharp side and is suited by 1m; acts on any going; tends to carry head high under pressure; blinkered at Newcastle. *I. Balding.*   **114**

KING OF MAN 4 gr.g. Three Legs 128–Auld Rogue (Tarqogan 125) (1982 8fg 9.4fg 11g² 12.3fg² 12g² 9s 12v⁴ 12d 1983 12d³ 12.2g 10f 12f 13f) neat, quite attractive gelding; plater; stays 1½m; one paced; sold 2,600 gns Doncaster August Sales. *C. Thornton.*   –

KING OF NAPLES 2 b.c. Ile de Bourbon 133–Padrona 103 (St Paddy 133) (1983 6d⁴) Apr 28; attractive colt; closely related to winning stayer Al Nasr (by Green Dancer) and half-brother to 2 winners, notably high-class middle-distance performer Pelerin (by Sir Gaylord); dam won over 5f and 6f at 2 yrs; second favourite, put up a very pleasing first effort when making quite significant late headway to finish 8 lengths fourth of 17 to Cremets in maiden race at Newbury in October; had refused to enter stalls at Ascot a month previously; sure to leave this form behind over longer distances. *G. Wragg.*   **76 p**

KING OF ROCK 3 ch.c. Music Boy 124–Visitation 84 (Tarqogan 125) (1982 5fg 5fg 5g 7g⁴ 1983 7fg* 7.6g³ 7f² 7fg* 6f* 7f 7f) robust, well-made colt; won handicaps at Leicester in June (50/1) and Ayr and Hamilton in July, twice making all; didn't run well last 2 starts though; stays 7f; well suited by a firm surface; blinkered once at 2 yrs (valuable seller). *P. Haslam.*   **77**

KING OF SPEED 4 b.c. Blue Cashmere 129–Celeste 83 (Sing Sing 134) (1982 6s 7fg 7f* 7.3fg 7d 8f⁴ 8g 7d* 7fg 7s 7d 1983 7s 6f 7fg 7f 7f 7f 8d 7.6fg 7g) lengthy, quite attractive colt; quite modest at his best; below form in 1983; best at 7f; seems to act on any going; good mount for an apprentice; blinkered sixth start; sold 3,200 gns Newmarket Autumn Sales. *D. Weeden.*   –

KING PERSIAN 2 ch.c. Persian Bold 123–Naiad Queen (Pampered King 121) (1983 6f* 6fg* 7d)   **104**
Previously the only five-furlong Group 1 event restricted to two-year-olds, the Heinz '57' Phoenix Stakes was run over an extra furlong in 1983. The £16,674 prize failed to attract a single foreign challenger and, as in previous years, took little winning for an event of its status. King Persian was one of only two unbeaten juveniles in a thirteen-runner field; Gala Event, the other, who had won the Woodford Stud Stakes by three lengths on her previous outing, started 2/1 favourite. King Persian, an 8/1-shot following an easy maiden race success at Gowran Park the previous month, stumbled leaving the stalls and lost several lengths as Gala Event and Grey Dream set a blistering early gallop. With two furlongs to run they were still clear of their rivals, but their exertions began to take their toll inside the final furlong, and King Persian, who had lain some way off the pace, ran on strongly to snatch the verdict by a short head from Gala Event, with Grey Dream three quarters of a length back in third. King Persian didn't fulfil the promise of this run when second favourite for the BBA (Ireland) Goffs National Stakes at the Curragh in September, never troubling the leaders and being beaten over five lengths into fifth place behind El Gran Senor in a race run over a furlong more and on much softer ground than he'd encountered before.

King Persian (ch.c. June 14, 1981)	Persian Bold (br 1975)	Bold Lad (b 1964)	Bold Ruler
			Barn Pride
		Relkarunner (b or br 1968)	Relko
			Running Blue
	Naiad Queen (b 1970)	Pampered King (b 1954)	Prince Chevalier
			Netherton Maid
		Invermore (ch 1961)	Anwar
			Luggeen

King Persian, a 29,000-guinea yearling in Ireland, is the fifth foal and third winner of his dam Naiad Queen, a fairly useful winner at up to seven furlongs in

Mr Seamus McAleer's "King Persian"

Ireland. Her two other winning foals were both useful: Inishannagh (by St Alphage) and Rising Tide (by Red Alert) were successful two-year-old sprinters who failed to win at three. Naiad Queen's dam, Invermore, a winner at five furlongs, has bred four winners including Hobby, a successful five-furlong performer who is herself the dam of the leading 1980 American grass filly, Just A Game. King Persian's breeding suggests he is likely to prove best at up to a mile. His liability to a penalty for his Group 1 success will make him difficult to place at three, though as a late foal he may have more than normal improvement in him. *L. Browne, Ireland.*

KING'S CLASSIC 3 ch.g. Kinglet 98–Classical Air (Melodic Air 111) (1982 NR 1983 11f) first foal; dam never ran; 50/1 when last of 9 behind Yuhzuru in maiden event at Hamilton in August. *H. Bell.* –

KING'S COLLEGE BOY 5 b.g. Andrea Mantegna–The Guzzler 69 (Behistoun 131) (1982 18.4fg 16g 20fg 22.2fg 18.4g³ 19f 16.1g³ 18.8fg* 17.4d 19s* 18d 20g⁴ 18s³ 1983 17.1v 17d⁴ 18.8v 20fg 18.4fg 19f³ 17fg* 18.8f⁴ 17d* 19g² 17.1g² 16.1s² 20fg⁴) big, rangy gelding; fair handicapper on his day; won at Wolverhampton in August and September; suited by a stiff test of stamina; acts on firm going but is well suited by some give in the ground; best in blinkers; hasn't always been consistent. *N. Vigors.* **82**

KING'S FOREST 4 b.g. Realm 129–Pardina 98 (Pardao 120) (1982 5f³ 6g 7f³ 7g* 7.6g³ 7fg³ 10fg 8g 8s 1983 6d 7fg 7s 6d 8fg) big, well-made, attractive gelding; good mover; quite moderate; best form at around 7f and isn't sure to stay 1¼m; acts well on firm going; blinkered fourth start (slowly away); sold 2,800 gns Ascot 2nd June Sales to L. Kennard. *R. Hollinshead.* –

KING SHARA (FR) 2 ch.c. Iron Duke 122–Shanella (Skegness) (1983 7f 8s 7g) Mar 29; 135,000 francs Y (approx £11,250); third foal; half-brother to French 3-y-o Sharana (by Free Round) and French 7f and 1¼m claiming races winner Snow Rose (by Gift Card); dam won over 10.5f in France; 10 lengths eighth of 12 to Talk Posh in 1m maiden race at Beverley in September; sold to Mrs M. Nesbitt 1,600 gns Doncaster November Sales. *P. Kelleway.* –

KING'S HOLT 4 b.c. Royal Palace 131–Lady Rowley 114 (Royal Levee) (1982   58
10d 7fg 8g* 8s⁴ 7g⁴ 1983 10g 8s 8.5g 6h 8f³ 7f 8fg* 7f 7f 8f) big, rangy colt; made
all to win minor event at Brighton in August; stays 1m but isn't sure to get further
unless he learns to settle; acts on firm going; blinkered fifth and sixth starts (very
reluctant to go down on first occasion); trained most of season by M. McCormack.
F. Watson.

KING SINBAD 3 ch.c. Dublin Taxi–Richo's Melody 57 (Double Jump 131) (1982   –
5fg 5fg³ 5g⁴ 5d 1983 6s 5.1fg) useful-looking colt; lightly-raced maiden plater;
should stay 6f; best form on a sound surface. *P. Haslam.*

KINGS ISLAND 2 ch.c. Persian Bold 123–Gerardmer (Brigadier Gerard 144)   107
(1983 6d³ 6d* 6fg* 6fg 6f 6fg³ 6g 6fg² 6fg⁴) May 3; 14,000Y; strong, useful sort;
second foal; dam unraced half-sister to very useful Potemkin and Tants; won
11-runner maiden race (apprentice ridden) at Doncaster in May and 9-runner minor
event at York in June, drifting left both times; ran extremely well subsequently,
particularly when third of 6 behind easy winner Precocious in Gimcrack Stakes at
York in August and when beaten a head by Cutting Wind under 9-7 in Golden Gates
Nursery at Ascot in September; should stay 1m; acts on a firm and a soft surface;
best with strong handling. *C. Brittain.*

KING'S MARCH 4 b.g. Moulton 128–Walk By 113 (Tower Walk 130) (1982 8g   –
10s⁴ 10g⁴ 1983 18f) lengthy gelding; plater; stays 1¼m; acts on soft going. *A.
Madwar.*

KINGS OFFERING 8 b.g. Frankincense 120–Ribble Girl 96 (Trouville 125)   44
(1982 5g 5fg 5fg 5f 5fg 5g⁴ 5g³ 5fg 5d 1983 5v 5s² 5d 5fg 5f 5f 5f 5f 5s) strong,
good-topped gelding; sprint handicapper; has been beaten in a seller; best at 5f;
acts on any going; good mount for an inexperienced rider; effective with or without
blinkers; has worn bandages; best on a sharp track. *R. Ward.*

KINGS PARADE 5 ch.h. Realm 129–La Lidia 78 (Matador 131) (1982 12f² 1983   –
14s) strong, well-made horse; good walker and mover; stays 1½m well; seems to
act on any going; useful hurdler; racing in USA. *G. Thorner.*

KINGS SOLDIER 4 b.g. Queen's Hussar 124–Albertina 102 (Great Nephew   –
126) (1982 8fg 10fg³ 10f² 10d* 10f 11g* 11.1fg 12f² 1983 10d) lengthy,
useful-looking gelding; good walker; tailed off only start at 4 yrs in October; stays
1½m; seems to act on any going. *J. Jenkins.*

KING VIV 3 b.c. Shirley Heights 130–Miss Tweedie 114 (Aberdeen 109) (1982   –
NR 1983 10g) 15,500Y; half-brother to quite useful 1977 2-y-o 5f winner Knight
(by Realm); dam very useful at 6f and 7f; unquoted when towards rear in 16-runner
amateur riders race won by Kuwait Team at Goodwood in September. *S. Mellor.*

KINNITY MARY 2 b.f. Mandrake Major 122–Saucy Moll 94 (Hard Sauce 131)   ?
(1983 6d 6f 6f) Apr 22; 1,700Y; leggy filly; half-sister to 3 minor winners by
Firestreak; dam stayer; poor form, including in sellers, in this country; winner in
Milan. *H. Blackshaw.*

KINSKI (USA) 2 b.c. Nijinsky 138–Royal Kin (Sir Gaylord) (1983 7fg) Feb 14;   85 P
$240,000Y; big, rangy colt; half-brother to several winners, notably Taisez Vous
(by Silent Screen), a high-class winner at up to 9f; dam stakes-placed winner of 3
sprint races at 2 yrs; looked green both in paddock and on way to start when 9/1 for
Houghton Stakes at Newmarket in October and was very sympathetically handled
in race, in circumstances showing a great deal of promise in finishing 5¾ lengths
seventh of 14 to Condrillac; has enormous potential and will make a good 3-y-o. *J.
Tree.*

KINZ 2 br.f. Great Nephew 126–Alicia Markova 64 (Habat 127) (1983 7f) Mar 23;   –
21,000Y; second foal; dam, half-sister to Music Maestro, Saulingo and Outer
Circle, ran 3 times at 2 yrs; ninth of 11 in maiden race at Yarmouth in August. *N.
Callaghan.*

KIOWA 2 b. or br.c. Saritamer 130–Double Blush 76 (Double-U-Jay 120) (1983   –
6fg) Mar 12; 4,000Y; strong, workmanlike colt; fourth foal; half-brother to 3-y-o 6f
winner Saxham Breck (by Abwah); dam, half-sister to smart sprinter Son of Shaka,
won over 1m; backward, behind in 22-runner maiden race at Newmarket in July. *P.
Haslam.*

KIRCHNER 5 b.h. Kashmir II 125–Vwonica (Val de Loir 133) (1982 8g³ 8s 8g⁴   110
6.5d 7d² 8fg* 8g 8g 8fg 8s 7s 8v 8v² 1983 8v 6d* 6s² 6f 6s 6fg 5d³ 6fg*) compact
ex-French horse; first foal; dam won over 8.5f in France; won Thirsk Sprint Stakes
in May by 2 lengths from Tysandi and Group 2 Premio Umbria at Rome in
November by a neck from Coquito's Friend; ran well in between to be second to

Solimile in 7-runner £6,700 event at Lingfield, ninth of 28 to Polly's Brother in Ladbrokes (Ayr) Gold Cup on fifth start and 1½ lengths third to Massorah in Premio Omenoni at Milan; stays 1m but is better at shorter distances; acts on any going except possibly very firm; has won for an apprentice; trained by A. Jarvis first 4 starts. *G. Lewis.*

KIRMANN 2 br.c. Top Ville 129–Karmouna (Val de Loir 133) (1983 8fg) Apr 3; — lengthy, angular colt; half-brother to several winners, notably very useful French middle-distance performer Kareliaan (by Luthier); dam, placed over 9f, comes from same family as Blushing Groom; 20/1 but looking to have done a fair bit of work, prominent to past halfway in 28-runner maiden race at Newmarket in October. *F. J. Houghton.*

KIR ROYALE (USA) 3 b.f. Ack Ack–Old Gypsy (Olden Times) (1982 7f 7g 7d⁴ — 1983 9v² 9f 8f³ 10fg) lengthy, sparely-made filly; placed in minor event at Wolverhampton in May and poorish maiden event at Beverley in July (blinkered, found nothing); stays 9f; best form in the mud. *M. Stoute.*

KIRSOVA 2 ch.f. Absalom 128–Law and Impulse 104 (Roan Rocket 128) (1983 — 5g⁴) Apr 24; 12,500Y; workmanlike filly; half-sister to 2 winners, including useful 1974 2-y-o 5f and 6f winner Cardinal Wolsey (by Henry the Seventh); dam won over 5f at 2 yrs; backward, never-dangerous 5¾ lengths fourth of 7 to Be My Valentine in maiden race at Newmarket in April. *C. Brittain.*

KITTY COME HOME 3 b.f. Monsanto 121–Fair Kitty 73 (Saucy Kit 76) (1982   **61** 5fg 7fg 7fg 8.2d 8s 1983 10s 12s 12s⁴ 14f* 14f) deep-girthed filly; held up when winning handicap at Yarmouth in June; ran moderately only subsequent start; gives impression she'll stay well; seems to act on any going. *D. Dale.*

KITTY FRISK 3 b.f. Prince Tenderfoot 126–Claremont Girl (Will Hays) (1982 7s   **64** 7s 1983 8fg 9.4d 9.4f³ 10f² 10g³ 10fg 8g) quite well-made, attractive filly; suited by 1¼m; sold 4,100 gns Newmarket December Sales. *J. W. Watts.*

KITTY RIVERS 3 b.f. Rapid River 127–Kitty H (Takawalk II 125) (1982 5f 5f³ — 5fg 6f 6fg 1983 6f 8f) bad plater; blinkered final start. *S. Norton.*

KITTY WREN 3 b.f. Warpath 113–Turtle Dove (Gyr 131) (1982 NR 1983 10d   **55** 12fg 12fg 13s 12g³ 12.2d* 15fg) lightly-built filly; sister to 3 winners, notably successful middle-distance stayer Path of Peace; dam ran only once; narrowly won selling handicap at Catterick in October (no bid); should be suited by 1¾m; suited by some give in the ground; slipped up fourth start; sold 1,450 gns Doncaster November Sales. *C. Thornton.*

KLAIMAN 3 b.c. Riverman 131–Klaizia (Sing Sing 134) (1982 NR 1983 10g⁴ 7s) 47,000Y; strong, good-bodied, attractive colt; half-brother to smart French miler Lypheor (by Lyphard); dam smart sprinter in France; shaped promisingly when fourth to easy winner Monongelia in maiden race at Newmarket in August but disappointed when favourite in weaker company at Yarmouth on only subsequent start; possibly unsuited by soft going and may be worth another chance. *L. Cumani.*

KLAIROVE 4 b.f. Averof 123–Klaire 85 (Klairon 131) (1982 10.1g 10g 8s 8.2s   **60** 1983 8.2d³ 8s³ 7d² 8fg 8fg* 8f² 8.2fg³ 10h⁴ 10f) lightly-made filly; poor walker; plater; attracted no bid after winning at Warwick in June; stays 1¼m; probably acts on any going; sometimes bandaged; consistent. *B. McMahon.*

KNEBWORTH 3 b.c. Nebbiolo 125–Nice Tack 106 (Hard Tack 111§) (1982 NR — 1983 8s 10.1fg 10.1f 14f) 15,000Y, 360 2-y-o; lengthy colt; poor walker; half-brother to two 2-y-o winners by Red Alert; dam stayed 7f; soundly beaten in maiden and minor events. *N. Callaghan.*

KNIGHTHALL (USA) 5 b.h. King's Bishop–Midnight Hush (Sunrise Flight)   **40** (1982 10.2s³ 10fg 12g 10.4g 10f⁴ 8g³ 8fg³ 12.3g 9g 1983 10.2d 9s 10fg³ 8f 9f² 9fg⁴) plater; stays 1¼m; acts on any going; suitable mount for an inexperienced rider; has worn bandages. *A. W. Jones.*

KNIGHT'S BANNER (USA) 2 b.c. Star Spangled–Isle of Success (Fiddle Isle)   **95 p** (1983 7g*) Mar 18; $85,000Y; lengthy, lightly-made colt; third foal; half-brother to 2 winners, one stakes placed; dam, half-sister to Derby runner-up Hawaiian Sound, won 5 times at up to 1m; sire, son of Round Table, was very smart winner at up to 9f; second favourite, made headway from halfway to lead 1½f out and kept on well to win 18-runner maiden race at Leicester in October easing up by 2½ lengths from Sugar Palm; will probably stay 1¼m; likely to go on to better things. *M. Stoute.*

KNIGHTSBRIDGE GAME 4 gr.g. Abwah 118–Turnstone 83 (Sea Hawk II   **45** 131) (1982 8.2d 6f 8.3fg 8fg 10d² 8s 10g² 10s 10s* 10.2s 1983 8s² 10.1d 10v 10s

10d 10fg[4] 10g[3] 11s 10.8g[2]) plain gelding; plater; suited by 1¼m; acts well on soft ground. *D. Wilson.*

KNIGHT'S HEIR 2 b.c. Lord Gayle 124–Kazanlik 116 (Ommeyad 120) (1983 7fg 8g) May 24; IR 3,600Y; lightly-built colt, lacking in scope; half-brother to numerous winners, including high-class hurdler Gay George (by Prince Regent) and very useful Irish performers Darling Bud (by Whistling Wind) and Lark Rise (by Larkspur); dam second in Irish Guinness Oaks; 50/1, behind in quite valuable events at Doncaster and Newbury in September. *D. Arbuthnot.*   —

KNIGHTS SECRET 2 ch.c. Immortal Knight 103–Lush Secret 50 (Most Secret 119) (1983 5d* 6f[3] 5f* 6f[2] 6f* 5fg[2] 6g[2] 6g[4]) Apr 12; workmanlike colt; first foal; dam plater; successful in maiden race at Catterick in June and nurseries at Beverley in July and Redcar in August; promises to stay beyond 6f; consistent. *M. H. Easterby.*   **90**

KNOWING CARD 8 b.m. Green Shoon 102–Poker Face (Borealis) (1982 NR 1983 11.7fg 12f[3]) ex-Irish mare; stays very well; acts on any going. *P. M. Taylor.*   —

KNOXVILLE 2 b.c. Pitskelly 122–Cariole 84 (Pardao 120) (1983 5g[3] 5s[2] 5v[3] 7f 7f*) Apr 10; IR 30,000Y; good-bodied colt; half-brother to several winners, including fairly useful 5f to 7f winner Marking Time (by On Your Mark) and 3-y-o 5f winner Suffred (by African Sky); dam won over 7.6f; won Seaton Delaval Stakes at Newcastle in August, staying on strongly to beat Kalim (gave 7 lb) by short head; beaten in maiden events previously; needs at least 7f, and will be suited by 1m; best form on firm ground; off course 2 months after third outing, and not raced after Seaton Delaval having jarred a knee. *B. Hills.*   **114**

KOHINOOR DIAMOND 3 ch.f. Roman Warrior 132–Czar's Diamond 66 (Queen's Hussar 124) (1982 5h[4] 6s 1983 6v[4] 7s 7fg 10.1f 12f) workmanlike filly; only poor form in varied company; blinkered final start. *G. Kindersley.*   —

KOLOMELSKOY PALACE 2 b.f. Royal Palace 131–Russian Princess 99 (Henry the Seventh 125) (1983 7g[4]) Feb 21; 16,500Y; half-sister to numerous winners, including good French middle-distance stayer Paddy's Princess (by St Paddy); dam, half-sister to Connaught, won over 6f at 2 yrs; 12/1 and backward, 2½ lengths fourth of 7 to Test of Time in minor event at Sandown in October; certain to do better at 1m+. *B. Hills.*   **77 p**

KOMATCH (USA) 4 ch.g. Apalachee 137–Zambezi River (Pretendre 126) (1982 14fg 16fg[2] 16d[2] 16f[4] 16.9fg 12f[2] 10.1s[2] 16s[2] 1983 18.8v[2] 16f) plain gelding; good mover; stays very well; acts on any going but is suited by some give in the ground; blinkered twice at 3 yrs. *M. Pipe.*   **72**

KONDAIR 3 b.c. Record Run 127–Milk and Honey 102 (So Blessed 130) (1982 7f[3] 7s 1983 8d 8s[3] 10d[2] 10fg[3] 10f 10f* 12d* 10fg[3] 12d[4] 10fg) smallish, fair sort; won ladies race at Brighton in August (by 10 lengths) and handicap at Goodwood in September (beat Nunswood by ¾ length); stays 1½m; acts on any going; didn't handle track well and hung in closing stages at Epsom third start; has worn a tongue strap. *D. Arbuthnot.*   **87**

KOOLIBAR 2 br.g. Balidar 133–July Mist 79 (High Treason 126) (1983 5d 5fg 5f 6g 7d) Apr 7; 1,400F, 8,000Y; fair sort; half-brother to minor winners here and abroad; dam won 1¼m claiming race; plating-class maiden; probably stays 7f; gelded after final appearance; sent to Malaysia. *M. W. Easterby.*   **66**

KOORINGA 2 ch.g. Streak 119–Abercourt 89 (Abernant 142) (1983 6fg 7g) Apr 2; 3,000F, 11,000Y; quite attractive, well-made gelding; brother to a poor animal, and half-brother to 5 winners, notably smart sprinter Blue Courtier (by Blue Cashmere); dam won 4 times over 5f at 2 yrs; well beaten in maiden events at Ascot (unseated rider going to start) in September and Lingfield (prominent until veering left under pressure 2f out) in October. *M. McCormack.*   —

KORYPHEOS 4 b.g. He Loves Me 120–Silly Song (Silly Season 127) (1982 7.6f 8fg[3] 7f 6g 6s 1983 8d 7s* 7.6v[2] 7f[3] 7fg[4] 8.3fg[3] 7g) leggy, lightly-made gelding; well backed when winning handicap at Brighton in May; ran creditably several starts afterwards; stays 1m; acts on any going; sweated up on final outing. *P. Mitchell.*   **70**

KOYQIO 3 ch.c. Wolverlife 115–Sweet Foot (Prince Tenderfoot 126) (1982 NR 1983 9.4d 7fg 7f) IR 1,200F, 1,800Y; first produce; dam never ran; tailed off in maiden and minor events. *I. Jordon.*   —

KRAKOW 3 b.f. Malinowski 123–Fighting 105 (Aggressor 130) (1982 6f 6g 6fg   **85**
1983 7d* 8f 7fg³ 7f* 6fg 6f³ 7f² 7fg³ 8fg) big, lengthy filly; good walker and mover;
held up when winning handicaps at Epsom and Yarmouth in summer; ran creditably
most other starts; should stay 1m; yet to race on really soft going but acts on any
other. *M. Stoute.*

KRAYYAN 3 ch.c. Tower Walk 130–Mrs Moss 81 (Reform 132) (1982 5fg* 5f* 5f²   **109**
6g³ 6g³ 1983 6v 5g³ 5f 6fg) well-made, attractive colt; half-brother to numerous
winners, including very smart middle-distance stayer Jupiter Island (by St
Paddy), very smart 1983 2-y-o Precocious (by Mummy's Pet) and very useful
1980 2-y-o 5f winner Pushy (by Sharpen Up); dam 2-y-o 5f winner; won maiden
race at Haydock and National Stakes at Sandown as a 2-y-o and subsequently
showed smart form in defeat; ran easily best race of 1983 when 4 lengths third of
17 behind On Stage in Palace House Stakes at Newmarket in April, running on
well to be nearest at finish; stayed 6f but gave impression 5f was probably his
optimum trip; acted on firm going; reportedly suffering from a blood disorder
when in rear final start; standing at Irish National Stud, fee IR £1,750 (special live
foal). *G. Hunter.*

KRISTALLINA 4 b.f. Homeric 133–Go Friendly (Be Friendly 130) (1982 8d 8.5f   **–**
10fg² 10f³ 10fg 10g² 12f 13.8f* 14f 14g 14s 15.5fg 1983 10f) lengthy filly; tailed off
only start at 4 yrs in June; stays 1¾m; needs a sound surface; sometimes
blinkered; bolted on way to start once in 1982. *A. Bailey.*

KRISTEL JONTEE 2 ch.f. Manor Farm Boy 114–Flying Molly (Shiny Tenth   **–**
120) (1983 5v 6fg 5f 6fg) Mar 8; bad plater. *J. Holt.*

KRISTEN 4 ch.f. Sheshoon 132–Sweet Boronia 96 (Mandamus 120) (1982 12g⁴   **47**
10.1fg 10f 9g 10.1d³ 10.8fg* 10.1fg³ 12g⁴ 10f 10v 1983 10.1d 10v* 10s 10.2g 10.1f
17fg 16.5f 15.5f 11.5s 15.5fg) small filly; plater; attracted no bid after winning at
Folkestone in May; well beaten afterwards; yet to show she stays long distances;
seems to act on any going. *R. Hoad.*

KRUGERAMA 5 br.g. Amber Rama 133–Krugerrand 74 (Goldhill 125) (1982 10s   **–**
8.2g 8g 8fg 8.2v³ 8d³ 1983 6f 8.2fg 5f⁴ 8f 7g) plater nowadays; stays 1m well;
probably acts on any going; occasionally wears blinkers. *E. Weymes.*

KRUIDTVAT 3 gr.c. Broxted 120–Pinnacle 70 (High Perch 126) (1982 5fg³ 5f 5g   **65**
1983 6fg³ 6g) sturdy colt; good walker; close third in seller at Windsor in July;
behind in non-seller 2 months later; suited by 6f; joined A. Moore after final start.
C. Horgan.

KUMU 3 b.f. Streak 119–Fleur d'Amour 85 (Murrayfield 119) (1982 5d 5fg² 5fg   **–**
5.8f 5g 5v⁴ 5s 1983 6v 5v 5s 5s 6fg 6fg) poor plater; seemed to act on any going;
blinkered final outing; dead. *M. Bradley.*

KUNG FU MASTER 2 ch.g. Import 127–Miss Kung Fu 70 (Caliban 123) (1983   **67**
5v² 5s² 5v⁴ 5fg⁴ 5f 6fg 6f) Mar 17; tall, workmanlike gelding; second reported
foal; dam won 7f seller; plating-class maiden; stays 6f; acts on any going; exported
to Singapore. *C. Williams.*

KUROSAWA (USA) 3 ch.c. Giacometti 130–Tebaldi 103 (Astec 128) (1982 NR   **83**
1983 12v 14d⁴ 12s 16fg³ 12f 12g⁴ 12fg* 12d 12g³) smallish, lengthy colt;
half-brother to 2 minor winners in USA; dam, 2-y-o 5f and 7f winner, stayed 1½m;
won handicap at Folkestone in October; probably stays 2m, but best form at 1½m;
best form on a sound surface; blinkered last 3 outings. *R. Sheather.*

KUSHSHOON 3 b.g. Sheshoon 132–Kushbehar 80 (Behistoun 131) (1982 7g   **–**
8.2d 1983 12.2g 12f⁴ 13.8f 12f 12fg 12.2d 10f) poor middle-distance plater; last
when blinkered fifth outing. *S. Wiles.*

KUWAIT BEACH (USA) 3 gr.c. Grey Dawn II 132–Horsing Around   **–**
(Advocator) (1982 6s 7g 1983 8f 8f 11.7fg 12d 13fg 12d) big colt; little worthwhile
form in varied races; trained until after second start by J. Sutcliffe. *R. Laing.*

KUWAIT DAY 2 ch.c. Tower Walk 130–Sara's Star 70 (Sheshoon 132) (1983 6f   **76**
6f³ 7f³ 7f) May 5; 8,600F, 15,500Y; useful-looking colt; brother to useful and very
tough 5f to 1m winner Venus of Stretham and half-brother to several winners; dam
quite moderate at 2 yrs; third in summer maiden races at Hamilton and Yarmouth;
suited by 7f. *G. Huffer.*

KUWAIT PALACE 2 b. or br.c. Julio Mariner 127–Flying Escape 74 (Hook   **85**
Money 124) (1983 6g 7fg 8g* 8.2s⁴) May 13; 5,600F, 9,200Y; tall, rather leggy
colt; half-brother to 2 winners, including fairly useful miler Chop-Chop (by
Birdbrook); dam at her best at 2 yrs; favourite when staying on well to beat

Shervani by 1½ lengths (pair clear) in 15-runner maiden race at Edinburgh in September; 5½ lengths fourth of 7 in minor event won by Trouvere at Hamilton the following month; will stay beyond 1m. *G. Huffer.*

KUWAIT SKY 2 br.c. African Sky 124–Darling Bud (Whistling Wind 123) (1983   **75** 5d³ 5fg* 7.2fg⁴ 6fg 6f⁴ 6fg 5.3fg⁴ 5fg) Feb 20; IR 24,000Y; half-brother to 3 winners, including fairly useful 5f to 7f winner A Star Is Born (by Tudor Music); dam useful Irish 2-y-o; landed the odds by a length from Fleet Builder in maiden race at Edinburgh in May; stays 7f; acts on firm going and a soft surface; blinkered fifth to seventh outings. *G. Huffer.*

KUWAIT SUN 3 gr.c. Bruni 132–Countess Decima (Sir Gaylord) (1982 7fg 1983   **101** 12f 10fg* 10d* 10d* 12g) close-coupled, good sort with plenty of scope; showed a deal of promise, though unplaced, before winning minor events at Salisbury (2 ran), Goodwood and Yarmouth in September; landed the odds comfortably by 1½ lengths from Only A Pound on last-named course; should stay 1½m; sold to M. Tate 19,500 gns Newmarket Autumn Sales. *G. Harwood.*

KUWAIT TAXI 2 b.f. Dublin Taxi–Gay Maria (Tacitus 124) (1983 6f 5s) May 28;   **–** 6,800F, 3,700Y; half-sister to useful 7f performer Jenny Splendid (by John Splendid) and 1½m to 2m winner Aniece (by Ballymoss); dam never ran; showed some ability first time out, but none at all second. *G. Huffer.*

KUWAIT TEAM (USA) 3 ch.c. Graustark–D'Arqueangel (Raise A Native)   **77 ?** (1982 7g 8s³ 1983 11.7s 12f 8f 12d 10g* 12g) quite useful-looking colt; good walker; mainly disappointing, easily best effort when 33/1-winner of amateur riders race at Goodwood in September; suited by 1¼m; wears a hood nowadays and has also worn a small bandage on his near-fore; trained until after second start by G. Harwood. *R. Laing.*

KUWAIT TOWER (USA) 3 gr.c. Little Current–Gris Vitesse (Amerigo 116§)   **120** (1982 7fg* 7fg² 8s⁴ 1983 8g⁴ 8f) $55,000Y; attractive, well-made colt; good mover; half-brother to several winners, including Derby third and Irish Sweeps Derby runner-up Silver Hawk (by Roberto) and very useful French 1m to 11f winner Blast Off (by Graustark); dam won Prix Jacques le Marois; was green as a 2-y-o but showed smart form nevertheless; 50/1 when excellent 3½ lengths fourth of 16 behind Lomond in 2000 Guineas at Newmarket in April on reappearance, running on well and showing improved form; missed Derby, reportedly because of coughing, and made only other appearance in Sussex Stakes at Goodwood in July when losing at least 6 lengths at start and eventually coming in ninth of 11 behind Noalcoholic; should stay middle distances; appears to act on any going. *J. Sutcliffe.*

KUWAIT WIND 2 br.f. Tumble Wind–Succeed 85 (Parthia 132) (1983 5s) May   **–** 11; 7,000Y; quite attractive filly; sister to Tumble Belle, a winner at up to 1m in Ireland, and half-sister to 3 winners, including fairly useful 1982 2-y-o 5f and 6f winner Escart Bay (by Stradavinsky); dam, winner at 1m, is half-sister to Observer Gold Cup winner Approval; 14/1 but fit and well, soon-struggling last of 9 in maiden race at Haydock in May. *G. Huffer.*

KWA ZULU (USA) 3 ch.g. Naskra–Sweet Nothings (Promised Land) (1982 6fg   **62** 6v 6d 1983 9s 11g 8fg⁴ 12.2f² 10f² 10d 8g 10fg) sparely-made, fair sort; poor walker; quite modest form in varied company; appears to stay 1½m; blinkered final outing; retained by trainer 5,000 gns Ascot December Sales. *G. Hunter.*

KYLE-HELEN 4 b.f. Orange Bay 131–Kyle Keep 73 (Ballymoss 136) (1982   **–** 13.1f 10.2s 8s 12s 1983 17.1g) little worthwhile form in varied company, including selling. *Dr A. Jones.*

KYNASTON 3 b.f. Pals Passage 115–Kelly Green (Kelly 122) (1982 5fg³ 5g² 6s   **76** 6d 5d² 6s 1983 5s⁴ 6d* 6d³ 5f⁴ 6f³ 6g 6f 6fg) lengthy filly; not a good mover or walker; won maiden race at Hamilton in May; soundly beaten in seller final start (very fractious in preliminaries); stays 6f; acts on any going; usually blinkered nowadays; apprentice ridden; sold 510 gns Ascot September Sales. *J. Berry.*

KYOTO 5 b.g. Averof 123–Klondyke Fire (Klondyke Bill 125) (1982 8f 10f 8d 8.2g   **–** 1983 12s) big, lengthy gelding; has shown no form on flat for a long time; stays 1¼m; occasionally blinkered; sometimes goes too fast for his own good. *J. Jenkins.*

KYROOTA 3 b. or br.g. Reliance II 137–Anna Barry 76 (Falls of Clyde 126) (1982   **66** 7g 7fg⁴ 1983 12d 12g 10v 7f 10.6fg³ 8f* 10.6f 8d 9d) lengthy, strong, workmanlike gelding; won apprentice maiden race at Yarmouth in August; didn't run particularly well afterwards, but had some stiffish tasks; stays 1¼m and should get further; acts on firm going. *M. Tompkins.*

443

L

LA BIRD 4 b.f. Le Johnstan 123–Bird 80 (Firestreak 125) (1982 12g 13.8f 12g 13.8f³ 12f³ 10d 1983 10g² 10f* 11f² 12f) lengthy filly; poor mover; plater; bought in 1,700 gns after scoring at Nottingham in June; stays 1½m; seems to act on any going but goes well on firm; suitable mount for an apprentice; sometimes bandaged behind; does best when ridden up with pace. *H. Wharton.*   **39**

LABOOSHA 2 b.f. Tarboosh–Flattery (Atan) (1983 5d 5s⁴ 7fg 6f 5f 5g 5g) Jan 11; 700F; leggy, narrow filly; poor mover; sister to a moderate plater; dam won over 5f at 2 yrs in Ireland; poor maiden; form only at 5f. *J. Gilbert.*   **53**

LACEFIELD 2 b.f. Quiet Fling 124–Remould 83 (Reform 132) (1983 5s³ 7.2fg 7f 7.2g 10d) Mar 30; 1,500Y; neat filly; second foal; sister to middle-distance winner Deal On; dam won over 5f at 2 yrs; poor maiden; ran in sellers last 2 outings; should stay 1¼m. *D. Arbuthnot.*   **58**

LACEWOOD 2 ch.f. Tap On Wood 130–Amablai (Levmoss 133) (1983 7g) Apr 14; 14,000Y; half-sister to Balu (by Ballymore), a useful winner at up to 15f in Ireland and France, and to disqualified 7f winner Red Fantastic (by Red God); dam, half-sister to Derby third Oats, won at up to 2m in Ireland; ninth of 13 in maiden race at Lingfield in October. *A. Ingham.*   **–**

LACEY'S LANE 2 b.c. Nebbiolo 125–Lavender Royale (Royal Palace 131) (1983 7d) Feb 28; third foal; half-brother to a winner in Belgium; dam unraced daughter of very useful 6f and 7f winner Sea Lavender; twelfth of 13 in maiden race at Yarmouth in September; exported to Malaysia. *P. Feilden.*   **–**

LACKBRIDGE 3 ch.g. Mansingh 120–Talsaana (Crepello 136) (1982 6f 6f 6g 6s 1983 8s 8s) useful sort; showed some ability final outing as a 2-y-o, but was well beaten in handicaps both efforts in 1983 (spring); should stay beyond 6f; acts on soft going; blinkered final start. *G. Balding.*   **–**

LA CONGA 3 b.f. Dance In Time–Pop Music (Val de Loir 133) (1982 6s 1983 8d 7f 12.2f³) rather a lightly-built filly; a twin; no worthwhile form in maiden and apprentice races. *E. Incisa.*   **–**

LAC ROYALE 3 b.f. Lochnager 132–Jubilee Year 63 (Red God 128§) (1982 8s 1983 12d 14g 12f) quite an attractive filly; good walker; shaped with a bit of promise in maiden race at Yarmouth in June but was well beaten at Carlisle later in month on only subsequent outing; seems suited by a test of stamina. *D. Arbuthnot.*   **–**

LADENDA 3 b.f. Bold Lad (Ire) 133–Brief Agenda (Levmoss 133) (1982 7d 8g³ 1983 8.2s³ 7g² 6d 7f 6fg* 6g 6s³ 6g 6fg⁴ 6f⁴ 7g) smallish, lengthy filly; won minor event at Ayr in July; effective at 6f and stays 1m; acts on any going; blinkered nowadays; has run well for an apprentice; sold 30,000 gns Newmarket December Sales. *J. W. Watts.*   **69**

LA DI DA 3 b.f. Cawston's Clown 113–Leylandia 69 (Wolver Hollow 126) (1982 5g⁴ 5s³ 5fg 5fg 5fg⁴ 6d² 5g 5d² 1983 9f⁴ 9f³ 8fg⁴ 7f) leggy filly; in frame in sellers; seems to stay 9f; probably acts on any going. *W. Storey.*   **44**

LA DIVA 2 ch.f. Orchestra 118–Madrilon (Le Fabuleux 133) (1983 5fg 6g) Feb 1; IR 3,000F, IR 5,200Y; smallish filly; half-sister to 2 winners in Ireland, including stayer Pouyelo (by Rheffic); dam never ran; in rear in maiden race at Leicester in June and minor event at Pontefract in October; sold 900 gns Ascot December Sales. *C. Nelson.*   **–**

LADY ABINGER 2 br.f. Owen Dudley 121–Smokey's Sister (Forlorn River 124) (1983 6g 6f 7d) Apr 28; rather leggy filly; half-sister to 2 winners over hurdles; dam won 6 races in Scandinavia; behind in maiden and minor events. *H. O'Neill.*   **–**

LADY ARPEGE 5 b. or br.m. Swing Easy 126–Giglet (Frankincense 120) (1982 6s 7fg 8f 7g² 6fg³ 6fg² 6g⁴ 8g* 8fg⁴ 8s 8g³ 1983 8v 10s 10g 11g 12s² 12fg* 12g² 11.7f⁴ 12f³ 14g 10fg² 12f 11s³ 10fg² 10fg⁴) workmanlike mare; former plater; decisively won apprentice handicap at York in June; ran well most subsequent starts, including when going down by ¾ length to Oratavo in valuable handicap at Ascot in October on penultimate outing; suited by middle distances; seems to act on any going; good mount for an apprentice; blinkered twice in 1982; tough. *W. Musson.*   **68**

LADY AURA 2 ch.f. Sallust 134–Red Chip 105 (Red God 128§) (1983 6g* 7g²) Apr 21; IR 46,000Y; first foal; dam useful winner at up to 1½m in Ireland; kept on to finish 2½ lengths second to Ballet de France in C. L. Weld Park Stakes at Phoenix Park in October; easy winner of maiden race at Navan the previous month; will probably stay 1¼m; sure to win more races. *E. O'Grady, Ireland.*   **95**

LADY BENNINGTON 3 b.f. Hot Grove 128–Honey Buzzard (Sea Hawk II 131) —
(1982 NR 1983 10g 12.2f 10g) lengthy filly; poor mover and bad walker; second
foal; dam, second 3 times at up to 2m at 4 yrs in Ireland, is daughter of Italian 1000
Guineas and Oaks winner Dolina; well behind in maiden races and a seller; sold out
of G. Huffer's stable 500 gns Doncaster August Sales after second outing. *P.
Bevan.*

LADY BETTINA 2 ch.f. Bustino 136–Lady Rhapsody 101 (Northern Dancer) —
(1983 7f) 24,000Y; third foal; half-sister to plating-class animals by Royal
Palace and Relkino; dam won over 1m and 1¼m; backward, last of 14 in maiden
race at Goodwood in July; sold 11,500 gns Newmarket December Sales. *B. Swift.*

LADY BLANROID 3 b.f. Haveroid 122–Blandford Lady (Blandford Lad 96) —
(1982 7s 1983 9fg) lengthy non-thoroughbred filly; showed signs of ability only
outing as a 2-y-o but was last in a seller only appearance in 1983. *M. H. Easterby.*

LADY CARA 3 br.f. Lochnager 132–Gold Cheb 88 (Chebs Lad 120) (1982 6g 5fg   82
5g 1983 5v* 5s³ 6d 5fg 5fg⁴ 5f 5g⁴ 5g* 5g 5fg²) fair sort; accounted for biggish
fields when winning maiden race at Wolverhampton in April and handicap at
Pontefract in October; good second to Singing Sailor after getting outpaced in
handicap at Doncaster in November; best at 5f; acts on firmish ground but is ideally
suited by some give. *J. Berry.*

LADY CAROL 3 b.f. Lord Gayle 124–Winter Serenade (Whistling Wind 123) —
(1982 NR 1983 6fg 8fg 6f 7f 8d 7.6d) 8,200Y; half-sister to a 2-y-o winner and a
winner in Hong Kong; dam well behind in maiden races; little worthwhile form,
although not entirely disgraced in a handicap at Lingfield in October on final start;
sold to J. Benstead. 2,100 guineas Newmarket Autumn Sales. *J. Benstead.*

LADY CLAREMONT 3 ch.f. Hittite Glory 125–Gulistan (Sharpen Up 127) —
(1982 NR 1983 8fg 12fg) first foal; dam poor daughter of smart stayer Turf; last in
2 sellers. *R. Thompson.*

LADY CLEMENTINE 3 b.f. He Loves Me 120–In The Clover (Meadow Mint   68
120) (1982 6g 6fg 7f 1983 6d 6v 6f 6fg 5g³ 5h 5fg 5g* 6d 5g) well-made filly; won
maiden race at Kempton in September but showed worthwhile form on only one
other occasion; should stay 6f. *B. Swift.*

LADY COX 4 b.f. Sun Prince 128–Lady Rowe 97 (Sir Ivor 135) (1982 8d 5.8g⁴ 6s —
6s 1983 6v 6fg 6f) lengthy, attractive filly; poor walker; moderate at her best; well
beaten in 1983; will be suited by 7f; taken down very quietly final start. *B. Hills.*

LADY CYNARA 5 b.m. Starch Reduced 112–Golden Perch 79 (Sovereign Lord —
120) (1982 NR 1983 8v 10.1d⁴ 7s 8g) plater; stays 1¼m; has run respectably for
an apprentice. *C. Wildman.*

LADY CYNTHIA 3 ch.f. Welsh Pageant 135–Petulant (Petingo 135) (1982 6f 7fg —
7fg 8.2d 1983 6s 6s 8f) leggy, lengthy filly; little worthwhile form in varied
company, including claiming; sometimes blinkered. *P. Cundell.*

LADY DARA 3 b. or br.f. Lord Gayle 124–Tanndara (Venture VII 129) (1982 7fg⁴ 102
7fg* 7f 1983 8f³ 8fg² 8.5f* 12d 8fg 9g³) strong, compact filly; landed the odds by 5
lengths from Anne's Dance in minor event at Gowran Park in August; placed in
minor event at Navan and Cornelscourt Stakes at Leopardstown (beaten a head by
Tea House) earlier and in another minor event at Naas afterwards; should be suited
by 1¼m+ (had stiff task and finished last of 6 behind Sun Princess in Yorkshire
Oaks at York when tried over 1½m); acts on firm going and wasn't disgraced on a
soft surface on penultimate start. *M. O'Toole, Ireland.*

LADY DONARO 3 br.f. Ardoon 124–Lady Kasbah (Lord Gayle 124) (1982 5g 5g   76
5g 5f 6s 1983 8d 8fg* 8g⁴ 8f 8f⁴ 8f 7.2g 8.2fg⁴ 8.2g 8d* 8g² 8fg) compact filly;
successful in maiden race at Edinburgh in May and seller at Wolverhampton in
October; good second when blinkered in non-selling handicap at Pontefract later in
October; suited by 1m; acts on any going; moved poorly to post seventh outing. *J.
Berry.*

LADY EN DOUCE 4 gr.f. Ballynockan 112–Clare Blue 83 (Blue Streak 106) —
(1982 8fg 8f 8fg 8f 1983 10d 6fg 8.3f 10f) plain filly; of little account; sometimes
blinkered. *J. Bridger.*

LADY EVER-SO-SURE 5 ch.m. Malicious–Time of Hope 98 (Matador 131)   58
(1982 10d 11s 12g 10.2s 1983 15.8d 11fg² 16s 12v* 10.6s 10f² 12fg 10.6fg² 12d⁴
12fg* 12g⁴ 12fg 10g*) strong, compact mare; plater; won at Wolverhampton
(bought in 1,200 gns), Beverley (no bid) and Redcar (no bid); stays 1½m; acts on
any going; usually wears blinkers. *J. Etherington.*

LADY FAWLEY 2 b.f. He Loves Me 120–Little Angle (Gulf Pearl 117) (1983   86
6d 7s³ 8d*) Apr 5; IR 6,800Y; half-sister to 4 winners, including fairly useful 1977
staying 2-y-o Duchess (by Electrify); dam once-raced twin; improved with
experience and battled back after being headed close home to beat Out And About
in a maiden race at Leopardstown in October; well suited by 1m. *N. Meade,
Ireland.*

LADYFISH 3 ch.f. Pampapaul 121–Tuna 63 (Silver Shark 129) (1982 6g 6f 6g 8fg*   78
8.2s 7d 1983 6s⁴ 7fg⁴ 6fg³ 8fg* 8h⁴ 8f³ 7f 8d⁴ 8fg) quite attractive filly; in frame
most starts and was successful in handicap at Leicester in July; suited by 1m;
probably acts on any going. *B. Hanbury.*

LADY GERARD 3 b.f. Brigadier Gerard 144–Sirnelta (Sir Tor) (1982 7d 6fg⁴   83
6s² 1983 10s² 10.6v* 12f 9.4f 10f* 10f* 10g³ 10fg) quite attractive filly; saw her
race out really well in the testing conditions when winning handicap at Haydock in
May; ran poorly in blinkers next 2 starts but returned to form without them to win
similar events at Brighton and Epsom in August, finding rare turn of foot both
times; tends to finish strongly in races over 1¼m and is well worth another chance
over further; acts on any going. *F. J. Houghton.*

LADY HICKLETON 2 b.f. Lochnager 132–Pronuba (Sica Boy 132) (1983 5.1fg   –
6fg 5g) Jan 31; 4,000Y; fair sort; half-sister to a winning plater and several winners
abroad; dam placed over 1¼m in Ireland; poor form, including in maiden auction
events; off course 3 months after second start. *G. Fletcher.*

LADY JOPLIN 2 ch.f. Scott Joplyn 108–Cyn's Gem (Spur On 104) (1983 5v 5s   –
6fg) Mar 22; first foal; dam last of 3 in selling hurdle on only appearance; of no
account. *P. Butler.*

LADY JUSTICE 5 ch.m. Status Seeker–Alldyke (Klondyke Bill 125) (1982 10f*   73
10fg⁴ 10g³ 10f* 11.7g² 10fg* 10.2g 10g 10g 10d* 10g³ 8s 1983 10s 10fg⁴ 10f 10f³
10g³ 10f³ 10.2fg² 11s 10fg 11d 10fg) workmanlike mare; in frame in handicaps on
several occasions but was rather disappointing nevertheless; best form at 1¼m;
acts on any going, except perhaps really soft. *J. Winter.*

LADY KAMINA 4 gr.f. Dragonara Palace 115–Miss Carvin (Carvin 127) (1982   65
9g 8g 10f* 10.6h⁴ 8fg 8g 8.3g² 10fg³ 8g* 8g* 7d³ 10s⁴ 1983 12d³ 8s² 10g* 12g 10d
10d² 12fg) workmanlike filly; plater; goes well at Brighton and won non-selling
handicap there in May; stays 1½m; acts on any going; blinkered once; good mount
for an apprentice; retained 5,600 gns Newmarket Autumn Sales. *P. Haynes.*

LADY KNIPHOFIA 4 b.f. Sparkler 130–Flora Day 92 (Floribunda 136) (1982   –
7fg 8fg 10fg 9s 10s 1983 8s³ 8v 8s) robust, sturdy filly; plater; promises to stay
1¼m; retained 560 gns Ascot January Sales; sold to C. Wildman 750 gns Ascot
May Sales. *P. Makin.*

LADY LIZA 2 b.f. Air Trooper 115–Liza Paul 66 (Ron 103) (1983 5fg 6fg 7d 7g)   69
May 20; fourth reported foal; dam won 1¼m seller; not raced until the autumn, and
showed nothing until finishing fifth of 13 behind wide-margin winner Royal Halo in
maiden event at Lingfield in October on final appearance; will stay 1¼m. *B.
Stevens.*

LADY LOCKET 2 b.f. Comedy Star 121–Hodsock Venture (Major Portion 129)   64
(1983 5fg 6f 6f 6h 7g) Apr 14; 4,300Y; strong, lengthy, good-bodied filly; carries a
lot of condition; first foal; dam showed no worthwhile form; poor maiden; no form
after second outing. *M. Lambert.*

LADY MOON 3 b.f. Mill Reef 141–Moonlight Night 112 (Levmoss 133) (1982   101
7g⁴ 1983 10.2v 12.3f* 12f* 11f² 11.1g*) leggy, sparely-made filly; successful in
maiden race at Newcastle, quite well-contested minor event at Leicester and
handicap at Kempton; stayed on to beat Gloria Mundi by a length on last-named
course in September; gives impression she'll be very well suited by 1¾m or
more; acts well on firm going. *H. Cecil.*

LADY MURFAX 4 b. or br.f. Ercolano 118–Golden Storm 95 (Golden Cloud)   –
(1982 7.2g 8g⁴ 6fg 6g 7fg⁴ 8d⁴ 8.2g² 7f² 7s² 8s* 10d 1983 10.8v 22.2f 17f 9fg
10.8g) leggy filly; good mover; plater; well beaten at 4 yrs; stays 1m; acts on any
going; effective with or without blinkers. *J. Howell.*

LADY OF IRELAND 3 ch.f. Be My Guest 126–Lantern Light 86 (Le Levanstell   82
122) (1982 6g 6g 5fg³ 6s 1983 8s⁴ 7v 10fg* 11.7fg³ 10f² 10f) strong, quite
attractive filly; won maiden race at Brighton in June; placed in handicaps
afterwards, missing break and having a shocking run when 1½ lengths second to
Lady Gerard on same course in August; ran badly final outing however; probably
stays 1½m; seems to act on any going; has run creditably for 5-lb claimer; ran
respectably in blinkers second outing. *M. Stoute.*

LADY OF LEISURE 2 ch.f. Record Run 127–Gold Pension 76 (Compensation 127) (1983 5f2 5f4 5f2 5f2 5g3 5s 5g*) Mar 27; 900Y; not a good mover in her slower paces; half-sister to 2 minor winners; dam best at 5f; made all in 9-runner nursery at Edinburgh in October; evidently regarded as 5f performer; acts on firm going. *I. Vickers.*   **70**

LADY OF SHONA 2 ch.f. Be Friendly 130–Connington 52 (Connaught 130) (1983 5v 5f 5fg 7f 5f3 5g) Apr 27; lengthy, heavy-bodied filly; first foal; dam half-sister to very useful 1981 2-y-o 5f My Lover; plating-class maiden; form only on fifth outing; acts on firm going. *P. Felgate.*   **61**

LADY OF THE HOUSE 2 b.f. Habitat 134–Relfo 124 (Relko 136) (1983 6fg4 7.9f* 6d) Mar 20; second foal; dam won Ribblesdale Stakes and was second in Prix Vermeille; landed the odds by 3 lengths from Finuge Lady in 10-runner maiden race at Dundalk in July; 14/1, wasn't disgraced when never-dangerous eighth of 20 to Gala Event in Moyglare Stud Stakes at the Curragh 2 months later; should stay 1¼m; a very well-bred filly who's likely to continue improving. *K. Prendergast, Ireland.*   **85 p**

LADY OF THE LAND 2 b.f. Wollow 132–Land Ho (Primera 131) (1983 6f 5f) Apr 28; 36,000Y; rather sparely-made filly; half-sister to several winners, including 3-y-o 5f winner Dry Land (by Nonoalco) and very useful 1976 2-y-o 5f winner Easy Landing (by Swing Easy); dam daughter of very smart sprinter Lucasland; poor form in maiden events at Yarmouth and Beverley (third favourite) in August. *M. Albina.*   **60**

LADY ORYX 3 b.f. Hotfoot 126–Hum 69 (Crooner 119) (1982 8s 7d 1983 8v 10s 7fg) rangy, useful sort; no form in maiden and minor events. *M. McCourt.*   **—**

LADY PRETENDER 2 b.f. Dragonara Palace 115–Gresham Girl 99 (Right Tack 131) (1983 5v* 5s 6fg 7f) Mar 20; workmanlike filly; good mover; second foal; dam, daughter of very speedy Granville Greta, won 3 times over 6f; won 10-runner minor event at Newbury in May; fifth of 9 in Cherry Hinton Stakes at Newmarket 2 months later, third outing and best subsequent effort; not raced after August; probably stays 7f; best form on a firm surface. *M. McCourt.*   **86**

LADY REEFIFI 2 b.f. Take a Reef 127–Sovereign Help 98 (Sovereign Lord 120) (1983 5f 5g 5fg 5fg 5g 6fg) May 12; small filly; half-sister to 2 modest 2-y-o winners; dam won five 5f races; poor form in maiden races and a seller. *J. Spearing.*   **—**

LADY SAPPHIRE 3 b.f. Amboise 113–Lady Advocate 116 (King's Bench 132) (1982 6fg 6fg 5s 1983 8s 8.3s) poor plater. *R. Simpson.*   **—**

LADY SAXON 4 b.f. Track Spare 125–Il Regalo (Meadow Mint 120) (1982 7fg 6f 7s 7d 1983 6fg) fair sort; poor plater; has worn blinkers. *R. Simpson.*   **—**

LADY SCOTT 2 br.f. Scott Joplyn 108–Deciduous 65 (Shiny Tenth 120) (1983 5f 7f 5.1f 6fg 8fg) Apr 13; first reported foal; dam sprint plater; in rear in maiden races and sellers. *H. Collingridge.*   **—**

LADY SEVILLE 2 ch.f. Orange Bay 131–Nevilles Cross 67 (Nodouble) (1983 5f 5f 8f2) Mar 30; 980F, 800Y; tall, rather leggy filly; half-sister to 1981 6f winner Marilena (by Rolfe); dam stayed 1m; 2½ lengths second of 23 finishers behind Tophams Taverns in maiden auction event at Redcar in September; beaten in seller previous outing; suited by 1m, and will stay further. *D. Smith.*   **62**

LADY SIAN 3 br.f. Tycoon II–Super Sian (Supreme Sovereign 119) (1982 5f 7f 6fg 5g 5v2 1983 5fg4 7s 6d 6g4 5f2 6g 6f3 6h 5fg 6g 6fg 6f 8fg3) neat filly; maiden plater; stays 1m; acts on any going; sold privately to C. Wildman 1,600 gns Doncaster November Sales. *D. Smith.*   **55**

LADY SO AND SO 2 ch.f. High Award 119–Casbar Lady 79 (Native Bazaar 122) (1983 5v 5v4 6fg 5f) May 21; first foal; dam won 4 times over 5f; bad plater; blinkered final outing; sold 360 gns Ascot October Sales. *S. Matthews.*   **44**

LADY SPEY 3 b.f. Sir Gaylord–Spey 88 (Jimmy Reppin 131) (1982 NR 1983 10s4 12s 12fg 10fg 11.7g) well-made, deep-girthed filly; second foal; dam 1½m winner; plating-class maiden; should stay beyond 1¼m. *F. J. Houghton.*   **—**

LADY TIPPINS (USA) 2 b.f. Star de Naskra–Strait Lane (Chieftain) (1983 6fg 6f2) Mar 22; $65,000Y; third foal; dam unraced half-sister to 2 stakes winners; sire, top American sprinter of 1979, won at up to 9f; caught close home and beaten a neck by Affair in 23-runner maiden event at Lingfield in August; stays 6f. *H. Cecil.*   **77**

LADY TOPKNOT 2 b.f. High Top 131–Knightside (Graustark) (1983 7f) Mar 31; half-sister to 3-y-o Sonic Meteor (by Star Appeal) and middle-distance winner   **—**

Justin Thyme (by Rheingold); dam won over 6f at 3 yrs in USA; last of 12 in maiden race at Yarmouth in August. *L. Cumani.*

LADY TUT 3 b.f. Fine Blade 121–Tutty 62 (Hotfoot 126) (1982 7fg* 7f 7.2s 1983 8v* 10.2v³ 8s³ 13fg² 10f⁴ 12g 13fg) fair sort; bought in 2,000 gns after winning seller at Warwick in April by 7 lengths; ran creditably in non-sellers afterwards; stays 13f; probably acts on any going; genuine. *T. Bill.* **62**

LADYVILLE 3 b.f. Lord Nelson 107–Vaudaville 77 (Vigo 130) (1982 NR 1983 7g 6d 8g 8.2fg) half-sister to 2 winning sprinters by Most Secret, including fairly useful Broon's Secret; dam ran only at 2 yrs; in rear in maiden and minor races and a handicap. *W. H. H. Williams.*

L'AFFAIRE DISCREET 2 b.f. Bay Express 132–Evening Venture 111 (Hopeful Venture 125) (1983 6g 6f 5f 6g 6fg) Apr 13; 9,000Y; second foal; half-sister to 1980 2-y-o 7f winner Rocket Venture (by Roan Rocket); dam won Galtres Stakes; poor maiden; form only on third outing; should stay 6f. *D. Dale.*

LAFONTAINE (USA) 6 b.h. Sham–Valya (Vandale) (1982 10.6s 12fg* 10f³ 10.2f* 10f² 12f⁴ 10d* 10.5f 12fg 12f² 11.7d² 12s² 12d* 1983 12d 12d 12f 10f 12fg 12fg⁴ 12f* 11.1g³ 11.7fg³ 12fg 12fg 12d 12fg) big, strong horse; a very tough and genuine performer at his best who won 10 races, including Cumberland Lodge Stakes at Ascot in 1982; gained only success at 5 yrs when making all to beat Looking For by a length in 6-runner £3,800 event at Lingfield in August; creditable 2 lengths third to Lyphard's Special in 6-runner September Stakes at Kempton next start; well beaten most other outings; stayed 1½m; not at his best on really soft going but acted on any other; suited by strong handling and forcing tactics; retired to Kilteelagh Stud, Co. Tipperary, fee IR £1,500 (Oct 1st). *C. Brittain.* **108**

LAFROWDA 2 b.f. Crimson Beau 124–Ballinkillen (Levmoss 133) (1983 6g 6fg 6f 7h 7g) June 9; second live foal; dam, daughter of smart Windy Gay, won over 1¼m in Ireland; plating-class maiden; should stay 1¼m. *R. Hoad.* **59**

LA GAVINA 4 b.f. Sagaro 133–Private Collection 70 (Whistling Wind 123) (1982 11g 12f 12fg 10g 1983 10d 10.1d 13.6f) big, rangy filly; poor plater; sometimes blinkered; sold out of W. Wightman's stable 1,000 gns Ascot May Sales after second start; resold to H. Bell 1,000 gns Doncaster October Sales. *M. McCausland, Ireland.* **–**

LA GRIGIA 3 ch.f. Habat 127–Wimosa 92 (Mossborough 126) (1982 6g⁴ 1983 8v³ 8g 10v* 10g⁴ 12g 10f³ 10g) neat filly; good walker; landed the odds comfortably in minor event at Lingfield in May; also in frame in BonusPrint Masaka Stakes at Kempton in April (knocked right back in straight and ran well), minor event at Newbury in June (shade disappointing) and Nassau Stakes at Goodwood in July (moved up a place after finishing about 4½ lengths fourth of 6 to Acclimatise); good seventh of 18 behind Ma Biche in 1000 Guineas at Newmarket on second start but ran poorly final outing; stays 1¼m; acts on any going; trained by R. Boss first start; sold 50,000 gns Newmarket December Sales. *J. Winter.* **102**

LAGSKONA 3 ch.f. Be Friendly 130–Super Anna (Super Sam 124) (1982 6g 1983 7.2fg 7f 5f 6f 12g 6fg) sparely-made filly; soundly beaten in varied races. *D. Morrill.* **–**

LAHAB (USA) 3 ch.c. The Minstrel 135–Playmate (Buckpasser) (1982 5g 6g² 7d³ 1983 11.5fg³ 9f* 10.1f⁴ 9f⁴ 10.2s 8g 10fg 9fg⁴ 9fg³) narrow, short-backed, active sort; waited with when beating Cash or Carry by a neck in maiden race at Newcastle in July; stays 11.5f, but is evidently regarded better at shorter distances; seems to act on any going; probably ran too freely for his own good fifth start. *F. Durr.* **73**

LA JEUNESSE 2 br.f. Young Generation 129–Parez 67 (Pardao 120) (1983 6f 6f) Feb 11; half-sister to 4 winners, including fairly useful 1982 2-y-o 6f winner Sparkling Moment (by Hot Spark); dam seemed not to stay 1m; soundly beaten in July in minor event (last of 6) at Salisbury and maiden race at Nottingham. *J. Dunlop.*

LAKE VALENTINA 2 b. or br.c. Blakeney 126–La Levantina (Le Levanstell 122) (1983 7f* 8fg) Feb 26; 39,000Y; small, quite attractive colt; third foal; dam won 6 times in Italy; won 17-runner maiden race at Newbury in August by a length from Bassett Boy; 5 lengths fifth of 9 to Alphabatim in William Hill Futurity at Doncaster 2 months later, making running until beaten for speed in last 2f; will stay well. *B. Hills.* **108**

LAK LUSTRE 2 ch.c. Mandalus 110–Slinky 71 (Salvo 129) (1983 5d* 5d* 5s* 5s² 5fg⁴ 8.2f 6g 6g² 5s²) Mar 27; IR 3,500F, 5,000Y; rather leggy, angular colt; third foal; half-brother to Irish middle-distance winner Slinky Persin and Irish bumpers **99**

race winner Sly Grin (both by Jupiter Pluvius); dam apparently of little account; successful in early-season minor events at Catterick, Pontefract and Ripon; did nothing much during the summer (off the course for a time) but came back to his best in the autumn, on final outing failing by only a head to catch Be There Baby when top weight in nursery at Haydock; should be suited by 7f and 1m; needs an easy surface; showed signs of temperament in preliminaries on seventh and eighth starts. *R. Fisher.*

LAKSHMI LADY 2 b.f. Kala Shikari 125–Jade Princess (Green God 128) (1983 5f 5.8h 6f 6fg 5g) May 4; good-quartered, quite attractive filly; first foal; dam poor maiden; poor form, including in a valuable seller. *R. Holder.*   **51**

LALA 2 br. or gr.f. Welsh Saint 126–Garland Song (My Swanee 122) (1983 6fg² 6f³ 6fg* 6g³ 6g³) Mar 18; 30,000Y; rather leggy, quite attractive filly; first foal; dam plating-class half-sister to Cajun and Ubedizzy; made all to win 10-runner maiden race at Brighton in August by 1½ lengths from Woodfold, the pair clear; ¾-length third of 10 behind Speak Nobly in minor event at Chester later in the month, next outing and better subsequent effort; acts on a firm surface. *R. Laing.*   **91**

LALLAX 2 ch.f. Laxton 105–Pallmonta 82 (Pall Mall 132) (1983 7f² 7fg* 8f 7.3d³) May 13; useful-looking filly; sister to 3-y-o Pallax and half-sister to 1m seller winner Maymonta (by Maystreak); dam placed several times at 2 yrs; put up an impressive display in 10-runner maiden race at Chester in August, forging clear in last 2f to win by 10 lengths; far from disgraced in much stronger company subsequently, finishing 4 lengths fifth of 7 to Almeira in Prix Marcel Boussac at Longchamp and 1¾ lengths third of 14 to Betsy Bay in Rochford Thompson Newbury Stakes; better suited by 1m than by 7f; acts on firm going and a soft surface. *B. Hills.*   **109**

LA MARINELLA 2 b. or br.f. Julio Mariner 127–Nonsensical 99 (Silly Season 127) (1983 5v⁴ 5v 5d³ 5d³ 6f) Feb 16; 4,000F; rather leggy, lightly-built filly; half-sister to 2 winners, including useful 1975 2-y-o Drop Of A Hat (by Midsummer Night II), successful at up to 7.2f; dam won at up to 1¼m; bad plater; trained first 4 starts by A. Young; raced in Italy after fifth outing. *N. Tinkler.*   **44**

LAMBOURN BOY 2 b.g. Cawston's Clown 113–Danabella (Dumbarnie 125) (1983 5g 7g 7d) Apr 25; IR 3,500F, 7,400Y; useful-looking gelding; half-brother to several winners, including quite useful middle-distance performer Rodney (by Saint Crespin III); dam placed at 3 yrs; soundly beaten in maiden races; dwelt final outing. *S. Mellor.*   **–**

LAMBWATH FLYER 4 b.g. Red Alert 127–Powder Box (Faberge II 121) (1982 8f 5f⁴ 8g 7fg 7s* 6s 1983 8s 7d 6d 8s 8g) big gelding; plater; stays 7f; acts well on soft going; usually blinkered. *A. Smith.*   **–**

LA MERCURIEL 2 br.f. Lucky Wednesday 124–Fiery Flo 78 (Firestreak 125) (1983 5d 5s* 6fg 5f³ 5fg) Mar 14; lightly-made filly; half-sister to 4 winners, including 5f to 1¼m winner Dad (by Constable); dam sprint maiden; won 11-runner maiden race at Catterick in June; should stay 6f; probably acts on any going; exported to Algeria. *M. Lambert.*   **64**

LAMLASH 4 gr.g. Habat 127–Iona 92 (Kalydon 122) (1982 7g² 7fg 8f* 7f 8f* 7f² 9fg 8g 9g 8f 8.2g 8fg 8s³ 8d 1983 8f 8h³ 8fg) strong, round-barrelled gelding; good walker but poor mover; inconsistent handicapper; stays 1m; acts on any going but goes well on fast ground; suited by forcing tactics. *T. Bulgin.*   **57**

LANCASTRIAN 6 b.h. Reform 132–Rosalie II 66 (Molvedo 137) (1982 10v* 10.5g² 12fg 12.5d² 1983 10v 10.5d* 12.5fg² 12fg 12s 12f)   **126**
    The outcome of the Prix Ganay at Longchamp in May could be seen as lending considerable support to that common-sense phrase 'If at first you don't succeed, try, try again.' The winner Lancastrian had collected three pattern races, the Prix du Lys, Grand Prix d'Evry and Prix d'Harcourt, over the previous three years, but had not managed to pick up a Group 1 event until the Ganay despite having contested seven and gained places in three. With his record thus improved Lancastrian, who will be standing at the Haras de Roiville in 1984 at 30,000 francs straight, ought to be more attractive to French breeders and it will be interesting to see how his stud career develops.
    Lancastrian's prospects of breaking his duck in the Ganay did not look at all bright beforehand since his six opponents included Welsh Term, Cadoudal and Mulaz Palace, who had finished a long way ahead of him when occupying the first three places in the Prix d'Harcourt on the same course in April. As Lancastrian grew older he seemed to get wiser with the result that in almost all his races as a six-year-old he started slowly and had to be ridden along fairly vigorously to keep up in the early stages. This is exactly what happened in the Ganay as he came under

the whip in last place after half a mile, made up ground hand over fist in the second half of the race to deprive Mulaz Palace of the lead at the distance and then battled on gamely to hold Cadoudal's late flourish by a short head with Welsh Term a never-dangerous third.

The Ganay form looked more reliable than most as far as the older French middle-distance horses were concerned and although the going was on top for the Grand Prix de Saint-Cloud, conditions which did not suit him ideally, Lancastrian seemed to have a reasonable chance of winning the race at the fourth attempt. Fourth in 1980, third in 1981 and a head second to Glint of Gold in 1982, he found Glint of Gold's brother Diamond Shoal too good for him on this occasion but proved more than a match for the other runners, including the good three-year-olds Jeu de Paille and Esprit du Nord, Zalataia, Lemhi Gold and two who admittedly ran below form, All Along and Electric. Behind early on, Lancastrian moved through from the final turn to take second place behind Diamond Shoal a furlong out but could not present a serious threat to the British colt who took the prize rather cleverly by three quarters of a length.

For one reason or another Lancastrian failed to run up to his best in the four races he contested on this side of the Channel during his career. On all known form he could not have won the King George VI and Queen Elizabeth Diamond Stakes at Ascot three weeks after the Grand Prix anyway, but he ought to have finished closer than he did to Time Charter, coming home nearly nine lengths behind her and eight lengths behind Diamond Shoal in fifth after being hopelessly outpaced until making some late headway. It was the same story in his last two races, the Prix Foy and Trusthouse Forte Prix de l'Arc de Triomphe, both at Longchamp. In the former he had only one behind him entering the straight and ran on to be sixth of eleven to Time Charter while in the Arc, wearing blinkers to try and sharpen him up, he walked out of the stalls, stayed last despite being strenuously ridden for a mile and then proceeded to finish as well as anything, ending up about four lengths ninth of twenty-six to All Along. The decision to retire Lancastrian after the Arc was probably a wise one for had he continued racing it is conceivable his attitude to the game would have become completely soured.

Reform, Lancastrian's sire, died in 1983. A grand little colt who won eleven of his fourteen starts including the Sussex Stakes and Champion Stakes, he has sired the winners of getting on for four hundred races here and abroad, notably the classic winners Polygamy and Roi Lear and the tip-top middle-distance gelding Admetus. Lancastrian's dam cost the equivalent of 10,000 guineas at the Deauville Yearling Sales and Sir Michael Sobell cannot regret the investment in the slightest. Successful in a mile-and-a-quarter maiden event at Salisbury from only three starts, Rosalie II has done well as a broodmare, her four other winners on the flat including the high-class Cistus (by Sun Prince), winner of the Nassau Stakes and

Prix Ganay, Longchamp—veteran Lancastrian keeps on gamely to hold off the strong-finishing Cadoudal (No. 2) by a short head

Sir Michael Sobell's "Lancastrian"

second in the Prix de Diane in 1978. The second dam, who dead-heated in the Prix de la Salamandre at two and ran placed in the Prix de la Grotte and Prix de Minerve at three, produced one other winner from a total of just three foals.

Lancastrian (b.h. 1977)	Reform (b 1964)	Pall Mall (ch 1955)	Palestine
			Malapert
		Country House (br 1955)	Vieux Manoir
			Miss Coventry
	Rosalie II (b 1965)	Molvedo (br 1958)	Ribot
			Maggiolina
		Lovely Rose III (b 1956)	Owen Tudor
			Galatina

Lancastrian, a big, strong horse with a markedly round action of the type often associated with a soft-ground performer, stayed a mile and a half well and towards the end of his career gave the impression he might have been suited by a return to a mile and three quarters, a trip over which he had been well beaten in the 1980 St Leger. Despite the slight wilfulness he displayed in 1983 he was genuine and consistent. *D. Smaga, France.*

L'ANCRESSE LODGE 5 ch.m. National Trust 89–Rosy Moll (Vermeil II 104) — (1982 10f 16.5f 7fg 1983 15.5f) small, fair sort; soundly beaten in varied races. *J. Long.*

LANDING LANE 3 b.f. Hittite Glory 125–Noor Jehan (Taj Dewan 128) (1982 — 6fg 6s 6d 6s 6d 1983 7v 6v 6f) plater; stays 6f. *M. Lambert.*

LANDSEER 3 br.g. Lochnager 132–Parlais 101 (Pardao 120) (1982 6fg[2] 6f* 6f 75 6f[4] 7.3g 6d 1983 6d 6g 6f* 7fg 5.8h 6f 6fg 6g 7fg) strong, well-made gelding; favourite when narrowly winning small handicap at Chepstow in June; little other form; not sure to stay 7f; acts well on fast ground; below form in blinkers sixth outing. *D. Sasse.*

LANGLEY COURT 4 gr.g. Saritamer 130–Marypark 93 (Charlottown 127) –
(1982 12f 12f 16d 7fg³ 8g 7g 8d 7d 1983 16s 16g) big, leggy gelding; good walker;
poor plater; usually wears blinkers. *D. Oughton.*

LANGTON LAD 3 br.g. Tudor Rhythm 112–Golden Linnet 96 (Sing Sing 134) –
(1982 6fg 7g 6g 1983 8s) leggy, light-framed gelding; no sign of ability. *A. Fisher.*

LANHYDROCK 2 b.g. Tower Walk 130–Tremellick 87 (Mummy's Pet 125) (1983 **68**
6f 6fg 8s) May 13; rather leggy gelding; first foal; dam won 3 times over 5f;
unquoted and sweating badly, 6½ lengths fifth of 12 to Talk Posh in 1m maiden race
at Beverley in September; subsequently gelded. *M. Camacho.*

LAOIS PRINCESS 3 ch.f. Crash Course 128–Laois Lady (Windjammer) (1982 **95**
7.5f* 7f 7d³ 7d⁴ 1983 8v 7s³ 7s² 8s³ 10s 8f³ 8fg² 7fg² 8fg 7f³ 7fg² 7f) strong,
lengthy, attractive filly; ran creditably in goodish company on several occasions,
including when length second of 10 behind Flame of Tara in Athasi Stakes at the
Curragh in April on third start and 1½ lengths third of 13 to Burslem in Coolmore
Hello Gorgeous Stakes on same course in June on sixth outing; faded in last 2f when
ninth of 10 behind Silverdip in Strensall Stakes at York in August on final start
(blinkered first time); best form at up to 1m; acts on any going; has run well for an
apprentice; free-running sort. *L. Browne, Ireland.*

LA PEPPER 2 b.f. Workboy 123–La Vickstan 72 (El Gallo 122) (1983 6f 5f 5f⁴ 5f **63**
5f 6f 8d* 8fg 7fg) Mar 12; compact filly; seventh foal; dam plating class at 2 yrs;
won 12-runner selling nursery at Beverley (no bid) in September; suited by 1m;
sometimes sweats up. *J. Etherington.*

LA PERRICHOLI (FR) 3 b.f. Targowice 130–Belle Margot (Counsel 118) **75**
(1982 5f 6g 6g³ 7g² 6f 7f 6d* 8d 1983 7v⁴ 6d² 6s 7g⁴ 6d² 8.2g 8d) tall, leggy,
workmanlike filly; in frame several times, best effort when runner-up to Overtrick
in minor event at Brighton on last occasion; stays 7f; probably acts on any going;
well beaten last 2 outings (blinkered on first occasion). *D. Marks.*

LA PIAF 2 ch.f. Great Nephew 126–La Mome 109 (Princely Gift 137) (1983 5v³ **75**
5d⁴ 6f⁴ 6h⁴ 6g) Apr 27; leggy, narrow filly; half-sister to fairly useful 5f to 10.2f
winner La Lutine (by My Swallow) and winners in Italy and Sweden; dam stayed
1¼m; in frame in maiden races; will be better suited by 7f+. *B. Hobbs.*

LA PRIMA 2 b.f. Captain James 123–Saint Veronica (Saint Crespin III 132) (1983 **56**
5s⁴ 5s² 5f 6f) May 3; 4,100Y; leggy, sparely-made filly; half-sister to Irish 1982
2-y-o 6f winner Blue Image (by Touch Paper), 6f to 1m winner Saint Motunde (by
Tyrant) and 2 winners abroad; dam probably of little account; won poor maiden race
at Hamilton in April; well beaten in valuable seller at York in July on final
appearance; should stay at least 1m; acts on any going; apprentice ridden. *J.
Berry.*

LARA (USA) 2 b.f. Lyphard 132–Valtama (Val de Loir 133) (1983 6d² 6fg⁴) May **87**
30; neat filly; dam French 12.5f winner; fair form in maiden events at Yarmouth
(beaten neck) and Newmarket (fourth of 29) in September; bred to stay middle
distances; bandaged off-hind at Newmarket; should win a race. *M. Albina.*

LA REINE ROSE (USA) 3 b.f. King Pellinore 127–M'lle Cyanne (Cyane) (1982 –
5fg 6g⁴ 7f³ 7g³ 7fg⁴ 8f 8s⁴ 1983 8.5d 12.2fg 12g 10g 10.2g) lengthy,
good-quartered filly; good mover; well beaten in 1983, having stiff task when
blinkered on second occasion; stays 1m; probably acts on any going. *J.
Ciechanowski.*

LARINE 2 b. or br.f. Lombard 126–Wow 106 (Baldric II 131) (1983 8g) –
lightly-made filly; half-sister to useful 1979 2-y-o 5f and 6f winner Why Not (by
Dancer's Image) and fairly useful 1982 Irish 2-y-o 6f winner Wish You Luck (by
Faraway Son); dam won over 1¼m; distant seventh of 8 in £3,400 event at
Goodwood in September. *P. Kelleway.*

LARIONOV 3 br.c. Balidar 133–Double Finesse 97 (Double Jump 131) (1982 6f **120**
6fg 6s* 6g 1983 8v² 8v³ 7v* 8v³ 7v⁴ 7f 7.2g⁴ 7fg 7g* 7fg) quite attractive colt; first
foal; dam won at up to 1m; developed into a very smart performer and won £10,800
Norwest Holst Trophy at York in May (always going smoothly and quickened up
impressively to beat Merely A Secret by 5 lengths) and 9-runner Harroways Stakes
at Goodwood in September (led in last furlong and showed improved form to beat
On Stage by ¾ length); ran respectably in between when fifth behind Tecorno in
Jersey Stakes at Royal Ascot and when fourth of 11 behind Major Don in £6,700
handicap at Haydock; stays 1m but best at 7f; acts on any going, but is very well
suited by some give; had stiffish task sixth outing, and possibly needed race after a
2-month lay-off. *J. Winter.*

L'ARISTOCRAT 3 b.g. Le Johnstan 123–The Rose Royale (Takawalk II 125)   –
(1982 NR 1983 10s 10.1s 8g 12g) 3,500Y; good-bodied gelding; fourth foal;
brother to modest 1978 2-y-o 5f winner Bart; dam once-raced half-sister to smart
miler My Drifter; soundly beaten in varied races, including a gentleman riders
event on final start (blinkered and sweating); trained by J. Sutcliffe first 3 starts. *P.
Haynes.*

LASSITHI 2 b.f. Tanfirion 110–Native Love 77 (Native Prince) (1983 6f 7s 7fg)   –
Jan 23; 840F; lengthy filly; half-sister to a winning plater and a winning hurdler;
dam placed over 6f; well beaten in maiden events. *P. Makin.*

LAST DEVICE 6 b.g. Grey Mirage 128–Gorgeous Device 88 (Falls of Clyde   –
126) (1982 8f* 7.6g* 8f 8.5f* 8fg² 8f 8f⁴ 7.6d 8.2f 7d 1983 8d 8.5g 8d 7.6fg 8.2fg⁴
7.6g³ 8f 9d) compact gelding; stays 1m; probably acts on any going; suitable
mount for an apprentice; suited by front-running tactics; sweated up and looked
unimpressive third outing. *C. Crossley.*

LAST GUNBOAT 3 b.f. Dominion 123–Sounion 69 (Vimy 132) (1982 NR 1983   **50**
8v 12g 13fg 12.2f 9.4f 7h 10f 12g 10.8g³) 7,000Y; closely related to 1½m winner
Suniti (by Derring-Do), and half-sister to numerous winners, including Oaks third
Suni (by Crepello); dam won at 1½m; close third in seller at Warwick in October,
probably best effort; suited by middle distances. *A. Ingham.*

LASTIQUE 3 b.g. Tobique 116–Blast's Queen (Blast 125) (1982 NR 1983 11.7h)   –
first foal; dam of no account on flat and over hurdles; bandaged when behind in
maiden race at Bath in August. *N. Kernick.*

LAST MOUNTAIN 6 ch.g. Mountain Call 125–Last Dew (Blast 125) (1982 NR   –
1983 6s 10.2g 8fg) of little account. *M. Wintle.*

LAST SEASON 2 b.g. Silly Season 127–Braemore 60 (Major Portion 129) (1983   –
7fg 6f 7f 7g 7.2s) Apr 29; 780F, 1,300Y; small, lightly-built gelding; of no account;
blinkered final outing; sold 360 gns Ascot December Sales. *Mrs J. Reavey.*

LAST SECRET 2 ch.f. Most Secret 119–Belle of Sark (Daybrook Lad 104) (1983   –
5d 5s 5fg 5f 5g 6fg) Apr 25; 1,350Y; lengthy, workmanlike filly; half-sister to Irish
7f winner John of Sark (by Le Johnstan); dam won over 9f in Ireland; no form,
including in a seller. *D. Chapman.*

LA TAJARAH (USA) 3 b.c. Elocutionist–Queens Turf (Round Table) (1982 7g   **62**
8s 1983 12s 13.3g 15.5f² 12f 16f) neat colt; second in small maiden race at
Folkestone in August, best effort; suited by a test of stamina; blinkered nowadays;
sold to CBA 1,400 gns Newmarket Autumn Sales. *J. Bethell.*

LATE HOUR 4 br.f. Reform 132–Midnight Melody 92 (Linacre 133) (1982 8fg² 7f   **54**
8.2fg 8g 7s 6d 6s 1983 6f 7f 7fg 7g 7fg4) small filly; poor handicapper; has been
beaten in a seller; will stay 1¼m; acts on a firm and a soft surface; blinkered fourth
to sixth starts in 1982; reportedly broke a blood vessel once at 3 yrs. *R.
Hollinshead.*

LATE SALLY 2 ch.f. Sallust 134–Late Summer (Habitat 134) (1983 6v⁴ 5s* 6g²   **93**
5fg³ 6f² 7f² 6.3f²) Mar 25; second living foal; dam, half-sister to outstandingly
prolific 1980 2-y-o winner Spindrifter, won over 5f at 3 yrs in France; always
prominent when winning 15-runner maiden race at Leopardstown in May by a neck
from Sign-of-Life; second subsequently in minor event won by Paymaster at Naas,
valuable race won by Captain Freddie at Phoenix Park, nursery at Galway and
valuable Ballsbridge-Tattersalls Anglesey Stakes won by Gala Event at the
Curragh, beaten no more than 1½ lengths each time; probably stays 7f; seems to
act on any going. *M. Cunningham, Ireland.*

LATIN FORT 3 br.c. Comedy Star 121–Rosy Glow 60 (Hotfoot 126) (1982 5g 5fg   **76**
7s² 1983 10g 8.5s 8d⁴ 10s² 8d 8s 7v 8g⁴ 11.7v 11f⁴ 8f* 9f 12fg 10s 11g) attractive
colt; very poor walker; second at Cagnes-sur-Mer early in year; often had stiffish
tasks afterwards and showed very mixed form, but won a handicap at Newcastle in
August; stays 1¼m; acts on any going; blinkered last 5 outings; trained by R.
Hollinshead until after tenth outing. *D. Smith.*

LATIN LIGHT 4 b.f. Roman Warrior 132–Spanish Lantern 92 (Don Carlos) (1982   –
7f 7g 8.3g 8fg 8s 1983 9v 6v 6fg 7g 10h 8g 8fg) useful sort; poor performer
nowadays; has been beaten in a seller; possibly stays 1m; acts on firm going. *C.
Wildman.*

L'ATTRAYANTE (FR) 3 br.f. Tyrant–Camerata (Klairon 131) (1982 5.5d*   **123**
7.5g* 7.5fg² 7g³ 8s³ 1983 8v³ 8d* 8v* 8g⁴ 10d* 10f² 9g)
    The top French three-year-old fillies were a much stronger force in
international competition than their male counterparts and in L'Attrayante and

Smuggly trainer Douieb had two of the very best, a pair worth mentioning in the same breath as the other good fillies he's had, the 1980 Prix de l'Arc de Triomphe winner Detroit and the top-class sprinter/milers Kilijaro and Sanedtki. In 1983 L'Attrayante completed a unique double when winning both the French and Irish One Thousand Guineas while Smuggly won her first three races, including the Prix Saint-Alary, and was run out of the Prix de Diane Hermes by Escaline only in the last thirty yards or so.

Neither L'Attrayante's nor Smuggly's two-year-old form measured up to classic-winning standard although L'Attrayante was placed only just outside the top half-dozen French-trained fillies in the official classification. After winning narrowly at Evry and Deauville she'd been beaten three times, on the last two occasions into third behind Maximova in the Prix du Calvados at Deauville again and into fourth, subsequently moved up a place, behind Goodbye Shelley in the Prix Marcel Boussac at Longchamp. L'Attrayante was rather sparely made and wiry as a juvenile though, and by the spring she'd made some physical progress. Her form in finishing third behind Mysterieuse Etoile and Take A Step on her reappearance in the Prix de la Grotte at Longchamp in April didn't entirely reflect that progress but she put up a promising effort considering she probably needed the outing; and it wouldn't have come as a complete surprise to many of those who saw the Grotte when she turned the tables on that pair in the Poule d'Essai des Pouliches over the same course and distance the following month. Held up and always travelling well in a field of ten, L'Attrayante came with a good run to challenge between Mysterieuse Etoile and English-trained Silverdip at around the distance, was on top about a hundred yards from home, and won by half a length and one and a half lengths from Mysterieuse Etoile and the strong-finishing Maximova. Later in the month she completed the double at the Curragh, an achievement that was barely practical in recent times until a change in the programme in 1980 extended the breathing space between the two races to nearly three weeks. In the 'seventies, when they'd been less than a fortnight apart, there hadn't been a single instance of a filly running in both races, but in 1983 there were three, L'Attrayante being joined by Maximova and Goodbye Shelley, the last-named reportedly in season when a disappointing seventh at Longchamp. In a much bigger field L'Attrayante was always going well, and three furlongs from home she moved up to dispute the lead with little apparent effort. So strongly was she travelling that her rider kicked for home in the testing conditions sooner than planned, and in the last two furlongs L'Attrayante never looked likely to be caught. Maximova finished strongly again but L'Attrayante had a length and a half to spare at the line, with Annie Edge a further length back in third, Flame of Tara fourth, Goodbye Shelley only seventh again and Habibti, having her last race at a mile, ninth. The following day at Longchamp Smuggly won the Prix Saint-Alary and the stable very nearly pulled off a third Group 1 win in quick time when Indian Prince went down to Karkour in the Prix du Cadran.

Goffs Irish One Thousand Guineas, the Curragh—a smooth victory for L'Attrayante from Maximova (rails) and Annie Edge (blaze)

Poule d'Essai des Pouliches, Longchamp—L'Attrayante comes with a strong run to beat Mysterieuse Etoile; Maximova (No. 5) finishes third

With no race of similar stature for L'Attrayante in the offing it was decided to rest her until the Prix du Moulin at Longchamp in September. By that time Luth Enchantee had emerged as a major force over the distance in France and L'Attrayante, probably short of peak fitness, was soundly beaten by her into fourth, finishing behind the colts L'Emigrant and Wassl also. Shortly afterwards it was announced that she'd been sold for a reported two million dollars to the American aircraft manufacturer Allen Paulson, a buyer on a significant scale at the yearling sales, and L'Attrayante continued her racing career on the other side of the Atlantic. She made a successful first appearance there in the E. P. Taylor Stakes at Woodbine in mid-October, beating the five-year-old If Winter Comes readily by half a length, and was then sent on for the hotly-contested Yellow Ribbon Invitational at Santa Anita where she finished a length-and-a-half second to the former French-trained mare Sangue, who was recording her tenth win in the States. Reportedly she hadn't relaxed so well as usual and had had little left in the closing stages, but she'd done nothing to be critical of. Far from it. She ran extremely well, far better than the other recent distinguished imports from Europe Flame of Tara, Luth Enchantee and Royal Heroine, each of whom finished towards the rear. She didn't fare quite so well against Sangue in her only subsequent race, the Matriarch Invitational Stakes at Hollywood Park, coming home only fifth.

			Bold Ruler (b 1954)	Nasrullah
L'Attrayante (Fr) (br.f. 1980)	Tyrant (b 1966)			Miss Disco
			Anadem (b 1954)	My Babu
				Anne of Essex
	Camerata (b 1959)		Klairon (b 1952)	Clarion III
				Kalmia
			Java Sea (br 1949)	Winterhalter
				Argovie

L'Attrayante is the best winner sired so far by Tyrant who began his stallion days in Ireland, was moved to France and has now been returned to stand in the United States. The majority of Tyrant's noteworthy winners have been fillies, among them River Dane who won the 1977 Child Stakes, Sutton Place who was successful in the following season's Coronation Stakes and Trevita, a smart performer here who has since done extremely well in the States; Tyrant is also the sire of the smart ex-Italian miler Bold Run, who for part of 1983 was in the same stable as L'Attrayante. The dam Camerata was twenty-one when she foaled L'Attrayante, and in view of her well-established producing record it is perhaps a little surprising that L'Attrayante fetched the equivalent of less than £12,000 as a yearling. Camerata won at Fontainebleau as a two-year-old and was placed in useful

Mr A. Paulson's "L'Attrayante"

company before embarking on her long career as a broodmare. L'Attrayante is her thirteenth foal and her eleventh individual winner, the others including Camerante, also by Tyrant, who won a minor eleven-furlong race and the grand stayer Campo Moro (by Bel Baraka) who at the ripe old age of seven won five races, including La Coupe and the Prix Gladiateur. The grandam Java Sea also did well at stud and produced eight winners besides Camerata, including Deboule, second to Relko in the French St Leger, and Corbara II, the dam of Red Johnnie and Tickled Pink.

We understand that L'Attrayante's new owner is keen to continue racing her as long as she's doing well, and we'll be surprised if more good prizes aren't forthcoming. Her American form suggests that she stays a mile and a quarter and acts on firm going, but in Europe she was undoubtedly very well suited by a mile and the mud. It's worth adding that she's thoroughly genuine and consistent. *O. Douieb, France.*

LAUGHING EMBERS 3 ch.f. Hot Spark 126–Tickled To Bits (Sweet Revenge —
129) (1982 NR 1983 10.2v 8f) 4,000Y; small, strong filly; second foal; dam poor maiden; in rear in minor events at Doncaster; sold 700 gns Ascot 2nd June Sales. *D. Morley.*

LAUGHING GRAVY 3 b.c. Monsanto 121–Poppy Time 77 (Hook Money 124) —
(1982 NR 1983 5f 6h 9d) small, strong, compact colt; half-brother to 2 winning platers; dam stayed 1m; little form, including in a seller. *Mrs B. Waring.*

LAUGHING LAD 3 br.c. Bold Lad (Ire) 133–Laughing Girl 110 (Sassafras 135) —
(1982 7d 8g 1983 9v 7d 12g 7fg) lengthy, quite attractive colt; good walker; fifth of 21 to Schuss in maiden race at Newmarket in April on second outing; acted as a pacemaker for stable-companion Teenoso at York in August next time; possibly unsuited by heavy ground. *G. Wragg.*

LAURA'S CHOICE 2 b.f. Abwah 118–Muninga 108 (St Alphage 119) (1983 5s 5g   59
5g 6f 5s 5g⁴ 5g 5fg³) Mar 13; 2,000Y; third reported foal; dam 5f sprinter; poor

maiden; often runs in sellers; apparently best at 5f; suited by a sound surface. *N. Bycroft.*

LAURA'S COTTAGE 3 b.f. Habitat 134–Lauretta 111 (Relko 136) (1982 NR 1983 8d 10fg 7h) smallish filly; half-sister to 9f winner Maypole Lane (by Grundy) and fairly useful 1¼m winner Brinkley (by Moulton); dam won over middle distances; behind in maiden races at Newmarket, Sandown and Chepstow (last of 8); sold to BBA (Italia) 24,000 gns Newmarket December Sales. *G. Wragg.* —

LAUREL EXPRESS 2 gr.f. Bay Express 132–Sea Lavender 114 (Never Say Die 137) (1983 6fg) Mar 5; quite attractive, useful-looking filly; half-sister to fairly useful 1981 2-y-o 5f winner Lavender Dance (by Dance In Time) and to winners in France and Belgium; dam, sister to smart miler Casabianca, won at up to 7.3f; 20/1, showed up well until beaten and eased considerably after 4f when eighth of 13 to disqualified Bluff House in minor event at Goodwood in August; sure to do better. *J. Dunlop.* — p

LAURENBEL 2 b.g. Dublin Taxi–Betbellof 65 (Averof 123) (1983 5g 6f³ 7f 6f 6f 7fg 7fg) May 17; quite attractive, rangy gelding; first foal; dam 2-y-o 5f winner; plating-class maiden; stays 7f, but may prove better at 6f; acts on firm going. *R. Hannon.* **68**

LAURENCE MAC 4 br.g. Grey Ghost 98–Mactavish 90 (St Alphage 119) (1982 6s⁴ 7g³ 6g⁴ 6f* 5g² 6g³ 5fg⁴ 1983 6s 5d 6g) compact gelding; well beaten in 1983; best at sprint distances; acts on firm going; sold 570 gns Doncaster August Sales. *T. Barron.* —

LAURENCIN (USA) 2 b.f. Accipiter–Our Own Hit (Bold Hitter) (1983 5g³ 6f* 6f³ 5f²) Apr 18; fair sort; fourth foal; dam, placed at 2 yrs, is daughter of Irish 1000 Guineas second Owenello; won 19-runner maiden race at Windsor in July; beaten ½ length by Double Room under 9-7 in nursery at Redcar in September; stays 6f; acts on firm going; sent to USA. *H. Cecil.* **89**

LAURETTE 3 ch.f. Artaius 129–Army Court (Court Martial) (1982 NR 1983 7d 7d 8.2fg 9d 8g) well-made filly; half-sister to 2 winners in France; dam, out of sister to Bold Ruler, was very smart winner at up to 1¼m in France; showed a little ability on second and third outings; gives impression she'll be suited by 1¼m or more. *G. Huffer.* —

LAURIE'S PANTHER 2 br.c. Jaazeiro 127–Mulattin (Henry the Seventh 125) (1983 6g 6fg⁴ 6f 6f 7fg⁴ 7g² 7g⁴ 8.2s*) Apr 27; lightly-built colt; half-brother to smart and tough 1979 2-y-o Sonnen Gold (by Home Guard) and middle-distance winner Cooks Corner (by Martinmas); dam never ran; won 6-runner maiden event at Haydock in October gamely by a head from Briarean; stays 1m well; probably acts on any going; genuine. *D. Elsworth.* **84**

LAUTREC 5 b.g. Wolver Hollow 126–Night Vision 100 (Yellow God 129) (1982 10.2g 13d 10.6f 1983 8v² 8v 10g 7f 8f 8f 8h 8fg 12g) tall gelding; stays 1¼m; probably acts on any going but goes well in the mud. *P. M. Taylor.* **55** d

LAVENDER GRAY 4 b.f. Bay Express 132–Ma Belle Amie (Never Say Die 137) (1982 7d* 8f⁴ 8f* 8f⁴ 8.2g 8f³ 1983 8g 8f 10d 8fg) useful-looking filly; well beaten at 4 yrs; stays 1m; seems to act on any going; sold to BBA 1,500 gns Newmarket Autumn Sales. *J. Winter.* —

LAVENHAM BLUE 5 b.m. Streetfighter 120–Brighton Girl 96 (Right Boy 137) (1982 NR 1983 12.2s⁴ 10f) big mare; poor maiden. *J. Wilson.* —

LAVINIA'S PET 2 b.f. Record Token 128–Forest Flower 91 (Fine Blade 121) (1983 6g 5fg 7.6d 7g) Apr 27; 7,000Y; second foal; dam 2-y-o 5f winner; in rear in autumn maiden and minor events at Lingfield. *P. K. Mitchell.* —

LAW BIRD 4 b. or br.g. Legal Eagle 126–Altarnum (Alcide 136) (1982 15.5v 1983 9s 12v 12s) workmanlike gelding; of little account; has worn blinkers; pulled up final start; cost 700 gns Doncaster January Sales. *Mrs N. Macauley.* —

LAWERS 4 ch.c. Hot Spark 126–Aspara 58 (Crimson Satan) (1982 6fg 6g 5g 6g 5fg 8.3g 6v 6g 1983 6v* 6v 7s² 6g 7s 6fg³ 7g⁴ 6fg 6fg 7fg* 8g² 7g 8fg³) compact colt; plater; won at Folkestone in March (no bid) and Brighton in August (bought in 1,650 gns); stays 1m; seems to act on any going; sometimes blinkered but not when successful; has run respectably for an apprentice; sold 2,500 gns Ascot October Sales. *Mrs N. Smith.* **51**

LAWNSWOOD AVENGER 2 b.c. Gulf Pearl 117–Passage Falcon (Falcon 131) (1983 5s 5d 6f* 6f* 7h* 7fg⁴ 8s 8fg) Apr 3; IR 5,400Y; useful-looking colt; second foal; half-brother to successful Irish 5f performer Just A Shadow (by Laser Light); dam unplaced 4 times in Ireland; won seller (bought in 2,100 gns) at **80**

457

Doncaster, minor event (apprentice ridden) at Carlisle and nursery (by short head from Floating Joker) at Beverley in summer; stays 1m; seems to act on any going; genuine. *R. Hollinshead.*

LAWNSWOOD MISS 5 b.m. Grey Mirage 128–Lor Darnie 65 (Dumbarnie 125) (1982 12g 1983 12s 12s) strong mare; probably of little account on flat nowadays. *R. Hollinshead.* —

LAWYERS CHOICE 2 b.c. Northfields–A Star Is Born 91 (Tudor Music 131) (1983 5s 5.3f³ 5fg) Apr 3; 25,000Y; lengthy, quite attractive colt; first foal; dam won 6 times from 5f to 7f; quite a moderate maiden; not seen out after June. *P. Cole.* **69**

LAXAY 2 ch.f. Laxton 105–Mayab 100 (Maystreak 118) (1983 6fg 6d⁴ 6fg) Mar 14; big, good-topped filly; first foal; dam won three 5f races; creditable fifth in minor event at Redcar in September and maiden race at Doncaster in October; favourite, wandered badly left under pressure when 8 lengths fourth of 18 behind Fill The Jug in valuable seller at York in between; stays 6f; suited by a firm surface; wears bandages in front. *H. Wharton.* **66**

LEADBURN (USA) 2 b.c. Mr Leader–Done Good (Impressive) (1983 8g*) Feb 24; $200,000Y; first foal; dam, winner 3 times at up to 1m, is half-sister to very useful 2-y-o 6f stakes winner Invincible Dooley; 10/1, looked a very useful colt in the making when winning 15-runner maiden race at Sandown in October, overcoming his inexperience to lead in final furlong and score by 2½ lengths from Runaway Lover; stays 1m well. *G. Harwood.* **94 p**

LEADENHALL BOY 2 b.g. Oats 126–Starduster (Lucifer) (1983 5s⁴ 7fg 6f* 7f 6fg 6d² 7fg) Mar 2; IR 9,200F, 7,200Y; smallish, close-coupled gelding; first living foal; dam useful winner from 9f to 1½m in Ireland; comfortable 4-length winner from Sambola in seller at Thirsk (bought in 1,650 gns) in July; 5 lengths second of 12 in selling nursery at Brighton 2 months later; should be suited by 7f; seems to act on any going; usually blinkered; sold 1,000 gns Doncaster October Sales. *R. Boss.* **59**

LEAPAWAY LAD 3 gr.g. Decoy Boy 129–Consula 88 (Privy Councillor 125) (1982 NR 1983 9s 12v 14g 11.5f) 2,300Y; workmanlike gelding; seventh foal; half-brother to a minor winner in France and fairly useful 1978 2-y-o maiden Sahibson (by Sahib); dam stayed 1m; well behind in maiden races; sold 900 gns Doncaster August Sales. *K. Ivory.* —

LEAP BRIDGE 5 b.g. King's Leap 111–The Tower (High Treason 126) (1982 7g* 6f 8f 7f⁴ 7f 6f 7f 1983 6fg 7f 7f 6g 6fg³ 7g) small gelding; poor handicapper; stays 7f; acts on firm going; blinkered fourth start; often sweats up. *Miss L. Siddall.* **51**

LEARCTIC 3 br.f. Lepanto–Ballyarctic (Arcticeelagh 119) (1982 NR 1983 14.7fg⁴ 15.5fg) fourth foal; half-sister to 1¼m winner Bali George (by Balidar); dam won over hurdles in Ireland; on backward side when staying on steadily to finish about 16 lengths fourth of 17 behind Neorion in minor event at Redcar in September; ran badly in a seller only subsequent start. *J. Toller.* —

LEAR FAN (USA) 2 b.c. Roberto 131–Wac (Lt Stevens) (1983 7f* 8fg* 7g*) **130**

No doubt in the fervent hope that they will take on some of the more desirable characteristics of their namesakes, horses have frequently been named after 'flying machines'. In recent seasons Olympic sprinters Wells and Mennea have had colts named in their honour; there are no fewer than fifteen animals listed in the volumes of the General Stud Book named after the legendary winged horse Pegasus; and since 1970 there have been winners in Britain, Malaysia and the USA called Shadowfax, the wondrously fast horse of *Lord of the Rings.* Others have had a mechanical derivation: Lear Jet was one of France's fastest two-year-olds in 1968, Super Concorde the champion juvenile there nine years later; the 1971 Stewards' Cup fell to Apollo Nine; and in 1983 possibly the most exciting youngster of the

Fitzroy House Stakes, Newmarket—a most impressive Lear Fan

Laurent Perrier Champagne Stakes, Doncaster—Lear Fan eases up, clear of Kalim

season was Lear Fan, namesake of the radical all-carbon-fibre business aircraft being developed at Reno, Nevada.

Lear Fan the racehorse looked well out of the ordinary from his very first outing, in the Isleham Maiden Stakes at Newmarket in August for which he started a 2/1-favourite to beat his nineteen opponents. He didn't just beat them, he left them grounded, quickening clear in a matter of strides below the distance to come home eight lengths ahead of Millside. Millside in turn was clear of Plaits and My Volga Boatman, both of whom later ran well in a pattern race. Lear Fan, a strong, good-topped, rangy colt, had looked beforehand to have bags of scope for improvement and afterwards was blowing much harder than the runner-up. He missed his next intended race, the Solario Stakes, because the ground was considered too firm but when returned to Newmarket towards the end of August he showed the expected improvement, putting up a top-class display in the first one-mile two-year-old race of the season, the Fitzroy House Stakes. He started at 11/4 on despite having to give 11 lb or more to the five other runners, all of whom had shown distinct promise: Gold And Ivory had shaped very nicely when third in the Sandwich Stakes; Speedwell had easily accounted for all except On Oath in a maiden at Haydock; Tropare had put up a good first effort when fifth in the Acomb Stakes; and the outsider Action Time had been beaten only a length in a Newbury maiden on his last appearance. Lear Fan moved in terrific style to the start, showing a long, raking stride which he reproduced in the race to gallop his rivals silly. After taking a very strong hold in second place, he went on approaching halfway and soon afterwards produced an exhilarating burst of speed which took him well clear of his toiling opponents within the space of a furlong. From then on the race was as good as over and his young rider Clark, who took the mount because first-jockey Starkey was riding Sandhurst Prince at Goodwood, was able to ease him right up inside the last hundred yards. Despite being eased to such an extent, Lear Fan still had a wide margin to spare over the runner-up Gold And Ivory, a margin the judge made eight lengths and we made eleven; and his timefigure of 0.87 fast was bettered by only eight two-year-olds during the year.

Clark again had the mount when Lear Fan reappeared in the Laurent Perrier Champagne Stakes at Doncaster less than two weeks later; Starkey was suspended. Following the late withdrawal of his main rival Trojan Fen, Lear Fan started at 4/1 on to beat Handstand, Kalim, a colt who had emerged the best horse at the weights on his two previous outings in pattern company, and Creag-An-Sgor, the Richmond Stakes runner-up who later won the Middle Park. Although he never managed to establish as commanding a lead as he'd done on his last start, Lear Fan was still impressive, having the others in trouble as soon as he went for home passing halfway. Kalim kept in touch for a while but by the distance Lear Fan had forged into an unassailable five-length lead, a lead reduced to three lengths as he was eased close home. The only blemish on an otherwise faultless display was Lear Fan's behaviour at the start; he seemed to be distracted—and who wouldn't be?—by the appearance nearby of a pony with a small terrier on its back, and he had to be blindfolded before he consented to enter the stalls.

Lear Fan had now won three races in the space of little more than a month by a total of nineteen lengths, a total which would have been even more impressive had he been ridden right out. Incidentally, we find it surprising that jockeys are prepared to risk jeopardising a colt's chance of establishing himself as the best of his age by easing up before the line, especially as the title of champion two-year-old carries considerable prestige as well as boosting the holder's value significantly. We're not for a moment suggesting that immature two-year-olds should be subjected to unnecessarily hard races but would it have taken any more out of Lear

459

Mr A. Salman's "Lear Fan"

Fan had he been pushed out on his last two starts? We think not. Sadly Lear Fan was considered to have done enough for the season and he missed the Dewhurst Stakes. Theoretically his presence there would have served the extremely useful purpose of establishing the relative merits of Lear Fan, El Gran Senor and some other leading two-year-olds, though had Lear Fan turned out for the Dewhurst El Gran Senor would in all probability have stayed at home. The evidence we have suggests that El Gran Senor was marginally the better two-year-old.

Lear Fan (USA) (b.c. Feb 2, 1981)	Roberto (b 1969)	Hail to Reason (br 1958)	Turn-to
			Nothirdchance
		Bramalea (b 1959)	Nashua
			Rarelea
	Wac (b 1969)	Lt Stevens (b 1961)	Nantallah
			Rough Shod
		Belthazar (br 1960)	War Admiral
			Blinking Owl

Lear Fan may well make the better three-year-old. Geoff Lawson, Guy Harwood's assistant, certainly thinks there is further improvement in him and he was quoted after Doncaster as saying 'I rode him myself after he had won at Newmarket first time and he had a leg in every parish. But he has never stopped improving and will be a different horse altogether next season. He has plenty of filling out to do'. Lawson added that, while both Starkey and Clark consider him primarily a Guineas horse, he sees no reason why Lear Fan shouldn't get the Derby trip. There is more than one reason to question Lear Fan's stamina potential. Admittedly his sire Roberto won the Derby and has sired plenty of good winners who stay a mile and a half, Critique, Silver Hawk, Touching Wood, Real Shadai and

Slightly Dangerous among them, but the other side of his pedigree isn't so stout. His dam Wac won two sprint races at three, as well as finishing second in the six-furlong Ashland Stakes, and her one success the following year came over a mile; neither of Wac's two other winners from five previous foals, the Vaguely Noble colt Invincible and the Buffalo Lark filly Flying Fortress, won beyond a mile; and Wac's stakes-placed sisters, Bel Sheba and Lady Lt, gained their victories at up to seven furlongs and a mile respectively. Wac herself is by Ridan's brother Lt Stevens, who never won beyond eight and a half furlongs although second in the ten-furlong American Derby, out of Belthazar, an unraced granddaughter of a good filly called Baba Kenny who won the one-mile Acorn Stakes back in 1931. The only other notable animal from the family in recent years, Bel Sheba's son Port Master, was a smart winner at up to nine furlongs in Canada.

We have learnt over the years that it can be misleading to use American animals' performances as guidelines when assessing the stamina potential in a European racehorse's pedigree, so perhaps too much shouldn't be made of these facts. But Lear Fan's attitude and style of racing must be highly relevant. He is a hard-pulling, extremely powerful galloper who impresses as far more likely to be suited by the straight mile of the Guineas than the switchbacked mile and a half of the Derby. On the debit side, he is considered by his stable to be a top-of-the-ground performer and a very wet spring could both hinder his preparation for the Guineas and, if the stable is correct, his performance in the race. We regard him as having a splendid chance of emulating his stable's To-Agori-Mou, winner of the race in 1981. Like To-Agori-Mou, Lear Fan was extremely well bought as a yearling, costing no more than 64,000 guineas. Incidentally his dam also changed hands in 1982; she was sold in foal to Matsadoon for 50,000 dollars, 15,000 dollars more than her colt foal by Honest Pleasure which followed her into the ring. The buyers of her colt struck a very good bargain; they resold him at the 1983 Highflyer Sales for 125,000 guineas. *G. Harwood.*

LEASE OF LIFE 3 ch.f. Tower Walk 130–Voucher Book 96 (Good Bond 122)   **78**
(1982 5s 7d³ 8d³ 1983 8d* 10.5s 7.2g 8s⁴ 7s) smallish, strong, fair sort; showed a fair turn of foot when readily winning maiden event at Thirsk in April; ran respectably in handicaps last 2 starts; stays 1m; acts well on soft ground and has yet to race on a firm surface. *C. Thornton.*

LEAVE EM LAUGHING 2 gr.c. Swing Easy 126–Janylou (St Chad 120) (1983   **50**
5s 6g 6fg³ 6fg 7f 7f 8g 8.2fg) Apr 9; 1,100Y; narrow, plain colt; first live foal; dam won over 9.5f at 2 yrs in French Provinces; poor plater; probably stays 7f; blinkered sixth outing. *Mrs B. Waring.*

LEAVE IT TO BALLY 3 ch.c. Ballymore 123–Time To Leave (Khalkis 127)   –
(1982 NR 1983 8v 8s 12s 10v 13s 16g 14f 14f 15.8g 16d) IR 33,000Y; ex-Irish colt; half-brother to 3 winners, all at least useful, including Foiled Again (by Bold Lad, Ire), a very useful winner at up to 1¼m; dam, winner at up to 9f in Ireland, is half-sister to dams of Pistol Packer and Saritamer; little worthwhile form, including in a seller on final start; blinkered last 3 outings. *M. McCormack.*

LE BRIND 2 ch.g. Be Friendly 130–Sweet Singer 128 (Roan Rocket 128) (1983 6fg   **66**
8s) Apr 3; plain gelding; third living foal; half-brother to 1975 2-y-o 5f winner Sweet And Naughty (by Connaught); dam won at up to 1m; backed at long odds, 10 lengths fifth of 14 finishers behind Flame Bearer in 1m maiden race at Beverley in September. *N. Tinkler.*

LE CANETON (USA) 2 b.c. Quack–Princess Teamiga (Tumiga) (1983 7fg) Apr   – p
25; $50,000Y; has a fluent action; third foal; half-brother to a winner by Marshua's Dancer; dam stakes-placed winner of 5 sprint races at 3 yrs; 12/1, showed early pace and wasn't knocked about when in mid-division in 30-runner maiden race at Newmarket in August; should improve. *G. Harwood.*

LECTOR (USA) 2 br.c. Elocutionist–Asroula (Assagai) (1983 6f 6f 8d) May 18;   –
$35,000Y, resold 17,000 gns Y; lengthy colt; good mover; fifth foal; half-brother to a winner in USA; dam unraced half-sister to very smart Wittgenstein; soundly beaten in races won by fairly useful colts at Goodwood, Salisbury and Newbury. *D. Elsworth.*

LEDNATHIE 2 b.f. Bay Express 132–Blue Rag 70 (Ragusa 137) (1983 6d³) Feb   **75 p**
25; quite attractive filly; third foal; half-sister to 2 winning 2-y-o's; dam 9f winner; 33/1 and in need of race, going on in good style when 3½ lengths third of 16 to Turn The Key in maiden race at Newbury in October; promises to stay 7f; should improve. *G. Pritchard-Gordon.*

LEEKMORE 4 br.c. Welsh Saint 126–Carnmore (Breakspear II) (1982 5d 5d* 5f³ 5f* 5f 5g 5s 5s 1983 6v⁴ 6s 5v 5g 5.8fg 5g 5fg) quite attractive colt; sprint handicapper; stays 6f; acts on any going; sometimes blinkered. *S. Matthews.*   —

LEGAL BEAU 4 ch.c. Legal Tender 94–Sunny Belle (Windsor Sun 116) (1982 NR 1983 10fg) in rear in varied company, including selling; has been blinkered. *P. Allingham.*   —

LEGAL LAD 2 b.c. Legal Eagle 126–Miltown Lass (Panaslipper 130) (1983 5s 6f 6f 7f 8g) Jan 24; 4,600Y; brother to fairly useful 1980 Irish 2-y-o 7.9f winner Miltown Eagle and half-brother to another winner; dam Irish 1m winner; poor maiden; should stay 1m. *P. Rohan.*   —

LEGALLY BINDING 2 ch.f. Beau of Paree–Full Swing 71 (Ballyciptic 122) (1983 7g 7.6fg 7.6d 6fg) Mar 21; sister to a poor animal; dam, half-sister to smart Lord Helpus, won over 5f at 2 yrs; behind in the autumn in £5,000 event and 3 maiden races. *P. Haynes.*   —

LEGAL SOUND 4 b.f. Legal Eagle 126–Sound Recordo 95 (Sound Track 132) (1982 6f 7f 6fg* 6fg⁴ 6g³ 6s² 6d* 6s³ 1983 6v 6d* 6f³ 7f 6fg 6f 6f² 6g² 6g 6g⁴ 6s* 6fg*) smallish filly; sprint handicapper; won at Carlisle in May and Haydock and Nottingham in October; best at 6f; acts on any going; suitable mount for an apprentice. *J. Etherington.*   **85**

LEGENDARY QUEEN 3 b.f. Wolver Hollow 126–Miss Legend (Bold Legend) (1982 5fg 6g 1983 6v³ 7g 7h 5f) well-made, attractive filly; third in minor event at Kempton in May; should be suited by 7f; blinkered last 2 starts. *A. Ingham.*   —

LEGEND OF FRANCE (USA) 3 b.c. Lyphard 132–Lupe 123 (Primera 131) (1982 6v 1983 8g* 8fg*)   **123**

    The excellent miler Lyphard, whom many British racegoers will best remember for his hopeless failure to come round Tattenham Corner properly in the 1972 Derby, has so far made more of a mark as a sire in France than in Britain. His French runners include the top-class Bellypha, Dancing Maid, Pharly, Reine de Saba and Three Troikas while in Britain the best of his representatives have been Durtal, Lyphard's Special and Monteverdi of whom only the first two were trained here. Arguably 1983 revealed two more to be added to the list in the shape of a pair of colts trained by Cecil for M Wildenstein, Vacarme and Legend of France. The former showed himself one of the best two-year-olds around and the latter, by his performance in the Petition Stakes, indicated that he wasn't far behind the top three-year-old milers on this side of the Channel.

    After running promisingly in the Duke of Edinburgh Stakes at Ascot on his only start at two Legend of France was off the course for eleven months, reportedly because of a badly pulled muscle, and reappeared in a maiden race at Yarmouth in September where he wore small bandages in front. His reputation preceded him and starting favourite he trounced twelve ordinary opponents, winning by six lengths from Habitassa. A fortnight later Legend of France, again bandaged in front, lined up against Spanish Place and Persian Glory for the Petition Stakes at Newmarket. Neither of his opponents could be regarded as a pushover–Spanish Place had finished second in the Craven Stakes and Persian Glory second in the Jersey Stakes—but Legend of France still started a warm favourite and put up a sensational display. Switched to the outside a quarter of a mile from home after tracking the other two, he accelerated in devastating fashion and strode away to beat Spanish Place in a canter by a dozen lengths. Unfortunately he did not race again since he had not been entered in the late-season pattern events and there was a lack of suitable alternatives. The smallish, quite attractive Legend of France, who will stay a mile and a quarter, certainly strikes us as the type to make up for lost time as a four-year-old, especially as he'll receive no penalty in races such as the Earl of Sefton Stakes and Westbury Stakes in the spring.

		Northern Dancer	Nearctic
		(b 1961)	Natalma
Legend of France (USA)	Lyphard	Goofed	Court Martial
(b.c. 1980)	(b 1969)	(ch 1960)	Barra II
		Primera	My Babu
		(b 1954)	Pirette
	Lupe	Alcoa	Alycidon
	(b 1967)	(ch 1957)	Phyllis Court

    The Oaks and Coronation Cup winner Lupe has produced three winners besides Legend of France, notably the smart Leonardo da Vinci (by Brigadier Gerard), successful in the White Rose Stakes before winning in the States where he is now at stud, and L'Ile du Reve (by Bold Lad, USA), who gained a runaway win

LEM

in the Cheshire Oaks. The grandam Alcoa, an out-and-out stayer that ran second in the Cesarewitch, foaled several other winners, including the Horris Hill winner Alcan, while the third dam was a half-sister to the Irish Derby winner Your Highness. *H. Cecil.*

LEGS OF MAN 4 ch.g. Hotfoot 126–Colony 93 (Constable 119) (1982 10s⁴ 7f⁴ 8f 11fg 8.2g 11g 11fg 12.3fg 8g 8.2g 8.2v 1983 8d) sturdy gelding; has a round action; quite a modest handicapper at his best; seems to stay 11f; has run respectably on firm going but is evidently best on soft; suitable mount for an apprentice; has twice run moderately in blinkers. *O. Brennan.*

LEIGHMOR 3 b.f. Connaught 130–Lidmoor (Caerdeon 98) (1982 6d 1983 8d 7g⁴ 7fg 8g² 10g⁴ 8fg 9f) rather a lightly-built filly; quite a moderate maiden; below form last 2 starts (looked as though she had lost a fair amount of condition on final outing); stays 1¼m; trained by C. Brittain until after third start. *D. Smith.* — 64

LEILANI 2 b.f. Fair Season 120–Sailing Along 104 (Crooner 119) (1983 5s 6s³ 6f* 7f 6f 6fg) Apr 18; 2,000Y; leggy filly; good walker; half-sister to a winner in Barbados; dam best at 2 yrs, when winner over 6f and 7f; won 18-runner maiden auction event at Ripon in June despite starting slowly; good fifth in minor event won by King of Clubs at Newmarket the following month, next outing and easily best subsequent effort; suited by 7f; acts on any going; suitable mount for an apprentice; racing in USA. *N. Guest.* — 81

LEIOS 3 ch.g. Singh–Smooth Siren (Sea-Bird II 145) (1982 7d 7f 7fg 1983 10s) close-coupled gelding; lightly-raced maiden; sold 1,750 gns Ascot May Sales. *H. Candy.* —

LEIOTRICHOUS 4 b.g. Nonoalco 131–Helmsdale 107 (Habitat 134) (1982 8fg 8fg 7f³ 7.6f 7.2g 7.6g⁴ 7fg 7f 7fg² 7fg 8d 10d 10s 1983 8d 7s 7s 7g 8h⁴ 8f² 10g 8fg 8d³) strong, compact, good-bodied gelding; poor walker and mover; plater; stays 1m; seems to act on any going; blinkered once; trained by T. M. Jones first 4 starts. *M. Blanshard.* — 46

LEIPZIG 2 b.f. Relkino 131–Fighting 105 (Aggressor 130) (1983 6f* 7f² 7fg²) Apr 7; 25,000Y; half-sister to several winners, including 3-y-o 7f winner Krakow (by Malinowski) and 7f winner Charming Life (by Habitat); dam miler; dead-heated with Collegian in 15-runner minor event at Ripon in August; won Tankerville Nursery at Ascot 2 outings and 6 weeks later by neck from Alnood, but badly hampered runner-up when edging right in final furlong and was disqualified; will be suited by 1m; acts on firm going. *M. Stoute.* — 107

LEISURE GIRL 4 b.f. Native Bazaar 122–Westerlands Prism (Primera 131) (1982 NR 1983 7d³ 8f 7g) plater; has a round action; stays 7f; blinkered once; sold 950 gns Ascot 2nd June Sales. *P. Cundell.* — 46

LEITH SPRING 4 b.f. Silly Season 127–Jane Escart (Escart III) (1982 6g 6fg² 6f 6g 6fg 6d⁴ 1983 6fg³ 6f 7f² 7f⁴ 8g 8f* 8fg 8d²) plater; sold out of M. Francis' stable 1,500 gns after trouncing 8 opponents at Salisbury in September; stays 1m; seems to act on any going; blinkered once in 1982 and on fourth start; sold to W. Stubbs 640 gns Ascot December Sales. *M. Pipe.* — 59

LE LEVADOR 4 br.g. Levanter 121–Adored (Aggressor 130) (1982 11g 13.3f 1983 16d) workmanlike gelding; beaten some way in maiden races and a seller. *Mrs R. Lomax.* —

LEMELASOR 3 ch.f. Town Crier 119–Broadway Lass 70 (March Past 124) (1982 5d* 6g² 5f⁴ 6g² 6g⁴ 7d² 7d 1983 7d 6d² 6s³ 6s 6fg 6fg 8g 8d³ 7s²) small, lightly-made filly; poor mover; moved down a place after beating Saqqara a head in 17-runner handicap at Wolverhampton in October on final start; twice beaten in sellers previously; possibly stays 1m; acts on soft going; blinkered eighth outing. *D. H. Jones.* — 68

LEMHI GOLD (USA) 5 ch.h. Vaguely Noble 140–Belle Marie (Candy Spots) (1982 8.5fg² 8.5fg³ 9f* 12f* 14f* 12f² 12f* 9fg⁴ 10f⁴ 10fg* 12fg* 12f 1983 9.7d 12.5fg⁴ 12fg) second foal; half-brother to smart 8.5f stakes winner Cajun Prince (by Ack Ack); dam smart stakes winner at 8.5f; a genuine, consistent and tip-top performer in USA who won 6 times, earned $1,066,375 and was voted Eclipse Award as Champion Handicap Male in 1982; gained his most important successes in San Juan Capistrano Handicap at Santa Anita, Marlboro Cup Invitational Handicap at Belmont and Jockey Club Gold Cup at Belmont again, winning the 3 races by an aggregate margin of 20 lengths; made running and kept on well once headed to be 2¼ lengths fourth of 9 to Diamond Shoal in Grand Prix de Saint-Cloud in July; well beaten both other outings in Europe, in Prix Dollar at Longchamp and King George — 123

463

VI and Queen Elizabeth Diamond Stakes at Ascot, sweating up each time and misbehaving at start in latter event (led for over 9f); stayed 1½m; did most of his racing on fast ground and was possibly unsuited by soft; retired to Gainesway Farm, Kentucky, at $50,000 live foal. *O. Douieb, France.*

L'EMIGRANT (USA) 3 b. or br.c. The Minstrel 135–Suprina (Vaguely Noble 129 140) (1982 6g² 8f* 8s² 7s* 1983 7v* 8v* 10.5v* 12fg² 9.2d³ 8f² 8g² 11s³)

The Poule d'Essai des Poulains is rarely anywhere near as strongly contested as the Two Thousand Guineas yet is occasionally won by a better horse, as in 1983. L'Emigrant's record compares favourably with Lomond's. He was a leading two-year-old, and after the Poulains he went on both to add to his reputation as a miler in the season's most exacting races and to perform creditably over a longer trip, including in the French Derby. His finishing second to the filly Luth Enchantee in the Prix Jacques le Marois and the Prix du Moulin, decisively ahead of a foreign challenge which included Noalcoholic and Montekin in the former and Wassl and Horage in the latter, suggests he was Europe's top miler except perhaps for Luth Enchantee; at a mile and a half he was three lengths behind Caerleon. He was retired never having been worse than third and only twice out of the first two in twelve starts, eight of them as a three-year-old.

L'Emigrant received 9-2 in the European Free Handicap, 4 lb less than Saint Cyrien who'd beaten him only a length in the Grand Criterium; L'Emigrant had comfortably accounted for the English-trained Drumalis afterwards when winning another of France's major two-year-old races, the Criterium de Maisons-Laffitte. Saint Cyrien stood in L'Emigrant's way in the Poule d'Essai des Poulains at Longchamp the following April but appeared slightly less formidable an obstacle after each had completed his preparation in the spring, for Saint Cyrien most unexpectedly lost to Castle Guard in the Prix de Fontainebleau whereas L'Emigrant won the Prix Djebel at Maisons-Laffitte with ease from Ginger Brink. Saint Cyrien still started favourite for the Poulains ahead of L'Emigrant and pacemaker Conerton but he turned out to be no obstacle at all for any classic horse worth the name. L'Emigrant, who impressed us enormously in the paddock beforehand (as also did Saint Cyrien) and on the way down, won very decisively. The American jockey Asmussen rode boldly, sending L'Emigrant on at the home turn after covering his pacemaker closely, and comfortably fending off all the challengers in the straight. Crystal Glitters, who'd been third to L'Emigrant and Drumalis in the Criterium de Maisons-Laffitte, took second a length behind. The fast-finishing Margouzed looked unlucky to be only third, three quarters of a length down on Crystal Glitters and a length ahead of Sackford. Saint Cyrien finished only sixth, Ginger Brink seventh and Castle Guard ninth. The winner gave trainer Boutin his first success in the Poulains; he is no stranger to success in the Two Thousand Guineas and has usually sent his best horse to Newmarket (as a matter of interest the stable's runner there in 1983 was Allverton).

After the Poulains L'Emigrant's main objective was the French Derby, the Prix du Jockey-Club, at Chantilly in June. He'd never been engaged at Epsom. His immediate objective was the Prix Lupin over ten furlongs or so at Longchamp, normally the strongest-contested of all the colts' classic trials in France and often the most reliable pointer to the French Derby. The latest affair attracted a somewhat disappointing turnout against L'Emigrant–his form and the very heavy ground would tend to discourage some of the others running. Nevertheless L'Emigrant barely scraped home by half a length and three quarters from the Prix Greffulhe runner-up Lovely Dancer and the Prix de Guiche winner Pluralisme; Lovely Dancer finished strongest, while the winner seemed to tire having led from

Poule d'Essai des Poulains, Longchamp—L'Emigrant wins comfortably from Crystal Glitters and Margouzed

Prix Lupin, Longchamp—another win for L'Emigrant. Lovely Dancer and Pluralisme finish in close attendance

two out. Castle Guard, Margouzed, Nile Hawk and the pacemaker Rodwell completed the field. Up to this point we'd never had the slightest doubt about L'Emigrant's staying a mile and a half but his performance in the Lupin clearly brought his stamina under suspicion. In the light of this it's surprising that Asmussen should have received the amount of criticism he did for saving L'Emigrant for a late run in the Prix du Jockey-Club. L'Emigrant came from behind to challenge on the outside without quite getting to grips with Caerleon; in the end Caerleon was too strong for him. Other local apologists who afterwards unreasonably condemned the run-up to the Prix du Jockey-Club in France for excessive toughness, had a sounder point when they moved on to contrast the first two's programmes: Caerleon had been given much the easier time. Nevertheless it's virtually certain that the race went to the better horse over the distance. L'Emigrant's connections apparently suspected he had failed to last out, and they abandoned middle distances in favour of a mile until trying him over eleven furlongs in the Man o' War Stakes at Belmont Park in New York in October. He didn't run up to his best on that occasion, gradually fading into third behind Majesty's Prince and Erins Isle, beaten half a length and five and a half lengths, after making the running for a mile in testing conditions.

L'Emigrant's return to shorter distances following the French Derby wasn't immediately a happy one. Asmussen gave him a poor ride in the Prix d'Ispahan, leaving him with so much to do that the horse did extremely well to finish third of twelve to Crystal Glitters. Much happier was their showing in the two most strongly-contested mile races in Europe during the year, the Prix Jacques le Marois at Deauville in August and the Prix du Moulin de Longchamp in September, though, unusually for him, L'Emigrant sweated up on the former occasion. L'Emigrant fared better against Luth Enchantee when ridden with a modicum of restraint: he went down by a length and a half at Deauville and by half a length at Longchamp. At Deauville he took on Noalcoholic for the lead and had proved the master by the time the winner swept past running into the last furlong. L'Emigrant finished two lengths ahead of third-placed Montekin; Ma Biche was fourth and Noalcoholic fifth. At Longchamp Asmussen let Horage and Wassl cut out the running. When he gave L'Emigrant his head halfway up the straight L'Emigrant shot several lengths clear of Horage, Crystal Glitters, Wassl and L'Attrayante, with Luth Enchantee making her run past those horses. L'Emigrant appeared to have the race won. Then Luth Enchantee began to gain ground, and she went on in the last hundred yards despite L'Emigrant's determined efforts which took him eight lengths clear of third-placed Wassl.

French breeders have been desperately short of the services of horses of L'Emigrant's quality, type and breeding of late. They won't have easy access to his services, either, since he remained in the United States to stand at Gainesway; he was syndicated at a reported figure which puts a valuation of 13 million dollars on him and his fee will be 65,000 dollars, live foal. A very attractive colt and an excellent mover, who cost 360,000 dollars as a yearling at the Keeneland Sales, L'Emigrant is closely related to another American bred, Salpinx (by Northern Dancer), who had a notable racing career in France. Salpinx won the Prix du Conseil de Paris in 1979 and was placed in several more big races, including the

465

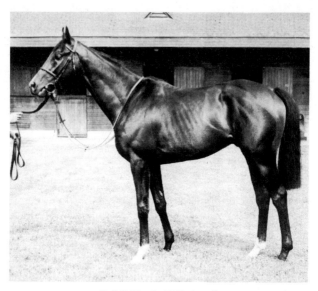

Mr S. S. Niarchos' "L'Emigrant"

Prix Vermeille and the Prix Saint-Alary. The dam's other living foals—Wainscott (by Raise A Native), Mexican Circle (by Circle Home) and Stonewall Champ (by Crimson Satan)—all won small races in the States. The dam Suprina, by one of the best Prix de l'Arc winners out of a seven-furlong winner, never ran. She is a

L'Emigrant (USA) (b. or br.c. 1980)	The Minstrel (ch 1974)	Northern Dancer (b 1961)	Nearctic
			Natalma
		Fleur (b 1964)	Victoria Park
			Flaming Page
	Suprina (b 1970)	Vaguely Noble (b 1965)	Vienna
			Noble Lassie
		Perfecta (bl 1965)	Swaps
			Cosmah

granddaughter of a smart and tough racemare, Cosmah, who foaled nine winners all told, among them Tosmah, the best American three-year-old of 1964; the high-class two-year-old Father's Image (a brother to Perfecta); the good middle-distance horse Halo; and Queen Sucree, the dam of the Kentucky Derby winner Cannonade. What's more, Cosmah was a half-sister to Natalma, the dam of Northern Dancer.

L'Emigrant was a versatile racehorse with a striking turn of foot, best at a mile but capable of high-class form at up to a mile and a half. He acted on any going. *F. Boutin, France.*

LEMON PIE 3 b.c. Saulingo 122–Stop Thinking (Divine Gift 127) (1982 6s 1983   – 10f) workmanlike colt; tailed off in claiming race and amateur riders event; exported to Malaysia. *P. Feilden.*

LEMSIP 2 ch.f. Hot Spark 126–Romancing 82 (Romulus 129) (1983 5v² 5d 5g⁴   71 5fg 5fg 5fg³ 5g 5.3fg 6fg) Apr 27; 4,500Y; half-sister to numerous winners, including fairly useful 7f and 9f winner Imagination (by Relko); dam won over 6f at 2 yrs; placed in maiden auction event at Kempton in April and nursery at Windsor (apprentice ridden at 3 lb overweight) in September; probably best over 5f; seems to act on any going; blinkered last 5 starts; sent to Trinidad. *B. Swift.*

LEODEGRANCE (USA) 7 b.g. King's Bishop–Reasonably (Hail to Reason) (1982 14fg* 12g 12f³ 16fg³ 14f² 13.1g² 1983 17.1v 17f 17.1h³ 14f* 14f²) well-made gelding; tended to hang left when narrowly winning handicap at Salisbury in August; stays well; ideally suited by firm ground; blinkered once at 3 yrs; front runner. *C. Nelson.*　**63**

LEONA STAR 2 b.f. Hotfoot 126–Harriny 94 (Floribunda 136) (1983 6fg 5fg 5g 6fg³) Mar 29; close-coupled filly; fifth foal; dam stayed 7f; beaten 2 lengths in 20-runner maiden race won by Tug Top at Doncaster in November; will be suited by 7f. *S. Matthews.*　**78**

LEONIDAS (USA) 5 ch.g. Exclusive Native–Double Think (Double Jay) (1982 10.2g⁴ 10g 12.2d 10f* 11.7fg 10fg² 10fg 10fg⁴ 10fg 1983 9v 8fg⁴ 10f² 10h* 10f* 10f 10f 10f 10f) workmanlike gelding; hasn't always looked genuine but did nothing wrong when making all to win handicaps at Chepstow and Folkestone in July; well beaten afterwards; stays 1¼m; acts well on fast ground; blinkered once in 1982; sometimes sweats up; often races with tongue tied down. *D. Arbuthnot.*　**71**

LEOPARDO 3 b.c. Busted 134–Naughty Party (Parthia 132) (1982 8g 1983 12f) robust, deep-girthed colt; ran on steadily when 8½ lengths fifth of 11 behind subsequently-demoted Prince of Peace in minor event at Newmarket in July, only outing as a 3-y-o; sold to CBA 3,000 gns Doncaster November Sales. *R. Williams.*　**–**

LEOPARD'S ROCK 9 b.g. Huntercombe 133–Reina Cristina 84 (Tamerlane 128) (1982 10f* 10.8fg* 12fg* 12g² 12f* 11.7g 12g² 12f³ 12d 10d 1983 10f³ 12fg 12f³) middle-distance handicapper; acts on any going but goes particularly well on top-of-the-ground; very good mount for an inexperienced rider; ran poorly second start. *J. Dunlop.*　**62**

LEPARDA 3 ch.f. Lepanto–Balisarda 82 (Ballymoss 136) (1982 6fg 1983 12.2g) leggy filly; behind in sellers. *H. Wharton.*　**–**

LE PRETENDANT 9 b.h. Prince de Galles 125–Reine d'Etat 53 (High Hat 131) (1982 NR 1983 17.1g) poor stayer; sometimes blinkered. *D. Hanley.*　**–**

LESLIE STONE (USA) 3 br.f. Bold Bidder–Drop the Pigeon (No Robbery) (1982 5fg³ 5f 6fg* 6f² 6g* 7g 7d³ 1983 8f 7fg 7f) lengthy filly; lightly raced and rather disappointing; best form at 6f. *J. Hindley.*　**–**

LETCHWORTH 2 b.c. Beau of Paree–Cool Spirit (Hot Brandy 119) (1983 7g) Apr 30; half brother to fairly useful stayer Wait and See (by Biskrah) and a winner in Holland; dam never ran; unquoted, distant ninth of 15 in maiden race at Lingfield in October. *C. Horgan.*　**–**

LET ME PLAY (FR) 3 b. or br.c. Sir Gaylord–Let Me Win (Fathers Image) (1982 NR 1983 8d 9v² 11d³ 12f 13.4fg) 1,150,000 francs Y (approx £104,000); good-topped, quite attractive colt; second foal; half-brother to a winner in the French Provinces by Roi Lear; dam won over 7f at 2 yrs in France; placed in maiden races; broke a leg and was destroyed at Chester in July; blinkered last 2 starts. *S. Norton.*　**73**

LETSGOMO 4 b.g. Royben 125–Veinarde (Derring-Do 131) (1982 5d 5f 6fg⁴ 7f 7fg 6f* 5fg 6g 6fg 6f 6d 1983 12.2g 12f 8.2fg) workmanlike gelding; poor mover; plater; stays 6f (unlikely to get 1½m); suited by a sound surface; has run respectably when sweating up; blinkered second start; has given trouble in preliminaries. *A. Watson.*　**–**

LEW HEATH LADY 3 br.f. Roman Warrior 132–Samia 73 (Galivanter 131) (1982 5s 1983 8d 6v 5fg 5f 6fg) tall, rather leggy, workmanlike filly; behind in varied races, including a seller, twice finishing last; sold 400 gns Ascot August Sales. *J. Bosley.*　**–**

LEXIS (USA) 2 b.f. One For All–Lexacon (Verbatim) (1983 7.6fg* 7.3d) Feb 27; $80,000Y; medium-sized, quite attractive filly; second foal; dam, successful 6 times at up to 1m, is half-sister to very smart 9f and 1¼m stakes winner First Albert; won 19-runner maiden race at Lingfield in October at 20/1; led 2½f out until outpaced in closing stages when 3¼ lengths fifth of 14 to Betsy Bay in Rochford Thompson Newbury Stakes later in month; will be suited by 1m+; acts on a firm and a soft surface. *P. Walwyn.*　**99**

LEYDENE LAD 2 b.g. John de Coombe 122–Andrew's Girl 84 (Quorum 126) (1983 5s 5v² 5d 5fg 6f 7g) Apr 2; lengthy gelding; half-brother to a winner in Malaya; dam 2-y-o 6f winner; plating-class maiden; form only at 5f, but should stay further; acts on heavy going; sweated up final outing. *Mrs R. Lomax.*　**61**

LEYSH 2 b.c. Ahonoora 122–Lucasta (High Hat 131) (1983 6g 6fg 6fg² 7g*) Apr   **93**
9; 27,000Y; compact colt; half-brother to 3 winners, including Cambridgeshire
winner Braughing (by Martinmas); dam never ran; made nearly all in 15-runner
maiden at Lingfield in October, winning by a length from Triple Tower; suited by
7f; acts on a firm surface. *G. Huffer.*

LIANA LOUISE 3 b.f. Silly Season 127–Red Ranger 102 (Red God 128§) (1982   –
6f 7g 7d 1983 10f 10f) fair sort; no worthwhile form, including in sellers. *D.
Weeden.*

LIBEL BY JEALOUSY 2 b.g. Legal Eagle 126–Second Thoughts (Calpurnius   **50**
122) (1983 5d³ 5v³ 6f) Feb 28; 800Y; lengthy, workmanlike gelding; poor plater;
trained by H. Westbrook first 2 starts; sold 1,700 gns Newmarket July Sales and
exported to Malaysia. *N. Callaghan.*

LIBERATED GIRL 3 b.f. Free State 125–St Gay 77 (St Chad 120) (1982 NR   –
1983 8s 8v 11.5fg 10f 6fg) 2,500Y; good-bodied filly; fourth foal; poor mover;
half-sister to winners in Switzerland and Malaya; dam won over 6f; no sign of
ability, including in sellers. *R. Boss.*

LIBERTY TREE 3 ch.f. Dominion 123–Enlighten (Twilight Alley 133) (1982 7f²   **85**
7fg* 6fg* 6g* 6fg* 8g⁴ 1983 8h* 8fg 8fg) useful-looking filly; good walker; game
and genuine as a 2-y-o but became highly strung in 1983 and tended to sweat up and
run very freely; overcame difficulties in running and put up best effort when getting
home by a short head from Black Falcon in apprentice event at Bath in July; stays
1m; has raced only on a sound surface. *Sir Mark Prescott.*

LIBERTY WALK 4 b.g. Free State 125–Path Of Pride (Sovereign Path 125)   **54**
(1982 8f 8fg 10f 10d 11.5fg* 12f⁴ 1983 12d 12s⁴ 16fg² 14.6f 16.1fg 15.8f* 13.8f⁴
17fg 15.8f 15.8g) big, rather narrow gelding; won handicap at Catterick in July;
stays 2m; seems to act on any going; blinkered once at 3 yrs; suitable mount for an
apprentice; suited by forcing tactics; sold 2,600 gns Ascot November Sales. *H.
Wharton.*

LIBRATE 2 ch.c. Mill Reef 141–Lyric Dance 106 (Lyphard 132) (1983 8d*) Apr   **91 p**
19; 220,000Y; first foal; dam won Free Handicap; justified favouritism in promising
style in 19-runner maiden event at Warwick in October, quickening in final furlong
to win by 2 lengths from Crisp with rest well beaten off; will stay 1¼m; looks sure
to win more races. *G. Harwood.*

LICHEN GREEN 5 b.m. Welsh Saint 126–Lichen 93 (Tyrone 130) (1982 8g 9fg   –
8.2g 8d³ 8s 8g⁴ 1983 7f 8f 8.2fg⁴ 8f) lengthy mare; poor mover; plater; stays
1m; probably acts on any going; has worn bandages. *Mrs C. Lloyd-Jones.*

LICHINE (USA) 4 b.c. Lyphard 132–Stylish Genie (Bagdad) (1982 9d* 11g* 10v   **113**
9d³ 10fg 8f 8s⁴ 1983 8v³ 8d³ 9.2v* 8f⁴ 8fg 7f² 7fg⁴ 9g³) $1,700,000Y (the most
expensive yearling sold at auction up to end of 1980); compact, good-bodied colt;
second foal; dam, stakes winner, won at up to 9f and is half-sister to top-class 1m to
1½m colt Artaius; won 80,000 francs race at Longchamp in May by nose from
Naishakar; in frame in pattern races several other starts, notably in Prix de
Ris-Orangis at Evry (third to Princes Gate), Prix du Muguet at Longchamp (1¾
lengths third to Prospero), Prix du Chemin de Fer du Nord at Chantilly (fourth to
Pampabird) and Prix de la Foret at Longchamp (over 4 lengths fourth to Ma Biche);
stayed 11f but was better at shorter distances; acted on any going; retired to Haras
de Fresnay-le-Buffard at 25,000 francs (live foal). *F. Boutin, France.*

LIDADORA 3 b.f. Monsanto 121–Hedwige (African Sky 124) (1983 5fg 6g 7d 7fg   **73**
9f) Mar 25; IR 13,000Y; neat filly; first foal; dam ran only once; quite a modest
maiden; stays 7f. *G. Pritchard-Gordon.*

LIDO ISLE (USA) 3 b. or br.f. Far North 120–She is Gorgeous (Drop Volley)   **95**
(1982 7d 1983 10g³ 11g* 12f 12f*) tall, leggy filly; half-sister to 3 winners,
including stakes winner Diamond Lover (by Shecky Greene); dam, smart stakes
winner, won at up to 7f; won maiden event at Ayr in July and handicap at Beverley
in August; awarded latter after being beaten on merit by Bucklow Hill; had stiff
task in between; stays 1½m; acts on firm going. *M. Stoute.*

LIFE GUARD 2 ch.g. Absalom 128–Queen's Parade (Sovereign Path 125) (1983   **85**
5d 6f⁴ 6g 7f² 7d) Mar 16; deep-girthed, fair sort; first foal; dam poor maiden;
beaten ½ length by Coping in maiden race at Redcar in September; suited by 7f;
acts on firm going and is possibly not at his best on a soft surface; gelded after final
appearance. *J. W. Watts.*

LIFE TIME WARRIOR (USA) 2 b.c. Lyphard 132–Morelle (Vitelio) (1983   **91 p**
5.5g 5.5fg² 6.5fg⁴ 7fg*) Mar 23; half-brother to modest 3-y-o Fast Torpido (by
Wajima); dam best sprinting mare of 1971 generation in Argentina; decisive winner

of maiden race at Longchamp in September by 1½ lengths from John John; will be suited by 1m; likely to make a better 3-y-o. *M. Saliba, France.*

LIGHT AND SHADE 4 ch.f. High Line 125–White Light (Amber Light 114) (1982 11.7f 12f² 13.8f² 16h³ 17.1f 14f* 14fg 12fg² 14fg 1983 12s 14s 16d 13.3g 11.7f 18.4fg) fair sort; staying handicapper; below form in 1983; probably needs a sound surface and acts on hard going; blinkered fifth start; does best when ridden up with pace; has run creditably for an apprentice; sometimes bandaged. *K. Brassey.* —

LIGHT ANGLE (USA) 2 b.f. Angle Light–Syntactic (Forward Pass) (1983 6s 6fg 5fg 5g 5g³) Mar 13; $19,000Y; lengthy filly; third foal; half-sister to 2 minor winners; dam unplaced in 8 starts; quite a modest maiden; stays 6f; apparently suited by some give in the ground; blinkered fourth outing. *A. Jarvis.* 75

LIGHTLY POACHED 3 ro.f. Runnymede 123–Monumental Moment 91 (St Paddy 133) (1982 5f³ 5fg² 5f³ 5fg 5fg³ 5fg 5f 5fg 5f 5d 5g⁴ 1983 5s 5d 6g 5g 5f 6f 6fg 5fg 5g) neat filly; maiden plater; not sure to stay beyond 5f; has run creditably in blinkers; sold 380 gns Doncaster October Sales. *K. Stone.* —

LIGHTNING GIRL 2 b.f. African Sky 124–Tenderly (Prince Tenderfoot 126) (1983 6f²) Apr 7; IR 17,500Y; quite attractive, neat filly; fourth foal; half-sister to 2 winners in Ireland, including fairly useful 5f to 7f winner Lord Trendy (by Lord Gayle), subsequently successful in USA; dam fairly useful from 5f to 9f in Ireland; favourite when 1½ lengths second to Forelie in 9-runner newcomers event at Ascot in June. *P. Kelleway.* 84 p

LIGHTNING JANE 3 b.f. Morston 125–Grain of Truth 84 (Mill Reef 141) (1982 6d 1983 10.1f 8h 8g 10fg) little worthwhile form in maiden and minor races and a handicap. *R. Laing.* —

LIGHTNING LEGACY (USA) 2 b.f. Super Concorde 128–Leave It To Me 112 (Levmoss 133) (1983 5fg 6f² 6f 7f⁴) Mar 24; $23,000Y; quite attractive filly; half-sister to 3 minor winners in USA; dam, 2-y-o 6f winner, stayed 1½m; in frame in maiden race (beaten head by Miss Kuta Beach) at Yarmouth in June and nursery at Lingfield in August; will stay 1m; has raced only on firm ground. *L. Cumani.* 78

LIGHT OF ZION 6 br.m. Pieces of Eight 128–Romardia 75 (Romulus 129) (1982 NR 1983 13.1h 16h) of little account nowadays. *J. Old.* —

LIGHT SHOW 3 b.g. Swing Easy 126–Laser Song 69 (Laser Light 118) (1982 7d³ 7fg 7g 7s 1983 10s³ 11v 12v 10.8v⁴ 7fg² 8f³ 8f³) strong, lengthy, heavy-bodied gelding; placed in maiden races and a handicap; stays 1¼m; blinkered last 3 starts, and doesn't look at all genuine. *R. Laing.* 82 §

LIGHTS OF SLANE 2 b.f. Touch Paper 113–Starlight Express 76 (Pals Passage 115) (1983 5fg 5g⁴ 7s 6fg) first foal; dam won from 5f to 1m and also over hurdles; poor maiden; form only at 5f. *J. Spearing.* 57

LILAC CHARM 3 b.f. Bustino 136–Rose Dubarry 127 (Klairon 131) (1982 7d 1983 12fg* 12f 14d 12fg) rather lightly-made filly; good walker and mover; won maiden race at Lingfield in August; fifth in minor events at Leicester and York on next 2 starts; stays at least 1½m; trained by H. Cecil until after second start. *R. Williams.* 87

LILY BANK 2 b.f. Young Generation 129–Jolisu 110 (Welsh Abbot 131) (1983 5d² 5s 5f 5fg) Apr 5; neat filly; half-sister to several winners, including 1982 2-y-o Sparkling Suzie (by Hot Spark) and fairly useful 1½m to 2¼m winner Jolimo (by Fortissimo); dam miler; quite a modest maiden; not raced after July; acts on a soft surface. *K. Brassey.* 73

LILY OF LAGUNA 2 gr.f. Warpath 113–Sweet and Lovely 111 (Prince Tenderfoot 126) (1983 7s 9g⁴ 10fg) Jan 29; lightly-made filly; first foal; dam ran only at 2 yrs, winning 3 sprint races from 6 starts; 12 lengths fourth of 13 to My Tootsie in maiden race at Wolverhampton in October; shapes like a stayer. *C. Thornton.* 64

LINANHOT 3 ch.f. Hot Spark 126–Anatevka (Privy Councillor 125) (1982 5v⁴ 5f 6f 6f 5d 1983 6v³ 8d³ 8s⁴ 7v³ 8g 7d 8d 8f 7f 7f) lightly-made filly; plater; seems to stay 1m but pulls hard and is probably better at shorter distances; best form with some give in the ground; has worn blinkers and bandages; trained by A. Young until after eighth outing. *G. Harman.* —

LINDA DUDLEY 3 gr.f. Owen Dudley 121–Tanara 93 (Romulus 129) (1982 5g 6fg 8f 7g 1983 6v 10v) sturdy, short-legged, attractive filly; moderate form in varied company; finds 6f inadequate and is bred to stay 1¼m. *B. Hobbs.* —

LINDA'S DESIGN 2 ch.f. Persian Bold 123–Piculet 69 (Morston 125) (1983 6f 6fg 6d) May 2; 15,500Y; smallish, sparely-made filly; first foal; dam disappointing

Mr John Bray's "Linda's Fantasy"

half-sister to very smart animals Prominent and Dominion; soundly beaten in 2 maiden races and a minor event. *R. Armstrong.*

LINDA'S FANTASY 3 ch.f. Raga Navarro 119–Loch Leven 87 (Le Levanstell 122) (1982 5fg 5g4 6fg 6fg* 6g* 6g* 7g* 7f* 1983 6d 6f 7fg2 8g3 7f 7f3 8f* 7f 8g2 10fg) smallish, well-made filly; good walker; won Atalanta Stakes at Sandown in August, quickening clear in good style to beat Remembering by 7 lengths after taking a little time to warm up; had earlier put up 2 excellent performances at Newmarket, going down by ½ length to Thug in 12-runner Van Geest Stakes and finishing 3½ lengths third of 8 to Royal Heroine in Child Stakes; also ran creditably when ¾-length second to Spanish Place in quite well-contested minor event at Goodwood in September, but was most disappointing on fifth, eighth and last starts; stays 1m; form only on a sound surface; capable of a useful turn of foot. *R. Armstrong.* **108**

LINDA'S REBEL (USA) 2 b.c. Restless Wind–Vellum (Mongo) (1983 5.1g) Mar 27; $8,500Y; big colt; fifth foal; half-brother to 3 minor winners; dam won 12 races at up to 1m, including claiming events; backward, seventh of 10 in maiden race at Yarmouth in June. *R. Armstrong.* –

LINDA'S ROMANCE (USA) 3 b.f. Restless Restless–Red Skies 84 (Skymaster 126) (1982 7d 8.2s 6s 1983 10.1fg 7f 6fg) lengthy filly; well beaten in varied races, 3 times last. *R. Armstrong.* –

LINDA'S ROMEO (USA) 3 b.g. Gallant Romeo–Strike Command (Royal Serenade 132) (1982 NR 1983 8d 8v 10fg 8fg 7f3 7f3 8f 8d) compact gelding; brother to useful American sprinter Gallant Serenade; third in 2 handicaps at Yarmouth; stays 7f; acts on firm going. *R. Armstrong.* **46**

LINDA VISTA 3 b.c. Ballymore 123–Petipa 115 (Habitat 134) (1982 NR 1983 8d 7d4 10fg 7f4) workmanlike colt; third foal; half-brother to 2 winners, including Irish 7f winner Bustineto (by Bustino); dam sprinter; fourth in maiden race at Sandown in May and small handicap at Redcar in August; should stay beyond 7f. *R. Baker.* **67**

LINDRICK PASSION 2 b.f. Silly Season 127–Speedy Willow 81 (Frankincense 120) (1983 5f) neat filly; first foal; dam won over 5f and 6f; backward, always behind in 16-runner maiden race at Beverley in August. *G. Harman.* –

LINDRICK ROSE 2 ro.f. Radetzky 123–Rosy Morn (Roan Rocket 128) (1983 5f) May 16; lightly-built filly; half-sister to 3 winners, including useful 1978 2-y-o 5f to 7f winner Nicholas Grey (by Track Spare), subsequently second in Italian Oaks; dam showed no form; behind in maiden race at Thirsk in June. *A. Young.* –

LINDRICK VICTOR 2 b.g. Rapid River 127–Annie-Jo (Malicious) (1983 6f 5f 5f3 7f 6h3 5f 6f 8f 7g 9fg 8.2g2 7.2s 10d4) Apr 17; fair sort; poor plater; stays 1¼m; acts on hard going and a soft surface. *G. Harman.* **50**

LINDRICK WHITSUN 2 b.c. Whitstead 125–Phaedima 76 (Darius 129) (1983 8s 8fg 7d 8g) Feb 26; big, workmanlike colt; half-brother to 3-y-o On Tour (by Queen's Hussar); dam won at up to 2m and is half-sister to Coup de Feu and Peleid; plating-class maiden; should stay long distances. *G. Harman.* **66**

LINDSAY'S GIRL 2 b.f. Meldrum 112–Devon May 58 (Maystreak 118) (1983 5f) May 26; second foal; dam placed over 7f at 2 yrs; tailed-off last of 8 in maiden race at Hamilton in August. *R. Johnson.* –

LINE ABREAST 4 b.f. High Line 125–Filiform 76 (Reform 132) (1982 10fg 11.7f 16.9fg4 15.5fg2 16s3 1983 13s3 14.7d3 18.8v 15.8f3 12f3 13f4 12fg3 15.8f2 16f 15g) lightly-made filly; poor mover; staying maiden; acts on any going; has sweated up; blinkered 3 times at 4 yrs. *S. Norton.* **48**

LINE OF REASON 3 b.f. High Line 125–Kofiyah 95 (Petition 130) (1982 NR 1983 10s 12s 12f4 16g 12fg 10f 10g) 2,800Y; big, sparely-made, workmanlike filly; sister to 1m winner Princess Kofiyah and fair 6f to 1¼m winner Tidal Water; dam, a miler, is sister to high-class sprinter French Plea; made running when fourth behind 15-length winner Queen of Night in maiden race at Brighton in June; well beaten afterwards (blinkered final start). *B. Swift.* –

LINER 2 b.g. Star Appeal 133–Fluke 117 (Grey Sovereign 128§) (1983 7fg 8f) June 4; well-made, good sort; brother to fairly useful 1¼m winner Sextant, and half-brother to 2 winners, including useful 7f and 1m winner Main Sail (by Blakeney); dam won from 5f to 7f, and is half-sister to high-class Buoy and Oaks winner Bireme; well beaten in big fields of maidens at Newmarket and Leicester; sold 3,300 gns Ascot December Sales. *R. Hern.* –

LINE SLINGER 4 b.f. High Line 125–Snow Tribe 94 (Great Nephew 126) (1982 10f 12f 12fg2 12.2f3 16g2 16.5f2 14.6g* 12g2 12g2 14s2 14g* 18s 1983 14v* 18d2 20f 16fg4) fair sort; not the best of movers; surpassed herself in 10-runner **110**

Yorkshire Cup, York—Line Slinger springs a surprise and wins from Khairpour

Mr N. Hetherton's "Line Slinger"

Yorkshire Cup at York in May, making virtually all and battling on with great gusto to beat Khairpour (who spoiled his chance by veering badly right) by 1½ lengths; kept on splendidly to be ½-length second to Broken Seal in handicap at Doncaster later in month; well beaten in Gold Cup at Royal Ascot and Jockey Club Cup at Newmarket subsequently; suited by a test of stamina; ideally suited by some give in the ground; very game; sold to NBA 72,000 gns Newmarket December Sales. *W. Elsey.*

LINGA LONGA 2 gr. g. Town Crier 119–Go Baby Go 81 (Takawalk II 125) (1983 6g 6d) Mar 22; brother to fair sprinter Town Flier; dam won 19f hurdle race; 12 lengths seventh of 14 to Angleman in minor event at Lingfield in September, first outing. *N. Vigors.*   —

LINGRETA 4 b.f. Pitskelly 122–Sheralanth (Pontifex) (1982 7f 7f⁴(dis) 8.3fg 7fg 8.2s 7d 8d 1983 8s 7fg) narrow filly; poor mover; plater nowadays; stays 7f; has run respectably on firm going but is ideally suited by plenty of give in the ground; has been tried in blinkers; has run well for an apprentice. *Peter Taylor.*   —

LINKLIGHTER 3 b.f. Busted 134–Gay Trinket 72 (Grey Sovereign 128§) (1982 7d 6fg* 6g 1983 7f³ 10f* 10f⁴ 8fg) well-made, good sort; favourite, quickened clear halfway up straight but didn't appear to have much left at finish when beating Elysian by 1½ lengths in handicap at Newbury in July; in frame in 2 similar events at Salisbury; stays 1¼m; acts on firm going; held up and never on terms final start. *G. Harwood.*   **89**

LINNET SONG 2 b.f. Derrylin 115–Progress (March Past 124) (1983 6f 7f 8g) Apr 8; sixth foal; dam poor maiden on flat but won a point-to-point; no sign of ability; broke a knee at Leicester in September; dead. *N. Vigors.*   —

472

LINPAC GOLD 4 b.f. Rheingold 137–Purple Goddess 69 (Red God 128§) (1982   –
10.5fg 12fg 12.2f² 12f³ 12g 15d 16s⁴ 12s 12d 12d 1983 12.2fg) sturdy filly; poor
maiden; stays 1¼m; acts on firm going; blinkered only start at 4 yrs; one paced; has
twice started slowly. *J. Peacock.*

LINPAC LEAF 2 b.f. Tower Walk 130–North Page 81 (Northfields) (1983 5f³ 6fg   **70**
6fg) Mar 13; sturdy filly; good walker; first foal; dam placed several times at up to
10.6f; quite a modest maiden; will stay 7f; acts on firm going; off course for 3
months after first outing. *W. Elsey.*

LINTON VILLAGE 2 b. or br. g. Arapaho 108–Rosecon 66 (Typhoon 125) (1983   –
6d 7g) Mar 14; IR 2,400F; half-brother to a minor winner and a bumpers winner;
dam stayed 1¾m; well beaten in maiden events at Lingfield in October, on debut
last of 24. *J. O'Donoghue.*

LION CITY 4 b.g. Simbir 130–Fille Sifflante §§ (Whistler 129) (1982 10s 12fg   **98**
10.6fg² 10f 8fg* 8fg⁴ 8f* 9fg³ 8g⁴ 8.2g* 8d* 9s² 8s² 1983 8d 8d³ 8v³ 10s 8d 10.5f⁴
10f* 10.6fg³(dis) 8g² 8fg* 8d* 10fg⁴) fairly useful handicapper; poor mover; won
handicaps at Sandown in July, Ascot in September (£5,800 event from
Worlingworth) and York in October (narrowly beat Florida Son in Hong Kong
Marlboro Cup); stays 1¼m; acts on any going; effective with and without blinkers;
has won when sweating up; ideally suited by strong handling though has won for an
apprentice; suited by waiting tactics; tough. *E. Eldin.*

LISAILY (USA) 3 ch.c. Raja Baba–Controlled Landing (First Landing) (1982   **71**
7d 1983 8v 8f 8f 10h² 12g⁴ 11.5g 14g) good-looking colt; in frame in maiden races
at Nottingham in August and Kempton (gentleman riders) in September; stays
1½m; a good-moving colt who seems suited by a sound surface; sold to N. Bycroft
11,500 gns Newmarket Autumn Sales. *H. T. Jones.*

LITTLE ANGEL 2 b.f. Shack 118–Nordic Maid 84 (Vent du Nord) (1983 5s 6fg   **43**
7f 7g 7f) May 2; neat, stocky filly; first foal; dam won 1m amateur riders race; bad
plater; stays 7f. *W. Wharton.*

LITTLE ATOM 6 gr.h. The Go-Between 129–Native Nymph 97 (Indigenous   **40**
121) (1982 6f 6f⁴ 6f 6f³ 6g³ 6d³ 5f³ 6f 7f 6f⁴ 6g 5fg 5d 7f³ 7d 1983 7f 7f 7f⁴ 6f² 6g)
poor handicapper; stays 7f; goes well on top-of-the-ground; has worn blinkers. *D.
Yeoman.*

LITTLE BOY 3 b.g. Free Boy 96–Sousocks (Soueida 111) (1982 5fg 7d 7fg 1983   –
12fg 16f) compact gelding; of little account; has worn blinkers. *P. Burgoyne.*

LITTLE CHANGE 3 ch.f. Grundy 137–Pennycuick 101 (Celtic Ash) (1982 5f⁴   –
5g³ 6f 7d 1983 6d 8d⁴ 10d⁴ 8f) neat filly; in frame in maiden events and handicaps;
yet to prove she stays 1¼m; ran respectably in blinkers final start; sold 42,000 gns
Newmarket December Sales. *F. J. Houghton.*

LITTLE EAGLE 2 gr.f. Rupert Bear 105–Keenland (Weensland 121) (1983 5g   –
5.8g 5.8f 6g 6g) May 1; 230Y; third foal; dam bad hurdler; no form, including in
sellers. *Peter Taylor.*

LITTLE EGRET 2 b.f. Carwhite 127–Miss Speak Easy (Sea-Bird II 145) (1983   **71**
6f 7f⁴ 7fg 8.2fg 8.2fg) Apr 23; 17,500 gns Y, 140,000 francs Y (approx £11,600);
half-sister to French 3-y-o Shameless (by Vitiges) and 2 winners, including very
useful French middle-distance winner Natchitoches (by Pontifex); dam minor
French 9f winner; quite a moderate maiden; form only on second outing; should
stay 1¼m. *R. Armstrong.*

LITTLE EMPRESS 3 b.f. Cavo Doro 124–Empress of England (Constable 119)   –
(1982 NR 1983 8h 8fg) 390 2-y-o; half-sister to a winner over hurdles; dam never
ran; behind in maiden race at Chepstow and seller at Bath. *M. Bradley.*

LITTLE-FAWN 2 b.f. Kala Shikari 125–Glengarry 72 (High Hat 131) (1983 5f 5f   –
5f 7g) June 4; 500F, 800Y; plain filly; half-sister to 7f and 11f winner Luigi's Glory
(by Hittite Glory); bad plater; not raced after July. *W. Clay.*

LITTLE GRIMALDI 3 b.c. Cawston's Clown 113–Coymount (Goldhill 125)   –
(1982 5.3g 5d 5fg 5f 5fg 7g 1983 10d 8f 7fg 7h) close-coupled colt; no worthwhile
form, including in a seller; blinkered final start; sold 500 gns Doncaster August
Sales. *S. Matthews.*

LITTLE HUNGARIAN 3 b.c. Gunner B 126–Cotton Lavender (Sassafras 135)   –
(1982 NR 1983 5f 6h 6f 5g) 2,000F; strong, good-quartered colt; first produce;
dam, half-sister to smart stayer Realistic, never raced beyond 7f; ran respectable
first race in maiden event at Nottingham in July but showed little form afterwards;
will be suited by further; apprentice ridden; sold 640 gns Newmarket Autumn
Sales. *R. Simpson.*

LITTLE LOOK (USA) 2 gr.c. Little Current–Come Hither Look (Turn-to)   **98**
(1983 7.6fg³ 8d² 7g²) Apr 20; $380,000Y; close-coupled colt; good walker and
mover; brother to very smart Prize Spot, winner of Hollywood Oaks, and
half-brother to numerous winners, including very useful English miler Pass A
Glance (by Buckpasser); dam very useful 2-y-o winner of 5.5f Blue Hen Stakes;
1½ lengths second of 14 to Corinth in £4,000 event at Newbury in October; failed
to land the odds in maiden at Lingfield later in the month, but ran well all the
same; better suited by 1m than by 7f, and will stay 1¼m; sure to win a race. *G.
Harwood.*

LITTLE MADAM 3 ch.f. Habat 127–Obedience (Reliance II 137) (1982 5g 5fg*   –
5g 5g 5f² 6fg⁴ 5fg³ 6s 1983 6s 6s 5g³ 5fg³ 6g 5f 5f⁴ 5fg 5fg 5g) small filly; possibly
best at 5f; had very stiff task sixth outing. *D. Wilson.*

LITTLE-MAUREEN 2 b.f. Cavo Doro 124–Golden Opinions (So Blessed 130)   –
(1983 5s 8.2f 8g) May 21; 340Y; small filly; poor mover; third foal; half-sister to a
winner in Belgium; well behind in minor event and 2 sellers. *W. Clay.*

LITTLE MEADOW (FR) 3 b.f. Carmarthen 130–Andelle (Spy Well 126) (1982   **114**
6s 6.5g* 7.5g³ 7.5fg 8fg⁴ 8g 8d 8d³ 9d 8s² 8v³ 1983 11v⁴ 8v⁴ 9s* 8v* 10.5v 9.5s³
8d⁴ 10v 10.5f 8g 10f 8g² 10fg 9.2f³ 8d) light-bodied filly; successful in minor event
at Evry and 80,000 francs race at Saint-Cloud, both in March; in frame on several
other occasions during a busy campaign; in Poule d'Essai des Pouliches at
Longchamp in May (2¼ lengths fourth to L'Attrayante) and Prix de l'Opera on same
course in October (1¾ lengths third of 18 to Royal Heroine, staying on); probably
stays 11f; acts on any going. *R. Collet, France.*

LITTLE MERCY 5 gr.m. No Mercy 126–Petite Rock (Goldhill 125) (1982 8fg*   **90**
8f* 8g² 8fg* 8f² 8g² 7g* 7f* 8g³ 7g² 1983 7s⁴ 8f⁴ 7f 7f* 7f* 7f³ 7f* 7f 7s² 6fg 6g³)
big, strong, good-topped mare; good walker and mover; won handicaps at
Catterick and Newmarket in July and at Brighton in August; best at 7f or 1m; acts
on any going, but is ideally suited by a sound surface; suited by forcing tactics;
game and consistent. *J. Winter.*

LITTLE MISS HORNER 2 b.f. Sit In The Corner–Argostone (Rockavon 120)   **63**
(1983 5d 5d 5s² 5d⁴ 5s 5s 5s³ 6g 5f 6f 7fg⁴ 5f³ 7h 5f 6fg 6g) Mar 17; workmanlike
filly; fourth foal; dam well beaten, including in a seller; had hard season, but stood
up to it pretty well until showing nothing under low weights in nurseries on last 3
appearances; best effort when third in nursery at Beverley in July on twelfth
outing; seems to stay 7f; acts on any going. *G. Harman.*

LITTLE NIECE 2 ch.f. Great Nephew 126–Anzeige (Soderini 123) (1983 7g 7s³   **74**
7g³) Mar 11; rangy, quite attractive filly; fourth foal; half-sister to Irish 3-y-o
Sparkeige (by Hot Spark) and top Dutch filly Libelle (by Arratos); dam, daughter of
German Oaks runner-up Ankerette, won over 1m in Germany; placed in October
maiden events at Leicester and Lingfield; will be suited by 1m+; acts on soft going.
J. Dunlop.

LITTLE STARCHY 5 b.h. Starch Reduced 112–Misty Morn 70 (Worden II 129)   **85**
(1982 5s³ 5g² 5fg 5.3g⁴ 5g 5fg² 5fg 5.3f³ 5g 5fg 5fg* 5s³ 5s² 1983 6s⁴ 5.8s* 5d*
5.8g 6g² 6f 5h 5f 5fg 5g 6fg 5g 5fg⁴) fair sort; made virtually all to win handicaps at
Bath in May and Epsom in June; beat Bonne Baiser ¾ length on latter; stays 6f;
acts on any going. *J. O'Donoghue.*

LITTLE STEEL 4 ch.c. Steel Heart 128–Nagin 120 (Pretense) (1982 5f 1983   –
6fg 8f) neat, dipped-backed colt; poor plater; sold 440 gns Ascot October Sales. *B.
Gubby.*

LITTLE TEMPEST 4 ch.c. Tumble Wind–Miss Pumpkin 62 (Silly Season 127)   –
(1982 9v 8s 9s 12f 13g⁴ 7.5f³ 8fg⁴ 16fg 12.8fg 7.9g 12f 12fg⁴ 16f⁴ 1983 16g 16d 9d²
9g) ex-Irish colt; dam showed only poor form; plating-class maiden on flat though
has won over hurdles; effective at around 1m and seems to stay 2m; seems to act
on any going; has been tried in blinkers; trained by J. Kennedy first 3 starts. *W. A.
Stephenson.*

LITTLE TOPPER 2 gr.f. Warpath 113–Yours and Mine 83 (Tin Whistle 128)   –
(1983 5s³ 5s 5d) Jan 20; 4,200Y; lengthy filly; sister to 2 winners, including
successful 1977 staying 2-y-o Sioux and Sioux; dam stayed 9f; of no account;
blinkered final outing. *D. Morley.*

LITTLE TOWN FLIRT 2 b.f. Quiet Fling 124–Clarity 98 (Panaslipper 130)   –
(1983 6g 7f) Mar 27; 16,000Y; half-sister to numerous winners, including quite
useful 1979 2-y-o 5f winner Loyal Manacle (by Manacle) and fairly useful stayer
Amity (by Amber Rama); dam, winner at up to 1½m, is half-sister to Santa Claus;

showed up for some way in maiden race at Yarmouth in July, second outing; likely to need a stiff test of stamina. *R. Laing.*

LITTLE TYRANT 6 br.g. Tyrant–Tadorna 81 (Sea-Bird II 145) (1982 NR 1983   –
    10f) poor plater; has worn blinkers and bandages. *B. Richmond.*

LITTLE WIZARD 2 b.g. Roman Warrior 132–Song's First 82 (Song 132) (1983   55
    5g 5v 5f 6fg 5f 5f) Feb 16; 2,000F; strong, compact, sprint type; second foal; dam
    won 8 sprints; poor form in maiden and minor events. *Mrs M. Nesbitt.*

LITTLE WOLF 5 ch.h. Grundy 137–Hiding Place 109 (Douttele 128) (1982 14f³   127
    12g* 12g² 16d* 15.5v 1983 12d² 14v 20f* 21f*)

'This', said Groucho of Harpo in a Marx brothers film, 'is the brains of our outfit. Now you know what kind of an outfit we've got'. By the same token, if Little Wolf was, by some way, the best out-and-out stayer in training in 1983 it's clear what kind of a staying division we had. Those behind Little Wolf in the Gold Cup and the Goodwood Cup were, taken collectively, a substandard bunch and although Little Wolf put up high-class performances in both races he isn't in the same class as those outstanding long-distance horses of recent years Sagaro, Buckskin, Le Moss, Gold River and Ardross.

The Gold Cup attracted small fields in Ardross' years—five in 1982 and four in 1981 (the latter the smallest Gold Cup field for more than sixty years)—but with no outstanding contender in the line-up in 1983 there were twelve runners, the biggest field for the race since 1950. The ex-Irish Ore, winner of the Queen Alexandra Stakes and runner-up in the Goodwood Cup as a four-year-old, started favourite; he had won both his races in the current season, including the Henry II Stakes at Sandown in May in which Khairpour and Centroline, two other Gold Cup runners, were among those behind. Khairpour, third at Sandown, had also finished second to Line Slinger, another Gold Cup runner, in the Yorkshire Cup, in which Little Wolf was only sixth. Little Wolf's poor showing in the Yorkshire Cup—and in the previous year's Prix Royal-Oak—was undoubtedly accounted for by the holding conditions. His overall record was one of steady improvement and his performance in the Jockey Club Cup as a four-year-old had convinced us that there would be few with as good prospects in the Cup races in 1983; giving weight all round at Newmarket Little Wolf beat Halsbury by six lengths with Ore third,

Gold Cup, Ascot—a grand performance from Little Wolf, beating
Khairpour by five lengths. Indian Prince (broad blaze) finishes third,
and Ore (partially hidden) fourth

finishing so strongly that we were left in no doubt that he'd get extreme distances, given the chance. The French sent two of their best out-and-out stayers to Royal Ascot, the Prix du Cadran runner-up Indian Prince and the subsequent Prix Gladiateur winner Balitou, but Little Wolf—who had shown he had trained on when second to Diamond Shoal in the John Porter Stakes on his reappearance—started second favourite. Line Slinger went off at a cracking pace, setting a gallop which coupled with the prevailing firm ground resulted in one of the fastest winning times—4m 24.36sec—for the Gold Cup since electrical timing was introduced in the 'fifties. When the runners reached the entrance to the final straight Indian Prince was in front, with Little Wolf, close up most of the way, poised just behind. Pushed along to take the lead early in the straight Little Wolf drew away in great style, clearly relishing the underfoot conditions, to win, kept up to his work, by five lengths and one and a half lengths from Khairpour and Indian Prince.

Before we leave the Gold Cup, the importance attached by some to Little Wolf's winning time is worth comment. Some used Little Wolf's time—the fastest in a Gold Cup since Zarathustra's 4m 23.93sec in 1957—to argue Little Wolf into a prominent position alongside his immediate predecessors Le Moss and Ardross. As we have said before, a record or near-record time is a dubious prop for anyone to make recourse to when assessing the merit of a racehorse. A fast time for a race usually means no more than conditions were ideal for the setting up of a fast time—as they were in the Gold Cup. Anyone who needs convincing that a fast time and an outstanding performance aren't necessarily the same thing should make reference to the list of record holders on the major courses: in some cases top-class animals hold the record, in others lesser animals have the honour. The electrically-timed record for Ascot's Gold Cup course, for example, is held, not by a Gold Cup winner, but by the handicapper Tubalcain who won the 1966 Ascot Stakes in 4m 21.36sec. Little Wolf's time, furthermore, was fractionally slower than that taken by the latest Ascot Stakes winner Right Regent, who carried only 6 lb less than Little Wolf, in conditions which weren't quite so fast as on Gold Cup day.

None of those that took on Little Wolf at Royal Ascot turned out against him at Goodwood six weeks later. The pick of the opposition in the seven-strong line-up for the Goodwood Cup looked to be Santella Man and Karadar who had fought out the finish of the Queen's Vase at Royal Ascot. So it proved. In another strongly-run race, Little Wolf took the lead three furlongs out but was pressed strongly by Karadar (who received 7 lb) in the closing stages and had to struggle to land the odds by half a length, with Santella Man six lengths away third. Carson dismounted soon after passing the post and Little Wolf was afterwards found to have jarred a joint in his near-fore, an injury which didn't clear up in time to allow him to contest the Doncaster Cup, the third leg of the so-called stayers' triple crown. Ground conditions at Goodwood's July meeting were extremely fast and Little Wolf lowered the existing record for the Goodwood Cup course and distance by almost three seconds; Noalcoholic also set a time record in the previous day's Sussex Stakes.

Little Wolf's victory in the Goodwood Cup helped to put his trainer on top of the trainer's list by the end of July. He remained there to become the leading trainer in Britain for the fourth time, with earnings of £549,598. Hern's stable, which concentrates on producing second- and third-season horses, had surprisingly never previously won the Gold Cup or the Goodwood Cup. Hern recovered from an unusually slow start in 1983 to saddle the winners of fifty-seven races, three of them to the credit of the season's leading money-earner in Britain Sun Princess who completed the Oaks-St Leger double, a feat last achieved by Dunfermline, also trained by Hern, in 1977.

		Great Nephew	Honeyway
	Grundy	(b 1963)	Sybil's Niece
	(ch 1972)	Word from Lundy	Worden II
Little Wolf		(b 1966)	Lundy Princess
(ch.h. 1978)		Doutelle	Prince Chevalier
	Hiding Place	(ch 1954)	Above Board
	(ch 1963)	Jojo	Vilmorin
		(gr 1950)	Fairy Jane

The achievements of Little Wolf in 1983 went some way to arresting a decline in the fortunes of his sire Grundy who, after occupying eighth place in the sires list in 1980, dropped to twentieth in 1981 and fortieth in 1982. However, Little Wolf accounted for more than half of Grundy's total earnings in 1983 and the news, announced at the end of the season, of Grundy's sale to Japan didn't come as a complete surprise. At the time of his sale only three applications for the National

*Goodwood Cup—Little Wolf stumbles, and Karadar rallies;
Little Wolf wins by half a length*

Stud's eleven 1984 nominations had been received. Grundy is the eighth post-war Derby winner to finish up in Japan and his departure, following the disappearance of Shergar (kidnapped in February) and the death of Troy (through natural causes in May) means that the services of the three best Derby winners of the past decade or so were lost to European breeders within the space of a year. Royal Palace, Blakeney, Mill Reef, Morston, Shirley Heights, Henbit and Golden Fleece are Derby winners still available.

Whether Little Wolf will eventually be given a chance as a sire in Europe remains to be seen. There is only limited demand for the stud services of long-distance performers nowadays. On the dam's side, Little Wolf comes from an excellent family. He is the ninth winner bred by the miler Hiding Place, dam of the very smart Smuggler (by Exbury), who won the Princess of Wales's Stakes, the Yorkshire Cup, the Henry II Stakes and the Gordon Stakes; Hiding Place is also the dam of two very useful racehorses, the Horris Hill winner Disguise (by Klairon) and the Hyperion winner Elusive Pimpernel (by Blakeney). Hiding Place's dam Jojo was a most successful broodmare, dam of twelve winners on the flat from fourteen foals including Brigadier Gerard's sire Queen's Hussar.

Little Wolf is a strong, close-coupled, quite attractive horse. He is genuine and consistent and stays in training with the Gold Cup again his principal objective. If he gets to post fit and well his chance will have to be respected. Although he acts on any going except heavy, firm ground on Gold Cup day would be very much in his favour, especially as such conditions might count strongly against Carlingford Castle who looks at this early stage one of the biggest stumbling blocks to further Cup honours for Little Wolf. *R. Hern.*

LITTLE WORKER 3 br.f. Workboy 123–Little Singer (Sing Sing 134) (1982 5g 5f² 6f 5d 5f 6fg⁴ 5g⁴ 6d 8fg 1983 5v³ 5fg 6g 6fg 6s⁴ 6fg) small filly; plater; stays 6f; acts on any going; blinkered fifth outing in 1982. *P. Calver.* — **43**

LIVELY ROSE 4 ch.f. Wolverlife 115–Baby Rose (Our Babu 131) (1982 5f 5.8f 6g 1983 6f 6fg 5h⁴ 5g 5g) leggy filly; sprint handicapper; seems to act on any going; blinkered final start. *N. Vigors.* — **–**

LIVE WITH ME 3 b.f. Free State 125–Pied A Terre (Ribocco 129) (1982 NR 1983 7fg 7.2fg 8f 7f 8f 7g) useful-looking filly; half-sister to 2 winners, including 1980 2-y-o 7f winner Salon Privee (by Dragonara Palace); dam daughter of sister to Reform; quite a moderate maiden; stays 7f. *R. Baker.* — **–**

L J'S PARROT 2 ro.c. Lombard 126–Grey Miss 72 (Grey Sovereign 128§) (1983 5fg 5f 6fg) Apr 30; leggy, lightly-made colt; half-brother to successful 5f performer Will George (by Abwah) and a winner in Switzerland; dam stayed 7f; no worthwhile form; blinkered in valuable seller at Doncaster in September on final appearance. *B. McMahon.* — **–**

LLANDWYN 2 ch.c. Jaazeiro 127–Peach Melba 96 (So Blessed 130) (1983 5v² 5f 5fg* 5fg 5fg 5g) May 21; 12,000Y; neat colt; excellent mover; second foal; dam won over 5f at 2 yrs; won maiden event at Pontefract in August; out of his depth as often as not; very slowly away when apprentice ridden final appearance. *M. Jarvis.* — **86**

LLINOS 2 ch.f. Camden Town 125–Roller Bird 69 (Ribocco 129) (1983 5s⁴ 6s 7f **64**
6g) Feb 27; quite attractive, well-made filly; half-sister to a winner in Jersey;
dam disappointing daughter of Park Hill Stakes winner Cursorial; plating-class
maiden; disappointing favourite in race won by Maruthayoor at Lingfield in June
on second outing; off course over 3 months after next appearance; should stay at
least 1m; acts on soft going. *C. Horgan.*

LOAD THE CANNONS (USA) 3 b.c. Cannonade–Hurry Harriet 129 (Yrrah **120**
Jr) (1982 NR 1983 10v³ 10.5d* 12f* 12fg* 12.5g* 13.5fg 13d 12g³ 11g)
half-brother to American claiming race winner Free Port (by Thatch); dam won
Champion Stakes; won 4 of his 6 races in France and developed into a very smart
performer; always in first 3 and took command early in straight when beating
Terreno by a length in 15-runner Prix Maurice de Nieuil at Saint-Cloud in July;
successful earlier in 20-runner race at Evry and in small races at Maisons-Laffitte
and Longchamp, on last-named course making all to beat Olindo by a length when
5/1 on; ran badly when last of 11 behind Zalataia in Grand Prix de Deauville in
August and when only ninth to All Along in Rothmans International at Woodbine in
October, but returned to form when 2 lengths third of 9 to Zalataia in Oak Tree
Invitational at Santa Anita in November; stays 1½m; seems to act on any going.
O. Douieb, France.

LOBKOWIEZ 4 b.c. Radetzky 123–Fulcrum Miss (Fulcrum) (1982 7d 8.5fg **86**
12.3g³ 12f 10fg² 12f² 12f4 12g 10f 10d 1983 10v⁴ 8v 10d 10fg 10f 8f² 8g⁴ 8fg 10.8d²
10fg) neat colt; smart and genuine performer at his best who ran particularly well
on fifth and sixth starts at 3 yrs, going down by short head to Kind of Hush when
carrying 8 lb overweight in Prince of Wales's Stakes at Royal Ascot and by 4 lengths
to Kalaglow in Coral-Eclipse Stakes at Sandown; hasn't reproduced that form;
stays 1½m but best form at 1¼m; acts on any going; blinkered sixth outing;
possibly best on a galloping track. *C. Brittain.*

LOCHAN ORA 2 br.f. Queen's Hussar 124–Lutine Belle 82 (Luthier 126) (1983 **—**
8fg) Apr 4; fourth foal; half-sister to middle-distance winner Inchgower (by
Ribero); dam stayed well; twelfth of 13 in £3,900 event at Salisbury in September.
Mrs N. Smith.

LOCHBOISDALE (USA) 3 b.g. Stage Door Johnny–Blue Law (Tom Rolfe) **82**
(1982 8s⁴ 1983 10s 10v* 10d² 12f 12d) good-bodied, quite attractive gelding;
showed improved form in spring with blinkers and front-running tactics, beating
Bahoor by ¾ length in minor event at Nottingham and finishing good second in
similar race at Brighton; gelded after latter and was subsequently lightly raced
and disappointing; should stay 1½m; acts well on heavy going; sweating final
start; sold to J. King 7,000 gns Ascot November Sales. *J. Tree.*

LOCHFEN 2 b.g. Lochnager 132–Ensign Steel 57 (Majority Blue 126) (1983 5s **66**
5d² 5g³ 5g) June 1; strong, compact gelding; brother to 2 winners, including fair
sprinter and useful hurdler Benfen; dam, placed over 6f, is half-sister to very useful
sprinters Red Track, Sovereign Set and Burwell; disappointing maiden; blinkered
at Hamilton in June on final appearance; acts on a soft surface. *K. Stone.*

LOCHLINNHE 4 b.g. Lochnager 132–Sunbird II (River Chanter 121) (1982 10g **52**
12.3g⁴ 14.7f 12v³ 12d³ 1983 13s4 15fg 12f² 14.7f² 12s) good-topped gelding;
plating-class maiden on flat though has won over hurdles; stays 1¾m; acts on any
going; has sweated up; sold out of Miss S. Hall's stable 14,500 gns Doncaster
August Sales after fourth start. *Ronald Thompson.*

LOCH LOUISE 3 br.f. Lochnager 132–Fair Louise 72 (Blakeney 126) (1982 NR **—**
1983 10f) big, lengthy filly; first foal; dam, from speedy family, stayed 2m; dwelt
and was always behind in maiden race at Ripon in August (apprentice ridden). *M.
W. Easterby.*

LOCH LOVER 2 b.f. Lochnager 132–Strike On The Box (Busted 134) (1983 5s **—**
5v 6g) May 25; 1,550F, 1,300Y; second foal; dam disappointing maiden; soundly
beaten in maiden races, on final outing last of 12; probably of little account. *R.
Allan.*

LOCHOW 2 b.f. Lochnager 132–Sunshine Holyday 96 (Three Wishes 114) (1983 **56**
5s 6g 7f 6f 8fg) May 1; leggy, lightly-built filly; half-sister to 3 winners, including
fairly useful 1982 2-y-o 7f winner Wargame (by Warpath) and fairly useful 1977 2-y-o
1m winner Westwood Boy (by Saintly Song); dam stayer; plater; best effort on final
start, when 2 lengths seventh of 16 to High Reef at Redcar in October; stays 1m;
retained 380 gns Doncaster October Sales. *C. Gray.*

LOCH PEARL 3 b.c. Lochnager 132–Dusky Pearl 68 (Gulf Pearl 117) (1982 6fg **81**
5s⁴ 1983 6v* 6s*) rangy colt, with a good, long stride; won maiden race at Ayr in
March (by 12 lengths) and minor event at Ripon in April, on latter course landing
the odds by 4 lengths from Kano Flower after making all; seemed to be developing
into a useful performer but wasn't seen out again; will stay at least 7f; has run
respectably on a firm surface, but clearly goes very well in the mud. *M. H.
Easterby.*

LOCHTILLUM 4 b.c. Song 132–Spring Storm 74 (March Past 124) (1982 5d 6d **65**
5fg⁴ 5fg⁴ 5fg 5g* 5fg³ 5g 6d 5d 6fg 5s 1983 5v² 5v* 5.8s⁴ 5fg² 5f* 5f 6fg² 5.6f 5f)
good-quartered colt; poor mover; sprint handicapper; won at Newcastle in May and
Beverley in June; stays 6f; acts on any going. *J. Douglas-Home.*

LOCKETTS DREAM 3 ch.f. Jolly Good 122–Solatia 75 (Kalydon 122) (1982 **–**
NR 1983 14g) third foal; dam won over 1½m; 50/1, behind in minor race won by
Childown at Sandown in October. *A. Hide.*

LOFTY 3 b.c. High Top 131–Enchanted 116 (Song 132) (1982 5g² 6f* 7fg⁴ 7fg³ **117**
8fg* 7v² 7s² 1983 7s³ 8g 8.5s* 9fg⁴ 11g 8fg² 7g) strong, good-bodied colt; carries
plenty of condition; third foal; half-brother to fair 1981 5f performer Pleasant
Dream (by Sharpen Up); dam smart sprinting 2-y-o; ran remarkably well when 5½
lengths sixth of 16 behind Lomond in 2000 Guineas at Newmarket in April
(200/1-chance) and confirmed his improvement when beating Aragon (gave 6 lb) by
a short head after a good battle in Pacemaker Diomed Stakes at Epsom in June; also
in frame in Salisbury 2000 Guineas Trial, Grosser Preis von Dortmund and
Oettingen-Rennen at Baden-Baden, finishing ¾-length second to Drumalis in
last-named in August; suited by 1m; acts on any going; game and consistent,
although below his best final start. *H. T. Jones.*

LOGAN 6 b.g. Biskrah 121–Amber Star (Amber Rama 133) (1982 10g 14f 12g⁴ **–**
12fg⁴ 16d 16f² 16.5f⁴ 16g* 16.5fg³ 16fg 1983 16v 16v⁴ 15.5v 12v 16g) rather
lightly-made gelding; poor handicapper; stays 2m; acts on any going; usually
blinkered nowadays. *M. Masson.*

Mrs H. T. Jones's "Lofty"

LOLLY DOLLY 2 b.f. Alleged 138–Lady Gold (Sir Gaylord) (1983 8s* 8fg⁴)   **104**
sister to plating-class French 3-y-o Princesse Legere; dam, very useful French
middle-distance performer, is sister to good North American stakes winner
Morold; favourite, finished well when under 3 lengths fifth to Boreale in Prix des
Reservoirs at Longchamp in October (promoted to fourth); successful by 2½
lengths from Arneda in minor event at Evry the previous month; will be suited to
middle distances. *J. Cunnington, jnr, France.*

LOMOND (USA) 3 b.c. Northern Dancer–My Charmer (Poker) (1982 6g* 7d³   **128**
1983 7s* 8g* 8v² 12s 8f)
Few milers of championship-winning standard stay in training after their
three-year-old days. There isn't much incentive for them in Britain: the Sussex
Stakes, elevated to the position of a semi-classic in 1963, is the only Group 1
pattern race at around a mile open to horses above the age of three. By contrast,
France has four Group 1 pattern races at around a mile open to older horses—the
Prix d'Ispahan, the Prix Jacques le Marois, the Prix du Moulin and the Prix de la
Foret. There's a good case, you might think, for at least one other open-aged
championship event at a mile or thereabouts in the British Calendar. So when
Lomond's owner approached us about a £700,000 sponsorship—£100,000 a year for
seven years—for the Timeform Charity Day programme at York, we devised what
we thought would be a race acceptable to the turf authorities and a prime draw for
spectators. The proposed Swettenham Stud Stakes, for three-year-olds and
upwards over nine furlongs, would have been the first championship race created in
Britain since the Benson and Hedges Gold Cup more than a decade ago. At the time
it was the biggest sponsorship offered to British racing but it didn't meet with
Jockey Club approval. We believed the timing of the race—mid-way between the
Guineas and the Sussex Stakes and suitable also for horses going on to contest the
Coral-Eclipse, the Benson and Hedges and the Dubai Champion—was ideal. But
the Stewards of the Jockey Club turned it down because 'to introduce this race with
its conditions, value and timing would unquestionably be harmful to established
pattern races.' They cited principally the Queen Anne Stakes (Group 3), the St
James's Palace Stakes (Group 2) and the Prince of Wales's Stakes (Group 2), all run
at Royal Ascot in the week following Timeform Charity Day. They added—in
confidence at the time—that the open-aged Queen Anne Stakes was likely to
receive an injection of prize money and an increase in status (to Group 2) in 1984.
'We have been aware for some time,' they said, 'that there was a need to improve
opportunities for older horses over a mile to encourage owners to keep these
horses in training.' If the Stewards succeed in this aim by tinkering with the Queen
Anne Stakes it will rate as one of the administrative miracles of all time.
Condemning, at this stage, the decision to turn down the Swettenham Stud Stakes
is rather like throwing a pebble after an avalanche, so much criticism did it receive
in the Press at the time. The Stewards somehow managed to convey an impression
to most critics of combining the politics of the ivory tower with the economics of
the madhouse.
Like the vast majority of his predecessors, the latest Two Thousand Guineas
winner Lomond was packed off to stud after his three-year-old campaign. Of the
last twelve Guineas winners, only Roland Gardens and Known Fact remained in

*Two Thousand Guineas Stakes, Newmarket—Lomond runs the race of his life, going clear
to beat Tolomeo (partially obscured by winner), Muscatite and the grey Kuwait Tower*

Mr R. E. Sangster's "Lomond"

training the next year in Europe. Lomond wasn't a good Guineas winner and the subsequent records of most of those that finished behind him confirmed that he beat a substandard field. Lomond himself didn't manage a single win in three outings after Newmarket, which is no recommendation for the Guineas form; and the performances of the Guineas principals in the Sussex Stakes—which was won for only the third time since 1963 by an older horse—did little to retrieve the reputation of the classic generation of milers. Lomond's own reputation took a knock in the Sussex Stakes: blinkered for the first time in public, he finished in the ruck behind six-year-old Noalcoholic and shortly afterwards the decision was taken to keep him out of the big mile races in the autumn. He has been retired to the Coolmore Stud complex in Ireland.

Vincent O'Brien's two-year-olds, as usual nowadays, dominated the 1982 Irish Free Handicap. They filled eight of the top fifteen places, Lomond and Solford just scraping into the top fifteen on 8-6, 15 lb below top-rated Danzatore with Caerleon, Glenstal, Ancestral, Beaudelaire and Heron Bay also officially rated above them. The O'Brien stable's prospects in the top three-year-old events looked bright. However, one of the pitfalls of long-range ante-post betting was illustrated by Lomond's Two Thousand Guineas success. Danzatore was widely regarded as his stable's number-one Guineas hope and, with seemingly more obvious replacements than Lomond on hand should anything go amiss with Danzatore, Lomond didn't figure in the winter betting on the Two Thousand Guineas. He wasn't even listed among the probable runners a week before the race, his next intended target after his victory over the older horses Patroon and Erin's Hope in the Gladness Stakes at the Curragh on his reappearance being the H.M. Hartigan Tetrarch Stakes, a Group 3 pattern race at the Curragh a week before the Guineas. The decision that Lomond should deputise for Danzatore—whose withdrawal from the Guineas eight days before the race had been widely anticipated in betting circles—was taken after Lomond reportedly performed very well in a gallop two days after the announcement of Danzatore's defection. Lomond's prospects were difficult to weigh up: his only defeat in three races, at 7/2 on in the National Stakes at the Curragh where he came third to Glenstal, had been put down to a throat infection discovered after the race; in his other races he had done all that could be expected of him, winning comfortably without showing form approaching classic standard. Two-year-old form is usually the most reliable guide to the Newmarket classics and the colts with easily the best first-season form, Diesis and Gorytus, headed the market at 100/30 and 7/2 respectively, with the Clerical, Medical Greenham winner Wassl at 9/2. Lomond came next at 9/1, with Muscatite, winner of the Craven Stakes from three other Guineas runners Spanish Place, Guns of Navarone and Tolomeo, at 12/1 and the only other foreign-trained challenger Allverton at 16/1. Gorytus and Wassl were among those that stood out in the sixteen-horse parade, the exceptionally handsome Gorytus particularly taking the eye in a field which contained a number of more commanding individuals than Lomond, a sturdy colt of around medium size.

Both Diesis and Gorytus ran way below their best two-year-old form in the Guineas, Diesis who had been plagued by training troubles never getting into the firing line after moving poorly on the way to post. Gorytus showed in front running into the Dip, the outsiders Tecorno and Lofty having done most of the donkey-work, but Lomond, making smooth progress towards the leaders after being waited with, looked the likely winner at the foot of the hill. Lomond's run carried him to the front inside the final furlong and kept him there, strongly ridden, to hold off the fast-finishing Tolomeo by two lengths, with Muscatite three quarters of a length away third, the same distance ahead of fourth-placed Kuwait Tower, with Gorytus fading to fifth. Diesis finished eighth and the disappointing Wassl ninth. Tolomeo, in last place for a long way, was gaining on Lomond as the post was reached, seemingly having been set with far too much to do. Whether or not Tolomeo would have won ridden with more enterprise no-one can say for certain, but whereas he appeared to receive a poor ride, Lomond certainly couldn't have been given a better one. Only Wassl of Lomond's opponents at Newmarket renewed rivalry with him in the Airlie/Coolmore Irish Two Thousand Guineas at the Curragh a fortnight later when the runner-up in the Poule d'Essai des Poulains (French Two Thousand Guineas) Crystal Glitters looked easily Lomond's most formidable rival. Lomond started at 4/7, with Crystal Glitters at 9/2; they bet 12/1 bar. Lomond managed to beat Crystal Glitters—Lomond finished second and Crystal Glitters fourth—but he couldn't peg back an in-form Wassl, going down by three quarters of a length after having more ground to make up on the leaders at the two-furlong pole than he'd had at Newmarket. Lomond took longer than at Newmarket to find his stride when asked for his effort and he met with a little interference when making his run. But he had every chance from a furlong out and was well held by the winner at the line. Lomond's participation at the Curragh had been in some doubt following the discovery of an abscess on a hind hoof the day before the race, but we can't believe he'd have been risked had there been any doubt about his ability to do himself justice.

Lomond (USA) (b.c. 1980)	Northern Dancer (b 1961)	Nearctic (br 1954)	Nearco
			Lady Angela
		Natalma (b 1957)	Native Dancer
			Almahmoud
	My Charmer (b 1969)	Poker (b 1963)	Round Table
			Glamour
		Fair Charmer (ch 1959)	Jet Action
			Myrtle Charm

Lomond will be standing in 1984 at a fee of IR 65,000 guineas with the October 1st concession. His pedigree will probably recommend him to breeders as much as his racing record. He's that most fashionable of all present-day stallion commodities, a classic-winning son of the great Northern Dancer. He's also a half-brother to the brilliant American triple crown winner Seattle Slew (by Bold Reasoning) who won fourteen of his seventeen starts and was voted the champion of his generation in each of his three seasons to race. In addition to the Kentucky Derby, the Preakness Stakes and the Belmont Stakes—the races that constitute the triple crown in the States—Seattle Slew won five other Grade 1 events, the Champagne Stakes (as a two-year-old), the Wood Memorial Stakes and the Flamingo Stakes (at three), and the Marlboro Cup and the Woodward Stakes (at four); he was North America's Horse of the Year in 1977. Lomond's sire Northern Dancer won two legs of the American triple crown—the Kentucky Derby and the Preakness—and his influence as a stallion on European racing has become legendary. Lomond's trainer in particular has met with enormous success with the offspring of Northern Dancer, notably with the triple crown winner Nijinsky and with The Minstrel who won the Derby, the Irish Sweeps Derby and the King George. Lomond, who was bought privately as a foal from his American breeders, is out of a minor stakes-winning daughter of Poker, a half-brother by Round Table to O'Brien's 1972 St Leger winner Boucher and himself a winner of the prestigious

Bowling Green Handicap over one mile, five furlongs. If there were only breeding considerations to go on it would seem reasonable to have expected Lomond to get at least a mile and a quarter: the average distance of races won at three years and upwards in Britain and Ireland by the progeny of Northern Dancer is nine and a half furlongs, and Lomond's dam, successful herself at a mile, is also the dam of the fairly useful Clandestina (by Secretariat) who won at a mile and a quarter in Ireland as a three-year-old. However, after dismounting from Lomond after the Two Thousand Guineas Eddery stated that he considered Lomond's stamina would be fully stretched by a mile and a quarter and that he had no prospects of staying the Derby trip. Lomond was actually entered for the five-furlong King's Stand Stakes at Royal Ascot, entries for which closed on March 16th. His presence in the Derby field therefore came as a surprise to many; after being in doubt about his Derby mount until the morning of the race, Eddery eventually deserted Lomond in favour of Salmon Leap. Lomond was trailing from a long way out at Epsom and came home sixteenth of the twenty finishers. The Derby was Lomond's only attempt on the racecourse at a distance beyond a mile. Lomond's only other poor performance—in the Sussex Stakes—came when he encountered firm ground for the only time in his career, and prompted the supposition that he might have needed some give in the ground to show to best advantage. Before we leave Lomond, it may be of interest to record that his once-raced two-year-old half-brother Argosy (by Affirmed), also under the care of O'Brien, is regarded by the trainer as one of his leading classic hopes for 1984. *V. O'Brien, Ireland.*

LONACH COTTAGE 2 b.f. Manor Farm Boy 114–Little Bird 87 (Only for Life 126) (1983 5fg 6f 6fg⁴ 5f 6d) May 11; 4,100Y; lightly-built filly; half-sister to several winners, including very useful sprinter Geopelia (by Raffingora); poor plater; retained 620 gns Ascot October Sales. *J. Douglas-Home.* —

LONELY STREET 2 b.f. Frimley Park 109–Abalone (Abwah 118) (1983 5g 5fg² 5g² 6f 5fg 5d 6fg) May 19; leggy, close-coupled filly; first foal; dam never ran; second in July maiden races at Warwick; best at 5f; sweated up third and fourth starts. *R. Laing.* 71

LONE RAIDER 6 b.g. Shantung 132–Love Resolved (Dan Cupid 132) (1982 14fg⁴ 18.8fg 1983 14fg) big, workmanlike gelding; lightly raced nowadays; stays 2m; acts on going and is probably unsuited by very soft. *J. Harris.* —

LONGBOAT 2 b.c. Welsh Pageant 132–Pirogue 99 (Reliance II 137) (1983 8fg²) Mar 24; half-brother to winning stayer Admiral's Barge (by Brigadier Gerard) and very useful 3-y-o Sailor's Dance (by Dance In Time); dam, closely related to good stayer Torpid, won over 1m; unquoted, came up against some promising, more-experienced animals in 21-runner maiden race at Newmarket and did very well to finish 4 lengths second to Alphabatim; will stay beyond 1m; a useful colt in the making. *R. Hern.* 97 p

LONGCROSS 2 ch.c. Dom Racine 121–Miss Carefree 99 (Hill Clown) (1983 6fg⁴) Apr 4; 27,000Y; good-bodied, useful-looking colt; third reported living foal; half-brother to useful sprinter Pencil Point (by Sharpen Up), subsequently a stakes winner in USA; dam 2-y-o 7f winner; unquoted and ridden by apprentice unable to claim his 5-lb allowance, showed up throughout and ran with distinct promise when 4 lengths fourth of 23 to stable-companion Optimistic Lass in maiden race at Newmarket in October; will stay at least 1m; sure to win in similar company. *M. Stoute.* 90 p

LONG MICK (FR) 2 b.c. Gay Mecene 128–Lunadix (Breton 130) (1983 9f* 10d*) 121

In our notes on L'Emigrant in *Racehorses of 1982* we pointed out that several sons of Vaguely Noble had proved failures at stud, adding that Exceller and Gay

Prix de Conde, Longchamp—a good staying performance from Long Mick, who beats Cold Feet

Mecene might make amends when their first runners appeared in 1983. Although it's far too soon to tell whether Exceller will succeed as a stallion—he has so far sired several minor winners in the States—there is every indication that Gay Mecene will make the grade. Despite being a late-maturing animal, whose own career at two was limited to a narrow victory in an end-of-season newcomers race at Maisons-Laffitte, Gay Mecene has sired five winners from a limited number of runners in Britain and France, four of them showing above-average ability: Van Dyke Brown won by a wide margin at Yarmouth; Arriance was considered good enough to take her chance in the Prix Marcel Boussac, a race won by another of his daughters, the Prix du Calvados winner Almeira; and Long Mick's success in the Prix de Conde at Longchamp in October was so impressive that he was officially rated France's best two-year-old.

In a field of five for the Conde, Long Mick was second choice in the betting behind Cold Feet, an odds-on shot on the strength of his short-head second to the subsequent Grand Criterium runner-up Truculent in the Prix Lord Seymour at Longchamp earlier in the month. Long Mick had made his only previous appearance in a newcomers race at the same meeting, when getting home by a nose from Plucky Dancer after holding a good place throughout. He didn't have to work nearly so hard in the Conde: after racing in second place behind the outsider Miss Boran until early in the straight, he lengthened his stride so impressively that Cold Feet could never land a blow. Long Mick's winning margin was three lengths and it was another eight lengths back to Ina Seville, a filly who had run Mendez to two and a half lengths in the Prix des Chenes; Dow Jones, who won a maiden race next time out, was a further eight lengths behind in fourth. This splendid effort by Long Mick suggests he may eventually reach heights similar to those scaled by Le Fabuleux, Phaeton, La Lagune, Margouillat, Top Ville and The Wonder, all previous winners of the Conde.

		Vaguely Noble	Vienna
Long Mick (Fr) (b.c. Apr 1, 1981)	Gay Mecene (b 1975)	(b 1965)	Noble Lassie
		Gay Missile (b 1967)	Sir Gaylord
			Missy Baba
	Lunadix (gr or ro 1972)	Breton (br 1967)	Relko
			La Melba
		Lutine (gr 1966)	Alcide
			Mona

Long Mick is owned by his breeder Jean-Luc Lagardere, who is in the fortunate position of being the owner-breeder of another very promising colt, the Prix Thomas Bryon winner Polly's Ark. Long Mick's dam Lunadix also carried the Lagardere colours to success, winning over six furlongs at two and over a mile at four; she was also placed in the Prix du Calvados and the Prix de Sandringham. Lunadix's only other winner from three previous foals is the Bolkonski colt Moonbeam, a useful performer at up to a mile and a quarter. Lunadix herself is one of two winners bred by Lutine, the winner of a mile-and-a-quarter maiden race at Windsor. Long Mick gives the strong impression he'll be suited by the Derby distance. However, before anyone backs him for the Epsom race they would do well to take note of the assessment of his rider in the Conde, Asmussen, that the colt 'possesses a long, supple action and, for me, will prefer a mile and a half and a level track.' *F. Boutin, France.*

LONGVIEW LADY 2 b.f. Tarboosh–Hellspear (Breakspear II) (1983 5v 6fg   **50** 5.8h 6fg 5fg 5fg) Apr 30; IR 420F, 1,700Y (privately); small, good-quartered filly; sister to 1982 2-y-o 7f winner Commodore Bateman; quite a modest plater; should stay 7f; blinkered last 3 starts; sold 880 gns Doncaster September Sales. *D. H. Jones.*

LOOKALIKE 3 br.g. Dancer's Image–Without Reproach 102 (Above Suspicion   **–** 127) (1982 7f 8d 8s 1983 10v 10s 10fg 14f³ 16g⁴ 14g) strong, workmanlike gelding; 33/1 when staying on quite well to be 3 lengths third of 12 to British in maiden race at Sandown in July, best effort; suited by 1¾m+. *P. Haynes.*

LOOKING FOR 5 b.h. High Top 131–Love You (Linden Tree 127) (1982   **121** including 15v* 10g³ 14v² 1983 12f² 12fg² 14g³)

Had Anthony Hope, author of that classic tale of mistaken identity *The Prisoner of Zenda*, been alive today it is likely he would have found intriguing the confusion caused by mix-ups in the identity of racehorses over the last couple of years. In the period since it was discovered early in 1982 that the supposed dam of Kalaglow had been confused with another filly at least ten years previously quite a few similar instances have come to light. During 1983 *The Racing Calendar*

Dr M. Boffa's "Looking For"

included details of pedigree alterations involving more than a dozen named horses, the most serious concerning the mares Habanna and Moon Min who had been confused before foaling in 1977 and in the interim had produced eleven foals between them. It seems logical to assume that this sudden upsurge is in part at least a direct result of the revelations about Kalaglow's dam, with horses' passports being examined rather more closely in some places than in the past. Whatever the rights and wrongs of the issue it has some interesting if not disturbing implications—Habanna, for instance, was unwittingly mated with her sire Habitat in 1978—and there must be reason to think there could easily be further examples of mistaken identity yet to be uncovered.

1983 in fact revealed an additional example to those contained in *The Racing Calendar*, one that turned out to be a rare witch's brew and showed how serious the repercussions of human error or negligence can be in this area. In 1979 two yearling colts, one by Thatch out of Dorilea and one by High Top out of Love You, were sent to Italy by plane from Ireland where they had been bred. During the flight, it is believed, the colts were accidentally switched with the outcome that each raced erroneously under the other's pedigree for the wrong owner. Both showed above-average ability in Italy up to the end of 1982 with the Thatch colt, called Looking For, winning eight races worth over £20,000 and the High Top colt, named Dentz, winning nine races worth nearly £64,000, including the Premio Roma in 1981 and the Coppa d'Oro di Milano at four. At the end of 1982 the so-called Looking For was sold and early in 1983 the so-called Dentz was sent to be trained in France where a discrepancy between the horse and his passport was noticed. After a lengthy inquiry the Italian turf authorities acknowledged that a mix-up had occurred and Dentz and Looking For reverted to their proper identities with Looking For, previously known as Dentz, being sent to England by his owner-breeder Dr Boffa for whom ironically he had yet to race. Both the horses involved are bay with a white sock on the near-hind, but their head markings apparently differ slightly and it is astonishing they were able to run for so long in Italy without the mistake coming to light—ideally in any country a horse should have its identity papers checked thoroughly every time it runs. As a matter of interest, at the time of writing the parties concerned have reportedly shelved all the financial considerations arising from the switch, notably prize money, breeders' premiums and the fact that Dr Boffa had sold Dentz, previously known as Looking For, before the çolt's true identity had been revealed.

The real Looking For was clearly one of the best of his age in Italy and on the form he showed on his last two starts at five he was well up to winning good races over here as well. His first outing for Cumani came in a well-contested £3,800 event at Lingfield in August in which he started the outsider of six and finished a creditable length second to Lafontaine, a short head in front of Zilos. The Cumberland Lodge Stakes at Ascot the following month presented Looking For with a much stiffer task but he stepped up on his Lingfield performance and ran a cracking race. Opposed by seven horses including the improving three-year-old Band, the September Stakes winner Lyphard's Special, the smart Khairpour, Lafontaine and Zilos, he was held up in last until halfway and still had only two behind him, one of them Band, turning for home. Showing a good burst of speed Looking For came through to deprive Zilos of the lead over a furlong out, left behind Lyphard's Special who had started his run at the same time and lost out to the strong-finishing Band in only the last fifty yards, going down by a length.

Looking For's one remaining race saw his making a third successive appearance in the Premio Roma at the start of November. As in 1981, when he won, and 1982, when he ran second, he put up a good display, and in a fairly rough race looked a shade unlucky. Moving through on the rail in the straight he had very little room from a furlong and a half out and according to his rider he was twice hit on the head by other jockeys' whips. Considering this he did well to be beaten a short head and a neck by High Hawk and Balitou after finally getting a run near the finish.

		Derring-Do	Darius
	High Top	(br 1961)	Sipsey Bridge
	(br 1969)	Camenae	Vimy
Looking For		(b 1961)	Madrilene
(b.h. 1978)		Linden Tree	Crepello
	Love You	(ch 1968)	Verbena
	(b 1973)	Toi	Shantung
		(gr 1968)	Teodora

Looking For's breeding, by High Top out of a mare by the Derby second Linden Tree, is rather more in keeping with a horse that stayed at least a mile and three quarters than is that of Dentz since a good proportion of High Top's progeny are effective at a mile and a half or more whereas few of Thatch's are. The dam Love You won three times in Italy and is a daughter of an unraced half-sister to the high-class sprinter Three Legs whom Cumani trained to win the Duke of York Stakes and run second in the July Cup in 1978. A compact, rather lightly-built horse, Looking For acted on any going and was genuine. He has reportedly been retired to stud in Italy. *L. Cumani.*

LOOKS A MILLION 3 b.f. Wollow 132–Grange Fire (Allangrange 126) (1982 7.6v 8g 1983 9s 12s) leggy, lengthy filly; beaten some way in maiden races and a handicap; sold 5,400 gns Newmarket July Sales. *W. Musson.*   –

L'ORANGERIE (USA) 2 b.f. J. O. Tobin 130–Liska (Lyphard 132) (1983 7fg[3] 5d* 6.5fg*) Jan 13; first foal; dam, very useful French miler, is half-sister to top-class Irish River; ran on well to lead inside final furlong when winning 2 races in the autumn, a maiden race at Maisons-Laffitte (by ½ length from Tea And Scandals) and an 80,000-franc all-aged event at Évry (by 2 lengths from Kaysama); will be suited by 1m. *Mme C. Head, France.*   115

LORD AND MASTER 4 gr.g. Scallywag 127–Look Twice (Mossy Face 98) (1982 NR 1983 12fg 16g) second reported foal; dam poor hurdler; tailed-off last in minor event at Leicester and maiden race at Lingfield in June. *W. Turner.*   –

LORD BUTCH 2 b.c. Royal Blend 117–Acquire 105 (Burglar 128) (1983 7f[3] 7f[3] 8d 8g[2] 8g) May 4; medium-sized, quite attractive colt; good walker and particularly good mover; half-brother to 3 winners, notably smart 5f performer Chellaston Park (by Record Token); dam won twice over 5f at 2 yrs; disappointed after showing fair form in useful company at Goodwood and Salisbury on first 2 outings; possibly does not stay 1m; acts on firm going. *J. Dunlop.*   88

LORD CHANTICLEER 3 ch.g. Oats 126–Linbel (Linacre 133) (1982 7f 7fg 7f⁴   **59**
7g 8fg 8d 8d 1983 12s 12v 12v⁴ 12.2g² 12g⁴ 12f³ 10f*) short-coupled gelding; has
no near eye; plater; bought in 1,250 gns after winning by 5 lengths at Beverley in
July; gives impression he'll stay beyond 1½m; acts on any going, but is suited by
firm; wears an eye-shield; sold to M. Pipe 840 gns Newmarket Autumn Sales. *D.
Morley.*

LORD JOHNSTAN 3 b.g. Le Johnstan 123–Pamora (Blast 125) (1982 6g 6g 6f   **–**
5g 6s 5d 1983 5s 5f 5fg 8fg 6f) tall gelding; bad plater; sold 360 gns Ascot
September Sales. *R. Whitaker.*

LORD LUDO 2 ch.c. Owen Dudley 121–Hotazur 52 (Hotfoot 126) (1983 6g³ 7g   **76**
7g 7f 8f 7g³ 7fg) Apr 2; 3,100F, 4,600Y; third produce; half-brother to 1982 2-y-o
5f winner Palace Beau (by Dragonara Palace); dam, poor plater, comes from good
family; acquitted himself well in maiden and nursery company after being beaten in
seller on debut; stays 1m; acts on firm going; trained first outing by W. Musson. *D.
Garraton.*

LORD LUX (USA) 2 br.c. Fluorescent Light–Dreamy (Windy Sands) (1983 6f   **77**
7f* 7fg⁴ 7g) Apr 8; $50,000Y; close-coupled colt; half-brother to several winners,
including very useful 1977 2-y-o My Little Maggie (by Tell); dam never ran; sire,
son of Herbager, was high-class middle-distance grass performer; won 9-runner
maiden race at Yarmouth in August by a short head from Adeeb; will be well suited
by 1m; below form in blinkers third outing (dwelt from flag start); sold BBA 7,000
gns Newmarket Autumn Sales. *M. Stoute.*

LORD MINTON 2 b.g. Auction Ring 123–Alpina 82 (King's Troop 118) (1983 6fg   **–**
6fg) Apr 1; 10,500Y; useful sort; brother to a prolific winner in Italy and a winner in
Malaya, and half-brother to 2 winners; dam, 1m winner, is sister to dam of French
Oaks winner Madam Gay; well beaten in late-season maiden events at Newmarket
and Doncaster (blinkered). *M. Jarvis.*

LORD OF MISRULE 9 gr.h. Supreme Sovereign 119–Mirth (Tamerlane 128)   **–**
(1982 12g 12fg⁴ 10f⁴ 12f 1983 10d 10g) poor handicapper; has been beaten in a
seller; usually wears blinkers; suitable mount for an inexperienced rider; sold out
of M. Haynes's stable 450 gns Ascot July Sales after first start. *D. Jermy.*

LORD OF TRILLORA (USA) 2 b.c. Majestic Light–Song Title (Jaipur) (1983   **117**
8s* 8f) Mar 3; $65,000; leggy, rangy colt; fourth foal; half-brother to a winner by
Tom Rolfe; dam won 7 times at up to 7f, earning over $112,000; won a newcomers
race at Longchamp in September by 5 lengths from Dictalino; creditable 3¼ lengths
sixth to Treizieme in Grand Criterium at same track the following month; should
stay 1¼m. *J. Fellows, France.*

LORD PROTECTOR (USA) 3 b. or br.c. Vaguely Noble 140–April Bloom 108   **99**
(Bold Lad, Ire 133) (1982 7g* 7v³ 1983 8g³ 10g 8f* 8fg³) attractive, rangy colt;
beat Timber Tycoon comfortably by 5 lengths after being held up in minor event at
York in July (didn't impress on way to post); third in £4,100 race at Newbury the
previous month (4½ lengths behind Orixo) and 21-runner ladies race at Ascot later
in July (saw daylight all way, ran too freely and was beaten 3¾ lengths by Sheriff
Muir); should stay beyond 1m; possibly not at his best on heavy ground; swallowed
his tongue second outing and subsequently raced with it tied down; sent to USA.
H. Cecil.

LORD SCRAP 7 ch.g. Tower Walk 130–La Concha (Le Levanstell 122) (1982   **58**
5d⁴ 6fg 6f² 6f 6fg² 6g* 6f 6g² 5fg* 5.8f* 5d² 6s 1983 5v 5v 6v 6g⁴ 5.8g³ 6g 6fg² 6f
6f 5.8h 6fg⁴ 5h* 6f⁴ 5.8fg 6fg) good-looking gelding; sprint handicapper; won at
Chepstow in August; stays 6f; acts on any going, except possibly really soft; has
won in blinkers but is better without; excellent mount for a boy. *B. Swift.*

LORD WIMPY 5 gr.g. Dragonara Palace 115–My Worry 72 (March Past 124)   **–**
(1982 6fg² 5fg 6f* 5.8f* 7f* 6f* 1983 6f 6fg 7d) strong, sprint type; best at up to
7f; acts on any going but is very well suited by firm; blinkered once; has sometimes
tended to hang and is not the easiest of rides. *J. Bethell.*

LORIOT 6 ch.g. Lord Gayle 124–Golden Moss 91 (Sheshoon 132) (1982 NR 1983   **–**
12fg) tumbling gelding; poor performer on flat nowadays; stays 1½m; probably acts
on any going. *D. Dale.*

LOR MOSS 3 ch.g. Mossberry 97–Lor Darnie 65 (Dumbarnie 125) (1982 8.2s   **65**
8d 1983 12v 9.4d 12f*) tall, narrow, close-coupled gelding; dropped in class when
gamely winning selling handicap at Wolverhampton in June; sold 3,900 gns
afterwards; suited by 1½m; acts on firm going; tends to sweat up. *J. Etherington.*

LORNA-BLY 2 b.f. Captain James 123–Princess of Nashua (Crowned Prince 128) —
(1983 5fg 5f) Apr 24; 580Y; small filly; first foal; dam unraced granddaughter of
high-class filly Victoria Cross; behind in maiden races at Nottingham and Pontefract
(auction event) in June. *W. Clay.*

LOST COUNTRY 2 b.f. Town and Country 124–Lost Riches 75 (Forlorn River —
124) (1983 5f 5f) Mar 13; plain filly; sixth foal; dam stayed 6f; behind in maiden
race at Salisbury in June and minor event at Warwick in August. *M. Pipe.*

LOST VALLEY 6 b.m. Perdu 121–Long Valley 71 (Ribero 126) (1982 NR 1983 —
8h) small mare; has badly enlarged off-hind; poor maiden on flat though has won
over hurdles. *R. Keenor.*

LOTTESVILLE (FR) 2 b.c. Guadanini 125–Lottie's Charm (Charlottesville —
135) (1983 7.6fg 8.2fg) Mar 20; 15,000Y; half-brother to 3 winners, including very
useful 1½m and 13f winner Taher (by Weavers' Hall); dam showed little worthwhile
form in Ireland; behind in October in maiden race at Lingfield and £3,400 event at
Nottingham. *C. Austin.*

LOTTIE LEHMANN 7 br.m. Goldhill 125–Sing High 85 (Sound Track 132) —
(1982 NR 1983 12f³ 12f³ 10f⁴ 16f) strong mare; middle-distance handicapper;
seems to act on any going; used to wear blinkers; suitable mount for an apprentice.
Mrs G. Reveley.

LOTUS DANCER 4 b.f. Midsummer Night II 117–Kushbehar 80 (Behistoun —
131) (1982 8f 7g 8f 5g 5.3f 6fg 5fg 10d 12v 1983 12f) small, lightly-made filly; poor
plater; has worn blinkers. *R. Howe.*

LOTUS LADY 2 b.f. Malinowski 123–Bordelaise 96 (Above Suspicion 127) (1983 45
6fg 7f 8g³ 8.2fg 8d) May 28; 2,600Y; fair sort; half-sister to several winners,
including 6f and 1m winner Love Supreme and useful Italian 3-y-o sprinter Conan
(both by Sallust); poor plater; stays 1m; slowly away when blinkered and
apprentice ridden final outing. *R. Akehurst.*

LOTUS PRINCESS 2 ch.f. Camden Town 125–Karlaine 86 (Tutankhamen) 72
(1983 5g 5f 5fg² 5fg 5fg⁴ 5g 6fg⁴) May 16; IR 5,000Y; useful-looking,
close-coupled filly; half-sister to 1982 2-y-o 5f winner Minie O'Neill (by Pitskelly), a
winner in Italy and a bumpers winner; dam won over 1¼m; in frame in maiden races
and a nursery; will be better suited by 7f+. *R. Hannon.*

LOUDMOUTH 4 b. or br.g. Mummy's Pet 125–Fortissimaid 75 (Fortissimo 111) —
(1982 NR 1983 10s 8f) small gelding; of little account; has worn blinkers; sold 500
gns Doncaster September Sales. *W. C. Watts.*

LOUISA ANNE 3 b.f. Mummy's Pet 125–Lucinda Anne (Abernant 142) (1982 6h 66
6g 5g 5f³ 6d 1983 6d 5g² 5fg 5f² 6fg² 6g) narrow filly; second in handicap and 2
maiden races. *P. Rohan.*

LOUISE MARIE 2 ro.f. Rolfe 77–Sweet Marilyn (Runnymede 123) (1983 6fg 8d —
6fg) small filly; first foal; dam only ran twice; apparently of no account. *G.
Thorner.*

LOUISE MOILLON 2 br.f. Mansingh 120–Ma Griffe (Indian Ruler 89) (1983 79
5v* 5f) Mar 25; 1,700F; rather leggy, attractive filly; half-sister to numerous
winners, notably very smart English and German winner Whip It Quick (by
Philemon); dam never ran; had little to beat when running away with Wilkinson
Memorial Stakes at York in May, and could finish only eighth of 15 when
co-favourite for Queen Mary Stakes at Royal Ascot the following month; will stay
6f; sent to France. *P. Kelleway.*

LOUISIANA LIGHTNING 2 ch.f. Music Boy 124–Summer Mist 57 —
(Midsummer Night II 117) (1983 6fg) Apr 6; first foal; dam won 1½m seller; in rear
in 14-runner maiden race at Yarmouth in June. *E. Eldin.*

LOUVIERS 5 br.g. Vitiges 132–Vive la Reine (Vienna 127) (1982 10s² 12.3g —
1983 10v³ 12fg) compact, good-bodied gelding; stays 1¼m; possibly needs some
give in the ground; has worn blinkers; has run respectably for an apprentice. *G.
Richards.*

LOVE ANOTHER 7 gr.m. Grey Love 103–Khaki (Martial 131) (1982 NR 1983 —
13.4fg) poor selling hurdler; staying-on fifth to Dancing Daughter in 13-runner
maiden event at Chester in July, first outing on flat. *M. Eckley.*

LOVE BITE 3 ch.f. Malicious–Kist 53 (Lucky Symbol 82) (1982 NR 1983 12v 8v —
8d) sturdy filly; second foal; dam second in 5f seller at 2 yrs; tailed off in sellers;
blinkered last 2 starts. *P. Asquith.*

LOVE EXPRESS 3 ch.c. Bay Express 132–Sweet Season (Silly Season 127) 67
(1982 5d 5d³ 6g 1983 6v 8fg³) medium-sized, good-topped colt; third in

apprentice maiden event at Warwick in June; stays 1m; sold 4,400 gns Newmarket September Sales. *B. Hills.*

LOVELY DANCER 3 b.c. Green Dancer 132–Janthina 118 (Petingo 135) (1982 7.5fg 8s* 7.5s 9d⁴ 10v³ 10v⁴ 1983 10v* 10.5v² 10.5v² 12fg 10d 10f⁴ 10g* 10s* 12f 12d) **130**

Lovely Dancer bore the distinction of being the first French-trained colt to cross the line when seventh of twenty-six behind All Along in the Trusthouse Forte Prix de l'Arc de Triomphe at Longchamp in October. He was virtually unconsidered in the betting at 45/1, despite having won his last two races and being partnered by Head, previously associated with both All Along and Zalataia during the season, yet was beaten only about two lengths. He made up a deal of ground on the outside in the straight along with Salmon Leap, the only colt to finish in front of him, and was gaining fast on the placed horses at the end. This was outstandingly Lovely Dancer's best performance in a season not noted for his consistency: he ran nowhere near so well on his only subsequent start, trailing in last of eight behind All Along in the Washington International at Laurel.

Lovely Dancer was a smart two-year-old and began 1983 by smoothly winning the Prix de Courcelles at Longchamp and finishing second on the same course to Dom Pasquini in the Prix Greffulhe and L'Emigrant in the Prix Lupin; he ran particularly well in the latter, going down by three quarters of a length. Lovely Dancer lost his form in mid-season, finishing well down the field in the Prix du Jockey-Club and the Prix Eugene Adam, but regained it when blinkers were fitted in the autumn. It wasn't until Head took over the ride and Lovely Dancer was dropped a little in class that he actually regained winning ways, but an easy win over Dayzaan in the Prix Ridgway at Deauville in August probably did his confidence the world of good. He gained his first pattern-race win when beating the four-year-old Darly by three quarters of a length in the seven-runner Prix du Prince d'Orange at Longchamp a fortnight before the Arc, presumably impressing Head more than All Along had done in the previous week's Prix Foy.

Lovely Dancer (b.c. 1980)	Green Dancer (b 1972)	Nijinsky (b 1967)	Northern Dancer / Flaming Page
		Green Valley (br 1967)	Val de Loir / Sly Pola
	Janthina (br 1972)	Petingo (b 1965)	Petition / Alcazar
		Jalanda (b 1966)	Sicambre / Japonica

Lovely Dancer is one of the best colts sired by Green Dancer who is now standing in the United States. The dam Janthina was one of the leading French two-year-old fillies of 1974, when an impressive winner of a newcomers race and second to Broadway Dancer in the Prix Morny; she ran only once at three, however, finishing down the field in modest company at the back-end of the season. Janthina's only previous foal Quouki (by Zeddaan) was a useful winner over nine furlongs as a two-year-old in 1981 and she has since had a colt by Nonoalco and a filly by Pharly. The grandam Jalanda, placed over a mile as a two-year-old, was a sister to the very smart middle-distance performer Jacambre, a stable-companion of Sea-Bird II.

A mile and a quarter and soft ground appeared to suit Lovely Dancer ideally at one time but his run in the Arc shows plainly that he's suited by a mile and a half and equally at home on firm. He wore bandages early in his career but raced without them through most of 1983. *O. Douieb, France.*

Prix du Prince d'Orange, Longchamp—Lovely Dancer accounts for Darly

LOVELY LEANA 3 gr.f. Town Crier 119–Set Piece 69 (Firestreak 125) (1982   **51**
5.8f 5g 6f 6g⁴ 7f⁴ 6s 7.2s 1983 5s⁴ 5g 6fg 5fg 12fg⁴ 10.4g 9d² 9g²) leggy,
lightly-made filly; plater; stays 9f and wasn't totally disgraced over 1½m; acts on
any going; blinkered final outing at 2 yrs; sold 1,050 gns Doncaster October Sales.
P. Brookshaw.

LOVELY LUCY 3 ch.f. Grundy 137–Romany 87 (King's Bench 132) (1982 6d 6s   **–**
1983 12.2d 12f 12.2f⁴ 12f) fair sort; promises to stay 1½m; blinkered final start. *J.
Winter.*

LOVE OF A GUNNER 3 ch.c. Gunner B 126–Prevailing Love 82 (Prevailing)   **67**
(1982 NR 1983 8.2s 12.2s* 12f 13.8f³ 13.8f 13.8f⁴ 16.5f 16d 15.8d² 18fg) tall,
rather narrow colt; second foal; dam best at 5f; won minor event at Catterick in
June; broke a leg and was destroyed at Nottingham in October; stayed well; acted
on any going; wore blinkers. *S. Norton.*

LOVERS BID 2 b.f. Auction Ring 123–Lover's Rose (King Emperor) (1983 6f²   **81**
6fg 6s* 6g) Feb 28; 31,000Y; well-made filly; poor mover; first foal; dam,
half-sister to very smart middle-distance stayer Swell Fellow, won at around 9f in
Ireland; won 10-runner minor event at Ayr in September by 3 lengths from Half
Shaft; fair sixth of 16 in £9,100 nursery at York the following month; should stay
beyond 6f; acts on any going. *J. Hindley.*

LOVER'S CLASH 2 br.g. Owen Dudley 121–Crash (Ballymoss 136) (1983 6fg   **71**
6fg 8g³ 8.2fg) May 7; 1,000F, 7,800Y; half-brother to 2 winners abroad; 6½
lengths third of 15 to Kuwait Palace in maiden race at Edinburgh in September; will
stay beyond 1m. *K. Brassey.*

LOVE WALKED IN 2 ch.g. Hotfoot 126–Love Resolved (Dan Cupid 132) (1983   **75**
6fg 6f 8d 10.2fg⁴) Mar 16; 44,000Y; deep-girthed, good sort; half-brother to 3
winners, including Lingfield Derby Trial winner Riberetto (by Ribero) and fairly
useful 5f and 7f winner Tribal Warrior (by Tribal Chief); dam placed over 13f in
France; showed little (off course for 2 months after second outing) until finishing
fourth of 24 behind easy winner Raami in minor event at Doncaster in November;
suited by 1¼m. *J. Winter.*

LOVING DOLL 3 gr.f. Godswalk 130–Le Levandoll 92 (Le Levanstell 122) (1982   **–**
5g 5fg 6s³ 1983 6s⁴ 6v 7fg 7s 8g 6g) sturdy filly; plating-class maiden; will be
suited by further (dam won at up to 1½m). *A. Hide.*

LOYAL SUBJECT 3 b.c. Mill Reef 141–Reine Dagobert 76 (Roi Dagobert 128)   **82**
(1982 NR 1983 12fg² 11g² 12f² 14f 15.8g* 14.7fg³ 12d 15.8g³) fourth foal;
half-brother to Irish 1½m winner Buoyant (by Lyphard) and useful 7f to 1¼m
winner Mauritzfontein (by Habitat); dam, half-sister to Grand Prix de Paris winner
Matahawk, won over 1½m; placed most starts and was a 6-length winner of maiden
event at Catterick in September, making most and staying on strongly; suited by
long distances and enterprising riding tactics; best form with some give in the
ground; sweated up seventh start; sold 9,000 gns Newmarket Autumn Sales. *W.
Elsey.*

LOYAL SUPPORTER 4 b.g. Scottish Rifle 127–Miss Moss Bros 69 (Sparkler   **69**
130) (1982 10.1g³ 11.7g³ 10.2s³ 10d³ 1983 12f 10f² 10g* 10d² 8fg 12fg 10g)
plater; made all to win at Lingfield in September; bought in 1,550 gns afterwards;
should stay 1½m; acts on any going; has run respectably for a lady rider. *A.
Davison.*

LUCIEN LASAGE 3 b.c. Brigadier Gerard 144–Photo Flash 119 (Match III   **60**
135) (1982 NR 1983 8g 8fg 8f 7f⁴ 8f³ 8g 8d) 1,500 2-y-o; good-bodied colt; turns
his front feet in; half-brother to 4 winners, including very useful stayer Golden
River (by Rheingold); dam second in 1000 Guineas and half-sister to Welsh
Pageant; showed a bit of ability fourth and fifth starts but was behind in a seller final
outing; stays 1m; blinkered third to fifth outings; wears bandages. *D. Ringer.*

LUCIETES 2 b.c. Julio Mariner 127–Rose Copse (Floribunda 136) (1983 7fg) Apr   **–**
6; 15,500Y; rangy, quite attractive colt; half-brother to 3 winners here and abroad,
including very smart 7f to 1½m winner Saros (by Sassafras); dam won over 4.5f at
2 yrs in France and stayed 1m; decidedly backward, behind in 20-runner maiden
race at Newmarket in August; the type to do better in time. *F. Durr.*

LUCK PENNY 3 b.f. Bustino 136–Thrifty Trio 116 (Groton) (1982 6fg² 6f 6fg 5s   **87**
1983 6d 5v² 5v² 5s* 6g⁴ 5f² 5f 5h* 5fg* 5.6fg) leggy, lengthy, shallow-girthed filly;
a progressive sort who won handicaps at Wolverhampton, Bath and Pontefract;
quickened up well to beat Bella Travaille a length in last-named in August; stays 6f;
acts on any going; has a good turn of foot; genuine and consistent, although didn't
run up to her best final start. *I. Balding.*

LUCKY APPEAL 3 b.f. Star Appeal 133–Lucky Omen 99 (Queen's Hussar 124)   —
(1982 7d 1983 7d 8f 11.5g 9d) quite well-made filly; little worthwhile form in
maiden and minor races, although was sixth of 12 on final start; retained 1,100 gns
Newmarket Autumn Sales. *C. Brittain.*

LUCKY BLOW 6 b.g. St Paddy 133–Breathalyser (Alcide 136) (1982 NR 1983   —
8h 11.7h 16f) probably of little account. *D. C. Tucker.*

LUCKY BOARDMAN'S 2 ch.c. Touch Paper 113–Lucky Poem (Lucky Guy   **83**
121) (1983 5s 5s*(dis) 5v⁴ 5fg 6f 5f* 5s² 6g 6g) Apr 25; IR 2,400F, IR 3,100Y,
resold 3,900Y; small, sturdy colt; brother to Irish 7.5f winner Scrahan's Best and
half-brother to a winner; dam never ran; won maiden auction event at Beverley in
September; also passed post first in maiden race at Hamilton in April, only to be
disqualified some time afterwards for failing dope test; appears best at 5f; acts on
any going; suitable mount for an apprentice. *J. Berry.*

LUCKY BROXTED 4 gr.f. Broxted 120–La Danza (Lucky Sovereign) (1982   —
NR 1983 11d) third foal; dam moderate hurdler; tailed-off last in maiden race at
Edinburgh in April. *A. W. Jones.*

LUCKY CHOICE 4 br.g. Lucky Wednesday 124–Pams Choice 87 (Mandamus   —
120) (1982 8s 9.4fg 9fg² 8g⁴ 9g² 10fg³ 10d 10.2f⁴ 1983 12d 10g 10fg 10f 10f 10f)
strong, good-bodied gelding; poor handicapper; stays 1¼m; acts on any going; one
paced and needs to lie up with leaders; best in blinkers; has sweated up; has run
respectably for an apprentice; not the heartiest of battlers. *C. Spares.*

LUCKY DUTCH 4 b.g. Lucky Wednesday 124–Dutch May 109 (Maystreak 118)   —
(1982 8f 8g 5d² 1983 5f 5f 6d 5f 8g 5fg³ 5d 6fg 7fg) fair sort; sprint handicapper;
has been beaten in a seller; sometimes sweats up. *M. W. Easterby.*

LUCKY ENGAGEMENT (USA) 2 b. or br.f. What Luck–Fiancee (Round   **75**
Table) (1983 6g 7s²) Mar 2; $65,000Y; third foal; dam, placed twice from 11
starts, is sister to very useful stakes winner Sphere; 4 lengths second of 19 to
Eljazzi in maiden race at Leicester in October; stays 7f. *P. Haslam.*

LUCKY FEN 3 br.g. Lucky Wednesday 124–Ensign Steel 57 (Majority Blue 126)   —
(1982 NR 1983 10f 15.8g) big, useful sort; third foal; half-brother to 2 winners by
Lochnager, including sprinter Benfen; dam, placed over 6f, is half-sister to several
very useful sprinters; behind in minor event at Ripon in August (dwelt) and maiden
race at Catterick in September. *M. H. Easterby.*

LUCKY FINGERS 3 ch.f. Hotfoot 126–Tilt Guard 75 (Crepello 136) (1982 7d⁴   —
1983 10v³ 10fg 10f 12fg 12f⁴ 10fg) well-made filly; suited by 1½m; acts on any
going; blinkered third start; reluctant to go down final outing; sold to R. Holder
940 gns Newmarket Autumn Sales. *C. Brittain.*

LUCKY IVOR (USA) 4 b.g. Sir Ivor 135–Carnival Queen (Amerigo 116§) (1982   **76**
12g 14g* 16.5fg* 14g⁴ 16.5s 18d 1983 16v 15.5v⁴ 17.1g* 16g 16f* 18.4fg³ 19f⁴
16h² 16fg 18fg) big, rangy gelding; out-and-out staying handicapper; won at Bath
in June and Beverley in July; needs a sound surface; suited by strong handling; sold
out of J. Dunlop's stable 11,000 gns Newmarket September Sales after eighth start
and was virtually pulled up first outing for new connections. *R. Hoad.*

LUCKY JENNIE 3 b.f. Lucky Wednesday 124–Miss Cameron 76 (Decoy Boy   —
129) (1982 5d 5g 6fg 6d 6g 1983 7g 6fg 5f 6f 6fg 5g 6fg) leggy, rather narrow filly;
poor maiden; towards rear in a seller fifth outing; stays 6f; has run creditably in
blinkers. *M. Haynes.*

LUCKY JOKER 4 br.f. Cawston's Clown 113–Charlie's Double (Fighting Charlie   —
127) (1982 12d 12f 8f 10d 10f³ 12fg⁴ 11g 10.4d⁴ 10.6f⁴ 13d 12d 10.2s 1983 12d⁴)
lengthy, rather dipped-backed filly; poor handicapper; has been beaten in a seller;
stays 1½m; acts on any going; has run respectably for an apprentice. *J. Wilson.*

LUCKY KNIGHT 3 b.c. Rarity 129–Emerin 85 (King Emperor) (1982 7fg 1983   **62**
8.5v³ 10s 12g 10s² 10.1fg 8f 10f 10g 10g) smallish, useful-looking colt; stays 1¼m;
form only with some give in the ground; often blinkered nowadays. *B. Swift.*

LUCKY LOCHE 2 b.g. Lochnager 132–Reignon 74 (Lucky Brief 128) (1983 6f   —
8fg 7fg) Apr 19; half-brother to 2 minor winners by Rapid River; dam, useful
hurdler, stayed 1½m; in rear in maiden races in the North, once last; gelded after
final appearance. *M. Camacho.*

LUCKY MADAM 3 b.f. Lucky Wednesday 124–Polistina 106 (Acropolis 132)   —
(1982 6g 1983 9d 7fg 8f) plater; sold 410 gns Doncaster September Sales. *D. H.
Jones.*

Burr Stakes, Lingfield—Lucky Scott wins from Nasr (right) and Quick Work

LUCKY MISTAKE 6 gr.m. Averof 123–Kingdom Come 77 (Klondyke Bill 125) (1982 10.2g 8g 8fg² 12f² 11.5fg 10g 1983 8f) strong mare; plater; stays 1½m; acts on hard going; has been tried in blinkers; has worn bandages; sometimes sweats up; suitable mount for an inexperienced rider. *R. Hodges.* —

LUCKY ORPHAN 3 b.f. Derrylin 115–Sinkit (Sing Sing 134) (1982 6fg 6fg³ 8s 1983 6h³ 7f 7fg 6d² 7s² 7fg) close-coupled, lightly-made filly; quite a moderate maiden; stays 7f; tends to sweat up. *R. Boss.* **72**

LUCKY SARAH 10 b.m. Fine Bid 106–Ensign Rouge (Magic Red) (1982 NR 1983 10.4g 12g 10.6s) plain mare; of no account. *R. Griffiths.* —

LUCKY SCOTT 2 b.c. Crimson Beau 124–Soft Pedal 92 (Hotfoot 126) (1983 7f 7g* 7.6g* 8f) Apr 7; rangy colt; carries plenty of condition; first foal; dam won 5 times at around 6f; made most of running to win 2 good races in September, keeping on most gamely to beat Macarthurs Head by a length in Chertsey Lock Stakes at Kempton and then having 1½ lengths to spare over Nasr in 5-runner Burr Stakes at Lingfield; disputed lead to turn into straight when just over 5 lengths eighth of 9 to Treizieme in Grand Criterium at Longchamp in October; suited by 1m; acts on firm going; a game and improving performer. *P. Cole.* **113**

LUCKY WEDDING 4 b.f. Lucky Wednesday 124–Lilmi Love 82 (Miralgo 130) (1982 8f³ 7g 8.3fg 8g 8fg 10fg 1983 8.2d 8fg 10g) plater; stays 1m; has twice been blinkered. *A. Young.* —

LUCY PLATTER (FR) 3 br.f. Record Token 128–Luciennes 108 (Grey Sovereign 128§) (1982 5s 5s 5v³ 1983 6g 7s 8g⁴ 7f 8f 10f 9f 9f) fair sort; should stay at least 6f; blinkered fourth outing; didn't look all that keen seventh start. *M. W. Easterby.* —

LUCY RAYNALDS 3 b. or br.f. So Blessed 130–Ciao (Mandamus 120) (1982 6fg 7f² 7g 7fg 1983 7s 10v 9f² 8f 8fg³ 8f⁴ 10s) leggy, light-framed filly; good mover; quite a moderate maiden; stays 1¼m; acts on any going; tended to hang and ran bit below her best when blinkered sixth start; sold 800 gns Newmarket December Sales. *P. Kelleway.* **71**

LUDERIC (USA) 3 b.c. Cornish Prince–Dols Jaminque (Kennedy Road) (1982 8v⁴ 8s² 1983 8v² 8v* 8f⁴ 9fg² 10fg) first foal; dam very lightly-raced half-sister to Seximee, the dam of Nonoalco and Stradavinsky; won maiden race at Saint-Cloud in May by 2½ lengths from Soliloquy; ran extremely well and finished clear of rest when short-neck second of 7 to Glenstal in Prix Daphnis at Evry in July, but ran a long way below form final outing (August); stays 9f; acts on any going. *G. Sauque, France.* **117**

LUIGI'S GLORY 3 b.g. Hittite Glory 125–Glengarry 72 (High Hat 131) (1982 5d 5fg 6g 5fg 7g* 8.2v² 1983 10v⁴ 11v 11.7s² 12v³ 11.7fg* 14f² 14f 12f 12g² 12g³ 10.5d³ 12fg³) quite an attractive, small gelding; won handicap at Windsor in June; placed 5 times afterwards, on last 2 occasions in valuable sellers; stays 1¾m; acts on any going. *R. Williams.* **76**

LUMINATE 2 b.c. Busted 134–Lora (Lorenzaccio 130) (1983 7.6fg² 7fg³) May 11; big colt; half-brother to 2 winners, including 1000 Guineas winner On The House (by Be My Guest); dam closely related to high-class sprinter D'Urberville; shaped like a sure future winner when running on strongly to be length second of 16 to Judex in maiden race at Lingfield in October and when finishing in great style to be 2¼ lengths third of 14 to Condrillac in Houghton Stakes at Newmarket later in month; will stay beyond 1m; certain to improve and win good races. *J. Dunlop.* **93 p**

LUMINIST 3 b.c. Majestic Light–Canterbury Tale (Exbury 138) (1982 NR 1983 –
10g) fair sort; half-brother to 2 winners in USA, including Knight's Tale (by Hail to
Reason), successful at up to 9f and earner of over $120,000; dam, very useful in
USA, won 1m stakes race; 20/1 but looking well when eleventh of 20 to Staravia in
maiden race at Sandown in October, making some progress in straight after getting
well behind; should benefit from the experience. *I. Balding.*

LUNARIS 2 b.f. High Top 131–Lady Of The Moon 89 (Crepello 136) (1983 6f 8g^3 **79**
7.6fg 7s) Apr 30; good-topped, close-coupled filly; has a round action; third foal;
half-sister to 3-y-o Firmament (by Relkino); dam, sister to Derby fourth Great
Wall, won 3 times over 1¼m; 3¼ lengths third of 17 to Senane in maiden race at
Leicester in September; stays 1m well; sold BBA (Italia) 15,000 gns Newmarket
Autumn Sales. *M. Smyly.*

LUNAR WIND 8 ch.g. Windjammer (USA)–Lunar Star (Star Gazer 123) (1982 –
7fg 8f 8f 8f^2 9fg 8fg 1983 10f 8d) leggy, narrow gelding; best at up to 9f on
top-of-the-ground; has worn blinkers and bandages; good mount for an apprentice.
J. Parkes.

LUSUS 2 b.c. Court Circus 97–Valpolicella (Lorenzaccio 130) (1983 7f) May 27; –
second foal; dam bad plater; tailed-off last of 6 in seller at Newcastle in July. *D.
Chapman.*

LUTH ENCHANTEE (FR) 3 ch.f. Be My Guest 126–Viole d'Amour (Luthier **130**
126) (1982 8s^2 7.5s 1983 8v^2 9s 8v^2 8s^2 8s* 7d^4 8fg* 8f* 8g* 12f^3 10f)
    The old saying 'winter rides on the tail of the last horse in the St Leger' seems
to contain the implication that once the Leger has been run the season is virtually
over. If this sentiment was ever intended it could not be proposed nowadays, when
there is so much still to come after the second week in September even in England.
Internationally, autumn stretches on and on; it has become one of the busiest and
most important periods of the year for racing, filled to overflowing with top races,
partly as a result of the United States and Japan becoming within reasonable
travelling time for European-trained horses. Possibly the most competitive
middle-distance event of the year confined to fillies and mares took place the day
after the flat closed in England, at Santa Anita in California. The event, the Yellow
Ribbon Invitational, was contested by twelve runners drawn from Europe, America
and New Zealand of whom seven were Group 1 winners and another three Group
1-placed. In such a contest none could afford to be at anything less than her best, as
several were for one reason or another. The outcome was rather different from
that which most followers of European racing would probably have expected since
the winner was the ex-European Sangue (favourite, incidentally), who beat the
French and Irish One Thousand Guineas winner L'Attrayante by a length and a half,
with the One Thousand Guineas runner-up Royal Heroine, the Dubai Champion

*Prix Jacques le Marois, Deauville—Luth Enchantee produces a good turn of foot to beat
L'Emigrant*

Stakes third Flame of Tara and the Trusthouse Forte Prix de l'Arc de Triomphe third Luth Enchantee among the distinguished also-rans. On her record there was no better filly to represent Europe in such a contest than Luth Enchantee, who unfortunately had a poor run in what turned out to be a rough race and, to make matters worse, was afterwards found to be coughing.

French-trained fillies, in particular improving three-year-olds, have played a big part in recent Prix de l'Arc de Triomphes. Luth Enchantee, who was the first French-trained three-year-old home in 1983 and ran third of twenty-six behind All Along and Sun Princess, beaten just over a length after making up at least eight lengths on the leaders in the straight, travelled a different road from most of her predecessors to the Arc: she was raced as a miler, and didn't take part in the Prix Vermeille. Luth Enchantee was an improving filly all right. She'd blossomed suddenly into as good a miler as there was in Europe with the possible exception of the colt L'Emigrant after taking until her seventh start, in a maiden at Saint-Cloud in June, the Prix des Dahlias, to get off the mark. The race after that she'd been beaten by three below top-flight four-year-olds, African Joy, Geral and Mir Bal, when favourite for the Prix de la Porte Maillot at Longchamp. Then she'd really begun to climb the ladder, and she went to the Arc without further defeat in three starts. When she won the Prix d'Astarte at Deauville early in August in good style by a length and a half from the Royal Hunt Cup winner Mighty Fly she hadn't quite reached her best, and would have had more to do if Saint-Martin had ridden a slightly more enterprising race on the runner-up and if Ma Biche hadn't needed the outing after a long lay-off through training setbacks. But she was magnificent in accounting for very strong fields in the Prix Jacques le Marois on the same course later in the month and the Prix du Moulin de Longchamp in September. The turn of foot Luth Enchantee showed in the d'Astarte was even more in evidence in the Marois and Moulin—one of the abiding memories of the two races, actually, as it was also in the Arc.

The Marois is featured as the top race at the month-long Deauville meeting and, as on most occasions, the latest came well up to expectations. In such a race Luth Enchantee started at 13/1. The French Two Thousand Guineas winner L'Emigrant was favourite at 11/4; next came the One Thousand Guineas winner Ma Biche at 3/1, followed by Noalcoholic (7/2) who'd recently won the race that has grown to be regarded as the one-mile championship in England, the Sussex Stakes; next the Premio Emilio Turati winner Bold Run coupled with a pacemaker Sea's Valley (4/1), and Crystal Glitters (12/1) who'd beaten an unlucky L'Emigrant and Bold Run in the Prix d'Ispahan. The English-trained Montekin started at 20/1. Montekin, a pretty good horse on his day, excelled himself here, turning Sussex Stakes tables on Noalcoholic. Nevertheless he was no match for the two leading

Prix du Moulin de Longchamp—Luth Enchantee gets the better of L'Emigrant again, this time by half a length

Paul de Moussac's "Luth Enchantee"

French horses. After the confirmed front-runner Noalcoholic and L'Emigrant had disputed the advantage for a long way Crystal Glitters, Ma Biche and Luth Enchantee came at them at the distance. In a few strides Luth Enchantee took over in front, and although she crossed Noalcoholic in the process she went on to win with complete authority by a length and a half from L'Emigrant; Montekin deprived Ma Biche of third place, two lengths further back; Noalcoholic came fifth. Luth Enchantee's performance in the Prix du Moulin three weeks later, though she had only half a length to spare over L'Emigrant this time, left one correspondent of the leading French turf newspaper unusually lost for words. It was an outstanding performance, breathtaking in its manner of achievement. Despite the presence in the eight-runner field of the Airlie/Coolmore Irish Two Thousand Guineas winner Wassl and the St James's Palace Stakes winner Horage, in addition to that of L'Attrayante and Crystal Glitters again, the finish concerned only Luth Enchantee and L'Emigrant: Wassl was a clear third, eight lengths down. In a truly-run race (Horage, Wassl and the pacemaker Conerton saw to that) Luth Enchantee gave three or four lengths start to L'Emigrant running towards the last furlong and still beat him; she had been at the rear from the start, detached from the others until closing up towards the foot of the hill before the home turn, and while making the rest look small beer as she moved through in the straight she seemed to have found one too fast for her in L'Emigrant who possessed indisputably the best turn of foot of all the French colts running at a mile to a mile and a half. L'Emigrant shot into a clear lead halfway up the straight, looking all over a winner, but eventually Luth Enchantee caught him under pressure and stayed just ahead in an exciting finish. There is no doubt that holding Luth Enchantee for a late run in these two important races was deliberate policy, executed with typical Gallic audacity on the second occasion. Her coming from behind in the Arc was, therefore, entirely predictable, but we formed the impression that on this occasion she, most surprisingly, experienced difficulty going the early pace. Be that as it may, the fact remains that she had more horses in front of her than behind when she began a great run on the outside early in the straight which would have taken her past Sun Princess into second place in another stride or two. Another tremendous performance!

Luth Enchantee (Fr) (ch.f. 1980)			
	Be My Guest (ch 1974)	Northern Dancer (b 1961)	Nearctic
			Natalma
		What a Treat (b 1962)	Tudor Minstrel
			Rare Treat
	Viole d'Amour (b 1972)	Luthier (br 1965)	Klairon
			Flute Enchantee
		Mandolinette (b 1963)	Yorik
			Malveillante

Be My Guest made the start every stallion owner dreams of with the classic winners Assert and On The House in his first crop. His second would look poor by comparison without Luth Enchantee, but in her he has sired a horse of similar stature to those two. The dam and her family are solidly, recognisably French. Viole d'Amour, a half-sister to several winners out of the middle-distance winner Mandolinette, was a very useful racemare. She won over eleven furlongs at Saint-Cloud and over a mile and a half at Longchamp as a three-year-old. Luth Enchantee is her second foal and so far her only runner. Mandolinette's dam Malveillante won over hurdles and fences in France; she was a half-sister to a smart French miler of the 'sixties called Malfaiteur.

Luth Enchantee was returned to France after the Yellow Ribbon Invitational and will be in training as a four-year-old. Apparently there are going to be more top-class older horses competing in 1984 than for a long time, promising some fine racing ahead. If she trains on satisfactorily Luth Enchantee, a lightly-built filly, is certain to win more good races when conditions are in her favour. Since she's effective at a mile to a mile and a half there should be plenty of alternatives for her connections, though their choice may be restricted by the weather if, as seems probable, she is better on a sound surface than a soft one. One obvious target, the Prix Ganay, for example, is more often than not run on soft going, and so is the Prix de l'Arc come to that. Luth Enchantee is a genuine filly with an exceptional turn of foot and a style of racing that may lull her jockey into over-confidence one day; we hope it doesn't. *J. Cunnington, jnr, France.*

LUTHERANNE 3 b. or br.f. Luthier 126–Yole Tartare (Captain's Gig) (1982 NR 1983 7s) 46,000Y; attractive filly; second produce; dam, minor 9f winner at 2 yrs in France, is half-sister to smart French filly Premiere Harde; 33/1 but fairly straight when tailed-off last of 20 behind Shore Line in maiden race at Newmarket in April, dropping out quickly from halfway. *P. Walwyn.*   –

LUXURIATE (USA) 6 b.g. Tom Rolfe–Dee Dee Luxe (Cavan) (1982 16.1g 17.1g³ 1983 16f) staying maiden; acts on firm going; used to wear blinkers; sold 3,000 gns Ascot November Sales. *I. Wardle.*   –

LUXURY 4 b.f. Ragapan 118–Vanessa's Queen (Faberge II 121) (1982 12fg 12f 16.1h⁴ 13.8f² 13.8f³ 14g 14.7fg² 16s² 15.8d* 16s³ 15d 1983 12v 12d 14.7f 15.8f² 16f⁴ 14.6f⁴ 15.8f⁴ 16s* 15.8d* 18fg³) lightly-made filly; has a round action; won handicaps at Beverley in September and Catterick in October; stays 2m but possibly not 2¼m; acts on any going but is ideally suited by some give underfoot; sometimes sweats up and rarely impresses in paddock. *J. Carr.*   63

LYMINSTER 3 gr.c. Hittite Glory 125–January (Sigebert 131) (1982 7g 8fg 8s² 8s 9s² 1983 8s 10d 9.5s* 10d³ 10g 11.7f 11.5f 12f 12fg 13fg 12s⁴) compact colt; beat Trocadero by ½ length at Cagnes-sur-Mer in February; unplaced on his return, but ran respectably on occasions; promises to stay 1½m; ideally suited by some give in the ground and acts well on soft going; sold to J. Jenkins 12,500 gns Newmarket Autumn Sales. *J. Dunlop.*   79

LYMOND 4 b.g. Rapid River 127–Gill Breeze (Farm Walk 111) (1982 7g 6f 7f² 8f 8f 6f 8g 7f 8g 10d 8fg³ 8.2g 9s⁴ 8.2s² 8s 8s⁴ 1983 7g* 7g 7fg 7f 7f) fair sort; poor walker; decisively won handicap at Thirsk in April; well beaten most starts afterwards; stays 1m well; acts on any going; blinkered twice at 2 yrs. *N. Tinkler.*   58

LYPHANESS (USA) 2 b.c. Lyphard 132–Ridaness 113 (Ridan) (1983 6fg) Feb 1; 80,000Y; quite well-made colt; first foal; dam best at up to 1m; 7/1, failed to recover from slow start in 17-runner maiden race at Newmarket in August. *B. Hills.*   –

LYPHARD'S PRINCESS (USA) 3 b.f. Lyphard 132–Avum (Umbrella Fella) (1982 6g² 6.5g² 7s* 8s 1983 8v 5s 7d 6.5fg³ 8fg² 8f 6fg² 6fg² 7f4) $375,000Y; second foal; dam won 10 races at up to 1m, including stakes, and is half-sister to Lord Avie and stakes winner Jolly Johu; won 80,000-franc race at Longchamp as a   114

2-y-o; placed in 1983 at Evry in July, Deauville (twice) in August and Maisons-Laffitte in September, finishing 2½ lengths second of 6 behind Maximova in Prix de Seine-et-Oise on last-named course; finds 5f too sharp and stays 1m; acts on any going; sent to USA. *J. de Chevigny, France.*

LYPHARD'S SPECIAL (USA) 3 b.c. Lyphard 132–My Bupers (Bupers) **121**
(1982 6f* 6d* 7f* 7f² 8s² 8d³ 1983 8s 7.6fg* 10f 11.1g* 12fg³ 10fg) good-bodied, attractive colt; good mover; half-brother to useful 1981 French 2-y-o Embarrassed (by Blushing Groom) and several winners in USA, notably champion sprinter My Juliet (by Gallant Romeo); dam placed several times; won first 3 of his 6 races as a 2-y-o and was placed in the others, including in Royal Lodge Stakes at Ascot and William Hill Futurity at Doncaster; not so consistent in 1983, although accounted for smallish fields in £8,200 Truman Bitter Stakes at Lingfield in July (having first outing for 3 months, beat I'll See You by 1½ lengths) and September Stakes at Kempton; looked in very good shape when beating Hot Touch readily by 2 lengths in latter race, and had race sewn up almost as soon as he took lead entering straight; gained only other placing when 3½ lengths third of 8 behind Band in Cumberland Lodge Stakes at Ascot later in September (sweating and unimpressive in paddock); below best in Craven Stakes at Newmarket, Prix de la Cote Normande at Deauville and Dubai Champion Stakes at Newmarket again; probably stays 1½m; acts on any going. *G. Harwood.*

LYPHARD'S TRICK (USA) 2 b.or br.c. Lyphard 132–Honor Tricks (Bold **110**
Bidder) (1983 8f⁴ 8g² 9g* 9f) Feb 23; first foal; dam unraced half-sister to several very good animals, including Tosmah and Halo, and to dam of Kentucky Derby winner Cannonade; easy winner of minor race at Evry in September by 5 lengths from Oldoway; about 2 lengths fifth to Truculent in Prix Lord Seymour at Longchamp the following month; will stay 1¼m+. *F. Boutin, France.*

LYPHNAP (USA) 3 b.f. Lyphard 132–Smooth 114 (Sound Track 132) (1982 5g⁴ **89**
6g³ 1983 6v* 6v³ 6s⁴ 6fg) smallish, strong, good-bodied, attractive filly; beat Je T'Aime very easily by 5 lengths in £3,200 event at Kempton in May; in frame in minor events at Newbury and Brighton (5/2 on) later in month, better effort on former course; gives impression she'll be suited by 7f; acts on heavy going. *J. Tree.*

Lady Harrison's "Lyphard's Special"

Duchess of Kent Maiden Stakes, York—Maazi wins in good style from Idolized

LYPTOSOL VELVET 2 b. or br.f. Daring March 116–Songonara 59 (Dragonara Palace 115) (1983 6f 5g 6fg) May 10; lengthy filly; first foal; dam sprint plater; behind in maiden and minor events; blinkered last 2 starts. *P. Calver.* –

LYSIMACHUS 3 b.or br.c. Lypheor 118–Grenadiere 111 (Right Royal V 135) (1982 NR 1983 12.3fg 10d 8.2g) 12,000Y; lengthy colt; half-brother to smart middle-distance stayer Stetchworth (by Nijinsky) and very useful Battlecry (by Bold Lad, Ire), a winner at up to 15f; dam, very useful stayer, is half-sister to good winners Full Dress II, Reload and Boulette; in mid-division in maiden races at Newcastle, Beverley and Haydock in second half of season. *M. W. Easterby.*

LYSISTRA 4 b.f. Owen Anthony 102–Freezing Point (March Past 124) (1982 NR 1983 11.5f 12f 12fg² 14f 18.1d 16fg 18g*) 420 3-y-o; poor mover; first foal; dam winning hurdler; plater; attracted no bid after winning at Pontefract in October (tended to hang left); suited by a test of stamina; has worn bandages. *R.Hobson.* 52

LYSITHEA 2 ch.f. Imperial Fling 116–Luscinia 73 (Sing Sing 134) (1983 7f³ 7g³ 7f 5g² 6g²) Mar 9; half-sister to 2 winners, including 5f and 6f winner Nariz (by Brigadier Gerard); dam won over 1m; plater; stays 7f; acts on firm going; blinkered on final appearance; consistent. *Sir Mark Prescott.* 63

M

MAAJID (USA) 2 b.c. Topsider–Your Nuts (Creme dela Creme) (1983 5g³ 5d* 6d² 5fg² 5f* 6fg* 6fg³ 5f* 6f² 5d* 5fg) Apr 14; $50,000Y; small, well-made colt; good walker; third foal; dam, 2-y-o 6f winner, is half-sister to very smart 2-y-o fillies Bundler and Picture Tube; sire, son of Northern Dancer and top-class filly Drumtop, was smart sprinter in USA; had excellent season, winning small races at Newmarket, Beverley (2) and Chester, and Bayford Fuels Horn Blower Stakes at Ripon; also placed 5 times, including good second to Idolized in Champion Two Yrs Old Trophy at Ripon in August; equally effective at 5f and 6f and promises to stay 7f; seems to act on any going; thoroughly genuine and consistent. *H. T. Jones.* 110

MAAZI 2 br.c. Ahonoora 122–Grangemore (Prominer 125) (1983 6f* 6g³ 7.3g² 7fg) Feb 5; IR 41,000Y; big, strong colt; good walker; half-brother to 2 winners by 94

498

Ballymore, including Irish 7f winner More Treasure; dam, Irish 7f winner, is half-sister to leading 1960 2-y-o filly Kathy Too; won valuable 13-runner maiden race at York in June by a length from Idolized; beaten favourite next 2 starts (ran well both times) in minor event at Lingfield in July and nursery at Newbury in September; stays 7f; acts on firm going. *P. Cole.*

MABELLA 3 b.f. Julio Mariner 127–Dorabella 88 (Rockefella) (1982 7g 1983 12s 12.2d 13d 14fg 18fg) fair sort; little show in maiden races and handicaps; blinkered final start; trained by W. Elsey until after third outing. *M. Francis.*   —

MA BICHE (USA) 3 b. or br.f. Key To The Kingdom–Madge (Roi Dagobert 128) (1982 5s³ 5.5g* 7g* 5.5g* 6fg³ 6g* 1983 7v* 8g* 8fg 8f⁴ 7fg*)   **125**

One of the wettest springs in living memory, which hampered the preparation of classic contenders in Britain, Ireland and France into Derby week, didn't prevent the One Thousand Guineas going to form. The favourite Ma Biche won the race decisively, and the next three in the betting filled the rest of the places though not in betting order, the second favourite Favoridge dividing the co-third favourites Royal Heroine and Habibti in a close finish for what remained. As a result of training problems during the summer Ma Biche was able to race only three times afterwards; she ended up having fewer outings as a three-year-old than as a two-year-old. Even so she did enough to confirm she was well up to standard for a One Thousand Guineas winner through her performance in the Prix de la Foret on her final appearance. She has now been retired and will begin her new career with a visit to another of the season's lightly-raced classic winners, Shareef Dancer. What may the result of the union be worth? Ma Biche herself was reportedly valued at three million pounds when changing hands after her first season.

By and large two-year-old form has proved the soundest guide to the Guineas: the race comes too soon for the slower developer. Far and away the best long-range pointer to the outcome of the One Thousand Guineas since the war has been the Cheveley Park Stakes, sponsored in recent years by bookmakers William Hill Limited. The race, for two-year-old fillies run over the last six furlongs of the Rowley Mile, had been won since the war by thirteen who had gone on to finish in the first three in the One Thousand Guineas. Six of them—Belle of All, Zabara, Night Off, Fleet, Humble Duty and Waterloo—had won both, and five further, including Ma Biche's grandam Midget II who split Honeylight and Arietta in 1956, had finished second. However, eleven years had passed since Waterloo did the double. Ma Biche won the Cheveley Park in 1982 by three parts of a length from the smaller Favoridge. She was an excellent two-year-old, the best of her age and sex in Europe; besides the Cheveley Park she won one of France's most important events for sprinting two-year-olds, the Prix Robert Papin, plus two other races including one over seven furlongs at Evry in which she accounted for seven previous winners. Her only defeat as a two-year-old after her first appearance was in the Prix Morny when she was third to the Papin runner-up Deep Roots and another colt, the English-trained On Stage, on ground firmer than she'd encountered before.

The Cheveley Park form stood up well in the spring. In the first week of April Ma Biche came out in the seven-furlong Prix Imprudence at Maisons-Laffitte and,

One Thousand Guineas Stakes, Newmarket—Ma Biche (second right) goes on from Royal Heroine, Favoridge (extreme left) and Habibti (stripes)

Prix de la Foret, Longchamp—Ma Biche goes out in style; she accounts for Pampabird, with Aragon third

at 5/2 on, won easing up in testing conditions by a length and a half from one of the previous season's better two-year-olds, Dancing Display, and five other opponents. There was no doubt whatever about her getting a mile. Favoridge, about whom there had been plenty of doubt during the winter concerning both her stamina and her prospects of training on, came out the following week in the seven-furlong Nell Gwyn Stakes at Newmarket and beat a stronger field than the Imprudence's; she too won easing up by a length and a half, from Annie Edge and Royal Heroine both of whom were also allowed to take their chance in the Guineas. Altogether sixteen fillies opposed Ma Biche and Favoridge in the Guineas, a surprisingly large number in view of the credentials of the principals; as usual some of the runners had no business in a classic field. Ma Biche started at 5/2, Favoridge at 7/2, Habibti and Royal Heroine at 10/1; half the field started at 40/1 or upwards, among them the Papin third Crime of Passion. In the paddock Ma Biche was more forward in her coat than the English fillies (there was no Irish challenger on this occasion), alone looking really bright and well, but though she impressed with her well-being she didn't physically dwarf her rivals as she'd done before the Cheveley Park.

Crime of Passion, by temperament and breeding a sprinter, refused to settle early on and she took them along at a good clip until she gave way to Annie Edge and Royal Heroine after five furlongs or so. At this stage the field remained fairly well bunched, with 100/1-shot Rare Roberta surpassing herself and challenging hard, and the jockeys on Ma Biche and Favoridge shadowing each other about three lengths off the lead. A furlong later it seemed as though in watching one another they'd perhaps overlooked Royal Heroine, for she'd slipped into a handy lead. Then Ma Biche began to make her run on the stand side, while Favoridge began hers more towards the middle of the track on the outside of Royal Heroine, Rare Roberta and Annie Edge. Ma Biche had always been moving strongly, always slightly ahead of Favoridge, and she quickened well to make her challenge running into the Dip. Almost as soon as she struck the rising ground Ma Biche had the race won. She went past Royal Heroine into the lead and held off the latter's renewed efforts with a very strong finish that saw her home by a length and a half. Favoridge weakened towards the end after having every chance; in contrast Habibti ran on into fourth place—in so doing delaying her return to sprinting. Ma Biche became the first French-trained winner of the One Thousand Guineas since 1976 and only the third in twenty years, following Flying Water, who was afterwards well beaten in the Prix Saint-Alary as a three-year-old, and the brilliant Hula Dancer who was beaten only once in nine races and afterwards won the Prix Jacques le Marois, the Prix du Moulin de Longchamp and the Champion Stakes. Through Ma Biche her trainer became the first licensed woman trainer of an English classic winner; Mme Head had trained some notable horses previously, the best of them the Prix de l'Arc winner Three Troikas.

Ma Biche was beaten in the Marois and had to miss the Moulin; it was never the intention to run in the Saint-Alary or the Champion Stakes over a mile and a quarter. She also had to forego an excellent opportunity in her first objective after the Guineas, the Coronation Stakes at Royal Ascot won narrowly by Flame of Tara from Favoridge, and wasn't ready to run again until August. Even then she wasn't at her best. Giving weight all round in the Prix d'Astarte at Deauville she ran as though she needed the race, flattering for a few strides below the distance then weakening quickly into sixth place behind Luth Enchantee. Beforehand she looked bigger than at Newmarket, well in herself and very much on her toes; she failed to impress on the way down, moving as though feeling the firmish ground. She ran better in the Prix Jacques le Marois later on at the meeting without quite reaching her best, finishing fourth of ten to Luth Enchantee, beaten just over four lengths. Again she challenged only to fall back. She needed to be on top form to have any chance of winning such a strongly-contested race. Ma Biche did not reappear until late October, when she ran in the seven-furlong Prix de la Foret at Longchamp. With Luth Enchantee and L'Emigrant out of the way in the United States and Salieri a last-minute withdrawal because of a bruised foot, her chances of picking up her fourth Group 1 win had obviously improved considerably, and she really took the eye in the paddock, belying the lateness of the season; but the opposition was still fairly strong (she met her elders on terms 3 lb worse than the weight-for-age in England) and the ground still on the firm side of good, which her record suggested might be against her. She won by half a length from Pampabird, the best older miler in France, making her effort in the straight, striking the front over a furlong out and running on just as strongly as in the Guineas. Aragon, having his first outing since Royal Ascot, finished third, three lengths behind Pampabird; the heavily-backed favourite Sackford finished fifth, outpaced throughout.

Ma Biche (USA) (b. or br.f. 1980)	Key To The Kingdom (b or br 1970)	Bold Ruler (b 1954)	Nasrullah / Miss Disco
		Key Bridge (b 1959)	Princequillo / Blue Banner
	Madge (b 1975)	Roi Dagobert (b 1964)	Sicambre / Dame d'Atour
		Midget II (gr 1953)	Djebe / Mimi

Like Shareef Dancer Ma Biche was bred in the United States, sired by a North American-bred stallion; her dam is French, though, whereas his is North American. Ma Biche's sire Key To The Kingdom is half-brother to two top-class middle-distance horses in the States, the dual Washington International winner Fort Marcy

Maktoum Al-Maktoum's "Ma Biche" (F. Head)

MAC

and the champion 1972 three-year-old Key To The Mint, the latter the sire of the latest Royal Lodge Stakes winner Gold And Ivory. Key To The Kingdom wasn't so good as his half-brothers on the racecourse but was a stakes winner at up to nine furlongs. The 1982 Arlington-Washington Lassie winner For Once'n My Life is the best of his runners in the States; in England his son the sprinter Flash N Thunder won the Duke of York Stakes in 1980.

Ma Biche is her dam's first foal. The second, a colt called North Madgic (by Far North), was sold as a yearling for 260,000 guineas at the Newmarket Sales and is in training in France with Boutin. Madge, the dam, won over eleven furlongs in France; her main task was to act as pacemaker for the top-class fillies Reine de Saba and Dancing Maid, either of whom will do well to equal its pacemaker's success as a broodmare. Madge's dam Midget II produced nine winners from twelve foals, the pick of them Mige, who shared with her dam and with Ma Biche the distinction of winning the Cheveley Park Stakes. For Midget as for Ma Biche winning the Cheveley Park was not the high point of her career: in an eventful three years she also picked up the Coronation Stakes, the Queen Elizabeth II Stakes, the Prix de la Foret, the Prix Maurice de Gheest and the Prix de Meautry; she finished third in the Prix de Diane as well as second in the One Thousand Guineas. These were the days before the pattern-race system blighted racing, when top-class horses might be found in handicaps, and on one occasion as a four-year-old racegoers had the privilege of seeing her contest the Royal Hunt Cup: she started favourite with 9-2 and ran second to Retrial giving him a stone. The third dam also bred the King George VI and Queen Elizabeth Stakes winner Vimy and the Oaks third Noemi. A splendid family!

Ma Biche was one of the most imposing of the classic fillies of 1983—a most taking individual, big, rangy and good-bodied. Her short, round action was nothing to write home about, though. Probably some give in the ground suited her action ideally, but she managed to win the Foret on good to firm. Fast enough as a two-year-old to win top races over sprint distances, Ma Biche at three years was effective at seven furlongs and ran as though she'd stay further than a mile. She was nearly always held up. *Mme C. Head, France.*

MACARTHURS HEAD 2 ch.c. Dom Racine 121–Mother Brown 103 (Candy Cane 125) (1983 7g² 8g*) Apr 1; rangy, attractive colt; good mover; half-brother to 1980 2-y-o 1m seller winner Orkney Annie (by Scottish Rifle), subsequently successful in Guernsey; dam genuine handicapper at up to 1¼m; had to be kept up to his work when landing the odds by a length from Marlion in 18-runner maiden race at Ayr in September; had previously put in a determined challenge in last 2f when failing by only a head to peg back more-experienced Lucky Scott in £5,000 event at Kempton; will be well suited by 1¼m+; a useful handicapper in the making. *J. Dunlop.* 88 p

MAC KELLY 9 b.g. Irish Ball 127–Gala Honey 66 (Honeyway 125) (1982 NR 1983 18fg) lightly raced on flat nowadays but is a useful jumper; stays well; needs plenty of give in the ground; ran abysmally when tried in blinkers. *T. Bulgin.* –

MACMILLION 4 br.c. So Blessed 130–Salsafy 81 (Tudor Melody 129) (1982 7fg³ 8fg 6d 8g² 7.3g 7g 8s² 1983 8s 8d 8g 7g 8d 7f) workmanlike colt; useful on his day but has deteriorated; suited by 1m; acts on any going; blinkered second start; often taken down early; usually ridden up with pace; trained by A. Bailey first 2 outings. *Mrs B. Waring.* –

MACPHAIL 3 b.g. Captain James 123–Sadie Thompson 82 (Sheshoon 132) (1982 6g 1983 10fg 11.7f⁴ 11.5g) tall, well-made gelding; remote fourth of 7 behind Gildoran in minor event at Bath in July; should be suited by middle distances; sold 2,000 gns Newmarket Autumn Sales and exported to Malaysia. *P. Walwyn.* –

MAC'S HUSSAR 2 ch.g. Queen's Hussar 124–Ryehaven (Sea Hawk II 131) (1983 7fg) Apr 27; 3,500Y; half-brother to very good Scandinavian winners Opatia and Sister Sala (both by Double-U-Jay); dam never ran; thirteenth of 15 in minor event at Brighton in September. *J. Old.* –

MAC'S OR MINE 2 ch.g. Connaught 130–Cropfall 79 (Acropolis 132) (1983 6fg 7fg 7g) Mar 31; 7,600Y; sturdy gelding; third reported foal; dam 1¾m winner; in rear in maiden events. *J. Old.* –

MAC'S PALACE 3 gr.c. Dragonara Palace 115–Swan Ann 84 (My Swanee 122) (1982 5f³ 5fg* 5fg* 6fg* 5g 6f² 5g² 7g 5v² 5d³ 1983 6v 5g² 5f 6f 5f 5.3fg⁴) rangy, useful-looking colt; very useful at 2 yrs when trained by W. O'Gorman; ran best race of 1983 when 2½ lengths second of 11 to Touch Boy in quite well-contested race at Beverley in June; had stiffish tasks next 2 starts and disappointed 104

502

on his final one (blinkered); effective at 5f and 6f; acts on any going; often bandaged in front at 2 yrs. *M. Blanshard.*

MADAGASCAR 3 ch.g. Warpath 113–Jasmin (Frankincense 120) (1982 6g 6g **81** 7g 1983 9.4d* 8g* 9g* 10g⁴ 8.2fg 8d 10f 8.2fg) workmanlike gelding; good walker; won 20-runner maiden race at Carlisle in May and handicaps at Beverley and Hamilton in June; put up best subsequent effort in a handicap on seventh start; stays 1¼m; suitable mount for an apprentice; sold 10,000 gns Doncaster November Sales. *C. Thornton.*

MADAM BREEZE 3 br.f. Tumble Wind–Golda (Red God 128§) (1982 5fg⁴ 6g 6fg **66** 6g 1983 9v³ 10.6v 7fg 8g² 7fg³ 8d 8d) leggy filly; placed in a minor event at Wolverhampton and 2 selling handicaps at Newmarket; promises to stay at least 9f; doesn't find much off bridle; sold 4,200 gns Newmarket December Sales. *M. Jarvis.*

MADAME DANCER (CAN) 3 ch.f. Northern Dancer–Madame Royale (Forli) **66** (1982 NR 1983 10.4g* 11.7g⁴) sturdy, good-bodied filly; half-sister to a minor stakes winner in USA by Crowned Prince and French middle-distance winner Zante (by Sir Gaylord); dam, from an extremely successful American family, ran only 3 times; second favourite but in need of a race, kept on well to be 7 lengths second of 14 to Guess Who in maiden race at Chester in August; awarded race 2½ weeks later as rider of winner had drawn wrong allowance; heavily-backed favourite when creditable fourth behind Statesmanship in handicap at Bath in October, only other outing; stays 1½m; sold to BBA 240,000 gns Newmarket December Sales. *B. Hills.*

MADAME DE COOMBE 2 gr.f. John de Coombe 122–Tassel (Ragusa 137) **54** (1983 6f 7f 7.6d 10fg) Mar 3; 1,050Y; strong, good-topped filly; fifth foal; dam poor maiden; poor maiden; form only on second outing. *C. Horgan.*

MADAME MIM 3 b.f. Artaius 129–Spring Valley (Val de Loir 133) (1982 6g 7d **57** 1983 7s 10.5s 12d³ 13.8s 12.2fg 10fg 8.2g 10fg) big filly; third of 18 behind impressive Celestial Air in maiden race at Thirsk in May, best effort; suited by 1½m; blinkered third to sixth starts. *B. Hanbury.*

MADAM FLUTTERBYE 3 ch.f. Quiet Fling 124–Balgreggan (Hallez 131) **82** (1982 7fg 8f⁴ 1983 9v⁴ 10.1fg 10f 10f³ 12fg² 12f* 12g⁴ 13.3g 16fg) tall, sparely-made filly; in frame several times and won handicap at Leicester in August with a bit in hand; suited by 1½m and should get further; best form on firm going; appeared to get bumped on final start. *N. Vigors.*

MADAM IMPORT 3 ch.f. Import 127–Chinese Falcon 81 (Skymaster 126) **–** (1982 5s³ 5g⁴(dis) 5f 5g 5g 1983 6fg 6g 7g 7g) fair sort; carries plenty of condition; plating-class maiden; ran best race of 1983 on first outing (September); blinkered final start in 1982. *T. Barron.*

MAESTRETTE 3 b.f. Manado 130–Camogie (Celtic Ash) (1982 6fg³ 7g³ 8s² **77** 8d² 1983 8v* 9s 10g 9f 8.2g 8.2s) leggy, lightly-made filly; beat Steps by 4 lengths in maiden event at Warwick in April (apprentice ridden) but showed little afterwards (blinkered fifth start); should be suited by 1¼m; seems to act on any going, but is clearly well suited by plenty of give. *S. Norton.*

MAFOO'S IMAGE 2 b.c. Pitskelly 122–Amiga Mia 71 (Be Friendly 130) (1983 **92** 7f 5f 7fg* 7fg³ 8d³ 7fg) Mar 11; IR 12,000F, 18,000Y; well-made colt; first foal; dam 6f winner; won 12-runner maiden race at Salisbury in September by 6 lengths from Corncharm; good third in nursery at York in October, penultimate outing and best subsequent effort; suited by 1m; acts on a firm and a soft surface. *R. Laing.*

MAFOO'S MANOR 2 ch.c. Manor Farm Boy 114–Flora Leigh 94 (Floribunda **60** 136) (1983 5v 5fg 7f 6f 6fg 10d³) May 17; 2,000F, 7,000Y; fair sort; plater; stays 1¼m; blinkered third to fifth outings; sold German International Bloodstock 8,000 gns Newmarket Autumn Sales. *J. Bethell.*

MAFOO'S MESSAGE 3 gr.g. Moulton 128–Queens Message 93 (Town Crier **–** 119) (1982 8s 1983 10s 14.6f 8f 10.5d) tall, workmanlike gelding; no worthwhile form in maiden races and a £4,000 seller; sold to CBA 4,000 gns Newmarket Autumn Sales. *J. Bethell.*

MAFOO'S TOKEN 3 ch.g. Record Token 128–Pall Nan 86 (Pall Mall 132) (1982 **79** NR 1983 8f 8f 8g² 8f³ 8.2g²) IR 10,000Y; workmanlike gelding; half-brother to several winners, including fairly useful 1979 2-y-o 7f winner Appleby Park (by Bay Express); dam best at 5f; placed in maiden races; gives impression he'll be suited by a bit further than 1m. *M. Smyly.*

MAGANYOS (HUN) 3 br.f. Pioneer–Marimba (Indikator) (1982 6g* 6g⁴ 7g⁴ **112** 1983 6v* 10s² 10.5v 10d 12.2fg* 12fg⁴ 12g* 10f 11g⁴ 12g⁴ 10.5g 12g* 10g) Hungarian-bred filly; won in Hungary on first outing as a 2-y-o and was subsequently fourth twice at Baden-Baden; did well in 1983, winning at

M D. Wildenstein's "Magdalena"

Evry, Frauenfeld (Swiss Derby), Chantilly and Nantes; picked up quite a good prize
on last-named course in November, beating Garthorn by a nose (pair clear) in
14-runner Grand Prix de Nantes; in frame on several other occasions, on tenth
outing finishing 12 lengths fourth of 8 behind Diamond Shoal in Grosser Preis von
Baden; stays middle distances (also won over 6f in modest company at start of
year); probably acts on any going; badly hampered final start. *Y. Porzier, France.*

MAGDALENA (USA) 3 ch.f. Northern Dancer–Madelia 127 (Caro 133) (1982   **119**
NR 1983 7d² 7v* 8g² 8f³) attractive, neat filly; first foal; dam, half-sister to
Mount Hagen and Monsanto, won all her 4 starts, including Poule d'Essai des
Pouliches, Prix Saint-Alary and Prix de Diane; shaped most promisingly when
going down by a head to What A Pity in newcomers race at Newbury in April and
justified favouritism without much fuss in maiden race at Goodwood the following
month, hacking over her 16 opponents 2f out and quickening up very smoothly to
beat Princess Zita easily by 2 lengths; ran only twice more over here, finishing 2
lengths second to Gaygo Lady when conceding nearly a stone all round in £4,100
race at Sandown later in May and just over a length third of 6 behind Flame of Tara
and Favoridge in Coronation Stakes at Royal Ascot in June; ran on extremely well
and put up a smart performance in last-named race, a particularly good effort
considering she was much the least experienced of the principals; suited by 1m;
acts on any going; sent to USA. *H. Cecil.*

MAGDOLIN PLACE 2 ch.g. Dublin Taxi–Watch Lady (Home Guard 129) (1983   **74**
5v⁴ 5f*) May 2; 1,300Y; fair sort; second foal; dam ran only twice; won 10-runner
maiden auction event at Pontefract in June by 4 lengths from Natina-May; last of 4
in seller at Newcastle in April previously; evidently goes well on firm going;
exported to Hong Kong. *D. Garraton.*

MAGIC 2 ch.f. Sweet Revenge 129–No Delay 72 (Never Say Die 137) (1983 5d³   **71**
5v² 5d* 5d³ 7f⁴ 6fg³ 8.2fg 7fg) Mar 8; IR 2,250Y; big, strong, workmanlike filly;
half-sister to several winners, including stayer and successful hurdler Sandalay (by
Sandford Lad); dam, suited by a test of stamina, is daughter of Nassau Stakes
winner Cracker; won weakly-contested minor event at Pontefract in April; off
course over 2 months after next outing, and didn't show much on return, although
impressing physically; probably stays 7f; seems to act on any going. *W. Wharton.*

MAGIC FORMULA 5 b.m. St Paddy 133–La Levantina (Le Levanstell 122)   –
(1982 NR 1983 16fg 20fg 15fg) lengthy mare; poor maiden; has worn blinkers;
cost 2,100 gns Ascot August Sales. *W. Musson.*

MAGIC MINK 3 ch.c. Record Token 128–Cowbells (Mountain Call 125) (1982 7d   **54**
7fg 7fg 8g 1983 7v 8f⁴ 7.6fg 8h⁴ 7h⁴ 8f² 8h 8h³) lengthy, useful-looking colt; good
walker; in frame in varied races; stays 1m; acts on hard ground; often blinkered;
suitable mount for an apprentice; trained by C. Nelson until after first outing. *R.
Holder.*

MAGIC MUSHROOM 2 gr.c. Rupert Bear 105–Circumstance 72 (Bleep-Bleep   **63**
134) (1983 5d⁴(dis) 5g 5f 6f³ 6g* 7fg 6f 6d) Mar 22; 620Y; lengthy, good-topped
colt; half-brother to 1m winner Peter The Butcher (by Autre Prince); fair
plater; bought in 2,700 gns after winning 6-runner event at Ayr in August; suited by
6f; acts on firm going. *D. Garraton.*

MAGNAMALA 4 ro.g. Runnymede 123–Mala Mala (Crepello 136) (1982 5f 5f   –
5f² 7f 5fg² 5fg 5g* 6fg³ 5f⁴ 5d 6s 5d⁴ 5d 1983 10.2d 6v 5g 5d 7d 6fg) lengthy, quite
useful sort; good walker; best at 5f; seems to act on any going; usually wears
blinkers. *M. Lambert.*

MAGNETIC FIELD 3 b.c. Northfields–Maid of Iron (Crozier USA) (1982 6f*   **109**
7g² 1983 10.1s⁴ 8f* 8f* 10.5fg 8fg) well-made, deep-girthed, quite attractive colt;
put up best effort in 18-runner £4,800 handicap at Goodwood in July, quickening
clear 2f out and holding on by 1½ lengths from Prego; landed the odds decisively by
1½ lengths from 50/1-chance Monaco Lady in 17-runner minor event at Salisbury
the following month; best form at 1m; acts well on firm going; very useful. *H.
Cecil.*

MAGUS 3 b.c. Solinus 130–Singing Witch 71 (Sing Sing 134) (1982 NR 1983 6v 6s   **61**
8f 8f 7f* 8f⁴ 7fg³ 7g 8g 8.2fg) 9,200Y; lengthy colt; half-brother to 1980 2-y-o 5f
winner La Belle Sorciere (by Sparkler) and 1978 2-y-o 5f and 6f winner Rose of
Shenfield (by Upper Case); dam half-sister to smart sprinter Vilgora; showed signs
of ability, though unplaced, before beating Emperor's Palace a neck in handicap at
Yarmouth in August; stays 7f; acts on firm going; soundly beaten in blinkers final
start. *M. Tompkins.*

MAHARALI (USA) 3 ch.g. Sauce Boat–Princess Grundini (Prince John) (1982   –
5fg 5f* 7f⁴ 5d 6g* 1983 6v 6g) stocky gelding; speedy, and possibly does not stay
7f; wears blinkers; exported to Malaysia. *R. Smyth.*

MAHOGANY 2 ch.f. Tap On Wood 130–Red Jade 82 (Red God 128§) (1983 7g*   **114** p
7fg*)

    Tap On Wood's stud career wasn't very far advanced before he hit the
headlines when the blood-typing tests carried out by Weatherbys proved that two
of his first-crop foals were not in fact by Tap On Wood. The finger of suspicion was
pointed firmly in the direction of the stud's teaser, a Connemara pony, and Tap On
Wood was subsequently moved from the Kildangan Stud to the Irish National Stud.
He received publicity of a much more favourable kind in 1982 when his son out of
Innocent Air, now named At Tarf, fetched 400,000 guineas, the year's top price for
a yearling in Britain and Ireland. And now that Tap On Wood's first runners have
appeared he has again hit the headlines. As many as eleven managed to win in
Britain and Ireland, with several showing plenty of potential: Red Russell was third
to El Gran Senor in the National Stakes; My Tootsie trotted up in two races in the
autumn; Rappa Tap Tap won the Blue Seal Stakes; Tapaculo took third place in the
Waterford Candelabra Stakes; Keep Tapping had the reputation of being one of the
best of Barry Hills's large string of two-year-olds; the Irish filly Park Lady won her
only completed race in good style; and Mahogany retired for the winter unbeaten in
two races and favourite for the One Thousand Guineas.

    Mahogany didn't make her first appearance until mid-September when one of
twenty-one runners in the Stable Stud and Farm Stakes at Newbury. She started at
10/1 in a market dominated by the only winner in the field, Seattle Siren, and gave
the impression beforehand that she wasn't fully wound up. Fully wound up or not,
she proved more than a match for the others. After moving into the lead coming to

Rockfel Stakes, Newmarket—Mahogany runs on in splendid style

the last quarter mile, she looked sure to be swamped as Seattle Siren drew alongside but she fought back so well that in the end she won going away by half a length. The eight-length margin back to the third-placed horse suggested strongly that the first two were way above average. Mahogany's trainer supported this view, naming the Royal Lodge as a possible target (he later claimed she was superior to her stable-companion Creag-An-Sgor). Mahogany missed the Royal Lodge in favour of the Rockfel Stakes at Newmarket in October, for which she started second favourite to the record-priced filly Kanz, who had looked a potential champion against lesser opposition at Leicester. Mahogany put up a display which confirmed her exceptional promise without proving her the equal of Creag-An-Sgor. Kanz's supporters knew their fate as soon as Mahogany swept past her into the lead two furlongs out and from then on Mahogany was never in danger despite the game efforts of Capricorn Belle, the winner of a twenty-nine-runner maiden race at Newmarket on her only previous start. At the line Mahogany was three lengths clear with the promising newcomer Sing Swing pipping Capricorn Belle for second. The next to finish, Vidalia, went on to win a good race in Italy by six lengths and

Mrs W. Tulloch's "Mahogany"

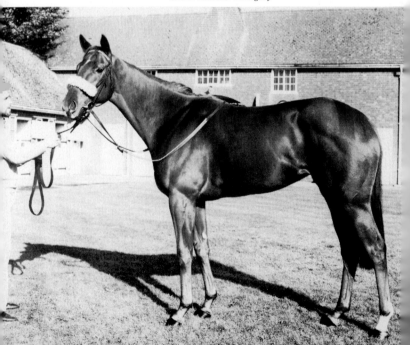

we're sure that several of the other runners will make their mark at three, especially the Mill Reef filly Sandy Island who shaped extremely well.

Mahogany (ch.f. Apr 19, 1981)			
	Tap On Wood (ch 1976)	Sallust (ch 1969)	Pall Mall
			Bandarilla
		Cat O'Mountaine (ch 1967)	Ragusa
			Marie Elizabeth
	Red Jade (ch 1975)	Red God (ch 1954)	Nasrullah
			Spring Run
		Tanzanite (ch 1968)	Mongo
			Bright Bauble

Mahogany's price as a yearling, 20,000 Irish guineas, compares very favourably with those paid for some of her Rockfel Stakes rivals—Kanz, Khwlah and Celtic Assembly cost nearly 3,000,000 dollars between them. Her three-year-old half-brother Red Minstrel, by Averof, has also proved a shrewd buy, more than recouping his purchase price of 6,000 guineas with four successes from a mile to a mile and a quarter. Red Minstrel and Mahogany are the first foals of Red Jade, whose own career consisted of five races at two, her one win coming in a five-furlong maiden race at Carlisle. Red Jade is herself one of four winners produced by the stakes-placed American filly Tanzanite; the others include the mile-and-a-half winner Lipstick and the fairly useful 1976 two-year-old one-mile winner Mined Illusion. Tanzanite won twice in the States, over four furlongs at two and over a mile at three, while her dam Bright Bauble won a division of the Ashland Stakes over six furlongs at three. Mahogany has already shown she stays seven furlongs and she gives the impression a mile will suit her very well. Whether she'll justify her position of favourite for the One Thousand Guineas is hard to say, but her form at two was little if any better than that of half a dozen other fillies. However, she's a sizeable, useful-looking filly, with plenty of further improvement in her and she looks sure to give an extremely good account of herself. *C. Nelson.*

MAHOGANY HALL 2 b.g. Red Alert 127–Wish A Dee (Wishing Star 117) (1983 6f 7f) Apr 9; IR 3,000Y; sturdy gelding; first foal; dam appeared of little account; behind in maiden auction events at Ripon in June and Catterick in July. *P. Calver.*   –

MAIDA VALE 4 br.f. Furry Glen 121–Gifted Samanta (Divine Gift 127) (1982 10f 11.7g 10f 12fg 10.1d 8g 8fg³ 10f² 12g³ 10fg² 10fg 10fg² 12fg² 7d² 8s 10s² 1983 10d 8fg³ 10f 10f³ 10f³ 8g³ 8fg⁴) small, lightly-made filly; plater; stays 1½m; acts on any going. *S. Woodman.*   38

MAIDEN HELL 2 b.g. Sagaro 133–Belinda Mede 86 (Runnymede 123) (1983 8.2fg) May 30; second living foal; brother to a plating-class animal; dam fair sprint maiden at 2 yrs; ninth of 16 in £3,400 event at Nottingham in October. *R. Laing.*

MAIDEN'S DANCE 3 b.f. Hotfoot 126–Rhine Maiden 106 (Crepello 136) (1982 5fg 6g 1983 9d³ 9f 10.2h 8.2h 8f 8g³ 8g³) lengthy filly; quite a moderate maiden; should be suited by 1¼m+; seems a little temperamental; sold 16,000 gns Newmarket December Sales. *P. Walwyn.*   60

MAID OF MILAN 3 ch.f. Home Guard 129–Farfisa 86 (Sassafras 135) (1982 7f 7d 8s² 1983 9v* 12f³ 10h 11.5g² 12d 10f) quite attractive filly; has a round action; decisively won 11-runner maiden event at Wolverhampton in May; probably ran best subsequent race when second in handicap at Yarmouth in September; stays 1½m; acts on any going, but is best with some give underfoot. *M. Stoute.*   78

MAILMAN 4 ch.g. Malacate 131–Sallail (Sallust 134) (1982 8.2fg⁴ 8g² 11.7f² 9f* 10.6h² 10.1fg* 8f² 8fg⁴ 8g* 10fg² 9d* 9d 1983.8v³ 8v 8.5g² 8d 10f* 10f² 11g* 10.2fg³ 10.2fg³ 9d* 8d* 10g*) tall, useful-looking gelding; good mover; had a splendid year, winning handicap at Beverley, valuable Prix de President et de Madame Max Dugniolle at Ostend, quite valuable handicaps at York (apprentices) and Newbury (beat Gouverno easing up) and Trofeo Cino del Duca at Milan; landed odds from Charlo Mio in last-named in November; stays 11f; acts on any going; good mount for an apprentice; consistent. *I. Balding.*   100

MAINTOP 6 b.g. High Top 131–Jujube 103 (Ribero 126) (1982 10f² 12fg* 12f⁴ 10d 12fg* 14g 13.3g 12g 1983 10f 10g 12f 10f² 11.7fg² 12fg² 10.2fg* 12fg 11d) strong gelding; fair handicapper on his day; won at Bath in September; stays 1½m; acts on a soft surface, but is much better suited by top-of-the-ground; blinkered last 4 starts in 1981; not particularly consistent. *M. Smyly.*   79

MAISSAN 2 ch.c. Nebbiolo 125–Spice Road (Gallant Man) (1983 7fg) Mar 25; IR 44,000Y; medium-sized, workmanlike colt; brother to smart Irish 3-y-o Burslem, a winner at up to 1m, and half-brother to numerous winners here and abroad, notably smart 1979 Irish 2-y-o 6f winner Noble Shamus (by Royal and Regal); dam won at   – p

507

up to 1m in USA; no show in 30-runner maiden at Newmarket in August; should do better. *P. Walwyn.*

MAJESTIC ENDEAVOUR (CAN) 3 b.c. Sham–Majestic Kahala (Majestic 108 Prince) (1982 NR 1983 8d* 10.5s 10fg* 10.5f³ 12f³) $170,000Y; lengthy, good-topped, quite attractive colt; first foal; dam one of best Canadian fillies in 1977 and 1978, winning at up to 1¼m; successful in 17-runner Wood Ditton Stakes at Newmarket in April and £6,100 Esal Handicap at Sandown in June, putting up a useful effort when beating Nestor decisively by 2½ lengths on latter course; third afterwards in John Smith's Magnet Cup (Handicap) at York (beaten 2 lengths by Bedtime) and Gordon Stakes at Goodwood (dead-heated with Russian Roubles, 4½ lengths behind easy winner John French), both in July; possibly doesn't quite stay 1½m; acts on firm going; said possibly to have ricked his back when tailed off second start. *M. Stoute.*

MAJESTIC FLIGHT 3 ch.c. Royal and Regal–Black Butterfly 78 (Prince —
Tenderfoot 126) (1982 6f 6g 1983 6v 5.1s 6fg 5g 6fg) compact, deep-girthed, quite attractive colt; behind in varied races, including an apprentice seller; sold 500 gns Ascot December Sales. *E. Eldin.*

MAJESTIC LAD 2 br.g. Royalty 130–Jane Bond 59 (Good Bond 122) (1983 8f 8s) 65 May 15; 1,100Y; lengthy gelding; second foal; half-brother to 1982 2-y-o 7f seller winner Water Pistol (by Scottish Rifle); dam won 5f seller at 2 yrs; 10½ lengths sixth of 14 finishers behind Flame Bearer in maiden race at Beverley in September, second outing. *M. Lambert.*

MAJESTIC PEACE (USA) 2 ch.c. Hold Your Peace–Sa Majeste (Majestic 82 Prince) (1983 7f 7g 8s³ 8fg) Mar 29; $42,000Y; good-looking colt; half-brother to 2 minor winners by Explodent; dam, 7f winner, is half-sister to high-class 1971 2-y-o Governor Max; moderate maiden; stays 1m; acts on soft going and a firm surface. *G. Pritchard-Gordon.*

MAJESTIC STAR 6 b. or br.g. Star Appeal 133–Vivante 87 (Bold Lad, Ire 133) —
(1982 10s 8d* 7fg 8d* 8d 8s² 10v 1983 8d 8g) neat, strong, good sort; good walker; very useful handicapper at 5 yrs in Ireland; needed run on reappearance in March; not seen out again until September and had very stiff task; stays 1¼m; acts on any going; suitable mount for an apprentice. *R. Simpson.*

MAJESTIC TOWER 4 ch.c. Tower Walk 130–Tzu-Hsi 66 (Songedor 116) (1982 8g —
5fg⁴ 6f 6g⁴ 6f 7g 6f⁴ 6g 6g² 5g 1983 6v 6d 5f) workmanlike colt; plater; stays 6f; acts on firm going; sometimes blinkered. *C. Gray.*

MAJICA 3 b.f. Morston 125–Seein Is Believin (Native Charger) (1982 7g 6g 1983 —
10s³ 12.2fg 10.1f⁴ 12g 12g 12f) leggy filly; plating-class maiden; should be suited by 1½m; sweated up fourth outing. *B. Hobbs.*

MAJNOON LEYLA 4 b.g. So Blessed 130–Anna Barry 76 (Falls of Clyde 126) —
(1982 NR 1983 5.3fg³ 8fg 8g 7.6g 6fg) 15,000Y; good sort; half-brother to 3 winners, including useful 5f performer Heywood Hardy (by Tribal Chief) and sprinter Swan Ann (by My Swanee), herself dam of very speedy Swan Princess (by So Blessed); dam 5f sprinter; only plating class; seems to stay 1m; blinkered fourth outing. *M. Masson.*

MAJOR ANTHONY 3 b.c. Dublin Taxi–Chiltern Miss 85 (Hook Money 124) —
(1982 6fg 6g³ 6fg 7v 1983 8v⁴ 8s 8d 10g³ 12f 11.7fg⁴ 10.1f⁴ 10.1f 8f 8g 10g) tall, strong, good-topped colt; has a round action; in frame in varied races; probably stays 11.7f; seems ideally suited by some give in the ground; usually ridden up with pace. *J. Bosley.*

MAJOR BREW 3 b.g. Brigadier Gerard 144–Light Lager 91 (Crepello 136) (1982 —
6f 1983 6d 8s 7v⁴ 8v² 12d 8s) workmanlike gelding; poor mover; maiden plater; suited by 1½m; sold 460 gns Ascot October Sales. *P. Rohan.*

MAJOR DECISION 2 b.c. Mandrake Major 122–Ritratto (Pinturischio 116) 61 (1983 5v³ 6d 6f 6f 6f³) May 17; workmanlike colt; half-brother to 7f and 8.2f winner Italian Master (by Workboy); dam never ran; plating-class maiden; will stay 7f; acts on any going; usually sweats up; blinkered second outing; exported to Algeria. *M. H. Easterby.*

MAJOR DON 3 ch.g. Mandrake Major 122–Kindling (Psidium 130) (1982 6fg 109 7s² 1983 9.4d 8f² 7.2g* 7f* 7f⁴ 8f* 8fg³ 8fg* 7fg² 8d⁴) big, strong, good-bodied gelding; improved and developed into a useful performer; won £6,700 Sporting Chronicle Handicap at Haydock, £4,100 handicap at Leicester, minor event at Thirsk and £6,300 Julio Mariner Handicap at Doncaster; ran on strongly to beat Video King by 1½ lengths in last-named race in September and ran another sound race when 1½ lengths second to Never So Bold in £9,600 handicap at Ascot later in month; effective at 7f and 1m; acts on any going, but is well suited by a sound surface; game and genuine; ran too freely for his own good on final start. *E. Weymes.*

MAJOR DRAKE 4 ch.g. Mandrake Major 122–Lametta 94 (Alycidon 138) (1982 NR 1983 8.3fg 10h 10fg) good-bodied, plain gelding; no form in maiden races and sellers; has been tried in blinkers; cost 750 gns Ascot March Sales. *C. V. Miller.* —

MAJORIAN 5 b.g. Majority Blue 126–Tinker Lass (Tin Whistle 128) (1982 11s⁴ 10.2f 9fg 5fg 8f 11s 10.6s 8.2v 1983 8v 10fg 8fg) poor handicapper nowadays; stays 1¼m; evidently acts on any going; inconsistent and possibly needs things his own way; hooded once. *J. Harris.* —

MAJOR MARK 2 ch.c. Mandrake Major 122–Lochville 83 (Charlottesville 135) (1983 6fg 5g) June 6; 2,000Y; brother to 1982 2-y-o 1m seller winner Prolific Major, and half-brother to 3 winners; dam won over 8.7f; in rear in maiden races at Brighton and Warwick (auction event) in October. *C. Horgan.*

MAJOR MUSIC 2 b.g. Music Boy 124–Wendela (Manacle 123) (1983 5s 5fg 5f) Mar 13; 6,200Y; sturdy gelding; first foal; dam Irish 1m winner; no form in varied company. *A. Jarvis.*

MAJORS CAST 3 gr. or ro.c. Morston 125–Be Easy 110 (Be Friendly 130) (1982 6f 6g³ 1983 10s³ 10fg 12.3f⁴ 14f⁴ 12fg* 12f³ 11f) close-coupled, workmanlike colt; stayed on well to beat Haute Hat by 3 lengths in 7-runner maiden race at Redcar in August; stays 1¾m; probably acts on any going; possibly not entirely genuine; sold 7,400 gns Newmarket Autumn Sales, probably for export to Italy. *G. Wragg.* **78 §**

MAJOR SETBACK 4 b.g. Brigadier Gerard 144–Bedfellow 104 (Crepello 136) (1982 11.5fg 1983 12s⁴ 13v³ 16g 14s 8d 12f³ 13d* 13fg² 13f³) strong, lengthy gelding; good mover; showed much more resolution than runner-up when beating Two Minutes ½ length in slowly-run handicap at Ayr in June; stays 13f; acts on any going; blinkered first 4 starts; sold to R. Holder 4,000 gns Newmarket September Sales. *M. Naughton.* **61**

MAJOR'S REQUEST 2 b.g. Mandrake Major 122–Arkadia 74 (Larkspur 128) (1983 7f 7f 7g² 7g³ 7.2fg* 8s) May 15; 2,500Y; big, workmanlike gelding; half-brother to fair middle-distance winner Alexanda the Great (by So Blessed) and a winner abroad; dam, 1¼m winner, is half-sister to very smart Tesco Boy; won maiden auction event at Haydock in August by 4 lengths from Nashville Sandy but didn't look particularly enthusiastic, ducking left soon after leading 1f out; should stay 1m; acts on a firm surface and finished last on only outing on soft ground. *E. Weymes.* **82**

MAJUBA HILL 2 ch.c. Tap On Wood 130–Manfilia 95 (Mandamus 120) (1983 7fg 7fg 7g³) Apr 2; IR 46,000Y; half-brother to several winners, notably high-class 5f to 1¼m performer Kilijaro, smart French 9f to 13f winner African Hope (both by African Sky) and very useful 1981 2-y-o Codrington (by Malinowski); dam won at up to 1¼m; showed ability on all starts, on final one wearing blinkers when 5½ lengths third of 15 to Bold Patriach in minor event at Chepstow in October; will be suited by 1m. *J. Hindley.* **78**

MAJUSCULE (USA) 2 b.c. Majestic Light–Royal Stance (Dr Fager) (1983 8fg*) Apr 13; $275,000Y; second foal; dam unraced half-sister to very good animals Awaasif, Konafa and Akureyri; favourite, made all to account for Dow Jones comfortably by 2 lengths in minor event at Maisons-Laffitte in September; will be suited by middle distances; an interesting prospect. *F. Boutin, France.* **106 p**

MAKE ME HAPPY 2 gr.f. Saritamer 130–Quortina 83 (Quorum 126) (1983 5s⁴ 7fg 7s⁴) Apr 7; leggy filly; half-sister to 1978 2-y-o 6f seller winner Ben's the Boy (by Burglar); dam successful middle-distance handicapper; 4 lengths fourth of 19 to Ophrys in maiden race at Leicester in October; beaten in sellers previously; suited by 7f; sure to win a seller. *J. Holt.* **73**

MAKE YOUR BID 2 b.f. Auction Ring 123–Valeur (Val de Loir 133) (1983 6f) May 12; second foal; half-sister to 1982 2-y-o 6f winner Royal Valeur (by English Prince); dam second over 10.5f in France; behind in 23-runner maiden race at Lingfield in August. *J. Dunlop.* —

MAKING HAY 2 ch.f. Gay Fandango 132?–Belle Viking (Riverman 131) (1983 5f³ 5fg² 5fg² 5g) Feb 22; 7,000Y; tall, lightly-made filly; first foal; dam, from family of Vitiges, won over 1m and 1¼m in France; second in maiden races at Pontefract and Wolverhampton (beaten short head) in August; bred to stay a good bit further than 5f. *K. Brassey.* **78**

509

MALAAK (CAN) 2 ch.f. The Minstrel 135–Majestic Kahala (Majestic Prince) 110
(1983 5d⁴ 5f 6f² 6f* 6f² 6fg² 6fg) Mar 2; $650,000Y; well-made, attractive filly;
has a round action; second foal; half-sister to useful 1m and 1¼m winner Majestic
Endeavour (by Sham); dam of one of the best Canadian fillies in 1977 and 1978,
winning at up to 1¼m; readily landed odds of 6/4 on in maiden race at Redcar in
August; good second subsequently in useful company at Ripon and Salisbury, and
excellent fifth, running on, 1¾ lengths behind Desirable, in William Hill Cheveley
Park Stakes (blinkered) at Newmarket; will be extremely well suited by longer
distances; acts on firm going; carried her head bit high at Salisbury. *M. Stoute.*

MALACCA STREET 3 b.g. Wolverlife 115–Magic Lady (Gala Performance) 81
(1982 NR 1983 7d³ 6s³ 7f² 7.6fg 7f) 7,600Y; rather lightly-made gelding; fifth foal;
half-brother to a winner in Hong Kong; dam placed over 1½m in Ireland; quickened
up quite well when winning newcomers race at Doncaster in March; didn't run well
last 2 starts (blinkered final outing in July); finds 6f on the sharp side and will stay
1m; acts on any going; usually reluctant to go down. *W. O'Gorman.*

MALADHU 4 b.g. Malacate 131–Mhairi Dhu 88 (Great Nephew 126) (1982 8g 60
10.1f 8fg 13.1f⁴ 1983 9f 12f³ 10.6g 8.2s* 12fg³) fair sort; won handicap at
Hamilton in October; stays 1½m; acts on any going; suitable mount for an
inexperienced rider. *J. Fitzgerald.*

MALANG-LOU 2 br.f. Auction Ring 123–Relic Spirit (Relic) (1983 5g² 5s* 6v² 98
6s⁴ 6f³ 5f³ 6fg) Apr 27; fifth foal; half-sister to 3 winners, including useful 1980
Irish 2-y-o 5f performer Heart n' Soul (by Bold Lad, Ire); dam second 4 times
over sprint distances in Ireland; ran creditably most outings, including in pattern
company last 2 starts when 1¼ lengths third to Safe Home in Nishapour Curragh
Stakes in July and just over a length fifth to King Persian in Group 1 Heinz '57'
Phoenix Stakes the following month; had earlier won maiden race at Phoenix Park
by 2 lengths from Sharp Roi; not sure to stay 7f. *J. Bolger, Ireland.*

MALEK 3 ch.c. Be My Guest 126–Ananiyya (Faristan 123) (1982 NR 1983 12v 8f –
8fg) big, strong colt; third foal; dam French 2-y-o 1m winner; behind in maiden and
minor events; wore blinkers and was trained by W. O'Gorman first start. *Mrs B.
Waring.*

MALEVOLENT 3 b.f. Bustino 136–Namecaller 83 (Malicious) (1982 6v 1983 –
12s) rangy, quite attractive filly; showed a lot of promise at Ascot on only outing as
a 2-y-o; 25/1 and just in need of race, refused to settle and weakened quickly in last
2½f when tenth of 14 behind subsequently-disqualified stable-companion Civility in
minor event at Salisbury in May, only race at 3 yrs; sold 8,400 gns Newmarket
September Sales. *J. Tree.*

MALIBU BEACH 2 ch.c. Quiet Fling 124–Hi Jay (Double-U-Jay 120) (1983 67 p
10.2fg) Apr 16; 4,500F; fourth live foal; half-brother to a winning plater; dam won
5 times from 9f to 1¾m in Ireland; backward, 12½ lengths eighth of 24 behind
Raami in minor event at Doncaster in November; will stay well. *E. Eldin.*

MALIBU LAD 2 b.g. Malinowski 123–Beaume (Faraway Son 130) (1983 5v 5d –
6fg⁴ 6f) Apr 26; 2,600Y; compact gelding; bad plater; not raced after June;
blinkered final start. *E. Eldin.*

MALLARD SONG 9 b.g. Tudor Melody 129–Romping (Sir Gaylord) (1982 12d –
12f 16fg² 17.1s 1983 16s 12f) poor staying handicapper; has been beaten in a
seller; best on top-of-the-ground; has worn bandages; has run respectably for an
amateur rider. *Dr A. Jones.*

MALTESE PET 3 b.f. Dragonara Palace 115–Miss Carvin (Carvin 127) (1982 7d 74
1983 8g³ 8s² 8s 10g 9d 7fg* 8g 10f 8f 8fg) smallish, lightly-made filly; beat Princess
Zita by a length in minor event at Salisbury in June, but only fairly modest on
balance of her form; stays 1m and should get further; possibly not at her best on
really firm going but acts on any other; blinkered final start; sold 3,300 gns
Newmarket December Sales. *R. Baker.*

MALVAN 7 b. or br.g. Decoy Boy 129–Khanum 81 (Soueida 111) (1982 11f 10fg 12f –
8d⁴ 8g² 8fg³ 8fg² 10g* 8fg 8fg 12.2s² 1983 10s 11.7d 11v 10.8v 10f) quite a
moderate handicapper at his best; well beaten in 1983; stays 1½m; acts on any
going, but is well suited by some give underfoot; effective with or without blinkers;
good mount for a boy; changed hands 1,550 gns Ascot March Sales; sold 1,050 gns
Ascot 2nd June Sales. *J. Bosley.*

MALVERN BEAUTY 3 b.f. Shirley Heights 130–Perfect Picture 78 (Hopeful 100
Venture 125) (1982 NR 1983 10.5s* 12fg 14.6fg 12fg) rangy, rather unfurnished
filly; third foal; dam lightly-raced daughter of 1000 Guineas second Photo Flash;
easy in market but looking pretty fit when staying on strongly to beat Peaceful Run

by 5 lengths in 12-runner minor event at York in May; had much stiffer tasks when towards rear in Ribblesdale Stakes at Royal Ascot, Park Hill Stakes at Doncaster and Princess Royal Stakes at Ascot again afterwards; should be suited by 1½m; acts on soft going; sold 21,000 gns Goffs November Sales. *H. Cecil.*

MAMIE 3 ch.f. Roman Warrior 132–Shady Desire 88 (Meldrum 112) (1982 5f 5s 7f 5s 6s 1983 10fg) strong, sturdy filly; of little account and probably temperamental. *M. McCormack.* —

MAMUNIA (USA) 3 b.f. Cutlass–Sparkling Spear (Raise A Native) (1982 6f 7fg* 7g* 7fg³ 6d 1983 8v 8g 7fg 7fg 7f) lengthy filly; fairly useful at 2 yrs but didn't recover her form in 1983; needs at least 7f; pulled hard on way down fourth outing and unseated rider when saddle slipped final start. *L. Cumani.* —

MAMUT 2 b.c. Comedy Star 121–Bonsella 68 (Carlemont 132) (1983 5s³ 5d 6d) Feb 26; 8,200F, 18,000Y; attractive colt; half-brother to a winning plater and a winner abroad; dam placed at up to 1¼m; disappointing maiden; not raced after June; exported to Malaysia. *W. O'Gorman.* — 72

MANAGERESS 3 br.f. Mandamus 120–Fire Hawk 70 (Firestreak 125) (1982 5.1g 6f* 6g 8.2s 1983 10s 8f 10f 8f 11.7f 12f) close-coupled, workmanlike filly; no form in 1983; should stay 1m. *P. Feilden.* —

MANCHESTERSKYTRAIN 4 b.g. Home Guard 129–Aswellas 93 (Le Levanstell 122) (1982 5d 5f 6f 8fg 8fg 1983 7s 8f 6h³ 6f³ 7f 6fg³ 6f 8fg 8fg 6d) strong, well-made gelding; stays at least 6f; acts on fast ground; blinkered final start. *G. Cottrell.* — 61

MANDARIN BAY 2 b.c. Orange Bay 131–Ardice 91 (Hard Tack 111§) (1983 6d) Mar 11; 3,300Y; workmanlike colt; half-brother to 3-y-o Drum Maker (by Scottish Rifle) and 2 winners, including 1¼m winner Morice (by Morston); dam fed to 1m performer; ninth of 11 in maiden race at Doncaster in May. *M. Lambert.* —

MANDELSTAM (USA) 3 b.c. Vaguely Noble 140–Abergwaun 128 (Bounteous 125) (1982 7g* 7d⁴ 1983 8s² 8d) useful-looking colt; shows traces of stringhalt; won maiden race and finished fourth in Houghton Stakes, both at Newmarket, as a 2-y-o; needed race and ran well when second to Hawkley in handicap at Newbury in April but was never dangerous at Newmarket later in month on only subsequent outing; suited by 1m; yet to race on a firm surface. *H. Cecil.* — 89

MANDOWN LAD 3 ch.c. Sexton Blake 126–Lanata 64 (Charlottown 127) (1983 5s* 5s² 6d 6f 7f 7f³ 7fg³ 7fg 7g) May 16; IR 1,200Y (privately); small, good-quartered colt; half-brother to a winner in Holland; dam placed over 5f at 2 yrs; won 9-runner maiden race at Newbury in April; apprentice-ridden third in small race at Catterick and nursery at Redcar in the summer; will stay 1¼m; acts on any going. *K. Brassey.* — 82

MANDRAKE BELLE 4 ch.c. Mandrake Major 122–Janabelle 101 (Gentle Art 121) (1982 5f 5fg 5g 5fg 5g 5fg² 5d 5d 1983 5v 5s 5v 5fg* 5.3f 5f⁴ 5.8h⁴ 5f⁴ 5g³ 5g) compact colt; won handicap at Warwick in June; acts on any going; effective with or without blinkers; has run respectably for an apprentice; has worn a brush-pricker on near-side of bridle; has been taken down early. *B. Gubby.* — 61 d

MANDRIANO 4 ch.g. Manado 130–Indian Runner (Sallust 134) (1982 8fg 8fg 8g 1983 8s 10.1d 8f) workmanlike gelding; of little account nowadays; has been blinkered; sold 450 gns Ascot September Sales. *W. R. Williams.* —

MANDY ANN 3 ch.f. Sweet Revenge 129–Pompadour (Levmoss 133) (1982 NR 1983 6v 6s 6d) 900F; fourth produce; dam unplaced 5 times in Ireland; well behind in 3 races in Scotland, first of them a seller. *W. H. Williams.* —

MANDY'S TIME 7 b.m. High Time 96–Mandy's Melody (Highland Melody 112) (1982 10.2g 1983 13.8g 10f) poor performer; had worn blinkers; dead. *J. Harris.* —

MANERLY 2 b. or br.c. Mansingh 120–Vaguely Hopeful 65 (Fortino II 120) (1983 5fg 5fg⁴ 6f* 6f 6fg*(dis) 6g) Mar 28; 5,000Y; robust colt; half-brother to 3 winners here and abroad, including quite useful 1m to 1¼m winner Doubly Hopeful (by Double Jump); dam ran only 3 times; won 17-runner maiden race at Thirsk in July and £4,500 nursery at Redcar in September, only to be disqualified on second occasion for hampering 2 of his rivals at start; suited by 6f; acts well on firm going and has yet to race on soft surface. *H. T. Jones.* — 87

MANGALA'S PRIDE 2 b.f. Mandrake Major 122–Lingala (Pinturischio 116) (1983 5v 6f 7fg 6f) Apr 26; big, workmanlike filly; half-sister to a winner in Malaya; dam lightly raced on flat and over hurdles; plating-class maiden; form only on second outing; should stay 7f; played up second and third appearances. *P. Rohan.* — 64

MANGO MAN 2 br. g. Mansingh 120–Pearl Drop 86 (Gulf Pearl 117) (1983 6fg 7f 74
7fg 7d 7fg⁴) Apr 15; 7,000Y; strong, well-made gelding; second living foal; dam
2-y-o 7f winner; blinkered first time, 6 lengths fourth of 15 to Muckle Roe in minor
event at Brighton in September; stays 7f. *R. Smyth.*

MANHATTEN MISS 3 b.f. Artaius 129–Habanna 107 (Habitat 134) (1982 6d³ 94
7d² 1983 6fg* 8fg 6f 6fg⁴ 6d² 7g³ 6d) IR 24,000F, 64,000Y; raced under wrong
pedigree first 4 starts with dam incorrectly shown as Moon Min (by First Landing);
fourth foal; half-sister to Irish 7f and 1¼m winner Millrock (by Bustino); dam Irish
2-y-o 5f and 6f winner; won £4,000 race at Phoenix Park in June, starting second
favourite and beating Beat The Drum by a length; ran best subsequent races when
in frame in 2 quite valuable races on same course and in handicap at the Curragh, in
last-named event finishing 3 lengths second of 20 behind Checker Express under
9-10; bred to stay 1m. *T. Curtin, Ireland.*

MANILOW 6 ch. g. Singing Bede 122–Lease Lend 96 (Cash and Courage 116) 85
(1982 6d 6g 5f³ 5fg² 5f 5.1f* 5g 5f³ 5g 5fg 5fg 1983 6s 5s 5d 5g* 5f 5.3f² 5f 5fg³
5fg³ 5f² 5f* 5fg) strong, good sort; sprint handicapper; made all to win at Lingfield
in June and landed the odds in apprentice race at Chepstow in September; best at
5f; needs a sound surface; good mount for an apprentice; wears a tongue strap;
usually taken down quietly. *B. Swift.*

MANIMSTAR 3 b.c. Martinmas 128–Reddish Radish (Red God 128§) (1982 6f 6fg 92 d
6g⁴ 1983 6v² 6s² 6d* 6g* 6fg 6f 6fg 6g) rangy, useful sort; in good form in first half of
season and was held up when winning handicaps at Kempton (in very good style from
Matou) and Newbury (by a head from Vino Rosso); fairly lightly raced afterwards;
stays 6f; well suited by some give in the ground; usually blinkered nowadays; sold to
P. Makin 6,200 gns Newmarket Autumn Sales. *M. Jarvis.*

MAN IN GREY 3 gr.c. Bonne Noel 115–Little Fuss (Sovereign Path 125) (1982 80
NR 1983 8f 10g 11.5g 12d* 10g³) good-bodied, quite attractive colt; brother to
smart 1¼m winner Noelino and high-class 1m to 1½m filly Little Bonny, and
half-brother to a winner; dam never ran; well-backed favourite, showed improved
form to win 12-runner maiden race at Newbury in October by ¾ length from
Maprang, coming from well back to lead going into last 100 yds; had stiff task when
third to Sunoak in amateur riders event at Lingfield later in month; very well suited
by 1½m and will also be suited by further; the type to win more races as a 4-y-o.
G. Pritchard-Gordon.

MAN IN THE MIDDLE 7 ch. g. Good Bond 122–Sharp Work 110 (Beau Sabreur —
125) (1982 7.5g 8s 10v³ 9.5g* 10d 8g 10.4g* 10g⁴ 8f 8g 8v³ 8.2s* 8s⁴ 1983 8s
9.5g* 10v² 10v 8d 8v 10s 8fg 9d 11d) big gelding; won at Pisa and was second on
same course in March; showed little afterwards; stays 1¼m well; suited by some
give in the ground and acts well in the mud; effective with and without blinkers;
sometimes starts slowly. *D. Sasse.*

MANIX 2 b.c. Manado 130–Ixee (Breton 130) (1983 6fg 7f 7fg 8fg) Mar 30; IR —
2,000F, 2,000Y; leggy, lengthy colt; second foal; dam never ran; no sign of ability,
including in valuable sellers; blinkered final start; sold 1,000 gns Ascot November
Sales. *I. Walker.*

MANLIGHT 3 b.c. Manado 130–Lady Habitat (Habitat 134) (1982 5g³ 5s² 1983 ?
6s² 6v) smallish, sparely-made colt; ¾-length second to odds-on Solimile in minor
event at Leicester in March; ran poorly in blinkers next time and was subsequently
sent to Italy (winner there); will be suited by 7f. *L. Cumani.*

MAN OF SPIRIT 4 b.g. Vitiges 132–Dauphine 102 (Pampered King 121) (1982 —
10f 13fg* 12g³ 13.8f* 16f* 16f 15.8d 19s³ 16v* 1983 18d⁴ 16g 17.1v) attractive,
well-made gelding; stays very well; acts on any going; has run respectably for an
apprentice. *J. Dunlop.*

MAN O'MAGIC 2 br.c. Manado 130–Garrucha 117 (Prince Taj 123) (1983 7f 7fg) —
May 7; 7,400F; tall, slightly leggy colt; half-brother to numerous winners,
including top 1975 Italian 2-y-o Northern Spring (by My Swallow) and useful
sprinter Peranka (by Klairon or Palestine); dam sprinter; in rear in good-class
events at Salisbury in August and Ascot (with leaders 5f) in September. *D. Sasse.*

MANOR FARM DOUBLE 2 ch.f. Decoy Boy 129–Teresa-Hernandez (Queen's —
Hussar 124) (1983 5d) Apr 3; 300F; half-sister to winning sprinter Vaquero (by
Burglar); dam never ran; remote last of 6 in seller at Hamilton in May. *M.
Tompkins.*

MANOR FARM LADY 2 gr.f. Manor Farm Boy 114–Lob (Master Sing 109) 48
(1983 5s 6g 6f 6f² 7fg 7h) Mar 20; 2,000Y; neat filly; poor plater; blinkered fourth
and fifth outings; dwelt last 2 starts; exported to Algeria. *G. Blum.*

MANOR FARM LEGACY 6 b.g. Royalty 130–Winklepicker (Hotfoot 126) (1982 NR 1983 10fg) plater; tailed-off last in non-seller only start at 6 yrs in June; stays 11f; acts well on soft going. *B. Richmond.* —

MANOR FARM TOOTS 4 br.f. Royalty 130–Winklepicker (Hotfoot 126) (1982 8fg 10g 10g 1983 13d* 12g4 12d* 15fg3 16.1fg3 16.1fg 13s) leggy filly; poor mover; decisively won handicaps at Hamilton in May and Carlisle in June; also ran well on fifth start; suited by a test of stamina; seems to act on any going; has run creditably for an apprentice; has shown signs of temperament. *M. Tompkins.* **63**

MANSERIN 3 b.g. Mansingh 120–Kaiserin (Carapalida) (1982 5fg 5fg 6g 8.2fg 1983 8s 10.2g 12f4 13.8f2) smallish, workmanlike gelding; plater; seems suited by a test of stamina; has been tried in blinkers. *J. Bethell.* **35**

MANTEL OAK 2 b.c. Mummy's Pet 125–Aunt Augusta 90 (Counsel 118) (1983 5d3 6fg 5f 6g 5fg2 5d2 5g) Feb 6; 21,000Y; robust, good sort; second foal; brother to 5f winner Augusta's Pet; dam won over 1½m and 1¾m; moderate maiden; best form at 5f; acts on a firm and a soft surface; blinkered last 3 outings; exported to Malaysia. *G. Hunter.* **80**

MANX 3 ch.c. Riverman 131–Dorignies (Yelapa 130) (1982 NR 1983 12f* 12f4 15s) $50,000Y; small colt; second foal; dam won small races from 9f to 11f in France; only lightly raced, but won maiden race at Redcar in July, staying on well; promises to stay further than 1½m, but was never going well when tried at 15f on final start; sold 1,300 gns Newmarket Autumn Sales. *J. W. Watts.* **78**

MANX GOD 2 b.g. Welsh Saint 126–White Goddess 65 (Red God 128§) (1983 5v 5d 5g2 5d3 5f 6fg4 5f 5f 5g 5g 5g) Apr 2; 820Y; 6,200 2-y-o; neat gelding; half-brother to quite moderate middle-distance performer China God (by Cumshaw) and a winner abroad; dam stayed 1m; plating-class maiden; suited by a sharp 5f; seems to act on any going; best in blinkers; sold 430 gns Ascot December Sales. *D. Chapman.* **62**

MANX SWALLOW 4 b.c. Habitat 134–Swallow (Forli) (1982 6s 8fg 8fg 7g 7.2g 7fg 8f 7s 1983 8d 8f4 10.4fg 10fg 10s 10.6g) useful sort; poor maiden; stays 1m; sold 520 gns Doncaster November Sales. *R. Hollinshead.* —

MA PIERRETTE 4 b.f. Cawston's Clown 113–Wigeon 80 (Divine Gift 127) (1982 6fg 6g 7fg4 7d* 7d 7f4 8f* 8g 8g4 8g4 9s3 8g 8s 1983 10v 8g2 10s 8f4 9f4 10fg* 8f 10g 8f 10d2 9fg 8g 10.2fg) leggy, light-framed filly; poor mover; quite a moderate handicapper; won at Ripon in July; suited by 1¼m; acts on any going; suitable mount for an apprentice; has run creditably when sweating up. *D. Dale.* **77**

MAPRANG 3 b.c. Mill Reef 141–First Huntress (Primera 131) (1982 7f 8g 7g4 1983 10.1fg 12g 10.8d3 12d2) well-made, attractive colt; looked all over a winner when taking up running 3f out in maiden event at Newbury in October but flashed his tail when challenged, refused to struggle near finish and went down by ¾ length to Man in Grey; suited by 1¼m+; wears blinkers; sold 26,000 gns Newmarket Autumn Sales, probably for export to Australia. *R. Hern.* **79 §**

MAPUTO PRINCESS 3 b.f. Raga Navarro 119–Buggles 66 (Kelly 122) (1982 5g 6f 1983 5v 6s 7f 7f 7fg) smallish filly; behind in varied company, including selling; often bandaged on off-hind. *K. Stone.* —

MARALINGO 3 br.g. Saulingo 122–Rose Marullah 104 (Valerullah 113) (1982 5s4 5f 5fg3 5f* 7f2 5fg4 6f3 6g3 6d 1983 8d2 8d 9.4f 8fg2 7f) rather leggy, close-coupled gelding; inconsistent plater; stays 1m; probably acts on any going. *A. W. Jones.* **51**

MARAMI 2 ch.f. Bay Express 132–Cala Blava (Moulton 128) (1983 6fg) Apr 19; 9,000Y; fair sort; second foal; dam unraced half-sister to Give Thanks; in mid-division in 29-runner maiden race at Newmarket in September. *G. Huffer.* —

MARASALI (FR) 5 b.h. Tennyson 124–Monique (Tanerko 134) (1982 12d 12d3 12fg 10.5g 12s 15g* 15fg3 13.5g 20s 12v* 15.5v 1983 12s* 12s 12v3 12f) strong, good-bodied, deep-girthed horse; smart performer on his day; won Prix d'Hedouville at Longchamp in April by 1½ lengths from Terreno; creditable 2¾ lengths third to Welsh Term in Prix Jean de Chaudenay at Saint-Cloud in May; not seen out again after finishing well beaten in La Coupe at Chantilly in June; one paced and stays well; revels in the mud; blinkered once at 4 yrs. *O. Douieb, France.* **119**

MARCH AT DAWN 3 ro.f. Nishapour 125–Mansi (Pardao 120) (1982 NR 1983 7d 9f 5fg) IR 3,000Y; lengthy, sparely-made filly; fourth foal; dam 2-y-o 7f winner in France; behind in minor events and a maiden race; sweated up second start. *B. McMahon.* —

MARCHING TIME 2 b. g. Stanford 121§–Lydja 75 (Hethersett 134) (1983 5s 6g 8d) Apr 28; IR 13,000F, 21,000Y; fair sort; half-brother to several winners, including Troms (by Wolver Hollow), useful winner at up to 1¼m in France; dam stayed 1¼m; little form in maiden races; off course 4 months after second outing; sold 2,500 gns Newmarket Autumn Sales for export to Malaysia. *H. Candy.*   –

MARCH SONG 2 b. c. Blakeney 126–Penitent 85 (Sing Sing 134) (1983 6fg⁴ 7fg⁴ 7g² 7g*) Mar 30; 4,000Y; half-brother to several winners, including fairly useful sprinter Penumbra (by Wolver Hollow); dam closely related to top sprinter Song; improved with racing and led 2f out to win maiden race at Naas in September by 2 lengths from Foscarini; will probably stay 1m+; likely to make a useful 3-y-o. *L. Browne, Ireland.*   **91 p**

MARCOSFABLES 2 b. c. Royal Palace 131–Moaning Low 75 (Burglar 128) (1983 6fg 7f⁴ 7f 7f⁴ 7d² 6fg 7fg 10fg⁴) Feb 3; 10,000Y; third foal; half-brother to 7f winner Jolly Burglar (by Jolly Good); dam 6f winner; modest maiden; stays 1¼m; acts on firm going and a soft surface; blinkered fifth and sixth outings; sold German International Bloodstock 8,600 gns Newmarket Autumn Sales. *C. Brittain.*   **82**

MARDI GRAS 4 gr. g. Martinmas 128–Miss Pimm 88 (Gentle Art 121) (1982 6s² 6d 7.6fg³ 8fg 10fg⁴ 8.2fg 5fg 6f⁴ 6v 6d 1983 8v 8g 10f 7g 8d 10fg) neat, strong gelding who carries plenty of condition; disappointing maiden; seems to stay 1¼m but races mainly at shorter distances; acts on any going; has shown a tendency to hang and may need strong handling; sometimes blinkered. *B. Hobbs.*   –

MAREEMA 2 b. f. Monsanto 121–Wayleave (Blakeney 126) (1983 6g 5f 5.1f³ 6g 6fg) Feb 12; 3,000F, 4,000Y; close-coupled filly; first living foal; dam ran only once; quite a moderate plater; will be much better suited by 7f. *D. Thom.*   **51**

MARGO'S STAR 4 ch. g. Fleece 114–Miss Starch 64 (Lucky Sovereign) (1982 NR 1983 10s 7s 8.3f) sturdy gelding; of little account; retained 900 gns Ascot July Sales. *J. O'Donoghue.*   –

MARGOUZED (FR) 3 br. c. Margouillat 133–Belle Zed (Zeddaan 130) (1982 5fg³ 8s 7v³ 1983 10s³ 10.5v 9.2v 8v⁴ 8v* 8v³ 8v* 10.5v 10v² 12fg 15fg 10g 10s⁴ 8g) medium-sized colt; first foal; dam won over 1m; successful in 65,000 francs race at Saint-Cloud in April and 80,000 francs race on same course in May, beating By The River by 3 lengths in latter event; rather mixed form over a variety of distances on his other starts but ran well on occasions, notably when 1¾ lengths third of 10 behind L'Emigrant in Poule d'Essai des Poulains at Longchamp in between (finished very fast indeed) and short-neck second to White Spade in Prix la Force on same course later in May; stays 1¼m; seems well suited by plenty of give in the ground; tends to start slowly and get a long way behind; blinkered first outing as a 2-y-o. *Y. Porzier, France.*   **117**

MARIAKOVA (USA) 3 ch. f. The Minstrel 135–Mofida 115 (Right Tack 131) (1982 6f³ 1983 8f²) strong-quartered, attractive filly; close-up last of 3 behind Key Tothe Minstrel in John Courage Stakes at York as a 2-y-o, and 5 lengths second of 11 behind easy winner Remembering in minor event at Newmarket in July, her only 2 starts; kept on well after showing signs of greenness in latter event (looked fit and well); suited by 1m. *B. Hills.*   **79**

MARICOURT (USA) 2 b. c. One For All–Empress of Canada (Accomplish) (1983 7fg² 8d³ 8fg*) Apr 19; $22,000F, $50,000Y; strong, medium-sized colt; third foal; half-brother to a minor winner; dam won 6 times at up to 7f; won 8-runner maiden race at Beverley in September; stays 1m well; acts on a firm and a soft surface; exported to Italy. *M. Jarvis.*   **82**

MARIE CATH 2 ch. f. Owen Dudley 121–Beetroot 89 (Psidium 130) (1983 8.2g² 8g* 8g²) Apr 7; 2,000Y; neat filly; closely related to 1½m winner Salsafy (by Tudor Melody) and half-sister to 2 other winners; dam stayed well; won 10-runner maiden race at Edinburgh in October; good second to Strathearn in minor event at Redcar the following month; will be suited by 1¼m+. *S. Norton.*   **92**

MARIE DE CONCORDE (USA) 2 b. f. Super Concorde 128–Marie de Sarre (Queen's Hussar 124) (1983 6g) Jan 17; 62,000Y; shapely filly; good walker; first foal; dam, minor French 11f winner, is half-sister to high-class French and American middle-distance stayer Dom Alaric; 9/1, fairly fit and one of nicest individuals in field, never dangerous in 27-runner maiden race won by Desirable at Newmarket in July; sure to do better, especially over longer distances. *M. Stoute.*   **– p**

MARIE DE FLANDRE (FR) 3 b. f. Crystal Palace 132–Primula (Petingo 135) (1982 NR 1983 10.5f 10.5g* 10fg 12g³) 840,000 francs 3-y-o (approx £79,000); second foal; half-sister to French 10.5f winner Marie de Russy (by Sassafras); dam   **109**

useful French miler; started second favourite for Prix de Diane Hermes at Chantilly in June on debut but finished well beaten behind Escaline; short-priced favourite when beating Ruler On A Lark by 2½ lengths in 7-runner minor event at Saint-Cloud in July; beaten over 6 lengths when sixth of 13 behind Sharaya in Prix de la Nonette at Deauville in August and almost 3 lengths when third of 7 behind Asnelles in Prix Joubert at Evry in September on only other starts; stays 1½m. *P-L. Biancone, France.*

MARIE DE LITZ (FR) 3 ch.f. Dictus 126–Mohair (Blue Tom 127) (1982 NR **122** 1983 10v* 10d³ 10.5fg* 10g⁴ 10fg 12s⁴ 12f 15.5f) 82,000 francs 3-y-o (approx £7,500); first known foal; dam, daughter of smart Imberline, never ran; proved a bargain after being purchased at the Mathet dispersal sale in March and was successful in newcomers race at Longchamp in April and 11-runner Prix de Royaumont at Chantilly in June; came from back of field in latter event to lead near finish and beat Brillante by a short neck; ran creditably in top company at Longchamp on 3 outings in autumn, finishing about 3 lengths fourth of 12 behind Sharaya in Trusthouse Forte Prix Vermeille, under 5 lengths tenth of 26 behind All Along in Trusthouse Forte Prix de l'Arc de Triomphe and about 6 lengths fifth of 14 behind Old Country in Prix Royal-Oak; effective at around 1¼m and evidently stays quite well; acts on any going; sold out of D. Smaga's stable 4,200,000 francs Arc de Triomphe Sale before penultimate start. *R. Collet, France.*

MARIES PARTY 5 ch.m. The Parson 119–Vulnavada (Vulgan 123) (1982 NR §§ 1983 11.7h) ex-Irish mare; placed in bumpers races and over hurdles in Ireland; refused to race in maiden event at Bath in July; sold 1,500 gns Doncaster October Sales, resold 1,050 gns Ascot December Sales. *O. O'Neill.*

MARINE 5 b.g. Hittite Glory 125–Seaside (Mossborough 126) (1982 NR 1983 – 8d) well-made, quite attractive gelding; lightly raced on flat nowadays; will be suited by 1¼m; blinkered twice at 3 yrs. *G. Balding.*

MARINERA 3 b.f. Julio Mariner 127–Mimika 85 (Lorenzaccio 130) (1982 7f 8s **60** 1983 12d 10v² 16fg⁴ 12f) angular filly; in frame in minor event at Ripon and maiden race at York in June; sold 2,900 gns Newmarket September Sales and sent to Algeria. *C. Brittain.*

MARINER'S DREAM 2 br.c. Julio Mariner 127–My Ginny 83 (Palestine 133) – (1983 5fg 7fg 7d) Mar 18; 4,500Y; fair sort; half-brother to 1979 2-y-o 5f winner Auntie Bessie (by No Mercy); dam 2-y-o 6f winner; last in maiden and minor events. *R. Morris.*

MARION'S DREAM 2 b.c. Homeboy 114–Cute 75 (Hardicanute 130) (1983 7fg – 6fg 6fg) May 15; smallish, sturdy colt; half-brother to successful 3-y-o stayer Priors Cutie (by Mr Bigmore) and another winner; dam disqualified winner over 6f at 2 yrs; in rear in late-season maiden and minor events, on debut last of 12. *D. Thom.*

MARITIME ENGLAND 3 b.c. Tumble Wind–Summer's Lease (Soderini 123) **75** (1982 5.8f² 5.8f² 5g* 6fg 1983 8f³ 8f 8h 8g 10f) quite attractive, well-made colt; suited by 1m; acts on firm going; usually sweats up; exported to Singapore. *C. Nelson.*

MARJOEMIN 3 b.f. Import 127–French Joy (French Beige 127) (1982 7s 1983 – 7f 7f 8f) big, backward-looking filly; seems only plating class. *J. Etherington.*

MARJORAM 4 ch.f. Warpath 113–Jasmin (Frankincense 120) (1982 7f 8f 7fg² – 8.2g 7f 7s 1983 8v⁴ 8.2s³) lightly-made filly; plater; possibly stays 1m; seems to act on any going; blinkered twice in 1982. *C. Thornton.*

MARK EDELSON 6 ch.g. Menelek 114–Game Cherry (Domenico Fuoco 82) – (1982 NR 1983 12fg 16f) second foal; dam won over jumps in Ireland; winning hurdler; well beaten on flat. *M. Jefferson.*

MARKELLA (FR) 2 br.c. Green Dancer 132–Frenetique (Tyrant) (1983 5v) – Feb 16; $80,000Y; lengthy, good-bodied, quite attractive colt; second foal; half-brother to minor 3-y-o French 9.2f and 1¼m winner Volitile (by Arctic Tern); dam very useful at around 1m in France; last of 6 in minor event at Lingfield in May. *G. Balding.*

MARKET MELODY 6 b.m. Highland Melody 112–Sandalshoon 103 (Red God **51** 128⁵) (1982 12f 8g 9fg² 12f 10g³ 10d² 9g 11s 1983 10.2d 9s 8v* 9d³ 8g* 8d* 10.2f 8f 10f 9fg 8fg) lengthy mare; good walker; won handicaps at Newcastle (apprentices) and Redcar in May and at Carlisle in June; stays 1¼m; has run respectably on a firm surface but is ideally suited by some give in the ground; suitable mount for an apprentice; doesn't always impress in paddock. *D. Smith.*

MARKHAM GIRL 2 b.f. Sovereign King–Markham Lady (Athens Wood 126) **66** d
(1983 5d 5g² 5s 5d 5f 5f 5d 6fg 10fg) Apr 23; lightly-made filly; first foal; dam poor
plater on flat and over hurdles; plating-class maiden; no form after second
appearance; blinkered fifth outing. *Ronald Thompson.*

MARKIE 7 br.g. On Your Mark 125–Jeannette (Whistler 129) (1982 10.2g 12g³ –
10f² 12f³ 12fg 12f 12fg 8fg 1983 12f 13.8f 12f 12fg 14fg 10.6fg 16f) well-made,
attractive gelding; poor middle-distance handicapper; acts on firm going;
sometimes blinkered; usually apprentice ridden; usually wears bandages. *R. E.
Peacock.*

MARK KELLY 2 ch.c. On Your Mark 125–Kelfresco 59 (Kelly 122) (1983 5fg 5g –
5d 5g) Feb 21; IR 4,800F; short-legged, sturdy colt; fifth reported produce; dam
poor half-sister to top-class German sprinter Pentathlon; poor form in maiden and
minor events; blinkered final outing. *P. Mitchell.*

MARK OF RESPECT 3 ch.c. North Stoke 130–Scarcroft 66 (King's Bench **73**
132) (1982 7g 8s 1983 10.2v 10f* 10g 11.5f³) leggy, rather lightly-made colt;
readily beat Star Charter in handicap at Nottingham in June, first form and best
effort; suited by 1¼m; acts on firm going; said by trainer to have had back trouble
in the spring; sold 7,600 gns Newmarket Autumn Sales. *R. Armstrong.*

MARK'S CHOICE 2 ch.c. Swing Easy 126–Piper's Gold 71 (Jimmy Reppin 131) **62**
(1983 5d 5d 6f 6f 8s 7f) May 1; well-grown colt; first living foal; dam placed over
1m; plating-class maiden; form only on fourth outing; not sure to stay 1m; trained
by P. Feilden first 4 starts. *M. Ryan.*

MARLEYCOMBE HILL 4 b.g. Sagaro 133–L'Anguissola 102 (Soderini 123) –
(1982 10s 6fg 16d 15.5f 15.5fg³ 15.5fg³ 1983 17.1v 16g 15.5f 13.1h 14f⁴) smallish
gelding; staying maiden; blinkered once in 1982; sometimes sweats up; sold 1,900
gns Newmarket September Sales. *W. Wightman.*

MARLION 2 b.c. Julio Mariner 127–Rose Mullion 82 (Tudor Melody 129) (1983 6f **86**
8g² 8fg²) May 6; rather leggy colt; excellent mover; brother to 3-y-o Shanmullagh
and closely related to 1978 2-y-o 5f winner Regina Magna (by Blakeney); dam won
over 5f at 2 yrs; good second in autumn maiden events at Ayr and Newcastle; will
be suited by 1¼m; sure to win maiden race. *E. Weymes.*

MARLOWSWOOD 3 ch.g. Hittite Glory 125–Thieves Honour (Hook Money **68**
124) (1982 7fg 8g 1983 9f⁴ 10f⁴ 10f 10fg³ 8.2s*) strong gelding; good mover;
plater; won at Hamilton in October (no bid); probably stays 1¼m; acts on any
going; sold 10,000 gns Newmarket Autumn Sales. *Sir Mark Prescott.*

MARNIE'S GIRL 4 br.f. Crooner 119–Philmarnie 66 (Klondyke Bill 125) (1982 –
8f 8s 8f 8g 10d 10fg 10d 1983 7f 8f 10f 10s) lengthy, workmanlike filly; poor form,
including in a seller. *A. Smith.*

MARRONESSE 2 ch.f. Tachypous 128–Louise 71 (Royal Palace 131) (1983 5v³ **61**
6s 6d 6s 6g 7.6d) Feb 27; 2,700F; 3,700Y; close-coupled, workmanlike filly; first
foal; dam won twice over 1½m; plating-class maiden; should stay at least 1¼m. *R.
Voorspuy.*

MARSHALDIRECTORY 2 ch.c. Exdirectory 129–Ginnies Pet 106 (Compen- –
sation 127) (1983 6f 7g) May 11; 6,600Y; sturdy colt; third foal; half-brother to a
winning plater; dam game sprinter; behind in maiden races at Yarmouth in August
and Leicester in October. *A. Jarvis.*

MARSHALLA 3 b.f. Cawston's Clown 113–Abbey Rose 84 (Lorenzaccio 130) **81**
(1982 6h 1983 9.4d 9.4d 9f 7f 7f³ 8.2fg* 10.6fg* 9fg³ 8h* 8s* 8g³) tall, leggy,
lightly-made filly; improved and, after smoothly winning 2 sellers at Haydock in
August (attracted no bid either time), stepped up in class to win non-selling
handicaps at Pontefract and Ayr in September; beat Comedy Fair readily by 3
lengths in £3,900 event on last-named course; stays 1¼m well; acts on any going.
J. Wilson.

MARSHALL RED 3 br.g. Lochnager 132–Miss Marvel 59 (Palestine 133) (1982 **64**
NR 1983 6g² 6f 7f 5f 6s⁴ 5f) big, good-bodied gelding; half-brother to successful
sprinter Miss Redmarshall (by Most Secret) and fair middle-distance performer
Boy Marvel (by Richboy); dam won 6f seller; in frame in maiden race and a handicap
at Ayr, best efforts; blinkered third and last 2 starts. *J. Mason.*

MARSHAL OSTHOFF 4 ch.c. Royal Match 117–Compliment (Tudor Music **46**
131) (1982 8.2fg 8f 10f 1983 12fg 9d 8g 7fg 7f 6fg 6g 6g² 6fg 5s³ 6f 5g) small,
useful sort; poor mover; poor handicapper nowadays; should stay 1m; best form
with some give in the ground. *T. Craig.*

MARSH HARRIER (USA) 2 b.c. Raise A Cup–Belle de Jour (Speak John)   – p
(1983 7fg) May 7; $125,000Y; big, strong, rangy colt; fourth foal; half-brother to a
winner by Giacometti; dam won 6f claiming race; eighth of 12 behind easy winner
Mafoo's Image in maiden race at Salisbury in September; has the scope to improve.
G. Harwood.

MARSH TRACK 3 br.g. Palm Track 122–Miss Warwick (Stupendous) (1982   **48**
6fg³ 6f 7f² 6d 6g 7fg 6s 1983 7d² 8s 7d 7f³ 7f⁴ 8f³ 8h 9f⁴ 8.2g) leggy gelding;
plater; possibly best at 7f; probably acts on any going; hung and didn't look all that
genuine third start. *W. Haigh.*

MARTHA SPANKS 3 br.f. Home Guard 129–Amazer (Mincio 127) (1982 5f   **60**
5.3fg* 6fg⁴ 5f 6fg 6fg⁴ 7g 1983 6s 6fg 7f 8.3fg 7f 7g³ 7g 8g 7.6d) leggy, fair sort;
mainly disappointing as a 3-y-o, but not disgraced in handicaps in latter part of
season; promises to stay 1m; acts on a firm surface; sold 14,000 gns Newmarket
December Sales. *J. Benstead.*

MARTIAL FITZGERALD 3 b.c. Tower Walk 130–Capsville (Cyane) (1982 5s   **67**
5s 1983 5v 6d 5.1fg⁴ 5f² 5g⁴ 5f² 5fg 5g² 5g* 5.1s 5g) lengthy, strong, good-bodied
colt; landed a gamble in 16-runner handicap at Goodwood in September; soundly
beaten afterwards; should stay 6f; slipped and fell second start. *N. Guest.*

MARTIN-LAVELL NEWS 2 ch.f. Song 132–Blue Promise 95 (Red Alert 127)   **90**
(1983 5f* 5g* 5f 5fg³) Apr 30; 12,000Y; short-legged, powerful, sprint type; good
walker; second foal; half-sister to quite useful 3-y-o sprinter Shanleys Style (by
Balidar); dam won over 5f from 3 starts at 2 yrs; successful in maiden race at
Carlisle in June and nursery at Warwick in July; creditable third of 6 to Sing To Me in
nursery at Goodwood in August; a grand sort, sure to win more races at the minor
meetings. *Sir Mark Prescott.*

MARTON MAID 3 b.f. Silly Season 127–Marton Lady 103 (March Past 124)   **59**
(1982 6g 6fg 7s 6d⁴ 6s 1983 8v 7fg³ 7f 9f⁴ 8f 8f² 8g² 9s⁴ 8g 8fg) neat filly; placed
in maiden and minor events; stays 9f; blinkered final start. *S. Wiles.*

MARUTHAYOOR 2 ch.f. Sallust 134–Carose (Caro 133) (1983 5v 6s* 6f 7fg   **104**
8.2h³ 8fg* 8fg² 7.3d⁴) Jan 31; IR 42,000Y; well-made, quite attractive filly;
carries plenty of condition; not a good mover in her slower paces; second foal;
half-sister to French 3-y-o 10.5f winner Pomme du Rhin (by Rheingold); dam
plating-class half-sister to very smart French middle-distance colt Noir et Or;
won maiden race at Lingfield in June and 17-runner nursery at Bath in September;
ridden by apprentice unable to claim, finished well when good fourth to Betsy Bay
in Rochford Thompson Newbury Stakes in October; better suited by 1m than by
shorter distances; acts on any going; genuine. *P. Cole.*

MARY MAGUIRE 6 b.m. Rapid River 127–Flicka (Balidar 133) (1982 5d 6f³ 6f²   **63**
6f 5fg² 5fg⁴ 6fg 6d² 6g* 6f² 6fg³ 6g² 6d 6f² 5g³ 6s* 6s 6s 1983 6g 6s³ 6s 6g 6f² 6f
6f 6f* 6f 6fg 6f 6h 6g 6fg 6f) strong-quartered mare; sprint handicapper; won at
Carlisle in July; acts on any going; sometimes sweats up; suitable mount for a
claimer; slipped away ninth start. *Mrs M. Nesbitt.*

MARY ROSE 2 b.f. Music Maestro 119–Sea Green 93 (Meadow Court 129) (1983   **43**
5v⁴ 5v 7.2fg 7h 8g 7d) Mar 19; 2,000Y; workmanlike filly; half-sister to a winner in
Holland; dam won over 1½m; poor form, including in sellers. *C. Williams.*

MARZIA'S HOLLOW 2 b.f. Wolver Hollow 126–Marzia Fabbricotti (Ribero   **86**
126) (1983 5fg 7fg* 7.6g 8fg) big filly; third reported foal in Ireland; dam won
twice in Italy; won 11-runner maiden race at Chester in August comfortably by 3
lengths from Angleman; in rear in Burr Stakes at Lingfield and £5,200 nursery at
Newmarket subsequently; should stay 1¼m. *N. Guest.*

MARZOOGA 3 ch.f. Bold Lad (Ire) 133–Lady Astronaut (Polly's Jet) (1982 6g   **–**
6s* 1983 6s 8.3fg) good-quartered filly; good walker; behind under stiff weights
both starts in 1983; should stay beyond 6f; acts on soft going. *G. Huffer.*

MASARIKA 2 b.f. Thatch 136–Miss Melody 110 (Tudor Melody 129) (1983 5.5v*   **117**
5fg* 5.5g* 6g³ 8f²)
Alain de Royer Dupre wasted little time in proving his worth as successor to
the Aga Khan's principal trainer in France, the legendary Francois Mathet. He won
good middle-distance races with the three-year-old fillies Rajpoura and Sharaya,
notably the Trusthouse Forte Prix Vermeille, and showed similar skill with his
two-year-olds, winning one of the longest pattern races, the Criterium de
Saint-Cloud, and two of the shortest, the Prix du Bois at Longchamp
and the Prix Robert Papin at Maisons-Laffitte, with Masarika.
Masarika became her owner's third winner of the Papin, following Zeddaan in

1967 and Blushing Groom in 1976. Like Zeddaan she came to the race unbeaten in two starts; she had slammed thirteen others in a newcomers event over the Papin course and distance in May, scoring by five lengths and the same; and a month later she had accounted for four others, successful in four of their five starts, in the Prix du Bois, which she took by three lengths from Sicyos after matching strides with him to the distance. Masarika started odds on for the Papin in a field completed by two other unbeaten French fillies, Harifa and Ruby Green, and two foreign raiders, the July Stakes winner Superlative from Britain and the filly Elegant Act from Canada. In the race she settled nicely, as Elegant Act and then Harifa made the running, and took the lead only entering the last furlong. She then tended to idle in front, in the end having only half a length to spare over the persistent Superlative after looking likely to win well. Good though Masarika's performance was, it came as a surprise to see her rider Saint-Martin claim 'She's undoubtedly the best two-year-old I have ever ridden. I won much more easily than the official margin suggests'. Considering that such performers as Allez France, Zeddaan, Amber Rama, Broadway Dancer, Texanita and Silver Shark are other two-year-olds Saint-Martin has ridden to big-race successes his claim seemed somewhat premature.

By the end of the season it also seemed highly extravagant. Masarika followed in the footsteps of the previous Papin winner Ma Biche by finishing only third at a short price in the Prix Morny at Deauville in August. Although she came to challenge the front-running Siberian Express at the distance she never looked likely to peg him back and she lost second place on the line to the strong-finishing Ti King; Siberian Express beat her two lengths. Masarika was said to have suffered a slight leg injury between the Papin and the Morny and it's possible she was still feeling its effects; we noticed her change her legs several times in the closing stages. Our Deauville race-reader thought the Cheveley Park a highly suitable autumn target for Masarika. Unfortunately she had never been entered for the race and a surprising alternative was found for her over a mile, the Prix Marcel Boussac at Longchamp on Arc day for which she started a 6/4 favourite. Although she ran well Masarika gave the impression a mile was just beyond her as a two-year-old. She took a very strong hold, pulling her way to the front after only a furlong, and her exertions took their toll in the closing stages where the Prix du Calvados winner Almeira quickened away to beat her two lengths.

Masarika's pedigree also raises doubts as to whether a mile will prove her optimum trip. Her dam Miss Melody raced exclusively over five furlongs as a juvenile, winning at Newbury before finishing second in both the Molecomb and Seaton Delaval Stakes, and she didn't show such good form when tried over six and seven furlongs as a three-year-old. Miss Melody was sold at the end of her racing career for 34,000 guineas at the December Sales, a figure bettered by only two other fillies in 1973; three years later she was bought by her present owner for 51,000 guineas. Her appeal stemmed as much from her pedigree as her racing record. Her dam The Veil was not only a half-sister to the Cheveley Park winner

Prix Robert Papin, Maisons-Laffitte—Masarika wins from Superlative

H. H. Aga Khan's "Masarika" (Y. Saint-Martin)

Lady Sybil, the Jockey Club Stakes winner Black Peter and the top sprinter Welsh Abbot, but also to the dam of the leading Canadian horse Nearctic and the grandams of St Paddy and Great Nephew. In addition Miss Melody is a half-sister to numerous winners, notably the Champion Stakes third Lord David and the very useful 1969 two-year-old filly Red Velvet, who later became the dam of the Mill Reef Stakes winner Red Cross. Masarika is the fourth winner from Miss Melody's first five living foals, with the Rheingold horse Maiymad, a very useful middle-distance

		Forli	Aristophanes
	Thatch	(ch 1963)	Trevisa
	(b 1970)	Thong	Nantallah
Masarika		(b 1964)	Rough Shod
(b.f. Mar 19, 1981)		Tudor Melody	Tudor Minstrel
	Miss Melody	(br 1956)	Matelda
	(b 1970)	The Veil	Nimbus
		(b 1953)	Sister Sarah

winner in France who has done extremely well over jumps, easily the best of the others. Masarika is by the Irish stallion Thatch, a top-class miler who was also fully effective over six furlongs as a three-year-old. Sadly Thatch's death was reported just a few days before his daughter's Robert Papin victory but the Irish have his son Thatching who promises to make an even better sire. It will be interesting to see whether Masarika is trained as a sprinter or a miler. The chances are she'll start over a mile and she should give Almeira and Treizieme plenty to do in the Poule d'Essai des Pouliches, provided she can be persuaded to settle better than in the Marcel Boussac. She acts on any going. *A. de Royer Dupre, France.*

MASHIN TIME 4 b.f. Palm Track 122–Baggin Time 91 (Pinsun 108) (1982 9f 7f⁴ 8f* 8g* 8fg* 8g* 8g* 1983 7v 8g 7f 8f 8f 8f) narrow, leggy filly; not the best of movers; won 5 handicaps in succession at 3 yrs; didn't find her form in 1983; suited by 1m; possibly needs a sound surface. *M. H. Easterby.* —

MASKED BALL 3 b.c. Thatch 136–Miss Mahal (Taj Dewan 128) (1982 NR 1983 8f 9f 10f³ 11f²12fg 12g*) fair sort; second foal; dam never ran; 25/1-winner of 77

519

20-runner maiden race at Redcar in November, running on strongly to beat Reham by 4 lengths; had run respectably in a valuable seller previous start (bandaged); suited by 1½m; yet to race on a soft surface; tends to sweat a bit. *P. Calver.*

MASKELL GOLD 3 br.c. On Your Mark 125–Mulattin (Henry the Seventh 125) (1982 6v 1983 8fg³ 8f 7g 7g) sturdy, compact colt; third in maiden event at Edinburgh in May, best effort; stays 1m; blinkered third outing; trained by C. Nelson first start. *H. O'Neill.* **72 d**

MASPIN LADY 2 b.f. Garnered 95–Debysue 47 (Red Pins 114) (1983 5f 6f 8d) May 28; short-backed filly; fifth live foal; dam bad plater; in rear in maiden races and a seller. *Mrs M. Nesbitt.* **—**

MASSIMO 4 b.c. Blakeney 126–Never a Fear 121 (Never Say Die 137) (1982 10fg² 10f² 12f³ 10fg⁴ 12f 8fg⁴ 9g* 10fg² 10g* 9s 1983 8g 8fg 10f 11.7f⁴ 8.3fg 10g 10g 9d 12d 12fg⁴) stocky, strong, attractive colt; poor handicapper nowadays; beaten in valuable seller final start; stays 1½m; needs top-of-the-ground; blinkered fifth and seventh outings; sold 3,200 gns Ascot November Sales. *P. Cundell.* **—**

MASSORAH (FR) 3 ch.f. Habitat 134–Marala (Sir Khalito) (1982 5s³ 7v 1983 7v⁴ 6.5s 5fg² 6f* 6fg³ 5d*) French filly; third reported living foal; half-sister to French 1979 2-y-o 6.5f winner Massalia (by Targowice); dam won over 1¼m from only 3 starts; won 20-runner handicap at Chantilly in June and picked up an important prize when accounting for Swing Fire by ½ length in Premio Omenoni at Milan in October; also placed in Prix du Gros-Chene at Chantilly again and valuable handicap at Deauville, finishing 2 lengths second of 11 to Gem Diamond in former; best at sprint distances; seems to act on any going; acted as a pacemaker for stable-companion Ma Biche on reappearance. *Mme C. Head, France.* **108**

MASTER ABBOT 3 b.c. Whitstead 125–Elton Abbess 86 (Tamerlane 128) (1982 8.2s 1983 10s) small, quite well-made colt; no show in minor and maiden races; sold 900 gns Newmarket September Sales, for export to Norway. *R. Boss.* **—**

MASTER-BLOW 4 ch.g. Roi Soleil 125–Surfacing (Worden II 129) (1982 6f 5f 5g⁴ 6g 6g* 7d⁴ 7s 1983 6v* 6v 6s* 6g³ 7fg 7f) leggy gelding; won handicaps at Ayr in March and Ripon in May; stays 7f; suited by some give in the ground; not seen out after June. *W. Elsey.* **75**

MASTER BOATMAN 4 ch.g. Riverman 131–Ya Ya 84 (Primera 131) (1982 10.6s³ 12fg³ 12.2f² 14fg³ 12g 14fg² 15d* 14g² 1983 12s 12v 16.1fg 15fg³ 16.1fg 13s² 18fg) narrow gelding; good walker; quite a modest handicapper; should be suited by 2m+; seems to act on any going; blinkered last 4 starts; sold 6,400 gns Newmarket Autumn Sales. *G. Wragg.* **78**

MASTER BROKER 3 b.c. Mummy's Pet 125–Ardent Runner 94 (Runnymede 123) (1982 5f 5fg 6g 6s 5d* 1983 5g 6v 5f 6fg 5f 5f) plater; was tubed; acted on a soft surface; was sometimes blinkered; dead. *M. W. Easterby.* **—**

MASTER CARVER 3 b.c. Sharpen Up 127–Climbing Rose 81 (Pirate King 129) (1982 NR 1983 10g 10.1f² 10.1fg² 9d⁴) 90,000Y; good-bodied colt; half-brother to several winners here and abroad, including smart middle-distance colt Criterion (by Royal Palace) and smart 1m to 1½m performer Saint Jonathon (by Welsh Saint); dam 2-y-o 5f winner; second in minor event and maiden race at Windsor in August; suited by 1¼m. *G. Harwood.* **72**

MASTER CAWSTON 4 ch.g. Cawston's Clown 113–Teresa Way 66 (Great White Way) (1982 6fg 6fg⁴ 6f² 6f 6g 6g⁴ 5s 6s 1983 6g* 5v 6f 6f 6f³ 6d* 6s 6fg 6d²) tall, useful sort; good mover; sprint handicapper; won at Newmarket in April and York in August; led near finish to beat Oyston Estates a neck in Harewood Handicap on latter; suited by 6f; probably unsuited by very soft going but acts on any other; sometimes blinkered but is better without; suited by strong handling; sold 20,000 gns Newmarket Autumn Sales. *G. Wragg.* **95**

MASTER DOLPHIN 2 b.g. Le Dauphin 73–Water Baby 104 (Clear River 114) (1983 5v 5d) Mar 26; 1,600Y; half-brother to fairly useful 1½m winner Tom (by Aureole); dam, who ran only at 2 yrs, is half-sister to Queen's Hussar; bad plater; not raced after May. *D. Smith.* **—**

MASTER DRIVER 2 gr. or ro.c. Absalom 128–Shelton Song 60 (Song 132) (1983 6d 6f 6fg 5f² 5s) May 5; 20,000Y; rather sparely-made colt; third foal; half-brother to 3-y-o 5f winner Stereos (by Tachypous); dam 5f winner at 4 yrs; quite a modest maiden; usually shows early pace and may be better suited by 5f than 6f; blinkered third and fourth outings. *D. Smith.* **70**

MASTER HEADLEY 2 ch.c. Status Seeker–Second Venture (Thirteen of Diamonds 126) (1983 5g* 5v⁴ 6v³ 6g 6f 5f) short-backed, good-quartered colt; **86**

half-brother to winning hurdler Reckless Philip (by Bargello); dam won over 9f and 1¼m in Ireland; won 11-runner maiden race at Navan in April by 2 lengths from Malang-Lou; ran creditably most subsequent outings, on last finishing 3¾ lengths fifth of 6 to Safe Home in Nishapour Curragh Stakes in July; stays 6f, and should get further; acts on any going. *R. Cotter, Ireland.*

MASTER LAD (USA) 2 b.c. Sir Ivor 135–Misukaw (Northern Dancer) (1983 7f 7.6fg) Apr 22; third foal; half-brother to Northern Majesty (by His Majesty), a very useful stakes winner at up to 9f, and to Share The Fantasy (by Exclusive Native), a leading 2-y-o filly in USA in 1982; dam stakes-placed winner of 3 sprint races; behind in autumn maiden races at Redcar and Lingfield. *G. Huffer.*   –

MASTER LEONARD 2 br.c. Record Run 127–Mistress Meryll 61 (Tower Walk 130) (1983 5s⁴ 5v² 6fg 8fg 7f) Mar 16; rather lightly-built colt; first foal; being placed over 6f; modest plater; stays 7f; sold 2,300 gns Doncaster November Sales. *J. W. Watts.*   47

MASTER LINE 2 ch.c. High Line 125–Fair Winter 111 (Set Fair 129) (1983 7fg) Feb 18; small, sparely-made colt; good walker; brother to 3 winners here and abroad, notably top-class middle-distance colt Master Willie, and half-brother to 3 others; dam very useful at up to 1¼m; third favourite, kept on very well without being knocked about to finish 6¼ lengths fifth of 21 behind Chelkov in maiden event at Newmarket in September; will be suited by 1¼m+; sure to do better and win races. *H. Candy.*   75 p

MASTER LOCKWOOD 3 b.g. Mummy's Pet 125–Tzu-Hsi 66 (Songedor 116) (1982 5d 5.8g 6fg² 6d 1983 6v² 6d 7v 8f 8fg 5h) tall, good-quartered gelding; disappointing maiden; stays 6f; blinkered last 2 starts; exported to Malaysia. *G. Hunter.*   –

MASTER PEPPER 2 b.c. Latest Model 115–Miss Pepper 61 (Arctic Chevalier) (1983 5s³ 5v) Apr 24; plain colt; eighth foal; half-brother to a winning point-to-pointer; dam won 5f seller at 2 yrs and 2 selling hurdles; poor maiden; unseated rider going to start and gave trouble at stalls at Warwick in April on second outing. *B. Forsey.*   58

MASTER PLUMBER 2 br.g. Monsanto 121–Suli (Morston 125) (1983 7fg 7fg) Mar 7; 3,800Y; workmanlike gelding; first foal; dam poor staying maiden; behind in September in maiden race at Salisbury and valuable seller at Newmarket; sold C. Wildman 420 gns Ascot October Sales. *J. Sutcliffe.*   –

MASTER SILCA KEY 3 b.c. Homing 130–Blaskette 99 (Blast 125) (1982 NR 1983 8f⁴) 41,000Y; fair sort; third foal; half-brother to 7.6f winner Wynnwith Boy (by Music Boy) and middle-distance winner D'Lo (by Sovereign Path); dam useful middle-distance handicapper; shaped promisingly when fourth of 16 to Tetron Bay in minor event at Salisbury in June; sold to J. King 4,100 gns Newmarket September Sales. *G. Harwood.*   –

MASTER WIT (USA) 2 ch.c. Master Derby–Witchy Woman (Strate Stuff) (1983 6f 6f 7g*) Feb 23; $130,000Y; smallish, useful-looking colt; has a long stride; fourth foal; half-brother to Coronation Cup winner Be My Native (by Our Native); dam won 5 times over sprint distances; won 16-runner maiden race at Leicester in September by a neck from Laurie's Panther; will be suited by 1m+; possibly needs some give in the ground. *H. Cecil.*   85

MATAFAO (USA) 2 b.c. Naskra–Pago Dancer (Pago Pago) (1983 7g 8fg) Feb 25; $62,000Y; fair sort; rather unfurnished; third foal; half-brother to French 1m winner Mr Badger (by Mr Leader); dam stakes-placed winner at up to 7f; showed modest form in fair company at Leicester (favourite) and Newmarket (gave trouble in stalls) at the back-end; sent to USA. *H. Cecil.*   85

MATARANY 3 ch.g. Mansingh 120–Nelion 102 (Grey Sovereign 128§) (1982 7fg 7s² 1983 8s 10g 8f 10.2f 10h 8fg² 8d³ 8g) big, sparely-made, workmanlike gelding; placed in amateur riders races at Goodwood; promises to stay 1¼m; blinkered last 4 starts; sold to H. Beasley 7,800 gns Newmarket Autumn Sales. *I. Balding.*   63

MATAWA 3 ch.f. Royal Match 117–Dance Away (Red God 128§) (1982 6fg 6g 6g 8fg 1983 12s) sturdy filly; behind in varied races. *D. Morley.*   –

MATCH MASTER 4 ch.g. Roman Warrior 132–Giglet (Frankincense 120) (1982 7fg 7.6f⁴ 7f³ 8g² 6fg 6g³ 6f² 8g 1983 7fg³ 8f⁴ 8fg² 7f² 7h 7d) quite well-made, good sort; carries a lot of condition; good walker and mover; useful at his best but has deteriorated markedly and is disappointing; stays 1m; seems to act on any going; sometimes blinkered; possibly ungenuine and has a tendency to hang left. *C. Nelson.*   54 §

Bradford and Bingley Handicap, York—Mauritzfontein beats Romoss (noseband)

MATCHROOM 2 br.f. Tower Walk 130–The Danstan 66 (The Brianstan 128) (1983 6f 6f 7f 7f 6fg) Apr 1; 2,400Y; fair sort; third foal; half-sister to 2 minor 2-y-o winners; dam won 5f seller at 2 yrs; behind in maiden races, 3 of them auction events. *D. Morrill.* —

MATHEMAGICIAN (USA) 3 b.g. Minnesota Mac–Margaritaville (Tom Rolfe) (1982 7.9f 7s 1983 7s 8v 8f 10fg) quite an attractive ex-Irish gelding; blinkered when seventh of 18 behind Tender Sovereign in handicap at Wolverhampton in June on third start, probably best effort; sold 1,550 gns Newmarket September Sales. *F. Durr.* —

MATIN 3 b.f. Rheingold 137–Remeta 67 (Reform 132) (1982 NR 1983 12d 16g 12.2f³ 16f³ 17.1h⁴ 16.5f² 16fg) compact filly; has a round action; first foal; dam won over 1¼m and 1½m; staying maiden; acts on firm going; blinkered last 5 starts. *M. Camacho.* **64**

MATOU 3 b.c. Mummy's Pet 125–Great Optimist 55 (Great Nephew 126) (1982 6f 6fg³ 6d 6g* 1983 7s³ 7g⁴ 6d² 6fg⁴ 6fg* 6fg* 6s 7fg 6fg) strong, well-made colt; finished very strongly to win quite valuable handicaps at Newmarket in July (beat Alakh a short head) and August (accounted for All Is Forgiven by a neck); carried 3 lb overweight when about 1½ lengths sixth of 28 behind Polly's Brother in Ladbrokes (Ayr) Gold Cup in September on seventh outing; suited by a stiff 6f, and stays 7f; probably acts on any going. *G. Pritchard-Gordon.* **101**

MATTAGIRL 2 ch.f. Music Boy 124–Green Chartreuse 91 (French Beige 127) (1983 6g 6g 5g² 6fg 6fg) Apr 28; sturdy, fair sort; sister to Middle Park Stakes winner and 2000 Guineas second Mattaboy and half-sister to 2 winners; dam won over 5f and 7f at 2 yrs; 3 lengths second of 16 to Kazarow in maiden race at Sandown in October; stays 6f; blinkered final outing. *C. Brittain.* **78**

MATTS MUSIC 3 ch.f. Music Boy 124–Ventrex 95 (Henry the Seventh 125) (1982 6g 5v 5s 1983 5g 8g) workmanlike filly; little worthwhile form. *K. Cunningham-Brown.* —

MAUJENDOR 3 b.c. Rose Laurel 125–Mark My Word (On Your Mark 125) (1982 7g 6g⁴ 7fg 7v 7d 1983 10h 8f 8f⁴ 9d*) small, stocky colt; sold to M. Tate 3,200 gns after winning seller at Wolverhampton in September; stays 9f; suited by some give in the ground; blinkered once. *C. Brittain.* **57**

MAUMANN (FR) 2 b.f. Sir Gaylord–Nabua (Le Fabuleux 133) (1983 6g⁴ 7g) rather leggy filly; half-sister to several winners, notably very smart French stayer Adam van Vianen (by Abdos); dam never ran; quite modest form in the autumn in fair company at Goodwood and York; will be better suited by 1m+; may improve. *B. Hills.* **70 p**

MAURITZFONTEIN 4 b.c. Habitat 134–Reine Dagobert 76 (Roi Dagobert 128) 93
(1982 8fg³ 7f² 8.3fg² 7f* 8fg 1983 8d 7fg 8fg 8f² 8f* 8g* 8fg 10g* 9fg) neat,
attractive colt; shows a bit of knee action; won handicaps at Goodwood in July,
York in August (beat Romoss 2½ lengths in Bradford and Bingley Handicap) and
Newbury in September (quickened well to account for Airfield by 3 lengths in
Peter Hastings Handicap); suited by 1¼m; acted on firm going; suited by a
strongly-run race; twice ran moderately at Newmarket, sweating up on second
occasion; stud in South Africa. *H. Candy.*

MAURMAX 3 b.g. Dragonara Palace 115–Lochness Lass (Track Spare 125) (1982 —
5fg² 5g 5g⁴ 5f⁴ 7g 6fg 5fg 6s⁴ 1983 7.6v 6s 6s 10.1fg 10g 7f 7fg) fair sort; no form
in 1983 (tailed-off last when blinkered in seller final outing); suited by 6f; acts on
any going. *P. K. Mitchell.*

MAVOURNSKI 3 b.f. Malinowski 123–Judy Green (Green God 128) (1982 6g 6f⁴ —
6f² 7fg 8fg 7.6v² 8.2s⁴ 7g 1983 8v) good-bodied filly; tailed off only outing of 1983
(April); stays 1m; seems to act on any going. *W. O'Gorman.*

MAWAL 6 b.h. Tudor Melody 129–Rebus 97 (Busted 134) (1982 NR 1983 12v* 50
14s³ 12fg 12d³ 12.2fg 12d 13g 12s³) attractive horse; decisively won handicap at
Thirsk in April; possibly stays 1¾m; needs some give in the ground; occasionally
blinkered but is better without; suitable mount for an apprentice; wears bandages.
N. Guest.

MAWATEA 3 ch.f. Meldrum 112–Bon Feu 75 (Blason 109) (1982 8.2fg² 7.2s 10d —
10.2s 1983 13.8s 9f) smallish, workmanlike filly; plater; stays 1¼m; probably acts
on any going. *Mrs A. Cousins.*

MAXIMAIN 3 ch.g. Monsanto 121–Long Valley 71 (Ribero 126) (1982 6f 8.2fg 7fg —
8d 6s 7g 1983 7s 5s 5s) bad plater; has twice been blinkered; sold 900 gns Ascot
2nd June Sales. *P. Burgoyne.*

MAXIMOVA (FR) 3 b.f. Green Dancer 132–Baracala (Swaps) (1982 6s* 6d* 121
6fg* 7g* 7f* 8s⁴ 1983 8v 8d³ 8v² 6fg 6.5fg² 6f* 6fg* 5d⁴)
We were somewhat surprised when Maximova was switched to sprinting
following her good efforts over a mile in the spring. She had stayed the distance
when placed in the mud behind L'Attrayante in both the Poule d'Essai des Pouliches
and the Goffs Irish One Thousand Guineas, and since the very best of her excellent
two-year-old form had been shown on a sound surface there were grounds for
thinking she'd have improved even on those two efforts over similar distances, or
possibly still further, when the ground dried out. Perhaps having Ma Biche in the
stable for the top mile races was at the root of the matter. Switching Maximova to
sprinting yielded two minor pattern-race victories yet left us unconvinced of its
wisdom.

Maximova was last into the straight at both Longchamp and the Curragh, and
in the circumstances did well to finish as close as she did. At Longchamp, in a field
of ten, she was brought with a trouble-free run on the outside to finish third, beaten

Prix de Meautry, Deauville—Maximova holds on by a head from Gabitat

two lengths, but at the Curragh there were almost twice as many runners and, by the time Maximova had threaded her way through, the winner had been kicked clear; Maximova came out clear second best though, ahead of Annie Edge and Flame of Tara, and was beaten only a length and a half.

Maximova didn't make an immediate success of sprinting, but considering the magnitude of her task in the William Hill July Cup at Newmarket on her first venture she wasn't disgraced in finishing seventh of fifteen behind Habibti and Soba; she wore blinkers there incidentally, but they weren't fitted again. At Deauville the following month she did better, travelling strongly most of the way and running the improving Beaudelaire to half a length in the half-furlong longer Prix Maurice de Gheest. And when faced with second-rate opposition in the Prix de Meautry at Deauville later in August and in the Prix de Seine-et-Oise at Maisons-Laffitte in September she was able to regain the winning thread. In the Meautry she was outpaced early on but got up on the line to beat the English-trained four-year-old Gabitat by a head while at Maisons-Laffitte, in one of the weakest of pattern-race fields, she was able to make just about all the running and win easily by two and a half lengths from Lyphard's Princess. Maximova finished only fourth to Bold Apparel in the Prix du Petit Couvert at Longchamp in October on her only subsequent start, outpaced throughout over five furlongs, and was then retired to stud.

		Nijinsky	Northern Dancer
	Green Dancer	(b 1967)	Flaming Page
	(b 1972)	Green Valley	Val de Loir
Maximova (Fr)		(br 1967)	Sly Pola
(b.f. 1980)		Swaps	Khaled
	Baracala	(ch 1952)	Iron Reward
	(ch 1972)	Seximee	Hasty Road
		(ch 1966)	Jambo

Maximova is a big, attractive, imposing filly; she looked magnificent in the paddock before the Prix Maurice de Gheest. Her sire Green Dancer did so well in his first few seasons at stud in France that his sale to the United States in 1981 was almost inevitable. Some of Green Dancer's fillies have done particularly well, with Aryenne and The Dancer in his first crop, Anitra's Dance and Premiere Danseuse in his second, Dancing Rocks in his third and Maximova, Brillante and Green Lucia in his fourth. All except Maximova showed form over middle distances, and so did Maximova's older sister Disco Girl who won over a mile and a half from only three outings. Disco Girl and Maximova are the first two reported foals produced by Baracala, a useful mile winner and a half-sister to the Two Thousand Guineas winner Nonoalco and the very smart Stradavinsky. *Mme C. Head, France.*

MAYAMA 2 ch.f. Vitiges 132–Friendly Goddess 80 (Green God 128) (1983 8g 7g* 7g) Feb 9; second reported foal; sister to a placed animal in France; dam, half-sister to Bay Express, was second over 5f at 2 yrs; creditable fifth, beaten about 3½ lengths, to Procida in Criterium de Maisons-Laffitte in October; had run on from distance to lead close home and account for Tranchard by ¾ length in maiden event on same track earlier in month; not sure to stay further than 1m. *P. Laloum, France.*   **105**

MAYBEHANDY 5 b.m. Some Hand 119–Unpredictable 103 (Pardal 130) (1982 7.2s 7fg³ 7f 7fg³ 7f* 7fg² 7g 1983 7.2v 7v 6fg 6f⁴ 8.2fg 8g 7g) leggy mare; plater; suited by 7f and 1m; probably acts on any going; needs holding up. *M. Camacho.*   **–**

MAY BE THIS TIME 2 ch.c. Be My Guest 126–Honeybuzzard (Sea Hawk II 131) (1983 5s 5g 6d⁴ 7f² 7fg 7fg 10fg*) Jan 31; big, rangy colt; second foal; half-brother to a middle-distance winner in Australia by Malacate; dam Irish 1¼m winner; awarded maiden race at Nottingham in October on disqualification of ¾-length winner My Aisling; suited by 1¼m, and will stay 1½m; seems to act on any going; blinkered third to fifth outings; trained by B. Hobbs first 5 starts. *J. Hardy.*   **74**

MAYLANDS 3 b.f. Windjammer (USA)–Toblerone (Honeyway 125) (1982 NR 1983 8f 10f 10d 8fg⁴ 10fg) 18,000Y; tall, rather lightly-made, fair sort; sister to smart French and Italian miler El-Muleta and half-sister to 2 winners, including very smart Irish sprinter Cinerama Two (by Sound Track); dam never ran; showed a little ability on several occasions; promises to stay 1¼m; brought down final start. *C. Brittain.*   **–**

MAYO BOY 3 b.g. Decoy Boy 129–Hethabella 62 (Hethersett 134) (1982 5f 6g² 5fg⁴ 6g 6d⁴ 6g 1983 7s 8d 8s² 8v 8f 8fg) good-topped gelding; stays 1m; best   **61**

form with some give in the ground; blinkered final start; sold to G. Blum 3,000 gns Newmarket September Sales. *W. Wharton.*

MAYOTTE 8 ch.m. Little Buskins 118–Jill Scott (Jock Scot 121) (1982 14g 11.7d 12fg³ 16.1s* 16.1s* 20g* 18s² 1983 18d* 16v³ 18.8v 15g² 18fg4 20fg*) smart staying hurdler and fair handicapper on flat; routed her rivals in Doncaster Town Plate in March, beating Cheka 15 lengths, and was a game winner at Newmarket in October, beating Moon Mariner by 2 lengths; in frame most starts in between, on last occasion coming home 1¾ lengths fourth to Bajan Sunshine in Tote Cesarewitch, also at Newmarket; suited by a thorough test of stamina; probably acts on any going, but is well suited by soft; has won for an apprentice; genuine. *R. Holder.*   **82**

MAYPOLE DANCER 2 b.c. Dance In Time–Spring Clump 87 (Mount Hagen 127) (1983 7f 7fg 8d* 8g³) Mar 16; tall, useful-looking colt; first foal; dam best at 2 yrs; made all in 16-runner maiden race at Warwick in October; creditable 4½ lengths third of 5 to Ashgar in minor event at Leicester later in month; suited by 1m and an easy surface; sold 14,000 gns Newmarket Autumn Sales. *J. Dunlop.*   **87**

MAYSARA 2 b.c. Be My Guest 126–Bentinck Hotel 74 (Red God 128§) (1983 7fg) Feb 16; 80,000Y; big, strong colt; second foal; brother to 3-y-o 5f winner Conrad Hilton; dam 2-y-o 5f winner; short-priced favourite, hampered leaving stalls and eased once chance had gone when out of first 11 of 26 behind Alleging in maiden race at Newmarket in September; sure to do better. *G. Harwood.*   **– p**

MAZIMMA 2 ch.f. Vitiges 132–Manushka (Sheshoon 132) (1983 8g 7s) May 3; fair sort; good mover; half-sister to 2 winners, including 1¼m winner Manntika (by Kalamoun); dam, minor 11f winner, is sister to very useful French long-distance horse Croque Monsieur; little sign of ability in big fields of maidens at Leicester in the autumn. *F. J. Houghton.*   **–**

MAZYOUN (USA) 2 gr.f. Blushing Groom 131–She's Decided (Decidedly) (1983 6fg 6f) Mar 21; $170,000F; half-sister to 3 winners, including stakes-placed Hill Fox (by Hillary); dam, stakes-placed winner, is half-sister to smart Hill Shade, the dam of Mysterious and J. O. Tobin; soundly beaten in August maiden races at Brighton and Folkestone; probably needs further. *P. Walwyn.*   **–**

MEADEWAY 3 b.f. Roi Soleil 125–Cotillion 73 (Gala Performance) (1982 5.3fg 5fg 5fg² 6f4 1983 7s 6s 7v² 7fg 8f 8g4 8g 10g) small, sparely-made, plain individual; plater; probably stays 1m; has run creditably on firm going, but seems better suited by some give. *H. Westbrook.*   **64**

MEADOWBROOK 2 b.c. Mill Reef 141–Hurlingham 102 (Harken 113) (1983 8.2fg 10.2fg²) Feb 20; 155,000Y; big, rangy colt; third foal; half-brother to useful 1979 2-y-o 6f winner Roehampton (by Sharp Edge); dam won over 7f and 1¼m; 16/1, came through strongly in closing stages, after being under pressure long way out, to finish second of 24 behind easy winner Raami in minor event at Doncaster in November; very much a stayer, and looks sure to win races at 1½m+. *I. Balding.*   **83 p**

MEAN FRANCINE 4 b.f. African Sky 124–Levrosa (Levmoss 133) (1982 8g4 7.3g4 7g4 8f 10g 1983 6g) tall, good-topped filly; put up a highly creditable effort on second outing at 3 yrs when fourth of 10 to Pas de Seul in Hungerford Stakes at Newbury; didn't reproduce that form; should have stayed 1m; blinkered only start of 1983 in April; sold, covered by Tyrnavos, 5,400 gns Newmarket December Sales. *P. Kelleway.*   **–**

MEASLES 2 ch.f. Tickled Pink 114–Outburst 57 (Articulate 121) (1983 5s 5v 5.1fg 5g 6f 6g) May 24; neat filly; has a round action; third foal; half-sister to a winning plater; dam won over 11f; poor form, including in a seller; blinkered last 3 starts. *G. Blum.*   **46**

MEAUME 3 b.c. High Line 125–Cissac (Indian Ruler 89) (1982 8s 8.2s 1983 8v 12v² 12v² 14s4 13.3g 14d) neat, strong, close-coupled colt who carries a fair bit of condition; came up against useful horses each time when in frame in maiden and minor events at Wolverhampton, Kempton and York in spring; stays well; seems to need plenty of give in the ground; needed race after a 4-month lay-off final start. *D. Ancil.*   **65**

MEDAALA 3 b.f. Owen Dudley 121–Mathilde 84 (Whistler 129) (1982 5g* 5g* 5f² 5f4 1983 6v 5f 5f 5.6f) lengthy, light-framed filly; broke a knee bone as a 2-y-o and was soundly beaten on her return (bandaged and very unimpressive on second outing); in foal to Sonnen Gold. *K. Stone.*   **–**

MEEKA GOLD (USA) 4 b.c. Ward McAllister–Locklear (First Landing) (1982 7g 7g 10.4fg4 10f² 10f² 10g 10f 10.4d* 10.5g4 11d² 10g 10.8s* 1983 10.6v³ 10v 10.2v4 10s 12v 12fg³ 10f4 12f* 12.3g² 12g² 11g 10.8d* 10.2fg² 12fg) strong, good sort; fairly useful performer; readily justified favouritism in slowly-run amateur   **96**

riders race at Thirsk in July and minor event at Warwick in October; beat Lobkowiez 4 lengths on latter; stays 1½m; acts on any going; suitable mount for an inexperienced rider; ran creditably when tried in blinkers on tenth outing, though pulled very hard early on; sent to USA. *S. Norton.*

MEESON GRANGE 2 b.c. Miami Springs 121–Hello Amy 70 (Forlorn River 124) (1983 5d⁴ 5g* 6f⁴ 7f⁴ 7f 7f⁴ 7.2g⁴ 6g 7fg) Apr 26; IR 15,500F, 15,000Y; tall, lengthy colt; half-brother to useful sprinter Touch Boy (by Touch Paper); dam placed over 5f at 2 yrs; won 6-runner maiden race at Ayr in May; creditable fourth under big weights in nurseries at Yarmouth and Haydock on sixth and seventh outings; stays 7f; often blinkered. *J. Berry.*   **86**

MEESON KING 2 b.c. Space King 115–Meeson Girl (Tyrant) (1983 5d* 5d* 5f⁴ 7d 5d) Apr 27; leggy, workmanlike colt; first foal; dam won three 5f races in Ireland; won sellers at Wolverhampton (retained 7,300 gns) and Redcar (bought in 3,000 gns) in May; off course for over 2 months after next outing; acts on firm going and a soft surface. *J. Berry.*   **57**

MEGAN 7 b.m. Mandamus 120–Brown Sugar (Presentiment) (1982 NR 1983 12s) non-thoroughbred mare; well beaten in lady riders race at Lingfield in June, first outing on flat. *Dr A. Jones.*   **–**

MEGASTAR (USA) 2 b.c. Star de Naskra–Lady Katie G (Amberoid) (1983 6d²) Mar 19; $35,000F, $135,000Y; smallish, quite attractive colt; half-brother to 2 winners in USA; dam, half-sister to high-class middle-distance performer Golden Don, won twice at up to 1m; sire, winner from 5f to 9f, was best sprinter of 1979; 10/1, moved badly to start when 3 lengths second of 16 to Turn The Key in maiden race at Newbury in October; will be suited by 7f and 1m; should improve. *G. Hunter.*   **79 p**

MEHRAGAN 3 gr.f. Dance In Time–First Watch (Primera 131) (1982 7d 7s 1983 9f 7.2fg 9fg 6h 8d 5g 8fg) good-bodied filly; poor mover; no worthwhile form, including in sellers. *R. Hollinshead.*   **–**

MEIG 2 b.c. Hotfoot 126–Pamagilan 89 (Pall Mall 132) (1983 5s⁴ 5v⁴ 7f* 7.2g 7fg² 7d 7fg³ 8s² 8fg 8g) Mar 27; 9,600Y; lengthy, rather narrow colt; good mover; brother to prolific Italian winner Lady Marmalade and half-brother to several winners; dam won over 5f at 2 yrs; won 9-runner maiden event at Wolverhampton in June; close second subsequently in minor event won by Falstaff at Chester and £4,300 nursery won by Courting Season at Doncaster; suited by 1m; acts on any going; genuine. *F. J. Houghton.*   **94**

MEIKLEOUR 4 b.g. Reliance II 137–Videmanette (High Perch 126) (1982 12fg⁴ 14.6g³ 14fg 16s 1983 14fg² 17.4g 16.1s) good-bodied gelding; ran creditably first start but poorly afterwards; should stay long distances; a strong puller. *J. W. Watts.*   **63**

MEIO LEME 2 b.f. Porto Bello 118–Starboard Belle 85 (Right Tack 131) (1983 5f 5g) Apr 17; lightly-built filly; fifth foal; half-sister to 1982 2-y-o 1m winner Mick's Star (by Orange Bay); dam won over 6f and 7f at 2 yrs; showed ability without being dangerous in minor events at Warwick in August and Redcar in November; will probably be better suited by 6f. *A. Jarvis.*   **65**

MEIS EL-REEM 2 b.f. Auction Ring 123–Tavella 98 (Petingo 135) (1983 5d 5g* 5fg*) Feb 9; IR 23,000Y; well-made filly; half-sister to 2 winners, including fairly useful Italian filly Swing Faster (by Swing Easy); dam at her best at 2 yrs when 6f winner; put up an impressive display in 20-runner maiden race at Warwick in October, leading over 1f out and drawing right away to beat Pendona by 10 lengths; didn't have best of runs when getting home by a head (value 2 lengths) from Deccan Queen in more strongly-contested race at Doncaster later in month; will stay 6f; a very useful sprinter in the making. *M. Albina.*   **102**

MELAURA BELLE 2 br.f. Meldrum 112–Aur (Aureole 132) (1983 5f 5f² 5f* 6f³ 6g*) May 13; strong-quartered filly; second foal; dam ran only twice; won maiden race at Catterick in August and very valuable Sha Tin Nursery (beating Ideal Home going away by ½ length) at York in October; suited by 6f and may stay further; has raced only on a sound surface. *T. Barron.*   **91**

MELBA TOAST 9 br.g. Meldrum 112–Ivory Coast 90 (Poaching 115) (1982 5fg 6g 5fg² 5g 5fg 5fg 1983 5v 6d⁴ 5fg 5fg) strong gelding; sprint plater; acted on any going; often wore blinkers; sometimes gave trouble at start and was banned from racing by Stewards of Jockey Club in July. *T. Taylor.*   **§§**

MELCOMBE REGIS 3 b.c. Red Alert 127–Alcinea 93 (Sweet Revenge 129) (1982 5g 5f³ 5s 1983 6v) small, good-bodied colt; tailed off in seller, only outing of 1983 (April); sold 330 gns Doncaster November Sales. *M. McCormack.*   **–**

Wokingham Stakes, Ascot—the tiring Melindra (left) just holds Milk Heart's late flourish

MELINDRA 4 b.f. Gold Form 108–Welsh Spear (Welsh Saint 126) (1982 5f³ 5g 5g 83
7d 5g² 5f* 5.8f 1983 6v* 6f* 6f 5.6fg³ 6s 5d) strong, lengthy, workmanlike filly;
sprint handicapper; beat Piencourt comfortably in £5,300 event at Kempton in May
and Milk Heart by a neck in Wokingham Stakes at Royal Ascot; favourite, made all
and was clear at halfway in latter but tired in closing stages and only just held on;
good third to Out of Hand and Ismore in Portland Handicap at Doncaster in
September; stayed 6f; acted on any going; sweated up when well beaten final start;
reportedly visits Glint of Gold. *D. Elsworth.*

MELISSA CLAIRE 2 b.f. Camden Town 125–First Bleep (Bleep-Bleep 134) –
(1983 5f 5f 6f) Mar 18; IR 12,000Y; strong, workmanlike filly; half-sister to Irish
3-y-o Godspell (by Godswalk) and useful sprinter Poldhu (by Manado); dam Irish
2-y-o 5f winner; in rear in maiden races and a minor event in the South. *J.
Benstead.*

MELISSA JANE 5 gr.m. No Mercy 126–Rich Harvest (Bounteous 125) (1982 7f 82
8f 8f 7.6f* 6fg 8g 8g 7s⁴ 8v 8s 7d 1983 8d 8f* 8.3fg⁴ 8g 8.3fg² 8fg³ 8fg) lengthy
mare; good mover; fairly useful at her best but was inconsistent; 20/1 when
decisively winning apprentice handicap at Ascot in July; stayed 1m well; seemed
to act on any going, but clearly went well on firm; sometimes gave trouble at
start; trained part of season by R. Thompson; in foal to Imperial Fling. *N. Vigors.*

MELLITE 3 ch.f. Diamonds Are Trump 108–Ziobia 78 (Tribal Chief 125) (1982 –
NR 1983 7.2fg 8fg) first foal; dam placed at up to 7f; behind in maiden race at
Haydock (backward) and minor event at Thirsk. *K. Stone.*

MELLOW DANCE (FR) 2 b.c. Fabulous Dancer 124–Red Murmaid (Riverman 91
131) (1983 5s⁴ 5v⁴ 6f 7.2g² 7f 7g*(dis) 8s 8fg) Feb 23; 270,000 francs Y (approx
£22,500); neat colt; second foal; half-brother to American 3-y-o 8.5f winner Red
Palace (by Crystal Palace), second over 7.5f and 1¼m at 2 yrs in France; dam minor
French middle-distance winner; won £5,200 nursery at Chester in August but was
later disqualified because his apprentice rider drew the wrong allowance; placed
only once otherwise, but on last 2 appearances ran creditably, though soundly
beaten, in Prix La Rochette at Longchamp and Royal Lodge Stakes at Ascot; will
stay 1¼m; blinkered fourth and fifth outings. *P. Kelleway.*

MEL MIRA 3 ch.f. Roi Soleil 125–Hei'land Mary 76 (Highland Melody 112) (1982 68
6g 6g² 6d³ 8f 8.2d 1983 8v 9s² 7fg* 7fg 8f 6fg 6fg² 7fg² 6f 8.2g* 7fg) good-bodied

filly; bought in after winning sellers at Leicester in June (1,100 gns) and Haydock in October (3,100 gns); sold privately out of D. H. Jones's stable 3,500 gns Doncaster October Sales and ran respectably in a non-seller the following day; stays 9f; probably acts on any going; best in blinkers; sometimes bandaged. *T. Craig.*

MELOWEN 3 ch.f. Owen Dudley 121–Gambit (King's Troop 118) (1982 5fg 5f² 6f³ 5fg² 7f 7f² 6g² 7fg 7d² 8f 6v² 7d⁴ 1983 6s 8v 8f² 8f 10f³ 10f 10f 10f 8g 7s² 6g 7g) leggy filly; second in handicap at Doncaster and minor event at Ayr, best efforts; behind in valuable seller on one occasion; not sure to stay 1¼m; acts on any going; sometimes blinkered. *D. Plant.*   **53**

MELROSE VALE 3 ch.f. Runnymede 123–Premier Bond 90 (Good Bond 122) (1982 NR 1983 6s 7s) 1,700Y; second foal; dam stayed 1m well; tailed off in maiden and minor races at Ayr. *J. S. Wilson.*   **–**

MEL'S CHOICE 5 b. or br.g. Birdbrook 110–Port Meadow 83 (Runnymede 123) (1982 5f* 5f⁴ 5fg³ 5fg* 5fg* 5s³ 1983 5f³ 5g² 5f² 6f⁴ 5fg 6d 6f 5f⁴ 5g² 6s⁴ 5fg⁴ 6g⁴ 6fg 6fg) good-topped gelding; sprint handicapper; in frame most starts, running particularly well when fourth in William Hill Stewards' Cup at Goodwood (3½ lengths behind Autumn Sunset) and Ladbrokes (Ayr) Gold Cup (just over a length behind Polly's Brother) on fourth and tenth; stays 6f; acts on any going; effective with and without blinkers; genuine. *D. Plant.*   **81**

MELTHEMI (USA) 3 ch.c. Restless Wind–Surfboard Betty (Bold Commander) (1982 5fg 5fg⁴ 5fg³ 5f* 6g* 6f² 6g 5g 1983 8d 6d 6f⁴ 6fg³ 6fg* 6f) useful-looking colt; good mover; easily landed the odds from only 3 opponents in £9,500 Tote Sprint Trophy (Handicap) at Ayr in July, beating Grey Desire by 2½ lengths after being held up; had run creditably in similar events at Newmarket (2) and York on his 3 previous starts; suited by 6f and promises to stay further; yet to race on very soft going but acts on any other; had stiffish task and found little off bridle final outing (August). *M. H. Easterby.*   **98**

MELTON ROSS 3 br.g. Dawn Review 105–Boudella 101 (Rockefella) (1982 6d 6fg⁴ 7f 7fg 5g 5g 7d 7s 1983 6fg 10f 8fg 18fg) leggy, lightly-made, close-coupled gelding; plating-class maiden; should stay at least 1m; blinkered third start. *D. Morrill.*   **–**

MEMORIA IN ETERNA 3 br.g. Rheingold 137–Fighting Lady 104 (Chebs Lad 120) (1982 7fg⁴ 7g 1983 7s 8s 6f² 6fg* 6fg² 6f² 6f 6d 6d) fair sort; won handicap at Nottingham in July and was narrowly beaten next 2 starts; stays 7f; suited by a firm surface; sold 1,700 gns Newmarket Autumn Sales. *R. Baker.*   **79**

MENALEE 3 b.g. Gracious Melody 117–Miss Della (Chinese Lacquer 96) (1982 NR 1983 11d 12f 12f) 420 2-y-o; second foal; dam ran only twice on flat; behind in maiden races at Redcar (2) and Beverley. *R. Ward.*   **–**

MENDEZ (FR) 2 gr.c. Bellypha 130–Miss Carina (Caro 133) (1983 6f 5.5fg* 8g* 8f³ 8fg²)   **121**

Although only Green Dancer has won the William Hill Futurity for France— and he did it back in 1974 when the race was known as the Observer Gold Cup—several other French challengers have come with excellent qualifications. Of the French runners in the last dozen years Choucri had won the Robert Papin, Earth Spirit the Criterium de Maisons-Laffitte, Mississipian the Grand Criterium and both Stanleyville and In Fijar the Prix des Chenes, while Kalamoun, Mount Hagen and Northern Baby were others to have shown abundant promise. Mendez, the 1983 challenger from France, was also very well qualified: he had justified favouritism in great style in a minor event at Evry in July on his second start, winning easily after being clear at halfway, before acquitting himself very creditably in two pattern events at Longchamp, the Prix des Chenes in September and the Grand Criterium in October. In none too strong a field for the Chenes Mendez started an even-money favourite, with only Green Paradise, an improving half-brother to Green Forest, backed to beat him. Once again his regular rider Asmussen made plenty of use of Mendez, taking him to the front at a modest gallop from the start, and none of the others was able to land a blow as he quickened the tempo in the straight; the filly Ina Seville chased Mendez home at a distance of two and a half lengths. Carson had the mount on Mendez in the Grand Criterium, as Asmussen was aboard the other Boutin runner Seattle Song, winner of the Prix de la Salamandre. Whether Carson was riding to orders we don't know but this time the colt was held at the back, pulling hard, as Lucky Scott and Green Paradise set what looked a very fast gallop. Unfortunately for Carson most of the eight other runners were still in with a chance when he asked Mendez to improve in the straight and the horse had anything but a clear run, being forced to check when full

Prix des Chenes, Longchamp—Mendez comfortably lands the odds from Ina Seville

of running at the distance. Once Mendez finally saw daylight he ran on so strongly he snatched third place, only a length and a half behind Treizieme.

Mendez was made a short-priced favourite at Doncaster to succeed where so many French colts had failed; understandably, since he was the only one of the nine runners to have gained a place, let alone a win, in pattern company. Strangely Mendez was pulled back to the rear by Asmussen despite once more showing signs of resenting restraint—he tended to race with his head up. He was still at the rear early in the straight, with little room to manoeuvre, and he began to cut back the deficit only when switched outside entering the last three furlongs. He looked likely to overcome his difficulties as he loomed up alongside Ilium and Alphabatim at the distance but he then drifted left under pressure, losing a little momentum, and was half a length adrift of Alphabatim at the post. We can't help thinking Mendez would have won had he been allowed to stride along.

Mendez (Fr) (gr.c. Apr 2, 1981)	Bellypha (gr 1976)	Lyphard (b 1969)	Northern Dancer Goofed
		Belga (gr 1968)	Le Fabuleux Belle de Retz
	Miss Carina (gr 1975)	Caro (gr 1967)	Fortino II Chambord
		Miss Pia (br 1965)	Olympia Ultimate Weapon

At 1,000,000 francs, or approximately £83,000, Mendez was the most expensive of Bellypha's first yearlings sold at auction. He has proved well worth the money and several of his sire's other representatives have done enough to suggest that Bellypha will soon be joining the numerous top-class French stallions now at stud in the States. Betsy Bay, Boreale and Misbehaving, all by Bellypha, established themselves among the leading staying two-year-old fillies in their respective countries and Don Basile, a winner twice in the autumn, showed plenty of potential. Bellypha was a top-class performer at around a mile who stayed well enough to finish fourth of eleven in the Prix du Jockey-Club. Mendez's dam Miss Carina was also a notable performer, the highest-rated filly in the 1977 Italian classification of two-year-olds after winning two important mile events, the Premio Dormello and the Criterium Femminile, and two other races from six starts. Significantly Miss Carina made all when gaining her two important successes, earning the description in the *Italian Breeding Bulletin* of 'a fast but one-paced filly who is at her best when taking her field along.' She wasn't so good at three, though successful once and third in the one-mile Premio Royal Mares. Mendez is her second foal; her first, the Nonoalco filly Miss Victoria, won in Italy as a two-year-old and her third a colt by Green Dancer which fetched 1,800,000 francs at the 1983 Deauville Yearling Sales. Miss Carina is a half-sister to numerous minor winners produced by the unraced Miss Pia. The next dam Ultimate Weapon is another who didn't race but she was a daughter of a very good filly, Outer Space, the winner of such important events as the Mother Goose Stakes and the Beldame, Bed O'Roses and Vagrancy Handicaps.

Mendez, a tall colt, undoubtedly has plenty of ability and should win more good races at around a mile. There must be a question about his temperament, though, and it is interesting that his trainer, when asked to compare his Grand Criterium runners, said 'in terms of sheer class, Mendez is the better but Seattle Song appears the tougher.' Perhaps a return to more enterprising tactics will prove the answer to Mendez; also his round action suggests he'll be more at home on softer ground than he's met so far. *F. Boutin, France.*

MEN

MENDICK ADVENTURE 2 b.f. Mandrake Major 122–Open House 91 (Road   **72**
House II) (1983 5v³ 5s² 5s³ 5fg³ 5f²) Apr 18; 750F; well-grown filly; fourth
reported foal; dam best at up to 7f; placed in maiden events; blinkered at Newcastle
in June on final appearance. *D. Smith.*

MEND IT 5 ch.g. Patch 129–Startop 72 (Divine Gift 127) (1982 9f 10f 8f 10fg 12fg   **40**
1983 17.1h³ 15g² 16.1g 15.8d) leggy, close-coupled gelding; former plater; clearly
suited by a stiff test of stamina; has been blinkered; suitable mount for an
apprentice. *N. Bycroft.*

MENINGI 2 ch.c. Bustino 136–Miss Filbert 95 (Compensation 127) (1983 7fg)   **– p**
Mar 1; 34,000F; strong, attractive colt; third foal; half-brother to 5f winner Prison
Payment (by Song); dam quite useful 7f to 1m handicapper; 20/1, never showed in
Houghton Stakes at Newmarket in October; likely to do better. *M. Jarvis.*

MENTON 3 b.g. Relkino 131–Antimacassar 86 (Tudor Melody 129) (1982 7fg 7g   **–**
8g 1983 8s 11.5f) well-made, quite attractive gelding; no worthwhile form in
varied races; sold 2,000 gns Newmarket September Sales. *R. Armstrong.*

MERAVAL 2 ch.c. Ahonoora 122–Sea Swallow 90 (Dan Cupid 132) (1983 5g² 5s³   **96**
6g* 6f² 7g 6f 6fg 7g* 7.3d) Feb 25; 24,000Y; close-coupled, good-quartered colt;
good mover; closely related to 1979 2-y-o 7f winner Good Companions (by
Lorenzaccio) and half-brother to 3 winners; dam won over 1¼m; won maiden race
at Yarmouth in June and £4,900 event at Goodwood in September; stays 7f;
probably acts on any going. *M. Ryan.*

MERCIA SOUND 4 b.c. Wishing Star 117–Audition (Tower Walk 130) (1982   **–**
12g³ 12s 12f³ 10.6fg⁴ 12f⁴ 12f⁴ 1983 12v 11f 10g 10.6g 12d) lengthy, useful sort;
poor middle-distance handicapper; acts on firm going; tends to pull hard. *R.
Hollinshead.*

MERCREDI 4 b.g. Mount Hagen 127–Amorce 81 (Le Levanstell 122) (1982 8d   **–**
10fg 11f 10f 11.7d 1983 11.7fg) lengthy gelding; beaten some way in varied races;
has given trouble at start. *M. Madgwick.*

MERDON MONARCH 2 ch.g. Relko 136–Palmavista 120 (Royal Palm 131)   **–**
(1983 7d 7fg 7g) May 15; 10,000Y; fair sort; brother to 3-y-o Sausage and useful 6f
to 1½m winner Limone, and half-brother to 3 winners, including useful middle-
distance performers Bigribo (by Ribero) and Crested Grebe (by Blakeney); dam
good winner at up to 1m; well beaten in autumn maiden events. *R. Sheather.*

MERELY A SECRET (USA) 3 ch.c. Secretariat–Lady Mere 118 (Decoy Boy   **78**
129) (1982 6d 7d 7g* 7g 8g² 7.6fg 1983 8s³ 8s* 7v² 8v⁴ 8f⁴ 8f 8f² 8h² 8.2h³ 8fg)
robust, short-legged, good-looking colt; first past post in handicaps at Salisbury in
May and Wolverhampton in August, but placings were reversed after beating
Monetarist by ½ length on latter course on seventh start; in frame on most other
starts; lacks pace and will be suited by 1¼m; acts on any going; game and genuine.
P. Walwyn.

MERIKA 3 gr.f. Morston 125–Mariko (Dancer's Image) (1982 6s 1983 8.5d 10fg)   **–**
plain filly; behind in maiden races. *D. Whelan.*

MERION 2 b.g. The Brianstan 128–Hope Baggot (Hopeful Venture 125) (1983 5f   **69**
5fg³ 6fg 6fg) May 9; 2,300Y; strong, quite useful-looking gelding; good walker;
third foal; dam never ran; plating-class maiden; best form at 5f, but probably stays
6f; acts on firm going. *R. Sheather.*

MERITOUS 8 b.g. Decoy Boy 129–Welsh Huntress 106 (Big Game) (1982 6d 6f   **55**
7.6g 5fg 7g⁴ 6g 7.6fg 7f² 8g² 6d² 7g* 7g* 7d³ 6s 1983 7v 7s 7fg 7g 7f 8g³ 7f 7fg
7.2g 7g 8.2s) big, lengthy gelding; poor handicapper; stays 1m; acts on any going
but is suited by some give in the ground; has worn blinkers and bandages. *T.
Taylor.*

MERMAID 3 br.f. Furry Glen 121–Wavy Navy (Hardicanute 131) (1982 7fg 7g 8s   **58**
1983 9s³ 11.7v 10fg 10f 9d 12fg⁴) tall, angular filly; plating-class maiden; suited by
1½m. *D. Ringer.*

MERRIE DANCE 3 ch.f. Tobique 116–Machrihanish 71 (King's Company 124)   **§§**
(1982 NR 1983 8fg) first living foal; dam second over 5f at 2 yrs; refused to race in
seller at Wolverhampton in August. *T. Bill.*

MERRY SHARP 2 ch.f. Sharpen Up 127–Just Married 96 (Habitat 134) (1983   **–**
5g) Mar 4; robust filly; has a round action; first foal; dam, out of half-sister to very
smart stayer May Hill, won over 5f at 2 yrs and later won Norwegian 1000 Guineas;
behind in 14-runner maiden race at Haydock in September. *P. Cole.*

MERRY TASSE 3 ch.c. Rymer 121–Fragrant Coffee 80 (Frankincense 120) (1982   **60**
5g 5f² 5g² 5fg* 6fg 5f 5fg⁴ 5g* 5g 5f 5g³ 6d 5g 1983 5s 5s* 5g 6f 5f 5f 9fg)

530

compact, lightly-made colt; narrowly won handicap at Catterick in June, best effort; should stay further than 5f; acts on firm going, but is probably better with some give nowadays; none too consistent; bandaged fifth start. *W. Bentley.*

MERRY TOM 3 ch.g. Jimmy Reppin 131–Fluent 73 (Florescence 120) (1982 NR 1983 7v 8v 8.5d³ 10.1fg⁴ 8.3f² 9fg* 10fg 10d 10f⁴ 10g² 10fg²) 1,650F, 24,000Y, 2,600 2-y-o; lightly-made gelding; first living foal; dam, placed over 1m, is half-sister to good 5f sprinter Caterina and Eclipse winner Scottish Rifle; bought in 5,300 gns after winning seller at Redcar in August; ran well in non-sellers last 3 outings, particularly when head second to Road To The Top in minor event at Leicester in October on last; stays 1¼m well; acts on firm going; good mount for an apprentice. *A. Bailey.* 75

MERRYWREN 2 br.f. Julio Mariner 127–Hat Girl (High Hat 131) (1983 6fg 6fg 8g 8d) Mar 3; 6,400Y; compact filly; half-sister to several winners here and abroad, including useful sprinter Laldheer (by Swing Easy); dam of little account; no form in varied company. *R. Whitaker.* –

METCALFE FLEET 2 ch.g. Wollow 132–Time Was 76 (Crowned Prince 128) (1983 7f⁴ 8s) Feb 16; 2,000Y (privately); second foal; dam 1¼m winner; soundly beaten in minor race at Redcar in August and maiden event at Beverley in September. *M. W. Easterby.* –

METELSKI 2 b.c. Rusticaro 124–Wadowice (Targowice 130) (1983 7fg) Apr 23; IR 11,000Y; good-bodied colt; first foal; dam in rear in 2 outings at 2 yrs in Ireland; backward, scratched down to start when behind in 21-runner maiden race at Newmarket in September. *G. Huffer.* –

METUCHEN 3 ch.f. Star Appeal 133–Merchantmen's Girl 58 (Klairon 131) (1982 5f 6f 7f 7f 8fg 7v⁴ 1983 12s 10v 7fg 7h 8f 8f 8.2fg 8d 8g 8g) smallish, sturdy, quite attractive filly; poor maiden; stays 1m; sometimes blinkered; trained by D. Elsworth until after sixth outing. *Mrs M. Nesbitt.* –

MEZIARA 2 b.g. Dominion 123–Abertywi 87 (Bounteous 125) (1983 5fg 5f 7f 7g) Mar 29; 6,200Y; good-bodied gelding; fourth living foal; dam, winner over 7f and 1m, is sister to high-class sprinter Abergwaun; behind in minor and maiden events; gelded after final appearance. *P. Burgoyne.* –

MIAMI DANCER 2 ch.f. Miami Springs 121–Place To Place (No Robbery) (1983 7.6d) Apr 22; IR 4,800Y; half-sister to several winners, including 1981 2-y-o 5f winner Pass No Remarks (by Wolverlife); dam won at up to 6f in USA; behind in 18-runner maiden race at Lingfield in October. *D. Wilson.* –

MIAMI DOLPHIN 3 br.f. Derrylin 115–Magibbillibyte 77 (Constable 119) (1982 5fg³ 5fg² 5f² 5f 7g² 6f⁴ 5fg⁴ 7fg 1983 5v 8g⁴ 7fg³ 7fg⁴ 5g) small, workmanlike filly; good walker; in frame in varied races but didn't reproduce her 2-y-o form; probably stays 1m; acts on firm going; off course almost 3 months before running poorly final start; sold 1,350 gns Newmarket December Sales. *P. Kelleway.* 78

MIAMI HOLIDAY 2 b.g. Miami Springs 121–Targos Delight (Targowice 130) (1983 6f 6f 6f 6f⁴ 8fg) Apr 11; big, workmanlike gelding; second foal; dam unraced half-sister to top 1974 Irish 2-y-o Sea Break; plating-class maiden; stays 6f; blinkered fifth outing, and again when withdrawn after giving trouble at stalls on next intended appearance. *M. W. Easterby.* 67

MIAMI PRINCE 2 b.c. Miami Springs 121–Jessamy Hall 77 (Crowned Prince 128) (1983 5.8f 6f 5.8h⁴ 7fg 5f² 5fg 6d* 6fg* 6g) May 4; 3,800Y; big, good-quartered colt; has a round action; first foal; dam 1m winner; showed much improved form to win 12-runner selling nursery at Brighton (no bid) in September by 5 lengths from Leadenhall Boy; made light of 10 lb penalty in 18-runner nursery at Nottingham later in the month; apparently best at 6f; acts on a firm and a soft surface. *P. Cole.* 78

MIAMI STAR 2 b.f. Miami Springs 121–Corr Lady (Lorenzaccio 130) (1983 6s 7f 8d² 9g² 8g³ 8fg*) Mar 27; 4,000F; quite attractive, lightly-built filly; first foal; dam never ran; won maiden race at Edinburgh in November; stays 9f; acts on a firm and a soft surface. *J. Winter.* 80

MIANDRA 3 ch.f. Porto Bello 118–Moral (Aureole 132) (1982 5fg 6f 5f 7fg 7f*(dis) 8.2fg 8.2s 1983 7d 6d 8d) sturdy filly; plater; no form in 1983 (ran wide when blinkered final start); suited by 7f; acts on firm going; sold 580 gns Ascot May Sales. *N. Tinkler.* –

MICHARRO 2 b.g. African Sky 124–Make a Signal 76 (Royal Gunner) (1983 6fg 6fg⁴) Mar 26; 15,000F; quite attractive gelding; second foal; half-brother to a poor animal by Sparkler; dam successful stayer (won 7 times) from family of Raise You Ten; blinkered, ran on strongly under pressure from halfway to finish 2 lengths 85 fourth of 24 behind Native Charmer in maiden race at Doncaster in November; subsequently gelded; will be suited by 7f+; acts on a firm surface. *B. Hobbs.*

MICHEAL RICE 2 ch.c. Manado 130–Allegretto (Preciptic 122) (1983 5s 5d 5v* 5d² 5v* 6fg 5fg 5f 5g) May 4; 6,000Y; rather leggy, lightly-made colt; half-brother to several minor winners; dam of little account; successful in May in sellers at Newcastle (no bid) and Lingfield (bought in 2,500 gns); didn't show much afterwards, including in 3 nurseries; should stay 6f; probably needs a soft surface and acts well on heavy going. *J. Berry.*   **60**

MICKEY TIM 6 br.g. Gay Fandango 132–Amicable 73 (Bold Ruler) (1982 NR 1983 13.1h) tall, attractive gelding; fair handicapper at his best but is unreliable and probably ungenuine; suited by middle distances; acts on firm going; has twice worn blinkers. *J. Baker.*   **– §**

MICKS BABY 3 b.f. Roi Soleil 125–Andy's Girl 65 (Court Feathers 120) (1982 5g 6g 5fg⁴ 5g 5s 5s 1983 6d 6fg 5fg 5f 6fg⁴ 6fg 6fg* 8d⁴ 7fg) compact filly; sold out of D. Ancil's stable 1,700 gns after winning apprentice seller at Windsor in August; stays 6f; apparently requires a firm surface. *M. Tate.*   **49**

MICK'S RITUAL 4 ch.g. Malacate 131–Aurabella 113 (Aureole 132) (1982 10g 10d 14.7f 9s 1983 11d) leggy, lengthy gelding; poor maiden on flat though has won over hurdles; has worn blinkers. *M. W. Easterby.*   **–**

MICK'S STAR 3 br.g. Orange Bay 131–Starboard Belle 85 (Right Tack 131) (1982 6g 7f 8f² 8d* 1983 12f⁴ 12f 12d 8d) big, rather leggy gelding; has rather a round action; little worthwhile form in 1983 (probably flattered first outing); should stay at least 1¼m; seems to act on any going but may prove best with some give in the ground; suitable mount for an apprentice; wears bandages. *M. W. Easterby.*   **–**

MICKY FOX 2 ch.c. Porto Bello 118–Pertelot 63 (Falcon 131) (1983 5d 5f 6h 6fg 5d 5s) Apr 3; rangy colt; third foal; brother to quite useful 5f performer Jack Fox; dam won sellers over 7f and 1m; bad maiden; tailed off under a low weight in nursery final start. *T. Taylor.*   **–**

MIDAAN 2 ch.f. Sallust 134–Some Thing (Will Somers 114§) (1983 6d) Mar 13; 32,000Y; half-sister to 2 winners by Realm, including smart 1979 French 2-y-o 6.5f and 1m winner Light of Realm; dam won at 1m and 10.5f in France, and is sister to 4 winners, notably very smart 1m to 1¼m filly La Troublerie; ninth of 10 in maiden race at Yarmouth in September. *A. Stewart.*   **–**

MIDDLE VERDE (USA) 2 b.f. Sham–Sailingaway (Sail On-Sail On) (1983 6f 6f 6f) Jan 12; $62,000F, 30,000 gns Y; quite attractive filly; first foal; dam, sister to stakes winner Sailingon, was a stakes-placed winner at up to 6f; soundly beaten in varied company in the South, twice last. *G. Hunter.*   **–**

MIDDLIN THRANG 5 b.g. Farm Walk 111–Darling Do (Derring-Do 131) (1982 8fg⁴ 9g² 11fg* 12g* 12g² 12fg 11f² 12.2f* 10.6s 11s 12s 1983 12.2g 12fg³ 11d* 12f 12f* 12h 12f³ 12f³) small, workmanlike gelding; won handicaps at Ayr in June and Hamilton in July; stays 1½m; acts on any going, but is ideally suited by a sound surface; has run respectably for an apprentice; suited by waiting tactics; has sometimes looked none too resolute; sold to R. Carter 3,800 gns Doncaster September Sales. *Miss S. Hall.*   **62**

MIDNIGHT COMMANCHE 3 b.c. Julio Mariner 127–Argentina 115 (Nearco) (1982 NR 1983 10d) half-brother to numerous winners, including very smart Averof (by Sing Sing), a winner at up to 1¼m, very useful 1¼m winner Tierra Fuego (by Shantung) and good stayer Falkland (by Right Royal V); dam stayed 1½m; never-dangerous seventh of 13 behind Somerset Bridge in maiden race at Beverley in September; sold 560 gns Doncaster October Sales. *R. Boss.*   **–**

Royal Hunt Cup, Ascot—Mighty Fly wins her third handicap of the season. Fandangle beats Christmas Cottage (blinkers) for second place

MIDNIGHT FLIT 3 b.f. Bold Lad (Ire) 133–Tawny Owl 123 (Faberge II 121)   89
(1982 6f 7fg^2 7s^4 7s^4 1983 7f* 8f^2 8f^4 8.3f 8fg) neat, attractive filly; excellent
walker but has a sharp action; held on by ½ length from High Fandango in 20-runner
maiden event at Newcastle in June; ran well in handicaps next 2 outings; stays 1m;
acts on any going; well beaten last 2 starts. *H. T. Jones.*

MIDNIGHT MARY 8 b.m. Celtic Cone 116–Sweet Tyrolean (Tyrone 130) (1982   –
NR 1983 12f) of little account on flat though has won a selling hurdle. *R.
Hollinshead.*

MIDNIGHT MOUSE (USA) 3 gr.f. Silver Series–Hada Say (Sadair) (1982 5s^3 60
5fg^3 6fg^2 6g 8.2g^3 8f 7g 1983 7fg 7fg 10.1f^2 12f^2 10f* 12fg* 12g 10g^2 16d*) small
filly; bought in after winning sellers at Lingfield (1,700 gns), Newmarket (4,200
gns) and Lingfield again (3,400 gns); stays 2m; seems to act on any going; blinkered
first outing. *P. Cole.*

MIDNIGHT PROMISE 3 b.f. Homeboy 114–Hey There (I Say 125) (1982 NR   –
1983 8f) second foal; dam of no account; backward when tailed-off last of 13 in
maiden race at Salisbury in September. *Mrs J. Reavey.*

MIDWEEK SPECIAL 3 b. or br.f. Lucky Wednesday 124–Cherry Cake (Pieces   –
of Eight 128) (1982 6f 7f 7g 8f 1983 12s 7d 8fg 5f 13.8g) leggy filly; little
worthwhile form, including in sellers; should be suited by middle distances; sold out
of G. Pritchard-Gordon's stable 1,800 gns Ascot 2nd June Sales after second start.
T. Kersey.

MIFAWI 3 b. or br.f. Nonoalco 131–Lighted Lamp (Sir Gaylord) (1982 NR 1983   73
8g 8g^3 8f 10g^2 9.4f 10f^2) 54,000Y; leggy, quite attractive filly; ninth foal;
half-sister to 7 winners, including smart middle-distance stayer Torus (by Ribero);
dam half-sister to Crocket; placed in maiden and minor races at Ayr (2) and Ripon in
summer; will possibly stay beyond 1¼m; blinkered third to fifth starts; not much of
a battler; sent to USA. *J. W. Watts.*

MIGHTY FLUTTER 2 br.c. Rolfe 77–Lettuce 60 (So Blessed 130) (1983 8g)   –
May 5; third foal; half-brother to smart miler Mighty Fly (by Comedy Star); dam,
half-sister to Grand National winner Rubstic, was placed over 1½m; ninth of 15 in
maiden race at Sandown in October. *D. Elsworth.*

MIGHTY FLY 4 b.f. Comedy Star 121–Lettuce 60 (So Blessed 130) (1982 7fg   117
10.1fg 8d* 8g* 8fg^4 8fg^3 8fg^4 8g^2 8g^4 8g* 8s 1983 8d* 10v 8v^4 8s^4 8d* 8f* 8fg^2
8fg^3 8d*)
    There is something peculiarly pleasing about any horse's rise from the status
of ordinary handicapper to that of leading participant in pattern races. Jupiter Island
managed the feat in 1983 yet in all the justified publicity given to his splendid
achievement there was a tendency to ignore a runner who had improved even more
during the season, namely Mighty Fly. Successful in handicaps at Salisbury, Bath
and Newmarket at three, Mighty Fly was on the go from March to September as a
four-year-old and made tremendous strides, ending up running three fine races in
Group 3 events.
    Regrettably the Lincoln Handicap, first run in 1853 and formerly a major focus
of attention over the winter with a strong ante-post market, no longer occupies so
important a position, this despite the sponsorship it has received since 1969 from
the Irish Sweeps Board and the William Hill Organization. Possibly one reason for
the relative decline in interest is the unpredictable influence of the draw at
Doncaster, which took over the race in 1965 on the closure of the Lincoln track,
since these days it is not until the meeting starts that any idea can be obtained as to
which side, if either, is favoured. The 1983 running showed that those that raced on
the far side, including Mighty Fly, had a decided advantage. Set to receive weight
from more than half her rivals, Mighty Fly, some way back at halfway, came with a
strong run that took her to the front about a furlong out and enabled her to win
convincingly by two and a half lengths from Paperetto; though a long way clear on
the stand side the fourth home, Crossways, was still nearly four lengths adrift of
the winner.
    Mighty Fly stayed in handicap company for another five races and ran
consistently well. In the frame in the Jubilee at Kempton and the Hambleton
Handicap at York, looking unlucky after getting no sort of run in the latter, she
picked up the Whitsun Cup at Sandown by a neck from Fandrange before going to
Royal Ascot in an attempt to complete the Lincoln-Hunt Cup double. While plenty
of horses had tried to win both races in the same season over the previous hundred
and thirty years none had succeeded, so Mighty Fly's success in the Hunt Cup

broke new ground. Carrying 9-3—she had understandably risen markedly in the weights since March—Mighty Fly once again showed how powerful a weapon her turn of foot could be, moving through in the second half of the race, leading inside the final furlong and bursting clear to beat Fandangle decisively by a length and a half.

Soon after the Hunt Cup Paul Mellon purchased Mighty Fly privately and she left the stable of Elsworth, who deserves praise for his handling of her, to join Balding. She immediately stepped up in class, travelling to Deauville to compete in the Prix d'Astarte in August. There is a world of difference between cutting down handicappers after using waiting tactics and cutting down high-class performers, and Saint-Martin unquestionably overdid things on Mighty Fly. Last with a quarter of a mile to travel she finished to some purpose without ever looking likely to reach Luth Enchantee, who had taken it up a furlong and a half out, eventually going down by a length and a half. Luth Enchantee had not yet reached the form she was to show later in the year but with Mighty Fly finishing ahead of such as the classic fillies Mysterieuse Etoile and Ma Biche, both admittedly carrying penalties, the British filly had obviously put in a splendid effort. She returned to the French course for the Prix Quincey later in the month and confirmed her improvement despite not having much luck in running. Held up in last place Mighty Fly had just been switched to begin her run two furlongs out when she received a hefty bump from the weakening Castle Guard which completely unbalanced her; though eating up the ground once she had recovered, the post came too soon and she finished third to Great Substence and Pampabird, beaten just over a length. The older French milers were not a particularly good collection but Pampabird and the fourth, African Joy, won four pattern races between them during the year while Great Substence went on to finish a fine third to Time Charter in the mile-and-a-half Prix Foy, so there is no reason to question the quality of Mighty Fly's performance.

After these excellent displays Mighty Fly looked to have a marvellous opportunity of winning a pattern race in the Gilltown Stud Stakes at the Curragh in September and she started a short-priced favourite to beat fourteen opponents including the Brownstown Stakes winner Bay Empress and the very useful English filly Fenny Rough. In the event Mighty Fly had to struggle to gain the spoils, perhaps because she was beginning to feel the effects of her tough season. Ridden nearer the pace than in France she challenged Bay Empress for the lead a couple of furlongs from home but had difficulty going past and in a driving finish it required all her courage to win by a neck and a short head from the fast-finishing El Kantaoui

Gilltown Stud Stakes, the Curragh—Mighty Fly (noseband) flies higher and beats El Kantaoui (right)

'Mr Paul Mellon's "Mighty Fly"

and Bay Empress. The Gilltown Stud Stakes turned out to be Mighty Fly's final race; she visits Mill Reef and however able the product of this mating may be it ought to lack for nothing in gameness.

Mighty Fly (b.f. 1979)	Comedy Star (b 1968)	Tom Fool (b 1949)	Menow / Gaga
		Latin Walk (br 1960)	Roman Tread / Stall Walker
	Lettuce (b 1972)	So Blessed (br 1965)	Princely Gift / Lavant
		Leuze (b 1963)	Vimy / Over the Border

Comedy Star, a very smart and genuine performer at up to one and a quarter miles, has sired winners over all sorts of distances since being retired at the end of 1972, including sprinters of the calibre of Solinus and On Stage, the smart if moody stayer Another Sam, the high-class hurdler Starfen and Mighty Fly herself. Mighty Fly is the second foal and first winner out of the oddly-named Lettuce who ran six times without showing much ability. Until Mighty Fly came along the family was notable more for producing good jumpers than flat performers—the unraced second dam foaled four winners, among them the Grand National winner Rubstic and the useful chaser Bennachie. Mighty Fly, a strong filly, showed her best form at a mile and acted on any going. *I. Balding.*

MIGHTY STEEL 3 b.g. High Top 131–Shortwood 90 (Skymaster 126) (1982 6g 7g 1983 7g 6d[4] 8.2g 8d 8.2fg 8f[4] 8fg 9fg 10s 11g[4] 8g[4] 8g 12fg) strong gelding; poor maiden; promises to stay 11f; acts on any going; has been tried in blinkers. *T. Craig.*

MIGRATOR 7 b.g. My Swallow 134–Houbichka (Swoon's Son) (1982 14fg⁴ 12fg   56
12fg⁴ 1983 11.7s² 17.1v) rangy ex-Irish gelding; stays 1½m; acts on any going;
suitable mount for an inexperienced rider; smart hurdler. *L. Kennard.*

MIJAS GOLF 2 b.c. Nonoalco 131–Arburie (Exbury 138) (1983 6fg 7f 8d 7g) May   73
23; IR 10,500Y; good-bodied colt; half-brother to Irish 3-y-o Ask The Wind (by Run
The Gantlet), a useful winner at up to 1¼m there and in France, and to a winner in
USA; dam, half-sister to very smart French middle-distance winner Armos, won
over 13f in Ireland; eighth of 14 behind easy winner Chief Singer in Coventry Stakes
at Royal Ascot, first outing and best effort; off course for 3 months after second
appearance; should stay at least 1m. *P. Cole.*

MIKEV 2 ch.g. Manado 130–Tagik (Targowice 130) (1983 5v 5.1f² 7fg 6f 5f 5f³   55
5.1f) Jan 8; lightly-made gelding; first foal; dam, half-sister to high-class sprinter
Green God, won 3 times in Italy; modest plater; not raced after August; form only
at 5f; acts on firm going; has worn a net muzzle; exported to Malaysia. *A. Bailey.*

MIKI MIKI MOTOR 2 ch.g. Red Alert 127–Starlina (Star Gazer 123) (1983 5v   61
5d 6f⁴ 7f 6fg 7f* 7g⁴ 7.2s 8.2fg) May 12; 7,400Y; strong gelding; plater; attracted
no bid after slamming his 21 opponents at Redcar in September; fourth of 11 in
nursery at Edinburgh the following month; suited by 7f; none too well away first 2
starts; sometimes blinkered (was when successful); fell eighth outing; trained by
C. Nelson first 2 appearances. *T. Craig.*

MIKRO POULAKI 3 b.f. Julio Mariner 127–Sandfly (French Beige 127) (1982   84
7d 1983 12f* 13fg) close-coupled filly; 50/1-winner of fast-run minor event at
Leicester in August, improving her position steadily and winning going away by 2½
lengths from Coyor; got going all too late on only other start; will be suited by
1¾m; acts on firm going. *C. Brittain.*

MILANION 4 ro.g. Roman Warrior 132–Fleora 61 (Fleece 114) (1982 6g 7d 10.6fg   –
8f 9g 9.4fg 1983 10.2d 10d³ 11fg 12v) workmanlike gelding; plater nowadays;
stays 1¼m but probably not 1½m; needs some give in the ground and acts on
heavy going; has run respectably for an apprentice; sold 420 gns Doncaster
September Sales. *J. Wilson.*

MI LAST FLING 2 ch.c. Quiet Fling 124–Matala 65 (Misti IV 132) (1983 5d 5v²   63
5v² 5d 7fg) Apr 7; tall, close-coupled colt; half-brother to 1½m winner Prince of
Kashmir (by Blue Cashmere) and to a winning hurdler; dam winning hurdler; plater;
not raced after early July; should be well suited by 7f+; form only on heavy going.
P. Feilden.

MILDRED 2 ch.f. Milford 119–Wandoo 79 (Hard Sauce 131) (1983 5g² 5g* 6g*   ?
6g* 7g* 7.5g 8fg) May 8; IR 7,000Y; lengthy, strong-quartered ex-Italian filly;
good walker; half-sister to 3 winners, all at least fairly useful, including sprinter
Springy (by Realm) and Irish 1m winner Petringo (by Pitcairn); dam daughter of
smart stayer Stephanie; won 4 of her 6 starts in Italy, picking up her most
important success in Premio Alessandro Perrone at Rome in June on fourth start,
winning by 2 lengths; gained her 3 other victories at Milan; 11/1 and blinkered,
dropped out after leading to straight when last of 8 in Hoover Fillies Mile at Ascot in
September; should be suited by 1m; fell sixth outing; trained in Italy by A. Botti. *D.
Sasse.*

MILITARY BAND (FR) 5 b.h. Sassafras 135–Melody Hour 105 (Sing Sing 134)   –
(1982 14g 16fg⁴ 12fg⁴ 12g² 12fg² 14g 1983 14s) tall, fair sort; fairly useful
handicapper at his best; soundly beaten only start at 5 yrs in May; seems best at
around 1¾m although stays further; acts on firm going; useful hurdler. *J. Gifford.*

MILITIA MAID 2 ch.f. Home Guard 129–Holernzaye 93 (Sallust 134) (1983 5fg)   –
Mar 7; 16,000Y; first foal; dam, half-sister to Rheingold, won over 5f and 6f at 2
yrs; tailed-off last of 16 in maiden race at Lingfield in October. *G. Lewis.*

MILK HEART 4 ch.c. Steel Heart 128–Cafe au Lait 98 (Espresso 122) (1982 5d²   100
6d* 7fg* 6g 7f 6g⁴ 6f 6d² 6g 1983 6v 6v⁴ 6v⁴ 6g 6f² 5h 8fg 6.5g² 5fg 6fg⁴)
compact, quite attractive colt; joint second favourite, just failed to get up when
neck second of 27 to Melindra in Wokingham Stakes at Royal Ascot on fifth start;
ran respectably on occasions afterwards; best at up to 7f though seems to stay 1m;
acts on any going; used to wear blinkers. *G. Lewis.*

MILLAINE 2 b.f. Formidable 125–Christine 102 (Crocket 130) (1983 8.2fg⁴) Apr   69 p
20; half-sister to several winners in France and Italy, notably 1981 Criterium
Femminile winner Smageta (by High Top); dam won from 7f to 1¼m; staying-on
8¾ lengths fourth of 16 to Alleging in £3,400 race at Nottingham in October; sure
to improve. *M. Jarvis.*

High Steward Stakes, Yarmouth—an impressive win for Millbow

MILLBOW 2 ch.c. Mill Reef 141–Makeacurtsey (Herbager 136) (1983 6f² 7f* **114**
7f³) Apr 13; 110,000Y; strong, good sort; good walker and mover; closely related
to useful 3-y-o middle-distance winner Civility (by Shirley Heights) and half-
brother to smart 1976 2-y-o 5f performer Piney Ridge (by Native Prince) and very
useful 1¼m winner Hill's Yankee (by Thatch); dam, placed in USA, is half-sister to 3
good stakes winners, including very smart grass horse Knightly Manner; won
7-runner maiden race at Yarmouth in July, coming from last 2f out to win
impressively by 5 lengths; evens, going well until outpaced in last 2f when 1½
lengths third of 6 to Knoxville and Kalim in Seaton Delaval Stakes at Newcastle the
following month; will be suited by 1¼m+; acts on firm going; likely to make smart
3-y-o. *H. Cecil.*

MILLE BALLES (FR) 3 b.c. Mill Reef 141–Elezinha (Tourangeau 99) (1982 **112**
6g³ 8g² 7v* 1983 8d² 9fg* 10fg* 10f 8g³ 10d³) French colt; successful in 80,000
francs race at Maisons-Laffitte and Prix de la Ville de Trouville at Deauville, putting
up a good performance to beat Piermont by 3 lengths in latter race in August (burst
clear when an opening appeared); put up best subsequent effort when 2½ lengths
third of 8 behind Pampabird in Prix du Rond-Point at Longchamp in September on
penultimate start; stays 1¼m; probably acts on any going. *A. Fabre, France.*

MILLER'S DAUGHTER 2 b.f. Mill Reef 141–Pirate Queen 77 (Pirate King —
129) (1983 6f 7f) May 26; attractive, well-made filly; half-sister to 3 winners,
notably Goodwood Cup winner Tug of War (by Reliance II); last in valuable newcomers race at Ascot in July and minor event at Brighton in
August. *D. Whelan.*

MILLFIELD LAD 6 b.g. Jimmy Reppin 131–Alexa (Runnymede 123) (1982 8f —
10fg³ 10g 10g 1983 8v 9g) poor handicapper nowadays; stays at least 1m; ideally
suited by some give in the ground; has run respectably in blinkers and for a claimer.
J. Charlton.

MILLFONTAINE 3 b.c. Mill Reef 141–Mortefontaine (Polic 126) (1982 NR **114**
1983 8d 8g² 10g* 10.1fg* 10.1fg* 10f* 12f* 11.7fg*)
Millfontaine won his last six races. He finished lame in the last of them, but he
stays in training and is the type to do well in stronger company than he met in 1983:
he has already shown himself a very useful horse and could be a better one.
Millfontaine's run of success began with a seven-length defeat of Underbid in a
Brighton maiden and continued with two wins in minor events at Windsor. His
fourth win, in Goodwood's Extel Handicap, was a much more important one and it
turned out to be his most valuable. The usual highly competitive field for the Extel
included the Magnet Cup second Gay Lemur, who started favourite ahead of the
lightly-weighted Northern Trial, previously runner-up in a valuable Ascot maiden,
Millfontaine and the well-backed Both Ends Burning. Millfontaine was never far
behind the leaders, though he was being ridden a long way from home. He
eventually took the lead inside the last furlong and stayed on really well to beat Gay

537

Extel Stakes, Goodwood—Millfontaine gets up to beat Gay Lemur, Both Ends Burning (No. 19) and Rangefinder (rails)

Lemur a length and a half with Both Ends Burning a head further away third. Two weeks later in the Associated Tyre Specialists Handicap at Newbury, Millfontaine was favourite to beat Gay Lemur again on roughly the same terms over a two-furlong longer trip. Four of the eight other runners had won on their previous start, including Paris North, one of only two horses in the race to have won over a mile and a half. Here Millfontaine led before two furlongs out; having gone to the front he started to idle, though he always looked the winner. He beat Paris North three quarters of a length, with Gay Lemur a length further back in third. Millfontaine's final start, in the Winter Hill Stakes at Windsor, was his first against

Mr S. S. Niarchos' "Millfontaine"

older horses. Though never a particularly valuable race, the Winter Hill Stakes seldom fails to attract at least one useful performer, its winners in the last twelve years including Parnell and Orange Bay, who were both placed in the King George VI and Queen Elizabeth Diamond Stakes, Fool's Mate, Sol'Argent and Knockroe. There were two English pattern-race winners against Millfontaine in the latest race, Zilos and Lafontaine. Significantly, Millfontaine won hard held by half a length and four lengths from that pair; the New Zealand Guineas winner My Sir Avon, who never really became acclimatized to English conditions, finished fourth. On this performance Millfontaine himself had earned a run in pattern company, and it's a pity injury cost him his chance in the autumn.

		Mill Reef (b 1968)	Never Bend (b 1960)	Nasrullah Lalun
Millfontaine (b.c. 1980)			Milan Mill (b 1962)	Princequillo Virginia Water
		Mortefontaine (br 1969)	Polic (br 1953)	Relic Polaire
			Brabantia (br 1953)	Honeyway Porthaven

Millfontaine, a medium-sized, attractive colt and a good mover, who cost 106,000 guineas as a yearling, is the fourth produce of Mortefontaine, the first being Polifontaine (by Bold Lad, USA), a winner over six furlongs and a mile at Deauville and Saint-Cloud at two years. The dam, who was placed in eighteen of her twenty-nine starts, but won only once, also over a mile at Saint-Cloud, is a sister to the good sprinter Polyfoto and to the dam of the dual Cambridgeshire winner Baronet. Brabantia, the second dam, was of little account on the racecourse, while the third dam Porthaven won once over five furlongs and was half-sister to the winners of twenty-four races in Britain. *G. Harwood.*

MILL HOUSE LADY 2 b.f. Junius 124–Right Dress (Baldric II 131) (1983 6f 7g 8fg) Apr 9; IR 9,200F, IR 6,000Y (privately); leggy, lightly-made filly; fourth foal (second to Northern Hemisphere time); dam never ran; apparently not fully wound up, well beaten in maiden races and a valuable seller. *W. Musson.* —

MILLIE GREY 3 gr.f. Grey Ghost 98–Nelka (Counsel 118) (1982 NR 1983 13.8g 12.2d 16f⁴ 16g 16f⁴ 15.8g) leggy filly; second living foal; dam won over hurdles and fences; plating-class maiden; needs a test of stamina. *T. Barron.* —

MILLISLES 3 gr.f. Pongee 106–Growing Leisure 81 (Constable 119) (1982 5f 6fg 6g 1983 8v 9d 9f) of little account. *N. Chamberlain.* —

MILL PLANTATION 4 b.c. Northfields–Fairly Hot 109 (Sir Ivor 135) (1982 8g³ 9g* 9fg 11f³ 12f 10f² 12f² 10f* 12g³ 10g 12s 1983 10v 10d 10f 10f) neat, attractive colt; fairly useful at his best; didn't show much at 4 yrs and looked a bit unenthusiastic on final start; stays 1½m; acts well on firm going; usually blinkered. *G. Wragg.* —

MILLS ALLEGIANCE (FR) 3 br.c. Habitat 134–Trottel (Exbury 138) (1982 NR 1983 11d 11.5fg 8f 8f 7h² 8.2h 10f 12g) 15,000Y; big, strong, lengthy colt; second foal; half-brother to French 1m winner Soufflot (by Kashmir II); dam, half-sister to very smart middle-distance colt Olantengy, won small 14.5f race at 4 yrs in France; had stiff task when second behind easy winner Myra's Best in minor event at Beverley in July, only semblance of form; promises to stay beyond 7f; sometimes blinkered; sold 5,200 gns Newmarket Autumn Sales. *C. Brittain.* —

MILLSIDE 2 b.c. Mill Reef 141–Heatherside 80 (Hethersett 134) (1983 7fg² 8s*) Apr 10; 60,000Y; well-made, good sort; brother to 1½m winner Heather's Reef and half-brother to a winner in Italy; dam, half-sister to several very useful animals, won over 1¾m; had to be ridden along to land the odds by a head from Peter Martin in 13-runner maiden race at Yarmouth in September; had had remainder well beaten off when second of 20 behind runaway winner Lear Fan in similar event at Newmarket the previous month; will be suited by 1¼m+; a useful 3-y-o in the making. *H. Cecil.* — 88 p

MILLY MOLLY MANDY 2 ch.f. Crimson Beau 124–South Georgia 80 (Ballymoss 136) (1983 7g 7.6fg) Feb 6; second reported foal; dam well suited by long distances; behind in big fields for £4,100 event at Newbury and maiden race at Lingfield. *P. Haynes.* —

MILNSBRIDGE 2 gr. or ro.f. Dragonara Palace 115–Janabelle 101 (Gentle Art 121) (1983 8d 8g) May 17; half-sister to 3 winners, including sprinter Kelso Belle —

(by Town Crier); dam won at up to 7f; in rear in autumn maiden races at Beverley and Edinburgh. *E. Weymes.*

MILORD (USA) 2 ch.c. Raise A Native–Evening (Up All Hands) (1983 5g 5g⁴ 5fg* 6f* 5fg 6fg³) Mar 20; $500,000Y; strong, well-made, attractive colt; good walker; third foal; half-brother to 2 winners, one stakes placed; dam, unplaced in 5 starts, is half-sister to high-class Twixt, a winner of 26 races at up to 9f; won maiden race at Windsor in June and £4,200 nursery at Goodwood in July; good third of 12 behind Forzando in nursery at Doncaster in September; not certain to stay beyond 6f; yet to race on a soft surface; blinkered second, third and sixth outings. *J. Tree.* **107**

MILTON BURN 2 b.c. Sexton Blake 126–Neasden Belle 66 (Sovereign Path 125) (1983 6f 8d 7g) Apr 7; 14,000Y; second foal; dam ran only at 2 yrs; little worthwhile form in maiden and minor events. *D. Hanley.* **–**

MIND OUT 3 br.f. Gay Fandango 132–Deer Leap 106 (Deep Diver 134) (1982 6fg 5s 1983 6f 5f) little worthwhile form in minor and maiden races. *N. Vigors.* **–**

MINE AT LAST 3 gr. or ro.f. Nishapour 125–Mrs Binks (Whistling Wind 123) (1982 6fg 1983 6v 9f 7f 8f) compact filly; soundly beaten in maiden and minor events; sold 1,000 gns Goffs November Sales. *J. Bethell.* **–**

MINGASH 2 br.c. Mansingh 120–Sarong 97 (Taj Dewan 128) (1983 5v 5s² 5s* 5fg* 6f³ 5f² 5fg² 5g4) Feb 3; 15,000Y; quite attractive, well-made colt; third foal; half-brother to useful 5f and 1m winner Hindi (by Mummy's Pet); dam 1m winner; won minor events at Windsor and Sandown (made virtually all) in June; beaten neck in Leicester nursery on penultimate start; not raced after July; best at 5f; acts on any going; genuine. *P. Cole.* **93**

MING VILLAGE 3 b. or br.g. Persian Bold 123–Wild Orchid (Sassafras 135) (1982 5fg 6f 7fg 7fg 7g 1983 8g 8.5s 8s 7f4 7f 6f 7s 7g 7fg 7g) well-made, quite attractive gelding; stays 7f; acts on a firm surface; below form last four outings. *R. Armstrong.* **–**

MINIBANK 5 b.h. Saritamer 130–Tilt Guard 75 (Crepello 136) (1982 7s 8fg 8g 1983 12.2v 11.7s 12s) good-topped, workmanlike horse; poor performer nowadays; sometimes blinkered. *M. Bradley.* **–**

MINICA 6 ch.m. Prince des Loges 73–Mink Mini 103 (Martial 131) (1982 8fg 10fg 5.3f 6s4 1983 8s 10s 10f 10f 6fg) poor maiden; stays 1m; blinkered second and third starts; unquoted first 4 outings. *M. Blanshard.* **–**

MINIE O'NEILL 3 b.f. Pitskelly 122–Karlaine 86 (Tutankhamen) (1982 5s 5d* 5f³ 6f 7g 1983 8.2v 7v 8v 7fg 7f 8fg) sturdy filly; keen walker; plater; probably stays 1m; blinkered last 2 starts. *W. Wharton.* **–**

MINISTERIAL (USA) 2 b.c. The Minstrel 135–River Rose 116 (Riverman 131) (1983 7fg* 7fg² 7fg* 7fg) Jan 30; 200,000Y; good-topped, attractive colt; has a round action; first foal; dam won 5 races over 5f in France; proved a very difficult ride on first 3 starts, swerving about badly, but managed nevertheless to win on 2 occasions, in maiden race at Salisbury in September and in Hyperion Stakes at Ascot in October (beat newcomer Ilium 2½ lengths in latter); every chance when 10 lengths fifth of 10 behind El Gran Senor in William Hill Dewhurst Stakes at Newmarket on final appearance; will probably stay 1m; acts on a firm surface. *G. Harwood.* **104**

MINMAX 5 b.h. Record Run 127–Paddy's Tickle (Shooting Chant) (1982 8d 7fg 7f 7f4 7g 7fg 7fg³ 8v 7g²(dis) 7d 1983 7.6v² 8v² 7.6fg 8fg 6g) leggy, good-topped horse; off course over 4 months after second start and didn't recover his form; stays 1m; probably acts on any going but is ideally suited by some give underfoot; suitable mount for an apprentice; wears blinkers nowadays. *P. K. Mitchell.* **76**

MINNE LOVE 4 ch.f. Homeric 133–Late Love 107 (Great White Way) (1982 6f 6g² 5fg² 5g³ 6fg 6f 6d 10v 1983 6v 8s* 8f 8f² 7f) small filly; plater; attracted no bid after winning narrowly at Wolverhampton in April; suited by 1m; acts on any going; has run respectably when sweating up. *H. O'Neill.* **50**

Hyperion Stakes, Ascot—an assertive victory for Ministerial from Ilium (braces)

MINNIE FULLER 2 ch.f. Derrylin 115–Mrs Paddy 69 (Acropolis 132) (1983 5g   –
5d 6g 6g) Mar 28; sturdy filly; half-sister to 3 minor winners in France; dam placed
over 1½m; poor form in maiden races; dwelt first start. *E. Incisa.*

MINSHAANSHU AMAD (USA) 4 br.c. Northern Dancer–Tappahannock   61 §
(Chieftain) (1982 9fg 11.7f⁴ 10f³ 8fg 16g 1983 13v 10v 10fg³ 12f³ 12.2fg² 16f³
14fg) small, attractive colt; good walker and mover; probably stays 2m; form only
on a sound surface; has been tried in blinkers and is possibly ungenuine; has run
respectably for an amateur rider. *J. Ciechanowski.*

MINTALA (USA) 3 ch.g. Key To The Mint–Tatallah (Tatan) (1982 6f 7fg 1983   69
8.5v 8f 8fg³) quite attractive gelding; quite a moderate maiden; stays 1m; veered
right and left in closing stages on final start; sold 4,500 gns Newmarket Autumn
Sales. *P. Walwyn.*

MINUS MAN 5 b.g. Firestreak 125–Cheb's Honour 70 (Chebs Lad 120) (1982   54
8.2s 9fg 10f 10fg 8g 8f 8f 8d² 8fg² 8g³ 7s⁴ 1983 8v 10g 10d* 10f 10f4 10fg³ 8fg*
10g) lengthy gelding; plater; awarded non-selling handicap at Leicester in June and
won seller at Brighton in September (attracted no bid); stays 1¼m; acts on any
going; has run respectably for an apprentice. *W. Holden.*

MIRALOVE 2 ch.f. Mount Hagen 127–Miralife 103 (Miralgo 130) (1983 6fg³ 6fg   91
7fg 6fg 7fg² 7fg³) May 20; 60,000Y; lightly-built filly; half-sister to 4 winners,
notably Irish 1000 Guineas winner Miralla (by Allangrange) and smart Irish 5f to 1m
winner Wolverlife (by Wolver Hollow); dam, third in Irish 1000 Guineas, is
half-sister to top-class Dickens Hill (by Mount Hagen); put up best efforts when
placed in good-class nurseries in October, going down by ½ length to Free Guest at
Newmarket and finishing 2 lengths third of 15 to Bastille, after missing break, when
well-backed favourite at Doncaster; will be suited by 1m; yet to race on a soft
surface. *R. Armstrong.*

MIRAMAR REEF 4 b.c. Mill Reef 141–Thalassa 94 (Appiani II 128) (1982 9fg⁴   ?
10fg 10.4fg 12fg 10fg² 12f 10f* 10f 10.5fg 10.5g 12fg 10g 9d 1983 10g² 11v 10fg*
10f² 10.5f 10f³ 10f⁴ 10f⁴ 11g 9fg 10fg³ 10fg²)
It would not have been that surprising if the ground at Newmarket had been
littered with discarded form-books after the Dubai Champion Stakes, an event
that has provided more than its share of shocks over the years. The first three
home, Cormorant Wood, Tolomeo and Flame of Tara, admittedly were all well
qualified to run in a race of this quality but the fourth, Miramar Reef, definitely
was not. Seemingly there merely to make up the numbers he ran the race of his
life to be beaten under two lengths, this after being hampered by the runner-up
with the result that the stewards moved him up to third following an inquiry.
We are still at a loss to explain how Miramar Reef, whose 200/1 starting price
appeared an accurate reflection of his chance, came to run so well. Apparently
fully exposed as no more than a useful handicapper and a temperamental one as
well with doubtful courage and a tendency to put his head in the air in a finish, he
had run ten times during the current season, winning once, when beating Hill's
Pageant by three quarters of a length at Sandown in June. It had required all
Piggott's skill to get Miramar Reef home that day, producing him in the final
furlong then forcing him to the front before he knew what had happened, and until
Baxter rode the colt in the Champion it had looked as if Piggott alone could get the
best out of him. The sole piece of form Miramar Reef had to suggest he might be
smart had come five outings after his win when he ran fourth of eight to General
Holme in the Prix Gontaut-Biron at Deauville, but this race is highly suspect since
several second-raters finished close up, and on his two starts immediately before
the Champion Miramar Reef could do no better than finish last in the Doonside
Cup at Ayr and sixteenth of thirty under the modest weight of 8-5 in the William
Hill Cambridgeshire.
These were hardly the credentials of a colt likely to play a significant part in
the Champion Stakes but optimism sometimes reaps its due reward in racing, as
the £16,750 Miramar Reef collected at Newmarket proved. Instead of dropping
out as expected when towards the rear with three furlongs to go he began to
make steady headway up the rail, greatly assisted by a gap two weakening rivals
left as they drifted right. Running well, Miramar Reef reached fifth place at the
distance where Tolomeo impeded him and though keeping on to take third halfway
through the final furlong he could do no more from that point and was beaten a
head, short head and length and a half behind Cormorant Wood; those further
back included such high-class colts as Sackford, Adonijah, Montekin and Hot
Touch. Lamentably an already rather murky picture wasn't clarified in the
slightest by Miramar Reef's final appearance in the Tia Maria Autumn Handicap on

Mrs Audrey Richards' "Miramar Reef"

the same course. Running off his old handicap mark he reproduced to the ounce his form prior to the Champion, going down by three lengths to Bahoor. His attitude was none too attractive either since he behaved mulishly in the preliminaries, as on several previous occasions, and yet again looked unenthusiastic when asked to go about his business.

		Never Bend (b 1960)	Nasrullah Lalun
	Mill Reef (b 1968)	Milan Mill (b 1962)	Princequillo Virginia Water
Miramar Reef (b.c. 1979)		Appiani II (b 1963)	Herbager Angela Rucellai
	Thalassa (ch 1971)	Templeogue (gr 1965)	Prodomo Tilla

Miramar Reef is the second foal of the fairly useful Thalassa who won over middle distances in England and France, gained places in the Lingfield Oaks Trial and Prix de Pomone and also ran four times in the States. Thalassa was the best of several winners here and abroad produced by the fair Irish mile- to mile-and-a-half handicapper Templeogue, a sister to Tigerin who showed herself the best German three-year-old filly of 1965. A strong, good sort who often impresses in appearance, and a good mover, Miramar Reef stays a mile and a quarter well and has form only on a sound surface. He needs holding up—the lack of daylight he saw in the Champion Stakes ironically helped as well as hindered him—and requires strong yet patient handling. *C. Brittain.*

MIRANOL 2 b.c. Full of Hope 125–Tabarka (Dicta Drake 126) (1983 7f 7fg) May   –
4; half-brother to 2 winning sprinters, including fairly useful Last Sale (by Royben);
dam of little account; in rear in maiden race at Newbury in July and minor event
(last of 17) at Lingfield in August. *R. Hannon.*

MIR BAL (FR) 4 br.c. Kashmir II 125–Balna (Baldric II 131) (1982 8s 8g³ 9d³   117
8s⁴ 8d* 9g 10fg 9.2f 8v³ 8s* 8s 10.5v 1983 8.5v 8v³ 8s 8v* 7d³ 8fg) 160,000
francs Y (approx £16,000); third foal; dam, winner over 4f at 2 yrs in France, is
sister to smart stayer Zab; put up an improved performance in Badener-Meile at
Baden-Baden in May, accounting for Solo Dancer comfortably with such as
Princes Gate well beaten; kept on well to be ½-length third to African Joy in Prix
de la Porte Maillot at Longchamp in June; stays 1m; revels in the mud; best in
blinkers. *P. Lallie, France.*

MIRROR BOY 6 ch.h. Pieces of Eight 128–Knocknashee 70 (Astec 128) (1982   –
12g 16s⁴ 14f 16fg 1983 10v 12d) well-made horse; fairly useful handicapper at his
best but has deteriorated; possibly stays 2m; probably acts on any going but is
suited by some give in the ground; ran poorly in blinkers once. *D. Oughton.*

MISBEHAVING (FR) 2 b.f. Bellypha 130–Lean On (Turn-to) (1983 7fg³ 7.5fg²   109
7.5d⁴ 8s⁴ 8fg* 8fg²(dis)) Mar 24; 540,000 francs Y (approx £45,000); fifth foal;
half-sister to a winner over jumps in France; dam, half-sister to Nonoalco's dam,
won 6f claiming race; made all to win minor event at Maisons-Laffitte in September
by 2 lengths from Sara Lee; led briefly inside final furlong when head second to
Boreale in Prix des Reservoirs at Longchamp the following month (later
disqualified on a technicality); suited by 1m; acts on firm going. *J. Fellows,
France.*

MISDIRECTED 3 ch.f. Ardoon 124–Grecian Palm 78 (Royal Palm 131) (1982   72
5fg 5f³ 5g² 5g4 5g 6d⁴ 1983 6f4 6fg 6f³ 6fg² 6s* 7fg* 7fg²) small, good-bodied
filly; has a short, sharp action; won seller at Ayr in September (bought in 2,000 gns)
and apprentice handicap at Lingfield in October; stays 7f; acts on any going; sold to
NBA 8,600 gns Newmarket Autumn Sales. *G. Pritchard-Gordon.*

MISFIRE 2 ch.f. Gunner B 126–Brookfield Miss 73 (Welsh Pageant 132) (1983   –
7s) May 19; sparely-made filly; second foal; half-sister to 3-y-o Inver Brae (by
Vitiges); dam showed a little ability at 2 yrs; blinkered, failed to recover from slow
start in 19-runner maiden race at Leicester in October. *R. Williams.*

MISGUIDED 3 b.f. Homing 130–Miss By Miles 91 (Milesian 125) (1982 6f 6g²   102
5fg² 5g* 6s* 6d* 1983 6d² 6f 6fg³) well-made, attractive filly; good mover;
placed in valuable handicap at Newmarket in May (3 lengths second to Bold
Secret) and £3,200 event at Salisbury in September (just over 2 lengths third to
Coquito's Friend); didn't run well in between, although not entirely disgraced
second outing; bred to stay beyond 6f; not at her best on really firm ground and
acts very well on soft. *H. Cecil.*

MISHA 3 b.f. Never Return 121–Blue Shawl (Bluerullah 115) (1982 NR 1983 8g   51
8g 8fg⁴) rangy filly; third foal; dam placed over 1½m in Ireland; 100/1 when about 3
lengths fourth of 25 finishers to Scoutsmistake in minor event at Doncaster in
November, first form; will be well suited by further. *J. Wilson.*

MISINSKIE (USA) 3 b.f. Nijinsky 138–Kankakee Miss (Better Bee) (1982 6g⁴   –
7f² 6f³ 7fg³ 1983 11g 10f 11.7f⁴ 10fg 12g) attractive, well-made filly; didn't run up
to her 2-y-o form; promises to stay middle distances. *P. Walwyn.*

MISS A BEAT 2 b.f. Song 132–Careless Flyer 66 (Malicious) (1983 5s 5g³ 6d 5f   73
6f⁴ 7fg*) Mar 23; 5,000F, 2,600Y; small, light-framed filly; first living produce;
dam won over 6f; blinkered first time, won 15-runner £2,600 seller at Newmarket
in July by 3 lengths from Musical Love; sold 7,400 gns afterwards to race in Italy,
and won in France; better suited by 7f than shorter distances. *R. Williams.*

MISS A BID (USA) 2 ch.c. Raise A Bid–Miss Morning Storm (Dust   78
Commander) (1983 5v 6g² 5.8h³) Feb 19; $12,000F, IR 57,000 gns Y; strong,
compact, useful-looking colt; first produce; dam won at up to 1m in USA; looked to
have race won when leading after halfway in 12-runner maiden at Haydock in July
but drifted right and failed by a short head to hold off Benz; favourite, beaten over 7
lengths into third place behind Rio Riva in 13-runner similar event at Bath later in
the month; should stay 1m; possibly not at his best on hard going. *P. Cole.*

MISS ABWAH 4 b.f. Abwah 118–Ladies Night 65 (Midsummer Night II 117)   –
(1982 6f 5d 7f⁴ 8fg 9f² 10f³ 10d 8.2v 10s 7s 1983 11fg 8v 8g³ 8fg 8f 10fg⁴ 9f³ 8g
12g⁴) fair sort; has a round action; plater; seems to stay 1½m; acts on firm going;
has worn blinkers; races with head in air; cost 1,700 gns Doncaster March Sales;
sold 1,250 gns Ascot December Sales. *J. S. Wilson.*

MISS ADMIRAL 3 ch. f. Native Admiral–Running Mate (Track Spare 125) (1982 —
5v 1983 6fg 5f) little worthwhile form in maiden races; sold to NBA 1,000 gns
Newmarket Autumn Sales. *R. Simpson.*

MISS ANNIE 3 b. or br. f. Scottish Rifle 127–Ryoanji 100 (Lyphard 132) (1982 60
6d² 7f* 7f 8fg² 7.6fg³ 1983 10s 12f 11fg² 12fg 14f* 18.1d⁴ 13fg) close-coupled filly;
good mover; won handicap at Yarmouth in August; evidently stays quite well; acts
on firm going; hasn't always looked the most genuine of fillies and ran in snatches
final start. *P. Haslam.*

MISS ANNIVERSARY 2 b. f. Tachypous 128–Unexpected 84 (Laser Light 118) 55
(1983 5s² 5g 5g 6f) Apr 23; 1,500Y; rather leggy filly; second foal; dam won over
7.6f at 4 yrs; showed form only when second in maiden auction event at Salisbury
in May; slowly away third outing, and blinkered at Nottingham in June on final
appearance; should be suited by 6f; possibly needs soft ground. *C. Williams.*

MISS BALI BEACH 3 b. f. Nonoalco 131–Miss Bali 95 (Crepello 136) (1982 7d* 87
1983 10fg 10h 8fg² 8g 10fg) big, rangy, attractive filly; has a fluent but slightly
rounded action; didn't fulfil her 2-y-o promise in 1983, best effort when ¾-length
second of 12 to Dinner Toast in £10,800 handicap at Ascot in September;
promises to stay 1¼m; seems to act on any going but goes well on soft ground; to
be trained by W. Hastings-Bass in 1984. *M. Stoute.*

MISS BEAULIEU 2 b. f. Northfields–Miss Monaco 107 (Crepello 136) (1983 85 p
6g*) Apr 25; rather lightly-built filly; half-sister to 3 winners here and abroad;
dam, a sprinter, at her best at 2 yrs; won 23-runner newcomers event at Goodwood
in September, making up lot of ground in final furlong to beat New Dimension short
head; will stay 7f. *G. Wragg.*

MISS BELLA 2 b. f. Floriferous–San Estrella (Star Gazer 123) (1983 5d² 5d⁴ 5g* 58
6f⁴ 5fg* 5fg² 6f 5s⁴) Apr 24; 800Y (privately); smallish filly; half-sister to fair
1970 2-y-o 6f performer Star of Lavant (by Le Levanstell) and a winner abroad;
dam maiden Irish sprinter; ridden by apprentice S. Morris, won two 4-runner
sellers at Hamilton in June (bought in 1,600 gns on second occasion); best form at
5f; acts on any going. *J. Berry.*

MISS BLACK GLAMA 3 br. f. Derrylin 115–Decatullus (Catullus) (1982 7v 54
7.6v 7d 1983 10v 12s³ 10v³ 11.7fg 14f) workmanlike filly; plating-class
middle-distance maiden; blinkered fifth start; sold to S. May 2,400 gns
Newmarket July Sales. *N. Callaghan.*

MISS BRODIE (FR) 3 ch. f. Margouillat 133–Brodie (Bryan G) (1982 9g 10g —
1983 9.1g 10g 10g 11.7h) 180,000 francs Y (approx £16,000); half-sister to 3
winners in France and USA; dam, from same family as Riva Ridge, won 6f claiming
race in USA at 2 yrs; no form in French Provinces when trained by J. P. Pelat,
including in 3 apprentice events; last of 9 in maiden race at Bath in August, only
outing over here. *C. Austin.*

MISS CANNIBAL 2 gr. f. Buckskin 133–No Nonsense (Nonoalco 131) (1983 7s) —
Feb 26; 5,200F; workmanlike filly; first produce; dam poor French maiden; 50/1
and bandaged behind, tailed off in 19-runner maiden race at Leicester in October.
M. Smyly.

MISS CARINE 3 b. f. Cawston's Clown 113–Lucy 83 (Sheshoon 132) (1982 7g —
8d* 8s 8d 1983 10g 12.3g 12d 13.8g⁴ 12g⁴ 12g) lightly-made filly; plater; stays
1¾m; well beaten in blinkers final start; retained 600 gns Doncaster October
Sales. *J. Wilson.*

MISS CARLA 2 ch. f. Dominion 123–Amerella (Welsh Pageant 132) (1983 5f 6f 71
7fg 6fg²) Feb 22; 17,000F, 700Y; smallish filly; first foal; dam, winner of 1¼m
ladies race in Ireland, is daughter of Molecomb Stakes winner Lowna; 7/1, kept on
well and finished 10 lengths clear of third horse when ½-length second of 14 to Top
Ranker in claiming race at Nottingham in October; claimed £1,521 afterwards to
race in Scandinavia; will stay 1m. *P. Rohan.*

MISS DIAWARD 6 br. m. Supreme Sovereign 119–Gay Pretendre (Pretendre 74
126) (1982 13s* 12f³ 13fg* 12fg 13g² 13fg* 12fg 14.6g 13d 12s³ 14s* 18s 1983
12.3v³ 12v² 12d² 12d³ 13g³ 12fg 13s³ 12g 14d⁴ 14.7fg) quite attractive, lengthy
mare; good walker, but poor mover; won handicap at Ripon in August; stays
1¾m; acts on any going; usually bandaged nowadays; needs to be brought very
late. *Miss S. Hall.*

MISS DUNSTER (USA) 3 b. f. Nizon 120–Janie V. (Dewan) (1982 7d 7g* 7s 84
1983 8f 10g³ 10f³ 10fg) quite attractive, lightly-made filly; third in handicaps at
Newmarket and Yarmouth (sweated up) in summer; stays 1¼m; acts on firm going;
went freely to post final start. *L. Cumani.*

MISS EGLANTINE 2 br.f. Shiny Tenth 120–Four Lawns 77 (Forlorn River 124)   **58**
(1983 5s³ 6fg 6fg³ 6d) Apr 15; second live foal; dam 5f winner; modest plater; third
at Lingfield in June and Windsor in August; promises to stay 7f; slowly away final
start. *D. Marks.*

MISS ENRYCO 2 ch.f. Enryco Mieo 77–Ludorum's Praise (Song of Praise 68)   –
(1983 5v 5s⁴ 6f 6f) May 2; neat filly; bad plater; not raced after August; blinkered
last 2 appearances. *M. Tompkins.*

MISS FELHAM 2 b. or br.f. Malinowski 123–Remission 75 (Sing Sing 134) (1983   –
6d 7f 7h) Mar 1; 5,000 2-y-o; strong, lengthy filly; fourth foal; half-sister to Irish 5f
winner Ching A Ling (by Pampapaul); dam quite moderate at 2 yrs; in rear in
maiden races at Doncaster, Yarmouth and Chepstow; not seen out after August. *A.
Cawley.*

MISS FLASH 3 b. or br.f. Scottish Rifle 127–Flashing Light (Sky Gipsy 117)   –
(1982 5f⁴ 5g⁴ 5fg 6g 1983 5fg 8f 8g 12fg) fair sort; should stay at least 6f; well
beaten in a seller when blinkered and bandaged final start. *W. A. Stephenson.*

MISS GEMINA 2 b.f. Levanter 121–Tonela (Manacle 123) (1983 6f 6fg) May 3;   –
first foal; dam never ran; little form in fair company at Brighton and Windsor; dead.
R. Hannon.

MISS GOLDINGAY 2 ch.f. Hot Spark 126–Patois (I Say 125) (1983 5f 6fg 5g   –
6g) June 13; 3,900F; angular filly; half-sister to middle-distance winners by Royal
Palace and Morston; dam twice-raced half-sister to very smart stayer Petty
Officer; well beaten in the North in varied races, including a valuable seller. *M. W.
Easterby.*

MISS GUENEVERE 2 gr.f. Brittany–Subtle Queen (Stephen George 102)   –
(1983 6s 5g) Apr 1; dipped-backed filly; second living foal; dam of little account; in
rear in autumn minor events at Ayr and Edinburgh. *T. Craig.*

MISS HAMILTON 2 b.f. Quiet Fling 124–Miss Silly (Silly Season 127) (1983   –
7.6d 7g) June 2; 3,500F, 2,000Y (privately); fourth foal; dam won 6 times in Italy
and is daughter of very useful sprinter Cease Fire; well beaten in October maiden
events at Lingfield. *P. K. Mitchell.*

MISS HATTIE 2 br.f. Kala Shikari 125–Wontell 90 (Buisson Ardent 129) (1983   –
6g) May 3; 2,500F (privately), 3,400Y; smallish filly; half-sister to very useful
sprinter Mummy's Darling (by Mummy's Pet) and a winner in Belgium; dam ran
only at 2 yrs; well behind in 27-runner maiden race at Newmarket in July. *P.
Haslam.*

MISS HENRY 3 b.f. Blue Cashmere 129–Rhodia (Parthia 132) (1982 6s 5fg 5g   **78**
1983 6d 6s 7fg³ 7h² 7f 7f 6f⁴ 7fg* 8d) lengthy filly; beat odds-on Eye Dazzler by
2½ lengths in 7-runner minor event at Salisbury in September; stays 7f; form
only on a firm surface; blinkered final outing in 1982; none too consistent. *J.
Benstead.*

MISS HIPPO 2 b.f. Wollow 132–Sound Type 92 (Upper Case) (1983 6f 7f) Mar   –
25; first foal; dam won over 7f and 1¼m; ninth of 12 in summer maiden races at
Nottingham and Yarmouth. *M. Stoute.*

MISS HOT FOOT 3 b.f. Hotfoot 126–Petite Case 76 (Upper Case) (1982 6s   –
1983 7fg 7h 6f) lengthy filly; behind in maiden and minor events; sold 400 gns
Newmarket Autumn Sales. *M. McCourt.*

MISS HYVER HILL 3 b.f. Reform 132–Meryl (Bold Lad, Ire 133) (1982 NR   –
1983 11.5fg 12g 10fg 10.2h) 24,000Y; quite attractive, well-made filly; first foal;
dam unraced daughter of St Leger second Patti; towards rear in maiden races in
first half of season. *P. Cole.*

MISS IMPORT 5 ch.m. Import 127–Chinese Falcon 81 (Skymaster 126) (1982   **101**
5g² 5d⁴ 5f 5fg 5f³ 5f* 5g³ 5g* 5g* 5fg* 5fg 5d 1983 5g² 5fg 5f 5g 5f* 5f*)
workmanlike mare; useful sprint handicapper; has won 10 races in her career, all
over 5f, and has shown improvement virtually throughout; had another excellent
year in 1983; led near finish to beat Mummy's Treasure by ¾ length in quite
valuable event at York in July and came virtually all to account for African Tudor
unchallenged by 3 lengths in Rous Memorial Stakes at Ascot later in month; had
earlier run creditably in similar races, particularly when 1½ lengths second to
Rambling River in Northern Sprint Handicap at Redcar in May and fifth of 16 to
Jonacris in Gosforth Park Cup at Newcastle in June; speedy and is best at 5f; yet to
race on really soft going but acts on any other; sometimes sweats up badly;

Mrs I. M. Raine's "Miss Import"

successful with and without blinkers (doesn't wear them nowadays); suited by strong handling; sent to USA. *T. Barron.*

MISS INDISCRETION 2 br.f. Mr Bigmore 123–Office Party 81 (Counsel 118) —
(1983 6f 9g 8f) May 2; small, lightly-made filly; second live foal; dam won over 1m; well beaten in maiden races. *P. Burgoyne.*

MISS INIGO 4 b.f. Sagaro 133–Parradell 104 (Pandofell 132) (1982 10h 10.2g —
1983 12.2s² 12f 12f) small, lightly-made filly; poor maiden; well beaten in seller final start; will stay well; best run on soft going. *M. McCormack.*

MISSISSIPI BLUES (USA) 4 b.g. Mississipian 131–Conga (Sword Dancer) 39
(1982 10s 10s 1983 10.2d 13v 12d 8s 10s³ 10.1fg 10fg 12f) plater; stays 1¼m; acts on soft going; has been blinkered; sometimes bandaged; sold to D. Wintle 1,025 gns Ascot August Sales. *K. Ivory.*

MISS JAY CEE 2 b.f. Record Run 127–Xynias 78 (Kythnos 126) (1983 5d 5d 5d) —
May 15; 600Y; sturdy filly; half-sister to a winner in Denmark; dam won over 6f at 2 yrs; beaten some way in minor and maiden events, at Carlisle in May on final start last of 15. *J. Parkes.*

MISS KUTA BEACH 2 ch.f. Bold Lad (Ire) 133–Miss Bali 95 (Crepello 136) 78 p
(1983 6f*) Apr 6; half-sister to 3 winners, including very useful 1m and 9f winner Bali Dancer (by Habitat) and 1982 2-y-o 7f winner Miss Bali Beach (by Nonoalco); dam won over 1½m and is half-sister to smart Welsh Harmony; very weak in market, got up close home to win 14-runner maiden race at Yarmouth in June by a head from Lightning Legacy; will stay 1m. *M. Stoute.*

MISS LIBERTY 2 br.f. Condorcet–Sea Scold (Sea Hawk II 131) (1983 6f 6fg⁴ 7f 71
7fg*) Mar 17; IR 2,800Y; big, deep-girthed filly with quite a lot of scope; third foal; dam never ran; sold 14,000 gns after winning valuable 28-runner seller at

Newmarket in September by ½ length from Bon Hommage; will be suited by 1m; exported to Italy. *R. Hannon.*

MISS LOVE 6 ch.m. Ragstone 128–What's Left (Remainder 106) (1982 NR 1983 12.3v² 12.2g* 12v³ 11g² 11d³ 12f) tall, rather narrow mare; apprentice ridden when winning handicap at Catterick in May; suited by 1½m and should get further; acts on heavy going and is possibly not at her best on firm; winning hurdler. *D. Smith.* **58**

MISS MAINA 2 br.f. Thatching 131–Indian Bird 79 (Relko 136) (1983 5d 7g) Apr 4; 44,000Y; stocky filly; second foal; half-sister to a winner in USA by Be My Guest; dam, daughter of Oaks runner-up Maina, won over 1½m; well beaten in minor event at Windsor in May and £4,100 race at Newbury in September. *G. Lewis.* **–**

MISS MALINOWSKI 3 ch.f. Malinowski 123–Vaguely Related (Pall Mall 132) (1982 6fg 6fg 7fg 7g 7.2s 8g⁴ 8d* 1983 12v 11v² 11.7s³ 11d 10f⁴ 10.1fg 10fg 8fg³) leggy filly; placed in handicaps at Wolverhampton and Windsor in spring and a minor event at Doncaster in November (ran well in blinkers); stays 1½m; acts on a firm surface but is possibly ideally suited by some give in the ground; has worn bandages behind; stumbled and unseated rider on first outing. *N. Guest.* **63**

MISS MATILDA 3 b.f. Jimmy Reppin 131–Ysemeopit 64 (Town Crier 119) (1982 6fg 5g 6d 6s 1983 12v 7d 7fg) small, lengthy filly; behind in varied races, including sellers. *W. Clay.* **–**

MISS MAUD 2 b.f. Tennyson 124–Kereolle (Riverman 131) (1983 5d 5d⁴ 6fg 7f 8g 7g) Feb 24; small filly; has a pronounced round action; first foal; dam, half-sister to very good broodmare Miss Manon, was second over 6f at 2 yrs in France but proved very disappointing; plating-class maiden; should be suited by 1m; possibly needs give in the ground; sold 5,000 gns Newmarket Autumn Sales. *E. Weymes.* **57**

MISS MINT 2 br.f. Music Maestro 119–Pop Gun 85 (King's Troop 118) (1983 5d² 5fg 6g³ 7g 6f 5f 7d 5fg) Mar 16; 4,000Y; lengthy, good-quartered, attractive filly; good walker; half-sister to 2 winning platers; dam best at 5f; most disappointing maiden; best left alone. *J. Winter.* **§§**

MISS MO 2 br.f. Swing Easy 126–Trigamy 112 (Tribal Chief 125) (1983 5d 5s 5v² 5g* 5g) May 8; 400Y; small, lightly-made filly; half-sister to 1982 2-y-o 5f seller winner Wayward Polly (by Lochnager) and 1980 2-y-o 5f winner Rathmoy's Sparkle (by Sparkler); dam 5f performer; made all in maiden auction event at Edinburgh in May; not seen out after May; speedy and isn't sure to stay beyond 5f; yet to race on a firm surface; exported to Malaysia. *M. W. Easterby.* **61**

MISS MOPS 7 br.m. Saulingo 122–Arcticanute 69 (Hardicanute 130) (1982 NR 1983 10f 12f) poor plater; has worn blinkers. *D. Mills.* **–**

MISS MULAZ (FR) 3 ch.f. Luthier 126–Mulaz Bregand (My Swanee 122) (1982 8s 10s³ 10v 1983 10s² 12v* 11v² 10.5v 10.5fg 12g⁴ 8s 12g² 12.5d 12d* 10v⁴) 500,000 francs Y (approx £45,000); tall filly; second live foal; half-sister to very useful French middle-distance winner Mulaz Palace (by Crystal Palace); dam won over 10.5f in France; won 65,000 francs race at Saint-Cloud in April (made all and came home 10 lengths clear) and 80,000 francs event at Evry in October; in frame on several other occasions, including when close second to Brillante in Prix de la Seine at Longchamp later in April and about 2¼ lengths fourth of 7 to Karkisiya after being hampered in Premio Roma Vecchia in November; suited by 1½m; acts well on soft ground; blinkered seventh start (went off very fast indeed and was presumably acting as a pacemaker for her successful stable-companion). *R. Collet, France.* **114**

MISS OLDHAM 3 b.f. Lochnager 132–Hi Baby 102 (High Treason 126) (1982 6h 5g⁴ 6g 5g 6d⁴ 5d 1983 8v 7f 8f 9fg) smallish, lengthy filly; plater; no form in 1983; sold 5,400 gns Newmarket September Sales. *J. Fitzgerald.* **–**

MISS OMAHA 2 ch.f. Vitiges 132–Panena (Thatch 136) (1983 5d 5v² 6fg⁴ 5.8h 6f⁴ 6d) Mar 11; 3,800F, 1,100Y; quite a moderate plater; stays 6f; blinkered final outing; sold 620 gns Ascot October Sales. *R. Akehurst.* **49**

MISS PERFECT 4 ch.f. Beau of Paree–Perfect Harmony (Darling Boy 124) (1982 8g 10.1d 1983 12fg) good-bodied individual; bad plater; has worn blinkers. *J. Bridger.* **–**

MISS PLASI 2 b.f. Free State 125–Welsh Jane 71 (Bold Lad, Ire 133) (1983 5fg² 5f* 5f* 5fg* 6f*) Feb 26; sturdy, good-bodied filly; not the best of movers; first reported foal; dam, daughter of speedy Abbot's Isle, seemed to stay 1m; won small **86**

races at Pontefract, Edinburgh and Hamilton (2) in June and July; suited by 6f; has raced only on fast ground. *Sir Mark Prescott.*

MISS POINCIANA 6 br.m. Averof 123–Miss Twomey (Will Somers 114§) (1982 5g² 5g* 5d* 5f² 5fg* 5f⁴ 5g⁴ 5fg 5fg⁴ 5d⁴ 5fg² 5d 5d 1983 5d* 5v 5f 5g) strong mare; sprint handicapper; won at Doncaster in March; stays 6f but races exclusively at 5f nowadays; acts on any going; often sweats up; usually held up; occasionally blinkered; well beaten last 2 starts. *M. Camacho.* — 70

MISS PRUDENT 4 b.f. Jolly Me 114–Acca Larentia (Romulus 129) (1982 NR 1983 8d 7d⁴ 8d 7fg⁴ 7f²) leggy, light-framed filly; good mover; stays 7f; acts on any going; has run respectably for 7-lb claimer. *C. Gray.* — 62

MISS PUDDLEDUCK 2 b.f. Mummy's Pet 125–Goosie-Gantlet 63 (Run The Gantlet) (1983 6f 5f) Apr 16; close-coupled, useful-looking filly; third foal; half-sister to 3-y-o middle-distance winner Rikki Tavi (by Monsanto) and fairly useful 7f and 1m winner Paperetto (by Godswalk); dam, daughter of very useful Goosie, stayed well; well beaten in modest company at Newbury and Warwick in August. *B. Hills.* — –

MISS RAPID 2 br.f. Rapid River 127–Miss Peebles (Twilight Alley 133) (1983 5f 7g 7f) Apr 20; 420Y; half-sister to a winning 2-y-o plater; dam never ran; modest plater; stays 7f. *W. A. Stephenson.* — 53

MISS REALM 3 b.f. Realm 129–Saltana 101 (Darius 129) (1982 5fg* 5f* 5fg³ 6fg 6f⁴ 1983 8s 8f 8f 6f) compact, quite attractive filly; good walker; fair performer as a 2-y-o; no form in 1983 (trained part of season by J. Fort); should stay beyond 5f; blinkered once as a 2-y-o. *D. Plant.* — –

MISS RITZY 3 b.f. Headin' Up–Ritzy Dreamer (High Line 125) (1982 NR 1983 5d 8s 7fg 5fg) smallish, workmanlike filly; second foal; dam deteriorated after finishing close second in 1m maiden race; poor form, including in a seller. *L. Barratt.* — –

MISS SADDLER 7 ch.m. St Paddy 133–Beech Tree 67 (Fighting Ship 121) (1982 NR 1983 16s³ 12f 12f) plater; stays well; has worn blinkers. *R. Hodges.* — –

MISS SAINT-CLOUD 2 br.f. Nonoalco 131–Miss Paris 111 (Sovereign Path 125) (1983 7fg*) May 4; rather leggy filly; good walker; fourth foal; half-sister to 2 winners, including 7.2f and 1m winner Miss Longchamp (by Northfields); dam, third in Cheveley Park, stayed 1m; ridden by 7-lb claimer, landed a gamble when leading inside final furlong to win 12-runner minor event at Doncaster in October by ½ length from Sindos; will stay 1m; should go on to better things. *M. Stoute.* — 90 p

MISS SHAMROCK 3 br.f. Saritamer 130–Miss Osprey 93 (Sea Hawk II 131) (1982 5.8g 5fg 5f 1983 11.7s 6fg) little worthwhile form, including in a seller; sold 580 gns Ascot August Sales. *K. Brassey.* — –

MISS SHAPE 5 ch.m. Reliance II 137–Shipshape (Shantung 132) (1982 8g 8fg 10fg 8g 12.2d³ 12d 1983 10s 9s) poor maiden; has worn blinkers. *G. Fletcher.* — –

MISS SILCA KEY 2 b.f. Welsh Saint 126–Tremiti 84 (Sun Prince 128) (1983 6f 6fg⁴ 6f² 6fg*) Feb 26; IR 8,000Y; big, rangy filly; first produce; dam won over 5f and 6f at 2 yrs; made experience tell when narrowly beating Hatim and Pagan of Troy in £6,000 Clarence House Maiden Stakes at Ascot in September; previous form only modest; failed to justify favouritism at Windsor in July on third outing; will stay 7f; has raced only on fast ground. *D. Elsworth.* — 99

MISS SINCLAIR 3 br.f. Warpath 113–Lush Pool 70 (Dumbarnie 125) (1982 7fg² 7.2g² 7d 1983 8d 10.4fg 10.4g 12f 15.8g 10.5d 12.2d) fair sort; poor mover; no form in 1983, including in a £4,000 seller; blinkered final start. *M. Lambert.* — –

MISS SMART SHOES 2 b.f. Kala Shikari 125–Ardent Runner 94 (Runnymede 123) (1983 5s 5f 5fg 5fg) Mar 18; 4,300Y; small, compact filly; second foal; half-sister to 1982 2-y-o 5f seller winner Master Broker (by Mummy's Pet); dam sprinting 2-y-o; poor maiden; showed form only on third outing. *P. Haynes.* — –

MISS ST ANDREWS 4 ch.f. Sassafras 135–Miss Scotland 111 (Henry the Seventh 125) (1982 10g 1983 8d 9d) rangy filly; poor maiden. *H. Blackshaw.* — –

MISS STANFORD 2 ch.f. Stanford 121§–Halfalook (Whistling Wind 123) (1983 5d 5f 5g 5g² 5d* 6fg²) Apr 27; 2,700F, 2,000Y; fourth foal; half-sister to Irish 1½m winner Killenaule (by Nebbiolo); dam placed at up to 9.5f in Ireland; blinkered first time, won 13-runner maiden auction event at Wolverhampton in October by a short head from Mummy's Chick; stays 6f; acts on a firm and a soft surface; sold 2,200 gns Doncaster November Sales. *J. Etherington.* — 71

548

Clarence House Maiden Stakes, Ascot—Miss Silca Key (centre) puts up her best effort in narrowly beating Hatim and Pagan of Troy (right)

MISS TANARAVE (USA) 2 b.f. Mr Prospector–Tananarive (Le Fabuleux 133) (1983 7f²) May 2; $550,000Y; useful-looking filly; good walker; half-sister to leading 1979 2-y-o filly and top-class middle-distance 3-y-o Mrs Penny (by Great Nephew) and American 3-y-o Seligman (by Habitony); dam won from 6f to 1¾m in France; third favourite; put in best work in second half of race, after having to be scrubbed along, when promising 1½ lengths second of 18 to New Generation in maiden event at Salisbury in September; will stay 1¼m; likely to make a useful performer and seems sure to win races. *H. T. Jones.*   **87 p**

MISS TANTAN 3 gr.f. Native Admiral–Tantanoola 75 (Swing Easy 126) (1982 6s) rather lightly-made filly; little worthwhile form; sold 500 gns Newmarket Autumn Sales. *Mrs A. Cousins.*   **–**

MISS TETO 3 b.f. African Sky 124–Texly (Lyphard 132) (1982 6f 6f 6g² 5d⁴ 6g 6d 1983 8d 7f 6fg 7f⁴ 8g 7.2g 7s 8g) strong, deep-girthed, sturdy filly; probably best at around 7f; well beaten when blinkered seventh start. *J. Toller.*   **–**

MISS THAMES 3 b.f. Tower Walk 130–Ebb and Flo 82 (Forlorn River 124) (1982 5.1f² 6g* 1983 6d² 8.5g⁴ 8f* 7f 7f* 7d* 7fg) lengthy, rather sparely-made filly; good walker; successful in slowly-run handicap at Beverley in July, fast-run handicap at Newbury in August (ridden by 7-lb claimer) and 4-runner minor event at Goodwood in September; quickened up very nicely and was soon clear when beating Page Blanche by 4 lengths on last-named course; below her best fourth and final starts however; stays 1m; yet to race on really soft going but acts on any other; useful. *M. Stoute.*   **105**

MISS TRILLI 4 ch.f. Ardoon 124–Grecian Palm 78 (Royal Palm 131) (1982 5g³ 5g 5f 5.1g 5fg 5f* 5fg⁴ 5d² 5d³ 1983 5.1fg³ 5fg² 5f* 5f³ 5f³) smallish, attractive filly; sprint handicapper; made all to win at Windsor in July; acts on any going; has run respectably when sweating up; game. *G. Pritchard-Gordon.*   **83**

MISS TURNBERRY 2 b.f. Mummy's Pet 125–Pleasure Boat 91 (Be Friendly 130) (1983 5v 5s³ 6fg² 7f* 7g³ 7d²) Apr 28; IR 21,000Y; half-sister to 2 winners,   **94**

including fairly useful 1979 2-y-o 5f winner Launch (by Tower Walk); dam won over 5f at 2 yrs; put up best performance when under 3 lengths third to Ballet de France in CL Weld Park Stakes at Phoenix Park in October (kept on inside last); 4/7 favourite, slightly disappointing when headed inside final furlong and beaten neck by stable-companion Egidia in minor event at Naas later in month; had earlier landed the odds by a length from Silky Touch in 11-runner maiden at Leopardstown; evidently stays 7f; acts on any going; blinkered last 2 starts. *D. K. Weld, Ireland.*

MISS WENDY (FR) 2 br.f. Homing 130–Cassoway 82 (Kashmir II 125) (1983   –
5fg 7g) sister to 3-y-o 9f winner Sunday Sport and half-sister to 2 winners; dam, daughter of Park Hill winner Cursorial, placed over 1¼m; little sign of ability in October maiden races at Folkestone and Lingfield. *J. Sutcliffe.*

MISS WHIZZ 3 ch.f. Artaius 129–Dame Buckle (Buckpasser) (1982 5g   1983 8f³   –
7fg 8f 8d⁴ 7s) sparely-made filly; quite a moderate maiden; stays 1m; blinkered fourth outing. *P. Cole.*

MISS ZHIVAGO 3 b.f. Gay Fandango 132–Jilly Winks (Blakeney 126) (1982 6f 6f   71
1983 8s 9s* 10.2v² 12v⁴ 10d) fair sort; showed a little promise in maiden races before winning one at Hamilton in April; ran easily best subsequent race next time; stays 1¼m; acts on heavy going; ridden by 7-lb claimer last 3 starts; sold 3,000 gns Newmarket July Sales and resold 2,800 gns same venue in December. *N. Callaghan.*

MISTANDO 2 b. or br.c. Monsanto 121–Fairfields 73 (Sharpen Up 127) (1983 6g   –
7fg 8fg 7g) Mar 13; 7,400F; strong, quite attractive colt; second produce; dam won 5f seller at 2 yrs and also won twice in Holland; behind in maiden races; blinkered final outing. *E. Eldin.*

MISTER ACCORD 3 ch.g. Nishapour 125–Welshpool 75 (Henry the Seventh   70
125) (1982 5f 8f 7g² 1983 7d⁴ 8.2s 9s³ 7v* 7fg 7g 9g* 8d 8f) lengthy gelding; successful in handicaps at Thirsk in May and Hamilton in June; stays 9f; suited by some give in the ground; best in blinkers; sent to Hong Kong. *H. Bell.*

MISTER AVATAR (USA) 3 ch.g. Avatar–Bitter Boredom (Nearctic) (1982 7g   –
6g 1983 10s⁴ 10s 10f 10f 8fg 10g) good-topped gelding; has a round action; poor walker; only poor form; dead. *M. Albina.*

MISTER FEATHERS 2 b.g. Town and Country 124–Nikali 89 (Siliconn 121)   –
(1983 7g 8d) May 14; fair sort; fourth foal; dam second twice over sprint distances at 2 yrs; in rear in autumn maiden races at Leicester and Warwick; subsequently gelded. *J. King.*

MISTER GOLDEN 3 ch.c. Diamonds Are Trump 108–St Pet (St Chad 120)   –
(1982 6g³ 7d² 1983 10s³) tall, useful-looking colt; placed in minor and maiden races, giving impression he didn't last out 1¼m in soft going when third of 17 behind Tinoco at Leicester in March on only outing of 1983. *G. Harwood.*

MISTER KILO 2 b.g. Leander 119–Miss Kilo (King Log 115) (1983 8.2f 7.2g 6fg)   –
workmanlike gelding; first foal; dam quite a moderate hurdler; well beaten in 2 sellers and maiden race. *A. W. Jones.*

MISTER KRUDGER 2 b.c. Jimsun 121–Demi Rock (Double-U-Jay 120) (1983   –
7fg 8g⁴ 7f) May 11; big, rangy colt; second foal; dam second in bumpers races and won over hurdles in Ireland; backward, well beaten in autumn maiden and minor events. *R. Hannon.*

MISTER LORD (USA) 4 b.g. Sir Ivor 135–Forest Friend (Linacre 133) (1982   81
12s 14f 9fg³ 12.8fg* 12d* 1983 13v 9s⁴ 12v* 15g) rangy ex-Irish gelding; won amateur riders race at Thirsk in May; suited by 1½m but finished well beaten over 15f; seems to act on any going. *S. Mellor.*

MISTER LUCKY 6 br.g. Royalty 130–Fair Songstress 100 (Compensation 127)   –
(1982 10fg 12f 12v⁴ 1983 12v³ 16v 12g 12g) poor middle-distance handicapper; acts on any going; suitable mount for a boy; trained part of season by M. Haynes. *D. Jermy.*

MISTER MERLIN 2 b.c. Kala Shikari 125–Maeanders Penny (Royal Palace 131)   78
(1983 6g 6g 6d 6fg*) Mar 25; 1,700F, 5,000Y; small; second foal; dam unraced daughter of very useful 1966 2-y-o Maeander; second favourite, showed much improved form to win 15-runner claimer at Nottingham readily by 2 lengths from Miss Stanford; claimed £4,502 afterwards to race in Scandinavia; stays 6f. *J. Sutcliffe.*

MISTER PITT 4 b.c. Pitskelly 122–High Command (High Hat 131) (1982 10d   –
8fg⁴ 8g 7.6d 8fg 8fg 8s 12v 1983 16v 12g) compact, quite attractive colt;

plating-class maiden; should stay 1¼m; best run on soft going; blinkered nowadays. *T. M. Jones.*

MISTER PRELUDE 3 gr. or ro.c. Warpath 113–Mitsuki 79 (Crowned Prince   **78**
128) (1982 8.2s 10g³ 1983 10.5f³ 10.2f 10g) fair sort; got well behind early on and seemed to carry his head high when 3½ lengths third of 8 behind Seymour Hicks in slowly-run £5,000 race at York in June, easily best effort of 1983; will be suited by further. *M. Jarvis.*

MISTER VALENTINO 3 b.g. Wollow 132–Bernice Clare 68 (Skymaster 126)   **77**
(1982 6fg 6g² 6g 7g 8d* 7d⁴ 1983 8.2v 12f 12f³ 13g 12f 18f 17.4g) smallish, useful-looking gelding; good walker; 5 lengths third of Scottish Dream in quite valuable handicap at Carlisle in June, best effort; stays 1½m; yet to show he can handle really soft going, but acts on any other; sold 5,800 gns Doncaster September Sales. *J. Hanson.*

MISTICAL NAT 2 b.c. Mishgar–Narrate (Narrator 127) (1983 7f⁴ 7f³ 7f⁴ 8d)   **48**
Apr 2; sturdy colt; poor plater; blinkered final outing; dead. *J. Fitzgerald.*

MISTOFFOLEES 3 b.g. Solinus 130–Poquito (Major Portion 129) (1982 5fg⁴ 5f   **75**
5f 6g 7fg 8d³ 1983 9d 9.4d² 12f 10.4g 10g³ 9.4f* 9f 9f* 9f) workmanlike gelding; won maiden race at Carlisle in July and apprentice event at Ripon in August, on latter course being strongly ridden to beat Valerio by a short head; acts on any going; sometimes sweats badly (did at Ripon); sent to USA. *J. Fitzgerald.*

MISTRESS GOSSIP 3 b.f. Le Bavard 125–New Arrival (Master Owen) (1982   **–**
NR 1983 12fg 10f 12s) seventh foal; dam never ran; behind in maiden races; dead. *Mrs A. Cousins.*

MISTRIAL 2 ch.f. Godswalk 130–Supreme Punishment (King of the Tudors 129)   **–**
(1983 5fg) May 4; 5,200Y; second foal; half-sister to 6f winner Moufide (by African Sky); dam Irish 9f winner; behind in 19-runner maiden race at Windsor in July. *A. Hide.*

MISTY FANTAN 7 ch.g. Habat 127–Misty Cat (Misty Flight) (1982 NR 1983   **46**
10.2g³) plater; stays 1¼m. *M. Pipe.*

MISTY FOR ME 3 gr.f. Roan Rocket 128–Rana (Welsh Pageant 132) (1982 5fg   **–**
5fg³ 5fg 5d* 5fg² 5fg* 5f* 5g³ 5v 1983 7s 6v) big, rangy, workmanlike filly; useful 5f performer as a 2-y-o; soundly beaten over further in spring; has won on a soft surface but goes really well on firm ground; sold 24,000 gns Newmarket December Sales. *M. McCourt.*

MISTY HALO 4 b.f. High Top 131–Ringed Aureole 77 (Aureole 132) (1982 12fg²   **86**
13fg² 14g³ 10g* 15.5fg² 10f* 12d* 12.2d* 12s* 1983 12f* 12f* 13fg² 12fg² 12fg*
16f² 12f* 12fg³ 10.2g² 16.5fg* 10g²) lengthy filly; an admirably consistent filly who has been well placed by her trainer to win 12 races from 24 starts; won amateur riders race at Beverley and small race at Pontefract in July, minor event at Pontefract again in August, lady riders race at Chepstow in September and minor event at Redcar in October; stays well; acts on any going but is ideally suited by some give in the ground; excellent mount for an inexperienced rider; tough and genuine. *Sir Mark Prescott.*

MISTY MIRAGE 3 b.g. Grey Mirage 128–Will She Win 57 (Arcticeelagh 119)   **–**
(1982 NR 1983 10.4fg 9.4f 12.2f) big, workmanlike non-thoroughbred gelding; dam won over hurdles; behind in maiden races in summer. *J. Berry.*

MISTY ROCKET 2 gr.f. Roan Rocket 128–Fiji Express (Exbury 138) (1983 5v   **75**
5s 5g⁴ 6g 5f 7f 7d³ 7d 7.6d) Apr 11; small, workmanlike filly; good walker; fourth foal; half-sister to successful sprinter Countach (by Balidar) and a winner in Italy; dam won over 7f and 1¼m in Ireland; quite a moderate maiden; should stay 1m; best form on soft surface; blinkered seventh and ninth outings; trained by P. Ashworth first 5 starts. *D. Elsworth.*

MITILINI 3 ch.c. Julio Mariner 127–Charming Thought (Stage Door Johnny)   **96**
(1982 7g 7g 8g 8.2s* 10g 1983 12v⁴ 12v 12s 16f) strong, short-coupled colt; close up throughout and kept on gamely when excellent 2 lengths second of 8 to Harly in Warren Stakes at Epsom in April; in rear afterwards in Highland Spring Derby Trial at Lingfield, Derby at Epsom (in front for a long way when twelfth of 20 finishers) and Queen's Vase at Royal Ascot; should be suited by further than 1½m; acts well on heavy going. *R. Boss.*

MOBERRY 2 br.f. Mossberry 97–Golden Palermo 80 (Dumbarnie 125) (1983 5s   **54**
5d 6d 7f 8d 8d) Mar 26; smallish, deep-girthed filly; half-sister to numerous winners, notably useful miler Greenwood Star (by No Mercy),later a good 9f winner in USA; dam won 5f seller; poor maiden; stays 1m. *J. Etherington.*

MODERN MAN 3 ch.c. Bold Lad (Ire) 133–Dominica (Zank) (1982 7f 7.9f 10g³   **–**
10s 9v 10v 1983 12g) IR 20,000Y; second foal; dam won over 9f and 1½m in

Ireland; showed a little ability in Ireland as a 2-y-o when trained by C. Collins; well beaten only start of 1983; stays 1¼m; sold to M. Bradley 600 gns Doncaster October Sales. *R. Simpson.*

MODUPE (USA) 3 b. or br.c. Bold Hour–Lost For Words (Verbatim) (1982 6f 7g 1983 8f 10g 10f 7g) leggy, close-coupled colt; poor maiden; well beaten in a seller final start. *I. Walker.*   —

MOFFAT 3 gr.g. Abwah 118–Ardeur (Roan Rocket 128) (1982 NR 1983 6s 6s 8f) big gelding; second foal; brother to 6f and 7f winner Mrs Buzby; dam poor maiden; showed signs of ability first 2 outings but ran badly final start (June). *H. Wharton.*   —

MOHAR 2 b.g. Mansingh 120–Pearlinda (Gulf Pearl 117) (1983 5g) June 19; well-made gelding; first foal; dam poor maiden; backward, behind in 20-runner maiden race at Newbury in September. *P. Makin.*

MOLOKAI 3 b.f. Prince Tenderfoot 126–Cake (Never Say Die 137) (1982 6fg⁴ 6g³ 7d* 1983 7fg 7.6fg⁴ 8f 7.6g 7f³ 8d² 8fg) smallish, lengthy, good-quartered filly; none too good a walker; in frame in handicaps at Chester, Epsom (made running) and Brighton; stays 1m; yet to race on really soft going, but acts on any other; well beaten final start. *J. Hindley.*   82

MOLON LAVE 6 b.g. Welsh Pageant 132–Another Princess 83 (King Emperor) (1982 8g 8fg* 7.6g 7fg² 8fg² 7f⁴ 7f 8fg 8fg² 8g 8fg 7fg 7g 7s 1983 8fg 8fg 8.2fg 8f 7f 8f 8fg 8fg) big, strong gelding; quite a modest handicapper at his best; stays 1m; ideally suited by top-of-the-ground; sometimes blinkered; sold 3,500 gns Newmarket Autumn Sales. *C. Brittain.*

MOLOVE 3 ch.f. Cawston's Clown 113–Charmelaine (Sheshoon 132) (1982 6s 1983 7.2fg 6fg 8.2g) strong filly; poor walker; behind in maiden races. *J. Edmunds.*

MOMENT IN TIME 3 b.f. Without Fear 128–Heavenly Bounty (Captain's Gig) (1982 6f 7f* 7g* 8g⁴ 8g 1983 10d) leggy, lightly-built filly; quite useful at 2 yrs; tailed off in Pretty Polly Stakes at Newmarket in April on only outing of 1983; sold, covered by Anfield, 5,000 gns Newmarket December Sales. *M. Stoute.*

MOMMETS LASS 2 b.f. Royben 125–Unpredictable 103 (Pardal 130) (1983 6f 6fg² 5g 5g) Jan 26; half-sister to 2 winners, including 7f and 1m winner Maybehandy (by Some Hand); dam useful 2-y-o 6f winner; modest plater; better suited by 6f than 5f; acts on a firm surface. *P. Cole.*   56

MONACO LADY 3 b.f. Manado 130–Perfect Bid (Baldric II 131) (1982 NR 1983 8f² 8h² 8.2g) 21,000Y; light-framed, unimpressive sort; second foal; half-sister to Chris's Lad (by Sandford Lad), a useful winner at up to 1m; dam poor daughter of smart middle-distance filly Pretty Puffin; seemed to run well when second of 17 to easy winner Magnetic Field in minor event at Salisbury in August, but disappointed both subsequent starts; stays 1m. *C. Nelson.*   83

MONARCHS MISS 4 ch.f. Royal Match 117–Fyjia (Hula Hul 124) (1982 7fg 8g 1983 10h⁴) of no account; has been blinkered. *Mrs N. Macauley.*   —

MONCLARE LADY 3 b. or br.f. Red Regent 123–Easy Path (Swing Easy 126) (1982 NR 1983 7v) compact filly; second reported foal; dam never ran; showed nothing when in rear in 17-runner maiden race won by Magdalena at Goodwood in May (backward). *A. Pitt.*

MONCLARE TROPHY 4 ch.c. Sandford Lad 133–Blue Warbler (Worden II 129) (1982 6s 5f 6f 6g 6g 6d³ 6f 8s 1983 8s* 8v 8s² 8s* 8d 8g² 7d 10f³ 10f* 10f* 10d) lightly-made colt; useful in plating company and was bought in after winning at Leicester in March (1,700 gns), Brighton in May (1,250 gns), Folkestone in August (1,050 gns) and Folkestone again in September (2,600 gns); suited by 1m+; acts on any going; blinkered twice in 1982. *A. Pitt.*   62

MONDAY BLUES 3 b.g. Workboy 123–Monday Morning (Royal Record II) (1982 5g 5g⁴ 6fg 5f 6f 6g 6d 1983 9s 8.2g) sturdy gelding; bad plater; temperamental into the bargain; sometimes blinkered; sold 360 gns Ascot September Sales. *R. Whitaker.*   — §

MONDOODLE 2 ch.f. Monsanto 121–Doodle 87 (Doudance 99) (1983 5s 5s 5s 6fg⁴ 6f* 6f 7f 7h 6d) Mar 15; quite attractive filly; half-sister to a winner in Belgium by Comedy Star; dam won from 9f to 11.7f; won 11-runner seller at Brighton (no bid) in June by ½ length from Jameena; showed a little in race either side, but nothing otherwise; should stay at least 1m; acts on firm going. *N. Mitchell.*   63

MONETARIST 3 ch.g. Monseigneur 127–Elated 80 (Sparkler 130) (1982 7d 7f² 7fg* 7fg⁴ 7d 7.3g³ 8d 7d 1983 8s 8v 8s 8f⁴ 8f³ 8f 8f*) fair sort; good walker;   94 awarded race after going down by ½ length to Merely A Secret in 7-runner handicap at Wolverhampton in August; stays 1m; suited by top-of-the-ground; sent to Hong Kong. *J. Dunlop.*

MONINSKY 2 ch.c. Monseigneur 127–Golden Number (Goldhill 125) (1983 5d²   **74** 5d² 5v³ 6fg 5f³ 5f 8fg 7g) May 1; 5,200Y; sparely-made colt; half-brother to very useful 5f performer Bucco Bay (by Deep Diver) and a winner abroad; dam ran twice; disappointing maiden; best form early in the season; best at 5f; acts on any going; blinkered sixth outing. *M. H. Easterby.*

MONKEY TRICKS (USA) 2 b.c. Honest Pleasure–Oraza (Zank) (1983 6d* 6f   **83** 7fg 7h 7g² 8g) May 19; small, strong colt; half-brother to 3 winners, including fairly useful 1m and 1½m winner Countess Palotta (by Brigadier Gerard); dam won German 1000 Guineas and Oaks; 20/1, led inside final furlong to win 16-runner minor event at Leicester in June by a neck from Moody Girl; good second in nursery at Leicester 3 months later; should stay 1¼m; suited by some give in the ground; suitable mount for an apprentice; sold 10,000 gns Newmarket Autumn Sales. *H. Candy.*

MONKS GOLD 3 b.g. Habat 127–Golden Dolly 76 (Golden Horus 123) (1982 5f   **– §** 5f 6f 7d³ 6fg* 7f 5g 6d 1983 7d 6f 7f) neat gelding; unreliable sprint plater; usually wears blinkers. *J. Carr.*

MONONGELIA 3 ch.f. Welsh Pageant 132–Bird of Dawning (Sea-Bird II 145)   **91** (1982 7f² 7fg² 7g³ 1983 10f² 9f² 10g* 9f* 10g 12g⁴) lengthy, lightly-built, rather plain filly; good mover; won maiden race at Newmarket and handicap at Ripon in August, latter by a neck from Boccaccio after making all; respectable fourth of 14 to Ounavarra in £4,700 event at Leopardstown in October; stays 1½m; has raced only on a sound surface; trained most of season by H. Cecil. *J. Bolger, Ireland.*

MONSANTO LAD 3 br.g. Monsanto 121–Swallow of Flandre (Flandre II 83)   **–** (1982 5f 5f 5f³ 6f 7f 7d 8g 7g 8g² 8d⁴ 1983 10v 8.2s⁴ 9.4d 8f 8f 7f 7f 8f 12.2g) small, short-backed gelding; disappointing maiden; should stay beyond 1m; tried in blinkers penultimate start. *K. Stone.*

MONSETTA 2 b.f. Monseigneur 127–Miss Etta (King's Troop 118) (1983 7f 7f 5fg   **55** 6fg 6g) Apr 17; 2,000F; workmanlike filly; half-sister to several winners, including useful sprinter Maccaboy (by Will Somers); dam unraced sister to very useful 5f to 1m performer Majetta; modest plater; best run at 5f. *P. Makin.*

MONS LAD 3 ch.c. Manado 130–Cabermaid (Shoemaker 121) (1982 8g 8.2s 1983   **–** 8v 7g 8f 8g) little worthwhile form in varied races; trained until after first start by C. Nelson. *H. O'Neill.*

MONSOON 2 ch.f. Royal Palace 131–Sooner Or Later (Sheshoon 132) (1983   **66** 8.2fg 7g) Mar 21; 4,000Y; half-sister to middle-distance winners Solatia (by Kalydon) and Salian (by Salvo), to winning stayer Sunny Look (by Lombard) and to 2 winners abroad; dam lightly-raced half-sister to Oaks third Suni; about 3½ lengths fifth of 13 behind Talk of Glory in 7f maiden event at Lingfield in October; should stay quite well. *Peter Taylor.*

MONSWART 2 b.c. Monsanto 121–Queen Swallow 58 (Le Levanstell 122) (1983   **80** 5v* 5s⁴ 5d 6f³ 6fg³ 7g 6fg³ 7.2g 8d) Feb 11; 6,000Y; sturdy colt; second reported foal; half-brother to a winning plater by The Brianstan; dam, closely related to My Swallow, was unplaced from 5f to 2m; won 4-runner maiden race at Haydock in April; third in minor event and 2 nurseries subsequently; best form at 6f but probably stays 7f; acts on any going. *M. H. Easterby.*

MONTANA DAWN 2 ch.f. Tumble Wind–Montana Moss (Levmoss 133) (1983   **–** 5d 5v 5.1f 6f 5f 5f 8g) Apr 6; 4,200Y; leggy, lengthy filly; of no account; has worn blinkers. *K. Ivory.*

MONTE ACUTO 9 ch.g. Mountain Call 125–Island Woman 76 (King's Troop 118)   **47** (1982 8f 8fg 8h³ 8g 8fg⁴ 8g 8g² 8fg² 10.2f 9g 1983 8v 8s 10.2g⁴ 10f⁴ 10h³ 10f 12h) strong, well-made gelding; poor handicapper nowadays; sometimes runs in sellers; stays 1¼m; acts on any going; has twice run below form in blinkers; good mount for an apprentice. *G. Cottrell.*

MONTEKIN 4 b.c. Mount Hagen 127–Sweet Relations (Skymaster 126) (1982   **125** 7fg 8fg 10.5f 8g² 10.8s² 10d⁴ 8s 8v² 1983 8s³ 8v² 8d 8v 8fg² 7fg³ 8fg² 8f⁴ 8f³ 8fg* 8fg³ 10fg 8g⁴)
      If mere habit had been his guide Montekin's lad easily might have taken the colt into the part of the unsaddling enclosure reserved for the second or third rather than the winner after the Waterford Crystal Mile at Goodwood in August.

Waterford Crystal Mile, Goodwood—Montekin gains his first success for two seasons, accounting for Adonijah (centre); Sandhurst Prince (rails) finishes fourth

Successful in three races at two, one of them the Horris Hill Stakes, and viewed by many, including ourselves, as having classic potential, he had been pretty disappointing as a three-year-old. Well beaten early on in the Clerical, Medical Greenham, Two Thousand Guineas and Mecca-Dante, in the last of which he had injured a hind joint, he had made a come-back in the autumn and astonishingly been beaten in a mile-and-a-quarter minor event at Warwick before partly salvaging his reputation when in the frame in the Dubai Champion Stakes and Premio Ribot.

The first part of Montekin's four-year-old campaign showed no appreciable improvement in his consistency. He ran well enough to be placed in the Doncaster Mile and Prix de Ris-Orangis at Evry, going down by four lengths to Princes Gate in the latter, yet in the Prix du Muguet at Longchamp and Lockinge Stakes at Newbury he put up substandard displays, particularly at Newbury where he wore blinkers. The Queen Anne Stakes at Royal Ascot saw a different Montekin, for after challenging Noalcoholic a furlong out he ran on well though always fighting a losing battle against Valiyar to be beaten a length and a half, six lengths ahead of Noalcoholic. Montekin finished in the frame on his next four starts too, running near his Royal Ascot form when fourth to Noalcoholic in the Sussex Stakes, where he again finished well without threatening the winner, and third to Luth Enchantee and L'Emigrant in the Prix Jacques le Marois.

Clearly running more consistently than in the past and moreover showing the best form of his career, Montekin looked to have a respectable chance of ending his seventeen-race losing run in the Waterford Crystal Mile in August. The five other runners consisted of Montekin's old rival Noalcoholic (they had met seven times already in 1983) carrying an 8 lb penalty which seemed to put him out of it; the winner of the race in 1982, Sandhurst Prince, making his seasonal reappearance after training troubles; the improving three-year-old Adonijah; and two from the Hern stable, Gorytus, attempting to redeem his by then somewhat tarnished

554

reputation, and Schuss. Montekin is not an easy ride—he needs to be held up and on occasions has looked in two minds about going through with his effort—but Rouse rode him with great dash at Goodwood. Dropped out as Sandhurst Prince and Noalcoholic fought for the lead, Montekin soon recovered after momentarily looking in danger of colliding with the rails when clipping the heels of Gorytus at almost halfway, and at the furlong pole he could be seen poised in fourth on the rails awaiting an opening. Luckily a gap rapidly appeared and showing a good turn of foot Montekin was forced through between Sandhurst Prince and Noalcoholic to lead a hundred yards out; running on strongly he held the powerful late surge of Adonijah, who had encountered considerable trouble in running, by half a length with Noalcoholic third. Although there is little doubt that Adonijah must be regarded as unlucky—when Montekin ran third to Sackford in the Queen Elizabeth II Stakes the following month Adonijah finished four lengths ahead of him in second—Montekin has to be given credit for at last seizing an opportunity to play the leading role in a good race after looking destined to remain a permanent understudy. Unfortunately it was back to normal on his last two starts for he came home seventh to Cormorant Wood in the Dubai Champion Stakes and fourth to the German colt Nandino in the Premio Ribot at Rome, a race he really ought to have won without much fuss.

Montekin, a 29,000-guinea foal resold for 14,500 guineas as a yearling, comes from a family that produced plenty of winners for the late Major Holliday. His dam, the twice-raced Sweet Relations, has also produced the Italian winner Night Relations (by Lochnager) and the two-year-old Good Relations (by Be My Guest) who won over seven furlongs at Limerick Junction in August and later ran respectably in two pattern races. Sweet Relations is one of five foals out of the Cheveley Park and One Thousand Guineas winner Night Off; three of the others won, notably the Dewhurst third Baldur and the smart Madame's Share, a winner in

Mr Peter S. Winfield's "Montekin"

England and France where she picked up the one-mile Prix d'Astarte. The third dam, like Montekin, won the Horris Hill and subsequently showed form from six

Montekin (b.c. 1979)	Mount Hagen (ch 1971)	Bold Bidder (b 1962)	Bold Ruler
			High Bid
		Moonmadness (ch 1963)	Tom Fool
			Sunset
	Sweet Relations (b 1973)	Skymaster (ch 1958)	Golden Cloud
			Discipliner
		Night Off (b 1962)	Narrator
			Persuader

furlongs to a mile and a quarter before developing into an excellent broodmare, foaling numerous winners including Night Off's brother No Argument, a useful sprinter. Montekin is a fine stamp of animal, strong, lengthy and attractive, and though he has sweated up on occasions he usually impresses greatly in appearance. While his best form is at a mile, he stays one and a quarter miles and acts on any going. *J. Dunlop.*

MONTEREEF 3 b.g. Take a Reef 127–Montage 64 (Polyfoto 124) (1982 7g 7fg 7d 1983 7fg 8fg 10.1fg 8h 6fg) small, close-coupled gelding; soundly beaten in varied races, including a seller. *D. Ancil.* —

MONTICELLI 3 b.g. Radetzky 123–Sovereigns Whistle 67 (Sovereign Path 125) (1982 7g 6g 6g 1983 6s 7.6v⁴ 8s 8f 8g 9f) fair sort; not the best of movers; poor maiden; ran in sellers last 2 starts; should stay 1m; has been tried in blinkers. *C. Brittain.* —

MONTREVIE 3 b.f. Monseigneur 127–Tack 88 (Tacitus 124) (1982 6f² 7g³ 8.2fg³ 7s 1983 7g² 8.5d 8f³ 8g²) leggy, very narrow filly; in frame on most outings, but didn't fulfil her 2-y-o promise; stays 1m; probably not suited by soft ground. *H. T. Jones.* — **75**

MOOBER STAR 2 ch.f. Master Sing 109–Mutchkin 65 (Espresso 122) (1983 5s 6f) Apr 21; 320Y; leggy filly; sister to a poor animal; dam won 1¼m seller; behind, slowly away, in minor event at Pontefract in May and seller at Thirsk in June. *T. Kersey.* —

MOODY GIRL 2 b.f. Relko 136–Moment To Remember (Assagai) (1983 6d² 6f 8f⁴ 7fg⁴ 7s² 7fg) Feb 27; 2,700Y; strong, lengthy filly; second foal; half-sister to Emma Royale (by Royal and Regal), a winning plater over 1½m; dam second over 5f and 1½m in Ireland; quite a moderate filly; placed at Leicester in June and October; ran badly in nursery on same course in October on final appearance; should stay 1½m; appears to need give in the ground. *R. Hollinshead.* — **78**

MOON CHARTER 2 gr.f. Runnymede 123–Moonscape 87 (Ribero 126) (1983 5v 5g 5.8g 5.1fg 5.8h 7f⁴ 8d) Mar 20; 960Y; first foal; dam, fair stayer, is half-sister to Derby fourths Great Wall and Moon Mountain; poor plater; suited by 7f; trained by K. Brassey first 6 starts. *Mrs W. Sykes.* — **45**

MOONDAWN 2 b.c. Dance In Time–Schoolhouse Dale 72 (Reform 132) (1983 5d 6g 5f 6f 5g 5g 5fg) Feb 22; third foal; brother to 9f winner Time Wind and half-brother to a winner in Italy; dam won over 1½m; plating-class maiden; needs further than 5f and should be suited by 7f+; blinkered last 2 outings; sold 1,350 gns Ascot November Sales. *W. Elsey.* — **59**

MOONDUSTER 4 b.f. Sparkler 130–Go Gracefully 85 (Jolly Jet 111) (1982 8d⁴ 9fg 12.3g³ 16g* 15d³ 16.1s 1983 15g² 20fg 18.4fg⁴ 20f 17.4g 16.1g) leggy filly; staying handicapper; acts on a firm and a soft surface. *G. Thompson.* — **63**

MOON JESTER 3 gr.c. Comedy Star 121–Castle Moon 79 (Kalamoun 129) (1982 7fg 7g 7g 7g 7fg 8g⁴ 8s* 1983 10v² 10s 12v² 12d² 11g* 12f² 13.3f⁴ 14f 10f⁴ 12f 10s 11.7g) fair sort; overcame considerable difficulties in running when just getting up to beat Gaelic Jewel a short head in handicap at Newbury in June; second in 4 other handicaps, including when going down by ¾ length to Dazari in 20-runner King George V Stakes at Royal Ascot; finds 1¼m on sharp side and stays 13f; acts on any going; tough and game; has run creditably in blinkers. *M. Usher.* — **91**

MOONLIGHT BAY 3 ch.f. Palm Track 122–Moonbay (Ovid 95) (1982 6g 8.2fg 7g 6s 1983 8f* 12g) plain, short-legged filly; showed only form when winning selling handicap at Beverley in August (no bid); suited by 1m and firm ground. *M. Lambert.* — **53**

MOONLIGHTING 3 b.f. Workboy 123–Ashen Light 76 (Shiny Tenth 120) (1982 6s 1983 8g 13d 12fg 16f 12fg) strong filly; in rear in maiden and minor events. *P. Calver.* —

MOON MARINER 3 ch.c. Julio Mariner 127–Maroukh (Kashmir II 125) (1982   84
8fg 8s 10s* 10.2s⁴ 1983 12s 12d² 10v 12f 12f³ 13.3f 16h* 15.8fg 18f³ 15s² 18fg
20fg²) well-made, quite attractive colt; beat Lucky Ivor by 4 lengths in small
handicap at Nottingham in August; ran well on occasions afterwards, on final outing
finishing best of all when 2 lengths second to Mayotte in handicap at Newmarket in
October; ideally suited by a thorough test of stamina; acts on any going; blinkered
and sweating fourth start. *C. Brittain.*

MOON MELODY 2 b.g. Silly Season 127–Melody Song 74 (Saintly Song 128)   66
(1983 5g 5f³ 6g 6f 6s) May 16; fair sort; first foal; dam won over 5f and 6f at 2 yrs;
modest plater; should stay beyond 6f; acts on firm going. *W. Haigh.*

MOORES METAL 3 b.c. Wolverlife 115–Torino (Firestreak 125) (1982 6g³ 6fg   94
6g³ 6d 6d⁴ 7d⁴ 7s 1983 7d 8f 7.2g³ 8fg* 8f 8fg 8g 10fg 8g) rather lightly-made,
quite attractive colt; led inside last furlong and held on gamely to beat Prego by ¾
length in 14-runner £8,700 Addison Tools Handicap at Newmarket in July; mainly
disappointing afterwards, although ran respectably over 1¼m; possibly not at his
best on very firm going; well suited by a strong pace (didn't get one fifth and sixth
outings); unreliable. *R. Hollinshead.*

MOORLAND MAIDEN 2 b.f. Saunter–Vetsera (Hopeful Venture 125) (1983 7f   —
7d 10fg) Apr 3; half-sister to Ascot Stakes winner Right Regent (by Kambalda);
dam never ran; well behind in autumn maiden races. *M. Pipe.*

MOP FAIR 2 b.f. Fair Season 120–The Mop 59 (Vilmorin) (1983 5f 5fg 7h) Apr   60
16; small, lightly-made filly; tenth foal; dam poor maiden; plating-class maiden; not
raced after August. *P. Cole.*

MOPSY LOVEJOY 3 b.f. Tudor Rhythm 112–Friendly Sylvan (Be Friendly 130)   55
(1982 5fg 5fg⁴ 6g 7g 6g 1983 9fg 8.2fg² 10h² 10h³ 10fg 12g⁴ 11s* 10.8g) plain
filly; poor walker; plater; won at Wolverhampton in October (no bid); stays 1½m;
acts on any going; blinkered last 3 outings. *D. H. Jones.*

MOQUETTE 4 b.f. Moulton 128–Miss Tweedie 113 (Aberdeen 109) (1982 12d⁴   —
13.4g 16.9fg 12g 1983 10d) lengthy filly; poor form, including in a seller. *L.
Barratt.*

MORALITY STONE 6 b.h. Ragstone 128–Miss Casanova 84 (Galivanter 131)   70
(1982 10.2f 11.5f³ 12g 11.7g³ 11.5g 10v 10s 1983 12g 12s 10s 12g 12s 8d* 10v 8s⁴
8d 10d 7f 8f* 8f 10g) robust, well-made horse; inconsistent handicapper; won at
Newbury in April (50/1 when beating Portogon a neck in Mellowes Metfab Spring
Cup) and Redcar (apprentices) in July; effective at 1m and stays 1½m; acts on any
going; suitable mount for an inexperienced rider. *P. Mitchell.*

MORCON 3 ch.c. Morston 125–Conciliation 98 (St Paddy 133) (1982 7f² 1983   120
10g 12s* 12s 12fg 10f* 10f² 10g* 10fg)
    Morcon made such an impression when winning the Schroder Life
Predominate Stakes at Goodwood in May that he started third favourite for the
Derby, in the absence of stable-companion Gorytus. Yet despite this and two more
wins at Goodwood before the end of the season, his eleventh of nineteen in the
Dubai Champion Stakes, for which he started 33/1, provides a more accurate
reflection of his standing among the top middle-distance performers. He's a smart
performer, but a stone or so behind the very best.
    Morcon's all-the-way six-length win over Rock's Gate in the Predominate
(Troy had won the corresponding race by only a length more in 1979) appeared a
promising Derby trial, at the same time misleadingly giving the impression that he
was extremely well suited by a mile and a half and soft ground. Ultimately the race
proved very little: the opposition was none too exacting and the field went no gallop
in the early stages. In the Derby itself Morcon never showed with a winning
chance, and he finished over twenty lengths behind Teenoso in eighth; and when
tried over a mile and a half for a third time in the Princess of Wales's Stakes at the
Newmarket July Meeting he ran very much as though he didn't get the trip in a
strongly-run race—he was in front half a mile from home but dropped out with fully
a furlong still to run and finished only fifth to Quilted.
    Put back to a mile and a quarter in the Trident Chesterfield Cup at Goodwood
later in July, a hotly-contested handicap in which he carried 9-0, Morcon returned
to form in no uncertain fashion. After impressing us with his coolness in the
paddock and with the way he went to post on the firm ground he simply outclassed
his fourteen opponents, romping in by four lengths from the useful four-year-old
Favoloso under hand riding. This was one of the best performances of the season in
a handicap, and the shorter distance clearly suited him ideally. Stepped up in class

Lord Rotherwick's "Morcon"

again in the Prix de la Cote Normande at Deauville a fortnight later Morcon went down by three lengths to the good French colt Mourjane, despite getting weight, but he regained winning form when returned to Goodwood once more for the Valdoe Stakes in September, his last race before the Champion Stakes. Prominent throughout in a somewhat muddlingly-run contest, Morcon just held on by a short head from the unlucky Guns of Navarone after being sent for home two furlongs out. It was a very game performance but not good enough to put him in the reckoning for the Champion.

Morcon (ch.c. 1980)	Morston (ch 1970)	Ragusa (b 1960)	Ribot
			Fantan II
		Windmill Girl (b 1961)	Hornbeam
			Chorus Beauty
	Conciliation (ch 1973)	St Paddy (b 1957)	Aureole
			Edie Kelly
		Mitigation (ch 1963)	Milesian
			Allegation

Morcon is a lengthy, quite attractive colt by Morston out of the quite useful top-of-the-ground performer Conciliation who won at Chepstow and Windsor as a two-year-old. Conciliation is a half-sister to the smart middle-distance horse Colum and closely related to the three-year-old Contester, whose remarkable finishing burst in the Tote Cesarewitch would have taken him to the front in another fifty yards or so. Morcon is Conciliation's third foal, following the two-year-old winners Briar (by Brigadier Gerard) and Woodcutter (by Wollow); she has since produced colts by High Top and Bustino and a filly by Troy. Morston hasn't been outstandingly successful at stud but Morcon's trainer Hern did well with two more of his progeny, More Light and Valentinian. If Morcon takes after that pair he'll improve a bit as a four-year-old. He'll probably need to in order to be placed to

558

advantage, for he'll be eligible for few handicaps and on his three-year-old form will find it difficult to win pattern races. *R. Hern.*

MOREAN 3 b.f. Mr Bigmore 123–Rhythm 64 (Bleep-Bleep 134) (1982 NR 1983 8f 12d) non-thoroughbred filly; half-sister to 3 winners, including useful 1979 2-y-o 5f and 6f winner Pink Blues (by Tickled Pink) and Vocalist (by Crooner), a useful winner here and in USA at up to 1m; dam seemed to stay 1½m; behind in maiden races at Salisbury (backward) and Lingfield in September. *A. Turnell.*   —

MORE CANDY 2 b.f. Ballad Rock 122–Zepha 88 (Great Nephew 126) (1983 5f 6g³ 6fg⁴ 6fg⁴) Mar 20; 25,000Y; first foal; dam handicap winner from 1m to 9.4f; 50/1, excellent length fourth of 13 to King Persian in Heinz '57' Phoenix Stakes in August, running on well inside final furlong; didn't obtain a clear run when over 2 lengths fourth to Grey Dream in Oldtown Stud Stakes at same track later in month; promises to stay 1m. *L. Browne, Ireland.*   **98**

MORE IGRA 3 ch.f. Mljet–Final Game 83 (Pardao 120) (1982 NR 1983 10f 10h) third foal; half-sister to 2 winners, notably very smart sprinter Mummy's Game (by Mummy's Pet); dam won over 1¼m; last-but-one in sellers at Lingfield and Chepstow in August. *W. Turner.*   —

MORENE 2 br.f. Lochnager 132–Podzola 77 (Royal Prerogative 119) (1983 5v 5s 5d 6fg 6fg 7g*) Apr 24; fair sort; first foal; dam won over 1m at 4 yrs and also won over hurdles; landed a gamble by a short head from Holme River in 16-runner seller (no bid) at Catterick in September; needs 7f and will stay 1m; acts on a firm surface; exported to Malaysia. *M. W. Easterby.*   **55**

MORESBY 2 b.g. Mount Hagen 127–Inch (English Prince 129) (1983 7g 8s⁴ 8g) Mar 7; IR 15,500Y; neat, strong gelding; good walker; first foal; dam fair performer at up to 1½m in Ireland; quite a modest maiden; will probably stay beyond 1m; acts on soft going; gelded after final outing. *B. Hills.*   **69**

MORE TENDER 2 ch.c. Ashmore 125–Lady Bequick 81 (Sharpen Up 127) (1983 8g) Mar 21; 3,600Y; second foal; dam ran only at 2 yrs when successful twice at around 5f; in rear in 11-runner minor event at Goodwood in September. *I. Wardle.*   —

MORE WIT 3 ch.f. Whitstead 125–Misty Echo (Mountain Call 125) (1982 6g 5g 7d 1983 10s 8.3s 8g³ 10.8fg³ 10.1f 10f⁴ 10f² 8f³ 10.6g 9g²) workmanlike filly; plater when trained by P. M. Taylor; blinkered when second in small race at Marseille, better effort in France; stays 1¼m. *J. Baldassari, France.*   **48**

MORGAN'S CHOICE 6 ch.h. Reliance II 137–Piave (Alcide 136) (1982 7s 16g* 18.4fg 17.1f* 17f⁴ 17.1f* 16fg* 16.1g³ 17.1g* 16fg⁴ 14.6g³ 13.3g 17.1s 18d 1983   **85**

Pimm's Goodwood Stakes—a comfortable win for Morgan's Choice from Cheka

16v 11.7s 17.1v[4] 17.1g 16f* 16f 16f* 17.1h* 16f* 19f* 14f[3] 14g[3] 14.6fg 16fg 18fg) small, well-made horse; in magnificent form in summer when he decisively won handicaps at Ascot, Sandown, Bath (fifth course win), Ascot again (Brown Jack Stakes from Voyant) and Goodwood; beat Cheka comfortably by 5 lengths in Pimm's Goodwood Stakes on last-named; had stiffer tasks afterwards but ran well several times, including when 4½ lengths third to Jupiter Island in Tote-Ebor at York in August; needs a test of stamina; acts on any going but is ideally suited by top-of-the-ground; has won in blinkers, but is better without; often bandaged on off-fore; has a useful turn of foot; tough and genuine. *J. Hill.*

MORICE 5 b.g. Morston 125–Ardice 91 (Hard Tack 111§) (1982 10s 12fg 13.3g 1983 12d 11.7d[3] 12v 12f[4] 11.7f) well-made gelding; stays 1½m; acts on any going; has run respectably for an amateur rider. *R. Hannon.*   **46**

MORSE PIP 4 b.c. Bay Express 132–Code of Love 99 (Bleep-Bleep 134) (1982 5g* 6fg[2] 5fg 5g[4] 5d[3] 6s* 1983 5s[2] 5v[4] 6g[3] 6g 6f[3] 6f* 6f 6f 5h[4] 7fg[3] 7.3g[4] 5g[4] 6fg) fair sort; not the best of movers; sprint handicapper; won at Salisbury in July; had run well previous start to be 2¾ lengths third to Melindra in Wokingham Stakes at Royal Ascot; finds 5f too sharp when going is on top and a stiff 7f stretching his stamina to the limit; acts on any going; good mount for an apprentice; has worn bandages. *S. Woodman.*   **84**

MORSTONIA 2 ch.f. Morston 125–Cigarette Case 89 (Faberge II 121) (1983 7fg[4]) Mar 1; smallish, lightly-built filly; sister to 1½m winner Latakia, closely related to 1½m and 1¾m winner Smoke Screen (by Blakeney) and half-sister to 2 other winners; dam won from 1m to 11f; 33/1, 2 lengths fourth of 14 to Claude Monet in minor event at Doncaster in October; bound to leave this form behind over middle distances. *M. Stoute.*   **77** p

MORSTONS MAID 4 ch.f. Morston 125–Dairy Queen 76 (Queen's Hussar 124) (1982 12f 12.2f[4] 12fg 15fg 12g 12.2f[4] 1983 12.3v 16f 18f 15f 15.8f 12f[3] 10fg[3] 10h[2] 12d 10g) leggy, lightly-made filly; plater; suited by 1½m; acts on hard going; has run respectably when sweating up; sometimes blinkered. *E. Alston.*   **40**

MORTON THE HATTER 7 b.g. Galivanter 131–Andromache 112 (Delirium 126) (1982 NR 1983 16v) staying handicapper; acts on a soft surface; has won for an amateur rider. *M. Masson.*   **–**

MORVA SONG 5 b.m. Drumbeg 94–Melodius Charm 98 (Prince Chevalier) (1982 NR 1983 12g) half-sister to several winners; showed own 5f at 2 yrs; tailed off in modest maiden race at Brighton in May; dead. *T. Hallett.*   **–**

MORVERN 4 b.g. Thatch 136–Sleat 112 (Santa Claus 133) (1982 10.4g 12f 11.5f[4] 14g[3] 16.5fg[3] 15.8d[4] 1983 12d 12fg) strong, compact gelding; staying maiden on flat though has won over hurdles; acts on a firm and a soft surface; has twice been blinkered. *J. Jenkins.*   **–**

MORWRAY BOY 3 b.g. Workboy 123–Lyn's Pride 85 (Star Moss 122) (1982 5f 6fg 5.8f[3] 6g[2] 7f[3] 7fg[4] 6g[2] 6f 6s[3] 6v 6g 1983 6s[2]) useful-looking gelding; excellent mover; good second to Vatican Way in maiden race at Pontefract in May on only outing of 1983; stays 7f; acts on any going; blinkered once in 1982. *S. Norton.*   **79**

MOSES SAMPSON 5 b.g. Bold Lad (Ire) 133–Countess Decima (Sir Gaylord) (1982 6f 8.3g 7f* 8fg 7g[2] 7g 7.6f* 7f[4] 7f 7g 7fg 1983 7s 7g 5f 6h 6g) stocky gelding; didn't find his form in 1983; stays 7f well; acts on any going; seems best in blinkers; has won for an amateur; occasionally starts slowly. *T. Taylor.*   **–**

MOSOF 2 b.g. Oats 126–Hail to Vail (Hail to Reason) (1983 10fg) Mar 13; 5,400Y; half-brother to several winners, including very useful middle-distance performer Prince Rheingold (by Rheingold); dam never ran; behind, slowly away, in 19-runner maiden race at Nottingham in October. *D. Oughton.*   **–**

MOSSBLOWN 3 b.f. Warpath 113–Montana (Mossborough 126) (1982 5f 7d 8fg[4] 1983 12fg[2] 12g[3] 12.2g) fair sort; will be suited by further than 1½m; sold 1,350 gns Doncaster November Sales, probably for export to Scandinavia. *C. Thornton.*   **57**

MOSS WALK 5 b.m. Private Walk 108–Moss Ville (Levmoss 133) (1982 10.1g 1983 10.2g 11.7h) ex-Irish mare; probably of little account; sold 500 gns Ascot November Sales. *J. King.*   **–**

MOSSWERN 4 ch.f. Towern 96–Mossy's Delight 44 (Mossy Face 98) (1982 10f[2] 8f[2] 8fg 1983 8d 8d[4] 7v 8fg) leggy, lightly-made filly; stays 1¼m; acts on any going; blinkered final outing; ran poorly first start. *A. Young.*   **–**

MOSSY BELL 3 gr.f. Town Crier 119–Miss Moss 54 (Mossborough 126) (1982 NR 1983 13.1fg) half-sister to 2 winners, including moderate middle-distance   **–**

handicapper Mudgedown (by Murrayfield); dam half-sister to top-class Nagami; unquoted when tailed-off eighth of 9 behind Insular in minor event at Bath in September. *R. Holder.*

MOSSY CONES 4 gr.g. Roan Rocket 128–Mossy Glade (Levmoss 133) (1982 7s 12f⁴ 16fg⁴ 14f² 13.4f 12d 1983 12f) ex-Irish gelding; first foal; dam never ran; modest staying maiden; acts on firm going. *W. A. Stephenson.* —

MOST FUN 5 b.h. Morston 125–Darling Bud (Whistling Wind 123) (1982 22.2fg 8fg 8fg 16fg 1983 14fg 18.8f) rather lightly-built horse; ran creditably at 3 yrs in Ireland; poor form on flat over here, probably best effort over 2m; has been bandaged behind. *J. Old.* —

MOST HONOURABLE (USA) 3 b.f. Exclusive Native–Princess Marshua (Prince John) (1982 NR 1983 7s 7.6v² 7v 8f² 7h* 10f 10.8g* 9fg² 10g) $500,000Y; rather leggy, angular, plain filly; first foal; dam, placed at 3 yrs, is daughter of CCA Oaks winner Marshua; successful in maiden race at Chepstow and handicap at Warwick in July; held up when beating Childown by 2 lengths on latter course; suited by 1¼m+; acts on any going; had stiffish task but was disappointing nevertheless final start (sweated and looked rather light). *F. Durr.*   93

MOTORWAY MADNESS 3 b.f. Thatch 136–Ringed Aureole 77 (Aureole 132) (1982 6s* 7f 7g 8f 8d 1983 8.2v 9s* 12v 12d 10v) leggy, close-coupled filly; 25/1-winner of amateur riders race at Ripon in April, only form of 1983; stays 9f well; acts well on soft going; sold 6,000 gns Ascot September Sales and exported to Algeria. *J. Berry.*   61

MOUHANNED 5 b.h. Ashmore 125–French Bird (Guersant 129) (1982 12d 1983 10.2d 12fg 12g) compact, good sort; disappointing handicapper; usually a front runner. *J. Old.* —

MOUHRA (USA) 3 b.f. Night Invader–Fiery Kiss (Irish Ruler) (1982 6fg 1983 7f) soundly beaten in maiden and minor events; sold 720 gns Newmarket July Sales; dead. *P. Cole.* —

MOULETTA 3 b.f. Moulton 128–Violetta III 110 (Pinza 137) (1982 NR 1983 7f 8f) quite an attractive filly; good walker; sister to 1979 2-y-o 6f winner Good Lassie, and half-sister to numerous winners, including Oaks second Furioso (by Ballymoss) and Irish 1000 Guineas winner Favoletta (by Baldric II); dam dead-heated in 1961 Cambridgeshire; never on terms in maiden events at Leicester (seventh of 12) and Warwick (started slowly) in summer. *G. Wragg.* —

MOULTON BOY 2 b.c. Moulton 128–Romara 105 (Bold Lad, Ire 133) (1983 6f 6f³ 6f⁴ 6fg 6fg²) Apr 16; quite an attractive colt; first foal; dam won over 7f and 1m; staying-on 3 lengths second of 13 to Mr Mccka in nursery at Newmarket in October, easily best effort; will be suited by 7f and 1m; yet to race on a soft surface. *G. Wragg.*   94

MOUNTAIN BEAR 2 b.f. Welsh Pageant 132–Eldoret 100 (High Top 131) (1983 6g 6fg 6d) neat, strong filly; first foal; dam won over 6f and 1m; not fully wound up, showed up in first 2 of 3 autumn races in varied company; should do better at 7f+. *J. Dunlop.*   79

MOUNTAINEER 4 br.g. Legal Eagle 126–Madzoro (Combat 123) (1982 NR 1983 12g) sturdy gelding; poor maiden; has worn blinkers; has worn a tongue strap. *J. Leigh.* —

MOUNTAIN LODGE 4 b. or br.f. Blakeney 126–Fiddlededee 94 (Acropolis 132) (1982 11.7f³ 16fg² 16d* 16g* 14fg 17.4d* 18d* 1983 16g⁴ 16f 18fg³ 14s* 15.5f)   120

Statements to the effect that history has been made by a certain event are frequent and often inaccurate, but there is no refuting the claim that the Curragh on October 8th did indeed see history being made. As Mountain Lodge passed the post a clear-cut winner of the Jefferson Smurfit Memorial Irish St Leger she became the first horse above the age of three to win a classic in Britain or Ireland with the blessing of the turf authorities—the ineligible four-year-old Maccabaeus had been disqualified after winning the 1844 Derby as Running Rein—and into the bargain proved the decision to run her at four had been a sensible one.

For much of the year it had looked as if Mountain Lodge would be retired to the paddocks without adding to the four wins she had gained in 1982 when a convincing victory under 7-10 in the Tote Cesarewitch had provided her finest moment. In fact if Henry Fielding was right in asserting that patience is a virtue very apt to be fatigued by exercise, the filly's connections' patience might well have been near exhaustion by October since it had been tested at a gallop rather than walking pace. Kept in training principally to try and win the Gold Cup, Mountain

Lodge had run just three times before the Irish St Leger, missing an opportunity of meeting the soft going that suited her so well when the Mono Sagaro Stakes at Ascot was abandoned owing to waterlogging, finishing a respectable staying-on fourth to Ore in the Henry II Stakes at Sandown and then missing Royal Ascot too because she bruised a foot on the day of the race. The very firm ground on which the Gold Cup took place would not have been in Mountain Lodge's favour anyway and after a moderate display on similar going in the Miner's Northumberland Plate at Newcastle towards the end of June she had a two-and-a-half-month lay-off, reappearing in the Doncaster Cup. Even then conditions were not in her favour but despite this she ran creditably, keeping on well after being given plenty to do in the straight—hardly a wise policy with a filly whose long suit was stamina—to finish over four lengths third to Karadar and Gildoran.

Ridden more enterprisingly Mountain Lodge would probably have been second at Doncaster so she had obviously improved from three to four, yet it still required great optimism to envisage her winning a Group 1 event in normal circumstances since Karadar and Gildoran are not top-class stayers by any means. Normal circumstances, though, do not apply with regard to the Irish St Leger which scarcely ever matches its British counterpart in the quality of the field contesting it. The 1983 race proved to be no exception to this rule, and while at least three of Mountain Lodge's nine opponents, the Cumberland Lodge winner Band, Grand Prix de Paris winner Yawa and four-year-old Geoffrey Freer Stakes winner Khairpour, had form demonstrably better than hers, she was not friendless in the market, being backed down to fourth favourite behind Band. Presumably one reason for the confidence in Mountain Lodge was the fact that heavy rain had made the going extremely testing, and in what turned out to be a real slog she revelled in the conditions. A thick mist made visibility atrocious, worse than the photograph of the finish suggests, and so far as could be seen early on Mountain Lodge was kept much closer to the leaders than at Doncaster as another British challenger High Cannon made the running. Turning into the straight High Cannon had been replaced by the Irish colt Arctic Lord and Yawa, closely followed by Band and then Mountain Lodge, and under two furlongs out Band took it up. Clearly tiring—he was almost out on his feet at the end—Band showed a tendency to hang left in front and had no reserves left with which to meet the persistent challenge of Mountain Lodge who wore him down well inside the last furlong and went clear to win by two lengths. Khairpour finished fairly well to be a length and a half back in third with Arctic Lord fourth and Yawa a disappointing sixth. Mountain Lodge thus became the fourth filly to win the race since the war, following Morning Madam, Lynchris and Pidget.

In retrospect the Irish St Leger would have been a very one-sided affair without the two four-year-olds and in as much as their decision to open the race to older horses increased its competitiveness the Irish Turf Club evidently succeeded in one of their aims. For all that, we do not think that Mountain Lodge would have made the first three in the Doncaster St Leger had she been eligible to run, and despite the injection of cash the Irish St Leger has received over the past two years from the Smurfit Organisation—Mountain Lodge collected the equivalent of £43,000 for her win—it remains to be seen whether there will be any marked improvement in the race's quality in the long run. As for Mountain Lodge, she ran once more, in the Prix Royal-Oak at Longchamp, where with the ground again on top it came as no surprise to see her finish well beaten behind Old Country and Band, dropping out after being within striking distance of the leaders two furlongs out.

		Hethersett	Hugh Lupus
	Blakeney	(b 1959)	Bride Elect
	(b 1966)	Windmill Girl	Hornbeam
Mountain Lodge		(b 1961)	Chorus Beauty
(b. or br.f. 1979)		Acropolis	Donatello II
	Fiddlededee	(ch 1952)	Aurora
	(ch 1967)	Eyewash	Blue Peter
		(ch 1946)	All Moonshine

Few horses racing purely on the flat have more stamina in their breeding than Mountain Lodge: of the fourteen horses shown in her pedigree all but three stayed a mile and a half and a good proportion stayed further. Her sire Blakeney ran second in the Gold Cup and her dam, sold for 13,000 guineas at the 1979 Newmarket December Sales, ran third in the Park Hill after scoring over a mile and a half at York. Fiddlededee has foaled two other winners, Fiddle-Faddle (by Silly Season), who stayed well, and Governor's Camp (also by Blakeney) who won at a mile and a half and showed promise over hurdles before being killed in a race at Ayr. The next two dams were prolific broodmares, producing twenty winners between them. Eyewash, given away carrying Fiddlededee, won the Lancashire Oaks and her

Jefferson Smurfit Memorial Irish St Leger, the Curragh—with conditions in her favour Mountain Lodge shows herself a very smart stayer, beating Band by two lengths going away

offspring included Collyria and Varinia, successful respectively in the Park Hill and Lingfield Oaks Trial; All Moonshine, a half-sister to Hyperion, numbered the high-class Mossborough among her winners. There have been plenty of other good horses from this family, for example Raise You Ten and the champion Australian sire Sir Tristram, and providing she is mated with stallions less well endowed with stamina than herself the game Mountain Lodge, a smallish, good-quartered individual, ought to maintain the tradition. *J. Dunlop.*

MOUNT CEDAR 2 ch.c. Mount Hagen 127–Mettle 107 (Pretendre 126) (1983   **81** p
7fg) Feb 3; 36,000F; tall, angular, rather plain colt; half-brother to several winners, notably 3-y-o Polished Silver (by Try My Best), a smart winner over 7f and 1m at 2 yrs; dam won twice over 5f at 2 yrs and stayed 1¼m; 33/1, got the hang of things in closing stages when 4 lengths seventh of 13 to All Hell Let Loose in £4,300 event at Newmarket in October; will be suited by 1m+; clearly good enough to win in maiden company. *M. Jarvis.*

MOUNTCOUT 4 ch.f. Manado 130–Beaume (Faraway Son 130) (1982 10v 12s   **–**
1983 12f 15.5f) leggy, lightly-built filly; bad plater; has been tried in blinkers. *H. Beasley.*

MOUNT IMPERIAL 2 b.c. Imperial Fling 116–Sacred Mountain 74 (St Paddy   **100** ?
133) (1983 5s 6fg* 7fg 6fg³ 6.3f³ 5g) Mar 31; 10,000Y; half-brother to 3-y-o Captivating Lady (by Averof), a winner over 6f at 2 yrs, and a winner in Norway; dam sister to very smart 1m to 1¼m performer Calpurnius; third of 5 runners twice in August, beaten under 2 lengths each time, behind So Fine in V'Soske Carpets Stakes at Phoenix Park, and Gala Event in Ballsbridge-Tattersalls Anglesey Stakes at the Curragh; had earlier won a maiden event at Phoenix Park; bred to stay middle distances but ran as though he didn't stay when tried over 7f; blinkered final start. *J. Oxx, Ireland.*

MOUNT KELLETT 3 b.g. Pitskelly 122–Belmullet (Bold Lad, Ire 133) (1982   **92**
6d 5g 6fg² 7g 6fg 5d³ 6d 1983 6v* 6d 5.6f² 6fg 5g³ 6fg 7fg²) lengthy gelding; grand walker; beat Timsah a shade cleverly by a length in handicap at Kempton in April and was placed on 3 other occasions; stays 7f; acts on any going; sent to Hong Kong. *R. Armstrong.*

MOUNT MAGIC 7 ch.g. Mount Hagen 127–Magical Music (Sing Sing 134) (1982   **–**
10s³ 12g* 12fg² 10.4g² 11fg² 12g 10g 1983 10v 12d 11s 11fg⁴ 11g) leggy gelding; plater; stays 1½m; ideally suited by top-of-the-ground; good mount for an apprentice; usually makes running; sometimes bandaged; sold 1,000 gns (privately) Doncaster May Sales. *R. Allan.*

MOUNT RULE 3 b.c. Manado 130–Angkor Vat (Vienna 127) (1982 5f 6g 5s 6d   **62**
1983 7v³ 8.2s 8.2fg² 8f 8f 7g) strong colt; inconsistent maiden; stays 1m; blinkered at 2 yrs; trained until after fifth start by R. Hollinshead. *D. Yeoman.*

563

MOUNT TUMBLEDOWN 2 b.c. Tumble Wind–Dowdy (Sea Hawk II 131)   **63**
(1983 6s⁴ 7g) Mar 25; IR 10,000F, 25,000Y; strong, heavy-topped colt; half-
brother to winners here and abroad, including Italian St Leger runner-up Baldog
(by Lord Gayle); dam never ran; shaped promisingly in first of 2 autumn races in
modest company; will probably by suited by 1m+. *C. Thornton.*

MOURJANE 3 br.c. Pitskelly 122–Affaire d'Amour (Tudor Music 131) (1982 8v³   **125**
8v² 1983 9s³ 8v* 10.5g* 10d* 10f* 12s²)
    The French colt Mourjane may be not be over familiar to the average British
racegoer but we shouldn't mind betting trainers Hern and Walwyn won't forget him
in a hurry. Their decent colts Morcon and Naar encountered him in the Prix de la
Cote Normande at Deauville in August and were given 6 lb and a thrashing;
Mourjane burst through a furlong or so out in a fast-run race and beat them in great
style by three lengths. This was a really good performance on Mourjane's part, and
was his fourth successive win in a spell that had seen him improve significantly with
every outing. He'd had the better of another Walwyn-trained colt Hawa Bladi in the
Prix Eugene Adam at Saint-Cloud the previous month, beating him by three
quarters of a length, and had earlier won a maiden race at Longchamp and a minor
event at Saint-Cloud.
    Mourjane seemed to be developing into a candidate for top honours in the
major middle-distance races of the autumn but his run was brought to an end in the
mile-and-a-half Prix Niel at Longchamp in September and he wasn't seen out again.
Odds on, but racing on much softer ground than at Deauville and over a distance
which his pedigree suggested might be beyond him, Mourjane was beaten three
lengths into second by another fast-improving colt Sagace, the outsider of five.
Since Sagace was receiving weight and went on to finish close up in the Arc despite
none too clear a run on his next start, there was no disgrace in Mourjane's defeat;
nevertheless we'd hesitate to say that he got the trip. His finishing burst was
missing and he had little chance with the winner from halfway up the straight.

	Pitskelly	Petingo	Petition
	(br 1970)	(b 1965)	Alcazar
Mourjane		French Bird	Guersant
(br.c. 1980)		(b 1959)	Golden Pheasant
	Affaire d'Amour	Tudor Music	Tudor Melody
	(ch 1974)	(br 1966)	Fran
		Fair Darling	Darling Boy
		(ch 1965)	Fair Astronomer

    Mourjane was well bought as a yearling for 16,000 guineas at Goffs. He is the
best winner sired by the seven-furlong performer Pitskelly since Pitasia, a member
of his first crop, who won the Prix Robert Papin and the Criterium des Pouliches as
a two-year-old and was one of the leading middle-distance fillies at three. The dam
Affaire d'Amour is an unraced granddaughter of the very good filly Fair
Astronomer. Mourjane, her second foal, is easily the family's best winner in recent
years.
    There are more good races to be won with Mourjane at around a mile and a
quarter if he remains in training and he'd be worth another chance over a mile and a
half on faster ground. He can produce a fine turn of foot when the going is on top
and would not be out of place in the best of company. *A. Fabre, France.*

MOUSIL 3 br.f. Moulton 128–Fusil 105 (Fidalgo 129) (1982 NR 1983 8d 10fg   **84**
10.1fg 10f* 10h³) robust filly; half-sister to several winners, notably 1000
Guineas winner Full Dress II (by Shantung) and smart staying fillies Reload (by
Relko), Boulette (by Nasram II) and Grenadiere (by Right Royal V); dam stayed
1½m; showed first form when getting home by a neck from Childown in maiden
race at Yarmouth in August; backed from 100/30 to 8/11, although facing stiff task,
when 5 lengths third of 5 behind Onaizah in minor event at Chepstow later in
month; will stay 1½m; acts on firm going; sold 80,000 gns Newmarket December
Sales. *G. Wragg.*

MOUSLAT (USA) 3 b.c. Golden Ruler–Fleeing Countess (Count Amber) (1982   **73**
7f 7fg 1983 8v 8fg² 7f* 8f² 8.2h 8g²) rather a sparely-made colt; ridden along
nearly all way when narrowly winning maiden race at Thirsk in July; second in
handicaps at Sandown (apprentices) and Bath, best subsequent efforts; stays 1m;
acts on firm going. *P. Cole.*

MOYSPRUIT 4 br.g. Import 127–River Moy (Niagara Falls 104) (1982 7g 6fg³   –
8fg 8g 10d 8.2s 1983 6v 8.2g) big, strong gelding; plating-class maiden; not sure
to stay 1¼m; refused to enter stalls once in 1981. *G. Richards.*

Prix de la Cote Normande, Deauville—Mourjane puts up a tremendous performance to win decisively from Morcon and Naar

MPEEPEE 2 ch.f. Gay Fandango 132–Slavissima (Sea Hawk II 131) (1983 7fg 8f3) Apr 24; IR 5,400Y; good-topped filly; closely related to winning 3-y-o stayer Frantonius (by Thatch) and half-sister to 3 winners, including fairly useful 1m and 1¼m winner Bold Hawk (by Bold Lad, Ire); dam never ran; apprentice ridden, 3 lengths third of 23 finishers behind Tophams Taverns in maiden auction event at Redcar in September; will stay beyond 1m. *G. Pritchard-Gordon.*   **76**

MR BIG JOHN 3 b.c. Martinmas 128–Supreme Song (Supreme Sovereign 119) (1982 6g 7d 7d2 6s2 7d 1983 6s2 6s* 6s3 7s4 6s* 6s4 8v) good sort; third foal; half-brother to useful 1981 Irish 2-y-o Philip Martin (by Tumble Wind); dam ran once; won handicap at the Curragh in March (by 4 lengths) and maiden event at Naas in April; ran creditably on all his other starts but tended to hang when 6¾ lengths fifth of 10 to Wassl in Airlie/Coolmore Irish 2000 Guineas at the Curragh in May on last of them; stays 1m, but will possibly prove best at sprint distances; yet to race on a firm surface; blinkered third start. *L. Browne, Ireland.*   **106**

MR CARACTACUS 2 b.c. Hittite Glory 125–Carol Service 64 (Daring Display 129) (1983 5d 5v 5v 6d 6fg2 6f 5g 7g2 7h 7fg 7f2 8f 7g) Mar 18; 2,000Y; leggy, light-framed colt; inconsistent plater; stays 1m; possibly needs a sound surface; blinkered seventh to ninth outings; sweated up very badly and ran badly ninth and tenth starts. *K. Ivory.*   **51**

MR CHEDDAR 3 ch.c. Gentilhombre 131–Lady Councillor (Privy Councillor 125) (1982 NR 1983 10fg) 1,200F; half-brother to a winning plater; dam ran only 3 times; 33/1 and apprentice ridden, dwelt when behind in minor event won by Road To The Top at Leicester in October. *R. Hannon.*   **–**

MR CHIDHAM 2 b.g. Imperial Crown 96–Greasby Girl (John Splendid 116) (1983 6fg 8d 7g) Mar 18; second foal; dam bad plater; in rear in maiden and minor events. *J. Smith.*   **–**

MR CHROMACOPY (USA) 2 b.c. Tell–A Runner (First Family) (1983 5g 5.8s2 6f 7f3 7f 7h2 8d4 7d 7d4 7fg2 7f* 7fg4) Mar 7; $55,000Y; tall, rangy, quite attractive colt; has a good, long stride; second foal; dam, winner at up to 1m, is half-sister to smart 2-y-o stakes winners Mamzelle and Uncle Fudge; sire, son of Round Table, won 1¼m Hollywood Derby; second 3 times previously, going down by a neck to Barnum in 13-runner nursery at Bath in August on sixth start; best at 7f on fast ground; twice ran below his best at Brighton; wears blinkers; sold 18,000 gns Newmarket Autumn Sales to race in USA. *G. Harwood.*   **95**

MR COLTSFOOT 4 gr.g. Cavo Doro 124–Lune Royale 77 (Sovereign Path 125) (1982 NR 1983 16g 11.5f 10.1fg 8f) tailed off in varied company, including selling; blinkered final start. *J. Scallan.*   **–**

MR COPPER 2 ch.c. Music Boy 124–Karen Scott (Our Babu 131) (1983 7f 5fg) Mar 19; non-thoroughbred colt; half-brother to 1m winner Pick Your Own (by No Mercy); dam, placed over 5f at 2 yrs, is half-sister to high-class sprinters Silver Tor and Prince Tor; behind in maiden races at Newbury (wore bandages and boots behind) in July and Windsor (slowly away) in August. *P. M. Taylor.*   **–**

MR FABULEUX (USA) 4 ch.g. Le Fabuleux 133–Miss Blue Norther (Pronto) (1982 10fg 1983 12d 10s 9f) rangy gelding; has a round action; well beaten on flat though has shown ability over hurdles; blinkered final start; sent to France. *R. Armstrong.*   **–**

MR FRESHNESS 5 ch.g. Tumble Wind–Beba Saint (Welsh Saint 126) (1982 NR 1983 10f 10f 10.2g) rather a plain gelding; poor performer nowadays; has once worn blinkers. *E. Carter.*   **–**

Mrs S. R. Brook's "Mr Meeka"

MR GREGORY (USA) 2 b.c. Dactylographer 119–Lar's Theme (Noor 123)   **74**
(1983 7fg 8g 7.6fg 8d) Feb 7; $5,000Y; fair sort; half-brother to 3 minor winners;
dam minor stakes winner at up to 1m; showed ability only when about 12 lengths
fifth of 14 to Corinth in £4,000 event at Newbury in October, final outing; should
stay beyond 1m. *G. Balding.*

MR KEY (USA) 2 b.c. Key To The Kingdom–Funny Diplomat (Diplomat Way)   **–**
(1983 7d 7.6fg) Apr 14; $25,000Y; first foal; dam ran only twice; 16/1, 8¾ lengths
seventh of 16 to Judex in maiden race at Lingfield in October, second outing; may
improve. *G. Lewis.*

MR MCGIFF 3 ch.g. Malicious–Night Lark (Larkspur 128) (1982 NR 1983 12v   **60**
13.8g 16g 12f³ 16.5f³ 16.5fg⁴ 16f) lengthy, rather sparely-made gelding;
half-brother to a minor winner; dam ran only twice; plating-class maiden; placed
over 2m, but pulls hard and may not truly stay long distances. *S. Norton.*

MR MEEKA (USA) 2 ch.c. To The Quick–Locklear (First Landing) (1983 6g 6fg   **110**
6f* 7d² 7f³ 6f* 6g² 6fg* 6g*) Apr 3; $50,000Y; tall, useful-looking colt; second
foal; half-brother to useful 6f to 1½m winner Meeka Gold (by Ward McAllister);
dam, winner twice over 6f, is daughter of sprint stakes winner Coppahaunk; won
maiden race at Hamilton in July, nurseries at Redcar in September and
Newmarket (7 lb penalty) in October, and minor event at Redcar in November;
put up very useful performance at Newmarket, leading all the way (well suited by
forcing tactics) to win by long 3 lengths from Moulton Boy; best at 6f; acts on firm
going and a soft surface; best in blinkers. *S. Norton.*

MR MISCHIEF 5 ch.g. Sharp Edge 123–Talarea 76 (Takawalk II 125) (1982 NR   **–**
1983 7fg 10h 12f 12f) poor maiden; sometimes blinkered. *C. Wildman.*

MR MUSIC BOY 2 ch.g. Music Boy 124–Spanish Chestnut (Philip of Spain 126) — (1983 5v 5fg 5f 5f 5g) Apr 10; 4,200Y; fair sort; good walker; no worthwhile form; last in a maiden race and a valuable seller on third and fourth starts; blinkered last 2 outings. *M. W. Easterby.*

MR MUSIC MAN 9 br.g. March Past 124–Merry Melody 68 (Counsel 118) (1982   **51** 10.2g 12g 8f 10.6f² 8f 12fg* 11.7g⁴ 10fg⁴ 12g⁴ 12f⁴ 12s 1983 12s 10d* 10.6s* 10.2g* 10f 12f⁴ 10f 13.1h 12fg 10.6fg 10.2g 8g) plater nowadays; won at Brighton (no bid), Haydock (no bid) and Bath; bought in 2,150 gns after winning on last-named in June; stays 1½m; acts on any going. *Mrs J. Reavey.*

MR PEAPOCK 7 b.g. Pieces of Eight 128–Cedar Tree (Alcide 136) (1982 NR 1983 12g) poor maiden on flat but is a fairly useful jumper. *T. Hallett.*

MR PORTIA 3 gr.g. The Go-Between 129–Saucy Councillor 64 (Privy Councillor   **54** 125) (1982 5d 6g 1983 6s 5v 5f 6f* 7fg 6g) fair sort; attracted no bid after winning small seller at Hamilton in July; no other worthwhile form; blinkered third start; sold 1,000 gns Doncaster August Sales. *A. W. Jones.*

MR ROCHESTER (USA) 2 b.c. George Navonod–Buck's Fizz (Barbizon)   **94** (1983 5s 5s 5v 6g 6f² 5.8h⁴ 6f 6f* 6g⁴ 6fg⁴ 6f⁴ 7g² 7fg 7fg) Feb 13; $10,000Y; well-made colt; has a round action; half-brother to 3 minor winners; dam never ran; sire very smart winner from 5f to 1¼m; won nursery at Folkestone in August; good second to Meraval in £4,900 race at Goodwood the following month; stays 7f; best form on a sound surface; seemed best in blinkers until finishing creditable fifth of 15 without them in nursery on final appearance. *G. Balding.*

MR ROSE 3 b.g. Whistlefield 118–Berganza 83 (Grey Sovereign 128§) (1982 6fg   **58** 5fg 6d 1983 8v 10.1fg 10f 10.1f 8g⁴ 8fg 8.2h⁴ 7f* 7f² 8h 7g⁴ 6fg 7g) sturdy, workmanlike gelding; improved in second half of season and won handicap at Folkestone; tends to run freely and doesn't seem to get 1m in a strongly-run race; acts on firm ground; sold out of R. Price's stable 1,700 gns Ascot January Sales. *L. Lightbrown.*

MRS BATEMAN 3 ch.f. Porto Bello 118–Salvo Of Conkers 79 (Salvo 129) (1982 — NR 1983 7s 8s 6d⁴ 6f 8f) workmanlike filly; good walker; third produce; dam won twice over 1½m; soundly beaten, including in 3 sellers; best run at 6f. *P. Feilden.*

MRS BENNET 2 br.f. Mummy's Pet 125–Sarasingh 93 (Mansingh 120) (1983 6fg   **89** 5g* 5g⁴ 6d³) Apr 28; 12,500Y; lengthy, lightly-made filly; third foal; dam 2-y-o 6f winner; won 20-runner maiden race at Newbury in September by 2 lengths from Yallah; co-favourite, tended to put head in air under pressure when moderate third of 12 to Redhouse Charm in £4,300 nursery on same course the following month. *D. Elsworth.*

MRS BUZBY 4 b.f. Abwah 118–Ardeur (Roan Rocket 128) (1982 7g 8fg 7d 1983   **71** 7d³ 6d³ 8s 6s* 7fg* 7g³ 8fg 7fg*) compact filly; plater; attracted no bid when winning at Catterick in June and Doncaster in November; won non-seller at Edinburgh in between; stays 7f; probably acts on any going. *Miss S. Hall.*

MR SEAGULL 5 ch.g. Deep Run 119–Marsa (Roi de Navarre II 123) (1982 NR — 1983 8fg 14f) ex-Irish gelding; dam sister to winning jumper; behind in amateur riders race at Warwick and maiden race at Sandown in summer. *M. Pipe.*

MRS FEATHERS 2 b.f. Pyjama Hunt 126–Inca Girl (Tribal Chief 125) (1983 5d   **57** 5s 5g 5f 6f) May 10; small, fair sort; first foal; dam placed over 5f and 7f in Ireland; poor maiden; should stay 6f; has worn bandages; not raced after early July. *R. Hannon.*

MR SHOON 2 b.g. Workboy 123–My Shoon (Sheshoon 132) (1983 5v³ 5d) Feb   **64** 27; IR 3,000Y; big, lengthy gelding; second foal; half-brother to 3-y-o Happy Season (by Silly Season); dam never ran; showed up well in large fields of maidens at Thirsk in May, on second occasion co-second favourite; subsequently gelded; will stay 1m. *J. Etherington.*

MRS KING (USA) 2 b.f. Icecapade–Social Column (Swoon's Son or Vaguely   **— p** Noble 140) (1983 5d 5fg) Apr 8; $87,000F, $95,000Y; first foal; dam, placed once from 2 starts, is half-sister to top-class filly Chris Evert; showed only a little ability in October maiden races at Wolverhampton and Folkestone; likely to do better over further. *J. Sutcliffe.*

MRS MEYRICK 2 b.f. Owen Dudley 121–Social Bee 108 (Galivanter 131) (1983   **—** 6fg 7s) May 15; 5,000Y; half-sister to very smart sprinter Brave Lad (by Bold Lad, Ire) and 2 winners in Italy; dam best at 5f; well beaten in autumn maiden events at Newmarket and Leicester. *G. Pritchard-Gordon.*

MRS POPELY 2 ch.f. Monsanto 121–Leaplet (Alcide 136) (1983 5v² 5d⁴ 5v 5s²)   **60**
Mar 20; medium-sized, deep-girthed, fair sort; plater; second at Bath in May and
Lingfield in June; trained by D. H. Jones first 3 starts; dead. *R. Howe.*

MRS THREE SHOES 2 ch.f. Redundant 120–Baby Flo 67 (Porto Bello 118)   **51**
(1983 6s 5g 5f² 5.3f⁴ 6d) Mar 25; first foal; dam sprint plater; modest plater; form
only at 5f; acts on firm going. *D. Jermy.*

MR TAGG 3 ch.c. Jimmy Reppin 131–Mrs Paddy 69 (Acropolis 132) (1982 NR   —
1983 9.4f 10g 8f 8.2g) big colt; half-brother to 3 minor winners in France; dam
placed over 1½m; in rear in minor and maiden events; sold to H. Bell 2,300 gns
Doncaster November Sales. *E. Incisa.*

MR TEASIE WEASIE 2 ch.c. Owen Anthony 102–Addis Ababa 102 (Pardal   —
130) (1983 6d 7f 7g 7f) Mar 29; 2,000Y; compact colt; of little account; blinkered
final appearance. *N. Tinkler.*

MR WILLIAM 2 br.g. Royal Palace 131–Pretty Fast 74 (Firestreak 125) (1983   —
5d 8d 9s) Apr 10; lengthy colt; second foal; dam won over 1¼m and also over
hurdles; in rear in maiden and minor events, on final outing tailed off. *T. Taylor.*

MUBARAK OF KUWAIT 4 b.c. Morston 125–Dominant 86 (Behistoun 131)   **97**
(1982 11.7f* 12f² 12f² 16g* 15fg 16d* 18d 1983 12d 14v 16.1fg 14g 14.6fg) quite
attractive colt; not a good walker but is a good mover; very useful handicapper with
a good turn of foot as a 3-y-o, winner 4 times; rather disappointing in 1983, best
effort on third start; stays well; seems to act on any going; often used to be coltish
in paddock but is more settled nowadays. *G. Harwood.*

MUCH BLEST 2 b.f. Mummy's Pet 125–La Mirabelle 92 (Princely Gift 137)   **85**
(1983 5fg* 5g³) Feb 27; small filly; good mover; sister to a disappointing animal
and half-sister to several winners, notably smart 6f and 7f performers Mirabeau
and Jeroboam (both by Sharpen Up); dam won over 6f; won 9-runner maiden race at
Chester in August by a neck from Innocent Maid; favourite, beat 3 of 3 in minor event
won by Stats Anna at Goodwood the following month; lacks scope. *G. Wragg.*

MUCH MISSED 3 b. or br.f. Royalty 130–Miss Wilhemina 84 (Quorum 126)   —
(1982 NR 1983 11s 12s 16g) tall, close-coupled filly; behind in maiden and minor
events, twice last; dead. *Miss A. Sinclair.*

MUCK ABOUT 3 b.f. Sweet Revenge 129–Messie (Linacre 133) (1982 6g 7s   —
1983 7d 8f) rather lightly-made filly; well beaten in 1983, including in a claiming
race; sold 500 gns Newmarket September Sales. *G. Pritchard-Gordon.*

MUCKLE ROE (USA) 2 ch.c. Far North 120–Sunswick Maid (Restless   **88**
Native) (1983 5s 7g² 7fg* 7g²) Feb 28; $51,000F, $65,000Y; tall, good-topped,
close-coupled colt; first produce; dam won 6f maiden race; won 16-runner minor
event at Brighton in September by a head from River Scape; beaten at odds on at
Chepstow the following month; will stay 1m; acts on a firm surface; none too well
away first 2 outings; sold 25,000 gns Newmarket Autumn Sales, reportedly for
export to USA. *G. Harwood.*

MUGASSAS (USA) 2 b.c. Northern Dancer–Petit Rond Point (Round Table)   **75** p
(1983 6fg) Mar 23; $1,100,000Y; quite attractive colt; good mover; fourth foal;
half-brother to middle-distance maiden Petita (by Nashua) and a minor winner;
dam, who ran 6 times unplaced, is out of half-sister to high-class French colts
Faraway Son and Liloy; odds on, under pressure soon after halfway and eventually
eased when 5¾ lengths fifth of 20 behind Saturnian in maiden race at Newmarket in
October; probably needs further; clearly thought to have plenty of ability and can
be expected to do better. *H. Cecil.*

MUKHULI 3 b.c. Nonoalco 131–All Beige (Ballyciptic 122) (1982 7fg 7fg 8s⁴ 10s   **63**
1983 12d 12.2g* 18fg) good-topped, strong colt; 33/1 when beating Fluella by ¾
length in handicap at Warwick in October; last next time; suited by 1½m. *K.
Brassey.*

MULAZ PALACE (FR) 4 b.g. Crystal Palace 131–Mulaz Bregand (My Swanee   **110**
122) (1982 10.5v* 12d² 12d* 12g³ 12v⁴ 12g 10.5d³ 1983 12s* 12g* 10v³ 10.5d⁴ 12f
12.5fg⁴) 360,000 francs Y (approx £36,000); first live foal; dam won over 10.5f in
France; twice won over hurdles at Auteuil during winter; successful in 80,000
francs event at Saint-Cloud and valuable race at Cagnes-sur-Mer (beat Thimpu) in
March; in frame next 2 starts at Longchamp in Prix d'Harcourt (6 lengths third to
Welsh Term) and Prix Ganay (7½ lengths fourth to Lancastrian); moved short to
post and finished tailed-off last of 10 to Stanerra in Hardwicke Stakes at Royal
Ascot, and ran below form in Prix de Reux at Deauville on final outing in August;

MUR

subsequently gelded; stays 1½m; acts well on soft going and is probably unsuited by firm. *P.-L. Biancone, France.*

MULLENAN 6 br.g. Master Buck–Midgy (Polyfoto 124) (1982 NR 1983 10g) staying maiden on flat though has won over hurdles. *J. Perrett.* —

MULLET 3 b.f. Star Appeal 133–Grandpa's Legacy 102 (Zeus Boy 121) (1982 6g3 7g 1983 10s 10f* 10.1f3 10.1fg2 10f4 8.2h2 8d4 8.2fg) won maiden race at Folkestone in June, making all; stays 1½m well; yet to prove she can handle really soft going but acts on any other. *P. Walwyn.* 75

MULTI GUARANTEE 3 b.g. Riboboy 124–Prudent (Silly Season 127) (1982 7.6v 7s 6s 1983 7.6v 8.5v) quite well-made gelding; well beaten in varied company, 3 times last; wears blinkers. *J. O'Donoghue.* —

MUMMY'S CHICK 2 gr.f. Mummy's Pet 125–Chick 106 (My Swanee 122) (1983 5v 5v4 5fg 5fg 6f3 5g2 5d2 5g2 5fg*) May 25; 3,600Y; leggy, light-framed, rather plain filly; third foal; closely related to winning sprinter Dawn Ditty (by Song) and half-sister to fairly useful 1979 sprinting 2-y-o Wren Rocket (by Roan Rocket); dam won over 6f and 7f at 2 yrs; improved late in the season, and slammed her 7 opponents in maiden race at Edinburgh in November; best form at 5f; acts on a firm and a soft surface; trained by P. K. Mitchell first 5 starts. *K. Brassey.* 77

MUMMY'S FANCY 2 b.f. Mummy's Pet 125–Lady From Aske 82 (French Beige 127) (1983 6fg 6d) Mar 19; 10,500Y; rather leggy, lightly-built filly; half-sister to 1976 2-y-o 5f and 6f winner Northern Lady (by The Brianstan) and fairly useful 5f to 7f winner Good Tune (by Crooner); dam, second 3 times at 2 yrs, is sister to useful stayer; last in September in £4,000 event at York and maiden event at Yarmouth. *C. Spares.* —

MUMMY'S GLORY 3 b. or br.f. Mummy's Pet 125–Maria Da Gloria (St Chad 120) (1982 5g2 5g* 5fg2 5f3 5g 5fg 1983 5f 5f4 5g 5f* 5d 5g) neat, strong filly; won handicap at Catterick in September; has raced only at 5f; acts on firm going; blinkered last 4 outings. *E. Weymes.* 64

MUMMY'S MAGASAS 2 b.c. Mummy's Pet 125–Relicia (Relko 136) (1983 5s 5fg2 5f3 6fg 6fg 5g) Mar 10; 15,000Y; good-bodied colt; has a round action; half-brother to several winners, including Irish 5f and 1m winner Delicia (by Sovereign Path); dam, from a very successful family, showed smart form over middle distances in France; quite modest maiden; ran poorly fourth outing and was then off course over 3 months; form only at 5f. *J. Benstead.* 73

MUMMYS PLEASURE 4 b.c. Mummy's Pet 125–Par Bloom (Pardal 130) (1982 7d3 6f* 6h4 6g3 5.8g3 5fg4 6f4 6fg* 5.6g 6g 1983 6g 6fg* 6g3 7fg* 6f 7f 7fg4 7fg) tall, rather leggy colt; won handicaps at Leicester in June and Newmarket in July, picking up a valuable prize when accounting for Gamblers Dream by a neck in Ward Hill Bunbury Cup on latter; suited by 6f+; acts on firm going; has won for an apprentice. *P. Haslam.* 97

MUMMY'S PRIDE 5 b.m. Mummy's Pet 125–Wontell 80 (Buisson Ardent 129) (1982 NR 1983 5d 8d 10.6g) compact mare; plater; not without ability but is temperamental and untrustworthy; often blinkered. *K. Bridgwater.* —

MUMMY'S TREASURE 5 b.h. Mummy's Pet 125–Gold Bloom 72 (Klondyke Bill 125) (1982 5.8f 5g 5fg 6g2 5g2 5g 5fg* 5fg* 5f2 5s 1983 5g 5s4 5.1g3 5f 5f2 5f* 5f2 5f) strong-quartered horse; poor mover; sprint handicapper; made all to beat Durandal decisively by 3 lengths in quite valuable event at Sandown in July; also ran creditably to be second in Gosforth Park Cup at Newcastle (neck behind Jonacris) and fairly valuable race at York (beaten ¾ length by Miss Import); best at 5f; best form on a sound surface; usually blinkered; has run creditably for an apprentice; genuine. *C. Spares.* 84

MUMTAZ TAJ 2 br.c. Mansingh 120–Spring Girl (Crowned Prince 128) (1983 6f 5fg 6d 6s) May 5; 1,500F; 3,100Y; close-coupled colt; no form, including in good-class sellers; sold 340 gns Ascot November Sales. *I. Walker.* —

MURDIF (USA) 3 b.c. Bold Bidder–Typha (Tantieme 136) (1982 7g 1983 8.2s4 7f 6fg3 6fg 6d 7g) compact, quite attractive colt; none too good a walker; disappointing maiden; in frame at Haydock and Ayr; stays 1m; blinkered last 3 starts; tends to pull hard. *H. T. Jones.* 65 §

MURILLO 7 b.g. Windjammer (USA)–Fuiseog (Eudaemon 129) (1982 7d4 6fg 7fg3 6fg3 6g3 6g 6s 6d 8s 1983 7v 7s3 8v4 8s3 7d 9fg 8f 8f4 6f 9g 10.2fg 8g 8d) neat gelding; fairly useful handicapper at his best; third in £5,100 event at Leicester in April and Hambleton Stakes at York in May; stays 1m; acts on any going but is very well suited by some give in the ground; wears blinkers, and a small bandage on his off-fore. *P. Asquith.* 95 d

569

MURLESSA 2 b.f. High Top 131–Cribyn 96 (Brigadier Gerard 144) (1983 7fg) **74** p
Feb 24; stocky, long-backed filly; second foal; half-sister to 3-y-o Crymlyn (by
Welsh Pageant); dam, winner over 7.2f and 1m on only starts, is half-sister to
Caergwrle and St Chad; 25/1, 8 lengths seventh of 22 to Travel Away in maiden
race at Newmarket in October; should do better. *C. Brittain.*

MURTHLY-BREEZE 2 b.f. Persian Breeze 121–Frau 60 (Frankincense 120) –
(1983 6g 5g 5s) Mar 15; second living foal; dam placed in 1m seller; in rear in
autumn maiden and minor events in Scotland. *W. H. Williams.*

MUSCATITE 3 b.c. Habitat 134–Takette (Takawalk II 125) (1982 7f³ 7fg* 7f* **122**
8d⁴ 1983 8s* 8g³ 8fg4 10f² 8f² 8f 10g 10fg)
Muscatite's record as a three-year-old divides conveniently into two parts. In
the first he ran with great credit in top company, winning the Craven Stakes and
being placed in both the Two Thousand Guineas and the Coral-Eclipse. In the
second his form declined disappointingly and after being beaten at odds on in a
handicap he failed even to reach the frame in three races which he'd have had an
outside chance of winning on his best form.
Muscatite put up a good performance when beating Spanish Place by a neck in
the five-runner Craven Stakes at Newmarket in April, but the race is a notoriously
unreliable guide to the Guineas nowadays and Muscatite wasn't on our short list for
the big race itself at the end of the month. In finishing two and three quarter lengths
third to Lomond Muscatite not only put up the performance of his life but also the
best of any Craven Stakes winner since Petingo came second to Sir Ivor in 1968.
Muscatite was never far off the front, racing towards the far side but no sooner had
he got the better of Gorytus for the lead than Lomond and Tolomeo came by in the
last furlong. Muscatite was never able to get in a blow when only fourth of seven to
Horage in the St James's Palace Stakes at Royal Ascot next time but ran much
better when second to Solford in the Coral-Eclipse at Sandown in July. Ridden by
Piggott there, in place of the suspended Taylor, Muscatite was dropped out at the

Mr H. Kais Al-Said's "Muscatite"

start and held up until making ground on the inside in the straight. For a moment or two he looked in danger of getting boxed in but he was extricated in plenty of time and under strong driving failed by only a head to peg back the winner in a five-horse finish, which also featured Tolomeo, Stanerra and Guns of Navarone. It was a fine effort on Muscatite's part though the result probably flatters him slightly, since the false pace at which the race was run was very much against both Stanerra and sixth-placed Time Charter.

We were surprised to see Muscatite in handicap company at Newmarket only a fortnight later, and even more surprised when blinkers were declared. No doubt connections regret running him for although Muscatite appeared to face a fairly simple task with only five opponents, all of whom were handicapped below the minimum permitted weight, he went down by half a length to El Gitano. He failed to take the eye in the preliminaries, refused to settle in a race run at no more than a steady gallop, and got into top gear all too late. This race marked the turning-point in Muscatite's fortunes. Again he didn't impress us in appearance when fifth to Noalcoholic in the Sussex Stakes at Goodwood at the end of the month. Afterwards he finished a disappointing eighth of fourteen to Tolomeo in the Budweiser Million at Chicago in August and fifteenth of nineteen behind Cormorant Wood in the Dubai Champion Stakes at Newmarket in October; in the last-named event he dropped out quickly after showing prominently until about two furlongs from home.

Muscatite (b.c. 1980)	Habitat (b 1966)	Sir Gaylord (b 1959)	Turn-to
			Somethingroyal
		Little Hut (b 1952)	Occupy
			Savage Beauty
	Takette (b 1967)	Takawalk II (b 1961)	Native Dancer
			Ampola
		Pamette (b 1962)	Pampered King
			Finette

Muscatite is a lengthy colt who made 40,000 guineas as a foal and 132,000 guineas when resubmitted as a yearling. Despite figures quoted to the contrary in several publications at the end of the season his sire Habitat and not Home Guard was the leading sire in Britain in 1983, thanks mainly to Habibti. The dam Takette won over six furlongs at Naas as a two-year-old and was placed at up to nine furlongs at four. She has produced several other winners, including the versatile Decent Fellow (by Rarity) who won five races on the flat and eight over hurdles, including the John Porter Stakes and the Irish Sweeps Hurdle in 1977. Muscatite remains in training, but as things stand he couldn't be followed with much confidence. If he should recapture his best form though he ought not to be too hard to place, for he won't have to carry harsh penalties in pattern races and he's seemingly indifferent to the state of the ground. *J. Hindley.*

MUSICAL BOX 2 ch.c. Grundy 137–Contralto 100 (Busted 134) (1983 7fg 8fg)   **89**
Feb 13; quite attractive colt; first foal; dam, closely related to smart Rhyme Royal, won over 6f and 7f at 2 yrs; showed promise in autumn maiden races at Newmarket, particularly on second start when running on strongly on far side to be seventh of 28 to Bob Back; will stay 1¼m; the type to win races. *R. Hern.*

MUSICAL LOVE 2 b.f. Music Maestro 119–Your Love 67 (Blakeney 126) (1983   **66**
5g 5v³ 5v² 6fg* 6f² 7fg²) Feb 11; compact, quite attractive filly; first foal; dam won over 15f; fair judged; made all to land odds readily at Nottingham (bought in 4,600 gns) in June; claimed after finishing good second at Newmarket in July on final appearance; suited by 7f; acts on any going; has raced with tongue tied down; genuine and consistent. *B. Hanbury.*

MUSICAL ROSE 2 ch.f. Music Boy 124–Tudor Cream 72§ (Tudor Melody 129)   **59**
(1983 5d⁴ 6fg 5f 5f³ 6f) Mar 21; 1,900Y; workmanlike filly; poor mover; half-sister to several winners here and abroad; dam disappointing; poor maiden; beaten in sellers first 2 outings; apparently best at 6f; acts on firm going. *D. Plant.*

MUSIC CITY 5 gr.h. Town Crier 119–Floating Melody 101 (Tudor Melody 129)   **62**
(1982 7s 8d 8g 8g 10s 1983 8v 8s⁴ 7s³ 8fg³ 7f⁴ 8h⁴ 10.2fg) well-made horse; stays 1¼m; acts on any going but goes well on soft. *M. Bradley.*

MUSIC FESTIVAL 2 gr. or ro.f. Music Boy 124–Two Friendly 54 (Be Friendly   **48**
130) (1983 5v 5d 5g 5.3f) Mar 21; 4,400Y; close-coupled, quite attractive filly; first foal; dam won 5f seller at 2 yrs; poor plater; looks a short runner; sold 1,900 gns Newmarket September Sales for export to Norway. *B. Swift.*

MUSIC LOVER 4 b.c. Gay Fandango 132–In The Clover (Meadow Mint 120)   **93**
(1982 6fg* 6f 6fg 5g 7d 8v 1983 7v 7g 7v 7d 9fg 9f* 10.6fg³ 9g² 10fg*) quite

attractive colt; good mover; fairly useful handicapper; beat Claudius Secundus by ½ length at York in July (33/1) and Lady Arpege by a short head in quite valuable apprentice event at Newmarket in August; stays 1¼m; probably acts on any going but goes well on fast ground; ran poorly in blinkers once in 1982. *P. Calver.*

MUSIC MY SON 2 b.g. Tumble Wind–Negante 68 (Negotiation) (1983 5v 5fg 5f 5fg 5g) May 21; IR 3,200Y, 9,000 2-y-o; fifth foal; dam won 7f seller at 2 yrs; well beaten in maiden events; blinkered last 2 outings. *M. Bradley.*   —

MUSIC NIGHT 6 ch.h. Jukebox 120–Directrice (Zank) (1982 5fg 5g* 5fg 5fg³ 6fg 6g 6d 6d 6fg 5g 5fg 5s 6s³ 6s* 1983 6d 6g⁴ 6f 6f 6f⁴ 5f² 6f 5f 7g 5g 6f 6fg* 7g) sturdy horse; former plater; 20/1-winner of claiming race at Nottingham in October; stays 6f; acts on any going; best in blinkers; has run respectably for an apprentice and an amateur; suited by enterprising riding tactics; sold 2,500 gns Doncaster November Sales. *D. Garraton.*   57

MUSIC SEASON 3 ch.g. Baragoi 115–Tide and Time (Easter Island 101) (1982 6fg 1983 10s 8v 9f 17f 10g) tall, leggy, plain gelding; seems of little account. *D. Leslie.*   —

MUSLAB (USA) 4 ch.c. Stage Door Johnny–Forever Amber (Bold Lad, Ire 133) (1982 10s⁴ 12f³ 14fg² 14f 16fg 14f² 13f* 14g* 14fg 12fg² 14.6f 14s 15.5v 1983 12v 16g⁴ 14s 14.7f 13.3g 13g* 14g⁴) good-bodied colt; fairly useful at 3 yrs; didn't run up to his best in 1983 though made much of running and stayed on strongly to win handicap at Hamilton in September; acts on any going; blinkered nowadays; has won for an amateur rider; didn't impress in paddock third start; sold 18,500 gns Newmarket Autumn Sales. *H. T. Jones.*   85

MUZNAH 3 b.c. Royal and Regal–Ballinavail (Rarity 129) (1982 6f² 7.2g 7d* 7fg 7.2s 1983 8f⁴ 8f* 10f 12fg³) good-bodied, fair sort; got up close home after being among first off bridle when beating Full Rainbow by a neck in handicap at Yarmouth in July; not disgraced afterwards; seems to stay 1½m; probably acts on any going. *H. T. Jones.*   92

MY AISLING 2 gr.f. John de Coombe 122–Bryony Ash 67 (Ribero 126) (1983 6f 7h*(dis) 7d⁴ 8g³ 8d 10fg³) Mar 24; 4,900Y; big, plain filly; first foal; dam placed over 6f and 1m; successful, only to be disqualified for interference, in 15-runner seller at Sandown in August and 19-runner 1¼m maiden race (demoted to third) at Nottingham in October; stays 1¼m really well; trained by P. Cole first 2 starts. *M. Pipe.*   72

MY BLONDIE 4 ch.f. Vulgan Slave–Kay II (Kadir Cup 97§) (1982 NR 1983 12g 12f 12f 19h) strong, workmanlike non-thoroughbred filly; first reported foal; dam never ran; of little account. *R. Hollinshead.*   —

MY BRIGHT EYES 2 ch.f. Roman Warrior 132–Apple Of My Eye 83 (Silver Cloud 121) (1983 6f 6fg) Mar 9; 1,750Y; smallish, fair sort; second foal; dam won 4 middle-distance races and was useful staying hurdler; last in maiden races at Yarmouth in June and Ayr (apprentice ridden, hung badly) in July. *J. Gilbert.*   —

MY CHALLENGE 5 b.g. Copte–Wolfsburg (Neckar) (1982 NR 1983 17f 14.6f) narrow, light-framed gelding; poor form in varied company, including selling; sometimes blinkered. *K. Bridgwater.*   —

MY CHARADE 2 ch.f. Cawston's Clown 113–Schull (Yorick II 127) (1983 5g² 5f* 5g 6f³ 7h 8.2h² 7.3g 8d) Apr 30; 4,800Y; leggy, lightly-built filly; half-sister to several winners, including very useful 6f to 7f performer Step Ahead (by Continuation); dam never ran; won maiden race at Nottingham in June; placed in nurseries subsequently, running very well when neck second of 9 to Noblesque at Nottingham in September; suited by 1m; acts on hard going. *Mrs B. Waring.*   79

MY CHERIE 2 b.f. Cool Guy–Polish Polish (Clairefontaine 74) (1983 5d 5d 6fg 7fg 7.6d) May 3; third foal; dam poor plater; no form including in a seller. *R. Voorspuy.*   —

MYDELLA 3 b. or br.f. Rymer 121–Mydel Field 66 (Abwah 118) (1982 5f 5g* 6g 1983 6d) fair sort; stays 6f. *J. Berry.*   —

MY DITTY 2 br.f. The Ditton 93–Fresh Tune (Romany Air 118) (1983 7f 9g) Mar 22; lengthy filly; first foal; dam never ran; in rear in maiden races at Brighton (last of 15) in August and Wolverhampton in October. *D. Weeden.*   —

MYDRONE 4 b.c. Mummy's Pet 125–Wordrone (Worden II 129) (1982 8.2fg² 8f 8g 8g 8d 8s 1983 7v⁴ 8v 7fg 8d 9f³ 10fg³ 10.6fg 9g 10s 10.6g⁴ 11fg 8fg) workmanlike colt; useful at his best but has deteriorated and is inconsistent and unreliable; stays 1¼m; acts on any going; blinkered final outing; has run creditably   72 for an amateur rider; takes a good hold nowadays; bandaged off-fore third start; sent to USA. *M. H. Easterby.*

MY FANCY 4 ch.f. Roi Soleil 125–Pat's Fancy 82 (Falcon 131) (1982 5g 5f² 5g³ 5fg 5f 5g 6g 6g 7d 1983 6v⁴ 5d 8d 8fg) workmanlike filly; poor maiden; has been beaten in a seller; possibly stays 1m; probably acts on any going; blinkered final start. *J. Berry.*   —

MY GODDESS 4 ch.f. Palm Track 122–Captain Frances (Captain's Gig) (1982 12f 15.8f 16.5f 10.4d 12fg 1983 15.8g) plain filly; poor maiden; has been blinkered. *G. Richards.*   —

MY HABAT 4 gr.g. Habat 127–Wake Island 101 (Relic) (1982 8g 11g 8f⁴ 8.2g⁴ 7f* 1983 12g 8fg 10g⁴) strong gelding; poor mover; plater; promises to stay 1½m; acts on firm going; sometimes blinkered; has shown a tendency to hang. *F. Watson.*   52

MY HAVEN 2 br.f. Godswalk 130–Hopeful Subject 82 (Mandamus 120) (1983 7fg* 7d 8f 8.2g) Apr 4; sparely-made, workmanlike filly; fourth live foal; half-sister to fairly useful 5f to 7.6f winner Paulager (by Lochnager); dam won over 1m at 2 yrs; upset by ½ length odds laid on James Winkle in 5-runner maiden race at Ayr in July; showed little in nurseries afterwards; stays 7f; acts on a firm surface. *M. H. Easterby.*   77

MY LADY MURIEL (USA) 3 ch.f. Visible–Lady Muriel (Prince John) (1982 NR 1983 8v 9s⁴ 12d 11.5fg) $16,500Y; short-coupled, quite attractive filly; first foal; dam won 1m maiden race; showed a little ability on first 2 outings. *G. Huffer.*   —

MY LOUIE 2 b.f. Music Boy 124–Jetwitch 56 (Lear Jet 123) (1983 5v* 5s³ 5s³ 5v² 5g² 5f 6fg 5f) Jan 30; 3,800F; big, robust filly; third produce; half-sister to 2 minor winners; dam stayed at least 1m; won poor maiden race at Kempton in April; ran well subsequently until ground firmed up, on fifth start finishing second to Nophe in Acorn Stakes at Epsom; not seen out after July; should stay 6f; suited by an easy surface; races with her head held high. *A. Ingham.*   79

MY MUSIC 3 b.f. Sole Mio–Brazen 83 (Cash and Courage 116) (1982 5f⁴ 6fg 5fg² 5fg 5d 5g 1983 8.2s 8f 8.2fg³ 7f³ 7.6g 7.2g) lengthy filly; plating-class maiden; probably stays 1m; blinkered last 3 starts, running poorly on last 2. *W. Elsey.*   59

MY NAUTILUS 3 ch.g. Free State 125–Naiche (Tribal Chief 125) (1982 7fg 1983 8f) strong, rangy gelding; last in maiden events at Salisbury as a 2-y-o and Sandown in July. *B. Swift.*   —

MYRA'S BEST 3 ch.f. Pampapaul 121–Matcher (Match III 135) (1982 5f² 5fg* 5g* 6fg⁴ 6g* 6g 1983 8g 7fg 7fg 7h* 7f) well-made filly; ran respectably at Newmarket, finishing tenth of 18 to Ma Biche in 1000 Guineas in April and less than 4 lengths sixth of 12 behind Thug in Van Geest Stakes in June, starting at 25/1 and 50/1 respectively; made all and landed the odds easily by 8 lengths from Mills Allegiance in minor event at Beverley in July; soundly beaten final start however; promises to stay 1m; has raced only on a sound surface; genuine. *R. Williams.*   98

MYRICAGALE 2 b.f. Wollow 132–Regency Gold (Prince Regent 129) (1983 7fg) Apr 29; rather leggy filly; good walker; sister to 3-y-o Woolooware and closely related to 1m winner Mianach Oir (by Wolver Hollow); dam won from 7f to 2m in Ireland; eleventh of 14 in minor event at Doncaster in October. *F. J. Houghton.*   —

MY-RIKI 2 ch.c. Riki Lash 77–My Foresight (Your Fancy 106) (1983 8s 8fg 7fg) workmanlike colt; ninth living foal; dam winning chaser; in rear in Northern maiden races, twice last. *N. Tinkler.*   —

MY SINGH 2 b.c. Mansingh 120–Sun Approach 84 (Sun Prince 128) (1983 5s 5d 7fg 7fg 7f 6fg³) Mar 21; 5,600Y, 2,100 2-y-o; rather lightly-made colt; well-backed favourite, hung badly left and was found to have split a pastern when 5 lengths third of 15 to Iran Flyer in seller at Lingfield in August; not sure to stay 7f; blinkered third, fourth and final outings; sold 440 gns Ascot October Sales. *P. Mitchell.*   59

MY SIR AVON (NZ) 6 ch.h. Avon Valley 111–Ballometes (Philoctetes 111) (1982 including 12g* 12d² 7f 12g³ 13g 10f³ 16f⁴ 12.5fg* 1983 10s 12d 12f 11.7fg⁴) small New Zealand-bred horse; not a good mover; first foal; dam unplaced 5 times; won New Zealand 2,000 Guineas in 1980; raced in Australia in 1982 and did well there, winning races at Randwick (7f event), Rosehill (W. J. McKell Cup) and Flemington (Queen Elizabeth II Stakes) and finishing in frame on several occasions, notably when fourth of 23 to Gurner's Lane in Melbourne Cup at Flemington again; didn't show a great deal over here at 6 yrs, best efforts on last 2 starts when over 15 lengths fifth of 10 to Stanerra in Hardwicke Stakes at Royal Ascot (sweated up   ?

slightly) and 5 lengths fourth of 5 behind Millfontaine in quite well-contested minor event at Windsor in September; seems to stay 2m; goes well on fast ground and is probably unsuited by soft. *R. Armstrong.*

MY SON MY SON 2 gr.c. Absalom 128–Idover 95 (Fortino II 120) (1983 6g 5fg 6fg) Jan 31; 5,600F, 19,000Y; workmanlike colt; half-brother to several winners, including fair 5f to 7f winner Hamdani and useful 3-y-o 1¼m winner Welsh Idol (both by Welsh Pageant); dam sprinter; little worthwhile form in autumn maiden events. *K. Brassey.*

MYSTERIEUSE ETOILE (USA) 3 b.f. Northern Dancer–Gulanar (Val de   122
Loir 133) (1982 6.5g* 8s² 1983 8v* 8d² 10v 10.5f 8fg 10fg 9.2f) small, good-quartered filly; first foal; dam won 5 races in Italy, including 2 useful prizes at around 1¼m; won maiden race at Deauville and was second in Prix Marcel Boussac at Longchamp as a 2-y-o; put up a good display when winning 11-runner Prix de la Grotte at Longchamp in April, taking over from pacemaker 2f out and having to be only shaken up to beat Take A Step by 1½ lengths; caught near finish when ½-length second to L'Attrayante in Poule d'Essai des Pouliches on same course in May (reportedly returned with a cut on her near-hind); mainly disappointing afterwards, but reportedly wasn't herself fourth outing and wasn't entirely disgraced when less than 4 lengths fifth of 12 behind Luth Enchantee in Prix d'Astarte at Deauville in August on fifth start; stayed 1m; ideally suited by some give in the ground and acted on heavy; sometimes raced with her tongue tied down; stud in USA. *M. Saliba, France.*

MYSTERIOUS ARTHUR 6 b.g. Baragoi 115–High In The Sky (Above   92
Suspicion 127) (1982 16g 10g* 10g 16s 12s 10d* 1983 8d* 8s⁴ 8s* 10v³ 10d) Irish gelding; third foal; dam once-raced half-sister to very useful sprinter Ballynockan; won handicaps at Leopardstown in March and Phoenix Park in April, beating Better Portion a length in quite valuable event on latter; never promised to take a hand when last of 10 to Stanerra in Brigadier Gerard Stakes at Sandown in May; stays 1¼m; acts on heavy going; fairly useful hurdler and did quite well chasing in USA in second half of year. *J. Feane, Ireland.*

MYSTERY SHIP 2 b.f. Decoy Boy 129–Impregnable 66 (Never Say Die 137)   105
(1983 5v² 5s* 6fg 6f⁴ 7g* 6fg 6s² 7fg 7.3d) Apr 9; close-coupled filly; half-sister to 1m winner Karima (by Song) and a winner in Norway; dam won over 1½m; won maiden race at Catterick in June and Sweet Solera Stakes (beating Calpoppy a neck) at Newmarket in August; good second to Rocket Alert in Firth of Clyde Stakes at Ayr in September; stays 7f well; apparently suited by an easy surface. *M. Usher.*

MYSTIC BOY 2 ch.g. Music Boy 124–Mystic Halo (Aureole 132) (1983 6g 5fg   75
6fg) Apr 4; neat, strong gelding; fifth foal; half-brother to 1981 2-y-o 5f winner Sy Oui (by The Brianstan); dam of no account; quite a modest maiden; best effort on first outing; stays 6f; possibly requires some give in the ground; sold 2,600 gns Newmarket Autumn Sales; subsequently gelded. *G. Harwood.*

MYSTIC MARGARET 4 b.f. Realm 129–Primed (Primera 131) (1982 10d 12f   60
9g 10.1d⁴ 10f* 10g 11.1fg 12fg² 10d 1983 10v 10fg 12f 10f² 10f³ 10h 10f⁴ 10fg* 10f² 12g⁴ 10fg 10.2fg³) strong filly; poor walker; former plater; won handicap at Newcastle in August; stays 1½m; acts well on firm going; suitable mount for an apprentice. *A. Hide.*

MY SWEET BABY 2 b.f. Stanford 121§–Geodesy (Linacre 133) (1983 5s 6fg 7f   42
8.2fg 10d 6fg³) Feb 24; IR 5,600F, 4,000Y; good-bodied filly; first foal; dam won over 1¾m in Ireland at 4 yrs and also won over hurdles; bad plater; sometimes sweats up; gave a lot of trouble in preliminaries fourth outing; sold out of N. Vigors' stable 400 gns Newmarket July Sales after second start, and resold 340 gns Ascot November Sales. *A. Ingham.*

MY SYMBOL 2 ch.f. Brigadier Symbol‡–My Path (Sovereign Path 125) (1983 5g   –
5g 5fg) small filly; half-sister to a winner in Holland; dam well beaten on 4 outings; behind in autumn maiden and minor events. *Mrs N. Kennedy.*

MYTINIA 3 b.f. Bustino 136–Mineown 85 (Roan Rocket 128) (1982 7g 1983 12v²   94
12g 10f⁴ 12fg³ 11.7h* 11.7fg³) lengthy, light-framed filly; in frame in varied races, including Lupe Stakes at Goodwood in May (favourite, 6 lengths second to Current Raiser), before winning maiden event at Bath in August by 5 lengths from Gloria Mundi (blinkered first time); well below her best when blinkered again final start; stays 1½m; unseated rider on way down and pulled hard third outing. *R. Hern.*

MY TONY 3 ch.c. Be My Guest 126–Pale Gold (New Chapter 106) (1982 7fg 7fg   73
7s 1983 8g 7f² 8f 8fg 8g 8g⁴ 10fg³) rangy, good-bodied colt; ran respectably in

varied races, on last occasion when close third to Road To The Top in minor event at Leicester in October; suited by 1¼m; acts on firm going. *G. Lewis.*

MY TOOTSIE   2 b.f. Tap On Wood 130–Malmsey (Jukebox 120)   (1983 6g 6d 9g* 7.2s* 10fg)   May 4; 19,000Y; well-grown, rather leggy filly; has a round action; third foal; closely related to 3-y-o Priors Mistress (by Sallust) and half-sister to 1981 2-y-o 5f winner Lockwood Girl (by Prince Tenderfoot); dam won over 1¼m and 1¾m in Ireland; wide-margin winner in October of maiden race (gambled on) at Wolverhampton and minor event at Haydock; one of first beaten when favourite for £7,900 event at Newmarket later in month; effective at 7f, at least when conditions are testing, and stays 9f well; almost certainly needs some give in the ground and revels in the mud. *M. Ryan.*   **88**

MY VOLGA BOATMAN (USA)   2 b.c. Riverman 131–Belle Sorella 99 (Ribot 142)   (1983 7fg⁴ 7fg² 7g* 7.3d²)   Apr 26; $185,000Y; smallish, strong, close-coupled colt; half-brother to French 3-y-o State Your Case (by Lyphard) and several winners, including useful French stayer Bel Sorel (also by Lyphard); dam, sister to Dewhurst winner Ribofilio, won three 1½m races; beat Muckle Roe decisively by 3 lengths in 14-runner maiden race at Leicester in September; easily bettered that effort in Horris Hill Stakes at Newbury the following month, giving Elegant Air a good fight before going down by 2½ lengths; will stay 1½m; looks sure to win more races. *M. Stoute.*   **108**

MZURI   3 b.f. Captain James 123–Mrs Bee 74 (Sallust 134)   (1982 5d* 5fg⁴ 5s 1983 5.8v 5.8f³ 5h 6h 5fg 5h² 5.8fg)   quite well-made filly; sprint handicapper; probably acts on any going; often apprentice ridden; sweated badly third outing. *C. Nelson.*   **65**

N

NAAR   3 b.c. North Stoke 130–Kye-Hye 61 (Habitat 134)   (1982 6fg* 6f* 7fg 1983 8d* 12s 10fg 11g 10f³ 9g⁴)   neat, attractive colt; first foal; dam placed at up to 1¾m; ridden by G. Lewis when easily landing the odds in 19-runner trainers race   **114**

Yazid and Ahmed Ltd's "Naar"

at Kempton in May; ran well in far stiffer races on occasions afterwards, including when sixth behind Teenoso in Derby at Epsom in June (beaten 16½ lengths, but would have finished closer except for being slightly hampered when well placed inside last 2f) and just over 3 lengths third of 14 behind Mourjane in Prix de la Cote Normande at Deauville in August; beaten 8 lengths when moderate fourth of 8 behind Salmon Leap in Pacemaker International Whitehall Stakes at Phoenix Park in September on final start; suited by middle distances; acts on any going; didn't run particularly well in blinkers third outing. *P. Walwyn.*

NADIA NERINA (CAN) 2 b.f. Northern Dancer–Shake A Leg 106 (Raise A Native) (1983 6f 7fg 7s² 7g²) Mar 6; $1,400,000Y; big, strong, rangy filly; carries plenty of condition; sister to top 1982 Irish 2-y-o Danzatore, closely related to useful but disappointing London Bells (by Nijinsky) and half-sister to 2 winners, including 8.5f stakes winner Vaguely Modest (by Vaguely Noble); dam, useful Irish 2-y-o 5f winner, subsequently won 3 stakes races over 6f in USA; placed in autumn maiden races at Ayr (beaten short head) and Lingfield; will be suited by 1m; probably acts on any going. *J. Dunlop.*   **82**

NADIRAH 2 ch.f. Mill Reef 141–Light O'Battle 97 (Queen's Hussar 124) (1983 6f 6f 7d 7fg³) Feb 16; 210,000Y; quite attractive filly; good mover; first foal; dam, winner over 7f at 2 yrs from only 2 starts, is sister to 1000 Guineas and French Oaks winner Highclere (dam of Milford) and very useful Light Duty (dam of Paradise Bay and Special Leave); placed in nursery at Edinburgh in November; will be suited by 1¼m+; acts on a firm surface, and is possibly not at her best on a soft one. *H. T. Jones.*   **71**

NAGALIA 4 br.f. Lochnager 132–La Gallia 70 (Welsh Saint 126) (1982 6s 6g 6f² 6h² 6d 1983 5v 6s 6s 6d 6fg 7f 7g) lengthy, lightly-made filly; not the best of movers; stayed 6f; probably acted on any going; ran moderately in blinkers once; in foal to Sonnen Gold. *K. Stone.*   **–**

NAHAWAND 3 b.f. High Top 131–Welsh Jewel 72 (Welsh Pageant 132) (1982 6g 1983 8f 6h 6fg 6fg) good-topped filly; plating-class maiden; not disgraced when blinkered in a claiming race final start. *A. Hide.*   **–**

NAJAM (USA) 4 b.c. Graustark–Spring Adieu (Buckpasser) (1982 7.6f 10g 10.2g³ 10fg⁴ 10g 1983 12g 12fg 10f 10f 11.7fg 11.7f 11.7f 12fg) quite attractive, well-made, robust colt; plating-class maiden; stays 1¼m; yet to race on a soft surface; wore blinkers at 3 yrs. *J. Benstead.*   **–**

NAJMA 3 ch.f. Stradavinsky 121–Garrucha 117 (Prince Taj 123) (1982 6g 1983 8v* 9f* 9.4f³ 12f) sparely-made filly; successful in maiden race at Warwick in May (apprentice ridden) and minor event at Wolverhampton in June, on latter course beating Dancing Daughter a head; below form afterwards; stays 9f (given plenty to do when tried over 1½m); acts on any going; genuine. *F. Durr.*   **71**

NAKTERJAL 3 b.f. Vitiges 132–Kilavea 69 (Hawaii) (1982 6g 6d 6s 1983 7fg 7f 9fg 8fg 10.6g) strong-quartered filly; poor maiden; stays 7f; tailed-off last third and final starts, wearing blinkers on former occasion; sold to BBA 210,000 gns Newmarket December Sales. *J. Dunlop.*   **–**

NANGA PARBAT 2 b.f. Mill Reef 141–Queen of the South 98 (Gallant Man) (1983 7.6d) Mar 9; fourth foal; dam won four 1m races; last of 20 behind stable-companion Risk All in maiden race at Lingfield in October. *J. Dunlop.*   **–**

NANUSHKA 4 b.f. Lochnager 132–Monashka 73 (Sica Boy 132) (1982 7.2g 8g 6d 6g 6d 5g* 6s 1983 5d² 5d⁴ 5s 5s³ 5d 5.1g 5f⁴ 5g 5g 5g 5d⁴ 5d 5g² 5g) big, lengthy, workmanlike filly; sprint handicapper; best at 5f; acts on any going but is suited by some give in the ground; blinkered nowadays; suitable mount for an apprentice; has worn bandages. *R. Hobson.*   **51**

NAOMAS 2 b.c. Northfields–Gorse Bush (Hallez 131) (1983 7f) Mar 26; 30,000Y; quite well-made, attractive colt; third foal; half-brother to 2 minor winners; dam won twice over 1¼m in Ireland; last of 12 in maiden race at Salisbury in June; a bit above himself beforehand. *J. Dunlop.*   **–**

NARBORO BOY 3 gr.g. Dragonara Palace 115–Judolyn 87 (Canisbay 120) (1982 5d 8s 1983 8fg 6f 10f) tailed off in maiden races and a handicap. *A. Fisher.*   **–**

NARROW AND SHORT (USA) 3 b.c. Riva Ridge–Waltz Me Sue (Olden Times) (1982 7g 5d 1983 6d 5d 6d 7fg 8fg 9f² 9f 9fg) smallish, quite attractive colt; suited by 9f and will get further; acts on firm going; blinkered fourth start; sold 720 gns Doncaster October Sales. *M. H. Easterby.*   **52**

NASHAAB 3 b.c. Sharpen Up 127–Falcon Bess (Falcon 131) (1982 5fg 7s 1983 8d 8v 8s⁴ 10v* 10d* 10fg³ 10g⁴ 8f 10g 10.1fg⁴ 10g 10g) big, quite attractive colt;   **75 d**

won handicaps at Folkestone and Leicester in May; stays 1¼m; acts on any going with possible exception of very firm; has a tendency to hang; runs some moderate races, and did so on last 2 starts. *J. Benstead.*

NASHVILLE SANDY 2 ch.f. Morston 125–Immaculate (Sovereign Path 125)   70
(1983 6g 7f 7.2fg² 8.2h) Mar 21; 2,600Y; useful-looking filly; half-sister to several winners, including Spanish Oaks winner Delfica (by Hardicanute) and very useful Irish middle-distance filly Slap Up (by Gala Performance); dam lightly raced; quite moderate form, including in a nursery; will stay 1¼m. *R. Akehurst.*

NASHWAH (USA) 2 ch.f. Banquet Table–Gun Hour (Bold Bidder) (1983 5f 6f   73
6fg⁴ 8d) Apr 9; $14,000Y, $65,000 2-y-o; neat filly; third foal; sister to 3-y-o Kates Banquet and half-sister to a winner in USA; dam third twice from 13 starts; quite a moderate maiden; should stay 1m; acts on firm going. *P. Walwyn.*

NASR 2 ch.c. Double Form 130–Malagangai (Nonoalco 131) (1983 6fg⁴ 6f 6f* 6g   106
7.6g² 8g⁴ 7fg) Feb 11; IR 22,000F, 37,000Y; big, strong, attractive colt; first foal; dam won over 1¼m from only 4 starts; won 4-runner maiden race at Yarmouth in August, beating newcomer Tocave Botta short head; good second following month to Lucky Scott in Burr Stakes at Lingfield, and creditable fourth 3 weeks later behind Northern Tempest in Gran Criterium at Milan; stays 1m; best form on good ground; not particularly consistent, and disappointed at Chester on fourth outing. *N. Callaghan.*

NASSIPOUR (USA) 3 ch.c. Blushing Groom 131–Alama (Aureole 132) (1982   95
8s 1983 10.1f 10.1f 12f* 12f⁴ 12g* 12fg⁴ 12d³ 14g*) quite attractive colt; not the best of movers; successful in maiden race at Brighton and handicaps at Kempton and Sandown in second half of season; came from behind to beat Karablake decisively by 2 lengths in a fast-run race on last-named course in October (mulish in preliminaries); well suited by 1¾m and will stay further; acts on any going, except possibly very soft; blinkered nowadays; sent to USA. *M. Stoute.*

NATHANIEL 6 b.g. Shantung 132–Pink Standard 81 (Tudor Melody 129) (1982   –
10f 12f 10s* 12g² 10d 10g* 10fg 10g 10.6s 10d 1983 10s) sturdy gelding; poor handicapper; has run creditably over 1½m but is probably better at around 1¼m; acts on any going, but is well suited by give in the ground. *M. W. Easterby.*

NATINA-MAY 2 b.f. Mandrake Major 122–Kildare Honey 79 (Khalkis 127) (1983   59
5d 5f² 6f 7f 6fg* 7f*) May 19; 2,800F, 1,900Y; fair sort; half-sister to a minor winner in France; dam 2-y-o 7f winner; won sellers at Ripon (bought in 2,600 gns) and Redcar (no bid) in July; stays 7f; acts on firm going; ran freely in blinkers fourth start. *T. Fairhurst.*

NATIONAL IMAGE 6 b.g. Sassafras 135 Pepi Image 111 (National) (1982 NR   57
1983 7s⁴ 10.8v 8h* 8g 11f 13.1h²) strong ex-Irish gelding; won handicap at Bath in July; stays 13f but is effective at much shorter distances; acts on any going but goes well on fast ground. *M. Tate.*

NATION WIDE 10 b.g. Irish Ball 127–Misylda 100 (Faubourg II 127) (1982   58 §
16.1s³ 14f 18.4fg 16.1g 15.8d³ 16d² 16d³ 16d 18s 1983 12d 14s³ 14fg 17.4g 16fg 18fg⁴) poor handicapper nowadays; suited by a strong gallop and stays really well; acts on any going but seems suited by some give in the ground; has been tried in blinkers; often gets himself well behind in early stages and is not the most genuine of animals. *G. Wragg.*

NATIVE BIDDER (USA) 3 b.c. Raise A Native–Cautious Bidder (Bold   63
Bidder) (1982 NR 1983 10f 10f⁴ 8g) big colt; half-brother to a stakes-placed winner in USA; dam, winner at up to 6f, was one of best American fillies of 1971; fourth in maiden race at Ripon in August; tailed off only subsequent outing; stays 1¼m. *M. Stoute.*

NATIVE CHANT 2 ch.f. Gone Native–One To Rose 44 (Huntercombe 133) (1983   –
5s 6f 6f) May 17; first foal; dam ran only twice; in rear in maiden and minor events; not seen out after July. *R. Thompson.*

NATIVE CHARMER 2 b.c. Gay Fandango 132–Nativity 91 (Native Royalty)   90
(1983 7fg 6fg² 6fg² 6fg*) Mar 30; quite a useful-looking colt; second foal; dam lightly-raced 2-y-o 5f winner; won 24-runner maiden race at Doncaster in November by 1½ lengths from Adam's Peak; good second previously in similar events at same course and at Newmarket; stays 6f well; acts on a firm surface; should win more races. *R. Hollinshead.*

NATIVE HERO 2 b.c. African Sky 124–Santa Chiara 79 (Aztec 128) (1983 5f 6g³   76
7.6fg⁴ 8g 6fg) May 30; IR 7,800Y; big colt; good mover; half-brother to 3-y-o Tapiz (by Pitskelly) and a winner in Jersey; dam a stayer; in frame at Lingfield in the

autumn in maiden race and minor event, on latter occasion favourite; stays 7.6f. *P. Mitchell.*

NATIVE LAW 3 ro.g. Native Admiral–Distant Display (Daring Display 129) (1982 NR 1983 12v 12.3v) 500Y; big gelding; first foal; dam never ran; tailed-off last in maiden and minor events in May. *R. Hobson.* —

NATIVE RECORD 3 ch.f. Record Token 128–Friendly Native (Native Dancer) (1982 7.6v 5v 1983 8v 6v 8g 12f 12f 5g) of no account; dead. *O. Jorgensen.* —

NATIVE RING 2 gr.c. Formidable 125–Elfinaria 79 (Song 132) (1983 5s 5v² 5s² 5.8s² 5d² 5fg³) Feb 3; 16,000Y; strong, good-bodied colt; carries plenty of condition; second foal; dam sprinting half-sister to smart Fair Season; modest colt; placed early in season in modest company at Bath (twice), Windsor (twice) and Leicester; winner over 6f in Italy. *I. Balding.* **78**

NATIVE SON (FR) 4 b.g. Faraway Son 130–Noble Native 98 (Indigenous 121) (1982 7d 8g 10f 7f 6f⁴ 1983 8s 10.2g 8fg) fair sort; poor walker; plater nowadays; stays 1m; sometimes blinkered; has run respectably when sweating up; sold 525 gns Ascot July Sales. *D. Hanley.* —

NATIVE SPELL (USA) 2 b.c. Our Native–Ninety Day Wonder (Lt Stevens) (1983 7g 8g³ 8g) Apr 24; $50,000Y; well-made colt; sixth foal; half-brother to 2 winners by Al Hattab, including minor stakes winner Posturist, successful at up to 9f; dam won over 5f and 1m; moderate maiden; beaten 11 lengths when placed in maiden event at Goodwood in September; stays 1m. *R. Armstrong.* **83**

NATIVE TIMES (FR) 3 b. or br.f. Faraway Times 123–Noble Native 98 (Indigenous 121) (1982 5g 8fg 7.6v³ 6d 1983 7v 7d 5f 10fg³) tall, leggy filly; ran best race of year when close third in claiming race at Deauville in August; suited by 1¼m; probably acts on any going; trained until after third start by C. Brittain. *C. Austin.* **?**

NATURAL LOVE 2 br.f. Mummy's Pet 125–Natural Flora (Floribunda 136) (1983 6f 7f 7f 6d) May 22; well-grown, workmanlike filly; half-sister to several winners here and abroad, including quite useful 1976 Irish 2-y-o 6f winner Fairhaven Lady (by Runnymede); dam never ran; behind in maiden races and a minor event; not certain to stay 7f; blinkered final outing. *R. Hobson.* —

NATURALLY ORIS 3 b.f. Lypheor 118–Scarletta 103 (Red God 128§) (1982 5f 6s 1983 5v 6d³ 7d* 7f 7fg 7f 8.2fg) leggy, light-framed filly; dropped in class when winning seller at Ayr in June (bought in 3,300 gns); ran moderately afterwards (usually blinkered); suited by 7f; acts on a soft surface; sold 3,500 gns Ascot October Sales. *C. Booth.* **52**

NAUGHTY TWINKLE 4 b.f. Red Alert 127–Sapphire Lady (Majority Blue 126) (1982 7d³ 5fg 6fg 7fg 6d 5g³ 6s 6s⁴ 1983 6v 6d 6s² 5f 6g⁴ 7f 6f² 6f³ 5f 5d 6fg) stocky filly; plater; stays 7f; acts on firm going but is ideally suited by some give in the ground; usually blinkered nowadays. *A. Balding.* **43**

NAUTEOUS 4 b.g. Nonoalco 131–Sassabunda 108 (Sassafras 135) (1982 8f² 10f* 10f³ 12d⁴ 12f* 12fg² 12g² 12g 12s 1983 11.1v 12d⁴ 12g³ 12f³ 12f³ 12f² 12h³) deep-girthed, quite attractive gelding; will stay 1¾m; acts on firm going and is probably unsuited by soft; blinkered once at 2 yrs. *P. Walwyn.* **75**

NAUTICAL WAY 3 ch.f. Captain James 123–Keep Walking (Continuation 120) (1982 6fg 1983 7fg 7.2fg) sparely-made filly; poor maiden; sold 410 gns Ascot September Sales. *M. Smyly.* —

NAVAJO BRAVE (USA) 5 br.g. Navajo–Rosy Lark (T. V. Lark) (1982 16d 1983 12g 6d 16fg) tall gelding; poor performer nowadays; stays well; has been bandaged. *R. Hoad.* —

NAVARINO BAY 3 br.f. Averof 123–Black Fire 92 (Firestreak 125) (1982 5fg* 5g² 6f² 1983 7v 8f 10g⁴ 10f⁴ 8fg) strong filly; useful performer as a 2-y-o, but reportedly sustained a stress fracture after last race; fourth behind 6-length winner Cumrew in £4,800 handicap at Newmarket in July, third outing and best effort of 1983; stays 1¼m; acts on firm going and may well be completely unsuited by heavy; blinkered final outing. *J. W. Watts.* **93**

NAVIGATIONAL AID 6 b.g. Blind Harbour 96–Tiny Clanger 73 (Sky Gipsy 117) (1982 14g 1983 12v) big, rangy gelding; fair handicapper at his best but is lightly raced nowadays; stays 2m but not 2¼m; acts on any going; blinkered once in 1980; suited by strong handling. *W. Holden.* —

NAWAL 2 b.f. Song 132–Devon Night 100 (Midsummer Night II 117) (1983 5.1fg³ 6g 5fg³ 6f* 6f² 6f² 7f⁴) Feb 18; 26,000Y; smallish, active sort; sister to 2 winners, **84**

including top 1978 2-y-o filly Devon Ditty, later a good winner at up to 9f in USA, and half-sister to several others; dam won at up to 7f at 2 yrs; showed improved form when running on well to beat Miss Silca Key by a length in 20-runner maiden event at Windsor in July; creditable second following month in nursery at Leicester and minor event at Epsom; suited by 6f; acts on firm going. *H. T. Jones.*

NAWARA 3 ch.f. Welsh Pageant 132–Bright Decision 108 (Busted 134) (1982 6fg 8fg[3] 8s[3] 1983 8g 9f 10.2h* 9fg 11.7fg) smallish, lightly-made, fair sort; ran best race when beating Kaysariyya by ¾ length in 20-runner maiden race at Bath in July; suited by 1¼m and should stay further; acts on any going. *P. Walwyn.* **70**

NAZEEH 2 br.c. Auction Ring 123–St Louisan 109 (St Chad 120) (1983 6fg 5g[2] 6fg[4]) Apr 6; IR 17,000Y; good-quartered, attractive colt; half-brother to winners here and abroad, including French middle-distance winner Vale of Tears (by Val de l'Orne); dam useful over 5f at 2 yrs; in frame in autumn maiden races at Catterick and Brighton; better suited by 6f than 5f; acts on a firm surface. *A. Stewart.* **73**

NEARDOWN BOY 2 ch.c. Hotfoot 126–Whip Finish 77 (Be Friendly 130) (1983 7.6fg 6d 7fg) Apr 24; 5,800F, 24,000Y; third foal; half-brother to fairly useful 1982 2-y-o Day of Judgement (by Bay Express); dam won twice over 5f at 2 yrs; 7½ lengths seventh of 14 to Claude Monet in minor event at Doncaster in October, third outing and only indication of merit; evidently stays 7f. *C. Horgan.* **67**

NEARDOWN LAD 2 ch.c. Hot Spark 126–All Shy 64 (Alcide 136) (1983 5fg 6f) Mar 20; 6,200F, 8,800Y; half-brother to several winners, including middle-distance performer Graf Metternich (by High Top); dam stayed at least 1½m; behind in June maiden races at Nottingham (slowly away) and Folkestone. *M. Blanshard.* **–**

NEARLY A NOSE (USA) 2 b.c. Cox's Ridge–Drury Nell (Bold Lad, Ire 133) (1983 6fg) $375,000Y; big, good sort; half-brother to Irish 6f winner Drama (by Sir Ivor) and 1981 American 2-y-o 7f stakes winner Taylor Park (by Sir Gaylord); half-sister to Typhoon and outstanding broodmare Moment of Truth; sire top-class winner of 16 races up to 9.5f; 16/1 and in need of race, seventh of 23 to Optimistic Lass in maiden race at Newmarket in October; has scope and is certain to do better. *P. Walwyn.* **– p**

NEBIHA 3 ch.f. Nebbiolo 125–Roses 103 (Ribero 126) (1982 6fg 7f 7fg 8fg[2] 1983 10.5s 12d[2] 12.2d[2] 12fg* 14f 12f* 10f 12d 12fg) well-made filly; won maiden race at Edinburgh and handicap at Thirsk in summer, latter staying on by 2½ lengths from Regal Steel; didn't run well afterwards; suited by 1½m and is worth another chance at 1¾m; ought to show she acts on really soft going, but acts on any other. *G. Huffer.* **81**

NEEDWOOD LEADER 2 br.c. Averof 123–The Doe 87 (Alcide 136) (1983 7fg 8s 9s) Apr 2; leggy colt; fourth reported foal; half-brother to a winner in Brazil; dam stayed at least 1¼m; plating-class maiden; seems to stay 9f. *B. Morgan.* **67**

NEEYEF 2 b.c. Formidable 125–Tetrazzini 70 (Sovereign Path 125) (1983 6g[3] 6fg*) Apr 17; 62,000Y; quite a useful-looking colt; half-brother to 2 winners, including useful 1979 2-y-o 5f to 7f winner Lady Downsview (by Prince Regent); dam placed over 6f; had his 11 opponents well strung out when all-the-way winner of maiden race at Folkestone in October; promising ½-length third of 23 to Miss Beaulieu in newcomers event at Goodwood the previous month; will stay 7f; a cut above the usual Folkestone winner and will win more races. *P. Walwyn.* **95 p**

NEGUNDO (FR) 3 b.c. Tyrant–Nuit Fabuleuse (Le Fabuleux 133) (1982 8g[3] 9s 7v* 1983 9.2v 11v 8s[2] 7d[2]) 350,000 francs Y (approx £32,000); fourth foal; half-brother to winners by Tarbes and Iron Duke; dam unraced granddaughter of Carrozza; won maiden race at Maisons-Laffitte as a 2-y-o; not seen out after May in 1983, best efforts when second in valuable 19-runner handicap at Evry (top weight) and 13-runner Prix du Palais Royal at Longchamp (went down by 2 lengths to Honeyland); best form at up to 1m; acts on heavy going and has yet to race on a firm surface. *F. Boutin, France.* **118**

NEKHBET 2 b.f. Artaius 129–Supreme Lady 86 (Grey Sovereign 128§) (1983 6f[4] 5g[3]) Apr 30; 44,000Y; good-topped filly; half-sister to several winners, including Irish St Leger winner M-Lolshan (by Levmoss) and useful sprinter Chemin (by Steel Heart); dam 2-y-o 5f performer; in frame in maiden races at Newbury in August and Wolverhampton in September. *G. Pritchard-Gordon.* **74**

NELLIE BLY 2 gr.f. Dragonara Palace 115–Arctic Dream 75 (Arctic Slave 116) (1983 5d[4] 5d* 5v) Apr 26; 660F, 3,600Y; sturdy non-thoroughbred filly; sixth reported foal; dam best at sprint distances; won 4-runner maiden race at Newmarket in April; blinkered when last of 5 in minor event at York the following month; possibly not suited by heavy going. *M. H. Easterby.* **80**

NELSONS DOCKYARD 2 ch.c. Thatching 131–Be Gyrful 89 (Gyr 131) (1983   **89**
7.2fg* 8.2fg²) Apr 5; IR 4,200Y; has a round action; half-brother to 3-y-o 1m and
9f winner Country Charm (by Northfields) and a winner in Italy by Habitat; dam,
winner over 5f and 1m, is daughter of Gimcrack winner Be Careful; beat Quaker
Bridge by 5 lengths in 8-runner maiden auction event at Haydock in August;
excellent 3 lengths second of 16 to Alleging in £3,400 event at Nottingham 2
months later; stays 1m well; acts on a firm surface, but has action of horse likely to
be better on an easy one. *P. Cole.*

NELSON'S LADY 2 gr.f. Native Admiral–Out of Depth 65 (Deep Diver 134)   **–**
(1983 5fg 5g) May 13; third foal; dam 5f winner; behind in October maiden races at
Lingfield and Warwick. *C. Horgan.*

NEORION 3 ch.c. Busted 134–Ship Yard 107 (Doutelle 128) (1982 8s² 8d 1983   **98**
9d 10v² 12v 12s 12f² 12h² 10f³ 14f* 14.6s 14.7fg*) big, strong colt; good mover
and walker; brother to Bustino; did well when given a test of stamina and beat
Jackdaw both times when winning maiden race at Haydock and minor event at
Redcar in September, latter by 2 lengths after travelling strongly throughout;
beaten about 20 lengths, but ran well nevertheless, when sixth of 10 behind Sun
Princess in St Leger at Doncaster in between; had run creditably most previous
starts and been second in slowly-run Guardian Classic Trial at Sandown, Churchill
Stakes at Ascot and Welsh Derby at Chepstow; finds 1¼m inadequate and stays
well; acts on any going. *C. Brittain.*

NEPHRITE 2 gr.f. Godswalk 130–Gradiva 110 (Lorenzaccio 130) (1983 5s 5g 5f³   **87**
6fg³ 6f* 6f² 6s 6g) Mar 6; lightly-made filly; third foal; sister to disappointing
Gravina and half-sister to 3-y-o 6f and 7f winner Gradille (by Home Guard); dam,
half-sister to top sprinter Double Form, won from 5f to 1m; won 13-runner nursery
at Windsor in August by a head from Baffle Bay; will be well suited by 7f; acts on
firm going and is probably unsuited by soft; wears blinkers. *F. J. Houghton.*

NEPULA 2 ch.f. Nebbiolo 125–Alata (Le Levanstell 122) (1983 5d 6g² 7f* 7f* 8fg²   **105**
8fg*)
Nepula improved with every run, so much so that having finished second in a
Hamilton maiden race on her second start, she ended her first season winning the
Hoover Fillies Mile at Ascot. Much improved though she is, Nepula will need to
continue to make more than normal progress if she's to match the achievements
of any of the last four winners of the Hoover Fillies Mile, Quick As Lightning,
Leap Lively, Height Of Fashion and Acclimatise, all of whom won further pattern
races as three-year-olds. However, she's a stayer in the making, so the distance
at least won't stop her emulating Quick As Lightning, Leap Lively and Acclimatise
by reaching the frame in the Oaks.

*Hoover Fillies Mile, Ascot—Nepula (rails) quickens well to beat Nonesuch Bay and Circus
Plume*

Mr Sulaiman Al-Qemlas' "Nepula"

Nepula gained her first success when tried over seven furlongs in a Wolverhampton maiden race, and followed up with an impressive victory in a nursery at Yarmouth. Stepped up considerably in class for her first attempt at a mile in the May Hill Stakes at Doncaster, she started at 20/1 but stayed on well to finish second to Satinette with the favourite Shoot Clear third. Nepula would have met Satinette on terms 7 lb better in the Hoover Fillies Mile had the latter not been withdrawn with a temperature. As it was, Nepula started second favourite to the comfortable Goodwood winner Girl Friday, with Circus Plume who had overcome eighteen other maidens to win at Salisbury also well fancied. Nepula ran a similar race to that at Doncaster: fourth into the straight, she ran on well after having to be switched to get a clear run two furlongs out, to win by three quarters of a length from the newcomer Nonesuch Bay, whose striking debut attracted even more attention than Nepula's victory; Circus Plume, who had every chance, finished a length behind Nonesuch Bay in third.

			Yellow God	Red God
		Nebbiolo	(ch 1967)	Sally Deans
		(ch 1974)	Novara	Birkhahn
Nepula			(b 1965)	Norbelle
(ch. f. Mar 16, 1981)		Alata	Le Levanstell	Le Lavandou
		(ch 1972)	(b 1957)	Stella's Sister
			Altamura	Tenerani
			(ch 1957)	Aldousa

Nepula is a smallish filly. Her sire, the Two Thousand Guineas winner Nebbiolo, ran only once beyond a mile, but has sired a Queen's Vase winner in Santella Man and plenty of animals who stay quite well. Nepula is Alata's second foal, following Alata Girl (by Mount Hagen) who won a good prize over eleven furlongs in Belgium. Alata herself won a nine-and-a-half-furlong maiden race at Dundalk and is out of a mare whose only other winner stayed extreme distances over hurdles. Alata's grandam, Aldousa, was a half-sister to a number of winning stayers, notably Alycidon. Nepula acts well on firm going. *G. Huffer.*

NERAIDA 3 br.f. Royalty 130–Run The Risk (Run The Gantlet) (1982 7.6v 1983   **52** 12f 12g 15.5fg* 12f 16g) workmanlike filly; bought in 960 gns after winning seller at Folkestone in October; suited by a test of stamina. *I. Walker.*

NESTOR 3 gr.c. Nishapour 125–Meadow Rhapsody (Ragusa 137) (1982 7fg 7.6s   **97** 8s² 1983 12v 10v 10d* 10fg² 12f³ 11.7f³ 12fg⁴ 12g² 13.3g 12fg³ 12d²) strong colt; needed to be driven along whole way when making virtually all to win 5-runner maiden race at Epsom in June; placed afterwards at Sandown, Ascot (twice), Bath, Kempton and York, finishing 4 lengths second of 5 to Gay Lemur in £3,000 event on last-named course in October; suited by 1½m; acts on any going; genuine; ran respectably in blinkers ninth start; sold to D. Nicholson 35,000 gns Newmarket Autumn Sales. *G. Lewis.*

NESTOR MAN 3 b.g. Lepanto–Ewelme (Ribomar 108) (1982 NR 1983 11.7v   **–** 12fg 16g 14f) sturdy, lengthy gelding; first reported thoroughbred foal; dam bad plater; behind in maiden and minor events and a handicap. *G. Balding.*

NET CORD 2 b.f. Auction Ring 123–Fenland Queen (King's Troop 118) (1983   **94 p** 8fg) Mar 24; 17,000Y; half-sister to several winners, including fairly useful 1977 2-y-o 7f winner Fosterfridge (by St Chad); dam unraced half-sister to high-class miler Belmont Bay (by Auction Ring); outsider of party but fairly fit, made stiff task for a newcomer and in circumstances ran creditably when 5 lengths fifth of 8 to Nepula in Hoover Fillies Mile at Ascot in September; well up to winning a maiden race. *P. Kelleway.*

NETSUKE 2 br.f. Tachypous 128–Merchantmen's Girl 58 (Klairon 131) (1983 5s³   **94** 5d 5f² 5f* 6f 7fg⁴) Mar 24; medium-sized, quite attractive filly; good mover with a light action; half-sister to 3-y-o Metuchen (by Star Appeal) and fair sprinter Lindsey (by Mummy's Pet), subsequently a useful winner at around 1m in USA; dam placed over 5f; won 11-runner maiden race at Sandown in June; also in frame in 2 pattern races, 2½ lengths second of 15 to Night of Wind in Queen Mary Stakes at Royal Ascot in June and 5½ lengths fourth of 8 to Shoot Clear in Waterford Candelabra Stakes at Goodwood in August; suited by 7f; acts well on firm going. *D. Elsworth.*

NEVER ENOUGH 5 b.m. Sandford Lad 133–Suffice 84 (Faberge II 121) (1982   **–** 8d 10fg* 10f 10.8fg 10f* 10g 1983 12f 12fg) strong, well-made mare; good walker; plater; stays 1¼m; acts on firm going; has worn bandages; sold 840 gns Ascot December Sales. *J. Yardley.*

NEVER SAY YES 3 ch.f. Import 127–Tinella 87 (Nelcius 133) (1983 6f 6f 7.6fg⁴   **68** 6g) Apr 4; 7,200Y; sparely-made filly; half-sister to 1980 2-y-o 6f winner Petrinella (by Mummy's Pet); dam, half-sister to Alverton, won over 1m and 11.2f; quite a modest maiden; best effort in third outing; evidently suited by 7f; blinkered last 2 starts. *C. Nelson.*

NEVER SO BOLD 3 b.c. Bold Lad (Ire) 133–Never Never Land (Habitat 134)   **100** (1982 6g 1983 7s⁴ 6d³ 7.3v³ 7fg* 8f 6f* 7s 7fg*) big, rangy, good-looking colt; has a round action; quite a useful handicapper on his day and won at Sandown in June, Ripon in August (Great St Wilfrid) and Ascot in September; ran on strongly to beat Major Don by 1½ lengths in £9,600 Pearce Duff Stakes on last-named course; stays 7f; acts on any going, but has done all his winning on fast ground. *R. Armstrong.*

NEVER TURN BACK 2 ch.f. Tumble Wind–You Never Can Tell (Never Say Die   **§§** 137) (1983 5s 5g⁴ 5.1fg 6f 5f⁴ 5fg⁴ 5fg³ 6fg 5g) Apr 7; IR 3,100F, 5,000Y; compact, well-made filly; good walker; half-sister to a minor winner in France; dam never ran; unreliable maiden; twice ran well in useful company, and often ran indifferently in bad; trained by A. Jarvis first 3 starts; one to leave alone. *J. McNaughton.*

NEW COINS (USA) 3 b.f. New Prospect–Estaciones (Sonny Fleet) (1982 6h⁴   **110** 7f³ 7d³ 7g² 6s* 7s* 1983 10.5s³ 12g³ 12g 12fg 12fg 12g⁴ 12g³)
    There can't be many horses about that have won as much as £30,000 in a season without finishing better than third, as New Coins did in 1983. This sum was gained through three third places—in the Oaks, the Musidora Stakes and the Grand Prix de Bordeaux—and one fourth place, in the Grand Prix de Nantes. At Epsom, New Coins started at 66/1: she had been beaten a long way by Give Thanks in the Musidora and her two-year-old form was unexceptional. Although no horse stood an earthly chance with Sun Princess once she went for home, New Coins ran with considerable credit. She was never far off the lead and was fourth when Sun

582

Mr S. T. Wong's "New Coins"

Princess came past her. New Coins then looked to be outpaced and dropped back to sixth with three furlongs to run, but she fought back extremely well to take third place, beaten twelve lengths and two and a half lengths by Sun Princess and Acclimatise, with Shore Line a further length and a half away fourth.

New Coins's next three runs were lack-lustre; disappointing in fact, for an Oaks third. She was well beaten behind Give Thanks again in the Lancashire Oaks, well beaten in the Prix de Minerve at Evry and last of eleven to Sylph in the Princess Royal Stakes at Ascot after a fairly lengthy spell off the course. She wore bandages at Haydock. New Coins was unlucky to find the ground firm at Ascot; she would have been far better suited by the easier surface more normal at that time of year. New Coins was kept in training into November with the unusual objective of races in the French Provinces. She finished fourth to the Hungarian-bred Maganyos in the Grand Prix de Nantes, the most valuable race run in Western France, beaten a shade over ten lengths. A week later she ran better in finishing third to the odds-on Full of Stars at Bordeaux. There she led till headed two furlongs out, and, as in the Oaks, kept on well to gain third place in the closing stages. She wore blinkers on both occasions.

New Coins (USA) (b.f. 1980)	New Prospect (b 1969)	Never Bend (b 1960)	Nasrullah
			Lalun
		Hasty Act (b 1960)	Hasty Road
			Saracen Flirt
	Estaciones (b 1975)	Sonny Fleet (b 1960)	Son of Alpen
			Fast Fleet
		Estacion (b 1953)	British Empire
			Lesina

New Coins is a close-coupled, fair sort and a good mover. She is the only British winner sired by the Florida-based stallion New Prospect, who has sired

583

nine stakes winners in the States since 1975. New Prospect won seven times at distances up to a mile and is by Never Bend, the sire of Mill Reef. New Coins is the first foal of Estaciones, who won over a mile in America. The grandam Estacion won four races in Argentina, then proceeded to win thirteen races in the next five seasons in the United States. At stud she produced ten winners, including three minor stakes winners British Commander, British Ross and British Fleet, the last named a brother to Estaciones, and two stakes-placed horses, one of whom is another brother to Estaciones. New Coins is ideally suited by a mile and a half and some give in the ground. *B. Hanbury.*

NEW DIMENSION 2 b.f. Sharpen Up 127–Millvera 94 (Mill Reef 141) (1983 6g2 6g* 6d4) Mar 7; first foal; dam, half-sister to smart Home Run, won 5 times over 7f and 1m; won 19-runner maiden race at Goodwood in September; disappointing favourite in minor event at Lingfield the following month; will be better suited by 7f+; apparently not at her best on a soft surface. *G. Harwood.*   **88**

NEWELLA 2 ch.f. New Member 119–Brackens Marella (Rugantino 97) (1983 7.6d) Feb 18; first foal; dam never ran; behind in 18-runner maiden race at Lingfield in October; sold 410 gns Ascot November Sales. *A. Ingham.*   **–**

NEW EMBASSY (USA) 6 b.g. Dynastic (USA)–Joys Will (Yes You Will) (1982 5g* 5s4 5f 5fg 5g 1983 5fg 5fg 5d 5fg) strong, well-made, good-quartered gelding; sprint handicapper; has shown no form for a long time; acts on any going; slowly into stride once in 1982. *G. Balding.*   **–**

NEW EXPRESS 4 br.c. Bay Express 132–Natasha 87 (Native Prince) (1982 5fg* 5fg* 6g4 5f 5g 1983 5v4 5f3 5f3 5h 5f3 5.6fg 5fg*) strong, lengthy colt; poor walker and mover; sprint handicapper; beat Cree Bay at Redcar in September; also first past the post at Ostend on third start but was relegated to third by stewards; best at 5f; acts on any going. *G. Huffer.*   **95**

NEW GENERATION 2 b.f. Young Generation 129–Madina 119 (Beau Prince II 131) (1983 7f* 6fg*) May 12; deep-girthed filly; half-sister to several winners, including very smart French miler Nonoalco (by Nonoalco) and leading French hurdler Mazel Tov (by Sigebert); dam won Prix Morny; successful in September in 18-runner maiden race at Salisbury and 23-runner minor event at Redcar, without accomplishing great deal on either occasion; will stay 1m; has raced only on fast ground. *Sir Mark Prescott.*   **91 p**

NEWMARKET SAUSAGE 2 ch.c. Owen Dudley 121–Manoeuvre 105 (Mountain Call 125) (1983 5g* 5f4 6f 7.2g2 8.2g3 8d 8.2fg) June 11; quite a useful-looking colt; fourth foal; half-brother to a winner in Austria; dam won from 5f to 7f at 2 yrs; won maiden race at Hamilton in June by 2 lengths from Gauhar, producing a powerful late run after getting behind; placed 3 months after in nurseries at Haydock (again taking long time to get going) and Hamilton; stays 1m; best form with some give in the ground; blinkered last 4 starts. *S. Norton.*   **81**

NEW RECRUIT 4 b.f. New Member 119–Cressandra (Polic 126) (1982 NR 1983 10.2g 8f) plain filly; sister to a winning jumper; dam 2m chaser; probably of little account; sold 400 gns Ascot August Sales. *O. O'Neill.*   **–**

NEWS 2 gr.f. Town Crier 119–Currency (Crepello 136) (1983 5g 5s4) Apr 24; tall, rather lightly-made, quite attractive filly; third foal; half-sister to 3-y-o Penybont (by Welsh Pageant) and very useful 1¼m filly Fee (by Mandamus); dam never ran; 6½ lengths fourth of 10 to Rizla Blue in minor event at Newmarket in May; will be much better suited by 6f+; sold to BBA 2,000 gns Newmarket December Sales. *B. Hobbs.*   **61**

NEWSELLS PARK 2 ch.c. Anne's Pretender 124–Fernelia 73 (Royalty 130) (1983 7fg) Apr 14; 6,200Y; big, strong colt; first foal; dam disappointing half-sister to Gold Cup winner Shangamuzo; in rear in 14-runner Houghton Stakes at Newmarket in October. *J. Winter.*   **–**

NEWSHAM 3 ch.g. Dublin Taxi–Whoops (Farm Walk 111) (1982 NR 1983 7f 8f 8.2f3 8g3 8g) neat gelding; first foal; dam, sister to very useful Move Off, virtually took no part on only appearance; plating-class maiden; stays 1m; bandaged off-hind on first outing; retained 3,200 gns Doncaster November Sales. *Miss S. Hall.*   **56**

NEW STRAND 2 ch.f. Music Boy 124–Junior Belle 71 (Swinging Junior 118) (1983 6f 6g 6s) Feb 24; first foal; dam won sellers over 6f and 7f; apparently of no account; blinkered last 2 outings. *W. Stubbs.*   **–**

NEW ZEALAND 2 b.f. Dominion 123–Freely Given 69 (Petingo 135) (1983 6g 6f 7s4) Mar 5; well-made filly; first foal; dam lightly-raced half-sister to very useful stayer Tom Cribb; 6 lengths fourth of 19 to Eljazzi in maiden race at Leicester in October; will probably stay 1¼m. *P. Walwyn.*   **71**

NIALAN 3 b.g. North Stoke 130–Buffy (French Beige 127) (1982 8g 8g³ 1983 11s   —
13.1fg⁴ 12g) well-made, quite attractive gelding; looked promising at 2 yrs but
didn't show much as a 3-y-o; having first race for 5 months when remote fourth to
Insular in minor event at Bath in September; played up at start and missed break on
first outing of 1983. *J. Sutcliffe.*

NIBABU (FR) 3 b.f. Nishapour 125–Noah's Acky Astra (Ack Ack) (1982 6v³   101 §
1983 7.3s² 10.5s⁴ 10v 8f³ 8f³ 8fg 6f 8g³ 8s 8fg⁴ 7d 10f 8g) lengthy, strong-
quartered filly; capable of running well in good company, as she showed when 3
lengths second of 9 to Goodbye Shelley in Gainsborough Stud Fred Darling Stakes
at Newbury in April, but was mainly disappointing and ended season still a maiden;
not certain to stay 1¼m and ran reasonably well in goodish company over 6f on
seventh start; trained until after seventh outing by B. Hills; not one to trust
implicitly. *D. Smaga, France.*

NICALINE 5 b.m. High Line 125–Ardema 63 (Armistice 131) (1982 21f 12s 1983   50
10s² 16f) plain mare; should be suited by further than 1¼m; has run respectably
for an apprentice; has given trouble at start. *R. Sturdy.*

NICE FELLA (USA) 3 b.c. Raise A Cup–Imalulu (Black Beard) (1982 7.6v 8s   —
1983 12v 10fg) well-made colt; showed promise as a 2-y-o but was behind both
starts in 1983. *M. Jarvis.*

NICELY NICELY 2 ch.c. Tumble Wind–Rushkey (Bullrush 106) (1983 5fg) Apr   —
12; IR 9,200Y; half-brother to several winners here and abroad, including fairly
useful 1976 2-y-o sprinter Rush Bond (by Good Bond); dam never ran; fifteenth of
17 in minor event at Windsor in June. *S. Mellor.*

NICE ONE ANDY 2 ch.c. Ahonoora 122–Star Set (Sunny Way 120) (1983 6f 6h²   74
5fg 5d) May 3; IR 5,700F, 6,000Y; fair sort; half-brother to 3 winners, including
1979 2-y-o sprinter Rosette (by Red Alert); dam never ran; quite moderate;
beaten ¾ length in 12-runner maiden event at Nottingham in August; clearly
suited by 6f. *G. Huffer.*

NICE VALUE 9 ch.g. Goldhill 125–Sinecure (Parthia 132) (1982 5fg 5fg 6fg 6s⁴   —
1983 8d 6v 6v 6d 6d) sprint handicapper; acts on any going but is suited by some
give in the ground; blinkered once. *R. Hollinshead.*

NICK NICK 3 br.f. Garda's Revenge 119–Prancer 70 (Santa Claus 133) (1982   58
5fg³ 5g³ 6f 5g³ 6g 6fg 6fg 6g 1983 6s⁴ 7v⁴ 8v 7f 8.2h 7fg⁴ 7.6d 6g* 7fg 7f) leggy
filly; poor walker; 33/1-winner of handicap at Leicester in October; in frame in
varied company previously, including selling; stays 7f; occasionally blinkered. *D.
Dale.*

NICKY NICK 2 br.g. Hotfoot 126–Ribbon Dancer 82 (Sharpen Up 127) (1983 6g   72
7g⁴ 7.2fg³ 7g) Mar 23; 4,200Y; compact, rather lightly-built gelding; first foal;
dam 2-y-o 7f winner; quite a modest maiden; will stay 1m; acts on firm going;
tended to hang on final appearance. *M. Usher.*

NICOLE'S CHIEF (USA) 2 b.c. Chieftain–Beautiful Design (Traffic Judge)   66
(1983 7s 8s 7fg) Feb 4; $30,000F; quite attractive colt; closely related to a winner
by Wajima and half-brother to 3 more; dam ran 3 times unplaced; plating-class
maiden; showed form only on first outing. *J. Hindley.*

NIEKA 2 b.f. Jellaby 124–Jamra 69 (Upper Case) (1983 6f 5.8h 5g⁴) May 31;   71
good-topped filly; first foal; dam won 3 times at around 1m in Scandinavia; quite a
modest maiden; should stay 7f+ but is a free-running sort and may not do so. *M.
McCormack.*

NIGEL'S ANGEL 2 b.f. Sit In The Corner–Pampered Angel 97 (Pampered   —
King 121) (1983 7.6d 6fg) Apr 12; half-sister to 2 winners, including smart miler
Pirate Dream (by Breeders Dream); dam won over 5f and 7f and stayed 1½m;
behind in October maiden events at Lingfield and Leicester. *A. Bailey.*

NIGHT CLOWN 4 b.g. Cawston's Clown 113–Night On (Narrator 127) (1982 5g   62
5g* 5.8f* 6f⁴ 6f 6fg 5fg³ 6f 5g 5s 1983 5d 6v 7s 6fg 6f 7g² 7g² 6g 6fg 7g³)
dipped-backed gelding; second in sellers at Yarmouth and Edinburgh in September;
stays 7f; acts on firm going; often blinkered; has won for an apprentice; sold 1,500
gns Ascot November Sales. *A. Bailey.*

NIGHT EYE (USA) 3 ch.c. Crow 134–Four Bells (Quadrangle) (1982 NR 1983   90
14f 14f³ 15.5f* 16f* 17.1h* 16fg⁴ 16.5fg² 18fg) $175,000Y; angular colt; third foal;
half-brother to minor winners in USA by Quack and Tom Rolfe; dam very useful
winner at up to 1m from 3 yrs to 5 yrs; a splendidly genuine and enthusiastic colt
who won maiden race at Folkestone, 2 handicaps at Newcastle and minor event at

Pontefract; beat Powersaver Lad by a length at Newcastle in October on last occasion; suited by a test of stamina; has raced only on firm ground; below form final outing. *F. Durr.*

NIGHT OF WIND 2 b.f. Tumble Wind–Night of Gladness 98 (Midsummer Night II 117) (1983 5d⁴ 5s⁴ 5s² 5f* 6fg) Apr 8; IR 6,000F, IR 11,000Y; rangy, quite attractive filly; half-sister to a 2-y-o winner by My Swanee; dam won from 5f to 1m; 50/1, showed markedly improved form when winning 15-runner Queen Mary Stakes at Royal Ascot in good style by 2½ lengths from Netsuke, always going pretty well, leading 1f out and quickening clear; looked a bit slack when 4/1 for Cherry Hinton Stakes at Newmarket the following month and dropped out rapidly in final furlong to finish 8½ lengths seventh of 9 behind Chapel Cottage; seems best at 5f; well suited by firm ground; exported to USA. *M. McCormack.*   **101**

NIGHT WARBLER 2 ch.f. Whistlefield 118–Night Work (Burglar 128) (1983 5.8h) Apr 20; second foal; dam well beaten in 2 juvenile hurdles; tailed-off last of 6 in maiden race at Bath in July. *J. Hill.*   –

NIGHT WATCH (USA) 9 br.g. Stage Door Johnny–Lucretia Bori (Bold Ruler) (1982 13fg 16d 12fg 14fg 12fg* 12d 12g 13.8d 1983 12v 14s 12g 12f) strong, good-looking gelding; not the force he was; stays well; appears to act on any going; very good mount for an inexperienced rider. *I. Balding.*   –

NIKARA (FR) 3 b.f. Emerson–Demokratia (Luthier 126) (1982 5.5d 6d 5.5d* 6.5g* 7s² 5.5g⁴ 8v⁴ 7s 8v 1983 7s 8d⁴ 6v 6f 5fg 8d 6d 7g 7fg 5s 6fg) smallish, workmanlike ex-French filly; first foal; dam unraced daughter of high-class 6f to 7f filly Democratie, herself a sister to Fleet and half-sister to Display and Pourparler; won claiming races at Evry and Deauville (claimed approx £6,500) as a 2-y-o; little form in 1983, including in sellers; acts on soft going; sometimes sweats up; occasionally blinkered; sold 2,000 gns Newmarket December Sales. *C. Austin.*   –

NIKIFOROS 4 ch.c. Music Boy 124–Contadina (Memling) (1982 8fg 10fg* 10fg³ 10g* 12f 10g² 10f³ 14f 12fg* 13.3g 10g² 10g 1983 12s 12v³ 12g³ 12f 11.5f³ 10g 12g³ 11.7fg* 12f³ 12fg² 10.5d⁴ 12fg 11d⁴) rangy, quite attractive colt; not the best of movers; fairly useful handicapper; won at Windsor in August; creditable ¾-length second to Free Press in Red Deer Stakes at Ascot in September; stays 1½m; acts on any going; has run creditably when sweating up; blinkered sixth and seventh outings; bandaged off-hind first start; suited by strong handling; often ridden up with pace; sold to R. Atkins 19,000 gns Newmarket Autumn Sales. *C. Brittain.*   **88**

NIKOS 2 b. or br.c. Nonoalco 131–No No Nanette 118 (Sovereign Path 125) (1983 6.5fg³ 6.5fg² 8s⁴ 7d* 7g²) Mar 20; third foal; half-brother to French 11f winner Neomeris (by Pharly) and very smart French middle-distance stayer No Attention (by Green Dancer); dam won 4 races at up to 10.5f, including Prix de Flore, and is closely related to high-class miler Nadjar; finished strongly after being hampered 1f out when neck second to Procida in Criterium de Maisons-Laffitte in October; comfortable winner of maiden race at same track earlier in month; had previously finished creditable fourth (beaten just over 2 lengths) to Cariellor in Prix La Rochette at Longchamp; should stay 1¼m; should win good races at 3 yrs. *J. C. Cunnington, France.*   **116**

NILE EMPRESS (USA) 2 b.f. Upper Nile–I Assume (Young Emperor 133) (1983 5s 6fg* 6f* 6f⁴ 6g³) May 22; $100,000Y; compact, quite attractive filly; bad mover in her slower paces; half-sister to a minor winner; dam, second once from 12 starts, is sister to dam of Cheveley Park winner Sookera; won 2 races in July, 12-runner maiden at Haydock and 5-runner John Smith's Brewery Centenary Stakes at York; good third to Melaura Belle on latter course 3 months later in very valuable nursery; will be suited by 7f; acts on firm going, but possibly better with some give in the ground. *B. Hills.*   **98**

NILSTONE RIDGE 2 b.f. Comedy Star 121–Little Grey Rabbit (Runnymede 123) (1983 6f 8f 7fg) Apr 20; 500Y; small, lightly-made filly; has a round action; second foal; dam ran only 3 times; well beaten in maiden events; apparently of little account. *J. Carr.*   –

NIMBLE DOVE 7 b.m. Starch Reduced 112–Red Dove (All Red 110) (1982 NR 1983 16v) smallish, lightly-made mare; staying handicapper; seems to need some give in the ground; game. *G. Price.*   –

NIMBLE IMP 2 b.g. Import 127–Aqua Nimba (Acropolis 132) (1983 6f 6f 8.2f 8fg) June 11; strong gelding; half-brother to 2 winners, including fair 1978 2-y-o miler Top Stream (by Highland Melody); no worthwhile form; wears blinkers; sold Norsk Jockey Club 850 gns Doncaster November Sales. *P. Asquith.*   –

NIOULARGO 4 b.c. Pitskelly 122–Morzine (On Your Mark 125) (1982 8g² 8fg   80
8fg* 8fg² 7g 8f 10.5g 10g* 10g 1983 10.2v 8d 8f 9f 10f 8f⁴ 8f) quite attractive colt;
useful at his best; mainly disappointing at 4 yrs; stays 1¼m; acts on firm going;
blinkered fourth start; sold 26,000 gns Newmarket September Sales, reportedly
for racing in Saudi Arabia. *R. Armstrong.*

NIPEGON 4 gr.g. Sir Albert 72–Valli 81 (Vigo 130) (1982 NR 1983 16f)   –
workmanlike gelding; sixth reported living foal; brother to a poor plater; dam
showed ability at 2 yrs; unquoted and blinkered when in rear in maiden race at
Newcastle in June. *Miss L. Siddall.*

NOALCOHOLIC (FR) 6 b.h. Nonoalco 131–Alea II (Galivanter 131) (1982   128
9.2s* 8f² 7g* 8d* 8g 8s² 7g* 1983 8s² 8d 8v* 8fg³ 8fg³ 6fg 8f* 8f 8fg³ 7fg²)
Protracted visits are not always beneficial or agreeable to a host but Gavin
Pritchard-Gordon has no reason to regret that Noalcoholic remained in his stable
much longer than anticipated. Trained by Douieb in France until May 1982,
Noalcoholic came to England for a theoretically brief stay in order to fulfil
quarantine regulations before going to stud in Australia, yet at the end of the
season he was still here having improved considerably and shown himself one of the
best milers around. Prevailed upon to keep Noalcoholic in training as a six-year-old,
Mr Du Pont had the pleasure of seeing his horse do even better, winning two top
prizes including the Sussex Stakes which has developed into a virtual British mile
championship in the last decade.
    There weren't many grander sights on the racecourse over the past couple of
years than Noalcoholic enthusiastically bowling along in front playing catch-me-if-
you-can with his opponents. Though usually held up in France, spending most of his
time racing at around a mile and a quarter, Noalcoholic really required forcing
tactics at seven furlongs or a mile to be seen to best advantage and his two
successes in 1983 showed how formidable a competitor he could be when
everything went right. The Lockinge Stakes at Newbury was his third start of the
year following a respectable second to Princes Gate in the Doncaster Mile and a
best-forgotten run in the Prix du Muguet at Longchamp in which he finished eighth
to Prospero, who isn't in the same league, after seeing no daylight at all because
the French jockeys seemed intent on hemming him in the whole way. At Newbury
things went much more according to plan. Front runners usually do best when they
have a rail to race against, since this helps stop their wandering, and after breaking
smartly from his outside draw Noalcoholic moved across in front of his rivals
towards the far rail. Kirchner kept him company to beyond halfway but over a
quarter of a mile out Duffield kicked Noalcoholic on and in a trice they had a lead of
five lengths. Battling on with great gusto though visibly tiring in the very deep
going—he acted on any—Noalcoholic never looked like relinquishing his lead and
came home a length and a half ahead of Valiyar who had come out of the pack in the
last furlong after being waited with.
    By the time he ran in the Sussex Stakes over two months later Noalcoholic
had failed to add to his tally in three races, finishing third to Valiyar on much faster
ground in the Queen Anne Stakes at Royal Ascot, third of five to Burslem in the
Guinness Golden Fleece Stakes at Phoenix Park and a creditable fifth of fifteen to
Habibti over a trip on the sharp side for him in the William Hill July Cup at
Newmarket. The Sussex Stakes, the only Group 1 event over a mile in Britain in
which older horses have the opportunity of meeting three-year-olds, predictably
attracted a strong field and with Noalcoholic under a slight cloud after his defeats
he started at 18/1 behind the first two in the Two Thousand Guineas, Lomond and
Tolomeo, the Irish Two Thousand winner Wassl, Kuwait Tower, fourth in
Lomond's classic, Muscatite, second in the Coral-Eclipse, Montekin and The
Noble Player. To an impartial observer the race proved a pleasure to watch.
Noalcoholic quickly took it up ahead of Wassl and The Noble Player and when
Duffield asked him to quicken the tempo at halfway he extended the lead from one
length to three. Most of the others were already under pressure and getting
nowhere, and by the furlong pole the contest seemed all over bar the shouting
since Noalcoholic, with three lengths to spare over his pursuers, showed no signs
of stopping. Galloping on resolutely he passed the post virtually unchallenged,
two and a half lengths in front of Tolomeo, who finished well, with Wassl a head
away third, Montekin in fourth and Muscatite fifth. Unlike those who wishfully
claimed Noalcoholic had won largely because his rivals' jockeys had given him too
much rope, we could see no possible excuse for any of the beaten horses apart
from the blinkered Lomond who ran well below his best for some reason. The
other jockeys knew Noalcoholic's style of racing full well and had they been able
to prevent his setting up a decisive lead they would have: their mounts simply
could not keep up despite vigorous urgings. In passing, Noalcoholic became the

Sussex Stakes, Goodwood—Noalcoholic runs the legs off his rivals and wins from Tolomeo (right) and Wassl (centre)

longest-priced Sussex Stakes winner since Queen's Hussar in 1963 and the first horse above the age of four to win the race, but too much should not be made of the latter fact since five-year-olds and upwards were made eligible to run only in 1975 and none of Noalcoholic's calibre had taken part since then.

Noalcoholic ran three more times. A respectable fifth to Luth Enchantee in the Prix Jacques le Marois at Deauville after being crossed by the winner when she took up the running about a furlong out, he returned to Goodwood for the Waterford Crystal Mile late in August and ran right up to his best under a sizeable penalty, coming home two lengths third to Montekin. His final appearance saw Noalcoholic trying to repeat his 1982 victory in the Bisquit Cognac Challenge Stakes at Newmarket; though beaten two lengths by Salieri, who accelerated past him as if he was standing still, he saw off the rest of a fairly strong field headed by Sandhurst Prince and Rare Roberta. Pritchard-Gordon's comment after the Sussex—'If it was up to me we would keep him until he is ten'—had been understandable, but after an honourable career encompassing twenty-eight races, more than double the number most horses of his ability contest these days, Noalcoholic has been retired. He hasn't yet finished his duties in England, though, for until June 1984 when he will at last make his fortunately delayed departure for Australia he'll be standing at the Side Hill Stud in Newmarket at a fee of £5,250 live foal. Stallions with Noalcoholic's ability, gameness, toughness, consistency and looks—he is a big, strong, good sort—aren't exactly two a penny and it will be surprising if he does not have a full book of mares.

Noalcoholic (Fr) (b.h. 1977)	Nonoalco (b 1971)	Nearctic (br 1954)	Nearco
			Lady Angela
		Seximee (ch 1966)	Hasty Road
			Jambo
	Alea II (ch 1967)	Galivanter (br 1956)	Golden Cloud
			Lycia
		Alleged (ch 1959)	Alycidon
			Plain Justice

Noalcoholic's sire Nonoalco has been represented by two other good milers since being sent to Japan, the Sussex Stakes third Noalto and Poule d'Essai des Poulains winner Melyno. On the distaff side, Noalcoholic is the fifth foal out of the champion Italian two-year-old filly and Italian One Thousand Guineas winner Alea II who cost Mr Du Pont 25,000 guineas carrying Noalcoholic at the 1976 Newmarket December Sales. One of Alea II's three winners in Italy before Noalcoholic, Amiel, was also by Nonoalco and the other two demonstrated clearly how tough her progeny are since between them Alceo (by Molvedo) and Alato (by Bold Lad, USA)

Mr William Du Pont III's "Noalcoholic"

ran one hundred and nineteen times for thirty-eight successes. Alea II's 1980 foal, the Riverman colt Alluvia, fetched about £53,000 as a yearling and has shown very useful form at up to eleven furlongs in France. The unraced grandam produced three other winners and was a sister to Allegation, dam of the smart stayer The Accuser and third dam of Morcon who, coincidentally, picked up three good prizes on the course where Noalcoholic showed his top form, Goodwood, in 1983. *G. Pritchard-Gordon.*

NOBLE BLOOD (USA) 3 b.f. Bold Forbes–Pleasant Noble (Vaguely Noble 140) (1982 NR 1983 8f 7f 8f² 8f* 8d² 7s) 6,800Y; strong, good-bodied filly; first foal; dam never ran; 4-length winner of maiden race at Warwick in August; creditable second to Dodgy Future in amateur riders race at Goodwood the following month; stays 1m well; probably acts on any going; sold to BBA 9,600 gns Newmarket December Sales. *L. Cumani.* **64**

NOBLE CAMEL (USA) 3 b.c. Bold Forbes–Vaguely Deb 113 (Vaguely Noble 140) (1982 NR 1983 10f³ 8g 10fg* 10.2fg) big, rangy colt; dam third in Oaks; finished strongly when beating Tivian by a short head in maiden race at Beverley in September; sweating when behind in a handicap only subsequent start; will be suited by 1½m; sold to NBA 14,000 gns Newmarket Autumn Sales. *L. Cumani.* **78**

NOBLE GIFT (USA) 4 br.c. Vaguely Noble 140–Queenly Gift (Princely Gift 137) (1982 10.5f² 10f* 10.5fg* 1983 12g 12fg² 11g 10f³ 12f³ 12f²) attractive colt; good walker and very good mover; ran well to be neck second to Say Primula in minor event at Beverley in June and just over 1½ lengths third of 7 to Seymour Hicks in Alycidon Stakes at Goodwood in July; no match for Cooliney Princess when odds on for Moet and Chandon Silver Magnum (gentleman riders) at Epsom in August and went down by 5 lengths; subsequently sent to race in USA, and won there; suited by 1½m; yet to race on a soft surface. *M. Stoute.* **111**

NOBLE LANCER 2 b.c. Queen's Hussar 124–Redeemer 62 (Supreme Gift 121)   –
(1983 8g) Apr 5; first foal; dam placed over 1m; last of 15 in maiden event at
Sandown in October. *D. Wilson.*

NOBLE MOUNT 2 b.g. Monsanto 121–Roanello 102 (Roan Rocket 128) (1983   75
6fg 7f 7fg 7d) Mar 10; fair sort; fourth foal; dam, half-sister to very smart Tudor
Mill, won over 6f and 7f at 2 yrs; quite a moderate maiden; will stay 1m; acts on
firm going. *G. Pritchard-Gordon.*

NOBLE PATIA (USA) 3 b.f. Vaguely Noble 140–Patia 119 (Don II 123) (1982   –
7g 1983 10d 12fg 14f) rangy filly; ran creditably in maiden race at Newmarket as a
2-y-o and when about 15 lengths fifth of 17 to Jolly Bay in Pretty Polly Stakes on
same course in April; soundly beaten in minor event at Leicester and maiden race
at Sandown subsequently; should stay 1½m. *J. Hindley.*

NOBLE PHILIP (USA) 6 b.h. Noble Decree 127–Quezette (Test Case 125)   –
(1982 NR 1983 7h 8fg 7g) quite moderate at his best; stays 1m; seems to act on
any going; blinkered once; sometimes bandaged; trained by D. O'Donnell in the
Isle of Man first 2 starts. *N. Guest.*

NOBLESQUE 2 b. or br.c. Pitskelly 122–Noble Lass (Wolver Hollow 126) (1983   93
5s³ 6fg 6h* 8.2h* 8.2fg² 8d² 10fg) May 17; IR 8,600Y; leggy, rather lightly-made
colt; first foal; dam unraced daughter of half-sister to Vaguely Noble; won maiden
race at Nottingham in August and nursery on same course in September; stays
1¼m; probably acts on any going. *A. Jarvis.*

NOBLE TRAMP 2 b. or br.c. Town and Country 124–La Dolce Vita 78   100
(Sallymount 125) (1983 7fg 7f* 7f⁴ 6fg² 8d* 7fg) Apr 11; 3,500F, 5,000Y; big,
useful sort, with plenty of scope; half-brother to winning plater and a winner in
Norway; dam won over 5f at 2 yrs; won auction event at Thirsk in July and nursery
under top weight at Yarmouth in September; suited by 1m; best form on a soft
surface; likely to make useful handicapper. *W. O'Gorman.*

NOBLE WAY 3 b.c. Monsanto 121–Marble Alley (Psidium 130) (1982 6g 5fg 6g   45
6g 1983 9fg 12.2d⁴ 12fg² 10f) sturdy colt; in frame in sellers; has a round action
and is probably ideally suited by some give in the ground. *G. Lockerbie.*

NOBLISSIMO (FR) 6 ch.h. Sanctus II 132–Nobla (Dicta Drake 126) (1982   49
16.1s⁴ 16v 12d 18s 1983 12g 12s³ 16fg⁴) close-coupled, good-looking horse;
ideally suited by a thorough test of stamina; acts well on soft going; has run
respectably for an apprentice. *N. Guest.*

NOBODY'S PERFECT 2 ch.f. Vitiges 132–La Troublerie (Will Somers 114§)   76
(1983 6f² 6f 7f) Mar 1; tall, workmanlike filly; sister to a modest animal and
half-sister to 2 minor middle-distance winners in France; dam won 7 times at up to
1¼m, including Prix d'Ispahan; quite a moderate maiden; showed little after first
outing; should stay 1¼m. *D. Marks.*

NO BUTTS 3 b.g. Monsanto 121–Lay Aboard (Sing Sing 134) (1982 8.2s 8s 1983   45
12v 8fg 12f 12g 11.7g 12f³) quite well-made gelding; poor walker; plating-class
maiden; stays 1½m; slowly away in apprentice event second start. *R.
Hollinshead.*

NO CONTEST 4 ch.c. Nonoalco 131–Never So Lovely 87 (Realm 129) (1982   75
8.2d 7fg 8f² 8fg³ 7.2f* 7d⁴ 6g* 6.5fg² 6f³ 6f⁴ 6fg⁴ 7fg* 7fg 7s 7s 1983 including 7f
6f 7f 10v 7.2s 5f 7g³ 7.6fg 7fg) workmanlike colt; good mover; fair handicapper at
his best; unplaced 4 times on dirt in USA early in season, including in claiming
races, and ran below form most starts on his return; best at distances short of 1m;
acts on any going; suited by forcing tactics; trained by M. Ryan most of season. *E.
Eldin.*

NO DEFECT 4 ro.g. No Mercy 126–Ruby's Chance 71 (Charlottesville 135)   50
(1982 10s 7f³ 7f² 7f³ 7f* 8g 7fg² 7f 6fg 9f³ 7h) 1983 6v 7fg 8g* 8fg²) lengthy, rather
unfurnished gelding; good mover; plater; bought in 1,100 gns after narrowly
winning at Edinburgh in May; subsequently won in Jersey; possibly stays 9f; acts
on firm going; has worn blinkers. *J. S. Wilson.*

NO FAULT (USA) 3 b. or br.c. J. O. Tobin 130–Gallant Trial (Gallant Man)   –
(1982 NR 1983 8d) $350,000Y; good-bodied, attractive colt; fourth foal;
half-brother to modest 1¼m and 1¾m winner Steel Kid (by Caro) and a minor
winner by Vaguely Noble; dam very useful winner at up to 1m; showed a bit of
promise when seventh of 17 behind Majestic Endeavour in newcomers race at
Newmarket in April, but wasn't seen out again. *H. Cecil.*

NO FLUKE 3 br.c. Averof 123–Daisy Warwick 91 (Ribot 142 or Sir Gaylord)   –
(1982 5fg 5.8f* 6f² 6fg 6g 6g 1983 8f 8fg 9d 10.6g) fair sort; poor plater nowadays;
should stay 1m; acts on firm going; has worn blinkers; fell final outing. *J. Yardley.*

NO HACK 4 ch.c. High Line 125–Cut and Thrust 78 (Pardal 130) (1982 12g 14g   –
1983 12s 8f 7fg 8fg 10f) tall, lightly-made colt; poor maiden; sometimes blinkered.
A. Moore.

NOHALMDUN 2 b.g. Dragonara Palace 115–Damsel 86 (Pampered King 121)   **79**
(1983 6d² 7fg⁴ 6g) Feb 20; rangy gelding; half-brother to a winning plater by
Mummy's Pet; dam 2-y-o 1m winner; in frame in maiden race at Doncaster in May
and £3,900 race at York in September; stays 7f; sold NBA 12,000 gns Newmarket
Autumn Sales; subsequently gelded. *M. H. Easterby.*

NO INK 4 b.f. No Mercy 126–Inklet (Never Say Die 137) (1982 7.6f 5.3f² 5f 5fg   –
6g 1983 10g) fair sort; poor handicapper; best at sprint distances; acts on firm
going. *D. Grissell.*

NOISY BOYSIE 3 br.c. Supreme Sovereign 119–Black Mink 83 (Gratitude 130)   –
(1982 5fg⁴ 1983 6v 5f) workmanlike colt; soundly beaten in maiden races at
Nottingham in April and July; should stay 6f; trained by M. Blanshard first start. *D.
Sasse.*

NOKURU 3 ch.g. Simbir 130–Polly Duckins (Dike) (1982 7s³ 1983 10s³ 8f)   **96**
attractive gelding; showed promise at the Curragh on only outing as a 2-y-o and
was worn down only in last furlong when excellent third behind Evening M'Lord
and Karol in 10-runner Rogers Gold Cup Ballymoss Stakes on same course in April,
beaten a neck and same; last behind Burslem in Coolmore Hello Gorgeous Stakes
at the Curragh again in June on only subsequent outing; gelded afterwards; suited
by 1¼m; possibly unsuited by firm going. *L. Browne, Ireland.*

NOMADIC STAR 7 b.g. Comedy Star 121–Roving Eye 63 (Galivanter 131) (1982   –
NR 1983 18f 14f) poor handicapper; stays 7f. *M. Chapman.*

NONABELLA 2 b.f. Nonoalco 131–Fiordiligi 109 (Tudor Melody 129) (1983 6f²   **81**
7f² 8d⁴) Apr 17; lengthy, rather sparely-made filly; second foal; dam game and
useful staying 2-y-o; disappointed after showing promise on first outing, failing to
justify favouritism in minor event (odds on) at Redcar in August and maiden race at
Beverley in September. *M. H. Easterby.*

NONESUCH BAY 2 b.f. Mill Reef 141–Vestal Virgin 91 (Hail to Reason) (1983   **103 p**
8g²) Mar 3; strong, most attractive filly; second foal; sister to 1982 2-y-o 1m
winner Saba; dam, winner over 1m and 1½m, is out of half-sister to Irish classic
winners Reindeer, Santa Tina and Atherstone Wood; impressed enormously both in
paddock and in race when 16/1 for Hoover Fillies Mile at Ascot in September,
putting in an excellent run in straight to finish ¾-length second of 8 to Nepula;
likely to develop into a good filly over middle distances and must be noted in any
company. *I. Balding.*

NONNITA 2 b.f. Welsh Saint 126–Summer Day 117 (Golden Cloud) (1983 5fg²)   **62 p**
Mar 2; half-sister to several winners, including useful 7f performer Heave To (by
Pirate King); dam won six 5f races at 2 yrs; co-favourite, second of 8 behind easy
winner Mummy's Chick in poor maiden race at Edinburgh in November. *Sir Mark
Prescott.*

NON NOBIS 2 b.c. Nonoalco 131–Explorelka (Relko 136) (1983 7fg) Apr 10;   **– p**
quite attractive colt; half-brother to 3-y-o River Baby (by Riverman) and 2 winners
in France, including very smart middle-distance performer Explorer King (by Roi
Dagobert); dam once-raced daughter of sister to Bold Ruler; in need of race, not
given hard time when twelfth of 20 behind wide-margin winner Lear Fan in maiden
event at Newmarket in August; has plenty of improvement in him. *P. Cole.*

NONO ALGEA 3 ch.f. Nonoalco 131–Majan 67 (Brigadier Gerard 144) (1982 8s⁴   –
8.5v 1983 10s 12.5v 10f 10.8d 10fg) 40,000Y; first foal; dam, half-sister to Irish
Sweeps Derby winner Weavers' Hall, was placed over 1¾m from 2 starts at 3 yrs;
ran probably best race of 1983 when fifth of 18 behind Karkisiya in 65,000 francs
race at Saint-Cloud in April; soundly beaten over here in minor event at Warwick
and maiden race at Newmarket in October; formerly trained by G. Bonnaventure;
retained 14,000 gns Newmarket December Sales. *P. Mitchell.*

NONPAREIL (FR) 2 ch.f. Pharly 130–Norme (Dark Tiger) (1983 7fg² 6fg) Feb   **92 ?**
12; fair sort; fourth foal; half-sister to French 1½m winner Norlero (by
Caracolero); dam won over 1m in France; 25/1; put up a fine first effort in
22-runner maiden race at Newmarket in October, bowling along in lead until caught
near finish by stable-companion Travel Away; odds on, most disappointing tenth of
20 in similar event at Doncaster the following month; almost certainly needs further
than 6f, but ran poorly all the same. *B. Hanbury.*

NONSENSE 2 b. g. Stanford 121§–Becassine (El Gallo 122) (1983 5fg⁴ 6fg²) Apr 9; IR 31,000Y; half-brother to useful Irish sprinter Entre Fancy (by Entrechat) and useful Irish 2-y-o 5f and 6f winner Phils Fancy (by Irish Love); dam ran only at 2 yrs; beaten length by Bezara, staying on, in maiden race at Folkestone in October; better suited by 6f than 5f. *Sir Mark Prescott.*   **77**

NONSTOP 4 ch. g. Nonoalco 131–Fast Motion 86 (Midsummer Night II 117) (1982 8g 8f*(dis) 8f⁴ 8g 8fg 8.2g³ 8.2s* 8s 7d 1983 8.2fg² 8.2f³ 8g 7f) tall, rangy gelding; not the best of movers; stays 1m well; acts on any going; has shown a tendency to hang; occasionally blinkered; sold 6,400 gns Newmarket Autumn Sales. *J. Etherington.*   **66**

NON-WET 3 b. c. Sallust 134–Maggie's Pet 74 (Coronation Year 124) (1982 5d² 6v² 6g 1983 7d 7fg 6fg² 6g* 6fg 6f 6fg 5g) strong, good-bodied colt; made all in handicap at Lingfield in July; had stiffer tasks next 2 outings; promises to stay 7f; last of 18 when blinkered final start. *J. Ciechanowski.*   **77**

NOPHE (USA) 2 b. f. Super Concorde 128–Fiorita (Princequillo) (1983 5g* 5f⁴ 6fg² 7g 6g³ 6s⁴) Mar 6; $300,000Y; good-topped, attractive filly; has a markedly round action; half-sister to numerous winners, including Liberal (by Arts and Letters), a very useful winner at up to 9f; dam unraced half-sister to dam of Lianga; made winning debut in Acorn Stakes at Epsom in June, beating My Louie 1½ lengths; ran well in useful company afterwards, reaching frame in Queen Mary Stakes at Royal Ascot, Cherry Hinton Stakes at Newmarket (4 lengths second to Chapel Cottage), Moet and Chandon Zukunfts-Rennen at Baden-Baden (2¼ lengths behind Water Moccasin) and Firth of Clyde Stakes at Ayr; should stay 1m; seems to act on any going; genuine and consistent. *H. T. Jones.*   **95**

NORDAN CENTRE 3 b. f. Saulingo 122–Sapphire Red (Red Alert 127) (1982 5fg 5f 5s² 5g³ 5fg* 5f⁴ 5f 5g² 5g* 5fg³ 5s* 1983 5s 5g 5s 5f³ 5f² 5fg⁴ 5g 5g 5d) strong, good-bodied filly; only just stayed 5f; acted on any going; blinkered last 2 starts; dead. *M. Camacho.*   **69**

NO REPROACH 2 ch. f. Northfields–Our Reproach 103 (Our Babu 131) (1983 6f³ 6f³ 7g³) Mar 6; neat filly; half-sister to 2 minor winners; dam 2-y-o 5f winner; third in big fields at Newbury on first and third starts and in maiden race (running moderately) at Epsom in between; will be suited by 1m; possibly needs a galloping track. *B. Hills.*   **74**

NORFOLK FLIGHT 6 br. g. Blakeney 126–First Light 82 (Primera 131) (1982 10f 10d 10fg⁴ 10fg 12f 10d³ 10g³ 10fg 10f² 10s 10d 8s 1983 10g 10g 10g 10fg 10f 10g 10f⁴ 10f² 10f 12f³ 10f² 12d* 12d 10.2g 10fg²) strong gelding; quite a modest handicapper; won apprentice race at Brighton in September; suited by middle distances; acts on any going; suitable mount for an inexperienced rider; ran creditably when tried in blinkers once; often makes running; hasn't always been consistent or reliable; trained part of season by R. Carter. *M. Tompkins.*   **73**

NORFOLK PAGEANT 4 b. g. Welsh Pageant 132–Norfolk Light 86 (Blakeney 126) (1982 8fg 10fg 8fg 10.1fg 10g 12f 10.8fg 10g 1983 12fg) neat, attractive gelding; soundly beaten in varied company; usually blinkered; winner over hurdles. *B. Swift.*   **–**

NORFOLK REALM 5 b. h. Realm 129–Norfolk Light 86 (Blakeney 126) (1982 8fg² 8g⁴ 9fg² 8fg³ 7.6g* 8fg 8fg 8d³ 9g 8g² 7s 1983 7s* 7s² 8fg⁴ 8.3f 7g 7g² 7fg 7f) rangy horse; brilliantly ridden by L. Piggott when scoring narrowly at Wolverhampton in May; best at up to 1m; probably acts on any going; blinkered once; has run well when sweating up. *P. Makin.*   **71**

NORFOLK SERENADE 3 b. f. Blakeney 126–Brave Ballard (Derring-Do 131) (1982 6s⁴ 1983 11.7v* 10.6v² 12fg 11.1g⁴ 13.3g 14fg²) well-made filly; good walker; won maiden race at Bath in May; creditable second in handicaps at Haydock and Newmarket afterwards, finishing strongly when going down by 2 lengths to Statesmanship on latter course in October; will stay 2m; acts on a firm surface, but is very well suited by plenty of give in the ground. *J. Bethell.*   **83**

NORMIA 2 gr. f. Northfields–Mia Pola 120 (Relko 136) (1983 8g² 8d*) closely related to useful French filly Keep In Step (by Dance In Time), a winner at up to 9f, and smart American horse Regal Bearing (by Viceregal), successful at up to 1½m, and half-sister to 3 other winners; dam, half-sister to top French winners Grey Dawn II and Right Away, won 3 of her 4 starts at 2 yrs; all out to hold Ibadiyya by short neck in maiden race at Saint-Cloud in November; nose second to Reine Mathilde in newcomers event at same track the previous month; will stay 1¼m; a very useful three-year-old in the making. *F. Boutin, France.*   **104 p**

NORROY 6 ch. g. Northfields–Tzaritsa 113 (Young Emperor 133) (1982 8f³ 8g³ 8d **61**
8f² 8g³ 8fg² 8fg³ 8d 1983 8fg² 8f* 8f) robust gelding; led last strides when
winning handicap at Salisbury in July; suited by 1m and is worth another chance
over further; seems to act on any going; blinkered once in 1980; has been bandaged
in front; sold 1,350 gns Ascot October Sales. *D. Elsworth.*

NORTHAIR (USA) 3 b. c. Northern Dancer–Bold Melody (Bold Reason) (1982 **80**
6f² 6f² 7f³ 6g* 6d 1983 6d² 7d 6fg³ 6h² 6f⁴ 6d 6fg) quite attractive colt; placed in
2 handicaps at Newmarket and apprentice event at Nottingham; seems better at 6f
than 7f; yet to race on really soft going but acts on any other; ran moderately last 2
starts; sent to USA. *P. Walwyn.*

NORTH BRITON 4 b. c. Northfields–Juliette Marny 123 (Blakeney 126) (1982 **67**
11g 10fg⁴ 8f 7fg⁴ 1983 12s* 12f³ 13.3g 14.6f 12f* 12h² 12f² 12.3g⁴ 12g 12g 14d
12fg) neat, attractive colt; good walker; won handicaps at Lingfield in May and
Salisbury in July; suited by 1½m; acts on any going; blinkered last 3 starts in 1982.
C. Brittain.

NORTHERN ADVENTURE (USA) 3 b. c. Far North 120–Liz. Piet (Piet) **93**
(1982 6v* 7d* 7s* 1983 8.2v 10g 8g³ 10g) good-looking colt; looked a smart
performer in the making when unbeaten in his 3 races as a 2-y-o; showed first form
of 1983, but didn't run up to his best, when 1½ lengths third of 9 behind Tetron Bay
in £5,600 handicap at Ascot in October; respectable fifth of 15 to Folly Hill in
handicap at Sandown later in month; may be suited by further than 1¼m; acts on
heavy going; seems to have been difficult to train. *G. Harwood.*

NORTHERN BEAU 3 b. g. North Stoke 130–Beaume (Faraway Son 130) (1982 –
8d 8g 10s³ 1983 10v 12s⁴ 16v) lengthy gelding; not disgraced in handicaps first 2
outings; looks short of pace and should stay beyond 1½m; acts on soft going;
blinkered last 2 outings. *J. Hindley.*

NORTHERN COMFORT 2 b. f. Ile de Bourbon 133–Fardo 86 (Tudor Melody –
129) (1983 7f) Jan 7; half-sister to 7f winner Qualuz (by Royal Palace); dam won
over 7f; never-dangerous sixth of 11 in maiden race at Yarmouth in August. *M.
Stoute.*

NORTHERN CONQUEST (USA) 4 b. g. Far North 120–Easy Conquest –
(Royal Charger) (1982 8f 1983 10f 10.6fg) fair sort; has a round action; well
beaten in maiden races in the North. *L. Barratt.*

NORTHERN DYNAMITE (USA) 2 b. f. Northern Prospect–Royal Crescent –
(Third Brother) (1983 6fg) Apr 26; half-sister to 6 winners, including stakes-
placed Solid Performer (by Jim J.); dam unplaced 5 times; sire, son of Mr
Prospector, was very useful stakes winner at up to 7f; never-dangerous ninth of 22
in maiden race at Leicester in October. *P. Calver.*

NORTHERN HALO 2 ch. c. Northfields–Halomata 68 (Hallez 131) (1983 6d 7f –
7fg 7.6fg) Feb 1; 36,000Y; compact, well-made, quite attractive colt; third foal
(first to Northern Hemisphere time); dam, winner over 2m from only 4 starts, is
half-sister to high-class French stayer Matahawk; in rear in varied company. *B.
Swift.*

NORTHERN HILLS 2 ch. c. Raga Navarro 119–Affectionately 82 (Mark-Ye- **73**
Well) (1983 5v⁴ 5fg³ 5f² 5f 5f 5f 5f⁴ 5g³ 5d) Apr 11; 4,200F; compact colt;
half-brother to winners here and abroad, including useful 5f and 1m winner King
Oedipus (by Gala Performance); dam ran 4 times at 2 yrs; quite moderate; should
stay 6f; probably acts on any going; blinkered sixth, eighth and ninth starts. *W.
Haigh.*

NORTHERN LAKES 2 b. c. Northfields–Aureoletta 118 (Aureole 132) (1983 –
7fg) Feb 20; neat colt; fourth foal; half-brother to fairly useful 1¼m winner
Milloletta (by Mill Reef) and a winner in France; dam third in Oaks became most
disappointing; backward, always behind in 12-runner minor event at Doncaster in
October. *B. Hills.*

NORTHERN PROSPECT 2 ch. c. Music Boy 124–Legal Treasure 46 (Quorum **67**
126) (1983 5f 6g²) Mar 3; 2,700Y; neat colt; half-brother to 4 winners, 3 fairly
useful, including sprinter Single Gal (by Mansingh); dam plater; claimed 3,000
gns after finishing ¾-length second of 17 to Strawberry Fields in seller (favourite)
at Yarmouth in September; stays 6f; sold 1,600 gns Ascot November Sales. *D.
Garraton.*

NORTHERN SCRIPT (USA) 3 br.f. Arts and Letters–My Nord (Vent du   95
Nord) (1982 5f 8fg² 7s³ 1983 8s 8f* 8f² 8f 8fg⁴ 8g) strong, lengthy, quite
attractive filly; beat Page Blanche by 2½ lengths in £6,000 Vernons Fillies' Stakes
at York in June, travelling well throughout and quickening up nicely; in frame in
minor event at Salisbury and valuable handicap at Ascot afterwards, in latter
event keeping on at one pace to be 3¾ lengths fourth of 12 to Dinner Toast; will
be suited by 1¼m; acts on any going. *J. Tree.*

NORTHERN TEMPEST (USA) 2 ch.c. Northern Jove–Extreme Turbulence   120 ?
(Swaps) (1983 6fg 7f* 7f² 7g² 7.6g⁴ 8g*)
    The Gran Criterium at Milan, the only Group 1 pattern race for two-year-olds
run in Italy, is not a race that has attracted much attention in Britain until recently.
Before 1980 few of the winners were of note outside Italy, though there were
exceptions—Ribot, Molvedo, Tadolina, who went on to finish second in the 1965
Champion Stakes, Gay Lussac and Sirlad who were fancied contenders for the King
George VI and Queen Elizabeth Diamond Stakes in their day (the former finished
fifth to Brigadier Gerard and the latter was injured on the gallops a few days before
the race) and the high-class sprinter New Model. The years 1980 and 1981 again
produced winners who would also prove top-class as older horses, Glint of Gold and
Grease. Underlining the increasing awareness of British trainers of the useful
prizes within reach overseas, four English-trained horses challenged for the Gran
Criterium in 1983, perhaps the pick of them on form Executive Man who'd already
won in Italy. Northern Tempest had won once from four starts in England, gaining a
comfortable victory over Anything Else in a minor event at Sandown. After failing
by a short head to beat Quick Work in Ayr's Heronslea Stakes, he finished only
fourth behind Lucky Scott in the Burr Stakes at Lingfield where Nasr, another of
the challengers in Milan, was second. King of Clubs from Glint of Gold's stable
completed the quartet. The Italians had high hopes of victory, chiefly through
course-and-distance winner Malevic, a son of Hawaiian Sound. However, Malevic
finished last of ten runners and only Lord Brummel, a four-and-a-half-length third,
prevented a British clean sweep. Northern Tempest ran out a comfortable
two-and-a-half-length winner from King of Clubs with Nasr two lengths behind
Lord Brummel in fourth. Executive Man started slowly and ran a below-par fifth.
Given that Northern Tempest improved on his previous form he still appears some
way short of the best to race in Britain, Ireland or France, and unless he makes
more than normal progress he will be difficult to place in this country with his
penalty for winning a Group 1 race.
    Northern Tempest, a well-made, attractive colt, is by one of the lesser known
sons of Northern Dancer, Northern Jove, out of a stakes-placed mare. Northern
Jove was a stakes winner at sprint distances; his two sons to be placed in British

Milburn Stakes, Sandown—Northern Tempest accounts for Anything Else

pattern races, Indigo Jones and Pacific King, were both placed in sprints. Extreme Turbulence is the dam of three winners in Puerto Rico, including Princess Carimar, the champion two-year-old there in 1980, who later won a six-furlong stakes race in

		Northern Dancer (b 1961)	Nearctic
			Natalma
	Northern Jove (ro 1968)	Junonia (ro 1961)	Sun Again
Northern Tempest (USA)			Pavonia
(ch.c. Jan 16, 1981)	Extreme Turbulence (b 1969)	Swaps (ch 1952)	Khaled
			Iron Reward
		Ya Es Hora (b 1961)	Nashua
			La Sylphide

the States. Extreme Turbulence also won on her only start in Puerto Rico and is a half-sister to stakes winners in the USA, Argentina and Venezuela. The third dam, La Sylphide, was a half-sister to the 1953 Prix de Diane and Prix de l'Arc de Triomphe winner La Sorellina. Northern Tempest has raced only on a sound surface. He's no sprinter and the chances are he'll stay a shade further than a mile. *M. Stoute.*

NORTHERN TRIAL 3 ch.g. North Stoke 130–Bare Costs (Petition 130) (1982 5f 5g 7fg 1983 7d⁴ 6d 8f 7fg 11g 10f² 10f) rangy gelding; turns his front feet out; showed rather mixed form over a variety of trips in 1983, but ran very well first 2 starts over middle distances, finishing about 2 lengths fifth of 11 behind Dazari in Mecca Bookmakers' Scottish Derby at Ayr and 1½ lengths second of 9 behind Realistic in well-contested maiden race at Ascot in July; disappointed under an extremely lenient weight in Extel Stakes at Goodwood later in July and was subsequently gelded; acts on firm going and has run creditably on a soft surface; ran poorly in an apprentice handicap when blinkered fourth start; not to be relied upon. *P. Kelleway.*   ?

NORTHERN TRIP 3 ch.c. North Stoke 130–Tripoli 70 (Great Heron 127) (1982 7fg 8fg 7fg³ 1983 10s² 11.7s⁴ 11.7fg² 12g² 10g 12.2d³ 10g) tall, close-coupled, quite attractive colt; runner-up in handicaps at Salisbury and Windsor and in gentleman riders maiden race at Kempton, finding nothing off bridle on last-named course in September; suited by 1½m; seems to act on any going; disappointing; sold to NBA 8,200 gns Newmarket Autumn Sales. *G. Harwood.*   82

NORTHGATE LADY 2 b.f. Fordham 117–Pay Roll 94 (Burglar 128) (1983 5f 5g 6fg 7.2g) Apr 2; IR 2,000Y; big, angular filly; shows signs of stringhalt; third foal; half-sister to 3-y-o Burglars Walk (by Godswalk); dam won 8 times over 6f and 7f; 10 lengths tenth of 23 to New Generation in minor 6f event at Redcar in September, only sign of ability, including in a seller; stays 6f. *D. Plant.*   54

NORTHGATE LODGE 5 b.g. Warpath 113–Pall Nan 86 (Pall Mall 132) (1982 16fg 1983 12s 16fg 20.4g 16f) leggy gelding; no form in handicaps since winning maiden race as a 3-y-o; stays well; acts on a firm surface; has been bandaged; trained by J. Fort first 2 starts; pulled up lame final outing. *D. Plant.*   –

NORTHGATE VENTURE 2 gr.g. Habat 127–Helm 81 (Royal Palace 131) (1983 8g 10fg 10.2fg) Apr 7; 5,200Y; third foal; dam, lightly-raced winner over 1¼m, is half-sister to Bireme, Buoy and Fluke; well beaten, twice last, in big fields in the autumn; subsequently gelded. *D. Plant.*   –

NORTH KEY 3 ch.g. North Stoke 130–Pukekohe (Larkspur 128) (1982 7g 7fg 8.2fg 1983 9s 9v⁴ 11g 7d 15s) rather leggy, narrow gelding; little worthwhile form in varied company, including plating; needs further than 7f. *M. Naughton.*   –

NORTH LADY 3 b.f. Northfields–Larosterna (Busted 134) (1982 6g 7g 1983 12f 8.2f 8.2g) small filly; little worthwhile form in maiden races and handicaps; sold 4,000 gns Goffs November Sales. *P. Haslam.*   –

NORTHORPE 4 b.g. Mummy's Pet 125–Jaragua (Flaneur 109§) (1982 6g 7f³ 6g⁴ 6f* 6fg 6d⁴ 6g² 6fg* 6g 6g* 6g 6g³ 6g 6s 1983 6g 6s 6g² 6fg³ 7f 7fg 7fg* 8.2fg 7f³ 8fg 7g) big, rangy gelding; poor walker; won handicap at Redcar in August; appears not to stay 1m; ideally suited by top-of-the-ground; has won for an apprentice; sometimes sweats up; blinkered third to sixth starts; retained 9,400 gns Newmarket September Sales. *G. Huffer.*   80

NORTH PINE 2 b.f. Import 127–Miss Barbara 87 (Le Dieu d'Or 119) (1983 6fg 7fg 5g) June 7; fair sort; half-sister to 3 winners, notably top-class sprinter Lochnager (by Dumbarnie); dam stayed 7f; behind in autumn minor and maiden events. *J. Etherington.*   –

NORTH STAR SAM 2 ch.c. Busted 134–Sweet Reproach 94 (Relic) (1983 8g 8d) May 16; 7,200Y; big, workmanlike colt; half-brother to 2 winners, including 7f   77 winner Dunham Park (by Manacle); dam 2-y-o 6f and 1m winner; 12 lengths sixth of 14 to Corinth in £4,000 race at Newbury in October, second outing; will stay beyond 1m. *R. Akehurst.*

NORTH STOKE BOY 3 b.c. North Stoke 130–My Grace (Sahib 114) (1982 5.8f —
5fg 6g 7fg 1983 8s 8s 10v 10.1fg) lengthy colt; no worthwhile form; blinkered final start. *K. Cunningham-Brown.*

NORTH STREET 3 ch.c. Solinus 130–Lady North 103 (Northfields) (1982 5f4 —
5g² 5f* 7fg 1983 8g 7fg 8f 8fg 6fg) IR 18,000Y; big, strong, rangy ex-Irish colt; good walker; second foal; dam useful at up to 1½m in Ireland; easily won 4-runner maiden race at Mallow as a 2-y-o when trained by J. Bolger; well beaten here, including on final start (blinkered); promises to stay 1m; sold to Mrs N. Smith 1,250 gns Newmarket Autumn Sales. *J. Hindley.*

NORTHSUN (USA) 2 ch.c. Northfields–Dickies Rising Sun (Roi Dagobert 128)   **91** p
(1983 6f 7d*) Apr 24; $45,000Y; second foal; dam, winner in Norway, is half-sister to useful sprinters Walter Osborne and Eagle Boy; 20/1, successful in minor event at Naas in October by 2½ lengths from Realgo, leading inside final furlong and running on well (had been off course almost 4 months); should stay 1¼m; a very useful 3-y-o in the making. *K. Prendergast, Ireland.*

NORTH WEST 8 ch.g. Welsh Pageant 132–Heather Grove (Hethersett 134)   **49**
(1982 12d 15.5g* 15.5fg² 18f² 16fg 15.5f³ 14fg⁴ 16.5f 1983 15.5v³ 15.5f) tall, short-backed gelding; genuine and consistent staying handicapper at his best; seems to act on any going; used to wear bandages; goes well at Folkestone. *M. Masson.*

NORTON CROSS 5 gr.g. Realm 129–Zameen (Armistice 131) (1982 8f 1983 8v)   —
sturdy gelding; good mover; modest handicapper at his best on flat and a useful jumper; probably stays 1¼m; possibly needs some give in the ground; blinkered only start at 5 yrs; does best when ridden up with pace. *M. H. Easterby.*

NORTON PRINCESS 2 gr.f. Wolver Hollow 126–Princess Ayesha (Bold Lad,   **76**
Ire 133) (1983 6f³ 6g* 7fg 7f 8fg⁴ 8s 7d³ 7fg) Mar 17; 7,200Y; rather lightly-built, quite attractive filly; third foal; sister to 1982 5f winner Hollering; dam Irish 1½m winner; won maiden race at Ayr in July by 4 lengths from Dora's Rocket; beaten in nurseries subsequently, best effort 4½ lengths third of 16 to Great Western at York in October; possibly best at distances short of 1m; suited by some give in the ground; blinkered fifth and sixth outings. *M. H. Easterby.*

NORWICK (USA) 4 b.c. Far North 120–Shay Sheery (A Dragon Killer) (1982   **?**
8g 12fg 12f 12f 11g² 10.5fg² 14.6f4 12v⁴(dis) 1983 including 10s 12d 12f* 12s 10f 13d) smallish, well-made, good-looking colt; has a sharp action; didn't win in 1982 but ran well on a number of occasions, notably when fifth to Golden Fleece in Derby, second to Assert in Benson and Hedges Gold Cup at York and fourth to Touching Wood in St Leger at Doncaster; ran moderately both starts at 4 yrs in Europe, finishing ninth of 16 to Imyar in Prix Exbury at Saint-Cloud in March and tailed-off seventh of 8 to Diamond Shoal in John Porter Stakes at Newbury in April; subsequently sent to Canada and won first 2 outings there, including Grade 3 Niagara Stakes at Fort Erie in August by 3½ lengths from Jacksboro (set new track record); stays 1¾m; acts on any going but goes well on soft; does best when ridden up with pace; hung badly final start at 3 yrs; trained by G. Harwood first 2 starts; syndicated at $30,000 a share and will eventually stand at Beechwood Farm, Ontario. *P. England, Canada.*

NO SALE 4 b.c. Nonoalco 131–Salote 109 (Forli) (1982 10.1d 10.1fg 11.7f 10v   —
10.8s 1983 12d 11.7d 8g 8f 16g 10.1fg 10fg) poor maiden; sometimes blinkered. *R. Atkins.*

NOSEY 2 b.f. Nebbiolo 125–Little Cynthia 76 (Wolver Hollow 126) (1983 5v 5f*   **96**
6f* 5fg³ 5g* 6g²) Mar 11; IR 7,600Y; third foal; half-sister to Irish 3-y-o 13f winner Little Kelly (by Pitskelly) and Irish 1¾m winner Saint Cynthia (by Welsh Saint); dam won over 1m; had a good season and won maiden race at Bellewstown, minor event at Naas and nursery at the Curragh in the summer, giving weight to all but one of her 9 rivals when scoring by a head at the Curragh; 3 lengths second of 9 to Andress in valuable nursery at Phoenix Park in October; bred to stay 1m but her style of racing suggests she may prove best at sprint distances; acts on firm going. *K. Prendergast, Ireland.*

NO SHARING 2 ch.f. Young Generation 129–Sharondor 84 (Matador 131) (1983   —
5d 5fg 6s) May 2; tall, lightly-made, narrow filly; half-sister to several winners, including useful 1972 2-y-o Altiora (by Taj Dewan); dam 6f sprinter; no sign of ability in maiden and minor events; blinkered final outing; sold 1,700 gns Ascot November Sales. *H. Candy.*

NOSTER PUER (USA) 3 ch.g. Quid Pro Quo–Rose Cloud (Toulouse Lautrec)   **81**
(1982 7d³ 7g² 7fg 1983 10s³ 11v 11.5fg* 16f³ 11.7f*) rangy gelding; game winner
of maiden race at Sandown in June and handicap at Windsor in July; stays 2m, but
possibly better at shorter distances; seems to act on any going; usually sweats
up; pulls hard nowadays. *D. Elsworth.*

NO SWEAT 4 b.g. Ashmore 125–Phantasmagoria 65 (Le Haar 126) (1982 10s 12f
12f³ 12f³ 14f* 14fg* 12.8f* 1983 12fg) IR 3,000Y, resold IR 6,000Y; ex-Irish
gelding; fourth live foal; half-brother to a winner in Malaya; dam placed over 1½m;
won maiden race at Tramore and handicaps at Ballinrobe and Wexford at 3 yrs; well
beaten only outing in this country in minor event at Pontefract in August (needed
run); stays 1¾m and will probably get further; acts well on fast ground; has won for
an amateur; does best when ridden up with pace. *J. Old.*

NOT EASY 3 ch.f. Warpath 113–Virginia (Pirate King 129) (1982 NR 1983 10d   **48**
12fg⁴ 13.8g* 16d 15.8d 12f) big, workmanlike, rather sparely-made filly; half-sister
to 2 winners, including 1m and 9.4f winner Nun (by Amber Rama); dam
lightly-raced sister to very useful stayer Avast; plater; sold out of C. Thornton's
stable 2,700 gns after winning at Catterick in September; well beaten afterwards;
should stay 2m; showed signs of temperament final start. *D. Chapman.*

NOTHING BLUE (USA) 3 ch.c. Cyane–Rienza (Graustark) (1982 6f* 7.2f²   **94**
1983 8s³ 8f 8.2fg* 8fg 8g 8g) quite attractive colt; good walker and mover;
awarded race after going down by a neck to Royaber in handicap at Haydock in
August, although wasn't interfered with himself; ran moderately afterwards,
including in a gentleman riders race; suited by 1m and may well stay further; acts
on any going; blinkered last 2 outings. *H. T. Jones.*

NOT SO DEAR 4 ch.f. Dhaudevi 127–Dimione (Tompion) (1982 11g 10g 10g   **—**
11.5g² 11g* 12g* 11g 10.5g 1983 10g 8fg 6fg 10d 15.5fg² 16d) big, workmanlike
ex-French filly; has stringhalt; has a round action; fourth foal; dam won twice over
9f in France at 3 yrs; won maiden race and handicap in French Provinces at 3 yrs;
plater over here; stays well; effective with and without blinkers. *A. Davison.*

NOTTA POPSI 2 ch.g. Nearly A Hand 115–Swaynes Lady 76 (St Alphage 119)   **—**
(1983 6d 7g) May 22; 1,450Y; second foal; half-brother to 1982 2-y-o 6f winner
Leadenhall Lad (by Comedy Star); dam 2-y-o 5f winner; well beaten in modest
company at Lingfield in October. *M. Haynes.*

NOT TO WORRY (USA) 3 b.f. Stevward–Lovely Barbizon (Barbizon) (1982   **—**
7g 6d 1983 10g 15f² 14.6f 12d 9fg⁴ 10fg) lengthy filly; staying maiden; second at
Edinburgh, best effort; blinkered fourth start. *B. Hanbury.*

NOUNOU 3 b.f. Nonoalco 131–Dame Foolish 121 (Silly Season 127) (1982 NR   **—**
1983 8f 8g) third foal; half-sister to modest sprinter Strapless (by Bustino); dam at
her best at 2 yrs when second in Cheveley Park Stakes; little worthwhile form at
Yarmouth (trained by H. Cecil) and Edinburgh; sold to BBA 12,500 gns Newmarket
Autumn Sales. *E. Weymes.*

NOUREEZ 2 b.c. He Loves Me 120–Noureen (Astec 128) (1983 7f 7fg 8d 7f) Apr   **—**
21; well-made colt; half-brother to 2 winners, including very useful 5f to 1m winner
Nasseem (by Zeddaan); dam unraced half-sister to very smart Tajubena, a winner
at up to 1½m; poor form in maiden and minor events; blinkered final outing. *F. J.
Houghton.*

NOURIYYA 3 b.f. North Stoke 130–Noureen (Astec 128) (1982 5fg 5fg 6fg 7g   **—**
8.2s 1983 8s 7fg 10f) small, plain, fair sort; should stay 1¼m; acts on a firm surface;
blinkered last 2 starts, starting slowly first occasion; sold 50,000 gns Newmarket
December Sales. *F. J. Houghton.*

NO-U-TURN 5 b.g. Nonoalco 131–Raffmarie 78 (Raffingora 130) (1982 10.2g   **79**
12fg² 9fg* 12f² 10fg³ 8g³ 10fg 8g 10fg⁴ 9g 10g² 12fg³ 10d 1983 10v 8g 8fg* 12g*
11.7f³ 10g² 12f 10fg* 11.7fg³ 12f² 10g*) attractive, well-made gelding; enjoyed an
excellent season and won amateur riders race at Warwick and handicaps at Lingfield
(2) and Goodwood; beat Steel Kid very smoothly by 3 lengths on last-named in
September; effective at 1m and stays 1½m; acts on any going. *S. Mellor.*

NOVELLO 2 b.c. Double Form 130–Roda Haxan 67 (Huntercombe 133) (1983   **113**
5s* 5d³ 6fg³ 6g⁴ 6fg 7s⁴) Feb 2; 45,000Y; strong, good sort; second foal; dam
poor sister to high-class Pyjama Hunt; had his sights raised considerably after
winning maiden race at Newmarket in April by 6 lengths on first outing, and
although running well failed to win again, finishing third in Coventry Stakes at Royal
Ascot, fourth in BonusPrint Sirenia Stakes at Kempton, fifth in William Hill Middle
Park Stakes at Newmarket, and fourth, fading in closing stages, in Criterium de
Maisons-Laffitte; probably best at 6f; seems to act on any going; genuine and
consistent. *J. Winter.*

R. E. A. Bott (Wigmore St) Ltd's "Novello"

NOVEMBER EVENING 2 gr.f. Martinmas 128–Sovereign Sunset 65 **39**
(Sovereign Path 125) (1983 5s 5v 5f⁴ 6fg 7f 7g) May 14; IR 4,000F, 5,000Y;
lightly-made, sharp sort; fifth foal; dam temperamental maiden; bad plater; acts
on firm going. *Mrs J. Reavey.*

NOVEMBER NIGHT 2 b.g. Midsummer Night II 117–Edith de Firfol (Noble **53**
Descent) (1983 5s 5v 5g) May 8; sparely-made gelding; first foal; dam placed from
1m to 1¼m in French Provinces; poor maiden; not raced after May; became very
upset in stalls second outing; sold 900 gns Doncaster November Sales. *K. Stone.*

NOVEMBER SUNSHINE 2 b.c. Gold Form 108–Lady Cortina 80 (Cortachy **64**
107) (1983 5f 6fg) May 15; 600Y; big, quite useful-looking colt; brother to two
2-y-o winners and half-brother to a winner; dam won at up to 1m; little worthwhile
form in minor event at Beverley in August and valuable seller at Doncaster in
September. *D. Garraton.*

NOW AND AGAIN (USA) 3 b.c. Ack Ack–My Violet (Warfare) (1982 6f* 7g* **107**
8s³ 1983 8f* 11.1g 8g³) tall, quite attractive colt; excellent mover; somewhat
immature as a 2-y-o, but was useful nevertheless; made a successful
reappearance in minor event at Newcastle in August, beating sole opponent
Lobkowiez easily by 2½ lengths; ran better subsequent race when 1¼ lengths
third of 6 to Spanish Place in quite well-contested minor event at Goodwood in
September; stays 1m (never really a threat over 11f); acts on firm going and is
possibly unsuited by soft; sent to Kuwait. *H. Cecil.*

598

NUDGE NUDGE 3 br. g. Windjammer (USA)–Veneziana 91 (Tiger 125) (1982 6d — 6g 7d 1983 8s) neat, strong gelding; appeared to run well when less than 4 lengths sixth of 10 to Rock's Gate in minor event at Wolverhampton in April; not seen out again; probably stays 1m. *S. Mellor.*

NUI NUI 2 b. or br. f. Vitiges 132–Liangold (Rheingold 137) (1983 5d 6g 8.2f* 8.2g **61** 7.2s) Mar 18; leggy filly; second foal; half-sister to a winning plater; dam ran once at 2 yrs in France; showed ability only when winning 11-runner seller at Haydock (bought in 1,800 gns) in September; will stay 1¼m; possibly requires a firm surface. *J. Etherington.*

NUMISMATIST 4 b. g. Vitiges 132–Mile By Mile 92 (Milesian 125) (1982 7.6f 8fg **87** 8d 8f³ 8fg⁴ 9g 7fg⁴ 10fg² 11.7s 1983 10.2d 8s 7s³ 7.6g² 6h* 6f* 6f³ 6fg* 7fg 6s³ 6g³ 6g³) lengthy gelding; showed much improved form at 4 yrs, winning handicaps at Chepstow and Nottingham in July and at Lingfield in August; also ran very well to be third in William Hill Stewards' Cup at Goodwood (to Autumn Sunset) and Ladbrokes (Ayr) Gold Cup (narrowly beaten behind Polly's Brother); best at up to 7f; acts on any going but goes very well on fast ground; blinkered twice in 1982; wears a tongue strap; game. *J. Bosley.*

NUNSWALK 6 ch. m. The Parson 119–Vital Error 105 (Javelot 124) (1982 NR — 1983 17f 13.1h) middle-distance plater; has worn blinkers and is possibly ungenuine. *M. Bradley.*

NUNSWOOD 3 ch. c. Solinus 130–Cafe Au Lait 98 (Espresso 122) (1982 5g 7fg **81** 8g 1983 10.1fg² 12fg² 11f⁴ 11.7h² 12f² 12d²) good-topped colt; runner-up in minor and maiden races (one of them an apprentice event), and in a handicap; stays 1½m; yet to race on really soft going, but acts on any other. *P. Cole.*

NUTTY SLACK 5 gr. g. Saritamer 130–Mary Mullen 88 (Lorenzaccio 130) (1982 — NR 1983 17.1g 12fg 16.5f) poor handicapper; has worn blinkers. *G. Thorner.*

NYPUS 3 b. c. Lypheor 119–Lady Kyth (Kythnos 126) (1982 6f 7fg 6s 7g⁴ 7g 10g **62** 1983 10.5v 10d 8s⁴ 10s 7v 10.1fg³ 12f*) smallish colt; sold to R. Carter 4,200 gns after winning selling handicap at Pontefract in July very easily indeed; suited by 1½m and firm going; blinkered fifth start. *D. Wilson.*

O

OAKAPPLE 4 ch. f. Connaught 130–Syringa 98 (Set Fair 129) (1982 8d³ 12fg **74** 10d* 11s² 14g 1983 12fg⁴ 12v⁴ 12fg 11f² 11g² 12s* 12fg) strong filly; won handicap at Hamilton in October; stays 1½m; acts on a firm surface but is ideally suited by some give in the ground; one paced. *J. W. Watts.*

OAK POOL 2 ro. f. Mandrake Major 112–Silver Teal 79 (Meldrum 112) (1983 5s **64** 5f 5f³ 5f 5f) Apr 15; very small filly; half-sister to fairly useful 1981 2-y-o 6f winner Strath of Orchy (by Lochnager); dam won over 5f and 1½m; plating-class maiden; will stay 6f; acts on firm going. *N. Tinkler.*

OAK RIDGE (FR) 3 b. c. Shirley Heights 130–Oak Hill 119 (Sheshoon 132) (1982 **69** NR 1983 12s⁴ 14f) 165,000Y; robust, good sort; second reported foal; half-brother to very useful French 1½m winner Oak Dancer (by Green Dancer); dam won Criterium des Pouliches; showed some promise when fourth behind Amber Heights in maiden race at Doncaster in May; favourite when towards rear in similar race at Yarmouth in August on only other start; sold 3,600 gns Goffs November Sales. *G. Harwood.*

OAK RUN 3 br. g. Wolfsbane 91–Precious Love (Precipice Wood 123) (1982 5g 7d — 1983 8v 10.8g 9fg 13.8f) small, unimpressive gelding; of little account. *J. Smith.*

OAKWOOD PARK 2 b. c. Balidar 133–Windy Sea 105 (Sea Hawk II 131) (1983 **88** 6g 6g³ 6g 6fg³) Mar 28; 16,500Y; big, well-made colt; third foal, half-brother to 3-y-o Sharp Sea (by Sharpen Up), a fairly useful 6f and 1m winner at 2 yrs; dam won over 7f and 1¼m; placed in big fields of maidens at Newmarket in August and October; will stay 7f; acts on a firm surface; should win a race. *B. Hobbs.*

OBADIAH 4 b. or br. c. Joshua 129–Ripatip 68 (Indigenous 121) (1982 8g 10fg **61** 11.5fg 1983 12d² 10g² 12d² 12fg⁴) big, rangy colt; bad mover; suited by 1½m and will get further; acts on a firm and a soft surface. *H. Westbrook.*

OBSERVATORY HILL (USA) 3 ch. c. Vaguely Noble 140–Extra Place (Round **96** Table) (1982 NR 1983 8s⁴ 9s² 8s³ 10v* 12v⁴ 11d) $70,000Y; half-brother to numerous winners, including stakes winners Bold Place (by Bold Bidder), Out To Lunch (by Hawaii) and Card Table (also by Bold Bidder); dam won over 6f and 7f; in frame 3 times at Phoenix Park before beating Ard Boyne by 8 lengths in 20-runner maiden race at Navan in May; beaten nearly 10 lengths when fourth of 6 behind Carlingford Castle in Gallinule Stakes at the Curragh later in month and was off course almost 5 months afterwards; should stay 1½m; has raced only on soft ground. *M. O'Toole, Ireland.*

OCHIL HILLS STAR 10 b.g. Chebs Lad 120–Turkish Maid 58 (Menelek 114) (1982 8s 11s 11fg 8fg* 8g 8f 7g 1983 8.2s 7fg 8g 9d 7f⁴ 8f) plater; stays 1¼m; acts on any going; has been tried in blinkers; good mount for an inexperienced rider. *Mrs A. Bell.*

OCTANORM 2 ch.f. Remainder Man 126§–No Man's Land (Salvo 129) (1983 5.8f 7fg 8.2f 7fg 7.2s 10d) May 15; 1,000Y; small filly; dam poor half-sister to very useful middle-distance stayer No Bombs; quite a moderate plater; sold NBA 1,100 gns Newmarket Autumn Sales. *R. Hannon.*   51

OCTAVIA GIRL 3 b.f. Octavo 115–Jane Shaw (Galivanter 131) (1982 6fg* 6fg³ 7fg³ 8g 8g 1983 8v² 8g 10v 12fg 8fg 8f 10g 8g 8g) good-quartered filly; went down by 1½ lengths to Sul-El-Ah after quickening into lead below distance in 9-runner BonusPrint Masaka Stakes at Kempton in April; in rear all subsequent starts, but usually had stiff tasks (including in 1000 Guineas and Ribblesdale Stakes); stayed 1m; probably acted on any going; blinkered on 3 of last 4 outings; sold for stud 31,000 gns Ascot December Sales. *D. Elsworth.*   104

ODARD 3 gr.g. Roan Rocket 128–Sparkling Jewel (Faberge II 121) (1982 NR 1983 12f) 8,400Y; half-brother to useful 6f to 9f winner Champagne Willie (by The Brianstan) and a winning hurdler; dam of little account; 33/1 when remote tenth of 15 finishers in maiden race at Redcar in June; sold 1,000 gns Doncaster October Sales. *M. Camacho.*   —

ODILE 2 b.f. Green Dancer 132–Water Frolic 92 (Sir Ivor 135) (1983 5f) Feb 16; neat filly; second foal; dam, daughter of 1,000 Guineas winner Waterloo, stayed 1¼m; in need of race, out of first 9 of 16 in maiden event at Beverley in August; bred to need 7f+; sold 17,000 gns Newmarket Autumn Sales. *E. Weymes.*   —

OFF THE CUFF 3 b.c. The Brianstan 128–Mystic Halo (Aureole 132) (1982 5g² 5fg³ 6fg 6g 5fg⁴ 1983 5s³ 6fg) fair sort; in frame in maiden and minor events; form only at 5f; seems to act on any going; retained 8,200 gns Ascot 2nd June Sales after first outing but resold only 725 gns at same venue in November. *I. Walker.*   64

OFF THE SEAM 2 b.f. Swing Easy 126–Rosalia (Tower Walk 130) (1983 5fg 5f) Mar 7; 360Y; well-grown, leggy filly; first foal; dam never ran; behind in sellers; dead. *M. W. Easterby.*   —

OFF YOUR MARK 3 ch.c. On Your Mark 125–Sparkling Diamond (Thirteen of Diamonds 126) (1982 5g⁴ 5f³ 6d 1983 7d 6d 6g³ 6f* 5f 6g⁴ 6f² 6f² 5f 5.6fg 5g) lightly-made colt; made all in apprentice maiden race at Pontefract in June; suited by 6f; acts on firm going; blinkered last 2 starts (tended to hang left on first occasion) *J. McNaughton.*   61

OH MISS BIGMORE 2 b.f. Mr Bigmore 123–Oh Well 61 (Sahib 114) (1983 5v 5d³ 5v 6fg 7g³) Mar 1; smallish, useful-looking filly; half-sister to 2 winners, including fair 1982 2-y-o 5f winner Jolie Courtisane (by Owen Dudley); dam stayed 1m; third in 5-runner maiden race at Newbury in April and 7-runner seller at Wolverhampton in July; slowly away first and third outings and wore blinkers on last 2. *P. Cundell.*   48

O. I. OYSTON 7 b.g. Martinmas 128–Last Lap 75 (Immortality) (1982 8g* 7.2s 7.6g 8g 8d 7.6fg 13g 8f⁴ 7.6d* 8f 8fg 7.2s 8.2s⁴ 7d³ 7g* 7d² 8s* 1983 8d 7d* 8v* 8v 8s 8g 8fg 7f 7.6fg³ 8.2f 7.6g 7g 10s 8fg 8.2s 7fg* 7g 8fg) big gelding; won handicaps at Catterick in March (apprentices), Newcastle in April and Doncaster in October; well beaten most other starts; stays 9f; acts on any going, but is very well suited by some give underfoot; has worn blinkers but is better without; has won for an apprentice; suited by front-running tactics, but has occasionally gone too fast for his own good; goes particularly well on turning tracks; tough. *J. Berry.*   83

OKLAHOMA CITY 4 b. or br.g. Tachypous 128–Exeat (Quartette 106) (1982 6f⁴ 1983 8fg 8d 8f) well beaten in varied company; has been tried in blinkers. *R. Simpson.*   —

OKLAHOMA KID 2 gr.c. Miami Springs 121–Tarpon Springs (Grey Sovereign 128§) (1983 6f 6g 7.6fg) Apr 24; IR 6,800Y; big, rangy colt; half-brother to several winners, including fair 1979 2-y-o winner I'm Grand (by Martinmas); dam closely related to No Mercy; little form in maiden events late July onwards; looks the type to do better in time. *E. Eldin.*   —

Prix Royal-Oak, Longchamp—the visitors Old Country, Band and Another Sam dominate proceedings

OLD COUNTRY 4 b.c. Quiet Fling 124–Little Miss 92 (Aggressor 130) (1982 **122** 12fg* 12v* 12f³ 1983 12d⁴ 12d³ 12f 15.5f*)

The Prix Royal-Oak, the French equivalent of the St Leger, has been open to four-year-olds and upwards since 1979. The race attracted only two older horses, neither of them outstanding, for its first running with changed conditions but subsequent runnings have attracted good-class representatives of the older stayers, Ardross and Gold River being notable examples. Ardross became the first

Mrs O. Abegg's "Old Country"

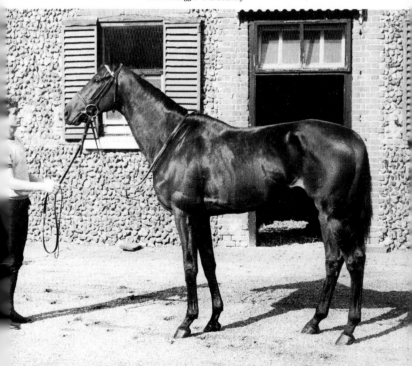

older horse to win, beating Proustille and Gold River in 1981, and four-year-old Old Country followed in his footsteps in 1983. Old Country was one of a four-strong British-trained challenge for the Royal-Oak which also comprised the six-year-old Another Sam (runner-up in the Jockey Club Cup), the four-year-old Mountain Lodge (winner of the Irish St Leger, opened for the first time to four-year-olds and upwards in 1983) and the three-year-old Band (runner-up to Mountain Lodge at the Curragh). Old Country had given us the overwhelming impression in a short season as a three-year-old that he would be a better proposition at a mile and three quarters than at a mile and a half. His running in the Jockey Club Stakes in April and the Coronation Cup in June strongly confirmed that impression: he stayed on very well when fourth to Electric at Newmarket and when third to Be My Native at Epsom, beaten about two lengths by the winner on each occasion. Old Country's reputation suffered set-backs after Epsom: he ran moderately in the Hardwicke Stakes at Royal Ascot and, after being off the course for three and a half months, was withdrawn at the start after playing up badly before the Jockey Club Cup. Old Country started at 27/1 for the Prix Royal-Oak. Always close up, he quickened clear in impressive style rounding the home turn and ran on strongly to hold off the strong-finishing Band and Another Sam by a neck and a length; Band had a desperately unlucky run and must have made up all of five lengths on the winner in the last two furlongs.

		Nijinsky	Northern Dancer
	Quiet Fling	(b 1967)	Flaming Page
	(b 1972)	Peace	Klairon
Old Country		(ch 1966)	Sun Rose
(b.c. 1979)		Aggressor	Combat
	Little Miss	(b 1955)	Phaetonia
	(b 1963)	Violetta III	Pinza
		(b 1958)	Urshalim

Old Country is a tall colt, and a good mover in all his paces with a long, sweeping action. Extensive details of his pedigree appeared in *Racehorses of 1982*. He is a half-brother to several minor winners on the flat, all of which were successful at a mile and a half. Old Country's sire Quiet Fling was a good-class horse over a distance of ground and his dam Little Miss, a half-sister to the dam of Teenoso, won at up to a mile and a half. Old Country stays well and acts on any going. He sometimes sweats up. *L. Cumani.*

OLD DOMINION (USA) 6 b.g. In Reality–Virginia Green 83 (Nashua) (1982 6d 6fg³ 6fg⁴ 6fg² 6g 6f² 5.8f* 6fg* 6f² 6g 5fg² 6g⁴ 6g 1983 6s³ 6g 5v 6g 6g 6g⁴ 7f³ 6fg* 6fg² 6fg 7d* 6.5g* 6fg 6d³ 6fg²) strong, good sort; good mover; fairly useful performer; won handicaps at Pontefract and Brighton and gentlemen riders event at Evry; trotted up from Milk Heart on last-named in September; stays 7f; acts on any going; suitable mount for an inexperienced rider; tough and genuine. *I. Balding.* **96**

OLD HUBERT 2 ch.g. Gulf Pearl 117–Wise Counsel (Counsel 118) (1983 7g 6fg) Apr 19; IR 5,400Y; workmanlike gelding; half-brother to several winners, including fair 1976 2-y-o 5f performer Karella (by Jukebox); dam plating-class half-sister to top 1963 2-y-o Talahasse; apprentice ridden, little worthwhile form in minor events at Newmarket in July and Nottingham in September. *A. Bailey.* **–**

OLD MACDONALD 5 ch.g. Scottish Rifle 127–Persian Belle 77 (Darius 129) (1982 NR 1983 22.2f⁴ 21f 16g) half-brother to a winner abroad; dam 2-y-o 5f winner; winning hurdler; showed first form on flat when under 10 lengths fourth of 9 to Sandalay in Queen Alexandra Stakes at Royal Ascot; tailed off in Goodwood Cup in July on next start; stays well. *D. Fitzgerald, Ireland.* **–**

OLD ROWLEY 5 b.h. Copte–Cennen-Olive (Wolver Hollow 126) (1982 12d 12g³ 12f 15.5f 1983 12s⁴ 14s 12.2fg) narrow horse; poor handicapper; stays 1½m; acts on soft going; trained part of season by Mrs J. Pitman. *D. Arbuthnot.* **–**

OLD STAGER (USA) 5 b.g. Forli–Queen of the Stage (Bold Ruler) (1982 NR 1983 8d 8fg 12f 12fg) tall, narrow gelding; no form in varied company. *D. Grissell.* **–**

OLIVIAN 2 ch.f. Hotfoot 126–Sandray's Palace (Royal Palace 131) (1983 8fg³) Apr 20; rather dipped-backed filly; second foal; sister to 13f winner Sandifoot; dam showed no ability; 3 lengths third of 12 to Raami in maiden race at Redcar in October; will be suited by 1¼m+; likely to improve. *J. W. Watts.* **79 p**

OLYMPIC CARNIVAL (USA) 4 b.c. Greek Answer–Streamer (Jet Jewel) (1982 6f 6fg 1983 5.3f³) quite well-made colt; stays 6f; acts on firm going; has been taken down early. *P. Butler.* **49**

OLYMPIC CHARM 3 ch.c. Filiberto 123–Pink Goddess (Yellow God 129) (1982   **87**
5g³ 5f* 5fg⁴ 6fg² 7f² 7f³ 6f 7g 6fg 6v³ 1983 10v* 7v 10.2s² 12f*) big, lengthy,
workmanlike colt; successful in handicaps at Ayr in March and Thirsk in June,
quickening up to beat Halyard by 1½ lengths in a slowly-run affair on latter course;
suited by middle distances; acts on any going; ran very wide on bend at Catterick
once as a 2-y-o; apprentice ridden in 1983. *D. Smith.*

OMAR MUKHTAR 2 b.c. Faraway Times 123–X-Data 93 (On Your Mark 125)   **86 p**
(1983 6.3f 6g*) June 8; 4,500Y; first foal; dam won over 5f and 6f; landed a gamble
when leading close home to account for Flight Plan by a head in maiden race at Naas
in November (had been off course over 3 months); will stay 7f. *K. Prendergast,
Ireland.*

OMINOUS 3 ch.f. Dominion 123–Safety Measure 68 (Home Guard 129) (1982 5g   **84**
5f³ 5g² 5f⁴ 7d² 7fg⁴ 7g* 7g³ 1983 8s 10.2v 10d* 10g² 7fg 8f 10f⁴ 10d) tall, quite
attractive filly; returned to form in handicap at Epsom in June, being sent off in
front for first time as a 3-y-o and just lasting home from fast-finishing Kondair; ran
creditably next time but then rather lost her form again; suited by 1¼m; seems to
act on any going but is possibly best with a little give in the ground; sold 18,000 gns
Newmarket December Sales. *R. Smyth.*

ONAIZAH (USA) 3 b. or br.f. Bold Bidder–Forest Friend (Linacre 133) (1982   **103**
6fg 6s* 1983 7.3v 7.2g² 8f 7f² 10h* 10s² 8fg* 8d⁴) compact filly; beat Thessaloniki
easily by 5 lengths in 5-runner minor event at Chepstow in August and
Remembering decisively by 1½ lengths in 7-runner Marlborough House Stakes at
Ascot in October; in frame most other starts, notably when under a length fourth to
Lina Cavalieri in Premio Bagutta at Milan later in October; stays 1¼m; acts on any
going; tends to flash her tail under pressure. *H. T. Jones.*

ONCE BITTEN 4 b.f. Brave Invader–Rathcolman (Royal Buck) (1982 NR 1983   **–**
10g 10.8g⁴) third foal; dam pulled up in a hurdle race; well-beaten fourth of 7 in
seller at Warwick in July. *O. O'Neill.*

ONE DEGREE 4 b.f. Crooner 119–Rhythm 64 (Bleep-Bleep 134) (1982 8f 7fg   **76**
8f³ 8g² 8.3g 7fg 7.2f² 7g 1983 7s 7s 6g* 6fg 5f 6f 7f² 7fg 6d⁴ 7.3g 6g) small,
strong, sturdy non-thoroughbred filly; beat Piencourt by ½ length in handicap at
Epsom in June; stays 1m; seems to act on any going but is ideally suited by a sound
surface; has run well for an apprentice; blinkered final start; game. *A. Turnell.*

ON EDGE 8 gr.g. Sharp Edge 123–The Country Lane 90 (Red God 128§) (1982   **88**
8d 8fg³ 8g 8f 8f² 8f³ 8.5fg 8fg³ 8.2fg² 8fg² 1983 9v 8g 8f³ 8f³ 8fg 8.2fg* 8.3fg³

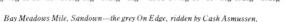

*Bay Meadows Mile, Sandown—the grey On Edge, ridden by Cash Asmussen,
holds the strong challenge of Gamblers Dream; the Americans won the
annual USA versus UK Jockey Challenge*

9fg³ 8g⁴ 8fg 8fg 8.2s 8g*) small, lengthy gelding; fair handicapper; made all to beat Barooq 2 lengths at Windsor in August and Gamblers Dream a short head at Sandown in October; stays 9f; suited by top-of-the-ground; blinkered once at 2 yrs; suitable mount for a claimer. *J. Spearing.*

ONE FOUR TODAY 2 b.c. Dominion 123–School Road 88 (Great Nephew 126) (1983 8f) Apr 27; 1,700Y; big, strong colt; second foal; dam, sister to smart miler Saher, ran only at 4 yrs when winner over 6f and 7f; last of 23 in maiden auction event at Redcar in September; dead. *Hbt Jones.* —

ONE O'CLOCK JUMP 3 b. or br.c. Hotfoot 126–Chiltern Red (Red God 128§) (1982 6fg 7g 7.6v² 7g³ 6g 1983 8s* 7s² 7d 7fg 8fg 8f² 8s³ 9d 8g* 8fg) strong, well-made, attractive colt; good walker; won maiden event at Doncaster in March and handicap at Sandown in October, being produced fairly late on to beat Spanish Bold by a length on latter occasion; stays 1m well; acts on any going, although scratched down to start and didn't look entirely at ease on firm on sixth outing; inconsistent; sold to H. Wharton 10,500 gns Doncaster November Sales. *F. Durr.* 95

ONESSILOS 3 ch.c. Saint Paul 106–Turnbeam (Hornbeam 130) (1982 6g 7f⁴ 8s 1983 7s 10v⁴ 10fg* 11fg3 12f⁴ 10d 10d) fair sort; won handicap at Leicester in June; stays 11f; probably acts on any going; sold to M. Masson 9,200 gns Newmarket Autumn Sales. *J. Dunlop.* 68

ONE WAY STREET 2 b.f. Habitat 134–Guillotina 118 (Busted 134) (1983 6fg) Apr 13; sister to a disappointing animal and useful 1977 2-y-o 7f winner Shorthouse, and half-sister to a winner; dam smart middle-distance stayer; 33/1, slow-starting twelfth of 15 behind odds-on stable-companion Athenia in maiden race at Doncaster in October. *H. Cecil.* —

ONLY A POUND 3 ch.c. Sharpen Up 127–Double Lock 104 (Home Guard 129) (1982 8g 10s² 1983 10d² 10fg* 9fg* 8f* 10fg) rangy colt; not seen out until September but did well, winning minor events at Brighton, Newcastle and Redcar; led 2f out and beat Perfect Host impressively by 2 lengths (value 5) on last-named; had every chance when sixth of 19 to Bahoor in valuable handicap at Newmarket on final outing; stays 1¼m; acts on any going. *J. Hindley.* 93

ON MANOEUVRES 3 br.f. Mandrake Major 122–Wandering On (Klairon 131) (1982 5f² 5fg⁴ 1983 7g³ 6s 8f 7.6g 7f* 7g) lengthy filly; not a good walker; dropped in class when decisively winning seller at Beverley in August (bought in 3,000 gns); never in race in non-seller only subsequent start; stays 1m; acts on firm going; sold 2,800 gns Doncaster September Sales. *Miss S. Hall.* 63

ON OATH 2 b.c. Monsanto 121–Cry of Truth 129 (Town Crier 119) (1983 6f³ 6fg* 6fg²) Mar 13; 40,000Y; compact, deep-girthed colt; good mover; third foal; half-brother to useful sprinter Integrity (by Reform) and 5f winner Truth Will Out (by Blakeney); dam best 2-y-o filly of 1974; won 7-runner maiden race at Haydock in August by ¾ length from Speedwell; beaten 3 lengths in minor event at Goodwood later in the month; a taking individual likely to win more races. *B. Hobbs.* 99

ONSLOW (USA) 3 b.c. Banquet Table–Hi Tam (Bold Tactics) (1982 7f³ 8s* 8g⁴ 1983 9d² 12v⁴ 9fg 10f 10s* 9fg) neat, quite attractive colt; good mover; put up a very useful performance under 9-7 when beating Vintage Toll by 5 lengths in £4,300 handicap at Ayr in September; had run very well when neck second of 8 to Zoffany in Gerry Feilden Memorial Stakes at Newmarket and been far from disgraced on other occasions; possibly stays 1½m, but best form at shorter distances; has run creditably on firm going but is much better with plenty of give in the ground. *J. Dunlop.* 109

ON STAGE 3 b.c. Comedy Star 121–Last Case 109 (Firestreak 125) (1982 6fg² 6g* 6d* 6f² 7fg* 6f* 6fg² 7fg³ 6g* 1983 6g* 5g* 6v⁴ 6v* 5f³ 6fg³ 7.3f 6g³ 7g²) 123
The decision to run Habibti in the William Hill July Cup instead of continuing at a mile was to bring to light one of the outstanding sprinters of recent years; at the same time it severely damaged the prospects of horses of the calibre of On Stage winning the remaining top races. Before Habibti arrived on the scene On Stage had had a very successful time, winning three of his five races during the season. His first defeat during that period came in the Duke of York Stakes behind Vorvados, when for the only time in his career he ran without blinkers, and was below par as a result. On Stage is a thoroughly genuine and consistent performer but he does require blinkers to show to advantage. On Stage won the Thirsk Hall Stakes on his reappearance, when he had the opposition struggling soon after halfway, finishing a length and a half ahead of Hello Cuddles. On his fourth outing he won another race

Palace House Stakes, Newmarket—On Stage is not extended to account for Fearless Lad

in the North, the Sandy Lane Stakes on very heavy ground at Haydock, gaining a ten-length victory over five rivals headed by Henry's Secret. His best run during this period came in the Palace House Stakes at Newmarket on his first attempt at the minimum trip. The weights were very much in his favour—he met runner-up Fearless Lad on terms 12 lb better than weight-for-age—and he was in command at halfway; he had only to be pushed out up the hill to beat Fearless Lad most decisively by two and a half lengths, with Krayyan third.

On Stage was at five furlongs again in the King's Stand Stakes at Royal Ascot, and he started favourite ahead of Fearless Lad, who in the meantime had won the Temple Stakes at Sandown. The field also included Soba, who had been running below her best, Chellaston Park, runner-up to Fearless Lad in 1982, and Sayf El Arab, On Stage's stablemate. On Stage struggled for much of the race and only began to gain ground on Soba after Sayf El Arab had gone clear. On Stage was beaten three lengths and three quarters of a length, which was as near as he got to Soba. He finished a length behind her when third in the July Cup, for which he again started favourite, and three quarters of a length behind her when third again in the Vernons Sprint, both races going to Habibti. On Stage who had won over seven furlongs in his first season, was twice tried over the trip in 1983. In the Hungerford Stakes at Newbury in August he was held up, found nothing under pressure and was soundly beaten behind Salieri. His final outing in the Harroways Stakes at Goodwood had a better result. He was ridden more enterprisingly, which seemed to suit him, and he led inside the distance before narrowly failing to hold off Larionov. On Stage was afterwards sold to race in South Africa, where he ought to pick up some useful prizes before he goes to stud.

		Comedy Star (b 1968)	Tom Fool (b 1949)	Menow
On Stage (b.c. 1980)				Gaga
			Latin Walk (br 1960)	Roman Tread
				Stall Walker
		Last Case (ch 1963)	Firestreak (b 1956)	Pardal
				Hot Spell
			Court Case (b 1949)	Court Martial
				La Petite

On Stage was a major contributor, along with Mighty Fly, to Comedy Star's most successful season as a stallion to date. He has proved a versatile sire as details of some of his offspring given in Mighty Fly's commentary show. As a racehorse he was a good, genuine handicapper. On Stage's dam Last Case won nine races including the Newbury Spring Cup. She has produced three other winners, among them the useful Court Clown; she is herself half-sister to four winners. The third dam La Petite won at a mile and a quarter, and was a sister to Saucy Sal, the Coronation Stakes winner. *W. O'Gorman.*

ON THE FOAN 3 b.c. Sallust 134–Fenland Queen (King's Troop 118) (1982 NR 74
1983 9.4d 10.1f 12f² 10.1fg³ 10f* 10fg 10.1fg 10s⁴ 10g⁴ 8fg 10f) 9,200Y; lightly-built
colt; half-brother to 3 winners, including fairly useful 1977 2-y-o 7f winner
Fosterfridge (by St Chad); dam unraced half-sister to high-class miler Belmont
Bay; placed in varied races and won a maiden event at Yarmouth in August; stays
1½m; probably acts on any going; none too consistent; sold 5,800 gns Newmarket
Autumn Sales. *F. Durr.*

ON THE SPOT 4 gr.g. Town Crier 119–Creolina 72 (Quorum 126) (1982 8.5fg –
6.5v 8d 7f⁴ 7g² 7fg⁴ 8g⁴ 10fg 10.1fg 9fg 10g² 10fg 10g 9f⁴ 10f 8v 10.2s 1983 8d 8g
8g 10.1f⁴) quite attractive gelding; good walker; plater; stays 1¼m; sometimes
blinkered. *C. Brittain.*

ON THE SPREE 3 b.f. Wolverlife 115–Red Lark (Larkspur 128) (1982 7d 7g –
1983 8f 10.1f 14f) good-topped filly; little worthwhile form in maiden and minor
races. *D. Morley.*

ON THE WARPATH 4 ro.g. Bustino 136–Cheyenne 83 (Sovereign Path 125) 51
(1982 11s⁴ 16f 12.3g 16g⁴ 14fg 16s 1983 13s² 17d 13d 13h 16fg) rangy gelding;
staying maiden; acts on soft going and wasn't disgraced on hard ground fourth
start; blinkered third outing; sold 10,500 gns Doncaster November Sales. *C.
Thornton.*

ON TOUR 3 b.f. Queen's Hussar 124–Phaedima 76 (Darius 129) (1982 6g 7d 7g² –
1983 12.2d 12.2d 9f 10fg 12fg) compact filly; plater; should stay middle distances;
blinkered final start; sold 490 gns Doncaster September Sales. *W. Haigh.*

ONWARDLEE (USA) 3 b.c. Ward McAllister–Stride Out (Impressive) (1982 77
6f³ 6f 7d 8d 8g² 9s 1983 12v* 12v² 12.3v 12f 12f³ 12f³ 12.2f³ 13s 11g* 12g² 12g)
sturdy colt; narrowly won maiden race at Wolverhampton in April and handicap at
Hamilton in September, latter from Oakapple; suited by 1½m; acts on any going.
S. Norton.

ON YOUR TOES 2 ch.c. On Your Mark 125–Lyrical Lion (Jukebox 120) (1983 5g –
5d 5f 5f 5f) Apr 8; IR 1,000Y; small, compact colt; of no account; sold 330 gns
Doncaster October Sales. *D. Plant.*

OO-LA-LA 4 b.g. Warpath 113–Croisette 95 (Sunny Way 120) (1982 10.2g 12.2f³ 55
10d 12fg 1983 11s 12d* 15.8d⁴ 12fg 12.2g) compact, quite well-made gelding;
poor mover; made all and stayed on strongly to win handicap at Carlisle in May;
probably stayed 2m; ideally suited by some give in the ground; dead. *C. Thornton.*

OOPS-A-DAISY 4 br.f. Warpath 113–Sunflower 96 (Paveh 126) (1982 10.2g –
12.2f 12g³ 12fg 1983 8s 10d 12v) useful-looking filly; poor plater; sometimes
blinkered; sold 800 gns Doncaster May Sales. *R. Hartop.*

OPALE 3 ch.f. Busted 134–Conning Tower 98 (Connaught 130) (1982 NR 1983 105
12.2d* 12f* 12fg* 12fg 12fg²) lengthy filly with scope; not the best of movers;
second foal; half-sister to fairly useful 7f and 1¼m winner Nureddin (by Brigadier
Gerard); dam best at up to 1m; a progressive sort who on first 3 outings won
maiden race at Catterick in June, 6-runner event at Wolverhampton in July and
handicap at Doncaster in September, last-named by 3 lengths from Gillies Prince;
stayed on strongly and ran a fine race in defeat when 1½ lengths second of 11
behind Sylph in Princess Royal Stakes at Ascot in October; will be suited by 1¾m;
seems to act on any going, but gives impression she'll be suited by some give in the
ground; saddle slipped fourth start and run can be ignored. *A. Stewart.*

OPARAU (NZ) 8 br.g. Stipulate–Hokonui Gold (Lomond 124) (1982 12f 1983 12g –
16f 12f) lengthy New Zealand-bred gelding; winner over jumps; no worthwhile
form on flat. *P. Felgate.*

OPENING BARS 2 b.g. Bruni 132–Tory Island (Majority Blue 126) (1983 5v 7f³ 89
7f²) May 2; 5,000Y; strong, quite attractive gelding; good walker; third foal
(second to Northern Hemisphere time); half-brother to winners in Australia and
Malaysia; dam poor sister to useful miler Votecatcher; placed in maiden events at
Salisbury in June and Sandown in July; subsequently gelded; will be suited by 1m+;
acts on firm going. *C. Horgan.*

OPEN THE BOX (USA) 4 b.g. Key To The Kingdom–T. V. Miss (T. V. Lark) 63 d
(1982 8.2s 7d 5.8g 6f 6f 6g 6g 6v 6d 7s* 1983 7g³ 7g* 6f 7f 7.6g 7g 7fg 7fg)
smallish, workmanlike gelding; won apprentice handicap at Lingfield in June;
didn't show much afterwards; should stay 1m; needs some give in the ground and
revels in soft going; best in blinkers; suited by forcing tactics. *G. Balding.*

OPEN UP 2 gr.f. Absalom 128–Opencast 97 (Mossborough 126) (1983 5f 6f³ 6f² 81
7g³ 7d) May 14; smallish, fair sort; half-sister to numerous winners, including very

useful stayer Kambalda (by Right Royal V) and useful 7f to 13f winner Oxslip (by Owen Dudley); dam 1¼m winner and half-sister to good winners Shaft and Bunker; placed in maiden races at Salisbury and Folkestone and in nursery at Goodwood; suited by 7f; acts on firm going; suitable mount for an apprentice. *H. Candy.*

OPHRYS 2 b.f. Nonoalco 131–Petrovna (Reliance II 137) (1983 6fg³ 7s*) May 19; big, lengthy, quite attractive filly; half-sister to several winners, including useful French sprinter Peymour (by Habitat); dam, winner over 1m in France, is daughter of French 1000 Guineas winner Pola Bella and half-sister to dams of Persepolis and Vayrann; 3/1 on, appeared not to have a lot to spare when ½-length winner from Perang's Niece in 19-runner maiden race at Leicester in October; had shaped very well when 2 lengths third of 29 to Capricorn Belle in maiden race at Newmarket the previous month; will stay 1m; possibly better on a firm surface than a soft one; has scope for improvement. *H. Cecil.* — 90 p

OPINEBO 3 b.f. Nebbiolo 125–Ops (Welsh Saint 126) (1982 6g³ 6d³ 6d 7g 1983 12v 10fg 12f² 12.2f² 14.6f² 16h* 12fg⁴ 12d 12g³ 14.7fg 12fg) lightly-made filly; gained a well-deserved success in maiden race at Nottingham in August, beating Whiskey Time by a neck; stays well; acts on hard ground. *D. Morley.* — 82

OPTIMISTIC DREAMER 4 b.g. Full of Hope 125–La Crima (Runnymede 123) (1982 7f 8fg⁴ 7fg* 7f 7fg 7d 7d 1983 9d⁴ 9d² 10g 8g 8h³) leggy, light-framed gelding; suited by 9f; probably acts on any going; blinkered once at 3 yrs; sold 2,500 gns Doncaster November Sales. *A. Bailey.* — 57

OPTIMISTIC LASS (USA) 2 b.f. Mr Prospector–Loveliest (Tibaldo) (1983 6fg*) Apr 26; $700,000Y; compact filly; third foal; half-sister to French 1m winner Rolando (by Giacometti); dam, half-sister to high-class American winner Arbees Boy, was very useful at up to 10.5f in France and won at up to 9f in USA; second favourite, squeezed through a gap on rails and quickened in tremendous style to win 23-runner maiden race at Newmarket in October by a length from stable-companion Balearica; will be suited by 7f+; sure to do better, and is probably a good filly in the making. *M. Stoute.* — 93 p

ORANELLA 3 ch.f. Orange Bay 131–Quick Dream (Crepello 136) (1982 7g 8s* 1983 12v⁴ 10d³ 11.5g) big, workmanlike filly; in frame in 2 handicaps in May; off course afterwards until September; probably stays 1½m; acts on soft going. *G. Pritchard-Gordon.* — 74

ORANGE BLOSSOM 3 b.f. Orange Bay 131–Aggrapina 79 (St Alphage 119) (1982 7g 8s⁴ 8d 1983 12.2d 12f 12.3f* 13.8f² 13h 12.2g⁴ 10.5d) sparely-made, leggy filly; got on top in last 100 yards when winning handicap at Newcastle in July; stays 1¾m; acts on any going; blinkered last 3 outings, finishing behind in a £4,000 seller on last occasion. *J. Etherington.* — 60

ORANGE NEST 2 b. or br.c. Orange Bay 131–Nest Builder 85 (Home Guard 129) (1983 7.6fg) Mar 7; first foal; dam won over 5f at 3 yrs; eighth of 17 in maiden race at Lingfield in October. *P. Walwyn.* — –

ORANGE REEF 3 ch.c. Mill Reef 141–Carrot Top 112 (High Hat 131) (1982 NR 1983 11s 12v* 14s 11g³ 11.7fg 12g³ 12fg³ 16fg³ 13.3d³) lengthy, quite attractive colt; good walker; half-brother to fairly useful 1978 2-y-o 5f winner Carrot Patch (by Habitat), subsequently a prolific winner in Italy; dam very useful at up to 1¾m; landed the odds without any fuss in minor event at Kempton in May, beating Meaume by 5 lengths; third in 5 handicaps afterwards, on last occasion to Insular at Newbury in October; stays well; yet to race on very firm going, but acts on any other; sold to G. Kindersley 40,000 gns Newmarket Autumn Sales. *J. Tree.* — 90

ORANGE SQUASH (USA) 3 ch.c. Unconscious–Doveland (Jet Man) (1982 5f⁴ 5fg* 6f 5f* 6fg* 5fg* 6f* 5v 1983 7d 6v 5fg 6fg 5h 5f 7g 8fg) good-bodied, quite attractive colt; didn't recapture his very useful 2-y-o form, but ran respectably on occasions; promises to stay 7f; acts on fast ground; sweated up fifth start; blinkered sixth outing. *R. Smyth.* — 104 d

ORATAVO 5 br.g. The Brianstan 128–Nimble Star (Space King 115) (1982 10fg 10fg² 10f* 12fg 10d* 8fg³ 10fg² 8fg 10g* 9d³ 10g 1983 10v 8d 8v 8f 10g 9fg 10fg* 10fg) lightly-made gelding; took time to find his form but did so when keeping on well to beat Lady Arpege by ¾ length in Bustino Stakes (Handicap) at Ascot in October; ran respectably only subsequent start; stays 11f; acts on any going; often apprentice ridden but hung when ridden by an inexperienced boy once. *J. Sutcliffe.* — 82

ORATION 4 gr.g. Rouser 118–Declamation 93 (Town Crier 119) (1982 11g* 12fg⁴ 10.1fg 10f² 10s 10g 12s 1983 10v 10.6fg 10fg) useful sort; fair performer at 3 yrs; — –

well beaten in 1983; stays 1½m; probably needs a sound surface; sold 1,450 gns Doncaster October Sales. *C. Thornton.*

ORCHARD ROAD 2 b.f. Camden Town 125–Little Apple (Sovereign Lord 120) **74** (1983 5fg³ 6f 5.8f² 7f³ 6f 6fg 7s) Mar 9; IR 4,200Y; lightly-made filly; half-sister to 3 winners, including useful 1980 2-y-o sprinter Red Russet (by Huntercombe); dam disappointing plater; placed in maiden race at Sandown in June and maiden auction events at Bath and Doncaster in July; below form last 3 outings; suited by 7f; acts on firm going. *R. Williams.*

ORE 5 ch.h. Ballymore 123–Minatonka (Linacre 133) (1982 10s 10s⁴ 16fg² 22.2fg* **114** 21f² 16g² 20s 16d³ 1983 13.3v* 16g* 20f⁴) big, strong, workmanlike horse; third foal; half-brother to bumpers race winner Karatonka (by Karabas); dam Irish 1m winner; smart stayer; held up when beating Future Spa in good style by 6 lengths in Aston Park Stakes at Newbury and Broken Rail decisively by 1½ lengths in Henry II Stakes at Sandown, both in May; respectable fourth to Little Wolf in Gold Cup at Royal Ascot; struck into there and wasn't seen out again; suited by a stiff test of stamina but has a fair turn of foot; acts on any going; blinkered once at 3 yrs. *W. Musson.*

OREGON TRAIL 3 b.c. Auction Ring 123–Oriental Star 94 (Falcon 131) (1982 **84** 8.2s 1983 8d 11v² 12s⁴ 12f 12d 12fg) strong, slightly hollow-backed colt; ran easily best races when 2½ lengths second of 17 behind Castle Rising in maiden race at Newbury in May and sixth of 20 behind Dazari in King George V Stakes (Handicap) at Royal Ascot in June, proving well suited by strong pace in latter event on fourth start; off course 4 months afterwards; will stay beyond 1½m; acts on any going. *D. Arbuthnot.*

ORIGINAL STEP 8 ch.g. New Linacre 82–Paddy's Walk (Admiral's Walk) (1982 **–** 12s 1983 12g 12s) fair hurdler; little worthwhile form on flat. *T. Hallett.*

ORIXO (USA) 3 ch.c. Our Native–Bold Fluff (Boldnesian) (1982 6f 6d⁴ 6fg* 6g² **107** 1983 8g* 8fg 7fg) good-bodied, attractive colt; has a round action; developed into a very smart performer as a 2-y-o; landed the odds impressively in £4,100 Hermitage Stakes at Newbury in June, quickening clear when shaken up around 3f out and winning easing up by 4 lengths from Hungarian Prince; favourite when disappointing later in month in St James's Palace Stakes at Royal Ascot (raced on only 3 shoes and finished tailed-off last of 7 to Horage) and Van Geest Stakes at Newmarket (eleventh of 12 to Thug); stays 1m; wore a tongue strap last 2 starts as a 2-y-o; sent to USA. *R. Hern.*

ORMOLU (USA) 4 b.g. Val de l'Orne 130–Donna Chere (Conestoga) (1982 11s³ **–** 12s 9f³ 9.4f 10f 12fg 11g³ 11g* 11g³ 11g 9fg 1983 12d 12d 12f 10f) tall, rather leggy gelding; bad mover; stays 11f; has been tried in blinkers; inconsistent and unreliable; bought 2,100 gns Doncaster March Sales. *K. Stone.*

OROFINO (GER) 5 br.h. Dschingis Khan–Ordinale (Luciano) (1982 12g* 11g* **121** 11g* 12g* 12d* 12fg² 1983 12d* 9.7d² 11g* 12g² 13.5fg³ 12f) first foal; dam, from an excellent family, was joint top-rated 2-y-o filly in Germany in 1974 and was third in Prix de Flore as a 3-y-o; an outstanding performer in his native country where he's won 12 of his 16 races; won Gerling-Preis at Cologne in May and Grosser Hansa Preis at Hamburg in July, easily beating Feuersturn in latter; also placed in Prix Dollar at Longchamp (short-neck second to Welsh Term), Grosser Preis von Berlin at Dusseldorf (second to Abary), and Grand Prix de Deauville (1¾ lengths third to Zalataia); effective at 1¼m and stays 13.5f; probably acts on any going; genuine and consistent; clearly very smart. *S. von Mitzlaff, Germany.*

Henry II Stakes, Sandown—Ore wins decisively from Broken Rail and Khairpour

ORRAVAN 2 b.g. Raga Navarro 119–Mink Fur (Victoria Park) (1983 5v⁴ 5s 6s 6fg 7f) Mar 1; IR 4,200F, 1,250Y; rather lightly-made gelding; third living produce; half-brother to 2 winners, including Austrian St Leger winner Idle Warrior (by Sandford Lad); dam unplaced once in France; bad maiden; not seen out after June. *R. Hoad.* **49**

ORVILLE'S SONG 2 b.c. Tarboosh–Mont Genevre (Sweet Revenge 129) (1983 7g 7.2fg 7fg 7g³ 8g² 7.2g* 7.2s) Mar 22; 700Y; leggy colt; first foal; dam, 2-y-o 5f winner in Ireland, is daughter of Irish Guinness Oaks winner Iskereen; plater; attracted no bid after beating Video Boom by ½ length at Haydock in September; stays 1m; from only on good going; suitable mount for an apprentice. *J. Wilson.* **68**

ORYX MAJOR 3 ch.g. Sandford Lad 133–You Never Can Tell (Never Say Die 137) (1982 7d 7g 8fg 8s 1983 13.1fg 16d) good-topped gelding; well beaten in 1983 (not seen out until September). *S. Mellor.* **–**

ORYX MINOR 3 br.g. Music Maestro 119–Minor Chord 88 (Major Portion 129) (1982 5fg 5fg 5d 5fg² 5fg 6fg 5d 1983 6s² 5g³ 5g 5fg 6s²) compact, fair sort; sprint maiden; yet to race on really firm going, but acts on any other; has run well in blinkers. *S. Mellor.* **69**

OTOTO (USA) 2 ch.g. Junction–Orlada (Dancing Moss 113) (1983 6g 6f 6f 5h³ 6f) Apr 14; $7,000Y; small gelding; good mover; first foal; dam won at 3 yrs and 4 yrs in Argentina but ran 13 times unplaced in USA; plating-class maiden; not seen out after running poorly in nursery at Windsor in August; bred to stay 7f+; acts on hard going. *R. Armstrong.* **64**

OTREBOR (USA) 2 b.c. Roberto 131–Flaxen (Graustark) (1983 7fg⁴ 8fg³) Feb 24; $260,000Y; quite attractive colt; closely related to 2 winners, including smart stakes-placed winner Executive Counsel (by Good Counsel), and half-brother to several others; dam twice-raced half-sister to smart 9f stakes winner Infuriator; very good third behind Alphabatim in big field of maidens at Newmarket in October; will be suited by 1¼m; acts on a firm surface; may show further improvement, and looks sure to win races. *M. Jarvis.* **97**

OTTERHILL 3 b.f. Brigadier Gerard 144–Lowna 120 (Princely Gift 137) (1982 5fg⁴ 6g 6fg 5g 1983 5f) neat, well-made filly; well bred, but apparently only a plating-class maiden. *C. Brittain.* **–**

OUI MONSIEUR 9 b.g. Levanter 121–Melody Call 55 (Tudor Melody 129) (1982 12d 15.5fg 12fg 12f 1983 11.7fg 13h) poor handicapper; stays 2m; acts on any going; suitable mount for an inexperienced rider. *J. Bosley.* **–**

OULA OWL 3 b.c. Tachypous 128–Oula-Ka Fu-Fu 67 (Run The Gantlet) (1982 7g 8g* 8g 1983 10v 8s 8s* 8f 7fg 8fg) well-made, attractive colt; good mover; beat Qemlas in great style by 8 lengths in small handicap at Leicester in May (ridden by 7-lb claimer); little other form in 1983, but is said to have been badly squeezed on fourth outing and came back with a bad shoulder and a bruised foot (off course over 3 months afterwards); suited by 1m, and should stay further; acts on soft going; inconsistent. *L. Cumani.* **96 ?**

OUNAVARRA 4 ch.f. Homeric 133–Montbretia (Aureole 132) (1982 7g 10g 8g 9g² 11.5s² 7.5s² 10s* 10v* 1983 12s⁴ 10s⁴ 8s⁴ 10s⁴ 10v² 12s⁴ 11g² 12g 12g* 12d* 16d²) IR 2,300F, 4,200Y; fourth foal; dam once-raced sister to Irish Guinness Oaks winner Aurabella; found her form in the autumn (as she had in 1982), winning valuable races at Leopardstown (beat Arctic Lord 2½ lengths) and Naas (November Handicap by a neck from Rosemore); ran well final start when length second to Gallant Royal in Leopardstown November Extended Handicap; suited by 1½m or more; yet to race on a firm surface and revels in the mud; tough and genuine; sold 90,000 gns Newmarket December Sales. *L. Browne, Ireland.* **100**

OUR BIRTHDAY 7 b.h. Great Nephew 126–Renoir Picture 90 (Relko 136) (1982 10d 10fg³ 10fg* 10d 8fg* 10f 10g 8fg 9g 8g 1983 10s 8s 8s 8f³ 10d) neat horse; poor handicapper; stays 1¼m; acts on any going; wears blinkers; sometimes starts slowly. *J. Benstead.* **51**

OUR CARO (USA) 3 b. or br.f. Caro 133–Irish Surprise (Linacre 133) (1982 NR 1983 8f 10.1f 12fg²) $36,000Y; big, lengthy filly; half-sister to several winners in USA; dam unraced half-sister to top-class Saritamer; 10 lengths second to Khyber in gentleman riders race at Brighton in October, first form; suited by 1½m; moved badly on first outing. *P. Cole.* **–**

OUR CHOICE 3 ro.g. Bustino 136–Betty Burke 95 (Prince Chevalier) (1982 7.2g 8d 1983 10fg) tall, narrow, leggy gelding; lightly-raced maiden; should stay 1¼m. *R. Hollinshead.*

OUR DAY (USA) 3 b.c. Judgable–Spanish Wind (Gushing Wind) (1982 6fg 7fg 5.8f⁴ 7f 1983 7s⁴ 6s 10d⁴ 10g 8.2f) robust, quite attractive colt; plating-class maiden; should stay 1m; acts on any going. *P. Cole.* —

OUR DYNASTY 2 b.c. Young Generation 129–Second Generation 95 (Decoy Boy 129) (1983 5s* 5g* 5d* 6d* 6fg 6fg⁴ 6g⁴ 5fg) Mar 26; 6,600Y; strong, useful-looking colt; not a good mover in his slower paces; first foal; dam a sprinter; trotted up, creating a most favourable impression, in minor events at Doncaster, Thirsk, Newmarket and Kempton in early part of season; had his limitations exposed in pattern-race company afterwards, best efforts when 8 lengths fourth behind Precocious in Gimcrack Stakes at York and 7½ lengths fourth to Vacarme in Mill Reef Stakes at Newbury; suited by 6f; acts on a firm surface, but is said to be better on a soft one. *M. Lambert.* **100**

OUR GOLD DIGGER 2 br. or ro.f. Saritamer 130–Gold Bloom 72 (Klondyke Bill 125) (1983 5s 5fg 5fg 5fg 5g) Mar 28; 2,400F, 3,800Y; close-coupled, sharp sort; half-sister to numerous winners, including tough 1976 2-y-o 5f and 6f winner Regency Bill (by Royalty); dam sprinter; poor maiden; blinkered third outing. *J. Gilbert.* **56**

OUR GRACIE 4 ch.f. Star Appeal 133–Tinkling Sound 93 (Sound Track 132) (1982 10h 9.4g⁴ 12f² 12v 1983 12f 12f 13.1h) poor maiden; stays 1½m; probably unsuited by heavy going; has worn bandages. *T. Bulgin.* —

OUR ISLAND STORY 2 b.f. Ile de Bourbon 133–Star Story 117 (Red God 128§) (1983 7f*) Apr 7; tall, rather angular filly; has an excellent, flowing action; half-sister to several winners, including useful sprinter Habitation (by Habitat); dam prolific winner at 5f and 6f; 14/1, soon travelling strongly in 18-runner maiden race at Salisbury in September and led inside final furlong, despite showing signs of inexperience, to win by 2 lengths from Allecta; will stay 1m; has scope and is certain to improve. *F. J. Houghton.* **88 p**

Mr Bill Hobson's "Our Dynasty"

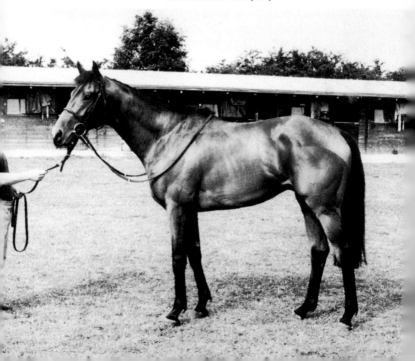

OUR KATY 3 gr. or ro.f. Dragonara Palace 115–Clouds of Gold (Goldhill 125) –
(1982 5.1f 6g 6g* 7g 6g 5s 1983 8s 6s 10f 7fg 8g 8d² 10g 6fg) lengthy, leggy filly;
plater; stays 1m; sold 1,200 gns Ascot November Sales. *K. Ivory.*

OUR LADY 2 br.f. Tachypous 128–Released 71 (Relko 136) (1983 6s 6f² 7f 7.2g **83**
7g² 8d² 8g² 8.2fg*) Mar 24; 9,400F; fair sort; second foal; dam poor maiden;
better right at the end of the season than at any time previously, and not least
appearance (blinkered) won 17-runner nursery at Nottingham; well suited by 1m
and may stay further; acts on a firm and a soft surface. *M. Jarvis.*

OUR-MARY-ROSE 2 ch.f. Record Run 127–Monica Rose (Forlorn River 124) –
(1983 6h 5g 5g) June 3; lengthy filly; poor mover; half-sister to 1¼m to 2m winner
Fata Morgana (by Grey Mirage) and a winner in Denmark; dam of little account; no
sign of ability, including in a seller. *G. Harman.*

OUR SHIRLEY 2 b.f. Shirley Heights 130–Coal Face 61 (Kalydon 122) (1983 **68 p**
7.6d³) Feb 24; 30,000Y; half-sister to 4 winners, notably smart 1m and 9f winner
Miner's Lamp (by High Top); dam, placed at up to 1¾m, is sister to very useful
stayers Shaft and Bunker; highly promising third, staying on, behind Risk All in
20-runner maiden race at Lingfield in October; sure to do better, and win races,
over further. *G. Lewis.*

OUR WHITE HART 3 br.c. Manado 130–Valiretta (Go Marching) (1982 NR –
1983 10v 10g 10.1fg⁴ 10.4fg 10.1fg 10fg 11.7fg) 9,200Y; rather leggy, useful-
looking colt; second foal; dam won 5 times over middle distances in France; poor
maiden; ran best race on third outing; ran freely in blinkers sixth start. *N. Vigors.*

OUT AND ABOUT 2 ch.f. Orchestra 118–Court Ballet (Barron's Court) (1983 **86**
7d 7s² 8d²) Apr 10; fourth reported foal; dam poor Irish maiden; kept on well when
¾-length second to Real Gold in maiden race at the Curragh, and headed on line
when short-head second to Lady Fawley in minor event at Leopardstown, both in
October; should prove suited by middle distances. *C. Collins, Ireland.*

OUT OF HAND 4 ch.c. Some Hand 119–Crusheen (Typhoon 125) (1982 7g* 8f **84**
7fg⁴ 7f³ 6fg⁴(dis) 6f 6g* 6g 6g 1983 7fg 6f 6fg 6f² 6f 6h* 5f 5.6fg* 5fg 5fg 6fg 5fg)
lengthy, useful sort; something of a character but won handicaps at Nottingham in
August and Doncaster in September; beat Ismore 1½ lengths going away in
Portland Handicap on latter; better suited by 6f than 5f, and stays 7f; yet to race on
a soft surface; used to wear a bandage on near-hind; suitable mount for an
apprentice; sometimes starts slowly. *D. Dale.*

OUT OF SHOT 2 b.f. Shirley Heights 130–Shooting Season 91 (Silly Season 127) **96**
(1983 7f* 7g⁴ 8fg⁴) Apr 1; lengthy filly; third foal; half-sister to 3-y-o 1m winner
Hollowell (by Wolver Hollow); dam stayed 1m well; won 15-runner maiden race at
Sandown in July by 2 lengths from Triagonal; creditable fourth subsequently in
Sweet Solera Stakes at Newmarket in August and May Hill Stakes (carried her
head a bit high) at Doncaster in September; will stay 1¼m; acts on firm going; a
pronounced tail-swisher. *J. Dunlop.*

OUT OF THE GLOOM 2 br.c. Netherkelly 112–Gloomy Portal 103 **73 p**
(Mossborough 126) (1983 8d) June 2; half-brother to several winners, including
very smart Conte Santi (by Sassafras) and very useful miler Grey Portal (by Grey
Sovereign); dam middle-distance performer; 50/1 and on backward side, 10 lengths
sixth of 12 to Corinth in £3,500 race at York in October; will probably do better. *R.
Hollinshead.*

OUT TO LUNCH 2 b.f. Anax 120–Spring Music (Silly Season 127) (1983 6f 7f) –
June 11; 2,000Y; sister to 3-y-o Sax and half-sister to 3 winners; dam never ran; in
rear in maiden auction event at Folkestone in August and 18-runner maiden race at
Salisbury (bandaged off-hind) in September. *S. Woodman.*

OUT TO PLAY 2 b.g. Music Boy 124–Royal Inheritance 78 (Will Somers 114§) **56**
(1983 5d 5fg 6f 5f 6fg) Apr 28; 3,200Y; small, sturdy, short-legged gelding; poor
walker; first foal; dam 2-y-o 6f winner; little worthwhile form; tried in blinkers in
seller at Newmarket in October on final appearance; subsequently gelded. *A. Pitt.*

OUTWARD'S GAL 2 b.f. Ashmore 125–Outward Bound 79 (Sing Sing 134) **78**
(1983 6g⁴ 6fg) Mar 4; lengthy filly; good walker and mover; half-sister to several
winners, including useful miler Morayshire (by Royal Palace); dam placed over
5f; 3¾ lengths fourth to At Talaq in 20-runner maiden race at Newmarket in
August and 6 lengths sixth of 17 to Seattle Siren in £4,000 event at York
(co-favourite) in September; will be better suited by 7f. *B. Hobbs.*

OVER AND OVER 4 b.g. Tumble Wind–Olvera (Molvedo 137) (1982 8fg 6f 7g –
6g 1983 6fg 7fg 10f 10g) lightly-made gelding; good walker; poor plater nowadays;
has been blinkered. *S. Woodman.*

OVER BOWLED 2 b.f. Bold Lad (Ire) 133–Sherapova (Baldric II 131) (1983 6g3   **72**
5fg4 6f4 5s) Apr 11; quite attractive filly; second reported foal; half-sister to a
winner in French Provinces; dam placed over 7.8f at 2 yrs in France; quite a
moderate maiden; stays 6f; acts on any going. *J. W. Watts.*

OVER THE RAINBOW 6 b.g. Song 132–Lady Matador 108 (Matador 131)   **71**
(1982 5d2 6f* 6f 6fg 5.1g2 6g3 6f 6f 1983 6d 6d 5.1g 6f 6fg4 6f 6fg 5f4 5f* 5fg 5g3
5g3) strong, compact gelding; has an enlarged near-fore; sprint handicapper;
always going well when scoring at Beverley in September; acts on any going; has
twice worn blinkers; sometimes sweats up. *J. Winter.*

OVERTRICK 8 b.h. Great Nephew 126–Jackyda 71 (Royal Palm 131) (1982 NR   **90**
1983 6fg 6d* 6g 6g 6fg) fairly useful handicapper; won minor event at Brighton in
September; stays 7f; suited by some give in the ground and revels in the mud;
usually held up; apprentice ridden at Brighton. *G. Huffer.*

OWENELLEN 5 b.m. Owen Anthony 102–Rimelo (Richard Louis 116) (1982 NR   ⌐
1983 10f) third foal; half-sister to 2m winner Cold Justice (by Arctic Judge); dam
poor point-to-pointer; very backward when tailed off in amateur riders event at
Newmarket in July. *M. Haynes.*

OWEN JOSEPH (USA) 2 b. or br.c. Proudest Roman–Prankesse   **75**
(Ambehaving) (1983 6f 7g 7f 6fg*) Apr 1; $52,000 2-y-o; rather lightly-built colt;
half-brother to 3 winners in USA and Mexico, one stakes placed; dam won claiming
races over 7f and 1m; dropped in class, made virtually all in 24-runner £4,200 seller
at Doncaster (bought in 5,200 gns) in September; easily best form at 6f; exported
to Malaysia. *M. Jarvis.*

OWEN ROCK 4 ch.g. Owen Dudley 121–Gillycan (Rockavon 120) (1982 12.2f   –
12.3g 12fg 16.5s 1983 14.7d) compact gelding; poor form, including in a seller; has
worn blinkers. *I. Jordon.*

OWENS FLAIR 2 b.f. Owen Dudley 121–Flaretown 63 (Town Crier 119) (1983   –
5d) May 15; second foal; half-sister to winning sprint plater Sweet Smile (by
Native Bazaar); dam third over 5f and 6f at 2 yrs; in rear in 14-runner maiden race
at Catterick in October. *S. Matthews.*

OWING STEVEN 2 b.c. Owen Dudley 121–Furley 91 (Decoy Boy 129) (1983 6d   **89**
5fg4 7f 6f 7.3g* 7tg3 7fg) Mar 25; 3,000Y; lengthy, useful-looking colt; second foal;
half-brother to winning 7f plater Shine Forth (by Shiny Tenth); dam 2-y-o 5f
winner; well ridden by 7-lb claimer L. Jones,led 3f out and ran on strongly to win
10-runner nursery at Newbury in September by 1½ lengths from Maazi; showed
nothing like that form in his other races; will stay 1m; evidently suited by some give
in the ground. *R. Hannon.*

OYSTON ESTATES 7 gr.g. Goldhill 125–Port Relic 90 (Relic) (1982 6g3 6fg*   **67**
6g4 8f2 6g3 8.2g 7d 8.2s 6s 1983 6s* 6v 6d 6g3 6g* 6fg2 6f 6g4 6d2 6h 7s3 6g 6fg)
strong gelding; has won 7 times at Hamilton, and gained successes there in
handicaps in April and June; has run creditably over 1m but is better at shorter
distances; probably acts on any going; effective with and without blinkers; good
mount for an apprentice. *J. S. Wilson.*

OYSTONS PROPWEEKLY 2 b. or br.f. Swing Easy 126–Spin Dry (High Top   **74**
131) (1983 5d2 5g* 5d4 6f 6fg 6s) Feb 9; 3,200F, 3,000Y; tall, leggy filly; first
foal; dam, daughter of very useful Paresseuse, showed little worthwhile form in
France; won 6-runner minor event at Ayr in May; ran moderately last 3 starts;
apparently best at 5f; sold 1,800 gns Doncaster November Sales. *J. Berry.*

OYSTON'S SPECIAL 2 ch.f. Music Boy 124–Aldbury Girl 79 (Galivanter 131)   **73**
(1983 5v* 5v3 5d 6g 5s) Mar 14; useful-looking filly; good walker; second foal;
half-sister to 3-y-o 6f seller Booth's Town Boy (by Decoy Boy); dam won over
5.9f at 2 yrs; had the reputation of good filly and the form of quite a modest one,
even though successful by 5 lengths in minor event at Newcastle in April on first
appearance; should have stayed 6f; off the course for over 4 months after third
outing; dead. *J. Berry.*

OZINSKY 2 b.c. Mansingh 120–Karenina 95 (Silver Shark 129) (1983 7g 7d 7fg)   –
Mar 12; 4,400Y; useful-looking colt; half-brother to several winners, including
3-y-o middle-distance winner Karablake (by Blakeney) and smart 1976 staying
2-y-o Sultan's Ruby (by Royal Palace); dam won twice from 4 starts at 2 yrs; no
worthwhile form; tried in blinkers in valuable seller on final appearance; sold 410
gns Ascot November Sales. *I. Walker.*

OZRA 3 b.f. Red Alert 127–March Malona 88 (Derring-Do 131) (1982 6fg 6s 1983   **63**
8.5s 8d 8s 8d4 7v* 7d* 6d* 6s2 6d2 6fg 7s) smallish, strong filly; in fine form in
first half of season and won sellers at Doncaster (no bid) and Newmarket (bought
in 4,600 gns) and handicap at Redcar; effective at 6f and probably stays 1m; well

suited by soft ground; blinkered nowadays; off course 4 months after ninth start. *C. Booth.*

P

PACIFIC KING (USA) 2 ch.c. Northern Jove–Distinctly Royal (Distinctive) **116**
(1983 5g 6v⁴ 5fg² 5f* 6g² 5f* 6f⁴ 6fg⁴ 6f* 5fg⁴ 5d² 5fg²)

It wasn't until his final start that Pacific King stamped himself as one of the season's best juvenile sprinters. Despite reaching the frame in ten previous races we could rate him no better than useful before he ran in the Group 3 Cornwallis Stakes at Ascot in October; he started at 14/1. The improving Petorius, winner of his previous three starts, the Windsor Castle Stakes winner Defecting Dancer and the consistent Maajid, a length winner from Pacific King in a mixed-aged race at Beverley the previous month, were among those preferred in the betting; Godstone, the OCL Richmond Stakes winner, was also in the field. Pacific King tracked the early leaders Godstone and Fawzi until his storming late run took him past Godstone close home; but Petorius finished even more strongly to deprive Pacific King of the spoils by a head with Godstone the same distance away third. Ascot was one of ten tracks on which Pacific King raced in 1983. He won at three of them: at Bath and Sandown in July and at Ripon in August, on each occasion making all the running. Pacific King also performed creditably when three lengths fourth in the Richmond at Goodwood in July (he finished fifth but was promoted a place on Vacarme's disqualification) and when around six lengths fourth to Sicyos in the Prix d'Arenberg at Longchamp in September.

It's no great surprise that Pacific King should turn out a sprinter. His sire Northern Jove won fourteen times at up to a mile from fifty-three starts but most of his wins were gained over five and six furlongs. The dam Distinctly Royal, a half-sister to the stakes winner Cyalo and several other winners, won over five fur-

Mrs P. L. Yong's "Pacific King"

longs as a two-year-old and the grandam Royalo won three races at up to six
furlongs. Pacific King, a tall, useful sort and a good walker, barely stays six furlongs
and his attitude to racing suggests he'll always be best at five. He'll probably

	Northern Jove (ro 1968)	Northern Dancer (b 1961)	Nearctic
			Natalma
Pacific King (USA)		Junonia (ro 1961)	Sun Again
(ch. c. Jan 31, 1981)			Pavonia
	Distinctly Royal (b 1973)	Distinctive (b or br 1966)	Never Bend
			Precious Lady
		Royalo (b 1962)	Royal Charger
			Topolo

be campaigned in the top sprint races at three but he's unlikely to prove good
enough to win any of them. Pacific King has done all his winning on firm going but he
acts on a soft surface. *W. O'Gorman.*

PACIFIC SPARKLER 4 ch. g. Sparkler 130–Shanghai Lady 87 (Crocket 130)   –
(1982 8g 8fg³ 9f⁴ 7f 8g 7f 8fg 1983 17.1v) small, strong gelding; poor handicapper;
stays 9f; seems to act on any going; has been tried in blinkers; inconsistent. *J. Thorne.*

PACIFICUS (USA) 2 b. f. Northern Dancer–Pacific Princess (Damascus) (1983
7fg) May 29; $200,000Y; small, close-coupled filly; third foal; sister to 3-y-o Sir
Seaward; dam, daughter of Coronation Stakes winner Fiji, was smart winner at up
to 9f; backward, in rear in 22-runner maiden race at Newmarket in October. *P. Walwyn.*

PACIVAL 3 b. g. Saulingo 122–Sweet Miss (Silver Cloud 121) (1982 6f 5fg 7g 5d   –
8d 6s 1983 8d 7d 6f) smallish, lengthy gelding; poor form, including in sellers;
has worn blinkers. *D. Garraton.*

PADDYS BELLE 3 b. f. St Paddy 133–Tycoons Belle 47 (Tycoon II) (1982 5f 7fg   47
6g 7fg 8s 1983 8s 6d³ 8d 8g 7d 8f³ 7fg³ 10.8fg⁴ 7fg⁴ 8f 7fg⁴ 6fg) small filly; plater;
possibly stays 1¼m; has worn bandages. *D. C. Tucker.*

PADDY'S FARE 2 b. c. Dublin Taxi–Deaney's Delight 63 (Sahib 114) (1983 5s 5g   54
6fg 6f⁴ 6fg 6f 6f 5fg 6s 6fg) May 13; 300Y; leggy colt; disappointing plater; possibly
not genuine; sold 1,000 gns Doncaster November Sales. *K. Stone.*

PADRE PIO 2 gr. c. Mummy's Pet 125–Tranquility Base 112 (Roan Rocket 128)   71
(1983 6g 6s³) Apr 6; 5,400Y; strong, workmanlike colt; half-brother to 2
winners, including fairly useful 1982 2-y-o 5f winner Shoeblack (by Hotfoot),
winner of 1983 Norsk 2,000 Guineas; dam at her best at 2 yrs when 5f and 6f
winner; 11 lengths third of 6 to Innamorato in small race at Leicester in October.
D. Arbuthnot.

PADYKIN 3 b. f. Bustino 136–Expadeo 82 (St Paddy 133) (1982 NR 1983 8d 12f)   –
small filly; second foal; dam won over 1½m; shaped with a bit of promise in
newcomers race at Newmarket in April but was well beaten in maiden race at
Redcar in July on only other outing; sold 1,100 gns Ascot August Sales. *R. Armstrong.*

PAGAN BAY (USA) 2 ch. g. Sadair–Fairy Isle (Pago Pago) (1983 5s 5s 5.3f 7f)   –
Mar 13; $11,000Y; smallish, light-framed gelding; first foal; dam second once
from 5 starts; soundly beaten in maiden races; subsequently gelded. *R. Armstrong.*

PAGAN OF TROY 2 b. or br. c. Troy 137–Scarcely Blessed 116 (So Blessed 130) 102 p
(1983 6g³ 6fg³) Apr 23; 240,000Y; strong, rangy, deep-girthed colt; has a long
stride; third foal; half-brother to 3-y-o 7f winner What A Pity (by Blakeney); dam
smart sprinter, from very good family; ran green but kept on steadily to finish 5
lengths third of 13 to Double Schwartz in £5,300 maiden race at York in August;
easily bettered that effort when narrowly-beaten third of 11 to Miss Silca Key in
Clarence House Stakes at Ascot the following month, rallying in good style after
disputing lead throughout; takes very much after his sire and is crying out for
longer distances; a grand sort who will eventually make a very useful performer.
R. Hern.

PAGAN SUN 2 ch. g. Mount Hagen 127–Europeana 84 (Dual 117) (1983 5s 5g 6d³   84
6f 7fg 8f 7g* 7fg² 7fg⁴ 7fg) Apr 22; IR 3,200Y; quite attractive gelding;
half-brother to several winners, including very useful Irish 6f to 1m winner Glanoe
(by Green God); dam, half-sister to smart stayer Wrekin Rambler, won from 6f to
1¼m; won 11-runner nursery at Edinburgh in October by 2½ lengths from
Coquito's Star; carried 1 lb overweight when short-headed by Bastille in 15-runner
similar event at Doncaster later in month; should stay 1m; acts on a firm surface;
not particularly consistent. *A. Bailey.*

PAGEANTIC 2 br.f. Welsh Pageant 132–Brig of Ayr 90 (Brigadier Gerard 144)   **83**
(1983 5s* 5f 6f² 6f 6d) Mar 15; 9,600F; lengthy, sparely-made filly; first foal; dam
won from 1m to 11f at 4 yrs; won minor event at Goodwood in May by 2 lengths
from Astral Dancer; showed little after finishing second to Deccan Queen in
similar race at Pontefract 2 months later; will be suited by 7f and 1m; acts on any
going; off course 3 months before final outing. *F. J. Houghton.*

PAGE BLANCHE (USA) 3 gr.f. Caro 133–Pixie Tower 116 (Songedor 116)   **101**
(1982 NR 1983 7.3s 7.6v 8d² 8f² 8f² 8g 8f* 8f⁴ 7d² 7fg) good-topped,
close-coupled filly; very good mover; half-sister to high-class 1981 staying 2-y-o
Paradis Terrestre (by Empery), subsequently successful at up to 10.5f in France,
and very smart American middle-distance winner Premier Ministre (by
Cannonade); dam, smart sprinter, is half-sister to brilliant filly Cawston's Pride;
gained a well-deserved success in £4,200 Surplice Stakes at Goodwood in July,
winning decisively by 4 lengths from Sunoak; had made running and held off
Gaygo Lady by a head in 17-runner £6,100 Fern Hill Stakes (Handicap) at Ascot
on fifth outing, but hung right under pressure and placings were reversed; ran
well on other occasions too, but was well beaten final start; stays 1m; probably
acts on any going. *P. Kelleway.*

PAIR-OF-DEUCES 4 b.f. Some Hand 119–Lost in Silence (Silent Spring 102)   **74**
(1982 8f³ 7f³ 8d 8g³ 8fg² 8.3fg 8fg³ 7.2f 7.3g* 7s 8s 8s³ 1983 8v⁴ 10v² 10s 8g 8g⁴
10fg) fair sort; stays 1¼m; acts on any going but goes well in the mud; sold 720 gns
Newmarket July Sales. *R. Hannon.*

PAJANJO 4 ch.g. Northern Flash–Quick Draw 70 (Kalydon 122) (1982 NR 1983   **94**
16.5f² 14f* 10fg* 12f4) third foal; dam 1¼m winner; won 6-runner minor event at
Limerick Junction in August by a length from odds-on Steel Duke and quite valuable
race at Phoenix Park later in month by a neck from odds-on Camisado; remote
fourth of 8 to Cooliney Princess in valuable gentleman riders event at Epsom later
in August; effective at 1¼m and stays well; yet to race on an easy surface; winner
over hurdles; sent to USA. *L. Browne, Ireland.*

PALACE GOLD 4 b.c. Rheingold 137–Palace Rose 88 (Aureole 132) (1982   **105**
10.6s² 10fg³ 10.5f² 12f 11g⁴ 12g² 12g 14.6f 1983 14v 12fg) strong, workmanlike,
good-bodied ex-French colt; smart at his best though is still a maiden; sustained
small fracture of cannon bone final start in 1982; not disgraced at 4 yrs in Yorkshire
Cup at York in May (fifth of 10 to Line Slinger) and Princess of Wales's Stakes at
Newmarket in July (moved poorly to post when sixth of 11 to Quilted); stays 1¾m;
acts on any going but goes well on firm; blinkered last 3 starts in 1982. *W.
O'Gorman.*

PALACE GUEST 2 ch.f. Be My Guest 126–Palace Rose 88 (Aureole 132) (1983   –
6g 7f) May 14; lengthy, lightly-made filly; good walker; half-sister to smart 1982
3-y-o Palace Gold (by Rheingold); dam 1½m winner; behind in maiden races at
Lingfield in June and Sandown (last of 13) in July; sold BBA 11,000 gns Newmarket
Autumn Sales. *F. J. Houghton.*

PALACE OF LOVE 3 ch.f. Dragonara Palace 115–Lovelorn 56 (Forlorn River   **60**
124) (1982 6g 7fg 8s 1983 6v 6f 6fg⁴ 6f⁴ 8f 8h³ 8f 7fg) tall, lightly-made filly;
maiden plater; stays 1m; sometimes blinkered. *R. Laing.*

PALACE ROCKET 2 ch.g. Roan Rocket 128–River Palace (Royal Palace 131)   **64**
(1983 5d 5d⁴ 5g 6fg 6f 6fg³ 6f* 6f 6g³) Apr 3; leggy, rather narrow gelding;
half-brother to 1½m winner Bazz's Boy (by Dragonara Palace) and a winner in
Denmark; attracted no bid after winning seller at Hamilton in August by 1½ lengths
from Josceline Winifred; should stay beyond 6f; acts on firm going; went very freely
to start penultimate outing; sold to T. Craig 2,000 gns Doncaster October Sales.
P. Brookshaw.

PALACE TOR 3 b.f. Dominion 123–Tortola § (Narrator 127) (1982 NR 1983 8g   –
10fg) 44,000F, 1,700 gns 2-y-o; closely related to useful 1980 2-y-o 5f winner Doobie
Do (by Derring-Do) and half-sister to 3 winners; dam half-sister to high-class
stayer Almeria; behind in maiden races at Edinburgh and Nottingham in October.
W. A. Stephenson.

PALLAVICINA 3 b.g. Radetzky 123–Fulcrum Miss (Fulcrum) (1982 6f 7g 7fg   **66**
7fg 7g 8g 1983 8s² 8v 9s³ 10g 12f 10g 8f 10f³ 11.7fg 11.7fg 9d³ 10fg) compact,
sturdy gelding; placed in varied company in 1983 but mainly disappointing; one to
be wary of; retained by trainer 6,600 gns Newmarket Autumn Sales. *C. Brittain.*

PALLAX 3 b.g. Laxton 105–Pallmonta 82 (Pall Mall 132) (1982 6d 1983 8f) strong   –
gelding; behind in maiden races at Doncaster; sweats up and has given trouble at
start. *H. Wharton.*

PALLETINE 2 b.c. African Sky 124–Pro Patria 86 (Petingo 135) (1983 5fg 6fg 7fg 7g) May 1; IR 4,400Y; first foal; dam, sister to smart miler Patris, won over 5f and 6f at 2 yrs from 4 starts; poor maiden; blinkered final outing. *D. H. Jones.*   **57**

PALLOMERE 4 b.f. Blue Cashmere 129–Pallona 62 (Royal Palm 131) (1982 7fg 8f* 10f 7g 7s 7s³ 7d² 8s³ 1983 8f 8h 7fg 7f) lengthy, lightly-made filly; stays 1m; acts on any going; blinkered second start; has been taken down early, often takes a strong hold and isn't an easy ride. *W. Musson.*   **–**

PALMERO 6 b.g. Palm Track 122–Duresme 76 (Starry Halo 122) (1982 NR 1983 13s* 14s 13g4 12d 20.4g) big gelding; has been fired; won poor maiden race at Hamilton in April; stays 1¾m; acts well on soft going; has worn bandages. *K. Stone.*   **48**

PALMER'S GOLD 2 b.g. Palm Track 122–Golden Pinelopi 62 (Sovereign Lord 120) (1983 7f 6fg) Feb 10; sixth foal; dam half-sister to very smart Relpin; in rear in sellers at Beverley and Haydock in the summer. *R. E. Peacock.*   **–**

PALM THE ACE 5 b.g. Palm Track 122–Aces High 62 (Acer 123) (1982 6d² 8d* 8g 7fg* 7f 6fg 8g 8fg 7f 8g 8s 6g² 8d² 7s 1983 8d 6v³ 8v 8s³ 7s 8g 6fg 7g 8.3f 5f 8.3fg 7g) small gelding; plater; stays 1m; probably acts on any going; has worn blinkers and bandages. *R. Hoad.*   **–**

PALS DELIGHT 2 b.f. Idiot's Delight 115–Palmyrrha 98 (Palestine 133) (1983 6fg 6f 8g 7.6fg) Mar 8; rather sparely-made filly; half-sister to 3 winners; dam 2-y-o 5f winner; plating-class maiden; best effort on first outing. *R. Champion.*   **61**

PAMBAZUKO 2 b.c. African Sky 124–Merette 63 (Runnymede 123) (1983 6fg) Apr 4; 4,500Y; half-brother to middle-distance winner French Knot (by Take a Reef) and 3-y-o 7f winner Shercol (by Monseigneur); dam second twice over 1m; slow-starting tenth of 14 in claiming race at Nottingham in October. *R. Akehurst.*   **–**

PAMELA JANE 2 b.f. Abwah 118–Baggage 86 (Zeus Boy 121) (1983 5v* 5v 5d*) May 18; 1,200Y; robust, useful sort; has a round action; half-sister to 2 winners, including fair sprinter Bunny Boy (by Right Boy); dam stayed 1m; successful in sellers at Newcastle in April (bought in 4,100 gns after making all) and Thirsk the following month (attracted no bid after showing considerable courage to get up close home); will stay 6f; exported to Italy. *N. Tinkler.*   **52**

PAMELA'S JET 3. b.f. The Brianstan 128–Brighton Jet 69 (Jolly Jet 111) (1982 5f² 5fg² 5f 5fg 5fg4 5fg 5fg² 5f² 5d 1983 5d 5s 5f³ 5g 5h 5f) small, sturdy, good-quartered filly; good walker; plating-class maiden; seems to need an easy 5f; well served by firm going; has run well for apprentice. *R. Hollinshead.*   **–**

PAMPABIRD 4 b.c. Pampapaul 121–Wood Grouse 56 (Celtic Ash) (1982 7s² 8.5d³ 8v 7s* 6.5g³ 8d² 8g4 8s² 7s 1983 8s* 8f* 9.2d 8fg* 6.5fg4 8fg² 8g* 7fg²)   **124**

Beset by training troubles at various stages of his career Pampabird at last had the chance to show what he was made of in 1983 and seized it with enthusiasm, winning four of his eight starts and being only once out of the frame, that when running over a trip arguably too far for him in the Prix d'Ispahan. While the older milers in France were not particularly strong as a group Pampabird has undoubted claims to be regarded as the best and most consistent of them, and his owner was fortunate to have had him as well as Luth Enchantee carrying his well-known gold and black colours.

Pampabird always did best when ridden up with the pace and his first two races at four saw his making all to win a well-contested 90,000 francs event at Saint-Cloud in May from the ill-fated Vieux Carre and the Prix du Chemin de Fer du Nord at Chantilly the following month decisively by two and a half lengths from Darly after being in complete command in the last quarter of a mile. Pampabird's moderate display in the Prix d'Ispahan next time represented only a minor hiccup in his progress for in the Prix Messidor at Maisons-Laffitte in mid-July he returned to winning ways with a three-quarters-of-a-length success over Geral, taking over at the distance after tracking Schuss most of the way and galloping on keenly to score with a bit in hand.

Pattern-race wins often result in penalties being carried in similar events and in his next three starts Pampabird had to give weight to most of his opponents. A creditable fourth to Beaudelaire in the Prix Maurice de Gheest at Deauville over a trip too sharp for him, he made a bold attempt to win the Prix Quincey on the same course three weeks later but as in 1982 had to settle for second place, going down by a head to Great Substence after a fine tussle. Pampabird came out of the Quincey rather sore and missed the Prix du Moulin (which his owner won with Luth Enchantee) before reappearing in the Prix du Rond-Point at Longchamp. On the book he had a first-rate chance since he had already shown himself superior to

Prix du Rond-Point, Longchamp—Pampabird beats Propositioning

African Joy, Kebir and Prospero on more than one occasion and looked to have little to fear from the three-year-olds either. A short-priced favourite, he took over from African Joy halfway up the straight and accounted for Propositioning comfortably by a length and a half. A month later Pampabird was returned to Longchamp to contest the Prix de la Foret. With Salieri withdrawn on the day the race had a reasonably open look to it and in a tight market Pampabird started third favourite behind Sackford and Ma Biche. He ran his usual game race without being quite good enough, challenging Ma Biche strongly in the final furlong before going down by half a length; Aragon, heading the remainder, was three lengths further away so this can be regarded as one of Pampabird's finest efforts. The Foret let down the curtain on Pampabird's career and he has been retired to the Haras du Mesnil at a fee of 10,000 francs plus 25,000 francs October 1st.

Pampabird (b.c. 1979)	Pampapaul (b 1974)	Yellow God (ch 1967)	Red God
			Sally Deans
		Pampalina (br 1964)	Bairam II
			Padus
	Wood Grouse (ch 1967)	Celtic Ash (ch 1957)	Sicambre
			Ash Plant
		French Bird (b 1949)	Guersant
			Golden Pheasant

Pampabird, like Sandhurst Prince, is a son of the Irish Two Thousand Guineas winner Pampapaul who unfortunately died in 1979. His dam, a half-sister to the very smart six- and seven-furlong performer Pitskelly, stayed thirteen furlongs and has produced two other winners at stud, notably Great Sound (by Meadow Mint) who won at up to seven furlongs at two in Ireland before collecting three stakes races at around nine furlongs in the States. The grandam French Bird won twice over sprint distances in Ireland and was one of numerous winners out of the unbroken Golden Pheasant. Pampabird, a strong, attractive colt bought for 29,000 guineas as a foal and resold for 25,000 guineas as a yearling at the Newmarket Houghton Sales, stayed a mile and acted on any going. Usually bandaged, he clearly had problems with his legs but couldn't have shown more courage. *J. Cunnington, jnr, France.*

PAMPAS 3 b.f. Pampapaul 121–Ribotingo 78 (Petingo 135) (1982 6f 6g 1983 7g² 6fg⁴ 5f* 5g² 6d² 5g⁴ 5g³ 5s²) quite a well-made, lengthy filly; won maiden race at Mallow in August and ran well in competitive handicaps next 4 starts, finishing excellent second twice at the Curragh; well below best when 2 lengths second to 20/1-chance Celtic Bird in minor event at Haydock in October on final outing; stays 7f but seems better at shorter distances; possibly not at her best on very soft going, but acts on any other; usually apprentice ridden, but not on fifth and sixth starts. *A. Moore, Ireland.*   **90**

PAMPERED GIPSY 4 b.g. Pampapaul 121–Gipsy Heart (Skymaster 126) (1982 6f 7fg 7f 6g 6f 7f² 7f³ 6g⁴ 6g⁴ 7fg² 7.3g³ 8d 8fg 7.2s 7s⁴ 6d 1983 11.7h) poor walker and mover; stays 7f; acts on any going; wears blinkers; good mount for an apprentice. *A. Bailey.*   **–**

PAMPERMEE 3 b.f. Pampapaul 121–Quantas 91 (Roan Rocket 128) (1982 NR 1983 12fg 17f) 3,800F, 6,400Y; half-sister to 2 winners, including sprinter Stepping   **–**

Gaily (by Gay Fandango); dam won over 6f at 2 yrs; no sign of ability in minor events (pulled up second outing); sold 740 gns Newmarket September Sales. *R. Hollinshead.*

PAMRODENA 6 b.m. Pamroy 99–Lerina Park (Le Lavandou 111) (1982 NR 1983 16s³ 10s 10f) sturdy mare; third in race in Isle of Man in May; stays well; sold 720 gns Doncaster October Sales. *J. Townson.* —

PAMYA (USA) 3 b.f. Bold Forbes–Pause 76 (Aureole 132) (1982 5f 5fg² 5g 5f 5d⁴ 5f 1983 7fg 7f 7f 5g) neat filly; no form in 1983; bred to stay 7f+ but is a free-running sort. *J. Ciechanowski.* —

PANBEL 2 gr.f. Dragonara Palace 115–Pakpao 77 (Mansingh 120) (1983 5v 5d 6s) Apr 5; second foal; half-sister to 1982 2-y-o 5f seller winner Pandan (by Blue Cashmere); dam 2-y-o 5f winner; soundly beaten in maiden races, wearing blinkers when last of 17 at Leicester in May on final start. *T. Fairhurst.* —

PANDAN 3 br.c. Blue Cashmere 129–Pakpao 77 (Mansingh 120) (1982 5g³ 5s 5f 5f* 5f* 6g 5f 1983 7f 7f 6g 6fg) leggy colt; has a round action; plater; soundly beaten in 1983; blinkered last 2 starts; sold 1,800 gns Ascot December Sales. *K. Morgan.* —

PANGULO 3 ch.c. Realm 129–Blue Draco (Majority Blue 126) (1982 5g² 5s³ 5fg⁴ 5fg³ 6f³ 6g⁴ 6g 6g 7g 1983 9v 6g 5f 6f 6f 7.6g 6fg 6s²) rather lightly-built colt; plater; stays 6f; often wears blinkers; sold 900 gns Doncaster September Sales. *T. Fairhurst.* 57

PANIC STATIONS 2 b.f. Red Alert 127–Dariana (Reform 132) (1983 5d 5fg 5g⁴ 5f* 6f² 6f* 6f⁴ 7g 5g⁴ 5d⁴) Apr 23; 3,000F; small, fair sort; has a sharp action; second produce; dam won in Norway; fair plater; successful at Folkestone (no bid) in July and Ripon (bought in 5,800 gns) in August; effective at 5f and 6f; yet to race on very soft going but acts on any other; blinkered third outing; genuine and consistent. *P. Makin.* 70

PAPAGENO 2 gr.c. Bruni 131–Amberwood 95 (Amber Light 114) (1983 6fg) May 18; big, useful-looking colt; fourth foal; dam won 6 times from 1¼m to 19f; in need of race, behind in 24-runner maiden event at Doncaster in November; likely to need stiff test of stamina. *R. Hollinshead.* —

PAPERETTO 4 br.c. Godswalk 130–Goosie-Gantlet 63 (Run The Gantlet) (1982 8s² 7fg⁴ 8f³ 10g 8d⁴ 8f 7g² 8g* 8f 7f* 7g 1983 8d² 7v 10g 7s 7fg 8d 8g) useful-looking colt; fairly useful handicapper at his best but is inconsistent; kept on well to be 2½ lengths second to Mighty Fly in William Hill Lincoln at Doncaster in March; didn't reproduce that form; best at up to 1m; acts on any going; sweated up third start; suited by forcing tactics. *B. Hills.* 87

PAPIER MACHE 2 ch.f. Touch Paper 113–Eirene Oge (Green God 128) (1983 5d 5s 5s 5f³ 5fg 5fg 5fg 5f⁴ 5g⁴ 5g 5g⁴) Apr 16; IR 3,000C; leggy filly; dam Irish maiden; poor maiden; evidently considered a 5f performer; suited by a sound surface. *J. Wilson.* 59

PARABEMS 4 b.f. Swing Easy 126–Lunar Queen 96 (Queen's Hussar 124) (1982 6g² 5d² 5s⁴ 6f⁴ 6g 5d² 6fg 5d 6d 1983 5v* 6v 5s³ 5d 5fg) leggy filly; poor mover; sprint handicapper; won at Folkestone in March; stays 6f; acts on any going but is ideally suited by some give in the ground; blinkered in 1983; has run creditably for an apprentice though has shown a tendency to hang; sold 2,600 gns Newmarket September Sales. *K. Brassey.* 57

PARADISE ISLAND 2 b.f. Artaius 129–Diamond Star (Lyphard 132) (1983 7fg) Feb 24; 19,000Y; second foal; dam unraced daughter of Prix de la Foret winner Democratie; had a chance inside last 2f when 9½ lengths eighth of 14 to Claude Monet in minor event at Doncaster in October; should do better. *C. Brittain.* – p

PARADISE REGAINED 3 ch.f. North Stoke 130–All Souls 96 (Saint Crespin III 132) (1982 6fg 8s 1983 11s) lengthy, tall, narrow filly; in rear in minor event and maiden races. *M. Usher.* —

PARADISE STRAITS 3 ch.f. Derrylin 115–Flaming Peace 104 (Queen's Hussar 124) (1982 7g 7fg 7fg 7.6v 1983 12s⁴ 16s* 17f 19g) rather a plain filly; proved well suited by the stiff test of stamina when decisively winning small handicap at Chepstow in May; acts on soft going; had stiffish task and been off course almost 3 months final start. *S. Woodman.* 65

PARADISE WALK (USA) 2 b.c. Caucasus 127–Sweet Impression (First Balcony) (1983 6g) Feb 22; $50,000F, $95,000Y; third produce; dam won small 1m stakes race at 5 yrs; in rear in 20-runner maiden race at Yarmouth in June; sold 460 gns Newmarket Autumn Sales. *F. Durr.* —

PARADIS TERRESTRE (USA) 4 b.c. Empery 128–Pixie Tower 116   **112**
(Songedor 116) (1982 7g⁴ 8s 1983 8v² 8v* 9.2v* 10.5d 9.7d⁴ 10.5s*)
lightly-made, narrow ex-English colt; has a nice, easy action; high class at his best
in this country when trained by H. Cecil; successful in minor event at Evry (beat
Hayel) and 70,000 francs race at Longchamp (by a nose from Naishakar) in April
and 90,000 francs event at Saint-Cloud in June; beat Un Etendard a nose in
last-named; creditable 2½ lengths fourth to Welsh Term in Prix Dollar at
Longchamp fifth start; stays 1¼m well; yet to race on a firm surface. *P.-L.
Biancone, France.*

PARAMARIBO (USA) 2 b.c. Super Concorde 128–Thatch Mop (Raise A   **99**
Native) (1983 6f* 6f² 6h³ 7d* 7fg 7fg⁴) Mar 3; $45,000Y; lengthy, attractive colt;
second foal; dam won sprints at 4 and 5 yrs; won 20-runner maiden race at
Newmarket in July and 17-runner nursery under top weight at Wolverhampton in
October; will stay 1m; acts on hard going and a soft surface; exported to Hong
Kong. *M. Jarvis.*

PARAMOUNT (USA) 2 b.f. Full Out–Brilliant Touch (Gleaming) (1983 7f 7f 7g)   –
Mar 31; $15,500Y, $25,000 2-y-o; sturdy, quite attractive filly; first foal; dam
once-raced half-sister to dam of high-class filly Love Sign; no form in maiden
events. *D. Sasse.*

PARANG 2 b.c. Sharpen Up 127–Parmelia 118 (Ballymoss 136) (1983 8fg 7fg) Apr   –
14; big, good-looking colt; good mover; half-brother to 3 winners, including very
useful miler Rebec (by Tudor Melody) and useful stayer Ormeley (by Crepello);
dam, half-sister to St Paddy, won Park Hill Stakes; well beaten in useful company at
Newmarket in October, on second occasion slowly away; looks capable of better in
time. *P. Walwyn.*

PARCHESSI (USA) 3 b.f. Youth 135–Thill (Iron Ruler) (1982 NR 1983 13fg   –
12fg 12d) second foal; half-sister to American winner Cintula (by Ramsinga); dam,
daughter of top-class American sprinter Ta Wee, won 3 sprint races; weak in
market when in rear in maiden races at Nottingham and Lingfield (2); sold 25,000
gns Newmarket December Sales. *J. Dunlop.*

PARISIENNE LARK 3 b.f. Sir Lark 101–Lady Novus (Ben Novus 109) (1982   –
NR 1983 11.7fg) first foal; dam of no account over hurdles; unquoted when
well-beaten eighth of 11 behind Karablake in minor event at Windsor in September.
M. Scudamore.

PARISIO (USA) 4 b.g. Sham-Miralla 120 (Allangrange 126) (1982 11g 12fg 16h²   –
16fg* 14g² 15.5f* 1983 14fg 18f) rather narrow, lengthy gelding; has a rather
round action; bandaged when well beaten in 1983; suited by a test of stamina; yet
to race on a soft surface. *D. Morley.*

PARIS NORTH (CAN) 3 gr.c. Lucky North Man–Bye Bye Paris (Grey Dawn II   **86**
132) (1982 8fg 8s 1983 12g 10v 10f 12g* 12f* 12f² 12f 16fg 14fg⁴ 13.3d²) big,
sturdy colt; won handicaps at Lingfield and Goodwood (£4,000 event) in July; good
second in similar races at Newbury in August (to Millfontaine) and October (to
Insular); stays 13f (found little when let down over 1¾m and 2m); seems to act on
any going; reportedly broke a blood vessel third start; sold to J. Jenkins 23,000 gns
Newmarket Autumn Sales. *J. Sutcliffe.*

PARISSAUL 3 b. or br.f. Saulingo 122–Varinessa (Varano) (1982 5fg³ 6g² 8d   –
1983 9s⁴ 12g) strong, compact filly; should be suited by 1¼m+; sent to race in
USA. *S. Norton.*

PARK BRIDGE 6 ch.g. Park Lawn 111–Asa-Bridge 77 (Como 120) (1982 11.7f   **37**
8h⁴ 10.6h 8g 8fg 9f 8.3g³ 8d² 8fg 8g 1983 10s 7s 8h 8f 8f) compact gelding;
plater; stays 1m well; possibly not at his best on very soft going, but acts on any
other; has worn blinkers; sold 420 gns Ascot November Sales. *M. Pipe.*

PARKDALE 5 ch.h. Swing Easy 126–Miss McWorden 75 (Worden II 129) (1982   –
10f³ 10.2f 8fg³ 10g⁴ 10fg² 10g 12g 12fg 12fg 12g 8s 1983 12v 12v) big, strong,
well-made horse; excellent mover; mainly disappointing since his 2-y-o days;
seems to stay 1½m; seems to act on any going; sometimes blinkered. *J.
Fitzgerald.*

PARK JET 7 b.g. Lear Jet 123–Parallelogram 63 (Pardal 130) (1982 NR 1983   –
12f) of little account. *R. Morris.*

PARK LADY 2 ch.f. Tap On Wood 130–Pointe de Grace (Dapper Dan) (1983 6f   **82** p
6g*) Mar 3; 58,000 gns F, $140,000Y; second reported foal and first to Northern
Hemisphere time; dam won over 9f in France and is half-sister to smart American
horse Point du Jour; 5/1 when winning 19-runner maiden race at the Curragh in

619

Mr Patrick H. Burns's "Park Lady"

August by 1½ lengths from Ms Kelmoy; had been pulled up in a distressed condition when favourite for 10-runner maiden race at Phoenix Park earlier in month (trained by L. Browne at time); will stay 1m; a useful filly in the making. *J. Bolger, Ireland.*

PARK PARADE 2 b.f. Monsanto 121–Parthian Queen 92 (Parthia 132) (1983 7.6d) Apr 21; half-sister to minor winners in France and Italy; dam, winner over 11f, is sister to best 3-y-o staying filly of 1966 Parthian Glance; shaped nicely although beaten some way when seventh of 20 to Katies in maiden race at Lingfield in October; will be suited by further; sure to do better in time. *J. Dunlop.* — p

PARK SPRINGS 2 br.f. Brigadier Gerard 144–Park Covert 93 (On Your Mark 125) (1983 5v² 5d² 5d* 5f 6g*) Apr 13; leggy, rather sparely-made filly; first foal; dam stayed 1m; apprentice ridden, made virtually all in maiden race at Ayr in June and minor event at Catterick in September, on second occasion upsetting by neck odds laid on Knights Secret; bred to stay at least 1m; suited by an easy surface; hung badly first 2 starts (reportedly suffering from abscess on mouth) and also veered off a straight course at Catterick. *J. Berry.* 85

PARLIAMENT 3 ch.c. Lord Gayle 124–Harbrook 95 (Le Haar 126) (1982 7g⁴ 1983 8s* 8v³ 12f 10g 8d) IR 140,000Y; medium-sized colt; keen walker; third foal; half-brother to very useful 1981 2-y-o sprint winner End of the Line (by Saulingo); dam won over 7f at 2 yrs; beat High Notions in good style by 4 lengths in 12-runner maiden race at Phoenix Park in May; kept on strongly and ran tremendously well considering his inexperience when 1¾ lengths third of 10 behind Wassl and Lomond in Airlie/Coolmore Irish 2000 Guineas at the Curragh later in month; finished only tenth of 12 behind Shareef Dancer in Irish Sweeps Derby at the Curragh in June and was off course afterwards until September, when respectable fifth of 11 behind Stanerra in Joe McGrath Memorial Stakes at Leopardstown, beaten about 7 117

620

lengths; worth another chance at 1½m; acts well on heavy going. *D. K. Weld, Ireland.*

PARLOUR PRINCESS 3 ch.f. Gentilhombre 131–Dairy Queen 76 (Queen's — Hussar 124) (1982 5g 7f 7f 6g 7.6v 1983 6f 7f) workmanlike filly; last both outings in 1983; stays 7f. *R. Smyth.*

PARRE TRIA 4 b.g. Sparkler 130–Flotsam 67 (Rustam 127) (1982 8g 8f⁴ 10f 12f — 14g 13.1g⁴ 12.3fg 1983 12d) fair sort; poor form, including in a seller; probably stays 13f; acts on firm going; blinkered once at 3 yrs; has worn bandages; winner over hurdles. *D. Sasse.*

PARTAKE 2 b.f. Take a Reef 127–My Cervantes (Hill Clown or Nulli Secundus 46 89) (1983 5v³ 5v 6fg⁴ 6fg³ 5f 6f) Apr 28; lightly-built filly; half-sister to 2 minor winners; dam poor half-sister to smart miler Maystreak; poor plater; not raced after July. *J. Holt.*

PARVENO 2 ch.c. Abwah 118–Lichen Lady 70 (Pardao 120) (1983 5v 5v 5v 5.3f 80 5g* 5f 5.3f² 5h 5.3fg³ 6fg* 5fg 7fg) Apr 30; 2,300Y; tall, leggy colt; has a round action; half-brother to 2 winners, including fair 1½m winner Rushbeds (by Ercolano); dam won over 1½m; successful in sellers at Lingfield in July (made all) and Newmarket in October (led near finish); bought in 2,200 gns on first occasion and 13,000 gns on second; much better suited by 6f than 5f, and should stay 7f; acts on firm going; usually blinkered. *R. Hoad.*

PASQUIER 4 b.g. Shiny Tenth 120–Tweetie Pie (Falcon 131) (1982 10s 1983 8f) — poor form, including in a seller; has worn blinkers. *H. O'Neill.*

PASSING AFFAIR (USA) 2 b.c. Elocutionist–Flirtation (Fleet Feet) (1983 110 7fg* 7fg²) Mar 13; $150,000Y; tall, rather leggy colt; half-brother to 5 winners, including very useful sprinter La Belle Coquette (by Exclusive Native); dam very useful stakes winner at up to 1m; well-backed favourite, made a very encouraging debut in 17-runner maiden race at Salisbury in September, scoring by 1½ lengths from Adiyamann after being eased significantly when running green in closing stages; good second to Reflection under 9-7 in John Sutcliffe Trophy Nursery at Lingfield the following month; will stay 1¼m; sure to win more races. *G. Harwood.*

PASSING MOMENT (USA) 4 ch.g. Parade of Stars–Thelma Dear — (Ballydonnell) (1982 6s 10f 8f 9g 10d 12fg 1983 10d) lightly-built gelding; good walker; plater nowadays; isn't sure to get 1¼m; blinkered once; sold 550 gns Ascot October Sales. *J. Jenkins.*

PASSING STORM 2 ch.c. Manado 130–Lady Beck 104 (Sir Gaylord) (1983 6fg³ 95 6g² 6fg⁴ 5g*) Mar 25; lengthy, quite attractive colt; third foal; half brother to 1980 2-y-o 5f winner Malia (by Malacate); dam won over 1m at 2 yrs in France; had an easy task in maiden race at Warwick in October and won by 5 lengths and 4 lengths; had run well previous month in minor event at Doncaster (second to Round Hill) and £6,000 maiden race at Ascot; will stay beyond 6f. *F. J. Houghton.*

PASSING THROUGH 3 br.f. Be My Guest 126–Angel Row 96 (Prince Regent 64 129) (1982 6d 1983 6v⁴ 8g 6fg 5g³ 6g 6g) quite well-made filly; rather a disappointing maiden; should be suited by further than 6f. *G. Hunter.*

PASSIONNEL 3 br.c. So Blessed 130–Gallic Law 91 (Galivanter 131) (1982 5g — 5fg³ 6fg² 1983 6fg 6fg 5g 5g 6d 5g) stocky colt; poor maiden; probably stays 6f; blinkered fourth outing; trained most of season by D. Marks. *M. Blanshard.*

PASS NO REMARKS 4 b.f. Wolverlife 115–Place To Place (No Robbery) (1982 — 6f 5fg 5fg 5fg⁴ 7f 7g 7.2f 5d 1983 5.1g 5f 5fg) lengthy, lightly-made filly; has shown no form for a long time and ran deplorably second start; best form at 5f; blinkered final outing. *B. McMahon.*

PASS TO PARADISE (USA) 4 gr.f. Key To The Kingdom–Duke's Duchess 63 (The Axe 115) (1982 10g 12.3g² 14g³ 12v 10g² 12d² 1983 12s 12f 11.5f* 12f³ 14f 11f) leggy, narrow filly; not a good mover; narrowly won amateur riders maiden event at Yarmouth in July; ran badly final start; stays 1¾m; seems to act on any going. *G. Pritchard-Gordon.*

PASTUNI 2 b.f. Rapid River 127–Whistlewych 40 (Whistler 129) (1983 5s 5d 5f 7f — 6f 5f) Apr 7; small, lightly-made filly; bad plater; not raced after July; blinkered final outing. *J. Carr.*

PATERNOSTER ROW 4 b.c. Godswalk 130–Abergara (Abernant 142) (1982 — 10fg³ 12fg 12g 12g⁴ 12fg³ 1983 18d 13.3v³ 16.1v 12fg 11.5f 13fg 10.8d 10.2fg) big, rangy colt; good mover; disappointing handicapper; will stay 1¾m; seems to act on any going; trained by R. Morris first 6 starts. *D. H. Jones.*

PATH OF PEACE 7 br. g. Warpath 113–Turtle Dove (Gyr 131) (1982 18.4fg   **100**
12fg 15d* 13d³ 14s² 14s² 12s 1983 12v* 12g* 14.6fg 15g* 14d² 12fg) small,
strong gelding; useful handicapper; came with a strong run to beat Miss Diaward
a length at York in May, Cool Decision by 2½ lengths in Great Yorkshire Handicap
on same course in August and Mayotte by 2 lengths in amateur riders event at
Ayr in September; stays 2m; well suited by plenty of give in the ground; goes well
when fresh; genuine. *C. Thornton.*

PATINATION 3 br. f. Monsanto 121–Miss Brecqhou 58 (Linacre 133) (1982 6g   –
7fg 6s 1983 8f 7h³ 7f 5f 6fg⁴ 7s 6fg 6fg) close-coupled, workmanlike filly; poor
plater; best at up to 7f. *A. Bailey.*

PAT ON THE BACK 3 b. f. Mummy's Pet 125–Kalopia 80 (Kalydon 122) (1982   –
5g² 5fg 6d 6f 6fg 6d 8fg 1983 6v 7fg 6fg 6f) leggy, lightly-made filly; not sure to
stay 1m; has worn blinkers. *G. Blum.*

PATRICK JOHN LYONS 2 b. c. Cavo Doro 124–Latin Spice (Frankincense   **80**
120) (1983 7g 7fg 8d 9f⁴ 10.2fg) Mar 20; robust, compact colt; third foal; dam
last on only outing; 2½ lengths fourth of 13 to Cri de Coeur in maiden race at
Redcar in October; suited by 9f. *S. Matthews.*

PATROON 4 b. c. Thatch 136–Greedy 69 (Major Portion 129) (1982 10g² 7g 8d*   –
1983 8s² 7s² 8s³) IR 10,500Y; sparely-made colt; third live foal; half-brother to
1977 Irish 2-y-o 6f and 7f winner Needy (by High Top); dam, half-sister to smart
stayer Shatter, stayed at least 1¼m; favourite when beaten 3 lengths by Yankee's
Princess in Irish Lincolnshire Handicap at the Curragh in March; length second to
ready winner Lomond in Gladness Stakes on same course in April; stayed 1¼m;
acted on soft going; dead. *D. O'Brien, Ireland.*

PATSY PENNALL 3 ch. f. Celtic Cone 116–Clyde Bush 59 (Bullrush 106) (1982   –
5fg² 5d³ 5g² 5fg² 6g³ 7d 6f 5g³ 6d 5v 1983 5f 5s) small, sturdy filly; sprint plater;
best form on a sound surface; sometimes blinkered as a 2-y-o. *J. Yardley.*

PATTER (USA) 2 b. or br. g. Bold Bidder–Lucky Spell (Lucky Mel) (1983 7f   **67 p**
7fg) Apr 17; $190,000Y; strong, long-backed gelding; third foal; brother to very
useful 6f and 7f winner Merlins Charm; dam very smart winner of 12 races at up to
9f; had anything but a clear run and in circumstances showed promise when 6½
lengths ninth of 19 to Lake Valentina in maiden race at Newbury in August; stayed
on without being knocked about when out of first 9 of 30 behind stable-companion
Rainbow Quest in similar event at Newmarket later in month; gelded
subsequently; will stay 1m; better than his form suggests. *J. Tree.*

PAULAGER 5 b. g. Lochnager 132–Hopeful Subject 82 (Mandamus 120) (1982   **81**
7d³ 7f* 7fg² 7fg* 7f 1983 7fg 8f 7f 8fg 7.6g) strong gelding; quite useful
handicapper at his best; suited by a strongly-run 7f but seems to find 1m too far;
acts on any going. *D. McCain.*

PAUL MARINER 3 ch. c. Julio Mariner 127–Aruba 77 (Amber Rama 133) (1982   –
7g 7s 8s 1983 8d) no form in maiden and minor events; sold 1,850 gns Newmarket
July Sales. *R. Boss.*

PAUSE FOR THOUGHT 6 ch. g. Jukebox 120–Madlin 102 (Sovereign Path   **67**
125) (1982 8f² 7f 8g* 9fg² 8fg 8f⁴ 8fg⁴ 8f⁴ 8.2g 1983 7v 8g 7fg 8d 7f 10f⁴ 8.2f² 10f*
10.2fg⁴ 8fg 10.6g³ 9d 10.2fg) tall gelding; won handicap at Ripon in August; stays
1¼m; acts on any going; has occasionally worn blinkers; sometimes sweats up;
suitable mount for an inexperienced rider; suited by waiting tactics. *D. Smith.*

PAYMASTER 2 b. c. Dom Racine 121–Cash Flo 72 (Floribunda 136) (1983 5s³   **101**
5s⁴ 5s⁴ 6g* 6f* 7fg⁴ 8d 7g⁴) Apr 5; IR 1,000F, IR 12,000Y (privately); half-brother
to 2 winners abroad; dam 2-y-o 6f winner; led close home to win 2 races by a neck
in June, beating Late Sally in minor event at Naas and Productivity in Tyros Stakes
at the Curragh; over 3 lengths fourth to Executive Pride in Ardenode Stud Stakes
at Leopardstown in August and to Fiery Celt in Tap On Wood Stakes at Phoenix
Park in October; last of 7 in Group 3 Ashford Castle Stakes in between; should stay
1m; acts on a firm surface. *M. Connolly, Ireland.*

PAY THE FARE 3 ch. g. Dublin Taxi–Lizzylyn 84 (Tower Walk 130) (1982 5f 5fg   **68**
5f 1983 5d 5v 5s² 5f* 5f*) tall, robust gelding; second in a seller before winning
apprentice handicap at Beverley and handicap at Carlisle (by 5 lengths) in June; has
raced only at 5f; acts on any going, but clearly goes well on firm; tends to hang
right. *M. Camacho.*

PEACEFUL RUN 3 ch. f. Grundy 137–Peaceful 95 (Crepello 136) (1982 6s 1983   **76**
8s³ 10s⁴ 10.5s² 10s 10f 10f⁴ 10g³ 8h 10g² 9d 10fg³) quite attractive filly; good
walker; quite a moderate maiden; suited by 1¼m; tends to get behind; sold 15,000
gns Newmarket December Sales. *G. Wragg.*

PEACEHAVEN 2 ch.f. Home Guard 129–Quiet Harbour (Mill Reef 141) (1983 7f 6g[4]) Apr 28; 26,000Y; tall, rather leggy filly; third foal; dam lightly-raced half-sister to Quiet Fling, Peacetime, Intermission and Armistice Day; favourite following promising debut, could keep on only at one pace when 6½ lengths fourth of 18 to Real Silver in minor event at Pontefract in October; needs 7f+. *R. Laing.* **71**

PEACETIME (USA) 4 b.c. Nijinsky 138–Peace 113 (Klairon 131) (1982 10f* 12fg* 12f 10g[4] 10fg* 1983 9d[3]) strong, lengthy, attractive colt who did well physically over the winter; has been hobdayed and has had a soft palate operation; a high-class performer in 1982 when he won Guardian Classic Trial at Sandown, Schroder Life Predominate Stakes at Goodwood and Valdoe Stakes at Goodwood again; looked and ran as though needing race when 8½ lengths third of 7 to Ivano in Earl of Sefton Stakes at Newmarket in April (wore a tongue strap); not seen out again; stayed 1½m; acted on firm going; stud in South Africa. *J. Tree.* **–**

PEACE TREATY 3 gr.g. Warpath 113–Country Ramble 93 (Kribi 110) (1982 8s 1983 7g 8v) probably of little account. *W. Stubbs.* **–**

PEAK CONDITION 7 ch.m. Mountain Call 125–Saffron Hill 101 (Gulf Pearl 117) (1982 12f 1983 11.7fg) of no account. *Mrs N. Kennedy.* **–**

PEANDAY 2 b.g. Swing Easy 126–Parradell 104 (Pandofell 132) (1983 5v 5s[4] 5g[2] 5.8g[4] 6g 5f[4] 5f* 6f 5g 6d) Apr 14; 675Y; tall, good-topped gelding; half-brother to 2 minor winners; dam 1¼m winner and sister to very smart stayer Piaco; won 12-runner maiden race at Folkestone in August; stays 6f; probably acts on any going; often blinkered. *H. Beasley.* **70**

PEARL CITY 2 b.c. Camden Town 125–Pearl Barley 79 (Pinza 137) (1983 5s 5s 6g) May 29; 5,000Y; rather lightly-made colt; closely related to 1m winner Darley Dale (by Derring-Do) and half-brother to 3 winners here and abroad; dam second 4 times at up to 1¾m; plating-class maiden; not raced after May. *E. Eldin.* **60**

PEARL KING 2 ch.g. Gulf Pearl 117–Sky Green (Skymaster 126) (1983 5s 6d 5.8g[4] 6d 8fg) June 4; 1,500Y; workmanlike gelding; half-brother to 1m winner Gerpoora (by Laser Light); dam ran only twice; poor maiden; showed form only on third outing; out of first 11 in 16-runner Newmarket seller on final appearance; subsequently gelded. *R. Hannon.* **53**

PEARLPIN 3 ch.g. Grundy 137–Pearlesque 88 (Gulf Pearl 117) (1982 6g 7fg 8s 10s 1983 9s 10d 10.5f 8f 10.2f 12.2f[3] 12f[3] 12.3f* 14d 12g 12fg 11g[3] 16fg[3] 13.8g 18fg) small, fair sort; won 3-runner maiden race at Newcastle in August; often had stiff tasks afterwards; seems to stay 2m; acts on firm going. *R. Whitaker.* **71**

PEARL RUN 2 ch.c. Gulf Pearl 117–Deep Down (Deep Run 119) (1983 5v 5d 7fg 8g 8fg[3] 10d 8fg) May 17; IR 5,000Y; good-bodied colt; second foal; dam unraced sister to 2 winners; moderate plater; stays 1m; acts on a firm surface. *K. Stone.* **60**

PEARL THYME 3 b.f. Gulf Pearl 117–Wild Thyme 63 (Galivanter 131) (1982 5.1f 6f 6s[3] 7f 8d 8.2s 1983 8d 10s[3] 10s[4] 12f[4] 14f* 14f[2] 16fg) leggy filly; beat Quickening Dawn by 1½ lengths in maiden race at Yarmouth in July and ran well next time; suited by 1¾m (tailed off over 2m however); acts on any going, but best form on firm; sold 6,400 gns Newmarket Autumn Sales. *B. Hobbs.* **80**

PEARLY STEPS 4 ch.g. Gulf Pearl 117–Step You Gaily 71 (King's Company 124) (1982 8fg 10fg 12g[4] 11.7f 16g 12fg 1983 10.2d 12s) rangy gelding; plating-class maiden on flat though has won over hurdles; stays 1½m. *Mrs J. Pitman.* **–**

PEAR SUNDAE 4 b.f. Shiny Tenth 120–Alice Perrers (Twilight Alley 133) (1982 12f 12g 12g[2] 12fg 14g 14.6g 12fg 1983 12f 12f) leggy filly; plater; stays 1½m; sometimes blinkered; cost 680 gns Doncaster March Sales. *S. Wiles.* **–**

PEBBLES 2 ch.f. Sharpen Up 127–La Dolce 108 (Connaught 130) (1983 5d 6g* 6fg* 6g[4] 7fg 6fg[2]) **114**

Julio Mariner's St Leger win at 28/1, Radetzky's Royal Ascot wins at 16/1 and 25/1, and Lafontaine's Cumberland Lodge Stakes win at 22/1 are some of the more notable examples trainer Brittain could cite to justify what some see as his over-optimism in placing his horses. Pebbles could be cited as another, since she failed by only a neck to add the William Hill Cheveley Park Stakes at Newmarket in September to these successes at odds of 33/1; only stable-companion African Abandon, Malaak and Rare Gal started at longer odds for the race. The field for the Cheveley Park also contained Prickle and Desirable, first and second in the Lowther Stakes at York the previous month (in which Pebbles had finished over four lengths fourth after a two-month absence from the racecourse), and Gala

623

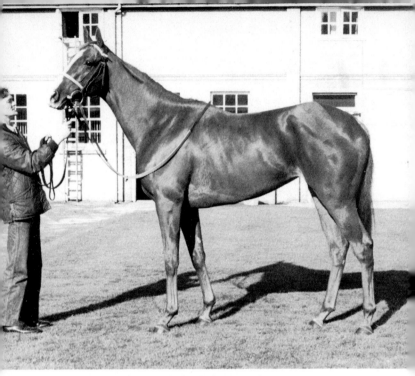

Captain M. Lemos' "Pebbles"

Event, the Moyglare Stud Stakes winner. Pebbles, who was sweating beforehand, came with a strong run in the final furlong and failed narrowly to catch Desirable, with Prickle a short head away third. Although this was Pebbles' best effort by far she'd won twice earlier. She'd quickened in good style to account for Refill by four lengths in the Kingsclere Stakes at Newbury, and when beating Sajeda by three lengths, giving weight to most of her twelve opponents, in the Childwick Stud Stakes at Newmarket later in the month. Pebbles finished a disappointing fifth when second-favourite for the seven-furlong Waterford Candelabra Stakes at Goodwood nine days after the Lowther: as in the Cheveley Park, she sweated up in the preliminaries, but she also raced too freely and hung badly when tired.

	Sharpen Up (ch 1969)	Atan (ch 1961)	Native Dancer Mixed Marriage
Pebbles (ch. f. Feb 27, 1981)		Rocchetta (ch 1961)	Rockefella Chambiges
	La Dolce (ch 1976)	Connaught (b 1965)	St Paddy Nagaika
		Guiding Light (ch 1965)	Crepello Arbitrate

After Pebbles' victory at Newmarket her trainer commented that she was one of the best fillies he's trained. Amongst the others must rank her dam, La Dolce, whose first foal Pebbles is. La Dolce won two races at a mile and finished fifth to Scintillate in the Oaks. The grandam Guiding Light, a middle-distance maiden bred by the Royal Studs, has produced three winners, notably the 1977 Queen Mary third Princess Zena and Port Ahoy, a winner at seven furlongs as a juvenile who has since produced the Rockfel Stakes winner Top Hope. Her sire Sharpen Up has made his name as a sire of fast-maturing two-year-olds who train on, although most of his stock have stamina limitations. Pebbles, a sparely-made filly who possibly won't stand a great deal of racing, should stay a mile if she learns to settle. She acts on a firm surface. *C. Brittain.*

PEG'S PETAL 3 ch.f. Ardoon 124–Abrill (Laser Light 118) (1982 5g 5f 5fg 5f²   – §
5f* 5d 5fg⁴ 5fg 5f 5s 1983 6s 5v 5.1fg 8f) of little account nowadays and isn't one to trust. *J. Gilbert.*

PEKING DANCER 3 ch.f. Orbit Dancer–Flying Bridge 71 (Bleep-Bleep 134)   –
(1982 5d 5fg 5fg³ 5fg 6g 5g⁴ 5f 6f 5v 1983 6v 10v 7g 7fg 10f 10f 8f 8g 10g) strong, lengthy filly; bad plater. *P. K. Mitchell.*

PELHAM LINE 3 ch.f. High Line 125–Pelham Wood 59 (Marmaduke 108) (1982   –
7f 7fg 1983 10fg 12g) quite well-made filly; has a round action; well beaten in maiden and minor events and a handicap. *W. Musson.*

PELION (FR) 3 b.g. Sassafras 135–Pallakis (Narrator 127) (1982 7g 8.2s 1983   58
16v⁴ 14.7d⁴ 13.8g*) well-made gelding; stayed on under pressure when narrowly winning maiden race at Catterick in May; suited by a test of stamina; sold to J. King 8,400 gns Ascot 2nd June Sales. *Sir Mark Prescott.*

PELLINORE'S POINT (USA) 3 b.c. King Pellinore 127–Bronze Point (Tobin   95
Bronze) (1982 6fg² 7fg 1983 8v⁴ 12d*) quite attractive, well-made colt; showed improved form when beating Moon Jester by ½ length in handicap at Thirsk in May; suited by 1½m; sent to race in USA. *S. Norton.*

PELOPONNESE (USA) 3 b.c. Bold Forbes–Snow Lady (Raise A Native) (1982   –
5fg 6fg 7f³ 8f⁴ 8d 1983 11.7s 11.7v 8f 10.1f 10fg) smallish, strong colt; should stay middle distances; acts on firm going and a soft surface; has given trouble at start; blinkered final start. *G. Kindersley.*

PEMELIA 3 b.f. Monsanto 121–Julie Be Quick (Selari) (1982 5s 8g 6s⁴ 1983   50
6.5g 8s⁴ 8s³ 8d³ 8v 8v 7d 12g 10f² 10f⁴ 10g⁴ 10g 8d) plater; in frame at Cagnes-sur-Mer early in year (trained by C. Milbank) and at Newmarket and Lingfield (twice); stays 1¼m; blinkered last 3 outings; sold 400 gns Doncaster October Sales. *R. Laing.*

PENARKSEA 3 ch.f. Privy Seal 108–The Festival Chat (Saucy Kit 76) (1982 5g   –
6s 1983 7.2fg 7f 10h) lightly-made filly; last in maiden races. *A. Fisher.*

PENCHETTA 3 gr.f. Sharpen Up 127–What A Picture 80 (My Swanee 122) (1982   –
5d⁴ 1983 5g 5fg⁴ 5f) plating-class maiden; has raced only at 5f. *C. Williams.*

PENDONA 2 b.f. Blue Cashmere 129–Calibina 101 (Caliban 123) (1983 5fg 5g²   72
6fg⁴) May 5; smallish, lightly-made filly; third foal; half-sister to 1982 2-y-o 6f winner Captain Tempest (by Manado) and successful 5f performer King Charlemagne (by Habat); dam, winner of Wokingham Stakes and Stewards' Cup, stayed 1m; in frame in October maiden events at Warwick and Leicester; best run at 5f. *W. Musson.*

PENDORI 2 b.f. Junius 124–Cresta 84 (Ribero 126) (1983 5fg 6f 6fg² 6fg² 6fg 7f   73
7f³) Apr 23; compact filly; second foal; half-sister to 1982 2-y-o 5f seller winner Cresta Swallow (by Hittite Glory); dam, half-sister to high-class Electric, won over 7f on only start at 2 yrs; placed in varied company in the summer, wearing blinkers when 4½ lengths third of 8 to Nepula in nursery at Yarmouth in August; stays 7f; has raced only on fast ground. *N. Callaghan.*

PENINSULA KING (FR) 2 b.g. Wolver Hollow 126–Baroness (Captain's Gig)   – §
(1983 7fg 7f 7d) Apr 26; 15,000Y; tall, slightly leggy, attractive gelding; second foal; half-brother to French 3-y-o Messagere du Soir (by Trepan); dam won over 6.5f in France at 2 yrs and is half-sister to high-class French colts Bellypha and Bellman; no worthwhile form; hung violently and flashed tail on debut and unseated rider when bolting on way to start on second appearance; evidently temperamental. *E. Eldin.*

PENITRAIT 2 b.f. Moulton 128–Sheinter (Sheshoon 132) (1983 7s 8d) Mar 18;   –
tall, leggy filly; half-sister to a winning plater and a winner abroad; dam ran only at 2 yrs; behind in maiden races at Beverley and Leicester (last of 18) in the autumn. *B. Morgan.*

PENLLYNE TROOPER 3 b.g. Tachypous 128–Fodens Eve 80 (Dike) (1982   81
5fg⁴ 5.8g² 6f 6s 6d⁴ 6g 6s² 1983 7.6v 8s⁴ 7d* 7fg 8.2fg³ 7fg² 7fg⁴ 8g 8g) big, tall gelding; won 16-runner maiden race at Sandown in May by 2 lengths from Amazon

Prince; also in frame in 4 handicaps; stays 1m well; probably acts on any going; occasionally blinkered; sometimes sweats up (did when successful). *R. Laing.*

PENNILESS DANCER 4 b.g. Impecunious–La Tango (Sailing Light 119) (1982 10.1fg⁴ 10.1fg 10.1fg 1983 10g) little worthwhile form; possibly stays 1¼m; bought 975 gns Ascot May Sales; sold to T. Kersey 925 gns same venue in July. *Mrs N. Smith.* —

PENNINE PRINCESS 3 br.f. Cawston's Clown 113–Firmpostie (Goldhill 125) (1982 NR 1983 6s 8d 7s 9f) lengthy, fair sort; half-sister to 6f and 7f seller winner Workshy (by Workboy); dam ran twice; behind in minor events and a maiden race. *W. Wharton.* —

PENNY RED 2 ch.f. Nebbiolo 125–Colourful 108 (Busted 134) (1983 9g³ 8fg) May 1; lengthy, rather sparely-made filly; third foal; half-sister to 3-y-o Irish 1¼m winner Tipperary Tartan (by Rarity); dam, closely related to smart Pink Gem, won from 1¼m to 1¾m; staying-on 5¾ lengths third of 10 to Penny's Double in maiden race at Wolverhampton in October; behind later in the month in valuable Newmarket seller; will stay 1¼m. *P. Cole.* 66

PENNY'S DOUBLE 2 b.f. Cavo Doro 124–Pennys From Heaven 60 (Royalty 130) (1983 6f 6f 7g⁴ 9g* 8d) Mar 11; rangy filly; moderate mover; first foal; dam won sellers over 6f and 7f; won 10-runner maiden race at Wolverhampton in October; suited by 9f. *N. Guest.* 80

PENNYWEIGHT 2 b.f. Troy 137–Hayloft 111 (Tudor Melody 129) (1983 7g) May 11; lengthy, attractive filly; third foal; half-sister to Irish 2000 Guineas winner Wassl (by Mill Reef); dam won Molecomb Stakes; weak in market and bit green, ran well until beaten and eased after 4f when 8½ lengths seventh of 10 to Troyanna in £3,800 race at York in October; sure to improve. *H. Cecil.* — p

PENSCYNOR 7 br.g. Lord Gayle 124–I Will (I Say 125) (1982 8d 9fg⁴ 9g⁴ 1983 8d⁴ 10.4fg³) lengthy ex-Irish gelding; poor performer nowadays; stays 1½m; acts on any going; sometimes blinkered and has worn a hood as well. *M. Lambert.* —

PENSYL-PAMSU 2 b.f. Streak 119–Belle Mere (Tacitus 124) (1983 5v 5.3fg 5g 6fg) June 3; 400Y; sister to 1m seller winner Party Trick; dam poor maiden; poor form, including in a seller. *C. Drew.* —

PENTLAND BEAUTY 2 ch.f. Remainder Man 126§–Long Drop 78 (Tower Walk 130) (1983 10fg 8f) Apr 24; 900Y; second foal; dam probably stayed 1m; little sign of ability in end-of-season maiden events at Nottingham and Leicester. *R. Hollinshead.* —

PENTLAND JAVELIN 3 b.c. Solinus 130–Georgian Girl 92 (Prince Tenderfoot 126) (1982 5g² 5g* 5f⁴ 5f³ 6fg³ 6fg* 6f² 6d 6g 6fg* 6d 1983 7s 6d 6f 6fg 6fg) attractive, good-bodied colt; useful performer on his day at 2 yrs; soundly beaten most starts in 1983 but had some stiffish tasks and was hampered at start second appearance; should stay 7f; best form on a firm surface. *R. Hollinshead.* 91

PENWOOD 8 b.m. Precipice Wood 123–Penview 73 (Pendragon) (1982 18g 1983 16v³) staying handicapper; revels in the mud; suitable mount for an apprentice. *N. Hall.* —

PENYBONT 3 ch.f. Welsh Pageant 132–Currency (Crepello 136) (1982 7g² 7fg 1983 8f 8fg² 9d4 10fg) rather lightly-made filly; in frame in minor event at Thirsk and maiden race at York in latter part of season; should stay 1¼m; slipped up final outing. *B. Hobbs.* 65

PEPPER'S COVE 2 b.g. Tanfirion 110–Fravelot (Javelot 124) (1983 8fg 8.2s 10fg) Apr 26; half-brother to The Very Thing (by Jupiter Pluvius), a fair middle-distance winner and useful hurdler; dam won over 1½m; well beaten in autumn maiden and minor events, on final outing blinkered. *S. Norton.* —

PEPPERWOOD 3 br.g. Tudor Rhythm 112–Calibre (Caliban 123) (1982 8s 1983 10.1s 11d 16g 14f) little worthwhile form; sometimes blinkered. *S. Matthews.* —

PERANG'S NIECE 2 b.f. High Award 119–Alumia (Great Nephew 126) (1983 6f 6fg 5fg² 5g²) Mar 28; big, strong filly; second foal; dam unplaced 3 times at 2 yrs; second in October maiden events at Lingfield and Leicester; finds 5f on sharp side and is suited by 7f; probably acts on any going. *K. Brassey.* 82

PERCASE 4 b.g. Tachypous 128–Pertinacity 106 (Aggressor 130) (1982 10d⁴ 11.7f² 12fg³ 13.1g³ 14f 11.7g* 12fg 12fg³ 11.7s³ 12s⁴ 1983 12.2v* 12d* 12v³ 12v 13.3g⁴ 12g² 12.2d*) neat gelding; quite a modest handicapper; won at Warwick and Newmarket (apprentices) in April and Warwick again in October; awarded race after going down by 5 lengths to Going Going on final occasion; suited by 1½m; acts 83 on any going but goes well in the mud; suited by waiting tactics; effective with or without blinkers; goes well when fresh. *I. Balding.*

PERFECT HOST 3 ch.c. Be My Guest 126–Popular Win 103 (Lorenzaccio 130) (1982 NR 1983 8f⁴ 7f² 8f³ 8.2g* 8f²) 25,000Y; quite an attractive colt; first foal; dam, daughter of Musidora winner Jakomima, won over 5f and 7f; in frame on all outings and won maiden race at Haydock in October; stays 1m; sold 7,800 gns Newmarket Autumn Sales and exported to Trinidad. *G. Harwood.* **85**

PERGODA 5 b.g. High Top 131–Saint Joan 63 (Grey Sovereign 128§) (1982 5f 6f 5fg 5f² 5g² 5fg 5fg² 5g² 5fg² 5s 5d 1983 6d⁴ 5d* 5g³ 5fg* 5f 5f 5f* 5f 5fg 5f 5fg 5g* 6fg 5d 7g) former plater; has been tubed; goes well at Edinburgh and won handicaps there in April (dead-heated), May, July and September; made all for last 2 successes; stays 6f but not 7f; acts on any going, except perhaps soft; usually blinkered nowadays; doesn't find much off bridle. *I. Vickers.* **68**

PERICULO LUDUS (FR) 7 ch.g. Timmy My Boy 125–La Beuvriere (Right Royal V 135) (1982 8f 8f⁴ 10d⁴ 10g³ 1983 11fg) workmanlike gelding; not a good mover; plater nowadays; stays 11f; seems to act on any going; sometimes wears blinkers. *J. Harris.* **–**

PERMABOS 4 b.g. Dubassoff–Blue Ann 60 (Road House II) (1982 12v 1983 14.7f) rangy gelding; has shown only a little ability in maiden races on flat, but is a winning hurdler. *K. Stone.* **–**

PEROVSKIA 3 b.f. Sagaro 133–Deep Blue (Deep Diver 134) (1982 5fg 6fg 8f 8fg² 9s 1983 8s 12.2d 12f³ 12.2f 12f* 13.8f³ 12fg* 8.2g 12f⁴ 12fg) neat, strong filly; plater; won in good style at Thirsk in July and September but didn't attract a bid either time; needs further than 1m and stays 1½m well; acts on any going; suitable mount for an apprentice. *J. Fitzgerald.* **61**

PERRY-BOY 3 b.g. Mon Cheval 71–Greatness (Pretty Form 97) (1982 NR 1983 12v) strong, good-topped gelding; first foal; dam never ran; 100/1 and in need of race when tailed-off last of 7 behind Dazari in minor event at Wolverhampton in May. *R. Morris.* **–**

PERSHING 2 ch.g. Gunner B 126–New Way 103 (Klairon 131) (1983 5f⁴ 6f³ 5h² 7f 7g) Mar 27; leggy, narrow gelding; poor mover; half-brother to 3 winners, including smart miler Star Way (by Star Appeal); dam won over 5f and 6f at 2 yrs; quite a moderate maiden; ran poorly in nurseries last 2 outings; should stay beyond 6f; acts on hard going. *J. Leigh.* **71**

PERSIAN EXPRESS 2 b.f. Persian Bold 123–La Pitore (Will Somers 114§) (1983 6f 7s 8d) Mar 29; 3,100Y; fair sort; closely related to fairly useful 1973 2-y-o 6f winner Lapis (by Bold Lad, Ire) and half-sister to 2 other winners; dam, half-sister to very smart Tacitus, won over 1m and 9f in Ireland; in rear in minor event and 2 maiden races. *D. Plant.* **–**

PERSIAN FRIEND 8 b.g. Be Friendly 130–Highland Rocket (Paveh 126) (1982 NR 1983 12g) thoroughly temperamental and must be avoided. *M. James.* **§§**

PERSIAN GILL 2 gr.g. Persian Breeze 121–Pippin Gill 77 (Ribston 104) (1983 6fg) Apr 6; first foal; dam stayed 7f; fifth of 6 in seller at Hamilton in July. *Mrs A. Bell.* **–**

PERSIAN GLORY 3 ch.c. Persian Bold 123–Painted Glen (Pall Mall 132) (1982 6d² 6fg* 7fg³ 7d⁴ 1983 7d⁴ 7f² 7fg 8fg³ 7fg) small, attractive, short-coupled colt; in frame in first half of season in Ladbroke European Free Handicap at Newmarket and Jersey Stakes at Royal Ascot, in latter event showing really good pace throughout and finishing excellent length second of 13 to Tecorno; didn't have best of runs next time and was subsequently off course 3 months; ran badly twice at Newmarket on his return, finishing last of 3 behind impressive Legend of France in Petition Stakes in September (moved atrociously to start) and ninth of 10 behind Salieri in Bisquit Cognac Challenge Stakes in October; stays 7f; acts on a soft surface but best form on firm; blinkered last 4 outings; sent to Scandinavia. *J. W. Watts.* **111 §**

PERSIAN ROYALE 3 ch.f. Persian Bold 123–Route Royale (Roi Soleil 125) (1982 6f 6d² 6s² 1983 10s⁴ 8f 10f* 8d*) IR 5,000Y; fourth foal; half-sister to 1979 2-y-o 6f winner Another Signcentre (by Pitskelly); dam never ran; won ladies race at Tralee and 25-runner Irish Cambridgeshire at the Curragh on last 2 of her 4 outings, beating Entre Nous by 2 lengths in latter in September; stays 1¼m; acts on any going. *E. Harty, Ireland.* **94**

PERSIAN THORNS 2 b.c. Persian Breeze 121–Silk Rose (Shantung 132) (1983 6f) Mar 5; first foal; dam of little account; tenth of 13 in maiden event at Redcar in June. *W. Wharton.* **–**

PERSIAN TIARA 3 ch.f. Persian Bold 123–Tarara Girl (Major Portion 129)   **98**
(1982 6g 1983 8g* 11d⁴ 11.7fg* 10g³ 12f⁴ 11.7fg* 12g* 12fg 12fg) IR 39,000Y;
useful-looking ex-Irish filly; half-sister to 3 winners in Ireland, including smart
1978 2-y-o 6f winner Martin Kelly (by Jukebox); dam lightly-raced daughter of
smart sprinter Tarara; had a good season and won minor event at Ayr and
handicaps at Windsor (2) and Haydock; beat Meeka Gold by 1½ lengths in a fairly
slowly-run affair on last-named course in September; stays 1½m; acts on firm
going; had stiff task final outing. *J. Hindley.*

PERSIS 2 ch.g. Persian Bold 123–Carol Day (Tudor Melody 129) (1983 6f 7g⁴ 7g*   **94**
8s³ 8fg³) Apr 29; IR 26,000Y; strong gelding; third foal; half-brother to a winner in
Italy; dam never ran; won 14-runner maiden race at Ayr in August; creditable third
following month in quite valuable nurseries at Doncaster and Newmarket; suited by
1m; acts on soft going and a firm surface; gelded after final start. *J. W. Watts.*

PERSONAL GUARD 5 ch.h. Home Guard 129–Fairly Flattered 73 (Pall Mall   **–**
132) (1982 NR 1983 6s 6s 5v⁴ 5s 6s) quite attractive horse; fairly useful at 2 yrs;
showed first form since when 2½ lengths fourth to Tilden in handicap at
Leopardstown in May; well beaten in minor event at Ripon previous start; should
stay 1m; acts on heavy going; tailed off in blinkers final outing at 3 yrs. *S.
Shields, Ireland.*

PETABELLA 2 gr.f. Absalom 128–Peta's Bay 67 (I Say 125) (1983 5f 5fg 8d) Jan   **–**
25; small filly; half-sister to several winners, including useful 5f performer Haditos
(by Averof); dam, half-sister to high-class Gold Rod, won over 7f; in rear in maiden
races; sold 750 gns Doncaster November Sales. *G. Pritchard-Gordon.*

PETCHANCE 2 b.f. Lucky Wednesday 124–Petploy 82 (Faberge II 121) (1983   **45**
5s 5s 5d⁴ 5f 6f³ 7f 6f 6f 6g) Apr 17; lightly-made, plain filly; poor plater; probably
needs 6f+; slowly away fourth start and unseated rider by rearing as stalls opened
on seventh; sold 350 gns Doncaster September Sales. *T. Fairhurst.*

PETER MARTIN 2 ch.g. Monsanto 121–Bouboulina (Hornbeam 130) (1983 5g   **88**
6d 8s²) Mar 17; 3,900F, 7,800Y; workmanlike, short-coupled gelding; half-brother
to a winning plater and a winner in Malaya; dam reportedly won in Greece; having
first race for 3 months, ran odds-on Millside to a head in 13-runner maiden event at
Yarmouth in September; suited by 1m at 2 yrs, and will stay middle distances; acts
well on soft going. *P. Kelleway.*

PETE ROCKET 4 ch.g. Roan Rocket 128–Devadara 73 (Royal Levee or Hill   **64**
Clown) (1982 8s 5g 6g³ 6f* 7fg* 5fg* 7g 7s 1983 5v 7.6v 6g 5.1g 7fg 6fg 8fg 5f
6g 6fg 6g⁴ 6fg* 7f) sturdy gelding; ran best races on last 3 outings, including when
winning claiming handicap at Newmarket in October; effective from 5f to 7f; acted
well on firm ground and was unsuited by soft; blinkered third start; had won for an
apprentice; unseated rider and bolted once in 1982; trained by J. Jenkins first 7
starts; dead. *D. Elsworth.*

PETER'S KIDDIE 2 b.f. Sallust 134–Jubilant 60 (Welsh Pageant 132) (1983 5s   **57**
5fg 5f 5g 5f 5f 5f² 6f 5g 5d 5d 5g) Mar 15; 5,000Y (privately); neat filly; first foal;
dam won over 1m; poor maiden; ran best races when dropped to selling company on
sixth and seventh outings; should stay beyond 5f; apparently suited by firm ground.
R. Hollinshead.

PETER'S QUARTER 8 b. or br.g. Ballyciptic 122–Rondanselle (Faust 122)   **–**
(1982 NR 1983 10.2g) ex-Irish gelding; won over 13f in Ireland in 1978; well
beaten in seller at Bath in June, first outing on flat since. *J. Fox.*

PETITE POMME 3 b.f. Be Friendly 130–Lady Phoenix (Lorenzaccio 130)   **–**
(1982 5f³ 5f 6g 5f³ 5f 5g 5d 5fg 5s 1983 7g 6s 6fg) sturdy filly; poor form, including
in sellers; sold 400 gns Doncaster November Sales. *D. Garraton.*

PETONG 3 gr.c. Mansingh 120–Iridium 78 (Linacre 133) (1982 7g 6d 6g⁴ 1983   **100**
5d* 5d 5.8v 5fg* 6h* 5g* 5fg* 5fg⁴ 6fg*) strong, compact colt; went from
strength to strength and was winning for sixth time when showing a good turn of
foot to beat Battle Hymn by ¾ length in £6,400 Doulton Energy Savers Handicap at
Doncaster in October; had earlier won at Pontefract (twice), Windsor
(apprentices), Ayr and Ascot (20-runner £6,300 Final Straw Handicap); effective at
5f and 6f; acts on any going, except possibly very soft; ran creditably in blinkers as
a 2-y-o; genuine; will win more races and may prove capable of holding his own in
better company. *M. Jarvis.*

PETORIUS 2 b.c. Mummy's Pet 125–The Stork 78 (Club House 110) (1983 5fg   **116**
6fg* 5fg* 5s* 5fg*)
    When the high-class sprinter Mummy's Pet retired to stud for the 1972 season
he possessed most of the qualities one looks for in a prospective sire of fast,

Harry Rosebery Challenge Trophy, Ayr—Petorius justifies favouritism, getting home by a length from African Abandon (near side) and Reesh

precocious animals: in addition to an excellent racing record, he boasted impressive looks and a pedigree which combined several of the most successful sprinting lines. His sire, the unbeaten two-year-old Sing Sing, topped the 1959 Free Handicap just a year after Tudor Melody, another son of the exceptional Tudor Minstrel, had done so. Sing Sing, like Tudor Melody, proved a highly influential stallion and sired such as Manacle, John Splendid, Jukebox, African Sky, Song, Saulingo and Averof. The distaff side of Mummy's Pet's pedigree makes equally impressive reading: he's a half-brother to the excellent sprinters Parsimony and Arch Sculptor and his dam Money for Nothing is by Grey Sovereign, twice champion sire of two-year-olds, out of a half-sister to another champion sire of two-year-olds, Whistler. Mummy's Pet hasn't let his forebears down. He topped the list of sires of two-year-olds from 1979 to 1981 in terms of races won, and had seventeen individual juvenile winners in 1980. 1983 was another highly successful year for Mummy's Pet: his youngsters, headed by the unbeaten Gimcrack winner Precocious and Petorius, earned more than any other stallion's.

Petorius won four of his five starts, and his one defeat was no fault of his own—he was badly hampered on his debut when seven of his opponents came down after halfway in a maiden race at Windsor in June. Petorius showed he'd suffered no ill-effects when returned to Windsor soon afterwards, winning a six-furlong event in a manner which suggested he would play a prominent part in the important two-year-old sprints. Unfortunately Petorius' win came on July 11th, five days after the closing date for the Flying Childers, Mill Reef and Middle Park Stakes and he hadn't been entered for any of them; nor was he in the Richmond or Gimcrack Stakes which had closed on May 4th and June 1st respectively. Thankfully Petorius will be one of the last horses to suffer in this way as it was announced in October that the early-closing pattern races would close at a more realistic date from 1984 onwards (the first four classics will close on February 29th in 1984 instead of the preceding November 9th). Petorius certainly made the most of the opportunities that were left to him, winning two important listed races, the Prince of Wales's Stakes at York and the Harry Rosebery Challenge Trophy at Ayr, and the

Cornwallis, Stakes, Ascot—a last-stride victory for Petorius from Pacific King (right) and Godstone

Mrs I. Phillips' "Petorius"

Cornwallis Stakes at Ascot, a pattern race which didn't close until September 21st.

Petorius, a strong, good sort, a good walker and excellent mover, impressed us greatly in the preliminaries at York. He was similarly impressive in the contest where, despite having those speedy animals Rocket Alert, African Abandon, Milord and Clantime among his seven opponents, he was clear by halfway and cruised home six lengths ahead of Rocket Alert. At Ayr Petorius started at 15/8 on to become only the third horse in fourteen years to complete the Prince of Wales/Harry Rosebery double, following Abdu in 1978 and Jester in 1981. He did so, but not so impressively as anticipated against opposition of the calibre of Reesh, Jeema, Brega Boy and African Abandon. He got home by only a length from African Abandon, after needing to be driven along to assert himself a furlong out, and raised doubts as to whether he was at his best on soft going. He again had to fight hard on much faster ground in the Cornwallis at Ascot in October, where he started favourite ahead of Defecting Dancer, Fawzi, Maajid and Pacific King, the winners of sixteen races between them. He looked in trouble a furlong and a half out, where Godstone held the lead as he'd done from the start, but Petorius responded well to strong driving and both he and Pacific King forced their heads in front of Godstone close home, the verdict going narrowly to Petorius. Petorius' victories proved he's a match for the vast majority of the younger sprinters but he has yet to prove himself in the same class as Precocious and, like all the other two-year-olds, he faces an uphill task now that Habibti stays in training. However, he's an individual we like very much and he's definitely one to keep on the right side, especially when given further chances of tackling six furlongs.

Petorius must have been quite an impressive individual even as a yearling; he fetched 25,000 Irish guineas although out of a Club House mare, The Stork, who failed to win in eight races and whose dam Cryhelp produced only two minor sprint winners from five living foals. Petorius' third dam, the five-furlong winner Lavant, made a significant mark at stud, producing the top sprinters So Blessed and

Lucasland. Cryhelp was also a sprinter, her one success coming over five furlongs as a two-year-old, but The Stork did most of her racing over further, finishing second twice over seven furlongs and twice over a mile. Petorius is The Stork's

Petorius (b.c. Mar 18, 1981)	Mummy's Pet (b 1968)	Sing Sing (b 1957)	Tudor Minstrel
			Agin the Law
		Money for Nothing (br 1962)	Grey Sovereign
			Sweet Nothings
	The Stork (b 1976)	Club House (b 1970)	Pall Mall
			Country House
		Cryhelp (ch 1963)	Martial
			Lavant

first foal; her second is a colt foal belonging to the first crop of Runnett who, interestingly, looks to be a pure-breeding bay like his sire Mummy's Pet. *M. Stoute.*

PETRIZZO 2 b.c. Radetzky 123–Perianth (Petingo 135) (1983 7g 6g 8s⁴ 8d⁴ 8fg) Mar 27; tall colt; first foal; dam never ran; appeared quite moderate until finishing highly-creditable seventh, 6 lengths behind Alphabatim, in William Hill Futurity at Doncaster in October on final outing; stays 1m well; evidently suited by a firm surface. *C. Brittain.*   105 ?

PETRODOLLAR 2 ch.c. Be My Guest 126–Marylove (Kalydon 122) (1983 7fg*) Mar 29; third foal (first to Northern Hemisphere time); half-brother to a placed animal in Australia by Solinus; dam, Irish middle-distance winner, is closely related to very smart Ksar; favourite, kept on well to beat Derryvale by 1½ lengths in maiden event at Tralee in August; wasn't seen out again; should be suited by middle distances. *D. O'Brien, Ireland.*   81 p

PETSY 2 b.f. Mummy's Pet 125–Madame Quickly 80 (Saint Crespin III 132) (1983 6f 6fg* 6fg 7g) Mar 7; fair sort; half-sister to several winners in France, including useful 1980 2-y-o 1m winner Kisty (by Kashmir II); dam won at up to 7f; won maiden race at Haydock in August in close finish with Birdwood and Calaloo Sioux; stays 6f; acts on a firm surface. *W. Elsey.*   84

PETTAZ 2 b.c. Mummy's Pet 125–Mumtaz (Sheshoon 132) (1983 5s 5v 5.1g) May 17; 9,000Y; well-grown, rather leggy colt; half-brother to numerous winners in France, including French 1¼m winner, is daughter of half-sister to Petite Etoile; little worthwhile form; blinkered second outing; dead. *G. Blum.*   —

PETTISTREE 5 ch.g. Sallust 134–Kokuwa (Klairon 131) (1982 6s³ 5s³ 6d⁴ 1983 7s 6g) small, fair sort; sprint handicapper; stays 6f; acts well on soft going; blinkered once. *O. O'Neill.*   —

PETT VELERO 4 b.g. Pitcairn 126–Naval Artiste (Captain's Gig) (1982 NR 1983 6v) 13,500Y; third foal; dam Irish 2-y-o 5f winner; unquoted when tailed off in minor event at Folkestone in May. *J. O'Donoghue.*   —

PETWICE 3 b.f. Mummy's Pet 125–Twice Shy (Lord of Verona 120) (1982 5g 1983 6d 5v⁴ 7g 6s³ 6d 5f 7.6g) compact filly; finds 5f on sharp side. *W. Haigh.*   62

PETWORTH 3 b.g. Mummy's Pet 125–Gambela 88 (Diplomat Way) (1982 5d 1983 7d 8.2s 8f 10d) workmanlike gelding; has a round action; ran with a bit of promise in 5f maiden race as a 2-y-o but showed little over longer distances in 1983; sold 640 gns Doncaster October Sales. *M. Camacho.*   —

PETWORTH PARK 4 br.f. Mummy's Pet 125–Lancashire Lass 73 (King's Troop 118) (1982 5d 1983 14s 16f 16f) lightly-made filly; good walker; has ability but is clearly temperamental and races only from flag starts; not sure to stay 1¾m. *S. Woodman.*   —

PHANJO 3 b.g. Record Token 128–Silk Willoughby (Pirate King 129) (1982 5f 6f 7fg 10s 1983 12f) poor maiden. *J. Hardy.*   —

PHARLIOU (USA) 2 b.c. San Feliou–Q Up (Distinctive) (1983 5g⁴ 6fg 6g³) Apr 16; $50,000Y; neat, quite attractive colt; third foal; half-brother to a stakes-placed winner by Our Native; dam won 4 sprint races, one a claimer; sire, son of Lyphard, was useful winner over 9f and 10.5f in France; improved with his races, on final outing 5 lengths third of 6 to Jamais Derierre in £2,900 event at York in October; will be suited by 7f and 1m. *R. Armstrong.*   85

PHAROAH'S TREASURE (USA) 2 ch.c. Upper Nile–Sulenan (Tompion) (1983 8g 8g⁴ 8.2s⁴) Feb 21; $155,000Y; tall, quite well-made colt; half-brother to numerous winners, including Swinging Lizzie (by The Axe), a smart winner at up to 7f; dam won 2 sprints at 3 yrs; quite a modest maiden; best effort on second outing; stays 1m. *D. Elsworth.*   80

PHILATELIST 3 b.g. Dubassoff–Chaddy (St Chad 120) (1982 5f 7g 5g 6s 1983 6f 5fg 5s⁴ 7fg 6fg) tall, leggy, lengthy gelding; plater; not disgraced over 7f, but best run at 5f; changed hands from Doncaster March Sales; dead. *C. Williams.*　–

PHILCROP 2 b.g. Forlorn River 124–Spanish Crop (Philip of Spain 126) (1983 5v 5v³ 6fg 5f² 5f 6fg² 6fg 7f) May 22; first foal; dam never ran; modest plater; suited by 6f; best form on a firm surface; gelded after final appearance. *T. M. Jones.*　56

PHILIPS HUSSAR 3 ch.c. Queen's Hussar 124–Princess Story 64 (Prince de Galles 125) (1982 8s 8s 7s 1983 8v 10.1d 10s 10g 8fg) small, workmanlike colt; poor plater; sometimes blinkered. *K. Cunningham-Brown.*　–

PHILPRIDE 3 br.c. Rheingold 137–Canelle (Sassafras 135) (1982 8d 8.2s² 1983 11g⁴ 12g) strong, useful-looking colt; lightly-raced maiden; in need of race and having first outing since May when fifth of 20 behind Masked Ball at Redcar in November; will be suited by 1¾m. *W. Elsey.*　68

PHILSTAR 2 b.c. Stradavinsky 121–Allanooka 94 (Be Friendly 130) (1983 5s 5s⁴ 5d 5fg* 5d³ 5f³ 5f 5f² 6g 5fg²) Jan 16; 3,600F, 5,600Y; strong, good-bodied colt; not a good walker; brother to 3-y-o Angels Tune, and half-brother to 1m winner French Charisma (by Young Emperor); dam won twice over 5f at 2 yrs and is half-sister to very smart sprinter Royben; won maiden race at Edinburgh in June; good second subsequently in minor event at Beverley and 17-runner nursery at Newmarket; ran moderately at 6f; seems to act on any going, but has shown best form on a firm surface; wears blinkers. *W. Elsey.*　90

PHILYRA 2 b.f. Averof 123–Foxhorn (Hornbeam 130) (1983 8d 8fg) Apr 30; 5,600Y; half-sister to 2 winners, including fair 1980 2-y-o 5f to 7f performer Horncastle (by Hornbeam); dam never ran; well beaten in autumn maiden races at Beverley and Newcastle. *E. Weymes.*　–

PHOEBE ANN 2 gr.f. Absalom 128–Lowna 120 (Princely Gift 137) (1983 5d² 5g* 5s*) Apr 24; 11,000Y; strong, good sort; half-sister to several winners, including Gospill Hill (by Crepello), a smart performer at up to 1¼m; dam won Molecomb Stakes; won maiden race at Ayr in August and nursery (by short head) on same course in September; promises to stay 6f; yet to race on a firm surface. *C. Thornton.*　76

PHYSICAL (USA) 3 gr.c. Grey Dawn II 132–Student Leader (Personality) (1982 NR 1983 8f) big, good-topped colt; second foal; half-brother to Ecole d'Humanite (by Bold Forbes), winner of a 6f stakes race at 2 yrs in 1981; dam, stakes-placed, won at up to 1m; looked green but shaped with a little promise when sixth of 16 to Tetron Bay in minor event at Salisbury in June. *P. Walwyn.*　–

PIANOSO (FR) 6 b.g. Appiani II 128–Cosa Nostra 68 (Bel Baraka 120) (1982 NR 1983 12v 16s 13d 18f) poor plater; sold 600 gns Ascot July Sales. *H. O'Neill.*　–

PIARA SINGH 2 b.g. Mansingh 120–Love Is Blind 90 (Hasty Road) (1983 5f 5fg 6g⁴ 6fg 6s) Mar 19; workmanlike gelding; good walker; half-brother to a winning plater; dam 2-y-o 6f winner; quite a modest maiden; stays 6f. *N. Vigors.*　75

PICATAC 3 b.f. Tack On 114–Picarosa (Eborneezer 105) (1982 NR 1983 16g 10.1f 10.1f) first foal; dam slow point-to-pointer; tailed off in maiden and minor events in the summer. *M. Bolton.*　–

PICCARD 2 ch.c. Young Generation 129–Home and Away (Home Guard 129) (1983 6g 5h⁴ 6f 7d) Apr 21; 9,000Y; small colt; first foal; dam never ran; poor maiden; probably stays 7f; sold A. Neaves 400 gns Newmarket Autumn Sales. *C. Brittain.*　53

PICHINCHA 2 b.f. Pharly 130–Absaroka (Prince Tenderfoot 126) (1983 5fg³ 5fg* 6f 6g 6fg) close-coupled, fair sort; second reported foal; dam very useful French 1¼m winner; won 14-runner maiden race at Windsor in August by 4 lengths; showed little subsequently, including in 2 nurseries; should stay at least 1m; acts on a firm surface. *R. Armstrong.*　82

PICKET LINE 3 ch.c. Run The Gantlet–Calleva (Worden II 129) (1982 8g 7s 1983 12v 16v) compact, good sort; in rear in maiden and minor races; blinkered final start; sold to W. Clay 2,300 gns 2nd June Sales. *I. Balding.*　–

PICKLED PEACHES (USA) 2 b.f. Sauce Boat–High Renaissance (Acroterion) (1983 7fg 6g) May 5; $63,000Y; lengthy filly; second foal; dam, second once from 6 starts, is sister to dam of top-class Flying Paster; no worthwhile form in fair company at Newmarket and York in the autumn. *B. Hills.*　–

PICOTEE 5 br.m. Pieces of Eight 128–Gail Time (Arctic Time) (1982 NR 1983 12g) half-sister to smart staying hurdler Town Ship (by Behistoun); dam won from　–

9f to 1½m in Ireland; tailed off in amateur riders maiden race at Kempton in September. *J. Bosley.*

PICTORIAL 2 b.f. Homing 130–Picture 98 (Lorenzaccio 130) (1983 5g²) May 12; rather lightly-built, lengthy filly; second foal; half-sister to 1982 2-y-o 7f winner Bo-Peep (by Decoy Boy); dam, half-sister to Queen's Hussar, won over 6f at 2 yrs; 7/1, ran on extremely well under considerate handling, and appeared to show plenty of promise, when second of 15 behind easy winner Follow Me Follow in maiden event at Newbury in June; bred to be much better suited by 6f+. *I. Balding.* — **70 p**

PIENCOURT 5 br.h. Averof 123–French Bugle 71 (Bleep-Bleep 134) (1982 5g³ 5s² 6fg³ 5f* 6fg³ 6fg 6f 6s⁴ 5s 1983 5d 6v* 6v* 6v² 6g² 6f 5fg 6fg 7fg 8d 6fg³) compact, quite attractive horse; useful handicapper; beat Pusey Street at Epsom and Kempton (£6,100 event) in April; also ran well fifth and final starts, on latter finishing under a length third to Vorvados in £4,600 event at Doncaster in November; effective from 5f to 7f; acts on any going; had stiff task when blinkered once. *C. Austin.* — **100**

PIEROTH 5 b.g. Averof 123–Terex (Khalkis 127) (1982 7fg⁴ 10.8fg³ 7f² 8g 8fg⁴ 10f⁴ 12f² 10g³ 10fg 12g* 12v* 12d* 1983 12fg) fair sort; in good form in autumn of 1982, winning 3 handicaps; well beaten only start at 5 yrs in September; stays 1½m; acts on any going, but is clearly suited by some give underfoot; has run creditably in blinkers. *G. Kindersley.* — –

PIERROT AUGUST 3 b.g. Cawston's Clown 113–Canty Day 87 (Canadel II 126) (1982 7g 8s 10d* 10.2s 1983 12v 16s 13.1v 12g 12g) tall, leggy, lightly-made gelding; plater; yet to show he stays beyond 1¼m; yet to race on a firm surface; trained until after third start by R. Simpson. *H. O'Neill.* — –

PIETRU (FR) 3 br.c. Arctic Tern 126–Agila (Sicambre 135) (1982 7.5g² 7.5fg 8d² 10v* 10v³ 1983 10.5v³ 11s² 10.5v* 12fg 12g³) French colt; very useful staying 2-y-o in 1982; gained only success of 1983 when beating Port Saigon by 6 lengths in 5-runner race at Saint-Cloud in May; placed in 3 of his other starts, including when 2½ lengths second of 8 behind Jeu de Paille in Prix Noailles at Longchamp earlier in month and 5 lengths third of 12 behind Garthorn in Prix Max Sicard at Toulouse in November (first outing for more than 5 months); stays 1½m; best form with some give in the ground; acted as pacemaker for L'Emigrant in Prix du Jockey-Club penultimate start (trained by F. Boutin until that time). *P. Bary, France.* — **116**

PIG TAIL 3 ch.f. Habitat 134–Plencia (Le Haar 126) (1982 6g⁴ 1983 7f* 7f⁴ 8f) rather lightly-made filly; good mover; sister to useful 6f and 8.5f winner Petroleuse and half-sister to 3 winners, notably outstanding middle-distance filly Pawneese (by Carvin); landed the odds smoothly by 2 lengths from Queen To Be in maiden race at Leicester in July; had stiff task when about 4 lengths fourth of 6 behind Fenny Rough in £9,000 Oak Tree Stakes at Goodwood later in July, better subsequent effort; should stay 1m; acts on firm going; sold to BBA 320,000 gns Newmarket December Sales. *H. Cecil.* — **98**

PIGWIDGEON (USA) 2 b.c. For The Moment–Ghost Rider (Gray Phantom) (1983 8g 7.6fg*) Apr 25; $28,000Y, resold 15,000 gns Y; strong colt; fifth foal; half-brother to 3-y-o 7f and 1m winner Jhansi Ki Rani (by Far North) and to 2 winners in USA; dam won 6 times at up to 1m, including claiming events, and is half-sister to 2 stakes winners; readily landed the odds from Calaloo Sioux in 18-runner maiden race at Lingfield in October; promising fifth previous month in £4,100 event won by Rainbow Quest at Newbury; stays 1m. *G. Harwood.* — **91 p**

PIMMS PALACE 2 ch.f. Dragonara Palace 115–Miss Pimm 88 (Gentle Art 121) (1983 6f⁴ 5f² 6f³ 6fg⁴ 7.2s) Apr 25; 2,700F, 3,000Y; leggy, narrow filly; half-sister to several minor winners here and abroad; dam 2-y-o 5f winner; in frame in maiden company prior to finishing 3 lengths fourth of 24 to Owen Joseph in valuable seller at Doncaster in September; not sure to stay 7f; acts on firm going; sold 3,100 gns Newmarket Autumn Sales. *A. Stewart.* — **66**

PINCHAPENNY 4 gr.f. Scallywag 127–Denaria (Hook Money 124) (1982 NR 1983 16g 16g) half-sister to a winning jumper; dam won over hurdles; well beaten in maiden races at Lingfield in June and July. *K. Bailey.* — –

PINCOTE LANE 2 ch.c. Cavo Doro 124–Sweet Helen (No Mercy 126) (1983 5d⁴ 7fg 9s) Apr 4; strong, well-grown colt; first foal; dam ran only once; showed bit of promise in maiden race at Leicester in May, but was seen out only twice subsequently, in August and October; should stay at least 7f. *R. Hollinshead.* — –

PINE HAWK 2 b.c. Algora 110–Paridance (Doudance 99) (1983 5fg 7g) Apr 26; fair sort; second foal; dam of no account; behind in 17-runner maiden race at Leicester in September; brought down on previous appearance. *D. H. Jones.* — –

PINE RIDGE 3 b.f. High Top 131–Wounded Knee 78 (Busted 134) (1982 7d⁴   **80**
1983 10fg⁴ 12f² 12.2f² 12f* 12d³ 12fg 12.2g*) attractive filly; turns front feet out;
won maiden race at Beverley in August (by 6 lengths) and apprentice race at
Catterick in October (by ½ length from Realistic); stays 1½m; yet to race on really
soft going, but acts on any other. *M. Stoute.*

PINE VALLEY 2 b.c. Monsanto 121–Bronze Princess 72 (Hul a Hul 124) (1983   –
6fg 6g 7.6fg) Feb 27; 12,500Y; heavy-bodied colt; second foal; dam won twice
over 5f at 2 yrs; no form in the autumn in minor event and 2 maiden races;
exported to Malaysia. *R. Sheather.*

PINKIE 2 b.f. Tickled Pink 114–Trojan's Centenary 68 (Crooner 119) (1983 5g   –
5fg) Apr 28; first foal; dam winning hurdler; in rear in October in minor event at
Bath and maiden race at Folkestone; sold 370 gns Ascot December Sales. *B.
Gubby.*

PINK MEX 4 b.f. Tickled Pink 114–Mexilhoeira 66 (Bleep-Bleep 134) (1982 8g 6d   –
1983 6v 10f 8.3f) plain filly; little worthwhile form, including in a seller; promises to
stay 1m. *R. Thompson.*

PINK ROBBER (USA) 2 b.f. No Robbery–Julie Pink (Young Emperor 133)   **85**
(1983 5s 6g* 6fg 6fg 7d 6s³) Feb 18; $20,000Y; smallish, lengthy filly; sister to
useful 1979 2-y-o 6f winner Swift Arrest, and half-sister to 3 minor winners; dam
won 6f claiming race at 2 yrs; 20/1, won 23-runner maiden race at Lingfield in June
by 4 lengths from Telham; creditable third under 9-7 in nursery at Hamilton in
October; stays 6f; acts on soft going and a firm surface. *B. Hanbury.*

PINOLA 4 b.g. Sallust 134–Pavlova (Fidalgo 129) (1982 NR 1983 16d 16g)   –
compact, quite attractive gelding; seems of little account; has twice been
blinkered. *J. Fox.*

PINTIMES (FR) 3 b. or br.f. Faraway Times 123–Queen Pin (Sovereign Path   –
125) (1982 6fg 7g 7g 5fg 6s 6s 1983 8v 6.5s² 7s 7fg 7fg 5g⁴ 5g⁴ 6g 6g) big, tall
filly; ran easily best races when in frame at Evry (trained by C. Bartholomew at
time), Lingfield and Newbury; stays 6.5f; sometimes blinkered. *C. Austin.*

PIP 3 b.c. Captain James 123–Where Is It (Wolver Hollow 126) (1982 7d³ 1983 8v   **88**
8g 8f 10.1f* 10h² 10g 10g) leggy, narrow colt; has a round action; 25/1-winner of
15-runner minor event at Windsor in July, making much of running and beating
Dalmane by 3 lengths; got rather warm before going down by a length to Woodcote
in 3-runner £3,500 event at Sandown the following month, easily best subsequent
effort; suited by 1¼m; probably acts on any going. *J. Dunlop.*

PIPATUNE (FR) 2 b.f. Music Boy 124–Directissima (Devon III 125) (1983 5fg⁴   –
7.5fg 5fg 5s) Apr 10; lightly-built filly; second reported live foal; dam won over
1¼m in France at 2 yrs; little worthwhile form in varied company here and in
France; blinkered final start. *C. Austin.*

PIP'EM 3 ch.f. Jimmy Reppin 131–Marock Morley 59 (Most Secret 119) (1982 6fg   –
5g² 5g* 5f 5s⁴ 6v 1983 7d 6s 7v² 6d 6d 6f 6f 6fg 7g 8d 6fg) small, good-bodied
filly; plater nowadays; stays 7f; acts on any going; often blinkered. *S. Norton.*

PIRATE MAID 3 b.f. Auction Ring 123–Spring Blossom 85 (Queen's Hussar 124)   –
(1982 NR 1983 6fg) 7,600F, 13,000Y; half-sister to 4 winners, including fairly
useful sprinter Mr Minstrel (by Laser Light); dam won over 5f at 2 yrs; unquoted
when behind in 23-runner maiden race won by Rare Honour at Lingfield in July. *P.
Walwyn.*

PITRASI 4 b.g. Pitskelly 122–Princess Ru (Princely Gift 137) (1982 7d 7g 6f 7.2f   **58**
7f³ 8fg² 8g² 8.3g³ 11.1fg 8fg³ 1983 8d 8.2d 9f 8g² 8f² 8fg² 8g) smallish, fair sort;
plater; moved down a place after scoring at Wolverhampton in August on sixth
start; stays 1m; acts on firm going; effective with and without blinkers; suitable
mount for an apprentice. *D. Garraton.*

PITROYAL 3 br.f. Pitskelly 122–Regal Way (Sovereign Path 125) (1982 6g 7f³   **74**
7g⁴ 7g 7.6v 7d 1983 6s 8.5d³ 12f³ 12g² 10f 12fg⁴ 12f 12d* 13.3d) well-made filly;
placed in varied races before beating Gloria Mundi by ¾ length in a maiden at
Brighton in September; stays 1½m; acts on any going except perhaps heavy;
sometimes blinkered (wore them at Brighton); sweated up fifth start. *R. Smyth.*

PITTSFIELD 3 br.c. Pitskelly 122–Ida 95 (Jukebox 120) (1982 7g 1983 7.6v 7d   **66**
7.6g² 8f 10.5d) quite attractive, small, robust colt; 10 lengths second of 20 to
Hooligan in maiden race at Chester in August; towards rear in valuable seller final
start; should stay 1m; sold 780 gns Goffs November Sales. *B. Hills.*

PIT YOUR WITS 7 b.h. Pitskelly 122–Sweet Chupatti (Rustam 127) (1982   **42**
12.2d 12g* 10.4g 14.6g 12g* 11.7fg² 12.3d 12fg² 12fg 12g 12.2s 1983 12s³ 12.2v

12s 11.7d⁴ 12s 12fg³ 11.7f 11.7fg 12d⁴ 12d³ 12d) well-made horse; stays 1½m, but isn't certain to get 1¾m; acts on any going except very firm; has worn blinkers; wears bandages; suitable mount for an apprentice. *D. H. Jones.*

PITY THE LADY 3 br.f. Pitskelly 122–Lady Exbury 111 (Exbury 138) (1982 NR 1983 12f 11g) IR 11,000Y; third foal; half-sister to 1m and 1¼m winner Maybury (by Manado); dam, half-sister to very smart Boreen, stayed 1½m well; behind in maiden races at Redcar and Ayr in summer. *J. W. Watts.*   –

PIXIE'S PARTY 6 ch.m. Celtic Cone 116–Clever Pixie 69 (Goldhill 125) (1982 NR 1983 10.2g 12.2f) tailed off in seller and maiden race; bandaged both starts. *Miss A. King.*   –

PLACE OF HONOUR 2 ch.f. Be My Guest 126–Sutton Place 105 (Tyrant) (1983 6h) Feb 23; tall, lengthy filly; good walker; first foal; dam won Coronation Stakes and is half-sister to Captain James and Nikoli; eighth of 10 in maiden race at Nottingham in August; should do better in time. *P. Walwyn.*   –

PLAITS 2 b.f. Thatching 131–Silk and Satin 108 (Charlottown 127) (1983 5fg² 7fg³ 6g 6fg⁴ 6g²) Mar 25; big, rather unfurnished filly; third foal; half-sister to Irish 6f winner Valentia (by Vitiges); dam won from 6f to 1m; good fifth, 7 lengths behind Prickle, in Lowther Stakes at York in August on third outing; nowhere near that form on her other appearances, although placed 3 times; capable on her York showing of winning maiden event at least, but is evidently one to treat with caution. *R. Armstrong.*   93 ?

PLANTING RICE 2 b.f. Manor Farm Boy 114–Pangkor 76 (Tribal Chief 125) (1983 5d 5d 5fg 5f) Apr 20; small, lightly-made filly; of no account. *T. Fairhurst.*   –

PLATO'S RETREAT 4 b.f. Brigadier Gerard 144–Acte 80 (Alycidon 138) (1982 10fg³ 12fg² 10.6s 12v* 12g 1983 12f⁴ 14.6f 14fg 15.8g⁴ 16s 12s² 12fg) fair sort; poor mover; possibly doesn't get 2m; acts on any going but is ideally suited by some give in the ground; blinkered last 3 starts. *W. Elsey.*   –

PLAY OUR SONG 3 br.f. Persian Bold 123–Scented Air 92 (Derring-Do 131) (1982 5g* 6g 1983 5f 6f²(dis) 6d 5fg*) small, rather lightly-made filly; good second to Roysia Boy in handicap at Yarmouth in August, but was disqualified some time afterwards as her apprentice rider had drawn wrong allowance; put up a game effort when getting up to beat Sanu by a short head in £4,500 race at Newmarket the following month; suited by 6f; best form on a sound surface. *P. Kelleway.*   97

PLAYTEX 3 b.f. Be Friendly 130–Flitterdale 81 (Abwah 118) (1982 NR 1983 10f 5f³ 8fg* 7g²) first foal; dam 2-y-o 5f winner; beat Penybont by ½ length in 6-runner minor event at Thirsk in September; by no means sure to stay 1¼m; has raced only on firm ground. *T. Barron.*   67

PLAZA TORO 4 ch.g. Ashmore 125–Duke Street (Lorenzaccio 130) (1982 12f* 12fg² 12f³ 1983 11.7s⁴ 12f) lengthy gelding; poor performer; suited by 1½m and will stay further; acts on any going. *S. Pattemore.*   –

PLEASE REMEMBER 3 b.g. Sandford Lad 133–Sea of Light (Aureole 132) (1982 NR 1983 8v) 3,100F, 16,000Y; half-brother to middle-distance winner Java Lights (by Manado) and a winner in France; dam Irish 1¼m winner and daughter of Coronation Stakes winner Ocean; 33/1, apprentice ridden and blinkered when last of 14 in maiden race at Warwick in May. *R. Armstrong.*   –

PLEDGDON GREEN 3 gr.g. Broxted 120–Lynn Regis (Ballymoss 136) (1982 5g³ 6d 8f 8.2d² 10d* 10d² 1983 8.2v 10d⁴ 10.1fg³ 11d³ 11.7fg 10h²) workmanlike gelding; claimed by V. Thompson £3,500 after finishing second in seller at Nottingham in September; suited by 1¼m+; yet to show he can handle really soft going, but acts on any other; blinkered fifth start; sometimes looks none too enthusiastic. *N. Callaghan.*   59

PLIANT 3 ch.c. Tumble Wind–Roman Wall (Romulus 129) (1982 7s 1983 6v 7d 8f³ 8g 7.6d²) IR 3,000F, IR 26,000Y; rangy, useful-looking ex-Irish colt; closely related to a winner in Singapore by Windjammer; dam poor daughter of Gimcrack winner Precast; 20/1 when excellent 2 lengths second of 23 to Spanish Bold in handicap at Lingfield in October; stays 1m; acts on a soft surface; formerly trained by P. Prendergast. *C. Horgan.*   83

PLOUGHMAN'S 2 gr.c. Homing 130–Cottage Pie 106 (Kalamoun 129) (1983 5fg 6fg³ 7fg 7d) Jan 30; sturdy colt; first foal; dam, half-sister to Yorkshire Cup winner Riboson, was useful staying 2-y-o; quite a moderate maiden; best form at 6f, but should be suited by 7f; sold 8,200 gns Newmarket Autumn Sales. *I. Balding.*   75

PLUCKY DANCER (FR) 2 ch.c. Fabulous Dancer 124–Peronelle 115   **103** p
(O'Grady) (1983 9f²) half-brother to 4 middle-distance winners in France,
including 3-y-o handicapper Ponty Pool (by Kashmir II); dam smart at up to 13f in
France; headed on line when nose second to Long Mick in newcomers event at
Longchamp in October (pair clear); had rest well beaten off and looks sure to win
good middle-distance races. *P.-L. Biancone, France.*

PLURALISME (USA) 3 b.c. The Minstrel 135–Cambretta (Roberto 131) (1982   **119**
7.5fg² 8g* 8s* 1983 9.7s* 10.5v³ 12s 9.2d 10f 10d*) 130,000Y; medium-sized,
good-looking colt; shows a lot of knee action; first foal; dam, winner over 9f in
Ireland, is sister to high-class 1m to 1½m winner Critique; looked set for a good
season when holding off strong-finishing White Spade by 2 lengths in 7-runner Prix
de Guiche at Longchamp in April; didn't win again until October however, when
accounting for Conform by 1½ lengths in 6-runner Prix du Ranelagh on same
course; ran best race in between and finished clear of remainder when 1¼ lengths
third of 7 to L'Emigrant in Prix Lupin at Longchamp again; never really a threat
when about 17 lengths seventh of 20 finishers behind Teenoso in Derby at Epsom
on third start; suited by middle-distances; best form on soft ground, although ran
respectably once on a firm surface. *A. Head, France.*

POINT NORTH 5 b. or br.h. Lorenzaccio 130–Off Scent 92 (Faberge II 121)   **50**
(1982 13v 12fg 12f² 12.3fg* 13g³ 15g³ 12f² 13fg³ 12g* 13fg* 13fg² 12g⁴ 13d 11s⁴
15d 1983 10v 11s 15g 9g 11g 12.3f 13f* 13g³ 12f³) strong horse; showed first form
at 5 yrs when winning handicap at Hamilton in July; stays 15f; acts well on firm
going. *W. H. H. Williams.*

POKERFAYES (USA) 4 b.g. Poker–Faye's Delight (Barbs Delight) (1982 8f   **64**
9.4f 8fg 7g 6g³ 7.2g 5fg 6fg 6fg 6d 6fg 5g³ 5s* 6s 1983 5d 6d 6s 5fg 5fg 6fg⁴ 6f* 5f⁴
5f* 5f 6h² 6g⁴ 5fg 5fg² 5g² 5d² 5g* 5fg) neat gelding; won seller at Newcastle (no
bid) and handicaps at Beverley and Warwick; stays 6f; acts on any going; has
sweated up; best in blinkers. *B. McMahon.*

POLAR STAR 4 b.g. Rarity 129–Arctic Chimes (Arctic Slave 116) (1982 8fg* 8f   **77**
10.1fg4 10f³ 12fg² 11f* 12s² 12v⁴ 1983 10.6v⁴ 10s³ 10t 10d 10fg 10f² 11.7fg* 11.7fg²)
leggy gelding; excellent mover; quite a modest handicapper; won at Windsor in
July; suited by 1½m; acts on any going; blinkered nowadays; needs holding up; sold
to M. Pipe 6,000 gns Newmarket Autumn Sales. *H. T. Jones.*

POLESTAR 3 b.f. Northfields–Place d'Etoile 93 (Kythnos 126) (1982 NR 1983   **77**
10fg 10.1fg³ 10f 10g³ 10fg*) IR 115,000Y; quite a well-made filly; sister to 2
winners, notably Irish 2000 Guineas winner Northern Treasure, and half-sister to
several winners, including smart 6f and 7f winner Etoile de Paris (by Crowned
Prince); dam won at up to 1¼m; took time to warm up before beating Summer
Impressions decisively by 2½ lengths in 11-runner maiden race at Newmarket in
October; gives impression she'll be suited by 1½m; yet to race on a soft surface;
sold 160,000 gns Newmarket December Sales. *J. Dunlop.*

Prix Thomas Bryon, Saint-Cloud—Polly's Ark wins from Duke of Silver (rails),
Toll Teller (No. 5) and Emaline (No. 6)

Ladbrokes (Ayr) Gold Cup—Polly's Brother (right) finishes strongly to snatch victory from Amorous, Numismatist and Mel's Choice (checks)

POLISHED SILVER 3 ch.c. Try My Best 130–Mettle 107 (Pretendre 126) (1982 7d* 7f* 8g* 7g* 1983 10v⁴ 12s) strong, rangy colt; went from strength to strength as a 2-y-o and was unbeaten in 4 races, including Somerville Tattersall Stakes at Newmarket; kept on quite well and wasn't disgraced when about 3 lengths fourth to Gordian in very slowly-run Guardian Classic Trial at Sandown in April, better of 2 runs on really soft ground in spring; stays 1¼m; has won on both firm and dead ground, but has the smooth, easy action of a top-of-the-ground performer; sent to race in USA. *H. Cecil.*   –

POLITBURO (USA) 3 b.g. Maribeau–Lovely Guinevere (Round Table) (1982 6s 1983 8s 10.1fg) big, rangy gelding; little worthwhile form; sold out of B. Hills's stable 1,600 gns Ascot May Sales after first start. *J. Bridger.*   –

POLLY'S ARK (FR) 2 b.c. Arctic Tern 126–Polly's Harde (Lyphard 132) (1983 8g² 9fg* 7.5s*) Feb 6; second foal; half-brother to useful 1982 French 2-y-o 7f winner Pajalski (by Bolkonski); dam, out of sister to 2000 Guineas winner Right Tack, won over 1m in France; led over 1f out to win 6-runner Prix Thomas Bryon at Saint-Cloud in October by 1½ lengths from Duke of Silver (who gave 4 lb); had previously justified favouritism in excellent style in 13-runner maiden race at Evry in September, drawing away in straight to win by 4 lengths from Blue Whale; will stay at least 1¼m; the type to continue improving and win good races at 3 yrs. *F. Boutin, France.*   **113** p

POLLY'S BROTHER 5 ch.h. Roi Soleil 125–Polairia 66 (Polic 126) (1982 6fg 6f² 6g* 8fg² 6g⁴ 6g² 6d³ 6g² 6s 1983 6g 6s 6d³ 6f 7f 7s* 6s* 6g* 6fg²) smallish, fair sort; not a good mover; useful handicapper; in great form in the autumn and won Battle of Britain Stakes at Doncaster (beat Ta Morgan a neck), Ladbrokes (Ayr) Gold Cup (by a head from Amorous) and Coral Bookmakers Sprint Trophy at York (accounted for Karen's Star by ½ length); also finished good head second to Vorvados in £4,600 event at Doncaster on final start; stays 1m, but best form at up to 7f; acts on any going, but is ideally suited by some give in the ground; genuine. *M. H. Easterby.*   **104**

POLO BOY 3 ch.g. Red Alert 127–Bermuda 81 (Doutelle 128) (1982 5g 6f 6f 7s³ 1983 8s 8s 8g 8fg³ 8f⁴ 10d 8g²) compact, useful-looking gelding; in frame in gentleman riders race and handicap at Goodwood and maiden event at Salisbury in between; stays 1m; blinkered final start. *G. Balding.*   **71**

POLSEW 2 b. or br.c. Relkino 131–Petulant (Petingo 135) (1983 7fg 7d 7f⁴ 8fg) Apr 8; 3,200Y; rather narrow colt; fourth foal; dam never ran; poor plater; should stay 1m; acts on firm going. *I. Walker.*   **48**

POLYNESIAN BEAUTY (USA) 3 b.f. Hawaii–Bonnie Blink (Buckpasser) (1982 NR 1983 10.1f) first foal; dam unraced half-sister to St Leger winner Boucher; 33/1, started slowly when behind in 19-runner minor event won by Ven Matrero at Windsor in July; sold 27,000 gns Newmarket December Sales. *J. Dunlop.*   –

POLYNOR (FR) 2 b.c. Polyfoto 124–Sorea (La Varende 125) (1983 7fg 8g) Mar 8; 55,000 francs Y (approx £4,700); brother to successful French hurdler Nolynor,   **58**

and half-brother to a winner; dam 2-y-o 7.5f winner in French Provinces; 12 lengths fifth of 15 behind Kuwait Palace in 1m maiden race at Edinburgh in September; stays 1m. *N. Tinkler.*

POMADE 3 b.f. Luthier 126–Pot Pourri 97 (Busted 134) (1982 NR 1983 9s²)   79
smallish, fair sort; sixth foal; half-sister to 2 winners, including fairly useful middle-distance winner Pottinger (by Vitiges); dam stayer and half-sister to very smart Almiranta; beat Fluid Mechanics by a head in 7-runner event at Wolverhampton in April but hampered her close home when edging left and placings were subsequently reversed; not seen out again; would have been suited by 1¼m+; visits General Assembly. *H. Cecil.*

PONTCHARTRAIN (USA) 3 b.c. Lyphard 132–Mauna Loa (Hawaii) (1982 6d³   87
1983 8f* 10.1f²) small, lightly-made colt; lacks scope; won 19-runner maiden race at Pontefract in June, staying on under hard riding to beat Major Don by 1½ lengths; beaten a length by Ven Matrero in 19-runner minor event at Windsor the following month on only subsequent outing; stays 1¼m; sold to Susan Piggott Bloodstock 8,000 gns Newmarket Autumn Sales. *H. Cecil.*

PONTIN BOY 4 b.c. Prince Tenderfoot 126–Buenaventura II (Celtic Ash) (1982   –
8.2f 8d 10.1fg⁴ 10f² 12fg* 12fg² 12fg² 12s 1983 10s 11.7d 11.7f) strong, lengthy colt; suited by 1½m; acts on firm going and is possibly unsuited by soft; has won for an amateur rider. *H. T. Jones.*

PONTOS 4 b.g. Averof 123–Filandria 90 (French Beige 127) (1982 8g 8.2fg 9fg   –
11.5f 11.5fg 10.1g 10fg 1983 10.2fg 10.8d) leggy gelding; poor performer nowadays. *Miss S. Morris.*

POOL PLAYER 3 ch.g. Warpath 113–Snow Goose (Santa Claus 133) (1982 7g   73
1983 12v² 11.7s⁴ 15.5v 11.7fg) quite a moderate maiden; should stay beyond 1½m; ran moderately in blinkers final start (June). *K. Brassey.*

POPEMOBILE 2 b.g. Vitiges 132–Pope Joan (So Blessed 130) (1983 6fg 7f 8g 9f   72
7fg) Feb 20; fifth foal; dam placed over 5f at 2 yrs in France on only start; quite moderate; best run at 9f; sold 825 gns Ascot November Sales. *W. Elsey.*

POP PICKER 2 ch.c. Record Token 128–La Brigitte 87 (Gulf Pearl 117) (1983   85
6d 6fg²(dis)) Apr 7; 11,500F, 18,000Y; half-brother to fair 1978 2-y-o 5f and 6f winner Great Wonder (by Miracle), subsequently successful in Hong Kong; dam won over 5f at 2 yrs; 14/1, swerved left 1f out and caused interference when neck second of 20 to Tug Top in maiden race at Doncaster in November and was disqualified; stays 6f. *C. Horgan.*

POPPIDUK 3 ch.f. Quack-Popkins 120 (Romulus 129) (1982 NR 1983 8f 7f³ 8f⁴   64
10f⁴ 11.5g) rather a leggy filly; half-sister to 2 winners, notably high-class 1977 staying 2-y-o Cherry Hinton (by Nijinsky); dam very smart at up to 10.5f; rather a disappointing maiden; should be suited by further than 1m; last when blinkered final start; sold to BBA (Ire) 60,000 gns Newmarket December Sales. *G. Wragg.*

POPPY SEED 2 b.f. On Your Mark 125–Ardrionn (Wolver Hollow 126) (1983 5fg   65
5g 5.3fg) Mar 30; IR 1,400F, IR 9,000Y; leggy, plain filly; second foal; half-sister to 3-y-o County Broker (by Kashiwa), a useful winner at 5f in 1982; dam poor Irish maiden; plating-class maiden; showed form only on final outing. *A. Jarvis.*

POPSI'S JOY 8 b.g. Hill Clown–Popsie's Pride (Border Legend 119) (1982 18g²   93
14g³ 18f³ 18.4fg 14fg² 20fg* 16fg 16g 19f 16d 18d² 20g 1983 16v² 16s² 16g* 14s² 16g 16f³ 16.1fg⁴ 19f 16fg 18fg² 20fg³) big, strong gelding; staying handicapper; ran more consistently than in 1982 and beat Red Field 1½ lengths at Newmarket in April; also runner-up 4 times, putting up a good effort on final occasion when going down by ¾ length to Bajan Sunshine in Tote Cesarewitch at Newmarket in October (apprentice ridden); acts on any going; invariably held up; ran poorly eighth start and didn't find much off bridle final outing. *M. Haynes.*

PORTADORE 3 gr.c. Porto Bello 118–Golden Herb 80 (Goldhill 125) (1982 NR   –
1983 5g 10fg 8d) tall, workmanlike colt; half-brother to three 2-y-o winners; dam seemed to stay 1m; well beaten in minor events. *M. Usher.*

PORT ANITA 2 b.f. Roman Warrior 132–Port Meadow 83 (Runnymede 123)   –
(1983 7g) Apr 1; half-sister to several winners, including 1982 2-y-o 5f winner Belinda Brown (by Legal Eagle); dam probably stayed 1m; in rear in 14-runner maiden race at Lingfield in October. *P. Mitchell.*

PORTE DES LILAS (FR) 2 b.f. Sharpman 124–Gentop (High Top 131) (1983   109
10g² 10g*) Feb 20; 470,000 francs Y (approx £39,000); second foal; half-sister to French 3-y-o middle-distance winner Ghisoni (by Carwhite); dam, from family of Grease and Phydilla, won 4 small races from 9f to 11f; made all to win maiden event

at Saint-Cloud in November by 3 lengths from Branta; beaten a neck by Soaring on same track and distance previous month; will stay 1½m; promising. *A. de Royer Dupre, France.*

PORTER 4 b.g. Mummy's Pet–Morelia 76 (Murrayfield 119) (1982 7d 8.2v³ 8fg 10fg 8.2g² 9g³ 11g 10d 12g⁴ 12fg 10s 1983 10v⁴ 12d³ 11s 12v 10.6s³ 11g* 12f⁴ 13h 12g⁴ 12s 14.7fg) leggy gelding; poor mover and has a round action; plater; won non-seller at Hamilton in June; stays 13f; acts on any going; best in blinkers; suitable mount for an apprentice; has been bandaged on off-hind. *E. Carter.*   **57**

PORT ERROLL 2 ch.g. Import 127–Honey Season 66 (Silly Season 127) (1983 5d 5v 5v 6f) Mar 29; 360Y; tall gelding; of no account; blinkered final outing; exported to Malaysia. *M. W. Easterby.*   **–**

PORTERS GIRL 4 b.f. Broxted 120–Blue Friend 61 (Blue Streak 106) (1982 NR 1983 12.2f 9s) third live foal; dam plater; probably of little account. *J. Townson.*   **–**

PORTHAND 2 b.f. Hillandale 125–Portella 78§ (Porto Bello 118) (1983 6f 5f 5.8h 6fg 8d 6g) Apr 1; good-bodied filly; second foal; dam, placed several times over sprint distances, was very bad at start; modest plater; not sure to stay 1m. *R. Holder.*   **54**

PORTLAW (USA) 2 b.c. Mr Prospector–Wee Bit of Irish (Irish Ruler) (1983 6f³ 6g³) Apr 4; 110,000Y; lengthy, angular colt; second foal; dam, stakes placed at 2 yrs, won 9 times at up to 7f including claiming events; placed in fair company at York in June and Doncaster (hung badly left final 2f) in September; will stay 7f; seemingly a difficult ride but has the ability to win races. *J. Tree.*   **95**

PORT-O-CALL 2 b.f. Import 127–River Chimes 43 (Forlorn River 124) (1983 5v 5.1f 5g 5g) May 3; rather leggy filly; first foal; dam sister to high-class sprinter Rapid River; of no account; sold out of M. Tompkins' stable 330 gns Ascot July Sales after second outing and resold 350 gns Ascot November Sales. *P. Burgoyne.*   **–**

PORTOGON 5 gr.h. Porto Bello 118–Helgonet (Soueida 111) (1982 8g 6.5fg 6.5v² 7.5d³ 7s 8fg 7fg⁴ 8g 7g 8f 7f³ 7g* 7fg² 7fg* 7d² 7s 1983 8v 8d² 7s 7s³ 7d* 7g* 8d* 7f 8h 7fg 7s 7.2g) big, strong, workmanlike horse; won handicaps at Thirsk and Ayr (2); beat Cyril's Choice ½ length in Tia Maria Handicap in May for first Ayr success and held off Ring Bidder by short head in Long John Scotch Whisky Handicap in June for second; stays 1m; acts on any going; does best when ridden up with pace; genuine though finished well beaten last 5 starts. *M. Usher.*   **77**

PORTO IRENE 3 ch.f. Porto Bello 118–Irene Louise 65 (Match III 135) (1982 6fg 5fg 5.8g⁴ 5t bs 1983 5s 6d 5.8v³ 6s 5s 5g 5.8g 5f 6fg 7h 6fg 6f 5f² 6fg) small, compact filly; second in handicap at Beverley in September, best run for a long time; stays 6f; acts on any going; saddle slipped second start. *D. C. Tucker.*   **52**

PORTO LOUISE 4 ch.f. Porto Bello 118–Irene Louise 65 (Match III 135) (1982 6fg 8.5f 10g 1983 12f 10.1f) compact filly; poor plater. *D. C. Tucker.*   **–**

POUR MOI 2 ch.f. Bay Express 132–Orange Sensation 69 (Floribunda 136) (1983 5v³ 5v 6f 5f 6fg³ 7s⁴ 6fg) May 17; 12,500Y; neat filly; half-sister to numerous winners here and abroad, including useful 1976 2-y-o Swift Sensation (by My Swallow); dam placed at up to 7f at 2 yrs; quite a modest maiden; suited by 7f; probably acts on any going; wears blinkers. *R. Laing.*   **73**

POUSDALE-TACHYTEES 2 b.f. Tachypous 128–Teesdale 97 (Aggressor 130) (1983 5v² 5s⁴ 5s 6s 6s 6g⁴ 7f 7f 6f 7f 8f 8fg) May 8; 2,600F, 3,000Y; small, fair sort; half-sister to several winners here and abroad, including useful 1975 2-y-o 6f winner Blue Cavalier (by Queen's Hussar), subsequently successful in Italy; dam won twice at 1¼m; plating-class maiden; stays 7f; acts on any going; blinkered ninth outing. *Mrs J. Reavey.*   **60**

POWDER PUFF 2 b.f. Frimley Park 109–Our Melody 78§ (Song 132) (1983 5fg² 5fg*) first foal; dam placed numerous times over sprint distances; made all in 16-runner maiden race at Folkestone in October; previously failed by only a neck to hold off Ewe Lamb after leading nearly all way in 13-runner maiden at Lingfield; evidently quite speedy. *K. Brassey.*   **82**

POWERSAVER LAD 3 b.c. Jaazeiro 127–Guama 89 (Gulf Pearl 117) (1982 NR 1983 8g 12g² 11.5fg² 16f³ 15.5f³ 14fg³ 14f³ 14f³ 14g³ 16fg² 18fg*) lengthy, fair sort; second foal; dam 2-y-o 7f winner; usually finishes thereabouts, and got off mark at last when beating Basta readily by 3 lengths in minor event at Doncaster in October; suited by a test of stamina; acts on firm going and has yet to race on a soft surface. *M. Jarvis.*   **77**

639

PRACTICAL 3 b. or br.f. Ballymore 123–Prudent Girl 92 (Primera 131) (1982   **95**
7.5d 8g 8s 1983 7d² 8s² 8d² 10v² 7g³ 10s* 8s 9d* 10d*) half-sister to 3 winners,
notably top-class American middle-distance performer Providential (by Run The
Gantlet) and top 1981 French staying 2-y-o filly Play It Safe (by Red Alert); dam,
half-sister to Hethersett, won over middle distances; in first 6 in 3 maiden races in
France as a 2-y-o when trained by F. Boutin; did well when blinkered in latter part
of 1983, winning maiden race at Listowel, minor event at Phoenix Park and
16-runner handicap at Leopardstown; had been second 4 times in spring, including
in Warmlife Stakes at Leopardstown and Thomastown Castle Stud Race at Phoenix
Park; will stay 1½m; yet to race on a firm surface. *D. K. Weld, Ireland.*

PRAIRIE SAINT 3 b.f. Welsh Saint 126–Prairie Bar (Ballymore 123) (1982   –
5.3fg 5.1g² 5fg² 5f* 1983 7v) sparely-made filly; needed race only outing of 1983
(April); form only at 5f on a sound surface. *C. Spares.*

PRECIPICE WILL 2 gr. or ro.c. Precipice Wood 123–Eastern Dove   –
(Agamemnon 91) (1983 8g) May 21; lengthy, rather sparely-made colt; fifth foal;
dam never ran; always well behind in 18-runner maiden race at Ayr in September.
J. S. Wilson.

PRECIS (USA) 4 b.g. Pretense–Vaguely Familiar (Vaguely Noble 140) (1982 7g*   **89** d
6g² 8fg* 8f² 9d 1983 7v² 6g 8f 7f) big, strong, rangy gelding; has a slightly round
action; creditable second to Christmas Cottage in quite valuable handicap at
Newcastle in April; below form afterwards, including when blinkered final start;
apparently finds 6f too sharp and stays 1m; acts on any going; gives impression he
will always do best on a galloping track; sometimes pulls hard. *J. W. Watts.*

PRECOCIOUS 2 b.c. Mummy's Pet 125–Mrs Moss 81 (Reform 132) (1983 5g*   **126**
5g* 5f* 5f* 6fg*)

The big autumn two-year-old events both here and in France were deprived of
considerable interest by knee injuries to two highly promising colts: the Prix de la
Salamandre and the Grand Criterium would surely have been enriched by the
presence of Ti King, a fast-finishing second to Siberian Express in the Prix Morny;
and the Flying Childers Stakes and Middle Park Stakes would most probably have
fallen to Precocious had he not been side-lined by injury towards the end of August.

At the time of his injury Precocious was well on his way towards establishing a
string of victories similar to Horage's in 1982. He was unbeaten in five races, three
of them pattern events, and like Horage he had taken one of Royal Ascot's
important events as well as the Gimcrack Stakes at York. Whereas Horage was
having no less than his sixth race at Royal Ascot Precocious was having only his
third when justifying favouritism in the Norfolk Stakes. He had made an impressive
first appearance in the Philip Cornes Nickel Alloys qualifier at Newmarket on Two
Thousand Guineas day in April, although his early preparation had reportedly been
interrupted by a six-week spell on the easy list to give his knees time to mature.
The Philip Cornes race had been chosen in recent years for the debuts of such good
colts as Shearwalk, Prince Reymo, Lucky Hunter, Runnett and Final Straw, and
several of the 1983 field also looked very promising, none more so than Precocious.

Norfolk Stakes, Ascot—a smooth win for Precocious from Indigo Jones (left)

Gimcrack Stakes, York—Precocious stamps himself a high-class two-year-old, winning very impressively from Adam's Peak (left)

A rangy, deep-girthed, good sort, he started a very short-priced favourite to become his trainer's third winning two-year-old from as many runners, a feat he accomplished in style by three lengths. What looked a fine effort at the time looked even better later in the year as both the second and third home, King of Clubs and Maajid, developed into very useful colts and nine other winners emerged from those further behind. On his next start Precocious turned in a tremendously smooth display to beat four others in the National Stakes at Sandown and it was no surprise to see him as short as 11/4 on against the likes of Clantime, Indigo Jones, Stanley The Baron and Express Delivery at Royal Ascot. His supporters were given no cause for worry: Precocious began to improve after halfway, hit the front before the furlong pole and needed to do no more than the bare minimum to score by three lengths from the Epsom winner Indigo Jones. Precocious' record therefore stood at three wins from three starts without his being seriously tested.

Neither of Precocious' subsequent races produced a rival capable of extending him. Giving up to 7 lb to his six opponents in the Molecomb Stakes at Goodwood in July proved a task that didn't trouble him in the slightest: he cruised through to deprive the speedy Sajeda of the lead below the distance and eventually crossed the line two and a half lengths clear. His performance at Goodwood matched his physical condition which was impressive. He had obviously thrived in the six weeks since Ascot. When he reappeared in the Gimcrack in August he looked superb, completely outshining the five other runners in the paddock one of whom, his only serious market rival the unbeaten Al Mamoon, was contrastingly unimpressive, sweating up and becoming very edgy. Although this was Precocious' first attempt at six furlongs there was little doubt he would stay the trip, considering his placid temperament and amenability to restraint, and Piggott allowed him to take the lead much earlier than previously, letting him stroll clear soon after halfway. From then on the race was as good as over; Al Mamoon and Garrulous had shot their bolt before the final furlong and Adam's Peak, Kings Island and Our Dynasty were quite unable to prevent Precocious' drawing further and further ahead. The manner of his victory brought to mind those of Petingo and Mill Reef back in 1967 and 1970, although towards the finish Precocious' action became scratchy and he changed his legs abruptly just before the post. Although there was no suggestion afterwards that anything was amiss, within a fortnight an announcement was made that he was lame, possibly the result of being cast in his box.

Precocious (b.c. Apr 4, 1981)	Mummy's Pet (b 1968)	Sing Sing (b 1957) — Tudor Minstrel / Agin the Law
		Money for Nothing (br 1962) — Grey Sovereign / Sweet Nothings
	Mrs Moss (ch 1969)	Reform (b 1964) — Pall Mall / Country House
		Golden Plate (ch 1964) — Whistler / Good as Gold

In our commentary on the Queen Mary winner Pushy in *Racehorses of 1980* we mentioned what a bargain the Marchioness of Tavistock secured when she purchased the filly's dam Mrs Moss as a six-year-old for 2,100 guineas at the 1975 December Sales. The word bargain seems scarcely adequate now. Pushy's first foal, a filly by Irish River named Eye Drop, was sold by a partnership including the Tavistocks for 750,000 dollars at the 1983 Keeneland Summer Yearling Sales (and is to be trained by Henry Cecil). And all of Mrs Moss's three subsequent foals to race have proved way above average. The first, Jupiter Island (by St Paddy), had a magnificent season in 1983, earning over £70,000 as well as winning the Tote-Ebor and recording his first pattern-race victory in the St Simon Stakes; the second, Krayyan (by Tower Walk), developed into a smart two-year-old sprinter after being sold for 150,000 guineas as a yearling, and has now been retired to the Irish National Stud; and thirdly comes Precocious, comfortably the best of Mrs Moss's eight winners. Mrs Moss was barren for the only time when covered by Kris in 1981; she has since produced her ninth foal, a sister to Precocious, and is now in foal to the Italian Two Thousand Guineas winner Good Times.

Mrs Moss showed nowhere near so much ability as the best of her offspring, gaining her only victory from four starts in a five-furlong maiden race at Chester as a two-year-old. Coincidentally she was ridden at Chester by Piggott who partnered Jupiter Island and Precocious to their highly unusual double in the Ebor and Gimcrack. Mrs Moss ran only as a two-year-old, as did her disappointing dam Golden Plate and Golden Plate's very smart brother, the sprinter Whistling Wind. Mrs Moss's achievements provoked an interesting difference of opinion between those celebrated writers on bloodstock, Peter Willett and Tony Morris. Willett concluded in an article in *Horse and Hound* that 'a mare who can produce four such notable performers, each by a different sire, must be prepotent and have a measure of greatness.' Without denying Mrs Moss's merit Morris took exception to the word 'prepotent,' pointing out that her best offspring are much nearer in merit to their sires than their dam and that their racing characteristics were those of their sires. He added that 'if Mrs Moss had been transmitting her own heritage her products would all have been short-runners of the "here-today-gone-tomorrow" type, which certainly has not been the case.' Morris completed his arguments with an alternative description for Mrs Moss which strikes us as much nearer the mark than 'prepotent'—he called her 'a non-interfering receptacle for the best qualities of her mates.' Whatever the source of Precocious' ability, neither side of his pedigree contains much in the way of stamina and we doubt whether he'll be capable of lasting out the mile of the Guineas. Hopefully though he'll recover fully from his injury and prove himself a worthy opponent for the best older sprinters. As yet he has raced only on a sound surface. *H. Cecil.*

PREDOMINATE 2 ch.c. Thatch 136–Miss Noname 102 (High Top 131) (1983 7fg4 7.6fg4 9s) Mar 16; 42,000Y; strong, quite attractive colt; first foal; dam best at up to 1¼m; ran disappointingly in modest company after appearing to show promise behind Donzel in Mornington Stakes at Ascot in September on first appearance; not certain to stay 9f, at least not as a 2-y-o in testing conditions. *G. Harwood.* **83**

PREGO 3 ch.c. Be My Guest 126–Audrey Joan 118 (Doutelle 128) (1982 NR 1983 7d3 8f* 8fg2 8f2 8f* 8g* 9fg4) big, rangy colt; half-brother to several winners, including smart miler River Dane (by Tyrant) and very good Australian filly Pure of Heart (by Godswalk), winner of pattern races over 6f and 7f; dam sprinter; held up when winning £5,100 maiden race at York in June, £7,600 Esal Credit Handicap at Newbury in August and £5,200 handicap at Haydock in September; seemed to have plenty in hand when beating Silver Season a length at Newbury but only just managed to get up and beat Lion City by a short head at Haydock; in frame on all his other starts, finding little in closing stages when less than 2 lengths fourth of 30 behind Sagamore in William Hill Cambridgeshire at Newmarket in October (had **108**

642

Mr R. E. Sangster's "Prego"

stiffish task for 3-y-o and came out best horse at weights); stays 9f; yet to race on really soft going but acts on any other; needs waiting tactics and is a difficult ride. *B. Hills.*

PRELKO 8 br.g. Relko 136–Pretty Cage 110 (Cagire II 122) (1982 NR 1983   **45**
15.8d³ 15g) strong gelding; has been fired; staying handicapper; acts on any going; wears bandages. *J. Fitzgerald.*

PREMIUM WIN (USA) 2 b.f. Lyphard 132–Classic Perfection (Never Bend)   **111**
(1983 6fg* 6fg³ 7fg² 8f⁴) Apr 26; half-sister to 3 good-class winners in North America, including Classic Go Go (by Pago Pago), a very smart winner at up to 9f; dam, 2-y-o 6f winner, is half-sister to very smart Batonnier; won 59,000-franc event at Evry in July; ran well afterwards to finish ¾-length third to Greinton in 90,000-franc event and 2 lengths second to Almeira in Prix du Calvados, both at Deauville in August; creditable fourth, beaten over 3 lengths, to same horse in Prix Marcel Boussac at Longchamp in October; should stay 1¼m. *A. Fabre, France.*

PREOBRAJENSKA 2 b.f. Double Form 130–Pulcinella 95 (Shantung 132) (1983   **93**
5fg 6fg² 6d³ 6fg* 5g* 6d*) Jan 29; 12,500Y; lengthy filly; good walker; second foal; half-sister to a winner in Switzerland; dam 1m winner; did not see racecourse until mid-August, and showed marked improvement towards the back-end, winning maiden race (made most) at Nottingham and minor events (led all the way) at York and Lingfield; seems equally effective at 5f and 6f; acts on a firm and a soft surface. *R. Armstrong.*

PRESENT VALUE 3 ch.f. Whistlefield 118–Second Gift (Frankincense 120)   **71**
(1982 NR 1983 10v³ 12v 11.5fg 10f³ 10f 10.1fg 9d) second foal; dam ran twice; plating-class maiden; stays 1¼m. *N. Guest.*

PRESS BARON 4 b.c. Touch Paper 113–Miss Dorothy 87 (Major Portion 129)   **–**
(1982 6s 6d 7f 6f 1983 10.1f 10f 8g 10g 7fg 6fg 6fg) of little account; has been blinkered. *P. Ashworth.*

PRETTY FABULOUS (USA) 2 b.c. Effervescing–Pretty Part (Chieftain) –
(1983 6f 7f) Mar 3; $48,000F, $45,000Y; lengthy, narrow, unfurnished colt; second
foal; dam, sister to 2 stakes winners, won 2 sprint races at 3 yrs; behind in maiden
race at Newmarket in July and £3,500 event at Sandown in August. *R. Armstrong.*

PRETTY LASS 6 br.m. Workboy 123–Pretty Cage 110 (Cagire II 122) (1982 NR –
1983 16f) poor maiden; has worn blinkers. *R. Woodhouse.*

PRETTY PICTURE 4 ch.f. Grundy 137–Miss Pinkie 121 (Connaught 130) (1982 92
12f² 12.2f* 14g⁴ 12fg³ 1983 14fg⁴ 16fg* 18.1d* 16fg 19g*) smallish, lengthy filly;
apprentice ridden when winning handicaps at Thirsk, Yarmouth and Goodwood in
September, making all to beat King's College Boy 3 lengths on last-named; suited
by a test of stamina; appears to act on any going; does best when ridden up with
pace; ran poorly fourth outing. *P. Kelleway.*

PRETTY PISTOL 2 b.f. Malinowski 123–Striking Bell (Bold Hour) (1983 5s 5v 58
7f⁴ 7g 8d) robust, good-bodied filly; first known foal; dam second over 6f and 1m at
3 yrs in France; poor maiden; best effort in claiming race on third outing; should
stay 1m; acts on firm going. *B. Hills.*

PRETTY TOUGH 5 b.g. Firestreak 125–Idyll-Liquor (Narrator 127) (1982 NR –
1983 10s 10d) poor maiden; has been blinkered. *W. Clay.*

PREVAIL 4 b.g. Steel Heart 128–Lavendula Rose 108 (Le Levanstell 122) (1982 –
6s* 6d³ 7fg⁴ 6f* 6f* 6fg² 7.2g 6g⁴ 6g 7g 7d 1983 8d 6s 6f 7.6g) neat, strong,
attractive gelding who often impresses in appearance; good mover; fairly useful on
his day but hasn't run up to his best for some time; stays 7f but gives impression 6f
is his optimum trip; acts on any going but goes well on firm; suited by waiting
tactics; refused to enter stalls once; sold 2,900 gns Newmarket Autumn Sales. *W.
Elsey.*

PRICEOFLOVE 3 b.c. Blue Cashmere 129–Gay Donna (Tudor Jinks 121) (1982 5fg 84
5f⁴ 5d* 5g 6d* 6g 1983 6v 6v³ 5.8v² 6s 6s 6fg 7.3g³ 7g 6s 6d) strong, quite attractive,
well-made colt; stays 7f; suited by some give underfoot; often blinkered; none too
consistent; sold 9,200 gns Newmarket Autumn Sales. *R. Laing.*

PRICKLE 2 b.f. Sharpen Up 127–Jungle Queen (Twilight Alley 133) (1983 6f* 6g* 114
6fg³)
    Despite meeting with exceptional success in his fourteen years as a trainer
Henry Cecil still has some way to go before he matches Vincent O'Brien's
achievement of having won all bar one of Britain's Group 1 events. The Derby, the
King George VI and Queen Elizabeth Diamond Stakes, the Coronation Cup, the
Oaks, the King's Stand, the July Cup, the Dubai Champion Stakes and the William
Hill Cheveley Park are still on the wanted list. The stable's Prickle started clear
favourite for the Cheveley Park at Newmarket in October, a race in which Cecil had
previously saddled two seconds, Caspian and Dame Foolish, and a third, Pushy.
Unfortunately Prickle had a distinctly wintery look about her, as though she might
have passed her best for the season, and she failed by a head and a short head to
hold off Desirable and Pebbles after leading to the last strides.
    Prickle had accounted for both Desirable and Pebbles in very good style on
their previous encounter in the Lowther Stakes at York in August. She had started
favourite there too, although her racecourse achievements—she had won an
eighteen-runner maiden race at Nottingham a month earlier by a length from
Malaak—didn't come up to those of Chapel Cottage, Desirable and Pebbles,
winners respectively on their last outings of the Cherry Hinton, Princess Margaret
and Childwick Stud Stakes. Prickle justified her market position most convincingly,
making all the running. For a moment she looked in trouble as firstly Pebbles and
then Chapel Cottage challenged entering the final quarter mile but she quickened

*Lowther Stakes, York—Prickle quickens clear in fine style from Desirable,
Chapel Cottage (far side) and Pebbles (blaze)*

again to shake them off and then held Desirable's challenge comfortably by two and a half lengths. A smart display!

Prickle (b.f. Apr 13, 1981)	Sharpen Up (ch 1969)	Atan (ch 1961)	Native Dancer / Mixed Marriage
		Rocchetta (ch 1961)	Rockefella / Chambiges
	Jungle Queen (b 1969)	Twilight Alley (ch 1959)	Alycidon / Crepuscule
		Snap (b 1949)	Big Game / Jiffy

The story goes that Prickle's owner-breeders acquired her dam Jungle Queen for '£100 and a case of wine if she does any good' after she failed to produce a foal in her first two seasons at stud. Jungle Queen has done her owners proud, producing four winners from four foals to survive to racing age. Prickle is easily the best but the others, Sharp Deal (a brother to Prickle), Jungle Jim (by Hotfoot) and Equanaid (by Dominion), were all fairly useful winners over a mile. Sharp Deal, Jungle Jim and Equanaid were sold for a total of over 45,000 guineas and a further sizeable dividend is surely due if Jungle Queen's next produce, a colt foal by Final Straw, is also sold. Although Jungle Queen herself showed little ability in three outings, the last in a two-mile maiden, her dam Snap was a useful staying half-sister to the war-time Derby winner Ocean Swell and to the One Thousand Guineas third and Oaks runner-up Iona. Prickle should have little difficulty in staying the mile of the One Thousand Guineas, for which she must be considered one of England's leading hopes. We do have one reservation about her Guineas prospects, though; she's rather a leggy, tall, raw-boned individual, not the type which usually comes to hand early in a cold spring. She has a smooth, easy action which is admirably suited by fast going; she has yet to race on a soft surface. *H. Cecil.*

PRIMA VOCE (USA) 4 b.c. Elocutionist–Que Mona (Ribot 142) (1982 7fg 8fg **121** 8.5f* 8f⁴ 10g 10fg⁴ 11.1fg 10fg 10d² 1983 8v 10fg 10f 11f* 10.5d 12g³ 12s* 12f)

Captain J. Durham-Matthews' "Prima Voce"

well-made colt; a very smart colt at his best; returned to form when decisively beating Jalmood by 3 lengths in Grand Prix Prince Rose at Ostend in July and picked up another valuable prize when accounting for Rheinsteel by ½ length (pair clear) in Stockholm Cup at Taby in September; also ran respectably on second and sixth starts, finishing staying-on fifth to Stanerra in Prince of Wales's Stakes at Royal Ascot and 8½ lengths third to Diamond Shoal in Grosser Preis von Baden; suited by 1¼m+; acts on any going; sent to be trained by J. Sheppard in USA. *R. Armstrong.*

PRIME ASSETT 2 b.c. Welsh Pageant 132–Orange Squash 78 (Red God 128§) (1983 7d⁴) Mar 14; IR 31,000Y; second foal; half-brother to 1982 French 2-y-o 1¼m winner Voussac (by Great Nephew); dam, sister to very useful Irish colt Matuno God, won 3 times at around 1m; 5/1, respectable fourth of 13 behind easy winner Van Dyke Brown in maiden race at Yarmouth in September; sure to improve. *W. O'Gorman.* 72 p

PRIME STONE 2 b.c. Sparkler 130–Primage 99 (Primera 131) (1983 5v 8g 8d) Mar 7; 17,000F; rangy, good-bodied colt; half-brother to numerous winners, including very useful 1979 2-y-o 7f winner Swift Image (by Bay Express) and very useful Irish 1m to 1¼m winner Mitchelstown (by Sweet Revenge); dam won over 6f at 2 yrs; showed no worthwhile form; should do better in time if looks mean anything. *J. Etherington.* –

PRIMROSE LAD 3 b.c. Bold Lad (Ire) 133–Nighty Night (Sassafras 135) (1982 NR 1983 7d 10s 11.5fg⁴ 10.2f) 8,400Y; smallish, quite attractive colt; third foal; brother to a modest winner and half-brother to a winner abroad; poor maiden; seems suited by 11.5f; exported to Malaysia. *E. Eldin.* –

PRIMULA BOY 8 ch.g. Sallust 134–Catriona 96 (Sing Sing 134) (1982 6d 6f 5fg 6g 6f 6fg 6d³ 6g 6g 7d⁴ 6f 6fg 7f 6g 6s 7s 1983 6s 6s 7d 7d) fair handicapper at his best but has deteriorated and is inconsistent; stays 7f; acts on any going; has worn blinkers but is better without; has been bandaged in front; has won for an apprentice; broke a blood vessel once in 1982. *W. Bentley.* –

PRINCE AMADEO 3 ch.c. Sallust 134–Flaring Angel (Nentego 119) (1982 6s 8s³ 6d 1983 6s 6d 7fg 8f 10f 10.1fg 10f 8g 10g 7fg) medium-sized, close-coupled colt; plating-class maiden; has run respectably at 1¼m; seems to act on any going; blinkered last 4 starts; sold to H. Beasley 1,100 gns Newmarket Autumn Sales. *F. J. Houghton.* –

PRINCE BALIDAR 2 b.g. Balidar 133–Right View 75 (Right Tack 131) (1983 5g 5g 5d) Apr 17; 2,700Y; quite well-made gelding; third living foal; half-brother to a minor winner; dam early 2-y-o 5f winner; plating-class maiden; best effort on first outing; gelded after final appearance. *D. Arbuthnot.* 70

PRINCE BARRINGTON 3 b.c. Hotfoot 126–My Princess (King Emperor) (1982 7g 6d 1983 8v 8f 10.1f² 10.1f* 10.1f 10.1fg* 10.1f³ 10s 10fg) deep-girthed colt; not the best of movers; successful in minor events at Windsor in July and August, in latter event making virtually all and just lasting home from Holmbury; ran moderately in between; stays 1¼m; acts on firm going (never in race on soft ground, eighth start); sold 13,000 gns Newmarket Autumn Sales. *B. Hills.* 82

PRINCE BLESS 5 b.g. So Blessed 130–Pearl Star 110 (Gulf Pearl 117) (1982 NR 1983 12d) strong, attractive gelding; good mover; quite modest at his best; suited by middle distances; acts on a firm surface; useful hurdler on his day; possibly temperamental; sold 3,200 gns Ascot May Sales. *Mrs N. Smith.* –

PRINCE CONCORDE 3 b.c. Condorcet–Barstown Princess (Seminole II) (1982 5g⁴ 5f 7f⁴ 7f 7fg* 8f* 8d³ 8d 1983 12d³ 10d² 12f 12f² 11f 12f 11f⁴ 12g* 12g) leggy, light-framed colt; capably ridden by his girl apprentice when winning 16-runner handicap at Leicester in September; suited by 1½m; yet to race on really soft ground, but acts on any other. *E. Carter.* 78

PRINCE CROW (USA) 2 ch.c. Crow 134–Fashionably Timed (Pronto) (1983 8fg 9s*) Mar 8; $22,000Y; fourth foal; half-brother to a winner; dam twice-raced half-sister to good animals Beau Brummel, Dapper Dan and Pas de Deux); made all to win 10-runner maiden race at Wolverhampton in October by 4 lengths from Dereta's Dudley; should make a useful middle-distance 3-y-o. *M. Stoute.* 87 p

PRINCE GUARD 4 ch.c. Home Guard 129–Crassula (Canisbay 120) (1982 12f 8f⁴ 8s 8s⁴ 8s* 8s 1983 8s² 8d² 8fg³ 8f³ 8f 8.3fg 8fg⁴ 8fg 8g 8fg* 8.2fg³ 8fg) big, fair sort; won handicap at Newcastle in October; stays 1m; acts on any going but goes well on soft; usually blinkered nowadays; suited by forcing tactics; inconsistent. *S. Matthews.* 70

PRINCE HENRY 3 ch.g. Whitstead 125–Concern 63 (Brigadier Gerard 144) (1982 7g 7fg 1983 10v 12d 14.7d* 13.1v⁴ 18fg) small, strong gelding; made all 66

when 8-length winner of 15-runner maiden race at Redcar in May; off course 5 months after next start; evidently suited by a test of stamina. *M. Tompkins.*

PRINCE LAFITE 3 gr.g. English Prince 129–Haut Lafite (Tamerlane 128) (1982 7g 7fg 7fg 1983 11v 8.2v 7g 10s 9g 14f 8fg 7g) of little account. *K. Ivory.*   –

PRINCELY FIGHTER (USA) 3 b. or br.c. Fifth Marine–Sharon A. (Princely Gift 137) (1982 6f* 6g4 6g* 6g 1983 6d 5f) attractive colt; quite useful at 2 yrs, but behind both outings in 1983; should stay beyond 6f; acts well on firm going; sold 3,100 gns Newmarket Autumn Sales. *M. Stoute.*   –

PRINCELY HERO (USA) 2 ch.c. Princely Native–Rarin To Go (Traffic Beat) (1983 6g 7d 7g 7g) Apr 2; $6,000Y; first foal; dam won 3 6f races; little form in maiden and minor events, all when blinkered. *G. Balding.*   –

PRINCE MAJ (USA) 5 b.h. His Majesty–Lady Rosse (Hail to Reason) (1982 12d4 12.3fg 16g 16f* 16fg* 14g2 18.8fg3 18.1g4 16d3 18d 1983 17.71 20f 16.6fg 17.1h 16h4 18fg 18fg 20fg) well-made, attractive horse; poor mover; fairly useful handicapper on his day but is unreliable; suited by a test of stamina; has run creditably on softish going but is better on a sound surface; usually wears blinkers and a hood; needs strong handling. *M. Pipe.*

PRINCE OBERON 2 b.g. Dragonara Palace 115–Native Nymph (Indigenous 121) (1983 5f4 5g4 6g) May 16; well-grown gelding; half-brother to several winners here and abroad, including sprinter Little Atom (by The Go-Between); dam 2-y-o 7f winner; plating-class maiden; should stay 6f; acts on firm going. *W. Haigh.*   61

PRINCE OF FASHION 2 b.c. The Brianstan 128–Trust Ann (Capistrano 120) (1983 5s 5g 5d2 5d* 5s* 6d3) Jan 27; 960F, 7,000Y; good-topped, quite attractive colt; first foal; dam won over 9f in Ireland and also over hurdles; won small races at Hamilton and Leicester in May, Leicester one on a disqualification; not seen out again after finishing disappointing third in minor event at Catterick in June; should stay 6f; acts on soft going; best in blinkers; sold 15,000 gns Newmarket September Sales, reportedly for export. *G. Huffer.*   86

PRINCE OF KASHMIR 4 ch.g. Blue Cashmere 129–Matala 65 (Misti IV 132) (1982 8fg 10fg 8fg 8f3 10.2g 10fg3 8fg 10.1d 1983 10.8v 12.2fg*) good-bodied gelding; 33/1 when winning handicap at Warwick in July; not seen out again; suited by 1½m; needs a sound surface and acts on hard going. *P. M. Taylor.*   55

PRINCE OF LIGHT 11 b.g. Laser Light 118–Royal Escape 94 (King's Bench 132) (1982 11s3 12fg4 10f 11fg 8f 9fg4 9.4f 10fg 12fg 12.2f 11s 1983 8g3 12fg 10.6s2 10g* 10f 12h 8h 10.6fg) plater; changed hands 2,100 gns after winning at Beverley in June (apprentices); stays 1½m; acts on any going except heavy; good mount for an apprentice; suited by an uphill finish and has won 5 times at Carlisle. *D. Smith.*   44

PRINCE OF PEACE 3 b.c. Busted 134–Miel (Pall Mall 132) (1982 NR 1983 8v 12s* 12f2 16f3 13s*) well-made, attractive, ex-Irish colt; sixth foal; dam never ran; accounted for some fairly useful animals when winning 21-runner maiden race at Naas in April (trained by M. Connolly at time); first past post in 2 minor events over here, beating His Honour by ½ length at Newmarket in July (wandered badly under strong pressure and placings were reversed) and Viennese Waltz by 3 lengths at Ayr in September (wasn't particularly impressive); met problems in running when third in amateur riders race at Beverley in between; gives impression he's suited by a test of stamina; evidently acts on any going but doesn't move well in slower paces and is possibly ideally suited by give in the ground; tends to hang. *H. Cecil.*   94

PRINCE OF PRINCES 4 br.c. Bustino 136–Princess Runnymede 108 (Runnymede 123) (1982 12f 11.7g4 12f 11.7fg4 16f* 16.5f2 16f* 16f* 15d 1983 16v 16s 16d3 20fg2 16f3 16f* 17.4g) tall, rangy colt; staying handicapper; well-backed favourite when scoring at Lingfield in August; had previously run well when losing by a neck to Right Regent (pair clear) in driving finish to Ascot Stakes at Royal Ascot; never going well final start; ideally suited by fast ground; has won for an apprentice; game. *J. Dunlop.*   91

PRINCE OF SPAIN 8 b.h. Philip of Spain 126– Miss Meryl 80 (River Chanter 121) (1982 7s* 7h* 8g4 7f 7fg 7fg3 8fg4 1983 7fg 7f 8f 8h 8f) quite a modest handicapper at his best; stays 1m; acts on any going; suitable mount for an apprentice; blinkered once; sometimes bandaged. *P. M. Taylor.*   –

PRINCE PADRAIG 2 b.c. English Prince 129–Corbalton 103 (Milesian 125) (1983 6s 7f*) Mar 10; 10,000Y; brother to fairly useful 1980 Irish 2-y-o Silver Creek and Irish 1¼m winner Royal Priority, and half-brother to numerous winners, notably very smart middle-distance winner Knockroe (by Fortino II); dam winner at up to 11f; stormed clear in final furlong to win maiden race at Leopardstown in   92 p

June by 8 lengths but wasn't seen out again; will be suited by middle distances; should make a smart three-year-old. *L. Browne, Ireland.*

PRINCE PUMA 2 ro.c. Native Admiral–Firey Kim (Cannonade) (1983 7f 7fg) — Mar 20; plain, good-topped colt; first foal; dam never ran; behind in maiden races at Redcar and Newmarket in September. *D. O'Donnell, Isle of Man.*

PRINCE RAGUSA 2 ch. c. English Prince 129–Trapani (Ragusa 137) (1983 5s* 94 6v* 6f² 7g 6h 7fg⁴ 7fg) Mar 29; 2,000F, 1,600Y; rangy colt; third produce; dam ran only 3 times; won maiden auction race at Salisbury in May and 9-runner minor event (giving weight all round) at Ripon in June; will be suited by 1m+; acts on any going. *G. Fletcher.*

PRINCE RAMBORO 2 b.c. Blakeney 126–Lady's Walk (Pall Mall 132) (1983 7g — 8d 7g) Apr 24; 8,000Y; fair sort; half-brother to several winners, including prolific 1979 2-y-o 5f winner Davidgalaxy Affair (by Tower Walk) and fairly useful 3-y-o 5f winner Deportment (by So Blessed); dam lightly raced; apparently not fully wound up, showed little in modest company towards the back-end. *D. H. Jones.*

PRINCE REVIEWER (USA) 5 b. g. Reviewer–Belle Sorella 99 (Ribot 142) 64 (1982 7.2s² 8fg 10.6g 8fg 8fg 7g 8f 7d⁴ 10.6s⁴ 7s³ 8.2s 10.2d 1983 8.3s 7v 9d 12v* 10g 12g 13s 12fg 12s) trotted up in ladies race at Ripon in June; stays 1½m well; acts on heavy going; sometimes sweats up; never going well when tried in blinkers once; inconsistent. *A. W. Jones.*

PRINCE REYMO 3 b.g. Jimmy Reppin 131–Honey Thief 77 (Burglar 128) (1982 102 5fg² 5f* 6f* 5f* 6f 1983 7d 5g 5f 5f 6f⁴ 6fg⁴ 6s 7fg) strong, full-quartered gelding; good walker and excellent mover; won 3 races in a row as a 2-y-o, including Windsor Castle Stakes at Royal Ascot; reportedly suffered from a back problem afterwards and was running best subsequent races when fourth to Maximova in Prix de Meautry at Deauville and to Gabitat in Goldene Peitsche at Baden-Baden, both in August; stays 6f; acts on firm going; sometimes blinkered; gelded at end of season. *R. Armstrong.*

PRINCE SANDRO 6 br. g. Hotfoot 126–Otra 88 (Sayajirao 132) (1982 NR 1983 61 12v 11.7s 12s 10s 12s 10.2g²) big, well-made gelding; fairly useful at his best but has deteriorated; second in seller at Bath in June; stays 13f; suited by some give in the ground; blinkered fifth outing and wore a hood on sixth; wears bandages nowadays; sold 450 gns Ascot 2nd June Sales. *P. Cundell.*

PRINCE SANTIAGO (USA) 4 b.g. Cougar II–Hasty Aysha (Hasty Road) 72 § (1982 12fg² 12fg 14f³ 14g* 14g* 16fg² 14f 16g³ 15d³ 16d 1983 12v 13d³ 16f² 15fg 14.7f⁴ 16f³ 14.6fg 13s⁴ 12fg 16.1g* 14d³) tall, attractive gelding; has a round action; won apprentice handicap at Haydock in October; creditable ½-length second to Weavers' Pin in Miner's Northumberland Plate at Newcastle earlier; stays well; acts on any going; effective with or without blinkers; inconsistent and doesn't find much off bridle. *D. Smith.*

PRINCES GATE 6 br.h. Realm 129–Consensus (Majority Blue 126) (1982 8g* 125 9fg 10f* 9g² 10f 8d² 8d* 10d 8v 1983 8s* 8v* 8.5g² 8v⁴ 8fg⁴) strong, workmanlike horse who usually impressed in appearance; very smart performer; gained second successive win in Doncaster Mile in March, accounting for Noalcoholic decisively by 2½ lengths, and wasn't troubled to beat Montekin by 4 lengths in Prix de Ris-Orangis at Evry in April; strong-finishing neck second to Mister Rock's in Grosser Preis von Dusseldorf later in April; stayed 1¼m well; acted on any going but put up best efforts with some give in the ground; genuine and consistent; stud in New Zealand. *H. T. Jones.*

PRINCE'S HEIR (USA) 3 ch.c. Princely Native–Lady Bencraft (Crafty 79 Admiral) (1982 5f⁴ 5g³ 5.8f⁴ 7d 7fg⁴ 6fg 1983 8g² 8.5d 8f 8f⁴ 8fg* 8. 2f* 8fg* 8.3f³ 8h² 8d* 8. 2g 8g) quite well-made colt; good mover; bought in 3,700 gns after winning seller at Leicester; subsequently proved much better than a plater, winning handicaps at Nottingham, Pontefract and Brighton; stays 1m; yet to race on really soft ground but acts on any other; ridden when successful by apprentice T. Quinn; sometimes blinkered; sold 14,000 gns Newmarket Autumn Sales, probably for export to Italy. *P. Cole.*

PRINCE SPY 3 b. c. Ballad Rock 122–Bay Laurel (Habitat 134) (1982 5g² 5f² 5d⁴ 117 5s* 5g* 6g* 1983 6v³ 6d* 6v³ 6f⁴ 6fg 7g⁴) smallish, robust colt who often impresses in appearance; came storming through to beat Miss Thames decisively by 2½ lengths, despite drifting right, in £8,100 handicap at Newmarket in April; in frame subsequently in Duke of York Stakes in May (had difficulty getting a run when 2½ lengths third to Vorvados), Cork and Orrery Stakes at Royal Ascot in June (about 2½ lengths fourth of 17 to Sylvan Barbarosa) and Harroways Stakes at Goodwood in September; favourite in last-named, following a very promising fifth to Salieri in Diadem Stakes at Ascot the previous month, ran as if possibly finding

Mr S. Powell's "Prince Spy"

7f beyond him and finished almost 6 lengths fourth of 9 to Larionov; stays 6f well; seems to act on any going, but has done all his winning with some give in the ground; has an excellent turn of foot; off course 3 months before fifth outing, reportedly with a hairline fracture of a sesamoid. *J. Sutcliffe.*

PRINCESS BRIONY 4 b.f. The Brianstan 128–Mernian 100 (Counsel 118) (1982 5fg 6d 8s 1983 7.6g 5fg 6f 10g) of little account; sold 420 gns Ascot November Sales. *C. James.*   –

PRINCESS HENHAM 3 gr.f. Record Token 128–Bog Oak (Sassafras 135) (1982 5fg 6fg³ 6g 7fg 7fg⁴ 8.2g* 8.2d 8d 8d 8.2s* 7s 1983 10d 12v⁴ 12v* 12d⁴ 12s² 12f 10g⁴ 12g⁴ 16.1fg⁴ 15.8fg 12g³ 16fg 12fg 10.2fg⁴) lengthy, rather sparely-made filly; raced alone in straight when winning handicap at Kempton in May; not disgraced on most other starts, on fifth finishing length second to Promindante in ladies event at Lingfield in June; stays 2m; acts on a firm surface but is well suited by soft ground. *N. Callaghan.*   **79**

PRINCESS MARTARA 3 b.f. Kala Shikari 125–Soft Moss (Santamoss 110) (1982 NR 1983 5v 5s 6d) IR 600F, 1,800Y; leggy filly; half-sister to 1981 Irish 2-y-o 6f winner Duncor (by Furry Glen); dam poor Irish maiden; behind in maiden races and a seller; sold 460 gns Ascot 2nd June Sales. *J. Douglas-Home.*   –

PRINCESS MONA 4 br.f. Prince Regent 129–Monaspear (Breakspear II) (1982 8fg 7d 7fg 8fg 8g 8f² 8d 1983 8g 7s 8f 10f 10f 10f 10g 8fg 10g) quite robust filly; poor plater; probably stays 1¼m; acts on firm going; has sweated up; not an easy ride and has shown signs of temperament. *J. Benstead.*   –

649

PRINCESS NABILA (USA) 2 b.f. King Pellinore 127–Guile Princess (Native – Guile) (1983 7fg) Apr 7; $75,000Y; tall, rather unfurnished filly; second foal; dam smart French 5f to 10.5f winner and also won over 1m in USA; in need of race, behind in 22-runner maiden event at Newmarket in October. *H. T. Jones.*

PRINCESS NAVARRO 3 ch.f. Raga Navarro 119–Gorgeous Gael (Atan) (1982 – 5g 5d 6g 5g 5v² 5s³ 5g 1983 5v⁴ 5s 5s 5fg 5f 6g³ 6f⁴ 6f 5.3fg) neat filly; good walker; plater; should stay 6f; acts well on soft going; often blinkered and has worn a bandage on off-hind. *W. Stubbs.*

PRINCESS PATI 2 b.f. Top Ville 129–Sarah Siddons 122 (Le Levanstell 122) **83 p** (1983 7g³) third foal; half-sister to high-class middle-distance performer Seymour Hicks (by Ballymore); dam won Irish 1,000 Guineas and Yorkshire Oaks; headed inside final furlong when under 3 lengths third of 18 to Princess Tracy in maiden race at Leopardstown in September; will be suited by 1¼m+; promising. *C. Collins, Ireland.*

PRINCESS POSSUM 2 br.f. Prince Tenderfoot 126–Macaw 85 (Narrator 127) – (1983 7f 8g) Feb 21; heavy-bodied filly; half-sister to several winners, including prolific 6f to 1m winner Northleach (by Northfields) and fairly useful 1980 2-y-o 7f winner Supreme Fjord (by Targowice); dam won over 1m; backward, well behind in maiden races at Salisbury and Leicester. *P. Mitchell.*

PRINCESS RIVA 2 ch.f. Riva Ridge–Cheveley Princess 120 (Busted 134) (1983 – p 6fg 7s) Mar 7; tall, lengthy, sparely-made filly; half-sister to fairly useful middle-distance winner Lakenheath (by Northfields); dam very smart winner from 7f to 1¼m; behind in autumn maiden events at Newmarket and Leicester; likely to do better in time. *G. Wragg.*

PRINCESS SHARPENUP 2 b.f. Lochnager 132–Sharpenella 72 (Sharpen Up **63 p** 127) (1983 5s³) Mar 16; second foal; dam won over 5.8f at 2 yrs; 5 lengths third of 8 to Addaana in maiden race at Hamilton in October; will probably stay 6f. *Mrs A. Cousins.*

PRINCESS SUNSHINE 2 b.f. Busted 134–Princess Biddy 86 (Sun Prince 128) – (1983 6g 6fg) May 4; IR 24,000Y; light-framed filly; second foal; dam, half-sister to top-class animals Double Jump and Royalty, won over 5f at 2 yrs; soundly beaten in September in 15-runner minor event at Doncaster and 29-runner maiden race at Newmarket. *R. Hollinshead.*

PRINCESS TRACY 2 b. or br.f. Ahonoora 122–Princess Ru (Princely Gift 137) **97** (1983 5s 5v 6g² 6f³ 6fg³ 6f² 6fg³ 6d⁴ 7g*⁴ 7g⁴) Mar 2; IR 16,000Y; workmanlike filly; half-sister to several winners, including National Stakes winner Trasi Girl (by Le Levanstell); dam poor maiden; won 18-runner maiden race at Leopardstown in September; put up several fair efforts in useful company previously, including third of 12 behind easy winner Vacarme in Erroll Stakes at Royal Ascot, ½-length third of 10 to Grey Dream in Oldtown Stud Stakes at Phoenix Park, and 4 lengths fourth of 20 behind Gala Event in Moyglare Stud Stakes at the Curragh; best form at 6f but stays 7f; acts on firm going and a soft surface. *M. Cunningham, Ireland.*

PRINCESS VIRGINIA 4 br.f. Connaught 130–Virginia Wade 116 (Virginia Boy **§§** 106) (1982 10f 8g 5f² 6h* 6f² 6d 6f 6f 6v² 6d 1983 10.6v 5s 9v 6d 6f 6f 7f* 7f³ 6fg 7f) rangy non-thoroughbred filly; good walker and mover; won handicap at Catterick in July; best at up to 7f; acts on any going; blinkered last 2 starts in 1982; thoroughly temperamental (refused to race last 2 starts) and is best left alone. *R. Hollinshead.*

PRINCESS ZITA 3 ch.f. Manado 130–Karmala (Tanerko 134) (1982 6g 6fg² **90** 1983 8g 7v² 7g* 7fg² 10f 8.3f⁴ 8.5f⁴ 8g 8.2s) tall, rather narrow filly; good mover; good second to Magdalena at Goodwood before beating Alawir by 1½ lengths in minor event at Epsom in June; mainly disappointing afterwards; should stay at least 1m; seems unsuited by really firm going, but acts on any other; blinkered eighth outing. *J. Dunlop.*

PRINCETON 6 gr.g. Sun Prince 128–Queen's Castle 98 (Sovereign Path 125) – (1982 NR 1983 10h) quite moderate at his best on flat and also a winner over jumps; should have stayed 1¼m; sometimes blinkered; dead. *M. Pipe.*

PRINCE WARREN 6 b.g. Pieces of Eight 128–Bobelle 62 (Pirate King 129) – (1982 12d 8.2s⁴ 10fg³ 10.1fg 12d 10g* 12fg 8fg 1983 10fg) plater nowadays; suited by middle distances; acts on any going but is particularly well suited by soft; sometimes sweats up; has worn blinkers; sometimes bandaged in front; pulled up lame only start at 6 yrs in June. *D. Wilson.*

PRINGLE 4 ch.g. Blue Cashmere 129–Word Perfect (Worden II 129) (1982 8fg⁴ – 8d³ 8fg* 7.6d 8fg 1983 8f) lengthy, sparely-made gelding; plater; stays 1m; acts well on firm ground; blinkered last 2 starts; has shown a tendency to put head in air. *J. Hindley.*

PRINGLE BAY 2 ch.g. Dublin Taxi–Motionless 109 (Midsummer Night II 117) (1983 6v 5f 7.2g) May 5; 3,300Y; leggy, rather lightly-made gelding; half-brother to 1m winner Speedy Tack (by Right Tack); dam third in English and Irish 1000 Guineas; behind in minor event and 2 sellers. *M. W. Easterby.* — –

PRINTAFOIL 3 b.f. Habat 127–Breathalyser (Alcide 136) (1982 6s 1983 12d 12g) fair sort; lightly raced and no sign of ability. *M. Jarvis.* — –

PRIONSAA 5 ch.h. Crowned Prince 128–Frame Up (Alycidon 138) (1982 7fg4 8f4 8g 8f2 6g2 11g4 9d 5d2 6s3 5d 5g 1983 6v3 6s 5g4 5d4 6g2 6g2 6f4 5fg3 6f 6g 8.2f 5g4 5g2 6g 5d 5g4) poor handicapper; effective at 5f and stays 1m; acts on any going; blinkered final start; has run creditably for a boy; has raced with tongue tied down; possibly ungenuine. *W. H. H. Williams.* — 48

PRIORS CUTIE 3 b.f. Mr Bigmore 123–Cute 75 (Hardicanute 130) (1982 8g 1983 8d 12d 17v* 15.5v* 20fg 16.1fg) rangy, workmanlike filly; won maiden race at Wolverhampton (by 8 lengths) and handicap at Folkestone (wandered in lead), both in May; well beaten afterwards, but had stiff task on first occasion and needed run on second; suited by a thorough test of stamina; ideally suited by plenty of give in the ground. *A. Madwar.* — 80

PRIORS DEAN 2 br.f. Monsanto 121–Varvel (Falcon 131) (1983 5fg 6f 5fg 7.6d) May 10; sturdy filly; second foal; sister to fairly useful 3-y-o Hawkley, a winner at up to 1m; dam not of much account on flat or over jumps; plating-class maiden; best effort on second outing. *K. Brassey.* — 61

PRIORS MISTRESS 3 b.f. Sallust 134–Malmsey (Jukebox 120) (1982 6fg4 7fg 8s 1983 8.5d 10fg) big, raw-boned filly; disappointing maiden; bred to stay beyond 6f; sold 12,000 gns Newmarket Autumn Sales. *I. Balding.* — –

PRIORY COURT 2 ch.c. Remainder Man 126§–Claral Star 71 (Top Star 96) (1983 6fg) Mar 27; 1,500Y; rangy colt; half-brother to 2 winners, including sprinter Brian's Star (by The Brianstan); dam won sellers over 6f and 1m; behind in 24-runner maiden at Doncaster in November. *F. J. Houghton.* — –

PRISONER OF ZENDA 11 b.g. Manacle 123–Ruritania (Pampered King 121) (1982 NR 1983 8d) of little account and probably temperamental. *F. Sutherland.* — –

PRIVATE LABEL (USA) 3 ch.g. Silent Screen–Summer Time Music (What A Pleasure) (1982 6g 5f2 6s3 5g* 5s* 5d2 5g3 1983 5s2 5v 6d 7f 8f 5d3 8fg) lengthy, quite attractive gelding; not a good walker or mover; had some stiffish tasks, but was placed in handicap at Doncaster in March and all-aged race at Beverley in September; best form at 5f; suited by some give in the ground. *M. Jarvis.* — 92

PRIVATE SPRING 2 ch.f. Miami Springs 121–Private Enterprise (Hopeful Venture 125) (1983 6f 5fg4 6f 5fg 6g) May 1; IR 6,200F; small filly; first foal; dam lightly-raced half-sister to smart miler Saher; plating-class maiden; showed form only when apprentice-ridden 3½ lengths fourth of 19 to Killycurra in maiden race at Windsor in July; evidently best at 5f; sold NBA 2,400 gns Newmarket Autumn Sales. *R. Sheather.* — 69

PRIX DE LA JOUTE (CAN) 2 b.f. Sir Ivor 135–Prix (Vaguely Noble 140) (1983 6fg 7fg4) strong, good-topped filly; half-sister to a winner in USA; dam, half-sister to top-class Trillion, won over 9f at 2 yrs in France; 16/1, strong-finishing 1¾ lengths fourth of 22 to Travel Away in maiden race at Newmarket in October; will be well suited by 1m+. *J. Winter.* — 89

PROCEEDING 2 b.f. Monsanto 121–Swifter Justice 62 (King's Bench 132) (1983 6f4 7h4 7s 9g 7fg4) Feb 24; 4,000Y; quite a useful-looking filly; half-sister to a minor winner in Sweden; dam selling handicapper; quite a modest maiden; gambled on and blinkered first time when fourth of 14 to K-Battery in nursery at Redcar in October; suited by 7f; possibly not at her best on soft going. *A. Jarvis.* — 73

PROCERUS 3 ch.g. Roman Warrior 132–Pretty Girl 78 (Double-U-Jay 120) (1982 6s 5d 6s4 1983 10f 16g) poor maiden; stays 6f (not certain to get 1¼m, let alone 2m). *H. Westbrook.* — –

PROCIDA (USA) 2 b. or br.c. Mr Prospector–With Distinction (Distinctive) (1983 7g* 7g*) — 116 p

Only a very bold or foolhardy person would be prepared to predict that a horse trained by Francois Boutin will not win the 1984 Criterium de Maisons-Laffitte for since 1977, when he sent out the disqualified winner Cosmopolitan, the top French trainer has monopolised the contest, winning with Crowned Music, Viteric, Cresta Rider, Zino, L'Emigrant and Procida. Though not all of the first five colts proved out

*Criterium de Maisons-Laffitte, Maisons-Laffitte—Procida (No. 4)
beats Nikos and Harifa*

of the top drawer the success of Zino, who won the Two Thousand Guineas, and L'Emigrant, the top French performer of his sex in 1983, along with Boutin's expressed opinion that Procida is a very good horse who could well be aimed at the Guineas indicate that the career of the last-named should be one to watch with interest.

Procida did not win anything like so readily as either Zino or L'Emigrant, and indeed it is arguable that he might have been slightly fortunate to win at all. He was one of eight runners, all winners, to face the starter at Maisons-Laffitte near the end of October having readily beaten Davy Crockett in a ten-runner newcomers event at Saint-Cloud three weeks earlier. The others included several with very useful form, notably the Prix Robert Papin and Prix Eclipse third Harifa, the Prix La Rochette fourth Nikos and from England the Coventry Stakes third and Middle Park fifth Novello. Two furlongs out Novello and Harifa were disputing the lead with Procida not far behind and when asked to improve Procida did so smoothly, taking it up with about a hundred and fifty yards to go. Meanwhile Novello, seemingly finding the trip a shade too far, had begun to go off a straight line, causing some interference to Harifa and to Nikos whose path was completely blocked on the rail. By the time Nikos got clear Procida had a clear advantage and managed to hold on by a head from his unlucky rival whose powerful finish would have gained him the spoils in a few more strides; Harifa ended up a length and a half back in third with Novello fourth. Even if allowance is made for Nikos' ill-luck, Procida, who started favourite despite being the least-experienced member of the field, had put up a most encouraging display and there is no denying his promise.

Procida (USA) (b. or br.c. Mar 23, 1981)	Mr Prospector (b 1970)	Raise A Native (ch 1961)	Native Dancer
			Raise You
		Gold Digger (b 1962)	Nashua
			Sequence
	With Distinction (b 1973)	Distinctive (b or br 1966)	Never Bend
			Precious Lady
		Carrie's Rough (b 1965)	Rough 'n Tumble
			Carrie Louise

Procida fetched 300,000 dollars at the 1982 Keeneland July Sales and the money looks well spent. His sire, the sprinter Mr Prospector, has done consistently well at stud in America where his progeny have included the 1982 Horse of the Year Conquistador Cielo, and in Europe he has been represented by such good performers as Hello Gorgeous, Proclaim and the French colts Diamond Prospect and Miswaki. On the dam's side Procida is the second foal and winner out of With Distinction, successful in seven races at up to seven furlongs, including one

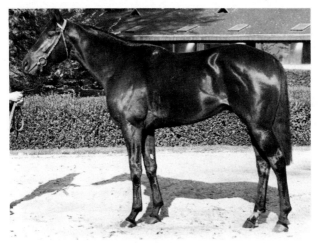

Mr S.S. Niarchos' "Procida"

stakes event, the Marlboro Nursery; her first foal, the Explodent colt Bold Uprising, won over four furlongs in the States in 1982. With Distinction is a daughter of Carrie's Rough who made up for failing to win on the track by producing five successful performers at stud, notably the Yellow Ribbon winner Country Queen, and the third dam won five times as well as gaining places in two stakes races at around a mile. Many horses by Mr Prospector stay a fair bit further than he did and Procida should have no difficulty getting the distance of the Guineas if not a shade further. *F. Boutin, France.*

PROCLAIMER 5 gr.m. Town Crier 119–Deck (Le Dieu d'Or 119) (1982 NR — 1983 8g) sprint plater; used to wear blinkers. *R. Woodhouse.*

PROCLAIM (USA) 3 b.c. Mr Prospector–Maybellene (Fleet Nasrullah) (1982   119 7g² 7fg* 7fg* 7fg² 8s* 1983 7s* 7s* 7d² 8g) rangy, rather sparely-made colt; second foal; dam won 6 races, 2 of them stakes events, at 3 yrs; won 3 of his 5 races at 2 yrs and did well again in a very short season in 1983; made most of running when landing the odds in £3,100 event at Leicester in March (by 1½ lengths from Drumalis and Able Albert) and Salisbury 2000 Guineas Trial in April (by ½ length from Aragon); well clear of remainder when ¾-length second of 5 to Wassl in Clerical, Medical Greenham Stakes at Newbury later in April; reportedly knocked a stifle and lamed himself at start when tailed-off last of 16 to Lomond in 2000 Guineas at Newmarket at end of month, only subsequent outing; stays 1m well; extremely well suited by soft going but has put up good efforts on firmish ground; consistent; exported to South Africa. *G. Harwood.*

PROFIT WARRANT 4 b.c. Ashmore 125–Stipa (Silver Shark 129) (1982 12fg   58 10f 11.7g² 10f* 10fg² 11.7fg* 10d* 11.7fg 10fg 11.1fg 12s 1983 12v 10v 12d 12s 10d 10g³ 10s* 10fg 12g 10f³ 10g 10f 10d 10d³ 10fg³ 10d² 10g 10g⁴) tall, lengthy colt; former plater; won handicap at Lingfield in June; stays 1½m; acts on any going; has run creditably for an apprentice; often sweats up. *P. K. Mitchell.*

PROLIFIC MAJOR 3 ch.g. Mandrake Major 122–Lochville 83 (Charlottesville — 135) (1982 5fg 6f 7f 8.2fg* 8d 8d 8.2s 1983 12s 12v 12d 9d) workmanlike gelding; plater; by no means certain to stay 1½m; acts on a firm and a soft surface; blinkered fourth start; exported to Malaysia. *K. Stone.*

PROMINDANTE 3 ch.g. Prominer 125–Hot Penny 105 (Red God 128§) (1982   80
7fg⁴ 7d 7d 7g 1983 8v 10s 11g* 12s* 12d 10g³) strong, heavy-bodied gelding;
showed improved form to win maiden race at Ayr in May and ladies race at Lingfield
in June; off course 3 months after beating Princess Henham a length in latter;
suited by 1½m; acts on soft going. *S. Mellor.*

PROMISED ISLE 2 b.c. Mill Reef 141–Parolee 88 (Sing Sing 134) (1983 6g 6g³   75
6d) Mar 20; rather sparely-made colt; ninth foal; half-brother to 8 winners,
including smart miler Trusted (by Crepello); dam sprinter; modest third in big
field of maidens at Goodwood in September; will probably be better suited by
7f+. *J. Dunlop.*

PROMISE OF SPRING 3 b.f. Ampney Prince 96–Wynter (Wynkell 88) (1982   –
5fg 5d 5fg 5g 1983 6d 8.3s 10.2g 8fg 8.3f) neat filly; poor plater. *P. Burgoyne.*

PRONUPTIA BRIDE 2 b.f. Red Johnnie 100–Crusheen (Typhoon 125) (1983   –
5fg 6f 6fg 6fg) Apr 13; small filly; half-sister to several winners, including sprinter
H. R. Micro (by High Award); dam ran twice at 2 yrs in Ireland; behind in maiden
races. *D. Dale.*

PROPOSITIONING (USA) 3 ch.f. Mr Prospector–Stay Over (Prove It)   111
(1982 7g* 8s 1983 8v 7fg* 8d* 8fg²) half-sister to a minor winner in USA; dam
won at up to 1m and is sister to smart 1969 American 2-y-o With Evidence; won
minor event at Clairefontaine in August and 60,000 francs event at Evry in
September, latter by 2 lengths from Conerton; stepped up in class and showed
improved form when 1½ lengths second of 8 behind Pampabird in Prix du
Rond-Point at Longchamp later in September; subsequently sent to USA and was
stakes placed there at around 1m. *O. Douieb, France.*

PROPRIETY 2 ch.f. Grundy 137–Fashion Club 95 (Tribal Chief 125) (1983 6g   77
6fg⁴) Mar 26; rather lightly-built filly; good mover; first foal; dam won four 6f
races; 4¼ lengths fourth of 14 to Really Honest in maiden race at Redcar in
October. *J. Hindley.*

PROPUS 9 b.g. Never Say Die 137–Amante 121§ (Tehran) (1982 NR 1983 11fg)   –
no longer of any account. *Mrs A. Bell.*

PROSPERO (FR) 6 b.h. Faraway Son 130–Golondrina (Sheshoon 132) (1982 8d   116
8d 8s⁴ 8g⁴ 8g⁴ 7g 6.5fg 8s 8f 8s 7s* 8v 1983 8v 8d* 8f 7d 8fg 8f 8g 8g) 32,000
francs Y (approx £3,800); second reported foal; half-brother to a minor winner in
France; dam French 1m winner; put up an improved performance when
accounting for Vieux Carre by 1½ lengths in Prix du Muguet at Longchamp in
May; well beaten most subsequent starts, though ran respectably in Prix
Messidor at Maisons-Laffitte on fifth; stays 1m; ideally suited by some give in the
ground. *C. Herve, France.*

PROUDEST DIANA (USA) 3 b.f. Proudest Roman–Time For Beauty   –
(Diplomat Way) (1982 7fg 6fg 6s 1983 10v 10v 12.2d⁴ 14g 16d⁴) rather a
lightly-built filly; poor maiden; ran respectably in a seller over 2m, tried in blinkers;
sold 1,250 gns Ascot November Sales. *I. Walker.*

PROVANHILL GIRL 3 ch.f. Gentilhombre 131–Lucky Pigeon (The Mongoose   39
108) (1982 5fg 5fg 5g 1983 5f 5g 5f 8f 8fg⁴ 10h³ 9d 10g 10fg 12g) leggy, plain filly;
poor plater; stays 1¼m. *T. Taylor.*

PUENTE ROMANO 2 gr.g. Dragonara Palace 115–Shari (Rustam 127) (1983   84
5s* 5s⁴ 5s 5s 5g 5g) Apr 8; 11,000Y; good-topped gelding; half-brother to several
winners, including very smart 5f filly Harem (by Tribal Chief); dam, sister to
Double Jump, won at 2 yrs in Italy on only start; landed the odds by 4 lengths from
Classical Vintage in maiden race at Leicester in March; didn't show much
afterwards, but was harshly weighted in nurseries on last 2 appearances; acts well
on soft going; sold 7,000 gns Newmarket Autumn Sales. *K. Brassey.*

PUFF PASTRY 3 ch.f. Reform 132–Shortbread 104 (Crisp and Even 116) (1982   70
5g 5s* 6f 5f 7v 8d 1983 8.2v⁴ 12s 11.7f 11.7f 12f⁴ 12f⁴ 12f 12d) compact filly; has a
round action; middle-distance handicapper; acts on firm going but is possibly
ideally suited by plenty of give in the ground. *D. Morley.*

PULHAM VENTURE 6 b.g. Tudor Music 131–Mille Fleurs (Floribunda 136)   –
(1982 NR 1983 8fg) small gelding; plater; stays 1¼m; has worn blinkers; cost 660
gns Doncaster March Sales and 500 gns Ascot July Sales. *M. James.*

PULSATE 2 gr.c. Orcis 79–Impulsive Lady 83 (Quorum 126) (1983 7g) Mar 12;   –
fourth reported foal; dam stayed 7f; distant seventh of 14 in maiden race at
Lingfield in October. *J. Benstead.*

PULSE RATE 7 b.g. Prince Tenderfoot 126–Florence Nightingale 78 (Above Suspicion 127) (1982 NR 1983 10.5d) quite an attractive gelding; genuine and useful performer in 1980; lightly raced on flat afterwards though showed himself a fairly useful hurdler; probably stayed 1½m; acted on any going; dead. *M. H. Easterby.* —

PUNCTURE 2 br.c. Goldhill 125–Midgy (Polyfoto 124) (1983 5v 5v³ 5d³ 6fg 8f 6fg) May 13; IR 740F, 2,800Y; robust colt; half-brother to a winning jumper; dam never ran; quite a modest plater; form only at 5f; acts on heavy going; sold 1,000 gns Doncaster November Sales. *K. Stone.* **46**

PUNTERS LAD 3 br.c. Home Guard 129–Arioza (Tambourine II 133) (1982 7f 7s 1983 7.6v 10fg) tall, useful-looking colt; good walker; showed definite signs of ability in maiden races at Lingfield (sixth of 19) and Sandown (seventh of 27) in first part of season; promises to stay beyond 1¼m. *C. Horgan.* —

PURE PERFECTION 3 b.f. So Blessed 130–Sardara 106 (Alcide 136) (1982 5g 1983 7g 6fg 9d) quite well-made filly; lightly raced and little worthwhile form. *G. Huffer.* —

PURIM 2 b.c. Comedy Star 121–Gossip (Sharp Edge 123) (1983 5s 5v 6fg³ 7fg³ 6f) Apr 6; IR 3,000F, 8,600Y; compact, quite attractive colt; third in maiden race at Brighton in June and in £2,600 seller (favourite) at Newmarket in July; stays 7f; form only on a firm surface; blinkered last 3 starts; exported to Singapore. *N. Callaghan.* **68**

PURNIMA 4 b.g. Prince Tenderfoot 126–Chandravati (Hard Tack 111§) (1982 6s 7g² 6g* 6fg 6fg 6g* 6f 6f 6g* 6s³ 6g 1983 6s 6v 6v 5f 6d) strong, good-bodied, attractive gelding; fair handicapper at his best; not disgraced on occasions at 4 yrs and very much caught our eye fourth start (easy in market); stays 7f; ideally suited by some give in the ground; suited by strong handling. *J. Sutcliffe.* —

PURNS MILL 3 b.f. North Stoke 130–Gavina (Val de Loir 133) (1982 NR 1983 10s 10s 12f² 10.2h 10f² 10g* 12g² 11.7g) workmanlike filly; first foal; dam second at 2 yrs in France; bought in 3,200 gns after winning maiden seller at Lingfield in September by 4 lengths; close second in claiming race at Leicester later in month, and would have won had her rider not taken things too easily in closing stages; below best final start; stays 1½m; acts on firm going. *P. Cole.* **65**

PURPLE 2 b.g. Anax 120–Plush 75 (Lombard 126) (1983 7fg 8s 8d) Mar 1; 2,700F, 7,000Y; first produce; dam in frame over 7f and 1½m; plating-class maiden; stays 1m; gelded after final appearance. *B. Hobbs.* **72**

PURPLE EMPEROR 3 b.g. Red Alert 127–Sea Sovereign (Sea Moss) (1982 5g 6fg 6d 1983 10f) narrow gelding; behind in maiden and minor events; dead. *G. Kindersley.* —

PURPLE FLASH 3 b.c. Nonoalco 131–Jolie Fleur 111 (Exbury 138) (1982 NR 1983 8d) good-topped colt; half-brother to 2 winners, including useful 1980 2-y-o 7f winner The Thatcher (by Thatch); dam, half-sister to Connaught, was very useful at 1m to 1¼m; 25/1 when in rear in 17-runner newcomers race won by Majestic Endeavour at Newmarket in April; sold to D. Ringer 2,700 gns Ascot 2nd June Sales. *H. Cecil.* —

PURPLE SONG 2 bl. or br.f. Mansingh 120–In The Purple (Tudor Melody 129) (1983 5f 5f 5fg³ 5g 5fg) Apr 14; 1,850 F, 400 2-y-o; lengthy, rather dipped-backed filly; fourth produce; half-sister to a winner in Holland; dam ran only once; 2¾ lengths third of 16 to Try Me in maiden race at Lingfield in October, first outing for over 3 months and only indication of merit; reared leaving stalls final appearance. *C. Drew.* **68**

PUSEY STREET 6 ch.m. Native Bazaar 122–Diamond Talk (Counsel 118) (1982 6f 5f² 5fg 5g³ 5f⁴ 5fg⁴ 5.8f 5g³ 5fg³ 5.8f 5d* 5d³ 6s* 5s 1983 5d 6v² 6s* 6v² 6v² 6v* 6f⁴ 6f 5h 6d³ 6s 5fg 6d 6g 6fg) leggy, light-framed mare; sprint handicapper; beat Return To Me 2 lengths at Salisbury in April and Sailor's Prayer 1½ lengths at Newbury in May; runner-up on three other occasions, notably when beaten a length by Sweet Monday in £3,700 event at Kempton on second start; acts on any going but revels in the mud; good mount for a boy; genuine. *J. Bosley.* **91**

PUSHKINIA (FR) 2 ch.f. Pharly 130–Shahinaaz (Venture VII 129) (1983 7g*) Apr 29; 720,000 francs Y (approx £60,000); half-sister to numerous winners, notably smart out-and-out stayer Karadar (by Rheingold), smart middle-distance filly Karamita (by Shantung) and smart middle-distance colt Kalidar (by Vienna); dam very useful winner at up to 13f in France; led 1f out when beating Lightsome a length in newcomers event at Saint-Cloud in October; will be suited by middle distances and should make a very useful 3-y-o. *M. Saliba, France.* **95** p

PUTNEY BRIDGE 3 b.c. North Stoke 130–Splash Down 103 (Sicambre 135) 94 d
(1982 8d* 1983 12s 12f⁴ 10g³ 14d 12fg³) big ex-Irish colt; looked very promising
when winning maiden race at Leopardstown as a 2-y-o; ran best race as a 3-y-o, but
hung as if possibly feeling the ground, when 3½ lengths fourth of 6 behind Society
Boy in Churchill Stakes at Ascot in June; third in amateur riders race at Lingfield
and handicap at Doncaster afterwards; suited by 1½m and is worth another chance
over further; blinkered last 2 outings. *M. Stoute.*

PYKESTAFF 6 b.h. Giacometti 130–Miss Melanie (Hard Ridden 131) (1982 45
7fg² 7h 6f 7g 7g 8fg³ 7f 7f 7fg 6g 7fg 1983 9d² 10g 10f 12f) leggy horse; former
plater; stays 9f; suited by firm going; often used to wear blinkers; sometimes
sweats up. *H. O'Neill.*

PYTHAGORIAN 2 br.c. Vilgora 113–Autumn Double 72 (Double Jump 131) 65
(1983 5s² 5s 5.1fg³ 6g) May 20; 1,050Y; well-grown, leggy colt; poor walker;
half-brother to winning sprinter Heavy Weapon (by Bay Express); dam won over
9f; plating-class maiden; not raced after August. *W. Stubbs.*

Q

QAMAR 2 br. or gr.c. Formidable 125–Abergrove 103 (Abernant 142) (1983 5fg –
6g) May 2; 35,000Y; half-brother to 3 winners, including fairly useful stayer
Marzook (by Blakeney); dam best at 6f; showed early pace in maiden race at
Goodwood in September; brought down in similar event at Windsor 3 months
previously. *J. Benstead.*

QEMLAS 3 gr.c. Town Crier 119–Grecian Charter (Runnymede 123) (1982 6f⁴ 76
5f³ 7fg⁴ 6v* 7d² 1983 7d 8v 7v³ 8s 8s² 7.2g 8.2f* 8.2fg 10fg 8.2fg) workmanlike
colt; beat Shoebutton in 2-runner handicap at Hamilton in July; stays 1m; has won
on firm going but is ideally suited by give in the ground; blinkered nowadays;
inconsistent. *G. Huffer.*

QUADRILLION 4 gr.c. Bruni 132–Quantas 91 (Roan Rocket 128) (1982 10.2g 60
14.6fg 10.6g² 12fg 12g 12fg⁴ 16s² 16s 12d³ 1983 14s 16fg* 16f 16.1fg³ 18.4fg) tall
colt; has rather a round action; won handicap at Beverley in June; stays well; acts
on a firm surface but is ideally suited by some give in the ground; has run creditably
for an apprentice. *R. Hollinshead.*

QUAESTOR 5 b.g. Track Spare 125–Syltung (Shantung 132) (1982 12g³ 13g² –
16d 14s 1983 12s 15g⁴ 12f) fair sort; poor mover; stays 13f; probably acts on any
going; often sweats up; trained by K. Stone first 2 starts; sold 440 gns Doncaster
November Sales. *J. Hardy.*

QUAFFING (USA) 2 b.c. Quadratic–Bluffing (Gentlemans Game) (1983 5s 6fg 56
7fg) Mar 16; $30,000Y; good sort; first foal; dam unplaced on all 19 starts; poor
maiden; showed ability only on second outing. *G. Pritchard-Gordon.*

QUAKER BRIDGE 2 b.c. Garda's Revenge 119–Dry Bridge (Welsh Saint 126) 66
(1983 6f 7f 7.2fg² 7.2g 8s 7fg 7g) May 12; IR 3,000Y, resold 3,500Y; rather
lightly-built colt; put up best effort when strong-finishing 5 lengths second of 8 to
Nelsons Dockyard in maiden auction event at Haydock in August; out of first 11 in
valuable seller at Newmarket in September on sixth start; stays 7f; acts on a firm
surface. *R. Hollinshead.*

QUAKER STAR 7 b.g. Blast 125–Star of Bethlehem 77 (Arctic Star) (1982 10fg –
1983 8s) neat gelding; poor handicapper; has been beaten in a seller; seems to stay
1¼m; acts on any going; ran poorly in blinkers once; has shown a tendency to hang;
has been bandaged; sold 540 gns Doncaster June Sales. *Ronald Thompson.*

QUALITAIR PRINCE 4 b.c. Saulingo 122–Sabra's Star 65 (Midsummer Night 68
II 117) (1982 8.2d 8fg⁴ 10d⁴ 8g⁴ 10d 12.3fg 9f⁴ 8g 8fg 8fg 8.2s 12d 1983 9d 10d
10f⁴ 10f 10f² 10f³ 11.7f⁴ 8f² 8fg 10f 9fg* 8d* 8d² 8.2g² 9d 8.2s⁴ 8g*) rangy colt;
poor walker and mover; former plater; won handicaps at Newcastle in August,
Yarmouth in September (both apprentice events) and Leicester in October; stays
1¼m; acts on any going; has been tried in blinkers. *M. Ryan.*

QUALITY CHORISTER 2 b.c. Music Boy 124–Blessed Beauty 97 (Rustam 76
127) (1983 5d² 6s³) Mar 5; 15,000Y; half-brother to 3 minor winners; dam won at
up to 7f; placed in maiden events at Wolverhampton and Hamilton (odds on) in
October; in retrospect, had lot to do at Hamilton, and didn't run badly although
soundly beaten into third place behind Track Deal; stays 6f. *Sir Mark Prescott.*

QUARRYMAN 2 ch.c. Le Johnstan 123–Ribbleston 75 (The Brianstan 128) 49
(1983 5s 5d⁴ 6g 7f 7h 7f³) Mar 25; good-bodied, workmanlike colt; second foal;
dam best at 5f; 5½ lengths third of 10 to Sky Mariner in seller at Redcar in August;
stays 7f. *W. C. Watts.*

QUDESA 4 ch. g. Swing Easy 126–Gambit (King's Troop 118) (1982 7g 8f 10d 11g 12fg² 16d 14.7fg 1983 14.7d) rangy gelding; poor maiden; best run at 1½m on a firm surface; blinkered once. *J. Mason.* —

QUEEN AND COUNTRY 2 b.f. Town and Country 124–Polairia 66 (Polic 126) (1983 7s 6fg) May 27; smallish filly; half-sister to several winners, including speedy Avon Valley (by Galivanter) and fairly useful 6f and 7f winner Polly's Brother (by Roi Soleil); dam stayed 1¼m; well beaten in maiden events at Leicester in October. *R. Williams.* —

QUEEN FORLI (USA) 2 ch.f. Forli–Bold Queen (Bold Ruler) (1983 6g 6fg) May 3; workmanlike filly; sister to a minor winner and half-sister to 3-y-o Epic Making (by Le Fabuleux) and several winners in USA; dam, smart stakes winner over 8.5f at 3 yrs, is sister to What A Pleasure and to dam of Quick As Lightning; behind in maiden races at Newmarket in August and Doncaster (last of 15) in October. *R. Armstrong.* —

QUEEN KONG 2 ch.f. Stanford 121§–My Stella (Pardao 120) (1983 6f 8.2fg) May 12; IR 6,000F; lengthy filly; fourth produce; dam daughter of Oaks third Myastrid; in rear in sellers at Yarmouth in August and Nottingham (very slowly away) in September; wears blinkers; sold 1,500 gns Newmarket Autumn Sales. *N. Callaghan.* —

QUEEN OF MUSIC 2 ch.f. Monseigneur 127–Sing a Song 115 (Sing Sing 134) (1983 5fg 6g⁴ 7d 6s² 6fg 6fg⁴) Apr 26; smallish filly; sister to Belgian 3-y-o Don Camillo and half-sister to 3 winners, notably smart 5f to 7f winner Hays (by Wolver Hollow); dam very speedy; moderate maiden; stays 6f; acts on soft going and a firm surface; best in blinkers. *S. Norton.* 80

QUEEN OF NIGHT 3 br.f. Grundy 137–Magic Flute 124 (Tudor Melody 129) (1982 NR 1983 10s 12f* 12f³ 14fg 12fg) rangy filly; good walker; half-sister to 4 winners, including very useful middle-distance performer Lost Chord (by Busted) and very useful 7f and 1m winner Pamina (by Brigadier Gerard); dam won Cheveley Park Stakes and was very smart at up to 1m; put up an impressive performance when winning 11-runner maiden race at Brighton in June by 15 lengths from Purns Mill; third to Lady Moon in quite well-contested minor event at Leicester the following month, best subsequent effort; suited by 1½m; acts on firm going. *P. Walwyn.* 89

QUEEN OF SONG 2 ch.f. Music Boy 124–Queen of Saba 105 (High Treason 126) (1983 5d 5v* 6fg) Mar 20; lengthy filly; closely related to 1980 2-y-o 5f winner Queen's Token (by Record Token) and half-sister to a winner; dam 5f sprinter; bought in 1,000 gns after winning 11-runner seller at Warwick in May; sold 1,550 gns Ascot 2nd June Sales; winner in Belgium. *Sir Mark Prescott.* 53

QUEEN OF THE NILE 3 b.f. Hittite Glory 125–Firella 56 (Firestreak 125) (1982 NR 1983 8f) lengthy, rather lightly-made filly; fifth foal; half-sister to a minor winner; dam fourth twice over 1m; 12/1 when never-dangerous eighth of 12 behind Kellathi in minor event at Doncaster in June. *J. W. Watts.* —

QUEENSBURY JOE 3 b.c. Rheingold 137–Strike on the Box 62 (Busted 134) (1982 8d 8g 10.2s 1983 12s 16s 16d) leggy colt; behind in varied races. *D. Dale.* —

QUEENSBURY LIZ 2 b. or br.f. Creetown 123–Dream Shared (Majority Blue 126) (1983 7fg 6fg) Apr 2; fourth reported foal; dam never ran; behind in valuable sellers at Newmarket in September and October. *D. Dale.* —

QUEENSBURY STAR 4 b.f. Wishing Star 117–Silent Mover (Burglar 128) (1982 6g 7f 6fg 6g 6h 7g 1983 7fg 10f) small, fair sort; has shown no form for a long time; stays 6f; acts on firm going. *D. Dale.* —

QUEEN'S CHASE 3 b.f. Manado 130–King's Chase (King's Leap 111) (1982 6g 8s 1983 7v) fair sort; behind in maiden races and a seller; sold 640 gns Ascot 2nd June Sales. *M. McCourt.* —

QUEEN'S GLORY 3 b.f. African Sky 124–Miss Millicent (Milesian 125) (1982 5s² 5f 1983 5fg 5fg 5f 5f) narrow, rather leggy filly; no form in 1983 (blinkered final start); sold 1,000 gns Newmarket September Sales. *C. Spares.* —

QUEEN'S HOME 4 b.c. Royal Palace 131–Come On Honey 94 (Never Say Die 137) (1982 12fg⁴ 12f 10f² 10f 10fg⁴ 1983 16s 13.3v) deep-girthed, attractive colt; fairly useful performer at his best; needs further than 1¼m and is bred to stay at least 1¾m; acts on firm going; winner over hurdles. *F. Winter.* —

QUEENS WELCOME 2 br.f. Northfields–Sweet Sound 74 (Sound Track 132) (1983 5.1fg⁴ 6f³ 6f 5f 5fg 5g 5d) Apr 16; 3,500Y; small filly; has a sharp action; half-sister to several winners, including high-class 1973 2-y-o sprinter The Blues (by Majority Blue); dam ran only at 2 yrs; plating-class maiden; at her best early in the season; stays 6f; acts on firm going; hasn't much scope. *J. Winter.* 60

QUEEN TO BE 3 ch. f. Nebbiolo 125–Petrovna (Reliance II 137) (1982 6g³ 1983   **76 §**
8f 7f² 9fg⁴ 10.4g 9d) smallish filly; good walker; in frame in maiden and minor
events at Leicester (bandaged near-hind) and Wolverhampton (tended to put head
in air); stays 9f; possibly none too genuine. *M. Albina.*

QUELLE CHANCE 2 b. f. General Assembly–Take A Chance (Baldric II 131)   **81 p**
(1983 6fg³ 5d*) May 17; 50,000Y; half-sister to several winners, including useful
7f and 1m winner That's My Son (by Busted); dam won Prix Yacowlef and is sister
to high-class French 2-y-o Without Fear; ran on strongly to lead close home in
maiden race at Phoenix Park in October, beating Salustrina a head; bred to stay 1m.
J. Costelloe, Ireland.

QUE MARIDO (USA) 2 b. c. Blushing Groom 131–Que Mona (Ribot 142) (1983   **95 p**
6fg*) Mar 14; $235,000Y; quite attractive colt; has a smooth action; half-brother
to 3 winners, notably Champion Stakes second Prima Voce (by Elocutionist); dam,
winner over 6f at 4 yrs, is daughter of Oaks winner Monade and half-sister to dam
of very smart Too Chic (by Blushing Groom); odds on, impressively beat a field
mainly of newcomers in 12-runner minor event at Nottingham in September,
leading 2f out and going clear to beat The Rotter 4 lengths (value 6); will stay 1m;
likely to go on to better things and looks a useful colt in the making. *H. Cecil.*

QUEMORA (FR) 3 b. f. Riverman 131–Moquerie 120 (Beaugency 126) (1982 NR   **114**
1983 10v 12v* 12v* 10.5fg 12.5fg³ 12g) second foal; half-sister to 10.5f winner
Avanie (by Avatar); dam dead-heated in Prix de Pomone and was suited by 1½m and
more; won 65,000 francs race at Saint-Cloud in April and 7-runner Prix des
Tuileries at Longchamp in May, latter readily by 1½ lengths from Alliance; finished
out of first 10 of 17 behind Escaline in Prix de Diane Hermes at Chantilly in June but
ran very much better (though flattered by proximity) when third of 10 behind High
Hawk and Radiance in Prix de Royallieu at Longchamp when next seen out 4
months later; suited by 1½m+; probably acts on any going. *A. Head, France.*

QUESTELLA 2 b. f. Star Appeal 133–Quaranta 83 (Hotfoot 126) (1983 7f* 7fg   **85**
8fg² 8s) Feb 7; compact filly; good mover; second foal; half-sister to fairly useful
3-y-o Quite A Night (by Midsummer Night II), a winner over 1m and 1¼m; dam,
2-y-o 5f winner, is half-sister to smart 5f to 7f performer Quy; won minor event at
Redcar in August, beating odds-on Nonabella by 2 lengths; beaten at odds on
herself in nursery at Thirsk the following month; stays 1m; acts on firm going, and
ran poorly on soft. *Sir Mark Prescott.*

QUIBISHAN (USA) 3 gr. c. Transworld 121–Lady Brava (Misty Day) (1982 NR   **–**
1983 12v 12d 14g) $55,000Y; rather leggy, close-coupled colt; half-brother to
several winners in USA, one a minor stakes winner; dam, stakes-placed winner of 4
sprint races, is daughter of Argentinian Oaks winner Contrabrava; behind in maiden
races in first half of season. *N. Callaghan.*

QUICKENING DAWN (USA) 3 b. f. To The Quick–Coral Dawn (Turn To   **78**
Mars) (1982 7g 7d³ 1983 10fg⁴ 11g³ 14f² 14fg³ 15.8g* 18fg) big, strong,
good-topped, attractive filly; narrowly won minor race at Catterick in October;
well beaten only subsequent start; stays 2m; best form with some give in the
ground; sold to CBA 23,000 gns Newmarket December Sales. *J. Hindley.*

QUICK FLING 2 b. g. Bay Express 132–Arrangement 72 (Floribunda 136) (1983   **63**
6fg 6d 7f) May 27; 6,000Y; fair sort; half-brother to sprint winners by Swing Easy
and Sweet Revenge and to a winner in Denmark; dam stayed 7f; plating-class
maiden; stays 7f. *R. Laing.*

QUICK KICK 3 b. f. Saritamer 130–Lichen Lady 70 (Pardao 120) (1982 NR 1983   **–**
9d 10fg) 1,250Y; rangy filly; third foal; half-sister to 2 winners, including fair
middle-distance stayer Rushbeds (by Ercolano); dam 1½m winner; never-
dangerous eighth of 20 finishers behind 6-length winner Road To The Top in 1¼m
maiden race at Nottingham in October. *F. Durr.*

QUICKSTEP 2 br. c. Hotfoot 126–Invitation 107 (Faberge II 121) (1983 7fg 7fg)   **–**
May 4; 15,000Y; tall, rather narrow colt; third living foal; dam, sister to Rheingold,
won at up to 13f; behind in maiden races at Newmarket in August and September.
C. Brittain.

QUICKTHORN 7 b. m. Owen-Kiz–Hawthorn III (Prince Bio) (1982 15.5fg 12d   **–**
1983 10.2d) sparely-made mare; winner over hurdles; no form on flat. *R. Hartop.*

QUICK WORK 2 ch. c. Sharpen Up 127–Tawny Owl 123 (Faberge II 121) (1983 6f*   **105**
6fg* 7g* 7h² 7.6g³) May 18; good-quartered colt; half-brother to 3 winners,
including 1m winner Bold Owl and 3-y-o 7f winner Midnight Flit (both by
Bold Lad, Ire); dam won at up to 1m in France and was placed in Poule d'Essai des
Pouliches; won his first 3 starts, beating Millbow comfortably in 19-runner maiden at

Doncaster in June, finishing alone in 2-runner event at Ripon in July, and holding off Northern Tempest by a short-head in 4-runner Heronslea Stakes at Ayr in August; placed subsequently in Solario Stakes at Sandown (beaten neck by Falstaff) and Burr Stakes at Lingfield; will stay 1m; yet to race on a soft surface; genuine. *H. T. Jones.*

QUIET CANNON 6 b.g. Connaught 130–Green Chiffon 83 (Crepello 136) (1982 13s 11s 12g 12f 1983 17.7g 16g 20.4g) good-bodied gelding; useful at his best but had deteriorated markedly; stayed 1½m; needed some give in the ground; sometimes blinkered; dead. *K. Bailey.*   —

QUIET COUNTRY 2 ch.c. Quiet Fling 124–Campagna (Romulus 129) (1983 7fg 7f4 7fg 8fg2 8g 8.2s2) Jan 27; big, good-topped colt; half-brother to several winners, including miler Druimfada (by No Mercy); dam won over 1¼m in France; second in the autumn in maiden race at Beverley and nursery at Hamilton; will be suited by 1¼m+; probably acts on any going; blinkered fourth and fifth outings; sold P. Makin 13,500 gns Doncaster October Sales. *M. Stoute.*   80

QUIET FALL 2 b.g. Quiet Fling 124–Falling Gold 77 (High Echelon) (1983 8g) Mar 28; third reported living foal; half-brother to winner in Argentina; dam won over 1m and 1½m; modest seventh of 12 in minor event at Redcar in November; subsequently gelded. *M. Camacho.*   66 p

QUIET FIELD (USA) 3 br.c. Stop The Music–Rock Garden 86 (Roan Rocket 128) (1982 NR 1983 7d 8f3 10fg 8f2) quite attractive, rangy colt; half-brother to useful 1981 staying 2-y-o Rockfest and winning hurdler Covent Garden (both by Stage Door Johnny) and to a winner in Scandinavia; dam, half-sister to very smart Glen Strae, won over 1m; placed in maiden races at York and Sandown in summer; stays 1m; sold to CBA 9,200 gns Newmarket Autumn Sales. *J. Tree.*   80

QUIET SOLICITOR 2 ch.c. Roan Rocket 128–Blesseen 71 (So Blessed 130) (1983 6f 7f*) Apr 10; angular colt; dam raced only at sprint distances; made all to beat Ride The Skies by 1½ lengths in 6-runner minor event at Doncaster in July; exported to Hong Kong. *B. Hanbury.*   84

QUIET STYLE 3 b.f. Oats 126–Cuba Libre (Rum) (1982 6f 7g 8f 1983 10s2 8d3 10f 10f 10g 10.8g 10g) plater; suited by 1¼m; acts on soft going; well beaten in blinkers third start. *W. Holden.*   47

QUILTED 3 b.c. Patch 129–Mill's Girl (Le Levanstell 122) (1982 7fg 6s 6s3 1983 6s 9s2 8s* 12f4 12fg*)   124

It is probable that we never saw the best of Quilted, who had to be retired after striking into himself while being prepared for the Benson and Hedges Gold Cup. At that time he'd just begun to show high-class form over middle distances. Quilted's first three runs of 1983 gave little notice of what was to come, since they amounted to an outing over a totally inadequate distance at Naas, a second to Danzatore in The Minstrel Stakes at Phoenix Park and a win in a mile maiden race at the Curragh by three lengths from Bonalma. Quilted's improvement coincided with his tackling a longer trip. He could hardly have had a much tougher first appearance at a mile and a half than in the Irish Sweeps Derby up against three classic winners, Caerleon,

Princess of Wales's Stakes, Newmarket—Quilted is driven out to account for Khairpour and John French

Teenoso and Wassl, the Derby runner-up Carlingford Castle and the King Edward VII Stakes winner Shareef Dancer. He started at 66/1. In the race Quilted was at the back of the field for much of the time and turning into the straight it appeared that he would not finish in the frame; however, he ran on to great effect to finish fourth, one and a half lengths behind Teenoso, three and a half behind Caerleon and six and a half behind Shareef Dancer. Ten days later Quilted was sent to Newmarket for the Princess of Wales's Stakes in which he faced strong competition including the Gold Cup runner-up Khairpour, the 1982 Arc third Awaasif and the smart three-year-old colts Morcon and John French. This time Quilted started favourite. He was held up as Lafontaine set his usual strong pace, and took quite a while to get into top gear when asked to improve running towards the final half mile. Gradually he made progress on the outside of the field and managed to wear down the two who'd gone on from Morcon two furlongs out, Khairpour and John French; he was driven out to hold Khairpour by half a length with John French two and a half lengths further back in third; the three finished a long way clear of the rest. Sadly this was Quilted's final race. Clearly a mile and a half suited him well, and both his style of racing and his breeding suggested a longer distance would have suited him even better. He was the wrong type of horse for the Benson and Hedges but could have developed into a leading St Leger contender.

		St Paddy	Aureole
	Patch	(b 1957)	Edie Kelly
	(ch 1972)	Palatch	Match III
Quilted		(b 1964)	Palazzoli
(b.c. 1980)		Le Levanstell	Le Lavandou
	Mill's Girl	(b 1957)	Stella's Sister
	(b 1970)	Mill Baby	Mazarin
		(b 1947)	Irreverence

Quilted is a strong, good-topped, useful-looking colt, though he isn't the best of movers. He is by some way the best son of Patch to race—the 1982 Irish Derby third Patcher, the November Handicap dead-heater Turkoman and the fairly useful stayer Sunley Builds being among Patch's previous best. Patch finished second to Val de l'Orne in the 1975 Prix du Jockey-Club and won the Lingfield Derby Trial and Great Voltigeur Stakes; but he was a great disappointment at stud in Ireland and was exported to Brazil in 1982. His progeny tend to stay well and he has had only five two-year-old winners in Britain and Ireland in four seasons. Quilted's dam Mill's Girl, who won a mile-and-three-quarters maiden race at Fairyhouse, has produced two other winners, Fair Siobahn (by Petingo), twice a winner in the USA, and the useful What A Riot (by Sun Prince) who won five races from seven furlongs to a mile and three quarters in Ireland including the Mulhuddart Handicap, a listed race over a mile and a half at Phoenix Park. Mill's Girl is a half-sister to the Irish St Leger winner Arctic Vale and another high-class stayer, Ragazzo. The second dam Mill Baby was a winner over two miles at the age of five; the third dam Irreverence was a half-sister to a smart handicapper, His Reverence, the 1936 City and Suburban winner. *M. O'Toole, Ireland.*

QUILTING 3 b.f. Mummy's Pet 125–Questa Notte 104 (Midsummer Night II 117) (1982 6g² 6s 1983 6s² 5fg 5fg⁴ 5h* 6f² 5.1s²) wiry filly; in frame most starts and carried top weight when winning handicap at Nottingham in August; stays 6f; acts on any going; sold 25,000 gns Newmarket December Sales. *B. Hobbs.*   80

QUINTA DO LAGO (USA) 2 br.c. Irish Castle–Tropical Way (Creme dela Creme) (1983 7fg 7.6fg 9s) Apr 25; $30,000Y; lightly-made colt; second foal; dam unraced sister to smart French middle-distance filly Tropical Creme; fifth of 8 behind Donzel in Mornington Stakes at Ascot in September, first outing and best effort; should stay beyond 7f. *A. Jarvis.*   72

QUISISSANNO 2 ch.f. Be My Guest 126–Mia Cosa 78 (Ragusa 137) (1983 7g 7fg 7f³ 8d) Apr 7; 20,000Y; tall, lengthy, angular filly; good mover; half-sister to a winning plater and a winner in Italy; dam, half-sister to good 1971 Irish 2-y-o Open Season, won 3 times at around 7f in Italy; quite a moderate maiden; should stay 1m; acts on firm going. *B. Hills.*   76

QUI SON (USA) 3 ch.c. To The Quick–Chief Song (Chieftain) (1982 7f 7fg 1983 6d 6v 5f³ 6fg³ 6f² 6f³ 6f 6f* 6g* 7f³) attractive, good-looking colt; good mover; placed in varied company before winning all-aged race at Folkestone in September and minor event at York in October; stays 7f; needs a sound surface. *J. Dunlop.*   79

QUISTADOR 7 ch.h. Le Johnstan 123–Little Bo Bleep 71 (Bleep-Bleep 134) (1982 12s 13fg 8.3fg 8.3fg 10.2d² 10s³ 12v 8fg 10g 8fg) workmanlike horse; poor performer nowadays; stays 1¼m; seems to act on any going; has been tried in blinkers; suitable mount for an inexperienced rider. *M. Chapman.*   –

QUITE ALERT 2 ch.f. Red Alert 127–Quiet Affair 88 (Prince Regent 129) (1983   **63**
5h³ 5f 5fg 6f 6f 7s 6fg 7fg) Jan 25; 5,200Y; smallish filly; second foal (first to
Northern Hemisphere time); dam, daughter of very useful Cease Fire, was placed
from 6f to 1m; plating-class maiden; stays 7f; blinkered fourth start. *A. Bailey.*

QUITE A NIGHT 3 b.c. Midsummer Night II 117–Quaranta 83 (Hotfoot 126)   **94**
(1982 5fg² 6f² 6g 8d* 7d 1983 10d* 10d⁴ 8f 8fg) lengthy colt; beat Hossam a neck
after a good battle in £4,100 Holsten Export Lager Handicap at Newmarket in May;
had stiffish tasks afterwards; suited by 1¼m; best form on a soft surface; sold
11,000 gns Newmarket Autumn Sales. *B. Hobbs.*

QUITE HOT 4 ch.g. Hotfoot 126–Quite Sweet 100 (Super Sam 124) (1982 8.2f   **65**
12fg 13.4g* 12.3fg⁴ 15.8d4 14.7fg 16s* 1983 12v³ 18d⁴ 20fg 18.4fg 12f³) strong,
rangy gelding; evidently suited by a test of stamina; suited by some give in the
ground and revels in the mud; suitable mount for an inexperienced rider; sold 3,000
gns Doncaster August Sales. *P. Rohan.*

QUORATE 2 b.c. General Assembly–River Craft (Reliance II 137) (1983 7fg)   **–**
May 30; 21,000FF, IR 38,000Y; rather unfurnished colt; half-brother to winning
stayer Wet Bob (by Run The Gantlet) and 1979 Irish 2-y-o 7f winner Private Craft
(by Private Walk); dam, sister to very smart 1m and 1¼m winner Rymer, was last
on only start; backward, never-dangerous tenth of 13 in £4,300 event at
Newmarket in October. *R. Armstrong.*

R

RAAMI 2 ch.c. Be My Guest 126–Fast Motion 86 (Midsummer Night II 117) (1983   **98**
7g² 8fg* 10.2fg* 10g) Mar 8; tall, lengthy colt; fourth foal; closely related to 1¼m
winner Alanood (by Northfields) and half-brother to a winner; dam won over 6f at 2
yrs; won maiden race at Redcar in October and 24-runner minor event (beating
Meadowbrook 4 lengths) at Doncaster in November; out of his depth subsequently
in Criterium de Saint-Cloud; stays 1¼m well; acts on a firm surface. *W.
O'Gorman.*

RAASHIDEAH 3 b.f. Dancer's Image–Monaco Melody 103 (Tudor Melody 129)   **–**
(1982 6g 6fg 6s* 1983 7v 7fg 7f) attractive, deep-girthed filly; lightly raced and no
form in 1983 (hampered at start when blinkered final start); should stay 7f; acts well
on soft going and is possibly not suited by a firm surface. *H. T. Jones.*

RABEEB 3 b.f. Home Guard 129–Mariinsky 69 (Nijinsky 138) (1982 7fg 8fg 1983   **–**
14.7d 11g 13g) big, unfurnished filly; lightly raced and little form in 1983; sold to A.
Balding 740 gns Doncaster November Sales. *M. H. Easterby.*

RABIRIUS 2 b.c. Mandrake Major 122–Richesse (Faraway Son 130) (1983 7f 7f³   **64** ?
7f⁴ 7f 8g 8fg 8fg) May 27; well-grown colt; first foal; dam ran once; plating-class
maiden; best race on final start; ran in sellers second and third outings; suited by
1m; slowly away fourth appearance. *W. Bentley.*

RACEMOSA 2 b.f. Town Crier 119–Daralina (Darius 129) (1983 7f 7.6fg) June 3;   **–**
lengthy filly; third living foal; dam poor half-sister to Petingo; showed up in first of 2
races in autumn maiden events. *M. Smyly.*

RACHELS GIRL 2 b.f. Malinowski 123–Propounder (Autumn Gold 101) (1983   **–**
7f 8d 7s) May 31; IR 9,000Y; half-sister to winning Irish stayer and useful jumper
Clash of the Ash (by Lord Gayle) and a bumpers winner; dam won twice over long
distances on flat in Ireland and also won over hurdles; well behind in maiden races.
W. Wharton.

RADIANCE (FR) 4 b.f. Blakeney 126–Sybarite (Royal Record II) (1982 10d*   **115**
10.5g 10.5fg⁴ 10g 13.5fg 12v* 1983 8.5v 10.5v* 10d⁴ 10fg 12.5fg² 10.5g) second
foal; half-sister to useful middle-distance performer Wild Oats (by Blakeney);
dam smart winner at up to 1½m in France; a smart filly who won Prix Corrida at
Saint-Cloud in April by 2 lengths from Rattle; ran creditably afterwards, putting up
a good display though flattered by proximity to winner when neck second to High
Hawk (whose jockey mistook winning post) in Prix de Royallieu at Longchamp in
October; suited by middle distances; probably acts on any going. *E. Bartholomew,
France.*

RADIANT ENERGY 2 br.c. Pitskelly 122–Little Hills (Candy Cane 125) (1983   **85**
6g 5d* 6.3g) May 26; IR 100,000Y; closely related to top-class 7f to 1¼m winner
Cairn Rouge (by Pitcairn) and half-brother to 2 winners, including 3-y-o 7.6f and 9f
winner Whisky Talk (by Wolverlife); dam won over 1½m in Ireland and also won
over hurdles; in front rank throughout and kept on well under pressure to win
20-runner maiden race at Leopardstown in June by ¾ length from Shubumi; not

seen out again until August when soundly beaten in P. J. Prendergast Railway Stakes won by El Gran Senor at the Curragh; should be suited by 6f+. *T. Curtin, Ireland.*

RADWHAW 2 gr. or ro. g. Abwah 118–Darwin Tulip (Campaign 106 or Pirate King 129) (1983 5d 6g 7f) Apr 16; workmanlike gelding; half-brother to 1½m to 2m winner High Rainbow (by High Line); dam never ran; no form in maiden and minor events; not seen out after July. *J. Etherington.*   –

RAFFLES TOWER 2 b. c. Tower Walk 130–Cloister Rose 70 (Track Spare 125)   64
(1983 5s 5d 5fg⁴ 6g 5fg⁴) Apr 30; 7,800Y; leggy, useful-looking colt; third foal; dam stayed 1½m; plating-class maiden; should stay beyond sprint distances. *W. O'Gorman.*

RAFT (USA) 2 br. c. Nodouble–Gangster of Love (Round Table) (1983 7f* 7f*)   114 p
Despite his huge investment in British racing, Khaled Abdulla has yet to finish higher than third in the list of leading owners, a feat he achieved in 1980 when Known Fact was awarded the Two Thousand Guineas. However, Abdulla's 1983 two-year-olds showed such potential that he must have excellent prospects of bettering that position in 1984: in addition to the William Hill Futurity winner Alphabatim, the Dewhurst runner-up Rainbow Quest and the Royal Lodge second Rousillon he owns the smart, progressive Attempt, the very promising maidens Duelling, Ensemble, Hatim, Kinski and Razyana, and others of promise in the lightly-raced winners Donzel and Librate. Then there is the unbeaten Raft, who could be the pick of the bunch. Unfortunately sore shins limited Raft's appearances to just two in the space of thirteen days in mid-summer, so we don't know as much about him as we'd like; nevertheless his successes were certainly gained in a style which suggested he would have proved a formidable contender for the big autumn events had he been able to take part.

The market for the Beacon Stakes at Newmarket in July suggested Raft wasn't greatly fancied to make a winning debut; he was fifth choice at 10/1 in a sixteen-runner field dominated by Beldale Lear, a highly promising second to

Mr K. Abdulla's "Raft"

Elegant Air over the same course and distance earlier in the month. In the race Raft was soon going well as Beldale Lear made the running; he came to dispute the lead inside the last two furlongs, quickly got the better of the favourite and won pushed out with hands and heels by a length with the third a further four lengths back. Considering that Raft had looked just in need of the run, this was a most encouraging display and he started favourite when tackling the dual winner Falstaff, the four-length Sandwich Stakes winner Harvard and twelve others in the Simonds Bitter Stakes at Salisbury in August. He confirmed his potential despite running green when asked to improve over a quarter of a mile out. Once he realised what was required of him he was most impressive, cutting down Falstaff below the distance then quickening away to win easing up by four lengths in a course-record time for two-year-olds; in so doing he recorded a highly respectable timefigure of 0.58 fast, and his performance was boosted still further by Falstaff's subsequent victories in the Solario Stakes and the Gilbey Champion Racehorse Futurity.

	Nodouble (ch 1965)	Noholme II (ch 1956)	Star Kingdom Oceana
Raft (USA) (br.c. Mar 31, 1981)		Abla-Jay (b 1955)	Double Jay Ablamucha
	Gangster of Love (b 1972)	Round Table (b 1954)	Princequillo Knight's Daughter
		Woozem (b or br 1964)	Hail to Reason Juliets Nurse

Raft's sire Nodouble was a tip-top performer in the States. He broke the track record under top weight in the Metropolitan Handicap, also carried top weight to success in the Californian Stakes, the Brooklyn Handicap and Hawthorn Gold Cup and won the Santa Anita Handicap; he earned a total of 846,749 dollars. He has done very well at stud, siring more stakes winners than any other stallion in 1978 and 1981 and topping the list of leading sires in 1981. Despite his success his stock isn't sought after to anything like the same extent as some leading stallions', such as Northern Dancer and Nijinsky. In 1982 only four of his twenty-six yearlings sold in North America fetched 100,000 dollars or more, with Raft the second-most expensive at 140,000 dollars. Raft is the third foal of Gangster of Love, an extremely well-bred filly who won three times at up to seven furlongs at three and once over six furlongs at four. His grandam Woozem, who has bred two other minor winners, was a much more able racemare than her daughter, winning four stakes races including the seven-furlong Golden Rod and the one-mile Demoiselle at two when she ranked among the best of her sex. Woozem's sister Dutiful was also a smart performer, winning the six-furlong Adirondack Stakes as a two-year-old, and her excellent half-brothers Run For Nurse and Gallant Romeo amassed twenty-two wins and fifteen wins respectively. Gallant Romeo became a successful stallion, numbering the Preakness Stakes winner Elocutionist and the champion sprinters My Juliet and Gallant Bob among his best offspring. Interestingly two other good winners from the family, the smart Irish mile-and-a-half filly Karelina and the high-class sprinter-miler Full Out, are out of Running Juliet, a mare bred on similar lines to Gangster of Love; Running Juliet is by Gangster of Love's sire Round Table out of her grandam Juliets Nurse.

As with so many American breds, it's difficult to assess Raft's stamina potential with any degree of certainty. However, we should estimate that Raft has fair prospects of staying a mile and a half; his maternal grandsire Round Table set a track record over thirteen furlongs and Nodouble, who stayed at least a mile and a quarter, has sired several excellent middle-distance winners, including the champion Canadian horse Overskate and the Japan Cup winner Mairzy Doates. As Raft is a stable-companion of the Two Thousand Guineas favourite Lear Fan and is in the same ownership as another leading candidate, Rainbow Quest, he may be trained more with an eye on the Derby, especially as his connections seem to think his fast, fluent action may prove best suited by top-of-the-ground conditions. Raft still has some way to go before he can be considered a potential Derby winner but he's a good-bodied colt, with scope for further improvement, and we're sure 1984 will see his making up for lost time. *G. Harwood.*

RAGASON 2 b.c. Raga Navarro 119–Miss Season (Silly Season 127) (1983 5s 5g 5s² 5.8g 6f) May 24; IR 2,200F, IR 3,000Y; sixth foal; half-brother to 3-y-o 5f winner Briavan (by Saulingo); dam never ran; poor maiden; not raced after June. *M. McCourt.* **58**

RAGE GLEN 6 gr.m. Grey Mirage 128–Septieme Ciel (Welsh Abbot 131) (1982 10s* 8.2s* 10f⁴ 8f 1983 9f³ 8f 8f³ 10h 8d) compact mare; stays 1¼m; acts on any **54**

going but is suited by some give in the ground; has worn blinkers; has run respectably for an apprentice; headstrong. *M. Lambert.*

RAGGED RASCAL 2 ch.g. Raga Navarro 119–Red Over Amber (Amber Rama 133) (1983 6f 8g) Mar 26; IR 3,500F, IR 11,000Y; well-made gelding; fourth produce; dam never ran; in rear in newcomers event at Goodwood in July and minor race at Bath in September. *C. Nelson.* —

RAGINDA 2 b.f. St Paddy 133–Alleyn (Alcide 136) (1983 7fg 8s 9g) Mar 15; 4,200Y; compact filly; second foal; half-sister to 1982 2-y-o 7f winner Enbyar Dan (by Porto Bello); dam showed no form on flat or over hurdles; in rear in maiden races. *I. Walker.* —

RAGTIME BLUES 3 b.f. Netherkelly 112–Blue Mountain (Mountain Call 125) (1982 5s 5d 5d 1983 8v 12f 12f 16f 13.8f 13.8f) of little account. *A. Potts.* —

RAGUSTAR 3 b.c. Dance In Time–Bamburi 93 (Ragusa 137) (1982 7fg 7fg 8d 1983 8f 10.1f 11.5f4 12d) robust colt; poor maiden; gives impression he'll be suited by a test of stamina. *D. Oughton.* —

RAHERE HUSSAR 3 ch.c. Queen's Hussar 124–Rahere Blackie (Richboy 117) (1982 5g2 6g2 5fg3 6fg* 6fg 6g 1983 7fg 10f3 10.8g 10f 11.7fg) workmanlike colt; suited by 1¼m; yet to race on a soft surface; blinkered last 2 starts. *C. Nelson.* 66

RAILROAD LADY 2 b.f. Rapid River 127–White House Lady (Saintly Song 128) (1983 5g 6fg2 6g3 6fg3) Apr 24; tall, rather narrow, sparely-made filly; first foal; dam poor maiden; placed in the autumn in maiden race and 2 minor events in the North; stays 6f; acts on a firm surface. *R. Hollinshead.* 78

RAINBOW DREAM (FR) 4 b.c. Riverman 131–Dellie Douglass (Mongo) (1982 8g2 8d 8s3 8s 9v 8v3 8v 1983 10s4 10s2 12s 10g 10f4 8h* 8d 10fg 8g 8.2fg) workmanlike ex-French colt; half-brother to 2 winners, including smart Diligo (by Petingo), successful at up to 7.5f in France; dam, daughter of top sprinter Secret Step, won over 6f at 4 yrs in USA; won apprentice handicap at Chepstow in August; stays 1¼m; acts on any going; has twice worn blinkers, including on final start. *A. Jarvis.* 70

RAINBOW QUEST (USA) 2 b.c. Blushing Groom 131–I Will Follow 117 (Herbager 136) (1983 7fg* 8g* 7fg2) 130

Finding a champion at the yearling sales is like finding the crock of gold at the end of a rainbow. The number of yearlings sold at public auction in 1982 in the USA and Canada, where a fair proportion of today's champions are bred, amounted to 8,174 and they fetched a total of 269,665,805 dollars. Only a very small percentage of that huge number will develop into top-class performers, but one that has already done so is the appropriately-named Rainbow Quest, at 950,000 dollars the second-highest priced of the 384 yearlings sold at the Fasig-Tipton Kentucky Summer Sales. He won his first two races most impressively and found only another unbeaten colt, El Gran Senor, too good for him in the other, Britain's most prestigious two-year-old race, the William Hill Dewhurst Stakes.

Rainbow Quest first appeared towards the end of August in the thirty-runner El Capistrano Stakes at Newmarket, a race which drew one of the biggest fields of the season—thankfully the days are long gone when anywhere near as many as fifty-eight horses lined up for one race, as they did once for the Lincolnshire Handicap. The runners for the El Capistrano Stakes promptly split into two groups with the first and second favourites, Bonjour Tristesse and Falstaff (USA), racing on the stand side and the third favourite, Rainbow Quest, on the far side. Even though Rainbow Quest led his group with two furlongs to run, he looked likely to find the two market leaders too strong at the final hill. However,

Haynes, Hanson and Clark Stakes, Newbury–Rainbow Quest wins quite readily from Duelling (grey) and Feasibility Study

Mr K. Abdulla's "Rainbow Quest"

he ran on so strongly when given a couple of slaps that not only did he win by two lengths from Bonjour Tristesse, he put seven lengths between himself and his nearest pursuer on the far side. Rainbow Quest also ran out a clear-cut winner when an even-money favourite for the Haynes, Hanson and Clark Stakes over a mile at Newbury the following month, despite having to give 5 lb to all except one of his twenty rivals. This time Eddery had no need to draw his whip: Rainbow Quest cruised into the lead below the distance, quickly established a decisive advantage when asked to race in earnest and was back on the bridle by the line. He was value for much more than the length-and-a-half margin over his unconsidered stable-companion Duelling. Rainbow Quest's victories were sufficiently impressive for him to start second favourite to the National Stakes winner El Gran Senor in the Dewhurst in October, ahead of Siberian Express, winner of the Prix Morny, Superlative, who numbered both the July and Flying Childers Stakes among his successes, and Ministerial, an impressive winner of the Hyperion Stakes. The market proved an extremely accurate guide, the first five in the betting taking the first five places in correct order. Rainbow Quest ran a splendid race despite having been brought back a furlong, proving the only one capable of giving the favourite a race. He made very smooth headway after halfway but soon had to get down to serious business as El Gran Senor moved easily past Siberian Express into the lead two furlongs out. Although from then on Rainbow Quest was fighting a losing battle he plugged on most determinedly, whittling down El Gran Senor's two-length advantage from the distance to half a length as the winner took things rather easily in the last strides. Rainbow Quest left Siberian Express and Superlative at least six lengths behind, proving beyond doubt that he's a top-class performer. Clearly El Gran Senor was the speedier two-year-old but it's Rainbow Quest we expect to see having the greater influence on the top middle-distance events. Indeed, Rainbow Quest's Dewhurst display entitles him to be considered a potential Derby winner.

Rainbow Quest is certainly bred well enough for almost anything, possessing a first-class pedigree combining stamina and speed. His sire Blushing Groom made his name as a top-class miler but he stayed well enough to take a third place in the Derby, and his first two crops contained several winners over a mile and a half or more, notably Jalmood, the smart French colts Coquelin and Un Etendard and the very smart North American performer Runaway Groom. Rainbow Quest's dam I Will Follow was suited by a mile and a half, gaining the more important of her two successes in the Prix de Minerve at that distance. I Will Follow was the first foal of the Oaks runner-up Where You Lead, herself a daughter of the brilliant Noblesse, winner of the 1963 Oaks by ten lengths. Where You Lead's third foal Slightly Dangerous found only Time Charter too good for her in the Oaks nineteen years

Rainbow Quest (USA) (b.c. May 15, 1981)	Blushing Groom (ch 1974)	Red God (ch 1954)	Nasrullah Spring Run
		Runaway Bride (b 1962)	Wild Risk Aimee
	I Will Follow (b 1975)	Herbager (b 1958)	Vandale Flagette
		Where You Lead (ch 1970)	Raise A Native Noblesse

later. Members of this family are naturally much sought after and Where You Lead and I Will Follow were sold for 1,000,000 dollars and 510,000 dollars respectively in 1981. I Will Follow was carrying her third foal at the time, a filly by Tromos which was sold for 270,000 guineas at the 1983 Highflyer Sales. Her first foal Red Comes Up, a three-year-old sister to Rainbow Quest, has been placed over a mile at Evry and over a mile and a half at Saint-Cloud. Rainbow Quest, an attractive, good sort, was rather a late foal and he could show more improvement because of that fact. He may well prove effective enough at a mile early in his second season to make a very bold show in the Guineas but we're more interested in him as a Derby candidate. Our one reservation about his prospects in the Derby is whether Epsom will suit his free, round action. *J. Tree.*

RAINBOW SPRINGS 3 b.f. Silly Season 127–Hod On 67 (Decoy Boy 129) —
(1982 6g4 6d3 6s2 1983 8f 6f 7g 6g 9fg 6fg) big, leggy filly; well below form in 1983, and ran appallingly when tried in blinkers in a claiming race on final start; should stay 7f; acts on soft going; sold 720 gns Doncaster November Sales. *M. Camacho.*

RAISE THE OFFER 4 b.f. Auction Ring 123–Raise The Roof (Raise You Ten —
125) (1982 12fg 17f3 12f3 16h* 12fg* 14g3 17fg3 14f 13g4 12f3 16g 12g2 12g 1983 18.8v 12fg) rangy filly; quite a modest handicapper at her best; stays well; acts on hard going; blinkered twice in 1982; inconsistent. *P. M. Taylor.*

RAJA KHAN (USA) 2 br.c. Raja Baba–Whole Wheat (Prince Mito) (1983 6fg —
6d) May 20; $63,000Y, resold $50,000Y; good walker and rein, easy mover; third foal; half-brother to a minor winner; dam, placed twice from 6 starts, is half-sister to dam of very smart Small Raja (by Raja Baba); behind in maiden races at Newmarket and Newbury (last of 16) in October. *B. Hills.*

RAJPOURA 3 ch.f. Kashmir II 125–Sparkling Rose (Luthier 126) (1982 8v3 118
10v* 10s3 10d* 10.5fg 12fg2 12fg* 13.5d2 12s 12.5fg 12g) tall, rangy filly; third foal; half-sister to 2 winners, including French middle-distance winner Roushaan (by Kalamoun); dam ran once; won 70,000 francs event at Longchamp in May and Prix de Minerve at Evry in July, starting favourite when beating Ghaiya by 2½ lengths in latter; ran well when 4 lengths second of 5 to Zalataia in Prix de Pomone at Deauville in August and subsequently finished in first 6 in Trusthouse Forte Prix Vermeille and Prix de Royallieu, both at Longchamp, and in Grand Prix de Nantes; suited by 1½m+; probably acts on any going. *A. de Royer Dupre, France.*

RAKE'S PROGRESS 3 ch.c. Vitiges 132–Invitation 107 (Faberge II 121) (1982 50
NR 1983 12v 12s 12v3 12s 13.3g 16f 10fg2 15.5f 12fg3) 9,600Y; strong, good-topped, fair sort; second living produce; dam, sister to Rheingold, won at up to 13f; placed in varied races, including a seller; stays 1½m; seems to act on any going; blinkered sixth to eighth starts; sold 3,100 gns Newmarket September Sales. *R. Laing.*

RAMBLING RIVER 6 b.h. Forlorn River 124–Who-Done-It 98 (Lucero 124) 97
(1982 6f 5fg4 5fg3 5f3 5fg 5fg2 5g3 5f 5g3 5fg* 5fg2 6d* 6fg4 5fg2 5s4 6g4 6d 5s 1983 5g 5g* 6f 5f 5g 5f 6f3 5f* 5fg4 6f3 5f* 5.6fg 5fg3 6g 5d*) strong, useful sort; sprint handicapper; had a good year and won at Redcar, Newcastle, Haydock and York; beat Relatively Sharp by ½ length in £4,800 race on last-named in October; possibly not at his best on really soft going, but acts on any other; blinkered

nowadays; has worn a bandage on near-fore; suited by waiting tactics; tough. *W. A. Stephenson.*

RAMONITA (USA) 2 b.f. Envoy–Spicy Reason (Hail to Reason) (1983 6f) Mar 1; $55,000Y; closely related to a minor winner by King Emperor and half-sister to French 1m winner Hot n' Spicy (by Don B); dam unraced daughter of Spicy Reason, winner of Mother Goose and Acorn Stakes; favourite, 3 lengths fifth of 14 behind Miss Kuta Beach in maiden race at Yarmouth in June. *H. Cecil.*   **69 p**

RAMO'S LADY 4 ch.f. Malinowski 123–Romp 67 (Romulus 129) (1982 10s 1983 16s4) fair sort; plater; stays well. *A. Bailey.*   —

RAMPAGING 3 b.g. Bold Lad (Ire) 133–Eleanor Clare 89 (Petingo 135) (1982 8d 1983 8d 10g 8f 8fg 10f) leggy, good-topped gelding; bad walker and mover; in rear in varied races; blinkered final outing. *G. Fletcher.*   —

RAMPANT 4 br.g. Reliance II 137–Glimmer of Hope 90 (Never Say Die 137) (1982 14fg 12f 16fg 14d 15.5fg4 16g 14.7f3 12g2 14g 14s 1983 16g) big, rangy gelding; stays well; sold 980 gns Doncaster August Sales. *W. Musson.*   —

RANAMAR 3 b.f. Fine Blade 121–Green Marvedo (Green God 128) (1982 5f2 5f 5fg 6fg 1983 7f 8.2f) tall, leggy filly; poor maiden. *J. Hardy.*   —

RANA PRATAP (USA) 3 b.c. Faliraki 125–Dodo S (Nagea) (1982 5fg 6g4 6g4 7g* 7d3 7s* 1983 7.3v 6d 7d3 8f 8f 8.3fg 8fg2 10g4 8d3) lengthy, good-looking colt; good walker; none too consistent but was in frame in 4 handicaps; gives impression 1m is on sharp side for him nowadays and wasn't disgraced over 1¼m; yet to show he can handle really firm ground but acts on any other; missed break sixth outing; bandaged last 3 outings and also blinkered on his last. *G. Lewis.*   **90**

RANGEFINDER 3 ch.c. On Your Mark 125–Battling Bessie (Typhoon 125) (1982 5g4 6fg4 5g 5s4 1983 9s2 8s* 10d3 8f 10f4 10f* 8g3 9fg) well-made, quite attractive colt; a courageous sort who won handicaps at Pontefract and Salisbury in good style; in frame in several other races, on last 2 occasions in valuable handicaps at Goodwood (fourth to Millfontaine) and York (third to Mauritzfontein after seeing little daylight); gives impression he'll stay beyond 1¼m; acts on any going. *B. Hills.*   **90**

RA NOVA 4 ch.c. Ragstone 128–Miss Casanova 84 (Galivanter 131) (1982 10fg 14d 12f3 14f 16g 1983 16s 14s 8h 10d* 10fg 10g*) small, quite well-made colt; won handicaps at Lingfield in September and Chepstow in October; best at middle distances; apprentice ridden when successful; trained by J. Jenkins first 2 starts; fairly useful hurdler. *Mrs N. Kennedy.*   **83**

RANT AND RAVE 3 ch.c. North Stoke 130–Libonia (Le Haar 126) (1982 7f 1983 8d 8v 8v 6fg 10.1f) small, well-made colt; well beaten all outings; blinkered third start. *J. Sutcliffe.*   —

RAPID BEAT 3 b.g. Rapid River 127–On Wings Of Song 51 (Jolly Jet) (1982 5f 5f 6g 5g 5g 6d 8.2fg 8fg4 7.2s 1983 7f 12fg3 14.7f3 15.8g) leggy, unfurnished gelding; plater; best at 6f as a 2-y-o and is far from certain to stay 1¾m. *W. A. Stephenson.*   **51**

RAPID LAD 5 b.g. Rapid River 127–Seacona (Espresso 122) (1982 7s3 8g 10.8fg2 8fg2 8fg* 8.2g 8f 1983 10s 8v4 10g 8s3 8fg* 10f* 10.2f 8f 10h3 10f* 10f4 8f2 8d* 8.2g4 8fg3 8g) compact gelding; former plater; goes well at Beverley and won handicaps there in July (2), August and September; stays 1¼m; acts on any going but is ideally suited by fast ground; occasionally blinkered (has run moderately in them); suitable mount for an apprentice; suited by waiting tactics. *J. Spearing.*   **72**

RAPID LADY 3 b.f. Rapid River 127–Princess Gretel 97 (The Phoenix) (1982 5g 5d2 5fg4 5f 5f 5fg* 5d4 6f 5g2 5g 6g 5d 5d 1983 5v2 5s* 5s2 6d 5s3 5f 5f3 6f 6f4 6f 8h) leggy filly; won small handicap at Hamilton in April and ran creditably most other starts; stays 6f; probably acts on any going; ran respectably in blinkers once; good mount for an apprentice. *Mrs M. Nesbitt.*   **52**

RAPID MISS 3 gr. or ro.f. Rapid River 127–Zellamaid 54 (Runnymede 123) (1982 6f 6f 5.1d3 6g* 5g2 5s 1983 5.1g 5f3 5f 6fg4 5h2 5fg 5f 5g) small, lengthy filly; ran creditably in non-sellers on occasions; stays 6f; acts on hard going and is possibly unsuited by very soft. *Mrs N. Macauley.*   **60**

RAPID PROGRESS (USA) 2 ch.c. To The Quick–Crafty Galise (Crafty Admiral) (1983 5v 6fg 7f 6fg) May 1; $39,000Y; compact colt; half-brother to several winners in USA, one stakes placed; dam won 2 sprint claiming races; no form, including in a claimer and a seller; blinkered last 2 starts; sold BBA 2,600 gns Newmarket Autumn Sales. *G. Hunter.*   —

RAPID RETURN 3 b.g. Rapid River 127–Grange Supreme (Keren 100) (1982 – NR 1983 7d 9v 9.4d 6fg 7f 6g) first foal; dam never ran; well beaten in maiden races and handicaps; blinkered final start. *F. Watson.*

RAPID SALLY 2 b.f. Rapid River 127–Brave Sally (Sallymount 125) (1983 5s 5f 46 5f) Feb 8; smallish filly; half-sister to 3 winners, including fairly useful 5f performer Erroll's Boy (by Bay Express); poor form, including in a seller; exported to Malaysia. *M. W. Easterby.*

RAPPA TAP TAP (FR) 2 ch.f. Tap On Wood 130–Reprocolor 114 (Jimmy Reppin 97 p 131) (1983 6d* 6fg*) Mar 12; active, quite well-made, useful-looking filly; first foal; dam won Lingfield Oaks Trial and Lancashire Oaks; won maiden race at Yarmouth in September and 12-runner Blue Seal Stakes (beating Spaced To Run ½ length) at Ascot later in the month; will be well suited by 7f+; likely to improve further. *M. Stoute.*

RARE DANCER 3 b.g. Rarity 129–Go Go Native (Native Dancer) (1982 8d – 1983 10v 13.3g) IR 3,600F, IR 33,000Y; ex-Irish gelding; half-brother to 2 winners in USA; dam never ran; lightly-raced maiden, best effort when fifth of 14 at Leopardstown as a 2-y-o; sold to Miss S. Morris 1,500 gns Doncaster October Sales. *R. Simpson.*

RARE FRIENDSHIP 3 b.f. Rarity 129–Hidden Hand (Ribocco 129) (1982 9s 65 1983 12v 12d 13d 12f 16.5f* 17f) big filly; ran easily best race when making all in small maiden race at Redcar in July; evidently stays well; acts on firm going (also ran respectably on soft as a 2-y-o); blinkered last 4 starts; sold to NBA 4,000 gns Newmarket December Sales. *E. Weymes.*

RARE GAL (USA) 2 gr.f. Caro 133–Rare Lady (Never Bend) (1983 5.1fg 5f* 79 5g² 6fg) Mar 23; well-grown, rather leggy filly; half-sister to 1982 American 2-y-o 6f winner Write Off (by Wajima); dam, lightly-raced 6f winner, is half-sister to Deceit, a high-class winner at up to 9f; backed from 7/1 to 5/2, won 16-runner minor event at Warwick in August by 2½ lengths from Clay Pigeon; favourite, beaten 2½ lengths by Biddour in small race at Catterick the following month; should stay 1m; acts on firm going. *G. Huffer.*

RARE GIFT 4 b.c. Rarity 129–Awash (Busted 134) (1982 8s* 8fg 10f 8g 8fg – 1983 8d 10v 8v 8d) tall, lengthy, sparely-made colt; good mover; disappointing handicapper; will stay 1½m; acts well on soft going; sold, reportedly for export to Malaysia, 3,200 gns Newmarket July Sales. *N. Callaghan.*

RARE HONOUR 3 br.f. Artaius 129–Honorary Member (Never Bend) (1982 84 7.6v 1983 7fg⁴ 7.2fg³ 6fg* 6f³ 6fg* 7.2g 6d) rangy filly; not the best of movers; successful in maiden race at Lingfield in July (made all) and handicap at Haydock in August; stays 7f, but best form at 6f; yet to show she can handle really soft going, but acts on any other; ran creditably in blinkers final start. *P. Cole.*

RARE ROBERTA (USA) 3 b.f. Roberto 131–Marketess (To Market) (1982 118 6fg² 7d³ 6g* 6d 6s* 1983 7.3s 8g⁴ 10v 7f 7.6fg³ 8fg 7fg² 7fg⁴ 8g*)
Rare Roberta's impressive win in the Prix Perth at Saint-Cloud in November kept up the remarkable strike rate of British-trained runners in the race: since 1970 British stables had won with Lord Gayle, Sparkler, Dominion, Jellaby, Princes Gate and Commodore Blake. The last-named, winner in 1982, took the field again in 1983 and, along with the favourite Aragon, had more obvious credentials than Rare Roberta who started at 38/1 in a field of fifteen, but neither got a look in. Rare Roberta made just about all the running from her draw near the inside rail and was virtually unchallenged in the straight, coming home two and a half lengths clear of the French filly Ask Lorna with another British-trained outsider Favoloso third, Aragon fifth and Commodore Blake sixth. This was a

Prix Perth, Saint-Cloud–Rare Roberta beats Ask Lorna and Favoloso (rails)

smart performance, all the more so since her rider Quinn, one of the season's leading apprentices, was unable to draw his allowance in so valuable a race.

Surprisingly the Prix Perth was Rare Roberta's first win in nine outings since her two-year-old days when she had won a maiden race at Lingfield and the Buggins Farm Nursery at Haydock. She'd shown some smart form though, and had run well above expectations when less than three lengths fifth of eighteen behind Ma Biche in the One Thousand Guineas, with Quinn again unable to claim; on Royal Heroine's disqualification she was moved up to fourth. In addition she had two recent good performances on the same course, finishing second to Wiki Wiki Wheels in a handicap under a stiff weight and just over five lengths fourth behind Salieri in the Bisquit Cognac Challenge Stakes. Consistency hadn't been her strong point, it's true, but on her best form she was by no means a forlorn hope at Saint-Cloud.

Rare Roberta (USA) (b.f. 1980)	Roberto (b 1969)	Hail to Reason (br 1958)	Turn-to / Nothirdchance
		Bramalea (b 1959)	Nashua / Rarelea
	Marketess (ch 1971)	To Market (ch 1948)	Market Wise / Pretty Does
		In The Green (b 1958)	Jet Pilot / Polka

Rare Roberta was bought for 58,000 dollars at Keeneland as a yearling. She's by Roberto, sire of the unbeaten two-year-old Lear Fan, and is the first foal of Marketess, who won six small races at up to six furlongs from more than fifty starts. The grandam In The Green, a minor winner, also bred the stakes winner Chenille. Rare Roberta will probably be at stud in 1984 and at the time of writing it was planned to mate her with Kings Lake. A big, strong filly, she stayed a mile well and acted on any going, with the possible exception of very firm. *P. Cole.*

RARE SCOTCH 5 ch.g. Rarity 129–Melody Ryde 90 (Shooting Chant) (1982 NR 1983 10.1f) poor maiden; has twice been blinkered. *Mrs N. Kennedy.* —

RARE SONG 2 b.f. Averof 123–Bird in the Hand 82 (Major Portion 129) (1983 6fg 5fg) May 15; half-sister to 2 winners, including fairly useful stayer Taffy (by Prince de Galles); dam won over 7f; well beaten in modest company at Windsor in July, on second occasion last of 19; sold 800 gns Newmarket December Sales. *F. Durr.* —

RASSEEMA (USA) 2 b.f. Youth 135–Ramanouche 112 (Riverman 131) (1983 7f[4] 8g[2]) Feb 1; well-made, good-topped, quite attractive filly; first foal; dam, daughter of very smart 9f to 13f filly Bubunia, was very useful winner at up to 7f in France; in frame in maiden events at Salisbury and Leicester in September; will stay 1¼m; should win a race. *F. J. Houghton.* — 81

RASTASEMEFAICH 5 b.g. Goldhill 125–May Slave (Arctic Slave 116) (1982 NR 1983 8f) second foal; dam lightly raced; unquoted when last in maiden race at Beverley in July. *H. Wharton.* —

RATHCANNON (USA) 2 b. or br.f. Irish Castle–Dumpty's Lady (Dumpty Humpty) (1983 6fg 6fg) May 8; $75,000Y: good-topped filly; good walker; half-sister to several winners, including useful 1981 French 2-y-o sprinter Baltimore Bullet (by Empery) and minor stakes winner Apalache Chief (by Apalachee); dam, smart winner at up to 1m, won 11 of her 51 races; little worthwhile form in maiden races at Newmarket in September and Doncaster in October. *B. Hills.* —

RATHDOWNEY MAY 3 ch.f. Derrylin 115–Angelica (Hornbeam 130) (1982 5fg 5d 5fg 5.8f[4] 7f 7g 1983 8s[2] 7fg 8g 8h 8fg) small, lengthy filly; poor plater; suited by 1m; sold 400 gns Doncaster November Sales. *M. McCormack.* — 42

RATHER EXCLUSIVE 2 b.c. Crimson Beau 124–Rather Warm 103 (Tribal Chief 125) (1983 7f 7fg) Mar 8; small, sturdy colt; good walker; first foal; dam won at up to 7.6f at 2 yrs; plating-class form in maiden events at Salisbury in June and Warwick in July. *P. Cole.* — 68

RATLEY LODGE 2 b.f. Daring March 116–Zaratella (Le Levanstell 122) (1983 5v 5v 5s) Mar 6; leggy, lengthy filly; third foal; dam ran 3 times; bad plater; not raced after May; blinkered final outing. *C. V. Miller.* —

RAWLINSON END 5 b.h. Song 132–Wong Way Girl 99 (Kibenka 119) (1982 8fg 8g* 7f[2] 8g 8f 8fg 8fg 8.3g 7fg[2] 7.3g 8g* 8g 1983 8v 8d 7s[4] 7.6v 7f[2] 8f 7f 7h 7d[4] 7.6fg[3] 6fg) neat, strong horse; good walker; inconsistent handicapper; stays 1m; — 52 acts on any going but seems well suited by top-of-the-ground nowadays; ran very badly in blinkers once. *R. Laing.*

RAY CHARLES 5 gr.g. Sun Prince 128–Ivory Gull 70 (Sea Hawk II 131) (1982 – 12d 1983 12v) tall, narrow gelding; none too good a walker or mover; ran consistently as a 3-y-o and showed fairly useful form; behind in both outings on the flat since; suited by 1½m; acts on any going; sold 2,100 gns Ascot May Sales. *D. Nicholson.*

RAZOR SHARP 3 ch.c. Sharpen Up 127–Pearl Star 110 (Gulf Pearl 117) (1982 6f **94** 6d 5fg³ 5.8f* 6s² 1983 8f 10f 8fg³ 7f² 7g) good-topped colt; stuck on gamely when placed in handicaps at Ascot (third to Steelworks) and Newbury (second to Miss Thames) in summer; promises to stay 1¼m; acts on any going; best in blinkers; reportedly broke a blood vessel final start. *C. Nelson.*

RAZOUMOVA 2 ch.f. Dominion 123–Rhodante (Busted 134) (1983 6g 7f⁴ 7f 7f **64** 8d) Apr 17; 18,000Y; rangy, useful-looking filly; not a good mover; second foal; dam Irish 1¼m and 1½m winner; plating-class maiden; best run at 1m; none too well away first 2 starts and wore blinkers on final appearance; sold 5,800 gns Newmarket Autumn Sales. *C. Brittain.*

RAZYANA (USA) 2 b.f. His Majesty–Spring Adieu (Buckpasser) (1983 7fg²) **87 p** Apr 18; $350,000Y; good mover; third foal; half-sister to 1982 2-y-o 6f winner You're My Lady (by Roberto); dam, winner of 3 small sprint races at 3 yrs, is half-sister to Northern Dancer; second favourite, led briefly 2½f out when promising 2½ lengths second of 26 to Alleging in maiden race at Newmarket in September; will stay 1¼m; sure to win in similar company. *J. Tree.*

R B BROTHER 3 gr. or ro.g. Broxted 120–Smokey Princess 83 (My Smokey – 125) (1982 NR 1983 8fg 10s 8fg) robust gelding; sixth reported foal; brother to 7f and 1m winner Royal Broxted; dam stayed 1¼m well; behind in maiden and minor races, twice last. *A. W. Jones.*

REACTION 2 b.f. Duc D'Orleans 76–Variety Act (Crooner 119) (1983 5f 6f 6h) – Feb 12; smallish, lengthy filly; of no account. *B. Richmond.*

READY WIT 2 br.c. Bay Express 132–Brevity 76 (Pindari 124) (1983 5s 6g 6fg **82** 7g*) Apr 17; 1,700F, 13,000Y; lengthy, workmanlike colt; half-brother to several winners, including fairly useful 1982 2-y-o 6f winner Stay Sharp (by Sharpen Up) and prolific 1975 2-y-o sprint winner Short Reign (by Tribal Chief); dam won over 7f at 2 yrs; won 10-runner minor event at Chepstow in October; suited by 7f. *R. Hannon.*

REAL COOL 3 ch.f. Record Token 128–Balante 90 (Balidar 133) (1982 5s 6d 6d – 1983 5s⁴ 5fg 5s 5fg 5g 5f 8d) lengthy, rather sparely-made filly; best at 5f; blinkered third to fifth starts. *P. Asquith.*

REAL GOLD 2 gr.f. Yankee Gold 115–Roman Folly (Pontifex) (1983 7s* 10g³) **113** Apr 8; first foal; dam last on second of only 2 starts; 20/1, all out to win 19-runner maiden event by ¾ length from Out And About at the Curragh in October; met with trouble in running and did really well to finish 2¼ lengths third to Darshaan in Criterium de Saint-Cloud the following month, running on strongly; clearly stays well; a very useful filly in the making and should win a good prize at 3 yrs. *J. Harty, Ireland.*

REALISTIC (USA) 3 b.c. In Reality–Powerful Katrinka (Beau Gar) (1982 NR **90** 1983 10g⁴ 10f* 10.1f³ 10h³ 12.2g² 11d* 12fg) $210,000Y; close-coupled, attractive colt; not a good walker; half-brother to 3 winners, including Toonerville (by Third Martini), a very smart winner at up to 1½m; dam ran 3 times; stepped up considerably on his first effort when beating Northern Trial by 1½ lengths in well-contested maiden event at Ascot in July; ran best subsequent race when getting home by ¾ length from Sikorsky in handicap at Newbury in October; stays 1½m; yet to race on really soft going, but acts on any other; has twice disappointed when sweating badly. *G. Harwood.*

REALLY HONEST 2 b.c. He Loves Me 120–Whitethorn (Gulf Pearl 117) (1983 **92** 7d 7fg 7g⁴ 6fg*) Mar 25; IR 20,000Y; good-topped colt; third foal; half-brother to 1½m winner Going Going (by Auction Ring); dam Irish 1½m winner; won 14-runner maiden race at Redcar in October easing up by 2½ lengths from Hello Gypsy; evidently suited by 6f. *B. Hanbury.*

REALLY REGAL 3 b.f. Relkino 131–Queen's Castle 98 (Sovereign Path 125) **90** (1982 NR 1983 8g⁴ 10f* 10d²) tall, rangy, sparely-made filly; half-sister to 3 winners, including smart 1976 French 2-y-o 7.5f and 1m winner Edinburgh (by Charlottown); dam stayed at least 1¼m and is half-sister to Reform; still bit green when landing the odds by 2 lengths from Honeybeta in 7-runner minor event at Salisbury in August; no match for sole opponent Kuwait Sun in minor event at Goodwood the following month; bred to stay beyond 1¼m; sold 42,000 gns Newmarket December Sales. *R. Hern.*

REAL MONTY 3 ch.g. Monsanto 121–Vila Real 76 (Town Crier 119) (1982 5g 5f 5f⁴ 6f⁴ 6fg 6g² 7fg 8f² 8.2s³ 8g* 1983 8fg* 8f 8fg 8g⁴ 8h) sturdy, compact gelding; good walker; won handicap at Edinburgh in June; suited by 1m; seems to act on any going; blinkered third outing; exported to Singapore. *M. H. Easterby.* 75

REAL SILVER 2 gr.f. Silly Season 127–Vila Real 76 (Town Crier 119) (1983 5fg⁴ 6f³ 6fg 6g* 7fg²) May 6; rather leggy filly; half-sister to 2 winners, including 1m winner Real Monty (by Monsanto); dam won 4 sellers over 7f and 1m; won 18-runner minor event at Pontefract in October; good second in Edinburgh nursery the following month; better suited by 7f than by 6f, and will stay further. *B. Hobbs.* 85

REAR ACTION 3 br.c. Home Guard 129–Matoa (Tom Rolfe) (1982 7g 7fg 7.6v 1983 10v 7fg 6g² 7f³ 5.3f 7f² 6f² 8g* 8g⁴) big, lengthy colt; placed in varied company before beating Ka Bu Nor by 3 lengths in 24-runner handicap at Leicester in September; suited by 1m; blinkered last 2 outings; retained 6,800 gns Newmarket Autumn Sales. *R. Smyth.* 78

REBOLLINO 4 b.c. Nebbiolo 125–Cloe (Shantung 132) (1982 7fg² 8fg 7fg 8f⁴ 7fg² 1983 8v³ 8fg 7fg 7s 7g) big, rangy colt; none too good a mover; stayed on well despite hanging right when 4½ lengths third of 10 to Noalcoholic in Lockinge Stakes at Newbury in May; soundly beaten afterwards in varied company; stays 1m and may get further; acts on any going; blinkered final start. *T. Fairhurst.* 108 d

RECEPTIVE 2 b.f. Decoy Boy 129–Reigning Grace 108 (Roan Rocket 128) (1983 8g) Mar 21; 700 2-y-o; fifth foal; dam winner in Austria; dam won at up to 1¼m; last of 12 in minor event at Redcar in November. *W. H. H. Williams.* –

RECORD DANCER 3 b.g. Dancer's Image–Treacle 85 (Hornbeam 130) (1982 8s² 8s² 1983 10d⁴ 10fg⁴ 10.6s²) close-coupled, useful-looking gelding; not seen out until September, but was in frame in maiden and minor races all outings; stays 1¼m; blinkered final start. *G. Pritchard-Gordon.* 73

RECORD HARVEST 2 ch.c. Record Token 128–Haybells (Klairon 131) (1983 5s⁴ 6v³ 7fg) May 8; 4,300F, 30,000Y; leggy, rather narrow colt; half-brother to 2 winners, including winning stayer Haywire (by Galivanter); dam lightly-raced half-sister to smart Haymaking; 1½ lengths fourth to Handstand in maiden race at York in May, best effort; not raced after August; should stay 1m; acts on soft going. *M. H. Easterby.* 73

RECORD RED 2 ch.f. Record Run 127–Flare Square (Red God 128§) (1983 6g 8g⁴ 8g 8fg) Mar 20; 1,200F; third produce; dam showed no ability; plating-class maiden; showed form only on second appearance. *D. Smith.* 61

RECORD SUPREME 2 gr.f. Record Token 128–Supremelos (Supreme Sovereign 119) (1983 5v³ 5.8f³ 6f² 6fg⁴ 6fg 6fg) Apr 4; 3,000Y; useful-looking filly; third foal; sister to fair 1982 2-y-o 5f winner Flying Disc; dam never ran; quite a modest maiden; stays 6f; acts on any going. *A. Pitt.* 69

RECORD WING 5 b.g. Record Run 127–O'Flynn (Prince Regent 129) (1982 10.1fg 8.3g³ 10f 7fg² 10d³ 8g* 8.3fg 8.3fg⁴ 12fg³ 10s⁴ 10.2s* 1983 10s* 8v⁴ 10s 10.6fg³ 11.7f⁴ 10fg 10.2fg 10d*) has been fired; former plater; won handicaps at Leicester in March and Lingfield in October; not disgraced over 1½m but best form at shorter distances; acts on a firm surface but is ideally suited by some give in the ground; blinkered once in 1981; usually bandaged. *D. H. Jones.* 61

RED 3 ch.g. Jimmy Reppin 131–Talis 79 (Tamerlane 128) (1982 5g 7d 7.2s 7g 1983 6s 6g 5g² 6v 5f 6f 8d 6fg) small gelding; sprint maiden; soundly beaten in sellers on occasions; trained much of season by W. Wharton. *P. Felgate.* 60 d

REDALCO 3 b.f. Nonoalco 131–Redowa 90 (Red God 128§) (1982 6fg 6f 6d³ 6s 1983 7g² 7s³ 8f 7f⁴ 7f 7f⁴ 6g⁴ 6fg) good-bodied filly; placed in varied races; should be suited by 1m; acts on any going; sold 11,000 gns Newmarket December Sales. *J. Winter.* 70 d

RED CLIP 9 b.g. Double Red 122–Barnstables 72 (Pay Up) (1982 8d 8f 8fg 5f 1983 8g) poor plater; has worn blinkers. *J. Gilbert.* –

RED COUNTER 2 ch.c. Red Alert 127–Night Encounter (Right Track 131) (1983 7f 7g) May 25; 7,200Y; smallish colt; first foal; dam, sister to Take a Reef, won at up to 12.5f in France; in rear in minor event at Doncaster in July and maiden race at York in October. *Hbt Jones.* –

671

REDDEN 5 ch.g. Red God 128§–Portden (Worden II 129) (1982 8g 10s 10fg⁴ 8g 10f* 8.5f² 10f³ 10fg² 12f 10f 10f* 10g 10g 10f³ 10d 1983 8v 10v 8s 10g 10fg 10f* 10f³ 10g 8fg 10f⁴ 10f² 10d⁴ 10.2fg 10fg) attractive, well-made gelding; returned to form when winning handicap at Brighton in June; also ran creditably eleventh start; stays 1¼m; needs a sound surface; has worn blinkers, but seems better without; has worn a tongue strap; goes well on switchbacked tracks; inconsistent. *B. Swift.* **83**

RED DIPPER 7 b.g. Seaepic 100–Grey Sport (Court Feathers 120) (1982 NR 1983 10.2g) blinkered when tailed off in seller at Bath in June. *O. O'Neill.* **–**

RED DUSTER 3 br.c. Luthier 126–Maroon 92 (Roan Rocket 128) (1982 7fg 1983 12s² 12s³ 16g* 14fg* 16fg 16.5fg³) tall, lengthy colt; landed odds from Faroor in maiden race at Warwick in July and justified favouritism by short head from Special Vintage in minor event at Haydock in August; below form afterwards, and seems not to be entirely genuine; suited by a test of stamina; yet to race on very firm ground, but acts on any other; blinkered final start; sold out of R. Hern's stable 12,000 gns Newmarket September Sales after fourth outing. *T. Fairhurst.* **93 §**

REDELLA 3 b.f. Red Regent 123–Amorella 106 (Crepello 136) (1982 NR 1983 7d 10s 10.1f 12fg) well-made filly; half-sister to numerous winners, including useful miler The Moorings (by Parthia); dam won Princess Elizabeth Stakes; little worthwhile form in varied races; sold 5,600 gns Newmarket Autumn Sales. *P. Walwyn.* **–**

RED FACE 2 b.c. Red Johnnie 100–Sygnome 53 (Precipice Wood 123) (1983 5s⁴ 6g 7f 7fg² 7f³) Mar 18; small, strong colt; third foal; dam poor stayer; moderate maiden; best effort when second in nursery at Newmarket in August; will stay 1m; exported to Hong Kong. *C. Brittain.* **78**

RED FIELD 5 b.h. Tudor Rhythm 112–Glebe 83 (Tacitus 124) (1982 16fg² 14.6g* 18.4g* 16fg⁴ 18.1g* 16d 1983 16.1v² 14s² 16g² 14s 16fg 16.1s 18fg) strong, lengthy horse; staying handicapper; acts on any going; seems to have a mind of his own these days (tried to savage winner first start and dwelt and took little interest sixth outing). *W. Holden.* **56**

RED GAY 2 ch.f. Red Alert 127–Gone Gay 86 (Crepello 136) (1983 7fg) Mar 13; 7,400F, 4,600Y; lengthy, robust filly; closely related to useful but disappointing 7f and 1m winner Ganimede and winning hurdler Ruby Wine (both by Red God) and half-sister to a winner; dam stayed 1½m; 6 lengths sixth of 12 to Miss Saint-Cloud in minor event at Doncaster in October; will stay 1m; likely to improve. *R. Sheather.* **76 p**

REDGRAVE ARTIST 2 b.c. Young Generation 129–Hardirondo 93 (Hardicanute 130) (1983 7fg 7fg³) Apr 26; 6,400Y; compact, sturdy colt; second foal; half-brother to a winner in Belgium; dam game stayer; length third of 14 to Claude Monet in minor event at Doncaster in October; will stay 1m. *R. Whitaker.* **83**

REDGRAVE CREATIVE 3 b.f. Swing Easy 126–Fair Sarita 95 (King's Troop 118) (1982 6g 5g⁴ 5fg 6fg² 6f³ 6g 1983 6s 7s** 7h 8g) big, rangy filly; won minor event at Catterick in June; behind both subsequent outings, including in a valuable seller; suited by 7f; probably acts on any going but goes well on soft; blinkered final start in 1982; sold 1,700 gns Doncaster October Sales. *R. Whitaker.* **67**

REDGRAVE DESIGN 3 b.f. Nebbiolo 125–Ribocana (Molvedo 137) (1982 5fg 5f³ 5g* 5d 5f 6g³ 6fg 1983 5f 5f 5f 6f 7.2g 6s 5s 5fg) smallish, fair sort; didn't recover her 2-y-o form in 1983; suited by 6f and should stay further; blinkered sixth and seventh outings; changed hands 1,300 gns Doncaster October Sales. *R. Whitaker.* **–**

REDHOUSE CHARM 2 ch.c. Swing Easy 126–Off The Mark (On Your Mark 125) (1983 5s** 5g 5fg² 6f² 6f 5g³ 6d*) Mar 4; 7,400Y; neat colt; fourth foal; half-brother to 2 minor winners; dam won over 1m in France; won minor event at Brighton in May and £4,300 nursery (just getting up) at Newbury in October; suited by 6f; better on a soft surface than a firm one; acts on any track; genuine; goes well for apprentice S. Whitworth. *R. Smyth.* **103**

RED INJUN 4 b.c. Mill Reef 141–Ardneasken 84 (Right Royal V 135) (1982 12f 14.7f* 18d⁴ 17.4d 1983 18d 20f 16f 16.1g 17.4g 16s² 16fg 20fg) medium-sized, quite attractive colt; out-and-out staying handicapper; acts on any going; often blinkered; ungenuine and inconsistent, and is one to be wary of. *C. Thornton.* **§§**

RED LINE FEVER 2 b.f. Bay Express 132–Bottom Line 90 (Double Jump 131) (1983 5s** 5fg² 5fg² 5s) Mar 29; small, rather lightly-built filly; first foal; dam won from 1¼m to 1½m; made all in 9-runner maiden race at Haydock in May; second subsequently in useful company at York and Thirsk; out of her depth in Flying **94**

Childers Stakes at Doncaster in September; speedy, and not certain to stay 6f, although bred to do so; acts on any going. *M. Jarvis.*

RED LORY 2 br.f. Bay Express 132–Powderhall 81 (Murrayfield 119) (1983 5s 5s* 5d² 5g 5fg) Mar 17; lightly-built filly; third foal; half-sister to 2 winners, including fair 1981 2-y-o 5f winner Run Like Mad (by Silly Season); dam won 4 races at up to 10.6f; won 12-runner minor event at Pontefract in May in very good style, making all and beating La Prima easing up by a long-looking 7 lengths; off course 4 months after next appearance, but ran well in Newmarket nursery second race back; acts on soft going and a firm surface. *R. Sheather.* — 87

RED MINSTREL 3 b.c. Averof 123–Red Jade 82 (Red God 128§) (1982 7d 7f 6fg² 7f 7f 6fg 1983 8g* 8f² 9.4f* 10f* 10.8g 9g 10.1fg* 10.2s² 10fg 8g) rangy, useful-looking colt; improved and won maiden race at Bath and handicaps at Carlisle, Pontefract and Windsor in game fashion; held on by a length from Il Pontevecchio on last-named course in September; soundly beaten fifth, sixth and last 2 starts however; stays 1¼m; acts on any going; blinkered once at 2 yrs; tends to sweat up; front runner; apprentice ridden for first 3 wins; sold 15,500 gns Newmarket Autumn Sales. *M. McCormack.* — 92

RED MUSTANG 2 ch.g. Red Alert 127–Wedding March (March Past 124) (1983 8g) May 5; IR 4,400F, 1,600Y; brother to 1m winner Hold Off, and half-brother to 2 winners; dam ran twice; in rear in 15-runner maiden race at Sandown in October. *H. Beasley.* — –

RED NORTH 3 ch.c. Dublin Taxi–Aberdeen Lassie 102 (Aberdeen 109) (1982 6f 5d 6s³ 1983 5d² 6d³ 5f 5f² 5g 5f) rather sparely-made, fair sort; probably finds 6f just beyond him; acts on any going; blinkered last 2 outings. *D. Garraton.* — 59

RED RIPPLE (FR) 3 ch.c. Anne's Pretender 124–Cup Cake (Dan Cupid 132) (1982 NR 1983 16v 14.7d 12fg) fair sort; third living foal; half-brother to Derby third Rankin (by Owen Dudley) and middle-distance winner Ransom (by Rose Laurel); dam won over 1m and 11f in France and also over hurdles; tailed off in maiden races in spring and in amateur riders event (carrying 18 lb overweight) in September; sold out of N. Tinkler's stable 720 gns Doncaster August Sales. *E. Alston.* — –

RED ROMAN 3 ch.f. Solinus 130–Dancer Signal 106 (Red God 128§) (1982 6g 5v* 1983 6f⁴ 6f 6d 6d 6g 5g) sturdy, good-quartered, quite attractive filly; good mover; mainly disappointing after finishing fairly promising fourth of 9 behind Coquito's Friend in £3,300 event at Newbury in July; stays 6f; started slowly in blinkers fourth outing. *J. Dunlop.* — 71

RED RUSSELL 3 ch.c. Tap On Wood 130–Granville Lady (High Hat 131) (1983 6v 6s 6g 7fg⁴ 7fg* 7d³ 8d⁴) Mar 16; IR 34,000Y; fourth living foal; dam, middle-distance winner in Ireland, is sister to Dewhurst winner Hametus; twice ran creditably at the Curragh in September, when 3¼ lengths third to El Gran Senor in BBA (Ireland) Goffs National Stakes and 4 lengths fourth to Without Reserve in Ashford Castle Stakes, lacking pace in closing stages each time; won a maiden event at Tralee by 6 lengths the previous month; will be suited by 1¼m. *C. Collins, Ireland.* — 100

RED TARA 2 b.f. Red Johnnie 100–Indian Wells (Reliance II 137) (1983 5d 5g 5f 5f³ 6f 6f 7.2g) Apr 7; workmanlike filly; half-sister to 3-y-o 11f seller winner Solares (by Free State); poor plater; blinkered sixth outing; sold 440 gns Doncaster October Sales. *D. Hanley.* — 45

RED VANITY 2 ch.f. Jimmy Reppin 131–Nordic Rose (Drumhead 122) (1983 5g) first foal in this country; dam, daughter of smart 1955 2-y-o The Rose of Sharon, finished in rear in 3 maiden races at 2 yrs; behind in 20-runner maiden race at Warwick in October. *G. Fletcher.* — –

REDWOOD CHEVALIER 2 ch.c. Proud Knight 83–Redwood Amber (Thunder Wild) (1983 5fg 7fg 8g 8d) Mar 27; good-topped non-thoroughbred colt; of little account; blinkered final outing. *R. Griffiths.* — –

RED ZEPHYR 3 b.c. Red Alert 127–Paduia (St Paddy 133) (1982 6f 5d 5d 1983 8s 10d 6v4 6f* 6f3 6fg3 6f 7g² 7fg* 7d) compact, deep-girthed colt; successful in minor events at Brighton in July and handicap at Salisbury (made all) in September; suited by 7f; best on fast ground; apprentice ridden; tends to sweat up; sent to Hong Kong. *R. Hannon.* — 91

REEFER MADNESS 3 b.c. Mill Reef 141–Parsimony 121 (Parthia 132) (1982 NR 1983 8d 10.1d² 11g²) 460,000Y; medium-sized, quite attractive colt; half-brother to 3 winners, including very useful 5f to 7f winner Petty Purse (by — 87

Petingo) and smart sprinter Scarcely Blessed (by So Blessed); dam won July Cup and is half-sister to good sprinters Mummy's Pet and Arch Sculptor; second in minor event at Windsor (beaten short head by Bedtime) and maiden race at Ayr (went down by ¾ length to Promindante when odds on), both in May; not seen out again; suited by 1¼m+. *J. Hindley.*

REEF GLADE 4 b.c. Mill Reef 141–Green Glade (Correspondent) (1982 7g³ **77** 12s² 11.7f* 12f 12f 13.1g 9fg* 9g 9d 1983 12d 11.7d 10.2f² 10f* 10g 10f² 10f 9fg 10.2fg 10fg) medium-sized, fair sort; not a good mover; made all to win handicap at Pontefract in July; stays 1½m; acts on any going; does best when ridden up with pace; inconsistent. *P. Haslam.*

REENY LEE 2 gr. or ro.f. Scallywag 127–War Bird (Warpath 113) (1983 5f 5f 6g) — Mar 13; smallish, lengthy filly; first foal; dam never ran; in rear in Northern maiden races; bred to need much further; hung badly second start. *R. Whitaker.*

REESH 2 b.c. Lochnager 132–Songs Jest (Song 132) (1983 5s² 5d² 5v* 6fg* 5s³ **105** 5s³ 5fg² 5fg 5fg³) Feb 3; 21,000Y; strong, compact, good sort; really good mover; second foal; half-brother to fairly useful 1982 2-y-o 5f performer Songroid (by Haveroid); dam, who never ran, is closely related to smart sprinter Jester; won minor event at Kempton in May and nursery at Windsor in August (reportedly off course with severe stomach trouble in between); placed subsequently in varied races, including Flying Childers Stakes at Doncaster, Harry Rosebery Challenge Trophy at Ayr and nursery under 9-7 at Newmarket; stays 6f; seems to act on any going; game and consistent. *W. O'Gorman.*

REFILL 2 br.f. Mill Reef 141–Regal Twin 77 (Majestic Prince) (1983 6g² 6fg⁴ 7f **88** 8fg) Mar 24; $220,000Y; good-looking, well-made filly; half-sister to useful 1981 2-y-o sprinter Corley Moor (by Habitat); dam won over 8.2f; best effort when fourth, 4½ lengths behind Chapel Cottage, in Cherry Hinton Stakes at Newmarket in July; well beaten subsequently in maiden race (favourite) at Goodwood and May Hill Stakes (blinkered) at Doncaster; should be well suited by 7f and 1m; disappointing. *I. Balding.*

REFLECTION 2 b.f. Mill Reef 141–Joking Apart 120 (Jimmy Reppin 131) (1983 **111** 5v² 5d 5f* 6f³ 5f 7h³ 7f* 7fg*) Mar 28; well-made, good sort; good walker and mover; half-sister to useful 1982 staying 2-y-o St Boniface (by Halo) and Galtres Stakes winners Sans Blague (by The Minstrel) and Deadly Serious (by Queen's Hussar); dam very smart at up to 1m; developed into a useful filly once given opportunity to bring her stamina into play, and on final appearance picked up valuable John Sutcliffe Trophy Nursery at Lingfield in October, beating Passing Affair 2½ lengths; successful previously in maiden race at Pontefract and minor event at Chepstow; hopelessly outpaced in 5f nursery at Goodwood on fifth outing; suited by 7f and will stay 1m; acts well on firm ground. *I. Balding.*

REFUELED 2 b.g. Reform 132–Fleeting Image 90 (Dancer's Image) (1983 5fg* **94** 6f² 6f³ 6f⁴ 5f³ 6d* 6s² 7fg³ 7f³) Feb 12; 7,400Y; neat, robust gelding; has a roundish action; half-brother to 3-y-o La Rosiaz (by Riboboy) and a minor winner; dam won 3 times at around 7f; won maiden race at Windsor in July and minor event at Catterick in October; stays 7f; appears to act on any going; blinkered fifth outing; consistent. *W. O'Gorman.*

REGAL BLISS (USA) 3 ch.f. Blood Royal 129–Bishop's Lady (High Echelon) **52** (1982 NR 1983 11fg 13fg 15f 12f 12fg⁴ 13.8f 12fg 13.8g 12g 18g³ 12.2d 12g²) $9,000Y, resold $11,000Y; workmanlike filly; second foal; dam never ran; slow plater; sometimes blinkered. *S. Norton.*

REGAL EXPRESS 3 gr.c. Royal and Regal–El-Al 104 (Palestine 133) (1982 NR **74 d** 1983 7d² 8d² 8.5v 8fg 7f 10f) IR 7,200F, IR 19,000Y; angular, fair sort; good walker; half-brother to 2 winners in Ireland by Supreme Sovereign; dam won at up to 7f and is sister to dam of Bay Express; ran best races when second in newcomers race at Doncaster and maiden event at Pontefract in spring, on both occasions being run out of it in closing stages; stays 1m; pulls hard and isn't the easiest of rides; sold to H. Wharton 6,200 gns Newmarket September Sales. *P. Kelleway.*

REGAL FAVOUR 3 b.f. Royal and Regal–Tiltress (Tiepolo II 121) (1982 NR — 1983 12f 11.5s) first foal; dam Irish middle-distance winner; behind in maiden race at Brighton and seller at Yarmouth. *A. Bailey.*

REGAL GIFT 3 ch.f. Royal Smoke 113–Friendly Gift (Be Friendly 130) (1982 5g — 5d 1983 5f 5f 6fg 5fg 5h 6fg³ 6fg) plater; third at Windsor in September, only form; blinkered final outing. *R. Thompson.*

REGAL MAY 3 b.f. Royal and Regal–Park Paddocks 92 (Hopeful Venture 125) — (1982 5fg 6f 7g 7fg 1983 7fg 8g) neat, lightly-made filly; poor mover; behind in maiden races and sellers; sold 600 gns Ascot October Sales. *P. Rohan.*

REGAL STEEL 5 ch.h. Welsh Pageant 132–All Souls 96 (Saint Crespin III 132) 87 (1982 12g⁴ 12f² 12fg² 12fg³ 12fg³ 12fg 12g⁴ 12fg³ 10.6g⁴ 12g 12fg⁴ 12fg⁴ 13d² 12s⁴ 14s⁴ 12g⁴ 14s⁴ 12s 1983 12g* 13d⁴ 12g² 12s* 12.3v* 12d³ 12f 12g* 12f² 12fg³ 12f² 12g 14g 14.6fg³ 13.3g 12fg 14g³ 12fg) compact horse; hasn't always been genuine or reliable but did well at 5 yrs, winning race at Cagnes-sur-Mer and handicaps at Doncaster, Newcastle and Haydock; picked up a valuable prize when holding off Voracity by ½ length in Old Newton Cup on last-named in July; stays 1¾m; acts on any going; usually comes from behind and is suited by a strongly-run race; tough. *R. Hollinshead.*

REGAL SYMPHONY 3 b. or br.c. Sovereign Bill 105–Pipers Tune (Jock Scot — 121) (1982 NR 1983 11.7f 12g) sixth known foal; dam never ran; tailed off in minor event and apprentice race at Chepstow. *A. Andrews.*

REGENCY BRIGHTON 5 ch.m. Royal Palace 131–Gay City 99 (Forlorn River — 124) (1982 NR 1983 12g) plain mare; behind in varied company; has twice dwelt. *M. Tate.*

REGENT LEISURE 4 b.g. Undulate–Happy Families 64 (Swaps) (1982 8fg — 10f³ 8fg 11.7fg 1983 10v 12d 12s 10s 11.5fg⁴ 12fg) well-made gelding; should stay 1½m; possibly needs a sound surface; blinkered final start. *R. Simpson.*

REGGAE 3 b.c. Gay Fandango 132–Some Dame 72 (Will Somers 114§) (1982 5fg 113 5f⁴ 5fg³ 5s² 5s³ 1983 5v³ 5.8v⁴ 5fg² 5f² 5.8f* 5f* 5f* 5f 5fg* 5f 5fg² 6fg) strong, lengthy colt; poor mover; improved dramatically in summer and was winning fourth handicap in little more than a month when beating Durandal by a short head in £6,800 Coral Bookmakers Handicap at Haydock in August; had earlier won at Bath, Windsor and Newmarket, on first 2 courses being ridden by 7-lb claimer; had stiff tasks in his later races but ran well twice, particularly when 2 lengths second to Soba in Scarbrough Stakes at Doncaster in September; bred to stay beyond 6f but is clearly a sprinter; acts on any going; genuine; sold to race in Australia. *R. Hannon.*

REGGAE DANCER 2 ch.f. Gay Fandango 132–Jazz Tune (Lyphard 132) (1983 67 6f 6fg 6d) Mar 10; workmanlike filly; good mover; first foal; dam never ran; plating-class maiden; best form on final outing; will be suited by further. *B. Hills.*

REHAM 3 b.f. Mill Reef 141–Loose Cover 106 (Venture VII 129) (1982 NR 1983 67 8f 8f 10f 10d³ 10.6g³ 12g²) strong, good-topped filly; half-sister to several winners, including Smoggy (by Run The Gantlet), a smart winner at up to 9f in France and USA, and Ribblesdale Stakes winner Dish Dash (by Bustino); dam miler; placed in maiden and minor events at Yarmouth, Haydock and Redcar, best efforts; stays 1½m. *H. T. Jones.*

REHOBOAM 5 b.g. Mummy's Pet 125–La Mirabelle 92 (Princely Gift 137) (1982 §§ 10g 6.5v 7.5d 6s 7fg 7f 6f 6fg 5f⁴ 6g 6fg⁴ 1983 8.3fg 12g 8d) lengthy, narrow gelding; has been hobdayed; unreliable plater; has been tried in blinkers. *R. Blakeney.*

REINE CAROLINE (FR) 2 ch.f. Pharly 130–Royal Model (Bold Lad, Ire 133) 117 (1983 5.5fg* 5f* 5fg² 6.5g²) second foal; half-sister to French 3-y-o 1¼m winner Royal Flush (by Tudor Music); dam lightly-raced sister to high-class 5f to 1m winner Daring Display; won 59,000-franc event at Evry in July by 5 lengths and Prix de la Vallee d'Auge at Deauville the following month; second subsequently in pattern races, namely Prix d'Arenberg (beaten 4 lengths by Sicyos) at Longchamp in September and Prix Eclipse (beaten a length by Diamada) at Saint-Cloud in October; should stay 1m. *J. C. Cunnington, France.*

REINE DE GRACE (USA) 2 b. or br.f. L'Enjoleur–Dame de Grace (Armistice 97 p 131) (1983 7g⁴ 8.5g²) Apr 16; $210,000Y; half-sister to several winners, notably 1976 French 2,000 Guineas winner Red Lord (by Red God); dam, winner over 1½m in France, is sister to French Oaks fourth Aglae (the dam of French Derby winner Val de l'Orne) and half-sister to Arc de Triomphe winner Soltikoff; finished strongly when nose second to Reve de Reine in minor event at Maisons-Laffitte in October; sure to win good races over middle distances. *J. Cunnington, jnr, France.*

REINE D'EGYPTE (USA) 2 b.f. Val de l'Orne 130–Reine de Saba 125 107 p (Lyphard 132) (1983 8g 8fg²) Feb 8; first foal; dam won Prix Saint-Alary and Prix de Diane; kept on well when ½-length second to Cedilla in maiden event at

Longchamp in October; certain to leave this form well behind over middle distances. *A. Head, France.*

REINE MATHILDE (USA) 2 b. or br.f. Vaguely Noble 140–Gay Matelda (Sir Gaylord) (1983 8g*) Mar 8; $525,000F; half-sister to several winners, notably smart sprinter Shelter Half (by Tentam); dam, out of half-sister to Tudor Melody, was high-class winner at up to 1¼m; led 1f out and held on well to win newcomers event at Saint-Cloud in October by a nose from Normia; very promising and will do well over middle distances. *Mme C. Head, France.*   **104 p**

REJUVENATOR 7 bl. or br.g. Reliance II 137–Juvenescence 87 (Golden Horus 123) (1982 15.8g 15f³ 20.4g* 19f⁴ 1983 15.8d²) strong gelding; needs a thorough test of stamina; has worn blinkers. *T. Barron.*   **46**

REKAL 5 gr.h. Busted 134–Idover 95 (Fortino II 120) (1982 8g 10f* 10.4g⁴ 10fg² 8f* 8g⁴ 8d 8f* 8fg 8f 8fg 10.2g⁴ 10d 1983 10v 10fg⁴ 10.2f³ 10h² 10f² 10f² 11.7fg 12f 10.2fg 10g* 10fg⁴ 10.2fg) quite well-made horse; narrowly won handicap at Goodwood in September; best at up to 1¼m; well suited by top-of-the-ground; not an easy ride and is suited by waiting tactics; sold to NBA 7,200 gns Newmarket Autumn Sales. *C. Brittain.*   **67**

REKINDLE 2 b. or br.f. Relkino 131–Land of Fire 99 (Buisson Ardent 129) (1983 6h 8d 9g) Feb 12; 1,700Y; good-topped filly; half-sister to 3 winners, including useful 1½m to 2m winner No Bombs (by St Paddy); dam genuine performer at up to 1m; plating-class maiden; should stay 1¼m; acts on a soft surface. *M. Lambert.*   **70**

RELATIVE EASE 12 ch.g. Great Nephew 126–Glider 83 (Buisson Ardent 129) (1982 6g³ 5d 6f⁴ 5f⁴ 5f 5fg 5g 5g 5.6f³ 5f 5g* 5fg 5d 5d 5d 1983 6f 5fg⁴ 5fg 5f² 5fg* 5f² 5f³ 5f 5fg 5g 5d) sprint handicapper; sometimes runs in sellers; won handicap at Ripon in July; best at 5f nowadays; acts on any going but is particularly well suited by top-of-the-ground; has worn blinkers; splendid mount for an inexperienced rider; has worn a tongue strap; best on an easy course; inconsistent. *D. Chapman.*   **51**

RELATIVELY SHARP 3 br.f. Sharpen Up 127–Alpine Niece 87 (Great Nephew 126) (1982 NR 1983 7fg 6fg 5f³ 5f* 5f² 5d² 5d 5fg) 50,000F, 22,000 2-y-o; second living foal; dam placed at up to 1½m; won maiden race at Warwick in August; close second in minor event at Redcar and handicap at York (to Rambling River) afterwards; best form at 5f; yet to race on really soft ground, but acts on any other. *P. Calver.*   **70**

RELATIVELY SMART 2 ch.f. Great Nephew 126–Ragirl (Ragusa 137) (1983 7fg) May 1; angular filly; half-sister to Cesarewitch winner Sir Michael (by Manacle) and very speedy 1974 2-y-o Fats Waller (by Sing Sing); dam never ran; 7¼ lengths sixth of 22 to Travel Away in maiden race at Newmarket in October; will be suited by 1m+; sure to improve. *M. Stoute.*   **76 p**

RELDA 3 b. or br.f. Relko 136–Rhodie (Rasper) (1982 6f² 7f 1983 12d 8f 9.4f² 9f 10f³ 10.2fg 12s 12g) tall, leggy filly; rather a disappointing maiden; should stay 1½m; trained by B. Hobbs until after third start. *R. Baker.*   **62**

RELIABLE VYNZ 3 b.c. Reliance II 137–Miss Bluetran (Levmoss 133) (1982 8s 9s 1983 11v 12s 12v 9g 7d 9f 8fg) quite a useful-looking colt; raced with dam incorrectly shown as Mazurka (by Hotfoot); first foal; dam poor plater; behind in varied company, including selling; blinkered final outing. *W. H. H. Williams.*   **–**

RELUCTANT HERO 4 br.g. Home Guard 129–Mia Cosa 78 (Ragusa 137) (1982 10f 8f 6f 7g 6g* 7fg⁴ 6fg 6g² 6g 1983 11.7d 7s) leggy, quite useful-looking gelding; plater; should stay 1m; wears blinkers. *A. Barrow.*   **–**

RELY ON GUY 3 b.f. Reliance II 137–Persian Lamb 108 (Rustam 127) (1982 NR 1983 8s 9s 10.5s 7d⁴ 7f* 7fg² 7f² 8g 7fg² 7g 7fg³ 7g²) big, rangy filly; half-sister to 6 winners, including prolific winning sprinter Swakara (by Porto Bello); dam useful at 2 yrs; made virtually all when winning handicaps at Doncaster in June and July, but was relegated to second after beating Vatican Way by short head in latter on seventh outing (tended to hang away from rails); showed up well most subsequent starts, usually being run out of it in closing stages; best at up to 7f; acts well on firm going, but has also run creditably on a soft surface; ridden by apprentice W. Ryan nowadays. *R. Hollinshead.*   **73**

REMAINDER GIRL 2 ch.f. Remainder Man 126§–Forlorn Leap (Forlorn River 124) (1983 8f) Feb 20; lengthy, angular filly; fourth foal; half-sister to sprint winners High Voltage (by Electrify) and Mindblowing (by Pongee); dam never ran; bandaged in front, well beaten in maiden race at Leicester in November. *M. Tompkins.*   **–**

REMAINDER LADY 2 b.f. Connaught 130–Solo Reign 84 (Space King 115) —
(1983 5.3fg) Mar 22; 6,200F, 2,100Y; first produce; dam, winner 9 times from 7f to
1½m, is half-sister to 2000 Guineas second and Derby third Remainder Man (by
Connaught); remote eighth of 13 in minor event at Brighton in September; likely to
need 1m+. *C. Horgan.*

REMAINDER LINE 3 b.c. High Line 125–Farida Jinks 106 (Tudor Jinks 121) —
(1982 6fg 5s 1983 8d 11.7s 12fg 9fg 7fg) fair sort; behind in varied company,
including selling; trained by P. Mitchell until after second start. *T. Kersey.*

REMEMBERING (USA) 3 b. or br.f. L'Enjoleur–Bold Memory (Disciplinarian) **100**
(1982 NR 1983 8f² 8f* 9f* 8f² 7f³ 8s⁴ 8fg 8fg²) $45,000Y; big, deep-girthed filly;
has a round action; half-sister to winners by Diplomat Way and Flush; dam,
stakes-placed sprint winner, was very useful at 2 yrs; successful in minor event at
Newmarket in July and modest race at Redcar in August, beating Mariakova in
great style by 5 lengths in former; improved afterwards and was in frame in
Atalanta Stakes at Sandown, Strensall Stakes at York (2 lengths third to Silverdip),
Sceptre Stakes at Doncaster (2 lengths fourth of 6 behind Royal Heroine) and
Marlborough House Stakes at Ascot; stayed 9f; acted on any going; stud in USA.
L. Cumani.

REMEMBRANCE 2 b.c. Martinmas 128–Prime Thought 69 (Primera 131) (1983 **74** +
6g 6fg 6fg) Mar 4; close-coupled, rather sparely-made colt; half-brother to useful
sprinter Chantry Bridge (by Porto Bello) and a bumpers winner; dam from good
family; had 3 races at Doncaster in the autumn, showing definite promise on 2
occasions; almost certainly better than we are able to rate him, and looks sure to
win races. *J. W. Watts.*

REMORSELESS (USA) 3 b.c. Accipiter–Joyeux Noel (Happy New Year) (1982 —
7g 7g³ 1983 10g) quite attractive, long-striding colt; showed promise as a 2-y-o;
not disgraced only outing of 1983 (October); may stay further than 1¼m. *J.
Ciechanowski.*

RENDSLEY BELLE 2 br.f. Kala Shikari 125–Ma Belle Amie (Never Say Die —
137) (1983 6fg) Mar 15; third foal; half-sister to 7f and 1m winner Lavender Gray
(by Bay Express); dam well beaten in maiden and minor events; behind in
20-runner maiden race at Lingfield in July. *N. Gaselee.*

RENEE BETTS 2 gr.f. Town Crier 119–Belle Berners 65 (Sharp Edge 123) **51**
(1983 7f 7.2fg 6g) Mar 19; 1,050Y; sparely-made filly; second foal; half-sister to
3-y-o Debayo (by Music Boy); dam poor maiden; poor maiden; stays 7f. *M.
Hinchliffe.*

RENO'S DREAM 2 ch.f. Rupert Bear 105–Peg Top 93 (Star Moss 122) (1983 5s **42**
7f 7h³ 8d 10d) Feb 9; lengthy, fair sort; half-sister to 1979 2-y-o 7f winner Tops (by
Club House); dam won over 1½m and over fences; bad plater; stays 7f. *W. Turner.*

RENOVATE 6 ro.h. The Go-Between 129–Touch It Up (Trojan Monarch) (1982 **62**
6g 6d 6f 6fg³ 6d 6g 6f 10fg 1983 7f² 7f) sturdy horse; poor mover; best at up to 7f;
acts on any going; often blinkered; bought for 4,000 gns Doncaster March Sales.
G. Huffer.

REO RACINE 2 ch.f. Dom Racine 121–Harbrook (Le Haar 126) (1983 6.3f³ 7fg² **92**
8g³ 7g⁴) Apr 13; IR 30,000Y; half-sister to Irish 2,000 Guineas third Parliament
(by Lord Gayle) and very useful 1981 2-y-o sprint winner End of the Line (by
Saulingo); dam won over 7f at 2 yrs; ran well to finish in frame behind Executive
Pride in Ardenode Stud Stakes in August and Shindella in Silken Glider Stakes in
September (both at Leopardstown), and Ballet de France in CL Weld Park Stakes
at Phoenix Park in October, beaten under 3 lengths each time; will probably stay
1¼m; sure to win races. *J. Oxx, Ireland.*

REPITCH 3 br.g. On Your Mark 125–Rosapenna (King's Leap 111) (1982 5g 5d⁴ —
5g⁴ 6d 5.8g 5.3f 5fg² 6fg 6f² 6v 1983 5v 6g 6d) sturdy, compact gelding; plater at
2 yrs; lightly raced and no form in 1983; stays 6f; suited by a firm surface; trained
by R. Hannon first outing. *J. Fox.*

RESEEKER 3 ch.f. Status Seeker–Fine Mesh (Match III 135) (1982 5g 5g 1983 —
10fg) in rear in maiden and minor races. *M. McCourt.*

RESIDE 7 ch.g. Quayside 124–Resurgence (Runnymede 123) (1982 8f³ 8f² 9.4f* —
8fg 8f* 10.6g 9g² 8d 8g 8d 1983 9d 9g⁴ 12f 8f 7f 8.2f 8f 10g 8fg) strong gelding;
well beaten most starts in 1983; has won over 1½m but is best at 1m or 9f
nowadays; best served by a sound surface; has run respectably for an apprentice;
usually held up and often starts slowly. *E. Carter.*

RESISTER 3 br.f. Monsanto 121–Irresistable (Siliconn 121) (1982 5f 5d 7fg 6fg   **41**
7f³ 6g² 8.2fg 1983 7d 8d* 8s) leggy filly; plater; won at Edinburgh in April (no
bid); stays 1m; seems to act on any going. *J. Berry.*

RESPIGHI 4 b.c. Sun Prince 128–Rotisserie 106 (Tesco Boy 121) (1982 8s⁴ 8d³   –
8d 8g* 8g* 8g³ 9d 1983 9v 9d 8f 8g 8g 8s 7g) strong, compact ex-French colt;
closely inbred to Princely Gift; half-brother to 2 winners, including useful 1½m and
1¾m winner Rowlandson (by Blakeney); dam won Fred Darling Stakes; won
handicaps at Evry and Vichy at 3 yrs; well beaten most starts in 1983, including in
ladies race at Doncaster (led 4f) and Harroways Stakes at Goodwood in September
on last 2; stays 9f; acts on heavy going; wears blinkers; trained part of season by C.
Bartholomew; sold 2,500 gns Newmarket Autumn Sales. *M. Smyly.*

RESTLESS CAPTAIN 5 ch.g. Sandford Lad 133–Kirkwall 74 (Sheshoon 132)   –
(1982 6s² 6s 8f 7f 1983 11.7h) workmanlike gelding; poor performer nowadays;
has been beaten in a seller; has run respectably over 9f but is possibly better at
shorter distances; probably needs some give in the ground; blinkered once. *R.
Hodges.*

RETSEL 4 ch.c. Scottish Rifle 127–Once For All (Quorum 126) (1982 11fg 8f 8g*   –
8fg 10f 8s 10v 1983 10s 16g) fair sort; poor handicapper; should stay middle
distances; suited by some give in the ground; blinkered once. *S. Woodman.*

RETURN MATCH 3 br.c. Sweet Revenge 129–Primrose 86 (Primera 131) (1982   **61**
6fg 1983 6s² 6s⁴ 6s 7d⁴ 7h 8h 6fg² 6f² 6d³ 6g 6g) dipped-backed colt; good
walker; in frame in varied races, including sellers; probably stays 7f; has run well
in blinkers; has occasionally looked ungenuine; sold out of J. W. Watts's stable
3,100 gns Ascot 2nd June Sales after fourth outing and resold 700 gns same venue
in December. *M. Pipe.*

RETURN-TO-JALNA 2 b.f. Abwah 118–Hareem Lady 77 (Firestreak 125)   **61**
(1983 5g 5fg 5s 5f 6h 6f 8f 6fg 5g³) Mar 18; 300Y; compact filly; poor walker;
second foal; dam plating-class maiden; placed in seller at Catterick in October;
evidently best at 5f. *E. Alston.*

RETURN TO ME 4 b.g. Music Boy 124–Perkasa 74 (Huntercombe 133) (1982   **71**
5fg* 5fg* 5fg 5g 6s 5d 5s 1983 6s² 6v 6g 5g 6f 6fg² 5f 6g 8fg 6fg⁴) strong, stocky
gelding; sprint handicapper; gambled on when second to Azaam at Newmarket in
August on sixth start; stays 6f; seems to act on any going; has worn a tongue
strap. *M. McCourt.*

REUVAL 2 ch.f. Sharpen Up 127–Sleat 112 (Santa Claus 133) (1983 6f³ 6f² 6f²)   **84**
May 10; half-sister to 2 winners, including fairly useful stayer Sligo Bay (by
Sassafras); dam, half-sister to St Leger winner Athens Wood, won over 6f and
1¼m; close second in maiden races at Carlisle in July and Redcar in August; will be
suited by 7f+; capable of winning maiden event. *B. Hobbs.*

REVE DE REINE (USA) 2 b. or br.f. Lyphard 132–Riverqueen 128 (Luthier   **97 p**
126) (1983 8g 8.5g*) second foal; half-sister to very useful 3-y-o French 1m and
1¼m winner Riviere Doree (by Secretariat); dam won French 1,000 Guineas and
Grand Prix de Saint-Cloud; all out to hold Reine de Grace by a nose in minor event
at Maisons-Laffitte in October; the type to make a much better filly over longer
distances. *Mme C. Head, France.*

REVELSTOKE 3 ch.f. North Stoke 130–Moomba 90 (Song 132) (1982 NR   –
1983 7d 8g 9v 10fg 8.3f 8f 8d) IR 4,500Y; sparely-made filly; first living foal; dam
sprint maiden; little worthwhile form, including in sellers; trained most of season
by R. Williams. *H. Fleming.*

REVENGED 2 ch.g. Sweet Revenge 129–Harridan 92 (Fighting Charlie 127)   –
(1983 8f 7f 7.2g) Mar 9; IR 1,500Y; seventh reported foal; dam stayer; behind in
maiden races and a seller in the North. *D. Plant.*

REVENUE 2 b.c. Habitat 134–Arkadina 121 (Ribot 142) (1983 6d) May 27; IR   – p
240,000F, 250,000Y; strong, useful sort; half-brother to 3 winners, including 1½m
Blandford Stakes winner South Atlantic (by Mill Reef) and smart Irish middle-
distance winner Encyclopedia (by Reviewer); dam, placed in 3 classics, is sister to
high-class stayer Blood Royal and closely related to Gregorian; burly and green,
little show in 16-runner maiden race at Newbury in October; bound to do a good bit
better in due course. *J. Tree.*

REX LAKE (USA) 2 b.c. Marshua's Dancer–Rufarina (Bold Hour) (1983 5g*   **99**
6s² 5g² 6h²) Mar 13; $35,000Y; quite attractive colt; good walker and mover;
half-brother to a winner by Best Turn; dam, a sprinter, won a minor stakes race;
won maiden race at Newmarket in April; good second subsequently in minor
event (beaten short head) at Goodwood, Berkshire Stakes (slowly away) at

Newbury, and well-contested race won by Fawzi at Pontefract; better suited by 6f than 5f; withdrawn, not under orders, when blinkered at Windsor in July on intended fourth start; sent to USA. *H. Cecil.*

RHAKI 3 ch.f. Relkino 131–Lady Rhapsody 101 (Northern Dancer) (1982 7d 6fg 7.6v 1983 9v 12g 10.1f 8f) strong filly; good mover; disappointing maiden; should stay at least 1¼m; acts on a firm surface; blinkered last 2 outings. *R. Laing.* –

RHAPSODIEN 3 b.c. Habitat 134–Sweet Rhapsody (Sea-Bird II 145) (1982 6g* 8s 1983 8s² 8g⁴ 8g²) French colt; won newcomers race at Chantilly and finished close up on his only other start as a 2-y-o; only lightly raced again in 1983, finishing second in Prix Omnium at Saint-Cloud in March (beaten 2 lengths by Castle Guard) and 90,000 francs race at Saint-Cloud in October, and 3 lengths fourth of 8 to Pampabird in Prix du Rond-Point at Longchamp in between (first outing for 6 months); stays 1m; acts on good going. *F. Boutin, France.* 111

RHEFFANOSA (FR) 4 gr.f. Rheffic 129–Zeddenosa (Zeddaan 130) (1982 10s 1983 12v 12f 16g 12g) lengthy filly; poor maiden; has given trouble at start. *Miss A. Sinclair.* –

RHEIN COURT 3 gr. or ro.f. Rheingold 137–Country Court 81 (Meadow Court 129) (1982 NR 1983 11.7v 10s 10.1f 12fg 10.6g 10fg) IR 4,800F, IR 7,000Y; rangy filly; half-sister to 2 minor 2-y-o winners by Jukebox and to a winner in Italy; dam, daughter of 1000 Guineas winner Abermaid, won over 5f at 2 yrs; towards rear in maiden and minor races; blinkered last 2 starts. *D. H. Jones.* –

RHEINFORD 7 gr.g. Rheingold 137–Florrie Ford 79 (Kelly 122) (1982 12s 12g⁴ 16f² 17.1f⁴ 14f 16fg³ 17.1s⁴ 16.1s⁴ 1983 16.1v 12d) staying handicapper; acts on any going; blinkered twice. *J. Old.* –

RHEINHEART 3 b.g. Rheingold 137–Bradden 77 (King Emperor) (1982 6f 6d 7fg⁴ 6f⁴ 6d² 6fg 6fg 7s 1983 10s 7v 7fg 10.4fg 7.6g) big, rangy gelding; plating-class maiden; bred to stay 1¼m but tends to race too freely; sold 2,300 gns Newmarket September Sales. *P. Brookshaw.* –

RHEINIEKEN 6 b.g. Rheingold 137–Priddy Maid 111 (Acropolis 132) (1982 13.8f 1983 12.2s 12g) strong gelding; poor maiden on flat though has won over hurdles. *E. Weymes.* –

RHEIN LAD 3 br.g. Rheingold 137–Bold Coleen (Bold Lad, Ire 133) (1982 NR 1983 12g 12s) 2,000F; first foal; dam Irish 5f winner; behind in minor and maiden races in May. *G. Richards.* –

RHEIN SILVER 3 b.f. Lypheor 118–Athene 64 (Supreme Court 135) (1982 7g 1983 12.3f 16g 16g 14f) rather sparely-made filly; ran best races on first and last starts; stays 1¾m, but isn't sure to stay 2m. *B. Hanbury.* –

RHINESTONE COWBOY 4 br.c. On Your Mark 125–Jeannette (Whistler 129) (1982 6s 7fg 6fg 6f³ 5fg² 7f⁴ 7.6g 1983 16g 10f⁴ 8f) strong, rangy, good sort; stays 1¼m; acts well on firm ground. *A. Madwar.* –

RHODONNA 3 b.f. Rhodomantade 110–Susan 88 (Hard Tack 111§) (1982 6g 7fg 7f 6s 6s⁴ 6s 1983 8d³ 8.2v 8s* 8.3s² 8v² 7d²) small, lengthy filly; good walker; plater; sold out of R. Hannon's stable 1,900 gns after winning at Bath in April; ran creditably afterwards; stays 1m well; acts on heavy going; blinkered fifth outing at 2 yrs. *O. O'Neill.* 57

RHYTHMICAL 2 ch.f. Swing Easy 126–Wrong Direction 90 (Young Emperor 133) (1983 6f 6f 7f 8g 6g) Mar 21; 7,200Y; rangy, workmanlike filly; third foal; half-sister to quite useful 1978 2-y-o 6f winner Village Voice (by Town Crier); dam won at up to 1m; plating-class maiden; stays 7f; retained 3,000 gns Newmarket December Sales. *J. Bethell.* 69

RHYTHMIC PASTIMES 3 ch.c. Dance In Time–Pass The Hat 88 (High Hat 131) (1982 7f 1983 11v³ 12g* 12fg⁴ 11f* 12fg³ 12g² 15g⁴ 13fg) well-made, quite attractive colt; apprentice ridden when making all in minor event and handicap at Edinburgh; ran creditably most other starts; best form at up to 1½m; acts on any going; sold to J. Jenkins 15,000 gns Newmarket Autumn Sales. *R. Williams.* 83

RIABOUCHINSKA 2 b.f. Sandy Creek 123–Golden Hind 90 (Aureole 132) (1983 7.6d) Apr 18; IR 9,600F, 15,000Y; half-sister to several winners, including very useful miler Mahler (by Great Nephew), and to dam of smart Super Sunrise; dam, half-sister to several good winners, needed at least 7f at 2 yrs; behind in 20-runner maiden race at Lingfield in October; sold 6,200 gns Newmarket Autumn Sales. *C. Brittain.* –

RIBBLE ROUSER 10 ch.g. Marcus Brutus 108–Ribble Reed 75 (Bullrush 106) (1982 15.8g⁴ 15.8f* 16f² 16fg 15.8f 19f 15.8f⁴ 16g 1983 15.8d 16fg 15fg⁴ 15.8f⁴ 35

16f³ 19h³ 16s) staying handicapper; poor mover; acts on any going; sometimes wears blinkers; suitable mount for an apprentice; inconsistent. *W. C. Watts.*

RIBBLE STAR 2 b.f. Mummy's Pet 125–Ribble Reed 75 (Bullrush 106) (1983 5s 5f 6f 5h 6f) May 31; leggy filly; half-sister to 2 winners, including 7f to 2m winner Ribble Rouser (by Marcus Brutus); dam sprint plater; poor form in maiden and minor events; not seen out after August. *W. C. Watts.*   **50**

RIBBONS OF BLUE 3 b.f. Jimmy Reppin 131–Lady Gaylord (Double Jump 131) (1982 NR 1983 9d 11g³ 9.4d³ 10g 10s 9fg 10f) strong filly; half-sister to 3 winners, including fair middle-distance winner Sage King (by Shantung); dam unraced half-sister to smart colt Romper; third in maiden races at Ayr and Carlisle in first half of season; stays 11f. *J. W. Watts.*   **60**

RIBERETTO 5 b.h. Ribero 126–Love Resolved (Dan Cupid 132) (1982 NR 1983 13g 12g 14g 16fg 12d 12fg) big, rangy horse; good mover; useful performer at 3 yrs; ran best races at 5 yrs on last 2 starts in St Simon Stakes at Newbury and William Hill November Handicap at Doncaster; should stay 2m; sweated up badly third start; does best when ridden up with pace. *A. Hide.*   **–**

RIBMIS 5 b.m. Simbir 130–Miss Parsons (Welsh Abbot 131) (1982 8s 6g³ 8f 8fg 10f² 8.2fg³ 8fg² 10fg 11g 10f³ 10fg 10fg 8g 10g 10f 1983 8.2v 8s 8g) poor mover; plater; stays 1¼m; sold 800 gns Doncaster June Sales. *M. Lambert.*   **–**

RIBOBELLE 2 b.f. Riboboy 124–Belle Royale 89 (Right Royal V 135) (1983 5f 6h 6d 6fg 6fg) Mar 15; 1,200Y; compact, plain filly; third living foal; dam, winner at up to 1½m, is out of Irish 1000 Guineas winner Shandon Belle; well beaten in varied company, including claiming; bred to need much further. *Ronald Thompson.*   **–**

RIBOBURG 2 b.g. Riboboy 124–Isthatchew 68 (Burglar 128) (1983 8g 7.6fg³ 9s) Apr 2; first foal; dam best at 6f; quite a modest maiden; stays 1m. *J. Dunlop.*   **77**

RIBODEN 5 b.g. Ribero 126–True Dresden 58 (Vilmoray 126) (1982 8f 1983 8s 7f 8f 9fg 10.6fg) plain gelding; plater; probably stays 1¼m; has been tried in blinkers; trained part of season by G. Fletcher. *J. Spearing.*   **–**

RIBOT STAR 4 b.c. Star Appeal 133–Ribo Pride 77 (Ribero 126) (1982 12d 12s⁴ 12fg 17f 14f 1983 17.1g 16fg) neat colt; good walker; poor maiden; best run at 1½m on soft ground. *J. Fox.*   **–**

RIBU DANCER 4 bl. or gr.g. Lock and Load 72–Panabu (Panaslipper 130) (1982 NR 1983 8fg 12fg 16d) of little account. *J. Long.*   **–**

RICCA GIRL 2 b.f. Riboboy 124–Captive Flower 99 (Manacle 123) (1983 5v* 5g⁴ 6f 6f³ 6g² 6s 7fg) Mar 31; 6,800Y; workmanlike filly; half-sister to useful 1m to 1½m winner Tesoro Mio (by Cavo Doro); dam won twice over 5f at 2 yrs; won maiden race at Newcastle in May by 2 lengths from Park Springs; good second in 13-runner nursery at Hamilton in September; suited by 6f; possibly best with some give in the ground; sometimes sweats up. *J. Etherington.*   **88**

RICHARDS BAY 2 b.c. Record Run 127–Gowyn (Goldhill 125) (1983 5v³ 5s³ 5g 8g 8.2g 7g) May 19; 1,200Y; half-brother to middle-distance winner Sealed Knot (by Most Secret); bad maiden; form only at 5f; blinkered final appearance. *R. Allan.*   **43**

RICHARD'S JOY 2 ch.f. Record Run 127–King's Caress 65 (King's Coup 108) (1983 5.1f) Mar 18; half-sister to 3 winners, including 1¼m winner The Sampson Boys (by Most Secret); dam, a plater, won over 6f and 1m; tailed-off last of 10 in seller at Yarmouth in August. *H. Westbrook.*   **–**

RICHARD'S RETURN 2 b.g. Rapid River 127–Dapple (Jukebox 120) (1983 5v 5d 5f 5f 5g 6d 5g⁴) Apr 11; strong, workmanlike gelding; 6½ lengths fourth of 9 behind El Gazebo in minor event at Redcar in November, easily best effort; capable of winning sellers. *Hbt Jones.*   **68**

RICH BENEFIT 3 b.f. Star Appeal 133–Grand Velvet 83 (Grand Roi 118) (1982 7d* 8d 1983 10.2s) compact, quite attractive filly; good walker; won maiden race at Chester as a 2-y-o; had stiff task when well beaten only outing in 1983 (May); should stay 1¼m. *J. W. Watts.*   **–**

RICH BLUE 2 ch.g. Blue Cashmere 129–Amberetta 72 (Supreme Sovereign 119) (1983 6g 6f 5h) Apr 20; leggy gelding; second foal; half-brother to 5f winner Tower of Strength (by Tower Walk); dam won 6 times at up to 9f; behind in maiden races, once last; not seen out after July. *J. Winter.*   **–**

RICH LANDING 5 b.g. Communication 119–Cabarita 88 (First Landing) (1982 6g 1983 10f) unfurnished gelding; poor form, including in a seller. *R. Cambidge.*   **–**

RICH LASS 3 gr.f. Broxted 120–Rich Girl 103 (Charlottesville 135) (1982 NR 1983 8g 7.6g³ 8f 8g 8.2g) small filly; second foal; half-sister to fairly useful 1978 2-y-o 5f and 6f winner Twice Rich (by Targowice); dam won over 11f and is half-sister to smart Richboy; mainly poor form, although was third of 20 in maiden race at Chester in August; sold 5,000 gns Newmarket Autumn Sales. *M. Smyly.* —

RICH VIRGINIA 7 b.g. Tycoon II–Smokey Joe (My Smokey 125) (1982 8f 8g⁴ 7.6fg² 8fg⁴ 8.2g 6d 7fg 7f 1983 7s 6fg⁴ 5f 7.6fg 6f) compact, good-quartered gelding; poor handicapper; has been beaten in a seller; gives impression he'll stay beyond 1m; suitable mount for an inexperienced rider. *J. Tierney.* —

RICKI LEE 2 ch.f. Monsanto 121–Quick Half (Quorum 126 or Caliban 123) (1983 5g 5g 7.2s 5g) May 24; tall filly; third foal; dam won over hurdles; of little account. *D. McCain.* —

RIDALS CHOICE 2 b.f. Royben 125–Edlin (Monet 127) (1983 5f 6f² 6h 6fg) Apr 15; half-sister to 2 winning platers; dam of no account; plating-class maiden; not sure to stay beyond 6f. *G. Hunter.* 61

RIDE THE SKIES (USA) 2 ch.c. Crow 134–Apalachee Lass (Apalachee 137) (1983 7f⁴ 7f² 7g³ 8fg 8.2fg³) Mar 10; $55,000Y; big, strong colt; first foal; dam stakes-placed winner at up to 1m; fair maiden; good third in nursery at Nottingham in October on final appearance; will be suited by 1¼m+; acts on firm going; sure to win a race. *M. Albina.* 88

RIDGEFIELD 5 br.g. Firestreak 125–Chebs Lass 84 (Chebs Lad 120) (1982 10d³ 10s³ 8g 12fg 11.7fg* 10fg³ 12fg 11.7g 11.7g 10d 11f³ 10.6s³ 10.5s³ 11s 1983 10.2d³ 10v* 10.6v* 10.2v 12v 11.1v² 10s 10fg 12fg 11.7f* 12f 12g) tall gelding; won handicaps at Kempton (Rosebery Stakes easily from Hill's Pageant) and Haydock in April and Windsor in July; stays 1½m; acts on any going; sometimes blinkered and hasn't always been genuine or reliable. *D. Thom.* 77

RIDGE THE TIMES (USA) 2 ch.f. Riva Ridge–Oath of Allegiance (Olden Times) (1983 5v 5g 5fg² 6f 6f⁴ 6f 5fg³ 5fg* 5g³ 5d) Apr 14; $75,000Y; quite well-made filly; has a smooth action; third foal; half-sister to 3-y-o State Duty (by Stage Door Johnny) and a winner in USA by What Luck; dam unraced half-sister to very smart 1975 French staying 2-y-o French Friend; won nursery at Hamilton in September; best form at 5f but has run respectably over 6f; acts on firm going; sold 25,000 gns Newmarket December Sales. *F. J. Houghton.* 78

RIDGEWAY BAY 3 b.f. Jimmy Reppin 131–Grange Park 73 (Derring-Do 131) (1982 NR 1983 8d) sixth foal; dam poor maiden; pulled up after saddle slipped in minor event at Warwick in October (bandaged). *Miss A. King.* —

RIDGEWAY GIRL 3 ch.f. Mr Bigmore 123–Starfold (Ratification 129) (1982 7.6v 7d 1983 9d 10.1fg 10.1f⁴ 12d 10g³ 16d 11s⁴) heavy-bodied, sturdy filly; in frame in minor event and 2 sellers; should stay at least 1½m. *P. Burgoyne.* —

RIDGEWAY PATH 3 ch.f. Scottish Rifle 127–Skiboule (Boulou) (1982 NR 1983 11.7s 12v 10f 12f 12d³ 12g) rather a lightly-built filly; third foal in this country; half-sister to useful middle-distance fillies Rollrights and Rollfast (both by Ragstone); dam won in Belgium; quite moderate form in maiden races; stays 1½m; ran badly when blinkered final start; sold to NBA 2,700 gns Newmarket December Sales. *J. Dunlop.* —

RIDINGS SUCCESS 2 gr.c. Dragonara Palace 115–Magic Maiden 97 (Magic Red) (1983 7f 6s) Jan 18; 8,400Y, 9,000Y; rather leggy colt; half-brother to several winners, including fairly useful 2-y-o's Hey Presto, Petulengra and Sunny Smile (all by Mummy's Pet); dam 7f winner; behind in the autumn in maiden race at Redcar and seller at Haydock; sold 2,000 gns Doncaster November Sales. *D. Garraton.* —

RIEVAUX RAVER 2 br.f. Decoy Boy 129–Hethabella 62 (Hethersett 134) (1983 5s* 5d* 6f 5f² 6fg 5s 5d) Apr 16; 1,500Y; rather leggy, workmanlike filly; sister to 3-y-o Mayo Boy and half-sister to a minor winner and a winning hurdler; dam 1½m winner; successful early in season in auction race at Leicester and minor event at Edinburgh; off course 2 months after fourth outing and showed nothing on return in valuable seller (bandaged) and 2 nurseries; should stay 6f. *W. Wharton.* 71

RIFLE SHOT 4 bl.g. Scottish Rifle 127–West Shaw 101 (Grey Sovereign 128§) (1982 8f 10f 1983 12v) compact gelding; poor maiden. *A. Smith.* —

RIGHT BANK (FR) 3 b.f. Luthier 126–Ask Gloria (Sir Ribot) (1982 7.5s* 8s* 8v² 1983 8.5s* 8g* 11v* 10.5f⁴ 9.2d 10fg³ 12s 10s* 12d²) 160,000 francs Y (approx £15,000); second foal; half-sister to French 10.5f winner and winning 121 jumper Left Bank (by Cavan); dam won over 1m in France; won 4 races in Italy, small race and Premio Regina Elena (Italian 1000 Guineas) at Rome in April, Oaks d'Italia at Milan in May and Premio Lydia Tesio at Rome again in October; beat What Lake by 2½ lengths in Premio Regina Elena and held off fast-finishing High Hawk by ¾ length in Oaks d'Italia; also ran very well to be less than 2 lengths fourth of 17 behind Escaline in Prix de Diane Hermes at Chantilly, 4 lengths third of 13 to Sharaya in Prix de la Nonette at Deauville and 6 lengths second to Awaasif in Gran Premio del Jockey Club at Milan later; probably stays 1½m, but best at shorter distances; acts on any going; game and consistent; trained by A. Botti in Italy until after fourth start. *J. Cunnington, jnr, France.*

RIGHT REGENT 5 ch.h. Kambalda 108–Vetsera (Hopeful Venture 125) (1982   **85**
18f* 18.4fg 16f* 20fg 16g 1983 16s³ 17.1v² 17d* 16d* 20fg* 16f 18fg) small, stocky horse; staying handicapper; won at Wolverhampton, Kempton and Royal Ascot; got the better of Prince of Princes by a neck in Ascot Stakes on last-named; acts on any going; races with enthusiasm; goes well for S. Cauthen. *M. Pipe.*

RIGIDSKI 2 br.c. Bolkonski 134–Unyielding 89 (Never Bend) (1983 5.1g⁴ 6fg 5f³   **84**
6g³ 7fg) Apr 4; 42,000Y; quite attractive colt; keen walker and good mover; first foal; dam, daughter of Irish 1000 Guineas winner Lacquer and half-sister to Bright Finish and Shining Finish, ran only 3 times; in frame in maiden races and a well-contested nursery; headstrong, but ran well over 7f; acts on firm going. *J. Winter.*

RIG STEEL 3 ch.c. Welsh Pageant 132–Fir Tree 90 (Santa Claus 133) (1982 7g   **79**
8s 7s³ 1983 10d 10s 9.5s 12d 16v 14s² 17v² 14f⁴ 16f³ 16f 15s 16fg) strong colt; in frame in varied company before beating Sabatash by a head in slowly-run maiden race at Newcastle in June; stays well; acts on any going; possibly not the greatest of battlers. *R. Hollinshead.*

RIGTON CORNER 4 b.f. Sit In The Corner–Rigton Caprice 69 (Straight Deal)   **–**
(1982 NR 1983 12v 13.8g 12.2s) sturdy filly; sister to a winner abroad and half-sister to 2 winners; dam won over 1¼m and over hurdles; in rear in varied company and is probably of little account. *R. Whitaker.*

RIGTON SALLY 3 b.f. Joshua 129–Rigton Caprice 69 (Straight Deal) (1982 NR   **–**
1983 10.6s 10fg 12g) lengthy filly; half-sister to several winners, including fair Irish 1½m and 2m winner It's Me Again (by Goldhill); dam stayed well and won over hurdles; towards rear in maiden and minor races in autumn. *H. Wharton.*

RIHAB 2 b.c. Imperial Fling 116–Heaven Knows 113 (Yellow God 129) (1983 6f   **86**
7g³ 7g² 7g* 8fg 7fg) Mar 14; 23,000Y; strong, good sort; excellent mover; third foal; dam won Lingfield Oaks Trial but was best at up to 9f; blinkered first time, showed improved form in 12-runner nursery at Catterick in September, making most of running and winning unchallenged by 5 lengths; creditable sixth of 15 to Bastille after running freely at Doncaster 2 outings later; suited by 7f. *M. Stoute.*

RIKKI TAVI 3 b.c. Monsanto 121–Goosie-Gantlet 63 (Run The Gantlet) (1982 6f   **80**
7g⁴ 8g 8s 1983 11.7s* 12v³ 12v² 12d 12f* 13.1f² 12f² 13.1h³ 12f* 12f 12g³ 13fg² 12.2d) quite attractive colt; won maiden race at Bath in April, apprentice handicap at Doncaster in June and handicap at Folkestone (by 7 lengths) in August, but ran moderately from time to time too; stays 13f; acts on any going. *B. Hills.*

RILIN 2 ch.f. Ribston 104–Lindosa 104 (Aureole 132) (1983 5s 5f 6f) May 3; small   **–**
filly; half-sister to a winner in Belgium; dam, from good family, won over 1m; behind in maiden races, on final outing last of 10. *N. Chamberlain.*

RILK 2 ro.f. Ribston 104–Queen's Silk (Pongee 106) (1983 7f 7f 7f) Mar 1;   **–**
compact filly; half-sister to a winning hurdler; dam last only outing; behind in sellers; of no account. *N. Chamberlain.*

RIMAH 2 b.c. Nishapour 125–Lady Simone (Realm 129) (1983 5s² 6d³ 7f* 7f³)   **81**
Apr 14; IR 36,000Y; attractive colt; second foal; dam, Irish 7f and 1m winner, is half-sister to smart 2-y-o's Pushy, Krayyan and Precocious; made all in 10-runner minor event at Newcastle in June; not raced after July; will stay 1m; acts on any going; consistent. *H. T. Jones.*

RINGARINGOROSES 2 b.f. Dance In Time–Sombreuil 95 (Bold Lad, Ire 133)   **–**
(1983 6f 6f 6g) Apr 10; smallish, robust, good sort; second foal; dam best at 1m; in mid-division in maiden and minor events; should be suited by further. *J. Dunlop.*

RING BIDDER 5 b.g. Auction Ring 123–Miss Holborn (Pall Mall 132) (1982 8g   **70**
7.2s 8fg⁴ 10fg 8f 7fg* 7.2f* 7fg 8fg* 8d² 7f 8fg³ 8fg⁴ 8g 8g 8f 7.3g⁴ 8g 1983 8d 8d 7s 8s 7fg 8d² 7f 8.2fg 8fg³ 7f³ 8g 8g 8f 8fg 8.2fg) useful-looking gelding; suited by

a stiff 7f or 1m (doesn't stay 1¼m); ideally suited by top-of-the-ground; does best when held up; well beaten when blinkered once; inconsistent. *R. Hollinshead.*

RING OF GREATNESS 3 b.c. Great Nephew 126–Fairy Ring 91 (Quorum 126) **98** (1982 7f 8fg³ 8s* 10s⁴ 1983 8s 10g 12v 12d³ 11g³ 12f³ 14d 14fg³) compact, quite attractive colt; good walker and mover; third in handicaps at Epsom and Goodwood, in Grand Prix de Bruxelles at Boitsfort in between, and in March Stakes at Goodwood again; possibly stays 1¾m; acts on any going; sent to race in Spain. *J. Dunlop.*

RING TRAVELSCENE 3 b.f. Auction Ring 123–Miss Hart 75 (Track Spare — 125) (1982 NR 1983 7f 7fg 8f 6fg) 3,100F; well-made filly; half-sister to 2 winners by Gulf Pearl and to a winner in Holland; dam stayed 1m; no worthwhile form, including in a claiming race (last of 17). *P. Makin.*

RIO BRANCO 2 br.f. Free State 125–Sewing Maid 68 (So Blessed 130) (1983 5f **68** 5f 5f 5g 5g 5g* 5g³) Feb 15; 1,000F; small filly; fourth produce; half-sister to a winner in Malaya; dam ran only at 2 yrs; 33/1-winner of 14-runner seller at Catterick (no bid) in October; creditable third in nursery at Edinburgh later in month; will stay 6f; suited by some give in the ground; wears blinkers. *W. Stubbs.*

RIO DEVA 5 b.h. Spanish Gold 101–Deva Rose 80 (Chestergate 111) (1982 10fg* **65** 10f² 10.4g 12f 12f⁴ 12f 12fg 10fg* 10s² 10g² 12.2fg³ 10f² 10f² 12f 1983 12fg 12f² 10.6fg* 10f² 10fg⁴ 12fg 10.5d 10fg 10.2fg²) small horse; led on post to beat Darting Groom a short head in handicap at Haydock in August; stays 1½m; acts on any going; suitable mount for an apprentice; finds little off bridle and is suited by waiting tactics and a strongly-run race. *R. Hollinshead.*

RIO JEM 2 b. or br.c. Forlorn River 124–Honey Thief 77 (Burglar 128) (1983 6f) — Mar 1; 3,600Y; smallish colt; fourth foal; half-brother to very useful 1982 2-y-o sprinter Prince Reymo (by Jimmy Reppin); dam won over 5f at 2 yrs; blinkered, last of 18 in maiden auction event at Ripon in June; sold 580 gns Doncaster August Sales. *R. Armstrong.*

RIO RIVA 2 b.c. Wollow 132–Elton Abbess 86 (Tamerlane 128) (1983 5fg³ 5.8h* **108** 6f² 6f* 6g² 5g² 6g³ 5fg) May 16; 5,000Y; quite attractive colt; good mover; second foal; dam won 3 sprint races; won maiden race at Bath in July and £3,100 event (on disqualification of short-head winner Keep Tapping) at Salisbury in August; ran well in varied company before, between and afterwards, on final outing finishing close-up fifth to Petorius (ridden by apprentice unable to claim) in Cornwallis Stakes at Ascot in October; stays 6f well; yet to race on a soft surface; usually blinkered; not an easy ride. *R. Laing.*

RISE AT DAWN 2 b.f. Hittite Glory 125–Beaute Royale (Duc de Gueldre 129) — (1983 5s 5v 6fg 5.1f 6f) Feb 3; 540F; small, dipped-backed filly; half-sister to 2 winners in France; bad plater; blinkered final outing; sold 390 gns Ascot July Sales. *G. Blum.*

RISING FAST 6 b.g. High Line 125–Sunny Sovereign 85 (Lucky Sovereign) — (1982 16g 12.2s 12d 1983 20fg) lengthy, good sort; staying handicapper; probably acts on any going; used to wear blinkers; has sweated up; sold 420 gns Doncaster November Sales. *M. Chapman.*

RISK ALL 2 b.f. Run The Gantlet–Pencuik Jewel (Petingo 135) (1983 7f 7g³ **84 p** 7.6d*) Mar 18; big, lengthy, good-topped filly; second foal; half-sister to a winner in Italy by Scottish Rifle; dam lightly-raced half-sister to Ragstone and Castle Keep; won 20-runner maiden race at Lingfield in October; will be suited by 1¼m+; promises to make useful 3-y-o. *J. Dunlop.*

RISKY MAC 2 b.c. Forlorn River 124–Sky Lustre 101 (Skymaster 126) (1983 7f — 7f 6fg) May 1; lengthy, lightly-made colt; half-brother to several winners, including useful sprinter Moneymaster (by Hook Money); dam useful over 5f at 2 yrs; poor form in maiden and minor events; not seen out after August. *C. Brittain.*

RITARIUS 4 ch.g. Wollow 132–Mellifont (Honey Money 124) (1982 5fg 7f³ 7g 7fg **60** 7d 1983 8f* 7g 10fg³ 10fg* 12fg 10g) tall, leggy gelding; plater; attracted no bid after winning at Yarmouth in August and Lingfield in October; stays 1¼m; acts on firm going; ran poorly when blinkered once; none too consistent. *C. James.*

RITSON 4 ch.g. Record Token 128–Florabette (Floribunda 136) (1982 8f 8d 7g — 1983 8v) smallish, workmanlike gelding; poor plater. *W. Storey.*

RITSURIN 2 ch.f. Mount Hagen 127–Ryoanji 100 (Lyphard 132) (1983 6f* 6f 7g **79** 7fg) May 15; 7,400Y; rather sparely-made, lengthy filly; third foal; half-sister to 3-y-o Miss Annie (by Scottish Rifle), a winner at up to 1¾m; dam ran only at 2 yrs when twice a winner over 7f; won 19-runner maiden race at Folkestone in June by a head from Mr Rochester; showed little subsequently in St Catherine's Stakes at Newbury and 2 nurseries; should be suited by 7f+. *R. Laing.*

RITZY GIRL 2 b.f. Relkino 131–Alpine Niece 87 (Great Nephew 126) (1983 8.2s) — Mar 8; 15,000F, 12,500Y; quite a useful-looking filly; third living foal; half-sister to 3-y-o 5f winner Relatively Sharp (by Sharpen Up); dam, sister to smart 1973 2-y-o Alpine Nephew, placed at up to 1½m; tailed-off last of 6 in maiden race at Haydock in October. *W. Wharton.*

RIVA BE GOOD (USA) 6 ch.g. Riva Ridge–Best Go (Mongo) (1982 NR 1983 — 12g) leggy, narrow gelding; has shown some ability in varied company, including selling; stays well; ran moderately in blinkers once. *O. O'Neill.*

RIVELLINO 4 b.c. Rheingold 137–Nothing On (St Chad 120) (1982 8s 10s 10g* 90 12g² 11g* 11f⁴ 12s 14.6f 1983 10s 20f 10fg 12g 10g³) IR 13,500Y; leggy colt; second foal; brother to fairly useful 1½m winner Amal Naji; dam unraced half-sister to 1,000 Guineas winner Nocturnal Spree; useful performer at 3 yrs; third to Sharp End in race at Baden-Baden in September; well beaten earlier in Rogers Gold Cup Ballymoss Stakes at the Curragh, Gold Cup at Royal Ascot (tailed off behind Little Wolf), Hessen-Pokal at Frankfurt (reportedly swallowed tongue) and Grosser Preis von Berlin at Dusseldorf; should stay beyond 1½m; trained by J. Oxx in Ireland first 3 starts. *H. Jentzsch, Germany.*

RIVENSKY 3 ch.c. Maystreak 118–Come North 72 (Track Spare 125) (1982 6d 80 1983 7d 8g 8s² 10g⁴ 8f 14.8fg⁴ 14.6s 10fg) shallow-girthed colt; quite a moderate maiden; was sometimes raced completely out of his depth; wasn't sure to have stayed 1¾m; destroyed after injuring a fetlock at Leicester in October. *H. Westbrook.*

RIVER CLEY 3 ch.f. Riverman 131–Cley 85 (Exbury 138) (1982 NR 1983 10g² 78 10fg) quite an attractive, lightly-made filly; half-sister to 3 winners, including fair middle-distance winner Bodham (by Bustino); dam, 1½m winner, is half-sister to Blakeney and Morston; 2 lengths second to Flout in maiden race at Sandown in May, easily better effort; dead. *J. Dunlop.*

RIVERHILL BOY 5 b.g. Manacle 123–My Grace (Sahib 114) (1982 8d 1983 8v — 6v 8s 8g 10fg) plater; stays 1m; has worn blinkers. *C. Wildman.*

RIVERJOY 2 b. or br.c. Riverman 131–Joy Land (Bold Ruler) (1983 8fg*) 99 p Mar 26; \$155,000Y; half-brother to several winners, including 6f to 1¼m winner Jin Jang (by Val de Loir) and smart French 9f winner Jalapa (by Luthier); dam won over 6f at 3 yrs; comfortable winner of newcomers event at Longchamp in October by a length from Double Sweep; will probably stay 1¼m; promising. *F. Boutin, France.*

RIVER MADAM 2 b.f. Dawn Review 105–Bally-Do (Ballymoss 136) (1983 5f 5f — 7h) Mar 10; robust filly; no form, including in a seller; dead. *M. Lambert.*

RIVER MAIDEN (FR) 3 b.f. Riverman 131–Naughty Marcia 97 (Connaught 86 130) (1982 7d 7f⁴ 7f² 7d 7d² 7s 1983 6v 6s⁴ 6f² 6f² 6fg 7fg² 7s* 7g 7g*) small, well-made, very attractive filly; has a sharp action; took a long time to get off mark, but narrowly won weakly-contested minor event and handicap at Catterick towards end of season; evidently thought best at up to 7f, but is bred to stay further; acts on any going. *J. Dunlop.*

RIVER OF KINGS 3 b.c. Sassafras 135–Miss Bangkok (Sovereign Path 125) 87 (1982 8g 8s² 1983 10v³ 10s² 10.5f 10g³ 10f* 10f* 11s² 12d) quite an attractive colt; good walker but poor mover; enterprisingly ridden when winning maiden and minor events at Ripon in August; had stiffish task when creditable second to Uplands Park in £7,500 handicap at Ayr the following month; stays 11f; acts on any going; ran poorly third start; sold to NBA 12,000 gns Newmarket December Sales. *G. Wragg.*

RIVER SCAPE (USA) 2 br.c. Riverman 131–His Squaw (Tom Rolfe) (1983 7f³ 93 7fg⁴ 7f 7g* 7fg² 8d) Feb 28; \$180,000Y; rather lightly-made, quite attractive colt; has a round action; first foal; dam, winner of 4 sprint races, is half-sister to smart American middle-distance performer Landscaper; blinkered first time, improved considerably to win 19-runner nursery at Leicester in September by 3 lengths from Monkey Tricks; beaten a head by Muckle Roe in minor event at Brighton later in the month; will be suited by 1m (slowly away when tried at trip); acts on a firm surface; sold 32,000 gns Newmarket Autumn Sales and is to be trained in Norway by T. Dahl. *J. Dunlop.*

RIVERS EDGE 5 b.g. Sharpen Up 127–Ebb and Flo 82 (Forlorn River 124) (1982 62 8f 7f 8.2g² 7f⁴ 7f* 7f 8.2s* 8s³ 8.2s² 8.2s² 1983 10.2fg 8d 8.2s⁴ 7g⁴) workmanlike gelding; stays 1m well; acts on any going; has worn a muzzle; has been tried in blinkers; usually apprentice ridden; has given trouble at stalls. *D. Smith.*

RIVERSIDE ARTIST 3 b.c. Ashmore 125–Sea Music 108 (Atan) (1982 5d 6g*   **93** 6f³ 7fg² 7.3g⁴ 7d 1983 7s⁴ 7g³ 8g⁴ 8f³ 8f² 8f⁴ 9g⁴) good-bodied colt; in frame all starts, running particularly well when third of 27 behind Teleprompter in Britannia Stakes at Royal Ascot in June and fourth of 18 to Magnetic Field in quite valuable handicap at Goodwood on fourth and sixth starts; stays 9f; probably acts on any going but goes well on firm; sweated up final start, but ran creditably; genuine and consistent; sent to USA. *N. Vigors.*

RIVERS LAD 5 ch.g. Rarity 129–Takette (Takawalk II 125) (1982 NR 1983 10s³   **49** 12g 12f) plating-class maiden; stays 1½m; has run respectably for an apprentice. *G. Balding.*

RI-WINE 4 b. or br.f. Free State 125–My Cousins 54 (My Swallow 134) (1982 6f   **§§** 8fg³ 7fg 9f 8d³ 8fg 7g 1983 8s 10h 10fg) small, close-coupled filly; plater; stays 1m; seems to act on any going; virtually refused to race second outing; sold out of P. Feilden's stable 700 gns Newmarket July Sales after first start. *T. Kersey.*

RIXIE 2 ch.c. Dominion 123–Miss Lollypop (St Paddy 133) (1983 7d³ 7f) May 22;   **82** 8,200F, 10,000Y (privately); half-brother to 3 winners, including stayer Morlolly (by Morston); dam unraced half-sister to some useful animals; beaten 3 lengths in maiden races at Yarmouth and Redcar in September; should stay 1m. *M. Ryan.*

RIX WOODCOCK 2 br.g. Lord Gayle 124–Silk Lady 97 (Tribal Chief 125) (1983   **82** 5v* 5s³ 5g 8fg 7fg) Apr 4; 16,000Y; small, rather lightly-made gelding; first foal; dam won three 5f races at 2 yrs; won 3-runner minor event at Folkestone in May; off course for nearly 3 months after third outing, and showed little in nurseries on return; not sure to stay 1m; best form on soft ground; gelded after final appearance. *P. Kelleway.*

RIZLA BLUE 2 b.f. Persian Bold 123–Tippity Top 56 (High Top 131) (1983 5g²   **83** 5s* 5s² 5f⁴ 5f 5fg 5g 5fg) Mar 8; 6,200Y; rather lightly-made, useful sort; second foal; dam won 5f seller at 2 yrs; won 10-runner minor event at Newmarket in May by ½ length from Rocket Alert; ran well in autumn nurseries on same course on sixth and eighth outings; evidently considered 5f performer; probably acts on any going; consistent; sold 10,500 gns Newmarket December Sales. *F. Durr.*

ROAD TO THE TOP 3 b.f. Shirley Heights 130–Silken Way 103 (Shantung 132)   **84** (1982 6fg 1983 12s 10.2h³ 12f³ 13.1fg² 10fg* 10fg*) tall, lengthy filly; in frame most starts, despite looking none too cooperative, and won twice in October; beat Arthur's Daughter by 6 lengths in maiden race at Nottingham and landed the odds by a head from Merry Tom in minor event at Leicester; stays 13f; probably acts on any going; tends to flash her tail and needs strong handling. *R. Hern.*

ROAN MIST 5 b.g. Roan Rocket 128–Barchessa 67 (Prince Chevalier) (1982 7s   **–** 7fg* 8fg 7f² 8d² 10g* 8fg 10fg 10s 1983 8fg) good-topped gelding; good mover; fair handicapper at his best; last only start at 5 yrs in September; stays 1¼m; possibly not at his best on really soft going, but acts on any other. *P. Haynes.*

ROBAND 3 br.g. Royal Smoke 113–Nushka (Tom Fool) (1982 7.6v 7g 8s 1983 10s   **–** 10.1fg 7.6fg 10g) big gelding; soundly beaten in varied races; retained 800 gns Ascot July Sales. *C. James.*

ROBBOE'S PET 3 b.f. Mummy's Pet 125–Regal Trial 93 (High Treason 126)   **–** (1982 5f 5f 5g³ 5fg 5fg 5s 1983 5fg 6f 5d) leggy filly; poor maiden; trained until after second start by J. Tierney; sold 460 gns Newmarket Autumn Sales. *B. McMahon.*

ROBERTS GIRL 3 gr.f. Mount Hagen 127–Deep Thought (Divine Gift 127)   **–** (1982 NR 1983 12v 8f 7h 7fg 7g 10g) rather leggy filly; first foal; dam Irish 9f winner; behind in maiden and minor events and a handicap. *K. Cunningham-Brown.*

ROBOUT (USA) 4 b.g. Full Out–Robustious (Rambunctious) (1982 12g 10d 1983   **–** 10g³ 8d 10f 10f 10f) smallish, compact gelding; poor middle-distance handicapper; sometimes blinkered; occasionally sweats up. *A. Cawley.*

ROCABAY BLUE 2 ch.g. Bay Express 132–Blue Bird 84 (Majority Blue 126)   **66** (1983 6fg⁴ 5f 5g 7d 7fg) Apr 2; big gelding; half-brother to several winners, including middle-distance stayer Sockburn (by My Swallow); dam stayed 1¼m; plating-class maiden; no form after second outing. *M. Camacho.*

ROCAMADOUR 4 b.c. Royal Match 117–Blakeney Belle (Blakeney 126) (1982   **105** 8fg⁴ 12f 10g³ 11g³ 14.6f 13d 1983 10v² 10s³ 12f 12fg 12f) quite attractive, full-quartered colt; put in a strong challenge and kept on gamely to be 2½ lengths second to odds-on Ivano (pair clear) in Westbury Stakes at Sandown in April; didn't reproduce that form, best effort when about 2 lengths third to Fine Sun in Clive Graham Stakes at Goodwood in May; acts on any going; blinkered last 2 starts; sold 64,000 gns Newmarket Autumn Sales and is reportedly to be sent to USA. *A. Pitt.*

ROCKET ALERT 2 b.f. Red Alert 127–Rocketina 57 (Roan Rocket 128) (1983 **110**
5s² 5g³ 5f* 6f* 5f³ 6f* 6fg² 5fg² 6s* 6fg) Apr 5; 14,500Y; useful-looking filly; second reported foal; dam won 1m seller; won at Beverley and Chepstow before picking up St Catherine's Stakes at Newbury and Firth of Clyde Stakes at Ayr; beaten only 2 lengths by Desirable when second in Princess Margaret Stakes at Ascot and sixth in William Hill Cheveley Park Stakes at Newmarket; no match for Petorius (rec 4 lb) in Prince of Wales's Stakes at York in August on eighth appearance; suited by 6f; acts on any going; tough and consistent. *W. O'Gorman.*

ROCKETONE 5 gr.h. Roan Rocket 128–Sweetstone (Honeyway 125) (1982 **49**
11.1g 17.1f⁴ 15.5g⁴ 16f⁴ 16.5f 1983 12s 12g 10f 12f⁴ 11.7f* 11.7fg⁴ 14f²) robust horse; won handicap at Windsor in July; suited by 1½m+; acts on firm going. *J. Benstead.*

ROCK'S GATE 3 b.c. Lord Gayle 124–Roxboro (Sheshoon 132) (1982 8s* 1983 **103**
8s* 10.2s* 12s² 12fg⁴ 13.3g) fair sort; successful in minor events at Wolverhampton and Bath in April, on latter course winning easily by 3 lengths from Sailor's Dance; in frame afterwards in Schroder Life Predominate Stakes at Goodwood in May (6 lengths second to Morcon) and Troy Stakes at Doncaster in September (poor fourth of 5 behind Trakady); stays 1½m well; form only on soft ground; races in a tongue strap and had a soft palate operation after Goodwood. *J. Tree.*

ROCKY'S GAL 2 b.f. Oats 126–Mallow Isle 64§ (Young Emperor 133) (1983 5s **–**
7s 6fg 6fg) Mar 31; IR 5,100F, 3,000Y; tall, leggy filly; third produce; dam won over 9f in Ireland; in rear in maiden and minor events. *W. Holden.*

RODNERS 3 b.g. Relko 136–Collateral 99 (Compensation 127) (1982 7fg **91**
7g*(w.o.) 8g² 1983 8d* 10v* 8fg 10.2s³ 9fg) strong, quite attractive gelding; beat Brave Memory by ¾ length in 29-runner maiden race at Newmarket in May and landed the odds in minor event at Ripon the following month; off course more than 2 months before finishing third behind easy winner Comedy Fair in £11,000 handicap at Doncaster in September (sweating, in trouble early in straight and simply plodded on); stays 1¼m; best form with give in the ground. *G. Pritchard-Gordon.*

ROEBUCK RUNNER 5 b.m. Maystreak 118–Rabelle (Rabirio) (1982 12d 16.5f **–**
1983 16.5f) good-bodied mare; poor maiden; has sweated up badly. *Miss L. Siddall.*

ROGER NICHOLAS 4 b.g. Immortal Knight 103–Lovesome Hill 57 **52**
(Murrayfield 119) (1982 10f 9.4f 5d 12f* 10g⁴ 12g 12.2f 10.6s 11s⁴ 13.8d 1983 12v 12.2g 12d 10f² 10f³ 10f 11fg* 12f³ 10fg⁴) lightly-made gelding; awarded handicap at Redcar in August; suited by 1½m; ideally suited by fast ground; has sweated up; has run respectably for an apprentice; rather reluctant to go down sixth start. *H. Wharton.*

ROIPAUL 3 b.c. Roi Soleil 125–Phileton 64 (Philip of Spain 126) (1982 NR 1983 **45**
6v 6v 8f 7g³ 7fg 6fg) fair sort; second foal; dam inconsistent plater at 2 yrs; poor plater; stays 7f; blinkered final outing. *S. Matthews.*

ROISINGH 3 b.c. Haveroid 122–Mansina (Mansingh 120) (1982 NR 1983 5s 6g) **–**
stocky colt; first foal; dam in rear in maiden and minor events; in rear in all-aged seller at Beverley and minor event at York (moved badly) in latter part of season. *M. W. Easterby.*

ROJO-ROCKET 2 gr.c. Roan Rocket 128–Amulree (Red Alert 127) (1983 5v 5d **45**
6g 5f² 6g 6f) May 24; smallish, lengthy colt; second foal; dam poor maiden at 2 yrs; poor plater; form only at 5f; blinkered final outing. *W. H. H. Williams.*

ROLL IN THE HAY (USA) 2 b.c. Honest Pleasure–Court Barns 101 (Riva **– p**
Ridge) (1983 6fg 7f 7g) Apr 24; medium-sized, quite attractive colt; good mover; first foal; dam, daughter of top-class Sovereign, won 3 times over 6f; showed no rateable form, but wasn't disgraced when in mid-division in big fields of maidens at Newmarket in July and Goodwood in September on last 2 appearances; likely to do a good bit better in due course. *G. Wragg.*

ROMACINA 3 b.f. Roman Warrior 132–Pilicina (Milesian 125) (1982 5f 6g 7fg 7g **–**
1983 10s 11.7f 10.2h) rangy filly; in rear in maiden and minor races. *P. M. Taylor.*

Firth of Clyde Stakes, Ayr—Rocket Alert defies top weight to beat Mystery Ship

ROMANARD 4 ch.g. Roman Warrior 132–Tackard 87 (Hard Tack 111§) (1982 8f — 8d 7g 10.6g 10g 8fg 9s 1983 16f³ 16f 14.7f) sturdy, compact gelding; poor walker; plating-class maiden; suited by 2m; acts on firm going; blinkered last 3 starts in 1982; sold 650 gns Doncaster November Sales. *W. C. Watts.*

ROMAN BEACH 3 b.c. Averof 123–Lovage (Linacre 133) (1982 6fg² 7f* 7d* **90** 1983 8d 8s* 8f⁴ 10f 10g⁴ 10fg² 10fg⁴ 8.2fg² 8fg²) lengthy colt; got up in last furlong to beat Star of Ireland by ½ length in handicap at Goodwood in May; in frame in similar events afterwards and was second at Ascot, Nottingham and Doncaster; stays 1¼m; acts on any going, but is ideally suited by soft. *W. Musson.*

ROMAN BONNET 2 ch.f. Roman Warrior 132–Sky Bonnet 72 (Sky Gipsy 117) **64** (1983 6g 6fg 6g) Mar 1; rangy, plain filly; second foal in this country; dam, winner over 1m and 1¼m, has been in Spain; 5½ lengths sixth of 12 to Soixante Quinze in maiden race at Hamilton in September, final outing and first indication of merit; may improve. *C. Thornton.*

ROMAN QUEST 4 b.c. Roman Warrior 132–Miss Richton 80 (Lauso) (1982 5fg **65** 6s* 6fg 6f 6f³ 7f 6fg 7.2g 6g 7fg³ 7.2g² 6g 8f 6fg 8fg 1983 7g 7v⁴ 8d 6g* 6f³ 7f⁴) big, useful sort; won handicap at Hamilton in June; stays 7f; acts on any going; good mount for an apprentice; sometimes blinkered but is effective without. *P. Rohan.*

ROMAN REALM 4 b.c. Realm 129–Breide's Wood (Le Levanstell 122) (1982 **74** 7fg 7g 7fg² 7g⁴ 8g* 1983 7v⁴ 7s 7fg 7f*) quite attractive, rather lightly-made colt; not the best of movers; returned to form when making all to win handicap at Yarmouth in June; subsequently sent to race in USA; stays 1m; acts on any going but goes well on fast ground; sweated up second start. *W. O'Gorman.*

ROMAN RULER 4 br.c. Roman Warrior 132–Broken Blossoms (Breakspear II) **79** (1982 6s 6d 6fg 5g⁴ 6f* 6f² 7g 7fg 6fg² 1983 6s 6d* 6fg 6g³ 6f² 6f 6f* 5.6fg 6fg⁴ 6fg 6d 6g) big, strong, good-bodied colt; sprint handicapper; won at Leicester in May and Brighton in August; ran well several other starts; suited by 6f; seems to act on any going; sweated up at Leicester; gives impression he'll always be best with strong handling; wears a tongue strap. *W. Wightman.*

ROMANTIC KNIGHT 3 b.c. Immortal Knight 103–Young Romance (King's **79** Troop 118) (1982 5f³ 5f² 6g² 6g 1983 8s 8.2s 8f⁴ 7f² 7f*) leggy, narrow colt; made all and beat Onaizah by 2½ lengths in small handicap at Thirsk in July; possibly doesn't quite stay 1m; best form on a sound surface. *M. H. Easterby.*

ROMANTIKI (USA) 3 b.f. Romeo or Giboulee–Dodge Me (The Doge) (1982 7g — 1983 7f 8f 8f 7fg) rangy filly; has shown only a little ability. *H. Candy.*

ROMANY BOY 3 b.g. Continuation 120–Mia Chico (Royal Palm 131) (1982 5f 5f² — 5f⁴ 1983 10f 10f) smallish, strong gelding; plater; not sure to stay 1¼m; blinkered second start. *J. Hardy.*

ROMILDO 3 b.c. Busted 134–Caprera 112 (Abernant 142) (1982 NR 1983 10.5d*   **114**
12f²) brother to 1981 French 2-y-o 9f winner Fabro and high-class middle-distance
colt Pevero, and half-brother to several winners; dam fourth in 1,000 Guineas;
created a most favourable impression when beating Playful River by 1½ lengths in
9-runner newcomers race at Longchamp in May; finished well when length second
of 6 behind Solford in Prix du Lys at Chantilly the following month on only
subsequent start; suited by 1½m; yet to race on really soft going, but acts on any
other. *F. Boutin, France.*

ROMOSS 5 ch.g. Royal Match 117–Pamela Rose 107 (Vilmorin) (1982 8g 8g² 8fg   **80**
8f 8f* 8f* 9.4f 9fg 8fg⁴ 8g* 8f² 8fg³ 9g³ 8d⁴ 10.2g 10d³ 8s² 7s 8s 1983 8d³ 8.2s*
8v² 8d* 10d⁴ 8f 8f 8f 8.2fg 8g² 8g 8g 8d 8.2g) strong, rangy gelding; won
handicaps at Hamilton in April and Thirsk in May; creditable 2½ lengths second to
Mauritzfontein in Bradford and Bingley Handicap at York in August; stays 1¼m;
probably acts on any going; has a fair turn of foot and is suited by waiting tactics;
not particularly consistent. *R. Whitaker.*

RONAN'S CABLES 3 b.g. Dublin Taxi–Sweet Sauce (High Perch 126) (1982 5g
5fg 6f* 6g 5fg² 5f 7f² 6fg⁴ 7d 7s³ 7s 1983 7g 7d 6f 8f⁴) robust, close-coupled
gelding; showed only form of 1983 on final outing; probably stays 1m; acts on any
going; sometimes blinkered; sent to Hong Kong. *R. Hannon.*

RONCESVALLES 3 br.c. Reform 132–High Ransom 88 (High Treason 126)   –
(1982 NR 1983 7f 8f 7f 12fg 10f) small, lengthy colt; half-brother to several
winners, including very useful 2-y-o sprinters Sanders Lad (by Amber Rama) and
Durandal (by Bay Express); dam won over 7f; no form, including in a seller. *D.
Wilson.*

RONNIYA 3 b.g. Home Guard 129–Palace Rose 88 (Aureole 132) (1982 6fg 7g   **57**
1983 8f 8.3fg 8f³ 8d) good sort; good walker; running-on third in apprentice
maiden race at Yarmouth in August, only form; will be suited by middle distances;
blinkered final start. *R. Armstrong.*

ROOKBARUGH 3 br.g. Lochnager 132–Good Form 54 (Deep Diver 134) (1983   **74**
6fg 6f 6fg 7g) Mar 7; big, strong, good-bodied gelding; second foal; dam stayed
1¼m; quite a moderate maiden; best effort on second outing; stays 6f; gelded after
final appearance. *M. H. Easterby.*

ROOM FOR JILL 2 b.f. Dragonara Palace 115–Ista Jil 97 (Gratitude 130) (1983   –
5v 5fg 5.1fg 5g 5.1f) May 28; 1,100Y; bad plater; sold 230 gns Ascot July Sales. *G.
Blum.*

ROSACEAE 4 b.f. Sagaro 133–Floradora Do 85 (Derring-Do 131) (1982 10d²   **101**
10.2f* 12fg* 12d* 13.3f⁴ 12g 12g 14.6g⁴ 12v 1983 12v* 12s) strong filly; stayed on
well to beat Forward by 1½ lengths in handicap at Kempton in April; behind in
Grosser Preis der Stadt Gelsenkirchen at Gelsenkirchen-Horst later in month;
suited by 1¾m; acted on any going; ran well in blinkers; stud. *I. Balding.*

ROSAGORE 3 ch.g. Bay Express 132–Monjenayr (Jukebox 120) (1982 5d² 5d³
5fg 5f 5fg 5g 5f 5fg⁴ 5d 6d 5v 5d 1983 5s 6f 6fg 6f 5f) lengthy, rather unfurnished
gelding; plater; acts on a soft surface; sold 560 gns Doncaster August Sales. *B.
Richmond.*

ROSANA PARK 2 b.f. Music Boy 124–Paddy's Tern 59 (St Paddy 133) (1983 5g³   **83**
5s² 6s² 5fg³ 6f⁴ 7f³ 6fg⁴) Mar 25; fair sort; second foal; dam suited by a test of
stamina; in frame in varied company, on final occasion 4 lengths fourth of 17 to
Seattle Siren in £4,000 event at York in September; stays 7f; seems to act on any
going; consistent. *E. Eldin.*

ROSE CHARTER 6 gr.g. Runnymede 123–Tavel (Tabriz 111) (1982 12f 13g 12f   **46**
11g⁴ 12g 12fg² 13fg² 12f 12.2f 12g 13.8d 1983 12fg* 11d⁴ 12f³) strong gelding;
middle-distance handicapper; won at Edinburgh in May; acts on any going; ran
moderately in blinkers once. *W. Bentley.*

ROSEDALE QUEEN 3 b.f. Silly Season 127–Queen's Rose 85 (Queen's Hussar   –
124) (1982 NR 1983 9f) 550F; small filly; half-sister to a winning plater and a
winning hurdler; dam won over 7f at 2 yrs and appeared to stay 1¾m; needed race
when last in seller at Redcar in September. *Mrs G. Reveley.*

ROSE D'ANJOU 2 ch.f. Relkino 131–Pink Sky 86 (Midsummer Night II 117)   **51**
(1983 5v³ 5s 7v 7f 7f) May 3; workmanlike filly; half-sister to 3 winners, including
useful 1½m winner Night Sky (by Star Moss) and fairly useful 1981 2-y-o 6f
winner Rosier (by Hotfoot); dam won over 6f at 2 yrs; poor maiden; no form after
first outing. *W. Holden.*

ROSE GERARD 3 b.f. Brigadier Gerard 144–Sombreuil 95 (Bold Lad, Ire 133)   53
(1982 6g 8f 6g 1983 10g 10fg 10.2h 8f³ 8d 10d) quite a moderate maiden; promises
to stay 1¼m; hampered fifth start; sold 2,000 gns Newmarket December Sales. *J.
Dunlop.*

ROSE GLOW 3 ch.f. Moulton 128–Blakewood 75 (Blakeney 126) (1982 5d 7fg   49
7f² 8.2fg³ 8fg* 8.2d* 8.2v 1983 12d 13.8s 12f 10fg* 12f 9fg⁴ 10.6fg⁴) small filly;
plater; attracted no bid after winning slowly-run affair at Ayr in July; should get at
least 1½m; probably acts on any going; veered right across course when ridden by
7-lb claimer once in 1982; sold 5,000 gns Newmarket September Sales. *J.
Fitzgerald.*

ROSE-LOVER 2 b.c. Ile de Bourbon 133–Grass Widow (Thatch 136) (1983 5s*   79
6fg 6f 6fg 7.3g) Mar 20; sparely-made, rather plain colt; third foal; half-brother to 2
winners, including 1982 2-y-o 5f winner Widow Bird (by Vitiges); dam unraced
half-sister to high-class 1973 2-y-o The Blues; favourite and very fit, won
14-runner maiden race at Salisbury in May by 1½ lengths from Son of Kandy; last of
10 in nursery on final appearance; should stay 7f; acts on any going; blinkered
fourth outing. *H. Candy.*

ROSENSKA 5 b.m. Arabian Sky 101–Moon Cruise (Ovid 95) (1982 NR 1983   –
12fg) small mare; first foal; dam never ran; tailed-off last in minor event at
Pontefract in August. *E. Alston.*

ROSE OF HARPENDEN 2 b.f. Mansingh 120–Golden Mullet (Star Moss 122)   –
(1983 6fg) May 5; 500F, 5,000Y; half-sister to a winner in Austria; dam of little
account; last of 23 in maiden race at Newmarket in October; sold 500 gns Ascot
November Sales. *I. Walker.*

ROSE OF THE NORTH 3 b.f. Sparkler 130–Twinkling Toes 70 (Prince   66
Tenderfoot 126) (1982 6g 6fg 7.2g 6d 7g 8.2s 1983 9v⁴ 8.2s 9.4d 8f 7.2fg⁴ 7.6fg
7.6g 8d 8g³ 8.2g⁴ 10.5d⁴ 10.2fg 9fg* 8fg) lengthy, unfurnished filly; in frame
several times, including in a £4,000 seller, before winning handicap at Redcar in
October; promises to stay 1¼m; blinkered last 3 outings. *J. Wilson.*

ROSE O'RILEY (USA) 2 b.f. Nijinsky 138–Rosetta Stone (Round Table) (1983   109 p
8g⁴ 8g*) Feb 7; sister to De La Rose, the best 3-y-o filly on grass in 1981 when
successful at up to 1¼m, and very smart 1¼m performer Upper Nile, and
half-sister to several other winners, one a stakes winner; dam winning half-sister
to high-class miler Rosalba; led entering straight when comfortable winner of
17-runner maiden event by ½ length from Jeromella at Saint-Cloud in November;
an extremely well-bred filly who is likely to improve further. *J. de Roualle,
France.*

ROSINKA 2 ch.f. Raga Navarro 119–Aggrapina 79 (St Alphage 119) (1983 5v² 5d⁴   62
5fg⁴ 5d* 6f* 5fg 6f 5g) May 9; 1,000Y; leggy, narrow filly; second foal; half-sister
to 3-y-o 1½m winner Orange Blossom (by Orange Bay); dam showed form only
over 5f; won sellers at Redcar in May and Thirsk in June without attracting a bid;
stays 6f; acts on any going; usually ridden by apprentice S. Horsfall; sold 940 gns
Doncaster October Sales. *J. Berry.*

ROSMINDLE 2 b.c. Jimsun 121–Dracaena 62 (Double Jump 131) (1983 8.2g) Apr   –
28; 2,600Y; brother to 2 winners, including quite useful 1980 2-y-o 6f winner
Veleso, and half-brother to a winner in Italy; dam won 7f seller at 2 yrs; distant
ninth of 10 in maiden race at Hamilton in September. *J. Townson.*

ROSOLIO 2 ch.f. Nebbiolo 125–Rose Girl (Thatch 136) (1983 6g 6fg² 6fg 7fg)   91
Apr 24; rangy, angular filly; second foal; dam, poor maiden, is half-sister to smart
sprinter Rambling Rose and very smart French colt Rose Laurel; 1½ lengths
second of 17 to Seattle Siren in £4,000 race at York in September; had fair bit to
do in useful company at Newmarket afterwards, but was nonetheless somewhat
disappointing; should stay 7f. *R. Armstrong.*

ROSSETT 4 ch.g. Jukebox 120–Flo Kelly (Florescence 120) (1982 6g 8fg 8fg* 8f   64
8g⁴ 7.6g² 8f 7.6d⁴ 8.2g 8g 8.2s³ 8d³ 1983 10v 7fg 8d⁴ 8g² 7fg³ 8d 6f³ 8f 8g 7f) fair
sort; suited by 1m; probably acts on any going; has run creditably for an apprentice.
T. Craig.

ROSSETTI (FR) 3 b.f. Bolkonski 134–Contarini Fleming 68 (Abdos 134) (1982   –
5fg 6s 1983 9v 10f 10.1fg 10fg 8f) well-made, quite attractive filly; no worthwhile
form at 3 yrs; should stay 1¼m. *B. Hills.*

ROSSY FOR SPORT 2 ch.c. Monseigneur 127–Red Roan (Roan Rocket 128)   –
(1983 7f) Mar 25; 950Y; big, heavy-topped colt; third foal; half-brother to 1979
2-y-o 6f winner Grey Mask (by Sallust); dam never ran; backward and bandaged,
last of 11 in minor event at Beverley in July. *A. Smith.*

ROTHERLEIGH 3 b.g. Workboy 123–Pickwood Sue 74 (Right Boy 137) (1982   –
5f* 5fg⁴ 5d 1983 5f 5f 7f 7g) leggy, quite useful-looking gelding; lost his form after
running respectably on reappearance; not certain to stay beyond 5f; bandaged
second outing; sometimes sweats up. *J. Leigh.*

ROUGH PEARL (USA) 2 b.c. Tom Rolfe–Jackie Pearl (Ruffled Feathers) (1983   80
6fg⁴ 7fg³ 8g) Mar 16; $100,000; good-topped, quite attractive colt; first foal; dam
very useful winner at up to 1m; placed in maiden race at Salisbury in September;
will stay 1¼m; acts on a firm surface. *G. Lewis.*

ROUGH STONES 2 b.c. Blakeney 126–Rockery 101 (Roan Rocket 128) (1983   80 p
8f²) Feb 4; fair sort; good walker; first live foal; dam 2-y-o 6f winner; 5/1, ran
odds-on Hidden Destiny to 2½ lengths in 14-runner maiden race at Leicester in
November; will be suited by 1¼m+; should have little difficulty in winning maiden
event. *R. Hern.*

ROUGH TIME BOY 3 b.g. Blue And Grey 93–Decoy Lady 70 (Decoy Boy 129)   –
(1982 NR 1983 8fg) first foal; dam second twice over 5f at 2 yrs; in rear in maiden
race at Edinburgh in May. *F. Watson.*

ROUND AGAIN 3 b.g. Decoy Boy 129–Shilly Shally 89 (Sallymount 125) (1982   –
5d 5g³ 5.8g 6d 6s 1983 7s 8f 10.1f) showed some ability at 2 yrs but was soundly
beaten in 1983; not sure to stay beyond sprint distances; blinkered final start. *A.
Turnell.*

ROUND HILL 2 br.g. Auction Ring 123–Hill Moss 87 (Priamos 123) (1983 6f³   111
6fg* 6g* 7fg* 7.3d³)
    Very few two-year-old geldings make a great mark on the racecourse in
Britain: the last one we can bring to mind is the 1973 National Stakes winner,
Daring Boy. In the years since then four geldings have been placed in
two-year-old pattern races in England—the Irish-trained National Wish in the
1975 Norfolk Stakes, Busaco in the 1981 Horris Hill Stakes and Fawzi and Round
Hill in 1983. Round Hill finished third in the Horris Hill Stakes though that was not
his best performance. He started favourite against the smooth Ascot winner
Donzel, the improving My Volga Boatman and Elegant Air, who had been beaten
less than three and a half lengths by El Gran Senor at the Curragh, but was never
going particularly well; he didn't quicken so well as previously and finished two
and a half lengths and a neck behind Elegant Air and My Volga Boatman. Prior to
Newbury Round Hill had won three of his four races, the first of them, the
Drawing Room Stakes at Goodwood, after being beaten on merit by Bluff House
who was later disqualified for hampering the fourth horse Passing Storm. There
was nothing fortuitous about Round Hill's other wins. In the six-furlong Mining
Supplies Stakes at Doncaster in September he beat Passing Storm by three
quarters of a length in a manner that suggested he would be better suited by
seven furlongs. The Somerville Tattersall Stakes at Newmarket later in the
month gave him the opportunity to prove the point. He faced his stiffest test so
far. Fawzi started co-favourite on the strength of his second to Vacarme in the
Mill Reef Stakes, and the opposition also included the highly-regarded pair
August and Get The Message, and the Northern trio Idolized, Daleside Redwood
and Golden Flute who had all won decent races. Round Hill was always chasing
the leaders and after being pushed along three furlongs out, he lengthened his
stride impressively on the rising ground to lead inside the final furlong. Despite
the determined challenge of Idolized, Round Hill won by a neck, with Get The
Message a length and a half third.

*Somerville Tattersall Stakes, Newmarket—the improving Round Hill holds a strong
challenge from Idolized (right)*

Round Hill is a well-made, attractive gelding, with a particularly nice, easy action. His sire, Auction Ring, was a very able though highly-strung sprinter, who won the July Stakes and the King George Stakes at Goodwood. He was entitled to stay a mile on breeding and his progeny have generally proved most effective at seven furlongs to a mile, notably the high-class Belmont Bay. The dam Hill Moss, trained like Round Hill and Auction Ring by Hern, won a mile maiden at Goodwood in 1975. She has produced a sister to Round Hill, Bid Fair, who has won three races

		Bold Bidder	Bold Ruler
	Auction Ring	(b 1962)	High Bid
	(b 1972)	Hooplah	Hillary
Round Hill		(b 1965)	Beadah
(br.g. May 12, 1981)		Priamos	Birkhahn
	Hill Moss	(b 1964)	Palazzo
	(b 1972)	Bandarilla	Matador
		(ch 1960)	Interval

at provincial tracks in France between a mile and a mile and three furlongs. Hill Moss is half-sister to five winners, including the top-class miler Sallust, the Britannia Handicap winner Strabo and the Extel Handicap winner Cupid. Her dam Bandarilla was a smart performer, a winner four times at distances up to six furlongs. Though his sister Bid Fair has won over further it seems likely that Round Hill will prove most effective at seven furlongs or a mile, and may well win his share of good races at that sort of trip. He acts well on a sound surface and may not be so effective on softer ground. *R. Hern.*

ROUSILLON (USA) 2 b.c. Riverman 131–Belle Dorine (Marshua's Dancer) 124 (1983 7fg* 8g* 8fg2)

The Royal Lodge Stakes at Ascot in September provided one of the season's most dramatic turnabouts. As the leaders swept towards the final furlong one of the co-favourites, Rousillon, seemed to have the race sewn up, having just taken a length advantage over the 25/1-shot Gold And Ivory. Hardly had he done so than Rousillon began to go to pieces: his stride shortened noticeably, his head started to go up and he looked a distressed horse as Gold And Ivory forged back to beat him by two lengths. As Rousillon had scratched down to the start on the firmish ground we fully expected to hear afterwards that he was sore or lame. However his stable quickly announced that no physical explanation had been found for his sudden flagging, so what could possibly have gone wrong with him? Had he simply found the testing Ascot mile too far? There may be something in this but we don't believe it fully explains Rousillon's display: he had already won over a mile, when trouncing the useful colts At Talaq and Finian's Rainbow in the Westhampnett Stakes at Goodwood earlier in the month. More likely the tactics used on him were to blame. Rousillon had been given a great deal to do, racing in fourth-of-five position as the 200/1-shot Mellow Dance set a very fast pace, and both he and the other co-favourite Trojan Fen had to be rushed up on the turn as it became clear that the pacemaker and Gold And Ivory were stronger than anticipated. Rousillon and Trojan Fen made up about half a dozen lengths in the space of a furlong, which was asking a lot of a two-year-old running at a mile. The effort took its toll of Trojan Fen, and by comparison Rousillon did very well to maintain his effort until inside the final furlong. Rousillon was mentioned as a possible runner in the William Hill Dewhurst Stakes but the Royal Lodge proved to be his last race. His first had been the Plantation Maiden Stakes at Newmarket in July, a race won by Troy, Vielle and Scintillating Air in recent years. He started a clear favourite in a twenty-five-strong field and justified the support in great style. After pulling over his rivals for a long way, he lengthened his stride to take the lead running into the Dip and won comfortably by two lengths from Timber Merchant.

		Never Bend	Nasrullah
	Riverman	(b 1960)	Lalun
	(b 1969)	River Lady	Prince John
Rousillon (USA)		(b 1963)	Nile Lily
(b.c. Apr 10, 1981)		Marshua's Dancer	Raise A Native
	Belle Dorine	(b 1968)	Marshua
	(b or br 1977)	Palsy Walsy	Sea O Erin
		(ch 1960)	Allie's Pal

Rousillon belongs to the first American crop of Riverman, the champion French stallion of 1980 and 1981. He was bought as a yearling at the Fasig-Tipton Kentucky Summer Sale for 100,000 dollars, 90,000 dollars less than his dam Belle Dorine had fetched as a three-year-old when carrying Rousillon. Belle Dorine, who

Mr K. Abdulla's "Rousillon"

ran once unplaced as a juvenile, is only the second of Palsy Walsy's first eleven foals to fail to win. Three of her dam's foals won stakes races, including the very useful Canadian sprinter-miler Captain's Party and the 1976 two-year-old five-furlong winner Who's That Lady. Palsy Walsy won only four small races but she was a half-sister to two stakes winners at up to eight and a half furlongs, notably the very useful filly Allie's Serenade, and her dam Allie's Pal won three stakes races at up to the same distance. As Belle Dorine's sire Marshua's Dancer gained all his nine successes over six furlongs it's possible a mile will prove the limit of Rousillon's stamina. It will be fascinating to see how he and his stable-companions Lear Fan, Alphabatim and Raft fare as three-year-olds. Lear Fan was certainly the best at two but the stable-jockey Starkey is said to be very keen on Raft, while the assistant trainer Lawson holds Rousillon in very high esteem. We think Rousillon will make an excellent three-year-old but anyone contemplating an ante-post bet on him or his stable companions would do well to listen to Lawson's advice. 'Back the stable not the individual. It's a long winter.' *G. Harwood.*

ROWA 2 ch. f. Great Nephew 126–Oh So Fair (Graustark) (1983 7fg) Apr 13; big,   **70** p
lengthy filly; half-sister to several winners, notably very smart 5f to 1¼m winner Roussalka and 1000 Guineas second Our Home (both by Habitat); dam won over 1¼m in Ireland; second favourite but a bit green, ran on without being knocked about to finish 5 lengths fifth of 14 to Claude Monet in minor event at Doncaster in October; sure to improve. *M. Stoute.*

ROYABER 7 ch. g. Sandford Lad 133–Honeymoon II (Ballymoss 136) (1982 8d 8f   **70** d
7fg 7fg3 8.5f4 7f4 8d* 8g3 8.3fg* 8fg 10g3 8fg2 8f* 8g3 10g 1983 8d 8v 11.7s 9v3 8.2fg 8fg 8.3fg 8.2fg*(dis) 7.6g2 8.3fg4 7.2g 9d 8g) big, strong gelding; hung left when winning handicap at Haydock in August and was disqualified; probably stays 1¼m; acts on any going; wears blinkers nowadays. *D. H. Jones.*

ROYAL ACADEMY ARMS 2 b.c. Ardoon 124–Miss Kalamaloo (Kalamoun 129) (1983 5g 5g 6fg) Mar 4; IR 3,600F, 4,200Y; workmanlike colt; first foal; dam never ran; little worthwhile form in end-of-season maiden races; blinkered final outing. *B. Gubby.* —

ROYAL AGENDA 2 b.f. Stradavinsky 121–La Pagode (Habitat 134) (1983 7f) Apr 16; 900F, 2,500Y; second produce; dam never ran; in rear in 16-runner maiden race at Wolverhampton in July. *M. Ryan.* —

ROYAL AND LOYAL 5 ch.g. Queen's Hussar 124–Lake of the Woods (Never Say Die 137) (1982 16s 17.1f³ 16d 14s³ 18d⁴ 16d 16.1s 1983 17.1v) compact gelding; staying handicapper; acts on any going; wears blinkers. *G. Cottrell.* —

ROYAL BRIGADIER 3 ch.c. Brigadier Gerard 144–Royal Pancake 104 (Crepello 136) (1982 6d 6f 1983 8v 8d 8f 10g 10g² 12g² 12d 10fg) deep-girthed colt; second in amateur riders race at Goodwood in September and gentleman riders race at Ascot in October; stays 1½m; ran poorly in blinkers seventh outing. *G. Balding.* **76**

ROYAL CONDOR 3 b.f. Moulton 128–Condora 99 (Matador 131) (1982 7d 1983 13fg 16g 8.2f 8f) of little account. *J. Spearing.* —

ROYAL CRACKER 2 b.c. He Loves Me 120–French Cracker (Klairon 131) (1983 7fg 7f) Mar 26; IR 20,000Y; lengthy colt; second foal; dam won over 1½m in Ireland; shaped nicely in good-class events won by stable companions at Lingfield and Sandown in August; sure to do better in time. *G. Harwood.* **68 p**

ROYAL CRAFTSMAN 2 b. or br.g. Workboy 123–Royal Huntress (Royal Avenue 123) (1983 7fg 7fg) May 23; fair sort; second foal; dam winning hurdler; in mid-division in maiden race at Redcar and minor event at Doncaster in October. *W. Elsey.* **71 +**

ROYAL DACHA 2 b.f. Averof 123–Beguiling 66 (Tower Walk 130) (1983 5v 5fg 7f 7d) useful-looking filly; third reported foal; closely related to a winning 2-y-o plater by Manacle; dam ran 4 times; soundly beaten in maiden races, twice last. *M. Blanshard.* —

ROYAL DAUGHTER 3 b.f. High Top 131–Pirate Queen 77 (Pirate King 129) (1982 7d 1983 10v 12s 10s 12f³ 12f 12fg 10.1fg) strong, deep-girthed filly; third to 15-length winner Queen of Night in maiden race at Brighton in June, best effort; sold to BBA 7,600 gns Newmarket December Sales. *D. Whelan.* —

ROYAL DIPLOMAT 6 ch.g. The Go-Between 129–Grace (Gratitude 130) (1982 6d 5d⁴ 6fg 5g 6g 6g³ 5g* 6fg 5fg 5s 5s* 6s³ 5s 1983 5d⁴ 5v⁴ 6v³ 6v 5v 6g 5.8g² 5g 5f⁴ 5g²) attractive gelding; sprint handicapper; has won on firm going but seems much better with some give underfoot; suitable mount for an apprentice; bandaged near-hind last 2 starts. *J. Holt.* **65**

ROYAL DUTY 5 b.g. Import 127–Lunar Queen 96 (Queen's Hussar 124) (1982 7f 7fg* 6f* 6f 6g* 7g⁴ 6f 7f 1983 7d 7d⁴ 7f 6f 6f² 6fg 7f² 6fg² 7f 6h 7g² 8fg) lengthy gelding; good mover; needs a stiff track when racing over 6f and stays 7f; probably acts on any going, but is well suited by firm; sometimes blinkered; goes well for Paul Eddery; trained most of season by E. Weymes. *N. Tinkler.* **69**

ROYAL EXPORT 3 b.f. Import 127–Rivachet (Forlorn River 124) (1982 5f³ 7g² 6f* 5g⁴ 1983 7d⁴ 7f 7f⁴ 7f 8g) lightly-made filly; won seller at Catterick in June (no bid) and occasionally ran respectably in better company; stays 7f; yet to race on really soft going, but acts on any other; tends to hang. *W. C. Watts.* **61**

ROYAL FLING 4 ch.c. Quiet Fling 124–Observer Royal (King's Troop 118) (1982 NR 1983 8fg) soundly beaten in maiden races; very troublesome in preliminaries once at 2 yrs. *C. Mackenzie.* —

ROYAL HALO (USA) 2 b.c. Halo–Lady Gordon (Royal Levee) (1983 7g*) Apr 9; $37,000F, $30,000Y; half-brother to 3 winners, one stakes placed; dam useful winner of 7 races at up to 1m; favourite, won 13-runner maiden race at Lingfield in October in great style by 6 lengths easing up from Nadia Nerina, leading approaching final furlong and quickening clear; will stay at least 1¼m; sure to win more races, and is an interesting prospect. *G. Harwood.* **100 p**

ROYAL HERITAGE (FR) 5 b.g. Welsh Pageant 132–Escorial 110 (Royal Palace 131) (1982 8.2fg 8fg 10f 10d 11s³ 12s⁴ 8s 1983 12.3v 10s) lengthy gelding; poor handicapper; stays 1½m; acts on any going. *E. Incisa.* —

ROYAL HEROINE 3 br.f. Lypheor 118–My Sierra Leone (Relko 136) (1982 6g⁴ 6f* 6fg* 6g² 1983 7d³ 8g²(dis) 12g 8g* 7.3f² 8s* 9.2f* 10f 9f*) **121**
Royal Heroine is another of those exceedingly tough and genuine high-class

fillies of which the latest season had more than the usual number. Prepared for the Guineas she kept her form well into November, ultimately achieving the distinction of winning a Derby after being beaten in the Guineas and the Oaks. At Hollywood Park in California on November 20th she won the first division of the Hollywood Derby, a race for three-year-old colts and fillies worth 87,150 dollars (approximately £59,000) to the winner, run over nine furlongs on turf. The names of none of her opponents apart from the good two-year-old filly of 1982, Bright Crocus, will mean much to the average British racegoer, but there were other more-than-useful animals in the field, including the favourite and three-quarter-length runner-up, the ex-French colt Interco. In winning Royal Heroine gained compensation for a most unlucky run in the more important Yellow Ribbon Stakes earlier in the month, when she did well to finish seventh of twelve to Sangue after meeting trouble and having to be snatched up so violently that her saddle slipped.

Royal Heroine's seven-race season in Europe was a fine one marred only by two things—a long-delayed inquiry into her positive test which led to disqualification from second place in the One Thousand Guineas, and her performance over a distance beyond her in the Oaks which saw her finishing a well-beaten seventh to Sun Princess. Royal Heroine ran an excellent race in the Guineas: she turned the Ladbroke Nell Gwyn Stakes tables on Favoridge and gave the favourite Ma Biche plenty to do. She was ridden with commendable enterprise by Swinburn who slipped her into what promised to be a decisive lead two and a half furlongs from home; in the end she hadn't the pace of the winner, but after being headed on her near-side by Ma Biche starting up the hill out of the Dip and being threatened on her off-side by Favoridge she rallied gamely under strong driving to snatch second place in the last fifty yards, a length and a half behind Ma Biche. Evidence given to the Jockey Club inquiry in September disclosed that her post-race urine sample contained traces of caffeine and theobromine, prohibited substances; the inquiry, while failing to establish the source of these substances, disqualified her and fined the trainer £600.

Upon Royal Heroine's revealing herself one of the best two-year-old fillies of 1982 through a clear defeat of Henry's Secret, Bright Crocus and Fenny Rough in the Princess Margaret Stakes at Ascot she had been purchased out of Mick Ryan's stable for a reported six-figure sum, later reported as £350,000. To recoup any six-figure sum on the racecourse, let alone £350,000, once the Oaks has been run is a very tall order with a three-year-old filly who doesn't stay a mile and a half and who, for all her ability, isn't the best around. Nevertheless her trainer left no stone

Sceptre Stakes, Doncaster—Royal Heroine runs on gamely to defeat Flamenco

Prix de l'Opera, Longchamp—Royal Heroine remains in good form

unturned in the attempt. He placed her to such advantage that until her unlucky bid for the Yellow Ribbon (worth 240,000 dollars, approximately £162,000, to the winner incidentally) she was beaten only once in four starts in good races, and that by the top-class colt Salieri at probably his optimum distance in the Hungerford Stakes at Newbury in August; on that occasion Salieri gave her 5 lb and beat her two and a half lengths. Royal Heroine won three races confined to fillies and mares, the Child Stakes at Newmarket in July, the Sceptre Stakes at Doncaster in September and the Prix de l'Opera at Longchamp on Arc day. She won the first two at the chief expense of Flamenco, by two lengths when receiving 3 lb and by a neck when conceding 4 lb; in the Child Stakes she again finished ahead of Favoridge and the Guineas sixth Annie Edge. She won the third at the chief expense of the injudiciously-ridden Fly Me who was nearly last of the eighteen runners into the straight at Longchamp. In contrast, Swinburn again excelled on Royal Heroine. If there was anything in the story that Royal Heroine had had a poor flight over she didn't show it. She looked as well as we'd seen her and she won in good style, moving strongly in about sixth place from the start and taking advantage of an opening her jockey found about two hundred yards from home to shoot clear and keep on to hold off Fly Me by a length and a half. The other English challengers Fluke, Ski Sailing and Goodbye Shelley played no part in the finish.

Royal Heroine (br.f. 1980)	Lypheor (b 1975)	Lyphard (b 1969)	Northern Dancer
			Goofed
		Klaizia (b 1965)	Sing Sing
			Klainia
	My Sierra Leone (ch 1971)	Relko (b 1960)	Tanerko
			Relance III
		Smeralda (gr 1966)	Grey Sovereign
			Brilliant Stone

Most stallions exported from Europe to Japan travel on a one-way ticket. But Lypheor, the Prix Quincey winner who was exported there after only one season at the Baroda Stud, has now been brought out of Japan to stand at Gainesway Farm in the United States where, as the sire of Royal Heroine and Tolomeo and as a grandson of Northern Dancer, he may be expected to appeal to breeders. He should get likelier mates, too, than Royal Heroine's dam was at the time Royal Heroine was conceived. My Sierra Leone, behind in two maiden races, had had only one previous living foal and no runner at that time. The foal, Betsy Red (by Mount Hagen), developed into a useful sprinter. My Sierra Leone is quite a well-bred filly, by a Derby winner out of a useful sprinter, Smeralda, who has produced several winners including the French miler Brittany. Smeralda was sold at the age of seventeen, covered by African Sky, for 52,000 guineas at Goffs Breeding Stock Sale in November. The third dam Brilliant Stone won the Blue Seal Stakes at Ascot. Since producing Royal Heroine My Sierra Leone has had another runner, the two-year-old Fahdi (by Manado); he has shown plenty of promise, and looks the sort to do well in handicaps in 1984.

That Betsy Red turned out to be a sprinter came as something of a surprise, but even so we couldn't entirely share the confidence of those who believed that

Mr R. E. Sangster's "Royal Heroine"

Royal Heroine would have sufficient stamina to run well in the Oaks (she started third favourite at 11/2). The facts suggest Royal Heroine is best at up to nine furlongs, though if she stays in training she deserves another chance at a mile and a quarter. A tall, lengthy filly, she acts on any going. Whilst in training in the United States she is handled by J. Gosden. *M. Stoute.*

ROYAL HOBBIT 5 b.h. Habitat 134–Royal Danseuse 111 (Prince Chevalier) **101**
(1982 5s² 5g* 5f⁴ 5d* 5f 5g 5fg⁴ 5g⁴ 1983 6v³ 5d 5g⁴ 5fg² 5g 7g 5g³ 5g² 5s* 6s*)
short-backed, smallish Irish horse; useful sprinter; won MacDonagh and Boland
Waterford Stakes at the Curragh in October by 2 lengths from Desert Walk and
accounted for Mothers Word by ½ length in handicap on same course later in
month; in frame most other starts, including when third to Curravilla in CBA
Greenlands Stakes at the Curragh; stays 6f; acts on any going but goes well in the
mud; effective with and without blinkers; consistent. *S. McGrath, Ireland.*

ROYAL HOLLOW 3 b.c. Wolver Hollow 126–Oubliette 68 (Crepello 136) (1982 —
NR 1983 8g 10h 10f 10g 8fg) 9,600F; big, useful-looking colt; third living foal;
closely related to Irish 1½m winner Wollowette (by Wollow) and half-brother to a
winner; dam 1¼m winner; in rear in maiden races and sellers; blinkered third start.
A. Jarvis.

ROYAL INSIGHT (USA) 4 ch.c. Majestic Prince–Foresight (Forli) (1982 11f **67**
10f² 10fg 12fg* 10g 12fg² 12g 12d* 12.2d² 1983 11.7f 14fg 14h³ 12fg 17d 19g⁴
17.1g) attractive colt; poor walker and mover; seems to stay well; seems to act on
any going; has twice worn blinkers (ran badly in them on first occasion); suitable
mount for an inexperienced rider. *R. Hannon.*

ROYAL OPPORTUNITY 3 b.g. Royal Palace 131–La Mome 109 (Princely Gift   –
137) (1982 7g 1983 8d 10s) robust, workmanlike gelding; behind in maiden races;
sold 940 gns Newmarket Autumn Sales. *M. McCourt.*

ROYAL QUESTION 4 ch.f. Grey Ghost 99–Royal Raintree (Royal Duet) (1982   65
6g 5fg⁴ 5g 5fg* 5fg³ 5f* 6g* 5g 5s 1983 5d² 6f 5f* 5fg⁴ 5f 5f 5g⁴ 5fg 5g 6f) rather
leggy filly; doesn't always impress in paddock; sprint handicapper; won at Thirsk in
July; stays 6f; best form on a sound surface; has run creditably for an apprentice. *T.
Barron.*

ROYAL RAINBOW 3 b.f. Space King 115–Bow Baby (Bowsprit 93) (1982 NR   –
1983 16f) sparely-made non-thoroughbred filly; sister to modest novice hurdler/
chaser Space Baby; dam never ran; unquoted, always behind when tailed-off tenth
of 12 behind Wordsworth in maiden race at Beverley in September. *M. H.
Easterby.*

ROYAL RASCAL 5 gr.g. Scallywag 127–Sea Queen (Ribomar 108) (1982 NR   –
1983 12f) has a high knee action; poor maiden on flat; has twice worn blinkers. *H.
Fleming.*

ROYAL RECOURSE (USA) 2 b.c. Valid Appeal–Lady Michael (Our Michael)   –
(1983 6fg) $15,500F; dam won 4 sprint claiming races; behind in 23-runner maiden
race at Newmarket in October. *R. Williams.*

ROYAL-RED 5 ch.g. Royal Fleece–Fortune's Red 65 (El Ruedo 91) (1982 NR   –
1983 9d 9d 12g 7fg 6fg 9f) plain gelding; no worthwhile form in varied races,
including a seller. *W. H. H. Williams.*

ROYAL REVENGE 4 ch.g. Sweet Revenge 129–Charley's Aunt 80 (Will   – §
Somers 114§) (1982 6g 6f 6f⁴ 8g* 7fg⁴ 8g 8d 8.2s 8s 10s⁴ 1983 7.3g 8fg 10.8d 10g)
big, rangy gelding; inconsistent handicapper; stays 1¼m; ideally suited by some
give in the ground; blinkered nowadays. *G. Cottrell.*

ROYAL REX 7 b.h. Royal Prerogative 119–Ballynulta 91 (Djebel) (1982 10d²   –
10fg 10f 10.6h 10fg⁴ 10g 12fg 12.3fg⁴ 12.2fg² 12fg 1983 10g) small horse; poor
middle-distance handicapper; has been beaten in sellers; seems to act on any
going; occasionally blinkered; bandaged only start of 1983. *J. Tierney.*

ROYAL SNAKE 2 b.f. Royal Blend 117–Snake 82 (The Brianstan 128) (1983   61
5.8h 6f 5.8h) Apr 7; second foal; dam won twice over 5f at 2 yrs; plating-class
maiden; not raced after August. *B. Palling.*

ROYAL TROUPER 4 b.g. Comedy Star 121–Dancing Class 75 (Compensation   87
127) (1982 6f 7d³ 7f² 7fg⁴ 7fg* 7s² 8g³ 1983 7.6v 7fg* 8f 8f 8f³ 8fg³ 7g* 7.6fg* 7fg
8d) big, rangy gelding; good mover; came with a strong run to win handicaps at
York, Doncaster (apprentices) and Lingfield; stays 1m; acts on any going. *A. Hide.*

ROYALTY MISS 4 b. or br.f. Royalty 130–Blue Delphinium 75 (Quorum 126)   –
(1982 16fg 10fg 12fg 15.5v 1983 12v 16s) of little account. *A. Neaves.*

ROYAL VALEUR 3 b.c. English Prince 129–Valeur (Val de Loir 133) (1982 6fg*   –
6d⁴ 6d² 6g 1983 10d 10.1fg 12f 10f 13s) tall, useful-looking colt; didn't recover his
2-y-o form; should stay middle distances; acts on a firm and a soft surface. *A.
Jarvis.*

ROYAL YACHT (USA) 2 b.f. Riverman 131–Regal Style (Cornish Prince) (1983   56
5g 5.1fg 5d⁴) Mar 24; $90,000Y; compact filly; fourth foal; half-sister to 1982
American 2-y-o 1m claiming race winner Crown the Emperor (by Empery); dam
unraced half-sister to high-class Traffic; having first race since June, modest
fourth in maiden race at Wolverhampton in October; not bred to be a 5f
performer; sold 25,000 gns Newmarket Autumn Sales. *J. Hindley.*

ROYBEN BOY 2 ch.c. Royben 125–Sweet Illusion (Decoy Boy 129) (1983 5d 5f   47
6f 5f) Apr 25; 300Y; compact colt; poor plater; not raced after August; wears
blinkers. *W. Clay.*

ROYSIA BOY 3 b.g. African Sky 124–For Keeps 57 (Track Spare 125) (1982 6g   92
1983 8g 7d 6fg² 6f* 6f* 6f* 6fg 5g 6g⁴) good-bodied, workmanlike gelding;
improved and was gaining fourth win in succession when making all to beat Legal
Sound a head in handicap at Newcastle in August; had won 3 times in fairly good
style at Yarmouth earlier; form only at sprint distances; acts on firm going; has won
for a 5-lb claimer; unlucky in running ninth outing. *G. Pritchard-Gordon.*

ROYSTON PLACE 2 b.f. Decoy Boy 129–Perfect Lady 85 (Sovereign Lord 120)   65
(1983 5s* 5s* 5f 5f⁴ 5fg) June 3; 1,100Y; small, rather lightly-made, good-
quartered filly; poor mover; sister to 1982 2-y-o 5f seller winner Mrs Chandler
and half-sister to 3 winners; dam won over 5f at 2 yrs; successful in sellers at

Leicester in April (no bid) and Ripon in May (bought in 2,400 gns); unlikely to stay 7f; acts on any going; exported to Algeria. *J. Berry.*

RUBABAY 3 b.g. Bay Express 132–Rubella (Buisson Ardent 129) (1982 6s 1983 **61** 8v 5f 6f 7f 8f 6h⁴) quite a moderate maiden; best form at sprint distances. *H. Candy.*

RUBY GREEN (USA) 2 b.f. J. O. Tobin 130–Uncommitted 101 (Buckpasser) **107** (1983 6g* 5.5g⁴) third foal; half-sister to useful 3-y-o French 1¼m winner Florenza (by Wajima) and very smart American horse Wavering Monarch (by Majestic Light), a stakes winner at up to 9f; dam, 2-y-o 7f winner in France, is half-sister to dam of Posse; beat Perdomi a length in newcomers event at Saint-Cloud in July; creditable fourth, beaten under 4 lengths, to Masarika in Prix Robert Papin at Maisons-Laffitte later in month; wasn't seen out again; should stay 1m. *M. Saliba, France.*

RUBY RED DRESS 6 b.m. Sparkler 130–Red Cape 84 (Matador 131) (1982 — 12.3g 12g* 12f 12s 12fg³ 12f³ 10g⁴ 9g 11f 1983 12s) big, well-made mare; stayed 13f; probably acted on any going; dead. *M. Camacho.*

RUCKLEY 3 b.g. Free State 125–Avahra 108 (Sahib 114) (1982 8.2fg 7fg 1983 — 10g 12.2g³) lengthy, fair sort; plating-class maiden; promises to stay 1½m. *P. Rohan.*

RUDOLFINA 4 b.f. Pharly 130–Rojanya (Petingo 135) (1982 10.5d² 10s* 12s⁴ **119** 10g* 9d² 10g 1983 10.5v³ 10.5v³ 10d* 10.5g² 8fg³ 8fg 10fg* 10f) fourth foal; half-sister to 3 winners in France, including useful middle-distance performer Rubino (by Gyr); dam never ran; smart filly; won Prix de la Pepiniere at Longchamp in May from Tudorville and Prix du Point du Jour on same course in October from Mondino; also ran well to be placed in Prix Corrida at Saint-Cloud (third to Radiance), Prix Fille de l'Air on same course (short-head second to Darine) and Prix Messidor at Maisons-Laffitte (third to Pampabird); best at up to 10.5f; probably acts on any going. *J-C. Cunnington, France.*

RUDRY PARK 4 gr.f. Blue Cashmere 129–Lenana (Never Say Die 137) (1982 — 10h 7fg 8f 8fg 9f 1983 10.6fg 8h 10h) lengthy filly; poor plater; has worn blinkers; pulls hard. *D. H. Jones.*

RUFCHA 2 bl. or br.g. Radetzky 123–Sharp Work 110 (Beau Sabreur 125) (1983 — 7f 7g) May 29; 2,000F; half-brother to several winners here and abroad, including fair 1m to 1¼m winner Man In The Middle (by Good Bond); dam, very useful at up to 7f at 2 yrs in England, also won 5 times at up to 1m in Italy; well beaten in maiden events at Newbury (last of 17) in August and Lingfield in October; subsequently gelded. *D. Sasse.*

RUFFO (USA) 4 b.c. Riva Ridge–Brave Lady (Herbager 136) (1982 6g 7.6f³ 7d³ — 8s³ 8s 1983 10f 11.7f) big, rangy colt; has a capped hock; none too good a walker or mover; disappointing handicapper; bred to stay middle distances; acts on any going; blinkered once. *R. Holder.*

RULA HULER (USA) 3 b.c. Chieftain–Native Go Go (Raise A Native) (1982 — 7g⁴ 6fg 1983 8v⁴ 7fg 10f 10f⁴ 12g 10g) big, rangy, good sort; has a really long stride; quite a moderate maiden; stays 1¼m; trained until after fourth start by L. Cumani. *A. Moore.*

RULE OF THE SEA (USA) 2 b.c. Accipiter–La Mer (Bosun) (1983 6g 6f⁴ 7f* **92** 7f³) Apr 19; $27,000Y; tall, quite attractive, good sort; fourth foal; half-brother to 2 winners, including smart 1982 American 2-y-o sprint winner Winning Tack (by Best Turn); dam won 6f claiming race; made all in 14-runner maiden race at Sandown in July; creditable 2¼ lengths third of 11 to King of Clubs in £4,100 event at Newmarket later in month; will probably stay at least 1m; acts well on firm going; suited by forcing tactics. *G. Lewis.*

RUMMANN (USA) 2 b.f. Lyphard 132–Regal Exception 126 (Ribot 142) (1983 **80 p** 7g 7fg²) Feb 5; $675,000Y; compact, attractive filly; half-sister to 4 winners, including 3-y-o 1½m winner Sikorsky (by Honest Pleasure), smart French 1m and 10.5f winner Twilight Hour (by Raise A Native) and stakes-placed Beyond Recall (by Roberto); dam won Irish Guinness Oaks and was fourth in Prix de l'Arc de Triomphe; didn't find her stride until too late when head second of 17 to Signorina Odone in maiden race at Beverley in September; will be better suited by middle distances; sure to improve. *M. Stoute.*

RUM MUSIC 2 b.g. Music Boy 124–Rum Year (Quorum 126) (1983 5d 6f 6fg 6f) — Apr 15; neat gelding; third foal; half-brother to a winner in Belgium; dam placed over hurdles; behind in maiden events and valuable sellers; not seen out after August. *K. Stone.*

RUMOUR HAS IT 2 b.f. Owen Anthony 102–Press Button 58 (Precipice Wood 41
123) (1983 6fg 6g 7g⁴ 8f) Mar 8; sparely-made filly; bad plater; sold 350 gns
Ascot September Sales. *M. Smyly.*

RUM RIVER 3 b.f. Forlorn River 124–Gilead 90 (Quorum 126) (1982 6g 1983 –
10.1s 11.5fg 10f³ 14f² 14g 14fg) leggy, sparely-made filly; second in maiden race at
Yarmouth in August, best effort; evidently suited by a test of stamina. *M.
Tompkins.*

RUMZ 3 ch.g. Gay Fandango 132–Double Eagle 71 (Goldhill 125) (1982 6fg 6g⁴ 5f² 73
5d³ 6g 6g² 1983 6s* 6d 5f 6f³ 6f 6f⁴ 6fg) workmanlike gelding; rather
disappointing after comfortably winning maiden race at Hamilton in April; stays 6f;
acts on any going; blinkered third to fifth outings; often ridden by claimer W. Ryan;
looks ungenuine. *N. Callaghan.*

RUNAWAY GIRL 2 ch.f. Music Maestro 119–Gay Donna (Tudor Jinks 121) 90
(1983 5fg* 5g³ 5s 5fg 5fg) May 11; IR 7,000Y; small, good-quartered
filly; half-sister to 6 winners, all successful at 2 yrs, including useful 5f performer
Happy Donna (by Huntercombe); dam of little account; won 18-runner maiden
race at Leicester in June pushed clear by 5 lengths from Ridge The Times; 7½
lengths fifth of 10 to Superlative in Flying Childers Stakes at Doncaster in
September, third outing and easily best subsequent effort; probably acts on any
going. *R. Laing.*

RUNAWAY LOVER 2 b. or br.c. He Loves Me 120–Divine Fleece (Status 92
Seeker) (1983 8g 8g² 7fg) May 7; IR 10,000F, 6,200Y; fair sort; second foal;
dam second over 7.9f and 9f in Ireland; well-backed second favourite, 2½ lengths
second of 15 to Leadburn in maiden race at Sandown in October; beaten little over
½ length when fifth of 13 to All Hell Let Loose in £3,800 event at Newmarket
later in month; sure to win a race. *R. Hannon.*

RUNNING BULL (USA) 2 ch.c. Believe It–Total Crash (Ambernash) (1983 88
7fg* 6g 7f) Apr 28; strong, rangy colt; good walker; half-brother to 2 winners,
including minor stakes winner Ice Cold Cutie (by Icecapade); dam won 4 sprint
races at 3 yrs; 20/1, put in a strong late run to win 23-runner maiden race at
Newmarket in June by 2½ lengths from James Winkle; last of 6 in 2 races on same
course the following month, 11 lengths behind Superlative in Anglia Television July
Stakes and virtually pulled up in Exeter Stakes; stays 7f. *B. Hanbury.*

RUNNING MELODY 3 b. or br.f. Rheingold 137–Fleet Serenade (Lorenzaccio 84
130) (1982 7fg 8fg³ 8s* 8.2s 1983 10f* 12f 11fg⁴ 12f) fair sort; soundly beaten
after winning small handicap at Newcastle in June (interfered with third start);
should stay beyond 1¼m; acts on any going; sold 9,400 gns Newmarket December
Sales. *J. W. Watts.*

RUNNING PRINCESS 2 ch.f. On Your Mark 125–Purple Princess 93 (Right 101
Tack 131) (1983 5g* 6f⁴ 6f 7f 7f⁴ 6fg² 7g 6fg) Jan 22; IR 19,000Y; medium-sized,
useful-looking ex-Irish filly; poor mover in her slower paces; second living foal;
half-sister to a winner in Italy; dam won 3 times at around 7f; won 10-runner maiden
event at Down Royal in May; in frame in a variety of races subsequently, running
easily best race when neck second of 12 to Forzando in nursery at Doncaster in
September; evidently best at 6f; yet to race on a soft surface; trained by M.
Kauntze in Ireland first 2 outings. *B. Hills.*

RUN NORTH 4 b.g. Run The Gantlet–Eranos (Arts and Letters) (1982 8g 10.6s –
12f³ 12f⁴ 14f* 14g 16f 14fg 1983 17.1g) strong gelding; good walker but poor
mover; has shown no form since winning maiden race at Yarmouth in June 1982;
suited by 1¾m and should get further; acts on firm going; cost 625 gns Ascot March
Sales. *A. Barrow.*

RUN RIOT 2 ro.g. Runnymede 123–Pasla Princess (Ben Novus 109) (1983 5s 5s³ 70
5s² 5v⁴ 5f 5fg 6fg 5fg 5d 5g²) Apr 23; 170F; leggy, fair sort; second produce; dam
never ran; placed in maiden races at Newbury and Lingfield in the spring and at
Warwick (blinkered) in October; usually races freely and isn't sure to stay 6f; best
form with give in the ground. *W. Wightman.*

RUPERT BLEND 2 b.c. Royal Blend 117–Scilly Isles 54 (Silly Season 127) (1983 –
6fg) May 19; 700F; smallish colt; half-brother to 3-y-o 1m winner Silly Boy (by
Decoy Boy), to 3 winning jumpers and a winner in Jersey; dam half-sister to smart
miler Murrayfield; 9½ lengths fifth of 7 behind On Oath in maiden event at Haydock
in August; dead. *J. Wilson.*

RUSE 2 ch.c. Jaazeiro 127–Bay Laurel (Habitat 134) (1983 5.3f* 6f² 7f² 7.3g) Feb 93
14; 19,500F, 34,000Y; fair sort; second foal; half-brother to very useful 3-y-o

sprinter Prince Spy (by Ballad Rock); dam won over 7f at 2 yrs in France; favourite, finished very strongly to beat Floating Joker by 2 lengths in 10-runner maiden event at Brighton in June; second 2 months later in nurseries at Salisbury and Epsom; best form at 6f, but stays 7f; acts on firm going; taken down early final start. *R. Smyth.*

RUSHBEDS 4 b.g. Ercolano 118–Lichen Lady 70 (Pardao 120) (1982 12fg 12fg* 14fg² 16fg 14f³ 1983 12v 12g) big, strong gelding; fair performer at 3 yrs; well beaten both starts in 1983; stays well; acts on firm going; lacks pace and is suited by forcing tactics; sold 1,000 gns Newmarket Autumn Sales. *B. Hobbs.* —

RUSH FOR HOME 3 ch.f. Homing 130–Desert Flame 96 (Baldric II 131) (1982 NR 1983 6s 7d) 15,000Y; half-sister to fair 1½m and 2m winner Frasass (by Sassafras) and 2 winners in France; dam, half-sister to very smart Popkins, stayed 1¼m; behind in minor events at Brighton and Leicester in first half of season; sold to BBA (Ire) 5,400 gns Newmarket December Sales. *B. Hobbs.* —

RUSSBOROUGH 2 ch.c. Astrapi 85–Melpo 73 (Hook Money 124) (1983 6g⁴ 7f 6fg 7h 7.6fg 8fg* 10.2fg) May 14; lengthy, plain colt; fourth live foal; dam 2-y-o 7f winner; plater; showed improved form when battling on gamely to beat Brewis a head in 20-runner selling nursery at Doncaster (bought in 6,100 gns) in October; ran very well in non-seller on same course the following month; suited by 1m+ at two years and will stay further than 1¼m; acts on a firm surface. *B. Wise.* — 67 ?

RUSSET (FR) 2 b.f. Relkino 131–Elizabethan 89 (Tudor Melody 129) (1983 7g) Feb 25; tall filly; third foal; half-sister to fairly useful 1982 2-y-o 6f winner Elysian (by Northfields); dam, from excellent family, won over 1m on only start; unquoted and backward, made up ground hand over fist, after being scrubbed along and having lot to do at halfway, to finish 9 lengths fifth of 21 behind Mahogany in £4,600 event at Newbury in September; will be well suited by 1m+; one to note in ordinary maiden company. *P. Walwyn.* — 73 p

RUSSET LADY 7 gr.m. Wolver Hollow 126–Portden (Worden II 129) (1982 NR 1983 12d) small mare; of little account; has been to stud. *J. Townson.* —

RUSSIAN DEBONAIR 4 b.f. Balidar 133–Cala Na Sith (Reform 132) (1982 6d 5fg³ 5f⁴ 5f⁴ 5f 5g 5.3fg 6f⁴ 5f⁴ 5f 1983 5v 5.1fg 5.3f 6fg) sturdy, compact filly; sprint maiden; has been beaten in a seller; best run at 5f on firm going. *D. Wilson.* —

RUSSIAN ROUBLES (USA) 3 b.c. Nijinsky 138–Squander (Buckpasser) (1982 7.6s 7d* 1983 10v 12f² 12h* 12f³ 10fg) good-looking, rangy colt; good mover; second foal; dam, from same family as Posse, was one of best 2-y-o fillies of 1976 but failed to win in 10 subsequent races; showed easily best form and put up a smart effort when length second of 7 to Shareef Dancer in King Edward VII Stakes at Royal Ascot in June, making up a lot of ground in closing stages and giving impression stamina is his strong suit; beat Neorion without much fuss in 3-runner Welsh Derby at Chepstow the following month; sweated up and was never going very well when evens favourite for 6-runner Gordon Stakes at Goodwood later in July, eventually dead-heating for third behind easy winner John French, and wasn't seen out again until October, when well beaten in Dubai Champion Stakes at Newmarket; runs as though he'll be suited by 1¾m or more; unsuited by really soft ground and acts on firm; sent to USA. *J. Dunlop.* — 116

RUSSIAN WINTER 8 b.g. King Emperor–Am Stretchin (Ambiorix 130) (1982 6f 5fg² 6f 5f 5fg 5fg* 5f 5.8f 5.1g 5fg 6fg² 5g² 5fg* 6d 5fg 5d³ 6s 5g 1983 5v 6d 5g 5f 5g⁴ 5f 6fg⁴ 5fg* 5f⁴ 5fg 6d 6f 5f 5.6fg 5g 5fg 6g) lengthy gelding; sprint handicapper; won at Ayr in July; unsuited by really soft going; wears blinkers; excellent mount for an inexperienced rider; best on a galloping track; inconsistent. *A. W. Jones.* — 68 d

RUST FREE 4 gr.f. Free State 125–Iridium 78 (Linacre 133) (1982 6.5s 8s 10d 8d 7fg 7.6fg 7g 10g³ 10.4fg⁴ 11f 9g 1983 10s) workmanlike filly; poor maiden; stays 1¼m; sometimes blinkered; cost 1,300 gns Ascot March Sales. *A. Pitt.* —

RUSTICATED 2 gr.c. Rusticaro 124–Shapely 84 (Parthia 132) (1983 6g) Apr 3; half-brother to several winners, including useful 5f to 1m winner Red Emerald (by Red God); dam stayed 1¾m; broke a leg in maiden race at Newmarket in August; dead. *A. Stewart.* —

RUSTIC CHARM 5 br.g. Palm Track 122–Polly-Ann Tanja (Cletus) (1982 7g 8f 8g² 8g³ 10fg³ 12f⁴ 8g⁴ 8fg 8fg 8.2s 1983 8v 8s 10f 6f 10fg⁴) smallish, workmanlike gelding; plater; possibly stays 1¼m; acts on a firm surface; usually blinkered; sold 550 gns Doncaster August Sales. *J. Carr.* —

RUSTICELLO 2 gr.f. Rusticaro 124–Parima (Pardao 120) (1983 6f* 6g 8fg) Feb 21; IR 62,000Y; compact filly; carries plenty of condition; second foal; half-sister to a winner in Italy by Wolver Hollow; dam won twice in Norway; won Virginia Water Stakes (newcomers event) at Ascot in July by ¾ length from Bustling Nelly; showed little afterwards in Lowther Stakes at York and May Hill Stakes at Doncaster; should stay 1m. *J. Tree.*   **94**

RUSTIC LACE 2 gr.f. Rusticaro 124–Lacey Brief (Roi Dagobert 128) (1983 7fg* 8g² 7g) Jan 20; IR 29,000Y; rather narrow, sparely-made filly; second foal; half-sister to a fairly useful winner in Italy by Run The Gantlet; dam won over 9f in Ireland; put up a very pleasing first effort when winning 11-runner maiden race at Tralee in September by 6 lengths from Probability; beaten favourite in pattern races afterwards, better effort when caught close home by Shindella after making much of running in Silken Glider Stakes at Leopardstown; reportedly struck into when sixth in CL Weld Park Stakes at Phoenix Park; should stay 1¼m. *J. Bolger, Ireland.*   **97**

RUSTIC TRACK 3 b.g. Palm Track 122–Polly-Ann Tanja (Cletus) (1982 5f 5f 5f 5fg³ 6f⁴ 7f 5f 8fg* 8s⁴ 8d 1983 9d² 9f* 9.4f⁴ 8fg⁴ 9f* 9f³ 10fg 9fg 7fg) smallish, lengthy gelding; successful in sellers at Redcar in June (bought in 3,000 gns) and Newcastle in August (no bid); stays 9f; seems to act on any going, but is well suited by top-of-the-ground; sometimes blinkered. *J. Carr.*   **59**

RUSTLE OF SPRING 4 ch.f. Leander 119–Geraghty Girl 54 (Frankincense 120) (1982 5h 1983 5s 5.8s 6d 5f 8f 7.6fg 9fg 8h) lengthy filly; poor plater. *R. Griffiths.*   **–**

Mr Ogden Mills Phipps's "Russian Roubles"

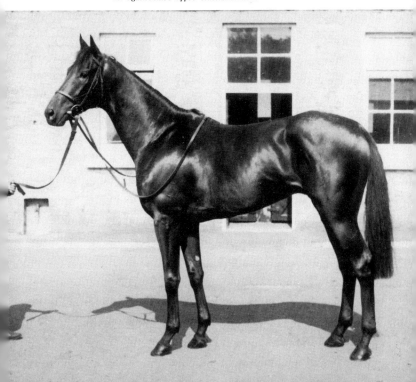

RUSTY BABY 3 ch.f. Patch 129–Edie's Court (Barrons Court) (1982 NR 1983   –
8.2fg 10f 12.2f 9g) 700Y; workmanlike filly; third foal; half-sister to 1m winner
Crown Counsel (by Simbir); dam never ran; little worthwhile form in maiden and
minor races. *E. Incisa.*

RUSTY BOY 4 ch.g. Rustingo 94–Cavalry Cloak (Queen's Hussar 124) (1982 NR   –
1983 8fg) second foal; dam never ran; well beaten in seller at Bath in September.
G. Price.

RUTHEFORD (FR) 3 b.c. Rheingold 137–Venetia (Luthier 126) (1982 9d²   110
8.5v⁴ 1983 12v* 12s³ 15d* 12.5fg) 200,000 francs Y (privately) (approx £18,000);
second foal; dam never ran; beat Diamond Rock decisively by 3 lengths in 65,000
francs event at Saint-Cloud in April and Homme de Paille by length in 7-runner Prix
de l'Esperance at Longchamp in May, getting on top inside last furlong on latter
course; suited by a test of stamina; best form on soft ground (soundly beaten first
outing on a firm surface at Deauville in August and wasn't seen out again). *A.
Fabre, France.*

RUTLAND 3 b.c. Mummy's Pet 125–Rennet 109 (King's Bench 132) (1982 5fg*   108
5f* 5g* 5f² 6d³ 1983 5g 5fg* 5f 6fg) lightly-made colt; good mover; won first 3 of
his 5 starts at 2 yrs; not so successful in 1983, best effort when beating 50/1-chance
All Is Forgiven by 2 lengths in 10-runner minor event at Sandown in June
(quickened up well when asked); behind in King George Stakes at Goodwood and
Orchardstown Stud Stakes at Phoenix Park afterwards; stays 6f; seems to act on
any going. *J. Dunlop.*

S

SAADA 2 b.f. Swing Easy 126–Sally Conkers (Roi Lear 126) (1983 5fg 5fg 7.6d)   –
Feb 11; 2,000Y; second foal; sister to 1982 2-y-o 6f winner Judy Conkers; dam in
rear all outings; no form in maiden races. *M. Haynes.*

SAB-AN 2 ch.c. Stanford 121§–Royal Tucson 87 (Henry the Seventh 125) (1983   71
6g⁴ 7fg⁴ 7fg) Jan 24; IR 4,400Y; quite attractive colt; half-brother to several
winners here and abroad, including quite useful 1975 2-y-o Tucsedo (by
Northfields); dam placed at up to 9f; quite a modest maiden; not raced after August;
stays 7f; blinkered final appearance; sold 1,600 gns Goffs November Sales. *W.
O'Gorman.*

SABATASH 3 b.c. Blakeney 126–Dominant 86 (Behistoun 131) (1982 NR 1983   79
12d 11d 12v 16f² 17f² 17g* 16f*) 24,000Y; compact colt; fourth foal; closely
related to very useful middle-distance stayer Mubarak of Kuwait (by Morston)
and half-brother to a winner in USA by Derring-Do; dam, winner at 1½m, is
half-sister to very smart English and American horse Dominion; improved when
given a test of stamina and a sound surface and won maiden race at
Wolverhampton and apprentice handicap at Thirsk; beat Summer Path
impressively by 8 lengths on latter course in July, but wasn't seen out again. *F.
Durr.*

SABHAN 3 b.c. Blakeney 126–Idiot's Delight (Bold Ruler) (1982 7g 7s 8d 1983   64
12g 12s³ 9g² 8.2fg³ 8.2f⁴ 10h⁴) strong, compact colt; promises to stay at least
1½m. *G. Huffer.*

SABI STAR 3 b. or br.f. Monsanto 121–Balandra Star 92 (Blast 125) (1982 6fg 5f   71
6g 5.8g 7.6v 1983 7fg 8.3fg 6fg 6f* 7.2g 8g 6fg²) workmanlike filly; plater; won
claiming handicap at Newmarket in July; should stay 1m; probably acts on any
going. *R. Hannon.*

SABLE ROYALE (USA) 3 ch.f. Real Value–Tiddlywinks (Court Martial) (1982   –
7d 7g 1983 6v³ 7v 8fg 7d) leggy filly; third in 6f minor event at Warwick in April,
only form; unseated rider leaving stalls next time; blinkered third start; sold 20,000
gns Newmarket December Sales. *N. Callaghan.*

SABRE DANCE 4 b.c. Dance In Time–Sarissa 105 (Reform 132) (1982 10.1fg²   114
10.1fg* 10.1fg* 10fg* 10.1g* 12fg* 12g 1983 10d⁴ 10fg² 10fg* 12f² 12f) big,
rangy, good-looking colt; landed odds convincingly by 1½ lengths from Commodore
Blake in 3-runner Land of Burns Stakes at Ayr in July; also ran well when 3¼
lengths fourth of 10 to Stanerra in Brigadier Gerard Stakes at Sandown, 4 lengths
second to same mare in Prince of Wales's Stakes at Royal Ascot and 1½ lengths
second to Seymour Hicks in Alycidon Stakes at Goodwood; poor last of 6 to
Lafontaine in £3,800 event at Lingfield in August; stays 1½m; probably acts on any
going; has a good turn of foot; sent to South Africa to be trained by H. Brown. *H.
Cecil.*

Queen Elizabeth II Stakes, Ascot—a notable performance from Sackford after five months off the course; he quickens away from Adonijah in fine style, the pair clear

SACKFORD (USA) 3 b.c. Stop the Music–Bon Fille (Ben Lomond) (1982 7.6v³ **129**
7s* 7s* 1983 8v* 8v⁴ 8fg* 10fg 7fg)

Sackford managed to salvage something from a season largely spoilt by
misfortune of one kind or another when he won the Queen Elizabeth II Stakes at
Ascot in September. That was only his third race as a three-year-old and his first
since finishing an unlucky fourth to L'Emigrant in the Poule d'Essai des Poulains in
the spring: he'd been kept off the course for five months by a viral infection and a
liver complaint. There wasn't much left for Sackford to go for afterwards. He ran
twice without further reward in different types of races from the Queen Elizabeth II
Stakes, coming fifth of nineteen to Cormorant Wood in the Dubai Champion Stakes
at Newmarket and fifth of eight to Ma Biche in the Prix de la Foret at Longchamp.
He appeared to have every chance in the Champion Stakes though there's just a
possibility that he suffered minor interference in a rough race; he definitely had
every chance in the Foret.

Sackford was so impressive in the Queen Elizabeth II Stakes that there's
every chance he's better than he showed later, and on his Ascot running he will be a
strong contender for the top mile races as a four-year-old. Despite his long absence
from the course Sackford was Starkey's choice of ride in the Queen Elizabeth II
Stakes in preference to Sackford's stable-companions Sandhurst Prince and Hays.
Sandhurst Prince himself had had a long time off but had finished a promising fourth
to Montekin in the Waterford Crystal Mile at Goodwood the previous month on his
return. Montekin was in the line-up at Ascot, as was the very unlucky second at
Goodwood, Adonijah, who started a short-priced favourite to gain compensation.
Other English-trained horses—the St James's Palace Stakes winner Horage and the
outsiders Commodore Blake, Welsh Idol and Lobkowiez—completed a field that
would have been improved by the presence of any leading overseas miler. With
several in the field suited by forcing the pace the gallop on the fast ground proved
every bit as strong as anticipated; in fact, the winner's time bettered the Ascot
round-mile record held by another Harwood-trained horse To-Agori-Mou.
Lobkowiez wasn't good enough to last long in the lead in this company, and he gave
way to Horage well before the home turn. For Horage there was to be no repeat of
his Royal Ascot performance; whereas he'd bravely hung on to his lead the length of
the straight in the St James's Palace Stakes he couldn't keep Adonijah at bay for
long on this occasion, and by the end had also given way to Sackford and Montekin.
Sackford tracked Adonijah into the straight. Before long the race had resolved itself
primarily into a contest between the pair and when the question came to be asked it
was Sackford who answered the better, quickening in very good style to lead inside
the final furlong and keeping on strongly to win by a length and a half. Montekin,
who'd finished an excellent third to Luth Enchantee at Deauville and a fair fourth to
Noalcoholic in the Sussex Stakes on his two outings prior to the Waterford Crystal
Mile, came in four lengths down on Adonijah, possibly being left with a little too
much to do but never looking like being any nearer. On the strength of this
performance Sackford started second favourite to Salmon Leap in the Champion
Stakes and a heavily-backed favourite ahead of Ma Biche in the Foret. It will hardly

703

be a surprise or consolation to the majority of his supporters to learn that we believe he failed to run within 10 lb of his best either time. Possibly the distance was too far for him at Newmarket where he was beaten about three lengths; it was certainly too short on the fast ground at Longchamp where he was beaten more than double that, outpaced throughout in the seven-furlong contest.

Sackford's form in the spring lived up to the promise of his two-year-old days when, after being slow to come to hand, he'd won minor events at Sandown and Leicester, the latter easing up by six lengths from Lofty. First time out at three he won the BonusPrint Easter Stakes at Kempton with any amount in hand by three lengths and two from Larionov and Guns of Navarone, then went for the Poule d'Essai des Poulains, the French Two Thousand Guineas, at Longchamp. Unfortunately for Sackford he was up against a much better horse there in L'Emigrant than anything the stable's winner in 1981, Recitation, faced; doubly unfortunately, he dwelt as the stalls opened and as a consequence had plenty to do on the turn, the winner well ahead. Sackford obtained a good run up the rails and went through under strong riding, but he lost ground to the even more unfortunate Margouzed in the last furlong; the impressive L'Emigrant beat him almost three lengths. Our first reaction was that he might not have stayed the distance but others thought he might need further, and the Mecca–Dante Stakes over ten and a half furlongs was announced as his next objective. Then illness began to interrupt his season.

There is a suggestion in Sackford's pedigree that he could stay further than a mile. His sire Stop the Music won over a mile and a quarter in the United States, his dam's sire Ben Lomond is a brother to the good middle-distance stayer High Perch and his dam Bon Fille is a half-sister to Royal Spirit, a good Canadian filly who twice won over nine furlongs. However, Bon Fille won only over sprint distances. Stop the Music has sired several stakes winners, and is also the sire of the latest season's Prix du Palais Royal winner Honeyland who stays a mile and a quarter.

Mr A. E. Bodie's "Sackford"

From her foals before Sackford Bon Fille had five winners in North America, including the very useful miler Good John (by Prince John), and one in France, Blacksmith (by Jacinto) a very useful performer at up to a mile. Her two-year-old French Story (by Speak John) has been placed in the United States. The next dam, a winner at three and four, bred several other winners besides Royal Spirit and Bon Fille, the best of them the Jerome Handicap winner High Tribute; she was a daughter of one of the best two-year-old fillies of 1935, Beanie M.

Sackford (USA) (b.c. 1980)	Stop the Music (b 1970)	Hail to Reason (br 1958)	Turn-to / Nothirdchance
		Bebopper (b 1962)	Tom Fool / Bebop II
	Bon Fille (ch 1962)	Ben Lomond (ch 1954)	Alycidon / Phaetonia
		En Casserole (ch 1952)	War Relic / Beanie M

Sackford, a well-made, quite attractive colt, has a slightly round action. After seeing him perform on soft going as a two-year-old we had reservations about his proving so effective on firm but he proved devastatingly effective on ground on the firm side of good in the Queen Elizabeth II Stakes. *G. Harwood.*

SACRED PATH 3 b.g. Godswalk 130–Crepe Rose (Crepello 136) (1982 6f⁴ 7fg 7fg³ 7.2f 8s 1983 10v⁴ 8g³) quite attractive, good sort; good walker; in frame in minor race at Kempton and maiden event at Bath in first half of season; stays 1¼m; acts on any going. *J. Bethell.* **68**

SADARA BOY 2 gr.g. Saritamer 130–Devadara 73 (Royal Levee or Hill Clown) (1983 6fg 7g) Mar 5; fourth foal; half-brother to 3 winners, including 5f to 7f winner Pete Rocket (by Roan Rocket); dam showed some ability at 2 yrs; behind in October in seller at Newmarket and minor event at Chepstow; subsequently gelded. *J. Holt.* **–**

SADARAR 2 gr.c. Absalom 128–Rockney 84 (Roan Rocket 128) (1983 5v² 7fg 6fg² 6fg 7d 7f 8g 6fg³) Mar 26; 12,500F, IR 14,000Y; small, lengthy colt; extremely good mover; half-brother to 3 winners, including useful sprinter Doc Marten (by Hotfoot); dam 2-y-o 5f winner; placed in varied company, on final occasion 2½ lengths third of 16 to Foot Patrol in claiming nursery at Newmarket in October; stays 7f; probably acts on any going. *R. Williams.* **78**

SADDAM 3 b. or br.c. Persian Bold 123–Peperonia (Prince Taj 123) (1982 NR 1983 10s 12v 12v 16g 14f 19h² 17fg² 16f 15.5f* 18f) IR 15,000Y; medium-sized, close-coupled colt; half-brother to winners here and abroad, including useful middle-distance winner Prince Pepe (by Prince Regent); dam minor winner over 1¼m in France; second in 2 handicaps before winning small maiden race at Folkestone in August; evidently needs a test of stamina; form only on firm ground. *F. Durr.* **65**

SADLER'S WELLS (USA) 2 b.c. Northern Dancer–Fairy Bridge 115 (Bold Reason) (1983 7g* 8s*) **110 p**
After El Gran Senor's victory in the William Hill Dewhurst Stakes Vincent O'Brien warned that anyone contemplating backing the colt for the Two Thousand Guineas would do better to back the stable as a whole, pointing out that any one of three other colts he holds in high esteem—Argosy, Capture Him and Sadler's Wells—could develop into the stable's leading contender. El Gran Senor was unquestionably the best of the bunch at two but no one can deny the vast promise of his three lightly-raced, unbeaten stable companions: Argosy, a half-brother to Seattle Slew and Lomond, ran out a decisive winner from some fairly useful colts on his only start; Capture Him was even more impressive on his sole appearance, slamming fifteen others in a Curragh maiden race; and Sadler's Wells did all that could be expected of him when winning both his starts by a wide margin.
Sadler's Wells started at 2/1 so when making his first appearance in a sixteen-runner race at Leopardstown in September, just half an hour after his rider, Eddery, had had a most uncomfortable ride without irons on Salmon Leap in the Joe McGrath Memorial. Sadler's Wells gave Eddery the smoothest of rides, racing in the first two until drawing right away in the straight to win by six lengths from Cyrano, an expensive newcomer from the David O'Brien yard. He was an even shorter-priced favourite for the Panasonic Beresford Stakes at the Curragh three weeks later. In a field reduced to four by the late withdrawal of the Coventry Stakes runner-up Hegemony and Sadler's Wells's stable-companion Grafton Street, he started at 7/2 on to beat Cerussite, runner-up in the Ashford Castle Stakes, Gimme

Mr R. E. Sangster's "Sadler's Wells"

Pleasure, who hadn't fulfilled the promise shown when winning his first two starts, and Shubumi, a fairly useful colt although still a maiden after seven races. Just as he'd done in the previous year's Beresford on Danzatore (another long odds-on shot by Northern Dancer) Eddery immediately sent Sadler's Wells to the front, and turned the race into a procession in the last quarter mile. Sadler's Wells shot clear to beat Cerussite six lengths, showing that soft going doesn't inconvenience him in the slightest. Some of the gloss was knocked off this display when Cerussite finished only eighth of nine in the Larkspur Stakes later in the month and a further sight of Sadler's Wells in one of Britain or France's big races should have given us a much clearer idea of his merit. Unfortunately he wasn't seen out against the top British and French colts—El Gran Senor represented the stable in the Dewhurst and Sadler's Wells was never entered in the Horris Hill, the William Hill Futurity or the Grand Criterium—so we are still a bit in the dark about him. But there's little doubt that Sadler's Wells has the potential to make an excellent three-year-old; only time will tell if he's good enough to replace El Gran Senor as the stable's Guineas candidate.

Sadler's Wells (USA) (b.c. Apr 11, 1981)	Northern Dancer (b 1961)	Nearctic (br 1954)	Nearco Lady Angela
		Natalma (b 1957)	Native Dancer Almahmoud
	Fairy Bridge (b 1975)	Bold Reason (b 1968)	Hail to Reason Lalun
		Special (b 1969)	Forli Thong

Hopefully Sadler's Wells will have a much busier racing career than many of his close relatives. His dam Fairy Bridge, whose first living foal he is, clearly had training troubles and was retired to stud at the end of her two-year-old days after racing only twice. She won both her races, sprints of no great importance at Phoenix Park by a head and five lengths respectively; after this it was a surprise to most when Fairy Bridge was assessed the equal of the Cheveley Park winner Sookera in the Irish Free Handicap, and a bigger one when she was described as 'champion filly at two in Ireland' in American racing magazines. Sadler's Wells's grandam Special, a sister to the top-class sprinter-miler Thatch and the Coronation Stakes winner Lisadell, ran only once (unplaced); her first foal, the five-furlong winner Kilavea, also ran only once. Another daughter, Wield, never made the racecourse but both Special's other foals of racing age did extremely well: Nureyev, by Sadler's Wells's sire, passed the post first in all his three races, only to lose the Two Thousand Guineas in the stewards' room, and Number, a tough filly by Northern Dancer's son Nijinsky, showed smart form to win two Grade 2 stakes races, the Firenze and Hempstead Handicaps, over nine furlongs. Other winners bred on similar lines to Sadler's Wells are the very useful Irish six-furlong performer Yeats, by Nijinsky out of Lisadell, and the disqualified July Cup winner Marinsky, by Northern Dancer out of Thong. Sadler's Wells, an attractive colt, has already shown he stays better than some of his relatives and he may well stay a mile and a quarter: his maternal grandsire Bold Reason won two good races over that distance, the Hollywood Derby and the Travers Stakes, as well as finishing third in the mile-and-a-half Belmont Stakes; and his grandam's half-brother King Pellinore was second in both the Irish Sweeps Derby and St Leger. *V. O'Brien, Ireland.*

SAFE HOME 2 ch.f. Home Guard 129–Azurn (Klairon 131) (1983 5s 5f* 6fg)   **94**
Mar 30; quite attractive filly; half-sister to several winners, including very useful sprinter Touch Paper (by Roan Rocket) and good 1978 Italian 2-y-o Nosy Be (by African Sky); dam half-sister to Blue Wind; having first race for over 3 months, never headed when winning valuable 6-runner Nishapour Curragh Stakes in July by a length from April Wind; beaten only 2 lengths when sixth of 13 to King Persian in Heinz '57' Phoenix Stakes the following month; should stay 1m. *J. Oxx, Ireland.*

SAFE PROCESS (USA) 3 b.f. Bold Forbes–Krassata 114 (Nijinsky 138) (1982   **105**
8.5g2 7fg2 1983 12v3 8v 10g* 11fg* 12f4 10fg3) second foal; dam fourth in Irish 1000 Guineas and Irish Guinness Oaks, and was very useful winner at up to 9f in USA; proved useful over middle distances, winning maiden event at Phoenix Park in June and handicap on same course the following month, and finishing in frame afterwards in Irish Guinness Oaks at the Curragh (6½ lengths fourth of 12 to Give Thanks) and £9,800 Shanbally House Stud Stakes at Phoenix Park again (5 lengths third of 7 to Homeowner); suited by 1½m; acts well on firm going. *D. K. Weld, Ireland.*

SAFFRON LADY 2 b.f. He Loves Me 120–Golden Gorse (Crepello 136) (1983   **39**
7f 8g 8d 10d) May 9; 1,000Y; leggy, lengthy filly; bad plater. *D. Ringer.*

SAFFRON POSER 3 b.f. Sagaro 133–Montelimar 108 (Wolver Hollow 126)   **–**
(1982 NR 1983 7.6g 8f 7s4 10.6g 8g4) 660 2-y-o; smallish, lightly-built filly; first foal; dam useful 5f and 6f winner at 2 yrs but didn't train on; quite a moderate maiden; stays 1m. *J. Berry.*

SAGACE (FR) 3 b.c. Luthier 126–Seneca (Chaparral 128) (1982 NR 1983 12s2   **127**
10fg2 10fg* 12s* 12f 12d*)
Few horses made such dramatic improvement in the autumn as Sagace who, if all goes well, will be a more than able back-up to his stable-companion All Along in the top middle-distance races in 1984. The season was two-thirds over by the time Sagace opened his account at Deauville but by the end of it he'd added decisive wins in the Prix Niel and Prix du Conseil de Paris at Longchamp and was firmly established among the top three-year-old colts.
Sagace's first run at Longchamp in April had been somewhat puzzling, for after looking likely to trot up he seemingly threw the race away by hanging violently across the finishing straight. Some observers were quick to condemn him as temperamental, but the explanation was that he'd torn a muscle in his back. There was no repetition at Deauville when he returned from a course of physiotherapy

Prix du Conseil de Paris, Longchamp—Sagace wins a shade cleverly from Galant Vert

and four months rest, and on the second of two outings at the meeting he beat the newcomer Garde Royale narrowly in a maiden event. Sagace was taking a big step up in class when contesting the Prix Niel at Longchamp in September and started the outsider of five, and he accomplished his task with surprising ease, producing a good turn of foot to beat Mourjane by three lengths. Mourjane, who had won his last four races, including the Prix Eugene Adam and the Prix de la Cote Normande, possibly found neither the distance nor the going ideal, but this was nevertheless a smart performance on Sagace's part. Jockey Saint-Martin was reportedly convinced that the colt had a good chance in the Prix de l'Arc de Triomphe over the same course and distance three weeks later, but as Saint-Martin was claimed for Sharaya Gibert took the ride. With only four races under his belt Sagace was much the least experienced of the twenty-six Arc runners, and in the circumstances he acquitted himself with great credit, racing in mid-field throughout and being beaten only about four and a half lengths into eleventh behind All Along. We've seen it said that he had an unlucky run; he certainly didn't have a great deal of room in the finishing straight but we doubt that it made much difference to the result. Unlucky or not, the experience did him a power of good and when returned to Longchamp a fortnight later he gained handsome compensation in the Prix du Conseil de Paris for which he started a short-priced favourite in the absence of any other Arc runner. Reunited with Saint-Martin and ridden with considerable confidence, Sagace quickened up really well on the outside from near the back of the field to take the measure of his chief opponent Galant Vert a furlong from home and win pushed out by a length and a half. The remainder, headed by Full of Stars, were well strung out at the finish and the four British and Irish challengers finished in the last six. Winning the Prix du Conseil de Paris provided a highly satisfactory conclusion to a season that had begun so inauspiciously for Sagace.

			Clarion III
Sagace (Fr) (b.c. 1980)	Luthier (br 1965)	Klairon (b 1952)	Kalmia
		Flute Enchantee (b 1950)	Cranach
			Montagnana
	Seneca (b 1973)	Chaparral (b 1966)	Val de Loir
			Niccolina
		Schonbrunn (b 1966)	Pantheon
			Scheherezade III

Sagace is from the penultimate crop of Luthier who missed the 1980 covering season owing to laminitis and died of a heart attack in September, 1981. Luthier's progeny did well again in 1983, despite Saint Cyrien's disappointing, and his winners included the Grand Prix de Paris winner Yawa and the Italian One Thousand Guineas and Oaks winner Right Bank; he's also the grandsire of Luth Enchantee. The dam Seneca descends from an outstanding German family. She's a daughter of Schonbrunn who after being purchased by M Wildenstein following wins in the German One Thousand Guineas and Oaks gained another valuable prize in the Grand Prix de Deauville as a four-year-old; interestingly the German One Thousand Guineas is named after Schonbrunn's great-grandam Schwarzgold who is said to be probably the best filly ever bred there. Seneca was reportedly rather delicate and made only one racecourse appearance, when a five-length winner of a small race over twelve and a half furlongs at Saint-Cloud. Both her previous foals have been only lightly raced: Spook (by Prince Tenderfoot) has been placed both on the flat and over jumps, the much better known Simply Great (by Mill Reef) won the 1982 Mecca-Dante Stakes and was ante-post favourite for the Derby when ruled out of the race by injury with less than a week to go.

We understand that Sagace will be aimed for some of the big prizes on offer in the first half of 1984 such as the Prix Ganay, with All Along likely to be saved once more for later on. He could do very well. Sagace seems indifferent to the state of the ground and certainly won't be inconvenienced by the muddy conditions that prevail in Paris most springs. Since he has been so lightly raced he may well have more than normal improvement in him and he has such a good turn of foot that he seems bound to win a good race or two. He's definitely one to keep on the right side. *P-L. Biancone, France.*

SAGAMORE 4 b.c. Sagaro 133–Veruschka (Turn-to) (1982 12fg² 12.3g 10f 16g³ **90** 12fg 11s* 16s 1983 10.2d* 12.2v² 12d 9s 12s 10fg 10f* 10g² 9g³ 8f 10.2fg² 9fg*) rangy colt; won amateur riders race at Doncaster in March, apprentice handicap at Newcastle in July and William Hill Cambridgeshire Handicap at Newmarket in October; made virtually all and held on well by a head from Teleprompter in last-named; best at middle distances; acts on any going; pulls hard, is suited by

William Hill Cambridgeshire Handicap, Newmarket—Sagamore holds on well by a head from Teleprompter

forcing tactics and isn't easiest of rides; has been taken down early; changed hands 31,000 gns Newmarket Autumn Sales. *F. Durr.*

SAGAR 3 ch.f. Habitat 134–Santa's Sister 104 (Middle Brother) (1982 NR 1983   **74**
7s 8g 10fg 10.1f³ 10fg⁴ 12g⁴ 10.5g* 10.5g) IR 140,000Y; good-bodied, fair sort; sister to stakes winner Placer Queen and half-sister to useful Irish 7f winner My Sister (by Nonoalco) and 2 winners abroad; dam won at up to 1m; blinkered for only time when narrowly winning minor event at Mont-de-Marsan in October; in frame at Windsor and Pontefract earlier in season when trained by B. Hobbs; stays 1¼m well. *M. Laborde, France.*

SAGARMATHA 3 b. or br.c. Shantung 132–Aberside (Abernant 142) (1982 6f   **–**
6fg³ 6f 6d 7s 1983 8s) lengthy colt; poor mover; no worthwhile form in varied company. *G. Balding.*

SAILING HIGH 2 ch.c. Take a Reef 127–Cloud Nine 97 (Skymaster 126) (1983   **84**
5g⁴ 7fg⁴ 6fg* 6d 7fg) Mar 10; 18,000Y; small, useful-looking colt; first living foal; dam won from 5f to 1¼m and is half-sister to Kilijaro's dam; won 11-runner maiden race at Hamilton in September by 3 lengths from Be There Baby; probably stays 7f; acts on a firm surface. *J. Bethell.*

SAIL LOFT 3 b.f. Shirley Heights 130–Set Free 90 (Worden II 129) (1982 NR   **74**
1983 7d 12s³ 12g 10d) quite an attractive filly; half-sister to numerous winners, notably classic winners Juliette Marny, Julio Mariner (both by Blakeney) and Scintillate (by Sparkler); dam won at 1m; pulled hard when 4 lengths third of 10 behind Shenton Way in maiden race at Haydock in May, best effort; suited by 1½m; blinkered final start. *J. Tree.*

SAILORMAN 2 br.c. Imperial Fling 116–Benedetta da Castello (St Paddy 133)   **79**
(1983 5s 5d 5s³ 5fg² 6fg 6f 5fg 5g* 5g⁴) May 27; 2,200Y; fair sort; good mover; half-brother to several winners here and abroad; dam never ran; won 19-runner maiden auction event at Warwick in September; creditable fourth of 12 to Broadwater Music in apprentice nursery at Sandown later same month; stays 6f; acts on any going except possibly very firm; blinkered seventh outing; trained by R. Thompson first 4 starts. *R. Hannon.*

SAILOR'S DANCE 3 b.c. Dance In Time–Pirogue 99 (Reliance II 137) (1982   **107**
7f* 8.2fg 1983 10.2s² 10f 10f² 12f 14.6s 12f) well-made, attractive colt; not a good mover in his slower paces; a useful colt who finished second in £3,100 events at Bath in April (went down by 3 lengths to easy winner Rock's Gate after making running) and Newbury in July (no match for rather clever 2-length winner Adonijah, but kept on well); had stiffish tasks on his other starts, and acted as pacemaker for stable-companion Sun Princess in St Leger and Prix de l'Arc de Triomphe on last 2 outings; should stay 1½m; acts on any going. *R. Hern.*

SAILOR'S PRAYER 5 gr.h. Martinmas 128–Coral Mermaid (Silver Shark 129)   **67**
(1982 6f 5f 6fg 5.8f³ 6fg 5g² 6f⁴ 5fg* 5g 5fg 5fg 5d³ 6s 6s 5s 1983 7s 6v² 6v 6f 6f 6h 5h 6fg 6s) leggy horse; poor walker; inconsistent sprint handicapper; acts on any going; trained by R. Thompson first 5 starts. *N. Vigors.*

SAINT ACTON (FR) 2 b.c. Phaeton 123–Sainte Maureen (Sanctus II 132)   **62**
(1983 8d 9s) Mar 17; 72,000 francs Y (approx £6,000); third foal; half-brother to French 3-y-o 1m and 9f winner Maurelock (by Gairloch) and minor French 9f winner

Marching Man (by Go Marching); dam won twice at around 1m at 4 yrs; showed little in October maiden races at Warwick and Wolverhampton. *A. Jarvis.*

SAINT BERNADINE 2 b.f. Welsh Saint 126–Crescentia (Crepello 136) (1983   **58** 6f 7f 6f 7.2fg⁴ 6fg) Apr 19; 4,000Y; fair sort; second foal; dam unraced daughter of Oaks third Pouponne; showed a little ability; dead. *S. Norton.*

SAINT CRESPIN BAY 4 ch.c. Bay Express 132–Crisp Piece 90 (Saint Crespin   **77** III 132) (1982 5d 5d 5fg² 5f3 5.3g 5fg 5g 5d 1983 6s 8v 7s 6g 6fg* 5f* 5.3f* 6f 5f* 5f² 6f 5f² 5.8fg 5g 5d³) workmanlike colt; sprint handicapper; ran more consistently than at 3 yrs and won at Nottingham, Wolverhampton (made all), Brighton and Sandown; beat Durandal gamely by ¾ length on last-named in July; acts well on fast ground; has run badly in blinkers. *R. Hannon.*

SAINT CYRIEN (FR) 3 b.c. Luthier 126–Sevres (Riverman 131) (1982 8g* 9d*   **110** 8s* 1983 8v² 8v 9fg) tall, attractive, imposing individual; first foal; dam, very useful winner at up to 9f, is half-sister to smart middle-distance filly Satilla; a high-class performer at 2 yrs when winning newcomers race at Evry and Prix Saint-Roman and Grand Criterium, both at Longchamp, last-named easing up by a length from L'Emigrant and The Noble Player after producing a magnificent burst of speed; met first defeat in Prix de Fontainebleau at Longchamp in April, looking tired at distance and having no answer to challenge of 2½-length winner Castle Guard; also disappointed both subsequent outings, finishing sixth of 10 to L'Emigrant in Poule d'Essai des Poulains on same course later in month (ran as though something was wrong with him) and sixth of 7 behind Glenstal in Prix Daphnis at Evry in July (never looked like getting on terms); stayed 9f; acted well on soft going; standing at Haras du Quesnay in 1984, at a fee of 35,000 francs. *Mme C. Head, France.*

SAINTE PARFAIT (FR) 3 b.f. Ben Trovato 128–Caecilia 76 (Skymaster 126)   **–** (1982 7g 8g 7d 1983 12s) workmanlike filly; in rear in varied races; sold 400 gns Doncaster August Sales. *D. Morley.*

SAINT JULIE 3 b.f. Monsanto 121–Tanzanite (Marino) (1982 6g 8d 1983 11.5fg   **50** 12f 10f² 11.5f 8.3f) tall, rather narrow filly; second in seller at Beverley in July; suited by 1¼m; sold 720 gns Newmarket September Sales. *C. Spares.*

SAINTLY LADY 8 b.m. Saintly Song 128–Melody Lady 74 (Highland Melody   **–** 112) (1982 9g 8.2g 9g 1983 12f) poor plater; has worn bandages. *M. Reddan.*

SAINTLY WAY 2 gr.f. Godswalk 130–Good Conduct (Sing Sing 134) (1983 5s³   **69** 5.8h⁴ 6h² 6fg) Feb 6; fair sort; half-sister to several winners, including useful French middle-distance filly Ho Han Wai (by Sassafras); dam never ran; quite a moderate maiden; stays 6f; sweated up third outing and was on toes on final appearance. *H. T. Jones.*

SAISON COQUETTE 3 ch.f. Silly Season 127–Frisky Molly 64 (Dumbarnie   **–** 125) (1982 NR 1983 12f 12f 8f) 1,600F, 610 3-y-o; rather sparely-made filly; half-sister to fair 5f winner Fingora (by Raffingora); dam won at up to 1m; tailed off in minor events and a maiden race. *A. Cawley.*

SAJEDA 2 ch.f. Mandrake Major 122–Siouxsie 90 (Warpath 113) (1983 5.1fg* 5f3   **94** 6fg² 6fg³ 5f² 5f3 6f 6g⁴) Mar 15; 15,500Y; quite attractive, lengthy, useful-looking filly; third foal; sister to fair 1982 2-y-o 5f and 6f winner Super Sioux and to Commissar, successful in a 6f seller at 2 yrs and subsequently a useful winner in Italy; dam 2-y-o 6f winner; won maiden race at Yarmouth in June by 2 lengths from Fairstead Belle; ran consistently well in useful company subsequently (third in Cherry Hinton Stakes at Newmarket, second in Molecomb Stakes at Goodwood, for example) until giving definite indications on last 2 outings of having trained off; usually races freely but stays 6f; has raced only on a sound surface; wears blinkers. *W. O'Gorman.*

SAKIMA (USA) 2 b.c. Sham–Exciting Divorcee (Candy Spots) (1983 6f) Apr   **–** 23; $75,000; half-brother to 5 winners, including fairly useful 1982 2-y-o 7f winner Rocky Marriage (by Riva Ridge), a stakes winner since in USA; dam, sister to dam of high-class Lemhi Gold, won at up to 6f; well-backed second favourite, last of 19 in maiden race at Folkestone in June. *C. Horgan.*

SAKLAWI 3 b.c. Sparkler 130–Princess Eboli 108 (Brigadier Gerard 144) (1982   **–** 6v* 1983 8v 12fg) no worthwhile form, including in an apprentice event; trained first start by M. Masson; sold 360 gns Ascot August Sales. *N. Callaghan.*

SALALA 2 b.f. Connaught 130–Mai Pussy 91 (Realm 129) (1983 7fg⁴) Apr 24;   **83 p** leggy, lightly-made filly; first foal; dam stayed 6f; 3 lengths fourth of 12 to Miss Saint-Cloud in minor event at Doncaster in October; will stay 1m. *B. Hanbury.*

SALAWA 2 ch.c. Mandrake Major 122–Tailor Donore 83 (Donore 119) (1983 6g   **76** 5.1fg 5g² 5g) May 4; 2,600Y; lengthy, useful-looking colt; half-brother to several winners, including Austrian 2000 Guineas and Derby winner Downholme (by Charlottown); dam 5f sprinter; 1½ lengths second of 13 to You Love Me in maiden race at Haydock in September; sold 5,000 gns Ascot November Sales. *I. Walker.*

SALDORO 4 ch.g. Cavo Doro 124–Salonica II (Ocarina 131) (1982 10.1fg 14g 16f³ 14fg 15.5f⁴ 15g 16.5fg³ 15.8d 14s 1983 12fg) neat, good-bodied gelding; moderate mover; staying maiden. *J. Winter.*   –

SALEAF 3 b. or br.f. Free State 125–Misfield 99 (Sahib 114) (1982 5fg 5d 5.1g³ 6g³ 6fg 6fg 6g² 5s³ 1983 5s 5v 7f 6g) lightly-built filly; below form in 1983 (pulled up second outing); stays 6f; possibly needs some give in the ground; blinkered nowadays; has run respectably for an apprentice; sold 500 gns Ascot July Sales. *B. Swift.*   –

SALIERI (USA) 3 ch.c. Accipiter–Hogan's Sister (Speak John) (1982 6fg* 6fg* 7fg² 6g* 1983 7d² 5f 6fg⁴ 7.3f* 7fg² 6fg* 7fg*) **131**

Thirteen of the one hundred and twenty-five two-year-olds in the Ladbroke European Free Handicap of 1982 belonged to the stable of the season's leading trainer Cecil. Pride of place went to the top weight and Guineas favourite Diesis (9-7); then Dunbeath (9-3), The Fort (9-1), Salieri (8-12), the filly Bright Crocus (8-11), Polished Silver (8-9), Now And Again (8-8), Fire-Thatch (8-7), John French (8-6), Alchise (8-5), Lord Protector (8-4), another filly Misguided (8-1) and Vaisseau (7-12). What a difference a year makes! Alone selected to do duty in the race, over seven furlongs at Newmarket in April, Salieri was beaten a length and a half by Boom Town Charlie; yet by the end of the season he had shown form in advance of any other three-year-old's in the stable and developed into one of the best of his age at seven furlongs and six furlongs in Europe. Such was his progress that missing the Prix de la Foret at Longchamp in October through a bruised foot may well have cost him his first Group 1 win: he had the best form of all those due to take part, better even than the eventual winner Ma Biche and the favourite Sackford, and on the day conditions were ideal for him.

Salieri produced his best form in the second half of the season, from the time he gave Royal Heroine 5 lb and beat her quite impressively by two and a half lengths in the Hungerford Stakes at Newbury in August. Hitting on his precise racing character took a while. The Free Handicap as usual represented good form—Salieri had given the winner 10 lb and the third horse Able Albert 9 lb—but apparently Salieri's rider Piggott formed the opinion that a shorter trip would suit him. However, though Salieri had been a relatively speedy two-year-old, speedier than his sire's first good horse in Britain, Beldale Flutter, and speedy enough to win the Mill Reef Stakes from Kafu, Krayyan, Horage and Fine Edge, dropping him down sharply to five furlongs proved no answer. He couldn't get near the likes of Sayf El Arab and Soba in the King's Stand Stakes at Royal Ascot on his next appearance, and was never higher than his finishing position of seventh. Six furlongs showed him in a better light. Not well drawn on the outside in the William Hill July Cup at Newmarket, he ran through gamely from halfway to finish fourth of fifteen to Habibti, beaten just over four lengths. Even so, Salieri's performance gave the impression that at six furlongs he was still being raced over a distance less than his optimum.

This impression persisted until Salieri won the Diadem Stakes at Ascot in September three outings later. In the meantime he at last received further opportunities of tackling seven furlongs, in the Hungerford Stakes (one of only two pattern races at the distance in Britain after Royal Ascot) and the Kiveton Park Stakes at Doncaster; he showed top-class form in both. The distance of the Hungerford Stakes is, to be precise, sixty yards further than seven furlongs: if Salieri had been a doubtful stayer he would have been found out in this, a fast-run, well-contested event. In fact he led from two furlongs out, taking it up smoothly after racing in fourth behind Horage, I'll See You and Gavo; from there he had only to be kept up to his work to hold off that good filly Royal Heroine, Tecorno and Drumalis. Winning at Newbury earned Salieri a 10-lb penalty at Doncaster. Despite his penalty he appeared to have an excellent chance and started at odds on in a slightly less competitive race than the Hungerford Stakes. But that was reckoning without Annie Edge's returning to her best. The filly reproduced her spring form—she'd been third in the Goffs Irish One Thousand Guineas and sixth to Ma Biche at Newmarket, don't forget—and in receipt of 13 lb from Salieri she managed to beat him in a tremendous finish. The result could have gone either way: Salieri fought back well after she'd thrown down a challenge at the distance, so well that there was only a short head in it.

The finish of the Kiveton Park derived added interest through featuring Piggott and his successor at Warren Place in 1967, Barclay. The latter, out of the limelight for the last few years, could claim a fair share of the credit for Annie

Diadem Stakes, Ascot—Salieri puts up an extremely game performance under inspired driving from Piggott to gain a head victory from Silverdip, with Soba in close attendance

Edge's win since without his strong driving she might well not have got up. When it comes to riding a finish Piggott has no superiors and few rivals among present-day jockeys. He and one of his outstanding contemporaries Eddery provided a memorable illustration of their art in the Diadem Stakes at Ascot later in September, Eddery on the three-year-old filly Silverdip who started third favourite behind Salieri and Soba. Soba was quickly into her stride as usual, not too quickly though for either Salieri or Silverdip who were both returning to six furlongs from seven. At the distance Salieri drew up to Soba's off-side and Silverdip drew up to her near, as they did so leaving the others struggling apart from the two-year-old Executive Man. By now Soba was becoming very tired; as she tired she rolled onto Salieri, giving Piggott an extra problem to deal with as he and Eddery went past Soba almost simultaneously and drove for the line for all their worth, each keeping himself and his mount beautifully balanced. The battle went Salieri's way by a head.

The Bisquit Cognac Challenge Stakes at Newmarket in October is the other seven-furlong pattern event staged in Britain after Royal Ascot. Perhaps the seven-furlong specialists deserve a slightly bigger slice of the cake. They are a small minority it's true, but their number might increase with more to go for: it's a debatable point, anyway. Silverdip was a late withdrawal from the Challenge Stakes. In her absence the race attracted less than a handful of horses known to be capable of extending Salieri at weight for age and sex, the best of them the improved previous year's winner Noalcoholic who started second favourite at 5/2 to Salieri's 13/8. Annie Edge received only 3 lb this time and started at 11/1. Noalcoholic used to earn most of his victories by galloping opponents into the ground. Here, as in 1982 when Motavato took him on, he had some difficulty in imposing his authority on the race, needing the best part of six furlongs to complete the job of shaking off the other would-be leaders, Sandhurst Prince, Rare Roberta and Annie Edge. He wasn't allowed to enjoy his lead for long, either: Salieri flew by him inside the last furlong to put him firmly in his place. In trouble early on and apparently none too promising just before halfway, Salieri was on the bridle three furlongs out; he hacked down into the Dip, and was ridden with supreme confidence to come and win going away by two lengths. Sandhurst Prince ran on to be third, a length behind Noalcoholic.

Contrary to expectations Salieri will not be racing as a four-year-old nor will he be at stud in England. He was bought by Tim Rogers, reportedly for two million dollars, to stand at the Widden Stud in New South Wales; he had, incidentally, changed hands previously for 37,000 dollars as a foal at Keeneland and for 8,000 guineas as a yearling at Newmarket. Salieri's departure leaves unanswered the interesting question of whether he was capable of staying a mile; at his best he was arguably superior to any in the Two Thousand Guineas field, or any of the European milers, come to that. Since he was never raced at the distance there must have been genuine doubts about his stamina, but it would have been interesting to see him given his chance in 1984. Salieri's sire Accipiter, now dead, won a mile stakes; the dam Hogan's Sister, unraced, is half-sister to several winners, including Father Hogan who won stakes events over nine and ten furlongs and stayed a mile and a half, and the three-year-old Northern Adventure who stays at least a mile. Hogan's Sister has had no other runner to date. Salieri is her first foal; her second, Key Lady (by Key To The Kingdom), was a two-year-old in training with Geoff Lewis in 1983; her third, a yearling by Dewan, was sold to Jeremy Hindley for 96,000 guineas at the December Sales. The family, well-established in the United States nowadays, traces to one of the Aga Khan's—the fourth dam was a sister to the Eclipse Stakes and Champion Stakes winner Rustom Pasha.

Salieri (USA) (ch. c. 1980)	Accipiter (b 1971)	Damascus (b 1964)	Sword Dancer / Kerala
		Kingsland (b or br 1965)	Bold Ruler / Landmark
	Hogan's Sister (b 1977)	Speak John (b 1958)	Prince John / Nuit de Folies
		Liz. Piet (b 1960)	Piet / Miss Elizabeth

Salieri is a lengthy, quite attractive colt, unusually unimpressive in his slower paces for a top-class animal. Equally effective at six furlongs and seven furlongs, he did all his racing apart from his outing in the Free Handicap on a sound surface, and nearly all of it on a firmish or firm one. He was a genuine and consistent sort, with a fine turn of foot. *H. Cecil.*

SALIX 3 b.g. Stradavinsky 121–Stipa (Silver Shark 129) (1982 6fg 6fg 1983 8v **67**
8d⁴ 9.4d 8d 12f³ 12fg 10d* 12g³ 12fg³ 10g²) big, lengthy gelding; bought in 1,050
gns after winning seller at Lingfield in September; ran creditably in non-sellers
last 2 outings, including in an amateur riders race; stays 1½m; blinkered fourth
start; sold out of J. W. Watts's stable 3,000 gns Ascot 2nd June Sales afterwards.
P. K. Mitchell.

Bisquit Cognac Challenge Stakes, Newmarket—much easier this time; Salieri beats Noalcoholic in good style

SALLAMETTI (USA) 5 b.m. Giacometti 130–Gay Sally (Sir Gaylord) (1982 8f   **45**
8f 11g* 12d 12g² 11fg 12.2f4 8.2s 1983 10f 10f⁴ 12f² 11f³ 12f³ 10fg 16f 15.8g 18g⁴
14.7fg² 15fg³) lengthy, lightly-made mare; poor handicapper; has been beaten in
sellers; stays well; acts on firm going; has run moderately in blinkers. *W. Bentley.*

SALLYALLY 2 gr.f. Warpath 113–Brandy Dip (Hot Brandy 119) (1983 10d) Apr   **–**
6; 3,000Y; fair sort; half-sister to fairly useful 6f to 1m winner Ziggy (by King Log);
dam never ran; last of 12 in seller at Leicester in October; sold 1,250 gns Ascot
December Sales. *Mrs J. Reavey.*

SALLY CHASE 2 ch.f. Sallust 134–Karen Chase 82 (Will Somers 114§) (1983   **101**
5.1fg 5f³ 5fg⁴ 6f² 5h* 6g* 5g* 6d* 6d) Apr 17; IR 9,000Y; compact filly; closely
related to 2 winners by Pall Mall, including fairly useful 6f and 7f winner Breathing
Exercise, and half-sister to several others; dam maiden sprinter; was in splendid
form August onwards, winning nurseries at Chepstow, Lingfield, Wolverhampton
and Lingfield again; suited by 6f; probably acts on any going; tough and genuine;
slowly away on final appearance. *A. Jarvis.*

SALLY'S RIVER (FR) 2 ch.c. Irish River 131–Sally's Wish (Sensitivo) (1983   **84** p
9s²) Mar 11; half-brother to 3 winners, notably very smart middle-distance
performer Lyphard's Wish (by Lyphard); dam ran 4 times; acquitted himself well
when beaten 1½ lengths by Flying Trove in minor event at the Curragh in October;
promises to stay 1½m. *K. Prendergast, Ireland.*

SALMON LEAP (USA) 3 ch.c. Northern Dancer–Fish-Bar (Baldric II 131)   **131**
(1982 8d* 1983 7s* 10s* 12s⁴ 9g* 10g 12f 10fg)
    It is more than coincidence that fillies and mares dominated the 1983
Trusthouse Forte Prix de l'Arc de Triomphe. The opposition from the colts was
much less formidable than usual, the weakest, taken overall, for many a year: apart
from Lancastrian and Sailor's Dance (who were linked for betting purposes with
Sun Princess) and Sagace (linked with All Along), Diamond Shoal and Salmon Leap
were the only colts to start at odds shorter than 21/1 on the pari-mutuel (there
were nine fillies at 18/1 or shorter). The cream of the three-year-old middle-
distance colts, the Derby winners of England, France and Ireland, were
conspicuous by their absence. In fact, of those that finished in the frame at Epsom,
Chantilly and the Curragh, Salmon Leap—fourth to Teenoso—was the only one to
take the field at Longchamp. Salmon Leap was the first colt home in the Arc, a
highly creditable fifth, less than two lengths behind the winner All Along, after
making up a tremendous amount of ground in the straight. Lovely Dancer, a
disappointment in the French Derby after finishing runner-up to L'Emigrant in the
Prix Lupin, came close behind Salmon Leap in seventh, the prominent showing of

Pacemaker International Whitehall Stakes, Phoenix Park—Salmon Leap wins from Chiavari

Mr R. E. Sangster's "Salmon Leap"

the pair restoring somewhat the reputation of the classic crop of middle-distance colts which, before the Arc, was widely held to be a moderate one by comparison with that of most other years.

Salmon Leap had remained unbeaten up to the Derby, winning a maiden race at Leopardstown in good style on his only start at two and taking the H.M.Hartigan Tetrarch Stakes at the Curragh in April (by two and a half lengths from Sir Prince John) and the Nijinsky Stakes at Leopardstown in May (by a head from the smart four-year-old Erin's Hope). Salmon Leap started second favourite behind Teenoso at Epsom, stable-jockey Eddery switching to Salmon Leap from the Two Thousand Guineas winner Lomond after heavy overnight rain. Eddery had Salmon Leap in a good position most of the way and turned for home about sixth or seventh on the inside, well enough placed, though not so well placed as Teenoso who was third with a clear opening to take up the running whenever his rider chose. Salmon Leap ran into a deal of trouble early in the straight, having first to be checked as one of

Salmon Leap (USA) (ch.c. 1980)	Northern Dancer (b 1961)	Nearctic (br 1954)	Nearco
			Lady Angela
		Natalma (b 1957)	Native Dancer
			Almahmoud
	Fish-Bar (b 1967)	Baldric II (b 1961)	Round Table
			Two Cities
		Fisherman's Wharf (ch 1959)	Alycidon
			Herringbone

the pacemakers Mitilini dropped back into his path and then switched to the outside to get a clear passage. Once extricated, Salmon Leap seemed to become unbalanced—perhaps through inexperience—and didn't really get into top gear until past the two-furlong marker. After depriving Guns of Navarone of third place inside the final furlong Salmon Leap was himself caught almost on the line by Shearwalk, the pair finishing six lengths behind Teenoso. Salmon Leap was off the course for three months after the Derby and won the Pacemaker International Whitehall Stakes at Phoenix Park on his return, starting at 11/4 on and beating Chiavari by two and a half lengths. Salmon Leap's performances in his races immediately before and after the Arc are best ignored: Eddery rode 'bareback style' most of the way in the Joe McGrath Memorial Stakes after an iron or leather

715

broke leaving the stalls; and Salmon Leap was probably feeling the effects of his exertions at Longchamp when weakening disappointingly to finish twelfth of nineteen in the Dubai Champion Stakes after looking dangerous three furlongs out.

Few of the inmates of Ballydoyle stables remain in training as four-year-olds nowadays. But the big, good-looking Salmon Leap will not be retired for at least another year. A successful campaign as a four-year-old—on his Prix de l'Arc form he should win good races—could boost Salmon Leap's stallion potential considerably. He is closely related to the top-class Kings Lake (by Nijinsky), one of Europe's most sought-after young stallions, and is a half-brother to four winners, including one of the fastest two-year-old fillies in our experience Cloonlara, herself the dam of the National Stakes winner Glenstal. Both Salmon Leap and Glenstal are sons of Northern Dancer. Salmon Leap stays a mile and a half well and is effective at shorter distances. He acts on any going. *V. O'Brien, Ireland.*

SALTATORE 3 b.g. Orange Bay 131–Sideshow 103 (Welsh Pageant 132) (1982 8g 10.2s 1983 12d 14s) tall, rangy, quite attractive gelding; lightly-raced maiden; looks very slow. *B. Hobbs.*   –

SALTCOTE MOSS ROSE 3 gr.f. Tudor Rhythm 112–Persian Kitty (Quorum 126) (1982 5s 5fg 5f 6fg⁴ 6fg 6s 1983 10v⁴ 11.7s 7fg 10f 11.5s 10g³ 9g) smallish filly; plater; stays middle distances; blinkered fourth to sixth starts. *M. Tompkins.*   51

SALTHOUSE 6 b.g. Blakeney 126–Grislе Run 94 (Stupendous) (1982 11g* 11s* 11.1g 10g 1983 12g) attractive, neat, strong gelding; poor handicapper; stays 1¾m; needs some give in the ground; has won for an apprentice. *A. Barrow.*   –

SALVINIA 3 ch.f. Mount Hagen 127–Aswellas 93 (Le Levanstell 122) (1982 6f 7g* 1983 7s* 7v³ 8.5g 7fg² 7s 6fg) rangy, quite attractive filly; justified heavy support in good handicap at Newmarket in April, beating One O'Clock Jump going away by ½ length; placed afterwards at York in May and Newmarket again in August (went down by a neck to Timber Tycoon when having first race for almost 3 months); ran poorly last 2 starts; stays 1m; probably acts on any going. *B. Hobbs.*   95

SAMANDAR (USA) 3 b.c. Decidedly–Dreaming (Bailarin) (1982 8g 1983 8d 8.2fg² 10f) close-coupled, workmanlike colt; second in maiden race at Hamilton in July, best effort (difficult to settle only subsequent start); stays 1m. *P. Haslam.*   66

SAMBOLA 2 gr.c. Absalom 128–Tritonia 69 (Tyrant) (1983 6f² 5f³ 6f 7f) Mar 3; 6,800F; small colt; poor mover; second foal; dam placed from 6f to 1m here and in Ireland; modest plater; best form at 5f. *J. Mason.*   64

SAM M (USA) 2 ch.c. Mr Prospector–Barbs Dancer (Northern Dancer) (1983 7f² 7fg⁴ 8f*) Feb 21; $375,000Y; tall, quite attractive, useful-looking colt; fourth foal; half-brother to 2 winners, including very useful sprint stakes winner Ruler's Dancer (by Irish Ruler); dam stakes-placed winner at up to 7f; won 18-runner maiden race at Leicester in November; pulled hard when disappointing fourth at odds on in similar event at Salisbury in September on previous appearance; stays 1m well; acts on firm going. *J. Dunlop.*   88

SAMMY BEAR 5 gr.m. Rupert Bear 105–Samba 69 (Sammy Davis 129) (1982 5d 5fg 6f 5f² 5g³ 5fg³ 5.6f 5fg 5g 5g⁴ 5fg 5d 1983 6v 5v² 5d 5fg³ 5fg 5g 5fg) strong, compact mare; speedy and best at 5f; acts on any going; sometimes sweats up. *W. Bentley.*   52

SAMMY WATERS 4 b.c. Rapid River 127–Sambell 71 (Sammy Davis 129) (1982 5fg 5fg⁴ 1983 5fg 6f 6f 6d 5f 5f 5g 5fg 5s) compact colt; sprint handicapper; acts on firm going; blinkered sixth and seventh starts; has sweated up and doesn't usually impress in appearance. *C. Booth.*   –

SAM PETE 2 ch.g. Runnymede 123–Dawn Wind (Tudor Jinks 121) (1983 6h⁴ 5f 5fg) May 6; poor maiden; sold K. Cunningham-Brown 850 gns Ascot October Sales. *N. Gaselee.*   –

SAM'S TAILOR 2 b.g. On Your Mark 125–Stand Off 61 (Murrayfield 119) (1983 5g) Mar 24; IR 4,200F, 4,600Y; compact gelding; third foal; half-brother to a winner in Belgium; dam won 5f seller at 2 yrs; 9 lengths sixth of 13 to Rex Lake in maiden race at Newmarket in April; afterwards raced with a lot of success in Italy, winning 6 times, including 7f Premio Mediterraneo at Rome. *B. Hanbury.*   ?

SAM'S TICKLE 3 b.g. Tickled Pink 114–Samoa Tan 89 (Pago Pago) (1982 6f 7.6v 6g 5d 1983 7.6v 8s 10v⁴ 10s* 10g 12f 16.5f) plater; bought in 2,000 gns after winning narrowly at Leicester in May; had stiff tasks in non-sellers afterwards; stays 1¼m; acts on soft going; occasionally blinkered at 2 yrs. *H. Beasley.*   42

SAMS WOOD 2 b.c. Jolly Good 122–Dust Sheet (Silly Season 127) (1983 5d 5g⁴ 6d⁴ 6d 6g⁴ 5.1f* 7f² 7f⁴ 7g³ 7g) May 31; well-grown, rather unfurnished colt; half-brother to 6f winner Chicken Again (by Royalty); dam ran twice; won claiming   84 race at Yarmouth in July; ran well in better races afterwards; suited by 7f; acts well on firm going; gives impression a galloping track will suit him; consistent. *T. Fairhurst.*

SAN BENITO 6 ch.g. Spitsbergen 103–Pollytooky (Polic 126) (1982 NR 1983   –
17.1g 17.1h) poor plater; has worn blinkers. *W. R. Williams.*

SAN CARLOS BAY 2 ch.c. Julio Mariner 127–Mimika 85 (Lorenzaccio 130)   **92**
(1983 7fg 8.2f⁴ 8d²) Feb 12; rather leggy, workmanlike colt; fourth foal; brother to
3-y-o Marinera; dam won over 5f at 2 yrs; showed improved form when staying-on
length second of 12 to Corinth in £3,500 race at York in October; will be suited by
1¼m; shouldn't be hard to place in ordinary company. *C. Brittain.*

SANDAAN 4 b.c. Zeddaan 130–St Louisan 109 (St Chad 120) (1982 6s² 5fg 8f   **57**
1983 8.3s⁴ 7s⁴ 7s 10.1fg² 8fg² 7.6fg 8.3f* 8h³ 8fg 8f³ 8fg* 7fg) tall, slightly
narrow colt; plater; won at Windsor in July and Bath (bought in 1,500 gns) in
September; stays 1¼m; acts on any going. *D. H. Jones.*

SANDALAY 5 ch.h. Sandford Lad 133–No Delay 72 (Never Say Die 137) (1982   **86**
16s² 12g* 13.3f* 16.1g* 18.4g² 18.8fg 1983 16g 14fg* 22.2f* 16f* 21f 16fg⁴) big,
rangy horse; put up an excellent display on third start when staying on dourly to
beat Heighlin 2½ lengths in Queen Alexandra Stakes at Royal Ascot; also
successful in handicaps at Sandown and Newbury; suited by a test of stamina; acts
on any going; has often made running; benefits from strong handling; never going
well when tried in blinkers once; genuine; useful hurdler. *P. Cundell.*

SANDCRACKER 4 b.g. Sandford Lad 133–Bubbly 61 (Busted 134) (1982 12.3f⁴   **47**
12f 12d 12g⁴ 16.5f³ 16.5f* 13.8f⁴ 16d 16g 15.8d 1983 12v 12d³ 16fg³ 14.6f 14fg³
16f 12fg 15fg) big, strong gelding; poor handicapper; has been beaten in a valuable
seller; suited by a test of stamina; seems to act on any going; usually blinkered
nowadays. *J. Etherington.*

SANDHAVEN 6 ch.g. Sandford Lad 133–Phobos 65 (Relko 136) (1982 NR 1983   –
12d) smallish gelding; poor handicapper; usually blinkered. *D. Grissell.*

SANDHURST PRINCE 4 ch.c. Pampapaul 121–Blue Shark (Silver Shark 129)   **124**
(1982 8s⁴ 8f² 8fg* 8f³ 8s 1983 8fg⁴ 8fg 7fg³)

Events conspired to make Sandhurst Prince's four-year-old campaign a brief
one, consisting of three races in a two-month spell towards the end of the year.
Successful in the Waterford Crystal Mile and placed in the Sussex Stakes and Prix
du Moulin at three, he suffered from the liver trouble that affected a number of
Harwood's horses in the first part of 1983 and consequently missed two of the races
in which his connections must have hoped to run him, the Sussex and the Jacques le
Marois. Though looking very well when he finally reappeared towards the end of
August in an attempt to gain a second victory in the Waterford Crystal Mile at
Goodwood, he ran as if needing the outing, soon pulling his way to the front, leading
by a length or so at the distance but being swamped in the closing stages as his
stride shortened, coming home just over two lengths fourth to Montekin.

Considering his long absence Sandhurst Prince had run a fine race yet Starkey
preferred another of Harwood's runners, Sackford, in the Queen Elizabeth II
Stakes at Ascot the following month and his judgement proved sound—Sackford
won readily with Sandhurst Prince back in fifth. The fact that he never reached the
front at Ascot as Lobkowiez and Horage set a strong gallop clearly did not suit the
rather headstrong Sandhurst Prince who always did best when able to blaze the
trail, and in the Bisquit Cognac Challenge Stakes at Newmarket in October Starkey
sensibly made no effort to restrain him. Battling for the lead with Rare Roberta and
Noalcoholic from the start, he had a slight advantage soon after halfway and fought
on well though headed first by Noalcoholic then by Salieri who cruised to the front
under a furlong out; at the line he was three lengths behind Salieri, two and a half
lengths ahead of the subsequent Prix Perth winner Rare Roberta. On this showing
Sandhurst Prince would probably have run well in the Prix de la Foret but the race
went by without him and he has been retired to the Cleaboy Stud in Ireland at a fee
of IR £6,000 (Oct 1st).

		Yellow God	Red God
	Pampapaul	(ch 1967)	Sally Deans
Sandhurst Prince	(b 1974)	Pampalina	Bairam II
(ch.c. 1979)		(br 1964)	Padus
		Silver Shark	Buisson Ardent
	Blue Shark	(gr 1963)	Palaska
	(b 1970)	Well Armed	Persian Gulf
		(ch 1961)	Armentieres

Though not so good as at three Sandhurst Prince ran well enough at Goodwood
and Newmarket to remind breeders of his ability and he should be popular as a

stallion especially as he is one of the most able runners from his successful immediate sire line available at stud – his grandsire Yellow God was exported to Japan in 1973 and both Yellow God's best sons, Nebbiolo and Pampapaul, died young. Sandhurst Prince is a half-brother out of Blue Shark to two winners, Saint Geran (by Red Alert), successful at up to a mile and a quarter, and the American winner Snake Hips (by Gay Fandango). Blue Shark, who showed little in four starts at two, is a daughter of the fair mile-and-a-half winner Well Armed whose half-sister Parlez-vous produced the smart colts High Game, Estaminet and Amboise. Sandhurst Prince, a rangy, quite attractive colt who showed a tendency to sweat up on occasions, stayed a mile and needed a sound surface to show his best form. *G. Harwood.*

SANDICLIFFE AGAIN (FR) 4 b.g. So Blessed 130–Never A Lady 112 (Pontifex) (1982 NR 1983 8v 7s 12s 12.2fg 10f 10.4fg) strong, lengthy, fair sort; showed fair form at 2 yrs; split a pastern in 1982 and finished well beaten at 4 yrs; blinkered final outing; sold out of B. Hills's stable 1,350 gns Ascot July Sales after fourth start. *M. Chapman.* —

SANDICLIFFE BOY 2 b.c. Jaazeiro 127–Almost (Levmoss 133) (1983 7fg 8fg) Apr 1; 12,500F, 20,000Y; big, angular colt; first produce; dam Irish 1¼m and 2m winner; showed up in first of 2 runs in big fields of maidens at Newmarket in the autumn; likely to do better in time. *B. Hills.* —

SANDIFOOT 4 ch.g. Hotfoot 126–Sandray's Palace (Royal Palace 131) (1982 8s 9g 12fg³ 13g* 12g 14.6f³ 12fg 12v 1983 13v) rangy, attractive gelding; poor handicapper nowadays; should stay 1¾m. *J. Haldane.*

SAND LADY 6 b.m. Sandford Lad 133–Ribocana (Molvedo 137) (1982 8fg 7g 10fg 8.3fg 8fg* 8g 1983 10d 8g 11.7f 11.7fg 8f*) ex-Irish mare; plater; backed from 10/1 to 2/1-favouritism when winning at Warwick in August; bought in 2,800 gns afterwards; probably stays 11f; probably acts on any going; used to wear blinkers. *J. Jenkins.* 54

SANDRA 2 gr.f. Saritamer 130–Balisarda 82 (Ballymoss 136) (1983 5v 5.1fg 7fg 7fg 7f 6f 6fg 6g) Apr 22; 800Y; small filly; bad plater; blinkered last 2 outings; retained 340 gns Doncaster September Sales. *G. Blum.*

SANDY CAP 2 b.f. Sandy Creek 123–Cappelle (Relko 136) (1983 5d³ 5fg 5d* 5d* 5f 6g 5fg 5g⁴ 6g 7g 6s) Feb 25; 1,700Y; small filly; half-sister to a winner in Scandinavia; dam never ran; successful in May in sellers at Hamilton (bought in 3,000 gns) and Carlisle (sold out of N. Tinkler's stable 3,200 gns); beaten in Scottish nurseries subsequently, running respectably most of the time; should stay 1m. *W. H. H. Williams.* 62

SANDY ISLAND 2 b.f. Mill Reef 141–Sayonara (Birkhahn) (1983 7fg) Mar 2; big, rangy filly; half-sister to 2 good winners in Germany, including German 2000 Guineas winner Swazi (by Herero); dam, winner of 5 races in Germany at up to 10.5f and second in German Oaks, is half-sister to German Derby winner Stuyvesant; 5/1, ran well to below distance when 5¼ lengths fifth of 13 behind Mahogany in Rockfel Stakes at Newmarket in October; will be much better suited by 1m+; sure to improve and win races. *H. Cecil.* 99 p

SANDYLA 2 ch.c. Quizair 103–Rosalind (Rosyth 94) (1983 5s 5g) Feb 19; 400Y; well-grown colt; first foal; dam last in novice hurdle on only start; in rear in maiden race at Leicester in April and maiden auction event at Brighton in May. *D. Dale.*

SANDY LOOKS 3 ch.f. Music Boy 124–Hannah Darling 108 (Match III 135) (1982 5fg 6h³ 7d 1983 8f 12.2f) well-made filly; has a capped off-hock; lightly-raced maiden; split a pastern at 2 yrs; not sure to stay 1m; acts on hard going; sold to R. Holder 2,400 gns Newmarket Autumn Sales. *C. Brittain.* —

SANDY RIVER 2 ch.c. Sandy Creek 123–Queen Of The Ice (Blue Prince 123) (1983 5d 5s 5s* 5d⁴ 6f³ 6fg⁴ 6fg 7g 7g) Feb 21; 8,400F, 6,200Y; small, sturdy colt; second produce; dam won at up to 1¼m in USA, including claiming races; ½-length winner from Kung Fu Master in 11-runner maiden race at Leicester in April; put up best subsequent effort when 7 lengths third to Gaius in 5-runner minor event at Pontefract in June; should be suited by 7f; acts on any going. *R. Hollinshead.* 75

SAN FERMIN 4 ch.g. Sallust 134–Ilsebill (Birkhahn) (1982 6s 7g 8fg 1983 12v 10h* 10fg² 12d² 12d 11fg*) compact gelding; won handicaps at Nottingham in August (backed from 20/1 to 11/2) and Redcar in October; stays 1½m; yet to show he can handle very soft ground but acts on any other; has run creditably for an apprentice. *J. Fitzgerald.* 59

Mr Roy Taiano's "Santella Man"

SANHEDRIN (FR) 6 ch.g. Satingo 129–India (Hautain 128) (1982 NR 1983 —
12g 12f) fair sort; poor middle-distance performer nowadays. *G. Balding.*

SANJARIDA 5 b.g. Sandford Lad 133–Caught In The Rye 97 (Manacle 123) (1982 **80**
6fg 6f 6fg* 6fg² 6fg 6f³ 6f² 6fg* 6g 5d 1983 6v 5.8g 6f⁴ 6f³ 6f 6fg⁴ 6d 5.8fg* 6g)
leggy, lightly-made gelding; sprint handicapper; won at Bath in September; stays
6f; ideally suited by a sound surface; blinkered once; suited by waiting tactics;
sold 6,200 gns Newmarket Autumn Sales and is to be trained by P. Haslam. *M.
Smyly.*

SANTELLA KING (USA) 3 b.c. King Pellinore 127–Timing (Bold Ruler) **87**
(1982 6fg 6f³ 7.2g⁴ 7f 8g 8g 1983 10s⁴ 12g³ 12f* 12.2fg³ 12f* 12f* 14d 12s) rangy,
attractive colt; in good form in summer and readily won 3 handicaps at
Folkestone; didn't have best of runs fourth start; stays 1½m; seems to need a
sound surface; useful young hurdler. *G. Harwood.*

SANTELLA MAN 4 ch.c. Nebbiolo 125–Belle Bretonne 90 (Celtic Ash) (1982 **117**
10f 12f⁴ 16fg² 16g* 14fg 14f* 18g³ 16d 18d 1983 16g 16f* 21f³ 16g 18fg⁴) smallish,
well-made colt; good mover; made up a deal of ground in straight when leading on
post to beat Karadar a short head in Queen's Vase at Royal Ascot; kept on at one
pace to be 6½ lengths third to Little Wolf in Goodwood Cup in July and 5 lengths
fourth of 8 to Karadar in Doncaster Cup in September; suited by a test of stamina;
acts on any going but is best served by a sound surface. *G. Harwood.*

SANTON BOY 2 b.c. Anton Lad 103–Sally Jane 86 (Royal Palm 131) (1983 5f) —
Apr 24; strong, workmanlike colt; has a long stride; second reported foal; dam

719

sprinter; eighth of 9 in valuable seller at York in August; sold 460 gns Doncaster November Sales. *C. Thornton.*

SANU 5 b.h. Steel Heart 128–Light Link 99 (Tudor Music 131) (1982 6f 6g 6fg³ 6f **86** 5g 5f 5.3f* 5fg² 6f 5d 5v 1983 5g 5s 6g 6f 5g³ 5f⁴ 5f⁴ 5fg 6f 5g 5fg² 5s) sprint handicapper; stays 6f; ideally suited by top-of-the-ground; blinkered fifth and final starts; sold 8,000 gns Newmarket Autumn Sales and has been sent to Trinidad. *F. Durr.*

SAQQARA 3 b.f. Persian Bold 123–Ballinteskin (Busted 134) (1982 6fg 6g 6s² **66** 1983 8v 8v⁴ 10f 8d 7.6fg 7s*) close-coupled, rather lightly-made filly; awarded handicap at Wolverhampton in October after going down by a head to Lemelasor; stays 1m; ideally suited by plenty of give in the ground; sold 3,000 gns Newmarket Autumn Sales, probably for export to Scandinavia. *P. Makin.*

SARAB 2 b.c. Prince Tenderfoot 126–Carnival Dance 69 (Welsh Pageant 132) **89** (1983 5fg* 5f* 5g 7fg) Apr 8; IR 2,200Y; lengthy, fair sort; first foal; dam beaten over 1m and 1¼m; won maiden auction race at Warwick in June and minor event at Beverley in August; should stay 7f. *P. Cole.*

SARACEN 3 b.c. Sharpen Up 127–Awash (Busted 134) (1982 6s² 1983 6g* 7f) **101** really good-looking colt; confirmed the promise of his only outing as a 2-y-o and was most impressive when beating Glorious Jane by 5 lengths in 13-runner maiden race at Phoenix Park in May; not seen out after finishing only seventh of 13 behind Tecorno in Jersey Stakes at Royal Ascot the following month (well-backed favourite); should stay beyond 6f. *D. O'Brien, Ireland.*

SARAH COURT 3 b.f. Rhodomantade 110–High Meadow 105 (High Treason **–** 126) (1982 5f 6fg 5fg 8f 8s 1983 10f) workmanlike filly; well beaten in maiden races. *H. Westbrook.*

SARAH GILLIAN (USA) 3 b.f. Zen–Kim's Song (Journalist) (1982 8g 1983 **–** 10d 12s 11.5fg 9f) tall, lightly-made filly; well beaten all outings, often in good company; sold 370 gns Ascot November Sales. *P. Kelleway.*

SARAH'S JOY 2 b.f. Full of Hope 125–Nicolene 91 (Nice Music 115) (1983 **–** 5.8h) small, close-coupled, deep-girthed filly; first foal; dam won over 1¼m and 1½m; never-dangerous 8 lengths seventh of 14 to Boezinge in maiden race at Bath in August; very on edge in paddock when withdrawn at Salisbury the following month; will be suited by longer distances. *R. Holder.*

SARAH'S VENTURE 4 br.f. Averof 123–Railway Hill (Guersant 129) (1982 **–** 7.6f 7fg 10fg 8g⁴ 8s² 1983 8g 7.6fg) small, fair sort; poor maiden; has been beaten in a seller; stays 1m; acts on any going; blinkered once; trained part of season by P. Mitchell. *C. Horgan.*

SARA LEE 2 ch.f. Little Current–Serenita (Lyphard 132) (1983 7s² 8fg² 8f² **105** 7d*) second foal; half-sister to useful French 3-y-o middle-distance filly Sorbonne (by Alleged); dam, from family of Sicambre, won twice at around 1m; showed promise in newcomers and maiden events before accounting for Margo's Mink and Maria Star by 2 lengths in maiden event at Saint-Cloud in November; should stay 1¼m; progressive sort. *Mme C. Head, France.*

SARANITA 4 b. or br.f. Thatch 136–Sarania 118 (Sassafras 135) (1982 7fg 8fg 8f **?** 8s 9s 7s² 1983 8g* 6.5d 8s) good sort; good walker; narrowly won race at Cagnes-sur-Mer in spring; well beaten next 2 outings; stays 1m; acts on soft going; sometimes blinkered but not when successful. *J. Dunlop.*

SARATINO 3 ch.c. Bustino 136–Sarah Siddons (Reform 132) (1982 7.6v 7d 1983 **77** 11s 11.7v 11.7v 8f² 8fg* 8fg 8h³ 8g) big, sparely-made colt; made all and stayed on strongly when winning maiden event at Ayr in July; should stay beyond 1m; acts well on firm ground; best in blinkers; sold to P. Mitchell 7,800 gns Newmarket Autumn Sales. *I. Balding.*

SARATOGA CHIP (USA) 5 b.m. Plenty Old–Saratoga Gal (Royal Orbit) (1982 **–** 8f 7fg³ 10.6f 8f 8.3fg 8.3g 7g⁴ 8s 8.2v 1983 10.1d 8f 7f 10f 10f 10f 14fg) lightly-made mare; poor plater; sometimes blinkered. *R. Voorspuy.*

SARAZIYR 4 ch.c. Sallust 134–Tazeem (Prince Taj 123) (1982 7d² 8.5g 10g* 9g² **84** 8g* 9.2fg 10d 1983 9s³ 12g* 12f 12.2f* 16g 15g 14d) rangy ex-French colt; good walker but moderate mover (had a round action); half-brother to several winners in France, including middle-distance filly Shahneez (by St Paddy); dam, daughter of 1,000 Guineas runner-up Tambara, won small 1m race in France; won amateur riders race at Hamilton in June and 4-runner apprentice race at Catterick in August; stayed 1½m well, but had been soundly beaten over further; acted on firm going; trained by A. Jarvis first 6 starts; dead. *S. Mellor.*

SARENA PLASTICS 3 b.g. Saulingo 122–Good Court (Takawalk II 125) (1982 —
5f⁴ 5fg 6s 7g 6d 6s 1983 7.6v 5.8g 5fg 6fg 7fg 10.1f) strong, compact gelding;
plater; best form at 6f; acts on a soft surface; blinkered final start. *S. Harris.*

SARITAMER LASS 2 b.f. Saritamer 130–Ann's Beam (Bold and Free 118) —
(1983 6g 8.2fg) Mar 10; third foal; dam well behind both starts; last in sellers at
Yarmouth and Nottingham in September; sold T. Kersey 380 gns Doncaster
October Sales. *B. Richmond.*

SARSFIELD 5 br.g. Lord Gayle 124–Sayann (Sayajirao 132) (1982 NR 1983 —
17.1g³ 16.1fg) strong, compact ex-Irish gelding; stays very well; looked
unenthusiastic second start; winning hurdler; sold to J. Roberts 3,000 gns Ascot
September Sales. *Mrs M. Rimell.*

SASCEROLE 2 b.f. Decoy Boy 129–Red Barrel 95 (Aureole 132) (1983 5.8g² 6f 73
5f² 5f⁴ 5fg 5s³ 6g 5g 5g³) Feb 20; 2,000Y; rather lightly-built filly; half-sister to
very useful 1976 2-y-o Cosy Bar (by Be Friendly) and useful stayer Reviver (by
Only for Life); dam won at 1¼m; in frame in a variety of races, penultimate
occasion beaten narrowly in nursery at Ayr in September; best form at 5f; acts on
any going; blinkered seventh and eighth outings. *M. Usher.*

SASHAMEL 4 ch.g. Tower Walk 130–Misty Echo 58 (Mountain Call 125) (1982 —
8fg 8fg² 8f⁴ 7fg³ 8g⁴ 8g 8s 1983 8s⁴ 7s 8f² 10f 8f) useful sort; poor mover;
former plater; stays 1m; probably acts on any going; blinkered twice in 1981;
suitable mount for an apprentice. *R. Hodges.*

SASSAGRASS (FR) 2 b.c. Thatch 136–Sassabunda 108 (Sassafras 135) (1983 95 p
7fg 9s* 8fg*) Mar 13; $110,000Y; big, good-topped colt; good walker; has a round
action; third foal; half-brother to middle-distance winner Nauteous (by Nonoalco)
and 3-y-o 1m to 10.2f winner Habitassa (by Habitat); dam short-head second in
Irish Guinness Oaks; won twice in October, beating Destroyer in fine style by 4
lengths in maiden race at Wolverhampton and then making nearly all under top
weight to win £3,200 event at Newmarket by a neck from Doubleton; will stay
1½m; has the scope to develop into a useful 3-y-o. *G. Harwood.*

SASSANOCO 2 b.c. Nonoalco 131–Sassanian (Sassafras 135) (1983 6fg³ 7fg) 79
Apr 19; big colt; third reported foal; dam, winner of 5 races in Spain, is sister to
smart 6f and 1¼m winner Sarania; showed up in minor events at Nottingham and
Doncaster in the autumn; lacks pace, and will be better suited by 1m+. *H. T.
Jones.*

SATCH 2 b.g. Music Maestro 119–Nicolina 97 (Matador 131) (1983 6g 6f 7d 7.2s⁴ 69
8fg) Feb 16; neat, strong gelding; sixth foal; half-brother to a winner over jumps;
dam, half-sister to High Line, probably stayed 1m; 4½ lengths fourth of 14
finishers behind Viva Lucia in selling nursery at Haydock in October; suited by 7f;
acts on soft going. *J. Dunlop.*

SATINETTE 2 b.f. Shirley Heights 130–Silk Stocking 109 (Pardao 120) (1983 6g 109
7f* 7fg² 8fg*)
     The excellent results obtained by Shirley Heights's first two crops show he is
passing on much of his ability to a good number of his offspring: among his first
three-year-olds are the Oaks runner-up Acclimatise and the high-class stayer High
Hawk, while as many as nine of his two-year-olds won in Britain or France, with
Darshaan, Elegant Air and Satinette picking up pattern races. Shirley Heights also
appears to be passing on a few other qualities and characteristics: all his stock, bar
the occasional grey out of a grey mare, are bay; most of his progeny stay well
(seven of his eight three-year-old winners in Britain and France gained their
successes over and mile and a quarter or more, the exception being the French
miler High Matinee, a daughter of the very speedy Matinee); and, oddly enough,
several of his daughters, notably Out of Shot, Road To The Top, Streamertail and
Satinette, have shown themselves pronounced tail-swishers. Tail-swishing is often
regarded as a sign of doubtful temperament, of a lack of honesty, but it isn't
necessarily so. That wonderfully game filly Gwen, runner-up in the 1964 One
Thousand Guineas, seemed almost to gain added propulsion from her tail; and no
one would dream of questioning the courage of Diamond Shoal who flashed his tail
repeatedly in the King George VI and Queen Elizabeth Diamond Stakes.
Interestingly Diamond Shoal shares the same sire as Shirley Heights who also
swished his tail to some extent when winning the Derby extremely pluckily.
     Satinette developed into a leading staying two-year-old filly in a non-vintage
year in that department. From the moment she first appeared on a racecourse, in
the Princess Maiden Stakes at Newmarket in July, it was obvious that Satinette was
a filly with a future; as well as being a rangy, good sort, she impressed as a good

May Hill Stakes, Doncaster—Satinette comfortably accounts for Nepula

walker and excellent mover. Although she started a clear favourite at 3/1 in a twenty-seven strong field, Satinette looked in need of the run and she finished only eighth behind Desirable, giving the impression six furlongs was too sharp. Less than three weeks later Satinette did much better over an extra furlong in the New Ham Stakes at Goodwood, and won by three quarters of a length from Exactly Like You after leading on the bridle early in the straight. However, her tail-swishing increased in proportion to her rider's pressure and it did so again when she was returned to Goodwood in August for the Waterford Candelabra Stakes in which she started fourth choice in the betting behind the very progressive Shoot Clear. Satinette proved the only one capable of giving the front-running Shoot Clear a race, chasing her all the way up the straight and going down by only a length. Surprisingly when the pair met again soon afterwards in the May Hill Stakes at Doncaster Shoot Clear was again made favourite although a mile was far more likely to favour Satinette, who had the added advantage of being 7 lb better off. With Shoot Clear being held up to get the trip, Satinette took charge fully three furlongs out and ran on far too strongly for the others, scoring by a length and a half from Nepula with Shoot Clear the same margin further away in third. Satinette was due to meet Nepula again on terms 7 lb worse in the Hoover Fillies Mile later in September but unfortunately she had to miss the race after developing a high temperature the day before, the same day her owner lost his admirable colt Falstaff in an accident on the gallops.

		Mill Reef	Never Bend
Satinette (b.f. Feb 23, 1981)	Shirley Heights (b 1975)	(b 1968)	Milan Mill
		Hardiemma	Hardicanute
		(b 1969)	Grand Cross
	Silk Stocking (ch 1970)	Pardao	Pardal
		(ch 1958)	Three Weeks
		Floss	Counsel
		(ch 1961)	Denturial

Satinette's dam Silk Stocking has a somewhat unusual record as a broodmare. Since producing the Queen's Hussar colt Blue Patrol, a winner over seven furlongs and a mile, in her first year at stud she has produced five fillies, the last two being a yearling by Blakeney and a foal by Final Straw. All four of her foals of racing age are winners, the others being the mile winner Organdy (by Blakeney) who was sold for 70,000 guineas at the end of her racing career and the three-year-old Silk Pyjamas (by Queen's Hussar), who put up good efforts as a juvenile to finish a close third in the Cherry Hinton Stakes and second in the May Hill. Silk Stocking was also a more-than-useful performer on the racecourse, making her first appearance as a three-year-old, when unbeaten in three races at up to a mile and a quarter, one of them the Strensall Stakes at York. Silk Stocking's half-brother Shiny Tenth won the Free Handicap, the Abernant Stakes and the Palace House Stakes among other races. Their dam Floss was a fairly useful staying two-year-old. Mile-and-a-half winners from this family are few and far between, but with Shirley Heights as her sire Satinette will probably be suited by middle distances. She acts well on fast ground and has yet to race on a soft surface. She should win more good races. *R. Hern.*

SATIN GRANGE 5 br. g. Satingo 129–Court Circular (Ambiorix 130) (1982   **51**
8.2s² 8f² 8g 8g 8fg 1983 8s³ 10g 10.2g² 10fg* 12fg) plater; attracted no bid after
winning at Yarmouth in June; stays 1¼m; acts on any going; blinkered once; has
shown a tendency to hang. *C. James.*

SATINO 2 b.c. Bustino 136–Salote 109 (Forli) (1983 7f 7f 7g) Apr 16; big, strong,   **64 p**
rangy, quite attractive colt; third foal; half-brother to French 3-y-o 1½m winner
River Isle (by Rheingold); dam suited by 1½m; improved with each outing, on final
one finishing 14½ lengths fifth of 18 to Gold And Ivory in maiden race at Goodwood
in September; will be much better suited by 1m+; sent to France. *R. Hern.*

SATURNIAN 2 ch.c. Sallust 134–Thrifty Trio 116 (Groton) (1983 5v 6d² 6fg*)   **92 p**
Apr 15; IR 35,000F, 41,000C; well-made, attractive colt; second foal; half-
brother to 3-y-o 5f winner Luck Penny (by Bustino); dam smart sprinter; having
first race since May, 2 lengths second of 17 to Cremets in maiden event at
Newbury in October; made virtually all in 20-runner maiden race at Newmarket
later in month, winning by ½ length from Native Charmer; acts on a firm and a
soft surface; promises to make useful 3-y-o. *R. Hern.*

SAUCY OLIVE 6 b.m. Gilded Leader 75–Olives Girl (St Xavier 77) (1982 NR   –
1983 12fg 10.6fg) lightly-made mare; tailed off both races, one of them a seller. *B.
McMahon.*

SAUCY SAPPHIRE 2 ch.f. Blue Cashmere 129–Saucy Jane 82 (Hard Sauce   –
131) (1983 6f 6f) May 29; 800Y; plain filly; sister to a minor 2-y-o winner and
half-sister to fair stayer C'est Afrique (by Behistoun); dam sprinter; remote eighth
of 10 in seller at Yarmouth in July; unseated rider when saddle slipped in similar
race at Windsor the following month. *M. Hinchliffe.*

SAUCY SERGENT 6 b.g. Home Guard 129–Kiss Me 82 (Tamerlane 128) (1982   –
NR 1983 12s 10h 12f) compact gelding; middle-distance handicapper; seems to act
on any going; sometimes blinkered; has won for an apprentice. *B. Richmond.*

SAULINGO LAD 3 br.g. Saulingo 122–Terina (Bold Lad, Ire 133) (1982 5s 5s   –
1983 5d 5d) lengthy gelding; well beaten in maiden and minor events; has been
tried in blinkers. *W. Stubbs.*

SAULINGO SONG 4 b. or br.g. Saulingo 122–Comino Song (Tudor Music 131)   –
(1982 6f 6f 5h² 7g 5g 5.3fg 1983 5f) fair sort; plater; yet to prove he stays 6f;
acts on hard going; blinkered nowadays. *R. Hodges.*

SAUNSON BOY (USA) 3 br.c. Honey Jay–Rulassah (Fleet Nasrullah) (1982   –
6g 1983 7s 8f 8g 8d) tall, lengthy colt; behind in varied races, including a seller;
blinkered second start; sold 1,400 gns Ascot November Sales. *I. Walker.*

SAUSAGE 3 ch.g. Relko 136–Palmavista 120 (Royal Palm 131) (1982 NR 1983   **69**
11.5fg 10.2f 12f 12f 12.2f 12.3f² 12f 16f³ 12f 13.8g⁴ 14g⁴ 12fg 12g³) 28,000Y, 2,000
2-y-o; short-coupled gelding; brother to Limone, a useful winner from 6f to 1½m,
and half-brother to 3 winners; dam good winner at up to 1m; quite a moderate
maiden; probably stays 2m.. *D. Morley.*

SAVIAL MIST 3 ch.g. Mr Bigmore 123–Eridantini (Indigenous 121) (1982 6f   –
7fg 7g 6d 1983 6f) lengthy, good sort; behind in varied races, including a seller
(gambled on). *T. Fairhurst.*

SAVING MERCY 3 b.f. Lord Gayle 124–Fair Darling 93 (Darling Boy 124) (1982   **94**
7g* 1983 7d 10g³ 10s⁴) small, lengthy, lightly-made filly; good walker; put up a
pleasing effort when winning Rockfel Stakes at Newmarket as a 2-y-o, but didn't
really fulfil the promise in 1983; off course well over 4 months before finishing in
frame in Intercraft Fillies Stakes at Kempton (creditable third to easy winner
Sedra) and minor event at Yarmouth (rather disappointing fourth to Elect) in
September; stays 1¼m; to be trained by D. K. Weld. *J. Hindley.*

SAVOIR VIVRE 2 b.g. Sagaro 133–Lilmi Love 82 (Miralgo 130) (1983 6fg 8s   **66**
8d) Apr 23; 3,400F; half-brother to 6f and 7f winner Love Me Two (by Double
Jump); dam won at 1¼m; plating-class maiden; will be better suited by 1¼m+; acts
on soft going. *M. W. Easterby.*

SAVONITA (USA) 3 ch.c. Prove Out–Catania II (Pride of Kildare 92) (1982 NR   **85**
1983 11.5fg⁴ 13fg² 12g² 12s* 12g*) $17,000Y, resold 17,000 gns Y; big, strong,
attractive colt; half-brother to several minor winners in USA; dam, rated second
best of her sex at 2 yrs and 3 yrs in New Zealand, won 7 times including Great
Northern Oaks; successful in maiden race at Hamilton and apprentice event at
Chepstow in October, on latter course getting home by a neck from Villars after

hanging left; will stay 1¾m; seems to act on any going; sold to T. Curtin 15,500 gns
Newmarket Autumn Sales. *G. Harwood.*

SAVOY RANGER 2 b.f. Free State 125–Kassiope 54 (Sir Gaylord) (1983 5.8g —
7fg 6f 7f 7h 7f 8.2fg 6g) Mar 8; 3,200Y; narrow filly; of no account; sold 330 gns
Ascot December Sales. *J. Douglas-Home.*

SAX 3 b.f. Anax 120–Spring Music (Silly Season 127) (1982 5fg² 6fg 5.8g⁴ 6f⁴ 5fg⁴ —
5s 5v 1983 6s 5g⁴ 7fg⁴ 10.2h 10f 8f 5g 5g 5d) leggy, narrow filly; in frame in varied
company; promises to stay beyond 7f; acts on any going; sometimes blinkered (ran
moderately in them in a seller sixth outing). *S. Woodman.*

SAXHAM BRECK 3 gr.c. Abwah 118–Double Blush 76 (Double-U-Jay 120) **95**
(1982 5f⁴ 5d 5fg 6d 5s 1983 8f 8f 6f* 6h⁴ 6f 6d* 6fg* 6fg⁴ 6g² 6fg² 6fg²) strong
colt; won maiden race at Folkestone in July and handicaps at Brighton and
Newmarket in September; second at Leicester, Nottingham and Doncaster
afterwards, showing good speed when going down by ½ length to Battle Hymn in
apprentice event on last-named course in November; stays 6f; yet to show he can
handle really soft ground, but acts on any other; sometimes bandaged. *F. Durr.*

SAXON FORT 3 b. or br.g. Manado 130–Thanks Edith (Gratitude 130) (1982 **61**
8.2s 1983 12d 12v 12s 12.3f 11.5g 10g³ 10.6g* 10fg) lengthy, workmanlike
gelding; 6-length winner of amateur riders handicap at Haydock in October; well
beaten only subsequent start; stays 1¼m; sold 10,000 gns Newmarket Autumn
Sales. *M. Jarvis.*

SAXON RADIO 2 gr.c. Town Crier 119–As Time Goes By (Calpurnius 122) (1983 —
6fg) Apr 13; 3,000Y; smallish colt; second foal; half-brother to 1982 2-y-o 5f and 6f
winner Time Is Time (by Broxted); dam, who never ran, is closely related to very
smart Sir Montagu; tailed-off last of 24 in £4,200 seller at Doncaster in September.
G. Huffer.

SAYF EL ARAB (USA) 3 b.c. Drone–Make Plans (Go Marching) (1982 5f⁴ **127**
5fg* 5f² 6g⁴ 6d² 5fg* 5f⁴ 1983 6v 5g 5s 5f* 6g 5fg 5f)

Royal Ascot winners seemed harder than ever to find in 1983 and Sayf El
Arab's 33/1-success in the King's Stand Stakes followed a series of shocks which
had seen four more of the meeting's most prestigious events fall to rank
outsiders—the St James's Palace Stakes to Horage at 18/1, the Coventry to Chief
Singer at 20/1, the Queen Mary to Night of Wind at 50/1 and the Cork and Orrery to
Sylvan Barbarosa at 20/1. Sayf El Arab's win was the biggest turn up in the King's
Stand since Squander Bug won in 1948, but there were no hard-luck stories this
time as there had been when the brilliantly speedy Careless Nora floundered in a
patch of bad ground and was caught in the last hundred yards. Sayf El Arab was
quite simply much the best horse on the day. He broke very fast and dominated the
race from start to finish, coming home three lengths clear of Soba; he even

*King's Stand Stakes, Ascot—a remarkable performance by Sayf El Arab, winning
unchallenged by three lengths from Soba (nearside)*

Mr Moufid F. Dabaghi's "Sayf El Arab"

appeared to be pulling further away at the finish. It's true that Soba had still to find her best form, but the race attracted just about the stongest field that could be mustered at the time and Soba was followed across the line by Sayf El Arab's stable-companion On Stage (favourite, having won three of his four previous races), Celestial Dancer and the 1982 winner Fearless Lad in a field of sixteen, the biggest for many years. To trainer O'Gorman, a most accomplished handler of sprinters, victory in the King's Stand, Britain's only Group 1 five-furlong race at that time, reportedly meant almost as much as winning the Derby would. It fulfilled a long-held ambition for him as his father had won the race twice, with Drum Beat in 1958 and with Majority Rule in 1963. The former, like Sayf El Arab, led throughout and won easily, putting up a very good performance indeed on the day. The latter, like Sayf El Arab, was recording easily his best performance and wasn't even placed in his other races as a three-year-old. Sayf El Arab's win must have been similarly important to jockey Thomas, who like most other lightweights has had a lean time in recent seasons; a bad fall at Ripon a month later put him out of action for a spell but he returned in the autumn to win another valuable prize on Sagamore in the Cambridgeshire.

Sayf El Arab hadn't finished closer than seventh in any of his races before Royal Ascot, the Quail Stakes at Kempton, the Palace House at Newmarket and the Prix de Saint-Georges at Longchamp, but he'd shown speed on occasions. The stewards rightly enquired into his improvement and accepted the explanation that 'the colt was wearing blinkers for the first time this season and had been suited by the very fast ground compared with the going in France and at Newmarket.' O'Gorman admitted surprise at the result to the Press but pointed out that he'd always thought a great deal of Sayf El Arab, who had been a very useful two-year-old at his best, but appeared not to have been using himself to full advantage since sustaining a tiny fracture to a cannon bone when beaten a head by Krayyan in the National Stakes at Sandown. He added that Sayf El Arab was the type to need a few runs to get fit.

Sayf El Arab wore blinkers in his remaining races but came nowhere near reproducing his best. In the Vernons Sprint Cup at Haydock in September the sixth furlong seemed to find him out and he weakened into fifth behind the very clear winner Habibti after leading for a long way. Both his other races were run under very similar conditions to those that had prevailed at Royal Ascot—five furlongs and firm ground—yet Sayf El Arab struggled to go the pace throughout in each. He wasn't beaten all that far when fifth to Soba in the Scarbrough Stakes at Doncaster later in the month but in the Prix de l'Abbaye at Longchamp he was receiving back-handers before the field had gone two furlongs and finished a well-beaten seventh of eight behind Habibti; his pari-mutuel price of 30/1 gives some indication of how far his reputation had fallen.

		Drone (gr 1966)	Sir Gaylord (b 1959)	Turn-to
Sayf El Arab (USA) (b.c. 1980)				Somethingroyal
			Cap and Bells (gr 1958)	Tom Fool
				Ghazni
		Make Plans (b or br 1971)	Go Marching (b 1965)	Princequillo
				Leallah
			Sister Antoine (b 1957)	Royal Serenade
				Our Patrice

Sayf El Arab was extremely well bought at only 37,000 dollars at the Keeneland September Yearling Sales. His sire Drone is a close relative of Sir Wimborne and Lady Capulet, both of whom are by Sir Ivor, another son of Sir Gaylord. Drone has done well at stud since his racing career was curtailed by injury after only four minor races as a three-year-old, all of which he won; he's had several high-class performers in the States, including Muttering and the short-lived Lets Dont Fight, and Weth Nan who was unbeaten as a two-year-old and finished third to Roland Gardens in the 1978 Two Thousand Guineas. The dam Make Plans was unplaced in three races as a two-year-old but has done reasonably well at stud, producing three other winners: two minor ones by Bagdad and another by Grey Dawn II. The grandam Sister Antoine was a far better racehorse, winning twelve races from sixty-eight starts, including the nine-furlong Santa Margarita Handicap, and several of her other daughters have also produced either stakes winners or stakes-placed winners.

Sayf El Arab remains in training and will probably have the King's Stand Stakes as his chief objective once more. A small, attractive colt who walks well but isn't the best of movers, he'd be sure to win another good race or two if reproducing his best form but he evidently can't be relied on to do so nowadays. *W. O'Gorman.*

SAY PRIMULA 5 ch.h. Hotfoot 126–Renoir Picture 90 (Relko 136) (1982 10s^4 10.5f* 10f* 10fg 10g^2 10.5fg 11d^2 10v 10g 1983 12g 10g^3 9s^2 10d 12fg* 12f 12f 12g^3 11g^2 12s^3 12fg) lengthy horse; useful performer on his day; beat Noble Gift a neck (pair 7 lengths clear) in 9-runner minor event at Beverley in June; 1½ lengths second to Balladier in Doonside Cup at Ayr in September; stays 1½m and has given impression he'll get further; evidently acts on any going; sometimes hangs and isn't the easiest of rides. *J. W. Watts.* **107**

SAYSABAN 4 ch.c. Sassafras 135–Side Step (Double Jump 131) (1982 9fg 10fg 11g^2 12g 1983 12v^2 13.3v 10g 10f^4 11.7f) strong, short-coupled ex-French colt; stays 1½m; acts on heavy going; blinkered last 2 starts in 1982. *G. Thorner.* **52**

SCALDANTE 2 ch.g. Hotfoot 126–Snow Goose (Santa Claus 133) (1983 5fg^3 7fg* 7fg^3 7g^4 7g^2 7fg) Jan 22; 22,000Y; good-topped, useful-looking gelding; has a long stride; half-brother to 3 winners on flat, including Obergurgl (by Warpath), successful over 1½m and 13f; dam never ran; won maiden race at Warwick in July; good second in nursery at Yarmouth 2 months later; should stay 1½m; acts on a firm surface; didn't have much luck in running on third and fourth outings; gelded after final appearance; exported to Hong Kong. *M. Stoute.* **98**

SCALLY BOY 3 gr.c. Scallywag 127–Grisbi 96 (Grey Sovereign 128§) (1982 NR 1983 12f) tall, leggy colt; half-brother to 3 winners, including fairly useful 1½m winners Bagshot (by Connaught) and Greats (by Great Nephew); dam, winner over 1m, is half-sister to smart Rouser; looked light when tailed-off last in maiden race at Redcar in July; sold privately 600 gns Doncaster November Sales. *E. Incisa.* **–**

SCARECROW 4 b.f. Thatch 136–Vaguely 92 (Bold Lad, Ire 133) (1982 NR 1983 8f) 1,500 3-y-o; first foal; dam won over 1m and 1¼m; tailed-off last in seller at Salisbury in September; sold 1,200 gns Newmarket December Sales. *P. Makin.* **–**

SCARLET O'HARLOT 2 ch.f. Nebbiolo 125–Pewsey 96 (Appiani II 128) (1983 5f* 6f^3 6fg 6fg^4) Apr 13; IR 2,500Y, resold 5,000Y; workmanlike, rather narrow filly; good walker; fourth live foal; half-sister to 1981 2-y-o 6f winner Puesdown (by **81**

Gay Fandango); dam won twice over 5f at 2 yrs; bought in 7,000 gns after easily justifying heavy backing in seller at Newcastle in June; ran well afterwards in nurseries at Goodwood and Newmarket (2); should stay 7f. *W. Musson.*

SCARLET PARTY 2 ch.f. Red Alert 127–Cait Ni Dhuibhir (Irish Love 117) (1983 7.2f 7f 5f 6g 5s) Mar 30; IR 2,600Y; stocky, workmanlike filly; dam unraced sister to useful 1978 2-y-o sprinter Phils Fancy; poor maiden; form only at 5f; sold 660 gns Newmarket Autumn Sales. *M. Jarvis.* — 53

SCARLET SAGA 4 gr.f. No Mercy 126–Leading Rose (Scarlet Ruler 93) (1982 NR 1983 10.2g 8f⁴ 8f) plater; stays 1m; has worn blinkers. *D. Ringer.* — –

SCARLET TOWN 5 b.h. Town Crier 119–Sindo 91 (Derring-Do 131) (1982 10.2g 8g³ 10f 8f³ 8f⁴ 10fg³ 9.4fg³ 10fg⁴ 10.2s⁴ 10d* 10g 10fg⁴ 10g² 10fg 10d² 8.2s² 8g* 8s 1983 8d 10s² 8.2s 9d 10v 10d 10f 8.2f 10g⁴ 11g 8.2s² 12fg) small, lightly-made, quite attractive horse; good walker; quite a moderate handicapper; stays 1¼m; acts on any going; suited by a strong gallop; ungenuine. *R. Hollinshead.* — 55

SCHEMING 5 ch.g. Great Nephew 126–Look Out 84 (Vimy 132) (1982 18.8fg² 18.8fg 16s 17.1s 1983 10.2g³ 18f) smallish, deep-girthed gelding; third in seller at Bath in June; stays well; probably acts on any going; blinkered last 2 starts. *P. Cole.* — –

SCHERZANDO 2 ch.f. Anax 120–Siren Sister (Red Alert 127) (1983 6f 6g 5g 5g) Mar 4; neat filly; first foal; dam never ran; plating-class maiden; suited by 6f. *M. McCormack.* — 67

SCHOLAR (USA) 2 b.c. Key To The Kingdom–Academic World 101 (Arts and Letters) (1983 7.6fg 9s⁴) Apr 5; half-brother to a winner in USA by Cougar; dam won 4 times at up to 1m here and later won 4 sprint races in USA; prominent both outings, on second beaten 6 lengths by Prince Crow in 10-runner maiden race at Wolverhampton in October. *P. Walwyn.* — 75

SCHULA 3 b.f. Kala Shikari 125–Golden Track (Track Spare 125) (1982 5g 5f³ 5f² 5f² 5fg³ 5fg* 1983 5s 5v³ 5g⁴ 5.1g² 5.1fg 5g 5d 5g) well-made filly; good walker; ran well when in frame in handicaps in first half of season; races only at 5f; acts on any going; trained by S. Mellor until after third outing. *H. O'Neill.* — 77

SCHUSS 3 b.c. High Top 131–Christiana 106 (Double Jump 131) (1982 6fg³ 1983 7d* 8.2v* 8fg⁴ 8fg) rather lengthy, quite attractive colt; has a long, raking stride; half-brother to Electric (by Blakeney); fulfilled his 2-y-o promise when decisively winning 21-runner maiden race at Newmarket in April and very competitive Cecil Frail Handicap at Haydock in May; dominated race from 3f out and put up a fine performance when beating Airfield in good style by 4 lengths in latter event; had every chance and ran respectably when 3 lengths fourth of 15 behind Pampabird in Prix Messidor at Maisons-Laffitte in July, but finished well-beaten last of 6 behind Montekin in Waterford Crystal Mile at Goodwood the following month (25/1-chance); suited by 1m; yet to race on really firm going but acts on any other; takes a good hold. *R. Hern.* — 109

Cecil Frail Handicap, Haydock—Schuss scores in fine style

SCINTILLO 2 ch.c. Hot Spark 126–Walk By 113 (Tower Walk 130) (1983 6g² 76
6fg) Feb 11; 7,200Y; strong, good sort; fourth foal; half-brother to a winner in
Belgium; dam, very useful sprinter, is half-sister to smart fillies Smarten Up and
Solar; second in minor event at Lingfield in September; capable of winning small
race. *B. Hobbs.*

SCOOP THE KITTY 2 b.f. Firestreak 125–Song Book 85 (Saintly Song 128) 72
(1983 6fg 5g⁴ 6g³ 5s⁴ 6fg) Apr 8; sturdy, quite useful-looking filly; second foal;
half-sister to 1982 2-y-o 5f seller winner Song to Singo (by Master Sing); dam
won 6f seller at 2 yrs; quite a moderate maiden; no show under 8-5 in claiming
nursery at Newmarket in October on final appearance; should stay at least 7f;
apparently suited by some give in the ground. *J. Etherington.*

SCORCHING 2 ch.g. Hot Spark 126–Nelion 102 (Grey Sovereign 128§) (1983 5v –
5s 8d 7g) May 21; 11,000Y; half-brother to several winners here and abroad,
notably high-class stayer Recupere (by Reliance II); dam won at 6f and 1m at 2 yrs;
no sign of ability in maiden and minor events; blinkered second and third starts;
sold 370 gns Ascot December Sales. *D. Elsworth.*

SCOT BENNETT 5 b.g. Tarboosh–Hell's Mistress (Skymaster 126) (1982 10d –
15.8f⁴ 12f 12f 10.6h 10d 10g⁴ 12d 15.5v* 1983 16s) fair sort; plater; stays well;
seems to act on any going; sometimes wears blinkers and isn't entirely genuine;
sold 1,150 gns Ascot October Sales. *J. Jenkins.*

SCOTCH RUN 3 ch.g. Nearly A Hand 115–Cithern 91 (Canisbay 120) (1982 NR 58
1983 13.8g 16g 12.3f 16.5f 16fg 18fg²) 980F; strong gelding; half-brother to fair
1981 2-y-o 5f and 6f winner Ten-Traco (by Forlorn River); dam, half-sister to Band
and Zimbalon, won over 7f at 2 yrs; springer in market when second in handicap at
Nottingham in October; suited by a thorough test of stamina; blinkered fifth outing;
dead. *K. Stone.*

SCOTTISCHE 3 b.f. Quiet Fling 124–Fatherless 63 (Ragusa 137) (1982 8fg 8s –
1983 12fg 8f 12g) workmanlike filly; poor form in varied races. *P. Haslam.*

SCOTTISH AGENT 7 gr.g. Porto Bello 118–Alys Grey 91 (Grey Sovereign 45
128§) (1982 6g 6d³ 6f 6f 5fg 6g 6f⁴ 7f⁴ 6fg 6d 7g⁴ 7f² 8fg 7g⁴ 7f 7fg 6f 6v 6v³ 8g
6s² 7s 1983 5d 5fg 6d 7fg 10f 8f² 7f 7g* 7fg 6fg 7g⁴ 7g) tall gelding; attracted no
bid after winning selling handicap at Yarmouth in September; stays 1m; acts on any
going; occasionally blinkered; often bandaged behind; inconsistent. *M. Ryan.*

SCOTTISH DREAM 5 ch.h. Palm Track 122–Captain Frances (Captain's Gig) 61
(1982 NR 1983 13v 12d⁴ 15.8d 12d³ 12.3f⁴ 12f* 16f² 13.8f² 13g) lengthy horse;
good walker; decisively won quite valuable handicap at Carlisle in June; stays well;
probably acts on any going but goes well on fast ground. *G. Richards.*

SCOTTISH GREEN 5 ch.g. Scottish Rifle 127–Nuque (Suceso) (1982 8f 8.3fg 48
8fg² 8.3g 1983 8g 10f 8f* 8f⁴ 7f 8fg) neat gelding; plater; attracted no bid after
winning at Yarmouth in August; stays 1m; acts on firm going; best in blinkers;
sometimes sweats up; sold 875 gns Ascot October Sales. *P. Makin.*

SCOTT'S HILL 2 ch.f. Dubassoff–Molvitesse 75 (Molvedo 137) (1983 8f 7f) Apr –
7; 800Y; half-sister to 3 winners, including 1982 2-y-o 6f winner Auburn Hill (by
Silly Season); dam won over 1m; well beaten in auction race and a seller. *Hbt
Jones.*

SCOUTSMISTAKE 4 b. or br.g. Prince Tenderfoot 126–Summer Serenade 96 69
(Petingo 135) (1982 8fg³ 8f 8f 8.3g 8d 8.2s 10.2s 1983 8.3f* 11fg*(dis) 10f 10fg
10.6g² 12g 8g³ 8fg*) lengthy, quite attractive gelding; gambled on when winning
seller at Windsor in July; ran well in non-sellers afterwards, winning slowly-run
handicap at Redcar (disqualified) and minor event at Doncaster; put up improved
display to beat Amazon Prince in latter in November; appears to stay 11f; acts on
firm going; has twice worn blinkers; has run creditably for amateur rider. *B.
McMahon.*

SCRAP HARRY 2 b.c. Derrylin 115–Radio Oxford 66 (Blakeney 126) (1983 5f 6f 58
7f 5f 5f 5g 6d 8fg) May 14; 3,100F, IR 2,000Y; strong, sturdy colt; second living
produce; dam disappointing daughter of very useful miler Radio Caroline; modest
plater; not bred to be effective at sprint distances; blinkered last 5 outings; sold
400 gns Doncaster November Sales. *R. Hollinshead.*

SCREES 2 gr.c. Precipice Wood 123–Chieftain's Lady (Border Chief 101) (1983 76
5fg 5d² 6d* 6fg 7g* 7f 7g³ 6g) Mar 10; 1,700Y; first foal; dam never ran; won
minor event at Catterick in June; awarded race over 2 weeks later after finishing
creditable length second of 11 to Mellow Dance in £5,200 nursery at Chester in

August; better at 7f than 6f, and should stay well; best form with some give in the ground; usually races freely and acts well on sharp tracks; dwelt sixth start. *J. Wilson.*

SCREW LOOSE 2 b.f. Homeboy 114–Love Seat (King's Bench 132) (1983 5fg 5f³ 5fg² 6f) May 6; neat filly; half-sister to 3 winners, including 1978 2-y-o 5f winner Flitterdale (by Abwah); dam never ran; poor plater; should be suited by 6f; blinkered final outing; sent to Italy. *J. Etherington.* **46**

SCRUMMAGE 5 b.m. Workboy 123–Broughton Flyer (Huntercombe 133) (1982 8s 8fg 8d 11g 6g 8g 7f 8.2v 1983 7d* 6g²) won apprentice handicap at Doncaster in May; little worthwhile form previously, including in sellers; stays 7f; acts on a soft surface; not seen out after June. *Mrs A. Cousins.* **44**

SCYTHE 2 ch.f. Sharpen Up 127–Wolverene 114 (Relko 136) (1983 7fg⁴ 7g) Apr 2; big, strong, rangy filly; half-sister to several winners, including useful middle-distance winners Shining Tor (by High Top) and Voracity (by Vitiges); dam game stayer; looked quite badly in need of race and in circumstances shaped extremely well when 7¾ lengths fourth of 18 to Seismic Wave in £5,000 event at Doncaster in September, showing plenty of speed to lead until lack of fitness told below distance; 6/1, running-on 5½ lengths fifth of 10 to Troyanna in £3,800 race at York the following month; will be well suited by 1m+; sure to win races. *G. Pritchard-Gordon.* **78 p**

SDENKA ROYAL 4 b. or br.f. Queen's Hussar 124–Sdenka 79 (Habitat 134) (1982 9f⁴ 10f² 10fg 10g² 10.2g² 1983 10f 10f 10.1fg³ 10f 12g 10d) fair sort; quite a modest maiden at her best; should stay 1½m; yet to race on soft ground; sometimes blinkered. *A. Hide.* **–**

SEA BALLET 2 ch.f. Pharly 130–Sea Singer 104 (Sea-Bird II 145) (1983 7.6fg) May 15; third live foal; dam won over 1¼m; 12/1, 8 lengths fifth of 17 to Taqdir in maiden race at Lingfield in October; should do better. *R. Hern.* **66 p**

SEABATTLE (USA) 4 b.c. Cannonade–Smooth Siren (Sea-Bird II 145) (1982 12fg 11.7f³ 11.7f² 12f* 12s 1983 12d 11.7s³ 14s 12d* 12f 14f² 16f 13.1h⁴ 12fg 12g³) tall, rangy colt; decisively won amateur riders race at Redcar in May; possibly stays 2m; acts on any going; blinkered seventh and last 2 starts (didn't look suitable mount for inexperienced apprentice on second occasion); sometimes sweats up; has been bandaged on off-fore. *P. Walwyn.* **77 d**

SEA BED 2 b.c. Sassafras 135–Feather Bed 111 (Gratitude 130) (1983 7fg 8fg) June 12; deep-girthed colt; has a nice, easy action; half-brother to numerous winners, including useful stayer Popaway (by Run The Gantlet) and smart middle-distance filly Cheveley Princess (by Busted); dam second in Irish 1000 Guineas; backward, behind in big fields of maidens at Newmarket in the autumn. *G. Wragg.* **–**

SEA BLUE 3 b.g. Blue Cashmere 129–Sea Magic (Hardicanute 130) (1982 NR 1983 9fg 9g 8fg) 2,600F, 4,300Y; half-brother to 2 winning platers; dam never ran; in rear in maiden and minor events, not beaten all that far on first occasion. *Miss L. Siddall.* **–**

SEA CHARM 3 b.f. Julio Mariner 127–Nyanga (Never Say Die 137) (1982 NR 1983 11d⁴ 13d³ 12.2f 14.7f) lengthy filly; half-sister to 4 winners, including high-class middle-distance stayer Mistigri (by Misti IV), useful stayer Tanaka (by Tapalque) and Cesarewitch winner Bajan Sunshine (by Reliance II); dam won twice over 1½m in France; in frame in maiden races at Redcar in May and Ayr in June; most disappointing final start; should stay at least 1¾m; possibly not at her best on firm ground. *J. W. Watts.* **70**

SEA DART 3 ch.f. Air Trooper 115–Major Isle (Major Portion 129) (1982 8s 7d 6s 1983 7s 10.8g* 12f²) workmanlike filly; dropped in class when winning selling handicap at Warwick in October (bought in 1,200 gns); suited by 1¼m+. *B. Morgan.* **55**

SEAFARING 2 b.c. Thatching 131–Sapphire Spray (Floribunda 136) (1983 6g*) May 22; 21,000F, 38,000Y; half-brother to several winners, notably smart 7f and 1¼m winner Warmington (by Home Guard); dam Irish 6f winner; drew clear in final furlong to beat Tomriland 2 lengths in minor event at Fairyhouse in October; will probably stay 1m; promising. *D. O'Brien, Ireland.* **88 p**

SEA FRET 3 gr.f. Habat 127–Fluke 117 (Grey Sovereign 128§) (1982 6g* 6fg² 7fg 1983 7d 8f 8g) quite attractive filly; quite useful at 2 yrs; had stiff tasks in 1983, but wasn't disgraced when fifth of 6 to Flame of Tara in Coronation Stakes at Royal Ascot in June on second outing; probably stays 1m. *G. Hunter.* **89**

SEA MIRACLE 2 b.f. St Paddy 133–Calm Sea 83 (Set Fair 129) (1983 6fg) – half-sister to several winners here and abroad; dam won over 5f at 2 yrs; behind in 20-runner maiden race at Newmarket in October. *J. Winter.*

SEAN BE FRIENDLY 3 b. or br.c. Clip Joint 101–Still Be Friendly (Be – Friendly 130) (1982 NR 1983 7g) first foal; dam of little account; last of 14 in minor event at Catterick in September. *M. Reddan.*

SEA PORT 3 br.f. Averof 123–Anchor 106 (Major Portion 129) (1982 NR 1983 – 7d⁴) rangy filly; half-sister to several winners, notably high-class stayer Sea Anchor (by Alcide); dam, useful 6f to 7f winner, is half-sister to Bireme and Buoy; third favourite but on backward side when about 9 lengths fourth of 11 to What A Pity in newcomers race at Newbury in April, staying on well after proving reluctant to settle. *R. Hern.*

SEA RAIDER (FR) 3 ch.c. Green Dancer 132–Sea Venture 98 (Diatome 132) **91** (1982 7fg 1983 8d 10s 12s² 12fg² 12f* 13.3f 10.6fg⁴) strong, rangy, attractive ex-French colt; third foal; half-brother to useful French 1980 2-y-o 6f winner Grecian Sea (by Homeric) and French 10.5f winner Venture To Say (by Luthier); dam, from same family as Reform, won over 6f at 2 yrs and stayed 1¼m; beat Count Derry decisively by 2½ lengths in slowly-run handicap at Salisbury in June; suited by 1½m; acts on any going, but clearly goes well on firm; wears blinkers; pulled hard final start; sold 10,000 gns Newmarket September Sales and exported. *R. Hern.*

SEA REPPIN 3 b.g. Jimmy Reppin 131–Sonseeahray 67 (March Past 124) (1982 – 6d 6f 7f 6d³ 8f³ 8.2s⁴ 7s 8.2v* 8.2s⁴ 10.2s 1983 8.2v 8d 8v 8s 8v³ 8g 12.2g) neat gelding; appeared not to go through with his effort but ran best race of year when third in handicap at Ripon in June; suited by 1m; acts on any going, but revels in the mud; often blinkered; trained most of season by K. Stone. *J. Leigh.*

SEA RHYTHM 3 ch.f. Manado 130–Music Mistress 83 (Guide 118) (1982 NR – 1983 8d 8g 7f 12f 9f 8d 10g 10f) 1,800 2-y-o; small, sparely-made, leggy, plain filly; half-sister to several winners, including useful 1977 2-y-o 6f winner Discreet (by Jukebox); dam ran only at 2 yrs; poor form, including in sellers. *G. Fletcher.*

SEA SALT 2 ch.g. Monsanto 121–Neptune's Treasure 65 (Gulf Pearl 117) (1983 **69** 6d 7fg 8fg³ 8f) Apr 13; 3,800Y; fair sort; first foal; dam, a maiden, best at 1¼m; 6 lengths third of 8 to Maricourt in maiden race at Beverley in September; suited by 1m. *M. Jarvis.*

SEASIDE SPECIAL 3 ch.f. Bay Express 132–Golden Mullet (Star Moss 122) – (1982 NR 1983 5f 6f 7fg) 3,200Y; half-sister to a winner in Austria; dam of little account; last in maiden and minor races in summer; sold 330 gns Ascot October Sales. *J. Douglas-Home.*

SEASONAL PICKUP (USA) 2 ch.f. The Minstrel 135–Bubinka (Nashua) **84 p** (1983 7g 6d*) first foal; dam, very useful winner over 1m in France and Italy, is sister to very useful 1m to 1½m winner Stoshka and half-sister to smart Taufan; showed signs of greenness when running on well to account for Lady Maureen by a length in minor event at Punchestown in October; will stay at least 1m. *D. K. Weld, Ireland.*

SEASONED EMBER 2 ch.f. Royal Smoke 113–Spring Vision 65 (Golden Vision – 105) (1983 5s 5s 6s 6g) Apr 2; first reported foal; dam won over 1½m at 5 yrs; soundly beaten, including in a seller; not seen out after June. *M. Bradley.*

SEASON'S GREETING 2 b.f. Martinmas 128–Arriva (Disciplinarian) (1983 – 5fg) Apr 6; half-sister to 4 winners, including fairly useful 2-y-o 5f winners King's Consort (by King's Company) and Quiana (by Huntercombe); dam unraced daughter of Californian Oaks winner Renova; in rear in 16-runner maiden race at Lingfield in October. *J. Sutcliffe.*

SEASONS LAST 2 b.f. Silly Season 127–Star Attention 91 (Northfields) (1983 – 5g) first live foal; dam best at sprint distances; backward, tailed-off last of 20 in small race at Catterick in September; unruly in paddock beforehand. *M. Reddan.*

SEATELL 3 ch.g. Guillaume Tell 121–Sea Dike (Dike) (1982 6fg 1983 10v⁴ 10v – 10v) tall, leggy, plain gelding; little worthwhile form in maiden and minor events; has been tried in blinkers. *W. Stubbs.*

SEATTLE ROSE (USA) 2 b.f. Seattle Slew–Sancta Rose (Karabas 132) (1983 **85** 5fg² 6f* 6fg 8f²) Mar 22; lengthy, rather lightly-made American-bred filly; good mover; dam Irish 7.5f and 1¼m winner; won 12-runner maiden race at Brighton in June; creditable 3 lengths second to odds-on Frisky Wharf in nursery at Warwick in August; will stay 1¼m; acts on firm going. *P. Walwyn.*

SEATTLE SIREN (USA) 2 b.f. Seattle Slew–Miss Ooh La La (Wallet Lifter)   **101** p
(1983 6fg* 7g²) Apr 12; $800,000Y; sparely-made but attractive filly; seventh foal;
half-sister to 2 winners, notably very smart middle-distance winner Pole Position
(by Draft Card); dam unraced half-sister to very good Californian performer New
Policy; won 17-runner £4,000 race at York in September by 1½ lengths from
Rosolio; good second to Mahogany, well clear of remainder, in 21-runner £4,600
event at Newbury later in the month; will stay 1m; sure to win more races. *R.
Hern.*

SEATTLE SONG (USA) 2 b. or br.c. Seattle Slew–Incantation (Prince   **123**
Blessed) (1983 7g* 7s* 8f)
    That there was no champion among France's juvenile colts is adequately
demonstrated by the fact that none of them managed to win more than one of the
fourteen two-year-old pattern races for which colts are eligible. Amazingly the
French failed to muster a single male representative in their first Group 1 race, the
Prix Robert Papin; and their next two Group 1 races, the Prix Morny and the Prix
de la Salamandre, attracted only four and three home-trained colts respectively.
The Salamandre at Longchamp in September looked something of a formality for
the impressive all-the-way Morny winner Siberian Express, a 5/2 on favourite in
the absence through injury of the Morny runner-up Ti King. Most danger was
expected to come from Ti King's stable-companion Seattle Song, a narrow winner
at 2/1 on of the Prix de Fontenoy, a newcomers event on the same course a
fortnight earlier on his only previous appearance. Seattle Song looked likely to fare
no better against Siberian Express than Ti King had done as he came to the final
furlong under the whip with two lengths to make up on that horse. However, the
whole complexion of the race changed dramatically as the front-running Siberian
Express began to weaken in the testing conditions. Steadily Seattle Song pegged
him back, showing plenty of determination under severe pressure, and forged past
in the last strides to win by half a length. The first two outclassed their three
opponents just as much in the race as they had in the paddock; the third horse, the
Ayr, Newmarket and York winner Blushing Scribe, was left six lengths back.
Seattle Song looked to have great potential for races over longer distances and he
started at odds on when returned to Longchamp the following month for the
one-mile Grand Criterium, in which he was coupled with his equally promising
stable-companion Mendez. Unfortunately he ran badly, coming home last of nine
behind the filly Treizieme after being the first beaten. The only explanation his
trainer could offer was that Seattle Song might not have recovered from his very
hard race in the Salamandre but it is at least as likely that he was unsuited by the
firm ground.
    Even if Seattle Song never wins another race, which seems highly unlikely, he
must be assured of a place at stud. His sire Seattle Slew has established himself as
one of the most promising of America's young stallions, possibly the most

*Prix de la Salamandre, Longchamp—the promising Seattle Song stays on strongly to account for
the Prix Morny winner Siberian Express*

promising. He is the sire of the tragically short-lived Landaluce, who was rated the joint-top two-year-old filly of 1982 after winning all her five starts; Slew O'Gold, who established himself as America's best three-year-old with a three-length success in the Jockey Club Gold Cup; Slewpy who added another Grade 1 victory to the one he'd gained in the Young America Stakes at two when winning the Meadowlands Cup over a mile and a quarter; and Swale, a contemporary of Seattle Song, who proved himself one of America's top two-year-olds with four stakes victories, two of them in Grade 1 events.

Seattle Song (USA) (b. or br.c. Feb 19, 1981)	Seattle Slew (b or br 1974)	Bold Reasoning (br 1968)	Boldnesian
			Reason to Earn
		My Charmer (b 1969)	Poker
			Fair Charmer
	Incantation (b or br 1965)	Prince Blessed (b 1957)	Princequillo
			Dog Blessed
		Magic Spell (br 1954)	Flushing II
			Subterranean

Although a really good-looking colt, Seattle Song was one of the cheaper yearlings from Seattle Slew's second crop, costing 'only' 320,000 dollars. None of his first three dams was a stakes winner but he does have one notable relative: his half-sister Lucky Spell (by Lucky Mel), one of eight previous winners produced by Incantation, was a very smart winner at up to nine furlongs and has herself produced the Jersey Stakes winner Merlins Charm. Incantation's three wins over six furlongs included two in claiming races, while her half-brother Brand Royal won the Los Feliz Stakes over half a furlong more. Seattle Song's grandam Magic Spell, a winner five times, gained her single placing in a stakes race over eight and a half furlongs at two and was herself a half-sister to the dams of the very smart colts Subpet and Atoll. Incantation's sire, Prince Blessed, won the Hollywood Gold Cup over a mile and a quarter; Magic Spell's sire, Flushing, was a winning stayer in France who also won over jumps (he is also the sire of the dam of the good chaser Tingle Creek). Seattle Song needed at least seven furlongs at two and should stay at least a mile and a quarter. Good colt though he is, he needs to improve still further if he's to hold his own against the top British colts. *F. Boutin, France.*

SEBAL 3 b.c. Prince Tenderfoot 126–Coral Lee (Le Levanstell 122) (1982 5f3 5fg* 6s 6s 1983 5s4 5s 5g 5g3 5g 5g2) lengthy, quite attractive colt; in frame in handicaps; should stay 6f; blinkered last 3 outings. *G. Hunter.*   **73**

SECLUSIVELY KNOWN (USA) 2 b.c. Seclusive–Favorably Known (Ways and Means) (1983 6fg 7g3 7g) first reported foal; dam won at up to 6f in USA; 4½ lengths third of 10 to Ready Wit in minor event at Chepstow in October; stays 7f. *D. Sasse.*   **72**

SECOND FLOWER 4 ch.f. Indian Ruler (USA) 104–First Flower (Floribunda 136) (1982 10f 9f 7g2 7fg 1983 8s 7s 8fg 8.3f4 6fg2 7fg2 6f2) workmanlike ex-Irish filly; plater; stays 1m; suited by top-of-the-ground; has run well for an apprentice. *D. Gandolfo.*   **50**

SECRET ASSIGNMENT 3 gr.f. Vitiges 132–Abettor 103 (Abernant 142) (1982 NR 1983 7s 8v3 8fg*) narrow filly; half-sister to several winners, notably very useful 7f to 1½m winner Sheer Grit (by Busted); dam, half-sister to good middle-distance horse Rehearsed, won over 1½m; not seen out after narrowly winning poorly-contested apprentice maiden race at Warwick in June; suited by 1m; missed break badly on first outing. *H. Cecil.*   **71**

SECRET BALLOT 9 ch.g. Reform 132–Illuminous 108 (Rockefella) (1982 NR 1983 12g*) smart performer over jumps; having first outing on flat since 1977 when winning 12-runner maiden race at Brighton in May; stays 1½m. *A. Turnell.*   **71**

SECRET FINALE 4 ro.g. Warpath 113–Fox Covert 82 (Gigantic 102) (1982 8g 10fg4 10.2g 11.5f 13.8f 10g2 10g 8.2s4 9s 1983 15.8d) sturdy gelding; not the best of movers; plating-class maiden; promises to stay 2m; has won over hurdles. *M. Lambert.*   **–**

SECRET GROUND 3 br.f. Grundy 137–Freeze The Secret 118 (Nearctic) (1982 NR 1983 10f 10f 14f3 12fg 16d) second foal; sister to a winner in USA; dam second in 1000 Guineas and Oaks; third in maiden race at Yarmouth in August, best effort; suited by 1¾m; apprentice ridden first 2 starts. *L. Cumani.*   **–**

SECRET MINSTREL 6 ch.g. Most Secret 119–Moreland Brandy 74 (Cash and Courage 116) (1982 NR 1983 9d 16f 12.3f) poor maiden. *J. Parkes.*   **–**

SECRETO (USA) 2 b.c. Northern Dancer–Betty's Secret (Secretariat) (1983 7d*) Feb 12; $340,000Y; first foal; dam unraced half-sister to French Derby   **83 p**

Luigi Miglietti's "Secreto"

winner Caracolero; 5/2 on when winning 7-runner minor event at Phoenix Park in October in good style by 2½ lengths from Antikitos; will be suited by middle distances; should have a bright future. *D. O'Brien, Ireland.*

SECRET PURSUIT 4 b.g. Ardoon 124–Shangara (Credo 123) (1982 8f² 8f³ 9.4fg* 1983 12d³ 12s* 13d 12h⁴ 12f⁴ 14fg 10f 11f 12d³ 12s 12fg²) small gelding; good walker; won handicap at Pontefract in May; second in valuable selling handicap at Doncaster in October; seems to act on any going; strong puller and has been taken to post early. *M. H. Easterby.* **69**

SECRET WALK 2 b.g. Tower Walk 130–Special Branch 83 (Acer 123) (1983 7d) May 4; 1,600F, 7,400Y; brother to useful 1976 5f to 7.6f winner Trossachs and half-brother to a winner abroad; dam won twice over 5f at 2 yrs; tailed-off last of 13 in maiden race at Yarmouth in September. *M. Tompkins.* **–**

SECRET WAY 2 ch.f. Troy 137–Silken Way 103 (Shantung 132) (1983 7g* 7.3d) Mar 29; lengthy, rather shallow-girthed filly; particularly good mover; fourth foal; half-sister to 3 winners, notably very useful 1980 staying 2-y-o Silken Knot (by Nonoalco); dam, daughter of smart Boulevard, won over 1¼m from 3 starts; won 19-runner maiden race at York in October by 1½ lengths from Hafeaf; outpaced early when creditable 5 lengths seventh of 14 to Betsy Bay in Rochford Thompson Newbury Stakes later in month; will be better suited by longer distances. *R. Hern.* **95 p**

SECURITY CLEARANCE 2 br.c. General Assembly–Freeze The Secret 118 (Nearctic) (1983 7fg⁴ 7f 8.5s 8d³) Apr 4; rather leggy, close-coupled, useful-looking colt; third foal; half-brother to a winner in USA; dam second in 1000 Guineas and Oaks; always about same place when 4¼ lengths fourth of 8 to easy winner Trojan Fen in minor event at Yarmouth in June, better of 2 efforts when trained by H. Cecil; kept on when 6 lengths third of 21 to Star Spartan in maiden event at Leopardstown in October; will stay 1¼m. *D. K. Weld, Ireland.* **80**

SEDGE 2 b.f. Oats 126–Shannon Princess (Connaught 130) (1983 6fg) May 22; second living foal; sister to fairly useful middle-distance winner Fitzpatrick; dam won over 1m and 1¼m in Ireland; always behind after dwelling in 22-runner maiden race at Leicester in October. *P. Walwyn.* **–**

Intercraft Fillies Stakes, Kempton—Sedra is given a confident ride, and accounts for Be My Darling in fine style

SEDRA 3 ch.f. Nebbiolo 125–Hispanica 85 (Whistling Wind 123) (1982 6f² 6f* 6fg² 6s² 7.2s⁴ 1983 8d² 7.3v* 8.5g* 8f 10f² 10g* 10fg² 8d²) useful-looking filly; half-sister to several winners, including Irish 1m winner Katie Roche (by Sallust); dam 2-y-o 5f winner; much improved and was ridden with great confidence when beating Be My Darling in good style by 3 lengths in 7-runner Intercraft Fillies Stakes at Kempton in September; had earlier won £4,500 handicap at Newbury and £7,300 Ebbisham Handicap at Epsom; also finished second 4 times, notably over 1¼m when going down by a neck to Green Reef in Prix de Psyche at Deauville and by a length to Cormorant Wood in Sun Chariot Stakes at Newmarket; acts on any going; genuine and consistent. *J. Dunlop.*   116

SEEK HIM HERE 6 b.g. Status Seeker–Nice One Jackie (Prince Tenderfoot 126) (1982 NR 1983 10g) poor plater; wears blinkers. *Mrs N. Macauley.*   –

SEIGNEUR 2 bl.c. Godswalk 130–Miss St Cyr 86 (Brigadier Gerard 144) (1983 6g 6d⁴) Apr 4; compact, quite attractive colt; has a quick action; first foal; dam 2-y-o 6f winner; staying-on 5 lengths fourth of 16 to Turn The Key in maiden race at Newbury in October; will be suited by 7f. *G. Wragg.*   74

SEISMIC WAVE (USA) 2 b.c. Youth 135–Shellshock 110 (Salvo 129) (1983 7fg*) Feb 16; smallish, sturdy colt; half-brother to 3 winners, including middle-distance stayer Sir Billy (by Sir Ivor); dam, half-sister to top-class Dibidale, was third in 1000 Guineas and stayed 13f; 12/1, won 18-runner £5,000 event at Doncaster in September in good finish with El Hakim, the pair coming away; will be much better suited by longer distances; sure to improve, and should make useful 3-y-o. *B. Hills.*   96 p

SELBORNE RECORD 5 ch.g. Record Run 127–Flatter Me (Palestine 133) (1982 15.8g 13v* 12f³ 12.3fg 12fg⁴ 1983 15.8d 15g) leggy, narrow gelding; poor performer on flat though is a fair hurdler; stays 13f; acts on any going. *H. Bell.*   –

SEL-BY-OYSTON 3 ch.g. Sagaro 133–I Don't Mind 97 (Swing Easy 126) (1982 6f³ 6g⁴ 7g³ 7f 7d 8f 1983 10v 9d 12s 12g 9f 12f 8.2s⁴) strong, good-topped gelding; plater nowadays; yet to show he stays beyond 1m; acts on firm going; sometimes blinkered; sold to W. Stubbs 1,800 gns Doncaster November Sales. *J. Berry.*   –

SEMPSTER 2 b.f. Habat 127–Slip Stitch 120 (Parthia 132) (1983 6s 6f 5f) Mar 3; half-sister to several winners, including fairly useful 1974 2-y-o 6f and 7f winner Moss Stitch (by Star Moss); dam good staying 2-y-o; behind in maiden races; not seen out after August. *W. Holden.*   –

SENANE 2 ch.f. Vitiges 132–Formulate 119 (Reform 132) (1983 7f 7f² 8g*) Feb 18; close-coupled, rather plain filly; first foal; dam top staying 2-y-o filly of 1978 but ran only twice afterwards; improved steadily, on final appearance justifying favouritism cleverly by ¾ length from Channel Affair in 17-runner maiden race at Leicester in September; better suited by 1m than by 7f, and should stay 1¼m; acts on firm going. *H. Cecil.*   86

SENANG HATI 4 b. or br.c. Nonoalco 131–Sweet Sound 74 (Sound Track 132) 59
(1982 8.2v 9.4f 7g 8g³ 10g 9fg³ 10fg⁴ 12.3g 1983 8v 7fg² 9f² 9.4f 7.6fg* 7f 7fg³
7.6g 7f) big, strong colt; won apprentice handicap at Chester in July; stayed 9f;
acted on firm going; retired to Louella Stud in Leicestershire. *D. Smith.*

SENG BRANCH 2 b.f. Bustino 136–Hide Out (Habitat 134) (1983 7s 7fg) Apr 71
18; 34,000Y; lengthy filly; good walker; second living foal; dam, bred on same lines
as Marwell, ran only once; 9 lengths eighth of 22 to Travel Away in maiden race at
Newmarket in October, second outing; will stay 1m. *J. Tree.*

SENIOR CITIZEN 4 br.c. Brigadier Gerard 144–Argent Soleil 68 (Silver Shark 108
129) (1982 8s* 7g² 10fg 8g* 9fg³ 1983 8s 7s⁴ 8s² 10d 8f 7f* 9fg*) 7,200Y; third
foal; dam won over 6f; won handicap at the Curragh (carried 10-5) and Coolmore
Be My Guest Stakes at Phoenix Park in August; apprentice ridden when getting
the better of Erin's Hope by a length in latter; in frame earlier in Gladness Stakes
at the Curragh (fourth to Lomond) and Coolmore/Pas de Seul Stakes at Phoenix
Park (length second to Captivator, pair clear); well-beaten sixth of 10 to Stanerra
after being prominent for a long way in Brigadier Gerard Stakes at Sandown on
fourth start; stays 9f; acts on any going. *C. Collins, Ireland.*

SENLIS (USA) 2 b.f. Sensitive Prince–Larceny Gal (No Robbery) (1983 8fg*) 101 p
Mar 1; $45,000F, $135,000Y; third produce; dam lightly-raced half-sister to dam of
very good American colts Stop the Music and Hatchet Man; made all to win
newcomers event at Longchamp in October, beating Lady Sharp a length in good
style; should stay 1¼m; promising. *F. Boutin, France.*

SENTROIA 2 ch.f. Troy 137–Sdenka 79 (Habitat 134) (1983 6f 7f 7g) Mar 27; 64
sturdy filly; fourth foal; dam placed over 7f; little worthwhile form in 2 maiden races
and minor event. *Mrs R. Lomax.*

SENTRY MAN 3 ch.g. On Your Mark 125–Lady Huzzar (Laser Light 118) (1982 —
6g 5d 6g 6v⁴ 1983 7fg 7g 7g 7f) strong, good-quartered gelding; poor form,
including in a £2,700 seller; should stay 6f; sometimes blinkered. *L. Lightbrown.*

Mr R. E. Sangster's "Seismic Wave"

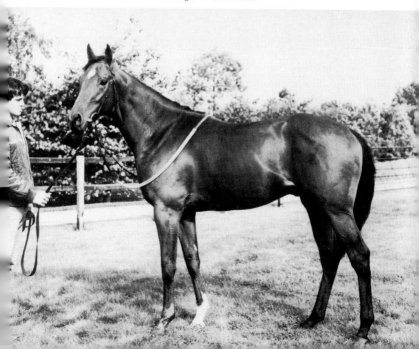

SERAPHIM 3 b.f. Oats 126–Saintly Angel 87 (So Blessed 130) (1982 NR 1983 **48** 12.2f 10f³ 12f 10g 7fg) strong filly; second foal; half-sister to fairly useful 1981 2-y-o 5f winner Shared Moment (by Bay Express); dam lightly-raced 2-y-o 5f winner; claimed out of Sir Mark Prescott's stable £4,000 after finishing third in seller at Lingfield in August; ran easily best subsequent race in 1¼m amateur riders race on penultimate start; should stay 1½m. *M. Haynes.*

SERENA MARIA 3 ch.f. Dublin Taxi–Slick Chick 89 (Shiny Tenth 120) (1982 **63** 5fg 6h 5g 5g⁴ 1983 6s³ 7v 7s 7fg² 6fg* 6h 8f 6s) workmanlike filly; sold out of M. McCormack's stable 3,400 gns after winning 22-runner seller at Windsor in July in a blanket finish; no subsequent form (blinkered final start); stays 7f; probably acts on any going; sold 540 gns Ascot October Sales. *A. Bailey.*

SERENDIPITY (USA) 3 ch.c. Terete–Gaska 110 (Gilles de Retz 132) (1982 **–** 7d 1983 10s 10f³ 12f 12g) quite a moderate maiden; promises to stay 1½m; tailed off final start. *R. Smyth.*

SERGEANT DECOY 3 b.g. Decoy Boy 129–Cedar Valley (High Perch 126) **–** (1982 NR 1983 11.5fg 16g) 1,900F, 4,200Y; lengthy gelding; half-brother to several winners, including good Italian horse De Hooch (by Dual); dam won over 7f at 2 yrs in Ireland; tailed off in maiden races at Sandown and Lingfield in June. *M. Smyly.*

SERGEANT JIM 9 b.g. Major Portion 129–Military Miss 72 (Martial 131) (1982 **–** NR 1983 8.2d) plater; very lightly raced nowadays. *R. Morris.*

SERGIADES 2 ch.g. Crimson Beau 124–Dea (Midsummer Night II 117) (1983 7g **69** 8d 10d²) Apr 22; 1,150Y; tall gelding; has a round action; half-brother to 3 winners in Italy, including Deimos (by Canisbay), a smart performer and a prolific winner; dam won in Italy; second favourite, beaten neck after dwelling in 12-runner seller at Leicester in October; gelded subsequently; stays 1¼m. *J. Holt.*

SERHEED (USA) 3 b.c. Nijinsky 138–Native Partner (Raise A Native) (1982 **80** 8g 1983 9d⁴ 10g 12v 10.1fg 9fg³ 12g⁴ 12g* 13.3d) tall, rangy, good sort; in frame in varied races before beating Savonita by 5 lengths in minor event at Lingfield in October; suited by 1½m and may stay further; has raced in a tongue strap. *P. Cole.*

SERPENTEL 2 b. or br.c. African Sky 124–Pendula 76 (Tamerlane 128) (1983 7f **86** 7f 8s⁴ 8g³) Mar 18; IR 18,000F, 11,000Y; rather leggy, useful sort; good walker and mover; half-brother to a winning plater and a winner in Sweden; dam won at up to 1¾m; showed progressive form, on final outing finishing good third in nursery at Pontefract in October; well suited by 1m. *L. Cumani.*

SET IT ALIGHT 2 b.f. Touch Paper 113–Rosey O'Leary (Majetta 115) (1983 5g **74** 5s* 5f³ 6fg 6fg³ 6f 8g) May 8; IR 2,000F, 9,600Y; workmanlike filly; third produce; half-sister to 9f to 1½m winner Gillies Prince (by Furry Glen); dam never ran; won 18-runner maiden race at Wolverhampton in May; ran poorly in nurseries last 2 outings; suited by 6f; acts on any going; blinkered fourth appearance. *N. Guest.*

SEVEN CLUBS 3 b.g. Some Hand 119–Sister Angelica (Song 132) (1982 6fg⁴ **71** 5d* 5s² 5s 1983 5fg 5f 5d 6g 6fg 6fg) sturdy gelding; seldom had ideal conditions in 1983, but wasn't disgraced fourth start; likely to prove best at 5f; acts well on soft going; blinkered last 2 outings. *M. Tompkins.*

SEVEN HEARTS 7 ch.h. Some Hand 119–Vienna Love 68 (Vienna 127) (1982 **79** 8g⁴ 8g* 8g 8g⁴ 8f³ 8fg 8d* 8g⁴ 8fg 8g 8.2f² 1983 7s⁴ 7s 7v² 7.2s 8.3fg 8g⁴ 8fg 7.2g 8d) strong horse; good mover; fair handicapper at his best; stays 9f; acts on any going but has done most of his winning when there's been some give in the ground; wears blinkers nowadays; wears bandages; suitable mount for an apprentice; front runner. *K. Brassey.*

SEVEN SWALLOWS 2 br.c. Radetzky 123–Polysee (Polyfoto 124) (1983 7g **–** 6fg) June 2; rangy colt; third living foal; dam ran only once; in rear in autumn maiden races at Leicester and Folkestone. *H. Collingridge.*

SEYL (USA) 2 br.c. Blushing Groom 131–Luxury (Jaipur) (1983 7f 7fg³) May **78 p** 19; $750,000Y; small, attractive, well-made colt; good mover; third foal; half-brother to a winner by Avatar; dam, very useful sprint winner, is sister to very smart 1969 2-y-o Forum and half-sister to very smart High Counsel; 6/1, wandered under pressure and was eased once held when 5½ lengths third of 17 to Passing Affair in maiden race at Salisbury in September; will stay 1m; sure to improve. *J. Dunlop.*

SEYMOUR HICKS (FR) 3 b.c. Ballymore 123–Sarah Siddons 122 (Le **125**
Levanstell 122) (1982 6fg³ 1983 8d² 7.6v* 8.2s* 10.5f* 11g² 12f* 12g* 12f)

The progressive Seymour Hicks had a very rewarding time in 1983, winning
five of his eight races, including the Great Voltigeur Stakes at York. He finished out
of the first two only once, when fourteenth to All Along in the Trusthouse Forte
Prix de l'Arc de Triomphe on his final start. Ignoring his first outing, when he wasn't
fully fit, Seymour Hicks might well have remained unbeaten up to the Arc: he was
very unlucky in running, finishing fast on the outside after being switched to obtain
a clear run, when narrowly beaten by Dazari in the Mecca Bookmakers' Scottish
Derby at Ayr in July, the most important event he had contested up to that time.
His first two victories, in maiden and minor events at Lingfield and Haydock, had
been followed by a win in the Daniel Prenn Royal Yorkshire Stakes over York's
extended mile and a quarter on Timeform Charity Day.

The Daniel Prenn Stakes has heralded the arrival in the first division of several
smart performers—Jimsun, Bright Finish and Prince Roland are other notable
winners—but a proposal to increase the prize money to £20,000 in 1984 and to
rename the event the Yorkshire Derby was rejected by the Stewards of the Jockey
Club. In their view the proposed race was too valuable—'it encroaches upon the
Group 3 parameters' they said—and they refused to allow the use of the word
Derby in the title. Quite why anyone should object to a Yorkshire Derby when there
is a Welsh Derby, Scottish Derby, and even a Dunstall Derby, is impossible to
fathom. Pills lose their bitterness with regular taking but the official attitude
towards efforts to rejuvenate the Timeform Charity Day programme took some
swallowing. Apart from rejecting the £100,000 Swettenham Stud Stakes—
discussed in the essay on Lomond—and the proposed Yorkshire Derby, the
Stewards also took a negative attitude towards a Timeform-sponsored apprentice
series. We had planned to run fifteen qualifying races for apprentices who had not
ridden a winner before the start of the season, leading to a Final on Timeform
Charity Day, the object being to give inexperienced boys a chance they might not
otherwise get. But the Stewards refused to give permission for the qualifiers to be
run in place of existing races, fearing that they might replace so-called 'much
needed' maiden races. We have complained before that the Jockey Club, through its
various committees, exercises far too rigid a control over the racing programme.
Clerks of courses are little more than licensed puppets nowadays, being told what
races they can have, what races they can't, what conditions they can have for their
races and what conditions they can't, even on occasions, as we have experienced,
how much prize money they can put up or what title they can use for a race. Flair is
stifled, fresh ideas looked upon with suspicion. It's an appalling situation, one that
wouldn't have been tolerated in Crocker Bulteel's day and Leslie Petch's day.
Bulteel and Petch, two of racing's greatest clerks of the course, were not afraid to

*Daniel Prenn Royal Yorkshire Stakes, York—Seymour Hicks quickens away from Airfield
and Mister Prelude (grey)*

step outside racing's established pattern and when they did so it usually turned out to be of benefit to racing—to racing as an entertainment, that is. Crocker Bulteel founded the King George VI and Queen Elizabeth Stakes which was immediately a resounding success; Leslie Petch built up York to a point where the August meeting became one of the season's major highlights. Like the theatre, racing needs impresarios, organisers of the entertainment. Put on a good show in the theatre and the public will give it their support. Put on a dull and dreary show and they will not. The same applies to racing programmes. Racing is not short of people with brains, enthusiasm and organising talent. But they are not being given the opportunity to exploit their ability. Progress is being inhibited and racing is becoming stagnated. The enthusiastic and talented brains we have in racing must be given some rein and allowed to show their worth.

To return to Seymour Hicks, he won the Daniel Prenn by two lengths from the favourite Airfield, showing a decisive turn of foot in the final stages. His first attempt at a mile and a half, in the Alycidon Stakes at Goodwood's July meeting, showed him to be well suited by the trip. He started favourite to beat six rivals, including the Land of Burns Stakes winner Sabre Dance and the Churchill Stakes winner Society Boy. Held up early on, Seymour Hicks again showed good acceleration to win decisively by a length and a half from Sabre Dance, with Noble Gift a head away third. So to the Great Voltigeur. A select field of five turned out, headed by Teenoso, the first Derby winner to contest the race since St Paddy, and the unbeaten Coral-Eclipse Stakes winner Solford; Dazari, Seymour Hicks and Teenoso's pacemaker Laughing Lad completed the field. Seymour Hicks was again settled at the back as Laughing Lad set a good pace to halfway. Teenoso took it up turning for home but Seymour Hicks was brought to challenge in the last furlong and a half, soon took command and steadily drew clear, kept up to his work, to beat Dazari by three lengths with Teenoso, conceding 7 lb to the first two, a head away in third.

		Ragusa	Ribot
	Ballymore	(b 1960)	Fantan II
	(b 1969)	Paddy's Sister	Ballyogan
Seymour Hicks (Fr)		(b 1957)	Birthday Wood
(b.c. 1980)		Le Levanstell	Le Lavandou
	Sarah Siddons	(b 1957)	Stella's Sister
	(b 1973)	Mariel	Relko
		(b 1968)	Ela Marita

Seymour Hicks is a small, rather unprepossessing individual. His sire Ballymore proved difficult to train and ran only five times, remarkably winning the Irish Two Thousand Guineas on his debut; his only other victory came in the Nijinsky Stakes, in which he beat Roberto. Ballymore made a good start at stud with the Irish One Thousand Guineas winner More So, the Irish Sweeps Derby runner-up Exdirectory and the Spanish Guineas and Derby winner Barilone among his first crop. With the exceptions of the dual pattern-race winner Ore, the very smart filly Racquette and the Park Stakes victress More Heather Ballymore had no further notable offspring until Seymour Hicks. Sarah Siddons, the dam of Seymour Hicks, was the best three-year-old filly of 1976, winning the Irish One Thousand Guineas and the Yorkshire Oaks. Seymour Hicks is her second foal; the first was unraced; the third, the two-year-old filly Princess Pati (by Top Ville), finished third on her only start. Sarah Siddons' yearling (by General Assembly) was sold to representatives of Khaled Abdulla at the Newmarket Highflyer Sales for a then-record price of 1,400,000 guineas. Seymour Hicks's grandam Mariel was in the frame in three classics in 1971 and her dam the Musidora and Fred Darling winner Ela Marita was a half-sister to Ragusa, the sire of Ballymore. Tim Rogers,

Great Voltigeur Stakes, York—Seymour Hicks puts up his best performance to win in commanding fashion from Dazari and Teenoso (rails)

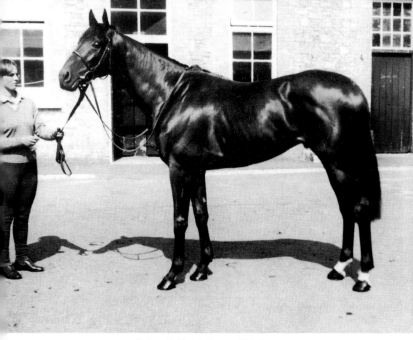

Mr Peter M. Brant's "Seymour Hicks"

whose death was reported in January, bought a half-share in Seymour Hicks after the Great Voltigeur and the colt will be in training with Whittingham in the United States in 1984. Tim Rogers, one of Ireland's most respected and influential owner-breeders, built the Airlie Stud complex into one of the biggest and most successful stallion operations in Europe; the management of the Airlie group of studs has been taken over by Rogers' widow assisted by his brother Mick who saddled the Derby winners Hard Ridden and Santa Claus. Seymour Hicks is a very genuine and consistent racehorse who is suited by a mile and a half and acts on any going. He is a quick-actioned colt whose good turn of finishing speed is a formidable weapon; he is well suited by waiting tactics. *J. Dunlop.*

S G S GLAZING 3 ch.g. Gunner B 126–Cherry Burton 79 (Kalydon 122) (1982 5fg 5f 6f⁴ 6f 7d 6f 7f 7f* 8fg⁴ 8.2s 8d 1983 11fg 12v 12.2g 9d) small, close-coupled gelding; plater; promises to stay 1¾m; suited by a sound surface; blinkered final start; sold 1,750 gns Doncaster June Sales, for export to Norway. *N. Tinkler.*   —

SHABNAM 3 br.f. Jimsun 121–Beychevelle (Sir Herbert 106) (1982 5g 5h³ 6f² 6fg 6g 6g³ 7g 8fg 8.2d 7g⁴ 7.2s² 1983 10fg⁴ 14f⁴ 10.2f³ 10f 8g 10g 10g 12f⁴) small filly; plater; in frame in non-sellers in summer; stays 1¾m; acts on any going; started none too well twice as a 2-y-o; sold 1,250 gns Ascot November Sales. *D. Gandolfo.*   48

SHACKLE PIN (USA) 3 b.g. Sir Wimborne 118–Countess Babu (Bronze Babu) (1982 6fg² 7.2g* 6g³ 8.2fg⁴ 8d 8d 1983 8g 8f 11g 12g 10.5d³ 8fg 10s) smallish gelding; usually faced stiff tasks and didn't show much in 1983; should stay at least 11f; best form on a soft surface; blinkered last 2 starts; sold 6,200 gns Doncaster September Sales. *J. Hanson.*   —

SHADAN 3 b.c. Cawston's Clown 113–Tudor Tilly 63 (Will Somers 114§) (1982 5fg 5g³ 5f* 5fg* 6fg* 7f⁴ 7g⁴ 6f* 7g* 6g 1983 7s 6s 7fg* 6fg 8f 7f⁴) small,   85

739

well-made colt; won 18-runner handicap at Warwick in June, getting up to beat Vatican Way in a blanket finish; not certain to stay beyond 7f; form only on top-of-the-ground; genuine; missed break fifth outing. *P. Haslam.*

SHADES OF BLUE 2 br.c. Blue Cashmere 129–Shades of Glory 80 (Queen's Hussar 124) (1983 5v 5s² 5s³ 5d²(dis) 6f 5fg 5f² 5f 6f² 6f 6fg² 5fg³ 5g³ 6fg⁴ 5d³ 6fg) Apr 14; 5,000Y; small, lengthy colt; has a round action; first foal; dam in frame at up to 1m; placed in varied races, including in 2 valuable sellers; stays 6f; acts on any going; often blinkered; disappointing, and possibly not entirely genuine. *M. Blanshard.* **73**

SHADES OF RED 3 ch.g. Whistling Deer 117–Positioned (Status Seeker) (1982 6fg 7g 6f 7f⁴ 7f 8f 8fg 8.2s³ 10d 1983 10v 12f 12f) leggy, lightly-made gelding; unreliable maiden plater; stays 1m; wears blinkers; sold 460 gns Doncaster August Sales. *D. Morley.* **– §**

SHADEY DOVE 9 b.m. Deadly Nightshade 107–Red Dove (All Red 110) (1982 16g 16f³ 16.1fg⁴ 17f 1983 17d² 18.8v³ 17.1d⁴ 16f 17f) staying handicapper; ideally suited by some give in the ground; game; doesn't always impress in paddock. *G. Price.* **51**

SHADHA 2 b.f. Shirley Heights 130–Plum Run 87 (Run The Gantlet) (1983 7h 6fg) Apr 27; first foal; dam won at up to 8.2f and comes from family of top-class American horse Arts and Letters; poor form in maiden events at Chepstow and Brighton. *H. T. Jones.* **57**

SHADILIYA 2 b.f. Red Alert 127–Shaara (Sanctus II 132) (1983 5f 7f² 6h³ 7f* 8fg) Mar 12; quite attractive sort; good walker; third foal; closely related to very useful 5f to 1m winner Shasavaan (by Red God); dam placed at up to 11f in French Provinces; won 12-runner maiden race at Yarmouth in August; stays 1m; acts on hard going; sent to France. *M. Stoute.* **90**

SHAHREEN 2 gr.f. Swing Easy 126–Palace Art 58 (Dragonara Palace 115) (1983 5s 5f 5.1fg* 5g 5h 5g) May 5; 800Y; leggy, lightly-made filly; first foal; dam won 5f seller at 2 yrs; backed from 20/1 to 12/1, made all in 11-runner maiden auction event at Yarmouth in June; showed nothing in nurseries afterwards; sold 580 gns Doncaster October Sales. *G. Blum.* **62**

SHAKA LASS 2 b.f. Home Guard 129–Mare d'Erba (Habitat 134) (1983 5fg 7f 7g 7.6d) Apr 7; IR 10,000Y; lengthy filly; third foal; sister to fairly useful 1981 2-y-o 6f winner Irish Grenadier, and half-sister to 3-y-o Be My Princess (by Try My Best); dam unraced granddaughter of smart 1964 2-y-o Unity; behind in maiden races; sold 1,150 gns Ballsbridge December Sales. *A. Ingham.* **–**

SHAKIRA GROVE 2 b.f. Hot Grove 128–Private Collection 70 (Whistling Wind 123) (1983 7s) Mar 28; 380Y; lengthy filly; fifth foal; dam stayed 1m; decidedly backward, 9 lengths sixth of 19 to Ophrys in maiden race at Leicester in October. *J. Spearing.* **–**

SHALLAAL (USA) 4 ch.g. Honest Pleasure–Grass Court (Herbager 136) (1982 10fg 10g 1983 12f 10h 8fg⁴ 10f* 10f 10d) strong, well-made, deep-girthed gelding; led near finish to win handicap at Folkestone in August; stays 1¼m; acts on firm going; has shown signs of temperament and is best in blinkers; not one to rely on. *J. Dunlop.* **54**

SHALLOT GIRL 3 gr.f. Spanish Gold 101–Shall Do (Passenger 122 or Derring-Do 131) (1982 NR 1983 7f 8f) small, plain filly; half-sister to a winner by Decoy Boy; dam ran twice; last to finish in a seller and a maiden race at Beverley. *F. Watson.* **–**

SHAMBOLIC 2 gr.f. Absalom 128–Shamba (Hornbeam 130) (1983 5v⁴ 5d² 5f 5fg³ 5f³ 5g 5fg³ 5g) Apr 7; 1,000F; small, strong, sturdy filly; half-sister to a placed animal in Sweden; dam won 3 times in Sweden; quite a modest maiden; should be suited by 6f; seems to act on any going. *R. Smyth.* **80**

SHAMROCK NAIL 4 b.c. He Loves Me 120–Come Aboard 82 (Whistler 129) (1982 7g 9fg⁴ 8f³ 8fg⁴ 8.2f 8g³ 8fg 8fg 7fg 8.2s 1983 10.1d³ 9h⁴ 7d 8f* 8h 8.3fg) rather leggy colt; poor mover; plater; bought in 1,600 gns after scoring at Pontefract in June; stays 1¼m; acts on any going; sometimes sweats up; has run respectably for an apprentice; raced alone when blinkered once; sold 1,800 gns Ascot September Sales. *D. Nicholson.* **57**

SHAMROCK PRINCESS 2 b.f. Manado 130–King's Chase (King's Leap 111) (1983 6f³ 6f 7f* 8f² 8g) Mar 17; 3,600Y; lightly-built filly; sister to poor 3-y-o Queen's Chase and half-sister to 9f and 1¼m winner Chaste Lady (by Sandford Lad); plater; bought in 1,700 gns after making all to beat Follow That Cab a head at Catterick in August; creditable second in selling nursery at Beverley the following **58**

month; stays 1m; acts on firm going; sold NBA 5,000 gns Newmarket Autumn Sales. *D. Morley.*

SHANAFONA   2 b.f. Flashback 102–Dumette 89 (Dumbarnie 125) (1983 5v 5v 5v 5s 6f) Apr 4; bad plater; not seen out after June. *A. Davison.*   —

SHAND   4 b.c. Saritamer 130–Stockingful (Santa Claus 133) (1982 7f 8s 9.4fg 10g 10fg 10d 12d 12v 1983 12s) strong, sturdy, good-bodied colt; well beaten in varied company. *P. Felgate.*   —

SHANIPOUR   3 ch.c. Nishapour 125–Forlorn Chance (Fighting Don) (1982 7fg 8g² 1983 10.6v³ 12v² 12g*) tall, lengthy colt; has a good stride; not seen out after battling on well to beat Grizabella a short head in 15-runner minor event at Newmarket in April; had shown plenty of ability previously, notably when good ¾-length second to Harly in Warren Stakes at Epsom earlier in month (had difficulty getting a run); suited by 1½m and will get further. *G. Harwood.*   94

SHANLEY'S STYLE   3 b.c. Balidar 133–Blue Promise 95 (Red Alert 127) (1982 5s* 5fg² 5fg⁴ 5h* 6fg⁴ 5g 6s 6s 1983 5s* 5s* 5s² 5.8v* 6s⁴ 5fg 5f 5g 5f 7g 5g⁴) lengthy, workmanlike colt; has a round action; in fine form early in season and won handicaps at Leicester, Salisbury and Bath in decisive fashion; ran respectably on occasions afterwards; stays 6f; acts on any going but is well suited by some give; blinkered final outing in 1982. *Mrs J. Reavey.*   97

SHANMULLAGH   3 b.f. Julio Mariner 127–Rose Mullion 82 (Tudor Melody 129) (1982 NR 1983 9f 7h) close-coupled filly; closely related to 1978 2-y-o 5f winner Regina Magna (by Blakeney); dam won over 5f at 2 yrs; soundly beaten in maiden and minor events in summer; sold 580 gns Doncaster November Sales. *J. Bethell.*   —

SHANOUSKA   3 b.c. He Loves Me 120–Khadija 69 (Habat 127) (1982 5fg 5.3g³ 5fg 5fg 7fg 7fg 6s 1983 5s³ 6s* 6s² 7g 6fg 7g 6f 5fg 6f 6fg⁴ 6fg) somewhat lightly-made, quite attractive colt; won apprentice handicap at Salisbury in May; stays 6f; acts on a firm surface but is probably ideally suited by some give in the ground. *J. Benstead.*   59 d

SHANTUNG LACE   2 b.f. Queen's Hussar 124–Shantung Lassie (Shantung 132) (1983 5s 5d 6f 6fg 6f* 6h⁴ 6fg) Mar 11; 820Y; lightly-built filly; half-sister to 7f seller winner Mount Eliza (by Welsh Saint); dam won at up to 1½m in France; changed hands 3,200 gns after winning 10-runner seller at Yarmouth in July by 2½ lengths from stable-companion Manor Farm Lady; should stay beyond 6f; acts on firm going; blinkered fourth outing; exported to Algeria. *G. Blum.*   55

SHARAYA (USA)   3 b.f. Youth 135–Shanizadeh (Baldric II 131) (1982 NR 1983 8v* 8v* 10v² 10g³ 10fg* 12s* 12f)   123

French-trained three-year-old fillies played less significant a part than we have come to expect in the Prix de l'Arc de Triomphe. Of four to line up only the top-class miler Luth Enchantee was in contention at the finish; Marie de Litz came in tenth, the French Oaks winner Escaline nineteenth and the Trusthouse Forte Prix Vermeille winner Sharaya twenty-first. Shortest priced of the four at 9/1, Sharaya ran below her best, fading after showing prominently on the outside from the number twenty-five draw (next to the winner) until into the straight. Although she undoubtedly ran below her best in the Arc Sharaya can't be regarded as the

Trusthouse Forte Prix Vermeille, Longchamp—Sharaya makes all the running and wins from Estrapade, Vosges (rails) and Marie de Litz

H. H. Aga Khan's "Sharaya" (Y. Saint-Martin)

equal of the majority of the Prix Vermeille winners of the last dozen years, an exceptional period during which San San and Three Troikas won the Arc and the Vermeille in the same season and Allez France, Ivanjica and All Along won the Arc the year after they won the Vermeille.

Unusually, none of the first three in the French Oaks, the Prix de Diane Hermes, ran in the Prix Vermeille: Escaline met with a last-minute mishap, cast in her box, Smuggly was out injured, and Air Distingue was racing in England with mixed results. In their absence Sharaya, who'd by-passed the French Oaks in favour of the Prix de Malleret at Longchamp two weeks later reportedly because she had taken time to get over her race in the Prix Saint-Alary, started favourite. She had been a disappointing third behind Chamisene and the Epsom Oaks favourite Alexandrie in the Malleret but had since won the Prix de la Nonette at Deauville with ease by two lengths and the same from two very useful fillies Green Reef and Right Bank, the latter fourth to Escaline in the French Oaks. And prior to the Malleret Sharaya had shown herself one of the leading three-year-old fillies in France: she had lost only once in three starts. Unraced as a two-year-old she won a maiden at Saint-Cloud (from Luth Enchantee) and a more valuable race at Longchamp, the Prix de Bagatelle, in the spring, the latter in excellent style; next she had finished second to Smuggly in the Prix Saint-Alary at Longchamp in May. The Saint-Alary is nearly always the best of the fillies' classic trials in France; Sharaya ran very well indeed in it, beating Escaline by four lengths for second place and going down by only two lengths to Smuggly after setting a steady pace and fighting back strongly when headed by the winner in the straight. At short odds coupled with Rajpoura, Sharaya also made the running in the Prix Vermeille. Saint-Martin her rider, champion jockey in France in 1983 for the fifteenth time, waited in front; he judged the pace soundly and kept enough in reserve both to fend off a challenge from Green Lucia and to produce a two-furlong spurt to win by two lengths, a short neck and short neck from Estrapade, Vacarme's half-sister Vosges and Marie de Litz, with the Yorkshire Oaks second Green Lucia seventh and Right Bank tenth of the twelve runners. Neither second nor third had a big-race victory to her name. The previously-unbeaten Estrapade, whose run from the back of the field petered out in the last furlong, was found to have suffered a fractured near-hind as a result of being struck into. Saint-Martin's reported post-race comment on Sharaya: 'She's a better horse now than Akiyda' proved wide of the mark; Akiyda, beaten by All Along in a much more strongly-contested Prix Vermeille (Grease, Harbour, Zalataia and Awaasif also ran in that race), went on to win the Arc.

			Ack Ack	Battle Joined
	Youth		(b 1966)	Fast Turn
	(b 1973)		Gazala	Dark Star
Sharaya (USA)			(br 1964)	Belle Angevine
(b.f. 1980)			Baldric II	Round Table
	Shanizadeh		(b 1961)	Two Cities
	(b 1974)		Safiah	St Paddy
			(b 1969)	Flaming Heart

Sharaya and Vosges are by the American-based Youth, the sire of the Derby winner Teenoso; all the first three in the Vermeille, incidentally, were foaled in the United States. Sharaya is her dam's first living foal, following dead twins by Caro. The dam Shanizadeh, by the Guineas winner Baldric II out of a mare who won an apprentice race over seven and a half furlongs and a handicap over nearly eleven furlongs in France, raced only four times; she was useful nevertheless, and won over six furlongs as a two-year-old and over a mile as a three-year-old. Shanizadeh's grandam Flaming Heart is a good-class winning daughter of Aimee, the grandam of Blushing Groom who stands alongside Youth at Gainesway Farm.

Sharaya is a rangy, very attractive filly. She stayed a mile and a half and acted on any going except, perhaps, going as firm as that on Arc day. She hasn't done much racing in her life, but it seems unlikely that she will be kept in training for another season. *A. de Royer Dupre, France.*

SHARAZOUR 3 gr.g. Nishapour 125–Scentless 88 (Floribunda 136) (1982 5.8g 6v 1983 6v 7s 7.6v 10fg 10f) neat gelding; has shown only a little ability, including in a seller; promises to stay 1¼m. *F. J. Houghton.* —

SHARED JOKE 2 b.g. Comedy Star 121–Betula 89 (Hornbeam 130) (1983 5fg 6f 6g 7fg 7.6fg) May 13; 4,200Y; half-brother to a minor winner; dam won at 6f and 1¼m; behind in maiden and minor events. *M. Bolton.* —

SHAREEF DANCER (USA) 3 b.c. Northern Dancer–Sweet Alliance (Sir Ivor 135) (1982 6f* 6fg⁴ 1983 8v² 12f* 12f*)   135

Sportsman: (fig) person who regards life as a game in which opponents must be allowed fair play, person ready to play a bold game (*Concise Oxford Dictionary*). How many of today's leading racehorse owners on the flat live up to this definition? Very few, one might think, judged by much of what is written on the subject in the racing Press. The popular media caricature of most of today's multi-millionaire owners is of the 'bad guys', people whose commercial instincts contrast sharply with the supposed sporting instincts of those at racing's grass roots. The handling of Shareef Dancer, for example, who wasn't raced after winning the Irish Sweeps Derby and was syndicated in late-summer for a world-record sum, created a good deal of controversy. His connections gained many more critics than friends by adopting a seemingly over-protective attitude towards Shareef Dancer after his victory at the Curragh. 'I offer no excuse—indeed there can be no excuse—for a man like Maktoum Al-Maktoum to chicken out of running Shareef Dancer in the Benson and Hedges Gold Cup and the weakly-contested September Stakes', wrote Tony Morris in *The Sporting Life* adding that to him Shareef Dancer's failure to turn out for these races constituted two defeats—'If the horse won't lay his reputation on the line, I have to suspect that his reputation is false'. Jonathan Powell wrote in *The Irish Field*: 'Where is the spirit of competition and challenge that once was an integral part of our racing? Regrettably, in flat racing it has gradually been eroded by an unhealthy fear of damage to reputations that, in some cases, have barely been established'. Powell contrasted Shareef Dancer's career with that of Sir Ivor, Mill Reef and Nijinsky. 'Did those final two defeats of Nijinsky harm his remarkable record or affect his future as one of the most important stallions this century? Not at all. Would that some of the so-called champions of the 'eighties were allowed to race with such freedom against the best'. There were less favourable reactions too than those of Morris and Powell to Shareef Dancer's inactivity after victory over the Prix du Jockey-Club winner Caerleon and the Epsom Derby winner Teenoso had established Shareef Dancer to most people's satisfaction as the champion-elect among Europe's three-year-old middle-distance colts.

As regular readers will appreciate, there is nothing new about our best horses being retired to stud at the end of their three-year-old days. Eighty years ago Sir

King Edward VII Stakes, Ascot—a greatly improved effort from Shareef Dancer, in beating Russian Roubles a length; Hawa Bladi is third

Theodore Cook wrote in *A History of the English Turf* that 'The services of fashionable sires are so much in request that a stallion with a first-class record and of high descent is sure to be sent early to stud . . . The high price of a good yearling in these days practically necessitates in most cases a quick return for the outlay of so much capital, and if that return is not secured by entering him for ten times more races than was the case a century ago, it must be reaped by getting early stud fees'. Cook also pointed out that the 'great prizes of our Turf are given to young horses', and the same applies today. The emphasis in the pattern of racing is on merit at two and three, as it almost always has been, and there is little chance of more top horses being kept in training at four so long as the racing programme fails to cater adequately for them. However, it is hard to counter accusations of faint-heartedness against a racehorse owner who doesn't even allow a supposed champion to fulfil a full racing programme as a three-year-old. A racehorse like Shareef Dancer is, of course, an extremely valuable commodity and an owner is perfectly entitled to do as he likes with his property, breaches of law and Jockey Club rules excepted. If Shareef Dancer's connections believed that it was in their best interests not to hazard the horse's reputation—and his capital value—by risking defeat then there was nothing anyone else could do about it. That said, one would like to think that in any field the paying public has some influence over the quality of entertainment offered to it. Those who bet on horse-racing contribute each year to prize-money through the levy while racegoers also contribute through admission fees to racecourses. And what of sponsors to whom racing, particularly at the top level, looks increasingly for support? Should the interests of these groups be ignored? It is tacitly accepted that the public cannot expect to see the top horses line up together more than a few times a season; but in recent times the games of musical chairs played around the racecourses of Europe with some of the top horses—particularly those in the highly-prestigious middle-distance category—have bordered on the farcical, with the racegoer often the loser. The handling of Shareef Dancer exemplifies, in extreme form, the approach of some of the current generation of leading owners. The withdrawal of Shareef Dancer from the Benson and Hedges Gold Cup at the last moment—because the going was deemed to have become unsuitable after morning rain—was, naturally enough, greeted with disappointment, even annoyance, by sections of the big crowd at the opening day of York's

August meeting. As we have said before, the situation in such circumstances so far as the public is concerned is to some extent comparable with that of a cricketer who declines to play in a Test match on the grounds that the wicket is so favourable to the bowlers that he will certainly harm his reputation and spoil his average by batting on it. The going for the Benson and Hedges was no worse than dead and although there were grounds for thinking that such conditions might not have been ideal for Shareef Dancer it is most unlikely he would have suffered physical damage by racing on it. Incidentally, the theory, widely held at the time, that Caerleon needed a sound surface to show his best form was shown to be erroneous when he won the Benson and Hedges in Shareef Dancer's absence. Although the York stewards imposed no fine on Shareef Dancer's connections, it has to be said that the decision to withdraw the horse seemed a craven one. Although admitting that a defeat at York might have raised one or two doubts elsewhere, in our book Shareef Dancer would have remained the best middle-distance three-year-old colt in Europe even if he had lost the Benson and Hedges. His Irish Sweeps Derby performance could not be assailed by defeat in another race over a shorter trip and on different going. Shareef Dancer's connections surely owed it to the horse to let him take part. Denied an opportunity to show that he could win a championship event on softish ground, Shareef Dancer was bound to fall short of the ideal. The complete racehorse should be capable of racing on any sort of going; by using Shareef Dancer's supposed inability to handle softish ground as an excuse for his withdrawal, connections were admitting a shortcoming in his make-up that might not have been there. Credit should go to Caerleon's connections on this occasion for at least allowing him to take his chance; in the event, Caerleon proved himself a more complete racehorse—though not a better one—than Shareef Dancer. The less said the better about Shareef Dancer's absence from the September Stakes at Kempton. No last-minute withdrawal here. Shareef Dancer, whose syndication was under way, was taken out overnight, reportedly because of 'an adverse weather forecast'. The going turned out to be as near perfect as you'd get. After this, hardly anyone believed Shareef Dancer would take the field for his next stated objective the Prix de l'Arc de Triomphe (which was run on ground as firm as it had been on Irish Sweeps Derby day). Shareef Dancer had become the ultimate absurdity, a racehorse seemingly too valuable to race.

The fact that Shareef Dancer wasn't seen out after June, and that he never had a chance to prove his worth against older horses or against some of the best representatives of a vintage collection of middle-distance fillies and mares, makes the job of accurately assessing his merit more difficult than if he had gone on to contest some of the season's top open-aged races for horses of his type. All we can say with any degree of certainty is that Shareef Dancer's Irish Sweeps Derby victory, a fine one as we have already intimated, still looked, at the end of the year the best performance put up by a three-year-old colt during the European season a a mile and a half. That Shareef Dancer looked poised to reach even greater heights

Irish Sweeps Derby, the Curragh—Shareef Dancer records an outstanding victory, striding away from French Derby winner Caerleon (right) and Epsom Derby winner Teenoso (rails)

after his success at the Curragh has now to be disregarded, of course: one must always guard against giving a horse credit for what he didn't do. So Shareef Dancer goes down in history as a good winner of the Irish Sweeps Derby, not so good as such recent winners as Troy and Shergar, but significantly above average nonetheless. The field that Shareef Dancer beat at the Curragh was a strong one, stronger than that for either the Epsom Derby or the Prix du Jockey-Club. Apart from the winners of those two events, Teenoso and Caerleon, the Irish Sweeps Derby also attracted the runner-up at Epsom, Carlingford Castle, and the first and third in the Airlie/Coolmore Irish Two Thousand Guineas, Wassl and Parliament. Shareef Dancer earned his place at the Curragh by winning the King Edward VII Stakes on firm going at Royal Ascot, quickening clear halfway up the straight after being held up and holding off the strong-finishing Russian Roubles by a length. Shareef Dancer's trainer had told us in the *Timeform Interview* for our Royal Ascot Issue that Shareef Dancer had been found to be suffering from a throat infection when beaten favourite for the Esher Cup at Sandown in April on his only previous outing in 1983 (he was beaten two lengths by 25/1-shot So True). 'We certainly haven't seen the best out of this colt yet . . . he's a wonderful little athlete with a great action and he'll be much better when he can get some bounce out of the ground', Stoute told us. Shareef Dancer's performance at Royal Ascot was easily his best up to that time—he had won a Newmarket maiden event and finished fourth in a minor event at Doncaster as a two-year-old—but the King Edward VII Stakes form looked some way below classic-winning standard and he started 8/1 third favourite for the Irish Sweeps Derby behind Caerleon (5/4) and Teenoso (2/1). Shareef Dancer was tremendously impressive in a strongly-run race at the Curragh, moving easily just behind the leading group from the start and pulling his way to the front two furlongs out when shown daylight. Pushed along soon after taking the lead, Shareef Dancer put the issue beyond doubt in a few strides and drew away to win by three lengths—we made it nearer five—from Caerleon, with Teenoso two lengths further away third. Quilted, who went on to win the Princess of Wales's Stakes at Newmarket's July meeting, came fourth, Wassl fifth, Carlingford Castle seventh and Parliament tenth of the twelve runners. It's rare to see a classic won in such fashion. It wasn't even necessary for Shareef Dancer's

Maktoum Al-Maktoum's "Shareef Dancer"

jockey to shake him up to send him to the front; as we have said, Shareef Dancer *pulled* his way into the lead. He was striding out in great style at the finish although a few were heard to crab his performance because he carried his head high in the closing stages. Contrary to what some appear to think, a high head carriage is not an automatic sign of ungenerosity; Bikala is a recent example of a really genuine sort who tended to race with his head high. Impressive though Shareef Dancer was on Sweeps Derby day, there were excuses for both his principal rivals. Caerleon didn't have the best of luck, having to be switched to the wide outside of the field after being trapped on the rails early in the straight; and Teenoso seemed unable to stride out freely on the firm ground in the closing stages, hanging sharply right when put under strong pressure.

		Nearctic	Nearco
	Northern Dancer	(br 1954)	Lady Angela
	(b 1961)	Natalma	Native Dancer
Shareef Dancer (USA)		(b 1957)	Almahmoud
(b.c. 1980)		Sir Ivor	Sir Gaylord
	Sweet Alliance	(b 1965)	Attica
	(b 1974)	Mrs Peterkin	Tom Fool
		(b 1965)	Legendra

Shareef Dancer has precisely the right sort of looks and pedigree antecedents to go with his classic victory. He is a most attractive individual, neat and well made, and he took the eye before all his races; he was an extremely good mover in all his paces. Northern Dancer is his sire, so there is no need to say anything further about the top half of his pedigree, except perhaps that Shareef Dancer was the third son of Northern Dancer to win the Irish Sweeps Derby, following Nijinsky (1970) and The Minstrel (1977). Shareef Dancer's dam Sweet Alliance, whose first foal he is, won six races including the Kentucky Oaks and the Jersey Belle Handicap. A daughter of Sir Ivor, Sweet Alliance comes from an excellent family. Her dam Mrs Peterkin, who won six races including the Chrysanthemum Handicap, is a half-sister to nine winners and has bred at least five other winners herself, among them Whydidju, who won six races including the California Oaks, and Dancing Champ, a winner of seven of his thirteen starts including the Massachusetts Handicap and the Woodlawn Stakes. Shareef Dancer cost 3,300,000 dollars (around £1.8m at the time) at the Keeneland Summer Select Yearling Sale; when he went into training he was the most expensive yearling ever to enter a British stable. He retires to the Dalham Hall Stud, Newmarket, valued by the terms of his syndication at 40,000,000 dollars (around £26.6m at prevailing exchange rates), having seen less than ten minutes action on the racecourse and repaid £138,383 of his purchase price in prize money. *M. Stoute.*

SHARLIE'S WIMPY 4 ch.c. Tumble Wind–Sweet Sharlie 77 (Fighting Charlie 127) (1982 6fg 8f² 8fg 8f 7g 8.5fg 8s 8v⁴ 8s 7s³ 6s 1983 8g 7f 7f 5.8h³ 6f³ 6f 6fg 6d 5.8fg) strong, attractive colt; good mover; fair handicapper on his day; stays 1m; acts on any going; usually blinkered. *J. Bethell.* **77**

SHARP AND READY 2 b.c. Sharpen Up 127–Ready and Willing 82 (Reliance II 137) (1983 8fg) Apr 7; 20,000Y; workmanlike colt; half-brother to fairly useful middle-distance winner Wollow Will (by Wollow) and a winner in Italy; dam won over 12.2f and comes from a good family; 33/1, disputed lead on far side for 5f in 28-runner maiden race won by Bob Back at Newmarket in October; sure to improve. *P. Haslam.* **– p**

SHARPEN UP BOY 3 b.c. Impecunious–Sharpenella 72 (Sharpen Up 127) (1982 8s 1983 10s 7f 12g) lengthy colt; beaten some way in maiden and minor events; sold 400 gns Newmarket Autumn Sales. *R. Simpson.* **–**

SHARP IMAGE 2 b.g. He Loves Me 120–Gravure (Zank) (1983 6g 7.6fg 8g) Apr 24; IR 6,200F, IR 11,500Y; useful-looking gelding; good walker; second produce; half-brother to Irish 9f winner Graviola (by Oats); dam, winner twice at 3 yrs in Germany, is closely related to top German sprinter Garzer; in rear in autumn maiden events. *G. Balding.* **–**

SHARPISH 3 ch.c. Sharpen Up 127–Restive 96 (Relic) (1982 6fg² 6fg 6fg³ 6d 6s 1983 5d* 6v 5g² 5fg³ 5f* 5f* 5g* 5fg² 5fg) quite an attractive colt; not a good walker; improved steadily and won minor event at Thirsk, £10,400 James Lane Handicap at Ascot, Singleton Handicap at Goodwood and Wykeham Handicap at York; beat Django in last 2 races, travelling strongly throughout both times and winning by ¾ length on latter course in August after tending to idle in front; also **105**

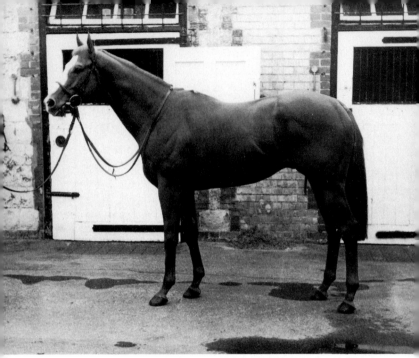

Mr R. N. Richmond-Watson's "Sharpish"

placed in handicaps at Sandown (2) and York; best at 5f; acts on a soft surface but is ideally suited by a sound one; tough and genuine. *B. Hobbs.*

SHARP MELODY 4 b.f. Hot Spark 126–Tulchan 95 (Tudor Melody 129) (1982 10f 1983 5v 10f 7fg 10f 8g 8fg) small filly; poor plater; has been blinkered. *H. Beasley.* —

SHARP REMARK (USA) 2 b.g. Clev Er Tell–Slogan (Lurullah) (1983 6f 7fg 6fg 7f³ 7fg 8d 7fg 7fg*) Mar 11; $17,000Y, $50,000 2-y-o; close-coupled, good-topped gelding; half-brother to several minor winners; dam won twice over 6f, including in a claiming race; won 12-runner nursery at Edinburgh in November; gelded subsequently; suited by 7f; acts on firm going. *B. Hanbury.* 77

SHARP ROI 2 ch.c. Roi Soleil 125–Simply Jane (Sharpen Up 127) (1983 5s⁴ 5s² 5v 6d*) Jan 27; 2,000F, 6,800Y; first foal; dam never ran; off course nearly 5 months before beating odds-on Waterville Lake 1½ lengths in maiden event at Phoenix Park in October; had earlier run creditably when 2 lengths second to Malang-Lou in similar race at same track in May; suited by 6f; yet to race on a sound surface. *K. Prendergast, Ireland.* 80

SHARP SEA 3 b.f. Sharpen Up 127–Windy Sea 105 (Sea Hawk II 131) (1982 6g³ 6f² 6f* 7f³ 6g 7.6s² 7s² 7g³ 1983 7s 8d 8s 10g 8fg 8f⁴ 8.3fg 8.2h*) robust, well-made filly; carries plenty of condition; mainly disappointing as a 3-y-o, but managed to win handicap at Nottingham in September, being produced late to head Mullet on post; suited by 1m; acts on any going; needs holding up; blinkered sixth and seventh starts. *B. Hobbs.* 84

SHARP SHOT 2 br.c. Sharpen Up 127–First Round 97 (Primera 131) (1983 6g 6f³ 6fg⁴ 7f⁴ 5s³ 5fg⁴) May 28; neat colt; half-brother to numerous winners, 77 including smart 5f and 7f winner Glenturret (by Habitat), useful sprinter Rollahead (by Tower Walk) and useful 7f and 1m winner Sheriff Muir (by Try My Best); dam won at up to 1¼m; quite a moderate colt; best run at 5f, but stays 6f; acts on any going; blinkered final outing; to be trained by J. Dunlop. *M. Stoute.*

SHARP SONG 2 ch.g. Sharpen Up 127–Mixed Melody 82 (Alcide 136) (1983 6f 6f 8.2g) May 3; second foal; dam, sister to smart stayer Flagon, won over 13f and also won Victor Ludorum Hurdle; in rear in maiden and minor events; off course nearly 3 months after second outing. *G. Richards.* —

SHARP STAR 5 ch.g. Sharpen Up 127–Sara's Star 70 (Sheshoon 132) (1982 8d 8f⁴ 10f⁴ 10fg 10f 8g 1983 10.8v 10fg 10f 12fg 11.7fg) leggy gelding; of little account nowadays; has worn blinkers. *G. Blum.* —

SHARP TAXI 2 ch.c. Dublin Taxi–Ibis 96 (Tamerlane 128) (1983 5d² 5v⁴ 7h⁴ 8d 9fg 8fg 7fg) Feb 11; 13,000Y; workmanlike colt; half-brother to 1976 2-y-o 1m winner Slick Chick (by Shiny Tenth); dam won over 6f at 2 yrs; fair plater; stays 9f; probably acts on any going; blinkered last 2 starts. *R. Williams.* 68

SHARP WIT (USA) 2 ch.c. Blade–I Cue (Crimson Satan) (1983 5s) Feb 16; $180,000Y; strong colt; half-brother to 3 winners, notably Italian Oaks winner Ilenia (by Navajo); dam, winner of sprint claiming races, is half-sister to smart stakes winner I'm On Top; third favourite, ninth of 12 in maiden race at Newmarket in April. *G. Harwood.* —

SHASTA SAM 3 b.c. Dragonara Palace 115–Deva Rose 80 (Chestergate 111) (1982 5f² 5g* 5g 5g 5g 1983 5s* 5s 5s) well-made, attractive colt; made much of running and beat Private Label gamely in handicap at Doncaster in March; well beaten afterwards (not seen out after May); has raced only at 5f; acts on any going; inconsistent. *R. Hollinshead.* 79

SHAWNEE 3 ch.f. Grundy 137–Catalpa 115 (Reform 132) (1982 NR 1983 12.2f* 13.8f³ 12d 10d) leggy, sparely-made filly; second foal; half-sister to Ribblesdale Stakes winner Strigida (by Habitat); dam and grandam won Ribblesdale Stakes; very weak second favourite, made a successful first appearance in 15-runner maiden event at Catterick in July, beating Tancred Walk by 2½ lengths; ran respectably on same course next time (bandaged near-fore), but didn't show much in Ireland afterwards; suited by 1½m+; acts on firm going; trained first 2 starts by H. Cecil. *M. Cunningham, Ireland.* 84

SHEARWALK 3 gr.c. Godswalk 130–Sairshea (Simbir 130) (1982 5fg* 5f³ 7.2g² 7f³ 7g³ 1983 8g* 10g* 12v² 12s³) 123

Shearwalk did best of the four runners to carry the Sangster colours in the Derby. He finished a highly creditable third, beaten three lengths and the same by Teenoso and Carlingford Castle, after being one of the worst sufferers in the scrimmaging that took place halfway down Tattenham Hill, when the rider of Yawa was unseated. Shearwalk was in a seemingly-hopeless position with only five behind him at Tattenham Corner but he ran on gamely up the centre of the track in the straight to snatch third place by a short head from the Sangster-owned Salmon Leap. Shearwalk was struck into at Epsom and was on the easy list for some time afterwards. He wasn't seen out again but we understand he is to be kept in training as a four-year-old. The John Porter Stakes and the Jockey Club Stakes, the conditions of which favour horses that haven't won pattern events, would be ideal targets for him in the spring.

That Shearwalk would make up into a classic contender was not to be anticipated on the evidence of his two-year-old career. He ran five times in his first season and was beaten in good-class races—won by Krayyan, Alchise and All Systems Go—after making a winning debut at Newmarket in the spring; Shearwalk's mark in the Ladbroke European Free Handicap—he received only 8-3—seemed an accurate reflection of his form. Shearwalk didn't grow much over the winter but he impressed when winning the Timeform Race Card Stakes at Thirsk in April on his reappearance. The latest running of the Timeform Race Card Stakes, conceived as a preparatory race for the Newmarket classics and won in 1979 by the subsequent Two Thousand Guineas winner Tap On Wood, attracted the ante-post fifth favourite for the Two Thousand Guineas Horage. Horage, subsequently found to have bruised a heel, could manage only third place; Shearwalk showed a useful turn of foot to get on top approaching the final furlong and won comfortably by five lengths from the outsider Ice Patrol. Twelve days later, in the Heathorn Stakes at Newmarket, Shearwalk took another notable scalp, that of Dunbeath, the winter favourite for the Derby; Shearwalk was sent to the front running into the Dip and ran on strongly up the hill to hold off Dunbeath by a length. In his only other race before Epsom Shearwalk was a clear

Timeform Race Card Stakes, Thirsk—Shearwalk shows a good turn of foot to land this classic trial

second to Teenoso in the Highland Spring Derby Trial at Lingfield, keeping up a determined challenge to the winner from some way out before going down by three lengths.

Shearwalk (gr.c. 1980)	Godswalk (gr 1974)	Dancer's Image (gr 1965)	Native Dancer / Noors Image
		Kate's Intent (b 1964)	Intentionally / Julie Kate
	Sairshea (ch 1975)	Simbir (ch 1970)	Shantung / Hevea
		Petit Chapeau (ch 1966)	High Hat / Armeria

Shearwalk is a compact, deep-girthed colt who usually impresses in appearance; he is also a good mover. His sire, the King's Stand winner Godswalk, never raced beyond six furlongs but judged on his pedigree he might well have stayed further and it's no surprise to us that he has sired a number of horses capable of getting at least a mile. Shearwalk's dam Sairshea, whose first foal he is, won three times over a mile and a half in Ireland and Shearwalk himself stays a mile and a half well. He acts on any going and is most genuine. *M. Stoute.*

SHEBA'S GLORY 5 br.g. Averof 123–Little Miss 92 (Aggressor 130) (1982   –
12g² 10d² 12fg* 12f4 11fg* 12f² 12fg 10fg³ 11g² 9g 12g 12g 1983 12fg 12f 10fg)
small, compact gelding; suited by 1½m; yet to race on very soft going but acts on any other; blinkered once; inconsistent. *F. Watson.*

SHEEOG 2 br.f. Reform 132–Sharifa 102 (Lombard 126) (1983 5f4 5fg* 5f3) Apr   **78**
29; 10,000Y; small, rather lightly-built filly; first foal; dam, from a very good German family, won over 7f and 1½m; made all in 8-runner maiden race at Wolverhampton in August; creditable third, ridden by 5-lb claimer, in 16-runner minor event won by Rare Gal at Warwick later in the month; will be well suited by 6f+. *D. Arbuthnot.*

SHEER HEIGHTS 2 br.c. Shirley Heights 130–Sheer Bliss 76 (St Paddy 133)   **96**
(1983 7f4 8fg² 8fg) Mar 8; 58,000Y; strong, rangy, deep-girthed colt; half-brother to several winners, including useful Irish middle-distance winner Sheringham (by Blakeney); dam showed only a little ability; showed plenty of promise, finishing 5¾ lengths fourth of 16 to Raft in maiden race at Newmarket in July, 2 lengths second of 13 to Carocrest in £3,900 event at Salisbury in September and 2½ lengths fifth of 28 to Bob Back, after coming out best of far-side group, in maiden race at Newmarket in October; will make a useful stayer. *P. Cole.*

SHEER MADNESS 3 ch.c. Wollow 132–Our Song 70 (Song 132) (1982 5d 6g   –
1983 7.6g 7g³ 5g) lengthy, workmanlike colt; poor plater; sold 1,300 gns Newmarket Autumn Sales. *Sir Mark Prescott.*

SHEK-O 2 b.c. Gay Fandango 132–Reproach Me Not (Connaught 130) (1983 8fg)   **81 p**
Mar 15; 16,500Y; good-bodied colt; half-brother to fairly useful 1979 2-y-o 5f and 1m winner Pieces of Gold (by Pieces of Eight); dam French plater; never-dangerous ninth of 28 to Bob Back in maiden race at Newmarket in October; sold 5,200 gns Newmarket Autumn Sales. *G. Harwood.*

SHELDAN 3 b.c. African Sky 124–Stickpin 74 (Gulf Pearl 117) (1982 5g 5fg² 5fg²   –
5g³ 5s² 6s² 1983 5v4 6fg 8.2g 7.6d 6g) neat colt; disappointing maiden; should stay 7f; best form with some give in the ground; sold to CBA 3,200 gns Newmarket Autumn Sales. *S. Mellor.*

SHENESTONE (FR) 2 ch.c. Sharpen Up 127–Fire And Ice (Reliance II 137)   –
(1983 6f 7g) Mar 24; smallish, rather lightly-made colt; first foal; dam, who showed
little sign of ability in 4 races in France, is out of sister to St Leger winner Boucher;
beaten some way in minor event at Windsor in August and maiden race at Leicester
in October. *B. Hills.*

SHENTON WAY (USA) 3 b.c. Silver Saber–Recia (Silver Moon III) (1982 8.2s   85
1983 11s 11.7v³ 12s* 14f² 14fg³ 17d) rangy colt; not the best of movers; beat Sea
Raider by 1½ lengths in maiden event at Haydock in May; ran well when
staying-on 1½ lengths second to Jowoody in £5,200 handicap at York in June but
below his best afterwards (off course 2½ months before final start); should stay
2m; acts on any going; sold to J. Jenkins 18,000 gns Newmarket Autumn Sales.
M. Jarvis.

SHENYOUP 2 ch.c. Sandy Creek 123–Roanoke (Charlottesville 135) (1983 5fg 5f   –
7fg) Feb 23; IR 115,000Y; useful-looking colt; half-brother to several winners,
including useful Irish 1m to 1¼m winner Old Oak Tree (by Ardoon); dam unraced
half-sister to Waterloo; well beaten in minor events; brought down on debut. *J.
Ciechanowski.*

SHEPHERD'S HYMN 2 ch.g. Cidrax–Lay Lady Lay (Celtic Ash) (1983 8s 8fg   76
9s³ 8f) Apr 13; IR 1,000Y, 2,100 2-y-o; plain gelding; has a long stride;
half-brother to 2 winners in Hong Kong, one a winning plater over here; dam well
beaten in 3 Irish maiden races; slow-starting 4 lengths third of 10 to Prince Crow in
maiden race at Wolverhampton in October; will be suited by 1¼m+. *B. Morgan.*

SHERCOL 3 ch.f. Monseigneur 127–Merette 63 (Runnymede 123) (1982 6d 7fg   69
7f 6g 5f³ 5s 6s 1983 8f 12f 9.4f³ 8f³ 7.6g 8f³ 7.2g* 8d 8.2g) leggy filly; made all and
won easing up in handicap at Haydock in September; stays 9f; possibly needs a
sound surface and acts on firm going; suitable mount for an apprentice. *R.
Hollinshead.*

SHERIFF MUIR 3 b.c. Try My Best 130–First Round 97 (Primera 131) (1982   94
5f² 6f³ 7fg* 7g² 7f 1983 10d 7f 8fg*) quite attractive colt; excellent mover;
possibly not entirely reliable, but did nothing wrong when beating Tender
Sovereign by ¾ length in 21-runner £3,600 races at Ascot in July; sixth in
handicaps at Newmarket and Sandown earlier; stays 1m; acts on firm going; tends
to get a bit warm; blinkered last 2 outings; sent to race in USA. *M. Stoute.*

SHERNAZAR 2 b.c. Busted 134–Sharmeen (Val de Loir 133) (1983 7g²) May 1;   84 p
quite a well-made colt; fourth foal; half-brother to 2 winners, notably Shergar (by
Great Nephew); dam, granddaughter of French 1000 Guineas winner Ginetta,
won over 10.5f in France; second favourite but on backward side, beaten a length
by Test of Time in 7-runner minor event at Sandown in October; sure to improve
enough to win over longer distances. *M. Stoute.*

SHERPA BOY 2 br.c. Mansingh 120–Skerne Glory 58 (Pinza 137) (1983 6f 6f⁴   46
6f 5.1f 6g 7g) May 26; fair sort; half-brother to winning stayer Intake (by
Malicious) and a winner over hurdles; dam won 1¼m seller; poor plater; wears
blinkers. *C. Spares.*

SHERVANI (USA) 2 b.f. Prince Dantan–Gay West (Chateaugay) (1983 7fg 7fg³   79
8g² 8g² 8fg³) Mar 20; $8,000Y; well-grown, useful sort; half-sister to a minor
winner; dam won over 6f at 3 yrs; sire, son of Graustark, won 1¼m Santa Anita
Handicap; 1½ lengths second in maiden races won by Kuwait Palace and Marie
Cath at Edinburgh in the autumn; will stay 1¼m. *S. Norton.*

SHES ANDREW 2 gr.f. The Brianstan 128–Another Spring 66 (Town Crier 119)   50
(1983 5s³ 5d 5d 5f 6f³) Feb 5; 940F, 2,200Y; neat filly; second foal; dam won 1m
seller and also won over hurdles; disappointing plater; stays 6f; sent to Italy. *N.
Tinkler.*

SHE'S LOUISE 2 b.f. Bay Express 132–Micklemere 82 (Blakeney 126) (1983   40
5.1fg 5fg 5.1f⁴ 6f 6fg 8g) Apr 7; 500F, 800Y; bad plater; sold 350 gns Ascot
November Sales. *K. Ivory.*

SHEZAJEM 2 b.f. The Brianstan 128–Zip Flip (Bleep-Bleep 134) (1983 5f 5fg 6fg   –
5fg) Apr 24; sister to 2 winners, including fairly useful 5f performer Brianstan
Zipper; dam well beaten in 3 races; in rear in varied company, including claiming;
blinkered final outing; sold 340 gns Ascot December Sales. *A. Bailey.*

SHICKLAH (USA) 3 ch.f. The Minstrel 135–Logette 79 (Forli) (1982 5f* 5f*   –
5fg 6f 5fg² 6g* 6g) 1983 5f) short-coupled, attractive filly; good walker; won 3
races at 2 yrs, including a valuable one at Baden-Baden; had stiff task when in rear
in valuable handicap at Ascot in June, only outing of 1983; suited by 6f, and is bred

to stay further; has won on firm going but is possibly better with some give in the ground. *H. T. Jones.*

SHIELDAIG 2 b.g. Shirley Heights 130–Crofting 102 (Crepello 136) (1983 7f 8g 8d) Mar 1; well-made, attractive gelding; third foal; dam stayed 1¼m; no form, including in Warwick maiden; sold to P. Cundell 6,200 gns Ascot November Sales and subsequently gelded. *R. Hern.*   —

SHIHAB 2 b.c. Nonoalco 131–Electric Flash (Crepello 136) (1983 7g) May 9; 10,500F, 30,000Y; half-brother to 6 winners, including useful Welsh Flame (by Welsh Pageant) and useful 6f to 8.5f winner Sofala (by Home Guard); dam lightly-raced half-sister to Parthia; last of 15 in maiden race at Lingfield in October. *M. Blanshard.*   —

SHIKANUM 2 b.f. Kala Shikari 125–Olibanum 61 (Frankincense 120) (1983 5d 5s 5d 5v⁴ 5s 5fg⁴ 5f) Apr 29; bad plater; wears blinkers; sold 300 gns Doncaster August Sales. *W. Stubbs.*   **42**

SHINDELLA 2 b.f. Furry Glen 121–Antipol (Polyfoto 124) (1983 5s² 5v* 5f³ 6d 8g* 8f) tall, wiry filly; sister to Irish 1m and 9f winner Borraderra; dam never ran; a useful performer who won twice at Leopardstown, beating Mayoress 6 lengths in maiden race in May and then finding a remarkable turn of foot under strong driving to beat Rustic Lace a neck in Silken Glider Stakes in September; ran creditably in between, notably when 3½ lengths third to Defecting Dancer in 10-runner Windsor Castle Stakes at Royal Ascot; soon struggling when 6½ lengths sixth of 7 to Almeira in Prix Marcel Boussac at Longchamp in October; suited by 1m; acts on any going; often ridden by apprentice M. Lynch. *R. Cotter, Ireland.*   **104**

SHINE FORTH 5 ch.g. Shiny Tenth 120–Furley 91 (Decoy Boy 129) (1982 5fg 7fg 8.2s 9g 8s 8g 1983 8v) lengthy, plain gelding; plater; stays 7f; has worn blinkers; sold 4,200 gns Ascot 2nd June Sales. *J. Edmunds.*   —

SHINER'S PAL 2 gr.c. Radetzky 123–Guiletta 63 (Runnymede 123) (1983 6f 7fg) May 15; 2,000Y; fair sort; half-brother to 3-y-o 12.3f and 13.8f winner Fiorenzo (by Filiberto) and to 2-y-o winners here and in France; dam ran only 3 times; in rear in maiden races at Nottingham in July and Salisbury in September. *Mrs B. Waring.*   —

SHINING OUT (USA) 3 b.c. Full Out–All Agleam (Gleaming) (1982 6fg⁴ 6g² 1983 7d 6s* 6v* 7d³ 6fg² 6f) strong, well-made, attractive colt; successful in handicap at Windsor and minor event at Folkestone in May, only scrambling home when odds on in latter event; not seen out after July; seems to find 7f too far; probably acts on any going. *G. Harwood.*   **91**

SHINY BARN 2 ch.g. Streak 119–Just Janie 84 (John Splendid 116) (1983 5fg 5g 5fg 5d 6g) Mar 8; 480Y; second foal; dam sprinter; no sign of ability, including in sellers; lost rider when hampered first outing; blinkered final appearance; trained part of season by S. Harris; sold 320 gns Doncaster November Sales. *G. Blum.*   —

SHINY BRIEF 2 ch.c. Shiny Tenth 120–Piney Lake 54 (Sassafras 135) (1983 6g) fair sort; first foal; dam placed over 1m and 1¼m; backward, behind in 23-runner newcomers event at Goodwood in September. *D. Marks.*   —

SHINY COPPER 5 b.g. Shiny Tenth 120–Comprella 54 (Compensation 127) (1982 NR 1983 12v⁴ 14s² 17d 15.5v 22.2f) strong, lengthy gelding; has shown ability on flat but is much better known as a jumper (won Daily Express Triumph Hurdle in 1982); stays 1¾m; acts on any going; blinkered fourth start; probably needs a galloping track. *Mrs N. Smith.*   —

SHINY HOUR 4 ch.c. Shiny Tenth 120–Lizzylyn 84 (Tower Walk 130) (1982 5d 6f* 6fg 6f³ 7fg 5.8g 5.8f 6f 6fg 6d 6g* 1983 6s 6d⁴ 6f 6f 6f 6f 6fg 7fg) rangy, workmanlike colt; sprint handicapper; best at 6f; seems to act on any going; has won for an apprentice; blinkered sixth start; sold 1,950 gns Ascot December Sales. *M. McCormack.*   —

SHIPWRIGHT 2 br.c. Hotfoot 126–Ripeck 90 (Ribot 142) (1983 7fg²) Mar 1; big, well-made colt; half-brother to numerous winners, notably Oaks winner Bireme (by Grundy), very good middle-distance stayer Buoy (by Aureole), smart sprinter Fluke (by Grey Sovereign) and smart 7.3f and 1m winner Boathouse (by Habitat); dam stayed 1½m; 25/1, put up a splendid first effort in 21-runner maiden race at Newmarket in September, lengthening stride in fine style from halfway and finishing very strongly indeed to take second place, 1½ lengths behind Chelkov; should make a good middle-distance 3-y-o. *R. Hern.*   **86 P**

SHIRAN 2 br.c. Dawn Review 105–Shirini 74 (Tehran) (1983 7f 8d) Mar 22; half-brother to several winners, including useful French sprinter Fortinella (by   —

Fortino II); dam won over 1½m; in rear in the autumn in maiden race at Redcar and £3,500 event at York. *M. Lambert.*

SHIRLEY CREPELLA 3 ch.f. Duc D'Orleans 76–Strudel (Vimadee 120) (1982 NR 1983 8v) 290F, 420 2-y-o; third foal; dam won a selling hurdle; tailed-off last in maiden race at Warwick in April. *K. Bridgwater.* —

SHIRLSTAR INVESTOR 3 b.f. Some Hand 119–Opal Fancy 83 (Kibenka 119) (1982 NR 1983 6s 7s 6fg) smallish, sturdy filly; first foal; dam placed over 1m; little worthwhile form in maiden and minor events; missed break badly first outing and in circumstances wasn't entirely disgraced. *H. Collingridge.*

SHIRLSTAR MISS 3 b.f. Lepanto–Mahnaz (Deep Diver 134) (1982 NR 1983 13f 15.8g 14.7fg 15.5fg) lengthy, workmanlike filly; first foal; dam never ran; little worthwhile form, including in a seller. *H. Collingridge.* —

SHMAIN 4 ch.g. Sheshoon 132–Maiden d'Or 87 (Songedor 116) (1982 12f 16fg* 12g 16d³ 15.8f 19f² 16.5g* 16f⁴ 16g⁴ 1983 15.8d 15g³) deep-girthed, useful sort; suited by a thorough test of stamina; seems to act on any going; has run respectably for an amateur. *G. Richards.* —

SHOEBUTTON 4 ch.f. Habat 127–Forgotten Dreams 82 (Shoemaker 121) (1982 12.2g 10f 12.2f³ 12f 12g 11g 11fg 1983 9g² 8f³ 8.2f² 9f³ 7f 9fg 9g 8.2s) leggy filly; half-sister to Italian Derby winner My Top (by High Top); placed in handicaps and an apprentice race; stays 1½m; acts on firm going; sold 8,000 gns Doncaster November Sales. *Mrs G. Reveley.* 51

SHOEMENDER 6 ch.g. Busted 134–Grey Shoes 104 (Grey Sovereign 128§) (1982 NR 1983 16f⁴) ex-Irish gelding; lightly raced on flat nowadays; stays 1½m; has worn bandages. *F. Watson.* —

SHOOT CLEAR 2 b.f. Bay Express 132–Unsuspected 95 (Above Suspicion 127) (1983 5fg² 5fg* 6f* 7fg* 8fg³) 109

Shoot Clear was the impressive winner of three of her five races in 1983, three in succession in fact. Her run began in a Warwick maiden race in early July where she scored an easy length-and-a-half victory from Lonely Street, and continued in a highly competitive nursery, the Tolly Cobbold Trophy at Newmarket, in which ten of the eleven runners were previous winners. Shoot Clear started favourite and won the race in great style, having travelled like a winner throughout. She was tucked in behind the leaders until leading inside the two-furlong marker and then quickened clear to win by three lengths from Forzando with Fair Dominion a length and a half further away in third. The runner-up had won his two previous races and would win his next three, each time carrying top weight, while Fair Dominion was otherwise unbeaten, easily winning a valuable Kempton nursery on her only subsequent start. Shoot Clear had her next run in a much more important event, the Waterford Candelabra Stakes at Goodwood in August. This race, which was first run under Waterford Crystal's sponsorship in 1975, has become a prime target for the trainers of some of the better staying two-year-old fillies: previous winners include the One Thousand Guineas winner Fairy Footsteps, Cistus, winner of the Prix de l'Opera and Nassau Stakes, and another smart filly, Triple First. Shoot Clear met a number of highly promising opponents at Goodwood including Inspire and Satinette who had won maiden races at the main Goodwood meeting. Shoot Clear led the eight runners from the start, and though strongly pressed by Satinette about two furlongs out, she stayed on really well and was increasing her lead at the finish where she was a length up on Satinette. Despite meeting that filly on terms 7 lb worse in the May Hill Stakes at Doncaster Shoot Clear started favourite (as she did on all her starts). It was not to be her race, however: held up this time, she was driven up to challenge two furlongs out, soon found herself getting nowhere and faded into third of nine behind Satinette and Nepula, beaten a length and a half and the same. Although she ran well Shoot Clear gave the impression that the distance of a mile was stretching her stamina to the limit.

Shoot Clear (b.f. Feb. 9, 1981)	Bay Express (b 1971)	Polyfoto (br 1962)	Polic / Brabantia
		Pal Sinna (ch 1966)	Palestine / Sinna
	Unsuspected (b 1972)	Above Suspicion (b 1956)	Court Martial / Above Board
		Chevanstell (b 1964)	Le Levanstell / Chevarctic

Shoot Clear's sire Bay Express was a top-class horse over five furlongs; he has produced very few runners that have won over a mile—only five of his offspring

Waterford Candelabra Stakes, Goodwood—Shoot Clear stays on really well to hold off Satinette

have won over a mile or more in Britain and they are all moderate. His other pattern race winner, All Systems Go, proved best over seven furlongs, while his other winners include a number of moderate sprint handicap winners, Cree Bay and New Express among them. Shoot Clear, a small, strong filly who carries plenty of condition, is the second foal of Unsuspected, a fairly useful winner of eight races between a mile and a mile and three quarters; the first, Warm Wind (by Tumble Wind), won three times at up to a mile and a quarter. Unsuspected is a half-sister to three minor winners, while her dam, Chevanstell, won over six furlongs and was a half-sister to five winners most notably the 1971 Phoenix Stakes winner Celtic Twilight. Shoot Clear is an enthusiastic, consistent filly who seems certain to win more races. Though she may well win at a mile as a three-year-old it is possible that she will be more effective at seven furlongs. She has so far raced only on fast ground. *M. Stoute.*

SHOOTING BUTTS 5 b.g. Tycoon II–Charlies Double (Fighting Charlie 127) (1982 12g 16d* 16fg 16d 17.1s 18d 18s 1983 16s⁴ 17.1v 17d 18.8v) workmanlike gelding; suited by a test of stamina; acts well on soft going; blinkered final start; inconsistent; sold 2,000 gns Newmarket Autumn Sales. *B. McMahon.* —

SHOOTING HIGH 4 b.f. Busted 134–Regal Miss 90 (Sovereign Path 125) (1982 10fg 10f² 12.2g 10.1fg 1983 10.2g⁴ 7.6fg 10g 10f³ 10f² 12g 12.2d) well-made filly; in frame in varied company, including selling; stays 1¼m; acts on firm going; sold 5,000 gns Newmarket Autumn Sales. *W. Musson.* — 52

SHOOTING MATCH 5 gr.g. Home Guard 129–Bundling (Petingo 135) (1982 8s 8.2s 11fg 8fg⁴ 8g 8f 7g 8fg 6fg 1983 7fg 8.2d 8f) workmanlike gelding; plater; stays 1m; probably acts on any going, but seems best on a sound surface; often blinkered; has run creditably for a boy. *Mrs A. Bell.* —

SHOOT THE RAPIDS 3 b.g. Rapid River 127–Weirdi 76 (Yrrah Jr) (1982 8f 1983 15f 12.2f) well beaten in maiden and minor races; far from certain to stay long distances. *W. A. Stephenson.* —

SHORE LINE 3 b.f. High Line 125–Dark Finale (Javelot 124) (1982 6fg 6g² 1983 7s* 8g 12g⁴ 12f 14.6fg) rather sparely-made filly; good mover and walker; sister to several winners, notably Park Hill Stakes winner Quay Line; really took the eye and battled on well when beating Floating Petal by a head in 20-runner maiden event at Newmarket in April; had stiff tasks afterwards in 1000 Guineas on same course later in month (twelfth of 18 to Ma Biche after being outpaced throughout), Oaks at Epsom (stayed on really well to snatch fourth, 16 lengths behind runaway winner Sun Princess), Irish Guinness Oaks at the Curragh in July (about 10 lengths sixth to Give Thanks) and Park Hill Stakes at Doncaster (fifth of 7 to High Hawk); should stay beyond 1½m; sold to BBA 250,000 gns Newmarket December Sales. *H. Candy.* 107

SHORELLA 3 ch.f. Kashiwa 115–Dorella (Zank) (1982 NR 1983 7fg 7fg 10fg 10.2h 10.1fg 8f 10g⁴ 8d 10g²) IR 3,000F; short-legged, heavy-topped filly; first foal; dam unraced sister to dam of Don, American Prince and Sovereign Dona; plater; stays 1¼m; wears blinkers; sold to NBA 2,500 gns Newmarket Autumn Sales. *J. Benstead.* 55

SHORT FUSE 2 b.f. Whitstead 125–Bright Spark (White Fire III) (1983 6fg 8g 8d) May 22; sparely-made, close-coupled, plain filly; has a sharp action; sixth produce; half-sister to a winner in Norway; dam poor half-sister to smart animals Ovaltine and Guillotina; plating-class maiden; best race on second outing; will stay 1¼m; sold 1,000 gns Newmarket December Sales. *R. Boss.* 65

SHOUT 3 b.c. Balidar 133–Cedar Tree (Alcide 136) (1982 5s 1983 10.1f 10f 10d) — tall, close-coupled colt; showed promise as a 2-y-o but was lightly raced and disappointing in 1983; sold to CBA 3,900 gns Newmarket Autumn Sales. *G. Harwood.*

SHOW OF HANDS 7 b.g. Royal Prerogative 119–Lindylee 69 (Grey Sovereign 67 128§) (1982 7fg* 7g* 8f⁴ 8fg* 8f³ 7g 7g 7g 1983 7fg* 7fg 7d² 8fg 8f 8f⁴ 7fg² 8f 7f 8fg⁴) tall gelding; goes very well at Edinburgh and won there in April; stays 1m, but probably best at 7f; acts well on firm going; blinkered once; ridden by apprentice N. Connorton for last 6 wins; often makes the running; ideally suited by an easy, turning track. *J. W. Watts.*

SHOWTIME 2 b.f. Bay Express 132–Girls Division 93 (Hotfoot 126) (1983 5f 6fg 70 5g 5g 5g 5g* 5g) May 19; 900Y; leggy filly; first foal; dam won over 1m; won 14-runner seller (no bid) at Catterick in October; bred to stay 6f; apparently suited by some give in the ground. *R. Whitaker.*

SHUBETTE 5 b.g. On Your Mark 125–Melka (Relko 136) (1982 NR 1983 13v) — ex-Irish gelding; poor maiden on flat though has won a selling hurdle; has been tried in blinkers. *A. Pitt.*

SHUBUMI 2 ch.c. Touch Paper 113–Belle Josephine (Beau Sabreur 125) (1983 6v 90 6v 5d² 6f⁴ 7fg² 7f² 7g² 8s³) Mar 31; IR 25,000F, IR 34,000Y; brother to useful Irish 5f to 1m performer Light Here and to Irish middle-distance winner and successful hurdler Joann's First, and half-brother to several winners; dam won over 6f and 7f at 2 yrs in Ireland; second in a variety of races, notably going down by 1½ lengths to Executive Pride in Hennessy V.S.O.P. Stakes at Leopardstown in June on fifth start and by 5 lengths to Blaze of Tara in Bright Highway Stakes at Phoenix Park in September on seventh; stays 7f and will probably stay 1m (9 lengths third of 4 to Sadler's Wells in Panasonic Beresford Stakes at the Curragh when tried at trip); probably acts on any going; wears blinkers. *M. O'Toole, Ireland.*

SHUKRIAA 3 b.f. Busted 134–Diplomatie (Val de Loir 133) (1982 NR 1983 — 11.5fg 9fg) 3,200Y; sparely-made, leggy filly; fourth foal; half-sister to French 6.5f

Mr R. Barnett's "Shore Line"

winner Dear Prince (by Sun Prince); dam, winner twice at around 1m, is half-sister to very smart French filly Diffusion; in rear in maiden and minor events in summer. *R. Boss.*

SHUMARD 3 b.g. Sweet Revenge 129–Miss Etta (King's Troop 118) (1982 NR 1983 9v* 14d 12d) 6,000F, 3,600Y; good-bodied, workmanlike gelding; half-brother to several winners, including useful sprinter Maccaboy (by Will Somers); dam unraced half-sister to some very useful animals; 5-length winner of maiden race at Mallow in May when trained by L. Browne; had stiff task and had been off course 4 months on only outing for present connections; stays 9f (far from certain to get 1¾m). *R. Fisher.*   ?

SHUTEYE 2 b.f. Shirley Heights 130–Sweet Hour 91 (Primera 131) (1983 6f 8d* 7g) May 15; slightly hollow-backed, good-topped filly; half-sister to 3 winners, including smart 3-y-o 1¼m winner Bedtime (by Bustino) and useful middle-distance performer Lake Naivasha (by Blakeney); dam 2-y-o 5f and 6f winner; won 15-runner maiden race at Beverley in September; will be suited by 1¼m. *R. Hern.*   84

SHUTLAR'S FLING (USA) 3 ch.c. Northern Fling–Nora Harvey (Le Fabuleux 133) (1982 7g 7.6v 1983 11g 16f³ 14f 15.5f 15.8g² 15.8g) leggy, sparely-made colt; staying maiden; acts on firm going. *I. Walker.*   73

SHUTTLE CRAFT 6 b.m. Sole Mio–Cindy O'Dea (Cintrist 110) (1982 8f 8d 6g 7f 1983 8d) strong non-thoroughbred mare; little worthwhile form. *R. Woodhouse.*   –

SHUTTLE D'OR 5 ch.g. Goldhill 125–Northern Flight (Borealis) (1982 10d 1983 8.2v 10d 10fg 10f) poor plater; has been bandaged. *M. Chapman.*   –

SHY DIANA (USA) 3 br.f. Vaguely Noble 140–Sporting Lass (Coursing) (1982 NR 1983 10fg 10fg 8g 8g 12g) small, lengthy filly; half-sister to several winners in USA, including stakes winner High Pheasant (by Ack Ack), successful at up to 9f; dam ran only at 2 yrs, when stakes winner over 8.5f; showed signs of a little ability third and fourth starts; should be suited by middle distances. *B. Hobbs.*   –

SHY MASTER 4 br.g. Saritamer 130–Harriny 94 (Floribunda 136) (1982 8d 5g 5fg² 5d 6s 1983 5v⁴ 5v 5.1g 7g 5f 5s 5g² 5d) smallish, fair sort; plater; best at 5f. *I. Walker.*   41

SHY RAMBLER (USA) 3 b.c. Blushing Groom 131–Roseliere 127 (Misti IV 132) (1982 NR 1983 8d² 10g) rather small, lightly-made colt; half-brother to 4 winners, including top-class 7f to 1¼m filly Rose Bowl (by Habitat), top-class middle-distance colt Ile de Bourbon (by Nijinsky) and 11f stakes winner Rose Crescent (also by Nijinsky); dam won French Oaks and Prix Vermeille; fractured his off-hind cannon bone in spring, 1982; second favourite and very fit, ran a good first race when ½-length second of 17 to Majestic Endeavour (pair clear) in Wood Ditton Stakes at Newmarket in April, looking an assured winner until run out of it in last 200 yards; split a pastern when only eleventh of 12 behind Shearwalk in Heathorn Stakes on same course later in month; stud in New Zealand. *I. Balding.*   88

SIBERIAN EXPRESS (USA) 2 gr.c. Caro 133–Indian Call (Warfare) (1983 6fg* 6g* 7s² 7fg³)   **122**

Few two-year-olds impressed us more in 1983 than did Siberian Express when he won the Prix Morny at Deauville in August. He had already stamped himself a very promising colt in a newcomers event earlier at the Deauville meeting on his only previous appearance, winning by six lengths after never being headed, but even so he looked to have it all to do in the Morny against three other unbeaten animals—the Prix Robert Papin winner Masarika, the Windsor Castle Stakes winner Defecting Dancer and the Prix des Yearlings winner Ti King—plus Sicyos, a winning son of the very speedy Sigy. Siberian Express led from start to finish after an extremely fast break. He needed only a couple of cracks in the last furlong to beat off the challenges of the favourites Masarika and Defecting Dancer and then held the fast-finishing Ti King by two lengths. The French Press was as impressed as we were, and compared Siberian Express to France's high-speed train, the TGV. What a horse he would be if he could go even a quarter as fast: neither Indigenous nor Raffingora managed to exceed an average speed of 42 mph when recording their memorable Epsom sprint victories.

Rather surprisingly Siberian Express was 'derailed' in his subsequent races, firstly at 5/2 on in the Prix de la Salamandre at Longchamp in September. Some observers had feared that Longchamp's bends and undulations would be against a powerful, raking stride such as his, but all seemed to be going smoothly as he came to the last two furlongs with the race apparently well sewn up. Siberian Express still looked to have matters under control a furlong later, although Seattle Song,

Prix Morny, Deauville—Siberian Express gains a very impressive success, unchallenged from Ti King (blinkers), Masarika (far side), Defecting Dancer and Sicyos

already under the whip, was beginning to emerge as a possible source of danger. However, the picture changed completely as Siberian Express began to find the combination of soft ground and seven furlongs too much for him. He virtually stopped to a walk in the closing stages, despite his rider's frantic efforts, and he failed by half a length to hold the determined Seattle Song. This display effectively ruled out the Grand Criterium as his next target, and the William Hill Middle Park struck us as an ideal alternative. Unfortunately Siberian Express hadn't been entered and instead he came to Newmarket in an attempt to become the first French-trained winner of the Dewhurst since Torbella III in 1957. The return to a straight course and fast ground made little difference to Siberian Express' performance and he fared no better against the best of his opponents than the last French challenger for the Dewhurst, the 1980 Prix de la Salamandre winner Miswaki, had done against Storm Bird and To-Agori-Mou. El Gran Senor easily took Siberian Express' measure after he'd led for five furlongs, and so did Rainbow Quest soon afterwards; Siberian Express was left six lengths behind as the leaders fought it out up the final hill. Incidentally he wore a piece of equipment here similar to a tongue strap.

Siberian Express (USA) (gr.c. Jan 25, 1981)	Caro (gr 1967)	Fortino II (gr 1959)	Grey Sovereign
			Ranavalo
		Chambord (ch 1955)	Chamossaire
			Life Hill
	Indian Call (b or br 1966)	Warfare (gr 1957)	Determine
			War Whisk
		La Morlaye (b 1958)	Hafiz II
			Manzana

Siberian Express' record suggests strongly he'll prove best at sprint distances although he has the looks—he's a fine, lengthy, attractive colt—and the pedigree of a horse who should stay quite well. His sire Caro stayed well enough to win the Prix Ganay over ten and a half furlongs and the average winning distance of Caro's stock in Britain, Ireland and France is around a mile and a quarter. Also Siberian Express is a half-brother to a very good American middle-distance performer Erwin Boy, a gelding by Exclusive Native who won three good stakes races on grass in 1976. After a limited racecourse career which saw her earn only a hundred dollars, his dam Indian Call has made ample amends as a broodmare, producing two other

Mr M. Fustok's "Siberian Express"

winners, including the minor six-furlong stakes winner Dancing Partner (also by Exclusive Native). Her yearling colt by Caro fetched exactly the same price as Siberian Express, 230,000 dollars. Indian Call's dam La Morlaye, another lightly-raced maiden who did much better at stud, produced the smart 1967 two-year-old filly Lady Tramp and another stakes winner. One of La Morlaye's half-sisters, the very useful two-year-old Journalette, did even better, producing the champion handicap mare Typecast. Siberian Express' paternal grandsire is the excellent French sprinter Fortino II. If Siberian Express does as well as Fortino as a three-year-old, when he'll be trained by A. Fabre, his connections will have no cause for complaint—Fortino won the Prix de Saint-Georges, the Prix de Meautry and the Prix de l'Abbaye de Longchamp. *M. Saliba, France.*

Prix d'Arenberg, Longchamp—Sicyos draws clear of Reine Caroline

SIBLEY 3 ch.f. Northfields–Suni 114 (Crepello 136) (1982 NR 1983 8g 10g² 10fg 12fg) quite an attractive, lightly-built filly; first foal; dam third in Oaks; ran easily best races in minor events at Sandown and Newbury (½-length second to Beach Light) in first part of season; suited by 1¼m and should stay further. *P. Walwyn.*   **84**

SICAMBRE PRINCESS 2 ch.f. Vitiges 132–Maroukh (Kashmir II 125) (1983 5s 6f 6f 7.6d) Mar 29; 2,100Y (privately); fourth foal; half-sister to 1¼m and 2m winner Moon Mariner (by Julio Mariner) and a winner in Barbados; dam ran only twice; no worthwhile form; trained by A. Jarvis first 3 outings; sold NBA 1,500 gns Newmarket Autumn Sales. *P. Mitchell.*   **–**

SICONDA 4 ch.f. Record Token 128–Quickmatch 89 (Match III 135) (1982 8d 8.2d 10f 11fg 9g 10fg 8fg 7g⁴ 8fg⁴ 6f 9fg* 8.2s⁴ 8d⁴ 1983 8fg 8f³ 8fg 9fg* 8fg 12d 8fg² 10fg 8d) small filly; plater; won apprentice event at Wolverhampton in August (bought in 900 gns); stays 9f; seems to act on any going; suitable mount for an apprentice; changed hands 980 gns Doncaster January Sales. *R. Hollinshead.*   **48**

SICYOS (USA) 2 ch.c. Lyphard 132–Sigy 132 (Habitat 134) (1983 5.5f* 5fg² 6fg² 6g 5fg* 5f³)   **126**
    Sicyos started a short-priced favourite to win the Prix d'Arenberg at Longchamp in September and complete a family double: the stable's Sigy, Sicyos' dam, won the race in 1978 at Chantilly. Of the eight other runners only the unbeaten Reine Caroline, winner of the Prix de la Vallee d'Auge at Deauville the previous month, was seriously backed to beat him. Quickly into his stride Sicyos tracked the leaders for three furlongs, burst clear below the distance and coasted home four lengths clear of Reine Caroline, the same winning distance, incidentally, as Sigy's. Asked about the comparative merits of Sicyos and Sigy their trainer said: 'He is as fast as she was,' boldly adding that she could not envisage his defeat in the Prix de l'Abbaye de Longchamp in October. Sicyos, who looked to be going in his coat afterhand, made a valiant attempt to emulate Sigy's win in the Abbaye five years earlier, but we can't help thinking he would have been better employed in the William Hill Middle Park Stakes. He kept on terms with the leader for three furlongs before finding Habibti and Soba too strong; nevertheless he was far from disgraced in finishing four lengths third to Habibti, and only three lengths behind Soba. Sicyos had begun his career with an easy victory in a newcomers race at Chantilly in June. He performed with credit in his other races though he didn't reach his peak until the autumn: he ran Masarika to three lengths in the Prix du Bois at Longchamp in June and finished a head second to Greinton, after meeting trouble, in the six-furlong Prix de Cabourg at Deauville in August. He faded in the final furlong when under three lengths fifth to Siberian Express in the Prix Morny on the latter track later in the month, encouraging his return to five furlongs, no doubt.

Sicyos (USA) (ch.c. Feb 28, 1981)	Lyphard (b 1969)	Northern Dancer (b 1961)	Nearctic
			Natalma
		Goofed (ch 1960)	Court Martial
			Barra II
	Sigy (b 1976)	Habitat (b 1966)	Sir Gaylord
			Little Hut
		Satu (b 1965)	Primera
			Creation

    Sicyos, a 210,000-guinea yearling, is Sigy's first foal. He very much resembles her in appearance—a typical sprinter, strong, muscular, good-bodied—and he has also inherited her speed. Sigy showed form only at five furlongs and was better at two years than three, though at the latter age she won the Prix du Gros-Chene; her sister Sonoma was also very speedy, the winner of the Gros-Chene and third in the William Hill July Cup. Sicyos' pedigree isn't entirely that of a sprinter, since Lyphard is his sire and his grandam is Satu, a smart middle-distance filly, winner of the Prix Fille de l'Air. Nevertheless it's a safe bet that Sicyos won't stay beyond six furlongs and a fair one that he'll be best at five. Providing he trains on he will take a lot of beating in the top French sprints. *Mme C. Head, France.*

SIDAB 3 b.g. Lochnager 132–Ritruda 95 (Roi Dagobert 128) (1982 5fg 6fg³ 5f* 6f 5fg* 5g* 5g³ 5g 5s² 1983 6d 6d 6d⁴ 6f 6fg 8f 7f³ 8s) strong, sturdy gelding; moderate walker and mover; often had stiffish tasks, but finished respectable third in handicap at Redcar in August; stays 7f; acts on any going. *W. Musson.*   **85**

SID'S MOB 3 b.g. Mummy's Pet 125–Native Nymph 97 (Indigenous 121) (1982 5f³ 5fg⁴ 5g³ 6g 6fg 5g* 1983 8.2v 5g 5g 5g⁴ 5f) leggy gelding; plater; evidently best at 5f; has run creditably in blinkers. *J. Berry.*   **–**

SIEBOLDII 3 b.c. Raga Navarro 119–Vale of Peace (Wolver Hollow 126) (1982 – NR 1983 6s 7s 7d 6fg 6f) IR 750Y; tall, rather leggy, angular colt; poor walker; second foal; dam never ran; in mid-division in maiden races on second and third outings, best efforts. *R. Armstrong.*

SI GABY (FR) 2 b.f. Sea Break 129–Gabrielle (Blockhaus) (1983 7fg 8d) May – 30; fair sort; first foal; dam unraced sister to good French miler Agy; backward, last in maiden races at Chester in July and Beverley in September. *S. Norton.*

SIGNALMAN 2 b.g. Stanford 121§–Battling Bessie (Typhoon 125) (1983 5v **74** 5.8s* 5fg) May 10; 13,500F; big, strong gelding; half-brother to several winners, including 1m and 1¼m winner Rangefinder (by On Your Mark) and French miler Miss Bessie (by Pitskelly); dam, half-sister to Roman Warrior, placed over 6f at 2 yrs in Ireland; had his opponents well strung out when winning 8-runner maiden race at Bath in May; well-backed favourite, disappointing fifth of 6 in minor event at Sandown the following month; gelded subsequently; suited by 6f; acts on soft going. *H. Candy.*

SIGN-OF-LIFE 2 br.f. Wolverlife 115–Gay Signal (Lord Gayle 124) (1983 5s² **103** 5s² 6g* 6f 6f⁴ 6.3g⁴ 7d² 7d⁴) Apr 30; leggy, rather narrow filly; third foal; half-sister to 2m winner Captain Oates (by Oats); dam won over 1m in Ireland; excelled herself when 33/1 for BBA (Ireland) Goffs National Stakes at the Curragh in September, making running at a good pace and keeping on so well she went down by only ¾ length to odds-on El Gran Senor; had previously won a maiden race at Phoenix Park in June by 6 lengths and run creditably in between in Tyros Stakes and P. J. Prendergast Railway Stakes, both at the Curragh, in latter finishing 5 lengths fourth of 9 to El Gran Senor on sixth outing; moved down to fourth place by stewards after finishing length second of 9 to Western Symphony in Larkspur Stakes at Leopardstown in October (hampered third-placed horse); clearly well suited by 7f, and will stay 1m. *M. Cunningham, Ireland.*

SIGNORINA ODONE 2 b.f. Vitiges 132–Duchy 99 (Rheingold 137) (1983 8d⁴ **80** 7fg*) Jan 23; second foal; dam placed over 1m and 1¼m from 3 starts in Ireland; won 17-runner maiden race at Beverley in September by a head from Rummann; will stay 1¼m. *C. Gray.*

SIKORSKY (USA) 3 b.c. Honest Pleasure–Regal Exception 126 (Ribot 142) **92** (1982 8g 1983 11v⁴ 10v 10.1fg 11.7fg² 12d* 10fg³ 11d² 12fg* 12fg³) strong, good-topped, quite attractive colt; poor walker; won maiden race at Lingfield in September and handicap at Newmarket in October, latter by 1½ lengths from Jackdaw after being held up; in frame most other starts and finished creditable third of 25 behind Asir (despite wandering a bit under pressure) in William Hill November Handicap at Doncaster on last day of season; suited by 1½m; yet to race on really firm going, but acts on any other. *J. Sutcliffe.*

SILCA STAR KEY (USA) 5 b.g. Majestic Prince–Who's to Know (Fleet – Nasrullah) (1982 8g 8d 7f⁴ 10g 8.5f 8fg 8f 8g 1983 9v 6g 7g) strong, well-made, attractive gelding; fair handicapper at his best but has deteriorated; stays 9f; seems to act on any going; sometimes bandaged; has raced with tongue tied down; blinkered once in 1982. *L. Lightbrown.*

SILENT DANCER 2 ch.f. Quiet Fling 124–Balgreggan (Hallez 131) (1983 8g **69** p 8g⁴) Feb 25; tall, workmanlike filly; third foal; sister to 3-y-o 1½m winner Madam Flutterbye and half-sister to useful 5f performer Street Market (by Porto Bello); dam twice-raced half-sister to smart stayer Golden Love; strong-finishing 8 lengths fourth of 10 to Gambler's Cup in minor event at Bath in October; will be suited by 1¼m+. *N. Vigors.*

SILENT POOL 3 b.f. Relkino 131–Idle Waters 116 (Mill Reef 141) (1982 7.6v 7d⁴ – 8s³ 1983 11.7s 12v 10fg 13fg) small, strong, lengthy, attractive filly; well beaten in 1983; looks slow. *F. J. Houghton.*

SILENT SUN 2 b.f. Blakeney 126–Crowdie 98 (Crepello 136) (1983 6f 8g³) Apr **79** p 7; tall, lengthy filly; closely related to 7f and 1½m winner Cordon (by Morston); dam 2-y-o 6f winner; 5/1, didn't find her stride until closing stages when 4 lengths third of 8 to Girl Friday in £3,400 event at Goodwood in September; will be well suited by 1¼m+; sure to improve. *R. Hern.*

SILENT TEARS 6 br.m. Weepers Boy 124–Skilla (Mexico III) (1982 5f 5fg 5f – 5fg 5fg 6g 5fg³ 5fg 5fg 7.6d 8fg 1983 5v 5s 9s 12v 5d 8s 5g 5f 5fg) small, strong mare; poor handicapper; stays 6f; acts on a firm and a soft surface; sometimes blinkered; has raced with tongue tied down. *M. James.*

SILK SARI (USA) 3 b.f. Raja Baba–Wisp O'Will (New Policy) (1982 5g 5fg 5f* – 6f³ 6fg² 6fg* 6g* 7.2f⁴ 7fg* 1983 7.3s 7fg 8fg⁴ 8fg) neat, strong filly; developed into a useful filly in 1982; lightly raced and disappointing in 1983; stays 7f; acts on firm going. *G. Harwood.*

SILK SASH (USA) 3 b. or br.c. Honest Pleasure–Silk Slipper 116 (Prince Tenderfoot 126) (1982 6.5g² 6fg⁴ 7.5g 1983 8g 8.2s³ 8f* 8f³) quite a well-made, attractive ex-French colt; first foal; dam smart winner at up to 1m in France; in frame twice as a 2-y-o when trained by J. Cunnington, jnr; showed quite a good turn of foot when beating Northern Script 2 lengths in minor event at Salisbury in June; creditable third at Haydock earlier and at Salisbury in August; gives impression he'll stay 1¼m; acts on any going, but is clearly very much at home on firm; sold 15,000 gns Newmarket September Sales. *R. Hern.*   **87**

SILLAGER 3 gr.g. Lochnager 132–Silly Sue 55 (Great Nephew 126) (1982 5g 6fg 5f⁴ 5d* 1983 7v 6v² 6s* 6f 8f 5fg 5d⁴) big, strong gelding; good walker; made all in handicap at Haydock in May; stays 6f; best form with some give in the ground; exported to Malaysia. *M. W. Easterby.*   **85**

SILLEY'S KNIGHT 7 b.g. Derring-Do 131–Silley's Maid 100 (Continuation 120) (1982 7g 7d 7.6g 7f³ 10f⁴ 8fg⁴ 8fg* 9f² 8g 8fg* 8fg 8g⁴ 8d⁴ 7d 8.2s 1983 8d 7fg³ 8v 8d 8f 8f 8f 10f³ 8fg* 11f³ 8g 10f 10f 8d³ 8fg 8.2s 8.2fg) strong, good-bodied, attractive gelding; poor mover nowadays; fair handicapper on his day; won at Pontefract in August; stays 11f; acts on any going; effective with or without blinkers; inconsistent. *D. Chapman.*   **71**

SILLY ABDULL 7 ch.g. St Alphage 119–Hirsova (Gulf Pearl 117) (1982 NR 1983 12.2g 8g 9g 8fg) poor performer nowadays; has been beaten in a seller; stays 1m; best served by firm ground; sometimes blinkered and has worn bandages; inconsistent; sold 500 gns Ascot October Sales. *F. Watson.*   **–**

SILLY BOY 3 ch.g. Decoy Boy 129–Scilly Isles 54 (Silly Season 127) (1982 6d 7f 8f⁴ 1983 8v* 8g 8v* 9s⁴ 7g³ 8f³ 9d) strong gelding; much improved in spring and won maiden race at Ayr (by 7 lengths) and handicap at Doncaster; off course nearly 4 months before final start; stays 1m well; acts on any going, but revels in the mud. *N. Bycroft.*   **83**

SILVERDIP (USA) 3 br.f. The Minstrel 135–Royal Dilemma (Buckpasser) (1982 7f 1983 7s* 8d 7d 8s 7fg* 7f² 7f* 6fg²)   **125**

There are few enough seven-furlong pattern races open to older horses in the second half of the season, and it was extremely unfortunate for Silverdip that injury robbed her of the chance of running in two of the most prestigious ones. She had to be retired after suffering a displacement of a hip caused by a muscular contraction while out cantering on the Berkshire Downs just before the Bisquit Cognac Challenge Stakes at Newmarket in October. She'd have had a good opportunity there of avenging her narrow defeat by Salieri in the previous month's Diadem Stakes, and in Salieri's absence she'd have had an even better chance of taking the Prix de la Foret at Longchamp later in October. Luckily Silverdip has been saved for the paddocks, but it is a great shame in view of the emphasis placed on winning pattern races by many breeders and buyers that she retires with the dubious distinction of being the best filly not to win one in 1983. She was a high-class filly, make no mistake, superior to all but a handful of her contemporaries and probably as much as two stone in front of some foreign pattern race winners.

Silverdip's second to Salieri in the Diadem over Ascot's stiff six furlongs on her final appearance was the closest she came to winning a pattern race. Waited with as usual, as Soba attempted to make all, Silverdip was produced with her challenge on the stand side approaching the last furlong by Eddery, who rode her particularly well; put under strong pressure she stayed on very gamely indeed, gradually wore down Soba and beat her by a length but, although making ground with every stride, couldn't quite peg back Salieri and went down by a head. She'd run the race of her life but for all that gave the impression that the distance was a little on the sharp side.

All Silverdip's previous races were at longer distances and each of her three wins was over seven furlongs. She'd made a successful reappearance in the mud in the Salisbury One Thousand Guineas Trial in April (only a listed race nowadays despite the continuing Group 3 status of the colts' equivalent) but after the Princess Elizabeth Stakes was washed out she wasn't seen again in England until the July meeting at Newmarket. In the meantime she had three races in France and put up a good effort there when sixth of ten behind L'Attrayante in the Poule d'Essai des Pouliches at Longchamp, fading out of contention only in the last furlong and being beaten little more than four lengths; she had such a poor run on her second outing in France in the Prix du Palais Royal that she was turned out again only three days later in the Prix de Sandringham, to no avail. Silverdip's chosen engagement

Mr George Strawbridge's "Silverdip"

the July meeting was the Montrose Handicap and by winning decisively under 9-7 she put up one of the season's outstanding performances in handicap company. With a strong pace to suit her and the firm ground proving no inconvenience Silverdip was produced with a smooth run on the outside to win decisively by a length and a half, despite drifting quite badly to the left once in front. At the weights she worked out 30 lb or more superior to the next three fillies home—Golden Rhyme, Krakow and Sweet Emma. The muddling pace was no use to her in the Oak Tree Stakes at Goodwood later in the month where Silverdip pulled hard early on and was beaten a length by Fenny Rough, but in the Strensall Stakes at York on her only other outing she turned the tables. She beat Fenny Rough by half a length, a margin that gives no true reflection of her superiority, for she was always going easily and made her challenge on the rails travelling so strongly that for a moment or two it looked as if she'd win by a wide margin. Once in front she tended to idle, rather as she had at Newmarket, and in the end she needed to be driven out to hold on. In all probability she'd have looked more impressive held up for a little longer.

	The Minstrel (ch 1974)	Northern Dancer (b 1961)	Nearctic
			Natalma
		Fleur (b 1964)	Victoria Park
Silverdip (USA) (br.f. 1980)			Flaming Page
	Royal Dilemma (br 1971)	Buckpasser (b 1963)	Tom Fool
			Busanda
		Queen Empress (b 1962)	Bold Ruler
			Irish Jay

Silverdip is quite an attractive filly, despite her tendency to sweat up at the races. We've had something to say before about the wide range of distances over which her sire The Minstrel's progeny are effective and in Balding's stable alone there were two quite different types from Silverdip—the useful middle-distance

762

filly Fields of Spring, winner of the Warwick Oaks and a Group 3 race in Germany, and the smart stayer Crusader Castle, successful in the 1982 Italian St Leger and in the Lonsdale Stakes at York. The dam Royal Dilemma is from another good American family. She's a daughter of Queen Empress, the champion 1964 American two-year-old filly and a sister to King Emperor. Queen Empress had fourteen races as a two-year-old (in marked contrast to Silverdip who was jarred up and put by after only one) and she was first past the post nine times, once being disqualified; she gained another seven wins over the next two seasons and retired with earnings of well over 400,000 dollars. Royal Dilemma wasn't in that class but she won twice over sprint distances and was stakes placed. All three of her previous foals are winners and two of them raced in Europe for trainer Thomson Jones. Her first foal, Imperial Fling, by The Minstrel's sire Northern Dancer, was a smart performer who won a Group 3 mile-and-a-half race in Germany and was sixth in the 1979 St Leger; he's now at stud. Her second, Imperial Dilemma (by Damascus), won over seven furlongs at Redcar as a two-year-old and has since done well in the States, where he is a minor stakes winner. Royal Dilemma has since had another filly, Nijinsky, by named Cor Anglais, a stable-companion of Silverdip's, who showed she's probably capable of winning when in the frame at Sandown and Brighton as a two-year-old. We shall be looking forward to seeing some of Silverdip's own offspring in a few years time and if they take after her they'll be worth waiting for. She is to be mated with Mill Reef. *I. Balding.*

SILVER EMPRESS 2 gr. or ro.f. Octavo 115–Quenelle 82 (Roan Rocket 128)   **63**
(1983 5f 6fg 7g 6g 7d) Apr 25; IR 15,000Y; lengthy, good-bodied filly; third foal; half-sister to a prolific winner in Italy by Amber Rama; dam, placed from 6f to 9f, is sister to smart Catherine Wheel; little worthwhile form; blinkered final start. *D. Elsworth.*

SILVER IKON 2 b.f. Godswalk 130–Mariinsky 69 (Nijinsky 138) (1983 7f⁴ 7h*   **90**
8d²) May 1; second foal; dam won over 1¾m; won 8-runner maiden race at Chepstow in August; excellent second, 1½ lengths behind Spitalfields, in 24-runner nursery at Warwick the following month; better suited by 1m than by 7f; probably acts on any going; sold German International Bloodstock 6,200 gns Newmarket Autumn Sales. *M. Stoute.*

SILVER KNIGHT 3 gr.c. Ardoon 124–Abanilla 115 (Abernant 142) (1982 5g 6f   **54**
5f 5f 1983 7f² 7f) rather leggy colt; second in seller at Beverley in July, only form; suited by 7f; blinkered once at 2 yrs; sold 900 gns Doncaster August Sales. *J. W. Watts.*

SILVER PROSPECT 2 ch.g. Roman Warrior 132–Red Form (Reform 132)   **–**
(1983 5s 5v) May 8; lengthy gelding; good walker; sixth living foal; dam of no account; soundly beaten in May maiden races at York and Newcastle; subsequently gelded. *K. Stone.*

SILVER RIBBON 3 gr.f. Legal Eagle 126–Gold Ribbon 106 (Blast 125) (1982   **–**
5s³ 5d⁴ 5fg² 5f* 5f* 5f 5fg 6d 1983 6d 6v 5fg 6f 5f) leggy filly; plater; best form at 5f on firm ground; often blinkered; sold 600 gns Ascot September Sales. *J. Berry.*

SILVER SEASON 5 b.h. Martinmas 128–Silver Ray 70 (Skymaster 126) (1982   **100**
8g² 8d 8g⁴ 8f³ 10f² 10fg⁴ 10g 8fg² 8f 8g³ 8d² 10g 8s 1983 8s 10s 8.5s⁴ 9fg 8f 8f 8f² 8g 8f³ 8fg 8fg 9fg) lengthy horse; has a round action; very useful performer; put up best efforts when battling on resolutely to be length second to Prego in Esal Credit Handicap at Newbury in August and when 1¼ lengths third to Steeple Bell in Ripon Rowels Handicap later in month; races mainly at up to 1¼m, but has run creditably over 1½m; acts on firm going but is ideally suited by some give in the ground; usually makes running; game and genuine; has run well with his tongue tied down; trained by C. Brittain first 5 starts; sold to C. Bell 12,500 gns Newmarket Autumn Sales. *M. McCormack.*

SILVER SNOW 5 gr.m. Abwah 118–Silver Yarn (Peter's Yarn 106) (1982 9fg*   **56**
9fg³ 9f³ 8.2g 8fg⁴ 10f 8fg* 8s* 8.2s 1983 8d 8fg³ 8f 8f 8s 7g 12.2d 8g) long-backed mare; stays 9f; acts on any going; has run respectably in blinkers and for an apprentice; successful 3 times at Hamilton; trained until after fourth outing by N. Tinkler. *J. Harris.*

SILVER STAND 2 ch.c. Stanford 121§–Silver Bullion (Silver Shark 129) (1983   **73**
5fg 6g 5fg² 5f²) Mar 23; IR 34,000Y; lengthy, good-quartered colt; good walker; half-brother to 2 winners, including useful 1981 Irish 2-y-o sprinter The Primate (by Godswalk); dam unraced half-sister to very useful sprinter Smooth; 4 lengths second of 14 to Pichincha in maiden event at Windsor in August; should stay 6f (stirrup leather broke when tried at trip); winner over 5f in Italy in the autumn. *L. Cumani.*

SILVER STONE 3 b.f. Derrylin 115–Chequered Flag 70 (King's Troop 118) (1982 —
6f 6fg⁴ 1983 8f 8f) lengthy, good-bodied filly; lightly raced and little worthwhile
form; blinkered final start. *B. Hobbs.*

SILVER STRINGS 3 b.g. Blakeney 126–Melody Hour 105 (Sing Sing 134) (1982 —
6f⁴ 1983 8v) rangy, attractive gelding; little worthwhile form; bandaged only start
in 1983. *B. Palling.*

SILVER TOKEN 2 b.c. Record Token 128–Moon Lover (Forlorn River 124)   83
(1983 5s 5s³ 6f 6g³ 6f³(dis) 7f* 6s⁴ 7fg² 7fg³) Apr 15; 6,000F, 7,200Y; lengthy,
full-quartered colt; second foal; half-brother to 3-y-o Lunar Harvest (by
Whitstead); dam well beaten both starts; did well physically through the season,
and improved accordingly; won nursery at Newcastle in August, and ran well on
last 2 appearances to be placed in similar events at Redcar and Doncaster; better
at 7f than shorter distances; acts on any going; wears blinkers. *T. Fairhurst.*

SILVER VENTURE 3 gr.g. Town Crier 119–Grecian Bridge 90 (Acropolis 132) —
(1982 7d 1983 7d 8v) little worthwhile form; dead. *H. Candy.*

SIMARA 3 b.f. Owen Anthony 102–Vulwell (Harwell) (1982 NR 1983 9f 10d 12f —
12fg) sturdy filly; second foal; dam selling hurdler; poor form in sellers and a
maiden race. *R. Whitaker.*

SIMBEAU 6 b.g. Simbir 130–Serendip (Sing Sing 134) (1982 NR 1983 8.3fg) —
winning hurdler; well beaten on flat, including in a seller. *H. O'Neill.*

SIMCOE STAR 2 b.g. Cawston's Clown 113–Miss Inglewood 61 (Dike) (1983 6fg   67
7g 8.2fg 8fg 10d* 10.2fg) May 15; rather plain gelding; first foal; dam second over
5f and 1m; plater; won 12-runner event at Leicester (bought in 1,700 gns) in
October easing up by 4 lengths; suited by 1¼m; blinkered last 3 starts. *W.
Wharton.*

SIMETTE 6 ch.g. Simbir 130–Machete (Macherio) (1982 14f 14fg² 13.3f⁴ 1983 —
12v 15g 10.6g) quite well-made gelding; staying handicapper; appears to act on any
going; used to wear blinkers; sold 520 gns Ascot November Sales. *C. James.*

SIMMIES LOVE 4 ch.f. Record Token 128–Love Is Blind 90 (Hasty Road) (1982 —
12.2g 8f 7f² 7g³ 8.2g⁴ 8g 8f* 7fg 8fg³ 9g 9g 8.2g 10f⁴ 8.2s 1983 8fg 10s⁴ 14.6f)
quite a well-made filly; bad mover; plater; stays 1¼m; acts on any going; suitable
mount for an apprentice. *W. Barrett.*

SIMON BOLIVAR 4 b.g. Grey Mirage 128–Penview 73 (Pendragon) (1982 NR —
1983 10s) 5,000 3-y-o; brother to a fairly useful hurdler; dam stayed well; behind
in apprentice event at Brighton in May, first outing on flat. *E. Wilts.*

SIMON (USA) 2 ch.c. Noholme II–So Vain (Drone) (1983 6d 5f⁴ 6g 7fg² 7fg²   87
7fg³ 6fg³ 6fg³ 6g² 7fg 7fg*) Apr 3; smallish colt; fifth foal; half-brother to a winner
in USA; dam unraced half-sister to stakes winner Dr Knighton; won maiden event
at Milan in November; form bit mixed previously, although placed many times;
better at 7f than shorter distances (beaten favourite last 3 outings over 6f); acts
well on a firm surface; disappointed when apprentice ridden third start. *B.
Hanbury.*

SIMPLY GREAT (FR) 4 b.c. Mill Reef 141–Seneca (Chaparral 128) (1982 8g⁴   114
10.5f* 1983 12d 10s⁴) well-made, deep-girthed colt; very smart performer at his
best; ran fourth in Ladbrokes Craven Stakes at Newmarket and accounted for
Palace Gold decisively, despite idling a bit in front, in Mecca-Dante Stakes at York
in 1982; subsequently sustained small fracture in a leg and didn't recapture his form
at 4 yrs, fading to be seventh of 11 to Electric in Jockey Club Stakes at Newmarket
in April (possibly needed run) and failing to find any extra pace after looking to be
going well 2f out when 2¼ lengths fourth of 8 to Fine Sun in Clive Graham Stakes at
Goodwood in May; subsequently injured a leg again; should stay 1½m; acts well on
firm going. *H. Cecil.*

SINACRE 2 gr.f. Saritamer 130–Canisburn 77 (Canisbay 120) (1983 5fg 6f 5.1f —
5.3f) Mar 2; small, sturdy filly; half-sister to 1981 2-y-o 5f and 6f seller winner
Eightpence (by Pieces of Eight); dam won over 11f; no form, including in 2
claimers. *M. Tompkins.*

SINDIANA 3 gr.f. Dancer's Image–Vardo 92 (Crepello 136) (1982 NR 1983 7s —
12d³ 12.2d) 6,800F, IR 16,000Y; robust, angular-topped filly; half-sister to 2
winners, including Irish middle-distance winner Great Decision (by Huntercombe);
dam stayed 1m; poor form in maiden races (last of 3 at Hamilton); looks slow; sold
to BBA 5,800 gns Newmarket December Sales. *J. Hindley.*

SINDOS 2 b.f. Busted 134–Sindo 91 (Derring-Do 131) (1983 6fg 7fg2) Feb 21; 89
31,000Y; big, rangy filly; half-sister to 2 winners, including 1m and 1¼m winner
Scarlet Town (by Town Crier); dam, closely related to Stilvi, won over 5f at 2 yrs;
½-length second of 12 to Miss Saint-Cloud in minor event at Doncaster in October;
will stay 1¼m; sure to win maiden race. *R. Hollinshead.*

SINGALONG JOE 5 ch.g. Sharpen Up 127–Captive Flower 99 (Manacle 123) –
(1982 10fg 8g4 8f2 9f3 8f 8g 8s2 1983 7s 8f 10fg 8h) leggy, light-framed gelding;
plater; probably stays 9f; acts on any going; blinkered final start (sweated badly);
sold 500 gns Ascot August Sales. *K. Bailey.*

SINGALONG LASS 2 ch.f. Bold Lad (Ire) 133–Tweezelnut (Charlottesville –
135) (1983 6fg) June 12; 7,400Y; workmanlike filly; third foal; dam Irish 1¼m
winner; behind in 23-runner maiden race at Newmarket in October. *M. Jarvis.*

SINGERMAN 2 b.g. Record Token 128–Mums Song 76 (Saintly Song 128) (1983 78
5d2 5fg2 5v 5d 5fg3 5f* 5fg2) May 30; 1,850Y; sturdy, compact gelding; second
living foal; dam 5f performer; won 11-runner maiden race at Newcastle in August;
failed by only a head to catch Jeema in nursery at Chester later in month; acts well
on firm going; ran very freely in blinkers fourth outing; exported to Hong Kong. *K.
Stone.*

SING GALVO SING 2 b.f. Music Boy 124–Aunt Winnie (Wolver Hollow 126) 64
(1983 5g 5f3 5fg 5fg 8f) May 9; 6,000F; plain filly; second produce; dam poor
maiden; plating-class maiden; not sure to stay 1m. *D. Oughton.*

SINGING BOY 2 b.g. Manor Farm Boy 114–Jailhouse Rock (Gulf Pearl 117) (1983 80
5s4 5v 5v 5.8g* 6fg 6fg4 6fg 7d 7fg) Feb 25; 1,000Y; lengthy, workmanlike gelding;
seventh foal; half-brother to a winning hurdler; dam ran only twice; won 13-runner
maiden auction event at Bath in June by 6 lengths; didn't show a lot afterwards; last
of 20 in nursery at Doncaster in November on final appearance; suited by 6f;
apprentice ridden all outings. *R. Williams.*

SINGING FOOL 7 gr.g. Singing Bede 122–Dilwyn 84 (Immortality) (1982 10.1d –
12fg 1983 10f 12f) sturdy gelding; plater; stays 1¼m; acts on firm going; has twice
worn blinkers. *A. Pitt.*

SINGING HIGH 3 b.f. Julio Mariner 127–Sing High 85 (Sound Track 132) (1982 87
7d3 1983 10.2v 8f 10g 9f3 8fg2 8f*) strong, useful-looking filly; leniently treated
when easily landing the odds in handicap at Ripon in August; promises to stay
beyond 9f; acts on firm going and has run creditably on a soft surface. *J.
Fitzgerald.*

SINGING JOHNNY 4 b.g. Record Run 127–Seasoning 74 (Silly Season 127) –
(1982 NR 1983 14.6f) workmanlike gelding; has a round action; in rear in maiden
races. *M. H. Easterby.*

SINGING SABRE 2 ch.g. Shiny Tenth 120–Crescent Dart 103 (Sing Sing 134) 71
(1983 6f 7fg) Feb 22; small, workmanlike gelding; half-brother to several winners,
including smart 1974 2-y-o sprinter Double Dart (by Songedor); dam sprinter;
prominent in large fields of maidens at Newmarket in July and September;
subsequently gelded. *G. Pritchard-Gordon.*

SINGING SAILOR 4 br.c. Mansingh 120–Sealady (Seaepic 100) (1982 5s3 5fg 100
5f 5fg 5g 5fg 5g4 5s 5v2 5s2 5s 1983 5v* 5v 5v 5d 5.8g 5f 6f 5f2 5.1s* 5fg2 5fg3 5d2
5fg*) small, quite well-made colt; useful handicapper; won at Doncaster in May
(£6,400 event from Batoni), Yarmouth in September and Doncaster again in
November; best at 5f; acts on any going but goes well in the mud; blinkered once in
1982; trained by R. Thompson first 6 starts. *R. Hannon.*

SINGING SOPRANO 3 b.f. Music Boy 124–Vanity (Vimy 132) (1982 5g 5fg 5d –
6s 1983 8g 7d4 8.3f) plater; stays 7f; sold to C. Wildman 1,300 gns Ascot
December Sales. *P. Bailey.*

SINGING TROOPER 4 ch.f. Air Trooper 115–Arne Melody (Romany Air 118) –
(1982 11.7g 12s 10s 1983 12s 10.2g 12f4 16g) plater; best run at 1½m on firm
going. *A. Andrews.*

SINGLE HAND 3 b.g. Solinus 130–Set-Elmal 80 (Tower Walk 131) (1982 NR 74
1983 6s 8d 6g3 6f3 6f4 7fg* 6s3 8fg 8g) IR 18,500Y; tall, rather lightly-made, quite
attractive gelding; first foal; dam won twice over 6f at 2 yrs; sold out of J. Hindley's
stable 5,200 gns after comfortably winning selling handicap at Newmarket in
August; promises to stay 1m; possibly best on a sound surface; sold to D. Chapman
1,700 gns Doncaster October Sales. *W. Musson.*

SINGLE PORTION 2 gr.f. Abwah 118–Shirwani 77 (Major Portion 129) (1983   **62**
5v⁴ 5.8s 6fg² 5g² 6fg² 5f⁴ 5f* 6f² 6f³ 5f³ 6d³ 5g) Apr 4; 3,000Y; smallish,
workmanlike filly; half-sister to 2-y-o sprint winners Better Portion (by Music Boy)
and Glenfield Portion (by Mummy's Pet); plater; made all to win by 3 lengths at
Hamilton (bought in 2,500 gns) in July; best form on firm ground; trained
by Mrs J. Reavey first 3 starts; tough, genuine and consistent. *M. Pipe.*

SING SWING 2 b.f. Relkino 131–Song God 96 (Red God 128§) (1983 7fg²) Apr   **103 p**
13; quite well-made filly; good walker; fourth foal; half-sister to French 3-y-o 9f
winner Rebecca's Song (by Artaius); dam 2-y-o 5f winner; 50/1, ran extremely well
in Rockfel Stakes at Newmarket in October, putting in a good run from halfway to
finish 3 lengths second of 13 to Mahogany; will stay 1m; clearly useful and should
have no difficulty winning races. *J. Hindley.*

SING TO ME 2 br.c. Lochnager 132–Sunset Song 87 (Song 132) (1983 5v 5s²   **75**
5d³ 5fg 5f 5f 5fg* 5g 5g 6fg) Apr 28; 3,600Y; big, useful-looking colt; third foal;
dam stayed 6f; put up best effort when blinkered in 6-runner nursery at Goodwood
in August, making all under bottom weight to win by short head from Crowfoot's
Couture; subsequently beaten in nurseries, wearing blinkers in 2; not sure to stay
6f; none too consistent. *R. Hannon.*

SIOUX PRINCESS 2 gr.f. Habat 127–Hillsquaw (Hillary) (1983 6fg 6f 5fg 5fg 5g   **—**
6d 7g) Apr 7; 3,600F, 6,000Y; half-sister to 1979 2-y-o 7f winner Nahane (by Porto
Bello); dam won over 7f in USA; soundly beaten in maiden and minor events. *Peter
Taylor.*

SIR BLESSED 4 b.g. So Blessed 130–Morinda 87 (Matador 130) (1982 8g 8fg   **73**
8.2f 10.4fg 8fg² 8g⁴ 9s 8s² 1983 10g⁴ 10f 10f³ 11.7f* 11.7f² 11.7f² 11.7fg² 11.7f²
11.7f 11.7fg 12fg 10fg 10fg) lengthy, rather sparely-made gelding; won handicap at
Windsor in July; stays 1½m; suited by top-of-the-ground. *R. Williams.*

SIR BUTCH 3 b.g. Record Token 128–Acquire 105 (Burglar 128) (1982 6f 6g* 6g   **74**
6g 1983 6v 6s* 7d 6f 7f 6f) strong, lengthy, good-quartered gelding; good
walker; ran best race when winning handicap at Goodwood in May; promises to
stay 7f; acts on soft going; blinkered final start. *J. Dunlop.*

SIR DOMINO 5 ch.g. Morston 125–Dominant 86 (Behistoun 131) (1982 NR 1983   **—**
10.1d) leggy gelding; probably no longer of any account. *J. King.*

SIRHANN 2 ch.c. Habitat 134–Molly Malone (Bold Lad, Ire 133) (1983 6d) May   **— p**
10; 68,000Y; strong, good sort; good walker; half-brother to 2 winners, including
fairly useful 1979 2-y-o 6f winner Live Ammo (by Home Guard); dam half-sister to
high-class animals Hot Spark and Bitty Girl (both by Habitat); 10/1, ran on after
being outpaced to finish 10½ lengths sixth of 17 to Cremets in maiden at Newbury
in October; has the scope to improve. *G. Harwood.*

SIR HUMPHERSON 2 b.c. Music Boy 124–Sweet Eliane (Birdbrook 110) (1983   **93**
6f³ 6fg² 6g* 6g³) Mar 20; 23,000Y; rangy colt; good walker and mover; first foal;
dam poor sister to very useful 7f and 1m performer Apple King; landed the odds in
excellent style in 14-runner minor event at Lingfield in September, winning by 5
lengths from Block of Granite; beaten favourite all other starts, finishing 2
lengths third of 14 to Angleman when 2/1 on in minor event at Lingfield later in
month; promises to stay 7f. *G. Harwood.*

SIR HUMPHREY 3 ch.g. High Line 125–Greek Money (Sovereign Path 125)   **66**
(1982 7s 1983 8s 8.5v 10g 10fg² 10.1fg 10g* 10f 10fg⁴ 12f³ 10f 12fg) lightly-made
gelding; none too consistent, but won handicap at Lingfield in June; stays 1½m;
blinkered nowadays. *B. Swift.*

SIR JOSHUA WYLEY 2 ch.c. Roman Warrior 132–Marchuna 96 (March Past   **—**
124) (1983 6h³ 7g) May 3; tall, rangy colt; second foal; half-brother to a winner
in Belgium; dam, half-sister to very smart miler General Vole, won 5 times at up
to 1m; 7½ lengths third of 7 to Golden Capistrano in newcomers event at
Chepstow in August. *N. Gaselee.*

SIR LUCKY 4 ch.g. Bonne Noel 115–Mount Gay (Divine Gift 127) (1982 8f 12f⁴   **—**
12g 12fg⁴ 11g 12d* 12d 12s⁴ 1983 12v 12d 11g 12g) lightly-made gelding; plater;
stays 1½m; best run on soft surface; usually blinkered. *C. Crossley.*

SIR MALA MALA (USA) 3 b.c. Seattle Slew–Mama Kali (Tom Rolfe) (1982 6f   **?**
1983 8v) well-made, attractive colt; no worthwhile form in goodish company at
Royal Ascot as a 2-y-o (finished very lame) and at Kempton in April (fifth of 6
behind Sackford in BonusPrint Easter Stakes); subsequently won in USA. *J.
Sutcliffe.*

SIR PRINCE JOHN 3 b.c. Prince Tenderfoot 126–Star of Sierra (Quisling 117)   **109**
(1982 6f 6d² 6s² 1983 6s 6s* 7s² 6v 6.3f² 6.3f² 6f² 6f² 8d 7g² 7fg) strong,
good-bodied colt; half-brother to Irish 7f winner Sierra Boy (by African Sky) and
Irish middle-distance winner Sam John (by Malinowski); dam Irish stayer; showed
improved form when beating Glenstal by a head after a ding-dong battle in £3,500
event at Phoenix Park in April; creditable second at the Curragh (3 times) and
Phoenix Park (also 3 times) afterwards; had stiff task and was never seen with a
chance when sixth of 10 behind Salieri in Bisquit Cognac Challenge Stakes at
Newmarket in October on final start; stays 7f; acts on any going; sometimes
blinkered nowadays; trained much of season by M. Connolly. *P. Daly, Ireland.*

SIR ROBERT 3 b. or br.c. Cavo Doro 124–Flowering (Reform 132) (1982 6d   –
1983 10v 8s) seemingly of no account; has been tried in blinkers; sold 1,550 gns
Ascot May Sales. *M. Haynes.*

SIR SIDNEY 2 ch.g. Morston 125–Giselle 104 (Pall Mall 132) (1983 6fg) Mar 19;   –
3,600Y; third foal; dam stayed 1¼m; distant seventh of 8 in minor event at Windsor
in August; subsequently gelded. *J. Holt.*

SISTER HANNAH 2 b.f. Monseigneur 127–Hannie Caulder (Workboy 123)   **70**
(1983 6g 6fg 5g²) Mar 28; lengthy, fair sort; first foal; dam unraced half-sister to
1000 Guineas winner Mrs McArdy; failed by a neck to catch Acka's Gem, after
stumbling inside final furlong, in 11-runner minor event at Edinburgh in October;
should stay 6f. *C. Booth.*

SITEX 5 b.h. Record Run 127–Glorious Light 53 (Alcide 136) (1982 5d 6g 5d 6fg   **49 d**
7g 7g 6fg³ 6g* 6g 6fg 6v 6s 1983 5v 6v 5v 6g 7s* 7s³ 6fg⁴ 7.6g 7fg 5f 6fg 6g 8fg 6fg
6g 6g) lengthy horse; poor handicapper; 50/1 when winning at Chepstow in May;
acts on a firm surface but is ideally suited by some give in the ground; has run
creditably in blinkers. *M. Bolton.*

SITICA 6 b.g. Siliconn 121–Time Call (Chanteur II 135) (1982 7d² 1983 6s 5s 7d   –
6f) narrow, fair sort; poor handicapper; stays 7f; goes well on a soft surface but is
unsuited by really firm going; has worn bandages; sometimes taken down very
quietly. *E. Alston.*

SIX O SIX AUCTION 3 b.g. Connaught 130–Honey Pot 111 (Hotfoot 126) (1982   **76**
6g 6d 8f⁴ 8g 1983 9.4d⁴ 9.4d 10.5d* 12fg²) neat gelding; showed improved form
when winning £4,000 selling handicap at York in October; bought in 6,000 gns
afterwards; suited by 1¼m+; probably acts on any going. *C. Thornton.*

SKATEBOARD 7 b.g. Tower Walk 130–Palgal (Le Prince 98) (1982 NR 1983   **45**
12d 12g 12f² 12.2fg 14f⁴ 13f²) lengthy, good sort; former plater; stays 1¾m; acts
on firm going; has run well for a lady rider. *D. Wilson.*

SKETCHMEAD BOY 2 ch.c. Manor Farm Boy 114–Ruby's Photo 77 (Polyfoto   **54**
124) (1983 5s 6fg 6fg⁴ 7g 6f 8f 8s 8fg) Apr 29; 5,000Y; leggy colt; second foal;
dam placed over 5f at 2 yrs; poor maiden; blinkered, well beaten in seller final
start; best at 6f. *N. Tinkler.*

SKEWHIFF 3 b.f. Gracious Melody 117–Winsan (Maystreak 118) (1982 NR 1983   –
7s 7f 7.2fg 6f 8d 6fg) smallish, sturdy filly; first foal; dam poor maiden; soundly
beaten in varied company, including selling; blinkered final start; trained by R.
Whitaker until after fourth outing. *H. Wharton.*

SKIATHOS 2 b.g. Creetown 123–Grecian Gift (Cavo Doro 124) (1983 5d) Mar   –
11; 2,200Y; first foal; dam never ran; last of 17 in maiden auction event at Redcar in
May. *M. Tompkins.*

SKI RUN 8 b.g. Workboy 123–Snow Rum (Quorum 126) (1982 12g² 10.6s* 12fg*   **78**
10.5f³ 10.2d 12s 1983 12v 12d 10d²) middle-distance handicapper; 2½ lengths
second to Free Press in Zetland Gold Cup at Redcar in May; not seen out again;
acts on any going; usually races with tongue tied down; has worn bandages;
suitable mount for a claimer; genuine and consistent. *P. Wigham.*

SKI SAILING (USA) 3 b.f. Royal Ski–Space Sailing (Sail On-Sail On) (1982 6v²   **115**
7g* 1983 8g 10v* 12g 12g² 10g³ 12fg 9.2f 10v) big, rangy filly; first foal; dam won
5f maiden race at 2 yrs; put up an impressive performance and looked a high-class
filly in the making when beating Sun Princess by 2 lengths (pair 25 lengths clear)
in 7-runner Sir Charles Clore Memorial Stakes at Newbury in May, quickening
into lead 2f out and striding out really well in the heavy ground; disappointed
behind same filly when second favourite for Oaks next time (soundly-beaten fifth
of 15) and didn't fulfil her promise, although was by no means disgraced when 2
lengths second of 13 to Give Thanks in Lancashire Oaks at Haydock in July and

Sir Charles Clore Memorial Stakes, Newbury—Ski Sailing strides out well in the heavy ground to beat Sun Princess, with the others trailing

about 2 lengths third of 6 to Morcon in rather slowly-run Valdoe Stakes at Goodwood in September; was particularly disappointing sixth and last starts, on latter occasion finishing only fifth of 7 in Premio Roma Vecchia; suited by middle distances; acts well on heavy going; changed hands privately before Oaks. *B. Hills.*

SKISKELTER 3 b.g. Malinowski 123–Skelmorlie (Blakeney 126) (1982 8s 8.2s 1983 12s 12f 16f 12g) strong, well-made gelding; little worthwhile form in varied company; gives impression he has a mind of his own; sold out of B. Hills's stable 1,100 gns Ascot July Sales after third outing. *C. Wildman.* —

SKITTISH (USA) 3 b. or br.f. Far North 120–Bright Merry (Speak John) (1982 8s 1983 12fg* 12fg³) tall, rather leggy filly; held up when winning maiden race at Wolverhampton in August; modest third at Hamilton in September on only other outing; suited by 1½m; probably acts on any going. *M. Stoute.* 73

SKYBOOT 4 b.g. African Sky 124–Sans Sabots (Whistler 129) (1982 6s² 6g 6d* 6g 6g 1983 6s⁴ 6v³ 7fg 7d² 7.2g 7fg) close-coupled, useful sort; suited by 7f; well suited by soft ground; has twice worn blinkers; sold to J. Townson 5,000 gns Doncaster November Sales. *A. Stewart.* 70

SKYBRIGHT 5 b.m. The Brianstan 128–Sky Hostess 72 (Skymaster 126) (1982 12fg 10fg 12fg 11.5fg 12g 10d 12d 1983 16s 15.5v) leggy mare; poor plater; probably stays 2m; sometimes sweats up. *G. Blum.* —

SKY HIGH GUY (USA) 4 b.g. Son Ange–Gay Minette (Sir Gaylord) (1982 10s² 11.7f² 12fg 12fg 13d 14g 12s 1983 12v 10.2g) strong, good-looking gelding; disappointing maiden; stays 1½m; acts on any going; has twice been blinkered. *I. Dudgeon.* —

SKY JUMP 9 ch.g. Double Jump 131–Damascus Sky (Skymaster 126) (1982 6d³ 6g 7f 7f² 7h 8f³ 7g 7f⁴ 7fg⁴ 8.3g* 7g*(dis) 1983 6v 8v 7s* 7d⁴ 8g 5.8h 7fg 8f 8.3fg* 8f 8fg) selling handicapper nowadays; bought in after winning at Brighton in May (1,750 gns) and Windsor in August (820 gns); made all on latter; stays 1m; acts on 56

768

any going; sometimes blinkered (wore them last 3 starts); good mount for a boy. *B. Swift.*

SKY LAWYER (FR) 5 b.h. Sea Lawyer–Medenine (Prudent II 133) (1982 8g 6.5v3 5s2 6g4 8g 7.6g 6g* 6s3 5fg 6s 5g* 6fg3 6g 5v2 1983 6v3 5s* 5fg4 5fg4 5f 5d2) strong, rangy horse; half-brother to 3 winners in France, including Over The River (by Luthier), useful on flat and over jumps; dam won over 7f; smart sprinter; made all and held off Kind Music by a head in Prix de Saint-Georges at Longchamp in May; in frame afterwards in Prix du Gros-Chene at Chantilly (behind Gem Diamond), William Hill Sprint Championship at York (moved up a place after finishing nearly 10 lengths fifth of 10 to Habibti) and Prix du Petit Couvert at Longchamp (½-length second to Bold Apparel); best at sprint distances, though stayed further; probably acted on any going; best in blinkers (didn't wear them at York); standing at Haras de Preaux, Calvados. *R. Touflan, France.* **119**

SKY MARINER 2 b.f. Julio Mariner 127–Sky Grove 47 (African Sky 124) (1983 5s 7f* 8s 7g 7d) compact filly; first foal; dam plater; bought out of J. W. Watts's stable 5,500 gns after winning 10-runner seller at Redcar in August in good style by 2½ lengths; showed nothing subsequently in nurseries; should stay 1m; acts on firm going. *J. McNaughton.* **59**

SKYMERIC 4 ch.f. Homeric 133–Skymarlin 75 (Skymaster 126) (1982 8d 8d 8fg 7g 10.4fg 10fg* 10.1g4 10.1fg 10d3 10d 1983 9v 10fg 10g 12f4 10f 12g 10fg) leggy, plain filly; plater; suited by 1¼m; acts on a firm and a soft surface; has run well for an apprentice; blinkered fourth start; has worn bandages in front; has had tongue tied down. *N. Guest.* **–**

SKYRAM 4 b.g. Sagaro 133–Molly Fay 69 (Faberge II 121) (1982 14fg4 13.8f2 12.3d2 12d 16g 12.2f* 1983 14.6f3 12f4 12fg 13.8f* 14.6f2 15.8f* 16f) strong, compact gelding; doesn't always impress in paddock; won handicaps at Catterick in July and August; stays well; seems to act on any going; bandaged in front nowadays; ran atrociously final start. *D. Morley.* **82**

Sheikh Mohammed's "Ski Sailing"

SKY

SKYTRICK 4 b.c. African Sky 124–Fascinating Trick (Buckpasser) (1982 8g — 1983 8f 8g 9fg) fine, big, rangy, attractive colt; useful at his best but is lightly raced and presumably difficult to train; not disgraced in William Hill Cambridgeshire Handicap at Newmarket in October on final start; promises to stay 9f; bandaged in 1983; sold to BBA 2,000 gns Newmarket December Sales. *L. Cumani.*

SLAINTHE MHATH 3 bl. or gr.f. Bruni 132–High Gloss (Super Sam 124) (1982 NR 1983 11d 16g 7f 8f) IR 2,200Y; smallish filly; half-sister to 2 winners; dam poor Irish maiden; well beaten in maiden races and an apprentice event. *D. Morrill.*

SLATE 4 gr.f. Ragstone 128–January (Sigebert 131) (1982 10f 1983 8g 12f 12f[4] 50 12g 12fg[2] 13.8g[3] 12fg) poor maiden; suited by 1½m and should get further; sweated up badly third start; sold 2,100 gns Newmarket Autumn Sales. *J. Dunlop.*

SLEDGE 2 b.f. Young Generation 129–Ride 71 (Sovereign Path 125) (1983 7f 80 8.2s[3] 8fg[4]) Mar 11; tall filly; good mover; half-sister to several winners, including high-class 6f and 7f performer Court Chad (by St Chad) and Lincoln Handicap winner King's Ride (by Rarity); dam lightly-raced daughter of smart Turf; 2 lengths third of 9 to All Fair in maiden race at Haydock in October; disappointing fourth in similar event at Edinburgh the following month; possibly not suited by firm surface. *K. Brassey.*

SLEEPLINE CONSORT 2 br.c. Vilgora 113–Sleepline Comfort 61 (Tickled — Pink 114) (1983 5g) Apr 6; useful-looking colt; first foal; dam won 5f seller at 2 yrs; behind in 20-runner maiden race at Newbury in September. *K. Brassey.*

SLEEPLINE PROMISE 4 b.f. Record Token 128–Herods Palace 95 (Palestine — 133) (1982 5d 7d 8g 8s 6s 1983 6v) useful sort; has been tubed; poor plater nowadays; has worn blinkers. *P. Cundell.*

SLEEPLINE SANDMAN 3 ch.c. Sandford Lad 133–Acropolita Mia 75 — (Acropolis 132) (1982 NR 1983 11.5fg 10f 11f 8f) 6,500Y; dipped-backed, workmanlike colt; brother to Mia Saint, 4 times a winner over 5f at 2 yrs in 1976, and half-brother to 1¼m winner and good hurdler Royal Vulcan (by Royal Match); dam won over 11.7f; seventh of 17 to Magnetic Field in 1m minor event at Salisbury in August, best effort. *S. Matthews.*

SLEWPY (USA) 3 b. or br.c. Seattle Slew–Rare Bouquet (Prince John) (1982 ? 5.5g* 6fg* 6.5fg 7fg 8.5fg 8.5fg* 9g 1983 7fg* 9fg[3] 8g[2] 9fg 8.5f[2] 12s 8.5d* 8g[4] 9fg* 10fg*)

Sending American-raced horses to be trained in Europe for a full season is not exactly a regular occurrence but there have been quite a few instances over the years including Omaha and Hill Rise, who both enjoyed highly successful campaigns, and Lemhi Gold, who regrettably did not. Equally, bringing a horse across for just one race is rare, mainly because American prize money is so high there is no need to seek rewards elsewhere, but not unprecedented, with such as Carry Back, Tom Rolfe, One For All, Intrepid Hero and Cunning Trick having run in the Arc, Topsider in the July Cup and That's A Nice in the King George. The fact that none of these colts, or for that matter Slewpy who contested the 1983 Derby, cut much ice is hardly likely to encourage American owners to try their luck in future, and we cannot envisage any great changes in the tendency for the traffic between Europe and the States to be one way in this area at least.

Owned by Equusequity Stable, Slewpy had shown very smart form at two, winning three races including the Grade 1 Young America Stakes decisively and being rated 7 lb below the joint top weights in the Experimental Free Handicap, Copelan and Roving Boy. With another fine son of Seattle Slew, Slew O'Gold, representing the same connections in two of the three American classics—he finished in the frame in the Kentucky Derby and Belmont Stakes—it appeared worthwhile to Equusequity to have a crack at the Derby with Slewpy who became the first good American-raced colt to compete in the race since Sir Martin who started favourite and had the misfortune to fall in 1909. Slewpy didn't start favourite or anything like it, going off at 100/1; bandaged behind he came in eighteenth of twenty to Teenoso, dropping back quickly after lying up with the pace to halfway. It goes without saying that Slewpy is much better than he showed at Epsom. His first five starts at three included a win in an allowance race at Gulfstream Park and creditable runs in the Louisiana Derby at Fair Grounds (third to Balbao Native despite a slipped saddle), a valuable allowance event at Aqueduct and, his first outing on grass, the Kingston Stakes at Aqueduct again (second to Thunder Puddles). It was in the autumn, though, that he revealed his true merit. Off the course for over three months on going back to the States, he returned to the scene of his Young America Stakes victory, Meadowlands in New Jersey, and proceeded to win three races on dirt, an

770

allowance event, the Grade 2 Paterson Handicap and Grade 1 Meadowlands Cup. In the Paterson Slewpy got the better of Bounding Basque (who had beaten him soundly in a division of the Grade 1 Wood Memorial at Aqueduct in April) by a neck, the pair clear. The Meadowlands Cup had a better field with Slewpy opposed by eight including the ex-English Bel Bolide, successful in three good races in 1983 among them the Grade 2 Carlton F. Burke Handicap by five lengths, Bounding Basque again and the top American two-year-old of 1981 Deputy Minister; the result was the same though, Slewpy scoring by a neck from Deputy Minister after finishing powerfully.

Slewpy (USA) (b. or br.c. 1980)	Seattle Slew (b or br 1974)	Bold Reasoning (br 1968)	Boldnesian
			Reason to Earn
		My Charmer (b 1969)	Poker
			Fair Charmer
	Rare Bouquet (ch 1963)	Prince John (ch 1953)	Princequillo
			Not Afraid
		Forest Song (br 1958)	Mr Music
			Sylvanaise

Slewpy, a tall, quite good-looking colt, is well bred—his sire has made a sensational start at stud and his unraced dam Rare Bouquet had eleven live foals, all winners, before he came along. Two of the eleven, My Old Friend (by Outing Class) and Fresh Pepper (by B. Major), won stakes races, My Old Friend showing smart form at up to eleven furlongs and Fresh Pepper collecting the eight-and-a-half-furlong Oak Leaf Stakes at two. The next dam, a minor winner, was also productive, with nine winners from seventeen foals. It would be folly to judge Slewpy's stamina capabilities on his Derby display and on breeding he ought to have reasonable prospects of staying a mile and a half. He wore blinkers in the Wood Memorial but the experiment was not repeated. *S. Watters, jnr, USA.*

SLINDON 3 b.g. Sagaro 133–Weeny Bopper 76 (Songedor 116) (1982 NR 1983 16g⁴ 16g 14f 12g 14g) useful-looking gelding; first foal; dam won over 7f and also several races at up to 25f over hurdles; remote fourth of 20 in maiden race at Lingfield in June, easily best effort; last twice afterwards. *S. Woodman.*   –

SLIP UP 3 b.g. Quiet Fling 124–Artemis 91 (King Emperor) (1982 7s 7s 1983 8v 10.1d) well-made, good sort; behind in maiden and minor events; sold 2,600 gns Ascot 2nd June Sales. *I. Balding.*   –

SLIX 3 b.f. High Top 131–Herbary (Herbager 136) (1982 6fg 6s 1983 7h² 10f² 10.1f* 10.1fg² 10fg³ 11d³) smallish, quite attractive filly; beat Master Carver easily by 7 lengths in 13-runner minor event at Windsor in August; placed all other outings; stays 11f; probably acts on any going; sweated badly fifth start; sold 8,600 gns Newmarket December Sales. *J. Dunlop.*   **87**

SMACKOVER 8 ch.h. Pontifex (USA)–Atanya (Atan) (1982 8f⁴ 8f* 8f* 8f³ 8fg³ 1983 8fg² 8f² 8f 8f* 8f 8fg³) strong, lengthy horse; poor walker; not the force he was but managed to win handicap at Pontefract in July; best at around 1m; acts on any going but is suited by top-of-the-ground; used to be blinkered; usually wears bandages; has won when sweating up. *B. McMahon.*   **61**

SMALL PRINCESS 3 gr.f. Godswalk 130–Stormy Princess 76 (Ballymoss 136) (1982 5v 1983 5fg 7f 8.2f 7g 9g) small filly; behind in varied company, including plating; sold 560 gns Newmarket Autumn Sales. *Mrs A. Cousins.*   –

SMART GAL 3 b.f. Martinmas 128–Galway Gate (Laser Light 118) (1982 6d 6g 7.2s 1983 8s 7d 12f) plain filly; poor form, including in sellers; sold 370 gns Ascot 2nd June Sales. *Mrs J. Reavey.*   –

SMART MART 4 ch.g. Jimmy Reppin 131–Fochetta (Fortino II 120) (1982 7f 8f² 8f 8f³ 8fg² 7f* 7fg² 8f⁴ 7f⁴ 7s 1983 8d 7.2s² 7f² 7f 8f 8fg 7f* 7f 7g⁴ 7g³) workmanlike, sturdy gelding; former plater; won handicap at Beverley in August; stays 1m; acts on any going; doesn't find much off bridle and is suited by waiting tactics; retained 2,600 gns Doncaster January Sales. *M. Camacho.*   **61**

SMILING LAUREL 4 ch.c. Young Emperor 133–Tom's Delight (Tom Rolfe) (1982 6fg⁴ 5fg 5g³ 7.2s 1983 8g 6fg 5f⁴ 7fg 6fg 6fg 5f³ 5g) strong, lengthy, useful sort; poor handicapper; should stay 7f; acts well on top-of-the-ground; usually blinkered nowadays. *Mrs B. Waring.*

SMITTEN 2 b.f. Run The Gantlet–Jantu 81 (Deep Diver 134) (1983 5fg 6f³ 7f³) Mar 23; third foal; half-sister to 3-y-o 6f seller winner Easy Star (by Red Alert); dam 6f winner; quite a moderate maiden; better suited by 7f than by shorter distances, and will stay 1m; acts on firm going. *B. Hanbury.*   **72**

SMOKEY LIN 2 b.f. Derrylin 115–Smoke Signal 77 (Bleep-Bleep 134) (1983 5v⁴   75
5s³ 6g 7f 6fg⁴ 6g 6fg²) Mar 24; IR 22,000Y; compact filly; half-sister to 2 winners
in Belgium, including 1976 2-y-o Flaming Temper (by Tyrant); dam won over 5f at
2 yrs; quite a modest maiden; stays 7f; suited by a firm surface; blinkered final
appearance. *A. Jarvis.*

SMOKEY SHADOW 6 gr.g. Dragonara Palace 115–Camdamus 83 (Mandamus   –
120) (1982 8g 7f³ 7f* 7f⁴ 7f³ 7g³ 8f² 10fg⁴ 8g 1983 8d 7s 7fg 8fg 8f 8s) fair sort;
ran poorly in 1983; seems to stay 1¼m; suited by firm ground; often blinkered;
usually ridden by a claimer or a lady nowadays. *E. Eldin.*

SMUGGLY (USA) 3 ch.f. Caro 133–Call Me Goddess (Prince John) (1982 8s³   121
7.5s* 1983 8v* 10.5v* 10v* 10.5f²)
    Smuggly started favourite for the French Oaks, the Prix de Diane Hermes at
Chantilly in June. Deservedly; though whether she represented value at a shade of
odds on in a field of seventeen when unproven on the prevailing firm going was
another matter. With Smuggly and L'Attrayante in the stable Douieb had a very
strong hand in the fillies' races in the first half of the season. The dual Guineas
winner L'Attrayante and Ma Biche had probably the best form of any of the French
three-year-old fillies up to the beginning of June but Smuggly herself had an
excellent record. She might have gone to Chantilly unbeaten except for being
hampered by a faller first time out as a two-year-old. She had won her three races
as a three-year-old, all of them of some importance—a 100,000-franc event and the
Prix Penelope at Saint-Cloud, and the Prix Saint-Alary at Longchamp—in so doing
accounting for several of her opponents in the Prix de Diane as well as two highly
regarded fillies who missed the big race, the Epsom Oaks favourite Alexandrie and
Sharaya.
    Smuggly won the first race at Saint-Cloud with a degree of ease. She was given
much more to do in the second, the Prix Penelope, particularly by Escaline who,
making her first appearance of the season, ran her to a short neck with Alexandrie
third. The Prix Saint-Alary is usually regarded as the most important Oaks trial in
France besides being a valuable race in its own right—it was worth the equivalent
of £38,726 to the winner in 1983, at that figure well ahead of the nearest British
counterpart the Musidora Stakes. In a field of eight Smuggly started third favourite
behind Sharaya and the French Guineas second Mysterieuse Etoile; the only
British runner Nibabu started the complete outsider and was outclassed. Sharaya
made the running, as she did later on when successful in another of France's top
events for three-year-old fillies, the Trusthouse Forte Prix Vermeille. On this
occasion she couldn't hold on to the lead in the straight. Smuggly came to challenge
shortly after the last turn and was soon able to get on top; she was never in danger
over the last two furlongs, running on to win most impressively by two lengths and
four from Sharaya and Escaline. On this form it was difficult to envisage Smuggly's
being beaten in the Diane. But beaten she was, by Escaline no less; on merit, too.
Smuggly tracked the pacemaker Quemora until going on with Air Distingue when
they straightened for home, and fought it out with Air Distingue for most of the rest
of the way. Just as she got the upper hand and seemed on the brink of winning,
Escaline came with an astonishing run on the outside which took her past in the last
thirty yards for a victory by three quarters of a length, going away.
    Of the large Diane field only the fourth, the Oaks d'Italia winner Right Bank,
won a race of any importance afterwards. Escaline ran once more in France when
nineteenth behind All Along in the Prix de l'Arc de Triomphe, while Smuggly was
prevented by injury from making any appearance whatsoever. Presumably Smuggly

Prix Saint-Alary, Longchamp—Smuggly is not extended to account for Sharaya

Mr E. Seltzer's "Smuggly"

will be at stud in 1984; if she does come back she is likely to have a tough time since some of the best middle-distance fillies will still be around, among them the first four in the Arc.

		Fortino II	Grey Sovereign
	Caro	(gr 1959)	Ranavalo
	(gr 1967)	Chambord	Chamossaire
Smuggly (USA)		(ch 1955)	Life Hill
(ch.f. 1980)		Prince John	Princequillo
	Call Me Goddess	(ch 1953)	Not Afraid
	(ch 1971)	Marshua	Nashua
		(b 1962)	Emardee

Smuggly is yet another American bred with strong European connections: her sire was exported to the United States after a fine racing career and a promising start at stud in France. The dam Call Me Goddess was a stakes-placed winner at up to a mile. She is just about as stoutly bred an American broodmare as one is likely to come across nowadays, by Prince John (sire of the Irish St Leger winner Transworld, Stage Door Johnny and Alleged's dam Princess Pout among others) out of Marshua, the winner of the ten-furlong CCA Oaks. This is an excellent family—Marshua is also a daughter of a stakes winner and Call Me Goddess is a half-sister to two others, Marshua's Dancer (sire of the dam of Rousillon) and Mashteen (the dam of the very promising French two-year-old Cedilla). With this background Smuggly was shrewdly bought at Saratoga as a yearling for 95,000 dollars, especially as the dam had produced a minor winner, With Elegance (by Exclusive Native), by that time. Call Me Goddess produced a colt foal by Caro the year after she had Smuggly.

Smuggly is a good-bodied, full-quartered filly; we regard her as very attractive also, though some think her too heavy and masculine to be described so. She would almost certainly have stayed a mile and a half. She acted on any going, particularly well on soft or heavy. *O. Douieb, France.*

SNAP TIN 5 ch.m. Jimmy Reppin 131–Hunu (Hul a Hul 124) (1982 8.2s 8f 1983   –
12.2f⁴ 10f) leggy mare; poor plater; sometimes wears blinkers; has worn
bandages; changed hands 500 gns Doncaster June Sales. *R. Ward.*

SNATCH AND RUN (USA) 3 b.c. Full Pocket–Running Fight (Degage) (1982   ?
5fg³ 5g⁴ 5fg* 5fg* 6fg² 1983 6d 6f* 5fg) well-made, quite attractive colt; made
all and held off Apoldream by a neck despite hanging in Group 2 Premio Melton at
Rome in May; well beaten in Abernant Stakes at Newmarket and Prix du
Gros-Chene at Chantilly on his only other starts over here; stays 6f; acts on firm
going; sent to race in USA. *M. Jarvis.*

SNATCH BACK 2 b.f. Mummy's Pet 125–Gambela 88 (Diplomat Way) (1983 6d)   –
Feb 1; 2,000 2-y-o; workmanlike filly; third foal; sister to a disappointing animal;
dam won over 1m; no show in 17-runner maiden race at Newbury in September. *R.
Baker.*

SNEAK PREVIEW 3 b.g. Quiet Fling 124–Glimmer of Hope 90 (Never Say Die   87
137) (1982 NR 1983 12d 12v⁴ 14d 13.3g 16f* 16fg 16.1g 18fg 18fg*) 10,000Y;
lengthy gelding; good walker; third foal; half-brother to 6f to 1¼m winner Moment
of Weakness (by Pieces of Eight); dam stayed well; ran best races when winning
maiden event at Nottingham in June and handicap on same course in October;
seems ideally suited by a test of stamina and top-of-the-ground conditions;
blinkered fifth, sixth and eighth starts. *H. Candy.*

SNOW CARD 2 b.c. Imperial Fling 116–Anjonic 56 (Le Levanstell 122) (1983 5v*   92
5v* 5v² 5s 6f 5fg⁴ 5f⁴ 5f² 5g 6fg³ 5fg* 6d) Mar 8; 21,000Y; attractive colt; has a
good, fluent action; half-brother to several winners, including 3-y-o 1m winner
Sul-El-Ah (by Tachypous) and speedy 1977 early-season 2-y-o Silk Lady (by Tribal
Chief); dam of little account; kept his form well, winning minor events at Lingfield
and Epsom in April and nursery (made all) at Folkestone in October; better at 5f
than 6f; acts on any going; tough and genuine; racing in USA. *G. Lewis.*

SNOW CHILD 2 br.f. Mandrake Major 122–Only Child 68 (Foggy Bell 108) (1983   84
5d⁴ 5f⁴ 6f* 6fg² 6fg² 5fg 6s) Apr 20; 800Y; small, close-coupled filly; sister to a
winner in Malaysia; dam 6f winner; made all in 20-runner maiden auction event at
Nottingham in June; better suited by 6f than 5f, and will stay 7f; acts on firm going
(last of 9 first outing on really soft ground); apprentice ridden all starts. *D. Smith.*

SNOW MALLARD 3 ch.g. Malinowski 123–Gulf Bird 71 (Gulf Pearl 117) (1982   84
NR 1983 12d 12v⁴ 14d 12f 15.5f* 16f² 16f*) 33,000Y; useful-looking gelding;
fourth foal; half-brother to 3 winners, including 1981 2-y-o 5f winner Ghawar (by
Malacate) and very useful 5f performer Blue Persian (by Majority Blue); dam
1½m winner; successful in handicaps at Folkestone and Thirsk in summer; suited
by a test of stamina; acts on firm going. *F. Durr.*

SNOW TREE 2 b.f. Welsh Pageant 132–Fir Tree 90 (Santa Claus 133) (1983 6fg)   – p
Apr 24; deep-girthed, short-coupled filly; sister to 3-y-o 2m winner Rig Steel and
half-sister to a winner in Malaya; dam, half-sister to smart stayer Celtic Cone,
stayed 1¾m; 50/1, never-dangerous seventh of 17 to stable-companion Telios in
maiden race at Newmarket in August; bound to do a good bit better over longer
distances. *B. Hobbs.*

SNOWY RIVER 3 ch.c. Sagaro 133–Lydiate 77 (Tower Walk 130) (1982 7fg 8s²   74
1983 9v² 11d² 14.7f 12f 12g) short-coupled colt; second in maiden races at
Newcastle and Redcar in spring; off course afterwards until September and rather
disappointing on his return; should stay 1½m; seems to need a sound surface. *R.
D. Peacock.*

SOARING (FR) 2 b.f. Pure Flight–Tanerkala (Tanerko 134) (1983 8s 10g* 10g⁴)   110
Mar 17; 26,000 francs Y (approx £2,100); sister to minor 1¼m winner The
Altimeter; dam useful winner at up to 13f; came with a late run when over 4
lengths fourth to Darshaan in Criterium de Saint-Cloud in November; beat Porte
des Lilas a neck in maiden event over same course and distance the previous
month; will be suited by 1½m. *G. Bridgland, France.*

SOBA 4 ch.f. Most Secret 119–Mild Wind (Porto Bello 118) (1982 5f* 6fg* 6fg* 7f*   127
6f* 5g* 6g 6f* 5fg* 6g2 6g* 5g* 6g² 6s* 1983 6d⁴ 6d 5f² 6fg² 5f* 5fg2(dis) 6g² 5fg*
6fg³ 5f²)
    All too often in racing as elsewhere a keenly-awaited future can turn into a
disappointing present. It is in the nature of things that each year should have its
share of good horses who do not train on or have their campaigns blighted by illness
or injury, and its clashes of giants that fail to live up to expectations even if they
occur—the three-year-old careers of Brondesbury, Danzatore, Diesis and Gorytus

King George Stakes, Goodwood—Soba gains a well-deserved pattern-race success, emphatically beating Fine Edge (No. 14), Chellaston Park (blinkers) and Fire-Thatch (hoops)

afforded vivid proof of this. It is consequently all the more pleasing to record that the hugely popular Soba, whose performances at three added so much to the good of the season, fully justified the decision to keep her in training by displaying even better form and picking up over £82,000 in prize money.

An end-of-year report on Soba in 1982 might have read as follows: 'Shows great enthusiasm and determination, has improved enormously and is now not far from the top of the class.' Her tally of eleven wins from fourteen starts, commencing in a lowly maiden event at Thirsk and moving on through a memorable triumph in the William Hill Stewards' Cup to success in races such as the Scarbrough Stakes and Coral Bookmakers Sprint, was a magnificent one, and her good second to Indian King in the Diadem Stakes suggested a pattern race could easily be within her capabilities. In the event, after Soba's first two appearances at four it looked very much as if this assessment of her prospects erred on the side of optimism, with doubts arising as to whether she had trained on. Racing without blinkers for the first time since September 1981 she didn't look herself before the Cammidge Trophy at Doncaster in March and finished fourth to Vorvados after wandering around under pressure in the closing stages, while in the Thirsk Sprint Stakes in May the restoration of blinkers, which she wore in all her remaining races, brought no apparent improvement as she came in a moderate sixth to Kirchner. It followed that for Soba at least the King's Stand Stakes at Royal Ascot assumed a significance to match its status as the only Group 1 contest run in Britain over the minimum trip. Happily her performance indicated she was on the way back for although unable to match the blistering pace of Sayf El Arab she kept on well to be three lengths second.

The King's Stand marked the start of Soba's renaissance and apart from Salieri and Silverdip who beat her into third in the Diadem Stakes at Ascot only the brilliant Habibti finished ahead of her during the remainder of the season. The first encounter of these two splendid fillies came in the William Hill July Cup in which Soba broke smartly as usual, had a couple of lengths in hand at halfway and battled on in typical never-say-die fashion once headed by Habibti at the furlong pole to go down by two and a half lengths. With On Stage, Salieri and Noalcoholic the next to finish Soba had evidently put up a first-rate display and later in the month she justifiably started favourite for the King George Stakes at Goodwood, the scene of probably her finest previous success in the Stewards' Cup. Though she acted on any going the very fast ground at Goodwood suited her ideally as did the five-furlong trip, and her supporters never had an anxious moment. Steadied behind the leaders as Brondesbury set a breakneck gallop from Crime of Passion, she improved immediately when asked about two furlongs out, hit the front at the distance as Brondesbury started to weaken dramatically and went clear to win comfortably by two and a half lengths from Fine Edge with Chellaston Park, who got no sort of run, a head away third.

The field for the King George was not an especially strong one—of the thirteen other runners only Sylvan Barbarosa managed to win a pattern race during the year—but Soba could do no more than win as she did and many believed she had a realistic chance of reversing Newmarket form with Habibti in the William Hill Sprint Championship at York; Habibti started at 13/8 with Soba at 7/4. In one sense the outcome of the race proved unsatisfactory. Though the course had dried out after rain two days before, Soba's jockey Nicholls, who rode her with great verve throughout 1982 and 1983, apparently believed the strip of turf on the stand side had more give in it than the rest of the straight and he determined to move his mount across from her stand-side draw as soon as possible to take advantage of the slightly firmer ground. There was nothing wrong with this plan; it was merely its execution that caused problems, for after being fast away Soba immediately shifted

775

Scarbrough Stakes, Doncaster—Soba lands the odds from Reggae

to her left under Nicholls' urgings, hampering Crime of Passion and Kind Music in the process. By halfway Soba had begun to draw away from Time's Time, Bold Bob and Sky Lawyer, but she couldn't shake off Habibti and as the two of them went clear it was obvious that all Soba's courage wouldn't be sufficient to carry the day. Pushed along to get on terms, Habibti took it up inside the final furlong and went away to win a shade comfortably by a length and a half. The rest hardly mattered; for the record Fine Edge finished six lengths back in third. An inquiry was swiftly announced and as the rules stand Soba's disqualification always looked likely although she had clearly been second best and would definitely have occupied the same position had she not interfered with Crime of Passion and Kind Music. Under rule 153 such considerations are immaterial, of course, and the stewards duly put Soba back to last place and suspended Nicholls for five days.

As in 1982 Soba's connections pursued an adventurous policy with her and when she returned to the winner's enclosure after the Scarbrough Stakes at Doncaster in September it was her second race within the space of five days. The first, the Vernons Sprint Cup at Haydock, had seen her run second to Habibti again, beaten seven lengths, after being completely outpaced in the final furlong of a race which we consider showed the winner one of the best sprinters in our experience. Apart from Sayf El Arab, who had not reproduced his King's Stand form, no high-class opponents faced Soba at Doncaster and showing no sign of her Haydock exertions she started at odds on. Soon bowling along sweetly in front she never looked in the slightest danger of defeat and came home a convincing two-length winner from Reggae.

By that stage of the season Soba and Nicholls must have been heartily fed up with the sight of Habibti's quarters, but this didn't stop Chapman giving his charge one last attempt at beating the champion sprinter elect in the Prix de l'Abbaye de Longchamp on Arc day. Soba's defeat in the Diadem, in which she tired perceptibly in the last hundred and fifty yards, possibly suggested she was beginning to feel the effects of her tough campaign, and her chances of winning the Abbaye were made to look even bleaker after she had a bad flight across to France. Travelling is nothing like so hazardous an operation for racehorses as in earlier days—in the nineteenth century, for instance, the Derby winners Blue Gown and Kingcraft both failed to survive journeys to the States—yet difficulties can still arise, and when the plane carrying Soba met with air turbulence not long after taking off the filly ended up with a gash on her near-fore that required five stitches. There was even talk of withdrawing her but she duly lined up, bandaged on both forelegs, and in spite of everything excelled herself. Settled in third as Sky Lawyer and the two-year-old Sicyos set a fierce pace, she kept on with the utmost determination in the closing stages and eventually went down by only a length to her old rival, a further three ahead of Sicyos. Though Habibti was going away at the end she knew she had had a race with the second who, incidentally, appeared so full of herself that it took Nicholls at least two furlongs to pull her up. There's a saying to the effect that first is first and second is nobody but this is far from the truth. No disgrace attaches to finishing second to a filly of Habibti's quality—quite the reverse, and we have little doubt that Soba's Abbaye run, along with that at York, put her among the top dozen or so of her sex aged three and above we have seen running over sprint distances.

This would have been a fine achievement for any performer; for a filly who started her career at two by failing to finish in the frame in eight races on courses varying from Stockton to Hamilton it was a feat as astounding as it was praiseworthy.

Soba (ch.f. 1979)	Most Secret (ch 1968)	Crocket (ch 1960)	King of the Tudors
			Chandelier
		Parysatis (b 1960)	Darius
			Leidenschaft
	Mild Wind (b 1972)	Porto Bello (ch 1965)	Floribunda
			Street Song
		Mile Cross (br 1967)	Milesian
			Cross Wind

Soba's breeding, though it has more of the plebeian than the patrician in it, is not without interest for she is the daughter of a twin. Twins seldom do much on the racecourse owing to their usually being undersized—the 1823 Two Thousand Guineas winner Nicolo is the only known example of a classic-winning twin—but there is no shortage of female twins who have done well at stud. Condell, successful in the Royal Whip Stakes in 1983, is out of a twin and the 1982 One Thousand Guineas winner On The House and, ironically, Habibti are granddaughters of the same twin, Courtessa; others descended from twins include the top-class American runners Spectacular Bid and Lemhi Gold. On the track Mild Wind showed nothing at all, finishing in the frame just once when fourth of five in a poor seller, and at stud she has produced only one other winner, the three-year-old Jo-Andrew (by Joshua) who won over five furlongs at Newcastle in May. Generally Mild Wind has not had the best of mates for apart from Joshua and Soba's sire, the tough and genuine sprint handicapper Most Secret, she has visited Timber King once and Court Circus three times without any live produce to show for it. Following Soba's success it is to be anticipated Mild Wind will be sent to better stallions and she is reportedly in foal to Absalom. The grandam, a fair maiden at up to a mile and a quarter, has foaled one winner on the flat (the useful five-furlong

Mrs M. Hills's "Soba"

performer Puza), another disqualified winner and two successful jumpers while the third dam, lightly raced and no great shakes as a broodmare, was a half-sister to the Park Hill winner Almiranta from the family of the talented but, in this country, temperamental Amerigo.

As tough and consistent a filly as one could wish to find, and a great credit to her trainer, the strong-quartered Soba has been retired. We shall not be alone in following her stud career, which begins with a visit to Golden Fleece, with interest. The great essayist William Hazlitt once noted that attending the performance of a play was generally 'A source of the greatest enjoyment at the time and a never-failing fund of agreeable reflection afterwards.' This comment can aptly be applied to Soba's career; the 1984 season will not be the same without her and we doubt if we shall see her like for a long time to come. *D. Chapman.*

SOBER SAM 3 gr.g. Lock And Load 72–Seldom Sober 58 (Vimy 132) (1982 NR 1983 11s 12s 14d) big, narrow gelding; fifth living foal; dam won over 2m and also over hurdles; behind in maiden and minor races. *R. Voorspuy.* —

SO BRAVE 5 b.g. So Blessed 130–Bravade 81 (Blast 125) (1982 NR 1983 10.6s) ex-Irish gelding; first foal; dam won 1m seller; lightly raced on flat nowadays; stays 1m well; acts on firm going; taken to post early only start at 5 yrs in October; winning hurdler. *S. Mellor.* —

SOBRIQUET 2 b.f. Roan Rocket 128–Nimble Gate 64 (Nimbus 130) (1983 7fg) Apr 4; 7,200Y; half-sister to several winners, including very useful 1976 2-y-o 5f performer The Andrestan (by The Brianstan); dam won 5f seller at 2 yrs; in rear in 13-runner maiden race at Redcar in October. *Miss L. Siddall.* —

SOCHER 2 ch.f. Anax 120–Sarasail 58 (Hitting Away) (1983 5v 6f2 6f4 6f 7.2s) Mar 20; 1,050F, 1,900Y; small filly; half-sister to a winner abroad and several jumping winners, including very useful Sea Merchant (by Idiot's Delight); modest plater; stays 6f well (brought down over 7f); trained by A. Young first 3 outings and by G. Harman on fourth. *C. Spares.* — 48

SOCIETY BOY 3 b.c. Sir Gaylord–Miss Petard 113 (Petingo 135) (1982 7fg* 7fg2 1983 10g4 12v 12f* 12f 13.3f) strong, rangy, quite attractive colt, with a good, long stride; good fourth behind Shearwalk in Heathorn Stakes at Newmarket in April; needed to be fairly hard ridden to get on top after travelling well most of way when beating Neorion by 1½ lengths in 6-runner Churchill Stakes at Ascot in June (heavily-backed favourite); had stiffish tasks last 2 outings; suited by 1½m and promises to stay further; acts on firm going and seems unsuited by heavy; sold privately after final outing. *J. Tree.* — 105

SOCKS UP 6 ch.g. Sharpen Up 127–Mrs Moss 81 (Reform 132) (1982 8g 7s 8f4 8fg 8g4 8g3 8fg2 8f2 8d4 9d 9s4 8.2s 1983 10.8v2 8g* 10f4 8fg2 10g 8fg4 10f 10f3 8g 8s3 9fg 9d2 10fg3 10fg) leggy, somewhat lightly-made gelding; good mover; modest handicapper; won at Newbury in June (apprentices); stays 1¼m well; acts on any going; blinkered twice in 1980; good mount for an inexperienced rider. *F. J. Houghton.* — 81

SOCRATIC (USA) 3 ch.c. Exclusive Native–La Jalouse (Nijinsky 138) (1982 7f3 1983 8g* 10.1d4 8.2v 7fg 8f4 7f 7f2) strong, deep-girthed, attractive colt; beat Millfontaine in good style by 3 lengths in 29-runner maiden race at Newmarket in April; sometimes disappointing subsequently, but ran reasonably well when second in handicap at Redcar in August (ridden by 7-lb claimer); best form at up to 1m; probably not at his best on a soft surface. *F. Durr.* — 93

SOFICA 3 b.f. Martinmas 128–Skymarlin 75 (Skymaster 126) (1982 5f3 5fg 6fg 6s3 5g2 6f 6s 6s 1983 6d 7fg 5fg 6f) leggy, lightly-made filly; plater; best form at 5f; probably acts on any going. *M. Hinchliffe.* —

SO FINE 2 b.f. Thatching 131–Face Lift (Herbager 136) (1983 6f3 6fg* 6fg2) Feb 10; IR 94,000Y; half-sister to 2 winners, including Takachiho (by Don II), a very useful sprint winner at 2 yrs in Ireland who subsequently won at up to 1½m; dam won at 2 yrs in USA; ran well in 3 races at Phoenix Park, notably when winning £4,100 race in August by a short head from Tartan Sea and finishing ½-length second of 10 to Grey Dream under top weight in Oldtown Stud Stakes later in month; will stay 7f; has raced only on fast ground; useful. *D. O'Brien, Ireland.* — 96

SOFT IRON (FR) 2 ch.c. Sanhedrin–Piber 53 (Saintly Song 128) (1983 6f 7g 8.2f) Apr 2; 8,000 francs Y (approx £700); compact, fair sort; half-brother to a winner in Belgium; dam well beaten in 3 races at 2 yrs; blinkered, 8 lengths fifth of 11 to Nui Nui in seller at Haydock in September, final outing; sold 600 gns Doncaster October Sales. *N. Tinkler.* — 50

SO GOOD (FR) 3 b.c. Sukawa 124–Sosti (Misti IV 132) (1982 9.5g⁴ 9.5g* 1983 **116**
10.5g² 10.5g* 11g* 10g* 11g* 12g* 12g* 10fg 15s² 12g²) French colt; brother to a
minor winner and half-brother to another; dam ran only 3 times; one of the leading
middle-distance performers in French Provinces and won successive races at
Toulouse, Mont-de-Marsan and Bordeaux (3, including Derby du Midi) before
winning minor event at Evry in June; second afterwards in Prix de Lutece at
Longchamp in September (beaten 5 lengths by Galant Vert) and Grand Prix de
Bordeaux (beaten length by Full of Stars) in November; seems to stay quite well;
trained by R. de Tauzia until after seventh outing. *A. Fabre, France.*

SOHO 2 b.f. Camden Town 125–Solitude 129 (Nosca) (1983 5s 6s 6d) Apr 14; IR **63**
23,000Y; rather leggy filly; half-sister to 5 winners, notably smart 1979 2-y-o 6f
winner Lavinsky (by Ridan) and very smart French 5.5f to 9f winner Flash Light (by
Relko); dam won Prix Morny and French 1000 Guineas; little worthwhile form in
minor event and 2 maiden races. *B. Hanbury.*

SOIE GENTILLE 3 ch.f. Shantung 132–Ma Reine 89 (Grand Roi 118) (1982 6fg **59**
8s 7d 1983 11.7fg³ 13.1f 11.7f 15.5f² 14f³ 15g 17.1g⁴ 16d) workmanlike filly; clearly
needs a test of stamina. *R. Baker.*

SOIGNEUSE (USA) 3 ch.f. Tom Rolfe–Trim and Tidy (Sea-Bird II 145) (1982 **109**
5s² 7fg* 7g² 7f 1983 9.5s² 10v⁴ 10.5f 10g 10f⁴ 12s 9.2f 8d³) attractive though
rather lightly-made filly; in frame on several occasions, including in Prix Vanteaux
(neck second to Escaline) and Prix Saint-Alary at Longchamp and Prix de Psyche
(about a length fourth of 12 to Green Reef) at Deauville; ran creditably when 5
lengths sixth of 17 behind Escaline in Prix de Diane Hermes at Chantilly on third
start and was noted going on strongly at finish when close-up seventh of 18 behind
Royal Heroine in Prix de l'Opera at Longchamp on penultimate outing; stays 1¼m
(blinkered when below best over 1½m); probably acts on any going; sent to USA.
F. Boutin, France.

SOIXANTE QUINZE 2 b.f. Gunner B 126–Gallic Law 91 (Galivanter 131) (1983 **79**
7s 6g*) Apr 23; rather leggy filly; half-sister to 3-y-o Passionnel (by So Blessed)
and 3 winners, including useful sprinter Ferriby Hall (by Malicious); dam won twice
over 7f at 2 yrs; won 12-runner maiden race at Hamilton in September; should stay
7f. *J. W. Watts.*

SOLARES 3 br.g. Free State 125–Indian Wells (Reliance II 137) (1982 5s 5f 6fg **56**
7g 8.2s 7.2s 1983 11d⁴ 11fg* 12v⁴ 10f 13.8g) big, rather leggy gelding; made all in
selling handicap at Edinburgh in April (bought in 1,600 gns); probably stays 1½m;
suited by top-of-the-ground; blinkered final outing at 2 yrs; below form last 2
starts. *J. Berry.*

SOLAR GRASS 8 b.g. Veiled Wonder–Fair Marilyn (Macherio) (1982 5fg 9fg 5f **–**
5fg 6f³ 6fg³ 7.6f 6fg 5g 6d 1983 9s 5g 6g 5f 5f 6fg 5f³ 5.8h 5fg 5f 5h 5h⁴ 5g 6fg)
strong, fair sort; sprint handicapper; acts on any going; often blinkered; virtually
refused to race penultimate start; trained part of season by W. Charles. *M.
James.*

SOLARIUM 5 br.g. Scottish Rifle 127–Daydreamer 78 (Star Gazer 123) (1982 **–**
12d 15.5v² 10g⁴ 12g 1983 16s 15.5v 12fg) poor staying plater; sometimes
blinkered; sold 2,100 gns Doncaster September Sales. *W. Musson.*

SOLAR LIGHT 3 br.c. Nonoalco 131–Madina 119 (Beau Prince II 131) (1982 8g⁴ **–**
8g 1983 8d 8f 8fg³ 12f 11fg 12s) strong, sturdy, good sort; good mover; very
promising as a 2-y-o; below form in 1983 (reportedly operated on for an intestinal
blockage in March); blinkered second outing; sold to Mrs N. Smith 6,400 gns
Newmarket Autumn Sales. *W. Elsey.*

SOLAR TEMPTRESS 3 b.f. Status Seeker–Sundalgo 82 (Fidalgo 129) (1982 **45**
6fg 7f³ 7f 8.2g 8g 13.8f³ 10f⁴ 12fg 12.2d²) big filly; second in seller at
Catterick in October; stays 1½m but possibly not 1¾m; sold 2,100 gns Newmarket
Autumn Sales. *D. Morley.*

SOLBELLA 3 b.f. Starch Reduced 112–Dear Sol (Dear Gazelle 113) (1982 6fg 6s **–**
1983 9fg 8f) lightly-made filly; of little account. *D. H. Jones.*

SOLCHER 2 ch.c. Welham 94–Dear Sol (Dear Gazelle 113) (1983 6fg 7f) May **–**
24; small colt; brother to 1976 2-y-o 5f seller winner Solchella; dam of little
account; in rear in August in sellers at Haydock (missed break) and Wolverhampton
(blinkered). *D. H. Jones.*

SOLDBY 3 b.g. Connaught 130–My Mary 93 (French Beige 127) (1982 6fg 6d **–**
8.2fg* 8.2s² 1983 12d² 14.7d⁴ 12.3f⁴ 10f⁴ 11f) useful-looking gelding; stays quite
well; seems to act on any going; blinkered fourth start. *M. H. Easterby.*

SOLDIER ANT 3 ch.c. Brigadier Gerard 144–Hants 111 (Exbury 138) (1982 6fg 101
6f 1983 10g 10v² 10.5s³ 8f 10f 10s² 10fg* 10fg² 10fg⁴ 12d) strong colt; got off
mark at last when beating Roman Beach decisively by 3 lengths in £5,900 William
Hill Handicap at Ascot in September; in frame afterwards in similar races at
Newmarket (flashed tail and tended to wander when second to Deutschmark) and
Ascot (had no sort of a run when close fourth to Oratavo); had run well in goodish
company on occasions in spring, but ran the odd moderate race too; suited by
1¼m+; probably acts on any going. *C. Brittain.*

SOLEROF 5 b.g. Averof 123–Solhoon 74 (Tycoon II) (1982 NR 1983 8g 12.2fg) –
big, workmanlike gelding; poor maiden on flat but is a winning hurdler; blinkered
both starts at 5 yrs, looking sour on first occasion. *J. Thorne.*

SOLFORD (USA) 3 b.c. Nijinsky 138–Fairness (Cavan) (1982 6fg* 7fg* 1983 127
10g* 12f* 10f* 12g⁴)
More often than not the Eclipse Stakes has been instrumental in bringing about
the first meeting of the season in England between top three-year-olds and their
elders over middle distances; the Prix d'Ishapan, run slightly earlier, usually fulfills
a similar function in France. In 1983 the Coral-Eclipse, as it is known nowadays,
attracted an excellent field and promised to be highly informative, since it set the
three-year-olds Tolomeo, Muscatite, Guns of Navarone and Solford against the
older Stanerra, Time Charter, Prima Voce, Lobkowiez and Lafontaine. Tolomeo
and Muscatite represented current classic form at a mile—they were second and
third respectively in the Two Thousand Guineas—and Guns of Navarone current
classic form at a mile and a half—he finished fifth in the Derby, giving the
impression in doing so that a slightly shorter distance would suit him better. Of the
best two older horses engaged in the race Stanerra had recently won both the
Prince of Wales's Stakes and the Hardwicke Stakes at Royal Ascot while Time
Charter had been outstanding the previous season, on one occasion winning the
Dubai Champion Stakes by seven lengths from Prima Voce and on another giving
weight and a beating to Stanerra in the Sun Chariot Stakes. Then there was
Solford.
Solford was an exciting prospect, but very much an unknown quantity for all
that he was unbeaten in four races, two as a three-year-old. While some of his
trainer's horses had been well and truly in the limelight Solford had been brought

*Coral-Eclipse Stakes, Sandown—Solford holds off Muscatite (third from right) for his fifth
consecutive win. Tolomeo (left), Stanerra (stripes) and Guns of Navarone (almost
hidden by winner), finish close up*

along steadily, more or less in their shadow. A horse typical of his stable in several respects, a really good-looking, well-bred, high-priced American import, he had narrowly won minor races at the Curragh and Leopardstown in 1982 at odds of 5/2 on each time. Deprived at the last minute of his planned first run of the new season in the Ballysax Race at the Curragh in April when he was seen not to be himself in the paddock (the vet found him very slightly raised in temperature and erupting in a skin condition), Solford was sufficiently recovered to take part in the Craddock Advertising Race at Phoenix Park in the last week in May. His stable-companion Caerleon, who had run poorly at the Curragh the same day that Solford had had to be withdrawn, was also in the field; Solford received 8 lb from Caerleon, was ridden by the stable's number-one jockey Eddery and started even-money favourite, five points shorter than Caerleon who was at longer odds than one of the eight other runners, Alleged's unraced brother Delgado. Both Solford and Caerleon ran very encouragingly. They and the previously-unbeaten Branch Line fought out the finish well clear of the rest, Solford beating his stable-companion by three parts of a length with Branch Line a neck away; Solford disputed the lead all the way and stuck on well. After this Solford and Caerleon were sent to run in France, at Chantilly, Caerleon on the first Sunday in June, and Solford on the next. Each achieved his chosen objective, Caerleon the French Derby decisively and Solford the markedly less well-contested Prix du Lys over the same distance. Solford faced only five opponents, one of them another stable-companion South Atlantic; at 2/1 on coupled with South Atlantic he won easily from animals who neither before nor after played any significant part in the season. Perhaps the most newsworthy feature of the race was that Solford wore blinkers for the first time; why he wore them we don't know, he never wore them again.

And so the Eclipse Stakes promised a most interesting and informative contest. In the event its promise was only partially fulfilled since although we were given as exciting a finish as anyone could possibly desire the race left some obvious questions unanswered, not least that of how good were the three-year-olds, Solford in particular. Solford kept his unbeaten record but most of the field finished in a heap. Unfortunately, and unsatisfactorily, the race was run at a slow, false pace; mainly as a result Stanerra and Guns of Navarone failed to find a clear run, on top of that Time Charter was set too much to do. We have to say that if the race were re-run at a true pace we should expect either Stanerra or Time Charter to win. Be that as it may, the records will show that Solford won the only race that counts, becoming the thirteenth of his age to succeed in the Eclipse since 1946, the third from his stable following Pieces of Eight and Artaius; Ballymoss also won the race for O'Brien as a four-year-old. Looking particularly well in himself, Solford made the most of a fine ride by Eddery and from the moment he got his head in front going to the last furlong after racing close up from the start he always looked like holding on. It was a close thing though, an extremely close thing. Muscatite, Tolomeo, Stanerra, Guns of Navarone and Time Charter all finished well. For all her efforts Time Charter remained a length and a half adrift of the others at the finish, where Solford held on by a head, a head, a neck and a neck again.

Unsatisfactory though the Eclipse may be in certain respects there's no escaping the fact that it provides by far the most important piece of evidence available for judging Solford's merit. On it we feel we have done fairly by him and Tolomeo in regarding the pair as equals. Solford was certainly considerably better than he showed in his only subsequent race, the Great Voltigeur Stakes at York in August, for which he started second favourite at 15/8 behind the Derby winner Teenoso. He hardly ran at all. Disappointing in his coat beforehand (he showed traces of a rash again), he was already being niggled at after the field had gone three furlongs—surprising for a horse who had the pace to win an Eclipse. He never promised to improve, and his jockey was understandably easy on him when his chance of catching the first three had disappeared in the final quarter mile, with the result that Solford was beaten fully fifteen lengths behind Seymour Hicks. Solford never ran again. He has now been syndicated and retired to Winfield Farm, Lexington, Kentucky.

Solford (USA) (b.c. 1980)	Nijinsky (b 1967)	Northern Dancer (b 1961)	Nearctic Natalma
		Flaming Page (b 1959)	Bull Page Flaring Top
	Fairness (ch 1963)	Cavan (ch 1955)	Mossborough Willow Ann
		Equal Venture (ch 1953)	Bold Venture Igual

Solford, as stated, is a really good-looking, well-bred colt. Big and strongly-built like his sire Nijinsky, he cost 1,300,000 dollars at the Fasig-Tipton Kentucky

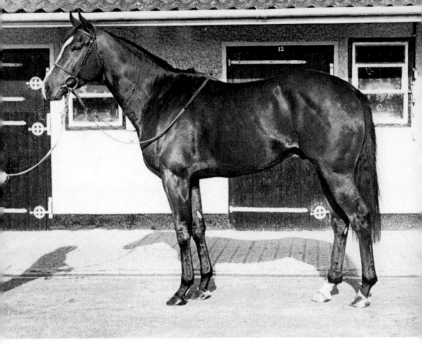

Mr R. E. Sangster's "Solford"

Selected Summer Yearling Sales. His dam, an unraced half-sister to the stakes winners Prove Out (a top-class middle-distance stayer), Saidam and Heartland, has produced six other winners. Among them are No Bias (by Jacinto), winner of the Grade 2 Vosburgh Handicap and San Carlos Handicap, and two fillies by Arts and Letters who were placed in the CCA Oaks, Equal Chance and No Duplicate. Fairness' foal of 1981, a filly by Vaguely Noble called No Designs, is in training in England with Hern having been purchased as a yearling for 550,000 dollars. There is a sister to Solford coming along called Ethics but there will be no more, for Fairness died in 1983. The second dam and third dam were also unraced half-sister or sister to stakes winners; the second dam Equal Venture, in fact, was a sister to an important horse in the history of the American Turf, the triple crown winner of 1946 Assault.

Solford was suited by middle distances. He raced on good ground twice and on firmer ground four times in a career that for its brevity resembles that of all too many high-class colts nowadays. Just as a matter of interest we looked up the complete racing records of all his American relatives named in the preceding paragraph. They provide food for thought. Prove Out made thirty-nine starts, Saidam twenty-eight, Heartland also twenty-eight; No Bias sixty, Equal Chance a mere eight, No Duplicate twenty-six; Assault no fewer than forty-two. Nijinsky, by the way, had thirteen races for Solford's stable, winning the first eleven. *V. O'Brien, Ireland.*

SOLIMILE 3 b.f. Solinus 130–Mile By Mile 92 (Milesian 125) (1982 5fg 5fg 7g 6s³ 1983 6s* 6s* 6d² 6d* 8g 7v 6s* 7f 6f 6s 7fg) smallish filly; improved and won small handicap at Doncaster, minor event at Leicester, handicap at Newmarket and £6,800 Leisure Stakes at Lingfield; made much of running on first 3 occasions, but **102**

got only up near line when beating Kirchner a head on last-named course in June; also finished good eighth of 18 to Ma Biche in 1000 Guineas at Newmarket but didn't run up to her best on her other starts; stays 1m but has plenty of pace and is effective at 6f; acts well on soft going; blinkered nowadays; off course almost 2 months before tenth start. *P. Kelleway.*

SOLITAIRE 3 br.f. Warpath 113–So Precious 100 (Tamerlane 128) (1982 6g 7d **49** 1983 12.2d³ 16v³ 14.7d 13.8g⁴ 16g 12f 18d² 16d³ 12g³ 12f) rather lightly-made filly; in frame in maiden races and sellers; needs a test of stamina; looked ungenuine final start; sold 1,600 gns Doncaster November Sales. *C. Thornton.*

SOLITARIO 2 ch.c. Derrylin 115–Mossy Girl (Ballymoss 136) (1983 8f) Mar 23; **–** 6,600F; sturdy, workmanlike colt; third produce; half-brother to 1m seller winner Poporinio (by Porto Bello); dam of little account; eighth of 14 in maiden race at Leicester in November. *A. Hide.*

SOLOMON (SPA) 6 b. or br.g. Old and Wise 121–Donna Callis (Don Carlos) **–** (1982 NR 1983 10f) Spanish-bred gelding; poor novice hurdler; tailed-off last in minor event at Brighton in July. *R. Howe.*

SOLVA 2 gr.f. Manado 130–Zelotta 87 (Zeddaan 130) (1983 5s 5d* 5d 5v 6f 5fg 7f* **62** 7h) June 3; 1,000F, 1,400Y; leggy, narrow filly; has a round action; fourth foal; dam won twice over 1m; successful in 5-runner maiden race at Newbury in April and in 17-runner claimer at Leicester in August; suited by 7f; blinkered fifth outing; sold 4,400 gns Newmarket September Sales, for export to Italy. *Mrs J. Reavey.*

SOLWAY WINDS 5 b.g. Windjammer (USA)–Maggie Mine 85 (Native Prince) **63 d** (1982 7f 7f 9g 8d 7f 1983 6d² 7d 6f³ 7f 6fg 8fg 8g 8f 10.2fg) strong, useful-looking gelding; poor handicapper; stays 1m; seems to act on any going; sold 1,500 gns Doncaster November Sales. *B. Wilkinson.*

SOME JET 5 ch.g. Some Hand 119–Jetador 73 (Queen's Hussar 124) (1982 8f 8g **53** 6g 7.6fg 8g⁴ 8fg⁴ 8.2v⁴ 1983 8.2v 10.6s 8d³ 9f⁴ 7.6fg⁴ 8g 10.4fg² 8.2f* 8d) neat gelding; plater; made all to win non-seller at Hamilton in August (apprentice ridden at 7-lb overweight); stays 1¼m; acts on any going; has run creditably when sweating up. *C. Crossley.*

SOMEL 5 b.g. Averof 123–Sygnome 53 (Precipice Wood 123) (1982 NR 1983 **–** 15fg) poor maiden; has worn blinkers. *J. S. Wilson.*

SOME OPTIMIST 3 b.f. Sousa 97–Craigallian Brig (New Brig 120) (1982 NR **–** 1983 9s 6d 5f) 380 2-y-o; small, strong filly; fourth foal; dam never ran; last in varied company, including selling. *K. Bridgwater.*

SOMERFOLDS 4 ch.f. Some Hand 119–Florica 80 (Floriana 106) (1982 8fg* 10f **–** 8.3g 8g 10v 1983 8f 10.1fg 10.8fg) dipped-backed filly; plater; stays 1m; sold 220 gns Ascot July Sales. *H. O'Neill.*

SOMERSDAY 4 b.f. Some Hand 119–Spring Day (Vic Day 126) (1982 10d³ 12g **–** 14f 14s 1983 12d) workmanlike filly; plating-class maiden; best run at 1¼m on soft ground. *M. Francis.*

SOMERSET BRIDGE (USA) 3 b. or br.f. Advocator–Harbour Queen (Young **70** Emperor 133) (1982 7d 8g³ 1983 9s 9d 10.8v 10.4g² 8f 10d*) lengthy, lightly-made filly; 20/1-winner of maiden race at Beverley in September (tended to hang right under pressure); evidently suited by 1¼m and some give in the ground; blinkered second, fourth and fifth starts; sent to USA. *S. Norton.*

SOMERS HEIR 8 b.g. Will Somers 114§–Treatisan 67 (Milesian 125) (1982 7s **40** 8d 8f 9g 8g 1983 8v 12s² 11.7d 12s 10f 10h) poor handicapper nowadays; evidently stays 1½m; goes well in the mud; occasionally wears blinkers; suitable mount for a boy. *D. Wintle.*

SOME SPARE 4 b.g. Track Spare 125–Some Say (I Say 125) (1982 8fg⁴ 8fg⁴ **–** 10fg 9g 10d 8s 1983 9d 10g 8fg) compact gelding; disappointing maiden; has twice been blinkered. *M. Smyly.*

SOME SUNNY DAY 3 br.f. Radetzky 123–Derry Willow (Sunny Way 120) (1982 **64** 5fg 6fg 7f 7g 8f² 8s⁴ 8.2s 1983 8s³ 10.2v⁴ 8s 8.5d⁴ 7h³ 8h 7fg 8h* 8d³ 8g) compact filly; beat Monaco Lady by ½ length in small maiden race at Chepstow in August and ran well next time; probably stays 1¼m; acts on any going; sweated badly and pulled hard in blinkers sixth start. *J. Benstead.*

SOME WOULD (USA) 2 b.f. One For All–Woodsome 117 (Runnymede 123) **86** (1983 5g² 6fg*) May 2; $20,000Y; small, slightly hollow-backed filly; second foal; closely related to 3-y-o Musical Sally (by The Minstrel); dam won 5 times at up to 6f at 2 yrs in USA and was a very useful stakes winner over 8.5f at 4 yrs in USA; ridden by 7-lb claimer, won 14-runner maiden at Brighton in October by 1½ lengths from Bobbie James; will be suited by 7f and 1m. *H. Candy.*

SOME YOYO 3 b.g. Lochnager 132–Katira 83 (Paveh 126) (1982 5f 5fg3 5g2 6f 5f3 5g 5g 1983 6s 5v2 7g* 6d* 5g4 6g 7fg 8f) strong gelding; good walker; won maiden race at Edinburgh and minor event at Hamilton in May; in rear last 3 outings, but twice had stiffish tasks; suited by 6f and 7f; probably acts on any going. *H. Bell.* **65**

SONDRIO 2 b.c. Nebbiolo 125–Needy (High Top 131) (1983 6f2 7fg4 6.3f 7s* 6d 8g*) Mar 22; third foal; half-brother to very useful 1982 2-y-o 5f winner Time's Time (by Whistling Deer); dam fairly useful winner over 6f and 7f at 2 yrs in Ireland; improved late in season and won 2 nurseries, beating Martina's Pearl 3 lengths at the Curragh and Royal Santa 2½ lengths at Leopardstown; had earlier run prominently for a long way when under 4 lengths fifth to Gala Event in Ballsbridge-Tattersalls Anglesey Stakes at former track in August; suited by 1m. *K. Prendergast, Ireland.* **101**

SONG MINSTREL 5 b.g. Song 132–Tribal Festival 65 (Tribal Chief 125) (1982 6f 6fg 6fg 6f* 6s 6d 6d 6fg2 6f4 7s 6s 7d* 1983 6s 7d 7d 6f 7f2 6f 7f 7f 9d 8.2fg 7g) strong, compact gelding; stays 7f; yet to prove he can handle very soft going, but acts on any other; usually blinkered; inconsistent. *M. Camacho.* **57**

SONG OF THE DAWN 2 b.f. Song 132–Gentildonna (Pieces of Eight 128) (1983 5s2 5g4 6f 6fg 8s) Apr 29; 9,000F, IR 22,000Y; rangy filly; good walker; long-striding mover; first produce; dam unraced half-sister to top-class sprinter Gentilhombre; plating-class maiden; probably stays 6f. *P. Cole.* **67**

SONGROID 3 b.f. Haveroid 122–Songs Jest (Song 132) (1982 5fg* 5fg 5f3 5f* 5g2 5d* 5g 1983 6s 5g 6d4 6s 5f 5f 6f 5f4 5g) lengthy, workmanlike filly; not so consistent as in 1982, but ran creditably occasionally; probably stays 6f; probably acts on any going; blinkered seventh outing. *A. Jarvis.* **80**

SONG TO SINGO 3 b.f. Master Sing 109–Song Book 85 (Saintly Song 128) (1982 5f 5d 5f 5g* 5d4 5g 5d 6s2 5d4 1983 6d 7v 6s 6f4 5f 6f 7f 7f 7g4 6fg 7fg3) small filly; plater; stays 7f; acts on any going; sometimes blinkered; sold out of J. Etherington's stable 1,100 gns Doncaster September Sales after ninth outing. *R. Carter.* **49**

SONIC METEOR 3 b.c. Star Appeal 133–Knightside (Graustark) (1982 8s2 10s 8d4 1983 8d 10fg 10.1f 8d) close-coupled, workmanlike colt; behind in varied company, wearing blinkers on last occasion; stays 1m; sold to BBA 400 gns Newmarket Autumn Sales. *J. Ciechanowski.* **–**

SON OF A GUNNER 3 ch.g. Gunner B 126–Swakara 92 (Porto Bello 118) (1982 5fg 6d 5fg3 7g 5d 6g 1983 6v* 7v 7fg4 7fg2 7f 8g 8g) compact colt; 4-length winner of minor event at Warwick in April; good second in apprentice handicap at Lingfield in July; stays 7f; acts on any going. *S. Mellor.* **65**

SON OF KANDY (USA) 2 br.c. Our Native–Brief Escar (Up Spirits) (1983 5s2 5v3 5fg* 5f 6f* 5f 6fg4 6d) Feb 20; $55,000Y; compact, quite attractive colt; good walker; half-brother to 2 winners in North America, including a useful Canadian stakes winner; dam stakes winner at up to 1m in Canada and is sister to 2 stakes winners, one the dam of good French sprinter Bold Apparel; won minor events at Windsor (made virtually all) in June and Salisbury in July; blinkered, poor last of 6 in Lingfield nursery in October on final appearance; stays 6f; best form on fast ground. *D. Elsworth.* **87**

SON OF MANADO 3 br.g. Manado 130–Pigmy (Assagai) (1982 5fg 5fg3 6f 7f 1983 10s 10fg 12f) leggy gelding; disappointing maiden; behind in seller final start; has been tried in blinkers. *A. Jarvis.* **–**

SON OF RAJA (USA) 3 ch.c. Raja Baba–Couronne de Fer (Iron Ruler) (1982 5fg 5g2 5f2 6d 5fg2 1983 5s 5fg 5fg 5f3 5h 6fg 8f 8f3 8h2 8f2 8g 8g) really strong colt; has a sharp action; still a maiden, but capable of fair form on his day; suited by 1m on top-of-the-ground nowadays; hampered eleventh start. *J. Bethell.* **80**

SOOLYN 4 b.f. Dominion 123–Lyndy Sue 70 (Major Portion 129) (1983 5s 5fg 6f 6f) Mar 15; robust, good sort; half-sister to several winners here and abroad, including quite useful 1m to 1¼m handicapper Kildoon (by Kalydon); dam disappointing; soundly beaten in minor and maiden events; not seen out after August. *D. Whelan.* **–**

SOOSJOY 2 ch.f. Sexton Blake 126–Perennial Twinkle (Continuation 120) (1983 7g* 8g3) Apr 22; IR 13,000Y; lightly-built filly; half-sister to 1m to 1½m winner Indulgence and winning Irish middle-distance stayer Always Smiling (both by Prominer) and to a winner abroad; dam Irish 2-y-o 5f winner; won 10-runner minor event at Catterick in October; odds on, beaten 2 lengths by Strathearn in 12-runner similar race at Redcar the following month; will stay 1¼m. *Sir Mark Prescott.* **89**

Esher Cup, Sandown—So True stays on well to land this valuable handicap from Shareef Dancer

SOOTY'S PAL 2 b.c. Tachypous 128–Myna Tyna 85 (Blast 125) (1983 5d 5d³ 5d **45**
5s 5d³ 6d 6f 6fg⁴ 7h⁴ 7f 8f 8d) Feb 6; 320Y; dipped-backed colt; poor plater;
stays 1m; often blinkered. *J. Parkes.*

SORELLANO (USA) 2 b.c. Soy Numero Uno–Miss Arellano (Sadair) (1983 7g) **72 P**
Apr 21; $62,000Y; big, rangy, good sort; has a good, long stride; second foal; dam,
sister to smart French middle-distance performer Air Peruvian, was smart sprinter
in USA, looked very green when short-priced favourite for 17-runner maiden race
at Leicester in September and was beaten 7½ lengths into fifth place behind All Hell
Let Loose after missing break; fine type of colt, bound to be better for the
experience, and must be noted for a similar event. *G. Harwood.*

SORREL LADY 2 b.f. Forlorn River 124–Belle (Continuation 120) (1983 5f 5f 6f **–**
7g 6fg) May 10; 300Y; lightly-built filly; in rear in varied races, including in a seller;
blinkered final outing. *T. Kersey.*

SO TRUE 3 b.f. So Blessed 130–Veracious 86 (Astec 128) (1982 5f² 5d* 7fg 7v³ **116**
6g 1983 8v* 10.5s² 12fg 11g 12d² 12fg) tall, lengthy, rather narrow filly;
25/1-winner of Esher Cup (Handicap) at Sandown in April, staying on well to beat
Shareef Dancer by 2 lengths; ran on steadily when second in Musidora Stakes at
York in May and St Simon Stakes at Newbury in October, going down by 8 lengths
to Give Thanks in former and by 2 lengths to Jupiter Island when 20/1 and having
first race for 3 months in latter; apparently well in at weights, couldn't quicken on
the firmish ground when tenth of 25 behind Asir in William Hill November Handicap
at Doncaster on final outing; suited by 1½m; goes particularly well in the mud. *G.
Balding.*

SOUND AND HAPPY 3 br.f. Diamonds Are Trump 108–Safe And Happy (Tudor **–**
Melody 129) (1982 6g 6fg 5v 1983 6d 8s⁴ 8.3s) good-topped filly; plater; stays
1m. *A. Ingham.*

SOUNDING 2 b.f. Mill Reef 141–Never Can Tell (Tambourine II 133) (1983 6h **–**
7f⁴) Mar 21; leggy, rather unfurnished filly; fifth foal; half-sister to a winner in Italy
by Bustino; dam from family of Never Too Late II; showed only a little ability in
maiden race at Nottingham and minor event at Brighton in August. *M. Stoute.*

SOUND OF THE SEA 4 b.f. Windjammer (USA)–Running Cedar (Bryan G.) **89**
(1982 6f² 6f² 6g 5fg⁴ 6f 5fg 6fg 6f* 6s 1983 6s 7s³ 6g 5.3f² 6h 6f* 5h*)
useful-looking filly; won handicaps at Goodwood in July (from Memoria In Eterna)
and Sandown in August (made most to beat Young Inca by ¾ length); stays 7f but is

785

better at shorter distances; acts on any going but is particularly well suited by fast ground; effective with and without blinkers; has won for an apprentice. *W. Wightman.*

SOUNDS BEAUTIFUL 2 b.f. Music Boy 124–Rare Coral (Rarity 129) (1983 5g 6fg 5g 5d) Mar 7; 2,100Y; good-bodied filly; first foal; dam poor maiden; in rear in autumn maiden races. *G. Blum.* —

SOURCE OF SUCCESS 3 b. or br.f. Balidar 133–Sweet Shop 62 (Sweet Revenge 129) (1982 5f 7d* 1983 6s* 7g² 7s³ 6.3f⁴ 5fg 6fg 5g 7g³ 6d³ 7g 6d⁴) IR 1,550Y; first foal; dam won over 13f; 16/1 and apprentice ridden when beating Hot Princess by 1½ lengths in 10-runner BBA Sprint Stakes at Phoenix Park in May; ran creditably afterwards, and was placed in varied company on same course (3 times) and at the Curragh; stays 7f; acts on any going; sold 25,000 gns Newmarket December Sales. *L. Browne, Ireland.* 101

SOUTH ATLANTIC 3 b.c. Mill Reef 141–Arkadina 121 (Ribot 142) (1982 8fg² 6s* 1983 10g 12f 12f⁴ 12f*) 640,000Y (record price for yearling sold in Europe to end of 1981); well-made, medium-sized colt; half-brother to smart Irish middle-distance winner Encyclopedia (by Reviewer) and useful 1979 Irish staying 2-y-o Forlene (by Forli); dam, placed in 3 classics, is sister to high-class stayer Blood Royal and closely related to Gregorian; favourite when making all to beat Steel Duke by a head, pair clear, in 8-runner Blandford Stakes at the Curragh in August; had also made running when less than 2½ lengths fourth of 8 finishers behind Condell in Royal Whip Stakes at the Curragh the previous month, best previous effort; suited by 1½m; acts on any going; sent to USA in autumn and was reportedly being syndicated, eventually to stand at Barracks Stud, Virginia. *V. O'Brien, Ireland.* 99

SOUTHERNAIR 3 b.g. Derrylin 115–Port La Joie (Charlottown 127) (1982 7fg 7g 7fg 1983 10v 10fg) quite attractive, well-made gelding; ran respectably when fifth of 21 behind Hawa Bladi in minor event at Kempton in May; soundly beaten only subsequent start (September); stays 1¼m. *P. Haynes.* 67

SOUTHERN DANCER 4 b.c. Connaught 130–Polyandrist 92 (Polic 126) (1982 8g⁴ 8f⁴ 10f 12fg 7fg 1983 8fg³ 8.2s 8fg⁴ 7v³ 6s 7fg⁴ 6d 7d 10f) tall, fair sort; has a round action; stays 1m; suited by some give in the ground. *J. Parkes.* 55

SOUTHERN DYNASTY 2 b.f. Gunner B 126–Northern Dynasty 65 (Breeders Dream 116) (1983 5s 5g 6g 7g³ 7.6d²) Mar 30; first foal; dam won over 1m; quite a moderate filly; placed in modest company at Lingfield in September and October; will be suited by 1m; blinkered second outing; trained by J. Winter first 2 starts. *P. Mitchell.* 77

SOUTHERN SMILES 2 b.f. Orange Bay 131–Shaky Puddin (Ragstone 128) (1983 8g) June 11; tall, sparely-made filly; first foal; dam poor daughter of sister to smart sprinter Ubedizzy; eighth of 17 in maiden race at Leicester in September. *M. Usher.* —

SOUTHERN VENTURE 2 b.f. Sandy Creek 123–Latona (Royal Record II) (1983 5f³ 5f² 5fg 5g² 6g 5g) May 18; IR 8,000Y; small, fair sort; half-sister to Norwegian 2000 Guineas and Derby winner Rheinsteel (by Rheingold), also successful over 1½m in this country; dam, half-sister to useful sprinter Trillium, won in Norway; runner-up in maiden race at Catterick in July and nursery at Edinburgh in September; should be suited by 6f; blinkered final start. *S. Norton.* 72

SOVEREIGN CELLAR 5 gr.g. Sovereign Path 125–Kessella (Le Levanstell 122) (1982 12d 1983 10g 10f² 8f 10f 10f) plater; stays 1¼m; acts on firm going. *Miss L. Siddall.* —

SOVEREIGN FLAME 5 ch.m. Supreme Sovereign 119–Flaming Peace 104 (Queen's Hussar 124) (1982 7g 8f² 1983 7d) poor performer; stays 1m; acts on any going; suitable mount for an apprentice; has been tried in blinkers; has worn bandages; sold 400 gns Doncaster October Sales. *A. Hide.* —

SOVEREIGN HONEY 2 ch.f. Royal Match 117–Agio (Aglojo 119) (1983 6fg 8g 8.2g* 8fg) Apr 22; IR 1,800F; workmanlike filly; third living produce; half-sister to a bumpers winner by Crash Course; dam won twice at 1½m in Ireland and over hurdles; trotted up by 10 lengths in 7-runner seller (bought in 2,600 gns) at Hamilton in September; will stay 1¼m. *N. Guest.* 69

SOVEREIGN ISLAND 4 gr.g. Supreme Sovereign 119–Practicality (Weavers' Hall 122) (1982 8s 7g 1983 12s 12d 13d 10g 8g 9g) tall, leggy gelding; poor handicapper; blinkered last 3 outings; has worn bandages; sold 1,750 gns Newmarket Autumn Sales. *N. Guest.* —

SOVEREIGN LACE 3 gr. or ro.f. Oats 126–Sovereign Sunset 65 (Sovereign — Path 125) (1982 5f 5fg 6f 6fg 6d 6s⁴ 1983 8d³ 10.5v 8f 8f 8f 8.2h 10.4g 10f 8h 13g 12s) rather lightly-made, fair sort; plating-class maiden; appears to act on any going; sometimes blinkered; inconsistent; trained until after fourth start by R. Hollinshead. *D. Smith.*

SOVEREIGN PAUL 4 gr.g. Supreme Sovereign 119–Joshua's Daughter 61 **58** (Joshua 129) (1982 NR 1983 7s 8s² 10.2g*) fair sort; plater; bought in 1,050 gns after winning at Bath in June; stays 1¼m; acts on soft going. *J. Fox.*

SOVEREIGN PEARL (FR) 3 b.f. Nonoalco 131–Perla 107 (Young Emperor — 133) (1982 6g 6d² 7d² 1983 7v 7f 7f 7fg) compact filly; didn't recover her 2-y-o form in 1983; stays 7f; blinkered final outing. *H. T. Jones.*

SOVEREIGN REEF 2 ch.c. Take a Reef 127–Brocton Queen (Supreme **63** Sovereign 119) (1983 5v* 5d³ 6fg 7f 7fg 8.2h 8fg³ 8.2g 8d 8fg⁴ 7fg) Mar 1; 1,250Y; fair sort; third foal; dam showed little worthwhile form; sold out of B. McMahon's stable 2,700 gns after winning 13-runner seller at Bath in May by 5 lengths; in frame in varied races afterwards, including a selling nursery; stays 1m; probably acts on any going; blinkered ninth outing; sold 2,600 gns Doncaster November Sales for export to Barbados. *J. Bethell.*

SPACED TO RUN (USA) 2 b.f. Run Dusty Run–Space Sailing (Sail On-Sail On) **89** (1983 6fg² 6fg³ 7.3d) Mar 29; neat, attractive filly; has a quick action; second foal; half-sister to smart 3-y-o middle-distance filly Ski Sailing (by Royal Ski); dam won 5f maiden race at 2 yrs; placed in quite useful company at Ascot in the autumn, notably ½-length second to Rappa Tap Tap in Blue Seal Stakes; ran poorly (thirteenth of 14) in Rochford Thompson Newbury Stakes; should stay 1¼m. *B. Hills.*

SPACEMAKER BOY 3 br.c. Realm 129–Glounanarrig (Dike) (1982 5fg* 5d² **67** 5f³ 5f⁴ 7g 6fg 7g 5s 6g³ 6s 1983 5s² 5s* 5s 5g² 5.1g⁴ 5f 6g 5.1s³ 5fg) good-bodied colt; poor walker; has a round action; odds-on winner of small handicap at Ripon in April; best at sprint distances; acts on any going, but is well suited by soft; blinkered last 2 outings. *G. Fletcher.*

SPACE ROCKET 3 gr.g. Roan Rocket 128–Davina (Darius 129) (1982 7g 6g 7fg — 8s 1983 8d 8.2v 12v) big, plain gelding; seemingly of little account. *M. Pipe.*

SPANISH BOLD 3 b.f. Tower Walk 130–Jill Somers 76 (Will Somers 114§) (1982 **78** 8f 6d 1983 8v* 8d³ 10fg 10.1fg 8.3f 8.3fg 8d³ 8g 8.2g 7.6d* 8g² 8.2fg) fair sort; good mover; accounted for big fields when winning maiden race at Kempton in April and handicap at Lingfield in October; inconsistent however; promises to stay 1¼m; yet to prove she can handle really firm ground, but seems to act on any other; sometimes bandaged. *M. Ryan.*

SPANISH CAVALIER 3 ch.g. Grundy 137–Escorial 110 (Royal Palace 131) **72** (1982 NR 1983 11.7v 10.1f³ 11.7h* 12f⁴) big, lengthy, workmanlike gelding; half-brother to 2 winners, including fairly useful 1980 2-y-o 7f and 1m winner Royal Heritage (by Welsh Pageant); dam very useful at up to 10.5f; very comfortably landed the odds in poor maiden race at Bath in July; about 8 lengths fourth of 5 to Asir in minor event at Salisbury the following month; will stay beyond 1½m; acts on hard going; sold to J. Baker 4,400 gns Newmarket September Sales. *R. Hern.*

SPANISH ESTATES 3 b.f. Firestreak 125–Lead Me On (King's Troop 118) **65** (1982 7g 7g 1983 8d 10.8g⁴ 9f² 12fg 10g) neat filly; second in 9f handicap at Ripon in August, best effort. *J. Toller.*

SPANISH LINE 2 b.c. Gay Fandango 132–Ottoline 59 (Brigadier Gerard 144) — (1983 8fg) Feb 10; IR 5,000Y; lengthy colt; first foal; dam stayed 1½m; behind, slowly away, in 28-runner maiden race at Newmarket in October; sold 3,400 gns Newmarket Autumn Sales. *J. Hindley.*

SPANISH PLACE (USA) 3 b.c. Greek Answer–Candy Aglo (Candy Spots) **110** (1982 6d* 1983 8s² 8g 7fg 6fg 7f 7g² 8g* 8fg² 9d*) rangy, attractive colt; beat Linda's Fantasy by ¾ length in quite well-contested minor event at Goodwood in September (always appeared to be going just the best) and landed the odds rather unimpressively in 3-runner event at York the following month; second on 3 other occasions, in Craven Stakes at Newmarket (beaten a neck by Muscatite), City of York Stakes (went down by ½ length to Able Albert) and 3-runner Petition Stakes at Newmarket again (beaten 12 lengths by Legend of France); stays 9f; possibly unsuited by very firm going but seems to act on any other. *B. Hills.*

SPANISH POINT 4 ch.g. Malacate 131–Bracken Girl (Skymaster 126) (1982 5g **64** 6.5g 6.5v 5s 5g³ 5d³ 5d³ 6fg 5f² 6g² 5fg* 5h³ 5g 5g 5.8f 6g 5d 5g⁴ 6s 5s 1983 6v 6v 6v 6g* 6g⁴ 5f 5f³ 6f 5fg 6fg³ 6d 6g) big, heavy-bodied gelding; has a round action;

won handicap at Brighton in May; stays 6f; seems to act on any going; best in blinkers; inconsistent. *D. Sasse.*

SPANISH RAINBOW 2 b.f. Ribston 104–Spanish Lamp (Don Carlos) (1983 5g) — first foal; dam of little account; backward, tailed off in small race at Catterick in September. *M. Reddan.*

SPANISH WAR 7 br.m. Warpath 113–Corrida 96 (Matador 131) (1982 NR 1983 — 16s 12g) of little account. *R. Voorspuy.*

SPARKABLE 3 br.g. Sparkler 130–Amicable 73 (Bold Ruler) (1982 NR 1983 8g — 8f 8fg 12.2d 12g) 8,200F, 6,000Y; little worthwhile form; tailed off when blinkered final outing; sold to C. Read 975 gns Ascot December Sales. *M. Usher.*

SPARK CHIEF (USA) 4 b.c. Chieftain–Heavenly Spark (Habitat 134) (1982 92 second on only start in USA 1983 5g 7f 8f 5.3fg* 5f* 5h3 5f* 5fg) sturdy, good-quartered ex-American colt; first foal; dam ran once at 2 yrs; had a good year, winning minor event at Brighton and Epsom; quickened well to beat Manilow decisively by 1½ lengths in valuable Vladivar Vodka Trophy on last-named in August; clearly best at around 5f; acts on hard going. *F. Durr.*

SPARKLER SPIRIT 2 b.g. Mandamus 120–Swallow Street (My Swallow 134) 82 (1983 6fg 6f 8d 7.6fg3 7g) Mar 28; fair sort; first foal; dam poor maiden; 3 lengths third of 19 to Lexis in maiden race at Lingfield in October; should stay 1m. *A. Pitt.*

SPARKLING BROOK 2 ch.f. Sparkler 130–Partridge Brook 109 (Birdbrook 57 110) (1983 5fg 5fg 5f 7h 6g4 7.2g3) Mar 23; smallish filly; has a sharp action; second foal; half-sister to 1m and 10.8f winner Fort Garry (by Relkino); dam won from 5f to 1¼m; modest plater; should stay 1¼m. *B. Hills.*

SPARKLING FORM 4 ch.g. Gold Form 108–Light Spark 73 (Twilight Alley 133) 63 (1982 5f 7g4 5g 5f3 6fg4 5f4 5fg 5fg 6f 7f 5g* 6s* 5s 5d 6s 1983 6g 6s 6s 5d3 6g 5fg 6f4 5g3 6fg 6h 5f3 6d 5f 5f 5f 5g 5fg 6f 6fg 7fg2) strong gelding; poor handicapper; second in seller on final start; only just stays 7f; acts on any going; sometimes blinkered; exported to Barbados. *R. Whitaker.*

SPARKLING MOMENT 3 ch.c. Hot Spark 126–Parez 67 (Pardao 120) (1982 82 5fg 5.8g2 6f* 6f3 6fg2 6fg* 6f* 6d 7d 6g 1983 6g 6f4 7f 7g) small colt; suited by 6f; acts well on firm going and is possibly unsuited by dead. *D. Arbuthnot.*

SPARKLING SIN 4 b. or br.c. Sparkler 130–Sinkit (Sing Sing 134) (1982 10f4 — 8f3 8.2f* 8fg 8g 8d 8.2f* 8g3 8.2g 8d4 1983 10f) tall, good-bodied colt; stayed 1¼m; acted on any going; dead. *J. Hardy.*

SPARKLING SONG 2 b.f. Sparkler 130–Song of Gold 85 (Song 132) (1983 5v4 67 5v4 5f* 5.1f4 5.8h* 7h 7g) Mar 24; 3,200F, IR 4,200Y; small, sharp sort; first foal; dam sprinter; won sellers at York (bought in 5,200 gns) and Bath (retained 1,750 gns); suited by 6f; acts well on very firm ground; inconsistent. *P. Cole.*

SPARKS 3 ch.g. Hot Spark 126–Arethusa 94 (Acropolis 132) (1982 7f* 6g2 7fg 8f 94 1983 7s 6s 8f*) good-bodied, quite attractive gelding; returned to form in handicap at Newmarket in July, winning gamely by ½ length from Airship; evidently needs a sound surface; often blinkered; won over 9f in USA. *W. O'Gorman.*

SPARKY 3 ch.g. Sparkler 130–Nyota 97 (Reform 132) (1982 5f3 5.8f 7f 7g 1983 — 12s 8s) compact gelding; no worthwhile form. *Dr A. Jones.*

SPARTAN BAZAAR 2 ch.c. Native Bazaar 122–So Unlikely 60 (Blast 125) — (1983 5d 6g 7f) May 8; lengthy, rather sparely-made colt; brother to winning sprinter Casbar Lady; little worthwhile form in maiden races. *S. Matthews.*

SPARTAN FLAME 3 ch.f. Owen Anthony 102 or Saucy Kit 76–Spartan Lass — (Spartan General 109) (1982 NR 1983 12g 10fg 12g) third foal; dam novice hurdler/chaser; tailed off in minor events. *J. Gifford.*

SPEAK NOBLY (USA) 2 b.c. Speak John–No Clouds (Noblesse Oblige 99) 96 (1983 5d 6g 6f 5f2 5f* 6g* 6fg) Apr 7; lengthy colt; good mover; first foal; dam stakes-placed winner of 3 sprint races; successful twice in the summer, landing the odds by ¾ length from Melaura Belle in maiden event at Ripon and putting up a game effort under top weight to beat Caerhagen a short head in £2,600 race at Chester; suited by 6f; acts on firm going. *N. Guest.*

SPECIAL FRUIT 2 b.f. Monsanto 121–Fleurs 106 (Green God 128) (1983 5v* 60 5d 5g) Jan 15; neat filly; first foal; dam useful 2-y-o sprinter; won maiden race at Ayr in March; trained by A. Young first 2 starts; exported to Algeria. *M. Lambert.*

SPECIAL LEAVE 3 b.c. Mill Reef 141–Light Duty 113 (Queen's Hussar 124) — (1982 7g3 7g3 7v* 1983 10v) attractive, well-made colt; showed considerable

788

promise in 1982 and won Hyperion Stakes at Ascot; ran only once at 3 yrs, finishing about 6 lengths sixth of 7 behind Gordian in very slowly-run Guardian Classic Trial at Sandown in April; injured on gallops in August and destroyed. *I. Balding.*

SPECIAL SETTLEMENT (USA) 2 b.c. Riva Ridge–Laura Bell (Jacinto) 72
(1983 6f 7f 7g 7fg) Apr 7; $105,000Y; quite attractive colt; half-brother to several winners, one a minor stakes winner and another stakes placed; dam won 5 sprint races; quite a modest maiden; form only on second outing. *G. Hunter.*

SPECIAL TREAT (USA) 3 b.f. Elocutionist–Beerbohm Special (Beau Max) 80
(1982 NR 1983 9s 12d* 12fg⁴ 13fg⁴ 14fg 12g 11g*) tall, rather leggy filly; half-sister to 4 winners, including Special Tiger (by Terrible Tiger), a smart stakes winner at up to 1¼m; dam ran 4 times unplaced; successful in maiden and minor races at Hamilton; stayed 13f (blinkered when well beaten over 1¾m); was sometimes bandaged; dead. *S. Norton.*

SPECIAL VINTAGE 3 ch.c. Nebbiolo 125–La Cita (Le Levanstell 122) (1982 93
NR 1983 16g 12f² 14.6f* 14fg² 14fg*) IR 25,000Y; 5,800 2-y-o; smallish, sturdy colt; first foal; dam won from 1½m to 1¾m in Ireland; gamely won maiden race at Doncaster in July and handicap at York in September; suited by a test of stamina; acts on firm going, but gives impression he'll be seen to even better advantage on easier ground; likely to win more races. *J. Fitzgerald.*

SPECTACULAR BEAUTY 2 ch.f. Monseigneur 127–Juhayna 78 (Diplomat 84
Way) (1983 5f 5g* 5g* 6fg⁴ 6d⁴ 5fg) Apr 19; quite attractive, useful-looking filly; second foal; half-sister to American 3-y-o 6f claimer winner Nashwane (by Balidar); dam in frame twice over 7f from 3 outings; won 10-runner maiden race at Warwick in July; ran well in nurseries on next 2 outings; suited by 6f. *G. Lewis.*

SPECTACULAR SKY 5 b.g. African Sky 124–Orient Queen (King's Troop 118) –
(1982 5fg³ 6g 6f 6f 6g 5g 1983 6d 5v 5.1g 5fg 6h 6fg 6g) rangy gelding; poor handicapper; unlikely to stay beyond sprint distances; blinkered fifth start; often has tongue tied down; sold 360 gns Doncaster November Sales. *M. Chapman.*

SPEED BABY (USA) 3 b.f. Diplomat Way–Stormy Ruler (Sir Ruler) (1982 5g* –
5f³ 6f 6f 1983 6s 10.2f) tall, useful sort; little form since winning at Windsor as a 2-y-o; not sure to stay 1¼m; possibly not suited by firm ground. *P. Cole.*

SPEEDO 4 ch.g. No Loiterer 90–Dominique III (Evening Trial 94) (1982 NR 1983 –
10.2d 10fg 12g 12g) seems of little account. *W. Wharton.*

SPEED OF MUSIC (USA) 3 b.c. Pago Pago–Baby Lullaby (Royal Serenade 89
132) (1982 5s² 8s³ 1983 7d³ 7s* 7g* 8f 7f) compact, attractive colt; apprentice ridden when successful in maiden race at Leicester in April (made all and beat Welsh Glory by 5 lengths) and minor event at Brighton in May (beat Montrevie by ½ length); stays 7f; evidently needs some give in the ground. *P. Cole.*

SPEED OF SOUND (USA) 3 br.g. Super Concorde 128–Chatter Box 118 70
(Ribot 142) (1982 7g 7s⁴ 7g 1983 8g 10fg 7f 8f³ 8f 7fg 7s) strong, rangy gelding; possibly stays 1¼m; exported to Singapore. *B. Hanbury.*

SPEEDPOST 2 ch.g. Dublin Taxi–Berostina 88 (Ribero 126) (1983 5g 6fg 6f) –
Mar 8; 6,800F; rather lightly-built, compact gelding; half-brother to 1980 2-y-o 6f winner Holdall (by Manacle); dam, winner over hurdles, was at her best at 2 yrs on flat; behind in maiden races, twice last. *E. Eldin.*

SPEED UP 3 ch.f. Mount Hagen 127–Lady Bequick 81 (Sharpen Up 127) (1982 –
NR 1983 6fg 8f 10.2g 6g) useful-looking filly; first foal; dam ran only at 2 yrs when successful twice at around 5f; sixth of 17 behind Magnetic Field in 1m minor event at Salisbury in August; sold out of J. Tree's stable 3,500 gns Newmarket September Sales; behind afterwards (blinkered final start). *I. Wardle.*

SPEEDWELL 2 ch.f. Grundy 137–Bluebell 103 (Town Crier 119) (1983 6fg² 8fg) 85
Feb 4; lengthy, rather lightly-made filly; good mover; first foal; dam, out of half-sister to Queen's Hussar, ran only at 2 yrs when successful over 6f and 7.3f; ¾-length second of 7 to On Oath in maiden race at Haydock in August; sweating, had stiff task and never threatened when 14 lengths last of 5 to Lear Fan in £6,000 event at Newmarket later in month; should be well suited by 1m. *R. Hern.*

SPERRIN MIST 2 ch.f. Camden Town 125–Miss Maverick 76 (Vilmorin) (1983 83
5d* 5f 6fg⁴ 6g 7g) Mar 31; IR 6,000Y; close-coupled, fair sort; half-sister to numerous winners, including useful 1968 2-y-o Mistral (by Whistling Wind); dam placed at 2 yrs; won 17-runner maiden race at Sandown in May at 50/1; well beaten in nurseries last 2 outings; stays 6f; acts on a firm and a soft surface. *R. Williams.*

SPEY BRIDGE 2 ch.g. Mill Reef 141–Strathspey 105 (Jimmy Reppin 131) (1983 75
7f 7.2g³ 7fg) Mar 14; quite attractive gelding; first foal; dam, winner from 6f to

1m, is sister to very smart Joking Apart; quite a moderate maiden; will be better suited by 1m+; possibly requires some give in the ground; gelded after final outing. *I. Balding.*

SPICE MARKET 2 ch.c. Native Bazaar 122–Mustardflower (Mustang) (1983 **60** 5v 6g 6f 7g 7g) Feb 4; fair sort; brother to Chancery Bloom, successful at up to 1m; dam won over jumps; showed a little ability in varied company; blinkered final start. *S. Matthews.*

SPICY STORY (USA) 2 b.c. Blushing Groom 131–Javamine (Nijinsky 138) (1983 **98** p 8fg 8d²) Feb 25; big, well-made colt; good mover; second foal; half-brother to American 3-y-o Java Coast (by Forli); dam very smart stakes winner at up to 11f; put up a very pleasing effort when head second of 9 to Gambler's Cup in £4,400 event at Goodwood in September, holding a good position throughout; will stay at least 1¼m; the type to continue improving and is sure to win races. *I. Balding.*

SPIDERS WEB 8 b.m. Big Deal 105–Dreynes Valley (Irish Dance 120) (1982 – NR 1983 12f²) winning jumper; having first race on flat when remote second to Misty Halo in lady riders race at Chepstow in September. *J. Webber.*

SPIGOT SHAFT (USA) 3 b.c. Upper Nile–Reckless Date (Nashua) (1982 NR **89** 1983 10.6v 12d 10.5s 10.2v³ 8.2g* 12f 10.6fg² 12s 10.2fg 12fg) $33,000Y, resold 21,000 gns Y; strong, compact, good-bodied colt; has a round action; second foal; half-brother to Irish 1½m and 2m winner Proven Date (by Prove Out); dam, from same family as Malinowski, Gielgud and Try My Best, won 2 sprint races; landed the odds in maiden race at Hamilton in June; also placed in minor event at Doncaster and handicap at Haydock; stays 1½m; probably unsuited by really firm going, but acts on any other; had very stiff task third start and was off course more than 3 months before eighth (moved poorly to start). *J. Hanson.*

SPIKEY BILL 6 ch.g. Souvran 98–Whitton Lane (Narrator 127) (1982 12d 10g³ – 15.5f 10f 1983 8.2v) tall gelding; plater; possibly stays 1½m; acts on soft going; blinkered once. *H. O'Neill.*

SPILL THE BEANS 2 ch.f. Import 127–Miss Buckingham (Royal Palace 131) **49** (1983 5v² 5f³) Apr 23; poor plater; dead. *R. Hannon.*

SPILT MILK 3 ro.f. The Go-Between 129–Dick's Yarn 80 (Peter's Yarn 106) – (1982 5fg 5g 5f 1983 5s) small filly; evidently of no account. *D. Ringer.*

SPINDLE BERRY 3 gr.f. Dance In Time–Chokeberry (Crepello 136) (1982 **89** 5fg² 5fg* 6f 5g 7.6s³ 7v⁴ 1983 8.5g 8f 10f) quite attractive, rangy filly; had stiff tasks and ran respectably in well-contested handicaps at Epsom and Ascot in June; beaten when hampered only subsequent start; should stay 1¼m; seems to act on any going; sold to BBA (Ire) 44,000 gns Newmarket December Sales. *C. Horgan.*

SPINELLE 2 ch.f. Great Nephew 126–Jacinth 133 (Red God 128§) (1983 7g⁴) **73** P Feb 19; rangy, deep-girthed filly; third live foal; half-sister to 2 winners by Habitat, including fairly useful 6f winner Jacquinta; dam best 2-y-o of 1972 and a high-class miler at 3 yrs; weak in market, given a very easy time once first 2 were beyond recall but kept on very nicely to finish nearly 9 lengths fourth of 21 to Mahogany in £4,600 event at Newbury in September; the type to improve a good deal and win races. *G. Harwood.*

SPINNAKER RUN 3 b.c. Sassafras 135–Golden Windlass 79 (Princely Gift 137) – (1982 NR 1983 8d 10d 10.1fg 8f 7.6g) 3,400Y; stocky colt; half-brother to 2 winners, including miler Haddfan (by Lorenzaccio); dam won over 1m; in rear in varied races; blinkered final outing; sold 560 gns Ascot November Sales. *P. Haynes.*

SPINNER 4 b.f. Blue Cashmere 129–Penny Pincher 95 (Constable 119) (1982 7f **52** 5g³ 5fg* 5f² 5fg 5g 6s 1983 5d 6f² 6f 5f 6f² 6fg 7f) sturdy non-thoroughbred filly; good mover; sprint handicapper; stays 6f; acts well on fast ground; blinkered last 3 starts; sometimes starts slowly. *S. Norton.*

SPIN OF A COIN 5 bl.h. Boreen (Fr) 123–Lovely Linan (Ballylinan 118) (1982 **83** 12s 11f³ 14fg² 12fg* 12g 11f² 12g⁴ 12.5g² 12g 12s 1983 12v 11v⁴ 12g 12f³ 11.5f⁴ 11f 16fg 12d 12g) strong, rangy, attractive horse; fair handicapper; running-on 5½ lengths third to Grand Unit in Bessborough Stakes at Royal Ascot; suited by 1½m+ and a strongly-run race; acts on any going; blinkered at Royal Ascot and on penultimate outing; trained by C. Horgan first 6 starts. *A. Moore.*

SPIRAL 3 b.f. Auction Ring 123–Primed (Primera 131) (1982 NR 1983 11f) – 26,000Y; half-sister to 3 winners, including 1¼m and 1¾m winner Georgian Girl (by Prince Tenderfoot); dam well bred but of little account; in rear in maiden race at Newbury in July; sold 10,000 gns Newmarket December Sales. *M. Smyly.*

SPIRITED GALA (USA) 2 br.f. Cutlass–Baggala (Bagdad) (1983 5f 5g) —
$17,500Y; first foal; dam ran only once; soundly beaten in maiden races at Sandown
in July and Warwick in October. *H. Candy.*

SPITALFIELDS (USA) 2 b.c. Icecapade–Engaged (Promise) (1983 5s 7f⁴ 7f   98
8d* 8fg 8g³ 8d*) Mar 16; $120,000Y; big colt; walks well; third foal; half-brother to
fair 1982 2-y-o 5f winner Hadi's Hope (by Run Dusty Run); dam, winner of 6 small
races at up to 1m, is half-sister to smart 1978 French 2-y-o Ice Cool (by Icecapade);
made short work of his 10 rivals in maiden race at Brighton in September; won
24-runner nursery at Warwick the following month; suited by 1m; best form on an
easy surface; sold 32,000 gns Newmarket Autumn Sales, reportedly to race in
Florida. *G. Harwood.*

SPIV'S RIGHT 2 ch.f. Mount Hagen 127–Right Minx (Right Tack 131) (1983 7f   66
8d* 7fg⁴) Apr 21; IR 3,000Y; second foal; dam won 7 times at up to 9f in France;
justified favouritism in good style in 19-runner apprentice maiden seller at Warwick
(bought in 850 gns) in October, winning by 2½ lengths from Free Light Laser;
respectable fourth in nursery at Leicester later in month; suited by 1m. *G. Huffer.*

SPLASH OF RED 2 gr.f. Scallywag 127–Our Swanee 62 (My Swanee 122) (1983   —
5s 5v 5s 7h 7f 8g) big, workmanlike filly; first known foal; dam second in 5f seller at
2 yrs; behind in maiden and minor events. *D. C. Tucker.*

SPLIT ACES 2 b.c. Vilgora 113–Primeapple (Primera 131) (1983 6h 6g³ 6s*)   73
Mar 13; fair sort; half-brother to 2 winners, including stayer Our Bara Boy (by
Baragoi); dam of little account; bought in 1,650 gns after winning 20-runner seller
at Haydock in October by 2½ lengths from Goldliner Bonus; may well stay 7f; acts
well on soft going. *P. Brookshaw.*

SPOILT FOR CHOICE 5 b.g. The Brianstan 128–Song of May 79 (Sing Sing   65
134) (1982 6s* 6g³ 6fg 6f⁴ 6f² 7g 6g 6f³ 7f 7g 6f 6s 6g 7s³ 1983 8v 6v 8s* 8v 6d 8fg
7f³ 6f² 6f² 7f² 7f³ 6fg 7f* 7f 6h³ 6g² 6fg² 6f³ 7g) neat gelding; poor mover; plater;
attracted no bid after winning at Ripon in April; won non-selling handicap at
Catterick in August; effective at 6f and stays 1m; acts on any going; sometimes
blinkered but is effective without. *D. Chapman.*

SPORTS HEADLINES 2 b.f. Take a Reef 127–Vilna 81 (Vilmorin) (1983 5s 6s   64
8fg) Jan 27; 2,400F; sparely-made filly; half-sister to several minor winners; dam
won over 1¼m; having first race since May, 7-length fifth of 11 to Miami Star in 1m
maiden event at Edinburgh in November; should stay 1¼m; trained first 2 outings
by J. Spearing. *J. Etherington.*

SPOT THE PATCH (USA) 3 b.c. Mr Leader–Spotter (Double Eclipse 125)   88 d
(1982 6fg 1983 12d 12g 12s² 10g 12f 11g 10.6s 12d) close-coupled colt; heavily
gambled-on second favourite in minor event at Lingfield in May but was caught
close home and beaten ½ length by High Hawk (near 20 lengths clear); faced stiff
tasks on some of his other starts too, but was well beaten in ordinary maiden
company last time out; stays 1½m; probably acts on any going. *M. Haynes.*

SPRIGHTLY WILLOW 4 b.f. Native Bazaar 122–Woodland Promise (Philemon   —
119) (1982 6f³ 5f 5fg 5fg 5fg 1983 5.8g 7.6g 6fg 6f) poor maiden; best run at 6f. *P.
M. Taylor.*

SPRING-ANN 2 b.f. Workboy 123–Elspeth Anne 68 (Pardao 120) (1983 5fg 5g   58
5d³ 5fg 5f* 5fg⁴ 5f 6f 5g 5g) Apr 15; 1,550Y; fifth living foal; dam showed a little
ability at 2 yrs; won 10-runner seller at Catterick in July (no bid); showed form
subsequently only on next outing; should stay 6f; acts on firm going; often sweats
up; blinkered 3 times, including when successful; has also worn a hood; retained
380 gns Doncaster October Sales. *W. H. H. Williams.*

SPRING COTTAGE 3 b.g. Rouser 118–Flying Florrie 74 (I Say 125) (1982 NR   —
1983 8s 12v 12d) small gelding; second live foal; half-brother to winning stayer
Chemin de Guerre (by Warpath); dam successful hurdler; appeared to shape quite
well in 1m seller at Thirsk in April, but ran as if failing to see trip out over 1½m on
both subsequent outings (despite his stout pedigree). *M. H. Easterby.*

SPRING CRACKER 8 ch.m. George Spelvin–Whizzbang 56 (Roan Rocket 128)   —
(1982 NR 1983 9f) poor plater. *J. Townson.*

SPRING FREE 3 ch.f. Godswalk 130–Living Free 81 (Never Say Die 137) (1982   69
5g 1983 7.2fg* 9fg 8.5f 7fg 8g) small, lightly-made ex-Irish filly; half-sister to 3
winners, including fairly useful 1981 2-y-o 6f winner Atossa (by Artaius); dam,
half-sister to Free State, stayed 1½m; quickened up well when winning maiden
event at Haydock in July, only form; should stay 1m; blinkered final outing; sold
10,000 gns Newmarket December Sales. *D. Arbuthnot.*

SPRINGLASS 3 ch.f. Redundant 120–Olibanum 61 (Frankincense 120) (1982 5fg 6f 1983 14fg 12f) leggy, sparely-made filly; tailed off in maiden and minor races. *W. Stubbs.* —

SPRINGLE 2 b.f. Le Johnstan 123–Summersoon 89 (Sheshoon 132) (1983 6s 6f 6f 7f⁴ 7fg 8g* 8.2s 7fg) Apr 19; 3,000Y; poor mover; half-sister to a minor winner and 2 winning hurdlers; dam stayed 1½m; stayed on well to win 13-runner maiden race at Edinburgh in October by 1½ lengths from Carado; suited by 1m; possibly not at her best on soft going. *R. Hollinshead.* **83**

SPRING PASTURES 2 b.g. Thatching 131–Jenny 99 (Red God 128§) (1983 5g 5d* 6d³ 5fg⁴ 5f* 6f³ 5f³ 6fg 5g² 5fg³ 5fg) May 13; 20,000F; robust, good-quartered gelding; good walker and mover; half-brother to 3 winners, including fairly useful middle-distance performer Inishlacken (by Connaught); dam won at up to 7f in England and France; successful in maiden race at Leicester in May and nursery under top weight at Folkestone in July; also placed 5 times, on penultimate appearance good third in £5,600 nursery at Newmarket in September; better suited by 5f than 6f; yet to race on very soft ground but acts on any other; tough and consistent; gelded at end of season. *J. Winter.* **102**

SPRING PURSUIT 2 b.c. Bay Express 132–April Days 75 (Silly Season 127) (1983 6f) Apr 25; 6,200Y; second living foal; dam, daughter of Oaks second Maina, won over 10.4f; badly hampered at start and in circumstances ran creditably when remote eighth of 17 to Water Moccasin in minor event at Windsor in August; will stay 7f; should leave this form behind. *P. Cole.* – p

SPRING ROSE 2 br.f. Blakeney 126–Saulisa 108 (Hard Sauce 131) (1983 6f 6f 7f) Apr 30; 72,000Y; neat, strong filly; half-sister to 5 winners, notably good sprinters Saulingo (by Sing Sing) and Music Maestro (by Song) and smart 1975 2-y-o Outer Circle (by My Swallow); dam sprinter; no sign of ability in maiden events. *J. Benstead.* –

SPRINGS TO MIND 2 b.f. Miami Springs 121–Racy Lady (Continuation 120) (1983 6f) May 13; IR 2,500F, 1,000Y; second foal; dam won over 9f and 1½m in Ireland; always well behind in 13-runner seller at Doncaster in July. *D. Thom.* –

SPRINGTIME DOUBLE 2 br.g. Take a Reef 127–Linton Spring 84 (Khalkis 127) (1983 5v 5d 6f 7f 6f 9fg 7.2s 8fg) May 17; 600F, 2,000Y; fair sort; poor plater; stays 7f (pulled hard over 9f); probably unsuited by firm going; blinkered seventh start. *M. Lambert.* **49**

SPRITEBRAND 3 br.g. Workboy 123–Benedetta da Castello (St Paddy 133) (1982 5f⁴ 5f³ 5fg³ 7f 7f⁴ 7d 8f³ 8f 1983 10d 8f 8f* 10g* 9f 10f² 11s 10.6g) lengthy gelding; won maiden race at Beverley in July and handicap at Ayr in August; stays 1¼m; acts on firm going; blinkered once in 1982; suited by forcing tactics. *M. H. Easterby.* **74**

SQUASH COURT 3 b.g. Orange Bay 131–First Court 82 (Primera 131) (1982 NR 1983 16g) half-brother to 1981 2-y-o 7f winner Garfunkel (by Music Boy); dam 1½m winner; close up for 1¼m when eighth of 19 to Glenanna in maiden race at Lingfield in July. *Mrs R. Lomax.* –

SQUIRES GOLD 2 br.c. Broxted 120–Squires Girl (Spanish Gold 101) (1983 5d 5fg 6f) May 16; heavy-topped colt; second foal; brother to smart sprinter Jonacris; dam never ran; behind in June maiden races at Leicester, Nottingham and Doncaster. *P. Felgate.* –

STACEY'S FOLLY 2 b.f. Queen's Hussar 124–Corneater (Skymaster 126) (1983 5v 5fg 5f 7f 6fg 7f) Apr 19; 620Y; fair sort; in rear in sellers and a maiden auction event. *D. Chapman.* –

STAFFORDSHIRE KNOT 8 ch.g. Welsh Pageant 132–Wrekinianne 96 (Reform 132) (1982 NR 1983 12s) poor handicapper; used to wear blinkers. *D. Gandolfo.* –

STAGE COACH 3 b.c. Luthier 126–Glass Slipper 100 (Relko 136) (1982 7d 1983 11s⁴ 12g) tall, close-coupled colt; showed promise when fourth to Balladier in maiden race at Newbury in April (trained by H. Cecil at time) but was well beaten in an apprentice event at Chepstow in October on only subsequent start. *B. Palling.* **94** ?

STAGE LIGHTS 2 br.f. Connaught 130–Dazzling Light 116 (Silly Season 127) (1983 6fg) May 15; half-sister to fairly useful 7f to 1¼m winner King's Glory (by Royal and Regal); dam, smart over 7f and 1m, is half-sister to Welsh Pageant; backward, out of first 10 of 23 in maiden race at Newmarket in October; should do a good bit better in time. *H. Cecil.* – p

STALY'S PET 4 b.f. Mummy's Pet 125–Stalybridge 88 (The Brianstan 128) (1982   **51**
5fg 5fg[3] 6d 5d[3] 7g 6f* 6g 6f 7d 1983 5d 5fg[4] 6f 6f 7f 5f[4] 5f[2] 5f 6g 5fg* 5d[3] 6f 7fg)
strong filly who carries plenty of condition; narrowly won handicap at Beverley in
September; has been beaten in sellers; stays 7f but is better at shorter distances;
seems to act on any going; best in blinkers. *Hbt Jones.*

STAMINA 2 b.f. Star Appeal 133–Swift Harmony 107 (Elopement 125) (1983 7f[4]   **78**
8g[3]) Feb 26; close-coupled filly; good mover; sister to Hungarian Oaks and St
Leger winner Star and half-sister to winners here and abroad, including Harmonise
(by Reliance II), a very useful performer at up to 1½m; dam middle-distance
handicapper; in frame in maiden races at Salisbury and Leicester in September;
shapes like a thorough stayer, and will be well suited by 1¼m+. *R. Hern.*

STAMPY 2 ch.c. Sallust 134–Caer-Gai 103 (Royal Palace 131) (1983 7.6fg 7g[4] 8f)   **62**
Apr 9; 6,000Y; close-coupled colt; third foal; dam, daughter of 1000 Guineas
winner Caergwrle, won over 1m; 8 lengths fourth of 10 to Ready Wit in minor event
at Chepstow in October; should stay 1m. *C. Brittain.*

STANERRA 5 ch.m. Guillaume Tell 121–Lady Aureola (Aureole 132) (1982 10s[2]   **128**
10s 8g 10fg[4] 10g* 10f[4] 12f[3] 12fg[3] 12g[3] 10fg[4] 10g[2] 12v 12f[4] 1983 9d 10d* 10fg* 12f*
10f[4] 10g* 12f 12f*)
    To a list of things that improve with age including, according to a Spanish
proverb, oil, wine and friends, can now be added the name of Stanerra who has
worthy claims to be regarded as one of the best of her sex trained in Ireland over
the last twenty-five years. Unbroken at two and seen out only twice at three when
trained by Bolger, Stanerra has since improved out of all recognition and as a
five-year-old showed form not far behind that displayed by the outstanding
Irish-trained Gold Cup winner Gladness at the same age in 1958. Overall the career
of this admirably tough, consistent and enthusiastic performer has been an object
lesson in the value of keeping horses in training until they reach full maturity, and it
would be pleasant, though probably naive, to think her fine record might encourage
some owners in future not to pack their horses off to stud prematurely.
    Immense credit for Stanerra's achievements must be given to her owner-
trainer Frank Dunne, a successful businessman who took out a licence to train in

Prince of Wales's Stakes, Ascot—Stanerra accounts for Sabre Dance decisively

1982 and has pursued a marvellously adventurous policy with his mare. The easy winner of a handicap at the Curragh early on at four, Stanerra ran in top company for the rest of the season and did well, finishing in the frame in seven races, notably the Hardwicke Stakes (third to Critique), the Sun Chariot Stakes (three quarters of a length second to Time Charter) and the Japan Cup (fourth behind Half Iced). Though we rated her a smart filly at the end of the year it would have required the qualities of a clairvoyant to forecast the extent to which she would come on over the winter. Her first start as a five-year-old, in the Earl of Sefton Stakes at Newmarket, revealed no improvement at all for she ended up tailed-off last to Ivano, but the Brigadier Gerard Stakes at Sandown in May showed a very different Stanerra. Ridden for the first time by Rouse who gets on with her so well, she was never far behind, came with an impressive run to lead a couple of furlongs out and always had the measure of Ivano in the closing stages, winning by a length. Incidentally, quite why the stewards did not see fit to inquire into this turn round in form is beyond our understanding. It is reasonable to assume Stanerra hadn't come to herself in time for the Newmarket race, yet it would still have been worthwhile to ask Dunne for an explanation to clarify a matter that might look inexplicable to those not well versed in the peculiarities of racehorses and the difficulties of training them.

Good as Stanerra's victory was it could hardly be seen as exceptional since she received 9 lb from the runner-up, and in the Prince of Wales's Stakes on the first day of Royal Ascot she started equal third favourite in a market headed by two who finished behind her at Sandown, Sabre Dance (fourth) and Erin's Hope (third). The fast ground clearly suited Stanerra (one of the best movers we saw all year) extremely well and she put up a spectacular performance. Towards the rear until half a mile from home after a rather tardy start, she then made rapid progress, luckily obtaining a clear run up the rails, and once in front under two furlongs out soon left the others for dead, beating Sabre Dance with great ease by two lengths. The Prince of Wales's Stakes had evidently taken little out of Stanerra and to the surprise of some commentators Dunne decided to bring her out again three days later for the Hardwicke Stakes. The Hardwicke field was a good one, the nine other runners including the Coronation Cup winner Be My Native, the Jockey Club Stakes winner Electric, Jalmood, fresh from a Group 1 success in Italy, and Old Country, but Stanerra won in scintillating style, showing herself just as effective at a mile and a half as at a mile and a quarter. We have seldom if ever seen a runner cut down the leaders in a top race as Stanerra did rounding the home turn; while all her opponents were being pushed along she cruised past Old Country and Lafontaine on the bridle and went for home with a relish that was a joy to behold. Electric, under very strong pressure, tried his hardest to reduce the deficit and drew twelve lengths clear of third-placed Be My Native without ever presenting a serious threat to Stanerra who had only to be pushed out for a thoroughly convincing length-and-a-half success. The time broke the course record set by Grundy in his magnificent duel with Bustino in the 1975 King George, and it speaks volumes for Stanerra that she was able to travel smoothly throughout a race run at such a punishing gallop.

The extent to which racing has changed over the past century is highlighted by the fact that Stanerra's two wins at Royal Ascot, and the enterprise of her trainer in running her twice, appeared altogether out of the ordinary. The shape of the Royal meeting has admittedly altered over the years, for in the nineteenth century some

Hardwicke Stakes, Ascot—a second Royal Ascot win for Stanerra, who produces a tremendous turn of foot to beat Electric

Joe McGrath Memorial Stakes, Leopardstown—another victory for the tough Irish mare; Eddery on Salmon Leap (behind Wassl on the rails) has to ride without irons

of the races were relatively uncompetitive with small fields, but even so it seems remarkable that in only one year during the period 1875 to 1899, namely 1892, did a horse fail to chalk up a double. Indeed, on a number of occasions more than one managed the feat – in 1876 four did – and the list of horses concerned includes such great performers as Doncaster, Isonomy, Tristan (twice) and Ormonde (twice), while as a matter of interest in 1896, when the Prince of Wales's Stakes was restricted to three-year-olds, Shaddock carried off the two races Stanerra was to win. Many more horses, of course, ran twice or even three times without achieving a double. Compare this with the position nowadays under which it is increasingly rare for a horse to run, let alone win, more than once at any Royal meeting – from 1946 to 1982 only Trelawny and Mountain Cross, both out-and-out stayers, entered the winner's enclosure there twice in the same week although Arthur, successful in the Prince of Wales's Stakes and fourth in the Hardwicke in 1971, came within striking distance of the double Stanerra was to achieve. The common belief that when things change they usually change for the worse seems all too true in this particular area, and although it is to be hoped Stanerra's successes and the fighting policy adopted with her may do something to persuade more owners and trainers to follow suit there is certainly no reason for confidence on that score. Those involved with thoroughbreds today tend to pamper the best horses in a way that would have been incomprehensible to their nineteenth-century predecessors and is, as far as we can see, highly undesirable, for with certain reservations there is much to be said for an ancient Arab adage that goes 'The horse is created to run; without this he is as worthless as a wooden frame.'

On the crest of a wave, Stanerra next lined up for the Coral-Eclipse at Sandown but in a rather unsatisfactory race her run of success came to an end. Though it can be dangerous making excuses for beaten horses we are far from convinced that the Eclipse would have had the same result on a re-run since the best member of the field, Time Charter, could finish only sixth after being given too much to do in a race run at a false gallop to halfway while Stanerra failed to find a clear run in the straight, eventually finishing strongly to be under a length fourth to Solford. Stanerra missed the King George VI and Queen Elizabeth Diamond Stakes owing to slight muscle trouble and when reappearing in the Joe McGrath Memorial Stakes at Leopardstown in September – the only time racegoers in Ireland saw her at five – she reportedly needed the run. The race proved otherwise for she produced her usual bright turn of foot once round the home turn, led a furlong and a half out and went on to defeat the Irish Two Thousand Guineas winner Wassl

795

emphatically by two and a half lengths going away. The good French colt General Holme came in third with the odds-on Salmon Leap, attempting to maintain the O'Brien family's stranglehold on the contest, back in fifth after an unhappy run which had seen his jockey riding without irons because one of them or a leather had broken as the stalls opened. On the evidence of the Trusthouse Forte Prix de l'Arc de Triomphe Salmon Leap would have given Stanerra something to do at Leopardstown but for this mishap. Soon close up after overcoming another slowish start, Stanerra lay second to Sun Princess for much of the Longchamp straight but could do no more in the last hundred and fifty yards and ended up about two lengths behind All Along, beaten also by Sun Princess, Luth Enchantee, Time Charter and Salmon Leap who caught her in the last strides.

Dunne planned an ambitious late-autumn campaign for his mare, taking in the Rothmans International, Turf Classic, Washington International and Japan Cup but because of continuing muscle trouble and a blood disorder Stanerra ran in just the last which provided a memorable conclusion to her season. The Japan Cup, inaugurated in 1981, has attracted quite a few good non-Japanese contestants, among them Mairzy Doates, successful in 1981, Frost King, John Henry and the first four in 1982, Half Iced, All Along, April Run and Stanerra. Besides Stanerra the field of sixteen in 1983 included seven local horses, notably the Emperor's Cup winner Kyoei Promise, the good New Zealand colt McGinty, the Park Hill and Premio Roma winner High Hawk from England, the St Leger second Esprit du Nord from France and Half Iced and Erins Isle from the States. As in the previous year spectators were treated to a tremendous finish with Stanerra, only third favourite behind High Hawk and Esprit du Nord, producing a storming run in the straight to lead near the line and win from Kyoei Promise (who broke down towards the end), Esprit du Nord, Half Iced and McGinty; the distances were a head, the same, half a length and a neck. This victory took Stanerra's earnings for the season to over £294,000—not bad pickings for a mare who cost 5,000 guineas as a yearling in Ireland.

Stanerra (ch.m. 1978)	Guillaume Tell (ch 1972)	Nashua (b 1952)	Nasrullah
			Segula
		La Dauphine (b 1957)	Princequillo
			Baby League
	Lady Aureola (ch 1964)	Aureole (ch 1950)	Hyperion
			Angelola
		Lady Godiva (ch 1948)	Royal Charger
			Princess Toi

Fortunately the rangy Stanerra is considerably tougher than her sire Guillaume Tell who won his first three starts, including the Churchill Stakes and Gordon Stakes, before breaking down in the Prix Foy. He has not been a great

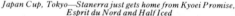

Japan Cup, Tokyo—Stanerra just gets home from Kyoei Promise, Esprit du Nord and Half Iced

Mr F. Dunne's "Stanerra"

success at stud, with the good Irish miler Tellurano his best other runner, and in 1981 he was sent to the States where he has been standing at Manor Brook Farm in Kentucky at a fee of 5,000 dollars. Stanerra is a half-sister to two French winners, including the smart middle-distance colt Padarek (by Sanctus), out of the French mile-and-a-quarter winner Lady Aureola. The grandam, one of six winners out of the unraced Princess Toi, seemed best at six furlongs though she ran second in the Irish One Thousand Guineas; her eight winners included No Fiddling, successful in the Blue Riband Trial.

Not long after the Japan Cup Dunne talked of retiring Stanerra and sending her to either General Assembly or Mill Reef, but in the event he has decided to keep her in training with the Coral-Eclipse as one of her principal targets providing all goes well. As a matter of interest Gladness, though she finished second to Alcide in the King George, did not run up to her best as a six-year-old and it is to be hoped Stanerra doesn't follow her example. That is in the lap of the gods; what can be said is that if Stanerra trains on and keeps her form more big races look sure to come the way of a mare who has already done a magnificent job in brightening up racecourses all over the world. *F. Dunne, Ireland.*

STANLEY THE BARON 2 b.c. Monsanto 121–Petard 112 (Mummy's Pet 125) **91** (1983 5v* 5d* 5s* 5s⁴ 5f 5f 5fg) Mar 14; IR 14,000Y; well-grown, rangy colt; good mover; second foal; dam won five 5f races, including 3 at 2 yrs; made much of running to win 3 times in the spring, maiden race at Nottingham (by 3 lengths), minor event at Brighton (by 5 lengths) and Salisbury Stakes (held on by ¾ length from odds-on Carabineer after being 3 or 4 lengths clear entering final furlong); beat only one home in his subsequent races; evidently needs the mud; sold BBA 8,000 gns Newmarket Autumn Sales. *K. Brassey.*

STAR ALLIANCE 5 b.m. Big Morton 85–Wet and Windy (Babu 117) (1982 — 8.2s* 8f⁴ 7f 10.6f 9g 1983 7d 9d 8d 12fg) plater; stays 1m well; probably acts on any going. *R. Morris.*

STARAVIA 3 b.c. Star Appeal 133–Fire Dance (Habitat 134) (1982 NR 1983 7d **83** 12d 10s 8.5d 7fg 8fg 10f³ 12fg⁴ 9f 10f 10g*) medium-sized, fair sort; third foal; half-brother to 1980 2-y-o 5f winner Disco Dancing (by Record Token); dam never ran; 40/1 and ridden by 7-lb claimer, seemed to show much improved form when beating Waterhead a length in 20-runner maiden race at Sandown in October (carried head very high); inconsistent previously, and had run in sellers; suited by 1¼m+; blinkered sixth outing; retained by trainer 5,400 gns Newmarket Autumn Sales. *F. Durr.*

STAR BREAKER 2 ch.c. Nebbiolo 125–Clearing Mist 62 (Double Jump 131)   **68** (1983 6f 6h 7fg 8fg³) Mar 26; IR 16,000F, 6,200Y; lengthy, useful-looking colt; half-brother to 3 winning sprinters, including fair Wyddial Park (by Tarboosh); dam half-sister to high-class sprinter Mountain Call; showed ability in maiden races and a valuable seller; stays 1m; acts on hard going. *P. Cole.*

STAR CHANCE 2 b.c. Comedy Star 121–Rue Talma § (Vigo 130) (1983 5v 6f⁴   **53** 6f) May 27; 2,600F, IR 2,100Y; half-brother to a minor winner and a winner abroad; dam left at start on 3 of her 4 outings; plating-class maiden; not seen out after August. *R. Hannon.*

STAR CHARTER 3 gr.g. Comedy Star 121–Charter Belle 60 (Runnymede 123)   **59** (1982 5f² 6f⁴ 6f 8.2fg⁴ 7s 8d 1983 10f² 10.8g³ 10h) leggy gelding; good mover; suited by 1¼m+ and a sound surface. *J. Hardy.*

STAR COVE 4 ch.f. Porto Bello 118–Your Star (On Your Mark 125) (1982 6g 6fg   — 6fg 5d 1983 5f) workmanlike filly; poor plater; sold 380 gns Doncaster August Sales. *A. Balding.*

STARELA 3 gr. or ro.f. Starch Reduced 112–Anthela 76 (Acropolis 132) (1982 6d   — 8f 6fg 6d 5g 1983 6fg 6f) lengthy, rather lightly-built filly; no worthwhile form; fell when blinkered final outing. *J. Wilson.*

STAR FLEET 5 ch.g. Record Token 128–New Way 103 (Klairon 131) (1982 11.5f   **61** 14g 16g 1983 10s 14fg 12f 15.5f² 15.5f* 16.5f) compact, lightly-made gelding; useful at his best but has deteriorated; comfortably won small race at Folkestone in July; suited by a test of stamina; seems to act on any going; inconsistent; front runner. *P. Kelleway.*

STARGAZE 3 b.c. Busted 134–Star of Bagdad 95 (Bagdad) (1982 7d 1983 10.5s⁴   **75** 11d* 12fg 13fg) strong, lengthy, good-bodied colt; beat Snowy River a neck in maiden race at Redcar in May; probably stays 1½m; yet to race on really firm ground but probably acts on any other; not seen out after July. *P. Calver.*

STARGON (FR) 2 b.c. Sandy Creek 123–Cramond 105 (Porto Bello 118) (1983   — 6fg 6d) Jan 17; IR 10,000Y; second foal; dam won Queen Mary Stakes but failed to train on; behind in October maiden races at Newmarket and Newbury; sold BBA 960 gns Newmarket Autumn Sales. *F. Durr.*

STARJAY 2 b.g. Comedy Star 121–Lady Jay 61 (Double Jump 131) (1983 6f 6f 7f⁴   **56** 7f 6f* 8d 9fg⁴) Mar 27; 2,100Y; fair sort; second foal; half-brother to Prix du Petit Couvert third Little Vagabond (by Ampney Prince); dam second in two 1m sellers; attracted no bid after winning 12-runner selling nursery at Ripon in August by 2 lengths from Brooklands Belle; probably stays 9f; gelded after final outing. *M. H. Easterby.*

STAR KID 8 ch.g. Stardao 83–Babulass (Babu 117) (1982 NR 1983 5g 5g 5d 5s)   — poor sprint handicapper; best at 5f with some give in the ground. *W. Stubbs.*

STAR LIFE 3 ch.f. Star Appeal 133–Alive Alivo 77 (Never Say Die 137) (1982 6f   **68** 6f 5f 1983 9.4d* 11d 9f 10.6f⁴) lightly-made filly; 33/1 and apprentice ridden when decisively winning 19-runner maiden race at Carlisle in June, easily best effort; suited by 9f and should get further. *T. Fairhurst.*

STARLIGHT LADY (USA) 2 b.f. Verbatim–Whatta Season (What A Pleasure)   — (1983 7f) Apr 16; $32,000F, $80,000Y; third foal; dam placed twice in 24 starts; third favourite, never-dangerous tenth of 11 in maiden race at Yarmouth in August; exported to Kuwait. *H. Cecil.*

STARLIGHT LASS 2 b.f. Mummy's Pet 125–Star of Light 85 (Counsel 118)   **64** (1983 5s 5s⁴ 5d³ 6fg 6s⁴ 6fg) Apr 16; leggy filly; half-sister to 2 winners, including Starlight Lad (by Willipeg), a winner at up to 1¼m and quite a useful chaser; dam won at 9f and over hurdles; plating-class maiden; will stay beyond 6f; probably acts on any going. *P. Calver.*

STARLIT SKY 3 b.f. Radetzky 123–Young May Moon (Hopeful Venture 125)   **78** (1982 6f 1983 8d 7g 7fg² 8f 7s⁴) attractive, rangy filly; second to Golden Rhyme in a blanket finish in maiden event at Sandown in June, best effort; stays 7f; sold 2,400 gns Newmarket December Sales. *J. Winter.*

STAR OF A GUNNER 3 ch.c. Gunner B 126–Starkist 81 (So Blessed 130) (1982   **85**
5fg 5fg 6g⁴ 8fg 8.2g⁴ 7f 8.2d⁴ 7g⁴ 7g 1983 8.2v* 8s* 8v⁴ 8s 8f 10d 8fg*) fair sort;
showed improved form in spring, winning handicaps at Nottingham and Salisbury;
returned to form at Doncaster on last day of season, getting up in last strides after
being outpaced, to beat Roman Beach in 27-runner handicap; should stay 1¼m;
acts on a firm surface but revels in the mud. *R. Holder.*

STAR OF ANAX 3 b.f. Anax 120–Starlit Coach 66 (Sandstone 105) (1982 5.8f   –
5f³ 6fg⁴ 5g 5f² 5f² 5.3f³ 5g⁴ 5d³ 5fg 6s² 5v 6s* 6s 1983 7fg 6fg 6f 6fg⁴ 6fg 5.8fg)
plain filly; plater; suited by 6f; acts on any going, except perhaps heavy; blinkered
once as a 2-y-o. *M. Blanshard.*

STAR OF IRELAND 3 b.c. Star Appeal 133–Belligerent 74 (Roan Rocket 128)   **82** d
(1982 6g 6f 7g 1983 8.5v² 7v* 8s² 7g³ 7d 8f 7.6d 10fg 7g) good-topped, quite
attractive colt; ran well in varied races in spring and won handicap at Kempton by 4
lengths from Averon; lost his form afterwards; stays 1m well; acts well in the mud;
blinkered last 2 outings. *A. Jarvis.*

STAR OF SALFORD 5 gr.h. Town Crier 119–False Evidence 53 (Counsel 118)   –
(1982 8d 10.1fg 10f 10.6f 8g 10.8fg 1983 16s 10f 12f 12f 10f) poor plater. *J. Long.*

STAR PATRICK 2 b.f. St Paddy 133–Ma's Baby 90 (Ashford Lea 95) (1983 6v 6g   –
6g) Apr 7; 1,500Y, 4,800 2-y-o; short-backed filly; second foal; half-sister to a
minor 2-y-o winner; dam at her best at 2 yrs when winner twice over 5f; in rear in
minor events and a maiden race, twice last. *D. Chapman.*

STAR REVUE 2 b.f. Comedy Star 121–Gingermede 76 (Runnymede 123) (1983   **66**
6g 6f 6fg 6fg) Apr 23; close-coupled, fair sort; third foal; plating-class maiden; no
form after first outing. *H. Westbrook.*

STAR ROUTE 2 b.f. Owen Dudley 121–Fleet Fen 74 (St Paddy 133) (1983 7fg 8g   **57**
6g 6fg) Mar 21; sturdy filly; first foal; dam second over 6f at 2 yrs; poor maiden;
form only at 6f. *H. Collingridge.*

STAR SPARTAN 2 b.c. Sparkler 130–Star Girl (Sovereign Gleam 117) (1983 7g   **93**
7d 9s³ 8d*) Mar 13; third foal; brother to Irish middle-distance winner Star Spark;
dam once-raced half-sister to Star Appeal; an improving sort who made all to win
going away by 3 lengths from Cyrano in maiden event at Leopardstown in October;
will be suited by middle distances; should make a decent 3-y-o. *J. Oxx, Ireland.*

STAR SPRAY (USA) 2 b.c. Star de Naskra–Princess Surfspray (Tamao) (1983   **97**
5d 6d 7f³ 7fg* 7d 7fg* 7fg* 8h* 7g* 8d⁴) Apr 6; $60,000Y; good-topped, quite
attractive colt; half-brother to 3 winners, including 8.5f stakes winner Bound
Green (by Vitriolic); dam never ran; won nurseries at Redcar, Goodwood,
Salisbury, Pontefract and Yarmouth in the space of 43 days in August and
September; turned out again at Yarmouth 2 days after his success there, but found
ground conditions had turned against him, and could finish only fourth of 5; suited
by 7f and 1m; acts on good surface; dead. *G. Harwood.*

STARTING POINT 2 b.f. Vilgora 113–Prim Dot (Primera 131) (1983 7f 6fg) Mar   –
18; 1,000 2-y-o; compact filly; half-sister to 2 winners, including useful stayer
Outpoint (by Fighting Charlie); dam never ran; behind in late-season maiden events
at Redcar and Doncaster. *N. Tinkler.*

STAR VENTURE 7 br.g. Swing Easy 126–Street Vendor 60 (High Perch 126)   –
(1982 6fg 8d 6f 8f 7.6fg 8fg 11.7fg 1983 8g 7.6g) strong gelding; of little account
nowadays; has been blinkered; has worn bandages; has raced with tongue tied
down; retained 520 gns Doncaster March Sales. *M. Chapman.*

STARWIND 2 b.g. Star Appeal 133–Mill Wind 68 (Blakeney 126) (1983 7fg 7f 8g⁴   **84**
8f²) lengthy gelding; good walker; first foal; dam stayed 1½m; showed
progressive form, on final outing finishing strongly when length second of 18 to Sam
M in maiden race at Leicester in November; will be suited by 1¼m+; acts on firm
going; gelded at end of year. *J. Winter.*

STATE AFFAIR 2 b.f. Dominion 123–Omentello 91 (Elopement 125) (1983 7g)   – p
Apr 1; closely related to smart 7f performer Tudor Mill (by Derring-Do) and
half-sister to numerous winners; dam won over 13f; third favourite, 10 lengths
sixth of 13 behind Talk of Glory in maiden race at Lingfield in October; should do
better. *M. Jarvis.*

STATE BALL 3 b.f. Dance In Time–Crystal Palace 121 (Solar Slipper 131) (1982   **61**
5f 5.3fg 6g 1983 9.4d 11fg³ 11f³ 12.3f³ 12.2g³ 13g² 13.8g) smallish, sparely-made
filly; gives impression she needs a test of stamina, and may well prove suited by
more give in the ground too; gave a bit of trouble at start as a 2-y-o. *W. Elsey.*

STATE BUDGET 2 b.g. Free State 125–Novelista 101 (El Gallo 122) (1983 6f 6fg 7fg) Feb 23; 2,000F, 4,600Y; workmanlike gelding; good walker; half-brother to 9f winner Noble Legend (by Noble Decree) and a winner in Australia; dam successful 2-y-o 5f performer; modest plater; gelded after final outing. *W. Musson.*   **59**

STATE HIGHWAY 3 br.g. Free State 125–Liebeslied 91 (Dike) (1982 NR 1983 6g 8f) 600Y; smallish gelding; first foal; dam won over 5.9f and 1m at 2 yrs, and also won over hurdles; soundly beaten in minor events at York and Redcar in October. *D. Garraton.*   **–**

STATE HOUSE (USA) 4 ch.c. Full Pocket–Star Empress (Young Emperor 133) (1982 5fg 6g 6g 7fg 6s 1983 5s 6d) lengthy, rather sparely-made colt; poor plater; sometimes blinkered. *R. Griffiths.*   **–**

STATELY MAIDEN 3 b.f. Free State 125–Namur (Amber Rama 133) (1982 5d4 6f 5fg 7f2 7g 7.2s 8d 1983 8s3 7v4 8.5d 10fg 8.3f 10f3 12fg4 10g4) neat, strong filly; plater; possibly stays 1½m; acts on any going; races with her head high and looks none too genuine; blinkered final start in 1982. *D. Weeden.*   **48**

STATESMANSHIP (USA) 3 b.c. Quadratic–Ocracoke (Cyane) (1982 7fg 8fg 8g* 1983 12v3 12f 11.7g* 14fg*) deep-girthed colt; good mover, with a long stride; only lightly raced but is a useful performer; improved in autumn and on last 2 starts won handicaps at Bath and Newmarket; quickened into lead 3f out and held on by 2 lengths from Norfolk Serenade on latter course; stays 1¾m; best form on a sound surface. *G. Harwood.*   **100**

STATE TROOPER 6 ch.h. Status Seeker–Sarah Pipellini (French Beige 127) (1982 NR 1983 8d 10v4 8v4 8.2s 8v) strong horse; fairly useful handicapper at 4 yrs; didn't show much in 1983; stays 1¼m; acts on any going; has run well for an apprentice; suited by front-running tactics; blinkered fourth start; cost 3,000 gns Doncaster January Sales. *W. Stubbs.*   **–**

STATS ANNA 2 b.f. Thatch 136–Lavendula Rose 108 (Le Levanstell 122) (1983 5f3 5g* 6fg) Apr 2; good-quartered, compact filly; excellent walker; half-sister to numerous winners, including useful 1980 2-y-o 5f and 7f winner Stats Emmar (by Steel Heart) and Miss Mars (by Red God), a very useful stakes winner at up to 9f in USA; dam, third in Irish Guinness Oaks, is half-sister to Wrekin Rambler; having first race for 2 months (had changed stables), quickened very well to lead over 1f out when winning 3-runner £3,400 event at Goodwood in September comfortably by 2½ lengths from Betsy Bay; 6 lengths seventh of 12 to Desirable in William Hill Cheveley Park Stakes at Newmarket later in month; will stay 7f; formerly trained by C. Horgan. *G. Hunter.*   **99**

STAY SECRET 6 b.g. Most Secret 119–Sayvanter (Galivanter 131) (1982 6g 5f 6f 5f3 5fg 5d 5g 5d 5g 1983 6d 6d2 5g2 5d 5f 5f 6fg) poor mover; plater; stays 6f; acts on any going; best in blinkers; has run well for an apprentice. *W. Bentley.*   **42**

STAY SHARP 3 ch.g. Sharpen Up 127–Brevity 76 (Pindari 124) (1982 6f* 6f3 5.5g 7fg 1983 8g 8g) rather leggy, lightly-made gelding; quite useful on his day at 2 yrs but ran badly both outings in 1983; yet to prove he stays beyond 6f; acts on firm going. *P. Kelleway.*   **–**

ST BONIFACE 3 ch.c. Halo–Joking Apart 120 (Jimmy Reppin 131) (1982 7f* 7f4 8s 1983 10.5d2) strong, well-made, quite attractive colt; very useful as a 2-y-o; disappointed in 3-runner High Line Stakes at York in August, making fairly heavy weather of getting on top of a 33/1-chance and then being completely overwhelmed by 10-length winner Adonijah; should stay 1½m; acts on firm going and probably isn't at his best on soft ground; sold to NBA only 1,200 gns Newmarket Autumn Sales. *R. Hern.*   **?**

ST CONAL 4 ch.c. Status Seeker–Irish Picture (Dual 117) (1982 6.5g4 8s 7d 6f4 6g 7g3 8fg 8fg 1983 11d 7g 11g2 9d3 10s 8fg 9fg4) fair sort; stays 11f; blinkered once at 2 yrs; cost 2,000 gns Ascot March Sales. *J. Parkes.*   **45**

STEADILY 3 b.f. Whitstead 125–Fearless 77 (Derring-Do 131) (1982 NR 1983 10d) half-sister to 7f to 1¼m winner Gibbon (by Swing Easy); dam, winner over 7f, is half-sister to More Light and Shoot A Line; ninth of 13 behind Fluella in maiden race at Beverley in September. *R. Hern.*   **–**

STEADY DUDLEY 3 br.g. Owen Dudley 121–Ready Steady Go 87 (On Your Mark 125) (1982 7fg 7g 1983 8f 11f 12fg) good-bodied, quite well-made gelding; has shown a little ability but ran appallingly under top weight in selling handicap at Newmarket in August on final start; sold 925 gns Ascot September Sales. *P. Cundell.*   **–**

STEADY MUSIC 3 b.f. Music Boy 124–Gin and French 71 (Poaching 115) (1982 —
5f⁴ 5f⁴ 6f 6g* 5fg 6fg³ 6fg 7fg 6s 1983 6d 6fg 6f 7h) close-coupled filly; little form
in 1983; suited by 6f; acts on firm going; blinkered third start. *C. Nelson.*

STEADY THE BUFFS 4 b.f. Balidar 133–Dinant 114 (Abernant 142) (1982 8d —
8d 7f 7fg³ 8f 8fg 8s⁴ 10.8s 10s⁴ 10g³ 1983 10.2d 10s 12s 10d 10fg 13.8g) big,
rangy filly; poor walker; has a round action; poor maiden; stays 1¼m; bought
4,000 gns Ascot January Sales; sold 8,600 gns Newmarket December Sales. *J.
Old.*

STEAL A GLANCE 3 b.c. Nishapour 125–Parthian Song (Parthia 132) (1982 —
6fg 7fg⁴ 7fg 1983 10v 7d 7g 8f) well-made, quite attractive colt; disappointing
maiden; should stay at least 1m. *B. Hills.*

STEAL THE SHOW 2 b.f. Comedy Star 121–Main Chance 63 (Midsummer —
Night II 117) (1983 6f 7s) Apr 8; first live foal; dam won twice over 11f; in rear in
minor event at Windsor (last of 17) in August and maiden race at Leicester in
October. *J. Fox.*

STEAMY 2 ch.g. Hot Grove 128–Adorit 76 (Habat 127) (1983 6f 7f 6fg 6f³ 6fg 8d) 64
Mar 30; 26,000Y; smallish, quite attractive gelding; first foal; dam best at 5f;
plating-class maiden; form only at 6f; blinkered fourth and fifth outings. *R.
Armstrong.*

STEAUA ROMANA 3 b.f. Pitskelly 122–Makura (Pampered King 121) (1982 6f —
8fg 1983 8f 7g) useful-looking filly; in rear in maiden and minor races; blinkered
final start. *W. Wharton.*

STEEL CHARGER 6 b.h. Steel Heart 128–Belaying Pin (Iron Peg §§) (1982 78 d
5f³ 5f* 5fg 5fg* 5f* 5fg 1983 5s 5f 5f⁴ 5f 5f 5fg 5f 5g 5g) strong, compact, good
sort; poor walker; sprint handicapper; has run respectably on soft going but is
clearly well suited by top-of-the-ground; blinkered once. *A. Hide.*

STEEL COMMANDER 5 b.g. Steel Heart 128–Commander Ali (Bold 102
Commander) (1982 8s 8s 6fg* 6.3g 5d 6.3fg 7fg 5fg⁴ 6f 7fg³ 6d³ 6d 1983 6s 6s*
6g³ 6v³ 5g³ 6fg³ 5g* 5g* 5g* 6s) Irish gelding; useful sprinter who won handicaps
at Phoenix Park in April (dead-heated), the Curragh in August (beat Pampas a neck
in Philips Electrical Stakes), Leopardstown in September and Phoenix Park again in
October; accounted for Royal Hobbit by a length in quite valuable event for final
success; stays 7f but is better at shorter distances; probably acts on any going;
best in blinkers. *D. K. Weld, Ireland.*

STEEL DUKE 7 b.g. Calpurnius 122–Corrie Royal (Fury Royal 108) (1982 8s 8s 97
16fg* 16g³ 16fg 9g 14f* 11.5f* 12fg² 11.5g 10fg 1983 12s 10g 14fg 12f 11.5 14f²
12f² 13f 11.5g² 16d* 16s 16s) strong Irish gelding; useful performer on his day;
narrowly beat Kalaminsky in minor event at Limerick Junction in October; had put
up best previous effort on seventh start when going down by a head to South
Atlantic (pair clear) in Blandford Stakes at the Curragh in August; stays well but
has run creditably at around 1m; acts on any going. *N. Meade, Ireland.*

STEEL KID (USA) 4 b.c. Caro 133–Gallant Trial (Gallant Man) (1982 14g 14d³ 83
12f⁴ 14f* 10.1g⁴ 10g* 12g³ 10.6f 1983 10g 11.7d 12s 10s 10.2f* 10.6fg* 11.7f³ 10f*
12f³ 10fg³ 10f 10g² 9fg 10fg) strong, stocky colt; not a good mover; won handicaps
at Doncaster, Haydock and Nottingham; ridden with great artistry by L. Piggott
when beating Rekal 3 lengths on last-named in July; stays 1¾m but is better at
shorter distances; seems to act on any going but goes well on top-of-the-ground;
hurdling with D. Nicholson. *R. Armstrong.*

STEEL PASS 5 b.g. Steel Heart 128–Senorita Rugby 86 (Forward Pass) (1982 —
6fg 6d 7f 6f 6f 6f⁴ 8f 8g³ 7s 7g 1983 5.8s 5fg 6fg 8h) hasn't run up to his best for
some time; stays 1m, but best form at shorter distances; acts on any going; has
often been blinkered; often pulls hard and is not the easiest of rides; has run tubed.
M. Usher.

STEEL VENTURE 4 b.c. Full of Hope 125–Grove Star (Upper Case) (1982 8g* 78 §
12fg³ 12.3fg 10f 8g* 8d² 8f 9s 1983 8g 8s 8d 8v 10.6v 10s² 10g⁴ 11v 12v 12d 10.2fg
10g 10.2fg 8fg) rather lightly-made, lengthy colt; poor mover; fair on his day but is
inconsistent; appears not to stay 1½m; suited by some give in the ground;
sometimes blinkered and has run moderately in them; has run well when sweating
up; has a tendency to hang, is possibly ungenuine and is not an easy ride. *M. Ryan.*

STEELWORKS 5 ch.h. Steel Heart 128–Hariota 73 (Hook Money 124) (1982 8d 85
7f 7.6g³ 8.5f 9fg* 10d 9f* 8f 8fg* 9g 9d³ 8g 10.2f 1983 8s 10g² 10s 10f³ 9f 8fg* 10f
9g 10f) compact, sturdy horse; made all to beat That's My Son by 2 lengths in quite
valuable handicap at Ascot in July; stays 1¼m; acts on a soft surface, but is well

suited by firm going; blinkered first 3 starts as a 3-y-o; inconsistent and unreliable; sold 4,900 gns Ascot November Sales. *B. Hills.*

STEEPLE BELL 7 b.g. Tower Walk 130–Nine Lessons 101 (Santa Claus 133)   97
(1982 8d 8fg 7g* 7fg³ 8d* 8d 8s⁴ 1983 8v³ 7s* 8f 7fg 8f* 8fg 7g*) lengthy, quite attractive gelding; good walker; a grand performer who maintains his form and enthusiasm extremely well; won handicaps at Epsom in June, Ripon in August (beat Gavo in Ripon Rowels Handicap) and York in October (accounted for Anstruther by ½ length); stays 1m; acts on any going; often apprentice ridden; genuine. *M. Stoute.*

STEERS 4 b.c. He Loves Me 120–Mile Cross 88 (Milesian 125) (1982 6fg 6g 5f 6g   –
1983 6v 5v 5v² 7.6v 5.8g 5g 6f 6f 6f 7.6fg) smallish, quite attractive colt; plater; stayed 6f; acted on any going; effective with and without blinkers; fell at Lingfield in October; dead. *J. Bridger.*

STELLARIS 3 ch.f. Star Appeal 133–Love-Knot (No Mercy 126) (1982 NR 1983   –
9f 10f 14.7f 14.7fg) 5,600Y; sturdy filly; second foal; half-sister to fair 7f and 1m winner Rapid Knot (by Rapid River); dam ran only twice; little worthwhile form, but is quite a nice type and showed a bit of promise when still on backward side third start. *Miss S. Hall.*

STEPHALOTUS 3 br.f. Coded Scrap 90–Stephandre 94 (Derring-Do 131) (1982   68
5fg 5s 6d* 6d⁴ 1983 7v 8s 6d 6f 6f 6h³ 6s* 7g 6fg 7g 6f) big, rangy filly; has a capped hock; apprentice ridden, overcame difficulties in running to win handicap at Ayr in September; promises to stay 7f; acts on any going; gives impression she needs holding up; sold 3,000 gns Newmarket Autumn Sales. *T. Fairhurst.*

STEPHANYS DREAM 3 b.f. American Beauty 74 (Mill Reef 141)   118
(1982 7v 8.5v³ 8s² 7v² 7v* 1983 8v 9s* 8v² 8s⁴ 10.5fg 8s* 9.2f 8d) small, quite well-made filly; beat Aunty by 1½ lengths in Prix Finlande at Evry in April and Princesse Timide by 1½ lengths in Prix de Liancourt at Longchamp in September, in latter event making up an immense amount of ground in straight; 4 lengths second to Sharaya in Prix de Bagatelle at Longchamp in between; stays 9f; acts well on soft ground. *R. Collet, France.*

STEPOUT 4 b.f. Sagaro 133–Pepstep 66 (Polic 126) (1982 10f 12f³ 12f* 12f 12g   –
10g² 11.7s* 12g 1983 12v 12g 11.5f 11.7f⁴ 11.7f) small, fair sort; good walker; stays 1½m; acts on any going. *M. Smyly.*

STEPS 3 b.f. Dance In Time–Miss Justice 87 (King's Bench 132) (1982 6fg³ 6g³   68
5.8g 1983 8v² 8d³ 10s⁴ 8fg³ 8f 8g) deep-girthed, fair sort; best form at up to 1m; seems to act on any going; blinkered final outing; sold to BBA 10,500 gns Newmarket Autumn Sales. *H. Candy.*

STEREOS 3 b.g. Tachypous 128–Shelton Song 60 (Song 132) (1982 NR 1983 5s*   86
5fg⁴ 6fg 6f² 6fg⁴ 5f) 19,000Y; 720 2-y-o; tall, workmanlike gelding; second foal; dam 5f winner at 4 yrs; 4-length winner of maiden race at Bath in May; ran respectably in handicaps afterwards; stayed 6f; acted on any going; apprentice ridden; didn't look ideally suited by course at Chester on fifth outing and was slightly hampered final start; dead. *H. Candy.*

STERLING VIRTUE (USA) 2 b.c. Silver Series–Virgin 114 (Zeddaan 130)   68
(1983 6f 7fg 7fg⁴ 7fg 7g) Mar 1; strong, good sort; has a round action; dam won from 5f to 9f in France; plating-class maiden; lacks pace and will be suited by 1m+; sold B. McMahon 2,300 gns Doncaster November Sales. *G. Pritchard-Gordon.*

STERN 7 br.g. No Mercy 126–Rudder (Reliance II 137) (1982 6f 6f 6fg 6g 6f 6g⁴   73
7fg* 6fg* 6f² 7.2s* 7d 1983 7s 7g 7f 7f³ 7f³ 6fg 7h² 6f* 7.2g 6fg* 6f 7f) quite a modest handicapper; won at Chepstow in September and Redcar in October; effective at 6f and 7f; good mover who evidently acts on any going; blinkered once at 3 yrs; genuine though was reluctant to go down tenth and eleventh starts and was taken down early final outing; sold to Mrs G. Reveley 3,100 gns Ascot November Sales. *I. Walker.*

STEVIE CEE 3 ch.f. Roi Soleil 125–Senna (Sica Boy 132) (1982 5fg 1983 6v 9s   –
11.7s 13fg 16.5f 10f 10g) of little account. *S. Harris.*

STEVULA 2 ch.c. Tarboosh–Countess Angelique (Sun Prince 128) (1983 5d⁴ 5d*   62
5d 5v 7f 5f 6fg 6d 5s 7fg 7fg) Apr 19; IR 2,000F, 1,000Y; narrow, leggy colt; first foal; dam unraced half-sister to smart 1¼m performer Jumpabout; won maiden race at Catterick in March; soundly beaten afterwards, including in a valuable seller; should stay 7f. *A. Smith.*

STEWARTS RISE 6 ch.m. Good Bond 122–Devadara 74 (Royal Levee or Hill Clown) (1982 10fg 8d[2] 8f 12f* 10.6f 10fg* 10fg[4] 10d 12fg 10.2s 12s 1983 13v[4]) leggy, light-framed mare; plater; stays 1½m; acts on any going; tends to sweat up; suitable mount for an inexperienced rider. *B. McMahon.* —

ST HELENA 2 b.f. Monsanto 121–Ergo 82 (Song 132) (1983 5s 5s 6g) Apr 3; small, quite attractive filly; second foal; half-sister to 1982 2-y-o 5f winner Henceforth (by Full of Hope); dam won once over 5f from 3 starts at 2 yrs; poor form in 3 early-season races; winner in Italy. *H. Candy.* ?

STIMLER 6 b.h. Charlottown 127–Pardalina 69 (Pardal 130) (1982 10fg 7.6f[2] 7f[2] 7g 8fg 9g 1983 8s 8g[4] 8f 7g 10f 7fg 7fg 7f 8.3fg 8fg) lightly-made horse; plater; stays 1m; probably acts on any going; often blinkered; suitable mount for an inexperienced rider. *M. Bolton.* —

STINGING NETTLE 2 b.f. Sharpen Up 127–Nettlebed 84 (Hethersett 134) (1983 6fg*) Feb 8; half-sister to 3 winners by Roan Rocket, including very smart 7f to 1¼m winner Gairloch and smart miler Whistlefield; dam won over 7f; 4/1, won 5-runner Duke of Edinburgh Stakes at Ascot in October by a neck from Chaumiere after running green; will probably stay 1m; a useful filly in the making. *G. Hunter.* **90 p**

STINGO 4 b.c. Mansingh 120–Quita II 105 (Lavandin 128) (1982 7d 6fg 7fg 10g 1983 12s 10.1f) poor maiden. *A. Moore.* —

STOCK HILL LAD 2 b.c. John de Coombe 122–Bella Rosetta 58 (Willowick) (1983 5.8s[4] 5s* 6fg* 5f 6fg[4] 7h 6f 6fg 5d) May 12; neat colt; third foal; dam, a plater, placed from 6f to 1¼m; won sellers at Lingfield (bought in 1,750 gns) in June and Haydock (no bid) in July; should stay beyond 6f; acts on any going; ran badly in blinkers fourth outing. *M. Blanshard.* **64**

STOCKSIGN (USA) 2 b.c. King's Bishop–Ruff Up (Rough'n Tumble) (1983 7g) Mar 28; $40,000F; tall, useful sort; half-brother to 5 winners, including sprint stakes winner Ruffast (by Fast Fellow); dam won claiming races at up to 7f; behind in 18-runner maiden race at Leicester in October. *G. Hunter.* —

STONEHENGE 6 gr.g. Great Nephew 126–Fairy Ring 91 (Quorum 126) (1982 10f 10fg 10.8fg 10d[3] 11.7fg[3] 10f 10g 10fg 10s 10.8s 1983 10d 10s 8g* 10.2g 10f 8.3f[3] 10f[3]) strong, compact gelding; plater nowadays; bought in 2,600 gns after winning at Yarmouth in June; stays 11.7f; probably acts on any going; blinkered second start. *P. Burgoyne.* **46**

STONEY 3 ch.f. Balidar 133–Sweetstone (Honeyway 125) (1982 6f 6f[4] 7f 1983 8v 7s 7fg 7f[3]) workmanlike filly; stays 7f; acts on firm going. *J. Winter.* **69**

STONEY BOAT INN 2 br.g. Orange Bay 131–Sallusteno 80 (Sallust 134) (1983 6f 7g 9s) May 19; first foal; dam stayed 1m; little worthwhile form in maiden races; gelded after final outing. *R. Hollinshead.* —

STORMCHASER 2 b.c. Abwah 118–White Cliffs (Hill Rise 127) (1983 5v 5v 5g 6fg 6f*) Mar 17; 1,550F, 1,900Y; big, good-topped colt; fourth foal; dam poor daughter of very useful Victoria Quay; won 10-runner maiden auction event at Folkestone in July; suited by 6f; acts well on top-of-the-ground; sweated up badly fourth outing (ran well). *H. Beasley.* **72**

STORM FOOT 2 b.f. Import 127–Matloch 70 (Matador 131) (1983 5d 5g 6f[3] 6f 6fg[2]) Apr 14; 10,000F, 41,000Y; big, robust, close-coupled filly; grand mover; half-sister to several winners, including smart 1973 2-y-o 5f performer Eveneca (by Frankincense) and useful 1981 2-y-o 6f winner Bless The Match (by So Blessed); dam sister to useful sprinter Spanish Sail; placed in maiden race at Windsor in July and nursery at Nottingham in September; stays 6f; acts on firm going. *B. Hills.* **76**

STORMING 4 ch.g. Red Alert 127–Winbeam (Hornbeam 130) (1982 8s* 12fg 11.7d 11.7fg 1983 16v) strong gelding; plater; stays 1m; acts on soft going; usually blinkered; winner over hurdles. *D. Dale.* —

STORM RULER 2 b. or br.c. Bay Express 132–Finest View 66 (Bold Lad, Ire 133) (1983 6fg 8s) May 12; 6,000Y; rather leggy, fair sort; half-brother to useful 3-y-o sprinter Bold Bob (by Sharpen Up); prolific Italian winner Miss Vermont (by Sandford Lad) and a winner in Argentina; dam stayed 7f; beaten some way in maiden races at Newmarket in August and Yarmouth in September; not sure to stay 1m. *E. Eldin.* —

STORMY GULF 2 ch.g. Gulf Pearl 117–Wild Thyme 63 (Galivanter 131) (1983 6v 7f 7.2fg 7g* 8.2g[2] 8.2fg) Apr 30; 3,000F, 5,000Y; leggy gelding; brother to 3-y-o 1¾m winner Pearl Thyme; half-brother to 3 winners, including useful 1975 2-y-o sprinter Rampion (by Pall Mall); dam won 7f seller; won 19-runner **72**

claiming race at Yarmouth in September; 5 lengths second of 13 to Tophams Taverns in nursery at Hamilton later in month; will stay beyond 1m; suited by some give in the ground; gelded after final outing. *M. Tompkins.*

STORMY KESTREL 2 gr. or ro.f. Monsanto 121–Sea Kestrel 82 (Sea Hawk II 131) (1983 6s 7f 7g 7.6d⁴) Apr 6; workmanlike filly; first reported foal; dam genuine stayer; 12 lengths fourth of 18 to Channel Affair in maiden race at Lingfield in October; will be better suited by further. *Mrs R. Lomax.*   57

STORMY MONARCH 2 b.g. Fordham 117–Stormy Queen 64 (Typhoon 125) (1983 6d 7fg) Apr 29; 29,000Y; half-brother to winning sprinter Queen's Bidder (by Auction Ring); dam, Irish 2m winner, is half-sister to top-class sprinter Sandford Lad; behind in minor event at Leicester in June and maiden race at Newmarket (last of 25) in July. *C. Brittain.*   –

ST PEDRO 5 b.h. St Paddy 133–Jinkin (King's Troop 118) (1982 8g 8g⁴ 8f² 8g* 10d³ 8fg 9g 8f⁴ 8g³ 9d 8s³ 10g 1983 8d 8v 8v 8g² 10g* 10f⁴ 8f 8f³ 8fg⁴ 8g⁴ 8fg² 10g) quite an attractive, robust horse; modest handicapper; won at Yarmouth in June; stays 1¼m; acts on any going; has run creditably for an apprentice; blinkered nowadays; sold 3,600 gns Newmarket Autumn Sales. *E. Eldin.*   77

STRACEY 3 ch.f. English Prince 129–Mellow Girl 88 (Mountain Call 125) (1982 NR 1983 12f 12fg 16g) sturdy filly; first foal; dam won over 5f and 6f at 2 yrs; well beaten in maiden and minor events, finishing tailed off on last 2 starts. *P. Felgate.*   –

STRACOMER NURSE 3 ch.f. Ardoon 124–Si (Ragusa 137) (1982 7fg³ 6d 1983 7s* 8v 7s 8fg⁴ 7h 10.4fg* 8.2fg* 11s) IR 20,000Y; neat, rather lightly-built ex-Irish filly; has a round action; sister to Irish 9f winner Sir Lee and half-sister to 2 winners, including Irish Guinness Oaks third Stracomer Queen (by Prince Tenderfoot); dam unraced daughter of smart 5f winner Acquiesced; successful in maiden race at Down Royal in May, apprentice event at Chester in August and handicap at Hamilton in September; won last 2 races readily after being held up, but ran moderately only subsequent start; stays 1¼m; acts on any going; formerly trained by T. Gallagher. *G. Lockerbie.*   74

STRAEKER 4 ch.c. Sharpen Up 127–Princess Tavi (Sea Hawk II 131) (1982 7fg 7f 6f 8f 1983 10g 10.8d) compact, fair sort; fairly useful at his best but has shown no form for a long time; should stay 1m; suited by some give in the ground. *P. Felgate.*   –

STRAIGHT MAN 2 ch.g. Homing 130–Farce (Bon Mot III 132) (1983 7fg 8fg) May 3; rangy, good sort; good mover; half-brother to very useful middle-distance winner Lindoro (by Sun Prince) and to Whitehall Bridge (by Auction Ring), a useful winner over 1½m here and in France; dam unplaced 3 times in France; 33/1, very much caught the eye when 9 lengths eighth of 26 to Alleging in maiden race at Newmarket in September, coming through in most pleasing style from halfway; 16/1, weakened very quickly after looking to be going strongly when in mid-division in another Newmarket maiden the following month; gelded afterwards; should be well suited by 1m+; a taking individual, certain to do better in due course. *R. Hern.*   76 p

STRAIGHT TO BED 3 b.f. Dominion 123–Burning Love 78 (Buisson Ardent 129) (1982 6g 7g 1983 7fg 10.1f 10f 10.4g⁴ 8f 9d) strong, fair sort; poor walker; plating-class maiden; promises to stay 1¼m; blinkered fifth start; sold 1,100 gns Newmarket Autumn Sales. *M. Smyly.*   –

STRATFORD PLACE 3 ch.c. Moulton 128–Wild Words 95 (Galivanter 131) (1982 6g⁴ 8d 1983 8v² 8d 10g 10f³ 10fg² 12g³ 10fg) big, strong, rangy colt; placed in varied races; stays 1½m; looks a bit short of pace. *R. Laing.*   77

STRATFORD (USA) 3 b.c. Hoist the Flag–Thong (Nantallah) (1982 6d 7s* 1983 7s 8s 8f⁴ 10fg³ 10fg) half-brother to 5 good winners, including Thatch (by Forli), King Pellinore (by Round Table) and Marinsky (by Northern Dancer); ran respectably at the Curragh first and third starts, coming home just over 3 lengths fifth of 8 to odds-on stable-companion Lomond in Gladness Stakes in April and 2½ lengths fourth of 13 to Burslem in Coolmore Hello Gorgeous Stakes in June; set slow pace when 4 lengths last of 3 behind Sabre Dance in Land of Burns Stakes at Ayr in July (had stiff task); promises to stay 1¼m; acts on any going; blinkered last 3 outings; sent to race in USA. *V. O'Brien, Ireland.*   107

STRATHCONON 2 br.c. High Top 131–Antonietta Corsini (Herbager 136) (1983 9f 10.2fg) Mar 31; useful-looking colt; good walker; half-brother to 3-y-o Feather Flower (by Relkino) and several winners, including very smart middle-distance stayer Relay Race (by Relko); dam won 8 races in Italy and is sister to Italian Derby winner Appiani II; had 2 races right at the back-end, on second occasion running   69 p well for long way when 11 lengths seventh of 24 behind Raami in minor event at Doncaster; sure to improve and should win maiden race. *Sir Mark Prescott.*

STRATHEARN 2 b.c. Connaught 130–Poquito (Major Portion 129) (1983 7f 8g*) **89** May 5; 5,800Y; sturdy colt; brother to very useful 6f and 1¼m winner Senorita Poquito, and half-brother to 3 winners; dam won from 5f to 1¼m in Ireland; apparently bit backward, won 12-runner minor event at Redcar in November by ½ length from Marie Cath; will be suited by 1¼m. *J. Fitzgerald.*

STRATH OF ORCHY 4 br.f. Lochnager 132–Silver Teal 79 (Meldrum 112) (1982 **66** 7s⁴ 7g 6fg³ 5fg 5fg³ 5fg 6f 5fg⁴ 6s 6s 5s³ 1983 7d 5fg 6f 5fg³ 5f 5g 5g) compact filly; good walker; sprint handicapper; ideally suited by some give in the ground; blinkered last 3 outings at 3 yrs; often bandaged in front; sold 2,800 gns Doncaster October Sales. *M. W. Easterby.*

STRATOSPHERE 3 b.f. Solinus 130–Marsville (Trouville 125) (1982 5.5s* **112** 1983 6.5s* 5s⁴ 5.5v) French filly; won minor event at Evry in April; good ½-length fourth of 10 to Sky Lawyer in Prix de Saint-Georges at Longchamp in May, easily better subsequent effort; will stay 7f; acts on soft going but is possibly unsuited by heavy; sent to USA. *O. Douieb, France.*

STRAVAGANZA 3 b.f. Busted 134–Scala di Seta 85 (Shantung 132) (1982 NR **–** 1983 8f 10g 12fg³ 14fg) tall, plain filly; half-sister to fair stayer To Kamari Mou (by Moulton) and 3 winners abroad, including high-class Italian 5f to 1½m winner Stone (by Moulton) and good 1978 Italian 2-y-o Stouci (by Upper Case); dam won over 1½m; modest third in 1½m maiden race at Wolverhampton in August, best effort; looks on slow side. *G. Wragg.*

STRAVARNEY 6 ch.m. The Go-Between 129–Riotous 97 (Silver Cloud 121) **–** (1982 NR 1983 7s) bad plater. *M. Bradley.*

STRAW 2 b.c. Thatch 136–Cooliney Dancer (Dancer's Image) (1983 5s 6d 6fg* **93** 7f⁴ 6fg* 6f³ 6fg³) Mar 20; 25,000Y; first foal; dam Irish 2-y-o 5f winner; successful in maiden race at Brighton in June and nursery at Windsor in July; far from disgraced over 7f but is better suited by 6f; form only on a firm surface and in blinkers; sweated up final appearance. *C. Nelson.*

STRAWBERRY FIELDS 2 b.f. Song 132–Silver Berry (Lorenzaccio 130) **66** (1983 6h 6g* 6d) Feb 27; first foal; dam poor half-sister to very smart 1¼m filly Cranberry Sauce; sold out of Sir Mark Prescott's stable 1,900 gns after winning 17-runner seller at Yarmouth in September; stays 6f. *C. Spares.*

STRAWFELLA 2 ch.c. Thatching 131–Golden Glimpse (Gallant Man) (1983 5v **60** 6f 5.8h³ 7fg) Apr 17; 5,200F; IR 6,000Y; half-brother to useful 1978 French 2-y-o winner Silver Glimpse (by Petingo); dam, winner over 1m in USA, is daughter of sister to Habitat; modest plater; should stay 7f; acts on hard going; blinkered on all but second outing; sold 1,700 gns Newmarket September Sales. *Mrs J. Reavey.*

STREAKING LADY 2 b.f. Streak 119–Pictynna (Polic 126) (1983 6g) Apr 19; **–** seventh live foal; dam ran only at 2 yrs; last of 19 in maiden race at Goodwood in September. *N. Mitchell.*

STREAMERTAIL 2 br.f. Shirley Heights 130–Sabrewing 105 (Petingo 135) **78** (1983 6fg 7f 8g⁴) Mar 28; strong, deep-girthed filly; fourth foal; half-sister to 2 winners, including fairly useful 6f to 1½m winner Bluethroat (by Ballymore); dam won over 6f at 2 yrs; quite a modest maiden; better suited by 1m than by shorter distances, and will be suited by 1¼m+; flashed tail under pressure final outing. *B. Hobbs.*

STREAMON 4 b.f. Rapid River 127–Reignon 74 (Lucky Brief 128) (1982 10.2g **58** 8g 1983 10d* 12d 10.6s) lengthy, lightly-made filly; plater; attracted no bid after winning at Pontefract in April; suited by 1¼m (well beaten over 1½m); sold 1,550 gns Doncaster October Sales. *M. Camacho.*

STREATLY 3 gr.f. Town Crier 119–Camusky 77 (Charlottown 127) (1982 5fg 6g⁴ **–** 7fg³ 7g 7.2f 6s 1983 8v 11v 12f⁴ 14.7f) strong-quartered filly; seems to stay 1½m; best form on a sound surface; blinkered fifth outing in 1982. *W. Wharton.*

STREET LEVEL 2 b.f. Swing Easy 126–Street Vendor 60 (High Perch 126) **69** (1983 5v³ 5s² 5s² 6s 7g 7d 5g) May 16; big, plain filly; sister to 6f winner Star Venture and half-sister to 2 winners abroad; dam won 5f seller at 2 yrs; narrowly beaten after missing break in spring maiden races at Wolverhampton and Salisbury; off course 4 months after fourth outing, and showed nothing on return; stays 6f; acts on very soft going; a difficult ride. *H. O'Neill.*

STRIDE 3 b.c. Tachypous 128–Span (Pan II 130) (1982 8g² 1983 10fg⁴ 12d) **78** robust, good-bodied colt; gave impression he'd have been suited by a good test of stamina; dead. *B. Hobbs.*

STRIDENT NOTE 2 b.f. The Minstrel 135–Furioso 116 (Ballymoss 136) (1983 **89**
6f 6fg 7.3d) Apr 3; attractive filly; good walker and mover; half-sister to 3
winners, notably Derby winner Teenoso (by Youth) and very smart Topsy (by
Habitat), successful at up to 1¼m; dam, half-sister to 1000 Guineas winner
Favoletta, was second in Oaks; 3½ lengths sixth of 29 to Capricorn Belle in maiden
race at Newmarket in September, second start; looked very light and sweated up
when respectable ninth of 14 in Rochford Thompson Newbury Stakes the following
month; should be well suited by 1m+; acts on a firm and a soft surface. *G. Wragg.*

STRIKE AGAIN 5 ch.g. Redundant 120–Kimolina (Ki Myth 96) (1982 NR 1983 **–**
13s 16f) lightly raced and probably of little account nowadays; sold 3,000 gns
Doncaster October Sales. *F. Watson.*

STRIKE LUCKY 3 ch.c. Royal Match 117–Chance Belle 85 (Foggy Bell 108) **69**
(1982 6f 6v⁴ 1983 10s² 10d⁴ 10d) well-made colt; off course well over 3 months
after finishing in frame in maiden events in first part of season; will stay 1½m; sold
5,000 gns Newmarket Autumn Sales. *A. Pitt.*

STRIKE THE BELL 2 b.g. Foggy Bell 108–P P Strikes Again (Kibenka 119) **–**
(1983 7d) second foal; dam well beaten in varied company; behind in 16-runner
maiden race at Brighton in September. *D. Hanley.*

ST TERRAMAR 8 b.h. St Alphage 119–Terramar Lass (Tom Rolfe) (1982 6f **65**
5.8f³ 5.8f 5g 6g³ 5g 5fg 7f 5s 6s 1983 6g 6fg 5.3f* 5fg³ 5f* 5f³ 6f 6f 5h 5f 5g) small,
good-bodied horse; poor mount; sprint handicapper; won at Brighton in June and
Leicester in July; ideally suited by fast ground; acts on any track; suitable mount for
a boy; best in blinkers; sometimes bandaged on off-fore; often starts slowly;
bought 500 gns Ascot May Sales. *D. Jermy.*

STUBBINGTON GREEN 6 br.g. Swing Easy 126–Lake Victoria 94 **–**
(Stupendous) (1982 8f 8f 1983 10g) leggy gelding; plater; stays 1¼m; acts on any
going; wears blinkers. *D. Yeoman.*

STUCK FOR WORDS 6 ch.m. Some Hand 119–Clear Speech (Articulate 121) **–**
(1982 NR 1983 10d 10g 8g 8fg⁴ 8f 8.3f³ 10fg 8d) plater; stays 1¼m; seems to
act on any going; suitable mount for an inexperienced rider. *A. Moore.*

STYLISH MOVER 4 b.g. Martinmas 128–Fuiseog (Eudaemon 129) (1982 7fg³ **–**
6f⁴ 8fg 7f 6fg⁴ 8g* 7f 8fg² 1983 7.6v⁴ 7s 8.5g 7fg⁴ 8f 7f⁴) close-coupled, fair sort;
poor walker and mover; suited by 1m; acts on any going; suitable mount for an
inexperienced rider; has been tried in blinkers. *M. Haynes.*

STYLOGRAM 2 ch.f. Record Token 128–Monagram 77 (Mon Fetiche 120) (1983 **75**
5f 5f* 6f 7fg 8f 7g 6g 6g²) May 3; 8,400Y; smallish filly; half-sister to several
winners, including useful 1976 2-y-o 5f winner Japora (by Raffingora) and 1m and 9f
winner Himorre (by Song); dam won over 1m; won 10-runner maiden race at
Newcastle in June; best form at 5f and 6f, but should stay further; acts on firm
going. *J. Etherington.*

SUCCESSFUL BIDDER 2 b.c. Auction Ring 123–Autumn Flush 57 (Rustam **95**
127) (1983 5fg 6f³) Mar 19; IR 30,000Y; tall, quite attractive colt; half-brother to
winners here and abroad; dam won over 1¼m; backed from 16/1 to 10/1 although
apparently in need of race, creditable 1¾ lengths third of 11 to Keep Tapping in
£4,500 maiden event at Goodwood in July; hampered and unseated rider on
debut; will stay 7f. *P. Haslam.*

SUE CLARE 3 ch.f. Busted 134–Hariota 73 (Hook Money 124) (1982 NR 1983 **–**
12g 11f 12.3fg⁴ 12g) 11,500Y; rather leggy, sparely-made filly; half-sister to
several minor winners; dam middle-distance winner; quite a moderate middle-
distance maiden. *P. Kelleway.*

SUELIZELLE 3 b.f. Carnival Dancer 113–Cathro (Appiani II 128) (1982 5d 5d **–**
5f² 6f³ 6f 6f 6d 1983 6fg) lightly-made filly; sprint plater; usually blinkered. *W.
Storey.*

SUFFRAGE 3 b.f. Reform 132–Sindo 91 (Derring-Do 131) (1982 NR 1983 6fg **–**
8d) fourth foal; half-sister to 2 minor winners, including Scarlet Town (by Town
Crier), successful at up to 1¼m; dam won over 5f at 2 yrs; in rear in big fields at
Nottingham in September and Warwick in October. *R. Laing.*

SUFFRED 3 b.f. African Sky 124–Cariole 84 (Pardao 120) (1982 6fg⁴ 6f² 6g⁴ 6g² **66**
7d 1983 6d⁴ 5g* 6f 6f 6f 6fg 5f) robust, useful sort; won handicap at Brighton in
May and ran respectably on other occasions; stays 6f; best on a sound surface;
sweated up and ran moderately sixth start. *J. Benstead.*

SUGAR LOCH 3 b.f. Lochnager 132–Quite Sweet 100 (Super Sam 124) (1982 7g **79**
7d⁴ 6g 1983 8.2v² 8d* 8s³ 8.5g 8f³ 7f 8f 10g 8.2g 10.2fg) lengthy, good-quartered

filly; beat Sedra in great style by 2½ lengths in £4,200 handicap at Newmarket in April; also placed in similar events at Haydock, York and Ascot, but subsequently lost her form completely (tried in blinkers seventh outing); suited by 1m; acts on any going; trained by J. Hindley first 7 starts. *D. Francis.*

SUGAR PALM 2 b.c. Gay Fandango 132–Get Ahead 58 (Silly Season 127) (1983 · 7f 7f 7g² 7f²) Apr 4; IR 8,200Y; quite attractive colt; first foal; dam poor daughter of smart middle-distance stayer Guillotina; good second twice in fair company at Leicester late in the season; will stay 1m; can win a maiden race. *R. Hannon.* **89**

SUGARVILLE JET 3 br.f. Warpath 113–Conchita 113 (Matador 131) (1982 6fg 6s 6d 1983 7s 6fg) big, lengthy filly; seemingly of little account; sold 600 gns Ascot August Sales. *P. Haynes.* **–**

SUL-EL-AH 3 b.f. Tachypous 128–Anjonic 56 (Le Levanstell 122) (1982 6s³ 1983 8v* 7d 10v 12v⁴ 12g 10f 10g⁴ 8fg) attractive, lightly-made filly; got up under strong pressure to beat Octavia Girl by 1½ lengths in 9-runner BonusPrint Masaka Stakes at Kempton in April; not disgraced when fourth in Lupe Stakes at Goodwood and Intercraft Fillies Stakes at Kempton, nor when eighth of 15 behind runaway-winner Sun Princess in Oaks at Epsom in between; seems to stay 1½m; acts on heavy going (didn't run well first outing on firm); sold to NBA 32,000 gns Newmarket December Sales. *P. Kelleway.* **99**

SULLY'S CHOICE (USA) 2 b.g. King Pellinore 127–Salute the Coates (Solar Salute) (1983 6f 6fg 7f² 7h* 6f* 6f 5s 7fg) Apr 11; $27,000Y; sturdy, fair sort; second foal; dam very useful sprinter; awarded good-class seller at Sandown (bought in 9,400 gns) in August on disqualification of My Aisling; sold out of J. Hindley's stable 7,400 gns after making all in similar event at Newcastle later the same month; equally effective at 6f and 7f; acts well on very firm going; best in blinkers. *D. Chapman.* **76**

SULZANO 5 b.g. Rheingold 137–Ribasha (Ribot 142) (1982 12fg² 16g³ 12fg⁴ 19f 16g 12s³ 12d 1983 12s 12d 15.8g 14d 18fg) compact gelding; has an enlarged knee; poor and inconsistent handicapper; stays 2m; probably acts on any going; blinkered when successful; has run creditably for an apprentice; bandaged in 1983; cost 1,000 gns Doncaster January Sales; trained by H. Fleming first 2 starts. *J. Leigh.* **– §**

SUMAYA (USA) 2 b.f. Seattle Slew–Merely (Dr Fager) (1983 7.3d) Feb 12; $1,600,000Y; lengthy filly; third foal; half-sister to Not A Flaw (by T. V. Commercial), a very useful stakes winner over 8.5f, and to Polite Rebuff (by Wajima), a very useful stakes winner at up to 9f; dam unraced daughter of high-class Politely; 14/1, started slowly when twelfth of 14 to Betsy Bay in Rochford Thompson Newbury Stakes in October; sure to do better. *J. Dunlop.* **76 p**

SUMMER FLING 2 b.f. Abwah 118–Triole (Charlottown 127) (1983 6fg 7fg 6fg) Apr 9; 1,200F; dipped-backed filly; first produce; dam winning hurdler; behind in October in varied races, including Newmarket seller; sold 400 gns Doncaster November Sales. *N. Guest.* **–**

SUMMER HOUSE 4 gr.f. Habat 127–Autumn Double 72 (Double Jump 131) (1982 8d 6d 6s 1983 12fg 8fg) big, lengthy filly; of little account nowadays; has worn blinkers and bandages. *W. Wharton.* **–**

SUMMER IMPRESSIONS (USA) 3 ch.f. Lyphard 132–Roussalka 123 (Habitat 134) (1982 5fg 1983 7d 10g 9d 10fg²) quite attractive filly; extremely well bred but lightly raced and rather disappointing; didn't look all that genuine when 2½ lengths second of 11 behind Polestar in maiden race at Newmarket in October; stays 1¼m; tends to sweat up. *H. Cecil.* **70**

SUMMERLAND 3 b.g. Warpath 113–Croisette 95 (Sunny Way 120) (1982 6g 1983 9.4d 9.4d 12.3fg 17.1h) quite well-made gelding; good walker; poor maiden; sold to R. Thompson 6,100 gns Doncaster November Sales after winning over hurdles. *C. Thornton.* **–**

SUMMER LIGHTNING 3 b.f. Hot Spark 126–Carrigeen 94 (Royalty 130) (1982 7.6v 7s 1983 10s 11.7s 8f 8f 10fg 10fg 12d³ 10g 12fg) strong, good-topped filly; poor maiden; best run at 1½m; blinkered fourth to sixth starts. *W. Wightman.* **–**

SUMMER PATH 6 gr.m. Warpath 113–Summersoon 89 (Sheshoon 132) (1982 12g² 12f 12fg³ 12f³ 12.3g 10g⁴ 13.8f 16g² 15.8f* 18d 16g⁴ 15.8d 1983 15.8d 15.8d 16fg 18f 16f² 15.8f) strong, compact mare; bad mover; former plater; probably stays 2m; acts on any going; has run respectably for an apprentice. *M. Camacho.* **–**

SUMMER SINGER 3 b.c. Silly Season 127–La Scala (Royben 125) (1982 6s 1983 6s 6v³ 6v 6fg 5s 5s 8fg) strong colt; bad mover; poor plater; trained part of season by Mrs J. Reavey; sold 320 gns Doncaster November Sales. *W. H. H. Williams.*

SUMMER STAR 6 ch.m. Midsummer Night II 117–Sounding Star 71 (Bleep- —
Bleep 134) (1982 NR 1983 8fg) of little account; has worn blinkers. *J. Bridger.*

SUMMER STOP 2 b. or br.c. Silly Season 126–Belinda Ann (High Treason 126) —
(1983 7.6fg 8g 7g) Mar 12; half-brother to 3 winners in France, including very
useful performers Dancing Marquess (by St Paddy) and Hopeful Bindy (by Hopeful
Venture), successful at up to 1½ m and 1m respectively; dam won over 5f at 2 yrs;
poor form in October maiden and minor events. *D. Elsworth.*

SUNAPA'S OWLET 2 br.f. Derrylin 115–Village Lass (No Mercy 126) (1983 5f 69
5f²) Apr 14; 2,200F, 5,000Y; tall, close-coupled, useful sort; first foal; dam never
ran; second favourite, ½-length second of 8 to Jesters Pet in maiden event at
Redcar in July; should stay 7f. *A. Jarvis.*

SUNDAY SPORT 3 b.f. Homing 130–Cassowary 82 (Kashmir II 125) (1982 NR 64 §
1983 9s* 10.2v 10.6v) 64,000Y; good-topped filly; half-sister to 1¼m winner
Flying Vixen (by Ragstone) and a fair winner in Italy; dam, daughter of Park Hill
winner Cursorial, placed over 1¼m; won weakly-contested maiden race at
Wolverhampton in April; tailed-off last in handicaps subsequently and is possibly
temperamental; should stay at least 1¼m. *P. Walwyn.*

SUNDHOPE LYNN 4 bl.g. Rapid River 127–Read Aloud 57 (Town Crier 119) 48
(1982 6fg 8g 9fg 1983 8fg3 9.4f 7f* 8f 8g3 6f 6g² 8.2fg) plater; won at Edinburgh in
July (no bid); stays 1m; acts on firm going; blinkered nowadays; has had tongue tied
down. *H. Bell.*

SUNFLOWER LAD 4 b.g. Jimsun 121–Floral Palm 69 (Floribunda 136) (1982 —
12.2f 12g3 12.2f 10s4 10fg4 10g3 10.2d 1983 10.2fg) big, strong gelding;
plating-class maiden on flat though is a winning hurdler; will be suited by a return to
1½m; seems to act on any going. *R. Holder.*

SUNLEY BUILDS 5 ch.h. Patch 129–Dance Mistress (Javelot 124) (1982 16s3 74
16fg4 18.4fg4 16.1f3 20fg4 16g 13.3g 12d² 18d 12s4 1983 16d 13g 16f3 16fg 16fg)
quite attractive, rangy horse; fairly useful at his best; lacks pace and stays well;
acts on any going; blinkered once. *G. Hunter.*

SUNNY LOOK 4 ch.f. Lombard 126–Sooner or Later (Sheshoon 132) (1982 12f3 —
12f3 16.1h² 16fg* 15d² 18d 1983 16v) leggy, fair sort; fairly useful at 3 yrs;
backward only start of 1983 in April; sold 4,000 gns Newmarket December Sales.
J. Hindley.

SUNNY REEF 3 b.g. Take a Reef 127–Sunny Bloom 71 (Forlorn River 124) —
(1982 5fg 5f3 7g 5fg 6g4 6s 1983 8s 10h 11s) smallish, leggy gelding; of little
account. *L. Barratt.*

SUNOAK 3 b.c. Averof 123–Blue Queen 54 (Majority Blue 126) (1982 7g 1983 100
8v3 8f* 8f² 9fg 10g*) tall, lengthy, quite attractive colt; landed the odds
impressively by 10 lengths from Quiet Field in maiden race at Sandown in July;
didn't really fulfil that promise and got home by only ½ length from Misty Halo in
amateur riders event at Lingfield in October; stays 1¼m; has a light action and is
suited by fast ground; still on weak side. *G. Harwood.*

SUN PRINCESS 3 b.f. English Prince 129–Sunny Valley (Val de Loir 133) (1982 130
6s² 1983 10v² 12g* 12fg3 12d* 14.6s* 12f²)
Even before she proved it beyond all reasonable doubt by finishing second in
Europe's most important middle-distance race the Prix de l'Arc de Triomphe, Sun
Princess was widely regarded as one of the best British-trained middle-distance
fillies of the now-extensive post-war era. Her record before the Arc was a fine one:
on only her third racecourse appearance she ran away with the Oaks, winning by
the widest margin officially recorded in an English classic for the best part of thirty
years; she also won the Yorkshire Oaks and the St Leger and came a credible
third in the King George VI and Queen Elizabeth Diamond Stakes. Whether Sun
Princess or the outstanding four-year-old Time Charter was the best British-
trained filly to race over middle distances in 1983 is a moot point. There is no
answer that isn't controversial—Time Charter won the King George but finished
two places behind Sun Princess in the Arc—but the choice lies, indisputably,
between the pair. They stood head and shoulders above their contemporaries. That
both are to remain in training for another year is excellent news. If they retain their
ability they will again prove formidable obstacles to any of Europe's middle-distance
horses.
Like so many of the top-class horses produced by the West Ilsley stables Sun

Oaks Stakes, Epsom—Sun Princess storms home in breathtaking fashion. Acclimatise (rails) does best of the remainder

Princess had only a light two-year-old campaign. In fact she made only one racecourse appearance, finishing a good second in the Blue Seal Stakes at Ascot in September, and was still a maiden when she took the field for the Oaks, having gone down by two lengths to Ski Sailing, looking in need of the outing, in the Sir Charles Clore Memorial Stakes in May. Sun Princess stuck to her guns in good style at Newbury without ever getting to grips with Ski Sailing and finished twenty-five lengths in front of third-placed Zeeza. Largely on the strength of this performance and of her trainer's and jockey's recent record in the Oaks—Dunfermline and Bireme had won for them in the previous six-year period—Sun Princess started fourth favourite at Epsom, behind the French-trained Alexandrie, Ski Sailing and the One Thousand Guineas runner-up Royal Heroine. In retrospect it was a substandard Oaks field: the majority of Sun Princess' fourteen rivals didn't manage a win of any sort after the Oaks and only two subsequently won at around a mile and a half (Fields of Spring won the Warwick Oaks and Sun Princess' stable-companion Mytinia won a maiden event at Bath); easily the two best fillies in the field apart from Sun Princess—Cormorant Wood and Royal Heroine—turned out to be much more effective at shorter distances. Furthermore, the competition was considerably diminished by the absence of the Irish-trained Give Thanks who had slammed her rivals in the Esal Bookmakers Oaks Trial at Lingfield and the Musidora Stakes at York. That said, Sun Princess couldn't have beaten her Oaks rivals in more impressive or devastating style; she gave one of the most striking performances seen all season. Sun Princess took a strong hold in the early stages as she was kept under restraint towards the rear and, after being checked for a few strides when hampered going up the hill, Carson eased her towards the outside of the field after the mile post and let her go as the field began to descend the hill to

809

Tattenham Corner. She quickly turned the race into a procession. Sailing into the lead, still on a tight rein, with more than half a mile left, Sun Princess presented a grand sight when set alight in the straight, leaving her rivals floundering and increasing her lead with every stride as Carson drove her out to win by twelve lengths from Acclimatise, with New Coins two and a half lengths further away third, Shore Line fourth and Ski Sailing fifth. No good judge watching Sun Princess stretching out in the closing stages of the Oaks could have been in much doubt that he or she was witnessing a really good performance, and plenty were convinced that Sun Princess would have been capable of winning the Derby with the weight-for-sex allowance of 5 lb, a view with which we concur. Sun Princess routed her field in a manner rarely seen in any flat race, let alone a classic. Not since Never Say Die in the 1954 St Leger had an English classic winner been officially credited with a twelve-length victory and, according to our research, Sun Princess' Oaks win stands in the record books as the most prodigious in the race for at least one hundred and forty years. Official distances were first published for the Oaks in 1842 and since that year only Formosa (1868) and Noblesse (1963), both of whom were returned ten-length winners, have approached Sun Princess' winning margin.

Sun Princess was the first maiden to win an English classic for thirty-three years, although the Irish and French classics have provided examples in the period between the Epsom Oaks successes of Asmena and Sun Princess, most recently those of Ballymore in the Irish Two Thousand Guineas of 1972, of Lady Capulet and Olwyn in the Irish One Thousand Guineas and Irish Guinness Oaks of 1977, and of Madam Gay in the 1981 Prix de Diane (neither Ballymore nor Lady Capulet had any previous racecourse experience). Sun Princess' limited experience was one of the factors which had to be taken into account when deciding her next objective. Should her connections send her to the Curragh for the Irish Guinness Oaks, seemingly the logical step, or take a much bolder course and saddle her for the King George? The redoubtable Dahlia won both races on consecutive Saturdays in 1973 but it was never thought that Sun Princess would attempt the double. In the end Sun Princess' meeting with Give Thanks—acclaimed in some quarters as 'the champion filly of Europe' after adding the Guinness Oaks to her impressive string of victories—waited for another day. Sun Princess became only the second Epsom Oaks winner to contest the King George VI and Queen Elizabeth Stakes in the year of her classic victory, following Pawneese who won both races in 1976. Pawneese won the Oaks in effortless style by five lengths and by the time she took the field at Ascot she had also won the Prix de Diane (French Oaks) and was unbeaten in five races as a three-year-old. The difference in the quality of the opposition to Sun Princess in the King George to that in the Oaks was as striking as it had been in Pawneese's year. Whereas both Sun Princess and Pawneese had their rivals labouring a long way out in the Oaks, in the King George—an event little behind the Arc as a test of a middle-distance horse—there were always other horses moving well around them. Pawneese made every yard of the running at Ascot but her closest pursuers were never far behind and she got home, with others closing on her at the finish, by a length from Bruni, with Orange Bay, Dakota and the Irish Sweeps Derby winner Malacate not far behind. We estimate that Sun Princess encountered opposition of very similar calibre to that faced by Pawneese so it goes almost without saying that we regard her third place, beaten three quarters of a length and a length by Time Charter and Diamond Shoal, as less meritorious than Pawneese's King George victory. By the end of the season we regarded Sun Princess as almost the equal of Pawneese but on King George day Sun Princess' relative inexperience tilted the scales against her. She undoubtedly contributed to her defeat by being too impetuous early on, pulling hard for her head and bounding forward in an effort to avoid the restraints of her rider; Carson had a hard job, even harder than at Epsom, to get her settled and she wasted energy that would have been valuable conserved for the end of the race. Sun Princess improved her position approaching the final straight and put in a strong challenge in the final two furlongs, battling on extremely well under strong riding without ever getting her head in front.

So to the Yorkshire Oaks at York's August meeting—and the eagerly-awaited clash between Sun Princess and Give Thanks. The presence in the field of Acclimatise, third to Give Thanks in the Lancashire Oaks after finishing second at Epsom, and of the Irish Guinness Oaks third Green Lucia provided added interest but Sun Princess (6/5 favourite) and Give Thanks (7/4) dominated the betting. For the exceptionally tough Give Thanks it was the eighth race of the season—she had suffered her only defeat at the hands of the Derby runner-up Carlingford Castle in the Gallinule Stakes—and, unfortunately, she didn't give her best running at York. Green Lucia convincingly turned the tables on Give Thanks and kept her out of second place by three lengths; Sun Princess beat Give Thanks by seven lengths.

The most significant thing about Sun Princess' performance was that she showed herself more amenable to restraint. Allowed to go to the front almost from the start, Sun Princess set a tremendous gallop but Carson was able to steady her after a quarter of a mile or so and keep enough up his sleeve to enable Sun Princess to stretch again when challenged by Give Thanks early in the straight; Sun Princess had the race sewn up from two furlongs out and, again kept up to her work, strode out with tremendous zest in the closing stages.

Once again Sun Princess' connections were in a quandary about her next engagement. With a Prix de l'Arc challenge the top priority, was it to be the Trusthouse Forte Prix Vermeille at Longchamp, a race with an outstanding record in recent years as a guide to the Arc, or the St Leger? The St Leger isn't our idea of an ideal preparatory race for the Arc—the two races are designed to try different attributes in the racehorse—and if Sun Princess had been ours she would have run in the Vermeille. But, after much deliberation, Sun Princess was announced as a definite runner for the final classic early in St Leger week – with the proviso that she would not run if the going became soft. The announcement, followed shortly afterwards by a similar one that the Prix du Jockey-Club winner Caerleon would also be in the field, added considerable interest to a St Leger which had seemed, at one time, likely to attract a disappointing field. Hopes that the St Leger would be made memorable by a clash between Sun Princess and Caerleon were dashed when Caerleon was withdrawn on the excuse of the rain that fell on the Thursday of the St Leger meeting. The announcement of Caerleon's withdrawal looked premature when the track dried out well on the Friday, but further heavy rain, which turned the going soft, threatened in the end to rob the St Leger of Sun Princess' presence also. Reportedly, Sun Princess was close to being withdrawn an hour before the race, her owners apparently wishing to scratch her while her trainer was said to be emphatically in favour of letting her take her chance. Thankfully for the Doncaster executive and the large crowd, Hern was able to persuade the owners to allow the filly to start, having convinced them that the Doncaster going had not become so testing that it might prejudice Sun Princess' Arc prospects. Sun Princess started 11/8 favourite in a field of ten which included the Derby runner-up Carlingford Castle, the Grand Prix de Paris winner Yawa and the Prix du Jockey-Club third Esprit du Nord. Aware no doubt of the possibility that the somewhat-impetuous Sun Princess might not get the St Leger trip in a race from end to end, and also of the desirability of her having as easy a race as possible with the Arc only three weeks away, Sun Princess' trainer devised a plan which produced the desired result—a victory for Sun Princess achieved without her taking any more out of herself than was absolutely necessary. Hern's plan called for Sun Princess' pacemaker Sailor's Dance to set only a fair gallop in order to prevent the St Leger developing into a gruelling test of stamina. Mercer on Sailor's Dance executed the plan to perfection, denying the early lead to Esprit du Nord and then settling back to a steady pace. How moderate a gallop Sailor's Dance set can be judged from the fact that the

Yorkshire Oaks, York—Sun Princess wins from Green Lucia and the disappointing Give Thanks

field, which included the modest maiden Rivensky (a 500/1-shot), was still closely grouped turning for home. Esprit du Nord, pressed by Carlingford Castle, took over from Sailor's Dance with more than three furlongs to go, Sun Princess giving chase after being waited with in the middle of the field. Sun Princess drew up in impressive style to complete the lead inside the two-furlong marker and held the renewed challenges of Esprit du Nord and Carlingford Castle in the final furlong to win by three quarters of a length and a short head. Fourth-placed Dom Pasquini was six lengths further back and the rest well strung out. Sun Princess was a decisive winner but she had to fight harder for her victory than many had anticipated; Carson had to show her the whip in the closing stages.

For master trainer Dick Hern it was the second time in seven years that he had saddled a filly to complete the Oaks–St Leger double, Sun Princess' achievement matching that of Dunfermline. Only two other fillies, Sun Chariot and Meld, have won the Oaks and St Leger in the past three quarters of a century. Very few Oaks winners contest the St Leger nowadays—Ginevra, third in Boucher's year, was the only one between Meld and Dunfermline, and there was none between Dunfermline and Sun Princess. Sun Princess was Hern's sixth St Leger winner, following Hethersett, Provoke, Bustino, Dunfermline and Cut Above and he has now sent out the winners of thirteen English classics, having also won the Oaks three times, the Derby twice, with Troy and Henbit, and the Two Thousand Guineas and the One Thousand Guineas with Brigadier Gerard and Highclere respectively. Only Vincent O'Brien among present-day trainers has a better record: he has saddled six Derby winners, three Two Thousand Guineas winners, three St Leger winners, two Oaks winners and also a winner of the One Thousand Guineas, a total of fifteen. Hern, whose career began in 1958 when he was appointed private trainer to Major L. B. Holliday, shares with O'Brien the distinction of having saddled a winner in each of the English and Irish classics.

Both Dunfermline and Sun Princess went for the Prix de l'Arc de Triomphe (sponsored in 1983 by Trusthouse Forte) after success at Doncaster. Dunfermline ran very well at Longchamp, finishing fourth to Alleged with whom she had fought out the finish of a very strongly-run St Leger in splendid isolation from the eleven other runners. Dunfermline's performance at Doncaster was exceptional—in our view, as good as any by a British-trained filly since the days of Petite Etoile and superior, strictly in terms of merit, to anything achieved so far by Time Charter or Sun Princess. But Dunfermline had her limitations in that she required a good test of stamina to be seen to best advantage; she needed all the length of the straight, or almost as long, to get up in the Oaks and was beaten for finishing speed in a muddling Yorkshire Oaks. Sun Princess looked a much better proposition for the Arc than Dunfermline had done and she gave a cracking display, keeping in close touch with her pacemaker Sailor's Dance—sent about his business from the start this time—until taking over before the final straight and sustaining a long run for home to hold off all except All Along. Sun Princess went down by a length, running on most courageously and giving a performance which, in our view, bettered even her Oaks-winning effort. We were astonished to hear criticism of Carson's handling

St Leger Stakes, Doncaster—Sun Princess holds Esprit du Nord (right) and Carlingford Castle

of Sun Princess in the Arc. Some critics expressed the view that he made too much use of her but we thought he rode her to perfection. Sun Princess is a long-striding, resolute galloper, the type that usually requires time and space to get opened out. She is not at all the sort of horse to be switching about in a race from one place to another. She hasn't the instant acceleration and handiness of a Time Charter, the type that can be whisked about as circumstances demand, take her opening when it comes and accelerate clear. Waiting tactics would have been wholly inappropriate on Sun Princess in the Prix de l'Arc field and Carson did the right thing to get her opened out a long way from home. His enterprise ensured that she was kept clear of interference and that her stamina and her ability to sustain her top pace for a long way were brought fully into play. Willie Carson is an excellent jockey, not least of his attributes being his boundless energy and enthusiasm: he rides every race as if it were the Derby or the Prix de l'Arc. He was champion jockey in Britain for the fifth time, reaching 159 winners in spite of spending twenty-six days on the side-lines as a result of suspensions received for riding offences. The penalties imposed on Carson—he received three separate suspensions, one of six days, another of eight and a third of twelve—were the subject of much comment in the racing Press, the majority view being that they were too harsh. Cauthen (twenty days), Starkey (nineteen days), Reid (eighteen days), Cook (fourteen days) and Hide (twelve days) were others to suffer lengthy absences from the racecourse because of riding offences. Allegations were made in some sections of the Press of a so-called 'crackdown' by the authorities on riders, but in fact the number and severity of suspensions for careless and reckless riding was not markedly different from other recent seasons. Thirty-eight individual suspensions (averaging 6.1 days) were imposed on jockeys and apprentices in the 1983 Flat season, compared to thirty-five (at an average of 5.2 days) the previous season, the figures for which include a six-day suspension on an amateur. Perhaps the fact that some of the big names were the worst offenders in the latest season—Baxter (twenty days), Robinson and the apprentice Dawson (fourteen days each) topped the list in 1982—had much to do with the publicity the subject received, although the automatic 'totting up' process, introduced in 1983, whereby successive offences were treated with increasing severity, has been dropped.

Sun Princess (b.f. 1980)	English Prince (b 1971)	Petingo (b 1965)	Petition
			Alcazar
		English Miss (b 1955)	Bois Roussel
			Virelle
	Sunny Valley (b 1972)	Val de Loir (b 1959)	Vieux Manoir
			Vali
		Sunland (ch 1965)	Charlottesville
			Sunny Gulf

The rangy Sun Princess doesn't carry any spare flesh when in training but she is quite attractive nonetheless and is a good mover in all her paces; she went down to post like a filly on top of the world before all her races as a three-year-old, a tremendous credit to her trainer and those who handled her at West Ilsley. Sun Princess was English Prince's second classic-winning offspring, following the ill-fated 1982 Irish One Thousand Guineas winner Prince's Polly. English Prince won the Irish Sweeps Derby and was retired to stud at a time when his sire Petingo was on the crest of a wave. Unfortunately, English Prince proved a rather disappointing sire for a horse of his ability and his own popularity waned after only a few seasons. He was sent to Japan in 1980, leaving six European crops behind him, and died there in 1983. Most of English Prince's progeny stay and there is plenty of stamina on the distaff side of Sun Princess's pedigree. Sunny Valley, whose first foal was the smart mile- to mile-and-a-quarter filly Dancing Shadow (by Dancer's Image), won in France as a three-year-old at ten and a half furlongs and at a mile and a half, showing useful form. She hasn't been the most fertile of broodmares and has produced only three foals—Sun Princess is her second and the unraced two-year-old Troyanos (by Troy) her third—up to the end of 1983. Sunny Valley is bred on the same lines as Shergar's dam Sharmeen, by the French Derby winner Val de Loir out of a Charlottesville mare. Sunny Valley's dam, the useful winner Sunland, proved extremely well suited by a distance of ground, coming third in the Park Hill Stakes, and she was a half-sister to the 1960 Park Hill winner Sunny Cove and to a couple of other fairly useful stayers. The family has been at the Ballymacoll Stud in Ireland since the days when the stud was owned by Miss Dorothy Paget; Sun Princess' owner acquired the stud in the late-'fifties. Sunny Valley and Sunny Cove, the dam of that grand old warrior Crucible and grandam of the high-class miler Sun Prince and the Canadian International Championship winner Great Neck, are among the best broodmares from the family to date.

Sun Princess has better prospects of doing well at four than Dunfermline

Sir Michael Sobell's "Sun Princess"

appeared to have. As we have said, the overwhelming impression of Dunfermline as a three-year-old was that she was first and foremost a stayer; but with the St Leger open only to three-year-olds there wasn't a top race in the British Calendar which catered for a horse of her type and, raced over distances short of her best, she failed to reproduce her St Leger form as a four-year-old. It is not necessary to give more than a passing nod of attention to the question of the limit of Sun Princess' stamina (she is bred to stay well but her performance in the St Leger was a little way removed from her best) because she is most unlikely to tackle distances beyond a mile and a half from now on. To our eyes she has developed into a true mile-and-a-half horse and is just the late-developing, progressive type one would expect to continue to train on. She's a really grand, courageous filly and we wish her well. *R. Hern.*

SUNRULLAH 4 ch.g. Sun Prince 128–Fleet Serenade (Lorenzaccio 130) (1982 12fg 12fg 8.2g 15d 12.2d 1983 13v 8g) tall, leggy gelding; poor maiden; possibly temperamental. *W. H. H. Williams.* —

SUNSHINE GAL 5 br.m. Alto Volante 109–Chinese Princess (Sunny Way 120) (1982 12.2g 10.1fg[4] 10f 8g 10.1fg* 10fg[2] 10g[4] 12s* 10s[3] 1983 12s 12fg[2] 11.7f[3] 10fg 15.8fg* 12f) neat mare; stayed on well to win handicap at Chester in August; suited by a test of stamina; acts on any going; has won for an apprentice. *N. Guest.* **68**

SUPER BEES 2 b.c. Manor Farm Boy 114–Monolyn (Happy Monarch 109) (1983 6f 8.2f 5g 5g) Mar 12; non-thoroughbred colt; third known foal; dam never ran; soundly beaten in maiden races and sellers; sold 460 gns Doncaster November Sales. *J. Berry.* —

SUPERBIA (USA) 2 b.f King Pellinore 127–La Duena (Jacinto) (1983 8g[2] 9g[2] 7f) Mar 30; $35,000Y; workmanlike filly; good mover; fifth foal; half-sister to 1981 **81**

814

2-y-o 5f winner Wodonga (by Shecky Greene); dam minor stakes winner at up to 1m; runner-up in 8-runner £3,400 event at Goodwood in September and 13-runner maiden race (favourite) at Wolverhampton in October; suited by 1m+; possibly not at her best on firm going; sold 15,000 gns Newmarket December Sales. *H. Candy.*

SUPERBOWL 2 br.c. Sexton Blake 126–Ruffled Bird 79 (Relko 136) (1983 7f 7f³ 8d 7d) Mar 22; 31,000Y; smallish, lengthy colt; has a round action; half-brother to several winners here and abroad; dam won over 1½m and 13f; quite a modest maiden; will be well suited by 1¼m+; acts on firm going and a soft surface; blinkered final outing. *J. Dunlop.*   **76**

SUPERB PRINCESS 2 ch.f. Roman Warrior 132–Super Princess 85 (Falcon 131) (1983 5.1fg 5f 5fg 6f 6f³ 5f³ 5s 5d³ 6g 6fg) May 5; 400F; strong, lengthy filly; third foal; sister to 3-y-o 5f winner Super Warrior and half-sister to a winning plater; dam won over 7f at 2 yrs and also over hurdles; modest plater; best form at 5f; acts on firm going and a soft surface; wears blinkers; has worn bandages. *K. Ivory.*   **62**

SUPER DIP 2 b.g. Golden Dipper 119–Miss Twist 84 (Major Portion 129) (1983 6g 5g 6fg 7g 6g) May 14; of no account; blinkered last 2 outings. *R. Hoad.*   **–**

SUPER EXPRESS 2 ch.c. Hotfoot 126–Gwynfa 65 (Welsh Pageant 132) (1983 7f 7fg 10fg) Mar 5; IR 22,000F, 23,000Y; big, strong, lengthy colt; first produce; dam lightly-raced half-sister to Royal Lodge Stakes winner Adios; little worthwhile form; favourite in poor maiden event at Nottingham in October on final outing. *M. Jarvis.*   **–**

SUPERFLOSS 3 gr.f. Supergrey 90–Gazelle V (Tynwald 98) (1982 NR 1983 12fg 10.1f) non-thoroughbred filly; fourth reported foal; dam never ran; tailed-off last in maiden and minor events. *R. Howe.*   **–**

SUPERFLUOUS 3 b.g. Track Spare 125–Super Jennie 80 (Stephen George 102) (1982 6g 6s 1983 7fg 11fg*) useful-looking gelding; held up when winning small handicap at Ayr in July; little previous form, including in a seller; suited by 11f; acts on a firm surface; sold 7,200 gns Newmarket Autumn Sales. *Sir Mark Prescott.*   **64**

SUPERIOR MAID 2 ch.f. Gay Fandango 132–Rounceval 79 (Ridan) (1983 6fg 8fg) Mar 20; 18,000Y; rangy filly; second foal; half-sister to a winning plater; dam won twice at around 1m; showed up in fair company at Redcar in September and October; may improve. *D. Garraton.*   **–**

SUPERIOR QUALITY 3 ch.f. Star Appeal 133–Lavington 64 (Ratification 129) (1982 6g 7.2s 8g 1983 10d 8.2g 12f 8f 14.7fg 8f) big, lengthy filly; plating-class maiden; blinkered final start; sold 9,000 gns Newmarket December Sales. *D. Garraton.*   **–**

SUPERLATIVE 2 ch.c. Nebbiolo 125–Clariden 82 (Hook Money 124) (1983 5v* 5g* 6fg 6g* 5.5g² 5s* 6fg² 7fg4)   **118**

No two-year-old had a harder time at the top level in 1983 than Superlative: he ran in no fewer than six pattern races in Britain and France. It speaks volumes for his toughness and enthusiasm, as well as his ability, that he managed to reach the frame in all but the first of them, winning the Anglia Television July Stakes and the Flying Childers Stakes.

The July Stakes at Newmarket marked Superlative's second attempt at winning a pattern race. Three weeks earlier he had started second favourite to

Anglia Television July Stakes, Newmarket—Superlative holds Kalim in a driving finish

Flying Childers Stakes, Doncaster—Superlative justifies favouritism from Defecting Dancer to record another important victory

Our Dynasty in the Coventry Stakes at Royal Ascot, on the strength of victories in a maiden race at Doncaster and in the Massey Europower Trophy at Beverley, in the latter of which he had beaten Maajid comfortably. He never promised to justify the support at Ascot, turning in his one poor effort; he was always behind and finished in the rear behind the impressive Chief Singer, who was to start an odds-on favourite for the July Stakes. Whatever the reason, he proceeded to turn the form-book upside down at Newmarket with a sharply contrasting display: in front from the start, he quickened for home with a vengeance two furlongs out and then battled on most gamely to hold Kalim's challenge by a head. Chief Singer was only fifth, beaten over nine lengths. Less than three weeks later Superlative confirmed his improvement with a fine effort in the Prix Robert Papin at Maisons-Laffitte, sticking on so well that he went down by only half a length to the unbeaten Masarika, who admittedly was allowed to take things rather easily in the the closing stages.

Superlative's next target was said to be the seven-furlong Laurent Perrier Champagne Stakes at Doncaster in September but his connections seemed to decide that discretion was the better part of valour once it became clear Lear Fan and Trojan Fen were intended runners, and switched him to the following day's Flying Childers Stakes over five furlongs. He started favourite to beat Defecting Dancer who had narrowly lost third place to Masarika in the Prix Morny the previous month. With the third favourite, the Cherry Hinton winner Chapel Cottage, running into all sorts of trouble the two market leaders had the finish to themselves. Superlative, who seems never to do more than is necessary, always had the edge in a good last-furlong tussle, and got the verdict by half a length with Chapel Cottage and Reesh sharing third place three lengths further away. Superlative's last two outings came in William Hill sponsored events at Newmarket in the autumn, the Middle Park and Dewhurst Stakes. Although he wasn't at all disgraced over seven furlongs in the latter, when fourth of ten, just over seven lengths behind El Gran Senor, he made a much bolder showing when second favourite to Vacarme in the Middle Park over six. After finding Creag-An-Sgor travelling just too well throughout, Superlative also looked likely to find Vacarme too strong up the final hill. He refused to give in though, fighting back so well he regained second place near the line, a length and a half behind Creag-An-Sgor.

Superlative is a strong, imposing individual with plenty of scope. He invariably impressed in the paddock and his condition throughout a hard season reflected great credit on his trainer. Superlative must also have taken the eye as a younger horse; he fetched 18,000 guineas at the Ballsbridge Sales in Dublin as a foal and 22,000 guineas at Newmarket as a yearling. His sales took place before his sire, the Two Thousand Guineas winner Nebbiolo, had made much impact as a stallion—Nebbiolo finished down in forty-third place in the 1982 list of leading sires.

However, 1983 saw numerous horses by Nebbiolo winning good races, Executive Man, Nepula, Annie Edge, Burslem, Glowing Embers, Sedra and Santella Man among them. Most of these stay at least a mile but the distaff side of Superlative's pedigree, in addition to his performance in the Dewhurst, suggests he'll prove better at short distances. Superlative's grandam Matterhorn was a speedy five-furlong performer at two, winning three of her seven starts, and both her winners in Britain, Gisela and Mattock, gained their victories over five furlongs at two. Superlative's dam, the moderate maiden Clariden, was placed twice over five furlongs as a juvenile.

		{ Yellow God	{ Red God
		(ch 1967)	Sally Deans
	{ Nebbiolo	{ Novara	{ Birkhahn
	(ch 1974)	(b 1965)	Norbelle
Superlative		{ Hook Money	{ Bernborough
(ch. c. May 3, 1981)		(ch 1961)	Besieged
	{ Clariden	{ Matterhorn	{ Matador
	(ch 1966)	(b 1961)	Priory Hill

She has fared much better as a broodmare, producing five other winners from nine previous foals, notably the very tough and useful sprinter Yonge St Clare (by Queen's Hussar) and the useful 1976 two-year-old Cambridge Star (by Dike), a winner at up to seven furlongs. Interestingly only one of Clariden's winners here and in Canada has won over a distance as great as a mile. We doubt whether Superlative will become the second to do so. Excellent though his two-year-old form was, he has a fair amount of improvement to make if he's to reach the top of the tree. However he's such a grand sort, and is in such capable hands, that the possibility cannot be ruled out. *W. O'Gorman.*

SUPERSHOE WONDER 2 gr.f. Abwah 118–Moulton Star (Moulton 128) (1983   –
5.3f) Mar 25; 300Y, 300 2-y-o; first foal; dam in rear in maiden and minor events; seventh of 9 in claiming race at Brighton in August. *R. Simpson.*

SUPER SIOUX 3 ch.f. Mandrake Major 122–Siouxsie 90 (Warpath 113) (1982   81
5g² 5v* 5f* 5fg² 6f* 5fg³ 6d² 6g* 6fg4 1983 7v² 6v 8v4 8f 8f) sturdy filly; had stiffish tasks when in frame in handicaps in spring; ran moderately final start (July); possibly stays 1m; acts on any going. *J. Berry.*

SUPER SOMETHING 2 b.f. Tower Walk 130–Water Pageant 58 (Welsh   –
Pageant 132) (1983 5g 5g) Mar 9; 6,000Y; second foal; half-sister to fair 1982 2-y-o sprinter Tinker's Image (by Dancer's Image); dam middle-distance maiden; behind in maiden races at Warwick in October. *G. Hunter.*

SUPER SUNSHINE (USA) 3 ch.c. Nodouble–On With It (On-and-On) (1982   –
5fg 6f 7d* 7g 7v 1983 7f 8f 7fg 7h 6f) shapely, attractive colt; good mover; disappointing since winning at Chester as a 2-y-o; should stay at least 1m. *G. Hunter.*

SUPERTRIM 3 ch.g. Continuation 120–Sassanian Queen 71 (Sassafras 135)   –
(1982 5f 5f³ 6f 1983 6fg 7f) lengthy gelding; no worthwhile form, including in sellers. *J. Hardy.*

SUPER TRIP 2 b.c. Windjammer (USA)–Esker Rose (Sunny Way 120) (1983 7fg   85
7g 6fg) May 12; IR 500F, 880Y, 8,800 2-y-o; useful-looking colt; half-brother to 2 minor winners; dam never ran; 2 lengths fifth of 24 to Native Charmer in maiden race at Doncaster in November, final outing and best effort; should stay 1m; looks sure to win a race. *G. Hunter.*

SUPER WARRIOR 3 b.g. Roman Warrior 132–Super Princess 84 (Falcon 131)   47
(1982 5g* 5g 5f 5fg4 6f³ 6fg 6g 5f4 5g 5. 1fg² 1983 5v* 5s 5s³ 5s 6v 6v² 7fg 5fg 6fg 5s 6fg) sparely-made gelding; made all in small handicap at Ayr in March and was second in a seller, but ran poorly later in season; stays 6f; acts on any going, but seems best with some give in the ground nowadays; occasionally blinkered. *K. Ivory.*

SUPPER'S READY (USA) 5 br.g. Nalees Man–Irish Wedding (Advocator)   81
(1982 NR 1983 12d4 14s* 14s* 16d4 16f) quite a moderate handicapper; won at Salisbury and Goodwood in May; stays 2m; form only with some give in the ground; suitable mount for an apprentice; blinkered last 3 starts at 3 yrs. *H. Candy.*

SUPREME CHALLENGER 3 br.c. Coded Scrap 90–Celtic Gwen 60 (Celtic   –
Ash) (1982 7.2s 5d 5d 1983 8v4 8g 9d 8d) poor form in sellers; blinkered last 2 starts; sold 1,050 gns Doncaster June Sales, for export to Norway. *T. Fairhurst.*

SURAJ 3 b.c. Pitskelly 122–Miss Wittington (Red God 128§) (1982 6fg 6f⁴ 8fg   — 8.2s³ 1983 10.1fg 10g 12.2d) small, leggy, lightly-made colt; lightly raced and little form in 1983 (bandaged final start); promises to stay beyond 1m; sold 2,600 gns Newmarket Autumn Sales. *P. Haslam.*

SURE FIT 3 b.f. Reliance II 137–Diorina 91 (Manacle 123) (1982 NR 1983 7fg 11f   — 10fg 10fg 7fg) second foal; half-sister to sprint winner Cheri Berry (by Air Trooper); dam at her best at 2 yrs when winner over 5.3f; behind in varied races, twice last. *W. Wightman.*

SURELY 2 b.f. Martinmas 128–Jane Shaw (Galivanter 131) (1983 6d) Mar 17; IR   — 6,500F, 11,000Y; tall, workmanlike filly; sister to 6f and 7f winner Priory Lane and half-sister to numerous winners, including useful 1982 2-y-o 6f winner Octavia Girl (by Octavo); dam poor maiden; behind in 16-runner maiden race at Newbury in October. *M. Smyly.*

SURFING ERA 2 b.f. Young Generation 129–Tidal Water 85 (High Line 125)   **69** (1983 5v 5.8s 6fg³ 6g* 7h 7fg 7fg 6s) Apr 16; tall, fair sort; first foal to Northern Hemisphere time; half-sister to winner in Australia; dam won over 6f and 7f at 2 yrs; plater; bought in 6,000 gns after making virtually all at Lingfield in June; off course for 2 months afterwards, and no form on return; should stay 7f; acts on a firm surface. *Mrs J. Reavey.*

SURPRISE ATTACK 2 gr.c. Town Crier 119–Pearl Harbour 83 (Martial 131)   — (1983 8s 7g 10.2fg) Feb 27; 8,600Y; strong, plain colt; closely related to fair 1980 2-y-o 6f winner Sovereign Landing (by Sovereign Path) and half-brother to 2 other winners; dam won over 6f at 3 yrs; no form in autumn maiden and minor events. *E. Eldin.*

SURREY RAINBOW 3 gr.f. Warpath 113–Brandy Dip (Hot Brandy 119) (1982   — NR 1983 12v 12s 12s 11.5fg) fair sort; half-sister to fairly useful 6f to 1m winner Ziggy (by King Log); dam never ran; well beaten in varied company; sold 400 gns Newmarket July Sales. *D. Wilson.*

SUSAN'S SUNSET 5 br.m. Welsh Saint 126–Honi Soit (Above Suspicion 127)   **47** (1982 7f 8g 7f² 7fg* 8fg² 7fg³ 7g 7f 7f⁴ 7g³ 7f 7g 7fg 6fg³ 7f 7g 1983 5v 8s 6fg 7f 6fg³ 6f 8fg³ 7f 7f 7g 7.6fg 6fg) neat mare; former plater; effective at 6f to 1m; probably acts on any going; usually blinkered nowadays. *S. Woodman.*

SUSA STEEL 2 ch.c. Thatching 131–Extra La (Exbury 138) (1983 5.1g³ 5f*   **95** 5fg* 5f³ 5fg⁴ 5fg³ 5fg) Mar 13; 17,000Y; fair sort; good walker but not a good mover; first foal; dam Irish 7f and 1m winner; justified favouritism in maiden race at Thirsk in June and nursery at Lingfield in July; apparently better at 5f than 6f; acts on firm going; consistent. *J. Hindley.*

SUSIE'S BABY 3 b.f. Balidar 133–Game Girl 85 (Abernant 142) (1982 5d 5s   — 1983 6fg 6f) small filly; behind in maiden races and a minor event. *R. Laing.*

SUSSEX QUEEN 4 ch.f. Music Boy 124–Counsel's Opinion 83 (Counsel 118)   **50** (1982 6fg³ 6fg 6f 6fg 7fg³ 8d⁴ 8.2s⁴ 7d 1983 9s 8v 8s 9f 11.7f 11.7f 11.7f³ 12f⁴ 12f 11g) fair sort; quite a moderate handicapper at her best; seems to stay 1½m; acts on any going; blinkered final start; sometimes bandaged on near-hind; sold 2,000 gns Newmarket Autumn Sales. *W. Musson.*

Abernant Stakes, Newmarket—Sweet Monday keeps on strongly

SUZY MANDEL 8 ch. g. Our Mirage 123–Sparkling Jewel (Faberge II 121) (1982 NR 1983 15.8d) strong gelding; staying maiden; has had tongue tied down. *R. Allan.* –

SUZY MARIE 3 b.f. Swing Easy 126–Betony 76 (Sovereign Path 125) (1982 5s 5fg 1983 5fg 6f 6f 5h⁴ 5f 5fg) compact filly; showed signs of a little ability third and fourth starts; pulled up final outing. *R. Hollinshead.* –

SWALEDALE (USA) 3 gr.c. Al Hattab–Door Star (Stage Door Johnny) (1982 7d³ 8f 1983 11.5g 12g* 15.8g) close-coupled colt; made virtually all when winning claiming race at Leicester in September; stays 1½m; appears to act on any going; sold 5,000 gns Newmarket Autumn Sales, and exported to Malaysia. *M. Stoute.* 71

SWEEP UP JACK (FR) 3 b.g. Giacometti 130–Sweep Up 82 (Relko 136) (1982 NR 1983 12v 12s 10g 12f) quite a well-made gelding; first foal; dam stayed well; well beaten, including in a seller; blinkered second outing; sold 420 gns Ascot July Sales. *C. Austin.* –

SWEET ANDY 4 br.c. Ardoon 124–Black Honey 91 (March Past 124) (1982 6s 6d 9f 7.6fg⁴ 8.2f 8f 7f 7.6d 10g 12f³ 1983 16s 8v 8s² 8fg 8g) neat colt; plater; seems to stay 1½m; acts on any going; usually wears blinkers; sometimes bandaged; suitable mount for an apprentice. *J. Gilbert.* 47

SWEET AS PIE 7 b.m. Andrea Mantegna–Mernian 100 (Counsel 118) (1982 NR 1983 16.5f) poor maiden; has been to stud. *K. Bailey.* –

SWEETCAL 6 b.m. Caliban 123–Honey House (Road House II) (1982 NR 1983 10s* 12f 12g) tall, angular, plain mare; sister to poor hurdler; dam of little account; winning hurdler; easily won 20-runner apprentice event at Brighton in May; bandaged when tailed off the following month, and wasn't seen out again until September; should stay 1½m; probably needs some give in the ground. *P. Cundell.* 54

SWEET COLLEEN 3 ch.f. Connaught 130–Tirana 101 (Ragusa 137) (1982 NR 1983 10d 9fg 12.2g) 1,250 3-y-o; closely related to winning middle-distance stayer Scutari (by St Paddy) and half-sister to 2 winners; dam won over 6f and 7f at 2 yrs; behind in maiden and minor races in autumn. *M. W. Easterby.* –

SWEET DIPPER 6 br.g. Golden Dipper 119–Sharp and Sweet (Javelot 124) (1982 7fg 7fg 7fg 8.3g 9g 7d 1983 8g 8g) poor handicapper nowadays; stays 7f; probably acts on any going; has run creditably for an apprentice; blinkered last 2 starts in 1982. *W. Wightman.* –

SWEET ECSTASY 4 ch.f. Rarity 129–Acrasia 74 (Bold Lad, Ire 133) (1982 8fg 7d 10fg 10.8fg 10g 10g 11 7s² 12.2s* 10s 12g* 1983 11.7d 12v 14fg 11.7fg 12fg 12f 13.3g 12d⁴ 12d) small, close-coupled filly; good walker; didn't find her form at 4 yrs; suited by 1½m and should get further; acts well on soft going; sold to C. Tinkler 3,200 gns Newmarket December Sales. *W. Wightman.* –

SWEET EMMA 3 b.f. Welsh Saint 126–Gang Plank 84 (Tower Walk 130) (1982 5s* 5s* 5fg* 6d⁴ 6g 1983 6s³ 8f⁴ 7fg⁴) lengthy, attractive ex-Irish filly; won her first 3 races as a 2-y-o, including Heinz '57' Phoenix Stakes at Leopardstown; finished very close third to Solimile and Kirchner in £6,800 event at Lingfield in June on first outing for new connections but was subsequently a quite soundly-beaten fourth in Coronation Stakes at Royal Ascot and in £6,600 handicap at Newmarket (sweated badly and pulled hard); stays 6f; acts on any going. *P. Walwyn.* 95

SWEET FRAGRANCE (USA) 3 ch.f. Forli–Oh So Sweet 90 (Ballymoss 136) (1982 NR 1983 11v 11.5fg 10g 14g 12fg*) $122,000 2-y-o; big, lengthy, lightly-made filly; half-sister to 3 minor winners here and in USA; dam, placed from 1m to 1½m, is sister to very smart 1m to 1½m horse Sweet Moss and half-sister to top 2-y-o filly Soft Angels; showed signs of a little ability before winning minor event at Edinburgh in November; stays 1½m. *R. Williams.* 67

SWEETHEART 3 b.f. Reform 132–Cupid's Delight 84 (St Paddy 133) (1982 8f 8g⁴ 1983 9g) compact filly; bred to be suited by 1¼m+. *W. Haigh.* –

SWEET JUDICIARY 3 b.f. Legal Eagle 126–Sharp and Sweet (Javelot 124) (1982 6g 5fg 1983 11.7v 11.7v) small, close-coupled filly; in rear in varied races. *W. Wightman.* –

SWEET MILLION 3 ch.f. Sweet Revenge 129–Cendrillon (Sound Track 132) (1982 6s 1983 8d 7d³ 10fg 10f) lengthy filly; lightly-raced maiden; best run at 7f; sold 1,100 gns Doncaster September Sales. *R. Sheather.* –

SWEET MONDAY 5 b.h. Sweet Revenge 129–Solly Graham 82 (Romulus 129) (1982 5s 6d⁴ 5fg 6f² 5fg 6f² 6f 5g⁴ 5g 5g 6g* 6f 6g 5d 1983 6v* 6d* 6v 5d⁴ 6fg 7.3f 119

7g) lengthy horse; has had a soft palate operation; smart performer; beat Pusey Street a length in £3,700 event at Kempton in April and made all and kept on strongly to account for Toast of the Town by 4 lengths in Abernant Stakes at Newmarket later in month; also ran well to be length fourth to Fearless Lad in Temple Stakes at Sandown in May and just over 4 lengths sixth to Habibti in 6f William Hill July Cup at Newmarket; suited by 6f but ran moderately over 7f final start; acted on any going; usually sweated up; ran below form when tried in blinkers; tended to hang third start; standing at Vine House Stud, Lancashire. *J. Holt.*

SWEET SAVAGE 3 ch.f. Gay Fandango 132–Cronk Bourne (Brigadier Gerard 144) (1982 7fg 5f⁴ 6s 1983 7fg 7f 7f) lengthy filly; should have stayed 7f; dead. *M. W. Easterby.*   —

SWEET SLEW (USA) 3 b.f. Seattle Slew–Trick Chick (Prince John) (1982 6fg 6g² 1983 8f² 8f) big, lengthy filly; good mover; looked promising when second behind Trakady in maiden race at Newbury in July but didn't run particularly well when heavily-backed favourite at Newmarket later in month; will stay beyond 1m; sent to USA and won 7f stakes there. *J. Sutcliffe.*   ?

SWEET SMILE 3 b.f. Native Bazaar 122–Flaretown 63 (Town Crier 119) (1982 5d 5d* 5d 1983 5g 5s* 5g 5d 5g) leggy filly; decisively landed a gamble in all-aged seller at Beverley in September; bought in 3,200 gns afterwards; best form at 5f; acts well on soft going. *S. Matthews.*   61

SWEET SOLICITOR 4 ch.g. Legal Eagle 126–Sharp and Sweet (Javelot 124) (1982 5f 7.6f 10.8fg 10.1g 10.1g 12g) smallish, workmanlike gelding; good mover; behind in varied company; sometimes blinkered; sold to J. King 1,450 gns Ascot 2nd June Sales. *W. Wightman.*   —

SWEET SOLUTION 3 ch.f. Sweet Revenge 129–Age Old 70 (St Alphage 119) (1982 NR 1983 7s 7v 7v 9f) IR 500F; small, fair sort; fourth live foal; dam won over 5f at 3 yrs; little worthwhile form, including in sellers; blinkered last 2 outings. *C. Spares.*   —

SWEET SONJA 2 b.f. Raga Navarro 119–Cheap and Sweet (Rising Market) (1983 6f 6g⁴ 6f* 7fg 6g* 6g 5s) June 6; 3,000Y; small, lightly-made filly; third foal; half-sister to 2 winners including fair sprinter Boatrocker (by African Sky); dam ran twice in France; successful in maiden auction event at Folkestone in August and nursery at Hamilton in September; seems not to stay 7f; acts on firm going. *G. Huffer.*   80

SWEET SOPRANO 2 ch.f. High Line 125–Be Sweet 117 (Reform 132) (1983 7f 7s*) Mar 27; quite a well-made filly; first foal; dam, half-sister to Royal Hive and Attica Meli, showed smart form at up to 1½m; improved from halfway and ran on really well to win 18-runner maiden race at Leicester in October by a length from Moody Girl; sure to show better form when given a stiffer test of stamina; acts on soft going. *P. Walwyn.*   80 p

SWEET TOOTH 2 b.f. Condorcet–Candy Flake (Dionisio 126) (1983 6fg 5.1f⁴ 6f 8d) June 2; 1,050Y; small filly; of no account. *G. Blum.*   —

SWELL SOUND 3 b.c. Undulate–Clatter 67 (Songedor 116) (1982 7s 1983 10.1fg 8f 8f 14f 13.8g) big colt; soundly beaten, including in a seller; looks very slow. *M. McCormack.*   —

SWIFT ENCOUNTER 4 b.g. Owen Dudley 121–Pop Gun 85 (King's Troop 118) (1982 11s² 10d 11.7g 13.8f⁴ 14g 13.8f⁴ 16.5f 1983 12v²) small gelding; poor mover; second in seller at Wolverhampton in May; stays 1¾m; suited by some give in the ground; blinkered last 3 starts. *J. Jenkins.*   50

SWIFT PALM 6 b.g. Some Hand 119–March Stone 84 (March Past 124) (1982 8f³ 8g 8d³ 8f⁴ 8.3g² 8fg 8g² 9g 8.2s 8.2s⁴ 8s 1983 8d* 8v⁴ 8d 10s 8g 8g³ 8f³ 8fg 9d 10fg) lengthy gelding; finished strongly to win apprentice handicap at Doncaster in March; not disgraced on occasions afterwards; stays 1¼m; acts on any going but is ideally suited by some give in the ground; has won for an apprentice but sometimes gives himself a lot to do and isn't an easy ride. *P. Cundell.*   61

SWIFT REPRISAL 2 b.g. Tachypous 128–More Or Less 64 (Morston 125) (1983 7f) Jan 23; first foal; dam winning stayer; in rear, slowly away, in 15-runner maiden race at Redcar in September. *M. Camacho.*   —

SWIFT RETURN 2 br.f. Double Form 130–Keep Going 113 (Hard Sauce 131) (1983 6fg 5g³ 6fg*) Apr 16; fair sort; half-sister to several winners, including smart 6f and 7.3f winner Skyliner (by African Sky) and useful 5f to 1m filly Slip the   79

Ferret (by Klairon); dam won 6 times over 5f at 2 yrs; favourite, won 13-runner maiden race at Leicester in October; suited by 6f; acts on a firm surface. *J. Winter.*

SWIFT SERVICE 3 ch. c. Captain James 123–November (Firestreak 125) (1982 8g⁴ 10g² 1983 12v 12d² 14f 14f⁴ 13.4fg3 17g² 14f 15.5f⁴ 14fg⁴ 18fg) smallish, fair sort; disappointing staying maiden; sometimes sweats up. *R. Williams.* **66**

SWIFT TEMPO 2 b. f. Junius 124–Harp (Ennis 128) (1983 5g 5g 5g³) Apr 3; IR 6,200F, IR 5,400Y; compact filly; half-sister to 3 winners, including 1980 Irish 2-y-o 5f winner Harp Auction (by Auction Ring); dam never ran; 10 lengths third of 20 to Meis El-Reem in maiden race at Warwick in October. *R. Hannon.* **71**

SWIFT TO CONQUER 3 b. f. Solinus 130–Wilhelmina (Proud Chieftain 122) (1982 6g² 6d* 6fg³ 1983 7d 7.3s 8g³ 8.5g 12.2fg) light-framed, lengthy filly; well beaten after finishing close third in handicap at Brighton in May; stays 1m; blinkered final start; sold 4,800 gns Newmarket December Sales. *R. Williams.* **87**

SWIFT TURTLE 4 ch. f. Le Bavard 125–Eileen (Milesian 125) (1982 9.5g³ 9.2g 9f 12f⁴ 10g³ 12f 9g 9d 12s 1983 10f² 10f* 10f 10f⁴) IR 560F; ex-Irish filly; half-sister to 1976 Irish 2-y-o 6f winner Donna's Delight (by On Your Mark); dam never ran; plater; favourite when winning at Folkestone in August (no bid); stays 1½m; acts on firm going; blinkered once at 3 yrs; suitable mount for an apprentice. *J. Fox.* **53**

SWINGIN' COWBOY (USA) 3 b. g. Parade of Stars–Tara Blue (Bold Bidder) (1982 5f⁴ 6f* 6fg* 7f² 7fg 7fg 8.2d 8.2v 1983 7d² 7g 7v 7g 8f 7g 7.2g² 8d 7g 8.2fg) strong, deep-girthed, attractive gelding; second in handicaps at Doncaster in March and Haydock in September; best form at up to 7f; possibly unsuited by really soft going, but acts on any other; often blinkered; none too consistent; sold 6,800 gns Newmarket Autumn Sales. *S. Norton.* **79**

SWINGING BABY 4 br. f. Swing Easy 126–Hi-Baby 102 (High Treason 126) (1982 5v³ 5g* 5f² 6f⁴ 6f 6h³ 5fg 5s 7d 1983 5d 6d 6g 5f 8f 13f⁴ 7f) lengthy, useful-looking filly; poor mover; well beaten in 1983; stays 6f; acts on any going; blinkered third start; dwelt once in 1982. *R. Woodhouse.* **–**

SWINGING CHRISTMAS 2 b. f. Swing Easy 126–Ermine Beauty (Young Emperor 133) (1983 8g 6fg) Apr 21; 600Y; fourth foal; half-sister to Irish 1¾m winner Surprising Queen and a winning hurdler (both by King's Company); dam won 1m claiming race at 4 yrs in USA; well behind in maiden races at Sandown and Leicester (slowly away) in October. *Mrs N. Kennedy.* **–**

SWINGING MOON 4 ch. c. Swing Easy 126–Moon Gem (Moontrip) (1982 7fg 10.1fg 12f⁴ 10g⁴ 12v³ 12.2s⁴ 14s³ 1983 12v* 16v³ 12d* 12v⁴ 12s* 12s³ 12f 12f 19g 14g) lengthy, shallow-girthed colt; won minor event at Folkestone and handicaps at Brighton and Chepstow early in year; stays 2m; acts on any going but is ideally suited by soft ground; blinkered last 3 starts in 1982; has worn bandages. *A. Ingham.* **74**

SWINGING REBEL 5 br. h. Swing Easy 126–Rebecca (Quorum 126) (1982 8fg 8g 7f 7f* 7g 7g* 8.2f 7f² 7s³ 1983 7.2v² 7s 7s 7f* 8fg⁴ 7f 7f² 7f* 7f 7d³ 7fg 7fg) lengthy horse; has had a soft palate operation; fair handicapper; won at Brighton in June and Lingfield in August; best at 7f; acts on any going; usually held up; ran badly on second start and is inconsistent. *N. Vigors.* **87**

SWINGING SOUND 3 ch. g. Swing Easy 126–Mary Connor 99 (Royal Avenue 123) (1982 NR 1983 6f) IR 3,100F, 4,600Y; half-brother to 9f and 1¼m winner Blakenor (by Blakeney), subsequently successful in France, and a winner in Trinidad; dam won 4 times over 1m; well behind in maiden event at Folkestone in July; sold 460 gns Ascot November Sales. *J. Holt.* **–**

SWING TO ME 3 br. c. Swing Easy 126–Françoise 109 (French Beige 127) (1982 6fg³ 7f 1983 8s 8v² 7v 8v³ 10fg* 8f³ 10f* 10f³ 12f⁴ 10g) big, rangy colt; occasionally proves reluctant, but nevertheless won handicaps at Yarmouth in June and Newmarket in July; probably stays 1½m; acts on any going; blinkered fourth start; sold to M. Bradley 10,500 gns Doncaster November Sales. *C. Brittain.* **80**

SWISS FRANC (USA) 3 ch. c. Annihilate 'Em–Worthy Charm (Boldnesian) (1982 NR 1983 7d 7fg⁴ 8f) fair sort; brother to 2 winners, including fair 1980 2-y-o 6f winner Glyndebourne, and half-brother to another winner; dam won 6f claiming race at 2 yrs; only lightly raced, but gave signs of a little ability first 2 outings. *G. Balding.* **–**

SYCAMORE SAGA 3 b. f. Sagaro 133–Phoenix Rose 85 (Frankincense 120) (1982 7s 9s 1983 12d 9.4d) rather lightly-built filly; in rear in maiden and minor events. *R. Woodhouse.* **–**

SYDETZKY 3 br.c. Radetzky 123–Sygnome 53 (Precipice Wood 123) (1982 5g⁴ 5d 6fg 7g 7f 7g 7g 8g 8d 10.2s 1983 10s 12f 12g 16d 10g) plater; probably stays 1¼m; sometimes blinkered in 1982; sold 700 gns Doncaster October Sales. *J. Harris.*

SYLPH (USA) 3 b.f. Alleged 138–Society Column (Sir Gaylord) (1982 NR 1983 10fg⁴ 10g* 12fg 14.6fg³ 12fg*) $270,000Y; quite an attractive filly; has a markedly round action; closely related to 2 winners by Hoist the Flag, namely Crown Thy Good, a winner at up to 9f and Present The Colors, a stakes winner at up to 11f; dam, stakes-winning half-sister to top-class mare Typecast, won at up to 1¼m; successful in 19-runner maiden race at Newmarket in July (won in great style by 5 lengths) and 11-runner Princess Royal Stakes at Ascot in October; favourite and blinkered first time, came through under hard driving to lead near finish and beat Opale by a length in latter; just over 4 lengths sixth of 11 behind Rajpoura in Prix de Minerve at Evry and 3¾ lengths third of 7 to High Hawk in Park Hill Stakes at Doncaster in between; stays 1¾m; has raced only on a sound surface; sent to USA. *J. Tree.* 110

SYLVAN BARBAROSA 4 ch.c. Native Bazaar 122–The Silver Darling 75 (John Splendid 116) (1982 5f³ 6fg² 5f³ 6fg* 5fg 5g 6f 5.6g 6g 1983 6v 5g 6v 5d 6f* 6fg 5f) strong-topped, sturdy colt; not a good mover; showed much improved form when 20/1-winner of Cork and Orrery Stakes at Royal Ascot, leading 1f out and holding on gamely by short head from Curravilla in driving finish; not disgraced earlier in Palace House Stakes won by On Stage at Newmarket, in CBA Greenlands Stakes won by Curravilla at the Curragh and Temple Stakes won by Fearless Lad at Sandown; well beaten in William Hill July Cup at Newmarket and King George Stakes at Goodwood on last 2 starts; effective at 5f and 6f; best form on a sound surface. *P. Mitchell.* 111

SYLVAN BARNUM 2 b.c. Comedy Star 121–The Silver Darling 75 (John Splendid 116) (1983 5v* 5v* 6s³ 6fg 7g 7f² 7h⁴ 7.3g 6fg 7fg) Apr 27; 10,000Y; strong, quite attractive colt; fourth foal; half-brother to Cork and Orrery Stakes winner Sylvan Barbarosa (by Native Bazaar); dam second in this country before winning in Belgium; won 6-runner events at Epsom and Lingfield in the spring; apprentice ridden, good second in nursery on latter course in August, best subsequent effort; better suited by 7f than shorter distances; acts on any going. *P. Mitchell.* 85

SYLVAN NAVARRO 3 b.c. Raga Navarro 119–Tinsel 95 (Right Boy 137) (1982 5f 5g 5g³ 5f² 5fg⁴ 5g³ 5f 6g⁴ 7fg 6g 7v 6s⁴ 1983 6d* 6s³ 5g 6fg* 5f² 6fg 6f⁴ 6f 5fg 5d³ 6d 6fg) compact colt; short-head winner of handicaps at Windsor in May and June; ran creditably on occasions afterwards; stays 6f; seems to act on any going; blinkered nowadays. *P. Mitchell.* 94

SYLVAN PARK 2 b.f Frimley Park 109–Frimley Grove (Tower Walk 130) (1983 5f 5.8h) May 24; compact filly; first foal; dam never ran; in rear in August in St Hugh's Stakes at Newbury and maiden race at Bath. *S. Matthews.* –

SYMBOLIC 3 ch.c. Simbir 130–Panetona (Pan II 130) (1982 NR 1983 10d 14g 12g*) 7,200Y; half-brother to several winners, including smart French middle- 79

Princess Royal Stakes, Ascot—Sylph comes through to beat Opale (rails) and Honeybeta

Mrs B. E. Wade's "Sylvan Barbarosa"

distance performer Mazus (by Major Portion) and very useful French and American 1m to 1½m winner Planing (by Daring Display); dam won over 10.5f in France; showed promise on both outings prior to beating Hazel Bush in good style by 6 lengths in 17-runner apprentice event at Chepstow in October; will stay 2m; could well have improvement in him. *G. Harwood.*

SYMPATIQUE 5 b.g. Simbir 130–Fun of the Fair (Skymaster 126) (1982 12fg² 10fg⁴ 12fg² 16s 12.2s 1983 12v 12.2v 12d 11.7d) strong, good sort; moves well; unreliable handicapper; stays at least 1½m; suited by some give underfoot; has worn blinkers. *N. Gaselee.* — §

SYNCOPATE 7 br.m. Highland Melody 112–Manipulation 90 (Appiani II 128) (1982 12g 18.4fg 12f 12.2f 1983 12v 13d 12.2g 10v 15.8d 13.8g) neat mare; mainly disappointing since 1981; stays 13f; best with some give underfoot; bandaged nowadays; didn't look keen fifth start; sold 875 gns Ascot December Sales. *D. Yeoman.* — §

T

TABASCO ROYAL 3 b.g. Royal Blend 117–Pensong 84 (Pendragon) (1982 5f 5f⁴ 5f 7fg 8.2fg⁴ 8fg 7.2s 1983 9v 12v 12s 12.2g 15.8g) rather leggy non-thoroughbred gelding; plater; should be suited by 1¼m+; sometimes sweats up; changed hands 2,000 gns Doncaster May Sales after third start; sold 720 gns same venue in October. *J. S. Wilson.* —

TABASCO STAR 3 ch.c. Grundy 137–Laxmi 108 (Palestine 133) (1982 5f 5f 7fg 8s 1983 8v 7d 6d 6g 8g 11f 9fg 7g) strong, short-coupled colt; only poor form; blinkered third outing in 1982; sold 800 gns Ascot December Sales. *D. Chapman.* —

TABERNACLE 10 b.g. Manacle 123–Tabarka (Dicta Drake 126) (1982 8g 12fg 16g 1983 12fg) poor plater; dead. *K. Bridgwater.* —

823

TACHADOR 2 ch.c. Tachypous 128–Adored (Aggressor 130) (1983 8g) Mar 21; third foal; dam showed no form; ninth of 10 in minor race at Bath in October. *R. Hodges.* —

TACHEO 2 ch.f. Tachypous 128–Camusky 77 (Charlottown 127) (1983 5v* 5v2 5g3 6d 6g 7.2s4 6fg) Feb 22; sturdy filly; half-sister to 7.5f and 10.6f winner Lonely Signorita (by Hotfoot); dam placed over 1½m; made all in maiden race at Warwick in April; placed the following month in £3,000 event at York and minor event at Catterick; off course 3 months after fourth outing; best form at 5f, but bred to stay at least 1m; acts on heavy going. *W. Wharton.* 64

TACHERON 2 b.c. Tachypous 128–Miss Cameron 76 (Decoy Boy 129) (1983 7g) May 7; second foal; dam won over 5f; in rear in 14-runner maiden race at Lingfield in October. *M. Haynes.* —

TACHEUR 2 b.g. Tachypous 128–Ribofleur 74 (Ribero 126) (1983 7.2fg 8g 7f) Mar 31; big, good sort; third foal; brother to a plating-class maiden; dam placed from 7f to 1¾m; soundly beaten in maiden and minor events. *M. Lambert.* —

TACHYLINE 2 b.f. Tachypous 128–Top Line 99 (Saint Crespin III 132) (1983 5f 5f 6f 8d 7.2g) Mar 14; rather leggy, fair sort; sister to 3-y-o 6f winner War War, and half-sister to a winning plater and a winning hurdler; dam won at 1m and 1½m and is daughter of smart Reel In; bad plater; should be suited by 7f+; blinkered final start. *M. W. Easterby.* —

TACHYROS 3 b. or br.g. Tachypous 128–Russellia (Red God 128§) (1982 7g 7g 1983 7d 9s 9.4d 10.1fg 10f 8f2 8g4 10d4) strong, quite attractive gelding; stays 1¼m; yet to show he can handle really soft going, but acts on any other; blinkered final start; sold 5,200 gns Doncaster November Sales. *M. Ryan.* 68

TACTFUL BOY 3 b.c. Tachypous 128–Baggage 86 (Zeus Boy 121) (1982 6fg 6g 5d 1983 6v 6s 8s) small colt; in rear in varied company, including selling. *T. Craig.* —

TACTIC 3 ch.g. Tachypous 128–Lively Lassie (Never Say Die 137) (1982 7g 7fg 7d 8.2s3 1983 8s 12v4 12f4 12fg4 14.7f 12g 12fg 12d) good-bodied gelding; promises to stay middle distances; probably acts on any going; blinkered fifth outing; has worn a bandage on off-hind. *E. Eldin.* —

TACTIQUE (FR) 3 ch.f. Anne's Pretender 124–Torre Blanca (Sailor) (1982 6fg 1983 10s 7d) lengthy, dipped-backed filly; soundly beaten in varied company; should be suited by 1¼m+; sold 560 gns Newmarket July Sales and resold 910 gns Doncaster September Sales and 500 gns Doncaster November Sales. *P. Cole.* —

TAELOS 2 gr.g. Godswalk 130–Quality Blake 91 (Blakeney 126) (1983 7fg 7g 8f) Mar 7; fair sort; second foal; dam won at up to 15f; soundly beaten in big fields of maidens; gelded after final outing. *A. Stewart.* —

TAGIO 3 b.g. Martinmas 128–Harford Belle 97 (Track Spare 125) (1982 6fg 1983 8v 6v 6g 6f 6fg4 7f* 10.8d) lightly-made gelding; sold out of G. Hunter's stable 1,700 gns after winning seller at Leicester in August (always going well); had stiff task and seemed to run well in much better company only subsequent outing; promises to stay 11f; possibly not at his best on really soft ground, but acts on any other. *M. Tate.* 65

TAHICHE (USA) 2 b.f. Topsider–Super Show (Knightly Manner) (1983 6fg3 5fg2 5g2) Apr 24; $65,000Y; quite attractive filly; half-sister to 3 minor winners; dam very useful winner at up to 1m in USA; runner-up in maiden races at Folkestone and Warwick in October; should stay 1m. *H. T. Jones.* 81

TAI FU KWAI 4 gr.g. Sagaro 133–Rebecca (Quorum 126) (1982 10s 9f* 10f* 11g* 12h 11.7d4 10.8fg2 10fg3 10.1d3 10g 1983 12d 10f2 10f* 11.7f2 10f* 8fg 10f 10s) compact gelding; moderate handicapper; won at Chepstow in June and Leicester in July; stays 1½m; acts on any going but goes well on firm; best in blinkers; suited by waiting tactics. *C. Williams.* 75

TAIGA 2 b.f. Northfields–Question Mark 83 (High Line 125) (1983 7.6d) Apr 22; 7,600Y; second foal; dam, sister to Park Hill winner Quay Line, won twice over 1½m; 8/1, behind in 20-runner maiden race at Lingfield in October; should do better. *G. Harwood.* — p

TAI SING KUNG 4 b.f. Hot Spark 126–Miss Kung Fu 70 (Caliban 123) (1982 10s 12f 12fg 1983 8.3s) useful sort; in rear in varied company, including selling. *C. Williams.* —

TAKACHIHO'S GIRL 2 br.f. Takachiho 111–Turkish Suspicion (Above Suspicion 127) (1983 7s 8g 8g) neat filly; half-sister to Irish middle-distance —

winner Geraldville (by Lord Gayle) and a winner in Brazil; dam poor half-sister to 1000 Guineas third and Irish Oaks runner-up Indian Melody; soundly beaten in autumn maiden races in Scotland. *T. Craig.*

TAKE A CARD 4 ch.g. Tachypous 128–Cigarette Case 89 (Faberge II 121) (1982   **86** 7f* 1983 7g 7s 10f 10fg 10d 10g⁴ 10.6g 10fg*) tall, rather lightly-made gelding; good mover; returned to form when winning apprentice handicap at Newmarket in October from Norfolk Flight; stays 1¼m; acts on firm going; blinkered seventh start; sold to BBA 14,000 gns Newmarket Autumn Sales. *M. Stoute.*

TAKE A STEP 3 b.f. Ashmore 125–Truly Thankful 111 (Majority Blue 126) (1982   **119** 7v* 1983 8v² 8d 8f 9fg³ 8g) rangy, attractive filly; won maiden race at the Curragh as a 2-y-o when trained by D. O'Brien; showed herself a very useful filly when going down by 1½ lengths to Mysterieuse Etoile in 11-runner Prix de la Grotte at Longchamp in April; well beaten behind L'Attrayante in Poule d'Essai des Pouliches at Longchamp next time (slowly away) and became disappointing, gaining only other placing when length third of 10 to Val Danseur in 55,000 francs race at Clairefontaine in August; stays 9f; best form on heavy ground. *P.-L. Biancone, France.*

TAKEN FOR GRANTED 5 b.g. Martinmas 128–Romanee Conti (Will Somers   – 114§) (1982 8.3fg 8g 1983 8d) tall, lengthy gelding; has shown no form for a long time; stays 1¼m; ideally suited by the mud; sold 1,500 gns Ascot May Sales. *R. Carter.*

TAKING MESSAGES (USA) 2 b.f. In Reality–Protectora (Prologo) (1983 9g)   – Apr 2; plain filly; half-sister to Doncaster Cup and Irish St Leger winner Protection Racket (by Graustark); dam, top filly in Chile, winning 9 races from 6f to 1¼m, subsequently showed very useful form in North America, winning at up to 1¼m; backward, slow-starting eighth of 13 in maiden race at Wolverhampton in October. *J. Hindley.*

TALKABOUT 6 b.g. Articulate 121–Avadera (Aurelius 132 or Primera 131) (1982   – NR 1983 22.2f 17.1h 18fg³) big, rangy gelding; stays well; winning hurdler. *G. Fletcher.*

TALK OF GLORY 2 b.c. Hittite Glory 125–Fiddle Faddle 85 (Silly Season 127)   **78** (1983 5f⁴ 7g*) Mar 31; 8,800Y; strong, rangy colt; first foal; dam, half-sister to Cesarewitch and Irish St Leger winner Mountain Lodge, won over 1½m and 2m; off the course since June, made all in 13-runner maiden event at Lingfield in October, winning by a head; will probably stay 1m. *H. Candy.*

TALK POSH (USA) 2 b.c. Elocutionist–Joyous Lass (Lurullah) (1983 7fg 8s*   **82** 7fg) Apr 3; $80,000Y, $50,000 2-y-o; sturdy colt; good walker; half-brother to 2 winners, including very useful 1978 2-y-o sprinter Maui Lei (by Rainy Lake); dam, 2-y-o 4f winner, is half-sister to Joachim, a very smart winner at around 9f; won 12-runner maiden race at Beverley in September, leading close home to beat Taqdir ½ length after none too good a run; third favourite, twelfth of 15 in nursery at Doncaster the following month; suited by 1m; acts on soft going. *M. Jarvis.*

TAMARIND GEM 7 ch.m. Salvo 129–Twisette (Alcide 136) (1982 NR 1983   – 15.8d) poor maiden; has worn blinkers and bandages. *R. Johnson.*

TAMDOWN FLYER 5 b.h. Hotfoot 126–Swing The Cat (Swing Easy 126) (1982   **83** 7f* 7f⁴ 7f* 6fg* 7f³ 5.8f⁴ 7d 8.2f³ 7f* 9d 8s 1983 6fg* 7fg 7f 8.3fg) leggy, light-framed horse; fair handicapper; won at Windsor in June; effective at 6f and stays 1m well; has run respectably on soft going but is much better on firm; well beaten in blinkers final start; suited by waiting tactics; sold, reportedly for export to Norway, 2,000 gns Newmarket September Sales. *W. O'Gorman.*

TAMERTOWN LAD 2 b.c. Creetown 123–Gay Tamarind (Tamerlane 128) (1983   **66** 6s 7.6fg 7g) Apr 2; 12,500Y; first reported foal; dam, half-sister to very useful 1m to 1¼m winner Words and Music, was tailed off only start; plating-class maiden; form only on second outing. *C. Horgan.*

TAMINO 2 b.c. Tap On Wood 130–Pamina 110 (Brigadier Gerard 144) (1983 7f   **81** p 7g³) Mar 7; well-made colt; first foal; dam, very useful at up to 1¼m, is daughter of very smart Magic Flute; odds on, 2¾ lengths third of 12 to Lucky Scott in £5,000 event at Kempton in September; will stay 1m; probably has improvement in him. *H. Cecil.*

TA MORGAN 5 b.g. Targowice 130–Sericana (Petingo 135) (1982 6g* 7f* 7f*   **91** 7.6f² 8g 1983 7s 5v 7.6v² 7f² 7s² 7fg) tall, lengthy gelding; second in handicaps at Lingfield in May (to Teamwork), Brighton in August (behind Little Mercy) and Doncaster in September (to Polly's Brother); effective at 6f and stays 1m; acts on any going; successful with blinkers and without; has won for an apprentice; genuine front runner. *G. Lewis.*

TAMWORTH TRACK 3 b.f. Palm Track 122–Rumbar (Meldrum 112) (1982 NR 1983 9s) 300 2-y-o; sparely-made filly; first foal; dam never ran; started slowly when tailed off in amateur riders race at Ripon in April. *K. Bridgwater.*

TANCRED WALK 4 b.g. Farm Walk 111–Darling Do (Derring-Do 131) (1982 8fg 1983 10v 12f² 12.2f² 12g* 13.8g) smallish, fair sort; quite moderate; had little trouble winning small race at Edinburgh in September (long odds on); suited by 1½m; acts on firm going; has run respectably when sweating up; takes a good hold; sold 4,000 gns Doncaster November Sales. *Miss S. Hall.* — 72

TANFEN 2 b.c. Tanfirion 110–Lady Mary (Sallust 134) (1983 5g²) Mar 22; IR 3,200F; workmanlike colt; first living produce; dam third over 5f and 9f in Ireland; second favourite, 5 lengths second of 6 to odds-on Our Dynasty in minor event at Thirsk in April. *M. H. Easterby.* — 71

TANG DANCER 2 ch.f. Junius 124–Ballinteskin (Busted 134) (1983 5.8f* 6f 6fg 5d) May 2; 4,700F, 4,000Y; useful-looking filly; half-sister to 3-y-o 7f winner Saqqara (by Persian Bold) and a useful winner in Scandinavia; dam never ran; won maiden auction event at Bath in July; subsequently in rear in nurseries; should stay 7f; apprentice ridden first 2 starts. *P. Makin.* — 76

TANNED MAN 2 b.c. Tanfirion 110–Emanuela (Lorenzaccio 130) (1983 6fg 7f³ 7.2g) May 19; fair sort; fourth foal; dam twice-raced half-sister to smart French middle-distance stayer El Mina; modest plater; best effort on first outing; should stay 1m. *C. Booth.* — 55

TAPACULO 2 gr.f. Tap On Wood 130–Sunbittern 112 (Sea Hawk II 131) (1983 6f² 6f² 7f* 7fg³ 8fg) Apr 25; rather wiry, plain filly, lacking in scope; half-sister to several winners, including high-class middle-distance stayer High Hawk (by Shirley Heights) and useful miler Herons Hollow (by Wolver Hollow); dam 6f and 7f winner at 2 yrs but became temperamental; won 11-runner maiden race at Yarmouth in August; good third in Waterford Candelabra Stakes at Goodwood later in the month; should stay 1m; acts on firm going. *B. Hanbury.* — 94

TAPIOLA 2 b.f. Tap On Wood 130–Head First 91 (Welsh Pageant 132) (1983 6f 5.8h³ 7h* 8fg 8fg) Apr 21; 28,000Y; small filly; second foal; dam, daughter of smart Guillotina, won twice over 1½m; won 11-runner maiden race at Chepstow in August; well beaten in nurseries afterwards, once favourite; should be suited by 1m. *B. Hills.* — 71

TAPIZ 3 b.g. Pitskelly 122–Santa Chiara 79 (Astec 128) (1982 6f 7fg 7g 1983 8fg 12f) rather leggy gelding; soundly beaten in maiden and minor events; bought out of C. James's stable 1,250 gns Ascot May Sales. *P. Mitchell.* — —

TAP-O-STRATH 3 br.f. Mandrake Major 122–Duck Walk (Farm Walk 111) (1982 6g 1983 8g) no sign of ability, including in a seller; sold 340 gns Ascot 2nd June Sales. *J. S. Wilson.* — —

TAPOUSCHA 2 ch.f. Tachypous 128–Marphousha (Only for Life 126) (1983 5f 6fg⁴ 5f 7g 7f² 7.2g² 7.2s³) Apr 13; 580Y; fair sort; sister to 3-y-o Cruncher, and half-sister to a minor winner and a winning hurdler; modest plater; will be suited by 1m+; probably acts on any going; usually blinkered. *W. Haigh.* — 60

TAPPING WOOD (USA) 2 b.c. Roberto 131–Unity 115 (Tudor Melody 129) (1983 6fg 6g) May 16; $1,300,000Y; well-made, attractive colt; half-brother to numerous winners, including smart but irresolute performer Open Season (by Sea-Bird II) and smart stakes winner Tilt Up (by Olden Times); dam miler; showed quite modest form in newcomers race at Ascot in July and maiden event at Newmarket in August, both occasions co-favourite; will probably improve over 1m+. *M. Stoute.* — 72 p

TAQA 3 b.f. Blakeney 126–Gliding 94 (Tudor Melody 129) (1982 7.6v 1983 12fg⁴ 10s* 10.6g* 10fg 10g) sturdy, lengthy filly; won minor events at Ayr and Haydock in September, beating Soldier Ant by 2½ lengths on former course; well below best afterwards; suited by 1¼m and is worth another chance over further; acts on soft going. *J. Hindley.* — 85

TAQDIR (USA) 2 b.c. Cox's Ridge–Etincelante (Le Fabuleux 133) (1983 8fg 8s² 7.6fg* 8.2s³) Mar 6; $175,000Y; tall, quite attractive colt; sixth foal; half-brother to 2 minor winners; dam unraced half-sister to high-class French sprinter/miler Sky Commander; favourite, made much of running and rallied splendidly to beat Bobby Dazzler by ¾ length in 17-runner maiden race at Lingfield in October; 4 lengths third of 7 to Trouvere in minor event at Hamilton later in month; will stay 1¼m; seems to act on any going. *G. Harwood.* — 87

TARANTA (GER) 4 br.f. Hotfoot 126–Traumspiel (Celadon II 125) (1982 –
including 10.5g⁴ 11v⁴ 10.5v* 1983 12d 12f³ 8.3fg) leggy, rather sparely-made
ex-German filly; fourth foal; half-sister to 2 winners in Germany, including useful
miler Torgos (by Upper Case); dam won 7 times in Germany; won 3 races over
10.5f from 10 starts in Germany in 1982; soundly beaten in varied company,
including selling, in Britain; should stay 1½m; acts on heavy going; has been
bandaged. *G. Blum.*

TARAS CHARIOT 2 ch.c. Dublin Taxi–Laura Reppin (Jimmy Reppin 131) (1983 –
6g 6fg) 1,350Y; third foal; dam never ran; apprentice ridden, behind in September
in 23-runner newcomers event at Goodwood and £6,000 maiden race at Ascot. *S.
Matthews.*

TARA'S CHIEFTAIN 5 b.g. African Sky 124–Hillberry Corner 70 (Atan) (1982 –
8h 7f 7g 8g 8g³ 8.3fg 8g⁴ 10fg³ 10s 1983 10d 10.1d) compact gelding; plater;
stays 1¼m; often blinkered; sometimes starts slowly. *R. Atkins.*

TARGET PATH 5 b.h. Scottish Rifle 127–Florabette (Floribunda 136) (1982 11g² **61**
12fg* 13s 12g 12v⁴ 1983 13v² 11s³ 13d² 12fg² 11g³ 12fg² 12f² 12f³ 11f4) strong
horse; stays 13f; acts on any going; has worn blinkers but seems better without;
suitable mount for an amateur; sent to Italy. *C. Nelson.*

TARIFA 3 gr.f. Pitskelly 122–Slap Up (Gala Performance) (1982 5g 5f 6d 6s* **73**
1983 6s³ 6v³ 6f* 6fg* 6f 6f² 6f4) good-topped filly; successful in 2 handicaps at
Brighton in June; subsequently sent to race in USA and won there; will stay 7f; acts
on any going. *J. Sutcliffe.*

TARISTEAC 3 ch.c. Be My Guest 126–Sans Culotte (Roi Dagobert 128) (1982 –
7g 6s 8d⁴ 7s 1983 7d 8v 10.1d 11d 10f4 16.5fg 12.2f) 26,000F, 28,000Y; small,
strong ex-Irish colt; poor mover; first foal; dam unraced half-sister to smart French
and American performer Golden Eagle; showed some ability in above-average
maiden company in Ireland at 2 yrs; modest fourth in maiden race at Folkestone in
June, best effort over here; seems to stay 1¼m; sometimes blinkered; trained first
5 starts by M. Kauntze. *G. Lockerbie.*

TARLETON 6 b. or br.g. Workboy 123–Lady Jester 108 (Bleep-Bleep 134) (1982 **44 d**
8g 8fg 10fg 9fg³ 12f 8fg 1983 8v* 8.2v³ 8v 8d 8fg 8f 8g 10g) strong gelding; plater;
attracted no bid after winning at Ayr in March; stays 9f but seems better at shorter
distances; acts on any going; suitable mount for an inexperienced rider; finds little
off the bridle. *P. Rohan.*

TARLETON ELM (USA) 3 br.c. Tarleton Oak–Nuthatch (Young Emperor 133) –
(1982 7fg 1983 8s 6g 8g 8f 6f 8f 7f 10f 7g 7fg) workmanlike colt; has shown little in
varied company, including selling; has been tried in blinkers and a hood; sold to Mrs
N. Smith 825 gns Ascot October Sales. *I. Walker.*

TARQUIN 2 br.c. Mansingh 120–Mildura 98 (Vilmorin) (1983 5fg) May 29; –
brother to 3-y-o 5f winner Captivate and useful 5f performer Pontin Lad, and
half-brother to speedy animals Gourmet (by Grey Sovereign) and Gauleiter (by
Mummy's Pet); dam 5f sprinter; behind in 15-runner maiden race at Warwick in
June. *A. Hide.*

TAR'S HILL 2 gr.g. Hill Farmer–Tar's Tart (Rosyth 94) (1983 6h 5fg 8d 7g) Apr **61**
8; third foal; dam never ran; plating-class maiden; gelded after final outing. *G.
Cottrell.*

TARSUS (FR) 4 ch.g. Hotfoot 126–Yole Tartare (Captain's Gig) (1982 7fg 10fg 7f –
10.1fg 10d 12f 1983 8v 10s 12f) medium-sized, attractive gelding; plating-class
maiden; stays 1¼m; blinkered last 4 starts in 1982; winner over hurdles; sold to J.
Harris 3,100 gns Newmarket September Sales. *B. Swift.*

TARTAN SEA 2 b.c. Artaius 129–Tigeen (Habitat 134) (1983 6v³ 5d 5fg* 5f4 **90**
6fg² 6fg 6.3g) Feb 19; first foal; dam, sister to high-class performers Bitty Girl and
Hot Spark, won twice over 5f in Ireland; won 8-runner maiden event at
Leopardstown in July by 2½ lengths from Formalist; in frame in Nishapour Curragh
Stakes later in month and 5-runner £4,100 race at Phoenix Park in August, going
down by short head to So Fine in latter; stays 6f. *D. K. Weld, Ireland.*

TARTAR TUDOR 2 b.c. Mister Tudor–Tartarbee 72 (Charlottesville 135) (1983 –
6g 8g) Mar 29; tall, lengthy colt; half-brother to 7f to 1½m winner Made My Day
(by Double Jump); dam, a plater, stayed 1m; well beaten in maiden race at
Leicester in May and minor event on same course in November. *A. Cawley.*

TARTEEN 2 br.f. Tarboosh–Fourteen (Will Somers 114§) (1983 6fg 7g 8.2g) **65**
Apr 5; IR 320F; leggy filly; third foal; dam never ran; plating-class maiden; stays
1m. *N. Guest.*

TASKFORCE VICTORY 2 ch.g. Record Token 128–Thorganby Victory 82   **77**
(Burglar 128) (1983 6fg 6f 6fg³ 6g 6s) Apr 20; sturdy, workmanlike gelding;
carries plenty of condition; first foal; dam 2-y-o 5f winner; quite a modest maiden;
s ays 6f; acts on a firm surface; gelded after final outing. *M. Tompkins.*

TAТIBAH 3 b.c. Habitat 134–Three Tees (Tim Tam) (1982 6f* 6d 6s 5v* 1983 **117** d
5v³ 5g 5s³ 6v 6fg 6.5fg) big, well-made, handsome colt; ran creditably first 3
starts in spring, finishing third to Fearless Lad in Field Marshal Stakes at Haydock,
fifth to On Stage in Palace House Stakes at Newmarket and strong-finishing third to
Sky Lawyer in Prix de Saint-Georges at Longchamp; hung badly when asked for his
effort (reportedly faltered on a patch of false ground) when last of 6 to On Stage in
Sandy Lane Stakes at Haydock in May, and was soundly beaten afterwards in
William Hill July Cup at Newmarket and Prix Maurice de Gheest at Deauville; may
prove best at 6f; evidently acts on any going; far from consistent. *F. J. Houghton.*

TAVARGOS 2 b.g. Bruni 132–Keino (Kautokeino) (1983 10d 10fg 10.2fg) Apr
18; close-coupled gelding; fourth foal; half-brother to 1¼m winner The Owls (by
Pieces of Eight); dam never ran; poor form, including in a seller. *C. Spares.*

TAWAAG (USA) 3 b.c. Hoist the Flag–Sarsar (Damascus) (1982 7d 8g 8d 1983   **59**
10g 10fg² 12f) strong, medium-sized, attractive colt; second in handicap at
Leicester in June, best effort; tended to run in snatches next time; suited by 1¼m
and should stay further. *J. Ciechanowski.*

TAW CROSSING 3 b.f. High Line 125–Taw Court 58 (Lear Jet 123) (1982 5.8g   –
6fg 1983 8v 8s) unattractive filly; no worthwhile form, including in a seller. *J. Hill.*

TAXIBUL 2 ch.c. Dublin Taxi–Cowbells (Mountain Call 125) (1983 5f 5f⁴ 5fg   **69**
5.3f* 6fg 6d 5d* 6g 6fg) Mar 24; smallish, deep-girthed colt; half-brother to 3-y-o
Magic Mink (by Record Token); successful in claiming race at Brighton in August
and nursery at Warwick in October; best at 5f; yet to race on very soft going but
acts on any other; blinkered final start. *R. Hannon.*

TAYGETUS 2 br.c. Tower Walk 130–Faviola 68 (Averof 123) (1983 6g 6fg 5fg⁴)   **65**
Apr 12; lengthy colt; has a good, long stride; first foal; dam, out of half-sister to So
Blessed and Lucasland, was placed at up to 1m; plating-class maiden; stays 6f;
went to post very freely last 2 starts. *C. Brittain.*

T. BELLE 4 br.f. Foggy Bell 108–Susan 88 (Hard Tack 111§) (1982 8fg 10fg 10d⁴   –
12.2f³ 12fg 1983 16f) sparely-made filly; plating-class maiden; suited by 1½m and
should stay further; acts on firm going; sold 300 gns Doncaster November Sales. *J. Yardley.*

TEA BISCUIT 3 ch.f. Cranley 75–Gay Desire (Dragonara Palace 115) (1982 5f 5f   –
5g 1983 6d 5s³ 8fg 8s 12f 12f) small filly; of little account. *J. Townson.*

TEA DANCE 3 ch.f. Vitiges 132–Rose Girl (Thatch 136) (1982 5d 7f 8fg 10s 1983   –
10s 11.7h 12fg 10f 15.5f) lengthy, rather sparely-made filly; well beaten in maiden
races and an amateur riders event; twice none too well away. *M. Blanshard.*

TEA HOUSE 3 ch.f. Sassafras 135–House Tie (Be Friendly 130) (1982 6g* 1983   **107**
7s⁴ 10s 8fg³ 8f* 8fg* 9g⁴ 8fg*) first foal; dam, Irish 1m winner, is daughter of
high-class filly Mesopotamia; made all when 3-length winner of minor event at
Navan in June and 8-runner £4,300 event at Phoenix Park the following month
(from Laois Princess); only fourth of 5 behind Verria, beaten 7½ lengths, in Prix
Chloe at Evry later in July, but regained winning form in 10-runner Cornelscourt
Stakes at Leopardstown in August, beating Lady Dara by a head; should stay
beyond 1m; acts on any going, but goes particularly well on firm; sent to race in
USA. *M. Kauntze, Ireland.*

TEALA 2 b.f. Troy 137–Kuwaiti 77 (Home Guard 129) (1983 6g) Apr 1; second   –
foal; dam, from excellent family, won over 5f at 2 yrs; out of first 11 of 27, after
showing reluctance to go to post, in maiden race at Newmarket in July. *L. Cumani.*

TEAMWORK 6 br.h. Workboy 123–Affirmative 96 (Derring-Do 131) (1982 8g 8g   **96**
8g* 8f* 8f⁴ 8fg 8f⁴ 8fg³ 8f* 8g³ 8fg⁴ 10.2g 9d 1983 7.6v* 8f 7f³ 7fg 8f* 8fg⁴ 8f 8fg)
strong, good-bodied horse; fairly useful handicapper; beat Ta Morgan a length in
£4,700 event at Lingfield in May and Alpine Way 1½ lengths at Thirsk in July; ran
well most other starts; suited by 1m; acts on any going; usually held up and has a
useful turn of foot; suited by a strongly-run race; goes well for apprentice S.
Jewell; consistent. *R. Sheather.*

Jersey Stakes, Ascot—Tecorno beats Persian Glory (left) comfortably

TECORNO (USA) 3 b.c. Tentam–Nimble Deb (Lucky Debonair) (1982 6f 7g² **119**
7s² 1983 8g 7d³ 7f* 8fg 7.3f³ 7fg)
    The maiden Tecorno's receiving all the allowances in the Jersey Stakes at
Royal Ascot detracted slightly from the value of a pattern-race victory gained in
good style: Tecorno received weight from all his principal rivals, a stone from
Aragon who'd won a similar event in France, the Prix de la Jonchere, the previous
month. Tecorno, looking tremendously well, came through smoothly on the bridle
to take up the running inside the final furlong and win by a length from the long-time
leader Persian Glory with Aragon a further three lengths behind. At this stage
Tecorno's record suggested he would stay a mile, and this was supported by the
fact that he is by Tentam, second to Secretariat in the mile-and-a-half Man o'War
Stakes. Because of soft going he was withdrawn on the morning of the race from
the seven-furlong Prix de la Porte Maillot a week after Royal Ascot and went
instead for a valuable handicap at Newmarket in which he got his second chance of
tackling a mile. On his seasonal reappearance Tecorno had been allowed to dispute
the lead in the Two Thousand Guineas; he had faded after six furlongs and finished
well back. On this occasion he was held up in a strongly-run race. He looked like
winning when brought through to challenge at the distance but, conceding upwards
of 20 lb to such as Teleprompter, Prego and the winner Moores Metal, he couldn't
quite sustain his effort; eventually he finished sixth of fourteen. Brought back to a
distance only sixty yards more than seven furlongs in the Hungerford Stakes at
Newbury in August Tecorno ran his best race. Again looking very well indeed, he
finished third of ten to Salieri and Royal Heroine, beaten two and a half lengths and
one and a half giving the runner-up 3 lb and receiving only 2 lb from the winner. He
was towards the rear as they turned into the straight, but under pressure made
very good ground and was going on strongly at the finish, in a manner that
suggested once again that he would stay a mile. Tecorno reopposed Salieri in the
Kiveton Park Stakes at Doncaster in September but ran unaccountably poorly,
dropping out under pressure some way from home to be last of eight behind Annie
Edge.

Tecorno (USA) (b.c. 1980)	Tentam (b or br 1969)	Intentionally (bl 1956)	Intent My Recipe
		Tamerett (b or br 1962)	Tim Tam Mixed Marriage
	Nimble Deb (b 1969)	Lucky Debonair (b 1962)	Vertex Fresh as Fresh
		Nimble Feet (br 1957)	Spy Song Throttle Wide

    Tecorno, purchased at the Saratoga Summer Select Yearling Sale for 120,000
dollars, is the best of four winners out of the unraced Nimble Deb; the others,
Hopto M'Lou (by Groton), Natashua (by Marshua's Dancer) and Royal Privilege (by

Countess Marianne Esterhazy's "Tecorno"

Dynastic) each won small races in the United States. His sire Tentam, now dead, won eleven races at up to nine and a half furlongs. Tecorno himself has been returned to the States, to be trained by John Gosden. A strong, good-bodied, attractive colt with a high knee action, Tecorno acts on any going but is well suited by fast. On the evidence available, seven furlongs is his optimum distance. *R. Hern.*

TEDDINGTON JEWEL 3 ch.g. Import 127–Welsh Cape (Abernant 142) (1982   – 6d 6f 5fg 1983 10.1fg 8f 10f 12g) of little account. *H. O'Neill.*

TEEJAY 4 b.g. Jimmy Reppin 131–Billingsgate 82 (High Perch 126) (1982 8g 7g⁴   65 8g⁴ 8g* 8fg⁴ 8.2s² 8d² 1983 8d 8d 8g 8d⁴ 8.2fg* 8h) strong gelding; won handicap at Nottingham in July; ran poorly next time; stays 1m; acts on any going with possible exception of very firm; blinkered last 3 outings; has given trouble at start. *M. Camacho.*

TEENOSO (USA) 3 b.c. Youth 135–Furioso 116 (Ballymoss 136) (1982 6fg 7g   132 8g⁴ 1983 10.6v² 12d* 12v* 12s* 12f³ 12g³)

The secret of the weather as a staple topic of British conversation, someone once wrote, is that it is not political; rain and snow are inevitable and absolute, in the same category as death and therefore a subject for poetry and piety, not for politics. Spells of extreme weather serve to remind everyone, especially politicians, of their essential powerlessness to do more than observe and experience many of the changes in the world. The weather eclipsed almost all other topics in the first part of the 1983 flat-racing season. Whether the spring was more wet than dry or more dry than wet was a matter of fine calculation. According to the weathermen it was the wettest since records began and if there has been a worse start to a flat season, no-one could recall it. The racing programme was badly affected: twenty-six of the eighty-one meetings scheduled before the York May meeting were lost and conditions at most of the meetings that went ahead varied between the unfriendly and the almost impossible, with heavy ground mostly the order of the day. None complained about conditions more than those trying to prepare contenders for the first four classics. Some yards were brought to a virtual standstill at times as gallops became waterlogged. Proper evaluation of classic contenders was extremely difficult and at one stage, with seventy-eight still left in the Derby, it seemed that the Jockey Club handicappers might be called upon for the first time in a classic to draw up assessments of those still engaged to enable eliminations to be made. The safety maximum for the Derby course is thirty-three.

Rain has never caused the abandonment of Derby Day but it came close to doing so in 1983. After overnight storms, the latest Derby was the first for more than half a century to be run on going described officially as heavy. Our representatives returned the going as soft but there's no doubting that conditions were extremely testing. Teenoso's winning time—2m 49.07sec—was the slowest since Common's in 1891 and almost fifteen seconds slower than that of Golden Fleece twelve months earlier. The 1891 Derby was run in a deluge and the jockeys drew 2 lb overweight on returning to scale. The overnight downpour in 1983 caused the withdrawal of the William Hill Futurity runner-up Cock Robin (his rider Swinburn switching to stable-companion Shearwalk) and of the outsider Northern Trial. Twenty-one went to post in what was widely regarded as one of the most open races for the Derby in recent years. The Derby is usually won nowadays by a horse that has been a leading two-year-old; it comes too soon in the season for many of the later-maturing types. But the latest Derby field lacked an outstanding representative from the previous season's juveniles. Among those with pretensions to stay, Saint Cyrien (9-6 European Free Handicap) and Danzatore (9-5) were under a cloud by Derby time; the winter favourite Dunbeath (9-3) did not take part after being well beaten into third place behind Teenoso's stable-companion Hot Touch and Guns of Navarone in Britain's most important Derby trial, the Mecca-Dante Stakes at York; Gorytus (9-5), fifth in the Two Thousand Guineas on his reappearance, missed Epsom because of fears of soft ground; L'Emigrant (9-2) wasn't entered and Caerleon (9-0) waited for the Prix du Jockey-Club—which he won from L'Emigrant—on the Sunday after Epsom. Of the top forty in the Free Handicap only the doubtful stayer The Noble Player (8-13), ranked joint-sixteenth, and French-trained Pluralisme (8-10), who had finished third to L'Emigrant in France's most important classic trial the Prix Lupin, were in the Derby field. Among the abandoned preparatory races whose results could have had a bearing on Derby calculations were the Blue Riband Trial at Epsom and the Chester Vase and the Dee Stakes. The Chester Vase, won by Henbit and Shergar before success at Epsom, had been on Teenoso's programme, but when Chester's three-day meeting fell victim to the

Highland Spring Derby Trial Stakes, Lingfield—Teenoso accounts for Shearwalk and Yawa

weather Teenoso was sent to Lingfield for the Highland Spring Derby Trial run, like the Chester Vase, over the full Derby distance. Teenoso had an undistinguished two-year-old career—he earned only £262 from three starts—and was beaten in a maiden event at Haydock in April on his reappearance, giving the impression that a mile and a quarter was on the sharp side for him. He confirmed that impression when spreadeagling a big field of maidens over a mile and a half at Newmarket eleven days later, quickening clear three furlongs out and running on strongly to win with something in hand by eight lengths from Khyber. Teenoso started third favourite for the Highland Spring Derby Trial behind Shearwalk who had won both the Timeform Race Card Stakes at Thirsk and the Heathorn Stakes (from Dunbeath) at Newmarket in April. Teenoso ran a good trial at Lingfield, one whose significance increased almost daily

Derby Stakes, Epsom—rounding Tattenham Corner, Mitilini leads from Neorion (outside) and Teenoso. They are followed by (right to left), Tivian, Guns of Navarone, Carlingford Castle and Wassl. Salmon Leap (white blaze, on inside) is next

as the rain continued: always close up, he went to the front over five furlongs from home and stayed on strongly in the heavy ground to hold the determined challenge of Shearwalk by three lengths, with the rest strung out like washing. By the time the last of Britain's recognised Derby trials—the Schroder Life Predominate Stakes at Goodwood—came to be run Piggott, with an unchallenged riding record in the Derby, had still to finalise his mount. When Dunbeath's possible deputy Polished Silver finished only fifth of six to the runaway winner Morcon at Goodwood, Piggott was left free to take an outside ride. After his name had been linked with a variety of candidates, including the Two Thousand Guineas runner-up Tolomeo, he was eventually booked for Teenoso who was backed down to 9/2 favourite. Second favourite at 11/2 was the unbeaten O'Brien-trained Salmon Leap, another subject of a last-minute change of jockey, Eddery switching from the Two Thousand Guineas winner Lomond after the overnight rain. After Teenoso and Salmon Leap they bet: 17/2 Morcon, 9/1 Lomond, 10/1 Wassl (winner of the Airlie/Coolmore Irish Two Thousand Guineas) and 14/1 Tolomeo and Carlingford Castle, who had been successful in the mud over the Derby distance in the Gallinule Stakes at the Curragh, beating Give Thanks. Some added interest was provided by Slewpy, the first North American-trained runner to be flown over specially to make the challenge; Slewpy had been ranked among the top eleven colts and geldings in the States as a two-year-old but had done nearly all his racing on dirt and was 100/1 at Epsom.

The partnership of Teenoso and Piggott looked completely at ease at every stage of the Derby. Piggott gave his mount a superb ride, jumping him smartly out of the stalls and taking up a position among the leaders from the start, perfectly placed to avoid the scrimmaging that often takes place in a big Derby field after about two and a half furlongs, when the field comes back to the left-hand rail after negotiating the right-hand bend soon after the start; Tolomeo and Yawa, both towards the rear, were among the sufferers at this point in the latest Derby. From the top of the hill to Tattenham Corner Teenoso waited in third place, tracking the rank outsiders Mitilini and Tivian, always with a clear opening to pass them whenever his rider chose. Rounding Tattenham Corner, the leaders were pressed by the stable-companions Neorion and Guns of Navarone, then came a group comprising Carlingford Castle, Wassl, Salmon Leap, Naar and the improving Tolomeo. Tolomeo had caused trouble halfway down Tattenham Hill, crossing to the rails and hampering the no-hoper Holmbury and Shearwalk which resulted in the hapless Yawa clipping the heels of Shearwalk and unseating his rider. Once into the straight Teenoso set sail for home, building up a useful lead while at least two of his most serious rivals were running into trouble. Carlingford Castle became pocketed at a crucial stage when making his run through the middle of the field and Salmon Leap, hugging the rails, had first to be checked, as the fading Mitilini dropped back into his path, and then switched to the outside to get a clear passage. Guns of Navarone was Teenoso's closest pursuer until approaching the final furlong where Carlingford Castle, galloping on resolutely, moved past him. But the race was over—or rather that for first place was! Teenoso, gone beyond recall, kept on in good style to pass the post with three lengths to spare over Carlingford Castle who was steadily cutting into his lead in the closing stages. Shearwalk, who had only five behind him at Tattenham Corner, did remarkably well to deprive Salmon Leap of third place by a short head, three lengths behind Carlingford Castle. Guns of Navarone finished two and a half lengths further back in fifth, after which there was an eight-length gap to Naar who was put out of the reckoning for a place when squeezed between Salmon Leap and Morcon just inside the two-furlong marker; Pluralisme and Morcon came next, while Tolomeo, Wassl and Lomond, each clearly much less of a force at a mile and a half than at shorter distances, finished even further back.

Lester Piggott demonstrated yet again why there is always a clamour for his services, particularly in the big races—and especially on Derby Day. He seems somehow to grow neither older nor less effective as the years go by—Teenoso was his thirtieth ride in the Derby—and his mastery of the Derby course in particular is complete. His great strength, demonstrated so effectively on Roberto and The Minstrel at Epsom, wasn't called into play in 1983 but his handling of Teenoso was an object lesson in how to ride a proven stayer in the Derby. Piggott's contribution

Derby Stakes, Epsom—Teenoso races home clear of Carlingford Castle. The grey Shearwalk gets up to beat Salmon Leap for third place; Guns of Navarone is fifth

to racing has been colossal and his place in the sport's Hall of Fame is secure. Teenoso took his number of Derby winners to nine, three more than any other rider in history, and left him one short of equalling Frank Buckle's record total of twenty-seven classic winners. Never Say Die, Crepello, St Paddy, Sir Ivor, Nijinsky, Roberto, Empery and The Minstrel were Piggott's Derby winners before Teenoso; he has also finished second on Gay Time, Meadow Court, Ribocco and Cavo Doro.

Teenoso doesn't rank, on his three-year-old form at any rate, among the best of Piggott's Derby winners. Shearwalk was struck into in the Derby and didn't race again but the fact that Teenoso, Carlingford Castle, Salmon Leap and Guns of Navarone achieved only two wins and four other placings between them from a total of fifteen outings after Epsom tells its own story about the strength of the Derby field in 1983. Neither Teenoso nor Carlingford Castle won a race after Epsom, Carlingford Castle putting up easily his best subsequent performance in the St Leger when a close third to Sun Princess on soft ground. The St Leger seemed an ideal target for both Teenoso and Carlingford Castle—stamina had been the keynote of their performances in the Derby—and but for sustaining a leg injury when third to Seymour Hicks (who received 7 lb) in the Great Voltigeur Stakes in August Teenoso would have been in the St Leger line-up, only the second Derby winner to go on to Doncaster since Nijinsky in 1970. Teenoso returned home from York lame on his off-fore, his trainer suspecting at first that the injury was a stress fracture of the shin. Thankfully, the injury turned out to be nowhere near so serious as feared and Teenoso was reported fully sound and back in steady work by late-autumn. He stays in training with the John Porter Stakes, the Ormonde Stakes, the Coronation Cup and the King George VI and Queen Elizabeth Diamond Stakes his intended programme in the first half of the season. How will he fare? Well, a lot of water will have passed under the bridge by the time the King George comes round again, but in a normal year we wouldn't be sanguine about Teenoso's chances of beating the best of the rising generation of middle-distance three-year-olds—and he'll also face a very strong challenge from the older horses. As we have said, there have been better Derby winners than Teenoso and the overwhelming impression of him as a three-year-old was that he is first and foremost a stayer. A really good middle-distance horse will always have the edge on Teenoso at a mile and a half, except in very testing conditions—which he is unlikely to find at Ascot at the end of July. Both Teenoso and Carlingford Castle were found wanting for finishing pace in the Irish Sweeps Derby; they were swamped by Shareef Dancer, Teenoso eventually finishing third, beaten decisively also by the Prix du Jockey-Club winner Caerleon. Teenoso finished four places in front of Carlingford Castle at the Curragh but the pair were separated by about the same distance as at Epsom. Teenoso hung sharply right when put under strong pressure in the closing stages of the Irish Sweeps Derby, giving the impression that he couldn't stride out freely on the firm ground. To say that Teenoso is unsuited by firm ground is too strong—he was, after all, third in the best field of middle-distance colts assembled for a classic during the European season—but he is clearly very well suited by plenty of give in the ground. He is very genuine.

	Youth (b 1973)	Ack Ack (b 1966)
		Battle Joined Fast Turn
		Gazala (b 1964)
		Dark Star Belle Angevine
Teenoso (USA) (b.c. 1980)		
	Furioso (b 1971)	Ballymoss (ch 1954)
		Mossborough Indian Call
		Violetta III (b 1958)
		Pinza Urshalim

Teenoso is a rangy, useful-looking colt and a good mover. He is the ninth American-bred Derby winner in the last sixteen years—his sire the Prix du Jockey-Club winner Youth stands at Gainesway Farm, Kentucky. On the distaff side, Teenoso comes from a family that has served his connections extremely well over the years. Teenoso and his winning half-sisters Topsy (by Habitat) and Palmella (by Grundy), the former a very smart performer who won the Sun Chariot Stakes and two other pattern races, are among a seemingly-endless stream of winners produced in the last thirty years by descendants of Horama, the famous foundation mare of the Moller brothers' White Lodge Stud. The Wragg family—son Geoffrey took over the licence from father Harry before the opening of the 1983 season—has trained for the Mollers for more than thirty years and has handled many good members of the Horama family. Speed has been the dominant characteristic of most of Horama's descendants including Teenoso's great-grandam Urshalim and her illustrious Wragg-trained daughters. Lacquer, Sovereign and Violetta III, all of whom raced in the Moller colours. Urshalim was a smart

Mr E. B. Moller's "Teenoso"

racemare, a sprinter pure and simple like her dam Horama, only one of whose nine winners won over a longer distance than six furlongs. Sent to stallions who were an influence for stamina Urshalim produced the Irish One Thousand Guineas winner Lacquer and Teenoso's grandam Violetta, both of whom stayed well enough to win or share a Cambridgeshire; their half-sister Sovereign was the fastest two-year-old filly of 1967 and won the Coronation Stakes over a mile at three, while Sovereign's brother Funny Fellow showed smart form at up to a mile and a half. Adhering strictly to the best family tradition Violetta has bred ten winners including Favoletta (the dam of Amaranda and Favoridge) who followed in Lacquer's footsteps by winning the Irish One Thousand Guineas, and two other fillies good enough to reach the frame in a classic, the 1974 Oaks runner-up and Irish Guinness Oaks fourth Furioso, who became disappointing towards the end of her racing career, and the 1976 Oaks fourth Laughing Girl. Two of Violetta's other offspring were also responsible for Group 1 pattern-race winners in 1983—Parthica (the dam of Give Thanks) and Little Miss (the dam of Old Country). Teenoso is the only colt among Furioso's seven foals to date. Furioso wasn't covered in 1983 but she has fillies by Mill Reef and Habitat following on after her 1983 two-year-old Strident Note (by The Minstrel); Strident Note had three outings in her first season without troubling the judge but she's a taking filly who, like Teenoso, could leave her two-year-old form well behind given time and longer distances. *G. Wragg.*

TEIGH 3 b.c. Gold Form 108–Palmural 111 (Palestine 133) (1982 5f 5g 5g 5d 1983 7f) compact, sturdy colt; poor plater; blinkered final start at 2 yrs. *A. Cawley.*   —

TELEGRAPH BOY 5 b.g. Bay Express 132–Code of Love 99 (Bleep-Bleep 134) (1982 5f 5.8f 5g² 5fg² 5fg² 5fg² 5d 5s 5d 1983 5v 5.8g 5f² 5f⁴ 5.3f⁴ 5f 5g⁴)   **47**

strong, close-coupled gelding; best form at 5f; acts on any going; blinkered sixth start; has worn bandages in front; often gets outpaced in early stages. *S. Woodman.*

TELE-LINK 2 b.c. Dominion 123–Canaan (Santa Claus 133) (1983 6g) June 15; half-brother to several winners, including useful 1½m to 2¼m winner Majestic Maharaj (by Sparkler); dam unraced half-sister to St Leger winner Cantelo; remote tenth of 19 in maiden race at Goodwood in September. *D. Arbuthnot.* —

TELEPATHY 4 b.c. He Loves Me 120–Clear Belle (Klairon 131) (1982 10.2g 9fg⁴ 8g 10fg 1983 11g) fair sort; poor form, including in a seller. *T. Barnes.*

TELEPHONE NUMBERS (USA) 3 b.c. Annihilate 'Em–Tims Flirt (Tim Tam) (1982 6g² 6f 6s² 7.6v* 1983 8s 12g) rangy, attractive colt; quite useful at 2 yrs; well beaten in 2 handicaps in 1983; should be suited by further than 1m; acts on any going; hurdling with D. Oughton. *C. Horgan.* —

TELEPROMPTER 3 b.g. Welsh Pageant 132–Ouija 104 (Silly Season 127) (1982 7g 1983 7d⁴ 8fg* 8d* 8f* 8fg³ 10f² 8g² 9fg²) big, strong, useful-looking gelding; improved with virtually every race in first part of season and won maiden event at Edinburgh and handicaps at Carlisle and Royal Ascot, beating Amazon Prince by 1½ lengths in 27-runner £9,600 Britannia Stakes at Royal Ascot (got up under strong driving after being among backmarkers at halfway); placed in 4 handicaps afterwards, on final start failing by only a head to peg back Sagamore in 30-runner William Hill Cambridgeshire at Newmarket in October (favourite); stays 1¼m; yet to race on very soft ground but acts on any other; tends to hang and needs strong handling. *J. W. Watts.* **104**

TELHAM (USA) 2 b.f. No Robbery–Hyacinth (O'Calaway) (1983 6g² 6f 7f 6fg 6g⁴) Feb 22; $30,000F, 6,200 gns Y; small, sparely-made filly; not a good mover; half-sister to 3 winners in USA; dam won claiming races at up to 9f; quite a modest maiden; best run in nursery on final appearance; should stay 1m. *H. Candy.* **77**

TELIOS 2 ch.c. Mill Reef 141–Stilvi 126 (Derring-Do 131) (1983 6fg* 7fg³) Feb 11; well-made colt; good walker; seventh foal; half-brother to 5 winners, all at least smart, notably Middle Park winner and 2000 Guineas second Tachypous (by Hotfoot), top 1978 2-y-o Tromos (by Busted), Irish Sweeps Derby winner Tyrnavos (by Blakeney) and 1000 Guineas second Tolmi (by Great Nephew); dam extremely speedy and game; ran green early in 17-runner maiden race at Newmarket in August but steadily wore down leaders to win by ¾ length; favourite although giving weight all round, couldn't quicken in final 2f when 5¼ lengths third of 18 to Seismic Wave in £5,000 event at Doncaster the following month; will be better suited by 1m+; should win more races. *B. Hobbs.* **94 p**

Britannia Stakes, Ascot—Teleprompter wins under strong driving

TELSMOSS 7 b.h. Levmoss 131–Elakonee Wind 110 (Restless Wind) (1982 12g* — 16s 12fg 12fg* 13.3f 12f 11.7d³ 13.3g 12g 1983 16s) small horse; poor walker; fair handicapper at his best; was retired after injuring himself only start at 7 yrs in April (bandaged); stayed 1¾m; acted on any going; genuine. *P. Mitchell.*

TEMPLE BAR 3 b.c. Tower Walk 130–Miss Jovian (Busted 134) (1982 NR 1983 70 7d 8d 7d 9f 10f 10d³ 14g³) angular colt; walks well; first foal; dam poor maiden; third in maiden races at Beverley and Sandown in autumn; suited by 1¼m. *C. Brittain.*

TEMPLE BAR MAID 3 ch.f. Decoy Boy 129–Razia 97 (Martial 131) (1982 6fg 54 5f 5fg³ 5f 5g 5fg⁴ 5v* 5v³ 5g 1983 6d 5s 5g 5f 5fg³ 5g 6f 5fg 6d 5g 5g 6fg⁴) lengthy, good-quartered filly; plater; possibly best at 5f; seems to act on any going but revels in the mud. *D. Wilson.*

TENACIOUS LADY 2 br.f. Forlorn River 124–Double Reception (Siliconn 121) 61 (1983 6f 5f) Mar 24; 680Y; second living foal; dam never ran; 4½ lengths fifth of 19 to Costalotta in maiden race at Folkestone in September, second outing. *P. Mitchell.*

TENDER BENDER 3 b.f. Prince Tenderfoot 126–Too Soon 73 (Sheshoon 132) 77 (1982 6fg 6fg 7.6v 8.2s³ 1983 9s* 11.7s 8d* 9fg³ 8h 8d 8.2g*) smallish, quite attractive filly; successful in maiden race at Wolverhampton in April and handicaps at Ayr in June and Haydock in September; stays 9f (had stiff task when tried at 1½m); best form with some give in the ground; blinkered last 2 outings in 1982; sold 12,000 gns Newmarket December Sales. *G. Pritchard-Gordon.*

TENDER GIFT 3 b. or br.f. Prince Tenderfoot 126–Hung Pao 75 (Cumshaw 111) 49 (1982 6g 5s 6s 1983 6d 7fg 5.8f⁴ 6fg 6f 7fg 6fg 7fg²) plater nowadays; stays 7f; sold to BBA 860 gns Newmarket Autumn Sales. *J. Benstead.*

TENDER GODESS 3 b.f. Prince Tenderfoot 126–Fairy Goddess (Yellow God — 129) (1982 5fg 5fg 5fg 6d 5d 1983 8.5d 10f) compact filly; poor plater. *D. Whelan.*

TENDER INCH 2 b.c. Prince Tenderfoot 126–Starrio 82 (Ribero 126) (1983 6g 66 7f 6f 6f 5fg 5fg 6g 6fg 6g) Mar 1; 5,400Y; close-coupled colt; first foal; dam, daughter of smart sprinter Star Story, stayed well; plating-class maiden; stays 6f. *M. Usher.*

TENDER LORD 3 b.g. Prince Tenderfoot 126–Monaspear (Breakspear II) (1982 — NR 1983 10f) IR 15,000Y; third foal; half-brother to Irish 6f to 1m winner Kaksi (by Prince Regent); dam won three 1¼m races; unquoted when last-but-one in 16-runner minor event at Brighton in June; sold 925 gns Ascot July Sales and resold 600 gns Doncaster October Sales. *M. Haynes.*

TENDER LOVE 2 b.f. Prince Tenderfoot 126–Charley's Aunt 80 (Will Somers — 114§) (1983 6f) May 3; IR 6,000Y; good-topped filly; half-sister to several winners, including 5f and 1m winner Royal Revenge (by Sweet Revenge); dam won at 1m to 1½m; in rear in 13-runner maiden race at Goodwood in July. *M. Smyly.*

TENDER MOON 2 ch.f. Vitiges 132–Amber Moon (Amber Rama 133) (1983 5fg 77 7g 7s³ 8g 6fg*) Mar 22; good-bodied filly; second foal; half-sister to a winning plater; dam poor half-sister to Sharpen Up; favourite, won 22-runner maiden race at Leicester in October; stays 7f. *B. Hanbury.*

TENDER PET 3 b.c. Mummy's Pet 125–Tender Courtesan 90 (Primera 131) — (1982 6d 1983 8f 8f 7f) big, lengthy colt; little worthwhile form. *N. Vigors.*

TENDER SEEKER 2 b.c. Status Seeker–Folle Remont (Prince Tenderfoot 75 § 126) (1983 5v⁴ 5s 5v 6f 6fg² 6fg² 7f 7h 7fg* 8.2fg) Apr 25; 6,400Y; compact, attractive colt; has a long stride; second foal; brother to a winning plater; dam never ran; blinkered first time, made all in nursery at Wolverhampton in August; most inconsistent previously, and beaten in 4 sellers; suited by 7f; not one to trust. *G. Lewis.*

TENDER SOVEREIGN 3 b.c. Prince Tenderfoot 126–Yellow Lotus (Majority 92 Blue 126) (1982 5fg⁴ 5.3g 6v³ 1983 6v 6s⁴ 6s 5g 8f* 8f³ 8f* 8fg²) quite attractive, well-made colt; narrowly won handicaps at Wolverhampton in June and July; finished strongly and came clear of remainder when excellent ¾-length second of 21 to Sheriff Muir in ladies race at Ascot later in July, only subsequent start; runs as if he'll be suited by a bit further than 1m; acts on any going, but goes particularly well on firm. *G. Lewis.*

TENDER SPRING 2 br.c. Prince Tenderfoot 126–Spring Spray (Silly Season 69 p 127) (1983 6fg) Feb 8; quite attractive colt; very good mover; first foal; dam unraced half-sister to high-class sprinter King of Macedon; 7/1 and in need of race,

7 lengths seventh of 22 to Chicago Bid in maiden event at Newmarket in July; sent to France. *R. Hern.*

TENDER TRADER (USA) 4 ch.g. Our Michael–My Roue (Hilarious) (1982   **79** 7fg 7.6f 6f 5h* 6fg* 5.8g* 6g 6d 6f 1983 6v 5.3f 6fg 6f⁴ 6f 6fg² 6h* 6g*) strong, attractive gelding; good mover; sprint handicapper; won at Nottingham (apprentices) and Leicester (again apprentice ridden) in September; needs a sound surface; sometimes wears bandages or boots in front. *G. Lewis.*

TENDER VENTURE 4 br.g. Prince Tenderfoot 126–Hopeful Maid (Hopeful   **–** Venture 125) (1982 7g 8fg 8fg 8fg 8fg 1983 11.7d 8.3s 7d) neat gelding; fair at his best; has shown no form for a long time and finished well beaten in sellers last 2 starts; not certain to stay beyond 7f unless he learns to settle; acts on a firm surface; best in blinkers; sold to W. Clay 2,000 gns Ascot 2nd June Sales. *G. Hunter.*

TENNIS PENNY 2 br.f. Auction Ring 123–Blessingtonia 79 (So Blessed 130)   **92** (1983 5g* 5g³ 5g 5f 7f 6g 8.2fg⁴ 8.2fg²) Apr 23; 9,400Y; tall, leggy, rather lightly-made, quite attractive filly; first foal; dam raced only at 5f, winning once at 2 yrs; won 8-runner minor event at Brighton in May; good second in nursery at Nottingham in October, easily best subsequent effort; suited by 1m; blinkered sixth start; possibly requires strong handling; inconsistent. *P. Kelleway.*

TENNIS TUNE 3 ch.c. Music Boy 124–Bonny Bertha (Capistrano 120) (1982   **66** 5g² 5fg* 5d² 5g³ 6fg 5g³ 5g² 1983 5g 5g 5f 5f³ 6g* 6f 6f) smallish, strong colt; good walker; won handicap at Ayr in July (ridden by 7-lb claimer); stays 6f; exported to Singapore. *D. Garraton.*

TENTH OF OCTOBER 4 b.g. Shiny Tenth 120–Seam 100 (Nearula 132) (1982   **–** 8g 10.6fg 8fg³ 10f⁴ 1983 12g 10g) useful-looking gelding; fair handicapper at his best on flat and a smart hurdler; stays 1¼m; acts on any going with possible exception of very firm; ran moderately in blinkers once. *S. Mellor.*

TENTRACO LADY 2 b.f. Gay Fandango 131–Dauphine 102 (Pampered King   **65** 121) (1983 6fg 7fg 7f 7.6d⁴ 6fg) Feb 12; 14,000Y; strong, compact filly; half-sister to several winners, including Free Handicap winner Man of Harlech (by Welsh Pageant) and stayer Man of Spirit (by Vitiges); dam genuine stayer; showed modest form, best effort on fourth outing; will be suited by 1m+; acts on a soft surface; may improve sufficiently to win small race. *D. H. Jones.*

TENTWORT 6 ch.m. Shiny Tenth 120–Pinguicula (Pinza 137) (1982 15g² 16fg⁴   **62** 16fg 16fg² 16g* 16d³ 17.4d 16.1s³ 18d 18s 1983 15g* 15.8d* 16f² 16f³ 16f 17.4g² 16fg 18fg) strong mare; staying handicapper; won at Ayr in May (easily) and Catterick in June; ran creditably sixth start; acts on any going but goes well on soft. *W. Elsey.*

TEPELENI 3 b.c. Averof 123–Starbright (Petingo 135) (1982 7fg³ 1983 10v²   **74** 10fg 10f 10f³ 8fg 8g) rangy, good-bodied colt; placed in maiden races; suited by 1¼m; sold 5,000 gns Newmarket Autumn Sales. *C. Brittain.*

TERN 2 b.g. Blakeney 126–Marcela 107 (Reform 132) (1983 6v) Mar 22; 5,200Y;   **–** compact, workmanlike gelding; half-brother to 2 minor 2-y-o winners; dam won three 6f races at 2 yrs; well beaten in minor event at Ripon in June; subsequently gelded. *M. H. Easterby.*

TERRENO 5 gr.h. Vaguely Noble 140–Ileana 113 (Abernant 142) (1982 10.5s*   **120** 10.5d³ 12s 10.5g* 12v* 12g* 12g³ 12v 1983 12s² 10.5d 12fg³ 12.5g² 12g* 13.5fg⁴ 12fg⁴ 12g 11g) French horse; smart performer; easily won Grand Prix de Vichy in August by 5 lengths from Margello; ran creditably several other starts, including when in frame in Prix d'Hedouville at Longchamp (second to Marasali), Prix Maurice de Nieuil at Saint-Cloud (length second to Load the Cannons), Grand Prix de Deauville (fourth to Zalataia) and Preis von Europa at Cologne (fourth to Esprit du Nord); ran in USA late in year; stays 13.5f; seems to act on any going; below form second start. *F. Boutin, France.*

TEST OF TIME 2 br.c. Bay Express 132–Brilliant Reay 74 (Ribero 126) (1983   **86** 7fg 7g 7g*) May 5; medium-sized colt; fourth foal; half-brother to fair 1979 2-y-o sprinter Braconda (by So Blessed) and a winner in USA; dam won over 10.4f; sweating badly, made nearly all in 7-runner minor event at Sandown in October, winning by a length; evidently stays 7f well. *H. Candy.*

TETRON BAY 3 b.c. Nonoalco 131–Tanella 103 (Habitat 134) (1982 5f 5fg 8fg   **107** 8.2s 7g² 7s² 1983 7g 8g² 8f* 8f² 8f* 8f 7.2fg³ 7f³ 8.5f* 8g* 10.2s 9fg 8g*) strong, lengthy colt; good mover; improved and had a fine season; won at Salisbury (twice), Epsom, Kempton and Ascot; made all and just lasted home from The

Ripleyite in £5,600 handicap on last-named course in October; stays 1m well; best form on a sound surface; suited by forcing tactics; genuine and consistent. *R. Hannon.*

TEUCER 3 ch.g. Dance In Time–Rose and the Ring (Welsh Pageant 132) (1982 5fg 5fg 8s 1983 11.5fg³ 14f 13.8f² 12f² 12fg*) big, lengthy gelding; made all, despite wandering around violently under pressure, in claiming event at Newmarket in August; stays 1¾m; blinkered last 4 starts; suited by forcing tactics. *A. Ingham.* — 77

TEZ SHAHZADA 3 b.c. Mummy's Pet 125–Eastern Romance 73 (Sahib 114) (1982 6fg 1983 5v 7f 7f 8d) rather lightly-made colt; plating-class maiden; promises to stay 1m. *P. Haslam.* — –

THAHUL (USA) 6 b.h. Nijinsky 138–Queen City Miss (Royal Union) (1982 16d 16f* 14fg* 14fg* 16g 12fg 1983 16s 14s 14fg³ 16f) deep-girthed, rangy horse; good walker; suited by 1¾m+; has won on a soft surface but is much better suited by top-of-the-ground; wears blinkers; ran as though something was wrong with him second start. *F. J. Houghton.* — 70

THANK YOU FANS 2 ch.f. Be My Guest 126–Send The Fleet (Bold Hour) (1983 7h³ 8g⁴) Feb 25; 10,000Y; light-framed filly; third foal; dam second over 6f and 8.6f in Ireland; in frame in maiden races at Chepstow in August and Leicester in September; stays 1m. *P. Kelleway.* — 67

THARALEOS (USA) 3 ch.c. Junction–Right About (Citation) (1982 7fg 7g 1983 8d 8.2s 8fg 10d 9g³ 8.2fg 9fg² 9f⁴ 10g² 10f* 10s 9fg³ 10f) robust, heavy-topped colt; won 18-runner maiden race at Ripon in August; stays 1¼m; acts on firm going. *F. Watson.* — 69

THARSUS GIRL 4 br.f. Blakeney 126–Just Larking (Sea-Bird II 145) (1982 12f 17f 12f 16fg 12.3d* 13.8f³ 12g 12g³ 16fg² 17f 16s³ 15.8d³ 18s 1983 12v 12.3v² 12.2g² 15.8d 12.3f* 12f 14.7f³ 16f⁴ 16fg⁴ 13s) workmanlike filly; has a round action; won handicap at Newcastle in June; stays well; acts on any going but is ideally suited by an easy surface; effective with and without blinkers; reportedly sent to India. *P. Rohan.* — 68

THARUS O'RILEY 2 b.c. Brianston Zipper 97–Dawn Express (Pony Express 85) (1983 5fg) May 7; second foal; dam never ran; well beaten in minor event at Windsor in June; sold 400 gns Ascot September Sales. *N. Kernick.* — –

THATCH CABIN 3 b.c. Thatch 136–Saccato (Bagdad) (1982 NR 1983 5d 5fg 8f 7f⁴) strong, quite attractive colt; brother to fairly useful 1980 Irish 2-y-o 6f winner Omer, and half-brother to another winner; dam won at up to 1½m in Ireland; poor form in maiden races; blinkered final start; dead. *J. W. Watts.* — –

THATCHINGLY 2 gr.c. Thatching 131–Lady Rushen (Dancer's Image) (1983 6fg³ 6fg⁴) Apr 7; 5,400Y; compact colt; first foal; dam fairly useful 2-y-o 6f winner in Ireland; in frame in October maiden races at Folkestone and Doncaster. *M. Albina.* — 85

THAT'S INCREDIBLE 3 b.c. Oats 126–Lively (Run The Gantlet) (1982 6f 6f 6v 1983 10d 11.7s 10v 10fg 11.7fg 10g 14f 12g 12f* 8f 12fg² 12d 10d 16fg 10d 12g) neat, strong, quite attractive colt; dropped in class, won selling handicap at Newmarket in July decisively despite wandering violently left under pressure (bought in 3,600 gns); needs further than 1m and should stay 1¾m; acts on firm going; has run creditably when sweating badly. *P. K. Mitchell.* — 64

THAT'S MY SON 4 b.c. Busted 134–Take a Chance (Baldric II 131) (1982 8s 10f 8f² 8fg² 8f 8g² 8fg* 7f* 8f* 8g 8g 7g 1983 7s 8fg 8fg² 8f 8g 8fg 7s 7f) big, strong, attractive colt; excellent walker; fairly useful on his day but is inconsistent; will stay 1¼m; acts on firm going; has sweated up; suited by waiting tactics and isn't an easy ride; sold to P. Cole 15,000 gns Newmarket December Sales. *C. Brittain.* — 93

THATS ODD 3 ro.g. Warpath 113–Broughton Flyer (Huntercombe 133) (1982 5s³ 5fg 6fg 5g 5g 5d 1983 6s⁴ 8d 7d 8f 6f³) leggy, workmanlike gelding; good walker; poor form, including in sellers; should stay beyond 6f; blinkered last 2 starts. *J. Berry.* — –

THA (USA) 2 ch.c. Jungle Savage–Calyptra (Le Fabuleux 133) (1983 7fg 7f³ 7f 6fg 6d³ 6fg³) Mar 4; $42,000Y; strong, good sort; first foal; dam placed twice from 4 starts; modest maiden; stays 7f; acts on firm going and a soft surface; blinkered last 2 starts. *M. Jarvis.* — 82

THE ADRIANSTAN 8 ch.g. Sparkler 130–Riberta 89 (Ribot 142) (1982 8f 10f 1983 12fg) one-time useful handicapper but is completely unreliable and best left severely alone; sold 625 gns Ascot December Sales. *B. Stevens.* — §§

THE ASPEL 5 b.g. Pongee 106–Stephela (Young Stratford 92) (1982 10g 1983 12f 12f 10fg) workmanlike gelding; well beaten in varied company, including selling; sometimes blinkered; sold 3,100 gns Ascot November Sales. *D. Chapman.* —

THE AZADSTAN 5 gr.g. Saritamer 130–The Dupecat 75 (Javelot 124) (1982 NR 1983 12g 17.1g) poor performer; has run in a seller; used to wear blinkers; quite a modest hurdler. *I. Dudgeon.* —

THE BABE (USA) 3 b.f. Fleet Mel–Babe's Wind (Windy Sands) (1982 5fg 6f³ 6f* 6g 7s 1983 10v 7f 8f 7g 7s) close-coupled filly; disappointing in 1983, although not entirely disgraced final start; should stay 1m. *G. Wragg.* —

THE BEGINNING 5 ro.m. Goldhill 125–Histoun (Behistoun 131) (1982 8.2s³ 8f 12f 9.4fg 12fg 15.8f 10d 12g⁴ 1983 8v 15.8d 15fg) fair sort; plater; probably stays 1½m. *W. Storey.* —

THE BONDERIZER 3 gr.g. Tennyson 124–Zeddenosa (Zeddaan 130) (1982 7g 7fg 8s 1983 12v 12s 10f) short-headed, plain gelding; plating-class maiden; sold 720 gns Ascot July Sales. *M. Blanshard.* —

THE BOSSMAN 2 br.g. Orchestra 118–Shoshoni Girl (Winning Hit) (1983 7g 7.6fg 6d) Mar 28; IR 5,000Y; third foal; half-brother to 2 winners in Ireland, including 5f winner Arabian Squaw (by Tarboosh); dam in frame at up to 7.5f at 2 yrs in Ireland; quite a modest maiden; best effort on third outing; gelded subsequently; should stay at least 1m. *J. Sutcliffe.* 71

THE BRADFORD 4 b.g. Connaught 130–Mockbridge 106 (Bleep-Bleep 134) (1982 8.2f 9fg 5fg 8.2s 6s 1983 12v) big, strong, workmanlike gelding; has a round action; plating-class maiden on flat though has won over hurdles; stays 1m. *L. Barratt.* —

THE BRU 3 b.g. Welsh Saint 126–Mrs Bizz (Status Seeker) (1982 5f⁴ 5fg 6f 8d⁴ 10d 1983 9d³ 12f² 13.1h 10f² 10h⁴ 10g²) unimpressive, leggy, dipped-backed gelding; plater; probably stays 1½m; sometimes blinkered; trained by J. Fitzgerald first 2 starts. *M. Pipe.* 57

THE BUSINESS 4 b.f. Young Emperor 133–Shenan (Dunce) (1982 7g 11.5fg 1983 8fg 8g) strong, plain filly; behind in maiden races; sold 850 gns Doncaster September Sales. *J. W. Watts.* —

THE BYSTANDER 4 b.g. Owen Anthony 102–Pearl River (Bourbon Prince) (1982 6d 7fg 6g³ 1983 6v 7s 7d* 8fg 7f 8.3f 6fg 6fg 8.3f 8f 8d*) smallish, lengthy gelding; plater; attracted no bid when winning at Leicester in June and Warwick in October; stays 1m; suited by some give in the ground; blinkered at Warwick; has run well for an apprentice but seems suited by strong handling. *J. Holt.* 56

THE CATISFIELD KID 4 br.c. Comedy Star 121–Pure Gold (Pieces of Eight 128) (1982 6s 8d 7.6f 5f 10g 1983 10g 10s 12f 12.2fg 13.1h 17fg³ 16.5f⁴ 14fg 12d) quite well-made colt; poor maiden; suited by a test of stamina; sometimes blinkered. *W. Wightman.* 35

THECCAN 2 b.f. Thatch 136–Pilacombe 73 (Huntercombe 133) (1983 7g 7f⁴) Feb 5; quite attractive filly; first foal; dam won over 1¼m; 6½ lengths fourth of 19 to Mr Chromacopy in maiden race at Redcar in October; will be suited by 1m. *J. W. Watts.* 71

THE CLIFTONIAN 5 b.g. Firestreak 125–Ile de France 84 (French Beige 127) (1982 10g 12fg 10d 10.8s 1983 8d 8g 8f) workmanlike gelding; disappointing and inconsistent handicapper; beaten in a seller second start; cost 1,450 gns Ascot January Sales. *P. Butler.* —

THE CLOSER 2 gr.c. Busted 134–Pearl Grey (Gulf Pearl 117) (1983 8f) May 18; IR 18,500Y; half-brother to Irish 8.5f winner Love Tangle (by Wollow) and a winner in USA; dam, Irish 1½m winner, is half-sister to Belmont Stakes winner Celtic Ash; ninth of 14 in maiden race at Leicester in November. *M. Jarvis.* —

THEDA 2 b.f. Mummy's Pet 125–Kiara (Great Nephew 126) (1983 7f³ 6f 7s 7fg) May 19; rather leggy, useful-looking filly; second foal; sister to 3-y-o Cray; dam of little account on flat and over hurdles; poor maiden; form only on first outing; stays 7f; blinkered final start. *W. Bentley.* 61

THE DIPLOMAT 5 gr.g. The Go-Between 129–Serene Thought (Burglar 128) (1982 8f 12f⁴ 11g 1983 10g) big gelding; little worthwhile form; not certain to stay 1½m. *D. Ringer.* —

THE DOWNS 7 b.g. Blast 125–Princess Lorna 63 (Royal Palm 131) (1982 NR 1983 6v 10fg 8d) poor plater; has been blinkered; has sweated up; sold out of H. O'Neill's stable 500 gns Ascot July Sales after second start. *D. Jermy.* —

THE ENID 3 b.f. Tudor Rhythm 112–Flora Leigh 94 (Floribunda 136) (1982 5fg 5fg 6g 5g 5.1f⁴ 1983 10v 8v) lengthy filly; poor form in varied races; blinkered once at 2 yrs. *C. Mackenzie.* —

THE FORT 3 ch.c. Sallust 134–Fortlin 95 (Fortino II 120) (1982 6fg³ 7g* 7fg* 7s* 1983 7d 7fg) good-bodied, full-quartered, quite attractive colt; brother to top-class French and American 6.5f to 9f winner Sanedtki; developed into a very smart performer as a 2-y-o and won his last 3 races decisively, including Intercraft Solario Stakes at Sandown and Limekiln Stakes at Goodwood (made all both times); disappointing as a 3-y-o in Clerical, Medical Greenham Stakes at Newbury in April and Van Geest Stakes at Newmarket in June, but almost certainly needed race in former and was hit over head by another rider's whip in latter; would have been suited by 1m; probably acted on any going; stud in Australia. *H. Cecil.* —

THE FOUR AYS 2 b.c. Kala Shikari 125–Polygon (Tarboosh) (1983 7fg 6f² 6f* 6fg⁴) Apr 12; 1,000Y; workmanlike colt; first foal; dam winning hurdler; won 13-runner seller at Doncaster (no bid) in July; respectable fourth in nursery at Windsor the following month; suited by 6f; exported to Algeria. *R. Akehurst.* — 67

THE FRIEND 5 ch.h. Run The Gantlet–Loose Cover 106 (Venture VII 129) (1982 12s² 13d⁴ 12f³ 12f* 12fg 1983 12d 12f 12f* 12h* 12g⁴ 12d⁴) lightly-made, quite attractive horse; poor walker; won handicaps at Doncaster (amateurs) and Chepstow in summer; best at 1½m though gets further; evidently acts on any going; blinkered nowadays; suitable mount for an amateur rider; hasn't always looked genuine. *H. T. Jones.* — 64

THE GAME'S UP 2 b.c. Cawston's Clown 113–Mandetta (Mandamus 120) (1983 7g 7fg) Mar 21; IR 6,200F; big, workmanlike colt; half-brother to 3 winners here and abroad, including 1980 2-y-o 6f winner Bugatti (by Arch Sculptor); dam plater on flat and over hurdles; little worthwhile form in September maiden events at Leicester and Newmarket. *P. Haslam.* —

THE GREY BUCK 3 gr.g. Grey Ghost 98–Mactavish 90 (St Alphage 119) (1982 NR 1983 5v 6d² 6g⁴ 7f 8f 7f* 7fg⁴ 8f³ 7f) big gelding; second foal; brother to 6f winner Laurence Mac; dam won over 6f and 7f at 2 yrs and also won 4 times over hurdles; 5-length winner of modest maiden race at Thirsk in July; also in frame in varied company; stays 1m; acts on firm going and a soft surface. *T. Barron.* — 74

THE HIGH DANCER 3 b.f. High Line 125–Sovereign Help 98 (Sovereign Lord 120) (1982 NR 1983 8g) half-sister to 2 modest 2-y-o winners; dam won five 5f races; unquoted; dwelt when last-but-one in 16-runner maiden race at Warwick in October. *J. Spearing.* —

THE HILL TARGET 2 ch.c. Mount Hagen 127–Benita 94 (Roan Rocket 128) (1983 5fg⁴) May 19; IR 10,000F, IR 6,400Y; half-brother to 3 winners, including fairly useful sprinter Red Rosie (by Red Alert); dam sprinter; 10 lengths fourth of 15 to Welsh Willie in maiden race at Windsor in July. *J. Sutcliffe.* —

THE HOMAN 2 b. or br.c. Manado 130–Hommage 69 (Tamerlane 128) (1983 7fg 7fg 7f 8.2fg² 8fg⁴ 8.2fg) Mar 19; IR 4,200Y; lightly-made, shallow-girthed colt; first foal; dam won over 10.6f; beaten head in 18-runner seller at Nottingham in October; will stay 1¼m; capable of winning a seller. *N. Callaghan.* — 67

THE HOUSE BUILDER 3 b.c. Sharpen Up 127–Via Tritus 103 (Sovereign Path 125) (1982 6v 5s³ 1983 6s⁴ 7s² 8d* 8f) strong, good-topped colt; beaten ½ length by Corston Lad in maiden race at Ayr in June but was slightly hampered in last furlong and placings were reversed; stays 1m; acts on soft going; racing in Italy. *M. Jarvis.* — 77

THE HUYTON GIRLS 5 ch.m. Master Sing 109–Artway 82 (Articulate 121) (1982 6s 6s² 5fg 5f 6fg⁴ 5g 5d 5s 1983 5s 5v 5d³ 6v 5g 5d³ 5g² 5g* 6fg⁴ 5f 5fg 5f 5f³ 5g 6g 5d) fair sort; sprint handicapper; won at Haydock in July; best at 5f nowadays; acts on any going but is ideally suited by some give in the ground; often apprentice ridden; often blinkered; sweated up badly ninth start; ducked left leaving stalls and virtually took no part fourteenth outing. *T. Taylor.* — 60

THE IRISH RHINE 5 b.g. Ragapan 118–At The King's Side (Kauai King) (1982 12s³ 15.5fg 12f 12s 1983 14fg* 18f* 16f² 19f 14fg) lengthy ex-Irish gelding; won handicaps at Yarmouth and Pontefract in June; suited by a test of stamina; seems to act on any going but goes well on fast ground. *D. Wilson.* — 56

THE KNIFE 5 b.g. Fine Blade 121–Mary Kanga 67 (Charlottesville 135) (1982 15.5fg 1983 15g) small, lightly-made gelding; poor plater; occasionally blinkered; bought 1,800 gns Ascot January Sales. *M. James.* —

THE KRACK 3 b.g. Forlorn River 124–Malpighia (Mourne 126) (1982 NR 1983   –
12f 10h3 14.7fg) big, lengthy, rather sparely-made gelding; half-brother to
several winners in France; dam won over 11f in France; third in seller at
Chepstow in August; had stiff task when bandaged in front only subsequent start;
stays 1¼m. *J. Yardley.*

THE LIQUIDATOR 3 b.c. Busted 134–Teleflora 89 (Princely Gift 137) (1982   93
8d* 1983 12v 14fg 13.3g) rangy, attractive colt; looked very promising when
winning at Newmarket on his only start as a 2-y-o, but was only lightly raced in
1983; weakened only in last 1½f or so and ran better than finishing positions
suggest when last of 5 behind Band in March Stakes at Goodwood and ninth of 16
behind Jupiter Island in Coral Autumn Cup (Handicap) at Newbury on last 2 outings
however; promises to stay 1¾m. *B. Hobbs.*

THE MANOR 2 ch.g. Manor Farm Boy 114–Fond Farewell 83 (Proud Challenge)   60
(1983 5d 5d 6g 6f 8f 8g) Mar 26; 1,300F, 2,500Y; tall, useful-looking gelding; first
foal; dam 1½m winner; poor maiden; form only at 5f; possibly needs a soft surface;
blinkered fourth and sixth starts; gelded after fourth outing; sold to E. Alston 740
gns Doncaster October Sales. *J. Berry.*

THE MAZALL 3 br.g. Persian Bold 123–Dance All Night 106 (Double-U-Jay 120)   –
(1982 7.2g 6g 1983 5f 6f 5f 5f 5fg) small gelding; plating-class maiden; should be
suited by 6f+. *Miss L. Siddall.*

THE MILKMAN 2 b.g. Daring March 116–Dairy Queen 76 (Queen's Hussar 124)   53
(1983 5f 6fg 5f 6f4 6g) Apr 4; neat, strong gelding; half-brother to 2 winners by
Birdbrook, including useful 7f and 1m performer Parlour Game; dam placed from
6f to 1¾m; poor maiden; should stay 7f; ran very wide into straight at Epsom
when apprentice ridden on fourth start; blinkered final appearance. *R. Smyth.*

THE MILLER (FR) 2 gr.c. Mill Reef 141–Turkish Treasure 111 (Sir Ivor 135)   92 p
(1983 7g*) Mar 16; third foal; half-brother to useful 1982 Irish 2-y-o 6f and 7f
winner Treasure Trove (by Try My Best) and useful 1981 staying Irish 2-y-o Sun
Worship (by Nonoalco), subsequently a stakes winner over 8.5f in USA; dam ran

Mr S. S. Niarchos' "The Miller"

only at 2 yrs when very useful winner over 6f and 7f; accounted for largely more-experienced individuals when justifying favouritism in very pleasing style in 14-runner maiden race at Phoenix Park in October, scoring by 2½ lengths from Cyrano; will stay at least 1¼m; the type to make a smart performer. *V. O'Brien, Ireland.*

THE MINSTER (USA) 3 b.c. The Minstrel 135–Play at Home (Round Table) (1982 6g² 7g² 1983 8g 6f* 6fg⁴) strong colt; good walker and mover; having first race for 4 months when narrowly winning maiden race at Yarmouth in August; had much stiffer task when creditable 3¾ lengths fourth of 7 behind Coquito's Friend in minor event at Salisbury the following month; should stay 1m; blinkered and wore tongue strap on reappearance, and reportedly has his own ideas about the game. *M. Albina.* **95**

THE MOOCHE 2 b.g. Swing Easy 126–Cress (Crepello 136) (1983 7fg 7fg 8fg) May 7; IR 10,000Y; rather leggy gelding; half-brother to 3-y-o 1¼m winner Dhofar (by Octavo) and 2 other winners, including speedy 1976 2-y-o Self Portrait (by Jukebox); dam ran only 3 times; quite a modest maiden; stays 7f. *G. Pritchard-Gordon.* **72**

THE MUMMER 2 b.g. Song 132–Ringaround (Martinmas 128) (1983 5s 5v 5d³ 6fg² 7fg) Apr 27; lengthy gelding; second foal; half-brother to a winner in Austria; dam never ran; fair plater; stayed 6f; acted on a firm and a soft surface; trained by I. Balding first 4 starts; dead. *H. Collingridge.* **66**

THE NOBLE PLAYER (USA) 3 ch.c. The Minstrel 135–Noble Mark 120 (On Your Mark 125) (1982 5g³ 5f* 5f* 6f² 7.2g³ 6g² 8.2fg* 8s³ 8s³ 1983 10.5s⁴ 7d* 12s 9.2d 8f 10g) well-made, attractive colt; half-brother to 3 middle-distance winners; dam very smart sprinter; kept his form and condition well through a busy first season in 1982 and won 3 times, showing high-class form; gained only win of 1983 and put up a good performance when beating Diesis (gave 3 lb) by ¾ length in Heron Stakes at Kempton in May, travelling strongly from start, leading at halfway, and rallying really well when joined by runner-up 1½f out; weakened in closing stages when about 4 lengths fifth of 12 behind Crystal Glitters in Prix d'Ispahan at Longchamp in June and when about 5 lengths sixth of 11 behind Noalcoholic in Sussex Stakes at Goodwood in July on fourth and fifth starts; never got in a challenge when last of 14 behind Tolomeo in Budweiser Million at Arlington Park, Chicago, in August and subsequently remained in USA; best at up to 1m; has run well on all types of going, but has shown his very best form with some give in the ground. *B. Hills.* **120**

THEODAS 2 br.g. Heres 81–Kaolin 98 (Kalydon 122) (1983 8d 7g) Apr 26; half-brother to 2 winners by Sharpen Up, notably very useful Belgian and French performer Epsiba, a winner at up to 15f; dam won over 9f and 1¼m; behind in October in maiden race (slowly away) at Warwick and minor event at Chepstow; subsequently gelded. *G. Cottrell.* **–**

THE OWLS 4 b. or br.g. Pieces of Eight 128–Keino (Kautokeino) (1982 10d* 12f 11.7d³ 11g⁴ 10fg³ 10fg³ 13d² 12g 12d² 16s 1983 12v 12fg³ 14fg) narrow, workmanlike gelding; stays 13f; acts on a firm and a soft surface; has run creditably for an apprentice; ran badly in blinkers once. *M. Tompkins.* **–**

THE PAWN 4 b.c. Malinowski 123–Skelmorlie (Blakeney 126) (1982 12f* 12f³ 10g 10g³ 16.5g³ 14f 12f* 13g 18d 12s 10s 1983 17d 14fg 18f² 17f 20.4g² 19h* 17fg⁴ 18f⁴ 18.1d³ 16fg 16fg² 18fg) smallish ex-Irish colt; out-and-out staying handicapper; easily won at Beverley in July; acts well on fast ground; best in blinkers; didn't look too keen third start; inconsistent. *M. Ryan.* **60**

THE PIRATE 3 b.c. Bay Express 132–Rosaura 105 (Court Martial) (1982 NR 1983 5v 6d) half-brother to several winners, including useful 1m and 11.7f winner Roses (by Ribero); dam, sprinter, is daughter of 1000 Guineas winner Belle of All; towards rear in maiden race at Thirsk and minor event at Hamilton in May. *C. Nelson.* **–**

THE POWVEE 2 b.g. Tudor Rhythm 112–Porto Novo (Sovereign Lord 120) (1983 5.8g 7fg 7d 10d) Mar 20; 900Y; good-topped gelding; half-brother to several winners, including 5f to 7f winner Jahil (by Song); dam unraced half-sister to very smart sprinter Kala Shikari; in rear in maiden races and a seller; retained 520 gns Ascot November Sales. *P. Haynes.* **–**

THE PROFESSOR 6 br.g. Welsh Pageant 132–Pulchra 107 (Celtic Ash) (1982 NR 1983 17.1g) staying handicapper; has shown no form since 1980; probably acts on any going; has been tried in blinkers; suited by strong handling; sold 2,300 gns Ascot July Sales. *J. Roberts.* **–**

THE RANEE 3 b.f. Royal Palace 131–Gingerale (Golden Horus 123) (1982 6g 7g   –
1983 8fg) lengthy filly; behind in maiden races at 2 yrs and in gentleman riders race
at Goodwood in August (bandaged in front); will be suited by further than 1m. *W.
Holden.*

THERAPEUTIC (USA) 2 ch.c. Unconscious–Instant Therapy (Going Straight)   – p
(1983 6fg) May 27; $57,000Y; second foal; dam won two 6f claiming races; 7/1, last
of 5 in Duke of Edinburgh Stakes at Ascot in October. *M. Jarvis.*

THEREON 2 b.f. Nonoalco 131–Thereby 99 (Star Moss 122) (1983 6fg 7g) Feb   –
18; 36,000Y; half-sister to numerous winners, notably top-class 7f performer Pas
de Seul (by Mill Reef); dam won at up to 1m; backward, in rear in September in
£3,500 race at Salisbury and £5,000 race at Lingfield. *H. Candy.*

THE RIPLEYITE 4 ch.c. Northfields–Red Ruby 113 (Tudor Melody 129) (1982   92
7g⁴ 8g² 8f² 8fg* 8fg 8.5f³ 8f³ 8fg³ 8f² 8.5fg³ 8fg³ 8d² 8s 8s 1983 8d 8v 8d 8v 8.5g³
8f 8f* 8fg³ 8f 8fg⁴ 8f 8h⁴ 8fg³ 8fg 8fg³ 8g² 8d 8fg⁴) lightly-made, quite attractive
colt; quite a modest handicapper; won at Brighton in June; stays 8.5f; probably acts
on any going but is ideally suited by top-of-the-ground; doesn't find much off bridle
and is suited by waiting tactics; sent to USA. *G. Balding.*

THE ROTTER 2 ch.g. Thatching 131–Bobbins 70 (Bold Lad, Ire 133) (1983 6fg²   88
6fg 7fg³) Mar 20; 14,000F, 18,000Y; good-bodied, quite attractive gelding; third
foal (first in this country); dam, half-sister to top 1977 2-y-o filly Cherry Hinton,
won over 1¼m and has been in Australia; placed in minor events at Nottingham and
Doncaster in October; suited by 7f. *B. Hills.*

THE SALTINGS (FR) 3 b.f. Morston 125–Eltisley 82 (Grey Sovereign 128§)   –
(1982 NR 1983 10s 10.1fg⁴) fourth foal; half-sister to useful 7f winner Applemint
(by Sir Ivor) and useful sprinter Dare Me (by Derring-Do); dam 2-y-o 5f winner;
soundly beaten in maiden race at Chepstow in May and minor event (fourth of 8) at
Windsor in August; sold 8,000 gns Newmarket December Sales. *R. Hern.*

THE SHINER 3 b.g. Julio Mariner 127–Wolver Valley 72 (Wolver Hollow 126)   –
(1982 7f 7g 7g 8g 1983 10fg) leggy gelding; ran best race when blinkered on first
start at 2 yrs; should be suited by 1¼m. *D. Nicholson.*

THE SIXTIES 2 ch.g. Monseigneur 127–Wigeon 80 (Divine Gift 127) (1983 5.8g   68
7f 5fg²) Mar 25; 4,000Y; third produce; half-brother to 5f to 1¼m winner Ma
Pierrette (by Cawston's Clown); dam won 5 times at up to 1¼m; 6 lengths second
of 11 to Anton Pillar in minor event at Windsor in August; should stay 7f; exported
to Singapore. *P. Cole.*

THE SMALL MIRACLE 5 gr.g. Most Secret 119–Grey Aglow 89 (Aglojo 119)   63
(1982 10d* 10d 12.3fg 10.5s 12d 1983 13v² 12d² 11s* 12fg) workmanlike gelding;
won apprentice handicap at Hamilton in April; stays 13f; has run creditably on a firm
surface, but revels in the mud; effective with and without blinkers; suited by
waiting tactics; not seen out after April. *N. Bycroft.*

THE SOLENT 7 ch.g. Exbury 138–West Side Story 127 (Rockefella) (1982 12g⁴   §§
15.8f 12fg² 12s 10g 10fg² 16d 8fg 1983 12f 14fg 8s) workmanlike gelding;
occasionally runs respectably but is temperamental and best left alone; blinkered
last 3 starts in 1982. *D. Chapman.*

THESPIAN 2 b.f. Ile de Bourbon 133–Artemis 91 (King Emperor) (1983 5s³ 5d   69
6g 6f) Apr 24; strong, deep-girthed, medium-sized filly; closely related to 3-y-o
Slip Up (by Quiet Fling) and half-sister to 2 winners, including useful Italian filly
Adolfina (by Gay Fandango); dam 2-y-o 7f winner; quite modest form in maiden
races; not seen out after August. *B. Hobbs.*

THESSALONIKI 3 ch.f. Julio Mariner 127–Camina Bay 109 (Whistling Wind   85
123) (1982 6fg⁴ 8g 8f² 6g⁴ 7g² 7s 1983 7s⁴ 10.5s⁴ 11.5fg³ 12fg 10fg³ 10g* 12f
10h² 10h* 10g* 10fg 12fg) small, close-coupled filly; successful in maiden race at
Ayr, minor event at Nottingham and handicap at Yarmouth; staying-on sixth of 14 to
High Hawk in Ribblesdale Stakes at Royal Ascot on fourth start; suited by 1¼m+;
ran creditably on soft going as a 2-y-o, but is ideally suited by a sound surface. *C.
Brittain.*

THE TARGE 2 ch.g. Town and Country 124–Hazelwood 71 (Lucky Brief 128)   71
(1983 5.8g 6f 7f 7h² 8s 8fg 7fg⁴ 8fg) May 10; 3,500Y; big, quite useful-looking
gelding; half-brother to winning jumper Tuffnut Prince (by Prince Consort); dam
placed over 5f and 7f at 2 yrs; quite useful plater; best form at 7f, but should stay
1m; acts on hard going; wears blinkers; gelded at end of year. *C. Nelson.*

THETFORD CHASE 3 b.f. Relkino 131–Boscage 104 (Queen's Hussar 124)   63
(1982 NR 1983 10f 12fg 14f 10fg 9d 10fg 10fg) leggy, rather narrow filly; fourth

foal; half-sister to fair 7f winner Thatching Time (by Thatch); dam won 3 races at 2 yrs, and stayed 1m; quite a moderate maiden; promises to stay beyond 1¼m. *F. Durr.*

THE THRESHER 2 ch.c. Oats 126–Kew 110 (Princely Gift 137) (1983 6g 6f⁴ 5g 7fg) June 3; lengthy colt; half-brother to numerous winners, including very useful 6f and 7f winner Haunt (by Habitat); dam, sister to Floribunda, showed very useful form over 5f at 2 yrs; quite a moderate maiden; stays 6f. *R. Armstrong.*   **75**

THE THUNDERER 3 gr.g. Town Crier 119–Fair Measure (Quorum 126) (1982 7s 8s 1983 6v 8fg 6f 6f⁴ 10.1fg) tall, leggy, short-backed colt; good mover; has shown ability in varied races, including a claimer; finds 6f too sharp and should stay 1m. *P. M. Taylor.*   **–**

THE WARRIOR 3 ch.c. Roman Warrior 132–Spanish Lantern 92 (Don Carlos) (1982 5.3g 5s 1983 5v 7.6v 6v 6f³ 6fg 6f) strong, rangy colt; poor walker; quite a moderate maiden; should stay beyond 6f; seems to need a sound surface. *G. Lewis.*   **–**

THE WAY SHE MOVES 3 b.f. North Stoke 130–Lovely Clare 106 (Sing Sing 134) (1982 7fg 8s 1983 9fg 8h⁴) fair sort; little worthwhile form at the minor meetings. *P. Cole.*   **–**

THIEVES HOLLOW 2 ch.f. Some Hand 119–Errichel (Sweet Revenge 129) (1983 6g 6d 6fg) small filly; second foal; dam never ran; well beaten in autumn maiden and minor events, on final outing last of 20. *G. Balding.*   **–**

THINKLUCKYBELUCKY 3 b.f. Maystreak 118–Rugby Princess 82 (El Gallo 122) (1982 5v 6s 1983 8v 5s 6g 6fg 6fg³) sprint plater; trained first start by J. Howell. *B. McMahon.*   **–**

THINK ON (USA) 3 b.g. Habitony–Native Mistress (Nearctic) (1982 6d 6f 6fg³ 6f⁴ 6g⁴ 5g 5g 6g 1983 8d 8f) small, fair sort; disappointing maiden; should stay 7f+; has been tried in blinkers; sometimes starts slowly and is a poor mover nowadays. *M. Tompkins.*   **–**

THIRD REALM 4 b.g. Realm 129–Such Moor 77 (Santa Claus 133) (1982 8f 7fg 12g⁴ 10fg 1983 12fg 16fg 12.2g) compact gelding; plating-class maiden; suited by 1½m; winner over hurdles. *M. Lambert.*   **52**

THISTLEFIELD 2 ch.f. Whistlefield 118–Sion Hill 60 (The Go-Between 129) (1983 5.8h 7f) fair sort; first foal; dam won 6f seller at 4 yrs; backward, last in seller and a minor event. *J. Hill.*   **–**

THOMAS A BECKET 4 ch.g. Record Token 128–St Gay 77 (St Chad 120) (1982 8d 9f 8f² 10.1d 8fg 9f 9fg 1983 10g 8fg) compact gelding; plater; stays 1m; acts on firm going; used to wear blinkers. *Mrs N. Smith.*   **–**

THORNDOWN 4 b.c. Busted 134–Sky Fever 108 (Skymaster 126) (1982 8fg² 8fg⁴ 8f* 8fg² 8f² 10fg* 10g 1983 10g 10s 12f 11.5f* 12g 12fg* 12fg 12fg²) very attractive, well-made colt who often impresses in appearance; won handicaps at Sandown in July (quite valuable event from Wiveton) and Salisbury in September (overcame trouble in running to beat Maintop by ½ length); suited by 1½m and may get further; needs top-of-the-ground; a rather lazy individual who is ideally suited by strong handling; wore a tongue strap last 2 starts. *L. Cumani.*   **94**

THORNTON LADY 2 gr.f. Shiny Tenth 120–Follow The Brave 68 (Owen Anthony 102) (1983 7.2g 8fg) Feb 9; second foal; sister to 1981 2-y-o 6f seller winner Next Decade; dam plating class at 2 yrs; showed ability in autumn sellers at Haydock and Redcar; sold BBA 5,800 gns Newmarket Autumn Sales. *Sir Mark Prescott.*   **53**

THOR'S DAUGHTER 3 b.f. Import 127–Matsui 61 (Falcon 131) (1982 NR 1983 9v 9d 9.4d 8.2fg⁴ 8g 8g 8.2s 7g 8fg) compact dam poor staying plater; poor form, including in sellers; blinkered final outing. *T. Craig.*   **–**

THOUGHTLESS (USA) 3 b.c. Alleged 138–Riverside (Sheshoon 132) (1982 NR 1983 10s² 12d³ 11.7s³ 14d³ 16fg*) $750,000Y; close-coupled, quite attractive colt; half-brother to numerous winners, including smart French middle-distance winner River River (by Riverman) and top-class 1m to 1½m filly Riverqueen (by Luthier); dam very smart winner at up to 13f; made fairly heavy weather of winning small maiden race at York in June; in frame all previous starts; stays 2m; yet to race on really firm ground but acts on any other; blinkered third start; lacks pace; sold 8,000 gns Newmarket September Sales and exported. *J. Tree.*   **84**

THRONE OF GLORY 2 b.c. Hittite Glory 125–Another Princess 83 (King Emperor) (1983 5g 5s 5fg² 6f* 6fg² 6f* 6fg² 6g⁴ 6f* 6fg) Mar 3; good-topped,   **103**

845

robust colt; third foal; half-brother to 7.6f and 1m winner Molon Lave (by Welsh Pageant); dam won over 1m; won 20-runner maiden race at Newmarket in July and nurseries under sizeable weights at Salisbury in August and September; suited by 6f; acts well on firm going and is possibly unsuited by soft; has run well when sweating up; thoroughly genuine and consistent. *F. Durr.*

THROW ME OVER 3 ch.g. Roman Warrior 132–Sultry One (Tropique 128) (1982 5g 1983 8.2s 8.2g 8f 6fg 7g 6f* 7f⁴ 7g* 6fg 7g 7g³ 7g² 8fg) big, workmanlike gelding; showed little until winning handicap at Ripon in August and minor event at Catterick in September; ran creditably in handicaps afterwards; stays 7f; acts on firm going. *R. Whitaker.* **74**

THUG 3 ch.c. Persian Bold 123–Spring Azure 98 (Mountain Call 125) (1982 7f* 1983 7fg* 7.6fg 7f⁴ 8f 7fg 7fg) well-made, attractive colt; good walker; met with minor setback after winning his only race as a 2-y-o and was having first subsequent race when getting up in last furlong to beat Linda's Fantasy by ½ length in 12-runner £11,600 Van Geest Stakes at Newmarket in June (25/1-chance); didn't really progress, although ran respectably on occasions, including when 8 lengths fourth of 7 to Beaudelaire in Beeswing Stakes at Newcastle; stays 7f (had particularly stiff task over 1m); acts on firm going. *J. Hindley.* **110**

THUNDERBRIDGE 4 br.g. Rapid River 127–Sayvanter (Galivanter 131) (1982 5fg 6f 5fg³ 6s 6s 5g 5s 1983 5d 6v 5g 5g* 5fg² 5f² 5f* 6fg³ 5g³ 5fg 5g 6fg) smallish, strong gelding; sprint handicapper; won amateur riders events at Ayr in May and Wolverhampton in August; stays 6f; ideally suited by a sound surface; blinkered last 2 starts in 1982; good mount for an amateur. *S. Norton.* **75**

THUNDER ROCK 2 b. or br.c. Royalty 130–Sweet Louise 67 (Sweet Revenge 129) (1983 6g 7.6fg) May 24; first foal; dam placed over 5f at 2 yrs; well beaten in autumn in newcomers race at Goodwood and maiden event at Lingfield. *H. Candy.* **–**

TIBOUCHINA 4 gr.f. Runnymede 123–Reproach Me Not (Connaught 130) (1982 5f 1983 5v 5s 5.1g 5f) lengthy filly; sprint maiden. *A. Hide.* **–**

TICKLED WIND 2 b.c. Tickled Pink 114–Head Scarf 59 (Tumble Wind) (1983 5.3f 5fg) May 30; first foal; dam won 7f seller; in rear in June maiden races at Brighton (slowly away) and Warwick. *H. Westbrook.* **–**

TIDDLYEYETYE 2 ch.c. Roman Warrior 132–Eridantini (Indigenous 121) (1983 6fg) Apr 18; 3,800Y; half-brother to prolific sprint winner Offa's Mead (by Rathlin); dam never ran; last of 11 in maiden event at Hamilton in September. *I. Vickers.* **–**

TIDWORTH TATTOO (USA) 4 ch.g. Native Charger–Beautiful World (Dr Fager) (1982 7d 12s⁴ 12fg 12f 10fg* 12d 10d 1983 16v 16g) tall, long-striding gelding; fair at his best; well beaten at 4 yrs, running badly second start; stays 1½m; sometimes bandaged; changed hands 1,100 gns Ascot August Sales. *D. Elsworth.* **–**

TIEBOLT 3 b.g. Native Bazaar 122–Contented Sole 77 (Gulf Pearl 117) (1982 5fg 6g 7s 1983 6d) lightly-made gelding; no worthwhile form, including in valuable seller; has been blinkered; sold 400 gns Ascot August Sales. *P. Burgoyne.* **–**

TIGER SCOUT (USA) 3 b.f. Silent Screen–Indian Tigress (Terrible Tiger) (1982 7f 7d⁴ 7fg* 7g⁴ 1983 8s 10.2v 10.6v 8f⁴ 8f² 8fg 8g³) quite attractive filly; in frame in handicaps in summer, making running on first 2 occasions; subsequently won an allowance race over 8.5f at Belmont, USA; best form on a sound surface; blinkered third start. *I. Balding.* **67**

TIGERWOOD 2 b.c. Lombard 126–Smokey Dawn 68 (March Past 124) (1983 6g 7fg² 7f 8d 7g) workmanlike colt; good walker; third reported foal; half-brother to winning hurdler Guywood (by Tudor Rhythm); dam won over 1¼m as a 5-y-o; quite a modest maiden; off course 2 months after running poorly in claimer (favourite) at Leicester in August on third outing; should stay 1m. *P. M. Taylor.* **69 ?**

TIGRETTA 3 ch.g. Persian Bold 123–One Rose (Pall Mall 132) (1982 5s 7d 6g 8.5g⁴ 10s 8s 8g 1983 10d) sturdy, good-topped, smallish gelding; quite a moderate maiden as a 2-y-o; tailed-off last only outing of 1983 (wore a small bandage on his near-hind); isn't sure to stay 1¼m; sold to Miss S. Morris 1,000 gns Doncaster October Sales. *R. Simpson.* **–**

TI KING (FR) 2 ch.c. Arctic Tern 126–Ilrem (Prudent II 133) (1983 7.5fg* 6g²) Having accounted for the useful Misbehaving readily by two and a half lengths in the seven-and-a-half-furlong Prix des Yearlings at Deauville in August **116**

on his first racecourse appearance it was rather surprising to find Ti King dropped back to six furlongs for the Group 1 Prix Morny at the same track later in the month on his next. Ti King started a relative outsider at 12/1 to win France's top two-year-old race over six furlongs: his six rivals included the Prix Robert Papin winner Masarika, the unbeaten English horse Defecting Dancer and the promising Siberian Express, all of whom were proven at sprint distances. Ti King was outpaced behind Siberian Express in the early stages of the race but he ran on strongly in the final two furlongs to snatch second place from Masarika in a driving finish for the minor placings, two lengths behind the comfortable winner Siberian Express. At that Ti King's first season came to an end: a chipped bone in his left knee unfortunately prevented him from running in the top staying events in the autumn.

Ti King (Fr) (ch.c. Apr 19, 1981)	Arctic Tern (ch 1973)	Sea-Bird II (ch 1962)	Dan Cupid
			Sicalade
		Bubbling Beauty (ch 1961)	Hasty Road
			Almahmoud
	Ilrem (ch 1966)	Prudent II (ch 1959)	My Babu
			Providence
		Persepolis (ch 1956)	Caracalla
			Fille de Soleil

Ti King, the fourth-highest priced yearling at the Deauville August Sales, was bought for 2,050,000 francs (approximately £171,000). He is the eighth foal of Ilrem, a mare who ran only four times and was placed once over a mile as a two-year-old; he is a half-brother to several winners, notably the Grand Prix de Saint-Cloud winner Guadanini (by Luthier) and the very smart stayer Kemal (by Armistice). His second dam Persepolis won the Prix de Royallieu as a three-year-old and is a half-sister to the successful broodmare Bellatrix, grandam of the Poule d'Essai des Pouliches winner Rajput Princess and the Irish Derby runner-up Exdirectory and great-grandam of the Irish Oaks winner Regal Exception. Ti King will be suited by a return to longer distances and will stay at least a mile and a quarter. A big, good-looking colt who wore blinkers on both outings, he should win more races provided his injury has no lasting ill-effects. *F. Boutin, France.*

TILDEN 5 br.h. Tyrant–Bright Sign 116 (Firestreak 125) (1982 5f 6g 6.3fg 5fg³ 5g 5fg* 6v 1983 5v* 5d³ 5g* 5fg* 6f³ 5fg* 5g 5f⁴ 5d) Irish horse; smart sprinter; had a good year, winning handicaps at Leopardstown and Phoenix Park (2) and Barronstown Stud Stakes at Phoenix Park again; beat Royal Hobbit by 3 lengths in last-named; also ran well to be third in Ballyogan Stakes at Leopardstown (to Bri-Eden) and Baroda Stud Seven Springs Sprint at Phoenix Park (behind Jester) and finished fine 4½ lengths fourth of 8 to Habibti in Prix de l'Abbaye de Longchamp on penultimate start; acted on any going; blinkered once in 1982; consistent; retired to Burgage Stud, Co. Carlow, fee IR 1,500 gns straight or IR 2,500 gns Oct 1st. *B. Kerr, Ireland.* **120**

TILKEY FRED 3 b.c. Fine Blade 121–Riberina (Ribero 126) (1982 7s 1983 10s 8g) small, hollow-backed colt; lightly raced and of little account. *A. Moore.* **–**

TIMBER CREEK 3 b.c. Hot Grove 128–Krafty Kate 73 (Klairon 131) (1982 5f 6f 6f 6f² 7fg³ 7f 7.6v 7s* 1983 8v 10v 8s 10d 8f 11.7fg 12g 8.2h 8.5f 8g 10.8d) close-coupled colt; promises to stay 1½m; acts on any going, but best on soft; sometimes sweats up; sold to Susan Piggott Bloodstock 4,500 gns Newmarket Autumn Sales. *D. Whelan.* **–**

TIMBER MERCHANT 2 b.g. Decent Fellow 114–Naturally Enough (Aglojo 119) (1983 7fg² 7fg) Apr 13; IR 3,200F, 27,000Y; lengthy, good-topped gelding; third foal; dam never ran; ran in well-contested maiden races at Newmarket in July and August, running well on first occasion and not so well (moved badly to start) on second; will stay 1m; gelded at end of season. *J. Winter.* **87**

TIMBER TYCOON 3 gr.c. Dragonara Palace 115–Sabala 93 (Tribal Chief 125) (1982 6f² 1983 8f³ 8f² 8f* 8f⁴ 7fg* 7g⁴ 8g 7fg 7fg⁴ 8d) tall, fair sort; good walker; tended to put head in air when winning maiden race at Yarmouth in July (by 1½ lengths from Remembering) and handicap at Newmarket in August (showed a decent turn of foot to beat Salvinia by a neck after being held up); had stiffish tasks towards end of season; stays 1m; acts on firm going and wasn't disgraced first outing on softish ground. *R. Armstrong.* **94**

TIME-BEE 2 ch.g. Manado 130–Alli-Bee 57 (Violon d'Ingres) (1983 5d³ 5d 7f 8.2fg 8g) Apr 10; IR 3,800F, 9,000Y; lengthy gelding; fifth foal; dam plater; plating-class maiden; stays 1m; gelded after final appearance. *R. Hollinshead.* **65**

King George VI and Queen Elizabeth Diamond Stakes, Ascot—the consistent Time Charter comes with a strong run on the outside to catch Diamond Shoal and Sun Princess

TIME CHARTER 4 b.f. Saritamer 130–Centrocon 112 (High Line 125) (1982 **130**
8d* 8fg² 12f* 10fg² 10g* 10d* 1983 12d² 10f 12fg* 12s* 12f4)

When asked once about the type of thoroughbred a breeder should aim at producing Federico Tesio, who bred such as Donatello II, Nearco and Ribot, facetiously remarked 'Very long ones, (because) if you could breed a horse a thousand metres long you would have won a five-furlong race before the other horses had even started'. Such humour aside, the structure of European racing with its regrettably heavy concentration upon middle-distance events—of fifty-five Group 1 races for horses above the age of two in 1983 no fewer than thirty-one were run between a mile and a quarter and a mile and a half—ensures that the 'ideal' horse for an owner or breeder is one having the acceleration associated with a miler allied to the ability to stay at least ten furlongs in the best company. Ideals are seldom attainable, of course, but Time Charter comes near it for although at a mile a top specialist would always beat her, at middle distances her sparkling turn of foot has made her an outstanding competitor during the last two years and will, with luck, continue to make her very hard to beat in 1984.

Since 1918 seventeen Oaks winners have run at four and only Brulette, Quashed, Petite Etoile, Lupe and now Time Charter can be said fully to have maintained their reputation. This indicates how speculative a venture keeping a good filly in training can be in so far as there is no guarantee the animal concerned will make normal progress or be up to beating the colts at the regulation 3-lb allowance. Even with Time Charter it wasn't all plain sailing, for an internal abscess and bad weather in the spring meant she did not come to hand early, while just before the Coronation Cup she knocked a leg on a stone, causing fairly severe bruising which resulted in her being withdrawn. By the time she lined up at Ascot in July for the King George VI and Queen Elizabeth Diamond Stakes Time Charter had in fact run twice, suffering a defeat each time. In the Jockey Club Stakes at the Guineas meeting she clearly had not come in her coat and in going down by a head to Electric, handled sympathetically by Newnes who didn't use the whip at all after bringing her with a strong run to lead halfway through the final furlong, she ran a most encouraging race. Subjected to maximum pressure Time Charter would probably have won at Newmarket, as she might have done given a more enterprising ride in the Coral-Eclipse at Sandown in July. Being waited with suits Time Charter well over middle distances—when second to On The House in the One Thousand Guineas she had been up with the pace throughout—but on occasions circumstances dictate that a rigid adherence to one set of riding tactics can be unhelpful. This particularly applies in races which, like the 1983 Eclipse, are run at a muddling gallop. Both Time Charter and Stanerra were given plenty to do; with not much more than two furlongs to run Time Charter still lay last of the nine

848

runners and although making headway from that point she never looked like reaching the leaders, coming home over two lengths sixth to Solford.

Newnes did not ride Time Charter at Ascot three weeks later having been the victim of a singularly nasty accident on the gallops nine days before the race when the three-year-old Silver Venture died under him, giving him a fall which necessitated his receiving the kiss of life. Mercer, who had won the King George on Brigadier Gerard eleven years previously, came in for the ride. Designed principally to provide a first-rate mid-summer test for horses from different generations, the King George has entirely achieved the purpose and in 1983 it attracted a rattling good field with the three-year-old classic winners and joint favourites Caerleon and Sun Princess, the Derby second Carlingford Castle, the top older horses of their sex in Britain and France, Diamond Shoal and Lancastrian, the 1982 Arc third Awaasif, the top-class American horse Lemhi Gold, Rocamadour and Time Charter herself. Another intended runner, Khairpour, was withdrawn at the start apparently because of a wasp sting which made him kick out and cut his legs. Looking much better than at Newmarket—she had put on weight and seemed altogether brighter in her coat—Time Charter stayed towards the rear until the final turn as Lemhi Gold made the running from Diamond Shoal, Awaasif and Sun Princess, and when Diamond Shoal slipped through to take a two-length advantage with over a quarter of a mile to go she still had at least five lengths to make up on him. Diamond Shoal was never an easy colt to peg back once in front; Awaasif tried and failed and Sun Princess, though she managed to reach his quarters halfway up the straight, could make no further progress. At the furlong pole it was obvious that only Time Charter had any chance of catching the leader, for she had begun a strong run on the outside, sweeping past Carlingford Castle and Awaasif to take her upsides Sun Princess, a length behind Diamond Shoal. Maintaining her run, Time Charter soon gained the upper hand, hitting the front a hundred and fifty yards out and keeping on powerfully to account for Diamond Shoal by three quarters of a length with Sun Princess a length away third, Awaasif two lengths further back in fourth and Lancastrian another five lengths behind in fifth. Caerleon, who had the misfortune to lose both front shoes during the contest, finished a poor last but we do not think he would have beaten the winner even at his best. Time Charter thus went one better than the 1959 Oaks winner, Petite Etoile, who ran second to Aggressor in the King George at four, and became the fifth of her sex to win the race following Aunt Edith, Park Top, Dahlia and Pawneese.

Immediately after Time Charter's victory Candy mentioned the Benson and Hedges Gold Cup as one of two possible targets for his filly before a shot at the Trusthouse Forte Prix de l'Arc de Triomphe. In the event she bypassed the York race and went instead for the Prix Foy run over the Arc course and distance. The decision to run her at Longchamp seemed sensible because it gave the now-recovered Newnes a chance to get acquainted with the track, and Time Charter's performance, along with Newnes's handling of her, left nothing to be desired. Odds on to account for such as Lancastrian, All Along, Welsh Term, Khairpour and Great

Prix Foy, Longchamp—Time Charter beats subsequent Arc winner All Along and Great Substence

Substence, she was surrounded by a wall of horses entering the straight but skilfully taken to the outside produced a smooth run to cut down the leaders, heading Great Substence inside the final furlong and holding off the tenderly handled All Along, who received 7 lb, fairly readily by three quarters of a length. For our money no horse put up a better Arc trial and on the day Time Charter started favourite ahead of the coupled Lancastrian and Sun Princess, and Diamond Shoal. Oddly, non-French-trained favourites are becoming almost commonplace in the Arc: since Youth and Exceller headed the market in 1976 only Le Marmot (coupled with Ela-Mana-Mou) and Akarad have interrupted an Irish and British monopoly exercised by Alleged (twice), Troy, Assert and Time Charter. It is asking a great deal of any horse to win both the King George and the Arc given that they are the two most strongly-contested middle-distance events run all year in Europe, are separated by two and a half months and are often run on very different ground—not every horse resembles Time Charter in being indifferent to the state of the going. Of the fourteen King George winners to have run in the Arc prior to Time Charter only Ribot, Ballymoss and Mill Reef had won both races though Right Royal V, Park Top, Nijinsky, Troy and Ela-Mana-Mou had all been placed. Time Charter came within a whisker of gaining a place too. Soon close up as the pacemaker Sailor's Dance set a strong gallop, she was perfectly positioned in third behind Sun Princess and Diamond Shoal turning for home and kept on gamely without mustering the pace needed to reach the front, ending up fourth behind All Along, Sun Princess and Luth Enchantee (who caught her on the line), beaten a length, a short neck and a nose. Unlike some commentators who seem to hold the foolish belief that a horse cannot run well in defeat and who consequently looked for excuses on behalf of Time Charter, we see no reason for thinking she ran anything other than a fine race. The three that beat her are all superb performers, and those behind included many of the top middle-distance horses in Europe.

At Longchamp Time Charter appeared to be going in her coat, and though invited to participate in the Washington International she did not run again. Happily her owner has decided to continue racing her and it is to be hoped this plan meets

Mr R. Barnett's "Time Charter"

with success. Very few Oaks winners this century have been campaigned at five; two that were, Quashed and Petite Etoile, failed to show their best form though Petite Etoile admittedly won four races including the Coronation Cup. Whether or not Time Charter will be as tough a nut to crack in her fourth season on the racecourse as in 1982 and 1983 only time will tell. Either way, her scintillating seven-length win in the Dubai Champion Stakes at three and her victory in the King George have already ensured she will long be remembered.

		Dancer's Image	Native Dancer
	Saritamer	(gr 1965)	Noors Image
	(gr 1971)	Irish Chorus	Ossian II
Time Charter		(b 1960)	Dawn Chorus
(b.f. 1979)		High Line	High Hat
	Centrocon	(ch 1966)	Time Call
	(ch 1973)	Centro	Vienna
		(b 1966)	Ocean Sailing

Without Time Charter the stud career of Saritamer, who showed top form over sprint distances, winning the Cork and Orrery, July Cup and Diadem, would have to be regarded as abysmal and at the end of 1981 he was sent to Saudi Arabia. Time Charter is the first foal of Centrocon, a game and very useful performer who won four races at up to two miles including the Lancashire Oaks. Her two subsequent foals have been the unraced two-year-old colt Larchmont (by Home Guard) who cost 92,000 guineas as a yearling and another colt, reportedly a very nice one, by the promising stallion Tap On Wood. The grandam, successful over seven furlongs at two, has been a regular partner of Centrocon's sire High Line at stud, producing another three winners by him, notably the very smart and genuine middle-distance stayer Nicholas Bill and the Jockey Club Cup winner Centroline. The next dam, a useful mile-and-a-half handicapper, foaled three other winners, among them Sea Music who picked up eight races as a two-year-old. Courage, enthusiasm and ability seem to be the watchwords of this splendid family and they are qualities Time Charter, a strong, well-made filly and an excellent walker, has in abundance. *H. Candy.*

TIME FOR A LAUGH 3 b.c. Cawston's Clown 113–Picnic Time (Silly Season   **64**
127) (1982 5g³ 6fg 5g 5g 5d 1983 7d 6v 7fg³ 7fg 6f² 8fg* 7f⁴ 8g⁴ 8fg* 9fg² 8f 10h*
9d³) neat, strong colt; plater; attracted no bid after winning at Ayr in July, Redcar
in August and Nottingham in September; stays 1¼m; acts on any going, with
possible exception of very soft; exported to Algeria. *R. Hollinshead.*

TIME MACHINE 2 b.c. Connaught 130–River Music (Riverman 131) (1983 5v²   **102**
5v² 5s* 5s² 6f⁴ 5f* 5g² 5fg*) Mar 18; 11,500Y; neat colt; first live foal; dam won
over 5f from 3 starts at 2 yrs in Ireland; won maiden race at Brighton in May, minor
event at Windsor in July and nursery at Lingfield in August; creditable second in 4
of his other races, once under top weight in nursery at Warwick; best at 5f; acts on
any going; suited by sharp tracks; tough, genuine and consistent. *J. Winter.*

TIMES 2 ch.f. Junius 124–Sardinia (Romulus 129) (1983 7f 6f 6f 5f⁴ 7g 7.2s 8fg)   **55**
May 9; 14,000Y; small, lightly-made filly; half-sister to 3 minor winners; dam won
over 5f and 1m in Ireland; disappointing plater; blinkered fourth outing. *W.
O'Gorman.*

TIME'S TIME 3 ch.g. Whistling Deer 117–Needy (High Top 131) (1982 5fg⁴ 5s²   **111**
5f* 5f* 5f* 5fg* 5fg* 5f* 5g 1983 6f³ 5f 5fg 5fg) compact, fair sort; improved
dramatically as a 2-y-o and won 6 successive races; 25/1 but looking fit, ran very
well when very close third of 17 behind Sylvan Barbarosa in Cork and Orrery
Stakes at Royal Ascot in June, showing good speed throughout and being mastered
only near finish; didn't show much afterwards, but continued to face stiff tasks;
speedy, but stays 6f; not disgraced on soft going but is very well suited by a sound
surface. *W. Wharton.*

TIME TO REFLECT 4 gr.c. Roan Rocket 128–Game Girl 85 (Abernant 142)   **50**
(1982 6f⁴ 6f 6fg 8g 8g 7f 8.2s 6s⁴ 1983 7d* 8d 6d 6g) rather leggy gelding; not the
best of movers; plater; sold out of M. Camacho's stable 3,200 gns after comfortably
winning at Catterick in March; stays 1m; suited by some give in the ground; has
worn a bandage on near-fore. *E. Incisa.*

TIMINALA 2 b.f. Mansingh 120–Karens Pet 63 (Mummy's Pet 125) (1983 5g⁴   **58**
5s³ 5f³) Feb 15; lengthy filly; first foal; dam 2-y-o 5f winner; plating-class maiden;
not raced after July; acts on any going. *K. Stone.*

TIMMY BOY 3 ch.c. Timolin 81–Cabarita 88 (First Landing) (1982 7fg 5fg 5g 5d   –
7fg 8d 1983 9fg 8fg) workmanlike colt; of little account. *R. Cambidge.*

TIMSAH 3 b.c. Solinus 130–Haco 104 (Tribal Chief 125) (1982 5g 5d 6f 6fg 6g⁴   **64** d
1983 6v² 7v³ 7.3v 6d³ 6fg 7f 6g 7f 7g 7fg⁴ 6g) tall, quite attractive colt; placed in 3
handicaps at Kempton in spring; stays 7f well; seems to act on any going; blinkered
nowadays. *J. Benstead.*

TIMURS DOUBLE 2 b.c. Double Form 130–Timur's Daughter 103 (Tamerlane   **72**
128) (1983 6fg 6f⁴ 6g) Apr 7; big, lengthy colt; good walker; closely related to
useful 6f to 1¼m winner Heir Presumptive (by Habitat) and half-brother to 3
winners; dam stayed at least 9f; quite a moderate maiden; not raced after July;
will probably be suited by 7f; acts on firm going. *F. J. Houghton.*

TINA'S EXPRESS 2 b.f. Bay Express 132–Aventina 83 (Averof 123) (1983 5f*   **96**
5f² 5fg³ 6g 5fg 6d² 5g²) Apr 4; 12,000Y; lightly-built filly; first foal; dam,
half-sister to Italian Derby winner Ruysdael II, won over 7f at 2 yrs; won 16-runner
maiden race at Wolverhampton in June by 3 lengths; ran well in varied company
afterwards; on fifth outing seventh of 14, 6 lengths behind Petorius, in Cornwallis
Stakes at Ascot; stays 6f; sold 54,000 gns Newmarket December Sales. *J. Winter.*

TIN BOY 4 br.c. Welsh Pageant 132–Tin Mary 96 (Tin King 126) (1982 7g 8f 8g   **73**
7fg 7f 6s 7g 1983 6.5d 8s 6.5d 5d² 5g 5d 7s² 7s³ 7d² 7s 8fg 8f⁴ 7f 8f 8h* 8fg) quite
a useful sort; dropped in class when landing odds in seller at Bath in August; bought
in 6,400 gns afterwards; suited by 7f and 1m; acts on any going; sometimes
blinkered; tends to sweat up and is usually taken quietly to start; inconsistent;
trained by C. Milbank first 5 outings; sold 11,000 gns Newmarket Autumn Sales. *I.
Balding.*

TINKERSFIELD 2 ch.g. Tap On Wood 130–Night Vision 100 (Yellow God 129)   **72**
(1983 6fg 6fg³ 7d 7f 7fg) Apr 18; 7,500Y (privately); sturdy gelding; half-brother to
7f and 1m winner Lautrec (by Wolver Hollow); dam, half-sister to high-class Take a
Reef, won over 6f at 2 yrs; quite a modest maiden; best effort on second outing; off
course for 3 months afterwards; should stay 7f; gelded after final appearance. *Sir
Mark Prescott.*

TINKER'S TRIP 8 ch.g. Royal Trip–Bohemian Girl (Pardao 120) (1982 NR   –
1983 11.7h) winning hurdler; tailed off in maiden race at Bath in July. *O. O'Neill.*

TINOCO 3 b.c. Bustino 136–Consistent 90 (Connaught 130) (1982 7f 7.2g⁴ 7g 8f³   **74** §
8f⁴ 1983 10s* 10v 12s 13fg⁴ 12f² 12f⁴ 12g 13h² 12g 13fg³ 16fg 18fg) small, strong
colt; beat Thoughtless by 1½ lengths in 17-runner maiden event at Leicester in
March and was placed on several other occasions; stays 13f; acts on any going;
possibly not the heartiest of battlers. *R. Hollinshead.*

TINTED BLONDE (USA) 3 ch.f. Charles Elliott–Color Me Blonde   –
(Craigwood) (1982 5fg 1983 7d 7f) lengthy, strong-quartered filly; towards rear in
maiden race and minor events. *D. Ringer.*

TINTERELLO 4 ch.g. Continuation 120–Polly Bellino 56 (Dadda Bert 95) (1982   –
8f 8fg² 8fg* 10fg 1983 10fg) compact gelding; plater; suited by 1m on fast ground.
J. Hardy.

TIPO STYLE 2 b.g. Cawston's Clown 113–Hasten Slowly (Mark-Ye-Well) (1983   –
6fg) Apr 11; 5,200Y; half-brother to useful 5f to 1m winner Darwood (by Sallust)
and 2 other winners; dam won at 6f to 1m in Ireland; in rear in 12-runner maiden
race at Folkestone in October; subsequently gelded. *G. Huffer.*

TIP THE BALANCE 3 b.c. Realm 129–Dialogue (Diatome 132) (1982 NR   –
1983 7d³ 8d 6v 10f) quite an attractive colt; first foal; dam unraced half-sister to
very smart animals I Titan and Favorita; third in newcomers race at Doncaster in
March, only form. *P. Cole.*

TIPTONIAN 4 gr.g. Royalty 130–Pretty Fast 74 (Firestreak 125) (1982 7fg 10s   –
1983 12.2f 12f) behind in varied company; has worn bandages. *T. Taylor.*

TIRAWA (USA) 4 b.c. Majestic Prince–Imalulu (Black Beard) (1982 8f 10f³ 10f   **70**
11.7fg* 11fg* 12g³ 1983 12s 12d 12f 12fg 12fg³) good-looking, lengthy colt; carries
plenty of condition; poor mover; cracked a cannon bone after winning twice at 3 yrs
and showed little worthwhile form in 1983; will stay 1¾m; bandaged first 2 starts;
sold, probably for export to Italy, 840 gns Newmarket September Sales. *M.
Jarvis.*

TIRWADDA 2 ch.c. Troy 137–Lys River 119 (Lyphard 132) (1983 8fg²) Feb 23;   **82** p
good walker; second foal; half-brother to fairly useful 7f winner Blushing
River (by Blushing Groom); dam smart French middle-distance filly; second
favourite, 3 lengths second of 12 to odds-on Raami in maiden race at Redcar in
October; should win over middle distances. *H. T. Jones.*

TISLAMEE 2 gr.f. Absalom 128–Lapis Lazuli 84 (Zeddaan 130) (1983 5d² 5s 5g³   **79**
5f² 5h* 5f² 5f*) Apr 18; 11,000F, 17,500Y; compact filly; half-sister to smart 1m
and 1¼m winner Farioffa (by Hotfoot) and a winner in Malaya; dam won over 5f at 2
yrs and is half-sister to smart sprinter Bas Bleu; successful twice in July, beating
odds-on Tudor Enterprise in small race at Chepstow and dead-heating with Trim
Taxi in nursery at Thirsk; suited by a sharp 5f; acts well on fast ground; genuine.
G. Hunter.

TITIANELLO 2 ch.f. Porto Bello 118–Titian Princess (Ballymoss 136) (1983 6g   **60**
6f 5.8h 8g⁴ 8d³) first foal; dam poor on flat and over hurdles; modest plater; stays
1m. *J. Holt.*

TIVIAN 3 b.c. Busted 134–Jovian 88 (Hardicanute 130) (1982 8g 7s³ 7v² 1983   **91** d
10g 12s³ 12s 14f 12f 10d² 10fg² 10g⁴) lengthy colt; showed useful form in smart
company in spring, but on last 3 starts was beaten in maiden races (second twice at
Beverley); out of his depth twice, including in Derby; stays 1½m; acts on a firm
surface, but best form with some give in the ground. *C. Brittain.*

TIVOLI GARDENS 4 b.f. Flashback 102–Jean's Joy 74 (Specific 102) (1982   **42**
12g 12fg 12v 1983 17.1g 16g 10.1f* 12d) good-topped, lengthy filly; dropped in
class and apprentice ridden when narrowly winning seller at Windsor in July;
bought in 860 gns afterwards; stays 1¼m; acts on firm going. *J. Fox.*

TIZZY 2 b.f. Formidable 125–Penny Blessing 112 (So Blessed 130) (1983 5fg 5f   **76**
5fg³ 6fg 6g 8fg³ 8d) Apr 1; smallish filly; first foal; dam, from family of Mummy's
Pet, Arch Sculptor and Parsimony, at her best at 2 yrs when successful over 5f;
quite a modest maiden; suited by 1m; acts on a firm surface; blinkered last 3
outings. *F. J. Houghton.*

TO ASTERI (USA) 2 ch.c. Big Burn–Bridal Shower (Hail to Reason) (1983 7f   –
8g 8g) May 10; $8,700F; workmanlike colt; half-brother to numerous minor
winners; dam, placed once from 26 starts, is half-sister to 2 stakes winners; behind
in 2 races at Newbury and one at Goodwood. *P. Mitchell.*

TOAST OF THE TOWN 4 b.f. Prince Tenderfoot 126–Truly Thankful 111   **90**
(Majority Blue 126) (1982 6s³ 7g 7s³ 6fg 7g² 1983 6s 6d² 6g⁴ 6s 6s⁴ 6f 6fg)
lengthy, good-bodied filly; has a sharp action; third reported foal; dam won at up to
6.5f, including Queen Mary Stakes; ran creditably to be 4 lengths second to Sweet
Monday in Abernant Stakes at Newmarket in April and 1¾ lengths fourth to On
Stage in Thirsk Hall Stakes later in week; about 4½ lengths fourth of 7 to Solimile in
£6,700 event at Lingfield in June; blinkered when behind in Cork and Orrery Stakes
at Royal Ascot sixth start; stays 7f; suited by some give in the ground. *F. Dunne,
Ireland.*

TOBACCO 3 b.g. Import 127–Prime Venture (Derring-Do 131) (1982 NR 1983   –
6g 8.2g 5f 5f 5g 5g) first foal; dam showed little worthwhile form; no worthwhile
form, including in a seller; sold 410 gns Doncaster October Sales. *T. Craig.*

TOBERMORY BOY 6 b.g. Mummy's Pet 125–Penny Pincher 95 (Constable   **85**
119) (1982 5f³ 5g 5f* 6fg² 5fg 5fg 5.6g 1983 5f 5f 5.6f³) neat gelding; fair
handicapper at his best; stays 6f; acts on any going. *J. Hardy.*

TOBINA'S GUEST 3 ch.g. Be My Guest 126–Happy Tobina (Tobin Bronze)
(1982 7f 7g² 8s 1983 12d) attractive gelding; good second at York as a 2-y-o, best
effort; tailed off in modest company at Lingfield in September, only outing of 1983;
should stay at least 1m. *B. Hills.*

TOBY LEGER 3 br.g. Record Token 128–True Dresden 58 (Vilmoray 126) (1982   –
6fg 6f 1983 10.1f) stocky gelding; in rear in maiden and minor races. *M.
Madgwick.*

TOBY'S LUCK 2 b. or br.g. Lucky Wednesday 124–Welcome Sara 66 (Lucky   –
Brief 128) (1983 6fg 7fg) Apr 12; rather leggy gelding; second foal; half-brother to
a winning hurdler; dam plating class; in rear in minor event at Windsor in August
and maiden race at Salisbury in September. *P. Bailey.*

TOCAVE BOTTA (USA) 2 ch.c. Northern Dancer–Thirty Years (Bold Hour)   **103**
(1983 6f² 6g² 7d²) Mar 11; $1,250,000Y; strong, good-topped, attractive colt;
good mover; third foal; half-brother to 2 winners, one stakes placed; dam, from
family of top-class Jaipur, won 8.5f stakes race; second in maiden events,
disappointing at 11/4 on at Yarmouth in September on final appearance; had run
Double Schwartz to short head in good race at York the previous month on second
outing; should be well suited by 7f+; possibly not at his best on a soft surface. *M.
Stoute.*

853

TOCKALA 2 b.g. Kala Shikari 125–Toccata (Kythnos 126) (1982 8g⁴ 8fg 9f)   **76**
May 25; leggy, close-coupled gelding; has a very round action; half-brother to
several winners, including fairly useful 1m to 1½m winner Abercata (by
Aberdeen); dam never ran; put up best effort in maiden race at Ayr in September,
running on well to finish 5½ lengths fourth of 18 to Macarthurs Head; possibly
needs some give in the ground. *E. Weymes.*

TOCODESU 2 b.c. Town and Country 124–Devil Sun (Midnight Sun II 131) (1983   **52**
5v 5s 7fg 10d) Mar 27; leggy, narrow colt; fifth foal; half-brother to a winning
hurdler; dam poor staying maiden; poor maiden; suited by 1¼m. *W. Turner.*

TOKAIDO 3 b.f. Bay Express 132–Perkasa 74 (Huntercombe 133) (1982 NR   **71**
1983 5d 5s 5f* 5fg 5fg 5.1s⁴ 5g) smallish, attractive filly; second foal; half-sister to
winning sprinter Return To Me (by Music Boy); dam won two 5f sellers; showed
good speed when beating Captivate by 1½ lengths in 22-runner maiden race at
Nottingham in July, easily best effort; possibly needs firm going. *J. Toller.*

TO KAMARI MOU 4 ch.g. Moulton 128–Scala di Seta 85 (Shantung 132) (1982   **–**
12fg 13.3f 14d² 16f² 14fg* 16g 14fg* 16g 14s 1983 17d) chunky gelding; fair at 3
yrs; bandaged when well beaten only start in 1983; suited by a test of stamina;
seems to act on any going; usually blinkered in 1982; inconsistent and probably
none too genuine. *R. Fisher.*

TOLLERS GOLD 5 ch.g. Roan Rocket 128–Hurly Burly (Sing Sing 134) (1982   **–**
NR 1983 10f 10f 5f) no worthwhile form. *D. Jermy.*

TOLL TELLER 2 ch.f. Sharpman 124–Distant Bells (Mount Hagen 127) (1983   **105**
8d 7fg* 8s 7g² 6.5g 7.5s³ 7g) first foal; dam won over 7.5f at 2 yrs in France; won
maiden event at Clairefontaine in August by ½ length; subsequently ran creditably
when ½-length second to Boreale in 90,000-franc event at Longchamp in
September and when 2 lengths third to Polly's Ark in Group 3 Prix Thomas Bryon
at Saint-Cloud in October; well beaten in pattern company on third, fifth and
seventh starts; should stay 1¼m. *R. Collet, France.*

TOLLYMORE 4 b. or br.g. Pitcairn 126–Maggie's Pet 74 (Coronation Year 124)   **–**
(1982 6s 7g 6f³ 7g* 9g* 7g² 7g⁴ 1983 10.2d 5v 9s 7s 6g) IR 21,000Y;
good-bodied ex-Irish gelding; half-brother to 2 winners, including useful 5f to 7f
winner Maxi's Taxi (by Klondyke Bill); dam won 5f seller at 2 yrs; won at Sligo
and Mallow at 3 yrs; no form in Britain in 1983; suited by 7f+. *P. Calver.*

TOLOMEO 3 b.c. Lypheor 118–Almagest 72 (Dike) (1982 7d² 7g² 7g* 1983 8s⁴   **127**
8g² 12s 8fg² 10f³ 8f² 10g* 10g⁴)
    In sharp contrast to the fervour shown by some of their French counterparts,
the leading British-based trainers seem to frown on campaigning their top horses in
North America in the autumn. But they have taken more interest than the French in the
recently-instituted Budweiser Million, run over a mile and a quarter on turf at
Arlington Park, Chicago at the end of August. As the name suggests the Budweiser
Million has a million-dollar purse—making it the world's most valuable race—and
horses representing England have picked up some of the prize money in each of its
first three runnings. Madam Gay finished third in 1981; Be My Native and Motavato
second and third in 1982; and Tolomeo carried off the first prize of 600,000 dollars
(£400,000 at prevailing exchange rates) in 1983. Tolomeo was one of four
British-trained runners in 1983—Be My Native, Muscatite and The Noble Player
were the others—while the French were represented by the ex-Italian four-year-
old Bold Run. Tolomeo's victory was, amazingly, the first by a British-based horse
in a major North American event on the flat since Karabas' in the 1969 Washington
International.
    Most of North America's major races are run on dirt and, notwithstanding its
value, the Budweiser Million has so far failed to attract the best American dirt
specialists, their trainers being understandably reluctant to run them on an
unfamiliar surface. Some of the best grass horses in North America in recent years
have been imported after successful careers in Europe and the home-trained
contingent for the Budweiser Million has included each year a sprinkling of such
types. The Bart, formerly trained in Ireland, came second to John Henry in the
inaugural running; the ex-French Perrault was the winner in 1982; and the 1983
field included The Wonder, Erins Isle and Trevita, each of whom had won major turf
races since being transferred permanently to the United States. The veteran
gelding John Henry, America's champion grass horse in 1980 and 1981 and still
among the best in 1983, started favourite for the Budweiser Million; none of the
five European challengers in the fourteen-strong field started at odds shorter than
17/1 and only the six-year-old mare Trevita started at longer odds than 38/1-shot
Tolomeo. In a slowly-run race the front-running Nijinsky's Secret, John Henry and

Budweiser Million, Arlington Park, Chicago—Tolomeo gains a well-deserved success, beating prolific winner John Henry with Nijinsky's Secret close up

Tolomeo filled the first three places throughout. Tolomeo had the immense good fortune to be presented with a clear run along the rails in the final straight when Nijinsky's Secret drifted off a true line and he accelerated superbly to take the lead inside the final furlong. John Henry was closing in the last few strides but Tolomeo held him off by a neck with Nijinsky's Secret half a length away third; there was a further two-length gap to fourth-placed Thunder Puddles; Bold Run came seventh, Muscatite eighth, Be My Native eleventh and The Noble Player last.

Tolomeo's victory in the Budweiser Million took him, at a stroke, into second place in the list of leading British-based money winners, his career earnings in first-prize money soaring to £404,432 (his only other victory so far was gained in a maiden race at Newmarket as a two-year-old); only Troy (£415,735) has won more. Inflation demeans prize-money statistics but, for readers interested in such figures, the list of leading European-based money winners (disregarding place money) is now headed by All Along (£813,207), Dahlia (£497,741), Allez France (£493,100) and April Run (£469,168), all fillies who remained in training after their three-year-old days; All Along's total would be boosted by £675,676 if the bonus she earned for landing North America's International Classic Series was included (Dahlia's total does not include money earned after her permanent transfer to the United States). Tolomeo's victory and that of Old Country in the Prix Royal-Oak earned for their trainer the trophy put up by the International Racing Bureau for the most successful trainer on foreign soil; in a season when British-based horses earned more than £2,000,000 abroad in total prize-money, Cumani led the field from Balding, Dunlop, Stoute and Hern. Tolomeo remains in training with good prospects of at least overtaking Troy's prize-money total; he is a high-class performer at a mile and a mile and a quarter—we think he's slightly better at the longer trip—and he is a genuine type. Another crack at the Budweiser Million is said to be at the top of his programme for 1984 and he could also go well in races such as the Coral-Eclipse and the Dubai Champion Stakes.

No horse with a victory in the world's richest race among his seasonal achievements can be said to have had an unlucky campaign. But it's true to say that things didn't always go right for Tolomeo as a three-year-old. His connections endured several near-misses in major races before Tolomeo won at Arlington Park: he came second in the Two Thousand Guineas, second in the St James's Palace Stakes (beaten a head), third (beaten a head and the same) in the Coral-Eclipse, and second in the Sussex Stakes. Tolomeo appeared to receive a poor ride at

855

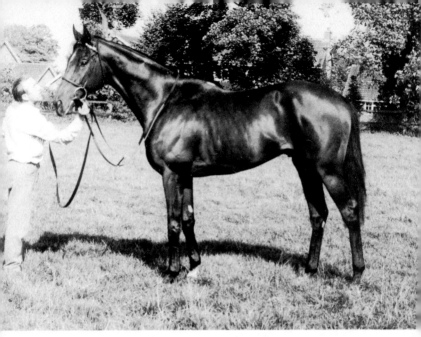

Mr C. d'Alessio's "Tolomeo"

Newmarket, languishing in last place for a long way and being set with an unnecessarily stiff task in the second part of the race. Tolomeo finished strongly and went down by two lengths to Lomond; whether he would have won ridden with more enterprise no-one can say for certain, but he'd surely have given Lomond a much harder fight. Tolomeo's trainer, incidentally, refutes any suggestion that Tolomeo was wrongly ridden in the Guineas—Tolomeo was eased back after the start on his instructions because he felt it was essential that the horse be covered up. That said, when the first four in the Two Thousand Guineas met again in the Sussex Stakes three months later Tolomeo wasn't allowed to get so far behind and he came out best of the three-year-olds, going down by two and a half lengths to Noalcoholic, with Lomond back in seventh place. Tolomeo stayed on strongly at Goodwood but never threatened to reach the front-running Noalcoholic. Tolomeo also appeared to have every chance when narrowly beaten by Solford and Muscatite in the Coral-Eclipse but he looked a shade unfortunate in the St James's Palace at Royal Ascot. Coming from well back, Tolomeo finished fast and would have caught the enterprisingly-ridden Horage in a few more strides. Tolomeo showed that he had suffered no lasting ill-effects from his 14,000-mile round trip to Chicago when running a fine race in the Dubai Champion Stakes at Newmarket in October on his final outing; he was always in the first six, took the lead at the Bushes and went down by a head to Cormorant Wood in a blanket finish, though he was adjudged to have caused some interference in the closing stages and was relegated to fourth by the stewards.

Tolomeo is a big, attractive colt who usually impresses in appearance; he is a very good mover. He was well bought as a yearling—he cost only IR 17,000 guineas —as, in retrospect, was another of his sire's offspring the subsequently-disqualified One Thousand Guineas runner-up Royal Heroine, who fetched only 5,600 guineas. Lypheor, a grandson of Northern Dancer, gained his most important win in the one-mile Prix Quincey at Deauville and has been much travelled as a stallion. He stood only one season in Ireland before being sent to Japan and is now standing at

Gainesway Farm, Kentucky. Tolomeo is the first foal of the mile-and-a-half winner Almagest who gained her only victory in a Leicester maiden event. Almagest's dam Celestial Sun was fairly useful on the racecourse, a thoroughly game and consistent animal who was well suited by a distance of ground. Tolomeo has been tried only once at a distance beyond a mile and a quarter, in the Derby when, after a rough

Tolomeo (b.c. 1980)	Lypheor (b 1975)	Lyphard (b 1969)	Northern Dancer
			Goofed
		Klaizia (b 1965)	Sing Sing
			Klainia
	Almagest (ch 1975)	Dike (ch 1966)	Herbager
			Delta
		Celestial Sun (ch 1965)	Sunny Way
			Heavenly Story

passage in the early stages, he came ninth of twenty finishers, earning notoriety as the main culprit in the scrimmaging that took place towards the back of the field halfway down Tattenham Hill (Tolomeo's rider Dettori received a six-day suspension for careless riding). Except in the Derby and in his Guineas preparatory race the Craven Stakes, Tolomeo raced only on a sound surface as a three-year-old, conditions which suit him well. *L. Cumani.*

TOM DOWDESWELL 7 br.g. Balidar 133–Georgian Princess 75 (Tamerlane 128) (1982 5d³ 5f 6f³ 5f 5fg 5g 5fg 5fg 5fg 5d 1983 5d 5g 5fg 5h) strong, good sort; sprint handicapper; ideally suited by top-of-the-ground; often used to wear blinkers. *A. W. Jones.* —

TOM FORRESTER 2 gr.c. Absalom 128–Blak-En-Bloo 72 (Blakeney 126) (1983 5v* 5v² 5v² 5fg 5f 6fg 6fg² 6f 5g 7fg) May 19; 2,000F, 2,500Y; useful-looking colt; fourth foal; dam stayed 1½m; won minor event at Folkestone in March; off course for almost 3 months after that outing, and showed form only spasmodically on return; should stay 7f; acts on any going except very firm. *A. Pitt.* 69

TOMMY TIMBOU 2 b.c. Jolly Good 122–Bright Brook (Deep Diver 134) (1983 7d 6fg) June 10; neat colt; first foal; dam unplaced 3 times in Ireland; bandaged in front, showed a little ability in seller at Newmarket in October on second appearance, starting joint-second favourite and finishing 7 lengths seventh of 22 behind Parveno. *B. Hobbs.* 55

TOMMY TROUBLE 3 ch.c. Native Bazaar 122–Copthorne Polly (Double-U-Jay 120) (1982 NR 1983 5f) third foal; half-brother to a winner in Belgium in Manacle; dam showed no worthwhile form; tailed off in minor event at Chepstow in June. *Dr A. Jones.* —

TOMMY TUDOR 3 b.g. Tudor Rhythm 112–Wheatley (Town Crier 119) (1982 6f 6d 7fg 7fg 8d 8.2d 8s 1983 8s 12v³ 12.2g 12f 12f) smallish, well-made gelding; plater; stays 1½m; has worn blinkers; sold 2,700 gns Ascot September Sales to K. Bailey. *J. Douglas-Home.* —

TOM OKKER (USA) 3 b.c. Tom Rolfe–Grass Court (Herbager 136) (1982 6f 7fg 1983 12v* 10s* 12v² 12d* 12f³ 12g) good-looking colt; has a round action; impressive winner of maiden race at Doncaster, minor event at Brighton and £4,400 handicap at Epsom; held up on first 2 courses but at Epsom in June made all in a rather slowly-run race and won by 5 lengths from Wagoner; also placed behind Dazari in minor event at Wolverhampton and King George V Stakes (close third of 20) at Royal Ascot; disappointed after a 2-month lay-off on final outing; promises to stay beyond 1½m; acts on any going but is possibly ideally suited by some give underfoot; genuine; sent to Italy. *L. Cumani.* 98

TOM SEYMOUR 3 b.c. Grundy 137–One Over Parr 114 (Reform 132) (1982 8g 1983 12d⁴ 12g⁴ 14d* 16f⁴ 15g 16g 14.6fg 14g² 14g 14s² 11.2v*) good-bodied ex-English colt; good walker; won maiden race at Newmarket in May (by 2½ lengths from Khyber) and Premio Unire at Naples in December (by ½ length from Command Respect); in frame in between in Queen's Vase at Royal Ascot (about 5 lengths fourth of 17 to Santella Man) and St Leger Italiano at Milan (led 1f out but was beaten a neck by Celio Rufo in a slowly-run race); suited by a test of stamina; acts on any going; trained most of season by M. Jarvis. *U. Pandolfi, Italy.* 108

TOM SHARP 3 b.g. Martinmas 128–Prellgo (El Gallo 122) (1982 8s 8.2s 1983 13fg 17g³ 16.5fg³ 17f³ 16f³ 16f 16d* 18fg³) close-coupled gelding; apprentice ridden when winning handicap at Warwick in October; suited by a test of stamina; probably acts on any going. *W. Wharton.* 78

TOM'S NAP HAND 2 b. or br.f. Some Hand 119–Fleet Street Fifty 51 (I Say 125) (1983 5v 5.8s 5g 5.8h 5g 5d) Apr 17; workmanlike filly; bad maiden. *W. R. Williams.* —

TOM'S WHATSISNAME 2 ch.g. Levanter 121–Je Dit 52 (I Say 125) (1983 5v 5.8s) May 12; fourth foal; dam, of little account on flat, won over hurdles; last in maiden and minor event at Bath in May. *W. R. Williams.* —

TO-NISAKI-MAS 3 ch.c. Sharpen Up 127–Skyey 70 (Skymaster 126) (1982 7f 7f 7g 1983 6f⁴ 6f 8f) deep-girthed, good sort; plating-class maiden; stays 7f; sold 1,800 gns Newmarket Autumn Sales. *C. Brittain.*

TONS OF MONEY 3 br.g. Hot Spark 126–Krugerrand 74 (Goldhill 125) (1982 NR 1983 12.2f) strong gelding; second foal; half-brother to 1980 2-y-o 5f winner Krugerama (by Amber Rama); dam won over 9f; 50/1 and backward when last of 6 behind Detente in minor event at Catterick in July. *R. D. Peacock.* —

TOO DO 3 br.f. Manado 130–Topa (Dark Tiger) (1982 5f⁴ 5fg 6f 6fg 7g 7fg 1983 6v) rather lightly-made filly; should stay 7f; blinkered once at 2 yrs (unseated rider). *K. Ivory.*

TOO FAMILIAR 3 ch.f. Oats 126–Born Friendly (Takawalk II 125) (1982 5fg 6d 5f 7f* 1983 10d 7d) lengthy filly; plater; should stay at least 1¼m; acts on firm going; sold 900 gns Newmarket July Sales. *D. Ringer.*

TO ONEIRO 2 gr.f. Absalom 128–Dissipation 83 (Disciplinarian) (1983 5g 6fg 6fg) Feb 9; small filly; half-sister to 3 minor winners; dam won over 5f at 2 yrs; plating-class maiden; better suited by 6f than 5f, and promises to stay further. *R. Armstrong.* 64

TO-ONERO-MOU 3 br.c. Wolver Hollow 126–Emma Canute 93 (Hardicanute 130) (1982 8d 8s⁴ 1983 11.5fg² 14f⁴ 11.7h³ 12f 12fg) well-made, quite attractive colt; excellent walker; in frame in maiden races at Sandown (2) and Bath; stays 1¾m; gives impression he'll always do best on top-of-the-ground; sold 8,200 gns Newmarket Autumn Sales. *G. Harwood.* 77

TOO OFTEN (USA) 3 br.c. J. O. Tobin 130–Frequently (Decidedly) (1982 NR 1983 10g) $600,000Y; half-brother to 3 winners by Hillary, including Royal Hunt Cup winner Jumping Hill, subsequently a very smart winner at up to 1¼m in USA; dam won at 1m; 25/1, when in rear in 20-runner maiden race at Sandown in October. *J. Dunlop.*

TOP CREATOR 4 b.c. High Line 125–Corneater (Skymaster 126) (1982 9fg 10fg⁴ 11f² 13.3f 10.1g³ 12g³ 12g³ 10d² 14g³ 1983 14s* 14v⁴ 20v) strong, rangy colt; spreadeagled his field in 8-runner handicap at Newmarket in April, leading 3f out and drawing steadily clear to beat Red Field easing up by 12 lengths; respectable staying-on 7½ lengths fourth of 10 to Line Slinger in Yorkshire Cup at York in May; suited by 1¾m and wasn't disgraced over further when fifth of 6 to Karkour in Prix du Cadran at Longchamp; acts on any going but goes well on soft; not seen out after May. *B. Hills.* 106

TOPHAMS TAVERNS 2 ch.c. Remainder Man 126§–High Density 66 (Pall Mall 132) (1983 5f 6f 6f³ 6fg 7h 6fg 8h² 8f* 8.2g* 8d*) Apr 22; 2,100Y; strong, workmanlike colt; half-brother to fair 1981 2-y-o sprint winner Knight Security (by Swing Easy) and winners in Italy and Hungary; dam won 1m seller; front runner, much improved in the autumn, winning 24-runner maiden auction event at Redcar, and defying penalties in nurseries at Hamilton and York; suited by 1m; yet to race on very soft going but acts on any other; game. *T. Fairhurst.* 87

TOPLEIGH 3 b.g. High Top 131–Nom de Plume 70 (Aureole 132) (1982 8s 9s³ 1983 15.8g 12f⁴ 12s 12g*) strong, lengthy gelding; sold 3,900 gns after readily landing the odds in seller at Edinburgh in October; not sure to stay 2m (pulled hard when tried at trip). *Sir Mark Prescott.* 68

TOP MATCH (FR) 2 b.c. Top Ville 129–Contestation (Abdos 134) (1983 8s* 8.5d*) Mar 20; 460,000 francs Y (approx £38,000); half-brother to several winners, including fairly useful miler Grand Conde (by Sun Prince); dam won over 1¼m in France and is half-sister to Prix Saint-Alary winner Scala; beat Palace Panther a length in maiden event at Longchamp in September and led 1f out to account for Districking easily by 2 lengths in 80,000-franc event at Maisons-Laffitte the following month; will be suited by middle distances; a smart three-year-old in the making. *F. Boutin, France.* 108 p

TOP OF THE MILLS 3 br.c. High Top 131–Bourton Downs 74 (Philip of Spain 126) (1982 NR 1983 8f) 17,000Y; narrow colt; first foal; dam 2-y-o 5f winner but didn't train on; in rear in 16-runner minor event at Redcar in October. *C. Brittain.* —

TOP OF THE MARK 5 ch.g. On Your Mark 125–None-So-Pretty (Never Say 49
Die 137) (1982 5.8f 8g 8fg 8g 5.8f 8f 8g 1983 8h² 7f⁴ 8h* 8f⁴ 10.2fg) strong
gelding; poor handicapper nowadays; made all to win at Bath in August; suited by
1m; acts on any going but goes well on firm; has been tried in blinkers. *N. Kernick.*

TOP OF THE STRETCH 2 ch.g. Whistling Deer 117–Princess Pixie 106 74
(Royal Captive 116) (1983 5s 5v 7f³ 7f) Apr 28; IR 11,000Y; strong, well-made
gelding; second foal; brother to Irish 3-y-o Whistling Pixie; dam won twice over 5f
at 2 yrs in Ireland; quite a moderate maiden; showed form only on third outing;
always well behind at Epsom in August on final appearance; suited by 7f; acts well
on firm going; gelded at end of season. *R. Hannon.*

TOPORI 4 br.g. High Top 131–Lady Oriana 91 (Tudor Melody 129) (1982 8d 8fg 59 d
8.5f* 8g 7f 8.3g 10fg 10v 1983 12d² 12v⁴ 12g 10s 10g) sparely-made gelding;
good mover; stays 1½m; seems to act on any going; well beaten last 3 starts. *S.
Woodman.*

TOP O'THE NORTH 3 b. or br.c. High Top 131–Gold Poulet 84 (Goldhill 125) –
(1982 5fg⁴ 5fg 6fg* 6g 6d* 7fg⁴ 5v³ 1983 6g 6v 6d 5f 7f 6s 6g 5d 6fg) big, strong,
lengthy, attractive colt who carries plenty of condition; developed into a very useful
performer as a 2-y-o, but was most disappointing in 1983; best at 6f; best form with
some give in the ground; tried in blinkers sixth and seventh starts. *M. W.
Easterby.*

TOP O'TH' LANE 6 b.g. Palm Track 122–Poachings Folly (Poaching 115) (1982 70
7.2f² 7fg⁴ 8fg 6f² 1983 8v 7d* 6f³ 7f 6f 7f² 7.2g 7g 7fg⁴ 7g*) lengthy gelding; won
handicaps at Redcar in May and November; stays 9f but runs mainly at shorter
distances; has won on a soft surface but acts well on firm going; ran moderately
when blinkered once; unreliable; sold out of W. Haigh's stable 5,200 gns Doncaster
October Sales before final start. *N. Bycroft.*

TOPPLE (FR) 2 b.f. High Top 131–Boswellia 109 (Frankincense 120) (1983 7f* 91
6f⁴ 7g⁴ 7d²) Jan 27; 35,000F, 44,000Y; quite attractive filly; good mover;
half-sister to 2 winners, including 1m winner Cape Chestnut (by Bustino); dam
won William Hill Gold Cup; won maiden race at Yarmouth in August; good second
to Great Western in 16-runner nursery at York in October; will be suited by 1m;
acts on firm going and a soft surface. *M. Ryan.*

TOP RANKER (USA) 2 ch.g. Lt Stevens–Greater Miracle (Great Mystery) 78
(1983 7g⁴ 7d 6fg 6fg*) Apr 3; $45,000Y; smallish, quite attractive gelding; good
walker; third foal; half-brother to a winner; dam won 6f claiming race at 2 yrs;
won 14-runner claimer at Nottingham in October; stays 7f; blinkered last 2 starts;
gelded after first outing. *J. Hindley.*

TOPSIOLA 2 ch.f. Thatching 131–Hariota 73 (Hook Money 124) (1983 5fg 5d 7g) –
Feb 14; 2,000F, 5,000Y; narrow, fair sort; half-sister to several winners, including
1m and 9f winner Steelworks (by Steel Heart); dam middle-distance winner;
soundly beaten in maiden races and a minor event August onwards. *R.
Hollinshead.*

TOP SPADE 3 b.g. Precipice Star 90–Diddy Duck 53 (Dicta Drake 126) (1982 8d –
1983 10.1f) fair sort; no show in sellers. *W. Turner.*

TOP THAT 2 br.g. Legal Eagle 126–Zellamait 54 (Runnymede 123) (1983 5f 5g 63
5d) Mar 14; 2,100Y; strong,good sort; second foal; half-brother to 1982 2-y-o 6f
seller winner Rapid Miss (by Rapid River); dam plater on flat and over hurdles;
plating-class maiden; disappointing favourite in auction event at Warwick in
October on final appearance. *T. Barron.*

TOP TOUCH 3 b.g. Touch Paper 113–Candy Flake (Dionisio 126) (1982 5f² 5fg 5f –
5fg 5g 5g 1983 8.2s 8f 9.4f 10.4fg) big gelding; plating-class maiden; sometimes
blinkered; trained until after first start by J. Berry. *D. McCain.*

TORONTO STAR 3 b.c. Ardoon 124–Bristol Milk 88 (Raise You Ten 125) (1982 46
6g 6f 7.2s 6s 8d 1983 8v 9d* 9d³ 7g 8fg) strong, stocky colt; well-backed winner
of seller at Redcar in May (no bid); had stiffer tasks afterwards; will stay 1¼m.
A. Potts.

TORREY (USA) 4 ch.c. Torsion–Deltaville (Delta Judge) (1982 7f 7d⁴ 1983 8fg) –
rather leggy, light-bodied colt; good walker and mover; only lightly raced but is a
fairly useful performer at his best; may stay 1m; blinkered first outing in 1982. *R.
Hern.*

TORRIDGE CROSSING 3 b.g. High Line 125–Night Work (Burglar 128) (1982 –
NR 1983 11.7s 8f) rangy, workmanlike gelding; first foal; dam well beaten in 2
juvenile hurdles; tailed-off last in maiden race at Bath in April and minor event at
Salisbury (veered left after 2f) in August. *J. Hill.*

TORRIE ANN (CAN) 2 b.f. Blushing Groom 131–Cailey Jane (Right 104 p
Combination) (1983 8d* 8fg³) half-sister to 3 winners, including very smart
French 1m to 13.5f winner Glenorum (by Prove Out) and very useful Canadian
stakes winner North Downs (by Hoist the Flag); dam stakes-placed sprint
winner; never threatened the leaders but finished well when over 2 lengths fourth
to Boreale in Prix des Reservoirs at Longchamp in October (promoted to third);
earlier successful in newcomers race at Deauville; promises to stay 1¼m; sure to
go on to better things. *D. Smaga, France.*

TORSKI 2 br.g. Abwah 118–Piethorne 86 (Fine Blade 121) (1983 5s 5d 5fg⁴ 5f² 7f²   53
6fg³ 7h* 7f³ 7f) June 10; small gelding; first foal; dam won over 11f; plater;
short-head winner at Beverley in July (bought in 1,200 gns); suited by 7f; acts on
hard going; blinkered when successful; ran poorly final start (subsequently gelded).
M. W. Easterby.

TOSCANA 2 ch.f. Town and Country 124–Constanza 94 (Sun Prince 128) (1983   – p
6fg) Apr 3; second foal; half-sister to 3-y-o Alimony (by Sallust); dam won over
1½m from 2 starts; second favourite, started slowly and was hampered 1f out when
seventh of 13 in maiden race at Leicester in October; will be better suited by
further; sure to improve. *R. Hern.*

TOT 3 ch.g. Dragonara Palace 115–Silver Cygnet 71 (My Swanee 122) (1982 7f 7g   –
7g 1983 10d 12f 7f 7g 7g) small, lengthy, lightly-made gelding; plating-class
maiden; by no means certain to stay middle distances; blinkered third start; trained
until after third outing by J. Carr. *D. Smith.*

TOTAL LINE 3 ch.f. High Line 125–Saving Season (Silly Season 127) (1982 NR   –
1983 9s 9d⁴ 10fg) lengthy, sparely-made filly; fourth living foal; dam poor maiden;
lightly-raced maiden; ran best race second outing (sweating). *J. Old.*

TOUCH BOY 7 b.h. Touch Paper 113–Hello Amy 70 (Forlorn River 124) (1982 5g   100
5s 5f 5fg 5g² 5g* 5fg* 6f 5fg 5fg³ 5.6g³ 5d 5d 1983 5v⁴ 5v 5g* 5f 5f 5f⁴ 5f 5f² 5f
5.6fg 5fg 5fg) compact, robust horse; useful sprint handicapper at his best
who won 11 races, notably Portland Handicap at Doncaster in 1981; gained his
only success at 7 yrs when beating Mac's Palace by 2½ lengths in £2,700 event at
Beverley in June; acted on any going, but seemed best on a sound surface
towards end of career; effective with or without blinkers; standing at Norton
Grove Stud, Malton, at £500 n.f. n.f. *J. Berry.*

TOUCHEN END 2 b.f. Diamonds Are Trump 108–Kilteelagh Lady (King's Leap   –
111) (1983 5s 5f 6f 6f) IR 8,600Y; tall, lightly-made filly; very good mover;
first foal; dam 2-y-o 6f winner in Ireland; in rear in minor and maiden events,
finishing last in blinkers third start. *R. Howe.*

TOUCHEZ LE BOIS 2 b.c. Habitat 134–Milly Moss 112 (Crepello 136) (1983 8fg)   80 p
Apr 15; 175,000Y; brother to 3-y-o Mossy Manor and half-brother to 3 winners,
including smart 6f to 1m winner Kashmir Lass (by Kashmir II); dam won Cheshire
Oaks and is sister to very smart Mil's Bomb; tenth of 21 behind Alphabatim in maiden
race at Newmarket in October; sure to be better for the experience. *H. Cecil.*

TOUCH OF RHYTHM 2 ch.g. Record Token 128–Halkissimo 61 (Khalkis 127)   –
(1983 6f 8g) Mar 24; half-brother to 3 minor winners and unbeaten hurdler The
Grey Bomber (by Scallywag); dam won over 1m; well beaten in minor event at
Carlisle in June and maiden race at Edinburgh in September. *D. Smith.*

TOUCH TENDER 3 b.g. Prince Tenderfoot 126–Touch of Dutch 54 (Goldhill   –
125) (1982 7fg 7g 1983 11s 8v 7g 6f 10f 13.8f) big, strong, good-bodied gelding;
behind in varied races, including sellers; sometimes blinkered. *A. Ingham.*

TOUCHY MISS 2 b.f. Tachypous 128–Miss Portal (St Paddy 133) (1983 5s 6f)   –
May 24; 1,250F, 820Y; fair sort; second produce (dam poor maiden); last in
11-runner maiden auction event (swerved quite badly leaving stalls) at Salisbury in
May and 19-runner maiden race at Windsor in July. *P. Mitchell.*

TOUGH COMMANDER (USA) 3 b. or br.c. Bold Commander–She's Tuff   –
(Royal Gem II) (1982 6f 6fg³ 7g 7g³ 1983 9d 10d 8v 10fg 14f 12f 12f 12f 10f) small,
shallow-girthed colt; disappointing maiden; evidently flattered considerably on final
outing as a 2-y-o; should stay at least 1m; blinkered third and fourth starts;
exported to Singapore. *R. Armstrong.*

TOUGH CUSTOMER 3 gr.g. Lucky Wednesday 124–Silver Swallow (My   –
Swallow 134) (1982 5fg 1983 10fg 10f) behind in maiden races and a minor event.
H. Westbrook.

TOUR DE FORCE 3 ch.g. Reliance II 137–Set to Work (Workboy 123) (1982   62
7s³ 1983 10fg 12f 10d 9d⁴ 10f 10g) workmanlike gelding; promises to stay at least
1¼m. *P. Makin.*

TOURNAMENT LEADER 3 ro.c. Dance In Time–Implacable (Never Say Die   –
137) (1982 6fg² 1983 10g) very lightly-raced maiden; fifth of 15 behind
wide-margin winner Bahoor in amateur riders race at Lingfield in October. *R.
Akehurst.*

TOVERIS 3 gr.f. Homing 130–Smeralda 105 (Grey Sovereign 128§) (1982 7d 7g*   –
1983 8s⁴ 8.3f 8g 8.2fg) good-topped filly; good mover; quite useful at 2 yrs, but
didn't recover her form; should stay 1m; blinkered final outing; sold 12,000 gns
Newmarket December Sales. *M. Stoute.*

TOWER HOPE 2 b.c. Tower Walk 130–Montcall (Mountain Call 125) (1983 6fg   –
6g 7g) Feb 6; 5,000F, 9,000Y; sturdy colt; fifth foal; half-brother to a winning
hurdler; dam unraced half-sister to French Champion Hurdle winner Hardatit; little
form, including in a claiming race; blinkered last 2 outings. *W. O'Gorman.*

TOWERING 4 br.g. Tower Walk 130–Up And At It 72 (Tamerlane 128) (1982 8g²   73
10fg 9g 8.2g 9g* 9s³ 8.2v* 1983 8v* 8v² 10v² 9v²) big, good-topped gelding;
quite a modest handicapper; decisively won at Wolverhampton in April; ran
creditably afterwards; stays 1¼m; acts on any going but is particularly well suited
by soft; suitable mount for an apprentice; has run respectably when sweating up;
sold to R. Blakeney 12,200 gns Ascot 2nd June Sales. *Sir Mark Prescott.*

TOWER JOY 9 b.h. Tower Walk 130–Great Joy (Kythnos 126) (1982 8g 7fg 7f³   85
8fg³ 7f 8g 1983 8v 7s 8g³ 8f⁴ 7fg³) strong, good-looking horse; fair handicapper;
ran creditably last 2 starts when fourth to Mighty Fly in Royal Hunt Cup at Royal
Ascot and fourth (moved up to third) behind Mummy's Pleasure in Ward Hill
Bunbury Cup at Newmarket; stays 1m; acts on any going; used to be an excellent
mount for an apprentice but tends to get behind nowadays and sometimes has
trouble getting through. *L. Cumani.*

TOWER OF STRENGTH 4 b.g. Tower Walk 130–Amberetta 72 (Supreme   75
Sovereign 119) (1982 5f* 6g 5f 6fg³ 6f 6f 6g 5fg³ 7d³ 8.2s 1983 6v³ 7d³ 6d² 6f 7f
6f³ 6f² 6fg⁴ 6fg 6g 6fg 6fg) quite attractive, well-made gelding; not the best of
movers; suited by 7f; acts on any going. *J. Winter.*

TOWER WIN 6 ch.h. Tower Walk 130–Takawin 109 (Takawalk II 125) (1982 8d   47
10f⁴ 8f³ 8g 10f 10f 10fg⁴ 8g* 10d³ 10d 1983 10g⁴ 8g⁴ 8fg 10h⁴ 10f 10f² 10f 10f*
10fg) quite attractive horse; apprentice ridden when winning handicap at
Chepstow in September; stays 1¼m; acts on any going; blinkered 3 times in 1980;
sometimes sweats up. *J. Benstead.*

TOWN BUSTER 2 b.g. Broxted 120–Cry of Joy 50 (Town Crier 119) (1983 5g)   –
Mar 12; workmanlike gelding; first foal; dam of little account; seventh of 9 in minor
event at Redcar in November. *H. Wharton.*

TOWNSVILLE 2 br.g. Camden Town 125–Lady d'Arbanville (Luthier 126) (1983   –
7fg) Apr 6; 5,200F, IR 32,000Y; lengthy gelding; fifth foal; closely related to minor
French 3-y-o 8.5f winner Clonsella Lady (by High Top); dam, minor 2-y-o winner, is
granddaughter of top-class La Sega; eleventh of 12 in maiden race at Salisbury in
September; subsequently gelded. *J. Sutcliffe.*

TRAA-DY-LIOOAR 3 b.c. Wollow 132–Parengeta 74 (So Blessed 130) (1982 5g   53
5g³ 6f² 7g² 7d³ 6fg³ 1983 8v 7fg⁴ 9d 8.2g⁴ 12fg 8.2fg 10fg³ 10g⁴ 11f³ 10s 10g)
leggy colt; plater; stays 11f; seems to act on any going except possibly very soft;
not particularly reliable. *W. H. H. Williams.*

TRACK DEAL (USA) 2 b.c. Elocutionist–Exotic Garden (Bold Ruler) (1983 7d   110 ?
5fg 6s* 7fg² 6fg*) May 4; $65,000Y; half-brother to 3 winners in USA, notably
very smart sprinter Lines of Power (by Raise A Native); dam once-raced half-sister
to 2 very useful stakes winners; was in good form at the back-end, winning maiden
race at Hamilton and Premio Brianza (defeating Old Dominion 5 lengths) at San
Siro, Milan; in between finished excellent second to Jabaraba, caught close home,
in nursery at Doncaster; stays 7f but is probably better at 6f; acts on soft going and
a firm surface; wears blinkers and bandages; sure to win more races. *B. Hanbury.*

TRACK ROYAL 2 ch.g. Track Spare 125–Get Set 65 (Stupendous) (1983 5v 5g³   65
5fg 6f 5f* 5f 5fg) Feb 4; 1,000Y; leggy gelding; brother to a winning plater; dam
won over 1¼m; won 8-runner nursery, making all, at Hamilton in July; stays 6f; acts
on firm going; often sweats up; sold 880 gns Doncaster October Sales, and
subsequently gelded. *P. Calver.*

TRACK SECRET 4 b.f. Palm Track 122–Secret Folly 83 (Infatuation 129) (1982   –
12.2f 12.2f 12d 10f³ 9f⁴ 12s² 12d 1983 12.3v 12d 12v 12d 12f) lengthy filly; plater;
suited by 1½m; acts on any going; blinkered final start; has worn bandages. *E.
Weymes.*

TRACK SHARP 4 b.g. Palm Track 122–Chrystal Sky 68 (Skymaster 126) (1982   –
NR 1983 12f 10f 12f² 16f 13g 10fg 8fg) sturdy gelding; fourth foal; half-brother to
1978 2-y-o 1¼m seller winner Jo-Anne (by Beatic); dam poor maiden; little
worthwhile form; blinkered final start. *Mrs M. Nesbitt.*

TRACY'S 2 b.g. Imperial Fling 116–Croomedale (Alcide 136) (1983 7g 8f) May
11; 8,400Y; small, strong, close-coupled gelding; half-brother to several winners
here and in France; dam, successful over 11f in France, is daughter of smart
Mirnaya; last late in the season in minor event (slowly away) at Chepstow and
maiden race at Leicester; subsequently gelded. *J. Old.*

TRADE 3 b.c. Great Nephew 126–Grove Star (Upper Case) (1982 8s 1983 8v
10g) lightly-made, quite attractive colt; no show in maiden races. *M. Ryan.*

TRADE HIGH 4 b.g. Tower Walk 130–Lucky Deal 93 (Floribunda 136) (1982 8g   62
7f 7.6d 8.2g⁴ 8.2s³ 8.2v² 6s⁴ 1983 6s² 6v² 8d 6d 7d⁴ 8d² 6f* 6f³ 8g 6g³ 8d 8.2s 7fg
7fg) lightly-made gelding; won handicap at Carlisle in June; beaten in seller final
outing; stays 1m; acts on any going; suitable mount for an apprentice; blinkered
fourth start. *G. Richards.*

TRADE LINE 2 b.c. High Line 125–Dark Finale (Javelot 124) (1983 7fg 7g⁴)   72 p
May 6; fair sort; has a round action; brother to several winners, including Oaks
fourth Shore Line, Park Hill Stakes winner Quay Line and very useful French filly
Ancholia, and closely related to another winner; dam won at up to 1½m in Ireland;
stayed on after having lot to do at halfway to finish 7 lengths fourth of 16 to Barry
Sheene in maiden race at Leicester in September; will be much better suited by
further; sure to improve. *H. Candy.*

TRADESMAN 3 br.g. Workboy 123–Song of May 79 (Sing Sing 134) (1982 5fg 5g   50
5g 5g 5f⁴ 7g 1983 5fg 5g 5fg 5fg* 5f⁴ 5f⁴ 5fg 5g) neat, sturdy gelding; made most
and rallied gamely when winning selling handicap at Edinburgh in June (bought in
1,100 gns); had some stiffish tasks afterwards; best form at 5f; yet to race on a
soft surface. *J. Haldane.*

TRAFFITANZI 2 b.c. Busted 134–Mrs McNicholas 74 (Tudor Music 131) (1983   83 p
8d³) Mar 6; 7,000Y; first foal; dam 2-y-o 7f winner; 16/1, staying-on 2 lengths third
of 16 to Maypole Dancer in maiden race at Warwick in October; shouldn't be hard
pressed to win in similar company. *R. Boss.*

TRAKADY 3 b.c. Relkino 131–Much Pleasure (Morston 125) (1982 NR 1983 8f*   117
8f³ 12fg* 12fg*)
    Three wins from four starts is the progressive Trakady's record to date and
since he did not have his first race until July it is reasonable to assume he has
further improvement in him. His reputation preceded him onto the racecourse;
starting a warm favourite for a twelve-runner maiden event at Newbury he
overcame greenness and a slow start to account for Sweet Slew convincingly by
four lengths. Trakady's defeat behind Page Blanche in the Surplice Stakes at
Goodwood later in the month indicated that a mile was too sharp for him in better
company and he stepped up in distance for his last two appearances. Up against the
odds-on Gay Lemur and three others in the Troy Stakes at the St Leger meeting,

		Relko	Tanerko
	Relkino	(b 1960)	Relance III
	(b 1973)	Pugnacity	Pampered King
Trakady		(b 1962)	Ballynulta
(b.c. 1980)		Morston	Ragusa
	Much Pleasure	(ch 1970)	Windmill Girl
	(ch 1975)	Ambrosia	Alcide
		(ch 1965)	Bride Elect

he made headway early in the straight, came to challenge the favourite entering the
final furlong and got the better of him by a neck under strong driving. The Choke
Jade Stakes at Newmarket later in September appeared to present Trakady with an
altogether stiffer task since his opponents were Zoffany, Farioffa, Forward,
Lafontaine and Dancing Affair, all at least very useful. We thought the slow early
pace might damage his prospects but events proved otherwise as he came through
in the last quarter of a mile with Carson again hard at work to wear down Zoffany
gamely and win by a head, the pair three lengths clear of Fariofffa. Judging by his

Troy Stakes, Doncaster—Trakady wins narrowly from Gay Lemur (right)

style of racing Trakady is likely to find a mile and a half a minimum trip at four and we anticipate his being suited by a mile and three quarters.

Trakady is the first foal of an unraced half-sister to Hard Fought, a high-class colt at up to a mile and a quarter who numbered the Westbury Stakes and Prince of Wales's Stakes among his successes. The grandam, a half-sister to Hethersett and Royal Prerogative out of the second-best two-year-old filly of 1954 Bride Elect, produced three other winners including the useful middle-distance performers London God and St Briavels. This is a fine family and there is a strong likelihood that Trakady, a close-coupled, quite attractive colt who has raced only on firm ground, will add to its reputation in 1984. *R. Hern.*

TRANSFLASH 4 br.c. Auction Ring 123–Gwen Somers (Will Somers 114§) (1982 5f 6g² 6f³ 7fg 8g 6v 6s³ 6s² 1983 5v 6v³ 6d⁴ 6f 6f⁴ 7f 6fg³ 6g 6fg 6fg³) leggy, useful-looking colt; stays 7f; acts on any going; blinkered in 1982; suitable mount for an apprentice. *I. Walker.* **55**

TRANSIENT (USA) 4 gr.c. For The Moment–Cutalong (The Axe 115) (1982 8fg 10.1fg 8d* 8d² 8f⁴ 8f 8.3g* 8fg⁴ 8s² 1983 8d⁴ 8v 8v² 9v* 10g 8f 10f 9fg) lengthy, useful-looking colt; won handicap at Wolverhampton in May; stays 9f; acts well on soft ground; sometimes blinkered but is effective without; has shown a tendency to hang and isn't an easy ride; sold to BBA 11,000 gns Newmarket Autumn Sales. *D. Oughton.* **84**

TRANSONIC 4 br.f. Continuation 120–Sassanian Queen (Baragoi 115) (1982 5f* 5fg 7f 5f 6s 1983 6d 6fg 6fg 6fg 5h 7g 5.8fg) lengthy, dipped-backed filly; poor sprint handicapper; well beaten in sellers on occasions; acts on firm going. *R. Thompson.* **–**

TRAPEZE ARTIST 2 b.c. High Line 125–Maternal 93 (High Top 131) (1983 7g 7g³) Apr 20; 6,200F, 9,400Y; close-coupled colt; third foal; half-brother to 1½m winner Channing Girl (by Song) and fair 1982 2-y-o 5f winner Grenfell Boy (by Sharpen Up), subsequently a winner in Singapore; dam 2-y-o 5f and 6f winner; 3½ lengths third of 18 to Knight's Banner in maiden race at Leicester in October; will be suited by 1¼m+. *N. Vigors.* **86**

TRAVEL AWAY 2 ch.f. Tachypous 128–Sugar Cookie 71 (Crepello 136) (1983   **93** p
7fg*) Mar 23; 12,000Y; strong, good-topped filly; third foal; closely related to
quite useful 7f and 1¼m winner Hayakaze (by Hotfoot); dam placed at up to 13f;
responded gamely to pressure when wearing down stable-companion Nonpareil
close home to win 22-runner maiden race at Newmarket in October by ½ length;
will be suited by 1m+; the type to train on. *B. Hanbury.*

TRAVEL FAR 3 b.f. Monseigneur 127–Sinella 93 (Sing Sing 134) (1982 NR   –
1983 7d 7v 7fg 6f 7.6g⁴ 7s) 25,000Y; fair sort; good walker; half-sister to 2
winners, including fairly useful 1975 2-y-o sprinter Sindo (by Derring-Do); dam,
winner over 5f at 2 yrs, is half-sister to top-class sprinter and broodmare Stilvi;
fourth behind wide-margin winner Hooligan in 20-runner maiden event at Chester
in August; tailed off only subsequent start; promises to stay 1m; sweated up
fourth start. *P. Walwyn.*

TRAVELGUARD 3 gr.c. Nishapour 125–Sequoia 87 (Sassafras 135) (1982 6fg²   **108**
7fg³ 8s³ 7d* 7s* 1983 7g² 7v⁴ 8fg 7g 7g⁴ 7s⁴ 7fg³) well-made colt; ran really well
when ¾-length second of 12 behind Bid Again in £8,300 handicap at Newmarket in
April; in frame afterwards at York (twice), Doncaster and Newmarket, finishing 2½
lengths third to Wiki Wiki Wheels on last-named course in October; had stiff task
third outing; stays 1m and may well get further; acts on a firm surface but is well
suited by soft ground; genuine; sent to race in USA. *J. W. Watts.*

TRAVEL HUNTER 2 b.f. Tap On Wood 130–Bananaquit 103 (Prove It) (1983   – p
6fg) Mar 14; IR 10,500Y; half-sister to 3 winners, including middle-distance
winner Bicentennial (by Blakeney); dam won twice over 5f at 2 yrs; in mid-division
in 29-runner maiden race at Newmarket in September; should improve. *P.
Walwyn.*

TREAGLE 3 ch.c. Legal Eagle 126–Teresa Way 66 (Great White Way) (1982 NR   –
1983 6s 8f 8f) workmanlike colt; third foal; half-brother to fairly useful sprinter
Master Cawston (by Cawston's Clown); dam placed over 5f at 2 yrs; behind in
maiden races; sold to W. Clay 600 gns Ascot August Sales. *G. Wragg.*

TREASONABLE 2 b.g. Creetown 123–Anjamadi (Buff's Own 113) (1983 7fg)   –
Apr 18; 920F, 1,700Y; smallish, rather narrow, fair sort; turns front feet out; first
produce; dam never ran; tailed off in 25-runner maiden race at Newmarket in July;
sold 390 gns Ascot November Sales. *I. Walker.*

TREASURE HUNTER 4 br.c. Full of Hope 125–Antigua 100 (Hyperion) (1982   **72**
7f 8d 9g 1983 10v* 12f* 12f 13g 13g 12s 15fg*) quite attractive, strong colt;
showed improved form, winning handicaps at Ripon and Ayr and minor event at
Thirsk; stays well; acts on any going; pulled hard and ran moderately sixth start. *J.
Fitzgerald.*

TREBERTH 2 b.f. Gay Fandango 132–Clouds 70 (Relko 136) (1983 7g) Apr 15;   –
half-sister to Irish middle-distance winner Clouds Daughter (by Rheingold) and 2
winners in Italy; dam, half-sister to Mountain Call, stayed 1¼m; remote eighth of
13 in maiden race at Lingfield in October. *R. Laing.*

TREE FELLA 6 br.g. King Log 115–Gold Reid (Le Dieu d'Or 119) (1982 6f⁴ 5fg   **67**
5fg³ 6g³ 6f³ 6f 6g* 6f 6d 6fg 7.2s 1983 7fg 6f⁴ 6fg* 6f 6fg² 7f⁴ 7g 7.2g³) leggy
gelding; goes well at Chester and won handicap there in July; stays 7f; acts on any
going; suitable mount for a boy. *C. Crossley.*

TREE MALLOW 5 b.m. Malicious–Potentilla 89 (Nearula 132) (1982 16f 12fg   **64**
12f 18d 13s 1983 18f* 15.8g* 16fg³ 16.1s* 20fg) compact mare; showed improved
form, winning handicaps at Ripon, Catterick and Haydock; well-backed favourite
when beating King's College Boy ½ length on last-named in October; suited by a
test of stamina; acts on any going; sometimes sweats up; has been tried in blinkers
but is better without; below form final outing. *M. Lambert.*

TREIZIEME (USA) 2 ch.f. The Minstrel 135–Belle Pensee (Ribot 142) (1983   **121**
8g* 8f*)
    When a filly manages to beat the colts in the Grand Criterium, France's most
valuable two-year-old event, her victory proves that she is exceptional, that the
colts are below standard, or both. Of the five fillies to have achieved this notable
feat since the war, the first three confirmed as three-year-olds that they were
indeed exceptional: the 1955 winner Apollonia afterwards won the Poule d'Essai
des Pouliches and the Prix de Diane by four lengths; the 1957 winner Bella Paola
took the One Thousand Guineas and Oaks, the Prix Vermeille and the Champion
Stakes; and Hula Dancer, the winner in 1962, won the One Thousand Guineas, the
Prix Jacques le Marois, the Prix du Moulin and the Champion Stakes. On the other

Grand Criterium, Longchamp—Treizieme beats the colts; the next four home
are Truculent, Mendez, Executive Pride and Green Paradise (No. 2)

hand Silver Cloud, who appeared to beat a substandard field in 1966, later won only the Prix de la Nonette from five outings. Now we have Treizieme, the first of her sex to win the Grand Criterium for seventeen years. As the Criterium was only the second race of her career Treizieme may well be an exceptional filly in the making, one capable of matching the achievements of Apollonia, Bella Paola or Hula Dancer. At the same time the signs are that the 1983 Grand Criterium took less winning than usual and Treizieme, for what it's worth, has been placed 11 lb below El Gran Senor in the International Classification, 6 lb below the top-ranked French colt Long Mick and 3 lb below the top-rated French filly, the Prix Marcel Boussac winner Almeira. We don't take quite so moderate a view of her form but we can't rate her so highly as the four other fillies, most of whom had at least one other first-class victory to their name: Apollonia had won the Morny, Bella Paola the Criterium de Maisons-Laffitte and Hula Dancer the Salamandre (by eight lengths).

Treizieme's only other appearance came in a newcomers race at Longchamp in September, the Prix de la Cascade, a race of nothing like the importance of the Morny or the Salamandre but which frequently attracts a budding star—such good fillies as First Bloom, Regal Exception, El Mina, Ivanjica, Paint the Town, Nonoalca and Salpinx made their debuts in it during the 'seventies. Treizieme started a short-priced favourite to beat her six rivals, a task she accomplished in style by a length and a half after leading throughout. She clearly deserved a crack at the best of her age but the top race for fillies, the Prix Marcel Boussac, came a little too soon, just a week after her debut. Incidentally the Marcel Boussac (formerly the Criterium des Pouliches) is probably the main reason why no filly has won the Grand Criterium for so long: since its inception in 1969 only eight fillies have taken on the colts, whereas five ran in the 1968 Grand Criterium alone. Maurice Zilber is one of the few who considers it worthwhile running a filly in the Grand Criterium and Treizieme became his third female challenger since 1969, following Nobiliary in 1974 and Pink Prism in 1980. Such was her reputation that Treizieme was backed down from 13/1 to third favourite at less than 7/2 behind the odds-on stable-mates Seattle Song, winner of the Prix de la Salamandre, and Mendez, winner of the Prix des Chenes. Lord of Trillora, a five-length winner of a newcomers race on his only start, was next in the betting ahead of the first two in the Prix La Rochette, Cariellor and Truculent, the latter of whom had since won the Prix Lord Seymour. Making up the field were the outsiders Green Paradise from France, Lucky Scott from England and Executive Pride from Ireland, and it was Green Paradise and Lucky Scott who ensured a fast pace. Treizieme, the last to break, was pushed along at the rear and was still only sixth of nine turning into the straight, where her rider wisely began to switch her outside. While Mendez was running into all sorts of trouble as he tried to improve towards the inside, Treizieme quickly closed on the leaders, Green Paradise, Truculent and the weakening Lord of Trillora. Truculent was the first to head Green Paradise but his moment of glory was brief: Treizieme cut him down soon afterwards and maintained her run to beat him going away by three quarters of a length. The highly unlucky Mendez, who snatched third place the same distance further back, later did little to advertise the form, failing to justify favouritism in a below-par William Hill Futurity. Nor does the proximity in fourth place of the dead-heaters Executive Pride and Green Paradise, beaten little more than two lengths, do much to advertise it: Executive Pride had previously cut little ice in pattern races in England and Ireland (and he was badly hampered here) and Green Paradise had been beaten five lengths by Mendez on his last start. One man with no doubts about Treizieme's merit is her trainer who is convinced she will develop into a champion—he regards her as superior to Dahlia at the same stage of her career, a claim we shouldn't disagree with. There was talk after the Criterium of Treizieme's attempting an even more remarkable feat, against the top American two-year-olds in the Hollywood Futurity on December 18th. One of her owners was said to be very keen on her taking her chance, not just because the race carries guaranteed prize money of 1,000,000 dollars but also because it would provide Treizieme with valuable experience of the Hollywood track, where the Breeders' Cup races are to be run in 1984. However the talk came to nought.

Treizieme (USA) (ch.f. Mar 10, 1981)	The Minstrel (ch 1974)	Northern Dancer (b 1961)	Nearctic Natalma
		Fleur (b 1964)	Victoria Park Flaming Page
	Belle Pensee (ch 1972)	Ribot (b 1952)	Tenerani Romanella
		Solid Thought (ch 1957)	Solidarity Unforgettable

Treizieme, a very attractive filly with an excellent action, possesses a fine pedigree, so much so that when sold as a foal she equalled the then-record price for a filly foal, 500,000 dollars. Her dam Belle Pensee, a mile-and-a-quarter winner at Deauville, is a half-sister to Junius, winner of the Middle Park Stakes, Gentle Thoughts, the leading Irish two-year-old filly of 1973 who won both the Flying Childers and the Cheveley Park Stakes, and Injunction, a minor stakes winner over six furlongs and nine furlongs in the States. Their dam, Solid Thought, was a very useful three-year-old, scoring in the Santa Ynez Stakes over six and a half furlongs and the Honeymoon Stakes over a mile. Belle Pensee produced two foals before Treizieme, the winning fillies Quest and Good Thinking. Good Thinking (by Raja Baba) gained her one success over seven furlongs at Gowran Park as a two-year-old, whereas Quest, a sister to Treizieme, scored once over nine furlongs and twice over a mile and a quarter in England, without ever fulfilling the promise of her third in the Queen Mary Stakes on her debut. We see no reason why Treizieme shouldn't stay at least as well as Quest and she may even get a mile and a half, a distance we always believed would suit Quest. She's another fine advertisement for her American-based sire The Minstrel who is doing well at stud, although he has sired only one American stakes winner and has yet to finish in the top seventy stallions in the USA. The explanation for this seemingly contradictory statement is simple: most of The Minstrel's offspring find their way to Europe, where he has sired such good performers as L'Emigrant, Chem, Longleat, Malaak, Ministerial, Peterhof, Pluralisme, Sharp Singer, Silverdip and The Noble Player. Eight of his nine two-year-old winners in 1983 won outside the USA, and European demand for his stock is likely to increase still further if Treizieme does as well as we think she will. She's the one they all have to beat in the Poule d'Essai des Pouliches and the Prix de Diane. Perhaps Treizieme will be sent over for the Derby by her adventurous trainer in an attempt to become the first filly to win the race since Fifinella in 1916—Zilber's Nobiliary found only Grundy too good for her in 1975. *M. Zilber, France.*

TREKKING 2 b.f. Homing 130–Tekatrack 81 (Track Spare 125) (1983 5.8h 7f 7g) — Apr 30; 4,000Y; second living foal; dam lightly-raced 2-y-o 5f winner; well behind in maiden races and a £5,000 event; sold 1,600 gns Ascot December Sales. *Mrs J. Reavey.*

TRENDY PHILLY 3 b. or br.f. Ballymore 123–Twaddle II (Tim Tam) (1982 7g 8s² 1983 12.2d⁴ 8s 9f² 8f 10.2h⁴) fair sort; in frame in maiden and minor events; stays 1¼m; acts on any going; tends to get behind; sent to USA. *B. Hanbury.*   67

TRENGALE 2 b.f. Shack 118–Snow Path (Warpath 113) (1983 5f 6f² 6f 7.2g 5g) May 8; small filly; second foal; half-sister to 1982 2-y-o 5f winner Flashpoint (by Red Alert); dam of no account; plater; showed no form after finishing second to Bantel Bandit in valuable race at York in July; blinkered last 2 outings. *M. Camacho.*   62

TRENTULLO BLUE 2 b. or br.f. Decoy Boy 129–Orseniga 97 (Privy Councillor 125) (1983 5g) big, workmanlike non-thoroughbred filly; half-sister to 1½m sellers winner Malors (by Malicious); dam stayed at least 13f; last of 7, badly away, in minor event at Wolverhampton in July. *P. Felgate.*   —

TRIAD TREBLE 2 ch.g. Sweet Revenge 129–Treble Cloud (Capistrano 120) (1983 5g³ 5s 5fg 7fg 5fg³ 7d 6d 6g⁴) Apr 19; IR 5,400F, 10,000Y; lengthy, fair sort;   65 second reported produce; half-brother to 1981 2-y-o 5f and 7f winner Welsh Cloud (by Welsh Saint); dam ran twice in Ireland; plating-class maiden; stays 6f; sometimes sweats up and gets above himself; gelded after final appearance. *Hbt Jones.*

TRIAGONAL 2 b.f. Formidable 125–Triple First 117 (High Top 131) (1983 5s 6s⁴ 7f² 6f* 7g³) Mar 19; well-made, quite attractive filly; third foal; half-sister to French 9f to 1½m winner Triple Dancer (by Dance In Time); dam thoroughly game winner of 7 races from 5f to 1¼m, including Musidora, Nassau and Sun Chariot Stakes; won 15-runner maiden race at Salisbury in July, forging away in closing stages to beat Deposit 6 lengths; finished very strongly when ¾-length third of 7 to Mystery Ship in Sweet Solera Stakes at Newmarket the following month; will stay 1m; acts well on firm going. *P. Walwyn.* **89**

TRIAL BY ERROR (USA) 2 b.c. Caro 133–Perfect Pigeon (Round Table) (1983 7d*) half-brother to 2 minor winners; dam, unplaced in 13 starts, is daughter of very smart middle-distance performer Pink Pigeon; won slowly-run 14-runner maiden race at Yarmouth in September by 1½ lengths from odds-on Tocave Botta; will be suited by 1¼m+; likely to go on to better things. *L. Cumani.* **89 p**

TRICKSHOT 4 br.g. Workboy 123–Lemoncilla (Philemon 119) (1982 12f 12.3d 13g² 16f 12g 16d⁴ 17.4d 16s 1983 12s 12fg 16.1fg⁴ 16f⁴ 16fg³ 17.4g⁴ 16s⁴ 20fg) useful-looking gelding; stays well; best form on soft ground but has run respectably on firm; blinkered twice in 1982; has been bandaged; inconsistent. *K. Stone.* **57**

TRIM TAXI 2 b.f. Dublin Taxi–Coldron Mill 64 (The Brianstan 128) (1983 5d² 5g² 5f² 5f* 5f* 5f) Feb 3; 620Y; fair sort; first foal; dam won 1¼m seller at 4 yrs; showed much improved form in 13-runner maiden race at Catterick in July, winning by 5 lengths; ridden by 7-lb claimer, dead-heated with Tislamee in nursery at Thirsk later in month; suited by a sharp 5f; acts well on firm going; always struggling after rearing as stalls opened on final appearance. *T. Barron.* **87**

TRIPLE JUMP 3 ch.g. Orbit Dancer–Crisp Piece 90 (Saint Crespin III 132) (1982 6fg 6g 8.2fg³ 8g 8.2s² 8g* 8.2s 1983 12s² 11v³ 12v* 13.1v² 14d³ 17.1g² 12f⁴ 14fg³) workmanlike gelding; in frame all starts and got up near finish to beat Moon Jester by ¾ length in handicap at Newbury in May; suited by a test of stamina; has run creditably on a firm surface, but probably ideally suited by some give underfoot. *R. Hannon.* **79**

TRIPLE TOWER 2 b.c. Tower Walk 130–Merry Yarn 64 (Aggressor 130) (1983 5v 6g 6g 6g 7g³ 7g²) Mar 22; 20,000Y; quite attractive colt; brother to a useful Italian winner and half-brother to useful middle-distance winner Lamb's Tale (by March Past) and a winning hurdler; dam won over 2m and is half-sister to top Australian winner Raffindale; placed in maiden events at Leicester and Lingfield in October; will be suited by 1m; exported to Singapore. *R. Smyth.* **90**

TRISH-TRASH 2 b.f. Music Boy 124–Rubbish (Major Portion 129) (1983 6f 5.1fg³ 6f³ 5fg 5fg² 5fg³ 5g) Feb 22; 3,700Y, 3,500Y; half-sister to winning sprinter Ratan Boy (by Workboy) and to a winner in Sweden; dam ran twice; placed in maiden company at Folkestone, Bath and Lingfield; best form at 5f. *F. Durr.* **69**

TRISKELION 4 b.c. Three Legs 128–Maynooth Belle (Busted 134) (1982 6f 6f 8f 7g³ 8.3g 8g 1983 6d 8fg 10.8fg) small colt; plater; stays 7f; blinkered once; has run respectably for an apprentice. *J. Howell.* **–**

TRISTRAM 2 gr.g. Nishapour 125–Court Dame (Court Fool) (1983 6fg) Apr 11; IR 7,800F, IR 2,600Y: tall gelding; second reported produce; dam won over 5f in Ireland; no show in 13-runner minor event at Goodwood in August; subsequently gelded. *K. Brassey.* **–**

TROCADERO 4 b.g. Sagaro 133–True Love 89 (Princely Gift 137) (1982 10d² 11g 12f² 11fg³ 13g 8g² 9g 10d 8g 1983 11g 12fg⁴ 15fg 15f³ 16f 16f 10h 12fg) neat gelding; poor maiden; has been behind in sellers; doesn't quite get 2m; seems to act on any going; trained by C. Thornton most of season. *D. Yeoman.* **–**

TROIS VALLEES 2 gr.f. Ile de Bourbon 133–Baccalaureate 109 (Crowned Prince 128) (1983 7s) Mar 30; 62,000Y; angular, unfurnished filly; first foal; dam, daughter of smart sprinter Bas Bleu, won over 7f and 1m; second favourite, made up ground in final furlong to finish 8 lengths sixth of 19 to Eljazzi in maiden race at Leicester in October; will do better over further. *M. Stoute.* **66 p**

*Lanson Champagne Stakes, Goodwood—Trojan Fen fights off the challenge of Elegant Air;
Captain Singleton is third*

TROJAN FEN 2 b.c. Troy 137–Fenella 91 (Thatch 136) (1983 7fg* 7f* 7f* 7f* **118**
8fg³)

The breeding industry in Britain and Ireland had barely had time to recover
from one debilitating blow, the theft of one of the greatest Derby winners, Shergar,
than it was dealt a second, the death in May of another truly outstanding Derby
winner, Troy. At the time of his disappearance Shergar had spent only one season at
stud, siring over thirty foals, but thankfully Troy had had more opportunities to
pass on his sterling qualities before he succumbed to the effects of a perforated gut
at the age of seven. In addition to thirty two-year-olds, none of which had run at the
time of his death, Troy had at least thirty-four yearlings and thirty-three foals, and
had already covered thirty-five mares in 1983. Troy's loss looks no less serious
after his first runners have had a chance to show their worth: of the fifteen which
ran in Britain, Ireland and France, Corinth, Hidden Warning, Secret Way, Trojan
Fen, Tropular and Troyanna won at least once, while others to show plenty of
promise were Glimmering, Ilium, Pagan of Troy and Tirwadda.

Trojan Fen became Troy's second runner and first winner when effortlessly
landing the odds in a minor event at Yarmouth at the end of June. He was also to
land the odds decisively in three much better races before the middle of August,
starting with a very smooth defeat of Carabineer and four others in the Donnington
Castle Stakes at Newbury. So impressive was he that he started as short as 11/4 on
against the July Stakes third Captain Singleton, the unbeaten Elegant Air and the
previous winners Hit The Heights and Altdorfer in the Lanson Champagne Stakes
at Goodwood, a race won by Troy five years earlier. Although he justified the
support, Trojan Fen needed to work quite hard entering the final furlong to take the
measure of Elegant Air, whom he eventually beat by a length and a half. He didn't
have to work nearly so hard to account for the Chesham Stakes winner Head For
Heights, the Cock of the North Stakes winner Hoyer and Finian's Rainbow in the
Washington Singer Stakes at Newbury; he had all three in trouble well below the
distance and won easing up by three lengths from Head For Heights, who was to
make Falstaff pull out all the stops in a valuable race at York later in August. Trojan
Fen was therefore unbeaten in four starts and the stage looked set for a fascinating
encounter with another unbeaten colt, the spectacular Lear Fan, when both were
declared to run in the Laurent Perrier Champagne Stakes at Doncaster in
September. Unhappily Trojan Fen's trainer changed his mind about running, fearing
that predicted wet weather would make the ground too soft for the colt. Cecil's
fears proved unfounded: good to firm at the time of declaration, the ground had
softened only slightly by the time the Champagne was run, to good on the straight
course and good to firm on the round course. There is no racecourse evidence that
Trojan Fen is unable to handle soft ground: the colt has yet to race on anything
other than firm or firmish ground. Cecil had told us some time before Doncaster
that he felt Trojan Fen would be of little account on soft, but the circumstances of
Trojan's Fen's withdrawal led the more cynical observers to wonder whether it was
brought about more by a fear of his losing his unbeaten record against a patently
top-class colt. Ironically Trojan Fen lost his unbeaten record on fast ground in the
Royal Lodge Stakes at Ascot a fortnight later. In our opinion neither he nor the
other unbeaten co-favourite, Rousillon, was ridden to best advantage; they were
given a lot to do as the rank outsider Mellow Dance set a very fast pace ahead of
Gold And Ivory. Both Trojan Fen and Rousillon were rushed up on the turn, as it
became clear the leaders weren't weakening, and the effort soon took its toll on
Trojan Fen. He couldn't keep on quickening and in the end he finished

third, four and a half lengths behind Gold And Ivory and two and a half lengths behind Rousillon. Coincidentally Troy also ended his first season with a defeat in the Royal Lodge.

Trojan Fen (b.c. Feb 14, 1981)	Troy (b 1976)	Petingo (b 1965)	Petition
			Alcazar
		La Milo (ch 1963)	Hornbeam
			Pin Prick
	Fenella (b 1975)	Thatch (b 1970)	Forli
			Thong
		Abanilla (gr 1958)	Abernant
			Nella

Will Trojan Fen emulate his sire by winning the Derby? We don't think so. For one thing his form so far is about a stone below that required to win the Derby in an average year; for another he isn't certain to be suited by a mile and a half. His dam Fenella, by the sprinter-miler Thatch, ended her racing career running unplaced over five furlongs, after gaining her one success over a little less than a mile; and his grandam Abanilla, by the brilliantly speedy Abernant, was at her best as a two-year-old, when successful in the five-furlong Princess Margaret Stakes and third in the Cheveley Park. Other members of the family, by sires who are much stronger influences for stamina than either Thatch and Abernant, have stayed well; Abanilla's half-brothers Parnell and Miralgo were both top-class middle-distance stayers, while her half-sister Tiarella produced the Cesarewitch winner Shantallah; and Fenella is a half-sister to three useful performers, Arenaria, Offenbach and Evvia, who stayed a mile and a quarter. Trojan Fen should stay as far as the last three, and the possibility of his staying further can't be ruled out. Trojan Fen, a close-coupled, good-topped colt, is Fenella's second foal, following the plating-class Irish sprint maiden Barely Hot (by Bold Lad, Ire). He was sold as a yearling for 115,000 guineas, just 3,000 guineas less than his dam had fetched at the 1980 Newmarket December Sales when carrying Trojan Fen. Fenella has since produced a yearling filly by Ile de Bourbon which fetched 90,000 guineas at the Highflyer Sales, and a colt foal by Mill Reef. The Mill Reef colt must surely sell extremely well if consigned to the sales, especially as Trojan Fen looks certain to figure prominently in more good races as a three-year-old. *H. Cecil.*

TROJAN SECRET 5 br.g. Averof 123–Camina Bay 109 (Whistling Wind 123) (1982 12d 10.2g³ 10fg³ 10f 8g 8fg 8s 1983 10v⁴ 12f) sparely-made gelding; disappointing maiden; stays 1¼m; sold 1,600 gns Newmarket July Sales. *C. Brittain.*   –

TROLL LADY 6 b.m. Crisp and Even 116–Fire Hawk 70 (Firestreak 125) (1982 10.6f 12d 12fg 16.5f 12g⁴ 1983 12f) leggy mare; plater; stays 1½m; probably needs some give in the ground; sometimes sweats up; has been bandaged on off-hind. *P. Feilden.*   –

TROMEROS 2 b.c. Camden Town 125–Silky Starlet (Silky Sullivan) (1983 7fg 7f³ 7fg) Mar 29; 8,800F, 10,500Y; good-bodied colt; half-brother to 3 winners here and abroad, including Irish 2000 Guineas third Mister Niall (by Ridan); dam never ran; showed up in useful company at Sandown and Newmarket in August on last 2 appearances; will stay 1m. *C. Brittain.*   **79**

TROOPER SERGEANT 4 b.g. Queen's Hussar 124–Grass Widow (Thatch 136) (1982 8.2fg⁴ 7f 7g 8f⁴ 8.5f³ 8d⁴ 7g* 6fg* 6f³ 6fg* 6d 6g 1983 7f⁴ 6fg) workmanlike gelding; quite a modest handicapper; stays 1m but seems better at shorter distances; seems to act on any going; doesn't find much off bridle. *G. Huffer.*   –

TROOP LEADER 4 b.g. Queen's Hussar 124–Lizzie Lightfoot (Hotfoot 126) (1982 NR 1983 12fg³ 11fg² 11.5f³) workmanlike gelding; moderate mover; second foal; dam, who never ran, is closely related to very useful 1¼m colt Light Fire; placed in minor event and maiden races, including an amateur riders race; stays 1½m. *C. Nelson.*   **74**

TROPARE (CAN) 2 b.c. The Minstrel 135–Renounce (Buckpasser) (1983 7d 8fg³ 8d⁴) May 21; rather lightly-made, quite attractive colt; good mover; fifth foal; half-brother to 3 minor winners in USA; dam lightly-raced half-sister to high-class Intrepid Hero; showed ability in good-class company, notably 8½ lengths third of 5 to Lear Fan in Fitzroy House Stakes at Newmarket in August; should stay 1½m; sure to win a race. *B. Hills.*   **87**

TROPICAL DREAM (FR) 2 b.f. Free Round 127–Tropical Queen (Creme dela Creme) (1983 7f 8g 7fg) Mar 3; lengthy, rather shallow-girthed filly; first known foal; dam plating-class sister to smart French 6f to 10.5f winner Tropical Cream;   **69**

TRO

showed a little promise on first outing but none at all afterwards; should stay 1¼m.
B. Hills.

TROPICAL MIST (FR) 3 b. or br. g. Faraway Son 130–Tropical Cream (Creme   85
dela Creme) (1982 8.2s³ 1983 8d 8d³ 10s* 10fg² 10g² 9.4f² 10f 10h² 11.1g³
11d) tall, rather leggy, fair sort; won maiden race at Leicester in May and was
placed in varied races, including an amateur riders event; will stay 1½m; acts on
any going; ran poorly seventh and final starts; sold to BBA 16,500 gns
Newmarket Autumn Sales. *P. Walwyn.*

TROPICAL RED 3 ch. c. Red Alert 127–Desert Pet 77 (Petingo 135) (1982 8s*   57
1983 8.2v³ 8s 8s² 8s² 8s³ 8.2h 10.1fg 8g) rather leggy, lengthy colt; placed in
handicaps in spring; worth another chance at 1¼m; seems to need plenty of give in
the ground, although has had stiffish tasks on firm. *C. Wildman.*

TROPICAL STORM 2 ch. f. Swing Easy 126–Dibby's Cousin (Be Friendly 130)   66
(1983 5fg 6f 8g* 7.2g 8fg 8fg³ 7fg) Mar 9; narrow filly; fourth foal; dam never ran;
apprentice ridden, won 22-runner seller at Leicester (bought in 1,700 gns) in
September; third in selling nursery at Doncaster the following month; suited by
1m; blinkered fourth and sixth starts. *A. Bailey.*

TROPICAL WAY (FR) 2 ch. c. Pharly 130–Tropical Cream (Creme dela Creme)   – p
(1983 6fg) May 4; useful-looking colt; good mover; closely related to useful French
1¼m winner Tropical Lightning (by Lyphard) and half-brother to 3-y-o 1¼m winner
Tropical Mist (by Faraway Son) and smart French 1m winner Tropicaro (by Caro);
dam, smart at 2 yrs and 3 yrs, won 10.5f Prix Cleopatre; behind in 20-runner
maiden race at Newmarket in October; should do better over longer distances. *P.
Walwyn.*

TROPINGAY 3 b. f. Cawston's Clown 113–Summer Sales 94 (Tropique 128) (1982   –
6fg 5s 1983 10s 10.1f) well beaten in maiden and minor events. *D. Elsworth.*

TROPWEN WINBOURNE 3 b. f. Arcadian Memories 89–Proud Bess (Blublue   –
Too) (1982 NR 1983 10fg) non-thoroughbred filly; first known foal; dam never
ran; slowly away when tailed-off last of 22 in minor event at Nottingham in June. *J.
Tierney.*

TROUBADOUR 3 b. c. Hotfoot 126–Beryl's Song 86 (Sing Sing 134) (1982 5f 5fg   66
5fg 5g³ 6fg 6g 5g 1983 5s 6d 8s 5f⁴ 5fg 5g 5.3f⁴ 5h 9d 7.6d) fair sort; should stay
at least 6f; often blinkered; sold to BBA 3,300 gns Newmarket Autumn Sales. *W.
Wightman.*

TROUVERE 2 b. c. Free State 125–Astral Suite 82 (On Your Mark 125) (1983 7d   84
8.2g³ 8g⁴ 8.2s* 9fg) Apr 26; 4,800Y; first foal; dam 6f and 7f winner; ridden by
7-lb claimer, won 7-runner minor event at Hamilton in October by 2½ lengths from
For Sure For Sure; beaten in Italy the following month; stays 1m well; acts on soft
going. *B. Hanbury.*

TROYANNA 2 b. f. Troy 137–Moon Min (First Landing) (1983 7f² 7g*) May 2;   91 p
60,000Y; good-bodied, attractive filly; good walker and mover; half-sister to 3-y-o
Fondu (by Nonoalco) and quite useful Irish 7f and 1¼m winner Millrock (by
Bustino); dam unraced half-sister to very smart 1963 American 2-y-o Traffic;
showed a lot of potential when justifying favouritism in 10-runner Malton Stakes at
York in October, quickening into a decisive lead 2f out and keeping on to win
comfortably by 2½ lengths from Ascot Strike; had signed on nicely to finish 3
lengths second of 19 to Circus Plume in maiden race at Salisbury a month
previously; will stay 1¼m+; one of the nicest 2-y-o fillies we saw all year and looks
sure to make her mark in good company. *I. Balding.*

TRUCULENT (USA) 2 b. c. Val de l'Orne 130–Minstrel Girl 115 (Luthier 126)   123
(1983 8f* 8s² 9f* 8f²)
Alec Head must have had high hopes of training his first Grand Criterium
winner since Satingo in 1972 when his latest challenger Truculent deprived the
front-running Green Paradise of the lead approaching the final furlong. Any such
hopes were short-lived: the filly Treizieme was bearing down on Truculent on the
outside and no matter how hard he tried, he couldn't prevent her sweeping past to
win by three quarters of a length. Truculent's trainer will no doubt be hoping that
history will repeat itself: Truculent's sire Val de l'Orne, after finishing second in the
Grand Criterium, went on to become Head's second winner of the Prix du
Jockey-Club. Truculent may well rise to similar heights though in our opinion his
first-season form is nearly half a stone inferior to Val de l'Orne's and he is also,
perhaps, less likely to have abnormal improvement in him, having already had two
more races than his sire, whose only other appearance at two was a victorious one
in a newcomers race.

Truculent also started his career with a win in a newcomers event, a five-runner affair at Deauville in August which he took by half a length from Vercors, finishing strongly. The betting here suggested that his connections were entertaining an angel unawares—he was only fourth choice at 9/1—and Truculent again started at a generous price, 8/1, when taking on Cariellor, a ten-length winner of a Deauville maiden race, in the Prix La Rochette at Longchamp in September, over the same course and distance as the Grand Criterium. Truculent failed by half a length to catch the all-the-way winner Cariellor, but he was given a great deal to do and his storming late run finally convinced observers of his merit: next time out he started a short-priced favourite for the nine-furlong Prix Lord Seymour at Longchamp on the day before the Arc. This race, formerly known as the Prix Saint-Roman, has been renamed in honour of Lord Henry Seymour who founded the Societe d'Encouragement, France's equivalent of the Jockey Club, a hundred and fifty years ago. Also in the Lord Seymour field were Duke of Silver and Daily Busy, winners of fairly valuable races at Deauville. However, Truculent's most serious rival proved to be the impressive Evry winner Cold Feet who hit the front halfway through the final furlong, shortly after Truculent had himself taken the lead from Duke of Silver. To his credit Truculent fought back well, showing his slightly greater experience, and narrowly got the verdict. He also showed here that he was as much at home on firm ground as he'd been on soft in the Prix La Rochette.

Truculent (USA) (b.c. Mar 15, 1981)	Val de l'Orne (b 1972)	Val de Loir (b 1959)	Vieux Manoir
			Vali
		Aglae (b 1965)	Armistice
			Aglae Grace
	Minstrel Girl (b 1976)	Luthier (br 1965)	Klairon
			Flute Enchantee
		Mige (b 1966)	Saint Crespin III
			Midget II

Truculent comes from a family which has served the Head family magnificently over the years. He's a great-grandson of the One Thousand Guineas runner-up Midget II who put up numerous high-class performances on the racecourse, over distances as different as six furlongs and a mile and a quarter, before proving equally successful at stud. Among her daughters are Madge, the dam of Ma Biche; Midou, who finished a good fourth in both the Poule d'Essai des Pouliches and the Prix de la Foret; and Mige, Truculent's grandam, who won the Cheveley Park at two and the Grand Handicap de Deauville at three, as well as finishing an excellent second to Habitat in the Prix Quincey. All Mige's four runners are winners, with Truculent's dam Minstrel Girl easily the best. Despite winning just one of her thirteen starts, Minstrel Girl was a smart performer; she was beaten only a length and a half when placed in such important races as the Prix d'Aumale, the Criterium des Pouliches, the Prix de la Grotte and the Prix de Minerve. Although her

Prix Lord Seymour, Longchamp—Truculent accounts for Cold Feet by a short head

M J. Wertheimer's "Truculent"

performance in the Minerve satisfied us that she stayed a mile and a half, Minstrel Girl was never asked to tackle so long a distance in five subsequent races. Truculent, an attractive colt, is Minstrel Girl's first foal. He should prove very well suited by a mile and a quarter or more and whatever his fate in the Prix du Jockey-Club he must have excellent prospects of developing into the best European performer by Val de l'Orne, better than Father Rooney, Ideal Point and Ruscelli, runners-up respectively in the Irish St Leger, the Prix Royal-Oak and the Prix Jean Prat. Incidentally Val de l'Orne hasn't proved a great loss to French breeders since being sent to the States in 1977 after just one season; even in his most successful year, 1983, he finished out of the top seventy-five stallions in North America. Significantly his fee has remained unchanged at 15,000 dollars, live foal, since his arrival there. *A. Head, France.*

TRUE FIRE (USA) 2 b.f. In Reality–Burning Pleasure (What A Pleasure) (1983   **74**
6f 6h 5f[4]) Mar 11; $150,000Y; small, close-coupled filly; has a sharp action; first foal; dam, half-sister to 4 stakes winners including very smart 5f to 8.5f winner Night Invader, won 3 sprint races; quite a modest maiden; best race on second outing; needs at least 6f; blinkered last 2 starts; sold NBA 16,000 gns Newmarket Autumn Sales. *J. Hindley.*

TRUE HERITAGE 4 br.c. Lord Gayle 124–Azurine 108 (Chamossaire) (1982   **71**
NR 1983 10v 10f 10f[2] 12f[4] 12g 11.5g* 12fg[3] 12s* 12fg) IR 17,500Y, 10,500 3-y-o; compact colt; brother to Oaks winner Blue Wind and half-brother to numerous winners; dam third in Irish 1,000 Guineas; won handicaps at Yarmouth in September and Haydock in October; stays 1½m; acts on any going. *A. Hide.*

TRUMPS 3 ch.g. Grundy 137–Good Try 92 (Good Bond 122) (1982 6g 6g 7fg 6g   **68**
1983 5v 6s 7g 7d 7fg 7f 7f[2] 6g[4] 7f* 8fg 7fg[3] 8.5f[2] 8f* 10d 7.6d 8g) strong, compact, attractive gelding; successful in handicaps at Folkestone in July and Chepstow in September; stays 1m; acts on firm going; blinkered final start at 2 yrs; tends to sweat up. *B. Swift.*

TRUSTY TROUBADOUR (USA) 3 ch.c. The Minstrel 135–In Trust   **79**
(Buckpasser) (1982 6f 7g[3] 7s 7g 8s[2] 1983 8g 10.1fg 10f[2](dis) 12f 10.6f* 10fg 10f)

lengthy, attractive colt; good walker; somewhat temperamental, but managed to beat Home Secretary by ½ length in small handicap at Haydock in September when blinkered first time; well beaten in blinkers afterwards; stays 1¼m; acts on any going; sold 30,000 gns Newmarket Autumn Sales. *F. J. Houghton.*

TRWYN CILAN 2 b.f. Import 127–Welsh Cape (Abernant 142) (1983 6fg) Feb 12; 5,000Y; sister to a poor animal and half-sister to Irish 1½m winner Evolution (by Upper Case); dam ran only twice; 50/1, ran on nicely under sympathetic handling in 3 lengths sixth of 24 behind Native Charmer in maiden race at Doncaster in November; sure to improve. *G. Balding.*   **79 p**

TRY ME 2 ch.f. Try My Best 130–My Lynnie 74§ (Frankincense 120) (1983 5f⁴ 5fg 5fg* 5g³ 5fg) Apr 5; 9,200Y; neat filly; first foal; dam unreliable 2-y-o 5f winner; having first race for nearly 3 months, won 16-runner maiden event at Lingfield in October by a neck from Perang's Niece; odds on when 1½ lengths equal-third to Lady of Leisure in nursery at Edinburgh later in the month; will be suited by 6f. *M. Ryan.*   **77**

TRY TIFFANY 2 ch.f. Tachypous 128–Liberation 63 (Native Prince) (1983 5g) Apr 4; 5,200Y; half-sister to 2 winners, including 1978 2-y-o 6f winner Maryoma (by Rheingold); dam half-sister to good sprinter Tudor Grey; 10 lengths sixth of 14 to Passing Storm in maiden race at Warwick in October. *R. Baker.*   **–**

TRY TO REMEMBER 3 b.f. Music Boy 124–Beech Tree 67 (Fighting Ship 121) (1982 6g 7d 1983 7fg 7fg 6f 6fg 8d⁴ 10f) big filly; plater; best run at 1m. *J. Toller.*   **–**

TRY TROFFEL 3 b.g. Golden Dipper 119–Floral 82 (Floribunda 136) (1982 5f⁴ 5f⁴ 5fg³ 5d³ 6f 5fg* 5d 5g 5s 1983 5g 5.8g⁴ 6f⁴ 5fg* 6f³) strong, sturdy gelding; led close home when winning handicap at Warwick in June; stays 6f; seems suited by top-of-the-ground; exported to Hong Kong. *P. Haynes.*   **76**

TRY YOUR BEST 3 b.c. Try My Best 130–Limuru 83 (Alcide 136) (1982 7s 1983 7d 8f 8fg 10f 10d 8d) fair sort; has a round action; quite a moderate maiden; should stay 1¼m; often blinkered; has worn a tongue strap; trained by P. Haslam until after fourth outing; sold 1,500 gns Ballsbridge December Sales. *M. Jarvis.*   **–**

TUBES CARE 4 b.f. Moulton 128–Drury Lane 82 (Gala Performance) (1982 12fg 12f 16fg 12fg 9f* 9g² 1983 10.2f 8f 10.6fg) big, strong filly; plater; should stay 1¼m; acts on firm going; best in blinkers; sometimes sweats up. *Hbt Jones.*   **–**

TUDOR BELL STAR 4 b.g. Wishing Star 117–Affectionately 82 (Mark-Ye-Well) (1982 9fg 9f 9g 8.3fg 8fg 12g 10fg³ 9fg 1983 10.2g 8fg 10.8fg* 10.1f³ 10h 8h² 12d) lengthy, sparely-made gelding; plater; springer in market and apprentice ridden when making all to win decisively despite wandering around at Warwick in July; bought in 1,550 gns afterwards; stays 1¼m well; acts on hard going; best in blinkers. *D. Wintle.*   **51**

TUDOR BOB 5 b.g. Tudor Rhythm 112–La Belle 118 (Vilmorin) (1982 NR 1983 17.1d⁴ 10fg 8fg 11.7f 14f) tall gelding; poor handicapper; sold out of D. Morley's stable 2,000 gns Ascot May Sales after first start. *R. Atkins.*   **–**

TUDOR CALL 5 b.m. Tudor Rhythm 112–Lucky Number (River Chanter 121) (1982 NR 1983 10f) lengthy mare; poor mover; half-sister to winners in Malaysia and Belgium; dam well behind in 3 races; tailed-off last in poor maiden race at Pontefract in June. *C. Gray.*   **–**

TUDOR DREAM 5 b. or br.m. Averof 123–So Smooth (Pall Mall 132) (1982 6f 1983 6d 5d 5fg) leggy, lengthy mare; poor plater nowadays; usually apprentice ridden; sometimes blinkered. *T. Cuthbert.*   **–**

TUDOR ENTERPRISE 2 b.c. Tudor Rhythm 112–Swannery 94 (My Swanee 122) (1983 5d³ 5d² 5d* 5h² 5fg 5fg) Mar 8; 6,600Y; smallish, fair sort; brother to 2 winners, including useful 1979 2-y-o 6f winner Atlantic City, subsequently successful in USA; dam 2-y-o 5f winner; made all in maiden race at Leicester in June; not seen out after August; will be suited by 6f; yet to race on very soft going but acts on any other; hung right in closing stages first and third outings (quite badly on latter); blinkered last 4 starts; sold 7,000 gns Newmarket September Sales. *G. Huffer.*   **82**

TUDOR GATE 3 b. or br.g. Tachypous 128–Shikra (Sea Hawk II 131) (1982 5f 7g 7g 7d 1983 12s⁴ 12s* 11d* 14.7d* 14f³) smallish, good-topped gelding; improved and won handicaps at Ripon, Hamilton and Redcar in May, beating Contester easily by 6 lengths on last-named course; bit mulish in preliminaries when 1½ lengths third to Jowoody in £5,200 handicap at York in June, only subsequent start; suited by 1½m and more; acts on any going, but is probably ideally suited by some give underfoot. *M. Tompkins.*   **75**

TUDOR PAGEANT 3 b.g. Welsh Pageant 132–Latin Verses (Appiani II 128) –
(1982 NR 1983 9.4d 9.4d 10g) 10,500Y; half-brother to 2 winners, including useful
6f winner Blessed Soandso (by So Blessed); dam Irish 1½m winner; well beaten in
maiden races; sold 1,165 gns Ascot August Sales. *C. Thornton.*

TUDOR ROOT 3 br.f. Tudor Rhythm 112–Beetroot 89 (Psidium 130) (1982 7f⁴ 55
7fg 8s⁴ 8.2s⁴ 1983 11.7v 11.7v 10.2g 12g 12g²) medium-sized, lengthy filly;
plater; claimed £2,500 after finishing second at Wolverhampton in October; suited
by middle distances. *R. Laing.*

TUDOR SINGER 2 b.c. Tudor Rhythm 112–Miss Meryl 80 (River Chanter 121) –
(1983 5s 7f 7f) Apr 18; tall, leggy colt; closely related to 6f and 7f winner Prince of
Spain (by Philip of Spain); dam showed a little ability; in rear in maiden races, twice
last. *P. Feilden.*

TUDY 3 b.f. Welsh Saint 126–Truly A Princess 90 (Prince Regent 129) (1982 6g 6f 61
6f 1983 8d 9g 8d 7f⁴ 8g*) smallish filly; bought in 2,600 gns after getting up on
post to win selling handicap at Newmarket in August (swished tail repeatedly under
pressure); suited by 1m; blinkered second outing; sold 4,100 gns Newmarket
September Sales. *G. Pritchard-Gordon.*

TUFTED LOCKS 2 b.f. Mandrake Major 122–Chubby Ears (Burglar 128) (1983 –
5s 8g 7fg) May 13; first foal; dam ran twice; in rear in maiden and minor events.
Miss S. Hall.

TUFT HILL 2 b.f. Grundy 137–Narration (Sham) (1983 6f* 6fg 6f⁴ 6g) Mar 27; 92
leggy filly; second foal; dam won over 6f at 2 yrs in Ireland and stayed 1m; won
15-runner maiden event at Doncaster in July; ran creditably in nurseries on next 2
starts, notably 2 lengths fourth of 16 to Mr Meeka at Redcar in September; will be
suited by 7f and 1m; acts on firm going. *J. Etherington.*

TUGAWAY 3 ch.c. Tug of War 117–Living Legend 88 (Derring-Do 131) (1982 5fg 72
7d 7fg 7f 8fg 1983 8.5v 10.1d 10d² 10f 12f⁴ 13f² 14f 10f⁴ 12g) small, close-coupled
colt; middle-distance maiden; blinkered final start at 2 yrs; sometimes sweats up;
bandaged off-fore when running badly final start; sold to J. King 1,300 gns
Newmarket Autumn Sales. *D. Whelan.*

TUGBOAT 4 ch.g. Grundy 137–Pirate Queen 77 (Pirate King 129) (1982 NR 1983 44
12g 16fg⁴ 15.8g² 15.8d⁴) rangy, quite attractive gelding; suited by a taste of
stamina; best in blinkers; winning hurdler. *P. Mitchell.*

TUGELA 4 br.f. Rapid River 127–Medodosusu 59 (The Brianstan 128) (1982 NR –
1983 8fg 9s 5g 8f 8f) lightly-made filly; first foal; dam, a plater, placed over 1½m;
beaten a long way in varied company. *N. Tinkler.*

TUG TOP 2 b.f. High Top 131–Heave (Kashmir II 125) (1983 6d³ 6fg*) Mar 2; 83 p
quite attractive filly; keen walker; first foal; dam won over 8.5f in Italy at 4 yrs; won
20-runner maiden event at Doncaster in September, getting up close home after
being hampered; will be much better suited by 7f and 1m; sure to win more races.
I. Balding.

TULA FANCY 5 b.g. Roan Rocket 128–Becassine (El Gallo 122) (1982 13v 1983 –
11d) ex-Irish gelding; has shown no worthwhile form for a long time; sold 1,000 gns
Ascot May Sales. *J. S. Wilson.*

TULSA FLYER 4 b.c. He Loves Me 120–Happy Thought 57 (Kauai King) (1982 91
8f* 10fg³ 8f³ 10g³ 8d⁴ 10fg³ 8g⁴ 7g² 8f 8g 1983 10v³ 10v* 10d* 10s 8f 10f 10f)
compact, quite attractive, rather hollow-backed colt; fair handicapper; beautifully
ridden by L. Piggott when winning at Lingfield and Kempton in May; well beaten
most starts afterwards, including when blinkered on fifth; suited by 1¼m; acts on
any going. *J. Bethell.*

TUMBLER 8 b.g. Tumble Wind–La Roquette (Sammy Davis 129) (1982 NR 1983 –
10s 12f) poor handicapper; has been beaten in a seller; used to wear blinkers. *O.
Jorgensen.*

TUNN'S PRIDE 2 ch.g. Goldhills Pride 105–Monjenayr (Jukebox 120) (1983 5s –
5d 5d 6fg) May 17; small gelding; of little account. *M. Hinchliffe.*

TURBO 8 gr.g. Song 132–Field Mouse 108 (Grey Sovereign 128§) (1982 NR 1983 –
8g) strong gelding; poor handicapper; beaten in seller only start of 1983; stays 7f;
acts on any going; has worn blinkers; has had tongue tied down. *A. W. Jones.*

TURCY BOY 2 gr.c. Godswalk 130–Claddie (Karabas 132) (1983 5v³ 5v² 5v⁴ 5v² 71
5d 6fg 7f 7fg⁴ 8fg⁴ 7fg) Mar 19; 12,000F, 7,000Y; strong, good-bodied colt;
brother to 3-y-o 6f winner Groszewski; dam, from good family, never ran; in frame
in varied races, including nurseries; stays 1m; acts on any going. *J. Benstead.*

TURKISH DELIGHT 2 b.f. Vitiges 132–Criss Cross (Clever Fella 117) (1983   85
6fg 7f 5fg 6fg*) May 1; 7,000Y; strong, compact filly, with plenty of scope; second
foal; dam, second over 1½m and 1¾m at 4 yrs in Ireland, is half-sister to dam of
Shirley Heights; 7/1, showed much improved form in blinkers to win 17-runner
nursery at Nottingham in October by ½ length from Ewe Lamb; should stay at least
1m. *P. Cole.*

TURKOMAN 4 b.g. Patch 129–Arctrullah (Great Captain) (1982 9g 10fg 10s⁴   –
10v* 10s* 12s* 10d* 12.3fg³ 10f⁴ 12g 10g 10v 10g 12s* 1983 12d 12g 10s² 16v⁴
14s) strong, compact gelding; fairly useful handicapper at his best; in frame in race
at Pisa in March and Queen's Prize at Kempton (fourth to Alpha Omega) in April;
promises to stay 2m; probably acts on any going, but revels in the mud; does best
when ridden up with pace; blinkered twice in 1981; not seen out after April. *D.
Sasse.*

TURN AND FLY (USA) 2 b.c. Best Turn–R. Thomasina (Nadir) (1983 5v³ 5g*   96
6f 6g) Apr 21; $95,000Y; good-looking, powerful colt; eighth foal; half-brother to
3-y-o R. Awacs (by Key To The Mint), second in $100,000 Holywood Prevue
Stakes at 2 yrs, and to 5 winners, one stakes placed; dam, placed twice in 4 starts,
is sister to high-class sprinter/miler R. Thomas; improved a good deal on first
effort when quickening clear in closing stages to win 5-runner Berkshire Stakes at
Newbury in June by 1½ lengths from slow-starting Rex Lake (gave 7 lb); ran
moderately subsequently in Erroll Stakes at Ascot and BonusPrint Sirenia Stakes
at Kempton; probably best at 5f; tends to sweat up. *G. Lewis.*

TURN SHY (USA) 2 b.c. Blushing Groom 131–Misty Bend 107 (Never Bend)   –
(1983 6g) Feb 8; $220,000Y; half-brother to 2 minor winners in USA; dam won
over 5f and 6f at 2 yrs in Ireland; thirteenth of 14 in minor event at Lingfield in
September. *J. Ciechanowski.*

TURN THE KEY 2 br.f. Home Guard 129–St Padina 91 (St Paddy 133) (1983 6fg   84 p
6d*) Apr 2; 10,500Y; compact filly; sister to useful 1¼m winner Double Lock, and
half-sister to 2 winners; dam, half-sister to Irish Guinness Oaks winner Celina, won
over 1m; made short work of her 15 rivals in maiden race at Newbury in October,
winning by 3 lengths from Megastar; will be suited by 7f+; certain to show further
improvement. *J. Winter.*

TUSITALA (USA) 2 b.c. Clev Er Tell–Cool Pleasure (What A Pleasure) (1983   71
5s² 5g 6d 7f⁴) Mar 17; $15,000Y; robust, short-backed colt; fifth foal; half-brother
to a minor winner; dam won 5 times at up to 7f as a 3-y-o; quite a modest maiden;
not seen out after June; best form at 5f, but probably stays 7f; races very freely. *G.
Lewis.*

TWICE AS FRESH 4 ch.c. Free State 125–Rose Mullion 82 (Tudor Melody   –
129) (1982 8g⁴ 10fg 8fg 8fg 10fg⁴ 15.8d 1983 12d 12g 11.5fg 12f 16g) fair sort;
plating-class maiden; stays 1¼m; often blinkered. *A. Moore.*

TWICE FRAGRANT 2 b.f. Double Form 130–Scented Air 92 (Derring-Do 131)   92
(1983 5g 5f 5f* 5fg² 5fg 5fg* 5g³) Mar 9; 6,800Y; lengthy, dipped-backed filly;
second foal; half-sister to winning 3-y-o sprinter Play Our Song (by Persian Bold);
dam, 2-y-o 5f winner, is daughter of very fast 1971 2-y-o filly Rose Dubarry;
successful in maiden race at Edinburgh in July and nursery (making all) at Windsor
in September; very good third under 10-lb penalty in nursery at Wolverhampton
later in September; seems unlikely to stay beyond 5f; ran poorly (possibly unsuited
by course) at Chester on fifth outing. *N. Callaghan.*

TWIDALE 10 ch.g. Twilight Alley 133–Leadendale Lady 90 (Damremont 120)   –
(1982 NR 1983 16f) fairly useful jumper at his best; poor maiden on flat. *J.
Wilson.*

TWIN HAPPINESS 2 ch.g. Sweet Revenge 129–Recapped (Sallust 134) (1983   –
6g 7g) Apr 28; IR 500Y; third foal; dam unplaced 3 times in Ireland; last in 2
late-season races at Lingfield; exported to Malaysia. *P. Burgoyne.*

TWIN SPARKLER (USA) 3 ch.f. Effervescing–Split Screen (Silent Screen)   70
(1982 NR 1983 10s 10fg 7h* 7f) $175,000Y; third foal; half-sister to 2 minor
winners; dam, from same family as Junius and Gentle Thoughts, was stakes-placed
winner at up to 6f; sire high-class winner at up to 1½m in USA; ridden by 5-lb
claimer when winning maiden race at Chepstow in July, best effort; evidently better
suited by 7f than by 1¼m. *P. Cole.*

TWO HIGH 4 b.f. High Top 131–Two's Company (Sheshoon 132) (1982 7fg³ 8g³   85
10.2g⁴ 10fg² 10f² 12fg* 12g* 12v* 12s² 10.2d² 1983 10.6v² 12s 12v* 12d 12f) quite
attractive filly; won handicap at Lingfield in May; rather disappointing afterwards
and wasn't seen out after June; suited by 1½m; acts on any going. *F. J.
Houghton.*

TWO MINUTES 4 ch.g. High Line 125–Elm Park (Aberdeen 109) (1982 9g – §
10fg³ 12d* 1983 12d⁴ 13d² 12fg) lightly-made, useful sort; suited by 1½m+;
possibly unsuited by very soft going but acts on any other; tends to sweat up
nowadays; looked none too keen second start; sold 1,600 gns Newmarket
September Sales. *G. Pritchard-Gordon.*

TWO UP 2 b.g. Auction Ring 123–Dance Away (Red God 128§) (1983 6fg 7f 6f 5g³ 79
6fg) Apr 10; IR 15,000F, 20,000Y; robust, rangy gelding; brother to 2 winners,
including useful 1981 2-y-o 6f winner Risk Taker, and half-brother to several
winners; dam fairly useful Irish 2-y-o 5f winner; moderate maiden; best effort on
fourth start; should be suited by 6f; sweated up and ran freely second and third
outings; gelded after final appearance. *F. J. Houghton.*

T W S HOMES 2 b.c. Comedy Star 121–Square Note 85 (High Top 131) (1983 6f 61
5fg 6f 6h 7g 7.2g 8fg² 10fg 8f) Apr 14; strong, workmanlike colt; second foal;
half-brother to 13.8f winner Avenita Lady (by Free State); dam 2-y-o 6f winner;
plater; showed form only on seventh outing; suited by 1m; blinkered final
appearance. *B. Richmond.*

TYMAPALI 3 b.c. Native Bazaar 122–The Blessing (Yrrah Jr) (1982 5fg 5g 5d 6s –
1983 7v 5f 5fg 5g 5f 5h 5fg⁴ 6h 5d) lightly-made colt; plating-class sprint maiden;
sold 900 gns Ascot December Sales. *J. Spearing.*

TYNDRUM 3 gr.f. Habat 127–Grilse Run 94 (Stupendous) (1982 5fg² 5g 6f³ 6g 73
6f² 7f³ 7g 1983 8fg³ 8g⁴ 6f² 6f³ 6g* 6d 6g) close-coupled, fair sort; made
virtually all when winning handicap at Yarmouth in September; below best
afterwards; stays at least 7f; acts on firm going; wears blinkers; sold 7,400 gns
Newmarket Autumn Sales. *R. Williams.*

TYPECAST 4 br.g. Tachypous 128–Ile de France 94 (French Beige 127) (1982 7g –
6f³ 6f 9f 1983 7d 6d 6s 6f 5f 6f) workmanlike gelding; good mover; poor sprint
plater; often blinkered; sold 1,200 gns Doncaster September Sales. *D. Yeoman.*

TYPESET 3 b.g. Status Seeker–Folle Remont (Prince Tenderfoot 126) (1982 5g –
5f 5fg 6fg² 6g 5f* 6f² 6g³ 6f³ 6d³ 6g 7fg² 1983 10.2s⁴ 6fg 8f 10.2f) strong,
compact gelding; no worthwhile form in 1983; stays 7f; probably acts on any going;
usually wears blinkers; has run creditably for a 7-lb claimer. *J. Baker.*

TYPHOON POLLY 4 ch.f. Lord Gayle 124–Polinesia (Takawalk II 125) (1982 –
8d³ 8g² 10v⁴ 9d 1983 8d) ex-French filly; smart performer at 3 yrs when in
frame in 3 good races, including Poule d'Essai des Pouliches at Longchamp; ran
moderately in £3,100 event at Brighton in April on only outing of 1983; stayed
1¼m; acted on heavy going; stud. *P. Walwyn.*

TYPO (USA) 2 ch.c. Secretariat–Pearl Necklace (Ambernash) (1983 7fg 8fg) Apr –
26; tall, rather unfurnished colt; first foal; dam, high-class winner of 21 races at up
to 1¼m from 48 starts, was sold for $925,000 carrying this colt; little show in
maiden races at Salisbury and Newmarket in the autumn. *F. J. Houghton.*

TYRANNOS 10 ch.h. Tyrant–Orange Sash (Sica Boy 132) (1982 8h 8fg 11.7g –
1983 10.2g) poor performer; dead. *M. Pipe.*

TYR O'GWIL 3 gr.c. Supreme Sovereign 119–Alidante 65 (Sahib 114) (1982 NR –
1983 7d 8fg) tall colt; first foal; dam plating-class maiden; behind in maiden races;
dead. *K. Brassey.*

TYSANDI 3 ch.f. Sharpen Up 127–Tikki Tavi 92 (Honeyway 125) (1982 5fg³ 5f* 93
5fg² 5fg 5fg 6g³ 6fg² 7d² 1983 6d² 8.2v³ 7f 6f 7f 6s 5f³ 6g) lengthy, fair sort;
excellent 2 lengths second of 11 behind Kirchner in Thirsk Sprint Stakes in May;
rather mixed form afterwards; probably stays 1m, but has the pace to be effective
at shorter distances; acts on any going; blinkered once at 2 yrs; sold to BBA 27,000
gns Newmarket December Sales. *W. Bentley.*

U

UBIQUE (USA) 2 b.c. In Reality–Golden Way (Diplomat Way) (1983 6h² 5fg*) 84
Feb 1; $200,000Y; half-brother to several winners, including La Soufriere and
Explosive Bid (both by Explodent), very useful stakes winners at up to 1m; dam
placed twice from 9 starts; won 15-runner maiden race at Bath in September in
good finish with His Dream; sold Mrs G. Forbes 14,500 gns Newmarket Autumn
Sales for export to Trinidad. *J. Tree.*

UDALE 2 b.f. Park Lane–Maries Girlie (Auld Brig O'Doon 88) (1983 6g 8g) first —
known foal; dam tailed off only start; in rear in Scottish maiden races in the autumn,
on second outing last of 13. *T. Cuthbert.*

ULCOMBE 3 gr.f. Native Admiral–Barmer (Colonist II 126) (1982 NR 1983 —
10.1fg 12g 12d) second foal; dam quite a useful staying chaser; behind in maiden
races. *H. O'Neill.*

ULTIMATE PRIDE (USA) 3 ch.c. Lyphard 132–Classicist (Princequillo) (1982 **97**
6fg 7.6s* 7d 1983 8.2v³) big, rangy, good-looking colt; excellent mover;
accounted for some useful animals when winning Burr Stakes at Lingfield as a
2-y-o; far from disgraced under stiff weight in £7,500 handicap at Haydock in April
on only outing of 1983, making early running and keeping on well to finish 2
lengths third of 7 to Equanaid; gives impression he'll stay beyond 1m; acts on
heavy going. *G. Harwood.*

ULTRASONIC 4 br.g. Prince Tenderfoot 126–Native Charm (Red God 128§) §§
(1982 7g 6s 5fg 6fg 5fg 5f³ 6f 5fg 5f 5fg 6s 6g 1983 6d 6s 8f 6fg³ 7f 6g 5fg⁴ 6f 5f 5f⁴
5f 5fg 7g 6fg 5s) workmanlike gelding; sprint plater; suited by top-of-the-ground;
effective with or without blinkers; sometimes conveyed to start prematurely; has
been unruly in preliminaries; headstrong and isn't one to rely on; sold 410 gns
Doncaster October Sales. *D. Chapman.*

UNBEKNOWN 3 br.f. Most Secret 119–Wits End (Salerno) (1982 5g 5f² 5f 1983 **62**
6d 7s 5g* 5f 7.6fg 6g) smallish, lengthy filly; ran best race when winning handicap
at Hamilton in June; has run respectably over 7f; sometimes blinkered; trained by
R. Woodhouse until after fifth start. *M. W. Easterby.*

UNBRIDLED PLEASURE (USA) 3 b.f. Honest Pleasure–Hempens Song **68**
(Hempen) (1982 5f 1983 7s³ 6d 7fg) quite well-made filly; third in maiden event
at Leicester in March, best effort; will stay 1m. *I. Balding.*

UNCLE DAI 4 ch.g. Import 127–Silver Cherry 69 (Silver Cloud 121) (1982 NR —
1983 6h 8h) tall, slightly hollow-backed gelding; probably of little account
nowadays; blinkered last 3 outings in 1981. *B. Palling.*

UNCLE OLIVER 2 b.c. Monsanto 121–Miss Merlin 79 (Manacle 123) (1983 5g **63**
5s 7d) Apr 19; 4,500Y; rather leggy, workmanlike colt; first foal; dam won twice
over 6f; plating-class maiden; best effort on first outing; off course for 4 months
between second and third; sold 5,400 gns Newmarket Autumn Sales. *H. T. Jones.*

UNDEB 3 ch.g. Winden 109–Spanish Ruler (Indian Ruler 89) (1982 5fg 8s 7g 1983 —
8v 8f) of no account. *M. Bradley.*

UNDERBID 3 ch.c. Sallust 134–Lady Minstrel (Tudor Music 131) (1982 7.6v **85**
1983 8v 10s 10g² 10f* 10.1f² 10f³ 10g) good-topped colt; has a round action; won
maiden race at Pontefract in June, placed at Windsor and Brighton (ladies race),
best subsequent efforts; suited by 1¼m; acts on firm going; seems best in
blinkers; sold 16,500 gns Newmarket Autumn Sales. *I. Balding.*

UNDEREAVES 2 b.c. Thatching 131–Miss Pudge 92 (Green God 128) (1983 6d) — p
Feb 19; 35,000F, 54,000Y; strong, good-topped colt; first foal; dam, sister to very
smart Irish sprinter Baby Brew, stayed 1m but was best at around 6f; 7/1 but
decidedly burly and hopelessly green, well beaten in 16-runner maiden race at
Newbury in October; looks capable of better. *C. Nelson.*

UNDER THE HAMMER 3 b.c. Auction Ring 123–Threadneedlestreet (Bold **80**
Lad, Ire 133) (1982 5.8f⁴ 5g 7d 6g³ 7.2s* 7v* 7d³ 1983 7d 8s 8s 7.3v⁴ 7fg 8f³ 8f³
8.2f² 9f³ 10f 8fg 8.2g 8d*) small, stocky colt; in frame in 5 handicaps before
running on well to beat Axkernish by 1½ lengths in one at York in October
(blinkered first time); stays 9f; acts on any going, but revels in the mud; genuine.
D. Arbuthnot.

UNICHEQ LAD 3 ch.g. Legal Eagle 126–Miragold 73 (Grey Mirage 128) (1982 —
NR 1983 8v 10v 16f) IR 1,000F, 3,600Y; strong, workmanlike gelding; first
produce; dam won twice over 5f at 2 yrs; behind in maiden race and 2 minor events;
sold 950 gns Ascot October Sales. *K. Cunningham-Brown.*

UNIT TENT 5 bl.g. Double-U-Jay 120–Signal Melody 70 (Bleep-Bleep 134) (1982 **43**
11.7fg 12f⁴ 8.3g 10fg 10v 12v 10.2s 1983 10d⁴ 10g 10d³ 10f 10f³ 8f³ 10g 8fg) neat,
quite attractive gelding; plater; stays 1¼m; acts on any going but goes well on
soft; found very little under pressure third start. *G. Lewis.*

UP BROADWAY (USA) 2 b.f. Alleged 138–Sarah Bernhardt (Buckpasser) **69**
(1983 6fg 7f 7g 7s) Mar 28; tall, rather leggy filly; half-sister to Irish 3-y-o 7f
winner Accentor (by The Minstrel) and 3 winners in USA, one stakes placed; dam
unraced daughter of best 2-y-o filly of 1967 Queen of the Stage; plating-class
maiden; should stay 1m; acts on any going. *R. Armstrong.*

UPLAND GOOSE 2 ch.f. Porto Bello 118–Bombay Duck 65 (Ballyciptic 122)   –
(1983 5fg 7fg) Mar 3; big, rather plain filly; second foal; half-sister to 7f and 1m
winner Bombil (by The Brianstan); dam won over 13f; in rear in maiden races at
Chester in July and August. *P. Rohan.*

UPLANDS MAYBLOSSOM 2 b.f. Native Bazaar 122–Woodland Promise   –
(Philemon 119) (1983 6g 7.6fg) Feb 12; sister to very useful sprinter Crofthall;
dam unplaced on flat and over hurdles; little worthwhile form in autumn maiden
events at Goodwood (backward) and Lingfield. *S. Matthews.*

UPLANDS PARK 4 b.c. Rheingold 137–God Sent 75 (Red God 128§) (1982   **86**
10.4g2 11f 10.4fg3 10g2 8f 9g2 8.5fg* 8f4 8s4 8s3 8.2s 1983 10v3 10v4 8v 8s 8.5g*
8fg 10g* 8f 10fg 10fg3 10f 8g 11s* 10g) rangy colt; fairly useful handicapper on his
day; decisively won at Epsom in June, Lingfield in July and Ayr in September; beat
River of Kings by 3 lengths in Ladbrokes Ayrshire Handicap on last-named; stays
11f; acts on any going; ran moderately in blinkers once in 1982; inconsistent; sold
to BBA 15,500 gns Newmarket Autumn Sales. *C. Brittain.*

UPLANDS SO SO 3 b.g. Native Bazaar 122–So Unlikely 60 (Blast 125) (1982 6f   –
5.3g 6f 1983 6v 5v 6s 7v 5s 6fg 5fg 5f) leggy, workmanlike gelding; poor form in
varied races, including sellers; blinkered last 2 starts; trained by P. M. Taylor first
5 outings; sold 600 gns Ascot October Sales. *S. Matthews.*

UP THE ANTE (USA) 3 b.c. Properantes–Mini Midi Maxi (Promised Land)   **67**
(1982 6f 7g 7fg3 8s3 7s 1983 12v 10v 12f 16g3 14f) lengthy, quite attractive colt;
has a round action; quite a moderate maiden; suited by a good test of stamina; sold
to CBA 4,500 gns Newmarket Autumn Sales. *G. Wragg.*

UPTOWN 3 b.g. Creetown 123–Groovy Granny 69 (Rheingold 137) (1982 NR   –
1983 8d 12fg 10.1fg) 3,600F, 5,200Y; first produce; dam stayed well; plating-class
maiden; best run at 1½m; sold 2,000 gns Newmarket Autumn Sales. *B. Hanbury.*

UR-NINA 2 b.f. Derrylin 115–Susan Slummers (Song 132) (1983 6fg) Mar 31;   –
5,000Y; workmanlike filly; second foal; dam never ran; backward, in rear in
20-runner maiden race at Newmarket in October. *R. Armstrong.*

V

VACANI 4 b.f. Dance In Time–Italian Sky 94 (Skymaster 126) (1982 9s 1983 8d)   –
leggy filly; poor maiden; has given trouble at start. *E. Incisa.*

VACARME (USA) 2 ch.c. Lyphard 132–Virunga 115 (Sodium 128) (1983 6f*   **118**
6f*(dis) 6g* 6fg3)
Sponsorship from Overseas Containers Ltd boosted the value of the first prize
for Goodwood's Richmond Stakes to £34,760, making it the season's sixth most
valuable race for two-year-olds in Britain. The new sponsors certainly received
value for money: the disqualification of first-past-the-post Vacarme, who started at
3/1 on, was one of the season's longest-running talking points. The incident that led
to Vacarme's disqualification occurred after Piggott on Vacarme had got himself into
a position where it appeared that only barging a way through could save him from
defeat. Hopelessly pocketed at the distance, but with his mount full of running,
Piggott sat and sat, awaiting an opening, until, showing great skill, he managed to
find a way through in the closing stages as one of the leaders Pacific King began to
falter. Bearing over sharply to the rails, in front of Pacific King, Vacarme produced
a fast finishing flourish to snatch the race almost in the shadow of the post. He showed
an excellent turn of foot—and also displayed considerable courage and dexterity—
to win virtually without coming off the bridle by three quarters of a length and a
length from Creag-An-Sgor and Godstone. How far Vacarme would have won given
a trouble-free run and made to show the full measure of his superiority over the
opposition is a matter for conjecture, but we think few would argue with the
contention that it would have been upwards of three lengths. At the subsequent
stewards' inquiry, held when Godstone's rider objected to Creag-An-Sgor for
bumping and boring inside the last furlong, Vacarme was found to have interfered
with fifth-placed Pacific King. The stewards considered Piggott guilty of careless
riding and suspended him for five days. The objection to Creag-An-Sgor was
sustained, but interference by him was deemed accidental. The amended result
read: Godstone first, Creag-An-Sgor second, Indigo Jones third and Pacific King
fourth.
Under the terms of the now-infamous rule 153 the stewards at Goodwood had
no option but to place Vacarme behind Pacific King once they had decided that any
interference was the result of careless or improper riding. Rule 153 was amended

Erroll Stakes, Ascot—Vacarme trots up from Hoyer

slightly in 1983, giving stewards more flexibility when dealing with cases of careless or improper riding. Mandatory disqualification to last place no longer applies in such cases—although it remains for reckless riding—but the stewards must still place the horse behind any horses with which it has interfered, *irrespective of whether such interference has had any effect on the result of the race.* We have sought, through various channels over the years, to persuade the Jockey Club to reform rule 153 and have covered the subject fully in previous Annuals—most recently in the essay on Nureyev in *Racehorses of 1980*—and we have no intention of wearying readers by dealing with the matter in detail again. Suffice to repeat that, in our view, the disciplining of jockeys for breaches of the rule and consideration of the equity of a race-result which may have been affected by interference, are two quite different matters which should be dealt with separately. Vacarme's disqualification was an illustration of the unsatisfactory nature of some parts of rule 153. Vacarme, much the best in the field on the day, won manifestly on merit—Pacific King's effort was petering out when Vacarme interfered with him (minimally in our view)—and equity could have been served only by leaving Vacarme's placing unaltered. If jockeys transgress in their riding, they should be disciplined for so doing by penalties that fall upon them, and them alone, by fines or suspensions of severity appropriate to the nature and the iniquity of the offences. Alterations of the placings should be made only with a view to restoration of the validity of the result. It is unjust to demote a winner or placed horse, depriving its innocent owner—and backers of the horse—of their rewards, on account of an incident in running which did not affect the result of the race.

Even before he contested the Richmond Stakes, Vacarme was widely regarded as a likely candidate for top honours among the two-year-olds. He had made a most impressive debut in the Erroll Stakes at Ascot in June, travelling strongly throughout and moving smoothly through the field when given a little rein to win with plenty in hand by six lengths from another newcomer Hoyer. Vacarme was put by for an autumn campaign after Goodwood and he was next seen out in the Mill Reef Stakes at Newbury in mid-September, his task being made easier when Double Schwartz was withdrawn on race-day because of a high temperature.

Mill Reef Stakes, Newbury—Vacarme beats Fawzi

Starting at 7/2 on, Vacarme won decisively by two and a half lengths and the same from Fawzi and Water Moccasin but Piggott had to nudge him along after taking the lead and Vacarme didn't win with the authority most had anticipated. His trainer explained afterwards that he had been fairly easy on Vacarme since Goodwood and expected him to benefit from the race. After the Mill Reef Stakes Vacarme was quoted as short as 7/1 in ante-post betting on the Two Thousand Guineas, his trainer announcing the William Hill-sponsored Middle Park and Dewhurst as further targets for him in the interim. Vacarme ran only in the Middle Park, in which he finished a disappointing third to Creag-An-Sgor and Superlative, beaten a little over a length and a half by the winner; Mercer, who took the mount on Vacarme after a widely-publicised rift between Piggott and Vacarme's owner, rode a waiting race and arguably asked a little too much of Vacarme although his challenge was being held throughout the last hundred yards.

		Northern Dancer	Nearctic
	Lyphard	(b 1961)	Natalma
	(b 1969)	Goofed	Court Martial
Vacarme (USA)		(ch 1960)	Barra
(ch.c. Mar 26, 1981)		Sodium	Psidium
	Virunga	(b 1963)	Gambade
	(b 1970)	Vale	Verrieres
		(ch 1959)	Calliopsis

On what he has achieved in public so far the much-vaunted Vacarme is not up to classic-winning standard, but those who rushed to back him for the Two Thousand Guineas before his failure in the Middle Park might still get a run for their money if, as we expect, Vacarme shows improvement when given the opportunity to race over distances more in keeping with his pedigree. We were surprised that he was never tried beyond six furlongs as a two-year-old. Vacarme's sire Lyphard—who sires quite a few animals who stay a mile and a half—won at a mile as a two-year-old and over a mile and a quarter at three; while Vacarme's dam, the quite stoutly-bred Virunga, unraced at two, stayed a mile and a half. The very attractive Virunga, a half-sister to Champion Stakes winner Vitiges, was unfortunate enough to be foaled in the same year as Allez France and Dahlia (who beat her into third in the Prix de Diane) but she was genuine and consistent and won three races at around a mile and a quarter as a three-year-old, including the Prix de Malleret, and came second in the Prix Saint-Alary (to Dahlia) and the Yorkshire Oaks (to Mysterious); Virunga gained a further success at a mile and a quarter as a four-year-old. Two earlier foals out of Virunga stayed well: the fairly useful Video Tape (by Cannonade), trained on the flat by Cecil, won over a mile as a two-year-old and subsequently achieved distinction as a hurdler in France; the three-year-old Vosges (by Youth), who didn't see a racecourse at two, proved very well suited by a mile and a half and finished third to Sharaya in the Prix Vermeille. The quite attractive, short-legged, good-bodied Vacarme will stay at least a mile and a quarter and has good prospects, judged on his pedigree, of getting a mile and a half. An exceptionally good mover, he has done all his racing so far on a sound surface. *H. Cecil.*

VACHTI (FR) 3 b.f. Crystal Palace 132–Valseuse (Tyrant) (1982 7v 8s⁴ 8v 1983   **114** 10.5s 10.5v 8s 10.5s² 8fg 10fg* 10.5d* 10f³ 10fg⁴ 12s) French filly; second living foal; dam unraced half-sister to smart French sprinter River Rose; took a long time to find her form but developed into a very useful filly; won handicaps at Evry and Saint-Cloud (130,000 francs event) in July, latter in good style by 4 lengths; ran well in much better company afterwards, finishing less than a length fourth to Sharaya in Prix de la Nonette on same course and just over 3 lengths fifth to Sharaya again in Trusthouse Forte Prix Vermeille at Longchamp again; needs 1¼m+; acts on any going. *G. Brillet, France.*

VAGRANT MAID (USA) 3 b.f. Honest Pleasure–Vigia 115 (Tiziano) (1982 7g   **85** 1983 10.2v⁴ 12f² 12.2f* 12.2f² 12f² 10.1fg³ 10fg) strong filly; won maiden event at Catterick in July by 4 lengths from Pine Ridge (pair 10 lengths clear); second twice afterwards, not looking entirely enthusiastic on first occasion; suited by 1½m; probably acts on any going, but seems well suited by firm; sold to BBA 125,000 gns Newmarket December Sales. *H. Cecil.*

VAIGLY REL 3 ch.c. Relkino 131–Dervaig 90 (Derring-Do 131) (1982 6g 5d 1983   **79** 8v* 8f 8.2f³ 8f 8d) useful sort; won maiden race at Warwick in May; ran best subsequent race third start; stays 1m; acts on any going; sold to P. Mitchell 9,000 gns Newmarket Autumn Sales. *M. Stoute.*

VAIGLY STAR 4 b.f. Star Appeal 133–Dervaig 90 (Derring-Do 131) (1982 7fg⁴   **114** 6f² 6f² 6f² 5f³ 5g 6f* 6g⁴ 5d² 1983 6v² 6f 6fg) compact, good-quartered filly; good walker; smart sprinter; looked sure to win when leading 1f out in Duke of York Stakes in May but was caught near finish and beaten ½ length by Vorvados; never going well when sixth to Sylvan Barbarosa in Cork and Orrery Stakes at Royal Ascot in June and in rear behind Habibti in William Hill July Cup at Newmarket; best at 6f; acted on any going; visits Kings Lake. *M. Stoute.*

VAIN DEB 4 b.f. Gay Fandango 132–Saint Mildred 89 (Saint Crespin III 132)   **66** (1982 7fg 7g⁴ 8g* 8fg² 8.2fg* 8g⁴ 8d* 8fg 9s* 1983 8v 8s³ 9v 10fg² 8f* 8.2f* 8fg⁴ 8fg⁴ 9d 9d) sparely-made filly; won handicaps at Carlisle in June and Hamilton in July; stays 1¼m; acts on any going; blinkered third outing; has run respectably for an apprentice and when sweating up; genuine. *P. Haslam.*

VAISSEAU (USA) 3 ch.c. Far North 120–Valhalla (New Chapter 106) (1982 7d*   **–** 7d² 1983 10.5f) lengthy colt; looked promising as a 2-y-o when winning maiden race at Leicester and finishing second in Houghton Stakes at Newmarket; had stiffish task, looked a bit light and ran far too freely when behind in John Smith's Magnet Cup (Handicap) at York in July on only outing of 1983; bred to stay 1¼m; sent to France. *H. Cecil.*

VAL CLIMBER (USA) 5 b.g. Val de l'Orne 130–Hardy Climber (Never Bend)   **61** (1982 12d 11.7d³ 16fg 12fg* 1983 12d 12s 15.5v 14fg² 14.7f³ 12f⁴ 14f* 14f* 14f⁴ 18fg 16g) tall, close-coupled gelding; won handicaps at Yarmouth in July and August; stays 1¾m; acts on any going; has run well when sweating up; blinkered third start; found nothing under pressure fifth outing and is suited by waiting tactics. *D. Oughton.*

VALDAMOSA 2 b.f. Jolly Me 114–Spaniard's Darling (Darling Boy 124) (1983 7f   **–** 6fg 7g 7f) May 31; has an enlarged near hock; bad plater. *T. Kersey.*

VALEDICTION 3 b.f. Town Crier 119–Golden Thoughts 86 (Golden Cloud)   **71** (1982 6fg 6g 1983 8.5d 10f 12fg² 12f 10fg 14fg² 16d 12.2g) close-coupled, rather lightly-made filly; excellent mover; second in maiden race at Haydock in August and apprentice event at Newmarket in September, easily best efforts; evidently suited by 1½m+; doesn't look particularly genuine. *H. Candy.*

VALERIO (USA) 3 b.c. Raise A Cup–Erin O'Connell (Dondeen 123) (1982 7g 1983 10fg[3] 10.2f[2] 10f 8f* 9f[2] 7fg* 8g* 8g[4] 8fg) well-made, attractive colt; won maiden race at Doncaster, minor event at Goodwood and small handicap at Yarmouth, getting up on line to beat Teleprompter by a head on last-named course in September; in frame most other starts, including in an apprentice event; stays 1¼m; acts on firm going; ran moderately third start. *L. Cumani.* **89**

VALIANT DANCER 2 ch.f. Northfields–So Valiant 80 (So Blessed 130) (1983 5d[3] 6s 7fg 7f 8.2h 7g 6fg) Apr 24; 7,000Y; rather sparely-made filly; half-sister to 3 winners, including fairly useful but temperamental 1979 2-y-o 5f winner Heroic Air (by Song); dam 2-y-o 5f winner; poor form in varied company; stays 1m; blinkered final outing. *Peter Taylor.* **53**

VALIYAR 4 b.c. Red God 128§–Val Divine (Val de Loir 133) (1982 8fg[2] 8s* 8d* 10g 1983 7s* 8v[2] 8.5s[3] 8fg*) **129**

The Vanian brothers have good reason to congratulate themselves for purchasing Valiyar from the Aga Khan at the end of the colt's three-year-old campaign. An extremely well-bred individual, Valiyar had shown useful form trained by the late Francois Mathet, winning a maiden race at Longchamp and an 80,000 francs event at Saint-Cloud before finishing a respectable seventh of ten to What A Guest in the Prix Eugene Adam, but nothing he had achieved suggested he would develop into probably the best older miler in Europe. His career, following those of Lucky Wednesday, Gunner B and Belmont Bay, was yet another example of the extraordinary success Cecil has had over the years with colts that have come to him from other stables.

Valiyar's four-year-old season turned out to be all too brief, ending with a sparkling victory in the Queen Anne Stakes at Royal Ascot. His three starts prior to the Queen Anne had resulted in a single success, in the Leicestershire Stakes at Leicester in April in which he faced one smart, if inconsistent, opponent, Jester, and a bunch of second-raters. He scored with great ease, leading on the bridle two furlongs out and quickening away to account for Jester by five lengths. This display impressed us greatly despite the generally inferior quality of the opposition, and though up against much better horses in the Lockinge Stakes at Newbury the following month Valiyar looked to have reasonable prospects of taking a hand in the finish. Coming from behind tends to be more difficult on heavy ground than on a sound surface, and at Newbury, where conditions were exceptionally testing, Valiyar had an almost impossible task in the last furlong and a half. When the front-running Noalcoholic went clear with over a quarter of a mile to go Valiyar lay fourth and a furlong later he still had some six lengths to make up on the leader;

Queen Anne Stakes, Ascot—Valiyar is most impressive in beating Montekin

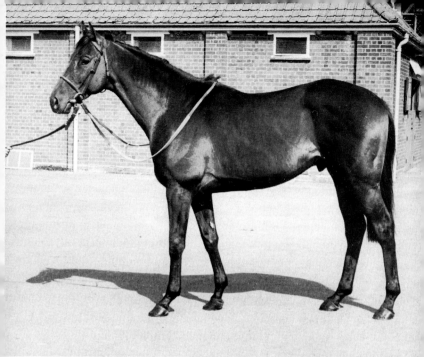

Mr Garo Vanian's "Valiyar"

though staying on powerfully and cutting back the deficit as Noalcoholic tired in the closing stages, he went down by one and a half lengths, finishing clear of the remainder.

The front-running tactics Piggott employed on Valiyar in the Pacemaker Diomed Stakes at Epsom on Derby Day next time failed completely since once the colt lost the lead over a furlong out he was left behind by Lofty and Aragon, coming home seven lengths third to the former, and with Piggott deciding to ride Cecil's other runner, Ivano, in the Queen Anne Eddery came in for the mount on Valiyar. Meeting eight opponents besides his stable-companion, including three that had run at Newbury, Noalcoholic, Montekin and Rebollino, Valiyar was once more ridden from behind, staying last to beyond halfway as Noalcoholic made the running. Given a little rein after being switched to the outside, he produced a delightfully smooth run that took him past Ivano then Noalcoholic at the furlong pole and thereafter Eddery scarcely had to move a muscle as Valiyar cruised home by a length and a half from the strongly-ridden Montekin. Noalcoholic finished six lengths further back in third with Ivano fourth. The Queen Anne suggested Valiyar would be a formidable competitor in the rest of the season's top mile races, but to the regret of everyone save, we suspect, the connections of the other good milers he did not have the chance to use his fine turn of foot again. A blood disorder kept him out of the Sussex Stakes, won by Noalcoholic, and with Cecil unable to get him right he also missed the Waterford Crystal Mile, won by Montekin, and the Queen Elizabeth II Stakes. In the autumn the announcement came that he had been retired and would be standing alongside Posse and Glint of Gold at the Derisley Wood Stud in 1984 at a fee of £6,000 plus £6,000 October 1st.

Valiyar, who stayed a mile and acted well on fast ground, is bred in the purple. His sire Red God was tremendously successful as a stallion, siring some fifty stakes winners, and colts from this line, for example Yellow God, Nebbiolo, Pampapaul

883

and Blushing Groom, have also done well at stud even if some of them have been short lived. On the dam's side Valiyar comes from a magnificent family. Val Divine, successful in a small race at around a mile and a quarter at Maisons-Laffitte, produced three winners before Valiyar, the best of them the top-class Vayrann who gained what turned out to be a controversial victory in the 1981 Champion Stakes.

	Red God (ch 1954)	Nasrullah (b 1940)	Nearco / Mumtaz Begum
		Spring Run (b 1948)	Menow / Boola Brook
Valiyar (b.c. 1979)		Val de Loir (b 1959)	Vieux Manoir / Vali
	Val Divine (b 1971)	Pola Bella (br 1965)	Darius / Bella Paola

The grandam Pola Bella and third dam Bella Paola were both first rate on the track—Pola Bella won the French One Thousand Guineas and Prix du Moulin, Bella Paola a host of top races including the One Thousand Guineas, Oaks and Champion Stakes—and both proved to be good broodmares. Pola Bella is also the grandam of Persepolis, arguably the best French three-year-old over middle distances in 1982, and Bella Paola produced eight winners, notably the good French middle-distance performers Beau Persan and Bubunia. With his pedigree and his impressive looks—he is a big, strong, good-bodied, handsome colt—Valiyar has the makings of a successful stallion. *H. Cecil.*

VALKYRIE 2 b.f. Bold Lad (Ire) 133–Sarissa 105 (Reform 132) (1983 5s⁴ 5v* 6g³ 5f³ 5f² 5h³) Apr 29; strong, well-made, quite attractive filly; second foal; half-sister to smart middle-distance performer Sabre Dance (by Dance In Time); dam won over 5f and 6f at 2 yrs; won maiden race at Warwick in May; disappointing favourite in nursery at Nottingham in August on final appearance; best form at 5f; acted on any going; to be mated with Cure The Blues. *H. Cecil.*   **87**

VALLEE DES ROSES 4 b.f. Dubassoff–Double Powered (Double Jump 131) (1982 NR 1983 13.4fg) third foal; dam daughter of very useful High Powered; behind in maiden race at Chester in July. *M. Eckley.*   —

VALLEY MILLS 3 ch.g. Red Alert 127–Haunting 79 (Lord Gayle 124) (1982 6g 6g 6fg⁴ 7d 7g³ 6d² 7g 6s 1983 8d 6v 6d³ 7.6fg 6g 6g 6fg 6g) lengthy, strong gelding; placed in varied company, including claiming; stays 7f; acts on a soft surface; wears blinkers; sold 750 gns Doncaster October Sales. *S. Wiles.*   —

VALOROSO 3 b.g. Young Emperor 133–My Plucky Lady 64 (Cash and Courage 116) (1982 6g 6fg 1983 6g 8.2fg) neat gelding; little worthwhile form. *C. Thornton.*   —

VAL'S DELIGHT 3 ch.f. Cawston's Clown 113–Sweet Hortense 71 (King's Troop 118) (1982 5fg 5f 5fg 5fg 1983 8g 9d 7fg 6f 8g 7fg) leggy filly; poor plater; has twice worn blinkers; sold 520 gns Newmarket September Sales. *C. Spares.*   —

VAL'S PRIDE 2 b.f. Owen Dudley 121–Isomer 60 (Runnymede 123) (1983 5v 5s 6fg 6f⁴ 7fg* 7fg 7g⁴ 8fg) Mar 11; lengthy, lightly-made, plain filly; third foal; dam won sellers over 6f and 7f; plater; attracted no bid after showing much improved form to win 8-runner event at Newmarket in August by 3 lengths; 1¾ lengths fourth of 19 to Stormy Gulf in claiming race at Yarmouth the following month; well suited by 7f; best form on a sound surface; ran poorly for 7-lb claimer sixth start; blinkered fourth outing. *M. Ryan.*   **61**

VALUABLE WITNESS (USA) 3 b.g. Val de l'Orne 130–Friendly Witness (Northern Dancer) (1982 NR 1983 10s* 14d² 16f 14.6fg⁴ 16fg² 14d*) $40,000Y; lengthy, quite attractive gelding; has a round action; half-brother to 3 winners, including useful Canadian stakes winner Leading Witness (by Mr Leader), successful at up to 1¼m; dam won over 1m; successful in maiden race at Salisbury in May and minor event at York in October, making all when odds on in latter; second in between in handicaps at Sandown (went down by neck to Jowoody) and Ascot (no match for 2-length winner Another Sam); stays well; acts on a firm surface but is probably ideally suited by some give in the ground; useful, and could well win another race or 2. *J. Tree.*   **109**

VAMMELERTS QUILP 3 ch.f. Orange Bay 131–Friendly Chorus 71 (Be Friendly 130) (1982 6f 1983 8f 10.1fg) plain filly; last or last-but-one in maiden races; sold to NBA 620 gns Newmarket Autumn Sales. *D. Thom.*   —

VANDA JOAQUIM 3 gr.f. Busted 134–Joking 81 (Ribero 126) (1982 NR 1983 8d 10f 12fg) 30,000Y; rather sparely-made filly; third foal; dam, half-sister to

Queen's Hussar, won over 1½m; showed signs of ability first 2 starts but ran poorly on her only other. *M. Jarvis.*

VAN DYKE BROWN 2 b.c. Gay Mecene 128–Latin Melody 109 (Tudor Melody 129) (1983 7fg 7f 7d* 8g²) strong, rangy, attractive colt; good walker and mover; half-brother to useful 5f and 1m winner Nelbi and useful 1978 2-y-o sprinter Innini (both by Cavo Doro); dam best at sprint distances; showed much improved form when winning 13-runner maiden race at Yarmouth in September by 5 lengths from Marcosfables; odds on, beaten 2½ lengths (value 1½ lengths) by Ashgar in 5-runner minor event at Leicester the following month; stays 1m; suited by an easy surface. *H. Cecil.*   **94**

VAN EYCK (USA) 2 ch.c. Dewan–Exclusive Secret (Exclusive Native) (1983 5v 5s* 5s 7f 6fg) Feb 6; $85,000Y; big, well-made colt; first foal; dam unraced half-sister to Triumphant, a very smart winner at up to 9f; won maiden race at Lingfield in May; showed little otherwise; blinkered when last of 8 in nursery at Windsor in August on final appearance; should stay 7f; acts on soft going; sold T. Curtin 6,600 gns Newmarket Autumn Sales. *G. Harwood.*   **76**

VANISHING TRICK 2 gr.f. Silly Season 127–Flitterdale 81 (Abwah 118) (1983 5f 5fg² 5g² 5f* 5g* 6d⁴) Mar 17; strong filly; second foal; half-sister to 3-y-o 1m winner Playtex (by Be Friendly); dam won twice over 5f at 2 yrs; won maiden race at Hamilton in August and nursery at Edinburgh in September; should stay 1m; acts on firm going and a soft surface. *J. Etherington.*   **83**

VARUSHKA 2 b.f. Sharpen Up 127–Varishkina 103 (Derring-Do 131) (1983 5fg⁴) Apr 19; well-grown filly; dam useful from 7f to 10.5f; 5 lengths fourth of 7 to Chapel Cottage in minor event at York in June. *J. Etherington.*   **74** p

VATICAN WAY (USA) 3 br.f. J. O. Tobin 130–Gayway (Sir Gaylord) (1982 6fg³ 7.6v³ 7d³ 1983 6s* 7fg² 8f² 7f* 7f² 7f²) lengthy filly; not the best of movers; won maiden race at Pontefract in May; second in 5 handicaps afterwards, and at Doncaster in July when apprentice ridden was awarded race after going down by a short head to Rely On Guy; stays 1m; acts on any going. *M. Stoute.*   **90**

VEDUTA 3 b.f. High Top 131–Broad Horizon 89 (Blakeney 126) (1982 NR 1983 7d 9d* 10g³ 8f 10f4) 40,000Y; well-made filly; good walker; first foal; dam, 2-y-o 7f winner who stayed 1¾m, is closely related to Rarity; won minor event at Wolverhampton in May and was in frame in similar race at Newbury (good third to Beach Light) and Virginia Stakes at Newcastle (had stiff task); last in a handicap fourth outing; stays 1¼m; tends to flash her tail. *H. Candy.*   **84**

VEE BEE 4 b.c. High Award 119–Ritual 79 (Right Royal V 135) (1982 8g 5g 6f 5fg 6f 5s 6s 6s 1983 5v³ 6v³ 7s⁴ 6fg 6fg 5f³ 5f⁴ 5fg 6g⁴ 6fg* 6f*) robust colt; poor mover; won handicaps at Folkestone (apprentices) and Redcar in October; stays 7f; acts on any going; blinkered fourth and fifth starts; suitable mount for an inexperienced rider. *D. Leslie.*   **59**

VEILLEUSE (USA) 2 gr.f. Halo–Via Maris (Dancer's Image) (1983 5d 5fg⁴) Apr 20; smallish, robust filly; second foal; half-sister to 3-y-o Vestal Queen (by Val de l'Orne); dam very useful winner at up to 9f in USA; showed little in early-season maiden events at Thirsk and Leicester; bred to require further; sent to France. *H. Cecil.*   **62**

VELA ROSSA 2 b.f. Julio Mariner 127–Rudella 95 (Raffingora 130) (1983 9g 7s) May 19; 2,100F; big, short-coupled filly; third foal; dam won over 5f at 2 yrs; modest seventh of 18 in poor maiden race at Leicester in October, second outing. *N. Gaselee.*   **–**

VELESO 5 b.g. Jimsun 121–Dracaena 63 (Double Jump 131) (1982 15.5fg 14fg 10.2s⁴ 1983 16v⁴ 17.1v³ 18.8v⁴) staying handicapper; acts on heavy going; sometimes sweats up; sometimes blinkered. *J. King.*   **–**

VELOCIDAD 3 ch.f. Balidar 133–Sun Lamp 76 (Pall Mall 132) (1982 5g² 6f 5fg² 5fg⁴ 5g 1983 6s 11.7v 8f⁴ 7fg³ 8d) tall, leggy filly; in frame in lady riders handicap at Redcar and minor event at Salisbury in June; promises to stay 1m but is unlikely to get middle distances; acts on a firm surface; ran poorly in blinkers on final appearance in 1982; sometimes bandaged in front. *M. Ryan.*   **67**

VELVET EXPRESS 2 b.f. Run The Gantlet–Drawing Room Car (Chingacgook 128) (1983 7.6d 10fg) Apr 26; 28,000F; half-sister to several winners in France, including 1m winner Lip Service (by Lyphard); dam, placed twice over 1¼m in France, is half-sister to smart French filly Sybarite; behind in sizeable fields of maidens at Lingfield and Nottingham in October. *P. Cole.*   **–**

VELVET SCOTER 3 b.f. Haveroid 122–March Poulet (March Past 124) (1982   –
NR 1983 7f 7f 14.7f) lengthy filly; half-sister to several winners, including useful
sprinter Golden Mallard (by Goldhill); dam of no account; in rear in maiden races;
sold 460 gns Doncaster October Sales. *J. Carr.*

VENETIAN PRINCESS 2 ch.f. Porto Bello 118–Ventrex 95 (Henry the   –
Seventh 125) (1983 6fg) Mar 7; second foal; dam won over 1¾m and 2m; 33/1 and
decidedly green, started slowly and swerved violently right before halfway when
behind in 20-runner maiden race at Newmarket in October. *J. Winter.*

VENJA 5 ch.h. Native Bazaar 122–Avengeress 73 (Aggressor 130) (1982 11.7fg   –
7g 7.6g³ 1983 11.7fg) leggy, light-framed, lengthy horse; plater; stays 1m;
probably acts on any going. *A. Moore.*

VEN MATRERO (USA) 3 b.g. Advocator–Short Cake (Fleet Nasrullah) (1982   **94**
NR 1983 10s 10fg 10f* 10.1f* 10.1f* 12g 12d 12fg 10fg³ 10fg 10g² 10fg) $30,000Y;
strong, rangy, good sort; good walker; half-brother to several minor winners; dam,
unplaced in 12 starts, is half-sister to 2 stakes winners; improved in summer and
won maiden race at Folkestone (by 12 lengths after making all) and 2 minor events
at Windsor in space of a fortnight; placed in handicaps at Ascot and Sandown in
October, best subsequent efforts; best at 1¼m (finished last on all 3 attempts at
1½m); acts well on firm going. *G. Harwood.*

VENTIMIGLIA 2 ch.f. Bruni 132–Princess of Verona 95 (King's Leap 111) (1983   –
6g 7g 7.6d) Mar 1; third foal; dam, half-sister to Music Boy, was best at 5f; remote
eighth of 20 in maiden race at Lingfield in October, third outing and only sign of
ability. *J. Sutcliffe.*

VERACITY 2 ch.f. Hittite Glory 125–Falls of Lora 107 (Scottish Rifle 127) (1983   **56**
5fg 5f 7f 6fg 7g) Apr 9; 1,600Y; tall, short-backed filly; first foal; dam won from 6f
to 1½m; poor maiden; best effort on final appearance; will probably stay 1m;
blinkered fourth outing. *M. Usher.*

VERAMENTE 8 b.g. Sassafras 135–Quelle Blague (Red God 128§) (1982 10.6f   –
12fg 16d 10f 1983 10d 12s) poor plater nowadays; has been tried in blinkers;
suitable mount for an inexperienced rider; has worn a tongue strap. *D. Grissell.*

VERBARIUM (USA) 3 br.c. Verbatim–Havre (Mister Gus) (1982 7g³ 7f* 7fg⁴   **71**
7f 8g 1983 8s 8s 8f 10.8g 8f 12d 10.5d² 10f³) close-coupled, workmanlike colt;
placed at York (£4,000 seller) and Redcar in October, best efforts for a long time;
suited by 1¼m; acts on any going, except possibly very soft; sold to BBA 8,000
gns Newmarket Autumn Sales. *P. Cole.*

VERCHININA 2 ch.f. Star Appeal 133–Sociable (Be Friendly 130) (1983 6fg 8fg   **78**
8g⁴) Feb 3; 22,000Y; rangy, quite attractive filly; half-sister to fairly useful sprint
handicappers Fashion Club (by Tribal Chief) and Geary's For Strip (by Mansingh);
dam ran only twice; quite a modest maiden; stays 1m; acts on a firm surface; raced
with head in air on final outing. *B. Hills.*

VERNAIR (USA) 2 ch.f. Super Concorde 128–What A Pannie (What A   **73**
Pleasure) (1983 7f 6f² 5fg⁴) Feb 28; $90,000F, $107,000Y; fair sort; first foal;
dam won 6 times at up to 6f at 3 yrs in USA; staying-on 4 lengths second of 13 to
Collegian in maiden race at Yarmouth in August, best effort; needs further than 5f,
and should stay 1m; acts on firm going. *J. Hindley.*

VERRIA (USA) 3 ch.f. Blushing Groom 131–Via Venise (Shoemaker 121) (1982   **118**
8f* 8s⁴ 1983 8f* 9g* 8fg 10fg) French filly; half-sister to very useful 1980 French
2-y-o 6f to 1m winner Vorias (by Cannonade); dam, useful winner at up to 1½m,
comes from same family as Val de Loir; won 100,000 francs race at Chantilly in June
and 5-runner Prix Chloe at Evry in July, in latter race quickening up impressively to
beat Alexandrie by 4 lengths; towards rear subsequently in Prix d'Astarte and Prix
de la Nonette, both at Deauville in August, better effort when eighth of 13 to
Sharaya in latter; stays 9f; acts on any going; sent to USA. *F. Boutin, France.*

VICEROY LAD 2 ch.g. Miami Springs 121–Lilac Lass (Virginia Boy 106) (1983   **91**
5s 5s 5.8s 7f 6fg³ 7.2fg³ 7f* 7.2g³ 7g 7g³ 7fg³ 7fg) Mar 26; IR 4,000Y; strong,
good-topped, fair sort; first foal; dam never ran; showed quite modest form until
making all (clearly well suited by forcing tactics) to win 8-runner nursery at Epsom
in August running away by 7 lengths; stays 7f well; acts on firm going; usually
wears blinkers (ducked left and right when running moderately without them on
eighth start); gelded after final appearance. *R. Hannon.*

VICEROY LASS 2 b.f. Certingo–Goldfoot (Prince Tenderfoot 126) (1983 6s 5f   –
7f 6f 7.6d) Apr 21; IR 2,800Y; sparely-made filly; fourth foal; half-sister to a
winner in Belgium; dam never ran; well beaten in maiden races; blinkered fourth
outing. *R. Hannon.*

VICEROY PRINCESS 3 gr.f. Godswalk 130–Black Crow 72 (Sea Hawk II 131) –
(1982 5f 5f 7d 7fg* 8d 1983 7.6v 8f) neat filly; showed only form when winning a
seller as a 2-y-o; suited by 7f; acts on a firm surface. *C. Williams.*

VICKIDORA 2 gr.f. Cavo Doro 124–Vicki Ann (Floribunda 136) (1983 7.6fg) Apr –
16; half-sister to fair 1976 2-y-o 5f winner Rushley Bay (by Crooner); dam of little
account; tailed-off last of 19 in maiden race at Lingfield in October. *H. Westbrook.*

VICTORIAN PRINCE 3 ch.g. English Prince 129–Victorian Habit 101 (Habitat –
134) (1982 5s² 5f³ 6d 7f 5s 8d 7s 1983 12v 8d 6f 8f 13.8f) short-coupled gelding;
disappointing maiden; well beaten in sellers on occasions; should stay at least 1m;
has been tried in blinkers. *H. Bell.*

VICTORY HOUSE 4 ch.c. Habitat 134–Star Court 102 (Aureole 132) (1982 **100**
6g* 1983 6g³) neat colt; having only third race in 3 seasons when keeping on
gamely without having clearest of runs to be 1¾ lengths third to On Stage in Thirsk
Hall Stakes in April; not seen out again; will be suited by 7f; clearly difficult to train;
sold to W. O'Gorman 7,000 gns Newmarket September Sales. *H. Cecil.*

VICTORY WARRANT 3 b.g. Pitskelly 122–Woo 72 (Stage Door Johnny) (1982 –
7f 7.2g 10s 1983 10s 10s 10fg 10f) little worthwhile form, although sixth of 15 in a
handicap final start. *C. Williams.*

VIDALIA (USA) 2 b.f. Nijinsky 138–Waya 116 (Faraway Son 130) (1983 6f³ 7g **108**?
7fg⁴ 8fg*)

There weren't many better-bred two-year-olds in training in 1983 than Vidalia.
Her sire, the triple crown winner Nijinsky, has matched his superb career on the
track at stud, siring over seventy stakes winners, and her dam Waya, whose first
foal she is, proved out of the top drawer in the States after showing smart form in
France, winning eleven races worth over 700,000 dollars and receiving the Eclipse
Award as best older filly or mare in 1979. Vidalia has a long way to go before she
matches the record of her parents but she has started in promising fashion and
definitely looks one to keep on the right side in 1984.

Vidalia's sole success came in the Group 3 Criterium Femminile at Rome in
November, a race which has been won by some pretty good Italian fillies over the
years including in 1978 by Maria Waleska who went on to pick up the Gran Premio
d'Italia and Italian Oaks at three. The six other runners included two that had won
listed events, Clair Matin and Philyra, but none of them could live with the
British-trained filly as she strode away in the last quarter of a mile to beat Clair
Matin by 6 lengths. In England Vidalia had run three times, putting up her best
effort in the Rockfel Stakes at Newmarket in October on the final occasion.
Previously third in a valuable newcomers race at Ascot and a disappointing sixth of
seven to Mystery Ship after giving some trouble at the start when favourite for the
Sweet Solera Stakes at Newmarket, she was one of the 50/1-shots for the Rockfel
but ran much better than her odds indicated, staying on strongly after being
outpaced to finish over four lengths fourth of thirteen to Mahogany.

			Northern Dancer	Nearctic
	Nijinsky		(b 1961)	Natalma
	(b 1967)	Flaming Page	Bull Page
Vidalia (USA)			(b 1959)	Flaring Top
(b.f. Mar 13, 1981)		Faraway Son	Ambiopoise
	Waya		(b 1967)	Locust Time
	(b 1974)	War Path	Blue Prince
			(b 1963)	Alyxia

Although Vidalia's form so far is no better than useful it is worth noting that
Balding regards her as a potential Oaks filly and it looks long odds on her improving
markedly as a three-year-old. On breeding as well as the way she races she will be
well suited by middle distances. Nijinsky stayed a mile and three quarters and
Waya, a half-sister to the smart French middle-distance stayer Warsaw, won the
Man o'War Stakes over eleven furlongs and the Turf Classic over a mile and a half.
Waya's dam War Path, successful at around nine furlongs in France, is one of six
winners out of Alyxia, a very attractive filly who failed to train on after winning the
Blue Seal Stakes at two. Vidalia, a well-made, good-looking individual, has raced
only on a sound surface. *I. Balding.*

VIDEO AFFAIRE 2 b.f. Godswalk 130–Ribots Affair 100 (Ribot 142) (1983 6g –
6f) Apr 15; IR 6,400F; well-grown, good-topped filly; half-sister to winners in
France and Malaysia; dam Irish 2-y-o 6f winner; last in July in maiden races at
Newmarket and Salisbury; sold D. Murray-Smith 7,400 gns Newmarket December
Sales. *B. Hills.*

VIDEO BOOM 2 b.c. Averof 123–Lady R.B. (Gun Shot) (1983 5v 5v 5fg 6fg **67** 7fg⁴ 6f 6f⁴ 6f 6fg 8d 7.2g² 6s⁴ 6fg⁴ 6fg) Apr 27; 4,600F, 6,500Y; rather leggy, short-backed colt; half-brother to several winners here and in USA, including 1m and 1½m winner Rifle Brigade (by High Top); fair plater; ½-length second of 12 to Orville's Song at Haydock in September; best form at 7f; didn't handle Catterick track well on ninth start. *R. Hollinshead.*

VIDEO KING 4 b.c. Blue Cashmere 129–Florintina 104 (Floribunda 136) (1982 **90** 7d² 6s² 8fg* 7.3fg* 8fg* 8f* 8fg⁴ 7fg⁴ 1983 7fg 7fg 7f³ 8f³ 8.3fg² 8fg² 7s*) rangy, quite attractive colt; beat Little Mercy 1½ lengths in handicap at Yarmouth in September; had run creditably earlier; stays 1m well; acts on any going; genuine and consistent; sold, probably for export to Italy, 5,000 gns Newmarket Autumn Sales. *C. Brittain.*

VIDEO LAD 2 ch.g. Cawston's Clown 113–Donegal Tweed (Allangrange 126) – (1983 6fg 7f 5f 8fg 6fg) Apr 21; IR 800F, 1,200Y; neat gelding; second reported foal; dam ran 3 times in Ireland; poor plater; form only at 5f. *R. Hollinshead.*

VIDEO MAN 3 b.c. Guillaume Tell 121–Pennycress 99 (Florescence 120) (1982 **88** 5f⁴(dis) 6d 6g⁴ 7fg² 7f* 1983 8d² 10f* 10f* 11f 10g) strong colt; won handicaps at Yarmouth and Redcar in July, latter decisively from Darting Groom; fifth of 15 behind easy winner Ormus in valuable handicap at Ostend the following month but finished last on final start; suited by 1¼m+; acts on a soft surface but is well suited by a firm one; game front runner. *G. Huffer.*

VIEILLE FEMME 2 b.f. Wolver Hollow 126–Old Gal 100 (Relko 136) (1983 **58 p** 7fg³) May 18; IR 10,500F, IR 23,000Y; rather unfurnished filly; half-sister to a winner in Spain; dam 1½m winner; 3 lengths third of 4 to Bonne Ile in Newmarket Challenge Cup in October; should improve. *B. Hills.*

VIENNESE WALTZ 4 b.f. High Top 131–Austria 93 (Henry the Seventh 125) **79** (1982 10.2g* 12fg 13d⁴ 16.5s* 18d² 18s 1983 18d³ 20fg 16.1fg 13s² 16.1g 18fg⁴) rangy filly; bandaged when creditable second to Prince of Peace in minor event at Ayr in September; suited by a test of stamina; needs some give in the ground; blinkered final start. *J. W. Watts.*

VIERGE D'OR (USA) 3 b.f. Secretariat–Vincennes 111 (Vieux Manoir 132) – (1982 NR 1983 10d 11.5fg 10fg) tall, lengthy, rather plain filly; half-sister to very useful 1m and 1¼m winner Vadrouille (by Foolish Pleasure); dam, second in Irish Guinness Oaks, is daughter of Valoris; showed signs of ability first 2 outings when trained by H. Cecil, but was off course nearly 5 months afterwards and soundly beaten on her return. *P. Kelleway.*

VIEUX CARRE (FR) 4 b. or br.c. Mississipian 131–Masque Bleu (Priamos **113** 123) (1982 6v⁴ 8s⁴ 8d² 8fg 8g* 8g² 8fg 8g 8s 1983 8v* 8d² 8s² 8f) first foal; dam, half-sister to French 1,000 Guineas winner Mata Hari, won over 6f at 3 yrs in USA; useful handicapper at 3 yrs, winning at Longchamp; improved in 1983, winning small race at Saint-Cloud in April and finishing good second in Prix du Muguet at Longchamp in May (1½ lengths behind Prospero) and 90,000 francs event at Saint-Cloud later in May (beaten a neck by Pampabird); had a heart attack during Prix du Chemin de Fer du Nord at Chantilly in June and died; stayed 1m; acted well on soft ground. *H. van de Poele, France.*

VIEW 2 br.f. Shirley Heights 130–Press Corps (Realm 129) (1983 6f³ 7fg² 6fg* 6s **86** 6fg 7fg) Feb 19; sturdy filly; second foal; dam 2-y-o 6f winner; won 8-runner minor event at Windsor in September; stays 7f; acts on any going. *B. Hanbury.*

VIEWERS CHOICE 2 b. or br.g. The Brianstan 128–Champagne Party (Amber – Rama 133) (1983 5d 5d 6f 6fg 6f 6f 5g 6s) May 3; 500Y; rangy, workmanlike gelding; bad plater; sometimes blinkered. *R. Ward.*

VIGOROUS VIGORS (USA) 3 gr.c. Vigors–Libelinha 123 (Hodell 120) (1982 **79** 7f 7g 7s 1983 10v 10fg 13fg³ 12f²) well-made, quite attractive colt; placed in handicaps in summer; won in USA afterwards; suited by 1½m+; acts well on fast ground. *R. Armstrong.*

VIKING CENTRE 3 ch.g. Owen Dudley 121– Another Clare (Blason 109) (1982 – 5.8g 6f 6f³ 6f* 1983 7d 8s) small, short-legged, strong-quartered gelding; plater; stays 6f; possibly needs a sound surface; blinkered nowadays. *D. Garraton.*

VIKING JACK 3 ch.c. Sallust 134–Erica (Ballyciptic 122) (1982 NR 1983 8d – 7d) 10,000Y; sturdy colt; half-brother to 1978 Irish 2-y-o sprint winner Gomera (by Young Emperor); dam lightly raced but showed a little ability; little worthwhile form in newcomers race at Newmarket (eighth of 17) and minor event at Leicester in spring; sold to D. Jermy 500 gns Ascot August Sales. *N. Callaghan.*

VICEROY PRINCESS 3 gr.f. Godswalk 130–Black Crow 72 (Sea Hawk II 131)   –
(1982 5f 5f 7d 7fg* 8d 1983 7.6v 8f) neat filly; showed only form when winning a
seller as a 2-y-o; suited by 7f; acts on a firm surface. *C. Williams.*

VICKIDORA 2 gr.f. Cavo Doro 124–Vicki Ann (Floribunda 136) (1983 7.6fg) Apr
16; half-sister to fair 1976 2-y-o 5f winner Rushley Bay (by Crooner); dam of little
account; tailed-off last of 19 in maiden race at Lingfield in October. *H. Westbrook.*

VICTORIAN PRINCE 3 ch.g. English Prince 129–Victorian Habit 101 (Habitat
134) (1982 5s² 5f³ 6d 7f 5s 8d 7s 1983 12v 8d 6f 8f 13.8f) short-coupled gelding;
disappointing maiden; well beaten in sellers on occasions; should stay at least 1m;
has been tried in blinkers. *H. Bell.*

VICTORY HOUSE 4 ch.c. Habitat 134–Star Court 102 (Aureole 132) (1982   **100**
6g* 1983 6g³) neat colt; having only third race in 3 seasons when keeping on
gamely without having clearest of runs to be 1¾ lengths third to On Stage in Thirsk
Hall Stakes in April; not seen out again; will be suited by 7f; clearly difficult to train;
sold to W. O'Gorman 7,000 gns Newmarket September Sales. *H. Cecil.*

VICTORY WARRANT 3 b.g. Pitskelly 122–Woo 72 (Stage Door Johnny) (1982   –
7f 7.2g 10s 1983 10s 10s 10fg 10f) little worthwhile form, although sixth of 15 in a
handicap final start. *C. Williams.*

VIDALIA (USA) 2 b.f. Nijinsky 138–Waya 116 (Faraway Son 130) (1983 6f³ 7g   **108**?
7fg⁴ 8fg*)
There weren't many better-bred two-year-olds in training in 1983 than Vidalia.
Her sire, the triple crown winner Nijinsky, has matched his superb career on the
track at stud, siring over seventy stakes winners, and her dam Waya, whose first
foal she is, proved out of the top drawer in the States after showing smart form in
France, winning eleven races worth over 700,000 dollars and receiving the Eclipse
Award as best older filly or mare in 1979. Vidalia has a long way to go before she
matches the record of her parents but she has started in promising fashion and
definitely looks one to keep on the right side in 1984.
Vidalia's sole success came in the Group 3 Criterium Femminile at Rome in
November, a race which has been won by some pretty good Italian fillies over the
years including in 1978 by Maria Waleska who went on to pick up the Gran Premio
d'Italia and Italian Oaks at three. The six other runners included two that had won
listed events, Clair Matin and Philyra, but none of them could live with the
British-trained filly as she strode away in the last quarter of a mile to beat Clair
Matin by 6 lengths. In England Vidalia had run three times, putting up her best
effort in the Rockfel Stakes at Newmarket in October on the final occasion.
Previously third in a valuable newcomers race at Ascot and a disappointing sixth of
seven to Mystery Ship after giving some trouble at the start when favourite for the
Sweet Solera Stakes at Newmarket, she was one of the 50/1-shots for the Rockfel
but ran much better than her odds indicated, staying on strongly after being
outpaced to finish over four lengths fourth of thirteen to Mahogany.

		Nijinsky (b 1967)	Northern Dancer (b 1961)	Nearctic Natalma
Vidalia (USA) (b.f. Mar 13, 1981)			Flaming Page (b 1959)	Bull Page Flaring Top
		Waya (b 1974)	Faraway Son (b 1967)	Ambiopoise Locust Time
			War Path (b 1963)	Blue Prince Alyxia

Although Vidalia's form so far is no better than useful it is worth noting that
Balding regards her as a potential Oaks filly and it looks long odds on her improving
markedly as a three-year-old. On breeding as well as the way she races she will be
well suited by middle distances. Nijinsky stayed a mile and three quarters and
Waya, a half-sister to the smart French middle-distance stayer Warsaw, won the
Man o'War Stakes over eleven furlongs and the Turf Classic over a mile and a half.
Waya's dam War Path, successful at around nine furlongs in France, is one of six
winners out of Alyxia, a very attractive filly who failed to train on after winning the
Blue Seal Stakes at two. Vidalia, a well-made, good-looking individual, has raced
only on a sound surface. *I. Balding.*

VIDEO AFFAIRE 2 b.f. Godswalk 130–Ribots Affair 100 (Ribot 142) (1983 6g
6f) Apr 15; IR 6,400F; well-grown, good-topped filly; half-sister to winners in
France and Malaysia; dam Irish 2-y-o 6f winner; last in July in maiden races at
Newmarket and Salisbury; sold D. Murray-Smith 7,400 gns Newmarket December
Sales. *B. Hills.*

a good turn of foot to lead near finish and win handicaps at Newmarket in April (by neck from Miramar Reef) and Ascot in July (beat Grand Unit a neck in quite valuable event); second in between at Newbury (ran rather in snatches) and Haydock (wandered about under pressure when beaten ½ length by Regal Steel in Old Newton Cup); suited by 1½m and promises to stay further; yet to race on a soft surface; needs strong handling; gelded at end of season. *J. Winter.*

VORVADOS 6 gr.h. The Go-Between 129–Keravnos 64 (Ionian 128) (1982 6d* **118** 6d² 7fg 6f 6f 6g 5g* 5fg² 6f* 5.6g* 6g 6g* 1983 6d* 6g 6v* 5d 6f 6fg 6g⁴ 6fg 5f 6fg 6fg*)

Surprisingly, as many as nine horses aged six years or more managed to win European pattern races in 1983. Our subject here, that interesting character the six-year-old Vorvados, won the Duke of York Stakes to be one of the number; the others were Bri-Eden (Ballyogan Stakes), Noalcoholic (Lockinge Stakes and Sussex Stakes), Princes Gate (Prix de Ris-Orangis), the French-trained quartet of Bylly The Kid, Kelbomec, Lancastrian and Prospero, and the German-trained Torgos. Most of the 'aged' pattern winners of recent years that spring to mind are stayers, notably Ardross and Sagaro, though there was another sprinter that won at six like Vorvados—Creetown, the 1978 Diadem Stakes winner, who raced in a similar manner. Few of the horses mentioned can be said to have improved as much as Vorvados from five to six. A highly successful though no more than useful handicapper in 1982 (he won the Portland with 8-13) Vorvados did well on several occasions in non-handicap races in 1983 and besides the Duke of York Stakes he picked up valuable events at the opening and closing meetings of the season at Doncaster. Although he failed to reach the first three in eight other runs, five were in top-class company, and he did finish a creditable fourth of six to Habibti in the Vernons Sprint Cup, two and a quarter lengths behind the runner-up Soba; two other runs were under big weights in competitive handicaps.

In the Duke of York Stakes at York in May Vorvados met some tough opponents including Prince Spy, On Stage and Sweet Monday who had already picked up five valuable races between them in 1983, and the smart four-year-old filly Vaigly Star. As he nearly always does, Vorvados got behind early on, being last at halfway, and no-one unfamiliar with his manner of racing would have given much for his chance. But he was produced with a strong run in the final two

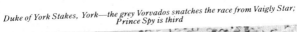

Duke of York Stakes, York—the grey Vorvados snatches the race from Vaigly Star; Prince Spy is third

VITTEL 3 b.g. Vitiges 132–Klaxonette 88 (Klairon 131) (1982 7f 1983 8v³ 10v⁴ 8v³ 8g 11.5f 7f) rather leggy, fair sort; rather a disappointing maiden; gives impression he'll prove best at distances short of 1¼m; sold to I. Wardle 4,300 gns Newmarket September Sales. *J. Winter.* —

VIVA LUCIA 2 b.f. Coded Scrap 90–Andalucia 57 (Rheingold 137) (1983 5g 5g 5f 6f³ 7f³ 6f⁴ 7f² 7f² 6f⁴ 8.2f⁴ 8d³ 9fg* 7.2s*) Apr 19; smallish, fair sort; first foal; dam won 1¼m seller; plater; won autumn nurseries at Redcar and Haydock without attracting a bid; will probably stay 1¼m; acts on any going but is particularly well suited by soft; blinkered fifth outing; game and genuine. *T. Fairhurst.* 73

VIVRE POUR VIVRE (ITY) 3 ch.g. Great Nephew 126–Velatura (Acropolis 132) (1982 6fg 7g 1983 9s 12g 8f 8f³ 8fg 10fg 10h 10f 8g) short-coupled gelding; good walker; plating-class maiden; best run at 1m on firm going; apprentice ridden nowadays; sometimes blinkered; sold out of P. Kelleway's stable 2,400 gns Newmarket September Sales after eighth start and resold 1,600 gns Doncaster November Sales. *M. Chapman.* 62 d

VLASSOVA (FR) 2 ch.f. Green Dancer 132–Victory Tune (Dr Fager) (1983 7fg) Apr 1; tall, sparely-made, narrow filly; third foal; sister to French 3-y-o Vulture; dam, French 11f winner, is half-sister to smart 1m to 1½m winner Volcanic; second favourite, never a factor in 22-runner maiden race at Newmarket in October; clearly thought to have ability. *H. Cecil.* – p

VODKATINI 4 b.g. Dubassoff–Olympic Visualise 84 (Northfields) (1982 14s 1983 12fg) big, strong gelding; winning hurdler; lightly raced on flat. *P. Haynes.* —

VORACITY 4 ch.g. Vitiges 132–Wolverene 114 (Relko 136) (1982 8fg 10f³ 10f² 11.5fg* 12g* 12g⁴ 1983 10g* 12g² 12g² 12fg* 14.6fg 12fg 12fg) tall gelding; found 106

Lord Derby's "Voracity"

subsequent outings, on final occasion finishing creditable 3¼ lengths third of 19 behind Bahoor in valuable handicap at Newmarket in October; stays 1¼m; probably acts on any going; tends to carry his head in air, but races consistently enough. *J. Fitzgerald.*

VIOLET BOUQUET (USA) 3 gr.f. Vigors–Boheme (Exbury 138) (1982 7g 1983 10fg 10g 16g⁴ 12d 12.2g) big, strong, lengthy filly; poor maiden; not sure to stay 2m. *R. Armstrong.*   –

VIOLINO DORO 4 b. or br.f. Cavo Doro 124–Morning Cloud 79 (Hard Tack 111§) (1982 7s 10s 12f 12.2f 1983 13s 16fg) neat ex-Irish filly; beaten some way in varied company, including selling; sold, for export to Norway, 860 gns Doncaster June Sales. *E. Carter.*   –

VIOLINO FANDANGO 5 b.g. Gay Fandango 132–Parkhurst (Sing Sing 134) (1982 8g 7f 10fg 8g 10fg 8.3g 6f 1983 8.2d 7.6g 7f² 7fg) tall gelding; plater; stays 7f well; acts on any going; has worn blinkers. *H. O'Neill.*   **44**

VIOLINO (USA) 3 b.f. Hawaii–Gay Violin (Sir Gaylord) (1982 NR 1983 10.2f 11g⁴ 12fg³ 12f) lengthy, quite attractive filly; half-sister to several winners, notably top-class miler Gay Fandango (by Forli) and Cellist (by Bagdad), a smart stakes winner at up to 1m in USA; dam won at up to 1m; in frame in maiden races. *J. W. Watts.*   **59**

VIRGIN ISLE 2 b.g. Free State 125–Saintly Princess 76 (Prince Tenderfoot 126) (1983 6fg) Mar 21; 6,200F, 10,000Y; strong, sturdy gelding; first produce; dam won over 5f and 6f at 2 yrs; backward, behind in 22-runner maiden race at Newmarket in July; subsequently gelded. *P. Haslam.*   –

VIRGIN SOLDIER 7 b.g. Queen's Hussar 124–Saintly Miss 63 (St Paddy 133) (1982 NR 1983 12d) lightly raced on flat nowadays; stays 1½m; acts on a firm and a soft surface; suitable mount for an inexperienced rider; has reportedly broken blood vessels over jumps. *J. Old.*   –

VIRGIN'S SMILE 3 b.f. Shirley Heights 130–Catherine Wheel 116 (Roan Rocket 128) (1982 NR 1983 10s² 13.3g⁴ 12f⁴ 16h⁴ 16d² 18fg) 41,000F, IR 90,000Y; leggy, sparely-made filly; half-sister to 2 winners, including Hunston (by Blakeney), a useful middle-distance winner here and a stakes winner over 9.5f in USA; dam, smart and tough, stayed at least 1¼m; second in maiden race at Chepstow in May (apprentice ridden) and handicap at Warwick in October, best efforts; stays well; evidently needs a soft surface. *P. Walwyn.*   **76**

VISIBLE FORM 2 b.f. Formidable 125–Look Out 84 (Vimy 132) (1983 6fg⁴ 6d* 6g*) May 22; lengthy, quite attractive filly; half-sister to several winners, including 2m winner Scheming (by Great Nephew) and out-and-out French stayer Second Watch (by Paveh); dam half-sister to very smart stayer Raise You Ten; showed promise in minor event at Newmarket in late August, and following month won maiden race at Yarmouth and well-contested minor event (beating Fair Test 1½ lengths) at Goodwood; will be suited by 7f and 1m; seems sure to win more races. *L. Cumani.*   **99**

VISIONTIM 3 ch.c. Royben 125–Godmother (So Blessed 130) (1982 NR 1983 10.1fg 10.1fg 11.7fg) second foal; dam ran 3 times in France, including in a claiming event; soundly beaten in minor events at Windsor. *D. Oughton.*   –

VITAL INTERESTS 3 ch.g. Sagaro 133–Rosalina 71 (Porto Bello 118) (1982 7fg 7s 1983 7f 7f 5.6f) compact gelding; behind in maiden races; blinkered second start; sold to D. Morrill 840 gns Doncaster August Sales. *B. Wilkinson.*   –

VITANGES 2 ch.g. Vitiges 132–Nyota 96 (Reform 132) (1983 6fg) Feb 28; 2,000Y; second foal; dam won over 7f and 1½m; remote seventh of 12 in maiden race at Folkestone in October; will need further. *R. Simpson.*   –

VITIGESON 3 ch.c. Vitiges 132–Piccadilly Etta 76 (Floribunda 136) (1982 5f 5fg³ 6g 5f 5f 5g² 5s 1983 5s 5d² 5g4 8d 8f* 7.2g 8fg* 8f* 10f 8fg4 8.2h 8s) good-topped, strong colt; not a good walker; improved and was in fine form in summer; successful in handicaps at Doncaster, Ripon and Redcar, on last-named course beating Aries Do by 1½ lengths; never going comfortably last 2 starts; suited by 1m and firm going (seems not to stay 1¼m); ran moderately in blinkers in 1982; has a fair turn of foot; reportedly returned lame sixth start. *T. Fairhurst.*   **87**

VITINGO 4 ch.c. Vitiges 132–Petlady 81 (Petingo 135) (1982 10s 9g 10f 8f 8s 10.1d4 11fg4 12f 10f 12.2f 10fg 10d 1983 12.2g 10f) fair sort; has shown only a little ability in varied company; stays 11f; sometimes blinkered; cost 1,300 gns Ascot March Sales. *J. Parkes.*   –

VIKING RAIDER 2 b. or gr.c. Native Admiral–Royal Celandine (Royal Palace 131) (1983 6h) Mar 30; first foal; dam ran twice; last of 7 in newcomers race at Chepstow in August. *D. O'Donnell, Isle of Man.* —

VILLACANA 4 b.f. Lord Gayle 124–Etoile Freda (Florescence 120) (1982 10f 11.7fg 8f 8fg 8d 1983 8f 10h 10.8g 13.1h) close-coupled filly; poor form, including in a seller. *J. Bosley.* —

VILLAGE LEADER (CAN) 3 ch.f. Vice Regent–Stone Cottage (New Providence) (1982 NR 1983 7s 9f 11.5f² 12f 10f³ 12f 12f⁴ 10d) $70,000Y; tall, leggy, angular, plain filly; third foal; half-sister to very useful Canadian filly Pensioner (by Irish Stronghold); dam, half-sister to smart filly Glenaris, won at up to 1m; second in amateur riders maiden event at Yarmouth in July; inconsistent however, and isn't one to rely on; suited by 11.5f; sold to BBA 19,500 gns Newmarket December Sales. *F. Durr.* 63

VILLAGE POSTMAN 2 b.c. Morston 125–Paperwork (Brigadier Gerard 144) (1983 6d 7fg² 7fg³) fair sort; second foal; dam won over 8.5f in France and over hurdles in this country; placed in maiden race at Chester in July and minor event at Lingfield in August; will stay 1¼m. *N. Guest.* 84

VILLAGE SCENE 4 br.c. Blakeney 126–Hayloft 111 (Tudor Melody 129) (1982 8.2f 8fg 1983 12g 13.8g) neat, attractive colt; bad maiden on flat though won over hurdles; twice wore blinkers; dead. *W. A. Stephenson.* —

VILLAJOYOSA (FR) 5 b. or br.m. Satingo 129–La Ramee (White Label II 126) (1982 8d 8v 8g 8s 8.2g² 8d⁴ 8fg 8fg* 8g 8fg 8d 7.5s 1983 7s 8s 6fg 7.6g 8.3f 8fg 8fg⁴ 8d 8f) ex-French mare; poor walker; plater; stays 1m well; probably acts on any going; best in blinkers. *C. Austin.* —

VILLANOVAN 4 b.f. Martinmas 128–Floatingonair (Whistling Wind 123) (1982 NR 1983 12fg 8fg 16g 12f 8f 6fg) 1,000Y; fourth foal; half-sister to Irish 13f winner Could It Happen (by Double-U-Jay); dam placed over 6f and 7.9f in Ireland at 2 yrs; seems of little account. *M. Chapman.* —

VILLARS 3 ch.f. Home Guard 129–Telamonia (Ballymoss 130) (1982 7f 7s³ 1983 12s 12v 10g 7h⁴ 8f 10f² 12f* 10d 10fg⁴ 12fg² 12g² 12fg⁴) big, rangy filly; in frame in maiden races before winning one by 6 lengths at Folkestone in September; second in handicap on same course and apprentice event at Chepstow in October; suited by 1½m; acts on any going. *J. Winter.* 84

VIMY ROSE 3 br.f. Soldier Rose 98–Wee Jennie (Vimadee 120) (1982 NR 1983 7f 12f 9d) sturdy filly; second foal; dam never ran; well behind in minor events; swerved at start first outing and dwelt on second. *M. Tate.* —

VINDANGO 2 ch.c. Manor Farm Boy 114–Alpine Damsel 46 (Mountain Call 125) (1983 6fg 6g 6fg⁴ 6d³) Apr 15; 3,200F, IR 4,000Y; 6,800 2-y-o; workmanlike, good-bodied colt; first produce; dam plater; showed little until finishing 2½ lengths third of 11 to Refueled in minor event at Catterick in October; promises to stay 7f; suited by soft surface. *P. Mitchell.* 83

VINDICATION (USA) 3 b.f. Advocator–Jani Nasrullah (Amastar) (1982 5fg² 6fg³ 5g⁴ 5f 7f³ 8.2s 7g² 8s 7d³ 1983 8s 7d² 7fg² 7g 8g 9g⁴ 8f 7f 7g 6fg 7s 7g 7g) neat, strong, attractive filly; second twice at Edinburgh in April but ran moderately later in season; suited by 7f; acts on a firm surface, but possibly better on an easy one; blinkered once as a 2-y-o; sent to USA. *S. Norton.* —

VINO FESTA 4 ch.f. Nebbiolo 125–Madrilon (Le Fabuleux 133) (1982 NR 1983 14.7fg 15.8g⁴ 18fg 12g) 640 3-y-o; rather sparely-made, workmanlike filly; half-sister to Irish 1980 2-y-o 1m winner My First Chance (by Bold Lad, USA) and a bumpers winner; dam unraced; winning hurdler but is only plating class on flat; stays well. *J. Parkes.* —

VINO ROSSO 3 b.g. Nebbiolo 125–Magic Quiz (Quisling 117) (1982 5fg³ 1983 8v 7s* 6v 6g² 6fg 6fg³ 5.8fg 6fg 5d) sturdy, lengthy gelding; has a round action; beat The House Builder easily by 5 lengths in maiden race at Leicester in April; placed in handicaps at Newbury and Newmarket afterwards, but was bit disappointing last 3 starts; stays 7f; yet to race on really firm going, but acts on any other. *H. Candy.* 86

VINTAGE TOLL 3 ch.c. Nebbiolo 125–Vesper Bell (Larkspur 128) (1982 NR 1983 8.2s² 8f 8f⁴ 10.6fg* 10f³ 10s² 8.2s³ 10fg³) IR 10,500Y, 3,600 2-y-o; short-backed colt; good walker; half-brother to useful 7f and 1m winner Mou-Ferni-Tychi and very useful French 7f winner Glittertind (both by Royal and Regal), and to another winner; dam ran once; won maiden race at Haydock in August; placed all 86

furlongs, and was switched outside Vaigly Star, who had taken up the running from Gabitat shortly after halfway, with a furlong to go; keeping on the better, he beat the filly half a length with the favourite Prince Spy two lengths further away third. Vorvados' Doncaster wins, in the Cammidge Trophy in March and the Remembrance Day Stakes in November, owed a good deal to his receiving the strong handling he needs to be seen to best advantage. In the Cammidge Trophy a vintage Piggott ride made the difference between victory and defeat: Vorvados came through to get up by a neck and a short head from Famous Star and Camisite; it was Starkey's turn to shine in the Remembrance Day Stakes, when Vorvados had a head to spare over the Ayr Gold Cup winner Polly's Brother.

Vorvados (gr.h. 1977)	The Go-Between (gr 1970)	Runnymede (gr 1961)	Petition
			Dutch Clover
		Game Girl (ch 1959)	Abernant
			Game Laws
	Keravnos (b 1968)	Ionian (b 1960)	Milesian
			Persian View
		Candlelight (ch 1959)	Gratitude
			Aurabora

Vorvados, a lightly-built horse, is the best son of the now Cyprus-based stallion The Go-Between who in his racing days started out as a typical early-season two-year-old and progressed to win the Cornwallis Stakes at Ascot. Vorvados is his sire's only pattern winner to date. Vorvados' dam Keravnos, who won a six-furlong seller at Windsor as a three-year-old, has produced only one other winner Alf's Folly (by Lear Jet) a winner in Jersey. The second dam Candlelight produced numerous other minor winners and was herself fairly useful over five furlongs. Vorvados is suited by six furlongs or five on a stiff track; he acts on any going, though he has done most of his winning on easy ground. Like old Popsi's Joy he is a credit to his trainer. *M. Haynes.*

VOSGES (USA) 3 b.f. Youth 135–Virunga 115 (Sodium 128) (1982 NR 1983 **117** 10.5g² 10.5g* 12s³) half-sister to 1980 2-y-o 1m winner Video Tape (by Cannonade), subsequently very successful over hurdles in France, and to smart 2-y-o Vacarme (by Lyphard); dam third in French Oaks; finished strongly when 1½ lengths second of 18 to Conform in maiden race at Evry in June and had opposition well strung out when beating Cave des Rois by 4 lengths in similar race at Deauville in August; stepped up considerably on that form when just over 2 lengths third of 12 behind Sharaya in Trusthouse Forte Prix Vermeille at Longchamp in September; very well suited by 1½m; acts on soft going. *P.-L. Biancone, France.*

VOX 3 br.g. Quiet Fling 124–Pollster 101 (Majority Blue 126) (1982 7f 7f 7g 1983 — 10s) smallish, quite well-made gelding; soundly beaten in maiden and minor events; blinkered first start at 2 yrs; sold 1,150 gns Doncaster May Sales. *W. O'Gorman.*

VOYANT 4 ch.c. Star Appeal 133–Vernier 94 (High Hat 131) (1982 10s* 14fg³ 16g **109 §** 14f³ 12g* 12fg³ 12g³ 1983 13.3v⁴ 13.3g² 16.1fg² 16f² 16g² 14.6fg) smallish, rather lightly-built colt; very useful performer when in the mood; runner-up in 3 handicaps and in Lonsdale Stakes at York; put up an astonishing display in last-named in August, making up ground hand over fist in straight to be beaten 2½ lengths by Crusader Castle after tailing himself off after 6f; stays 2m; seems to act on any going; coltish in paddock at York; pulled himself up final start and clearly has a mind of his own; sold 5,800 gns Newmarket December Sales. *B. Hobbs.*

VYNZ GIRL 3 b.f. Tower Walk 130–Mayo Girl 110 (Connaught 130) (1982 7g 7d⁴ **82** 8s³ 7d 10.2s³ 1983 10s² 10s⁴ 10d 12.2d* 12d⁴ 10.5s) rangy filly; in frame twice at Cagnes-sur-Mer before making virtually all to win maiden race at Catterick in March by 10 lengths; had stiffer tasks afterwards; suited by 1½m; acted on soft going; showed a tendency to hang at 2 yrs; retired to stud. *C. Booth.*

VYNZ SUPREME 3 b.c. Supreme Sovereign 119–High Drama 90 (Hill Clown) — (1982 6s⁴ 1983 8f 7f⁴ 9f 12fg) plating-class maiden; ran best race of 1983 over 7f. *W. Haigh.*

W

WAADI HATTA (USA) 3 b.f. Upper Nile–Q Up (Distinctive) (1982 NR 1983 9d 10g 8d) $175,000Y; second foal; half-sister to a winner; dam won 4 sprint races, including a claiming event, and is half-sister to smart 1973 French 2-y-o sprinter Colourman; little worthwhile form, possibly best effort when eighth of 16 in 1¼m amateur riders race; sold to BBA (Ire) 6,000 gns Newmarket Autumn Sales. *J. Ciechanowski.*

WAGA BAY 3 ch.c. Roi Soleil 125–Purple Queen 88 (Grey Sovereign 128§) (1982   –
7g 6s 6s 5s 1983 6s 8s 9s 7s 7s³ 6s 7g³ 9g 7g 7g 7.5d 8fg⁴ 8fg) 1,100F, IR 4,800Y; half-brother to several winners, including fairly useful sprinter Georgie Girl (by Crocket); dam 2-y-o 5f winner; in frame in maiden race at Down Royal, apprentice handicap at Sligo and seller at Edinburgh; stays 1m; trained most of season by M. Cunningham in Ireland. *S. Norton.*

WAGGISH 2 ch.c. Sagaro 133–Facetious 88 (Malicious) (1983 5v* 7f 7g) June 9;   **66**
light-framed, angular colt; second foal; half-brother to fairly useful 1982 2-y-o 5f performer Bottesford Boy (by Record Token); dam disappointing maiden; won 20-runner maiden race at Thirsk in May by a head at 33/1; last in Seaton Delaval Stakes at Newcastle and Catterick nursery afterwards; should stay at least 7f. *J. Leigh.*

WAGONER 3 b.c. Rheingold 137–Tranquilly (Sea-Bird II 145) (1982 8s 1983   **99**
12v* 12d² 16f) nice, big, well-made colt; pick of paddock when winning maiden race at Kempton in April; didn't handle bend well but ran creditably when 5 lengths second to Tom Okker in handicap at Epsom in June (would have done better with a stronger gallop) and ran another fair race when about 11 lengths sixth of 17 behind Santella Man in Queen's Vase at Royal Ascot in June; not seen out again; stays well; acts on any going. *P. Walwyn.*

WAHED 8 gr.g. Red God 128§–Welsh Crest 86 (Abernant 142) (1982 8g⁴ 7fg² 8f   **59 §**
8f² 7g² 8f 8f 8d³ 8fg 8g 10f* 10g 10g* 10g 10g² 10d 1983 8g 11g 10f 8f² 10f* 8g 10f² 10f³ 10f⁴ 10f 10s 8fg 10g) strong gelding; won handicap at Newcastle in July; has been beaten in selling company; suited by 1¼m; probably acts on any going but goes well on fast ground; has worn blinkers; suitable mount for an inexperienced rider; needs to be covered up; inconsistent and unreliable. *F. Watson.*

WALDRON HILL 3 ch.g. Hotfoot 126–Ankole 85 (Crepello 136) (1982 6f 7d 6d   –
6v³ 1983 7g⁴ 7fg 11g 12fg⁴ 8.2f 9f⁴) fair sort; good walker and mover; plater; stays 9f; trained first 2 starts by S. Norton. *R. Allan.*

WALHAN 3 b.c. Captain James 123–The Cosmos (Windsor Sun 116) (1982 NR   –
1983 10f 10f 8g) IR 24,000Y; half-brother to 4 winners, including quite useful 1969 2-y-o 5f winner Miralgo Lad (by Miralgo), subsequently successful in Australia; dam unraced half-sister to Irish 1000 Guineas winner Royal Danseuse; little worthwhile form in maiden races; sold 3,900 gns Ascot December Sales. *J. Hindley.*

WALJAT 3 b.g. Bay Express 132–Giglet (Frankincense 120) (1982 5.1f³ 5d 5g⁴   **75**
6g³ 1983 6v³ 7d³ 8v* 8f 7.6fg³ 8.3fg) fair sort; returned to form when beating Hooligan a neck in handicap at Doncaster in May; far from disgraced next 2 starts, but wasn't seen out after being hampered and well beaten at Windsor in July; suited by 1m and will stay a bit further; acts on any going. *W. Musson.*

WALK ALONG 4 ch.g. Farm Walk 111–Leger Bar 63 (French Beige 127) (1982   – §
10f 12d 1983 10s 10.2f 12f 12f⁴ 12f⁴ 12f⁴ 10h 10s⁴ 10g⁴) lightly-made gelding; has a round action; plater; stays 1½m; probably ungenuine and isn't an easy ride. *W. Haigh.*

WALK IN RHYTHM 2 b.c. Tower Walk 130–Maiden d'Or 87 (Songedor 116)   –
(1983 5d 6fg) May 16; fifth foal; half-brother to winning stayer Shmain (by Sheshoon); dam won at up to 1m; behind in maiden races at Hamilton (last of 7) in May and Doncaster (backward) in November. *A. Balding.*

WALTER-KOHRING 2 gr.c. Homing 130–A-Bye 116 (Abernant 142) (1983 6fg   **63**
5g 5g) Mar 30; strong, good-topped colt; poor walker; closely related to useful 1976 2-y-o 5f winner Abode (by Habitat) and half-brother to another 2-y-o winner; dam smart 5f performer at 2 yrs and sister to good sprinter Abwah; showed a little ability last 2 outings in September maiden events at Haydock and Newbury. *M. Ryan.*

WALTER'S WEDNESDAY 2 ch.f. Lucky Wednesday 124–Fiery Comet 82   –
(Star Moss 122) (1983 5f 7f 7.2g 6fg) Mar 19; leggy, narrow filly; bad plater. *J. Etherington.*

WALTON HEATH 3 b. or br.g. Persian Bold 123–Faa Paa (Skymaster 126)   **62**
(1982 5d 5fg⁴ 5f⁴ 7d² 7g 7g 7fg 8f* 7g 1983 7v 7v 8.5d* 7s 7fg 7f 8.3fg 8g) leggy, lightly-made gelding; bought in 4,800 gns after winning seller at Epsom in June;

894

suited by 1m; seems to act on any going; inconsistent; usually blinkered. *A. Ingham.*

WANGAROO (USA) 4 b.g. Charles Elliott–Saratoga Gal (Royal Orbit) (1982 – 10g 1983 10.1d 10g) sturdy gelding; of little account. *R. Hartop.*

WANG FEIHOONG 3 b.c. Sagaro 133–Tulchan 95 (Tudor Melody 129) (1982 **88** d 6fg 7f 8g² 1983 11.7s 11.7fg 12fg* 11f* 14fg 13s⁴ 12fg) neat colt; good walker; won 2 small handicaps at Hamilton in July; suited by 11f and more (never got into race and finished last over 1¾m); ideally suited by fast ground; set much too fast a pace for his own good final outing. *P. Haslam.*

WAR AND PEACE 4 br.g. Red Alert 127–Swinging Nun (Tudor Melody 129) – (1982 7.6f 10.2g 10.1fg 7g 1983 10f 12f 16g 16fg 16d) poor walker; of little account. *D. Mills.*

WARBIOLA 3 ch.f. Nebbiolo 125–War Lass 100 (Whistler 129) (1982 5d 1983 – 8d 8s) light-framed filly; little worthwhile form, including in sellers; sold 660 gns Newmarket September Sales. *W. Musson.*

WARDAH (USA) 2 b.f. Break Up The Game–Skate Back (Carry Back) (1983 – 7fg) Apr 21; $40,000F, $50,000Y; half-sister to numerous winners, including very smart Frosty Skater (by Diplomat Way), a winner at up to 1m; dam won 4 races at up to 1m in USA; tenth of 17 in maiden race at Beverley in September. *M. Albina.*

WARFLIGHT 4 b.c. Warpath 113–Brief Flight 108 (Counsel 118) (1982 9g 10.6fg **52** 9.4fg 9g* 8.2g* 8f² 8d³ 10.6s² 12v* 12g 12s 1983 12v 8d 8fg 11d² 12f 12f² 12f 11f³ 13g⁴ 10.6g 12fg) big, useful-looking colt; poor handicapper; has been beaten in a valuable seller; needs further than 1m and stays 1½m well; acts on any going but goes well in the mud; blinkered once; suitable mount for an amateur rider; wears a tongue strap; sold to J. Yardley 3,600 gns Doncaster November Sales. *C. Thornton.*

WARGAME 3 ch.g. Warpath 113–Sunshine Holyday 96 (Three Wishes 114) (1982 – 6fg 7g* 7s 7d³ 1983 8d 12d 12fg 8f 13.8f 7g 8d) rangy, good sort; good walker; didn't recover his 2-y-o form, though not entirely disgraced in big fields on last 2 outings (blinkered final start); should be suited by middle distances; sold 3,300 gns Doncaster October Sales. *C. Gray.*

WAROOKA 6 gr.g. Veiled Wonder–Grey Parrot (Abernant 142) (1982 6g 5d 5g – 5.8f 6fg 7.6g 6g 5g 5fg 5fg 1983 5.8s) strong gelding; has a round action; disappointing sprint handicapper; suited by some give in the ground; blinkered last 2 starts in 1982. *J. O'Donoghue.*

WARPLANE 3 b.g. Warpath 113–Glider 82 (Buisson Ardent 129) (1982 NR 1983 **74** 8f 9g* 11f² 12f 8s 8.2g³ 9fg* 9fg⁴) useful-looking gelding; half-brother to several winners, including very useful performers Aliante (by Busted), Donello (by Crepello) and Juggernaut (by Ragusa); dam won over 1m; held up when winning maiden race at Hamilton in June and handicap at Redcar in October; best form at up to 9f but stays further; probably acts on any going. *C. Thornton.*

WAR WAR 3 ch.g. Tachypous 128–Top Line 99 (Saint Crespin III 132) (1982 7g **63** 7g 8d 1983 8.5v⁴ 10s 12v⁴ 12v 6g* 8f⁴) heavy-bodied gelding; dropped in class when winning seller at Ayr in July (bought in 2,800 gns); should be suited by further than 6f; blinkered fourth start. *A. Ingham.*

WARWICK AIR 4 b.f. True Song 95–Maid of Warwick 96 (Warwick 110) (1982 – NR 1983 10.1f) second foal; dam sprinter; tailed off in minor event at Windsor in August. *Mrs A. Finch.*

WARWICK BLUE 3 b.g. Raga Navarro 119–Allegretto (Preciptic 122) (1982 – 5fg 7g 5g 1983 6v 8s 8.3s) leggy, close-coupled gelding; bad plater; sold to L. Kennard 1,150 gns Ascot 2nd June Sales. *J. Holt.*

WASHBURN FLYER 2 b.f. Owen Dudley 121–Blaeberry 100 (Hook Money **46** 124) (1983 5v 5v 6s 6g 7fg 5.1f 6g 8.2fg 10d 6fg) Feb 24; 4,000F; lengthy, workmanlike filly; poor plater; stays 1m. *K. Ivory.*

WASSL 3 b.c. Mill Reef 141–Hayloft 111 (Tudor Melody 129) (1982 6fg* 1983 7d* **125** 8g 8v* 12s 12f 8f³ 8g³ 10g² 10fg)
    It was always on the cards that Wassl's ideal distance would be hard to find. His sire Mill Reef tends to be an influence for stamina, although there are notable exceptions, and among his outstanding runners are the middle-distance performers Acamas, Diamond Shoal, Glint of Gold and Shirley Heights (the last-named an influence for stamina at stud). The dam Hayloft on the other hand is by the exceptionally speedy Tudor Melody and gained all her three wins over five furlongs

Airlie/Coolmore Irish Two Thousand Guineas, the Curragh—Wassl (left) turns the tables on Lomond (right); Parliament (noseband) is third

as a two-year-old, including in the Molecomb Stakes at Goodwood; she was placed over a mile at three but was returned to sprint distances before being retired to stud. A mile is pretty sure to be within Wassl's scope, so stamina was unlikely to be a problem in the Guineas, but beyond that was anybody's guess. Trainer Dunlop therefore had little option but to experiment after Wassl won the Airlie/Coolmore Irish Two Thousand Guineas; he was tried with varying results over a mile and a half and, after a return to a mile, at a mile and a quarter.

As a two-year-old Wassl reportedly showed tremendous speed at home, more even than Rutland and Aragon according to his trainer, and he was an impressive winner over six furlongs at York in mid-summer before being kept off the course by a pulled muscle, sustained when he was cast in his box. Apparently he worked very lazily the following spring and was thought sure to need the race when making his reappearance in the Clerical, Medical, Greenham Stakes at Newbury in April. That proved not to be the case. Wassl won without having at all a hard time, getting up to beat Proclaim by three quarters of a length despite having stumbled and swerved when leaving the stalls. The Greenham was generally considered a good Guineas trial, and Wassl started third favourite in the big race itself, but he ran most disappointingly and came home only ninth behind Lomond. His running was considered so out of character that he was risked against Lomond again at the Curragh, where Wassl and Boom Town Charlie were the English challengers in a field of ten. Murray, riding Wassl for the first time, had him close up throughout and sent him up to dispute the lead from halfway. Wassl, staying on really well in the very testing conditions, was on top in the last furlong and had three quarters of a length to spare over Lomond at the finish. Lomond didn't have the best of runs and the proximity of Parliament in third casts doubts over the value of the form; nevertheless Wassl had obviously made substantial improvement on his Newmarket running, and Dunlop was asked by the stewards to account for the same. The *Irish Racing Calendar* records that 'Dunlop could offer no firm explanation, but said that at Newmarket (where Wassl was drawn one) he had to race on his own and, being a lazy sort, he may have lost interest. Certainly Murray said that Wassl had to keep having something to race with'. The trainer added that he'd been disappointed with Wassl at Newmarket. For Dunlop Wassl was a third Irish classic winner, following Black Satin and Shirley Heights (Mountain Lodge gave him a fourth in the autumn); for Murray, for whom Wassl was a chance ride, it was a fourth Irish classic win, following those on Dickens Hill, Cairn Rouge and Tyrnavos.

In our opinion Wassl's pedigree and, perhaps as importantly, his relaxed style of running suggested that there were reasonable prospects of his staying the Derby distance; but, as it always will, fact counted for much more than opinion. He came to the end of his tether shortly after rounding Tattenham Corner, and he eventually trailed in only fourteenth behind Teenoso. Given another chance to prove the matter one way or another, Wassl ran in the Irish Sweeps Derby and finished a modest fifth to Shareef Dancer, giving the impression once again that the distance was beyond his best.

With the Coral-Eclipse just a week later and the Benson and Hedges a long way off Wassl was brought sharply back to a mile in his next race, the Sussex Stakes at Goodwood late in July. He was sent in pursuit of Noalcoholic virtually from the start but lacked the pace to get to grips and was just run out of second by Tolomeo. Similarly in the Prix du Moulin de Longchamp in September he was no match at all for the outstanding French milers Luth Enchantee and L'Emigrant and was beaten comprehensively, by more than eight lengths into third. Both these efforts were reasonable enough considering the strength of the opposition, but they left the impression that a mile, at least on fast ground, had become too sharp for Wassl. The Joe McGrath Memorial at Leopardstown later in September provided an ideal opportunity to try him out at a mile and a quarter, and, in finishing two and a half lengths second to Stanerra, he put up a really good showing, even allowing for the mare's lack of a recent race. Wassl took up the running fully a furlong and a half out and kept on well to finish a further two and a half lengths clear of third-placed General Holme. It seemed, at last, as if his best trip had been found, and given this performance we'd be inclined to ignore his contrasting display in the following month's Dubai Champion Stakes at Newmarket. In all probability Wassl had had enough by then. He finished last but one behind Cormorant Wood.

Mill Reef's stud fee in 1984 is double that of 1983: £40,000 July 1st plus £40,000 live foal. The latest season was probably his best since 1978, so even at his increased fee he is likely to continue in great demand. It is interesting to note, however, that the average price paid for his yearlings in 1983 had fallen to 90,000 guineas from a peak in 1981 of 213,613 guineas. His colt out of Arkadina, subsequently named South Atlantic and a useful winner in Ireland, went for a European record yearling price when sold for 640,000 guineas that year, the same year that Wassl himself cost 300,000 guineas. Wassl's dam Hayloft was a very useful filly, as we've seen, and the grandam Haymaking was even better. Haymaking was successful at two, three and four and won both the Coronation

Sheikh Ahmed Al-Maktoum's "Wassl"

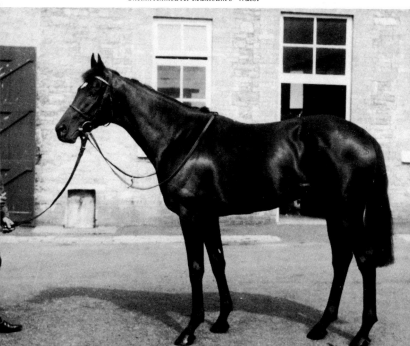

Stakes and the Nassau Stakes by the convincing margin of three lengths. Looking further back in the pedigree we find that Wassl's fifth dam was a half-sister to Hyperion. Hayloft's only foal prior to Wassl was the Blakeney colt Village Scene who showed nothing on the flat but won two weakly-contested novice hurdles before his death in the autumn. Hayloft has since produced two fillies by Troy: the first, Pennyweight, was in training with Cecil as a two-year-old; the second was bought by Dunlop for 500,000 guineas at the Highflyer Sales in September.

		Never Bend	Nasrullah
	Mill Reef	(b 1960)	Lalun
	(b 1968)	Milan Mill	Princequillo
Wassl		(b 1962)	Virginia Water
(b.c. 1980)		Tudor Melody	Tudor Minstrel
	Hayloft	(br 1956)	Matelda
	(b 1973)	Haymaking	Galivanter
		(br 1963)	Haytime

Wassl remains in training as a four-year-old, likely to face tough opposition from such as Tolomeo, Stanerra and Time Charter as well as the new generation of classic horses. We can't help thinking that Dunlop will have his work cut out to find worthwhile opportunities for him in England, but Wassl will no doubt be finishing in the money again in top company. A neat, most attractive colt—altogether a bonny type—he should be assured a place at stud in due course. *J. Dunlop.*

WATER CANNON 2 b.g. Gunner B 126–Awash (Busted 134) (1983 8fg 9f 10fg⁴) May 11; 18,000Y; strong, quite useful-looking gelding; third foal; half-brother to useful Irish 3-y-o 6f winner Saracen (by Sharpen Up) and 1m winner Rare Gift (by Rarity); dam modest daughter of smart 5f to 7f winner Fluke, a half-sister to Buoy and Bireme; staying-on 2½ lengths fourth of 9 to High Debate in Jennings The Bookmakers Zetland Stakes at Newmarket in October, easily best effort; gelded subsequently; will be suited by 1½m; sure to win a race. *J. Hindley.*   **87**

WATER DRAGON 3 gr.g. Dragonara Palace 115–Leger Bar 63 (French Beige 127) (1982 NR 1983 7f⁴ 8fg 7h⁴ 7.6g 8h 12g²) 6,000 2-y-o; leggy gelding; half-brother to 2 winners, including fair 5f and 7f winner Water of Life (by Mummy's Pet); dam plater; little worthwhile form (poor second of 3 in slowly-run race final start); blinkered fourth outing. *E. Witts.*   **—**

WATER EATON GAL 3 ch.f. Legal Eagle 126–Little Run 89 (Silver Cloud 121) (1982 NR 1983 10.1fg 11.7h 9d 6fg 6g) second foal; dam won several times at up to 1m and was also successful over hurdles; behind in varied races. *M. Tate.*   **—**

WATERHEAD 3 b.c. High Top 131–Djimbaran Bay (Le Levanstell 122) (1982 7s⁴ 1983 8d³ 8v² 8f 8d² 10g²) medium-sized, lengthy colt; good walker; has a round action; in frame in maiden and minor races; will be suited by further than 1¼m; needs some give in the ground; sold to CBA 13,000 gns Newmarket Autumn Sales. *J. Tree.*   **85**

WATER MARGIN 2 gr.f. Dragonara Palace 115–Madame Birwood (Constable 119) (1983 6f 6g) Mar 30; 2,000F, 4,800Y; tall, leggy filly; half-sister to several winners here and abroad, including very useful 1978 2-y-o 6f and 7f winner Birwood Lad (by Mummy's Pet); dam ran only twice; 5/1 and blinkered, led to 2f out when 7½ lengths fifth of 17 to Strawberry Fields in seller at Yarmouth in September, second outing; again blinkered, crashed into rails leaving paddock at Beverley later in September and was withdrawn. *W. O'Gorman.*   **—**

WATER MOCCASIN (USA) 2 br.c. Topsider–Surf (Hawaii) (1983 5f 5.8h² 5.8h* 6f² 6f* 6g* 6g³ 6fg) Feb 13; quite well-made, attractive colt; first foal; dam, very useful stakes winner over 8.5f at 4 yrs, is half-sister to very smart middle-distance stayer Anifa; sire smart American sprinter; won Moet and Chandon Zukunfts-Rennen at Baden-Baden in September by 2¼ lengths from Any Business; had previously landed the odds in maiden race at Bath and minor event at Windsor; gave 4 lb all round and was far from disgraced when 5 lengths third of 7 to Vacarme in Mill Reef Stakes at Newbury later in September; looked past his best when well beaten subsequently in William Hill Middle Park Stakes at Newmarket; will be very well suited by 7f; has raced only on a sound surface. *I. Balding.*   **108**

WATER PISTOL 3 br.g. Scottish Rifle 127–Jane Bond 59 (Good Bond 122) (1982 6d 6f² 7f* 7fg³ 7g² 8g 8.2s 1983 7d 6d⁴ 8s⁴ 6d 7f) compact, lightly-made gelding; probably stays 1m; yet to show he can handle really soft going, but acts on any other. *M. Lambert.*   **64**

WATERS END 2 br.f. Rapid River 127–Sue's Last (Como 120) (1983 5d 6fg) Mar 11; 260F; rather narrow filly; of no account. *Mrs N. Macauley.* —

WATERVILLE LAKE 2 b.c. Thatch 136–Abella 121 (Premonition 130 or Abernant 142) (1983 6d²) May 3; brother to 3 winners, notably top-class sprinter Thatching and smart sprinter Golden Thatch, and half-brother to a winner; dam very smart Irish sprinter; 4/1 on, found no extra in final furlong when beaten 1½ lengths by Sharp Roi in maiden event at Phoenix Park in October; not sure to stay 7f; evidently thought to have plenty of ability and is certain to improve and win races. *V. O'Brien, Ireland.* 76 p

WATSON'S BOY 3 b.c. Rolfe 77–Jezebel's Fancy (Dairialatan 111) (1982 NR 1983 10g 10fg) evidently of little account. *P. Ashworth.* —

WATTLEFIELD 4 b.c. Red God 128§–Short Commons 109 (Hard Tack 111§) (1982 8g 7.2h 1983 8d 8fg) a grand individual; walks well and moves with an extravagant, light action; smart performer at his best with a good turn of foot, but had training troubles and ran only twice in 1982 and 1983; having first outing for almost a year when respectable sixth to Mighty Fly in handicap at Sandown in May (well there 7f); tailed off in Queen Anne Stakes at Royal Ascot following month; stayed 7f; won on a soft surface but needed top-of-the-ground to show to best advantage; retired to Southcourt Stud, Bedfordshire at £500 + £1,000 Oct 1st. *M. Stoute.*

WAULKMILL 3 ch.f. Grundy 137–Guiding Light 78 (Crepello 136) (1982 7fg 8g 1983 10fg) sturdy filly; soundly beaten in minor event and maiden races; sold 23,000 gns Newmarket December Sales. *W. Holden.* —

WAY OF THE WOLD 5 b.g. Sandford Lad 133–Tatty Kay (Tarqogan 125) (1982 NR 1983 13v 12d 12.3v 13d 12d 15fg² 18f³ 14fg) small gelding; has been hobdayed; good mover; suited by a test of stamina; ideally suited by top-of-the-ground; sometimes blinkered; has sweated up; suitable mount for an inexperienced rider; didn't look keen seventh start. *S. Norton.* 49

WAYSIDE INN 4 b.g. Thatch 136–Holiday Inn (Le Haar 126) (1982 NR 1983 9f 10f 12.3fg³ 12g) IR 43,000Y, 1,800 3-y-o; robust, good sort; third foal; dam unraced half-sister to smart French miler Gracious Knight and very useful 9f and 1¼m winner Christmas Box; staying-on third of 17 to Karablake in maiden race at Newcastle in August, easily best effort; suited by 1½m+; bandaged final start. *B. Wilkinson.* —

WAYWARD GLANCE 2 b.f. Bold Lad (Ire) 133–Cliona (Ballymore 123) (1983 6f³ 6g 6g 6fg² 6fg 6fg) May 31; rangy, good-bodied filly; second foal; dam, useful French 1¼m winner, is out of Kew, a very useful sister to Floribunda; quite moderate maiden; will stay 7f; blinkered fourth and fifth outings. *R. Armstrong.* 79

Miner's Northumberland Plate, Newcastle—Weavers' Pin beats Prince Santiago, Karadar (right) and Crusader Castle (blaze) in a driving finish

899

WAYWARD POLLY 3 br.f. Lochnager 132–Trigamy 112 (Tribal Chief 125) (1982   –
5fg 5f 5f³ 5g 5d* 5g 1983 6fg) smallish, lengthy filly; won a seller as a 2-y-o; tailed
off only outing in 1983; evidently suited by a soft surface. *N. Callaghan.*

WEAVER'S DAUGHTER 2 b.f. Captain James 123–Weavers' Lane (Weavers'   **63**
Hall 122) (1983 5fg 6f 5fg) Mar 15; 6,000F, IR 3,000Y (privately); first foal; dam
won over 1¼m in Ireland; plating-class maiden; form only on first outing; will be
suited by 7f+. *C. Horgan.*

WEAVERS' PIN 6 b.g. Weavers' Hall 122–Priceless Pin (Saint Crespin III 132)   **90**
(1982 13fg² 16g⁴ 14f 12f* 12fg³ 1983 11.7s 12v³ 13.3g* 12f⁴ 16f* 16.1fg
15fg² 16f³) small, fair sort; fairly useful performer; won handicaps at Newbury and
Newcastle in June, leading near finish to beat Prince Santiago by ½ length in
Miner's Northumberland Plate on latter; 3 lengths second to Forward in Tennent
Trophy at Ayr in July; effective at middle distances and stays 2m; best form on
top-of-the-ground; good mount for an inexperienced rider; reportedly injured
suspensory ligament in August. *M. Francis.*

WEAVERS WAY 3 b.c. Weavers' Hall 122–Corneater (Skymaster 126) (1982   –
8d 1983 17v 12s 7f 9fg) big, workmanlike colt; has a round action; little
worthwhile form; sold to R. Cambidge 1,100 gns Ascot December Sales. *H.
Collingridge.*

WEBBS JEWEL 4 b.f. Shiny Tenth 120–Prompt Delivery (Catullus) (1982 6s*   **56**
6f 7f* 6fg 7d 7f 7fg 6f⁴ 6d 8s 1983 5s* 7s 7d 8f² 8fg² 6fg 7fg) fair sort; plater;
successful in small race in Isle of Man in May; stays 1m; acts on any going;
trained most of season by D. Marks. *M. Blanshard.*

WEDDED BLISS 7 b.m. Relko 136–True Home 89 (Princely Gift 137) (1982   –
13s⁴ 16.1s 12f⁴ 18f⁴ 15.8f⁴ 13.8f 14g⁴ 15.8f² 15.8d* 16d 1983 15.8d) sturdy
mare; stays well; seems to act on any going; suited by a strong pace and waiting
tactics; has given trouble on way to post. *D. Chapman.*

WEDNESDAY BOY 4 ch.g. Lucky Wednesday 124–Hutton Barns 92 (Saintly   –
Song 128) (1982 6s 6g* 6g 7fg 6fg³ 7fg³ 6d 1983 7s 8g) plater; poor mover;
should be suited by 1m; acts on any going; has been tried in blinkers; sold 645 gns
Ascot 2nd June Sales. *M. Hinchliffe.*

WEE FROSTY 2 gr.c. Absalom 128–Polly Darling 80 (Darling Boy 124) (1983   –
5v⁴ 5s 5d) Feb 3; 7,200F, IR 8,000Y; small colt; half-brother to a winning plater
and a winner abroad; dam won at up to 6f and was placed at up to 1½m; poor form in
maiden and minor events; sold 1,400 gns Doncaster June Sales, probably for export
to Norway. *P. Calver.*

WELCIANA 4 b.f. Welsh Pageant 132–Damiana 84 (Mourne 126) (1982 NR 1983   –
10g) seems of little account on flat though has won a selling hurdle. *R. Atkins.*

WELLAND TOWER 3 b.f. Comedy Star 121–Two On A Tower 89 (Nulli   –
Secundus 89) (1982 NR 1983 8v 8g 8f) fourth foal; dam won at up to 1½m and was
also successful over hurdles; in rear in maiden and minor races. *D. Elsworth.*

WELL COVERED 2 b. or br.c. Thatch 136–Tirana 101 (Ragusa 137) (1983 7f*   **83** +
7d) Apr 18; leggy, close-coupled colt; half-brother to 3 winners, including fairly
useful middle-distance winner and useful hurdler Brave Hussar (by Brigadier
Gerard); dam won over 6f and 7f at 2 yrs; won 20-runner maiden event at Newbury
in July, coming through strongly from halfway to beat Careen 1½ lengths; looked to
have stiffish task under top weight when favourite for quite valuable nursery at
York the following month and never got in a blow, finishing ninth of 16 to Blushing
Scribe; stays 7f well; acts on firm going; probably better than we are able to rate
him. *H. Cecil.*

WE'LL MEET AGAIN 6 b.h. Song 132–Coaster 61 (Right Tack 131) (1982 10s   **78**
10g 10fg 10fg 10s⁴ 10v² 12s 1983 10v⁴ 10s* 10v⁴ 10s* 10d² 10d 10g) workmanlike
horse; won handicaps at Leicester in April and Goodwood in May; stays 1¼m; acts
on any going but goes particularly well on soft; has run creditably for a boy; needs
to be held up. *J. Benstead.*

WELL RIGGED 2 ch.c. Windjammer (USA)–Topless Dancer (Northfields) (1983   **84**
6f² 6f 7f² 7f² 7f³) Mar 23; IR 9,800F, 13,000Y; lengthy, rather narrow colt; first
living foal; dam won over 1m in Ireland and also won over hurdles; placed in fair
company in the North; will stay 1m; should win a small race. *M. H. Easterby.*

WELSH DANCER 2 b. or br.f. Welsh Saint 126–Dancing Princess 99 (Prince   **94**
Regent 129) (1983 5s 5v² 5fg*) Apr 20; leggy, lightly-made filly; not a good
walker; fourth foal; sister to Irish 3-y-o 7f winner Welsh Light; dam stayed 1m;
picked up a valuable prize when beating April Wind a length in 5-runner Goffs
Silver Flash Stakes at Phoenix Park in July; had previously run well when length

second to Black Country in M. C. Collins Marble Hill Stakes at the Curragh in May; got loose at start and was withdrawn from Queen Mary Stakes at Royal Ascot in between; should stay 6f; probably acts on any going. *J. Oxx, Ireland.*

WELSH EVE 2 ch.f. Welsh Pageant 132–Crockeve 77 (Crocket 130) (1983 7.6d) — Mar 14; fourth foal; half-sister to a minor winner in France; dam, placed over 5f and 6f, is closely related to Queen Mary Stakes winner Farfalla; apprentice ridden, behind in 18-runner maiden race at Lingfield in October. *J. Dunlop.*

WELSH GLORY 3 ch.g. Welsh Pageant 132–Fairy Fans (Petingo 135) (1982 7s[3] 83 1983 7d[2] 7s[2] 8f[2] 8f) quite attractive gelding; good walker; second in maiden races at Newmarket, Leicester and Beverley, on last-named course in July giving impression he'd be suited by further than 1m; acts on any going; ran moderately final start and was subsequently gelded. *H. Cecil.*

WELSH IDOL 3 gr.c. Welsh Pageant 132–Idover 95 (Fortino II 120) (1982 7f 115 d 1983 10.6v* 10v[3] 10.5s 9fg[2] 9.2d 10d 10.5d 8fg) 18,000Y; rangy, good-bodied colt; brother to 5f to 7f winner Hamdani and half-brother to several winners; dam sprinter; won well-contested maiden event at Haydock in April, holding on by a neck from Teenoso after running very green in front; also ran creditably when 3 lengths third of 7 to Gordian in very slowly-run Guardian Classic Trial at Sandown later in month and when going down by ¾ length to Ginger Brink in 10-runner Prix Jean Prat at Chantilly in June; well beaten facing very stiff tasks on his other outings; stays 10.6f; seems to act on any going; blinkered last 2 starts. *P. Kelleway.*

WELSH MASTER 2 b. or br.g. Welsh Captain 113–Miss Albalist (Traditionalist) — (1983 5f 6f) May 11; IR 800F, IR 880Y; leggy gelding; first produce; dam ran once; behind in sizeable fields of platers at Ripon and Newcastle in August; sold 320 gns Doncaster October Sales. *D. Plant.*

WELSH NOBLE 5 b.h. Welsh Saint 126–Just A Glimmer 75 (Dumbarnie 125) 50 (1982 6fg[2] 6f[2] 6fg[4] 6fg[2] 6fg 1983 6s 6v 6fg 6f 6fg[3] 5.6f[4] 6fg 6f[2] 6fg) good-topped horse; sprint handicapper; suited by 6f; acts on any going; suitable mount for an apprentice; has worn blinkers. *A. Balding.*

WELSH ROSRAY 2 br.f. Welsh Saint 126–Primrose 86 (Primera 131) (1983 5fg[4] 78 5f*) May 14; IR 18,000Y; quite well-made filly; half-sister to 2 winners, notably useful 1980 2-y-o 7f winner Engulf (by Gulf Pearl); dam 2-y-o 5f winner; favourite, won 16-runner maiden race at Salisbury in June by 1½ lengths from Hot Melody; not sure to stay 6f. *R. Smyth.*

WELSH SPY 2 ch.g. Welsh Pageant 132–Spey 88 (Jimmy Reppin 131) (1983 6f 7f — 7fg 7g) Feb 22; 1,000Y; rangy, workmanlike gelding; third foal; dam 1½m winner; no worthwhile form; blinkered third outing; gelded after final appearance. *N. Guest.*

WELSH TERM 4 b.c. Welsh Pageant 132–Trinity Term 100 (Primera 131) (1982 126 8.5v* 8v[2] 10.5fg 10v* 12s* 12s* 1983 10s[2] 10v* 10.5d[3] 12v* 9.7d* 12s[4] 12f 13d 12g[4] 12d[2] 11g)

Unlike a number of his fellow trainers Robert Collet tends not to treat the horses in his care with kid gloves. For example, in 1983 Coleman and Tumulto ran twenty-two times apiece, Dear Prince twenty times, Black Tie eighteen times before being claimed out of the stable in June and the two-year-old Melodie Lidye an astonishing twenty-two times. Nor is it just the lesser lights who have fully to earn their keep, for the good three-year-old Dom Pasquini won a minor event two days before picking up the Prix Greffulhe and the high-class Welsh Term gained victories in two Group 2 races in the space of six days in May.

Prix Dollar, Longchamp—Welsh Term pegs back Orofino

Welsh Term was the best performer in the stable and a match over middle distances for any older horse of his sex in training in France. A convincing winner of the Prix d'Harcourt at Longchamp in April, beating Cadoudal four lengths, he also gained places in the Prix Exbury at Saint-Cloud (second to Imyar) and the Prix Ganay at Longchamp (five lengths third to Lancastrian) before going to Saint-Cloud for the Prix Jean de Chaudenay towards the end of May. There were no three-year-olds among the eight contestants and Welsh Term started a short-priced favourite ahead of Brezzo, second to Diamond Shoal in the Grand Prix d'Evry, and Zalataia. The last-named, unsuited by the deep going, ran below form in sixth and Brezzo, despite finishing quite well to be second, had no chance with Welsh Term who led a furlong and a half out and scored smoothly by two and a half lengths. Although the Prix Dollar at Longchamp, run later the same week, is over two furlongs shorter than the Jean de Chaudenay this proved no problem to Welsh Term as he came with a decisive run to peg back the good German horse Orofino in the last hundred yards for a short-neck win; the front-running Darly, later to run well in the Prix d'Ispahan and Prix du Prince d'Orange, finished a length and a half away third.

After the Dollar Collet announced that Welsh Term would be aimed at the Coral-Eclipse and Budweiser Million but in fact he wasn't seen out again until the autumn and spent most of the rest of the year in unavailing attempts to get to grips with the brilliant All Along. A creditable fourth to Time Charter in the Prix Foy at Longchamp, he ended up towards the rear in the Trusthouse Forte Prix de l'Arc de Triomphe—a poor display that can be ascribed to his being unsuited by the very fast ground—and was then sent to the American trainer Sonnier for a crack at some of the top events in Canada and the States. Eighth to All Along in the Rothmans International at Woodbine, he ran a similar race when a well-beaten fourth to her in the Turf Classic at Aqueduct and then put up a bold show in the Washington International at Laurel, battling on gamely once he lost the lead to All Along half a mile out to go down by just over three lengths. On his final start Welsh Term ran unplaced behind John Henry and Zalataia in the Hollywood Invitational Turf Cup at Hollywood Park.

		Tudor Melody	Tudor Minstrel
	Welsh Pageant	(br 1956)	Matelda
	(b 1966)	Picture Light	Court Martial
Welsh Term		(b 1964)	Queen of Light
(b.c. 1979)		Primera	My Babu
	Trinity Term	(b 1954)	Pirette
	(b 1968)	Hilary Term	Supreme Court
		(b 1962)	Spring Running

Purchased for 29,000 guineas as a foal, Welsh Term is one of five winners out of the easy Chesham Stakes winner Trinity Term. The others include his sister Orchestration, successful in the 1977 Coronation Stakes, and Bishop of Orange (by English Prince) who showed useful form over middle distances in Ireland. Trinity Term's dam, who had only two foals, both winners, won over a mile after running fifth in the Oaks and was a granddaughter of the French Oaks and Grand Prix de Paris winner Bagheera. Welsh Term, a tall, well-made, attractive individual, unquestionably needs some give in the ground and revels in the heavy going he encountered in the Harcourt and Jean de Chaudenay. *R. Collet, France.*

WELSH WARRIOR 3 ch.g. Welsh Pageant 132–Brave Lass 114 (Ridan) (1982   **95**
6f 1983 8d* 8f⁴) rangy gelding; heavily-backed favourite, although having first race for 16 months, beat Waterhead in quite good style by 4 lengths in 24-runner minor event at Warwick in October; odds on, didn't look at ease on firm going when 4½ lengths fourth of 16 to Only A Pound in similar race at Redcar later in month; stays 1m well; wears small bandages in front nowadays. *H. Cecil.*

WELSH WILLIE 2 ch.c. Young Generation 129–Rose Spring 72 (High Top 131)   **81**
(1983 6fg² 5fg* 6f 6g³) Feb 17; 10,000F, 14,000Y; lengthy, useful-looking colt; first live foal; dam 1¼m winner; got up close home to win 15-runner maiden race at Windsor in July by ¾ length from Bold Realm; beaten favourite in nurseries afterwards; stays 6f but has shown better form at 5f; acts on a firm surface. *M. Stoute.*

WELSH WOMAN 2 b.f. Welsh Saint 126–Devil Woman (Prince Regent 129)   **105**
(1983 5fg 5f³ 5f* 5f* 6d³) Mar 1; IR 15,000Y; useful-looking filly; third foal; dam Irish 2-y-o 5f winner; made all when easy winner of 2 races at Limerick Junction in August, accounting for 3 fairly useful winners in good style when beating Jingo Ring 2½ lengths in Ballsbridge-Tattersalls Stakes on fourth start; looked particularly

well when 14/1 for Moyglare Stud Stakes at the Curragh the following month and put up a performance to match, finishing length third of 20 to Gala Event after bowling along in lead for long way; may prove best at 5f; seems to act on any going; should win more races. *K. Prendergast, Ireland.*

WENSUM LASS 2 b.f. The Brianstan 128–Screen Goddess 65 (Caliban 123)   –
(1983 5f 7fg 5g 5g 7s 8f) Feb 12; strong, plain filly; second foal; dam, placed at up to 1½m, is half-sister to Cambridgeshire winner Negus; behind in varied company; apparently of little account. *B. Richmond.*

WEST ASHLING 3 b.f. Firestreak 125–Beseech 84 (Petition 130) (1982 NR   –
1983 10g 8f⁴ 8fg 8f) stocky, heavy-bodied filly; sister to 2 poor animals and half-sister to several winners, including 1981 2-y-o 5f winner Begham Bay (by Bay Express) and fairly useful 1978 2-y-o Man of the Sea (by Mansingh); dam won over 11f; fourth of 17 to easy winner Magnetic Field in minor event at Salisbury in August, only sign of ability; stays 1m; has worn bandages. *P. Haynes.*

WESTERN CIRCUIT 3 br.f. Undulate–Quick Draw 70 (Kalydon 122) (1982 5d   –
1983 6d 6g) neat filly; in rear in maiden and minor events; bred to need 7f+. *J. Mason.*

WESTERN DANCER 2 b.c. Free State 125–Polyandrist 92 (Polic 126) (1983   **83**
6d² 6fg 6fg) May 21; lengthy colt; half-brother to several winners, including very useful 5f performer Trigamy (by Tribal Chief); dam best at up to 1¼m; strong-finishing 3 lengths second of 24 to Preobrajenska in minor event at Lingfield in October, easily best effort; probably needs 7f+, particularly when conditions are not testing. *C. Horgan.*

WESTERN SYMPHONY (USA) 2 b.c. Nijinsky 138–Millicent (Cornish   **112**
Prince) (1983 7f³ 5g* 7g² 6d* 7d*)
    The Larkspur Stakes run at Leopardstown in October rarely fails to attract a fancied runner from Ballydoyle. 1983 proved no exception: Western Symphony

Mr R. E. Sangster's "Western Symphony"

started the eighth O'Brien-trained favourite for the race and became his fifth winner in the last ten years. Although he can't compare with the best of his stable's previous winners, The Minstrel, Try My Best and Storm Bird, Western Symphony beat a substandard field in useful style. Tracking the leader Sign-of-Life for most of the trip, he forged through in the final furlong to pass the post a length clear of the subsequently demoted runner-up. In winning this Group 3 event Western Symphony avenged his defeat by Fiery Celt in the Tap On Wood Stakes at Phoenix Park earlier in the month—on terms 5 lb worse Fiery Celt could finish only sixth at Leopardstown. In the interim Western Symphony had beaten Anita's Prince by three lengths under top weight in the Birdcatcher Nursery at Naas, again quickening clear in the final furlong after holding a good position. These three performances amply confirmed the promise he'd shown in his two earlier races: he'd finished under three lengths third to stable-companion El Gran Senor on his debut, and was odds on when beating Formalist by a head in a valuable maiden event at Phoenix Park.

		Northern Dancer	Nearctic
	Nijinsky	(b 1961)	Natalma
	(b 1967)	Flaming Page	Bull Page
Western Symphony (USA)		(b 1959)	Flaring Top
(b.c. May 4, 1981)		Cornish Prince	Bold Ruler
	Millicent	(br 1962)	Teleran
	(b 1969)	Milan Mill	Princequillo
		(b 1962)	Virginia Water

Western Symphony is the sixth winning foal of his dam Millicent, an unraced half-sister to Mill Reef. The best of these is Western Symphony's close relation Peterhof (by The Minstrel), winner of the Flying Childers Stakes and now standing at stud in the United States. Of the others two were successful at a mile or more—the In Reality filly Marston's Mill was a stakes-placed winner at up to a mile, and Beverley Mill (by Tom Rolfe) scored at up to nine furlongs in modest company. Western Symphony gave the impression on his second start that five furlongs was too sharp; he should stay a mile. Obviously he needs to improve to match the best of his generation but he will no doubt be placed to win a decent race in Ireland at three years. He acts on soft ground, and wore blinkers on his last two starts. *V. O'Brien, Ireland.*

WESTGATE LADY 2 gr.f. Sandy Creek 123–Mariko (Dancer's Image) (1983 5fg 5f⁴ 5g 6fg 5s² 5fg⁴) May 11; 8,200Y; small, workmanlike filly; second foal; dam Irish 5f winner; plating-class maiden; ran badly (last of 18) over 6f; acts on any ground; blinkered last 2 starts. *C. Booth.*   **69**

WESTGATE STAR 4 b.g. He Loves Me 120–Sea Swallow 90 (Dan Cupid 132) (1982 7g⁴ 10f⁴ 11g³ 10.1fg 11g 8fg³ 9g⁴ 8f³ 10.6s 8s 1983 8v⁴ 8g 8fg² 9d 8g 8g* 8fg) rangy gelding; won minor event at Edinburgh in October; stays 9f; acts on a soft surface but has shown best form on top-of-the-ground; good mount for an inexperienced rider; has sweated up. *P. Calver.*   **63**

WESTMOUNT SQUARE (USA) 2 b.c. Icecapade–Mean Katrine (Hasty Road) (1983 6h³ 6fg⁴ 7g 6fg⁴) Mar 20; $70,000Y; workmanlike colt; third foal; dam won over 6f at 2 yrs; ran fair race second outing and moderate ones on other 3; should stay 7f; blinkered final start; disappointing; sent to USA. *H. Cecil.*   **88**

WESTVIEW 3 b.f. Shirley Heights 130–West Two 104 (Connaught 130) (1982 NR 1983 12d⁴ 14g² 13fg* 14f 13fg* 14fg) strong, lengthy filly; third foal; dam 2-y-o 6f winner; successful in maiden race at Nottingham in July and handicap on same course in September, staying on well to beat Rikki Tavi decisively by 1½ lengths in latter; stays 1¾m; acts on a firm surface; genuine; sold 12,000 gns Newmarket December Sales. *H. Cecil.*   **84**

WEST WELLOW 3 ch.g. Red Alert 127–Jodees Gift (On Your Mark 125) (1982 5f 5f 5d 6f⁴ 6fg 6f⁴ 6g⁴ 6fg* 7v 1983 7s 7s³ 7f 7f² 7f⁴ 7.3g) robust, useful-looking gelding; in frame in handicaps, best effort when second to impressive Major Don in quite valuable event at Leicester in July; stays 7f; probably acts on any going. *G. Balding.*   **74**

WESTWOOD DANCER 4 b.f. Home Guard 129–Great Bounty (Tarqogan 125) (1982 10s 8fg³ 10f³ 8f³ 11g 8f 8fg 7f² 7f⁴ 9g 8.2g 7f² 7d 7g² 6s 1983 7fg² 7d 8fg 8f* 8f⁴ 7f 7g 7g* 9d 7g) strong, quite well-made filly; poor mover; poor handicapper; won at Edinburgh in July and Catterick in September; doesn't stay 11f; seems to act on any going; best in blinkers; sold 2,300 gns Ascot November Sales. *T. Fairhurst.*   **64**

WET BOB 5 ch.g. Run The Gantlet–River Craft (Reliance II 137) (1982 11.7fg **62**
12d 12fg 12fg 16d 15.8d 1983 12s* 16v* 16s* 17.1v 18fg 18fg) small, stocky
gelding; in great form in spring and won handicaps at Leicester (made virtually all),
Warwick and Newbury; stays well; revels in the mud; best in blinkers. *R. Holder.*

WETHBA 2 b.f. Artaius 129–Lareyna 98 (Welsh Pageant 132) (1983 5v³ 6s 5fg³ **64**
7f 6fg 6f 6g) Feb 8; 24,000Y; neat filly; first foal; dam won over 5f and 6f at 2 yrs;
plating-class maiden; stays 6f. *M. Blanshard.*

WHANGAREI 5 b.m. Gold Rod 129–Vilmainder 78 (Remainder 106) (1982 7g **–**
8fg 8g 8fg 8fg 8.2g 8g² 8fg 10d* 8.2s 10g³ 1983 10.1d 10.6s 8f 10fg) plain mare;
has stringhalt; plater; stays 1¼m; acts on any going. *D. Wintle.*

WHAT A PITY 3 b.f. Blakeney 126–Scarcely Blessed 116 (So Blessed 130) (1982 **97**
NR 1983 7d* 9v³ 7f 8f) small, attractive filly; second foal; dam, smart sprinter,
from very good family; beat Magdalena by a head in 11-runner newcomers race at
Newbury in April, racing close up throughout and running on courageously under
pressure; didn't act on the heavy ground when 12½ lengths third of 11 behind Maid
of Milan in minor event at Wolverhampton in May and was off course afterwards
until July (soundly beaten, facing stiffish tasks, both outings on her return); should
stay at least 1m; sold 185,000 gns Newmarket December Sales. *F. J. Houghton.*

WHAT EXCITEMENT 3 gr.f. Dragonara Palace 115–Gold of the Day 72 (Bing **–**
II) (1982 5f 5.3g³ 5s⁴ 1983 6v 6s 6d 6fg 6f⁴ 8g 7f 5h 6f) lightly-made filly; poor
maiden; should be suited by 6f. *E. Witts.*

WHAT LAKE (USA) 3 br.f. What Luck–Placid Lake (Terrang) (1982 5g² 6g* **110**
5v⁴ 1983 7d⁴ 8g² 6f⁴ 8s) well-made, quite attractive filly; never reached leaders
but nevertheless ran well when 4½ lengths fourth of 9 to Favoridge in Nell
Gwyn Stakes at Newmarket in April; in frame twice at Rome afterwards, finishing
3½ lengths second of 8 behind Right Bank in Premio Regina Elena (Italian 1000
Guineas) and about 1½ lengths fourth of 9 to Snatch And Run in Premio Melton;
stays 1m; probably acts on any going. *B. Hanbury.*

WHAT'S IN STORE 2 b.f. Captain James 123–Half Pint (Blakeney 126) (1983 6f **–**
7h 7s) Mar 11; 6,300F, 2,000Y; well-grown filly; fourth foal (first to Northern
Hemisphere time); dam never ran; no form in maiden company. *C. Nelson.*

WHEATFIELD 2 br.c. Camden Town 125–Hell's Angels 109 (Hook Money 124) **70**
(1983 6d 5.8g³ 6f 7f) May 11; IR 3,000Y; leggy, light-framed colt; half-brother to
2000 Guineas third Thieving Demon (by Burglar) and a winner over hurdles; dam,
useful Irish 2-y-o, is sister to good sprinter Daylight Robbery; showed ability in
maiden auction events, best effort when 2¾ lengths third of 13 to Janicolane at
Bath in June; not seen out after July. *P. Kelleway.*

WHEELWRIGHTS LADY 2 b.f. Porto Bello 118–Her Worship 61 (Privy **58**
Councillor 125) (1983 5d 5g 6fg 6g 7fg 8d 8.2fg³ 8d 10d) Feb 22; leggy,
dipped-backed, shallow-girthed filly; moderate plater; suited by 1m; acts on a
firm surface. *M. Haynes.*

WHEN I DREAM 2 gr.f. Sparkler 130–Grey Home 110 (Habitat 134) (1983 6f 7f **–**
6g) Apr 14; 3,700Y; lengthy, fair sort; half-sister to 3-y-o middle-distance winner
Jinny Beaumont (by Blakeney) and 7f and 1m winner Hiya Judge (by Ashmore); dam
very useful 5f winner from only 3 starts; little worthwhile form in maiden and minor
events. *G. Balding.*

WHENYOURTRAINSGONE 4 b. or br.g. Free State 125–Great Blue White **–**
73 (Great Nephew 126) (1982 9fg² 8fg² 10f 10d* 10f 9g² 8g 9d 8.2s 10s* 1983 8d
8d) fair sort; well beaten both starts in 1983; ideally suited by 1¼m; suited by
some give in the ground; blinkered once; dead. *F. Watson.*

WHERE YOU WILL 3 gr.f. Great Nephew 126–Bundling (Petingo 135) (1982 **48**
7g 1983 9s³ 10s 10s 8f 8f 8d) good-topped filly; poor maiden; should stay 1¼m;
sometimes blinkered; sold to BBA (Italia) 2,200 gns Newmarket December Sales.
I. Balding.

WHINSTONE 3 ch.c. Great Nephew 126–Irma Flintstone 110 (Compensation **–**
127) (1982 5g 6fg 1983 5v 5v 7f 10f) compact colt; poor form in minor and maiden
events; dead. *T. Fairhurst.*

WHIRLABOUT 2 b.g. Tumble Wind–Rahesh 111 (Raffingora 130) (1983 5s 5g 5f **–**
6s⁴ 7g) Feb 2; 20,000Y; robust, good-bodied, quite attractive gelding; first foal;
dam very useful and speedy at 2 yrs; soundly beaten in maiden and minor events;
blinkered final start; subsequently gelded. *D. Hanley.*

WHISKEY EYES 2 ch.c. Stanford 121§–Lepello (Le Levanstell 122) (1983 5v **–**
7g) Feb 10; IR 5,400Y; workmanlike, good-bodied colt; half-brother to 1980 Irish

2-y-o 7.5f winner Le Boosh (by Tarboosh) and to 1½m winner Master Carl (by Pitskelly); dam never ran; showed up in big fields of maidens at Kempton (auction race) in April and Leicester in September; may be capable of improvement. *S. Mellor.*

WHISKEY TIME 3 b.g. Filiberto 123–Glebe 83 (Tacitus 124) (1982 NR 1983 **84** 12v³ 12.3v 12g⁴ 16g² 16f 14f² 14.6f³ 16h² 16f*) 2,000Y; lengthy gelding; has a round action; half-brother to 4 winners, including 7f winner Cannon Hall (by Singing Bede); dam, winner over 2m, is half-sister to high-class filly Bringley; in frame most outings and won a maiden race at Beverley in August after being given quite an enterprising ride; stays 2m; acts on firm going, but gives impression he'll be best served by some give in the ground; moved and ran poorly when blinkered fifth start. *C. Brittain.*

WHISKY TALK 3 b. or br.c. Wolverlife 115–Little Hills (Candy Cane 125) (1982 **102** 6d³ 1983 7.6v* 10.5s² 8.5s 8fg 8fg 9g* 8s 8fg³ 8fg³) tall, quite attractive colt; good walker and mover; won 4-runner minor event at Lingfield in April and 17-runner Falmouth Handicap at York in August, latter pushed out by 3 lengths from Music Lover after travelling well throughout; also ran creditably when ½-length second of 7 to Gay Lemur in £4,500 event at York in May (raced freely in lead much of way), third of 18 behind Torgos in Elite-Preis at Cologne in October (narrowly beaten) and third of 8 to Nandino in Premio Ribot at Rome in November; rather disappointing on his other outings, including in 2 ladies races; stays 10.5f; yet to race on very firm going, but acts on any other; probably suited by a strong gallop and waiting tactics; blinkered fourth outing; inconsistent. *I. Balding.*

WHISPERING GRASS (USA) 2 b.c. Key To The Mint–Hill Whisper (Hillary) **–** (1983 8fg) Mar 20; $200,000Y; tall, lengthy colt, with plenty of scope; half-brother to 2 winners, including very useful 8.5f stakes winner Madera Sun (by Montparnasse II); dam, winner over 1m, is closely related to smart Hill Shade, the dam of J.O. Tobin and Mysterious; last of 7 in £3,200 event at Newmarket in October. *G. Harwood.*

WHISTLEDOWNWIND 2 b.g. Saritamer 130–Rippling Wind 87 (Jimmy **– p** Reppin 131) (1983 7d) Apr 1; 3,600Y; first foal; dam winning sprinter; 7 lengths fifth of 19, finishing well, to Dorset Venture in maiden race at Warwick in October; subsequently gelded; should improve. *M. Usher.*

WHISTLE HILL 3 b.g. So Blessed 130–Sera Sera 88 (Hill Clown) (1982 6fg 6d **62** 7fg⁴ 8s 1983 6f³ 6fg⁴ 8f⁴ 8f* 9g) won maiden race at Beverley in September; stays 1m; acts on firm going; sold 4,700 gns Doncaster November Sales. *C. Thornton.*

WHITEHALL BRIDGE 6 b.h. Auction Ring 123–Farce (Bon Mot II 132) (1982 **–** 12g 10.5g 14d 10.5s 1983 16d 14fg 17d) strong, good-bodied ex-French horse; useful performer at 4 yrs but has deteriorated; suited by 1½m+; goes well on soft ground; effective with or without blinkers; winning hurdler. *J. Edwards.*

WHITEMANS DREAM 7 b.g. African Sky 124–Kirkwall 74 (Sheshoon 132) **–** (1982 NR 1983 8fg 9.4f 8g 8f) of little account. *J. Smith.*

WHITE MORNING 4 ch.f. Swing Easy 126–Carina Janie 88 (Silver Cloud 121) **–** (1982 8f 8g 8fg 1983 8fg) poor plater; has worn blinkers. *R. Keenor.*

WHITE NILE (USA) 3 b.c. Upper Nile–Popaway (Cyclotron) (1982 5fg³ 7d **–** 1983 7s 7.6v 8f 8f 12.3f³ 10f⁴ 10.1fg 8f 8d 8f) neat, strong, quite attractive colt; disappointing maiden; should be suited by 1m+; sold to C. Booth 5,200 gns Newmarket Autumn Sales. *F. Durr.*

WHITE SPADE 3 b.c. Brigadier Gerard 144–Mattinata 90 (Matador 131) (1982 **115** 5g² 5.5s² 6fg² 6.5g³ 8d* 10v⁴ 10v² 1983 9.7s² 8v 10v* 9fg 10d³ 10f) strong colt; half-brother to several winners, including useful 1978 2-y-o 7f winner Chalumeau (by Relko); dam 5f sprinter; quickened well to go a length clear 1½f out in Prix La Force at Longchamp in May and kept on gamely to hold off Margouzed by a short neck; not beaten far on most other starts, including when placed in Prix de Guiche at Longchamp (2 lengths second to Pluralisme) and Prix Eugene Adam at Saint-Cloud (third to Mourjane) and when fifth of 10 behind L'Emigrant in Poule d'Essai des Poulains at Longchamp on second start; suited by 1¼m and may well stay further; probably acts on any going but is well suited by plenty of give; sent to USA. *D. Smaga, France.*

WHITEWALLS 3 b.g. Pitskelly 122–More The Perrier (Rarity 129) (1982 5f 5g **61** 6f 5g 5d⁴ 6s 5d³ 1983 7g 6g* 6g³ 6f³ 7f³ 6fg³ 6fg* 6s) sturdy gelding; poor walker and mover; won handicap at Catterick in May and seller at Windsor in September; bought in 2,900 gns after latter; stays 7f; acts on any going. *D. Garraton.*

WHITSTAR 3 b.f. Whitstead 125–Reita 87 (Gilles de Retz 132) (1982 8g 10.2s* 1983 12d³ 10d 12s 12f 12g) strong, well-made filly; quite useful as a 2-y-o; gained only placing of 1983 when 8 lengths third of 8 to High Cannon in minor event at Thirsk in April; one paced and stays well; acts on soft going and moved poorly on firm fourth start; sold 7,000 gns Newmarket December Sales. *M. Jarvis.* —

WHITTINGTON (USA) 5 b.g. Best Turn–Novee (Judgable) (1982 8g 8g³ 12fg⁴ 1983 10f 12f 12f) workmanlike gelding; plater; stays 1½m; acts on any going; sold 3,000 gns Ascot August Sales. *G. Balding.* —

WHO KNOWS THE GAME 2 ch.f. John de Coombe 122–Long Valley 71 (Ribero 126) (1983 5v³ 5d² 5d² 5fg* 6fg² 5f 6f⁴ 6fg² 5f* 5fg* 5fg 5g* 5s*) May 5; 800Y; workmanlike filly; half-sister to a winning plater; dam showed a little ability at 2 yrs; did very well in second half of season, winning nurseries at Newcastle, Wolverhampton and Beverley, last 2 by narrow margins under penalties; had earlier won sellers at Beverley in June (no bid despite winning by 8 lengths) and Ripon in August (bought in 3,400 gns); speedy and best at 5f; acts on any going; tough, game and consistent; sold 8,000 gns Doncaster November Sales. *B. McMahon.* **81**

WHY THE BUSTLE 2 b.f. Bustino 136–Polly Packer 81 (Reform 132) (1983 7fg) Apr 14; 46,000F; first produce; dam, daughter of very useful miler Vital Match, was second over 7f and 1m; backward, out of first 9 of 30 in maiden race at Newmarket in August; likely to do better. *B. Hobbs.* — p

WIBIS RANGE 4 b.c. Wolver Hollow 126–Polonaise (Takawalk II 125) (1982 7g* 8fg⁴ 10f 8.2f 8d 7.2g⁴ 8g 7fg⁴ 10f³ 8g⁴ 10.6f 1983 8s 10v² 7g 8v* 8g² 9fg² 8d³ 8fg² 9g) tall colt; held off Romoss by short head in Thirsk Hunt Cup in May; ran creditably most subsequent outings; best at up to 9f; acts on any going; blinkered second and third starts; has run creditably for an apprentice. *M. Naughton.* **77**

WIDD 6 b.g. Derring-Do 131–Tin Mary 96 (Tin King 126) (1982 7fg 7g 8fg⁴ 1983 12v⁴ 16v 12d 12s 12s² 12s* 12g² 14fg² 12f⁴ 12fg) workmanlike gelding; easily won handicap at Brighton in May; ran creditably next 2 starts; stays 1¾m; seems to act on any going; blinkered once at 3 yrs; has run creditably for an apprentice; swerved left 2f out on ninth outing. *D. Mills.* **61**

WIDDICOMBE FAIR 2 b.f. Fair Season 120–Calgary 63 (Run The Gantlet) (1983 6f 8d 9g) Mar 29; rather sparely-made filly; first foal; dam, middle-distance maiden, is half-sister to Cesarewitch winner Centurion; soundly beaten in maiden races, best effort when over 14 lengths fifth of 13 to My Tootsie at Wolverhampton in October on final appearance. *I. Balding.* **59**

WIDE MISSOURI 3 br.c. Warpath 113–Shenandoah 88 (Mossborough 126) (1982 6d 6s 1983 10v 16fg² 16f² 18f 15g 16.1s 18fg) sturdy colt; good walker; runner-up in maiden races; stays well; sold to R. Champion 5,200 gns Doncaster November Sales. *C. Thornton.* **72** d

WIKI WIKI WHEELS 3 ch.c. Import 127–Falcrello 61 (Falcon 131) (1982 6d⁴ 5.8g* 6fg* 6fg 5g* 6f² 5g* 5v 1983 5s⁴ 6d³ 6d³ 6f 5f⁴ 6f 7f⁴ 7f* 6s 7fg* 7fg*) strong, quite attractive colt; a grand sort who won handicaps at York in August and Newmarket (2) in October, beating Rare Roberta and Worlingworth respectively by 2 lengths on latter course; suited by 7f nowadays; acts on any going; genuine; blinkered last 4 outings. *C. Nelson.* **105**

WILBY 4 ch.g. Ribston 104–Kist 53 (Lucky Symbol 82) (1982 NR 1983 8fg) first foal; dam second in 5f seller at 2 yrs; tailed-off last in maiden race at Edinburgh in April. *M. Ryan.* —

WILDHORN 3 ch.g. Midsummer Night II 117–She's the One (Sword Dancer) (1982 8fg 7d 7fg³ 7g² 7g 1983 8v 8v 11.7fg² 10g³ 12f⁴ 12f² 11.7h³ 11.7fg) well-made gelding; in frame in handicaps and maiden races in summer; gives impression he'll be suited by further than 1½m; suited by a sound surface; not particularly consistent; blinkered second and seventh starts. *H. Candy.* **81** d

WILDRUSH 4 b.g. Free State 125–Ribble Reed 75 (Bullrush 106) (1982 8g 8.2v 8f 10fg 1983 12d* 12s 12fg⁴ 12.3f³ 12f⁴ 16f) big gelding; apprentice ridden, always prominent when decisively winning minor event at Pontefract in April; suited by 1½m; seems to act on any going; sometimes sweats up. *W. C. Watts.* **60**

WILD SIDE 2 ro.c. Record Token 128–Stroppy Lou (Shantung 132) (1983 5v 5d 5f⁴ 6f 6fg* 5f² 7f) Mar 25; 4,500Y; strong colt; good walker; half-brother to 5f to **80**

10.6f winner Bright Charlie (by Saintly Song); dam never ran; made all in 14-runner minor event at Nottingham in July; stays 7f; acts on firm going; best in blinkers; exported to Hong Kong. *M. W. Easterby.*

WILGOR 2 b.c. Relkino 131–Jarama (Amber Rama 133) (1983 5g 5g 7f 8.2g³ 6s 8fg 8g) May 31; 600 2-y-o; neat colt; poor plater; stays 1m; sold 700 gns Doncaster November Sales. *J. Berry.* — 47

WILL BE WANTON 3 b.f. Palm Track 122–Immodest Miss 73 (Daring Display 129) (1982 6f 6f 6fg 8fg 7.2s 6s 6s³ 6s 6s 1983 6s 6v 5.3f 5g 5.3f 6f 6f 6fg 10f⁴ 10g 10g 10fg³) small filly; plater; seems to stay 1¼m; inconsistent; blinkered eighth outing. *P. K. Mitchell.* —

WILLERBY 6 b.g. Great Nephew 126–Sera Sera 88 (Hill Clown) (1982 11fg* 13fg 8f³ 11g 12fg⁴ 11fg 10fg 1983 10v 12d 11g 10f 10f) neat gelding; poor handicapper; stays 11f; acts on firm going; trained part of season by T. Craig. *J. Parkes.* —

WILL GEORGE 4 br.g. Abwah 118–Grey Miss 72 (Grey Sovereign 128§) (1982 5f 5f 5f 5f 5fg³ 5fg 5g 5f 5fg* 6f 5s* 1983 5v³ 5v 5.8s 5g² 5g⁴ 5g) good-topped gelding; poor mover; sprint handicapper; speedy and is best at 5f; acts on any going; usually blinkered; suitable mount for an apprentice. *G. Harwood.* — 74

WILLIAM BLAKE 4 b.g. Blakeney 126–Parthian Glance 120 (Parthia 132) (1982 10.5v 10.7g 12g 12fg 11g 12g² 12g⁴ 11d 15.5v 1983 12v 13v 12g³ 12f* 16.5f* 14fg* 15.8fg² 18.8f²) quite attractive ex-French gelding; fifth foal; half-brother to useful stayer Knight Templar (by King Log) and another winner; dam best 3-y-o staying filly of 1966; much improved and won handicaps at Salisbury in June, Folkestone in July and Haydock in August, 2 of them amateur riders races; stays very well; acts on any going; blinkered fifth start at 3 yrs. *J. Dunlop.* — 85

WILLIE GAN 5 ch.g. McIndoe 97–Queen's Bay 73 (King's Troop 118) (1982 11s 7f³ 6f* 6fg* 6f⁴ 6g 1983 7d 6s 6v⁴ 6s 6f* 6f² 6fg³ 6f³ 6fg* 6f³ 5fg 6g 6fg) quite a useful sort; won handicaps at Thirsk and Redcar in June and Ripon in August; best at 6f; ideally suited by a sound surface; good mount for an apprentice; often makes the running; consistent. *D. Smith.* — 78

WILLOWBED 3 gr.f. Wollow 132–Abergrove 103 (Abernant 142) (1982 6d 1983 7s 8.5d 10fg² 10fg³ 10f* 9d 10g³) fair sort; won maiden event at Brighton in August; difficult to settle previous start; suited by 1¼m; possibly needs a sound surface. *J. Dunlop.* — 66

WILLOW TWIG 2 ch.g. Bruni 132–Willow Walk 74 (Farm Walk 111) (1983 7fg) Apr 10; first foal; dam won over 1½m and also won over hurdles, fences and in point-to-points; in need of the race, ran well when 5 lengths fifth of 12 behind Miss Saint-Cloud in minor event at Doncaster in October; subsequently gelded; should prove capable of winning in the North at 1½m or more. *Miss S. Hall.* — 81 p

WILLY JAMES 3 br.c. Blue Cashmere 129–Seadora 68 (Sea Hawk II 131) (1982 5fg⁴ 5f² 5.1g* 5fg³ 5fg³ 5fg⁴ 6d 7s 1983 5g 6.5g* 5d³ 5s³ 6d) lengthy, quite attractive colt; not a good mover in his slower paces; won at Cagnes-sur-Mer and was third on same course and was third at Doncaster (beaten 2 short heads) in spring; stays 6.5f; acts on any going. *R. Armstrong.* — 75

WILLYPOUS 3 b.c. Tachypous 128–Daughter of Song 73 (Song 132) (1982 6d 6fg 7d 7g 5d 7g 6d 1983 7s 9s 7fg 8f 8g) sturdy colt; plating-class maiden; stays 7f; sold 1,250 gns Ascot August Sales. *R. Hollinshead.* —

WILLY WITEFOOT ESQ 4 ch.g. Hotfoot 126–Mountain of Mourne 76 (Mountain Call 125) (1982 10d 12.3fg⁴ 10f 1983 12.3fg 14fg⁴ 16fg⁴ 15.8d 18fg 15fg⁴) rather lightly-made gelding; staying maiden; pulls hard. *M. Lambert.* — 59

WILTSHIRE YEOMAN 3 ch.c. Derrylin 115–Ribo Pride 77 (Ribero 126) (1982 8s³ 1983 11.7v 10.1fg 14f 14f³ 15.5f⁴ 12f) lengthy colt; quite a moderate maiden; stays 1¾m (not beaten far but ran below form over further). *D. Elsworth.* — 71

WIMPY FRANKHART 3 b.g. Relkino 131–Colony 93 (Constable 119) (1982 7g 6g 7fg 1983 10v 8v) rangy gelding; behind in varied races, including a seller; sold 925 gns Ascot May Sales. *D. Elsworth.* —

WINART 5 br.h. Scottish Rifle 127–Alice (Parthia 132) (1982 8g³ 8fg³ 8f 8g² 8s² 8.2s 1983 8v 8d 8d 10s* 10fg) neat horse; poor mover; won minor event at Pontefract in May; off course afterwards until October; stays 1¼m; acts on a firm surface but is well suited by some give underfoot; sometimes blinkered (has won in them) and is possibly ungenuine. *G. Pritchard-Gordon.* — 77§

WINDCOTE 2 ch.f. Import 127–Tin Pan 58 (Tin Whistle 128) (1983 5v² 5s 5fg)   **42**
Apr 24; 3,200Y; leggy filly; poor form in maiden events; pulled up at Edinburgh in
June on final outing; dead. *J. Berry.*

WIND FROM THE WEST 2 b.c. Creetown 123–Bonandra 82 (Andrea   **54**
Mantegna) (1983 6g 6g 5g) Apr 14; 2,200Y; second foal; dam won over 6f and
1¼m; poor maiden; should stay 7f. *N. Vigors.*

WINDOW SHOPPER 2 b. or br.f. Town and Country 124–Watch Em Go   –
(Hidden Treasure) (1983 6d 6fg) Feb 26; 2,000F; half-sister to French
middle-distance winner Go Swallow (by My Swallow) and a winner in USA; dam
won 6f claiming race in North America; behind in October maiden races at Newbury
and Leicester. *G. Balding.*

WINDPIPE 5 ch.g. Leander 119–Whiffle 105 (King's Troop 118) (1982 8f 8g² 8f   **69**
8fg² 8fg² 8d³ 8d² 7s 1983 8v³ 8g⁴ 8f² 9f 8g³ 9fg 8g* 8fg² 8.2s) workmanlike
gelding; won £4,300 handicap at Ayr in September by a neck from Bold Fort; has
won over 1¼m, but races mainly at 1m; acts on any going; occasionally wears
blinkers (has won in them). *J. W. Watts.*

WINDS ALOFT (USA) 3 br.f. Hoist the Flag–Pressing Date (Never Bend)   **75**
(1982 NR 1983 10g 11f) big, good-quartered, rather plain filly; has a markedly
round action; first foal; dam, daughter of Oaks winner Monade, was smart winner
at up to 1m in USA; bandaged in front when fifth in biggish fields of maidens at
Newmarket (left in stalls) and Newbury (had every chance), both in July; stays 11f.
R. Hern.

WINDYHAUGH 3 b. or br.g. Porto Bello 118–Carolinda 63 (Grand Roi 118) (1982   –
5d 7g 6g 1983 7v) behind in varied company, finishing last 3 times. *Miss A. King.*

WINDY LAD 4 ch.c. Tumble Wind–Bold Bird (Bold Lad, Ire 133) (1982 5d 5d 8f   **39**
5.3g 5fg 5d 1983 5v³ 5v 5v 6fg) compact colt; poor sprint handicapper nowadays;
revels in the mud; has twice worn blinkers. *S. Matthews.*

WINDY RED 2 ch.c. Windjammer–Ciel Rouge 98 (Red God 128§) (1983 5g 5g   –
5g) June 18; IR 800Y; compact colt; half-brother to a minor winner by Runnymede;
dam won over 7f and 1m at 2 yrs; no form in 3 races, one a seller, at the back-end.
D. Plant.

WINDY WEATHER 2 b.g. Bay Express 132–Firente 85 (Firestreak 125) (1983   –
6d 7f 6s⁴) Mar 10; strong gelding; second foal; dam 1½m winner; no worthwhile
form; didn't keep a straight course first 2 starts (unseated rider on debut) and wore
blinkers on third; subsequently gelded. *J. Fitzgerald.*

WING AND A PRAYER 2 b.c. Oats 126–Matcher (Match III 135) (1983 7f   –
8.2fg) Apr 26; IR 5,200F, 6,600Y; tall, short-backed colt; half-brother to several
winners, including useful 5f to 7f winner Myra's Best (by Pampapaul) and useful
1977 French 2-y-o 5f winner Oncle Riton (by Daring Display); dam daughter of
smart miler Lachine; behind in maiden race at Newmarket in July and £3,400 event
(last of 16) at Nottingham in October. *A. Bailey.*

WINGINGIN 2 ch.f. Absalom 128–Florabette (Floribunda 136) (1983 5f 6g) Apr   –
9; 7,000Y; half-sister to 3 winners, including 9f to 1½m winner Target Path (by
Scottish Rifle); dam never ran; in mid-division in 12-runner maiden races at
Folkestone in August and Hamilton in September. *C. Nelson.*

WIN GREEN HILL 7 b.m. National Trust 89–Bibbernette (Vasant) (1982 NR   –
1983 12g) novice hurdler; tailed off in amateur riders maiden race at Kempton in
September. *J. Old.*

WINGS OF THE MORN 3 ch.g. North Stoke 130–March Wonder 99 (March   **72**
Past 124) (1982 NR 1983 10.1f 12f 10.1fg 12g* 15.8g 12f*) 9,200F; lightly-made
gelding; keen walker; half-brother to several winners, including useful Yunkel (by
Amber Rama), successful at up to 7.6f; dam won 5 races at 1¼m; tended to hang
when winning claiming races at Leicester in September and November, latter by 6
lengths; well beaten in between; stays 1½m; has raced only on a sound surface. *J.
Dunlop.*

WINNING BIRTHDAY 3 gr.f. Tudor Rhythm 112–Spartan Queen (Matador   –
131) (1982 NR 1983 9.4f) ninth foal; half-sister to a winning hurdler; dam poor
half-sister to Precipice Wood and Spartan General; in rear in minor event at Carlisle
in June. *A. W. Jones.*

WINNING FLUSH (USA) 2 b.c. Poker–Bold Saffron (Bold Hour) (1983 6d)   –
Mar 15; $110,000Y; brother to a winner, and closely related to 2 more, notably

smart 1982 2-y-o 6f and 1m winner Bright Crocus (by Clev Er Tell), subsequently a good stakes winner in USA; dam, half-sister to 1000 Guineas third Kesar Queen, won 3 sprint races; slow-starting tenth of 11 in minor event at Catterick in October; subsequently sold 4,800 gns Doncaster October Sales, reportedly for export to Norway. *H. Cecil.*

WINNING STYLE 2 ch.f. Sagaro 133–Quibble 59 (Quisling 117) (1983 5v⁴ 7f²) **69**
May 1; 1,950Y; rather leggy filly; half-sister to several winners, including 1978 2-y-o 5f winner Quibbling Streak (by Maystreak); dam of little account; favourite, beaten length by Courting Season in 14-runner maiden auction event at Catterick in July. *M. H. Easterby.*

WINNING TENDER 3 br.f. Mansingh 120–Godhood 86 (Green God 128) (1982 –
5fg⁴ 5f² 5g 6f 5.8f 5g² 5.1d⁴ 5g 1983 5s 6d) leggy, narrow, lightly-made filly; plater; seems best at 5f; acts on firm going. *K. Bridgwater.*

WINTERREISE 5 b.g. Fine Blade 121–Pouilly Fuse (Tudor Music 131) (1982 **46**
12g 11f 12d 12f³ 11g* 12g 1983 12d 12f 12.3v⁴ 12d 12s 11g 12.3f² 12f² 12f 13s) strong gelding; stays 1½m; acts on firm going; sold to M. Tate 850 gns Doncaster November Sales. *W. Bentley.*

WINTER SPORT 3 b.c. Lochnager 132–Nelski 83 (Skymaster 126) (1982 NR –
1983 8v 11v 12v 8v² 7fg 10.2f 8g 9d) neat, strong colt; brother to 7f and 1m winner Christmas Cottage, and half-brother to 2 winners; dam best at up to 7f; hung left when second in 1m maiden race at Warwick in May, only form; last in big fields on last 2 starts. *M. Usher.*

WINTER WIND 7 b.h. Tumble Wind–Northern Beauty (Borealis) (1982 6g* 6d* **100**
6f 6d* 6g 6s 1983 5d³ 5v³ 5v⁴ 5g 6v 6d³ 5d 6s 5f) very attractive horse; good mover with a nice, easy action; useful sprinter; ran well several starts, notably when fourth to Fearless Lad in Field Marshal Stakes at Haydock in April, sixth to Vorvados in 6f Duke of York Stakes in May on fifth start and fifth to Fearless Lad in Temple Stakes at Sandown next time; acts on any going but seems suited by some give in the ground nowadays; blinkered once at 3 yrs; needs to be held up; sent to USA. *W. O'Gorman.*

WINTER WORDS 4 b.c. Wollow 132–Prinia 77 (On Your Mark 125) (1982 7g³ **67**
7fg³ 7f 7g 1983 7.2v 7s 9v 7.2s 6f⁴ 7fg 8f 7.6g 7g³) close-coupled colt; none too good a mover; suited by 7f; form only on a sound surface; has run creditably for an apprentice; sometimes makes the running. *Mrs C. Lloyd-Jones.*

WISE CROWN 2 ch.c. Thatch 136–Sapientia (Prudent II 133) (1983 6fg 6f⁴) Apr **81**
27; 11,000F, 30,000Y; tall colt; half-brother to 3-y-o Mothers Word (by Mummy's Pet), a useful winner over 5f in Ireland at 2 yrs, and 2 winners in France; dam won at up to 1¼m and comes from Great Nephew's family; favourite, ran green when 3½ lengths fourth of 20 behind Throne of Glory in maiden event at Newmarket in July; looked certain to be better for the experience, but wasn't seen out again. *L. Cumani.*

WISE MAN 7 ch.g. Frankincense 120–Sans Gene 77 (Songedor 116) (1982 NR –
1983 8d 10.6s) probably of little account nowadays; sold 740 gns Doncaster September Sales. *Ronald Thompson.*

WISE OWL 6 ch.h. Crowned Prince 128–Tawny Owl 123 (Faberge II 121) (1982 – §
10d⁴ 8f 10.1d² 9g 1983 8d 8d³ 10fg 8fg) good-looking horse; disappointing and ungenuine maiden; stays 1¼m; acts on a firm and a soft surface. *G. Wragg.*

WISE SPECULATION (USA) 3 ch.f. Mr Prospector–Wisdom (Hail to –
Reason) (1982 5d 5fg 1983 8f) rather a leggy filly; well beaten in maiden races as a 2-y-o; behind when falling only outing of 1983. *P. Calver.*

WISE WARNING 3 b.f. Red Alert 127–Balabukha (Sayajirao 132) (1982 NR –
1983 8d 8f 10f) 2,800Y; quite an attractive filly; closely related to winners here and abroad, including Irish 7f and 1m winner Bay God (by Yellow God), and half-sister to 2 winners; dam never ran; soundly beaten in sellers; sold 390 gns Ascot August Sales. *C. Nelson.*

WISH YOU WERE HERE (USA) 2 ch.f. Secretariat–Summer Guest (Native **81**
Charger) (1983 7f 7d* 8g) Jan 20; big, rangy filly; third foal; half-sister to a minor winner; dam top-class middle-distance performer, winner of 13 races and over $480,000; won 9-runner maiden race at Brighton in September by a length from Dashing Light; co-favourite, well beaten in nursery at Pontefract following month; will stay 1¼m. *I. Balding.*

WITCH'S POINT 4 br.c. Lochnager 132–Vacation 102 (Remainder 106) (1982 5f **54**
5f 7f² 8fg 7f⁴ 7g³ 7fg* 7f³ 7g 7fg 7d 7d 1983 7g² 8f 6f 7f 8fg 8.2fg 7f⁴ 8f 8g 7f 8fg)

useful-looking colt; blind in near-eye; poor handicapper; stays 1m; acts on any going; often blinkered; has run creditably for an apprentice; sold 680 gns Doncaster October Sales. *M. H. Easterby.*

WITCHY WOMAN 3 gr.f. Broxted 120–Minibus 77 (John Splendid 116) (1982 6s 1983 8s 9d 7.6fg 10.4g 8d 6fg) fair sort; poor walker; ran easily best race in 6f apprentice event; well beaten previously, including in a seller; sometimes slowly away; blinkered last 2 outings. *C. Crossley.*   –

WITH A LITTLE BIT 3 b.c. High Top 131–Willow Song 78 (Tudor Melody 129) (1982 NR 1983 10v 10fg³ 10.4fg⁴) small, quite attractive colt; second foal; half-brother to fairly useful 1979 2-y-o 5f performer Sing Willow (by Sharpen Up); dam, placed over 6f, is daughter of top-class Park Top; bit short of room when close third of 22 behind Hoorah Henry in minor event at Nottingham in June; seemed unsuited by Chester course only subsequent start; stays 1¼m. *M. Stoute.*   **76**

WITHOUT RESERVE 2 b.c. Auction Ring 123–Fear Naught 99 (Connaught 130) (1983 5fg³ 7fg* 6.3g 8d* 7g³ 7d²) Apr 17; first foal; dam won Royal Hunt Cup; always going well and led 1f out when beating Cerussite 1½ lengths in Group 3 Ashford Castle Stakes at the Curragh in September; found no extra in final furlong when over a length third to Fiery Celt in Tap On Wood Stakes at Phoenix Park and when 2½ lengths third (promoted to second) to Western Symphony in Larkspur Stakes at Leopardstown, both in October; had earlier accounted for Foscarini by 1½ lengths in maiden event at Leopardstown; well suited by 1m; wore blinkers last 3 starts. *L. Browne, Ireland.*   **108**

WIVETON 5 br.g. Blakeney 126–Wolverene 114 (Relko 136) (1982 10.6g* 11.5f² 10.6g* 12g² 12fg* 12g 10g 1983 10fg 12f* 11.5f² 12fg² 12.3g* 12f 12g³ 10.2fg⁴) useful-looking gelding; fairly useful handicapper; beat Goumi a length (pair well clear) at Brighton in June and Meeka Gold ¾ length at Chester in August; suited by 1½m+; yet to race on very soft going, but acts on any other; has run well for an apprentice; game. *G. Pritchard-Gordon.*   **100**

WIZZARD ART 2 b.f. Wolver Hollow 126–My Sweetie (Bleep-Bleep 134) (1983 6f 7f 7f* 8f⁴ 7g) May 9; 3,300Y; leggy, narrow filly; third reported foal; dam lightly-raced half-sister to smart Air Trooper; won 16-runner maiden event at Doncaster in July; showed little in her other races, one a claimer; stays 7f well; inconsistent. *I. Walker.*   **71**

WOA (FR) 2 b.f. Wolver Hollow 126–Teku San (Welsh Saint 126) (1983 5f 5f 7g) Mar 7; robust filly; good walker; first foal; dam placed at up to 9f in Ireland and France; bad maiden. *S. Norton.*   –

WOJO 3 b.g. Royal Palace 131–Spring Running 91 (Nearula 132) (1982 6f 7f 8.2fg 6g⁴ 10d² 10s⁴ 1983 16v 12s 14g⁴ 13fg* 12f 14f 14f² 14.6f 14f⁴ 16d 14.7fg³) sturdy, good sort; made nearly all when winning handicap at Nottingham in June; ran easily best subsequent races when placed at Yarmouth and Redcar; needs plenty of driving and stays 1¾m; acts on soft going, but best form on a sound surface; usually blinkered nowadays. *M. Ryan.*   **63**

WOLFIE 4 ch.g. Wolverlife 115–Apair (Red Slipper 126) (1982 8g⁴ 8f³ 9.4f³ 8fg 1983 7d 8.2v 8fg* 8s⁴ 8fg 10fg 8g) leggy, unfurnished gelding; seldom impresses in appearance; plater; bought in 1,300 gns after winning at Edinburgh in May; stays 9f; form only on a sound surface. *R. Woodhouse.*   **47**

WOLLOW MAID 3 ch.f. Wollow 132–Maid In Love (Sky Gipsy 117) (1982 6d 7g 1983 8f³ 8f⁴ 8g³ 10f* 10f⁴ 9d³ 10s 9fg 10g) rather a plain filly; won maiden race at Yarmouth in August; suited by 1¼m; acts on firm going and ran respectably on dead ground sixth start; blinkered seventh outing; refused to race penultimate start and dwelt on her last; sold 6,000 gns Doncaster November Sales. *M. Ryan.*   **72**

WOLVER PLUME 2 b.f. Wolver Hollow 126–Nom de Plume 70 (Aureole 132) (1983 5v 5s 7f 8g) Apr 10; 10,000Y; useful-looking filly; half-sister to several winners, including useful 1981 2-y-o 5f to 7f winner French Gent (by Sassafras); dam ran only at 2 yrs when winner over 7f; bad maiden. *Peter Taylor.*   –

WOLVERSINE 2 b.g. Wolverlife 115–Iresine (Frontal 122) (1983 8.2fg 6fg) May 7; IR 3,900F, 4,300Y; workmanlike gelding; dam, granddaughter of German 1000 Guineas and Oaks winner Ivresse, ran twice in Germany; showed little in fair company at Nottingham and Newmarket right at the back-end. *W. O'Gorman.*   –

WONDERFUL SURPRISE 6 b.h. Run The Gantlet–Ashling's Lass 89 (Levmoss 133) (1982 12.3g⁴ 12fg 13fg⁴ 14.6fg² 12fg* 14f* 12f* 14f* 12g* 14.6g 12s 12g 12s 1983 12s 12v 14.6f* 12fg² 13fg* 16f⁴ 14g 14.8fg 13.3g³ 12g*) quite   **93**

attractive horse; fairly useful performer; won handicaps at Doncaster in June, Ayr in July and Haydock in September; stays 2m; ideally suited by top-of-the-ground; blinkered once; usually wears bandages in front; suitable mount for an apprentice. *E. Eldin.*

WONDER WOOD 4 ch. g. High Line 125–Alice (Parthia 132) (1982 12fg 12fg² 12f* 13.8f 13d 12.2d² 16s⁴ 15d³ 1983 17.1v 15.8g² 16fg* 16.1s 14.7fg⁴) strong, lengthy gelding; narrowly won handicap at Nottingham in September; stays 2m; acts on any going; has run respectably for an apprentice; sold to R. Holder 8,800 gns Newmarket Autumn Sales. *Sir Mark Prescott.*   **64**

WONGCHOI 4 b. c. Bustino 136–Lady of Chalon (Young Emperor 133) (1982 8g² 8fg 12f 7fg 7g⁴ 7fg⁴ 8fg 8.2s 7g² 7d 1983 8f* 8f) tall, most attractive colt; good mover; useful at his best but is inconsistent; accounted for Windpipe by 1½ lengths in £4,100 handicap at Newcastle in June; ran in void race next start; stays 1m; seems to act on any going; blinkered once at 3 yrs and is possibly ungenuine; sent to Hong Kong. *E. Eldin.*   **71**

WOODCARVER 2 ch. c. Tap On Wood 130–Cocarde (Red God 128§) (1983 6f) Feb 10, 33,000Y; strong, heavy-bodied colt; half-brother to several winners, including French 1¼m and 1½m winner Edward French (by Jim French); dam, winner over 1¼m in France, is half-sister to Caro; 9/2, 3¼ lengths fifth of 20 to Paramaribo in maiden race at Newmarket in July; will be better suited by 7f and 1m; sure to improve. *H. Cecil.*   **78 p**

WOODCOTE 3 b. or br. c. Blakeney 126–Fragrant Air 94 (Frankincense 120) (1982 6f 7fg 7g⁴ 8g 1983 10fg 10f 10.1f 9f* 10f* 10h* 10.5fg³ 10g² 10d⁴) neat, attractive colt; usually a good mover; improved and won maiden race and a handicap at Newcastle (both slowly run) and 3-runner £3,500 race at Sandown; beat Pip quite comfortably by a length in last-named race in August; will probably stay 1½m; acts on firm going; held up and has a good turn of foot. *G. Pritchard-Gordon.*   **90**

WOODCOTE BELLE 3 ch. f. Connaught 130–Pamagilan 89 (Pall Mall 132) (1982 6g 7g⁴ 7f³ 7.6v* 1983 7s² 10d 12s 8g) workmanlike filly; backed from 12/1 to 4/1 when 2 lengths second to Silverdip in 8-runner Salisbury 1000 Guineas Trial in April; in mid-division in Pretty Polly Stakes at Newmarket and Esal Bookmakers Oaks Trial at Lingfield on next 2 starts; not seen out after May; finds 1m on sharp side now and seems to stay 1½m; clearly revels in the mud. *R. Smyth.*   **89**

WOODFOLD 2 br. f. Saritamer 130–Beryl's Jewel 86 (Siliconn 121) (1983 5s⁴ 5f⁴ 5f² 6fg² 6f² 5fg 5g) Feb 19; 4,000Y; well-made, quite attractive filly; first foal; dam beat at 5f; disappointing maiden; failed to land odds of 9/2 on in auction race at Folkestone in August on fifth outing, and did nothing at all after that; stays 6f; acts on firm going; best left alone. *J. Winter.*   **79 §**

WOODLANDS JET 3 b. f. Mljet–Woodlands Girl (Weepers Boy 124) (1982 NR 1983 12g) first foal; dam won over hurdles; tailed off when pulled up in apprentice race at Chepstow in October; dead. *D. C. Tucker.*   **–**

WOODPECKER BOY 2 b. or br. c. Kala Shikari 125–La Chunga (Queen's Hussar 124) (1983 5s 6fg 7f² 7f⁴ 6f 6fg) May 9; big, strong, lengthy, plain colt with scope; first living foal; dam poor plater; moderate plater; stays 7f; trained most of the season by K. Stone. *N. Guest.*   **56**

WOODWAY 2 ch. c. Tap On Wood 130–Clarina (Klairon 131) (1983 6f⁴ 8g 8d³) Feb 9; attractive, close-coupled colt; half-brother to 3 winners, including good English and German performer Claddagh (by Bold Lad, Ire) and Italian 1000 Guineas winner Rosananti (by Blushing Groom); dam won twice over 1½m in Ireland; improved with his races, on final outing finishing creditable third of 12 behind Corinth and San Carlos Bay in £3,500 event at York in October; promises to stay 1¼m; sure to win a race. *J. Dunlop.*   **86**

WOOLAW 4 b. f. Golden Mallard 103–Calaburn 72 (Caliban 123) (1982 NR 1983 6d 5d) bad plater. *Hbt Jones.*   **–**

WOOLOOWARE 3 br. g. Wollow 132–Regency Gold (Prince Regent 129) (1982 7d 7f³ 7f⁴ 8s⁴ 1983 10v 10d 8f 11.7f 12f 12g³ 12f 12g²) quite well-made, attractive gelding; in frame in varied races, including a gentleman riders event and a seller; stays 1½m; best form on a sound surface; not one to rely on. *G. Balding.*   **53**

WOOTTON GIRL 3 ch. f. Legal Eagle 126–Zerosa (Zeus Boy 121) (1982 NR 1983 10.2f 16g) small, plain filly; fifth foal; dam won over hurdles; well beaten in maiden races in summer. *Miss A. King.*   **–**

WORD OF HONOUR 2 ch. f. Absalom 128–Voucher Book 96 (Good Bond 122) — p
(1983 6fg) May 4; second foal; half-sister to 3-y-o 1m winner Lease of Life (by
Tower Walk); dam won 8 times at up to 13.8f; in need of race, 13 lengths fourteenth
of 23 to New Generation in minor event at Redcar in September; sure to be better
for the experience. *C. Thornton.*

WORDSWORTH 3 br. c. Warpath 113–April 107 (Silly Season 127) (1982 7s 1983 **75**
11d³ 13d⁴ 16f* 15s³ 16fg 18fg) neat, strong colt; beat stable-companion End of the
Road by 3 lengths in maiden race at Beverley in September; favourite although
facing stiffer task when respectable 6 lengths third of 8 behind High Cannon in
minor event at Ayr in September; suited by a test of stamina; probably acts on any
going, although didn't move well in the soft at Ayr; sold privately to D. Wilson
11,000 gns Doncaster November Sales. *C. Thornton.*

WORLING DUKE 3 b. g. Great Nephew 126–Derring Maid (Derring-Do 131) —
(1982 NR 1983 11v 11.5fg 10.2f) quite an attractive, well-made gelding; fourth
foal; half-brother to fairly useful 5f to 1m winner Worlingworth (by Jimmy Reppin);
dam of little account; well behind in maiden races; sold 700 gns Newmarket July
Sales. *M. Ryan.*

WORLINGFOOT 3 br. g. Hotfoot 126–Taormina (Windjammer) (1982 7g 7d **73**
1983 10s 8f 8fg² 8f* 8f² 8.2h² 8f² 9fg 10d) strong gelding; good mover; won
handicap at Yarmouth in July; second in 4 other races, finishing fast after being
trapped on rails when apprentice ridden at Nottingham on penultimate occasion;
suited by 1m but has yet to show he stays 1¼m; acts on hard going. *M. Ryan.*

WORLING GOLD 2 ch. f. Connaught 130–Derring Maid (Derring-Do 131) (1983 —
5g 5s) Apr 18; neat filly; fifth foal; half-sister to fairly useful 5f to 1m winner
Worlingworth (by Jimmy Reppin); dam of little account; behind in maiden races at
Newmarket in April and Wolverhampton in May; sold to O. Jorgensen 680 gns
Newmarket July Sales. *M. Ryan.*

WORLING-PEARL 2 b. f. Radetzky 123–La Marsa 82 (Royalty 130) (1983 7fg —
7fg) Apr 2; rangy filly; first foal; dam won over 7f and 1½m; ran in 2 maiden races
at Newmarket in the autumn, showing a little promise on first occasion (bandaged
behind) and none at all on the second; should stay 1¼m. *F. Durr.*

WORLINGWORTH 4 ch. c. Jimmy Reppin 131–Derring Maid (Derring-Do 131) **77**
(1982 5g* 6s 5f 5f 6fg 6g² 6h² 6fg 6g 6fg 6d 5.6g 6g³ 7s* 6g 8s 8s* 1983 8d 8v 8v 8s
8d 8.5g 8f 7f 8fg 7s 8fg² 9fg 8g⁴ 7fg² 7fg) short-backed colt; inconsistent
handicapper; stays 1m; acts on any going but revels in the mud; blinkered once in
1982; bandaged in front first outing. *M. Ryan.*

WORLINGWORTH WALTZ 4 b. g. Connaught 130–My Polyanna 81 (Polyfoto —
124) (1982 8f 12f 8s 8fg 8f 8g 10fg⁴ 10s 7g 8s³ 1983 12d 8.3s 7d 8fg⁴ 8f 8g)
compact gelding; plater; promises to stay middle distances; has been taken down
early. *D. Jermy.*

WORRELL (USA) 3 gr. g. Cougar–Lily Marlene 76 (Drone) (1982 5s 5f³ 7g 6fg **78**
6fg² 7fg² 6fg⁴ 6s* 1983 8s 7g 7d 6f² 6fg) neat, attractive gelding; ran best race of
1983 when close second in handicap at Chepstow in June (blinkered first time);
didn't wear blinkers next time; stays 7f; acts on any going. *G. Lewis.*

WORTH AVENUE 7 ch. h. Busted 134–Lavenham Rose 85 (Floribunda 136) **47**
(1982 16.1s² 16fg 16g⁴ 16d 1983 16v 14s 13g 13.8g 16g²) good-bodied horse;
staying handicapper; acts on any going; sold to M. Chapman 2,100 gns Ascot
November Sales. *I. Walker.*

WORTH WHILE 2 b. f. Sexton Blake 126–Darinda (Darius 129) (1983 7f 5f 8g² **82**
10fg* 10.2fg) Apr 14; IR 3,000Y; lightly-built filly; has a very round action;
half-sister to 3 winners, including very useful sprinter Bold Image (by Balidar);
dam well bred but showed only poor form; improved dramatically once given a
test of stamina, going down by ¾ length to Adiyamann in minor event at Bath in
October and winning 13-runner maiden race at Nottingham later in month by a
neck from Connaught Prince; yet to race on a soft surface. *C. Spares.*

WOW WEE WOO 2 gr. f. Dragonara Palace 115–Love Always (Be Friendly 130) **76**
(1983 5s 5s 5s 5f² 5fg* 5f 5h⁴ 5fg 5s² 5g³ 5g) May 20; 7,500Y; narrow, rather
leggy filly; none too good a mover; second foal; half-sister to a winner in Sweden;
dam poor maiden; speedy in her class and made all in 6-runner maiden race at Ayr in
July; good second in nursery on same track in September; suited by sharp 5f; acts
on any going. *E. Witts.*

WRONG AGAIN 4 gr. f. Grey Ghost 98–Fashionable Lady (Prince Rois) (1982 —
NR 1983 7f 10f 10.1fg) half-sister to 2 winners over jumps; dam quite moderate
hurdler; soundly beaten in minor events and a maiden race. *E. Witts.*

WUNDERKIND (USA) 2 ch.c. Nijinsky 138–Wonderful Gal (The Axe 115)   **89**
(1983 7fg 7g² 8g⁴) Feb 17; lengthy colt; half-brother to minor stakes winner
Hattab Voladora (by Dewan) and fairly useful 1982 2-y-o 5f and 7f winner Ridge
Heights (by Riva Ridge), subsequently winner of Austrian 2000 Guineas; dam,
winner at up to 1m, is sister to very smart American colt Al Hattab; ran odds-on
Barry Sheene to a neck in 16-runner maiden race at Leicester in September, easily
best effort; favourite when fourth of 15 behind Leadburn in similar event at
Sandown the following month; will stay 1¼m; capable of winning maiden race. *H.
Candy.*

WUSANAME 2 gr.c. Saritamer 130–Dulcidene 71 (Behistoun 131) (1983 7g 7.2g   **54**
8fg 6fg⁴) Apr 4; good-bodied colt; second foal; dam won sellers at around 1¼m;
modest plater; stays 7f; blinkered final appearance; sold 2,000 gns Ascot
December Sales. *R. Hannon.*

WYE LEA 4 ch.g. Crash Course 128–Blue Fragrance (Blue Prince 123) (1982 NR   **–**
1983 15.8g 12g⁴) IR 1,650F, IR 6,000 3-y-o; fifth reported foal; dam won twice at
up to 6f in USA; winning hurdler; modest fourth of 16 finishers to Symbolic in
apprentice race at Chepstow in October, better effort on flat. *J. Edwards.*

WYLDWYCH LASS 2 b.f. Streak 119–Paddyswitch (St Paddy 133) (1983 5d 5g   **–**
6fg) Apr 2; second foal; dam poor half-sister to smart sprinter Vilgora; in rear in
minor event and 2 sellers; not raced after early August; blinkered final outing. *M.
Haynes.*

WYNNWITH SOVEREIGN 5 br.g. Sovereign Path 125–Sheer Bliss 76 (St   **–**
Paddy 133) (1982 NR 1983 10.1d 12v 10.6s 10.2g 12f) plater; stays 1½m; has
been tried in blinkers; trained part of season by J. Roberts. *J. Jenkins.*

X

XARELI 2 b.f. Diamonds Are Trump 108–Khios (Khalkis 127) (1983 6g) Apr 24;   **–**
IR 2,000F; fourth reported produce; dam placed in a bumpers event; ninth of 12 in
maiden race at Hamilton in September. *P. Haslam.*

XENIA 5 b.m. High Line 125–Zugela 90 (Zucchero 133§) (1982 16d 12.2g 17.1f 12f   **45**
12g³ 12.2fg 12fg⁴ 14fg 12d 17.1s 15.8d 1983 16s² 10.1d* 14s 18.8v 12g 10h 10f 10f²)
lengthy mare; plater nowadays; bought in 3,000 gns after winning readily at
Windsor in May; stays 2m; acts on any going; has twice worn blinkers. *D.
Elsworth.*

XMAS TREE 2 b.c. Flatbush 95–Carol H. (Lucky Leaprechaun) (1983 6f 6g 7f)   **–**
Mar 30; sturdy colt; second foal; dam tailed-off last on only completed outing over
hurdles; in rear in maiden and minor events. *F. Watson.*

XUANDE 3 b.f. High Line 125–Zugela 90 (Zucchero 133§) (1982 NR 1983 13.3g   **–**
12d 8fg 14g) big, plain filly; sister to 2 winners, including fair 1¼m and 1¾m winner
Xarfina, and half-sister to several winners here and abroad; dam stayer; well
behind in varied races. *W. Wightman.*

Y

YAA SALAAM 2 b.f. Imperial Fling 116–Mauritania 74 (The Brianstan 128)   **–**
(1983 6fg 6f 7s) May 12; 8,400F, 17,000Y; useful-looking filly; good mover; third
foal; half-sister to winning Italian 3-y-o Brave Ivy (by Decoy Boy); dam placed at
up to 1m; little worthwhile form; off course for over 2 months after second
outing. *P. Walwyn.*

YALLAH 2 b.c. Bold Lad (Ire) 133–Never Never Land (Habitat 134) (1983 6f 6fg³   **90**
5g² 5g² 5g² 5fg⁴) June 1; 10,500Y; strong, quite attractive colt; has a round
action; fourth foal; brother to 3-y-o 6f and 7f winner Never So Bold; dam unraced
half-sister to Bruni's dam; second in maiden races at Haydock and Newbury in
September and in apprentice nursery at Sandown in October; best form at 5f, but
should be suited by 6f; blinkered last 2 outings; sure to win race. *W. O'Gorman.*

YANGTSE-KIANG 3 ro.g. Rapid River 127–Au Pair 68 (Runnymede 123) (1982   **72**
5f 5f⁴ 5fg² 5fg 6fg* 6g 5g 1983 5.8s 8s 6h 5h³ 6fg* 7h² 6f 7f 7h 5.8fg² 5g 6g) leggy
gelding; improved with blinkers and won handicap at Windsor in July; stays 7f;
suited by top-of-the-ground conditions; sold out of J. Carr's stable 3,500 gns
Doncaster March Sales. *M. Bradley.*

YANKEE BOND (USA) 2 b.c. Giboulee–Glitter 70 (Reliance II 137) (1983 6s⁴   **91** ?
6f 7f 7g 7d 7fg 10fg²) Feb 26; 25,000Y; leggy, narrow colt; first foal; dam, closely

related to high-class stayer Proverb, won over 10.8f on first of only 2 starts; seemed only plating class until finishing strongly to be ½-length second of 9 to High Debate in Jennings The Bookmakers Zetland Stakes at Newmarket in October; evidently extremely well suited by 1¼m, and will stay further. *C. Brittain.*

YANKEE HONEY 3 gr.f. Yankee Gold 115–Honey For Tea 70 (Hul a Hul 124) – (1982 6g 5fg 1983 5d) light-framed filly; well beaten, including in sellers. *W. Stubbs.*

YARBOROUGH 2 b.g. Dawn Review 105–Summer Rain (Palestine 133) (1983 **80** 6fg 7d 10fg³ 10.2fg) fair sort; half-brother to a winning plater by Lauso and a winner in Malaya; dam tailed-off both outings; ¾-length third of 13 behind Worth While in maiden race at Nottingham in October, easily best effort; suited by 1¼m; sold privately at end of season. *D. Morrill.*

YASHGAN 2 br.c. Hot Grove 128–Val Divine (Val de Loir 133) (1983 8g*) Apr 3; **101** p fifth foal; half-brother to 4 winners, notably Champion Stakes winner Vayrann (by Brigadier Gerard) and Queen Anne Stakes winner Valiyar (by Red God); dam won over 10.5f in France and is daughter of high-class Pola Bella; favourite, led early in straight and held on well to account for Bare Minimum by ¾ length in 15-runner newcomers race at Saint-Cloud in October (pair clear); will stay 1½m; certain to improve and is one to keep an eye on. *A. de Royer Dupre, France.*

YASMEEN 3 b.f. Mansingh 120–Western Vale (Milesian 125) (1982 6g 6f 5fg 5f 5v – 5d³ 1983 5d 5s 5g 5f) small, lengthy filly; plater; sometimes blinkered; sold to T. Kersey 600 gns Newmarket July Sales. *C. Spares.*

YASU NAFTI 3 b.g. Octavo 115–Russalka (Emerson) (1982 5d 5d 5f³ 5f 6f 7g – 8.2g 8f 8.2d³ 10d⁴ 10d 1983 11v 10s 10v³ 10.2g 12f 12f) smallish, fair sort; poor mover; plater; stays 1¼m; has run creditably on firm going, but is probably better suited by some give in the ground; sometimes blinkered; sold 525 gns Ascot July Sales. *D. Sasse.*

YAWA 3 ch.c. Luthier 126–Lucky For Me 116 (Appiani II 128) (1982 8.2s 1983 8v **122** 8d 11.7s* 12v³ 12s 15g* 13.3f³ 14.6s 14s)
Yawa's Derby, for which he started at 50/1 following his fifteen-length win in a maiden race at Bath and his seven-length third to Teenoso in the Highland Spring Trial at Lingfield, ended abruptly on the descent of Tattenham Hill. He was so badly hampered along that stretch that his jockey became unshipped. By then Yawa had shown enough to provide a clue to a facet of his character that became crystal clear before the end of the season: he is a stayer not a middle-distance horse, slow to warm up, a horse who needs a man on his back. At the time of his departure from the Derby he hadn't succeeded in getting out of the tail-end division, having been scrubbed along virtually all the way to keep up. Even over fifteen furlongs in the Grand Prix de Paris at Longchamp next time out Yawa was off the bridle from the start. On that occasion, though, events took a far happier turn, since he emerged as one of the few English-trained horses ever to win the once-famous race.

The status of the Grand Prix de Paris has fallen considerably, or rather been allowed to fall considerably, in recent years. In 1983 the French fielded only two runners against five challengers from abroad, the Prix Hocquart third Fubymam du Tenu and the Prix de l'Esperance second Homme de Paille, neither discernibly in the top flight of French three-year-olds. The foreign challenge consisted entirely of English-trained horses—Yawa, Brogan, Jasper, Castle Rising and Tom Seymour. Brogan, winner of the Prix Berteux and third in the Esperance, a length and a half behind Homme de Paille, on his last two visits to France started favourite at 2/1. Yawa was only sixth in the betting at 11/1. The race could hardly have been run in more inclement weather for June, attended by a thundery downpour throughout, but there is no doubt that the best horse won. Yawa, indeed, was so superior to the rest that he won by two lengths from Fubymam du Tenu despite coming near to throwing the race away in astonishing fashion. The incident happened halfway up the straight where Yawa had moved ahead surprisingly easily after a couple of cracks of the whip; almost immediately he began to swerve violently all over the course, first to the left, then to the right and then to the left again. His jockey Waldron did well to stay on board, let alone keep him running to the finish. Yawa's trainer afterwards offered the plausible explanation that Yawa had attempted to make for the gate he'd been using for access to the course at exercise.

As logic dictated, Yawa was trained for the St Leger on his return from France. On his only appearance before Doncaster he ran an excellent Leger trial over a distance just short of a mile and three quarters in the Geoffrey Freer Stakes at Newbury in August. His finishing third, staying on, behind the four-year-old Khairpour and Castle Rising on most unfavourable terms was so encouraging that he started third favourite for the Leger behind Sun Princess and Carlingford Castle at 11/2. He looked well enough on the day to run the race of his life, too, but failed to do so. The tactical gallop set by Sailor's Dance on Sun Princess' behalf was all against a horse of Yawa's character: once the pace quickened turning for home Yawa's lack of acceleration was cruelly exposed, and he struggled the length of the straight, sinking from a close third to a modest fifth, almost thirteen lengths behind Sun Princess. The opposition to Yawa in his final race, the Jefferson Smurfit Memorial Irish St Leger, was much less exacting but he was beaten further and was placed lower than at Doncaster: he finished only sixth to Mountain Lodge after dropping back in the last three furlongs like a tired horse.

		Klairon	Clarion III
	Luthier	(b 1952)	Kalmia
	(br 1965)	Flute Enchantee	Cranach
Yawa		(b 1950)	Montagnana
(ch.c. 1980)		Appiani II	Herbager
	Lucky For Me	(b 1963)	Angela Rucellai
	(b 1972)	Lucky Day	Vic Day
		(ch 1958)	Something Win

Luthier has sired a surprisingly large percentage of animals who stay better than he apparently did. Among his better winners in 1983 alone were the Italian Oaks winner Right Bank and the fifteen-furlong Prix de Lutece winner Galant Vert. Yawa's dam Lucky For Me, a smart middle-distance filly who won the Galtres Stakes at York, produced horses with more pace than Yawa in Strike It Rich and Euclid when sent to Rheingold and Lyphard respectively. Strike It Rich won over nine and ten furlongs in Ireland; Euclid was a very useful Irish two-year-old, winner of the Beresford Stakes. The dam's yearling of 1981 Alnood (by Habitat) won quite valuable nurseries over six and seven furlongs in the latest season. The best horse produced by the family in recent years apart from Yawa is Lucky For Me's

Elisha Holding's "Yawa"

half-brother, the Irish Sweeps Derby fourth Nor, Yawa's equal on his subsequent form in the United States.

There isn't much of Yawa: he's a smallish, narrow, rather lightly-made colt. A good walker, he acts on any going. Yawa's future lies in long-distance racing; from what we've seen of him, the stiffer the test of stamina the better for him. He will have to avoid the likes of Carlingford Castle and Little Wolf if he is to win major races. *G. Lewis.*

YAZEED (USA) 2 br.c. J.O. Tobin 130–Smooth 114 (Sound Track 132) (1983 – p
6h) Feb 28; $200,000Y; half-brother to several winners, including 3-y-o 6f winner Lyphnap (by Lyphard) and very useful 1979 2-y-o 6f winner Suavity (by Personality); dam game sprinter; second favourite, seventh of 12 in maiden race at Nottingham in August; will probably improve. *P. Walwyn.*

YELED 5 br.g. Youth 135–Lalibela 123 (Honeyway 125) (1982 12g 13d* 12fg³ 12f* **80**
12f* 12fg 12d² 12fg 14g 12fg* 10.6s 1983 13v³ 12v 12v² 12f 13f* 12f* 12f*(dis) 14f²(dis) 16h* 14fg 12fg 20fg) lengthy, angular gelding; first past post in handicaps at Nottingham in July and Ripon (2) and Chepstow (amateur riders) in August; disqualified some time after second win at Ripon, and from his next race, his rider having drawn wrong allowance; stays 2m; acts on any going but ideally suited by fast ground; front runner; excellent mount for an inexperienced rider. *P. Kelleway.*

YELLOW DOMINO (FR) 2 ch.c. Sanhedrin–Sofa (Penhurst) (1983 6g³ 6fg 6g **83**
5fg* 5g³) Feb 27; 120,000 francs Y (approx £10,000); useful-looking colt; third foal; half-brother to very smart French sprinter Trio Boy (by Trio); dam won 3 times at up to 9f in French Provinces; sire, smart performer at 2 yrs and 3 yrs in USA, was third in Kentucky Derby and Belmont Stakes; made all in 15-runner maiden race at Nottingham in September; fair third in apprentice nursery at Sandown the following month; bred to be suited by longer than sprint distances; acts on a firm surface. *P. Kelleway.*

YONBERRY BOY (USA) 2 ch.c. Twogundan–Careful Juror (Bandit) (1983 8s **70**
8fg) Apr 10; $4,000 2-y-o; rather leggy colt; half-brother to 2 minor winners; dam won 9 races at up to 9f, including claiming events; sire smart performer at around 1m; 8½ lengths fifth of 12 to Raami in maiden race at Redcar in October, second outing; exported to Malaysia. *M. Jarvis.*

YOOHOO 9 ch.g. Mountain Call 125–Dreamy Idea 68 (Double Jump 131) (1982 –
6f² 6f³ 6g 6g² 6d⁴ 6fg 7f 6s 1983 6v 6f 6fg 7f 7f) sprint handicapper; acts on any going; usually wears blinkers. *C. Booth.*

YORKSHIRE MOORES 3 ch.c. Sagaro 133–Taffytina 106 (Caerdeon 98) (1982 **57**
6g 1983 12v 10.1d 12.2fg³ 14f⁴ 12f) small, lightly-made colt; looks one paced and is well worth another chance at 1¾m; sold 3,300 gns Newmarket September Sales, probably for export to Italy. *R. Armstrong.*

YOU CHEEKY 2 ch.c. Morston 125–Another Treat 92 (Derring-Do 131) (1983 –
6g 7g) Feb 6; 6,000F, 7,000Y; second foal; brother to 1½m winner Another Thrill; dam, daughter of smart Fab, won over 1¼m and 1½m; in rear in modest company at Lingfield in the autumn. *P. K. Mitchell.*

YOU LOVE ME 2 br.f. He Loves Me 120–Youee 66 (Buisson Ardent 129) (1983 **77**
5d 5v² 5s⁴ 5f 6f³ 5f² 6fg 6fg 5g³ 5g* 6g 5fg) Mar 7; leggy, sharp sort; half-sister to several winners, including fairly useful 1976 2-y-o 5f winner Michael Arlen (by Green God); dam ran only at 2 yrs; won 13-runner maiden race at Haydock in September; stays 6f; acts on any going. *R. Hollinshead.*

YOUNG BRETT 2 ch.f. Import 127–Lady Helen 63 (Majority Blue 126) (1983 5s –
5s 5f 5f 6f) May 8; 1,400F; small, sturdy filly; no sign of ability, final start last of 13 in a seller; sold 420 gns Doncaster September Sales. *Ronald Thompson.*

YOUNG BUCKERS (USA) 2 b.c. Full Out–Scuffling (One For All) (1983 6g 7f) –
Jan 27; $65,000Y; sturdy colt; good walker; second living foal; dam unraced half-sister to 2 stakes winners; well beaten in modest company at Goodwood and Redcar in the autumn. *A. Jarvis.*

YOUNG CROFTIE 6 b.g. Sit In The Corner–Open Arms 77 (Dignitary 121) –
(1982 6g 7g 7f 8fg 6fg 8fg 1983 10.2g 10f) poor plater; dead. *N. Mitchell.*

YOUNG DANIEL 5 b.h. Dragonara Palace 115–Pepperita 79 (Nelcius 133) (1982 **89**
8d 7fg⁴ 8g 7fg 8g 8fg 8fg 7f 7fg² 1983 7s 8s 7.6v³ 8fg* 7f* 7fg 7f 8f* 8f⁴ 7f 8fg 8fg³ 8g 8g³) well-made horse; successful in 3 handicaps at Sandown, being waited with

when scoring first 2 successes but making virtually all to account for Mauritzfontein by ¾ length on final occasion in July; stays 1m; acts on any going; has won for an apprentice. *A. Moore.*

YOUNG INCA 5 gr. g. Young Emperor 133–Sunny Eyes (Reliance II 137) (1982 **89** 7fg³ 8fg 7h 5fg 5.8f 5g⁴ 5fg* 5fg 5.8f² 5d² 1983 5v 5.8g* 6f 6f* 5.8h* 5f² 5h² 5f* 5.8fg⁴ 5fg³ 5fg* 5d) leggy gelding; had a fine season and won handicaps at Bath (2), Salisbury (2) and Ascot; dead-heated with Debaj in Bovis Stakes in last-named in October; best at sprint distances; ideally suited by top-of-the-ground; has won in blinkers but is better without; genuine and consistent. *G. Cottrell.*

YOUNG KNIGHT 2 b.g. Immortal Knight 103–Young Romance (King's Troop **81** 118) (1983 6g 5f 8s 7g⁴ 7f 7fg) Apr 8; strong, compact gelding; fourth foal; brother to 3-y-o 7f winner Romantic Knight; dam pulled up only outing; sweated up profusely when 3½ lengths fourth of 19 to Secret Way in maiden race at York in October, easily best effort; should stay 1m; also sweated up final start. *M. H. Easterby.*

YOUNG LUNAR 3 ch.g. Ashmore 125–Lunar Star (Star Gazer 123) (1982 NR   **–** 1983 8v⁴ 9s 12.3v 10d) 1,000Y; half-brother to several winners, including moderate 7f winner Big Blonde (by Ballymore); dam won over 9.5f in Ireland; poor maiden; should be suited by middle distances. *A. Young.*

YOUNG MONARCH 3 gr. g. Young Emperor 133–Trapani (Ragusa 137) (1982   **–** NR 1983 7d) 2,100F, 8,200Y; slightly dipped-backed gelding; second produce; dam ran only 3 times; tailed-off last in newcomers race at Doncaster in March; sold 1,050 gns Doncaster June Sales, for export to Norway. *A. Balding.*

YOUNG PRETENDER (FR) 2 b.c. Anne's Pretender 124–Chere Madame   **?** (Karabas 132) (1983 5g⁴ 5.8s⁴ 5fg⁴ 5f 6.5fg 7d* 7g² 8f 8fg² 8fg 6fg⁴ 7.5g* 7.5s 8d) May 14; 10,000Y; third foal; half-brother to French 3-y-o Girl Friday (by Faraway Times) and a winner in Belgium; dam, winner from 6f to 1m in France, is half-sister to Santa Anita Derby winner Habitony; won claiming races at Clairefontaine in August and Maisons-Laffitte in November; will stay 1¼m; acts on a firm and a soft surface; blinkered last 4 outings; trained by D. Hanley first 4 starts, was claimed out of C. Austin's stable after seventh outing and out of P. Bary's after ninth. *S. P. Perruchot, France.*

YOUNG TURK 2 br.c. Bold Lad (Ire) 133–Rosalie II 66 (Molvedo 137) (1983 7f* **101** 7d⁴) Mar 19; quite attractive colt; brother to useful hurdler Cut A Dash and half-brother to several winners, notably very smart 6f to 1¼m winner Cistus (by Sun Prince) and high-class French middle-distance performer Lancastrian (by Reform); dam won at 1¼m; 25/1, put up a splendid first effort in 13-runner Foxhall Maiden Stakes at Goodwood in July, soon travelling strongly in a good position and drawing away very smoothly from distance to win by 4 lengths from Carocrest; disappointing 5 lengths fourth of 13 to Elusive (received 10 lb) in Acomb Stakes at York the following month; will stay 1m; possibly not at his best on a soft surface. *I. Balding.*

YOUR CHOICE 2 b.c. Hot Grove 128–Brush (Laser Light 118) (1983 5g² 6f⁴ **63** 6fg* 6f³ 7f³ 8s³ 8.2g 8.2s) Mar 19; first foal; dam never ran; won 6-runner seller at Hamilton in July; ran creditably in nurseries on next 3 appearances; stays 1m; acts on any going; blinkered all but sixth outing. *W. H. H. Williams.*

YOUR SONG (FR) 3 br.g. Sassafras 135–Bell Song 101 (Tudor Melody 129)   **–** (1982 NR 1983 12s 14g 12g 14g) 1,050,000 francs Y (approx £95,000); strong, compact gelding; half-brother to very smart 1981 2-y-o 6f winner Circus Ring (by High Top) and 3 other winners; dam stayed 1¼m; poor form in maiden and minor races; sold to M. O'Toole 6,400 gns Newmarket Autumn Sales. *G. Harwood.*

YOU'RE SO VAIN 2 ch.c. Music Boy 124–Vanity (Vimy 132) (1983 5s 5s 6g 5fg **74** 5.3fg 5g 5g) Apr 25; 5,200F; good-topped, workmanlike colt; brother to a poor animal and half-brother to several winners in Ireland and Belgium by No Mercy; dam never ran; blinkered first time, close-up fifth of 16 behind Fluctuate in maiden race at Warwick in October, final outing and easily best effort; should stay beyond 5f. *H. Beasley.*

YOUTHFUL MISS 3 b.f. Youth 135–Billante (Graustark) (1982 NR 1983 10s **58** 9.4d⁴ 8g 8.2s 10f²) first foal; dam unraced half-sister to 1000 Guineas winner Waterloo; lightly-raced maiden plater; will be suited by 1½m; sold 16,000 gns Newmarket December Sales. *W. Holden.*

YUHZURU 3 b.f. Thatch 136–Joie de France (Reliance II 137) (1982 7g 1983 **63** 10fg³ 11f* 12fg⁴ 12fg³) lengthy, angular filly; won maiden race at Hamilton in August; stays 1½m; acts on firm going; blinkered final start. *Sir Mark Prescott.*

Z

ZABEEL 3 b.c. Habitat 134–Never So Lovely 87 (Realm 129) (1982 6fg³ 6f³ 6g⁴   **85**
1983 6v 5s⁴ 10fg 11f³ 10f 10f* 10fg³ 9d² 10fg 10.5d² 10g) a grand-looking
individual, who walks and gallops with an extremely long, raking stride; possibly
not entirely genuine, but won maiden race at Ripon in August fairly comfortably and
ran creditably afterwards; seems best at middle distances; has run respectably on
soft going but is possibly better on firm; blinkered second outing. *F. J. Houghton.*

ZACCIO 5 ch.g. Lorenzaccio 130–Hepash 81 (Henry the Seventh 125) (1982 12d   **42**
15.5fg 1983 10s 12f 14.7f²) poor handicapper; unplaced in sellers on occasions;
stays 1¾m; suited by firm going; blinkered once in 1981. *P. Mitchell.*

ZAHAV (ISR) 2 b.c. Verre Dore–Wise Company 65 (King's Company 124) (1983   **39**
5v⁴ 5s 6f⁴ 5f 6f 7h) Apr 15; leggy, narrow, sparely-made colt; bad plater; not
raced after July; often blinkered. *K. Ivory.*

ZAHEENDAR 3 gr.c. Welsh Saint 126–Zaheen (Silver Shark 129) (1982 6fg⁴ 6f²   **110**
6g² 7g³ 7fg* 7d 1983 7v 8s² 8f* 8fg 7.2fg* 8fg* 8g⁴) lengthy, workmanlike colt;
good mover; very useful handicapper on his day; was kicked clear 2f out and ran
on strongly to hold Gaygo Lady by ¾ length under 9-7 in £8,000 Northern
Goldsmith's Handicap at Newcastle in August; had been ridden by apprentice R.
Lines when winning handicaps at Thirsk and Haydock earlier; stays 1m; acts on
any going; sent to race in USA. *M. Stoute.*

ZAHEER 3 b.c. Nonoalco 131–Red Berry 115 (Great Nephew 126) (1982 7fg 7g   **89**
7g³ 1983 5s 7.6v² 8s 8s 7g³ 10fg* 10f 12fg⁴ 10f 11.1g 10g) big, rangy colt;
overcame difficulties in running when beating Good as Diamonds by 1½ lengths in
27-runner maiden event at Sandown in June; rather disappointing afterwards,
although not entirely disgraced final start; suited by 1¼m; acts on heavy going, but
best form on a sound surface; sometimes blinkered; sold to BBA 16,500 gns
Newmarket Autumn Sales; blinkered fifth and final outings. *G. Lewis.*

ZAIDE 2 b.f. English Prince 129–Hemlock Cup 89 (Sweet Revenge 129) (1983 6f   **82 p**
7f²) Apr 11; robust filly; first foal; dam 2-y-o 6f winner; 25/1 and in need of run
after a 4-month absence, made good progress in last 2f when 2 lengths second of 19
to Mr Chromacopy in maiden event at Redcar in October; will stay 1m; sure to
improve further and win a race. *R. D. Peacock.*

ZALATAIA (FR) 4 ch.f. Dictus 126–Tapioquerie (Tapioca 123) (1982 10d² 12d*   **124**
12s* 11fg³ 10.5g² 12d² 13.5fg* 12f 1983 10.5v 12v 12f* 12.5fg³ 13.5d* 13.5fg* 12f
12g* 11g²)
    In a season which saw one in eight of the three hundred and fifty or so North
American graded stakes races won by horses that had spent at least part of their
careers running in Europe, French-raced performers did particularly well,
collecting eleven Grade 1 events. All Along dominated her rivals in the Rothmans
International, Turf Classic and Washington International, The Wonder annexed the
Century Handicap and Californian Stakes, Sangue the Yellow Ribbon Invitational
and Matriarch Invitational Stakes, Nijinsky's Secret the Hialeah Turf Cup,
Palikaraki the Arlington Handicap, Ginger Brink a division of the Hollywood Derby
and, on the day of the Washington International, Zalataia put up arguably the best
performance of her career to win the Oak Tree Invitational at Santa Anita.
    The Oak Tree attracted a strong field of nine including, besides Zalataia, the
odds-on favourite John Henry attempting to win the prize for the fourth year in a
row, the Rothmans International and Turf Classic runner-up Thunder Puddles, the
Maurice de Nieuil winner Load the Cannons, the good ex-South African horse
Prince Florimund and Awaasif. Zalataia would have been a decidedly unlucky loser,
for about three furlongs out she had just begun to make ground when severely
baulked by two of her opponents coming together immediately in front. Fortunately
all was not lost. Switched outside, Zalataia recommenced her run and ate up the
ground in the closing stages to catch John Henry near the finish for a half-length
success with Load the Cannons a length and a half away third and Prince Florimund
fourth. A month later Zalataia failed to confirm the form with John Henry (whose
trainer McAnally was then after being sold for an undisclosed sum early in
December) in the Hollywood Invitational Turf Cup at Hollywood Park, but she ran
an excellent race nonetheless, going down by half a length after a fine tussle with
the grand old gelding. For these two displays Zalataia picked up something in
excess of £230,000, getting on for four times what she had earned in a successful
season in Europe.
    Zalataia's previous form had shown her one of the best middle-distance
performers in France. Like so many of her sex she took time to come to hand at

M F. Baral's "Zalataia"

four but did so with a vengeance in La Coupe at Chantilly in June, using her good turn of foot to beat Flower Prince by two lengths, breaking the course record in the process. A creditable run in the Grand Prix de Saint-Cloud, in which she couldn't maintain the momentum of an apparently-dangerous challenge halfway up the straight and came in a length-and-a-half third behind Diamond Shoal, preceded two successes within eight days at Deauville. In 1982 Zalataia had won a muddling race for the Prix de Pomone from Akiyda and the unlucky-in-running April Run; this time there were no excuses for the beaten horses who were simply outclassed as Zalataia cantered home by four lengths from the Prix de Minerve winner Rajpoura. The Grand Prix de Deauville had a better field than the Pomone with Dom Pasquini, Orofino and Terreno among the ten trying to prevent Zalataia from achieving a notable double. None of them managed to trouble her for, after being waited with as usual, she moved up rounding the home turn, soon accelerated into the lead and readily accounted for Dom Pasquini by one and a half lengths with Orofino a neck back in third. Zalataia's final start in Europe came in the Trusthouse Forte Prix de l'Arc de Triomphe, a race in which the previous two Grand Prix de Deauville winners, Perrault and Real Shadai, had run well. She performed creditably without being good enough to make the frame, always chasing the leading group on the rails, struggling into sixth place over a furlong and a half out but making no further progress, eventually finishing about three and a half lengths eighth to All Along.

				Fine Top
	Dictus	Sanctus II		Sanelta
	(ch 1967)	(b 1960)		Worden II
Zalataia (Fr)		Doronic		Dulzetta
(ch.f. 1979)		(ch 1960)		Vandale
	Tapioquerie	Tapioca		Semoule d'Or
	(ch 1968)	(b 1953)		Cernobbio
		La Hauquerie		Capeline
		(b 1964)		

Dictus, a high-class colt who won the Jacques le Marois, was sent to Japan in 1980. At stud he has been notable more for the quantity of his winners than their quality—he has headed the French stallion list in terms of races won in five of the last six years—and the best of his progeny apart from Zalataia have been the Prix du Rond-Point winner Daeltown, Palikaraki, the three-year-old Prix du Royaumont winner Marie de Litz and Diamada, successful in the Prix Eclipse in October. On the whole the distaff side of Zalataia's pedigree is unimpressive and she reportedly changed hands for a derisory 6,000 francs as a yearling. The dam Tapioquerie, now dead, had one winner in the Provinces from four previous foals and her 1980 foal, Don't Mary (by Matahawk), won over a mile and a quarter during 1983. Tapioquerie, who stayed a mile and a half, failed to win in thirteen starts; the next dam, unraced, died after producing Tapioquerie, her only foal; and the third dam, a half-sister to the Vermeille and Jacques le Marois winner Astaria II, finished in the frame just once from nine outings before producing one minor winner. Zalataia, a strong, attractive filly and a genuine and consistent one too, is suited by a mile and a half or more. Whereas her sire seemed to need some give underfoot she is ideally suited by top-of-the-ground conditions. *A. Fabre, France.*

ZARIYA (USA) 3 ch.f. Blushing Groom 131–Zahra (Habitat 134) (1982 6g³ 7fg 7f* 7d* 1983 10d) close-coupled, fair sort; fair performer at 2 yrs; didn't settle and ran moderately only outing in 1983 (May); bred to stay at least 1m; probably acts on any going. *M. Stoute.* —

ZARKOS 2 b.c. Mummy's Pet 125–Frenchouan (Jim French) (1983 5g 5s 5fg³ 6f 7f 7d³ 8fg⁴ 6d³) Mar 25; 23,000Y; compact, well-made colt; good walker; first foal; dam, daughter of very smart French 6f to 9f winner Ouananiche, won over 10.5f in France and also won over jumps; moderate maiden; good fourth in Rowley Mile Nursery at Newmarket in September on seventh outing; better suited by 1m than by shorter distances; acts on a firm and a soft surface; sold German International Bloodstock 11,000 gns Newmarket Autumn Sales. *B. Hobbs.* 84

ZARNINA 3 b.f. The Brianstan 128–Cham-Ol Bazaar 85 (Native Bazaar 122) (1982 5d³ 5fg* 5f⁴ 5f² 5g⁴ 1983 7fg 6fg) small, lengthy, lightly-made filly; poor sprint plater. *J. Long.* —

ZAYLIANNE 3 br.f. Diamonds Are Trump 108–Andromeda Nebula (Arctic Star) (1982 NR 1983 9v 12d 16f 16f 10.8g) lightly-built filly; seems of little account; trained much of season by G. Lockerbie. *E. Eldin.* —

ZAYTOON 2 b.c. Formidable 125–Lady Constance 118 (Connaught 130) (1983 6g) Feb 21; 58,000Y; lengthy, good sort; good walker; first foal; dam smart winner over 5f and 7f at 2 yrs; unquoted, in touch to halfway when behind in 23-runner newcomers event at Goodwood in September. *J. Ciechanowski.* —

ZEEZA (USA) 3 b.f. His Majesty–Azeez (Nashua) (1982 7g 7s 1983 10d⁴ 10v³ 8f 8.2g⁴) wiry filly; in frame in spring in Pretty Polly Stakes at Newmarket (under 9 lengths fourth of 17 to Jolly Bay) and Sir Charles Clore Memorial Stakes at Newbury (completely outpaced by Ski Sailing and Sun Princess and beaten over 25 lengths); ran moderately both subsequent outings; bred to be suited by 1½m. *J. Dunlop.* 86

ZELDA'S FANCY 8 b.g. Touch Paper 113–Lady Aylmer (Nice Guy 123) (1982 NR 1983 8fg) ex-Irish gelding; lightly raced on flat since winning over 9f at Gowran Park in 1980, though has won several times over jumps. *H. O'Neill.* —

ZENJEBEEL 2 ch.c. Home Guard 129–Street Light 120 (St Chad 120) (1983 7fg 7fg⁴) Apr 18; 58,000Y; quite attractive colt; brother to useful 5f and 6f winner Highland Light and half-brother to 2 winners; dam smart sprinter; unquoted, 3 lengths fourth of 14 to Condrillac in Houghton Stakes at Newmarket in October; stays 7f; sure to win a race. *J. Hindley.* 92

ZENYATTA 3 gr.g. Town Crier 119–Soldier Girl (Queen's Hussar 124) (1982 5g² 5fg* 5f² 1983 5g 6d 5s 5f) rather lightly-made gelding; has been fired; had stiff task and ran best race of 1983 on third start; form only at 5f; acts on any going. *D. Smith.* 73

ZERO 2 b.g. Impecunious–Fleder Maus (Clear River 114) (1983 7g) second foal: dam never ran; tailed off in minor event at Chepstow in October. *C. Austin.* —

ZERO OPTION 3 ch.f. Privy Seal 108–Destarte (Royal Levee) (1982 7.6v 5v 6s 1983 10s) no form, including in a seller; sold 420 gns Ascot 2nd June Sales. *R. Hannon.* —

ZETA (USA) 3 gr.f. Zen–Aries Kiss (Power Ruler) (1982 8s 1983 10s 11.5fg 11.5f 12fg) tall, lengthy filly; well beaten in varied company, including claiming; blinkered last 2 starts; sold 680 gns Newmarket September Sales. *A. Hide.* —

ZIGGURAT 2 b.c. Pitskelly 122–High Lake (Quisling 117) (1983 7f 7fg 7f 7f 6fg*   **102**
8g⁴ 7.3d⁴ 7fg²) Mar 11; IR 16,000Y; lengthy, useful-looking colt; second produce;
dam won 5 times from 9f to 13.5f in Ireland; won maiden race at Brighton in August
by a neck from Sadarar; in frame subsequently in nursery at Pontefract, Horris Hill
Stakes at Newbury and minor race at Brighton (failed by a short head to catch All
Hell Let Loose after making up lot of ground in final furlong); will be well suited by a
return to 1m; acts on a firm surface but is apparently better with some give in the
ground. *F. Durr.*

ZILOS 4 b.c. Grundy 137–Sandarey 94 (Darius 129) (1982 10f⁴ 12.3g⁴ 12f 12fg   **110**
14fg³ 14f³ 14.6f² 15.5v 1983 12d 12f³ 16g 11.7fg² 12fg⁴) big, well-made colt; ran
easily best race of his career on penultimate start in 1982, when second to Touching
Wood in St Leger at Doncaster; in frame in varied races at 4 yrs, probably best
effort when 5 lengths fourth of 8 to Band in Cumberland Lodge Stakes at Ascot in
September; suited by 1¾m+; has won on a soft surface but goes best on fast
ground; blinkered nowadays; hung and looked unenthusiastic third start. *B.
Hobbs.*

ZIMAM 3 b.f. Free State 125–Once For All (Quorum 126) (1982 5fg 5fg² 5.3fg   **–**
1983 7d 7fg 7f 7h 7g) small, quite well-made filly; poor maiden; gives impression
she'll stay 1m; sold to NBA 1,100 gns Newmarket Autumn Sales. *J. Winter.*

ZINABAR 2 b. or br.f. Jolly Good 122–Marista (Mansingh 120) (1983 6fg 7g 7fg   **–**
8.2g) Apr 25; lengthy, dipped-backed filly; first foal; dam, lightly-raced sister to
useful sprinter Cedar Grange, looked rather temperamental; no form, including in
Hamilton nursery when carrying 7-12; evidently of little account. *K. Stone.*

ZIO PEPPINO 2 ch.c. Thatch 136–Victorian Habit 101 (Habitat 134) (1983 5g   **79**
6f⁴ 6f* 7f⁴ 6f) May 10; IR 2,000Y; neat, sturdy colt; none too good a mover in his
slower paces; fourth foal; half-brother to French 3-y-o 1m winner Ya Sater (by
Sassafras); dam 2-y-o 5f winner; made all in 6-runner maiden auction event at
Newcastle in July; gives impression 6f is his distance (ran much too freely when
tried over 7f); acts on firm going. *A. Jarvis.*

ZIPCODE 2 gr.c. Abwah 118–Mixed Up Kid 53 (Track Spare 125) (1983 5g) Apr   **–**
30; 580F, 5,000Y; second produce; dam won 3 times at up to 1m at 4 yrs; 6/1,
never-dangerous seventh in 13-runner maiden race at Haydock in September;
likely to need further. *C. Thornton.*

ZIRCON'S SUN 4 b.g. Roi Soleil 125–Zircon (Pall Mall 132) (1982 11.7f 12f 11.7d   **–**
14f 15.5fg* 13.1g 16fg 1983 16v 12s 15.5f 16.5f) lightly-made gelding; suited by a
test of stamina; blinkered first start. *R. Laing.*

ZOFFANY (USA) 3 b.c. Our Native–Grey Dawn Girl (Grey Dawn II 132) (1982   **119**
6f² 6g* 7fg* 7s² 1983 9d* 10g³ 12s 12fg² 12d) tall, good-bodied colt; good
mover; evens favourite and outstandingly the pick of paddock when beating
Onslow a neck in 8-runner Gerry Feilden Memorial Stakes at Newmarket in April,
getting through a furlong out after having a very bad run; placed twice on same
course afterwards, finishing 2½ lengths third of 12 to Shearwalk in Heathorn
Stakes later in month (tended to hang under pressure) and head second of 6 to
Trakady in slowly-run £4,500 race in September (having first outing for almost 4
months, tended to put his head in air once in front); well below form both other
starts, finishing tailed-off last when tried in blinkers in Derby at Epsom; probably
stays 1½m; probably acts on any going; has a good turn of foot but isn't the most
enthusiastic of battlers; sent to USA. *G. Harwood.*

*Gerry Feilden Memorial Stakes, Newmarket—Zoffany (rails) lands the odds from Onslow and
Hungarian Prince (blaze)*

ZOIROS (GR) 4 ch.c. Tachypous 128–Sils Maria (Midsummer Night II 117) (1982   **86**
10g 8fg^2 8fg* 1983 10s^4 8fg^2 8f^3 8f* 8f^3) attractive, well-made colt; easily
justified favouritism in handicap at Chepstow in June; slightly disappointing next
time; best form at 1m on a sound surface. *B. Hobbs.*

ZORN 3 ch.c. Riboboy 124–Pearlemor 93 (Gulf Pearl 117) (1982 7f^2 7d 8s* 8g^3 **86**
1983 10v 12v 10.1fg* 12f 11.7fg^3 12f^3 12d* 12fg 13.3d) quite well-made colt; readily
won handicaps at Windsor in June and Beverley in September, but also ran the odd
moderate race; stays 1½m; acts on any going, except possibly heavy; has raced in a
tongue strap; sold 13,000 gns Ascot November Sales, reportedly for export to
Italy. *J. Dunlop.*

ZULU CHIEFTAIN 2 b.c. Native Admiral–Practicality (Weavers' Hall 122)   –
(1983 7f) May 2; third foal; dam once-raced half-sister to very smart miler
Poacher's Moon; behind in 17-runner maiden race at Redcar in September. *D.
O'Donnell, Isle of Man.*

ZULU WARRIOR 4 ch.g. Cawston's Clown 113–Miss Taurus 79 (Bullrush 106)   –
(1982 11fg 7f 8g 9g 7g 6g 12g 1983 12fg) workmanlike, dipped-backed gelding;
poor plater; sometimes blinkered. *A. W. Jones.*

TIMEFORM
CHAMPIONS OF 1983

HORSE OF THE YEAR (RATED AT 136)
HABIBTI
3 br.f. Habitat–Klairessa (Klairon)
Owner Mr M. A. A. Mutawa   **Trainer** J. Dunlop

BEST TWO-YEAR-OLD COLT (RATED AT 131)
EL GRAN SENOR (USA)
2 b.c. Northern Dancer–Sex Appeal (Buckpasser)
Owner Mr R. E. Sangster   **Trainer** V. O'Brien

BEST TWO-YEAR-OLD FILLY (RATED AT 121)
TREIZIEME (USA)
2 ch.f. The Minstrel–Belle Pensee (Ribot)
Owner Mr T. P. Tatham   **Trainer** M. Zilber

BEST SPRINTER (RATED AT 136)
HABIBTI
3 br.f. Habitat–Klairessa (Klairon)
Owner Mr M. A. A. Mutawa   **Trainer** J. Dunlop

BEST MILER (RATED AT 130)
LUTH ENCHANTEE (FR)
3 ch.f. Be My Guest–Viole d'Amour (Luthier)
Owner M P. de Moussac   **Trainer** J. Cunnington, jnr

BEST MIDDLE-DISTANCE HORSE (RATED AT 135)
SHAREEF DANCER (USA)
3 b.c. Northern Dancer–Sweet Alliance (Sir Ivor)
Owner Maktoum Al-Maktoum   **Trainer** M. Stoute

BEST STAYER (RATED AT 127)
LITTLE WOLF
5 ch.h. Grundy–Hiding Place (Doutelle)
Owner Lord Porchester   **Trainer** R. Hern

1983 STATISTICS

The following tables show the leading owners, trainers, breeders, jockeys, horses and sires of winners during the 1983 season, under Jockey Club Rules. Some of the tables are reproduced by permission of *The Sporting Life*.

OWNERS

		Horses	Races Won	Stakes £
1.	R. E. Sangster	25	40	461,488
2.	E. B. Moller	8	13	271,837
3.	Sir M. Sobell	10	16	265,663
4.	Sheikh Mohammed	38	61	191,320
5.	K. Abdulla	26	37	161,442
6.	Lord Porchester	6	13	140,990
7.	R. Barnett	2	2	136,958
8.	R. J. McAlpine	3	5	129,417
9.	H. H. Aga Khan	13	22	126,842
10.	M. Mutawa	2	5	124,827
11.	S. Niarchos	15	29	121,715
12.	P. Mellon	11	21	119,732

TRAINERS

		Horses	Races Won	Stakes £
1.	W. Hern	31	57	549,598
2.	J. Dunlop	57	89	475,324
3.	H. Cecil	57	92	440,022
4.	G. Harwood	56	104	423,159
5.	M. Stoute	56	89	398,125
6.	B. Hills	35	58	348,630
7.	G. Wragg	18	27	307,967
8.	M. V. O'Brien	5	5	306,682
9.	I. Balding	34	60	253,073
10.	H. Candy	25	34	230,427
11.	W. O'Gorman	24	39	191,468
12.	C. Brittain	29	45	175,280

BREEDERS

		Horses	Races Won	Stakes £
1.	White Lodge Stud	8	13	282,223
2.	Ballymacoll Stud	10	16	263,491
3.	John P. Costello	5	10	152,745
4.	Marquess and Marchioness of Tavistock	3	11	146,404
5.	H. H. Aga Khan	14	24	146,180
6.	W. and R. Barnett	2	2	136,953
7.	R. A. McAlpine	3	5	129,417
8.	Lord Porchester	5	11	123,079
9.	Paul Mellon	10	18	114,521
10.	Claiborne Farm	5	9	114,339
11.	Pillar Stud Inc.	3	8	95,136
12.	King Ranch	5	9	91,471

JOCKEYS

		1st	2nd	3rd	Unpl	Total Mts	Per Cent
1.	W. Carson ..	159	90	98	385	732	21.72
2.	L. Piggott ..	150	109	64	318	641	23.40
3.	Pat Eddery ..	122	113	82	345	662	18.42
4.	G. Starkey ..	103	71	61	318	553	18.62
5.	S. Cauthen ..	102	92	68	348	610	16.72
6.	G. Duffield ..	98	69	86	464	717	13.66
7.	T. Ives	71	60	74	369	574	12.36
8.	W. R. Swinburn ..	62	61	41	258	422	14.69
9.	P. Cook	62	83	67	393	605	10.24
10.	B. Rouse	58	51	53	431	593	9.78
11.	J. Mercer ..	55	49	55	386	545	10.09
12.	E. Hide	53	70	65	324	512	10.35

HORSES

		Races Won	Stakes £
1.	Sun Princess 3 b.f. English Prince–Sunny Valley	3	221,356
2.	Teenoso 3 b.c. Youth–Furioso	3	186,343
3.	Time Charter 4 b.f. Saritamer–Centrocon	1	133,851
4.	Cormorant Wood 3 b.f. Home Guard–Quarry Wood	3	123,883
5.	Habibti 3 br.f. Habitat–Klairessa	3	122,404
6.	Caerleon 3 b.c. Nijinsky–Foreseer	1	93,980
7.	Solford 3 b.c. Nijinsky–Fairness	1	81,718
8.	Precocious 2 b.c. Mummy's Pet–Mrs Moss	5	79,395
9.	Noalcoholic 6 b.h. Nonoalco–Alea II	2	76,504
10.	Lomond 3 b.c. Northern Dancer–My Charmer	1	73,462
11.	Ma Biche 3 br.f. Key To The Kingdom–Madge	1	71,472
12.	Give Thanks 3 b.f. Relko–Parthica	3	67,566

SIRES OF WINNERS

		Horses	Races Won	Stakes £
1.	Habitat (1966) by Sir Gaylord	15	28	234,305
2.	English Prince (1971) by Petingo	2	5	224,517
3.	Youth (1973) by Ack Ack	4	9	205,925
4.	Nijinsky (1967) by Northern Dancer	6	6	205,453
5.	Mummy's Pet (1968) by Sing Sing	24	38	195,200
6.	Home Guard (1969) by Forli	16	22	192,905
7.	Nebbiolo (1974) by Yellow God	19	34	158,281
8.	Shirley Heights (1975) by Mill Reef	13	21	149,263
9.	Northern Dancer (1961) by Nearctic	5	5	146,606
10.	Saritamer (1971) by Dancer's Image	2	2	136,475
11.	Nonoalco (1971) by Nearctic	14	24	130,711
12.	Comedy Star (1968) by Tom Fool	11	22	117,151

AN INTERNATIONAL CLASSIFICATION 1983

The following ratings for horses which ran in France, Great Britain or Ireland were allotted jointly by the official Handicappers concerned and published on 15th December. The rating given to each horse represents the official assessment of its merit against a norm of 100.

TWO-YEAR-OLDS, 1983

El Gran Senor	88	Defecting Dancer	77	Duke of Silver	75
Rainbow Quest	87	Masarika	77	Executive Man	75
Lear Fan	84	Raft	77	Executive Pride	75
Long Mick	83	Satinette	77	Feerie Boreale	75
Siberian Express	82	Treizieme	77	Green Paradise	75
Creag-An-Sgor	81	Alphabatim	76	Greinton	75
Sicyos	81	Darshaan	76	Ilium	75
Almeira	80	Eastern Dawn	76	Mahogany	75
Seattle Song	80	Forzando	76	Ministerial	75
Gold and Ivory	78	Kalim	76	Petorius	75
Sadler's Wells	78	Mendez	76	Polly's Ark	75
Shoot Clear	78	Boreale	75	Precocious	75
Superlative	78	Cariellor	75	Prickle	75
Ti King	78	Chapel Cottage	75	Procida	75
Truculent	78	Chief Singer	75	Trojan Fen	75
Vacarme	78	Desirable	75	Western Symphony	75
Cold Feet	77	Diamada	75		

THREE-YEAR-OLDS, 1983

Shareef Dancer	93	Cormorant Wood	83	Beaudelaire	81
Habibti	91	Crystal Glitters	83	Chamisene	81
Caerleon	90	Escaline	83	Jeu de Paille	81
L'Emigrant	89	Horage	83	John French	81
Luth Enchantee	89	Hot Touch	83	Seymour Hicks	81
Sun Princess	89	Lomond	83	Shearwalk	81
Teenoso	88	Mourjane	83	Air Distingue	80
Tolomeo	87	Wassl	83	Dom Pasquini	80
Sackford	86	Burslem	82	Estrapade	80
Salmon Leap	86	Flame of Tara	82	Gorytus	80
Lovely Dancer	85	Give Thanks	82	Green Lucia	80
Adonijah	84	L'Attrayante	82	High Hawk	80
Carlingford Castle	84	Ma Biche	82	Maximova	80
Esprit du Nord	84	Quilted	82	Muscatite	80
Salieri	84	Sagace	82	Pluralisme	80
Sharaya	84	Sayf El Arab	82	Right Bank	80
Solford	84	Smuggly	82	Silverdip	80

FOUR-YEAR-OLDS AND UPWARDS, 1983

All Along	92	Montekin	83	Terreno	81
Diamond Shoal	89	Soba	83	Fearless Lad	80
Time Charter	88	Welsh Term	83	General Holme	80
Noalcoholic	87	Zalataia	83	Ivano	80
Lancastrian	86	Be My Native	82	Kelbomec	80
Stanerra	86	Lemhi Gold	82	Kind Music	80
Electric	85	Orofino	82	Little Wolf	80
Valiyar	84	Pampabird	82	Old Country	80
Cadoudal	83	Awaasif	81	Sandhurst Prince	80

THE FREE HANDICAPS

TWO-YEAR-OLDS OF 1983

The following are the weights allotted in the Ladbroke European Free Handicap published on 15th December. The race is to be run over seven furlongs at Newmarket on 18th April, 1984.

Horse		st	lb	Horse		st	lb	Horse		st	lb
El Gran Senor	..	9	7	Petorius	..	8	8	Novello	..	8	1
Rainbow Quest	..	9	6	Polly's Ark	..	8	8	Pigwidgeon	..	8	1
Lear Fan	..	9	3	Precocious	..	8	8	Water Moccasin	..	8	1
Long Mick	..	9	2	Prickle	..	8	8	Carocrest	..	8	0
Siberian Express	..	9	1	Procida	..	8	8	El Hakim	..	8	0
Creag-An-Sgor	..	9	0	Trojan Fen	..	8	8	Harvard	..	8	0
Sicyos	..	9	0	Western Symphony	..	8	8	Head For Heights	..	8	0
Almeira	..	8	13	Double Schwartz	..	8	7	Lucky Scott	..	8	0
Seattle Song	..	8	13	Maajid	..	8	7	Round Hill	..	8	0
Gold and Ivory	..	8	11	Nepula	..	8	7	Tapaculo	..	8	0
Sadler's Wells	..	8	11	Pacific King	..	8	7	Ashgar	..	7	13
Shoot Clear	..	8	11	Pebbles	..	8	7	Captain Singleton	..	7	13
Superlative	..	8	11	Rousillon	..	8	7	Elusive	..	7	13
Ti King	..	8	11	Elegant Air	..	8	6	Idolized	..	7	13
Truculent	..	8	11	Godstone	..	8	6	Macarthurs Head	..	7	13
Vacarme	..	8	11	Seattle Siren	..	8	6	Night Of Wind	..	7	13
Cold Feet	..	8	10	Beldale Lear	..	8	5	Northern Tempest	..	7	13
Defecting Dancer	..	8	10	Bob Back	..	8	5	Quick Work	..	7	13
Masarika	..	8	10	Condrillac	..	8	5	Sheer Heights	..	7	13
Raft	..	8	10	Donzel	..	8	5	Boezinge	..	7	12
Satinette	..	8	10	Corinth	..	8	4	Cutting Wind	..	7	12
Treizieme	..	8	10	Malaak	..	8	4	Keep Tapping	..	7	12
Alphabatim	..	8	9	Rocket Alert	..	8	4	Lallax	..	7	12
Darshaan	..	8	9	Blushing Scribe	..	8	3	Milord	..	7	12
Eastern Dawn	..	8	9	Fair Dominion	..	8	3	Out of Shot	..	7	12
Forzando	..	8	9	Falstaff	..	8	3	Passing Affair	..	7	12
Kalim	..	8	9	Trial By Error	..	8	3	Reesh	..	7	12
Mendez	..	8	9	Attempt	..	8	2	Reflection	..	7	12
Boreale	..	8	8	Bluff House	..	8	2	Rio Riva	..	7	12
Cariellor	..	8	8	Capricorn Belle	..	8	2	Sassagras	..	7	12
Chapel Cottage	..	8	8	Falstaff (USA)	..	8	2	All Agreed	..	7	11
Chief Singer	..	8	8	Fawzi	..	8	2	Alnood	..	7	11
Desirable	..	8	8	Indigo Jones	..	8	2	Gambler's Cup	..	7	11
Diamada	..	8	8	Millside	..	8	2	Innamorato	..	7	11
Duke of Silver	..	8	8	San Carlos Bay	..	8	2	Inspire	..	7	11
Executive Man	..	8	8	Young Turk	..	8	2	Jamais Derierre	..	7	11
Executive Pride	..	8	8	Betsy Bay	..	8	1	King's Island	..	7	11
Feerie Boreale	..	8	8	Chicago Bid	..	8	1	Lake Valentina	..	7	11
Green Paradise	..	8	8	Circus Plume	..	8	1	Leipzig	..	7	11
Greinton	..	8	8	Fan Club	..	8	1	Sam M	..	7	11
Ilium	..	8	8	Feasibility Study	..	8	1	Throne of Glory	..	7	11
Mahogany	..	8	8	Girl Friday	..	8	1	Vidalia	..	7	11
Ministerial	..	8	8	My Volga Boatman		8	1				

THREE-YEAR-OLDS, 1983

The following handicap published on 15th December is for information only. The figures shown against each horse represent the official assessment of its merit against the norm of 100.

Horse		st	lb	Horse		st	lb	Horse		st	lb
Shareef Dancer	93	10	0	Cormorant Wood	83	9	4	Seymour Hicks	81	9	2
Habibti	91	9	12	Horage	83	9	4	Shearwalk	81	9	2
Caerleon	90	9	11	Hot Touch	83	9	4	Air Distingue	80	9	1
Sun Princess	89	9	10	Lomond	83	9	4	Green Lucia	80	9	1
Teenoso	88	9	9	Wassl	83	9	4	High Hawk	80	9	1
Tolomeo	87	9	8	Flame of Tara	82	9	3	Muscatite	80	9	1
Sackford	86	9	7	Give Thanks	82	9	3	Silverdip	80	9	1
Adonijah	84	9	5	Ma Biche	82	9	3	Morcon	79	9	0
Carlingford Castle	84	9	5	Quilted	82	9	3	On Stage	79	9	0
Esprit du Nord	84	9	5	Sayf El Arab	82	9	3	Proclaim	79	9	0
Salieri	84	9	5	Beaudelaire	81	9	2	Royal Heroine	79	9	0
Solford	84	9	5	John French	81	9	2	Aragon	78	8	13

Diesis	78	8	13	Flamenco	71	8	6	Orixo	65	8	0
Guns of Navarone	78	8	13	Larionov	71	8	6	Schuss	65	8	0
Yawa	78	8	13	Rutland	71	8	6	St Boniface	65	8	0
Band	77	8	12	Tecorno	71	8	6	Autumn Sunset	64	7	13
Reggae	77	8	12	Zoffany	71	8	6	Brogan	64	7	13
The Noble Player	77	8	12	Funny Reef	70	8	5	Linda's Fantasy	64	7	13
Acclimatise	76	8	11	Gay Lemur	70	8	5	New Coins	64	7	13
Drumalis	76	8	11	Millfontaine	70	8	5	Travelguard	64	7	13
Dunbeath	76	8	11	Thug	70	8	5	Balladier	63	7	12
Favoridge	76	8	11	Welsh Idol	70	8	5	Now And Again	63	7	12
Goodbye Shelley	76	8	11	Bid Again	69	8	4	Zaheendar	63	7	12
Dazari	75	8	10	Boy Trumpeter	69	8	4	Henry's Secret	62	7	11
Lyphard's Special	75	8	10	Fenny Rough	69	8	4	His Honour	62	7	11
Prince Spy	75	8	10	Trakady	69	8	4	Magnetic Field	62	7	11
Ski Sailing	75	8	10	Able Albert	68	8	3	Major Don	62	7	11
Tatibah	75	8	10	All Systems Go	68	8	3	Bahoor	61	7	10
Boom Town				Jonacris	68	8	3	Bold Connection	61	7	10
Charlie	74	8	9	Sedra	68	8	3	Gildoran	61	7	10
Fine Edge	74	8	9	Shore Line	68	8	3	High Cannon	61	7	10
Legend of France	74	8	9	Sylph	68	8	3	Opale	61	7	10
Magdalena	74	8	9	Time's Time	68	8	3	Prego	61	7	10
Majestic				Bedtime	67	8	2	Sailor's Dance	61	7	10
Endeavour	74	8	9	Jolly Bay	67	8	2	Shanipour	61	7	10
Russian Roubles	74	8	9	Onslow	67	8	2	Tetron Bay	61	7	10
Gordian	73	8	8	So True	67	8	2	Asir	60	7	9
Hawa Bladi	73	8	8	Spanish Place	67	8	2	Bumpkin	60	7	9
Jasper	73	8	8	Coquito's Friend	66	8	1	Dancing Affair	60	7	9
Rare Roberta	73	8	8	Harly	66	8	1	Down Flight	60	7	9
Annie Edge	72	8	7	Krayyan	66	8	1	Honeybeta	60	7	9
Castle Rising	72	8	7	Persian Glory	66	8	1	Rock's Gate	60	7	9
Curravilla	72	8	7	Stratford	66	8	1	Solimile	60	7	9
Lofty	72	8	7	Naar	65	8	0	Whisky Talk	60	7	9

FOUR-YEAR-OLDS AND UPWARDS, 1983

The following handicap, published on 15th December, is for information only. The figures shown against each horse represent the official assessment of its merit against a norm of 100.

Diamond Shoal	89	10	0	Indian Prince	75	9	0	Santella Man	66	8	5
Time Charter	88	9	13	Ore	75	9	0	Condell	65	8	4
Noalcoholic	87	9	12	Sweet Monday	75	9	0	Karadar	65	8	4
Stanerra	86	9	11	Amyndas	74	8	13	Forward	64	8	3
Electric	85	9	10	Erin's Hope	74	8	13	Jester	64	8	3
Valiyar	84	9	9	Sabre Dance	74	8	13	Top Creator	64	8	3
Montekin	83	9	8	Vorvados	74	8	13	Cyril's Choice	63	8	2
Soba	83	9	8	Chellaston Park	73	8	12	Camisite	62	8	1
Be My Native	82	9	7	Jalmood	73	8	12	Famous Star	62	8	1
Fearless Lad	80	9	5	Jupiter Island	73	8	12	Line Slinger	62	8	1
Ivano	80	9	5	Mighty Fly	73	8	12	Noble Gift	62	8	1
Little Wolf	80	9	5	Cannon King	72	8	11	Rocamadour	62	8	1
Old Country	80	9	5	I'll See You	72	8	11	Another Sam	61	8	0
Sandhurst Prince	80	9	5	Sylvan Barbarosa	72	8	11	Lafontaine	61	8	0
Commodore Blake	78	9	3	Broken Rail	70	8	9	Voracity	61	8	0
Looking For	78	9	3	Vaigly Star	70	8	9	Voyant	61	8	0
Princes Gate	78	9	3	Farioffa	69	8	8	Hollywood Party	60	7	13
Khairpour	76	9	1	Zilos	68	8	7	Kirchner	60	7	13
Mountain Lodge	76	9	1	Fine Sun	67	8	6	Rebollino	60	7	13
Gabitat	75	9	0	Crusader Castle	66	8	5	Say Primula	60	7	13

1948

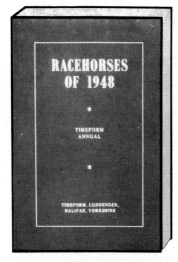

— the year of Abernant, Alycidon, Black Tarquin, My Babu, My Love, Petition, Sayajirao and Tenerani — and of the first Timeform Annual!

In response to requests, the much sought-after first edition of the 'Racehorses' series — the Timeform Annual of 1948 — has been reprinted from the original in a limited edition. Copies are available at £45 (post free in UK). A number of mint copies of 'Racehorses' of 1959, 1974, 1976, 1979, 1980, 1981 and 1982 are also available, priced at £45.

AN IRISH CLASSIFICATION

TWO-YEAR-OLDS, 1983

Published on 15th December, for information only.

El Gran Senor	..	9	7	Shindella	..	8	0	Anita's Prince	..	7	9
Sadler's Wells	..	8	11	Welsh Woman	..	8	0	Malang-Lou	..	7	9
Executive Pride	..	8	8	Real Gold	..	7	13	Sondrio	..	7	9
Western Symphony		8	8	Ballet de France	..	7	12	Cerussite	..	7	8
Capture Him	..	8	7	Sign of Life	..	7	12	Field Dancer	..	7	8
Gala Event	..	8	5	Grey Dream	..	7	11	Jackie Berry	..	7	8
King Persian	..	8	4	So Fine	..	7	11	More Candy	..	7	8
Without Reserve	..	8	3	Black Country	..	7	10	Arranan	..	7	7
Andress	..	8	1	Fiery Celt	..	7	10	Deasy's Delight	..	7	7
Argosy	..	8	1	Paymaster	..	7	10	Final Thatching	..	7	7
Atlantic Salmon	..	8	1	Prince Padraig	..	7	10	Photo Copy	..	7	7
Hegemony	..	8	1	Red Russell	..	7	10	Princess Tracy	..	7	7
Blaze of Tara	..	8	0	The Miller	..	7	10	Secreto	..	7	7

THREE-YEAR-OLDS, 1983

Published on 15th December, for information only. The rating given to each horse represents the official assessment of its merit against a norm of 100.

Shareef Dancer	..	93	Beaudelaire	..	81	Stratford	..	66
Caerleon	..	90	Green Lucia	..	80	Tea House	..	66
Salmon Leap	..	86	Danzatore	..	78	Committed	..	65
Carlingford Castle		84	Glenstal	..	75	Ankara	..	64
Solford	..	84	Curravilla	..	72	Homeowner	..	64
Lomond	..	83	Glasson Lady	..	68	Arctic Lord	..	63
Wassl	..	83	Parliament	..	68	Colonial Flag	..	63
Burslem	..	82	Ancestral	..	67	Safe Process	..	61
Flame of Tara	..	82	Captivator	..	67	Aras An Uachtarain		60
Give Thanks	..	82	Ask The Wind	..	66	Countess Candy	..	60
L'Attrayante	..	82	Glowing Embers	..	66	Iron Leader	..	60
Quilted	..	82	Sir Prince John	..	66	South Atlantic	..	60

FOUR-YEAR-OLDS AND UPWARDS, 1983

Published on 15th December, for information only. The rating given to each horse represents the official assessment of its merit against a norm of 100.

Stanerra	..	86	Mountain Lodge	..	70	Senior Citizen	..	62
Tilden	..	75	Jester	..	66	Steel Commander	..	61
Erin's Hope	..	70	Condell	..	65	Ounavarra	..	60

THE FRENCH FREE HANDICAPS

TWO-YEAR-OLDS, 1983

The following are the weights allotted in the Handicap Libre, published on 31st December.

Name	st	lb	Name	st	lb	Name	st	lb
Long Mick	9	10	Executive Pride	9	1	Lallax	8	11
Siberian Express	9	8	Feerie Boreale	9	1	Cedilla	8	10
Sicyos	9	7	Green Paradise	9	1	Daily Busy	8	10
Almeira	9	6	Greinton	9	1	Fargaze	8	10
Seattle Song	9	6	Polly's Ark	9	1	Misbehaving	8	10
Superlative	9	4	Procida	9	1	Ruby Green	8	10
Ti King	9	4	Grand Orient	9	0	Thatville	8	10
Truculent	9	4	Lord of Trillora	9	0	Vercors	8	10
Cold Feet	9	3	Nikos	9	0	Bountiful	8	9
Defecting Dancer	9	3	Pacific King	9	0	Enoch Arden	8	9
Masarika	9	3	Premium Win	9	0	Equinol	8	9
Treizieme	9	3	Reine Caroline	9	0	Ina Seville	8	9
Darshaan	9	2	Dance Quest	8	13	L'Orangerie	8	9
Eastern Dawn	9	2	Lyphard's Trick	8	13	Perdomi	8	9
Mendez	9	2	Top Match	8	13	Philnaka	8	9
Boreale	9	1	Don Basile	8	11	Porte des Lilas	8	9
Cariellor	9	1	Grausberry	8	11	Reine d'Egypte	8	9
Diamada	9	1	Harifa	8	11			
Duke of Silver	9	1	Keyala	8	11			

THREE-YEAR-OLDS, 1983

The following are the weights allotted in the Handicap Libre, published on 31st December.

Name	st	lb	Name	st	lb	Name	st	lb
Habibti	10	3	Vosges	9	4	Falling Star	9	0
Caerleon	10	2	Green Reef	9	4	Fly Me	9	0
Sun Princess	10	1	Mysterieuse Etoile	9	4	Glenstal	9	0
L'Emigrant	10	1	Royal Heroine	9	4	Karkisiya	9	0
Luth Enchantee	10	1	Tatibah	9	4	Looking West	9	0
Salmon Leap	9	12	Romildo	9	3	Mille Balles	9	0
Sackford	9	12	Rare Roberta	9	3	Saint Cyrien	9	0
Esprit du Nord	9	11	Aborigine	9	2	Garthorn	8	13
Lovely Dancer	9	11	Brogan	9	2	Rutheford	8	13
Sharaya	9	11	Load The Cannons	9	2	Youdjin	8	13
Solford	9	11	Rajpoura	9	2	Alexandrie	8	13
Crystal Glitters	9	10	Aragon	9	2	Aunty	8	13
Escaline	9	10	Sedra	9	2	Bal des Fees	8	13
Mourjane	9	10	Stephany's Dream	9	2	Bid For Bucks	8	13
Sagace	9	8	Verria	9	2	Bourbonnais	8	13
L'Attrayante	9	8	White Spade	9	2	Luderic	8	13
Ma Biche	9	8	Homme de Paille	9	1	Val Danseur	8	13
Smuggly	9	8	Vachti	9	1	Miss Mulaz	8	11
Jeu de Paille	9	7	Allverton	9	1	Pietru	8	11
Beaudelaire	9	7	Alzao	9	1	Alluvia	8	11
Chamisene	9	7	Ice Hot	9	1	Cheers	8	11
Dom Pasquini	9	6	Interco	9	1	Compte Rendu	8	11
Estrapade	9	6	The Noble Player	9	1	Conform	8	11
High Hawk	9	6	Welsh Idol	9	1	Margouzed	8	11
Air Distingue	9	6	Woozley	9	1	Morcon	8	11
Pluralisme	9	6	Fubymam du Tenu	9	0	Propositioning	8	11
Right Bank	9	6	Full of Stars	9	0	Rodwell	8	11
Maximova	9	6	Tintern Abbey	9	0	Tearing	8	11
Galant Vert	9	5	Angela Serra	9	0	Bold Apparel	8	11
Marie de Litz	9	5	Ask Lorna	9	0	Flower Vase	8	11
Ginger Brink	9	5	Brillante	9	0			
Band	9	4	Castle Guard	9	0			

FOUR-YEAR-OLDS AND UPWARDS, 1983

The following are the weights allotted in the Handicap Libre, published on 31st December.

All Along	..	10 4	Tilden	..	9 4	Marasali	..	8 13
Diamond Shoal	..	10 1	Another Sam	..	9 3	Mulaz Palace	..	8 13
Time Charter	..	10 0	Great Substence	..	9 3	Riz au Lait	..	8 13
Noalcoholic	..	9 13	Bylly the Kid	..	9 3	Cost Control	..	8 13
Lancastrian	..	9 12	Sky Lawyer	..	9 3	Favoloso	..	8 13
Stanerra	..	9 12	Denel	..	9 2	Kebir	..	8 13
Welsh Term	..	9 10	Dayzaan	..	9 2	Lichine	..	8 13
Zalataia	..	9 10	African Joy	..	9 1	Nickel Ange	..	8 13
Cadoudal	..	9 10	Naishakar	..	9 1	Rudolfina	..	8 13
Montekin	..	9 10	Terson	..	9 1	Amarkson	..	8 11
Soba	..	9 10	Balitou	..	9 0	Flower Prince	..	8 11
Lemhi Gold	..	9 8	Karkour	..	9 0	Indian Prince	..	8 11
Orofino	..	9 8	Oak Dancer	..	9 0	Le Niragongo	..	8 11
Pampabird	..	9 8	Bell Tempo	..	9 0	Mariacho	..	8 11
Terreno	..	9 7	Bold Run	..	9 0	Petit Montmorency	..	8 11
Kelbomec	..	9 6	Commodore Blake	..	9 0	Roi Guillaume	..	8 11
Old Country	..	9 6	Geral	..	9 0	Coquelin	..	8 11
General Holme	..	9 6	Imyar	..	9 0	Darine	..	8 11
Kind Music	..	9 6	Mighty Fly	..	9 0	Paradis Terrestre	..	8 11
Gem Diamond	..	9 5	Princes Gate	..	9 0	Water Melon	..	8 11
Darly	..	9 4	Radiance	..	9 0			
Gabitat	..	9 4	Campero	..	8 13			

NIZON
(PREMIO ROMA 1978
GROUP ONE)

POLICEMAN
(FRENCH DERBY 1980
GROUP ONE)

ARGUMENT
(WASHINGTON D.C.I 1980
PRIX GANAY 1981
BOTH GROUP ONE)

DEEP ROOTS
(PRIX MORNY 1982
PRIX DE LA SALAMANDRE
1982
BOTH GROUP ONE)

Photo: Bernard Gourier

We have decided not to participate in the recession...

CONTACT: **Patrick Barbe**
Bloodstock Agent

 259, avenue Charles de Gaulle
60260 LAMORLAYE-FRANCE
24h/24: (4) 421.23.51 Telex: BARBE 150980F

THE BROWNSTOWN STUD
CURRAGH, CO. KILDARE

One of the World's Great
Breeding Establishments

BROWNSTOWN mares have produced many top horses
including winners of the following Group 1 races.

Prix de l'Arc de Triomphe
Derby
Gold Cup (3 times)
Irish Sweeps Derby (twice)
Irish Oaks
Irish Two Thousand Guineas
Irish One Thousand Guineas
Irish St Leger
Champion Stakes
Prix de Diane
Yorkshire Oaks
Prix du Cadran (twice)

Brownstown is the only stud farm to have bred the winners of all
the Irish classics; Breeders of the most individual winners in 1978 and
1979; 2nd Leading Irish stud (money earnings) in 1978.

**All enquiries to The Manager, Brownstown Stud, Curragh,
Co. Kildare. Tel. Curragh 41303
Telex 91039**

SELECTED PATTERN RACES 1983

1 PRIX D'HARCOURT (Gr 2) 1¼m
£18,349 Longchamp 4 April

Welsh Term 4-8-12 YSaint-
Martin **1**
Cadoudal 4-9-2 J-LKessas ... 4.**2**
Mulaz Palace 4-8-12
LPiggott 2.**3**
Imyar 4-9-0 ABadel ¾.4
Alfred's Choice 4-8-12
GDoleuze ¾.5
General Holme 4-9-0 FHead .. 4.6
Mariacho 5-8-12
CAsmussen ½.7
Brezzo 4-8-12 DLawniczak ... 8.8
Lancastrian 6-9-2 ALequeux. 2½.9
Oui Mon Capitaine 4-9-4
MPhilipperon 10.10
5/4 General Holme, 42/10 WELSH
TERM, 21/4 Lancastrian, 9/1 Imyar, 11/1
Alfred's Choice, Mulaz Palace, 12/1
Cadoudal, 21/1 Brezzo, 28/1 Oui Mon
Capitaine, 50/1 Mariacho.
O. Helman (R. Collet) 10ran 2m 21.2
(Heavy).

2 PREMIO PARIOLI (Gr 1) (3y c) 1m
£22,727 Rome 10 April

Drumalis 9-2 PEddery **1**
Beldale Concorde 9-2
SCauthen 1.**2**
Benjamin Baker 9-2
GDettori 1½.**3**
Hasty Flirt 9-2 PRobinson 1.4
Okay for Sound 9-2
SFancera s.hd.5
Shenable 9-2 MDepalmas 5.6
Quintero 9-2 GFois 4.7
Batoni 9-2 ASauli 5.8
Colback 9-2 LBietolini 2.9
2/5 DRUMALIS, 2/1 Beldale Concorde,
5/2 Hasty Flirt, 7/2 Benjamin Baker and
Colback, 8/1 Shenable, 25/1 Okay for
Sound, 33/1 Quintero, 100/1 Batoni.
Greenland Park Ltd (I. Balding) 9ran
1m 39.3 (Good).

**3 POULE D'ESSAI DES 1m
POULAINS (Gr 1) (3y c)**
£43,592 Longchamp 24 April

L'Emigrant 9-2 CAsmussen ... **1**
Crystal Glitters 9-2 AGibert. 1.**2**
Margouzed 9-2 ALequeux .. ¾.**3**
Sackford 9-2 GStarkey 1.4
White Spade 9-2
YSaint-Martin nk.5
Saint Cyrien 9-2 FHead 2½.6
Ginger Brink 9-2 GGuignard ½.7
Castle Guard 9-2
MPhilipperon ¾.8
Conerton 9-2 OMongelluzzo .. 2.9
Ice Hot 9-2 GDubroeucq ... d.ht.10

6/4 Saint Cyrien, 28/10 L'EMIGRANT
and Conerton, 7/2 Sackford, 19/4 Castle
Guard, 15/1 White Spade, 19/1
Margouzed, 33/1 Crystal Glitters, 44/1
Ice Hot, 55/1 Ginger Brink.
S. Niarchos (F. Boutin) 10ran 1m 46.3
(Heavy).

**4 PREMIO REGINA ELENA 1m
(Gr 1) (3y f)**
£21,978 Rome 24 April

Right Bank 8-11 SFancera **1**
What Lake 8-11 LPiggott.. 3½.**2**
Lida Perelli 8-11
MDepalmas 1½.**3**
Gisele 8-11 LFicuciello 1.4
Stemegna 8-11 PPerlanti .. s.nk.5
Lina Cavalieri 8-11 SDettori .. ½.6
Tajwind 8-11 GDettori nk.7
Captivating Lady 8-11 PCook 8.8
Evens RIGHT BANK and Tajwind, 6/5
What Lake, 7/2 Stemegna, 8/1 Lida
Perelli, 9/1 Lina Cavalieri, 20/1 Gisele,
33/1 Captivating Lady.
Scuderia Cieffedi (A. Botti) 8ran 1m
40.3 (Good).

**5 ONE THOUSAND GUINEAS 1m
STAKES (Gr 1) (3y f)**
£71,472 Newmarket 28 April

Ma Biche 9-0 FHead **1**
Royal Heroine 9-0
WRSwinburn 1½.**2**
Favoridge 9-0 PEddery hd.**3**
Habibti 9-0 WCarson ½.4
Rare Roberta 9-0 TQuinn ¾.5
Annie Edge 9-0 JReid 3.6
La Grigia 9-0 BTaylor hd.7
Solimile 9-0 TIves s.hd.8
Ski Sailing 9-0 SCauthen 1½.9
Myra's Best 9-0 LPiggott.... hd.10
Henry's Secret 9-0 GStarkey. 6.11
Shore Line 9-0 WNewnes ... nk.12
Flamenco 9-0 PCook ¾.13
Octavia Girl 9-0 BRouse ... 1½.14
Dancing Meg 9-0 JMercer .. 2.15
Indian Lady 9-0 PWaldron 0
Acora's Prediction 9-0
IJenkinson 0
Crime of Passion 9-0 GDuffield 0
5/2 MA BICHE, 7/2 Favoridge, 10/1
Habibti, Royal Heroine, 11/1 Ski Sailing,
12/1 Shore Line, 16/1 Annie Edge, 20/1
Flamenco, 25/1 Myra's Best, 40/1
Henry's Secret, 50/1 Octavia Girl, 66/1
Crime of Passion, La Grigia, Solimile,
100/1 Dancing Meg, Indian Lady, Rare
Roberta, 500/1 Acora's Prediction.
Royal Heroine was subsequently
disqualified.
Maktoum Al-Maktoum (Mme C. Head)
18ran 1m 41.71 (Good).

6   JOCKEY CLUB STAKES   1½m
(Gr 3)
£18,786   Newmarket   29 April

Electric 4-8-10 WRSwinburn .. **1**
Time Charter 4-8-9
WNewnes hd.**2**
Amyndas 5-8-7 AMurray 1.**3**
Old Country 4-8-12 SCauthen ¾.**4**
Diamond Shoal 4-8-10
PEddery 1½.**5**
Zilos 4-8-7 GBaxter 5.**6**
Simply Great 4-8-10 LPiggott.. 4.**7**
Mubarak of Kuwait 4-8-7
GStarkey 3.**8**
Henricus 4-8-7 BTaylor 2.**9**
Easter Sun 6-8-12 BRaymond 1.**10**
Future Spa 4-8-7
PRobinson 2½.**11**

5/2 Diamond Shoal, 7/2 Simply Great,
4/1 Time Charter, 6/1 Old Country, 12/1
ELECTRIC, 14/1 Amyndas, 16/1 Zilos,
25/1 Easter Sun, Mubarak of Kuwait,
66/1 Future Spa, Henricus.
  R. Clifford-Turner (M. Stoute) 11ran
2m 39.14 (Dead).

7   TWO THOUSAND GUINEAS 1m
STAKES (Gr 1) (3y c+f)
£73,462   Newmarket   30 April

Lomond 9-0 PEddery **1**
Tolomeo 9-0 GDettori 2.**2**
Muscatite 9-0 BTaylor ¾.**3**
Kuwait Tower 9-0 JMercer.... ¾.**4**
Gorytus 9-0 WCarson s.hd.**5**
Lofty 9-0 TRogers 2.**6**
Drumalis 9-0 BRaymond 1.**7**
Diesis 9-0 LPiggott s.hd.**8**
Wassl 9-0 SCauthen 1½.**9**
Spanish Place 9-0
YSaint-Martin nk.**10**
Guns of Navarone 9-0
PRobinson 4.**11**
Allverton 9-0 CAsmussen 1.**12**
All Systems Go 9-0
GDuffield ½.**13**
Tecorno 9-0 WRSwinburn s.hd.**14**
Rivensky 9-0 WNewnes 5.**15**
Proclaim 9-0 GStarkey t.o.**16**

100/3 Diesis, 7/2 Gorytus, 9/2 Wassl,
9/1 LOMOND, 12/1 Muscatite, 16/1
Allverton, 18/1 Drumalis, Tolomeo, 20/1
Proclaim, 25/1 Spanish Place, 33/1 All
Systems Go, 50/1 Guns of Navarone,
Kuwait Tower, Tecorno, 200/1 Lofty,
Rivensky.
  R. Sangster (V. O'Brien, Ireland)
16ran 1m 43.87 (Good).

8   POULE D'ESSAI DES   1m
POULICHES (Gr 1) (3y f)
£42,772   Longchamp   1 May

L'Attrayante 9-2 ABadel **1**
Mysterieuse Etoile 9-2
AGibert ½.**2**
Maximova 9-2 FHead 1½.**3**
Chamisene 9-2 AMurray nk.**4**

Little Meadow 9-2
YSaint-Martin d.ht.**4**
Silverdip 9-2 PEddery 2.**6**
Goodbye Shelley 9-2 JLowe... ½.**7**
Dancing Display 9-2
GGuignard 4.**8**
Take A Step 9-2 GStarkey 6.**9**
Sea Symphony 9-2 ELegrix dist.**10**

2/1 Mysterieuse Etoile and Chamisene,
Goodbye Shelley, 15/4 Maximova, 6/1
Take A Step and Sea Symphony, 12/1
L'ATTRAYANTE, Little Meadow, 25/1
Dancing Display, Silverdip.
  Mme. C. Thieriot (O. Douieb) 10ran
1m 42.5 (Dead).

9   PRIX GANAY (Gr 1)   1m2½f
£38,494   Longchamp   1 May

1   **Lancastrian** 6-9-2 ALequeux...**1**
1² **Cadoudal** 4-9-2
J-LKessas s.hd.**2**
1* **Welsh Term** 4-9-2 YSaint-
Martin 5.**3**
1³ Mulaz Palace 4-9-2
GStarkey 2½.**4**
1   Mariacho 5-9-2 AGibert ... ½.**5**
Paradis Terrestre 4-9-2
ELegrix 2.**6**
Terreno 5-9-2 CAsmussen.. 5.**7**

5/4 Welsh Term, 5/2 Cadoudal, 5/1
Mulaz Palace and Paradis Terrestre,
21/4 Terreno, 54/10 LANCASTRIAN,
25/1 Mariacho.
  Sir M. Sobell (D. Smaga) 7ran 2m
16.9 (Dead).

10   DERBY ITALIANO   1½m
(Gr 1) (3y c+f)
£43,956   Rome   8 May

My Top 9-2 PPerlanti **1**
Brogan 9-2 PEddery 1½.**2**
High Cannon 9-2 JLowe 2½.**3**
Truth Detector 9-2
GDettori ½.**4**
Nuzzi 9-2 ASauli 5.**5**
Maladonte 9-2 ADiNardo ... 1.**6**
Mount Fire 9-2 SDettori 3.**7**
Green More 9-2 SFancera .. 2.**8**
Celio Rufo 9-2 LBietolini ... 2.**9**
Tintern Abbey 9-2
CAsmussen **10**
Balkny 9-2 LFicuciello **11**

Evens Tintern Abbey, 3/1 Celio Rufo,
7/2 MY TOP and Balkny, 4/1 Brogan,
5/1 Truth Detector, 8/1 High Cannon,
25/1 Nuzzi, 40/1 Mount Fire, 45/1
Green More, 50/1 Maladonte.
  Scuderia Siba (A. Botti) 11ran 2m
28.59 (Firm).

11   AIRLIE/COOLMORE   1m
IRISH TWO THOUSAND
GUINEAS (Gr 1) (3y c+f)
£60,628   The Curragh   14 May

7   **Wassl** 9-0 AMurray **1**
7* **Lomond** 9-0 PEddery ¾.**2**

Parliament 9-0 JDeegan... 1.**3**
32 Crystal Glitters 9-0 AGibert 3.**4**
Mr Big John 9-0 MJKinane .. 2.**5**
Boom Town Charlie 9-0
TIves nk.**6**
Cremation 9-0 DMcHargue 2.**7**
Aras An Uachtarain 9-0
CRoche 1½.**8**
Fighting Falcon 9-0 GCurran 3.**9**
Thionville 9-0 JCoogan 2.**10**

4/7 Lomond, 9/2 Crystal Glitters, 12/1 Parliament, WASSL, 14/1 Aras An Uachtarain, 16/1 Fighting Falcon, 20/1 Boom Town Charlie, 66/1 Cremation, Mr Big John, Thionville.
Sheikh Ahmed Al-Maktoum (J. Dunlop) 10ran 1m 51.00 (Heavy).

12 PRIX LUPIN (Gr 1) 1m2½f
(3y c+f)
£43,290 Longchamp 15 May
3* **L'Emigrant** 9-2 CAsmussen ... **1**
Lovely Dancer 9-2 ABadel ½.**2**
Pluralisme 9-2 FHead ¾.**3**
3 Castle Guard 9-2
YSaint-Martin 5.**4**
33 Margouzed 9-2 ALequeux 4.**5**
Nile Hawk 9-2 LPiggott ... 10.**6**
Rodwell 9-2 OMongelluzzo 8.**7**

7/10 L'EMIGRANT and Rodwell, 9/4 Pluralisme, 29/4 Lovely Dancer, 15/2 Margouzed, 12/1 Castle Guard, 14/1 Nile Hawk.
S. Niarchos (F. Boutin) 7ran 2m 19.3 (Heavy).

13 OAKS D'ITALIA (Gr 1) 1m3f
(3y f)
£26,293 Milan 15 May
4* **Right Bank** 8-11 GDettori .. **1**
High Hawk 8-11 WCarson ¾.**2**
Barussa 8-11 FDessi ¾.**3**
Louise de Lorraine 8-11
MJerome 2½.**4**
Retrousse 8-11 AMurray ... 2.**5**
Notte Chiara 8-11 SFancera 3.**6**
Fresh 8-11 BRaymond 4.**7**
Emerald Reef 8-11 JMatthias.. **8**
Stemegna 8-11 PPerlanti **9**
Stand By Me 8-11 AParravani **10**

6/4 High Hawk, 2/1 RIGHT BANK, 13/2 Fresh, 7/1 Emerald Reef, 9/1 Stemegna, 12/1 Notte Chiara, 14/1 Barussa, 30/1 Louise de Lorraine, 50/1 Retrousse, 100/1 Stand By Me.
Scuderia Cieffedi (A. Botti) 10ran 2m 28.1 (Heavy).

14 GOFFS IRISH ONE 1m
THOUSAND GUINEAS
STAKES
(Gr 1) (3y f)
£48,348 The Curragh 21 May
8* **L'Attrayante** 9-0 ABadel ... **1**
83 **Maximova** 9-0 FHead ... 1½.**2**
5 **Annie Edge** 9-0 JReid 1.**3**

Flame of Tara 9-0
DGillespie 1½.**4**
Glasson Lady 9-0 PVGilson ¾.**5**
Beat The Drum 9-0
CRoche 1½.**6**
8 Goodbye Shelley 9-0
JLowe 1¼.**7**
Joanne's Joy 9-0 PEddery .. 7.**8**
5 Habibti 9-0 WCarson s.hd.**9**
Anne's Dance 9-0
MJKinane ¾.**10**
Bay Empress 9-0 GMcGrath **11**
Natural Sunshine 9-0
DJMurphy **12**
Safe Process 9-0 DMcHargue **13**
Nova Express 9-0 SCraine .. **14**
Stracomer Nurse 9-0
RCarroll **15**
Saraday 9-0 GCurran **16**
Persian Polly 9-0 JDeegan ... **17**
Top Rated 9-0 LPiggott **18**

4/1 L'ATTRAYANTE, 5/1 Flame of Tara, Goodbye Shelley, 6/1 Habibti, 8/1 Maximova, 10/1 Glasson Lady, 12/1 Joanne's Joy, 14/1 Beat The Drum, 16/1 Annie Edge, 20/1 Top Rated, 33/1 Anne's Dance, Safe Process, 50/1 Bay Empress, Natural Sunshine, Nova Express, Persian Polly, Saraday, Stracomer Nurse.
Mme. C. Thieriot (O. Douieb, France) 18ran 1m 49.2 (Heavy).

15 PRIX SAINT-ALARY (Gr 1) 1¼m
(3y f)
£38,726 Longchamp 22 May
Smuggly 9-2 ABadel **1**
Sharaya 9-2 YSaint-Martin .. 2.**2**
Escaline 9-2 MPhilipperon .. 4.**3**
Soigneuse 9-2 CAsmussen ... ½.**4**
Brillante 9-2 FHead ½.**5**
8 Little Meadow 9-2 LPiggott .. ½.**6**
82 Mysterieuse Etoile 9-2
AGibert hd.**7**
Nibabu 9-2 SCauthen 10.**8**

6/4 Sharaya, 7/2 Mysterieuse Etoile, 37/10 SMUGGLY, 7/1 Brillante, 10/1 Escaline, Soigneuse, 11/1 Little Meadow, 26/1 Nibabu.
E. Seltzer (O. Douieb) 8ran 2m 19.7 (Heavy).

16 PRIX DU CADRAN (Gr 1) 2½m
£25,818 Longchamp 22 May
Karkour 5-9-2 FHead **1**
Indian Prince 4-9-2
ALequeux hd.**2**
Denel 4-9-2 J-LKessas 5.**3**
Facq 5-9-2 MPhilipperon ... 4.**4**
Top Creator 4-9-2 SCauthen 3.**5**
Pas Si Fou 5-9-2 PAngot dist.**6**

4/5 Denel, 2/1 KARKOUR, 4/1 Facq, 6/1 Top Creator, 9/1 Indian Prince, 42/1 Pas Si Fou.
Ecurie Manhattan (J. Audon) 6ran 4m 49.6 (Heavy).

17   PREMIO PRESIDENTE   1¼m
      DELLA REPUBBLICA (Gr 1)
£21,786   Rome   22 May
      Jalmood 4-9-7 WCarson **1**
      Bater 4-9-7 MJerome ... 1½.**2**
      Great Boss 4-9-7
        LFicuciello 6.**3**
      Teofane 4-9-7 LBietolini ... nk.4
      Camille Bloch 3-8-6
        SDettori ½.5
10   Nuzzi 3-8-6 ASauli 1.6
      How To Go 4-9-7 SFancera ½.7
      Phebis 4-9-7 MDepalmas ... 6.8
      Realistic Boy 4-9-7 ALuongo 4.9
7/10 JALMOOD, 3/1 Bater, 6/1
Teofane, 8/1 Phebis, 10/1 Great
Boss, 12/1 Camille Bloch, 14/1 Nuzzi,
16/1 How To Go, 33/1 Realistic Boy.
      Sheikh Mohammed (J. Dunlop) 9ran
2m 0.6 (Good to Firm).

18   PRIX DOLLAR (Gr 2)   1m1¾f
£20,576   Longchamp   29 May
9³   **Welsh Term** 4-9-3
        YSaint-Martin **1**
      Orofino 5-9-5 PAlafi s.nk.**2**
      Darly 4-8-12 ALequeux 1½.**3**
9   Paradis Terrestre 4-8-12
        GStarkey ¾.4
      Coquelin 4-9-1 CAsmussen .. ns.5
      Great Substence 5-9-1
        MPhilipperon 2.6
      Bell Tempo 4-8-12 J-CDesaint 3.7
      Lemhi Gold 5-9-5 FHead nk.8
      Singing Boy 5-8-12
        GGuignard ¾.9
14/10 WELSH TERM, 9/4 Lemhi Gold,
11/4 Orofino, 12/1 Darly, 14/1 Coquelin,
17/1 Paradis Terrestre, 23/1 Bell
Tempo, 25/1 Great Substence, 33/1
Singing Boy.
      O. Helman (R. Collet) 9ran 2m 0.3
(Dead).

19   DERBY STAKES (Gr 1)   1½m
      (3y c+f)
£165,080   Epsom   1 June
      Teenoso 9-0 LPiggott **1**
      Carlingford Castle 9-0
        MJKinane 3.**2**
      Shearwalk 9-0 WRSwinburn 3.**3**
      Salmon Leap 9-0 PEddery.. s.hd.4
7   Guns of Navarone 9-0
        PRobinson 2½.5
      Naar 9-0 JMercer 8.6
12³   Pluralisme 9-0 FHead ½.7
      Morcon 9-0 WCarson 4.8
7²   Tolomeo 9-0 GDettori hd.9
      Gordian 9-0 CAsmussen 1.10
      The Noble Player 9-0
        SCauthen nk.11
      Mitilini 9-0 GBaxter 12
      Neorion 9-0 BRouse 13
11*   Wassl 9-0 AMurray 14
      Tivian 9-0 ABarclay 15
11²   Lomond 9-0 WShoemaker 16

      Appeal To Me 9-0 JReid 17
      Slewpy 9-0 YSaint-Martin 18
      Holmbury 9-0 MMiller 19
      Zoffany 9-0 GStarkey 20
      Yawa 9-0 PWaldron .... u.r
9/2 TEENOSO, 11/2 Salmon Leap, 17/2
Morcon, 9/1 Lomond, 10/1 Wassl, 14/1
Carlingford Castle, Tolomeo, 16/1 The
Noble   Player,   18/1   Pluralisme,
Shearwalk, 20/1 Guns of Navarone, 25/1
Gordian, 28/1 Zoffany, 50/1 Yawa, 100/1
Naar, Slewpy, 150/1 Neorion, 500/1
Appeal To Me, Mitilini, Tivian, 1,000/1
Holmbury.
      E. Moller (G. Wragg) 21ran 2m 49.07
(Soft).

20   CORONATION CUP (Gr 1)   1½m
£42,338   Epsom   2 June
      Be My Native 4-9-0 LPiggott .. **1**
6*   **Electric** 4-9-0 WRSwinburn ¾.**2**
6   **Old Country** 4-9-0
        SCauthen 1½.**3**
6   Diamond Shoal 4-9-0 PEddery ¾.4
      My Sir Avon 6-9-0 WCarson 15.5
      Lafontaine 6-9-0 BRaymond 25.6
7/4 Electric, 9/4 Diamond Shoal, 3/1 Old
Country, 8/1 BE MY NATIVE, 25/1
Lafontaine, 100/1 My Sir Avon.
      K. Hsu (R. Armstrong) 6ran 2m 45.38
(Dead).

21   OAKS STAKES (Gr 1) (3y f) 1½m
£99,788   Epsom   4 June
      Sun Princess 9-0 WCarson **1**
      Acclimatise 9-0 GBaxter .. 12.**2**
      New Coins 9-0 PYoung 2½.**3**
5   Shore Line 9-0 WNewnes .. 1½.4
5   Ski Sailing 9-0 SCauthen ¾.5
      Cormorant Wood 9-0 LPiggott ¾.6
5   Royal Heroine 9-0
        WRSwinburn ¾.7
      Sul-El-Ah 9-0 PWaldron 2½.8
      Current Raiser 9-0 TIves .. 2½.9
      Ghaiya 9-0 BRouse 7.10
      Alexandrie 9-0 FHead 6.11
      Mytinia 9-0 PCook nk.12
      Fields of Spring 9-0 GStarkey 2.13
5   Acora's Prediction 9-0
        IJenkinson 14
      Hagen's Holly 9-0 JHBrown 15
11/4 Alexandrie, 7/2 Ski Sailing, 11/2
Royal Heroine, 6/1 SUN PRINCESS,
11/1 Cormorant Wood, 16/1 Shore Line,
20/1 Acclimatise, 25/1 Current Raiser,
50/1 Ghaiya, Fields of Spring, Mytinia,
66/1 New Coins, 100/1 Sul-El-Ah, 500/1
Acora's Prediction, Hagen's Holly.
      Sir M. Sobell (R. Hern) 15ran 2m
40.98 (Good).

22   PRIX DU JOCKEY-CLUB   1½m
      (Gr 1) (3y c+f)
£82,169   Chantilly   5 June
      Caerleon 9-2 PEddery **1**
12*   **L'Emigrant** 9-2 CAsmussen...3.**2**

Esprit du Nord 9-2
LPiggott ½.**3**
Jeu de Paille 9-2 HSamani ¾.**4**
Galant Vert 9-2 FHead.......... 3.5
Jasper 9-2 WCarson 2.6
Fabuleux Dancer 9-2
MPhilipperon 4.7
Dom Pasquini 9-2
YSaint-Martin 1.8
Cock Robin 9-2 WRSwinburn.. 5.9

Pietru 9-2 OMongelluzzo .. 1½.10
12   Margouzed 9-2 ALequeux 0
12[2] Lovely Dancer 9-2 ABadel 0

14/10 CAERLEON, L'Emigrant and
Pietru, 3/1 Dom Pasquini, 15/4 Galant
Vert and Jeu de Paille, 33/4 Lovely
Dancer, 12/1 Esprit du Nord, 14/1
Margouzed, 17/1 Fabuleux Dancer, 23/1
Cock Robin, 24/1 Jasper.
R. Sangster (V. O'Brien) 12ran 2m
27.3 (Good to Firm).

23   PREMIO EMILIO TURATI   1m
(Gr 1)
£25,042   Milan   5 June

Bold Run 4-9-3 GDettori **1**
7   **Drumalis** 3-8-7 SCauthen .. ns.**2**
17[2] **Bater** 4-9-3 MJerome s.nk.**3**
Bold Brigadier 5-9-3 EHide ... 2.4
Hitchock 5-9-3 SDettori ½.5
2   Okay for Sound 3-8-7
PPerlanti ¾.6
2[2]   Beldale Concorde 3-8-7 PCook 2.7
Emkar 4-9-3 GFois 2.8
Escalente 4-9-3 SGorli 2.9

Evens Drumalis, 6/4 Bater, 7/2 Beldale
Concorde, 4/1 BOLD RUN, 12/1
Hitchock, 15/1 Escalente, 20/1 Bold
Brigadier, 30/1 Okay for Sound, 33/1
Emkar.
Scuderia Cieffedi (A. Botti) 9ran 1m
33.5 (Good to Firm).

24   PRIX DE DIANE   1m2½f
HERMES (Gr 1) (3y f)
£67,170   Chantilly   12 June

15[3] **Escaline** 9-2 GWMoore **1**
15*   **Smuggly** 9-2 ABadel ¾.**2**
Air Distingue 9-2 WCarson. ½.**3**
13*   Right Bank 9-2 MPhilipperon. ½.4
Bid For Bucks 9-2 LPiggott...
2½.5
15   Soigneuse 9-2 CAsmussen ... ¾.6
8   Dancing Display 9-2
GGuignard 2½.7
14   Goodbye Shelley 9-2 JLowe s.nk.8
15   Little Meadow 9-2
YSaint-Martin nk.9
Aunty 9-2 J-CDesaint 2½.10
Blue River 9-2 PBruneau 0
Don't Mary 9-2 PEddery 0
Heron Cove 9-2 DVincent 0
Marie de Flandre 9-2 ELegrix .. 0
Marqueuse 9-2 MPlanard 0
15   Mysterieuse Etoile 9-2 AGibert 0
Quemora 9-2 FHead 0

9/10 Smuggly, 7/1 Marie de Flandre, 9/1
Blue River and Quemora, 11/1
ESCALINE, Right Bank, 12/1 Little
Meadow, 15/1 Air Distingue, 18/1
Soigneuse, 23/1 Mysterieuse Etoile,
24/1 Heron Cove, 28/1 Bid For Bucks,
33/1 Aunty, 60/1 Goodbye Shelley, 65/1
Don't Mary, 68/1 Dancing Display, 84/1
Marqueuse.
Mme. J. Fellows (J. Fellows) 17ran 2m
7.8 (Firm).

25   GRAN PREMIO DI   1½m
MILANO (Gr 1)
£42,644   Milan   12 June

20   **Diamond Shoal** 4-9-7
SCauthen **1**
6   **Easter Sun** 6-9-7 BRaymond 4.**2**
9   **Terreno** 5-9-7 MDepalmas... ¾.**3**
6[3]   Amyndas 5-9-7 GBaxter 2½.4
23[3] Bater 4-9-7 MJerome 1.5
10*   My Top 3-8-6 PPerlanti ½.6
10   Celio Rufo 3-8-6 WRSwinburn 3.7
Tebaldo Brusato 3-8-6 LSainati . 8

6/5 DIAMOND SHOAL, 6/4 My Top and
Tebaldo Brusato, 4/1 Amyndas, 7/1
Easter Sun, 9/1 Terreno, 14/1 Celio
Rufo, 15/1 Bater.
P. Mellon (I. Balding) 8ran 2m 26.3
(Good to Firm).

26   QUEEN ANNE STAKES   1m
(Gr 3)
£15,544   Ascot   14 June

Valiyar 4-9-5 PEddery **1**
Montekin 4-9-5 BTaylor .. 1½.**2**
Noalcoholic 6-9-8
GDuffield 6.**3**
Ivano 4-9-8 LPiggott 2½.4
Bali Dancer 4-9-5
WRSwinburn ½.5
Iron Leader 3-8-5 DMcHargue 3.6
Travelguard 3-8-5 EHide 5.7
Rebollino 4-9-5 RPElliot ½.8
Wattlefield 4-9-5 GStarkey ... 20.9
That's My Son 4-9-5 PRobinson 10

7/4 Ivano, 9/4 Noalcoholic, 10/1 Bali
Dancer, VALIYAR, 14/1 Iron Leader,
Rebollino, 16/1 Travelguard, 20/1
Montekin, 40/1 Wattlefield, 50/1 That's
My Son.
G. Vanian (H. Cecil) 10ran 1m 42.29
(Good to Firm).

27   PRINCE OF WALES'S   1¼m
STAKES (Gr 2)
£22,310   Ascot   14 June

Stanerra 5-8-12 BRouse **1**
Sabre Dance 4-8-11 LPiggott. 4.**2**
Commodore Blake 6-9-4
WRSwinburn hd.**3**
Cannon King 7-9-1 WCarson 1½.4
Prima Voce 4-9-1 SCauthen .. ¾.5
Farioffa 4-9-1 BRaymond ... 1½.6
Erin's Hope 4-8-11
DGillespie 2½.7
Lobkowiez 4-8-11 TIves ¾.8

945

19   Naar 3-7-10 RFox 1½.9
Fine Sun 6-9-1 PEddery nk.10
By Decree 3-7-10 AClark .. nk.11

9/2 Sabre Dance, 6/1 Erin's Hope, 7/1 Farioffa, Fine Sun, STANERRA, 9/1 Naar, 10/1 Commodore Blake, 12/1 Prima Voce, 14/1 By Decree, 16/1 Cannon King, 20/1 Lobkowiez.

F. Dunne (F. Dunne, Ireland) 11ran 2m 6.51 (Good to Firm).

---

28   ST JAMES'S PALACE   1m
STAKES (Gr 2) (3y)
£27,060   Ascot   14 June

    Horage 9-0 SCauthen 1
19   Tolomeo 9-0 GStarkey hd.2
    Dunbeath 9-0 LPiggott 4.3
7³   Muscatite 9-0 BTaylor nk.4
22   Cock Robin 9-0 WRSwinburn.. 10.5
    Glenstal 9-0 PEddery 25.6
    Orixo 9-0 WCarson 7

100/30 Orixo, 4/1 Muscatite, 9/2 Dunbeath, Glenstal, 6/1 Tolomeo, 12/1 Cock Robin, 18/1 HORAGE.

A. Rachid (M. McCormack) 7ran 1m 40.08 (Good to Firm).

---

29   CORONATION STAKES   1m
(Gr 2) (3y f)
£22,910   Ascot   15 June

14   Flame of Tara 9-0 DGillespie... 1
5³   Favoridge 9-0 PEddery nk.2
    Magdalena 9-0 LPiggott 1.3
    Sweet Emma 9-4 JMercer 8.4
    Sea Fret 9-0 PCook 1.5
14³ Annie Edge 9-0 JReid 4.6

Evens Favoridge, 5/1 Magdalena, 11/2 FLAME OF TARA, 6/1 Annie Edge, 14/1 Sweet Emma, 40/1 Sea Fret.

Miss P. O'Kelly (J. Bolger, Ireland) 6ran 1m 42.16 (Firm).

---

30   GOLD CUP (Gr 1)   2½m
£43,146   Ascot   16 June

    Little Wolf 5-9-0 WCarson 1
    Khairpour 4-9-0 JReid 5.2
16² Indian Prince 4-9-0
    ALequeux 1½.3
    Ore 5-9-0 LPiggott hd.4
    Prince Maj 5-9-0 SCauthen 6.5
    Centroline 5-9-0 WNewnes ... 2.6
    Red Injun 4-9-0 JBleasdale.. 1½.7
19   Appeal To Me 3-7-8 DMcKay.. 3.8
    Disturbance Money 4-9-0
    DGillespie 10.9
    Line Slinger 4-8-11 EHide 2.10
    Rivellino 4-9-0 PEddery 11
    Balitou 4-9-0 GStarkey 12

7/4 Ore, 4/1 LITTLE WOLF, 9/2 Indian Prince, 11/1 Balitou, Centroline, 14/1 Khairpour, 16/1 Line Slinger, 33/1 Disturbance Money, Rivellino, 40/1 Prince Maj, 100/1 Appeal To Me, Red Injun.

Lord Porchester (R. Hern) 12ran 4m 24.36 (Firm).

---

31   HARDWICKE STAKES   1½m
(Gr 2)
£22,596   Ascot   17 June

27* Stanerra 5-8-9 BRouse 1
20² Electric 4-8-12
    WRSwinburn 1½.2
20* Be My Native 4-9-0
    LPiggott 12.3
    Criterion 4-8-9 GStarkey 1.4
20   My Sir Avon 6-9-0 BRaymond ¾.5
    Say Primula 5-8-9 EHide ... 2½.6
20³ Old Country 4-9-0 PEddery 7
17* Jalmood 4-9-0 WCarson 8
20   Lafontaine 6-8-9 SCauthen 9
9   Mulaz Palace 4-8-9 JMercer ... 10

3/1 Electric, 4/1 Jalmood, STANERRA, 6/1 Be My Native, 15/2 Old Country, 20/1 Lafontaine, Mulaz Palace, 25/1 Criterion, 33/1 Say Primula, 100/1 My Sir Avon.

F. Dunne (F. Dunne, Ireland) 10ran 2m 26.95 (Firm).

---

32   KING'S STAND STAKES (Gr 1) 5f
£34,208   Ascot   17 June

    Sayf El Arab 3-8-9 MLThomas 1
    Soba 4-9-0 DNicholls 3.2
    On Stage 3-8-9 TIves ¾.3
    Celestial Dancer 4-9-3
    AMurray ¾.4
    Fearless Lad 4-9-3 EHide 1.5
    Fine Edge 3-8-9 PEddery nk.6
    Salieri 3-8-9 LPiggott 2.7
    Prince Reymo 3-8-9
    SCauthen 1½.8
    Chellaston Park 4-9-0 PCook nk.9
    Another Risk 3-8-9
    BCrossley 1½.10
5   Crime of Passion 3-8-6
    WNewnes s.hd.11
    Kind Music 4-9-3 GDubroeucq.. 0
    Steel Charger 6-9-3
    WRSwinburn 0
    Touch Boy 7-9-3 WCarson 0
    Jonacris 3-8-9 MMiller 0
    Krayyan 3-8-9 GStarkey 0

11/4 On Stage, 7/2 Fearless Lad, 6/1 Salieri, 10/1 Kind Music, 11/1 Soba, 12/1 Jonacris, Krayyan, 14/1 Touch Boy, 16/1 Chellaston Park, Fine Edge, 25/1 Celestial Dancer, Crime of Passion, 33/1 Another Risk, Prince Reymo, SAYF EL ARAB, Steel Charger.

M. Dabaghi (W. O'Gorman) 16ran 1m 0.06 (Firm).

---

33   IRISH SWEEPS DERBY   1½m
(Gr 1) (3y c+f)
£109,289   The Curragh   25 June

    Shareef Dancer 9-0
    WRSwinburn 1
22* Caerleon 9-0 PEddery 3.2
19* Teenoso 9-0 LPiggott 2.3
    Quilted 9-0 DGillespie 1½.4
19   Wassl 9-0 AMurray 1.5
    Kalaminsky 9-0 CRoche ... s.hd.6

19^2 Carlingford Castle 9-0
            MJKinane ½.7
        Sir Simon 9-0 JCoogan 8.8
        Avalanche Way 9-0 KMoses ... 3.9
11^3 Parliament 9-0 JDeegan nk.10
        Heron Bay 9-0 GMcGrath 6.11
        Slaney Prince 9-0 GCurran t.o.12

5/4 Caerleon, 2/1 Teenoso, 8/1
SHAREEF DANCER, 17/2 Carlingford
Castle, 16/1 Wassl, 20/1 Parliament,
66/1 Avalanche Way, Heron Bay, Quilted,
Sir Simon, 200/1 Kalaminsky, 500/1
Slaney Prince.
    Maktoum Al-Maktoum (M. Stoute)
12ran 2m 29.4 (Firm).

34   GRAND PRIX DE PARIS   1m7f
        (Gr 1) (3y c+f)
£38,462   Longchamp   26 June
19   **Yawa** 8-11 PWaldron **1**
     Fubymam du Tenu 8-11
        ALequeux 2.**2**
22   **Jasper** 8-11 LPiggott 2.3
        Castle Rising 8-11 WCarson .. hd.4
        Homme de Paille 8-11
            CAsmussen 2½.5
        Tom Seymour 8-11 BRaymond 10.6
10^2 Brogan 8-11 PEddery 15.7

2/1 Brogan, 11/4 Homme de Paille, 4/1
Jasper, 19/4 Castle Rising, 6/1 Fubymam
du Tenu, 11/1 YAWA, 21/1 Tom Seymour.
    Elisha Holding (G. Lewis) 7ran 3m
24.0 (Good).

35   PRIX D'ISPAHAN (Gr 1)   1m1¼f
£38,462   Longchamp   26 June
11   **Crystal Glitters** 3-8-9
        YSaint-Martin **1**
18^3 **Darly** 4-9-6 ALequeux 3.**2**
22^2 **L'Emigrant** 3-8-9
            CAsmussen hd.3
23* Bold Run 4-9-6 ABadel ½.4
19   The Noble Player 3-8-9
        SCauthen ½.5
19   Pluralisme 3-8-9 FHead 3.6
        Alluvia 3-8-9 HSamani 6.7
23^2 Drumalis 3-8-9 PEddery 2.8
        Pampabird 4-9-6 MPhilipperon 2.9
24   Right Bank 3-8-6 DVincent ... 3.10
        Soliloquy 3-8-9 OMongelluzzo... 0
        Welsh Idol 3-8-9 LPiggott 0

7/10 L'Emigrant and Soliloquy, 31/4
Pampabird and Right Bank, Pluralisme,
9/1 Bold Run, 10/1 CRYSTAL
GLITTERS, 11/1 The Noble Player, 16/1
Welsh Idol, 23/1 Alluvia, Drumalis, 27/1
Darly.
    M. Fustok (M. Saliba) 12ran 2m 0.8
(Dead).

36   CORAL-ECLIPSE   1¼m
        STAKES (Gr 1)
£81,718   Sandown   2 July
    Solford 3-8-8 PEddery **1**

28   **Muscatite** 3-8-8 LPiggott .. hd.**2**
28^2 **Tolomeo** 3-8-8 GStarkey ... hd.3
31* Stanerra 5-9-4 BRouse nk.4
19   Guns of Navarone 3-8-8
            PRobinson nk.5
6^2 Time Charter 4-9-4
            WNewnes 1½.6
31   Lafontaine 6-9-7 ABarclay 4.7
27   Prima Voce 4-9-7 PTulk 2½.8
27   Lobkowiez 4-9-7 WCarson ... 10.9

11/4 Stanerra, 3/1 SOLFORD, 100/30
Time Charter, 9/2 Tolomeo, 11/1
Muscatite, 25/1 Guns of Navarone, 33/1
Prima Voce, 50/1 Lobkowiez, 66/1
Lafontaine.
    R. Sangster (V. O'Brien, Ireland) 9ran
2m 6.36 (Firm).

37   GRAND PRIX DE   1m4½f
        SAINT-CLOUD (Gr 1)
£84,890   Saint-Cloud   3 July
25* **Diamond Shoal** 4-9-8
            SCauthen **1**
9*   **Lancastrian** 6-9-8
            YSaint-Martin ¾.**2**
        Zalataia 4-9-5 GDubroeucq ¾.3
18   Lehmi Gold 5-9-8 FHead ¾.4
22   Jeu de Paille 3-8-9 HSamani.. 1½.5
22^3 Esprit du Nord 3-8-9 LPiggott.. 1.6
        All Along 4-9-5 GStarkey 3.7
1   Brezzo 4-9-8 DLawniczak 2.8
31^2 Electric 4-9-8 WRSwinburn s.hd.9

2/1 Lancastrian, 9/2 Electric, 23/4 All
Along, 6/1 Jeu de Paille, 8/1 Esprit du
Nord, 9/1 Lehmi Gold, Zalataia, 96/10
DIAMOND SHOAL, 33/1 Brezzo.
    P. Mellon (I. Balding) 9ran 2m 34.9
(Good to Firm).

38   PRINCESS OF WALES'S   1½m
        STAKES (Gr 2)
£23,944   Newmarket   5 July
33   **Quilted** 3-8-0 WNewnes **1**
30^2 **Khairpour** 4-9-0
            SCauthen ½.**2**
        John French 3-8-0
            PCook 2½.3
        Awaasif 4-9-6 BRaymond ... 8.4
19   Morcon 3-8-0 WCarson ¾.5
        Palace Gold 4-9-0 TIves 2½.6
21   Cormorant Wood 3-7-11
            RFox 7
        Aberfield 6-9-0 Pd'Arcy 8
31^3 Be My Native 4-9-9
            LPiggott 9
        Condell 4-9-0 DGillespie 10
36   Lafontaine 6-9-3 BTaylor........ 11

7/2 QUILTED, 9/2 Morcon, 15/2 John
French, 8/1 Awaasif, Be My Native,
Khairpour, 12/1 Cormorant Wood, 14/1
Condell, 20/1 Palace Gold, 33/1
Lafontaine, 66/1 Aberfield.
    J. Fluor (M. O'Toole, Ireland) 11ran
2m 32.75 (Good to Firm).

39   WILLIAM HILL JULY   6f
     CUP (Gr 1)
£41,644   Newmarket   7 July
14   **Habibti** 3-8-8 WCarson **1**
32² **Soba** 4-9-3 DNicholls........ 2½. **2**
32³ **On Stage** 3-8-11 TIves 1.**3**
32   Salieri 3-8-11 LPiggott........ ¾. 4
26³ Noalcoholic 6-9-6
       GDuffield s.hd.5
     Sweet Monday 5-9-6
       JMatthias s.hd.6
14² Maximova 3-8-8 FHead......... 2.7
32   Celestial Dancer 4-9-6
       EHide 7.8
32   Fearless Lad 4-9-6
       GStarkey nk.9
     Fire-Thatch 3-8-11
       JMercer 1½. 10
     Vorvados 6-9-6
       PEddery 1½. 11
     Tatibah 3-8-11
       SCauthen .... ¾. 12
     Sylvan Barbarosa 4-9-6
       BRouse .... nk. 13
     Vaigly Star 4-9-3
       WRSwinburn 7.14
32   Krayyan 3-8-11 PCook......... 2.15

5/1 On Stage, 7/1 Fearless Lad, 15/2
Soba, 8/1 HABIBTI, Maximova, 17/2
Salieri, 10/1 Celestial Dancer, 12/1
Vaigly Star, 20/1 Noalcoholic, Sylvan
Barbarosa, 28/1 Tatibah, 33/1 Fire-
Thatch, Krayyan, Sweet Monday,
Vorvados.
  M. Mutawa (J. Dunlop) 15ran 1m 12. 11
(Good to Firm).

40   IRISH GUINNESS   1½m
     OAKS (Gr 1) (3y f)
£48,166   The Curragh   16 July
     Give Thanks 9-0
       DGillespie **1**
13² **High Hawk** 9-0
       PEddery 2½. **2**
     Green Lucia 9-0
       DHogan 2½.**3**
14   Safe Process 9-0
       DMcHargue 1½.4
     Countess Candy 9-0
       MJKinane ¾.5
21   Shore Line 9-0 JMatthias 3.6
     Hocus Pocus 9-0 SCraine nk.7
     Osmunda 9-0 CRoche 1.8
     Glowing Embers 9-0
       JDeegan nk.9
     Salacious 9-0 GCurran 7.10
14   Bay Empress 9-0 PVGilson..... 11
     Simmay 9-0 PShanahan 12

7/4 GIVE THANKS, 9/4 High Hawk, 6/1
Shore Line, 11/1 Safe Process, 14/1 Bay
Empress, Green Lucia, 16/1 Osmunda,
20/1 Countess Candy, 33/1 Glowing
Embers, Salacious, 100/1 Hocus Pocus,
Simmay.
  Mrs O. White (J. Bolger) 12ran 2m
32.3 (Firm).

41   KING GEORGE VI AND   1½m
     QUEEN ELIZABETH DIAMOND
     STAKES (Gr 1)
£133,851   Ascot   23 July
36   **Time Charter** 4-9-4
       JMercer **1**
37* **Diamond Shoal** 4-9-7
       LPiggott .... ¾. **2**
21* **Sun Princess** 3-8-5
       WCarson 1.**3**
38   Awaasif 4-9-4 BRaymond 2.4
37² Lancastrian 6-9-7
       ALequeux 5.5
33   Carlingford Castle 3-8-8
       GStarkey 3.6
     Rocamadour 4-9-7 BRouse ... 10.7
37   Lemhi Gold 5-9-7 FHead 2.8
33² Caerleon 3-8-8 PEddery t.o.9

9/4 Caerleon, Sun Princess, 5/1 TIME
CHARTER, 8/1 Diamond Shoal, 15/1
Awaasif, 16/1 Lemhi Gold, 25/1
Carlingford Castle, 33/1 Lancastrian,
150/1 Rocamadour.
  R. Barnett (H. Candy) 9ran 2m 30.79
(Good to Firm).

42   PRIX ROBERT PAPIN   5½f
     (Gr 1) (2y c+f)
£25,168   Maisons-Laffitte 24 July
     Masarika 8-9 YSaint-Martin ... **1**
     Superlative 8-11 TIves ..... ½. **2**
     Harifa 8-9 LPiggott 2½.**3**
     Ruby Green 8-9 GDubroeucq ¾.4
     Elegant Act 8-9 GStahlbaum .. 6.5

7/10 MASARIKA, 7/4 Harifa, 7/1
Superlative, 9/1 Ruby Green, 16/1
Elegant Act.
  H. H. Aga Khan (A. de Royer Dupre)
5ran 1m 5.3 (Good).

43   SUSSEX STAKES (Gr 1)   1m
£63,032   Goodwood   27 July
39   **Noalcoholic** 6-9-7
       GDuffield **1**
36³ Tolomeo 3-8-10 LPiggott .. 2½. **2**
33   Wassl 3-8-10 WCarson hd.3
26² Montekin 4-9-7 BRouse ½.4
36² Muscatite 3-8-8 BTaylor ¾.5
35   The Noble Player 3-8-10
       SCauthen 1.6
19   Lomond 3-8-10 PEddery 3.7
35   Drumalis 3-8-10 JMatthias ... ½.8
7   Kuwait Tower 3-8-10
       JMercer 1½.9
     Thug 3-8-10 TIves 4.10
     Hays 4-9-7 GStarkey 5.11

9/4 Lomond, 11/4 Tolomeo, 7/1 Wassl,
10/1 Kuwait Tower, 11/1 Muscatite, 16/1
Montekin, The Noble Player, 18/1
NOALCOHOLIC, 33/1 Drumalis, Hays,
Thug.
  W. du Pont III (G. Pritchard-Gordon)
11ran 1m 37.51 (Firm).

44 GOODWOOD CUP (Gr 2) 2m5f
£23,348   Goodwood   28 July

30*	**Little Wolf** 5-9-7 WCarson	**1**
	Karadar 5-9-0 WRSwinburn.. ½.	**2**
	Santella Man 4-9-3	
	GStarkey	6.3
	Crusader Castle 4-9-5	
	SCauthen	15.4
	Sandalay 5-9-0 PEddery	20.5
	Old Macdonald 5-9-0 LPiggott	15.6
	Fishleigh Gamble 8-9-0 JMercer .	7

4/9 LITTLE WOLF, 15/2 Karadar, Santella Man, 11/1 Sandalay, 25/1 Old Macdonald, 40/1 Crusader Castle, 300/1 Fishleigh Gamble.
Lord Porchester (R. Hern) 7ran 4m 32.28 (Firm).

45 PRIX MAURICE DE GHEEST (Gr 2) 6½f
£16,556   Deauville   7 August

	Beaudelaire 3-8-7 PEddery ..	**1**
39	**Maximova** 3-8-4 FHead ..... ½.	**2**
	African Joy 4-9-1	
	ALequeux .... 1½.	3
35	Pampabird 4-9-3	
	MPhilipperon .... hd.	4
	Mister Rock's 5-9-3 AGibert. 1½.	5
	Altina 3-8-7 YSaint-Martin	1.6
	Deep Roots 3-8-7 WCarson.. 1½.	7
	Curravilla 3-8-10 AMcGlone..1½.	8
	Jester 4-9-1 MJKinane	2.9
39	Tatibah 3-8-7 JReid .... nk.	10
	Gem Diamond 5-9-1 ABadel	0
	Geral 4-8-11 GDubroeucq	0
35	Alluvia 3-8-7 HSamani	0
	Faith Guest 3-8-7 CAsmussen ..	0

18/10 BEAUDELAIRE, 25/4 Pampabird, 13/2 Maximova, 8/1 Deep Roots, 17/2 Geral, 15/1 Mister Rock's, Jester, 16/1 Altina, 18/1 Alluvia, 19/1 Gem Diamond, 20/1 African Joy, 42/1 Tatibah, 44/1 Curravilla, 85/1 Faith Guest.
R. Sangster (V. O'Brien, Ireland) 14ran 1m 16.3 (Good to Firm).

46 PRIX JACQUES LE MAROIS 1m (Gr 1)
£28,759   Deauville   14 August

	Luth Enchantee 3-8-6	
	MPhilipperon	**1**
35³	**L'Emigrant** 3-8-9	
	CAsmussen .... 1½.	**2**
43	**Montekin** 4-9-2 PEddery .... 2.	**3**
5*	Ma Biche 3-8-6 FHead .... ¾.	4
43*	Noalcoholic 6-9-2 GDuffield... ½.	5
35	Bold Run 4-9-2 ABadel ..... 1½.	6
35*	Crystal Glitters 3-8-9 AGibert nk.	7
45	Deep Roots 3-8-9	
	YSaint-Martin	3.8
	Prospero 6-9-9 HSamani	20.9
	Sea's Valley 6-9-2 J-PLefevre.	5.10

11/4 L'Emigrant, 3/1 Ma Biche, 7/2 Noalcoholic, 4/1 Bold Run and Sea's Valley, 12/1 Crystal Glitters, 13/1 LUTH ENCHANTEE, 15/1 Deep Roots, 20/1 Montekin, 31/1 Prospero.
P. de Moussac (J. Cunnington, jnr) 10ran 1m 35.9 (Firm).

47 PRIX DE LA COTE NORMANDE (Gr 2) (3y) 1¼m
£16,434   Deauville   15 August

	Mourjane 9-1 AGibert	**1**
38	**Morcon** 8-9 LPiggott	3.**2**
27	**Naar** 8-9 JMercer nk.**3**
22	Lovely Dancer 8-9 ABadel ... ¾.	4
12	Castle Guard 8-12	
	YSaint-Martin	2.5
	Mille Balles 8-9 HSamani ..... ns.	6
	Lyphard's Special 8-9	
	GStarkey	1.7
35	Pluralisme 8-12 FHead .... ½.	8
	Hawa Bladi 8-10 SCauthen ... ½.	9
	Ankara 8-9 PEddery .... ¾.	10
	White Spade 8-12 PPaquet	0
	Regal Step 8-9 CAsmussen	0
7	All Systems Go 8-9 GDuffield ...	0
	Pontfol 8-9 GDubroeucq	0

11/4 Ankara, 13/4 Mille Balles, 23/4 Morcon, 66/10 MOURJANE, 33/4 Hawa Bladi, 11/1 Pluralisme, 14/1 Regal Step, 17/1 Lovely Dancer, 18/1 Lyphard's Special, 22/1 White Spade, 26/1 Castle Guard, 45/1 Pontfol, 86/1 Naar, 91/1 All Systems Go.
M. Dabaghi (A. Fabre) 14ran 2m 6.7 (Firm).

48 BENSON AND HEDGES GOLD CUP (Gr 1) 1m2½f
£93,980   York   16 August

41	**Caerleon** 3-8-10 PEddery	**1**
	Hot Touch 3-8-10 SCauthen nk.**2**
38³	**John French** 3-8-10	
	LPiggott .... 1½.	**3**
7	Gorytus 3-8-10 WCarson ...... hd.	4
37	Electric 4-9-6 GStarkey ...... ¾.	5
36	Guns of Navarone 3-8-10	
	PRobinson .... nk.	6
36	Prima Voce 4-9-6 GDuffield ...	5.7
	Burslem 3-8-10 GCurran	2.8
35	Welsh Idol 3-8-10 EHide	.9

100/30 CAERLEON, 7/2 Gorytus, 5/1 Hot Touch, John French, 10/1 Electric, Guns of Navarone, 13/1 Burslem, 20/1 Prima Voce, 100/1 Welsh Idol.
R. Sangster (V. O'Brien, Ireland) 9ran 2m 16.35 (Dead).

49 YORKSHIRE OAKS (Gr 1) (3y f) 1½m
£39,588   York   16 August

41³	**Sun Princess** 9-0 WCarson	**1**
40³	**Green Lucia** 9-0 PEddery ... 4.**2**
40*	**Give Thanks** 9-0 DGillespie	3.**3**
21²	Acclimatise 9-0 GBaxter	5.4
21	Current Raiser 9-0 LPiggott...	30.5
	Lady Dara 9-0 GStarkey	30.6

6/5 SUN PRINCESS, 7/4 Give Thanks,

949

10/1 Acclimatise, 12/1 Green Lucia, 16/1 Current Raiser, 25/1 Lady Dara.
Sir Michael Sobell (W. Hern) 6ran 2m 36.12 (Dead).

50   GREAT VOLTIGEUR   1½m
      STAKES (Gr 2) (3y c)
£34,136   York   17 August
    Seymour Hicks 8-7 WCarson   **1**
    Dazari 8-7 WRSwinburn 3.**2**
33³   **Teenoso** 9-0 LPiggott hd.**3**
36*   Solford 9-0 PEddery 12.4
    Laughing Lad 8-7 TIves dist.5
Evens Teenoso, 15/8 Solford, 11/2 SEYMOUR HICKS, 10/1 Dazari, 200/1 Laughing Lad.
Peter M. Brant (J. Dunlop) 5ran 2m 33.97 (Good).

51   LOWTHER STAKES   6f
      (Gr 2) (2y f)
£15,832   York   17 August
    Prickle 8-11 LPiggott **1**
    Desirable 8-11 SCauthen .. 2½.**2**
    Chapel Cottage 9-2 EHide.. nk.**3**
    Pebbles 8-11 PRobinson 1½.4
    Plaits 8-11 WCarson 3½.5
    Bryony Rose 8-11 JLowe .. s.hd.6
    Tina's Express 8-11 GStarkey.. 4.7
    Rusticello 8-11 PEddery ½.8
    Calpoppy 8-11 TIves 1½.9
11/4 PRICKLE, 3/1 Chapel Cottage, 9/2 Desirable, 11/2 Pebbles, 15/2 Rusticello, 16/1 Bryony Rose, 25/1 Tina's Express, Plaits, 33/1 Calpoppy.
P. D. Player (H. Cecil) 9ran 1m 12.24 (Good).

52   WILLIAM HILL SPRINT   5f
      CHAMPIONSHIP (Gr 2)
£40,660   York   18 August
39*   **Habibti** 3-8-7 WCarson **1**
32   **Fine Edge** 3-8-10 PEddery **2**
32   **Chellaston Park** 4-8-11
    JMercer ¾.**3**
    Sky Lawyer 5-9-0 PPaquet . 1½.4
    Time's Time 3-8-10 SCauthen.. 5.5
32   Jonacris 3-8-10 GStarkey 7
32   Crime Of Passion 3-8-7
    WNewnes 8
    Bold Bob 3-8-10 PRobinson 9
32   Kind Music 4-9-0 LPiggott 10
39²   Soba 4-8-11 DNicholls .... disq.
13/8 HABIBTI, 7/4 Soba, 13/1 Chellaston Park, Fine Edge, 15/1 Kind Music, 16/1 Time's Time, 20/1 Sky Lawyer, 22/1 Jonacris, 50/1 Bold Bob, 66/1 Crime Of Passion.
Soba finished second, 1½ lengths behind Habibti and 6 lengths in front of Fine Edge, but after a stewards' inquiry was disqualified. Fine Edge was promoted to second place and Chellaston Park to third.
M. Mutawa (J. Dunlop) 10ran 57.99 (Good to Firm).

53   GIMCRACK STAKES   6f
      (Gr 2) (2y)
£41,181   York   18 August
    Precocious 9-0 LPiggott **1**
    Adam's Peak 9-0 BRouse 6.**2**
    King's Island 9-0 WCarson.. ¾.**3**
    Our Dynasty 9-0 PEddery .. 1½.4
    Al Mamoon 9-0 TRogers ... 2½.5
    Garrulous 9-0 NConnorton 3.6
8/11 PRECOCIOUS, 5/2 Al Mamoon, 13/2 Our Dynasty, 18/1 Garrulous, 33/1 King's Island, 40/1 Adam's Peak.
Lord Tavistock (H. Cecil) 6ran 1m 11.88 (Good to Firm).

54   PRIX MORNY (Gr 1) (2y c+f)   6f
£24,793   Deauville   21 August
    Siberian Express 8-11
    AGibert **1**
    Ti King 8-11 CAsmussen 2.**2**
42*   **Masarika** 8-8 YSaint-Martin nk.**3**
    Defecting Dancer 8-11
    LPiggott hd.4
    Sicyos 8-11 FHead nk.5
    Indigo Jones 8-11 JMercer 8.6
    Red and Silver 8-11 PPaquet .. 2.7
5/4 Defecting Dancer, Masarika, 53/10 SIBERIAN EXPRESS, 9/1 Sicyos, 12/1 Ti King, 30/1 Indigo Jones, 39/1 Red and Silver.
M. Fustok (M. Saliba) 7ran 1m 10.1 (Good).

55   WATERFORD CRYSTAL   1m
      MILE (Gr 2)
£27,520   Goodwood   27 August
46³   **Montekin** 4-8-13 BRouse **1**
    Adonijah 3-8-6 LPiggott ½.**2**
46   Noalcoholic 6-9-7
    GDuffield 1½.3
    Sandhurst Prince 4-8-13
    GStarkey hd.4
48   Gorytus 3-8-4 WCarson hd.5
    Schuss 3-8-4 JMercer 15.6
6/4 Gorytus, 11/4 Adonijah, 13/2 Sandhurst Prince, 8/1 MONTEKIN, Noalcoholic, 25/1 Schuss.
P. S. Winfield (J. Dunlop) 6ran 1m 39.27 (Good to Firm).

56   GRAND PRIX DE   1m5½f
      DEAUVILLE (Gr 2)
£20,747   Deauville   28 August
37³   **Zalataia** 4-9-5 FHead **1**
22   **Dom Pasquini** 3-8-10
    YSaint-Martin 1½.**2**
18²   **Orofino** 5-9-8 PAlafi nk.**3**
25³   Terreno 5-9-8
    CAsmussen nk.4
    Oak Dancer 4-9-0
    J-CDesaint................. s.hd.5
    Glenorum 6-9-0 PPaquet ... 1½.6
    Flower Prince 4-9-0
    WCarson 1½.7
    Rians 5-9-0 YTalamo 2½.8

Ponty Pool 3-8-5 GGuignard .. 3.9
Load The Cannons 3-8-10
  ABadel ¾.10
22 Fabuleux Dancer 3-8-5
  MPhilipperon 11

17/10 ZALATAIA, 7/2 Load The Cannons, 13/2 Terreno, 15/2 Orofino, 11/1 Oak Dancer, 13/1 Dom Pasquini, Fabuleux Dancer, 16/1 Glenorum, Rians, 20/1 Flower Prince, 50/1 Ponty Pool.

F. Baral (A. Fabre) 11ran 3m 1.6 (Good to Firm).

57	BUDWEISER MILLION	1¼m
£400,000	Arlington	28 August

43²	**Tolomeo** 3-8-6 PEddery 1
	John Henry 8-9-0
	CMcCarron nk.2
	Nijinsky's Secret 5-9-0
	JVelez ½.3
	Thunder Puddles 4-9-0
	ACordero 2.4
	Erins Isle 5-9-0 LPincay nk.5
	Hush Dear 5-8-10
	JVasquez nk.6
46	Bold Run 4-9-0 GStarkey 7
43	Muscatite 3-8-6 EFires 8
	Trevita 6-8-10 JVelasquez 9
	Rossi Gold 7-9-0 PDay 10
38	Be My Native 4-9-0 LPiggott .. 11
	Majesty's Prince 4-9-0 EMaple 12
	The Wonder 5-9-0
	WShoemaker 13
43	The Noble Player 3-8-6
	SCauthen 14

C. d'Alessio (L. Cumani) 14ran 2m 04.2 (Good).

58	VERNONS SPRINT CUP	6f
	(Gr 2)	
£40,100	Haydock	3 September

52*	**Habibti** 3-8-9 WCarson 1
52	**Soba** 4-9-0 DNicholls 7.2
39³	**On Stage** 3-8-12 TIves ¾.3
39	Vorvados 6-9-3 SCauthen .. 1½.4
32*	Sayf El Arab 3-8-12 MBirch.. 2½.5
45*	Beaudelaire 3-8-12 EHide 6.6

8/13 HABIBTI, 3/1 Beaudelaire, 6/1 Soba, 11/1 On Stage, Sayf El Arab, 33/1 Vorvados.

M. Mutawa (J. Dunlop) 6ran 1m 15.31 (Good).

59	PRIX DU MOULIN DE	1m
	LONGCHAMP (Gr 1)	
£33,058	Longchamp	4 September

46*	**Luth Enchantee** 3-8-8
	MPhilipperon 1
46²	**L'Emigrant** 3-8-11
	CAsmussen ½.2
43³	**Wassl** 3-8-11 WCarson 8.3
14*	L'Attrayante 3-8-8 ABadel.. 2½.4
28*	Horage 3-8-11 YSaint-Martin ½.5
46	Prospero 6-9-2 CRamonet ... ¾.6

46	Crystal Glitters 3-8-11
	AGibert ½.7
3	Conerton 3-8-11
	OMongelluzzo 15.8

Evens L'Emigrant and Conerton, 48/10 LUTH ENCHANTEE, 11/2 Crystal Glitters, 23/4 L'Attrayante, 6/1 Wassl, 10/1 Horage, 24/1 Prospero.

P. de Moussac (J. Cunnington, jnr) 8ran 1m 38.9 (Good).

60	GROSSER PREIS VON	1½m
	BADEN (Gr 1)	
£43,533	Baden-Baden	4 September

41²	**Diamond Shoal** 4-9-6
	SCauthen 1
	Abary 3-8-9 GBocskai 3½.2
48	**Prima Voce** 4-9-6 PRobinson 5.3
	Maganyos 3-8-5
	DRichardson 3½.4
	Dzudo 6-9-6 PRemmert 3½.5
	Stornello 5-9-6 SEccles dist.6
	Fall 4-9-6 ESchindler 7
	Arszlan 5-9-6 DWildman 8

P. Mellon (I. Balding) 8ran 2m 28.0 (Good).

61	PARK HILL STAKES	1¾m127y
	(Gr 2)	
£19,255	Doncaster	7 September

40²	**High Hawk** 9-0 WCarson 1
49³	**Give Thanks** 9-0 DGillespie ¾.2
	Sylph 9-0 PEddery 3.3
	Civility 9-0 SCauthen 1.4
40	Shore Line 9-0 WNewnes .. 2½.5
	Malvern Beauty 9-0 LPiggott...3.6
49	Current Raiser 9-0 GBaxter 7

7/4 Give Thanks, 2/1 HIGH HAWK, 5/1 Sylph, 7/1 Shore Line, 12/1 Malvern Beauty, 25/1 Civility, Current Raiser.

Sheikh Mohammed (J. Dunlop) 7ran 3m 8.9 (Good to Firm).

62	LAURENT PERRIER	7f
	CHAMPAGNE STAKES (Gr 2) (2y)	
£31,940	Doncaster	9 September

	Lear Fan 9-0 AClark 1
	Kalim 9-0 JReid 3.2
	Handstand 9-0 EHide 6.3
	Creag-An-Sgor 9-0 PEddery 2½.4

1/4 LEAR FAN, 9/2 Kalim, 16/1 Creag-An-Sgor, 50/1 Handstand.

A. Salman (G. Harwood) 4ran 1m 28.16 (Good).

63	FLYING CHILDERS STAKES	5f
	(Gr 2) (2y c+f)	
£12,888	Doncaster	10 September

42²	**Superlative** 9-0 TIves 1
54	**Defecting Dancer** 9-0
	LPiggott ½.2
	Reesh 9-0 EHide 3.3
51³	**Chapel Cottage** 8-11
	WCarson d-ht.3

Runaway Girl 8-11 WNewnes.. 4.5
African Abandon 8-11
  YSaint-Martin 3.6
Brega Boy 9-0 RP Elliott ... 1½.7
Red Line Fever 8-11
  BRaymond ½.8
Bossy Boots 9-0 JMercer 2.9
Follow Me Follow 8-11
  WRSwinburn 10

7/4 SUPERLATIVE, 11/4 Defecting
Dancer, 9/2 Chapel Cottage, 6/1 Red
Line Fever, 20/1 Brega Boy, Reesh, 33/1
African Abandon, Follow Me Follow,
Runaway Girl, 100/1 Bossy Boots.
  Mrs P. L. Yong (W. O'Gorman) 10ran
1m 2.69 (Soft).

64   ST LEGER STAKES   1¾m 127y
  (Gr 1) (3y c+f)
£81,980   Doncaster 10 September
49* **Sun Princess** 8-11 WCarson ... **1**
37 **Esprit du Nord** 9-0
  GMoore ¾.**2**
41 **Carlingford Castle** 9-0
  LPiggott s.hd.**3**
56² Dom Pasquini 9-0
  YSaint-Martin 6.4
34* Yawa 9-0 PWaldron 6.5
19 Neorion 9-0 PRobinson 7.6
  Dancing Admiral 9-0 TIves 7
50² Dazari 9-0 WRSwinburn 8
  Sailor's Dance 9-0 JMercer 9
7 Rivensky 9-0 JLowe 10

11/8 SUN PRINCESS, 9/2 Carlingford
Castle, 11/2 Yawa, 8/1 Dazari, 17/2 Dom
Pasquini, 11/1 Esprit du Nord, 100/1
Neorion, Sailor's Dance, 150/1 Dancing
Admiral, 500/1 Rivensky.
  Sir M. Sobell (R. Hern) 10ran 3m
16.65 (Soft).

65   MOYGLARE STUD STAKES 6f
  (Gr 1) (2y f)
£39,404   The Curragh 10 September
  Gala Event 8-11 KMoses **1**
51² **Desirable** 8-11 SCauthen ... ¾.**2**
  Welsh Woman 8-11
  DMcHargue nk.**3**
  Princess Tracy 8-11 SCraine .. 3.4
  Shindella 8-11 MLynch s.hd.5
  Saffron Ring 8-11 RCarroll .. ½.6
  Merry Life 8-11 PVGilson 7
  Lady of the House 8-11 GCurran.. 8
  Ms Kelmoy 8-11 DManning 9
  Yellow Creek 8-11 DJMurphy .. 10
  Ispahan 8-11 PEddery 11
  Foolhardy Secret 8-11 JDeegan 12
  Nina John 8-11 AJNolan 13
  Bold Meadows 8-11 CRoche ... 14
  Ballet de France 8-11 CRoche .. 15
  Afef John 8-11 MJKinane 16
  Warning Sound 8-11 PShanahan 17
  Black and Beauty 8-11 JCoogan 18
  Sharpwinds 8-11 GMcGrath 19
  Ivorysguest 8-11 KFO'Brien ... 20

9/4 Desirable, 9/2 GALA EVENT, 7/1
Ballet de France, Ispahan, Shindella,

12/1 Bold Meadows, 14/1 Welsh Woman,
Lady of the House, Princess Tracy,
Warning Sound, 16/1 Afef John, 20/1
Foolhardy Secret, Ms Kelmoy, 25/1
Black and Beauty, Ivory Guest, Merry
Life, Nina John, Saffron Ring,
Sharpwinds, Yellow Creek.
  F. Groves (T. Curtin) 20ran 1m 14.7
(Dead).

66   B.B.A. (IRELAND) GOFFS   7f
  NATIONAL STAKES (Gr 2) (2y)
£28,602   The Curragh 10 September
  El Gran Senor 9-0 PEddery ... **1**
  Sign-of-Life 8-11 SCraine ... ¾.**2**
  Red Russell 9-0 PShanahan 2½.**3**
  Elegant Air 9-0 SCauthen... s.hd.4
  King Persian 9-0 MJKinane ... 2.5
  Executive Pride 9-0
  DMcHargue 1¼.6
  Cerussite 9-0 GCurran 7
  Berni John 8-11 DGillespie 8

4/5 EL GRAN SENOR, 4/1 King
Persian, 6/1 Executive Pride, 7/1
Elegant Air, 10/1 Red Russell, 25/1
Cerussite, 33/1 Sign of Life, 100/1 Berni
John.
  R. Sangster (V. O'Brien) 8ran 1m 27.8
(Dead).

67   PRIX NIEL   1½m
  (Gr 3) (3y c+f)
£13,300   Longchamp 11 September
  Sagace 8-12
  YSaint-Martin **1**
47* **Mourjane** 9-2
  ALequeux 3.**2**
  Full of Stars 8-12
  CAsmussen 1½.**3**
37 Jeu de Paille 9-2
  HSamani ½.4
  Guidup 8-12 LPiggott........... 8.5

9/10 Mourjane, 6/4 Jeu de Paille, 6/1 Full
of Stars, 9/1 Guidup, 99/10 SAGACE.
  D. Wildenstein (P-L Biancone) 5ran
2m 43.5 (Soft).

68   TRUSTHOUSE   1½m
  FORTE PRIX VERMEILLE
  (Gr 1) (3y f)
£58,188   Longchamp 11 September
15² **Sharaya** 9-2 YSaint-Martin **1**
  Estrapade 9-2 LPiggott 2.**2**
  Vosges 9-2 FHead s.nk.**3**
  Marie de Litz 9-2 HSamani s.nk.4
  Vachti 9-2 GDoleuze 1.5
  Rajpoura 9-2 GWMoore ½.6
49² Green Lucia 9-2 PEddery 4.7
  Angela Serra 9-2 PPaquet ... ¾.8
24 Soigneuse 9-2 CAsmussen ... nk.9
35 Right Bank 9-2
  MPhilipperon 1½.10
  Aborigine 9-2 AGibert 0
  Conform 9-2 ALequeux 0

14/10 SHARAYA and Rajpoura, 13/4
Estrapade, 19/3 Green Lucia, 7/1 Right

Bank, 35/4 Vosges, 19/1 Aborigine, Vachti, 21/1 Soigneuse, 29/1 Angela Serra, 36/1 Marie de Litz, 44/1 Conform.

H. H. Aga Khan (A. de Royer Dupre) 12ran 2m 42.1 (Soft).

69 PRIX FOY (Gr 3) 1½m
£13,300 Longchamp 11 September

41*	**Time Charter** 4-9-1 WNewnes	**1**
37	**All Along** 4-8-8 FHead	¾.**2**
18	**Great Substence** 5-9-0 AGibert	½.**3**
18*	Welsh Term 4-9-2 CAsmussen	2.4
1	Alfred's Choice 4-8-12 GDoleuze	1.5
41	Lancastrian 6-9-4 ALequeux..	ns.6
16*	Karkour 5-9-4 MPhilipperon..	hd.7
38²	Khairpour 4-9-2 YSaint-Martin	1½.8
16³	Denel 4-9-0 J-LKessas	2.9
30³	Indian Prince 4-8-12 LPiggott	¾.10
	Acamas 8-8-12 GDubroeucq ...	11

9/10 TIME CHARTER, 11/2 Lancastrian, 6/1 All Along, 9/1 Welsh Term, 12/1 Khairpour, 16/1 Acamas, 19/1 Great Substence, 20/1 Alfred's Choice, Indian Prince, 22/1 Denel, 23/1 Karkour.
R. Barnett (H. Candy) 11ran 2m 40.6 (Soft).

70 JOE MCGRATH 1¼m
MEMORIAL STAKES (Gr 1)
£16,086 Leopardstown 17 September

36	**Stanerra** 5-9-2 BRouse	**1**
59²	**Wassl** 3-8-11 AMurray	2½.**2**
1	**General Holme** 4-9-5 FHead	2½.**3**
38	Condell 4-9-5 DGillespie	2.4
19	Salmon Leap 3-8-11 PEddery..	2.5
33	Parliament 3-9-1 DMcHargue	s.hd.6
	Homeowner 3-8-11 CRoche..	1¼.7
	Clouds Daughter 4-9-2 MDuffy	2½.8
	Ranapour 5-9-5 ALequeux	0
	Captivator 3-8-11 GMcGrath ...	0
	Rare Horizon 3-8-11 GCurran ..	0

1/2 Salmon Leap, 9/2 General Holme, 7/1 STANERRA, Wassl, 20/1 Parliament, 25/1 Homeowner, 33/1 Captivator, Clouds Daughter, Condell, Ranapour, Rare Horizon.
F. Dunne (F. Dunne) 11ran 2m 9.5 (Good).

71 PRIX DE LA SALAMANDRE 7f
(Gr 1) (2y c+f)
£24,719 Longchamp 18 September

	Seattle Song 8-11 CAsmussen.	**1**
54*	**Siberian Express** 8-11 AGibert	½.**2**
	Blushing Scribe 8-11 LPiggott	6.**3**

Depechez Vous 8-11 J-PLefevre 1½.4
53² Adam's Peak 8-11 BRouse 10.5

4/10 Siberian Express, 32/10 SEATTLE SONG, 29/4 Blushing Scribe, 10/1 Adam's Peak, 17/1 Depechez Vous.
S. Niarchos (F. Boutin) 5ran 1m 24.3 (Soft).

72 DIADEM STAKES (Gr 3) 6f
£14,728 Ascot 22 September

39	**Salieri** 3-9-3 LPiggott	**1**
8	**Silverdip** 3-9-0 PEddery ...	hd.**2**
58²	**Soba** 4-9-4 DNicholls	1.**3**
	Executive Man 2-7-10 DMcKay	2½.4
	Prince Spy 3-9-3 SCauthen ...	nk.5
52³	Chellaston Park 4-9-4 JMercer.	5.6
58	Vorvados 6-9-7 WCarson	7
	Azaam 5-9-7 TIves	8
	Reggae 3-9-3 BRouse	9
	Autumn Sunset 3-9-3 WSwinburn	10
	Kirchner 5-9-7 PWaldron	11
	Gabitat 5-9-7 RCurant	12

9/4 SALIERI, 5/2 Soba, 7/1 Silverdip, 11/1 Gabitat, 16/1 Chellaston Park, 20/1 Autumn Sunset, Prince Spy, Reggae, Vorvados, 50/1 Executive Man, Kirchner, 66/1 Azaam.
C A B St George (H. Cecil) 12ran 1m 14.8 (Good to Firm).

73 CUMBERLAND LODGE 1½m
STAKES (Gr 3)
£13,888 Ascot 22 September

	Band 3-8-5 WCarson	**1**
	Looking For 5-9-3 PEddery..	1.**2**
47	**Lyphard's Special** 3-8-8 GStarkey	2½.**3**
6	Zilos 4-9-0 GBaxter	1½.4
	Voracity 4-9-0 LPiggott	3.5
69	Khairpour 4-9-5 JReid	1.6
38	Lafontaine 6-9-3 TIves	7
21	Ski Sailing 3-8-4 SCauthen	8

100/30 BAND, 4/1 Lyphard's Special, 9/2 Ski Sailing, 5/1 Khairpour, 13/2 Voracity, 14/1 Looking For, Zilos, 25/1 Lafontaine.
R. Hollingsworth (R. Hern) 8ran 2m 33.5 (Good to Firm).

74 QUEEN ELIZABETH II 1m
STAKES (Gr 2)
£21,386 Ascot 24 September

3	**Sackford** 3-8-7 GStarkey	**1**
55²	**Adonijah** 3-8-7 LPiggott ..	1½.**2**
55*	**Montekin** 4-9-4 BRouse	4.**3**
59	Horage 3-8-11 SCauthen	1½.4
55	Sandhurst Prince 4-9-4 JMercer	¾.5
27³	Commodore Blake 6-9-4 WRSwinburn	1½.6
48	Welsh Idol 3-8-7 EHide	7
43	Hays 4-9-0 WCarson	8
36	Lobkowiez 4-9-0 PRobinson	9

5/4 Adonijah, 11/2 SACKFORD, 7/1 Montekin, Sandhurst Prince, 9/1 Horage, 20/1 Commodore Blake, 33/1 Hays, 66/1 Lobkowiez, Welsh Idol.
A. Bodie (G. Harwood) 9ran 1m 39.8 (Good).

75	ROYAL LODGE STAKES (Gr 2) (2y)	1m
£32,686	Ascot	24 September

Gold And Ivory 8-11 SCauthen.	1
Rousillon 8-11 GStarkey	2.2
Trojan Fen 8-11 LPiggott..	2½.3
Great Western 8-11 WCarson.	5.4
Mellow Dance 8-11 PWaldron..	7.5

6/5 Rousillon, Trojan Fen, 12/1 Great Western, 25/1 GOLD AND IVORY, 200/1 Mellow Dance.
P. Mellon (I. Balding) 5ran 1m 41.6 (Good to Firm).

76	WILLIAM HILL CHEVELEY PARK STAKES (Gr 1) (2y f)	6f
£41,918	Newmarket	28 September

65²	Desirable 8-11 SCauthen	1
51	Pebbles 8-11 PRobinson	nk.2
51*	Prickle 8-11 LPiggott	s.hd.3
65*	Gala Event 8-11 KMoses	¾.4
	Malaak 8-11 WRSwinburn ...	¾.5
	Rocket Alert 8-11 TIves ...	s.hd.6
	Stats Anna 8-11 BRouse	4¼.7
	Jameelapi 8-11 JMercer	2.8
	Fortysecond Street 8-11 WCarson	s.hd.9
63	African Abandon 8-11 PEddery	5.10
	Island Smile 8-11 CAsmussen	1¼.11
	Rare Gal 8-11 GStarkey	12

11/8 Prickle, 6/1 Gala Event, 15/2 Island Smile, Jameelapi, 12/1 DESIRABLE, 14/1 Fortysecond Street, 20/1 Stats Anna, 25/1 Rocket Alert, 33/1 Pebbles, 40/1 African Abandon, 50/1 Malaak, Rare Gal.
Mrs J. Corbett (B. Hills) 12ran 1m 14.84 (Good to Firm)

77	WILLIAM HILL MIDDLE PARK STAKES (Gr 1) (2y c+f)	6f
£38,402	Newmarket	29 September

62	Creag-An-Sgor 9-0 SCauthen	1
63*	Superlative 9-0 TIves	1½.2
	Vacarme 9-0 JMercer	s.hd.3
72	Executive Man 9-0 DMcKay.	1½.4
	Novello 9-0 LPiggott	nk.5
	Hegemony 9-0 PEddery	2½.6
	Godstone 9-0 PWaldron	nk.7
	Water Moccasin 9-0 JMatthias	½.8
53	Al Mamoon 9-0 PCook	8.9

8/13 Vacarme, 4/1 Superlative, 10/1 Hegemony, 14/1 Executive Man, 16/1 Novello, 20/1 Al Mamoon, Water Moccasin, 33/1 Godstone, 50/1 CREAG-AN-SGOR.
Mrs W. Tulloch (C. Nelson) 9ran 1m 13.24 (Good to Firm).

78	PRIX DE L'ABBAYE DE LONGCHAMP (Gr 1)	5f
£25,381	Longchamp	2 October

58*	Habibti 3-9-7 WCarson	1
72³	Soba 4-9-7 DNicholls	1.2
54	Sicyos 2-8-8 FHead	3.3
	Tilden 6-9-10 WNewnes	½.4
52	Sky Lawyer 5-9-10 HSamani	3.5
45³	African Joy 4-9-10 ALequeux..	2.6
58	Sayf El Arab 3-9-10 MLThomas	4.7
72	Vorvados 6-9-10 LPiggott	¾.8

2/5 HABIBTI, 5/2 Sicyos, 12/1 Soba, 18/1 African Joy, 19/1 Vorvados, 30/1 Sayf El Arab, 31/1 Sky Lawyer, 36/1 Tilden.
M. Mutawa (J. Dunlop) 8ran 54.3 (Firm).

79	TRUSTHOUSE FORTE PRIX DE L'ARC DE TRIOMPHE (Gr 1)	1½m
£211,506	Longchamp	2 October

69²	All Along 4-9-1 WRSwinburn ..	1
64*	Sun Princess 3-8-8 WCarson	1.2
59*	Luth Enchantee 3-8-8 MPhilipperon	s.nk.3
69*	Time Charter 4-9-1 WNewnes	ns.4
70	Salmon Leap 3-8-11 PEddery.	½.5
70*	Stanerra 5-9-1 BRouse	hd.6
47	Lovely Dancer 3-8-11 FHead	s.nk.7
56*	Zalataia 4-9-1 GDubroeucq...	1½.8
69	Lancastrian 6-9-4 ALequeux.	½.9
68	Marie de Litz 3-8-8 HSamani	hd.10
67*	Sagace 3-8-11 AGibert	11
60*	Diamond Shoal 4-9-4 SCauthen	12
41	Awaasif 4-9-1 LPiggott	13
50*	Seymour Hicks 3-8-11 BRaymond	14
56³	Orofino 5-9-2 PAlafi	15
60³	Prima Voce 4-9-4 GBaxter	16
70³	General Holme 4-9-4 AMurray.	17
48	Guns of Navarone 3-8-11 PRobinson	18
24*	Escaline 3-8-8 GWMoore	19
	Dalby Jaguar 5-9-4 GNordling	20
68*	Sharaya 3-8-8 YSaint-Martin ...	21
69	Welsh Term 4-9-4 CAsmussen.	22
64	Dom Pasquini 3-8-11 ABadel ...	23
69	Acamas 8-9-4 J-CDesaint	24
60	Dzudo 6-9-4 AMcChesney	25
64	Sailor's Dance 3-8-11 JMercer.	26

13/4 Time Charter, 27/4 Sun Princess, Lancastrian and Sailor's Dance, 29/4 Diamond Shoal, 31/4 Stanerra, 9/1 Sharaya, 13/1 Awaasif, 15/1 Salmon Leap, 16/1 Zalataia, 17/1 Luth

954

Enchantee, 173/10 ALL ALONG and Sagace, 18/1 Escaline, 21/1 Seymour Hicks, 36/1 Welsh Term, 37/1 Orofino, 45/1 Lovely Dancer, 57/1 Dom Pasquini, 72/1 Marie de Litz, 78/1 Dzudo, 80/1 General Holme, 100/1 Acamas, Dalby Jaguar, Guns of Navarone and Prima Voce.

D. Wildenstein (P.-L. Biancone) 26ran 2m 28.10 (Firm).

80 PRIX MARCEL BOUSSAC 1m
(Gr 1) (2y f)
£25,381 Longchamp 2 October

	Almeira 8-9 DVincent	**1**
54³	**Masarika** 8-9 YSaint-Martin..	2.**2**
	Feerie Boreale 8-9	
	HSamani	s.nk.**3**
	Premium Win 8-9 WCarson ...	1.4
	Lallax 8-9 SCauthen	¾.5
65	Shindella 8-9 CRoche	2½.6
	Arriance 8-9 CAsmussen	2.7

6/4 Masarika, 2/1 ALMEIRA, 8/1 Feerie Boreale, 17/2 Arriance, 9/1 Lallax, 10/1 Shindella, 11/1 Premium Win.

Countess Batthyany (J-C Cunnington) 7ran 1m 38.8 (Firm).

81 PRIX DE L'OPERA 1m1¼f
(Gr 2) (3 + 4y f)
£16,920 Longchamp 2 October

21	**Royal Heroine** 3-8-12	
	WRSwinburn	**1**
	Fly Me 3-8-10 ALequeux ..	1½.**2**
24	**Little Meadow** 3-8-10	
	GDubroeucq	nk.**3**
24	Aunty 3-8-10 J-CDesaint	hd.4
	Ask Lorna 3-8-10 DVincent	hd.5
	Princesse Timide 3-8-10	
	GWMoore	s.nk.6
68	Soigneuse 3-8-10 CAsmussen	¾.7
	Tearing 3-8-10 J-LKessas..	s.hd.8
	Fluke 3-8-10 WCarson	s.nk.9
73	Ski Sailing 3-8-10	
	SCauthen	s.hd.10
68	Angela Serra 3-8-10 ABadel	0
	Green Reef 3-8-12	
	MPhilipperon	0
24	Goodbye Shelley 3-8-12 JLowe..	0
24	Mysterieuse Etoile 3-8-12	
	AGibert	0
21	Alexandrie 3-8-12 FHead	0
	Stephany's Dream 3-8-10	
	YSaint-Martin	0
	Overdose 3-8-10 SGorli	0
	Alma Ata 3-8-10 LPiggott	0

24/10 ROYAL HEROINE, 11/2 Green Reef, 7/1 Alexandrie, 15/2 Stephany's Dream, 9/1 Ski Sailing, 11/1 Princesse Timide and Soigneuse, 14/1 Alma Ata, Fly Me, 22/1 Aunty, Mysterieuse Etoile, 29/1 Overdose, 31/1 Goodbye Shelley, 36/1 Fluke, 54/1 Tearing, 59/1 Angela Serra, 70/1 Ask Lorna, 98/1 Little Meadow.

R. Sangster (M. Stoute) 18ran 1m 50.10 (Firm).

82 JEFFERSON SMURFIT 1¾m
MEMORIAL IRISH
ST LEGER (Gr 1)
£43,024 The Curragh 8 October

	Mountain Lodge 4-9-4	
	DGillespie	**1**
73*	**Band** 3-8-12 WCarson	2.**2**
73	**Khairpour** 4-9-7 JReid	1½.**3**
	Arctic Lord 3-8-12 CRoche ...	3.4
10³	High Cannon 3-8-12 JLowe ...	½.5
64	Yawa 3-8-12 PWaldron	7.6
	Colonial Flag 3-8-12 PEddery ...	7
	Liffey Locket 3-8-9 MJKinane ..	8
	Fork Ball 3-8-12 DMcHargue ...	9
	Labib John 3-8-12 KMoses	10

6/4 Band, 7/2 Colonial Flag, 5/1 Yawa, 13/2 MOUNTAIN LODGE, 12/1 Arctic Lord, Khairpour, 16/1 High Cannon, 33/1 Fork Ball, 66/1 Liffey Locket, 100/1 Labib John.

Lord Halifax (J. Dunlop) 10ran 3m 15.9 (Soft).

83 PREIS VON EUROPA 1½m
(Gr 1)
£60,102 Cologne 9 October

64²	**Esprit du Nord** 3-8-8 LPiggott	**1**
60²	**Abary** 3-8-12 GBocskai	nk.**2**
	Katapult 4-9-2 DRichardson	½.**3**
56	Terreno 5-9-2 OMongelluzzo..	1.4
	Belesprit 5-9-2 PSchade	nk.5
	Ordos 3-8-12 PAlafi	7.6
	Nandino 3-8-8 BRaymond	7
31	Jalmood 4-9-6 GStarkey	8

R. F. Scully (J. Fellows) 8ran 2m 31.2 (Soft).

84 GRAN CRITERIUM 1m
(Gr 1) (2y)
£21,052 Milan 9 October

	Northern Tempest 8-11	
	WRSwinburn	**1**
	King of Clubs 8-11	
	JMatthias	2½.**2**
	Lord Brummel 8-11	
	SFancera	2.**3**
	Nasr 8-11 PEddery	2.4
77	Executive Man 8-11 DMcKay ...	5
	Life on Mars 8-11 CBertolini ...	6
	Mantero 8-11 AParravini	7
	Caro Remuccio 8-11 ADiNardo..	8
	Sinio 8-11 MJerome	9
	Malevic 8-11 GDettori	10

Sheikh Mohammed (M. Stoute) 10ran 1m 38.2 (Good).

85 GRAND CRITERIUM 1m
(Gr 1) (2y c + f)
£41,771 Longchamp 9 October

	Treizieme 8-8 GDubroeucq ...	**1**
	Truculent 8-11 FHead	¾.**2**
	Mendez 8-11 WCarson	¾.**3**
66	Executive Pride 8-11	
	DMcHargue	¾.4
	Green Paradise 8-11	
	AGibert	d-ht.4

Lord of Trillora 8-11 GDoleuze 1.6
Cariellor 8-11 YSaint-Martin .. 1.7
Lucky Scott 8-11 JMercer 1.8
71* Seattle Song 8-11
CAsmussen 2½.9
8/10 Mendez and Seattle Song, 34/10
TREIZIEME, 25/4 Lord of Trillora, 29/4
Cariellor, 10/1 Truculent, 20/1 Green
Paradise, 38/1 Lucky Scott, 41/1
Executive Pride.
T. Tatham (M. Zilber) 9ran 1m 38.8
(Firm).

86   BISQUIT COGNAC   7f
      CHALLENGE STAKES (Gr 3)
£21,320   Newmarket   13 October
72* **Salieri** 3-9-2 LPiggott **1**
55³ **Noalcoholic** 6-9-6 GDuffield.. 2.**2**
74   **Sandhurst Prince** 4-9-6
     GStarkey 1.**3**
5   Rare Roberta 3-8-13
     SCauthen 2½.**4**
43   Thug 3-9-2 BTaylor 3.**5**
     Sir Prince John 3-9-2
     DGillespie nk.**6**
29² Favoridge 3-8-13 JReid **7**
29   Annie Edge 3-8-13 ABarclay **8**
     Persian Glory 3-9-2 EHide **9**
32   Prince Reymo 3-9-2 BRaymond **10**
13/8 SALIERI, 5/2 Noalcoholic, 8/1
Sandhurst Prince, 9/1 Favoridge, 11/1
Annie Edge, 14/1 Rare Roberta, 33/1 Sir
Prince John, Thug, 50/1 Persian Glory,
Prince Reymo.
C. A. B. St George (H. Cecil) 10ran
1m 24.34 (Good to Firm).

87   WILLIAM HILL DEWHURST   7f
      STAKES (Gr 1) (2y c+f)
£44,219   Newmarket   14 October
66* **El Gran Senor** 9-0 PEddery ... **1**
     Rainbow Quest 9-0
     SCauthen ½.**2**
71² **Siberian Express** 9-0
     YSaint-Martin 6.**3**
77² Superlative 9-0 TIves ¾.**4**
     Ministerial 9-0 GStarkey 2½.**5**
     Harvard 9-0 PCook 3.**6**
84   Nasr 9-0 WRSwinburn **7**
     Chelkov 9-0 LPiggott **8**
     Black Spout 9-0 GBaxter **9**
     Corncharm 9-0 JMercer **10**
7/4 EL GRAN SENOR, 7/2 Rainbow
Quest, 4/1 Siberian Express, 8/1
Superlative, 9/1 Ministerial, 20/1
Chelkov, 66/1 Harvard, Nasr, 150/1
Corncharm, 200/1 Black Spout.
R. Sangster (V. O'Brien, Ireland)
10ran 1m 24.90 (Good to Firm).

88   DUBAI CHAMPION   1¼m
      STAKES (Gr 1)
£91,610   Newmarket   15 October
38   **Cormorant Wood** 3-8-7
     SCauthen **1**

29* **Flame of Tara** 3-8-7
     DGillespie **2**
     Miramar Reef 4-9-3
     GBaxter **3**
57* Tolomeo 3-8-10 GDettori **4**
74* Sackford 3-8-10 GStarkey .. 1½.**5**
74² Adonijah 3-8-10 LPiggott ¾.**6**
74³ Montekin 4-9-3 BRouse 1½.**7**
     Alzao 3-8-10 AGibert ¾.**8**
48² Hot Touch 3-8-10 JReid nk.**9**
73³ Lyphard's Special 3-8-10
     PCook 4.**10**
47² Morcon 3-8-10 JMercer 3.**11**
79   Salmon Leap 3-8-10
     PEddery s.hd.**12**
     Russian Roubles 3-8-10
     BRaymond nk.**13**
79   Guns of Navarone 3-8-10
     PRobinson 2.**14**
57   Muscatite 3-8-10 BTaylor .. hd.**15**
59   Crystal Glitters 3-8-10
     YSaint-Martin 1½.**16**
74   Lobkowiez 4-9-3 TIves 2.**17**
70² Wassl 3-8-10 WRSwinburn ... 8.**18**
57   Be My Native 4-9-3 WNewnes **19**
5/2 Salmon Leap, 7/2 Sackford, 11/2
Adonijah,   10/1   Tolomeo,   18/1
CORMORANT WOOD, 20/1 Hot Touch,
Montekin, Muscatite, Wassl, 25/1
Crystal Glitters, Flame of Tara, 33/1
Guns of Navarone, Morcon, 40/1
Lyphard's Special, 50/1 Alzao, Be My
Native, Russian Roubles, 200/1
Lobkowiez, Miramar Reef.
R. J. McAlpine (B. Hills) 19ran 2m
7.95 (Good to Firm)
Tolomeo finished second a head behind
Cormorant Wood, and a short head and
1½ lengths in front of Flame of Tara and
Miramar Reef, but after a stewards'
inquiry was relegated to fourth.

89   GRAN PREMIO DEL   1½m
      JOCKEY CLUB (Gr 1)
£42,104   Milan   16 October
79   **Awaasif** 4-9-0 LPiggott **1**
68   **Right Bank** 3-8-8
     MPhilipperon 6.**2**
     Tombos 4-9-3 GBocskai ... 2.**3**
13   Retrousse 3-8-8 JMercer ½.**4**
25   My Top 3-8-11 GDettori **5**
     American-Baby 4-9-0 ADiNardo **6**
     Judd 5-9-3 PPerlanti **7**
     Feu de Guerre 3-8-11 CBertolini **8**
17   Teofane 4-9-3 MJerome **9**
25   Celio Rufo 3-8-11 MDepalmas **10**
10   Balkny 3-8-11 BSecci **11**
Sheikh Mohammed (J. Dunlop) 11ran
2m 29.2 (Good to Soft).

90   ROTHMANS INTER-   1m5f
      NATIONAL STAKES (Gr 1)
£168,768   Woodbine   16 October
79* **All Along** 4-8-11 WRSwinburn **1**
57   **Thunder Puddles** 4-9-0
     RPlatts 2.**2**
57   **Majesty's Prince** 4-9-0
     EMaple ¾.**3**

956

57[3] Nijinsky's Secret 5-9-0
     JVelez nk.4
     Palikaraki 5-9-0
     WShoemaker hd.5
     Norwick 4-9-0 GStahlbaum   2¾.6
79   Escaline 3-8-3 SHawley 2.7
79   Welsh Term 4-9-0 JFell ½.8
56   Load The Cannons 3-8-6
     MCastaneda 1¼.9
     Half Iced 4-9-0 DMacBeth 1¼.10
     What Nonsense 3-8-6 WBuick.. 11

5/3 ALL ALONG, 13/4 Majesty's Prince, 5/1 Escaline, 11/2 Nijinsky's Secret, 15/2 Palikaraki, 22/1 Thunder Puddles, 37/1 Welsh Term, 42/1 What Nonsense, 48/1 Half Iced, Load The Cannons, 75/1 Norwick.
    D. Wildenstein (P-L. Biancone) 11ran 2m 45 (Good to Soft).

91   WILLIAM HILL FUTURITY   1m
     STAKES (Gr 1) (2y c+f)
£46,529   Doncaster   22 October

     Alphabatim 9-0 GStarkey **1**
85[3] **Mendez** 9-0 CAsmussen ½.**2**
     Ilium 9-0 PCook hd.**3**
     Falstaff 9-0 WRSwinburn 2.4
     Lake Valentina 9-0
     SCauthen 2½.5
75   Great Western 9-0 LPiggott .. 1.6
     Petrizzo 9-0 TIves 7
     Beldale Lear 9-0 PEddery 8
     Bounty Hawk 9-0 BRaymond ... 9

11/8 Mendez, 9/2 ALPHABATIM, 6/1 Beldale Lear, 10/1 Falstaff, Great Western, Lake Valentina, 12/1 Ilium, 40/1 Bounty Hawk, 200/1 Petrizzo.
    K. Abdulla (G. Harwood) 9ran 1m 41.32 (Good to Firm).

92   PRIX DE LA FORET (Gr 1)   7f
£25,167   Longchamp   23 October

46   **Ma Biche** 3-9-7 FHead **1**
45   **Pampabird** 4-9-12
     MPhilipperon ½.**2**
     Aragon 3-9-11 SCauthen 3.**3**
     Lichine 4-9-12 CAsmussen ... ¾.4
88   Sackford 3-9-11 GStarkey 2.5
78   African Joy 4-9-12
     ALequeux 1½.6
     Larionov 3-9-11 BTaylor ... s.nk.7
59   Prospero 6-9-12 CRamonet 1½.8

2/1 Sackford, 22/10 MA BICHE, 5/2 Pampabird, 29/4 Lichine, 11/1 African Joy, 12/1 Aragon, 25/1 Prospero, 56/1 Larionov.
    Maktoum Al-Maktoum (Mme C. Head) 8ran 1m 22.6 (Good to Firm).

93   TURF CLASSIC   1½m
£239,838   Aqueduct   23 October

90* **All Along** 4-8-11 WRSwinburn **1**
90[2] **Thunder Puddles** 4-9-0
     J-LSamyn 8.**2**
57   **Erins Isle** 5-9-0 CAsmussen ¾.**3**

90   Welsh Term 4-9-0 JFell 1.4
     Moon Spirit 3-8-9 JVasquez .. ½.5
     Chem 4-9-0 WShoemaker 1.6
     Late Act 4-9-0 JBailey 9.7
     Ten Below 4-9-0 OVergara ... ¾.8
69[3] Great Substence 5-9-0 AGraell 9
     Sprink 5-9-0 FLovato 10

9/10 ALL ALONG, 32/10 Erins Isle, 7/1 Chem, 8/1 Thunder Puddles, 11/1 Late Act, 16/1 Moon Spirit, 39/1 Welsh Term, 45/1 Ten Below, 48/1 Great Substence, 50/1 Sprink.
    D. Wildenstein (P-L. Biancone) 10ran 2m 34 (Good).

94   PRIX ROYAL-OAK (Gr 1) 1m7½f
£25,041   Longchamp 30 October

31   **Old Country** 4-9-3 PEddery ... **1**
82[2] **Band** 3-8-11 WCarson nk.**2**
     Another Sam 6-9-3
     RCochrane 1.**3**
30   Balitou 4-9-3 YSaint-Martin ... 3.4
79   Marie de Litz 3-8-8
     CAsmussen 2.5
69   Karkour 5-9-3 MPhilipperon.. ½.6
56   Oak Dancer 4-9-3 J-CDesaint hd.7
67   Jeu de Paille 3-8-11
     HSamani d-ht.7
82* Mountain Lodge 4-9-0
     LPiggott s.hd.9
69   Denel 4-9-3 J-LKessas ½.10
     Kaiserstern 5-9-3 AGibert 0
     Petit Montmorency 4-9-3
     GDoleuze 0
     Ya Sater 4-9-3 JLicari 0
56   Ponty Pool 3-8-11 GDubroeucq 0

2/1 Balitou, 3/1 Jeu de Paille, 4/1 Mountain Lodge, 6/1 Band, 7/1 Marie de Litz, 11/1 Denel, 12/1 Karkour, 19/1 Petit Montmorency, 27/1 OLD COUNTRY, 31/1 Oak Dancer, 38/1 Ponty Pool, 55/1 Another Sam, 66/1 Kaiserstern, 99/1 Ya Sater.
    Mrs O. Abegg (L. Cumani) 14ran 3m 24.9 (Firm).

95   PREMIO ROMA (Gr 1)   1¾m
£24,948   Rome   6 November

61* **High Hawk** 3-8-6 WCarson **1**
94   **Balitou** 4-8-13
     MDepalmas s.hd.**2**
73[2] **Looking For** 5-8-13
     PEddery nk.**3**
83* Esprit du Nord 3-8-9
     LPiggott nk.4
     Lattanzio Gambara 4-8-13
     ADiNardo 5
94   Karkour 5-8-13 ABadel 6
34   Tom Seymour 3-8-9 BRaymond 7
94   Denel 4-8-13 J-LKessas 8
89   Celio Rufo 3-8-9 GDettori 9
89   Retrousse 3-8-6 JMercer 10
34[2] Fubymam du Tenu 3-8-9
     APerrotta 11

    Sheikh Mohammed (J. Dunlop) 11ran 3m 03.94 (Good).

96 YELLOW RIBBON 1¼m
INVITATIONAL (Gr 1)
£162,162 Santa Anita 6 November
  Sangue 5-8-11 WShoemaker … **1**
59 **L'Attrayante** 3-8-7
  EDelahoussaye ………. 1½.**2**
  Infinite 3-8-7 ACordero …… 2.**3**
  Sabin 3-8-7 EMaple ……….. ½.4
  Avigaition 4-8-11 TLipham . 2½.5
  Castilla 4-8-11 CMcCarron 1½.6
81* Royal Heroine 3-8-7
  WRSwinburn …………… 2.7
79³ Luth Enchantee 3-8-7
  MPhilipperon …………… nk.8
88² Flame of Tara 3-8-7
  DGillespie …………… 3½.9
  Fabulous Notion 3-8-7
  DPierce ………………… ¾.10
  Triple Tipple 4-8-11 LPincay …. 0
  Pride of Rosewood 5-8-11
  DPeake ………………… 0

2/1 SANGUE, 36/10 Castilla, Luth
Enchantee, 13/1 L'Attrayante, 15/1
Fabulous Notion, Triple Tipple, 16/1
Sabin, 22/1 Avigaition, Flame of Tara,
24/1 Infinite, 40/1 Royal Heroine, 58/1
Pride of Rosewood.
R. C. Parks (H. Moreno) 12ran 2m
02.2 (Firm).

97 WASHINGTON DC 1½m
INTERNATIONAL (Gr 1)
£101,351 Laurel 12 November
93* **All Along** 4-8-12 WRSwinburn **1**
93 **Welsh Term** 4-9-1 DMiller 3¼.**2**
90³ **Majesty's Prince** 4-9-1
  ACordero ……………… 2¾.**3**
57 Hush Dear 5-8-12 J-LSamyn hd.4
61² Give Thanks 3-8-5
  DGillespie ……………… hd.5
88* Cormorant Wood 3-8-5
  SCauthen ……………… hd.6
90 Palikaraki 5-9-1 WShoemaker 1.7
79 Lovely Dancer 3-8-8 FHead 4½.8

2/5 ALL ALONG, 11/2 Majesty's Prince,
15/2 Palikaraki, 16/1 Cormorant Wood,
Give Thanks, 20/1 Lovely Dancer, 26/1
Hush Dear, 44/1 Welsh Term.
D. Wildenstein (P-L Biancone) 8ran
2m 35 (Good to Soft).

98 OAK TREE 1½m
INVITATIONAL (Gr 1)
£162,162 Santa Anita 13 November
79 **Zalataia** 4-8-11 FHead ………. **1**
57² **John Henry** 8-9-0
  CMcCarron ……………… ½.**2**
90 **Load The Cannons** 3-8-10
  WShoemaker ………….. 1½.**3**

  Prince Florimund 5-9-0
  PValenzuela …………… 3½.4
57 Bold Run 4-9-0 LPincay ……… 5
83 Terreno 5-9-0 EDelahoussaye .. 6
  Pettrax 5-9-0 KBlack ………… 7
93² Thunder Puddles 4-9-0 RPlatts 8
  Awaasif 4-8-11 LPiggott ……… 9

F. Baral (A. Fabre) 9ran 2m 29.2
(Good).

99 JAPAN CUP (Gr 1) 1½m
£209,085 Tokyo 27 November
79 **Stanerra** 5-8-9 BRouse ……… **1**
  Kyoei Promise 6-8-13
  MShibata ……………… hd.**2**
95 **Esprit du Nord** 3-8-9
  GMoore ……………… hd.**3**
90 Half Iced 4-8-13 EMaple …… ½.4
  McGinty 4-8-13 RVance …… nk.5
  Amber Shadai 6-8-13 KKato 2½.6
  Miss Radical 4-8-9
  HOtonashi ……………… nk.7
95 Celio Rufo 3-8-9 GDettori .. 2½.8
93 Erins Isle 5-8-13
  CAsmussen …………… 1¼.9
  Daring Grass 5-8-13
  STakahashi …………… ¾.10
  Takara Tenryu 4-8-13 IShimada 11
  Mejiro Titan 5-8-13 MItoh …… 12
95* High Hawk 3-8-5 WCarson ….. 13
89³ Tombos 4-8-13 GBocskai ……. 14
  Canadian Factor 3-8-9
  GStahlbaum ……………… 15
  Hagino Kamui O 4-8-13 KItoh 16

F. Dunne (F. Dunne) 16ran 2m 27.6
(Firm).

100 HOLLYWOOD INVITA- 1m3f
TIONAL TURF CUP (Gr 1)
£188,356 Hollywood Park 11 December
98² **John Henry** 8-9-0 CMcCarron **1**
98* **Zalataia** 4-8-11 FHead ……. ½.**2**
97 **Palikaraki** 5-9-0 LPincay.. 1½.**3**
96* Sangue 5-8-11 CMcGunn … 1¼.4
  The Hague 4-9-0 FToro ………. 5
98³ Load The Cannons 3-8-10
  WShoemaker ………………… 6
  Sir Pele 4-9-0 JFell …………… 7
97³ Majesty's Prince 4-9-0
  EDelahoussaye …………… 8
  Exploded 6-9-0 SHawley …… 9
3 Ginger Brink 3-8-10
  CAsmussen ……………… 10
97² Welsh Term 4-9-0 DMiller ……. 0
98 Prince Florimund 5-9-0
  PValenzuela ……………… 0

Dotsam Stable (R. McAnally) 12ran
2m 16.6 (Good).

958

INDEX

961

963

Airlie....for
the best selection of stallions in Europe and the best care that money can buy

The Airlie studs comprise over 1,500 acres of fenced and watered lands. Each of the five main studs have a completely separate staff and are run independently. Of the two smaller studs one is used completely for isolation and the other for the resident yearlings. There are three private veterinary surgeons and a private laboratory staffed seven days a week during the covering season. For the convenience of overseas patrons we can offer accommodation for mares prior to the start of the covering season. This enables mares visiting the stallions **ARTAIUS, BALLAD ROCK, CUT ABOVE, DARA MONARCH, ELA-MANA-MOU, HABITAT, HENBIT, PRINCE BEE,** and **TUMBLE WIND** to settle in their new surroundings.

Under the management of Mrs S. M. Rogers assisted by Mr Michael Rogers

Airlie Stud
Lucan, Co. Dublin

Dowdstown Stud
Maynooth, Co. Kildare

Grangewilliam Stud
Maynooth, Co. Kildare

Loughmore Stud
Killeen, Dunsany, Co. Meath

Loughtown Stud
Donadea, Co. Kildare

Simmonstown Stud
Celbridge, Co. Kildare

Williamstown Stud
Clonsilla, Co. Dublin

TRAINERS

The figures in brackets are the number of winners each trainer has had over the past five seasons, from 1979 to 1983 inclusive. Quarters and telephone numbers are given after the trainer's name.

Akehurst, R. P. J. (14:9:1:1:5)
Upper Lambourn   Lambourn
(0488) 71871
Albina, M.H. (—:0:10:5:5)
Newmarket   Newmarket (0638) 661998
Allan, A. R. (1:0:3:3:1)
St Boswells   St Boswells (083 52) 2403
Allingham, P. B. (0:0:0:0:0)
Luton   Offley (046 276) 337
Alston, E. J. (—:—:—:0:0)
Preston   Longton (0772) 612120
Ancil, D. I. (2:2:0:0:1)
Banbury   Banbury (0295) 711006
Andrews, A. M. (—:—:0:0:0)
Taunton Bishops Lydeard (0823) 432 632
Arbuthnot, D. W. P. (—:—:—:4:8)
Newbury   Lambourn (0488) 72637
Armstrong, R. W. (38:29:45:43:26)
Newmarket Newmarket (0638) 663333/4
Armytage, R. C. (0:0:0:0:0)
East Ilsley   East Ilsley (063 528) 203
Ashworth, P. H. (0:1:3:4:0)
Epsom   Epsom (037 27) 20336
Asquith, P. (9:6:5:7:5)
Wetherby   Wetherby (0937) 62122
Atkins, R. A. L. (2:0:0:0:0)
Elstead   Elstead (0252) 702028
Austin, C. A. (2:4:2:2:3)
Wokingham   Wokingham (0734) 786 425

Bailey, A. (—:6:4:11:6)
Newmarket   Newmarket (0638) 661537
Bailey, K. C. (0:0:0:0:0)
East Ilsley   East Ilsley (063 528) 253
Bailey, P. G. (0:0:0:0:0)
Salisbury
Amesbury (0980) 22964 (Home)
and 22682 (Office)
Baker, J. H. (1:0:0:0:0)
Dulverton   Dulverton (0398) 820508
Baker, R. J. (—:—:6:6:5)
Marlborough Marlborough (0672) 54739
Balding, A. (5:4:8:7:5)
Doncaster   Doncaster (0302) 710221 or
0777-818407 (Stables)
Balding, G. B. (17:26:14:18:6)
Weyhill   Weyhill (026 477) 2278
Balding, I. A. (39:49:39:58:60)
Kingsclere   Kingsclere (0635) 298210
Barnes, T. A. (3:1:0:0:0)
Ousby   Langwathby (076 881) 379
Barons, D.H. (0:0:0:0:0)
Kingsbridge   Loddiswell (054 855) 326
Barratt, L. J. (2:1:0:0:0)
Oswestry   Queens Head (069 188) 209
Barrett, W. A. (—:—:0:0:0)
Lincoln   Fenton Claypole (063 684) 413
Barron, T. D. (0:0:5:11:10)
Thirsk   Thirsk (0845) 587 435

Barrow, A. K. (—:—:—:—:0)
Bridgwater   Bridgwater (0278) 732 522
Beasley, H. R. (—:—:—:0:3)
Lewes   Lewes (07916) 6619
Bell, Mrs. A. M. (—:—:1:2:0)
Biggar   Skirling (089 96) 273
Bell, C. H. (0:6:6:2:10)
Hawick   Denholm (045 087) 278
Benstead, C. J. (17:17:19:13:11)
Epsom   Ashtead (037 22) 73152
Bentley, W. (7:6:11:8:4)
Middleham
Berry, J. (11:15:19:26:43)
Lancaster   Forton (0524) 791179
Bethell, J. D. W. (15:19:14:15:16)
Didcot   Abingdon (0235) 834333
Bevan, P. J. (0:0:0:0:0)
Kingstone
Dapple Heath (088 921) 647 or 670
Bill, T. T. (—:—:—:1:1)
Ashby-de-la-Zouch
Ashby-de-la-Zouch (0530) 415881
Blackshaw, H. F. (0:0:0:0:0)
Wensleydale   Wensleydale (0969) 23295
Blakeney, R. E. (0:0:0:0:0)
Devizes   Cannings (038 086) 245
Blanshard, M. T. W. (0:4:5:8:9)
Lambourn   Lambourn (0488) 71091
Blum, G. (7:6:5:7:4)
Newmarket   Newmarket (0638) 662734
Bolton, M. J. (1:5:0:1:1)
East Grinstead
Dormans Park (034 287) 403
Booth, C. B. B. (5:1:6:6:13)
Flaxton
Whitwell-on-the-Hill (065 381) 586
or 239 (Stables)
Bosley, J. R. (2:1:4:7:7)
Bampton Bampton Castle (0993) 850 212
Boss, R. (14:21:9:16:3)
Newmarket   Newmarket (0638) 661335
Bradley, J. M. (4:2:0:0:1)
Chepstow   Chepstow (029 12) 2486
Brassey, K. M. (—:—:0:12:19)
Lambourn   Lambourn (0488) 71508
Brennan, O. (0:0:0:0:1)
Newark   Caunton (063 686) 332
Bridger, J. J. (—:—:—:0:0:0)
Chichester   Eastergate (024368) 3525
Bridgwater, K. S. (2:1:0:0:0)
Solihull   Knowle (056 45) 77026
Brittain, C. E. (34:25:54:53:45)
Newmarket
Newmarket (0638) 663739 and 664347
Brookshaw, P. T. (—:—:0:2:3)
Melton Mowbray
Melton Mowbray (0664) 813161
Bulgin, T. S. M. (—:—:—:0:0)
Salisbury Fontmell Magna (0747) 811648
Burgoyne, P. V. J. P. (—:—:—:0:1)
Sparsholt   Childrey (023 559) 623

965

Butler, P. (0:0:0:0:0)
Lewes Plumpton (0273) 890124
Bycroft, N. (—:—:0:2:7)
Brandsby Brandsby (034 75) 641

Callaghan, N. A. (34:14:29:15:9)
Newmarket Newmarket (0638) 664040
Calver, P. (7:2:2:5:8)
Ripon Ripon (0765) 700313
Camacho, M. J. C. (13:7:16:16:11)
Malton Malton (0653) 4901
Cambidge, B. R. (0:0:0:1:0)
Shifnal
   Weston-under-Lizard (095 276) 249
Candy, H. D. N. B. (39:28:30:32:34)
Wantage Uffington (036 782) 276
Cann, J. F. (0:0:0:0:0)
Cullompton Kentisbeare (088 46) 356
Carr, E. J. (4:3:4:4:4)
Hambleton Thirsk (0845) 597 288
Carter, E. (2:0:3:6:5)
Malton Malton (0653) 3522
Carter, R. (0:2:0:0:0)
Swaffham Gooderstone (036 621) 226
Cawley, A. N. (—:—:—:—:1)
Oakham Castle Bytham (078 081) 608
Cecil, H. R. A. (128:84:107:111:92)
Newmarket
   Newmarket (0638) 662192 or
   (Home) 662387
Chamberlain, N. (—:0:0:0:0)
West Auckland
   Bishop Auckland (0388) 832 465
Champion, R. (—:—:—:0:0)
Swindon Broad Hinton (079 373) 329
Chapman, D. W. (2:5:11:22:21)
Stillington Easingwold (0347) 21683
Chapman, M. C. (0:0:0:0:0)
Market Harborough
   Clipston (085 886) 255
Charlton, J. I. A. (—:—:0:0:0)
Stocksfield Stocksfield (0661) 843 247
Ciechanowski, J. M. S. (—:—:—:—:1)
Lambourn
   Lambourn (0488) 71368 and 71595
Clay, W. (0:2:0:0:0)
Uttoxeter
   Uttoxeter (088 93) 2068 and Dapple
   Heath (088 921) 613 (Home)
Cole, P. F. I. (61:48:50:39:41)
Lambourn Lambourn (0488) 71632
Collingridge, H. J. (9:3:7:4:2)
Newmarket Newmarket (0638) 665454
Cottrell, L. G. (2:2:2:4:6)
Cullompton Kentisbeare (088 46) 320
Cousins, M. A. (0:1:1:0:0)
Tarporley
   Little Budworth (082 921) 260 or 316
Cousins, Mrs S. A. (—:1:0:0:2)
Carnforth Carnforth (052 473) 3058
Craig, T. (10:5:5:5:3)
Dunbar Dunbar (0368) 62583
Crawford, W. H. (—:—:—:0:0)
Haddington Haddington (062 082) 2229
Crossley, C. C. (7:12:4:8:4)
Thurstaston Wirral (051 648) 1546
Crump, N. F. (3:2:3:1:0)
Middleham Wensleydale (0969) 23269

Cumani, L. M. (19:26:30:25:35)
Newmarket
   Newmarket (0638) 661569 and 665432
Cundell, P. D. (10:10:10:8:6)
Compton Compton (063 522) 267/8
Cunningham-Brown, K. O.
   (—:—:0:0:0)
Stockbridge Wallop (026 478) 611
Cuthbert, T. A. K. (—:0:0:0:0)
Carlisle Carlisle (0228) 60822

Dale, D. (4:4:7:7:5)
Newmarket Newmarket (0638) 661586
Davison, A. R. (6:0:0:0:1)
Caterham Caterham (0883) 43857
Delahooke, M. C. (0:0:0:—:0)
Cheltenham
   Bishops Cleeve (024 267) 2162
Dickinson, M. W. (—:1:1:0:0)
Harewood
   Harewood (0532) 886536 (Office) or
   886346 (Home)
Douglas-Home, J. T. A. (0:0:1:1:2)
Wantage East Hendred (023588) 247
Doyle, J. C. M. (—:5:0:0:0)
Wetherby
   Wetherby (0937) 63855 (Home) or
   65051 (Stable)
Drew, C. (—:—:—:—:1)
Potton Potton (0767) 260924 and 260491
Dudgeon, I. M. (0:0:0:0:0)
Warminster Codford St Mary (09855) 477
Dunlop, J. L. (96:91:67:87:89)
Arundel
   Arundel (0903) 882194 (Office) or
   882106 (Home)
Durr, F. (38:51:42:13:57)
Newmarket Newmarket (0638) 662090

Easterby, M. H. (74:63:37:43:30)
Malton Kirby Misperton (065 386) 600
Easterby, M. W. (31:17:26:18:11)
Sheriff Hutton
   Sheriff Hutton (03477) 368
Eckley, M. W. (—:0:0:0:1)
Ludlow Brimfield (058 472) 372
Edmunds, J. (0:0:0:0:0)
Birmingham Wythall (0564) 822334
Edwards, J. A. C. (0:0:0:0:0)
Ross-on-Wye
   Harewood End (098987) 259
Eldin, E. (0:11:11:27:23)
Newmarket
   Newmarket (0638) 662036 or 663217
Elsey, C. W. C. (12:26:11:18:10)
Malton Malton (0653) 3149
Elsworth, D. R. C. (10:12:10:17:24)
Fordingbridge
   Rockbourne (07253) 220 (Home) or
   528 (Office)
Etherington, J. (24:20:20:22:21)
Malton Malton (0653) 2842

Fairhurst, T. (20:11:13:13:26)
Middleham Wensleydale (0969) 23362

966

Feilden, P. J. (3:3:4:3:1)
Newmarket   Exning (063877) 637
Felgate, P. S. (0:1:0:7:1)
Melton Mowbray
        Melton Mowbray (0664) 812019
Finch, Mrs P. A. (0:0:0:0:0)
Shaftesbury   East Knoyle (074 783) 305
Fisher, A. L. (0:0:0:0:0)
Melton Mowbray
        Leicester (0533) 605907
Fisher, R. F. (—:—:0:0:3)
Ulverston   Ulverston (0229) 55664
Fitzgerald, J. G. (15:13:14:10:24)
Malton   Malton (0653) 2718
Fleming, H. (0:1:2:0:0)
Cleethorpes   Cleethorpes (0472) 695215
Fletcher, G. G. (2:3:4:2:3)
Clipsham Castle   Bytham (078081) 370
Forsey, B. (—:0:0:0:0)
Crowcombe   Crowcombe (098 48) 270
Forster, T. A. (0:0:0:0:0)
Letcombe Bassett
        Wantage (023 57) 3092
Fox, J. C. (—:—:0:0:4)
Amesbury   Shrewton (0980) 620 861
Francis, M. E. D. (3:3:3:1:4)
Lambourn   Lambourn (0488) 71700
Francis, W. D. (4:2:4:3:0)
Malpas   Tilston (082 98) 208

Gandolfo, D. R. (4:2:3:0:1)
Wantage   Wantage (023 57) 3242
Garraton, D. T. (—:1:3:3:7)
Malton   Rillington (094 42) 506
Gaselee, N. A. D. C. (2:5:6:1:1)
Lambourn   Lambourn (0488) 71503
Gifford, J. T. (3:1:0:0:0)
Findon   Findon (090 671) 2226
Gilbert, J. A. (—:1:1:1:0)
Oakham   Edenham (077832) 226 or 330
Gray, C. W. (—:1:4:4:5)
Beverley   Beverley (0482) 882490
Griffiths, R. D. (0:—:—:—:0)
Tenbury Wells
        Tenbury Wells (0584) 810 430
Grissell, D. M. (—:—:0:1:0)
Heathfield   Brightling (042 482) 241
Gubby, B. (2:4:2:4:2)
Bagshot   Bagshot (0276) 63282
Guest, W. N. (14:11:4:12:11)
Newmarket   Newmarket (0638) 661680

Haigh, W. W. (6:9:13:5:2)
Malton   Malton (0653) 4428
Haldane, J. S. (—:—:0:0:1)
Kelso   Kelso (0573) 24956
Hall, N. (0:2:0:0:0)
Burton-on-Trent
    Barton-under-Needwood (028 371) 2279
Hall, Miss S. E. (15:7:12:22:13)
Middleham   Wensleydale (0969) 40223
Hallett, T. B. (0:0:0:0:0)
Saltash   Saltash (075 55) 2064
Hanbury, B. (8:25:21:22:35)
Newmarket   Newmarket (0638) 663193
(Stable) Wickhambrook
        (0440 082) 396 (Home)

Hanley, D. L. (0:0:2:2:0)
Lambourn
        Lambourn (0488) 72169 and 72219
Hannon, R. M. (30:37:29:28:49)
Marlborough
        Collingbourne Ducis (026 485) 254
Hanson, J. (8:13:5:7:4)
Wetherby   Wetherby (0937) 62841
Hardy, J. (14:17:10:4:1)
Staunton Long Bennington (0400) 81212
Harman, G. R. (—:—:2:1:0)
Helmsley   Helmsley (0439) 70838
Harris, J. L. (2:1:0:0:0)
Melton Mowbray   Harby (0949) 60671
Harris, S. T. (0:1:0:1:0)
Amersham   Amersham (02403) 21718
Hartop, R. W. (—:0:0:0:0)
Newark   Mansfield (0623) 883081
Harwood, G. (48:69:97:120:104)
Pulborough
        Pulborough (079 82) 3011 or 3012
Haslam, P. C. (25:38:35:29:15)
Newmarket Newmarket (0638) 664523/5
Haynes, M. J. (16:12:9:8:6)
Epsom   Burgh Heath (073 73) 51140
Haynes, P. D. (—:—:—:9:2)
Chichester   West Ashling (024 358) 231

Henderson, N. J. (0:0:0:0:0)
Lambourn   Lambourn (0488) 72259
Hern, W. R. (16:65:64:44:57)
West Ilsley
        East Ilsley (063 528) 219 and 251
Hide, A. G. (5:4:8:10:13)
Newmarket   Newmarket (0638) 662063
Hill, C. J. (13:7:6:8:5)
Barnstaple   Barnstaple (0271) 2048
Hills, B. W. (56:61:82:55:58)
Lambourn   Lambourn (0488) 71548
Hinchliffe, M. J. (—:0:0:0:2)
Newmarket   Newmarket (0638) 665 293
Hindley, J. J. (41:46:32:39:38)
Newmarket Newmarket (0638) 664141/2
Hoad, R. P. C. (—:2:1:3:3)
Lewes   Lewes (079 16) 77124
Hobbs, B. R. (42:60:50:42:24)
Newmarket   Newmarket (0638) 662129
Hobson, R. (5:4:0:2:6)
Worksop
        Mansfield (0623) 822835 (Home)
        Worksop (0909) 475 962 or 475425
                            (Stables)
Hodges, R. J. (—:—:—:0:0)
Langport   Long Sutton (045 824) 340
Holden, W. (8:4:5:4:4)
Newmarket   Exning (063 877) 384
Holder, R. J. (—:—:—:3:10)
Portbury   Pill (027 581) 2192 and 9881
Hollinshead, R. (25:26:57:36:43)
Upper Longdon Armitage (0543) 490298
Holt, L. J. (12:9:10:9:10)
Tunworth   Long Sutton (025 681) 376
Horgan, C. A. (—:—:—:—:4)
Findon   Findon (090 671) 2872
Houghton, R. F. J. (39:42:29:38:29)
Blewbury   Blewbury (0235) 850480
Howe, R. E. (—:—:—:—:1)
Hassocks   Plumpton (0273) 890 331

967

Howell, J. M.   (—:—:—:—:0)
Kenilworth   Kenilworth (0926) 59260
Huffer, G. A.   (23:11:18:22:26)
Newmarket
   Newmarket (0638) 730391 (Home) and
                 667997 (Stable)
Hunter, G. H.   (22:30:29:18:19)
East Ilsley   East Ilsley (063 528) 250

Incisa, D. E.   (—:—:0:0:0)
Leyburn   Wensleydale (0969) 40653
Ingham, A. P.   (9:3:3:3:7)
Headley   Ashtead (037 22) 72859
Ivory, K. T.   (15:9:19:10:3)
Radlett   Radlett (092 76) 6081

James, C. J.   (3:10:3:1:3)
Newbury   Great Shefford (048 839) 280
James, M. B. C.   (—:0:3:0:0)
Whitchurch   Whitchurch (0948) 4067
Jarvis A. P.   (5:6:24:34:9)
Royston
Royston, Herts.   (0763) 47444 (Office)
               and 46611 (Home)
Jarvis, M. A.   (39:30:35:31:40)
Newmarket
   Newmarket (0638) 661702 and 662519
Jefferson, J. M.   (—:—:0:1:2)
Malton   Malton (0653) 7225
Jenkins, J. R.   (—:1:2:2:4)
Horsham   Lower Beeding (040 376) 606
Jermy, D. C.   (0:0:1:1:2)
Carshalton   (01-668) 3765 or 8814
Johnson, R.   (0:1:2:0:0)
Bishop Auckland
     Bishop Auckland (0388) 762113
Jones, Dr A.   (0:0:0:0:0)
Swansea
Clydach   (0792) 843504 (Home) and
               842303 (Stables)
Jones, A, W.   (3:8:5:5:4)
Oswestry   Oswestry (0691) 659 720
Jones, D. H.   (3:4:14:13:11)
Pontypridd   Pontypridd (0443) 202515
Jones, Hbt.   (5:9:1:6:4)
Malton   Malton (0653) 2630
Jones, H. Thomson   (13:40:40:45:42)
Newmarket   Newmarket (0638) 664884
Jones, T. M.   (1:0:1:0:0)
Guildford   Shere (048 641) 2604
Jordon, I. D.   (2:0:1:0:0)
Newcastle-on-Tyne
     Newcastle-on-Tyne (0632) 869 143
Jorgensen, O.   (—:0:0:0:0)
Heathfield   Heathfield (043 52) 2551

Keenor, R. F.   (0:0:0:0:0)
Chulmleigh   Chulmleigh (076 98) 432
Kelleway, P. A.   (21:23:11:22:25)
Newmarket   Newmarket (0638) 661461
Kennard, Mrs E.   (—:—:—:—:0)
Taunton   Williton (0984) 325 88
Kennard, L. G.   (0:2:1:0:0)
Bishops Lydeard
     Bishops Lydeard (0823) 432550

Kennedy, Mrs K. A. A.   (0:0:0:3:2)
Lambourn   Lambourn (0488) 71636
Kernick N.   (—:—:—:0:1)
Kingsteignton
     Newton Abbot (0626) 5899
Kersey, T.   (0:2:0:0:0)
West Melton   Rotherham (0709) 873166
Kindersley, G.   (0:0:1:0:0)
Newbury   Great Shefford (048 839) 301
King, Miss A. L. M.   (—:—:—:—:0)
Stratford-on-Avon
     Stratford-on-Avon (0789) 298 346
King, J, S.   (—:—:—:0:0)
Swindon   Broad Hinton (079 373) 481

Laing, D. R.   (7:17:12:18:12)
Lambourn   Lambourn (0488) 71825
Lambert, M. J.   (—:—:—:6:12)
Malton   Burythorpe (065 385) 440
Leadbetter, S. J.   (0:0:0:0:0)
Denholm   Denholm (045 087) 260
Leigh, J. P.   (0:1:0:1:2)
Willoughton, Lincs.
     Hemswell (042 773) 210
Leslie, D. M.   (7:7:5:0:3)
Leicester   Tugby (053 756) 257/357
Lewis, G.   (0:5:26:19:27)
Epsom   Ashtead (037 22) 77662 or 77366
Lightbrown, L.   (—:—:—:—:1)
Loughborough
     East Leake (050 982) 2288
Lloyd-Jones, Mrs C. F.   (—:—:0:0:0)
Willington   Tarporley (0829) 51143
Lockerbie, G.   (—:1:5:2:3)
Malton   Malton (0653) 3615
Lomax, Mrs R. A.   (5:2:2:2:0)
Baydon   Marlborough (0672) 40288
Long, J. E.   (0:0:0:0:0)
Canterbury   Elham (030 384) 229

Macauley, Mrs N. J.   (—:—:—:2:0)
Sproxton
Grantham   (0476) 860578 and Melton
     Mowbray (0664) 62943 (Office)
Madgwick, M. J.   (—:—:—:—:1)
Denmead, Hants
     Waterlooville (070 14) 583 13
Madwar, A. A.   (—:—:—:0:2)
Exning   Exning (0638) 77429
Makin, P. J.   (10:7:8:7:13)
Ogbourne Maisey
     Marlborough (0672) 52973
Mason, J.   (—:4:3:1:3)
Stockton   Stockton (0642) 580561
Masson, M. J.   (3:3:11:4:0)
Lewes   Lewes (079 16) 4984
Matthews, S. G.   (2:7:6:5:5)
Blewbury   Blewbury (0235) 850338
McCain, D.   (0:0:0:0:0)
Birkdale
     Southport (0704) 66007 and 69677
McCormack, M.   (—:3:3:13:11)
Wantage   Childrey (023 559) 433
McCourt, M.   (2:3:7:5:5)
Letcombe Regis   Wantage (023 57) 4456

McDonald, R. (—:0:0:0:0)
Duns   Chirnside (089 081) 218 or 446
McLean, D. B. (0:0:0:0:0)
Morpeth   Felton (067 087) 478
McMahon, B. A. (2:6:17:15:19)
Tamworth   Tamworth (0827) 62901
McNaughton, J. (—:—:—:—:1)
Richmond   Teesdale (0833) 27478
Mellor, S. T. E. (4:10:18:15:12)
Lambourn   Lambourn (0488) 71485
Miller, C. J. V. (0:0:0:0:0)
Stratford-on-Avon
    Alderminster (078 987) 296 and 232
Mills, D. W. (—:—:—:0:1)
Heathfield
    Rushlake Green (0435) 830 284
Mitchell, N. R. (—:—:0:0:1)
Sherborne
    Buckland Newton (030 05) 272
Mitchell, P. (7:12:14:11:13)
Epsom   Ashtead (037 22) 73729
Mitchell, P. K. (0:0:6:3:6)
Folkington   Polegate (032 12) 2437
Moore, A. (0:1:0:0:3)
Woodingdean   Brighton (0273) 681679
Morgan, B. C. (—:—:—:0:2)
Barton-under-Needwood
    Hoar Cross (028 375) 304
Morgan, K. A. (—:0:0:0:0)
Grantham   Knipton (0476) 870 738
Morley, M. F. D. (0:5:12:11:9)
Bury St Edmunds   Culford (028 484) 278
Morrill, D. (—:—:—:0:0)
Market Rasen
    Market Rasen (0673) 858595
Morris, R. W. (1:1:1:1:0)
Welshpool   Trewern (093 874) 378
Morris, Miss S. O. (0:0:0:0:0)
Chard   Chard (046 06) 3187 and 3379
Mulhall, J. (0:0:0:0:0)
York   York (0904) 706321
Musson, W. J. (2:4:3:13:12)
Newmarket   Newmarket (0638) 662380

Naughton, M. P. (0:5:3:2:2)
Richmond   Richmond (0748) 2803
Neaves, A. S. (1:0:0:0:0)
Faversham   Eastling (079 589) 274
Nelson, C. R. (16:31:9:22:19)
Lambourn   Lambourn (0488) 71391
Nesbitt, Mrs M. (—:—:—:7:4)
Middleham   Wensleydale (0969) 23645
Nicholson, D. (0:3:1:1:2)
Condicote
    Stow-on-the-Wold (0451) 30417
Norton, S. G. (14:14:29:29:41)
Barnsley   Bretton (092 485) 450

O'Connor, P. O. (—:—:—:—:0)
Ticknall Melbourn (Derby) (033 16) 3084
O'Donoghue, J. (1:1:0:1:2)
Reigate   Reigate (073 72) 45241
O'Gorman, W. A. (25:30:25:49:39)
Newmarket   Newmarket (0638) 663330
Old, J. A. B. (3:3:5:3:0)
Dundry   Bristol (0272) 642756 (Office)
    and 781340 (Ansaphone)

Oliver, J. K. M. (0:0:0:0:0)
Hawick   Denholm (045 087) 216
O'Neill, H. (2:5:4:1:2)
Coldharbour   Dorking (0306) 711723
O'Neill, O. (0:0:0:0:0)
Cheltenham
    Bishops Cleeve (024 267) 3275
Oughton, D. A. (—:—:—:0:4)
Findon   Findon (090 671) 2113

Palling, B. (0:0:2:1:0)
Cowbridge   Cowbridge (044 63) 2089
Parkes, J. E. (—:—:—:0:1)
Richmond, N. Yorks.
    Richmond (0748) 2118
Pattemore, S. P. (0:0:0:0:0)
Somerton   Somerton (0458) 73112
Peacock, J. H. (0:0:0:0:0)
Ludlow   Seifton (058 473) 217
Peacock, R. D. (3:3:6:9:5)
Middleham   Wensleydale (0969) 23291
Peacock, R. E. (2:1:0:0:0)
Tarporley   Tarporley (082 93) 2716
Perrett, A. C. J. (0:0:0:1:0)
Cheltenham Andoversford (024 282) 244
Pipe, M. C. (3:4:2:5:12)
Wellington, Somerset
    Craddock (0884) 40715
Pitman, Mrs J. S. (1:1:1:0:0)
Lambourn   Lambourn (0488) 71714
Pitt, A. J. (9:9:5:5:6)
Epsom   Epsom (037 27) 25034
Plant, D. G. (1:—:—:—:0)
York   Stamford Bridge (0759) 714 72
Potts, A. W. (0:0:0:0:1)
Barton-on-Humber
    Saxby All Saints (065 261) 750
Prescott, Sir Mark (30:34:36:35:33)
Newmarket   Newmarket (0638) 662117
Price, G. H. (0:0:3:0:1)
Leominster Steens Bridge (056 882) 235
Pritchard-Gordon, G. A.
    (58:47:36:43:37)
Newmarket   Newmarket (0638) 662824

Ransom, P. B. (0:0:0:0:0)
Leominster   Wigmore (056 886) 253
Reavey, Mrs C. J. (—:—:7:7:9)
Newmarket   Newmarket
Reddan, M. T. (0:0:0:0:0)
Houghton-le-Spring
    Houghton-le-Spring (0783) 844639
Reveley, Mrs G. (—:—:—:—:4)
Saltburn   Guisborough (0287) 50456
Richards, G. W. (14:19:12:8:2)
Greystoke   Greystoke (085 33) 392
Richmond, B. A. (1:1:0:1:0)
Wellingore   Lincoln (0522) 810578
Rimell, Mrs M. (—:—:0:1:0)
Kinnersley   Severn Stoke (090 567) 233
Ringer, D. S. (5:3:3:1:1)
Newmarket   Newmarket (0638) 662653
Roberts, J. D. (—:—:—:—:0)
Tiverton   Bampton (039 83) 626
Robinson, W. R. (—:—:—:0:0)
Scarborough Scarborough (0723) 862162
Rohan, H. P. (28:28:23:19:6)
Malton   Malton (0653) 2337/8

969

Ryan, M. J. (23:11:14:22:29)
Newmarket   Newmarket (0638) 664172

Sasse, D. J. G. (14:2:3:8:3)
Lambourn   Lambourn (0488) 71902
Scallan, J. J. (0:0:0:0:0)
Colchester   Nayland (0206) 262613
Scott, A. (2:1:1:0:0)
Alnwick   Wooperton (066 87) 252 or 288
Scudamore, M. J. (0:0:0:0:0)
Hoarwithy   Carey (043 270) 253
Sheather, R. (10:15:13:7:7)
Newmarket   Newmarket (0638) 664687
Siddall, Miss L. C. (—:—:0:3:2)
York   Appleton Roebuck (090 484) 291
Simpson, R. (5:3:5:10:6)
Upper Lambourn
        Lambourn (0488) 71850
Sinclair, Miss A. V. (1:0:0:0:1)
Tenterden   Tenterden (05806) 2076
Smith, A. (1:4:5:3:2)
Beverley   Hull (0482) 882520
Smith, D. (53:35:29:20:28)
Bishop Auckland
        Bishop Auckland (0388) 603317
Smith, J. P. (—:—:—:1:0)
Rugeley   Burntwood (054 36) 6587
Smith, Mrs N. (—:—:—:0:6)
Chichester   Chichester (0243) 683863
Smyly, R. M. (5:12:11:16:7)
Lambourn   Lambourn (0488) 71408
Smyth, R. V. (9:17:20:17:11)
Epsom   Epsom (037 27) 20053
Spares, C. W. (—:—:—:7:7:3)
Newmarket   Newmarket (0638) 664674
Spearing, J. L. (4:3:11:11:7)
Alcester Bidford-on-Avon (0789) 772639
Stephenson, W. A. (9:3:2:3:8)
Bishop Auckland
        Rushyford (0388) 720213
Stevens, B. (—:—:—:—:0)
Ringwood   Ringwood (04254) 2034
Stewart, A. C. (—:—:—:—:6)
Newmarket   Newmarket (0638) 667323
Stone, K. (9:17:14:17:6)
Malton
        Malton (0653) 4597 (Stable) and 3586
                                        (Home)
Storey, W. L. (—:—:0:0:0)
Consett   Edmundbyers (0207) 55259
Stoute, M. R. (80:101:95:103:89)
Newmarket   Newmarket (0638) 663801
Stubbs, R. W. (7:4:4:5:5)
Middleham   Wensleydale (0969) 22289
Sutcliffe, J. R. E. (21:19:24:20:17)
Epsom   Ashtead (037 22) 72825
Swift, B. C. (24:22:8:14:15)
Headley
        Leatherhead (037 23) 77209 and 77308
Sykes, Mrs W. D. (—:—:—:—:0)
Bishop's Castle
Bishop's Castle (0588) 638451 and 638263

Tate, F. M. (1:2:0:0:1)
Kidderminster
        Chaddesley Corbett (056 283) 243
Taylor, Peter (0:3:1:2:0)
Churt   Frensham (025 125) 3529

Taylor, P. M. (8:12:2:6:1)
Upper Lambourn
        Lambourn (0488) 71667
Taylor, T. (0:2:3:2:1)
Ashbourne   Rocester (0889) 590334
Thom, D. T. (5:7:0:3:8)
Newmarket   Exning (063 877) 288
Thompson, R. (—:—:2:2:2)
Colerne   Box (0225) 742471
Thompson, Ron (—:—:—:—:0)
Doncaster   Doncaster (0302) 842 857
Thompson, V. (0:0:0:0:0)
Alnwick   Embleton (066 576) 272
Thorne, J. (0:0:0:0:0)
Bridgwater   Holford (027 874) 216
Thorner, G. E. (—:—:0:0:0)
Letcombe Regis   Wantage (023 57) 3003
Thornton, C. W. (33:32:26:22:28)
Middleham   Wensleydale (0969) 23350
Tierney, J. (1:1:1:0:0)
Stafford
        Wheaton Ashton (0785) 840833
Tinkler, N. D. (—:0:3:7:10)
Malton   Burythorpe (065 385) 245
Toller, J. A. R. (—:0:3:7:4)
Newmarket   Newmarket (0638) 668503
Tompkins, M. H. (—:4:9:12:17)
Newmarket   Newmarket (0638) 661434
Townson, J. (—:—:0:0:0)
Blackburn   Whalley (025 482) 3412
Tree, A. J. (30:30:23:22:35)
Beckhampton
        Avebury (067 23) 204 and 244
Trietline, C. C. (—:—:—:—:0)
Welford-on-Avon
        Stratford-on-Avon (0789) 750 294
Tucker, D. C. (—:—:—:0:2)
Frome   Frome (0373) 62383
Turnell, A. (—:—:—:1:2)
Ogbourne Maisey
        Marlborough (0672) 52542
Turner, W. G. M. (1:0:0:0:0)
Tavistock   Mary Tavy (082 281) 237

Usher, M. D. I. (—:—:—:—:6)
Lambourn
        Lambourn (0488) 71025 (Home) and
                                72765 (Office)

Vickers, I. (2:1:0:0:5)
Darlington   Dinsdale (0325) 332450
Vigors, N. A. C. (13:13:21:12:12)
Lambourn   Lambourn (0488) 71657
Voorspuy, R. (—:—:—:—:0)
Polegate   Polegate (032 12) 2821

Walker, I. S. (14:16:13:12:9)
Newmarket   Newmarket (0638) 665 750
Walwyn, F. T. T. (1:0:0:0:0)
Lambourn   Lambourn (0488) 71555
Walwyn P. T. (44:78:53:48:26)
Lambourn   Lambourn (0488) 71347
Ward, R. C. (2:2:2:0:0)
Doncaster   Doncaster (0302) 700574
Wardle, I. P. (0:0:0:0:0)
East Horrington   Wells (0749) 73167

970

Waring, Mrs B. H. (0:0:1:0:1)
Malmesbury Crudwell (066 67) 238
Watson, A. (0:0:0:0:0)
Skipton Earby (028 284) 2228
Watson, F. (—:—:—:4:2)
Sedgefield Sedgefield (0740) 20582
Watts, J. W. (46:47:51:29:25)
Richmond Richmond (0748) 5811
Watts, W. C. (3:7:0:2:2)
Bridlington Bridlington (0262) 73719
Webber, J. H. (2:0:0:2:0)
Banbury Cropredy (029 575) 226
Weeden, D. E. (5:4:0:1:0)
Newmarket Newmarket (0638) 730 587
Westbrook, H. C. (3:2:1:7:1)
Newmarket Newmarket (0638) 667689
Weymes, E. (9:19:16:20:10)
Leyburn Wensleydale (0969) 40229
Wharton, H. (0:1:1:2:3)
Wetherby Wetherby (0937) 65002
Wharton, W. (15:24:10:12:10)
Melton Mowbray
Waltham-on-the-Wolds (066 478) 258
and Melton Mowbray (0664) 65225
Whelan, D. (3:1:1:1:0)
Epsom Epsom (037 27) 22763 and 21482
Whiston, W. R. (0:0:0:0:0)
Market Drayton Hodnet (063 084) 203
Whitaker, R. M. (0:5:4:10:12)
Leeds Leeds (0532) 892265
Wigham, P. (1:4:2:2:4)
Malton Rillington (094 42) 332
Wightman, W. G. R. (17:14:14:9:11)
Upham Bishop's Waltham (048 93) 2565
Wildman, C. P. (—:2:3:5:2)
Salisbury Durrington Walls (0980) 52226
Wiles, S. J. (0:0:0:0:1)
Flockton
Flockton (0924) 848 468 (Stables)
and 848 977 (Home)
Wilkinson, B. E. (0:0:1:0:0)
Middleham Wensleydale (0969) 23385
Williams, C. N. (—:0:2:5:4)
Reading
Bradfield (0734) 744265 (Office) and
744677 (Stables)

Williams, R. J. R. (—:—:12:22:14)
Newmarket Newmarket (0638) 663218
Williams, W. H. H. (19:15:2:4:4)
Ayr Ayr (0292) 266232
Williams, W. R. (0:0:0:0:0)
Idestone Exeter (0392) 81558
Wilson, D. A. (—:0:5:4:4)
Epsom
Ashtead (037 22) 77645 (Business) and
73839 (Home)
Wilson, J. H. (1:2:5:5:9)
Preston Hesketh Bank (077 473) 2780
Wilson, J. S. (—:0:1:3:7)
Motherwell Motherwell (0698) 62653
Winter, F. T. (5:0:1:0:0)
Lambourn Lambourn (0488) 71438
Winter, J. R. (31:13:19:30:28)
Newmarket Newmarket (0638) 663898
Wintle, D. J. (0:0:1:0:1)
Westbury-on-Severn
Westbury-on-Severn (045 276) 459
Wise, B. J. (1:0:0:0:1)
Polegate
Polegate (032 12) 3331 and 2505
Witts, E. E. P. (—:—:—:—:2)
Lower Basildon, Reading
Upper Basildon (049 162) 690
Woodhouse, R. D. E. (—:—:0:0:2)
York Whitwell-on-the-Hill (065 381) 637
Woodman, S. (4:4:4:5:3)
Chichester Chichester (0243) 527136
Wragg, G. (—:—:—:—:27)
Newmarket
Newmarket Office (0638) 662328 Home
(0638) 662846
Yardley, F. J. (2:1:2:0:0)
Ombersley Worcester (0905) 620477
Yeoman, D. (0:0:4:1:2)
Richmond Richmond (0748) 811756
Young, A. J. (—:—:—:5:1)
Malton Malton (0653) 5140

The following also held a licence for part of
the year:
Mackenzie, C. (—:0:0:0:0)
Sturdy, R. C. (—:1:0:0:4)

JOCKEYS

The figures in brackets show the number of winners each jockey has ridden in this country
during the past five seasons, from 1979 to 1983 inclusive. Also included are telephone
numbers and riding weights.

Atkinson, D. J. (5:3:0:0:0) 8   3
Wantage (023 57) 3164

Balding, J. (0:1:0:0:2) 8   8
Doncaster (0302) 710096
Ballantine, H. (—:1:1:0:0) 7   13
Lambourn (0488) 71700
Banner, M. A. (4:5:7:0:2) 8   3
Newmarket (0638) 664 971
Barclay, A. M. (—:—:—:—:6).....8   2
c/o Lambourn (0488) 713 68
and 715 95
Baxter, G. E. (64:52:57:52:39) ...8   0
Lambourn (0488) 71320
Beecroft, M. C. (0:1:9:8:2) 8   0
Wensleydale (0969) 23027

Birch, M. (77:71:56:69:51) 8   1
Hovingham (065 382) 578
Bleasdale, J. (41:41:18:26:26).....8   0
Bedale (0677) 22222 and
Wensleydale (0969) 23350
Bond, A. M. (16:16:12:9:5) 8   3
Stetchworth (063 876) 681
(Home) and Six Mile Bottom
(0638 70) 204
Bray, M. J. (—:—:0:0:0)............7   12
Malton (0653) 5690
Burns, D. (2:—:—:—:0) 7   12
Wensleydale (0969) 222 52
Butler, K. R. (0:0:1:1:0)............7   7
Littlehampton (090 64) 22431 and
c/o Pulborough (079 82) 3011

Carson, W. F. H.
(142:166:114:145:159) 7   9
Newmarket (0638) 663623, East
Ilsley (063 528) 348 and
Cirencester (0285) 68919

Cauthen, S. M.   8   6
(52:61:87:107:102) ....
Lambourn (0488) 72312

Charnock, L. (25:16:23:25:13) 7   8
Malton (0653) 5004

Cochrane, R. (6:21:22:25:20)......8   0
Newmarket (0638) 669142

Colquhoun, P. R. (12:7:11:4:2)...8   0
Exning (063 877) 216

Cook, P. A. (80:90:84:83:62).......8   1
Marlborough (0672) 20265

Crook, A. (—:1:0:0:1)................7   12
Ripon (0765) 700814

Crossley, B.G. (6:21:45:29:26)....7   8
Newmarket (0638) 730 708

Curant, R. D. (31:18:21:22:17) 7   13
Marlborough (0672) 40601

D'Arcy, P. W. (11:3:1:4:6)...........7   12
Newmarket (0638) 663857

Darley, K. P. (14:19:14:14:37) 7   9
Stamford Bridge (0759) 71882

Day, N. P. (1:13:35:22:17) 8   0
Newmarket (0638) 663 343

Dineley, D. B. (2:4:3:6:2)...........7   12
Lambourn (0488) 72712

Dixon, A. (—:—:—:—:0)............7   10

Duffield, G. P. (76:78:94:92:98)...7   13
Stetchworth (063 876) 544

Dwyer, C. A. (20:23:11:12:12) 8   6
Malton (0653) 3471

Dwyer, M. P. (—:—:—:—:1) 9   5
Malton (0653) 3961

Eddery, P. J. J.
(123:130:108:83:122) 8   4
Haddenham (0844) 290 282

Elliott, R. P. (0:0:0:4:14)...........8   0
Wensleydale (0969) 22884

Fox, R. D. S. (17:26:16:21:23) 7   8
Chieveley (063 521) 352

Francois, C. G. A. (0:0:2:0:0).....8   0
c/o Winchester (0962) 880808

Gibson, D. J. (0:0:1:0:2)............7   11
Newmarket (0638) 750653

Giles, M. S. (0:0:1:1:3) 8   4
c/o Newmarket (0638) 663801

Gosney, G. (5:1:2:1:2) 8   2
c/o Appleton Roebuck (090 484)
291

Gray, O. J. (10:8:10:9:4) 7   13
Wensleydale (0969) 22403

Guest, R. (1:7:6:7) 8   5
Newmarket (0638) 661508

Gunn, G. P. (2:1:6:0:1) 8   3
Newmarket (0638) 668724

Hamblett, P. A. (—:—:—:—:5)...7   10
Newmarket (0638) 662486 and
c/o 662 841

Henry, B. (0:0:0:—:0)...............8   0
c/o Lambourn (0488) 713 91

Hide, E. W. G. (53:106:106:65:53) 8   4
Malton (0653) 2132 and
Newmarket (0638) 750155

Higgins, J. J. (11:9:3:2:0) 8   2
Newmarket (0638) 750123

Higgins, W. F. (11:13:2:3:0) 7   11
Reading (0734) 868028

Hodgson, R. A. M. (0:1:0:1:1).....7   4
c/o Ashtead (037 22) 731 52

Hood, B. (0:0:0:—:0)................8   0
c/o Malton (0653) 2842

Ives, T. A. (38:53:42:82:71) 8   3
Newmarket (0638) 664605

Jago, B. (15:30:19:11:5)............8   2
Epsom (037 27) 21025

Jenkinson, I. P. (3:1:0:3:1).........7   7
Epsom (037 27) 24484

Johnson, E. (61:48:29:46:27)......7   8
Newmarket (0638) 663343

Johnson, I. E. (3:19:8:14:12) 8   3
Kintbury (0488) 58749

Kelleher, P. (2:3:6:2:0)..............8   0
Bishop Auckland (0388) 663837

Kelly, G. P. (—:—:—:—:0) 8   7
Flaxton Moor (090 486) 401 or
Sheriff Hutton (034 77) 368

Kersey, G. (—:—:—:—:0) 8   10
Rotherham (0709) 873 166

Kettle, M. (1:4:7:0:0) 8   1
Newmarket (0638) 668739
(Home) and 667624

Kimberley, A. A. (27:15:8:4:8)....8   3
Newmarket (0638) 663267

Launchbury, A. T. (—:0:0:0:0)....8   4
c/o Clydach (0792) 842303

Leason, K. M. (14:10:11:6:0) 7   11
Rotherham (0709) 548 170

Logie, J. (0:1:0:0:0) 8   0
c/o East Hendred (023 588) 247

Lowe, J. J. (49:54:69:57:52) 7   8
York (0904) 708 871

Mackay, A. (8:2:15:27:31) 7   8
Newmarket (0638) 669 008

Madden, P. J. (8:8:8:2:1)...........8   6
Newmarket (0638) 750603

Maitland, D. (3:0:1:0:0)............7   9
Newmarket (0638) 661615

Malham, M. S. T. (5:6:6:1:0) 7   10
c/o Lambourn (0488) 71767

Marshall, R. C. (9:1:0:—:0) 8   2
Newmarket (0638) 661 751

Matthias, J. J. (23:41:37:40;38)...8   4
Tadley (073 56) 2126

McGhin, R. (0:2:0:1:1)...............8   3
c/o Ashtead (03722) 73729

McKay, D. J. (23:11:26:20:13) 7   8
Lambourn (0488)71735

Mercer, J. (164:104:64:58:55)......8   4
Hermitage (0635) 200306

Miller, M. M. (19:14:19:24:14).....7   12
Newmarket (0638) 730374
Millman, B. R. (—:—:—:—:0)....8   11
Hele (039 288) 405
Mills, A. E. (—:0:0:0:0) 8   2
Wensleydale (0969) 23350
Moss, D. E. (0:—:—:—:0) 7   10
Compton (063 522) 584

Newnes, W. A. P.
(19:35:28:57:41).......................7   12
Lambourn (0488) 72397
Nicholls, D. (0:4:7:28:17)..........8   2
Collingham (0937) 72363
Nutter, C. (6:5:6:4:2)................7   10
Newmarket (0638) 668153

Oldroyd, G. R. (7:4:3:5:10) 8   3
Malton (0653) 5991
O'Leary, P. (1:1:0:0:0)...............7   7
01-979 6046
O'Neill, J. J. (7:3:—:0:0)...........9   3
Skelton (08534) 555

Perkins, P. (0:1:1:1:0)...............8   2
Ely (0353) 720895
Perks, S. J. (8:5:41:26:32) 8   5
Rugeley (08894) 4671
Piggott, L. K.
(77:156:179:188:150)...............8   6
Newmarket (0638) 662584
Powdrell, K. M. (0:0:1:1:0).........7   7
Lambourn (0488) 72419
Proctor, B. T. (3:3:1:5:1)...........8   3
East Ilsley (063 528) 596
Proud, A. (6:9:3:0:1) 7   7
Bingham (0949) 373 11
Pugh, D. A. (—:—:—:0:0) 7   11
01-391-0997

Ramshaw, G. (6:4:3:5:5)...........8   5
Burgh Heath (073 73) 53611
Rawlinson, A. C. (—:3:4:0:0)....8   6
Newmarket (0638) 669 174
Raymond, B. H. (63:73:74:51) 8   3
Newmarket (0638) 730387
Raymont, S. J. (26:4:5:0:1)........7   13
Seagry (0249) 812934
Reid, J. A. (72:79:54:63:30)........8   4
Boxford (048 838) 433 and
Abingdon (0235) 832603
Robinson, P. P. (51:59:30:48:52) 7   9
Newmarket (0638) 76414 or
750123
Rodrigues, C. (0:0:—:—:1)........7   5
c/o Newmarket (0638) 662129
Rogers, T. (16:39:18:19:12)........8   3
Thatcham (0635) 63047
Rouse, B. A. (42:43:65:54:58)....8   0
Rusper (029 384) 547

Seagrave, J. (25:24:23:35:27)....8   4
Malton (0653) 2692
Sexton, G. C. (16:9:23:8:11)......8   1
Newmarket (0638) 664367

Shrimpton, P. R. E. (0:0:0:0:0)...7   9
Armitage (0543) 490298
Shrive, A. H. (—:—:0:0:0).........8   5
Worcester (0905) 25807
Skeats, G. H. (1:—:1:1:0).........8   6
Bishop Auckland (0388) 720225
Skilling, J. F. (—:1:1:1:0) 8   4
Malton (0653) 2979
Sozzi, Miss T. L. (—:0:0:0:0)......8   2
Wensleydale (0969) 40653
Starkey, G. M. W.
(99:82:90:103:103)...................8   5
Mildenhall (0638) 714672
Still, R. W. (11:—:2:2:3)............7   7
Newmarket (0638) 750 755
Storey, C. V. (1:1:1:—:0) 7   12
Street, R. (13:3:8:9:3) 7   7
Lambourn (0488) 71412 and 71548
Swinburn, W. R. J.
(47:49:65:64:62) 8   3
Wickhambrook (044082) 277

Taylor, B. (56:32:48:53:48).........8   6
Newmarket (0638) 664605
Thomas, M. L. (49:27:15:24:10)...7   8
Fordham (0638) 720780
Tulk, P. F. (14:10:8:4:2).............8   2
Newmarket (0638) 663209

Waldron, P. (54:53:49:31:31) 8   1
Inkpen (048 84) 263
Weaver, R. I. (13:10:10:5:6)........8   4
Hungerford (048 86) 3884
Webster, S. G. (10:13:12:16:12) ...7   12
Wensleydale (0969) 23576
Welsh, G. (0:0:1:0:0)................7   10
c/o Lambourn (0488) 71368
Wernham, R. A. (—:—:0:1:4).....8   0
Kingston Blount (0844) 290282
Wharton, W. J. (18:15:4:2:1) 8   4
Melton Mowbray (0664) 60908
Wigham, M. (25:37:19:16:12)......8   2
Childrey (023 559) 467
Wilkinson, W. P. (0:1:0:0:0) 8   1
Epsom (037 27) 28788
Williams, C. N. (0:0:0:0:0) 8   3
Bradfield (0734) 744265
Williams, J. A. N. (0:0:0:0:0) 8   3
Clydach (044 15) 3407
Wood, M. (12:16:10:17:12) 7   9
Malton (0653) 5234
Woolard, R. G. (1:3:—:—:0).......8   3
Wantage (023 57) 67610

The following relinquished their licence during the season:

Clements, B. (—:—:—:—:5)......
Howard, P. T. (2:0:8:2:2)...........
Mercer, A. (18:14:11:1:2)...........
Moss, C. (9:2:0:—:1)................
Murray, A. P. (2:5:0:22:14) ....
Murray, J. A. (—:—:—:10:1) ......
Wigham, R. (—:—:0:2:1) ....
Young, P. J. (15:22:33:37:16) ......

APPRENTICES

The following list shows the employer and riding weight of every apprentice who held a licence at the end of the 1983 season, and the number of winners he or she has ridden, wins in apprentice races being recorded separately.

Apprentices may claim 7lb until they have won 10 races, 5lb until they have won 50 races and 3lb until they have won 75 races. Apprentice races are excepted in all these cases. The allowance each apprentice is entitled to claim is shown in brackets. The claim may be exercised in all handicaps and selling races, and in all other races with guaranteed prize money of not more than £3,500.

Adams, J. A. (7) 1+2 ap 8 0	(G. Lewis)	
Adams, N. M. (7) 3+1 ap 7 3	(M. Blanshard)	
Adams, R. B. (7) 7 0	(Miss A. King)	
Allen, C. N. (7) 2+1 ap 7 7	(M. Ryan)	
Alston, M. (7) 7 0	(W. Wharton)	
Anderton, Miss E. (7) 7 9	(H. Jones)	
Atkinson, C. B. (7) 8 3	(J. Etherington)	
Austin, G. P. (7) 7 4	(B. Stevens)	
Bacon, A. E. (7) 7 3	(R. Hern)	
Bardsley, D. A. A. (7) 7 12	(M. Ryan)	
Barford, P. A. (7) 8 7	(R. Thompson)	
Berry, M. (7) 2+3 ap 8 6	(J. Berry)	
Blake, J. W. (7) 2+5 ap 7 12	(L. Cumani)	
Bloomfield, P. S. (5) 19+13 ap 7 13	(A. Bailey)	
Boucher, R. (7) 7 9	(G. Lewis)	
Bourton, D. D. (7) 7 12	(R. Atkins)	
Bradshaw, K. (5) 12+4 ap 7 6	(M. Stoute)	
Bradwell, P. (5) 46+9 ap 7 8	(C. Brittain) Newmarket (0638) 667903 or 664347	
Breedon, P. A. (7) 2 ap 6 7	(B. Hills)	
Brennan, M. J. (7) 8 8	(O. Brennan)	
Brette, P. (7) 6 0	(A. Hide)	
Brown, D. (7) 2 ap 7 1	(S. Mellor)	
Brown, G. (7) 4+5 ap 8 0	(J. Fitzgerald)	
Brown, J. (7) 7 5	(B. Hobbs)	
Brown, J. H. (5) 13+13 ap 7 9	(I. Balding)	
Brown, R. A. (7) 1+1 ap 7 8	(J. Fitzgerald)	
Bryan, T. (7) 5 ap 8 0	(G. Balding)	

Burke, P. A. (7) 6 7
(J. McNaughton)
Burke, Miss T. I. (7) 7 13
(J. Toller)
Butler, P. S. (7) 7 9
(C. A. Austin)

Carlisle, N. A. 68 +3 ap 7 7
(R. Hollinshead)
Carr, J. M. (7) 2 .... 7 12
(E. Carter)
Carroll, J. (7) 2 ap 7 7
(G. Richards)
Carter, G. A. (7) 1 .... 6 7
(G. Blum)
Carter, J. P. (7) 7 0
(P. M. Taylor)
Carter, R. P. (7) 3 ap 7 7
(M. Tompkins)
Carter, Miss W. J. (7) 2+1 ap 7 9
(E. Carter)
Charlton, A. (7) 8 0
(M. Lambert)
Clark, A. S. 86+3 ap 7 11
(G. Harwood) Pulborough
(07982) 3354
Clements, B. E. (7) 8 6
(R. Hern)
Coates, C. (7) 3+1 ap 7 10
(T. Fairhurst)
Coates, S. P. (7) 7 2
(I. Balding)
Connorton, N. B. 82+9 ap 7 11
(J. W. Watts) Richmond (0748)
4059
Cooper, Miss S. J. (7) 1+1 ap 7 2
(F. J. Houghton)
Coughlin, C. (7) 1 ap 7 10
(A. Stewart)
Cox, C. G. (7) 2 .... 8 7
(S. Pattemore)
Coyle, Miss J. A. (7) 7 0
(D. Elsworth)
Crowley, D. P. (7) 7 10
(B. Gubby)
Cullen, E. M. (7) 1 .... 7 12
(C. Horgan)
Cunningham, A. (7) 6 8
(M. Lambert)
Currie, J. (7) 6 7
(W. H. H. Williams)

Davies, T. (7) 7 0
(R. Hollinshead)
Dawe, N. J. (5) 11+12 ap 7 12
(J. Dunlop)

Dawson, S. (5) 37+4 ap 7   3
   (N. Vigors)
Dennison, S. E. J. (7) 5+7 ap 8   4
   (R. Armstrong)
Derham, S. D. (7) 7   0
   (J. Bethell)
Dickie, G. (7) 5+6 ap 7   2
   (N. Guest)
Dicks, A. C. (7) 2 7   11
   (C. Wildman)
Dixon, I. (7) 1 ap 8   3
   (C. Thornton)
Donkin, S. (7) 5+5 ap 7   13
   (M. H. Easterby)
Doughty, P. A. (7) 1+1 ap 7   7
   (C. Crossley)
Downey, E. G. (7) 7   10
   (J. Yardley)
Duffy, A. J. (7) 8   0
   (G. Pritchard-Gordon)
Duffy, M. A. T. (7) 7   9
   (P. Haslam)
Dunster, Miss S. L. (7) 7   13
   (T. Hallett)

Eatwell, M. (7) 1 7   7
   (H. Candy)
Eddery, J. D. (7) 7   2
   (R. Hannon)
Eddery, Paul A. 77+6 ap 7   10
   (H. Cecil)
Eddington, P. V. (7) 8   4
   (C. Williams)
Edwards, S. D. (7) 1 ap 7   12
   (G. Blum)
Elden, M. J. (7) 7   7
   (P. Taylor)
Feilden, Miss J. L. (7) 1 ap 7   9
   (P. Feilden)
Fitzgerald, Z. (7) 7   8
   (C. Brittain)
Ford, T. J. (7) 7   11
   (K. Brassey)
Fotheringham, R. (7) 1 ap 7   7
   (J. W. Watts)
Fowler-Wright, D. J. (7) 1 ap 7   0
   (W. Musson)
Fozzard, M. G. (7) 2+6 ap 7   6
   (D. Chapman)
Frampton, Miss A. D. (7) 2+1 ap 7   7
   (J. Holt)
Fretwell, K. (7) 7+5 ap 8   6
   (D. Garraton)
Fry, M. J. (3) 52+8 ap 7   4
   (D. Smith) Bishop Auckland
   (0388) 606636

Geran, M. P. (7) 7   12
   (H. T. Jones)
Gilbert, Miss S. P. (7) 8   4
   (J. Gilbert)
Gilchrist, M. F. (7) 8   7
   (J. Jenkins)
Gilmour, S. H. (7) 1+2 ap 8   3
   (G. Balding)
Glenn, C. L. (7) 7   12
   (J. Hardy)
Glozier, A. D. (7) 1 ap 7   10
   (M. Tompkins)

Godden, T. P. (7) 7   7
   (C. Horgan)
Goldie, N. A. (7) 7   13
   (H. O'Neill)
Goldsborough, W. (7) 2 ap 7   10
   (C. Spares)
Gorman, A. W. (7) 7   0
   (J. W. Watts)
Grant, R. (7) 7   0
   (D. McCain)
Griffin, D. A. (7) 1 ap 7   12
   (P. M. Taylor)
Griffiths, S. P. (7) 4+4 ap 7   1
   (D. Chapman)
Guest, E. J. (5) 29+1 ap 8   4
   (M. Stoute)
Guest, Miss S. (7) 7   12
   (M. Stoute)

Hadley, S. R. (7) 1+3 7   8
   (R. Hern)
Haines, P. (7) 7   0
   (F. J. Houghton)
Harris, Miss V. M. (7) 8   7
   (J. Harris)
Harris, S. A. (7) 7   6
   (W. Clay)
Harrap, D. V. (7) 6   12
   (I. Balding)
Hayes, B. E. (7) 1 7   10
   (R. Hollinshead)
Hayes, P. G. 7   0
   (M. Ryan)
Hayes, S. M. (7) 7   7
   (B. Hills)
Heath, Miss C. A. (7) 8   0
   (J. Dunlop)
Hewitson, C. (7) 7   10
   (M. Usher)
Hill, P. D. (7) 1 ap 7   0
   (W. Wharton)
Hills, M. P. 72+7 ap 7   8
   (J. Hindley)
Hills, R. J. (3) 72+4 ap 7   6
   (H. T. Jones)
Hodgson, K. 81+11 ap 8   0
   (M. H. Easterby) Malton (0653)
   7376
Horsfall, S. S. (5) 12+2 ap 7   4
   (J. Berry)
Howe, N. J. (3) 55+12 ap 7   11
   (P. Walwyn) Wantage (02357)
   68227
Hughes, G. (7) 2 ap 8   4
   (P. Rohan)
Hunt, K. (7) 6   7
   (G. Lewis)

Jackson, G. N. (7) 7   11
   (J. Carr)
James, K. (7) 7   7
   (G. Wragg)
Jarvis, S. J. (5) 40+3 ap 8   5
   (A. Jarvis)
Jarvis, T. O. (5) 16+3 ap 8   12
   (A. Jarvis)
Jewell, S. (7) 7+5 ap 7   12
   (R. Sheather)

John, P. (7) 4 6   7
(G. Harwood)
Jones, D. (7) 8   7
(R. Hern)
Jones, L. (7) 6 7   7
(R. Hannon)
Jones, B. (5) 23+5 ap 6 12
(R. Whitaker)

Kaye, J. A. (7) 2 7   7
(P. Kelleway)
Keightley, S. L. (7) 5+5 ap 8   3
(W. Pearce) Thirsk (0845) 597373
Kelleway, Miss G. M. (5) 10+8 am 7 11
(P. Kelleway)
Kennedy, J. B. (7) 2 ap 7   6
(H. Candy)
King, G. N. (7) 7   3
(E. Eldin)

Landau, G. L. (7) 3 ap 7   6
(G. Harwood)
Lawes, S. D. (5) 15+1 ap 8   0
(A. Smith)
Lea, R. G. (7) 8   4
(F. Durr)
Leadbitter, D. (7) 3+4 ap 7   3
(D. Smith)
Lines, R. V. (5) 9 7   5
(M. Stoute) Newmarket (0638)
665063
Lockwood, D. (7) 7   7
(T. Taylor)
Lomax, G. (7) 7   7
(H. T. Jones)
Love, Miss M. P. (7) 7   0
(S. Harris)
Lynch, M. J. (7) 7   9
(C. Brittain)

Mann, P. A. (7) 7   0
(H. Candy)
Martin, J. S. (7) 7   5
(D. Wilson)
Mash, G. A. (7) 8   3
(K. Ivory)
Matthews, P. M. (7) 1 7   0
(C. Nelson)
McAndrew, M. A. (7) 8   0
(G. Huffer)
McDermott, P. (7) 2 8   4
(G. Balding)
McFeeters, D. M. (7) 2 ap 7   9
(S. Matthews)
McGiff, B. C. (7) 7   3
(W. Haigh)
McGlone, A. D. (3) 64+11 ap 7   7
(R. Hannon)
McGuinness, S. P. (7) 8   0
(R. Beasley)
McKeown, D. R. (3) 59+8 ap 7 12
(W. O'Gorman) Newmarket
(0638) 664314 or 750817
McLean, J. A. (7) 5+5 ap 7   0
(H. Candy)
McLellan, A. D. (7) 8   3
(C. Williams)

McNamee V. (7) 8   2
(P. Cole)
Meek, T. W. (7) 7   7
(M. Camacho)
Moore, D. P. (7) 7   8
(A. Bailey)
Morgan, G. P. (7) 7   8
(D. Elsworth)
Morell, Miss A. M. (7) 8   0
(J. Holt)
Morris, S. D. (3) 40 .... 7 12
(J. Berry)
Morris, W. A. F. F. (7) 1 ap 8   7
(G. Huffer)
Morse, R. R. (7) 7   0
(W. Holden)
Moseley, M. F. (7) 4 7   7
(R. Holder)
Mose, P. (7) 1 ap 7   7
(G. Harwood)
Murray, J. G. (7) 7   0
(M. W. Easterby)
Nesbitt, H. A. (3) 53+5 ap 7   2
(C. Thornton)
Nolan, C. D. (7) 7   4
(R. Hollinshead)
Nolan, P. M. (7) 8   2
(K. Bridgwater)

O'Brien, Miss C. E. (7) 8   7
(J. O'Donoghue)
Ollivier, C. G. (5) 23+4 ap 7 12
(S. Norton)
O'Reilly, A. J. P. (7) 3 ap 6 12
(Sir Mark Prescott)
O'Reilly, J. P. (7) 1 .... 6 10
(W. Stubbs)
Osborne, S. (7) 1 ap 7 10
(K. Brassey)
Osborne, W. (7) 1+1 ap 7   4
(J. Holt)

Parker, M. R. (7) 7 10
(K. Ivory)
Parrish, Miss J. T. (7) 7   7
(R. Voorspuy)
Payne, P. G. (7) 6 10
(H. O'Neill)
Potts, T. M. (7) 8   0
(A. W. Potts)
Price, D. J. (7) 4+2 ap 7 12
(F. J. Houghton)
Proctor, T. (7) 8   2
(W. O'Gorman)
Purchase, J. E. (7) 7   9
(M. James)

Quinn, T. R. (3) 53+4 ap 7   8
(P. Cole)

Radcliffe, K. (7) 1 ap 7   5
(R. Laing)
Radley, S. P. (7) 7   9
(D. H. Jones)
Rae, D. G. (7) .... 6 .7
(A. Hide)
Ramage, D. G. (7) 7   7
(P. Cole)
Rawlinson, A. (7) 2 ap 8   0
(L. Cumani)

Redhead, S. R. (7) 7 10
(R. Hollinshead)
Rees, S. P. (7) 8 0
(D. Dale)
Reid, M. (7) 8 0
(M. Stoute)
Richardson, M. A. (7) 1+1 ap 7 6
(N. Bycroft)
Rimmer, M. E. (3) 74+9 ap 8 1
(G. Huffer) Newmarket (0638)
730 374
Roberts, F. G. 7 12
(R. Johnson Houghton)
Robinson, S. (7) 1 .... 7 7
(H. T. Jones)
Rogan, M. S. (7) 1 ap 7 8
(P. Walwyn)
Rogers, A. M. (7) 1 .... 7 7
(L. Cumani)
Rutherford, S. (7) 1 ap 7 11
(C. Nelson)
Rutter, C. L. (7) 7 0
(H. Candy)
Ryan, S. L. (7) 7 0
(Mrs C. Reavey)
Ryan, W. (5) 30+1 ap 7 3
(R. Hollinshead)

Salmon, I. P. A. (7) 1+1 ap 7 12
(C. Horgan)
Saltmarsh, S. A. (7) 7 10
(P. Cundell)
Sargent, P. J. (7) 7 7
(B. Swift)
Scally, J. J. (7) 7 7
(P. Haslam)
Scobie, F. (7) 7 12
(G. Huffer)
Selby, S. (7) 1 ap 7 10
(G. Pritchard-Gordon)
Shoemark, I. W. (7) 1 ap 7 12
(I. Balding)
Shoults, A. F.(7) 7 0
(J. Hindley)
Sidebottom, R. (5) 41+9 ap 8 6
(R. Williams)
Silkstone, J. (7) 7 10
(P. Walwyn)
Simms, D. A. (7) 8 4
(I. Walker)
Simpson, A. (7) 7 9
(J. Tierney)
Smith, D. R. (7) 7 12
(W. Elsey)
Smith, V. (7) 1 ap 7 12
(M. Jarvis)
Spink, Miss K. A. (7) 7 10
(C. Booth)
Stead, A. D. P. (7) 8 0
(P. Wigham)
Steers, C. (7) 1+3 ap 7 4
(A. Jarvis)
Surrey, D. (7) 7 0
(G. Wragg)

Taylor, T. (7) 7 0
(A. Jarvis)
Tebbutt, M. (7) 6 7
(C. Thornton)

Telford, M. (7) 8 0
(H. T. Jones)
Thomas, G. (7) 1 .... 7 9
(A. Bailey)
Thompson, Miss J. S. (7) 8 6
(R. Thompson)
Thorpe, Miss G. M. M. (7) 1 ap ... 7 9
(R. Hollinshead)
Tilley, O. D. G. (7) 1 ap 7 12
(H. Cecil)
Tootell, J. D. (7) 1 .... 7 2
(C. Thornton)

Walker, Miss E. (7) 7 7
(J. Hardy)
Ward, G. I. (7) 8 0
(N. Callaghan)
Wardrope, B. M. (7) 1 .... 7 5
(R. Hollinshead)
Warner, J. A. (7) 1 ap 7 13
(E. Witts)
Watkins, A. M. (7) 1 ap 7 7
(I. Balding)
Weiss, A. L. (5) 11+10 ap 7 10
(F. Durr)
Whiffen, Miss L. M. (7) 8 0
(J. Parkes)
Whitehall, A. J. (7) 7 2
(R. Hollinshead)
Whiteside, A. (7) 7 3
(A. Ingham)
Whitworth, S. J. (7) 5+4 ap 7 9
(R. Simpson)
Wilkinson, Miss S. (7) 8 2
(M. Hinchliffe)
Willey, K. M. (5) 18+5 ap 7 12
(B. Hills)
Williams, C. (7) 8 0
(J. Berry)
Williams, K. E. J. (7) 3+11 ap 7 6
(Sir Mark Prescott)
Williams, T. L. (7) 4+4 ap 6 7
(H. Candy)
Wilson, L. (7) 1+2 ap 7 9
(I. Walker)
Winder, Miss S. A. (7) 7 3
(B. Hobbs)
Wood, M. A. (7) 7 11
(J. Wilson)
Woods, E. W. J. (7) 5+3 ap 7 3
(G. Harwood)
Woolnough, K. L. (7) 1 ap 7 10
(M. Haynes)
Woolward, A. (7) 7 0
(N. Guest)
Wooton, C. (7) 7 2
(N. Vigors)
Worral, M. A. (7) 7 0
(R. Hollinshead)

Yeo, G. A. (7) 7 7
(C. Thornton)

The following winning apprentices of
1983 relinquished their licences during the
season:
Hindley, M. G. (7) 7+8 ap
Marrin, P. (7) 1+1 ap

977

AYR

Scotland's Premier Racecourse

FLAT MEETINGS 1984

Monday and Tuesday   March 26 and 27
Friday (Evening) and Saturday   May 25 and 26
        The Tia Maria Handicap, 7f
        The P.G. Tips Tea Cup (Amateur Riders), 1m 2f
        The Philip Cornes Nickel Alloys Stakes (Qualifier), 5f

Friday and Saturday   June 22 and 23
        The Long John Scotch Whisky Handicap, 1m
        The Scottish Farm Dairy Foods Handicap 1m 3f
        The Belleisle Stakes, 2-y-o, 5f

Saturday, Monday and Tuesday   July 14, 16 and 17
        Mecca Bookmakers Scottish Derby, 1m 3f, 3-y-o only
          (£20,000)
        The Johnnie Walker Black Label Handicap, 1m 5f
        The John Barr Scotch Whisky Stakes, 7f
        The Tennent Trophy (Handicap), 1m 7f
        The Strathclyde Stakes, 2-y-o, 6f

Friday (Evening) and Saturday   July 20 and 21
        The Tote Sprint Trophy, 6f
        The Drambuie Handicap, 1m 5f
        The Land of Burns Stakes, 1m 2f

Tuesday and Wednesday   August 7 and 8
        The Heronslea Stakes, 2-y-o, 7f

THE WESTERN MEETING
(Royal Caledonian Hunt)

Wednesday, Thursday, Friday and Saturday—September 19, 20, 21 & 22
        The Eglinton & Winton Memorial Handicap, 2m 1f
        The Laurent Perrier Handicap, 5f
        The Doonside Cup, 1m 3f
        The Bogside Cup, 1m 5f
        The Harry Rosebery Challenge Trophy, 2-y-o, 5f
        The Ladbrokes (Ayr) Gold Cup, 6f (£25,000)
        The Weir Memorial Trophy (Handicap), 1m 2f
        The Ladbrokes Hotels Nursery Handicap, 6f
        The Ladbrokes Ayrshire Handicap, 1m 3f
        The First of Clyde Stakes, 2-y-o fillies, 6f
        The Ladbroke Strathclyde Handicap, 1m
        The Holsten Diat Pils Handicap, 7f

Free Stabling and Accommodation for Lads and Girls.
Landing facilities for Helicopters in Centre of Course.

Further particulars from

W. W. McHarg   Racecourse Office,
General Manager   2 Whitletts Road,
and Joint Clerk of the Course.   Ayr.
Telephone: Ayr (0292) 264179

CHARACTERISTICS OF RACECOURSES

ASCOT.—The Ascot round course is a right-handed, triangular circuit of 1m 6f 34yds, with a run-in of 2½f. There is a straight mile course, over which the Royal Hunt Cup is run, and the Old mile course which joins the round course in Swinley Bottom. All races shorter than a mile are decided on the straight course. From the 1½-mile starting gate the round course runs downhill to the bend in Swinley Bottom, where it is level, then rises steadily to the turn into the straight, from where it is uphill until less than a furlong from the winning post, the last hundred yards being more or less level. The straight mile is slightly downhill from the start and then rises to the 5f gate, after which there is a slight fall before the junction with the round course. Despite the downhill run into Swinley Bottom and the relatively short run-in from the final turn, the Ascot course is galloping in character; the turns are easy, there are no minor surface undulations to throw a long-striding horse off-balance, and all races are very much against the collar over the last half-mile. The course is, in fact, quite a testing one, and very much so in soft going, when there is a heavy premium on stamina. In such circumstances races over 2 miles to 2¾ miles are very severe tests.
DRAW: The draw seems of little consequence nowadays.

AYR.—The Ayr round course is a left-handed, oval track, about twelve furlongs in extent, with a run-in of half a mile. Eleven-furlong races start on a chute which joins the round course after about a furlong. There is a straight six-furlong course of considerable width. The course is relatively flat, but there are gentle undulations throughout, perhaps more marked in the straight. It has a good surface and well-graded turns, and is a fine and very fair track, on the whole galloping in character.
DRAW: In races over seven furlongs and a mile a low number is desirable. On the straight course the draw is ordinarily of little consequence.

BATH.—The Bath round course is a left-handed, oval track, just over a mile and a half in extent, with a run-in of nearly half a mile. There is an extension for races over five furlongs and five furlongs and 167 yards. The run-in bends to the left, and is on the rise all the way. The mile and the mile-and-a-quarter courses have been designed to give over a quarter of a mile straight at the start, and the track generally is galloping rather than sharp. The course consists of old downland turf.
DRAW: The draw seems of little consequence nowadays.

BEVERLEY.—The Beverley round course is a right-handed, oval track, just over a mile and three furlongs in extent, with a run-in of two and a half furlongs. The five-furlong track bends right at halfway. The general galloping nature of the track is modified by the downhill turn into the straight and the relatively short run-in. The five-furlong course is on the rise throughout, and so is rather testing even in normal conditions; in soft going it takes some getting, particularly for two-year-olds early in the season.
DRAW: High numbers have an advantage over the five-furlong course.

BRIGHTON.—The Brighton course takes the shape of an extended 'U' and is 1½ miles in length. The first three furlongs are uphill, after which there is a slight descent followed by a slight rise to about four furlongs from home; the track then runs more sharply downhill until a quarter of a mile out, from where it rises to the last hundred yards, the finish being level. The run-in is about 3½ furlongs, and there is no straight course. This is essentially a sharp track. While the turns are easy enough, the pronounced gradients make Brighton an unsuitable course for big, long-striding horses, resolute gallopers or round-actioned horses. Handy, medium-sized, fluent movers, and quick-actioned horses are much more at home on the course. There are no opportunities for long-distance plodders at Brighton.
DRAW: In sprint races a low number is advantageous, and speed out of the gate even more so.

CARLISLE.—Carlisle is a right-handed, pear-shaped course, just over a mile and a half in extent, with a run-in of a little more than three furlongs. The five-furlong course, of which the five-furlong course is a part, the mile course, and the mile and a half course start on three separate off-shoot extensions. For the first three furlongs or so the course runs downhill, then rises for a short distance, levelling out just beyond the mile post. From there until the turn into the straight the course is flat, apart from minor undulations. The six-furlong course, which bears right soon after the start, and again at the turn into the straight, is level for two furlongs, then rises fairly steeply until the distance, from which point it is practically level. The track is galloping in character, and the six-furlong course is a stiff test of stamina for a two-year-old.

DRAW: High numbers have an advantage which is more marked in the shorter races.

CATTERICK.—The Catterick round course is a left-handed, oval track, measuring one mile and 180 yards, with a run-in of three furlongs. The five-furlong course bears left before and at the junction with the round course. From the seven-furlong starting gate the round course is downhill almost all the way, and there is a sharp turn on the falling gradient into the straight. The five-furlong course is downhill throughout, quite steeply to start with, and less so thereafter. Catterick is an exceedingly sharp track with pronounced undulations of surface, and it is therefore an impossible course for a big, long-striding animal. Experience of the track counts for a great deal, and jockeyship is of the utmost importance.

DRAW: A low number gives a slight advantage over five furlongs, and a much more definite one over six furlongs but a quick start is essential whatever the draw. A slow beginner on the inside is almost certain to be cut off.

CHEPSTOW.—The Chepstow round course is a left-handed, oval track, about two miles in extent, with a run-in of five furlongs. There is a straight mile course, over which all races up to a mile are run. The round course has well-marked undulations, and the straight course is generally downhill and level alternately as far as the run-in, thereafter rising sharply for over two furlongs, and then gradually levelling out to the winning post. Notwithstanding the long run-in and general rise over the last five furlongs, this is not an ideal galloping track because of the changing gradients.

DRAW: High numbers have a slight advantage on the straight course.

CHESTER.—Chester is a left-handed, circular course, only a few yards over a mile round, the smallest circuit of any flat-race course in Great Britain. It is quite flat and on the turn almost throughout, and although the run-in is nearly straight, it is less than two furlongs in length. The Chester Cup which is invariably run at a very strong gallop all the way, is a testing race demanding exceptional stamina and is always won by an out-and-out stayer. Apart from extreme distance events, such as the Cup and other 2¼m races, the course is against the long-striding, resolute galloper and greatly favours the handy, medium-sized, sharp-actioned horse.

DRAW: A low number is of great importance in races at up to seven and a half furlongs and a quick beginning is essential. It is virtually impossible to overcome a slow start over sprint distances.

DONCASTER.—Doncaster is a left-handed, pear-shaped course, over 15 furlongs round and quite flat, except for a slight hill about 1¼ miles from the finish. There is a perfectly straight mile, and a round mile starting on an off-shoot of the round course. The run-in from the turn is about 4½ furlongs. This is one of the fairest courses in the country, but its flat surface and great width, its sweeping turn into the straight, and long run-in, make it galloping in character, and ideal for the big, long-striding stayer.

DRAW: The draw is of no importance on the round course. On the straight course high numbers used to have a considerable advantage, but nowadays low numbers are usually favoured.

EDINBURGH.—The Edinburgh round course is a right-handed oval track nearly a mile and a quarter in extent, with a run-in of half a mile. There is a straight five-furlong course. The track is flat, with slight undulations and a gentle rise from the distance to the winning post. The turns at the top end of the course and into the straight are very sharp, and handiness and adaptability to negotiate the bends is of the utmost importance. The big, long-striding, cumbersome horse is at a distinct disadvantage on the round track, especially in races at up to a mile and three furlongs, but to a lesser extent in races over longer distances.

DRAW: High numbers have an advantage in seven-furlong and mile races.

EPSOM.—Epsom is a left-handed, U-shaped course, 1½ miles in extent, with an interior unfenced track, known as the Metropolitan course, used only in 2¼-mile races. In these races the horses start at the winning post and proceed the reverse way of the course, branching off to the right just before reaching Tattenham Corner and rejoining the course proper just over 8½ furlongs from the winning post. The Derby course is decidedly uphill for the first half-mile, level for nearly two furlongs and then quite sharply downhill round the bend to Tattenham Corner and all the way up the straight until approaching the final furlong, from where there is a fairish rise to the winning post. The run-in is less than four furlongs. The 7f and 6f courses start on tangential extensions. The 5f course is quite straight and sharply downhill to the junction with the round course. Races over 2¼ miles are, of course, true tests of stamina, and races over 1½ miles can also be testing if the pace over the first uphill four furlongs is strong, as it frequently is in the Derby. Otherwise the track is not really testing in itself, and races up to 8½ furlongs are very sharp indeed, the sprint courses being the fastest in the world. Owing to its bends and pronounced downhill gradients, Epsom favours the handy, fluent-actioned, medium-sized horse: big horses sometimes handle the course well enough, but cumbersome horses, long-striding gallopers, or those with pronounced 'knee-action' are not suited by it and are frequently quite unable to act upon it, especially when the going is firm or hard. Any hestitation at the start or slowness into stride results in considerable loss of ground over the first furlong in sprint races. For this reason Epsom is no course for a green and inexperienced two-year-old, slow to realise what is required.

DRAW: In races up to eight and a half furlongs a low number is advantageous, but quickness out of the gate is of far greater importance, particularly in five-furlong, six-furlong and seven-furlong races.

FOLKESTONE.—The Folkestone round course is a right-handed, pear-shaped track, about ten and a half furlongs in extent, with a run-in of two and a half furlongs. There is a straight six-furlong course. The course is undulating, with the last part slightly on the rise, but notwithstanding its width, the easy turns and the uphill finish, it is by no means a galloping track.

DRAW: Low numbers have a slight advantage on the straight course.

GOODWOOD.—The Goodwood track consists of a nearly straight 6f course, with a triangular right-handed loop circuit. The Goodwood Cup, about 2m 5f, is started by flag in front of the stands: the horses run the reverse way of the straight, branch left at the first or lower bend, go right-handed round the loop and return to the straight course via the top bend. Races over 2m 3f, 1¾m, 1½m and 1¼m are also run on this course, but 1m races rejoin the straight course via the lower bend. Although there is a 5f run-in for races of 1¼m and upwards, the turns and, more specially, the pronounced downhill gradients from the turn make Goodwood essentially a sharp track, favouring the active, handy, fluent mover rather than the big, long-striding horse. This is of lesser importance in 2m 3f and 2m 5f races, where the emphasis is on sound stamina, and of greater importance in the shorter distance races, particularly in sprints and especially when the going is on top. The 5f course is one of the fastest in the country.

DRAW: A high number is regarded as advantageous in sprint races, but the advantage is not great. Alacrity out of the gate is certainly of importance in five-furlong races.

Catering
with style . . . . .
P. T. FAWCETT

Caterers Ltd., The Racecourse, Boroughbridge Road, Ripon.

Specialists in Outside Catering, Wedding Receptions,
Banqueting, Dinner Dances, Private House Parties

Specialist Catering Service for All Indoor and Outdoor Events,
Agricultural Shows, V.I.P. Marquees, Galas, Exhibitions etc.

Fully Licensed Bars

For Personal Service telephone Ripon (0765) 4295

HAMILTON.—The Hamilton track is a perfectly straight, six-furlong course, with a pear-shaped, right-handed loop, the whole being a mile and five furlongs in extent from a start in front of the stands, round the loop and back to the winning post. The run-in is five furlongs. The turns are very easy, and the course is undulating for the most part, but just over three furlongs from the winning post there are steep gradients into and out of a pronounced hollow, followed by a severe hill to the finish.

DRAW: Middle to high numbers are thought to have a slight advantage in races over the straight course.

HAYDOCK.—Haydock is a left-handed, oval-shaped course, about 13 furlongs round, with a run-in of 4½ furlongs, and a straight 5-furlong course. Races of 6 furlongs and 1½ miles start on tangential extensions to the round course. The course is rather galloping in character, with a rise of twenty-one feet throughout the straight.

DRAW: Horses drawn in the low numbers are regarded as having an advantage in races of six, seven and eight furlongs. On the straight course the draw is of no consequence when the going is sound, but when it is soft, horses racing under the stand rails (high numbers) seem to be favoured.

KEMPTON.—Kempton is a right-handed, triangular course, just over 13 furlongs round. The ten-furlong Jubilee course starts on an extension to the round course. Sprint races are run over a separate diagonal course. The Kempton track is perfectly flat with normal characteristics, being neither a sharp track nor a galloping one.

DRAW: On the sprint course a draw near the rails is advantageous when the ground is soft; when the stalls are placed on the far side a high draw is an enormous advantage nowadays whatever the going.

LEICESTER.—The Leicester round course is a right-handed, oval track, about a mile and three quarters in extent, with a run-in of four and a half furlongs. The straight mile course, on which all races of up to a mile are run, is mainly downhill to halfway, then rises gradually for over two furlongs, finishing on the level. The course is well-drained, the bends into the straight and beyond the winning post have been eased and cambered, and the track is galloping. For two-year-olds early in the season it poses quite a test of stamina.

DRAW: High numbers have an advantage in races at up to a mile and the advantage seems to be more marked when the going is on the soft side.

LINGFIELD.—The Lingfield round course is a left-handed loop, which intersects the straight course of seven furlongs and 140 yards nearly half a mile out and again less than two furlongs from the winning post. The run-in is not much more than three furlongs. For nearly half its length the round course is quite flat, then rises with easy gradients to the summit of a slight hill, after which there is a downhill turn to the straight. The straight course has a considerable downhill gradient to halfway, and is slightly downhill for the rest of the way. The straight course is very easy, and the track as a whole is sharp, putting a premium on speed and adaptability, and making relatively small demands upon stamina, though this does not, of course, apply to races over two miles. The mile and a half course, over which the Derby Trial is run, bears quite close resemblance to the Epsom Derby Course.

DRAW: On the straight course high numbers have a slight advantage.

NEWBURY.—The Newbury round course is a left-handed, oval track, about a mile and seven furlongs in extent, with a run-in of nearly five furlongs. There is a straight mile course, which is slightly undulating throughout. Races on the round mile and over the extended seven furlongs start on an extension from the round course. Notwithstanding the undulations this is a good galloping track, and excellent arrangements have been made for watering the course.

DRAW: A high number used to be a fairly considerable advantage over the straight course, but since the narrowing of the track the advantage seems to have disappeared.

Haydock Park

FLAT RACING FIXTURES 1984

APRIL
4th Wed.
Field Marshal Stakes; Freddy Fox Handicap.

21st Sat.
Valspar Paints Handicap; Philip Cornes Nickel Alloys (Qualifier); Holsten Diat Pils (Qualifier).

MAY
5th & 7th Sat. & Mon.
Fairey Engineering Spring Trophy; Sir Richard Fairey Memorial Handicap (Saturday); Tia Maria Handicap Hurdle (Monday).

25th & 26th Fri. & Sat.
John Davies Handicap (Friday); Cecil Frail Handicap; Sandy Lane Stakes (Saturday).

JUNE
8th & 9th Fri. (Evening) & Sat.
Burtonwood Brewery Handicap (Friday); Stones Best Bitter Handicap; John of Gaunt Stakes (Saturday).

JULY
6th & 7th Fri. & Sat.
Great Central Handicap (Friday); Lancashire Oaks; Old Newton Cup; Cock of the North Stakes (Saturday).

AUGUST
10th & 11th Fri. (Evening) & Sat.
Matthew Peacock Handicap (Friday); Better Bet Coral Handicap; Harvey Jones Handicap (Saturday).

SEPTEMBER
7th & 8th Fri. & Sat.
Claude Harrison Trophy (Friday); Vernons Sprint Cup; John Smith's Brewery Handicap (Saturday).

OCTOBER
5th & 6th Fri. & Sat.
Otis Handicap; Brooke Bond Oxo Final; Outland Handicap (Friday); Daily Mirror Apprentice Handicap.

17th & 18th Wed. & Thurs.
Oak Handicap (Wednesday); Beech Handicap (Thursday).

N.B. The details given above are correct at time of going to press, but factors outside the control of the Haydock Park Executive may result in alterations having to be made.

All enquiries to:
   **HAYDOCK PARK RACECOURSE, NEWTON-LE-WILLOWS, MERSEYSIDE
WA12 0HQ**
   Phone: Ashton-in-Makerfield (0942) 727345

NEWCASTLE.—Newcastle is a left-handed, oval-shaped course of 1m 6f in circumference. There is also a straight course, over which all races of seven furlongs or less are run. The course is decidedly galloping in character, and a steady climb from the turn into the straight makes Newcastle a testing track, particularly for two-year-olds early in the season. Ability to see the journey out thoroughly is most important.

DRAW: The draw is of no particular consequence.

NEWMARKET ROWLEY MILE COURSE.—The Cesarewitch course is two and a quarter miles in extent, with a right-handed bend after a mile, the last mile and a quarter being the straight Across the Flat. From the Cesarewitch start the course runs generally downhill to a sharp rise just before the turn. There are undulations throughout the first mile of the straight, then the course runs downhill for a furlong to the Dip, and uphill for the last furlong to the winning post. This is an exceedingly wide, galloping track, without minor irregularities of surfaces, so it is ideal for the big, long-striding horse, except for the descent into the Dip, which is more than counterbalanced by the final hill. Ability to see the trip out thoroughly is essential.

DRAW: The draw usually confers little advantage but in big fields low numbers are favoured at times and high numbers at other times.

NEWMARKET SUMMER COURSE.—The Newmarket Summer course is two miles and twenty-four yards in extent, with a right-handed bend at halfway, the first mile being part of the Cesarewitch course, and the last the straight Bunbury Mile. The course runs generally downhill to a sharp rise just before the turn. There are undulations in the first threequarters of a mile of the straight, then the course runs downhill for a furlong to a dip, and uphill for the last furlong to the winning post. This is an exceedingly wide, galloping track, ideal for the big, long-striding horse, except for the descent into the dip which is more than counterbalanced by the final hill. Ability to see the trip out thoroughly is essential.

DRAW: The draw confers little advantage.

NOTTINGHAM.—The Nottingham round course is a left-handed, oval track, about a mile and a half in extent, with a run-in of four and a half furlongs. There is a straight 6f course but no longer a straight mile. The course is flat and the turns are easy.

DRAW: High numbers are slightly preferred over the straight course.

PONTEFRACT.—Pontefract is a left-handed, oval track, two miles in extent. There is no straight course, and the run-in is only just over two furlongs. There are considerable gradients and a testing hill over the last three furlongs. The undulations, the sharp bend into the straight, and the short run-in disqualify it from being described as a galloping track, but there is a premium on stamina.

DRAW: A low number is advantageous particularly over five furlongs but it becomes a decided disadvantage if a horse fails to jump off well.

REDCAR.—Redcar is a narrow, left-handed, oval track, about a mile and threequarters in extent, with a run-in of five furlongs, which is part of the straight mile course. The course is perfectly flat with normal characteristics, and provides an excellent gallop.

DRAW: The draw confers no advantage.

RIPON.—The Ripon course is a right-handed, oval circuit of 13 furlongs, with a run-in of 5f, and a straight 6f course. Owing to the rather cramped bends and the surface undulations in the straight, the Ripon track is rather sharp in character.

DRAW: On the straight course the draw is of no importance but in races on the mile course, horses drawn in the high numbers seem to have an advantage.

SALISBURY.—The Salisbury track is a right-handed loop course, with a run-in of seven furlongs, which, however, is not straight, for the mile course, of which it is a part, has a right-handed elbow after three furlongs. For races over a mile and threequarters horses start opposite the Club Enclosure, and running away from the stands, bear to the left, and go round the loop. The course, which is uphill throughout the last half-mile, is galloping and rather testing.

DRAW: Low numbers are favoured in sprints when the going is soft.

SANDOWN.—Sandown is a right-handed, oval-shaped course of 13 furlongs, with a straight run-in of 4f. There is a separate straight course which runs across the main circuit and over which all 5f races are decided. From the 1¼m starting gate, the Eclipse Stakes course, the track is level to the turn into the straight, from where it is uphill until less than a furlong from the winning post, the last hundred yards being more or less level. The 5f track is perfectly straight and rises steadily throughout. Apart from the minor gradients between the main winning post and the 1¼m starting gate, there are no undulations to throw a long-striding horse off balance, and all races over the round course are very much against the collar from the turn into the straight. The course is, in fact, a testing one, and over all distances the ability to see the trip out well is of the utmost importance.

DRAW: On the five-furlong course high numbers have a considerable advantage in big fields when the ground is soft.

THIRSK.—The Thirsk round course is a left-handed, oval track, just over a mile and a quarter in extent, with a run-in of half a mile. There is a straight six-furlong course, which is slightly undulating throughout. The round course itself is almost perfectly flat, but though the turns are relatively easy and the ground well levelled all round, the track is on the sharp side, and by no means ideal for a horse that requires time to settle down, and time and space to get down to work in the straight.

DRAW: High numbers have an advantage on the straight course.

WARWICK.—Warwick is a broad, left-handed, oval track, just over a mile and threequarters in extent, with a run-in of about three and a half furlongs. There is no straight course, the five-furlong course having a left-hand elbow at the junction with the round course. Mile races start on an extension from the round course, the first four and a half furlongs being perfectly straight. This is a sharp track, with the emphasis on speed and adaptability rather than stamina. The laboured galloper is at a disadvantage, especially in races at up to a mile.

DRAW: A high number is advantageous in races up to a mile when the ground is soft, but a quick beginning is also important.

WINDSOR.—Windsor racecourse, laid out in the form of a figure eight, is 12½ furlongs in extent. In races of around 1½ miles both left-handed and right-handed turns are encountered, but in races over 1m 70 yds only right-handed turns are met. The last five furlongs of the course are straight, except for a slight bend to the right three furlongs from the finish. The six-furlong start is now on an extension of this straight. Although perfectly flat throughout, the bends make this track rather sharp in character. However, as there is a nearly straight 5f run-in the relative sharpness of the track is of no consequence in the longer races. Big, long-striding horses which normally require a more galloping course are at little or no disadvantage over these trips.

DRAW: In five- and six-furlong races horses drawn in the high numbers have an advantage provided they start well enough to be able to avoid being squeezed out or impeded at the slight right-hand elbow in the straight.

WOLVERHAMPTON.—The Wolverhampton round course is a left-handed, pear-shaped or triangular track, just over a mile and a half in extent, with a run-in of five furlongs. There is a straight course of five furlongs. The course is level throughout, with normal characteristics.

DRAW: The draw confers no advantage.

YARMOUTH.—The Yarmouth round course is a narrow, left-handed, oval track, about thirteen furlongs in extent, with a run-in of five furlongs. There is a straight mile course. Apart from a slight fall just before the run-in, the track is perfectly flat, with normal characteristics.

DRAW: High numbers have an advantage on the straight course.

YORK.—York is a left-handed, U-shaped course, 2 miles in extent, and quite flat throughout. There is also a perfectly flat straight course, over which all 5f and 6f races are run. 7f races start on a spur which joins the round course after about two furlongs. The run-in from the turn is nearly 5 furlongs. This is one of the best courses in the country, of great width throughout and with a sweeping turn into the long straight. The entire absence of surface undulations makes it ideal for a long-striding, resolute galloper, but it is really a splendid track, bestowing no great favour on any type of horse.

DRAW: The draw used to be of no consequence, but recently low numbers have had a marked advantage, particularly when the ground has been on the soft side.

ERRATA & ADDENDA
"RACEHORSES OF 1982"

Dazari	second foal
Dido	dam is <u>Correct</u> Approach
Drumalis	great grandam is <u>Mrs</u> Rabbit
Larionov	dam also won over 7f and 1m at 4yrs
Misty Glen	aged <u>7</u>
Muznah	dam half-sister to Hilal
Princess Saluki	changed hands <u>4,000</u> gns
Whiskey Go Go	should be Whisky Go Go

"One of the world's premier racecourses, consistently providing some of the best racing in Europe."

"15 days racing in 1984
-over £1,000,000 in prize money"

John Sanderson
York Race Committee
THE RACECOURSE
YORK YO2 1EX
TEL:YORK
(0904)20911

York Races

990

Stallion Section

Timeform Ratings quoted in the Stallion Section are those which appeared in the 'Racehorses' annuals except where otherwise stated.

DOMINION

SIRE OF GROUP & STAKES WINNERS in 1983

Sire of: **DOMYNSKY**—Winner of 7 races, including 5 races at 2 years in England. and the Hill Prince Stakes, Belmont, Gr. III; also 3rd Saranac Stakes, Gr. III, total £65,761. **BLACK COUNTRY**—LR Marble Hill Stakes, Curragh, at 2 years, 1983; also stakes placed. **EQUANAID**—Valspar Paints H., Haydock, £7,479; 2nd (hd) LR XYZ H., Newcastle. **FAIR DOMINION**—June Stakes, Sandown, etc. and £7,743 at 2 years, 1983. **OMINOUS**—Sun Life of Canada H., Epsom. **LIBERTY TREE**—5 wins to date. **DETENTE**, etc.
His first 2 crops won 30 races, £130,052.
DOMINION won 14 races (8-9f), £145,289 in England, France and U.S.A. incl. Gr. III Prix Perth (beating Gr. I winners incl. Arctic Tern). Gr. III Bernard Baruch H. Stakes, Saratoga; Rumson H. Stakes, Monmouth; and Jersey Blues H. Stakes, Meadowlands. 2nd Gr. II Lockinge Stakes, Gr, III Westbury Stakes (beating Gr I winner Anne's Pretender), Gr. III Earl of Sefton Stakes, Chicago H. Stakes (won in N.T.R.), etc. 3rd (to Bolkonski and Grundy) Gr. I 2,000 Guineas, Gr. II Queen Elizabeth II Stakes (won by Rose Bowl). 4th Gr. I Sussex Stakes (behind Bolkonski, Rose Bowl and Lianga).
DOMINION holds the 8½f. record at Gulfstream Park, and retired to stud perfectly sound after 46 races from 2-6 years).

			Dante
		Darius	Yasna
	Derring-Do	Sipsey Bridge	Abernant
	(b. 1961)		Claudette
DOMINION			Nasrullah
Bay 1972		Princely Gift	Blue Gem
	Picture Palace	Palais Glide	King Legend
	(b. 1961)		Side Slip

FULL EVERY SEASON AT STUD
The Property of a syndicate
Syndicate Chairman: R. J. McCreery, Stowell Hill, Templecombe, Somerset.
Tel: 0963 70212. Syndicate Secretary and Stud Manager: Mrs. A. J. Cuthbert, Aston Park Stud. Tel: 084 428 417 or 0844 51492 (Office).

Dual Group One Winner At Two
Prix Morny and Prix de la Salamandre
1982 leading two-year-old stakes winner in France

DEEP ROOTS

Br. 1980 Dom Racine — La Paqueline (Sassafras)

May 14	Won Prix Ossian (maiden), 5f, Maisons-Laffitte, 1m 1.80 sec
June 26	Won Prix du Bois, Group 3, 5f, Longchamp, 58.80 sec (subsequently moved back to third for interference)
July 27	2nd Prix Robert Papin, Group 1, 5½f, Maisons-Laffitte, 1m 5.40 sec
August 28	Won Prix Morny, Group 1, 6f, Deauville, 1m 11.10 sec
Sept 19	Won Prix de la Salamandre, Group 1, 7f, Longchamp, 1m 23.20 sec
Oct 10	4th Grand Criterium, Group 1, one mile, Longchamp, 1m 46.50 sec

Deep Roots convincingly defeated Ma Biche, the European filly of the year, by three lengths in the Prix Morny.

Deep Roots won the Prix Morny in a faster time than Blushing Groom, Super Concorde, Irish River and Green Forest.

Family of Frizette, also ancestress to Seattle Slew, Mr Prospector etc.

The property of a syndicate.
Fee for 1984: 30,000 fr straight plus 30,000 fr (1st Oct concession).
Standing at Haras du Petit Tellier, Sevigny, 61200 Argentan, France. (Stud owner: M. Patrick Chedeville, Tel. (33) 67 07 65.
Enquiries to: M. Patrick Barbe, 259 Avenue Charles De Gaulle, 60260 Lamorlaye, France, Tel: (4) 421 23 51. Telex 150980 F.

Electric sprints clear in the Gordon Stakes at Goodwood

AT WHITSBURY MANOR STUD,
NR. FORDINGBRIDGE, HAMPSHIRE

ELECTRIC

Winner of 4 Group Races, £111,567, (10-12f)

WON   Gr II Great Voltigeur Stakes, York, by ¾ length and 7 lengths from Diamond Shoal and Touching Wood.

WON   Gr III Jockey Club Stakes, Newmarket, beating Time Charter and Diamond Shoal (subsequently first and second in Gr I King George VI Queen Elizabeth Stakes).

WON   Gr III Gordon Stakes, Goodwood, by 3 lengths from Touching Wood and Jalmood.

WON   Gr III White Rose Stakes, Ascot.

2nd   Gr I Coronation Cup, Epsom, beaten ¾ length, beating Diamond Shoal and Old Country.

2nd   Gr II Hardwicke Stakes, Ascot, in course record time, to Stanerra, beating by 12 lengths Gr I winners Be My Native, Jalmood, Old Country etc.

2nd   Gerry Feilden Memorial Stakes, Newmarket, beaten a neck by Ivano.

2nd   Yattendon Maiden Stakes, Newbury, in a field of 24, on debut at 2 years.

3rd   Gr III Highland Spring Derby Trial, Lingfield.

Fee: £3,000 15th July and £3,000 n.f.n.f. 1st October.

All enquiries to: London Thoroughbred Services Ltd., 7 Phene Street, London SW3 5NZ. Tel: (01) 351 2181. Telex: 916950 *or:* C. J. Harper, Whitsbury Manor Stud, Nr. Fordingbridge, Hants. Tel: Rockbourne (07253) 283.

994

FINAL STRAW

A LEADING MILER

13 YEARLINGS SOLD IN 1983
AVERAGED 100,954 GNS

FIRST RUNNERS 1984

FULL 1981-1984 (inclusive)

All enquiries to: The Director, National Stud, Newmarket. Tel: Newmarket (0638) 663464 *or*: the Secretaries to the Syndicate: London Thoroughbred Services Ltd., 7 Phene Street, London SW3 5NZ. Tel: (01) 351 2181. Telex: 916950.

GLINT OF GOLD

Bay 1978 **MILL REEF** — CROWN TREASURE **(GRAUSTARK)**

At 2 years: won Gran Criterium Gr 1, Sandwich Stakes; 2nd Acomb Stakes.

At 3 years: won Derby Italiano Gr 1, Grand Prix de Paris Gr 1, Preis von Europa Gr 1, Great Voltigeur Stakes Gr 2; 2nd Derby, St Leger.

At 4 years: won Grand Prix de Saint-Cloud Gr 1, Grosser Preis von Baden Gr 1, John Porter Stakes Gr 2; 2nd Jockey Club Stakes, Hardwicke Stakes; 3rd King George VI and Queen Elizabeth Diamond Stakes. Total Earnings: £472,760.

His sire MILL REEF, winner of Derby, Eclipse, King George VI and Queen Elizabeth and Prix de l'Arc de Triomphe, is one of the world's leading sires — SHIRLEY HEIGHTS, ACAMAS, FAIRY FOOTSTEPS, PAS DE SEUL, WASSL, DIAMOND SHOAL, etc.

His dam CROWN TREASURE was a good 5f winner in USA. Her first two foals are GLINT OF GOLD and DIAMOND SHOAL (Grand Prix de Saint-Cloud Gr 1, Grosser Preis von Baden Gr 1).

Glint of Gold retired to stud in 1983, FULL BOOK OF TOP-CLASS MARES.

The Property of a Syndicate.
Standing at Derisley Wood Stud Farm, Woodditton Road, Newmarket, Suffolk CB8 9HF.
Apply to A. W. Johnson, The Manager, as above. Tel: Newmarket (0638) 730055 or 730100. Telex: 817886.
or: **Secretary to the Syndicate, Charles Rowe. Tel: (044083) 511.**

HIGH TOP

Br 1969 Derring Do—Camenae by Vimy
**PROLIFIC CLASSIC SIRE, GROUP ONE WINNING 2-Y-O
CLASSIC WINNING THREE-YEAR-OLD**

HIGH TOP won 5 races at 2 and 3 years (5f-8f), including 2,000 Guineas, Gr 1, (beating Roberto, Sun Prince) and Observer Gold Cup, Gr 1. 2nd Sussex Stakes, Gr 1, Prix Jacques le Marois, Gr 1.

FULL STUD RECORD	Year	Winners	Races	£
	1976	8	13	22,133
	1977	25	39	108,115
	1978	32	61	178,587
	1979	34	55	351,224
	1980	34	68	209,099
	1981	38	66	380,308
	1982	36	70	309,679
	1983*	33	55	244,483
	*1st October		427	1,803,628

Principal Winners: **TOP VILLE**—Gr 1 Prix du Jockey-Club, Gr 1 Prix Lupin and 2 other Group races; **CUT ABOVE**—Gr 1 St. Leger Stakes, Gr 3 White Rose Stakes; 2nd Gr 1 Irish Sweeps Derby; 3rd Gr 2 Geoffrey Freer Stakes; **CIRCUS RING**—Joint Champion European 2-year-old filly, 1981; Gr 2 Lowther Stakes, Princess Margaret Stakes, etc.; **MY TOP**—Gr 1 Derby Italiano, Gr 2 Premio Emanuele Filiberto; **LOOKING FOR**—Gr 1 Premio Roma, Gr 3 Coppa d'Oro; **TRIPLE FIRST**—Gr 2 Nassau Stakes, Gr 3 Sun Chariot Stakes; **MINERS LAMP**—Gr 3 Oettingen-Rennen; also Rose of York H. Stakes; **ALOFT**—Gr 3 Princess Royal Stakes; **SMAGETA**—Gr 3 Criterium Femminile, 3rd Gr 1 Italian 1,000 Guineas, 1982; **LOFTY**—Gr 3 Pacemaker Diomed Stakes; **CREWS HILL**—All American Handicap ($100,000 added), 1982, Stewards Cup, Goodwood, etc.; **COULSTRY** (Norwegian St. Leger, Gr 2), etc.
Enquiries to:
British Bloodstock Agency, Thormanby House, Falmouth Avenue, Newmarket (0638) 665021.   Telex 817157.   or 16/17 Pall Mall, London SW1Y 5LU.   Tel: 01-839 3393.   Telex: 27403

KIND OF HUSH

Bay, 16 hands ½ ins. by Welsh Pageant, out of Sauceboat, by Connaught

Kind of Hush winning the Prince of Wales's Stakes (Gr 2)

At 2 years — **4TH** Rous Memorial Stakes, **L**, 6 furlongs, Goodwood.
At 3 years — **WON** Ladbroke Craven Stakes, **Gr 3**, 1 mile, Newmarket
(beating To-Agori-Mou).
WON September Stakes, **L**, 11 furlongs, Kempton Park.
3RD Joe McGrath Memorial Stakes, **Gr 1**, Leopardstown.
At 4 years — **WON** Prince of Wales's Stakes, **Gr 2**,1¼ miles, Royal Ascot.
2ND Joe McGrath Memorial Stakes, **Gr 1**, 1¼ miles, Leopardstown.
2ND Westbury Stakes, **Gr 3**, 1¼ miles, Sandown Park.
3RD Earl of Sefton Stakes, **Gr 3**, 9 furlongs, Newmarket.

Earnings £58,444

1st Dam:
   SAUCEBOAT won 4 races, total £20,991, including Child Stakes (**Gr 3**) and
   Strensall Stakes (**L**), also second Nassau Stakes (**Gr 2**), twice, etc.
2nd Dam:
   CRANBERRY SAUCE won 4 races including Sun Chariot Stakes (**Gr 2**),
   Prix Fille de l'Air (**Gr 3**), Nell Gwyn Stakes (**Gr 3**), etc.
3rd Dam:
   QUEENSBERRY won 4 races including Cheveley Park Stakes (**Gr 1**), Mole-
   comb Stakes (**Gr 3**), Lowther Stakes (**Gr 3**), and 1,000 Guineas Trial Stakes, etc.

Fee: £3,000 live foal

All enquiries to: R. A. Fowlston at the stud (Tel: 0460-72255)
or: London Thoroughbred Services Ltd., 7 Phene Street,
London SW3 5NZ.   Tel: 01-351 2181.   Telex: 916950

Gold Cup—LE MOSS inflicts the first of 3 defeats on ARDROSS

Goodwood Cup—LE MOSS again beats ARDROSS

Doncaster Cup—LE MOSS and ARDROSS battle it out again

3 GREAT WINS BY A GREAT RACEHORSE

CHAMPION EUROPEAN MILER

KRIS

Chesnut 1976, 16h. 0½ in. by SHARPEN UP, out of DOUBLY SURE, by RELIANCE II
SET THREE COURSE RECORDS

WINNER OF 14 OF HIS 16 STARTS INCLUDING 8 PATTERN RACES: Sussex
Stakes, Lockinge Stakes, Queen Elizabeth II Stakes, St. James's Palace Stakes,
Waterford Crystal Mile, Clerical Medical Greenham Stakes, Bisquit Cognac Challenge
Stakes, Horris Hill Stakes and 2nd The 2,000 Guineas, Queen Elizabeth II Stakes.

10 YEARLINGS
SOLD IN 1983
AVERAGED 117,000 GNS

FULL 1981-84 (inclusive)   FIRST RUNNERS 1984

All enquiries to: J. F. Day (Manager), Thornton Stud, Thornton-le-Street, Thirsk.
Tel: Thirsk (0845) 22522. or: the Secretaries to the Syndicate:
London Thoroughbred Services Ltd., 7 Phene Street, London SW3 5NZ.
Tel: (01-351 2181). Telex: 916950.

POSSE

Ch. 1977 **FORLI**—IN HOT PURSUIT (**BOLD RULER**)

At 2 years: placed 2nd Houghton Stakes, Newmarket (to Night Alert, with Bireme (Oaks) 3rd) on his only start.
At 3 years: won Sussex Stakes, Gr 1, St James's Palace Stakes, Gr 2; 2nd 2,000 Guineas, Gr 1; 3rd Clerical Medical Greenham Stakes, Gr 3; 4th Airlie/Coolmore Irish 2,000 Guineas, Gr 1, all his starts. Total earnings £9ᴑ,652.
His sire FORLI was undefeated classic winner in Argentine. Horse of the Year at 3, Argentine Triple Crown, also a good winner in the United States. Sire of over 40 stakes winners including FOREGO, THATCH, INTREPID HERO, HOME GUARD, BOONE'S CABIN, FORMIDABLE, GAY FANDANGO. Also a leading broodmare sire (sire of the dams of NUREYEV and JAAZEIRO).
His dam IN HOT PURSUIT was only raced at 2 and won 3 races from 5 starts including Fashion Stakes Gr 3. Full sister to FULL OF HOPE, DISCIPLIN-ARIAN, BOLD SULTAN, etc., and half-sister to DISCIPLINE.
First crop runners 1984

The Property of a Syndicate.
Standing at Derisley Wood Stud Farm, Woodditton Road, Newmarket, Suffolk CB8 9HF.
Apply to A. W. Johnson, The Manager, as above. Tel: Newmarket (0638) 730055 or 730100. Telex: 817886.
or: Secretaries to the Syndicate, Rustons and Lloyd, High Street, Newmarket. Tel: Newmarket (0638) 661221. Telex: 817970.

Shareef Dancer

CHAMPION EUROPEAN 3-y-o 1983

SHAREEF DANCER (b.1980)				
NORTHERN DANCER (b. 1961) Champion 2 and 3-y-o; Horse of the Year, Champion Sire of 100 Stakes winners including Champions: NIJINSKY, THE MINSTREL, TRY MY BEST etc.	**NEARTIC** Stakes winner and Sire of 49 Stakes winners.	Nearco, 1935	Pharos	
			Nogara	
		Lady Angela, 1944	Hyperion	
			Sister Sarah	
	NATALMA Winner and producer of 3 Stakes winners.	Native Dancer, 1950	Polynesian	
			Geisha	
		Almahmoud, 1947	Mahmoud	
			Arbitrator	
SWEET ALLIANCE (b. 1974) Winner of 6 races, $179,219, including Kentucky Oaks Gr.2. Jersey Belle H.cap Gr.3.	**SIR IVOR** Horse of the Year, Champion 2 and 3-y-o. Sire of: IVANJICA, CLOONLARA, GODETIA, BATES MOTEL.	Sir Gaylord, 1959	Turn-to	
			Somethingroyal	
		Attica, 1953	Mr. Trouble	
			Athenia	
	MRS PETERKIN Winner of 6 races including Chrysanthemum H.cap Gr.3. Dam of 7 winners incl: WHYDIDJU (California Oaks).	Tom Fool, 1949	Menow	
			Gaga	
		Legendra, 1944	Challenger II	
			Lady Legend	

Enquiries to: R.P. Acton, **Dalham Hall Stud,** Duchess Drive, Newmarket, Suffolk. Tel: (0638) 730070. Telex: 818823

CHAMPION EUROPEAN SPRINTER

SHARPO

Chestnut, 15 hands 3¼ ins. by Sharpen Up, out of Moiety Bird, by Falcon

WINNER OF SEVEN PATTERN RACES

William Hill Sprint Championship, York—Sharpo wins Europe's most
valuable sprint; Marwell is second and Moorestyle third

At 3 years — **WON** William Hill Sprint Championship **(Gr II)** York.
WON Temple Stakes **(Gr III),** Sandown Park.
2ND Prix de l'Abbaye de Longchamp **(Gr I).**
2ND Cork and Orrery Stakes **(Gr III),** Royal Ascot.
3RD William Hill July Cup **(Gr I),** Newmarket.

At 4 years — **WON** William Hill Sprint Championship **(Gr II),** York.
WON Prix de Saint-Georges **(Gr III),** Longchamp.
2ND Prix de l'Abbaye de Longchamp **(Gr I).**
3RD Palace House Stakes **(Gr III),** Newmarket.

At 5 years — **WON** William Hill July Cup **(Gr I),** Newmarket.
WON Prix de l'Abbaye de Longchamp **(Gr I),** Longchamp.
WON William Hill Sprint Championship **(Gr II),** York.
3RD Palace House Stakes **(Gr III),** Newmarket.

Total Earnings: £231,994

Fee: £3,000 15th July + £3,000 N.F.N.F. 1st October

All enquiries to: London Thoroughbred Services Ltd., 7 Phene Street,
London SW3 5NZ. Tel: 01-351 2181. Telex: 916950
or the stud (Tel: 0638-663081 or 662258)

TOUCHING WOOD

				Royal Charger
	ROBERTO (b. 1969) Champion 2 and 3-y-o, winner of Epsom Derby Gr.1 etc. Champion sire of 36 stakes winners incl. champions **DRIVING HOME, SOOKERA, CRITIQUE** etc.	**HAIL TO REASON** Sire of sires incl. **MR LEADER, HALO** (sire of 1983 Kentucky Derby winner **SUNNY'S HALO**), **BOLD REASON, STOP THE MUSIC** etc.	Turn to	
				Source Sucree
			Nothirdchance	Blue Swords
				Galla Colors
		BRAMALEA Winner of 8 races at 2 and 3 years incl. Coaching Club of America Oaks Gr.1. Dam of 8 winners.	Nashua	Nasrulla
TOUCHING WOOD b.c. 1979 Winner of English and Irish St. Legers Group 1 2nd Epsom Derby to unbeaten Golden Fleece (fastest Derby since Mahmoud)				Segula
			Rarelea	Bull Lea
				Bleebok
	MANDERA (b. 1970) Winner of Princess Royal Stakes Gr.3, graded stakes placed 2nd twice. Dam of two foals to race, both winners.	**VAGUELY NOBLE** Champion 3-y-o, winner of Arc de Triomphe Gr.1, sire of 43 stakes winners incl. **DAHLIA, LEMHI GOLD, EXCELLER** etc.	Vienna	Aureole
				Turkish Blood
			Noble Lassie	Nearco
				Belle Sauvage
		FOOLISH ONE Unraced half sister to champion racehorse and sire **BOLD RULER.** Dam of **PROTANTO** and **FUNNY FELLOW.**	Tom Fool	Menow
				Gaga
			Miss Disco	Discovery
				Outdone

RECORD-BREAKING SON OF CHAMPION ROBERTO
stands at ASTON UPTHORPE STUD 1984

Enquiries to:

M. H. Goodbody,
Gainsborough Stud,
Newbury,
Berkshire.
Tel: (0635) 253273
Telex: 849436

R. P. Acton,
Aston Upthorpe Stud,
Nr. Didcot,
Oxfordshire.
Tel: (0235) 850300/850338

VALIYAR

Bay 1979 **RED GOD**—VAL DIVINE **(VAL DE LOIR)**

At 2 years: unraced.

At 3 years: won Prix Sica Boy, Saint-Cloud, Prix du Pre-Catalan, Longchamp, 2nd Prix de Baville, Evry (btn ¾l on debut).

At 4 years: won Queen Anne Stakes Gr 3 (beating Noalcoholic, Montekin, Ivano), Leicestershire Stakes (by 5l from Jester), 2nd Lockinge Stakes Gr 3, 3rd Pacemaker Diomed Stakes Gr 3. All but one of his starts. Total earnings £43,638.

His sire RED GOD is sire of over 50 stakes winners including BLUSHING GROOM (champion 3-y-o of Europe, sensational young sire in USA), YELLOW GOD (sire of Nebbiolo and Pampapaul), JACINTH, RED ALERT, GREEN GOD etc.

His dam VAL DIVINE, winner and stakes-placed, is dam of 4 winners from her first four foals including European champion VAYRANN (Champion Stakes Gr 1). Grandam is POLA BELLA, champion 2-y-o and winner of Gr 1 French 1,000 Guineas).

Valiyar retires to stud in 1984.

The Property of a Syndicate.
Standing at Derisley Wood Stud Farm, Woodditton Road, Newmarket, Suffolk CB8 9HF.
Apply to A. W. Johnson, The Manager, as above. Tel: Newmarket (0638) 730055 or 730100. Telex: 817886.
or: **Secretary to the Syndicate, Charles Rowe. Tel: (044083) 511.**

AIRLIE
STALLIONS
1984

1983 : Champion Sire   **(HABITAT)**

1982 : Champion Sire (Races Won)   **(HABITAT)**

1981 : Champion Sire (Individual Winners and Races Won)   **(HABITAT)**

1980 : Champion Sire   **(PITCAIRN)**
        Champion Broodmare Sire   **(HIGH HAT)**

1979 : Champion Sire   **(PETINGO)**
        Champion Sire of 2-Y-O's   **(HABITAT)**

1978 : Champion Sire (Races Won) (PETINGO)

For the stallions listed in
the following pages apply to:

Airlie Stud,
Lucan,
County Dublin,
Irish Republic.
Tel: Dublin 280267 or 281548
Telex: 31049 TROG E.1

ARTAIUS

**CHAMPION OF EUROPE AT A MILE & A MILE AND A QUARTER
IN 1977** when winner of Sussex Stakes, Gr 1 (beating Relkino, Nebbiolo, Mrs
McArdy, etc.), Eclipse Stakes Gr 1 (in course record time) and Classic Trial
Stakes Gr 3. Also 2nd in Prix du Jockey Club, Gr 1, Benson & Hedges Gold
Cup, Gr 1, and Beresford Stakes, Gr 2 (only start at 2). **Timeform 129.**
Stud Record: Full since retiring to stud in 1978. Yearlings have made up
to IR 400,000 gns. Sire of stakes winners FLAME OF TARA (Coronation
Stks Gr 2, 2nd Champion Stks Gr 1), DAY IS DONE (National Stks Gr 2),
CAPTIVATOR, NOTTE CHIARA, DELICES, etc.

			Prince Rose
	Round Table	Princequillo	Cosquilla
	(b 1954)		Sir Cosmo
ARTAIUS		Knight's Daughter	Feola
(bay 1974)		My Babu	Djebel
	Stylish Pattern		Perfume II
	(b 1961)		Hyperion
		Sunset Gun II	Ace of Spades

By ROUND TABLE, winner of 43 races, $1,749,869, Champion North American
Sire 1972. Sire of over 70 stakes winners incl. ARTAIUS, TARGOWICE
(a leading sire), BALDRIC, KING PELLINORE, APALACHEE, FLIRTING
AROUND etc.
Out of STYLISH PATTERN, dam of 7 winners, including ARTAIUS,
EMBROIDERY (Ascot 1,000 Guineas Trial Gr III), STYLISH GENIE (Fairway
Fun Stakes and $49,195) Her dam won at 3 years in England and bred 5 winners
including SPRING DOUBLE (22 wins, $438,317, Pimlico Futurity, etc.; stakes
sire in USA) and ARTHURIAN (Churchill Stakes, Ascot). Traces to PRETTY
POLLY.

Stands at: Airlie Stud, Lucan, Co. Dublin.
Apply: Airlie Stud, Lucan, Co. Dublin
(tel: Dublin 280267; telex 31049 TROG E. I.)

BALLAD ROCK

CHAMPION IRISH SPRINTER. Winner of 5 races from 10 starts including Mat Gallagher Sprint Stakes, Greenlands Stakes and Rockingham Hcap (by 2l car 9–12) also 2nd (btn head by Solinus) in Ballyogan Stakes, Gr 3.

Racehorses of 1978: 'After Ascot Ballad Rock continued to show form of a high order. A month later he contested the Matt Gallagher Sprint Stakes . . . Nothing had the slightest chance with Ballad Rock, even though he started slowly; he burst five lengths clear in the final furlong'.

Stud Record: 71.4% winners to runners with his first crop in 1982. Principal winners CHIEF SINGER (Coventry Stks, Gr 2 1983), PRINCE SPY (also Gr placed), SOLAR ROCK (also 2nd Richmond Stks Gr 2), FIERY CELT, MORE CANDY, etc.

			Nasrullah
		Bold Ruler	Miss Disco
	Bold Lad (Ire)		Democratic
	(b 1964)	Barn Pride	Fair Alycia
BALLAD ROCK			Buisson Ardent
(ch 1974)		Roan Rocket	Farandole II
	True Rocket		Hill Gail
	(b 1967)		Arctic Rullah
		True Course	

Sire: **BOLD LAD** (Ire) won 5 races incl Middle Park Stks, Gr 1, and was champion 2-y-o in England and Ireland. Sire of Waterloo (1,000 Guineas), **Boldboy, Daring Display, Persian Bold,** etc. Dam **TRUE ROCKET** (Timeform 116) won 5 races at 2 yrs and is dam of 5 winners. Her yearling of 1982 made 215,000 gns.

Stands at: Loughtown Stud, Donadea, Co. Kildare

Apply: Airlie Stud, Lucan, Co. Dublin (tel: Dublin 280267; telex 31049 TROG E.1.)

CUT ABOVE

CUT ABOVE WON THE Gr. 1 ST. LEGER (BEATING SHERGAR, GLINT OF GOLD, BUSTOMI), the Gr. 3 White Rose Stakes (by 3 lengths) and £124,066. He was also 2nd Gr. 1 Irish Sweeps Derby (to Shergar, beating Kirtling, Dance Bid, etc.) and Gr. 3 Horris Hill Stakes (btn ¾l); and 3rd Gr. 2 Geoffrey Freer Stakes. **Timeform 130.**
Stud Record
Cut Above retired to stud in 1982. Full 1982 and 1983.

			Darius
	High Top	Derring-Do	Sipsey Bridge
	(br 1969)		Vimy
CUT ABOVE		Camenae	Madrilene
(b. 1978)			Aureole
	Cutle	Saint Crespin III	Neocracy
	(ch 1963)		Donatello II
		Cutter	Felucca

By **HIGH TOP**, 5 races, £61,322, including Gr. 1 2,000 Guineas, Gr. 1 Observer Gold Cup. A leading European sire, including Top Ville (Gr. 1 French Derby), Cut Above, Circus Ring (unbeaten, Gr. 2 Lowther Stakes), Triple First, etc.
Out of **CUTLE**, 2 races, at 3 years. Dam of 5 winners, including Sharp Edge (Gr. 1 Irish 2,000 Guineas, sire of group and stakes winners in England and a leading sire of 2-y-o's in Australia with his first crop in 1981). She is half-sister to the sires Torpid, Sloop and Tepukei. Her dam won Gr. 1 Yorkshire Oaks and is half-sister to the dams of Hermes (outstanding sire in New Zealand), Eagle (classic sire in Japan), Mariner (a leading sire in Australia), etc. Family of Bireme, Buoy, Sea Anchor, Shoot A Line, etc.
Stands at: Dowdstown Stud, Maynooth, Co. Kildare
Apply: Airlie Stud, Lucan,
Co. Dublin (tel. Dublin 280267; telex 31049 TROG E.1.) *Airlie..*

DARA MONARCH

A LEADING EUROPEAN MILER, brilliant winner of Airlie/Coolmore Irish 2,000 Gns., Gr 1, and St. James's Palace Stakes, Royal Ascot, Gr 2, also won Anglesey Stakes, Gr 3, at 2 years and McCairns Trial Stakes, Gr 3, at 3 years.

Racehorses of 1982: 'It says a great deal for Dara Monarch that he should so quickly go so far clear of so many horses in a classic . . . . he looked far and away the best in the race passing the post (Airlie/Coolmore Irish 2,000 Guineas) . . . . an exhilarating performance by the winner (St James's Palace Stakes)'. **Timeform 128.**

Stud Record   Dara Monarch retired to stud in 1983.   FULL.

DARA MONARCH (b. 1979)	Realm (b 1967)	Princely Gift	Nasrullah Blue Gem
		Quita II	Lavandin Eos
	Sardara (ch 1969)	Alcide	Alycidon Chenille
		Plaza	Persian Gulf Wild Success

Sire **REALM** 5 races, incl. Gr I July Cup, Gr 3 Diadem Stakes, Gr 3 Challenge Stakes. Leading First Crop Sire, he is responsible for group-winners, **Dara Monarch, Hatta, Another Realm, Royal Boy, Light of Realm.**   Dam **SARDARA** 3 races and stakes-placed; half-sister to **INTERMEZZO** (Gr I St. Leger; successful sire in Japan).   Family of **Pharos, Fairway, Raffingora, Sandford Lad, Sweet Revenge, Alcibiades, Alcimedes,** etc.

Stands at: Grangewilliam Stud, Maynooth, Co Kildare

Apply: Airlie Stud, Lucan, Co. Dublin
(tel. Dublin 280267; telex 31049 TROG E.1.)

Airlie..

ELA-MANA-MOU

EUROPE'S RECORD-BREAKING MIDDLE-DISTANCE CHAMPION 1980.
In 1980 Ela-Mana-Mou won the King George VI and Queen Elizabeth Diamond Stakes,
Gr 1, Coral Eclipse Stakes, Gr 1, Prince of Wales's Stakes, Gr 2 and Earl of Sefton
Stakes, Gr 3, earning £236,332 in first-prize money, a record for a 4-y-o trained in England.
In a splendid career he also won Royal Lodge Stakes, Gr 2, (allotted 9-2 2-y-o Free
Handicap, ahead of Troy), King Edward VII Stakes, Gr 2, and was also 2nd Grand Prix
de Saint-Cloud, Gr 1, 3rd Prix de l'Arc de Triomphe, Gr 1, 3rd King George VI and
Queen Elizabeth Diamond Stakes, Gr 1, 4th Derby, Gr 1. **Timeform 132.**

Stud Record
Ela-Mana-Mou retired to stud in 1981; his first crop yearlings made up to IR 330,000 gns.

		Petingo	Petition
	Pitcairn		Alcazar
	(b 1971)	Border Bounty	Bounteous
ELA-MANA-MOU			B Flat
(b.c. 1976)		High Hat	Hyperion
	Rose Bertin		Madonna
	(ch 1970)	Wide Awake	Major Portion
			Wake Island

By **PITCAIRN**, Champion Sire 1980—also sire of CAIRN ROUGE (Champion
Stakes, Gr 1, Goffs Irish 1,000 Guineas, Gr 1) Flighting (Princess Royal Stakes, Gr 3) and
pattern-placed KAHAILA, PETRINGO and BONNIE ISLE.
Out of **ROSE BERTIN**, winner at 3 years. Her dam WIDE AWAKE won the Ebbisham
Stakes and was 3rd Nell Gwyn Stakes, Gr 3, traces to BELLE OF ALL, champion filly
of 1950 and 1951, 1,000 Guineas, Gr 1, Cheveley Park Stakes, Gr 1, etc.

**Stands at: Simmonstown Stud, Celbridge, Co.
Kildare, Ireland.
Apply: Airlie Stud, Lucan,
Co. Dublin, Ireland. Tel: Dublin 280267 or
281548. Telex: 31049. Trog E.I.**

HABITAT

CHAMPION EUROPEAN MILER OF 1969 when winner of Prix du Moulin de Long-champ, Gr 1, Lockinge S, Gr 2, Prix Quincey, Gr 3 and Wills Mile, Gr 3. **Timeform 134**
Stud Record
Champion sire of 2-y-o's 4 times and Leading Sire (individ. winners and races won) twice
Principal winners: HABIBTI (July Cup Gr 1, Prix de l'Abbaye Gr 1), FLYING WATER
(1,000 Guineas, Gr 1, Champion Stakes, Gr 1, Prix Jacques le Marois, Gr 1), ROSE BOWL
(Champion Stakes, Gr 1), DOUBLE FORM (King's Stand Gr 1, Prix de l'Abbaye Gr 1),
MARWELL (King's Stand Gr 1, July Cup Gr 1, Prix de l'Abbaye Gr 1, Cheveley Park
Gr 1), SIGY (Prix de l'Abbaye de Longchamp Gr 1), HABITONY (Santa Anita Derby,
Gr 1), HABAT (Middle Park Stakes, Gr 1), STEEL HEART (Middle Park Stakes, Gr 1),
HITTITE GLORY (Middle Park Stakes, Gr 1, Flying Childers Stakes, Gr 1), HOT
SPARK (Flying Childers Stakes, Gr 1), HOMING, CHALON, DALSAAN, STRIGIDA,
HARD FOUGHT etc.   Yearlings have made up to 350,000 gns.

		Turn-to	Royal Charger
	Sir Gaylord		Source Sucree
	(b 1959)		Princequillo
HABITAT		Somethingroyal	Imperatrice
(bay 1966)		Occupy	Bull Dog
	Little Hut		Miss Bunting
	(b 1952)		Challenger II
		Savage Beauty	Khara

By SIR GAYLORD winner of 10 races, Sire of SIR IVOR (Champion at 2 and 3 years,
winning Epsom Derby, Washington International, etc., a leading sire).   Out of LITTLE
HUT also dam of NORTHFIELDS (Louisiana Derby, classic sire with his first crop) and
GUEST ROOM (SW of $172,954).

Stands at: Grangewilliam Stud, Maynooth, Co. Kildare.
Apply: Airlie Stud, Lucan, Co. Dublin.
(tel. Dublin 280267; telex 31049 TROG E.I.)

1015

HENBIT

BRITAIN'S CHAMPION MIDDLE-DISTANCE THREE-YEAR-OLD 1980. Henbit won the Gr. 1 Derby (beating Master Willie, Pelerin, Hello Gorgeous, Nikoli, Water Mill, Tyrnavos, Monteverdi), the Gr. 3 Chester Vase (beating Light Cavalry) and the Gr. 3 Classic Trial Stakes (beating Master Willie, Huguenot etc.). He was also 4th in the Gr. 1 Dewhurst Stakes (beating Final Straw). **Henbit cracked his off-fore cannon bone when winning the Derby.**

Racehorses of 1980: 'Held onto his lead (in the Derby) extremely gamely.... There is little doubt that Henbit sustained his injury at the point he hung right; how much it affected his performance is impossible to say.... He must have been hampered to some extent'. **Timeform 130.**

Stud Record
Henbit retired to stud in 1982. Excellent first crop foals.

HENBIT (b. 1977)	Hawaii (b 1964)	Utrillo
		Ethane
	Chateaucreek (ch 1970)	Chateaugay
		Mooncreek

Toulouse Lautrec
Urbinella
Mehrali
Ethyl
Swaps
Banquet Bell
Sailor
Ouija

By HAWAII, won 21 races in South Africa and USA, $326,963, Gr. 1 Man O'War S., Gr. 1 United Nations H., etc. Champion Grass Horse. Also Champion at 2, 3 & 4 in S. Africa. Also sire of Hunza Dancer, Hawaiian Sound, Sun and Snow (Kentucky Oaks), Triple Crown, etc.

Out of CHATEAUCREEK won 6 races, $24,203 at 2 & 3 years, including Delta Queen H.; Henbit is her second foal. His grandam bred 5 winners and his third dam was a stakes winner and dam of Ouija Board (National Stallion S., etc. at 2; sire); grandam of Limit to Reason (Gr. 1 Champagne S.; sire of stakes winners).

Stands at: Airlie Stud, Lucan, Co. Dublin
Apply: Airlie Stud, Lucan, Co. Dublin
(tel. Dublin 280267; telex 31049 TROG E.1.)

Airlie..

PRINCE BEE

WINNER OF 5 RACES AND £132,214 including Great Voltigeur Stakes, Gr 2, Prix Niel, Gr 3, and Gordon Stakes, Gr 3, and second in Irish Sweeps Derby, Gr 1, Coronation Cup, Gr 1, Dee Stakes, Gr 3, and fourth in Champion Stakes, Gr 1.
Racehorses of 1981: 'Prince Bee, a strong, attractive colt and a good mover, acts on any going, and is genuine.' **Timeform 128** (in 1980 and 1981).
Stud Record Prince Bee retired to stud in 1983. FULL.

PRINCE BEE (b 1977)	Sun Prince (ch 1969)	Princely Gift	Nasrullah Blue Gem
		Costa Sola	Worden II Sunny Cove
	Honerko (b 1968)	Tanerko	Tantiéme La Divine
		Be A Honey	Honey's Alibi Neola

Sire **SUN PRINCE**, won 4 races, £47,644, including Gr 1 Prix Robert-Papin, Gr 2 St, James's Palace Stakes, Gr 2 Coventry Stakes, Gr 3 Queen Anne Stakes. Successful sire. including group winners **Prince Bee, Alia, Cistus, Royal Harmony, Sportscaster, Sungazer, Outpace,** etc. Dam **HONERKO**, stakes-winner; dam of **Balteus** (Gr 3 Prix Saint-Roman) and **Prince Bee,** her first two foals. Her grandam, **Neola,** winner of 5 races, 2nd Gr 1 Cheveley Park Stakes, is own-sister to Champion 2-year-old **Neolight,** and half-sister to Champion **Tudor Minstrel** (a leading sire, including Champions **Sing Sing, Tudor Melody** and **What A Treat**). The next dam is half-sister to Champion sire **Fair Trial** . Family of **Nasrullah, Royal Charger, Kalamoun, Shergar, On The House, Abernant, Kashmir II, Nishapour,** etc.

Stands at: Dowdstown Stud, Maynooth, Co Kildare
Apply: Airlie Stud, Lucan, Co. Dublin
(tel Dublin 280267; telex 31049 TROG E.1.)

TUMBLE WIND

WINNER OF 9 RACES FROM 2-4 YEARS INCLUDING HOLLYWOOD DERBY
Gr 1 BY SIX LENGTHS. Also won Argonaut Stks Gr 2, San Luis Obispo Hcp Gr 2,
Westchester Stks Gr 2, Haggin Stks Gr 2 and $249,175.
Stud Record: Tumble Wind sired the winners of 126 races and $638,895 in the States
and since coming to Ireland his winners include: HORAGE (10 races, £134,648 including
St James's Palace Stks Gr 2, Gimcrack Stks Gr 2, etc.), DRUMALIS (Italian 2,000
Guineas, Gr 1), NIGHT OF WIND (Queen Mary Stks Gr 2), TUMBLEDOWNWIND
(Gimcrack Stks Gr 2, 4th 2,000 Guineas Gr 1), MILLINGDALE LILLIE (Fred Darling
Stks Gr 3, 4th 1,000 Guineas Gr 1), COOLINEY PRINCE (McCairns Trial Gr 3),
PEPPONE (Criterium di Roma Gr 3), etc.

TUMBLE WIND (b 1964)	Restless Wind (b 1956)	Windy City II	Wyndham
			Staunton
		Lump Sugar	Bull Lea
			Sugar Run
	Easy Stages (b 1953)	Endeavour II	British Empire
			Himalaya
		Saturday Off	Kiev
			Mexican Tea

Sire. **RESTLESS WIND**, won 9 races £328,723 including National Stallion Stakes,
Arlington Futurity, Washington Park Futurity. A leading sire in North America
including **On Your Mark** (a leading sire of 2-y-o's). **Windjammer** (a leading sire of
2-y-o's) and **Process Shot** (champion 2-y-o filly). Dam **EASY STAGES** won 2 races and
dam of winners. Own sister to **Gone Fishin** (7 wins, 3rd Preakness) and to the dam of **Hul
A Hul** (successful sire).

Stands at: Loughtown Stud, Donadea, Co. Kildare

Apply: Airlie Stud, Lucan, Co. Dublin
(tel: Dublin 280267; telex 31049 TROG E.I.)

1018

COOLMORE STALLIONS 1984

BE MY GUEST ● CAERLEON ● CROFTER
DALSAAN ● GLENSTAL ● GODSWALK
GOLDEN FLEECE ● HELLO GORGEOUS
KINGS LAKE ● LAST FANDANGO ● LOMOND
PAS DE SEUL ● THATCHING ● TRY MY BEST
HOME GUARD ● LONDON BELLS

Bob Lanigan or Christy Grassick **Coolmore Stud,** Fethard, Co.
Tipperary, Tel: Clonmel (052) 31298 (office) (052) 31385 (C. Grassick, home)
Telex: 80695.
Tom Gaffney **Castle Hyde Stud,** Fermoy, Co. Cork,
Tel: Fermoy (025) 31689/31966 (office) (025) 32128 (T. Gaffney, home)
Telex: 28470.
Tommy Stack or Niall Power **Longfield Stud,** Cashel, Co. Tipperary,
Tel: Thurles (0504) 42234 (office) (062) 54129 (T. Stack, home)
Telex: 33003.
David Magnier or Joe Hernon **Grange Stud,** Fermoy, Co. Cork,
Tel: Fermoy (025) 31966 (office) 31465 (D. Magnier, home),
(022) 26275 (J. Hernon, home) Telex: 28470.

BE MY GUEST

Winner of 4 races at 2 and 3 years (6-8.5f.).
WON GR. 2 Waterford Crystal Mile, Goodwood **Gr. 3** Blue Riband Trial Stakes, Epsom. *(". . . a scintillating performance." Timeform)*. **Gr. 3** Desmond Stakes, Curragh. **Timeform rating 126.** (Racehorses of 1977). **Dam won 11 races and $321,608** including Alabama Stakes. **Gr. 1** and is half-sister to the dam of **GOLDEN FLEECE**, Horse of the Year, and unbeaten winner of Epsom Derby, **Gr. 1**. Retired to stud in 1978 and **sire of the winners of 139 races and over £1 million, with his first three crops** (to 1/10/83).
CHAMPION FIRST SEASON SIRE 1981
CHAMPION TRIPLE CLASSIC SIRE 1982

SIRE OF 37 INDIVIDUAL WINNERS IN 1983
Principal winners:
ASSERT (**Gr. 1** Irish Sweeps Derby **Gr. 1** Prix du Jockey Club, **Gr. 2** Gallinule Stakes, **Gr. 2** Beresford Stakes).
ON THE HOUSE (**Gr. 1** One Thousand Guineas, **Gr. 1** Sussex Stakes, 2nd **Gr. 1** Cheveley Park Stakes).
LUTH ENCHANTEE (**Gr. 1** Prix Jacques le Marois, **Gr. 1** Prix du Moulin, **Gr. 2** Prix d'Astarte).
WHAT A GUEST (**Gr. 2** Prix Eugene Adam, **Gr. 3** Prix de la Jonchere).
ANFIELD (**Gr. 3** Ashford Castle Stakes, **Gr. 3** Railway Stakes).
FAITH GUEST (**Gr. 3** Premio Primi Passi, **Gr. 3** Criterium Nazionale).
BE MY VALENTINE (St Hugh's Stakes), **PREGO.** etc.
His yearling made up to IR£168,000 in 1983.

BE MY GUEST (USA) ch. 1974	Northern Dancer	Nearctic	Nearco
			Lady Angela
		Natalma	Native Dancer
			Almahmoud
	What A Treat	Tudor Minstrel	Owen Tudor
			Sansonnet
		Rare Treat	Stymie
			Rare Perfume

COOLMORE   **Stands at COOLMORE STUD**

CAERLEON

Unbeaten at 2. Rated second on Irish Free Handicap.
Winner of 4 races £230,894 at 2 and 3 years (6-12f.).
WON Gr. 1 French Derby *(by 3 lengths, beating L'Emigrant, Lovely Dancer, Esprit du Nord)*.
Gr. 1 Benson & Hedges Gold Cup *(beating Electric, John French, Prima Voce, Gorytus)* **Gr. 3** Ballsbridge-Tattersalls Anglesey Stakes
LR Tyros Stakes *(by 2 lengths on debut)*
2nd Gr. 1 Irish Sweeps Derby *(beating Teenoso, Wassl, Carlingford Castle)*.
Timeform rating 139. (19/9/83).
"very attractive, medium-sized, compact colt . . . put up a top-class performance when beating L'Emigrant by 3 lengths in 12-runner Prix du Jockey-Club . . . put up another fine effort in 8-runner Benson & Hedges Gold Cup . . ."

Brother to **VISION** (1983 Pilgrim Stakes, **Gr. 3,** Aqueduct). By triple crown winner and Horse of the Year **NIJINSKY,** sire of 67 stakes winners, including **Golden Fleece, Kings Lake, Ile de Bourbon, Solford,** etc.
Out of **FORESEER** own-sister to **Royal Glint** (**Gr. 1** winner of $1,004,816), FORESEER won 3 races and placed second in **Gr. 2** Santa Ynez Stakes. Dam of **CAERLEON,** stakes winner **Palmistry** and classic placed **Good Thyne.** Her dam is Champion 2-year-old filly **Regal Gleam.**

			Nearctic
		Northern Dancer	Natalma
	Nijinsky		Bull Page
CAERLEON		Flaming Page	Flaring Top
(USA) b. 1980		Round Table	Princequillo
	Foreseer		Knight's Daughter
		Regal Gleam	Hail to Reason
			Miz Carol

CROFTER

Stakes winner of 3 consecutive races (7-8f.) at 3 years and placed second twice from 5 starts.
2nd Gr. 1 Prix de la Foret, Longchamp *(beaten 1 length by Horse of the Year Moorestyle at level weights and beating triple champion Kilijaro).*
Gr. 3 Prix Perth, Saint- Cloud
By Champion sire and sire of sires **HABITAT,** responsible for **Hard Fought, Steel Heart, Homing, Hot Spark** as well as the fillies **Marwell, Flying Water, Rose Bowl** and **Habibti.**
Dam, **MARIE CURIE,** group placed producer of 3 winners from her first 3 foals. She is half-sister t. **Mariel (Gr. 2** Pretty Polly Stakes, second **Gr. 1** Irish 1,000 Guineas; dam of **Sarah Siddons, Gr. 1** Irish 1,000 Guineas, herself dam of **Seymour Hicks).** 2nd dam multiple group winning half-sister to **Ragusa.**

A yearling by **CROFTER** fetched **420,000 francs** at the Deauville Select Sale in 1983, and another brought **26,000 gns** at the Tattersalls Highflyer Sales. Two o. his yearlings at Goffs were bought by B.B.A. (Ireland) for **42,000 gns** and Richard O'Gorman for **39,000 gns.**

CROFTER ch. 1977	Habitat	Sir Gaylord	Turn-To
			Somethingroyal
		Little Hut	Occupy
			Savage Beauty
	Marie Curie	Exbury	Le Haar
			Greensward
		Ela Marita	Red God
			Fantan II

COOLMORE

Stands at **GRANGE STU**

DALSAAN

Winner of 5 races, £63,189, from 2 to 4 years (6-7.3f.).

WON Gr. 3 Hungerford Stakes, Newbury *(by 2½ lengths, beating Star Pastures)*,
Gold Shield Windows Trophy Haydock *(beating Known Fact)*.

2nd Gr. 3 Challenge Stakes, Newmarket.

4th Gr. 1 Sussex Stakes, Goodwood, **Gr. 2** St. James's Palace Stakes, Royal Ascot, **Gr. 3** Queen Anne Stakes, Royal Ascot.

NEVER OUT OF THE FIRST FOUR.

Timeform rating 125. (Racehorses of 1981).

By Champion sire **HABITAT**, responsible for **Hard Fought, Steel Heart, Homing, Hot Spark,** as well as the fillies **Marwell, Flying Water, Rose Bowl** and **Habibti. Out of a winner of the French 1,000 Guineas, Gr. 1.** Grandam, a half-sister to **FLOSSY** (Champion Stakes, **Gr. 1**), is from the family of **DERRING-DO, HETHERSETT, ROYAL PREROGATIVE** (classic sire in South Africa, 1981), **HARD FOUGHT, PROVIDENTIAL.**

		Sir Gaylord	Turn-To
	Habitat		Somethingroyal
		Little Hut	Occupy
DALSAAN			Savage Beauty
b. 1977		Kashmir II	Tudor Melody
	Dumka		Queen of Speed
		Faizebad	Prince Taj
			Floralie

GLENSTAL

Winner of 3 races, £29,164, at 2 and 3 years (6.3-9f.).
WON Gr. 2 National Stakes (*beating Lomond, Burslem*), **Gr. 3** Prix Daphnis (*beating Saint Cyrien*).
Timeform "medium-sized, attractive colt; good walker".
Sire, Champion **NORTHERN DANCER,** the world's leading stallion with 100 stakes winners, including **Nijinsky, The Minstrel, Lyphard, Be My Guest, Nureyev, Lomond, Shareef Dancer.**
Dam, Champion Irish 2-year-old **CLOONLARA,** is half-sister to European Champion **Kings Lake** (by a son of Northern Dancer) and Triple Group winner **Salmon Leap** (by Northern Dancer).
"The best bred horse standing at stud today" — *Vincent O'Brien*

GLENSTAL (USA) b. 1980	Northern Dancer	Nearctic	Nearco
			Lady Angela
		Natalma	Native Dancer
			Almahmoud
	Cloonlara	Sir Ivor	Sir Gaylord
			Attica
		Fish Bar	Baldric II
			Fisherman's Wharf

COOLMORE   **Stands at LONGFIELD STUD**

GOLDEN FLEECE

Top rated three-year-old in his category in Europe.
Unbeaten winner of 4 races, £162,255, at 2 and 3 years (8-12f.)
WON Gr. 1 Epsom Derby, Epsom *(beating Touching Wood, Silver Hawk, Persepolis)*,
Gr. 2 Nijinsky Stakes, Leopardstown *(by 2½ lengths from Assert)*.
Gr. 2 Sean Graham Ballymoss Stakes, Curragh.
Timeform rating 133. (Racehorses of 1982).
NIJINSKY, sire of 67 stakes winners, including dual European Champion **Ile de Bourbon, Kings** Lake, Green Dancer, Caerleon, Princesse Lida, Night Alert, Solford etc.

Golden Fleece is half-brother to Stakes winner **Office Wife** from an unraced half-sister to Champion 3-Year-Old Filly **What a Treat,** herself the dam of Champion Sire **BE MY GUEST.**

			Nearctic
		Northern Dancer	Natalma
	Nijinsky		Bull Page
GOLDEN		Flaming Page	Flaring Top
FLEECE (USA)			Vienna
b. 1979		Vaguely Noble	Noble Lassie
	Exotic Treat		Stymie
		Rare Treat	Rare Perfume

COOLMORE   Stands at COOLMORE STUD

HELLO GORGEOUS

Winner of 4 races, £129,647, at 2 and 3 years (6-10½f.).
WON Gr. 1 William Hill Futurity Doncaster (*beating In Fijar*)
Gr. 2 Royal Lodge Stakes, Ascot
Gr. 2 Mecca-Dante Stakes, York (*beating Master Willie, Tyrnavos*)
Ballymore Stakes, York (*beating Millingdale Lillie*)
2nd Gr. 1 Eclipse Stakes, Sandown Park
(*beaten ¾ length by Ela-Mana-Mou*)
Heathorn Stakes, Newmarket
Rated 9st. 4lb. on Free Handicap at 2 years, above Henbit, Shoot A Line, Quick as Lightning, Tyrnavos, Master Willie, Night Alert, Moorestyle, etc.
Rated 9st. 9lb. on Free Handicap at 3 years, above Hard Fought, Final Straw, Cairn Rouge, etc.
Timeform rating 128. (Racehorses of 1980).
"*. . . attractive colt . . . thoroughly genuine.*"
MR PROSPECTOR — Leading U.S. Sprinter and sire. Sire of 1982 Horse of the Year **Conquistador Cielo** and 1982 Eclipse Award Winner **Gold Beauty,** as well as **It's In The Air** (Champion 2-y-o), Group 1 winners **Fappiano** and **Miswaki,** and the sensational first season U.S. stallion **Northern Prospect.**
HELLO GORGEOUS — Sire of **European record priced yearling** (1,550,000 gns) at Tattersalls Highflyer Sales.

			Native Dance
		Raise a Native	Raise You
	Mr. Prospector		Nashua
HELLO		Gold Digger	Sequence
GORGEOUS			Jet Pilot
(USA) ch. 1977		Jet Jewel	Crepe Myrtle
	Bonny Jet		Mr. Busher
		Bonny Bush	San Bonita

COOLMORE   **Stands at LONGFIELD STUD**

KINGS LAKE

Winner of 5 races, £147,847, at 2 and 3 years (6-10f.).
EUROPEAN CHAMPION MILER WON Gr. 1 Irish 2,000 Guineas, Curragh (*beating To-Agori-Mou, Dance Bid*)
Gr. 1 Sussex Stakes, Goodwood (*beating To-Agori-Mou, Belmont Bay, In Fijar*)
Gr. 1 Joe McGrath Memorial Stakes, Leopardstown (*beating Erins Isle, Blue Wind, Arctique Royale*)
2nd Gr. 2 St. James's Palace Stakes, Royal Ascot
3rd Gr. 1 Prix Jacques le Marois, Deauville
Gr. 2 Ballymoss Stakes, Curragh
Timeform rating 133. (Racehorses of 1981). *"neat, very attractive colt . . . an extremely genuine and courageous performer who raced with tremendous zest."*
His sire triple crown winner and Horse of the Year **NIJINSKY,** is already responsible for over 67 stakes winners, including 1982 Epsom Derby winner **Golden Fleece**, leading Sire **Green Dancer, Caerleon, Princesse Lida, Niniski, Czaravich, Solford,** etc.
Dam, stakes winner **FISH BAR,** is also dam of Champion 2-year-old **Cloonlara.**
KINGS LAKE is three parts brother to **SALMON LEAP** (Nijinsky Stakes, **Gr. 2**; Pacemaker Whitehall Stakes, **Gr. 3**; H.M. Hartigan Tetrarch Stakes, **Gr. 3**; 4th Epsom Derby, **Gr. 1**)

			Nearctic
	Nijinsky	Northern Dancer	Natalma
KINGS	(CAN)	Flaming Page	Bull Page
LAKE (USA)			Flaring Top
b. 1978	Fish Bar	Baldric II	Round Table
			Two Cities
		Fishermans	Alycidon
		Wharf	Herringbone

COOLMORE   **Stands at COOLMORE STUD**

LAST FANDANGO

Winner of 3 races, £62,985, at 3 and 4 years (7-8½f.).
WON Gr. 3 Ladbroke Blue Riband Trial Stakes, Epsom.
L.R. John of Gaunt Stakes, Haydock Park.
2nd Gr. 1 Airlie/Coolmore Irish 2,000 Guineas, Curragh (*beaten sht. hd. by Nikoli, beating Final Straw, Posse*),
Gr. 3 Queen Anne Stakes, Royal Ascot (*beaten a neck*).
3rd Gr. 2 St. James's Palace Stakes, Royal Ascot (*behind Posse and Final Straw*).
4th Gr. 2 Waterford Crystal Mile, Goodwood.

Timeform rating 125. (Racehorses of 1980).
"*. . . well made colt . . . races with tremendous enthusiasm.*"
WELSH GAME, group-placed winner of 5 races in France. From the immediate family of **MOUNT HAGEN, AMERIGO, HORNBEAM.**

		Forli	Aristophanes
	Gay Fandango		Trevisa
		Gay Violin	Sir Gaylord
LAST			Blue Violin
FANDANGO		Pall Mall	Palestine
ch. 1977			Malapert
	Welsh Game		Abernant
		Nantgarw	Lynsted

LOMOND

Winner of 3 races, £99,182, and 2nd 3 years (6-8f.).

WON Gr. 1 2,000 Guineas (*beating Tolomeo, Diesis, Gorytus, Vassl*).

L.R. Gladness Stakes.

2nd   Gr. 1 Airlie/Coolmore Irish 2000 Guineas (*beaten ¾ length, beating Crystal Glitters*).

3rd   Gr. 2 National Stakes.

Timeform rating 135 (19/9/83)
Medium-sized, sturdy colt . . . put up a top-class performance when convincingly winning 2000 Guineas . . ."

Sire, Champion **NORTHERN DANCER,** the world's leading stallion with 100 stakes winners, including, **Nijinsky, The Minstrel, Lyphard, Be My Guest, Nureyev, Shareef Dancer,** etc.

Dam, stakes winner **MY CHARMER,** dam of **LOMOND** and **SEATTLE SLEW** (U.S.A. triple crown, Champion first crop sire in U.S.A., 1983. His first two crops include Champion **Landaluce** and Gr. 1 winners **Slew o' Gold, Seattle Song, Swale** and **Slewpy**).

LOMOND (USA) b. 1980	Northern Dancer	Nearctic	Nearco
			Lady Angela
		Natalma	Native Dancer
			Almahmoud
	My Charmer	Poker	Round Table
			Glamour
		Fair Charmer	Jet Action
			Myrtle Charm

PAS DE SEUL

Winner of 4 races at 2 and 3 years (6.3-7.3f.).
WON Gr. 1 Prix de la Foret, Longchamp *(beating The Wonder, Tres Gate, Dara Monarch, etc.)*
Gr. 3 Hungerford Stakes, Newbury,
Gr. 3 Prix Eclipse, Saint- Cloud.
Timeform rating: 133 (Racehorses of 1982) *"he was a top class horse, probably as good as any at his distance trained outside France."*
By Champion Racehorse and Champion sire **MILL REEF**, whose progeny include the Group 1 winners **SHIRLEY HEIGHTS** (now a leading sire), **ACAMAS, FAIRY FOOTSTEPS, GLINT OF GOLD, DIAMOND**

SHOAL, WASSL etc.
MILL REEF is currently the leading sire standing in England in 1983 (1st October).
Dam, **THEREBY,** won 3 races at 2 and 3 years and is dam of 7 winners from her first 9 foals, including **PAS DE SEUL** and stakes winner **CAPTIVE DREAM.** She is half sister to 4 winners, including Group placed **Catch Penny, Costmary** (14 races) and the dam of **Girandole. FIRST FOALS 198**

PAS DE SEUL b. 1979			
	Mill Reef	Never Bend	Nasrullah
			Lalun
		Milan Mill	Princequillo
			Virginia Water
	Thereby	Star Moss	Mossborough
			Star of France
		Besides	Naucide
			Bees Knees

THATCHING

EUROPEAN CHAMPION SPRINTER
Winner of 4 races at 3 and 4 years.
WON **Gr. 1** July Cup,
Newmarket *(beating Vaigly Great, Greenland Park, Devon Ditty, Absalom, etc.)*,
Gr. 3 Cork and Orrery Stakes, Royal Ascot *(by 4 lengths)*,
Gr. 3 Duke of York Stakes.
Also won **Gr. 2** William Hill Sprint Championship *(beating Ahonoora, Double Form, etc., but disqualified)*.
Timeform rating 131. (Racehorses of 1979).
Dam Group placed winner of three races (**Timeform 121**).

Own-brother to **Golden Thatch** (Greenlands Stakes, **Gr. 3,** Ballyogan Stakes, **Gr. 3**). Half-brother to **Ashford Castle** (won over $100,000, in USA).
Family of **Reform, Val de Loir, Apalachee, King Pellinore, Thatch, Nureyev,** etc.
Sire of 12 winners of 16 races and £57,248 including:
HANDSTAND (also 3rd Laurent Perrier Champagne Stakes, **Gr. 2**)
HIT THE HEIGHTS, SO FINE, SUSA STEEL.
Sire of the top priced IR380,000 guinea yearling at Goffs Invitation Sales.

			Aristophanes
		Forli	Trevisa
	Thatch		Nantallah
		Thong	Rough Shod
THATCHING			Owen Tudor
b. 1975		Abernant	Rustom Mahal
	Abella		Darius
		Darrica	Erica Fragrans

TRY MY BEST

CHAMPION EUROPEAN TWO-YEAR-OLD
Winner of 4 races at 2 and 3 years from 5 starts.
WON **Gr. 1** William Hill Dewhurst Stakes, Newmarket **Gr. 3** Larkspur Stakes, Leopardstown **Gr. 3** Vauxhall Trial Stakes, Phoenix Park **Timeform rating 130p.** (Racehorses of 1977). Try My Best is own brother to Champion **El Gran Senor** (4 races at 2, 1983, William Hill Dewhurst Stakes **Gr. 1.** BBA (Ireland)/Goffs National Stakes **Gr. 2**, P.J. Prendergast Railway Stakes, **Gr. 3**) and half-brother to unbeaten **Solar** (3 races at 2 years, including Railway Stakes, **Gr. 3** and Park Stakes, **Gr. 3**). His dam is half-sister to **Blush With Pride** (6 races, $536,807, Kentucky Oaks, **Gr. 1,** Santa Susana Stakes, **Gr. 1**, 1982), Champion two-year-old **Malinowski** and Group winner **Gielgud**.

In 1982 and 1983, with very few runners, **sire of the winners**
POLISHED SILVER (winner of 4 races, including Somerville Tattersall Stakes, at 2 years and placed fourth in Guardian Classic Trial, **Gr. 3**, at 3 years.
TREASURE TROVE (Birdcatcher Nursery, Naas, also third in Curragh Stakes, **Gr. 3**, 1982).
CHIAVARI (2 races at 3 years, 1983, also placed third in Gallinule Stakes, **Gr. 2** and second in Pacemaker Whitehall Stakes, **Gr. 3**).
ATTEMPT (2 races and placed second 4 times from 7 starts at 2 years, 1983), **SHERIFF MUIR** and **HE WHO DARES.**
LEADING FIRST SEASON SIRE IN 3 CATEGORIES 1982.
His yearlings made up to IR£200,000 gns. in 1983.

			Nearco
		Nearctic	Lady Angela
	Northern Dancer		Native Dancer
TRY MY BEST		Natalma	Almahmoud
(USA) b. 1975			Tom Fool
		Buckpasser	Busanda
	Sex Appeal		Traffic Judge
		Best in Show	Stolen Hour

GODSWALK

CHAMPION SPRINTER
Winner of 8 races at 2 and 3 years (5-6f.).
WON **Gr. 1** King's Stand Stakes, Royal Ascot **Gr. 3** Norfolk Stakes, Royal Ascot **Gr. 3** Ballyogan Stakes, Curragh Airlie/Coolmore Castle Hyde Stakes, Curragh Waterford Testimonial Stakes, Curragh Marble Hill Stakes, Curragh *Top 2-y-o colt on 1976 Irish Free Handicap. Rated superior to The Minstrel, Pampapaul and Nebbiolo.* Timeform rating 130. (Racehorses of 1977).

Leading sire of 2-y-o's individual winners and joint leading sire of 2-y-o's races won with his first crop in 1981 Sire of the winners of 175 races, £553,772, (1/10/83) with his first three crops, including **GODSTONE** (Richmond Stakes, **Gr. 2**, 1983), **SHEARWALK** (Heathorn Stakes, Newmarket, **L**, 3rd Derby Stakes, **Gr. 1**, 1983), **CELESTIAL PATH** (Athasi Stakes, **Gr. 3**), **THE PRIMATE** (also second Gallaghouse Phoenix Stakes, **Gr. 1**, btn. sht. hd. by Achieved, and Curragh Stakes, **Gr. 3**), **PURE OF HEART** (George Ryder Stakes, **Gr. 1**, Autumn Stakes, **Gr. 3**, in Australia), **CHEEKY TROT** (Karrakata Plate, **Gr. 2**, in Australia), **CELESTIAL CITY, MAARIV.**

		Native Dancer	Polynesian
	Dancer's Image		Geisha
GODSWALK		Noor's Image	Noor
(USA) gr. 1974			Little Sphinx
		Intentionally	Intent
	Kate's Intent		My Recipe
		Julie Kate	Hill Prince
			Doggin' It

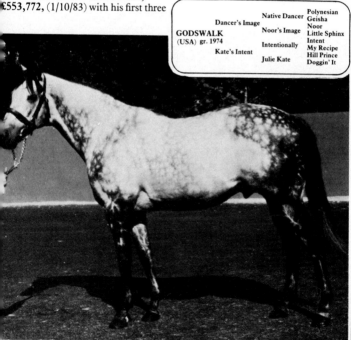

HOME GUARD

Winner of 7 races (5-7f.).
WON Gr. 3 Tetrarch Stakes,
Gr. 3 Diadem Stakes, Philips
Electrical Rockingham Stakes,
Curragh. **2nd Gr. 1** Prix de
l'Abbaye de Longchamp, Spillers
Stewards Cup *(beaten a head giving
winner 30lbs)*. **3rd Gr. 1** Eclipse
Stakes, Sandown Park *(to Brigadier
Gerard)*.
Timeform rating 129. (Racehorses
of 1972). From his first seven crops,
**sire of the winners of 296 races,
£1,000,330,** (1/10/83), including:—
CASTLE GUARD (Prix de
Fontainebleau, **Gr. 3,** 1983).
SAFE HOME (Curragh Stakes,
Gr. 3, 1983).

GOODBYE SHELLEY (Prix
Marcel Boussac, **Gr. 1** 1982,
Fred Darling Stakes, **Gr. 3,** 1983)
MARQUEE UNIVERSAL (Dix
Handicap, **Gr. 2,** Edgemere
Handicap, **Gr. 3,** 1980).
SONNEN GOLD (7 races,
Gimcrack Stakes, **Gr. 2,** second
Middle Park Stakes, **Gr. 1,** etc.,
sire).
MANJAM (Prix du Petit Couvert
Gr. 3).
CORMORANT WOOD (Dubai
Champion Stakes, **Gr. 1,**
Sun Chariot Stakes, **Gr. 2** etc.).

			Hyperion
		Aristophanes	Commotion
	Forli		Advocate
HOME		Trevisa	Veneta
GUARD (USA)			Nasrullah
b. 1969		Bold Ruler	Miss Disco
	Stay at Home		Polynesian
		Alanesian	Alablue

COOLMORE   Stands at **HARAS DE VICTOT** Apply: **Paul Nataf, Horse France,**
9 Rue de la Paix, 75002 Paris. Tel: 261.55.69 Telex: 670357.

LONDON BELLS

Winner of 4 races in Ireland and U.S.A., at 2 and 3 years (6-8.5f.).
WON Erne Plate, Curragh (in course record time, previously held by Nijinsky and The Minstrel).
2nd Gr. 2 Coventry Stakes, Royal Ascot, Gr. 2 National Stakes, Curragh, to Pampapaul (beating Final Straw by 3 lengths).
Rated 8st. 11lb. on Irish Free Handicap, above Smokey Lady, Night Alert, Nikoli, Cairn Rouge, etc.
Timeform. "big, strong, good-bodied, attractive colt".

NIJINSKY, sire of over 67 stakes winners, including dual European Champion Ile de Bourbon, Kings Lake, Golden Fleece, Green Dancer, Solford, Caerleon, Princess Lida, Night Alert, etc.
SHAKE A LEG, a Group winner of 9 races is also the dam of DANZATORE (Irish Champion 2-y-o 1982, Beresford Stakes, Gr. 2, Ashford Castle Stakes, Gr. 3, etc.), and VAGUELY MODEST (Selene Stakes, Gr. 3). By RAISE A NATIVE, sire and grandsire of Champions Exclusive Native, Affirmed, Alydar, Genuine Risk, Mr. Prospector (himself sire of Hello Gorgeous and Conquistador Cielo).

			Nearctic
		Northern Dancer	Natalma
	Nijinsky		Bull Page
		Flaming Page	Flaring Top
LONDON BELLS			Native Dancer
(CAN) b. 1977		Raise a Native	Raise You
	Shake A Leg		Fleet Nasrullah
		Fleeting Doll	Chinese Doll

COOLMORE Stands at PEGASUS STUD, Dr. and Mrs James D. Smith, Mt. Horeb, Lexington, Kentucky 40511 (606) 254-0186

Spendthrift-bred Smuggly, by Caro, winning the Prix Saint-Alary

Spendthrift-bred Siberian Express, by Caro, winning the Prix Morny

Spendthrift-sired Seattle Song, by Seattle Slew, winning the
Prix de la Salamandre from Siberian Express

GROUP PERFORMANCE!

Through November 6, 1983,
the Spendthrift stallions with progeny
of racing age had sired 151 stakes horses,
which had won or placed 273 times in
stakes races (73 of which were graded),
including European group winners.

SEATTLE SONG
(Prix de la Salamandre-Gr. I)

STRAMUSC
(Criterium di Roma-Gr. III)

NORTHERN TEMPEST
(Gran Criterium-Gr. I)

SMUGGLY
(Prix Saint-Alary-Gr. I, etc.) and

SIBERIAN EXPRESS
(Prix Morny-Gr. I, etc.)

Achieved
Champion 2-year-old colt and multiple group stakes winner.
Thatch—Last Call, by Klairon

Belted Earl
Champion sprinter and multiple group stakes winner.
Damascus—Moccasin, by Nantallah

Hilal
Top Miler and multiple group stakes winner of $270,447.
Royal and Regal—Whistling Rex, by Whistling Wind

Pilgrim
Stakes-winning full brother to THE MINSTREL and FAR NORTH.
Northern Dancer—Fleur, by Victoria Park

Security Council
Half-brother to sires STOP THE MUSIC and HATCHET MAN.
Secretariat—Bebopper, by Tom Fool

Solford
Group I winning son of NIJINSKY II
Nijinsky II—Fairness, by Cavan

Time to Explode
Graded stakes winner, equaled world record – 7 f., 1:19 ⅖.
Explodent—Timely Queen, by Olden Times

All Winfield stallions are eligible for the Breeders' Cup Series and Premium Awards.

Winfield_____

Mr. and Mrs. C. Gibson Downing
Inquiries to: C. Gibson Downing III, Mgr. Dir.
5075 Athens-Walnut Hill Road
Lexington, Kentucky 40515
(606) 269-8963 or 268-8706

irish NATIONAL STUD

kafu

(1981)

WON 3 RACES (2 years, 5f) incl.
FLYING CHILDERS STAKES, Gr. 2.
MOLECOMB STAKES, Gr. 3,
2nd COVENTRY STAKES, Gr. 2,
2nd MILL REEF STAKES, Gr. 2,
3rd ANGLIA TELEVISION JULY STAKES, Gr. 3,
4th WILLIAM HILL MIDDLE PARK STAKES, Gr. 1,

FEE Ire £3,750 (Special Live Foal)

African Sky	Sing Sing
	Sweet Caroline
Pampered Dancer	Pampered King
	Star Dancer

For further information and application forms apply:-
Irish National Stud Co. Ltd., Tully, Kildare.
Telephone 045/21251/21301/21377 Telex 31770.

1039

irish NATIONAL STUD

stallions available for 1984

indian king

(1978)

WINNER OF 8 RACES (3-4 years, 6-8f) incl.
CORK AND ORRERY STAKES, Gr. 2,
ROYAL ASCOT, in course record time.
VERNON SPRINT CUP, Gr.2, HAYDOCK,
DIADEM STAKES, Gr. 3, ASCOT,
PRIX DU PALAIS ROYAL, Gr. 3, LONGCHAMP
JOHN O'GAUNT STAKES, HAYDOCK,
in course record time, and
AUTOBAR VICTORIA CUP, ASCOT.
FIRST FOALS DUE 1984.
FEE Ire £8,000 (1st October Concession)

Raja Baba	Bold Ruler
	Missy Baba
Protest	Rash Prince
	Dynamis

lord gayle

(1965)

WON 8 RACES (3-5 years, 7-10f) incl.
PRIX PERTH, Gr. 3, ST CLOUD, and
WILLIAM HILL GOLD CUP.

Sires of winners incl. BLUE WIND,
DESIRABLE, STRONG GALE, EVENING
M'LORD, LADY SINGER, YANKEE GOLD,
PARLIAMENT, ISAAK BABEL, LORDEDAW,
CILL DARA, CROGHAN HILL, ELMAR,
BLONDY, ROCK'S GATE etc.
FEE Ire £7,500 (Special Live Foal)

Sir Gaylord	Turn to
	Somethingroyal
Sticky Case	Court Martial
	Run Honey

sallust

(1969)

WON 7 RACES (2-3 years, 5-8f) incl.
SUSSEX STAKES, Gr. 1,
PRIX DU MOULIN, Gr. 1, in course record time.
GOODWOOD MILE Gr. 2,
RICHMOND STAKES, Gr. 2,
Sire of winners, incl. TAP ON WOOD
SANEDTKI, GALA EVENT, EN AVANT,
AMERICUS, THE FORT, LATE SALLY, etc.
FEE Ire £6,000 (Special Live Foal)

Pall Mall	Palestine
	Malapert
Bandarilla	Matador
	Interval

ahonoora

(1975)

WON 7 RACES (2-4 years, 5-6f) incl.
WILLIAM HILL SPRINT CHAMPIONSHIP, Gr. 2,
KING GEORGE STAKES, Gr.3,
2nd KING STAND STAKES, Gr. 1, etc.
A LEADING FIRST SEASON SIRE
MERAVAL (2 WINS), MAAZI, PRINCESS TRACY
(ALSO PLACED IN MOYGLARE STUD STAKES Gr. 1.)
AHOHONEY (2 WINS), FINAL THATCHING etc.
FEE Ire £2,750 (Special Live Foal)

Lorenzaccio	Klairon
	Phoenissa
Helen Nichols	Martial
	Quaker Girl

For further information and application forms apply
Irish National Stud Co. Ltd., Tully, Kildare.
Telephone 045/21251/21301/21377 Telex 31770.

tap on wood
(1976)

WON 10 RACES (2-3 years, 5-8f) incl. 2,000 Gns
Gr. 1, NATIONAL STAKES, Gr. 2, KIVETON PARK
STEEL STAKES
THE LEADING FIRST SEASON SIRE OF 1983
Sire of 11 winners of 14 races
INCLUDING MAHOGANY, RAPPA TAP TAP (BLUE
SEAL STAKES, ASCOT – LISTED RACE), RED
RUSSEL (ALSO PLACED IN BBA (IRE), GOFF'S
NATIONAL STAKES, Gr. 2, (CURRAGH), TAPACULO
(ALSO PLACED IN WATERFORD CANDELABRA
STAKES, Gr. 3 GOODWOOD), PARK LADY,
MY TOOTSIE, etc.

Sallust	Pall Mall
	Bandarilla
Cat O'Mountaine	Ragusa
	Marie Elizabeth

crash course
(1971)

WON 5 RACES incl.
ASCOT STAKES, ROYAL ASCOT,
DONCASTER CUP,
2nd JOCKEY CLUB CUP, Gr. 2,
Sire of winners incl.
LAOIS PRINCESS, HOME AND DRY,
ALL EXPENSE, TEMPO ROSE,
THE GANGER MAN

Busted	Crepello
	Sans Le Sou
Lucky Stream	Persian Gulf
	Kypris

tug of war
(1973)

WON 10 RACES, incl.
GOODWOOD CUP, Gr. 3,
NORTHUMBERLAND PLATE (Twice)
FIRST CROP ARE 3 YEAR OLDS.

Reliance II	Tantieme
	Relance III
Pirate Queen	Pirate King
	Cantus

krayyan
(1980)

WON 2 RACES (2-3 years, 5f) incl.
NATIONAL STAKES (LR)
2nd NORFOLK STAKES, Gr. 3,
3rd WILLIAM HILL MIDDLE PARK STAKES, Gr. 1,
3rd MILL REEF STAKES Gr. 2,
3rd PALACE HOUSE STAKES Gr. 3.
FEE Ire £1,750 (Special Live Foal).

Tower Walk	High Treason
	Lorrikeet
Mrs Moss	Reform
	Golden Plate

B. B. A. STALLIONS 1984

ANFIELD
KING EDWARDS PLACE STUD,
WANBOROUGH, WILTSHIRE.

ARAGON
EGERTON STUD,
NEWMARKET, SUFFOLK.

ARDROSS
BEECH HOUSE STUD,
CHEVELEY, NEWMARKET,
SUFFOLK.

BALIDAR
MEDDLER STUD,
NEWMARKET, SUFFOLK.

BELDALE FLUTTER
BANSTEAD MANOR STUD,
NEWMARKET, SUFFOLK.

BUSTINO
WOLFERTON STUD,
SANDRINGHAM, NORFOLK.

BUSTOMI
NEW ENGLAND STUD,
NEWMARKET, SUFFOLK.

FREE STATE
BARLEYTHORPE STUD,
OAKHAM, LEICESTER.

GREAT NEPHEW
DALHAM HALL STUD,
NEWMARKET, SUFFOLK.

HIGH TOP
WOODLAND STUD,
NEWMARKET, SUFFOLK.

ILE DE BOURBON
BANSTEAD MANOR STUD,
NEWMARKET, SUFFOLK.

JALMOOD
EGERTON STUD,
NEWMARKET, SUFFOLK.

JULIO MARINER
ASHLEY HEATH STUD,
NEWMARKET, SUFFOLK.

KALAGLOW
BROOK STUD,
CHEVELEY,
NEWMARKET, SUFFOLK.

KING OF SPAIN
LOCKINGE STUD,
WANTAGE, OXON.

LOCHNAGER
EASTHORPE HALL STUD,
MALTON, NORTH YORKSHIRE.

MANSINGH
RED HOUSE STUD, EXNING,
NEWMARKET, SUFFOLK.

MILL REEF
NATIONAL STUD,
NEWMARKET, SUFFOLK.

B. B. A. STALLIONS 1984

MUMMY'S GAME
BARLEYTHORPE STUD,
OAKHAM, LEICESTERSHIRE.

MUMMY'S PET
BARLEYTHORPE STUD,
OAKHAM, LEICESTERSHIRE.

MUSIC MAESTRO
BEECHGROVE STUD,
BRIGG, LINCS.

NINISKI
LANWADES STUD,
NEWMARKET, SUFFOLK.

PERSEPOLIS
HARAS DE FRESNAY-LE-
BUFFARD, NORMANDY,
FRANCE.

RECORD TOKEN
LIMESTONE STUD,
WILLOUGHTON,
GAINSBOROUGH, LINCS.

RELKINO
BARTON STUD, BURY ST.
EDMUNDS, SUFFOLK.

SHIRLEY HEIGHTS
SANDRINGHAM STUD,
KINGS LYNN, NORFOLK.

STAR APPEAL
NATIONAL STUD, NEWMARKET,
SUFFOLK.

SWING EASY
HERRIDGE STUD,
COLLINGBOURNE DUCIS,
WILTSHIRE.

TOWER WALK
LIMESTONE STUD,
WILLOUGHTON,
GAINSBOROUGH, LINCS

WINDJAMMER
BRITTON HOUSE STUD,
CREWKERNE, SOMERSET.

The British Bloodstock Agency Ltd.
THORMANBY HOUSE, FALMOUTH AVENUE,
NEWMARKET

Telephone: Newmarket (0638) 665021   Telex: 817157

16/17 PALL MALL, LONDON SW1Y 5LU
Telephone: 01-839 3393   Telex: 27403

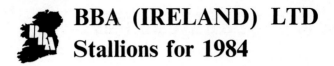

BBA (IRELAND) LTD
Stallions for 1984

At Corbally Stud, Celbridge, Co Kildare
(Dublin 288081/2)

Junius (USA)   b 1976 by **Raja Baba**
—Solid Thought (Solidarity)

Pitskelly   br 1970 by **Petingo**
—French Bird (Guersant)

Persian Bold   br 1975 by **Bold Lad**
—Relkarunner (Relko)

At Milford Stud, Milford, Co Carlow
(Carlow 46133)

On Your Mark
(USA)   ch 1964 by **Restless Wind**
—Super Scope (Swaps)

At Brownstown Stud, Curragh, Co Kildare
(Curragh 41303)

Le Moss   ch 1975 by **Le Levanstell**
—Feemoss (Ballymoss)

At Tara Stud, Tara, Co Meath
(Navan 25203)

Wolverlife   b 1973 by **Wolver Hollow**
—Miralife (Miralgo)

**BBA (Ireland) Ltd., 51 Lansdowne Road, Dublin 4.
Tel: Dublin 686222. Telex: 25599.**

ALEX CROSS'S
TRIAL
James
Patterson
& RICHARD DILALLO

arrow books

Published in the United Kingdom by Arrow Books in 2010

1 3 5 7 9 10 8 6 4 2

First published in Great Britain in 2009 by Century

Arrow Books
Random House, 20 Vauxhall Bridge Road,
London SW1V 2SA

www.randomhouse.co.uk

Addresses for companies within The Random House Group Limited
can be found at: www.randomhouse.co.uk/offices.htm

The Random House Group Limited Reg. No. 954009

A CIP catalogue record for this book
is available from the British Library

ISBN 9780099543022
ISBN 9780099543039 (export edition)

The Random House Group Limited supports The Forest Stewardship
Council (FSC®), the leading international forest certification
organisation. Our books carrying the FSC label are printed on FSC®
certified paper. FSC is the only forest certification scheme endorsed by
the leading environmental organisations, including Greenpeace. Our
paper procurement policy can be found at
www.randomhouse.co.uk/environment

Typeset by SX Composing DTP, Rayleigh, Essex
Printed and bound by
CPI Group (UK) Ltd, Croydon, CR0 4YY

For Susan of course

A PREFACE TO *TRIAL*

BY ALEX CROSS

A few months after I hunted a vicious killer named the Tiger halfway around the world, I began to think seriously about a book I had been wanting to write for years. I even had the title for it: *Trial*. The previous book I'd written was about the role of forensic psychology in the capture of the serial killer Gary Soneji. *Trial* would be very different, and in some ways even more terrifying.

Oral history is very much alive in the Cross family, and this is because of my grandmother, Regina Cross, who is known in our household and our neighborhood as Nana Mama. Nana's famous stories cover the five decades when she was a teacher in Washington—the difficulties she faced during those years of civil rights turmoil, but also countless tales passed on from times before she was alive.

One of these stories—and it is the one that stayed with me the most—involved an uncle of hers who was born and lived most of his life in the small town of Eudora, Mississippi. This man, Abraham Cross, was one of the finest baseball players of that era and once played for the Philadelphia Pythians. Abraham was grandfather to my cousin Moody, who was one of the most unforgettable and best-loved characters in our family history.

What I now feel compelled to write about took place in Mississippi during the time that Theodore Roosevelt was president, the early part of the twentieth century. I believe it is a story that helps illuminate why so many black people are angry, hurt, and lost in this country, even today. I also think it is important to keep this story alive for my family, and hopefully for yours.

The main character is a man my grandmother knew here in Washington, a smart and courageous lawyer named Ben Corbett. It is our good fortune that Corbett kept first-person journals of his incredible experiences, including a trial that took place in Eudora. A few years before he died, Mr. Corbett gave those journals to Moody. Eventually they wound up in my grandmother's hands. My suspicion is that what happened in Mississippi was too personal and painful for Corbett to turn into a book. But I have come to believe that there has never been a better time for this story to be told.

ALEX CR•SS

Part One

A GOOD MAN
IS HARD TO FIND

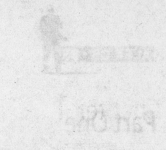

Part One

A GOOD MAN
IS HARD TO FIND

Chapter 1

"LET HER HANG until she's dead!"

"Take her out and hang her now! I'll do it myself!"

Bam! Bam! Bam!

Judge Otis L. Warren wielded his gavel with such fury I thought he might smash a hole in the top of his bench.

"Quiet in the court!" the judge shouted. "Settle down, or by God I will hold every last one of you sons of bitches in contempt."

Bam! Bam! Bam!

It was no use. Warren's courtroom was over-flowing with disgruntled white citizens who wanted nothing more than to see my client hang. Two of them on the left side began a chant that was soon taken up by others:

3

We don't care where. We don't care how.
We just wanna hang Gracie Johnson now!

The shouts from some among the white majority sent such a shiver of fear through the colored balcony that one woman fainted and had to be carried out.

Another bang of the gavel. Judge Warren stood and shouted, "Mr. Loomis, escort all those in the colored section out of my courtroom *and out of the building.*"

I couldn't hold my tongue another second.

"Your Honor, I object! I don't see any of the colored folks being rowdy or disrespectful. The ones making the fuss are the white men in front."

Judge Warren glared over his glasses at me. His expression intimidated the room into silence.

"Mr. Corbett, it is my job to decide how to keep order in my court. It is your job to counsel your client—and let me tell you, from where I sit, she needs all the help she can get."

I couldn't disagree.

What I once thought would be an easy victory in the case of *District of Columbia v. Johnson* was swiftly turning into a disaster for Gracie and her increasingly helpless attorney, Benjamin E. Corbett: that being myself.

Gracie Johnson was on trial for the murder of Lydia Davenport, a wealthy white woman who was active in Washington society at a level high enough to cause a nosebleed. Worse, Gracie was a black woman accused of killing her wealthy white employer.

The year was 1906. Before it was all over, I was afraid they were going to hang Gracie.

I had to be careful they didn't hang me while they were at it.

Chapter 2

"I WILL NOT TOLERATE another outburst," Judge Warren said to the spectators. He turned to look me in the eye. "And I suggest that you, Mr. Corbett, select your objections with greater care."

"Yes, Your Honor," I said, then immediately held my tongue in check with my teeth.

"Mr. Ames, you may resume questioning the defendant."

Carter Ames, the city attorney, was a little old man about five feet tall. He strode to the witness stand as if he were every inch of six-two.

"Now, Grace, let's go back to the afternoon in question, May twenty-third. In your testimony—before the unfortunate disruption occurred—isn't it true that you essentially admitted to murdering Mrs. Davenport?"

"Excuse me, sir, I said *no such thing*," Gracie shot back.

"The court stenographer will please read the testimony given by Miss Johnson a few moments before the courtroom interruption."

"Got it right here, Carter," the stenographer said.

Wonderful. Ames and the court stenographer were on a first-name basis. No telling which parts of Gracie's testimony had been left out or "improved."

The stenographer flipped back the pages in his tablet and began to read in a droning voice.

"Miz Davenport was always a mean old lady. Never had a nice word for anybody. Ask me, she had it coming to her. The day before she got killed, she told me she was fixing to fire me because I was too stupid to know which side of the plate do the fish fork go on. She was a mean old witch, she was. I'm telling you, she had it coming."

I jumped up from my chair.

"Your Honor, obviously my client did not mean—"

"*Sit down, Mr. Corbett.*"

I had one more thing to say—I just had to get it out.

"Your Honor, the prosecutor is deliberately twisting my client's words!"

7

Carter Ames turned to me with a smile. "Why, Mr. Corbett, I'm not twisting a thing. Your client has spoken for herself very clearly. I have no further questions, Your Honor."

"In that case, court will adjourn for a two-hour recess, so we can get ourselves a cold glass of tea and some dinner," the judge said. "I believe that Mrs. Warren said my personal favorite, chicken pot pie, is on the menu today."

Bam! Bam! Bam!

Chapter 3

THE TWO-HOUR DINNER BREAK before Carter Ames and I gave our closing arguments seemed to last at least twice that long. I never had much appetite during a case, so I spent the interval pacing the block around the courthouse square, mopping my face and neck with a handkerchief.

Washington was in the grip of a torturous heat wave, and it was only June. The air was as thick and swampy as any summer afternoon back home in Mississippi. Carriage horses were collapsing. Society ladies called off their afternoon teas and spent their leisure time soaking in cool tubs.

Back home in Eudora I rarely had to wear the full lawyer suit with high stiff-starched collar and all the snaps and suspenders. Down south, folks knew how to survive the heat: move slowly, and wear light clothing.

It must have been ninety-five degrees when we finally returned to the courtroom. The newfangled electric fans barely stirred a breeze. Gracie's face streamed with perspiration.

The judge entered. "Are you ready, gentlemen?"

Carter Ames sauntered toward the jury box. He put on a big friendly smile and leaned in close to the jury foreman. Ames was justly famous for the high drama and fancy oratory of his closing arguments in murder cases.

"Gentlemen, I want you to join me on an important journey," he said, in his orotund voice. "I'll let you in on our destination before we commence—the Kingdom of Truth. Few who set out on the journey toward the Kingdom of Truth ever reach their destination. But today, gentlemen, I can promise you, that is where we shall arrive."

The smoke from Judge Warren's after-dinner cigar wafted blue through the air around the dandyish little city attorney. He slowly paced the length of the jury box, turned, and paced the other way.

"We are not going to make this journey by ourselves, gentlemen. Our companions on this journey are not of the fancy kind. They don't wear fine clothes and they don't ride first class. Our companions, gentlemen, are the facts of this case."

As metaphors go, it seemed fairly simpleminded to me, but the jurors were apparently lapping it up. I made a mental note to lay on an even thicker layer of corn pone than I had originally intended. It was the least I could do for Grace and her chances.

"What do the facts of this murder case tell us?" Ames asked. His voice dropped a few notes on the scale. "The first fact is this: Grace Johnson has all but *confessed* to the crime of murder, right here in front of you today. You heard her admit to a most powerful motive, the hateful emotions and vitriolic resentments she bore toward her employer."

It was all I could do to keep from jumping up and shouting "Objection!" Judge Warren's earlier warning served to keep me in my seat.

"The second fact speaks even more loudly. Grace claims that Lydia Davenport shouted at her. Let me repeat that shocking claim, gentlemen. Lydia Davenport dared to shout at the woman who was a willing employee in her household. In other words, Mrs. Davenport deserved to die because she shouted at a *maid!*"

Ames was not just a skillful actor; when it came to the facts, he was also quite the juggler.

"Now let another fact speak to you, friends.

The fact is, the court has appointed one of the capital's finest young attorneys to represent Grace Johnson. Now mind you, this is as it should be. Let the least among us have the best defense money can buy—your tax money, that is. But don't let the young gentleman fool you. Don't let his pretty words bamboozle you. *Let me tell you what he's going to try to do.*"

He waved his hand indifferently in my direction, as if I were a fly buzzing around his head.

"Mr. Corbett will try to cast doubt upon these *obvious facts*. He will tell you that the Davenport house was bursting with employees who might have murdered Lydia Davenport."

Ames spun on his tiny heel and pointed a crooked finger at my client.

"But the *fact* is this: Only one person in that house admits out loud, in a clear voice, to having a motive for the murder. And *that person is seated right there! Grace Johnson!*"

He strode to the prosecution table and lifted a worn brown Bible. He opened it to a page he seemed to know by heart and began to read aloud.

"If you continue in my word, you are truly my disciples, and you will know the truth, and the truth will set you free."

He snapped the Bible closed with a flourish and held it high in the air.

"Gentlemen, we have arrived. Our journey is done. Welcome to the Kingdom of Truth. The only possible verdict is guilty."

Son of a bitch! Carter Ames had just destroyed my closing argument.

Chapter 4

THE DIMINUTIVE PROSECUTOR THREW a thin smile my way as he returned to his chair, his eyes dancing with the light of triumph. I felt a twinge in my stomach.

But now it was my turn to speak, and hopefully to save a woman's life.

I began with a simple declaration of the fact that no one had witnessed the murder, and then I discussed the other suspects: the Irish gardener, Mrs. Davenport's secretary, and her houseman—all of whom despised their employer and could have easily committed the murder. Of course, they were all white.

Then, since Carter Ames had stolen my thunder, I decided to finish up in another direction, a bold and risky one that brought tremors to my hands.

"Now, before you all go off to your jury room, I'm going to do something that's not often done. Mr. Ames claimed to have taken you to the Kingdom of Truth, but the *fact* is, he never even got close to his stated destination. He omitted the most important truth of all. He never mentioned the real reason Gracie Johnson is facing the possibility of losing her life.

"You know the reason. I don't even have to say it. But I'm going to say it anyway.

"*Gracie Johnson is colored*. That's why she's here. That's the only reason she's here. She was the only colored employee in attendance at the Davenport house that day.

"So there it is. She's a Negro. You gentlemen are white. Everyone expects that a white jury will always convict a black defendant. But I know that not to be true. I think—matter of fact, I truly believe—that you have more honor than that. You have the integrity to see through what the prosecutor is trying to do here, which is to railroad an innocent woman whose only crime was telling you honestly that her boss was a mean old woman.

"Do you see what we've found? We've turned up the most important *fact* of all. And that fact, the fact that Gracie's skin is black, should have no influence whatsoever on what you decide.

"That's what the law says, in every state in this Union. If there is a reasonable doubt in your mind as to whether or not Gracie Johnson is a murderer, *you…must…vote…to…acquit.*"

I started to go back to my chair, but then I turned and walked right up to Carter Ames's table.

"May I, Carter?"

I picked up his Bible, flipping through the pages until I appeared to find the verse I was seeking in the book of Proverbs. No one needed to know I was quoting from memory:

"When justice is done, it brings joy to the righteous."

I closed the Good Book.

Chapter 5

CARTER AMES PUSHED his silver flask of bourbon toward my face. "Have a swig, Ben. You deserve it, son. Well done."

What a sight for the funny pages we must have made—Ames barely five feet tall, me at six-four—standing side by side in the marble hallway outside the courtroom.

"No, thanks, Carter. I'd rather be sober when the verdict comes in."

"I wouldn't, if I was you." His voice was a curdled mixture of phlegm and whiskey. As he lifted the flask to his mouth, I was surprised to see half-moons of sweat under his arms. In the courtroom he'd looked cool as a block of pond ice.

"Your summation was damn good," he observed. "I think you had 'em going for a while there. But then you went and threw in that colored stuff. Why'd you have to remind them? You think they didn't notice she's black as the ace of spades?"

"I thought I saw one or two who weren't buying your motive," I said. "Only takes one to hang 'em up."

"And twelve to hang *her,* don't I know it."

He took another swig from his flask and eased himself down to a bench. "Sit down, Ben. I want to talk to *you,* not your rear end."

I sat.

"Son, you're a fine young lawyer, Harvard trained and all, gonna make a finer lawyer one of these days," he said. "But you still need to learn that Washington is a southern town. We're every bit as southern as wherever you're from down in Podunk, Mississippi."

I grimaced and shook my head. "I just do what I think is right, Carter."

"I know you do. And that's what makes everybody think you're nothing but a goddamned bleeding-heart fool and nigger-lover."

Before I could defend—well, just about everything I believe in—a police officer poked his head out of the courtroom. "Jury's coming back."

Chapter 6

THE CUMBERSOME IRON SHACKLES around Gracie Johnson's ankles clanked noisily as I helped her to her feet at the defense table.

"Thank you, Mr. Corbett," she whispered.

Judge Warren gazed down on her as if he were God. "Mr. Foreman, has the jury reached a verdict in this case?" he asked.

"Yes, we have, Your Honor."

Like every lawyer since the Romans invented the Code of Justinian, I had tried to learn something from the jurors' faces as they filed into the courtroom—the haberdasher, the retired schoolteacher, the pale young man who was engaged to Congressman Chapman's daughter and had cracked a tentative smile during my summation.

Several of them were looking directly at Gracie, which was supposed to be a good sign for a defendant. I decided to take it that way and said a hopeful little prayer.

The judge intoned, "How find you in the matter of murder against Grace Johnson?"

The foreman rose in a deliberate manner, then in a strong, clear voice he said, "We the jury find the defendant guilty as charged."

The courtroom erupted with exclamations, some sobs, even an ugly smattering of applause.

Bam! Bam! Bam!

"I will have order in my court," said the judge. Damned if I didn't see a smile flash across Judge Warren's face before he managed to swallow it.

I slid my arms around Gracie. One of us was trembling, and I realized it was me. My eyes, not hers, were brimming with hot tears.

"It be all right, Mr. Corbett," she said quietly.

"It *isn't* all right, Gracie. It's a disgrace."

Two D.C. blueboys were heading our way, coming to take her back to jail. I motioned for them to give us a moment.

"Don't you worry, Mr. Corbett," Gracie said. "Jesus works in mysterious ways."

"God bless you, Gracie. We'll file an appeal."

"Thank you, Mr. Corbett. But now I got to tell you something."

"What's that?"

She leaned close to me, dropping her voice to a whisper. *"I done the crime."*

"What?"

"I done the crime."

"Gracie!"

"I got five chillun, Mr. Corbett. That old lady, she don't pay me hardly nothing. I needed money. So I meant to take the silver."

"And...what happened?"

"I was coming through the dining room with the silver chest in my hands. Miz Davenport walk in. She 'posed to be having a nap. Well, she screamed at me like she the devil. Then she come a-running at me."

Gracie was composed, very calm, almost in a trance as she spoke to me.

"I had the bone-handle carving knife in my hand. Not for her—I don't know, just in case of something. When she run at me, I turned. She run straight up on that knife, sir. I swear I never meant to do it."

The policemen apparently felt they'd been patient long enough. They came up alongside us and, taking hold of Gracie's arms, began to lead her away.

"But I tell you, Mr. Corbett . . ."

"What, Gracie?"

"I would do it again."

Chapter 7

AS I WALKED all the way home from the court-house on that hot June day, I still had no idea what life-changing things were in store for me and my family. Not a hint, not a clue.

Our house was quiet and dark that afternoon when I arrived. I walked through the front parlor. No sign of Meg, Amelia, or Alice.

In the kitchen a peach pie was cooling on a table. Through the window I saw our cook, Mazie, sitting on the back stoop, shelling butter beans into a white enamelware pan.

"Has Meg gone out, Mazie?" I called.

"Yes, suh, Mr. Ben. And she took the littl'uns with her. Don't know where. Miz Corbett, she was in some bad mood when she went. Her face all red like, you know how she gets."

How she gets. My Meg, my sweet New England wife. So red in the face. *You know how she gets.* The gentlest girl at Radcliffe, the prettiest girl ever to come from Warwick, Rhode Island. Burning red in the face.

And she gets that way because of me, I couldn't help thinking. Because of my failure, because of my repeated failure. Because of the shame I bring on our house with my endless "charity cases" for the poor and disenfranchised.

I walked to the parlor and lifted my banjo from its shelf. I'd been trying to learn to play ragtime tunes since I first heard the new music that had come sweeping up from the South late in the old century. It was music as noisy and fast as one of the new motorcars that were unsettling horses all over the country.

I sat on the piano bench and tried to force my clumsy fingers to find the first offbeat notes of that skittering melody. The music seemed to be in such a hurry, but something about it took me back to a place and a time much slower, and maybe better, than any in Washington, D.C. The bumpy syncopation reminded me of the sound I used to hear coming from tiny Negro churches out in the country, in the woods outside Eudora, Mississippi, where I was born and raised.

As a boy I'd walked past those churches a thousand times. I'd heard the clapping and the fervent amens. Now that had all gotten blended in with a fast-march tempo and the syncopated melody of the old work songs. Mix it all together, speed it up, and somehow, from that corner of the South, down around where Louisiana, Mississippi, and Arkansas meet up, the music came out ragtime.

Whenever I heard that sound, whether issuing from a saloon on the wrong side of Capitol Hill or a shiny new phonograph in Dupont Circle, it sent me out of my Washington life and down the memory road to Mississippi.

And whenever I thought of Mississippi, I couldn't help seeing my mother's face.

Chapter 8

EUDORA, THE COUNTY SEAT, is located in an odd corner of southern Mississippi, sixty miles east of the Big Muddy and fifteen miles north of the Louisiana state line.

My father, the Honorable Everett J. Corbett, may have been the most important judge in town, but the only truly famous citizen in Eudora was my mother, Louellen Corbett. They called her "the Poetess of Dixie." She wrote sweet, simple, sentimental verses in such noted periodicals as *Woburn's Weekly Companion* and *The Beacon-Light* that captured the hearts of southern ladies. She wrote poems about everything dear to the southern heart—paddle wheelers on the Mississippi, moonlight on the magnolias, the lonely nobility of the aging Confederate widow.

But that one particular day in Eudora...

I am a boy of seven, an only child. I'm downtown with my mother on a summer afternoon.

Downtown consisted of the Purina feed and seed store, the First Bank, a few shops around the courthouse square, the Slide Inn Café, specializing in fresh seafood from the Gulf, and the Ben Franklin five-and-dime—about which my mother was fond of saying, "They sell everything you need and nothing you really want."

July was wide-open summer in south Mississippi, featuring a sun that rose early and stayed at the top of the sky all afternoon. The air near the Gulf is so humid at all times of year that you have to put your shoes near the stove at night to keep them from turning white with mildew.

I was wearing short pants, but Mama was "dressed for town"—a lacy flowing dress that swept the ground, a sky blue shawl with dark blue fringe, and her ever-present wide-brimmed straw hat. A boy always thinks of his mother as pretty, but on that afternoon, I remember, she seemed to be shining.

Our chore that day was to pick up eighteen yards of blue velvet Mama had ordered from Sam Jenkins' Mercantile for new dining room curtains.

"Mornin', Sam."

"Why, good morning, Miz Corbett," he said. "Don't you look nice today."

"Thank you."

For Mama, that was mighty few words to utter. I turned to look at her, but she seemed all right.

Sam Jenkins stood there peering at her too. "Is there something I can help you with, Miz Corbett?"

"Yeah," she said, "Sham. Oh. Excuse me."

Something *was* wrong. Why was my mother slurring her words?

"Did you come to pick up that fabric, Miz Corbett?" said Sam, Instead of answering, Mama squinted hard and rubbed the front of her head.

"Miz Corbett? You all right?"

Silence from my mother. Only a puzzled gaze.

Then that slurred, weak voice again.

"When doesh shoe...when..."

"Miz Corbett, have you been...have you been *drinking?*"

Mama shook her head slowly and kept rubbing her forehead. I felt the blood flush through my body.

"Don't be shilly. I sh...I...don't..."

I spoke very quietly. "Mama, what's wrong with you?"

"Ben, you better take your mama home now. Looks like she may have had a little touch o' the grape." He forced a laugh.

"My mama never drinks. She must be sick."

"I'm afraid she is, son. Whiskey sick."

Suddenly my mother's knees buckled. She drooped over to one side and then fell to the floor with a heavy thud.

Sam Jenkins turned to the back of his store. "Henry, come up here! I got a lady passed out drunk on the floor."

Chapter 9

FROM SEPARATE DIRECTIONS CAME two teen-age boys. One was white, with red hair. The bigger one was black, as tall as he was skinny.

"Y'all help this boy take his mama out of here," Sam Jenkins said.

The white boy leaned down to Mama and tried to lift her. She was small, but he couldn't find the right angle to maneuver her into a standing position.

"Marcus, you gonna help me?"

"Mist' Sam, I think this lady sick," said the black kid.

"Nobody asked your opinion," said Mr. Jenkins. "Just get her out of the store!"

They lifted my mother up and carried her out to the sidewalk, where they set her on a bench near the watering trough.

"Shit. She ain't sick," said the redheaded boy. "She's drunk as a monkey."

I was trying my best not to cry, but I couldn't stop the tears blurring my eyes. I was helpless and small, and something was terribly, terribly wrong with my mother. I believed that she might die right there.

The white boy disappeared back into the store, shaking his mop of red hair in disgust.

Then Marcus spoke very softly to me. "Want to hep me carry her down to the doctor?"

I remember nothing of how we got my mother to Dr. Hunter's house. I do remember hearing the doctor say, "Louellen isn't drunk. This is apoplexy. She's had a stroke, Ben. I'm so sorry."

I burst into tears.

Later on, when I understood what the doctor's words really meant, I wished Mama *had* been drunk. Everything in our lives was so different from then on. The next day she was in a wheelchair and looked twenty years older. Eventually she regained her ability to speak, but she left that chair only when she was lifted into the washtub or her bed.

She wrote a few poems about her condition — "A View from a Moving Chair" and "Words You May

Not Understand" were the most famous ones—but she was always weak and often distracted.

To my surprise, she sometimes enjoyed talking about that day in Jenkins's store. She would laugh at the idea that she had been mistaken for a drunk, but she always repeated the lesson she had learned that day: "Just remember one thing, Ben. That was a *black* boy who helped us. He was the only one who helped."

I did as she instructed. I remembered it through grammar school, high school, college, and law school. I remembered it whenever colored people came to my office in Washington with worried faces and tears in their eyes, asking for my help.

But sometimes I couldn't help them. The way I couldn't help Grace Johnson.

I rested the neck of the banjo against my arm and began to pick out the notes of "Bethena," the saddest rag Joplin ever wrote. Every note in that jaunty, quick tune is minor, every shading of the melody is dark.

For all that, it made me feel better—a little homesick, maybe, but what's so wrong with that?

Chapter 10

I HEARD THE CLICK of the front door, then the happy, giggly sounds of Amelia and Alice hurrying inside.

This was followed by Meg's icy voice.

"Say a quick hello to your father, girls. Then wash up for supper."

Amelia poked her head through the parlor door, a happy little angel of seven in a red-and-white gingham sundress, shortly followed by Alice, another helping of strawberry shortcake in an identical outfit.

Those dresses were the only thing identical about the girls. Although they were twins, they barely looked like sisters.

Amelia was small, with fine, dark, beautiful features exactly like her mother's. Alice was taller, blond and lanky, and had the misfortune of taking after her father, though I will say that our family looks had settled better on her face than on mine.

"Remind me again which one of you is which," I said with a stern expression.

"Daddy, *you know*," said Amelia. Alice squealed in delight.

"No, I've completely forgotten. How am I supposed to be able to tell the difference when you look exactly alike?"

To Amelia, that was a scream.

Meg walked into the front hall. "Come along, girls. You heard what I said."

I pointed at Alice. "Oh, *now* I remember. You are...Amelia." And then, pointing at Amelia, "So that means you must be Alice."

"And *you* must be Mommy!" Amelia pointed at me, giggling at her own cleverness. Was there any sweeter sound in the world?

I knelt down and kissed her, then her sister, and gathered them both for a big daddy-hug.

"Where have you two been causing trouble today?"

In a ridiculously loud stage whisper Alice said: "We're not allowed to say...but we were hiding in church."

Meg called again, with the business end of her voice: *"Girls!"*

"Mama says you're in trouble," Amelia reported. "She says you're in the doghouse."

"And we don't even have a dog!" Alice crowed with laughter.

"Girls!" That voice brooked no nonsense.

They ran from my arms.

Chapter 11

I WILL NEVER FORGET the rest of that evening, not a moment of it. Not a detail has been lost on me.

"You and I are living in two different marriages, Ben. It's the truth, a sad truth. I'll admit it," said Meg.

I was flabbergasted by this announcement from my wife of nearly eleven years. We were sitting in the parlor on the uncomfortable horsehair sofa Meg's father had given us as a wedding gift. We had just finished an awkward supper.

"Two different marriages? That's a tough statement, Meg."

"I meant it to be, Ben. When I was at Radcliffe and you were at Harvard I used to look at you and think, Now, this is the man I could always be with.

I honestly believed that. So I waited for you while you went to law school. All the time you were at Columbia, in New York, I was wasting away at my father's house. Then I waited some more, while you went to Cuba and fought in that war that none of us understood."

"Meg, I'm sorry. It was a war."

"But I'm still waiting!" She twirled around, her arms outstretched. And in that one gesture, in those few seconds, I realized the complete truth of what she was saying. Our house was not the one on Dupont Circle that Meg deserved, but a small frame bungalow on the wrong side of Capitol Hill. Cracks were visible in our plaster walls. The piano had broken keys. The roof leaked.

Through soft sobs Meg continued, "I'm not a selfish woman. I admire the cases you take, really I do. I want the poor people and the colored people to be helped. But I also want something for my girls and me. Is that so wrong?"

She wasn't wrong. Maybe I had let her down by worrying too much about my own conscience, not thinking enough about her expectations and the life she believed she was getting when she married me.

"I love you, Meg. You know I adore you." I

reached and touched her face. Her dark hair fell across my fingers. We could have been back in Harvard Yard or walking in the moonlight along the Charles.

A sudden knock, and Mazie entered the room. "'Scuse me, Mr. Ben. They's a man at the door. Says it's urgent."

"Who is it, Mazie?" said Meg.

"He say his name Nate, and…" She paused, reluctant to finish the sentence.

"Is he a colored man, Mazie?" I asked.

Meg said, "Of course he is, Ben. He's here to see you, isn't he?"

A pause.

"Please show the man in," I said.

Chapter 12

RIGHT THEN AND THERE, everything changed in our lives, certainly in mine. Meg looked at me with those big eyes of hers, as much in sorrow as in anger. I reached to touch her again, but she pulled away. She shook her head as if I were a child whose behavior had disappointed her. "You know this one by name?"

"I only know one man named Nate, and that's Nate Pryor. He was Tenth Cavalry. We rode together at San Juan Hill."

Nate appeared at the door just in time to hear Meg say, "The hell with you, Ben."

She walked past Nate and out of the room without so much as looking at him. Her passing set up the first decent breeze I'd felt all day.

"You can introduce us some other time," Nate said. His voice was deep, his enunciation precise. I shook his hand warmly and clapped his shoulder.

"I don't know what elixir you're drinking, Nate, but you look younger than you did the day Colonel Roosevelt drove us up old San Juan Hill."

"The only medicine I take is good old-fashioned hard work. The kind the Lord intended a man to make with his days. Maybe a little taste of 'shine once in a while, for a chaser."

I nodded, but then I looked into his eyes. "What brings you here, Nate? What's so urgent?"

"I'm here with a serious proposition. I wouldn't bother you, but it's something I believe only you can do."

Whatever the favor he was about to ask of me, I was fast losing the desire to hear about it. A sad tale, surely—hard times, ill health, someone's poor relative left penniless and in need of free legal assistance.

I tried to keep my voice gentle. "I've taken on about all the cases I can handle for a while."

"Oh, this is not a law *case*." He flashed a particularly charming smile. "Perhaps I should have mentioned that I came here today directly from the White House. This isn't *my* proposition. This is a request from the president."

I was astonished. "Roosevelt sent you here? To my home?"

"The man himself."

Chapter 13

THE FIRST TIME I EVER LAID eyes on Theodore Roosevelt—God, how he hated the nickname "Teddy"—I was surprised by how much he resembled the cartoons and caricatures with which the papers regularly mocked him. And now, on this fine summer day in the White House, I saw that the thick spectacles pinching his nose, the wide solid waist, and the prominent potbelly had only become more pronounced since he took up residence on Pennsylvania Avenue.

Roosevelt jumped up from his desk and charged across the room toward me before his assistant, Jackson Hensen, could finish his introduction.

"Captain Corbett, a pleasure to see you again. It's been too long."

"The pleasure is entirely mine, Colonel...uhm, Mr. President."

"No, no, no. I'll always prefer Colonel!"

The president waved me over to a green silk sofa near his desk. I sat, trying to contain my excitement at being in the Oval Office, a room that was airy and beautifully appointed but a good deal smaller than I would have imagined.

A door to the left of the president's desk glided open. In came a tall Negro valet bearing a tea tray, which he placed on a side table. "Shall I pour, sir?"

"Thank you, Harold, I'll do my own pouring."

The valet left the room. Roosevelt went to a cabinet behind his desk and took out a crystal decanter. "Except I'll be pouring *this*. What'll it be, Captain, whiskey or wine? I'm having claret myself. I never touch spirituous liquors."

That is how I wound up sitting beside TR on the green sofa, sipping fine Kentucky bourbon from a china teacup embossed with the presidential seal.

"I presume our old friend Nate Pryor has given you some idea why I wanted to see you," he said.

I placed my cup on the saucer. "He actually didn't say much, to be honest. Only that it was to do with the South, some kind of mission. A problem with the colored people? Danger, perhaps."

"I've been doing a little checking on you, Ben. It just so happens that the place you were born and raised is the perfect place to send you. *Assuming* you agree to this assignment."

"Mississippi?"

"Specifically your hometown. Eudora, isn't it?"

"Sir? I'm not sure I understand. Something urgent in *Eudora*?"

He walked to his desk and returned with a blue leather portfolio stamped with the presidential seal in gold.

"You are aware that the crime of lynching has been increasing at an alarming rate in the South?" he said.

"I've read newspaper stories."

"It's not enough that some people have managed to reverse every forward step the Negro race has managed since the war. Now they've taken to mob rule. They run about killing innocent people and stringing 'em up from the nearest tree."

The president placed the portfolio in my hand.

"These are papers I've been collecting on the situation: reports of the most horrible occurrences, some police records. Things it's hard for a Christian man to credit. Especially since the perpetrators of these crimes are men who claim to be Christians."

My first thought was that the president was exaggerating the problem. Northerners do that all the time. Of course I had heard of lynchings, but I hadn't known of any in Mississippi since I was a boy.

"They hang men, they hang women, for God's sake they even hang young children," Roosevelt said. "They do the most unspeakable things to their bodies, Ben."

I didn't say a word. How could I? He was talking about my hometown.

"I've tried discussing the matter with several southern senators. To a man, they claim it's the work of outsiders and a fringe element of white reprobates. But I know damn well it's the Klan, and in some of these towns that includes just about every respectable white man."

"But Colonel," I said, "the Klan was outlawed forty years ago."

"Yes. And apparently it's stronger than ever now. That's why you're here, Captain."

Chapter 14

I WAS GLAD when Roosevelt reached for the decanter again. This talk of the sins of my fellow southerners had me upset, even a little angry.

"Colonel, I haven't spent much time down home since I finished law school," I said cautiously. "But I'd be surprised if there's a problem in Eudora. Folks there generally treat the Negroes well."

When he spoke, his voice was gentle. "Open your eyes, Ben. Since April there have been two men and a fifteen-year-old boy allegedly lynched within a few miles of your hometown. It's on the way to becoming a goddamn epidemic, and I—"

"Excuse me, sir. Sorry to interrupt. You said 'allegedly'?"

"Excellent! You're paying attention!" He thwacked my knee with the portfolio. "In this file you'll see

letter after letter, report after report, from congressmen, judges, mayors, governors. Nearly every one
tells me the lynching reports are greatly exaggerated.
There *are* no lynchings in their towns or districts.
The Negro is living in freedom and comfort, and the
white southerner is his boon friend and ally."

I nodded. I didn't want to admit that had I been
asked, that would have been very much like my
own estimate of the situation.

"But that is *not* the story I'm hearing from certain
men of conscience," he said. "I need to know the
truth. I'm glad you don't automatically believe what
I'm telling you, Ben. I want a man with an open
mind, an honest and skeptical man like yourself
who can see all sides of the question. I want you
to go down there and investigate, and get to the
bottom of this."

"But sir, what is it you want me to find out?
Exactly what?"

"Answer these questions for me," he said.

"Are lynchings as common a fact of life as I think
they are?

"Is the Ku Klux Klan alive and thriving down
there, and if so, who is behind the outrageous
resurgence?

"What in hell is the truth—the absolute truth?

And what can a president do to stop these awful things from happening?"

He barked these questions at me in the same high, sharp voice I recalled from the parade ground in Havana. His face was flushed red, full of righteous anger and determination.

Then, softly, he asked, "Will you do it for me, and for this country, Ben?"

I did not hesitate. How could I? "Of course, I am at your service. I'll do what you ask."

"Bully! When can you go?"

"Well, sir, I do have a trial beginning next week in the circuit court," I said.

"Leave the judge's name with Mr. Hensen. We'll take care of it. I want you in Mississippi as soon as possible."

He clapped his hand on my shoulder as he walked me to the door. From the breast pocket of his jacket he removed a folded scrap of paper, which he handed to me.

"This is the name of a man who will assist you down there. I believe he'll be able to open your eyes to the way your good people of Eudora have been treating their colored citizens."

"Yes, sir." I tucked it away.

"One more thing…"

"Sir?"

"I must have secrecy. A cover story has been arranged for you: you're in Mississippi to interview possible federal judges. If your real mission is exposed, I will deny that I had anything to do with your trip. And Ben, this could be dangerous for you. The Klan murders people—clearly."

In the outer office I gave the judge's name to Mr. Hensen, then walked down the steps of the North Portico to the curving driveway. To be honest, I hoped some friend or acquaintance might happen along and witness my emergence from that famous house, but no such luck.

I stepped out onto Pennsylvania Avenue and turned toward my office. I would have to work late getting everything in order. It seemed I might be gone for a while.

I had just passed the entrance to Willard's Hotel when I remembered the slip of paper the president had given me. I pulled it out and took a step back to read it in the haze of gaslight from the hotel lobby.

Written in the president's own bold, precise hand were four words:

ABRAHAM CROSS
EUDORA QUARTERS

I thought I knew everybody in Eudora, but I'd never heard of Abraham Cross. "The Quarters" was the Negro section of town. This was the man who was going to teach me about southerners and lynching?

The fact was, I had not been completely honest with Roosevelt. Had he asked me, I would have told him the truth. I already knew more than I cared to know about the horror of lynching.

I had seen one.

Chapter 15

THE SUMMER WE BOTH turned twelve, my best friend, Jacob Gill, and I made it a practice to slip out of our houses after supper and meet at the vacant lot behind the First Bank of Eudora. Once out of the sight of grown-ups, we proceeded to commit the cardinal and rather breathtaking sin of smoking cigarettes.

We'd blow perfect smoke rings into the hot night air and talk about everything, from the new shortstop just sent down from the Jackson Senators to play with the Hattiesburg Tar Heels, to the unmistakable breasts budding on a lovely and mysterious eighth grader named Cora Sinclair.

More than anything, I think, we liked the ritual of smoking—swiping the tobacco from Jacob's father's humidor, bribing Old Man Sanders at the general store to sell us a pack of Bugler papers without a word to our mothers, tapping out just the right amount of tobacco, licking the gummed edge of the paper, firing the match. We considered ourselves men, not boys, and there was nothing like a good after-dinner smoke to consecrate the feeling.

Then came a Monday night, early August. The last night we ever smoked together.

I will tell you how the nightmare began, at least how I remember it.

Jacob and I were a little light-headed from smoking three cigarettes in quick succession. We heard noises on Commerce Street and walked down the alley beside the bank to see what was stirring.

The first thing we saw was a group of men coming out of the basement of the First Methodist Church. I immediately recognized Leon Reynolds, the "dirty man" who did the sweeping and manure hauling in front of the stores around the courthouse square. He had a hard job, a big belly, and a sour-mash-whiskey attitude.

Across Commerce Street, on the sidewalk in front of Miss Ida Simmons's sewing and notions shop, we saw three colored teenagers standing and shooting the breeze. Lounging against the wall of

Miss Ida's, they were facing the wrong way to see that there were white men bearing down on them.

I recognized the tallest boy as George Pearson, whose mother sometimes did washing and ironing for our neighbors the Harrises. Beside him was his brother Lanky. I didn't recognize the third boy.

If Jacob and I could hear their conversation this plainly, so could the men walking down the sidewalk toward them. George Pearson was doing most of the talking.

"Shoot, Lank, they couldn't do a damn thing 'round here without us," he said. "Let 'em try to get along without colored folks. Who'd curry their hosses and pitch their hay? Who'd they get to cut cane and pick cotton?"

Jacob looked at me. I looked back at him. We knew black boys were not supposed to talk this way.

The white men walked right past us and stepped down into the street. I don't think they even registered our presence. When they heard what George was saying, they started walking faster, and then they ran. They were almost upon the three boys when one of the men boomed, "Hell, George, you one smart little nigger to figure all that out by yourself!"

Chapter 16

GEORGE PEARSON TURNED, and I saw nothing but the whites of his eyes. It was stupid of him to be talking like that in the open on Commerce Street, but he quickly demonstrated that he was smart enough to run.

Jacob and I watched him leap the horse trough in one bound and take off sprinting through the skinny alley beside the church. Leon Reynolds and his pals gave chase, huffing and cursing and yelling "Stop, nigger!"

"We better go home, Ben," said Jacob. "I'm not kidding you."

"No," I said. "We're going after them. Come on. *I dare you.*"

I knew Jacob would lay down his life before taking off in the face of a dare. Sure enough, he followed me. We kept far enough back so as not to be seen. I had not been a very religious boy up till then, but I found myself praying for George Pearson to get away. *Please, God,* I thought, *make George run fast.*

The men chased him all the way to the end of Court Street, out past the icehouse. As they went along, a couple more men joined the chase. George seemed to be getting away! Then, from out of nowhere, a bucket came sailing out of the icehouse door, tangling his feet and tripping him up.

Within seconds the men were on George. Leon Reynolds punched him right in his face. The man next to him hocked up a big wad of spit and let it fly. Another man reached down, grabbed George by the testicles, and twisted his hand.

"Holy God," Jacob whispered in the bushes where we'd taken shelter. "They're gonna kill him, Ben. I swear to God."

The men yanked George up by one arm and set him stumbling in front of them. They taunted and teased and pushed him toward the swampy woods behind the icehouse. One of them had a torch. Then another torch was lit.

"We gotta do something," I said to Jacob. "We *gotta.* I'm serious, boy."

"You crazy? What in hell can we do? They'll twist our balls off too."

"Run home and get your daddy," I said. "I'll try to keep up with 'em."

Jacob looked at me, plainly trying to gauge whether his departure now would mean he had failed to live up to my earlier dare. But finally he ran for help.

Leon Reynolds yanked George up hard by his ear. I found my hand clutching at the side of my own head in sympathy.

Two men lifted George as easily as if he were a cloth doll. Blood poured from his mouth, along with a load of bile and vomit.

One man held George at the waist while another pushed and pulled his head up and down to make him perform a jerky bow.

"There you go, nigger boy. Now you're bowing and showing the respect you should."

Then, leaning in, with one firm tug, Leon Reynolds pulled George's ear clean off his head.

Chapter 17

I WANTED to throw up.

I stood ankle deep in the muck of the swamp, batting at the cloud of mosquitoes that whined around my face and arms. I was hiding as best I could behind a tangle of brambly vines and swamp grass, all alone and completely petrified.

In no time at all, the men had fashioned a rope into a thick noose with a hangman's knot. It took even less time to sling the rope over the middle fork of a sizable sycamore tree.

The only sound in those woods was the awful grunting of the men, the steady metallic chant of the cicadas, and the loud beating of my heart.

"You know why you being punished, boy?" shouted one of the men.

There was no response from George Pearson. He

56

must have fainted from the beatings or maybe the pain of losing his ear.

"We don't appreciate *boasting*. We don't appreciate it from no nigger boy."

"Now, come on, Willy, ain't it a little rough to throw a boy a rope party just for shootin' off his stupid-ass mouth?" said another.

"You got another suggestion, Earl?" Willy said. "What other tonic would you recommend?"

I looked around for Jacob. Surely he'd had time to get home and come back with his father.

The men carried George to the sandy ground underneath the sycamore. One of them held up his head while the others slid the rope around his neck.

I didn't know what I could do. I was just one boy. I wasn't strong enough to take on one of these men, much less all of them, but I had to do something. I couldn't just hide like a jackrabbit in the woods and watch them hang George Pearson.

So I finally moved out of the shadows. I guess the slosh of my feet in swamp water turned their heads. I stood revealed in the light of the moon and their torches.

"Would you looka here," said Willy.

"Who the hell is this?" said one of his friends.

"Ain't but a little old boy, come out to give us a hand."

I realized I was shivering now as if this were the coldest night of all time. "Let him go," I squeaked, instantly ashamed of the tremor in my voice.

"You follered us out here to hep this nigger?" said Willy. "You want us to string you up next to him, boy?"

"He did nothing wrong," I said. "He was just talking. I heard him."

"Willy, that's Judge Corbett's kid," said a tall, skinny man.

"That's right," I said, "he's my daddy. You're all gonna be in bad trouble when I tell what you did!"

They laughed as if I'd told the funniest joke they'd ever heard.

"Well, now, correct me if I'm wrong, young Master Corbett," said Willy, "but I believe the law in these parts says if a nigger goes to boasting, his friends and neighbors got every right to throw him a little rope party and teach him how to dance."

My throat was so dry I was surprised any sound came out. "But he didn't do anything wrong," I said again. For some reason I thought if I repeated myself, they would see the logic.

Willy put on a smile that held not a hint of

amusement. "Boys, I believe we have got ourselves a pure-D, grade-A, number one junior nigger-lover."

The other men laughed out loud. Hot tears sprang up in my eyes, but I willed them not to fall. I would not cry in front of these awful bastards, these cowards.

I recognized a tall, skinny one as J. T. Mack, the overseer at the McFarland plantation. He slurred his words as if he were drunk. "If this boy is half smart as his daddy, he'll just turn his ass around and march on back home. And forget he ever come out here tonight."

In two steps Willy was on me, gripping my arm, then my throat. J. T. Mack moved in to grab my other arm.

"Hold on, son. You can't go home to daddy yet. We need a souvenir of your visit. Come on out of there, Scooter," said J.T.

Out of nowhere came a dapper young man in a green-and-white-plaid suit, his hair slicked back with brilliantine. He looked about sixteen years old. He carried a wooden box camera on a large tripod, which he set up in the clearing about ten feet from the motionless body of George Pearson.

Scooter stuck his head under the black cloak attached to the camera and then pushed back out.

"I can't see nothing. It's too dark. Bring your light in close to his face," he said.

The two men with torches moved closer, illuminating the shining black skin of George Pearson's face. Scooter put his head back under the cloth.

With that, Leon pulled hard on the rope. George Pearson stood straight up and then he flew off the ground three or four feet. His eyes opened wide, bulging as if they might explode. His whole face seemed to swell. His body began trembling and jerking.

The horror of what I was seeing froze me in place. I felt something warm dripping down my leg and realized I had peed my pants.

No one was looking at me now or bothering to hold me. Slowly, slowly, I began to back away.

"Hope you got a good likeness, Scooter," said J.T. "We'll all be wanting a copy. Something to remember ol' George by."

Everybody hooted and laughed at that one. I turned and ran for my life.

Chapter 18

I SUPPOSE THERE might have been one good thing about the punishing southern-style heat wave that had settled over Washington: that night Meg had gone to bed wearing her lightest nightgown. As I opened the door to our room Meg was resting on our bed, pretending to read her leather-bound copy of the book of Psalms.

"Are you speaking to me?" I asked her.

"You weren't here to speak to until now," she answered without looking up.

I leaned down and kissed her and was relieved that she didn't turn away.

Meg was so lovely just then, and I wanted nothing more than to lie down beside her. But it wouldn't be fair, not with the knowledge running around in my head.

"Meg," I said softly, "I have something to tell you. I'm not sure how you're going to take it."

Her eyes hardened.

"I went to the White House tonight," I said.

Her eyes flashed. In one second the hardness melted into joy.

"The White House!" she cried. "Oh, I knew it! I *knew* Roosevelt would have to come around! You're one of the best young lawyers in town. How ridiculous of him to have waited this long to offer you a position!"

"It's not a position," I said. "The president asked me to…take on a mission for him. It could be for a month or two."

Meg sat straight up. The Psalms slid to the floor with a soft plop. "Oh, Ben, you're going to leave us again? Where?"

"Home," I said. "To Mississippi. To Eudora."

She exhaled sharply. "What could the president possibly want you to do in that godforsaken corner of nowhere?"

"I'm sorry, Meg," I said. "I can't tell you. I had to give Roosevelt my word."

Meg's rage exploded, and she cast about for a suitable weapon. Seizing the bottle of French eau de toilette I had given her for her birthday, she fired it against the wall with such force that it shattered. A dreamy scent of lavender filled the room.

"Meg, how could I say no? He's the president of the United States."

"And I'm your wife. I want you to understand something, Ben. When you go back to Mississippi, on your *mission*, you'd best be advised to purchase a one-way ticket. Because if you go, there's no point in coming back. I mean that, Ben. So help me, I'm serious. I can't wait for you any longer."

I heard a sound behind me. Meg and I turned to discover that we had an audience for this display: Alice and Amelia.

"Hello, girls," I said. "Mama and I are having a talk. An adult talk. Back to bed with both of you now."

Meg had already turned her face away from the door. I could see from the heaving of her shoulders that she was crying, and that made me feel awful.

I walked the girls back to their room, where I tucked them in, covering them gently with the light cotton sheets that sufficed on hot nights like this.

I kissed Amelia, then Alice. Then I had to kiss Alice again, and Amelia, in that order, to even things out.

As I rose to leave, Amelia threw her skinny arms around me and tugged me back down to her side.

"Don't go, Papa," she said in a voice so sweet it nearly broke my heart. "If you go, we'll never see you again."

The moment Amelia said it, I had the terrible thought that my little girl just might be right.

ALEX CR•SS

Part Two

HOMECOMING

Chapter 19

I WAS SOON ENOUGH reminded of the dangers of the mission I'd undertaken for the president of the United States. Two days into my journey south, I was in Memphis, about to board the Mississippi & Tennessee train to Carthage, where I would switch to the Jackson & Northern for the trip to Jackson. I had just discovered some truly disturbing reading material.

I had been waiting when the Memphis Public Library opened its doors at nine a.m. A kindly lady librarian had succumbed to one of my shameless winks. She agreed to violate several regulations at once to lend me a number of back issues of the local newspapers, which I agreed to return by mail.

I had carefully chosen the most recent issues that carried sensational stories of lynchings on their front pages. Many of those appeared in the *Memphis News-Scimitar* and the *Memphis Commercial Appeal*.

I was instantly confused by one headline that declared, "Colored Youth *Hung* by Rope AND *Shot* by Rope." The article explained that after the fifteen-year-old boy was strung up by his neck—he'd been accused of setting fire to a warehouse—the mob shot so many bullets at his dangling corpse that one bullet actually severed the rope. The boy's body crashed to the ground, a fall that would surely have killed him had he not already been dead.

Another article blaring from the *News-Scimitar* concerned the lynching of a Negro who was the father of two young boys. The man was taken forcibly from the Shelby County Jail and lynched within a few yards of the entrance. The unusual thing here? A member of the sheriff's department had gone to the man's home and brought his sons to view their daddy's lynching.

The "coverage" in these pieces read more like the review of a new vaudeville show or a lady pianist at a classical music concert. To wit:

> The Everett lynching was far more gruesome
> than the Kelly lynching of but two weeks

previous. Due to the unusual explosion of Thaddeus Everett's neck and carotid arteries, this hanging was both more extraordinary and interesting than the afore-mentioned Kelly death.

And from the *Memphis Sunday Times*, a "critique" of a different lynching:

Olivia Kent Oxxam, the only woman privileged to be present at "Pa" Harris's lynching in the River Knolls region, declared it to be "One of the most riveting events of my lifetime. I was grateful to be there."

These articles made the lynchings seem so engrossing that they must surely surpass the new Vitagraph "flicker" picture shows for their entertainment value.

I folded the papers carefully and stashed them in my valise. Then I decided that the heat inside the train carriage was worse than the soot and grime that would flow in from the stacks after I opened the window. I made my move, but the damn window wouldn't budge.

I was pushing upward with all my strength when the gentleman in the opposite seat said, "Even a strong young man like yourself won't be able to open that window—without pulling down on the side latch first."

Chapter 20

I LAUGHED AT MYSELF, then pulled on the latch. The window slid down easily. "I guess strength doesn't help," I said, "if you don't have some brains to go along with it."

My fellow traveler was middle-aged, paunchy, seemingly well-to-do, with a florid complexion and a gold watch fob of unmistakable value. He put out his hand.

"Henley McNeill," he said. "Grain trader. I'm from Jackson."

"I'm Benjamin Corbett. Attorney at law. From Washington."

"Miss'ippi?" he said.

"No, sir. Washington, D.C."

"Well, you are one very tall attorney, Mr. Corbett. I would bet those Pullman berths play havoc with the sleep of a man your size."

I smiled. "I've spent my whole life in beds that are too short and bumping into ceilings that are too low."

He laughed and put away the book he'd been reading.

"Are you a journalist, too?" Henley McNeill asked.

"No."

"Well, I only ask on account of I saw you reading all those newspapers."

I decided to see where the truth might take me. "I was doing a little research…on the history of lynching."

He blinked, but otherwise betrayed no reaction. "Lynching," he said. "In that case, newspapers might not be your best source of information."

"How do you figure?"

"Well, sir, in my view, the newspapers don't always tell the truth.

"Let me give you a point of observation," McNeill continued. "Now, this is just the opinion of one man. But I'm a man who's spent his whole life right here in Mississippi. And my daddy fought for the Confederacy alongside Braxton Bragg at Stones River."

Henley McNeill seemed like a sensible fellow.

This was the very type of man Roosevelt had in mind when he sent me down here to speak with the locals.

"The white man doesn't hate the colored man," he said. "The white man is just *afraid* of the colored man."

"Afraid?"

"Not afraid in the way you think. He's not afraid the colored man's going to rape his wife or his daughter. Although, let's be honest, if you turned a colored man loose on white women with no laws against it, there's no telling what might happen."

He leaned forward in his seat, speaking intensely. "What genuinely scares the white man is that the colored is going to suck up all the jobs from the whites. You just got out of Memphis, you saw how it is. It's the same in all the big cities—Nashville, New Orleans, Atlanta. You got thousands and thousands of Negroes running around looking for jobs. And every one of 'em willing to work cheaper than the white man, be they a field hand, a factory hand, or what have you."

I told McNeill that I understood what he was saying. In fact, it was not the first time I'd heard that theory.

"Yes, sir," he went on. "The black man has got

to figure out a way to get along peaceable with the white man, without taking his job away from him."

He paused a moment, then leaned in to tap the side of my valise with an insistent finger. A smile spread over his face.

"And if the black man don't come to understand this," he said, "why, I reckon we'll just have to wipe him out."

Chapter 21

HOME AGAIN.

Home to the town where I learned to read, write, and do my multiplication tables. Home to the town where my mama fell ill, stayed ill for many years, and died, and where my father was long known as "the only honest judge in Pike County."

My town, a little over three thousand souls, where I once set the Mississippi state record for the hundred-yard dash, shortly before I broke my leg in a fall from a barn roof. Where Thomas McGoey, the mail carrier, rang our doorbell and personally presented me with the letter announcing I'd been accepted at Harvard.

The last time I'd been home to Eudora was for my mother's funeral, six years ago. I remember being startled at the time by how much the town had changed. Most astonishing to me then were the two gas-powered motorcars parked beside the hitching posts.

Many other things had changed since that last mournful journey to my birthplace. But on this day, while I waited for Eudora Station's one ancient porter to summon the energy to unload my trunk, I found myself amazed to see how much this lazy little town resembled the one I knew when I was a boy.

The early-summer heat remained as overwhelming as I remembered, the whitish sun seeming to press down on everything under its gaze. The First Bank, Sanders' General Store, the Purina feed and seed, the Slide Inn Café— everything was just the same.

Eudora Town Hall still featured an oversized Confederate stars-and-bars hanging in the second-floor window above the portico. The same faded red-and-white-striped barber's pole stood outside the shop with the sign that said "Hair Cuts, Shaves, & Tooth Extractions"—although no one had gone to Ezra Newcomb for a bad tooth since the first real dentist moved to town when I was eleven.

One difference I noticed immediately was that many of the doorways—at the depot, at the little vaudeville theater, at the Slide Inn—now bore signs marking certain entrances as "White" or "Colored." When I was a boy, everyone knew which places were for whites and which for Negroes.

At last the porter approached with my trunk and valises, accompanied by a gangly colored teenager. The porter asked, "Will we be taking these to your father's house, Mr. Corbett?"

I frowned. "How'd you know my name?"

"Well, suh, the stationmaster tol' me to hurry up and go help Judge Corbett's boy with his trunk, so I purt' much figured it out from there."

I gave the old man a dime and offered another dime to the boy if he would carry my luggage on to my destination. He threw that heavy trunk up on his shoulders as if it contained nothing but air and picked up my pair of valises with one large hand.

"I'll be staying at Maybelle Wilson's," I said. "I'm here on business."

We crossed to the First Bank and turned left onto Commerce Street. It was right then that I had the feeling that I had entered into one of Mr. H. G. Wells's fabled time-transport machines. "My God," I said under my breath. *"How can this be?"*

Chapter 22

THERE BEFORE ME was my first sweetheart, Elizabeth Begley, instantly recognizable with her blond curls, her delicate face, a sweet young girl in a pretty pink-checked sundress.

I realized with a start this was neither a dream nor a memory. This really was Elizabeth Begley. *And she truly was eleven years old!*

Then I saw the very real and very grown-up Elizabeth Begley step out of Ida Simmons's notions shop and call out to the little girl standing before me.

"Emma? You wait right there for me."

I called out Elizabeth's name. She turned, and her face lit up instantly.

"Why, good Lord! Ben Corbett! The heat must have gone to my eyes. This cannot be you!"

"It's Ben, all right. Your eyesight is just fine."

As was everything else about her. Elizabeth looked as beautiful as when I used to sneak glances at her all through our school years together. If anything, she'd gotten even prettier as a woman.

"Well, Ben, what brings you back to our little nothing of a town?" she asked.

I told myself to close my mouth, which had fallen open in astonishment, partly at the chance meeting, but also at the sight of this lovely woman.

"Oh, just some work for the government. Interviewing candidates for the federal bench, potential judges. And I suppose I needed a breath of good old Mississippi fresh air."

"Honey, everybody in town is just gonna be beside themselves with excitement to see you," Elizabeth said and beamed. "The famous Ben Corbett, the one we all thought had gone off forever to be a Yankee lawyer, has finally come for a visit! I know your father must be thrilled."

"I hope he will be," I said. "It's a surprise. The job I'm on came up suddenly."

I doubted that many people in town—especially my father—would be all that happy to see me. But that wasn't the kind of information to share with Elizabeth. Instead I remarked that Emma was as pretty as Elizabeth had been as a girl, which happened to be true, and made both of them smile.

"I see you've still got honey on your tongue, Ben," she said, with a hint of a blush. And then a wink, to show her sense of humor was intact.

"I'm just speaking the truth," I said, smiling. It really was good to see her.

"Ben, I would love to stand here and visit with you and get more compliments, but Emma is going to be late for her dance class," she said. "I do want to talk to you. Where is Mrs. Corbett? Did you abandon her at the station?"

"She stayed home," I said. "The children are involved in their lessons."

"I see," Elizabeth said, with an inflection that suggested she didn't quite comprehend that version of events. "It's been too long, Ben," she went on. "I hope we'll see each other again?"

"Of course we will. Eudora is a small town."

"And that's why we love it."

She took her daughter's hand and headed off toward the shade of the oak trees surrounding the town square. I turned around and stood watching Elizabeth and Emma as they walked away.

Chapter 23

HERE'S SOMETHING I truly believe: a man should be able to walk through the front door of his childhood home without knocking. I was thinking this as I clutched the ring of the brass knocker on my father's front door. I may have spent the first eighteen years of my life here, but it was never *my* house. It was always *his* house. And he never let me forget it.

It was six years ago, at my mother's funeral, that I had last laid eyes on my father.

It hadn't gone well. I had just buried the most understanding parent a man could possibly have. When the service was over, I was left with a stern, distant, conservative father who had no use for a lawyer son who leaned the other way. After the funeral luncheon, after all the deviled eggs and potato salad and baked ham had been consumed, after the Baccarat punchbowl had been washed, dried, and put away, my father had an extra glass of whiskey and began to pontificate on the subject of my "Washington shenanigans."

"And if you don't mind, what might those terrible shenanigans be?" I asked. "How have I disappointed you?"

"Believe it or not, son, y'all don't have a lock on every form of human knowledge in that Yankee town you now call home," he said. "The news does travel down to Mississippi eventually. And everybody I know says you're the most *progressive* young lawyer in Washington." I had never heard that word pronounced with a more audible sneer.

I didn't answer. All the way down on the train, I had vowed to myself not to react to his temperamental outbursts.

"Your mother enjoyed that about you," he went on. "Your Yankee free-thinking ways. But she's gone now, God rest her soul. And I can tell you this, Benjamin. You're a fool! You're up to your knees in the sand, and the tide's approaching. You can keep trying to shovel as hard as you can, but that will not stop the tide from coming in."

"Thank you for the colorful metaphor," I said.

Then I went upstairs, packed my valise, and went back to Washington.

After that I heard from him only once a year, around Christmas, when a plain white envelope would arrive containing a twenty-dollar bill and the same handwritten note every year:

"Happy Christmas to yourself, Meg, and my granddaughters. Cordially, Judge E. Corbett."

Cordially.

Chapter 24

NOW HERE I WAS, STANDING at his door again. And as much as it galled me to knock on that door, I could not come home to Eudora without seeing my father. I was sure he already knew that I was back.

Dabney answered the door. He had been my father's houseman since before I was born.

"Good Lord! Mister Ben! Shoot, I never expected to open this door and find you on the other side of it. The judge is gonna be absolutely de-*light*-ed to see you."

"Dabney, it's good to know you're still the smoothest liar in Pike County."

He smiled brightly and gave me a wink. Then I followed him to the dining room, breathing in the old familiar smell of floor wax and accumulated loneliness.

My father sat alone at the long mahogany table, eating a bowl of soup from a fine china bowl. He glanced up, but his face did not change when he saw me—eyes icy blue, his lips thin and unsmiling.

"Why, Benjamin. How nice of you to grace us with your presence. Did somebody die?"

My father's gift for sarcasm had not diminished. Immediately I found myself wishing I hadn't come running over to his house my first day in town.

"How are you feeling?" I asked.

"Sound body, sound mind. As far as I can tell. Why? Have you heard otherwise?"

"Not at all. I'm glad to hear you're well."

"What wonderful Yankee manners. I trust you are healthy yourself?"

I nodded. The silence between us was almost painful.

"So, Ben, you still busy up there freeing the slaves?"

"I believe it was President Lincoln who did that."

"Ah, that's right," he said, a wisp of a smile coming to his face. "Sometimes I forget my history. Care for some turtle soup?"

Soup? On a ninety-degree night in Mississippi?

"No, thank you."

"No turtle soup? Yet another in a succession of foolish choices on your part, Benjamin."

My father did not ask me to take a seat at his table.

He did not ask what brought me to Eudora after six years, and I wondered if it was possible that he knew.

He did not inquire after Meg, or ask why my wife had permitted me to travel all this way by myself. He did not ask about Alice or Amelia.

I thought of Mama, how much she would have loved having two little granddaughters in this house. It was always too quiet in here. I remembered one of her favorite expressions: "The silence in here is so loud, I can hear my own heart rattling around in my ribs."

Judge Corbett looked me up and down. "Where is your baggage?" he asked.

"I'm not staying here," I said. "I've taken a room down at Maybelle Wilson's. Actually, I'm here on business for the government. I have to check out some candidates for the federal courts."

I could have sworn this news made him wince, but he recovered quickly enough.

"Fine," he said. "Be about your business. Maybelle's should suit you perfectly. Is there something else?"

I saw no reason to prolong this agony. "Oh, no. Nothing. It was pleasant to see you again."

He waved for Dabney to ladle more soup into his bowl. He dabbed at his lips with a starched linen napkin. Then he deigned to speak.

"We should arrange another visit sometime," my father said. "Perhaps in another six years."

Chapter 25

"YOU NEED SOMETHING for your belly, Mr. Corbett?" Maybelle called in a loud voice from the front parlor of her rooming house.

I had found the Slide Inn Café all closed up for the night, but still I declined Maybelle's invitation. "No, thank you, ma'am. I'm all taken care of."

"Just as well. Ain't nothin' in there but some old pone."

Maybelle's had never been known for luxury. In fact, the only thing the place was ever known for was a string of slightly disreputable boarders through the years. Now, I supposed, I was one of them.

The original Maybelle had died years ago, about the time the house was last given a fresh coat of paint. But Eudora tradition dictated that any woman who ran the place was referred to as "Maybelle."

Occasionally a shoe salesman or cotton broker spent a night or two at Maybelle's. Once or twice a year my father commandeered the place to sequester jurors during a trial. And there were, inevitably, rumors about women of uncertain morality using the rooms for "business."

A monk would have felt at home in my room: a narrow iron bed, a small oaken desk with a perilous wobble, and an equally wobbly cane-backed chair. On the bureau were an enameled-steel bowl and pitcher. And under the bed, a chamber pot for those times you didn't want to make the trip to the outhouse.

In the corner of the room was one small window, which somehow managed to admit all the hot air from outside during the day and to hold it inside all night.

I stripped down to my Roxford skivvies and positioned the chair directly in front of that window. I suspected there was no breeze to be had in town that night. Luckily, my room was provided with the latest advance in cooling technology: a squared-off cardboard fan with the inscription "Hargitay's Mortuary Parlor, The Light of Memphis."

A lonely man sitting with his bare feet propped up on a windowsill, waving a funeral fan at his face.

Welcome home, Ben.

Chapter 26

IT WAS TOO DAMN HOT for sleeping. I figured I might as well do some detective work in my room.

I had put aside two newspapers from the collection of "lynching reviews" I'd brought from Memphis. Now was as good a time as any for reading.

These particular articles were of special interest. From the pages of the *Jackson Courier,* they told the stories of lynchings that had taken place right here in Eudora, and within the past three years.

I unfolded the first paper:

Word of an horrific death by strangulation reached our office this morning. By the time this reporter visited the alleged scene, no trace of said hanging was evident, save for a bloodied rope tossed aside in a pile of swamp grass.

The unanswered questions were obvious. Who told "this reporter" that the death was "horrific"? Why was he so careful to use the word "alleged"?

I picked up the other newspaper.

We learned of the death by lynching of Norbert Washington today. A witness at the lynching site in that area of Eudora called "the Quarters" said that Washington, a tobacco tanner at a plantation in nearby Chatawa, had been heard making rude and suggestive comments to a white lady in the Chatawa Free Library.

Upon investigation it was discovered that the town of Chatawa did not have a library, free or otherwise. That information notwithstanding, the eyewitness stated, "The hanging was most exciting, gruesome and, I must add, satisfying in its vengefulness for the niggerman's impertinence."

I was glad that I kept reading, even though I

wanted to look away. The final sentences were, for me, the most startling:

> When interviewed, Chief of Police Phineas Eversman said that he was unaware of any lynching that previous evening in Eudora. A visitor in Chief Eversman's office, the respected Eudora Justice Everett Corbett, agreed. "I too know nothing about a lynching in Eudora," Judge Corbett said.

I let the newspapers fall to the floor. No wonder Roosevelt needed someone to sort out this tangle of contradictions, half-truths, and outright lies.

Loneliness also gives a man time for thinking. It broke my heart to be so far away from my family—and to have left on this trip without a single kind word between Meg and me. From my valise I drew a small pewter picture frame, hinged in the middle. I opened the frame and stared at the joined photographs.

On the left was Meg, her smile so warm, so bright and unforced, that I found myself smiling back at her.

On the right were Alice and Amelia, posed on the sofa in our parlor. Both of them wore stiff expressions, but I knew the girls were seconds away from exploding into laughter.

I studied the images for a few minutes, thinking only good thoughts. I wished there were some way I could blink my eyes and bring the pictures to life so that all three of them could be here with me.

Chapter 27

EARLY THE NEXT MORNING, I discovered that the current Maybelle, a pleasant and blustery woman, was not much of a cook. I sat at the dining room table, poking at breakfast: a biscuit as tough as old harness leather, grits that were more lumps than grits, and a piece of salt pork that was 100 percent gristle.

"Miss Maybelle, who belongs to that bicycle I saw leaning against the shed out back?" I finally asked. "I need to see a few people around town."

"I keep that for the boy runs errands for me after school," she said. "You welcome to borry it, if you like."

Five minutes later I was rolling up my pant legs to protect them from bicycle chain grease. Two minutes after that I was sailing down Commerce

Street. I felt like a nine-year-old boy again, keeping my balance with my knees while extending my arms sideways in a respectable display of balancing skills.

I was nine again, but everything I saw was filtered through the eyes of a thirty-year-old man.

I rode the bicycle two circuits around the tiny park in front of the Methodist church, took a left at the minister's house and another left at the scuppernong arbor. At the end of the vine-covered trellis stood a simple white wooden structure that was unsupervised by anyone's eyes and universally known among the young people of Eudora as the Catch-a-Kiss Gazebo.

It was here that I came with Elizabeth the summer I was fifteen. It was here, on that same wooden bench, that I leaned in to kiss Elizabeth and was startled down to my toes by an open-mouthed kiss in return, full of passion and tongue and spit. At the same moment I felt her hand running smoothly up the side of my thigh. I felt the pressure of her nails. My own hand moved from her waist to her small, rounded bosom.

Then Elizabeth pulled away and shook her head, spilling blond curls onto her shoulders. "Oh, *Ben*, I want to kiss you and kiss you. And more. I want to do everything, Ben. But I can't. You know we can't."

I had never heard a girl talk like that. Most boys my age were hopeless when it came to discussing such matters — at least, in Eudora they were.

There were tears in Elizabeth's eyes. "It's all right," I said, but then I grinned. "But we could kiss some more. No harm in that." So Elizabeth and I kissed, and sometimes we touched each other, but it never went any farther than that, and eventually I went away to Harvard, where I met Meg.

Now I rode that bicycle fast down the lane, leaning into the curve, rounding the corner at the preacher's house, faster and faster, remembering Elizabeth Begley and the first taste of sex that had ever happened to me anywhere but in my own head.

Chapter 28

I PEDALED THAT BICYCLE all the way from my growing-up years to the present day. And I began to see people I knew, shopkeepers, old neighbors, and I waved and called out "Hi." A couple of times I stopped and talked with somebody from my school days, and that was fine.

I rode over to Commerce Street, past the Slide Inn Café, past the icehouse where a bucket came flying out of the darkness just in time to trip up poor George Pearson and send him to his death by hanging.

The exhilaration of my first ride through town was fading under the glare of a morning sun that was beating down hard. I was out of training for Mississippi summers. My thirst was demanding attention, and I remembered a pump at the end of the cotton-loading dock at the gin, just down from the depot.

I pedaled down Myrtle Street to the end of the platform that ran from the cotton gin beside the tracks of the Jackson & Northern line. I leaned my machine against the retaining wall and turned to the pump.

As I worked the handle and reveled in the water—half drinking, half splashing my face—I heard a loud voice behind me, an *angry* voice.

"What the hell makes you nigger boys think you can come high-walkin' into our town looking for a job? All our jobs belong to white men."

At the other end of the platform were two large and burly men I recognized as the Purneau brothers, Jocko and Leander, an unpleasant pair of backwoods louts who had been running the cotton gin for Old Man Furnish as long as I could remember. The two of them towered over three scrawny black boys who looked to be fifteen years old, maybe even younger.

"Well, suh, we just thinking with the crop coming you might be needin' some mo' help round the gin," said one of the boys.

"That's the trouble with you niggers, is when you set in to tryin' to think," said Leander Purneau.

He spoke in a friendly, jokey voice, which put me, and the boy, off guard. But then he popped him a solid punch on the side of his face and sent the boy down onto his knees.

The other boys skittered away like bugs from a kicked-over log. Suddenly I really was back in the past, and the boy on the ground was in serious trouble, like poor George Pearson had been.

There was one difference now—I was not a timid little boy. I was a grown man. As I wiped my wet hands on my shirt, I considered what I was about to do.

If I caused a commotion, made a scene, called attention to myself, I might endanger my mission even before it started.

But if I did nothing?

Fortunately, the boy on the ground rolled over and jumped up. He sprinted off down the platform, holding his jaw, but at least he was getting away.

And at that very moment, I felt something cold and hard jammed against the side of my neck.

It felt an awful lot like the barrel of a gun.

A deep voice behind me: "Just put your hands in the air. Nice and slow, *high*, that's the way to do it."

Chapter 29

"NOW, I WANT you to turn around real slow, partner. Don't make any fast moves."

I did exactly as I was told. *Real slow*.

And found myself looking straight into the face of Jacob Gill. Jacob and I had been inseparable from as far back as I could remember, until the day I left Eudora for college.

"You son of a bitch!" I shouted at him.

Jacob was laughing so hard he actually held his stomach and doubled over. His laughter made him do a little jig of delight.

"You nearly gave me a goddamn heart attack," I said. "You're a jackass."

"I know," Jacob said, howling some more.

Then we hugged, seizing each other by the shoulders, stepping back to get a good look.

"How'd you even know it was me?" I asked.

"We don't have too many yellow-haired fellows ten feet tall hanging around," said Jacob. Then he added, "I saw you decide not to mix it up with Jocko and Leander. That was smart thinking on your part."

"I guess so," I said. I remembered the time Jacob left me in the swamp to watch what happened to George Pearson. I wished I could tell him why I'd held back this time.

"Hey, it's near dinnertime," Jacob said and lightly punched my shoulder. "Let's go get some catfish."

"That sounds good. Where we going?"

"Don't tell me you've turned into such a big-city boy you forgot Friday is catfish day at the Slide Inn?"

Chapter 30

I PUSHED THE BICYCLE between us down Myrtle Street, toward the town square. Jacob stopped twice along the way to take a nip of whiskey from a pint he kept in his worn leather toolbox, and I said hello to a couple more people I recognized, or who remembered me.

The Slide Inn was alive with the hum of conversation, the smell of frying fish, the smoke from the cigars of the old fellows who always occupied the front table, solving the world's problems on a daily basis.

"Why aren't you staying at your daddy's?" Jacob asked as soon as we sat down at a corner table.

"You know my father," I said. "It seemed like Maybelle's was the smart place to be. My father and I just don't get along."

"All right, then. But there is one question I been

dying to ask: *What in hell are you doing back in Eudora?*"

"Nothing much," I said. "I've got a little business to tend to."

"Lawyer business?"

"Just a simple job for the Justice Department. I have to interview a few lawyers in the county, that's all it is. In the meantime—it's catfish!" I said.

Pretty soon Miss Fanny came from behind the counter bearing plates of crispy fried fish, sizzling-hot hush puppies, and ice-cold sweet-pickle coleslaw. The first bite was delicious, and every bite after. I asked Miss Fanny what time the place opened for breakfast, and made up my mind never to suffer through another of Maybelle's breakfasts.

"Hell, I look old, but you still look like a high-school boy, Ben," said Jacob. "Like you could run ten miles and never even break a sweat."

"Oh, I did plenty of sweating just riding that bike a dozen blocks," I said. "It'll take me a while to get used to this heat again. How you been keeping yourself, Jacob?"

"Well, let me see...you probably heard I turned down the offer to be ambassador to England...and that was right after I passed on the chance to be president of the university up in Tuscaloosa. Well, sir, it was shortly after that I made up my mind that the profession I was most suited for was as a carpenter's assistant."

"That's good," I said. "Honest work."

"Yeah, me and Wylie Davis are the men you want to see if you need a new frame for your window screens, you know, or a new roof for your johnny house."

Then there was silence, a good and acceptable kind of silence—nothing nervous or uncomfortable about it. The kind of quiet that is tolerable only between old friends.

It was Jacob who finally broke it.

"They were good days, Ben. Weren't they?"

"They were *great* days."

"We were friends! Right through it all."

"The best," I said. "We were like brothers."

We clinked our iced-tea glasses. Then Jacob spoke.

"But there is one thing I need to make very clear to you, Ben."

"What's that?" I tried to keep the note of concern out of my voice.

"You said we were like brothers?"

"Yeah? That's what I said."

"I just need to remind you of something."

"Well, go ahead, Jacob," I said.

"I was *always* the pretty one."

Chapter 31

ENOUGH!

Enough idle thoughts about my long-ago romance with Elizabeth Begley.

Enough turning over in my mind the painful lack of affection between my father and me, the disgust in his face when he saw me for the first time in six years.

Enough reliving an old friendship like Jacob's and mine.

Theodore Roosevelt hadn't sent me to Eudora to take a rickety bicycle ride down memory lane. I had a job to do, and it might even help change history.

I paid the bill for our lunch, and Jacob left two bits for Miss Fanny. Then he headed off up Commerce Street to help Wylie frame a new roof for the front porch of the town hall.

An old black man stepped off the sidewalk as Jacob passed, not to avoid a collision, but simply making the customary show of respect. Black men of all ages had been stepping down off sidewalks to get out of my way since I was five years old.

I rode the bicycle back to Maybelle's, changed my shirt, and set off on foot for the Eudora Quarters. On my way out, I made sure to tell Maybelle I had some interviews to attend to.

I considered trying to hire a horse and buggy, and couldn't think of anywhere in town to do such a thing. My father had three perfectly good horses in his barn, of course, but I was determined to do what I came to do without him.

ABRAHAM CROSS, EUDORA QUARTERS said the slip of paper the president had given me.

It was time for me to meet this Mr. Cross.

Chapter 32

I KNEW THE STREETS of the Quarters almost as well as I knew the rest of Eudora. I knew the history of how it came to be. After the war, the slaves from all the plantations and farms in the vicinity of Eudora had been freed. Most of them had either left their previous lodgings or been turned out by masters who no longer wanted to provide housing for people they didn't own.

So the freed slaves built their homes where no one else wanted to live, in a swampy, muddy, mosquito-ridden low place half a mile north of the center of Eudora.

They gathered fallen logs from the woods and lumber from derelict barns to build their little houses. They laid boards across the swampy, pestilential ground to keep their children's feet out of the mud.

They stuffed rags and old newspapers in the chinks in the walls to keep out the wind in winter.

They ate squirrel and possum, poke sallet and dandelion greens. They ate weeds from the field, horse corn, the leftover parts of a pig, and whatever else they could get their hands on.

Walking along there now, as the neighborhood changed from poor white to poorer black, I saw a colored man sitting on the porch of a shack painted a gay shade of blue. He nodded at me.

I returned his nod. "Pardon me, do you know a man by the name of Cross? Abraham Cross?"

He never blinked. His eyes didn't move from mine, but I had the feeling he was deciding whether or not I was worthy of the information I sought.

"Yes, suh," he finally said. "If you just keep walkin', you will come on a house with a strong smell of onions. That will be Abraham's house."

The sight of a white man walking on this street was not a welcome one for most of the people I came across. They kept their eyes down as they passed, which seemed to be customary now in Eudora but had not been the case when I was a boy.

Within minutes I caught the sharp tang of onions on the air. I saw thick patches of the familiar blue-green stalks in the yard of a small red house.

Suddenly, from the space between two houses, one little boy came running, followed by two more, and two more in pursuit.

"He gonna snatch you and eat you," the lead boy shouted.

Then I saw what was chasing them—a wild pig, huge and hairy and grunting, bearing down on the boys with a pair of very bad-looking tusks.

"That ain't the most beautiful animal in the world," said a colored man standing on the porch of the red house.

I answered, "That is a face not even a mother could love."

I looked closer. The man was taller than me, by at least three inches, and older, by at least fifty years.

"But she sure is beautiful when she's angry," he said.

We both laughed.

Then he said, "Begging your pardon, sir, but I get the idea you might be looking for someone."

"Well, as a matter of fact, I *am* looking for a man. His name is Abraham Cross."

"Yes, sir. You lookin' at him."

I must have appeared surprised.

"You was expectin' some young fella, weren't you, Mr. Corbett?"

"No, I—I really had no idea who to expect…"

"Well, sir, I confess I was expectin' a young fella myself. So I guess at least one of us was right."

Chapter 33

MAYBE IT WAS because he looked like a picture of silver-haired wisdom. I just don't know. But the truth is, I liked Abraham Cross from the moment I met him.

When he shook my hand, he grasped my shoulder with his other hand, so that I felt well and truly gripped.

"From this moment, Mr. Corbett—"

"Call me Ben," I said.

"From this moment, Mr. Corbett," he said pointedly, "I am happy to be of service to you as a guide and advisor. With luck, we may also become friends."

I told him that I felt luck would be on our side.

He offered me a seat on his porch, which had a view of everyone passing along the boards from one end of the Quarters to the other. Abraham greeted everyone—man, woman, child—with a friendly wave and a personal word of greeting. I think if that hairy old boar had come back, Abraham would have waved and said howdy.

Abraham Cross had the way of a man at ease with himself. He wore dark woolen trousers, a neatly ironed white shirt, and a navy blue bowtie. I don't know if he'd dressed up because he was expecting me or if he dressed this way every day.

On his head was a faded blue baseball cap with the initial *P* faded to near invisibility. I asked him what the *P* stood for.

"Pythians," he said. "Does that mean anything to you?"

"Weren't they athletes in ancient Delphi?" I said.

"Well, sir, I may be old but I ain't as old as the Greeks in old Delphi," he said, laughing.

Then he explained.

His greatest love in his young life, he told me, was baseball. After the War between the States he headed north, where a few Negro teams played.

"Notice I said they 'played.' I didn't say they 'flourished.' Anyways, I made the team in Philadelphia. We was porters and butlers, iron

113

men, lawn mower men during the week. On the weekends we played baseball."

At Abraham's nod, I followed him off his porch and toward the little "downtown" of the Quarters.

We were passing the colored general store, Hemple's, where you could see the canned goods inside through gaps between the boards. By the front door stood a neat pyramid of beautiful peaches.

Abraham reached into his pocket for a couple of pennies, which he took inside to the old man at the cash box. He came back out and selected a nice fat peach from the side of the stack.

"Were you any good?" I asked the old man.

He smiled. He looked past me to a broom standing just inside the door. He asked me to hand it to him.

"You want to know if I was any good?"

He held the broom short, like a baseball bat. Then he tossed that beautiful peach into the air.

He swung.

He connected. Tasting a fine spatter of peach juice on my face, I watched it sail up and up, into the hot afternoon sky.

"Don't bother to go lookin' for that peach," he said.

"I believe it is gone," I agreed.

"In a minute or two it's gonna be in Loo-siana," he said with a grin. "They always said tall, skinny boys like you and me can't play baseball. They say we too far from the ground. I'll tell you something, I proved they don't know everything."

He wiped the broom handle on his shirt and put the broom back inside.

We walked a few minutes in silence. Then Abraham stopped, his face suddenly serious.

"I could talk baseball and swing at soft peaches all day," he said. "But you and I have some other business."

"Yes, we do," I said.

"This is serious business, Mr. Corbett. Sad business. My people are worse off now than they were the day Mr. Lincoln signed the Emancipation."

Chapter 34

"WE DON'T HAVE TO GO far to find a lynching tree," Abraham said. "But I know how tired you young fellas get from walking in the heat of the day. I reckon we'd best take the hosses."

The two "hosses" Abraham led out from a rickety blacksmith shop were mules—in fact, they were mules that had hauled one too many plows down one too many cotton rows. But those skinny animals proved their worth by depositing us, less than twenty minutes later, at a secluded swampy area that was unmistakably the site of a lynching.

Unmistakably.

A cool grotto tucked back in the woods away from the road. Big branches interlaced overhead to form a ceiling. The dirt was packed hard as a stone floor from the feet of all the people who had stood there watching the terrible spectacle.

Abraham pointed to an oak at the center of the clearing. "And there's your main attraction."

Even without his guidance, I would have recognized it as a lynching tree. There was a thick, strong branch barely a dozen feet from the ground. The low dip in the middle of the branch was rubbed free of its bark by the friction of ropes.

I walked under the tree. The hard ground was stained with dark blotches. My stomach churned at the thought of what had happened in this unholy place.

"Somebody left us a greeting," Abraham said. "That would be the Klan."

He was pointing behind me, to the trunk of a sycamore tree. About five feet up, someone had used an odd-looking white nail to attach a plank with crude lettering on it:

BEWARE ALL COONS!
BEWARE ALL COON LOVERS!

"I've never seen a nail that color," I said.

"You never seen a nail made out of human bone?" said Abraham.

117

I shuddered, reaching up to haul the plank down.

"Don't waste your strength, Mr. Corbett," he said. "You pull that one down today, there'll be a new sign up there next week."

His face changed. "We got *company*," he said.

Chapter 35

THE DOUBLE-BARRELED SHOTGUN pointed our way was almost as big as the girl holding it. It was so long and heavy I was more afraid she would drop it and discharge it accidentally than that she might shoot us on purpose.

Abraham said, "What you fixin' to do with that gun? That ain't no possum you aimin' at."

I was distracted by the fact that she was very serious *and* very pretty. She wore a simple cotton jumper, stark white against the smooth brown of her skin. A perfect face, with delicate features that betrayed the fierceness of her attitude. Deep brown eyes flashed a steady warning: *keep away from me.*

"What y'all doing messin' around the lynching tree?" she said.

"You know this girl, Abraham?"

"I surely do. This is Moody. Say hello to Mr. Corbett."

Moody didn't say a word to me. She kept her barrel trained on my heart. If she was going to stare at me this way, I couldn't help looking back at her.

"Well, if you know her," I said, "maybe you should tell her not to go around pointing firearms at people."

"Moody, you heard the man," said Abraham. "Put it down. Now, granddaughter."

"Oh, Papaw," she said, "what you bring this white man out here for?"

Abraham reached out and pushed the gun barrel away. Moody pulled back from him as if he were trying to take away her doll.

"She's your granddaughter?"

"That's right."

It struck me that the girl had seemed as willing to shoot her grandfather as to shoot me. She walked boldly up to me, around me, looking me over as if I represented some species of animal she had never observed before and already didn't like.

"Mr. Corbett is here from Washington," said Abraham.

"You working for him?" said Moody. "Why would you?"

"We working together," said Abraham.

"Well, if you ain't working for him, how come he calls you Abraham, and you call him Mr. Corbett?"

"Because he prefers it that way." Abraham knew that wasn't so, but he fixed me in place with a look that stifled the protest in my throat. "Mr. Corbett is here by the instructions of the president of the—"

"*Abraham,*" I said. "We're not supposed to talk about any of this."

He nodded, dipped his head. "You are right, Mr. Corbett," he said.

Moody gave me a disgusted look and said, "You should have let me shoot him while I had the chance."

Chapter 36

WHEN I WAS GROWING UP, gumbo was not something most white people would eat, unless they were Catholic and lived down on the coast. Gumbo was food for black people, or Creole people. Like chitlins and hog ears, it was the kind of thing mostly eaten out of necessity. Or so most people thought. My mother's cook, Aurelia, used to whip up a big pot of sausage-and-crawfish gumbo and leave it to feed us through Friday, her day off.

So when Abraham suggested we stop in at a little gray shanty of a saloon with a crooked sign on the door, GUMBO JOE'S, I was a happy man. Also along for the meal was Moody and her brother Hiram, a handsome boy of nineteen with aspirations to be a lawyer.

I was surprised at the idea of a Negro restaurant

in Eudora, but when I stepped inside the place, I saw it was 95 percent saloon, with a little cooker perched beside the open window in back. On the flame sat a bubbling pot.

An old black man came out from behind the rickety bar. I couldn't help flinching at the sight of him: he had no chin, and his right arm was severed just below the elbow.

Without our asking, he brought three small glasses and a bottle of beer. "Y'all want gumbo?"

"We do," said Abraham.

So much for a menu.

Abraham poured beer into all three glasses, and I took one. It wasn't cold, but it tasted real good.

"What happened to that man?" I said softly.

"The war," said Abraham. He explained that the old man had been a cook for Pemberton's army at Vicksburg. The Yankee mortar shell that crashed through the mess tent was no respecter of color or rank.

"He lost half his face fighting for the side that was trying to keep him a slave," I said.

"Wasn't fighting, he was cooking," said Abraham. "A lot of us did. The pay was good. Better than we got staying home. Those was good times, if you didn't get killed."

The War between the States had been officially over for forty-three years but had never actually ended in the South. The Confederate battle flag still flew higher than Old Glory, at least at our courthouse. There were Rebel flags hanging on the fronts of stores and from the flagpoles of churches. Ever since I was a boy I had recognized the old faded butternut cap as the sign of a Confederate veteran.

There had always been men with wooden legs or wooden crutches. I knew that an empty sleeve pinned up inside a suit jacket meant an arm had been left on a battlefield in Georgia or Tennessee. Maybelle's handyman, otherwise a handsome old gent, had a left eye sewn shut with orange twine. The skin around that eye burned to a god-awful dry red that would have scared me if I'd been a child.

"That old man behind the bar?" said Abraham. "Before the war, he was trying to become a professional fiddler."

I shook my head. "And now he has no chin to lean his fiddle on," I said.

Abraham's face broke open in a big smile. So did Moody's and her brother's. "Aw now, Mr. Corbett, I was fooling on you. Old Jeffrey wasn't no fiddler.

He was slingin' beer back before the war, and he been slingin' beer ever since."

Moody saw the look on my face and busted out with a guffaw. "Papaw, *Mr.* Corbett ain't too swift, is he?"

Chapter 37

THE CHINLESS OLD MAN RETURNED, bearing in his good hand a tray with three steaming bowls of dark gumbo.

"Look like we maybe gonna have some music too," Hiram said, and his face lit up in a smile.

Two or three men had drifted in, still shiny-sweaty from the field. They ordered beers and shot nervous looks in our direction. The more I thought about it, the more I realized how out of place I was in here. It was the Negroes' place; who was I to come in and sit down as if I belonged?

At least they had the courtesy to let me sit there, which would certainly not be the case if one of them tried to order a beer in a white barroom.

I was delighted to see a grizzled middle-aged fellow taking out a banjo, tuning it up while his buddy drummed his hands on an overturned gutbucket. The thin, listless woman between them waited for the banjo player to plink a little chord, and then without any introduction or ritual, she set in to wailing.

Lawd, I been blue
Since my man done left this town...

The little hairs on my neck prickled.

"You heard the blues before, Mr. Corbett?" asked Hiram.

"I have—one time," I said. "On Beale Street in Memphis."

Sho done been blue
Since my man done left this town...

"You like the way she sings?" Moody said.

"I do," I said. "I like it a lot."

Moody shrugged, like she didn't much care which way I answered her question.

"I'm a devotee of ragtime music," I told her.

"You a what?" said Moody. "A deevo—what did you say?"

"Admirer," I said. "I'm an admirer of ragtime."

"No, that word you used—what was it again?"

Moody had a bold way of speaking. I must admit I wasn't accustomed to being addressed by a colored girl without the customary "yes, sir" and "no, sir."

"Devotee," I said. "One who is devoted to something. I think it's from the French."

"That's a pretty word," she said, "wherever it come from."

He beat me, then he leave me
And now he ain't been coming round.

When that lament ended, the banjo man put down his instrument and brought out a battered guitar.

Once again I was swept up in the mournful repetition, the slangy bent notes from the singer echoed by the guitar, the way it all fell together into a slow, rhythmic chant of pure feeling. This music was made from leftover parts of old field songs and hymns and slave music, but to me it sounded like something entirely new, and something quite wonderful.

Chapter 38

MY BELLY WAS STUFFED full of gumbo and rice. My tongue still burned from the red pepper. I remarked to Abraham on the staying power of the cayenne.

"Here, take a chaw on this," said Abraham. From his satchel he brought forth a length of brown sugarcane. I smiled. That's what our cook Aurelia used to prescribe for a sore throat or any other minor childhood complaint: a suck on a piece of sweet cane.

"You got enough for family?" said Moody.

"I got plenty, but it don't look right for a gal to chew cane," Abraham said.

She put on such a pout that Abraham laughed and brought out a piece for her and another for Hiram.

"My granddaughter is incorrigible," said Abraham. "I hope you can forgive her."

"I don't need him forgiving me," she said.

Her grandfather's face darkened. "Moody? Watch your mouth."

She dropped her eyes. "Yes, sir."

"See now, Mr. Corbett, she got so comfortable settin' here next to you that she's done forgot how she s'posed to act. If you was any other kind of white man, she could be in big trouble right now, sassing you that way. Same thing goes for Hiram. *Even more so.*" I had the feeling he said this more for Moody's and Hiram's benefit than for mine. Moody kept her eyes riveted fiercely on the floor beside our table.

"See, when you're colored, you always about this close—" he held up his fingers, indicating a tiny space—"to sayin' the wrong word. Or lookin' the wrong way. And that means you this far from gettin' beat up, or kicked, or punched, or cursed. Or gettin' strung up and killed by the KKK."

I took a long sip from my beer.

"Everything a colored man does can be a crime these days," he said.

"I don't quite understand," I said.

Moody's eyes came up. "Let me tell him, Papaw."

He hesitated, but then he said, "All right."

130

"They's a young fellow called Whitney," she said, gazing intently at me. "He spent a day hoeing out the flowerbeds around ol' Miz Howard's house, then when she was done he told her how much it was. She didn't want to pay. Said he hadn't worked that many hours. Then she calls up the sheriff and says Whitney done said something dirty to her. Well, she got him arrested, but that wasn't enough for 'em. They come drug him out of the jail and hung him up. Killed him. All because he asked for his pay." Her eyes blazed.

"That's the *truth*," said Hiram.

"Sammy Dawkins brung his empty Co-Cola bottle back to Sanders' store to get his penny back. Ol' Mr. Sanders tells him niggers don't get the penny back, just white folks. Sammy argues with him and next thing you know he's in jail. *For wanting his penny!*"

"Keep your voice down," Abraham said.

"There was a couple boys sitting on the sidewalk downtown. They was talkin' to each other quiet like, telling about this strike of colored men up in Illinois. Well, sir, somebody overheard what they said, and next thing you know a bunch of men jump on these boys. One of 'em, they knocked out all his teeth."

"We get punished for 'boasting,' and for 'strutting,' and for talking too loud, and for casting the evil eye. We get arrested for 'walking too fast,' or 'walking too slow,' or taking too long to say *yassuh*."

Moody was furious now. Her voice carried to tables nearby. Some of the people stopped their own conversations to listen.

"Colored man looks at a white woman, they kill him just for thinkin' the thoughts he ain't even thought," she said. "If he even looks at a white woman, it must mean he wants to rape her or kill her. When they're the ones doing most of the raping and killing around here!"

"Now, calm down," Abraham said.

"Don't tell me to calm down! I know what it's like. It happens to me too, Papaw."

"I know, child."

"You don't know what happened yesterday. I was bringin' the basket of ironing back to Miz Cooper, you know she got that boy Dillard, he's not right in the head. Well, he out there pulling weeds in the kitchen garden. He looked at me. All I said was, 'Howdy, Dillard,' and he says somethin' real rude, like, 'Maybe you want to go with me, Moody' or somethin' like that. I just ignored him, Papaw. I just kept walking. But he come up behind me and grab me, like, you know, touching my titties."

"Hush," said Abraham sternly.

"It's what happened, Papaw," she said. "Then he says 'Aw come on, Moody, you a nigger girl, and ever'body knows that is all a nigger girl wants.'"

And with that, she couldn't keep the tears in. She folded her arms on the table and buried her head. Hiram stroked her neck.

I spoke softly: "We're going to do something, Moody. That's why I'm here with your grandfather."

There was silence. Then Moody looked up at me and she was angry.

"*Go home, Mr. Corbett.* That's what you could do. Just pack up your bag, and go home."

Chapter 39

"I GUESS YOU PRAYED for mail, Mr. Corbett," Maybelle said as I walked past the kitchen of the rooming house the next morning. "And the Lord answered."

She held out a plate with a pair of blackened biscuits and another plate with three envelopes. My heart lifted. But my happiness faded when I glanced through the letters and found that none of them had come from Washington.

I smiled down at the biscuits, thanked Maybelle, and put them aside for disposal later.

On my way over to the Slide Inn, I thumbed through the mail. First I opened a flyer inviting me to a "social and covered dish supper" at the Unitarian church in Walker's Bridge, one town west of Eudora. In the right-hand margin was a handwritten addition: *"Ben—Hope to see you at the supper. Elizabeth."*

The next envelope also held an invitation. This one was a good deal fancier than the first, engraved on heavy paper, wrapped in a piece of protective tissue.

Mr. and Mrs. L. J. Stringer
request the pleasure of your company
at supper on Saturday, July fourteenth,
nineteen hundred and six
at eight o'clock in the evening

Number One Summit Square
Eudora, Mississippi
R.S.V.P.

What was this world coming to? A fancy-dress invite from L. J. Stringer, of all people!

It was hard to believe that the sweet, kindly boy with whom I'd spent a good portion of my childhood was now in such a lofty position that he could send out invitations engraved on thick vellum. And that on his way to manhood, L.J. had invented a machine that shot twine around cotton bales in one-eighth the time it took four men to do the job.

The Stringer Automatic Baler. Without it, Cotton would no longer be King.

I eased into a rear table at the Slide Inn Café. I ordered coffee and a big breakfast of grits and eggs, patty sausage and biscuits. I thought about L. J. Stringer for a moment or two, but my heart was heavy at the absence of a single letter from home.

Why hadn't Meg written? I didn't really need to ask myself that. I knew the answer. But even if she was too angry—why hadn't she allowed the girls to write?

I decided to detour by the post office just to make sure no letters had been accidentally sent to Judge Everett Corbett's home.

Meantime I took a slurp of the Slide Inn's good chicory coffee and tore open the last of my three letters, the one without a return address.

At first I thought the envelope was empty. I had to feel around inside it before I found the card.

It was a postcard, like any other postcard. In place of a picture of the Grand Canyon or Weeki Wachee Springs, the card bore a photograph of a young black man dangling from a rope. His face had been horribly disfigured. The whip marks on his bare chest were so vivid I felt like I could touch them.

136

On the other side of the card was a handwritten message:

THIS IS THE WAY WE COOK COONS
DOWN HERE.
THIS IS THE WAY WE WILL COOK YOU.
WE KNOW WHY YOU ARE HERE.
GO HOME, NIGGER-LOVER.

Chapter 40

I DIDN'T GO HOME, of course; I couldn't—my mission was only just getting started. So I actually talked to some candidates for federal judgeships. And I continued my secretive investigation for Roosevelt. I even squeezed in a few hours at L. J. Stringer's party and remembered what a good friend he was.

A few weeks later, I felt I needed a haircut, and I knew where to go: Ezra Newcomb's.

During my visit, I congratulated Ezra, Eudora's only barber, on the sharpness of his blade. This resulted in my receiving a nine-point instructional course on the most important techniques involved in properly sharpening a straight razor. (The truth was, I had brought my own dull razor along, hoping to have Ezra sharpen it.)

"You got to start her off real slow, then you swipe down the strop real fast," he was saying.

This was exactly the lesson I had gotten from Ezra the last time he cut my hair, when I was a boy of eighteen.

"Just don't understand it," Ezra said. "A boy goes all the way up to Harvard and they don't teach him how to sharpen a razor."

"I must have been out sick the day they gave that class."

Ezra laughed and swept the bib off me with a dramatic flourish. He returned my sharpened razor to me. I handed him a quarter and told him to keep the change. He whistled at my generous big-city tipping habits.

Then I stood outside the barbershop in the bright September sun, admiring the dangerous gleam on the edge of the blade.

"Why, Ben, you're looking at that razor the way most men look at a pretty girl!"

I turned around to see Elizabeth Begley standing right there beside me. We were practically elbow to elbow.

"I was admiring Ezra's handiwork. In all my years of trying, I have never been able to put half as good an edge on a razor."

"Oh, Ben, I don't believe there's anything you can't do," she said, "if you decide to go after it."

Now what was this craziness? Was my old girlfriend flirting with me? Was I flirting right back?

I flicked the razor shut and slipped it into my pocket.

"Come walk me to Jenkins's store," she said. "I bought new boots for Emma and she's already been through the laces. That's not right."

We walked the sidewalk of Commerce Street, which was fairly deserted at this hour.

"A little bird told me you were the *guest of honor* at the Stringers' dress party the other night," she said.

"I wouldn't say guest of honor," I said. "But I guess some people are a little curious what I'm doing back here."

"You must tell them all you've come to visit *me*," Elizabeth said with a smile. "That will get their tongues wagging."

She laughed, and so did I.

"Speaking of people who love to talk behind other people's backs . . ." She nodded in the direction of Lenora Godwin, who was walking toward us on the sidewalk across the street, apparently lost in thought.

"Lenora was at the party," I said. "She's still as well dressed as ever."

"Did she look ravishing?" There was a slightly caustic edge to the question.

"She may still be the 'Best Dressed,'" I said, "but I was wondering why the 'Most Popular Girl' at Eudora High wasn't there."

"It's simple, Ben. She and her husband were not invited to attend."

I was surprised to hear this. I knew that Eudora "society," such as it was, was a small, intimate group. Surely Elizabeth would be included.

"I think you know my husband is Richard Nottingham, the state senator," Elizabeth said. "Richard is known to be the political kingmaker."

"I did know that," I said.

"Well, then, put it together. L. J. Stringer never sits down to dinner with anyone more important than himself. Some people say that Richard will be the next governor," she said.

"And what do you think, Elizabeth?"

"He certainly wants to be governor. But I...I don't want to leave Eudora."

We had reached Jenkins's store now. "Thank you for walking with me, Ben. And for our talk. Now I have boot laces to buy."

To my disappointment, she didn't invite me in with her. But Elizabeth leaned in and lightly kissed my cheek, then disappeared into the store—the same one where my mother had collapsed when I was just a boy.

Chapter 41

MY MOTHER USED TO SAY, "When you're truly in love, you see the face you love in your coffee cup, in the washstand mirror, in the shine on your shoes." I remembered those words as I sat at my regular table at the Slide Inn, sipping a cup of strong and delicious chicory coffee.

Miss Fanny brought my breakfast of fried eggs, creamy salty grits, a slice of cured ham, and buttermilk biscuits, but I only had eyes for my coffee cup, and Mama's words haunted me. I couldn't stop thinking about Elizabeth. *Yes, Mama. I see her face in the surface of my coffee.*

Elizabeth.

If I were not feeling so lonely and abandoned by my wife, would I be having these feelings? Probably not. But I was feeling lonely and abandoned, and worse — aroused.

Elizabeth.

My reverie was broken by Fanny's exclamation as she looked past me and out the window.

"That boy is like to drive me crazy, late as he is. Look at him, running up here like his shirttail's on fire!"

A gangly colored boy of about sixteen was headed for the café in a big, sweaty, arm-pumping hurry—such a hurry, in fact, that he almost dashed in the front door without thinking.

Then he saw Fanny and me staring at him. He remembered his place, ducked his head, and went around back.

Miss Fanny went to meet him. Through the window to the kitchen I saw the two of them in serious conversation, the boy gesticulating wildly.

I waited until Miss Fanny came back out front, then lifted my finger for more coffee. She brought the tin pot over to me.

"What's the trouble?" I said.

"Big trouble," she said quietly. "Seems like there was another hangin' party last night."

I kept my voice low. "You mean...a lynching?"

"Two of 'em," she said.

Chapter 42

I TOOK ANOTHER SIP of coffee and noticed that my hand was shaking some. Then I folded my napkin and headed back through the kitchen as if I intended to visit the privy. On the way I detoured to the side of the room where the boy stood over a sinkful of dirty dishes.

"What happened, son?" I said. "Please, tell me everything."

At first the boy just stared at me without speaking a word.

Fanny came up behind us. "It's okay, Leroy. This here's Mr. Corbett. He's all right to talk to."

At last the boy spoke. "You know who is Annie?" he said. "The one cook for Miz Dickinson? She got a girl, Flossie, little older than me?"

I didn't know who he was talking about, but I nodded so he would continue.

"Well, it was that Mr. Young," he said, "Mr. Jasper Young."

I knew Jasper Young, who owned the hardware and feed stores. He was a quiet, grandfatherly man who exercised some influence behind the scenes in Eudora.

"What does Jasper Young have to do with it?"

"I can't say." The boy stared down at his dishes.

"Why not?"

He shot a look at Miss Fanny. "Lady present."

"Aw, now, come on, Leroy. Not one thing in this world you can't say in front of me!"

He wiggled and resisted, but at last he turned his eyes away from Fanny and fixed them on me.

"Mr. Young want some lovin' from Flossie. She didn't want to go along with it. So he...he *force* the love out of her."

What an incredible way to put it.

He force the love out of her.

The rest of the boy's story came quickly.

Flossie had told her mother of the rape. Annie told her husband. Within minutes, her husband and son, crazed with rage, broke into Jasper Young's home. They smashed china and overturned a table. Then they beat Jasper Young with their fists.

A neighbor summoned a neighbor who summoned

another neighbor. Within an hour, no more than that, Annie's husband and her son were hanging from ropes in the swamp behind the Quarter.

"Where are they, exactly?" I asked the boy.

"Out by Frog Creek."

That was not the place I'd visited with Abraham, but I knew where it was.

I practically ran all the way back to Maybelle's. I didn't ask if I could borrow the bicycle, I just climbed on and rode out the old McComb Road, toward the swamp.

Toward Frog Creek.

Chapter 43

I CAME UPON A VISION of horror, all too real. Two men, one young, one older, naked and bloody, dangling from ropes. Already the smell of rotting flesh was rising in the morning heat. Flies were on the bodies.

On the ground beneath the stiff, hanging bodies, amid the cigar butts and discarded whiskey bottles, sat a woman and child. The woman was about thirty-five years old. The boy was no more than four. He was touching the woman's face, touching the tears on her cheeks.

The woman saw me and her face furrowed over in rage. "You go on, now," she shouted. "They already dead. You cain't do no more to hurt 'em."

I walked closer and she drew the boy to her, as if to protect him from me.

"I'm not going to hurt anybody," I said. "I'm a friend."

She shook her head fiercely. *No.*

I wanted to comfort her terrible sobbing, but I stayed back. "Are you Annie?"

She nodded.

Now that I was close to the dangling bodies, I saw the welts left by whips, the bloody wounds covering almost every part of their bodies. The older man's arm hung down from his shoulder by a few bloody tendons. As the younger man slowly twisted, I saw that his testicles had been severed from his body.

My voice finally came out choked. "Oh, I am so sorry."

I noticed a pink, rubbery thing in her hand, something she kept stroking with her finger as she wept.

She saw me looking. "You want to know what it is? It's my Nathan's tongue. They done cut his tongue out of his head. Stop him from sassin' them."

I looked up. Blood was thickly caked around the older man's mouth.

"Oh, Jesus!"

"Ain't no Jesus," she said. "There ain't no Jesus for me."

She wept so terribly I could not hold myself back. I knelt by her in the clearing.

For a moment all was quiet, but for her sobbing.

Then a noise. A rustling in the underbrush, a crackling of twigs. I saw birds fly up in alarm.

Someone was there.

No doubt about it.

Someone was watching us.

And then out came several people, some men but also women, black people from the Quarters come to cut down the father and son who had been murdered.

ALEX CR•SS

Part Three

SOUTHERN FUNERAL
FAVORITES

Chapter 44

COULD ANYONE POSSIBLY PEDAL a bicycle as slowly as I did going back to Eudora?

I looked all around me. Although my little town still looked much as it had when I was a boy, now it was stained and tattered almost beyond recognition.

Now the whole place was poisoned by torture and murder. The proof was still swinging from that oak tree out by the banks of Frog Creek. I thought about going to the police, but what good would it do? And besides, it would raise the question of why I had gone out to the scene of the lynchings.

"You all soakin' wet," Maybelle said as I trudged up onto her porch. "Set here with me and have a lemonade."

I put myself in a porch rocker and prepared to be disappointed, but the lemonade was cold, sweet, delicious.

"Oh, I almost forgot," Maybelle said. "You had a visitor while you were gone. Senator Nottingham's wife."

"Elizabeth? Did she leave any message?"

"No, she said she would stop by again. But that reminds me, I know how much stock you put in getting the mail, and you did get some today. I put it in the front hall."

On the hall table was a square, cream-colored envelope with my name written in Meg's delicate hand.

I took the stairs two at a time. Inside my room, I removed my jacket and settled into the chair at the window for a good read.

Dear Ben,
I know I ought to be ashamed for not having written sooner. The girls have done very little else but remind me. They have pestered me about you night and day. But I've been busy doing almost all the housekeeping, because Mazie had to go up to Trenton on account of her sister has been "ill."

Do not worry about me. Other than sore muscles from wringing out the wash and

from scrubbing the floors in the house, I am
in good physical shape.

These opening lines filled me with joy. My wife was still my wife. My fears were unjustified. The letter sounded so much like her—the teasing complaints, the emphatic descriptions, even the hint that she regarded Mazie's sister's problem as nothing more than a love of the grape.

Later on, when I reflected on this moment, I wished I had stopped reading at that point.

Ben, I might as well get to the point. I have
suffered and wept many nights over this.
Finally I have reached my decision. There is
no reason for me to delay the pain for both of
us, and pain there will surely be when I tell
you what is in my heart.

I think it would be best for all involved if I
move back in with my father.

I read that last sentence again . . . and again . . .

I doubt this will truly come as a surprise to
you. You know that we have not been in love,

as husband and wife must be, for some time now.

My hand was shaking now. The paper began to rattle and my eyes burned.

I rested my head back against my chair. "I'm still in love, Meg," I said out loud.

I have prayed much about this matter, and have spoken to my father about the situation.

I should have known. Meg had consulted the one god in her life, the almighty Colonel Wilfred A. Haverbrook, U.S. Army, Ret. No doubt the colonel had agreed with her that her husband was a miserable failure.

I know that my decision may strike you as a terrible mistake on my part. Yet I believe it is the only correct solution to our dilemma. We must be honest with each other and ourselves.

I think it best if you do not come home at this time. I will be in touch with you by post

*or wire, as I begin the steps necessary to bring
about a most painful but inevitable result.*

*Cordially, your wife
Meg*

I have often heard the expression "It hit him
like a punch in the stomach," but I had never felt
it myself. Suddenly I knew exactly what it meant.
The letter struck me a blow that caused a physical
ache so sharp I had to bend over. Then I sat up.
Perhaps I'd missed a word, or an entire sentence,
and reversed the meaning of the thing.

I grabbed the letter and read it again. I read it out
loud.

Eventually I turned it over and found another
message scrawled on the back in pencil, a child's
handwriting.

*Daddy, me and Alice miss you terrible, just
terrible. Pleas come home soon as you can. I
love you, your dauhgter, Amelia.*

And that is when I felt my heart break.

Chapter 45

I POURED COLD WATER from the pitcher into the basin, then washed my face with the coarse brown soap, scrubbing so hard I threatened to take the skin off.

Next I took a sheet of writing paper from my valise, along with a pen Meg had given me for the first anniversary of our marriage: a beautiful Waterman pen.

I pulled the wobbly chair up to the wobbly table and uncapped the pen. Immediately I felt all my lawyerly eloquence disappear.

> *Dear Meg,*
> *As your husband, and your friend, I must tell you that you have some things wrong. I do love you. You are simply wrong to say*

that I don't. A separation like this is a rash thing to do, especially considering that we have never even discussed these problems face to face.

I don't care about your father's opinion of our marriage. But I do care that our parting will break the hearts of everyone involved—Alice, Amelia, my own heart, even yours.

Before you take any further action, please, my darling Meg, we must discuss this—together, as husband and wife, as mother and father of our two little daughters, as Meg and Ben who always planned to spend our lives together.

Suddenly I came out of my writing trance...

"Mr. Corbett! Mr. Corbett!"

It was Maybelle, hollering from the foot of the stairs.

I quickly wrote,

> *Your loving and faithful husband,*
> *Ben*

"Mr. Corbett!"

I put down the pen and walked out to the landing.

"What is it, Maybelle?" I called.

"Mrs. Nottingham is here to see you. She's here on the porch. She's waiting on you, Mr. Corbett. Hurry."

Chapter 46

THERE ELIZABETH WAS, standing on Maybelle's wide wraparound porch. She had put on another bonnet and seemed even more attractive than she'd been this morning.

She reached out for my hand. "I came to apologize, Ben."

I took her hand. "What do you mean? Apologize for what?"

I said this for the benefit of Maybelle, whom I could see lingering in the parlor, trying not to be observed.

"Let's go look at Miss Maybelle's rose garden," I proposed. "It's in full bloom this time of year."

I made a motion with my eyes that disclosed my real meaning to Elizabeth. She nodded and followed me around the porch toward the backyard.

Maybelle's roses were actually in sad shape, a few blossoms drooping among a profusion of weeds.

"I'm sorry for this morning," Elizabeth said. "The way I ran off."

"You didn't run, you walked. I watched your every step," I said and smiled.

"You can still be funny, Ben."

"Sit on the bench," I said. "I won't bite you."

Smoothing her dress, she sat on the stained marble bench amid the raggedy roses.

Sitting close to her, I was fascinated by her every gesture, word, movement. I noticed the way Elizabeth touched her mouth with the knuckle of her second finger, giving herself a little kiss before coming out with an opinion. And the slow southern musical rhythm of her speech. *Lord, what was getting into me? Probably just loneliness. Or was it being rejected by my wife?*

"You were surprised I came to see you again so soon?" she said.

"I'm always glad to see you, Elizabeth," I said. Then added, "Yes, I'm surprised you're here."

"I do have an ulterior motive," she said. "We're having a luncheon after church on Sunday. Will you come?"

"*We?*"

"Richard and I."

"Sure, I'll come," I replied.

I caught the faint scent of rose water, and I noted the curve of her nose, and remembered being very young and in love with that little nose.

"Wonderful," she was saying. "Come about one, Ben. We'll have some nice people in. I'll try not to have any of those you were subjected to at L.J.'s."

She stood. "I can't be late picking up Emma from her lesson. She's quite the little pianist, and I guess I'm quite the doting mother."

I stood, and we smiled. This time, there was no kiss on the cheek.

But I watched Elizabeth walk away again, every step, until she finally disappeared behind the rooming house porch.

Chapter 47

That same afternoon, Senator John Tyler Morgan, Democrat of Alabama, stood in the lobby of the Willard Hotel, yelling at the general manager.

"I have never been refused service in my life! That insufferable man in the elevator had the nerve to tell me he was holding the car for an *important personage*. He told me to get off that car and wait for another car!"

Senator Morgan was so angry that specks of saliva were speckling the lapels of the general manager's morning coat.

"Senator, I am so sorry for the inconvenience—"

"Not an *inconvenience!* It's a goddamned *insult!* Who the hell was he holding the elevator for, the goddamned president of the United States?"

164

As he roared this question, the great glass doors of the lobby flew open at the hands of two uniformed guards. In walked Theodore Roosevelt.

He took one look at John Tyler Morgan in mid-rampage and the poor little cowering manager. Then Roosevelt thundered, "Unless my eyes deceive me, the man at the center of that ruckus is none other than the senior senator from the great state of Alabama. Good morning, John!"

The famous Civil War general and southern statesman was stunned into silence. No one had called him John in many years.

"Morning, Mr. President," he finally managed to say.

"Come ride the elevator with me, John!"

A few minutes later, having deposited the red-faced Morgan on his floor, Roosevelt had a good laugh at his expense. "And the newspapers call *me* a gasbag? Senator Morgan, my friends, is the royal and supreme emperor of gasbags! Did you see how quickly I deflated him simply by using his Christian name?"

Appreciative laughter from his aides trailed the president to his suite. Roosevelt grew serious the moment he passed through the door.

"Good morning, Mr. President. We're all ready

for your meeting," said Jackson Hensen, his capable assistant.

"Well, get them in here. No need to dawdle."

"Yes, sir. They're on their way up in the service elevator."

Roosevelt chuckled. "How did they take to that?"

"I understand the gentleman was ... displeased," Hensen said.

Chapter 48

THE INNER DOOR OPENED and a pair of adjutants appeared, escorting a distinguished-looking black man with a Vandyke beard and a wide woman of a darker, more African appearance, with a wise face and a spectacular sweep of hair that plainly was not entirely her own.

Mr. Roosevelt bowed to the man and kissed the lady's gloved hand. He could never be seen doing such a thing in public, but here in private he was all too happy to pay honor to W. E. B. Du Bois, the great Negro writer and crusader, and to Ida B. Wells-Barnett, the passionate antilynching campaigner, such a modern and audacious woman that she dared to append her husband's name to her own when she married.

"My sincere apologies for the indignity of

bringing you up in the...back elevator," the president said.

Du Bois bowed slightly. "It is not the first time I have ridden in the servants' car, Mr. President," he said. "I am fairly sure it will not be the last."

Mrs. Wells-Barnett perched her sizable self on the upholstered chair beside the fireplace.

"Now, Mr. Du Bois," said the president, "I have received quite a lot of correspondence from you about these matters. I want you to know that my administration is doing everything within our power to see that these local authorities start observing the laws as—"

Roosevelt was surprised when Ida Wells-Barnett interrupted.

"That's fine, Mr. President," she said. "We already know all that. You don't have to coddle us or pour on all that old gravy. We know what you're up against. We're up against the same. White men get away with killing black men every day."

Roosevelt's eyes flashed behind his spectacles. "Well, Madam, I think I may be able to do something finally," he said. "That's why I agreed to this meeting."

Du Bois said, "Yes, sir, but—"

"If you will try to refrain from interrupting your

president," Roosevelt demanded, "I will further explain that I am taking steps right now to learn the true situation in the Deep South. Once I have all the facts, I assure you I intend to act."

"I appreciate that," Du Bois said.

"We're not asking for public displays any more than you are," said Wells-Barnett, warming to the discussion. "As you recall, sir, when you invited Booker Washington to dine at the White House, it caused a political headache for you and accomplished absolutely nothing for the cause of colored people."

"Booker T. Washington is the whitest black man I know," grumbled Du Bois.

Roosevelt sat ramrod straight in a large leather armchair. Jackson Hensen loomed over a tiny French desk in the corner, taking down in shorthand everything that was said.

"Mr. Roosevelt, let me put this as simply as possible," said Wells-Barnett. "What we have at the present time is an epidemic of lynching in the South. The problem is getting worse, not better."

Jackson Hensen decided to speak up.

It was an unfortunate decision.

"I understand what you are saying, Mrs. Wells, Professor Du Bois," he said carefully. "But at the same time you are telling us these terrible stories of lynching, we have it on excellent authority that there is also an epidemic of white women being raped and molested by Negroes all over the South. I've seen the numbers. The crime of rape is at least as prevalent as the crime of lynching, is it not?"

"That simply isn't true, young man." Du Bois's voice was an ominous rumble. "I don't know where you're getting that insidious, completely inaccurate information."

Wells-Barnett interrupted. "Just this morning, Senator Morgan was telling people in the lobby of this hotel that he intends to repeal the antilynching laws now in effect."

Jackson Hensen made a skeptical sound. "With all respect, Mrs. Wells-Barnett, I seriously doubt Morgan can muster the votes to do such a thing."

Then Du Bois: "I disagree, young man. I disagree—vehemently!"

"That's enough!" said the president. He got to his feet and paced the floor behind his desk. "I've heard enough of this squabbling. I *am* determined to get to the bottom of the problem. And I will!"

The president's flash of anger silenced everyone. They all stared at him dumbly: the combative Du Bois, the passionate Wells-Barnett, the young and arrogant Hensen.

Now Roosevelt spoke, quietly and with purpose. "At this very moment I have sent a personal envoy to the Deep South on a dangerous mission, to investigate this entire question of lynching. He is a man I trust," Roosevelt continued. "A native of those parts. I have connected him with certain others who can show him the situation from all sides. I haven't told you his name because I'd rather this situation remain confidential until he's done his job. And then I will do whatever I deem necessary to *remedy* the tragic situation in the South."

Ida Wells-Barnett rose from the sofa. "Thank you, Mr. President. I gladly tell anyone who asks that you are the best friend the Negro has had in this office since Mr. Lincoln."

Roosevelt shook her hand enthusiastically.

Du Bois was forced by Mrs. Wells-Barnett's action to rise from the sofa and offer his own hand. "Thank you, Mr. President," he said.

"Yes. Thank you, sir." The president shook his hand. "Let's hope we can make progress on this."

"I've been hoping for progress all my life," Du Bois said.

Roosevelt kept the fixed smile on his face until the two were out of the room. Then he frowned and uttered an epithet.

"Sir?" said Hensen.

"You heard what I said."

"Is there something I should do about this?"

"Get a message to Abraham Cross. Tell him I want a report from him and Ben Corbett immediately—if not sooner."

Chapter 49

I WENT DOWN to Young's Hardware—the only such store in town—and bought myself a bicycle. Then I wheeled my purchase out into the hot sun. The machine was a beautiful silvery blue, with pneumatic tires to smooth out the bumps and ruts of Eudora's dirt streets.

I took my maiden voyage on my new machine out to the Quarters, to see Abraham Cross.

On this day Abraham and I did not head for the swamp. We rode his mules along the Jackson & Northern tracks, then turned east on the Union Church Road. This was fine open ground, vast flat fields that had been putting out prodigious quantities of cotton for generations.

Every mile or so we encountered a clump of trees surrounding a fine old plantation house. These plantations had been the center of Eudora's wealth, the reason for its existence, since the first slaves were brought in to clear the trees from these fields.

"You don't mean they lynched somebody right out here in the open?" I said.

"You stick with me," Abraham said, "and I'll show you things that'll make your fine blond hair fall out."

At that moment we were riding past River Oak, the McKenna family plantation. In the field to our left about thirty Negro workers were bent over under the hot sun, dragging the cloth sacks that billowed out behind them as they moved down the row, picking cotton.

We passed out of the morning heat into the shade, the portion of the road that curved close to the McKennas' stately home. On the front lawn two adorable white children in a little pink-painted cart were driving a pony in circles. On the wide front veranda I could see the children's mother observing their play and a small army of black servants hovering there.

This was a vision of the old South and the new South, all wrapped into one. There, gleaming in the drive, was a handsome new motorcar, brass fittings shining in the sun. And there, rushing across the yard in pursuit of a hen, was an ink-black woman with a red dotted kerchief wrapped around her head.

Abraham was careful to ride his mule a few feet behind mine, to demonstrate his inferior position in the company of a white man. I turned in the saddle. "Where to?"

"Just keep riding straight on ahead to that road beyond the trees," he said.

"You don't think that lady's going to wonder what we're up to?"

"She don't even see us," said Abraham. "She just happy to sit up on her porch and be rich."

We passed once more out of the shade and turned our mules down the long line of trees flanking the McKennas' pecan orchard.

Soon we arrived at another clump of trees shading an intersection with another dirt lane. The western side of this crossing formed a natural amphitheater, with a gigantic old black gum tree as its center.

Beneath this tree someone had built a little platform, like a stage. In a rough semicircle several warped wooden benches were arranged, their whitewash long faded. Obviously they had been hauled out of some derelict church and placed here for spectators.

"What is this, a camp revival?" I said.

Abraham pointed up at a sturdy low branch of the gum tree. The branch extended directly over the little wooden stage—or rather, the stage had been built directly under the branch. Three ropes were carefully knotted and hanging from the branch, three loops waiting for heads to be slipped in, waiting for someone to hang.

"Good God!" I said as I realized what I was seeing.

"For the audience," Abraham said as he gestured around at the benches. "They come to watch the lynching. And they need a place to sit. Nothing worse than having to stand while you waiting to watch 'em hang a nigger."

That was the first time I'd heard Abraham use that word, and his eyes burned fiercely.

I almost couldn't believe it. Across that fence was the McKennas' impeccable lawn, acres and acres of flawless mown grass. I could see beds of bright orange daylilies sculpted into the landscape from here to the big house.

To one side of the stage, I noticed a low table with a small bench behind it. Maybe that was for shotguns and rifles, to keep them out of the dirt.

"What's that table for, Abraham?"

He answered with a weak smile. "That's where they sell refreshments."

Chapter 50

IF I THOUGHT that obscene place was the worst abomination I was going to see — a serene amphitheater constructed for the pleasure of human beings torturing other human beings — I was wrong.

Our journey was just beginning.

We turned south, along back roads, until we were riding beside the fields of the Sauville plantation. I asked if they too had a theater for lynching.

"I don't believe so," said Abraham. "Why bother building your own when there's such a nice one already established in your neighborhood?"

We rode past the showy Greek Revival pile of the Sauville home, past miles of fields with colored folks in them, picking cotton.

After riding for most of an hour, we came to a

long, low cotton barn with a tall silo for storing grain at one end. The place was neatly kept and obviously much in use; the doors at one end stood open, revealing deep rectangular bays stuffed to the ceiling with the first bales of the new crop.

The most successful farmers used barns like this for storing their cotton from year to year, selling only as they needed cash or the price reached a profitable level.

"You telling me they've lynched somebody here?"

"I'm afraid so. This was where Hiram Frazier got hanged. And a couple more since."

"How on earth could you hang somebody in a barn this low? Looks like his feet would drag on the ground."

He pointed to the end of the barn by the silo. "The folks watch from in here. But they hang 'em inside the silo. Don't even need a tree."

I shook my head. I thought of Jacob Gill and the pint he kept in his leather toolbox. I wished for a taste of that whiskey right now.

Abraham led the mules to a slow, muddy stream, where they drank. The old man knelt down, cupped some water in his hand, and drank too.

"It don't look like much, but it taste all right," he said.

I was thirsty but decided I could wait.

We climbed up on the mules. Abraham's animal groaned as he brought his full weight down on its back.

"I declare, I don't know who's in worse shape," Abraham said, "this poor old mule or me."

I smiled at him.

"There's one more place I need to show you, Ben," he said. "Then I reckon we'll be ready to write an official report for Mr. President."

As his mule started off, I saw Abraham wince in pain and try to hide it. He saw that I had noticed and forced a smile.

"Don't worry about me, Mr. Corbett," he said. "I'm old, but I ain't even close to dyin' yet."

But as he turned away and the smile dropped from his face like a mask, I realized that Abraham was a very old man, and probably a sick man as well. His face had the hidden desperation of someone hanging on for dear life.

Or maybe just to make this report to the president.

Chapter 51

I SUPPOSE ABRAHAM WAS WISE to save the worst for last. We rode the mules through a peach orchard south of the Chipley plantation, making a roundabout circle in the general direction of town. The air was heavy with the smell of rotting fruit. For some reason no one was picking these peaches.

At the end of the orchard we emerged into a peaceful wooded glen. At the far side stood two huge old trees. From the fruit dotting the floor of the glen, I made out that these were black cherry trees; we had a nice specimen growing in back of the house the whole time I was growing up.

From the tree on the right hung a black man. At least, I think it was a man. It was mostly unrecognizable. Flies buzzed around it. It had been there a while.

I didn't want to go closer, but I found myself moving there as if my legs were doing all the thinking for my body. I could see that the man had been young. He was caked with blood, spit, snot, mud, and shit. His head was distended, swollen from the pressure of hanging. His lips were swollen too, like balloons about to pop.

I began to gag and I turned away. I fell to one knee and heaved.

"Go ahead, Ben," Abraham said. "It's good to be sick, to be able to get rid of it like that. I wish I could. I guess I'm just gettin' too used to seein' it. It's a bad thing to get used to."

I took out my handkerchief and wiped the edges of my mouth. The wave of nausea was still sweeping over me.

"That's Jimmy Patton up there," he said.

"What happened to him?"

"He worked over at the gin for Mr. Purneau," Abraham said. "Last Saturday he got drunk like he always does after he gets his pay. He was walkin' home and somehow he got hold of a gun. Don't know if he brung it with him, I never knowed Jimmy to carry a gun. Anyway he popped it off right there a couple of times on Commerce Street, down at the end there by the depot. He didn't hit anybody, but a couple of men saw him. They brought him here."

"We can't leave him up there," I said.

"Well sir, we have to," said Abraham.

"Why is that?"

"Because they told the people came to cut Jimmy down they wanted him left here as a warning for the others."

"You afraid to cut him down, Abraham? This man needs to be buried."

"We got no way to carry him."

"Across the mule's back," I said. "I can walk it, or I can ride with you."

"I'm an old man, Mr. Corbett. I can't climb that tree."

"Well, I can, but I don't have a knife," I said.

Abraham produced an excellent bowie knife with a bone handle.

It was only when I was directly under Jimmy Patton's body that I saw someone had severed his fingers and toes. Where his digits should have been there were bloody stumps.

I made quick work of climbing the cherry tree.

"Yes, sir," Abraham said. "Sometime they cut off pieces. To take for souvenirs. And sometimes they sell 'em, you know. At the general store. At the barber shop. Ten cent for a nigger toe. Twenty-five cent for a nigger thumb."

I waved my hand at the ugly explosion of blood on the front of Jimmy Patton's trousers.

"That's right," said Abraham. "Sometimes they don't stop at fingers and toes."

I felt light-headed and nauseated again. "Just—just stop talking for a minute, would you, Abraham?"

I sawed at the rope with a knife for what seemed like an hour. Jimmy Patton finally fell to the ground with a sickening thud.

Somehow I managed to climb down that tree. Somehow I got the Indian blanket out from under Abraham's saddle and wrapped it around the dead man. With Abraham's help I got Jimmy onto the mule. His body was so stiff from rigor mortis that I had to balance him just so, like a pine log.

"We better get out of here," Abraham said. "Somebody watching us for sure."

"Where? I don't see anybody."

"I don't see 'em," he said, "but I know they watching us, just the same."

We made it back through the peach orchard, onto the road, all the way back to town without meeting a soul. I walked the mule by its rope, hoping it would help to be out front. But there was nowhere to walk without breathing in the smell of Jimmy Patton's decomposing flesh, the coppery smell of his blood.

"I'm ready to write that report, Abraham," I said.

"Yes, sir," he said. "I imagine you are."

Chapter 52

SUDDENLY IT WAS SUNDAY, and I was back in a world I recognized. I didn't admit to myself why I felt so lighthearted. I splashed my face with lilac water and clipped a fresh collar to my shirt, but it wasn't until I was standing at the bright yellow door of Elizabeth Begley's white mansion that I admitted what had made me so happy yet apprehensive: *the prospect of seeing her again.*

The door swung open even before I could knock. At a house so grand, I naturally expected to be greeted by a servant, but instead I found the door opened by its owner, Elizabeth's husband, a short, bald man with an amiable smile. "You must be the famous Benjamin Corbett of Washington, attorney at law," he said.

"I am," I said. "And you must be the much more

famous Richard Nottingham, senator and man of influence."

He smiled. "You've got that just about right," he said, grabbing my hand. That hand had not been shaken so vigorously since Roosevelt operated it at the White House. Maybe it was a habit of politicians to inflict pain on new acquaintances, as an aid to memory.

"Lizzie talks so much about you I feel like we already know each other."

Lizzie. The familiarity of the nickname made me wince inwardly.

"I've been looking forward to meeting you," I said. "She speaks fondly of you."

"Oh, now, he's making that up," said Elizabeth, coming up behind her husband. "Don't lie, Ben. Richard knows I haven't spoken fondly of him in years!" She threw her husband a big stage wink. "At least, not in public."

Nottingham laughed. "Isn't she a delight?"

I agreed that she was, in a most unspecific murmur. Then I followed them into a small drawing room off the rear of the center hall.

"Ben, Richard and I are so happy you came. There may be a few people here you don't know—"

This looked a lot like the gathering at L. J.

Stringer's mansion: the same aging stuffed shirts, the same overstuffed dresses, a faint smell of mothballs.

Elizabeth led me to a stout couple on the fringed velvet loveseat. "This is Senator Oscar Winkler and his dear wife, Livia."

I noticed that state senators dropped the "state," turning themselves into real senators. Senator Winkler clasped my hand. "Nice to see you again, Ben."

I was surprised he remembered me. Many years ago, as political editor for the *Eudora High School Bugler*, I had interviewed Senator Winkler for a column entitled "Eudora Looks Forward." He had been warm to me and wise in his comments. One thing he said I had never forgotten. He said it, then asked me not to print it: "The southern man who figures out a way to bridge this terrible divide between the black and the white will enjoy all the blessings our Lord can bestow."

I shook the senator's hand and kissed his wife's. As I was straightening up I heard Elizabeth say, "And I do believe you already know this fellow."

I turned. To my astonishment, I found myself smiling and extending my hand to one Judge Everett Corbett.

He shook it quite formally and made a little bow. "Ben, always a pleasure," he said. "I hope your business down here is going well."

Richard Nottingham clapped his hands. "Lizzie, I heard just a bit too much preaching this morning, and presently I'm about to starve to death." Everything the man said had that odd quality of being humorously intended but not actually funny. "Could we *please* have our dinner?"

Chapter 53

I WAS PLEASED about two things immediately. One, Elizabeth seated me next to herself at the table; two, turtle soup was *not* on the Nottinghams' menu.

I'd eaten a skimpy breakfast, expecting the usual six- or seven-course southern exercise in dinnertime excess. Instead I found the food a touch on the dainty side: deviled eggs, shrimp rémoulade, cucumber sandwiches, various cheeses, and a big silver dish of pickles.

My father was also dishing it up: the personification of silver-haired charm, as he could be at those times when he let himself be roped into a social event.

"I really owe you and Elizabeth a debt of gratitude," he told Nottingham. "If it weren't for you, who knows if I'd even get to see my son again before he heads home!"

I recognized that as a clear signal. Now that we'd seen each other and been observed acting cordially toward each other, my job was done. I was welcome to go back to Washington anytime.

"Oh, I'm not going home yet, Father," I said over the back of the settee. I held up my glass of claret. "I'm grateful too, Richard. My father and I don't get to see each other enough. It's so rare to see him in such a cheerful and expansive mood."

My father gave out a little laugh. "Ben is quite a character," he said. "He's come down to tell us all where we went wrong. He thinks the South ought to be able to change overnight."

Richard Nottingham was glancing from my father to me, as if wondering whether this dispute was going to lead to blows among all this expensive china and crystal.

"I'm just hoping for a South that returns to the rule of law," I said. "I just want a place where the Ku Klux Klan is not hanging black men from every available tree." I knew that I was treading dangerously here, but I couldn't help myself.

"Now you're being plain ignorant," my father said. "You don't seem to remember that the Klan was outlawed about forty years ago."

"I remember it very well," said Livia Winkler.

"My daddy said it was the end of civilization."

Senator Winkler cleared his throat. "Now, Judge, you know as well as I do that outlawing something does not guarantee that it ceases to exist," he said. "As a matter of fact, that's one of the best ways to ensure its continuing existence—to forbid it!"

They glared at each other. It struck me that they'd had this argument before, when I was nowhere around. It also reminded me that there were many good men and women in the South, even here in Eudora.

I was about to say something in support of Winkler when a servant girl walked in bearing a large round cake, frosted white, on a silver platter.

Nottingham brightened. "Why, Lizzie, is that a hummingbird cake?"

"Of course it is. I had them make it just for you. Richard's going off to Jackson next week. We'll miss his birthday, but we can all celebrate tonight."

Something happened then that sent an electrical jolt through my body. It was all I could do to keep from bolting upright in my seat.

As she said these words to her husband, I felt Elizabeth's hand gently pat the inside of my thigh.

"Ben," she said, "you must try the cake."

Chapter 54

"NO, SIR."

"No, not today, Mr. Corbett."

"No, sir, nothing today."

Maybelle always had the same answer to the question I asked her at least once every day. First I would check the table in the front hall, then I'd convince myself that a letter had come and Maybelle was keeping it from me because she knew how anxiously I waited.

I would go ask her, and she would say, "No, sir."

It had been more than a week since I'd written to Meg. I'd imagined that my love had fairly leapt off the page when she read it and that she would write back immediately.

That letter had not yet arrived.

Meanwhile I was keeping someone else waiting:

President Roosevelt expected a report on what I had found out about lynching in and around Eudora. I had spent the past two evenings on a long letter to the president that gave precise locations, right down to the species of the hanging trees. I included the names of victims and the approximate times and dates of their murders.

Then I showed the letter to Abraham. He read it and said, "If it was me, I'd make it like a telegram. Short and sweet. 'Dear Mr. President, it's worse than you heard. Send the Army. Stop.'"

Abraham was right. I remembered years ago at Las Guasimas when Roosevelt spoke to me for the first time. He glared down from his horse. "Do we have provisions for an overnight, Captain?"

"Sir, I ordered the men to double their rations and to fill their canteens—"

"Stop!" Roosevelt commanded. "That was a yes-or-no question."

"Yes, sir," I said.

And now it took Abraham to remind me of Roosevelt's fondness for a concise report.

"Send it to him in a wire," he said.

"That's a good idea. But I can't send it from Eudora."

The telegraph operator in town was Harry

Kelleher, who was also the stationmaster. The moment I left the depot after sending my wire to the White House, Kelleher would personally see that the contents were passed on to every man, woman, and child in Eudora.

"Where can I go, Abraham?"

"Where's the closest place where everybody doesn't know who you are?"

I thought about that. "McComb," I said.

McComb was the nearest sizable town, a farm center and railroad hub ten miles north. When I was growing up, McComb was nothing but a crossroads, but when the Jackson & Northern railroad extended its line and located a terminus there, it outgrew Eudora. McComb was only an hour's carriage ride away, and it boasted Sampson's, a fine restaurant specializing in New Orleans–style food: Creole jambalaya, grits and grillades, steak Diane.

Most of all, it had something that was sure to lift my spirits. I had seen the handbill only the day before, hanging on the front wall of the *Eudora Courier* office.

TOMORROW! ONE NIGHT ONLY!

THE INIMITABLE AUTHOR, SATIRIST, & RACONTEUR

MR. SAMUEL LANGHORNE CLEMENS,

WHO MAY DECIDE TO APPEAR ALONGSIDE

MR. MARK TWAIN

DOORS OPEN AT 7 O'CLOCK

THE TROUBLE TO BEGIN AT 8 O'CLOCK

MCCOMB CITY LYRIC THEATRE

My favorite author in the world was just a carriage ride away.

And then another thought struck me. I didn't have a carriage, but I knew someone who did.

Chapter 55

WHEN I PUSHED my carefully composed telegram across the desk to the man behind the barred window at the McComb depot, his eyes bugged. "I ain't never sent a wire to the White House before," he said in a loud voice.

A few people waiting for the next train turned their heads to give me an appraising glance.

I smiled at the man. "Neither have I," I said gently. "Could you please keep it down?"

"I sent one to the president of Ole Miss one time," he bellowed, "but that ain't the same thing. You mean for this to go to the real president, in the White House, up in Washington?"

"That's the one," I said.

I would have to tell Abraham that his idea of coming to McComb for anonymity had failed. I wondered whether there was anyplace in the state of Mississippi from which you could dispatch a wire to 1600 Pennsylvania Avenue without causing a fuss.

"Yes, sir," the man was saying, "one time I sent one to Governor Vardaman, and there was this other time a fellow wanted to send one—"

"I'm glad you and I could make history together," I said. "Could you send it right away?"

"Soon as the station agent comes back from his break," he said.

I forced myself to remember that I was down South, where everything operated on Mississippi time, a slower pace than in other places. After the man's break would be soon enough.

I hurried out to Elizabeth's carriage, where she sat surveying the panorama of McComb.

Half the town had burned to the ground just a few years before, but a sturdy new town had already been put up to replace it. At one end of the business district stood a fine new depot and the famous McComb Ice Plant, which iced down thousands of train cars full of southern fruits and vegetables for the trip north.

All the way at the other end of downtown, on Broadway Street, stood the only other building that really interested me—the Lyric Theatre, where Twain would perform tonight.

First we repaired to Sampson's, where I ordered crab gumbo and Elizabeth ordered—what else?—turtle soup. We chatted and relived old times throughout the Pompano en Papillote and the Snapper Almondine, the bread pudding and the egg custard. It was the finest meal, and dining companion, I'd had since returning to the South.

With a rare sense of satisfaction, Elizabeth and I strolled down the new sidewalks of Front Street to the theater. Men in waistcoats and women in fancy crinolines were milling about the entrance, and I couldn't wait to go in.

"You look like a child on Christmas morning," Elizabeth said and laughed merrily.

I lifted my hat to the man I'd engaged to water our horse and keep an eye on the carriage. "It's better than that," I said. "Christmas comes once a year. But Mark Twain comes once in a lifetime."

Chapter 56

LET ME PUT THIS SIMPLY. Mark Twain remains to this day the funniest, most intelligent and entertaining person I ever saw on any stage or read in any book.

By then he was an old man, over seventy, but he wore his famous white suit, smoked his famous cigar, and constantly ran his long fingers through his famously unruly hair. His voice was as raspy as an old barn door. He sounded at all times as if he were about ten seconds away from erupting in a violent rage.

"Nothing needs reforming," he said by way of beginning, "so much as other people's habits."

The audience roared in recognition of a universal truth.

"Best forget about the animals. Man is the only one with the true religion..."

The audience waited. Sure enough, the rest of the sentence arrived with perfect timing.

"Yep...several of them."

He was amusing, biting, sarcastic, ferocious, and bitter in his repudiation of nearly everything and everyone. Elizabeth laughed as hard as I did—harder sometimes. I kept sneaking glances at her: shoulders shaking, handkerchief pressed to her mouth. I was happy she was having such a good time.

I was no author, no satirist, no raconteur, but I did know that the humor of this man Clemens was different. Besides being funny, every word he spoke was the absolute truth. The bigger the lies he pretended to tell, the more truthful the stories became.

When he talked about his struggles with trying to give up whiskey and his beloved cigars, we all laughed because we had struggles of our own, and he helped us see that they were ridiculous.

When he read from his book *Huckleberry Finn*, a passage in which Huck is bemoaning the fancy clothes the Widow Douglas has forced him to wear, we laughed because someone had once forced us into Sunday clothes too.

Occasionally Twain landed with both feet in an area that made this audience a little restless, as when he said:

"We had slavery when I was a boy. There was nothing wrong with slavery. The local pulpit told us God approved of it. If there were passages in the Bible that disapproved of slavery, they were not read aloud by the pastors."

Twain paused. He looked deadly serious. I saw men shifting in their seats.

"I wonder how they could be so dishonest..."

Another long pause. And then: "Result of practice, I guess."

The laughter came, and I saw Elizabeth dab at her eyes.

After more than an hour of effervescent brilliance, it became clear that Twain was exhausted, clinging to the podium. A man pushed an armchair in from the wings, and Twain asked our permission to sit down.

He sat down and lit a cigar, which drew another round of applause.

He was finishing up. When he spoke this time, I felt he was speaking directly to me.

"There's a question I'm interested in," he said. "You-all might have an opinion on this. Why does a crowd of people stand by, smitten to the heart and miserable, and by ostentatious outward signs pretend to enjoy a lynching?"

The room fell so quiet you could hear the nervous cough of one man at the back.

"Why does the crowd lift no hand or voice in protest?" Twain said. "Only because it would be unpopular to do it, I think. Each man is afraid of his neighbor's disapproval—a thing which, to the general run of the race, is more dreaded than wounds and death."

Still the audience sat rapt, unmoving.

"When there is to be a lynching, the people hitch up and come miles to see it, bringing their wives and children," he said. "Really to see it? No—they come only because they are afraid to stay at home, lest it be noticed and offensively commented upon.

"No mob has any sand in the presence of a man known to be splendidly brave. When I was a boy, I saw a brave gentleman deride and insult a mob, and drive it away.

"This would lead one to think that perhaps the remedy for lynchings is to station a brave man in each affected community. But where shall these brave men be found? That is indeed a difficulty. There are not three hundred of them on the earth."

That's exactly what Mark Twain said that night. I looked around and saw almost everyone in that audience nodding their heads, as if they all agreed.

Chapter 57

APPARENTLY ELIZABETH'S CARRIAGE HORSE had never encountered an automobile before, at least not after sundown, and not in such profusion.

With all the sputtering and clanging and light-flashing and honking in the streets around the Lyric Theatre, the frightened old horse bucked and snapped at the air. It took some fancy rein work to get us safely back on the road to Eudora.

The trip home made the trouble worthwhile. The stir of a breeze in the sultry night. A fat full moon that seemed stained yellow around its edges.

"I saw *Charley's Aunt* in that theater," Elizabeth said. "I saw Maude Adams in Jackson when she came through as Peter Pan. And they were both wonderful. But they didn't touch my heart the way Mr. Twain did. Or make me laugh until there were tears."

"It's a very special evening," I said. "Couldn't have been any better."

I waited. She didn't answer.

"It is," she finally said. "It's very special to me too."

These last words caught in her throat. I glanced at her: even in the faint moonlight, I could see the shine of tears in her eyes.

"What's the matter?" I asked.

"Oh, you know what it is, Ben," she said. "I should be riding home with Richard. I should be sharing memories of Mark Twain with him. I should be in love ... with Richard."

I knew what I wanted to do then. I wanted to tell Elizabeth my own troubles, Meg's and mine, tell her how lonely I felt, how devastated when Meg proposed (*by letter, no less!*) that we put an end to our marriage.

Instead, I drove along in silence. The breeze disappeared, and the moon went behind a cloud.

"Why did you ask me to go with you tonight?" she said.

"I thought you would enjoy it," I said. "And I guess I've been ... lonely."

"Oh, Ben," she said. "Oh, Ben." Then she took my hand in hers, and held it for a long moment.

We were riding past the town limits sign now. It was late; Commerce Street was deserted. The clip-clop of the horse's hooves echoed off the storefronts.

I finally pulled to a stop in front of the Nottingham home. I clicked open my watch. "Ten minutes till midnight," I said. "Very respectable."

"Respectable," she said with a little smile. "That is one thing you are. It's a good thing, Ben."

I walked her to the yellow door flanked by a pair of flickering gaslights.

"Thank you for a beautiful evening," she said. She pressed her lips to mine, her body soft against mine. The embrace lasted only a few seconds, but for those seconds, I was lost.

"Ben, do you want to come inside?" Elizabeth said in a whisper.

"I do," I whispered back. "I most certainly do. But I can't."

Then Elizabeth disappeared inside her house, and I went back to Maybelle's. I had never felt more alone in my life.

Chapter 58

I WAS STILL WAITING for an answer from the White House. Maybe my telegram had been *too* concise? Too curt or disrespectful to send to the president? Maybe Roosevelt had forgotten about me?

I walked downtown to get out of the rooming house, to do something other than wait. Pretty much every human being within ten miles came to town on Saturday. For a few hours in the morning, the sidewalks of Eudora buzzed with the activity of a much larger town.

I was standing in front of the Purina feed and seed, discussing the weather with Mr. Baker, when I saw an old lady and her grown daughter hurrying along the sidewalk toward us, as if getting away from something.

"I don't care what anyone says," the younger woman said as they passed, "they are human beings too. It isn't right! Those boys are acting like heathens!"

Mr. Baker and I tipped our hats, but the ladies failed to notice us.

I excused myself and walked up Maple Street, around the corner where they had appeared. What I saw made my heart drop.

Three white men, maybe my age, were holding the heads of two black boys under the surface of the horse trough in front of Jenkins' Mercantile.

They were *drowning* those boys. It scared me how long they were submerged after I came around the corner and saw them. Then, as if on cue, they were yanked up from the water. They spluttered out a desperate heaving breath, and then their heads were plunged into the water again.

Those boys were just kids—twelve or thirteen at the most.

When their heads came up out of the water again, they cried and begged the men to please let them go.

"Whatsa matter, you thought them white ladies was gonna save you?"

Their heads went back under.

I remembered the closing words of Mr. Clemens's address: *"Where shall these brave men be found? There are not three hundred of them on the earth."*

I took three long strides forward. "What's going on here? Let 'em up. Do it now."

The white men whirled around. In their surprise, they jerked the heads of their victims clear of the water. The boy on the left used the moment to make his escape, but the largest man tightened his grip on the other boy's arm.

He was a mean-looking fat man with red hair, bulging muscles, and a tooth missing in front. "These niggers was sassing us," he said.

"Turn him loose," I said.

"Shit, no."

"He's about twelve years old," I said. "You men are grown. And three of you against two little boys?"

"Why don't you mind your own damn bidness," said the second man, who had a greasy head of black hair and a face that even his mother could not have loved much. "These nigger boys was out of line. We don't allow that in this town."

"I'm from this town too," I said. "My father's a judge here. Let him go."

I guess I sounded just official enough for Big Red to relax his grip. The black boy took off like a shot.

"Look what we got here, men," said Red then. "A genuine nigger-lover."

Without warning he charged and struck me full force with the weight of his body. I went flying.

Chapter 59

I WAS SLAMMED DOWN on the hard dirt street, and before I could catch my breath Red jumped on top of me.

"Reckon I'll have to *teach* you how to mind your own business."

I was trying to figure a way out of this. I had once watched Bob Fitzsimmons demolish an opponent with a third-round knockout. That was one way to do it. But there was another way to win a fight.

I reached up and pressed my thumbs into the soft, unprotected flesh of the fat man's throat. I got my leverage, then slung him off me, right over my head. Red landed face-first in the dirt and scuffed up his lip. Blood was coming out of his nose too.

I jumped to my feet and his buddies charged at me. The first ran hard into a right uppercut.

He dropped like a rock and was out cold in the street.

Now there were two dazed bullies down, but the third got behind me and jumped on my back. He started pounding his fists into my ribs.

I knew there was a thick wooden post supporting the gallery in front of Jenkins' Mercantile, so I leaned all my weight into the man, propelling us backward, smashing him right into it. His arms unraveled from my neck and he lay on the ground twitching. He'd hit that post pretty hard, maybe cracked a couple of ribs.

"Nigger-lover," he spat, but then he struggled up and started to run. So did the other two.

It was quiet again, the street empty.

Well, almost empty.

Chapter 60

STANDING ON THE BOARD SIDEWALK beside Jenkins's display window was the dapper local photographer, Scooter Willems. Today he looked extra-fashionable in a seersucker suit with a straw boater. As always, he had his camera and tripod with him. I wondered whether he had just photographed me in action.

"Where'd you learn to fight like that, Ben?"

"Boxing team at college," I said.

"No, I mean, where'd you learn to put your thumbs in a man's throat like that? Looks like you learned to fight in the street," Scooter said.

"I reckon I just have the instinct," I said.

"Mind if I take your photograph, Ben?"

I remembered the night I first saw him, photographing George Pearson. "I *do* mind, Scooter. My clothes are a mess."

"That's what would make it interesting," he said with a big smile.

"Maybe for you. Not for me. *Don't take my picture.*"

"I will honor your wishes, of course." Scooter folded the tripod and walked away.

I tucked my shirt into my torn trousers, and when I brushed my hand against my chin, it came back bloody.

Moody Cross stepped out of Sanders's store with a sack of rice on one hip and a bag of groceries on her arm. She walked toward me.

"You are beyond learning," she said.

I used my handkerchief to wipe off the blood. "And what is it I have failed to learn, Moody?"

"You can go around trying to fight every white man in Mississippi that hates colored people," she said, "but it won't do any good. There's a lot more of them than there is of you. You can't protect us. Nobody can do that. Not even God."

She turned to walk away, but then she looked back. "But thank you for trying," she said.

Chapter 61

IN FOUR WEEKS OF LIVING at Maybelle's, I'd come to realize that my room was so damp, so airless, so overheated night and day, that nothing ever really dried out.

My clothes, my hand towel, and my shave towel were always damp. My hair was moist at all times. As much as I toweled off, powdered with talc, and blotted with witch hazel, my shirts and underclothes always retained a film of moisture. This stifling closet at the top of Maybelle's stairs was a punishment, a torture, a prison.

And besides, there was so much to keep me awake at night.

I longed for a letter from home.

And maybe because I didn't hear, I wrestled with

thoughts of Elizabeth. I could still feel our kiss in front of her house.

I wondered if Roosevelt had ever gotten my wire. Surely he would have sent some answer by now. What if that telegraph operator in McComb had taken exception to the facts as I was reporting them?

And here I was, quite a sight, if anyone happened in to see me. I lay crosswise on the iron bed, naked, atop sweat-moistened sheets. I had tied a wet rag around my head; every half hour or so, I refreshed it with cool water from the washbasin.

But no one could win the battle against a Mississippi summer. Your only hope was to lie low and move as little as possible.

"Mr. Corbett."

At first I thought the voice came from the landing, but no, it came from outside.

Beneath my window.

"Mr. Corbett."

A stage whisper drifting up from three stories below.

I swung my legs to the floor, wrapped the top sheet around myself, and walked over to the window. I couldn't make out anyone in the mottled shadows under Maybelle's big eudora tree.

I called softly, "Who's out there? What do you want?"

"They sent me to get you," the voice said.

"Who sent you?"

"Moody Cross," he said. "Can you come?"

I didn't think it was a trap, but it paid to be careful. "What for? What does Moody want?"

"You got to come, Mr. Corbett." The fear in the voice was unmistakable. "They been another lynchin'."

"Oh God—where?"

"Out by the Quarters."

"Who is it?"

"Hiram," the man said. "Hiram Cross. Moody's brother is dead."

Chapter 62

I FELT A DEEP SURGE of pain in my chest, a contraction so sharp that for a moment I wondered if I was having a coronary. Almost instantly I was covered with clammy sweat.

I heard the voice from outside again.

"Somebody overheard Hiram say that one day white folk would work for the black," the man whispered hoarsely. "Now Hiram swinging dead from a tree."

I felt the room beginning to turn—no, that was just my head spinning. I felt a strange chill, and a powerful force rising within me.

"Stand back," I said loudly.

"What's that, Mr. Corbett?"

"I said stand back. Get out from under this window!"

I heard branches strain and creak as the man obeyed.

Then I leaned my head out the window and threw up my supper.

Chapter 63

MOODY DID NOT SHED a tear at her brother's funeral. Her face was an impassive sculpture carved from the smoothest brown marble.

Abraham fought to stay strong, to stand and set a brave example for all the people watching him now. And although he managed to control his expression, he could do nothing about the tears spilling down his face.

Swing low, sweet chariot.
Coming for to carry me home.

It must have been the hottest place on earth, that little sanctuary with one door in back and one door in front and no windows at all. It was the Mt. Zion A.M.E. Full Gospel church, three miles out of town on the Muddy Springs Road, and it was jammed to overflowing with friends and relatives.

Early in the service, a woman fainted and crashed hard to the floor. Her family gathered around her to fan her and lift her up. A baby screamed bloody murder in the back. Half the people in the room were weeping out loud.

But Moody did not cry.

Nobody knows the trouble I've seen.
Nobody knows but Jesus.
Nobody knows the trouble I've seen.
Glory hallelujah!

"I knew Hiram from the day he was born!" cried the preacher. "I loved him like a father loves his son!"

"Yes, you did!" shouted an old lady in the front row.

"Tell it, brother!"

"Amen!"

"I carried the baby Hiram to the river," the preacher went on, "and I dipped him in the river of life. That's right, I held him under the water of Jesus until he was baptized, and he come up sputtering, and then he was lifted up in the Holy Spirit and the everlasting light of Jesus—"

"That's right, Rev!"

"—so that no matter what might happen to Hiram, no matter what fate might befall him as he walked the earth, he would always have the Lord Jesus Christ walking right there by his side!"

"Say it, brother!"

"Now, children," the preacher said with a sudden lowering of his tone, "we know what happened to our son and brother Hiram Cross! We know!"

"Hep us, Jesus!"

"The white man done come for Hiram, done took him and killed him," the preacher called.

"We should think of our Lord, and how brave he was on that last night when he set there waiting for the Roman soldiers to come. He knew what was gonna happen. He knew who was coming for him. But he did not despair."

Instantly I found myself wanting to disagree, wanting to cry out, to remind him of the despairing words of Jesus on the cross, *My father, my father, why hast thou forsaken me?*

"Hiram was just that brave," said the preacher. "He didn't bow down or beg them to spare his life. He went along without saying a word, without letting them ever get a look at his fear. We should all strive to be as courageous as our brother Hiram."

"That's right!"

"The white man killed Hiram!" he hollered again. "But my friends, we are not like the white man! We cannot allow ourselves to be like that. The Bible tells us what to do. Jesus tells us what to do. It's plain to see. We have to do as Jesus did, we have to turn the other cheek."

There were groans from the congregation. It seemed to me that most of them had been turning the other cheek their entire lives.

Abraham's head had drooped until his chin was nearly resting on his chest. Moody continued to gaze straight ahead at the plain wooden cross on the rear wall.

"As the Lord tells us in Proverbs, *'Do not say, "I'll pay you back for this wrong!" Wait for the Lord, and he will deliver you.'* God does not want us taking matters into our own hands.

"That is our charge, brothers and sisters. That is what the Lord tells us, in the book of Matthew: *'Love your enemies and pray for those who persecute you, that you may be sons of your Father in heaven.'* "

"How long, Brother Clifford?" came a voice from the back. "How long we 'posed to wait? Till the end of all time? How long?"

"We wait until the Lord makes his will clear," the

preacher said calmly. "We wait like the children of Isr'al waited, forty years out in that desert."

The insistent voice spoke again:

"But how long? How long do we go on forgiving? How many of us got to die before it's time?"

And that is when I saw one shining tear roll down Moody's face.

We shuffled along, following behind Hiram in his pine box, out the narrow front door. The choir took up an old hymn.

I sing because I'm happy.
I sing because I'm free.
For His eye is on the sparrow
And I know He watches me.
And I know He watches me.

Chapter 64

A BLINDING LIGHT CAME. Then another bright flash.

We were leaving the church, just making our way down the rickety steps.

Another stunning flash of light came.

At first I thought it was lightning, then I realized lightning doesn't come from a clear blue sky. I blinked, trying to regain my power of sight, and then saw what was causing it: Scooter Willems and his camera, with its flash-powder apparatus.

Beside him were three large men I did not recognize, white men with twisted smiles on their faces, guns at their sides.

Moody left the line of mourners and marched straight over to Willems, right up to him.

"Show some respect," she said to him. "This is my brother's funeral."

"Sorry, Moody," Scooter said, almost pleasantly. "I thought you might want a photograph for your memory book."

"I don't need no photograph to remember this," she said. "I'll remember it fine."

The pallbearers were sturdy young men about the same age as Hiram. They slid Hiram's coffin onto the back of a buckboard. I made my way over to where Moody was glaring at Scooter and his bodyguards.

Scooter turned to me. "Moody's all het up because I wanted to take a memorial photograph of the funeral."

"Too bad you didn't take a memorial photograph of the lynching," Moody said. She turned on her heel and fell in step with the other mourners behind the wagon.

"Leave her alone, Scooter," I said.

Scooter frowned. "Like I said, I just wanted to commemorate the event."

I turned to leave, but Scooter wasn't quite finished talking.

"Hey, Ben, how's about I take one of you against this ocean of colored folks."

I spun around at him. "Put your damn camera away. Go back to Eudora, where you belong. Leave these folks alone."

I noticed two little black boys listening to our conversation. As I turned to leave, Scooter spoke to them.

"Hey, little boys, I'll give you each a nickel to let me take your picture." He held out his hand with two nickels in it.

I pulled nickels out of my own pocket and handed one each to the boys. "Y'all run on," I said.

They did.

And I went to join Hiram's funeral procession.

Chapter 65

ABRAHAM HANDED ME a huge slice of chess pie. It was a southern funeral favorite because it could be made quickly, using ingredients most people kept on hand—milk, eggs, sugar, butter.

Abraham's house was overflowing with dishes and platters and baskets of food, and mourners eating as much as they could.

A question swam into my mind. How did Scooter Willems know Moody? I distinctly recalled him calling her by name, as if they were old friends. Were they? And how could that be?

I excused myself and threaded my way through the crowded little parlor, through the overpopulated kitchen, out the back door. I saw Moody sitting in the yard on an old tree stump, glaring at the ground.

"Moody," I said.

She did not acknowledge me.

I reached out to touch her shoulder. "Moody."

She pushed my hand away. "Don't put your *white* hand on my *black* shoulder," she said.

I drew back and put my hands in my pockets.

"Do you know Scooter Willems?" I asked.

She lifted her head and looked at me. "Who?"

"Scooter Willems. That photographer from outside the church."

"I never seen that man in my life. He ain't nothin' but a buzzard, pickin' the meat off of dead people's bones."

"If you've never seen him, how did he know your name?"

"I don't know."

Moody looked into my eyes. For the first time since we'd met, she didn't look the least bit feisty or defiant. She looked downtrodden. Defeated. The heartbreak of Hiram's death had drained all the anger from her.

I put my hand on her shoulder again. This time she reached up and patted my hand.

"I've been going to funerals since I was a baby," she said. "This one is different. Ain't no 'peaceable joy' around here."

"What do you mean?"

"We used to burying the old folks," she said. "You know—after they lived a whole life. After they married and had their own kids, maybe even their grandkids. But lately, all these funerals for the young ones. And Hiram…I mean, Hiram…"

Moody began to cry.

"He weren't nothing but a baby himself," she said.

I felt tears coming to my own eyes.

"Here." I thrust the pie under her nose. "Eat some of this. You need to eat."

It was useless advice, I knew, but it was what I remembered my father saying to people at funerals. *Eat, eat*…Now I understood why he'd said it: he just couldn't think of anything else to say.

Moody took the plate from my hand.

Chapter 66

MOODY WAS RIGHT. No "peaceable joy" came into Abraham Cross's house that day.

The bottle of moonshine was gradually consumed. The ham was whittled away until nothing but a knuckly bone was left on the plate. The pies shrank, shrank some more, then disappeared entirely. The afternoon lingered and finally turned into nighttime, with ten thousand cicadas singing in the dark.

I shook hands with Abraham. Moody gave me a quick little hug. I made my way through the remaining mourners, out the front door.

Fifty yards from the house, in front of the fig tree where I had parked the bicycle, stood three large white men. I couldn't make out details of their faces in that shadowy street, but I knew where I'd seen them: these were the same men who'd been standing with Scooter that afternoon at the Mt. Zion church when he took his photographs.

One of them spoke. "You looking for some trouble, Corbett?"

I didn't answer.

Looking back on it, I guess one man must have been smoking a pipe. I saw him move and smack something hard against the trunk of the fig. Sparks flew in a shower to the ground.

"We asked you a question," said the man in the middle. "Serious question."

"Abraham! Moody!" I yelled.

I don't know if they heard me. If they did, I don't know whether they came out of the house. In less time than it took for me to get my arms up, the three men were on me.

Kicked in the head. In the face. I tasted blood. I fell face-down on the ground, hard. A knee went into my stomach, fists whaling at me all over. Someone stomping on the side of my rib cage. I could not get my breath. Something tore into my neck. It felt like fire.

"Looks like you found it—*trouble!*" a man grunted, and drew back to get a better angle for kicking me. He delivered a stunning blow to my knee. I heard a cracking crunch and felt a wild sear of pain and thought he had shattered my right kneecap.

That was the last thing I remembered for a while.

Chapter 67

THE NEXT THING I was aware of—voices.

"You gotta use a higher branch. He's tall."

Something was in my eyes. *Blood.* I was blind from all the blood.

"Use that next branch, that one yonder," said a second man. "That's what we used when we hung that big nigger from Tylertown."

"He wasn't tall as this one. I can't hardly see up this high."

"Hell he wadn't. I had to skinny up the tree to put the rope way over."

Every inch of my body was experiencing a different kind of pain: sharp pain, dull pain, pain that throbbed with a massive pounding, pain that burned with a white-hot roar.

I thought, *It's amazing how much pain you can feel and still not be dead.*

"This nigger-lover is tall," the second man said, "but that 'un from Tylertown, he had to be six-foot-six if he was a inch."

I groaned. I think they were lifting me — hands under my armpits, digging into my flesh, cutting into me, dragging me off to one side.

A thud — something hurting my back. Then I felt the damp ground under me.

A crack — something landed hard on my left knee. I guessed that knee was shattered too.

"This rope is all greasy. I can't get aholt of it."

"That's nigger grease."

I felt the coarse hemp rope coming down over my face, dragging over my nose, tightening against my neck.

And I thought: *Oh, God! They're hanging me!*

Then I flew up into the air, like an angel — an angel whose head was exploding with terrible pain.

I could not see anything. I thought my eardrums had burst from the pressure in my skull.

But they hadn't tied the noose right. Maybe the one who thought I was too tall was inexperienced. The rope was cutting under my jaw, but it had not gone tight. I got my hand up, somehow worked my fingers between the rope and my neck. I dangled and kicked as if I could kick my way out of the noose. *They are hanging you, boy,* was the chant that went through my head, over and over, like a song, an executioner's song.

Crack! I felt a sting on my back. Was it a bull-whip? A buggy whip? A willow branch?

"He's done. Or he will be," the voice said. "We can go. Let's get out of here."

The air smelled of woodsmoke. Were they going to burn me? Was I going to go up in flames now?

That heat grew and grew. I struggled to see through the blood. *It sure is hot up here. Maybe I'm already in hell. Maybe the devil has come and got me.*

"We better get out of here, J.T.," said the voice.

"Not yet."

"Listen to me. They're still awake over in the Quarters. They're angry."

"Let 'em come out here," the other man said.

"They'll be looking for Corbett. He's just like one of them."

"Yeah, he is. Just like a nigger. Wonder how that is?"

I heard the crack of a branch. The voices began to fade. The heat that had burned me alive began to fade away. Then I was alone. There were iron hands around my neck, squeezing and squeezing. No air. No breath. No way to breathe.

Oh, God. My mouth was so dry.

And then I was gone from the world.

Chapter 68

A FEW MOMENTS OF CONSCIOUSNESS. Then I blacked out again.

Awake.

Asleep.

Awake.

The wakeful times were a nightmare of confusion.

Terrible pain. There was something snapping at my feet, something with fierce sharp claws. Raccoons? Possums? A rabid fox? I didn't know if I was still alive.

I was surely dead for a while, then the bugs woke me with their biting, sucking my blood, little no-see-ums biting my neck and arms, mosquitoes big as bats sucking the blood from my veins, and then rats jumped onto my legs and ran up and down my body, squeaking, snapping at my privates.

Then a flash of light, so bright I saw the spackle of blood outlined on my swollen eyelids.

Was I dead? Was I in a different world? In my delirium I heard something. Maybe the angels singing. Or was it a dog barking—

Another flash, so bright it nearly shook me.

The pain in my skull increased. I felt the blood pumping through a vein in my forehead. I imagined it bursting, the blood running in a stream down my leg.

I tried to make a fist. *My fingers are gone!*

Oh my God. Maybe not. I couldn't feel anything on that side.

I couldn't taste the air.

I could only feel my tongue swelling up in my mouth, choking me. And my fingers were gone.

In my overheated brain I saw Mama at her desk, in that flowing white gown she wore under her housecoat. The violet inkstand, the silver pen. Mama smiled at me. "I think you'll like this poem, Ben. It's about you, baby."

I sat on my little stool in the room off her bedroom that smelled like lavender and talcum powder. I saw myself sitting there as if I were a figure in a drawing—a precise, detailed sketch of Mama and me.

Then the pain came swelling up through my chest, through my neck, and up into my brain.

Another flash of light.

And once again, nothing.

Chapter 69

MORNING COMES TO A MAN hanging from a rope as it comes to a man sleeping in his bed—the chatter of birds, a faint breeze, the bark of a dog.

Then comes the pain again.

So much blood had clotted on my eyelids and eyelashes that I couldn't open them.

I breathed in short sharp intakes of air. The fingers of my right hand wedged into the rope had kept open just enough of a passage for a trickle of air down my windpipe. It had kept me alive. Or maybe somebody had spared me. Maybe the one who said I was too tall? Maybe someone I knew?

The rest of my body was pure pain: so intense, so complete, that the pain now seemed like my normal state.

"Look, Roy, ain't no colored man. That man white."

The voice of a child.

"Dang," said another voice. "Look like they done painted him red all over."

A dog barked.

"Worms!" the first boy yelled.

I could only imagine what kind of horrible creatures were crawling on my skin.

"Worms!"

I felt something licking my foot. Then it barked.

"Worms! Get away from him, he *dirty!*"

Ahhh. Worms was the dog.

It was so hot. I should surely be dead by now. I think the pain radiating from my knees was keeping me alive. It wasn't that I had a will to survive.

I thought of stories from the war, wounds so horrible or amputations so unbearable that men begged their comrades to shoot them, to put them away. If I could speak, I would ask these boys to fetch a gun and shoot me in the head.

I felt something sharp poking my stomach. I must have flinched or jumped a little, and gave out a groan. The boys shrieked in terror.

"Oh, Jesus, the man alive!"

"Run!"

I heard them running as fast as they could,

running away from the monster. I heard Worms barking as he ran after them.

I wanted to tell them to please come back and cut me down. Oh, how I wanted to lie on the ground just once more before I died.

That was not to be. I couldn't just hang here like this, waiting to die. The best I could hope for was to hasten it along.

I began wriggling my dead hand, trying to get it out from between the rope and my neck.

ALEX CR•SS

Part Four

"MY NAME IS HENRY"

Chapter 70

"MY NAME IS HENRY."

I could barely hear.

"Can you hear me? I said my name's Henry."

I could barely see.

I could, however, tell that the person speaking to me was a *woman*. An ancient, bent-over colored woman.

"*Henry.* My name is *Henry*," she said. "You in there, Mist' Corbett?"

Most of her teeth were missing, producing a kind of whistly lisp as she leaned closer and spoke to me.

"Come on now, eat this," she said. She held out a spoonful of something. I opened my mouth. She stuck it in. God, it was delicious: black-eyed peas cooked to death, mashed to a paste.

While moving the food around my sore, battered mouth, my tongue discovered the gaping hole on the left side where two teeth had been.

"Where am I?" I croaked.

"Abraham house," Henry said. She poised another spoonful in front of my mouth.

I will never forget the taste of those peas. They remain to this day the single most wonderful food I have ever encountered.

I heard a familiar voice: "Now would you look at Mr. Corbett, settin' up and eatin' baby food all by himself." Moody came around from the head of the narrow cot where I lay, at the center of their parlor, in exactly the spot where Hiram's coffin had been.

Perhaps I was still in the midst of my delirium, but I thought she looked happy that I was alive and awake.

"This is Aunt Henry who been looking after you," she said.

"Henry?" I asked.

"Don't you be calling me Henrietta," she said.

Moody sat on the little footstool beside my bed. "You been through a pretty rough time, Mr. Corbett," she said. "When they cut you down, we just knew you was dead. But Papaw felt a pulse on your arm. So he run and got Aunt Henry. She's the one with the healing touch."

"Don't make him talk now, child," Aunt Henry said. "He still wore out." Every time I opened my mouth she stuck in more of the black-eyed-pea mush that was bringing me back to life, a spoonful at a time.

"She been pouring soup in you with a funnel," Moody said. "She done washed you and powdered you, shaved your face. When your fever went up, she sent me to the icehouse for ice to put in your bed. When the cut places started to scab, she put salt water on 'em so they wouldn't scar."

"How long have I been here?"

"Eight days since they cut you down," she said.

I felt the dull pounding ache in both knees. I remembered how those men had kicked my feet out from under me, then gone after my knees with the toes of their boots.

"Did they break my knees?"

Aunt Henry frowned. "Near 'bout," she said. "But you got you some hard knees. All battered up and cut up. But ain't broke."

"That's good." I managed a weak smile.

"It *is* good," Aunt Henry said. "Soon as you finish this here peas, you gonna have one more little nap, and then we gonna see if we can get you walkin'."

Moody said, "You'd best get him up *running*, Aunt Henry."

I shifted onto my side. "What do you mean?"

"The ones that hanged you gonna find you," Moody said. "Then they gonna hang you again."

Chapter 71

AUNT HENRY WAS RIGHT. My knees weren't broken. But they certainly were not happy when called upon to do their job.

Armed with wobbly wooden crutches and a short glass of whiskey, I went for a late-afternoon stroll between Moody and Abraham. My body ached in a hundred different places, all tied together by the pain in my knees. When I bent my leg to take a step, the knee shot a white-hot arrow of pain to my hip. My neck was still raw from the rope, and the mangled fingers of my right hand were twisted and so blackish blue they might yet go gangrenous and have to come off. The sweat rolled down my back, into the swollen whip welts, stinging like fire ants.

But I kept on, hobbling down the muddy board walkway. I knew I was damned lucky to have survived, with no broken bones. My pain was nothing. It would be gone in a few days, or weeks at the worst. I could deal with that.

But inside, I felt another, more disturbing pain. I had been beaten and left for dead. I had disappeared from the world, and hardly anyone had come looking for me. I mattered to virtually no one. Meg. Elizabeth. My father. My daughters. Jacob, my childhood best friend. The entire town of Eudora. I had mostly been forgotten. A few people from town *had* come, good, kind folks. L. J. Stringer had actually visited a few times. But my own father hadn't come once.

"Abraham," I said. "Could I ask a favor?"

"Ask it," he said.

"Can you stop by Maybelle's and see if she's got any letters for me?"

He shook his head. "I went by this morning. Nothing there." Then he added, "Nothing for you from the White House, either."

I kept on, but the pressure of the crutches under my arms was getting to be too much to bear. Everything from my neck down was one big aching mass of bruises.

"Does Maybelle know what happened to me?" I asked.

"Mr. Corbett, everybody in Eudora knows what happened to you. I'll tell you something I believe. There's good and bad in Eudora Quarters, good and bad in the town of Eudora—probably in equal numbers. Problem is, there's cowards in both places. That's why the bullies can have their way, Mr. Corbett."

"Abraham," I said with a sigh. "For God's sake. We've been through a good bit together. Would you please call me Ben?"

He patted my shoulder. "All right, Ben."

"Thank you."

"You welcome." He smiled. "But now you got to call me Mr. Cross." Abraham laughed out loud at that.

As I picked my way past the door of Gumbo Joe's, two old ladies looked up and waved at me. "I pray for you, sir," one of them said to me.

"Thank you, ma'am."

We went on a few more yards. "The colored folks appreciate what you was trying to do, Mist—Ben," he said. "We know your heart is not the same as some the rest."

Moody spoke up. "Yeah, and the white folks know it too. That's why they goin' to kill him."

Chapter 72

"YOU JUST PLAIN don't need me no more." Aunt Henry said it straight out as she dabbed at the wounds on my back with one of her secret potions.

"Fact is, Mist' Corbett, you hardly even got any scabs left on you," she said. "These is all healed up real good."

I twisted around on my chair to pull on my shirt, wincing from the pain.

"Now don't you be foolin' with me," Aunt Henry said. "You walkin' good with no crutch."

I knew she was right. Aside from the occasional shock of pain in my neck, or in my knees, I was feeling almost human again. I had no further need for Aunt Henry's fussing and babying, which I had come to enjoy.

And it was time for me to go back to Eudora.

Frankly, I felt a bit reluctant to leave. There was something good about life as it happened in this modest little house. Certainly, the opportunity to see Moody every day was something I had enjoyed. But as much as that, I had enjoyed getting to know Abraham. With everything going against him—the death of his grandson, the increasing fear in the colored community, the lifetime of bigotry he had endured—Abraham was a man at peace with himself.

Just the night before, on a warm rainy evening when the mosquitoes were at their droning worst, we sat on a bench underneath the overhang of the porch.

We were working our way through a basket of hot corn muffins Moody had just brought out of the oven. I smiled up at her. She ignored me and turned back inside.

"Sometimes a man can sense something," Abraham said. "Something small that can blossom up into trouble."

"You mean, because we haven't heard from Roosevelt?" I asked. "I don't understand that at all. I almost got hanged for him."

"This got nothing to do with the president," he said, gazing off into the darkness. "I'm talking about another kind of business. Right here in my house."

I swallowed the rest of the muffin and wiped my mouth, inelegantly, on the back of my hand. I knew exactly what he was talking about. I had been hoping he wouldn't notice.

"Nothing has happened, Abraham," I said softly. "Nothing is going to happen."

He didn't look at me.

"I love that girl just about as much as I ever loved anybody," he said. "Including her mama. And including even my dear departed wife. As for you—well, I done took you into my house, hadn't I? That ought to show you, I hold you in high regard. You a fine man, Ben, but this just can't be. *It can't be.* Moody...and you? That is impossible."

"I understand that, Abraham. I don't think you ought to worry. Maybe you hadn't noticed, but Moody hasn't spoken a kind word to me since the day we met."

He put his hand on my shoulder.

"And maybe you hadn't noticed," he said, "but that's exactly how you can tell when a woman is in love with you."

Chapter 73

FROM THE DAY after my hanging, someone was always awake and on guard at Abraham Cross's house. During the day and the evening, Abraham and Moody took turns keeping watch from the front-porch rocker. Since I was the cause of all this, I took the dead man's shift, from midnight till dawn.

Some nights I heard Abraham stirring, and then he would come out to sit with me for an hour or two.

One night, along about four a.m., I thought I heard his soft tread on the floorboards.

I looked up. It was Moody standing there.

"Mind a little company?" she said.

"I don't mind," I said.

She sat down on the bench beside the rocker. A foot or two away from me—a safe distance.

We sat in our usual silence for a while. Finally I broke it. "I've been busting to ask you a question, Moody."

"Wouldn't want you to bust," she said. "What is it?"

"Is that the only dress you own?"

She burst out laughing, one of the few times I'd made her laugh.

It was the same white jumper she'd worn the day I met her and every day since. Somehow it stayed spotless, although she never seemed to take it off.

"Well, if you really want to know, I got three of these dresses," she said. "All three just alike. Of all the questions you could have asked me, that's the one you picked?" she said. "You are one peculiar man, Mr. Corbett."

"I sure wish you would call me Ben. Even your grandfather calls me Ben now."

"In case you hadn't noticed, I don't do everything he does," she said. "I'll just keep on calling you Mr. Corbett."

At first I thought it was moonlight casting that delicate rim of light around her face, lighting up her dark eyes. Then I realized that it was dawn breaking, the first streak of gray in the sky.

"I'll be moving back to Maybelle's tomorrow," I said. "It's time."

Moody didn't reply.

"It'll be better for Abraham once I'm out of here," I said. "And for you."

No answer.

I said, "The only reason those bastards come around is because I'm here."

Nothing. She stared out at the street.

"Thanks to y'all, I'm much better now. I'm feeling fine. I've got some decisions to make."

Her silence and stubbornness just went on and on, and I gave up trying to pierce it. I sat back and watched the gray light filling in all the blank dark spaces.

I think we sat another ten whole minutes without a word. The sun came up and cast its first shadows of the day.

At last Moody said, "You know I ain't never gonna sleep with you."

I considered that for a moment.

"I know," I said. "Is it because I'm white?"

"No," she said. "Because I'm black."

Chapter 74

"I AM JUST AS SORRY AS I can be, Mr. Corbett, but we simply have no rooms available at this time," Maybelle said to me. "We are full up."

The dilapidated rooming house seemed strangely deserted for a place that was completely occupied.

"But Abraham came by and paid you while I was incapacitated," I said.

"Your money is in that envelope on top of your baggage," she said, pointing at my trunk and valises in a dusty corner of the center hall. "You can count it, it's all there."

"You accepted my money," I said, "but now that I need the room, you're throwing me out? That makes no sense."

Up till now, Maybelle had maintained her best polite southern-lady voice. Now the tone changed.

Her voice dropped three notes.

"Look, I ain't gonna stand here and argue with the likes of you," she said. "I don't know how I could make it any clearer. *We got no rooms available for you.* So if you don't mind, I will thank you to go on and leave the house now."

"I can't carry this trunk by myself," I said.

"Why don't you get one of your nigger friends to help you," she snapped. "That's what I would do."

"I'll take the valises and send someone back for the trunk," I said.

I stuffed the envelope in my pocket, picked up a bag in each hand, and walked out into the blazing noonday sun of Eudora. Now what?

Sweet tea. That's what I needed, a frosty glass of tea. And time to think things through. I went to the Slide Inn Café and sat at my usual table. I sat there for almost twenty minutes. I could not seem to get the attention of a waitress. Miss Fanny wouldn't even meet my eye.

Oh, they saw me. The waitresses cast glances at me and whispered among themselves. The other customers—plump ladies in go-to-town dresses, rawboned farmers, little girls clinging to their mamas' skirts—they saw me too. When I dared to look back at them, they turned away.

And I remembered what Abraham had said: *There's cowards in both places. That's why the bullies can have their way.*

Finally, Miss Fanny approached with a glass of tea, dripping condensation down its sides.

She spoke in a quiet voice. "I'm sorry, Mr. Corbett. We don't all feel the same way about you. Personally, I got nothing against you. I like you. But I ain't the owner. So you'd best just drink this tea and be on your way. You're not welcome here."

"All right, Miss Fanny," I said. "Thanks for telling me."

I drank the tea in a few gulps. I put a quarter on the table. I hoisted my valises and walked out into the street.

As I passed Miss Ida's notions shop, I saw Livia Winkler coming out.

"Miz Winkler," I said, touching the brim of my hat.

She suddenly looked flustered. Averting her eyes, she turned around and hurried back into the shop.

I crossed the street, to the watering trough in front of Jenkins' Mercantile. I scooped up a handful of water and splashed my face.

"That water is for horses, mules, and dogs," said a voice behind me. I turned.

It was the same fat redheaded man who with his two friends had jumped me at this very place, when they were holding those boys' heads underwater.

This time he held a branding iron in his hand.

I was too exhausted to fight. I was hot. I was still a bit weak and wobbly from everything I had been through. But Red didn't know that. I straightened up to full height.

"Use your brain," I said. "Turn around and walk away. Before I brand *you*."

We stared each other down. Finally he broke it off—shook his head in disgust, spat on the sidewalk near my shoes, and walked away. He looked back once. I was still there, watching him go.

Then I turned and headed in the direction of the one person in Eudora I believed would help me.

Chapter 75

"WELL, DAMN, BEN! I could have used some warning, you know? I got about the biggest family and the littlest house in the whole town, and you want to move in here? Damn it all to hell, Ben!"

That was the warm greeting I got from Jacob Gill, my oldest friend in the world, my hope for a roof over my head that night.

"Sorry, Jacob," I said, "but I didn't know anywhere else to go."

He looked me over. I looked right back at him. Finally he crossed some line in his mind. He sighed, picked up one of my valises, carried it through the tiny parlor and into the tiny dining room.

"I reckon this is the guest room now," he said, and finally offered up a half smile. "I'll get some blankets;

we can make a pallet on the floor—unless you want to sleep out in the smokehouse. Got nothing hanging in there, it might be more private for you."

"This will be fine," I said.

Jacob's house was a sad sight on the inside. The few pieces of furniture were battered old castoffs held together with baling wire and odd ends of rope. The cotton batting was coming out of the cushions on the settee. In the kitchen, a baby's cradle gave off an unpleasant aroma. A skinny cat nosed around the pantry, no doubt hoping to meet a mouse for lunch. Jacob said, "You want a drink?"

"Just some water would be good for me."

"The pump's on the back porch," he said. "I need me a finger or two myself."

He didn't bother to pour the whiskey into a glass. He pulled the cork and took a big slug right out of the bottle.

"Well, that's just fine, ain't it? Drinking straight from the bottle, and it ain't even lunchtime yet."

This observation belonged to Charlotte, Jacob's wife, who came in from the back porch with an infant in one arm and a pile of laundry in the other.

"Hello, Charlotte. Ben Corbett."

"Yeah, I know who you are." Her voice was cool. "I heard you were back in town."

"Ben's gonna be staying with us for a few days," said Jacob. "I told him he could sleep in the dining room."

"That's grand," Charlotte said. "That's just wonderful. That oughta make us the most popular family in Eudora."

Chapter 76

THE SECOND NIGHT I WAS at the Gill house, after a supper of leftover chicken parts and grits, Jacob suggested we go for "a walk, a smoke, and a nip."

First he poured whiskey from the big bottle into a half-pint bottle, which he stuck in his trouser pocket.

He walked and drank. I walked and looked anxiously down every dark alley.

"You sure are one hell of a nervous critter tonight," Jacob said.

"You'd be nervous too, if they beat you half to death and strung you up and left you for dead," I said. "Excuse me if I tend to be a bit cautious after almost being lynched."

A man came down the steps of the First

Methodist church, looking as if he had been waiting for us.

I recognized him: Byram Chaney, a teacher at the grammar school. Byram had to be well up in his seventies by now; I had thought of him as elderly years ago, when he was teaching me how to turn fractions into decimals.

"Evening, Jacob," he said. "Ben."

Jacob turned toward the streetlight to roll a cigarette. "I hope Byram didn't startle you, Ben," he said.

"Glad you could join us this evening, Ben," Byram said. "I think getting a firsthand look at things will be worthwhile for you. Jacob spoke up for you."

Suddenly I realized that Byram Chaney had, in fact, been waiting for us. I turned to Jacob to find out why.

"I haven't told him yet," Jacob said to Byram.

"Told me what?"

"You'd best go on and tell him," said Byram. "We'll be to Scully's in a minute."

I knew Scully as a man who owned a "kitchen farm" on the road south of town. Everybody who didn't have his own garden went to Scully's for whatever vegetables were in season.

"What's going on here, Jacob?"

"Calm down, Ben. We're just going to a little meeting. Me and Byram thought it might be a good idea if you came along. I *did* speak up for you."

"What kind of a meeting?"

"Just friends and neighbors," he said. "Keep your mind open."

"Pretty much half the people in town," put in Byram.

"But they don't like to be seen by outsiders," said Jacob. "That's why you'll have to wear this."

From his knapsack he pulled a white towel.

Then I realized it wasn't a towel at all. It was a pointed white hood with two holes cut for eyes.

I stopped dead in my tracks.

"A Klan meeting?" I said.

"Keep your voice *down*, Ben," Jacob said. "We're standing right here beside you. We can hear."

"You must be insane," I said. "I'm not going to any Klan meeting. Don't you know it's illegal? The Klan's been outlawed for years."

"Tell the sheriff," said Jacob. "He's a member."

As soon as I got over my shock at finding that my old best friend was a Ku Klux Klansman, I knew Chaney was right. I *had* to go along. This was exactly the kind of information Theodore Roosevelt had sent me down here to uncover.

Chapter 77

THROUGH THE HOLES in my hood I saw at least fifty men in white hoods and robes, walking in loose ranks along the dirt road. Jacob, Byram, and I fell right in with their step.

No one said anything until we were all inside Scully's large old barn and the doors had been closed.

One man climbed up on a hay bale and ordered everyone to gather around. I followed Jacob toward the back wall of the barn.

"Our first order of business," he said, "is to announce that we have a special guest attending our meeting this evening."

He waved his hand—*was he waving in my direction?* There was no way he could know who I was, not under that hood.

Without a word Jacob reached over and snatched the hood off my head.

I stood revealed. The only man in the place without a mask covering his face.

A murmur ran through the crowd.

"Benjamin Corbett," said the man on the bale. "Welcome, Ben. You are among friends here. We're not the ones tried to hurt you."

I sincerely doubted that. But then he took off his hood and I recognized Winston Conover, the pharmacist who had filled our family's prescriptions for as long as I could remember.

One by one the men around me began taking off their hoods. I knew most of them. The Methodist minister. A farm products salesman. A conductor on the Jackson & Northern railroad. A carpenter's assistant. The county surveyor. The man who did shoe repairs for Kline's store. Sheriff Reese and his deputy. The man who repaired farm implements at the back of Sanders' General Store.

So this was the dreaded Ku Klux Klan. As ordinary a group of small-town men as you're likely to come across.

"Ben, we appreciate you showing up to let us talk to you." It was Lyman Tripp. Jovial, chubby Lyman had the readiest smile in town. He was the undertaker, so he also had the steadiest business of anyone.

"Maybe you'll see that we ain't all monsters," he said. "We're just family men. We got to look out for our women and protect what's rightfully ours."

I didn't quite know what he meant by "rightfully ours."

Byram Chaney tied a gold belt around the waist of his robe. He climbed up on the hay bale from which Doc Conover had just stepped down.

"All right, let's get it started," he said.

The men stood around in their white sheets with their hoods off, conducting the most ordinary small-town meeting. They discussed the collection of dues, a donation they'd recently made to a widowed young mother, nominations for a committee to represent the local chapter at the county meeting in McComb.

Just when it began to seem as harmless as a church picnic, Byram Chaney said, "Okay now, there must be a recognizing of new business related to the niggers."

Doc Conover spoke up. "I had two colored girls come into the drugstore last week. They said they was up from Ocean Springs visiting some kin of theirs. They wanted to buy tincture of iodine. I explained to 'em, just as nice as I could, that I don't sell to coloreds. Then one of 'em started to lecturin' me on the Constitution. When I told her to get the hell out of my store, she said she'd come back with her daddy and her brother, and they'd *make* me sell 'em iodine."

"You say they's from Ocean Springs?" said Jimmy Whitley, the athletic coach at Eudora High.

"That's sure what they said."

"Johnny Ray, ain't you got a cousin in the chapter down in Ocean Springs?"

"I do, that's Wilbur Earl," said Johnny Ray.

Byram Chaney said, "Johnny Ray, why don't you talk to your cousin, find out who those girls might have been. Then we can see about getting 'em educated."

The crowd murmured in agreement.

Another man spoke. "I only want to report that that old nigger Jackie, you know, the one that used to drive the carriage for Mr. Macy? He come into my store again, looking for work."

I recognized the speaker as Marshall Farley, owner of the five-and-dime.

Jacob leapt to his feet and spoke with passion. "There you go," he said. "Niggers looking for jobs that belong to us! That old coon's had a perfectly good job all this time, driving for one of the richest men in the county. Now he wants more. He wants a job that could go to a fella like me, a good man with a family to feed."

In place of the polite murmur, a wave of anger now rolled through the crowd. I understood something new about these men. They weren't filled just with hate; they were filled with at least as much *fear*. Fear that the black man was going to take everything away from them—their jobs, their women, their homes, all their hopes and dreams.

Then I realized Jacob was talking about me. "So if you ask me, I think it's high time we teach our guest a thing or two," he was saying. "He needs to know we aren't just a bunch of ignorant bigots. I make a motion that we give over the rest of our meeting to the proper education of Ben Corbett."

I looked around and couldn't believe what I saw. Half a dozen men, in a rough circle, were coming right at me. Then they were upon me, and they had me trapped for sure.

Chapter 78

FEELING SICK TO my stomach now, my brain reeling, I rode in the back of an open farm wagon with Jacob, Byram Chaney, and Doc Conover. I was the one with hands bound behind his back.

Cicadas made a furious racket in the trees, their droning rhythm rising and falling. We were driving south out of town into the swamp, an all-too-familiar journey by now.

I was almost as terrified as I was angry. When I spoke to Jacob, I could barely keep from screaming.

"How could you do this? The one man I thought I could trust!"

"Stay calm, my friend."

"I'm not your friend," I said.

"Ben, you can't help it if you got some mistaken ideas about us," he said. "You'll find out, we're nobody to be scared of. We're fair-minded fellows, like you. I just ask you to keep an open mind."

"By going to the swamp to watch you lynch another black man?"

"I said, *stay calm*."

After a time we came into a clearing. I could have sworn this was the place where somebody hanged me. Where I almost died. But it was a different spot altogether.

Two men in white robes stood near a crude wooden platform. Between them they held a man in place, with a rope around his neck.

His face was turned away from me.

"Let's go closer," Jacob said.

"This is close enough," I said.

But it wasn't my decision to make. Byram Chaney lifted his reins and drove the wagon into the clearing for a better view of the murder.

Slowly the man on the platform turned to face the crowd. He was a small man. Frightened. Pathetic. On his nose he wore gold-rimmed spectacles.

The man was white.

Chapter 79

"HIS NAME IS ELI WEINBERG," Byram Chaney told me in confidential tones. "He's a crooked little Jew from New Orleans. He talked three different widow ladies out of a thousand dollars each. He was selling deeds to some nonexistent property he said was down in Metairie."

"And he would have got away with all that money," Jacob said, "but the fellows found him yesterday, hiding in the outhouse at the McComb depot."

Eli Weinberg decided to speak up for himself. "Those are valid deeds, gentlemen," he said in a quavery voice.

"What are you doing?" I said. "You can't hang him, he might be telling the truth!" I felt my whole body shaking. "Why don't you look into what he says?"

"We did look into it," said Doc Conover. "We got word from our brothers that he's been fast-talking his way into towns all over this part of the country."

"So have him arrested," I said.

"This is better," Conover said. "We get the job done, no waiting, no money wasted on lawyers and trials and such. And we let them other Jews know they better think twice before coming to Eudora to steal from the likes of us."

"The likes of you?" I said. "Hell, you're all murderers!"

Eli Weinberg heard my voice. He twisted around in the hands of his captors to see who might have spoken in his defense. "Murderers! Yes, that man's right! You are all murderers!"

Jacob said, "You're missing the point, Ben. The Klan is here to fight against *all* injustice. We're not here just to educate niggers. We're here to educate anyone who needs educating."

I narrowed my eyes and shook my head. "You're crazy, Jacob. You and your friends are just a bunch of crazy killers."

Eli Weinberg shouted out, "Listen to him! He's right! You're all crazy killers!"

Those were the last words he spoke.

Someone jerked hard on the rope, and Eli Weinberg's body flew into the air. His cheeks inflated. His eyes bugged in their sockets. His face turned an awful dark crimson, then slowly faded to gray. Vomit spilled from his mouth. His body jerked and trembled horribly.

Within seconds he was dead.

A few seconds after that, the brilliant flash of Scooter Willems's camera illuminated the dark night.

Chapter 80

THE HANGMAN'S BOWIE KNIFE made quick work of the rope. They let Eli Weinberg's body fall to the ground with a thud. I had seen ailing farm animals put down with more respect.

"You reckon we oughta bury him?" a man said.

"Leave him where he lies," said Chaney. "He said he had a son in Baton Rouge. We'll get word to our brothers down there. The son can come fetch him."

"Jews are supposed to be buried before sundown on the day they die," I said.

"It figures you would know all about Jews," said Doc Conover.

Chaney climbed aboard the wagon and took the reins. As we jolted out of the clearing, Jacob reached down to untie my ankles. "Turn around and let me do your hands," he said.

I will confess it—I felt a wash of relief. They didn't intend to kill me tonight.

Without any warning a stiff breeze swept over us, along with a spatter of oversized raindrops. The breeze died for a moment, then the rain was on us, lashing us with windy sheets of water.

I noticed that Doc's wet white robe had become translucent, so I could read his name stitched on the pharmacist's jacket he wore underneath.

"What you think, Ben?" Jacob asked as the wagon wheels slogged through the mud. "Is the Klan making a little more sense to you now?"

If Jacob hadn't been a friend my whole life, I would have punched him right then. "Listen to yourself, Jacob. You just killed a man. Do you hear me? *You killed him.*"

I thought he was going to snap back at me, but the fire suddenly died in his eyes. He shook his head, in sorrow or disgust. He stared down at his callused hands.

"You...will...never...understand," he said. "I'm a fool to even try. You're not like us anymore. You don't understand how things have changed."

"Let me tell you what else I don't understand," I said. "How you—the one I always thought was my friend—how could you do this to me, Jacob? Jacob, *I was your friend.*"

"I did it to help you," he said. "To keep you alive." His voice was weak, pathetic.

The rain was beginning to slacken. The wagon slowed to a stop outside Scully's barn, where the evening's festivities had begun.

"Come on, Ben," Jacob said in a low voice. "Let's go home."

"I don't think so." I turned away and set off walking in the direction of Eudora.

"Where the hell you going?" he called after me.

I didn't answer or even look back.

Chapter 81

A SILK BANNER with elegant black letters ran the length of the wall.

WELCOME HOME, BEN

This was the banner that had hung in the dining room for the big family celebration the day I returned from my service in Cuba. Half the town turned out to cheer the decorated Spanish-American War veteran who had distinguished himself under the famous Colonel Theodore Roosevelt.

Now the banner was dingy, the silk stained brown with drips from the leaky roof. I was standing not in my father's house on Holly Street but in the "long house" out back, a former slave quarters.

It was to the long house that I had come after I left Jacob. It hadn't housed an actual slave since well before I was born. At the moment it seemed to be serving as a storage room for every piece of castoff junk my father didn't want in the house.

It was also home to the dogs, Duke and Dutchy, the oldest, fattest, laziest bloodhounds in all of Mississippi. They didn't even bother to bark when I opened the door and stepped inside.

I lit an old kerosene lantern and watched the mice scurry away into corners. As the shadows retreated, I realized that all the junk piled in here was *my* junk. My father had turned the long house into a repository of everything related to my childhood.

The oak desk from my bedroom was shoved against the wall under the welcome banner. Piled on top of the desk were pasteboard cartons and the little desk chair I had used before I was old enough to use a grown-up one.

I lifted the lid of the topmost carton. A musty smell rose from the books inside. I lifted out a handful: *A Boy's History of the Old South, My First Lessons in Arithmetic,* and my favorite book when I was a boy: *Brass Knuckles, Or, The Story of a Boy Who Cheated.*

Next to the desk stood my first bed, a narrow spool one decorated by my mother with hand-painted stars. It was hard to believe I'd ever fit on that little bed.

In the far corner was another pile of Benjamin Corbett's effects: football, basketball, catcher's mitt, slide trombone, the boxer's speed bag that once hung from a rafter in the attic.

I lifted the corner of a bedsheet draping a large object, and uncovered the most wonderful possession of my entire childhood: a miniature two-seater buggy, made perfectly to scale of white-painted wicker with spoked iron wheels. I remembered the thrill it gave me when our old stable hand Mose would hitch up the old mule, Sarah, to my buggy. He would lift me onto the driver's seat and lead the mule and me on a walk around the property. I must have been all of six or seven.

Before I knew what was happening, I was crying. I stood in the middle of that dark, musty room and let the tears come. My shoulders shook violently. I sank down to a chair and buried my head in my hands. I was finally home—and it was awful.

Chapter 82

A FAMILIAR VOICE brought me out of a deep sleep. These days I came awake instantly, and always with an edge of fear. It was only when I blinked at the two figures smiling down on me that I was able to relax.

"Near 'bout time for breakfast," said Yvella, my father's cook. Beside her was Dabney, the houseman. Each held a silver tray.

"Way past time," said Dabney. "In another hour it'll be time for dinner."

Among the items on Dabney's tray were a silver coffeepot emitting a tendril of steam from its spout and a complete place setting of Mama's best china.

Yvella's tray offered just about every breakfast item known to southern mankind: grits, fried eggs, spicy link sausage, homemade patty sausage, griddle cakes with sorghum syrup, a basket of baking-powder biscuits, butter, watermelon pickles, and fig preserves.

"Yvella, you don't expect me to eat all this?"

"Yes, suh, I sure do," she said. "You too damn skinny."

"I *have* lost some weight here recently," I said and rolled my eyes.

"Yeah, I heard all about it," she said.

"How'd y'all know I was here…*in the guest quarters?*"

"Duke come and told me," Dabney said.

I realized that I was standing in front of them shirtless, wearing only my drawers. I looked around for my clothes.

"Don't you worry about it, Mister Ben," Yvella said. "I seen plenty worse than that. I took your clothes to the wash."

Dabney brought over a filigreed iron tea table I remembered from Mama's flower garden.

"I didn't tell your daddy you's here," he said. "I figure you'd want to tell him yourself. But why don't you come on and sleep in the house, Mister Ben. That big old house just rattling around with hardly nobody in it, you out here sleepin' with the dogs."

"We'll see," I said. "Thank you for the invitation."

Along with the coffee, Dabney had brought me a straight razor, shaving soap, a tortoiseshell comb and brush, and a stack of fresh clothing—my old clothes, laundered and folded. I was probably skinny enough to fit into them now.

"God bless you both," I said.

"You the one that needs the blessin', from what I hear," Yvella said. "You best keep out of trouble."

"I will try," I said. "Listen, I have a favor to ask both of y'all."

"Your father don't need to know, and we ain't gonna tell him," said Dabney.

"The same goes for me," said Yvella. "And now I got a favor to ask of you."

"What is it?"

"Would you eat them damn biscuits before they get cold?"

Chapter 83

AS SOON AS I POURED the last of the coffee, Duke and Dutchy started barking—insistent, urgent, annoying barks. They ran up and down along the wall underneath the cobwebby window.

I went over and was astonished to see Elizabeth in the bushes and with her none other than L. J. Stringer.

I motioned for them to go around to the front door.

"Damn, Ben," L.J. said, "if we wanted to come through the front door, we would have done it in the first place."

I shut the door behind them. "How'd you even know I was here?"

They looked annoyed at my stupidity.

"Don't you think those Klan boys had somebody

follow you home last night after their meeting? The whole town knows, Ben. Everybody knows who you are and where you are. *All the time*."

I felt stupid. Of course they had followed me.

L.J. straightened. "Ben, let me put it to you as simply as I know how. *Your life is in danger*."

"He's right. Actually, it's a miracle you're still alive," said Elizabeth. She reached out and touched my shoulder, eyes wide with concern.

L.J. spoke in a no-nonsense voice. "People are really angry, Ben. I mean *angry*. You forget what a small town this is. Folks know you're up to something, and whatever it is, you ain't here to make them look good."

"I don't have to defend myself, L.J. There's murder going on in this town. Hell, I've seen six people with my own eyes who've been murdered, just in the short time since I got here! They nearly killed me, just for seeing what I saw."

Elizabeth spoke, her voice as gentle as L.J.'s was harsh.

"Ben, these are, or were, your neighbors," she said. "These are your friends. Most of them are good, decent people."

"Elizabeth, I don't see anything decent about men who murder innocent people. You put neighborliness ahead of simple humanity? Forgive me if I disagree."

I realized that I probably sounded like a defense attorney pleading a case. Another hopeless one?

L.J. seemed to read my mind. "No point in discussing it any further," he said. "We came here because we're afraid for you, Ben. We want to try to help. It's just a matter of time before they come for you again. And hang you good. I'll figure out some way to keep you safe."

"Thank you, L.J., Elizabeth. I really do appreciate your concern. More than you can possibly know."

"Until then, Ben, listen to me. *Do not trust anyone*. And that means *anyone*."

I knew that "anyone" included Jacob Gill, and even my father. It probably meant Dabney and Yvella too. But did it also mean the very people giving me this cautionary advice? Could I trust L.J. and Elizabeth?

"We'd best be on our way," L.J. said. "Isn't there a back door out of here?"

I pointed to it.

"Don't forget what I said, Ben. Keep your head down."

L.J. opened the little door that let onto the alley.

He glanced around, then turned back. "Nobody around. Let's go, Elizabeth."

She turned to me with a smile that spoke of her concern.

"Ben, please let us help. We're your friends. Maybe your only friends."

Chapter 84

ALMOST MIDNIGHT. Another knock came on the rear door of the long house.

I shot the bolt and the door swung open.

Moody Cross was standing there in a white jumper. And not a little terrified. She pushed past me and slammed the door shut.

"Papaw sent me."

"I guess my secret hiding place is the worst-kept secret in Mississippi," I said.

She was out of breath. "We need help. A lady from the Slide Inn sent her colored girl out to warn us. Said they's a group of men coming out to kill me and Papaw and Ricky."

"Who's Ricky?"

"My cousin, you met him at the funeral. He got run out of Chatawa, where he lived all his life. He been staying with us since you left—you know, like for protection."

Now I remembered him, a boy about the same age as Hiram, with a family resemblance to Hiram and Moody.

"What happened in Chatawa?" I asked.

"Two white men said they saw Ricky staring at a white woman. Said he was *thinkin'* evil thoughts. I guess some white folks can even see inside of a black boy's brain. There's this group of 'em—the White Raiders, is what they call 'em up there. They s'posed to be the ones coming to get us."

This seemed like more than coincidence. The horror raining down upon Abraham's family simply would not stop, would it?

"There's something else."

What else could there possibly be?

"Papaw is sick," she said. "He can't get out of his bed, got the fever and the shakes, and Aunt Henry's been there nursing him."

Moody started to cry, and I remembered something Mama always used to say: *When the time comes you want to start crying, that's the time to start moving.*

It was time for me to go get L.J. and Elizabeth.

Chapter 85

L. J. STRINGER'S six-seater spring wagon flew down the road, stirring the motionless air of a sticky-hot Mississippi night.

"You're going straight to hell, Ben Corbett, and you're taking me with you!" L.J. raised his crop to urge on his team.

As soon as I had gotten Moody to stop crying, we'd sneaked over to the Stringer place and surprised the whole household with our late-night knock on the kitchen door. I'd asked L.J. to help me protect Abraham, Moody, and Ricky. He'd listened and he hadn't hesitated. "I said I'd help you, Ben, and I will."

Yes, he'd heard of the White Raiders. Yes, he knew them to be a gang of killers. Finally he sighed heavily and sent his man Luther out to hitch up his team.

And now here we were, bumping and rolling our way out to Abraham's house in the Quarters. Crammed together on the back bench were Moody, Luther Cosgrove, and his brother Conrad.

Luther and Conrad were L.J.'s assistants — "my man Friday and his brother Saturday," he joked — on call twenty-four hours a day to do whatever the boss wanted done. They drove Allegra Stringer on her errands. They ran packages to McComb and Jackson and Shreveport. If L.J. needed anybody "brought into line," as he put it, it was the Cosgroves who did the bringing.

"What we're doing here is extremely foolish," said L.J. "You know that?"

"I know that," I said. "But if we don't help these people, nobody will. And they're all going to die."

L.J. shrugged and said, "Well, we can't have that. This has to stop somewhere. Might as well be right here and right now."

Chapter 86

POOR ABRAHAM WAS in the parlor of his house, sleeping fitfully when we arrived. Half a dozen men came from the Quarters, as volunteers, even though they had only a couple of rifles. "Guarding Father Abraham," that's what they called it. Abraham was that beloved here.

As it turned out, the White Raiders didn't come that first night, but we continued guarding Father Abraham. As the sun went down the second evening, L.J. and I took our places on the porch. We'd been friends for a long time, but he'd gotten better and better with the years, the exact opposite of Jacob.

I arranged the other men as carefully as a Civil War general planning his lines of defense. I put two of the new men on the roof, despite Moody's protest that the sheets of tin were so old and rusty that they would almost certainly fall through.

Then L.J. dispatched five of the men in an enfilade line among the old willow trees at the edge of the woods.

"Stay awake. Stay alert," he told everyone. "Don't leave your post for any damn reason. If you need to pee, just do it in place."

As the second night watch began, our fears were as high as on the first.

Around eleven L.J. and I decided a finger of sour-mash whiskey was what our coffee needed to take the edge off. After midnight Moody came out with a fresh pot. She told me Abraham was awake.

Through the window I saw him propped up on his pillow. Between his hands he held a bowl of steaming liquid, which he raised to his lips.

"How's he doing?"

"He's got a little more energy tonight. But I ain't getting my hopes up. Aunt Henry says he's on his way."

I nodded and walked inside.

"How are you feeling, friend?" I asked.

He smiled. "How are *you*, is the question," he said. "I ain't doing nothing but laying on this bed, trying not to die. You the one doing somethin'."

"I'll keep doing my job, as long as you do yours," I said.

I was surprised how sharp he seemed, and I seized the opportunity.

"Still no word from the White House, Abraham," I told him. "Makes me angry."

"The Lord and the president, they both work in mysterious ways," he said.

"How did you ever come to know him, Abraham?" I asked. "The president, that is."

"Mr. Roosevelt's mama was a southern lady, you know. Miss Mittie. From over where I'm from, in Roswell, Georgia. And see, my sister Annie went to work for Miss Mittie, eventually went with her up to New York. She was still up there, nursing Mittie, the day she died. Died the same day as Mr. Roosevelt's first wife, Alice. Did you know his mama died the same day as his wife? I was there that day, helping Annie. That was a terrible day. I guess he never forgot it."

"*Ben!*" L.J. shouted. "The sons o' bitches are here! They're *everywhere!*"

From all around the cabin came a clatter of hooves, then an explosion of gunfire.

I lunged for the front door. I was almost there when one of the Raiders came crashing through the roof, landing on my back.

Chapter 87

BULLETS WERE WHIZZING through the air as the confused-looking man picked himself up off the floor, still clutching a scrap of rusted tin he'd brought with him on his fall through the roof.

L.J. ran into the house and aimed a rifle at the fallen Raider. "Get the hell out of here or die. I see you again, you die!"

In the darkness outside I could see eight men wheeling about on horses. They wore no sheets, no hoods. They weren't bothering to hide themselves. I recognized the redheaded troublemaker I'd encountered at the trough in front of Jenkins' Mercantile.

One lout, on a big dappled quarter horse, must have weighed in at four hundred pounds. The horse struggled to keep from collapsing.

The fat man was agile, though, hopping down from his saddle like somebody a third his size. The other Raiders were getting down too, yoking their horses together.

One aimed his shotgun at the house. *Ka-blam!*

"Goddammit," L.J. grunted. He poked the barrel of his fine hand-carved rifle through the window, squeezed the trigger, and dropped the shooter in his tracks.

This was war, just like I remembered it from Cuba, except the enemy was from my own town.

L.J. called, "Take the back of the house, Ben!" So I ran to the tiny kitchen and onto the stoop.

Behind the trunk of a giant pecan tree stood Ricky, with his shotgun trained across the yard on an oak where a White Raider huddled with his rifle trained on him.

Neither of them had a clear shot, but they were banging away at each other, riddling each other's tree trunk with bullets and squirrel shot.

As I burst headlong onto that stoop, I presented a clear target for the White Raider.

He swung his gun toward me, and time seemed to slow down while I watched him turn. He squeezed off a shot. I saw the spark of the bullet strike a rock near the stoop.

The man ducked behind the oak, but he was big enough that the trunk didn't entirely conceal his belly. I braced my pistol hand on my other arm and fired.

I got him, and he hit the dirt with a thud, screaming, holding his abdomen.

His fellow Raiders had circled behind the house in a ragged line, and now attacked, sweeping the ground with gunfire, round after round. These men had come well armed; they were good with their guns. I remembered that Colonel Roosevelt called this kind of fighting "sweep in and sweep up," a strategy, he said, that was "generally used by butchers and fools."

These fools were shooting and yelling as they came, catcalling, "We got you now, niggers!" and "Run, boy! Look at him go!"

A shout came from the swamp: "They got Roy! Goddamn niggers done shot Roy!" This news provoked a fresh round of shooting. L.J. glanced at me; we had the same thought at the same instant.

We waited until the last shot, when all their weapons were unloaded at the same time.

Then we charged around the house, weapons leveled at the Raiders. *"Drop 'em!"* L.J. hollered.

They obliged, and I rushed to pick up the rifles, yelling, "Don't move — not one of you move!"

Soon two of the black men who'd been concealed along the fence line appeared, lugging a prone, struggling Raider they had lassoed and hog-tied.

"Where y'all want this one?"

"Put him down right here by the rest," said L.J.

When they came riding in, the Raiders hadn't realized they were outnumbered, but they were finding it out now. I saw a couple of smart ones leap on their horses and ride off.

But here came the huge fat man, lumbering around the side of the house with a shotgun in one hand, a pistol in the other.

"Drop your guns!" L.J. yelled.

The fat man did not obey. Instead, he pulled the trigger on the pistol. The bullet hit L.J. in the right cheek. I swear I heard the crack of his cheekbone breaking, then he fell to the ground.

I fired at the fat man and he went down hard. Stayed down, didn't move.

"L.J.! Are you all right?" I knew he was not.

"Oh, hell, yeah," L.J. said. "The damn thing just grazed me." I could plainly see that it had taken a sizable chunk of flesh out of his cheek; blood oozed down his chin. That side of his face was black with gunpowder.

I heard more commotion in front of the house,

then hoofbeats. The remaining Raiders had taken this opportunity to get the hell out of there.

"Moody!" I called.

There was no answer.

L.J. made a kind of whistling sound as he breathed through the new hole in his cheek.

"Moody, they're gone! Come on out now, I need you!"

Again all was silent.

"You'd better...go see...," L.J. mumbled.

I rushed through the back door and stopped short at the threshold of the parlor. Abraham lay on his bed with the long barrel of a pistol pointed at his head. The man holding it had his other arm around Moody in a choke hold.

"You stop right there, Corbett," said the Raider. "They's nothin' would give me more pleasure than to finish off this old troublemaking nigger, and then you."

I didn't move.

I didn't have to.

I watched Moody's hand gliding into the pocket of her jumper. She pulled out a kitchen knife and in one smooth motion plunged it into the White Raider's back.

Chapter 88

"BEN CORBETT HERE is a well-known nigger-lover, so I don't expect him to know any better—but L.J., *for the love of God*, I never in this world thought I would find *you* pulling such a stunt."

It was four in the morning, and we were standing in the dogtrot of the log cabin that belonged to Phineas Eversman and his family. Phineas was the chief of the Eudora police department, which consisted of him, Mort Crowley, and Harry Kelleher, who worked only part-time.

"Just hear us out, Phineas," L.J. said. When he lifted the bloody rag from his face, his voice had a sickening whistle in it. "Your town is out of control."

"Look, Phineas, you can call me every name in the book," I said. "You can hate me and everything

I stand for, but we still have five men in the back of our wagon who attacked and murdered innocent people in the Quarters tonight. We are witnesses, and we are here to swear out a formal complaint against these men. That means you are required by law to arrest 'em, hold 'em, and see that they're brought to trial for murder."

Eversman looked past me and out the front door. In the back of the wagon he saw five White Raiders tightly bound, hand and foot, by the very ropes they had brought with them for hanging Negroes.

Standing guard over these men were Cousin Ricky and eight of the ten surviving volunteer guards. Luther Cosgrove and a man named Jimmie Cooper had been gunned down. The captured men had laughed and hooted all the way downtown, promising us that their pal Phineas Eversman would soon set them free.

"Now, wait a minute, Corbett," said Phineas. "The first thing out of your mouth was that you and these Nigras killed some of the men."

"*They attacked us!*" I bellowed. "*We had to fight back or we'd all be dead! Are you listening?*"

"There's no need to get ugly," said Phineas. His voice was mild, but his eyes kept flicking outside to the tied-up men, as if he were weighing the risks on all sides.

L.J. pressed the bloody cloth against his cheek. "Phineas, you listen to me, now," he said quietly. "It's time, Phineas. It's time to put an end to it—the violence, all the hatred against coloreds in this town. These Ku Kluxer gangs are tearing Eudora apart, limb from limb. People are living in fear, black and white. You know me, Phineas. I've lived here all my life. I was there tonight. I saw what happened. I demand as a citizen of this town that you arrest these men for murder. Right now."

Eversman pulled his chenille bathrobe snug around his skinny body. He refashioned the knot in the belt, then made his way past us, outside to the wagon.

"Evenin', Phineas," said one of the Raiders with a chuckle. "I sure am sorry these bastards decided to wake you up for no good reason."

Eversman didn't laugh. He didn't even smile. I thought I heard a quiver in his voice, but he spoke loud and clear.

"You men are under arrest for . . . for trespassing, assault with a deadly weapon, and . . . and . . ."

He couldn't seem to get the words out, so I helped him.

"And first-degree murder."

Eversman glanced at me. He swallowed hard. "And first-degree murder," he said.

The men set up a howl. A dour, wiry man yelled, "Because that nigger-lover Corbett says so?"

Eversman's voice had lost its tremor. "And because his complaint is supported by our most upstanding citizen, Mr. Stringer," he said.

"Mr. Stringer is indeed upstanding," I said. "But Chief Eversman will also find that my complaint is fully and completely supported by a person even more esteemed than L. J. Stringer, if you can imagine that."

The wiry man in the wagon cast an ugly eye on me. "And who the hell that?"

"His name," I said, "is Theodore Roosevelt."

ALEX CR•SS

Part Five

THE TRIAL AT EUDORA

Chapter 89

JACKSON HENSEN, the harried senior personal assistant to the president, entered the Oval Office with a bloodred leather folder under his arm. He took one look at the president and dropped the folder. The morning's correspondence scattered all over the carpet—telegrams and official greetings from the king of England, the shah of Persia, and the Japanese ambassador, letters from congressmen, ordinary citizens, and all manner of federal bureaucrats.

"Har-de-har-har!" The president was laughing and singing. Also, he was dancing a jig. He was waving a golden Western Union telegram in the air as he capered in a circle behind his desk.

"Is anything the matter, sir?" Jackson Hensen asked.

"Does it look like there's anything the matter, Hensen?"

"Well, sir, I've never actually seen you dancing, except at state dinners. Never at your desk."

"This is the first time I've ever been happy enough to dance at my desk," Roosevelt said. "Read this." He thrust the telegram at Hensen and collapsed onto a sofa, out of breath, but still chuckling and congratulating himself.

Hensen scanned the telegram. It was stamped 11:50 p.m. of the previous night, signed CROSS AND CORBETT, and originated from a telegraph station in McComb, Mississippi. The report described in detail events that had occurred during the previous several days—lynchings, Klan meetings, the attack of the White Raiders, the gun battle, the arrest of three Raiders on charges of first-degree murder.

It was this last piece of information that so delighted the president.

"There it is!" Roosevelt shouted. "White men charged for killing black men, right down there in the heart of Dixie. Now let Du Bois and that Wells-Barnett woman try to tell me I have ignored the Negro problem!"

Hensen's eyes came up from the telegram. "It is excellent news, sir."

"Worth dancing about, Hensen?"

"Well, sir . . . certainly."

For a moment Jackson Hensen feared that President Roosevelt was going to make him dance.

"Do you know why I am *fortunate* enough to receive this most excellent news, Mr. Hensen?"

"Why is that, sir?"

Roosevelt peered around the sofa. "Where'd you go, Hensen?"

"I'm here, sir. Picking up the mail."

"Never mind that, Hensen. Get your pad, will you? I gave Margaret the afternoon off. I want to send my congratulations to Abraham Cross and Ben Corbett. What shall it be, then, a letter or a wire?"

Hensen took a little notebook and pencil from his vest pocket.

"Those men must have thought I'd forgotten all about them." He laughed, a big booming Roosevelt laugh. "I think I showed great wisdom *not* to respond to their first report, but to let them draw their own conclusions as to what should be done."

"Yes, sir, it most certainly was wise of you." Hensen was often amazed at the depth and breadth of the president's self-regard. He licked the point of his pencil. Roosevelt perched on the edge of his desk, mindful of the fine figure he cut as he dictated his message of congratulations.

"What a magnificent ending to this project!" the president exclaimed.

Chapter 90

PHINEAS EVERSMAN'S FIRST ACT was to release two of the five prisoners. He told us it was for lack of evidence, but I assumed there was some family connection. (There had to be; this was Mississippi.) I was so surprised and impressed that the chief had actually arrested the other three men that I offered no word of protest.

The three still in custody were named Chester Madden, Henry Wadsworth North, and, ironically enough, Lincoln Alexander Stephens, a man whose name evoked both the Great Emancipator and the dwarfish vice-president of the Confederacy. Henry North was the redheaded bully I'd encountered before, at Jenkins' Mercantile.

Some folks called it "the Niggertown Trial." Others called it "the White Raiders Trial." The

313

New Orleans Item dubbed it "That Mess in Eudora." Whatever people called it, everyone was obsessed with it.

The citizens of Eudora were divided on the issues, but they certainly weren't *evenly* divided. A small group welcomed the prospect of punishment for the violent, night-riding Raiders. But many folks, unbelievable as it might seem, thought the Raiders were being treated unfairly.

The *Eudora Gazette,* a weekly four-sheeter usually devoted to social notes, was now publishing five days a week, churning out a breathless new front-page report on the White Raiders Trial every day. The formerly lazy and slow-moving editor, Japheth Morgan, was a whirl of energy, placing expensive telephone trunk calls nearly daily to consult with his "unimpeachable sources of information in the capital."

Japheth Morgan had never worked this hard before. He was losing weight and smoking cigarettes, one after another. He had dark circles under his eyes.

"You'd best settle down a bit, Japheth," L.J. told him. "This trial could end up being the death of you."

"But you don't understand," Japheth answered.

"For me and for the *Gazette,* this isn't the opportunity of a lifetime, it's the trial of the century!"

The trial of the century.

As soon as he said it, I knew it was true. This *was* the trial of the century—not just for Eudora, not just for Mississippi, but for the entire country.

Chapter 91

"NOTICE HOW NOBODY COMPLAINS about the heat anymore," L.J. said to me one morning over breakfast at his home. "Nobody talks about the mosquitoes, or the price of cotton, or any of the things that mattered before. None of those things means a damn now. All anybody cares about is the trial."

I had to smile. "I wouldn't know what you're talking about, L.J., since nobody in this town speaks to me."

"Maybe they're like me, they just hate talking to a damn lawyer."

I'd been given a bedroom on the second floor at L.J.'s, with a sitting room attached and a small balcony where my first cup of coffee was served every morning. There were fresh sheets, starched and ironed, every day; the best sausages for breakfast, aged beef for supper.

Most important, L.J. posted three armed guards around the house: one at the front, one in the back, and one baking on the roof. At L.J.'s I'd gotten the first really good night's sleep I'd had since coming back to Eudora.

L.J.'s wife, Allegra, bustled into the dining room.

"Japheth Morgan insists on seeing you two right now," she said.

Indeed, Morgan did mean *right now*. He had followed Allegra and was standing directly behind her. In his hand was a fresh broadsheet, the ink still shiny. At the top of the page I saw in enormous type the word EXTRA!!!

"I thought you two gentlemen would want to be the first to read this," Morgan said.

L.J. shook his head. "What the hell have you done now, Japheth?"

Morgan began to read aloud. "The Mississippi Office of Criminal Courts has announced the venue and date for the proceedings currently known far and wide as the White Raiders Trial. Following a ruling by the Mississippi Supreme Court, the prosecutor's petition for change of venue has been denied, and the trial will be held in Eudora, Mississippi, scene of the alleged offenses."

"Well, hell, that's no big surprise," L.J. said. "We all knew nobody else wanted to grab hold of this hot horseshoe."

"I agree," I said. "It's disappointing, but it does provide the prosecution with its first proper grounds for appeal."

"Appeal to whom?" said L.J. "The Supreme Court has ruled."

"There's another Supreme Court, in Washington," I said with a wink.

Japheth looked relieved. "Do y'all want to hear this or not?"

"Please," L.J. said, straightening his face into a serious expression. "Please read on."

"Jury selection will begin on September the seventeenth at nine o'clock a.m.," he read.

"Goddamn, what is that, *next Monday*? That's six days from today," L.J. said. "Ben, you're gonna have to scramble."

"Wait. Wait. Wait," Japheth said.

He read slowly, emphatically:

"Further, the Supreme Court has exercised its judicial discretion to appoint a judge to oversee this important and much-noted trial. The judge appointed is..."

Japheth glanced over to make sure we were listening. We absolutely were.

Then he read on:

"The judge appointed is a lifetime citizen of Eudora, the Honorable Everett J. Corbett."

Chapter 92

SON OF A BITCH!

It was not illegal for the Mississippi Supreme Court to appoint my father to preside over a trial in which I was assisting the prosecution.

Not illegal, but wildly unusual, and absolutely deliberate.

I could have fought it, but I already knew that I wouldn't. It gave us a second, decent ground for the eventual, inevitable appeal.

Most people in town, Japheth reported, were positively *delighted* with the news. Everyone knew that Judge Corbett was "fair" and "honest" and "sensible." Judge Corbett "understands the true meaning of justice."

"That is exactly what I am afraid of," I said.

Having spent the first part of my life listening to

my father pontificate, I knew one thing for certain: he might cloak himself in eloquence, reason, and formality, but underneath it all he believed that although Negroes might be absolutely free, thanks to the detested Mr. Lincoln, nowhere was it written that Negroes deserved to be absolutely equal.

Judge Corbett and men of his class had gradually enshrined that inequality in law, and the highest court in the land had upheld its finding that "separate but equal" was good enough for everybody.

Now the trial was less than a week away, and one huge question was still outstanding: who would the state of Mississippi send to prosecute the case?

"My sources in the capital have heard nothing about it," Japheth told L.J. and me. "It's a big, holy secret."

Chapter 93

A WHILE LATER, the three of us were sitting on the west veranda of L.J.'s house, watching the sunset and sipping bourbon over cracked ice.

"Well, you gentlemen are always acting so all-fired high and mighty," Japheth said, "but you've yet to give me a single piece of information that I can use. Why don't you start by sharing the names of the prosecution witnesses?"

"Watch out, L.J., he's using one of his journalist's tricks to get you to spill it," I said.

"Me?" L.J. scoffed. "What do I know? I don't know anything. I've been cut off by the entire town. I'm almost as much persona non grata as Mr. Nigger-Lover Corbett. Everybody from here to Jackson knows whose side I'm on. And you know any friend of Ben Corbett's doesn't have another friend between here and Jackson."

I clapped his shoulder. "I appreciate what you've done, L.J."

It was right then that we heard a deep tenor voice, with a hint of something actorly in the round tones, accompanying a firm bootstep down the upstairs hall.

"If you need a friend from Jackson, maybe I can fill the bill."

We looked up to see a man whose appearance was as polished and natty as his voice. He wore a seersucker suit of the finest quality and a straw boater with a jaunty red band. He could not have been much more than thirty, and he carried a wicker portmanteau and a large leather satchel jammed with papers.

He introduced himself as Jonah Curtis and explained that he had been appointed by the state of Mississippi to prosecute the White Raiders.

"I had my assistant reserve a room at Miss Maybelle's establishment," he said. "But Maybelle took one look at me and it turned out she had misplaced my reservation. She suggested I bring myself to *this* address."

"Welcome to the house of pariahs, Mr. Curtis,"

said L.J. "You are welcome to stay here in my home for as long as this trial takes."

"I do appreciate that, sir. And please, call me Jonah."

Jonah Curtis was almost as tall as I. He was what anyone would call a handsome man.

And Jonah Curtis was one other thing besides.

Jonah Curtis was a black man.

Chapter 94

ONE IMPORTANT PIECE of the puzzle was still missing.

Who would be defending the White Raiders?

The next morning that puzzle piece appeared. L.J. came rushing into the house yelling, "Those goddamn leaky slop buckets have gone and got themselves the best goddamn criminal defense attorney in the South!"

Jonah looked up from his book. "Maxwell Hayes Lewis?"

"How did you know that?" L.J. asked.

"You said the best." Jonah turned to me. "Ben, if you needed a lawyer to defend a gang of no-good lowlifes who viciously attacked a colored man's house, who would you get?"

"Maxwell Hayes Lewis," I said.

"And why would you want him?"

"Because he got the governor of Arkansas acquitted after he shot his bastard son—his half Negro son—in full view of at least twenty-five people."

"So, our little pack of rats managed to get themselves 'Loophole Lewis,'" Jonah said.

Loophole Lewis. That's how he was known wherever lawyers got together and gossiped about others of their species. Lewis's philosophy was simple: "If you can't find a loophole for your client, go out and invent one."

Jonah carefully closed his well-thumbed copy of the *Revised Civil Code of the State of Mississippi*. "You know, I have always wanted to meet Counselor Lewis," he said.

Jonah must have made a special connection with the good Lord, because we were still sipping coffee ten minutes later when L.J.'s butler announced that a Mr. Maxwell Lewis was there to see us.

"I thought it would be the mannerly thing to do, to come by and introduce myself to you distinguished gentlemen of the prosecution," Lewis said, coming in.

He was plainspoken and plain-looking. My mother would have said he was "plain as an old corn stick." Then she would have added, "But that's just on the outside, so you'd better watch yourself."

We all told Mr. Lewis we were pleased to meet him. He said he was pleased to meet us as well. No, thank you, he said, no tea or coffee for him. Bourbon? Certainly not at this early hour, he said, although he asked if he might revisit the question somewhat later in the day.

This display of southern charm was not the reason for his visit, I was sure. Fairly soon he sidled up to the real reason.

"I must say, Mr. Corbett, I was a mite surprised when I saw that the trial judge will be none other than your distinguished father," he said.

"As was I," I said. Clearly he wanted me to say more, so I stayed silent.

"It's an unusual choice, and highly irregular," he continued on. "My first instinct was to try to get a new judge from the powers that be in Jackson, but then I got to thinking about it. This is an open-and-shut case. Why bother causing a fuss? I'm sure Judge Corbett will preside with absolute fairness."

"If there's one thing he's known for," I said, "it's his fairness. And already we find ourselves in agreement, Mr. Lewis. We also believe that this is an open-and-shut case. I'm just afraid the door will be shutting on you."

Lewis chuckled at my sally. "Ah! We shall see about that," he said. "I've been checking on your record in murder trials up in Washington, D.C. And yours too, Mr. Curtis. We shall certainly see."

Chapter 95

OVER THE NEXT DAYS we transformed the sitting room off my sleeping quarters into the White Raiders War Room, as L.J. soon nicknamed our paper-strewn maelstrom of an office.

Conrad, the Cosgrove brother who had survived the assault at Abraham's house, went up to McComb every morning to collect every newspaper and pamphlet having to do with the upcoming trial. We hauled an old chalkboard up from L.J.'s basement and made two lists of possibilities: "Impossible" and "Possible."

Among the latter were some terrifying questions:

What if Maxwell Hayes Lewis leads with a request for dismissal?

Bang, the gavel falls! The case is over!

What if Abraham is too ill to testify? What if he dies before or during the trial?

Bang! The case is over!

What if Lewis tampers with the jury? It wouldn't be too difficult in this town.

What if...?

We made our lists, erased them, improved and reworked them, and studied them as if they were the received word of God.

After spending a few days working beside him, I decided that Jonah Curtis was not only a smart man but a wise one. Jonah clearly had intelligence to spare, tempered with humor and a bit of easygoing cynicism—the result, I supposed, of growing up always seeing the other side of the coin toss we call Justice. He was the son of a sharecropper who spent most of his life as a slave, on a cotton plantation near Clarksdale, in the Mississippi Delta. When Jonah got his law degree and passed the bar examination, his father gave him a gift, the gold pocket watch for which he'd been saving since before Jonah was born.

It was a beautiful timepiece, but the chain, clumsily hammered together from old scraps of iron, didn't match its quality. Jonah told me that his father had made it himself, from a piece of the very chain that had shackled him to the auction block the last time he was offered for sale.

Sometimes Jonah got a little ahead of himself with his legal theories, at least as far as L.J. was concerned.

"A verdict depends on the culture of any given town," Jonah said. "A man held for killing a Negro in New York City will have a very different trial—and a very different outcome—than a man held for the same crime in Atlanta. Bring him to Eudora, and again the crime and the resulting trial would be different. We might say this White Raiders case is *sui generis.*"

L.J. sighed heavily. "Talk English, for God's sake," he said. "Down here, we say 'soo-ey' when we're calling hogs."

L.J. already considered me the worst know-it-all in the room, so I left this for Jonah to explain.

"Sorry, L.J., it's Latin," said Jonah. "*Sui generis*—'of its own kind,' literally, 'of its own genus.' In other words, this case...well, there's never been another one anything like it."

Chapter 96

THE CHANTING OUTSIDE L.J.'S HOUSE grew louder. The voices came closer and closer.

All white?
Not right.
All white?
We fight.

I hurried to the balcony off the War Room, with L.J. and Jonah at my heels. An astounding sight met our eyes. There were black people, scores of them—two hundred or more—slowly marching down the middle of Willow Street in Eudora, Mississippi.

This was almost unbelievable. In the South, black people were not supposed to assemble in these numbers.

L.J. let out a whistle. "That is one angry bunch of Negroes," he said.

"I think the word *I* would use is 'passionate,'" said Jonah.

Though I had never expected to see black people marching through the streets, I knew instantly what this was about. Tomorrow the trial would begin, and the first order of business was jury selection. No Negro had ever been permitted to serve on a jury in the state of Mississippi. Many of the liberal Yankee newspapers had declared it an outrage. They suggested that the White Raiders Trial might be just the occasion for the presiding judge to allow one or possibly even two colored men to serve as jurors.

We stood at the railing of the veranda, watching the marchers slowly pass. It was plain that they had taken a detour from Commerce Street to go past L.J.'s house. Some of them waved or lifted their hats to us.

Just when we thought we had seen the last of the marchers, another phalanx turned the corner onto Willow.

I was amazed. "Gentlemen. Are you seeing what I'm seeing?"

L.J. smiled. "Yessir, it's one hell of a crowd."

"Not just the *size* of the crowd," I said. "Take a look at who's *leading* it."

All white?
Not right.

L.J. squinted to see. "Those two old folks at the front?"

Jonah answered for me. "The lady is Ida Wells-Barnett," he said. "And the gentleman, if I am not mistaken, is Mr. W. E. B. Du Bois. This is history being made, indeed."

Chapter 97

WHEN I WAS A BOY, my mother would sometimes take me to watch my father conducting a trial.

"It's a *presiding* day," she'd say. "Let's go see Daddy scaring the pants off of everyone." And away we'd go to the courthouse.

To my child's eyes the old Pike County Courthouse looked exactly like a church. The second-floor gallery where the colored people got to sit was like the choir loft. The benches below were the pews. And my father stood at the high altar in the front of the room, delivering thunderous sermons and running the whole thing like a very strict minister who happened to wield a hammer instead of a Bible.

More than twenty years later, here I was, back in the church of Judge Everett Corbett.

But today, as L.J. and Jonah and I arranged our papers and books on the prosecution table, the old courthouse felt like something else entirely.

Not a church.

It was more like a theater now.

The upstairs colored section had been transformed into balcony seats. The benches on the main level were the orchestra seats, jammed to overflowing with an audience that had stood in line for hours to see the hottest entertainment in town. And that altar? Well, that was now center stage.

That was Everett J. Corbett's stage. He could be a dynamic, exciting performer, and I felt sure he would not let his audience down today.

Ringing the front steps of the courthouse were Scooter Willems and several dozen men like him, bristling with tripods and huge black accordion cameras. Accompanying the photographers were at least a hundred reporters flashing pencils and notebooks, trading tidbits with each other, rushing this way and that in pursuit of the latest rumors.

Inside, the colored spectators had dutifully filed upstairs to the cheap seats. The benches below were filled to maximum capacity by the white citizens of Eudora. Only the first two rows had been left empty, roped off for the pool of potential jurors.

Dominating the wall above the judge's bench was an enormous Fattorini & Sons regulator clock nearly as long as a grandfather clock, with a carved dark-wood case, elegant Roman numerals, and a pair of gleaming brass pendulums. Growing up, I always thought of it as the Clock of Justice.

Now every tick brought us closer to nine a.m.

Here came a pair of Chief Eversman's newly recruited deputies, leading in the defendants. Three White Raiders. No shackles, ropes, or handcuffs. The deputies chatted and laughed with the men as they led them to the defense table.

And then the great Maxwell Hayes Lewis strode from the back of the room to greet the Raiders and shake their hands so that everyone in the courtroom could see how normal, how average and amiable, these men were. After a moment's discussion the defendants turned to look at our table. They looked back at each other and grinned. The sight of Jonah, L.J., and me seemed to amuse them greatly.

The bailiff entered with a solemn expression, carrying the heavy cast-iron imprinting seal, which he placed at the right end of my father's bench. This was the seal he would use to mark evidence as it was admitted.

"All rise," the bailiff called. "The court is now in session, the Honorable Everett J. Corbett presiding."

Daddy's big entrance was always a highlight. Here he came through the door at stage left, his hair gleaming with brilliantine, his silky black robe pressed to perfection by Dabney.

He lifted the heavy mahogany gavel. I was surprised to see him using the gavel I had sent him on his sixtieth birthday, since I had never received a thank-you note.

He brought the gavel down with a thunderous bang.

"There will be order!" he commanded. "There will be silence! There will be justice!"

Chapter 98

NOW TO PICK A JURY.

That summer had been one of the hottest on record. It seemed to me that God had saved up all the excess heat and humidity in the world and brought it down upon Eudora today. It was already so hot in the courtroom that the hand fans were flapping like a flock of restless birds.

Judge Corbett had evidently taken measures to spruce up the courtroom for the national press, who were allowed inside between sessions to gather scraps of news. He had ordered all the spectator benches and tables and chairs sanded and revarnished, and indeed they all gleamed as if brand-new. But the new varnish turned soft and sticky in the heat and gave off fumes that set heads spinning. I breathed the sweetish, medicinal smell; the seat of my trousers stuck to my chair.

This was going to be a very long day.

I saw at once that Judge Corbett still ran an efficient courtroom. It took only ten minutes for the first three candidates to be interviewed, approved, and seated in the jury box: three middle-aged white men.

Jonah made little fuss over any of them. I assumed he was saving his objections for an occasion when they might prove persuasive.

It didn't take long.

The clerk read a name from the list: "Patton William Taylor."

Chapter 99

FROM THE FRONT ROW rose a mousy little man commonly known as Patsy-Boy Taylor. I knew him as a helper of Lyman Tripp, the undertaker in whose wagon I had ridden to the Klan meeting at Scully's barn.

I scribbled a note and passed it to Jonah.

Taylor served time in La. State Prison for assault of Negro girl. Believe he broke her leg.

Jonah scanned the note, nodding. It was his turn to question the prospective juror first.

"Good morning, Mr. Taylor," he said. "Tell me, sir, have you ever been to Louisiana?"

"Once or twice," said Patsy-Boy.

"How about the town of Angola? Ever been there?"

The man frowned. "I reckon I have."

"And how long was your most recent stay in Angola, Mr. Taylor?"

"I don't remember."

"Perhaps I can help refresh your memory, sir," Jonah said. "Mr. Taylor, did you recently finish a five-month term in the Louisiana State Penitentiary at Angola?"

"I might've," said Taylor. "I can't quite remember."

"Your Honor, if it please the court, could you direct Mr. Taylor to answer my question?"

The ice in my father's water pitcher had melted away, but there was plenty of it in his voice. "He *did* answer, Mr. Curtis," he said. "He said that he couldn't quite remember."

"Your Honor, with all due respect, I don't believe—"

"Your beliefs are of no interest to me, Mr. Curtis," my father said. He turned to the defense table. "Mr. Lewis, do you have any objection to this gentleman sitting on this jury?"

"None whatsoever, Your Honor."

"Mr. Taylor will be sworn in to serve," my father said. The gavel came down.

By reflex L.J. and I came up off our chairs. I can't say I couldn't believe what had just happened, probably because I'd watched justice being meted out in Mississippi for too long. But *still*.

"I most strenuously object, Your Honor," Jonah said in a loud voice.

A young colored woman in the gallery called out, "That ain't justice!"

My father pointed his gavel at her. "Contempt of court. Ten days in jail and a dollar fine. Get her out of here!"

Two of Phineas's deputies ran to do his bidding. Everyone heard the woman's noisy protest as they dragged her down the stairs.

Meanwhile, my father's attention was seemingly riveted by the sight of a fly trapped in the soft varnish of his bench. The insect was hopelessly stuck, its wings buzzing. The judge closed his thumb and forefinger on the fly, plucked it up, and placed it in the center of his desk.

Bang! He brought his gavel down on that fly.

"Let me tell you something, Mr. Curtis," he said. "Let me explain something to you. I would advise you to listen, and listen well. *I am in charge of this courtroom*. Did you hear what I said?"

"Yes, sir," Jonah replied.

"What did I say?" My father's voice was deadly calm. "Repeat it for me, please."

"You are in charge of this courtroom, Your Honor."

"You're damn right I am. Now, you may object to Counselor Lewis's comments. He is your opponent; he represents the defense. But you may not ever—*ever*—object to something I have said. For any reason."

The only sound in the courtroom was the ticking of the clock and the hum of the ceiling fans.

"Thank you, Mr. Curtis. And tell those two clowns you brought with you to sit themselves down, or I'll have them removed from my courtroom."

The trial of the new century—the proceedings known as the *State of Mississippi v. Madden, North, and Stephens*—was officially under way.

Chapter 100

THERE THEY SAT, three White Raiders facing *a jury of their peers.*

It was a true statement in every way. Once Judge Everett Corbett cut off all objections from our side, he quickly empaneled a jury of twelve middle-aged white men who looked just like the men they would be called upon to judge.

"We have a jury," the judge announced, "and so we will proceed to trial. Is the prosecution prepared to begin in the morning?"

"Yes, Your Honor," Jonah said.

"And I'm sure the defense is ready."

"Defense is certainly ready, Your Honor," said Maxwell Hayes Lewis.

"Then without further ado —" my father began.

Jonah Curtis stood up and dared to interrupt him again.

"Your Honor, begging the court's pardon, I feel compelled to state for the record that the prosecution has not seen a fair and representative jury selection here today."

My father's voice was dangerously soft. "All right. I have warned you, Mr. Curtis, and I will not warn you again. I am in charge of this trial. I am in charge of this courtroom. I have ruled that this jury is fit to serve."

"But Your Honor—"

Suddenly my father rose up and bellowed, *"And I will not warn you again!* Try me, my friend! Just try me once more! Challenge my jurisdiction again, and I will declare a mistrial here and summarily dismiss all the charges. Which, I remind you, is within my power."

My father turned on his heel and swept out of the room. I knew the drill: he would walk straight into his office and pull off his robe. His clothes would be damp with sweat. I pictured him settling into his swivel chair in that office lined with law books, oak filing cabinets, diplomas, and certificates of appreciation. On his desk he permitted himself one personal touch: the sad-beautiful honeymoon photograph of him and Mama, arm in arm on the boardwalk at Biloxi.

While the defendants stood shooting the breeze with their jailers, Lewis took a detour by our table.

"I guess they didn't teach y'all everything up in those Ivy League law schools," he said. "Down here, we believe the first responsibility of a good criminal attorney is to make friends with the judge."

"Oh, they tried to teach us that," Jonah said. "I guess I just didn't do a good job of learning it."

"Me either," I said. "And I've had decades of practice with the man."

Loophole Lewis chuckled genially and brought out a couple of cigars from an inside pocket. "May I offer you boys a Partagás? Best quality, fresh off the boat from Havana. I'm sure you enjoyed a few of these fellows when you were down in Cuba, Ben."

"No, sir," I said mildly. "We didn't have much time for smoking cigars." I was about to say more when I saw Conrad Cosgrove pushing into the courtroom through the crowd.

"Mr. Corbett," he said. "A messenger brought this to the house. I figured you'd want to see it right away."

Conrad handed over a small envelope.

On the front, in an elegant hand, were the words BENJAMIN CORBETT, PERSONAL CORRESPONDENCE.

The words engraved on the back flap were just as simple: THE WHITE HOUSE.

"If you gentlemen will excuse me," I said. I didn't wait for an answer.

Chapter 101

AS I WALKED down the courthouse steps, a reporter from the *New Orleans Item* took my elbow to ask how I thought the first day had gone.

"Exactly as expected," I said. "Justice will be served here." I took my arm back and kept walking.

I followed the cinder path around the side of the building. The giant oak trees in the square provided the only real shade in the center of town. I felt twenty degrees cooler the moment I stepped under their branches and took a seat on a bench.

I sliced the edge of the envelope with my fingernail. Inside was a single typewritten sheet on gold-embossed White House stationery.

Dear Capt. Corbett,
The eyes of America are upon you, and upon the proceedings in Eudora. I can assure you

that with my own (four) eyes I am personally watching you and the trial at every moment.

I know you will continue to do your best, and I know that you will succeed in this endeavor, as we succeeded together during the late War.

Ben, know that your president is with you every inch of the way.

Sincerely yours, I remain
Your obt. servant,
Theodore Roosevelt, Pres't.

I smiled at the president's little joke about his "four eyes," but when I realized the meaning of his subsequent words, my stomach took a nervous dive. As if I didn't have enough tension to deal with, now the president of the United States was "personally watching" me "at every moment."

I read the letter again and put it back in the envelope.

A voice called, "Mr. Corbett, sir."

I looked to both sides and saw no one.

Again the voice: "Mr. Corbett? Over here, sir, *behind you.*"

Chapter 102

I TURNED AROUND QUICKLY to find a tall, slender colored man standing on the sidewalk. He was perhaps ten years older than me and beautifully dressed, down to the club scarf in his pocket and the jeweled pin in his necktie.

"May I have a word with you for a moment, sir?" he asked.

"Well, of course," I said. "Come have a seat."

"I'm sorry, Mr. Corbett, I can't. That park is White Only."

I had forgotten—or maybe I'd never realized—that the old wooden benches, the little fountain, the shade of the big old eudoras, all were reserved for the exclusive use of white Eudora.

I walked across the grass to the man and extended my hand. "Ben Corbett."

"I'm a correspondent for the *Indianapolis Cross*," he said.

"Ah yes," I said. "I've read your paper. Y'all have published some of the best general reports I've seen on the question of lynching."

"Why, thank you, sir," he said. "I'm honored that you've heard of us."

"Welcome to Eudora," I said.

"Oh, it's not my first time," he said. "I grew up in Eudora."

I looked at him harder. I rattled around in my memory, but I couldn't place where I had seen him before.

"I used to work for Mr. Jenkins at the mercantile store," he said.

All at once I knew him.

I said. "Is that—*Marcus*? Is that you?"

His eyes lit up. "You remember me?"

"I'll be damned if I'll ever forget you, Marcus," I said.

I reached out my arms and embraced him. He was surprised, but he let me do it, and even patted me on the back.

"You were the only one who helped my mother," I said. "You helped me get her to Dr. Frederick. If you hadn't, she might have died."

Marcus told me that his family had left Eudora for the Midwest not long after the time of Mama's stroke. They wound up in central Indiana, where his father worked for a cattle farmer. Marcus went on to study English at the Negro teachers college in Gary and had landed a job with the largest colored newspaper in the state.

And now, he said, he had convinced his editors to send him to Mississippi to cover the White Raiders Trial because he had a personal interest in one of the defendants. "Henry North," he said. "I knew him. You did, too."

"I did?"

Marcus said, "Do you remember that redheaded boy that worked with me at Jenkins' Mercantile? He helped us carry your mama out that day. That boy is Henry North."

Sure, I remembered the loutish boy. He was thin and rawboned in those days. He had said Mama was drunk, to leave her where she lay.

"I remember the day your mama took sick," Marcus said, "like it was yesterday. You weren't more than about seven years old, but you acted like a grown man. You answered old Sanders back like he deserved. And you helped me carry her to the doc. I always knew you were going to turn into a fine man."

I was speechless. Marcus's words made me feel humble. The truth was that after years of remembering Marcus's example every day, as my mother had told me to do, I hadn't thought about him in quite a while.

"I've paid close attention to your law career, Mr. Corbett — helping people up in Washington, helping wherever you can. When I saw how you were turning out, I tell you, it gave me a little hope along the way."

Seeing Marcus again, hearing him speak like this, gave me a transfusion of energy. As if I'd just received new blood, a whole body's worth of it.

Without knowing it, I had given Marcus "a little hope along the way."

And now Marcus had given me hope for the difficult murder trial that lay ahead.

Chapter 103

AFTER CAREFUL DELIBERATION, Jonah Curtis had chosen to wear a navy blue suit, a crisp white shirt, and a bright red tie. He didn't look exactly like an American flag, but all the colors were there for the patriotic effect he intended for his opening statement to the jury.

"Gentlemen, I did not come to Eudora to make history," he began. "I was sent here by the Supreme Court of the state of Mississippi to seek justice. If in the name of justice you reach the verdict I truly believe you must reach, the state will ask you to assign a degree of punishment that you feel is appropriate for these crimes."

"Let us begin, though, not at the ending," he said, "but at the beginning. A hot summer night. You know what that means, surely I don't have to tell you. Talking to a Mississippi man about the heat is like talking to a fish about the water."

This little joke brought an involuntary smile to two or three faces among the jury.

"So there we are on that hot summer night. Sweltering. Down in the Quarters, inside a poor man's house.

"And here, on a bed in the parlor, an old man lies dying. His granddaughter is tending to him, his trembles and tremors, his rackety cough."

All the men on the jury were watching him now, even those whose expressions revealed their innate distaste for a Negro attorney dressed in a suit.

"On the porch of this home, there are two gentlemen standing guard. These are not fighters or thugs. One is an attorney, well known to the most powerful men in our nation's capital. The other is the inventor of the Stringer Automatic Baler, the most successful businessman in Eudora—heck, let's be honest—in all of south Mississippi."

There was a patter of quiet chuckling; everyone in the courtroom shot a look at L.J., beaming at this description of him.

"These gentlemen have come to the Quarters on this night," Jonah said, "because the dying man is their friend. They've heard rumors of trouble.

They have a well-reasoned fear that some kind of tragedy is in the offing.

"Lord, it's hot. The old man struggles to breathe. The granddaughter cannot help the tears that come to her eyes. The old man is all she has on this earth.

"Then there comes a sound, the sound of hoofbeats on the road. There are men on horses, raising a cloud of dust in the darkness."

A couple of the jurors looked ostentatiously bored, and a man in the back row was already dozing. But the others seemed attentive, and a few were even transfixed, as if Jonah were telling them a scary story.

And that's exactly what he was doing.

"Suddenly, gentlemen, all is pandemonium — uproar and violence and chaos. Men firing guns everywhere. Glass flying. Women screaming. Suddenly there are men all around the house, trying to shoot their way in. Trying to kill the old man. Trying to kill his granddaughter.

"The old man is terrified. The young woman throws herself over him, shielding his body with her own. The assault lasts only a few minutes, but it seems like hours and hours."

Jonah paused. He studied the faces of the jurors, each one in turn.

Finally he spoke again, in a hushed whisper.

"Two men lie dead on the ground. One is a man who's been a friend and neighbor to you all, all his life—Luther Cosgrove, an employee of Mr. Stringer for nearly thirty years. He lies dead in the side yard, shot in the face by the men on horseback. The other is a much younger man from out in the county, a fellow named Jimmie Cooper, who had come to that house of his own free will that night and volunteered to stand guard over that dying old man. Jimmie Cooper lies dead on the ground in front of the house."

Jonah paused and shook his head sorrowfully, as if he couldn't believe the price Jimmie and Luther had paid.

"But then there is a miracle," he said. "Three of the killers are arrested. For once, they are not allowed to pull on their Klan hoods and go riding off into the darkness, unmolested, unpunished. For once, there are men who are interested in capturing the killers, in bringing them to justice—in bringing them here today, to face trial before a jury of their peers. And that, of course, is where you gentlemen come into the story."

He turned, pointed his finger at the defendants. "There they are. Mr. Chester Madden. Mr. Henry North. Mr. Lincoln Stephens."

The defendants put on the smirk they had evidently practiced beforehand, but they couldn't hold it. Their nerves and the silence in the room got the best of them.

It was now time for the most difficult, delicate portion of the opening statement. Jonah and I had spent hours in the War Room going back and forth over this part, trying to find the best way to say what he needed to say.

"Gentlemen, you may have noticed there is one fact I left out of my account," Jonah said. "You may think it's the most important fact of all. And that is the fact that these defendants are white men. They attacked a colored family in a colored neighborhood. One of the men they killed was white. The other was black. I didn't mention any of this to you.

"And do you know why? I'll tell you why— because the pursuit of justice knows no color! The pursuit of justice admits only that which is fair, and honest, and true.

"This case is *not about race*. It is not about the black versus the white. This case is much easier than that. It's a simple matter of justice.

"Now, as the prosecutor representing the great state of Mississippi, it will be my job to show you how these three men attacked and pillaged, how they came to the Eudora Quarters planning to kill, intending to kill. How they planned and then executed the deliberate, premeditated murder of two men on a hot, awful night in the Quarters. On a night when these three men, and all the ones who got away, were hoping that justice had taken a holiday. *Well, justice has not taken a holiday here in Eudora!*"

I heard a sound from the jury box. Glancing over, I was astounded to see one of the jurors, old Lester Johnson, a retired teller from the First Bank of Eudora, clapping. So taken was he by Jonah's presentation that he was applauding. The sound was very loud in the room.

Then there was a louder sound: the gavel coming down *BANG!*

My father jumped to his feet. "Lester!" he shouted. *"Have you lost your goddamn mind?"*

Chapter 104

"WELL, WELL, WELL," Maxwell Hayes Lewis said slowly. Then he rose from his chair to begin his opening statement.

Those three words were all it took for me to realize what he was up to.

Lewis was appropriating the style of Clarence Darrow, a Chicago labor lawyer renowned all over the nation as the "lawyer's lawyer." Darrow was the most effective courtroom presenter of the day, his style casual, colloquial, at times downright homey, with ample doses of country wisdom and sentiment tossed in.

Lewis scratched his head, then slid his hand down, cupping his face in his hand, squeezing his cheek, as if he were sitting in his study, lost in thought.

Then he appeared to notice the jury for the first time, and ambled over.

"Now, Mr. Curtis here says, and I quote, 'the pursuit of justice knows no color. The pursuit of justice admits only that which is fair, and honest, and true.' "

He turned around and stared hard at Jonah. But when he spoke, his voice was gentle. "Thank you for saying that, Mr. Curtis. All I have to say to that is, Amen."

The jurors visibly relaxed. The lawyer had brought them to a point of tension, then eased up.

"But let me tell you fellows where Mr. Curtis and I are absolutely *not* in agreement," he said.

Lewis's face was glistening with perspiration, and he hadn't been talking a minute yet. He mopped his face with a handkerchief, a gesture that afforded him a dramatic pause.

"We are not in agreement *on the story itself.* Mr. Curtis tells a tale of night riders galloping in and shooting up a house in a frenzy of violent and lawless behavior. I have another version of that story to tell you. Now, the story I have to tell you is about eight upstanding white citizens of Pike County. Three of them were wrongly accused and arrested, the three gentlemen you see before you today.

"But on the night in question, there were eight. They climbed up on their horses, calmly, and in a neighborly way they rode over to Abraham Cross's house. Why did they go there? Were they looking for trouble? Well, no—the trouble had already come and found *them*."

He paused, turned around, and walked the other way along the jury box, meeting the eyes of each man in turn.

"Those eight men rode over that night to investigate a complaint against Mr. Cross's nephew, a Mr. Richard Cross, known as Ricky, a Negro who was suspected of molesting and raping a young white girl of the Cedar Bend community.

"Understand, my friends, that the prosecutor's story and this story fit together perfectly. The entire evening can be seen, from one perspective, as a gigantic misunderstanding. If the people in that house in the Quarters had not shot first and asked questions later—if they'd all been informed that they harbored a rapist in their midst, if they'd known about the assault on the girl, and the legitimate reasons my clients had for going to Mr. Cross's house that night—why, none of this would have happened.

"But even so, it *did* happen. And it is a tragedy.

"And yet, gentlemen, it is not murder. I am here to tell you about Abraham Cross—a dying man, according to Mr. Curtis, although just for your information he is still alive and well, and I wouldn't be surprised if you all get to meet him. I'm going to show you how Mr. Cross and his granddaughter and his hired gunmen, some of whom are in this room trying to intimidate you gentlemen here today..."

As he said this he was looking directly at L. J. Stringer and me.

"...I will show you how this armed band of Negroes and their white friends set about to deny my clients any access at all to the suspected man. How they, in fact, attacked my clients, and sought to visit great bodily harm upon them—even though my clients had *a written legal warrant* deputizing them and empowering them to question the accused, they were set upon by a pack of armed men.

"My clients fired their own weapons, gentlemen, in self-defense. The case is simple. It's what is known in our game as 'open and shut.' My clients are facing these terrible charges, they have been jailed and denied their most basic rights as Americans, as Mississippians."

You could see the jurors straightening with pride as he said this. "And all because of a story! A fable! A fiction, my friends. Mr. Jonah Curtis is a very eloquent lawyer, gentlemen, anyone can see that, but what he's telling you is nothing more than a bedtime story!"

Several jurors laughed out loud.

"That is right, gentlemen of the jury. A bedtime story. We have two versions being told here. Mr. Curtis has told you a fairy story, and I have told you the truth. *As God above knows it to be!*"

Chapter 105

"GODDAMN THEM, BEN. Goddamn them all to hell!"

L.J. slammed his fist on the dining room table, rattling the crystal goblets. "Goddamn their lying, cheating asses!"

L.J. was doing all the shouting. Jonah and I were standing back, watching him scream in a way only rich men can. We didn't try to stop him or calm him down.

"The biggest lie of all," L.J. said, "is when he says these White Raiders had some kind of official warrant to come into that house after Ricky."

Jonah looked at me. "All right, Ben, how is Lewis going to demonstrate that in a credible fashion?"

"Easy," I said. "He'll put Phineas Eversman on the stand."

"The policeman?"

"Chief of police, and the only full-time officer on the force," I reminded him. "He'll put Phineas on and Phineas will lie through his teeth."

Jonah looked quizzical. "I thought Eversman was on our side. Or at least neutral."

"He was on our side for exactly one night," I explained. "He only arrested those men because L.J. pushed him into it. He's been looking for a way out ever since."

I speared a slice of Virginia ham before passing the platter to L.J.

"It didn't look like it would rain tonight, did it?" said Jonah.

"Not to me," L.J. replied. "Why?"

"That sure does sound like thunder outside," Jonah said.

I walked over to the window and pulled back the drapes. First I was surprised; then I was frightened.

"What is it, Ben?"

"About thirty, forty fellows with guns," I said, "and a few with pitchforks. They appear to be just standing there, watching the house."

"That's a mighty big crowd for Eudora," L.J. said.

"No," I said. "It's a mighty big *mob*."

Chapter 106

THE MOB CAUSED US no trouble that night. For about an hour they watched us watching them through the windows, then they turned and went away. Every few minutes I peeked out the window, but the streets of Eudora stayed quiet and dark that night.

The next morning the trial began in earnest. I spent a long minute studying the face of Henry Wadsworth North, trying to match the man with what I remembered of the boy on the day Mama took sick. Too many years had intervened. This sallow, blotchy-faced fat man bore only a vague resemblance to the surly kid I remembered from Jenkins' Mercantile.

Jonah called his first witness: Abraham Cross.

Abraham was wearing his best church suit,

of speckled brown wool, and a matching fedora. He rolled in in a rickety wheelchair Moody had borrowed from a crippled neighbor of L.J.'s, a nice woman who sympathized with us.

"Now, Mr. Cross," Jonah said, "why don't you take us back to the night of August twenty-fifth. Tell us what you remember."

Abraham nodded. "Well, sir, I was in the parlor, a-layin' in my bed, and Moody was tendin' after me—"

"Excuse me, sir," Jonah said. "Who is Moody?"

"Moody Cross. My granddaughter. She looks after me."

"Thank you, sir. Please go on."

"Like I say, I was a-layin' in my bed. Not quite sure if I'd been sleeping or not. But then sure enough I come awake. Sound like the cavalry done showed up outside the house. A bunch of horses, I don't know how many. And men shootin' off guns, and yellin'. Like to scared me half to death—and I don't need to be any closer to dead than I already am."

Laughter rolled through the courtroom, from whites and Negroes. My father slammed down the gavel to kill it.

Abraham continued telling his story in precise,

unwavering detail. Without any prompting from Jonah, he pointed out and positively identified two of the defendants.

"That one there, I saw him through the front window," he said, pointing at the defense table.

Jonah asked him to be more specific.

"That one on the right," he said. "Stephens. He shot Jimmie Cooper dead."

"You're sure it was Mr. Stephens you saw?"

"No doubt about it," said Abraham. "And then that one there—Mr. Madden—he come into the parlor where I was, with another one of them Raiders. A man he called Harold."

"And what did Mr. Madden do?"

"He says to this Harold, 'You watch this old nigger real good. Keep your gun on his neck.' Then he went back outside, Madden did."

"And the one he called Harold—he stayed there with you?"

"Yes, he did."

"Did he keep a gun on you?"

"Yes, sir. Up against my skull. And he grabbed Moody too. Not in a nice way."

"And how did you respond to that, Mr. Cross?"

Abraham scratched his old head, closed his eyes for a moment. Then he spoke.

"Well, sir, to tell you the truth I didn't have to respond."

"And why is that?"

"Because a minute later, Ben Corbett come into the room, and my granddaughter Moody..."

He stopped.

"Please continue," Jonah said.

"She pushed a kitchen knife into Harold's back."

Chapter 107

"SO, LET ME SEE if I've got this straight, Mr. Cross."

Maxwell Hayes Lewis stood up to begin his cross-examination of Abraham.

"You were *lying* in your living room, half asleep. Or maybe you were asleep and dreaming part of the time, you're not really certain. You woke up...or you think you woke up...you looked out that window and saw a man you *thought* was Mr. Stephens pulling the trigger on a pistol."

Jonah said, "Your Honor—"

"Overruled," my father said.

"This is supposed to be a cross-examination," Jonah said. "Could he get to a question sometime today?"

"I said overruled," my father repeated.

"Oh, I'm asking him a question," Lewis said. "I'm asking him if I've got his story straight. Mr. Cross, you said you saw this man shooting a pistol. But in fact you never saw him shoot anyone. You never saw anyone take a bullet from Mr. Stephens's gun, did you? You can't follow the path of a bullet with your eyes."

"Your Honor—"

"Hush." My father waved his hand as if Jonah were a fly that needed swatting. He turned to Abraham. "Answer the question. Are you sure who you saw?"

Abraham worked his jaw, as if chewing a wad of tobacco. Then he spoke.

"I know it was Mr. Stephens shooting, 'cause I saw him clear as day. I heard Jimmie when he fell and hit the roof. I knew that's who it was 'cause I'd watched him climb up on the roof. And I saw him again, when he fell."

Good for you, Abraham, I cheered silently. *Give it back to him. Stick him with the truth.*

"And that's the way you remember it?" Lewis said.

"Yes, sir. But not only that. That's how it *was*."

"How is your memory these days, Mr. Cross?"

"Sharp as a serpent's tongue, sir," he said.

That got a chuckle from the spectators.

Lewis smiled too. "How old are you now, Mr. Cross, sir?"

"Mama always said I come into Miss'ippi the same year Miss'ippi joined up with the United States."

"And Mississippi became a state in 1817," said Lewis. "So that would make you..."

"Eighty-nine," Abraham said. "Same as Miss'ippi."

Another laugh. If the jury was anything like the audience, some of them had to be enjoying Abraham's company.

Lewis ambled over to his desk, picked up a piece of paper, and carried it to the bench. "Your Honor, if it please the court, I submit article number one as physical entry and evidence, a warrant from the chief of police to search the premises of one Abraham Cross in the Eudora Quarters."

"Very well," my father said. He took pleasure in sliding the document into the maw of his heavy iron stamp, bringing down the lever to imprint his seal and admit it into evidence.

He handed the warrant back to Lewis, who carried it to Abraham.

"Mr. Cross, would you please take a look at this document?"

Abraham slowly settled his spectacles onto the bridge of his nose and took the paper from Lewis.

"Mr. Cross, do you know how to read?"

Abraham straightened up and glared at him. "I've been reading the Good Book since I was five years old."

"In that case, would you please be so kind as to read that for me — the sentences printed at the top, in the heavy ink."

Abraham read: "'This warrant renders unto the bearers the unchallenged right to examine all house, home, and household goods of the residence denoted below, by order of the Chief of Police in the township of Eudora, Mississippi.'"

Abraham looked up at the attorney towering over his wheelchair.

Lewis said, "Please read the name on the line marked 'Residence.'"

"It's my name. 'Abraham Cross.'"

Lewis stuck his thumbs through his suspenders, a pose exactly like the photograph of Clarence Darrow I'd seen in the *American Legal Companion*.

"Now, Mr. Cross, when have you seen this document before?"

"Never in my life," Abraham said.

"Are you sure about that?"

Yes, sir, he said. He was sure. Lewis asked him the question five different ways. Jonah tried to object and was gaveled into silence.

"Didn't Mr. Stephens hand this document to you when he arrived at your house that night, Mr. Cross?"

Ah, here we go. Jonah jumped up. Objection overruled. He seemed to have reached a silent agreement with Judge Everett Corbett: he would be allowed to keep making objections as long as he understood he would be instantly overruled on every one.

"Mr. Cross, isn't it true that you saw this document, you read it, and you threw it on the ground?"

"No, sir."

"Didn't you tell Mr. Stephens that if he wanted to search your house, he'd have to shoot you first?"

"No, sir. I did not."

"Are you certain?"

"He didn't bring no paper. They rode up and started shooting. If Mr. Stephens said he did that, he is a liar. And if you say he did it, sir, you would be a liar too."

Chapter 108

AFTER ABRAHAM FINISHED testifying and Moody took him home to put him back to bed, Jonah challenged the admissibility of Phineas Eversman's search warrant.

My father looked mildly amused. "It's a search warrant, Mr. Curtis. It looks like a thousand others that I've seen over the years," he said.

Since his profane outburst in the direction of the applauding juror, I thought, my father had been unusually patient with Jonah. He must have realized how bad that eruption would look once all these "two-bit newspaper reporters" put it into print.

Jonah decided to tack in another direction. "Your Honor, I know you are well aware that under the rules of civil procedure, all documents entered as evidence must be shared with all counsel *before* commencement of trial," he said. "The first time I saw this was a few minutes ago."

My father peered down his nose at the spectacle of a Negro lawyer daring to cite civil procedure to him. "Now, Mr. Curtis, you being from up in Jackson and all, and educated up in the North, well, I'm sure you are accustomed to practicing before the big-city courts like they have up there, with your civil procedures and all that," he said. I had seen him perform this act before: the simple country judge, working his way through the facts of the case with nothing but his good ol' horse sense. "But down here in Eudora," he went on, "we do things in a simple and logical fashion. Mr. Lewis hands me a document, I take a look at it. I ask myself if it looks authentic. In this case I thought it did, and I admitted it into evidence. I'm sorry you didn't get to see it earlier—Mr. Lewis, you should've showed it to him—but I'm not going to throw it away or declare a mistrial on account of a thing like that. Mr. Curtis, is that all right with you? Yes? Let's proceed."

He was so folksy, so mock-reasonable, that it made my stomach queasy. It was obvious that this judge was not the least bit worried about being overturned on any appeal. That could only be because he knew there would never be an appeal: Sheriff Reese and his deputy were Klansmen, and Phineas Eversman, the only other law enforcement officer in Pike County, had crossed over to their side. The defendants would be acquitted, they would go free, and no one would ever disturb them on these murder charges again.

"Now, I want both sides to listen," my father said. "I'm going to recess this proceeding until tomorrow morning. Just because every reporter in America is interested in this case, doesn't mean I don't have other matters to adjudicate. This afternoon I will devote myself to the trial of a man who's been charged with public drunkenness and urination. I'm going to have to settle a fence-line dispute between a planter and one of his colored sharecroppers. And I'm going to listen to that old German butcher, Henry Kleinhenz, tell me one more time why Sam Sanders should not be allowed to sell chicken parts at the general store."

He banged his gavel once.

"Until tomorrow, nine o'clock. *Sharp*."

Chapter 109

"ALL RISE! THIS COURT stands adjourned!"

My father swept out of the room. Everyone in the courtroom started talking at once, the newspaper reporters pushing through the crowd, hastening to beat each other to the telegraph stations at the depot.

Through the window I saw that the sunny morning was giving way to dark-bottomed clouds. Everyone had been hoping for rain, if only to cool things off for an hour or two before the sun heated it all up again.

Maxwell Hayes Lewis stepped over to the prosecution table.

"Mr. Curtis, gentlemen—I just want to say, I am mighty sorry for forgetting to show that search warrant to you fellows before we got started this morning."

I looked him right in the eye. "Ah, Mr. Lewis, that is perfectly understandable. I'm sure you were too busy manufacturing that warrant this morning to bother showing it to us."

Lewis chuckled. "Ben, I am sorry to see you have become such a cynic."

"Let me tell you something, Mr. Lewis." I straightened all the way up so as to look down on him from the maximum height. "You got Phineas to fake a warrant for you, and you found some justice of the peace who was happy to sign it and postdate it, and you got my father to admit it into evidence with a wink and a nod. But Jonah has a whole bunch of witnesses who saw what your clients did that night. They saw the death and destruction. And they will testify."

The affable smile disappeared from Lewis's face. He was gathering his wits for a comeback when Conrad Cosgrove burst into the near-empty courtroom, shouting.

"Mr. Stringer! Mr. Corbett! Come on out here, you got to see this!"

I followed the others down the center aisle to the doorway. Outside, the trees in the square were swaying in the breeze from the oncoming storm. A soft patter of rain had just started to fall.

Right in front of the door, in the center of the lawn fronting the courthouse, was a sight I had never witnessed before.

A huge cross was planted there.

And it was burning.

Chapter 110

THAT EVENING A nervous and troubled prosecution team met for supper in the dining room of the Stringer home. Allegra, who usually took her meals with the children, decided to join us.

"Louie, isn't it just amazing how our Ella can turn one little handful of crabmeat into a she-crab soup worthy of Galatoire's in New Orleans?" Allegra said.

I was thinking, *I never knew his name was Louie. Even way back in grammar school, he was always L.J.*

L.J. had no time to answer. At that moment a rock exploded the glass of the window above the dining table and skipped across the room. A second rock smashed through the window beside it, then a third. Glass flew everywhere.

"The girls!" Allegra screamed and hurried up the stairs.

I ran after L.J. into the center hall. He opened his gun cabinet and took out three rifles: one for me, one for him, one for Jonah.

L.J. moved quietly along the walls of the front rooms, reaching up to cut off the gaslights so that we could see out and the people outside couldn't see in.

I saw at least fifty men milling about out there. They looked like the mob from the previous night, only larger. And they were chanting:

Free the Raiders!
Let 'em go!
Free the Raiders!
Let 'em go!

They carried rifles, pistols, and pitchforks, and torches to light their way. I saw some of them holding big branches they must have pulled down from trees along the way. One man had a bullwhip he kept cracking with a pop like a pistol shot.

Free the Raiders!
Let 'em go!

L.J. stuck his head around the window frame. "Let the jury decide who goes free," he shouted.

A rock came hurtling across the veranda to

shatter the porcelain urn on a pedestal behind me. Another rock crashed through a stained-glass panel beside the front door.

"L.J., get your head in!" Jonah cried. "Don't be a fool. Or a martyr."

L.J. stood in full view of the mob, waving his arms, trying to quiet them down, but soon realized that Jonah was right. He stepped back from the window.

"You've got to get Allegra and the girls out of here," I said.

He nodded. "I'll have Conrad hitch up the carriage. Allegra's got a sister up in Pricedale. This whole town has gone crazy."

As L.J. ran from the room, Jonah turned to me. "This town was crazy long before tonight," he said.

I was sorry to say that I had to agree.

Chapter 111

JONAH AND I watched from the rear balcony as L.J.'s carriage clattered down the back drive and onto the Old Laurel Road. The crowd in front continued chanting for another half hour or so, but then the rain picked up and extinguished their torches, and their anger, at least for tonight.

Before long I was seated in the ground-floor parlor with a snifter of brandy and a pot of coffee. Two of L.J.'s housemen were sweeping up the broken glass and bringing in planks to nail over the windows. Quite the sight. And quite the night.

A knock came at the door. I looked up to see Nelson, one of the houseboys.

"There's a Miz Begley here to see you, sir," he said.

I went and met Elizabeth in the front alcove.

Her bonnet was glistening from the rain, and she looked uncharacteristically disheveled.

She reached out and took my hand. "Oh, Ben, I was in the courtroom today," she said. "It's awful, just awful. We all see what's happening. How can I help?"

I led her to L.J.'s study, toward a green damask sofa, where we sat. Elizabeth untied the bow of her bonnet and shucked it off. Her hair went flowing onto her shoulders.

"I want to help you Ben. Please let me in. These hangings, all of it, has got to stop. Most of us in town want it to stop."

"I don't know what to say, Elizabeth. L.J. just took Allegra and their kids out of town."

"Don't push me away again. Please. I live here. I have more to gain, and to lose, than you do. *Ben?*"

After a brief silence, I told her about a plan that had been forming in my head. It was quite a daring one, and I wasn't sure if I could pull it off.

"Elizabeth," I said. "You already *are* a help to me. Just knowing that I have your support and trust means everything to me."

Chapter 112

SINCE THE NIGHT we had convinced Phineas to arrest the White Raiders, I'd known that if this trial ever came about, winning three guilty verdicts would be close to impossible. But this was the first time I had ever considered that it might be *completely* impossible.

I couldn't think of a way to combat all the lies, the false testimony, the faked documents, the bigoted jurors—and, of course, the overwhelming and nearly laughable prejudice of the presiding judge.

Jonah Curtis, on the other hand, seemed to be clinging to his little tiny ray of hope. He kept urging me to have the courage to stand by him; he intended to fight Loophole Lewis to the bitter end.

So it was that Jonah went after every scrap of

evidence with passion, intelligence, and no little amount of cunning. He did constant battle with my increasingly impatient father. On the third day of the trial, everyone was astonished when Judge Corbett actually upheld one of Jonah's objections. "Don't let that give you any ideas," my father growled.

The next day Jonah put an emotional Conrad Cosgrove on the stand.

"That's right, Mr. Curtis," Conrad said, "they was at least eight of 'em coming from all directions. They never said a word, they just started shootin' everything and everybody in sight."

And later: "Yes, sir, Mr. Curtis, I seen my brother Luther take that man's boot to his head at least six, seven times. Hard enough and long enough to kill him. I was standing closer to him than I am right now to you."

But then Maxwell Hayes Lewis always got his chance at rebuttal.

"Now, Mr. Cosgrove, my dear Mr. Cosgrove, would you say that your opinion of what happened that night is influenced at all by your sorrow at the death of your brother?"

Conrad pondered the question, then shook his head. "No, sir. I do feel sad that Luther is dead, but that doesn't have a thing to do with my opinion about what happened that night."

It was a small trap, but Conrad had walked right into it.

Loophole Lewis pounced. "So the testimony you gave to Mr. Curtis just now was your *opinion*, not fact?"

"Well, sir," Conrad said slowly, "it is my opinion, like you said, but it's based on what I saw. And that's just a fact."

"But you're not absolutely certain of those facts, are you? How could you be?"

Jonah climbed to his feet again. "Your Honor, Mr. Lewis is purposely trying to confuse this witness."

Judge Corbett looked over his spectacles. "If the witness is so easily confused," he said, "then perhaps you made a mistake *calling* Mr. Cosgrove to testify in the first place."

And so it went. In that steamy courtroom, ripe with the smell of sweat and Rose of Sharon eau de toilette, the good people of the Eudora Quarters took the stand and swore to tell the truth and nothing but the truth. And they did. And then Maxwell Lewis ripped them apart.

One by one, Loophole Lewis plowed his way through our witness list. Whether defiant or docile when they took the stand, every one of those witnesses eventually stepped down looking foolish, stupid, or wrong.

It happened every single time.

At last Jonah stood up.

"If it please the court, the people call Miss Moody Cross to the stand."

Chapter 113

MY GOD. She was dressed like a grown-up.

I had never seen her wearing anything but one of the three identical white jumpers she rotated through the laundry basket so that she always appeared to be wearing the same spotlessly clean dress. Today she looked like a grown woman: a formal blue skirt, a neat white blouse. On her feet were lace-up boots polished to a high shine. She wore white gloves and a straw hat.

Last night we had gone over and over the questions we would ask. "Just tell the truth," Jonah kept saying, "and everything will be fine."

"What are you talking about?" she scoffed. "In that courtroom the truth ain't worth a bucket of piss."

"Charming," I said. "Try not to say that."

Jonah said, "The truth is the only weapon we have, Moody. So we have to use it."

"Maybe so," she said.

I should have listened more carefully to that phrase of hers.

Under Jonah's patient questioning, Moody told the same story her grandfather had told. The same story Cosgrove told. The same story every one of the witnesses from the Quarters had told.

By the time Jonah turned to Maxwell Lewis and said, "Your witness," the gentlemen of the jury looked about ready for some dinner and a nice nap.

Lewis said, "Miss Cross, are you a permanent resident of the house where your grandfather lives, over there in the Quarters?"

"Yes, sir, that's right. I live with him and take care of him."

All morning I had been noticing that Moody sounded more mature. She had managed to hide the edge of anger that so often came into her voice. She was speaking carefully, politely.

"I wouldn't really call it a house, though," she added. "It's more like a shack. But we do all right."

"Now, would you say your first notice of the alleged intruders on that night was when they rode up, supposedly shooting their weapons and yelling?"

"Oh, no, sir," she said in a very clear voice. "I would say my first notice was when Mr. North there, and Mr. Stephens, knocked on the door and showed me their search warrant."

Chapter 114

SWEET JESUS IN heaven! Jonah and I had never discussed this with her. We had certainly never planned for her to say such a thing. But say it she had:

"...and showed me their search warrant."

With those words Moody changed the whole atmosphere of the courtroom and the direction of this entire murder trial.

Jonah looked at me wide-eyed. Together we stared at Moody on the witness stand.

I thought I detected a hint of amusement behind her serious expression. She watched Loophole Lewis swivel all the way around to shoot a goggle-eyed look at my father. She heard the defendants whispering frantically among themselves. She was aware that her words had set off a buzz of confusion in the gallery. Even the jurors had snapped to wakefulness.

And Moody was enjoying every minute of it. Maybe she knew our cause was lost, and she was out to confound everybody. To confuse us. To throw the whole trial up in the air and see where the pieces came down.

This was every lawyer's nightmare: the rogue witness, off on her own.

My father banged his gavel several times. "Order!" The buzz subsided. "Mr. Lewis?"

Lewis turned back to the witness stand. "Now, Miss Cross," he said, "every previous witness, including your grandfather, claimed that they never were presented with a search warrant that night."

"I know that, sir," she said. "Papaw's getting pretty old now; he doesn't always notice everything. And when those men came with the warrant, there wasn't anybody out in front of the house except me. I was the only one."

I'm sure that almost everyone else thought Maxwell Lewis looked as confident as ever, but I saw signs that he was flustered. He was forgetting to slouch casually against the railing of the jury box. He was standing at attention and speaking a little too quickly. His countrified Clarence Darrow lilt had all but vanished. Moody had rattled him.

"This is, to say the least, a most unusual bit of testimony, Miss Cross."

"Why is that, sir? You-all said they came there with a search warrant. You said they showed it to us. All I'm saying is...well, that's exactly what happened."

She was lying. I knew it for sure. I was with Abraham in the parlor that night, and I knew nobody came to the door with any warrant. All had been quiet, there was a clatter of horses, then the Raiders started shooting at anything that moved.

Maxwell Lewis put on an uncomfortable smile. "All right, they showed you the warrant," he said. "And then what happened next?"

Suddenly I knew where Moody was going with this, why she was lying. What she was hoping to demonstrate with her lie.

Damn! It was brilliant! Why hadn't I thought of it?

But of course, if I *had* thought of it—if I'd even asked her to do such a thing—I could have been disbarred.

As it was, she was on her own.

"Well, sir," she said to Lewis, "I was looking over the warrant, you know, and I said, 'I still don't think y'all have the right to do this. But if that's what the paper says, I reckon we've got no choice but to let you come on in.' "

"You said that?" Lewis turned to the jury, hoping they would share his skepticism.

None of them even noticed. Their eyes were on Moody. She had them under her spell, and they were finally listening.

"Yes, sir, I did, and I no sooner got the words out of my mouth than a bunch of 'em rode up on their horses and started shootin' and yellin' and everything. Just like Papaw said."

"If we can," Lewis said, "let's return to the issue of the search warrant."

"Yes, sir," said Moody, as proper and polite as I had ever heard her.

"Now, who showed it to you?"

"Mr. North was the one holding the paper," she said. "And Mr. Stephens was with him."

"You are absolutely certain they presented that warrant to you?"

"Well, yes, sir, I mean — that's what happened. Just like y'all said. Don't you believe me?"

She looked the very picture of confounded innocence.

Maxwell Lewis turned to my father and shrugged.

My father spoke from the bench in a dangerous growl: "Moody Cross. You have sworn to tell the truth in this court. Do you understand that?"

"Oh, I certainly do, Your Honor, that's just what I'm doing," she said. "For the life of me, I can't figure out why me telling the truth has got y'all so confused. It's almost like you're *angry* at me."

She even had the nerve to smile. I thought, *Don't get carried away now, don't go too far. You've got them right where you want them.*

Before she took the stand, Moody and her grandfather had been uncooperative liars, uppity Negroes, troublemakers. Agitators defying a legal search warrant. Now they were innocent citizens who had agreed to a search of their premises and then, without warning, were unfairly and savagely attacked. For no reason at all.

Chapter 115

THE MOMENT MOODY stepped off the witness stand, my father declared a recess until Monday.

I followed Moody, L.J., and Jonah down the steps of the courthouse into a barrage of questions accompanied by that acrid gunpowdery smell of flash powder exploding. Moody moved through that crowd of newsmen like a ship slicing through a wave, holding her head up, walking straight ahead.

We brushed off the last pesky reporters and walked three blocks to the Stringer house. We waited until we had Moody in the War Room before anyone spoke.

"What did you think you were doing?" I asked. "You got up under oath and told the biggest, fattest lie in the history of Mississippi. And all the time grinning like a fool!"

She was grinning like that now. "I tried to keep the smile off my face," she said.

"Why didn't you tell us you were going to do that?"

"'Cause if I had, you'd have told me not to do it. This way I could scare the devil out of that Loophole Lewis, *and* your daddy the judge, *and* Phineas Eversman, *and* everybody else who was in on the lie."

"But *you* lied in order to counter *their* lie," I shouted. "That's perjury!"

"So what?" she said. "You fight fire with fire. Lewis can't contradict me. If he does, he'll have to admit they made up that warrant out of thin air, a long time after the raid."

"Oh, I understand what you were doing, all right," I said. "I just want to know what gives you the right to—"

"Ben," said L.J. "I don't see how this hurts us. I think it can only help."

I sank onto a chair. "I think so too, as bad as that is. What do you think, Jonah?"

Jonah was looking out the narrow second-floor window.

"It must be six-thirty. The usual mob is beginning to form," he said.

Then he turned from the window and faced the three of us.

"So, what do you think?" I repeated.

"I think what Moody did was...interesting. I must say, I did enjoy watching Loophole Lewis and Judge Corbett squirming like worms on a hook..."

I smiled. We had all enjoyed that sight.

"...but it won't make any difference," Jonah finished. "I'm afraid it won't."

"Yes, it will," Moody protested. "It'll cast doubt in their minds. It'll make it seem like we tried to cooperate, and they attacked us anyway."

Jonah shook his head. "Oh, Moody. Those jurors have lived here their whole lives. They don't *care* who's telling the truth and who's lying! The phony warrant? Some of the jurors were probably down at the town hall when Eversman was writing it up."

There was silence then. A long minute of it.

The chanting outside began again.

Free the Raiders!
Let 'em go!

Moody stood and smoothed her blue skirt. She adjusted her straw hat and slipped on her white gloves.

"I got to go. Papaw is in bad shape. Coming to the court, he didn't hardly know who he was," she said.

Without thinking about it I leaned over and kissed her on the cheek. "Tell Abraham I'm coming out tomorrow to see about him."

Jonah said, "Thank you for trying to help, Moody. From the bottom of my heart."

Chapter 116

IT WAS TIME TO TRY OUT the plan I had concocted. Maybe it was even past time, too late. Moody and L.J. had come with me. Jonah wanted to but knew he couldn't. After all, he was representing the great state of Mississippi, and we were about to break the law in too many ways to count.

"Stinks bad in here," Moody said.

The awful smell was everywhere, a sharp, nauseating odor, like a cross between bad patent medicine and rancid moonshine. It was the foul scent of the chemicals Scooter Willems used to develop his photographs.

I had just climbed through an unlocked window, with Moody and L.J. behind me, into Scooter's old cabin off the East Point Road. Now we were in his studio, one large room with black curtains dividing it into three. The front part was a portrait studio, with a backdrop and a stool for the subject to pose on. In the middle section two large wooden tables held trays of foul-smelling chemicals. But it was in the last section that we found what we'd come for: boxes and boxes of Willems's photographs, with dozens more pinned to the walls.

There was one box full of nothing but photographs of lynchings. Scooter Willems had been busy these past months. Beside that box sat a stack of postcards manufactured from the photos, souvenir pictures of hanged corpses, burned bodies, twisted victims, like the one I'd received in the mail.

"God Almighty," Moody said. "The man has taken pictures of everybody who ever got hanged."

"Look here," said L.J., working his way along the wall. "These are all from the Bobby Burnett lynching."

I held up the lantern to see.

"First, take a look at poor old Bobby hanging there," L.J. said. "Now look who's standing next to him. *There*. By his feet."

There they were, plain as day in the flickering lamplight: Chester Madden and Lincoln Alexander Stephens, two of the three White Raiders on trial.

They grinned up at the bloated, bloody, bursting head of Bobby Burnett.

One by one I pulled the photographs down from the wall, gathering them in a manila folder I found on Scooter's desk.

"Look at this!" Moody exclaimed, holding a photo up to the light.

I came up beside her. There was her brother Hiram, dead on the ground, with a rope around his neck. His grinning killers each had a foot on his body, as if he were a prize lion they'd slain on safari.

L.J. pointed to the man on the end. "I'll be damned if that ain't Lester Johnson."

I almost stopped breathing. "And now he sits on our jury."

Then I recognized the man beside him. It was Jacob, Jacob Gill, with his foot resting on Moody's dead brother. I felt my eyes filling.

Scooter Willems was nothing if not thorough. Everyone who'd ever had a hand in a lynching in this part of Mississippi had been assiduously recorded, their faces plainly recognizable. Some of the lynchings were of victims I'd heard about, others were news to us.

The horror increased with just about every

picture. Before we were through, we'd seen the faces of many prominent Eudora citizens enjoying a night out, a night of murder and mayhem.

What a record of guilt! What amazing evidence! I couldn't take the pictures down fast enough.

"Just put 'em all in the box," I said. "We need to get out of here."

"No, y'all can stay," I heard.

Chapter 117

THE BLACK CURTAIN was yanked aside, and the studio flooded with light. At first I couldn't make out who they were, but there were five of them. Their torches were much brighter than our lantern, and they dazzled us.

"I don't recall inviting any of you folks here," a voice said. That high nasal whine had to be Scooter Willems's.

As he moved his torch I saw them all.

Two men with guns whom I didn't recognize.

Phineas Eversman, chief of police.

And Senator Richard Nottingham, Elizabeth's husband.

"Go ahead and finish packing up," said Nottingham, waving his pistol. "Saves us having to do it."

Another man stepped into the cabin. "Yeah, y'all get to work, would you?" I knew that voice. And that face. It was Jacob Gill.

"'Preciate you gathering 'em up for us, Ben," he said. "We were just gonna have ourselves a little evidence-burnin' party."

"We knew we'd find you here," Phineas said with a smirk on his face.

L.J. growled, "How did you know? Who the hell told you we were comin' here?"

There was a silence, then the others looked at Richard Nottingham. Finally he said, "My wife."

The words stabbed me in the heart. I felt my throat closing and thought I might be sick.

"Elizabeth was spying for me. She told us every word you ever said, Corbett. She's a good girl. Thanks for keeping us up to date. It was damn useful to Maxwell Lewis."

Phineas took the box of photographs from Moody. One of the pictures caught his eye. "We don't need this one," he said.

He handed it over to me. "In case you want a souvenir."

It was a picture of me—half naked, hanging from a lynching tree.

Scooter did a fine job with the picture. The detail

409

was crisp; you could see every leaf on the tree. The dog licking my bloody foot, the flies swarming over my face.

"You always took a nice picture, Ben," said Jacob Gill.

Chapter 118

"ALL RIGHT NOW, Ben, we tried your plan, and you might say it didn't work out so well. So now we're going to try my plan."

Jonah was not in the mood to butter me up.

"You know those photographs would have worked," I said bitterly. "All right, all right, tell me *your* plan."

"Well, it's not quite as audacious as yours. Matter of fact, it's very logical, very well thought out."

"Damn it, just tell us," L.J. said.

"Tomorrow," Jonah said, "I want Ben to give the summation to the jury."

L.J. didn't hesitate a beat before answering, "That is a fine idea."

"No, it isn't," I said. "I was there on the night of the murders. I'm a witness but you've chosen not to put me on the stand. You're the one who's been telling them the story of these crimes all along. Why change now?"

"You know why," said L.J.

"Because I'm white?" I said. "That's no reason!"

"It never hurts," Jonah said with a faint smile. "Look, you come from here," he explained. "You know these people. The judge is your father. These jurors will trust you more than they will me. And not because you're white—because you were there. You can give a summation that comes from your heart. For God's sake, you've been lynched yourself. You have to tell them a story, Ben. They need to hear it from you."

I dreaded the truth in what he was saying. The next thing he said cinched it for me:

"I tried the case. I fought the case. I pled the case. But all along, even before I got here, it was always your case, Ben."

Chapter 119

IT LOOKED AS IF half of America had come to tiny Eudora for the conclusion of the White Raiders Trial.

Outside the courthouse that morning, hundreds and hundreds of spectators jammed the town square. Little boys had climbed trees for a better view of the action. Photographers muscled their tripods through the crowds, jostling for the best angles. A few of the more enterprising had bought out Russell Hardware's entire stock of ladders to get an over-the-heads-of-the-crowd view.

Judge Everett Corbett had petitioned Governor Vardaman for state militiamen from Jackson to keep order. The soldiers had set up temporary wooden fences along the sidewalk in front of the courthouse to control the spectators who'd been

413

flooding into Eudora by train, carriage, horseback, and on foot.

Inside the courtroom there was no question who was in control: Judge Everett Corbett.

During the course of the trial, he had expelled four colored women from the gallery for reacting too loudly. He had found three reporters in contempt of court for referring in unflattering terms to his dictatorial ways. And he had sent an old colored man to jail for shouting, "The Lord hates a liar!" during one defendant's testimony.

The first thing my father did on the trial's last morning reaffirmed his imperial status.

"Now we are ready to deliver this case to the jury," he said. "The testimony has been passionate on both sides. Tempers have run high. Outside interest has been remarkable by any standard. And thus, gentlemen of the jury, we have come to the crux of the matter. You have to let the facts speak for themselves. You will now hear from the prosecutor, Mr. Curtis, his last and best argument about how you'll decide. Then you'll hear the same from Mr. Lewis. And finally, it will be entirely up to you, the jury, to make your decision, as the framers of the Constitution intended. Mr. Curtis?"

Jonah rose with an impassive face. "Your Honor,

the jury has heard quite a lot from me in this trial. More than enough, I think. So I'm going to let my colleague Mr. Benjamin Corbett deliver the summation for the state."

Chapter 120

I GOT TO MY FEET, a little wobbly in the legs. The dumbfounded faces of my father, Loophole Lewis, and his three murdering clients gave me at least some pleasure.

It took my father only a moment to make the calculation: I had the right to speak, and there was nothing he could do about it. He smiled, crossed his arms, and sat back in his chair.

"I wondered if we were ever going to hear from Counselor Corbett," he said. "Of course, as his father, I have heard a great deal from him over the years, and I look forward to sharing that pleasure with the rest of you."

Appreciative laughter rolled through the room. I had no choice but to smile and try for a little joke of my own. "And, of course, as the proud son of my father, I can only say I have done at least as much *listening* over the years as *talking*," I said. "I have learned a great deal that way."

"Please proceed, Mr. Corbett," my father said, "and let us decide for ourselves if that is true."

The audience laughed again. My old dad had definitely won the first round.

I wondered what he saw, peering down at me from his bench. Did he see a Harvard Law graduate, a well-known Washington defense lawyer? Did he see a man of passion, righteousness, ambition?

No. He saw a boy crying when he fell off his rocking horse, a child furiously resisting a spoonful of the hated mashed carrots. He didn't see me. He saw a powerless boy.

So I was determined that when I finished speaking, he would see a man; he might even see the real Ben Corbett.

"Thank you, Your Honor," I said. "I will try not to disappoint you."

Chapter 121

BENJAMIN E. CORBETT'S SUMMATION to the jury:

"Judge Corbett just told you that you have to let the facts speak for themselves. The only problem with that is, facts do not have voices of their own; they can't actually speak. So I'm the one who is standing here to give voice to the facts. That is my job today, and I appreciate your willingness to give me an ear.

"It's the middle of the night in the Eudora Quarters. Three men ride up to execute a search warrant. It's two o'clock in the morning—hardly the most traditional time to conduct a search of private premises—but that is what these men have decided to do.

"Ah, but wait. There's a girl in the house, granddaughter of the old dying man. She reads the warrant and accepts it. She doesn't like it, she says, but it's the word of the law, so she will not resist. Come on in, she says. Search our house. Torment us. Question us. Rifle through our belongings. We have committed no crime, there is no actual legal reason for you to want to search here. But she allows it. She opens the door. She lets them in.

"And yet even her total submission, her complete and immediate cooperation, are not enough for these men. The search warrant was simply a ruse to get in the door. They have not come here to do anything legal.

"They are here to torture and torment, and to kill, because they think it's their right to kill anyone who gets in their way. To skirt around the law and execute anyone they decide is guilty. To evade juries like the one you gentlemen are sitting on today. They are there to kill the idea of fair trial, a jury of a man's peers. They have come to get their way by using the gun, the knife, the rope. And the terrible rule of the mob."

Calmly, meticulously, I began to lead them through the events of that night—the shooting and wounding of the guards at Abraham's house, the death by kicking of Luther Cosgrove, the fatal shooting of Jimmie Cooper up on the roof, the spectacle of poor Abraham with a gun to his head.

And finally, I told them about my part in the whole thing: why I'd gone to Abraham's house that night, how I knew the Raiders were coming, what I did and thought and felt at every moment. I explained how lucky Abraham and I had been to avoid being killed and to manage to bring these three Raiders to Phineas Eversman so the law could work as it is supposed to work.

"Now, Chief Eversman did his duty that night as an officer of the law. Not only that, he stuck his neck out, gentlemen. He did the honest, moral, upright thing—and that's not always easy to do. He arrested these men and charged them, and he saw that they were brought to trial. He may have changed his mind since then about some things, but the fact remains that Chief Eversman knew instinctively that these men had to be stopped.

"He had no choice. He saw the blood. He smelled it—that's how fresh it was. The blood of their victims was on the defendants' hands when we brought them to him. It was on the toes of their boots.

"Now you gentlemen are in the same position the chief of police was in that night. You have heard the truth from the people of the Quarters who witnessed these brutal attacks, these murders. You have seen the blood.

"Let me put it to you frankly: the evidence has not been refuted, *because it cannot be refuted.*

"Gentlemen, outside this courthouse, there is a whole nation watching us. Reporters from all over the country have come to Eudora to see if our little town can rise above itself, rise above the customs and prejudices that have held sway down here.

"But that's not why I want you to deliver the verdict you know to be right: a verdict of guilty on all counts. I don't want you to do it because I think you should rise above your prejudices, whatever they may be. Or because I want you to show the world that Mississippi is not a place where murderers get away with their awful crimes.

"I don't want you to consider what the outside world thinks. Who cares about them? I want you to think about your own soul, your own self, *inside,* where you live, when there is no one else around.

"I hope that you will find these men guilty, because it has been proven beyond any reasonable doubt that they are. The only thing that might prevent your rendering such a verdict is fear—fear that some of your neighbors will think less of you if you send these guilty men, these murderers, to prison. You must conquer that fear. The people of this country are depending on you to prove yourselves worthy of the grave responsibility they have invested in you. Show them that here in Mississippi, the light of justice is still shining."

I saw Jonah and L.J. smiling at me. I glanced up to my father. For a moment I thought I saw the ghost of a smile on his face too. Or maybe I just wanted to see it.

I turned back to the jury.

"There's someone who said it better than I ever could. And he said it in the first book of Samuel."

I recited from memory. "For the Lord seeth not as man seeth; for man looketh on the outward appearance, but the Lord looketh on the heart."

Now it was Maxwell Lewis's turn.

Chapter 122

MAXWELL LEWIS'S SUMMATION to the jury:

"Eloquence like young Mr. Corbett's has rarely been heard in any courthouse in our nation," he said.

Then he turned to face the judge. "Wouldn't you say that's right, Your Honor?"

This time my father withheld his smile. "Let's just get on with it, Counselor."

I was anxious to see what tone Lewis would take now. Would he appear as the mighty Darrow? Would he try to play humble country lawyer? Would he be a preacher hurling fire and brimstone, or a kindly old grandpa proffering wise advice?

Of course he would be all those things.

"Gentlemen, I begin with a simple question... *Where is the evidence?* What the prosecution calls evidence is not what *I* would call evidence. If it seems to you that Mr. Curtis and Mr. Corbett have paraded the entire population of the Eudora Quarters in front of you, one after the other accusing these citizens of Eudora of murder, rioting in the streets, and general mayhem—well, sir, that's because that is exactly what they've done.

"But now, when you consider charges of this magnitude and gravity, you must, as Mr. Corbett told you, consider the evidence. The prosecution's evidence, mainly the statements of various witnesses, is like any kind of evidence: it's only as good as the people who give it.

"And where does this so-called evidence come from? Who are the people giving this testimony? What is the quality of these people that would lead us to believe their testimony? Well, I'll tell you.

"These allegations come from people who wash your clothes, and chop your weeds, and clean out your barns. They come from the old uncle who sits in front of the store all day, shooting the breeze. From the people who pick cotton all day. This is testimony from people who resent you because you happen to have the blessing and good fortune to be white, and therefore you have more privileges than they have."

A dramatic pause. Then he whipped around.

"And you are being asked to take their word as truth.

"Why on God's green earth would anyone suppose that you would take the word of this bunch of worthless rabble-rousers over the word of three gentlemen from Eudora?"

I shot a glance at my father, who was watching Lewis with the same contemptuous expression he'd been aiming at me since the trial began.

I wanted to shout, "The people who wash your clothes and pick your crops can tell the truth. The truth is not based on how much money you have. It's based on . . . the truth."

Of course, I did not interrupt the summation.

"Gentlemen," Maxwell Lewis continued. "Be aware. There are forces at work here that would like nothing better than to take away your freedoms, your right to live life the way you have always lived it here. I warn you to do what you must to make sure that does not happen. Gentlemen, be alert. *And acquit these three innocent men.*"

I turned to Jonah. He shrugged.

Lewis went on in a quiet, humble voice.

"Gentlemen, I am sorry for the rough times the people in the Quarters have had. But that gives them no license to come here and lie to you. And it gives you no license to ignore the plain facts in front of you."

What facts? I thought. Moody's dramatic lie had undercut the entire thrust of the Raiders' argument. They had no facts on their side. Lewis wasn't anything like a great lawyer; he hadn't even bothered to counter that revelation. He was counting on the famous prejudices of white juries to carry the day for him.

"Mr. Corbett quoted the Good Book to you. He quoted a verse from First Samuel. Well, I too would like to leave you with a phrase from God's holy word. The book of Exodus."

He paused, and then spoke in a clear, loud voice: "Thou...shalt...not...*lie!*"

That was it? That was Lewis's big dramatic finish?

I wanted to laugh, and I could swear I saw my father roll his eyes.

Chapter 123

JUDGE CORBETT'S INSTRUCTIONS to the jury:

"All right, that brings the evidentiary phase of this proceeding to a close," said the judge.

He rubbed his chin, then adjusted his spectacles. He took a sheet of paper from a folder and placed it in front of him.

"Gentlemen of the jury, I need not remind you that many people outside Eudora are watching our little town now, because of this case. You have seen the signs of it—the streets of our town are filled with strangers, including, but not limited to, the so-called gentlemen of the press. And I understand that over at the Slide Inn Café they keep running out of chocolate pie as fast as they can make it."

He paused, waiting for a laugh.

It didn't come.

The courtroom was too tense for frivolities now.

The sight of all those soldiers outside had made everyone nervous.

"You heard the testimony as it was presented," he said. "And now it is up to you to decide the truth as you see it, using the laws of our great state of Mississippi as your guide.

"Once you decide this case," he went on, "those reporters will write their stories, and then they'll leave. Once the circus is gone and the streets are quiet again, we folks in Eudora will be left with...each other."

I had heard my father give his charge to a jury many times. Usually his words were dry, precise, legalistic. Today, for some reason, he was being unusually lyrical.

"And what you decide in that jury room will influence...for a very long time...the way we live our lives in this town."

Suddenly he seemed to snap out of it. When he spoke again, he was all business.

"You will adjourn to the jury room now. I'll have the bailiff standing right outside your door, if there's anything you need."

The jury members looked at one another,

waiting for a signal that Judge Corbett had finished his instructions.

But he was not quite done.

"One other thing, gentlemen.... I know you enjoyed hearing the defense counsel just as much as I did, but I do want to give you my point of view on a matter he chose to address."

He claimed to be speaking to the jurors, but his eyes stayed on Maxwell Lewis the whole time.

"The people who wash your clothes and pick your cotton are every bit as capable of telling the truth as any other kind of people."

Lewis's face flushed so red I thought he might explode.

But I knew exactly what my father was up to. For the spectators and journalists, some of whom he had allowed into the courtroom to hear the closing arguments, Judge Corbett was showing himself to be a courageous man, boldly making a statement of racial tolerance.

I was neither a spectator nor a journalist, however. I wasn't buying his act for a minute. I had sat through fifty-four objections that were overruled fifty-three times. My father had systematically sabotaged the prosecution's chances of getting a fair trial in his court.

The judge banged the gavel I had given him. "Gentlemen, kindly repair to the jury room and do your job."

Chapter 124

I TRIED TO HURRY past the mob of reporters. I was becoming quite adept at avoiding them, but the more skilled ones—the fellows from New York and Washington—were relentless. They pulled at the sleeve of my jacket. Some actually planted themselves in the middle of my path.

Finally, I had to push them out of my way. It was the only way to get past these rude and opportunistic fellows.

"Mr. Corbett, do you think you have a chance?"

"Jonah, why'd you let a white man give your summation for you?"

"Mr. Stringer, what's your angle? What's in it for you?"

I felt someone push something into my hand and looked down to find a twenty-dollar bill.

A reporter I recognized from Washington was grinning at me. "That's for a private interview, and there's more if it's really good!" I wadded the bill and tossed it back at him.

I heard Jonah calling to me across the throng: "See you at the War Room, half an hour."

The reporters lost interest in me and turned on Jonah. *The War Room? What War Room? What war? Do you think of this trial as a war? Do you think you will lose?*

I used this opportunity to escape. I crossed Commerce Street and hurried downtown, to the platform by the nearly deserted depot. One old colored man was attaching a feedbag to a fine brown horse hitched to a flat truck.

I found a bench in the shade near the stationmaster's house from which I could survey most of Eudora.

The mob was still swirling around the courthouse, a jam of horses and wagons and honking automobiles.

Out on the edge of town, on the dirt road leading out to the Quarters, I saw columns of smoke rising into the sky, the campfires of Negroes who'd come from all over southern Mississippi to await the verdict. I had ridden through their camp yesterday, smelling the smoke of fatback, hearing the hymns they sang.

"Sing loud so He can hear you," I said to the distant columns of smoke.

This was the first time in weeks I'd been alone, without the trial looming in front of me. It was time I did something I had put off for too long.

I took out a sheet of paper, turned the satchel over my lap, and started to write.

Dear Meg,
I have waited weeks to write this letter.

I have waited because I kept hoping that you would reply to my last. I envisioned an envelope with your return address on it. I imagined myself tearing it open to discover that you had changed your mind, that the thought of us living apart was something you had come to believe was a mistake. That you once again believed in the two of us. But that letter never arrived. I am alone, as separated from you and Amelia and Alice as if I were dead—or, perhaps, as if I'd never existed.

Meg, much has happened in the time we have spent apart. I have been involved in a highly provocative trial here in Eudora. I'm sure you've read about it in the newspapers. I will not waste time in this letter describing the trial, except to say that as I write to you now, the jury is deliberating the outcome.

I know that this might anger you, but I must tell the truth. I am convinced beyond any doubt that I am doing the right thing when I try to use my skills as a lawyer to help those who can't find justice anywhere else.

Meg, I know that I alone cannot right the wrongs of this society. But I cannot and will not stop trying. I know you feel that effort takes too much energy and time away from you, our girls, and my love for the three of you.

Should you decide to continue our marriage, I promise I shall try to be a better husband and father.

But I must also warn you that I will not (and cannot) abandon my ideals. As much as you may long for it, I cannot become just another government lawyer.

Please, Meg, give it another chance. We have so much to lose if we abandon each other. We have so much to gain if we try to move forward together.

My time here in Eudora is drawing to an end. Soon I will be coming back to Washington, and to you. I know now—I have learned—that Washington is my home. You are my home, Meg. The girls are my home.

I pray that when I open that front door, I will hear your sweet voice again, and you will speak to me with love.

Till I see you again, I remain

Your loving husband,
Ben

Chapter 125

THE JURY HAD A VERDICT.

My father banged his gavel furiously, but it did no good. "Quiet!" he bellowed. "I will clear this courtroom!"

Spectators pushed this way and that, tripped over one another, stumbling to find seats. My father continued hammering away at his bench. The jurors began to make their way to the jury box, blinking nervously at the uproar their appearance had provoked.

"I will clear this courtroom!" my father shouted again, but this had no effect at all on the level of noise and excitement in the room.

"Very well," he said. "Bailiff, get 'em all out of here. *Get 'em all out!*"

Those were the magic words. Instantly the

courtroom came to perfect attention. The crowd fell silent, and everyone sank into the nearest available seat.

"Very well. That's much better," said Judge Corbett. "Mr. Foreman, has the jury reached a verdict?"

"Yes, Your Honor, we have."

The foreman handed a white slip of paper to the bailiff, who handed it up to my father. Though this took only seconds, it seemed much longer than that. Time was slowing, and my senses were unbearably acute.

My father opened the paper and read it with no visible emotion. He raised his head and looked my way, still betraying nothing about the verdict.

Then he spoke. "Mr. Foreman, in the matter of the *State of Mississippi versus Madden, North, and Stephens*, how does the jury find?"

In that moment, it seemed to me, all life stopped on this earth. The birds quit chirping. The ceiling fans stopped spinning. The spectators froze in midbreath.

The foreman spoke in a surprisingly high-pitched whine.

"We find the defendants not guilty."

As he uttered those impossible words, I was

staring at the piggish face of Henry Wadsworth North. The hardest thing of all was seeing the joy that broke out all over his hateful visage.

A smattering of cheers went up from the white audience. Reporters rose and sprinted for the doors. A collective groan, and then sobs, arose from the Negroes in the gallery.

My father banged his gavel again and again, but no one seemed to care.

Chapter 126

AFTER THE COURTROOM HAD CLEARED, I sneaked out a side entrance to avoid the crowd of journalists out front, and did what I had done so many times lately. I got my bike and headed for the Eudora Quarters.

The first person I saw was the old man in the blue shack who had showed me the way to Abraham's house the first time I came out here.

"You done your best, Mist' Corbett," he called. "Nobody coulda done better."

"My best wasn't good enough," I called back. "But thank you."

He shook his head. I continued down the dirt road.

A large brown woman was coming the other way, balancing a wicker basket of damp clothes on her head and carrying another under her arm. She picked up the conversation in midstep: "Aw, now, Mistuh Corbett, that's just the way things goes," she said.

"But it's not fair," I said.

She laughed. "Welcome to my life."

There I was, trying to explain the concept of fairness to a woman carrying two huge baskets of other people's washing.

At the crossroads in front of Hemple's store, I saw the usual two old men playing checkers. I stopped in front of their cracker barrel. "I'm sorry, gentlemen," I said.

One man looked up at me sadly. The other one said, "Well, suh, ain't nobody strong enough to beat 'em. And so what they did was, they got off scot-free. Nothin' new 'bout that."

"Ben." A soft voice, a hand on my arm. I turned. It was Moody.

She was wearing her white jumper again. She even had a little smile on her face.

"You planning to go door-to-door, explain to everybody in the whole Quarters what happened in the white man's courtroom?" she asked.

"I would," I said.

"Don't you worry your purty head about it," she

said. "All the explaining in the world won't change a thing." She took me by the elbow, leading me away. The men watched us go.

"Papaw is worse sick," she said. "I think the excitement of the trial done it. You want to see him? He wants to see you."

Chapter 127

ABRAHAM LAY in the narrow iron bed in the front parlor, just the way he was lying there the night the White Raiders attacked. His voice was so faint I barely heard him. His lips were cracked and dry. "I imagine you been going around beating yourself up pretty good about this verdict, eh, Ben?" he asked.

"I thought I could accomplish something," I said. "The country was watching, from the president on down. I thought we could make a little bit of progress."

"Who's to say we didn't?" he asked.

Moody gently dabbed his forehead with rubbing alcohol, then blew lightly to cool his skin. Every time she touched his face, Abraham's eyes closed in gratitude. I thought he must be seeing clouds, getting ready to dance with the angels.

"When you get to be as old as me, Ben, you can't help but remember a lot of things. I was thinking about my mama...one time I stole a nickel from her purse. She knew it before she even looked in there, just by peering in my eyes. She said, 'Abraham, I don't know what you guilty of, but you sho' nuff guilty of *somethin'*, so you might as well go on and confess.' I cried for an hour, then I give back that nickel."

Moody kept rubbing his face, rhythmically massaging the skin with her fingers. His eyes closed, then opened. He went on.

"I was just a young man during the war," he said. "You ever heard that expression, how they say the ground ran red with blood?"

I said I had heard it.

"I saw it with my own eyes," he said. "I saw the ground run red. I was up at Vicksburg, just after the fight. I saw...oh, Lord. Hurts to remember. I saw legs, you know, and arms, and feet, big heaps of 'em outside the hospital tent. All rottin' in the sun."

I could see the horror of it all in my mind's eye.

"But bad as it was," Abraham went on, "that's when things begun to change. A big change at the first, then they took it back. But what happened in that courtroom...that'll change it. You just wait. You'll live to see it."

He fell into such a deep silence that I thought he might have fallen asleep. Maybe he was beginning his passage into the next world.

But he had a few more words to say.

"Moody said you told the jury a saying from the book of Samuel," he said.

I nodded.

"That's one of my favorite passages," he said. "I sure hated to miss you. Would you say it out to me now?"

"Of course, Abraham," I said.

I cleared my throat.

"For the Lord seeth not as man seeth; for man looketh on the outward appearance, but the Lord looketh on the heart."

Then Abraham spoke the last words he would ever say to me.

"You did fine, Ben. You did just fine."

Chapter 128

"HE'LL SLEEP NOW," Moody said. "Maybe he won't wake up this time."

I followed her out to the little front porch. We sat in the chairs where L.J. and I had spent a long hot night waiting for the Raiders to come.

The worst heat had finally broken. You couldn't call it a cool day, exactly, but the wet blanket of humidity had lifted.

"I'm glad I got to talk to him," I said. "His words mean a lot to me."

Moody said nothing.

"I feel terrible about the way the trial turned out," I said.

I was hoping, I suppose, that Moody would say something like Abraham had said: that I had done my best and it wasn't my fault.

She turned to face me. "I know you're going to think I'm nothin' but a cold, ungrateful girl. But I don't just feel bad—I'm angry. Damn angry. Oh yeah, you did your best. And Mr. Curtis did his best. And Mr. Stringer spent all that money...but those murderers walked away free."

"You're right, Moody," I said. "They did."

"Papaw keeps saying it takes a long time for things to change. Well, that's fine for him—he's almost run out of time. I don't want to be old and dying before anything ever starts to get better."

I nodded. Then I did something I didn't know I was going to do until I did it.

I reached over and took Moody's hand.

This time she did not pull away.

We said nothing, because finally there was nothing left to say. After a few minutes she leaned her head on my shoulder and began to weep softly.

Then she pulled away and sat up. "Listen, Ben, do me a favor. I'm afraid Papaw's going to get bedsores, and Hemple's is all out of wintergreen oil. You reckon you could go into town and bring some?"

"Gladly," I said. "But only if you go with me. You've been trapped in this house for days."

"You are plain crazy, Ben Corbett," she said.

"You think the people of this town want to see you and me parading together downtown? You want to get yourself lynched again?"

"I don't care," I said. "Do you care about what the people of Eudora think?"

She pondered that a moment. "No. I s'pose I don't."

She wiped her eyes with a corner of the dishtowel. "Oh, hell, Ben, what goes on in that crazy brain of yours?"

I was wondering the same thing.

"Will you go with me?" I said. "I need to do something in town."

Chapter 129

I HELPED MOODY DOWN from the handlebars of the bicycle. She had hollered most of the way into town, threatening bodily harm if I didn't let her down off that contraption this instant! The noise we made was enough to turn heads all the way up Maple Street, onto Commerce Street, and into the center of town.

Eudora had just begun to settle down again. The last of the photographers and reporters had gone away on the one o'clock train.

I heard the rhythmic clang of iron from the blacksmith shop, and the *pop-pop* report of a motorcar doing a circuit around the courthouse square.

A few hours ago the eyes of the nation were upon Eudora. Now it was just another sleepy little southern town, happy to go back to living in the past, looking toward the future with nothing but suspicion and fear.

"Shall we?" I asked Moody.

"You're gonna start a riot," she said. "You know that, don't you?"

I clasped her hand tightly in mine. Then we began to walk down the sidewalk of the busiest street in Eudora.

To anyone who didn't know us, we would seem like lovers out for a romantic stroll on a late-summer afternoon.

But of course there was a complication: I was white, Moody was black. My hair was blond and straight, hers was black and tightly curled.

The citizens of Eudora had never seen anything like the two of us.

They stopped in their tracks. Some got down off the sidewalk to put some distance between us. Others groaned or cried out, as if the sight of us caused them physical pain.

Corinna Cutler and Edwina Booth came out of Miss Ida's store, a couple of plump old hens cackling to each other—until they laid eyes on our joined hands.

Both their jaws dropped.

"Afternoon, Miz Cutler," I said. "Afternoon, Miz Booth."

Their faces darkened and they hurried away.

Ezra Newcomb saw us through the window of his barbershop. He abandoned his lathered-up customer in the chair and stalked to the door. "Ben Corbett," he shouted, "I oughta take this razor to your damn throat!"

I relinquished Moody's hand and wrapped a protective arm around her shoulder. "Nice to see you too, Ezra."

Word of our coming spread down the street before us. About half the town stepped out onto the sidewalk to see what was causing the commotion.

At the drugstore I held the door for Moody.

Doc Conover stared down at us from his pharmacist's bench at the rear. "What do you want, Corbett?"

"A bottle of wintergreen oil, please," I said.

"We're fresh out," he said.

"Aw now, come on, Doc," I said. "It's for Abraham Cross. He's dying, and it would bring him relief. You've known Abraham all your life."

"I told you we're out," he said. "Now clear out of here."

"There it is, up there next to the camphor." I

pointed to the row of bottles on the shelf above his head.

"You callin' me a liar?" said Conover. "Take off, or I'll have the police throw you out of here."

Moody pulled at my sleeve. "Let's go," she said.

I followed her toward the front door.

There was a crowd waiting outside to point and jeer at us. We turned left and headed down the block. "Let's go to the Slide Inn and have some iced tea," I said.

"I can't go in there," she said.

"Sure you can. Who's going to stop you?"

"Get out of here, nigger-lover!" called a man in the crowd.

We came to Jenkins' Mercantile, passing the bench where Henry North and Marcus had carried my mother after she had had her stroke.

We walked the rest of the way to the Slide Inn, trailing our little mob of catcalling spectators.

Lunch service was over. There were only three customers in the café—two young ladies sipping coffee and an old woman chewing on a cheese sandwich.

I'd hoped Miss Fanny was on duty today, but it was another waitress who approached us. "Can'tcha read?" she said, poking her thumb at a brand-new sign posted above the cash register:

WHITES ONLY

"I'm white," I said.

Without a pause the waitress said, "You got a nigger with you. Now go on, get outta here."

"Where's Miss Fanny?" I said.

"She don't work here no more," the woman said. "'Cause of you."

We turned to the door. I felt something hit my sleeve and I glanced down. It was a gob of spit, mixed with what looked like cheese. It could only have come from the little old lady.

When we stepped out the door our audience had swelled to a couple of dozen angry people.

They gawked at us. They yelled. They mocked.

"Kiss me," I whispered to Moody.

She looked up at me as if I were insane, but she didn't say no.

I leaned down and brought my lips to hers.

A cry of pain ran through the crowd.

A woman's voice: "Look, he got what he wanted—a nigger girl to take to his bed."

A man's voice from behind me shouted, "Y'all goin' to hell and burn for all time!"

"Niggers! You're *both* niggers!"

"You make me sick in my gut!"
"Get out of here! Just get out!"
I whispered, "You ready to run?"
Moody nodded.
And we ran, and ran, and ran.

Chapter 130

WE WERE HALFWAY to the Quarters before the most persistent of our pursuers gave up. We stopped to catch our breath, but I kept an eye out, in case anyone was still following.

As it dawned on me what we had done, I realized that I was—well, I was *delighted*. Who would have thought two people holding hands could make so many wrong-minded people so very unhappy? We had put the citizens of Eudora in an uproar, and that realization warmed my heart.

I had abandoned my bicycle downtown. Maybe the mob had strung it up in a noose by now.

As Moody and I walked the muddy boards that passed for a sidewalk, folks began coming out of their houses to have a look at us. As fast as we'd run, news of our public display seemed to have preceded us.

"Y'all damn crazy," said one old lady.

"Naw, they in love," said a young man beside her.

"Well, hell, if *that* ain't crazy, I don't know what is!"

"No, ma'am," I said. "We're not crazy and we're not in love, either."

"You just tryin' to cause trouble then, white boy?" she demanded.

"All I did was kiss her," I explained. "But we did cause some trouble."

The old lady thought about it a moment, then she cracked a smile.

It was like a photographic negative of our march through Eudora. By the time we got to the crossroads by Hemple's store, we had a crowd of spectators tagging along with us.

One of the old men looked up from his checkerboard, his face grim. "*Now* see what you done," he said to me. "You done kicked over the anthill for sure. They comin' down here tonight, and they gonna lynch you up somethin' fierce. And some of us, besides."

"Then we'd better get ready for them," Moody said.

"Ready?" said the other checkers player. "What you mean ready, girl? You mean we best say our prayers. Best go make the pine box ourselves."

"You got a gun for shootin' squirrel, don't you?" said Moody. "You got a knife to skin it with, don't you?"

The old man nodded. "Well, sho', but what does that—"

"They can't beat all of us," Moody said. "Not if we're ready for them."

The people around us were murmuring to one another. Moody's words had started a brushfire among them. "Let 'em come!" cried a young man. "Let 'em come on!"

Moody looked at me with soulful eyes. And then she did something I will never forget. I will carry it with me my whole life, the way I have carried Marcus's kindness to Mama.

She took my hand in hers again. Not for show, because she wanted to. We walked hand in hand to Abraham's house.

Chapter 131

I THOUGHT I would be standing guard alone on the porch that evening, but at midnight Moody appeared—wearing a clean white jumper, of course.

"I couldn't sleep, thinking how you hadn't had nothing to eat the whole day long." She set before me a plate of butter beans, field peas, and shortening bread.

The minute I smelled it, I was starving. "Thank you kindly," I said.

"You're welcome kindly," she said, easing down to the chair beside me.

I dove in. "There was this old colored lady who raised me," I said, "and she always sang, 'Mammy's little baby loves short'nin'—'"

"Hush up, fool!" Moody said.

I held up both hands in surrender. "All right, all right," I said, laughing.

"You can't help it, I reckon," she said, shaking her head. "No matter how hard you try, you are always gonna be a white man, the whole rest of your life."

"I expect I am," I said, taking a bite of bread.

We watched the moon rising over the swamp from Abraham's front porch. We heard the *gank, gank* of the bullfrogs and the occasional soft call of a mourning dove staying up late.

We sat in silence for a while. Then Moody spoke.

"You think they coming tonight?"

I sighed. "You know they'll want to teach us a lesson."

We heard a groan from inside. Moody leaped up and I followed her into the parlor.

Cousin Ricky was there, at Abraham's bedside, reading from the open Bible on his lap. Abraham looked too peaceful to have given out that groan just a moment before.

"You are the light of the world," Ricky read. "A city set on a hill cannot be hid."

We crept back out to the porch. After a time Moody said, "You made Papaw's last summer a good one."

"He's one of the finest men I've met," I said. "Of course, you know that."

She touched the back of my hand. It crossed my mind that we might kiss each other now. Also it crossed my mind that we might not.

I'll never know what could have been.

Suddenly there was a gunshot, then another, the clatter of hoofbeats, lots of horses.

We stood up, unable to see the men yet, but we could hear their voices in the darkness. We hurried inside before they could drop us where we stood.

"There they go, Sammy," a man yelled. "Nigger-lovin' Yankee and his nigger whore."

It was unfolding just like the first White Raiders attack: gunfire everywhere, men jockeying their horses into position in the dark, the hatred in their voices.

This time though, there was a difference.

The Eudora Quarters was ready—at least I hoped so.

Chapter 132

THERE HAD NEVER BEEN A FIGHT like this one in the state of Mississippi, and maybe anywhere else in this country. One way or the other, we were about to make some history.

The Raiders must have thought we were too stupid to know what was going to happen or too scared to defend ourselves. It never occurred to them that Moody and my little stroll down the sidewalk might have been deliberate, a provocation, and that they were riding into a trap.

There were nine of them this time. That's how confident they were that we wouldn't resist. What arrogance—to come into the Quarters with this pack of their friends, nine of them among hundreds of Negroes.

"Ricky, go around!" Moody yelled through the window. "We'll meet you on the other side!"

"You stay here," I told her. "Your job is to guard Abraham." She started to argue but gave up when I placed a snap-load pistol in her hand.

I stuck a loaded pistol in each of my trousers pockets, lifted the shotgun, and swung around just in time to stop three men dead in their tracks at the door.

I recognized them at once. There was Roy, who'd been shot in the arm in the first White Raiders attack, and Leander Purneau from the cotton gin. Best of all was the fat redheaded man in the middle, the surprised-looking fellow at whose nose both barrels of my shotgun now pointed. This was none other than Henry Wadsworth North, former defendant, murderer.

In my mind I squeezed the trigger and watched his limited supply of brains spatter all over the screen door behind him. I felt a jolt of pleasure at the prospect of being the one to end Henry North's life.

But I couldn't shoot the man like this. It just wasn't in me.

His mouth twisted up into a smile. "What you gonna do, Corbett, have me arrested again?"

From out of nowhere he brought up a small pistol.

My finger tightened on the trigger. "Drop it or I'll blow your head off," I said. "Do not doubt me for a second! I *want* to shoot you!"

He let the pistol drop to the floor. All at once hands seized him and dragged him over backwards—

Here they were, the people of the Quarters, bearing guns and knives, pitchforks and sharpened sticks, clublike lengths of straight iron. A dozen men swarmed in from the porch, seizing the Raiders and dragging them outside.

Gunfire echoed, and I heard more horses—a second wave of Raiders. But here came our reinforcements too, pouring out of nearly every door in the Quarters, bearing weapons or no weapons at all, swarming down the street and around Abraham's house. They dragged Raiders down off their horses and set upon them with clubs, rocks, and farm implements.

Every blow they struck was violent payback for a lynching, a hanging, a beating, a murder. I heard the thud of club against flesh, the crack of rock striking bone. Terrible cries erupted as the colored men overwhelmed the Raiders, avenging the lynchings of their brothers, the oppression and torture and murder of fathers and friends.

I saw Doc Conover swinging a long rifle like a club at a woman who was down on her knees, covering her head with both arms. Then I saw a man knock Conover senseless with a fireplace poker to his skull.

Lyman Tripp, the undertaker, was on the ground, surrounded by men kicking him in the ribs. I remembered how happy he had been to hang a Jew, so I didn't feel sorry for him. Not for any of them.

But then, over the racket of punches and shouts, I heard more horses approaching. There were many horses, bearing reinforcements for the other side.

Chapter 133

"CORBETT!" A MAN SHOUTED at the top of his lungs.

I stepped out onto the porch to see none other than Phineas Eversman on a fine black mare, wearing his black cowboy hat with the badge pinned to the brim. "You are under arrest," he said, "and that nigger girlfriend of yours."

The fight was swirling all around us, defenders chasing and shouting, new waves of attackers coming in from the woods. It seemed unbelievable that Eversman would be trying to make an arrest in such a setting.

I trained my shotgun on his chest. "Get your ass down off that horse, Phineas."

"You put your gun down, Ben," said a voice behind me.

I turned to find a revived Doc Conover with a nasty twelve-gauge shotgun leveled at me.

"Hey, Ben," Doc said. "I meant to bring your oil of wintergreen, but I forgot." He chuckled.

A shot rang out and the gun flew from his hands. Conover screamed and grabbed his elbow. Ricky ran up and scrambled after his gun.

I glanced around to see who had fired the shot. Good God!—It was ancient Aunt Henry in the doorway of Abraham's shack, blowing smoke from the long barrel of a Colt revolver. She nodded at me and went back inside.

I heard a loud crack and turned to find Eversman down off his horse with a big bullwhip in his hand, a whip straight out of *Uncle Tom's Cabin*. It had a black leather-wrapped stick for a handle and three little stinger-tips at the end of the whipcord. Eversman cracked it again, with a report louder than a pistol shot.

His arm swept around, and the whip shot out and wrapped around my ankles with a sting as fierce as yellowjackets. It snatched me off my feet, and I landed hard on my back in the dirt. I felt blood running down where the whip was cutting into flesh and then Eversman was on me, hitting with both fists at once. But I was stronger, and angrier too. I managed to roll over and fling him on his back. Seizing the slack end of the whip, I wrapped it around his neck so tight that with one hard tug I could break his windpipe. He gurgled and coughed like the two men I had seen lynched—like the sound I must have made when they lynched me.

Eversman's eyes bugged out horribly. The leather cord bit into his neck, making a deep red indentation.

And then...

I let go of him. He would kill me if he could, but I couldn't kill him.

He fell into the mud. Somehow I had opened a big cut on his cheek just above his mouth. Blood oozed out. I began unwinding the whipcord from my ankles.

I stood over him, breathing hard. "You've cut your face, Phineas. Ask Doc if he's got any wintergreen for that."

Chapter 134

IN THE BACKYARD I FOUND the old checker players from Hemple's store tying up Byram Chaney, the retired teacher in whose wagon I'd been taken to the Klan rally. That rally and the lynching that followed seemed to have taken place a hundred years ago.

I heard an odd *glunk*ing sound behind me and turned to see two men with kerosene cans working their way along the side of Abraham's house, splashing fuel on the foundation.

The one nearest me was the renowned legislator Senator Richard Nottingham, Elizabeth's husband. The military jacket he wore for this night's action was too small for him; the fabric gaped open around the buttons.

"Bring a match to that fuel," I called out, "and I'll shoot you dead. Be my pleasure."

The other man was bent over, facing away from me. He whirled and pulled a handgun. To my horror, it was Jacob Gill.

"Drop your gun, Ben," he said. "I would shoot you dead too."

Around us swirled a madness of yelling, fighting, and dust, screaming, cursing, and gunfire. Yet at that moment it felt as if Jacob and I were facing off all alone in the middle of a giant, empty room.

"Why, Ben?" he croaked. "Why'd you have to come back and ruin our nice little town?"

Chapter 135

JACOB JUST KEPT walking toward me.

Finally, my face hovered inches from his, so close I could smell whiskey and bacon grease on his breath. His face was covered with stubble, the skin on his nose peppered with gin blossoms.

I lashed out and grabbed his gun hand and twisted it hard until the weapon dropped. Jacob had always been smaller, but he could whip me at least half the time when we were boys. He was wiry and strong, and not afraid to fight dirty. I remembered the venom he could turn on our enemies when we got together in a schoolyard scrap.

"Goddamn you, Ben!" he yelled. Then I saw he had a knife. I took his arm and held it with all my strength. It felt as if we stayed that way for hours, grappling, neither of us gaining an advantage, the razor edge suspended between us. My arms ached.

I looked Jacob in the eye. *"Jacob!"* I yelled at him. *"It's me, goddamn it! It's Ben!"*

But his eyes were bulging with rage, one hand now gripping my throat, the other inching closer with the blade. If he killed me here, amid all this noise and insanity, no one would ever know it was Jacob who'd done the deed. I would just be Ben Corbett, another victim in another senseless attack in a small town.

And then I *knew* that was not how it was going to happen. I was not going to die here, at the hand of Jacob Gill. That knowledge gave me strength, just enough to jerk his arm sideways and break his hold on the knife.

I kicked Jacob hard and wrenched the knife away. I got on him, kneeling on his chest with the blade an inch from his neck. I could have slit his throat right then, but instead I poked the knife into his Adam's apple, hard enough to draw blood. Jacob's eyes widened. God, I knew those eyes.

"You gonna kill me, Ben?" he said.

I flung the knife away and heard it crash into the bushes beside the smokehouse. Then I got up. There were no words for this. So I turned and walked away from the man who had once been my best friend in the world.

Chapter 136

WHILE I WAS FIGHTING JACOB, the rest of the fracas had begun to die down.

I watched Sam Sanders, owner of the general store, jump off his horse and run away into the darkness. I saw two other White Raiders flee in his wake, one of them limping badly.

"We'll come back for you, niggers," one yelled as he ran.

"You ain't won. You just *think* you won," another called.

A flurry of hoofbeats, and the Raiders were gone.

Colored people were scattered all over the yard, nursing wounds. Four white men lay trussed up in the dirt in front of Abraham's house. I remembered Abraham talking about the earth running red with blood—and I saw blood, tiny rivers of it, here on his home ground.

On the porch near the tied-up men, Aunt Henry was dressing the leg wound of Lincoln Alexander Stephens, another of the original White Raiders who'd come calling tonight. Aunt Henry would take care of anyone, I reflected, regardless of race, creed, or degree of idiocy.

There seemed to be only one fatality—Leander Purneau, who lay flat on his back in the mud across the road from Abraham's house. I wouldn't miss him for a second.

Cousin Ricky told the captured Raiders he could kill them. Or he could tar and feather them. Or he could do what he was going to do: drive them into town and leave them, tied up, for the citizens of Eudora to find in the morning. "Tell 'em what we did to you," he said. "Tell 'em there's as many of us in the Quarters as there is of you in town. Don't come out here again, not unless you're invited. Which ain't likely."

Richard Nottingham brought his flat-wagon out of the woods. Brown hands helped him lift Leander Purneau's body up into the bed. Nottingham's shoulder was bandaged.

The battle was over. Eudora Quarters had

won — at least for one night. It would not help me or the people of the Quarters to shoot one more bullet. It was finished.

And if I needed more proof, from around the house came Jacob Gill, his shirtfront stained red with blood from where I'd nicked his throat. He walked between two colored men to the wagon and climbed in the back without looking at me. So be it.

"Mr. Corbett!" I looked up. It was Ricky, standing at the front door.

"Come on back in," he said. "Abraham has passed."

At the door, Ricky put his hand on my shoulder. "You all right?"

"I am."

Moody glanced up as we came in, then went back to reading from the Bible:

"And he said, 'Jesus, remember me when you come into your kingly power.' And Jesus said to him, 'Truly I say to you, this day you shall be with me in Paradise.'"

Moody closed the Bible. She looked up and our eyes met.

We had already spoken our last words to each other.

Chapter 137

"ARE YOU STAYING for Abraham's funeral?" L.J. asked. "I'll go with you, Ben."

"I don't think so," I said. "Moody already knows how I feel about him. And it's definitely time for me to head back...you know..."

"North!" L.J. said. "Go ahead, say the word! You're headed back up to damn Yankeeland to become a damn Yankee again!"

We were standing near the table in the War Room, where we'd spent so many hours plotting our strategies for the White Raiders Trial. I was just finishing packing.

"I've gone around and around in my mind, L.J., and for the life of me I don't know what I would do differently," I said. "If I had the luxury of doing it over again."

"You did as much as you could, Ben. Most men wouldn't even have tried to help."

I slipped my razor and shaving brush into the little leather kit and tucked it in my valise. "Help," I said. "Is that what we did? I think some of the help I gave ended up hurting them."

"Go ask 'em. Go to the Quarters," L.J. said, "and ask 'em if they're worse or better off for what you did.

"I can have a man drive you up to McComb so you can get the earlier train to Memphis," L.J. went on.

"No need for that. I'll just take the good old two-oh-five." I snapped the catches on my valise. "I might stop over in Memphis tonight and hear a bit of that music I told you about."

"Sure you don't want to stay here a day or two more?" L.J. asked. "Rest up?"

I shook my head. "It's time to go. I've said my good-byes, and I suspect I've worn out my welcome in Eudora. In fact, I'm sure of it. My own father said as much."

Chapter 138

THREE DAYS LATER I stepped off the train in Washington. My soles squeaked on the station's marble floors when I walked across them, and I once again admired the acres of gold leaf and ranks of granite arches like victory gates. A man entering Washington through this portal was glorified and enlightened by the passage.

But one man, Ben Corbett, coming home after all these months, felt as lowly and insignificant as a cockroach scurrying along an outhouse floor.

My mind was a jumble, a clutter of worries. I couldn't stop thinking about everything that had passed, and all the terrible things that might yet happen.

Meg had never answered my letters. I thought it likely that I would return to an empty house, shuttered and forlorn, my wife and children having gone off to live with her father in Rhode Island.

I could imagine the walls empty of pictures, white sheets covering the furniture, our modest lawn overgrown with foot-high grass and weeds.

These were my dark thoughts as I made my way through happy families on holiday, returning businessmen, flocks of government workers, Negro porters in red coats, and bellboys in blue caps.

"Mr. Corbett, sir," a voice rang out down the platform. "Mr. Corbett! *Mr. Corbett!*"

I stopped, searching the oncoming faces for the source of the greeting—if indeed it was a greeting.

"Mr. Corbett. Right here. I'm so glad I found you."

He was a young man, short and slight, with wire-rimmed glasses and an intensely nervous stare. I had seen him somewhere before.

"Mr. Corbett, I'm Jackson Hensen. The White House?"

"Ah, Mr. Hensen," I said. "What a surprise to see you here."

He smiled hesitantly, as if not quite sure whether I'd made a joke. "Will you come with me, sir?"

"I'm sorry?" I looked down at his hand cupped on my elbow.

"The president would like to see you immediately."

"Oh. Yes. Of course," I said. "And I would like to see him. But first I thought I would see my family."

"I'm sorry, Mr. Corbett. The president is at the White House right now. He's waiting for you."

So I followed Hensen outside to a splendid carriage drawn by the handsomest quartet of chestnuts I'd ever seen. All the way to the White House I kept thinking, *Dear God, please see to it that Teddy Roosevelt isn't the only person in Washington who wants to see me.*

Chapter 139

THEODORE ROOSEVELT JUMPED UP from his desk and came charging at me with such high spirits I was afraid he might bowl us both over.

"Welcome home, Captain!" he roared. When he pumped my hand I recalled that Roosevelt didn't consider a handshake successful unless it resulted in physical pain.

"And all congratulations to you, sir, on a difficult job extremely well done," he exclaimed. "The White Raiders Trial was a smashing success."

"But Mr. President, we lost the case."

"Of course you did," he said. "I knew you would — technically — lose the case. But you won a tremendous victory all the same."

"I don't think I understand."

He sank onto the sofa to the left of his desk and

patted the seat cushion next to his, as if I were a faithful dog being summoned. I sat. The president continued.

"I don't know how much of our press you've seen while you've been away, Ben, but you've become something of a hero up here. The more progressive citizens see you as a kind of abolitionist, a figure of progress in the march of civilization toward full equality. And the coloreds in the South see you as some kind of protector, a hero. *It's damn good!*"

"Mr. President, I was just in the South," I said. "Believe me, I'm nobody's hero there."

"I'm meeting the newspaper boys in a few minutes," he said. "You'll be with me. I'll announce that I masterminded your adventure in the South. I'll disclose to them how I supported your efforts against the White Raiders. I'll pick up votes in New England, and I'll have the colored vote from now until the end of time."

"But you sent me to Eudora to investigate lynchings."

"Indeed I did. And if you'd reported back to me that lynching was a way of life among the leaders of the white South, I would have had to do something about it. Something that would enrage some white people, no matter how much it endeared me to the Negroes."

"That's why you didn't answer my telegrams?"

"It wasn't convenient for me to hear from you yet," he said. "But then we had the most magnificent stroke of luck when the Raiders Trial came along!"

He was bubbling, but I couldn't keep silent any longer.

"Luck? You call it a magnificent stroke of luck? People died. A town was torn apart."

He ignored me completely, and he was still grinning at his good fortune.

"I know there was pain, Captain. That's to be expected. Progress requires a certain amount of suffering. You did well, you worked hard, and eventually you managed to bring it all under control. I certainly chose the right man for the job." He stood up from the sofa.

I stood as well. "Is that all, Mr. President?" I said.

"The reporters are waiting, Ben. I need you to help me explain what happened."

"Is that an order, sir?" I asked.

He looked surprised. "Well, no," he said. "Don't you want to come?"

"No, sir," I said. "If I may, I respectfully decline."

Chapter 140

AS I LEFT THE WHITE HOUSE that day I noticed that my legs felt more limber, my body lighter. There was an actual spring in my step. To my astonishment I felt strangely, incredibly happy.

The White House was bathed in an intensely golden light, and as I walked northwest on the wide avenue, past the tattered rooming houses and saloons, I saw the Washington Monument sparkling in the distance like a gigantic diamond hatpin.

Certainly I was angry that Theodore Roosevelt had used me as a pawn in one of his electoral chess games. And I dreaded even more the moment when I returned home to find my house empty.

But still, there was something hopeful in the light sparkling on the monument, and the delightful smell of woodsmoke on the breeze.

I found myself remembering Abraham Cross a few nights ago, just before he drifted off to sleep.

"You did fine, Ben. You did just fine."

To have a man like Abraham say that...well, that's all anyone could ever ask for.

"You did fine, Ben. You did just fine."

I turned off South Carolina Avenue onto our street. Everything looked so familiar that I might have left home only a day or two ago. No one had taken a paintbrush to our peeling little house. The second-floor shutters still hung tilted and broken, and the brick walkway was still perilously uneven.

As I mounted the front steps, three months' worth of anxiety was twisting my insides into a hard knot.

I unlocked the door and stepped into the vestibule. All was still.

I walked to the bottom of the stairs and stood there a few moments. And then—

I heard Alice's little voice.

"I think I heard the front door," she said.

I knelt down to remove two identical boxes wrapped in brown paper from my valise. I shucked off the paper and opened them.

"Do you think it could be Papa?" Amelia asked.

Then—I heard Meg's voice.

"I certainly hope so," she said. "Wouldn't that be wonderful?"

I ran up those stairs clutching the gifts for my girls—identical brown, fuzzy teddy bears, the most popular dolls of the day, inspired by President Roosevelt himself.

"Daddy!" screamed my girls, all three of them.

I took the little ones into my arms. "Now, which of you is Alice, and which is Amelia?" I asked as they giggled and snuggled into my chest.

Then I reached out my free arm. "And you—you must be Meg. I've missed you so much." Then Meg came into my arms too. "I'll never leave you again," I whispered.

True to my word, I never did.

THE NEW ALEX CROSS NOVEL, COMING IN NOVEMBER 2010

Cross Fire

James Patterson

The Mastermind is back, and he's about to destroy everything – and everyone – Alex Cross loves.

Detective Alex Cross and Bree's wedding plans are put on hold when Alex is called to the scene of a perfectly executed assassination of two of Washington DC's most hated public figures: a corrupt congressman and a scheming lobbyist. All avenues of investigation lead Cross to dead-ends, and the prospect of finding the killer seems nearly impossible. As more crooked politicians are picked off with simliar long-range shots, public opinion is divided – is the elusive marksman a vigilante or a hero?

Media coverage of the case explodes and FBI agent Max Siegel battles Alex for jurisdiction. As Alex struggles with the sniper, Siegel, and the wedding, he receives a call from his deadliest adversary, Kyle Craig. The Mastermind is in DC and will not relent until he has eliminated Cross – and his family – for good. With a supercharged blend of suspense, action, and deception, *Cross Fire* is James Patterson's most exciting Alex Cross novel yet.

Century · London

Read on for a sneak preview of
Cross Fire

One

IT HAD BEEN eight months since Kyle Craig had killed a man. Once upon a time, he'd been the type who needed everything yesterday, if not sooner. But no more. If four years of hellish solitude in the Florence ADX in Colorado had taught him nothing else, it was how to wait for what he wanted.

He sat patiently in the foyer of his quarry's Miami apartment, weapon cradled on his lap, watching the lights of the harbor and biding his time. He was in no particular hurry, enjoying the view, maybe finally learning to enjoy life. He certainly looked relaxed—faded jeans, sandals, a T-shirt that said CONSIDER THIS FAIR WARNING.

At 2:12 a.m., a key sounded in the lock. Kyle

immediately rose to his feet and pressed his back against the wall, hanging there as silently as any other piece of art.

The man of the hour, Max Siegel, was whistling as he came in. Kyle recognized the melody, an old snatch from his childhood. It was *Peter and the Wolf.* The violin section—Peter's hunting theme. Ironically enough.

He waited for Mr. Siegel to close the door behind him and take a few more steps into the still dark apartment. Then Kyle leveled his red laser site and squeezed the trigger. "Hello, Mr. Siegel," he said. "Good to meet you."

A stream of electrically charged saline solution hit Siegel squarely in the back, carrying 50,000 volts with it. He grunted between clenched teeth. His shoulders seized up just before his body went completely rigid, and he fell like a tree to the floor.

Kyle didn't hesitate for a second. He slipped a nylon cord three times quickly around Siegel's throat and started to drag him—once in a small circle to sop up the saline solution on the floor —then straight through the apartment toward the master bath in the back. Siegel was too weak to struggle. Whatever effort he could muster was spent on the cord itself, trying not to be strangled.

"Don't fight me," Kyle finally said. "There's no point in it."

In the bathroom, Kyle lifted him into the oversized tub and tied off the ends of the cord to one of the chrome fixtures. It wasn't necessary, physically speaking, but it kept Siegel's head up where Kyle could see his face.

"You probably don't even know about these, do you?" he said, holding up the strange gun he'd carried in. "I know you've been underground a while, but trust me, they're going to be huge."

The thing looked like a Super Soaker, which it kind of was. Regular tasers could go for thirty seconds, at best. This baby could *run* and *run*, thanks to a two-gallon wearable water pack, strapped to his back.

"What…do you want?" Siegel finally choked out a response to the madness.

Kyle unpocketed a small Canon digital camera and started taking pictures. Full face, left profile, right profile.

"I know who you are, Agent Siegel. Let's start there, OK?"

A look of confusion crossed the man's face. Then fear. "Oh God, this is some kind of horrible mistake. My name is Ivan Schimmel!"

"No," Kyle said, snapping away—brow, nose, chin. "You're Max Siegel, and you're FBI. You've been deep undercover for the last twenty-six months. Worked your way up with the Buenez cartel until they trusted you enough to start making shipments.

"Now, while everyone's watching Colombia, you're running heroin from Phuket and Bangkok to Miami."

He lowered the camera and looked Siegel in the eye. "Never mind the moral relativism. It's all in the name of the big takedown at the end. Isn't that right, Agent Siegel?"

"I don't know who you're talking about!" he tried. "Please! Check my wallet!" He'd begun to struggle again, but another dose of voltage put a quick end to that. The electricity went right after the motor and sensory nerves. Siegel's pain tolerance was irrelevant. And the ammo, such as it was, ran right down the drain into Biscayne Bay.

"I suppose you might be forgiven for not recognizing me," Kyle went on. "Does the name

Kyle Craig mean anything to you? Or maybe *the Mastermind*? That's what they call me up at the Puzzle Palace in DC. As a matter of fact, I used to work there. Long time ago."

A flash of recognition came and went in Siegel's eyes, not that Kyle needed any kind of confirmation. His reconnaissance was still flawless.

But this Max Siegel was a pro, too. He wasn't about to stop playing the game now, *especially* now. "Please," he blubbered on, "what is this? Who are you? I don't know what you want."

"Everything, Max. Every last little thing."

Kyle took another half dozen pictures, and repocketed the camera. "You're actually a victim of your own good work, if that's any consolation. Nobody knows who you are down here, not even local FBI. That's why I chose you. I selected you out of all the agents working in the US. *You* — Max. Can you guess why?"

His voice had changed as he spoke. It was more nasal now, with the exact same shades of Brooklyn accent that laced the real Max Siegel's speech.

"This will never work! You're insane!" Siegel screamed at him. "You're fucking mad!"

"By some standards, I think that might be true," Kyle said. "But I'm also the most brilliant son of a bitch you'll ever have the pleasure to know." Then he pulled the trigger one more time and just let the thing *run*.

Siegel writhed mutely on the bottom of the tub. Eventually, he began to gag on his own tongue. Kyle watched, carefully noting every detail all the way to the end, studying his subject until there was nothing left to learn.

"Let's hope this works," he said. "Wouldn't want you to have died for nothing, Mr. Siegel."

Two

TWENTY-TWO DAYS LATER, a man bearing a striking resemblance to Max Siegel checked out of the Hotel Melia in the ritzy Miramar section of Havana, Cuba. Medical tourists were as common as pickpockets here; no one looked twice at the broad-shouldered man in the linen suit with bruises around his eyes and gauze over his nose and ears, as he came through the lobby.

He signed the bill with a perfectly replicated signature and kept the charges on Max Siegel's brand new American Express card. The surgeries, however, had been paid for in cash.

From the hotel, he caught a cab across town to Dr. Cruz's office, discreetly tucked into one of the city's endless neoclassical arcades. Inside was a full-service, fully staffed modern clinic that would have made a high-priced plastic surgeon in Miami or Palm Beach proud.

"I have to tell you, Señor Siegel, that I'm quite proud of this." The doctor spoke softly as he removed the last of the bandages. "It is some of the best work I've ever done, if I may say so." His manner was thoughtful, but crisp and efficient— very professional. You'd never know he was willing to cut so many ethical corners along with the skin and bones of his clients' faces.

Dr. Cruz had performed seven separate procedures, something that might have taken months, or even a year elsewhere. There was blepharoplasty for the eyelids; a template rhinoplasty for the nose, with a complete elevation of the skin and soft tissue in the nasal pyramid; new Medpor implants for a more prominent chin and cheekbones; a sliding genioplasty of the jawbone; a little silicone augmentation for the brow; and as a finishing touch, a nice little cleft in the chin —just like Max Siegel's.

At the patient's request, no electronic imaging had been taken, before or after the procedures. For the right rate, Dr. Cruz had been more than willing to work from a series of digital blowups in hard copy, no questions asked, no interest in any biophysical detail.

Now, when he held up the large hand mirror for Kyle to see, the effect was stunning. The implants, especially, were like a miracle of change.

Max—not Kyle—smiled back from the mirror. He felt a slight sting at the corners of his mouth, which didn't move quite the same way as before. In fact, he didn't recognize himself at all. It was a total mind fuck, in the best possible way. There had been other disguises in the past few months, including some very expensive prosthetics that had gotten him out of prison. But they were nothing compared to this.

"How long will the bruising last?" he asked. "And this swelling around my eyes?"

Cruz handed him a folder of aftercare information. "With proper rest, you should be looking completely normal in seven to ten days."

The rest he could do for himself—shave and dye the blond hair down to a dark buzz-cut, and put in a simple pair of brown contacts. If there was any disappointment at all, it was that Kyle

Craig had been so much better looking than Max Siegel.

But screw it. He needed to look at the larger picture here. Next time, he could be Brad Pitt if he wanted to.

He left the clinic in an excellent mood and took another cab straight to José Marti Airport. From there, he caught a flight back to Miami, with a connection to Washington that same afternoon. For the main event.

Already, his thoughts had begun to coalesce around one idea: meeting up with his old friend, and sometimes partner, Alex Cross. Had Alex forgotten the promises Kyle made to him over the years? That didn't seem possible. But had Cross grown just a little complacent in the meantime? Maybe so. In any case, the "great" Alex Cross was going to die, and die badly. There would be pain, but even more than that—regret. It would be a finale worth waiting for, no question.

And in the meantime, Kyle was going to have some fun. After all, as the new and improved Max Siegel, he knew better than anybody—that there was more than one way to take another man's life.

NOW AVAILABLE IN PAPERBACK

I, Alex Cross

James Patterson

A Cross family member is murdered, and the case catapults Alex into a world where power masks unfathomable evil.

Detective Alex Cross is pulled out of a family celebration and given the devastating news that his niece, Caroline, has been found brutally murdered. Cross vows to hunt down the killer, and soon learns that Caroline was mixed up in one of Washington's wildest scenes. And she was not this killer's only victim.

The search leads Cross to a place where every fantasy is possible, if you have the credentials to get in. Alex is soon facing down some very important, very protected, very dangerous people in levels of society where only one thing is certain – they will do anything to keep their secrets safe.

As Cross closes in on the killer, he discovers evidence that points to the unimaginable – a revelation that could rock the entire world.

'Sharp, sassy and guaranteed to send shivers down your spine, this is a tense thriller'
Woman

arrow books

DETECTIVE
MICHAEL BENNETT

If you enjoy following the Alex Cross series, you'll love James Patterson's newest bestselling series featuring Detective Michael Bennett.

THE *SUNDAY TIMES* NO. 1 BESTSELLING DETECTIVE MICHAEL
BENNETT NOVEL, AVAILABLE IN PAPERBACK FROM
NOVEMBER 2010

Worst Case

James Patterson
& Michael Ledwidge

**Alex Cross has Washington DC. The Women's Murder Club
have San Francisco. Detective Michael Bennett has
New York City – chaos capital of the world.**

The son of one of New York's wealthiest families is snatched off the
street and held hostage. His parents can't save him, because this
kidnapper isn't demanding money. Instead, he quizzes his prisoner
on the price others pay for his life of luxury. In this exam, wrong
answers are fatal.

Detective Michael Bennett leads the investigation. With ten kids of
his own, he can't begin to understand what could lead someone to
target anyone's children. As another student disappears, one
powerful family after another uses their leverage and connections
to turn up the heat on the mayor, the press, anyone who will listen,
to stop this killer. Their reach extends all the way to the FBI, who
send their top Abduction Specialist, Agent Emily Parker. Bennett's
work life – and love life – suddenly get even more complicated.

Before Bennett has a chance to protest the FBI's intrusion on his
case, the mastermind changes his routine. His plan leads up to the
most dreadful demonstration yet – one that could bring cataclysmic
devastation to every inch of New York.

arrow books

James Patterson

To find out more about James Patterson and his bestselling books, go to www.jamespatterson.co.uk